PRIVATE PROSECUTION IN AMERICA

ALSO BY JOHN D. BESSLER

Death in the Dark:
Midnight Executions in America

Kiss of Death:
America's Love Affair with the Death Penalty

Legacy of Violence:
Lynch Mobs and Executions in Minnesota

Writing for Life:
The Craft of Writing for Everyday Living

Cruel and Unusual:
The American Death Penalty and the Founders' Eighth Amendment

The Birth of American Law:
An Italian Philosopher and the American Revolution

Against the Death Penalty (editor)

The Death Penalty as Torture:
From the Dark Ages to Abolition

The Celebrated Marquis:
An Italian Noble and the Making of the Modern World

The Baron and the Marquis:
Liberty, Tyranny, and the Enlightenment Maxim
That Can Remake American Criminal Justice

PRIVATE PROSECUTION IN AMERICA

Its Origins, History, and Unconstitutionality in the Twenty-First Century

John D. Bessler

PROFESSOR OF LAW
UNIVERSITY OF BALTIMORE
SCHOOL OF LAW

CAROLINA ACADEMIC PRESS

Durham, North Carolina

LIBRARY OF CONGRESS CATALOGING-IN-PUBLICATION DATA

Names: Bessler, John D., author.
Title: Private prosecution in America : its origins, history, and unconstitutionality in the twenty-first century / by John D. Bessler.
Description: Durham, North Carolina : Carolina Academic Press, LLC, 2021. | Includes index.
Identifiers: LCCN 2021042793 | ISBN 9781531020064 (hardback) | ISBN 9781531020071 (ebook)
Subjects: LCSH: Private prosecutors—United States—History. | Prosecution—United States—History. | Indictments—United States. | Criminal procedure—United States.
Classification: LCC KF9640 .B47 2021 | DDC 345.73/05042—dc23/eng/20211006
LC record available at https://lccn.loc.gov/2021042793

Carolina Academic Press
700 Kent Street
Durham, North Carolina 27701
Telephone (919) 489-7486
www.cap-press.com

Printed in the United States of America

In memory of

TOM JOHNSON (1945–2020)

a thoughtful and dedicated public servant, a friend, trusted counselor, and man of compassion, and a champion of criminal justice reform who took a principled stand against capital punishment and who fought with integrity for human rights, racial justice, and equal protection of the laws throughout his life as a lawyer

The Trial of Daniel Sickles in Washington, D.C., 1859. Source: *Harper's Weekly*

"Justice is justly represented blind, because she sees no difference in the parties concerned. She has but one scale and weight, for rich and poor, great and small."

— William Penn, *Some Fruits of Solitude* (1693)

"We discover no error except in the allowance of assistance in the prosecution by the counsel of private prosecutors. We are not at liberty to overlook such an error from any impression that the conviction would have been had without him. The rejection of such prosecutors is in the public interest and the rule is one which should be enforced."

— *People v. Hurst*, 1 N.W. 1027, 1031–32 (Mich. 1879)

"Private prosecution has become obsolete."

— Roscoe Pound, "The Causes of Popular Dissatisfaction with the Administration of Justice" (1906)

"The prosecutor has more control over life, liberty, and reputation than any other person in America. His discretion is tremendous. He can have citizens investigated and, if he is that kind of person, he can have this done to the tune of public statements and veiled or unveiled intimations."

— United States Attorney General Robert Jackson (1940)

"The duty of the prosecutor is to seek justice, not merely to convict."

— American Bar Association Standards Relating to the Administration of Justice (3d ed. 1992)

CONTENTS

ACKNOWLEDGMENTS

This book came about as a result of an invitation from Roger Fairfax, now dean of American University's Washington College of Law, to speak about private prosecution at a 2020 conference sponsored by the Southeastern Association of Law Schools ("SEALS"). I had written on that subject in the *Arkansas Law Review* back in 1994 after getting the opportunity, as a new lawyer at Faegre & Benson in Minneapolis, Minnesota, to work with attorney Sandra Babcock on a legal research project involving that topic. Now a clinical professor specializing in international human rights litigation and the faculty director of the Cornell Center on the Death Penalty Worldwide, Sandra was then representing two Texas death row inmates, Wayne East and Joseph Stanley Faulder. Both East and Faulder had been convicted of capital murder in criminal trials involving the use of privately retained lawyers hired by the murder victims' relatives, more commonly known as "private prosecutors." After getting the invitation to speak at the SEALS conference, I began the process of updating my prior research, initially with a view to simply writing a new law review article to supplement what I'd written in 1994. It quickly became apparent, though, that the issue of private prosecution was worthy of a much longer treatment, prompting me to undertake to write the book you now hold in your hands.

I am grateful to Sandra Babcock for the opportunity, all those years ago, to delve into the myriad legal issues associated with private prosecutors, including those implicating the U.S. Constitution. In addition, I am grateful to Roger Fairfax, a former colleague of mine at the George Washington University Law School, for reaching out to me about the SEALS conference. Our panel, taking up the issue of "The Private Role in Criminal Justice," involved a lively exchange of views, one moderated by Professor Jelani Jefferson Exum of the University of Detroit Mercy School of Law. In addition to Roger and me, our fellow panelists, law professors Bennett Capers, Russell Gold, Veronica Root Martinez, and Maybell Romero, also spoke about their research—and offered their perspectives—at the SEALS conference. Likewise, I am indebted to Carolina Academic Press for agreeing to publish this book. This is the fifth book I've published with Carolina Academic Press, and I've been continually impressed with its leadership, its operation, and its whole team of people. Producing a high-quality book is no small task, and Carolina Academic Press does a fantastic job.

As I wrote the manuscript, a number of people sent along helpful information, including Robert Dunham, the Executive Director of the Death Penalty Information Center who spent 25 years litigating capital cases; Liz Vartkessian, a mitigation specialist and the Executive Director of Advancing Real Change, a national non-profit based in Baltimore, Maryland; and Steve Wells, a lawyer at Dorsey & Whitney in Minneapolis who has represented multiple death row inmates. I also had the chance to speak about the history and subject of private prosecution to my colleagues at the University of Baltimore School of Law. I am blessed to work with a wonderful group of people, and their comments as I workshopped this project were very insightful. Over the years, on a variety of issues pertaining to legal history or constitutional or criminal law, I've regularly consulted with many of them, including, among others, José Anderson, Amy Dillard, Garrett Epps, Nienke Grossman, Steve Grossman, Dan Hatcher, Mike Higginbotham, David Jaros, Rob Knowles, Bob Lande, Ken Lasson, Jane Murphy, Arnie Rochvarg, Tim Sellers, Colin Starger, Byron Warnken, and Kim Wehle. A special thank you to our leader, Dean Ron Weich, Associate Dean Vicki Schultz, and to everyone who offered their observations on this project. Meaghan Farnham and Sean Colgan, two University of Baltimore law students, provided first-rate citation and research assistant work as I finalized the manuscript. And Christine Stutz, the director of communications at the University of Baltimore School of Law, lent her superb editorial eye as the book moved into final page proofs.

I also want to thank Harvey Morrell, the Director of the law library at the University of Baltimore School of Law, and Ryan Greenwood, the Curator of Rare Books and Special Collections at the University of Minnesota Law School. Harvey and Ryan both provided useful guidance and information about databases as I began this project, and they were extremely helpful to me. Without the assistance of my librarian friends, this book would not be nearly as complete or accurate. As Neil Gaiman, an English author, once put it: "Google can bring you back 100,000 answers, a librarian can bring you back the right one." The material gathered for inclusion in this book came from a wide array of sources, including books, magazines, newspapers, and law review articles, and it was very helpful to have the assistance of librarians, especially during the COVID-19 pandemic that disrupted—and, in fact, took—so many lives. The digitization of books and newspapers has made writing legal histories a lot easier, though also more time-consuming as there is so much information to analyze.

In addition, I'd be remiss if I didn't thank my wife Amy, and our daughter Abigail, and some close friends of mine. This book consumed a lot of my time, and time spent on the book meant time away from family and friends. My law school classmate, Bruce Beddow, was a reader of portions of the manuscript and provided extremely helpful comments as I wrote the book. It has been a long time—1991—since we graduated together from Indiana University School of Law in Bloomington, but our friendship has been a constant since we first met—in the same small 1L section (through a fortunate circumstance, assigned alphabetically by last name)—in our first year. Friendships with Terry Anker and Greg Braun came about through that same fortuitous circumstance. Also, Judge Bill Fisher and another longtime friend, Andy Luger (a very talented lawyer who became the U.S. Attorney for the District of Minnesota), provided helpful information and valuable early feedback on the manuscript. Adam Scales, now a law professor at Rutgers Law School in New Jersey who I first got to know in Minnesota, likewise provided terrific insights as I did my research, as did Pete Crum and Michael Handberg, two of my friends from college. My executive assistant, Deborah Thompson, also gave me valuable assistance as I prepared the final manuscript, with Ryland Bowman and Kathleen Soriano-Taylor at Carolina Academic Press guiding me through the publication process. Thank you, everyone.

ABOUT THE AUTHOR

John D. Bessler teaches at the University of Baltimore School of Law and the Georgetown University Law Center. A two-time Minnesota Book Award finalist and the winner of an *Independent Publisher* book award and a Next Generation Indie Book Award for biography, he is the author of multiple books on capital punishment and in the area of American legal history. His 2014 book about Enlightenment thinker Cesare Beccaria, *The Birth of American Law: An Italian Philosopher and the American Revolution*, won the prestigious Scribes Book Award, an annual award given out since 1961 by the American Society of Legal Writers for "the best work of legal scholarship published during the previous year." He has also taught at the University of Minnesota Law School, the George Washington University Law School, Rutgers Law School, and the University of Aberdeen in Scotland, and is the editor of Justice Stephen Breyer's *Against the Death Penalty* (2016). In 2018, he was a visiting scholar at the University of Minnesota Law School's Human Rights Center and received the University System of Maryland Board of Regents' Faculty Award for Research, Scholarship and Creative Activity.

INTRODUCTION

In twenty-first century America, the topic of criminal justice reform has garnered a lot of public attention.[1] A number of prominent organizations and non-profits, along with countless individuals, have laudably sought to reform the country's criminal justice system, seeking to have it operate more fairly and equitably.[2] The American Civil Liberties Union, the Equal Justice Initiative, Families Against Mandatory Minimums, the Marshall Project, the Brennan Center, the Southern Center for Human Rights, and the Sentencing Project, among many others, have pushed for changes such as bail reform,[3] fairer sentencing outcomes,[4] and an end to what has been termed "mass incarceration."[5] With well-documented racial disparities and runaway sentencing severity in America's complex, multi-jurisdictional criminal justice system,[6] an array of books—Michelle Alexander's *The New Jim Crow*,[7] John Pfaff's *Locked In*,[8] Brandon Garrett's *End of Its Rope: How Killing the Death Penalty Can Revive Criminal Justice*,[9] and Paul Butler's *Chokehold: Policing Black Men*[10]—have, in recent years, called for major changes to criminal justice, policing, and sentencing policies.[11] George Floyd's 2020 murder in Minneapolis, along with other officer-involved killings or shootings, have sparked renewed focus on police brutality and the use of excessive force,[12] with the COVID-19 pandemic—affecting hundreds of thousands of prisoners who tested positive for coronavirus—drawing further attention to the large number of incarcerated individuals and the harsh conditions within U.S. jails and correctional facilities.[13]

Although bail, policing and sentencing reform, as well as the use of excessive force, solitary confinement[14] and the death penalty,[15] have gotten the bulk of the attention,[16] one aspect of American criminal justice—the use, albeit infrequent at this juncture,[17] of so-called "private prosecutors"[18]—has gotten relatively little, if any, attention. Private prosecution by interested parties is where the victim or the victim's family either initiates or directs a criminal case or hires a lawyer to manage or assist in a case's investigation or prosecution.[19] Private prosecutions were the norm in ancient Anglo-Saxon legal systems, and they were routinely used in England—America's mother country—well into the twentieth century.[20] Indeed, they still occur, if only sporadically and in limited circumstances, in American states[21] and under Canadian,[22] English,[23] Irish,[24] and Scottish law,[25] as well as under other nations' laws,[26] in some cases with much greater frequency.[27] "Private prosecution as an institution," one New Jersey superior court observed in 1998, "is rooted in the English common law practice which generally relied on the victim, or the victim's relatives and friends, to prosecute criminals."[28] "In past centuries in England, in the American Colonies, and in the United States," the late U.S. Supreme Court Justice John Paul Stevens wrote in a concurrence in *Steel Company v. Citizens for a Better Environment* (1998),[29] "private persons regularly prosecuted criminal cases."[30]

Private criminal prosecutions by interested parties were thus once an entrenched, deeply rooted part of Anglo-American common law,[31] and they were used in other legal systems, too, such as in Spain[32] and the Philippines,[33] where private prosecutors worked closely with the public prosecutor. "The Anglo-American criminal trial of the seventeenth and early eighteenth centuries," observes law professor Laura Appleman, "was a very different creature than that which we have today." After noting American colonists brought with them English criminal justice traditions that included private prosecution but did not guarantee the accused the right to the assistance of defense counsel, she points out: "The standard English common-law felony criminal trial was both brief and informal; usually, both the presentation of evidence and the return of a verdict lasted only a half-hour. Private parties brought criminal charges against a defendant, and the victim or friend or relative of the victim often pursued the case personally." As Appleman notes of a then-typical proceeding: "This private prosecutor would personally testify and question witnesses, and the defendant was permitted to respond to the evidence and question witnesses on his or her own behalf. In common-law felony criminal trials of that era, the judge served to referee the proceedings, although he could also examine witnesses and answer questions of law."[34]

A close examination of past practices reveals the clear differences between then and now in the conduct of criminal prosecutions, with Professor Appleman noting that a criminal defendant centuries ago "did not obtain a copy of the indictment pre-trial, was not informed of the evidence against him or her, and could not compel witnesses on his or her behalf."[35] In England and American locales, it was, in fact, once predominantly poorly compensated constables or private detective and policing organizations[36] who investigated alleged offenses, with a number of private prosecution associations formed to prosecute offenders.[37] "[I]n the overwhelming majority of criminal prosecutions the state played no role at all," writes historian Allyson May of the English system of justice that relied so heavily on crime victims or their next of kin to prosecute criminal activity.[38] The American justice system did, in time, part ways from English practice in allowing criminal defendants to retain counsel, with that procedural safeguard specifically included in the U.S. Bill of Rights. "[T]he long-standing English common law rule in effect at the time of the adoption of the Sixth Amendment," law professor Russell Christopher writes, "utilized a disproportional allocation: misdemeanor, but not felony, defendants enjoyed the right." That

English rule, which did not guarantee the right to counsel, had been looked upon disfavorably in colonial America, with Professor Christopher pointing out that "[t]welve of the original thirteen colonies granted a right to retained counsel for serious offenses and most also granted the right for all offenses." Although the U.S. Bill of Rights originally constrained only the federal government,[39] the Sixth Amendment—incorporated against the states in *Gideon v. Wainwright* (1963)—itself provides: "In all criminal prosecutions, the accused shall enjoy the right to ... have the Assistance of Counsel for his defence."[40]

Whereas a criminal defendant's right to counsel was once hotly disputed, the right of private parties to initiate prosecutions was quite clear in prior centuries. Eighteenth-century "private prosecutors" in the English-speaking world pursued both petty offenders[41] and serious felons[42] in individual cases,[43] including through capital charges[44] carrying life-or-death consequences for the accused.[45] Many nineteenth-century criminal prosecutions in American states were still being initiated and directed by private citizens, not lawyers or government-paid attorneys,[46] although it became commonplace for crime victims—commonly called "private prosecutors" in newspapers—to retain counsel to assist in such prosecutions if they could afford to do so.[47] For example, in Philadelphia, where district attorneys were not elected until the early 1850s,[48] assault and battery and petty larceny cases were typically private prosecutions[49] and, in the Commonwealth of Pennsylvania, victims directly prosecuted crimes throughout the nineteenth century.[50] In that locale, private prosecutions could be downright bizarre, with a husband's wife—as historian Allen Steinberg writes of her prosecution against her own husband in the state's early history—"prosecuting him for refusing to come to bed when called and making too much noise, preventing her from sleeping."[51] As UCLA law professor Stephen Yeazell writes of the character of private prosecutions and of how many petty offenses were litigated in that manner in nineteenth-century Philadelphia: "The overwhelming majority of these private prosecutions did not involve lawyers at all. Rather, they were brought before municipal courts in which both the prosecutor and the defendant represented themselves."[52]

In America's colonial and founding eras, state systems of criminal justice varied widely, sometimes with separate courts, as with one set up in Virginia in 1692 by virtue of "*An Act for the more speedy prosecution of slaves committing capital crimes*," for the punishment of enslaved persons.[53] All those centuries ago, ordinary citizens—whether they could afford it or not—were often tasked with seeking justice for themselves, or for their raped or murdered relatives, after being victimized by crime.[54] Only after public prosecutors' offices professionalized did private prosecutions in American states dwindle and become the exception rather than the norm.[55] At the federal level, the Judiciary Act of 1789—passed by Congress after the U.S. Constitution's ratification in 1788—took a somewhat different route, creating the positions of Attorney General and District Attorneys (now called U.S. Attorneys). Their power and prosecutorial responsibilities were explicitly divided—and dispersed and decentralized—between them, with public prosecutions being the standard practice. The

Attorney General was to "prosecute and conduct all suits in the Supreme Court in which the United States shall be concerned, and to give his advice and opinion upon questions of law when required by the President of the United States, or when requested by the heads of any of the departments." By contrast, District Attorneys in the various federal districts were to be persons "learned in the law". Their duty? To prosecute in their respective districts "all delinquents for crimes and offenses, cognizable under the authority of the United States." The vast majority of crimes were prosecuted at the state level, but the U.S. Congress, in its Crimes Act of 1790, provided for the punishment of treason, piracy, counterfeiting, and other offenses. Formally titled "An Act for the Punishment of Certain Crimes Against the United States," that law made an assortment of crimes punishable by death and authorized those found guilty of larceny to be publicly "whipped, not exceeding thirty-nine stripes," and fined not more than four times the value of the property stolen.[56]

In America, the administration of the criminal law—including the punishments authorized by it—has shifted over time, including at both the federal and state levels. "In the ensuring years," one legal commentator, Leslie Arffa, writes of the post-1789 period and the prosecution of federal crimes, "Congress took dispersion to a degree unthinkable in the modern era: it frequently delegated criminal law enforcement responsibility to individuals who were in no way subject to executive command, namely private citizens and state officials." As Arffa explains of early American law: "At the Founding, Congress allowed state officials to prosecute violations of federal law in state courts. Private citizens could also either 'contact[] [a] grand jury directly' or 'appear before a ... state judicial officer and swear out a complaint against a suspected criminal.'" "Further," Arffa observes, "Congress passed a variety of *qui tam* provisions, which directly authorized individuals to sue under criminal statutes to enforce the law."[57] In recent years, numerous courts have stressed that federal law does not permit private criminal prosecutions,[58] which are handled by the U.S. Department of Justice and U.S. Attorneys around the country.[59] But the practice in states—with some outlawing interested private prosecutors even as others continue to utilize them—varies widely, albeit with locally elected public prosecutors and state attorneys general handling the vast majority of criminal trials and appeals.[60] Although modern-day legal commentators speak of a prosecutor's duty of neutrality[61] and to do justice,[62] early American private prosecutors were often self-interested—even financially through related civil litigation matters—in the prosecutions they commenced and conducted.[63]

In truth, America's criminal justice system many decades ago bears little resemblance to what it looks like today.[64] What were once largely private affairs, with crime victims initiating and driving the judicial process while frequently being either unable to afford counsel or ultimately accepting compensation in lieu of convictions to avoid protracted disputes and further prosecution expenses, has turned into a highly public one. Prosecutions are now controlled almost exclusively by public prosecutors whose salaries are paid by the State, not by victims and their families, though public entities still often contract with private law firms to handle some criminal cases, usually misdemeanors or petty misdemeanors.[65] Naturally, questions have thus been raised about the propriety of private prosecutions by interested parties in the twenty-first century. "The unique nature of criminal law and the corresponding unique role of the prosecutor," the Supreme Court of South Carolina observed in 2010, "illustrate the danger in allowing private prosecutions." "Because a prosecutor is an attorney representing community, rather than private interests, the prosecutor's role is very different from that of a civil attorney," that state's supreme court emphasized, adding: "If a private party is permitted to prosecute a criminal action, we can no longer be assured that the powers of the State are employed only for the interest of the community at large. In fact, we can be absolutely certain that the interests of the private party will influence the prosecution, whether the self-interest lies in encouraging payment of a corporation's debt, influencing settlement in a civil suit, or merely seeking vengeance."[66]

Because the United States has a federal criminal justice system, as well as separate justice systems in the U.S. territories and all fifty states, it is, of course, hard to make sweeping generalizations about the state of the law due to considerable variations between jurisdictions. Over the centuries, though, there has certainly been a general and notable shift away from private prosecutions and toward public ones.[67] In some locales such as New Hampshire, New Jersey, Pennsylvania, Rhode Island, Virginia and Texas, whether by statute, rule of criminal procedure, or case law, private prosecutions are still authorized in limited circumstances or under certain specified conditions. For example, Rule 506 of the Pennsylvania Rules of Criminal Procedure allows a private criminal complainant to seek judicial review of the denial of his or her complaint by the district attorney.[68] Where the district attorney's denial is predicated on a legal evaluation of the evidence, the trial court undertakes a *de novo* review of the matter. But where the district attorney disapproves the private criminal complaint based on policy considerations, the trial court's standard of review of the DA's decision is "abuse of discretion." In a Rule 506 petition for review, "the private criminal complainant must demonstrate the district attorney's decision amounted to bad faith, fraud or unconstitutionality" and "must show the facts of the case lead only to the conclusion that the district attorney's decision was patently discriminatory, arbitrary or pretextual, and therefore not in the public interest."[69] In addition, judicial decisions in other American states, relying on common law precedent, still permit private prosecutors to conduct or assist public prosecutors—in some cases, only for misdemeanors or offenses not subject to imprisonment. For the most part, though, criminal prosecutions in the U.S. are no longer driven primarily by private actors, as they once were, although many private law firms across the country, operating under government contracts, regularly bill and get compensated for handling misdemeanor or petty misdemeanor cases.[70]

In Anglo-American law, the shift away from private prosecutions and toward public ones has actually been quite dramatic. "Criminal prosecution," Scott Ingram, a professor of criminal justice, writes of American history and the way it once was in light of imported, long-entrenched English norms, "had been largely a private pursuit." "Crime victims," he notes, "pursued offenders through the courts, pleading their own cases in minor matters and securing the services of attorneys in serious matters."[71] "At the time when the founding fathers gathered in Philadelphia to hash out the foundation and fabric of American law," notes another scholar, Major John Olson, Jr., a Judge Advocate for the United States Army, "the victim was the primary player in criminal trials."[72] Although modern-day crime victims have various rights, often guaranteed by state constitutional provisions or statutes,[73] it is no longer the case that crime victims are, themselves, preparing indictments or cross-examining the defendant or witnesses in court, though sometimes victims or their family members have been permitted to hire private lawyers to help pursue and prosecute criminal cases. That is not to say that private actors have not been actively involved in criminal matters and prosecutions in the last few decades. They certainly have, especially as eyewitnesses to acts of criminality. They have routinely appeared as witnesses in court, oftentimes offering victim impact statements. In addition, private attorneys—whether through a government contract or a more *ad hoc* arrangement—have been involved in criminal cases along with public prosecutors. As one commentator, Michael Edmund O'Neill, writes: "Perhaps the most notorious example of a state-hired private prosecutor was the prosecution of legendary former boxing heavyweight champion Mike Tyson. In Tyson's 1992 rape prosecution, the Indianapolis District Attorney's Office opted to hire a private attorney to lead the prosecution. The attorney was selected not by the victim, but, rather, the government prosecutor who would have otherwise initiated the case."[74]

There were, to be sure, a plethora of public prosecutions in early America, including, for example, of "delinquents for crimes and offences" in Georgia who were, by law, to be prosecuted by the attorney general or a solicitor general.[75] But it was a mixture of public and private prosecutions, with public prosecutions only growing in popularity over time. By the eighteenth century, one scholarly article notes, "most states had committed to the concept of public prosecutions," though "because of deficiencies in the office of public prosecutor, American citizens continued to prosecute private criminal actions in many locales during the nineteenth century."[76] Aaron Burr's highly publicized trial for treason, led by George Hay, appointed in 1803 to be the U.S. Attorney for the District of Virginia, is just one of many examples of early American public prosecutions.[77] But in those days, state and local private prosecutions, which, as in the English justice system, clearly favored the wealthy over the poor in terms of access to justice, were still common. "Private prosecutors," the victims of crime who often retained private lawyers (in some cases, more than one), conducted prosecutions of everything from murder,[78] assault and battery,[79] and trespass[80] to financial crimes,[81] defrauding creditors,[82] disturbing public worship,[83] stealing wood,[84] and causing property loss or destruction, however large or small (e.g., $17 of damage to a washing kettle).[85] Today, in sharp contrast, public prosecutors' offices routinely handle almost all serious criminal matters and, especially in urban centers, a large percentage of less serious offenses, too. Their highly skilled, licensed lawyers—educated in law schools and, in most cases, very seasoned after years of on-the-job training—specialize in the criminal law's administration and appear before courts of law to adjudicate criminal cases. Public prosecutors represent "the state," "the commonwealth," or "the people" and do not owe fidelity to private interests.[86]

Public prosecutions are now the norm in American society. But the remnants of the country's once-extensive private prosecution system, which began to be dismantled in the early eighteenth century, still remain. "In 1704," writes University of Virginia law professor Darryl Brown of the nation's heritage, "Connecticut established what was probably the first public prosecutor's office."[87] That initial step toward public prosecution then, over many generations, became a torrent of rushing water that flowed toward America's now-dominant public prosecution system. According to the U.S. Bureau of Justice Statistics, there are currently more than 2,300 public prosecutors' offices in the United States.[88] The National District Attorneys Association, based in Arlington, Virginia, was itself formed in 1950, and—according to its website—"has more than 5,500 members across the nation representing state and local prosecutors' offices from both urban and rural districts, as well as large and small jurisdictions."[89] In fact, America's tradition of public prosecution now dates back centuries, along with a much more recent tradition of public defenders' offices to represent indigent defendants accused of crimes.[90] With the U.S. Supreme Court's landmark decision in *Gideon v. Wainwright* (1963) accelerating the formation of public defenders' offices, such offices—like public prosecutors' offices—are now a fixture around the country. That decision put criminal defendants on a more level playing field with public prosecutors' offices, with *Gideon* holding that the U.S. Constitution's Sixth Amendment requires states to provide attorneys to indigent criminal defendants unable to afford them.[91]

American history is complex, full of both sordid and uplifting chapters, from slavery, lynchings, and state-sanctioned executions driven by racial prejudice in the former category to the civil rights and women's suffrage movements in the latter. Private prosecutions are, certainly, part of America's knotty past, and America's modern-day criminal justice system cannot be truly understood without analyzing the impact of racial prejudice and knowing about historical practices, including the now largely forgotten history associated with private prosecutions. As explained later in the book, overt racism shaped colonial and early American laws, with racial discrimination at times influencing the very *method* of prosecution—public versus private—selected by state officials. With Philadelphia's private prosecutors—the crime victims or their chosen representatives—taking on (as one description puts it) "the solemn and majestic" responsibility of prosecutors well into the nineteenth century,[92] history shows that only gradually did American public prosecutions surpass—and then, in time, far exceed—private ones.[93] In the modern era, criminal justice reform is still very much a work in progress.

American jurisdictions, historical records demonstrate, acted much earlier than the British Parliament in making the transition from largely private to mostly public prosecutions, though there are lots of variations in America, in terms of the exact timing of the switch, because of the country's system of federalism.[94] "[P]ublic prosecution in the common-law world," Vincent Chiao explains in *Criminal Law in the Age of the Administrative State*, "first arose in a systematic way in North America."[95] After the colony of Connecticut moved to public prosecutors in 1704, Virginia and other locales followed suit.[96] As Chiao writes of the Anglo-American world's transition—albeit an incomplete one, replete with scores of legislative enactments and judicial rulings over the years—from private to public prosecutions: "Private prosecutions remained the norm in England until much later: the office of the Director of Public Prosecutions was not created until 1879, and another century went by before the Crown Prosecution Service was created in 1986. Admittedly, the practice of private prosecution persisted in the United States well after the introduction of public prosecutors, 'because some wealthy crime victims did not trust the low-paid, often inexperienced, and understaffed public prosecutors.'" "[A]lthough private prosecutions remain possible today," Chiao adds of the current state of affairs, "that power is typically thoroughly circumscribed by official discretion."[97] The job of the prosecutor involves life-changing decisions and lots of discretion, and that is, obviously, one of the major concerns about putting such enormous power into private hands.

In hindsight, certain trends in the law reveal themselves and become clear. While a modern-day Pennsylvania federal judge has aptly observed that "private criminal prosecutions once characterized the common law,"[98] that system of private prosecution came under attack across the United States. In the late 1830s in Kentucky, when a private prosecutor was paid a $1,000 fee by the deceased's relations and friends in a high-stakes capital murder case, the defense attorney—in his argument to jurors—excoriated the practice of private prosecution as a violation of due process and the presumption of innocence.[99] And when New York congressman Daniel Sickles was famously put on trial for murdering his wife's lover, Philip Barton Key II, the District of Columbia's handsome District Attorney and the son of Francis Scott Key of "The Star-Spangled Banner" fame, in Lafayette Square, just across the street from the White House, one of his defense attorneys, Edwin Stanton, took a pointed swipe at the use of a private prosecutor. That, notably, was one of the earliest cases in which the "temporary insanity" defense was successfully invoked. The Key family had hired a private attorney, James Carlisle, to join the public prosecution team, and after questioning if the prosecution had engaged in "destruction of evidence," Stanton—in a loud, passionate voice—decried "private prosecutors" in a dig at Carlisle's role.[100] Two prosecutors—a public and a private one—actually handled the case, but the appearance of Mr. Carlisle, the private prosecutor, was said to have created "an unusual spectacle" in the courthouse. Stanton argued that the prosecution was trying to "lead" his client, Daniel Sickles, "to the gallows by those who are malignantly seeking for his blood."[101] Stanton, the talented lawyer, later became Abraham Lincoln's Secretary of War.[102]

The law's history traverses many eras—from medieval to colonial to modern times. The first U.S. civil rights acts were passed by Congress in 1866, 1870, 1871 and 1875,[103] and federal judges—in delivering grand jury charges—once frequently warned against the dangers of "private prosecutors."[104] In the nineteenth century, though, private prosecutions were still being used with considerable regularity in American states—and by the end of the nineteenth century, a number of state courts had blessed the entrenched practice in one fashion or another.[105] As historian Robert Ireland wrote in a 1955 article about the prior use of private prosecutors in American states: "By 1820, most states had established local public prosecutors known by a variety of names, including state's attorney, county attorney, district attorney, and commonwealth's attorney. Yet, because of deficiencies in the office of the public prosecutor, privately funded prosecutors constituted a significant element of the state criminal justice system throughout the nineteenth century." "Privately funded prosecutors," Ireland explained, "most often appeared in murder trials, including some of the most famous of the nineteenth century." "Perhaps the most famous," he noted, "involved the trial in Boston in 1850 of Harvard University professor, John White Webster, for the murder of Dr. George Parkman." Parkman's family had hired George Bemis, a prominent lawyer, to assist the attorney general, John Clifford, in the prosecution. As Ireland summed up the historical use of the practice: "Privately funded prosecutors appeared in many of the famous trials of the avengers of sexual dishonor including those of Daniel Sickles, Amelia Norman, Laura D. Fair, 'Little Phil' Thompson, Harry Crawford Black, George W. Cole, James Nutt, and Daniel McFarland. These celebrated trials and others, including relevant cases found in *American State Trials*, constitute the basic source of information about the realities of privately funded prosecution in the nineteenth century United States."[106]

Through the years, the American use of private prosecutors has created some unique constitutional law arguments and legal controversies—from whether private prosecutors should be forced to pay the costs of ill-founded prosecutions[107] to how much control, if any, a public prosecutor can cede to a private prosecutor.[108] In a recent case, *Rehberg v. Paulk* (2012), the U.S. Supreme Court observed that, "in 1871, it was common for criminal cases to be prosecuted by private parties," but that "private prosecutors, like private plaintiffs in civil suits, did not enjoy absolute immunity from suit." "Instead," the Supreme Court noted, "'the generally accepted rule' was that a private complainant who procured an arrest or prosecution could be held liable in an action for malicious prosecution if the complainant acted with malice and without probable cause." However, "[i]n the decades after the adoption of the 1871 Civil Rights Act," a piece of legislation passed to protect Black citizens from the Ku Klux Klan, the Court emphasized in *Rehberg* of the country's history, "the prosecutorial function was increasingly assumed by public officials, and common-law courts held that public prosecutors, unlike their private predecessors, were absolutely immune from the types of tort claims that an aggrieved or vengeful criminal defendant was most likely to assert, namely, claims for malicious prosecution or defamation." "This adaptation of prosecutorial immunity," the Court stressed in *Rehberg*, "accommodated the special needs of public, as opposed to private, prosecutors."[109] Today, it is estimated that there are approximately 5,800 federal prosecutors,[110] with scores of public prosecutors at the state and local levels.[111]

Current practices as regards the legality or illegality of private prosecutions (or restrictions on them) differ wildly among individual countries[112] and, in the U.S., among American states.[113] In a 2018 article in the *Minnesota Law Review*, scholar Darryl Brown writes: "[M]any countries continue to authorize private citizens to initiate criminal prosecutions when public officials do not, and others allow privately funded attorneys to assist or supplement public prosecutors in litigating criminal cases." "Canada, Australia, New Zealand, and England and Wales," he explains, "all continue to allow private prosecutions, and fifteen of the twenty-eight member states of the European Union grant victims some comparable authority." "Details vary across jurisdictions," Brown observes of such prosecutions, "but everywhere private prosecutors' authority is limited by oversight from public prosecutors and courts."[114] American states take far different approaches, with some outlawing them altogether while others embrace or tolerate them in one form or another. Another scholar, Mugambi Jouet, puts it this way of the use of private prosecutors in continental Europe, known for its inquisitorial civil law system: "In misdemeanor cases and, to a lesser extent, in felony cases, continental systems generally allow victims to act as private prosecutors, which enables them to directly summon the accused to court and seek to prove his guilt without the involvement of government prosecutors."[115]

For the moment, suffice it say that a wide variety of private prosecution mechanisms still exist around the world. In fact, within the context of the U.S. legal system, a specific distinction has been made by American scholars between "victim-retained private prosecution" and "outsourced prosecution." *Victim-retained private prosecution,* one source notes, refers to "the practice of allowing the victim of a crime to retain private counsel ... to bring a prosecution on the victim's behalf." In contrast, *outsourced prosecution* refers to "situations in which the Government hires a private lawyer or law firm (the 'outsourced prosecutor') to handle some portion of a prosecution."[116] "[V]ictim-retained prosecutors," Professor Roger A. Fairfax, Jr., then at the George Washington University Law School, has noted, "generally are authorized only to assist the public prosecutor or, in rare circumstances, to step in and perform the prosecutorial role when the government declines to do so in a given case."[117] In a 2010 law review article, Fairfax pointed out of the outsourcing of the prosecutorial function by local governments: "[A] significant amount of prosecution outsourcing already is being undertaken by smaller jurisdictions across the nation. These governments, with limited budgets for criminal justice administration, often turn to the private bar for prosecution services." "Rather than spend scarce resources on a traditional public prosecutor," Fairfax wrote, "some governments will pay private lawyers or law firms to prosecute criminal matters within the jurisdiction."[118]

Legal systems are not static, and over the centuries, prosecution methods have not remained the same. Throughout U.S. and world history,[119] private prosecutors undeniably played a significant role in countless criminal cases,[120] and they still appear in at least some places,[121] whether in capital or other felony cases, or for lower-level or petty offenses.[122] "Private prosecution dominated criminal justice during the colonial period," explains historian Allen Steinberg, who studied early American practices in Philadelphia's criminal justice system.[123] "Colonists who arrived on North American shores," legal commentator Carolyn Ramsey concurs, "brought with them a tradition of allowing crime victims to initiate and prosecute their own cases."[124] Such private prosecutions have included instances where the state's ultimate sanction—the death penalty—was sought and obtained. In Joseph Stanley Faulder's capital murder case in Texas, two private attorneys were paid approximately $90,000 to prosecute Faulder for the 1975 murder of an elderly widow. Although a public prosecutor was assigned to the case, that public prosecutor's participation was limited to jury selection, where he questioned a few prospective jurors, and to putting into the record a deceased hearsay declarant's testimony. That prosecutor even took a day off from the trial to go golfing.[125] Sentenced to death for the murder, Faulder—a Canadian citizen[126] known to his family and friends in Alberta as "Stan"—was executed by lethal injection in 1999 despite a legal challenge to the use of private prosecutors in his case.[127]

In another, even more recent capital case, in Kansas, a Wyandotte County judge, despite some personal misgivings, ruled in 2019 that private lawyers had to be allowed to assist in the death penalty prosecution of a man charged with killing two sheriff's deputies, Theresa King and Patrick Rohrer. Thirty-year-old Antoine Fielder was charged with capital murder after the fatal shooting in June 2018 of King and Rohrer while they were escorting Fielder back to jail after a court hearing in a robbery case. "Under Kansas law," *The Kansas City Star* reported, "crime victims can pay for lawyers to assist prosecutors as 'associate attorneys,' and the families of Rohrer and King have hired married law partners Tom Bath and Tricia Bath." Attorneys for the Kansas Death Penalty Defense Unit argued that the law in question had never been used in a capital case, contending that its application raised "novel constitutional, statutory and ethical issues." But the Baths cited Kansas Supreme Court precedents allowing crime victims to hire private attorneys. The Wyandotte County District Attorney had no objection to the Baths' participation, and District Judge Bill Klapper, though finding the private prosecutors' involvement in the case "inherently problematic," ruled that Kansas law allowed their participation.[128] While former Johnson County assistant district attorney Tom Bath, who, as a private prosecutor, had previously helped convict another man, university professor Thomas Murray, for killing his ex-wife,[129] Tricia Bath was an assistant Wyandotte County district attorney before going into private practice.[130]

Though its use has waned considerably in American life over the last century and a half, the antiquated practice of private prosecution thus continues to be a reality. "Private prosecution," one commentator, George Dession, observes of the idiosyncratic tradition that raises significant ethical, legal, and conflict of interest issues, "was a medieval institution, going back to a time when the civil and the criminal were not well differentiated and the chief purpose of the law was to preserve the peace by providing an orderly substitute for private vengeance through proceedings in the courts."[131] A "tort" is a wrong, with early English law not making a clear distinction between criminal and civil violations.[132] In medieval times, "kin vengeance" was common among Germanic peoples and in English and Scandinavian societies.[133] Yet, with private prosecutions by interested parties persisting in some American locales, court challenges—some successful and some not—have continued to be made to such increasingly rare prosecutions. Those challenges have come in capital cases, but also ones involving petty offenses. In a recent New Jersey case, a practicing lawyer, Howard Myerowitz, was convicted of a petty disorderly persons offense by the complainant's private counsel. In that case, *State v. Myerowitz* (2015),[134] the Appellate Division of the Superior Court of New Jersey held that the complainant's private counsel could not prosecute the harassment charge without completing a very specific private prosecution certification form required by New Jersey law.

To better understand private prosecution as it exists today in American states, whether for felonies or lesser offenses, one must explore its long history abroad and domestically, the subject of the first part of this book. Notably, England and Scotland diverged substantially in their approaches to handling prosecutions, and that diverse history informed the American experience. In the United States, private prosecution—the custom inherited from England—used to be a fairly routine practice in multiple places into the nineteenth century.[135] It would remain so until public prosecution became the American norm and public prosecutors' offices steadily grew in reputation and size and, under the leadership of elected county and district attorneys, professionalized.[136] "In the late eighteenth and early nineteenth centuries," one scholar notes of early American public prosecutors, "prosecutors were still part-timers who spent much of their practice on noncriminal matters."[137] In 1868, the year that the U.S. Constitution's Fourteenth Amendment was ratified, private prosecutions in Pennsylvania—the birthplace of the Declaration of Independence and the Constitution—were common.[138] Private prosecutions—as the book recounts—were frequent in other locales, too, with at least some states in the South moving to public prosecutions for very different reasons than their northern counterparts.

Professor Eric Freedman at Hofstra University observed in 2016 that a comprehensive account of America's gradual, as-yet-incomplete transition from private to public prosecutions has yet to be written, an assessment shared in Jason Twede's recent Ph.D. thesis, "Go Public: How the Government Assumed the Authority to Prosecute in the Southern United States."[139] But whatever this book may do to rectify that scholarly gap, it is already crystal clear from the existing scholarly literature and the history of crime and punishment that, over time, a number of U.S. states—whether legislatively or through judicial decisions—outlawed or restricted private prosecutions,[140] even as other states continued to allow their use[141] or turned aside legal challenges to privately retained lawyers conducting criminal trials.[142] Police departments, correctional and sentencing practices, and American public prosecutors' offices are being scrutinized more than ever in the modern era,[143] with many practices—from cash bail and chokeholds to other policing techniques, and harsh sentences for non-violent drug offenders—increasingly in the public spotlight. The use of capital charges that, upon offenders' convictions, send men and women to death row, have also come under intense scrutiny, especially as the federal government resumed the use of executions in 2020 and early 2021 after a 17-year hiatus, with the Trump Administration's Justice Department executing inmates—thirteen in all—in rapid succession even in the midst of the COVID-19 pandemic.[144] Flying under the radar, though, the lesser known practice of private prosecution—the legal tradition rooted in England,[145] used extensively in colonial[146] and early America[147] and elsewhere,[148] and still in use in select American locales—has largely escaped public scrutiny. That practice, as with the others, should be subject to reexamination and a fully developed critique.

A prosecutor's duty, it has been repeatedly emphasized, is to "do justice."[149] "Doing justice," as one source emphasizes, "means that the prosecutor should attempt to convict only those who actually are guilty, not simply those against whom a conviction can be obtained."[150] Public prosecution units must therefore serve the public interest, not private interests, and when individual prosecutors stray from that appointed mission and responsibility, courts do not—and should not—hesitate to find prosecutorial misconduct.[151] Yet when victims or their relatives retain private lawyers to prosecute an accused, it creates an inherent—a *structural*—conflict of interest,[152] raising serious ethical,[153] due process,[154] and equal protection[155] issues. The American Bar Association's Model Rules of Professional Conduct contain an entire provision—Rule 3.8—titled "Special Responsibilities of a Prosecutor," and those ethical rules contain separate provisions governing such topics as the attorney-client relationship and the duties of an attorney. Rule 1.2 of the Model Rules of Professional Conduct, for example, states in part that "a lawyer shall abide by a client's decisions concerning the objectives of representation."[156]

Although private prosecution is, to one degree or another, still in use in many regions of the world[157]—and thus in many individual countries,[158] from Argentina,[159] Montenegro,[160] and New Zealand,[161] to Russia,[162] Serbia,[163] and Spain,[164] and from China[165] Finland,[166] and Taiwan,[167] to Croatia,[168] Kenya,[169] and South Africa[170]—private prosecution now constitutes a small percentage of American criminal prosecutions, especially in felony cases. By contrast, back in the mid-1950s, the practice was relatively common, with sixty-two percent of public prosecutors responding to a survey indicating that they permitted privately hired attorneys to assist in criminal proceedings.[171] The questionable practice of private prosecution,[172] despite the long-standing efforts to put a stop to it, stubbornly remains a reality in various American states—sometimes only for misdemeanors or petty offenses[173]—as well as in specific countries in Africa,[174] Asia,[175] Europe,[176] and elsewhere in the Americas.[177] But the practice has already been outlawed in *some* American states, including heavily populated California,[178] and greatly restricted in others,[179] leading one to legitimately ask: should the practice[180] finally be outlawed altogether? It is that question that this book, *Private Prosecution in America*, seeks to address.

The U.S. Supreme Court has not been entirely silent on the subject, though it has yet to weigh in with the full weight of its authority to interpret the U.S. Constitution. In 1987, the Supreme Court, in *Young v. United States ex rel. Vuitton et Fils, S.A.*,[181] relied on its "supervisory authority" to overturn contempt convictions secured by counsel for an interested party.[182] In that case, in what could foreshadow a U.S. Supreme Court ruling that the use of private prosecutors violates the U.S. Constitution,[183] the Supreme Court ruled that the appointment of counsel for an interested party created opportunities for conflicts of interest to arise and at least an appearance of impropriety.[184] In making its decision, the Supreme Court in *Young* declined to rely on any provision of the U.S. Constitution,[185] instead using its "supervisory power," thus leaving open, for another day, the issue of the constitutionality of private prosecutions.[186] The U.S. Supreme Court and other courts have frequently invoked the "appearance of impropriety" standard in judicial proceedings,[187] and this book argues that, in assessing the practice of interested private prosecutions, courts should carefully examine the U.S. Constitution's Due Process and Equal Protection Clauses.

In 2010, in *Robertson v. United States ex rel. Watson*,[188] the U.S. Supreme Court again came close to addressing the constitutionality of private prosecutors. However, the Supreme Court—over a vigorous dissent, and the language of the U.S. Constitution's due process of law and equal protection guarantees notwithstanding—ultimately decided it was not the appropriate time to address the issue.[189] The U.S. Constitution's Fifth Amendment provides that "[n]o person shall ... be deprived of life, liberty, or property, without due process of law,"[190] and the Constitution's Fourteenth Amendment—making provisions of the U.S. Bill of Rights applicable to the States[191] after the Fourteenth Amendment's ratification in 1868[192] and a series of U.S. Supreme Court cases interpreting it[193]—also guarantees: "nor shall any State deprive any person of life, liberty, or property, without due process of law; nor deny to any person within its jurisdiction the equal protection of the laws."[194] In *Robertson*, writes Tulane University law professor Tania Tetlow, the Supreme Court "came tantalizingly close to addressing" the private prosecution issue but "a majority of the Court decided that the relevant issues were not clearly presented by the facts of the case, and the Court denied certiorari as 'improvidently granted.'"[195]

This book, an extended and much-expanded sequel to an *Arkansas Law Review* article I wrote on the topic of private prosecutors more than 25 years ago,[196] argues that the U.S. Constitution should, at long last, be read to bar interested private prosecutions as a matter of law. Certainly, much has changed in American law and society since the country's founding era and the nineteenth century when private prosecutions were once so prevalent. In this, the third decade of the twenty-first century, the U.S. Supreme Court must thus no longer turn a blind eye to the practice and all the obvious ethical red flags raised by it. Instead, the Supreme Court must give credence to the inherently problematic nature of interested private prosecutions, then act to ensure the criminal justice system's integrity. Given America's now long-standing tradition of using public instead of private prosecutions[197] to adjudicate criminal responsibility and to administer justice,[198] and given the infrequency of interested private prosecutions in terms of actual cases brought, adjudicated, or tried in court,[199] the U.S. Supreme Court should declare unconstitutional the increasingly arbitrary and rare use of such prosecutions as a violation of due process[200] and equal protection of the laws.[201]

Way back in 1783, before the U.S. Constitution's ratification, Benjamin Franklin—the American founder, inventor, polymath, and scientist—expressed a concern about "private Resentment" in the criminal justice system.[202] In the twenty-first century, there is simply no appropriate justification for continuing to allow interested private prosecutions. Some state legislatures and judicial systems have already outlawed interested private prosecutors, and more should do so.[203] Lawmakers certainly have the power to forbid them, and state supreme courts are also free to interpret their own state constitutions to protect individual rights in a manner that would bar interested private prosecutions. Prosecutors have immense power. Although grand juries were intended by America's founders to check abusive power, Chief Judge Sol Wachtler, of the New York Court of Appeals, warned in the mid-1980s that a prosecutor has such enormous influence that a grand jury could be convinced to "indict a ham sandwich."[204] That immense power necessitates that prosecutors not be biased or prejudiced. Allowing interested private prosecutions in capital cases and criminal matters where an accused's life or liberty is at stake is particularly egregious. At the next available opportunity, the U.S. Supreme Court—using the U.S. Constitution's Due Process and Equal Protection Clauses, and safeguarding the Eighth Amendment's protection against "cruel and unusual punishments" to avoid arbitrary and capricious results[205]—should itself thus explicitly hold that private prosecutions by interested parties are unethical, unconstitutional, and violate the fundamental rights of the accused.[206] A twenty-first century reading of the U.S. Constitution demands no less.

PRIVATE PROSECUTION IN AMERICA

1

PRIVATE PROSECUTION IN THE BRITISH ISLES

Criminal Procedure in English vs. Scottish Law

The English Common Law Origins of Private Prosecution

Several legal scholars, including Allen Steinberg and Joan Jacoby, have attempted to trace the historical origins of private prosecution in the United States.[1] These scholars, examining historical documents, observe that private prosecutions were once routine in common-law England, where the legal system primarily relied upon the victim or the victim's relatives to bring a criminal to justice.[2] According to these historians, and as the now centuries-old documentary record itself makes clear, private prosecutions developed in England as a means of facilitating private vengeance,[3] though a leading English jurist, Sir Edward Coke, the author of *The Institutes of the Laws of England*, professed and insisted in the seventeenth century that "no man for any injury whatsoever, ought to use private revenge; for revenge belongeth to the magistrate, who is Gods lieutenant."[4] The nineteenth-century British historian, Sir James Stephen, later put it this way in *A History of the Criminal Law of England* (1883): "The fact that the private vengeance of the person wronged by a crime was the principal source to which men trusted for the administration of justice in early times is one of the most characteristic circumstances connected with English criminal law, and has had much to do with the development of what may perhaps be regarded as its principal distinctive peculiarity, namely the degree to which a criminal trial resembles a private litigation."[5]

In medieval England and until quite recently in that country, private individuals played the dominant role in English life in instituting—and then driving, basically from start to finish—the criminal justice process.[6] "In Tudor and Stuart England," scholars Janelle Greenberg and Martin Greenberg of the University of Pittsburgh explain, "the machinery of the criminal justice system could be set in motion only by a private person, in the form of an appeal, or by the Crown, in the form of an indictment or an information." "Appeal of felony," they note, "was a private action brought by the victim or his or her relatives against the suspected offender" and was of "considerable importance" in the Middle Ages,[7] though its use "loomed less large in the 16th and 17th centuries." "Of far greater importance," they recount of the latter time period, "was prosecution by indictment or information." An indictment, initiating a prosecution for a felony or misdemeanor in the king's name,[8] was—they explain—"an accusation made by 12 or more laymen, usually sitting as a grand jury." "In noncapital cases, that is, those criminal offenses which were less than felonies and which were usually called misdemeanors," they add, the available criminal procedure "could be by information as well as by indictment." "Informations," they expound, "were accusations brought either by a private person or by a law officer, e.g., the attorney-general, and were frequently used to enforce economic regulations."[9]

A Complete Collection of State Trials and Proceedings for High Treason and Other Crimes and Misdemeanors from the Earliest Period to the Year 1783 (1816), shows that, in England, royal Crown prosecutors played a key role in trying high-profile offenses against the monarchy, such as acts of treason.[10] However, in prior centuries, *private prosecutors*—that is, the actual victims of crime or their family members—took on the weighty responsibility of initiating the vast majority of English criminal cases. Such private prosecutors charged offenders with everything from murder to manslaughter, to rape and robbery, as well as an array of other offenses.[11] In prominent state trials, of the kind compiled in *A Complete Collection of State Trials*, a prosecuting attorney such as the Attorney General regularly appeared. Historian John Langbein—after examining Old Bailey sessions papers from the late seventeenth century and early eighteenth century—found, however, that "[i]n ordinary felony trials at the Old Bailey," the prosecution was, in practice, unrepresented by counsel. For example, in one 1678 pamphlet reporting on thirty-two cases, Langbein notes "there is no mention of prosecuting counsel" in any of the cases, including those involving private prosecutors. "[T]echnically," Langbein explains, a private prosecutor was "anyone whom the JP"—the justice of the peace—"bound over to prosecute; in practice the victim or his kin."[12] The "Old Bailey" was the customary moniker for the Central Criminal Court of England and Wales, so named because of the London street on which it was located.[13] In the law, to "bind over" someone meant to place the person under a legal obligation to perform some act.[14] Langbein notes that the Old Bailey of the 1730s processed "a dozen and more cases to full jury trial in one day"; that a jury trial in those days was "*a summary proceeding*"; and that "[n]either prosecutor nor defense was represented in ordinary criminal trials."[15]

Private prosecutions have a long pedigree, and thousands of years ago, they were used in ancient Greece[16] and were an integral part of Roman law.[17] For example, in ancient Athens, prosecutions were typically brought by volunteers—private individuals who acted either out of a sense of civic duty or an attempt to advance a political career. As one history of Greek practices explains: "In case of conviction, the prosecutor might be entitled to a portion of the defendant's paid fine or confiscated property. Frivolous prosecution was discouraged by a law requiring the prosecutor to pay a fine himself if his case won less than one-fifth of the jury vote."[18] By contrast, one 1830 encyclopedia observes that the procedural mechanism of an *appeal* in English law (*i.e.*, "criminal prosecution at the suit of a private individual") "originated in those times when great offences were generally expiated by payment of a sum of money, called a *weregild*, to the person injured." "This custom," that encyclopedia noted, "seems to have been common to us with other northern nations, and to have been derived from the Germans" and "appears to obtain among most semi-barbarous nations, where the nature of criminal justice is but imperfectly understood, and where offences are regarded rather with a view to private injury than to public detriment."[19] Lord Chief Justice John Holt (1642–1710) called the then-existing *appeal of murder* criminal procedure "a most noble birthright of an Englishman," while Lord Ashburton—in the House of Commons—called it "that great pillar of the Constitution."[20]

A *weregild*—as one 1876 law dictionary puts it—was "[t]he fine formerly paid for killing a man, when such crimes were punished with a pecuniary mulct, and not with death." "This fine," that dictionary notes, "was paid partly to the king, for the loss of his subject, party to the lord whose vassal he was, and partly to the next of kin of the slain man."[21] In Germanic societies, a *weregild*—described by one historian as "the equivalent, material value of a man who was a victim of theft, insult, injury, or even murder"—was the fine "an offending party had to pay the offended," whether that fine was paid in cattle, furs, jewelry, land, produce or through other means. The contours of this ancient Anglo-Saxon custom varied over time,[22] with the *weregild* for homicide during the time of Tacitus in Rome said to be "due to the relatives of the deceased" and, for other offenses, "one-half to the injured party, and one-half to the state." "In the days of Edward the Elder the weregild had become a much more complicated penalty, the composition for homicide consisting of four different payments," one source notes of the concept's complexity, explaining that two of these payments went to the king, with the other two going to "the kindred to loosen the hand of the avenger of blood" and to "the overlord to compensate him for the loss of a vassal."[23] "This social institution, while perhaps strange to our eyes," that history relays, "did fill the function of helping end the ceaseless feuding that ultimately might destroy a society."[24] Like the deadly feud between the Hatfields and the McCoys that took place along the Kentucky and West Virginia border during the nineteenth century,[25] blood feuds or personal vendettas were not uncommon in medieval and Renaissance times.[26]

In the case of English homicides, a person with legal standing had the common-law right to bring a murderer to justice within a year and a day of the murder,[27] though a murder victim's family members, of course, were often not lawyers and might not have any relevant experience in initiating a criminal case, let alone in conducting a murder prosecution.[28] Professor James Barr Ames, a prominent legal historian at Harvard Law School, observed in 1913 that "[t]he common law is essentially of Teutonic origin, and came from two sources: Anglo-Saxon law and Norman law, Norman law being Frankish." In a lecture on the substantive law before the time of Henry de

Bracton (c. 1210 – c. 1268), Ames observed that, in prior centuries, "the law of torts included much that in modern times falls under the head of criminal law." "Thus," he emphasized, "killing, mayhem, robbery, and the like belonged principally to private law." As Ames described the law prior to Bracton's time: "There was no public prosecutor, and nothing corresponding to an indictment. If the party injured, or, in the case of killing, the kinsmen of the deceased, did not seek redress, the wrong went unpunished." "If the party injured proceeded against the wrongdoer," Ames observed, "the latter, in most cases, escaped with the payment of a pecuniary compensation and a fine, unless he refused to appear, in which case, as in any civil action, he was outlawed." "Of this fine," Ames noted, "the larger part, 'faidus,' went to the plaintiff and the smaller, 'fredus,' to the state."

In discussing the law of the Salic Franks, administered in town hall-style courts called Hundred Courts in which all freemen served as judges, James Barr Ames explained that the system of fines and pecuniary compensation was quite exact. As Ames recounted: "One could tell to a shilling just what it would cost to kill one's neighbor's cow, or even the neighbor himself. If the latter was a free man the compensation was two hundred shillings; if a slave, twenty-five shillings; if a royal official, six hundred shillings. Similarly there was a fixed price for a broken nose or an eye knocked out." After noting that Anglo-Saxon law was "similar to the Salic law," Ames pointed out that "[t]he Anglo-Norman law was a development" from the Normans—an ethic group that arose from contacts between Norse Viking settlers of Normandy and indigenous Franks and Gallo-Romans. As Ames stressed: "Actions for torts in the King's courts after the Norman Conquest were known as appeals, a Norman term. Thus there were appeals of battery, mayhem, robbery, larceny, arson, rape, homicide and murder, imprisonment, and sorcery." In the criminal law, *mayhem* was defined as "[t]he act of unlawfully and violently depriving another of the use of such of his members as may render him less able, in fighting, either to defend himself or annoy his adversary." "The cutting or disabling or weakening a man's hand or finger, or striking out his eye or foretooth, or depriving him of those parts the loss of which abates his courage," John Bouvier's nineteenth-century law dictionary emphasized, "are held to be mayhems."[29]

Giles Jacob (1686–1744), a leading British writer whose works also included a popular law dictionary, wrote an entire treatise, *The Laws of Appeals and Murder* (1719), in which he covered the then-existing, if somewhat byzantine, terrain of English criminal procedure.[30] In it, Jacob—a member of Lincoln's Inn, one of London's legendary Inns of Court where barristers trained and associated with one another—began by observing that the word *appeal* "is deriv'd from the French word *Appeller*, signifying to *accuse*." That word, he noted, "is frequently us'd in the Common and Civil Law, on the Removal of a Cause from an inferiour Judge to a Superior; but more commonly from the private Accusation of a Murderer, by a Person who had Interest in the Party kill'd." It was appeals of the latter kind—"Appeal of Murder,"[31] "Appeal of Homicide,"[32] appeals "of Maihem, Rape, Robbery, &c."—that Jacob's treatise discussed at length.[33] "*Appeal* in some of our Law-Books," Jacob continued, "is said to come from *Appello*, to call," pointing out that per Bracton, the thirteenth-century English jurist famous for *De Legibus et Consuetudinibus Angliae* (*On the Laws and Customs of England*), "*Appello* in the Common Law is as much as *Accusatio* with the Civilians: For as in the Civil Law, Cognizance of Criminal Causes is had either upon Inquisition, Denunciation or Accusation, so in ours it is taken upon Indictment or Appeal; Indictments comprehending both Inquisition and Denunciation."[34]

Until more modern times, prosecutions in the British Isles were routinely hampered by the lack of an organized police force. David Jones, in *Crime in Nineteenth-Century Wales* (1992), has observed that a crime victim was his own "policeman,"[35] with scholar Barbara Shapiro writing that "[t]he dominance of private prosecution created considerable inconvenience and expense for those who prosecuted,"[36] especially those without the requisite training or resources. "In our Ancient Books," Giles Jacob wrote of the standard legal terminology then in use, "he that appeals is call'd *Accusator*; but at this time he hath the Denomination of *Appellor* or *Appellant*, and is in legal Signification peculiarly applied to Appeals of three sorts: First, of Wrong to an Ancestor, whose Heir male he is, and that only of Death: The second is of Wrong to the Husband, and is prosecuted by the Wife for the Death of her Husband: And the third is of Wrongs done to the Appellants themselves, as Robbery, Rape and Maihem."[37] After defining *Appeal of Maihem*,[38] *Appeal of Rape*,[39] and *Appeal of Robbery*,[40] Jacob stressed that "[a]n Appeal is commenced two Ways, either by Writ or Bill." As he wrote in his legal treatise: "Appeal by Writ is when a Writ is purchased out of the Chancery by one to another to this End, that he appeal a third of some Felony committed by him, finding Pledges that he shall do it, and deliver this Writ to the Sheriff to be recorded. Appeal by Bill is where a man of himself gives up his Accusation in Writing to the Sheriff or Coroner, offering to undergo the Burden of Appealing the Person therein nam'd." In old English law, it was customary to get at least two pledges of prosecution.[41]

Over time, English norms for the handling of appeals by victims or their next of kin developed, though adjustments—as is so often the case when it comes to legal matters—were made in the law from time to time as Parliament deemed appropriate. In his treatise, Jacob—considering the effect of a finding of guilt in a criminal case—notes that "[i]n an Appeal of Murder, the Jury may find the Defendant guilty of Manslaughter, or not, as they shall see Cause; but if they find him guilty of Manslaughter, that shall be a good Plea to an Indictment for the same Murder."[42] "But if the Defendant be convicted of Manslaughter, on an Indictment, and is allowed the Benefit of Clergy, and read as a Clerk," he emphasized, referring to the once-in-use legal doctrine of *benefit of clergy*,[43] "it is a good Bar to Appeal of Murder."[44] "Benefit of clergy" allowed a first-time convicted felon (and eventually, in the seventeenth century, women)[45] to avoid the death penalty if the felon could recite a biblical verse—namely, Psalm 51. That psalm became popularly known as the "neck verse" because it could literally save one's neck. As one law dictionary observed of benefit of clergy: "In its original sense, the phrase denoted the exemption which was accorded to clergymen from the jurisdiction of the secular courts, or from arrest or attachment on criminal process issuing from those courts in certain particular cases. Afterwards, it meant a privilege of exemption from the punishment of death ...."[46]

The English criminal law had layers of complexity, and early English criminal procedure was particularly dense. "If upon an Indictment of Murder," Jacob continued, laying out the then-prevailing English law in thick prose, "the Party is convicted of Manslaughter, and immediately after at the same Gaol-Delivery the Wife or Heir of the Deceased shall put in an Appeal, the Convict is to be called to Judgment upon the Indictment, without taking notice of the subsequent Appeal, which cannot obstruct it, and to be allowed his Clergy, before he be put to answer the Appeal, and then he may plead the Conviction and Clergy in Bar."[47] "Appeals," Jacob further observed, noting the then-governing statute of limitations for private prosecutors to assert their claims, "are to be brought within a Year and Day after the Death of the Person; and if the next Heir of the Deceased who ought to prosecute, be within Age at the time of the Death of his Ancestor, he must nevertheless commence his Appeal within the Year, and proceed in his Minority."[48] "In former Times," Jacob pointed out, "there could be no Proceeding on an Indictment for Murder 'till the Year and Day was expir'd, in which time the Party might bring an Appeal; but this was not in *Provisione Legis*, but at the Discretion of the Justices, who apprehended that the Person most nearly related would be most zealous in prosecuting the Criminal."[49]

If one goes way back in time, disputes in England pertaining to crimes were once resolved by *trial by battle* or *trial by ordeal* until *trial by jury* became the standard method of resolving such disputes.[50] Trial by battle, also known as "judicial combat" or a "judicial duel," was an appeal to God's will and a customary practice in early Germanic life from approximately the year 500. "A judicial battle could be fought between men on horseback or on foot, armed with either lethal or non-lethal weapons," Hunt Janin writes in *Medieval Justice: Cases and Laws in France, England and Germany, 500–1500* (2004). Although a form of jury known as the Grand Assize became an option under English law, in a trial by battle a person could choose to fight himself or engage a "champion" to fight on his behalf. As Jain writes of this antiquated method of dispute resolution: "Champions were often family members or freeman retainers, but gradually a class of professional 'hired guns' came into being. These freelance champions sold their skills to the highest bidder." Englishmen used trial by battle to resolve land disputes, and even monks in monasteries were known to use this mode of prosecution, though not everyone was entitled to use it (*e.g.*, serfs could not challenge freeman). The penalty for defeat was death or some lesser, but nonetheless horrific, punishment. As Janin explains: "If a champion was defeated in a trial by combat, he might be punished by the amputation of a hand or a foot, or even by hanging."[51] The use of trial by battle, however, gradually dwindled over time and then became what one legal history describes as "a curiosity" because of the rarity of its use.[52] The practice of trial by battle, once entrenched in England and also known as *combat*, ultimately came to be seen as a barbarous practice.[53]

In a trial by ordeal, the accused—relying on divine intervention to determine the outcome—would submit to some physical test to establish his guilt or innocence. "The ordeal was based entirely on theology," writes Janin, noting that "[a]ccording to the thinking of the times, men did not judge other men by means of the ordeal: they simply relied on the will of God as revealed through it." Priests played a key role in such ordeals, with Janin observing that—in the days when ecclesiastical courts and canon law existed side by side with royal courts—these religious figures invoked "divine blessings on the ordeal before it began." In 1215, the same year that King John agreed to the charter of rights known as Magna Carta, though, the Fourth Lateran Council banned priests from participating in ordeals, thus leading to their ultimate demise. "As a general rule," Janin observes of the highly superstitious practice of fighting to determine God's will, "the ordeals themselves were used only when there seemed to be no other way of determining a person's innocence or guilt." "A legal maxim in twelfth-century England," Janin notes, "held that 'the ordeal of hot iron is not to be permitted except where the naked truth cannot otherwise be explored.'"

In medieval times, there were ordeals by hot iron, cold water, and hot water, with holy water—for the latter kind of ordeal—heated in a cauldron before the accused had to thrust his own hand into it, perhaps to retrieve a stone or a ring. The Anglo-Saxon king Athelstan (924–939) spoke of the ordeal by "boiling" water, done "by command of God" with a "kettle of iron or brass, or lead or of clay," with the accused's hand to be submersed once "up to the wrist." If the ordeal was for a serious offense, Athelstan explained, the arm had to be submersed three times and even deeper—in his words, "threefold, up to the elbow." Serious offenses involved plotting to assassinate the king, murder, arson, robbery, and other felonies such as counterfeiting. "The hand and, if necessary, the forearm, too, would then be bandaged and sealed," Janin writes of the immediate aftermath of the ordeal by hot water, noting the ultimate consequence of the ordeal: "If an inspection three days later showed that the injuries were healing well, the accused was pronounced innocent. If they were not, he was held to be guilty." While an ordeal by hot iron involved the same basic procedure as the ordeal by hot water—that is, prayer, fasting, a mass and a blessing, and the bandaging and inspection of the injuries three days later—a cold water ordeal involved the accused being bound and then thrown into a body of water that had been blessed by a priest. "The theology behind this ordeal," Janin notes of a time when criminals might be put to death in drowning pools,[54] "was that water was a pure element which, when blessed and therefore made holy, would *refuse to accept a guilty person*." As Janin describes the ordeal by cold water: "If the water accepted the accused, i.e., if he sank, he was innocent. If the water rejected him, that is, if he floated, he was of course guilty."[55]

While the English private prosecutor and the defendant were, respectively, once called the "appellor" and "appellee," actions were initiated in a county court, with trials held by royal justices as they traveled throughout the country. As USC law professor and historian Daniel Klerman writes of the transition that occurred in 1215, the year Magna Carta established, by law, the right to trial by jury: "Before 1215, the appellee could choose either trial by battle or trial by ordeal. After 1215, jury trial replaced the ordeals." The Magna Carta forbade depriving a free man of liberty or property "but by the lawful Judgment of his Peers."[56] Whereas male appellors, in the bygone era of trial by battle, were required to offer proof by battle, thus putting the appellors' lives in danger if the appellees opted to defend by battle, female appellors never waged battle. "Those accused by women," writes Daniel Klerman, "had to submit either to the ordeal (before 1215) or to jury trial (after 1215)."

More than a third of thirteenth-century private prosecutors were women, Klerman notes, explaining that, at a time when few attorneys were involved in England's prosecutions, "[w]omen brought nearly two-thirds of the homicide private prosecutions and all of the rape prosecutions." A "plausible explanation for women's dominant role in prosecuting homicide," Klerman offers, "is that, unlike men, women who brought appeals did not risk trial by battle"; "most likely," Klerman further explains, a woman's role in making the accusation "would spare male relatives the peril of trial by battle." As Klerman, after studying thirteenth-century English practices, reasons: "When a family had already had one member killed by the defendant, it would have been understandably reluctant to put another member at risk in judicial combat. The fact that married women sometimes brought appeals for their husbands' injuries and for property that legally belonged to their spouse may also reflect women's immunity from the peril of battle." A study of female plaintiffs in the King's Court in thirteenth- and fourteenth-century England, done by J. Savannah Shipman in a master's thesis, also found that women in medieval times frequently used the justice system "to gain compensation and justice for crimes committed against their families, their properties, or their bodies." The study's abstract observes that "[f]emale plaintiffs complained to the king and his justices of crimes including murder, assault, robbery, breaking and entering, and arson, and often gained convictions."[57]

In medieval England, the Normans regularly used the mechanism of private prosecution procedure known as *appeal of felony*[58] (*appellum de felonia*).[59] As Margaret Kerr, a Canadian lawyer and expert on ancient legal procedures, explains of that procedural tool: "It required the prosecuting party, the appellor, to make an oral accusation at a series of meetings of the county court, and the defending party, the appellee, to deny the accusations or to object to them on technical grounds. When the court decided that the accusation had been properly made and answered, the appeal was ready to be tried."[60] Medieval trials in England thus did not resemble modern ones, with *appeals of murder*—part of the English common law into the early nineteenth century—allowing a person to be tried, convicted, and executed quite speedily through prosecutions initiated by the victim or the victim's spouse or heir.[61] As Kerr adds of the now-antiquated English criminal procedure: "If the appellor was a man who was neither maimed nor too old to fight, trial was by battle; if the appellor was a man exempt from battle or a woman, trial was by ordeal. The judge was not the court, but God, and failure meant death or mutilation."[62] "Private prosecution took precedence over public prosecution," Kerr notes, writing that "[t]he court rolls of the late twelfth and thirteenth centuries make it clear that the king had no overriding right to proceed against offenders who were appealed by their victims."[63] "The appeal of felony, introduced into England by the Normans," Kerr observes of English history, "was the major if not the exclusive avenue of prosecuting criminal offenses when Henry II ascended the throne in 1154."[64]

Though it might be a little confusing to modern ears, an "appeal" in medieval times was not, depending on the context, necessarily the same thing as we think of one today. As law professor David Seipp writes: "An appeal was an ancient form of lawsuit brought by a victim, or the heir or widow of a slain victim, against a wrongdoer to prove the commission of a felony. 'Appeal' in this context is not an ancestor of our modern legal term."[65] Like other scholars, Seipp explains how the appeal of felony procedure worked: "Victims could bring appeals for any of the traditional common law felonies, including homicide, rape, mayhem (maiming), robbery, burglary, larceny, and arson. The consequences of a conviction were drastic. The usual sentence for felons after 1200 was death by hanging."[66] Also, Seipp observes, alluding to the now-antiquated legal concepts of *attainder*[67] and *corruption of blood*,[68] both referred to in the U.S. Constitution,[69] "conviction of felony deprived the felon's family of any inheritance or bequest that the felon would have left them."[70] As countless historical documents reveal, vengeance was frequently the motive for bringing appeals of felony—the common-law procedural mechanism by which the private prosecutors of yesteryear held criminal defendants accountable for their actions.[71] "[R]evenge," Seipp writes, taking note of the English practice centuries earlier, "was apparently such a powerful motive that some victims tried to bring appeals for wrongs that were not serious enough to meet the royal courts' standard for felonies."[72]

The *appeal of felony* and *appeal of murder* procedures—described, in effect, as authorizing "private criminal prosecutions"[73]—were not abolished in England until 1819, multiple decades after the American Revolution and the conclusion of America's Revolutionary War (1775–1783),[74] the same year of Walt Whitman and Herman Melville's births,[75] and the same year—1819—that Thomas Jefferson founded the University of Virginia.[76] In 1819, the British Parliament voted 64 to 2 to adopt the following law: "All appeals of treason, murder, felony or other offenses shall cease; nor shall issue be joined, nor trial be held by battle in any writ of right."[77] That reform represented a major shift in English law—a reform that came long after the Glorious Revolution of 1688–1689 and the landscape-changing English Bill of Rights (1689) in a society that still retained harsh punishments, including the death penalty and an array of corporal, or bodily, punishments, such as branding, lashes, and the pillory.[78] In 1688, England had approximately 50 capital crimes, a number that rose to more than 200 in the coming decades, leading to the country's criminal laws being referred to derisively, and collectively, as the English "Bloody Code." "Private prosecution remained the norm," historian Barbara Shapiro writes of the post-Glorious Revolution period, meaning that private prosecutors had within their power, if they pursued their cases and obtained convictions, to not only punish offenders, but to send them to their deaths on the scaffold.[79]

William Rogers, a former dean at the Cincinnati Law School,[80] recounted in 1911 how the *appeal of murder* and *appeal of felony* procedures finally came to an end in England in 1819. On the night of May 26, 1817, Mary Ashford had been raped and murdered after attending a dance in the village of Warwickshire, England. She had danced with Abraham Thornton, a farmer, at the village dance, and Thornton had left the dance with her. He was to escort her to her grandmother's home, but she never arrived there, immediately raising suspicions of foul play. After her dead body was found in a pond, Thornton was arrested, charged with her murder, and put on trial. Although "strong circumstantial evidence" was produced against Thornton, as Dean Rogers recounted in his article about the case, Thornton "established an alibi, and on account of the lack of direct evidence of his guilt was acquitted." Mary's distraught brother, William Ashford, thereafter hired counsel, who informed William of a means by which Thornton might yet again be brought to trial notwithstanding his acquittal. "It was," Rogers explained in *The Ohio Law Reporter*, "an obsolete legal remedy known as 'appeal of murder,' wherein an heir or near blood relative of a murdered person could demand that one charged with the murder might again be placed upon trial." According to Dean Rogers' account of the case: "William authorized his counsel to proceed with this ancient remedy against Thornton and he was soon thereafter rearrested and brought before the court of Kings Bench for retrial in November, 1817. The case created un[u]sual interest, as the 'appeal of murder' had not been resorted to in England for generations before this time."[81]

After the criminal case began, the defendant, Abraham Thornton, was asked to plead to the charge of murder. But in a surprise move, Thornton did not mundanely enter a formal plea of not guilty or move to quash the proceedings. Instead, he dramatically pulled a pair of leather gloves from his bag, placed one on his left hand, and threw the other on the floor in front of William Ashford, the murdered woman's grieving brother. Standing up and holding up his now-gloved left hand, Thornton declared, "I am not guilty and am ready to defend the same with my body." As Dean Rogers described the chaotic scene in the courtroom that followed Thornton's announcement: "For a time no one but himself and his counsel comprehended the meaning of his conduct. Upon inquiry from Lord Ellenborough and the other judges who sat with him they were informed that the defendant demanded trial by battle and was ready to enter upon that mode with young Ashford, the prosecutor, to determine his guilt or innocence." Ashford's counsel insisted that there was no law in existence justifying that mode of trial, but after listening to the arguments of counsel, the judges concluded that while they were averse to granting the right to trial by battle, that it was, in fact, the law of the land. After William Ashford, a rather frail man, and his counsel, thereafter refused to proceed with the private prosecution, Thornton was discharged from custody, though the intense controversy surrounding the case resulted in—as Dean Rogers put it—"the final repeal of the law authorizing this barbarous method of testing a person's guilt of the charge made against him." As Rogers wrote of the British Parliament's decision to abolish trial by battle along with all appeals of murder and felony: "Thus ended in the civilized world that strange proceeding by which force instead of reason had in England since the time of William the Conqueror been held to be a valid method of settling private disputes and determining individual rights."[82]

A contemporary account of the *Ashford v. Thornton* case, published in 1818 in *The Observer* of London, contained a discussion of "wager of battle." In reporting on the proceedings in the Court of King's Bench, *The Observer* noted: "This morning the defendant in this case was brought from the King's Bench prison, as on former occasions, when called upon to attend in court. He arrived about nine o'clock, and, as usual, Westminster Hall was crowded by persons anxious to witness his approach." The newspaper further noted that Mr. Chitty, "junior counsel on the part of the plaintiff," said that "[t]he right of the heir to appeal a party for the murder of his ancestor is recognized, established, and preserved" by English law. Citing a text written in 1272, Chitty quoted from a section titled "Concerning Appeals of Homicide" before quoting from another source, a sixteenth-century book containing a section on "Trial by Battle" that read in part: "Trial by battle is another trial which the defendant in appeal of felony may elect; that is, to fight with the appellant by way of trial whether he is guilty of the felony or not; and if the event of such battle be so favourable to the defendant that he vanquish the appellant, he shall ... bar him of his appeal for ever. And this is an ancient mode of trial in our law, and one much used in time past, as appears by divers[e] precedents in the times of Kings Edward III. and Henry IV; a mode which is not disused but may be brought into practice again at this day, if the defendant pleased, and there be nothing to support the counterplea of the other party." Additional discussion of appeals and trial by battle then followed.[83]

In medieval times, trial by combat, commenced after a formal proclamation by the judges, could go on for hours. As Dean Rogers, the legal historian, explained the barbaric custom that Parliament, at long last, did away with: "The combatants, stripped like a sea bather, with heads, arms and legs naked, were required to fight 'till one or the other was killed or vanquished, or till the stars came out at night.' If the plaintiff was defeated and gave up the contest, he became infamous and was deprived of the right of a free man. He was subject to many years' imprisonment and fine, and must pay damages to the defendant." If the defendant lost the trial by battle, though, his guilt was established, the officers of the law took him into their custody, and he was promptly executed. "There was no appeal, and no power to stay the hand of death," Dean Rogers emphasized, adding this of the antiquated custom's strange and sordid history: "Prior to the time when young Thornton invoked this procedure in 1817 it had probably not been enforced in England for more than two centuries, and while the court records give us absolute evidence of the enforcement of the law in this method, they indicate that other and more civilized methods kept it from taking deep root in English law, and early in the fourteenth century had pressed it far on the way of extinction." "The development of the jury system in which the hearing of evidence became the most important part of the trial, had more than anything else, to do in causing the abandonment of trial by battle," Rogers explained.[84] *Ashford v. Thornton* is said to have "led to the abolition the next year of both trial by battle and the appeal of murder."[85]

Public vs. Private Wrongs—and English vs. Scottish Law

In the very first chapter of volume four of his *Commentaries on the Laws of England* (1769), Sir William Blackstone divided "wrongs" into "*private*" and "*public*" ones." "Private wrongs ... are frequently termed civil injuries," he wrote, dedicating a separate volume of his *Commentaries*—volume four—to "the consideration of public wrongs, or crimes and misdemeanors; with the means of their prevention and punishment." In discussing "the *pleas of the crown*," Blackstone wrote that they were given that moniker "because the king, in whom centers the majesty of the whole community, is supposed by the law to be the person injured by every infraction of the public rights belonging to that community, and is therefore in all cases the proper prosecutor for every public offence." In considering "the general nature of crimes," Blackstone explicitly distinguished between *crimes* and *misdemeanors* before discussing how criminality itself constituted a public wrong. As Blackstone observed: "A crime, or misdemeanor, is an act committed, or omitted, in violation of a public law, either forbidding or commanding it." "This general definition," he wrote, "comprehends both crimes and misdemeanors; which, properly speaking, are mere synonymous terms: though, in common usage, the word, 'crimes,' is made to denote such offences as are of a deeper and more atrocious dye; while smaller faults, and omissions of less consequence, are comprized under the gentle name of 'misdemeanors' only."[86]

In his *Commentaries*, Blackstone explored at length the difference between civil injuries and criminal conduct.[87] "The distinction of public wrongs from private, of crimes and misdemeanors from civil injuries," he stressed, "seems principally to consist in this: that private wrongs, or civil injuries, are an infringement or privation of the civil rights which belong to individuals, considered merely as individuals; public wrongs, or crimes and misdemeanors, are a breach and violation of the public rights and duties, due to the whole community, considered as a community, in it's social aggregate capacity." Blackstone specifically mentioned treason, murder, and robbery as "properly ranked among crimes; since, besides the injury done to individuals, they strike at the very being of society; which cannot possibly subsist, where actions of this sort are suffered to escape with impunity." "In all cases," Blackstone added, "the crime includes an injury: every public offence is also a private wrong, and somewhat more; it affects the individual, and it likewise affects the community." "Thus treason in imagining the king's death," he used as one example, "involves in it conspiracy against an individual, which is also a civil injury: but as this species of treason in it's consequences principally tends to the dissolution of government, and the destruction thereby of the order and peace of society, this denominates it a crime of the highest magnitude."

As to the long-standing felonies of murder and robbery, Blackstone—a member of Parliament from 1761 to 1770 who later served as a Justice of the Court of King's Bench and as a Justice of the Common Pleas[88]—had this to say: "Murder is an injury to the life of an individual; but the law of society considers principally the loss which the state sustains by being deprived of a member, and the pernicious example thereby set, for others to do the like. Robbery may be considered in the same view: it is an injury to *private* property; but, were that all, a civil satisfaction in damages might atone for it: the *public* mischief is the thing, for the prevention of which our laws have made it a capital offence." "In these gross and atrocious injuries," Blackstone wrote, "the private wrong is swallowed up in the public: we seldom hear any mention made of satisfaction to the individual; the satisfaction to the community being so very great." "And indeed," Blackstone stressed, "as the public crime is not otherwise avenged than by forfeiture of life and property, it is impossible afterwards to make any reparation for the private wrong; which can only be had from the body or goods of the aggressor."[89]

In those days, English offenders were often punished corporally, whether by death or through ear cropping, whipping, the stocks, or the pillory.[90] And if an offender could not afford to pay a fine, he might end up in prison or paying with a part of his own body. The Latin maxim *qui non habet in crumena luat in corpora*, literally "who has nothing in purse, let him suffer in body," gave early English judges direction on how to punish destitute offenders, with debtors' prisons also still in use in England and early America.[91] Corporal punishments such as ear cropping and the pillory were once regularly put to use under English law.[92] As one book summarized the kinds of punishments previously inflicted by English courts: "convicted criminals were sentenced to stand a certain number of hours, fastened upon a platform, in some public place, to be gazed at, jeered, execrated, and pelted with mud, rotten eggs, dead cats, and other male-odorous missiles, by the London mob. Some were nailed by the ear to the post in the pillory; some, especially libellers, had their ears cut off. In rare cases, prisoners exposed in the pillory were pelted to death."[93] And such horrific punishments persisted for many years after Blackstone's *Commentaries*—a treatise containing a whole chapter on executions—first appeared in print in the 1760s. The pillory was abolished in England for all offenses except perjury in 1816, but the pillory was not abolished completely until 1837; public whippings persisted there until 1817; and the last use of the stocks in England occurred decades later, in 1872.[94] The chapter in Blackstone's *Commentaries*, titled "Of Execution," mentions hangings, burning to death, and beheading. "[I]t is clear," Blackstone concluded of the death penalty, "that if, upon judgment to be hanged by the neck till he is dead, the criminal be not thoroughly killed, but revives, the sheriff must hang him again."[95]

For public wrongs, Blackstone wrote that "besides the private satisfaction due and given in many cases to the individual, by action for the private wrong, the government also calls upon the offender to submit to public punishment for the public crime." "And the prosecution of these offenses," he pointed out, "is always at the suit and in the name of the king, in whom by the texture of our constitution the *jus gladii*, or executory power of the law, entirely resides." "Thus too, in the old Gothic constitution," Blackstone added, "there was a threefold punishment inflicted on all delinquents: first, for the private wrong to the party injured; secondly, for the offence against the king by disobedience to the laws; and thirdly, for the crime against the public by their evil example." "Any private person (and *a fortiori* a peace officer) that is present when any felony is committed, is bound by the law to arrest the felon; on pain of fine and imprisonment, if he escapes through the negligence of the standers by." Upon probable suspicion, Blackstone continued, a private person "may arrest the felon, or other person so suspected, but he cannot justify breaking open doors to do it." "There is yet another species of arrest, wherein both officers and private man are concerned, and that is upon an *hue* and *cry* raised upon a felon committed." "An hue (from *huer*, to shout) and cry, *hutefium et clamor*," Blackstone emphasized, tracing its long history, "is the old common law process of pursuing, with horn and with voice, all felons, and such as have dangerously wounded another."[96]

In chapter 23 of his *Commentaries*, William Blackstone laid out "the Several Modes of Prosecution." In particular, Blackstone discussed *presentments*, *indictments* and *informations*. "A presentment, *generally* taken," he wrote, "is a very comprehensive term; including not only presentments, properly so called, but also inquisitions of office and indictments by a grand jury." "A presentment, *properly speaking*," he added, "is the notice taken by a grand jury of any offence from their own knowledge or observation, (*a*) without any bill of indictment laid before them at the suit of the king: as the presentment of a nuisance, a libel, and the like; upon which the officer of the court must afterwards frame an indictment, (*b*) before the party presented can be put to answer it." The grand jury system had been in place for many centuries, with its name derived from the fact that it usually had more jurors than a trial—or petit—jury. "The Grand Jury is an old institution" that—as one source noted of its long history—occupies the time of "twenty-three gentlemen," with grand jurors taken away "from their homes and occupations" for "days together" to perform their assigned duties.[97]

For centuries, grand juries have indicted wrongdoers.[98] "An indictment," Blackstone continued, "is a written accusation of one or more persons of a crime or misdemeanor, preferred to, and presented upon oath by, a grand jury." Indictments, he observed, are brought "in the name of the king, but at the suit of any private prosecutor," with Blackstone adding that grand jurors "are only to hear evidence on behalf of the prosecution: for the finding of an indictment is only in the nature of an enquiry or accusation, which is afterwards to be tried and determined; and the grand jury are only to enquire upon their oaths, whether there be sufficient cause to call upon the party to answer it." "When the grand jury have heard the evidence," Blackstone observed, "if they think it a groundless accusation, they used formerly to endorse on the back of the bill, 'ignoramus;' or, we know nothing of it; intimating, that though the facts might possibly be true, that truth did not appear to them." "[B]ut now," Blackstone noted, grand jurors "assert in English, more absolutely, 'not a true bill,'" thus discharging the party without need of a "farther answer." Only if the grand jury was satisfied as to an accusation's truth did the grand jurors endorse the words "a true bill" upon it and the party in question then stood indicted. "[I]n case of murder," Blackstone wrote, reciting the traditional rule, "the time of death must be laid within a year and a day after the mortal stroke was given."[99]

After laying out "all the methods of prosecution at the suit of the king," Blackstone noted that "[t]here yet remains another, which is merely at the suit of the subject, and is called an appeal." As Blackstone wrote about this latter mode of prosecution in 1769—decades before the *Ashford v. Thornton* case—in the fourth volume of his *Commentaries*: "An appeal, in the sense wherein it is here used, does not signify any complaint to a superior court of an injustice done by an inferior one, which is the general use of the word; but it here means an original suit, at the time of it's first commencement. An appeal therefore, when spoken of as a criminal prosecution, denotes an accusation by a private subject against another, for some heinous crime; demanding punishment on account of the particular injury suffered, rather than for the offence against the public." "As this method of prosecution is still in force," Blackstone wrote of *appeals*, which he observed had, in fact, become extremely infrequent in English legal practice, "I cannot omit to mention it: but, as it is very little in use, on account of the great nicety required in conducting it, I shall treat of it very briefly; referring the student for more particulars to other voluminous compilations."[100]

After citing William Hawkins' book, *A Treatise of the Pleas of the Crown*,[101] first published in 1711,[102] Blackstone—observing that "throughout the kingdom, by statute 25 Geo. II. c. 37. it is enacted that, in case of murder, the judge shall in his sentence direct execution to be performed on the next day but one after sentence passed"[103]—wrote of the process to assert an appeal by which an execution might, ultimately, be obtained: "This private process, for the punishment of public crimes, had probably it's original in those times, when a private pecuniary satisfaction, called a *weregild*, was constantly paid to the party injured, or his relations, to expiate enormous offences. This was a custom derived to us, in common with other northern nations, from our ancestors, the antient Germans ...."[104] As Blackstone added in his now-famed *Commentaries on the Laws of England*, a popular text[105] not only in England but in colonial and early America: "An appeal of felony may be brought for crimes committed either against the parties themselves, or their relations. The crimes against the parties themselves are larc[e]ny, rape, and arson. And for these, as well as for may[h]em, the persons robbed, ravished, maimed, or whose houses are burnt, may institute this private process." "The only crime against one's relation, for which an appeal can be brought," Blackstone continued, "is that of killing him, by either murder or manslaughter. But this cannot be brought by every relation: but only by the wife for the death of her husband, or by the heir male for the death of his ancestor;

which heirship was also confined, by an ordinance of king Henry the first, to the four nearest degrees of blood."[106] "These appeals," Blackstone wrote, "may be brought, previous to any indictment; and, if the appellee be acquitted thereon, he cannot be afterwards indicted for the same offence." "In like manner as by the old Gothic constitution," he stressed, "if any offender gained a verdict in his favour, when prosecuted by the party injured, he was also understood to be acquitted of any crown prosecution for the same offence: but, on the contrary, if he made his peace with the king, still he might be prosecuted at the suit of the party."[107]

The type of crime—for example, whether it involved treason, murder, or assault and battery—usually determined whether the king's lawyers or a private party or that party's private counsel would be involved in a prosecution. "Although criminal prosecutions were carried on in the name of the king," writes Allyson May in *The Bar and the Old Bailey, 1750–1850*, "there was no system of public prosecution." "The state's involvement in prosecution," she writes, "was extremely limited: law officers of the Crown prosecuted those accused of treason, and in the eighteenth century they become increasingly involved in coining and forgery cases." "Murder," she explains, "occasioned another exception: homicide was a serious breach of the king's peace, and any violent or suspicious death was from the Middle Ages investigated by the coroner, who convened a jury to assist him." With respect to other crimes and homicides that did not attract the interest of the Crown's solicitors, though, the English executive branch took a largely hands off approach and had little role to play. As May explains: "Victims of crime bore the chief responsibility for bringing offenders to justice: a victim's pursuit and apprehension of a suspected felon and his willingness to take that person before a local magistrate were crucial to prosecution." "English criminal justice," May continues, looking back at the actual practice as reflected in historical documents, "was thus rooted in private prosecution, and while there was no rule forbidding private prosecutors to engage counsel, they did not do so until the opening decades of the eighteenth century. At midcentury the presence of counsel for the prosecution was still rare."[108]

In England, the records of London's Old Bailey—the courthouse where tens of thousands of criminal cases were conducted from the seventeenth to the nineteenth century—reflect instances where appeals, and thus private prosecutions, were pursued. A widow brought "an Appeal of Murder" in 1691 against Peter Ricaut, a man previously found not guilty of the murder of the woman's husband, Daniel Hill.[109] In 1724, Lewis Hussar, a laborer, "was try'd upon the Appeal of Solomon Rondeau, Brother and Heir of the Deceased, for the Murder of Ann Hussar, his wife, by cutting her Throat with a Razor."[110] Lewis Hussar, also referred to in Old Bailey records as Lovi Houssart, was eventually executed in December of that year.[111] In July of 1729, Old Bailey records also show that James Cluff "was Try'd upon an Appeal lodg'd against him last April Sessions, by the Appellant John Green, Heir and Brother of Mary Green after his being acquitted of the Murder of the said Mary Green, the 11th Day of April last." That case's outcome: "The Prisoner's Counsel pleaded strenuously on Behalf of the Prisoner, remarking on the Testimony of the Appellant's Witness whatsoever they thought might make to the Advantage of the Appellee; not withstanding which, the Jury upon a mature Deliberation of the Matter, found the Prisoner guilty of the Murther; whereupon the Appellant came into Court at the Time when Sentence was to be pass'd on the other Convicts, and demanded Judgment on the Appellee, which was accordingly pronounced upon him. Death."[112] As reflected in an ordinary's account dated July 25, 1729, the 32-year-old James Cluff—after being acquitted once, then convicted on the appeal of murder—was promptly executed at Tyburn, the site of London's notorious gallows, though Cluff went to his death asserting his innocence.[113]

Eighteenth- and nineteenth-century newspapers are, in fact, scattered with references to "private prosecutors." Such references can be found throughout the British Isles—in England,[114] Ireland,[115] Scotland,[116] and Wales[117]—in addition to such far-flung places as Australia,[118] British Columbia,[119] Jamaica,[120] Manitoba,[121] Ontario,[122] and Quebec,[123] which were, at one time, all colonies under British rule.[124] And that historical legacy of private prosecution from Great Britain would be reflected in the United Kingdom and its colonies for decades to come. In *The Gazette*, of Montreal, one October 1880 news item, titled "Court of Queen's Bench," contains this tidbit: "The Court commended the leniency displayed by the private prosecutor in this case. The criminal proceedings had evidently been instituted by him only to establish his innocence of the imputations levelled against him, but as soon as the defendant showed a disposition to repent, he had generously came forward and prayed the Court to inflict a light sentence." "Since the private prosecutor had so generously interfered to save the defendant from punishment proportioned to the gravity of the offence," it was reported, "the Court would merely inflict a nominal sentence, and fined the prisoner ten dollars."[125] Another news item from 1880, in the *Ottawa Daily Citizen*, noted that "[t]he Grand Trunk Railway are the private prosecutors" in "[t]he case of the Queen against the Hamilton Powder Company for having carried publicly and manufactured a dangerous explosive," with the complaint said to have grown out of "the terrible and fatal accident which occurred at Stratford from an explosion."[126] Over the years, private prosecutors in a variety of locales pursued criminal cases in a wide range of matters, everything from murder to the breaking of a pane of glass[127] to attempting to get public officials to clean up filthy streets.[128] It is also clear that the wishes of private prosecutors frequently played a role, often a big one, in judges' sentencing decisions.[129]

Private prosecutors showed up in cases big and small. *A Complete Collection of State Trials* (1816), compiled by T. B. Howell, contains multiple references to private prosecutors. For example, at the 1752 trial of James Stewart for the murder of Colin Campbell before the Circuit Court of Justiciary, held at Inverary, Scotland, Walter Stewart—James Stewart's defense lawyer—protested against his client's treatment by "the private prosecutors." With the accused referred to as the "pannel," as was the Scottish custom, Walter Stewart grumbled: "In the entry of this trial, my lord, I cannot help complaining of most intolerable hardships, which this pannel has undergone since May last, when he was first incarcerated." "The unjustifiable steps I am now to complain of," he said, lamenting that his client had been held in close confinement and not allowed to see anybody for six weeks, "I must therefore lay to the charge of the private prosecutors." There had been a long-running feud between the families of the man charged with murder and his victim, with the *London Evening Post* of December 5, 1752 reporting: "We are informed by a private letter from Argyleshire, that the ancient animosity between the Stewarts and Campbells is likely to revive, on the score of hanging James Stewart at Ballachelish, on account of the murder of Colin Campbell of Glenure."[130]

Before his client had been put to death, Walter Stewart had complained that even after the six-week time period his client had been held in close confinement that, aside from James Stewart's wife and one or two others, "any who could be thought proper persons to prepare defences for his trial, were carefully denied access to him." "By the precaution of this private prosecutor too," Walter Stewart complained, noting the extreme difficulty that James Stewart had in retaining counsel, "the bar has been in a manner shut up against this pannel; all the old experienced counsel, though not brought to maintain the charge against him, have been retained from giving him their assistance; otherways, in all probability, I had not now been employed to open his defense."[131] Facing an extremely hostile judge and jury and found to be an accessory to a murder committed near Appin, in the Scottish West Highlands, James Stewart—whose friends insisted was "hastily and unjustly condemned"—was gibbeted at Ballachulish, with his dead body publicly hung in chains for eighteen months before its burial in the Chapel of Kells. In what would be called a "mockery of justice," the presiding judge at Stewart's trial for Colin Campbell's murder was Archibald Campbell, the Duke of Argyll and the Chief of Clan Campbell, and 11 of the 15 jurors in the criminal case had the last name of Campbell.[132]

A private prosecutor, a Mr. Cornwall, also appeared at the 1765 trial of William Lord Byron, Baron Byron of Rochdale, for the murder of a distant cousin and neighbor, William Chaworth, before the Right Hon. House of Peers, in Westminster Hall, in full Parliament. A "*Serjeant at Arms*" opened the murder trial, at which the accused was charged with willfully, and with malice aforethought, killing Chaworth with a sword. "Oyez, Oyez, Oyez!" the serjeant at arms ceremoniously announced at the proceeding's outset. "Our sovereign lord the king," he said to a packed audience that included barons, bishops, viscounts, and clerks of the crown, "strictly charges and commands all manner of persons to keep silence, upon pain of imprisonment." "God save the king," he proclaimed after the Lord High Steward[133] stood up and spoke to the assembled peers about the indictment for murder issued upon the oath of twelve jurors in the county of Middlesex. "Oyez, Oyez, Oyez!," the serjeant at arms repeated, making the point that would be repeated more than once: "Our sovereign lord the king strictly charges and commands all manner of persons to keep silence, upon pain of imprisonment."

The gentleman usher of the black rod—the chief gentleman usher to the king who got his name from the black rod,[134] topped with a lion in gold, he carried in his hand—made three reverences and knelt before the Lord High Steward. "[T]he Clerk of the Crown, by direction of the Lord High Steward," the trial transcript reveals, then "read the Certiorari, and the Return thereof, together with the Caption of the Indictment, and the Indictment certified thereupon, against William lord Byron." William Bryon, a British nobleman born in 1722, had served in the Royal Navy and had become a member of the House of Lords in 1743;[135] later in life, he became known as the great uncle of George Gordon Byron, the Romantic poet popularly known simply as Lord Byron.[136] After the indictment was read to the House of Lords and to the presiding judge, Lord Mansfield, the serjeant at arms issued yet another command: "Oyez! Oyez! Oyez! Lieutenant of the Tower of London, bring forth William lord Byron, your prisoner, to the bar, pursuant to the order of the House of Lords." At that point, the detained prisoner—as the detailed transcript also reflects—"was brought to the bar by the deputy-governor of the Tower, having the axe carried before him by the gentleman-gaoler, who stood with it on the left hand of the prisoner, with the edge turned from him."

After the prisoner bowed before the Lord High Steward in a proceeding cloaked in formalities and solemnity, the Lord High Steward reminded Lord Byron of the homicide charges against him and he was arraigned. "Not Guilty, my lords," Lord Byron pled. At that point, the serjeant at arms issued the following command before the Lord High Steward allowed Mr. Cornwall, the private prosecutor, to proceed: "Oyez! Oyez! Oyez! All manner of persons that will give evidence, on behalf of our sovereign lord the king, against William lord Byron, the prisoner at the bar, let them come forth and they shall be heard; for now he stands at the bar upon his deliverance." "May it please your lordships; Willian lord Byron stands indicted by the grand jury of the county of Middlesex, for murder," Mr. Cornwall opened the case for the prosecution against the man who had been brought from the Tower of London—a place used to hold prisoners—to appear before the House of Lords. "I am likewise of counsel for this prosecution," the Attorney General continued, saying that "by the indictment which has been opened, your lordships have heard that the noble prisoner at the bar is charged with one of the highest offences that human nature is capable of committing, nothing less than shedding the blood of a fellow-creature." The Attorney General then laid out the series of events that led to the murder charge—a good-humored dinner of gentlemen at the Star-and-Garter tavern in Pall Mall that turned into a heated verbal dispute, and a perceived slight, over the best method of preserving game and dealing with poachers. There was a 100*l.* wager between Lord Byron and Mr. Chaworth, the Attorney General said, before Lord Byron and Mr. Chaworth got into a disagreement about Sir Charles Sedley's land holdings and manors, with their quarrel escalating and leading to the deadly sword fight in a small room crowded with furniture.

The Attorney General ended his own opening statement by noting the private prosecutor's role in representing the interests of the inheritor of the deceased man's estate. "I cannot sit down," he said, "without mentioning another circumstance, which further evinces his majesty's love of justice, and his inflexible resolution to do right, according to law, without favour or affection, however high and respectable the noble personage may be, who is concerned in this important cause." "Your lordships," the Attorney General said, referring to the 1760 murder trial of Lawrence Earl Ferrers,[137] "all remember, upon another very solemn and melancholy occasion, as the event proved, the then noble prisoner had killed a person of very inferior rank, who left neither a fortune nor relations equal to the expence of a prosecution of this sort." "His majesty from his love of justice," the Attorney General continued of that prior case, "sustained the whole charge, and committed the care of that prosecution to his own servants." "But in the present instance," he noted, "the deceased having a large fortune, and the inheritor of it being both able and willing to carry on this prosecution, his majesty, from the same love of justice, and that there might not be the appearance of partiality to the noble prisoner at the bar, has left the prosecution, and the intire management of it, in the hands of the private prosecutor, who, actuated by no motive of revenge, only hopes, that there will be a fair, but a strict and full enquiry for the blood of his deceased relation; being thoroughly satisfied that your lordships will hear with patience, deliberate with caution, and determine with wisdom, justice, and truth."

The prosecution witnesses were heard over two days, with Mr. Cornwall—the retained private prosecutor—being an active participant in the trial. Lord Byron, however, opted not to call any witnesses at all, asserting: "I have reduced into writing what I have to offer to your lordships; which, as my voice is very low, I am apprehensive of my not being heard by your lordships, and therefore desire it may be read by the Clerk." In his written statement, Lord Byron recited that Mr. Chaworth had, "without any cause, treated me in a slighting and contemptuous manner" and that towards the end of the dinner, Mr. Chaworth, "with some heat, said, There would be no game in the country; and that I should not have a single hare on my estate, if it was not for the care taken by himself and sir Charles Sedley, to preserve the game on their manors; and added, that he had more game on five acres than I had in all my manors." "The proposal of a bet followed, but some of the gentlemen interfered, and no bet was made," Lord Byron said, setting forth this version of events: "Mr. Chaworth again mentioned sir Charles Sedley's manors, and his care of the game; upon which I happened to ask what manors of sir Charles Sedley he meant; when he answered Nuttall and Bulwell; to which I replied, I did not understand how that could be, for though I knew Nuttall was sir Charles Sedley's, yet Bulwell-park was mine."

After more chatter about Sir Charles Sedley's manors, Lord Byron said that Mr. Chaworth suddenly blurted out: "Sir Charles Sedley, my lord, lives at Mr. Cooper's, in such a place, and I doubt not, will be ready to give your lordship satisfaction about his manors, and if you have any thing to say concerning them; and as to myself, you know where I live, and I shall be ready to answer your lordship whenever you will call upon me, if you have any thing to say to me." Lord Byron attested that Mr. Chaworth, after leaving the dinner table, then waited for him, and that the two men ended up in a sixteen-feet-square locked room where the deadly swordfight occurred. It was an impromptu, quasi-duel of sorts, though without all the prearranged, customary formalities normally carried out by "seconds," the gentlemen regularly chosen by the principal participants in a duel to make the arrangements for it. Ultimately, Lord Byron was found not guilty of murder but guilty of manslaughter. After claiming "the benefit of the statute of Edward the sixth," he was granted that statute's benefit and discharged, simply paying his fees.[138] Under the statute of Edward VI, a peer was entitled to benefit of clergy on a first conviction of a felony by asserting simply that he was a peer.[139] Benefit of clergy was not abolished in England until the 1820s—a time period when various progressive reform measures were being taken up and passed by Parliament.[140]

With the tradition of private prosecutors rooted in the common law, such prosecutors made appearances throughout the British Isles. In Scottish newspapers, they were frequently said to be acting in "concourse" or "concurrence" with His Majesty's Advocate, also known as the Lord Advocate.[141] The July 22, 1776 edition of Edinburgh's *The Caledonian Mercury* provides an illustration of how His Majesty's Advocate and private prosecutors might work together on criminal cases. That newspaper made this report: "This day, came on before the High Court of Justiciary, the pleadings on the relevancy of the indictment, at the instance of his Majesty's Advocate, and William Nicolson blacksmith in Dumfries, for the murder of Joseph Nicolson blacksmith there, brother of the said William, on the morning of the 7th day of September last." "The pleadings were opened, on the part of the pannel," it reported, "by Mr Alexander Ferguson Advocate, as counsel for the private prosecutor, who was followed by his Majesty's Advocate, on the part of the Crown, and the reply was made for the pannel by Mr. George Oglivie Advocate."[142] In Scotland, which had a decidedly different legal tradition than England, the *pannel*—or panel box—was the place of arraignment in a court of law, the dock, or the bar of the court.[143] The term *pannel*, in Scotch law, though, also commonly referred to the actual person accused of a crime or indicted.[144] As Dr. John Jameson, the Scottish lexicographer, defined "Pannel": "any person who is brought to the bar of a court for trial."[145]

In Scotland, if the Lord Advocate declined to act, a private prosecution could be brought.[146] But the *procurator fiscal*—the county-level public prosecutor, often just called the *fiscal*,[147] who was appointed by the sheriff but subject to the Lord Advocate's direction—conducted the vast majority of Scottish prosecutions.[148] Though relatively rare,[149] Scottish private prosecutors did appear before the High Court of Justiciary in criminal prosecutions,[150] including in a case involving a trial under a law for preventing and punishing duels.[151] In another instance, the High Court of Justiciary took up the fraud allegations of Henry Blandy, a shareholder-turned-private prosecutor who, after a Glasgow bank failure, alleged that the bank's directors had engaged in criminal wrongdoing.[152] In yet another case, the High Court of Justiciary wrestled with the question of whether the public prosecutor's promise of immunity to a man extended to a subsequent private prosecution.[153] Scotland itself has a long tradition of *public* prosecutions, with one modern legal commentator emphasizing of Scotland's prosecutorial system: "It is important to appreciate that criminal prosecutions are very much the responsibility of the Crown or the state. It is very rare (and highly unusual) for private prosecutions to be permitted in Scotland. In any case, the High Court of Justiciary must grant permission, by way of a Bill of Criminal Letters, for any private prosecution to proceed in the first place."[154]

Old newspaper accounts show that once Scotland's Lord Advocate authorized a private prosecution, the case could proceed to trial, even if the public prosecutor decided to withdraw from participation in the case. As one Scottish newspaper described a precedent: "[I]n the well known case of Charteris, where the Public Prosecutor withdrew his concourse after it had been given, the Court ruled that the trial should nevertheless proceed, and it did proceed accordingly, and was prosecuted to an issue. Now, the principle here indirectly recognised was, that the concourse was necessary to enable the private prosecution to come into court, but that once there, their continuance or withdrawl of it was equally indifferent, and that the Court were equally competent in either case to proceed with the trial of the libel before them."[155] In the case of Colonel Francis Charteris of Amisfield, tried for rape in 1723 at the instance of the woman's husband, the court ordered that the colonel pay the private prosecutor "L. 300 Sterling for damages and expences."[156] The indictment of Colonel Charteris recited that "notwithstanding" the victim's "cries for help," the colonel had "carried her some space off the highroad, and forcibly had carnal dealing with her." The jury found that the private prosecutor had proven the case, with the colonel "seen lying above the woman, and that while on the ground together, the latter was heard" to "cry out."[157]

The Scottish private prosecutors who pursued cases not only did pretrial preparation and conducted trials, but they weighed in at sentencing, too. In October 1773, in Edinburgh, for example, *The Caledonian Mercury* ran a news item about three women who had stolen potatoes being "called before the magistrates, when they all judicially acknowledged their guilt." The newspaper noted that "[t]he private prosecutors likewise appeared, and declared that the women had given them sufficient indemnification for the loss they had sustained, and therefore passed from any complaint against them." "The magistrates, however, in order to deter others from committing the like in time coming," the paper observed of the goings-on of the court, "sentenced Margaret Person and Elisabeth Pearson to suffer ten days imprisonment in the tolbooth" (a Scottish term for a town jail) and to be on "good behavior." The third woman, Katharine Macfarlane, had reportedly "been enticed by the other two" to participate in the theft and had her case dismissed on the condition that she record herself "in the council books, never to be guilty of any similar practices."[158] Other Scottish private prosecutors cut deals—or made special arrangements—with criminal defendants or "pannels," with such private discretion occasionally becoming the subject of public debate.[159] In 1803, two private prosecutors—individuals responsible for the maintenance of public lamps in Perth, Scotland—brought a case against Thomas Ogilvie and Mungo M'Pherson for breaking "no less than sixty-four of the street lamps." Found guilty after a trial and ordered to be imprisoned for two months, the two men were ordered to pay damages to the private prosecutors, with a fine also ordered to be paid to the procurator fiscal, the public prosecutor, for prosecutorial expenses.[160]

The use of private prosecutors in Scotland—as it was elsewhere—was sometimes challenged in court, though Scottish private prosecutions were very rare in comparison to English private prosecutions. For example, *The Caledonian Mercury* reported in December 1777 that "a pleading in the cause of George Smith" and two other men came on before the High Court of Justiciary arising out of the murder, in 1772, of Alexander Rule. "The question before Court was, Whether these people could now be tried at instance of Rule's father, the private prosecutor, who had, soon after the alledged murder, given a written obligation that he would not prosecute." As *The Caledonian Mercury* reported of what transpired that day: "The arguments on both sides were inserted in this paper when the cause came on before Lord Gardenstone at the Circuit Court of Jedburgh. His Lordship remitted it to the High Court of Justiciary, who, on Thursday, after very able pleadings, ordered informations upon the point."[161] In another case heard before the High Court of Justiciary in 1844, though, the Duke of Roxburgh was held to be precluded from acting as a private prosecutor because the duke's complaint "was deficient in an essential particular—in failing to set forth that interest in the private prosecutor which, if disputed, he would have been bound to prove."[162] In many legal systems, the aggrieved person must have legal standing—or *locus standi*—in order in appear in court as a private prosecutor.[163] "The requirement of *locus standi* is a further limitation on a private individual who wants to set in motion the machinery of the criminal law," one legal text notes.[164]

The Private Prosecutor in the British Isles

In *A Treatise on Various Branches of the Criminal Law of Scotland* (1811), John Burnett—an advocate—wrote a whole chapter on private versus public prosecutors. "The right to prosecute crimes belongs, by the Common Law of Scotland, either to the private party injured, or to his Majesty's Advocate," Burnett began Chapter XV of his treatise, with Burnett giving a full recitation—with lots of citations—about the history of, and the then-existing practices pertaining to, both private and public prosecutions. "[T]he right of the individual to prosecute, who felt himself aggrieved by the crime," Burnett wrote early on in his chapter, "was, with us at least, recognized in the fullest extent from a very early period, and gave rise, for a long time, to the only mode of prosecution then known." "At what precise period the office of *public* prosecutor, such as we now have, was introduced, does not appear," Burnett observed, citing language from "Act 1579, c. 78" and offering this informed speculation: "It undoubtedly existed previous to the year 1579; for in that year we find mention made of the case where 'the King's Majesties' Advocate is only pursuer.'" As Burnett added of the role of public officers even before 1579: "One thing however appears, that in the century preceding, the *Justice-Clerk* and *Sheriffs* were the officers, who, in the King's name, prosecuted all crimes affecting the individual, when the private party did not appear and insist. This is clear from the acts 1424, c. 20. and 1433, c. 140. and we know, that long after this, and when his Majesty's Advocate was an acknowledged officer, the Justice-Clerk framed the indictments and prepared cases for trial, even when private parties appeared and prosecuted."[165]

In recounting the centuries-old history, Burnett explained how His Majesty's Advocate came to be involved in crimes harming individuals. "The right, indeed, of his Majesty's Advocate to insist in the prosecution of crimes that did not immediately affect the public," Burnett recounted, "seems originally to have been introduced with the view of correcting the abuse of private parties agreeing not to prosecute, and *compounding* the crime; in short, as a *subsidiary remedy*, to ensure, at all events, the prosecution and conviction of offenders, while at that period, the right to prosecute all crimes affecting individuals, was understood to belong in the first instances to the private party injured." *Compounding a felony* was an indictable offense, though, over time, it essentially became a non-issue in Scotland—and no Scottish prosecutions for compounding a felony were needed—because public prosecutors instead of private prosecutors were entrusted with the prosecution of crime.[166] As John Bouvier's popular law dictionary defined the crime of compounding a felony: "The act of a party immediately aggrieved, who agrees with a thief or other felon that he will not prosecute him, on condition that he return to him the goods stolen, or who takes a reward not to prosecute." "This is an offence punishable by fine and imprisonment," that law dictionary stressed, "and at common law rendered the person committing it an accessory." "In an indictment for compounding a felony," the dictionary emphasized, citing case law for all of the entry's propositions, "it must be alleged that the felony was committed by the person with whom the corrupt agreement is made," with "[t]he agreement not to prosecute being the gist of the offense."[167]

As evidence of the long-established role of Scotland's public prosecutors, dating back to the sixteenth century,[168] John Burnett cited "act 1587, ch. 77" and McKenzie's "*Inquisition*." The 1587 act, Burnett observed, "goes far to show that such was the origin of the powers of the King's Advocate in these cases; and even then, they were not his exclusively, but belonged equally to the King's Treasurer." McKenzie, "in referring to this act and the prior enactment 1436," Burnett continued, "observes, that pursuits at his Majesty's instance are only subsidiary, and that from these acts 'two things may be concluded; 1*st*, that of old, it was doubtful if the King could pursue private crimes without an accuser; 2*d*, That pursuits at his Majesty's instance for *private* crimes, are *yet only* subsidiary and allowable, if parties be silent, or collude,' &c." "In many cases indeed, long after the institution of *King's Advocate*," Burnett emphasized, "we find it objected, that he could not prosecute without the concurrence of the party injured, or his kinsmen." "This at all events is clear," Burnett concluded, "that the proper and original form of prosecution with us, was in the name of the private party injured, who accordingly prosecuted, not merely for reparation and redress to himself as an individual, but for punishment and for reparation to the public; and hence it was, that this form of prosecution continued, and still subsists, with the same effect, and to the same conclusions, as to the full pains of law, as a prosecution at the instance solely of his Majesty's Advocate."[169] Eighteenth-century legal sources specifically describe how private parties could obtain His Majesty's Advocate's concurrence by seeking "a Bill for Criminal Letters."[170]

After discussing the origins of private prosecution, Burnett documented the Scottish legal system's transition to largely public prosecutions, noting that "the law ceased to indulge revenge, when it took the power of punishment out of the hands of the individual injured." "Private prosecutions," Burnett emphasized, "were *introduced* as the only mode then known of securing the punishment of offenders, and of maintaining the peace and good order of the community. They were *continued* as the most effectual mode of insuring the same object; while it appears, that the introduction of a public accuser in crimes against the individual, was merely a subsidiary remedy, in order more effectually to guard against the impunity of offenders, and to enforce the rule, which every community has so material an interest to maintain, *that crimes shall not go unpunished.*" In highlighting how Scotland made use of both private and public prosecutions to ensure accountability for criminal conduct, Burnett wrote: "It is indeed the union of these two modes of prosecutions, that constitutes the pre-eminence of the criminal jurisprudence of Scotland, and distinguishes it from that of most other countries in Europe." "It is by preserving *both* in due vigour," Burnett observed, "that public justice is effectually secured; that the remissness or partiality of the public accuser is on the one hand guarded against, and the too great lenity and forbearance of the individual corrected on the other."[171] Whether a prosecution would go forward, of course, depended on the facts and circumstances of each case, just as whether a prosecution would be a public or private one—or, perhaps, some combination thereof—also depended on the factual context.

The importance of Europe's Enlightenment, of which the Scottish Enlightenment was a major part, is well known. The Enlightenment, among other things, focused on legal reform and ensuring a separation of powers and fighting tyranny and abuses of power. One of its core maxims—laid down by Montesquieu, the French jurist, and later publicized by Cesare Beccaria, the Italian criminal-law theorist from Milan who, in the 1760s while still in his mid-twenties, wrote his much-celebrated book, *An Essay on Crimes and Punishments*—was that any punishment that goes beyond necessity is "tyrannical."[172] In a somewhat similar vein, Burnett's treatise specifically highlighted some of the restraints Scottish law "wisely" placed on private prosecutions, such as the interest required to commence one, the "oath of calumny," and "the paying of expences or penalties, when the prosecution is found to be groundless and malicious." These, Burnett wrote, served to "cure many of those evils that might result from lodging the power of prosecution in private hands; which, while it must in many instances occasion a remissness in the execution of the law, will in others often give rise to vexatious and oppressive proceedings." Preventing frivolous or vexatious private prosecutions was a goal frequently recited by various legal commentators, including in Scotland.

A private prosecution, Burnett pointed out, could be brought "as to every sort of crime, by which his person, his property, his *status*, his peace of mind, or his fame, is injured." "He may prosecute criminally for assaults, for injuries by *putting in fear* and *endangering* the person, for thefts, for frauds of all sorts, and for gross calumnies," as well as for "injuries that are done to us as members of a corporation or community" and for harms "by which our *interest*, either *personal* or *patrimonial*, may be affected," he explained. "[T]his right," he stressed, "extends to injuries done to others, if nearly connected with us; and which are held, as they truly are, as injuries done to ourselves, if they are of that atrocious and aggravated kind, which carry with them distress and anguish, as well to the sufferer as to his kindred and relations." "Such is the case," Burnett noted in this treatise, "in homicide, in rape, or attempts to ravish, and in other wrongs done to the person, of a highly aggravated nature, *e. g.*, the unlawful seizure, confinement, or forcible abduction of the person." The private party's interest, he pointed out though, could not be too attenuated—too "remote or feeble," in Burnett's words—or "one which does not affect him immediately, either as an individual, or as a member of some associated body."[173]

Burnett's treatise, capturing the state of Scottish criminal procedure at the time, observed that "while the Law thus gives its fullest sanction to prosecutions at the instance of the private party," the law guards against "the abuse of this right" by placing and imposing "proper limitations and restraints." One of those much-recited, much-vaunted restraints: the oath of calumny.[174] As Burnett explained this Scottish legal practice: "To guard against calumnious and malicious prosecutions by private parties, the Law allows the *oath of calumny* to be put by the party accused to the prosecutor, which if he refuse to take, the libel will be dismissed." "The oath," Burnett declared, "ought to bear, that the prosecutor '*believes* that the facts he alleges in his libel are true, and that he has good reason to insist in the prosecution;' and the reference would be made *in limine*, at all events before the assize are sworn." The taking of oaths has always been part of societies and judicial or legal systems in particular,[175] and that was true in Scotland, too. "It is owing to this privilege in the party accused," Burnett noted, "that the private prosecutor ought to be *personally* present at all diets of Court, at least previous to the commencement of the proof."

All oaths are designed to serve a purpose, and such was the case with the oath of calumny in criminal cases. According to the *Scottish National Dictionary*, the oath of calumny was "an oath taken at the outset of an action, by which both parties, either by themselves or through their counsel, swear that the facts pleaded are true." That dictionary, citing Hume's *Trial for Crimes* (1800) and Bell's *Dictionary of the Law of Scotland*, gave these representative uses: "The pannel may call on the prosecutor to swear the libel, as it is styled; that is, to give his oath of calumny." "This oath of calumny ... was in practice never put, unless the adverse party required it; and, when made, it was held as an oath of credulity or opinion merely."[176] *Calumny* is "the crime of accusing another falsely, and knowingly so, of some heinous offence,"[177] and it also means "the making of false and defamatory statements about someone in order to damage their reputation; slander."[178] "Private prosecutors at Roman law," one history notes, "were required to swear that they were not proceeding *calumnaie causa*, 'with blackmailing intent.'"[179]

Other existing safeguards against vexation private prosecutions that Burnett took notice of: monetary sanctions for malicious prosecutions and obtaining the *concourse*, or consent, of the Lord Advocate—the Scottish public prosecutor. "The Law also subjects the private prosecutor in expences, and even in penalties," Burnett wrote, "if he insist in a groundless or malicious accusation; and which penalties the Court have now a power to award, corresponding to the damage sustained by the party, to which the old statutory sum would be wholly inadequate." "Giving expences, however," Burnett cautioned, explaining Scots law, "is a mere matter of discretion with the Court, and does not necessarily follow in every case of an acquittal." "The Act 1587," he pointed out, "provides that they shall be awarded *where parties are maliciously* charged." "*Lastly*," Burnett reported, "[i]n no case can the *instance* of a private party be sustained, unless the *concourse* of the King's Advocate be given to it." "This, indeed," he wrote, "is an essential and necessary requisite in all indictments raised by a private party, and was originally introduced as a check to groundless and malicious prosecutions at his instance."[180] As another source, *Practice of the Criminal Law of Scotland* (1833), put it: "The prosecution at the private instance requires the concourse of the Lord Advocate, and cannot be insisted in without it; but his Lordship is not the uncontrolled judge of giving or refusing his concourse, but may be compelled to state his grounds for withholding his concourse to the Supreme Court, who will judge of their sufficiency."[181]

In Scotland, which formed a Union with England in 1707, private prosecution was defended[182] and put to use,[183] even as the practice—as newspaper accounts and legal commentators reveal—was subject to continual abuses[184] and, over time, gradually withered away and fell out of favor.[185] In a departure and break from England's long-standing common law practice, Scotland's Lord Advocate assumed the dominant position in criminal cases, with Scottish private prosecutions becoming extremely rare, though still, technically, legally permissible. "The Lord Advocate was the public prosecutor in almost all instances in Scotland," *The Morning Chronicle*, of London, reported in 1822, a little more than ten years after the publication of John Burnett's treatise on Scottish criminal law.[186] By 1858, *The Standard* of London reported on the parliamentary resolution of Mr. Baxter, who emphasized of Scotland's Lord Advocate: "The Lord Advocate was a member of the Faculty of Advocates, and was almost invariably the most distinguished member of his profession among his party, so that he had a most extensive private practice. He was the public prosecutor for

Scotland, and English members were not, perhaps, aware of the great amount of business which devolved upon him in that capacity." As Mr. Baxter stressed: "In Scotland private prosecutors were almost unknown, and great offenders were prosecuted by the Lord Advocate before the Court of Justiciary in Edinburgh. In Scotland there was no grand jury, and there was no coroner's inquest, and the Lord Advocate had the sole right of deciding who was to be tried for any offence."[187]

In fact, the Scottish system of public criminal prosecution was oftentimes—perhaps inevitably, given Scotland's close physical proximity to England—compared to the English system of criminal justice that relied so heavily on private prosecutors.[188] At an academic gathering in 1860, Scotland's Lord Advocate—James Moncreiff—himself spoke on the subject of jurisprudence, lecturing favorably, quite naturally, of the Scottish system of public prosecution while taking note of the long-standing reform efforts in England to put in place a similar system. In his address to the National Association for the Promotion of Social Science, delivered in the common hall of a university, the Lord Advocate—Scotland's chief prosecutor—had this to say: "I turn to another subject which your noble President last night invited our attention to—I mean the subject of a Minister of Justice, or public prosecutor, in the criminal department of the law. Now, this is a very large and very important matter, but more fitted to be dealt with by English hands than by mine." "As regards ourselves," he said, injecting a little humor, "I suppose I am hardly an impartial witness as to the usefulness of a public prosecutor. (Laughter, and great applause.) At the same time, I think I am entitled to say—because I speak now from very considerable experience of that office—that every year that I have had the opportunity of seeing the working of the system has increased my conviction that it would be very difficult indeed to devise a mode of prosecuting criminal business which would accomplish the twofold object which the prosecutor ought to have before him—the detection of the guilty and the protection of the innocent."

Lord Advocate James Moncreiff, a baron,[189] gave a lengthy recitation of his personal views. "No doubt," he offered, "a public prosecutor in an arbitrary state is very dangerous to the liberties of the people; but a public prosecutor, under the influence of public opinion and Parliamentary responsibility is, in my opinion, as far as the practical working of it is concerned, the best mode in which the criminal affairs of a country can be conducted." As Lord Advocate Moncrieff emphasized: "It is impossible to deny that as crimes are crimes against the public, so the public should be at the expense of prosecuting and punishing them. (Hear, hear.) And whatever may be the practical operation of it, it has no right to leave upon a private prosecutor—who may be supposed to prosecute only for the injury done to himself—the vindication of the great public law, the breach of which is truly at the ground-work of the proceedings. (Applause.) And, accordingly, it has been the desire in England for many years to accomplish, if possible, this most desirable change."[190]

In England, America's mother country, private prosecutions had long been in use, including in some very high-profile cases in the lead up to the American Revolution that produced the Declaration of Independence, the Articles of Confederation, and then the U.S. Constitution. For example, in the 1760s, after a prominent radical English politician and reformer, John Wilkes, the publisher of the *North Briton*, was fined and ordered to be jailed, his supporters—known as Wilkites—vehemently protested. The protests culminated in the "Massacre of St. George's Fields" on May 10, 1768, the date set for the opening of Parliament, when British soldiers fired on the protesters who'd gathered chanting "Wilkes and Liberty!" John Wilkes, a duly elected member of Parliament, had a long history of poking at King George III and his ministers and, in 1768, he was, though duly elected by his constituency, being prevented from taking his seat in Parliament by virtue of his conduct and a sentence of imprisonment. Five years earlier, in 1763, Wilkes had written an article in the *North Briton* that disparaged George III, leading to Wilkes' arrest for seditious libel. Benjamin Franklin closely followed John Wilkes' activities and what became known as the *North Briton* affair,[191] with Wilkes, in time, becoming a hero to American revolutionaries for standing up to George III and his ministers.[192]

After a judicial ruling that Wilkes—whom John Adams and other Sons of Liberty in Boston came to view as an "Illustrious Patriot" for "his strenuous efforts" to "preserve" the British Constitution[193]—had a parliamentary privilege, a ruling that outraged George III, Wilkes was discharged from custody. But Parliament then voted to amend the law so members of Parliament could be arrested on libel charges. Declared an outlaw, Wilkes had to flee to France, where he lived in exile before returning to England, eventually getting elected yet again to the House of Commons as an MP for Middlesex due to his popularity in his constituency. Before the large protests in south London in 1768 at St. George's Fields, with the gathered crowds variously estimated to be anywhere from 1,000 to 40,000 people, the protesters who'd assembled had been read the Riot Act of 1715 and been told, on threat of force, to disperse. The Riot Act was an attempt to bolster the power of civil authorities and it made it a crime for a group of twelve or more people to refuse to disperse within an hour of being ordered to do so by a magistrate.[194] After a London justice of the peace, Samuel Gillam, authorized the British soldiers to use their guns after being hit in the head with a stone, the scene at St. George's Fields turned deadly, with several people shot to death, including William Allen.

In a letter written by Benjamin Franklin from London in mid-May of 1768, he described what had happened to Wilkes' supporters. As Franklin wrote to Joseph Galloway on May 14, 1768: "Great mobs of his adherents have assembled before the prison, the guards have fired on them: it is said five or six are killed and fifteen or sixteen wounded, and some circumstances have attended this military execution, such as its being done by the Scotch regiment, the pursuing a lad and killing him at his father's house &c. &c. that exasperate people exceedingly, and more mischief seems brewing." "Several of the soldiers are imprisoned," Franklin added of the aftermath of the massacre at St. George's Fields, with Franklin observing: "If they are not hanged it is feared there will be more and greater mobs; and if they are, that no soldier will assist in suppressing any mob hereafter. The prospect either way is gloomy. It is said the English soldiers cannot be confided in to act against these mobs, being suspected as rather inclined to favour and join them."[195]

A spectator and the son of a Southwark publican, the proprietor of the Horse Shoe Inn on Blackman Street, William Allen found himself in the wrong place at the wrong time, as did another innocent bystander, William Redburn. Redburn, a journeyman weaver, was shot through the thigh and later died in a London hospital. In Allen's case, a soldier had been chasing one of the rioters but reportedly lost sight of him in the vicinity of a public house and then mistook Allen for the rioter. In response to the killing, William Allen's father commenced a private prosecution against a Scottish soldier, Donald Maclean (sometimes spelled Maclane or Macleane), believed to have been involved in his son's death. Maclean was tried at the Guildford Assizes in August 1768. But "being proved to have acted only in discharge of his duty," one source recounts, he was ultimately acquitted and two other alleged accomplices were discharged, too. As one history notes: "Maclean had been chasing one of the rioters but lost sight of him in the vicinity of a public house. Entering a shed at the rear of the building he had mistaken Allen for the rioter, bayoneted him and shot him dead. Maclean, who spent six months in prison awaiting his trial, was acquitted on a submission that he had acted in discharge of his duty as a soldier and in obedience to orders from a superior officer."[196]

William Allen's father, as an edition of the *North Briton* later reported, wanted vengeance and made that clear. He petitioned the House of Commons, and addressed a petition directly "To his MAJESTY" that read in part as follows: "Your Petitioner thinks it his duty to lay before your Majesty, with great humility, a short account of the unprovoked and outrageous murder committed by a Scotch officer, and three soldiers of the same regiment, upon the innocent body of your petitioner's only son; a youth, that all who knew him are ready to attest, was perfectly sober, temperate, humane, dutiful to his parents, and a sincere lover and worshipper of his God." "Your Majesty," the petition concluded, "can never be offended with your most afflicted petitioner for applying to your Majesty for justice against the cruel murderers of his beloved child, whose blood cries aloud for vengeance."[197] William Allen's grieving parents later erected a monument to their son at his tomb that recalled his "unspotted Life and amiable Disposition" and how he "was inhumanly murdered" near St. George's Fields "on the 10th Day of May 1768 by Scottish Detachments from the ARMY."[198]

The Wilkites also persuaded the widow of the innocent bystander, William Redburn, to bring a private prosecution against Samuel Gillam, the justice of the peace who had warned the protesters to stop throwing stones and who had given the troops the order to "Fire." Gillam had been indicted by a Middlesex grand jury for "the willful murder of William Redburn," with it alleged that Gillam had acted "feloniously, willfully, and of malice aforethought" and that, "on the 10th of May," he "was present, aiding, helping, abetting, comforting, and maintaining" the "unknown" person who "with a musket loaded with gunpowder and a leaden bullet" had discharged the gun that took Redburn's life.[199] Although Gillam—dressed in a black suit—was acquitted in front of a packed courtroom at a session of London's Old Bailey a few days later, the private prosecution in that case represented an effort by Redburn's grieving widow to hold the monarchical government in power accountable.

The History of the Reign of George III (1822) later captured the futility of the exercise of trying to take on the Crown, with that book summarizing the murder charge's outcome: "Samuel Gillam, esq. one of the justices, was tried on a charge of having murdered William Redburn by having ordered the soldiers to fire; in consequence of which, Redburn had been killed. The jury seeing the absurdity and the injustice of such a prosecution, would not suffer the accused to take the trouble of entering upon his defence; but, when the prosecutor's evidence was closed, pronounced a verdict of acquittal."[200] Another account of Gillam's prosecution, given in the House of Commons, summarized its outcome this way: "[T]he innocence of Mr. Gillam appeared so evident, that he was not put upon his defence; all the judges on the bench agreed that he had not only acted justifiably but commendably; the jury, without going out of Court, or hesitating a moment, pronounced him not guilty; and the Court granted him a copy of the indictment."[201] There were, of course, varied opinions on the case. One observation, published in 1770, was that the decades-old Riot Act had been invoked to justify "the murderers in St. George's-fields" but did not "give a commission for instant slaughter; or authorize a justice of the peace to say—fire."[202]

In England, early nineteenth-century private prosecutors—as had happened in some eighteenth-century state trials in the House of Lords, too—sometimes coordinated with the Attorney General, the country's chief legal officer.[203] The use of private prosecutors in Crown cases is apparent from accounts in nineteenth-century newspapers,[204] with the private prosecutor's role distinguished from that of public officials and grand juries.[205] A representative notice in a London newspaper—one that an English reader sipping tea might've encountered—read like this short one from 1843 in *The Morning Chronicle*: "The prosecution was conducted by Mr. B. Gallway, Crown prosecutor, assisted by Mr. George Gregg for the private prosecutor, Rev. Mr. Seymour."[206] "It was well known that in most cases in England there were private prosecutors," *The Sydney Morning Herald* in distant Australia proclaimed in 1843.[207] In Australia, established as an English penal colony in 1788, there were—as England itself would witness as well—ongoing public discussions in the 1840s about how prosecutions, including private ones, were being conducted.[208] Some disparaged private prosecutions, contending—as in one 1880 case against a tailor and a shoemaker for bribery at a borough election—that they should not have been brought in the first place.[209] Sensitive to that critique, private prosecutors were often themselves careful to point out that they were seeking "public justice," not "vengeance" or to "indulge personal vindictiveness."[210]

The Case of Henry Hunt—and the Fierce Debate Over Private Prosecution

Although England's Attorney General got involved in high-profile cases,[211] many private prosecutors, often with no formal legal training or insufficient financial resources to hire competent counsel, were essentially on their own as they tried to make use of the English legal system—a system of justice that prominent penal reformers, such as Jeremy Bentham, saw as problematic.[212] In November of 1819, in the Court of King's Bench, one man, Henry Hunt, who was not a member of the Bar but who had made unsuccessful runs for Parliament, sought to make a motion in court against "the Manchester Magistrates." A powerful orator, Hunt was a British radical and agitator who advocated for universal suffrage, an end to child labor, and the repeal of the Corn Laws—tariffs on imported food and grain designed to protect domestic producers but that intolerably raised food prices for working people. People were going hungry and working long hours, and at that time, only a small percentage of the population—just two percent in 1815, by one estimate—had the right to vote. Because of his oratorial skills, Hunt was invited to address what was to be a massive rally at St. Peter's Field in Manchester, England, as its featured speaker on August 16, 1819. But that rally turned deadly, and it later became known as the Peterloo Massacre, in what has been called "an ironic reference to the Battle of Waterloo."

On the morning of August 16th, the Manchester magistrates had met for breakfast at the Star Inn to decide how to deal with Mr. Hunt when he arrived, and they had pre-arranged for several hundred British troops and militiamen to be on hand to counter whatever rioting or unrest might occur at the mass meeting. After women dressed in white from the Manchester Female Reform Society escorted Hunt to the hustings, two carts lashed together for the speakers, William Hulton—the chairman of the magistrates who'd been watching the events unfold at a nearby house—decided to preemptively issue an arrest warrant for Hunt and the meeting's organizers. The local constable quickly decided that military assistance would be needed to execute the warrants, and as the cavalry and untrained yeomanry charged through the crowd—estimated to be around 30,000 to 60,000 people, some holding signs reading "No Corn Laws" and "Universal Suffrage"—chaos erupted as people frantically tried to get out of the way of the galloping horses, with the soldiers atop them wielding sabres. The crowd dispersed in a few minutes, but more than ten people were killed in the melee and hundreds were injured. Hunt himself was arrested on that hot summer's day, later to be convicted of seditious conspiracy at the York Lent Assizes in 1820 and sentenced to be confined in the Ilchester Gaol for thirty months.[213]

Before the Court of King's Bench at Westminster, Mr. Hunt, prior to his own conviction, sought in November 1819 "to move for Criminal Information" against the Manchester magistrates—a procedural mechanism to institute a criminal prosecution. The Chief Justice, however, told Mr. Hunt that such a motion "must be made by some Gentleman at the Bar." Although Mr. Hunt insisted that he had procured the necessary affidavits, the Chief Justice was unmoved and totally unreceptive. "That may be, but the motion which you propose to make," the Chief Justice told Hunt, "must be made on behalf of his Majesty, and should be made either by one of his Officers, or by some Gentleman at the Bar." "I can't hear any motion upon such a subject, except from a Gentleman at the Bar," the Chief Justice stressed, shutting down Mr. Hunt's efforts. "We will not allow you to make a motion for a criminal information," a clearly frustrated Chief Justice continued as his antagonist, Mr. Hunt, persisted in pleading his case. The Chief Justice's colleague, Mr. Justice Bayley, then weighed in, telling Hunt: "Every party has a right to come into a Court of Justice to conduct his own suit, or his defence, or to employ counsel on his behalf. In the distribution of justice, the public have certain rights, however, in which the King acts on their behalf: and in order to enable to act, certain officers are appointed—I mean the Attorney and Solicitor Generals; and it has been also the course for other gentlemen of the bar to stand in the same situation."

Justice Bayley offered Mr. Hunt reasons why, in the context of the case before the court, only members of the Bar should be allowed to address the jury. "Gentlemen at the Bar," Justice Bayley observed, "have received an education for the purpose, and they know what points they may, consistently with the rules of law, submit for the consideration of the Court: they know that certain rules exist which they will take care not to infringe; and, in conducting criminal prosecutions, where persons are to be tried capitally or for a misdemeanor, it is of the utmost importance that these rules should be known and observed—otherwise prejudices might be excited in the minds of Juries, which no subsequent effort of the Judge could remove." When Mr. Hunt continued to protest, saying "the case of the King on the prosecution of Lyon, Huskisson and others" provided an applicable precedent, Justice Bayley parried back, telling Hunt: "That is a case directly against this motion. After my Lord Ellenborough had suffered Mr. Pitt to make an address to the Jury, I took an opportunity of speaking to his Lordship, and represented to him that a private prosecutor could not, in point of law, address the Jury. I reminded him that what he had done in suffering Mr. Pitt to address the Jury as a prosecutor was contrary to law, and his Lordship ultimately affirmed what I had said, and admitted that what he had done was wrong."

The displeased Mr. Hunt nonetheless persisted, saying, "I have no Counsel nor Attorney, nor the means of getting any. I ask your Lordships, therefore, how am I to proceed." At that point, Mr. Justice Holroyd jumped in, explaining to Mr. Hunt: "This is an application on the part of a private individual for a criminal information on public grounds. No instance has been mentioned to justify such a proceeding, and it is never allowed except at the instance of Officers of the Crown—such as the Attorney and Solicitor Generals, authorised to act for the Crown, or Gentlemen at the Bar, who are in their nature public Officers." In the "[o]ne instance" identified in which "a private prosecutor, in the name of the King, was suffered to address the Jury," Justice Holroyd pointed out, cautioning the increasingly agitated Mr. Hunt not to interrupt him, on "that very occasion, the Learned and Noble Judge who permitted such a proceeding, admitted afterwards that what was done was not sanctioned by law, and that he had not done right in that respect." "I am clearly of opinion," Justice Holroyd said, "that it is not in the power of any individual who may think fit, to convert himself into Counsel for the Crown; and I think this application cannot be made at all by the person now applying."

After Justice Holroyd addressed Mr. Hunt, Mr. Justice Best decided to weigh in on the controversy as well. "In a criminal proceeding," Justice Best said, "no private individual can make himself a party, and therefore it is impossible that the person who now presents himself to the Court can become a party in this case." Justice Best distinguished between criminal and civil proceedings. "If this person had received an injury, and wished to obtain satisfaction for that injury," he continued, "he might become a party in a civil suit, and then present himself to the Court in his own name." "That, however, is not the question now before us," he said, adding of Mr. Hunt as he rejected the man's arguments: "He comes forward as the advocate of the King, which the law says he cannot be allowed to do, because the King will be the only party who can set the law in motion." As Justice Best remarked, explaining: "In criminal informations the King is one party and the defendant is the other, and the question is, whether this person is in a situation in which he can present himself to us as the advocate of the King? If any precedent could be cited in which such a proceeding had been allowed, I should have thought it right to consider whether we ought to be bound by that precedent. But there is no such precedent in which such a practice has been admitted, and no case can be cited in which such a proceeding can occur, but at the instance of the Attorney and Solicitor General, or of a gentleman at the bar."

The court proceeding went on and on, with the law-trained justices and Mr. Hunt—the non-lawyer—sparing and getting equally frustrated with each another. "As no case can be found to authorise this proceeding, shall we make a precedent? What right have we to say, that this person shall thus intrude himself as the person who is to inform this Court for the King?" Justice Best asked rhetorically. Justice Best's perspective: "I can see no reason for it, and I am sure that the replies made on the Court to-day by this person, are pregnant proof how extremely improper it would be to establish such a precedent. When a gentleman at the bar has stated what he thinks it is important for the Court to hear, he stops and receives the judgment of the Court. That, however, is not the case with such advocates as the person we have now before us, for they are never contented with any thing said by the Court." "It would be attended with dreadful inconvenience to the administration of justice," Justice Best stated, "if such persons could be permitted to discharge the important duties of advocates." "I am clearly of opinion," he concluded, "that this motion cannot be entertained at the instance of this present applicant." At that point, the transcript of the record indicates, "Mr. Hunt, in a discontented tone, left the Court, saying, I can only say that the Manchester Magistrates will have no application made against them by a Gentleman of the Bar."[214] Mr. Hunt either could not afford to hire one or knew that because of the controversial nature of his position none would step forward. Accordingly, Hunt left the courthouse feeling he had not been heard.

Hunt later complained that the affidavits that had been gathered to support the prosecution of the Manchester magistrates were not permitted to be read "on the novel ground that no one could be allowed to move in a proceeding which merely tended to establish a criminal prosecution except through his majesty's attorney or solicitor general, or other counsel; although this new rule of court is obviously contrary to the principle, which permits every man in person to accuse before a grand jury, and is direct violation of Magna Charta and the Bill of Rights." The Attorney General, the monarch's chief legal officer, had rebuffed Hunt and refused to take up the case.[215] In truth, Mr. Hunt did not stand much of a chance before the English judiciary in any event. The Prince of Wales—the man who became King George IV—sent a message to the Manchester magistrates thanking them "for their prompt, decisive, and efficient measures for the preservation of the public peace," and Hunt himself ultimately had to face charges that he was involved in a conspiracy to overthrow the government. Although Hunt was granted bail before trial, his conviction at the York Assizes in 1820—and the imposition of his 30-month sentence along with being bound over for £2,000 to keep the peace for five years—sent the clear and unmistakable message that protests against the English monarchy would not be tolerated and would be ruthlessly quashed. After the Peterloo Massacre, in fact, Parliament reassembled and passed the so-called Six Acts—legislation aimed at "curbing radical journals" and meetings "as well as the danger of armed insurrection." The new laws, which included the Seizure of Arms Act, the Seditious Meetings Act, the Blasphemous and Seditious Libels Act, and the Newspaper Stamp Duties Act, were all intended to clamp down on English radicals.[216]

The debate in England over whether to move from private prosecutors to public ones generated much discussion and debate in the years to come.[217] For example, in 1825, *The Morning Chronicle* of London observed that it had "often called the attention to our readers to the barbarous helplessness" of England's system of justice, emphasizing that "[n]o civilized country ought to be without an institution for securing the execution of the law." "In England," the newspaper noted in a verbose, long-winded fashion, "this task is thrown on the individuals injured by the criminal, or their relations, who are bound over to prosecute, that is those who have already suffered, are called on to suffer still more,—and put themselves to an expence of money and time, and to encounter a great deal of obloquy,—that is, a burden which ought to be borne by the whole community, through an officer commissioned and paid by that community, is thrown on the very persons in the community, who in consideration of their misfortune ought to bear less of the burden instead of more than others." *The Morning Chronicle* then raised a couple of pointed questions: "Can we wonder that many, through dread of the trouble to which they may subject themselves, cease to complain? Can we wonder that many of those who have complained, shrink from the labour of the task imposed on them?"

In its 1825 article, *The Morning Chronicle* delivered a blunt message. "In vain," it said, "Magistrates inveigh against the remissness of prosecutors; and remind them of the duty they owe to the public." "The natural unsophisticated sense of men tells them," the newspaper added of crime victims, "that instead of the Community having a further claim on them, they have a claim on the Community." "It not unfrequently happens," the paper reported, "that the prosecutor, besides escaping trouble and expence, can only hope indemnification for his loss, by conniving at the escape of the criminal." As *The Morning Chronicle* wrote: "What a shame to compound felony! exclaims some sapient Magistrate. The extent of absurdity, daily swallowed by persons even of decent parts, is really astonishing. A Banker is robbed of a 10,000*l.* parcel—he perceives that he has not the slightest chance of recovering any part of this property, except by an arrangement with the thieves, whom he allows to pocket 4,000*l.* on condition of receiving back 6,000*l.*" "Besides, the system allows the rich to escape," *The Morning Chronicle* lamented, editorializing: "A prosecutor, who cannot afford to forfeit his recognizances, tells the friends of the criminal, I am ready to forgive him, but I cannot afford to lose 50*l.* If the criminal is rich, or has rich friends, this difficulty is soon got over,—if he is poor, the law takes its course. Hence, we see the whole country laughing at the farce of Judges, with all due solemnity, wondering at the absence of prosecutors, when every one knew before hand that the matter had been arranged."

The subject of the criminal law, *The Morning Chronicle* conveyed to its readers, "is discussed in a sensible article in the forthcoming number of *The Edinburgh Review*," with the latter publication observing: "We cannot help (says the Author) classing the method of putting the criminal law in motion by private prosecutors as nearly akin to those remnants of most antique wisdom (Weregild, and Appeal of Battle), and manifestly smelling of the same age." As the author of *The Edinburgh Review* article stressed: "When any offence, however grave, is committed in England, the care of bringing the offender to punishment is in every case devolved upon the private party injured, or supposed to be injured; or in the rare cases of the party injured being killed, and having no relations, or of the injury being done to a pauper, then the prosecution is entrusted to the parish officers." After noting that "[t]he only practical exceptions to this are where towns have undertaken the care of prosecuting offences," *The Edinburgh Review* article author added that "[t]he general principle, however, is, that the private party voluntarily prosecutes, or is bound over to prosecute by the Magistrate who commits the offender."[218] In the eighteenth century, it is estimated that more than eighty percent of indictable offenses were prosecuted by either the victim of the crime or the victim's agents, with most of the remaining offenses prosecuted by individuals who held the rotating office of parish constable and who had been "bound over" by magistrates to prosecute the crimes because the victims were too poor or incapable of doing so.[219]

In many cases throughout English history, private prosecutors were thus more or less solely responsible for navigating the thicket of the legal system as they sought to secure the conviction and punishment of offenders, though they frequently used what power they possessed either in a vindictive manner or by seeking to extort favorable terms from the accused.[220] "Private prosecutors," London's *Morning Post* reported in 1851 of perjury cases, "often choose to incur considerable expenses beyond these allowed by the Court, on account of the importance to themselves of establishing the guilt of a person who has sworn falsely."[221] Five years later, in the Court of Queen's Bench, Lord Campbell—at "Sittings at Nisi Prius at Westminster," had this to say: "I believe that in the majority of cases, where there is a private prosecutor and a conviction, a compromise takes place between the prosecutor and the culprit, and the latter escapes the punishment which the law inflicts. And I believe there are also instances in which the prosecutor and the person convicted have shaken hands, after entering into some corrupt agreement, and become apparently friends."[222] There were, certainly, some strange occurrences. In one English court martial, Sir William Mansfield, the Commander-in-Chief of the Indian army, awkwardly appeared as *both* public prosecutor and private prosecutor.[223]

Putting the financial and time-consuming onus on private individuals to bring criminals to justice actually produced much injustice in the British Isles. Only those with means could afford to hire competent attorneys, and access to the criminal justice system depended largely on one's station in life. Although a system known as the *frankpledge* developed in England that involved pledges of mutual security[224] requiring males over a certain age to deliver up any neighbor who committed a crime[225] in an effort to preserve the public peace,[226] aristocrats and nobles could easily make use of the court system while the poor could not. England's private policing and private prosecution systems also placed accused suspects and criminal defendants in jeopardy of vindictive or malicious prosecutions. "For a very long time, really into the nineteenth century," historian John Langbein writes, "the English relied on a predominant, although not exclusive, component of private prosecutions." "The obvious drawback to any system of gratuitous citizen prosecution," he aptly points out, "is that it is unreliable." As Langbein explains: "There will be cases where there are no aggrieved citizens who survive to prosecute, and others where the aggrieved citizens will decline to prosecute, or be inept at it."[227] "The birth of widespread public policing did not occur in Great Britain until 1829," another scholar, law professor Ric Simmons writes, pointing to the passage that year of the Metropolitan Police Act, which created full-time, uniformed police officers who were independent of the courts.[228] England's approach to policing made possible the creation of Sir Arthur Conan Doyle's fictional private detective character, Sherlock Holmes, whose brilliant mind and speedy yet thorough investigations were needed to solve crimes.[229] But putting self-interested English subjects in charge of the criminal process plainly jeopardized the public interest and the rights of the accused.

The Quest to Reform England's Private Prosecution System

Over time, English public prosecutors accrued more and more power, with one London newspaper, *The Standard*, pointing out in 1829, with considerable hyperbole, that the "power of the public prosecutor" had, by that time, "superseded" that of "the private prosecutor." That may have been a gross overstatement of the reality in the same year, 1829, that saw the emergence of the Metropolitan Police in London,[230] but the need to protect the public interest—and to put the public's interest above private interests—was certainly coming into clearer view. "In law," *The Standard* reported, "there are two interests to be considered in the perpetration of crimes, the public and the private interests." "But those two interests are essentially different," the newspaper editorialized, adding: "It is not in the power of the private and individual prosecutor to defeat the ends of public justice, by any arrangement which he can make with the accused. No compact into which he can enter will be binding on the public prosecutor—but whatever the public prosecutor does is binding on the private."[231] In short, *The Standard*—recognizing that the public prosecutor had powers that private prosecutors did not—showed a need to ensure that public justice would be done, even though private prosecutions were still commonplace in English life.

While England's Attorney General or lower-level officials, such as constables, frequently handled specific criminal cases,[232] many prosecutions were, in the years to come, still said to have been "properly left with private prosecutors, or the parochial authorities."[233] In 1847, in *The Times* of London, one judge in Durham, in summing up English law, was quoted as telling a jury this in a case dealing with a malicious prosecution allegation: "It was part of the policy of our law, with some exceptions, to leave private prosecutors to take the initiative in proceedings for punishing offenders against the law. In some crimes, high treason for instance, proceedings were taken directly by the law officers of the Crown, but, generally speaking, it was left to private individuals to set the law in motion against offenders." "The law, therefore," the judge advised, "did not tolerate the idea that it was wrong in an individual to come forward to prosecute."[234] "In Great Britain, to this day," an American judge told a jury in a remark later published in New York's *Buffalo Enquirer* in 1893, "nearly all prosecutions for the Crown are conducted by counsel employed by private prosecutors."[235] In other words, even though particular concerns were raised about the conduct of private prosecutions (*e.g.*, solicitors for private prosecutors appearing before grand juries),[236] the English justice system remained bifurcated between public and private prosecutions, generating a considerable level of confusion and complexity and raising significant practical issues about *who* had the responsibility of—or who *should* take up the responsibility for—prosecuting individual cases.[237]

Because of their considerable cost, private prosecutions were, not surprisingly perhaps, most often brought by people of substantial means, resulting in two systems of justice—one for the rich and one for the poor. "There were heavy burdens on citizen-prosecutors," observes Fred McElrea, a New Zealand district court judge,[238] noting that "[t]he time, effort and cost involved in gathering witnesses and getting their evidence taken by the local magistrate"—the justice of the peace—"was a disincentive to many people, so that many crimes were not prosecuted." Justices of the peace were tasked with doing pre-trial depositions—the recorded statements of the accuser, the accused, and any relevant witnesses. In response to this reality of private prosecutions, scores of mutual associations for prosecuting felons were formed,[239] and English solicitors—often the clerks to justices of the peace—started to play a role in preparing criminal cases, drafting indictments, and doing the work necessary to prepare for the introduction of evidence at trial. "Solicitors," McElrea emphasizes, were "commonly used by those who could afford them, i.e. the wealthy, but were sometimes disreputable and unscrupulous—the 'Newgate solicitors.'" "Not until the 1750s did Parliament empower the courts to reimburse the costs of poor prosecutors and witnesses who secured the conviction of felons," McElrea notes.[240] "From the 1820s," one history points out, "police forces began to prosecute indictable offences themselves, and, where this was not the case, reimbursed private prosecutors part of their costs." That source adds, though, that the central government and local authorities desired "to keep the expense to a minimum, aware that increases in taxes and rates would damage their trust relationships with their electorates."[241]

In 1829, one American newspaper reprinted this telling item about private prosecution from London's *Morning Journal*: "The Duke of Wellington has at length descended from his ministerial character, and entered the Old Bailey Court against the proprietors of the *Morning Journal*, as a private prosecutor." "The object of his Grace," the London news item emphasized, "is clearly the ruin of the individuals whose property, whose liberty, and whose independence are at stake, because they have had the courage to speak unreservedly of the principles of their illustrious opponent, and the pernicious measures he has sanctioned." The Duke of Wellington, the London paper observed, "has entered the area with us a private antagonist; having on his side all the patronage of the Crown—all the influence of that wealth he has acquired from the country he has injured—all the servility of the slaves of office—all the treasurers of the Treasury—all the secret service money—while we have nothing to repose upon but our innocence, our consistency, our sterling principles, and a jury of our countrymen."[242] The clear import of the paper's critique: the system was unfair because of the huge imbalance of resources. The Duke of Wellington's well-funded prosecution of the London newspaper—as one source notes—"for libels against the King, the government, and himself" sprang, it was said, "in no small degree, from the political excitement of the times; and they were either so vague or so raving as to be nearly harmless," with one characterizing the Duke "as an ambitious, unprincipled, and dangerous minister."[243]

Private prosecutions were highly criticized in the press, in fact, because their use meant that the wealthy had access to a system of justice that was, in many cases, simply out of reach for the working class. "The law will always be open to the charge of pressing unequally on the rich and the poor till public prosecutors are charged with the duty of bringing offenders to justice," an 1841 editorial in *The Morning Chronicle* of London read. As that editorial observed: "There are a hundred ways of gaining over private prosecutors, who, feeling that they have no responsibility, are seldom proof against the inducements held out to them. One man is brought over, the feelings of another are appealed to, a third is intimidated. But a public prosecutor knows that if a case is not successfully conducted, he will suffer in his professional reputation, if not in his honour, and he holds out resolutely." "We repeat, then," the editorial concluded, "that the law will always be viewed as an instrument which the rich may manage at pleasure till public officers are made responsible for its execution."[244] In *The Age*, a newspaper in Melbourne, Australia, the law itself was described as an "expensive luxury," though it noted that "so far as criminal proceedings are concerned they have little attraction for private prosecutors, inasmuch as these have nothing to gain individually by ventilating an alleged wrongdoing in the criminal courts."[245]

High-profile cases involving wealthy private prosecutors—the kind of gossipy cases frequently reported in the English press—looked a lot different than cases in the justice system involving those without adequate means to employ reputable, competent counsel.[246] In 1850, *The Times* of London offered a particularly disturbing portrait of private prosecutions, even as it praised the judicial system while declining to call for the total abandonment of private prosecutors. The news item it ran related to "the administration of justice at the Old Bailey" and a petition that called upon the Home Secretary and Parliament to investigate and redress the injustices observed, with a Mr. Wakely contending that "a public prosecutor is absolutely necessary for the purpose of insuring a decent and orderly administration of criminal justice in the metropolis." "In English criminal jurisprudence," the newspaper editorialized, "great pains have been bestowed in perfecting the mode and conduct of the trial of a criminal charge." As the paper emphasized of its utmost respect for the judiciary and the jury system: "Our judges generally are above reproach; the tribunal, jury included, is almost universally impartial—no unfair influences affect the decision which it is called upon to make. The evidence is fairly extracted, and the rules according to which it is adduced are, for the most part, judicious and just." That "portion of the administration of justice," *The Times* stressed, "has consequently deserved, and has certainly won, the confidence of the public."

But that newspaper, writing in the mid-nineteenth century, had serious concerns about the pretrial process—one often controlled by private prosecutors. "The same praise," it wrote after lauding the integrity of English judges and juries, "cannot be awarded to the mode in which the various and necessary preliminaries to the trial are arranged amongst us." After pointing out that English trials, once started, continued to conclusion without break or interruption, the newspaper observed that "[i]t is evident, then, that if any mistake occur in preparing for the trial, there will be a failure of justice" and "[t]he verdict will be given of necessity after an imperfect investigation, and the truth will not be elicited." "And yet in our judicial system," it continued, "there is really no one who can be deemed officially responsible for the due performance of these most essential preliminaries." "In the case described by Mr. Wakely," it noted, "a man died in consequence, it was supposed, of improper medical treatment," with a "medical man" set for trial on a manslaughter charge after a coroner's jury investigated the patient's death. "The constable," the paper wrote, "appears to have had after this the whole conduct of the prosecution; he had to bear in the first instance the necessary expenses—to collect and marshal the evidence—to employ the attorney—and be, in short, the prosecutor." Private prosecutions were expensive to conduct, and to make matters worse, private prosecutors—on the risk for their costs—were often unable to fully recoup their considerable expenses.[247]

The Times was especially skeptical of a constable's ability to carry out such weighty responsibilities.[248] "However respectable a constable may be," the newspaper offered, "he is clearly not a fit officer for the performance of such a duty: he cannot have received the necessary education, and he is not placed above the many corrupt influences that may be brought to bear upon him while endeavouring to execute this difficult task." Most of all, *The Times*—the popular London newspaper that sent its gritty reporters out to gather the day's news—wanted the public to be better informed about the English criminal justice system and the actors operating within it. As the paper wrote: "[T]here appear to be results from this system not, indeed, generally known, but which, nevertheless, might have been expected to follow so unwise an arrangement." "An immense mass of petty cases," it wrote, "being after this fashion intrusted to the care of a constable and illiterate and humble private prosecutors, a class of persons has arisen calling themselves attorneys, who, in fact, are not attorneys, but who, nevertheless, perform in aid of the constable and the illiterate prosecutor the duty which can only be properly performed by a person possessed of a certain degree of legal knowledge and practical skill." Thanks to the popularity of Sir Arthur Conan Doyle's fictional stories, Sherlock Holmes—the famed detective at 221B Baker Street who first made an appearance in print in *A Study of Scarlet* (1887)—had a well-earned reputation for quickly solving the most perplexing cases. But in truth, the average criminal case in the English justice system decades ago was far less likely to be investigated properly, if at all, because of the financial burdens placed upon private prosecutors.

The Times wrote, in particular, of the criminal justice system's corruption and incompetence—topics that many English newspapers expressed concerns about, along with the potential for money-driven considerations, even bribery or extortion, to enter into the equation as regards private prosecutions.[249] Men "really on the roll of attorneys" were "usually employed" to handle private prosecutions, but there were charlatans just trying make money; "[a] horrible and complicated system of vice and misery" had arisen, the newspaper concluded. As *The Times* editorialized: "Charges are preferred simply to obtain the costs: and under the guise of seeking for justice, a set of degraded wretches make a living at the expense of the public." As the newspaper continued: "The mischief, unhappily, is not confined to one class or one branch of the legal profession. Instances have been known in which a criminal negligence has been evinced by counsel with respect to the persons from whom their briefs are received." "The tribe of pretended attorneys," it stressed, "know to whom they can safely apply, and thus there is in reality a disgraceful conspiracy to fleece the public, beginning with a constable and ending with a barrister." Of the corruption that was often widely unknown, *The Times* wrote: "The extent of this evil the public cannot easily appreciate. Important cases attract general attention, and are in consequence properly conducted; and as the public see only these cases, and perceive that they are skil[l]fully and honourably managed, they fancy the general system works well; but pains are seldom taken to ascertain what proportion these more important cases bear to the whole number brought before the various tribunals of the metropolis."

The Times specifically identified the myriad problems associated with private prosecutions, noting how those problems—often occurring in cases that did not get much press attention—frequently went unnoticed by the general public.[250] "The misery and vice connected with this imperfect mode of managing criminal trials for the most part, therefore, escape observation," *The Times* warned its readers, "as we regard with an almost criminal apathy a mass of evil which, in its aggregate, is immense, because the items of which it is composed happen to be minute." "[T]his evil," the paper observed, "has almost entirely arisen from there being no established officer upon whom the duty would devolve of preparing every case for trial, and on whom the responsibility would rest if the duty were not properly performed, or if charges were improperly preferred." But at that juncture, *The Times* was unwilling to see the English criminal justice system jettison private prosecutions altogether. "We do not, however, mean that there should be a public prosecutor to supersede all private interference," *The Times* noted. Reticent about wholesale reform, but simultaneously looking to the future, *The Times* observed of an all-powerful public prosecutor sought by some while making this somewhat vague, progressive-leaning suggestion: "An officer with such exclusive powers would not be agreeable to those habits of self-reliance to which we owe in a great measure our extraordinary success as a people; but a plan could easily be devised by which an effective check could be established upon the imposition to which at present the public purse is subject in the item of expense attendant upon our criminal jurisprudence."[251]

In fact, the House of Commons entertained serious proposals in the mid-nineteenth century to provide for the appointment of public prosecutors. In 1854, John George Phillimore made one such effort, standing up in that body to move for leave to introduce a bill to appoint a public prosecutor. "The Bill had for its object to simplify and facilitate the course of public justice which had been hitherto in a most discreditable state," he told his fellow MPs.[252] "Under the present neglected state of our law, after the proceedings before the magistrate closed," a public report of his speech observed, "it was left often to the ability or zeal of a private prosecutor whether the greatest criminal should be brought to justice, or whether he should escape scot free." "Prosecutions depend entirely on the arrangements between attorneys and police constables," he lamented, "and thus it happened that while on the one hand prosecutions were indefinitely multiplied, on the other any opulent criminal had a great chance of escaping altogether."

As the newspaper summary of Mr. Phillimore's speech explained: "He alluded to the trial of a nobleman for fighting a duel. The ground upon which the noble lord accused was acquitted was this—that, it being the case of a duel, the prosecutor failed in identifying the person shot at, notwithstanding there were persons who could easily have identified him." Calling that result disgraceful, Phillimore concluded: "Had the case been intrusted to a public prosecutor that could never have happened." In another case, Phillimore observed, "a person of high position was indicted and convicted of obtaining money under false pretences," but a new trial was sought, and "the prosecutor was poor, and could not support the expense of a new trial." "Had there been a public prosecutor," Phillimore said to cheers in Parliament of *Hear, hear*, "it would have been impossible that so scandalous a thing could have happened." "The object of the present bill," Phillimore emphasized, "was to withdraw from a sphere of private animosity, caprice, and revenge, that which ought never to be left to private animosity, caprice, and revenge, and to see that justice was properly administered."[253]

A General View of the Criminal Law of England (1863), penned by James Fitzjames Stephen, an Inner Temple barrister, captured the state of English law in the mid-nineteenth century after efforts to try to put in place a better public prosecution system had been made. "[T]he law of England, as it now stands," he wrote in his treatise, "makes no special provision either for the detection or for the apprehension of criminals." As Stephen explained: "It permits any one to take upon himself that office, whether or not he is aggrieved by the crime, and it authorizes, and, in some cases, requires, particular public bodies, such as the corporations of particular towns, and the Quarter Sessions for counties, to maintain at the public expense a police force for the purpose of exercising this right; but, speaking broadly, policemen as such can do nothing which private persons cannot do." "The only mode by which the public interest in the prosecution of criminals is secured," Stephen noted, "is that of binding over persons to prosecute who from any motive bring an alleged offender before justices of the peace, and persuade them to commit him for trial; but there is no power, either theoretical or practical, by which people can be compelled to bring cases before the magistrates, and if the prosecutor chooses to forfeit his recognisances, the public have no remedy."

Though Stephen stressed that the Attorney General's functions "constitute an apparent exception to this rule," he observed that it was apparently only because, although "[i]t is his official duty to prosecute in particular cases where the public interest is concerned," "he is under no legal obligation to do so." "Though no one is obliged by law to prosecute a crime, any one who chooses to do so has ample facilities for that purpose," Stephen nonetheless underscored, pointing to the existence of justices of the peace who, upon sworn information, could grant a warrant, and to the rule that "any one has a right to apprehend another, even without a warrant, upon a reasonable suspicion of his having committed a felony." "There is very little difference between the rights of a peace-officer and a private person in this particular," Stephen stressed, "except that in some cases a peace-officer incurs less responsibility than a private individual." "The whole of our system proceeds upon the supposition that the prosecutor is to prove his case, and the prisoner to arrange his defence in his own way," Stephen explained, adding that "it would be impossible to appoint in this country public prosecutors" unless "our whole system of criminal procedure were radically changed."

There were, of course, non-English models of criminal justice for English legal commentators to examine as they contemplated law reform. After carefully examining France's inquisitorial system of criminal procedure, Stephen wrote that "[a]lthough the introduction of the continental machinery for the detection of crime is out of the question, it cannot be denied that the absence of any system whatever is a great evil." Not only did "many crimes go undetected because it is nobody's business to detect them," he emphasized, but "prosecutions sometimes fail on account of the slovenly manner in which cases are prepared for trial when the prosecutors are poor, and the attorneys for the prosecution have nothing to look to beyond the county allowance." "[W]hen crimes are prosecuted in a proper manner," he added, alluding to properly resourced prosecutions and citing evidence gathered in 1855 before the Select Committee of the House of Commons on the subject of public prosecutors, "the prosecutor is not only frequently, but almost always, put to great expense by the prosecution." After providing a detailed, full-throated critique of England's then-existing system, Stephen observed that "[t]he prosecutor is often careless" and "the prisoner generally poor and ignorant." The consequence: "the case goes to the jury in an imperfect and unsatisfactory form."

In his treatise, Stephen took particular note of the fact that various remedies had been proposed to fix the system's defects. "They consist for the most part," he said, "in the proposal that there should be in every county an officer, whose duty it should be to institute inquiries into crimes, and to superintend the collection of evidence respecting them; and that there should also be a certain number of standing counsel for the Crown, charged with the duty of advising on evidence, and conducting some or all prosecutions." The "obvious objection" to that proposal, Stephen countered, playing the devil's advocate, "is the great expense which it would involve, and the great amount of patronage which it would produce." Offering that English prosecutorial reform might be achieved by simpler means, Stephen made this counterproposal contradicting the viewpoint previously offered by *The Times*: "The detection of crimes, which no private person has an interest in prosecuting, ought to be a branch, and a very important one, of the duties of the chief constable of the county or borough police." "In the counties especially," Stephen stressed, "these officers are generally men of education, intelligence, and experience, often military officers, and are perfectly competent, with the assistance of a few detectives, to inquire into the circumstances of any crime which may occur."

Stephen knew that prosecutions took considerable resources to conduct and he sought to increase the resources dedicated to them. "The preparation of the case for trial is simply a matter of money," Stephen observed, saying that "if the same class of attorneys were employed" in criminal prosecutions as in civil matters, "with the prospect of being paid at the same rate," criminal trials would get the same quality preparation as civil trials. "The fact is that criminal business is so unpleasant, and the fees paid for transacting it are so wretchedly small, that respectable attorneys generally refuse to take it, unless they happen to be clerks to the magistrates," he offered. "If the committing magistrates had the power to direct cases of importance to be entrusted to attorneys of their own selection, on the terms that the costs should be taxed on the same scale as in a civil cause," he suggested, "every object would be gained which could be attained by the appointment of public prosecutors, and at a much smaller expense." "The management of important prosecutions would become an object of ambition to attorneys, and they would have the ordinary professional motives to do them well," Stephen asserted.[254]

The Overend & Gurney Scandal and the Efforts of English Reformers

The harsh reality of the nineteenth-century English criminal justice system was that the sheer cost of private prosecutions, as well as people's unwillingness to take on the responsibility or unwanted public exposure that went along with them, deterred many English subjects from bringing them or continuing with them if asserted in the first place.[255] One private prosecutor, in a February 7, 1869 letter to the editor of *Lloyd's Weekly Newspaper* in London, appealed explicitly to the public for funding to help finance his white-collar prosecution—one that involved six directors of Overend & Gurney, a well-known bank, indicted in February 1869 for defrauding shareholders of £3 million.[256] "As private prosecutor in this national cause," the letter began, alluding to a cause affecting scores of workingmen, "I have already appealed in the daily papers to the community at large for pecuniary aid." "Permit me now, through your widely-circulated sheet," the letter continued, "more especially to address a few words to the class which has suffered perhaps more deeply than all the other classes put together, from the circumstances that have led to these criminal proceedings." Lots of money had been lost, and the letter writer was leading an effort to try to get compensation and to hold people accountable. The bottom line: he needed money, and he needed it badly, to conduct the private prosecution.

The letter writer's appeal was direct and to the point: "If the hundreds of thousands, whose assistance I thus invoke in a struggle which is really their own, come forward in their collective might, shop by shop, yard by yard, factory by factory, they will, at a merely nominal sacrifice to each individual, make their weight decisively felt in a question which to them is little less than a necessary of life." With the published letter signed "ADAM THOM" at "90, Gower-street, W.C.," the letter writer also called for another remedy—but one that would require Parliament's intervention. "Let 'a public prosecutor' be the cry at every election; let 'a public prosecutor' be the pledge for every member of parliament," he wrote, taking note of the Scottish example of public prosecution and asserting the potential relevance of his suggestion to the criminal case he had initiated: "If ever there has been a case for a public prosecutor it is this one, affecting, as it does, all the sections of society beyond even the limits of her Majesty's dominions. The propriety of engrafting such an officer on our penal judicature is, in fact, conceded by the rule, that formally every indictment shall emanate from 'the Queen.'"[257] Mr. Thom thus recognized the difficulty of one individual taking on the responsibility of prosecuting a complex criminal enterprise, and he had a proposal and a potentially potent remedy—a public prosecutor—in mind.

Mr. Thom's letter, essentially an advertisement seeking funds to finance the prosecution of Overend & Gurney's directors for their alleged role in defrauding the public of millions of British pounds,[258] even drew the attention of *The Economist* and *The Pall Mall Gazette* in London because of the scandal's nature and the letter's plaintive call for a public prosecutor.[259] At some point, Overend & Gurney's London partners realized they were holding £4 million in bad debt, and if their depositors found out it would bring down the firm. As one historical account observes of what happened next: "In a move that betrayed their Quaker origins, the London partners shored up Overend & Gurney in 1865 by floating it on the Stock Exchange as a limited liability company, hoping to trade out of trouble with new capital. But it was too late. They failed with over £5 million liabilities on 10 May 1866, triggering 'Black Friday' in the City the next day."[260] *The Times* of London, like *The Economist*, eagerly weighed in on the Overend & Gurney case, noting the decades-old quest for reform to create a public prosecutor's office.[261] Without the resources of a committed public prosecutor's office, it was clear that it was next to impossible to pursue a white-collar criminal case of such complexity and magnitude.

Individual cases can sometimes inspire collective action, and the high-profile Overend & Gurney scandal was one that garnered a lot of public attention. The issue of the prosecution of the Overend & Gurney's directors, in fact, made its way to the House of Commons, with a Mr. Eykyn of Windsor seeing the issue of one of "national importance" and opining that the prosecution's burden "should be borne by the Government, and the case conducted by the law officers of the Crown." Mr. Eykyn, the press reported, "made a strong appeal to the Government in the interests of justice and commercial morality, to take up the prosecution which had become too expensive a burden for a private prosecutor." Mr. Eykyn's speech in the House of Commons generated considerable debate, with two members—Mr. Fothergill and Mr. Dalrymple—immediately expressing their support for the Home Secretary's decision not to undertake the prosecution. Mr. Bruce, in turn, asserted that "there were ample means amongst the shareholders to conduct this prosecution," adding: "[I]f there had been a public prosecutor he would have sifted the case from the first, and might possibly have come to the opinion that there was no case at all, but now the Government was called upon to interfere without any previous knowledge of the facts, or opportunity of investigating them." Before the House of Commons adjourned at 2:00 a.m., the Attorney General also defended the sitting Government's actions. As a transcript of the parliamentary debate indicates: "The ATTORNEY-GENERAL thought it was most undesirable that Government should be called upon to take up a case, unless certain of a conviction. If the parties desired that course, they ought long ago to have forwarded the depositions of the law officers of the Crown, who would then have had time to have gone into it."[262]

Throughout the private prosecution, Mr. Thom had trouble financing the case, leading to speculation that his prosecution would collapse.[263] Eventually, no doubt due to all the publicity surrounding the high-profile matter, the trial of the Overend & Gurney case was postponed for a time to allow for additional preparation of the case.[264] It became a drawn out matter. After the Overend & Gurney directors were acquitted,[265] though, the breaking news generated yet another round of public debate and angst about the country's need for a public prosecutor's office modeled on Scotland's.[266] In 1870, England's Attorney General explicitly declared his public support for the concept behind a Public Prosecutor's Bill that had been introduced in Parliament. As he said at that time: "The system of public prosecutors was adopted in almost all continental countries, and also to some extent in Ireland and Scotland, and it therefore appeared to him that there was made out a conclusive case in favour of supplying what he regarded as a great omission in regard to the administration of the criminal law of this country." The Attorney General cited statistics to back up his statement, explaining: "Many offences were not prosecuted at all, while others were only prosecuted inefficiently." He had learned that "of 30,000 persons who were apprehended, 2000 were discharged because no one would appear against them, and of 20,000 prisoners who were committed for trial, the prosecutions failed in nearly 5000 cases."

In its own article titled "Moving Forward," *The Bradford Observer*, a newspaper in Bradford, England, added that such statistics "only touches one side of the evil." "Everybody knows," it wrote, "of scandalous cases of frauds and embezzlement and the like, which are daily hushed up because a private prosecutor will not risk the cost, trouble, and danger of a trial which, should it fail, would land him perchance in an action for damages and malicious prosecution." "Thousands of very bad cases," the newspaper reported, "are of such a nature that a private prosecutor cannot collect evidence or keep witnesses in hand as the public prosecutor could do." England's Attorney General also took note of other problems with private prosecutions: "Another class was that of collusive prosecutions, or those in which witnesses were bought off or induced to leave the country. In another class the criminal law was abused for the enforcement of civil rights, but further, it frequently happened that a prosecutor cared very little about his case, and it was taken up by a policeman, who acted not only as the principal witness, but also as the prosecutor." As *The Bradford Observer*'s editorial concluded: "The country is rich enough to pay for the proper administration of justice, and yet it is quite possible that by the vigorous enforcement of fines and forfeitures, the new office will sustain itself, or nearly so. Such is the case in Scotland; but the economical objection is hardly worth discussion."[267]

Other newspapers, even ones in the United States, joined in the spirited public debate over private versus public prosecution. In 1875, the *New York Daily Herald* ran a story headlined "Criminal Law in England" that noted yet another bill had been prepared for introduction in the House of Commons that sought the appointment of English public prosecutors. "England is the only country in Europe without a public prosecutor," its writer emphasized, making this first-person observation: "When I say so I do not except even the other portions of the United Kingdom; for in Ireland the Irish Attorney General and in Scotland the Scottish Lord Advocate are public prosecutors." The writer found it "astounding" that while England and Ireland shared the same "common and statute laws" and that "their administration generally is conducted on the same system in both countries," Ireland had a public prosecution system while England did not.[268] The writer observed that, "[i]n very special cases," prosecutions were "conducted by departments of the government," such as "the Post Office" and "the Treasury," with "Mint prosecutions" (*i.e.*, "prosecutions against persons for coining counterfeit coin or uttering it") conducted under the Attorney General's auspices. "But nineteen-twentieths of the prosecutions in England," the writer stressed, "are left to take care of themselves during one-half their process and go a-begging during the other half." As the article's writer relayed: "Thousands of people suffer the loss of property rather than attempt to bring the thieves to justice, so expensive is it for one to institute a criminal prosecution on his own account."

Calling private prosecutions "the very worst abuse" in England's criminal system, the writer had this to say: "Usurers and shopkeepers who find a difficulty in recovering their money allege false pretences on the part of their creditors, where there are really nothing of the kind, in order to bring the screw of criminal courts to bear as a more effective instrument of compulsion than any that can be found in civil proceedings." In Ireland, the writer explained, "[n]o prosecution can be carried to the District or Assize Court without the fiat of the Attorney General authorizing further proceedings." As the writer stressed: "By this means many abortive prosecutions are nipped in the bud and much expense saved to the country, as well as much injustice to accused persons. Moreover, the Attorney General is represented in every criminal court by barristers of his own selection, and thus there is some guarantee for the conduct of the prosecution by a competent person. For each of the four provinces of Ireland there is a Crown Solicitor, who is charged with the duty of preparing the cases for the criminal courts and drawing up the briefs for the prosecuting counsel."[269] Ireland—as one nineteenth-century report on criminal justice noted—had "to a very large extent" adopted the Scottish system of public prosecution, although certain categories of cases (*e.g.*, "prosecutions under the Bankruptcy Act," "for fraudulent bankruptcies," and "[e]xtensive frauds") had been "left to private prosecutors."[270]

The off-and-on, hot-and-cold debate in England over whether to establish a public prosecutor's office, often inspired by the Irish or Scotch systems,[271] went on for many decades, in fact, before one was finally established there. "The issue of public prosecution," scholar Allyson May explains in *The Bar and the Old Bailey*, "had been raised a number of times before the 1830s, although the term 'meant different things to different people.'" As May observes: "The introduction of some form of public prosecution was recommended by a select committee in 1798; Jeremy Bentham, who had compared the systems of prosecution in England and France in 1790, turned his attention to the issue twice in the early nineteenth century; Patrick Colquhoun likewise developed a plan to address the problems posed by private prosecution; and among the Old Bailey's bar William Fielding had argued in 1816 (by which time he had become a Westminster magistrate) for the institution of a 'public accuser.'" The prolific Jeremy Bentham, a utilitarian and penal reform advocate, became known for *A Fragment on Government* (1776), *An Introduction to the Principles of Morals and Legislation* (1789), and *Panopticon; or, The Inspection-House* (1790); Patrick Colquhoun was a Scottish merchant, economist, and superintending magistrate of the Thames River Police, a forerunner of the Metropolitan Police, whose works on policing—*A Treatise on the Commerce and Police of the River Thames* (1800), *A Treatise on the Functions and Duties of a Constable* (1803), and *Treatise on the Police of the Metropolis* (1806)—became influential texts; and William Fielding, a magistrate and the son of novelist Henry Fielding, testified in 1816 before the Select Committee on the State of the Police of the Metropolis and, in that forum, appealed for a public prosecutor.[272]

Other leading figures, seeking to reform England's prosecutorial system, also weighed in, offering their own preferred approaches. "Romilly," Allyson May continues, referencing Sir Samuel Romilly (1757–1818), the British lawyer and politician, "appears to have supported the concept of public prosecution, as did Denman and Sir Robert Peel." In 1826, Sir Robert Peel had asserted: "If we were legislating *de novo*, without reference to previous customs and formed habits, I for one should not hesitate to relieve private individuals from the charge of prosecution in the case of criminal offences justly called by writers upon law—public wrongs." "I would," Peel said, "have a public prosecutor acting in each case ... and not on the heated and vindictive feelings of the individual sufferer, on which we mainly rely at present for the due execution of justice ... and I would by the appointment of a public prosecutor guard against malicious or frivolous prosecutions on the one hand, and on the other, I would ensure prosecution in cases in which justice might require it."[273]

Likewise, in 1855, Lord Brougham—a British statesman who had served as the Lord High Chancellor of Great Britain in the 1830s[274]—recommended to the House of Lords "[t]hat the prosecution of offenders should be intrusted to an officer appointed by the Government, with such number of subordinate officers as may be required for conducting prosecutions in the counties and larger towns."[275] "The appointment of such an officer and his deputies," *The Times* said of that proposal, "would obviously be a great increase of patronage and expense, is not therefore to be justified on mere speculative grounds, but only because it would correct some great mischief or some pressing inconvenience." "Now, does any such practical grievance exist?" *The Times* pondered aloud, writing, "If so, it must touch either the private prosecutor or the administration of public justice."[276] In a speech Lord Brougham delivered in 1855 excoriating the practice of relying on private prosecutions, he offered this critique: "In truth, this plan of leaving the execution of the laws to the party injured alone—for I object not to it, if combined with a responsible functionary—comes down to us from very ancient and very barbarous times. It grew out of the irrational laws and customs of the dark ages."[277]

In 1856, a Select Committee of the House of Commons on the appointment of public prosecutors presented its report on the subject, recommending that agents "shall be appointed, one to each of a certain number of districts, for the purpose of preparing and conducting prosecutions to the time of trial"; that they be paid annual salaries of £700; and that "they shall devote their whole time to the duties of their office, abstaining altogether from private practice." "The duties of such district agents," it was recommended, "should be to prepare and conduct prosecutions through the stages preliminary to trial." "Where it comes to their knowledge that an offence has been committed, and that no steps have been taken to bring the offender to justice," the committee wrote, "it will be their duty to take the necessary steps for apprehending or for otherwise bringing the offender before a magistrate; or, if the party have already been apprehended, and the case is one of any difficulty or importance, it will be their business to intervene, and take upon themselves the further conduct of the prosecution." "Your committee," the report cautioned, "would not, however, go to the length of advising that individuals instituting prosecutions should be prohibited from employing their own attorneys and counsel, and be compelled to resort exclusively to the public prosecutors." "We think it should be left open to the private prosecutor to pursue the ordinary course, as at present practised," the committee recommended, seeking public prosecutions to supplement private ones. "[B]ut, with a view to prevent the compromises which the evidence we have taken shows are sometimes resorted to for purposes of private interest, and to ensure the effective administration of justice," the committee concluded, "we would make it compulsory on an attorney employed to conduct a prosecution to give notice to the district agent of his intention to prefer an indictment, and would give the latter authority to intervene, and, if necessary, to apply to the court for leave to take up the prosecution and conduct it to its close."[278]

The Select Committee's report highlighted a litany of problems with England's then-existing private prosecution system. After collecting "a large body of evidence" on the subject "from witnesses whose professional eminence and experience entitles their opinion to more than common weight," the Select Committee found: "It constantly happens that a wealthy person under prosecution buys off the witness." Lord Campbell was of the opinion that, in England, "the criminal law is often most shamefully perverted to serve private purposes" and that "[t]here is no sufficient control" over private prosecutions. As the Select Committee observed in one section of its report: "Prosecutions for conspiracy are set on foot with a view to get money, and conviction is followed by a compromise; sentence is pronounced, but not carried into effect. Those abuses necessarily flow from the virtual irresponsibility of prosecutors." "Collusions to defeat justice," the report said, "are frequent; criminal justice is resorted to, in a large class of cases, for the mere purpose of enforcing civil rights. Guilty persons escape at the last moment by making terms with their adversary, often in consequence of a pecuniary arrangement."

Other concerns were raised as well after the Select Committee's fact-finding mission was completed. "Policemen," the committee's report stated, "assume the functions of public prosecutors—a practice liable to abuse." As the authors of the report reasoned: "There may often be a good case for conviction, and no deficiency of evidence, yet acquittal ensures, because the prosecutor, acting with advice, is not sufficiently informed as to the precise nature of the proof required by law." "In the existing state of affairs," the Select Committee determined, the attorneys employed by private prosecutors "are over-zealous to obtain the professional triumph of a conviction—a fault from which permanent public officers employed for the same purpose would be free." The then-existing private prosecution system, the report further emphasized, "is irregular and anomalous" and "the practice of metropolitan districts is different from that of the counties." "Felonies," the report noted, taking the input of Charles Sprengel Greaves, Q.C., the drafter of the 1851 Criminal Procedure Act who had become a Queen's Counsel in 1850,[279] "are often committed without its being the personal interest of any one to prosecute." Greaves objected to prosecutions being conducted by constables and police officers, and he thought "means should be taken to prevent the mismanagement of cases" by a "low class" of attorneys. After hearing about the positive qualities of New York's and Scotland's public prosecution systems, the Select Committee noted that "[t]he proportion of convictions to acquittals is much greater in Scotland than in England; the system gives general satisfaction."[280] The fierce debate—between private and public prosecutions—would continue on both sides of the Atlantic in the decades to come.

2

THE MOTHER COUNTRY

England's Shift from Private to Public Prosecutions

The Appointment of England's Director of Public Prosecutions

In twenty-first century England, two public authorities, the Attorney General and the Director of Public Prosecutions, have now placed severe limitations on the ability of private citizens to prosecute criminal actions. The Attorney General, the country's chief legal advisor, has the power to instruct the Director of Public Prosecutions to take over any private prosecution, and private prosecutions can now be terminated by public officials.[1] This change in the law did not happen overnight. Indeed, the reform took decades to achieve. In 1879, after many years of debate, the British Parliament at long last established the Office of Director of Public Prosecutions, to be under the Attorney General's supervision.[2] It was, at the time, a very modest effort involving the authorization of just a few new government positions, and there was, in fact, no actual aim or desire at the time to do away with private prosecutions. The 1879 act, one scholar has noted, conferred no sweeping official powers, but merely gave the newly designated director powers of a "very technical nature, his duties under the act amounting to little more than those of a private prosecutor, duties formerly imposed upon various minor functionaries in the judiciary system."[3] In effect, the Director of Public Prosecutions would just supplement, not displace, private prosecutions, and in England, interested private prosecutions would remain the norm for decades to come.

As *The Huddersfield Daily Chronicle* in England reported of the then-newly adopted Prosecution of Offences Act, 1879: "This Act provides for the appointment ... of a Director of Public Prosecutions (a Barrister or Solicitor), with assistants not exceeding six (Barristers or Solicitors), whose duties, under the superintendence of the Attorney-General, will be to institute, undertake, or carry on such criminal proceedings, and to give such advice and assistance to chief officers of police, clerks to justices, and other persons concerned in any criminal proceedings respecting the conduct of that proceeding as may be prescribed by regulations under the Act, or directed in a special case by the Attorney-General." "Nothing in the Act is to interfere with the rights of private prosecutors," the newspaper reported, making this additional note in 1879 about the duties of the new position: "The regulations are to provide for the Director of Public Prosecutions taking action in cases which appear to be of importance or difficulty, or in which special circumstances, or the refusal or failure of a person to proceed with a prosecution appear to render the action of such director necessary to secure the due prosecution of an offender, and also to fix the districts for which the assistants shall respectively be appointed and act." "Where the Director of Public Prosecutions institutes, undertakes, or carries on any criminal proceeding," the paper observed of the new law, which took effect on January 1, 1880, "he is not to be bound over to prosecute or give security for costs."[4]

The Times of London itself marked England's legal reform at the end of December 1879, noting that "Mr. MAULE, Q.C., has been appointed Director of Public Prosecutions." Sir John Blossett Maule, the British barrister selected to serve, was educated at Oxford and after entering the Inner Temple in 1844 had been called to the bar in 1847, becoming a Queen's Counsel, or Q.C., in 1866.[5] "The office is a new one," *The Times* said, noting that "[i]t was created by an Act, passed last Session, intended to remove or diminish a striking blemish in the criminal law of this country." "[S]peaking generally," it reported after laying out, in broad outlines, the public officer's official duties, "it will be his business ... to see that offences are prosecuted more vigilantly and systematically than they are." Speaking highly of the newly appointed Director of Public Prosecutions, *The Times* had this to say of his qualifications and the task before him: "His duties are large and not too well defined by the statute. They will be sufficient for any one man. Mr. MAULE is a lawyer of considerable experience and repute. He has been engaged in many inquiries on behalf of the Government; and he is placed in a position in which a man of energy and ability may do much good, if not actually work wonders, and may save the country the sight of scandalous miscarriages of justice."

But *The Times* was also very cautious in its expectations, especially given the small size of the new office being created in relation to the country's size. As it observed: "Too much, however, must not be expected from the new machinery. The office of Public Prosecutor is at last established in deference to the opinion of all persons who are acquainted with the working of our criminal law. But it is not the precise form of the office which most persons have been asking. It is not all that which the Judicature Commissioners, for example, recommended." The Judicature Commission had issued its "Fifth and Final Report" in 1874, and that report dealt primarily with the subject of the appointment of a public prosecutor.[6] As *The Times* continued of the new office that would soon come into being: "When we have got our Director of Public Prosecutions, our system of criminal procedure will still be open to criticism, and will differ widely from those of most other civilized countries. There will remain the great anomaly that the State regards the prosecution of crime with something like unconcern, and that private individuals are free to gratify their passions in a field from which passion should be excluded." "In Scotland or in France," the newspaper pointed out by way of contrast, "a crime is viewed more as an offence against the State than the individual who happens to be wronged." It wrote that in Scotland it was "theoretically possible" for a private party "to institute proceedings if he obtains what is called the 'concourse' of the Lord Advocate," but added that, "in practice," the normal mode of bringing Scottish offenders to justice was prosecutions conducted by and in the name of the Lord Advocate.[7] "The sound principle that the punishment of crime is the affair of the State, and ought not to be committed to private persons, who are too often unsuited for this delicate duty," *The Times* further stressed of criminal prosecutions across the English Channel, "is rigorously carried out in France, and, in fact, all over the Continent."[8] The inquisitorial system in France, of course, was well known by anyone who had studied the matter.

Despite what it saw as the laudable change in English law, *The Times* wanted further reform. "The great fault of our existing system," it observed, "is that, while it is everybody's right to prosecute, it is nobody's business to do so." As the newspaper editorialized: "Many salutary laws passed for the terror of evildoers are thus quite inoperative. Parliament appends to them a battery of pains and penalties, but these are mere shots fired in the air—nobody is a bit the worse." As the paper wrote: "There are few persons who have the courage or the means to bring to justice the guilty authors of a complicated commercial fraud. Such prosecutions are generally arduous and protracted; the result is uncertain; and if the criminals have money with which to defend themselves, it would generally be downright folly for a private person to seek to bring them to justice." A private prosecutor, *The Times* contended, "will be sure to lose much time and money; he will be exposed to the bullying of counsel and the irksomeness of attendance at courts; he runs the risk of being sued for malicious prosecution; and, even if he succeeds, he will receive no thanks for his pains, but will be thought to have done a rather Quixotic act." "None but a fool or rogue, it has been said," *The Times* offered, "will prosecute in an English court of justice; and it is notorious that those who have done so once rarely repeat their example of public spirit."[9]

The modest English law reform that Parliament finally did approve in 1879 was, in general, nonetheless favorably reported on in the press. Indeed, with the first Director of Public Prosecutions appointed in England at the end of December 1879 so he could hit the ground running at the start of the new year,[10] word quickly got out about the new law, including through English grand jury charges which explained the law's provisions. For instance, a deputy-chairman, in charging a grand jury at the Autumn Quarter Session of the Peace for the County of Chester, was reported to have told grand jurors of the then-new Prosecution of Offences Act in October 1879: "This Act got rid of a question which had vexed the public mind for some time, namely the appointment of public prosecutors. The wholesale appointment of officers of that kind had the disadvantage, in the first place of being very expensive, and in the next place there were many objections to it which many entertained, and he thought the

Legislature had wisely steered clear of these difficulties, and had found an intermediate course, that, he hoped, would work satisfactorily."

As the deputy-chairman emphasized of the new law, which created a relatively small office, in the grand jury charge: "The Government of the day had power to appoint an officer who was to be called Director of Public Prosecutions, who would be assisted by not more than six gentlemen who were to be deputies to him in different parts of the country, and their duties would be to have a general superintendence of criminal prosecutions throughout the country." "There was no wish and no intention to interfere with private prosecutors in any way," the deputy-chairman stressed, adding: "So long as justice was administered in the hands of private prosecutors, who desired to conduct their own cases, the law would be allowed to take its own course." "[W]hile there was no desire to interfere with any prosecutor," the deputy-chairman concluded, "in cases where there was a suspicion of improper dealing, or tampering with justice, there would now be an officer to whom the public might report, whose duty it would be to see that prosecutions were carried out."[11] In other words, the Director of Public Prosecutions was seen as essentially as a gap-filler and being tasked with rooting out corruption in private prosecutions.

Despite all the genuine hopes and expectations about the newly appointed Director of Public Prosecutions, the new office—completely understaffed, with only one assistant to the Director appointed in the first three years—did not initially function very well, if for no other reason than because of the lack of adequate personnel. As *The Times* reported in April 1883: "More than three years have elapsed since the office of Director of Public Prosecutions was established in response to a general demand for a department intrusted with the duty of bringing offenders to justice. So far as experience has gone, there is disappointment as to the effect of the creation of the office; and even those who expected little from it were not prepared for the actual meagre results." "When we come to look clearer at the extent of the Director's powers," *The Times* noted, examining the authorizing statute's legal language, "their limitations are seen to be very great." As *The Times* observed of Parliament's law and the legal constraints placed upon the Director of Public Prosecutions: "The Act to which he owes his creation restrains him from interfering, unless in cases of 'importance or difficulty, or in which special circumstances, or the refusal or failure of a person to proceed with a prosecution, appear to render the action of such Director necessary to secure the due prosecution of an offender.' His hands are thus tied." As *The Times* continued with its critique, contrasting the new Director with Scotland's Lord Advocate: "He cannot take up every prosecution in which he is invited to intervene, even though he is convinced that a crime has been committed. He possesses no means of acquiring information other than that which is voluntarily laid before him or what he sees in the newspapers. He is not like the Lord Advocate, the centre of a number of converging lines of knowledge. He is not served, as that functionary is, by a number of experienced subordinates throughout the country."[12]

After the publication of this critique in *The Times*, members of Parliament earnestly renewed their vigorous debate about private versus public prosecutions.[13] The issue also got more attention in the press.[14] For example, in August 1883, London's *Morning Post* had this to say: "For many years the demand for a Public Prosecutor was universal, and the hope was entertained that if such a public functionary was called into existence many of the ever-recurring scandals in connection with the administration of the Criminal Law would be avoided. Under the then existing system the prosecution of criminals, save those charged with the most serious offences, rested practically with private individuals, and it depended in a large degree upon their sense of public duty, or their capabilities of self-sacrifice whether or not the law was put in motion." "In a great many cases," the *Morning Post* emphasized, "the offenders were permitted to go scot free because the sufferers declined to prosecute; while in others the persons aggrieved, however willing they might be to set the law in motion, were destitute of the means of doing so." "It is a misdemeanour to compound a felony," it reported, "as, for example, to forgive or to reward a thief in consideration of the restitution of the stolen property, but nevertheless by imposing on the various members of the community the duty of prosecuting offenders the law necessarily holds out the strongest temptation for the wholesale composition of felonies."[15]

Compounding a felony—as one 1835 law dictionary put it—occurred "where the party robbed not only knows the felon, but also takes his goods again, or other amends upon agreement not to prosecute." "It was formerly held to make a man an accessary," that dictionary prepared by Sir Thomas Edlyne Tomlins, a barrister of the Inner Temple, noted, tracking language from Blackstone's *Commentaries*, "but is now punished only with fine and imprisonment."[16] In his *Commentaries*, Blackstone wrote that "the offence of *theft bote*" is "where the party robbed not only knows the felon, but also takes his goods again, or other amends upon agreement not to prosecute," which "is frequently called compounding a felony."[17] Another English law dictionary, from 1876, contained separate entries for *compounding felony* and *compounding misdemeanors*. According to that dictionary, prepared by Herbert Newman Mozley, a fellow of King's College, Cambridge, and George Crispe Whiteley, a barrister at the Middle Temple, "COMPOUNDING FELONY" is "where a party robbed or otherwise injured by a felony takes a reward from the felon, or, in case of theft, takes back the stolen goods, upon agreement not to prosecute for the felony." "COMPOUNDING MISDEMEANORS," that dictionary observed, "signifies entering into an agreement not to prosecute, or to withdraw from a prosecution, for a misdemeanor." "It is said to be illegal, if done without leave of the court," the dictionary entry stated, adding this: "But it is not uncommon, when a person has been convicted of a misdemeanor more immediately affecting an individual,—as a battery, imprisonment, or the like,—for the court to permit the defendant to *speak with the prosecutor*, before any judgment is pronounced; and, if the prosecutor declares himself satisfied, to inflict but a trivial punishment."[18]

Writing in August 1883, London's *Morning Post* lamented the painfully slow start of the Director of Public Prosecutions. "[T]o the astonishment of every one," the newspaper reported, "the new official, who it was supposed would inspire almost universal terror, and whom the Legislature was careful to put under the severest restrictions lest he might prove too formidable, turned out to be one of the gentlest and most harmless of functionaries and almost as invisible as the QUEEN'S PROCTOR himself." "So far from harassing her MAJESTY's lieges with prosecutions, however lightly they might be found tripping," the paper editorialized, "he almost refused to take action under any circumstances whatever." As the newspaper honed in on the glaring problem with the Director of Public Prosecutions: "His discretion was found to be so completely fettered by the Legislature that the cases in which he could, or thought he could, interfere were of a very exceptional character. When demands were made for his intervention, compliance was not unfrequently refused on grounds which, however plausible or convincing to the mind of the Public Prosecutor, seemed extremely unsatisfactory to the general public." "Meanwhile," the paper said, "a conflict of authority arose between the new functionary and the Solicitor to the Treasury." "In the old days," the *Post* emphasized in its extended piece, "the latter invariably conducted all prosecutions which were undertaken by the Crown, and it would seem that when the office of Public Prosecutor was created Parliament had not been careful to draw the line between the separate domains ruled by the two officials." "Altogether," the newspaper relayed, summing it up, "what between the Director of Public Prosecutions declining to interfere in a great many cases when, according to the common-place ideas of the general community, it was his duty to interfere; and his assuming a jurisdiction in other cases which was claimed by another department of what in other countries would be called the Ministry of Justice, the public interests suffered, and scandals arose even more serious than those of the old regime."[19]

Despite Parliament's modest legislative act, private prosecutions thus continued to be an instrumental part of English law and life, with well-to-do private prosecutors—the victims of crime—regularly retaining private counsel to pursue such prosecutions. For example, in 1892, an English actress, Violet Gordon, was indicted on a charge of shooting at Harry Fischer, a well-known actor, at the Harrogate Railway Station. As *The Blackburn Standard and Weekly Express* observed of the subsequent commencement of that private prosecution: "Mr. John Strachan made an application. He said no bill had yet been sent to the grand jury, and he applied that Mr. Fischer, whom he represented, should have the conduct of the prosecution. Mr. Fischer was the complainant, but for some reason the magistrates bound over the police superintendent." As the newspaper's account continued: "Mr. Strachan cited the case of Regina v. Bushell, and said the question was the right of a private prosecutor to conduct his own prosecution. His Lordship, after reading the case, said the authority was one which he thought he ought to follow. Mr. Strachan afterwards asked permission to prefer a bill of common assault, and the Judge assented."[20] In discussing the country's administration of justice, a Mr. Justice Brett, in charging an English grand jury in

1875 in the Crown Court at Croydon, described how prosecutions were typically commenced. As he put it: "The law was set in motion either by the police or a private prosecutor, and the accused was taken before a magistrate, who determined whether there was a *primâ facie* case to go to a jury. The case, if the prisoner was committed for trial, then came before the grand jury, which was composed of gentlemen of position. It was shifted by them, and if a true bill were found, the prisoner was tried in open court by a jury who had the advantage of the advice of a judge."[21]

In its early years, the work of the office of the Director of Public Prosecutions was so low profile that in 1888, Lord Ellenborough rose in Parliament "to ask Her Majesty's Government what prospect there was of the appointment of a Public Prosecutor." As *The Times* reported Lord Ellenborough's inquiry: "A general opinion prevailed that such a public officer was necessary to prevent inequality in respect of the trial of persons under the criminal law, and he was prompted to ask the question by what had occurred in reference to one case in London and another in Birmingham."[22] "The LORD CHANCELLOR," as *The Times* reported the response to the parliamentary inquiry, "said he was not quite sure that he distinctly understood the question of the noble lord; it was not certain what he intended to convey by asking the question whether the Government were about to recommend the appointment of a Public Prosecutor." "If the noble lord meant by a Public Prosecutor a person charged with the duty of looking after any prosecution in which his intervention was required, such an officer was already in existence," the Lord Chancellor stated, explaining further: "By the Act of 1879 a Public Prosecutor was appointed, and by the amending Act of 1884 the office was vested in the Solicitor to the Treasury, who was charged to take up cases in which no private prosecutor was to be found, and who in fact often took cases out of the hands of private prosecutors." "Therefore," the Lord Chancellor said, "the answer to question was that there was a Public Prosecutor already existing." The Lord Chancellor went on to praise the "skill and ability" of Sir Augustus Stephenson, who was then performing the office's duties, adding that "he had not heard of any failure of justice by reason of the supposed absence of such an officer." "It was not the present intention of the Government to appoint an officer to look after all prosecutions," the Lord Chancellor emphasized.[23]

Despite the Lord Chancellor's spirited defense, England's Director of Public Prosecutions continued to come under fire for not doing enough to bolster the stature of the newly created office. As London's *Reynold's Newspaper* editorialized in 1892: "The Public Prosecutor is an official for whom nobody has any respect. He neglects in the grossest way his most obvious public duties, while fussing about some unimportant case which might well be left to a private prosecutor." "Our so-called Courts of Justice," that newspaper reported, "are becoming a byword of shame, on account of the terrible amount of perjury which takes place there every day. Yet the Public Prosecutor, whose duty it is to take up such cases, never interferes." As the *Reynold's Newspaper* harshly observed: "The perjury in the Divorce Court is notorious; indeed, in every court there is hardly a case tried in which perjury is not committed. If the Public

Prosecutor acted in one-tenth of the cases, he would inspire a wholesome terror in the bosoms of untruthful witnesses." "Again, in the case of fraudulent solicitors," the paper emphasized, "the Public Prosecutor never interferes, although case after case is brought to his knowledge by those who have suffered from the crimes of this thievish and dishonourable crew." The subject was one that the newspaper thought "ought to receive the attention of Parliament immediately" after "it reassembles."[24] Others also vehemently and publicly criticized the Director of Public Prosecutions for refusing to prosecute particular cases.[25]

Oscar Wilde vs. the Marquess of Queensberry

In spite of England's creation of the position of Director of Public Prosecutions, private prosecutions continued unabated. One that made big headlines in Europe and the United States was Oscar Wilde's private prosecution against John Sholto Douglas, the 9th Marquess of Queensberry, also popularly known as the Marquis of Queensberry or, simply, Lord Queensberry.[26] The Marquis of Queensberry had put in writing that Wilde had homosexual proclivities, and Wilde—who did not foresee all of the consequences that would flow from his decision to commence a private prosecution—decided to bring a criminal libel case against the Scottish aristocrat who'd been terrorizing and tormenting him.[27] An Irish playwright and poet known for his involvement in the philosophy of aestheticism, Oscar Wilde had moved to London where he traveled in rarified and elite circles and built his literary reputation. There, he had befriended and lavishly entertained several young men, and—as a prominent literary figure and playwright—famously penned the homoerotic Gothic novel, *The Picture of Dorian Gray*, and wrote successful plays.

Wilde's *Lady Windermere's Fan* premiered in February 1892 at St. James's Theatre,[28] and his next play, *A Woman of No Importance*, opened at the Haymarket Theatre in April 1893.[29] Although Wilde had a male lover, one of Lord Queensberry's sons, Wilde himself was married with children and his sexual activities, including with Lord Queensberry's son, Lord Alfred Douglas, were unknown to the public in the first half of the 1890s. Indeed, Wilde's third dramatic comedy, *An Ideal Husband*, had opened with much fanfare and publicity at London's Haymarket Theatre on January 3, 1895. *An Ideal Husband* deals with an attempt to blackmail a member of the House of Commons and explores issues of honor, with George Bernard Shaw—in reviewing Wilde's new play in the *Saturday Review* of January 12th of that year—making this observation: "In a certain sense Mr. Wilde is to me our only thorough playwright. He plays with everything: with wit, with philosophy, with drama, with actors and audience, with the whole theatre. Such a feat scandalizes the Englishman, who can no more play with wit and philosophy than he can with a football or a cricket bat." Wilde, the classical scholar, had a lifelong love of language and a penchant for wit. For instance, at age 16, while attending his first ball at Dublin Castle, he'd asked a woman to dance. When she replied, "Do you think I'm going to dance with a child?", Wilde teased: "Madame, if I had known you were in that condition, I never would have asked you."[30]

Like most theater productions, Wilde's plays got mixed reviews, with one critic writing on January 4, 1895 of *An Ideal Husband*: "Anyone happening to look in at the Haymarket on the fall of the curtain last night would have come to the conclusion that Mr. Wilde had written a brilliant play, and no doubt many of those who cheered so lustily were quite of that opinion." "But viewed dispassionately," that reviewer continued, "*An Ideal Husband* was a thing of shreds and patches, a stringing together of a number of inconsequent incidents whose only dramatic value was that they had been in use for years past, and are therefore to be borne with as we bear with ancient jokes of an elderly, highly respectable and, above all, wealthy member of one's family." "There is nothing in it," the reviewer wrote of the play, "which gives Mr. Wilde the right to class himself as a playwright either of promise or experience." A critic for the *Morning Post* gave this assessment of *An Ideal Husband*: "Not only had Mr. Wilde enjoyed the performance—the public had enjoyed it also. The minority, doubtless, had not been satisfied. There had been an *amari aliquid* [something bitter] in their cup." As that English critic bitingly critiqued the play in the context of Wilde's other theatrical works: "*An Ideal Husband* is as inferior to *A Woman of No Importance* as *A Woman of No Importance* was inferior to *Lady Windermere's Fan*. Mr. Wilde is not progressing in the dramatist's art."[31]

Just weeks after *An Ideal Husband* opened, Wilde's next play, *The Importance of Being Earnest*, was first performed in London on February 14, 1895. The premier, which garnered much public acclaim, occurred shortly before Wilde commenced *Regina v. Douglas*, his high-profile private prosecution against the Marquess of Queensberry for criminal libel. That private prosecution sought to stop Lord Queensberry, a bully in every sense of the word, from spreading rumors about Wilde's private life. The Marquess of Queensberry—the father of Wilde's lover, Lord Alfred Douglas—was described by his own son as a "brute or a crazy lunatic" who wrote "brutally abusive letters" to his estranged wife. After the marquess had come to suspect the true nature of Wilde's undisclosed sexual relationship with his son, the marquess demanded that the two stop seeing each other. "Your father," Wilde confessed to Lord Alfred Douglas in mid-1894, "is on the rampage again—been to the Café Royal to enquire for us, with threats etc. I think now it would be better for me to have him bound over to keep the peace, but what a scandal!" "Still," Wilde reflected, "it is intolerable to be dogged by a maniac."[32]

As the public acclaim for Oscar Wilde's plays was reaching new heights, Wilde's private life was in considerable turmoil by the beginning of 1895 due to Lord Queensberry's menacing behavior. Despite all the veiled and not-so-veiled threats by the Marquis of Queensberry to expose Wilde's private affairs, the Irish playwright—whose professional career was skyrocketing, even if theater critics did not uniformly like his plays—had decided not to take any legal action against the Marquis of Queensberry in 1894, a decision he revisited the following year. "No English play for many years has been the subject of so much competition among American managers as Oscar Wilde's latest farce, 'The Importance of Being Earnest,'" a New York newspaper editorialized on February 28, 1895 of Wilde's theatrical prowess, adding that Wilde's newest play at the St. James's Theatre in London had "proved such a great success."[33] Wilde had already become famous in the United States because of a North American lecture tour he had done years earlier, in 1882. "It is safe to say that after his 15,000-mile tour of North America," one historian explains, "neither Wilde nor his host countries would ever be quite the same." "Partly by intent, partly by instinct," that historian, Roy Morris, Jr., notes, "Wilde pioneered the way in which modern celebrities are created, cultivated, and commodified." On his tour, he met many prominent figures, including Louisa May Alcott, Oliver Wendell Holmes, Henry Wadsworth Longfellow, Walt Whitman, and even Ulysses S. Grant.[34]

The Marquess of Queensberry, with his intense hatred of Oscar Wilde, had diabolically plotted to spoil the opening night of Wilde's new play on Valentine's Day with a plan to throw a bouquet of vegetables, instead of flowers, on stage at the St. James's Theatre.[35] Lord Queensberry, a Scottish nobleman, had a reputation for bigotry, belligerence, and extreme intolerance and volatility, and he had even once rudely disrupted a play by the poet laureate Alfred Lord Tennyson.[36] As *The Daily Examiner* in San Francisco had reported back in November 1882 under the headline "TENNYSON AND QUEENSBERRY": "The Marquis of Queensberry attended during the week at a representation of Mr. Tennyson's new drama, conceded to be the worst play that has been brought out here in many years, and in which Mr. Tennyson holds up a freethinker to public odium as the motive of his play." "The Marquis," that news story reported, "promptly denounced the laureate during the first act, and on the fall of the curtain made a violently impassioned harangue to the audience. It made a great sensation, but the Marquis was put out of the theater." "The affair," the newspaper observed, "has become the occasion of a widespread discussion in print and out of it. Freethinkers are gathering to his lordship's support. Mr. Tennyson is abused more than he was by the dramatic critics, and we are having it out according to the new Queensberry rules."[37]

In early 1895, the St. James's Theatre had gotten wind of Lord Queensberry's premeditated plan to similarly disrupt Oscar Wilde's play. Taking precautions before the play's premiere, the theater refused to admit the marquess—the man who, in 1882, had been so notoriously ejected from the Globe Theatre for loudly interrupting Alfred Lord Tennyson's play, *The Promise of May*.[38] The St. James's Theatre did not want to see a repeat of what had occurred in 1882, with one source describing what the Marquess of Queensberry, Sir John Sholto Douglas, had so notoriously done: "At a performance on November 14, 1882, of Tennyson's play *The Promise of May* at the Globe Theatre, Douglas rose in the stalls and denounced the play, protesting that in the chief character, Philip Edgar (a freethinker, secularist, and hedonist), Tennyson had travestied true freethinkers. The Marquis of Queensberry made the protest twice, at the beginning and at the end of the play."[39] In Wilde's case, the thwarted marquess thus had to content himself with leaving his "floral arrangement"—a bunch of carrots and turnips—at the box office, though with his troubled mind he continued to plot—through his contacts and in whatever way he could—to destroy Wilde's life.[40] The volatile Marquis of Queensberry vehemently loathed Oscar Wilde's relationship with his son, Lord Alfred "Bosie" Douglas, and Lord Queensberry was determined to destroy Wilde's personal and literary reputation in spite of the fact that Wilde's fame was then at its apex. "'The Importance of Being Earnest,' Oscar Wilde's latest, just produced in London, is a colossal success, and Oscar's stock is booming," American newspapers like Ohio's *Akron Daily Democrat*, Indiana's *The Fort Wayne News*, and York, Pennsylvania's *Gazette* had proclaimed without hyperbole after the play's 1895 premiere at the St. James's Theatre.[41]

Lord Queensberry's petty plan to toss "a bunch of vegetables" on stage on the opening night of Oscar Wilde's play had been prevented by the theater's refusal to admit him.[42] But soon after the successful opening night of *The Importance of Being Earnest*, Wilde—the Trinity College- and Oxford-educated writer who'd married a woman, Irish author Constance Lloyd,[43] in 1884—became embroiled in an intense public controversy with the undeterred father of his male lover. His bitter antagonist: the Marquess of Queensberry. From 1872 to 1880, the marquess—an athlete, horse owner, and boxing enthusiast—had been a Scottish peer in the House of Lords, but he had announced himself a "free thinker" who refused to participate in any religious "tomfoolery," thus ending his political career. The marquess had a reputation for tirades, making threats, and outbursts of violence, and it was belligerent threats Lord Queensberry made against Oscar Wilde that ultimately caused Wilde to bring his private prosecution. "Oscar Wilde Sues for Libel," a headline in the *Scranton Times* of Pennsylvania read far from the English venue where the criminal case was filed, taking note that the marquess, a well-known aristocrat, had been "served with a summons on an alleged defamatory libel."[44] "It would be hard to find two more notorious men than Oscar Wilde and the Marquis of Queensberry, whose differences, as you have no doubt been informed by cable, have just culminated in a suit for libel brought by Wilde," a newspaper correspondent reported from London, noting that the criminal libel case "will no doubt add to their notoriety, if such a thing be possible."

By then, the marquess was already well known because of a set of famous pugilistic rules that bore his name—the so-called Queensberry Rules, which, in the 1860s, had codified regulations for the sport of boxing that were endorsed by the 9th Marquess of Queensberry. While Lord Queensberry's virulent temper was legendary, one newspaper correspondent covering the Oscar Wilde/Marquess of Queensberry controversy reported that Wilde's "chief characteristics are clever impudence and a willingness to do almost anything for money." "Who but a man of these traits," the correspondent offered of Wilde, "could have displayed the nerve he showed during his memorable tour through the United States when he attired himself in knee breeches and appropriate accompanying garments and lectured in stained glass attitudes with a sunflower in his hand?"[45] In 1882, Oscar Wilde—as a young poet—had extensively toured both the U.S. and Canada, making witty statements throughout his time in North America as he traversed thousands of miles. Upon arriving in New York, Wilde—when asked if he was carrying any contraband—told a customs officer: "I have nothing to declare but my genius."[46] In a PR blitz, Wilde gave nearly 150 lectures and did at least ninety-eight interviews on his tour between January and November of 1882—a tour in which he visited major cities such as Boston, New York and San Francisco but also smaller towns in Colorado, Iowa, Kansas and Utah. He called Nathaniel Hawthorne's novel, *The Scarlet Letter*, "the greatest work of fiction ever written in the English tongue," and when one interviewer asked him for details of his "private life," Wilde quipped: "I wished I had one."[47]

Because of his notoriety, Oscar Wilde's private prosecution—his criminal libel case—attracted massive attention on both sides of the Atlantic. Under the headline, "Mr. Oscar Wilde and the Marquis of Queensberry," the *Exeter Flying Post* explained that "the Marquis of Queensberry was charged with publishing a defamatory libel concerning Mr. Oscar Wilde." That paper further observed that Wilde's counsel, Mr. Humphreys, "said Mr. Oscar Wilde had been cruelly persecuted by Lord Queensbury for ten months past" and that "[t]he last act occurred on February 28th, when the Marquis left an open card at the Albemarle Club—of which both parties were members—with a vile epithet written on the back."[48] The referenced "epithet," one that other late nineteenth-century newspapers called "unfit for publication"[49] or suggestively said related to "unnatural practices" or "unnatural vices,"[50] pertained to Lord Queensberry's perception of Oscar Wilde's sexual proclivities. Although Oscar Wilde was married and he and his wife, Constance, had two sons, Wilde, in fact, had long had male lovers, including Lord Alfred Douglas, the 25-year-old son of John Douglas, the 9th Marquess of Queensberry.[51] Lord Alfred Douglas, referred to familiarly by Wilde and others as "Bosie,"[52] had struggled academically at Oxford, and his mother, Lady Queensberry, had asked Wilde—the brilliant scholar—for his advice. The poet John Gray had already been Oscar Wilde's lover, with Wilde agreeing to defray the publishing expenses of Gray's first book, *Silverpoints*. Wilde's relationship with Gray lasted nearly three years, but it ended after Wilde met and fell in love with Bosie.[53]

Oscar Wilde first met Lord Alfred Douglas in 1891, and Wilde immediately fell for Bosie and his charm. Oscar and Bosie soon became lovers,[54] spending much time together and exchanging intimate letters and poetry. Bosie and another young man, Alfred Taylor, also reportedly introduced Wilde to the clandestine world of gay prostitution in London.[55] "I am the love that dare not speak its name," Bosie would write in one poem. But his father, the Marquess of Queensberry, a boxer and a hunter, did not approve of his son's relationship with Wilde and was determined to put an end to it, with the marquess—the Scottish aristocrat so well known for his boxing rules—brazenly confronting and threatening Wilde. The Queensberry rules required boxing contestants to wear padded gloves and to fight for three minutes per round, with any fighter who got knocked down having to get up unaided within 10 seconds.[56] The conflict between Wilde and the marquess—destined to become a no-holds-barred legal brawl without gloves—only escalated after the London premier of *The Importance of Being Earnest.* Indeed, it was just weeks later that Wilde would bring his high-profile charge of criminal libel against the Marquess of Queensberry. Wilde was, by then, already a controversial figure in Victorian society because of his free-spirited lifestyle—and the libel case would only exacerbate his woes within the constraining, rule-bound society in which he lived. In a preface to *The Picture of Dorian Gray* (1891), parts of which had been censored, Wilde famously wrote: "There is no such thing as a moral or an immoral book. Books are well written, or badly written. That is all." Among Wilde's many aphorisms that had made him so famous: "The only way to get rid of a temptation is to yield to it." "I can resist everything except temptation."[57]

After Oscar Wilde's criminal libel action had been commenced, Sir George Lewis, a well-known Queen's Counsel, made an initial appearance on behalf of the marquess, telling the magistrate that "when the circumstances in the case were more fully known the magistrate would find that the marquis had acted under feelings of great indignation" and "upon abundant provocation." "We cannot go into that now," the magistrate, the Hon. Robert Milnes Newton, had replied, leaving public exposure of the salacious details of the case for another day.[58] "I don't wish this case to be adjourned without it being known that there is nothing against the honour of Lord Queensberry," George Lewis said. Earlier, Lewis had asked the magistrate that "before any evidence was taken the case should be adjourned, so that he might consult with his client, and have more time to consider the matter." "Extraordinary interest is being shown in the case of Mr. Oscar Wilde against the Marquis of Queensberry," a Scottish newspaper reported as Wilde's very public private prosecution got underway, editorializing that "[t]he case is unpleasant in the extreme, and the living sense of its gravity which the parties entertain is shown in the fact that the services of most eminent counsel have been secured."[59]

Because of Lord Queensberry's prominence and Oscar Wilde's flamboyant personality and celebrity, newspapers around the world followed the progress of Wilde's private prosecution with intense interest. "London sensation at the present moment is the libel suit which Oscar Wilde has brought against the Marquis of Queensberry," the *New York Recorder* and the *Indianapolis Journal* reported, adding that everyone "is talking of it."[60] Although Sir George Lewis initially appeared on behalf of the marquess, Lewis later cited a conflict of interest and stepped aside, likely out of his friendship with Wilde.[61] Wilde's lover, Lord Alfred Douglas, had actually initially wanted and advised Wilde to consult with Lewis—described by one history as "a prominent lawyer who specialized in settling awkward society cases out of court." But Lewis had, by then, already been retained by Lord Queensberry. Lewis reportedly knew "a great deal more about Wilde's private life" than the Q.C. and solicitor Wilde ultimately consulted with and retained, and it is speculated that Lewis may have dissuaded Wilde from attempting to prosecute Queensberry in the first place. With Lewis withdrawing from his representation of the marquess, Lord Queensberry's defense—as reported—was taken over by "Mr. E. H. Carson, Q.C., M.P., and Mr. C. F. Gill, instructed by Messrs. Day and Russell, of Norfolk-street, Strand." A barrister, Edward Carson had been appointed Queen's Counsel in England and Ireland, and Charles Russell—Lord Queensberry's chosen solicitor—was the son of England's Lord Chief Justice, Lord Russell of Killowen.[62]

The chronology of what led to the legal dispute between Oscar Wilde and Lord Queensberry—the latter described in his initial court appearance as "having no occupation and as residing in Carter's Hotel" on Dover Street—later came to light through the court proceedings. On February 18, 1895, the Marquess of Queensberry left his calling card with a hall porter, Sidney Wright, at the Albemarle Club with a quickly scrawled handwritten note. That note read, "For Oscar Wilde posing as somdomite" [sic]. The calling card with the misspelling would become Exhibit A in Wilde's libel action, though later published news reports about the card's handwritten note frequently left off its exact wording, saying, for example, that it contained "an expression which we are unable to print."[63] The Albemarle Club[64] was an exclusive private club in London in which Wilde and his wife—as well as Lord Queensberry—were members. On February 28th, the porter, Sidney Wright, gave the card, which he had thought best to enclose in an envelope addressed to "Oscar Wilde Esq.," to its intended recipient. "Lord Queensberry," Wright told Wilde, "left this for you" and he "desired me, sir, to hand this to you when you came into the club." The porter's act in relaying Lord Queensberry's calling card and hastily scrawled note, which *The Times* reported contained "epithets of the foulest nature," set in motion the sensational private criminal prosecution that garnered so much public attention around the world.[65]

Rejecting the advice of his friends, including critic and fellow playwright George Bernard Shaw and *Saturday Review* editor (and later *Vanity Fair* publisher) Frank Harris, Oscar Wilde responded to the calling card by commencing the criminal libel case. "Bosie's father has left a card at my club with hideous words on it," Wilde wrote to a friend, adding: "I don't see anything now but a criminal prosecution." After engaging a solicitor, Charles Humphreys, Humphreys had asked Wilde point blank—and "on his solemn oath"—whether there was any truth to Lord Queensberry's sodomy charge, to which Wilde assured him there was not. "If you are innocent," Humphreys had then told Wilde, "you should succeed." After getting Wilde's assurance (and Wilde had secured Humphreys' services), Humphreys took Wilde to the magistrate's court and they applied for a warrant for criminal libel. In particular, Wilde accused Lord Queensberry of making a "false scandalous malicious and derogatory" statement about Wilde, the "tenor and effect" of which was that "Oscar Fingal O'fflahertie Wills Wilde had committed and was in the habit of committing the abominable crime of buggery with mankind." In describing Wilde's motivation for pursuing a case that would require him to lie, Steven Lubet—a Northwestern University law professor—made this historical assessment: "Queensberry's pursuit of Oscar and Bosie eventually became nearly intolerable. He followed them to clubs and restaurants, and even accosted Wilde in his own home with an accusation of sodomy." As Lubet observed: "Queensberry had invaded Wilde's sanctuary, which was evidently a signal that he would stop at nothing. Wilde believed that his only recourse was to the law and Bosie agreed, anxious to strike back at his abusive and intimidating father."[66]

As a result of Oscar Wilde's decision to pursue a private prosecution, the arrest warrant was thus procured by Wilde and his chosen solicitor, Charles Humphreys. Lord Queensberry was thereafter promptly arrested by Thomas Greet, a detective-inspector of the "C" Division of the Police, at the beginning of March 1895 at Carter's Hotel.[67] The marquess was taken by authorities to the Vine Street police station, then transported to the Great Marlborough Street magistrates' court and arraigned on the charge of criminal libel—a crime carrying a sentence of up to two years in prison. Mr. Humphreys indicated that "Oscar Wilde was a married man, and lived on most affectionate terms with his wife and two sons" but "had been the object of a system of most cruel persecution at the hands of Lord Queensberry." Humphreys advised he had first been consulted ten months earlier, but noted that, "in consequence of the domestic affairs of the Queensberry family," Wilde had been "unwilling to take any steps of a criminal nature." But Humphreys added that matters had "come to a climax, and he felt bound to take steps in self-protection." There was some difficulty in deciphering Lord Queensberry's handwriting on the calling card, but the marquess—in open court—would freely interpret his own handwriting, interjecting during Humphreys' remarks, "The word is 'posing.'"[68] The magistrate, Robert Milnes Newton, after considering the matter, ordered that the case be adjourned for a week and that the marquess post bail in the sum of £1000 and provide an additional surety of £500, thus allowing him to be released on his own recognizance. William Tyser, a Gloucester Square merchant described as a "gentleman of military bearing with a fierce white moustache," immediately went into the witness box, tendered the £500, and agreed to act as the surety, offering the necessary bail to secure Lord Queensberry's release.[69]

Like the criminal libel charge itself, the Marquis of Queensberry's arrest made news around the world through transatlantic cables and telegraph wires. "The prosecution of a marquis for criminal libel is not a matter of everyday occurrence," the *Evening News* aptly observed. *The Marion Baptist* in faraway Kansas printed this of the London action: "Oscar Wilde has had the marquis of Queensberry arrested on a charge of criminal libel."[70] Lord Queensberry, as determined as ever, would not back down, though, and the matter proceeded through the London court system rather quickly and in due course. At the next step in the process, the preliminary hearing on March 9, 1895, the courtroom was packed with prominent people. At that hearing, the defendant, the marquis, was defended by Thomas Ward, a Queen's Counsel and the former consul general for Ireland. "Oscar Wilde, who wore a long dark blue overcoat with velvet cuffs, drove to the police court in great style, in a carriage and pair with footman and coachman," *The Times-Picayune* of New Orleans reported, also emphasizing that "[a]ccompanying Mr. Wilde was Lord Alfred Douglass," the Marquis of Queensberry's son and better known as "Bosie" to his family and friends. Bosie and his older brother had both come to court to support Oscar Wilde, not their father, although Bosie was not permitted to remain in court during Wilde's examination.[71] "The Marquess of Queensberry, on entering the courtroom, at once stepped into the dock," the *Western Mail* stressed, pointing out that the magistrate—after noticing the marquess standing—remarked, "Give Lord Queensberry a chair." A chair was quickly placed near the solicitor's table as the marquess, overly eager to give his testimony, left the dock, then sat down, making space for Oscar Wilde to take his place and start his testimony.[72]

After the preliminary hearing got underway, Oscar Wilde took the stand, entering the witness box and giving his full name as Oscar Fingal O'Flahertie Wills Wilde. When dutifully asked as part of the preliminaries if he was the author and dramatist, Wilde—accustomed to injecting as much wit as possible into his conversation and writings—replied: "I think I am well known." That prompted Magistrate Newton to sharply interpose: "Answer the question, please." "Yes," the admonished Wilde then answered.[73] In his testimony, Wilde went on to describe when he first became acquainted with the Marquis of Queensberry, the Scottish nobleman known as "an irascible peer" and for his "love of sport" and his "strong atheism."[74] Wilde's solicitor, Charles Humphreys, also asked Wilde, his client, when he had finished his studies at Oxford and about two lunches at Café Royal with Lord Alfred Douglas that the Marquis of Queensberry attended. At the second of those lunches, the three men had discussed Egypt, from which Lord Alfred Douglas had just returned, before Bosie handed Oscar a letter which came from Lord Queensberry. That letter was not read aloud in the courtroom, and the magistrate remarked that it should not be put in evidence. But solicitor Charles Humphreys alleged the letter contained libels other than the one alleged on the calling card that had been left at the Albemarle Club. At one point in the hearing, the magistrate specifically pointed out that Mr. Humphreys sought to indict Lord Queensberry for libels besides the one alleged on the card.[75]

Edward Carson, an M.P. and the Marquis of Queensbury's solicitor, said he did not object to the letter in question being put into evidence. But in response to Humphreys raising alleged libels outside the one on the calling card, Carson observed of Humphreys: "If he intends to do that, under the Vexatious Indictments Act there must be committal upon one, and of course I should take an objection at the trial if there was an indictment on a charge not enquired into here."[76] The Vexatious Indictments Act of 1859—as one barrister, Peter Solomon, later explained—"limited the right hitherto possessed by the private prosecutor to prefer before a grand jury a bill of indictment charging any offence whatsoever." Before that act became law, Solomon noted, Solicitor-General H. S. Keating had observed that indictments had been obtained against persons before grand juries for extortionate or oppressive purposes, with the bill providing that prosecutors—before preferring their bills of indictment—should be required to take proceedings before magistrates to give parties notice of accusations. Sir James Stephen, a prominent English legal commentator, had in fact once lamented that "in this country anyone and everyone may accuse anyone else, behind his back and without giving him notice of his intention to do so."[77]

At the preliminary hearing, Edward Carson—Oscar Wilde's classmate at Trinity College—gave Wilde and his attorney a preview of the Marquis of Queensberry's legal strategy. "I may say, on behalf of Lord Queensberry," Carson said, referring to letters not yet introduced into evidence, "I myself would call for these letters on cross-examination." "I am very anxious that they should be produced," Carson continued, adding shortly thereafter of Humphreys' discussion of one of the letters: "I really hope that the letter will be put in." "My point," he stressed, tantalizing courtroom spectators with his words, "is that Lord Queensberry was acting in the interests of his son and I am very anxious to have the letter which introduces the whole matter." "[Y]ou cannot go into that here," the magistrate cautioned Carson, tamping down Carson's enthusiasm, with Carson quickly replying, "I am quite aware of that." But Carson, telegraphing his intentions, then observed: "I think it affects the truth. I shall do it elsewhere." Wilde's counsel—who then "withdrew the letter" from consideration—said it was not his intention to read the letter in open court "as the names of exalted personages were mentioned it" and he "did not think it right that their names" be disclosed publicly.[78]

Edward Carson asserted that the defense sought to show that Lord Queensberry had exercised "a father's privilege" in "seeking to protect his son from Wilde's friendship." "I would be entitled ... to go into the question of the privilege of Lord Queensberry giving advice to his own son and if the ultimate charge arose out of that, it being a mere question of privilege," Carson told the magistrate, "that surely is a matter I could raise before you here."[79] After the magistrate ruled that this contention amounted to "a plea of justification," the Marquis of Queensberry was asked if he had anything to say. His short response, in which he expressed no regrets whatsoever: "I have only to say that I wrote the card complained of simply with the intention of bringing matters to a head, as I had been unable to see Mr. Wilde otherwise and to save my son from his influences. I abide by what I wrote."[80] When he was arrested by Inspector Greet, Lord Queensberry had said: "I have been wanting to find Mr. Oscar Wilde for nine or 10 days. This thing has been going on for almost two years." At the preliminary hearing, the Marquis of Queensberry then signed his deposition, just as Oscar Wilde signed his deposition moments earlier.[81]

In the midst of the hearing, the magistrate, Mr. Newton, had the lawyers assemble in his private "consulting room" and "strongly urged them to come to some settlement" in regard to the matter in controversy. "I suggest that you, Mr. Humphreys, and Mr. Carson should accompany me into the room here and have a word," Newton invited the advocates.[82] "Certainly, sir," Humphreys quickly agreed, with the lawyers spending a few minutes with the magistrate while Wilde remained in his seat.[83] At the hearing, Magistrate Newton had sought to avoid the public disclosure of the libels in question, suggesting to Humphreys that he simply say Wilde had "received libels from Lord Queensberry and mention the dates."[84] The magistrate's suggestion, however, prompted Carson to object to that mechanism of bringing libels to the court's attention. "Well, sir, I should, with very great respect," Carson said, "object to that course, unless they are produced, because to have a general statement that there are libels from Lord Queensberry is really begging the question." "You can have the dates," Magistrate Newton assured him. Still, Carson pressed: "Even with dates I should ask to have the documents put in, in fairness to Lord Queensberry, if they are to be gone into at all." If matters other than the card left at the Albemarle Club "are to be gone into, I ask to have the documents produced and the fullest investigation of them," Carson stressed. The letters "should not be read in public," Humphreys stressed, noting that "with reference to one particular letter the names of exalted persons are used and I don't think it would be right to them that their names should be called in question in matters of this description, and if the letter were used publicly, of course, those names must." The unmentioned names of those "exalted persons," as one history notes, "were deliberately kept out of the proceedings."[85]

The magistrate's effort to help the parties amicably settle their dispute proved to be—as one source put it—"apparently hopeless." "Queensberry," *The New York Times* reported on March 10, 1895, "is now quite dogged in his resolution to see the matter through."[86] On the other hand, Lord Queensberry's sons were equally determined to support Wilde in preference to their own father. Lord Alfred Douglas contended that "there was not the slightest truth in his father's allegations against Wilde and himself" and made this statement when he called upon the London office of the *Sun* and other news agencies: "My father is a madman. All the family are against him in this matter. My elder brother and I drove with Mr. Wilde to court to-day, and we shall do everything in our power to vindicate him from my father's charges." Because of his behavior, Lord Queensberry, certainly, had a knack for alienating those around him, including those closest to him. His first wife, Sibyl Douglas, had divorced him in Edinburgh in 1887, what's been called "a nearly unheard-of event in Victorian England,"[87] and just six days after his eldest son's tragic death, his second marriage to Ethel Weeden—which had taken place in November of 1893—was annulled in late October of 1894, "pronounced and declared to have been and to be absolutely null and void ... by reason of the frigidity, impotency and malformation of the parts of generation of the said Respondent [the Marquess of Queensberry]."[88]

The marquis's eldest surviving son, Lord Douglas of Hawick, recently back from a trip to Australia, reportedly made "an even more damaging statement against his father" than Bosie, also saying there was no truth to his father's charges. "My father," he offered, "has been a brute to his family." The Marquis of Queensberry—as noted—had divorced his first wife, whose maiden name was Sibyl Montgomery, in 1887, and then, a few years year later, gotten married to a younger woman, Ethel Weeden, a marriage that lasted less than a year.[89] In an especially painful moment, Lord Douglas of Hawick further asserted that his father was "responsible for the death of ... my eldest brother, and now seems bent on ruining my younger brother and me." "We shall do all we can to help clear Mr. Wilde of this infamous charge," Lord Douglas of Hawick asserted.[90] His late brother—Lord Queensberry's eldest son, Francis Archibald Douglas, Viscount or Lord Drumlanrig—had died on October 18, 1894, likely by suicide, in what was called elsewhere "a mysterious shooting accident."[91] "My father's so-called evidence," Lord Douglas of Hawick added of the Wilde-Lord Queensberry dispute, "consists of anonymous letters which he himself has written to my brother. One was that which was produced in court today and which the magistrate very properly suppressed." As Lord Douglas of Hawick observed: "These letters contain the wildest and most dreadful charges against many prominent people. I believe my father is of unsound mind, but there is a good deal of vice in his madness."

The late Lord Drumlanrig had been the private secretary to Lord Rosebery, Prime Minister William Gladstone's foreign secretary. Lord Drumlanrig, through Rosebery's efforts, had gotten an English peerage—something that his Scottish father had been refused due to his atheism. Lord Drumlanrig's elevation to a baronage—the 1st Baron Kelhead—gave the young, unmarried Lord Drumlanrig a seat in the House of Lords because of Lord Rosebery's patronage, something that enraged the previously slighted Lord Queensberry, who suspected a homosexual relationship between his son, Lord Drumlanrig, and Rosebery. Lord Queensberry had not been allowed to take a seat in Parliament because he'd refused to take a religious oath of allegiance to the Queen, and after his eldest son's violent death—in a communication to his ex-father-in-law, Alfred Montgomery—he blamed "the snob Queers like Rosebery" for his son's death. Lord Queensberry had sent hate mail to Rosebery and others complaining about his own humiliation in being excluded from the House of Lords, and in August 1893—in yet another fit of rage—he'd actually stalked Rosebery to Homberg and threatened to thrash him with a dog-whip. "It is a material and unpleasant addition to the labours of Your Majesty's service to be pursued by a pugilist of unsound mind," Rosebery later wrote to Queen Victoria about the incident. "Drumlanrig's death, ostensibly the result of a shooting accident," one history observes, "was widely suspected to be a suicide triggered by his homosexual relationship with the British foreign minister, Lord Rosebery." As another history reports: "On 18 October 1894 Drumlanrig was found dead during a shooting party at Quantock Lodge in Somersetshire. He was lying with his head in a bramble bush and the double-barrelled gun lay on his chest." "Though the doctor told the inquest that Drumlanrig had been shot through the mouth," that history notes, "the coroner decided that it was an 'accidental death', and that the gun had gone off while Drumlanrig was climbing the hedge to join his shooting chums."[92]

Under governing libel law, the ever-plotting Marquess of Queensberry sought to avoid conviction for libel by showing that his accusations on the calling card left at the Albemarle Club were true. As was then required by English libel law, Lord Queensberry further asserted that he had made his statements "for the public benefit and interest," with Lord Queensberry's representative, Edward Carson, preparing the plea of justification. That plea asserted that "Wilde was a man of letters and a dramatist of prominence and notoriety and a person who exercised considerable influence over young men," but whose writings "were calculated to subvert morality and to encourage unnatural vice."[93] To prepare for the trial, Lord Queensberry hired private detectives to try to undercover evidence of Wilde's lifestyle, relationships, and suspected homosexual acts. That team of private detectives was directed by none other than Edward Carson, the prominent Q.C. and a former solicitor-general for Ireland.[94] Although Wilde's precise libel allegations remained somewhat obscure to the public, the news reportage of the preliminary hearing focused on the bitter and salacious nature of the dispute, even though general attitudes during the Victorian era—to some extent—inevitably shaped how reporters covered the high-society scandal. For example, *The Sun* in New York wrote this after the preliminary hearing, treading somewhat lightly: "The case in which Oscar Wilde appears as prosecutor against the Marquis of Queensberry is of such a vile description that public comment upon it was impossible until to-day, when it assumed an extraordinary phase. The proceedings in court to-day furnished a slight indication of the peculiar features of the affair. The prosecutor produced proof of the libel which the Marquis is accused of bringing against Wilde. He also put in a letter in the Marquis of Queensberry's writing, containing fearful charges of immorality, not only against Mr. Wilde, but also against several eminent persons in public life." "The magistrate," *The Sun* emphasized, "would not permit this document to be read, and called the counsel on both sides into his private room for consultation." *The Sun* gave these final nuggets in its report of the hearing: "Upon returning to the court the Marquis, after being cautioned, admitted writing the libels complained of and declared that he would abide by and justify them. He claimed the right, as a father, to take the course which he had done in order to rescue his son from Mr. Wilde's influence. The defendant was committed for trial."[95]

After the preliminary hearing, rumors circulated that the Marquess of Queensberry and Oscar Wilde might fight a duel—the way in which aristocrats, politicians, and other elites had so frequently resolved their disputes in prior times. In condensing the news for its readers, one California newspaper summed up the two men's dispute in this way: "A very senseless row is going in London between Oscar Wilde and the Marquis of Queensberry. The latter is anxious to fight a duel with Wilde."[96] Reprinting a story from London, a newspaper in distant Topeka, Kansas, also eagerly informed its readers: "Oscar Wilde and Lord Alfred Douglass, son of the Marquis of Queensberry, have started for Monte Carlo. There is no question of a duel between Mr. Wilde and the marquis."[97] *The Boston Daily Globe* likewise ran a story from Monte Carlo titled "Oscar Wilde and the Marquis, It is Said, Will Fight on the Riviera—Arrival Causes a Sensation." The story said that the Marquis of Queensberry and Wilde "have arrived here simultaneously, and it is expected that a duel will shortly take place on the Riviera." "The prince of Monaco will not allow a duel to take place in his toy principality, but just beyond Monaco, on the Riviera," the newspaper reported, "are many wild spots, where a duel to the death might easily take place." "If a duel takes place—and nobody expects anything else—it will probably be of a very bitter and serious character," *The Boston Daily Globe* emphasized in its front-page story, adding:

"The marquis said only a few days ago he regretted that duelling was no longer permitted in England, where it flourished as late as the early part of the present century."

Taking note of the widely circulated rumor that "Wilde challenged" the Marquis of Queensberry to a duel, *The Boston Daily Globe* emphasized the belief that there was "no doubt in the mind of any one at Monte Carlo that the marquis and Wilde have come here from London with the determination of fighting."[98] The rumor about the imagined duel in Monto Carlo, however, was a complete fabrication, with the Marquis of Queensberry having remained in London,[99] where a grand jury—on March 25th—returned a "true bill" against him for libeling Oscar Wilde.[100] False rumors were floating around everywhere. Indeed, it was reported by the *Observer*, via a dispatch from Monto Carlo, in a story that was later retracted,[101] "that after Oscar Wilde and Lord Alfred Douglas, the second son of the Marquis of Queensberry, arrived at that place, they went to a hotel" but "after staying there a day the proprietor, at the request of the other English visitors, informed them that their rooms were engaged." Although the *Observer*, a week later, issued an apology to Oscar Wilde and Lord Alfred Douglass for that reporting after the two men denied the story's accuracy,[102] the *Observer*'s dispatch also reported on March 25th that "[b]oth Mr. Wilde and Lord Alfred are now in London."[103] The City of London always remained the focal point of the legal dispute, with distinguished legal counsel getting involved in the case on all sides as the parties lawyered up for their imminent courtroom battle. Following the proceeding at London's Central Criminal Court where the grand jury indicted the Marquis of Queensberry, it was reported that "Sir Edward Clarke, Q.C., and Mr. Charles Mathews are for the prosecution; Mr. Carson, Q.C., Mr. C. F. Gill, Q.C., and Mr. A. Gill have been instructed for the defense."[104]

The Criminal Libel Trial of the Marquess of Queensberry

In the lead-up to the libel trial, the public interest in Oscar Wilde's libel case against the irascible Lord Queensberry reached fever pitch. "Society will attend the law courts next week in order to hear the testimony in the suit of Oscar Wilde against the Marquis of Queensberry," one story reported in the buildup to the start of the trial.[105] With the libel trial just a day away, another article breathlessly observed: "It is rumored that Oscar Wilde left London suddenly this morning to avoid being present at the trial tomorrow of the suit for libel which he brought ... as a result of the allegations the Marquis made against him on a card in the Albemarle February 18th last."[106] But when the trial date arrived, both Oscar Wilde and the Marquess of Queensberry—with their high-powered teams of attorneys, both led by prominent Queen's Counsel—were on hand at the Old Bailey, London's Central Criminal Court, to duke it out in the bright light of a public courtroom. Lord Queensberry's Q.C., Edward Carson, reportedly possessed "rhetorical skills" that "outmatched Wilde's," while Edward Clarke, Wilde's Q.C., admitted later he felt "somewhat uneasy" about Carson's pointed questions during the libel trial.[107] As predicted, the courthouse was packed. "Every available inch of the Old Bailey was occupied this morning when the Marquis of Queensberry surrendered to bail and the libel suit brought against him by Oscar Wilde was opened before Justice Collins," came a report out of London on the trial's opening day.[108] Sir Richard Henn Collins, the presiding judge, had been educated at Trinity College Dublin and Cambridge before becoming a Queen's Counsel and then a judge.[109] In *Regina v. John Douglass*, Sir Edward Clarke, Q.C. and M.P.—as well as Charles Willie Mathews and Travers Humphreys, the son of Charles Humphreys—appeared for the prosecution, while Edward H. Carson, another Q.C. and M.P., appeared for the Marquis of Queensberry along with his co-counsel, Mr. C. F. Gill and Mr. A. E. Gill. Shorthand notes of the trial would be taken by Messrs Cherer, Bennett and Davis, with Lord Alfred Douglas and Lord Douglas of Hawick—the Marquis of Queensberry's sons—bringing their own legal counselors, Edward Besley, Q.C., and John Lionel Monckton, to monitor the proceedings. It may not have been the trial of the century, but it took place in a packed courtroom and still ranks among the nineteenth-century's most remembered, attracting massive press attention, as did other famous trials of that era.[110]

The reporters in attendance at the criminal libel prosecution provided countless details as the trial played out. Oscar Wilde, one source reported, arrived at the Old Bailey "faultlessly dressed in a long, black frock coat"; he "carried his gloves in his hands, showing his fingers to be covered with rings."[111] As the *Pall Mall Gazette*, in its news report, described the scene: "Mr. Oscar Wilde came down to the Old Bailey this morning to prosecute the Marquis of Queensberry for criminal libel. The Marquis was already on the spot prepared to do his best to justify that criminal libel." The general public "clamoured at the doors for admission soon after eight o'clock in the morning," though it was "only the privileged few who gained entry."[112] After noting that Justice Richard Henn Collins punctually took his seat at 10:30 a.m., the *Gazette* observed of the dramatic scene: "The Marquis wore a Cambridge blue hunting-stock instead of a collar and tie, and until his name was called as the signal for his surrender he stood a yard to two away from where Mr. Wilde sat at the solicitors' table. There was none of that tendency to flippancy on Mr. Wilde's part which some thought they detected at the police-court. He was intensely grave, and his first request was that a glass of water might be placed in front of him, and passed on to him in the witness-box."[113] Another report from London made these observations: "The aisle of old courtroom was crowded with lawyers. Admission was obtained by ticket only and the Sheriff in charge showed the representatives of the press a pile of applications a foot high, many of them being from well-known people."[114] In short, there was tremendous public interest in the private prosecution.

The Marquis of Queensberry was intent on proving that what he had written about Oscar Wilde was true. As the proceeding convened, the Clerk of Arraigns read aloud the indictment, which set the stage for the trial's start by charging that the defendant had maliciously published a defamatory libel.[115] The "plea of justification" interposed by the Marquis of Queensberry had, in fact, prompted the marquis to gather considerable evidence about Wilde, his compatriot and friend Alfred Taylor, and others for use in connection with that plea. "The Marquis of Queensberry, who wore a shabby overcoat," newspaper reports emphasized, "was placed in the dock" and answered "Not guilty" to the indictment, with the marquis adding: "The libel is true and was published for the public benefit."[116] "The Marquis seemed quite unconcerned," one report observed, noting that in replying to the questions put to him, "he spoke quietly and clearly."[117] At trial, letters written by Oscar Wilde to Lord Alfred Douglas would be presented in open court, with the Marquis of Queensberry alleging—and attempting to prove—that Wilde had homosexual proclivities and solicited persons to commit "indecent offenses."[118]

Sir Edward Clarke, representing Oscar Wilde's interests as the private prosecutor, opened the trial. "May it please your lordship, gentlemen of the jury," he began, "you have heard that the charge against the defendant is that he published a malicious libel with regard to Mr. Oscar Wilde." As Clarke emphasized: "The libel was published in the form of a card which was left by Lord Queensberry at the club to which Mr. Oscar Wilde belongs. It was a visiting card of Lord Queensberry with his name printed upon it and had written upon it the words 'For Oscar Wilde posing as sodomite', and in respect of the libel so published on that card this charge is brought against the defendant."[119] At that time, English law made sodomy a criminal act punishable by a long term of imprisonment. Indeed, in 1885, a British politician, Henry Labouchere, authored the notorious "Labouchere Amendment" of the Criminal Law Amendment Act that criminalized all homosexual conduct. That amendment read: "Any male person who, in public or private, commits, or is a party to the commission of, or procures or attempts to procure the commission by any male person of, any act of gross indecency with another male person, shall be guilty of a misdemeanor, and being convicted thereof, shall be liable, at the discretion of the court, to be imprisoned for any term not exceeding one year with or without hard labour." The Attorney General, Sir Henry James, had accepted that amendment, although the maximum penalty under the Labouchere Amendment had been increased in the legislation to two years instead of one, and it became part of English law on January 1, 1886.

England's Offences Against the Person Act (1861) had already criminalized acts of sodomy, with section 61 of that Act, titled "Sodomy and Bestiality," reading: "Whosoever shall be convicted of the abominable Crime of Buggery, committed either with Mankind or with any Animal, shall be liable, at the Discretion of the Court, to be kept in Penal Servitude for Life or for any Term not less than Ten Years." The Act's next section, section 62, titled "Attempt to commit an infamous Crime," provided: "Whosoever shall attempt to commit the said abominable Crime, or shall be guilty of any Assault with Intent to commit the same, or of any indecent Assault upon any Male Person, shall be guilty of a Misdemeanor, and being convicted thereof shall be liable, at the Discretion of the Court, to be kept in Penal Servitude for any Term not exceeding Ten Years and not less than Three Years, or to be imprisoned for any Term not exceeding Two Years, with or without Hard Labour." But while the Offences Against the Person Act criminalized both sodomy and attempted sodomy, the Labouchere Amendment broadened that criminalization by, more vaguely, prohibiting acts of "gross indecency," with no definition of that terminology. "The Labouchere Amendment also became known as the blackmailer's charter," one source notes, adding that "gross indecency" could "mean many things, and its interpretation was often up to the arresting officer and/or the courts." The combination of the Offenses Against the Person Act and the Labouchere Amendment, that source adds, "criminalised any sexual relationships between men."[120]

In his opening statement to everyone assembled in the courtroom, Sir Edward Clarke took note of the momentous nature of the legal proceeding. "Now, gentlemen," he stressed, "it is a matter of serious moment that such a word as Lord Queensberry had written on that card should in any way be connected with the name of a gentleman who has borne a high reputation in this country." As Clarke—in his lengthy remarks—argued to jurors: "It is not an accusation of that, the gravest of all offences—'posing as sodomite' indeed appears to suggest there is no guilt of the actual offence—but that in some way or another the person of whom those words are written as appeared to be—nay, desired to appear to be—a person guilty of or inclined to the commission of that gravest of all offences; and the publication of such a statement, the leaving of such a card with the porter of a club, of course, is an act most serious, likely gravely to affect the reputation and the position of the person as to whom that injurious suggestion is made." It was Oscar Wilde bringing the private prosecution against Lord Queensberry, but everyone knowledgeable about English law knew about the Offenses Against the Person Act and the Labouchere Amendment—an amendment that specifically targeted all forms of homosexual conduct beyond sodomy (e.g., oral sex). In short, everyone knew what was at stake in the criminal libel trial.[121]

In his opening, Clarke had this to say about the Marquis of Queensberry's plea of justification in relation to the words written on the card left at the Albemarle Club: "By the plea which the defendant has put before the Court today a much graver issue is raised. He says that that statement is true and that it was for the public benefit that that statement was made. He says that it is true, giving particulars in the plea of matters which, as he alleges, show that statement to be true with regard to Mr. Oscar Wilde." "The plea has not in full been read to you," Clarke said, "but I will state to you this: there is no allegation in the plea that Mr. Oscar Wilde has been guilty of the offence of which I have spoken, but there are a series of accusations, mentioning the names of certain persons—many persons—and it is said in regard to all those persons that Mr. Oscar Wilde has solicited them to commit with him the grave offence and that he has been guilty with each and all of them of indecent practices."[122] As a practical matter, Lord Queensberry's plea of justification put in issue whether the alleged libel on the calling card was true, with a common maxim or expression of the law being "the truth is no libel."[123]

As part of his opening statement, Sir Edward Clarke emphasized that Oscar Wilde "is the son of Sir William Wilde, a very distinguished Irishman, a surgeon and oculist, and a gentleman who did great public service as chairman of a Census Commission in Ireland." Although Oscar Wilde's father had died "some years ago," his mother, Lady Wilde, was still living, Clarke pointed out. Clarke further emphasized that Oscar Wilde had distinguished himself at Trinity College, Dublin and at Magdalen College at Oxford. "Leaving the university after a brilliant career," Clarke said of Wilde, "he devoted himself to literature and literature in its artistic side," with Clarke also observing that, in 1884, Wilde "had the happy fortune to marry the daughter of late Mr. Horace Lloyd, Queen's Counsel." Oscar Wilde and his wife, with their two sons, had lived at Tite Street in Chelsea, where they had received various friends, including Lord Alfred Douglas and Lady Queensberry, the defendant's ex-wife. As Clarke described Oscar's initial meeting and relationship with Lord Queensberry's son, Bosie: "Among the friends whom he saw at Tite Street was a gentleman whose name I mention—it is necessary I should mention—Lord Alfred Douglas, and in the year 1891 Lord Alfred Douglas came to Tite Street one afternoon, was introduced by a friend of Mr. Wilde and a friend of Lord Alfred's and from that time until now Mr. Oscar Wilde has been the friend not only of Lord Alfred Douglas but of Lord Alfred Douglas's brothers and Lord Alfred Douglas's mother Lady Queensberry, who was the wife of the defendant, but who some years ago obtained a release from the marriage tie in consequence of the defendant's conduct."[124]

Oscar Wilde, Sir Edward Clarke's opening continued, had lunched at the Café Royal with Lord Alfred Douglas and his father, the Marquis of Queensberry—something previously reported in the press. "The fashionable Café Royal on Regent Street," one scholar explains of Victorian London, was itself "one of several places in which Wilde captivated" younger companions such as Lord Alfred Douglas. As that historian, Joseph Bristow, writes: "It was here that Wilde was introduced to a man named Edward Harrington: a music publisher's clerk who most probably enhanced his income through sex work. And it was also at the Café Royal that Wilde lunched with another sex worker and blackmailer, Frederick Atkins (also known, both on stage and sometimes in court, as Fred Denny), who had been developing a music-hall career as both a comedian and cross-dressed sex worker." As Bristow further writes of the Café Royal: "It was there, too, that Wilde entertained respectable youths, such as Edward Shelley: a mentally unstable clerk who worked for the publisher John Lane, whose company The Bodley Head was located in nearby Vigo Street. Shelley was also one of Wilde's sex partners." "Most of these assignations," Bristow recounts, "took place in late 1892 or early 1893, and Wilde often followed up his liberal hospitality at the café by taking the young men out to one of his favourite restaurants—especially the Florence, Kettner's, or the Solferino—in neighbouring Soho."[125]

In November 1892, Oscar Wilde and the Marquis of Queensberry had shaken hands at one of those lunches, Clarke added, noting how Lord Alfred Douglas had, during that time, experienced extremely "strained feelings" with his father.[126] It was in

1893 that Oscar Wilde first heard that "his character was being impugned," with Clarke describing the backstory of what had led up to the criminal libel case. Specifically, Clarke spoke of Alfred Wood—a young, out of work clerk[127]—who had found four of Oscar Wilde's letters in the pocket of a coat that had been worn by Lord Alfred Douglas; Wood's subsequent request of money from Wilde for the letters; and how Lord Queensberry had left the by then infamous calling card at the Albemarle Club.[128] "This card," one news report emphasized, "was not read or shown to the press at the preliminary investigation, and its contents are known only to the principals and lawyers in the case."[129] Wood, Clarke observed of the effort to extract money for the personal letters, "represented himself as being in some distress and trouble and as wanting to go to America, and Mr. Wilde gave him fifteen pounds or twenty pounds in order to pay his passage to America and Wood handed to Mr. Wilde three somewhat ordinary letters which had been written by him to Lord Alfred Douglas." In describing what amounted to an effort to extort money from Wilde, Clarke noted that a fourth letter had been "retained," with Clarke then referring to "the set of people—Wood and a man named Allen and a man named Cliburn—who were taking part in this transaction."[130] At one point, a copy of the fourth letter had been given to Sir Herbert Beerbohm Tree, an actor, the manager of the Haymarket Theatre, and an acquaintance of Wilde,[131] with a note reading, "To Mr. Tree. Mr. Tree kindly give this to Mr. Wilde." "The original letter is in my hands now," Clarke said of the fourth letter, describing how the original had, in time, come back into Oscar Wilde's possession.

Clarke described how Oscar Wilde's letters, intended only for Lord Alfred Douglas's eyes, had inadvertently come into the possession of others. Wilde had admittedly given Alfred Wood the money to allow him to travel to America, but it was emphasized that Wilde had rebuffed other efforts to get an even larger sum of money for recovering the letters that Wilde himself had once written.[132] Clarke also noted for jurors how the prominent theatre manager, Sir Herbert Beerbohm Tree, had been unwittingly drawn into the blackmailers' scheme. In 1893, Clarke reminded the jurors, the Haymarket Theatre—managed by Sir Herbert Beerbohm Tree—was preparing Oscar Wilde's play, *A Woman of No Importance*, for its stage production. Noting that "some of you will remember" the "great success" of the play, Clarke observed how "Mr. Wilde was from time to time and very frequently seeing Mr. Beerbohm Tree, the actor and manger, and there came into his hands through Mr. Beerbohm Tree this paper, which purports to be and to some extent is a copy of a letter, which had been retained by these persons or some of them when the others were handed over to Mr. Oscar Wilde." Around that time, a copy of that letter—one that had been retained by Wood and two other men, Allan and Cliborn (sometimes spelled Allen and Cliburn)—had come into the hands of Sir Herbert Beerbohm Tree, the famed actor and Haymarket Theatre manager.[133]

The letter in question, written by Oscar Wilde, addressed to Lord Alfred Douglas, and handed to Justice Collins in the courtroom, read:

> My own Dear Boy,—Your sonnet is quite lovely, and it is a marvel that those red, rose-leaf lips of yours should be made no less for music of song than for madness of kissing. Your slim gilt soul walks between passion and poetry, I know Hyacinthus, whom Apollo loved so madly, was you in Greek days. Why are you alone in London, and when do you go to Salisbury? Do go there and cool your hands in the grey twilight of Gothic things, and come here whenever you like. It is a lovely place. It only lacks you. But go to Salisbury first. Always with undying love, yours, OSCAR.[134]

Lord Alfred Douglas's mother resided at Salisbury at a place called St. Ann's Gate, and Wilde had been one of her guests there.[135] In discussing that letter, Sir Edward Clarke said that the words of the letter "appear extravagant to those who are in the habit of writing commercial correspondence or those ordinary letters which the necessities of life force upon one every day." But—in a remark that generated laughter, including from Oscar Wilde himself—Clarke said that the letter's words constituted "mere poetry."[136]

A version of Oscar Wilde's letter had actually been published two years earlier, in 1893, albeit in a different form, in an Oxford-produced publication called *The Spirit Lamp*. That periodical, self-described as "An Aesthetic, Literary, and Critical Magazine," was edited by none other than Lord Alfred Douglas. An edited version of the letter, translated into French, had appeared as a "SONNET" in Volume 4, Issue 1 of *The Spirit Lamp*, with a publication date of May 4, 1893. Consistent with his lawyer's line of argument at the criminal libel trial, Wilde had told one of the men who tried to blackmail him that he looked upon his letter to Lord Alfred Douglas as merely a "prose sonnet," with the first page of *The Spirit Lamp* containing the French-language sonnet, signed by Pierre Louÿs, with the following editorial characterization before the start of the poem: "*A letter written in prose poetry by Mr. Oscar Wilde to a friend, and translated into rhymed poetry by a poet of no importance.*"[137] Pierre Louÿs was a friend of Oscar Wilde whom he'd met in Paris in 1891.[138]

A modern scholar, Xavier Giudicelli, has described the circumstances of the publication of the so-called "Hyacinthus sonnet" by Pierre Louÿs this way: "Wilde had written a passionate letter to Alfred Douglas, in which he praised the sonnet the latter had sent him ('In Sarum Close') and compared the young man to the classical figure of Hyacinthus—loved and unwittingly killed by Apollo, then turned into a flower." As Giudicelli writes, referencing Oscar Wilde's letter and Richard Ellmann's biography of Wilde: "This letter was later used in the trials as evidence to prosecute Wilde. According to Ellmann's biography, Wilde asked Pierre Louÿs, who had come to London in April 1893 to attend the opening night of *A Woman of No Importance* (hence the allusion to 'a poet of no importance' in the title of the poem in *The Spirit Lamp*), to translate the letter into French and turn it into poetry so as to escape possible blackmail." The poem, Giudicelli explains, "offers an illustration" of the use of a foreign language—making it inaccessible to some—"as a means of aestheticizing life and articulating otherwise unspeakable desires."[139]

At the trial, Wilde's counsel thus addressed the letter's contents head on in his opening statement, emphasizing how his client, Oscar Wilde, simply viewed the letter as "a sort of prose sonnet, an answer written to a piece of poetry written to Lord Alfred Douglas, a piece of poetry which is transcribed and paraphrased in the sonnet printed in this *Spirit Lamp* which I now hold in my hand." Wilde, Sir Edward Clarke said, had "preserved this letter and preserved it until today and produces it now saying to you it is a letter of which he was and is in *no* way ashamed; that it is a letter he was prepared to produce anywhere, a letter with regard to any imputation connected with which he was absolutely indifferent, a letter with regard to which he says that as an artist and a poet that letter is an expression of poetical feeling and has no relation whatever to the hateful suggestions—hateful to him as to all of you—which are made with regard to him in the plea in this case."[140] A juror asked Clarke for the letter's date, but Clarke said that the letter was undated, stressing that the French sonnet had been published in the literary magazine on May 4, 1893, and that the letter was written before that date. Clarke then handed a copy of the issue of *The Spirit Lamp* to the judge, adding, "I am told that the letter had been written in December 1892." After again referring to the publication of the sonnet in *The Spirit Lamp* "in the early part of the year 1893," Clarke told the jurors that "there is nothing with which I need trouble you with regard to the remainder of that year."[141]

It was shortly after a lunch Wilde had with Lord Alfred Douglas and Bosie's father at the Café Royal, Clarke observed, that "Mr. Oscar Wilde became aware that Lord Queensberry was writing letters which affected his character and contained suggestions injurious to him." "You may well understand," Clarke spoke to the jurors in the libel case, alluding to the nature of the case, "why Mr. Oscar Wilde would be extremely reluctant—not for his own sake for he had no question or no reason to hesitate at all with regard to that, but for the sake of others" to bring "to public notice the hideous and frightful suggestions which we are now forced in this court to discuss." Wilde, Clarke said, "abstained from doing so for reasons which I am not entitled to state, which I do not state, but which I am quite sure will be obvious to all of you before we have gone very far in the conduct of this case"; "and so the latter part of the year 1894 passed," he told the jurors. In his appeal to the jury, Clarke added: "I should tell you—I will not go into details about it—that there was an interview between Lord Queensberry and Mr. Wilde about the middle of the year 1894. The details of that interview I need not tell you, except that Mr. Oscar Wilde absolutely repudiated suggestions which he understood Lord Queensberry was making and called upon Lord Queensberry to leave his house and insisted that he should do so, and gave in Lord Queensberry's hearing directions that he should never again be admitted to that house."[142] With Clarke's opening statement describing how the Marquess of Queensberry had left the card at the Albemarle Club[143] and bringing up what he called the "curious allegations" in the marquis's plea of justification,[144] Lord Queensberry reportedly "sat glaring at Mr. Wilde." It was even reported that Lord Queensberry, obsessed in his hatred of Oscar Wilde, "made a movement as though he intended to attack him, and he undoubtedly would have done so had it not been for the persons between them."[145]

After Sir Edward Clarke's opening statement, the *Pall Mall Gazette* observed that "Mr. Oscar Wilde was called and examined." Clarke's direct examination of Wilde began after he "languidly arose from the solicitors' table at which he had been seated and entered the witness box." He was—according to news reports—"very pale" but "seemingly composed" and "spoke with his customary drawl, leaning his arms upon the rail of the witness box and replying distinctly to the questions addressed to him."[146] As one reporter put it, Wilde "lounged over the rail of the witness stand in graceful pose, and clasped his hands in front of him upon the gloves he held."[147] The jury, composed of "very intelligent men of elderly appearance, mainly prosperous tradesmen," one report emphasized, "eyed him with curiosity."[148] At the very beginning of his testimony, Wilde declared: "I am the Prosecutor in this case, and am 39 years of age. My father was Sir William Wilde, surgeon, of Dublin, and Chairman of the Census Commission. He died when I was at Oxford." Wilde then said of his academic background: "I was a student at Trinity College, Dublin, where I took a classical scholarship and the Gold Medal for Greek. I then went to Magdalen College, Oxford, where I took a classical scholarship, a first in 'Mods' and a first in 'Greats,' and the Newdigate prize for English verse." In his last year in college, Wilde had received the Sir Roger Newdigate Prize for English Verse for his poem "Ravenna." After relaying to jurors that he got his degree in 1878, Wilde spoke of his successful literary career and portrayed himself as a family man, observing: "From that time I have devoted myself to art and literature. In 1882 I published a volume of poems, and afterwards lectured in England and America. I have written many essays of different kinds, and during the last few years have devoted myself to dramatic literature. In 1884 I married Miss Lloyd, and from that date till now have lived with her in Tite-street, Chelsea. I have two sons, the eldest of whom will be ten in June, and the second nine in November."[149]

In the witness box, echoing what his counsel had already alluded to, Oscar Wilde also testified about a visit that the Marquis of Queensberry had paid to his (Wilde's) home with another gentleman. Upon their arrival at Wilde's house, the marquis had demanded that Wilde sit down, but Wilde retorted: "Lord Queensberry, I will not allow anyone to talk that way in my house. I suppose you have come to apologize for the statement you made about my wife and myself in a letter you wrote to your son. I should have the right any day I choose to prosecute you for criminal libel for writing such a letter." In their heated exchange, Wilde denied that he and the marquis's son, Lord Alfred Douglas, had been kicked out of the Savoy Hotel. "That is a lie," Wilde told Lord Queensberry after the marquis made this accusation at Wilde's home: "You were both kicked out of the Savoy Hotel at a moment's notice for your disgusting conduct." "Is it possible that you accuse me and your son of sodomy?" Wilde asked pointedly, knowing that sodomy was then prohibited by English law and carried stiff penalties.

At Wilde's home, the homophobic Marquis of Queensberry—in an era in which homosexuality, as Bosie later put it, was regarded as "far worse than murder"[150]—had replied: "I did not say it, but you look like it and appear like it."[151] On that occasion, Lord Queensberry had then directly threatened Wilde, saying, "[I]f I ever catch you with my son together again in any public restaurant I will thrash you." At that point, with the exchange becoming more heated and tense with each passing moment, Wilde had replied to the Marquis of Queensberry, alluding to the boxing rules that bore the latter's name: "I don't know the Queensberry rules, but the Oscar Wilde rules are shoot on sight. The letters you have written about me are infamous. You are trying to ruin your son through me." Wilde then told the Marquis of Queensberry to get out of his home, with Wilde testifying about the end of the encounter with the belligerent marquis: "Then when we were in the hall I said to a servant: 'This is the Marquis of Queensberry, the most infamous brute in London. Do not let him enter the house again.'"[152] Wilde told Lord Queensberry, "I will not have in my house a brute like you," with Wilde further instructing his servant that if the Marquis of Queensberry should ever attempt to enter the house, the servant "must send for the police."[153]

The specific events leading up to the criminal libel case at the Old Bailey were laid out in detail at the trial by both Oscar Wilde and his counsel. For example, Sir Edward Clarke asked Wilde about the estrangement between Lord Alfred Douglas and his father and about Wilde's conversation with the man to whom Wilde had given £15 or £20 to pay his passage to America. "I am aware that there had been some estrangement between the two," Wilde said, adding that in 1893 he had heard that some letters that he had written to Bosie "had come into the hands of certain persons." Alfred Wood, Wilde testified, saw him and told him that he had found some letters in a suit of clothes that Lord Alfred Douglas had given the young man. "I suppose you will think very badly of me," Wood had said upon meeting Wilde, with Wilde upbraiding the young man and responding: "I heard that you have letters of mine to Lord Alfred Douglas, which you certainly ought to have handed back to him."

After Alfred Wood handed Wilde "three or four letters," it was said, Wood cryptically declared that "they were stolen from him the day before yesterday by a man named Allan, and that he had to employ a detective to get them back." Wilde testified that he read the letters, but said that he then told Wood—a man of about 23 years of age—that he did not think them of any importance. "I am very much afraid of staying in London, on account of this man, and I want money to go to America," Wood had pressed Wilde, with Wilde testifying that he paid the young man 15*l.* but that another man, Allan, had then come to him with another of his own letters. "I felt that this was the man who wanted money from me," Wilde testified, "and said, 'I suppose you have come about my beautiful letter to Lord A. Douglas. If you had not been so foolish as to send a copy of it to Mr. Beerbohm Tree, I would gladly have paid you a very large sum of money for the letter, as I consider it to be a work of art.'" "A very curious construction could be put on that letter," Allan then said, making an ominous threat to Wilde in a society full of *de jure* discrimination and intense prejudice against homosexuals, with Wilde—trying to display a lack of concern in response to the not-so-subtle threat—replying: "Art is rarely intelligible to the criminal class."

Oscar Wilde—as widely reported in the press—further testified about his exchange with Allan: "The man told me he had been offered £60 for the letter and I advised him to immediately accept it."[154] Sir Herbert Beerbohm Tree had already given a copy of the letter to Wilde, with Wilde rejecting Allan's attempt to sell him the letter's original version. Wilde said, "I now have a copy"; "[t]he original is of no use." Wilde, consistent with his counsel's earlier assertion, reiterated that he viewed the letter, in fact, as nothing more than a "prose sonnet." In particular, Wilde said he told Allan after Allan had intimated he could get £60 for the letter: "If you take my advice you will go to that man and sell my letter to him for 60*l*. I myself have never received so large a sum for any prose work of that length; but I am glad to find that there is someone in England who considers a letter of mine worth 60*l*." Wilde reported that Allan was taken back. "The man is out of town," Allan said. After Wilde parried, "He is sure to come back," Allan—clearly disappointed—said he had not a single penny, clearly fishing for some cash.

At that point in the blackmail attempt, Wilde said he could not guarantee Allan's cab expenses, but that he would gladly give him half a sovereign—at which point Allan took the money and went on his way. Wilde further testified that, in just five or six minutes, another man named Cliborn came to his house. "I cannot bother any more about this matter," Wilde told him, with Cliborn then producing the original version of the letter out of his pocket. "Allan has asked me to give it back to you," Cliborn offered, adding that Allan wanted him to have it back because "you were kind to him, and that there was no use trying to rend you as you only laugh at us." Wilde noted that the letter was "extremely soiled" and remarked derisively: "I think it quite unpardonable that better care was not taken of the original manuscript of mine." Cliborn said he was sorry, observing that the letter than been in many hands, whereupon Wilde said, "I will accept it back, and you can thank Allan from me for all the anxiety that he has shown about it." After Wilde gave Cliborn half a sovereign for his trouble, Wilde remarked: "I am afraid you are leading a wonderfully wicked life." "There is good and bad in every one of us," Cliborn reportedly said before leaving.[155] At the very end of his direct examination, Wilde was specifically asked about Lord Queensberry's plea of justification. "Is there any truth in these allegations?" Wilde was asked. "There is no truth whatever in any one of them," Wilde answered.[156]

On cross-examination, Edward Carson—the Marquis of Queensberry's counsel—took pains to poke as many holes as possible in Oscar Wilde's direct testimony and to question his morality, trying to use Wilde's own words and works of literature against him. Carson wasted no time in trying to undermine Wilde's credibility. "You stated at the commencement of your examination that you were thirty-nine years of age," Carson began, adding, "I think you are over forty, isn't that so?" "I don't think so.

I think I am either thirty-nine or forty—forty my next birthday." "If you have my certificate there, that settles the matter," Wilde conceded after Carson held up a copy of Wilde's birth certificate. "You were born, I believe, upon the 16th of October, 1854?" "That makes you more than 40?" Mr. Carson pushed. "Ah!" Wilde acknowledged. "Yes, I have no intention of posing for a younger man at all. I try to be correct in the date," Wilde declared, with Carson then eliciting that Lord Alfred Douglas was much younger—only twenty-four years of age. Carson got Wilde to admit that he had, in fact, stayed at many places with Lord Alfred Douglas, Wilde's constant companion, and that he had spent time abroad with him, including most recently at Monte Carlo.

After asking Wilde about his views on works of literature that Carson viewed as blasphemous,[157] Carson then read passages from *The Picture of Dorian Gray*,[158] Oscar Wilde's novel first published in *Lippincott's Monthly Magazine* in 1890 and later printed in book form. When that story had first been published, the magazine's editor—fearing it might be viewed as indecent—had deleted approximately 500 words without Wilde's knowledge. Despite the publisher's censorship, *The Picture of Dorian Gray*—with its homoerotic overtones—had nonetheless still offended the sensibilities of many late nineteenth-century Victorian Era readers. "Do you think that the description of Dorian Gray, given on page 6, is a moral one?" Carson asked. "Yes," Wilde replied, "just what an artist would notice in a beautiful personality." "Did you ever adore madly, as described in 'Dorian Gray,' any person of the male sex younger than yourself?" Mr. Carson asked next. "I took the idea from Shakespeare's sonnets," Wilde shot back, eliciting loud laughter with a quip that "I have never given adoration to anybody except myself."[159] In an introduction to *The Picture of Dorian Gray*, Wilde—as Carson, who'd clearly combed through Wilde's writings, reminded him—had written, "There is no such thing as a moral or an immoral book. Books are well written or badly written." "That expresses my view on art," Wilde admitted. Asked about another work of literature, "The Priest and the Acolyte," Carson probed: "May I take it that you think 'The Priest and the Acolyte' was not immoral?" Wilde's jibe in response: "It was worse. It was badly written."

At trial, Wilde testified in detail about the letter he'd written to Lord Alfred Douglas, saying it was "merely poetical" and that he did have "undying love" for the young man he called "his best friend." "Why should a man of your age address a boy nearly 20 years younger as 'My own boy?'," Carson queried, asking if it was an "improper thing"? Wilde reported response: "Not if I was fond of him. I don't think so." As another source described Wilde's answer: "I was fond of him. I have always been fond of him." "Do you adore him?" Carson pressed. "No," Wilde answered, "but I have always liked him." After bringing up Wilde's letter making reference to "those red roseleaf lips of yours" and the "madness of kissing," Carson pressed Wilde: "Do you mean to tell me, sir, that was a natural and proper way to address a young man?" "Yes, I think it was a beautiful letter," Wilde replied, adding: "It is a poem. If you ask me whether it is proper you might as well ask me whether *King Lear* was proper or a sonnet of Shakespeare was proper," Wilde retorted, taking on his courtroom adversary, and observing that his letter "was written with the object of making a beautiful thing." Wilde spoke of being an artist, said he never repeated himself in his style and confidently parried that "Everything I wrote is extraordinary," spoke of his "great admiration for Lord Alfred Douglas," and parsed his words carefully, distinguishing at one point on cross examination between a "love letter" and "a letter expressive of love."[160] Wilde also specifically denied that he'd been guilty of any impropriety toward young men such as Alfred Wood, who, Wilde told Carson, was introduced to him by Alfred Taylor. Wilde befriended the out-of-work man, he said, at the request of Lord Alfred Douglas, with Wilde taking Wood to supper.[161]

Wilde was a smart and sophisticated man, and he did his best to charm the jury as Edward Carson continued going on the attack, asking about Wilde's relationships with a series of young men—not only Alfred Wood but also Edward Shelley, Alfonso Conway, and Charles Parker. Wilde testified that he knew that there had been an attempt to blackmail him with his letters, but that—in Alfred Wood's case—he'd given Wood money out of charitable impulses, saying that Wood told "the pitiful tale about himself." "Wood convinced me," Wilde said, that it was not his intention to engage in blackmail, though Wilde knew it was the intention of others.[162] "In answers to questions during the cross-examination," *The Brooklyn Daily Eagle* reported of the goings-on in London, "Mr. Wilde said that in writing he did not concern himself to produce morality or immorality" but was only concerned "with literature, beauty, wit and emotion." "The cross examination," that paper observed, "was very severe and brought out the great differences in the ages of Oscar Wilde and Lord Alfred Douglas" and how the two men had visited various towns together and met at the Savoy Hotel, with "Lord Alfred" visiting "Wilde's chambers in St. James place, which the plaintiff maintains in addition to his house at 16 Tite street, S.W."[163]

Mr. Carson's cross-examination of Oscar Wilde included very specific questions about the efforts to blackmail him and Wilde's acquaintances with other young men, including Edward Shelley, an 18-year-old "office boy" at Wilde's publishers whom Wilde dined with at the Albemarle Hotel. Wilde had given money to Shelley on three occasions. "I regarded him as a gentleman," Wilde said, denying he considered him a "good-looking boy" but saying he had "an intellectual face." "Did you ask this lad to dine with you?" Carson asked. "Oh, yes, he often dined with me," Wilde said. "Was that for the purpose of having an intellectual treat?" Carson followed up. "Well, for him, yes," Wilde replied to laughter. Asked about giving liquor to Shelley in Wilde's private suite, Wilde insisted nothing improper had happened. Wilde was also asked, for instance, about a newsboy, Alfonso Conway, whom Wilde said led "a happy, idle life." Wilde admitted given presents to Conway, buying a blue suit and a straw hat for him, and bringing him to Brighton's Albany Hotel. "I did not want him to be ashamed of his shabby clothes," Wilde explained. "Why did you seek the boy's society?" Carson queried Wilde about the teenager. "Was it for an intellectual treat?" "Oh, he was a bright, careless, amusing creature," Wilde observed. During his cross-examination, Carson produced a signed photograph of Wilde and a silver cigarette case and a silver-mounted walking stick that Conway had gotten from Wilde. Wilde expressly denied kissing Conway, and said that they had just stayed a night at the hotel with a sitting room and two bedrooms and eaten at a local restaurant.[164]

On cross-examination, it was suggested to Wilde that his friend, Alfred Taylor, notoriously introduced and procured young men for older men, with Carson referring to Taylor's heavily draped, perfumed rooms in which Taylor hosted tea parties. In his testimony, however, Wilde said that Taylor had done nothing wrong. Wilde himself commented: "I like the society of young men. I delight in it." At one point, Wilde confessed that iced champagne "is a favourite drink of mine—strongly against my doctor's orders." When Carson, trying to keep the focus on Wilde consorting with young men, replied, "Never mind your doctor's orders, sir," an undeterred Wilde shot back, "I never do," eliciting more laughter. Over the course of his testimony, Wilde talked about his stays at hotels and the giving of gifts to teenagers and young men in their early twenties, with Wilde admitting that he took Freddie Atkins, a bookmaker, to Paris (he said as a favor for a friend); that he gave Ernest Scarfe a cigarette case but never kissed him or did anything indecent; that a twenty-five-year-old, Sydney Mavor, had dined and stayed a night with him at the Albermarle but that nothing indecent happened on that occasion either; and that Charles Parker was one of the young men he became friendly with. "How old was he?" Carson probed of Parker, already knowing the answer. "I do not keep a census," Wilde retorted. "Never mind about a census. Tell me how old he was?" Carson pressed. Wilde's response: "I should say he was about twenty. He was young and that was one of his attractions, the attraction of youth." "He was seventeen," Carson relayed, adding that Parker was neither a literary personality nor an artist. "Was he an educated man?" Carson asked, trying to insinuate Wilde's real purpose in associating with Parker before the jury. "Culture was not his strong point," Wilde said, off-handedly delivering another *bon mot*.

Carson questioned Wilde, in particular, about meeting Charles Parker and his brother, William, at Alfred Taylor's and then taking them to a fancy restaurant. "I have a passion to civilize the community," Wilde offered, adding, "The pleasure to me was being with those who are young, bright, happy, careless, and free. I do not like the sensible and I do not like the old." Speaking of a sixteen-year-old boy who was a servant of Lord Alfred Douglas at Oxford, Carson asked: "Did you know Walter Grainger?" "Yes," Wilde replied, with Carson—in what had become a pattern—then asking, "Did you ever kiss him?" "Oh, no, never in my life; he was a peculiarly plain boy," Wilde asserted, what one modern-day commentator described as a "stumble" that prompted Carson to follow up relentlessly. "He was what?" Carson asked. "I said I thought him unfortunately ... very ugly—I mean—I pitied him for it," Wilde said, with Carson and Wilde having an extended exchange about the young man. Carson: "Very ugly?" Wilde: "Yes." Carson: "Do you say that in support of your statement that you never kissed him?" Wilde: "No, I don't; it is like asking me if I kissed a doorpost; it is childish." Carson: "Why did you mention his ugliness?" Wilde: "No, I said the question seemed to me like—your asking me whether I ever had him to dinner, and then whether I had kissed him—seemed to me merely an intentional insult on your part, which I have been going through the whole of this morning." Carson: "Why did you mention his ugliness? I have to ask these questions." Wilde: "I say it is ridiculous to imagine that any such thing could possibly have occurred under any circumstances." A persistent Carson: "Why did you mention his ugliness?" An agitated Wilde: "For that reason. If you asked me if I had ever kissed a doorpost, I should say, 'No! Ridiculous! I shouldn't like to kiss a doorpost'? The questions are grotesque." A still persistent Carson: "Why did you mention the boy's ugliness?" "I mentioned it perhaps because you stung me by an insolent question." "You make me irritable," Wilde told Carson, with Wilde saying that Carson had insulted him and was trying "to unnerve me in every way." "At times," Wilde conceded, "one says things flippantly when one should speak more seriously, I admit that, I admit it—I cannot help it."[165]

English and American newspapers, eager to sensationalize the trial and Wilde's lifestyle and witty testimony, put their own spin on everything. "They were of the class of servants, valets, etc., not belonging to Mr. Wilde's station in life, not interested in literature or art, yet they addressed this distinguished dramatist by his Christian name, Oscar, he in turn calling them Charlie, Freddie, etc.," one newspaper suggestively reported.[166] Wilde—it was reported—acknowledged that he knew Allan was "a blackmailer," and said that he only gave him 10*s*. "out of contempt." Wilde testified that he had seen Cliborn before at the stage door of the Haymarket when he (Cliborn) said that he wanted to speak with him (Wilde) about a letter in Allan's possession, at which time Wilde had informed Cliborn he was rehearsing, "could not be bothered," and "did not care two-pence" about the letter. At all times, Oscar Wilde tried not to appear defensive. "I gave him half a sovereign," Wilde admitted, saying that Cliborn had "made no attempt to blackmail me." As *The Brooklyn Daily Eagle* editorialized of the portion of Carson's cross-examination about Wilde giving a young man the cigarette case, a silver-mounted cane, and a book, *The Wreck of the Grosvenor*: "Wilde emphatically denied that he had done anything improper but he was troubled and confused under the terrible cross examination he was subjected to and frequently drank water." "In fact," the paper reported, Wilde seemed "ready to faint and a chair was placed inside the witness stand for his use." "Throughout the questioning of the plaintiff," it was also reported of the cross-examination, which was not yet finished when the court adjourned for the day at 5:00 p.m., "the Marquis of Queensberry stood facing him and did not take his eyes off of him." As Oscar Wilde, the private prosecutor, left the Old Bailey after his first day of trial testimony, testimony that had been dramatized in the press as a story might be dramatized in the theater, a large crowd of people were still assembled at the courthouse to see him make his way out.[167]

The criminal libel trial, which began at the Old Bailey on April 3, 1895,[168] ended up revealing many intimate details of Wilde's personal life—details that got widely reported in England and across the Atlantic. "Terrible Ordeal for Oscar Wilde—The Aesthetic Poet's Relations with Lord Alfred Douglass Aired in Court," a headline in *The Philadelphia Inquirer* blared.[169] "Oscar Wilde Is Pitilessly Scored," a *Chicago Tribune* headline declared.[170] Over the course of six hours of intense cross-examination that extended into a second day,[171] Wilde said he'd become friendly with "[a]bout five" young men, confessing that he "liked their society." "I have given money and presents to all five," Wilde conceded, admitting he attended "tea parties" in Alfred Taylor's "artistically furnished" rooms "in which perfumes were burning," though he denied he'd ever seen Taylor "in woman's costume." Alfred Taylor, the son of a cocoa manufacturer who had inherited £45,000 in 1883 and rapidly squandered it,[172] had, since coming into the fortune, no occupation but had, instead, "lived a life of pleasure." In 1894, Taylor and Arthur Marling, a "female impersonator," had been arrested at a party given by John Preston at 46 Fitzroy Street along with a number of other young men. In that police raid, Arthur Marling was taken away wearing what has been described as "a frock of black and gold lace" or "a fantastic female garb of black and gold."[173] During his cross-examination, an exasperated Wilde reportedly "lost his temper" and—according to one account—"confused and contradicted himself frequently."[174]

On Sir Edward Clarke's re-examination, Oscar Wilde specifically denied that his wife, Constance, was petitioning for a divorce, and Wilde discussed letters written by Lord Queensberry to Lord Alfred Douglas in which the marquis objected to Wilde's relationship with his son. Clarke read aloud portions of those letters, with the Marquis of Queensberry's words to his son including these: "[Y]our infamous intimacy with this man Wilde must cease, or I will disown you and stop all money supplies, and, if necessary, I will go personally and tell him so. I am not going to try to analyse this intimacy, and make no accusations, but to pose as a thing is as bad as to be it. With my own eyes from this window I saw you in disgusting and loathsome familiarity. It was proved by your manner and the expression of your countenance. It turned my blood cold. Never have I seen such a sight in human nature as I saw in your horrible faces. I hear now, on good authority, that his wife is petitioning for a divorce from him on the grounds of unnatural crime." Lord Queensberry's warning to his son: "If I catch you with this man Wilde I will make a public scandal in a way you little dream of. It is already a suppressed one; I prefer an open one. Unless this acquaintance ceases I shall carry out my threat, and stop supplies. I will cut you down to a mere pittance; so you know what to expect." "You are a reptile, and no son of mine," the letter concluded.[175]

As regards the Marquis of Queensberry's plea of justification, Mr. Carson—in his opening statement—said that the marquis had "tried, at all hazards, to save his son." "Mr. Wilde's character had been made known to Lord Queensberry," Carson asserted, alluding to "scandals connected with the Savoy Hotel." In cross-examining Wilde, Carson had specifically asked if Wilde had committed "an act of criminality" with a man at the Savoy in a private room after giving him "iced champagne"—a charge Wilde "absolutely denied." Carson had also pointed out that young men with whom Wilde associated had been arrested in a police raid in which men had been wearing women's clothes.[176] When he'd been asked why he associated with young men of a different social class, Wilde had tried to deflect the question by making this quip: "I recognise no social distinctions, and would sooner talk to a young man half an hour than be cross-examined in court." But Carson was intent on portraying Wilde in as negative a light as possible. As Carson said of Wilde to the jury in his opening statement on the plea of justification: "He had been going about with young men who were not his co-equals, he had been associated with men who, it would be proved, were well known as some of the most immoral characters in London." It wasn't long, in fact, before Oscar Wilde—under the intense pressure of the criminal libel trial and his cross-examination—would do an about-face and decide to drop the criminal prosecution entirely, leading to a "not guilty" verdict in the case.[177]

What Oscar Wilde began as a private (but highly publicized) prosecution to protect his reputation would, ironically, destroy it, with both American and English newspapers—in story after story—exposing the minute details of Wilde's lifestyle, including his associations with much younger men. The Marquis of Queensberry's counsel denounced Wilde in open court, announcing that he had the "painful task" to call to the stand "several young men to tell their tale." Carson made an allusion to "conduct at the Savoy Hotel and elsewhere, which could not be even indicated," and Wilde's offered explanations for his relationships with the young men—ones reported in the papers—had been closely questioned (and called into question) by Lord Queensberry's counsel, courtroom observers, and the public at large. As one newspaper, *The Pall Mall Gazette*, editorialized: "Mr. Wilde's absurd explanation of his friendship with these lads was that there something beautiful and charming about youth. Surely, if that were all, Mr. Wilde could have found youths of his own class and culture for his companionship, instead of these unemployed clerks, valets, and grooms who addressed the distinguished dramatist and litterateur as 'Oscar.'" As that newspaper continued, excoriating Wilde's behavior and reflecting the late nineteenth-century prejudices, biases and bigoted views of its writer: "[A]fter hearing the evidence they would have to hear, the jury would wonder not that the rumours and scandals reached Lord Queensberry's ears, but that this man Wilde had been tolerated in society in London so long as he had. More audacious stories than Wilde had told had never been related in a court of justice. Doubtless Wilde thought that in many of his answers he was making smart repartees and scoring off counsel, but underneath it all was the incredibility and the disgraceful audacity of Wilde's explanations."[178]

Oscar Wilde's private prosecution came to sudden end as it became apparent—indeed, crystal clear—where it was headed. On the libel trial's final day, one in which the court and galleries at the Old Bailey were "again thronged by half-past nine o'clock," it was reported that there were "printed broad sheets" visible everywhere with "the noisy rustling of the papers mingling with the incessant chatter going on as to the prospects of the case." After Mr. Carson had given short descriptions of what he intended to prove at trial, including that jurors would hear from witnesses who said they'd had sexual experiences with Wilde and that Alfred Taylor "acted as procurer" of young men for Wilde, Sir Edward Clarke—Wilde's counsel—grew increasingly concerned, interrupted his opposing counsel, and sprung into action to short-circuit the criminal libel trial.[179] Clarke, it was reported of an exchange between opposing counsel, "rather excitedly chatted with his colleague, and then hurried out of court." When Clarke returned to the courtroom a quarter of an hour later after conferring with his own client, then absent from the courtroom, Clarke whispered to, and spoke briefly with, Mr. Carson. Clarke—the British barrister who'd served as the Solicitor-General from 1886 to 1892, and who knew the English legal system as well as anyone—then announced that Oscar Wilde, the private prosecutor, was formally dropping the case. "The excitement caused by this sensational denouement was of the wildest description," the press reported. After the jury, under instructions from Justice Collins, found the Marquis of Queensberry not guilty, the verdict was reportedly received with "loud applause" that went unchecked by the presiding judge. Clarke tried to mitigate the damage, but to no avail. "[D]o you also find that the plea of justification was true in substance and in fact?" the Clerk of Court asked the jury. "We do," the foreman replied, adding on behalf of the jurors that the alleged libel "was published for the public benefit." In response to a request from Mr. Carson, Justice Collins ordered that Lord Queensberry—said to be "smiling and surrounded by his friends"—be discharged from custody.[180]

The press reported that the crowd assembled outside the Old Bailey eagerly awaited "any scraps of information as to the reason for so sudden a termination of the case, and long after the finish of the trial people loitered about the court discussing the verdict." In one day's time, Oscar Wilde, the much-celebrated playwright, suddenly became a pariah and "the disgraced author,"[181] with locales banning his writings and theaters quickly abandoning the production of his plays and removing Wilde's name from playbills. Even more troubling for Wilde, it was also soon announced that "the Public Prosecutor" had been consulted, and that a warrant had been issued for Oscar Wilde's apprehension. After Wilde had spent several hours in the company of Lord Alfred Douglass at a hotel in Holborn before they drove away, Wilde was located and arrested at the Cadogan Hotel on Sloan Street. The arrest warrant was executed by Inspector Richards of Scotland Yard and another detective, with Wilde "placed in a four-wheeled cab and conveyed to Bow-street" and arraigned before a magistrate. The application for Wilde's arrest was reportedly made by "Mr. Angus Lewis, of the Treasury," and "Mr. Charles Russell, Lord Queensberry's solicitor in the case which ended so dramatically." London's *Evening News* also reported that it had received the following letter from Oscar Wilde, written on notepaper from the Holborn Viaduct Hotel, which gave this explanation as to why Wilde had withdrawn his prosecution of the marquis: "It would be impossible for me to prove my case without putting Lord Alfred Douglas in the witness-box against his father. Lord Alfred Douglas was extremely anxious to go into the box, but I would not let him do so. Rather than put him in so painful a position I determined to retire from the case and to bear on my own shoulders whatever ignominy and shame might result from my prosecuting Lord Queensberry." Wilde had spent the prior night at the Holborn Viaduct Hotel because of its proximity to London's Central Criminal Court.[182]

The Aftermath of Oscar Wilde's Abandoned Private Prosecution

The end of Oscar Wilde's private prosecution brought swift consequences, including the imposition of court costs upon Wilde. After the trial ended with the Marquess of Queensberry's acquittal, Queensberry's solicitor—at Queensberry's directive—had taken the massive amount of information he'd compiled to the Director of Public Prosecutions, who then sent the file to the House of Commons and to the Attorney General, the Solicitor General, and the Home Secretary. A warrant was then prepared and issued for Wilde's arrest that very afternoon. Though his friend, Robbie Ross, advised Wilde to flee to France when he found him at the Cadogan Hotel in Knightsbridge, Wilde said dejectedly, "The train has gone. It's too late." "The arrest of Mr. Oscar Wilde last night," the *Glasgow Herald* reported of the "gross indecency" charges leveled against him pursuant to the Labouchere Amendment, "was the necessary result of the collapse earlier in the day of the prosecution of the Marquis of Queensberry for libelling him."[183] "Immediately after the House of Commons met yesterday," *The Standard* of London further observed, "a representative of the Public Prosecutor had an interview with the Home Secretary, the Attorney General, and the Solicitor General in regard to the case of Mr. Oscar Wilde."[184] The day after Oscar Wilde's arrest, Alfred Taylor—the wealthy young man with whom Wilde associated—was also arrested, with the police finding a large collection of female clothing in his room. Oscar Wilde's private prosecution having fizzled, Wilde and Alfred Taylor would both be put on trial later that month for violations of the Criminal Law Amendment Act (1885).[185]

As for Lord Queensberry, he reportedly sent Oscar Wilde this message at the end of the criminal libel trial: "If the country allows you to leave all the better for the country, but if you take my son with you I will follow you wherever you go, and shoot you." Under the headline "Branded Before All the World—An Indelible Mark of Shame Set Upon Oscar Wilde," the *St. Louis Post-Dispatch* gave this summary of the events of the last day of Wilde's private prosecution, which had attracted international attention throughout the trial: "The suit of Oscar Wilde against the Marquis of Queensberry came to a sudden and unexpected termination today shortly after the third day's proceedings were begun in the Old Bailey before Judge Collins."[186] Before taking the case from Wilde's solicitor, Charles Humphreys, Sir Edward Clarke—once described as a "veritable titan at the bar"—made a point of questioning his own prospective client. "I can only accept this brief, Mr. Wilde, if you can assure me on your honour as an English gentleman that there is not and never has been any foundation for the charges that are made against you." Wilde had told Clarke that the charges were "absolutely false and groundless," but Wilde—a man quite familiar with fiction—was known to make up stories to suit himself. Had Clarke known the truth, he would never have taken the case. Years later, Wilde's own grandson speculated that "arrogance born of social and literary success, and the belief that he was in some way immune from the law unquestionably played a part" in the decision to commence the private prosecution.[187]

Oscar Wilde's abandonment of that private prosecution made him responsible for the Marquess of Queensberry's considerable expenses in defending against the case. Not only did that ultimately bankrupt Wilde later in the year,[188] but his theatrical career was put into taters, with his play, *The Importance of Being Earnest*, forced to close after less than three months on stage. In addition, Wilde was immediately confined in Holloway Prison, where he remained prior to the criminal trial he would face. Both Wilde and Alfred Taylor were denied bail because of what Justice John Bridge termed the "gravity of the offence." There were, in fact, twenty-five counts brought under the Criminal Law Amendment Act. "The twenty-five counts," one historian notes, "included nine counts alleging misconduct with the brothers Charles and William Parker, three counts of misconduct with Frederick Atkins; five counts of misconduct with Alfred Wood; two counts of misconduct with unknown boys at the Savoy Hotel; two counts of misconduct with Sidney Mavor; one count of misconduct with Edward Shelley; and three counts of conspiracy with Alfred Taylor."

In the criminal libel trial against Lord Queensberry, Oscar Wilde had been asked about his relationships with these young men, but it was now Wilde who was facing the prospect of criminal consequences and the loss of his liberty. It was Alfred Taylor who had arranged Wilde's meeting with Wood, Wilde said, though on cross-examination Wilde had denied that Taylor was "notorious for introducing young men to older men." "I have never heard that in my life," Wilde had said even as he acknowledged that Taylor had, in fact, introduced Wilde to young men such as Fred Atkins and Charles Parker. As Wilde testified about his connections to Taylor and how he spent his leisure time: "I have dined with him and young men perhaps 10 or 12 times at Solferino's, Kettner's, and the Florence. We usually had a private room, as I prefer dining in private rooms." Charles Parker, Wilde testified, "was one of those I became friendly with," with Wilde giving this answer when asked about Parker's age: "Really, I do not keep a census. He may be about 20. He was young, and that was one of his attractions. I have never asked him his age. I think it vulgar to ask people their age." In asking Wilde about one of those dinners at Kettner's, Carson had inquired of Wilde if, after dinner, he (Wilde) had, in the presence of Taylor and William Parker, turned to Charles Parker and said, "This is the boy for me"? "Most certainly not," Wilde had replied.[189] Wilde's dinners with these young men would come up again when Wilde and Alfred Taylor were put on trial under the Criminal Law Amendment Act. Alfred Taylor, the public prosecutor asserted, "was a man closely connected with the prisoner Wilde, and the evidence would show that he was engaged in acting for Wilde in procuring for Wilde young men with whom" he (Wilde) afterwards committed "acts of gross indecency."[190]

Justice Arthur Charles, dressed in a scarlet robe and donning a small wig, presided over the prosecution of Oscar Wilde and Alfred Taylor for violation of the Criminal Law Amendment Act. Sir Edward Clarke, Charles Mathews and Travers Humphreys defended Oscar Wilde, while J. P. Grain and Paul Taylor represented Alfred Taylor. Because of Wilde's dire financial situation, Sir Edward Clarke—a man already invested in the details of the dispute—graciously offered to represent Wilde free of charge, an offer that a depressed Wilde, from the Holloway Gaol and suffering from insomnia, readily accepted.[191] With Wilde and Alfred Taylor tried together on charges of "gross indecency," the criminal trial in London began on April 26th before a packed courtroom. "There was a great eagerness on the part of the public to obtain admission to the court," the *Manchester Weekly Times* reported of the similarities to the criminal libel prosecution, observing: "As soon as the doors were opened, there was a rush for the public gallery, which was soon crowded. Barristers in wig and gown were also present in large numbers."[192] "The Old Court was thronged," another newspaper noted, observing that the courtroom's gallery "was from an early hour packed with a most unusually well-dressed crowd."[193] Although the trial's spectators sported attire befitting of those in high society, Wilde's appearance was described as "haggard" and he was said to be looking "ill" and to be suffering from "acute mental depression." The press, meanwhile, played up the nature of the criminal charges that had been leveled, going out of its way to describe Taylor as "effeminate" in demeanor.[194]

The lead prosecutor, Charles Gill, opened the case, observing at the outset that he was sure the jurors "had read and heard much" but "to dismiss from their mind anything they knew of the case, and listen to the evidence to be brought before them with impartiality." After noting that Wilde was charged with acts of indecency and Taylor with procuring men for Wilde and committing acts of indecency himself, Gill made this declaration in his opening statement: "Taylor was familiar with a number of young men, who were in the habit of giving their bodies, or selling them, to other men for the purpose of sodomy. It appears that there was a number of youths engaged in this abominable traffic, and that one and all of them were known to Taylor, who went about and sought out for them men of means who were willing to pay heavily for the indulgence of their favorite vice." "It will be shown," Gill said in his opening, "that Taylor himself was given to sodomy and that he has himself indulged in these filthy practices with the same youths as he agreed to procure for Wilde." London's *Reynolds's Newspaper* gave this account of the end of Gill's opening statement: "There was no sound in the court, except the moving of the people and their seats, when Mr. Gill sat down—no expression of feeling one way or the other, as so frequently marked the Queensberry trial."[195]

The first witness at the criminal trial: Charles Parker. He testified that when he and his brother, William, were out of work in February 1893, Alfred Taylor spoke to them at the St. James's Restaurant and "suggested to them the disgusting means whereby they might obtain plenty of money," offering "to introduce them to Wilde." Charles Parker further testified that, after a candlelit dinner at Kettnor's with plenty of champagne and then brandy and coffee, Wilde said to him, "This is the boy for me. Will you go to the Savoy Hotel with me?" After Charles said he consented, they drove in a cab to the hotel and drank whiskey and soda before Wilde asked Charles into the bedroom. While one newspaper story reported in brackets, "Witness here described certain acts of indecency which took place in the apartment," it was reported elsewhere that Charles testified that Wilde "committed the act of sodomy upon me," played with his "privates as a man might amuse himself with a girl," and that Wilde had asked him "to imagine that I was a woman and that he was my lover." "Before I left," Charles added of the encounter, "Wilde gave me £2, telling me to call at the Savoy Hotel in a week." Charles Parker then described other sexual encounters he had with Wilde, how Alfred Taylor had "gone through a form of marriage with a youth named Mason," and how he had ended his association with Taylor in August of 1894.[196]

Among other witnesses, William Parker corroborated his brother's testimony and Margaret Bancroft, a tenant, said she had seen Wilde leave Taylor's residence. In addition, Ellen Grant—who assisted Alfred Taylor with household chores—said that Taylor's rooms "were curtained and draped, and no daylight was admitted," and that she had seen women's shoes and stockings there. Grant also testified that she had seen at Taylor's residence at 13 Little College Street "several young men," including Alfred Wood, Sidney Mavor, Charles Mason and one Machlin, who ranged in age from sixteen to thirty. Mrs. Grant said Taylor and his male friends used to affectionately call one another "Charlie dear" and "My dear boy." Alfred Wood, who said he'd been a clerk, also testified that he had lived with Taylor for about three weeks and slept in the same bed with him. Wood said that he had met Wilde at the Café Royal about a month after he'd made Taylor's acquaintance, that Wilde offered him something to drink before he was invited to a dinner at which he drank champagne, and that after Wilde gave him £3 they went to Wilde's house and engaged in what a newspaper characterized as "an act of indecency." Wood also said that, at dinner, "Wilde would put his hand inside my trousers underneath the table and compelled me to do the same with him." Wood further testified that he had told Wilde he wanted to go away to America, and that Wilde had given him money for that purpose, with Wilde reportingly saying at the time: "You have some letters I should like to get back."

As the criminal trial extended into another day, the courtroom galleries remained as crowded as ever, with young barristers occupying "all the spare seats" and even sitting "on the stairs of the Court" or standing "at the sides of the seats." On Sir Edward Clarke's cross-examination, Alfred Wood said he had gone to America in 1893 before returning to England the following year, with Clarke getting Wood to admit that, in one instance, he and Charles Parker had gotten "£300 or £400" from a gentleman, with Wood getting £175 of that sum. And one by one, other witnesses took the stand. Thomas Price, a hotel waiter, said that Wilde had rooms there from October 1893 to April 1894, and that the rooms consisted of a bedroom and a sitting room. Price recognized Taylor and testified that Charles Parker had come to the hotel "five or six times" and was "shown into Mr. Wilde's rooms." Fred Atkins, describing himself as "a bookmaker's clerk and a comedian," said he dined at a restaurant with Wilde and Lord Alfred Douglas, saw Wilde kiss the waiter, and traveled to Paris once with Wilde at Wilde's request. A housekeeper, Mary Applegate, as well as Savoy Hotel workers, also said that Wilde's bed sheets had been "stained in a peculiar way." Other young men—namely, Sidney Mavor and Edward Shelley—also testified about gifts they'd received from Wilde, with Shelley specifically testifying that Wilde had kissed and slept with him.[197] "There is no truth whatever in any one of the allegations," Wilde told his counsellor, Sir Edward Clarke, in open court.[198]

After Clarke cross-examined the trial witnesses and Justice Charles made his evidentiary rulings, narrowing the case to four questions and instructing the jurors, the jury deliberated for almost four hours. Gill—the lead prosecutor—had urged jurors to "protect society from such scandals" no matter "however sorry you may feel yourselves at the moral downfall of an eminent man." Despite the prosecutor's appeal, the jury returned a "not guilty" verdict on one count while failing to reach a consensus on the other counts.[199] But the criminal case—as it might have—did not end there. "The prisoners will be brought up again at the next sessions," the *Liverpool Mercury* tersely reported of the prosecution's expressed intent to put the two defendants on trial again.[200] It was decided by Justice Charles and the lawyers involved in the case that a retrial would take place in May at the next Central Criminal Court session. Alfred Taylor and Oscar Wilde—both said to be fully committed to fighting the charges "to the end"[201]—were thus each put on trial for a second time. This time, however, their cases were tried separately, with Solicitor-General Frank Lockwood—in a move that would spell trouble for Wilde—successfully arguing that Taylor's trial should occur before Wilde's trial.[202]

At Taylor's trial, Taylor was called to the stand and denied the allegations of "improprieties between himself and persons whose names had been mentioned." He also denied going through a marriage ceremony "with a man named Mason." On cross-examination, however, Taylor admitted "that he had slept with young men on more than one occasion, and had attired himself in female Eastern costume."[203] With a crowded public gallery watching the proceedings, Taylor said he was first "introduced to Mr. Wilde by a friend named Schwabe," while Taylor's lawyer—Mr. Grain—asked the jury "to place no reliance upon the testimony of blackmailers and accomplices," contending that his client was "an innocent man." The result of Taylor's criminal trial on May 21st, one in which jurors deliberated for only about 20 minutes before reaching their verdict, was reported around the world.[204] *The Wilmington Messenger* in North Carolina, for example, conveyed that the jury—in very ominous news for Wilde, who was still awaiting his trial—"found Taylor guilty on two counts in regard to Charles and William Parker." Taylor's sentencing, it was noted, "was delayed until a verdict shall be reached in the trial of Wilde, which will begin tomorrow."[205] *The Standard Union* in Brooklyn, New York, likewise made a similar report after jurors were polled,[206] with *The Age* in Melbourne, Australia reporting that the jury returned a guilty verdict after hearing "the charge of criminal immorality." Taylor lacked Wilde's fame, but in the Victorian Era he was quickly branded as a criminal in less than a half hour.

With the judge deferring Taylor's sentencing to await the verdict of a different jury that would hear the criminal retrial of Oscar Wilde, it was simultaneously reported by *The Age*, under the headline "Peers at Fisticuffs," that "[a] disgraceful encounter, the news of which has caused a great sensation," took place in public in London on May 21, 1895. That encounter involved "the Marquis of Queensberry and Lord Douglas of Hawick, who was one of the bondsmen for Oscar Wilde." As the news item in *The Age*, about a fight that broke out, reported: "When the news of the conflict was first made public, wild rumors were circulated that the parties concerned were the Marquis of Queensberry and his son, Lord Alfred Douglas, and the accounts were garnished with most sensational details. It was made to appear that the father, meeting the son in a fashionable thoroughfare during the afternoon, had administered a severe chastisement, that the son had retaliated with great effect upon his parent, and that both had been arrested on a charge of disorderly conduct and to bail." The Marquis of Queensberry was, it seems, ever the pugilist, forever fighting, including members of his own family.

Although Lord Alfred Douglas was present for the interfamilial affray, the quarrel and "violent altercation" that broke out in the street in Piccadilly was, in fact, between the Marquis of Queensberry and Lord Douglas of Hawick even though some news outlets reported that it was between the Marquis of Queensberry and Lord Alfred Douglas.[207] According to the report in *The Age*, Lord Douglas of Hawick called his father "a liar and a slanderer" respecting the allegation made by the Marquis of Queensberry against Oscar Wilde and the relations between Wilde and Lord Alfred Douglas, whereupon Lord Queensberry hit Lord Douglas in the face, causing a bruise which soon developed into a black eye. After the police, with "great difficulty," managed to separate the two men, Lord Queensberry—in a highly agitated state—gave a speech to the crowd "setting forth the motives for his action." In it, which the gathered crowd on the street received with cheers, Lord Queensberry referred to "the filial disobedience of his son" and stated "that henceforward he would disown him."[208] The fistfight between father and son was later depicted in an artist rendering in the *Illustrated Police News*.[209]

After Alfred Taylor was convicted at his retrial,[210] Wilde's second criminal trial—putting the playwright in legal jeopardy once more—immediately followed, with one headline somewhat optimistically predicting that chances for Oscar Wilde's conviction were thought to be slight.[211] The same fact witnesses testified, but unlike at Wilde's first trial Sir Frank Lockwood—the country's Solicitor-General—took the reins as the lead prosecutor. Lockwood—as one historian notes—had "a reputation for ruthlessness" and "an even more aggressive prosecutorial style" than Charles Gill, the lead prosecutor at Wilde's first trial. Lockwood freely acknowledged that men had attempted to blackmail Wilde, but Lockwood asked the jury "to take care lest they enabled another vice as detestable and as abominable to raise its head unblushingly in this country." The origin of the blackmailing scheme, Lockwood said, "was a man who had committed these acts of indecency," calling Wilde's criminal case a "painful and shocking" one that "necessitated a cold and calm administration of justice." Wilde reportedly looked "ill and anxious" at his second trial, with Solicitor-General Lockwood asserting that Wilde "was closely intimate with Taylor" and that Wilde had "flaunted" Lord Alfred Douglas "at hotels in London and the country." Lockwood also commented upon Wilde's much-talked-about letter to Bosie, which referred to rose-leaf lips and the madness of kissing. "Sir Frank Lockwood," one report observed of the solicitor-general, "made such a strong appeal to the jury for a conviction that it drew forth the protest from Sir Edward Clarke that such conduct was unbecoming on the part of the Crown."[212]

In terms of the players, it was not only the lead prosecutor who differed at Oscar Wilde's retrial. The presiding judge at Wilde's second trial was Sir Alfred Wills, a 77-year-old who shared a Tite Street address with the defendant and who admitted evidence that the more congenial Justice Charles—at the first trial—had refused to admit into evidence. Justice Wills also gave a highly prejudicial summing up of the case to the jury, noting in one instance that the letters written by Wilde to Lord Alfred Douglas "were undoubtedly open to suspicion."[213] Fewer criminal charges were brought against Wilde at his second trial, but the *Star* called Lockwood and two of his fellow prosecutors a "destructive trio." The jury—after making pointed inquiries relating to Lord Alfred Douglas and after deliberating for more than two hours—ultimately convicted Wilde on all of the counts of the indictment. Edward Clarke's fear that a negative verdict against Taylor would unduly prejudice Wilde's trial proved to be prescient, and Justice Wills had further poisoned the proceeding against Wilde through his deleterious comments. Justice Wills' "summation of the case"—as one historian notes—"virtually commanded the jury to find Wilde guilty." Among other things, Justice Wills expressed his support for the aphorism that "a man must be judged by the company he keeps" and he said no valid reason existed for men as wealthy as Taylor and Wilde to ever share their beds with other men. The new indictment against Wilde had contained only eight, as opposed to twenty-five, counts, charging him—as historian Michael Foldy notes in *The Trials of Oscar Wilde* (1997)—with committing "indecent acts with Parker (four counts), Wood (one count), certain persons unknown at the Savoy Hotel (two counts), and Shelley (one count)." But the more aggressive prosecution team and the presiding judge's handling of the case sealed Wilde's fate. At Wilde's second trial, Lockwood was especially dismissive of Clarke's efforts to portray the blackmail scheme as the case's most serious issue, with Lockwood asserting: "[T]he genesis of the blackmailer is the man who has committed these acts of indecency with him, and the genesis of the man who commits these foul acts is the man who is willing to pay for their commission. Were it not for men who were willing to pay for the vice, there would be no blackmail."[214]

Prior to the jury giving its guilty verdict, the foreman of the jury had asked if a warrant for the arrest of Lord Alfred Douglas had ever been issued and whether, if jurors found Oscar Wilde guilty based upon his letters to Lord Alfred Douglas, it would affect the latter as well as the defendant before the court? No arrest warrant for Lord Alfred Douglas had ever been issued, the jury foreman was told, with the Solicitor-General's answer to the foreman's other question reported as follows: "His Lordship said he thought the receipt of these letters and the continued intimacy was as damaging to the reputation of the recipient as to the sender, but that had nothing to do with the present inquiry. The question was whether guilt was brought home to the man in the dock."[215] Solicitor-General Lockwood emphasized that if guilty, Lord Alfred Douglas would not be spared but that "[i]t might be there was no evidence against him" and that the only question before jurors was "whether the man in the dock had been guilty of immoral practices with certain persons, of whom Lord Alfred Douglas was not one."[216] The Marquis of Queensberry, whose own son, Bosie, was not a criminal defendant, attended Oscar Wilde's trial, with the Solicitor-General—in open court before the jury rendered its guilty verdict—having said that Oscar Wilde's answers to the charges "were not worthy of belief."[217]

After initiating his ill-fated private prosecution, Oscar Wilde had himself been criminally prosecuted (not once but twice) and was now at the mercy of the presiding judge—the same jurist who would sentence Wilde after his conviction for "committing acts of gross indecency with certain male persons." At the joint sentencing of Oscar Wilde and Alfred Taylor, Justice Wills pulled no punches and showed no mercy, referring to "the horrible crimes" of the two men. Justice Wills observed that Taylor "kept a kind of male brothel," and—in speaking to Oscar Wilde—said that "you, Wilde, have been the centre of a circle of extensive corruption among young men of the most hideous kind it is equally impossible to doubt." Wills' lead-in before his imposition of the sentences: "Oscar Wilde and Alfred Taylor, it has never been my lot to try a case of this kind before which has been so bad. One has to put a stern constraint upon oneself to prevent oneself from describing in language I ought not to use the sentiments which must arise in the breast of every man who has a spark of decent feeling in him, and who has heard the details of these two terrible trials." After stating, "That the jury have arrived at a correct verdict I cannot persuade myself to entertain the shadow of a doubt," Justice Wills observed of Taylor and Wilde: "People who can do these things must be deaf to every sense of decency which can influence conduct." "I shall, under the circumstances, be expected to pass the severest sentence that the law allows," he intoned, adding sternly: "In my judgment, it is utterly inadequate for such cases. The sentence upon each of you is imprisonment with hard labour for two years."[218] There were shouts of "Shame" in the courtroom, and *The Yorkshire Herald* observed: "The pronouncement of the sentence was followed by hisses in the gallery, which the ushers failed to suppress." Upon hearing the sentence, that newspaper reported, Wilde "seemed quite dazed, stood with fixed gaze and trembling hands, and looked as if about to faint." "Two warders were quickly at his side, but Wilde held up his hands as if to keep them off, and addressed the Court in a few unintelligible words," the paper further observed.[219]

After the two men's sentences were imposed, they were taken to cells in Newgate Prison, adjoining the Central Criminal Court, pending the preparation of legal warrants authorizing their detention for two years. Wilde was imprisoned in the Pentonville Prison, where he was transported via the same "prison van" as Taylor, and then at the Wandsworth Prison in London. Upon their arrival at the Pentonville Prison, both men had to exchange their regular clothes for prison garb and were—according to the terms of their sentences—to be isolated from their friends except for four occasions each year.[220] Wilde, like Taylor, was forced to do hard labor while subsisting on a meager diet,[221] and his health quickly declined, with Wilde growing thinner and more melancholy.[222] Wilde ruptured an ear drum in a fall, and he grew suicidal in the confines of prison life. Shortly after his arrest, Wilde had written to his lover, Lord Alfred Douglas, "Your love has broad wings and is strong, your love comes to me through my prison bars and … is the light of all my hours." "In prison," Wilde had written Bosie, "I am going to test the power of love." But Wilde grew increasingly dispirited by his plight.[223] "I am here for having tried to put your father in prison," Wilde lamented from his prison cell to Lord Alfred Douglas.[224] In November 1895, in the context of his bankruptcy proceeding, Wilde was brought from prison to be questioned about his assets and liabilities. "He looked dreadfully pale and worn and ill," one London newspaper observed, noting that Wilde's "face has shrunk and the skin hangs down from his cheek-bones, making ugly wrinkles on either side of his nose." His hair, it was noted, had been cut "in a shocking way," with Wilde said to have "a short, scrubby, unkempt beard."[225]

Oscar Wilde was later moved to Reading Gaol, the locale where he spent the last eighteen months of his sentence. The private prosecution Wilde had commenced had, in the Victorian society in which he lived, boomeranged back at him, ruining his life irretrievably. "At the time of his arrest in April 1895, two of his plays, *An Ideal Husband* and *The Importance of Being Earnest*, had been running to packed houses in London's West End," notes historian Nicolas Frankel in his book about Wilde's later years. "He was then at the top of his game and one of the most celebrated writers in the English-speaking world," Frankel explains, observing that prior to his arrest Wilde's plays alone had earned him approximately £10,000, equivalent to roughly £1 million today. But during his imprisonment, bailiffs had sold off his possessions; his wife, Constance, had separated from him after visiting him just twice, including one compassionate visit in February 1896 to let Wilde know of his mother's death; and Wilde decided to abandon his lover and was stripped of any right to see his children. Six months before his release, Wilde wrote that he had "lost wife, children, fame, honour, position" and "wealth," and in a letter written to a friend weeks before his release, he resolved to never have anything to do with Lord Alfred Douglas, whom Wilde called "ill-omened" and "so fatal to me and to my house." After his eventual release from prison in 1897, Wilde—in ill health—took on a new name, Sebastian Melmoth, to disguise his identity, and he traveled to France, where he died in late 1900 at the age of 46 at the Hotel d'Alsace in Paris.[226] Before his death, Wilde—in a period of self-loathing, clearly brought on by his bout of imprisonment—called his love for men a "monstruous sexual perversion" and "the most horrible form of erotomania" and reflected on his legal battles with the irascible Marquis of Queensberry and what had happened to him in the English courts: "Certainly no man ever fell so ignobly, and by such ignoble instruments, as I did. I say, in *Dorian Gray* somewhere, that 'a man cannot be too careful in the choice of his enemies'. I little thought that it was by a pariah that I was to be made a pariah myself."[227]

The Development of Modern Public Prosecution Practices in the United Kingdom

By the early twentieth century, precious little had changed in the way English prosecutions were generally conducted. As *The Government of England*, written by A. Lawrence Lowell, the president of Harvard University, put it in 1914: "The Director of Public Prosecutions makes to Parliament an annual report of his doings, enlivened by narratives of the most interesting cases. But in spite of his activity the vast bulk of the prosecutions are conducted as of old under private direction; for out of the many thousands of criminal cases tried every year, only from three hundred and fifty to five hundred are in his charge, and the number shows no marked tendency to increase."[228] It was not until 1985, in fact, that the duties of the Director of Public Prosecutions were fully delineated and set forth in the Prosecution of Offences Act, which created the now well-known Crown Prosecution Service.[229] Whereas private prosecutions had, in England, been seen as an "historical right" dating back to "the earliest days" of the English legal system, in parliamentary debate in the 1980s it was emphasized that "the need for prosecutions to be undertaken (and paid for) by private individuals has largely disappeared." "The right of private prosecution is an important element in the rule of law," Lord Simon offered in November 1984 as part of the debate, though research conducted for the Royal Commission on Criminal Procedure in 1980 found that only 2.4 percent of all non-police prosecutions were by private individuals.[230]

The main function of the Director of Public Prosecutions is, at this juncture, to head the Crown Prosecution Service.[231] According to the Prosecution of Offences Act, the Director of Public Prosecutions "shall be appointed by the Attorney General," with the Director to receive "such remuneration as the Attorney General may, with the approval of the Treasury, determine."[232] The Crown Prosecution Service, which is independent of the police, is now responsible for prosecuting most criminal cases in England and Wales. After the police or other government agencies investigate a case, it is referred to the Crown Prosecution Service to determine whether a criminal case should be brought. In that regard, the Crown Prosecution Service has tremendous discretion in deciding what cases to actually prosecute, though its lawyers must be fair and objective and follow the Code for Crown Prosecutors. For the Crown Prosecution Service to bring a prosecution there must—in its eyes—be a "realistic prospect of conviction."[233]

Today, British citizens maintain the right to institute private prosecutions.[234] As the Supreme Court of New Jersey put it of modern English practices in 1995: "Although uncommon in England today, private prosecution survives."[235] But in the era of the Crown Prosecution Service, the English right to bring a private prosecution is infrequently exercised by individuals[236]—and there are now various limitations to its exercise set forth by law.[237] In a modern English law firm's "Guide to Private Prosecution Procedure in England and Wales," it notes that "[a] member of the public can bring a private prosecution for any offence, unless the offence is one for which the consent of the Attorney General (AG) or the Director of Public Prosecutions (DPP) is required before a prosecution can take place." A private prosecution, that guide notes, "is commenced by laying an 'information' at, followed by the issue of a warrant by, a magistrate's court." This must be done in writing, and the written information must describe the offense in ordinary language, identify the legislation that makes the conduct an offence, and make clear the private prosecutor's allegations. In deciding whether to issue a warrant, the magistrate or the magistrate's clerk must ensure that an offense known to law has been alleged in a timely fashion and that the court has jurisdiction over it. In addition, the Attorney General or the Director of Public Prosecutions is always free to take over the conduct of the private prosecution at any stage of it and to discontinue that prosecution as may be appropriate.[238]

In their book about the English legal system, *Policing and Criminal Justice* (2010), Christopher Blake, Barrie Sheldon and Peter Williams summarize the material transformation from eighteenth-century England to the way English cases are prosecuted now. "If we look back some 300 years," they write, "the state would generally prosecute the more serious offences, such as treason." "Then," they explain, "minor criminality was accepted as part of everyday life and cases would be dealt with mainly through private prosecutions, and sometimes through community associations on payment of a fee." At that time, constables were unpaid and played only a minor role in law enforcement, and any victim of crime who wanted a constable to undertake activity on his or her behalf was expected to pay the expenses of doing so.[239] "While this enabled people to have their cases heard," they aptly observe, "it was usually the wealthy who benefited." In the eighteenth century, they note, the practice of "thief taking" became an accepted method of apprehending criminals and bringing them to justice. The use of bounty hunters and monetary rewards offered by the state for informers to identify criminals also led to many false accusations and instances of perjury,[240] with corruption in the criminal justice system becoming rampant at various points in the past.

For example, in the process of seeking to return stolen property for a fee, "thief-takers" frequently blackmailed felony suspects instead of bringing them to trial. As Blake, Sheldon and Williams observe: "This was largely because of the cost of bringing a prosecution and the risk of acquittal or conviction on a lesser charge for which no reward was offered." The testimony of one notorious thief-taker, Jonathan Wild, reportedly sent more than 60 thieves to the gallows, although, ironically, Wild himself was executed in 1725 after running a successful gang of thieves. "It was during the early part of the nineteenth century," Blake, Sheldon and Williams explain, "that the balance in bringing prosecutions shifted markedly towards the state, particularly after the emergence of the New Police in 1829." "The police," they explain, "gradually assumed responsibility for prosecution, but it wasn't until the enactment of the County and Borough Police Act 1856 that they were permitted to act formally as a prosecuting authority." "Before this," the authors stress, "most criminal cases were private prosecutions that didn't involve professional lawyers."

In their book, Christopher Blake, Barrie Sheldon and Peter Williams write that, with the creation of the Director of Public Prosecutions ("DPP"), "by the latter part of the nineteenth century, most cases were being prosecuted by a police prosecutor." In their timeline of key events, they highlight a few specific time periods of considerable interest for understanding the complex history. "After 1908," they first note, "although the most serious cases in England were being referred to the DPP, most charges continued to be investigated and prosecuted by police officers." "By 1981," they then observe, "a number of different provisions" had been developed for criminal prosecutions, with "three broad approaches" put to use for all "non-serious cases." As Blake, Sheldon and Williams, summarizing the practices that developed over time, emphasize of those three basic approaches: "In some areas a local authority prosecuting solicitor's department would prosecute all cases, while others retained one or more firms of private solicitors. The Metropolitan Police Service had its own solicitor's branch. However, the decision to prosecute, or to continue with a prosecution, ultimately remained with the Chief Constable." "Until 1986," they next offer, pointing out that each of 43 police services in England and Wales were allowed to bring their own prosecutions, "England was one of only a few countries that allowed the police to prosecute rather than a state agency, such as the US District Attorney or the Scottish Procurator Fiscal." It was only after concerns were raised about inconsistent charging standards that England's Crown Prosecution Service came into existence. The Crown Prosecution Service, with its representatives guided by its Code for Crown Prosecutors, is now the prime actor in initial charging decisions.[241] The Code for Crown Prosecutors specifically provides that "[t]he independence of the prosecutor is central to the criminal justice system of a democratic society."[242]

The English journey toward a robust and independent public prosecution system—and away from the use of private prosecutions—took centuries. Although by 1819 the antiquated *appeal of felony* procedure was no more, the English tradition of private prosecutions continued unabated—as the history shows—long after the abandonment of that peculiar criminal procedure mechanism. "In England," one early twentieth-century source reported, "it has been customary for all criminal prosecutions to be conducted by private citizens, except in rare cases of crimes directly affecting the sovereign, when the prosecution was conducted by the Attorney-General." As that source, *The New International Encyclopædia* (1916), emphasized, providing a snapshot of a time more than one hundred years ago: "In cases of private prosecution in England the person instituting the proceedings is usually required to give a bond conditioned upon his proceeding with the prosecution. He can be relieved from his obligation only by the court or on the entry of a *nolle prosequi* by the Attorney General. The prosecutor is required to bear all the costs of the prosecution, but the court will usually award him a sum sufficient to cover his necessary expenses."[243]

The Act of Parliament in 1879, designed to "more effectually" provide "for the prosecution of offenses in England," laudably brought into existence the Director of Public Prosecutions, who was duty-bound to institute and carry out prosecutions under the Attorney General's direction. But the initial authority of the Director of Public Prosecutions—as has been described—was "somewhat limited" and too vaguely defined. While private prosecutions in modern-day England are now very rare,[244] it took a very long time for England to move away from them and to get to where it is today—a prosecution system that promises that public prosecutors "must be fair and objective" and "must be even-handed in their approach to every case."[245] As *The New International Encyclopædia* pointed out in 1916, decades before the creation of the Crown Prosecution Service, "it is still true that under the English system there is no officer whose duty it is to prosecute for all crimes."[246] Only after much advocacy did English private prosecutors largely fall by the wayside and did the Crown Prosecution Service come into being, though there are still concerns in England about the continued, if somewhat limited, use of private prosecutions.

In an 2014 editorial titled "Justice for Sale," *The Independent* noted that "the use of private prosecutions in the British courts" had been increasing, even though it stressed that "most prosecutions are brought by the state." "In reality," that newspaper observed, "private prosecutions are mostly brought—and pretty much can only be brought—by companies and wealthy individuals, as they alone can bear the costs." With the Lord Chief Justice of England and Wales pointing out that private prosecutions were growing "at a time of retrenchment of state activity in many areas where the state had previously provided sufficient funds to enable state bodies to conduct such prosecutions," the newspaper worried aloud: "Ought it not to concern everyone if a small minority of the better-off can use their financial muscle to bypass this 'retrenchment', leaving the rest of us stuck in justice's slow lane?" "If a growing trend towards use of private prosecutions is indicative of a trend towards a privatised, two-tier justice system in general—which is what it seems—that should worry all of us, not just the Lord Chief Justice," the paper concluded.[247]

3

PRIVATE PROSECUTORS IN AMERICA

From Colonial Days to the Early Nineteenth Century

Private Prosecution in Colonial and Early America

Some American colonies moved toward public prosecutions in the early eighteenth century[1] and neither adopted nor fully embraced English common law practices respecting appeals of murder and other crimes.[2] But, not surprisingly, English settlers to the New World brought various aspects of the English common law and criminal procedures with them.[3] Private prosecutions were thus quite frequent on American soil in colonial times and before the onset of the Revolutionary War (1775–1783). For example, an analysis of records of the New Jersey Court of Oyer and Terminer from 1749 to 1762, written in cursive, found evidence of private prosecutions. Because there were no police departments in those days, Rutgers University law professor George Thomas III observes, "[l]aw enforcement was left principally in the hands of citizens," with community members acting as police "by means of the 'hue and cry' by which felons were caught 'red-handed.'" The grand jury, composed of freeholders, was the mechanism for commencing criminal charges to be heard by New Jersey's Court of Oyer and Terminer. In one case, that court convicted the defendant of larceny and ordered that restitution be made to the victim, a person referred to in the records as the "prosecutor."

There were colonial courts, and the Court of Oyer and Terminer functioned as New Jersey's court of general jurisdiction for serious criminal cases requiring an indictment or presentment for the Crown to proceed with the case. As Professor Thomas observes of the reference to the victim as the prosecutor: "That suggests what we know from other sources, such as treatises and commentaries, that while the king was represented in court by counsel, charges could be, and often were, laid by private citizens. Blackstone noted that indictments are 'preferred' to the grand jury 'in the name of the king,' but allowed at the suit of any private prosecutor."[4] As another scholar, Josephine Gittler, observes of colonial private prosecutions: "When the colonies were being settled in the seventeenth century, the English system of criminal prosecution was primarily a system of private prosecution, where the victim or interested individual had the right to bring and prosecute the case against a criminal offender." "Although it is difficult to generalize about colonial criminal prosecutions because of the differences between the colonies and the paucity of historical research," Gittler writes, "the system in most of the colonies resembled the English system of private prosecution."[5]

Private citizens in colonial America, in fact, regularly initiated the criminal process by bringing complaints before grand juries[6] and justices of the peace.[7] In short, localities relied largely on ordinary citizens to maintain peace and order.[8] If a crime victim sought the help of a sheriff, for instance, there was a fee to pay.[9] "Law enforcement in colonial America," two other scholars, Susan Gegan and Nicholas Rodriguez, emphasize, "was fashioned similarly to that of England."[10] "In colonial America, as '[i]n England,'" a federal district court wrote in 2014, "'victims prosecuted their own crimes *pro se*, without lawyers and at their own expense,' and 'American prosecutions remained private well into the nineteenth century.'"[11] "In colonial Pennsylvania," the Supreme Court of Pennsylvania has observed, "crimes were viewed 'as an offense against the individual victim[,]' and private prosecutions were the most common mode by which the criminal justice system functioned in the colonial era."[12] For example, the prosecution of sex crimes relied on the efforts of private prosecutors,[13] and when men were held in custody in Philadelphia in 1768 on the charge of murder committed on the high seas, the prospect of a private prosecutor coming forward was considered in advising English authorities.[14] "Proceeding on the basis that crime harms individuals," law professors Douglas Beloof and Paul Cassell write in the *Lewis & Clark Law Review*, summing up the now centuries-old history, "early American criminal prosecutions were (as in England) often brought by the victim—a private prosecutor—rather than by a government agency."[15]

In colonial times, law codes and the punishment of crime was often rooted in the text of the Bible or based on theological interpretations of it. Indeed, punishments in Puritan society were based almost entirely on religious beliefs and sought to suppress sin and immorality.[16] "[T]he law is like a halter to check the raging and otherwise limitlessly ranging lusts of the flesh," the religious leader John Calvin said, believing that the law imposes a "constrained and forced righteousness." "[R]eformers," John Witte and Thomas Arthur emphasize of perspectives from past centuries, looked to "natural or moral law—that compendium of moral rights and duties that transcend the positive laws of the state." "God, they believed," Witte and Arthur point out, "has written a moral law on the hearts of all persons, rewritten it in the pages of Scripture, and summarized it in the Ten Commandments." As Witte and Arthur specifically relay: "A long tradition of Anglo-American jurists and moralists, from the early seventeenth century onward, expounded and expanded the legal doctrine of the purposes of criminal law in an array of treatises, pamphlets, and sermons—in some instances, writing under the direct inspiration of Protestant theologians." In a 1687 sermon about an execution, Cotton Mather called the magistrate "a minister of God, a Revenger to execute wrath upon him that does Evil." Mather said "Private Reveng[e] is evil," but he preached that "publick Revenge on those that violate Laws of God, is good."[17] For centuries, in a criminal procedure practice that got replicated in the British Empire's far-flung colonies, English indictments—reflecting the close association of religion and punishment—recited that heinous crimes had been committed "by the instigation of the Devil."[18]

In colonial America, the basis of punishment was, written codes make clear, frequently grounded in biblical passages, with private citizens regularly initiating prosecutions. The 1641 Massachusetts criminal code, to give just one example of the law's intersection with religion, cited an array of Old Testament verses as the express authority for death sentences. In the Massachusetts Bay Colony, the following twelve prohibited acts—eleven of them based explicitly on Old Testament verses—were punishable by death under its 1641 legal code: (1) adultery, (2) bestiality, (3) blasphemy, (4) conspiracy and rebellion, (5) false witness in capital cases, (6) idolatry, (7) manslaughter, (8) man stealing, (9) murder, (10) poisoning, (11) sodomy, and (12) witchcraft. Capital punishment was, itself, overtly tied to the Bible and then-prevailing interpretations of Deuteronomy, Exodus, Genesis, or Leviticus, with Genesis 9:6—"Whoso sheddeth man's blood, by man shall his blood be shed"—being just one biblical verse regularly cited as justification for death sentences. "If any man after legal conviction shall have or worship any other god, but the lord god," the first capital offense in that code read, "he shall be put to death." Connecticut's 1642 colonial code also had twelve capital crimes, eleven of which were similarly rooted in scriptural passages.[19]

The religious basis of colonial laws has long been noted, with one scholar emphasizing that "[t]he court itself represented the government; individuals brought charges against lawbreakers."[20] In colonial Massachusetts, historian William Nelson writes, "[r]eligion 'was a way of life' for the early settlers of Massachusetts, and all of the Bay Colony's institutions reflected its religious values." The settlers equated crime with sin, he observes, recalling that they viewed the state "as the arm of God on earth." After reviewing extensive Massachusetts county records, Nelson identified 2,784 criminal prosecutions from 1760 to 1774, 38% of which charged individuals with sexual offenses (e.g., fornication) and 13% of which charged religious ones: blasphemy, the use of profanity, or failure to go to church. In those Massachusetts Bay Colony court records for that period, Nelson found that, in Middlesex County alone, there were 370 prosecutions, either in the Superior or General Sessions Courts, with 210 of that number for fornication, 27 for violations of the Sabbath, two for cohabitation, and one for adultery. In addition to those offenses, what the English jurist, Sir William Blackstone, categorized as offenses against God and religion, there were 32 larceny prosecutions and 15 prosecutions for burglary and breaking and entering in Middlesex County during that time. Of course, private prosecutions were then common, meaning that criminal cases—as Nelson asserts—"were in reality contests between subjects rather than contests between government and subject."[21]

In early America, the function of public prosecutors was not necessarily thought to be assigned exclusively to the executive branch. In a 2018 law review article, "George Washington's Attorneys: The Political Selection of United States Attorneys at the Founding," Scott Ingram writes that President Washington—the country's first leader—considered local U.S. Attorneys assigned to specific judicial districts to be "part of the judiciary.'"[22] The position of "attorney for the United States" was, in fact, created by the Judiciary Act of 1789. Section 35 of that law provided that—in addition to the position of "attorney-general for the United States"—"there shall be appointed in each district a meet person learned in the law to act as attorney for the United States in such district, who shall be sworn or affirmed to the faithful execution of his office, whose duty it shall be to prosecute in such district all delinquents for crimes and offences, cognizable under the authority of the United States...."[23] A "meet person" was not defined by the 1789 statute, though the term is thought to refer—based on other historical sources—to "a person who will act in the place of or in coordination with someone else."[24] Ingram points to these four pieces of evidence to demonstrate Washington's understanding of the U.S. Attorney role: (1) "traditional state practice made district attorneys judicial figures"; (2) by the inclusion of U.S. Attorneys in the Judiciary Act of 1789, Congress indicated its implicit concurrence; (3) Washington penned correspondence to Edmund Randolph, the first Attorney General of the United States, in September 1789 in which he spoke of "the due administration of justice" and the "arrangement of the judicial department as essential to the happiness of our country"; and (4) Washington included the U.S. Attorneys in the same appointment message as federal judges.[25]

In his law review article, Scott Ingram emphasizes that "[i]n the years preceding Washington's first United States Attorney appointments, prosecutors began shifting from purely private attorneys to government-appointed, sometimes by the local judiciary." "Criminal prosecution had been largely a private pursuit," he observes, adding that "[c]rime victims pursued offenders through the courts, pleading their own cases in minor matters and securing the services of attorneys in serious matters." Because many of the "moral offences" laid down in colonial times and early America "often only had society as victim" with no individualized "identifiable victim," Ingram writes, "some states hired local attorneys" to prosecute such offenses while, in others, the state's attorney general took up that role. "While state practice served as the model for the Judiciary Act and Congress identified the new United States Attorneys as judicial officers," Ingram recounts, "Congress debated who would appoint these attorneys." As Ingram describes and summarizes the hotly contested congressional debate: "Initial drafts granted the Supreme Court appointment power. Later, Congress changed the provision, giving it to the President with the Senate's advice and consent. While this might indicate a desire to make the District Attorneys executive officials, the judges were subject to the same process." Of President George Washington and late eighteenth-century legal practice, Ingram points out: "When Washington nominated United States Attorneys, he did so at the same time as judicial appointments.

For each judicial district, Washington nominated a judge, an attorney, and a marshal, all of whom served the court." At that time, when private prosecutions were still in widespread use at the state level,[26] a U.S. Attorney's job was a part-time position and U.S. Attorneys received a fee for each case they brought.[27]

Another legal scholar, Stephanie A.J. Dangel, assembling her own items of evidence, also writes that "[t]he history of colonial prosecution exhibits four characteristics in conflict with the assertion that prosecution is a core executive, or presidential, function." In her law review article, she points to these four characteristics from colonial times, even before the passage of the Judiciary Act of 1789: (1) "private individuals, not government officials," conducted the bulk of prosecutions; (2) "the primary work of attorneys general and district attorneys consisted of non-prosecutorial duties, with their prosecutorial discretion limited to ending, rather than initiating or conducting, prosecutions"; (3) "public prosecution was locally based, not centrally controlled"; and (4) "colonial and state constitutions did not classify prosecution as the exclusive province of any one branch." After noting the prevalence of private prosecution in the English common law system of the seventeenth and eighteenth centuries, one in which the aggrieved victim or interested party or family member initiated the prosecution, Dangel writes in the *Yale Law Journal* of the way in which the system functioned: "After investigation and approval by a justice of the peace and grand jury, a private individual would conduct the prosecution, sometimes with assistance of counsel."[28]

Noting historical records "confirm the relative insignificance of public prosecutors in the colonial criminal systems," Stephanie Dangel makes this telling observation of early American state constitutions: "Only five of the first thirteen constitutions mention a state attorney general, and only Connecticut mentions the local prosecutor." Because of the acknowledged prevalence of private prosecution assisted by local officials in various locales, "it is not surprising to discover," she writes, "that most state constitutions at the time of the Framing did not mention, let alone classify, the prosecutorial function." Indeed, Dangel explains: "Only the Connecticut and New York constitutions mentioned public prosecutors, both states providing for judicial appointment. Later state constitutions further distinguished prosecuting attorneys from officials with quintessentially executive duties, sometimes relegating prosecuting attorneys to a subsection of articles establishing the structure and officers of state courts." Five state constitutions—those of Georgia, Maryland, Massachusetts, New Jersey and Virginia—explicitly put the office of attorney general under the judicial article. Dangel further emphasizes that "the earliest judicial decision voicing disapproval of private prosecution" didn't actually appear until 1849 in a Massachusetts case, *Commonwealth v. Williams*, and that "[n]o decision affirming public prosecutors' virtually unreviewable discretion appeared before 1883," when an Illinois case, *People v. Wabash*, was handed down in that state.[29]

In today's America, prosecutors are typically seen as serving an executive branch function. "Prosecutors are members of the Executive Branch," the Superior Court of

Connecticut observed in 2015, adding: "The Court, of course, is the Judicial Branch. So despite the belief of a great many defendants, judges, in the form of courts, cannot tell prosecutors what they can charge."[30] "[T]he decision whether to prosecute a defendant rests with the executive branch, not the judicial branch," a Massachusetts court observed almost ten years earlier.[31] "Under the United States Constitution," it has been written, "it is the Executive Branch of the federal government, and not the Judicial Branch, that is responsible for conducting criminal investigations, and bringing criminal charges, if warranted."[32] In *State v. Matthews* (2019), the Court of Appeals of Wisconsin similarly ruled: "As part of the executive branch of the government, district attorneys 'have primary responsibility and wide discretion' in charging criminal offenses without judicial interference. The district attorney does not answer directly to any other state officer regarding charging decisions; he or she is ultimately answerable to the electorate."[33] And in *Brosky v. Miller* (2015), a U.S. District Court judge in the Western District of Pennsylvania—quoting the U.S. Supreme Court's decision in *Wayte v. United States* (1985)—put it this way: "It is well established that decisions regarding the filing of criminal charges are the prerogative of the executive branch of government, are consigned to the sound discretion of prosecutors, and under the separation of powers doctrine are not subject to judicial fiat. Indeed, it has long been recognized that the exercise of prosecutorial discretion is a matter, 'particularly ill-suited to judicial review.'"[34]

In their popular treatise on modern criminal procedure, Wayne LaFave, Jerold Israel, Nancy King and Orin Kerr observe that while America's republic was formed in 1776, the colonial period shaped the country's early customs, with some locales departing from English practices, including as to how prosecutions were conducted. "In the seventeenth century," they write, "colonial courts were given considerable room to depart from the usual processes of the English common law, but as the colonies matured, and the influence of lawyers grew, the English law was more faithfully followed." "The colonies," they note of the history, "retained a right of private prosecution, but superimposed a governmental official, the local prosecutor, who was to bear primary responsibility for the prosecution of serious offenses in the interests of the public." Although Scotland's system of criminal justice, those four legal scholars emphasize, had "expanded substantially the role of the public prosecutors," local county prosecutors' offices were "basically an American invention" supplementing, but not dislodging, private prosecutors. As they write in their treatise: "The colonial county prosecutor did not displace private initiative in the bringing of the prosecution. Private parties still bore the primary responsibility for investigation, and prosecutions were still initiated by the private citizens presenting a complaint before the magistrate." "It was only after the magistrate had issued a warrant and sent the case forward to the grand jury, and in some places, after the grand jury had issued an indictment," they add, "that the county prosecutor ordinarily took charge of the prosecution."[35] In fact, in some locales, the grand jury foreman was required to endorse the name of the private prosecutor on the indictment itself.[36]

Members of the U.S. Supreme Court have, over time, documented the English common-law origins of early American private prosecutions. "[T]he 18th century criminal prosecution at the common law," Justice William O. Douglas observed in a concurrence in *United States v. Marion* (1971), "was, in general, commenced in a completely different way from that with which we are familiar today." As Justice Douglas wrote: "By the common law of England which was brought to the American colonies, the ordinary criminal prosecution was conducted by a private prosecutor, in the name of the King. In case the victim of the crime or someone interested came forward to prosecute, he retained his own counsel and had charge of the case as in the usual civil proceeding." In that concurrence, joined by Justices William Brennan and Thurgood Marshall, Douglas explained: "Procedurally, the criminal prosecution was commenced by the filing of a lawsuit, and thereafter the filing of an application for criminal prosecution or rule nisi or similar procedure calling for the defendant to show cause why he should not be imprisoned." As the concurrence of Justice Douglas in *United States v. Marion* continued: "The English common law, with which the Framers were familiar, conceived of a criminal prosecution as being commenced prior to indictment. Thus, in that setting, the individual charged as the defendant in a criminal proceeding could and would be an 'accused' prior to formal indictment."[37]

Early American lawyers carefully studied English history, frequently making notes in their commonplace books, and the tradition of English private prosecutions was certainly not lost on American lawmakers and jurists. In his law lectures, Pennsylvania attorney James Wilson—a signer of the Declaration of Independence and the U.S. Constitution who became an Associate Justice of the U.S. Supreme Court—specifically addressed "the different steps which the law prescribes for apprehending, detaining, trying and punishing criminals." A warrant for someone's apprehension, Wilson said, "may be directed to the sheriff, constable, or to a private person; for the warrant constitutes him, for this purpose, an authorized officer." "All, of age, who are present when a felony is committed, or when a dangerous wound is given, are, on pain of fine and imprisonment," Wilson added, "bound to apprehend the person who has done the mischief." "If the crime has been committed out of their view," he noted, citing English legal commentators, "they are, upon a hue and cry, obliged to pursue with the utmost diligence, and endeavor to apprehend him who has committed it." "Hue and cry," he observed, "is the pursuit of an offender from place to place, till he is taken: all who are present when he commits the crime, are bound to raise it against him on his flying for it." "It is a general rule," Wilson asserted, "that, at any time, and in any place, every private person is justified in arresting a traitor or a felon; and, if a treason or a felony has been committed, he is justified in arresting even an innocent person, upon his reasonable suspicion that by such person it has been committed."[38]

In his law lectures, James Wilson also addressed "the next step"—the instituting of a criminal prosecution—after "the party is taken, and bailed or imprisoned." "This may be done," Wilson advised, "by four different methods—by appeal; by information; by presentment; by indictment." As for the first method, *appeal*, Wilson observed:

"An appeal is an accusation by one private person against another for some crime: it is a private action of the party injured, demanding punishment for the injury which he has suffered: it is also a prosecution for the state, on account of the crime committed against the public." Wilson explained that, in ancient times, "there were appeals for a breach of the peace, for a battery, and for false imprisonment, as well as for more aggravated injuries and crimes," but he added of appeals that "they have been out of use, and converted into actions of trespass, for many hundred years." In discussing the concept of appeals, Wilson added: "An appeal lies for mayhem, for larceny, for arson, for rape, for death. It is brought by the party ravished, robbed, maimed, or whose house was burned; or by the wife, or, if no wife, by the heir, of the person killed." "An appeal," Wilson advised, saying the procedural mechanism could be traced to Germany's ancient forests, "may be brought previous to an indictment; and if the defendant be acquitted, he cannot afterwards be indicted for the same crime: if he is found guilty, he shall suffer the same punishment as if he had been convicted on a prosecution by an indictment."[39]

Across the Atlantic from England, America's mother country, one actually finds reference to the criminal-law procedure of *appeal of murder* in a 1788 New York statute,[40] along with scattered references in American case law to *appeal of murder* and *appeal of felony*.[41] An appeal "[i]n criminal practice," one law dictionary containing terms and phrases from American and English jurisprudence emphasized, constituted "[a] formal accusation made by one private person against another of having committed some heinous crime."[42] Colonial New York's criminal justice system, it has been said, "was a mixed one of public and private prosecutions, depending on the location of the prosecution,"[43] with private prosecutors appearing in New York before and after the American Revolution.[44] In New York City, "private prosecutions made up much of the docket into the latter nineteenth century, well after establishment of the district attorney's office," notes scholar Darryl Brown, who points out that "[l]awyers for private prosecutors sometimes appeared alongside a public prosecutor or even in place of him, in which case they were compensated by the court."[45]

In *Hurtado v. People of State of California* (1884), the U.S. Supreme Court itself noted that, under English law, "appeals of murder, which were prosecutions by private persons, were never regarded as contrary to *Magna Charta*." "On the contrary," the Supreme Court stated in *Hurtado*, "the appeal of death was by Lord Holt 'esteemed a noble remedy, and a badge of the rights and liberties of an Englishmen.'" And the appeal of murder procedure was not seen as conflicting with the prohibition against double jeopardy—a prohibition that found its way into the U.S. Bill of Rights in the Fifth Amendment. "We are told that in the early part of the last century, in England," the Court in *Hurtado* stressed, "persons who had been acquitted on indictments for murder were often tried, convicted, and executed on appeals." "The English statutes concerning appeals of murder were in force in the provinces of Pennsylvania and Maryland," the Court added, observing that "no such appeal was ever brought in

Pennsylvania" but that "in Maryland, in 1765, a negro was convicted and executed upon such an appeal."[46]

That Maryland case makes clear that American colonists—at least by the time Parliament passed the Stamp Act (1765)—had not completely jettisoned the appeal of murder mechanism despite the infrequency of its use. In *Soaper v. Negro Tom* (1765), the Provincial Court for the Proprietary Province of Maryland thus explicitly sat in judgment in "an appeal of murder" case. In that instance, the sheriff of Frederick County gave a command—written in the prevailing legalese of the time—"that if *Sarah Soaper,* widow, who was the wife of *Thomas Soaper,* should make him secure of prosecuting her clamour, then he should attach *Negro Tom,* (the slave of *John Gantt,*) late of *Frederick* County, labourer, by his body, so that he might have him before the Justices of his Lordship's Provincial Court, to be held at the City of *Annapolis,* on the second *Tuesday* of *September* then next, to answer unto the aforesaid *Sarah,* for the death of the aforesaid *Thomas Soaper,* formerly her husband, wherewith she appealed him; and that he should have then and there that writ, &c." An attorney, Edmund Key, appeared for Sarah Soaper in the proceedings, and two individuals—"*John Cooke,* Esquire, and Major *Joseph Sim,*" of Prince George's County—are listed as "Pledges for prosecuting" in the sheriff's return of the writ to the court.[47] A declaration against Tom, the enslaved man, read in part: "*Maryland,* to wit: *Negro Tom,* late of *Frederick* County, labourer, formerly the slave of *John Gantt,* of *Prince George's* County, gentleman, but now the slave of *Samuel Swearingen,* of *Frederick* County, inn-holder, was attached by his body to answer unto *Sarah Soaper,* widow, who was the wife of *Thomas Soaper,* of the death of the aforesaid *Thomas Soaper,* formerly her husband, whereof she appeals him, the said *Negro Tom*...."

The enslaved man known only to history as Tom was, in fact, a tragic victim of double jeopardy, though the accusations against him by Sarah Soaper were in no way inconsistent with the then-prevailing Anglo-American legal practice of that time. In November 1764, a grand jury of fifteen men, acting on information provided by John Cooke, John Gantt, and Zachariah Evans, had indicted Tom, the enslaved man, for murdering Thomas Soaper. That same month, however, a petit jury of twelve men, after hearing the evidence, acquitted Tom of the capital charge. Tom stood accused of "feloniously" stabbing Thomas Soaper with "Malice aforethought" and "with premeditated Designs against the Peace of the said Lord Proprietary." Although Tom was found not guilty of stabbing Thomas Soaper with a knife worth one shilling sterling, Maryland law then allowed Sarah Soaper to bring a private prosecution: a post-acquittal appeal of murder. As one source describes it, "[t]he provincial court's permitting her to bring her appeal," thereby placing Tom in double jeopardy, "was in no way contrary to English law or to English practice."[48] A second jury of twelve men, contradicting the first jury's verdict, found that Tom had "feloniously Voluntarily and of his Malice aforethought killed and Murdered" Thomas Soaper in the manner charged by Thomas Soaper's widow, Sarah.[49]

The accusations in the appeal of murder brought by Sarah Soaper would lead to the execution of the man referred to in the court's caption only as "Negro Tom." The formal accusations in the case, again in legalese and reflecting the colonial use of private prosecutions, reads as follows: "[W]hereupon the said *Sarah,* by *Edmund Key,* her attorney, according to the form of the statute in such cases made and provided, within one year appeals[50] the aforesaid *Negro Tom* of this, that the aforesaid *Thomas Soaper,* being in the peace of God, and the Right Honourable the Lord Proprietary that now is, at the parish of *Queen Anne's* in *Prince George's* County, on the, &c. (as in an indictment for murder,) and if the aforesaid *Negro Tom,* the felony and murder aforesaid, upon him, the said *Negro Tom* in form aforesaid, imposed, will deny, she, the said *Sarah Soaper,* is here ready to prove the same, as the Court shall order and direct." "[T]he aforesaid *Negro Tom* being called," it was indicated of the man put on trial for murder in response to Sarah Soaper's accusation, pleaded "he is not in any wise guilty thereof." With the jury of twelve men ultimately concluding "on their oath that the said *Negro Tom* is guilty of the premises in the same declaration contained, in manner and form as said *S. S.* therein hath declared," Tom was committed to the custody of the sheriff of Anne Arundel County. Sarah Soaper thereafter appeared in person at the court asking for "judgment against the said *Negro Tom* on the verdict aforesaid" and "that he may be hanged by the neck on the 2d day of *November* next, until he, the said *Negro Tom,* is dead."

The Provincial Court's final judgment—sealing Tom's fate—consisted of four terse sentences: "[I]t is considered by the Court here, that the said *Negro Tom* be, for the offence aforesaid, hanged by the neck until he is dead, and that the execution of the said *Negro Tom* be on the 2d day of *November* next. And thereupon the said *Negro Tom* is committed to the custody of the sheriff of *Anne Arundel* County, to be re-delivered to the sheriff of *Prince George's* County. The sheriff of *A. A.* County being present, takes charge of him accordingly. In case the public should pay for the said *Negro Tom,* the Court value him at 53*l.* 6*s.* 8*d.* *Maryland* currency."[51] In other words, the condemned and enslaved man, Tom, was valued by the court at the precise but mere sum of fifty-three pounds, six shillings and eight pence.[52] Scores of enslaved persons were executed in colonial and early America, with methods of executions including breaking on a wheel, burning, gibbeting and hanging.[53] And southern legal codes—as one sources notes—"even compensated white slaveholders for the 'taking' of executed slaves," with public executions taking place in many locales.[54] In eighteenth-century South Carolina, the "cruel punishment" of enslaved persons could result in fines, though slaveholders were expressly permitted to exercise a number of corporal punishments. As a 1740 act in that state provided in bone-chilling language: "[I]n case any person or persons shall willfully cut out the tongue, put out the eye, castrate, or cruelly scald, burn, or deprive any slave of any limb, or member, or shall inflict any other cruel punishment, other than by whipping, or beating with a horse-whip, cow-skin, switch, or small stick, or by putting irons on, or confining, or imprisoning such slave; every such person shall, for each such offence, forfeit the sum of one hundred pounds, current money."[55]

Of "Appeals," Ducking and Duels, and Private Prosecutions

By and large, Americans inherited the English system of crime and punishment, as well as English modes of criminal procedure. To understand the origins of America's criminal justice system, one must thus understand English practice. In *Crime, Policing and Punishment in England, 1660–1914* (2016), historian Drew Gray notes that there are "three broad themes" worthy of note. "First," Gray writes, "many of the punishments that were in use at the start of our time period would have been familiar to inhabitants of late medieval and Tudor England: hanging, the pillory, whipping, the stocks, ducking and imprisonment were all used to discipline or punishment offenders." "Likewise," he explains, "many of the offences that were prosecuted from the late 1600s onwards had been prosecuted in previous centuries: murder, highway robbery, burglary, coining and several other forms of property crime all brought miscreants to court and to the gallows." "Third," he observes, "the nature of prosecution was victim led, and the players involved in the merry-go-round of criminal justice were, for the most part, ordinary citizens and not paid professionals." "In English towns and villages," Gray explains of the latter theme, "the onus was on individuals to catch and prosecute criminals and this meant that reactions to crime could be sporadic at best, especially in less populated areas." "This participatory system of prosecution," he discerns, "developed from the medieval period; it allowed individuals (at least for those men of some means) to confront those that had 'wronged,' and the law gave them an arena in which to settle their differences."[56]

Appeals, though by then rare, were still considered an option for victims around the time of the American Revolution. For example, in 1770, the notion of an appeal came up in the aftermath of the Boston Massacre in a letter written by Captain Thomas Preston of the 29th Regiment of Foot. Captain Preston was part of the British garrison in Boston, Massachusetts, and he was present when British troops, on the snowy evening of March 5, 1770, opened fire on American colonists who were throwing rocks, ice, and snowballs at Boston's Custom House on King Street. At that time, more than 2,000 British soldiers were occupying the City of Boston to help enforce English tax laws, and what began as a dispute between one British soldier, Private Hugh White, and angry colonists, soon escalated into what became known as the Boston Massacre after Captain Preston arrived at the scene with other British soldiers to defend the Custom House. After British soldiers opened fire, five colonists, including a dockworker, Crispus Attucks, were killed, and six others wounded. After Captain Preston and other soldiers were arrested, Captain Preston—ultimately represented by John Adams, the future President of the United States—was put on trial, as were others, after the appointment of prosecuting attorneys and the retention of defense attorneys.

Although the indictment was prepared by Jonathan Sewall, the King's attorney general, he left the city in the wake of the Boston Massacre and the court appointed a British sympathizer, Samuel Quincy, as a kind of special prosecutor. One diary entry from that time notes: "The People of the Province are at a loss to know what is become of the person reputed the King's Attorney, he not having been visible at the Superior Court now sitting in Boston for a considerable time past."[57] Samuel Adams and other Sons of Liberty, however, lacked faith in Samuel Quincy, the Tory and British sympathizer who had been admitted to the Suffolk bar on the same day as John Adams,[58] to vigorously pursue the murder case—one that had so inflamed Boston residents. Accordingly, on March 13th, it was resolved by local city leaders that "the Selectmen be desired to employ one or more Council to offer to the Kings Attorney as Assistance to him in the trial of the Murtherers now committed; and in case the Kings Attorney should refuse such Assistance, and the Relatives of those Persons who were murthered should apply for it, that then the Town will bear the Expence that may accrue thereby."[59]

Even before that vote, efforts had been made to secure the services of Robert Treat Paine, an experienced, Harvard-educated lawyer,[60] to assist in the prosecution of the British soldiers, including Captain Preston. William Molineux, a Bostonian merchant active in the Sons of Liberty,[61] thus wrote to Paine on March 9th to relay that "Yesterday in the Forenoon the Select Men met in Order to Consider what was Necessary to be done Relative to proper Council to be Appointed to Appear in behalf of the Relatives of the Deceased, the first was Murder'd by Richardson and Afterwards others per Capt. Preston and his Soldiers."[62] On February 22nd, before the Boston Massacre, Ebenezer Richardson—a British informer—had tried to take down a protest sign posted by members of the Sons of Liberty and got into a tussle with a group of boys, whereupon he retreated into his own house, eventually firing into the crowd of boys with a musket and wounding 11-year-old Christopher Seider. Seider died later that night, leading to a murder charge against Richardson.[63] In his March 9th letter to Robert Treat Paine, Molineux—seeking to recruit Paine to act as prosecutor—sent him 80 affidavits to read so he could "be fully Posses'd of Substance and fact." Molineux's letter also contained this nugget: "By a Vote of the Town You'l Observe they are to Pay the Expence of Prosecution, of Consequence You will be by them Amply Satisfyed. It is the Opinion of the Select Men, & also those that are Suppos'd to be better Acquainted in Law Matters, that it will not be in Character for the Town to Appear against the Criminals, but the Relatives of the Deceased, by whome & in whose Name You are the Gentleman pitched Upon in their behalf, & against the said Richardson & the Capt. & Soldiers."[64] Robert Treat Paine, later a signer of the Declaration of Independence, promptly agreed to take up the role of prosecutor and work alongside Samuel Quincy.[65]

The notion of an appeal came up after Captain Preston's dramatic trial, in which John Adams—in his opening statement, one said to have produced an "electrical effect" on courtroom observers—quoted the much-celebrated Italian aristocrat and

Enlightenment thinker Cesare Beccaria, whose book, *An Essay on Crimes and Punishments*, originally published in Italian in 1764, had called for the death penalty's abolition. "I am for the prisoners at the bar," Adams said in his initial courtroom remarks, "and shall apologize for it only in the words of the Marquis Beccaria: 'If by supporting the rights of mankind, and of invincible truth, I shall contribute to save from the agonies of death one unfortunate victim of tyranny, or ignorance, equally fatal, his blessings and tears of transport shall be sufficient consolation to me for the contempt of all mankind."[66] In a letter to Major General Thomas Gage, written from Boston on October 31, 1770, after Captain Preston had been acquitted by a jury's not guilty verdict, Preston wrote of those still angry about his role in the Boston Massacre: "They have endeavourd to lodge an Appeal against me, in behalf of one of the relations of the deceasd, but it won't lie, as there are not any near enough of kin now surviving, but their busy malice has found out another way to distress me, by sueing me for damages on acc^{t} of the wounded, & if taken wou'd involve me in endless lawsuits...."[67] At the time, the appeal of felony and appeal of murder procedures, though used very infrequently,[68] were thus still contemplated and in use, as well as spoken of by attorneys, in Anglo-American legal systems.[69] General Thomas Gage was the commander of British troops in North America and served as the Governor of the Massachusetts Bay Colony in 1774 and 1775 before the issuance of the Declaration of Independence (1776).[70]

Prominent American lawyers also mentioned the appeal of murder procedure in the course of their work. For example, in 1792, in delivering a grand jury charge in the District of Georgia in the Circuit Court of the United States, James Iredell—an Associate Justice of the U.S. Supreme Court—described the duties of grand jurors along with existing laws pertaining to crimes against the United States. In the course of his grand jury charge, Justice Iredell had this to say: "At Common Law there was no limitation of time for the prosecution of any offence. Limitations however have been prescribed in England by some acts of Parliament; but they extend only, I believe, to cases of treason and misprision of treason, with certain exceptions; to appeals for murder, which are in the nature of a private prosecution; and to informations for the breaches of penal statutes."[71] In colonial North Carolina, crime victims had long played a key role in criminal prosecutions, just as they long had in England. As historian Donna Spindel writes of North Carolina's justice system during the period from 1720 to 1740: "The prosecution of a crime depended first on victims or witnesses willing to describe their injury to a local justice of the peace. It is quite possible that many victims chose not to report an offense because they would be required to participate extensively in the process of bringing an offender to justice." After studying those two decades of the eighteenth century, Spindel concluded of those who controlled and were most likely to use the justice system: "The criminal court records clearly show that men of property administered and directed justice in colonial North Carolina."[72]

The *appeal of felony* concept—like the appeal of murder procedure Sarah Soaper used,[73] that Captain Preston alluded to, and that Justice Iredell referenced in his grand jury charge—was, despite the procedure's relatively atypical use, also a familiar one to other early American attorneys, lawmakers and jurists.[74] In 1795, for example, a bill was proposed in New York to abolish appeals of murder, rape, and other offenses, "the right to which"—as a Philadelphia newspaper put it—"must have been conceded to individuals, in compliance with ancient strong but barbarous prejudices."[75] The next year, in 1796, the New Jersey legislature not only abolished benefit of clergy, "corruption of blood," and capital punishment for most crimes, but it did away with the appeal of murder mechanism, with Vermont's *Rutland Herald* praising such developments as part of the "glorious work of reformation" in which the people "begin to learn that sanguinary punishments sprung from savage ignorance and revenge."[76] Section 77 of the New Jersey law, "An Act for the Punishment of Crimes," passed on March 18, 1796, read as follows: "That the suit or action of appeal for murder, manslaughter, rape, arson, larceny, mayhem, or other offence or wrong whatsoever, shall be, and the same hereby is abolished and for ever done away."[77]

Many decades later, in 1982, the Minnesota Supreme Court, in *Thompson v. Petroff's Estate*,[78] gave its own tutorial on the history of the *appeal of felony* practice. "At early common law no cause of action in tort in the modern sense existed," Chief Justice Douglas Amdahl wrote for a unanimous court, adding: "By the thirteenth century, a wrongdoer was dealt with by means of the appeal of felony."[79] As Chief Justice Amdahl explained: "At that time, a felony was a crime that could be prosecuted by an accusation in which the accuser was required to offer battle. The felon was likely to forfeit life or limb and his lands and goods would be confiscated by the king. No clear distinction was made, at least with respect to the punishment visited upon the wrongdoer, between civil and criminal actions."[80] "Because these early actions were intended more to punish the wrongdoer than to compensate the victim," Amdahl wrote of early English law, "the rule evolved that no one other than the wrongdoer should suffer for his misdeeds."[81] "According to some authorities," Amdahl's opinion added, "the appeal of felony eventually evolved into the writs of trespass."[82] Trespass has its roots in criminal law and procedure, and the appeal of felony procedure was only "slowly supplanted by indictment."[83] "The first trespassory writs (*vi et armis* from the late twelfth century)," one historian notes, "were intended to assist complainants to use existing remedies for wrong by securing on their behalf the appearance of their opponents in court."[84]

In *Crime and Punishment in American History*, the eminent historian Lawrence Friedman described the historical similarities between the English and early American common-law systems, though, to be sure, there were differences. "It took a two-step process to convict a criminal," Friedman observed of serious crimes such as murder and other felonies that, upon conviction, might bring death to an offender at the hands of the executioner. First, a person was indicted by a grand jury, an "ancient institution" that was "a panel of men drawn from the community who heard evidence about crimes." The grand jury, a body now consisting of 16 to 23 citizens,[85] had the responsibility to indict someone if the evidence supported it, with the grand jury returning a "true bill" (*billa vera*, in Latin) in such a circumstance. Only if the evidence was deemed insufficient would the grand jury return a "no bill," thus setting an accused and the detained individual free. Second, any indicted person would be tried before an ordinary or "petit jury." "One striking aspect of trial was the system of private prosecution," Friedman writes of England's common-law system, observing that "English law had no district attorney, no public prosecutor." As Friedman, using an illustrative example, explains: "If you were a shopkeeper, and you caught a thief robbing your store, it was *your* responsibility to bring him to justice. A constable might help you chase and catch the thief; but that was all. In any event, the money for the prosecution would have to come out of *your* pocket."[86] If the jury found for the defendant, the private prosecutor, in fact, could be expected to pay the defendant's costs.[87]

Each colony in America had its own system of justice tailored to the views of its early settlers, with Dutch settlers influencing New York's prosecutorial practices, Puritans shaping the Massachusetts Bay Colony, and Quakers molding the colony of Pennsylvania.[88] "The laws and legal customs in the colonies," Friedman writes, "were a mirror of what elites, magistrates, and leaders thought about the good, the true, and the right, about justice and order." "[C]ourt systems were bound to be simpler in the colonies than in the mother country," Friedman explains, noting that there were county courts in many colonies and "a single magistrate, the justice of the peace, who handled cases of petty crime in his locality." "Puritan justice had a strong *inquisitorial* flavor, at least in the seventeenth century," Friedman observes, noting the judges were religious and political leaders who "believed unswervingly in their right to rule in the name of God and according to the divine plan." As Friedman adds of the speedy colonial justice delivered after a criminal accusation was made: "The trial itself took place soon, quickly, and without jurymen or lawyers. Witnesses appeared and gave whatever evidence they had." "Colonial justice," he continues, "was a business of amateurs" who "dominated the system." Not only did lay magistrates decide most cases, he explains, but lay constables and watchmen, in places such as New York, were bound to detain anyone found to be "disturbing the peace" or "lurking about" any house or committing a theft. In the case of suspicious deaths, a coroner's jury, another ancient institution with English roots, would view a dead body to determine if the cause of death was murder, suicide, or accidental.[89]

Those historians who have closely studied colonial justice, such as Lawrence Friedman, take note of its "profoundly popular" or "democratic" character. For example, Friedman writes: "The thousands of pages of court records certainly breathe a popular flavor. Ordinary people *used* the courts, to get justice for themselves, vindication, restitution; and in criminal as well as civil matters." England's private prosecution system, Friedman editorializes, "seemed to suggest . . . a kind of indifference to the prosecution of criminals" because it left English subjects largely to their own devices. That system—as structured—"bent the administration of justice toward the interests of the rich and the powerful." Colonial trials, he recounts of the American experience, "were at first as lawyerless as trials in England," with Friedman writing that there were "very few trained lawyers in the colonies before the eighteenth century." Whereas attorneys were allowed to appear in felony cases, he writes, they could only assist with points of law, with one Virginia statute giving the accused the right to "counsel" in "all trials for capital offenses," if, in fact, such criminal defendants could afford to retain counsel in the first place.[90] "In Philadelphia, from colonial times through the middle of the nineteenth century," another scholar, Martin Alan Greenberg, writes, quoting the work of fellow historian Allen Steinberg, "private prosecution of crime—'one citizen taking another to court without the intervention of the police'—was the basis of law enforcement." This private prosecution system, Greenberg asserts, echoing Friedman, had "democratic and egalitarian aspects," though because its use required substantial resources, it worked much more to the advantage of the rich than the poor.[91] In short, there was an inequality of opportunity associated with private prosecutions.

In time, public prosecutions obviously did become a regular feature of American criminal justice, with an attorney general in each of the colonies—as well as individual local prosecutors—exercising vast discretion to decide what criminal cases to pursue.[92] Colonial attorneys general were tasked with protecting the Crown's financial interests and, if necessary, pursuing criminal cases. While the bulk of their legal work was civil, not criminal, in nature, Louis Palmer, Jr.—in *The Death Penalty in the United States* (2014)—observes that even though "[c]olonial attorney generals were also responsible for prosecuting criminal defendants," that duty was generally "neglected," with Crown prosecutors, following common-law practice, exercising "absolute discretion in deciding what course, if any, to take regarding a criminal offense." As Palmer writes: "Rarely did colonial attorney generals prosecute criminal defendants. They intervened in this area only when a notorious major felony occurred. A routine murder was not considered notorious, unless it affected a colonial aristocrat." But, Palmer notes, "[t]he fact that colonial attorney generals rarely prosecuted criminal defendants did not mean that vigorous criminal prosecutions were nonexistent in the colonies." "Crime was routinely prosecuted," he observes, pointing out that "[t]he citizens of the colonies prosecuted the vast majority of crimes."[93]

Because of the English heritage of private prosecution, the right of individuals to pursue criminal cases in colonial times thus persisted on American soil. Indeed, the right to pursue a private prosecution was passionately defended in the British Parliament along with England's unique system of criminal procedure. "As late as 1774, on the eve of the American Revolution," Harvard Law School graduate Cynthia Nicoletti writes in the *Law and History Review*, "several members of Parliament protested vehemently against a proposal that would have abolished the appeal of felony and the right to defend one's innocence through trial by battle in Massachusetts as a way to crack down on the unruly colonists." "MP John Dunning, later Lord Ashburton," Nicoletti notes, "insisted that even surly Americans could not be denied 'that great pillar of the Constitution, the Appeal for Murder,' for fear that such a statute would create a dangerous precedent and eventually cause Englishmen to lose this right as well."[94] Parliament in fact defeated that proposed measure,[95] and private prosecutions continued unabated even as American states—after the Revolutionary War—ceded greater control to public prosecutors. That control was placed in the hands of public prosecutors to deal with the varied problems and concerns associated with private prosecutions, or, much more nefariously—as in Georgia—to protect slaveholders' interests after abolitionists began using private prosecutions against slaveowners.[96] In antebellum Maryland, where the institution of slavery stubbornly persisted in spite of abolition efforts,[97] with enslaved African Americans outnumbering all other groups in Prince George's County,[98] private prosecutors employed by abolitionists were actually precluded from appearing in court altogether.[99]

Even though colonists and early Americans largely took private prosecutions for granted,[100] serious questions were raised about their propriety during the American Revolution—and, in particular, about their suitability for the new American republic. In *Sketches of the Principles of Government* (1793), Nathaniel Chipman—a federal judge in the District of Vermont—wrote specifically about the importance of grand and petit juries to the American system of justice. "In the administration of criminal law," he began, "the institution of a grand jury has a very leading influence, in a free government." "To guard the innocent from the infamy and oppression of a public accusation; and without partiality, without favor, to bring forward the guilty to trial for their crimes, constitutes the principal duty of a grand jury," Chipman explained of that ancient institution, adding of its composition and special purpose: "Taken from the body of the people, and having, in the prosecution of offences, no interests but the peace and welfare of the community, as far as they are secured by the prevention of crimes, they are placed as a shield between the accused, and the interested passions, or malicious attempts of private prosecutors." "This intervention between the people and the officers of the law, who, from the nature of their office, may, sometimes, be suspected of interested views, or at least of a want of feeling," he stressed, "gives a facility to the execution of criminal law, and reconciles to the sentiments of the people, the necessary punishment of offenders."[101]

A leading American jurist, Nathaniel Chipman saw a transition occurring within societies warranting a simultaneous evolution of prosecutorial methods.[102] "It may be made a question," Chipman wrote, "how far persons injured, ought to be admitted to prosecute for the end of punishing." "I apprehend," he observed, "this will depend much on the state of manners, and the principles of the government." As Chipman, making an extended argument, wrote in his treatise: "In a government, supported, in a great measure, by force, and in a state of manners, in which the mind is highly inflamed by private injuries, and the passion or revenge, is satisfied with nothing short of personal retaliation, it may be necessary to permit the person injured to prosecute his revenge, at law, to prevent the fatal consequences of private malice." "To restrain personal revenge, and subject it to general laws, is a great point in the progress of society," Chipman offered hopefully, further observing that "as prosecutions for the end of punishment, by the party injured, have a direct tendency to perpetuate a resentment of injuries, and to make the law instrumental in the exercise of personal enmity, the practice, by no means agrees with a general refinement of manners, or the humane principle of a democratic republic." "The right of punishment," he emphasized, echoing a familiar Enlightenment axiom, "ought to be exercised solely for the prevention of crimes, and to be permitted to those only, who are appointed and selected by law for that purpose, and who supposed to be capable of candor and moderation in their proceedings." "By refinement of manners," Chipman noted, "is not meant the etiquette of politeness merely, which may consist with many traits of barbarous manners." "It consists," he wrote, "with the modern point of honor; the practice of duelling to revenge personal affronts and imaginary injuries; a practice which still disgraces some of the American states." "We ought rather," Chipman stressed, "to place a refinement of manners in the sentiments of humanity, and a general spirit of accommodation."[103]

Duels—once a common, highly dramatic means of resolving quarrels or disputes in the 1700s and 1800s, especially among aristocrats and elites—were outlawed over time,[104] with libel suits largely taking their place.[105] Indeed, dueling—a practice that might end in death—came to be viewed as a violation of the common law.[106] King Henry IV of France outlawed dueling in 1602; English laws criminalized it during the seventeenth and eighteenth centuries; the 1804 duel between Alexander Hamilton and Aaron Burr that so famously took Hamilton's life sparked the formation of anti-dueling associations; and the District of Columbia statutorily banned dueling in 1839 after the death of a congressman, Jonathan Cilley, who fought a duel with another congressman, William Graves, on the afternoon of February 23, 1838. American states passed a variety of anti-dueling legislation (*e.g.*, making the offense punishable by death or that disqualified participants in duels from holding public office) both before and after the Civil War,[107] with Professor Bennett Capers, of Fordham Law School, noting that—in terms of prosecution practices—"by the time of the Civil War, private prosecution was becoming a memory" and "receding" with public prosecution becoming the norm."[108] "In an effort to subordinate the desire for personal vengeance aroused by insults," one source notes, "the legislatures of several southern states enacted anti-dueling statutes that authorized an award of damages for insulting language calculated to lead to a breach of the breach."[109]

Nathaniel Chipman, certainly, had a lot to say in his treatise about prosecutions. Criminal prosecutions were necessary to address wrongdoing, he believed, writing in *Sketches of the Principles of Government*: "Justice is administered for the redress of some evil, either public, or private. The evil is past, and sometimes uncertain, or at least of difficult investigation." After laying out his concerns about private prosecution and "private malice" in particular, Chipman asked: "Can we then hesitate to pronounce, that in the United States of America, the institution of criminal prosecutions, in the name, and under the direction of private persons, is contrary to the present state of manners, and the principles of their governments? And that the intervention of a grand jury ought to be secured in every constitution, as the sacred right of the people, in prosecutions for crimes?" Chipman added: "The observations made on the institution of grand juries, who, by their intervention between the ministers of the law, and the people, and their approbation of prosecutions, remove the odium of severity, and reconcile the execution of criminal law, to the sentiments of the people, apply with more force to petit juries, in proportion as the condemnation is of more consequence than the accusation."[110] At that time, the long-standing institution of the English common law—private prosecution—was still a predominant feature of American law, though it was coming under increasing attack from prominent jurists and other Enlightenment figures because of abuses associated with it.

Because the English legal system made such extensive use of private prosecutions, it is not surprising that, in North America, the use of private prosecutors continued with some regularity throughout the nineteenth century. Not only were private prosecutions customary and frequent in Canadian locales,[111] but private prosecutions were common in many American states long after the landscape-changing American Revolution.[112] Indeed, the structure of American institutions and the framework of government set up by America's founders left states to their own devices as regards the method of prosecution. The Second Continental Congress issued the Declaration of Independence in 1776, but the Articles of Confederation—ratified five years later, in 1781—did not provide for general federal criminal law enforcement.[113] Instead, states and private citizens were largely responsible for the criminal law's enforcement.[114] The U.S. Constitution, ratified in 1788, created a much stronger executive branch at the federal level, but—as University of Virginia law professor Harold Krent notes—that new frame of government "did not automatically end the participation of private citizens in enforcing the criminal law," which was then quite significant throughout the country. As Krent observes: "Although Congress never vested victims with a general right to prosecute defendants under federal criminal provisions, citizens in the first years under the Constitution evidently presented evidence of crimes directly to the grand jury." "More commonly," Krent adds, "individuals continued as at common law to bring evidence of crimes before magistrates and then, upon the magistrate's approval, to obtain a bench warrant for the defendant's arrest. Without any involvement from the district attorneys, therefore, grand juries issued presentments of crimes and judges ordered suspects arrested, pending trial."[115]

The common law proved to be resilient. "Private prosecution," observes Jeffrey Miller and Brooke Dorner, "carried over to the English colonies in North America and persisted in the new states to varying degrees after the Constitution went into effect." The notion that private individuals could prosecute crimes at that time, they explain, "is understandable, since most early crimes were common law crimes for injuries to individuals and their property."[116] In 1789, in its Judiciary Act, the United States Congress did create the office of U.S. district attorney, vesting the federal district attorneys in every judicial district with the authority to prosecute all federal crimes within their assigned territories. Krent notes that an early opinion by Attorney General William Bradford (1755–1795), the second Attorney General of the United

States,[117] shows that "the colonial practice of privately-initiated prosecutions continued at least for a brief period under the Constitution,"[118] though it became clear over time that federal courts would handle criminal cases in an entirely different manner than their state counterparts. For example, *The Scranton Republican* of Pennsylvania reported on a grand jury charge delivered at the opening of the March 1892 term of the U.S. District and Circuit Courts. Judge Joseph Buffington, who delivered the charge, discussed "the difference in the methods of prosecuting crime found in the Federal Courts and in the State Courts." "In the Federal Courts," Judge Buffington stated, "the District Attorney is the prosecutor for the Government, and if in his judgment, the public right demands a prosecution, he brings it before the Grand Jury, but if in his judgment, the public right does not demand such prosecution, he is perfectly free to refuse to prosecute." "The passion, whim or wish of no private prosecutor need be consulted," Buffington stressed, adding of the federal system: "All prosecutions being brought through the trusted officer of the Government, the Government bears the expense, and in cases of ignored bills, unlike the practice in the State Courts, the Grand Jury cannot put costs on the prosecutor."[119]

Daniel Webster and the Salem Murder Trials

In many American states, private prosecutions remained a common nineteenth-century occurrence,[120] though most criminal cases attracted little public attention outside of terse reports in local newspapers. But when leading lawyers, especially sitting politicians or former congressmen, got involved in prosecuting murder cases, the press took notice, giving lengthy reports of the proceedings. Indeed, in spite of the passage of state laws providing for public prosecutors, high-profile private prosecutors often stole the limelight from their public counterparts. Such was plainly the case at the 1830 murder trials of two brothers, John Francis "Frank" Knapp and Joseph J. "Joe" Knapp, Jr., in Salem, Massachusetts, when the famed American lawyer and politician, Daniel Webster, appeared as a private prosecutor for the Commonwealth of Massachusetts.[121] Although Webster had built his reputation arguing U.S. Supreme Court cases,[122] one of Webster's biographers notes of Webster's employment as a private prosecutor in those murder trials: "This was Webster's only appearance as a prosecutor in a criminal case, and the effort he put into gathering information and evidence showed, according to one contemporary, his extraordinary 'capacity for toil,' for 'at the appointed hour, Mr. Webster was completely ready.'"[123] When Daniel Webster showed up at the courthouse as one of the "conductors of the prosecution," there was reportedly "a tremendous rush for entrance, and the floor and gallery were instantly filled."[124]

It was a notorious crime in his home state that drew Webster into the murder prosecutions. In 1830, at one of the most opulent houses in Salem, Massachusetts, its wealthy, 82-year-old owner, Captain Joseph White, was found murdered in his bed. His lifeless body was discovered on the morning of April 7th with thirteen deep stab wounds and with a heavy blow to his left temple, causing a crushed skull. Mysteriously, nothing of value had been taken from the sea captain's house despite the fact that many valuable items, including a trunk of money, were kept at the home. It was a shocking murder that occurred right in the middle of town, and it sparked an uproar among the local populace—a level of panic not seen, likely, since the mass hysteria of the Salem Witch Trials in the 1690s.[125] As John Lawson, the editor of *American State Trials*, later described the murder's profound and immediate effect: "The perpetration of such an atrocious crime, in the most populous and central part of the town and under circumstances that indicated the utmost coolness, deliberation and audacity, deeply agitated and aroused the whole community. Large rewards for the detection of the murderer were offered by the heirs of the deceased and by the Governor of the State. The citizens held a public meeting, and appointed a committee of vigilance."[126] It was later reported in Boston that the Salem murder of Captain White had become "the late all-engrossing topic."[127]

Twenty-seven leading citizens made up the committee of vigilance—among them, Stephen White, the murdered man's nephew. Its purpose: to locate anyone responsible for the murder. A state senator and the brother-in-law of long-time U.S. Supreme Court Associate Justice Joseph Story,[128] who'd been appointed to the Supreme Court by James Madison in 1812, Stephen White was the principal heir to Captain White's fortune. Captain White—a slave trader—had never married, and he had amassed a large fortune, allowing him to build his stately mansion in Salem. Captain White's ships had hauled cargo such as codfish, shoes and tools, but they had also carried enslaved persons from Africa to be sold in the Caribbean for gold. The only individuals who'd slept in the house on the night of the murder other than Captain White—the wealthy mariner and shipowner—were a male servant, who discovered an open window and the captain's dead body in the morning, and a trusted maid. Footprints found in the garden outside following the murder matched neither of the servants, however. Also, Captain White's niece and long-time housekeeper, Mrs. Beckford, was seven miles away at Wenham on the night of the murder visiting her daughter, Mary, and her husband, Joe Knapp. The stab wounds, the examining physicians and a hastily assembled coroner's jury determined, were made by a sharp dirk or poniard, it appearing that Captain White had been dead for several hours by the time his lifeless body was found. Instead of making use of the normal law enforcement process, the committee of vigilance took control of the investigation, searching homes, doing interrogations, and bypassing the usual mode of conducting criminal investigations. Stephen White himself offered a $1,000 reward and contributed money to help defray the committee of vigilance's expenses.[129]

The sequence of events leading up to the murder and the apprehension of murder suspects in the case was complex and, at times, downright bizarre. For weeks, the investigation produced no promising clues. Captain White's house had not been ransacked, and a *rouleau* of doubloons in the iron chest in Captain White's bed chamber were all there, stumping Salem's committee of vigilance. The mass panic and palpable fear in the community, meanwhile, reached fever pitch. All of Salem's citizens—as one summary puts it—"were led to fear that the same fate might await them in the defenceless and helpless hours of slumber." "For several days," that source notes of precautions taken by the town's residents, "persons passing through the streets might hear the continual sound of the hammer, while carpenters and smiths were fixing bolts to doors and fastenings to windows." "While the public mind was thus excited and anxious," the summary of one of Salem's most notorious murder cases continues, "it was announced that a bold attempt at highway robbery was made in Wenham by three footpads, on Joseph J. Knapp, Jr. and John Francis Knapp, on the evening of the 27th of April, while they were returning in a chaise from Salem to their residence in Wenham." The Knapp brothers, the alleged victims of the reported highway robbery attempt, were young sea captains—"masters of vessels" who, it was noted, belonged "to a very respectable family."[130]

The Knapp brothers—known familiarly to their friends and family as "Joe" and "Frank"—appeared before the committee of vigilance and testified that, after 9:00 p.m. on the night in question, three men had approached them and attempted to rob them but that the highway robbers had been fended off with a sword and a whip before disappearing into the darkness. The account of the Knapp brothers, which led community members to fear that dangerous criminals were lurking about, appeared in the local newspapers, with *The Essex Gazette* noting of the Knapp brothers: "these gentlemen are well known in this town, and their respectability and veracity are not questioned by any of our citizens." Weeks later, after more information came to light that did question their character and veracity, it was reported, however: "The Knapps are the young men who a few weeks ago pretended to have been attacked by highwaymen near Wenham Pond. J. J. Knapp jr. now acknowledges that the whole was a fabrication."[131] Joseph Knapp Sr.—Joe and Frank Knapp's father—had once brought a ship, the *Revenge*, from Captain Joseph White, the murder victim who'd been a loyal British subject at the Revolutionary War's outset but who became the first privateer from Salem after the British had raided one of his ships.[132]

Ultimately, it came to the attention of Stephen White and the committee of vigilance that a petty criminal named Hatch, confined in the jail at New Bedford, Massachusetts, claimed to have material information about Captain Joseph White's murder. Hatch said that while frequenting gambling houses in February, he'd overheard two brothers, Richard and George Crowninshield, talking about their intent to steal Captain White's iron chest full of riches. After Hatch was brought in chains to testify before a Salem grand jury, the two brothers, Richard and George Crowninshield, were indicted for murder and abetting the crime and detained in the Salem Gaol, a structure made of granite blocks with iron-barred windows.[133] The Crowninshield family was a very prominent one in Salem, with the brothers' uncle having served as Secretary of the Navy under Presidents Madison and Monroe.[134] Supreme Court Justice Joseph Story himself had close political ties to the Crowninshields, with Story, in 1808, succeeding Jacob Crowninshield as a member of the U.S. House of Representatives from the 2nd District of Massachusetts before his elevation to the U.S. Supreme Court in 1812. Richard Crowninshield, Sr.—the father of the two implicated brothers, one of whom was known to frequent Salem's "haunts of vice"—was reportedly "not an outstanding member of the family." As a U.S. Supreme Court justice, Joseph Story had himself—before Captain White's murder—participated in a Supreme Court ruling against Richard Crowninshield, Sr. in *Sturges v. Crowninshield* (1819), a court case in which Richard Crowninshield attempted to free himself of business debts following the passage of a state bankruptcy law.[135]

Although Joseph Story had once served as a lawyer for the Crowninshield family, Story's connections to the White family ran especially deep. As one history of Salem notes of Joseph Story's strong familial connections to Joseph White Jr. and the whole White family: "A romance had developed between White and a Story sister, and then an engagement, and on January 19, 1808, at the bride's home, Joseph White Jr., twenty-seven, had married Elizabeth Story, twenty-three. It may have been on that occasion that Stephen White and Harriet Story, both twenty, announced their own engagement." Stephen and Harriet got married a few months later, on August 8, 1808, the sixty-first birthday of Captain Joseph White. "Through their double-sibling marriages," that history notes, "the Whites would become more than brothers." Those White brothers, prominent Salem merchants, owned ten ships, including the brig *Romp*, with a history of Salem noting that the ship, jointly owned by Joseph White Jr., Joseph J. Knapp, Richard Crowninshield, and others, had been seized in 1810 as a result of a French policy being invoked to confiscate American vessels and their cargoes. "The Crowninshield family of Salem," one book, *The Ships and Sailors of Old Salem*, observes, "earned very unusual distinction on salt water and a national fame as men of affairs and statecraft." That family, that book notes, was full of seafaring men involved "in the East India trade" who "commanded ships before they were old enough to vote."[136]

In early nineteenth-century Salem, Massachusetts, the Story family rose to great prominence, with Associate Justice Joseph Story—who taught law at Harvard from 1829 to 1845 and who served on the U.S. Supreme Court from 1812 until his death in 1845 at age 65—being one of its most prominent members. "In 1811, on adjoining lots overlooking the town Common," Robert Booth writes in his history, *Death of an Empire: The Rise and Murderous Fall of Salem, America's Richest City*, "Stephen and Joseph Jr. put up splendid three-story brick mansions; and their wives' brother, the lawyer Joseph Story, put up a third nearby." Joseph Story had practiced law in Salem after graduating from Harvard, and it was there that he had gotten into politics. "In a matter of a few years," Booth continues, "Joseph Story, still just twenty-eight, had risen to the head of the Essex bar, with a lucrative practice and political ambitions that had him serving alongside Joseph White Jr. as a representative in the state legislature." It was after the unexpected death of Congressman Jacob Crowninshield, at age 38, who had spit up blood while serving in the nation's capital, that Joseph Story had taken the Massachusetts House seat and become even more closed allied with the

White brothers. "Thereafter," Booth writes, "the White-Story faction would rule over Republican politics in Salem."[137]

There was, to say the least, much suspicion and intrigue involved in Captain Joseph White's murder investigation. Three years before the murder, one of the house's prior occupants, Mary Beckford, the daughter of Captain White's niece and housekeeper, had married Joseph Jenkins Knapp, Jr., more familiarly known as Joe Knapp. A shipping captain's son, Joe Knapp had once been a master of one of Captain White's sailing vessels. The aging Captain White had strenuously opposed Joe's marriage to Mary Beckford, with White—accusing Knapp of fortune hunting—threatening to fire Joe Knapp and cut Mary out of his will if they married. After they wed in spite of those warnings, Captain White made good on his threats, and he removed Knapp from his command and disinherited Mary. Joe Knapp, as he would later confess, then came up with an ill-informed, ill-fated murder-for-hire scheme. As one history describes his misimpression and twisted motive and the historian's take about the events surrounding Captain White's murder: "Joseph Knapp mistakenly believed that if the will could be destroyed, his mother-in-law would inherit half the fortune, so he hired Richard Crowninshield to murder White, while Knapp, still having the run of the house, was to steal the will. Crowninshield murdered White, and Knapp stole a document, but the wrong one. White's real will was safe in the keeping of his lawyers." "In the real will," that historian notes, "the major inheritor of a great fortune was the once-suspect nephew Stephen White, a Massachusetts state senator and the brother-in-law of Joseph Story."[138] But none of that information came out until later, with the investigation taking considerable time to play out.

Especially given the nature of the cold-blooded murder, the investigation to solve the crime naturally had a sense of urgency to it. After a coroner's jury of local citizens was convened after the murder, and a subsequent, and more thorough, autopsy was conducted, the vigilance committee immediately got to work trying to solve the crime, using whatever means it had at its disposal. There was a sizable inheritance at stake, and before Captain White's murder, there had been credible rumors or intimations that Captain White might change his will. It was Hatch, the petty criminal in custody seventy miles away in New Bedford for shoplifting, who eventually came forward to disclose that, while at a gambling spot run by Richard Crowninshield, he overheard him say "he would love to murder Captain White." In fact, the two brothers, Richard and George Crowninshield, were later indicted for Captain White's murder and abetting the crime. It was after John C.R. Palmer, another suspected accessory to the murder, was questioned, informing authorities that he'd overheard George Crowninshield tell his brother, Richard, that Frank Knapp wanted them to kill Captain White and that Frank's brother, Joe, had offered to pay them $1,000 to commit the crime, that the Knapp brothers—like the Crowninshield brothers—were taken into custody. Joe Knapp was reportedly angry that Captain White had recently changed his will, planning to leave most of his estate to Stephen White.

The Knapp brothers' own father, Captain Joseph J. Knapp, Sr., actually unwittingly set in motion the series of events that led to the arrest of the Knapp brothers. On May 14th, nine days after the Crowninshield brothers were indicted, the father of the Knapp brothers got a mysterious letter from Belfast, Maine, that was signed "Charles Grant, jun." and that demanded a $350 "loan" by May 22. The letter read in part: "It is useless for me to enter into a discussion of the facts which must inevitably harrow up your soul—no—I will merely tell you that I am acquainted with your brother Franklin, and also the business that he was transacting for you on the 2d of April last; and that I think you was very very extravagant in giving me one thousand dollars to the person that would execute the business for you—but you know best about that, you see that such things will leak out." Unable to decipher the letter's ambiguous and cryptic meaning, Captain Joseph J. Knapp, Sr. showed the letter to his son Phippen, a recent Harvard graduate and respected lawyer, and together they travelled to Wenham to talk to Phippen's brothers, Joe and Frank, about the mysterious letter. After Joe Knapp, the son, declared that the letter contained "a devilish lot of trash," his father—on Joe's advice—promptly turned it over to the vigilance committee.

When that committee got its hands on it, it sent an anonymous reply to "Charles Grant" enclosing $50 and promising to send more money later. Simultaneously, the committee cleverly dispatched one of its members to arrest whoever picked up the letter, and that turned out to be none other than John C.R. Palmer, a 23-year-old ex-convict who would eventually provide the incriminating information about the Knapp brothers. After being questioned, Palmer told the vigilance committee that, while at the Crowninshield house, he saw Frank Knapp and another man come to the house and meet up with Richard and George Crowninshield. George Crowninshield later said that Frank Knapp had asked them to kill Captain White and that Joe Knapp had, in return, promised to pay $1,000 for the dastardly deed.[139] The *Evening Post*, of New York City, would summarize what happened in this way: "It appears that the discovery of the real perpetrators of the crime was brought about in the following manner. The letter from Palmer was addressed to 'Joseph Knapp, Merchant, Salem,' and was taken out of the Post Office and opened by the father of him for whom it was designed, Mr. Joseph J. Knapp, a respectable merchant of that place, who supposed the letter intended for himself. Finding it to contain some dark hints and threats concerning the murder of Mr. White, the meaning of which he was totally unable to comprehend, he handed it over to the committee of vigilance, little thinking that his own sons were the murderers, and that he was thus, by the inscrutable decrees of Providence, to be made the avenger of his offspring's guilt. The incentive to this murder, was, as has been stated, the supposition on the part of J. J. Knapp Junr. that in the event of Mr. White dying intestate, he, in right of his wife, would inherit half of the estate."[140]

As a result of the incriminating revelations, the Knapp brothers were arrested and sent to the Salem Gaol, where Joe Knapp confessed to his role in the crime. The signed confession, prepared by Rev. Henry Colman, a minister of the Independent Congregational Church, was nine pages long, with Joe Knapp promised immunity from prosecution by Rev. Colman—a friend of the White family who was intimately involved with the vigilance committee. Not only was Stephen White a member of the congregation, but Rev. Colman had, ironically, performed the wedding of Joe and Mary Knapp—the latter being the daughter of Captain White's housekeeper.[141] The confession, which the vigilance committee refused to let the Harvard-educated lawyer Phippen Knapp read but portions of which were leaked to the press, stated that Joe Knapp knew Captain White had made a will that would bequest approximately $15,000 to Mrs. Beckford, but that if White died intestate (that is, without a will), Knapp expected her to inherit nearly $100,000. The confession further stated that a plan was hatched to steal and destroy the will, with Joe's brother, Frank Knapp, said to have tapped Richard Crowninshield—the man who climbed through Captain White's window and bludgeoned and stabbed the elderly sea captain to death—to carry out the murder for $1,000. The hiding place for the two-foot-long, lead-weighted bludgeon used to murder Captain White—a rat hole under the steps of Salem's Howard Street meeting house—was also revealed.[142]

An extra to *The Salem Observer* reported on "particulars of the confession of Capt. Joseph J. Knapp, Jr." As word of Joe Knapp's confession spread about the country, *The National Gazette* in Philadelphia relayed this summary of the confession: "Some months since Joseph J. Knapp, Jr. who married the grand niece of Captain White, and the daughter of his housekeeper, stated a hypothetical case to a lawyer, and from him understood that if Captain White died intestate, his mother in law, as the sole representative of Capt. White's sister, would inherit half the estate—all the heirs at law being representatives of Capt. White's brother." "In order to effect this project," it was reported, "Knapp proposed to his brother John F. Knapp, to murder Captain White. His brother replied that he would not do it, but he knew who would; he could get Richard Crowninshield, Jr." Richard Crowninshield, Jr., it was noted, "was employed, for that object, by John F. Knapp, at his brother's request, and was to receive, we understand, $1000 for accomplishing the object."

Of course, the confession was big news, especially since the mystery surrounding Captain White's murder had so captivated the public. As the *National Gazette* summarized other details from the damning confession: "On Friday, 3d April, J. J. Knapp, Jr. went into Captain White's chamber, and took from the iron chest a will, which he supposed to be Captain W.'s last will, carried it to Wenham, and kept it in his possession until he heard of Captain W.'s death, and then destroyed it. On the same day he procured the will, he unbarred the window, by which Crowninshield entered. Knapp returned to Wenham [the] same day; and did not return to Salem again until the murder was committed." "The murder was committed by Crowninshield alone. He alone was in the house. It was effected by a dirk, ... and by a bludgeon of hickory, with a large head, loaded with lead." "While the deed was doing, J. F. Knapp was watching in Brown street." "J. J. Knapp, Jr. acknowledges himself author of several infamous anonymous letters, which have been sent to the honorable Stephen White, and the Committee of Vigilance, since the murder."[143]

Before Joe Knapp gave and signed his confession and the vigilance committee completed its work, U.S. Supreme Court Justice Joseph Story—a man with a big familial interest in the case—had written to Daniel Webster, one of Massachusetts' sitting U.S. senators, about the murder. As Story wrote to Webster on April 17th: "An entire new direction was given to my thoughts by the horrible murder of Old Capt'n White at Salem. You are aware that he died childless and his principal heirs are Mr. Stephen White and my sister's children. It is altogether the most mysterious and dreadful affair that I ever heard of. Not the slightest trace has yet been found by which to detect the assassins (for I am satisfied that there was more than one) and we are yet in a darkness rendered darker by the utter defeat of every conjecture." "I have been obliged to go to Salem several times, and every thing there seems in inextricable confusion," Story confided. As Justice Story further reported of Captain White and the inheritors of his considerable estate before the investigation into the murder case was completed: "Mr. White left a will. He had given many legacies to his relatives; but the bulk of his fortune goes to Mr. Stephen White who will get from \$150,000 to \$200,000. Three of my nieces will receive about \$25,000 each." That will, naming Stephen White as executor and superseding an older one that divided up his estate more equally among his heirs, had been drawn up approximately three months before the captain's murder.[144]

The Knapp brothers—the sons of Joseph Knapp, Sr., the prominent Salem sea captain—would be tried separately before the supreme judicial court in Salem, Massachusetts. Frank Knapp's 1830 trial would take place after Richard Crowninshield, while in custody, committed suicide on June 15th, adding even more drama to the whole affair. Before hanging himself with two silk handkerchiefs tied to the bars of his cell, Richard—deeply depressed but hoping to save his brother, George—had consulted a lawyer, Franklin Dexter, on the subject of the law of principals and accessories. Through some legal advice about applicable Massachusetts law, Richard had come to understand that his brother, George, could not be put on trial as an accessory if Richard himself was never tried and convicted.[145] After Richard's suicide, the prosecution's job thus became a lot more difficult, as someone needed to be convicted as a principal in the murder lest others conspiring in the crime should get off scot-free. The common law of Massachusetts made clear that "unless there be a conviction of the principal there can be no trial of the accessory." In an attempt to punish those responsible for Captain White's murder, the grand jury, having been informed of that common-law rule, had chosen to indict Frank Knapp as principal and Joe Knapp and George Crowninshield as accessories.[146] The charges, at that time, carried the prospect of death sentences.

The gravity of the case—and what was at stake financially for Associate Justice Joseph Story's relatives—made it ripe for a private prosecution, and that is exactly what happened. For Frank Knapp's prosecution, the state's long-time attorney general, Perez Morton (1751–1837), got an advocate at the very top of the legal progression, obtaining U.S. Senator Daniel Webster's assistance to conduct it. Under Massachusetts law, the designated state prosecutors were Morton—then nearly 80 years of age—and Daniel Davis (1762–1835), the state's solicitor general and a man approaching 70 years of age. Because of their concerns about the murder case's complexity and the handling of the high-profile case, as well as their intense interest in the prosecution's outcome, Justice Joseph Story and Stephen White prevailed upon Daniel Webster, then 48 years of age and at the height of his powers, to get involved. Webster agreed to do so even though he had only recently remarried, to Caroline LeRoy, and had just finished a busy U.S. Senate session in Washington, D.C. Webster had served multiple terms in the U.S. House of Representatives before his election to the U.S. Senate in 1827, and Justice Story and Stephen White were friends. Webster himself was in debt, with one historical account observing that the prospect of a hefty fee "could not be ignored by a man periodically harassed by his creditors" as his "eight-dollar-a-day salary as senator would hardly have paid his wine bill."[147] Only days before the trial was set to commence, Webster—known for oratory, riveting summations, and effective cross-examinations—was thus recruited to take on the case.

The British writer Harriet Martineau, who wrote about prominent historical figures, later recalled how Daniel Webster was pressed into service: "A citizen of Salem, a friend of mine, was deputed to carry the request.... Mr. Webster was at his farm by the seashore. Thither, in tremendous weather, my friend followed him. Mr. Webster was playing checkers with his boy." Although Webster had initially declined to get involved, pointing to his "swollen bags of briefs lying in a corner," Martineau explained that "upon a little further explanation and meditation, he agreed to the request with the same good grace with which he afterward went through with his task." As Martineau reported of Webster: "He made himself master of all that my friend could communicate, and before daybreak was off through the woods, in the unabated storm." Stephen White, it turns out, had discretely promised Webster a $1,000 attorney's fee, which wasn't publicly disclosed at the time.[148] That handsome fee might well have prompted—and almost certainly influenced—the reversal of Webster's initial decision not to take up the case.[149] "Webster's appetite for wealth would lead him to land speculation," one biographical sketch recounts of the U.S. Senator's substantial investments, observing that Webster's "careless financing and the 1830s depression would cause him to remain debt-ridden the rest of his life."[150]

The prosecution of the Knapp brothers did not proceed as initially contemplated. The sudden death of Isaac Parker, the Chief Justice of the Massachusetts Supreme Judicial Court, on the night of July 25, 1830, had unexpectedly delayed the start of Frank Knapp's murder trial—a trial originally scheduled to begin on July 27th. It was only after Chief Justice Parker's death that Daniel Webster—in the midst of the storm—agreed to assist the commonwealth's prosecution, with Webster having little time to prepare for his participation in the case.[151] Mr. Morton, in his opening speech to the jury in August, took special note of that fact, addressing the gentlemen of the jury: "Since the adjournment of the court, the counsel for the Government have procured the services of a gentleman pre-eminent at the bar, to assist in the management of this cause, and at my request, from his superior physical strength, as well as for his acknowledged supremacy in the powers of mind, he has taken the more arduous duty of closing the cause, leaving to me the easier one of opening." "The charge against the prisoner at the bar," Morton said in his opening, "is for the murder of the late Mr. Joseph White—a murder of no ordinary character—a murder the most cold-blooded, unprovoked, and atrocious that has ever yet stained the annals of our Commonwealth, if not of any other country—a murder in the commission of which every personal security and safety which the law specially guaranties to the citizen in the asylum of his dwelling-house, and in the recess of his bed-chamber, has been outraged and violated." The prosecution knew it was up against a talented defense team, one made up Franklin Dexter, the son of Samuel Dexter, President John Adams's Secretary of the Treasury; William H. Gardiner, a prominent member of the Boston bar; and Robert Rantoul, then a 25-year-old lawyer from Salem who later rose to prominence as a penal reformer and staunch death penalty opponent.[152]

In his opening statement, Mr. Morton explicitly referred to Joe Knapp's confession. "After the two Knapps were arrested, at the request of several respectable citizens of Salem," he said, alluding to the vigilance committee, "I authorized in writing the Rev. Mr. Colman to receive the free and voluntary disclosures of any one of the individuals charged, without naming any one; and giving him authority to say that on condition of his disclosing the whole truth and nothing but the truth respecting the murder, I would call him as a witness on the trial, and that, being a witness, he would have the implied pledge of the Government, not to be prosecuted for that offense." "In consequence of this authority," Mr. Morton explained, "Mr. Colman received the voluntary disclosure of J. J. Knapp, Jr., in writing." After noting that Joe Knapp, acting under the advice of counsel, had subsequently refused to testify before the grand jury for fear of incriminating himself, Attorney General Morton said he would be calling Joe Knapp again at trial. "[I]f he again refuses to testify," Morton explained, "every one will acknowledge that the pledge of the Government will be completely redeemed, and his promised protection will be forfeited, and he must stand on his own original responsibility." Morton's opening—setting forth the Commonwealth's position—was intended to be a shot across the bow to young Joe Knapp, with Morton knowing that Joe Knapp's actions could result in a death sentence.

The trial of 19-year-old Frank Knapp lasted ten days, with U.S. Senator Daniel Webster actively involved in preparing for it—and then vigorously participating in it. In fact, the Commonwealth's closing statement—as promised by Attorney General Morton—was made by Webster. As the summation of events in *American State Trials* notes of Frank Knapp's trial: "The principal, John Francis Knapp, was first put on trial. As the law then stood, the accessory in a murder could not be tried until the principal had been convicted. The trial was long and arduous and the witnesses numerous. His brother Joseph, who had made his confession on the government's promise of immunity, if he would, in good faith, testify to the truth, was brought into court, called to the stand as a witness, but declined to testify." Though he plainly risked surrendering his immunity from prosecution, as Morton himself made clear in his opening, Joe Knapp was, ultimately, simply unwilling to testify against his own brother—even if it threatened his own life. In summing up Mr. Webster's role at Frank Knapp's trial, the editor of *American State Trials* further observes: "To convict the prisoner it was necessary for the government to prove that Frank was present, actually or constructively, as an aider or abettor in the murder. Mr. Webster's task in the prosecution was to convince the jury first that there was a conspiracy to commit the murder and that the prisoner was one of the conspirators; and secondly that, at the time of the murder, he was in the street at the rear of Mr. White's garden to aid and abet in the murder, ready to afford assistance if necessary."

The public interest in Frank Knapp's murder trial was incredibly high, with Mr. Dexter—representing the defendant—arguing to jurors that his client faced an "extraordinary array of counsel, active and inactive, brought in aid of the Government."[153] "The Court House," New York's *Evening Post* reported, "has been crowded within and thronged without" from the trial's commencement. Noting that "[a]n intense interest is manifested in the proceedings by all classes of citizens," the newspaper observed that "[t]he number of strangers in town, from always every quarter, is very large."[154] According to the local paper, the *Salem Gazette*: "After the Jury had gone to their lodgings for refreshments, many persons kept their stations about Court-street till a late hour in the evening, to which they were induced principally by a recollection of the circumstance that when S. M. Clark was capitally convicted, several years ago, the Jury did not return a verdict till eleven o'clock at night, at which time the court was called together to receive it." "The Court-room," the *Salem Gazette* emphasized, "has continually been thronged and filled, and multitudes have retired from inability to gain entrance." As the *Gazette* pointed out: "While Mr. Webster was closing the cause, we observed that the windows of the houses near the Court House were filled with attentive listeners. Hundreds of individuals were also gathered around the house, being enabled by the powerful voice and distinct enunciation of Mr. W. to hear the greater part of his address to the Jury from the street."[155]

In his argument for the Commonwealth of Massachusetts in the case of Frank Knapp, Daniel Webster began: "I am little accustomed, gentlemen, to the part which I am now attempting to perform. Hardly more than once or twice, has it happened to me to be concerned, on the side of the government, in any criminal prosecution whatever; and never, until the present occasion, in any case affecting life." As the famed lawyer, far more accustomed to arguing before the U.S. Supreme Court and serving in the role of defense counsel in criminal cases, said of his role at the Knapp trial: "Though I could well have wished to shun this occasion, I have not felt at liberty to withhold my professional assistance, when it is supposed that I might be in some degree useful, in investigating and discussing the truth, respecting this most extraordinary murder. It has seemed to be a duty, incumbent on me, as on every other citizen, to do my best, and my utmost, to bring to light the perpetrators of this crime." "Against the prisoner at the bar, as an individual, I cannot have the slightest prejudice," Webster assured the jury, adding: "I would not do him the smallest injury or injustice. But I do not affect to be indifferent to the discovery, and the punishment of this deep guilt. I cheerfully share in the opprobrium, how much soever it may be, which is cast on those who feel and manifest an anxious concern that all who had a part in planning, or a hand in executing this deed of midnight assassination, may be brought to answer for their enormous crime, at the bar of public justice." In other words, Webster portrayed his involvement in the case as driven by civic duty and the benevolence of public service, not by any monetary reward or remuneration.

Part of Daniel Webster's summation naturally focused on the facts of case. "An aged man, without an enemy in the world, in his own house, and in his own bed, is made the victim of a butcherly murder, for mere pay," Webster told the jurors, calling the murderer of Captain White an "assassin." But another part of his summation defended his own role in the case as a private prosecutor. "The learned counsel for the prisoner," Webster emphasized to jurors of their role before beginning his own defense of his participation in the case, "has said, truly, that it is your individual duty to determine his guilt or innocence—and that you are to weigh the testimony with candor and fairness. But much at the same time has been said, which, although it would seem to have no distinct bearing on the trial, cannot be passed over without some notice." As Webster continued: "A tone of complaint so peculiar has been indulged, as would almost lead us to doubt whether the prisoner at the bar, or the managers of this prosecution, are now on trial." "Great pains have been taken to complain of the manner of the prosecution," Webster said before making these spirited remarks: "We hear of getting up a case—of setting in motion trains of machinery—of foul testimony—of combinations to overwhelm the prisoner—of private prosecutions—that the prisoner is hunted, persecuted, driven to his trial—that everybody is against him—and various other complaints, as if those who would bring to punishment the authors of this murder were almost as bad as they who committed it."

Webster then went on offense, parrying defense counsel's intimations and trying to make the defense counsel look petty. "In the course of my whole life," Webster said, "I have never heard before, so much said about the particular counsel who happen to be employed. As if it were extraordinary, that other counsel than the usual officers of the government should be assisting in the conducting of a case on the part of the government." As Webster tried to reassure jurors, invoking a precedent: "In one of the last capital trials in this county, that of Jackman for the Goodridge robbery (so-called), I remember that the learned head of the Suffolk bar, Mr. Prescott, came down in aid of officers of the government. This was regarded as neither strange nor improper."[156] As the *Salem Gazette* reported on the closing argument, Webster contended in open court that "there was nothing uncommon or improper" about the Salem vigilance committee as "[i]n the case of Major Goodridge, not only was a large reward offered, but it was raised by subscription, and a committee was chosen to attend to the subject." "The respected head of the Boston Bar, Mr Prescott," Webster said, "had been called in on that occasion to aid the government in the prosecution; and in that case the counsel on the other side had occupied themselves rather in refuting his arguments than in carping at his presence."[157]

In his argument, Daniel Webster observed that "[t]he learned counsel have endeavored to persuade you that there exists a prejudice against the persons accused of this murder." "They," Webster said of opposing counsel, "would have you understand that it is not confined to this vicinity alone—but that even the legislature have caught this spirit, that through the procurement of the gentleman, here styled private prosecutor, who is a member of the senate, a special session of this court was appointed for the trial of these offenders; that the ordinary movements of the wheels of justice were too slow for the purposes devised." "The criminal law," Webster assured jurors, "is not founded in a principle of vengeance." As Webster spoke of his understanding of the criminal law in his lengthy argument: "It does not punish, that it may inflict suffering. The humanity of the law feels and regrets, every pain it causes, every hour of restraint it imposes, and more deeply still, every life it forfeits. But it uses evil, as the means of preventing greater evil. It seeks to deter from crime, by the example of punishment." "Gentlemen," Webster urged jurors, "your whole concern should be to do your duty, and leave consequences to take care of themselves." "Your verdict, it is true," he acknowledged, "may endanger the prisoner's life; but then, it is to save other lives." "If the prisoner's guilt has been shown and proved, beyond all reasonable doubt, you will convict him," Webster concluded.[158]

The prosecution of Frank Knapp was full of drama and recriminations, including about Daniel Webster's role in the case. The first jury, which deliberated for many hours on August 13 after hearing all the evidence, was unable to reach agreement about Frank Knapp's presence at the murder scene.[159] As a result, the jurors deadlocked and the prosecution ended in a hung jury. But the commonwealth's prosecution team was undeterred, and Frank Knapp was put on trial again—and he was convicted after a second jury was impaneled to hear the evidence.[160] While the jurors in the first trial deliberated for approximately 24 hours before announcing their inability to reach a decision,[161] causing the judge to declare a mistrial, the second trial took six days—and the second jury brought back a guilty verdict after just five hours of deliberations.[162] "In the interim between the two trials," one historian writes about the case, "the new jury had been exposed to newspaper accounts of the first hearing, as well as to heavy criticism leveled at the previous jury for its failure to convict." The lead defense lawyer, Franklin Dexter, explicitly attributed the guilty verdict to Daniel Webster's skillful advocacy, with many prominent figures taking note of Webster's performance. Henry Cabot Lodge called Webster's address to the jury "among the very finest masterpieces of modern oratory," and attorney Samuel McCall called Webster's speech "the greatest argument ever addressed to a jury." Nathaniel Hawthorne, the Salem-born writer, then 26, whose great-great-grandfather had overseen the Salem witch trials,[163] was himself riveted by the case, with his own father and grandfather having been sea captains. In letters, Hawthorne wrote of "the murder of Mr. White," "the execution of Frank Knapp," and Salem's "universal prejudice" against the Knapp family. "The force of Mr. Webster's argument," the editor of *American State Trials* reports of the Frank Knapp murder trial and the high-stakes legal issues associated with it, "convinced the jury that he was, in this sense, *present* at the murder, and he was convicted and hanged."

Frank Knapp was sentenced to death on August 21, 1830, and it was just a week after his twentieth birthday that he met his fate on the gallows in front of a crowd—at least per one estimate—of approximately 5,000 spectators.[164] At his sentencing in Salem, when Frank Knapp was asked if he had anything to say as to why a sentence of death should not be pronounced, he was resolute: "I have only to say that I am innocent of the charge—and I now declare to the world that I shall die innocent of the crime, for which I am to suffer." Judge Samuel Putnam, who delivered the sentence, was reportedly "greatly affected, and sobbed audibly after he had pronounced the judgment of the Court." Frank Knapp, meanwhile, remained "as unconcerned and immoveable as ever," putting "a quid of tobacco into his mouth with great nonchalance" as he left the bar of justice.[165] As one historian, Walker Lewis, later wrote of the young man's execution just weeks after the sentencing: "On Tuesday, September 28, 1830, Frank Knapp, just turned twenty, was hanged. He met the end with composure, coolly testing the drop of the scaffold with one foot before stepping on it, and then waiting quietly while the noose was adjusted."[166] "For a few seconds no movement was perceptible," the *Vermont Aurora* reported after "the drop fell," with the newspaper further noting "[a] slight convulsion of the limbs and heaving of the breast" before Knapp was pronounced dead.[167]

Another account of Frank Knapp's execution, estimating an even larger crowd size, observed that "[t]he people began to assemble about the prison in crowds at an early hour, and soon after 8 o'clock it is supposed that eight or ten thousand men women and children had collected to witness the scene." As that account reported: "By half past eight o'clock, Knapp had taken leave of his family in the cell where he had been confined from the day of his sentence, and appeared at the place of execution in the jailyard attended by the High Sheriff of Essex and four Deputies. He was also ministered unto by Rt. Rev. Bishop Griswold, and throughout the appalling catastrophe, maintained the same apathetic composure that he had manifested during his trial and sentence." Garbed in "a dark green frock coat, white vest, dark pantaloons and boots," Knapp declined to make a dying speech, simply replying "yes" when asked if he was ready to mount the scaffold. After a cap was drawn over his eyes and he dropped a handkerchief as a signal, he was "launched into eternity." "Thus perished a convicted principal in the midnight assassination of the late Capt. White," the paper reported.[168] Joe Knapp, Frank's brother, was still in custody, but he was given the opportunity to see his brother's corpse before its burial in the Branch Burial Ground, a scene said to be "truly a distressing one." In agony, Joe knelt "to embrace the lifeless features of his brother" and fainted after returning to his cell.[169]

The ensuing trial of Joe Knapp, accused of being an accessory to Joseph White's murder after his brother Frank had been tried, convicted and executed, got underway in Salem, Massachusetts, a little over a week after his brother died on the scaffold. The Honorable Samuel Putnam, Samuel Wilde and Marcus Morton presided as the judges at Joe's trial, while Daniel Webster, Attorney General Perez Morton, and Solicitor General Daniel Davis appeared for the Commonwealth of Massachusetts. And once again, Franklin Dexter and William Howard Gardiner served as the lead defense lawyers. As the prefatory remarks in *American State Trials* notes of Joe Knapp and the key events leading up to his trial: "He it was who had first made a full confession of the whole matter under a promise of pardon and who, when called to the stand to help convict his brother, refused to open his mouth. He had thereby forfeited the immunity promised him by the Government, and was now on trial himself for his life." Mr. Webster, *American State Trials* evocatively notes of what had happened before, had convinced the jury at the earlier trial that Frank Knapp "was *present* at the commission of the murder by Richard Crowninshield, who had hanged himself in his cell and was beyond any earthly tribunal."

Knowing that Daniel Webster had already helped to secure his brother's execution, Joe Knapp must have recognized the true peril he faced as the assembled team of prosecutors squared off against his defense team. The prosecution's strategy would be different, but the advocates seeking his execution would be the same as those who had already procured his brother Frank's death. At Joe Knapp's trial, the editor of *American State Trials* observes, "Mr. Webster's task was of an entirely different nature." That's because the defendant on trial—Joe Knapp—"could not be convicted without the use of the confession which he had made under the promise of a favor." The facts made clear that Joe Knapp had initially talked to Rev. Colman with the express understanding that communications with the clergyman were privileged, and that the written confession had been made on the promise of immunity, leading to questions about the voluntariness of his confession. "Mr. Webster," the editor of *American State Trials* wrote in retrospect, "had to satisfy the Court that the confession was admissible, although made under these circumstances."[170] As one contemporary account observed of how—and how effectively—the sitting U.S. senator handled his task: "Mr. Webster then proceeded to argue the point of admitting the confession made by Joseph J. Knapp to Mr. Colman in writing, as evidence against the prisoner. In the whole course of the trial Mr. Webster has never appeared with greater force of reasoning or more aptness of illustration."[171]

At the beginning of Joe Knapp's trial on November 9, 1830, Mr. Dexter—one of the defense lawyers, and the lawyer who attributed Frank Knapp's conviction to Daniel Webster's advocacy—explicitly objected "to the employment of counsel for the prosecution in addition to the law officers of the Government."[172] As a summary of the record reflects, an anxious Mr. Dexter "referred to St. 1807, c. 18, which requires county attorneys to act in behalf of the Commonwealth, "'provided, that the attorney general, if present, shall, in any court, have the direction and control of prosecutions and suits in behalf of the Commonwealth.'" "The second section" of that state statute, Mr. Dexter added, provides 'that no attorney general, solicitor general or county attorney shall receive any fee or reward from or in behalf of any prosecutors, for services in any prosecution, to which it shall be his official duty to attend.'" According to the trial record, Mr. Dexter "objected that as both the attorney general and solicitor general were present, and neither of them disabled to conduct the prosecution, Mr. Webster ought not be permitted to act in behalf of the Commonwealth."

Mr. Dexter couldn't change the facts of the case, but through his objection he sought to disqualify and silence Daniel Webster, the prosecution's most effective orator. Defense counsel, Dexter said, "understood" that Mr. Webster "was to receive a compensation for his services from a private prosecutor, and they questioned the right of a private individual to retain counsel to aid the law officers of the Government in effecting a conviction for a crime punishable with death." After Attorney General Morton, with all his decades of legal experience, chimed in and assured the court that "it was not a novel practice for the prosecuting officers to call in the aid of other counsel," Daniel Davis—the state's solicitor general, also a highly experienced attorney—added that "counsel for the Government would be greatly embarrassed if Mr. Webster were not permitted to act in the case, as the preparation for the trial had been made under the expectation of his assistance." "Mr. Webster," the record shows, "stated that he appeared solely at the request of the attorney general, and without any pecuniary inducement." Webster, apparently, treated the $1,000 fee from Stephen White as only applicable to his work in Frank Knapp's murder case, at which no formal objection had been lodged as to Mr. Webster's appearance.[173] The Court, tasked with making rulings on contested issues, offered "it would make a ruling" on the point of law "in the morning."[174]

It was ultimately agreed on November 10th that Daniel Webster could appear in the case—one in which there was much difficulty in choosing the jury because, by then, nearly everyone had an opinion already about Joe Knapp's guilt due to the published confession.[175] The presiding judge, Judge Samuel Putman, said that he had "considered the application of the Attorney General for the admission of Mr. Webster to assist him in the management of this Cause," and that he had come to the opinion that the state statute cited by Mr. Dexter "was not intended to prohibit the appointment of the Counsellors of this Court in aid of the law officers whenever the circumstances of the case should require the Court in the exercise of a sound discretion to make such appointment." As Judge Putnam, speaking for the three-judge panel, ruled: "It is one of the incidental powers of the Court, and has heretofore been exercised in cases within our own recollection. In cases where civil rights are in controversy and the form of proceeding is by indictment or information, the Court do not perceive any objection that the party in interest should employ Counsel in aid of the law officers." "The same reasons would not apply to cases involving public considerations only," Judge Putnam observed, adding that "[i]n such cases the statute supposes that the prosecution shall be conducted by the law officers, for their salaries, and without any other compensation whatsoever." Judge Putnam laid out some rules for the conduct of the case, but he made clear that Daniel Webster would be allowed to participate. "In the present case," Judge Putnam said, referring to Webster and his comments of the previous day, "the learned gentleman avows that he is induced to aid the Attorney General merely at his request, and without any other consideration."

Judge Putnam, clearly, was taken in by Daniel Webster's reputation, rhetoric, representations, and the lawyer's charm, public position, and powers of persuasion. "So," Judge Putnam observed, not insisting on a more fulsome examination of if or how Webster was being compensated, "this case presents the question whether a Counsellor may, at the request of the Attorney General, be admitted to aid him in the prosecution, without any pecuniary consideration being paid to him, or any other consideration which may be supposed to influence him, excepting a disinterested regard for the public good." "And we all think that under these circumstances the application should be granted," Judge Putnam concluded, taking note that at Frank Knapp's murder trial, "Mr. Webster was at the request of the law officers appointed to aid them" and "there was no objection then made by the prisoner or his Counsel." "And although that appointment," Judge Putnam said, "strictly was for the then pending trial, yet if the other trials had followed immediately, the Counsel for the Government would have had reason to suppose that they were to receive his assistance in those trials, unless good objections should have been made." "It is said by the law officers," Putnam emphasized, alluding to the attorney general and solicitor general's comments of the previous day, "that the preparations for this trial have been made under a similar expectation on their part, and no objection was made to this measure until the jury were empanelled." Judge Putnam—setting down his ground rules for the conduct of Joe Knapp's murder trial—advised that "two gentlemen only are to address the jury in the case in behalf of the Commonwealth." "It is further to be understood," Judge Putnam said, "that the 'direction and control of the prosecution' is to be with the Attorney General, who acts under oath, and upon his official responsibility."[176]

After Judge Putnam issued the court's ruling, defense counsel in the case remained skeptical and unsatisfied. William Howard Gardiner—another defense lawyer—said "that the statute required that there should be no fee or hope of reward to stimulate the exertions of the prosecuting counsel." "The objection in this case," he said, alluding to Daniel Webster, "arose from the belief that the assistant counsel was retained... by a private individual." "The objection falls to the ground," he conceded, "if this is not the fact." Mr. Gardiner's co-counsel, Mr. Dexter, then jumped in, observing that he "did not understand Mr. Webster to have said he received no fee from any private individual," but that, if he was wrong about that, he "should like to be set right." Judge Samuel Wilde—one of the three judges on the Supreme Judicial Court of Massachusetts sitting in judgment—piped up next. "Judge Wilde," the record reflects, "said he distinctly understood Mr. Webster to say that he came solely at the request of the Attorney General, and had no other inducement." At that point, a short colloquy took place between Mr. Dexter and Mr. Webster. After Mr. Dexter said he "should like to know whether Mr. Webster expected any fee from any private individual," Mr. Webster—as the record also reflects—replied to this effect: "if it would make it stronger, he would repeat it." Mr. Dexter then said he "was satisfied," and the trial thus proceeded with Mr. Webster's active participation.

Notably, shortly after being allowed to participate in Joe Knapp's murder trial, Daniel Webster wrote a private letter about the case to Joseph Story, who, by then, had served nearly two decades as an associate justice of the U.S. Supreme Court. In his letter, Webster wrote that "the P.M." of the day before was spent "mainly in debating whether the attorney-general had a right to bring in other counsel." "[O]n this question," Webster relayed, "their honors deliberated, and this morning agreed to let me in, I having stated to them that I appeared at the request of the attorney-general, and had not received, and should not receive, any fee in this case; which, of course, was and is true." Justice Story, whose two sisters had married Captain White's relatives, had himself drawn Daniel Webster's attention to Captain White's murder in a letter he wrote just ten days after the crime, so it was not too surprising that the two men would be corresponding about the murder case. As Justice Story had written to Webster: "[A]n entire new direction was given to my thoughts by the horrible murder of Old Capt'n White at Salem." "'Truth is stranger than fiction' has been often said—I never knew any case, which so completely illustrated the truth of the remark as this," Justice Story had observed, writing to Webster about the murder that must have frequently consumed his daily thoughts given his familial connections to the murdered man. As Story—as noted—wrote to Webster before the plot to murder Captain White had been exposed: "Not the slightest trace has as yet been found by which to detect the assassins, (for I am satisfied there was more than one) and we are yet in a darkness rendered still darker by the utter defeat of every conjecture."[177]

As it turns out, Daniel Webster was playing a little fast and loose with the facts—at the very least, omitting to tell the court the whole story about the financial arrangements made pertaining to his retention as counsel. For his role in Frank Knapp's murder trial, Stephen White paid Webster the promised $1,000 fee for agreeing to serve as a special prosecutor in the case. Although the first trial had ended in a hung jury, Webster had secured a conviction the second time around, thus proving—yet again—his persuasive powers as an orator and courtroom advocate. Indeed, Webster must have felt great pressure to secure a death sentence in the case, with the *New Hampshire Patriot and State Gazette* commenting: "It would be a sad joke if the immortal Daniel should not succeed in getting a culprit hanged who everybody knows deserves it."[178] But when inquiries were made about arrangements pertaining to attorney's fees, Daniel Webster—as his biographer, Robert Remini, notes—"certainly misled the court and the defense about his recompense." Webster neglected to mention that, far from acting as a volunteer or providing *pro bono* services to aid the public prosecutor, he had already received a fee of $1,000 from Stephen White in payment for his efforts at Frank Knapp's murder trial.[179] A receipt for $1,000, dated August 14th and in Webster's handwriting, pertaining to services in the case of "Jno. F. Knapp" (*i.e.*, John Francis "Frank" Knapp) was later found in the Webster Papers of the Massachusetts Historical Society.[180] Webster's "earnest assertion" that he "appeared without fee" in the Joe Knapp murder trial, Webster biographer Maurice Baxter notes of the material omission, "bypassed the pertinent fact that he had received a handsome fee from his friend Stephen White, nephew and principal heir of the slain shipmaster, to prosecute Frank in the preceding and closely related case."[181]

At Joe Knapp's murder trial, which quickly got underway after Daniel Webster was allowed to participate, William Howard Gardiner opened for the defense. In addressing the jury, he conceded that "this murder is most atrocious," but warned the jurors that "you are not to let the enormity of the crime and the general alarm that it has excited prevent a full and free exercise of your judgment." "The counsel for the prisoner," Gardiner said, describing what his nineteen-year-old client was up against, "is now opposed by the committee of vigilance, opposed by a private prosecutor, Mr. Stephen White, opposed by public opinion, opposed by the whole bar of Essex, and opposed by the learned officers of government." "But the whole bar of Essex, both of these experienced officers, together with the committee of vigilance to back them, is not enough; more strength is necessary," Gardiner acerbically editorialized, adding of Daniel Webster's role in the case: "The most distinguished orator of our time, the high representative of the rights of Massachusetts in the Senate of the United States, with his green and fresh-gained laurels wreathed upon his brow, comes here to aid the host already pressing down the hope and life of the prisoner, to overpower the jury with his eloquence and to 'nullify' the prisoner's defense. So determined seems to be the community to establish the guilt of the persons accused, that it is almost hazardous to appear in their defense." Emphasizing that "[t]he fact of guilt must be proved," Gardiner posed some pointed questions, hoping to plant reasonable doubt about Joe Knapp's guilt: "How many persons have been suspected of this murder—aye, and believed to be guilty? How many false hypotheses have been stated? How many persons falsely accused?" Gardiner pointed out that "even Stephen White—the private prosecutor"—had been examined "because he received the greatest benefit" following the elderly sea captain's murder.[182]

Ultimately, Joe Knapp's confession was read to the jury, with Daniel Webster—as the editor of the trial record in Joe Knapp's case observes—"then persuading the jury that the confession was true." The nine-page confession began: "I mentioned to my brother, John Francis Knapp, in February last, that I would not begrudge one thousand dollars that the old gentleman, meaning Capt. Joseph White of Salem, was dead." "I mentioned to him," Joe confessed of his conversation with his brother Frank, "that the old gentleman had a will, which if destroyed, half of the property would come on this side; that is, to my mother-in-law, Mrs. Beckford; that with the present will, the bulk of the property would go to Stephen White...." In providing a clear motive for the murder, the damning admissions of Joe Knapp—his first confession made in the Salem Jail on May 29, 1830 and a second confession made in the same locale two days later[183]—made clear Joe Knapp's belief that if Captain White died intestate (that is, without will) his considerable fortune would be divided among his close relatives. Joe Knapp, who still had access to Captain White's house through his marriage to Mary, the housekeeper's daughter, damningly admitted stealing what he believed to be Captain White's will four days before the murder—and to burning the stolen document a day after the murder. While at Captain White's house before the murder, it was revealed, Joe Knapp "unbarred and unscrewed" a window, thus allowing entry to the house. But in spite of all the meticulous planning that had taken place, Joe Knapp was unaware that Captain White's last will and testament was, in fact, in the office of the sea captain's lawyer. It was Frank Knapp who told his brother, Joe, that he "had not the pluck" to murder Captain White, leading to the hapless murder-for-hire scheme that unraveled after its execution. The Knapp brothers' childhood friends—Richard and George Crowninshield—had been drawn into the sinister plot, with Richard Crowninshield ultimately agreeing to murder the aging captain.

At Joe Knapp's trial, Mr. Gardiner—arguing for the defense—asserted that "[o]rdinary and extraordinary means were used to convict" Frank Knapp. "We have referred to the employment of Mr. Webster," Gardiner stressed, adding: "Our objections to Mr. Webster appearing in these cases is grounded on principle—they surely are not personal. We consider it illegal for counsel to appear in aid of the law officers of the Government, in behalf of a private prosecutor. This fact is denied in regard to the present case, but it was expressly admitted at the former trial." As Gardiner continued: "It delights me to see that gentleman represent the Commonwealth in the Senate Chamber of the United States; it would delight me to see him represent the Government here—but it does not delight me to see him representing a private prosecutor in the name of the Commonwealth. The prodigious power of this gentleman was exercised against the unhappy youth then put upon this trial." "The Government," Gardiner pointed out of Frank Knapp's first murder trial, "was aided by his great powers in closing the cause—yet, notwithstanding this great pressure of opinion and power brought to act against the prisoner, the first jury could not find the defendant guilty of the matter charged against him, and they were discharged by the Court."[184]

In his prosecutorial role, Daniel Webster urged jurors to consider the deliberate and malicious nature of the crime. "May it please Your Honors—Gentlemen of the jury," Webster began, "[t]he unhappy man who stands charged as being the original mover and promoter of the murder of Captain White, is now before you—it is your duty to pass upon his life." "His own brother allured by him into this dreadful crime," Webster appealed to jurors, noting Frank Knapp's role in the murder-for-hire scheme and observing that the brother "has already atoned by an ignominious death to the violated laws of his country."[185] The crime, Webster said, was "a cool, calculating, money-making murder." "An aged man, without an enemy in the world, in his own house and in his own bed," Webster observed, "is made the victim of a butcherly murder, for mere pay." "It was all 'hire and salary, not revenge,'" he said, adding: "It was the weighing of money against life; the counting out of so many pieces of silver, against so many ounces of blood." Ever the advocate, Webster—the sitting U.S. Senator—nailed home his points. "The deed was executed with a degree of self-possession and steadiness equal to the wickedness with which it was planned," Webster said, detailing the cruel, almost unspeakable way in which the murder was carried out in a room "uncommonly open to the admission of light." As Webster described the murderous act: "The face of the innocent sleeper was turned from the murderer, and the beams of the moon resting on the gray locks of his aged temple, shewed him where to strike—The fatal blow is given! And the victim passes, without a struggle or a motion, from the repose of sleep to the repose of death!" "Gentlemen," Webster concluded in his emotional appeal to jurors, "Your whole concern should be to do your duty, and leave consequences to take care of themselves."[186]

The result of Daniel Webster's advocacy for the prosecution: the jurors returned a verdict of guilty after a four-day trial and a few hours of deliberations. Joe Knapp was sentenced to death on November 15, once again by Judge Putnam. "The aged sufferer was a near relative to your wife," Judge Putnam said, intoning of her close relationship with Captain White: "She was nurtured at his house, and loved and cherished by him as a child." Judge Putnam then turned his attention to Joe Knapp's role, as found by the jury, in the murder victim's death: "You were admitted to partake of his hospitality—you availed yourself of the opportunities to visit at the house of the deceased, to prepare the way for the entrance of your hired assassin to the bed chamber of the victim. You were for months deliberately occupied in devising ways and means of his death. Horrible to think! while you were eating his bread at his own table, you were plotting against his life." "The execution of this awful conspiracy spread dismay, anxiety, and distrust throughout the country," Judge Putnam said before pronouncing "the Sentence of the Law, for the crime of which you have been convicted, which sentence is, and this Court doth accordingly adjudge, that you are to be taken from hence to the prison from whence you came, from thence to the place of Execution, and there be hanged by the neck until you shall be dead." "And may God of his infinite grace have mercy upon your soul," Judge Putnam proclaimed.[187] In Massachusetts, hanging was the standard method of execution.[188]

On Friday, December 31, 1830, Joe Knapp—like his brother, Frank, before him—was thus hanged in accordance with the then-prevailing law. As one newspaper reported it: "The execution of Joseph J. Knapp Jr. took place this morning in the prison yard, about 5 minutes past 9. To the surprise of all, he was as calm and firm, througout, as his brother Frank."[189] He appeared "haggard and dejected," one report noted, emphasizing that his "convulsive spasms continued about five minutes" and that his "body was cut down" about thirty minutes before being placed in a coffin.[190] "There is no chance of any error," Webster had told the jury, saying with confidence in his powerful voice: "His confession cannot be wrong—never was there a story more completely corroborated by external circumstances. Then there are the letters, do they not prove guilt? These letters, which with a most depraved heart he penned and sent to the post Office in order to ward off attention from himself, and fix suspicions upon the innocent, were the very means by which his own enormous guilt was first brought to light." Joe Knapp had planned the murder, Webster stressed, "for mere pieces of silver" and "to come earlier into possession of property." "There is not one bright spot to be discerned in his destiny," Webster had lamented to the jury, "and if it shall be illuminated even by a ray of penitence, it will be dreadful—dreadful—dreadful—all black."[191]

With Daniel Webster having stayed at Stephen White's house in Salem during his time there, his prosecution of the Knapp brothers drew decidedly mixed reviews. Webster's summation at Frank Knapp's murder trial—as Brook Thomas writes in *Cross-Examinations of Law and Literature* (1987)—has been called the "greatest ever delivered to an American jury." One critic, though, was clearly not impressed, calling Frank Knapp's conviction an "example of judicial murder." George Crowninshield—who'd previously been arraigned for his alleged role in the crime—was ultimately acquitted on the basis of an alibi (a woman with whom he'd spent the night), and he maintained to the end of his life, dying at age eighty-five in 1888, that Stephen White, not his brother who'd committed suicide, had murdered the elderly sea captain. "Some attributed his acquittal to the absence of Webster at this trial," notes Brook Thomas in summarizing the case, adding: "Enough Salem residents were outraged at Webster for helping hang two members of a prominent Salem family so that he was never again warmly welcomed by them in their town." "Others," Thomas records, "were understandably upset at the irregularity of having Webster brought in from outside to serve the prosecution, especially since, contrary to his official denial, he was paid one thousand dollars"—the same fee, ironically, paid to Richard Crowninshield to commit Captain White's murder. Such resentment only grew, Thomas observes, when Daniel Webster later received a gift of a yacht, *The Calypso*, from Stephen White, the murdered man's nephew who had been so involved in the committee of vigilance. It was later reported by the *Boston Gazette* in 1832 that Webster and Stephen White had other business dealings, with that newspaper noting that "the Hon. Daniel Webster, Stephen White, and Gen. Wm. H. Sumner, have purchased the Island in our harbor, called Williams' Island, for $70,000, for the purpose of erecting dwelling houses thereon, and building up a little City for summer residences." In a letter sent on August 2, 1832, less than two years after the Knapp brothers had met their fate on the gallows, Daniel Webster wrote to Stephen White: "I have not followed the seas at all, since I saw you last. I reserve the pleasure of renewing that sort of life till you come again, and until *The Calypso* makes her appearance on this coast."

4

PRIVATE PROSECUTIONS IN STATE COURTS

From Murder Charges to Petty Misdemeanors

The Use of Private Prosecutions in State Courts

Senator Daniel Webster's role in the 1830 murder trials of the Knapp brothers made them especially high-profile private prosecutions. But private prosecutors regularly appeared in less conspicuous cases in many places in nineteenth-century America, including in state and local courts in Pennsylvania, the birthplace of the Declaration of Independence and the U.S. Constitution. For example, private prosecutors routinely appeared in Philadelphia's mayor's court[1] and in Pennsylvania's Court of Quarter Sessions.[2] The latter court—modelled on England's, set up in the seventeenth century, and that met (as its name suggested) four times a year—heard all but the most serious cases, with its jurisdiction encompassing everything from cursing and fornication to selling beer without a license.[3] In 1839, one Pennsylvania newspaper pointed out that it was "often the case" that resort was had to the use of "[p]rivate prosecutors."[4] Indeed, a U.S. Senator from Pennsylvania, James Buchanan—a prominent lawyer from Lancaster, Pennsylvania, who became the President of the United States—had this to say in 1842 on the floor of the U.S. Senate: "Most criminal prosecutions are instituted by private prosecution; and the attorney general appears before the State court merely as the law officer of the Government."[5]

In what has been called "[t]he most thorough study of private prosecution in the United States,"[6] Professor Allen Steinberg examined the transformation of criminal justice practices in Philadelphia from 1800 to 1880. In his study, Steinberg found lots of private prosecutions extending long after the American Revolution,[7] with Steinberg concluding: "The discretion of the private parties in criminal cases was not checked by the public prosecutor. Instead, the public prosecutor in most cases adopted a stance of passive neutrality. He was essentially a clerk, organizing the court calendar and presenting cases to grand and petit juries. Most of the time, he was superseded by a private attorney or simply let the private prosecutor and his witnesses take the stand and state their case."[8] Steinberg recounts how the private prosecution system was used in Philadelphia since colonial times, and notes that a city recorder, in 1836, described how a "spirit of litigation" was "among the evils which our fellow citizens suffer, particularly among the poorer classes." In Pennsylvania, public prosecutors had certain powers that private prosecutors did not, but private prosecutions were initiated nonetheless. As *The Carbondale Journal* reported in 1839 of a special power given to the public prosecutor: "The power to enter a *nolle prosequi rests only*, according to the act of assembly, *with the Attorney General and the Court*. A private prosecutor has *no power* to enter a *nolle prosequi*, or take any steps preparatory thereto."[9] Latin for "we shall no longer prosecute," a *nolle prosequi* is an entry made on the record by a prosecutor in a criminal case stating that the prosecutor will no longer pursue the matter.[10]

In tracing the use of private prosecutions back to William Penn and the original settlers of Pennsylvania, Steinberg notes that by 1854 there were more than 50 aldermen in Philadelphia who, in a very decentralized manner, presided over a large docket of civil and criminal matters. "All day long, every day," Steinberg writes, "residents of a ward streamed in and out of the alderman's office, bringing him a variety of civil and criminal business ranging from marriage to murder." There were official state prosecutions, too, but private prosecutions were "overwhelmingly dominant" in the early nineteenth century, with a regular feature of such private prosecutions being pre-trial detention. "For a private prosecution," Steinberg observes of imprisonment, "it was a very powerful lever to use against a foe; for a policemen, an effective way to establish his authority; and for an alderman, a form of legitimate punishment and an unparalleled instrument of extortion."[11] "[P]rivate prosecution was the mainstay of criminal justice for Philadelphia's lower classes," another source emphasizes of the city's earlier days.[12]

Steinberg's study of the actual prosecutorial practices in nineteenth-century Philadelphia reveals some patterns. "Nonindictable offenses—primarily drunkenness, disorderly conduct, and vagrancy—were most often state-initiated," Steinberg writes, adding by way of contrast that "[i]ndictable offenses—mostly assault and battery or petty larceny—were usually private prosecutions." To be sure, there were critics of private prosecutions in Philadelphia, with John Binns, in *Binns' Justice*, asserting that justices of the peace should "prevent the name of the Commonwealth from being used as an engine to gratify private malice, rather than as an instrument to promote the peace and dignity of the Commonwealth." "During the first half of the nineteenth century," Steinberg explains, however, "private prosecution dominated criminal justice in Philadelphia." That was especially true with assault and battery charges, with Steinberg observing that such charges were "the most common private prosecutions" and often produced "cross-bills" by criminal defendants who sought to become private prosecutors themselves. Private prosecutions were frequently used in an attempt to resolve day-to-day disputes, including adultery cases, landlord-tenant matters, and even one case against a fortune teller who led a man's wife to believe that, for a fee, information about his marital infidelities could be revealed.[13] Although David Paul

Brown, a prominent attorney, advised lawyers to "never take blood money," suggesting that capital cases should be handled by the public prosecutor, his advice was not always followed.[14]

In Philadelphia, private prosecutions continued clogging the courts even as efforts were made to stem frivolous cases. They were specifically authorized by legislation, with one 1866 act specifically referring to "private counsel employed by the prosecutor" and providing that if, "at any stage of the proceedings, the district-attorney of the proper county and the private counsel employed by the prosecutor should differ as to the manner of conducting the trial, it shall be lawful for the prosecutor to present his or her petition to the court of the proper county, setting forth the character of the complaint." "[I]f the court shall be of the opinion that it is a proper case for a criminal proceeding or prosecution," that statute read, "it shall be lawful for it to direct any private counsel employed by such prosecutor to conduct the entire proceeding, and where an indictment is necessary, to verify the same by his own signature, as fully as the same could be done by the district attorney." "Between 1854 and 1874," Steinberg writes, "the major weapon used by grand jurors to discourage petty prosecutions was still the power to place the court costs in ignored cases on the prosecutors." Judges warned grand jurors that "by far the largest number of cases which will be submitted to you" belong to a class "originating in private spite." As grand jurors were instructed as to those cases: "With those public justice has no concern. Criminal courts were not created to foment or to pander to either malice or extortion. We do not sit for the collection of bad debts or the accumulation of costs. All cases which fall within this category should be promptly ignored and the prosecutors ordered to pay the costs." "Most of the complaints that come before our aldermen are brought by those who seek to gratify personal animosity and a sudden desire of vengeance rather than any wish to punish the wrong-doer for the sake of right," the Philadelphia Society for Alleviating the Miseries of Public Prisons lamented, with reformers advocating—unsuccessfully at that time—for an end to the private prosecution system. Even after the district attorney position was created in 1850,[15] the law passed in 1866—as noted—entitled a private party's attorney, with the court's permission, to conduct a case if the public prosecutor failed to do so in a manner consistent with the private prosecutor's wishes.[16]

Although duly elected district attorneys within American states took on greater responsibility for charging and prosecutorial decisions over time,[17] private prosecutors still regularly appeared in American courts, not only in Philadelphia[18] but in many other places, too.[19] Before Congress, in 1871, passed the law now codified at 42 U.S.C. § 1983 that provides a cause of action against state actors who violate an individual's rights under federal law, what are often viewed today as government functions were frequently carried out by a mixture of public employees and private actors. "At the time § 1983 was enacted," the U.S. Supreme Court observed in *Filarsky v. Delia* (2012), "private lawyers were regularly engaged to conduct criminal prosecutions on behalf of the State."[20] For instance, "private prosecutors"—or, oftentimes, privately retained counsel acting on their behalf—appeared in places as diverse as Idaho,[21] Illinois,[22] Iowa,[23] Kansas,[24] Kentucky,[25] Maryland,[26] Michigan,[27] Mississippi,[28] New York,[29] North Carolina,[30] Oregon,[31] Texas,[32] Virginia,[33] West Virginia,[34] and Wisconsin.[35] As the Supreme Court wrote in *Filarsky*: "In the mid-19th century, government was smaller in both size and reach. It had fewer responsibilities, and operated primarily at the local level. Local governments faced tight budget restraints, and generally had neither the need nor the ability to maintain an established bureaucracy staffed by professionals."[36]

In the 1850s in Illinois, Abraham Lincoln—the future president who was then a lawyer in private practice—was himself appointed to prosecute criminal acts. The May 14, 1853 edition of the *Springfield Daily Register* reported that "A. Lincoln, esq. was appointed prosecutor" in a rape case, a reference to his role in prosecuting Thomas Watlen for child rape,[37] and in 1857 Lincoln also helped the state's attorney prosecute a murder case—*People v. Wyant*—in which the defendant claimed insanity.[38] In the latter case, a grand jury, in 1855, had returned a "true bill," indicting Isaac Wyant for Anson Rusk's murder. "The indictment," a newspaper reported, "is in the old English form, and sets up that the 'aforesaid Isaac Wyant, not having the fear of God before his eyes, but being moved and seduced by the instigation of the devil,' etc." After seeing Rusk at the courthouse in DeWitt County, Wyant had drawn a revolver and shot Rusk four times. Wyant and Rusk, who had previously quarreled, had been neighboring farmers, and Rusk has previously shot Wyant in the right arm, leading to its amputation, for which Wyant harbored "a deadly hate against Rusk." When the case was initially called, Leonard Swett—Rusk's attorney—moved for and obtained a continuance.

After the venue of the case was transferred and the case was finally called up for trial in 1857, *The Weekly Pantagraph* in Bloomington, Illinois, reported in April of that year: "Great interest in the progress and result of the trial was manifested by the people, and the Court House was constantly thronged." The case was "taken up" on March 31st, with Ward Hill Lamon appearing for the State along with Abraham Lincoln and "C. H. Moore, Esq." The local newspaper pointed out that Judge David Davis presided over the case, with Ward H. Lamon acting as "the State's prosecuting attorney, assisted by Abraham Lincoln, who really conducted the case." As that newspaper reported: "Abraham Lincoln opened for the people, and Leonard Swett for the defense." Medical experts, including three physicians, testified that they believed the murderer was insane, with Swett closing for the defense and Lincoln closing for the prosecution. "The trial," the *Pantagraph* observed decades later of the tremendous public interest in the case, "was the absorbing theme of the time, and men of business and farmers neglected their duties to hear and see the great contest of intellectual giants."[39]

There was, at that time, a large degree of informality in how criminal cases were handled. As one source notes of Abraham Lincoln's relationship with Judge David Davis: "Between 1854 and 1859, Davis appointed Lincoln acting judge in his place to try cases or finish the term. Although this was not legal, it was common practice." As noted, Lincoln also provided assistance to the state's attorney, one of whom was his friend Ward Hill Lamon. As that source, Allen Spiegel's *A. Lincoln, Esquire*, observes: "Lincoln assisted and wrote documents for David Campbell, the state's attorney, and his successor Lamon. In the Logan County Circuit Court, Lincoln drafted an indictment for Lamon." "In *People v. Wyant*," Spiegel writes of that case, "Lincoln prosecuted a murderer when the defense plea was insanity caused by an overdose of chloroform." Although Lincoln believed that the defendant, Isaac Wyant, was "possuming" insanity, Wyant—represented by Leonard Swett, who worked with Lincoln at other times—was acquitted by a jury in McLean County. It was thereafter determined that Wyant should be sent to the Illinois State Hospital for the Insane.[40] The successful assertion of a plea of insanity—as one newspaper later reported—saved "the murderer's neck from the gallows."[41]

Private prosecutors appeared elsewhere, too, including before the Police Court and the Municipal Court in Boston, Massachusetts.[42] At the 1868 trial of Edwin Kelly, accused of murdering Thomas Sharpe, the *New York Daily Herald* gave this report of one such American private prosecution: "The trial of Edwin Kelly, charged with shooting Thomas J. Sharpe, was concluded yesterday. The court room was thronged during the day with members of the theatrical and minstrel profession." "The District Attorney," the newspaper reported, "had not presented the case, but had left it, which was right and proper, to the chosen counsel of the private prosecutor, who, while he nominally represented the people, in point of fact appeared for Mr. Sam Sharpe."[43] "Private citizens were actively involved in government work, especially where the work most directly touched the lives of the people," the U.S. Supreme Court has noted of that era.[44] In some instances, private prosecutors were immigrants who struggled with the English language, necessitating translation services that slowed down the courtroom drama as it unfolded.[45]

Private prosecutors who got convictions could be awarded their court costs.[46] But when unsuccessful, they might be required to foot the bill for those costs.[47] For example, in 1893, in an Oregon case, the costs were taxed to the private prosecutor where one man, Mr. Matney, had another man, Mr. Casson, arrested for tearing down a fence on a county road.[48] In a Vermont case, one community rose up to put an end to a private prosecution it saw as unfair. In that instance, a man named C. C. Doty was "engaged in the manufacture of patent medicine." During some liquor seizures in 1870 for selling alcohol in violation of the law, the authorities were "persuaded" by "Doty's enemies" to seize Doty's products. In a letter to the editor signed "Fair Play" and published in *The Vermont Union*, the letter writer observed: "The people here, on looking the matter over, came to the conclusion that there was too much of a vindictive spirit manifested in the case. It looked to them too much like a malicious prosecution, and, feeling that it would not be right to allow such a spirit to control the case, got up a petition to the State's Attorney, signed by more than one hundred of our citizens, without regard to party, to take the case out of the hands of these private prosecutors and conduct it himself, which he has done, by appointing his agent to take the case in charge, and the investigation is now going on under the control of the State's Attorney."[49]

Old habits die hard. In the nineteenth century, private prosecutors or their chosen attorneys either took charge of or aided or assisted in the prosecution of everything from murder, manslaughter and rape,[50] to fraud and embezzlement,[51] to assault and battery,[52] to assault with a dangerous weapon.[53] Private prosecutions also occurred in cases involving death threats,[54] trespass,[55] perjury,[56] violation of libel[57] and liquor laws,[58] and malicious mischief for tearing down and defacing posters for places of amusement,[59] as well as in a wide range of other matters, from indecent exposure and polygamy to small thefts and larceny.[60] For example, in a Pennsylvania case, *The Wellsboro Agitator* noted in 1866 that "a carpenter by the name of Harry Keissler" acted as the "private prosecutor" of Ernest Watkins, a man charged with stealing a trunk, a watch, old clothes, and a pair of boots.[61] Likewise, in Oregon in 1898, two bakers got into a dispute about a bicycle valued at $15, resulting in a private prosecution.[62] Although private prosecutors were involved in larceny cases where the amount in controversy might be just a few dollars or where the defendant faced time in the county jail,[63] private prosecutors also got involved in murder and manslaughter cases where the stakes were much higher—and might be death or long-term imprisonment.[64]

Private prosecutions sparked heightened emotions, with such prosecutions sometimes pitting relatives against one another. In rare instances, such prosecutions might actually cease with the death of the private prosecutor—a person subjected to the burden and stress of undertaking a prosecution. Such was the case with one criminal matter in Iowa in 1891. In a news item headlined "Taken to a Higher Court," *The Cedar Rapids Evening Gazette* reported on April 30th of that year that "[t]he usual monotony of taking testimony in a criminal case was broken yesterday morning by the announcement that the private prosecutor, G. W. Janes, had suddenly died with heart disease." "It was the case of the State vs. B. F. Ogden for perjury," the newspaper observed, adding: "The state had introduced its witnesses and the defendant, B. F. Ogden, had just commenced to testify in his own behalf, when a messenger announced that the prosecutor, G. W. Janes, was dead." "It was a startling incident in a remarkable case," *The Cedar Rapids Evening Gazette* reported, noting that the case arose out of a family feud between Janes and Ogden, his brother-in-law. Ogden was "visibly shocked," and the court adjourned, with the newspaper noting that "the case will now be dropped."[65]

In other instances, private prosecutors simply lost interest in prosecutions, got intimidated by the accused or the accused's friends,[66] or failed to show up altogether,[67] causing criminal cases to fall apart.[68] For example, on May 30, 1882, *The Times* of Philadelphia noted that "[t]he criminal suits of the Commonwealth against William Gallagher, William J. Gilmore and George Wood, charged with conducting a theatrical exhibition without having obtained a State license, came on for trial yesterday, before Judge Craig Biddle, for the third time." The newspaper observed that Assistant

District Attorney Warwick "asked for a postponement" because "the Commonwealth had not been able to secure the attendance of its witnesses." An attorney, J. S. Williams, described as "the private prosecutor," was then sent for, "but could not be found." After the judge insisted that the cases should proceed to trial because they were on "the printed list," "the Commonwealth's witnesses had been properly subpoenaed," and "there were no legal grounds for a continuance," the Commonwealth—as the newspaper editorialized—"thus pushed to the wall, called to the stand B. Frank Paris, the only witness present." "Mr. Paris," the paper reported, "said that he did not know anything about the matter," leading to the entry of a not guilty verdict.[69] In April 1884, *The Philadelphia Inquirer* also reported about another ill-fated private prosecution in this fashion: "The cases of George Brotherton, Budd Williams, Abram Marks and Charles Kane, charged with keeping gambling houses, were called for trial before Judge Finletter in the old court house yesterday, but as the private prosecutors, Henry Wesley, Benjamin B. Wiley, Henry C League and Fred. Winslow failed to put in an appearance... and verdicts of not guilty taken."[70]

It came to be understood in many places that the district attorney had to maintain control over the prosecution—and over any private attorney appearing in the case to assist the public prosecutor. That notion, in fact, goes back a long way. For instance, a treatise published in 1850—*The Law Student, or Guides to the Study of Law in Its Principles*—observed that although "[t]he private prosecutor may... invoke the aid of his own retained counsel," "this is always subject to the control of the public officer, who has power to check oppression." Noting that "[t]he most customary mode of exercising such control, is by entering a 'nolle prosequi' on the indictment," that treatise emphasized that "to the honor of those who have filled the office" of attorney general, district attorney or county attorney, "they have not hitherto been found remiss in using" their power to check abuse. As that treatise also observed: "In the United States, as in England, any one may accuse under the penalty attending a groundless prosecution. Our administration of the criminal law seems most safe, as it has the constant intervention of an impartial officer to restrain or defeat the malice of a prosecutor." "The effectual check, however, in both countries, to the abuse of criminal power by private malice," that treatise, *The Law Student*, pointed out, "is the action on the case for malicious prosecution."[71]

In 1851, to give but one example of the law requiring public prosecutors to control prosecutions in addition to the court ruling concerning Daniel Webster's assistance in Joe Knapp's 1830 trial in Massachusetts, *The Daily Delta* in New Orleans, Louisiana, reported on one matter, *United States v. Henderson*, before the U.S. Circuit Court. In summarizing Judge McCaleb's ruling in a case involving an alleged violation of "the Neutrality Laws," the newspaper made this observation about what Judge McCaleb said in rejecting a motion to force an assistant prosecutor, Mr. Benjamin, off the case: "The District Attorney would conduct this case under the supervision of the Court, who would see that the accused had a fair trial, that there was no oppression in the prosecution." The judge could not "deny the right of the District Attorney to call other counsel to his aid, in a case which would involve an amount of physical and intellectual labor beyond the capacity of one man." As the judge, speaking for the court (and as summarized by the newspaper), made clear: "The District Attorney would be responsible for this assistant counsel. This Court would not have anything to do with the fee of this counsel, and only looked to him as part of the prosecution,—an auxiliary employed by the District Attorney to aid him. Of course, the Court would not allow the District Attorney to employ too many counsel, or to oppress the accused in any manner." Judge McCaleb referred to many state court cases where "assistant counsel had been employed to aid the prosecutor."[72]

The Murder of "Big Jim" Fisk and the Trials of "Ned" Stokes

While the poor were often unable to afford to retain counsel to represent their interests, wealthy individuals commonly employed private prosecutors. An example of that can be seen in a series of bitter disputes—culminating in a murder case—in the 1870s between James Fisk Jr., a flamboyant stockbroker who was the senior partner in the Wall Street firm of Fisk & Belden, and Edward "Ned" Stokes, whose family owned a New York oil refinery and who was, for a time, a business partner of Fisk. Known as "Diamond Jim" and "Big Jim," James Fisk Jr.—a militia colonel who made a fortune in dry goods during the Civil War—had close ties to Tammany Hall, New York's Democratic Party's machinery. He also had close financial ties to Gilded Age robber baron and financier Jay Gould, the president of the Erie Railway. In 1869, Jay Gould's scheme to try to corner the entire U.S. gold supply—one in which Fisk actively participated—led to a stock market panic known as Black Friday on September 24, 1869.

A well-known womanizer whose wife, Lucy, lived apart from him in Boston, Fisk gave his New York mistress, Helen Josephine Mansfield, a four-story residence not far from his mansion along with access to servants, a carriage, clothing, and jewelry. But in 1870, much to Fisk's dismay, Mansfield—a former showgirl—announced that she had fallen in love with Ned Stokes, a handsome businessman she had met through Fisk himself. Fisk and Stokes were once fast friends who had profitable business dealings. In another financial scheme, the Erie Railroad—at Fisk's behest—had previously given Stokes' oil refinery in Brooklyn favored treatment. But jealousy over being jilted, combined with efforts to extract money from Fisk, eventually had deadly consequences.[73] After "Josie" Mansfield demanded a $25,000 cash payment from Fisk, with Mansfield and Stokes threatening to publish Fisk's love letters to Mansfield if Fisk did not comply, Fisk rebuffed those efforts. "Big Jim" would not be played or pushed around, and he decided to play hardball. Fisk cancelled lucrative deals between the Erie Railroad and Stokes' oil refinery, destroying Stokes' business, and Fisk publicly charged Mansfield and Stokes with blackmail, leading to a libel suit against Fisk.

This was just one of many legal proceedings that would occur, with Fisk having Stokes arrested—and put in handcuffs—for allegedly embezzling $250,000. Fisk alleged that Stokes stole the money from the oil refinery business in which Fisk and Stokes were partners. When Fisk lost that battle, Stokes sued Fisk for malicious prosecution, a suit later settled when Fisk agreed to purchase the Stokes family interest in Brooklyn Oil. A neutral referee also ordered Fisk to pay Stokes $10,000 in compensation for being imprisoned for one night on the wrongfully filed embezzlement charge. After Stokes sued Fisk for fraud and attempted to prove that it was Fisk who was stealing corporate assets, Stokes sought to introduce into evidence telegrams and love letters that Fisk had sent to Mansfield. The judge, however, decided to exclude the missives—a ruling that only further heightened the tension between the two men. "These letters," one history notes, "were of a nature that would have compromised many people and revealed important Erie secrets, besides making public many of Fisk's personal affairs that he did not care to have paraded." Eventually, Fisk relented and agreed to pay Stokes $15,000 for the letters. But after the money was paid, Stokes reneged on the bargain, leading Fisk to make a charge of blackmail against Stokes.

The bitter series of disputes eventually turned deadly. The evidentiary ruling on the letters was made on January 6, 1872, with Fisk—known as "the Prince of Erie"—leaving the Yorkville Police Courthouse feeling victorious. After court adjourned, a number of the lawyers went to eat lunch at Delmonico's at the corner of Broadway and Chambers Street. Stokes went there, too, with his lawyer, John McKeon. It was at Delmonico's that Stokes—always fashionably attired whenever he went out—learned from a judge that he'd been indicted by a grand jury for blackmail and would be arrested, sending him into an apoplectic rage. As one account reports of what transpired next: "Stokes armed himself with his Colt revolver, went to see Josie, and then left in search of Fisk. Learning that Fisk intended to visit some friends at the Grand Central Hotel, Stokes arrived there first and waited at the top of a staircase. He fired twice, wounding Fisk in his arm and stomach." Stokes' revolver was later found under a sofa in the parlor, although Stokes himself admitted to shooting Fisk and asked that a physician be called to the scene. Doctors tried unsuccessfully to remove the bullet from his chest, but Fisk died the next morning.

The shooting took place after Ned Stokes was seen "pacing back and forth in an agitated state" in the hotel's upper lobby. After Fisk arrived at the hotel, Stokes had confronted him on the stairway, with Thomas Hart, a bellboy, testifying that he saw Stokes standing at the top of the stairs pointing his gun at Fisk. "I've got you now," Stokes told Fisk, Hart testified. "For God's sake, will anybody save me?" Fisk yelled, but it was too late. After firing the two shots, Stokes fled while Fisk, reeling in pain, managed to walk down the stairs. Thomas Hart, the bellboy, reportedly "followed Stokes at a safe distance, saw him cross the second-floor lobby, pause at a sofa, then go down the main staircase to the first-floor lobby." But after Hart pointed out Stokes to H. L. Powers, the hotel's manager, Powers shouted, "Stop that man!" Powers and other citizens then managed to detain Stokes at the hotel's Mercer Street entrance near a barber shop. Stokes was quickly arrested for the shooting, with Fisk identifying Stokes as the shooter as he was being treated for the gunshot wound by Dr. Thomas

Tripler in Room 213 of the hotel. Stokes would assert at trial that he had acted in self-defense, claiming that Fisk had pointed a revolver at him—a claim that would be contested by Thomas Hart, the eyewitness to the shooting. Josie Mansfield's own father had been murdered in California during the Gold Rush when she was just seven years of age, and now Josie's former lover—Jim Fisk—would be killed, too, the result of an ill-fated love triangle.[74]

There actually ended up being three criminal trials, not just one, in the aftermath of the shooting, with Stokes retaining three lawyers—Willard O. Bartlett, John McKeon, and Elbridge T. Gerry—to represent him. At the initial inquest into the circumstances surrounding Fisk's death, held in the Tombs Building at the Court of Special Sessions, Ned Stokes was arraigned before a coroner's jury for the killing. The coroner, Nelson Young, presided over the inquest, and—as *The New York Herald* reported—"[t]here appeared for the accused Stokes four of the greatest lawyers in New York." Among them, John McKeon, a man described as having "white hair" and as having "all the chivalry of his impetuous nature aroused in this case, as he is celebrated life-long for taking the side of the under dog in the case." John McKeon was described elsewhere as "one of the keenest lawyers in New York."

At the inquest, three men—William Beach, William Fullerton, and Charles S. Spencer—sat to the left of the prisoner's counsel and were described as "THE ERIE LAWYERS." Their "part in the proceedings"—as the *Herald* noted—"did not seem to be clearly understood until John McKeon made them show their hands." James Fisk and Jay Gould had been close friends, and it was Fisk and Gould who had sworn out warrants and had Stokes locked up in Ludlow Street Jail.[75] It was rumored that those three lawyers "were appearing secretly to help District Attorney Sullivan, who sat directly under the Coroner, but they did not appear openly on behalf of the prosecution until John McKeon unmasked their batteries, and then he drew their fire immediately." As the *Herald* reported: "It seems that Beach and Fullerton had been writing out questions on slips of paper to be propounded to the lad Redman, the first witness summoned for the prosecution, and McKeon in his fiery way demanded from the Coroner that the name of each person sending a question to the Coroner or District Attorney should be appended to the paper as sent up, Coroner Young having already ruled that the prisoner's counsel must put all questions to the witnesses on slips of paper and then that he should decide if they were admissible." "Beach and Fullerton," the newspaper noted, "both were forced to 'rise and explain' and acknowledge that they had sent up the questions; but District Attorney Sullivan, who was advising the Coroner, refused to answer who had sent him the slips of paper."[76]

Ned Stokes, a man of considerable means, got favorable treatment during his pretrial detention. After being confined in Cell No. 50 at the Tombs, the notorious New York prison, Ned Stokes had the cell decorated at his expense pending trial. As one source reports of how Stokes transformed the cell's appearance: "It is richly carpeted, the walls are papered and hung with a few fine pictures, and a new hair mattress and new bed-clothing have been substituted for the coarse prison articles. Altogether, the cell now appears more like a young lady's boudoir." Although the coroner's jury had found against him, Stokes remained upbeat, telling reporters, "You newspapermen are all wrong about my case." "I have no more fears of the result than you have," he said, adding: "I am confident I will get out of it. That Erie gang is working against me. It is one of the worst the world ever knew, and the head of it is an astute villain—that little Jay Gould. They seem to have the newspapers, though I don't know how they can secure their influence." Stokes' first murder trial, in fact, ended in a hung jury—vindicating, at least to a decree, Stokes' air of confidence. That initial trial began on June 19, 1872, and the jurors were given the case on July 13th. They deliberated for 40 hours but were unable to reach a unanimous verdict. However, in a second trial, which began on December 18, 1872, Stokes was convicted of the capital charge of first-degree murder. Stokes was promptly sentenced to be hanged on January 6, 1873, the one-year anniversary of the shooting, but after he was taken back to the Tombs, which housed New York's death row inmates, his lawyers appealed the verdict.[77]

The role of the private prosecutors was attacked in the murder prosecution of Ned Stokes, though to no avail before the trial court. In 1872, John McKeon—Stokes's defense lawyer—vocally criticized the public prosecutor for associating with private counsel. "These law-books which I have before me," he said in an opening statement, "make prosecutions of this kind in the nature of public, official acts, to be conducted by public officers, and not to partake of the nature of a private prosecution." "In this case," McKeon said, "my charge is distinctly to the District Attorney, and to his face, that this is not a public prosecution but a private prosecution." As McKeon emphasized: "This display which has been made here of private counsel, has been, I say, but once before in the history of the administration of justice in this State. None of the gentlemen who preceded him in this high office have had alongside of them persons fed by private individuals. I challenge him to point to a single case which has been assisted by private counsel." "The only cases in which they have been allowed are those in which they took the place of the public prosecutor," he said, telling jurors: "Just think what power is wielded by that officer. The District-Attorney can at once convert a felon into an honest man by converting him into a witness, and he is a credible one if the jury choose to believe him. Further than that, I know the power has been exercised, and properly, too, of entering *nolle prosequis* in cases of life and death, and thus permitted persons to walk off the scaffold." In making his argument that no private prosecutor should have been allowed to associate with the district attorney in the case, McKeon asserted: "The District-Attorney can go into the Grand Jury room and tell the Grand Jury, 'If you indict this person I will immediately enter a nol. pros., and tell the man to go free.' He can hold all this power, and it is right. And when he holds that power, I deny that any public prosecutor should allow private prosecutors to be associated with him."[78]

In the second trial, the one in which Stokes was convicted of murdering James Fisk Jr., the accused, Ned Stokes, faced off in the New York Court of Oyer and Terminer against a prosecution team consisting not only of Assistant New York County District

Attorney John R. Fellows,[79] but two well-regarded private attorneys, William Beach and William Fullerton, both of whom had appeared at the inquest and the latter a former judge with considerable experience in criminal matters.[80] Beach and Fullerton knew Stokes, but—as one newspaper article put it—"announced themselves retained to assist the Public Prosecutor in putting the rope about his neck." The lead defense lawyer, John McKeon, vehemently objected to the presence of Beach and Fullerton in the courtroom, seeing the two private attorneys as agents hired to procure a death sentence. Beach had actually been Fisk's lawyer in Josie Mansfield's prior libel suit, and Fullerton was Beach's colleague. "These gentlemen now employed," McKeon said, "were hired for the purpose of producing a conviction." "It is a terrible spectacle," he emphasized, "to see private counsel arranging themselves on the side of the prosecution, and with blood-hound perseverance hound this man."

But in spite of John McKeon's objection, the private attorneys were allowed to participate in the trial for the prosecution, with Fullerton formally opening the prosecution's case. And that opening statement was widely hailed, described in the press an "an effective address."[81] Beach, too, did his job in a workmanlike manner. "The result of the second trial of Edward S. Stokes for the killing of James Fisk, Jr., will probably no less surprise the public than it astounded, last evening, the prisoner and his friends," the *New York World* and another paper reported, adding: "The first trial had been generally conceded to be unfair, or at least founded upon insufficient testimony; and when the new witnesses for Stokes—witnesses who swore so straight to the point that Fisk drew and dropped a pistol on the stairs—appeared, Thursday, there was a flood-tide of favorable feeling in the audience at court, and in the audience outside of court, toward the man whose death was a very short while ago insisted upon by a public sentiment which loathed an assassin."

The reaction to the jury's verdict was mixed. "We are not surprised at the verdict," the *New York Herald* editorialized, observing: "A year ago all but a day Fisk, bold, reckless, intriguer as he was, died by the hand of Stokes, a man with whom he had long been engaged in a bitter quarrel." "Though we have said above that Fisk was a bold and reckless intriguer," the paper emphasized, "we do not wish it for a moment to be understood that these traits of character were at all to be considered as arguments for or against the conviction of his murderer." "[W]hile all citizens are agreed that a murderer should, according to law, be hung," the *New York World* reported, "so singular a doubt as to who was the aggressor in this case will still linger in the public mind after the verdict." "To the score or so of alleged murderers who are awaiting trial in the Tombs," the venerable *New York Times* weighed in, adding its reaction, "the conviction of Stokes will be somewhat depressing news." "To the public who were gravely considering the problem whether the murderers and the criminal lawyers were not becoming too strong and too cunning for the regular process of law," that paper observed, "the news will be reassuring, and will put an end, for the present at least, to a good deal of wild talk, partially justified by recent deeds of violence."[82]

As University of Texas at Austin historian H. W. Brands, putting the unfolding action in the present tense for his readers, observed of the shocked reaction of Stokes to the jury's guilty verdict in that case: "He faces the private prosecutor. 'Mr. Beach,' he says bitterly, 'you have done your work well. I hope you have been paid for it.'" After Assistant District Attorney John Fellows declared that Beach had only reluctantly taken on prosecutorial responsibilities and without any fee from Jim Fisk's family or friends, Stokes asked: "Not from Jay Gould?" There was momentary silence. "This verdict is not in accordance with the facts: it is in accordance with the money of Jay Gould!" Stokes exclaimed.[83] When the sentence of death was imposed, it was reported that the courthouse "presented an unusually animated spectacle, long lines of men passing hurriedly and eagerly in, as though afraid that they were too late for something that was about to occur inside." As one newspaper reported: "At 11 a.m. Sheriff Brennan and his deputies, Stevens and Shields, entered the room with the prisoner, upon whose face was impressed the habitual look of weariness and despair. He was pale and gloomy, and took his seat apparently oblivious of everything around him." As that account noted: "Judge Boardman walked in directly afterward, but had no sooner taken his seat, and asked the crier to open Court, than a movement was observed in the group around Stokes, where sat, beside his own counsel, Mr. Beach and Mr. Fullerton." "Stokes," it was said, "was seen to rise and follow Sheriff Brennan outside," with the newspaper account observing: "The conjectures as to this move were many for the moment, and one of the rumors of the Court was that Mr. Beach, whose eye had been fixed steadily upon Stokes, feared a pistol shot from the man for whose conviction he had argued so forcibly and earnestly, and had whispered to the Sheriff the propriety of having the prisoner searched."[84]

Before being sentenced, Stokes professed his innocence, saying "the evidence of homicide on which I was convicted is false from beginning to end, and I believe the prosecution knew it, and the District Attorney knew it, and the counsel for the prosecution knew it when he summed up the case." But a death sentence was imposed nonetheless, with the judge observing at the outset: "You have been defended by the most eloquent and able counsel with extraordinary skill and devotion. You have been supported and sustained by the sympathy of your loving relatives and ardent friends. All that wealth, affection or industry could do for you has been cheerfully and well done." After noting that a "carefully selected" jury of "intelligent and upright gentlemen" had "listened patiently and kindly to your own account of this terrible act, as well as to the other evidence that has been put in your behalf," the judge observed that Stokes had been found "guilty of murder in the first degree—the highest crime known to our laws—in having caused the death of James Fisk, Jr., one year ago to-day." "This verdict," the judge said, "was wrung from their judgment—not prompted by their hearts." "Edward S. Stokes, in obedience to the requirements of the law," the judge intoned at the sentencing, "this Court orders and directs that you been taken hence, in the custody of the Sheriff of the City and County of New York, to the prison from whence you came; that you be there confined in close custody by said Sheriff until the 28th of February, 1873, and that on that day, between the hours of 11 o'clock in the morning and 3 o'clock in the afternoon, you be hanged by the neck until you are dead, and may God have mercy on your soul." In New York, hanging was the mode of execution until the passage of the Electrical Execution Act of 1888.[85]

After being sentenced, the death warrant was read to Stokes by the clerk before he was taken back to his cell.[86] Although Stokes had been scheduled to be hanged in February 1873, he was granted a stay and the Court of Appeals ultimately granted him a new trial. It was a third and final trial, which began on June 10, 1873, that led to a manslaughter conviction for Stokes and a six-year prison sentence to be served at Sing Sing. At that trial, in which the district attorney demanded a death sentence and called "Josie" Mansfield a "harlot," Stokes asserted that he had shot Fisk in self-defense, that Fisk had brandished a gun when they met on the staircase at the Grand Central Hotel, but that he (Stokes) had managed to shoot first. Mansfield testified that Fisk owned nearly a dozen pistols and had threatened to kill Stokes, with new witnesses testifying that Fisk did have a gun on the fateful day that he was shot.[87] In 1877, after serving four years of his sentence, Stokes was released from prison. Josie Mansfield reportedly "drifted about for some time" after the whole episode and ended up settling in Paris.[88]

The presence of meddlesome private lawyers was continually on the mind of Ned Stokes. In 1876, as he was pleading for his release from prison in a habeas corpus petition, Stokes was still complaining about his treatment by the private prosecutors. Essentially, in his petition, Stokes was seeking credit for the time he spent in prison—at the Tombs—prior to being convicted, in part because of the conduct of the private prosecutors. In addressing "THE HONORABLE JUDGES OF THE SUPREME COURT, SECOND DISTRICT," Stokes took the opportunity to describe his "unfortunate and remarkable case." "I was arraigned in the Oyer and Terminer, at the expiration of said ninety days, before Judge Cardozo, whom my prosecutors had selected to preside at my trial," Stokes recited, adding: "Private counsel was employed against me. Messrs. William A. Beach and ex-Judge Fullerton, who advised the District Attorney, S. B. Garvin, that the question as to the legality of the Grand Jury that indicted me should be determined by jury trial, which subjected me to additional delay." Samuel B. Garvin, the District Attorney, served in that position from 1869 to 1872.[89]

Although he had indisputably killed a man, Ned Stokes—having asserted he acted in self-defense—was furious about how he had been treated. "Upon the conclusion of said trial," Stokes noted, "Judge Cardozo resigned his official position, which delayed my trial still further until the month of June." "The manifest terrible injustice that outrageous verdict inflicted upon me is a matter of history," Stokes railed, "and I will not expatiate upon it further than to say that on the 10th of June the Court of Appeals by a unanimous vote reversed the judgment, declaring it illegal in every particular." "District Attorney Fellows, representing the people at that trial," Stokes added, "has since had the manhood and magnanimity to declare that subsequent information received from the police authorities fully satisfied him Fisk was armed." As Stokes described the new evidence and District Attorney Fellow's position: "Fisk's pistol was picked up on the staircase and spirited away, and further, that he fully indorses the opinion advanced by Mr. Bartholomew, the foreman of the final jury, that the principal witness, Thomas Hart, committed deliberate perjury." In an extended statement about his case written from Sing Sing in February 1874, Ned Stokes declared that "that Fisk brought about the conflict," and that "Erie Ring lawyers and Tammany Ring judges came near destroying me," with Stokes referring to "the manufactured story of Thomas Hart and his accomplices."[90]

Growing Skepticism and the Public Debate over Private Prosecutors

Although private prosecutions were still fairly common in many American states during the nineteenth century, a growing skepticism of private prosecutors' motives—ranging from concerns about corruption and malice,[91] to schemes to collect fees,[92] to the potential for extortion and blackmail[93]—led many American jurists to warn about the abuses associated with them. For example, in 1872 in the District of California, U.S. Supreme Court Associate Justice Stephen Field—nominated by President Abraham Lincoln—gave this pointed instruction to a grand jury: "You will not allow private prosecutors to intrude themselves into your presence, and present accusations. Generally such parties are actuated by private enmity, and seek merely the gratification of their personal malice." "If they possess any information justifying the accusation of the person against whom they complain," Justice Field said, "they should impart it to the district attorney, who will seldom fail to act in a proper case." "But if the district attorney should refuse to act," Field clarified of private prosecutors, "they can make their complaint to a committing magistrate, before whom the matter can be investigated, and if sufficient evidence be produced of the commission of a public offense by the accused, he can be held to bail to answer to the action of the grand jury."

In his charge to grand jurors, Justice Field emphasized the importance of the public prosecutor and the magistrate to administering the criminal laws. "When the court," Justice Field said, "does not deem the matter of sufficient importance to call your attention to it, and the district attorney does not think it expedient to submit the matter to your consideration, and the private prosecutor neglects to proceed before the committing magistrate, we think it may be safely inferred that public justice will not suffer, if the matter is not considered by you." "A preliminary examination of the accused before a magistrate, where he can meet his prosecutor face to face, and cross-examine him, and the witnesses produced by him, and have the benefit of counsel," Justice Field stressed, "is the usual mode of initiating proceedings in criminal cases, and is the one which presents to the citizen the greatest security against false accusations from any quarter." "And this mode," Field continued, "ought not to be departed from, except in those cases where the attention of the jury is directed to the consideration of particular offenses by the court, or by the district attorney, or the matter is brought to their knowledge in the course of their investigations, or from their own observations, or from disclosures made by some of their number." Justice Field took specific note of abuses by prior grand juries, observing that "an impression widely prevails that the institution of the grand jury has outlived its usefulness, an impression which has been created from a disregard of those limits, and the facility with which it has, unfortunately, often been used as an instrument for the gratification of private malice."[94] Although many Americans defended the grand jury system, seeing it as a check against "made up" accusations, there were, in fact, calls in the nineteenth century to do away with the grand jury system entirely because of abuses associated with it.[95]

Tracking the sentiments of Justice Field, and in some cases repeating his exact words,[96] many lower courts in the United States also warned grand jurors to be extremely wary of private prosecutors.[97] For example, in the State of Montana, Chief Justice Decius Wade—at the opening of Yellowstone County's district court in 1883—delivered what was described as an "exhaustive charge" to the grand jury about its duties. That charge included a warning "not to act at the instigation of any private prosecutor as, if this were allowed, grand juries might be made instruments of oppression and the tools of malice."[98] In Camden, New Jersey, in 1890, Judge Garrison's grand jury charge similarly instructed the grand jurors about a real and present danger: "the tendency existing in this county of private prosecutors appearing before the grand jury in the first instance to commence public prosecutions." "This course," he said, "is not only contrary to all established forms of procedure in criminal matters, but it is also to the entire spirit of the laws and is hostile to the proper procedure of the grand jury as will be shown if reference is made to the obligation just taken."[99] And in New Orleans, Louisiana, in 1892, Judge J. C. Moise instructed grand jurors: "You will not allow private prosecutors to intrude themselves into your presence and present accusations. Generally such parties are actuated by personal enmity, and seek merely the gratification of their personal malice. If they possess any information justifying the accusation of a person, they should impart it to the prosecuting officer, who will not fail to act in a proper case."[100]

Grand jury charges, in fact, became a common way for jurists to excoriate the ulterior motives of private prosecutors motivated by ill-will or principally by financial gain.[101] For instance, in 1893, in Missouri, the *St. Louis Post-Dispatch* summarized a grand jury charge as follows: "Judge Edmunds also warns the jurors to remember that it is not the intention of the law that the criminal courts be used to collect private debts, and instructs the jurors that when they have any reason to believe that is the intention of the prosecution not to indict." As the newspaper, summarizing the grand jury charge, asserted under the headline "Judge Edmunds Tells the Jury to Beware of Private Prosecutors Whom He Severely Scores": "This is to be judged mainly by the length of time that has elapsed after the offense was committed before the prosecution was began." The judge, the paper relayed, gave the following advice: "The private prosecutor is to be viewed by you with the utmost suspicion in all cases, but especially in cases of embezzlement. The private prosecutor who appears for the first time before you is as a rule a coward or a knave—too much of a coward to appear in the Court of Criminal Correction, which has preliminary jurisdiction in all cases of felony, but knave enough to sneak into the Grand-jury room and under the protection of the secrecy there enjoyed, gratify his malice."[102]

The institution of the grand jury was widely seen in those days as a check against malicious private prosecutors. "Grand juries in our times," the *Harrisburg Telegraph* observed in 1882, "serve as a barrier against friv[o]lous State prosecutions and a wholesome restraint upon private prosecutors and the malice of popular excitement."[103] Ten years later, in another newspaper, one published in Carbondale, Pennsylvania, the grand jury's responsibility—and a bit of information about its history—was laid out in this way: "The function and duty of a grand jury in this day and generation is a question that puzzles men of every degree, who know little or much of court practice and the machinery of the judicial mill. In ancient times the Grand Jury was an important body, composed in each county of representative citizens of the several hundreds. Their first and principal duty was to pass upon indictments presented to them in the name of the King (or Commonwealth), but at the suit of any private prosecutor."[104] A *hundred*—a Saxon designation consisting of "ten *tithings*, or groups of ten families of freeholders or frankpledges"—was an administrative division formerly used in England, Wales and elsewhere; each hundred was governed by a high constable and had its own court. In 1878, a Virginia attorney also specifically argued that grand juries "were a necessity as a bar to the malice of the private prosecutor."[105]

Serious concerns arose that private prosecutors—or their agents or representatives—were attempting to manipulate grand jurors and that such efforts might go unnoticed because of the secrecy of grand jury proceedings and deliberations. In 1891, *The Sun* in New York observed that "[i]n the course of his recent charge to the April Grand Jury in the Court of General Sessions, Judge RANDOLPH B. MARTINE made the following remarks: 'When the Grand Jury is sworn the names of the grand jurors appear in the newspapers. Friends of individual grand jurors who have grievances, real or imaginary, against some person have been in the habit of calling upon their friend on the Grand Jury and asking him to take up their grievance. I desire to say that this is not a proper practice. No grand juror should give attention to any such private complaint. All such complaints, or all the complaints of any character, should be laid before the Grand Jury as a body, and not before an individual member.'" *The Sun* then editorialized: "The Grand Jury can hardly be warned too often against allowing themselves to be made the agents of private prosecutions which are not designed to promote any public interest, but are intended in reality only to enforce the collection of claims or to accomplish some other purpose of a purely personal character with which the community at large has no concern." "Forty years ago," the newspaper continued, "the tendency to such abuses was pointed out in a report made to the Legislature by the Commissioners appointed to frame a Code of Criminal Procedure. . . ."[106] "When such information reaches a member of the Grand Jury," *The Sun* advised, "he should not take up the case as a prosecutor, but should cause the accuser to attend in person before the Grand Jury as a body, and tell his story to them. Then the other witnesses may be sent for, and the matter may be investigated in a proper manner."[107]

In individual cases and as matter of policy, the use of private prosecutors thus came under blistering attacks in the nineteenth century, including in American courtrooms, where attorneys and judges already had a healthy dose of skepticism toward them. In 1839, in antebellum Kentucky, Benjamin Hardin—one of the most prominent lawyers in the state—was paid $1,000 to act as a special private prosecutor in the highly publicized trial of three men—a judge, a physician, and one of their friends—accused of murdering two Louisville men, a bar-keeper, Alexander Meeks, and a hatter, John Rothwell. The $1,000 payment came from friends of the victims, and the courtroom was reportedly "crowded to the doors" for the murder trial, with "more than two hundred of the spectators being women." The men put on trial—Judge Wilkinson, Dr. Wilkinson, and John Murdaugh—were very prominent, so the case attracted considerable public attention prior to and during the trial. Judge Wilkinson, from Mississippi, had been a guest at the Galt House in Louisville, Kentucky, along with his brother, Dr. Wilkinson, and their friend, Mr. Murdaugh. A local tailor had been hired to make a suit for the doctor, but the coat didn't fit right, leading to a dispute in the tailor's shop.

In that dispute, Judge Wilkinson struck the tailor on the head with a poker and Dr. Wilkinson and Mr. Murdaugh both drew their Bowie knives. The tailor, Mr. Redding, later attempted to get a writ against the three men at the mayor's office, but he was told that he needed to get all of their names, so he and his brother-in-law, John Rothwell, went to the Galt House and obtained them from the bar-keeper. Meanwhile, what had happened to the tailor in his shop became known among his friends, and a butcher and Mr. Meeks began suggesting to others that they avenge the attack on their friend. When Judge Wilkinson entered the barroom, Redding denounced him as a scoundrel and a coward and threatened to "whip" all three of the Mississippians if they stepped out into the street. Judge Wilkinson promptly threatened to kill Redding if he laid a hand on him, with Judge Wilkinson retiring to his room before returning with his two friends for supper.

The conflict at the Galt House quickly escalated after the three men entered the barroom. "They are all three here now," Redding exclaimed, with Redding looking at Mr. Murdaugh and saying, "You are the gentleman who drew a knife upon me at my shop to-day." "Whoever says I drew a knife upon you, is a damned liar," Murdaugh replied, quickly brandishing in his right hand a white-handled dirk and threatening to kill anyone who touched him. "You are the damned little rascal," Alexander Meeks declared, striking Murdaugh over the head with the butt-end of a whip. John Rothwell also got into the action, striking Murdaugh with a hickory club. In the melee that followed, Murdaugh fatally stabbed Meeks, Judge Wilkinson was struck with a sword cane, and Dr. Wilkinson was knocked down and beaten. Judge Wilkinson stabbed

Rothwell in two places with a Bowie knife, leading to Rothwell's death, before retreating to his room while brandishing his knife. After a preliminary examination, a Louisville grand jury ultimately indicted Judge Wilkinson and his physician brother, along with Mr. Murdaugh, for the murder of the two men. But because of concerns about whether the Wilkinsons and Mr. Murdaugh could get a fair trial, the Kentucky state legislature passed a law allowing the venue of the case to be changed to Mercer Circuit court. While Meeks, whose family was from Indiana, had been a part-time hotel bar-keeper in Louisville, Rothwell—one report noted—was especially "well thought of by his neighbors" and his death caused a great deal of "melancholy gloom throughout the whole city."[108]

Because of its high-profile nature, the criminal case attracted top-notch legal talent. "The Commonwealth," *American State Trials* later reported, "was represented by the Prosecuting Attorney, and a venerable member of the Bar, Benjamin Hardin, was specially retained by the families of Rothwell and Redding." Hardin had been a member of the state legislature, serving as a state senator from 1828 to 1832. As *The Kentucky Encyclopedia* notes: "Hardin became one of the foremost trial lawyers of antebellum Kentucky, excelling in criminal law as both prosecutor and defense attorney. In the trial of the Wilkinsons and Murdaugh in Harrodsburg in March 1839 for the alleged murder of two Louisville artisans, friends of the victims paid Hardin a fee of $1,000 to act as special private prosecutor."[109] Despite Hardin's considerable talents as a lawyer, the defense attorney, John Rowan, gave what has been described as a "blistering attack on the tradition of private criminal prosecutors" and obtained acquittals. In the course of his representation, Rowan assailed Hardin for serving as a private prosecutor, challenging the very notion of private prosecution as violative of "due process and the presumption of innocence."[110]

At trial, Mr. Rowan's co-counsel, Colonel Robertson, opened the defense case, which rested on the theory of self-defense. "Judge Wilkinson," Colonel Robertson said, "had come to Kentucky at the time for the purpose of executing and consummating the most important and holy contract which man can enter into." "On the Tuesday of this bloody tragedy," Robertson observed of the judge, "he was to take to his bosom as his wife, one of the most lovely girls of Kentucky, and all the considerations which spring from such a prospect naturally prompted him to avoid all personal dangers." "A necessity forced upon him by a band of violent, athletic and lawless men," Colonel Robertson stressed of the asserted need for self-defense by his clients. "Before I take my seat, I beg leave to say one word to the distinguished gentleman who has been employed to aid in this prosecution," Colonel Robertson continued, making this line of attack: "I regret, most sincerely regret, to see the practice of hired counsel in criminal cases gaining ground in this Commonwealth. Under its influence the heart becomes corroded and steeled against all the sympathies of our nature. The learned gentleman who is aiding in this prosecution, is to receive one thousand dollars for his services, and from the very nature of his bargain, as it has been proven, he must have undertaken to convict, if he can, whether the accused be innocent or guilty." "The distinguished gentleman who aids in this prosecution," Colonel Robertson added, "has furnished us with some proof of the corroding influence upon the human heart, caused by a long indulgence in prosecution for alleged crimes."

In arguing for a not guilty verdict, Colonel Robertson took special aim at the private prosecutor and impugned his motives. "I do not doubt," Robertson said, speaking of the private prosecutor, "but he has so long lent his aid in prosecutions of this kind that he has brought himself 'to look on blood and carnage with composure.'" As Robertson spoke of Mr. Hardin: "He will doubtless make, as he has heretofore made, a bold and mighty effort to convict the accused, though in my judgment such conviction would be against both the law and evidence. Neither the shrieks nor the tears of the lovely Andromache, nor the groans and lamentations of the aged Priam, can stay him in his fierce pursuit; the wife and the father sink into nothingness when compared with the glittering fee that awaits his efforts; he had bargained for conviction, and he goes for his bond." "[I]n those ancient days," Colonel Robertson argued to the jury after referencing characters from *The Iliad*, "the gods were supposed to hold in *their* hands the fate of men and of nations" and those gods "invariably decided according to the principles of right and justice." "In more modern times, gentlemen of the jury," Robertson implored, "you have been substituted for the gods; you hold in your hands the fate of my gallant and much injured friends, and, not less just than the gods, you, too, will decide according to right and justice." "Do this, as I know you will," he added, "and we shall be content."[111]

S. S. Prentiss, Judge Wilkinson's friend, also assisted in the defense of the case.[112] In his address to the jury, he spoke of the "foul, bitter, and turbid torrent of private vengeance." "I fear," he said, "that a similar spirit still actuates that portion of this prosecution which is conducted, not by the State, but by private individuals." "I am not aware," he offered, "that the Commonwealth of Kentucky is incapable of vindicating her violated laws, or unwilling to prosecute the perpetrators of crime." "The District Attorney," he observed of the commonwealth, "has given ample proof that she is provided with officers fully capable of asserting her rights and protecting her citizens, and with the exception of one or two remarks, which fell from him inadvertently, I accord to his observations my most unqualified approbation." As Prentiss put it of the district attorney and, then, his views of the private prosecutor: "He has done equal justice to the State and the defendants; he has acquitted himself ably, honorably, and impartially. But, gentlemen, though the State is satisfied the Prosecutor is not. Your laws have spoken through their constituted agent; now private vengeance and vindictive malice will claim to be heard." "One of the ablest lawyers of your country, or of any country," Prentiss said, "has been employed to conduct the *private part* of this prosecution; employed, not by the Commonwealth, but by the real murderer; him whose forehead I intend, before I am done, to brand with the mark of Cain—that in after life all may know and all may shun him."

The defense team had a clear strategy, and part of that strategy was to attack the private nature of the prosecution. "The money of the Prosecutor," Prentiss said of Mr.

Redding, who Prentiss asserted had conspired with other men against his clients, "has purchased the talent of the advocate, and the contract is, that *blood* shall be exchanged for *gold*." Mr. Hardin's lawyering, Prentiss said, was "purchased wrath," with Prentiss concluding in his appeal to jurors: "Through you now flows the stream of public justice; let it not become turbid by the trampling of unholy feet. Let not the learned counsel who conducts the private part of this prosecution act the necromancer with you, as he did with the populace in the city of Louisville, when he raised a tempest which his own wizard hand could not have controlled." After praising his "respected friend, Colonel Robertson," for his remarks, Prentiss lauded his fellow defense lawyer, Mr. Rowan, as "a gentleman... who, better, perhaps, than any other man living, can give you, in his profound learning and experience, a just interpretation of the laws of your State."[113]

In his own argument to the jury, Mr. Rowan accused Mr. Hardin of representing "the *vengeful* feelings of the very near relations" of the deceased men and as having been "employed to convict." As Mr. Rowan put it of Mr. Hardin and those financing the private prosecution: "He has not appeared in this case as the Commonwealth's Attorney, nor under any appointment by the government, but as *hired counsel*—hired, too, by the incensed witness, Redding, upon whose testimony, mainly, it was hoped and desired by both to produce the conviction and ignominious death of the accused." Addressing the "Gentlemen of the Jury," Rowan attacked Mr. Hardin's appearance, saying: "I shall attempt to convince you that his appearance in this case, against the accused, is in contravention of the law of the land and the moral sentiment of all civilized communities—reprobated as well by the social sympathies of our hearts, as by the precepts of our holy religion." "Our constitution," Rowan stressed, "guarantees to every man, a *fair* and *impartial* trial by a jury of his peers, and proclaims that no man can be deprived of his life, liberty, or property, unless by the *judgment* of his *peers* or the *law* of the land; by the law of the land, we understand, as well the protective as the punitory laws of our code." "The punitory part relates to offenses and their punishment," Rowan observed, noting that while the guilty are to be punished, the innocent are to be protected.[114]

Rowan saw criminal prosecution as a governmental function. "In ascertaining and punishing guilt," Rowan argued to the jury, "the laws are construed and applied to the case of the accused by the functionaries of the government." "In the making of laws," he argued by analogy, "there are no *hired* legislators—they are all *elected* by the people—so, in the enforcing the laws, there are no hired *prosecutors*, Judges, jurors or Sheriffs." As Rowan continued: "They are all *appointed* and paid by the government. The machinery of judicial proceedings is altogether *official*. The agents are all *official*. There is no clubbing of official powers with that of any other individual, to bear down, oppress, or destroy another individual. The government, instead of assisting individuals to oppress, restrains them from oppressing each other." "The government," Rowan declared, making his pitch, "acts toward every man upon the presumption that he is innocent, until his guilt be ascertained by *official agency* according to the laws of the land." "This presumption, that every man is innocent until his guilt be fairly and legally proven," he added, "is the most essential element in the corporate structure of civil society, one, without which its parts could not cohere nor exist for a single day—it is not only the cement, by the very *basis* of the civil union." Like S. S. Prentiss, Mr. Rowan complimented the public prosecutor: "It gives me pleasure to say that the Commonwealth's Attorney (Mr. Bullock) has discharged his duty, faithfully and ably. He has acted upon the presumption, which I have been urging, that the accused should be considered innocent throughout the whole *progress* of their trial, and until its conclusion should evidence the contrary." But Rowan accused Mr. Hardin—the retained private prosecutor—of representing "the avenger of blood in this case."[115]

Mr. Hardin, Rowan offered, had "with his usual ability, and with somewhat unusual zeal, displayed great devotion to the interests and inclinations of his client." As Rowan put it of Hardin and his representation of private interests in the capital case: "He was bound by his undertaking to have the accused convicted and executed, unless they should be able to prove themselves innocent. His duty and his energies were to destroy them, guilty or innocent." Mr. Hardin's appearance in the case, Rowan told the jurors, "violates the rights of the accused, and especially their great right to be presumed innocent, and profanes the sacredness of the temple of justice, and all the sacred usages and forms of proceeding." As Rowan identified the problems associated with the private prosecutor's use: "It corrupts the streams of justice in their very fountains. It introduces and consecrates the sanguinary and long exploded claims of the next of kin to the slain." Synonyms for *sanguinary*—a word commonly used in the nineteenth century—are "cruel, bloody, murderous."[116]

"Gentlemen of the jury," Rowan implored, speaking to a mid-nineteenth century audience, "according to the rude and barbarous usage of man in his aboriginal state, the next of kin had a right to kill the slayer of his father, brother, etc., without regard to the character of the occasion—without inquiring whether it had been inflicted justifiably, excusably, by misfortune, or of malignant design." "This practice," he said, "prevailed even in our day among the Indians of North America," with Rowan calling it rooted in a "vengeful" and sanguinary principle, adding: "It crept into the codes of many semi-civilized nations as they advanced from barbarism." "The same principle," he argued, "insinuated itself into the code of England, but as she has advanced in civilization she wisely and humanely tamed and rendered it harmless in the shape of a civil action, denominated an appeal of murder, which she permitted the next of kin to institute against the homicide; and she humanely encumbered the action with such technicalities, and subjected it to such delays in its progress, as rendered it harmless to the accused, by affording time for the subsidence of the bad passions of the avenger; while she, in the meantime, proceeded to give the accused a fair and impartial trial by a jury of his peers." "[I]n the appearance and efforts of the hired counsel in criminal cases," Rowan emphasized, using the anti-Semitic and often bigoted language of the day, "we behold the re-appearance of that odious and exploded principle, in a more aggravated form than it was ever displayed among the barbarians, the Jews or the Anglo-Saxons."[117]

Rowan's argument to the jury in 1839, made on behalf of the defense, took pains to expose the injustice and unfairness of a private prosecution. "[I]f the avenger might lawfully employ the talented gentleman who represents *him*, and not the Commonwealth, in that case, might he not have employed any given number of our most distinguished lawyers and advocates, and at once overwhelm the accused by their combined talents, eloquence and weight of character?" As Rowan explained of the power of money: "The limits of his vengeful efforts are not to be found in the law, but in his purse. The security of the accused is no longer to be found in the laws and the institutions of the Government, but in his own wealth and the poverty of the avenger. Guilt or innocence, upon this principle, is to be decided not by the constitution and laws of the land, but by the comparative wealth or poverty of the avenger and the accused; and thus, instead of appealing to Heaven, for a decision of guilt or innocence, as in the days of yore in the trial by battle, between the avenger and the accused, we shall have the question decided by a conflict of their purses."

In arguing that private prosecution was at odds with a principled, well-functioning criminal justice system, Rowan sought to vindicate his client's rights in the courtroom. Rowan's penultimate concern? "And thus our beautiful system of criminal jurisprudence," he said, "will be so subverted and degraded that the liberty and life of the accused will depend, not upon his innocence, but whether he, or the avenger, can bid highest—the one to preserve, and the other to destroy it, by the instrumentality of hired lawyers, who, in competition with each other, for employment, will be seen hovering about the avenger and the accused, ready to be employed by either, and soliciting employment from both, regardless of the merits of the case, and regardful only of the amount of the fee which may be obtained." "Gentlemen," he observed, appealing to the jurors, "I leave you to contemplate the moral degradation, the widespread corruption, which would follow the practice if it were to prevail, which I am resisting as unfair and unlawful."[118]

In his argument to jurors, Rowan—like his co-counsel—then took specific aim at Mr. Hardin. "The venerable gentleman," Rowan offered, "has told you that he and myself practiced law together and abreast for nearly half a century." "It is true," Rowan conceded, but then pointed out of Mr. Hardin: "for the first twenty-five years of that period, he like myself declined all applications to appear against the lives of our fellow men." "His first departure from that course," Rowan lamented of Mr. Hardin's law practice, "was, as he tells us, in the case of the Commonwealth vs. Smith, charged with the killing of Dr. Brown." "That was a long time ago, and I am sorry to tell you that he has been at it ever since, and seems determined to keep at it," Rowan continued, alluding to the 1828 murder prosecution of Randal Smith. Smith had killed Dr. Brown, been captured in Missouri before being put on trial, and convicted of manslaughter.[119] Rowan contrasted his own approach to the practice of law as follows: "I take much pleasure and feel some pride in being able to say that I never have taken a fee or appeared as a lawyer against the life or liberty of my fellow man and that no amount of fee could, at any period of my life, have tempted me to do so. I refused a fee of one thousand dollars to do so when I was not worth that many cents."

Above all else, Rowan—the lawyer who provided vigorous advocacy[120]—saw private prosecutions as unethical. "Apart from its being unfair and unlawful, as I verily believe it to be," Rowan said of private prosecution, "I do, and always have, reprobated the practice, because of its tendency to indurate the heart and deprave the moral feeling." Rowan argued that if the $1,000 fee had been given to the sheriff, the judge, the Commonwealth's attorney, or to jurors, an impartial jury would not be impaneled, the judge would decide every question of law against the accused, the Commonwealth's attorney would invert the presumption of the law as to the innocence of the accused, and the jury would promptly render a conviction. "Would not all mankind reprobate it, and fasten shame and degradation upon all concerned in a transaction so corrupt?" Rowan asked, quickly answering his own question: "They certainly would."[121] In short, Rowan sought an impartial prosecution, not one driven by considerations of self-interest and money.

In focusing on the idea of a $1,000 fee being paid to a key actor in the criminal justice system, Rowan highlighted the corrupting influence of cash on America's justice system. "The odious effect of money so distributed," Rowan said, "consists in the pollution which it inflicts upon the pure streams of justice, to the prejudice of the accused." "The pith of its effect," he said, "is in its unfairness toward them." "Money," he stressed, "can not be given by the avenger to the Commonwealth's Attorney (nor to any of the judicial officers), because of its unfair influence against the accused." Rowan went on to argue that it was, in fact, worse to give $1,000 to Mr. Hardin, the private prosecutor, than it would have been to give it directly to the Commonwealth's attorney. A $1,000 fee paid to the Commonwealth's attorney would have led to "corruption," Rowan observed, but by paying the $1,000 to Mr. Hardin, a man of "experience, sagacity, and weight of character," the prosecution—and thus the prejudice against the accused—was "rendered worse." As Rowan told the jurors: "It is, gentlemen, in the contemplation of sober reason, unfair, and, therefore unlawful, that the effect and influence of this one thousand dollars should be thrown into the scales against them." "It is corruption," he said, "to an *undefined* extent—I say undefined extent, because, though we can ascertain the amount of the money, we can not ascertain precisely the degree of unfairness it produces—but as any, the least degree of it, is excluded by the laws of criminal procedure, we can, with confidence say that the influence of the one-thousand-dollar fee, most gratuitously and sagaciously exerted by the hired lawyer against the accused, is palpably unfair."[122]

As his argument continued, Rowan appealed to the jurors' sense of fairness. "There is, gentlemen of the jury, in the human heart an inherent love of fairness, which, when unbiased by passion, it is sure to display whenever occasions for its display are presented." "It pervades all ranks and grades of mankind," Rowan stressed, adding: "It is evinced in all their settled modes of contest—when a fight occurs among the multitude, you will hear the exclamation of 'fair play' from the mouths of all who are not engaged in it; and very many, in every crowd, are ready to maintain fairness at all hazards. Hence the popular apothegm, 'Fair play is a jewel.'" "Pugilism and dueling," Rowan said, "have their rules of fair play." "The sports of the people, as well as their fights," he continued, "have some settled rules of fairness, and even war between nations has its laws of fairness; these rules of fairness are legibly and indelibly written upon the human heart, and we perceive them intuitively; we feel their force in every fibre of our frame, in every pulsation our blood; they are venerated everywhere, and in reference to every subject." "Now, let me ask you," Rowan observed rhetorically, "does the attitude of the gentleman, and his one-thousand-dollar power, exerted against the accused, quadrate with this rule?" "What rule of fairness, within the verge of human conception, justifies his position here, and his exertions against them?" Rowan asked of Mr. Hardin's role in the capital case. Rowan compared Mr. Hardin to a "mercenary," calling his efforts "unauthorized" on behalf of "the representative of the avenger of blood." "Can the law, I would ask you, gentlemen of the jury," Rowan concluded, "license such a procedure against the accused?" "No, gentlemen, no," he emphasized, passionately calling private prosecution "a vicious and foul excrescence, which, like mistletoe upon the oak, deforms and distempers the trunk upon which it fastens itself."[123]

Mr. Rowan was, certainly, not alone in such views, and private prosecutors came under attack in other high-profile cases, too.[124] Yet, in the nineteenth century, private counsel—in spite of defense counsel's often vigorous objections—were frequently permitted to appear at counsel's table with the local public prosecutor. For example, in 1893, in Buffalo, New York, at "[t]he Criminal Term room" of City Hall at the Superior Court in a criminal case against a man accused of election fraud, it was reported that the district attorney, after taking a seat at "the little table directly before the jury box," was "quickly joined by Mr. Spencer Clinton, one of the counsel for the citizens' committee." The defendant, James Duggan, Jr., the chair of the election board for the Third District of the Second Ward, was accused of falsifying the returns by taking 42 votes from a candidate for Superintendent of Education and giving them to a rival candidate. After a grand jury had been convened, the District Attorney, Mr. Quinby, rose and stated that he had an order of the County Judge allowing Spencer Clinton and William Marcy—said to be "representatives of the Citizen's Committee"—to appear as associate counsel for the prosecution. The defense lawyer, Mr. Shire, objected to their appearance. "I claim," Mr. Shire said, "that the law discourages the employment of such parties, as it is inimical to justice in prosecutions of this character." Although Judge Titus ruled that Mr. Clinton and Mr. Marcy were entitled to appear in the case, Mr. Shire entered an exception to the ruling and tried to inquire—and to get on the record—as to what compensation was being paid to the attorneys who he understood "appear here as private prosecutors" and who had been "hired by the citizens' committee to push this case against the prisoner."[125]

The Rejection of Private Prosecutors in Some Locales

Occasionally, nineteenth-century judges did refuse to allow the participation of private prosecutors. For instance, in one 1873 first-degree murder case, an Iowa court refused to appoint a privately retained lawyer to associate with the public prosecutor because the public prosecutor would not attest that he was "exhausted with excessive labor." At that first-degree murder trial—of Nathan Yard, his wife Rachel Yard, and E. W. Smith for the killing Jack Jones—the prosecuting attorney asked the court "to assign Judge Phillips as additional prosecutor." That drew an objection from defense counsel, who argued that "the accused were unable to employ additional counsel, and that the Code specially declared that the Prosecuting Attorney alone should conduct criminal cases." The presiding judge took the matter under advisement until the jury was empaneled. "Immediately after dinner"—it was reported—defense counsel "presented an affidavit signed by Mr. Yard stating that Judge Phillips had been employed as private prosecutor against him by 'a private person actuated by hatred and ill will against him,'" and asking that he be debarred "from so appearing."[126]

The court thereafter ruled, on the defense motion, that "a more specific statement be made, which was done by stating that J. C. Jones employed Judge Phillips." John C. Jones was the deceased man's brother.[127] In the newspaper, the court's ruling was reported as follows: "The court held that there was little doubt that private persons have no right to employ an attorney for the State. In a case where the Prosecuting Attorney is exhausted with excessive labor, the court would have power to appoint assistance, but it will not make such appointment unless Gen. Given insists that he is physically exhausted and unable to give the case the attention and care that an attorney would ordinarily give it." "Gen. Given declining to make such statement," the paper emphasized, "the court declined to appoint, and the work of calling a jury was continued."[128] In a report on the murder trial, it was emphasized that "[t]he question of the admission of Judge Phillips, as additional prosecutor to assist the Counsel for the State, came up on a statement of Gen. Given that he had employed that gentleman on his own responsibility and at his own expense." The following appointment signed by Iowa Governor Cyrus C. Carpenter, dated November 29, 1873, had also been presented: "At the request of the District Attorney, and by the advice of the Attorney General, Wm. Phillips, Esq., of Polk County, is hereby appointed to assist the District Attorney, of the Fifth Judicial District, in the trial of the case of the State vs. Yard and others, indicted in said Polk County; the State to bear no expense on account thereof."[129]

In 1891, the *Camden Daily Courier* likewise covered a courthouse story about two private lawyers being excluded from participating in the prosecution of lawyer Floranc F. Hogate "for obtaining money under false pretences." Mr. Hogate had been indicted nearly a year before, and the State of New Jersey "was represented by Prosecutor Wilson H. Jenkins, Assistant Prosecutor Ridgway, General George M. Robeson and Lawyer Thomas E. French." The case attracted much interest, with *The Post* in Camden, New Jersey reporting that the courtroom was filled.[130] After the case was opened and the jury was seated, one of the defendant's lawyers, Fred Rex, objected when "Prosecutor Jenkins stated that as Lawyer French was better acquainted with the facts in the case than he was, that attorney would make the opening to the jury." "The defendant objects," interrupted Rex, "to either General Robeson or Lawyer French appearing for the State in this case." The specific grounds for Rex's objection: "First, because they are both paid by a private prosecutor to prosecute this case. This is contrary to the spirit of the criminal law, public policy and the statute." "Under the old common law," it was noted, "it was customary for private persons to conduct public prosecutions, but that they might be freely and impartially conducted public prosecutors were appointed, who are bound to present all facts in the cases." "Now," it was asserted, "if the counsel is to be paid by private parties he cannot freely and impartially try the case for the State."[131]

At that point, Mr. Rex read an excerpt "from one of the statutes, which recited that on and after the date of its passage the prosecutions must be exclusively conducted by the prosecutors of the various counties." According to the newspaper's extended account of Mr. Rex's argument: "He then said that, of course, the State's attorney could have assistants, but they must be sworn and then become liable to the same restrictions under the law as he, in event of accepting fees from persons interested in a prosecution, and would be guilty of bribery and malfeasance in office. He claimed, too, that there was no statute permitting outside counsel to appear, and said that what is not allowed by statute is denied. He then read opinions from the Supreme Courts of Michigan, Wisconsin, Massachusetts and Pennsylvania in which this question had been decided by the debarring of such private counsel." By then, some American judicial decisions interpreting state laws had either renounced or restricted the use of private prosecutors. Mr. Rex, hoping to convince the New Jersey court to adopt a similar rule and to exclude private counsel in criminal prosecutions, seized upon these precedents.

Later in the year, Mr. Rex would represent Floranc Hogate on other charges after Hogate was convicted of forgery[132] and it came to light that Hogate had pocketed alimony money of $12 a week that was owed to a client.[133] But the precedents Mr. Rex cited in court in his effort to exclude the participation of the private prosecutors were fairly recent ones. For example, in *Meister v. People* (1875), the Supreme Court of Michigan emphasized of that state's departure from the English tradition of private prosecutions: "The great scandals which have occurred from the abuse of criminal process to further purposes of gain or vindictiveness, have often demanded notice; and no better remedy has been suggested than the policy of our statute. It does not prevent any one from hunting up proofs, or furnishing every facility to the officers of the law." "But it will be very inefficient," the state supreme court observed, "if it is possible to allow those who have a direct pecuniary interest in convicting a prisoner, to take an active part in his trial." "Until the legislature see fit to restore the common-law rule, and leave cases to private prosecution," that court stressed, "it must be assumed that they regard it as unsafe, and opposed to even-handed justice."[134]

By contrast, in *Appeal of Nicely* (1889), a case that arose out of the first-degree murder convictions of Joe and Dave Nicely following a robbery and homicide in Jennertown, Pennsylvania, that occurred on February 27, 1889,[135] the Supreme Court of Pennsylvania had written these words: "It is difficult to measure the amount of zeal which is allowable, or at least excusable, on the part of counsel engaged in the defense of a man who is upon trial for his life. Writers upon professional ethics differ upon this subject, and I will not discuss it. We have no difficulty, however, in measuring the extent of zeal which counsel for the commonwealth may properly display upon such occasions." As the court in *Appeal of Nicely* explained: "The district attorney is a *quasi* judicial officer. He represents the commonwealth, and the commonwealth demands no victims. It seeks justice only,—equal and impartial justice,—and it is as much the duty of the district attorney to see that no innocent man suffers as it is to see that no guilty man escapes." "Hence," the court said of the district attorney, "he should act impartially." As the court continued of the district attorney's obligations: "He should present the commonwealth's case fairly, and should not press upon the jury any deductions from the evidence that are not strictly legitimate. When he exceeds this limit, and in hot zeal seeks to influence them by appealing to their prejudices, he is no longer an impartial officer, but becomes a heated partisan." "When that officer allows private counsel to assist him in the trial of a cause," the court added, "such counsel represents him to that extent, and should be governed by the same rules of propriety."[136] Although private counsel had aided the district attorney in the prosecution of Joe and Dave Nicely for a man's murder, the Supreme Court of Pennsylvania affirmed their murder convictions—and the two men, after escaping from jail but being recaptured,[137] were hanged in 1891.[138]

In the last quarter of the nineteenth century, some American jurists saw the need to abandon the use of private prosecutors. For example, in Philadelphia in 1877, it was reported in *The Times* that Judge Craig Biddle of the Court of Common Pleas "cut the Gordian knot of abuses against witnesses, prosecutors and defendants in the sessions, by peremptory notice to the District Attorney that he would not hear any case where the Commonwealth was not represented by its proper officer." In speaking of lawyers conducting prosecutions, Judge Biddle said: "They are not to be prosecutor to suit the vindictiveness of private suitors, but the demands of public justice. The officers of the Commonwealth are under the obligation of an oath to see that the prosecution is conducted with that view alone, and they are responsible to the law for its proper performance." "A prisoner in our State is entitled to impartiality from the prosecuting officer as well as from the judge and jury," Judge Biddle observed, recalling a decision of late Pennsylvania Supreme Court Chief Justice John Bannister Gibson in which it was held that the prosecutor's office is a "public trust" which involves "the exercise of an almost boundless discretion by an officer who stands as impartial as a judge." In that case, *Rush v. Cavenaugh* (1845), Chief Justice Gibson wrote: "[I]t might be doubted whether counsel retained by a private prosecutor, can be allowed to perform any part of his duty. Certainly not, unless in subservience to his will and instructions." As Gibson's decision in *Rush* emphasized: "With that restriction, usage has sanctioned the practice of employing professional assistants to whom the attorney-general, or his regular substitute, may, if he please, confide the direction of the particular prosecution; and it has been beneficial to do so where the prosecuting officer has been overmatched or overborne by numbers. In that predicament, the ends of justice may require him to accept of assistance."[139]

In praising Judge Biddle's decision, *The Times* editorialized: "This prompt departure of Judge Biddle will be received with universal satisfaction by all good citizens, and now that the question has been formally acted on by one of our judges, there can be no doubt that all of them will gladly join in the strict enforcement of the letter and spirit of the law that has, little by little, been disregarded until monstrous abuses have been reared upon its wreck." For many years, *The Times* emphasized, "it has been the custom for the District Attorney to yield the direction of cases in which private counsel have been employed; and the custom has become so established, through various administrations, that it would have been deemed an act of discourtesy, or perhaps an act of prejudice or partiality, had he attempted to assume his conceded authority in such cases." "Thus," *The Times* wrote, "the very class of cases which most of all require the sound discretion of an impartial prosecuting officer, who is sworn to conduct them only in obedience to 'the demands of public justice,' have been given over to private counsel who are employed solely with reference to their ability and willingness to display the attributes of the bully and the blackguard in the courts." "The prosecutions which grow out of individual, family or church quarrels are noted for their bitterness," the newspaper wrote, "and it is usual in such disputes for both sides to lavish money freely for the most malignant defamation they can employ to be hurled against each other." "And the evil," the paper continued, "has not been confined to social or business quarrels, but leading representatives of religious bodies have at times been among the most forgetful of charity and even decency in the direction of such judicial conflicts." The regrettable result, it emphasized, "has been the degradation of the bar; the serious wounding of popular respect for the court; the hesitation of truthful witnesses to enter the witness-box; the growth of perjury, and generally the embarrassment and often the absolute defeat of justice in her own sanctuary."[140]

Just three years before Mr. Rex's 1891 court appearance, the Supreme Court of Wisconsin, in *Biemel v. State* (1888), had expressly held that privately retained attorneys must not appear in criminal prosecutions. In particular, Wisconsin's highest court ruled that a municipal court judge had erred in refusing to permit a defendant convicted of third-degree manslaughter to show that R. N. Austin, a private attorney who appeared and assisted the district attorney, "was employed and paid by private parties to aid in such prosecution." As the Wisconsin Supreme Court ruled in that case: "We think public policy, and the fair, just, and impartial administration of the criminal law of the state, make it the duty of the courts to exclude the paid attorneys of private persons from appearing as prosecutors. That public policy is against permitting them to prosecute, is, we think, clearly indicated by the several provisions of our laws upon the subject of criminal prosecutions." "The statutes," the state's supreme court observed, "provide for the election in each county of a prosecuting attorney, and they make it his duty to appear and prosecute all persons informed against or indicted for crimes in the courts of his county, and when for any reason there is no public prosecutor in the county, the court in which the prosecution is pending, shall appoint some one to prosecute the accused."

The Wisconsin Supreme Court's opinion was a detailed one. "The question for determination," the court wrote, "is whether it is in accord with the statutes and laws of the state and with public policy that the court should permit an attorney employed by and expecting compensation from private parties to appear and aid in the prosecution of a person charged with a crime punishable by imprisonment in the state prison." "We think it is quite clear from the reading of our statutes on the subject, as well as upon public policy," it then ruled, "that an attorney employed and paid by private parties should not be permitted either by the courts or by the prosecuting attorney to assist in the trial of such criminal cases." As the state supreme court expressly held: "The laws have clearly provided that the district attorney, who is the officer provided by the laws of the state to initiate and carry on such trials, shall be unprejudiced and unpaid except by the state, and that he shall have no private interest in such prosecution. He is an officer of the state, provided at the expense of the state for the purpose of seeing that the criminal laws of the state are honestly and impartially administered, unprejudiced by any motives of private gain, and holding a position analogous to that of the judge who presides at the trial."[141]

In his argument, Mr. Rex cited precedents from four states—Michigan,[142] Massachusetts,[143] Wisconsin[144] and Pennsylvania[145]—that had specifically addressed the private prosecution issue. By then, there was a number of cases from around the country about private prosecutors, though such cases did not necessarily preclude their appearance in every single instance. For example, in one early case from Massachusetts, *Commonwealth v. Williams* (1849), a defendant had been tried and convicted in the Court of Common Pleas upon an indictment charging him with breaking and entering and stealing gold coins. On the district attorney's motion, George Farrar, a private attorney who had not received any compensation, had been permitted to examine and cross-examine witnesses in the case. In the *Williams* ruling, the court affirmed the conviction, observing that no showing had been made that Farrar had received "any pecuniary compensation, from any private individual, for the services he rendered," though the court opinion stressed that—as a general matter—"[i]t is undoubtedly the policy of our system of criminal jurisprudence, that the district attorney, or other public officer having official charge of the criminal department, should have the active superintendence and management of all criminal cases, on the trial of the same before the jury."

The *Williams* case was decided less than twenty years after Daniel Webster had acted as a private prosecutor in the murder trials of the Knapp brothers. "As a general rule," it was held in *Williams*, "the public prosecutor" must conduct the case, with the court adding this caveat: "But exceptions may occur to this rule, arising from peculiar circumstances applicable to particular cases, which would justify the court in associating with the public prosecutor, at his request, additional counsel to aid him in the conducting of a cause." "While we deem it our duty to say, that such additional counsel is not, under ordinary circumstances, to be permitted, yet, when sanctioned by the court, under the limitations suggested," the *Williams* decision declared, referencing the sound discretion of a judge in making its judgment, "it will not furnish any sufficient ground for setting aside a verdict."[146]

In *Biemel*, the Wisconsin Supreme Court had, itself, relied on such precedents as *Williams*, emphasizing in its 1888 opinion: "This question has been fully considered by the courts of Michigan and Massachusetts,—states in which the laws prescribing the duties of public prosecutor are substantially like ours,—and the courts of these states have uniformly held that attorneys employed by private parties ought not to be permitted to aid the district attorneys in the conduct of criminal cases." Although the Wisconsin Supreme Court took notice of contrary practices in Texas and Kansas as regards the employment of private prosecutors, the *Biemel* court had nonetheless ruled: "Among the conflicting opinions of the courts upon the propriety or impropriety of permitting counsel employed by private persons to assist the district attorney in the trial of criminal actions, where the punishment is imprisonment in the state prison, we are inclined to hold that under the laws of this state, since the legislature has given the trial judge the power of appointing assistant counsel, where they think the public interest requires it, and providing that such assistant counsel shall be paid out of the public fund, counsel should not be permitted to appear in the case even at the request of the district attorney, when it appears that such counsel have been employed to appear by private parties, at whose request such counsel appears in the case, and from whom he expects to receive compensation for his services."[147]

In the New Jersey dispute, General Robeson—an experienced lawyer—made an attempt to reply to Mr. Rex's arguments about private prosecutors, but Mr. Rex interposed the same objection to him taking part in the case. That prompted General Robeson, the ex-Secretary of the Navy, to offer with a smile, "Well, then, perhaps the court will hear me as *amicus curae*." "As a 'friend of the court,' certainly," Judge William Hugg[148] replied, letting General Robeson address him in open court in spite of Mr. Rex's objection. The *Camden Daily Courier* summed up General Robeson's responsive arguments—as well as Mr. Rex's reply to them—as follows: "The general stated that the statute in which the word exclusive occurred was passed to define the duties of the attorney general, and to prevent that officer from conducting trials and ousting the prosecutors, as had been the habit. He spoke at length on this, and when he resumed his seat Mr. Rex said that the court can only rule on the law as it finds it, and can not make the law. He added that the court must find this statute to be 'not the law' before it could overrule the objection." At that point, Prosecutor Jenkins interjected: "Mr. Rex, I think, has only been at the bar about two years and...." "Your Honor," Mr. Rex fired back, "I shall have to ask the gentleman not to indulge in personalities." Judge Hugg agreed. "That kind of argument," Judge Hugg told the state's prosecutor, "would have no weight with the court." "Some young lawyers," Judge Hugg observed, "know more than their elders." "Mr. Jenkins," the newspaper noted, "then urged the court not to decide rashly and asked that the objection be overruled, so that the defendant could carry the case to the Supreme Court for decision."

Mr. Rex, the young lawyer, was eager to make his mark on the law and to reply to his more elder opposing counsel, and Judge Hugg permitted him to do so. "While I may have only been at the bar two years," Mr. Rex offered, "my learned friend Jenkins has been a prosecutor a good many years and should have learned before this that he is assistant to the attorney general and that any law affecting the latter would, of course, relate to the prosecutor." After consulting at length with two of his colleagues, Judges Gaunt and McDowell, Judge Hugg prefaced his ruling on the matter with these words, taking note of how New Jersey's justice system had changed over time: "The Court of Common Pleas formerly, in the absence of a Supreme Court Justice, was composed of lay judges, who were supposed not to be acquainted with the law, but the Legislature in its wisdom subsequently created law judges, who are supposed to be learned in the law. These judges are in the court for the purpose of expounding the law, therefore, when questions of this kind arise it becomes their duty to decide the law as they find it, without reference to the right of either side to appeal to higher authority." "This word, 'exclusive,' in the opinion of the court," Judge Hugg then ruled on the substantive issue, "is meant to exclude all others with the attorney general." "Now, while there have been no decisions of the Supreme Court of this State on this subject," he said, "we must look to the decisions in other States for light and these decisions all seem to agree and to cover the point in controversy." In sustaining Mr. Rex's objection, Judge Hugg concluded: "So, however much we may regret having to exclude General Robeson and Mr. French from this case, yet, as we find the law so must we decide."[149]

In the late nineteenth century, there was, in fact, a fierce public debate percolating in multiple jurisdictions as to the efficacy or propriety of a private prosecution system.[150] Questions were raised, on the one hand, about whether private prosecutors were adequately incentivized to bring prosecutions.[151] On the other hand, there was significant concern about ill-founded private prosecutions. One nineteenth-century writer said he could conceive of "nothing more hazardous before a jury than a private prosecutor."[152] A private prosecutor was considered by some to be a "persecutor,"[153] and the costs associated with private prosecutions became a topical and familiar issue,[154] including before legislative bodies and courts.[155] For example, in an 1893 case in Pennsylvania in which C. C. Daggett was "charged with administering poison" to a horse belonging to C. H. Johnson, of Jackson township, Daggett was found not guilty, with the jury—in its verdict—initially dividing the $300 costs "between the county and the private prosecutor." After jurors were instructed that they could not divide the costs in that manner, they then "put the costs upon the county." As *The Wellsboro Agitator* editorialized of this result: "This was a very unfortunate case for the Commonwealth and ought never to have been brought to Court.... The only proof that the Commonwealth had against Mr. Daggett was that he lived near the barn where the horse was poisoned; that he and the prosecutor were on unfriendly terms, and that Daggett had uttered some threats of a general character against the prosecutor, Johnson, and had avoided arrest by going to Elmira after he learned he had been charged with the commission of the deed." As the paper added of the prosecution's circumstances: "The horse in question died October 26, 1891, from the effects of Paris green and pounded glass which some one had maliciously put in his feed-box during the night. The neighbors and friends of Mr. Johnson contributed sufficient money to purchase him a new horse, and Mr. Daggett was arrested upon mere suspicion."[156]

Despite the reticence about private prosecutions, a number of private associations were formed to urge, and to advocate for, the enforcement of criminal laws (*e.g.*, relating to cruelty to animals).[157] Indeed, when the sixth annual meeting of the National Law and Order League took place in Philadelphia in 1888, the *Philadelphia Press* staked out the position that there was a "necessity for private organizations to enforce public laws." The need, the newspaper editorialized, "lies in the fact that law-breakers have a direct and personal interest in breaking or evading the law, and they must be met by others who feel a like zeal in enforcing the law." "The general public do not feel this," the paper observed, adding: "What is everybody's business is nobody's business, unless there are some noble souls to come forward and make it their business, and this valuable public function the law and order organizations perform." As the *Philadelphia Press* stressed of its viewpoint and favored approach to law enforcement: "Judges, district attorneys and policemen are paid to enforce the law, but under our system of administration an official rarely makes the initiative in the punishment of crime unless the offense is committed in his presence. There must be a complainant, a private prosecutor, or the violated law is seldom vindicated, and it is as private prosecutors and the careful collectors of testimony that the law and order associations serve society and bring upon themselves the maledictions of all classes of wrong-doers."[158]

The tradition of private prosecutions was one that many people, including in America's heartland, fully embraced and did not want to see fall by the wayside. "Our Anglo-Saxon system of administering penal law," Nathan Cree wrote in *The Wyandott Herald* of Kansas City, Kansas, in 1888, "is through the agency of private prosecutors who bring accusations against offenders before magistrates or grand juries, and also furnish knowledge of the requisite witnesses to prosecuting officers." "With us," Cree observed, "the administration of that law is not, as in some countries, the sole business of certain paid functionaries." The "[m]ost important consequences" flowing from the Anglo-American system, Cree added, were these: "It leaves the administration of the criminal law in the last resort substantially to the feeling and opinion of the people. If any penal law be deemed unjust, oppressive, unnecessary, or is not desired by the people, it is practically abrogated by them, because private prosecutors will not come forward upon such a law and lodge the necessary sworn complaints, or give evidence before grand juries, and furnish the names of witnesses to prove the offense before the grand or the petty jury or court."

Nathan Cree thus saw the intimate involvement of victimized citizens in the prosecution of offenses as a check on governmental power and as a plus, not a negative. As Cree explained his perspective on the importance of localized self-government: "Legislatures may enact, but practically the public regulate the executions of the law according to the sense of society, and laws not grounded in the moral consciousness and in the convictions of the people are practically set aside in a silent, unseen and unavoidable way." "Under such a system," he offered, "the *people* themselves, mainly, and not officers *alone*, enforce the law, and any other system would require a vast body of officers,—including hired informers,—subservient to some central executive power to enforce criminal law." "Some countries, cursed with arbitrary governments," Cree continued, "have bodies of official prosecutors, charged,—and solely charged,—with the duty of detecting, arresting, committing and prosecuting offenders, with the necessary consequences of hordes of paid informers, the people having nothing to do with the laws but to obey them." Instead, Cree said that "[t]he common law conservators of the peace, the *posse commitatus*, or power of the county, the militia, and in case of extended domestic violence, the regular army, are all the agencies that we need in this country to preserve public order, together, of course, with the locally responsible police, standing upon the footing of an ordinary constabulary force."[159] Latin for "power of the county," *posse comitatus* refers to "[t]he power of the sheriff to call upon any able-bodied citizens to help keep the peace or apprehend a criminal." The Posse Comitatus Act was enacted in the wake of the Civil War and made it a felony offense to use the military to enforce civil law.[160]

Others, however, saw a real danger in ceding enormous prosecutorial power to private actors with financial interests or axes to grind, and they worried about frivolous or malicious private prosecutions. For example, in Oregon, justices of the peace were cautioned about the abuses and costs of private prosecutions,[161] and district attorneys were asked to help reduce such abuses.[162] Likewise, in 1898, San Francisco's *Examiner* editorialized in the context of libel cases: "The privilege to a private person of putting in his attorney as a special assistant to the Prosecuting Attorney in criminal cases should be allowed with extreme caution. There are cases when it is proper. Where intricate and important questions of law are involved, where the private wrong is also a great wrong to the public, and the case is one that requires more attention than the public prosecutor can well give it, there may be reason to allow the injured party to furnish his own private prosecutor." "But," the newspaper cautioned, "such cases are rare." "It is much more likely," the paper wrote, "that the special prosecutor comes forward to work out a private grudge that has no place in the system of public justice."[163]

Particularly litigious and belligerent private prosecutors were certainly not unknown. In 1890, for example, *The Corvallis Gazette* in Oregon reported on Morgan Lillard, who, the paper said, "was a quarrelsome man and of late years was almost constantly before the criminal courts, in the county, either as private prosecutor or an offender against the peace and dignity of the state." In its news story, headlined "Shooting at Big Elk," the newspaper reported that Morgan Lillard "had been shot and mortally wounded by his son-in-law, R. L. Feagles." Lillard and Feagles had quarreled "over some trifling matter" years earlier, and they had been on unfriendly terms since that time. Lillard and Feagles had ranches close to one another, and on a Saturday morning—as the newspaper reported—"Lillard found occasion over some fancied grievance, to continue his quarrel with Feagles on this account." Lillard ended up pointing and shooting his revolver at Feagles, hitting him in his right wrist, and an armed Feagles shot back with his own revolver, striking Lillard with a bullet slightly above his navel. Although Lillard was treated by a doctor, he died the next day, reportedly "surrounded by his family and regretted by few persons of his acquaintance." Lillard's "tragic death," *The Corvallis Gazette* observed, "should stand as a warning to neighborhood bullies."[164]

In that same year, Thomas Reed, a private prosecutor in Oregon, swore out a warrant against Nancy Slator, a tenant on Reed's ranch, leading to her arrest and arraignment. In an 1890 newspaper article about the case, there was said to be "bad blood" between Reed and Slator. The two had fought and both had been injured, but the newspaper reported that the 79-year-old Reed, who, it noted, had unsuccessfully brought civil and criminal suits in the past, was ultimately taxed $61 for his role as a private prosecutor in the case that he had brought under the caption "State versus Nancy Slator."[165] In Oregon, as in other states, the issue of who would pay the costs of a prosecution was frequently brought up.[166] In 1882, in fact, Oregon's legislature passed a law to discourage malicious or unfounded criminal prosecutions by private prosecutors. That legislation, titled "An Act Providing for Taxing Prosecutors with Costs and Disbursements of Criminal Actions when found to be Malicious or without Probable Cause," was approved on October 20, 1882.[167] Laws designed to force private prosecutors to pay costs or give security in advance for costs and disbursements impacted the poor more than the wealthy in terms of their ability to access the justice system.[168] Such laws, though, were plainly intended to prevent the real and known abuses of private prosecutors.[169]

Although it was not always clear in every individual case who was actually paying private attorneys to handle criminal prosecutions,[170] it is clear that the particularly wealthy could afford to finance such prosecutions and were also able to use them to take on union members, child laborers, or others without political or economic power.[171] "Justice," an 1892 article in Pennsylvania's *The Lancaster Intelligencer* began, "seems to have strange ways in Allegheny county, where men are arrested in large numbers on charges of murder, sworn to by one man, who is the secretary of the Carnegie Steel company, and are laid by the heels in jail, because Lovejoy insists upon having twenty-four hours' notice of an application for bail." "The men who are arrested," the Pennsylvania newspaper observed, "are the leaders of the striking workmen of the Carnegie company, and it is easily seen wherefore the officers of the company have an evil mind toward them, and wherefore they find it to their account to take them away from the leadership of the men with whom they are contending." "It doubtless seems to them," the paper editorialized of the corporate officers, "to be a very smart scheme to swear out warrants for murder against the leaders of the strikers and to hold them in jail as long as possible, and so it may be." "But the officers of justice of Allegheny county," the newspaper warned, "should not lend their aid to a plot of that kind." As the paper wrote of the action of Carnegie Steel's secretary, F. T. F. Lovejoy, that put labor leader Hugh O'Donnell and others behind bars: "Secretary Lovejoy's oath alone has sufficed to commit O'Donnell and his fellows to answer for the charge of murder, which is not bailable when of the first degree.... Clearly a private prosecutor should not have the power to imprison his foe; and he does not have it when the law is properly administered. It is only when the district attorney yields his official power to aid the private prosecutor's purpose that his malice can take effect."[172]

In that particular set of circumstances, the battle between Carnegie Steel and union workers was fierce, with Andrew Carnegie and his fellow industrialist, Henry Frick, desiring to break the steel workers' union. Hugh O'Donnell, the Chairman of the Advisory Committee of the Amalgamated Association of Iron and Steel Workers, was a labor leader during Pennsylvania's now-famed Homestead Steel Strike of 1892—an industrial lockout and strike that began on July 1, 1892. On the night of July 5, 1892, with Frick wanting to decrease union wages by more than twenty percent and having locked out union workers and made efforts to replace them with non-union workers, approximately 300 Pinkerton National Detective Agency employees arrived in the area. As tensions mounted, armed strikers opened fire at the tugboat pulling the barges loaded with Pinkerton agents and pistols and rifles as they were being pulled toward the Homestead steel mill. After the force of Pinkerton agents arrived at the Homestead mill and union workers and their families had flocked to the mill after strikers blew the plant's whistle at 2:30 a.m. on July 6th, a gun battle ensued and several strikers and Pinkerton agents were killed, with many also injured, including Hugh O'Donnell. It was disputed whether the strikers or the Pinkertons fired the first shots, but there was much bloodshed, with O'Donnell—in speaking to a crowd of strikers—urging that the Pinkertons be charged with murder.

The deadly gun battle attracted much attention. After O'Donnell himself was arrested in September of 1892 and charged with aggravated rioting, conspiracy, treason, and two counts of murder, he was tried on the murder charges in February of 1893 but acquitted by a jury. He was later released on bail, and all of the other charges were eventually dropped. A number of union leaders had, in July of 1892, already been charged with rioting, conspiracy and murder, with Carnegie Steel pressing charges. The union charged company executives with murder, too. Although both union and company men were ordered to post bonds, most of the union workers were unable to post bail, and thus were confined in jail, whereas the company's executives didn't have to spend any time behind bars. After a New York anarchist, Alexander Berkman, the lover of Emma Goldman, attempted to assassinate Frick on July 23rd, 1892, the union's strike collapsed. Ultimately, most of the charges were dropped on both sides, though three workers were tried and acquitted and one local leader of the Knights of Labor was found guilty of conspiring to poison non-union workers at the plant.[173]

In the nineteenth century, the services of highly skilled private lawyers were often sought after for criminal prosecutions, including in capital cases. For instance, in a Virginia murder trial captioned "*The Commonwealth vs. Charles B. Christian, for the Murder of Thomas Blackburn*," the defense lawyer, Robert L. Doyle, argued to the jury in 1854 that, because of the retention of a private prosecutor, "revenge had purchased with base lucre the services of an advocate to pursue the prisoner to his death." In what was described in one headline as the "Shocking Tragedy at Lexington, Virginia," Thomas Blackburn—a young Virginia Military Institute cadet, and the son of Dr. R. S. Blackburn of Charlestown, Virginia—had been killed on a Sunday by another young man, Charles Christian, a member of Judge John White Brockenbrough's local law school, known then as the Lexington Law School. According to an account of what transpired: "Christian had sought and obtained an introduction to a young lady, a cousin of Blackburn, and by her consent, had made an arrangement to accompany her to church. Blackburn informed the young lady that Christian was not a suitable person for her to associate with, whereupon she wrote the latter a note desiring to be released from her arrangement just named." After Blackburn acknowledged that he'd advised his cousin, that account notes, "Christian armed himself with a bowie knife, and went to the door of the church to wait the arrival of Blackburn." After asking Blackburn "to step aside with him," Christian—in a very unchristian act—proceeded to "cut him in the neck with the knife, entirely severing one of the carotid arteries, causing his death instantly." "This rash act," it was reported, "was no doubt committed in the heat of passion, as it is difficult to conceive how any man could, at such a place, on the Sabbath day, coolly and deliberately perpetrate so dark a deed."[174]

Hiring a private attorney didn't come cheap, especially in such a high-profile case. "Gold," Robert Doyle asserted, "had been given to purchase the blood of the prisoner, and the funds of the friends of the deceased, and the V.M.I. had been appropriated here to purchase this young man's blood." In that case, a private prosecutor, Thomas Johnson Michie, had been employed for a promised fee of $500[175] to assist the Commonwealth's prosecutor, including by the Virginia Military Institute, and Doyle argued that Michie "showed from his declarations that he should not have been here, and if he had known the motives of those who employed him, he never would have been here." "Those who employed him," Doyle said, "were actuated by no other motive" than a "spirit of revenge." This, Doyle suggested, made the prosecution unfair, with Doyle speaking of Thomas Michie as follows: "He, although faithful and able, always looked on his own side of a cause, and pursued it to the utmost extent, without seeing anything on the opposite side." "I would not be employed to assist to prosecute a prisoner for the wealth of Golconda's mines," Doyle offered by way of contrast, alluding to the legendary mines in India that had produced the finest and largest diamonds in the world.

Robert Doyle—the defense lawyer—observed that "[t]he court could appoint counsel to prosecute or to assist the prosecution, but the court would not employ a man to prosecute who had in his pocket a fee from the avenger of blood, or from the next of kin to him who was slain." As Doyle argued, invoking the Bible as he laid out his position: "The courts repudiate the doctrine of private vengeance. This doctrine of private vengeance is also repudiated by the divine law—it is there said that 'Vengeance is mine.' Under the Mosaic dispensation there were cities of refuge where the murderer remained until he could have a fair trial." If Thomas Blackburn's parents "have, as I learn they have, the proper christian spirit," Doyle observed, "they would not wish the prisoner offered up as a sacrifice to the remains of their departed son." Michie, because he'd been "hired by the friends of the deceased," Doyle pressed, "could not help but be biased in favor of those who employed him, and he could not occupy that impartial position that the law intended a prosecutor should occupy."

In an unexpected twist, after Charles L. Mosby—another defense lawyer in the case—fell ill on the tenth day of the trial, the presiding judge, Lucas P. Thompson, took it upon himself to ask another judge, Judge Brockenbrough, to fill in for Mr. Mosby. "Judge Thompson," the *Richmond Dispatch* noted, "remarked that under these circumstances there was nothing improper or illegal" about having a judge "taking his place in the argument." In addressing the jury, Judge Brockenbrough—the founder of the Lexington Law School, which opened in 1849 and educated more than two hundred lawyers until the Civil War forced its closure[176]—then attacked Mr. Michie's role in the case. Michie, Judge Brockenbrough said, "had been employed by the friends of the deceased and the V.M.I., to interpose his great intellect to sustain the cause of the Commonwealth." "The funds appropriated by the Legislature of the State to purposes of education, had been improperly contributed to add additional malignity and venom to this cause," Judge Brockenbrough lamented, adding: "This conduct in perverting these funds was worthy of all denunciation."

Although Judge Brockenbrough—the jurist and law school teacher—said Michie had a "noble" heart, Brockenbrough contended that Michie had "thrown out of the cause every circumstance and consideration that could weigh in behalf of the prisoner, and urged his conviction by every argument and every circumstance that could drive the minds of the jury to a conviction of the prisoner of murder in the first degree." Michie, Brockenbrough argued, "had his clients behind him urging him on, and a party to give a satanic laugh at his jests and jokes, and at the positions assumed by the defence," and "thus attempts, by that viper's breath of popular prejudice, which has pervaded this community, and even entered this sanctuary of justice, to give weight to the prosecution, and to the conviction of the prisoner."[177] The trial of Charles Christian in Lexington, Virginia, ultimately resulted in a hung jury, with eleven jurors favoring a conviction but a single juror favoring an acquittal. But at a subsequent, multiday trial in Liberty, Virginia—one attended by the defendant's mother, his sisters, and other members of his family—Christian was acquitted, devasting the Blackburn family. "The trial," a family friend wrote, "seems to have opened their wound afresh, & their hearts are bleeding with the same convulsive sorrow as that which characterized the earliest period of their grief."[178]

5

FROM PRIVATE TO PUBLIC PROSECUTORS

The Professionalization of District Attorneys' Offices

The Beginnings of Public Prosecution: Early Activity Amidst the Custom of Private Prosecution

Private prosecution has deep roots. By virtue of the English common law, the practice was imported to American soil by colonists, with a 1931 report of the U.S. National Commission on Law Observance and Enforcement emphasizing of the practice's heritage: "the ordinary criminal prosecution was conducted by a private prosecutor in the name of the King."[1] In America, though, public prosecutions gradually began to replace that long-standing custom, with some changes occurring even before the colonies gained their independence.[2] In 1704, Connecticut—moving away from England's common-law tradition—became the first colony to enact a statute specifically providing for a system of local public prosecution.[3] That statute, passed in May 1704 by the Connecticut Assembly in Queen Anne's reign,[4] and using the customary spelling of the time, provided: "Henceforth there shall be in every countie a sober, discreet and religious person appointed by the countie courts, to be atturney for the Queen to prosecute and implead in the lawe all criminals and to doe all other things necessary or convenient as an atturney to suppresse vice and immoralitie."[5] In 1711, the colony of Virginia, followed suit by establishing its own system of local prosecuting attorneys.[6] At that time, men were nominated from Virginia's county courts to serve as deputy attorneys general, and the Virginia Attorney General appointed such deputies in each county in the colony to prosecute both serious and more routine cases.[7]

American attorneys general had been in place before local public prosecutors were appointed and rose to prominence. For example, in 1643, Virginia—following the English custom of appointing a chief legal officer—had established the office of attorney general.[8] Patterned largely after its English counterpart, including with respect to the name given to its officeholder, this office allowed the colony's attorney general to initiate prosecutions of special importance to the Crown.[9] Predominantly Dutch settlements in the American colonies, including settlements in Connecticut, New York, New Jersey, Pennsylvania, and Delaware, meanwhile, had the services of a *schout*, a figure akin to a sheriff and public prosecutor.[10] As one scholar describes the position, the *schout* "was a combination sheriff, public prosecutor and financial agent for the Dutch West India Company."[11] "After 1732," another scholar, Stephanie Dangel, writes in the *Yale Law Journal*, "New York counties paid deputy attorneys general, many of whom settled in the counties and became local bar members." "This cooptation of nominally state officers by local government," Dangel explains of America's transition to locally controlled prosecutions, "continued after 1789 as state constitutions separated local prosecutors from the attorney general, culminating in the 1830's with the local election of public prosecutors."[12] Before district attorneys were elected, they were appointed, whether by state legislatures, county court judges, or governors.[13]

The transition to elected local prosecutors took place over time. In 1832, the State of Mississippi became the first American state to provide for the election of prosecutors, but other states—Ohio (1833), Maine (1842), Indiana (1843), and Iowa (1846)—followed suit in the years to come. By 1860, nearly three-quarters of U.S. states had given voters to right to elect public prosecutors, though poor pay gave rise to calls for increased salaries. "By the outbreak of the Civil War, twenty-five of thirty-four states had adopted elected prosecutors, and all but four would soon follow," writes Michael Ellis in *The Yale Law Journal*.[14] In the State of New York, the office of district attorney became an elective one instead of an appointed office in 1846, giving New York's district attorneys—as with elected DAs elsewhere—vast discretion over prosecutorial decisions.[15] Such changes in the law, giving the elected prosecutors around the country tremendous power over people's lives,[16] did not immediately halt private prosecutions, however. As scholar Yue Ma writes of how private prosecution coexisted with public prosecution: "In New York, for instance, in the early 1800s, private lawyers, despite the existence of the office of district attorney, commonly presented criminal cases in courts. It was not uncommon for experienced criminal lawyers to represent the victim in one matter and the defendant in another."[17]

In the 1850s alone, fifteen states—Kentucky, Michigan, Pennsylvania, Vermont, Texas, Maryland, Missouri, Virginia, Louisiana, Tennessee, Massachusetts, Georgia, Kansas, Minnesota, and Oregon—moved to elected prosecutors, most through the adoption of constitutional provisions and a few (*i.e.*, Pennsylvania, Texas, Georgia) by statute.[18] By 1912, it has been noted, American states had almost uniformly transitioned to elected prosecutors, with 38 of the 48 states then in the Union providing for them in their state constitutions.[19] As Yue Ma has written of the history: "By the early 20th century, of the 48 states in the Union, only Florida, New Jersey, and Connecticut did not have an elective system of prosecutorial selection. Not surprisingly, all three states also did not have elected judges." As Ma relays: "Florida amended its constitution in 1945 and shifted to the elective system of selecting judges and prosecutors. With Florida joining the rest of the states, New Jersey and Connecticut became the only two states that still retained the appointive system of selecting judges and prosecutors."[20]

At one time, public prosecutors in states such as Georgia relied on a "fee system" to be compensated. After 1841, for instance, the salary paid by the State of Georgia to solicitors general had been fixed at $250 per annum, making the primary source of their compensation fines, forfeitures and fees. By 1912, when elected public prosecutors had already become the norm, though, that "fee system" had come under criticism because of the belief that officers were receiving fees in excess of reasonable compensation for their services. The fee system was abolished in various places in 1917 and 1918, and—as one scholar, Charles Olson, explains in the *Journal of Southern Legal History*—Georgia's General Assembly "abolished the last vestiges of the fee system" in 1968 and "placed all district attorneys on a state salary of $18,000 per annum, which counties could supplement," also allowing a $4,800 "contingent expense." That legislation ending the fee system, Olson writes, "also made the district attorneys full-time prosecutors by prohibiting them from engaging in the private practice of law." "Making all of the state's district attorneys full-time prosecutors," Olson observes, "accelerated the process of professionalizing public prosecution in Georgia, a step that the American Bar Association would recommend in 1970 for all state and local public prosecutors."[21]

With the rise of elected public prosecutors, American jurists more closely scrutinized private prosecutions. Many nineteenth-century state courts nonetheless allowed private prosecutions,[22] with American citizens continuing to privately prosecute a significant number of criminal cases in many locales.[23] In Philadelphia, for example, all types of cases were privately prosecuted, with assault and battery prosecutions being the most common.[24] But a few state courts—obviously concerned about private prosecutions—criticized or outlawed them. For instance, in 1849, the Massachusetts Supreme Court suggested in dicta that a privately retained prosecutor might void a criminal conviction.[25] In 1855, Massachusetts formally prohibited the use of private prosecutors,[26] though a Massachusetts court case in 1925 allowed a privately retained attorney to sit with the public prosecutor at counsel's table to consult with him.[27] Likewise, Michigan prohibited the employment of private prosecutors in 1875.[28] Although the Michigan Supreme Court flirted with a retreat from that prohibition in an 1889 case, *People v. Schick*,[29] the ban on private prosecutors was reaffirmed only a year later, in an 1890 case, *People v. Hillhouse*.[30]

In the State of Wisconsin, the propriety of private prosecutors was left unquestioned until 1888 when the Wisconsin Supreme Court handed down its landmark decision in *Biemel v. State*.[31] In *Biemel*, the Wisconsin Supreme Court declared that "public policy, and the fair, just, and impartial administration of the criminal law of this state, make it the duty of the courts to exclude the paid attorneys of private persons from appearing as prosecutors."[32] According to the Wisconsin Supreme Court: "An attorney employed and paid by private parties should not be permitted either by the courts or by the prosecuting attorney to assist in the trial of such criminal cases...." The state supreme court in *Biemel* emphasized that while the prosecuting officer represents the public's interests, has a duty to disclose exculpatory evidence, and has the objective of doing justice, paid attorneys of private parties may act out of "passion" or "prejudice" and simply be desirous of securing a criminal conviction for a fee.[33] A subsequent Wisconsin judicial decision allowed a privately retained attorney to perform minor pretrial tasks,[34] but Wisconsin courts have—through the years—repeatedly reaffirmed the ban on the use of private prosecutors.[35]

With the rise of public prosecution in the U.S., nineteenth-century state legislators and jurists also began putting various constraints on private prosecutors. For example, legislators enacted statutes to deter malicious prosecutions,[36] with private prosecutors subject to sanctions for bringing frivolous or vexatious prosecutions. As the U.S. Supreme Court recounted the historical shift in *Rehberg v. Paulk*: "When § 1983's predecessor was enacted in 1871, it was common for criminal cases to be prosecuted by private parties. And private prosecutions, like private plaintiffs in civil suits, did not enjoy absolute immunity from suit. Instead, 'the generally accepted rule' was that a private complainant who procured an arrest or prosecution could be held liable in an action for malicious prosecution if the complainant acted with malice and without probable cause."[37] State judicial systems likewise subjected private prosecutors to liability for the payment of costs.[38] Private attorneys might be prohibited from accepting fees for prosecuting criminal cases,[39] and public prosecutors had to consent to private prosecutors[40] and retain control over criminal cases involving their assistance.[41] Some judicial systems also prohibited the participation of private prosecutors in related civil matters[42] or having financial stakes in the prosecutions,[43] and they prohibited private prosecutions altogether for certain types of offenses.[44] In New Jersey, while municipal courts still permit the use of private prosecutions, they are not permitted for serious crimes,[45] and the failure to complete a private prosecution certification form in municipal court renders a conviction void *ab initio*.[46]

While the origin of the American public prosecutor remains a "historical enigma,"[47] academics generally trace the public prosecutor's roots to one of three European antecedents: the English, the Dutch, or the French.[48] Those foreign influences include the Dutch *schout*, the English attorney general or justice of the peace, and the French *advocate general, procurer publique* or *procurer du roi*.[49] The American public prosecutor, in truth, has something in common with each of these foreign-born predecessors. According to scholar Joan Jacoby, a local American prosecutor "shares characteristics" with the *procurer*, in the sense that the American prosecutor possesses the power "to initiate all public prosecutions"; the *schout*, as the prosecutor is "a local official of regional government"; and the English attorney general, as the prosecutor "has the power to terminate all criminal prosecutions."[50] Even in civil law countries such as Austria, France, Germany and Spain, private prosecutions were permitted for certain categories of crimes.[51] It was only over time, as a U.S. district court judge has recently explained of American prosecutorial practices, that—though isolated pockets of private prosecution remain—"the state acquired a monopoly over a professionalized public prosecution process."[52]

One must go back multiple centuries, in fact, to glimpse the complex origins of America's current public prosecution system. In the Dutch system, the *schout* was the designated public prosecutor. That prosecutorial system made its way to North America when the Dutch emigrated and settled the colony of New Netherland, which comprised parts of modern-day Connecticut, Delaware, New Jersey, New York, and Pennsylvania.[53] As one source describes the Dutch approach: "Unlike the chaotic system of prosecution tolerated by the common law, Dutch law intrusted the task of prosecuting criminals to a single office—the office of schout. Dutch colonists did not haul their neighbors into criminal courts on real or imagined charges for monetary gain. If a criminal offense occurred, the office of schout prosecuted the crime." As that source further describes how public prosecutions came to be an entrenched part of American law: "When the English eventually took New Netherland from the Dutch, the term *schout* was buried, but the idea of entrusting a public prosecutor with the responsibility for prosecuting all crimes took root and blossomed in America. The public prosecutor of today is a distant cousin of the common law and the first cousin of the schout."[54]

A legal historian, W. Scott Van Alstyne, Jr., has described the Dutch system of prosecution that was introduced into New Netherland. As Van Alstyne wrote in the *Wisconsin Law Review*: "Dutch law, including criminal procedure, is, like the substantive law and procedure of other continental countries, essentially the product of Roman, Canon, and 'tribal' law. In their criminal prosecutions the Dutch have always employed a public prosecutor whom they call the schout." Noting that the Dutch brought their laws and legal customs with them, Van Alstyne explained in 1952 that the first court records for New Netherlands that have survived date back to 1653, and that those documents are for "the Court of Schout, Burgomasters and Schepens at New Amsterdam." "At this time," Van Alstyne observed, "one Cornelius van Tienhoven was the schout-fiscal" at New Amsterdam (now Manhattan), with the offices of schout and fiscal later separated and van Tienhoven, who served as the schout from 1653 to 1665,[55] replaced by another man, Nicasius de Sille. "Records of the New Netherlands colony," Joan Jacoby points out, "show that the office of the *schout* was also established in settlements in New Jersey, Delaware, and Pennsylvania."[56] As a schout, van Tienhoven successfully prosecuted many cases, including an assault charge brought in 1653 against defendant Stoffel Elsers for beating up Adam Roelantsen, a woodcutter. "In Connecticut," Van Alstyne emphasized, taking note of Dutch immigration to that locale, "the first public prosecutor appears to have been William Pitkin who was appointed in 1662 for the county of Hartford."[57]

But the presence of public prosecutors did not spell the demise of private prosecutions on American soil. Indeed, in early America, as in England, a tradition arose of private associations being formed to safeguard property and to aid in the law's enforcement. Between the mid-eighteenth and late-nineteenth centuries, private prosecution societies proliferated across England and the United States, with English societies said to have emerged "as one approach to coping with ineffective criminal law enforcement and making the existing criminal justice system more accessible in the face of a very expensive private prosecution procedure." In addition to what has been termed the "American crime-control vigilantism that involved citizens taking the law into their own hands," anti-theft organizations—ones that pursued criminal suspects and held them for trial by the authorities—operated throughout America in the eighteenth and nineteenth centuries.[58] For example, when two boys stole grapes in 1847 from John Lincoln's farm in Worcester, Massachusetts, the farmer did not contact the local police; instead, he notified the head of the Worcester Association for the Protection of Fruit, a private association that had been formed in 1843 for the purpose of protecting the property of its subscribers. "It is requested," John Lincoln wrote, "that such measures may be taken as may be thought most expedient for the reformation of these boys, and for the prevention of others to offend in like manner." The Worcester Association for the Protection of Fruit, writes scholar Ann-Marie Szymanski, "was but one of hundreds of local associations created during the nineteenth century to protect the private property of U.S. citizens." "At least seventy-two such protective societies, serving over one hundred towns," she observes, "existed in New England," with many of them located in rural areas.

These private associations included theft-detecting societies, most notably ones aimed at horse thieves—a class of offenders that drew the particular ire of early Americans. "Faced with a lack of police protection," Szymanski observes, "townspeople across the Northeast began to organize permanent voluntary associations to combat theft, especially of horses, during the last two decades of the eighteenth century." There were societies in Dedham and Milton, Massachusetts, for apprehending horse thieves, and there were the Newton, Needham and Natick Society for Apprehending Horse Thieves, the Framingham Thief Detecting Society, the Shrewsbury Thief Detecting Society, and the Westborough Thief Detecting Society. "By 1782, when citizens of Northampton, Massachusetts, founded the first American antitheft society," she notes, recounting how American towns emulated the English precedent of such private associations, "dozens of similar societies had already been formed in England." Rewards would be offered to those who helped retrieve stolen goods, with anti-theft societies relying on broadsides, handbills, and newspaper advertisements as part of their work. Most towns in New England, Szymanski points out, "appointed only a handful of constables—part-time, unsalaried officials who often rotated in and out of office" annually, receiving "some fees for their services" (*i.e.*, "rewarded for making arrests, serving warrants, producing witnesses, and performing other duties associated with their position as court officers").

From the founding period to the mid-nineteenth century, private law-enforcement associations played a major role in American life, assisting in the prosecution of everything from counterfeiting and property crimes to liquor law violations. For example, in 1793, in Connecticut, the Woodstock Theft Detecting Society proclaimed that it sought to "aid the State in the execution of its laws," emphasizing: "While government is doing what it can to keep the body of the people in order, and render secure the property of its citizens, the members of this Society design to co-operate with the plan of government, and by their private compact, to increase that security of property which the State endeavours to afford." Members of these anti-theft societies had to pay entrance fees and dues or assessments to remain in good standing. "In the late 1840s," Szymanski writes, "temperance reformers in New York and Massachusetts founded two organizations designed 'to plug the gaps created by inefficient and unwilling local authorities': the Carson League and the Temperance Watchmen, which helped enforce state prohibition statutes in the 1850s." By the late nineteenth century, she explains, a number of associations existed in New England, including "antiliquor 'law and order' leagues, societies for the prevention of cruelty to animals and children, and societies for the suppression of prostitution, pornography, and gambling."[59]

The origins of public prosecution in America is, in fact, a very complex story—one shaped by English law, other European legal systems, and some homegrown inventions. "With respect to prosecution," legal historian Yue Ma writes, "the English attorney general, the French *ministère publique*, and the Dutch *schout* all impacted the mode of prosecution in the early colonial days." "The office of the prosecuting attorney, typically in the form of the office of district attorney," Ma explains of the development of American prosecutorial practices, however, "is a product of American experience and a distinctive and uniquely American contribution." Although American colonists had imported English traditions, including sheriffs, justices of the peace, and private prosecutions, many colonists—as Ma observes—came to view private prosecution "as incompatible with their ideals of justice" and looked to public prosecutors to help repress crime. "The attorney general, being the official that performed a function resembling public prosecution," Ma notes, "was pushed to the center stage and began to play a more active role in criminal prosecution." As populations grew, deputy attorneys general were appointed in counties to better serve local communities and the desire for local autonomy laid the foundation for federal U.S. district attorneys and, at the state level, local solicitors and district or county attorneys.[60]

The Early Twentieth Century: The Practice of Private Prosecution Continues Amidst the Growth of Public Prosecutors' Offices

Despite the creation and funding of early American public prosecutors' offices, newspaper reports make clear that the common-law practice of private prosecution persisted—and, in some places, continued to thrive[61] in spite of the presence of public prosecutors handling many criminal matters. In the early twentieth century, "private prosecutors"—or individuals described as such by the press—appeared in places as diverse as Arizona,[62] California,[63] Colorado,[64] Georgia,[65] Illinois,[66] Indiana,[67] Iowa,[68] Kansas,[69] Louisiana,[70] Maryland,[71] Mississippi,[72] Missouri,[73] Montana,[74] Nebraska,[75] North Carolina,[76] Oklahoma,[77] Oregon,[78] Pennsylvania,[79] South Dakota,[80] Tennessee,[81] Texas[82] and Utah.[83] Although district attorneys, county attorneys, and solicitors—the varied names given to local public prosecutors—were taking more control of criminal matters,[84] including excluding private prosecutors from grand jury proceedings,[85] private prosecutions still frequently occurred in various locales, especially where they had a long tradition (*e.g.*, North Carolina,[86] Pennsylvania[87] and Texas).[88] Part of the rationale was that private prosecutions were thought to be necessary to supplement the efforts of public prosecutors in fighting crime. As one summary published in *The Yale Law Journal* described the 1931 *Report on Prosecution* and the Kefauver Crime Committee's work investigating organized crime in the early 1950s: "The United States National Commission on Law Enforcement concluded that the majority of suspects are never brought to trial for their alleged crimes even though there are convincing cases against them. More recently the Kefauver Crime Commission has charged that prosecutors in general are failing to suppress widespread crime."[89]

The Commonwealth of Pennsylvania—one of the places that utilized privately paid attorneys with considerable frequency—had, as noted in an earlier chapter, a particularly long tradition of private prosecutions. And that tradition continued unabated in the early twentieth century. In 1905, for example, *The Philadelphia Inquirer* reprinted this tidbit of advice for crime victims: "The District Attorney prosecutes all criminal cases either personally or by his assistants, but if you as private prosecutor are especially desirous of securing a conviction you should retain counsel to prepare your case and assist in its prosecution. The jury may, if it wishes, put the costs on you or on the county."[90] In fact, countless Pennsylvania cases over many decades involved private prosecutors,[91] including in murder cases.[92] In Philadelphia, the district attorney's responsibility was said in 1906 to begin only "when the grand jury passes along the cases to him."[93] In a 1913 news story out of Memphis, Texas, a newspaper likewise noted that in a case charging complicity in a murder an attorney had been "employed by the dead man's relatives as private prosecutor."[94] A 1916 report out of Goldsboro, North Carolina, similarly observed that, in a murder case against Hyman Epstein for the killing of Leonard Edwards, the state's solicitor gave up "his prerogative to be the last to address the jury to Victor S. Bryant, employed as private prosecutor by the Edwards family."[95]

In the City of Brotherly Love, the norm—as it had been for decades—was for private prosecutors to initiate criminal cases, with district attorneys largely deferring to citizens in deciding who, what, and when to prosecute. Indeed, Philadelphia's district attorney only rarely took the initiative and was the go-to official only when no private prosecutor would step forward to assume responsibility for a prosecution.[96] In a 1906 editorial in *The Philadelphia Inquirer*, the division of responsibility between private prosecutors and the district attorney's office was even the subject of commentary in the paper. "It is neither a rule of law nor of practice," the newspaper editorialized, "that the District Attorney shall in no case initiate a criminal prosecution, though the instances of such institution by him are extremely rare." As the paper's editorial continued: "The criminal law of the Commonwealth contemplates that there shall be a private prosecutor in every criminal action, a private prosecutor who is answerable in damages if the arrest be unwarranted and malicious. To this end, the law provides that a defendant need not plead to an indictment until the name of the private prosecutor be indorsed thereon." "Nevertheless," the editorial continued, "the law invests the District Attorney with power to initiate a criminal action without a private prosecutor in extraordinary cases; e.g., where great haste is necessary, as where the defendants are about to escape, or the statute of limitations will intervene, or other exigent circumstances make it necessary and proper that the District Attorney should act immediately, in order that justice may not be defeated." "In such cases," it was noted of the District Attorney's role, "he may present a Bill of Indictment, commonly called a District Attorney's bill, to the grand jury, without a preliminary hearing or binding over of the defendant by a magistrate."[97]

It was, at least in Philadelphia, thus an extremely unusual occurrence for the district attorney's office to take the initiative in commencing criminal prosecutions. "The cases in which a District Attorney begins proceedings before a magistrate are equally rare," *The Philadelphia Inquirer* noted, adding of former District Attorney George Graham: "Mr. Graham began such proceedings two or three times during his long term." There was, however, an accepted process for the district attorney's office to commence criminal prosecutions. "Where the District Attorney thus begins proceedings before a magistrate," the paper stressed, "he must, of course, procure some person—a detective in his office or a citizen—who will swear out the warrant the District Attorney draws up and has served." "Mr. Bell," the paper noted of then-in-office District Attorney John C. Bell, "has made it clear in his recent published statements that where a crime is committed which is not against a particular individual, but is against the whole community, and where the evidence of such crime as laid before him is sufficient in his judgment as a quasi-judicial officer to establish and prove the guilt of the persons accused, he should begin proceedings before a committing magistrate." "It was for this reason," it was reported, "that he began proceedings against the Ice Trust conspirators; a crime that affected the whole community, and where the evidence presented to him was sufficient in his judgment to establish the guilt of the accused."[98]

In 1955, an article published in *The Yale Law Journal* gave a detailed snapshot of private prosecution in America. As that article reported: "Despite widespread belief that criminal actions are conducted exclusively by public officials, private prosecutors in fact play an extensive role in criminal law enforcement. In thirty jurisdictions appellate courts have decided that privately employed attorneys may assist the public prosecutor, while only three have said that they may not."[99] Although Massachusetts, Michigan and Wisconsin had refused to permit private attorneys to assist in criminal prosecutions, "even in those states"—the 1955 article emphasized—"there have been exceptions where the private attorney participated in a limited manner or was not hired by interested parties."[100] As a practical matter, public prosecutors in the 1950s were allowing private prosecutors to appear in criminal cases, with private prosecutions "especially common before magistrates, municipal courts and justices of the peace."[101] The article further emphasized that "[m]ost states find authority for permitting private prosecution in the inherent power of the court to administer justice," with some jurisdictions using "the power of the public prosecutor to select assistants ... as the authority for permitting private attorneys to aid in criminal prosecution."[102] "The courts," the article concluded, "have approved of private assistant prosecutors even in actions for such serious crimes as murder, manslaughter, burglary, larceny and rape."[103]

In truth, district attorney offices (or their equivalents in other states) were gradually being professionalized. Over time, many public prosecutors came to see their assigned role as serving the public, not attempting to exact revenge for a crime. In 1835, just five years after the private prosecution of the Knapp brothers in Salem, Massachusetts, led by U.S. Senator Daniel Webster, a New York District Attorney, Ogden Hoffman, gave what was described as a "valedictory" address on the eve of his leaving his official duties. A graduate of Columbia, Hoffman served as New York's district attorney from 1829 to 1935. "May it please the Court," he began, observing that it would be the last time he appeared in court as part of his official duties. After noting "the solemnity of his oath of office," Hoffman added: "Nor can I refrain from here expressing, publicly, how much I am indebted to the active and efficient police department of our city, for their intelligent and zealous co-operation with me, in bringing offenders to justice, and for the powerful aid which they at all times have so cheerfully afforded me." Although Hoffman did not want to speak about himself on the occasion of his retirement, he did want to convey "one thought that will cheer me at parting," making these concluding remarks about his prosecutorial career: "I have never strained for a conviction through envy, hatred or malice; and on the other hand, I have never failed to use my utmost exertions to convict those whom I knew to be clearly guilty." As Hoffman told the court: "I have never omitted to carry out the pure ends of public justice through fear, favor, affection, or the hope of reward. During the time that I have had the honor to fill the office of public prosecutor, I have ever borne in mind that I was no less the counsel for the prisoner, than the advocate of the State; and that while my duty demanded that the criminal law should be administered justly as regarded the interests of the people, it also required me to act with mercy to the accused."[104]

In the twentieth century, though private prosecutions did not disappear in the jurisdictions that continued to authorize them, public prosecutors' offices began to more actively manage criminal cases, gaining more power and prestige as deputies or assistants were added to governmental payrolls. In reviewing Philadelphia District Attorney Samuel Rotan's first term in office, *The Philadelphia Inquirer*, in October 1909, highlighted endorsements for Rotan's reelection to the position. One former Assistant District Attorney, Frederick Shoyer, observed as part of the newspaper's profile: "[t]here is no more important office in the city or county of Philadelphia than that of District Attorney." After making reference to Sir William Blackstone's view that no man, however noble his birth, is free from the law's reach, Mr. Shoyer made this extrapolation on the importance of the office of district attorney: "If it be true that no man, be he high or lowly, is beyond the reach of the law, how important then, when forced to appear to plead to an indictment, to find that he is face to face with a public prosecutor who knows no rule but his oath of office. One who will not stoop himself or permit his corps of assistants to serve the personal or political ambition of private prosecutor; who will not with prejudice or passion urge the conviction of a defendant, other than on the evidence; who when public excitement runs high will not listen to noise and clamor, and mistake it for the voice of justice."[105]

In early twentieth-century Philadelphia, prosecutions might be likened to a public-private partnership. A Republican who served as Philadelphia's district attorney from 1906 to 1926, Samuel Rotan noted in a speech in 1909 that he had been endorsed by 974 Philadelphia lawyers and that his office had disposed of more than 20,000 cases in his first three years in office. In the disposition of cases, he said in a long-winded fashion, "we in every case send for the private prosecutor, and for the witnesses whose names were on the bill of indictment, and in a great many cases, trivial cases, like assault and battery, malicious mischief, instead of putting down those cases for trial and sending such a man to jail we made a study of the defendant, his habits from the time of his arrest until the time of the investigation, and where we found that the defendant had lived a decent life and had endeavored to make an honest living for his family and had not been a lawbreaker during that time, we sent for the defendant and for his counsel—if he had one—and we went into court before the judge sitting on the bench and before the jury sitting in the box, and we explained the facts as we had found him, and where the law justified it, and the facts were such, we openly in open court, before everybody made the statement that the great Commonwealth of Pennsylvania felt that this poor prisoner should not go to jail and that they had re-established themselves as good citizens and that they had had sufficient punishment, and we asked in those cases that a verdict of not guilty be taken and that they be found not guilty."[106] In making such recommendations, the public prosecutor no doubt heard in advance the very personal views of many private prosecutors.

The Work of Private Prosecutors: A Wide Range of Cases

A large number of early twentieth-century private prosecutions in America were, in fact, in assault and battery cases,[107] including instances involving domestic violence[108] or the abuse of alcohol.[109] In assault cases, the charge would typically be made by the victim,[110] or private prosecutor, which would then lead to the arrest of the accused by the constable or other local law enforcement official. One reported case from Oregon, in 1904, illustrates how the process would work: "Jacob Idlewine, a resident of North Salem, was, upon a warrant sworn out by one Clarence Bell, of this city, arrested by Constable John H. Lewis last evening, upon the charge of assault and battery, alleged to have been committed upon the person of the private prosecutor. He was arraigned before Justice of the Peace E. D. Horgan, entered a plea of not guilty, and his hearing was set for 10 o'clock this morning."[111] In another case, brought in Pennsylvania in 1905, *The Daily Notes* of Canonsburg, Pennsylvania, reported that the accused defendant in an assault and battery case was fined $10 along with the imposition of costs and sentenced to 30 days in jail. "The private prosecutor," the news report observed, "was Lucy Morris," who charged the defendant "with striking her on the back with a piece of ice and with attempt to kill her."[112]

A variety of people with different backgrounds and occupations served as private prosecutors. In addition to crime victims and their relatives, constables, sheriffs, chiefs of police, police officers, detectives, revenue officers, mayors, banks, corporations, bank cashiers, mine inspectors, mine superintendents or foremen, and coroners served—or were described—as private prosecutors.[113] For example, in one Pennsylvania case, Leo Logan, Monongahela's Chief of Police, was listed as the private prosecutor in a case where Clara Fields and her mother, Nancy Fields, were arrested and then charged with the murder of Clara's child and the concealment of the infant's body. While the grand jury refused to indict the mother and charged the costs to the county, the charges against the daughter, Clara, went forward.[114] At the trial itself, it was reported: "Assistant District Attorney C. L. V. Acheson is looking after the interests of the commonwealth. At the tables for the prosecution are Leo Logan, the private prosecutor, and Coroner W. H. Sipe."[115] Chief Leo Logan was also described as "the private prosecutor" in other matters, including in cases ranging from the theft of a hat[116] to one man, Henry Paul, being charged with murdering another man, David McCann.[117] In one news report, from 1911, when Monongahela had a new police chief, *The Daily Republican*—a newspaper of that city—similarly reported of a case alleging that a speakeasy was selling liquor without a license: "Chief of Police Harry Chester of this city was the private prosecutor...."[118] In another Pennsylvania case, one brought a year later, in 1912, a local junk dealer served as the private prosecutor in a perjury case. That case resulted in the defendant, John Leyds, being sentenced to pay costs, a $1.00 fine, and to serve a term of one year imprisonment in the workhouse.[119]

Although an assortment of individuals served as private prosecutors, at least one Pennsylvania grand jury condemned the practice of police officers serving in that role. As the *Pottsville Republican* reported on January 7, 1922: "The grand jury on Saturday morning in making its regular presentment to the court, condemned the action of police officers appearing as prosecutors on information received . . . ." In expressing concern about "trivial cases," the grand jury stated that the custom of police officers serving as private prosecutors "was to be strongly condemned, as it was apparent that these prosecutions by public officers are in many cases brought solely to relieve the private prosecutors from liability for costs." The court, in commenting on the grand jury's report, concurred that "too many people are indulging in the luxury of being in court." It specifically referenced "a recent occurrence where a justice has returned a case accusing a defendant of assault and battery upon a rooster." The court also took notice of instances where "police officers should not be assessed with costs, as they acted in good faith, without an opportunity to investigate," but then observed "that recently the practice of making officers the prosecutors had become quite common." In its news report, the *Pottsville Republican* cited some statistics that gave a snapshot of the grand jury's work. As the newspaper recited: "The grand jury acted upon 150 bills at the present time, ignoring 80 of the bills and furnishing indictments in balance. In 23 cases costs were placed on the county and upon the litigants in 57."[120]

Another local newspaper, the *Evening Herald* of Shenandoah, Pennsylvania, itself commented on the grand jury's report. Like the *Pottsville Republican*, the *Evening Herald* noted that the grand jury had condemned "the practice of borough and private officers becoming prosecutors for the sole purpose, apparently of relieving private citizens from becoming prosecutors in order to escape liability for costs." The grand jury's report, the *Evening Herald* noted, stated: "It has come to our notice that constables, borough police and even State Police officers have become prosecutors in cases upon information received. This practice and custom is to be condemned as it is apparent that these prosecutions by public officers are in many cases brought sole[l]y to relieve private prosecutors from liability from costs and also condemned that these public prosecutors have a personal and direct interest in costs." "The practice of Justices of the Peace and Aldermen in returning trivial cases when the costs in such cases should be disposed of by the Justice or Alderman," the grand jury's report added, "is also condemned."[121]

Despite such condemnation of behavior, there was often coordination or collaboration between a district attorney's office and the private prosecutor,[122] although where constables or officers made the arrests, those officials often acted as the private prosecutors.[123] In some criminal cases, attorneys retained by victims prepared the cases for trial by the public prosecutor's office.[124] In 1906, in Pennsylvania, Charles A. O'Brien, in laying out his eight-point platform in running for Allegheny County's district attorney, including this item in his list: "To aid the City Police and all other proper officers, as well as private prosecutors, in a due, regular and just enforcement of the law, with a view solely to the competency of the service and the eradication of all petty influences and frictions, which tend so greatly to thwart and defeat an efficient criminal administration."[125] Law firms, former judges or district attorneys, or private lawyers were frequently retained to represent the victim-private prosecutors.[126] In one Pennsylvania case, one constable unusually served as the private prosecutor in a criminal case against another constable.[127] In still other instances, government officials were urged to hire private prosecutors—in that category of case, meaning private attorneys—to bring criminal charges. For instance, in 1913, under the headline "City Urged to Hire Private Prosecutor in Reservoir Cases," the *Fort Worth Record* reported that, "if a recommendation made by the Chamber of Commerce advisory committee ... is followed by the city commission," that "private counsel" would "prosecute parties indicted for alleged crooked work in connection with the construction of the West Fork dam."[128]

Aside from assault and battery cases,[129] including felonious assaults with intent to kill,[130] private prosecutions were brought in many other types of cases, with larceny (*e.g.*, of goods, of a horse and buggy, a mule, a plow and cultivator, "of two love birds," etc.) being an especially frequent charge.[131] The private prosecutor and the defendant naturally had diametrically opposing interests, so they were regularly at odds—if not at their throats—in the courtroom. "There was evidence of ill feeling between the private prosecutor and the defendant," *The Daily Notes* of Canonsburg, Pennsylvania, reported in February 1906 after the jury brought in a guilty verdict in a case against one man charged with larceny and receiving stolen goods.[132] In other case, *The Daily Notes* reported that William Hoffman—the private prosecutor—got up during the criminal defendant's testimony, pointed a finger at the defendant, and exclaimed: "You're a liar by the clock." The defendant, Stephen Jeffers, had been indicted for an assault against Hoffman's daughter.[133] Of course, it is hardly surprising that there would be bad blood between an accuser and the accused. After all, an accuser is making an allegation of criminal activity on the part of the defendant.

Other times, private prosecutors had conflicts with county prosecutors about the proper handling of a case,[134] with one private prosecutor, in 1911, accusing the public prosecutor in Wilkes-Barre, Pennsylvania, of mishandling conspiracy cases and offering this striking rebuke: "The District Attorney was no more prepared to try those cases than I am of walking across the river without a bridge. He never investigated anything, but simply took what we told him for his evidence. He never even as much as walked to the corridor of this Court House to see if what we were saying was the truth. How could a man have much faith in a case that was handled in that manner?"[135] Sometimes, depending on the nature of the alleged offense, there were multiple private prosecutors to share in the responsibility for the prosecution. In early November 1909, *The Daily Republican* of Monongahela, Pennsylvania, gave this report on what it called "the leader of an organized gang that did not work, but lived off what they could extort to take from fellow countrymen, especially on pay day": "The grand jury yesterday found an indictment against Tony Calastro, an Italian, charged with robbery. There are thirteen separate counts in the indictment and that many different private prosecutors."[136]

Private prosecutions were brought in the most serious cases, including in murder[137] and manslaughter[138] cases, even where death sentences were sought.[139] For example, *The Evening Gazette* of Cedar Rapids, Iowa, reported on November 10, 1919 that "[t]he entire state of Iowa" would be watching "with more than passing interest next week" at the murder trial at West Union, of George Briggs, Jr., accused of James Wait's slaying. Wait was "a prominent citizen" of Edgewood, Iowa, who was a material witness against Briggs in an arson trial. "This promises to be one of the most sensational trials in the state's criminal annals," *The Evening Gazette* reported of the capital case, adding that "on the side of the state are the county attorneys of Fayette and Clayton counties and private prosecutors, D. D. Murphy and his sons, and Mr. Price of Elkader."[140] Likewise, in March 1921, *The Daily Times* of Davenport, Iowa, reported that a widow, Amanda Houghton, "planned to employ a private prosecutor to assist the state in prosecuting John Polos, who has been bound over to the grand jury for the charge of murder in the first degree in the specific case of Ray Houghton." "The county attorney," that newspaper added, "said he had no information on the definite appointment of a prosecutor, but that the state would welcome any such assistance offered to assist in bringing Polos to justice."[141]

In the twentieth century, private prosecutions were brought in many other types of cases, too. For example, they were commenced in rape,[142] arson,[143] rioting,[144] kidnapping,[145] perjury,[146] graft,[147] highway robbery[148] and nuisance cases.[149] In addition, they were employed in conspiracy,[150] fraud,[151] burglary,[152] robbery,[153] forgery,[154] bribery,[155] extortion,[156] false pretense,[157] trespass,[158] disorderly conduct,[159] accomplice liability,[160] election[161] and embezzlement matters.[162] And they were put to use for adultery;[163] desertion and non-support;[164] making and delivering worthless checks;[165] fornication;[166] aiding a prisoner's escape;[167] breaking and entering;[168] drunk and reckless driving;[169] receiving stolen property;[170] attempts to kill[171] and the making of death threats;[172] unlawful wounding;[173] and an assortment of gun crimes, such as felonious shooting,[174] assault with a dangerous or deadly weapon,[175] carrying concealed weapons,[176] illegally possessing a shotgun,[177] threats by brandishing a firearm,[178] wantonly pointing firearms,[179] and carrying firearms with intent to kill.[180] In one Pennsylvania case, a grocer, Katz Baskin, was charged with giving short weight in a bush of potatoes sold to another man. As *The Daily Notes* of Canonsburg, Pennsylvania, reported on that case, which was then still on appeal: "John F. Curran, scaler of weights and measures, was the private prosecutor. Baskin was arrested and taken before Justice Robinson, Meadow Lands, where he was fined."[181]

In addition, newspaper articles reveal private prosecutions for bigamy;[182] horse stealing[183] and driving a horse to death;[184] mayhem;[185] sodomy;[186] bank failures;[187] throwing trees and brush into a creek to interfere with logging operations;[188] grossly disturbing the public peace by transporting dynamite;[189] unlawfully whipping a school boy with a paddle;[190] promoting a prize fight in violation of law;[191] breaking up or disturbing a religious meeting;[192] attempting to defraud a creditor;[193] killing game out of season;[194] practicing optometry or veterinary medicine without a license;[195] distributing free samples of cooking soda without a permit;[196] operating a motor vehicle with insufficient brakes;[197] selling cigarettes to a minor;[198] contributing to the delinquency of a minor;[199] selling liquor without a license,[200] at a speakeasy,[201] or to a minor;[202] violating commodities,[203] mining[204] or liquor laws;[205] selling cocaine in violation of the law;[206] peddling shoes without a license;[207] illegal fishing[208] or hunting without a license;[209] libel;[210] unlawfully transacting business as an agent of a foreign corporation;[211] impersonating an officer;[212] violation of the pure food laws;[213] selling short weight butter in violation of state law;[214] insurance fraud;[215] malicious mischief,[216] including for breaking windows[217] and removing a tombstone and markers from a cemetery;[218] keeping a bawdy, disorderly or gambling house;[219] and selling liquor or keeping open a business or place of amusement on a Sunday.[220]

The private prosecutions not only covered a wide array of conduct, with one in Pennsylvania accusing a woman of being "a common scold,"[221] but they could—not surprisingly—be highly contentious. One Oregon news report from 1903, recounting a dispute over a 50-acre plot of land that devolved into a criminal case, gives an example of how a private prosecution might unfold: "James V. Springer, who was arrested Monday afternoon charged with threatening to kill J. W. La Follett, was tried at 2 o'clock yesterday, the principal object of private prosecutor J. W. La Follett, being to have him put under bonds to keep the peace."[222] In New York, another private prosecution sought to indict the president and officers of the Tammany Hall ice trust, but was stymied by the district attorney, who was said to owe his office "to Tammany, and probably had received his instructions in full."[223] In 1909, *The Daily Notes* of Canonsburg, Pennsylvania—in reporting on a case involving allegations that a bank was defrauded of $60,000—observed that "[y]esterday was practically consumed with a battle between the attorneys for the private prosecutor and the defendant." "Skirmish after skirmish was fought," the newspaper explained.[224]

Private prosecutions, which included private investigatory activities[225] and participation by private attorneys at trial, including on behalf of corporations,[226] thus ranged from the most violent offenses (*e.g.*, murder and rape)[227] to property offenses such as theft or larceny, often involving relatively small sums of money or property (*e.g.*, the theft of shoes valued at $4.00, watches, $20.00 bills, a mining pick and shovel, a meat cleaver, a horse blanket, chickens, sweet corn, lumber, coal, candy, a suit, pairs of trousers, other clothing items, an old leather belt, an overcoat and gloves valued at $3.00).[228] The bulk of private prosecutions, reflective of the type of crimes actually committed, naturally involved many lower-level offenses, with criminal charges precipitated, for example, by the theft of a bicycle tire[229] or by pickpocketing[230] or the removal of shrubbery from a mother's home after her death.[231] In 1903, one Oregon woman, Frances Bressler, swore out a warrant for the arrest of another woman, Minnie Ringwald, for assault and battery. Bressler, in the role of private prosecutor, alleged before Justice of the Peace E. D. Horgan that Ringwald, a neighbor, struck her on the head with an umbrella after they got into a dispute.[232]

The Critique of Private Prosecutors: Public Denunciations and Courtroom Confrontations

In the twentieth century, although public prosecutors were accused of being corrupt at times,[233] private prosecutors continued coming under scrutiny, including for their alleged misconduct, whether driven by money, malice, or a discriminatory purpose.[234] Defense counsel frequently questioned their motives[235] or attempted—sometimes successfully—to disqualify private prosecutors altogether.[236] Rebukes of private prosecutors were made in court,[237] in motions to quash indictments,[238] in dismissal and new trial motions,[239] on appeals,[240] in legislative proposals,[241] and in newspaper editorials,[242] letters to the editor[243] and speeches.[244] In one 1906 case in the Hawaii Territory, a motion to disqualify a private prosecutor was made, but the judge allowed the private prosecutor to continue in an "advisory capacity" while insisting that the Deputy Attorney General "shall conduct the case."[245] In a subsequent case in the Hawaii Territory, Judge Andrade, in a 1910 case, *Territory of Hawaii vs. Manuel Lewis*, in which a private prosecutor appeared in police court, had this to say when confronted with the specter of a private prosecution: "A great deal has been said in this case about private prosecutors but as far as I am aware there is no such thing as a private prosecutor. While a man may be privately employed to prosecute a case, from the time he obtains the consent of the County Attorney he becomes a public prosecutor and not a private prosecutor. He is representing the people and in that way representing the defendant."[246] New trials were sometimes granted in cases where private prosecutors made prejudicial arguments at trial.[247]

In some locales, the issue of private prosecution also became a political issue, coming up in political advertisements[248] and political campaigns.[249] For example, in 1930, in a newspaper advertisement in Oregon's *Corvallis Gazette-Times*, paid for "Denman's Committee for District Attorney," the candidate—George W. Denman—headlined it, "Taxpayers Pay $750.00 for Private Prosecutor in Case of State vs. Bryant." That ad then read, referencing the $750.00 bill for services submitted to, and paid by, Benton County in that particular case: "To the taxpayers and voters: The taxpayers of this county, are entitled to know the additional cost to them for the private prosecutor who conducted and tried the case of State vs. Lansy Bryant." After also referencing a $125.00 bill for services paid by Benton County in the case of State vs. Avery, the ad further noted that "[i]n addition to said sum it also cost the regular salary of the District Attorney $150.00 per month, and $30.00 a month for stenographer." "Geo. W. Denman," the ad concluded, "is pledged by one of his platform planks, to-wit: 'I will run the office on salary allowed by law, without additional expense to already overburdened taxpayers.'"[250] Another newspaper ad, seeking to reelect Washington County District Attorney Michael Hanna in Pennsylvania, noted of his prosecutorial record: "No case dismissed (nolle prossed) without WRITTEN consents of arresting officers or private prosecutors AND approval of court."[251]

Other candidates for local elective office also weighed in on the subject of private prosecutors. In 1931, Felix Bolowicz, in announcing his district attorney candidacy, had this to say: "I believe it the duty of the district attorney to prevent the clogging of trial lists and the imped[i]ment of court work, at great expense to the taxpayers, by the inclusion of a large number of petty violations where slight infractions are criminally prosecuted to vent the spleen or satisfy the personal vengeance of the private prosecutor." "This," Bolowicz said, "only serves to make the district attorney's office appear to be prosecuting a voluminous number of cases without effectively combatting crime."[252] Likewise, in 1932, Walter Petcsh, a candidate for county attorney in Kerr County, Texas, included the following text in a political advertisement appealing to voters there: "I pledge you that I will not permit private prosecution in any case where the Defendant is charged with a misdemeanor, because, if such practice is permitted the private prosecutor or his employer will or at least have a tendency to control the [county attorney's] office and for the further reason that private prosecution invariably, in this character of case, constitutes persecution rather than prosecution, in my judgment."[253]

Newspapers, taking notice of the problems associated with private prosecutions, also weighed in. In an editorial in *Carter's Weekly* titled "The Private Prosecutor," the North Carolina newspaper observed that the "custom or usage" of private prosecutions was "deeply rooted in the practice of our State courts" but was "highly pernicious." "We refer," the editorial emphasized, "to the practice that permits private interests to intermeddle in criminal prosecutions by employing counsel of their own selection to appear with the solicitor for the State." "This practice," the editorial noted, "has obtained in the courts of North Carolina so widely and for so long a time that our people generally have come to regard it as a matter of course and an indefeasible right." After correctly pointing out that the practice "is not tolerated" in federal courts, the newspaper editorial argued: "We offer no criticism of the individual lawyer who accepts employment for this character of service—to do so would be to stultify ourselves. The service can be rendered, so long as the practice obtains, without offense against any code of legal ethics; nevertheless, we do not hesitate to say that, taken in sum, we regard the practice as enormously prejudicial to the administration of justice." "Two principal evils," the paper said, "result from this practice, namely: (1) There is an inevitable tendency to degrade the issue arising upon the charge of an offense against society to the level of a mere controversy between individuals; (2) where the prosecution is entrusted largely to counsel subsidized by the vindictiveness of the injured party, there is always the temptation to seek conviction by questionable methods—methods that would not conceivably be resorted to by a public prosecutor standing alone and acting under the sanctions of an official oath." Although public prosecutors sometimes engage in misconduct, the editorial thus recognized that private prosecutors may have additional incentives to do so.

The editorial in *Carter's Weekly* also saw private prosecutions as problematic for another reason. "The vogue of private prosecution has yet another injurious tendency that ought not to be overlooked," the editorial stressed, with its writer observing: "The custom has grown so general that it has come to be felt as obligatory by persons of small means to whom the expense frequently is ruinous." "Crime is an offense against society," the editorial argued, "and as such it should be prosecuted by society; and it is only as society acts through its own sworn officials and holds its prosecutions inviolate against the intermeddling of persons having 'private griefs' that conviction and punishment can be reasonably assured." As the editorial continued: "When private persons, with motives of private injury, are allowed to intrude themselves into the counsels of the State the public character of criminal prosecution is gravely compromised, with the result that defendants frequently are enabled to hide their guilt behind a smoke-screen of persecution." "The vindictiveness of private prosecution has done as much perhaps as any other one cause to weaken the sanctions of the criminal law in North Carolina," the editorial concluded.[254] As it was, some North Carolina citizens disliked serving as private prosecutors,[255] though the formation of local law and order leagues—like one formed in Wilkes County—were designed to encourage private citizens to lend their aid to law enforcement.[256]

The term "private prosecutor" itself came, in at least some locales, to be viewed as derogatory in nature—in effect, a kind of epithet.[257] Often, it was the criminal defendant's defense attorney—or, periodically, the accused—who, in court, disparaged the use of private prosecutors or denounced them as acting in "bad faith."[258] For example, in 1913, Charles Pekor—a staff correspondent for the *Fort Worth Star-Telegram*—reported that the defense lawyer, William P. McLean Jr., "scored the private prosecutors in the case and commented on the little that District Attorney Spencer has had to do with the trial." McLean, Pekor reported, "said it would be the delight of the private prosecutors, hired to get victory, for the jury to send [John Beal] Sneed to the penitentiary."[259] Another defense lawyer, W. D. Berry, lamented of the case against his client: "it was not the case of the state of Texas against Beal Sneed, but the case of Odell, Cooper and the Boyces against Sneed." As the *Waco Morning News* reported of his argument for the defense: "Berry's denunciation of the private prosecutors was bitter, and he said the prosecution of Sneed showed a spirit of vindictiveness on the part of the Boyces."[260] In another Texas case, from 1914, A. W. Dumas, charged with incest, accused J. Frank Norris—himself only recently acquitted on an arson charge—of being out to get him after Norris employed a special prosecutor. At the third trial of Dumas for his alleged conduct, the two prior trials having resulted in hung juries, Dumas—while on the stand and speaking to Norris's lawyer in open court—"shook his finger at the private prosecutor and accused him of being employed by Norris." "I believe, before God," Dumas said, "Dr. J. Frank Norris is in a conspiracy against me and that he has employed you to try to send me to the penitentiary."[261]

Private prosecutors, perhaps not surprisingly, would often push for harsh sentences, up to and including the death penalty.[262] On rare occasions, though, they might later experience a change of heart and shift their views as to the propriety of a charge or the appropriateness of a particular sentence. Private prosecutors could cause a charge to be dropped, which happened not infrequently,[263] or a criminal defendant could be released from custody upon the private prosecutor's urging or recommendation.[264] In the Hawaii Territory, in February 1911, the *Hawaiian Star* gave this report: "Two charges were nolle prossed in the police court Saturday but, in making the necessary application, Deputy City and County Attorney Brown stated that it was another of those cases of a private prosecutor being employed who, after investigation, had decided not to go on with the charges. Judge Lymer remarked that such cases should not be put on the records of the County Attorney's office, as so many were nolle prossed."[265] In other instances, private prosecutors supported pardons or commutations for convicted criminals,[266] even joining—or adding their names to—executive clemency petitions.[267] In 1909, *The Gazette Times* noted that one Pennsylvania trial judge had observed that "[i]t is quite uncommon for the district attorney and for the private prosecutor's counsel to ask for leniency on behalf of a defendant."[268]

Even though private prosecutors were often employed by victims' relatives in murder or other felony cases for the express purpose of seeking the death penalty, it appears that even in such cases, they sometimes shifted their stances after the passage of time. In one early twentieth-century case in North Carolina, the private prosecutor of Jesse Whitehead, an African-American man convicted of the crime of burglary, publicly supported a commutation of Whitehead's original sentence—death by electrocution—to life imprisonment. D. E. Henderson, the private prosecutor, had this to say to North Carolina's governor in 1910 in support of the commutation: "It seems to be the consensus of opinion that this negro should not be put to death, but serve a sentence of life in the penitentiary. I think I am prepared to say that no criticism will arise from any source if you should commute the sentence to life imprisonment."[269] In a separate case, from Dallas, Texas, lawyer R. B. Allen, the private prosecutor in the case of Ed Christian, another African-American man convicted and given the death penalty, also asked the death sentence to be commuted to life imprisonment. In that 1914 case, Mr. Christian—then confined in the Dallas County Jail and awaiting execution—was scheduled to die on the scaffold later in the month.[270]

There were, throughout the twentieth century, conscious and thoughtful efforts to rein in the power of private prosecutors—efforts that would, in time, bear fruit in multiple jurisdictions.[271] Indeed, at the very beginning of the new century, in 1900, *The Pittsburg Press* reported that Judge John D. Shafer and District Attorney John C. Haymaker "sprung a big surprise in the form of a new order regulating the conduct of cases in criminal court." According to their order: "For several years it has been the custom of parties with a grievance, especially in petty assault and battery cases, to hire a lawyer to prosecute their case. This is done from the idea that more attention will be given their side of the case than if it were handled by the district attorney or one of his assistants, who possess also a kind of judicial power in determining whether or not the prosecution will be dropped. It also gives the alleged injured parties an opportunity to introduce personal malice and spite in their attempt to get even with the defendant, thus changing the prosecution into a persecution." "At the same time, especially during the closing term," the order continued, "an extraordinary amount of the time of the court has been misspent by private prosecuting attorneys, who, in nearly every case, failed to obtain a verdict for the commonwealth." After taking note of the ineffectiveness of private prosecutors, the order read: "It is to stop this practice that the district attorney, after consulting with the judges of the common pleas courts, has adopted an order which, in future, forbids the employment of counsel as prosecuting attorney, except with the special permission of the court or something particular in the case."

Judge Shafer, in publicly announcing the new order, had this to say to members of the bar: "There has grown up in this county, silently, and without its being observed particularly, a practice on the part of many private prosecutors, especially in actions of assault and battery and like cases, of hiring private counsel to conduct the prosecution. The practice appears to have been growing, of late years, and we have found from experience that it is subject to a number of serious objections." In laying out those objections, Judge Shafer emphasized that "it is notorious in this court, that a case in which private counsel represents the commonwealth is sure to take from one-third to one-half more time than if it was prosecuted by the district attorney, without any corresponding advantage." Also, Judge Shafer reported, "the fact that the private counsel of the prosecutor is paid by the prosecutor in the particular case, makes it necessary for him, in order to appear faithful to his client, and to give him something for his money, to urge the prosecution in a way that is not proper in an officer representing the commonwealth." Judge Shafer also emphasized that the district attorney represents the commonwealth and has a duty of determining "whether a case is one that should be prosecuted or not, and is bound by his office to act fairly with the prisoner, as well as the commonwealth." "When private counsel is employed," Judge Shafer observed, "the prosecution sometimes tends to turn into a persecution."

To curb private prosecution abuses, Judge Shafer—speaking for the local judges—relayed to members of the bar: "We have consulted with some of the judges of each of the courts of common pleas in regard to the matter, and all whom we have been able to consult are firmly of opinion that the practice should be changed." After delivering his diatribe against private prosecutors, Judge Shafer nonetheless said: "There is, of course, no objection to a prosecutor employing counsel to assist in preparing the case, and to communicate with the district attorney. That course would, in fact, frequently materially assist the district attorney in the discharge of his duties; but we think that in every case the cause should be tried by the district attorney, or one of his assistants, as leading counsel, having full control of the conduct of the case." "We have also consulted with the district attorney in regard to the matter, and he heartily concurs in these views," Judge Shafer observed, adding of the district attorney's position: "He has, therefore, upon our suggestion and request in view of what has been said, adopted a rule that no cause shall be tried for the prosecution by private counsel, without his leave and the leave of the court in the particular case, upon cause shown." The headline in *The Pittsburg Press* announcing the new order—"Private Lawyers Are Not in Favor"—reflected the growing skepticism about the use of private prosecutors.[272]

The Imposition of Court Costs: Deterring Malicious or Frivolous Private Prosecutions

The imposition of court costs was one well-recognized way to deter frivolous or improper private prosecutions, just as awarding successful private prosecutors a portion of fines was sometimes used to encourage such prosecutions.[273] Indeed, judges frequently resorted to the imposition of costs to deter vexatious private prosecutions. In many cases, unsuccessful private prosecutors were thus forced to bear the costs—or at least part of them—of their ill-fated prosecutions.[274] Examples abound, with one Pennsylvania news report emphasizing that "[i]n a criminal court where a jury acquits a defendant and directs the private prosecutor to pay the costs, the presumption is that the private prosecutor instituted the prosecution 'maliciously and without probable cause.'"[275] "In the case against Mrs. Rose Gilmore, charged with aggravated assault and battery," *The Daily Republican* in Monongahela, Pennsylvania, reported in 1904, "the grand jury ignored the bill and the court sentenced the private prosecutor to pay the costs and to give security to the sheriff for the payment of the same in 10 days."[276] In 1913, *The Daily Republican*—giving a good sense of the then-prevailing custom—observed: "In any of the trivial cases listed for this term of criminal court in which the defendant and private prosecutor are apparently both to blame, the juries are dividing the costs."[277]

In other Monongahela, Pennsylvania cases, costs were divided in many different ways—essentially to send a message, as desired, to the private prosecutor, the defendant, or both. For example, costs might be divided "in equal parts" between the private prosecutor and a defendant, or all the costs might be put on defendants even when acquitted—reflecting the wide discretion involved in the whole exercise.[278] In one Monongahela case, *The Daily Republican* emphasized that "the jury made a rather unusual division of the costs," finding the defendant not guilty but putting "one-eighth of the costs upon him." "The other seven-eighths," the paper noted, "were put on the private prosecutor, Steve Ban."[279] In 1904, under the headline "Costs were Divided," it was reported that after the defendants in a larceny case were found not guilty, the prosecutor was ordered to pay one half the costs while the defendants paid one sixth each.[280] In a 1905 case reported by *The Daily Republican* in Monongahela, it was emphasized that after a defendant was charged by the private prosecutor, George Elco, with hitting Elco with a brick, but where a not guilty verdict was returned, "the costs were divided."[281] In Pennsylvania, costs were thus split in sundry different ways, often down to the penny. In one 1922 case, 10 percent of the costs—or $10.27—was placed on a defendant acquitted of embezzlement, while the other 90 percent of the costs—a sum of $92.41—got divided equally between John E. Reagen and P. H. Toohey, the latter described as the "private prosecutor."[282]

In other Pennsylvania cases, the assignment of costs would likewise vary considerably, giving a snapshot of early twentieth-century practices. For example, in 1905, *The Daily Notes* in Canonsburg, Pennsylvania, reported that the private prosecutor "will pay one-third" of the costs while an acquitted defendant "will pay two-thirds."[283] The next year, in mid-November 1906, that same newspaper reported that after a not guilty verdict was returned in a case against Al Jennings alleging the larceny of a dog, the costs were placed on the private prosecutor, Peter Trenhauser, but that where an acquittal was obtained in a case charging a landlord's assault, three-fourths of the costs were still placed on the men charged with the assault while the remaining one-fourth of the costs were assessed to Ernest Hudertmart, the private prosecutor.[284] After 18-year-old Edward Warren was acquitted of a charge of assault and battery for striking an 11-year-old African-American boy, Joseph Weaver, the jury directed that Warren pay one half of the costs while putting the other half of the costs on the private prosecutor.[285] In yet another private prosecution, in which John Klinzey was indicted for felonious shooting after some "trouble" occurred "at a christening," *The Daily Notes* reported that after an acquittal the jury placed "one-twelfth of the costs on the defendant, and the remaining eleven-twelfths on the private prosecutor."[286] A review of newspaper articles consequently shows that, depending on the facts of a case,[287] costs might be imposed on the private prosecutor or divided equally—or in some other fashion as deemed appropriate—between an acquitted defendant and the private prosecutor.[288] "It has been clearly shown that James D. Evans is the private prosecutor," one defense lawyer, John F. Whelan, argued in Philadelphia in 1919, "and if you believe defendant's arrest was without warrant and unjustifiable then you can impose on James D. Evans the costs of this prosecution and acquit the defendant."[289]

Other private prosecutions were withdrawn or settled on amicable terms[290]—sometimes astounding or confounding courtroom observers—with some mutual agreement as to the payment of damages or costs[291] or to reduce a sentence.[292] For example, in Pennsylvania, the December 4, 1901 edition of *The Wellsboro Agitator* contains this front-page news item: "On Saturday morning the gambling case against W. H. Fretz, arising from a turkey raffle before Thanksgiving, was called for trial, but an arrangement was effected with the private prosecutors whereby the defendant paid the costs and agreed to stop the raffling, whereupon a *nolle prosequi* was entered and the defendant was discharged."[293] Likewise, in 1902, after John McDonald was arrested in Oregon for the theft of a bicycle belonging to Ed Coots, a private prosecutor, it was reported that after McDonald's arraignment "the case was dismissed upon motion of the district attorney, for the reason that the case had been amicably settled between the defendant and the private prosecutors." Coots decided he did not want to prosecute McDonald and withdrew the criminal charge after McDonald returned the stolen property and agreed to pay the costs.[294] "Settlement of criminal actions by way of reparations for injuries to individuals," a North Carolina newspaper reported in 1930, "seems to be popular."[295]

Private prosecutors, with many other things to do in their everyday lives, could be unreliable or simply lose interest in a criminal prosecution. On occasion, they did not even show up, leading to delays in the administration of justice or the dismissal of charges.[296] In other instances, private prosecutors who had previously levied charges against an individual abandoned them,[297] either because of a change in heart[298] or because a settlement or accommodation of the matter had been reached.[299] The latter practice was renounced by some public commentators despite it being a relatively common one. For example, C. C. Daniels, the solicitor of the Fourth Judicial District in North Carolina, prepared a pamphlet to mayors and justices of the peace in that district. "No magistrate has the right," he offered, "to allow a private prosecutor to withdraw the warrant" and "suppress the prosecution." "It is often the case," Daniels observed, "that after a warrant is sworn out before a magistrate the private prosecutor and the defendant get together and agree to stop the prosecution upon the payment of a sum of money, or for some other consideration." "The magistrate," he added, "is then requested to allow the warrant to be withdrawn on the payment of costs." Such settlements occurred in spite of the long tradition making it a criminal offense to compound a felony and, in at least some locales, to compound a misdemeanor.[300]

C. C. Daniels was clearly bothered by the practice of private settlements he had observed first-hand. "No reputable magistrate," Daniels editorialized, "should countenance such an agreement; to do so detracts from the dignity of the office and causes the people to question the motives of the magistrate, and to lose respect for the administration of the law." As Daniels concluded: "Every man should be 'equal before the law' and if it is proper to suppress a prosecution begun before a magistrate against a person who is able to satisfy with money or otherwise the private prosecutor, then it is proper to suppress prosecutions as to all." "Every man should be made to feel that when he enters a court of justice, that justice will be administered without fear or favor. The State is the prosecutor in every case and no person has the right at his pleasure to stop a criminal prosecution, and when a magistrate permits it to be done, he becomes a violator of the law himself."[301] In examining eighteenth-century practices in England, David Friedman wrote that "however corrupt such arrangements might have been from a legal standpoint, they helped solve the fundamental problem of private prosecution." As Friedman observed in 1995: "The possibility of compounding provided an incentive to prosecute—it converted the system into something more like a civil system, where a victim sues in the hope of collecting money damages. And while compounding might save the criminal from the noose, he did not get off scot-free. He ended up paying, to the prosecutor, what was in effect a fine."[302]

Judges and Grand Jury Charges: The Growing Skepticism of Private Prosecutors

In the early twentieth century, as in the late nineteenth century, judges around the country—in places like Alabama,[303] California,[304] Hawaii,[305] Kansas,[306] Maine,[307] Missouri,[308] Nebraska,[309] New Jersey,[310] New York,[311] Oklahoma,[312] Pennsylvania[313] and Wisconsin[314]—continued to warn grand juries about the dangers of private prosecutors.[315] For example, in the Hawaii Territory, one judge gave these grand jury charges in the first decade of the twentieth century: "[Y]ou should not allow private prosecutors to appear before you for the purpose of prosecuting accusations and you should carefully scrutinize all charges brought to your attention in order that you may not become the instruments of those persons who have invoked the criminal law for the purpose of collecting a debt or of punishing an enemy." "Private prosecutors shall not be permitted to enter your jury room nor to discuss with any of your members matters under investigation."[316] Likewise, in St. Louis, Missouri, Judge Selden P. Spencer gave this grand jury charge in April 1900, just after the turn of the century: "Private prosecutors should not be allowed to intrude themselves into your presence. If they have a just cause of grievance against any person the more orderly way for them to proceed is either to present the matter to the Circuit Attorney, whose sworn duty it is to act when a proper case is presented, or failing him, they may themselves make application for a warrant in the Court of Criminal Correction, which has power to examine and if necessary to commit the alleged offender."[317] Such admonitions against private prosecutors would continue to appear in the decades to come.[318]

In the federal courts, the use of private prosecutors continued to be renounced in the early twentieth century. Thus, when an attorney, Frederick Kahle, announced his intention to institute both civil and criminal proceedings against persons who wrecked a bank, the relevant United States Attorney, Mr. Dunkle, quickly let it be known that "[t]he criminal action in this case belongs to this office and in this court there is no such thing as a private prosecutor." "Mr. Kahle," Dunkle said, alluding to the variance of state and federal practice, "might try his action in the county courts, but he could not do it in the Federal court." "This office," he added, "will bring the criminal proceedings when the time comes."[319] Still, at the state level, the use of private prosecutors was defended—sometimes by privately retained lawyers or by the victims, the private prosecutors, themselves. At a criminal trial in Memphis, Texas, A. S. Moss, one of the private prosecutors, reportedly "defended his position as a private prosecutor, saying the bereaved had as much right to employ special counsel" as a defendant had "to employ lawyers to defend him."[320]

But in state courts, where private prosecutions had long been in widespread use, American courts—in a noticeable development—gradually began to shift their views on such prosecutions. For example, in 1911, the Nebraska Supreme Court reversed a convicted murderer's life sentence where a private prosecutor had been employed at the defendant's trial.[321] In that case, the defendant, Joe McKay, was convicted of first-degree murder in the district court for Antelope County for the killing of Albert Brown. On appeal, McKay insisted that the trial court erred in permitting M. F. Harrington, a private lawyer paid by Brown's brothers and sisters, to conduct part of the prosecution. The trial court had permitted Mr. Harrington to assist the county attorney in the prosecution, and the trial judge had overruled McKay's counsel's objection to Mr. Harrington's participation. Mr. Harrington made the closing argument in the case despite the fact that a Nebraska statute made it the county attorney's duty to prosecute cases and a portion of that law, while allowing the appointment of "one or more deputies" to "assist" the county attorney "in the discharge of his duties," expressly provided that "such assistant or assistants shall be allowed such compensation as the county board shall determine for his services." Mr. Harrington's compensation came from private parties, not a public source.

In its 1911 decision, the Nebraska Supreme Court observed that "[t]he question of the right of private counsel to appear in the prosecution of a criminal action has been before this court a number of times." It first noted that in 1883, under the then-existing Nebraska statute, the court had held that the district attorney in a criminal case could employ private counsel. The Nebraska Supreme Court then analyzed the Wisconsin Supreme Court's 1888 decision in *Biemel v. State*—a precedent which impressed Nebraska's highest court—and judicial decisions from the State of Michigan. The Nebraska Supreme Court, recognizing the realities of the early twentieth century, wrote: "We are not unmindful of the fact that in many cases, particularly in sparsely settled counties, young lawyers of little experience are ofttimes, from necessity, elected to the office of county attorney, and, if the prosecution of felony cases were left to such a county attorney alone, crime might go unpunished. In such cases it is to the interest of the state that such a county attorney should have the assistance of outside counsel...." While the Nebraska Supreme Court held that the state statute under consideration "provided for just such emergencies," the court—quoting a Michigan court decision—emphasized that "'[t]he prosecuting officer represents the public interest, which can never be promoted by the conviction of the innocent'" and that "'[h]is object, like that of the court, should be simply justice; and he has no right to sacrifice this to any pride of professional success.'"

In its decision, the Nebraska Supreme Court specifically ruled: "Counsel called to assist in the prosecution should govern his actions in like manner; and, when procured in the manner and for the compensation contemplated by the statute quoted, would doubtless do so, while counsel employed by outside parties and, in the case of a homicide, by relatives of the deceased, would not feel bound by any such rule or conduct. He appears as private counsel simply, to represent the wishes, prejudice and animosities of his clients; to secure a conviction at all hazards." Finding that the Nebraska legislature had rejected a policy allowing the appointment of such interested counsel, the Nebraska Supreme Court stressed: "In the case at bar there is nothing to show that the county attorney, who is a lawyer of known ability, requested the assistance of Mr. Harrington, nor that he had been in any manner previously consulted in reference thereto. The mere fact that the court permitted Mr. Harrington to assist in the prosecution cannot be held to be a compliance with the statute which provides that private counsel may be procured by the county attorney under the direction of the court." "Mere acquiescence in or assent to the appearance of private counsel," the Nebraska Supreme Court concluded, finding that Mr. Harrington's appearance violated state law, "does not constitute the affirmative action required by the statute and is not sufficient."[322]

Even where private prosecutions were common, such as Pennsylvania, serious questions were raised about them. For example, the case of John Tanger—charged with involuntary manslaughter not by the commonwealth in whose name the prosecution was brought, but by a private party—caused the *Reading Times* to call Pennsylvania's system of private prosecution "archaic and really iniquitous." "One private and necessarily prejudiced party, acting through his own private lawyer," the Pennsylvania newspaper emphasized in 1928, "swore out the warrant for Tanger and in the name of the commonwealth prosecuted him." "That and similar cases are morally wrong," the paper editorialized, adding: "We have elected officials whose duty it is to prosecute in the state's name and solely in the interests of justice, coldly and fairly and without passion. It is wrong when we allow prejudiced, private individuals to take power and authority to a greater or less extent from the hands of these disinterested officials to wreak their private vengeance." The newspaper noted the potential for life-and-death stakes in criminal cases, with the paper pointing out that "[w]e have had cases in this county when men have gone to the electric chair, prosecuted by lawyers in the private pay of hatred-mad individuals." As the paper concluded: "This is a prostitution of justice. It is the hateful part of lynch-law set to courtroom music." In calling for the abolition of Pennsylvania's private prosecutor system, the *Reading Times* stressed that "[m]any states have done away with this special prosecutor system" and that "[m]any states will not permit this abuse of power and degradation of law."[323]

In the years that followed, the *Reading Times* continued its crusade against private prosecutors. In 1829, in an editorial titled "Improving the Legal System," the newspaper wrote: "Scores of cases come to our criminal court because some lawyer has advised his client that it will be easier to force a settlement for civil damage if a criminal prosecution is brought." "This is what lawyers call the 'private prosecutor system,'" the paper emphasized, adding of the kind of cases—and behavior—it had witnessed in Pennsylvania: "A man's automobile collides with another. Instead of suing for damage as he should, one driver has a warrant sworn out against the other before an alderman for assault and battery. Then a private lawyer, acting as a special commonwealth prosecutor, asks for an indictment." "Unless the man agrees to buy off the prosecutor and make a settlement," the newspaper asserted, "this case will be dragged into our court and the man tried as a criminal." "Many, many times rather than go through the disgrace of a criminal trial and the danger of a jail sentence," the paper continued, "the innocent victims who were in no way to blame for the accident, pays his good money to avoid a criminal prosecution thus unjustly brought." "This whole system, if we are rightly informed," the *Reading Times* advised its readers, "should be done away with."[324]

In 1931, the *Reading Times* printed another editorial in which—only half in jest—it put forth its own idea for "a swell law": "AN ACT to stop the people of the Commonwealth of Pennsylvania from wasting their time and money in idle, petty, vicious law suits and to prevent them from misusing the criminal statu[t]es to wreak private vengeance." Using biting, satirical language, it proposed that the new act include these four sections: "SECTION ONE—It shall hereafter be unlawful for voracious aldermen to deliberately encourage litigation to buy shoes for the baby. It shall be their duty to endeavor to reconcile litigants instead of padding court costs to buy new tires for constables' cars." "SECTION TWO—It shall be unlawful for attorneys at the bar to bring cap-pistol, three-dollar wagon and dollar-and-a-half-stove case[s] before the county courts...." "SECTION THREE—It shall be unlawful for district attorneys to work in cahoots with private prosecutors for the purpose of extracting fees on the theory that these private prosecutors' lawyers are fellow members of the bar and thus practically Brothers Elks." "SECTION FOUR—It shall be the duty of presiding and associate judges of common pleas and quarter sessions courts to cultivate a sense of humor and a hearty horse laugh and when they see one of these cases coming it shall be their duty to line up the offending lawyers and after giving them a Brooklyn razzberry turn them over to the custody of the sheriff, under his direction to throw a real party at a good speakeasy for the litigants and the jury. And the newspapermen. PROVIDED—that ice cream shall be served to reporters who don't like gin."[325]

It was not just in Pennsylvania were law reform was sought—and where concerns existed about private prosecutions or the justice system's operation. In 1829, in North Carolina, a very serious bill was introduced in the state legislature to curtail the use of private prosecutors. As one newspaper summarized it, the bill "would limit the employment of private prosecutors in criminal actions to two, and then only when they are appointed by the judge on the written request of the solicitor." Before further discussing the legislation, that newspaper, *The Landmark* of Statesville, North Carolina, described the then-prevailing state of affairs in the state: "It is a custom for members of families and others interested in the prosecution to employ attorneys to assist the solicitor. In the federal courts the employment of private prosecutors is not permitted. In the State courts of North Carolina there is no restriction." In describing the bill, the newspaper noted that the employment of private prosecutors "is usually for the purpose of presenting the side of the prosecution on equal terms with the defense." Noting that "[t]he number of attorneys employed by the defense is unlimited" and that "[f]requently the solicitor has to fight a half dozen or more able lawyers," the paper observed that there was—in the state—a "frequent desire to give the prosecution a better showing by employing help for the solicitor." Restricting the employment of private prosecutors to two lawyers, *The Landmark* editorialized, "is not unreasonable," though it took issue with the legislation in these terms: "[B]ut the question is as to the right to restrict. That has a tendency to deny the right of anybody, for any reason, to aid and abet the prosecution of violations of the law except on official designation, and is questionable in that respect."[326]

By the 1940s, in the midst of World War II, some significant reforms were made, including in Pennsylvania, where private prosecutions had been so long entrenched, going all the way back to colonial times. For example, an order was issued in 1944 by Judge W. Russell Carr, and signed by two other judges, that addressed the practice of law before Fayette County's Courts of Oyer and Terminer and the Courts of Quarter Session of the Peace. That order provided: "The district attorney and assistant district attorneys shall prosecute all crimes and offenses against the Commonwealth. Private counsel shall not actively participate in conducting such trials except by special leave of Court for cause shown in writing, and in every case where such leave is granted, the trial, including the arguments of counsel to the jury, both for the Commonwealth and for the defense, shall be fully reported so as to become part of the record." As *The Morning Herald* of Uniontown, Pennsylvania, described the impact of the order: "In effect, the new ruling restricts the courtroom activity of private counsel or private prosecutors, paid by individuals, who can only sit at the table during criminal trials for the purpose of conferring with and aiding the district attorney's office in the prosecution of the cases." Only in "rare instances," the newspaper reported, would private attorneys be permitted to act beyond that scope after the court had a chance to carefully scrutinize the facts.

The new order governing Fayette County was not issued out of the blue. "The new rule," *The Morning Herald* observed, "has been advocated in various opinions of the Pennsylvania Supreme [C]ourt, particularly by Justice Frazer in the appeal from Westmoreland county courts in the murder case of Angelo Cicere who, in 1925, was electrocuted at Rockview for the slaying of Earl Shoup, steward of a club at Bradenville, near Latrobe." In that appeal, Justice Frazer wrote: "We take this occasion . . . to repeat what has frequently been said by this court, that the district attorney is a quasi-judicial officer, representing the Commonwealth, which seeks no victims, but only justice; that since he is invested with these grave responsibilities, he should, at all times, conduct the Commonwealth's case fairly, present it in an impartial manner and avoid seeking to influence the jury by arousing prejudice." "Where private counsel is permitted to assist the district attorney, in the trial of a case," Justice Frazer's opinion read, "such counsel represents that officer and should be governed by the rules of conduct applicable to the latter." "It is the duty of the district attorney," Frazer had determined, "to prosecute crimes against the Commonwealth and special counsel should not be permitted to actively participate in conducting such trials except in extreme cases; when permission is granted, it is the duty of both the district attorney and the court to see that counsel so appointed observes the rules of conduct required of the regular prosecuting officer."[327]

An Antiquated Practice in the Modern Era: From the 1950s to the Claus von Bülow Case and Beyond

Private prosecutions—whether for murder,[328] rape,[329] or assault and battery,[330] or for assault with a deadly weapon,[331] larceny[332] or other crimes[333]—continued in various locales in the years and decades to come.[334] For example, a review of newspapers shows that lawyers for private prosecutors appeared in places such as New Hampshire,[335] North Carolina,[336] Oregon,[337] Pennsylvania,[338] Tennessee,[339] Texas[340] and Virginia.[341] While some private prosecutions involved capital trials with life-or-death stakes, others involved reckless driving[342] or petty or lower-level crimes, such as writing bad checks.[343] The range of cases in which private prosecutors were employed is notable, but a fair number of private lawyers got retained to assist in high-profile murder cases—the most serious kind of cases, especially where the death penalty might be imposed. For example, a private prosecutor, Tim Valentine, was reportedly "retained by the dead man's family" in a North Carolina murder case.[344] In another case, Joan Little, a 21-year-old African-American woman, was charged in a capital case with the first-degree murder of a jailer, Clarence Alligood. She contended she had killed Alligood only after he had attempted to rape her, but the Alligood family hired a private prosecutor, John Wilkinson, to aid the local Beaufort County public prosecutor. Wilkinson himself had represented Little in a prior case in which she was charged with shoplifting and received a six-month suspended sentence.[345] And in yet another murder trial, one that arose out of a shooting that occurred after an argument over the price of two hot dogs, a private prosecutor was similarly employed by the family of the deceased man, drive-in owner Worth Howard Langley.[346]

In other instances, private attorneys continued to be hired or put to use for specific reasons or in specific cases, whether by public prosecutors or other government officials. In Salt Lake City, Utah, in the 1960s, a backlog of traffic cases in City Traffic Court led the Salt Lake County Bar Association to recruit a number of volunteer private prosecutors to help eliminate pending cases.[347] Likewise, in California, in 1970, private prosecutors were hired to temporarily handle the increased caseload following disturbances at Fresno State College after the firebombing of the school's $1 million computer center.[348] Conversely, private attorneys, whose legal bills were paid by the government, were also frequently retained (in an instance of outsourcing) to provide counsel to criminal defendants (*e.g.*, if a public defender's office was overburdened or had a conflict of interest). As one report from the 1980s noted: "Contract systems involve government contracting with individual attorneys, bar associations, or private law firms to provide services for a specified dollar amount. County agencies are usually responsible for the award of defender services contracts, and they are now frequently awarded to individual practitioners as opposed to law firms or other organized groups."[349] Contracts to outsource the prosecution function similarly came into vogue at different times in different places.[350]

Despite efforts to rein in their use, private prosecutions remained a mainstay in places such as Pennsylvania and North Carolina in the post-World War II era. In 1950, in Pittsburgh, for example, three leaders of the Communist Party in western Pennsylvania were arrested on sedition charges. Under the headline, "Pittsburgh's Red Leaders Are Held," it was reported that year that "Judge Thomas M. Marshall granted a petition by Judge Michael A. Musmanno, acting as a private prosecutor, padlocking the Communist Headquarters in the Bakewell building."[351] Judge Musmanno, the private prosecutor, also successfully petitioned to have the bond for Steve Nelson, a defendant in the case, raised from $10,000 to $100,000, even as Hymen Schlesinger, an attorney for the Communists, asserted that Judge Musmanno was conducting a one-man "witch hunt" to suppress political activity.[352] After the Pennsylvania Supreme Court, in a 4 to 1 decision issued in 1954, voided Nelson's state-law sedition conviction, Musmanno—who had served as a judge on the Allegheny County Common Pleas Court before being elevated to Pennsylvania's highest court—announced that he would file an official protest to the state supreme court's decision "as a citizen of the United States and as the private prosecutor in the case."[353]

A newspaper editorial from December 1954 gives a snapshot of the practice of private prosecutors in Philadelphia at that time. In that editorial, *The Gazette and Daily* of York, Pennsylvania observed that, for the year 1953, Philadelphia's district attorney had this to say about the then-prevailing state of affairs: "Neither Philadelphia custom nor your District Attorney's budget permit him to send Assistant District

Attorneys to hearings conducted in magistrates offices when warrants are sworn out by private citizens instead of by police officers. At the magistrates' hearing level these prosecutions are conducted in the name of the Commonwealth by private citizens or their lawyers. We pick the cases up only when and if the defendants are held for indictment by the Grand Jury." "Since approximately 6,000 such private warrants are issued in a year," Philadelphia's district attorney pointed out, "this is a real problem." "Persons who ought not to be held for the Grand Jury are held without our having a say in the matter," he said. After Philadelphia's DA professed to be "more than a rubber stamp" and said "that he must have the right not to place his signature on a bill of indictment, either where there is clearly no crime or the case is so petty that it is a disservice to the community to have trial courts devote their time to it while more important cases wait," he added: "Of course, any private prosecutor or victim of crime who disagrees with our decision not to indict should have the right to ask a judge to review our decision. The statutes of Pennsylvania contain a provision permitting exactly that."[354]

America's criminal justice system, the evidence shows, can be error-prone and produce wrongful charging decisions and wrongful convictions. But a private prosecution regime brings additional concerns than a public prosecution system. Private prosecutors have their own interests, whether personal or financial, and they may act in ways that a public prosecutor might not. In fact, history shows that in a number of twentieth-century drunk driving cases, private prosecutors either declined to press charges or failed to appear in court,[355] though some determined victims did charge and pursue such cases, testifying in court to get convictions.[356] In North Carolina, remedial actions were even taken to better ensure the appearance of crime victims who became private prosecutors, including arresting and fining them for malicious prosecution if they failed to show up after bringing criminal charges.[357] In Tennessee, judges sometimes dismissed charges (*e.g.*, for assault and battery, drunken driving, unlawful possession) if they believed that the state had no case. That power was wielded, among other things, to screen out unmeritorious cases brought by private prosecutors. Usually, Sessions Judge Alfred Frazier observed in 1955, "such dismissals have taken place because the private prosecutor has failed to show up."[358]

In the immediate post-World War II period and in the decades that followed, private prosecutors continued initiating prosecutions and appearing in court in various jurisdictions. Such prosecutions took place in quite varied circumstances—on charges ranging from assault and battery[359] to murder and kidnapping,[360] and from mistakenly shooting and wounding a person while deer hunting[361] to shoplifting from businesses.[362] In 1954, during the Red Scare and at the height of McCarthyism,[363] a private prosecutor even caused the arrest of a woman who was an officer for an organization collecting funds for the defense of Julius and Ethel Rosenberg, the husband and wife charged with violating federal espionage laws. Despite maintaining their innocence, the Rosenbergs were later executed in the electric chair at Sing Sing Prison in Ossining, New York, after being convicted of passing atomic bomb secrets to the Soviet

Union.[364] The woman was arrested for soliciting funds without a license, and counsel for the private prosecutor demanded the woman's indictment by a grand jury.[365] Because lawyers were privately retained, one could never predict, in fact, when an attorney for a private prosecutor might show up, because it was dependent on the interested party's willingness and financial ability to retain one. In some locales, it was hardly uncommon to encounter a private prosecution, with the types of prosecutions varying greatly. In 1962, in North Carolina, for example, a man who dynamited his estranged wife's home was privately prosecuted after the wife suffered severe injuries.[366]

While clusters of private prosecutions still could be found in some American locales by the mid-twentieth century, as the decades went by, public prosecutors took over the lion's share of prosecution work. This trend, naturally, was reflected in news reports. For example, in 1971, the *Iowa City Press-Citizen* ran a front-page story titled "Bartel Presses Efforts To Be 'Private Prosecutor.'" The story, about Iowa City's justice system, began: "Attempts by Richard Bartel, Sharon Township constable, to appear as a 'private prosecutor' before the 1971 Grand Jury here so far have been thwarted by a quagmire of ambiguities in Iowa law." "Attempts to become a private prosecutor appear to be rare in Iowa," the *Iowa City Press-Citizen* observed, adding nevertheless that Iowa law "refers to indictments found 'at the instance of a private prosecutor'" and thus "evidently allows a person under certain conditions to appear before the jury as a private prosecutor, presumably to present evidence as would a county attorney." "The private prosecutor," the newspaper reported, "is liable for the costs of the prosecution if the court trying the cause is 'satisfied from all the circumstances that the prosecution was malicious or without probable cause.'" The paper emphasized that while "[t]he outlet for complaints such as Bartel's" normally would be the county attorney, Bartel aspired to become a private prosecutor. The paper stressed that, for Bartel, "[a] main problem simply is how to make a request to appear as a private prosecutor" because "Iowa law imposes a maximum penalty of $1,000 and a year in prison for any attempts to improperly influence a grand jury, making any contact with grand jurors risky."[367]

In the 1970s, as in preceding decades, the use of private prosecutors continued to come under intense scrutiny, with one North Carolina state representative, Herbert L. Hyde, calling for the elimination of private prosecutors. Prosecution, he said, "is the state's responsibility."[368] In March 1976, a North Carolina district attorney, Herb Pierce, actually refused the services of a private attorney, Jerry Paul, in a rape case brought against Michael Sykes. Sykes, a former Burlington police officer, was charged with raping Mrs. Edna Leath on February 20th. Mrs. Leath's "emotional state," *The Daily Times-News* of Burlington reported on March 19th, following Pierce's rejection of the private prosecutor, "caused postponement" of a preliminary hearing that occurred just hours after Paul's services had initially been offered. Jerry Paul had successfully defended Joan Little in her high-profile murder trial the summer before, obtaining an acquittal in that case, but Pierce decided he didn't want Paul's legal services for the prosecution.[369] Three years later, another North Carolina public prosecutor, Guilford County District Attorney Mike Schlosser, would also decline an offer of services from a would-be private prosecutor, New York attorney William Kunstler, who had also represented Joan Little.[370] His defense of the Chicago Seven from 1969 to 1970 had vaulted William Kunstler into the limelight—and the ranks of America's best-known lawyers.[371]

In declining the legal services of Jerry Paul, the lawyer who had represented Joan Little, Alamance County District Attorney Herb Pierce expressed his own views as to why he would handle the rape prosecution of Michael Sykes. After initially declining comment, Pierce eventually "confirmed rumors that an attempt had been made" to retain Jerry Paul to prosecute Sykes but that the discussions in Pierce's office had not gone anywhere. "I am the elected district attorney," Pierce said, "and I choose who prosecutes for the State" as well as "the lawyers who appear." *The Daily Times-News* further reported of the controversy: "Regarding published reports that an associate in the office of Attorney General Rufus Edmisten had offered his unresearched opinion that Pierce had no right to refuse privately employed prosecution, Pierce said, 'If a private prosecutor appears in a case he appears at the pleasure of the district attorney.'" Alluding to T. Lawrence Pollard, the named associate in the attorney general's office, Pierce commented critically: "This man should have checked the law before giving an opinion off the top of his head." "He must be very young and he must not have much trial experience," Pierce said dismissively of Mr. Pollard, adding: "Obviously, he has not researched the law."

Pierce went on to say that the attorney's general's office "has no authority to tell me what I can and cannot do," specifically laying into Mr. Pollard for his "irresponsible" act in issuing "an opinion off the top of his head" without knowing "what the law is." "Ordinarily," Pierce said, "I accept private prosecutors, but in this case"—that is, the rape prosecution of Sykes—"I choose not to do so." According to *The Daily Times-News*, "Pierce said he told Paul his refusal to accept the law firm's services had nothing to do with Paul personally, 'But I chose not to have his firm participate in this case.'" Pierce gave these concluding comments to the paper: "I've tried many rape cases. I don't need Mr. Paul in this particular case. This case is going to be prosecuted by the State of North Carolina. Mrs. Leath understands that, and is agreeable with it." As to the prior postponement of the preliminary hearing, Pierce offered these comments: "I've never said the woman was sick. Her emotional state at that time was the reason for the continuance."[372]

Herb Pierce, who had run for office on a platform of "law and order for all" and for "the impartial administration of justice,"[373] actually declined the services of a private prosecutor on more than one occasion. In 1977, an article in *The Daily Times-News*, under the headline "Mebane's Parents Very Upset," began by quoting Bill Durham, an attorney hired by the Mebane family to observe the trial of William Wayne Roark. Roark was one of two men charged in the death of their son, Robbie. "Robbie Mebane's parents are very shocked and upset," Durham said after Roark was found not guilty of kidnapping and murder. Although Roark was found guilty of common-law robbery, Durham criticized District Attorney Pierce for his handling of Roark's trial and for his decision to negotiate a plea bargain in the case of Kenneth Warren Lawson, who pled guilty to second-degree murder, kidnapping, and armed robbery and who was sentenced to life imprisonment—plus two 15-year sentences—in December 1976. "We urged Mr. Pierce not to accept Lawson's plea," Durham said after Roark's acquittal on the most serious charges.

Bill Durham gave this perspective of his prior discussions with District Attorney Pierce: "We told him then that it would allow Lawson to testify to anything he wanted to in this trial and he, Lawson, would have nothing to lose." "If the two men had been tried together," Durham offered, "the evidence in the case against Roark would have been presented entirely different and he would have been convicted." Durham—the private lawyer—accused Pierce of "sloppily" handling the prosecution, with *The Daily Times-News* reporting that Durham said he had, at the Mebane family's request, "offered to assist the district attorney with the Roark trial as a private prosecutor but that his offer was refused." After Pierce had rejected Durham's involvement, Durham had simply observed the trial at the Mebane family's request. For his part, District Attorney Pierce said he rejected Durham's offer of assistance in the Roark case because Mr. Durham had, in open court, opposed his plea bargain agreement with Lawson. As Pierce explained his rejection of private assistance from Durham: "He tried to have the court reject a negotiated plea after it had been accepted and presented to the court. It was my considered opinion that this was in conflict with the total case and that he, Durham, should not appear with the state in this action." "When I feel there is a position of conflict, as I did in this case," Pierce said, "I can not and will not abdicate my position as a public official representing the public."[374]

On the judicial front, the issue of the propriety of private prosecutors continued to be litigated in the courts. For example, in one case in the 1990s, the Springfield District of the Missouri Court of Appeals unanimously reversed the conviction of James "Peterboy" Harrington for the murder of Kenneth Ellison in Sikeston during a dice game. That reversal was based in part—as the written opinion of Chief Judge William H. Billings made clear—on the participation in the prosecution "by a privately employed attorney." The hiring of the special prosecutor, Robert Dempster, by the deceased man's family was singled out in the appeal as a serious error. "During testimony," it was reported, "Max Ellison, father of the slain youth, was asked if his hiring Dempster was done with the intention that it would help ensure a conviction. Ellison said it was." Dempster, the lawyer, reportedly threatened a potential witness, Larry Johnson, with jail time if he would not testify in court, with Johnson contending that Dempster tried to "put words in my mouth ... trying to tell me what I did see, what I didn't see."

At the trial itself, the private prosecutor, Robert Dempster, played an active role, cross-examining the defendant and all of the defendant's witnesses, making objections at trial, and making the closing argument to the jury. The Missouri Court of Appeals emphasized the practice of employing special prosecutors "does violence to the statutes governing criminal prosecutions, creates an automatic conflict of interest for the privately employed attorney and gives rise to the issue of fundamental unfairness." "We think public policy and the fair, just and impartial administration of the criminal law of the state," the appellate court ruled, "make it the duty of the courts to exclu[d]e the paid attorneys of private persons from appearing as prosecutors." "It is our opinion," the court concluded, that "the private prosecutor's participation in the case cast a cloud of fundamental unfairness over the defendant's trial and conviction."[375] The Missouri Supreme Court, in a 1976 decision, later agreed, also voting to reverse Harrington's conviction on the ground that private prosecutors should no longer be permitted.[376]

In other states, the practice of private prosecution garnered additional public scrutiny from jurists, too. Some change even came to Pennsylvania through a new state-ordered judicial procedure, as reported by Pennsylvania newspapers at the very end of 1973. Before the rule change went into effect on January 1, 1974, it was reported that the system worked as follows: "Complainants appeared before the minor judiciary and swore out information. The minor judiciary issued a summons or warrant and it was served by police or constables."[377] "After January 1," by contrast, the *Evening Herald* of Shenandoah, Pennsylvania, observed, getting the word out to the public about the procedural change, "a private prosecutor cannot begin criminal prosecution without the district attorney's permission unless there is a danger, such as when a husband beats his wife and threatens to administer further beatings." "In all other cases," the paper observed, "if the district attorney does not give approval, the citizen has the right to appeal to court." As the newspaper described that process: "The court, if it overrules the district attorney, holds a preliminary hearing."[378] In short, a private citizen in Pennsylvania was allowed to go directly to court if the district attorney refused to prosecute.

The new rules generated controversy, including at a meeting of the Delaware County Magistrates Association, with one letter from Judge John V. Diggins to A. Evans Kephart—a state court administrator in Philadelphia—noting that "the application of this rule means that hundreds of business establishments who are plagued with cases such as bad checks or shoplifting will have to devote an enormous amount of time to get relief." Judge Diggins expressed the view that "it was a mistake to make the rule mandatory in all judicial districts." "It may," he said, speaking for Delaware County, "have justification in Philadelphia but I do not think the same can be said of this jurisdiction." After observing that the new procedure meant that the private prosecutor would have to "come to the DA's office" with the complaint properly filled out, Judge Diggins noted that sometimes the complaint would not be properly prepared, necessitating that the DA "rewrite the complaint." Writing in early January 1974, Judge Diggins said: "this has happened at least 40 times so far and the volume has made it necessary for residents to wait four or five hours to have the complaint processed." As Judge Diggins wrote in his letter: "We think this unfair and untenable and even if the District Attorney's manpower were increased to meet this demand, there would still be the long travel distance and loss of time." "I think the court should be more readily accessible on the district judge level to the private sector," he emphasized."[379]

Throughout the country, there was a growing awareness, though, that district attorneys had a particularly important role to play in the enforcement of the laws—one that many felt should be non-delegable. Speaking to the Freeport Rotary Club in Illinois in 1974, for example, the Stephenson County State's Attorney William E. Sisler said the "overriding yardstick" guiding a public prosecutor's judgments is "what will best serve the public interest." "The state's attorney," he stressed, "is not an attorney for any complaining witness nor for any individual. He is a representative of the people, not a private prosecutor." As Sisley told his audience of the state's attorney duty to the public: "He has a direct responsibility to uphold the spirit of the law as well as its letter. In a very important sense and one which I think is often overlooked or not understood is that the state's attorney is a lawyer for all the people, which includes the defendant."[380]

The concern about the ethics of private prosecutions continued into the 1980s, with the practice still called into question today. Indeed, in the not-too-distant past, the charge that a lawyer was acting as a "private prosecutor" was made in some especially high-profile cases. For example, Herald Price Fahringer—a New York lawyer representing Claus von Bülow, accused Richard Kuh, a former District Attorney of Manhattan, of acting as a "private prosecutor." A socialite, von Bülow had been accused of trying to kill his millionaire wife, Martha, better known as "Sunny," with insulin injections. "A private prosecutor was running the show," Fahringer charged in 1982 in a Rhode Island court of the investigation that had led to von Bülow's indictment for attempted murder. In that case, the mother, son and daughter of Martha von Bülow had gone to extraordinary lengths to have Claus von Bülow prosecuted. Kuh had been hired by Alexander and Ala von Auersperg and their grandmother, Mrs. Aitken, to investigate the circumstances surrounding Sunny's comatose condition. After he was hired to provide a legal opinion about whether Claus von Bülow had engaged in criminal conduct, Kuh, in turn, had hired others to assist in the investigation, including a private detective and multiple chemical-testing experts. Under Kuh's supervision, incriminating evidence, including a black bag, was gathered and examined before Kuh's findings were turned over to New York and Rhode Island authorities.[381]

Because of Kuh's involvement, Claus von Bülow's defense attorneys tried to have the attempted murder indictment dismissed. A superior court judge, however, denied the motion to dismiss, holding that the state's use of evidence gathered by Kuh's investigation did not technically constitute a "private prosecution." While Kuh himself did not oversee Claus von Bülow's criminal trial, he did appear as a witness for the state in the case. As one source summarizes Fahringer's courtroom examination of Kuh: "Fahringer got Kuh to describe hiring a private detective to accompany Alexander von Auersperg to Clarendon Court to find the black bag, its discovery in Von Bülow's closet, their bringing the bag to Kuh in New York, his turning it over to doctors for analysis, and his eventual turning over of all his evidence to the Rhode

Island police."[382] The Rhode Island Supreme Court ultimately agreed that Claus von Bülow's claim of a private prosecution was not meritorious, but it nevertheless vacated von Bülow's conviction on other grounds, holding, in part, that von Bülow had been denied access to certain evidence gathered by Kuh's privately conducted investigation. "We are of the opinion that defendant's claim of private prosecution was utterly without merit," the Supreme Court of Rhode Island ruled in 1984, adding dismissively: "We do not believe that this claim requires either discussion or extended analysis."[383] In that case, at least from the defense's perspective, the line between a public prosecution and a private one had been blurred—and according to defense counsel, crossed.

In 2021, the issue of private prosecution garnered national news with the criminal contempt prosecution of environmental lawyer Steven Donziger, a prosecution in New York led by three lawyers—Brian Maloney, Sareen Armani and Rita Glavin—associated with the law firm of Seward & Kissel LLP, which had previously represented Chevron. In a July 29, 2021 letter to the Honorable Roslynn Mauskopf, the director of the Administrative Office of the U.S. Courts, U.S. Senators Ed Markey and Sheldon Whitehouse observed that Donziger's case (which arose out of Donziger's representation of indigenous people in Ecuador against Chevron for harm caused by oil-drilling waste) had "shined a spotlight on private prosecutions of criminal contempt prosecutions." "These prosecutions," the two U.S. senators wrote in their letter, asking a series of pointed questions, "are highly unusual and can raise concerning questions of fundamental fairness in our criminal justice system."[384] In an article in *Slate*, one writer, Sofia Andrade, offered this perspective on the much-publicized case: "[T]he apparent conflict of interest the private prosecution had is directly at odds with Supreme Court precedent. In the 1987 decision of *Young v. United States ex rel. Vuitton et Fils*, the Supreme Court ruled that, when it comes to private prosecutors pursuing criminal contempt cases, they 'certainly should be as disinterested as a public prosecutor who undertakes such a prosecution.'" That article went on to quote University of Oklahoma law professor Guha Krishnamurthi on the matter. "Appearances," Krishnamurthi said, "are really functionally important for the rule of law, and for our judiciary." "I think it's such a clear abuse that it violates the defendant's constitutional right to due process," another law professor, Louis Raveson, of Rutgers Law School, commented of the conflict of interest at issue.[385] The role of private parties also drew headlines in 2021 after Texas adopted a patently unconstitutional anti-abortion law that, in effect, sought to turn private citizens into "bounty hunters."[386] With President Joe Biden saying the Texas law "blatantly violates" a woman's constitutional rights under *Roe v. Wade* (1973), multiple court challenges to the law, including by the Justice Department and abortion providers, soon followed.[387]

6

DIVIDED OPINIONS AND SPLIT DECISIONS

Jurisdictions Outlawing vs. Authorizing Private Prosecutors

A Divided Country: Different Norms of Prosecutorial Practice

The history of prosecution in America is marked by many changes over time, including a transition from private to public prosecutions. In 1931, the National Commission on Law Observance and Enforcement's "Report on Prosecution"—giving a snapshot and summary of American practice from an early 1930s vantage point—was transmitted to President Herbert Hoover by George Wickersham, the former Attorney General of the United States under President William Howard Taft. That report discussed the history of private and public prosecution, observing at the outset: "By the common law of England, which was brought to America by the colonists, the ordinary criminal prosecution was conducted by a private prosecutor in the name of the King. In case the victim of a crime, or someone interested, came forward to prosecute, he retained his own counsel and had charge of the case as in an everyday civil proceeding except that the Attorney General, as the representative of the King, might refuse to allow it to go on." "Private prosecution," the report relayed, "was a medieval institution, going back to a time when the civil and the criminal were not well differentiated and the chief purpose of the law was to preserve the peace by providing an orderly substitute for private vengeance through proceedings in the courts." "Bad features of this system of private prosecution," the report emphasized, "were pointed out by Lord Chief Justice Hale in the seventeenth century."[1]

In tracing the incomplete, still-in-progress transition from private to public prosecutions, the 1931 Report on Prosecution took notice of Connecticut's 1704 statute providing for public prosecution, as well as other eighteenth-century legal developments in Virginia and other colonies. In addition, the report took specific note of other countries' prosecutorial innovations, pointing out that in France, for instance, that country's public prosecutors—firmly established by the seventeenth century—had been hailed as "one of the best creations of the French genius." "The influence of the French *procureur du roi* in giving final shape to the American institution of an official prosecutor is obvious," the report stated, giving this explanation of the overall effect of the American Revolution, which France's king, Louis XVI, had supported: "After the Revolution, especially in the era of rising Jeffersonian democracy, things English were for a season discredited and things French regarded with enthusiastic interest." "The American official prosecutor, Federal and State," the report concluded, "is a compound of the English attorney general and the French *avocat general* and *procureur du roi*, on the basis of the colonial county attorneys."[2] Noting that the Judiciary Act of 1789 created the Attorney General of the United States and U.S. district attorneys "in language in which one may trace an echo of the Connecticut act of 1704," the Report on Prosecution—highlighting the federal prosecutorial system forged after the U.S. Constitution's 1788 ratification—emphasized how U.S. district attorneys were, until 1861, "legally and actually quite independent in the conduct of their office." "In 1861, because of the exigencies of civil war," the report stressed of a later change, taking note of a congressional act of August 2, 1861,[3] "the Attorney General of the United States was given by statute 'superintendence and direction of United States attorneys and marshals in all districts of the United States.'"[4] It was a technological advancement, in fact, that made that legal development possible. The invention of the telegraph made communications much quicker, allowing the Attorney General of the United States to more effectively control and supervise the actions of U.S. district attorneys in distant places.[5]

Throughout American history, a split of authority has existed—and in fact continues to this day—regarding public versus private prosecution and the propriety of private prosecutors. While the debate over private prosecution goes back to a far earlier time, in 1955, *The Yale Law Journal* published an article titled "Private Prosecution: A Remedy for District Attorneys' Unwarranted Inaction," giving a mid-1950s snapshot of American prosecutorial practices. That article observed that the appellate courts of thirty jurisdictions had decided that privately retained attorneys could assist the public prosecutor as opposed to only three jurisdictions which had determined they could not. "Massachusetts, Michigan and Wisconsin have generally refused to permit private attorneys to assist in criminal prosecutions," the article emphasized, noting that even in those three locales "there have been exceptions where the private attorney participated in a limited manner or was not hired by interested parties." The 1955 article, reporting on the results of a *Yale Law Journal* questionnaire, provided some telling statistics. "[S]ixty-two per cent of 151 public prosecutors from forty-five states who responded to a *questionnaire* on prosecution procedures stated that they permit privately hired attorneys to assist in criminal proceedings," the article observed, further noting that 25% of those responding public prosecutors stated that they did not have enough time or help to conduct necessary prosecutions. Of the prosecutors who responded to the survey, 60% of them stated that "they permit privately hired attorneys to aid in the prosecution of the case at trial with no restriction on the scope of his activity." In addition, the survey found that "[t]he private prosecutor is permitted to control the criminal action of 16% of the responding public officials with the sole limitation that a member of the prosecutor's staff be present at the trial," but that 3% of public prosecutors "would give private attorneys complete control of the criminal action." "*Questionnaire* responses," the article added, "disclosed that in at least twenty-eight states, it is a common practice for private attorneys to prosecute criminal actions in the lower courts."

In detailing real-world prosecution practices, the 1955 law review article noted of those lower courts: "Since these courts customarily have jurisdiction over all misdemeanors, private citizens may initiate criminal actions which result in jail terms up to one year." The article then gave this report based on a careful analysis of the questionnaire responses: "In many states the latitude of private prosecutors is extended by the fact that the public prosecutor need not attend such courts unless the presiding official requests his appearance. If the district attorney chooses, he can control the proceedings in these courts; in his absence, a private attorney is in complete charge of the prosecution." With state judicial systems relying on statutes or "the inherent power of the court to administer justice" to authorize the use of private prosecutors, the 1955 article emphasized that, while private prosecutions were used in many different types of cases, "some courts will reverse a conviction if the relationship between the accused and private prosecutor or hiring citizen might have produced unfairness" (*e.g.*, if the private prosecutor was hired on a contingent fee basis). "The courts have approved of private assistant prosecutors even in actions for such serious crimes as murder, manslaughter, burglary, larceny and rape," the 1955 *Yale Law Journal* article observed after taking stock of then-existing practices.[6] Through the years, state courts, through their judicial decisions, have placed certain guardrails around the conduct of private prosecutors.[7] Although those guardrails vary from state to state, their very existence highlights—in one sense—a kind of wariness or uneasiness about the use of private prosecutors.

Through the decades, a number of academics have studied the practice of private prosecution. In 1968, one scholar—citing the results of that earlier *Yale Law Journal* questionnaire—pointed out that "[a]lthough conclusive data is not available, there is little doubt that private prosecution is more widespread at the inferior court level than at the level of the general jurisdiction court." In other words, private prosecution was used to a much greater degree—at least in terms of frequency—for lower-level offenses than for more serious crimes. That scholar, Thomas Robinson, Jr., cited cases from a variety of states—Alabama, Florida, Georgia, Illinois, Kansas, Kentucky, Maine, Minnesota, Mississippi, Missouri, North Carolina, North Dakota, Ohio, Oklahoma, and Pennsylvania—where private prosecutors had been involved in prosecutions for all sorts of offenses (*e.g.*, armed assault with intent to rob, assault and battery, embezzlement, manslaughter, murder, and rape). At that juncture, the year of the Tet Offensive in Vietnam and the assassinations of Martin Luther King Jr. and Robert F. Kennedy, Robinson noted that there continued to be "at least three states, Massachusetts, Michigan, and Wisconsin, which refuse to permit private prosecution." "There seems to be a rule generally that any private prosecution must be in the discretion of the trial court, and at the instance or with the permission of the official prosecutor," Robinson observed. "Michigan and Massachusetts," he wrote of those two locales, "have made exceptions to this rule against private prosecution" where the private prosecutor was not retained or motivated by an interested party or when "the private counsel participated in only a very limited fashion."[8]

By 1976, when another legal scholar, Andrew Sidman, published "The Outmoded Concept of Private Prosecution" in *The American University Law Review*, there was little new to report in terms of change. As Sidman wrote in that piece of scholarship: "A majority of the states that have considered the question have ruled that privately employed prosecutors may assist the state's prosecutor in conducting cases. The two federal courts that have addressed the issue have also sustained the practice." Noting that jurisdictions generally allowed the privately retained lawyers to actively participate at trial, Sidman also reported on case law requiring that the public prosecutor "maintain ultimate control of the proceedings." Like other commentators before him, Sidman described how Massachusetts, Michigan and Wisconsin had prohibited private prosecutors, but also took note of a lesser-publicized private prosecution prohibition in Nebraska and how Iowa, too, looked unfavorably upon private prosecutors. "Other courts have struck down the practice of private prosecution under certain conditions," Sidman advised in the mid-1970s, noting how some convictions had been reversed where private counsel appeared before the grand jury and that courts had observed that it would be problematic for a public prosecutor to relinquish complete control of a prosecution to a private lawyer. "In one instance, when the defendant's motion to have the private prosecutor disclose his source of employment was overruled by the trial court, the conviction was reversed on appeal," Sidman observed, citing a 1924 case from West Virginia.[9]

Other law review articles have given snapshots of private prosecution in subsequent time periods,[10] with some American jurisdictions today continuing to prohibit interested private prosecutions entirely or, as in New Hampshire, for offenses that carry the possibility of imprisonment.[11] Private prosecutions by interested parties are now generally prohibited by law in Alaska,[12] California,[13] Georgia,[14] Idaho,[15] Massachusetts,[16] Minnesota,[17] Missouri,[18] Nebraska,[19] New York,[20] South Carolina,[21] and Wisconsin,[22] although, for example, Massachusetts allows private parties to seek criminal prosecutions for misdemeanors[23] and Michigan and other jurisdictions allow them to be brought in contempt cases.[24] Connecticut, North Dakota and other states make clear in their case law that a private party has no standing to prosecute another individual,[25] and New Jersey and Rhode Island are examples of states that only permit private prosecutions for lower-level crimes.[26] But whether by statute,[27] rule of criminal procedure,[28] or judicial decisions[29] reliant on the common law, many American states, including Alabama,[30] Arkansas,[31] Colorado,[32] Delaware,[33] Illinois,[34] Kansas,[35] Kentucky,[36] Louisiana,[37] New Hampshire,[38] New Jersey,[39] North Carolina,[40] Ohio,[41] Oregon,[42] Pennsylvania,[43] Rhode Island,[44] Tennessee,[45] Texas,[46] Virginia,[47] and

West Virginia,[48] continue to allow the appointment of private attorneys to assist or take charge of criminal prosecutions to one degree or another.[49] In places like Alabama and Texas, a number of litigated cases reflect the continued use and approval of the practice through the years. The Court of Criminal Appeals of Texas has, for instance, turned aside legal challenges to private prosecutors, including in homicide and capital cases.[50]

In some states, there are statutes that cover a very specific area of law. New Jersey has a state statute specifically authorizing private prosecution for election law violations. That New Jersey statute, adopted in 1930 and still on the books, provides: "Any citizen may employ an attorney to assist the prosecutor of the pleas to perform his duties under this title, and such attorney shall be recognized by the prosecutor of the pleas and the court as associate counsel in the proceedings." "No prosecution, action or proceeding," that statute continues, "shall be dismissed without notice to, or against the objection of, such associate counsel until the reasons of the prosecutor of the pleas for such dismissal, together with the objections thereto of such associate counsel, shall have been filed in writing, argued by counsel and considered by the court, with such limitation as to the time of filing such reasons and objections as the court may impose."[51] That statute has been put to use,[52] with a court ruling that it was intended to "guarantee a vigorous prosecution and prevent any attempts at a 'whitewash' of the charges."[53] The State of Minnesota, in 1988, had adopted similar laws pertaining to elections and campaign practices. "Anyone except the person under investigation or the person's agent," they read, "may employ an attorney to assist the county attorney in the investigation and prosecution of a violation of this chapter." But those laws were repealed in 2004, with the newly enacted replacement provisions providing simply: "A county attorney may prosecute any violation of this chapter."[54]

Where still permitted, interested private prosecutions are—as they have been for some time—typically subject to certain conditions, one of which is that the local district attorney's office (or the relevant jurisdiction's equivalent) supervise and retain control over the prosecutions.[55] The public prosecutor "should remain in charge of and responsible for the prosecution of criminal actions," the Court of Appeals of North Carolina explicitly ruled in 1974, adding: "Except for the most compelling reasons, the trial judge should not permit the solicitor to abdicate his duties and responsibilities in a criminal action and permit privately employed counsel to assume responsibility for the prosecution."[56] "Although the unfettered right of private prosecution is still recognized in some jurisdictions," one New York appellate court ruled in 2008, citing cases from Alabama, Montana, Ohio and Rhode Island, "the majority have either prohibited the practice altogether or limited the private prosecutor to acting under the control of the public prosecutor." In *State v. Riser* (1982), the Supreme Court of Appeals of West Virginia, citing its prior decision in *State v. Atkins* (1979), reiterated that state's requirement that "a private prosecutor" is "subjected to the same high standards of conduct in the trial of a case as a public prosecutor." That rule, the *Atkins* case determined, was necessary "to blunt the usual criticism that a private prosecutor would be overzealous to convict."[57] Thus, while occasionally private prosecutors may be allowed to participate without the district attorney's consent or supervision,[58] the vast majority of jurisdictions have at various times imposed restraints on their use and allowed participation, subject to certain articulated standards (*e.g.*, disclosure of requested evidence in discovery),[59] only with the public prosecutor's consent and retention of control over the case.[60]

In North Carolina, New Mexico and elsewhere, trial court judges have the discretion to determine whether a private attorney may assist a district attorney in a case's prosecution.[61] "[T]he trial court would have the right, for good cause, to refuse to permit an attorney to appear as a special prosecutor in any case," the Court of Criminal Appeals of Alabama observed in 1981.[62] In *Atkins*, the Supreme Court of Appeals of West Virginia had this to say on that matter: "The right to obtain a private prosecutor in this State was never absolute and was always subject to judicial control and review." "In *State ex rel. Moran v. Ziegler*," the *Atkins* court emphasized, citing one of its precedents from 1978, "we clearly established that a private prosecutor is subject to the same high standards of conduct in the trial of the case as is a public prosecutor." "This rule," the court in *Atkins* reiterated, "blunts, if it does not entirely dissipate, the major criticism of private prosecutors, that they will be overzealous to convict and consequently ignore the public prosecutor's fundamental obligation to do justice."[63] Only a few modern-day court decisions allow private prosecutors to retain unbridled discretion over a criminal prosecution,[64] with most states prohibiting the participation of private prosecutors in related civil matters.[65]

In American law, there is a significant difference in practice between the federal courts versus what is permitted in various state judicial systems. Federal courts, in fact, have expressly held that private individuals are prohibited from prosecuting criminal actions.[66] "A private citizen cannot prosecute a criminal action in federal court," a federal judge in the U.S. District Court for the Southern District of New York ruled in 2020, for example.[67] The U.S. District Court for the Eastern District of Pennsylvania, taking note of the federal practice, likewise made this illustrative declaration in 2014: "[I]n federal court, at least, a private individual cannot prosecute a criminal action; not only do federal criminal laws provide no basis for such prosecution, but under Article III of the Federal Constitution,[68] federal courts lack jurisdiction over such suits."[69] "As the Supreme Court has explained," that court stressed in its decision, "'a citizen lacks standing to contest the policies of the prosecuting authority when he himself is neither prosecuted nor threatened with prosecution." "*[A] private citizen*," the court stressed, *"lacks a judicially cognizable interest in the prosecution or nonprosecution of another*.'"[70] Various lower federal courts, including federal circuit courts, have consistently enforced this rule by dismissing private efforts to prosecute criminal activity,[71] so it is clear that a private individual cannot sue in federal court to compel a state government or the federal government to investigate or prosecute an alleged crime.[72]

In contrast to the federal system, American states have adopted their own approaches to private prosecution—approaches that vary considerably state by state. A number of cases decided in state courts before the U.S. Supreme Court's landmark decision in *Young v. United States ex rel. Vuitton et Fils S.A.* (1987)[73] either outlawed or restricted the use of private prosecutors on behalf of interested parties.[74] In *Young*, the Supreme Court held that "[a] private attorney appointed to prosecute a criminal contempt... should be as disinterested as a public prosecutor who undertakes such a prosecution."[75] In the wake of *Young*, additional American states have changed or modified their approach to private prosecutions, some in direct response to the Supreme Court's *Young* decision.[76] Meanwhile, American courts have grappled with a multitude of issues pertaining to prosecutorial misconduct;[77] prosecutorial immunity,[78] with prosecutors—by law—now enjoying far-reaching immunity from liability;[79] and malicious prosecution claims,[80] including against private prosecutors.[81] Other judges have held or reiterated that, in contempt cases, a public prosecutor should be sought out to conduct the prosecutions[82] and that private attorneys—in particular, disinterested ones—should be engaged only as a last resort to handle such matters.[83] "There is a strong government interest in dispassionate assessment of the propriety of criminal charges, particularly where there is a pending civil case which might benefit from the criminal prosecution," a Superior Court of New Jersey noted in 1997, citing *Young*.[84]

Change can be seen in many places. Georgia's common law, for instance, once allowed the use of private special prosecutors employed by murder victims' family members to assist district attorneys in prosecuting murder cases.[85] A provision of Georgia law, Uniform Superior Court Rule 42.1, titled "Private Special Prosecutors," changed that common law rule in 1985, however, even before the U.S. Supreme Court handed down its ruling in *Young*.[86] Rule 42.1 provides: "Private special prosecutors retained by the family or relatives of one named as a victim in an indictment or accusation may not participate in the prosecution of a criminal case."[87] Private attorneys in Georgia are permitted to perform certain acts, with section 15-18-5 of Georgia's code specifically allowing a "private attorney" to act as "district attorney pro tempore" when "a district attorney's office is disqualified from interest or relationship to engage in a prosecution."[88] In one case, the Court of Appeals of Georgia held that no violation of Uniform Superior Court Rule 42.1 occurred when a private attorney, representing the parents of a homicide victim in a pending civil suit against the defendant, helped to arrange the appearance of an expert witness for the State of Georgia in the defendant's prosecution. In that case, the attorney for the parents did not sit at counsel table, did not assist in the preparation of the State's case, and took no part in the actual trial of the homicide case. "There is no prohibition on private counsel merely referring the State to an expert," the appellate court declared of the nominal assistance provided, noting that "[t]he State was free to call the expert or not."[89]

In several post-*Young* cases in other locales, the families of crime victims nonetheless have been allowed to retain private counsel to prosecute the accused. For example, in *Commonwealth v. Hubbard*,[90] the Kentucky Supreme Court allowed an attorney for the decedent's family to prosecute a defendant charged with reckless homicide. Likewise, in *State v. Worley*,[91] the West Virginia Supreme Court of Appeals affirmed a murder conviction where a county prosecutor withdrew an offer to accept the defendant's plea of guilty to the charge of first-degree murder with a recommendation of mercy. This withdrawal came after a private prosecutor hired by the deceased's family relayed the family's wish that the case be vigorously prosecuted. It should, of course, be unsurprising that a paid attorney for the victim's family might take a different approach to a criminal case's prosecution than the public prosecutor might ordinarily be so inclined to take.[92] After all, while a private retained lawyer may be singularly focused on the expressed interests of a paying client, a public prosecutor is duty-bound to represent the public interest—a role that requires a delicate balancing of the interests of the accused, the victim, and the general public.

Multiple pre-*Young* cases, a review of case law confirms, expressly approved of the use of private prosecutors retained by crime victims or their families.[93] For instance, in *Woods v. Linahan*,[94] the Fifth Circuit held that a defendant charged with murder and armed robbery was not denied due process because of the participation at trial of a private attorney retained and paid for by the victim's family and friends. Although the private prosecutor's initial activities in *Woods* were said to "border on a constitutional violation" where the private prosecutor's initial activities included interviewing witnesses, filing motions, and developing trial strategy without the district attorney's knowledge and consent, the Fifth Circuit ultimately decided that the activities of a new district attorney, who took a more active role in the prosecution,[95] "cured any defect that may have occurred in the pretrial stages" of the case.[96] Although the use of a private prosecutor was approved in *Woods*, the Fifth Circuit's decision was not made without reservations. "While we find that no error is shown in this case," the Fifth Circuit wrote, "we note our concern about the practice of using a private attorney, paid by family and friends of the victim, to prosecute persons accused of murdering a person dear to the person paying the private prosecutor." "Human experience," the Fifth Circuit observed, "indicates that an attorney who is paid by a group of people to provide a service has some loyalty to those persons paying his fee." "This loyalty," it noted, "may serve to prejudice the well recognized rights of a defendant accused of committing a crime." "While we do not intimate that a defendant will always be prejudiced by the participation of a private attorney in a criminal prosecution," the Fifth Circuit concluded, "the chances are greater in this situation than where the state's attorney, or an attorney appointed and paid by the state, prosecutes the case."[97] As detailed in earlier chapters, private prosecutors were—as history shows—commonly approved in pre-*Young* cases for all types of prosecutions, including murder prosecutions.[98]

Private attorneys have been—and still are—intimately involved in the criminal justice system, whether because of public lawyers' conflicts or the way in which prosecutorial services are handled. In a large number of locales, for instance, municipalities (*e.g.*, in Idaho, Iowa, Michigan, Minnesota, New Hampshire, North Dakota, Texas, Utah, and Washington State) regularly send out requests for proposals ("RFPs") seeking prosecution services from private lawyers or law firms. These RFPs solicit bids for prosecution services for gross misdemeanors, misdemeanors, petty misdemeanors, contested traffic infractions, juvenile violations, criminal code enforcement, and animal control matters, whether on a contact (hourly, monthly retainer, per-case fee), as an "independent contractor," or through some other arrangement.[99] For example, Farmington City, Utah, recently sent out an RFP for prosecutorial services that included this language:

> The City is interested in receiving proposals to provide prosecuting attorney services from well-qualified vendors. The City will be contracting for these services. The City wishes to pay a single monthly flat fee to provide all prosecuting services. Duties include review of cases for filing, subsequent charging decisions, subpoena preparation, trial preparation. All court appearances to include arraignments, motions calendars, bench and jury trials, plea negotiations, forfeiture hearings and any appeals.[100]

A Fifty-State Survey: A Wide Range of Rules and Practices in American States

There is a wide range of practice and legal rules in the fifty states, with some states barring private prosecutions while others permit them, albeit often with certain restrictions or limitations. This section sets forth the law—and pertinent information, including historical snippets—on a state-by-state basis. It is difficult to be comprehensive in any fifty-state survey, but this section highlights various relevant state statutes and judicial rulings.

Alabama: Alabama permits private prosecutions, although the state's prosecutor must oversee and manage the criminal cases. In 1925, in *Handley v. State*, the Supreme Court of Alabama ruled that "[s]pecial counsel may appear in the prosecution as an assistant to the solicitor and with the consent of the court." In that case, Emma Handley was indicted for the murder of her husband, James Johnson, and at trial the solicitor referred to the husband's dying declaration about Handley's role in killing him. Life insurance policies made Handley the beneficiary, and Mr. Beddow, a special counsel, had been retained to assist with the prosecution. Following Handley's second-degree murder conviction, the state's supreme court emphasized that "[t]he management of the case remains with the official representative of the state, in whose name the special counsel appears." The court gave this justification for allowing private prosecutions: "The rule is founded upon the public policy that encourages the citizens to give aid in the detection and punishment of crime." "The consent of the state," the court observed, "is all the authority needed by special counsel; hence a motion by defendant to require special counsel to show his authority is properly overruled."[101]

In *Handley*, the special counsel appeared after the jury's selection and the trial had started. The insurance companies had a clear interest in the trial's outcome, with Emma Handley contending that she was entitled to know if those companies had retained Mr. Beddow, the special counsel. The Alabama Supreme Court, however, rejected her request, emphasizing that she had previously been advised that the state was contending that the insurance policies in question furnished a possible motive for the murder. Quoting other legal authorities, that court—in turning aside the appeal—specifically held: "'In the absence of a statute, the state cannot be compelled to disclose the names of private prosecutors or informers, especially where it is not shown that the defendant will be prejudiced by the want of such information.'" The court in *Handley* wrote this of a private prosecutor's prerogative: "He need not assume the role of a prosecutor, but, with the consent of the state authorities, render assistance in the name of the state." The *Handley* court specifically found that "[b]ringing to the attention of the jury the names of those employing or paying special counsel may work an injustice to the state or to the defendant, as the case may be." "Thus," the state supreme court opined, alluding to how private prosecutions had previously been financed, "if a popular subscription is raised to prosecute a man accused of crime, the publishing of the names of contributors might easily throw into the case a personal and popular influence highly injurious to the defendant." "In the absence of some reason to the contrary," the court ruled, "it is better that prosecutions proceed purely in the name of the state."

The *Handley* court laid out its concerns, but it refused to give weight to Handley's arguments. "We can easily conceive of abuses arising from unknown or secret interests employing counsel to prosecute in the name of the state," the Alabama Supreme Court acknowledged. But the state's supreme court found no prejudice because it found that the "interest of the insurance companies" and the "alleged relation" of the policies to the homicide were "fully known and in no sense a secret to defendant." "The official representative of the state has the first duty to see that no abuses arise," that court observed, noting that "a failure of duty in this regard will not be presumed unless made to affirmatively appear." "The protection of property rights involved in the commission of crime is a proper incentive to lending assistance to the state in detecting and punishing crime," the court stressed. "Assuming that a disclosure of the parties retaining Mr. Beddow as special counsel would have named" the relevant insurers, the *Handley* court found, "such fact would not, or should not, have influenced the jury in any way, and would have disclosed nothing material to the defense which was not already known." In affirming the second-degree murder conviction, the *Han-*

dley court added this coda: "If there was any personal relation between Mr. Beddow and any juror which put defendant at disadvantage in the matter of challenges, it is not made to appear; hence it is not shown there was abuse of discretion in denying the motion for continuance."[102]

Since *Handley*, the Alabama courts have continued to allow private prosecutions. "The appearance of additional employed counsel to aid in the prosecution of criminal cases has always been recognized in this State as legitimate and proper," the Alabama Supreme Court confirmed in *Oliver v. State* (1937)—a case in which Arthur Oliver was convicted of the first-degree murder of his wife, Vidie, and sentenced to death. At Oliver's trial, the private prosecutor was accused of "accepting blood money" and being a "persecutor," not a prosecutor.[103] In a more recent case, *McCrory v. State* (1986), the Alabama Court of Criminal Appeals—citing *Handley* and other Alabama cases—reiterated that a special prosecutor may appear as an assistant in a criminal prosecution with the trial court's consent. In that case, Charles McCrory—indicted for the intentional murder of his wife—complained on appeal after being convicted and sentenced to life imprisonment that he was deprived of a fair trial because the victim's family employed a special prosecutor to assist the district attorney.[104]

In Alabama, a special prosecutor—like a public solicitor—must abide by certain judicially prescribed minimum standards of conduct. In *McCain v. City of Montgomery* (1956), for example, the Court of Appeals of Alabama explicitly held: "A defendant in a criminal prosecution is entitled to a fair and impartial trial, and nothing more. So long as the conduct of the special prosecutor comports to due and orderly procedure a defendant is in no position to complain as to who conducts the prosecution." In that case, the Alabama appellate court found no abuse of discretion where a special counsel acted with the regular prosecutor's consent and the court's permission.[105] Historically, Alabama law has long permitted a public prosecutor to receive a private prosecutor's assistance. As the Court of Appeals of Alabama stated in *Johnson v. State* (1915): "The control of the prosecution, in so far as presenting the state's case is concerned, was in the hands of the solicitor, upon whom the statute imposes the duty of representing the state in the prosecution. There is nothing in the statute or the policy of the state as expressed therein which denies the solicitor the right to accept assistance from a duly licensed practicing attorney, who is a sworn officer of the court." "The acceptance of such assistance in a prosecution where he is not disqualified," that court stressed in the early twentieth century, "is entirely a matter within the discretion of the solicitor." "It is certainly not a matter in which the defendant has any voice," the court offered.[106] In recent decades, private attorneys and special prosecutors have regularly appeared in Alabama criminal prosecutions.[107]

Alaska: In *Cooper v. District Court* (2006), the Court of Appeals of Alaska held that a crime victim—the wife of man who pled no contest to a misdemeanor assault of her—had no standing or independent right to challenge a sentence imposed by the district court. In that case, the appellate court took note of the English private prosecution system that American colonists imported, but noted that "[t]his system obviously favored the rich and powerful—those with sufficient influence and resources to apprehend the purported wrongdoer and to pursue the case in court." In describing how societal views had changed over time, with criminal prosecutions "brought by the state on behalf of the community as a whole" instead of being seen as "a private injury to the victim," the *Cooper* court emphasized: "It became the government's task to bring the wrongdoer to justice: government prosecutors, not crime victims, decided whether charges should be filed; likewise, if charges were filed, government prosecutors directed the litigation of those charges." After discussing the implications of that shift, one that sometimes put the views of government prosecutors at odds with crime victims, the Alaska appellate court spoke of the perception that there were "societal benefits of having an objective governmental official, as opposed to a person whose personal interests were at stake, decide whether a citizen should be charged with a crime, and what that charge should be, and how that charge should be litigated or settled."

Following a discussion of state-level efforts, including in Alaska, to elevate the victim's role in the criminal process, the *Cooper* court discussed victims' rights as set forth in Article I, Section 24 of the Alaska Constitution and under the Crime Victims' Rights Act of 1989. Section 24 of the Alaska Constitution gives crime victims, among others, these rights: "the right to confer with the prosecution"; "the right to be treated with dignity, respect, and fairness during all phases of the criminal and juvenile justice process"; "the right to obtain information about and be allowed to be present at all criminal or juvenile proceedings where the accused has the right to be present"; and "the right to be allowed to be heard, upon request, at sentencing, before or after conviction or juvenile adjudication." In finding that Alaska law did not give dissatisfied crime victims the right to appeal a defendant's sentence, the court in *Cooper* made clear that "the fact that a person or organization is legally entitled to express their views in court does not necessarily mean that this person or organization is also entitled to appeal the court's decision if the court does not adopt their view of the facts or their view of the law."

In rejecting the argument that a crime victim should have standing to appeal a defendant's sentence, the Court of Appeals of Alaska in *Cooper* first observed: "Even though Alaska law requires sentencing judges to consider both the interests of the community at large and the interests of the people who have particularly suffered as a result of the defendant's conduct, a criminal prosecution is not a private lawsuit brought by the victim(s) against the defendant, nor is a sentencing hearing a community meeting in which all members of the public have a right to enter the discussion and, if dissatisfied, challenge the decision." The *Cooper* decision then explained: "[O]ur system of criminal justice is no longer based on the idea that individual victims should bring perpetrators to court in order to obtain retribution and restitution for the harm done to their personal interests. Rather, criminal conduct is seen as an injury to the community." "Criminal prosecutions," the *Cooper* court declared, "are undertaken in the name of the community, and the executive branch of government (as the representative of the community) has the sole responsibility and authority to initiate and litigate criminal cases—and, if necessary, to challenge a trial court's decisions by seeking appellate review."

In its decision, the Court of Appeals acknowledged that there would inevitably be differences in viewpoints between crime victims and public prosecutors (as well as sentencing judges) as to the appropriate sentences for specific defendants. But, it observed, for two hundred years "the people of this county have believed that the fairest way to resolve" differing views as to the proper handling of a case "is to put the responsibility in the hands of public officials—prosecutors and judges—who have no personal interest in the case." "Indeed," the *Cooper* court wrote, "some courts have held that the constitutional guarantee of due process of law includes the requirement that all decisions in a criminal prosecution be made by a prosecutor who has no personal stake in the outcome." The *Cooper* court's conclusion: "There will be times when a crime victim is dissatisfied with the way a case is handled or resolved. But we, as a society, have decided that it is fairer to let public officials make these decisions, rather than putting the victim in charge of making these decisions, or letting the victim second-guess or veto these decisions."[108]

Arizona: As in other states, Arizona prosecutors have ethical constraints. The Supreme Court of Arizona has stated that "[t]he role of a prosecutor is not to seek convictions and sentences but rather to seek justice."[109] As that court emphasized in *Pool v. Superior Court in and for Pima County* (1984): "[T]he prosecutor is not the representative of an ordinary litigant; he is a representative of a government whose obligation to govern fairly is as important as its obligation to govern at all. The prosecutor's interest in a criminal prosecution 'is not that it shall win a case, but that justice shall be done.' Thus, 'while he may strike hard blows, he is not at liberty to strike foul ones.'"[110] The Arizona Constitution vests in an elected county attorney "the power and the duty to represent the public's interest in the prosecution of those charged with crimes."[111]

In *Johnson v. Vederman in and for the County of La Paz* (2017), the Court of Appeals of Arizona exercised its discretion to accept jurisdiction of consolidated petitions for special action relief from criminal defendants challenging a superior court's orders. The superior court had denied motions to disqualify James Schilder, whom La Paz County Attorney Tony Rogers had appointed as a special deputy prosecutor to prosecute charges against the petitioners. According to the appointing document in each case, Schilder was "responsible for determining the necessity and manner of [the] prosecution." As the Court of Appeals noted of the case's unique circumstances: "There is no contention that the appointment was the result of a conflict of interest on the part of the County Attorney. Nor is Schilder formally employed or affiliated with any county attorney's office. Rather, the County Attorney accepted Schilder's volunteer offer to prosecute these and several other cases without pay." At oral argument in the superior court, Schilder had represented that he had "independent power without the day-to-day oversight" of the county attorney.[112]

Under those facts, the Court of Appeals of Arizona wrote that no authority had been cited for the proposition that an Arizona statute "requires Board approval" of volunteer deputies. "The broad scope of the power that may be implied by Schilder's appointment, however," that court observed, "may raise serious due-process concerns." "Not surprisingly," the court pointed out, "there is no Arizona case authorizing this arrangement or even addressing it." "In other jurisdictions, in the rare case where a similar arrangement has been undertaken," it noted, "courts have expressed grave concerns about attorneys simply taking over for properly elected or appointed prosecuting officers without supervision, absent any ethical conflict or statutory authorization." "In the usual case," it ruled, citing a 2015 Arizona precedent, "discretionary decision-making inherent in the power to prosecute may not be delegated to unelected private counsel." "To the contrary," the court pointed out, "important due-process rights are implicated when an elected prosecutor cedes all control over a prosecution to a private lawyer." Ultimately, the Court of Appeals of Arizona, in remanding the case back to the superior court to receive evidence on the scope of Schilder's authority over the cases and the nature and extent, if any, of the elected county attorney's supervision of Schilder, made this ruling:

> A lawyer's willingness to perform pro bono legal services is commendable. But when all responsibility for the prosecution of a criminal matter is ceded to an unelected special prosecutor, the resulting lack of accountability infringes the due-process rights of the accused, regardless of whether the special prosecutor is working for free. In such a case, the accused is deprived of his or her due-process right to prosecution by or under the supervision of an elected officer who owes "a special and enduring duty to 'seek justice.'"[113]

The La Paz County Attorney later appointed a different special prosecutor before appointing the Chief Deputy Attorney of Mohave County.[114]

Arkansas: Arkansas has permitted private prosecutions. In a 2008 case, *Olmstead v. Olmstead*, the Supreme Court of Arkansas—in a *per curiam* opinion—wrote:

> On April 10, 2008, Olmstead filed a petition for writ of certiorari with this court seeking to stay his trial, contending, inter alia, that he was being prosecuted by an unauthorized private prosecutor in violation of *Young v. United States ex rel. Vuitton et Fils S.A.*, 481 U.S. 787, 107 S. Ct. 2124, 95 L.Ed.2d 740 (1987). This court denied the writ without prejudice on April 10, 2008. The following day, Olmstead was tried and convicted of criminal contempt and

> sentenced to a one-year term of imprisonment in the Cleburne County Jail, and fined $1,000.[115]

Other courts have also considered and rejected challenges to private criminal contempt enforcement actions, with the Court of Appeals of Arkansas ruling in *Standridge v. State* (2012) that "[t]he law does not require that a trial court disqualify a duly-elected prosecutor unless there is some evidence of specific misconduct."[116]

California: California once considered private prosecutions to be lawful. In *People v. Turcott* (1884), the defendant was convicted of first-degree murder and sentenced to be hanged. Responding to an argument on appeal that the trial judge had erred in permitting private counsel to assist the district attorney in the case's prosecution, the Supreme Court of California had this to say:

> The practice of allowing district attorneys to have the assistance of other counsel in the prosecution of criminal cases has existed and been acquiesced in almost since the organization of the state, and this practice seems to have been sanctioned by legislative action. In prescribing the course of the trial the legislature has provided by the second subdivision of section 1093 of the Penal Code, that the district attorney *or other counsel for the people* must open the cause and offer the evidence in support of the charge, and by section 1095, that if the indictment or information be for an offense punishable with death, *two* counsel on *each* side may argue the cause to the jury. We think the point not well taken.[117]

In another case, *People v. Blackwell* (1864), the Supreme Court of California also considered whether it was permissible for a crime victim to employ private counsel to assist the prosecutor. In that case, the trial court, at the district attorney's request, permitted other counsel to assist him. Although the defendant excepted, that motion was overruled by the trial judge. On appeal, the state supreme court ruled: "It appears that the district attorney had the active superintendence and management of the case during the progress of the trial. Whether the State, through him, should be allowed to avail itself of additional professional aid, was a matter addressed to the discretion of the court, and there is nothing in the record showing that the court abused its discretion in granting the request of the attorney." The state supreme court, though, ultimately reversed the conviction because the defense lawyer—"[o]n the cross-examination of the prosecutrix"—was not permitted to ask her if she had employed the private attorneys at Budd & Carr and Heslep & Jenkins to assist in the prosecution.[118] A "prosecutrix" refers to a "female prosecutor" and was a term frequently used in criminal prosecutions to describe a sexual assault victim.[119]

Later court cases made crystal clear, however, that all California criminal prosecutions are conducted in the name of the people.[120] Indeed, a series of recent cases—among them, *People v. Subramanyan*,[121] *People v. Dehle*,[122] and *People v. Parmar*[123]—have held that California law forbids private prosecutions,[124] even though a number of victims' rights are articulated by Marsy's Law (setting forth a comprehensive bill of rights for victims)[125] and Megan's Law (requiring the registry of sex offenders).[126] One of the items in the victim's bill of rights: "A victim, the retained attorney of a victim, a lawful representative of the victim, or the prosecuting attorney upon request of the victim, may enforce the rights enumerated ... in any trial or appellate court with jurisdiction over the case as a matter of right. The court shall act promptly on such a request."[127] In *People v. Eubanks* (1996), the Supreme Court of California, writing under the heading "The Independence and Impartiality of the District Attorney," specifically ruled as to the current state of the law:

> In California, all criminal prosecutions are conducted in the name of the People of the State of California and by their authority. California law does not authorize private prosecutions. Instead, "[t]he prosecution of criminal offenses on behalf of the People is the sole responsibility of the public prosecutor ... [who] ordinarily has sole discretion to determine whom to charge, what charges to file and pursue, and what punishment to seek. No private citizen, however personally aggrieved, may institute criminal proceedings independently, and the prosecutor's own discretion is not subject to judicial control at the behest of persons other than the accused."[128]

"California law does not authorize private prosecutions," a federal district court reconfirmed in 2020.[129]

Colorado: Colorado district attorneys—who, in the past, have allowed the appearance of "special counsel"[130]—are considered part of the executive branch. As executive officers, they have broad discretion to perform their duties and the scope of their discretion extends to "'the power to investigate and to determine who shall be prosecuted and what crimes shall be charged.'"[131] That power, however, is constrained by a Colorado statute when there is an unjustified refusal to prosecute a person for crime. As that statute, titled "Judge may require prosecution," reads:

> The judge of a court having jurisdiction of the alleged offense, upon affidavit filed with the judge alleging the commission of a crime and the unjustified refusal of the prosecuting attorney to prosecute any person for the crime, may require the prosecuting attorney to appear before the judge and explain the refusal. If after that proceeding, based on the competent evidence in the affidavit, the explanation of the prosecuting attorney, and any argument of the parties, the judge finds that the refusal of the prosecuting attorney to prosecute was arbitrary or capricious and without reasonable excuse, the judge may order the prosecuting attorney to file an information and prosecute the case or may ap-

> point a special prosecutor to do so. The judge shall appoint the special prosecutor from among the full-time district attorneys, assistant district attorneys, or deputy district attorneys who serve in judicial districts other than where the appointment is made; except that, upon the written approval of the chief justice of the supreme court, the judge may appoint any disinterested private attorney who is licensed to practice law in the state of Colorado to serve as the special prosecutor. Any special prosecutor appointed pursuant to this section shall be compensated as provided in section 20-1-308, C.R.S.[132]

The State of Colorado, by law, thus allows crime victims to challenge prosecutors' decisions.

Connecticut: In Connecticut, a private citizen "lacks standing to contest the policies of the prosecuting authority" when that citizen "is neither prosecuted nor threatened with prosecution." Likewise, it has been held that "a private citizen lacks a judicially cognizable interest in the prosecution or nonprosecution of another."[133] Like many states, though, Connecticut recognizes a cause of action for malicious prosecution. An action for malicious prosecution against a private person requires a plaintiff to prove that: "(1) the defendant initiated or procured the institution of criminal proceedings against the plaintiff; (2) the criminal proceedings have terminated in favor of the plaintiff; (3) the defendant acted without probable cause; and (4) the defendant acted with malice, primarily for a purpose other than that of bringing an offender to justice."[134]

Delaware: The Supreme Court of Delaware, in *DiSabatino v. Salicete* (1996), permitted the private prosecution of a criminal contempt case but only if the private attorney was disinterested. In that case, the Family Court of New Castle County held a former husband in contempt for violations of a restraining order. The state supreme court found that the sanctions imposed were criminal in nature and were improperly imposed without affording the husband constitutional protections. In its ruling, the Supreme Court of Delaware—citing the U.S. Supreme Court's decision in *Young v. United States ex rel. Vuitton et Fils S.A.* (1987)—noted that "[s]ince courts possess 'inherent authority to initiate contempt proceedings for disobedience to their orders,' that authority 'necessarily encompasses the ability to appoint a private attorney to prosecute the contempt.'" "Ordinarily, however," the court in *DiSabatino* stressed, "a court 'should first request the appropriate prosecuting authority to prosecute contempt actions, and should appoint a private prosecutor only if that request is denied. Such a procedure ensures that the court will exercise its inherent power of self-protection only as a last resort,' just as it usually considers enforcing compliance with its orders through the imposition of civil contempt before it utilizes criminal contempt as a sanction." As the *DiSabatino* court—again quoting *Young*—made clear:

> A criminal contempt proceeding that arises out of civil litigation is "between the public and the defendant, and [is] not a part of the original cause." Consequently, in the event that a private attorney is appointed to prosecute a criminal contempt which arises from a civil proceeding, that attorney "should be as disinterested as a public prosecutor who undertakes such a prosecution." Therefore, the attorney for a party that is the beneficiary of a court order in a civil proceeding "may not be appointed as a prosecutor in a [criminal] contempt action alleging a violation of that order."[135]

By contrast, in another case, *Seth v. State* (1991), the Supreme Court of Delaware held that a "Lend-A-Prosecutor" program, by which attorneys employed and compensated by a private law firm were appointed by the state's attorney general as volunteer, part-time prosecutors to prosecute criminal cases for the State, was not prohibited by statute and did not violate the Lawyers' Rules of Professional Conduct. In that case, the state's supreme court held that Delaware's attorney general, in creating the Lend-A-Prosecutor program, "acted within the broad statutory power to act in the public interest." In rejecting the charge that the "Lend-A-Prosecutor program was "illegal," the state supreme court observed that the attorney general has "the broad authority to appoint assistants, provided they are residents of Delaware and authorized by this Court to practice law in Delaware." That authority, the court found, encompasses the authority to employ part-time as well as full-time assistants. The objection that the part-time prosecutors were being paid by Skadden, Arps, a large private law firm, was also rejected. The state supreme court found that part-time prosecutors could be compensated from private sources, affirming the trial court's finding that there was "no indication that the prosecutor" appointed under the Lend-A-Prosecutor "was faced with any conflict of interest."[136]

Florida: In *Gordon v. State* (2007), a Florida appellate court considered the assertion by Jay Gordon, an ex-husband, that a trial court judge had erred by appointing his ex-wife Elizabeth Savitt's attorney, Jonathan Root, as a special prosecutor to handle a criminal contempt charge. In the circuit court, Gordon had been found guilty of criminal contempt and been placed on probation for one year, with a special condition of 30 days in the county jail on weekends, with credit for time already served. In making his argument on appeal, Gordon relied on the U.S. Supreme Court's *Young* decision, in which the Court—using its supervisory powers—held improper a district court's appointing of attorneys who represented a trademark holder to prosecute a criminal contempt for violations of an injunction against trademark infringement. In concluding that it would not apply the *Young* ruling to the case before it, one involving the enforcement of a domestic violence injunction, the court in *Gordon* ruled: (1) "to require the appointment of an independent prosecutor in all cases would nullify a remedy provided in the domestic violence statute" (namely, allowing a party to compel enforcement "through a civil or criminal contempt proceeding"); (2) it would "cause a sea change in Florida practice," which allows a party to a civil case "to initiate and prosecute an indirect criminal contempt proceeding to enforce an order of the court"; (3) "if one of the parties in a civil case may initiate a contempt enforcement proceeding, it follows that the judge may appoint the attorney of the moving party to 'prosecute' the case, which is to call witnesses and present evidence at a contempt hearing"; (4) that "adequate procedural safeguards" were in place "to protect against abuse of the contempt sanction"; and (5) that "orders in family or domestic violence cases are different than the injunction at issue" in *Young*, the U.S. Supreme Court decision involving alleged trademark infringement.[137]

In distinguishing *Young*, the court in *Gordon* wrote that the *Young* decision "arose in a commercial trademark infringement case where a party with deep pockets secured the appointment of its attorneys to conduct a lengthy investigation and prosecution pertaining to counterfeit handbags." By contrast, the *Gordon* court observed, the criminal contempt proceeding in the Florida case involved a different context which outweighed the interest in having—as *Young* articulated—a private attorney "as disinterested as a public prosecutor who undertakes such a prosecution." As the *Gordon* court put it:

> Although the public has an interest in an order entered in a family law or domestic violence case, this interest is far outweighed by the interest of the party seeking the enforcement or protection of the order. The public interest in the authority or dignity of a court is abstract; a litigant's interest in receiving child support or being free from physical harm or harassment is real and immediate. For this reason, the law should not preclude such parties from using their own attorneys to prosecute indirect criminal contempts. To require the appointment of an independent prosecutor in all cases would inject delay and additional expense into proceedings where litigants are often of limited means. Although an indirect criminal contempt proceeding in a family law case is vitally important to the parties, such a case often has little interest to a professional prosecutor.[138]

The difference between a direct and an indirect criminal contempt has been articulated by Florida courts and a variety of other courts and commentators. "In order to be considered direct criminal contempt," the Supreme Court of Florida has ruled, "all of the acts underlying the contemptuous conduct must be committed in open court in the presence of the judge, 'where all of the essential elements of the misconduct are under the eye of the court [and] are actually observed by the court." In contrast, "[c]onduct committed outside the presence of the court is indirect criminal contempt." If a judge needs to rely on statements or testimony from others regarding their knowledge about contemptuous acts, the misconduct is no longer considered direct criminal contempt because additional explanation or testimony is necessary. "Criminal contempt," the Supreme Court of Florida observed in *Plank v. State* (2016), "is considered to be 'a crime in the ordinary sense.'" "A criminal contempt proceeding," the state's supreme court emphasized in that case, "is 'instituted solely and simply to vindicate the authority of the court [or] otherwise punish for conduct offensive to the public in violation of an order of the court.'"[139]

Georgia: In Georgia, a private citizen may not prosecute a criminal matter "on his or her own." Instead, in the public prosecutor's role as "an administrator of justice," the prosecutor "has broad discretion in making decisions prior to trial about whom to prosecute, what charges to bring, and which sentence to seek."[140] Indeed, as noted earlier in this chapter, Uniform Superior Court Rule 42.1, titled "Private Special Prosecutors," now specifically provides: "Private special prosecutors retained by the family or relatives of one named as a victim in an indictment or accusation may not participate in the prosecution of a criminal case."[141] In *Rogers v. State* (1986), the Court of Appeals of Georgia did note that there was no violation of Rule 42.1 where a private attorney, representing the victim's parents, merely assisted in arranging for the appearance of an expert witness in the defendant's prosecution where (1) the parents' attorney did not sit at counsel table, (2) the attorney took no part in the actual trial of the case, (3) the attorney did not assist in the preparation of the State's case and was not present when the expert witness was interviewed, and (4) the expert was paid by the State.[142]

Hawaii: In Hawaii, county charters determine a prosecutor's status.[143] For example, section 8-104 of the Revised Charter of the City & County of Honolulu sets forth the "Powers, Duties and Functions" of the "prosecuting attorney" in that locale. That section states that the prosecuting attorney shall (a) "[a]ttend all courts in the city and conduct, on behalf of the people, all prosecutions therein for offenses against the laws of the state and the ordinances and rules and regulations of the city"; (b) "[p]rosecute offenses against the laws of the state under the authority of the attorney general of the state"; (c) "[a]ppear in every criminal case where there is a change of venue from the courts in the city and prosecute the same in any jurisdiction to which the same is changed or removed"; and (d) "[i]nstitute proceedings before the district judges for the arrest of persons charged with or reasonably suspected of public offenses, when the prosecuting attorney has information that any such offenses have been committed, and for that purpose, take charge of criminal cases before the district judges either in person or by a deputy or by such other prosecuting officer or in such other manner as the prosecuting attorney shall designate with approval of the district court or in accordance with statute; draw all indictments and attend before and give advice to the grand jury whenever cases are presented to it for its consideration; and investigate all matters which may properly come before the prosecuting attorney." "Nothing herein contained," section 8-104(d) of that Revised Charter further states, "shall prevent the conduct of proceedings by private counsel before courts of record under the direction of the prosecuting attorney."[144]

The Supreme Court of Hawaii has interpreted Hawaii statutes (which allow each political subdivision to frame and adopt a charter and to provide for the prosecution of offenses) and section 8-104(d) of the Revised Charter of the City & County of Honolulu "as allowing the Prosecutor of the City and County of Honolulu, in his discretion, to hire private counsel to prosecute particular cases."[145] In *Okuda v. Ching* (1990), where a private attorney was retained to prosecute a man on misdemeanor charges, the state's supreme court rejected an argument that section 8-104(d), which reads "under the direction of the prosecuting attorney," requires the prosecuting attorney's "personal supervision." "This contention," the *Okuda* court ruled, "founders on the rock of common sense." "There is no way, given the volume of criminal cases handled by the prosecuting attorney" for the City and County of Honolulu, the court emphasized, "that the prosecutor can personally supervise each and every case." "Under Charter § 8–105," the court observed, "the prosecuting attorney is empowered to appoint deputies, and under the provisions of Charter § 8–104, it is obvious that it is intended that those deputies may perform the functions of the prosecutor."[146]

Idaho: In *People v. Biles* (1885), the Supreme Court of the Territory of Idaho considered the appeal of a defendant indicted, tried, and convicted for the crime of assault with intent to murder. The defendant alleged that the trial court had erred in allowing private counsel to assist in the prosecution, but the Supreme Court of the Territory of Idaho, rejecting that argument, ruled:

> While the statute does not specifically authorize the employment of private counsel to assist in the prosecution of persons charged with crime, section 354 of the criminal practice act distinctly and in terms recognizes the right of private counsel to appear and assist the prosecution. The second clause of said section states: "The district attorney, or *other counsel* for the people, must open the cause and offer the evidence in support of the indictment." The words "or other counsel" evidently mean private counsel; as otherwise there could be no other counsel for the people. Section 356, as amended in Eleventh Session Laws, 227, still more clearly authorizes the appearance of counsel to assist the prosecution, and his right to assist in the prosecution, as follows:
>
>> "If the indictment is for an offense punishable with death, two counsel on each side may argue the cause to the jury. If it is for any other offense the court may, in its discretion, restrict the argument to one counsel on each side."

> This recognizes the right of more than one counsel to appear and assist in the prosecution of any criminal cause, but authorizes the court to restrict the argument, in his discretion, to one counsel on each side, in offenses less than capital, but not in capital cases. These sections are not repealed nor affected by section 6 of the act creating the office of district attorney. The latter section reads:
>
>> "It shall be the duty of the district attorney to prosecute or defend all actions, applications or motions, civil or criminal, in the district court of his county, in which the people, or the territory or county, is interested as a party."
>
> It does not say that he shall do so unassisted or alone, but simply means the district attorney shall have the general management and control of all such cases. We see no reason why counsel may not be employed to assist the district attorney in the prosecution of criminal causes.[147]

The Supreme Court of Idaho in *Derting v. Walker* (1987) made clear that county prosecutors could maintain private law practices and private attorneys could handle misdemeanor prosecutions. As the court ruled in that case:

> Until relatively recent times the office of county prosecutor has been part-time in nature. It is common knowledge, and we take judicial notice of the fact, that county prosecutors maintain private law practices in addition to their duties in prosecuting criminal offenses. When the legislature provided for "full time" prosecutors in certain counties, it made clear that in such counties the prosecutors were permitted to enter into contracts with municipalities for the prosecution of city misdemeanors. The wisdom of such a policy decision by the legislature is not open to question by the courts in the absence of constitutional prohibition. As above noted, we find no such constitutional prohibition. Municipalities are free to enter into contract with private attorneys for the prosecution of city misdemeanors. By virtue of the legislation, they may adopt the alternative of contracting with the county prosecuting attorney for the prosecution of city misdemeanors. No question is raised concerning the ability of a part-time prosecutor to contract with municipalities for the prosecution of city misdemeanors and retain to himself the proceeds of such contract. Likewise, the legislature expressly permitted such practice to be utilized by municipalities with full-time prosecutors.[148]

More recently, however, the Court of Appeals of Idaho made clear that crime victims are not parties to criminal prosecutions and thus cannot, themselves, direct them. In that case, *State v. Johnson* (2020), the Court of Appeals reviewed a case in which a defendant, Roy Johnson, was convicted of a felony—aggravated driving under the influence of alcohol—in which the district court, following that conviction, granted a crime victim's motion for restitution. In his appeal, Johnson argued that the district court lacked the jurisdiction to grant the motion for restitution because it was filed by the crime victim, who was not a party to the criminal case. "Because the State was not seeking restitution on behalf of the crime victim and the victim did not have standing to file a restitution motion," the appellate court held, vacating the restitution order, "the district court lacked authority to consider the motion." "Under Idaho's current statutory scheme," the court noted, "crime victims are not parties to a criminal case even for the limited purpose of seeking restitution and therefore lack standing to pursue a motion independently of a party." Article V, section 1 of the Idaho Constitution provides: "every action prosecuted by the people of the state as a party, against a person charged with a public offense, for the punishment of the same, shall be termed a criminal action." Likewise, an Idaho statute, § 19-104, titled "Parties to criminal actions," reads: "A criminal action is prosecuted in the name of the state of Idaho, as a party, against the person charged with the offense." "At the core of these provisions," the *Johnson* court wrote, "is the belief that criminal prosecutions are public matters, sought by the State on behalf of its citizen[s], not contests between a defendant and a crime victim."

After making its ruling that a crime victim is not a party to a criminal case, the Idaho Court of Appeals in *Johnson* wrote: "No other rule, statute, or constitutional provision allows a crime victim to independently intervene within a defendant's criminal case." "Allowing a non-party to intervene in a defendant's criminal proceeding would bring complicated consequences, including the potential to undermine the critical and distinct role of the prosecutor," the court emphasized, adding: "Unlike private counsel, a prosecutor has the unique role as 'a minister of justice and not simply that of an advocate.'" The *Johnson* court further stressed: "[A]llowing counsel for a crime victim to file a motion for restitution within a criminal case and present the State's case for restitution without the support of the prosecutor's office may give rise to significant conflicts of interest and due process concerns." As the court wrote: "A defendant's right to due process may be violated when a person who is a victim of the crime or who has a personal, financial, or attorney-client relationship with the victim of the crime prosecutes the criminal case. As a result, it is generally recognized that '[a] private attorney who is paid by, or who has an attorney-client relationship with, an individual or entity that is a victim of the charged crime ... should not be permitted to serve as prosecutor in that matter.'"[149]

Illinois: Court approval of private counsel in Illinois to assist the state's attorney goes back more than a century. "[T]he power of the court to permit special counsel employed by private interests to assist the state's attorney" in prosecutions, the Supreme Court of Illinois ruled in *People v. Hartenbower* (1918), "has frequently been passed upon by this court, and in each instance the right of the court to do so has been sustained."[150] "While the practice of allowing private prosecutors, paid by parties interested in securing the conviction of a defendant, to appear before the grand jury and examine the witness is to be deprecated," the Appellate Court of Illinois noted in *People v. Wiggins* (1923), "yet it sometimes happens, by reason of the inability of the Attorney General to lend aid to the State's Attorney and the failure of the county board to provide sufficient assistance, that the ends of justice might be defeated were private parties not allowed to furnish the needed aid."[151]

Not only did the Supreme Court of Illinois, in *People v. Husband* (1954), approve the appointment of special counsel to assist the state's attorney in a murder prosecution,[152] but in *People v. Farnsley* (1973) that court reiterated: "[i]t has long been held that a trial court is vested with discretion in permitting privately retained counsel to assist a State's Attorney in the trial of criminal case."[153] Illinois courts have also held that criminal contempt proceedings may be instituted by private counsel.[154] For example, Illinois judges have noted that "[a] court's inherent authority to initiate contempt proceedings understandably includes authority to appoint an attorney to represent the public interest in vindication of the court's authority." "In fact," the Appellate Court of Illinois wrote in one case, "the private litigant who brings the facts of an indirect contempt, civil or criminal in nature, before the court, performs a valuable service to the court." In that case, *Del Dotto v. Olsen* (1993), the Appellate Court of Illinois observed: "In the instant case, the criminal contempt of court arose out of a civil matter. Plaintiff's counsel was retained to seek an injunction restraining defendant from harassing plaintiff. After the court entered the order, defendant continued to harass plaintiff. Plaintiff's counsel prosecuted the matter, thereby performing a valuable service to the court."[155]

Indiana: The Supreme Court of Indiana ruled in 1948 that private complainants cannot institute criminal actions.[156] But in *Sedelbauer v. State* (1983),[157] an Indiana appellate court upheld the conviction of an adult bookstore worker for distributing an allegedly obscene film depicting homosexual acts, despite the trial court's decision to allow a member of an anti-obscenity group, Citizens for Decency through Law, to act as the public prosecutor's co-counsel.[158] Indiana has a statute allowing for the appointment of special prosecutors,[159] although the courts will disqualify certain attorneys from serving in that role if there is a conflict of interest or an appearance of impropriety.[160] In 2009, the Court of Appeals of Indiana observed that "appointment of a special prosecutor may be required if the elected prosecutor will be a witness in the case, or if the elected prosecutor has a special interest in the outcome of the case."[161]

Iowa: The Supreme Court of Iowa, which once took note of America's colonial practice of trials being "informal affairs prosecuted by private parties,"[162] has long held prosecutors have special responsibilities.[163] In a recent case, the state's supreme court observed: "Prosecutors have a special role in our criminal justice system. A prosecutor is not an ordinary advocate, at least in the sense that 'a prosecutor owes a duty to the defendant as well as to the public.' Although a prosecutor should zealously and lawfully advocate on behalf of the state, 'the prosecutor's primary interest should be to see that justice is done, not to obtain a conviction.'"[164]

More than fifty years ago, in 1970, the Iowa Supreme Court—in *State v. Ronek*—held that a statutory provision that no prosecution for adultery could be commenced except on the injured spouse's complaint was not violative of any constitutional right of the defendant.[165] That statutory provision, no longer on the books, read: "Every person who commits adultery shall be imprisoned in the penitentiary not more than three years, or be fined not exceeding three hundred dollars and imprisoned in the county jail not exceeding one year; and when the crime is committed between parties only one of whom is married, both shall be punished. No prosecution therefor can be commenced except on the complaint of the husband or wife."[166]

Much more recently, in an Iowa Supreme Court case, *Venckus v. City of Iowa City* (2019), Justice Brent Appel wrote a separate opinion—concurring in part and dissenting in part—in which he discussed the state's history of private prosecutions. As Justice Appel recounted that history:

> In Iowa, public prosecutors have worked alongside private prosecutors since before the 1857 constitutional convention. At the constitutional convention, Mr. Harris noted that, oftentimes, private prosecutors were employed to initially present a case to a magistrate, after which they "let the matter go into court, when the State will take charge of it. They look to the prosecuting attorney to take charge of it in the courts." The framers discussed the ineptitude of some county attorneys and debated whether district attorneys would be preferable. Mr. Harris noted that the people of his district "desired only to see the law faithfully executed," while Mr. Gillaspy emphasized that incompetent public prosecutors had cost the state enough "to build a railroad from one end of the State to the other."[167]

Kansas: A statute in Kansas, adopted in 1901[168] but still on the books, authorizes private counsel to appear in criminal cases for the prosecution. That law provides:

> [T]he prosecuting witness in any criminal action or proceeding may, at his own expense, employ an attorney or attorneys to assist the county attorney to perform his duties in any criminal action or proceeding under any of the laws of the state of Kansas, and such attorney or attorneys shall be recognized by the county attorney and court as associate counsel in such action or proceeding, and no prosecution shall be dismissed over the objection of such associate counsel until the reason of the county attorney for such dismissal, together with the objections thereto of such associate counsel, shall have been filed in writing, argued by counsel, and fully considered by the court.[169]

A prior Kansas law, appearing in the session laws of 1885, read:

> Any citizen may employ an attorney to assist the county attorney to perform his duties under this act, and such attorney shall be recognized by the county attorney and the court, as associate counsel in the proceedings; and no prosecution shall be dismissed over the objection of any such associate counsel, until the reasons of the county attorney for such dismissal, together with the objections thereto, of said associate counsel, shall have been filed in writing, argued by counsel, and fully considered by the court.[170]

In fact, private attorneys have appeared in Kansas criminal cases for the prosecution. For example, in *State v. Baker* (1991),[171] the Kansas Supreme Court addressed the issue of whether the defendant's right to a fair trial was violated where it was alleged that an assistant private prosecutor exceeded the scope of his involvement permitted by Kansas law.[172] Noting that the attorney hired by the victims' families was an "assistant prosecutor," rather than a "special prosecutor," under Kansas law,[173] the *Baker* court held that an assistant prosecutor "may take an active role in the proceedings, and need not confine himself to taking notes and advising the district attorney . . . ."[174] The privately retained attorney in *Baker* performed (1) juror voir dire, (2) the direct and redirect examination of his client, (3) the direct and cross-examination of the psychiatric expert witnesses relative to the defendant's insanity defense, (4) the cross-examination of the defense witnesses, and (5) the second half of the State's closing argument. Rejecting the defendant's contention that the privately retained attorney was acting as the state's "lead" counsel,[175] the *Baker* court affirmed the defendant's conviction for, among other things, first-degree murder and kidnapping.[176]

Likewise, in *Pabst v. State* (2008), the Supreme Court of Kansas considered the case of Tod A. Pabst, convicted of premeditated first-degree murder in the shooting death of his finacée, Phoebe Harkins. Pabst's first conviction, in 1997, had been overturned by the state supreme court, but for the retrial that took place in 2000, the victim's attorney hired a private attorney, Pedro Irigonegaray, to act as associate counsel to assist the public prosecutor pursuant to Kansas Statute § 19–717. Irigonegaray actively participated in the retrial of the murder case even though, at the time, he was also employed to assist with civil litigation that would be impacted by the criminal trial's outcome. At that retrial, the jury again convicted Pabst of premeditated first-degree murder, and in 2002, the Kansas Supreme Court affirmed that conviction. In the 2008 case, the Kansas Supreme Court was considering the denial of Pabst's motion for post-conviction relief after an evidentiary hearing.[177]

At the evidentiary hearing, both Pabst and Irigonegaray testified—as did Assistant Attorney General Stephen Maxwell, the lead prosecutor. As the Kansas Supreme Court summarized Irigonegaray's and Maxwell's testimony:

> Irigonegaray related that he was retained by the victim's sister and parents to be an associate to the attorney general's office under K.S.A. 19–717 to assist with

> the prosecution of the murder trial. Irigonegaray admitted that he represented the victim's sister and her husband in a termination of parental rights and adoption case involving Pabst's child. At the time of the criminal retrial, Pabst had filed a motion to set aside the termination, and Irigonegaray was involved in the case. Irigonegaray's office was also involved in other civil cases involving the victim's family which were at least prompted by the murder, albeit the record is not altogether clear on the details of those cases or the extent of Irigonegaray's involvement.[178]
>
> Although Irigonegaray admitted involvement in the civil cases, he denied that he ever used information from the civil cases to gain an advantage in the criminal trial. However, he did admit that the murder conviction had some impact on the attempt to set aside his client's adoption of Pabst's child. Further, Irigonegaray did use the fact that Pabst had filed two civil cases involving property to argue for a hard 40 sentence based on murder for financial gain, although the sentencing court rejected the argument and refused to impose the enhanced minimum sentence.
>
> Assistant Attorney General Stephen Maxwell testified on the State's behalf, acknowledging that he was the lead attorney on the case and had assigned the handling of several parts of the trial to Irigonegaray. Specifically, he assigned Irigonegaray the opening statement, 7 out of 25 State witnesses, 1 or 2 of the defense witnesses, and a portion of the closing argument. However, Maxwell asserted that he controlled the case and everything that Irigonegaray did on the case was subject to Maxwell's prior approval.[179]

After that evidentiary hearing, the district court found that defense counsel knew of the potential conflict of interest issue but failed to timely object or raise the issue. The district court also reviewed cases that dealt with prosecutors facing a conflict of interest. The district court found Pabst's case to be distinguishable from the others, mainly because Pabst did not seek disqualification before the trial court and because Irigonegaray was not the sole or controlling prosecutor, but instead participated under the direct supervision of Stephen Maxwell, the assistant attorney general. The district court also concluded that it is not structural error when a private attorney has a conflict of interest "unless the private attorney effectively controlled critical prosecutorial decisions." The district court found that, under the facts of the case, any error that may have occurred was subject to harmless error analysis.[180]

In reviewing the district court's decision, the Kansas Supreme Court addressed Pabst's argument that the private attorney's alleged conflict of interest violated Pabst's rights under the U.S. Constitution's Due Process Clause. The state supreme court first noted that "Pabst's initial complaint about being placed in a position to be prosecuted by the victims is refuted in some measure by a specific statute authorizing a victim to be represented in the prosecution," namely Kansas Statute § 19–717. "It is noteworthy," the court pointed out, "that the statute contemplates that the outside attorney will be employed and paid by the prosecuting witness, obviously suggesting an attorney/client relationship between the victim and one of the prosecutors." As the court also observed of the statutory language: "Further, leave of court is not required, but rather the judge, as well as the county attorney, 'shall' recognize the victim's attorney as an associate prosecutor. Moreover, the victim's employment of an associate counsel places some restrictions on the county attorney's discretion to dismiss the case, which is ordinarily unrestrained."[181] In specifically rejecting Pabst's due process argument, the court had this to say:

> While the argument that concurrently serving two masters is a per se violation of defendant's due process rights has surface appeal, it dissipates upon closer scrutiny. First, defendant is not one of the clients that is directly subjected to the alleged divided loyalties; the alleged conflict is between the private attorney's duty to the victim on the one hand and to the State of Kansas on the other. Except to the extent that Pabst may be a beneficiary of the duties Irigonegaray owed to the State of Kansas, his own legal representation was not conflicted....
>
> Secondly, with or without employed counsel, a victim is involved in the criminal prosecution. Granted, we have said that a complaining witness is not a party in the criminal action. However, the legislature has clearly indicated that the views and concerns of a victim should be considered by the court under appropriate circumstances. See K.S.A. 74-7333 (creating a bill of rights for victims of crime). Moreover, this State has created a crime victims compensation fund, K.S.A. 74-7332, which recognizes that victims may be entitled to financial redress as a result of the defendant's actions. Obviously, that redress may well be sought through a separate civil action.
>
> Finally, K.S.A. 19-717 appears to implicitly set up an inherent conflict, regardless of the existence of concurrent civil litigation. As noted, the statute provides for the prosecuting witness to employ and pay for the "associate counsel." With regard to the loyalties owed because of that employment, we have said "[a]n attorney is obligated to act in the best interests of his or her client which, in the case of an attorney hired pursuant to K.S.A. 19-717, is the complaining witness who retained the attorney's services." Yet, *Dressel* also recognized that an attorney retained by the victim pursuant to K.S.A. 19-717 is "hired to *assist* the prosecution." As such, the *Dressel* court found the victim-retained associate counsel in that case to be subject to at least a portion of the ethical rules explicitly applicable to prosecutors, then designated as DR 7-103 and currently contained in Rule 3.8 of the Kansas Rules of Professional Conduct (KRPC) (2007 Kan. Ct. R. Annot. 525). *Dressel* recognized that the "peculiar role of an attorney who is privately retained by a complaining witness to assist in a criminal prosecution" would necessitate compromise and a balancing of the interests the attorney represents.

> Given that K.S.A. 19–717 implicitly authorizes a serving-two-masters scenario, we cannot find that the associate counsel's concurrent representation of the victim in a separate civil action creates a per se violation of the defendant's due process rights.[182]

The court in *Pabst*—applying the harmless-error rule—found "that Pabst has failed to establish that any conflict of interest that Irigonegaray may have had as a result of concurrently representing the victims in civil matters substantially affected the criminal prosecution so as to impair Pabst's right to a fair trial."[183] In *Pabst v. McKune* (2011), the U.S. Court of Appeals for the Tenth Circuit also held that the participation of a privately-retained attorney in the prosecution did not constitute a due process violation.[184]

Kentucky: In *Earl v. Commonwealth* (1978), the Court of Appeals of Kentucky held that it was not prejudicial error in a manslaughter prosecution for a private attorney employed by a victim's family to participate by assisting the commonwealth's attorney. In that case, the court emphasized: "A line of early cases in this Commonwealth held that privately employed attorneys may participate in trial of the Commonwealth's cases if done with the assent of the Commonwealth's attorney. Indeed, as early as 1864, the state's highest court held that the employment of private counsel to assist the public official was not against public policy."[185] In a more recent case, *Commonwealth v. Hubbard* (1989), the Supreme Court of Kentucky also ruled: "The employment of private counsel to assist the Commonwealth Attorney in the prosecution of a criminal case does not violate the due process clauses of the Fifth and Fourteenth Amendments to the United States Constitution. It has been previously held that it is permissible for the circuit court and the Commonwealth Attorney to permit a private attorney to assist the Commonwealth Attorney in prosecuting a criminal case." The state supreme court in *Hubbard* emphasized, however: "It should be noted that the ethical conduct of any private counsel should be measured by the same standard as applied to the Commonwealth Attorney. Private counsel who undertake the duties of prosecution may not become involved in any civil matter related to the criminal prosecution.[186]

Louisiana: In 1909, the Supreme Court of Louisiana observed that the state's bill of rights "provides that 'prosecutions shall be by indictment or information'" and that the provision's "object and purpose" was "made plain by the simple fact of its being found in the Bill of Rights." "It is," that court said of the provision's intent, "to secure the citizen against prosecution by private citizen, by Governor, or judge, or by any authority other than a grand jury or a district attorney."[187] Article 63 of the Louisiana

Code of Criminal Procedure nonetheless states: "The district attorney may employ or accept the assistance of other counsel in the conduct of a criminal case."[188] Louisiana case law establishes that private counsel may be employed to assist the state's attorney general or a district attorney in the trial of a criminal case.[189] In 1905, the Supreme Court of Louisiana ruled: "[I]t is well settled in this state that the Attorney General or a district attorney may be assisted in a prosecution by private counsel, and it has more than once been held that such counsel, with the permission of the official representative of the state, 'may lead or conduct the prosecution alone.'"[190]

Maine: Maine law allows courts in that state to "dismiss certain criminal prosecutions without the acquiescence of the prosecuting attorney" when the injured party has agreed to the dismissal.[191] Title 15, section 891 of the Maine Revised Statutes, titled "Dismissal on satisfaction of private injury," provides as follows:

1. General rule. When a person is charged with a Class D or Class E crime, or is the subject of a juvenile petition alleging a juvenile crime that would constitute a Class D or Class E crime if the juvenile involved were an adult, for which the party injured has a remedy by civil action, if the injured party appears before the court and in writing acknowledges satisfaction for the injury, the court, on payment of all costs, may dismiss the charge.
2. Exceptions. This section does not apply to the crime or juvenile crime of refusing to submit to arrest or detention as defined by Title 17-A, section 751-A, to any crime or juvenile crime in which the alleged victim is a family or household member as defined in Title 19-A, chapter 101 or to any juvenile who has previously been adjudicated of a juvenile crime or who has previously obtained relief under this section with respect to a juvenile petition.

Another provision of Maine law—as the Supreme Judicial Court of Maine has held—also gives to a citizen having personal knowledge of an indictable offense the opportunity to persuade a superior court justice to be allowed to present evidence to the grand jury so that an indictment can be issued. That provision—Title 15, section 1256 of Maine Revised Statutes—reads in full:

> Grand juries shall present all crimes for which by law they are given territorial authority to indict, and may appoint one of their number to take minutes of their proceedings to be delivered to the attorney, if the jury so directs. When they are dismissed before the court adjourns, they may be summoned again, on any special occasion, at such time as the court directs. Evidence may be offered to the grand jury by the Attorney General, the district attorney, the assistant

> district attorney and, at the discretion of the presiding justice, by such other persons as said presiding justice may permit.[192]

"By the very nature of our criminal system," the Supreme Judicial Court of Maine wrote in *Petition of Thomas* (1981), "the discretion thereby vested in the presiding justice needs to be exercised with the greatest circumspection." Not only must the justice "be satisfied that the petition on its face alleges sufficient facts to demonstrate a probability, or at least a substantial possibility, that the grand jury will be persuaded to indict," but "[i]f the presiding justice is satisfied that the petition is facially persuasive, he must next be satisfied that the public interest will be served by allowing the petitioner to present his case to the grand jury."[193]

Maryland: In Maryland, if a victim wants to pursue a criminal prosecution, a victim can—as a complainant—file an "Application for Statement of Charges."[194] The requisite form, which must include "a statement of facts" within the complainant's "personal knowledge (what you saw or heard, what someone said to you, etc.)," states that the signing individual is applying "for a statement of charges and a summons or warrant which may lead to the arrest" of another individual. The statement of facts must show that "there is probable cause to believe that a crime has been committed and that the defendant has committed it." The "Notice to Applicant for a Charging Document" gives this information to the complainant:

> You are applying for a charging document which may lead to the arrest and detention of the person you are charging. If the commissioner issues a charging document, neither you nor the commissioner may withdraw the charges later. The charge may only be disposed of by trial or by action of the State's Attorney.
>
> You must appear at the trial as a witness. Unless you are excused by the State's Attorney, failure to appear on the date set by the court could result in your arrest for failure to obey a court order.
>
> You are filing the application under oath. Criminal Law Article § 9-503, of the Annotated Code of Maryland makes it a crime to knowingly make a false statement in order to have charges brought or an official investigation started.
>
> Please give as much information as possible about the offense. *This form should enable the judicial officer who reads it to come to conclusions about what has happened. You should explain what you know about what has happened, and how you know it.*[195]

In describing Maryland's criminal justice process and the role of court commissioners, one secondary source puts it this way:

> If the police were not called at all or did not arrest the assailant at the time of the incident, and the victim wants to pursue criminal prosecution, the victim must

see a court commissioner. Commissioners are located in each of the district court buildings or police precincts. Their job is to review citizen complaints, determine if there is probable cause to believe a crime was committed, and, where appropriate, issue a summons or a warrant.

Commissioners are available to the public on a 24-hour basis. However, commissioners have many other duties, some of which, by law, take priority over reviewing citizen complaints. A victim of domestic violence can access a commissioner by going to any on-duty commissioner's office or by telephoning an on-call commissioner. Calling the commissioner's office in advance may give the victim an idea of the best time to see the commissioner. Commissioners also have the ability to issue interim protective orders when the courts are closed in the evenings, on weekends, and holidays. Interim orders can protect victims of domestic violence until the courts reopen.

In some instances, it is advisable to have an advocate or attorney accompany the victim to see the commissioner. Commissioners sometimes charge crimes incorrectly or try to dissuade the victim from pursuing criminal charges. In addition, the victim may have difficulty communicating or writing down their account of the incident. An advocate can help the victim overcome these obstacles.

Before meeting with a commissioner, the client needs to prepare a statement of charges where the client will provide information about the incident. These forms are available at the commissioner's office. The statement of charges should constitute a clear and succinct summary of the incident. It is imperative that the documents be complete and accurate because the complaining witness must swear to the truth of the document. If, at trial, the victim's testimony differs substantially from their sworn statement in the application for statement of charges, the victim will be discredited.

If the commissioner issues a criminal summons, the assailant will be served with the summons, requiring his or her appearance in court. Often the client and their attorney must assist the police in locating the assailant so the summons or warrant can be served. To facilitate matters, the client and their attorney should provide the commissioner and police with contact and location information for the assailant.[196]

Massachusetts: It has been held in Massachusetts that "the right to pursue a criminal prosecution belongs not to a private party but to the Commonwealth."[197] In *Bradford v. Knights* (1998), the Supreme Judicial Court of Massachusetts made this observation: "The right of a citizen to obtain a criminal complaint is itself something of an anomaly, because in modern times the formal initiation and prosecution of criminal offenses is usually the domain of public officials. Accordingly, even where the Legislature has given a private party the opportunity to seek a criminal complaint, we have uniformly held that the denial of a complaint creates no judicially cognizable wrong." "Nonetheless," that court ruled, "the Legislature has allowed private parties to seek criminal complaints in the case of misdemeanors."[198]

In *Commonwealth v. Ellis* (1998), the Superior Court of Massachusetts considered a motion of a criminal defendant, James Ellis, Jr., to disqualify prosecuting counsel after 42 indictments were returned against him. Ellis asserted that the indictments obtained against him violated his right to a "disinterested prosecutor" and invoked the U.S. Constitution's Fourteenth Amendment and Articles 5, 6, 7 and 12 of the Massachusetts Declaration of Rights. In particular, Ellis contended that a legislative scheme, which created an entity known as the Insurance Fraud Bureau ("IFB"), had led to the formation of the Office of the Attorney General's Insurance Fraud Division ("Fraud Division"), and had assessed the insurance industry to fund indirectly the Fraud Division, thereby injecting impermissible private interests into the Fraud Division's prosecutorial decisions. In December 1990, the Massachusetts General Court had enacted a statute authorizing the Automobile Insurers Bureau of Massachusetts ("AIB")—a voluntary, non-profit association of Massachusetts automobile insurance companies—to create the IFB. The AIB represents the interests of those companies in regulatory and rate-making proceedings. The IFB, a private investigatory agency, was established to prevent and investigate fraudulent insurance transactions.

In *Commonwealth v. Ellis*, Ellis sought an evidentiary hearing—a request opposed by the Commonwealth—to attempt to "prove the extent to which the prosecutors are encumbered by private interests and private influence." At the center of the controversy was a $100,000 annual assessment by the Commissioner of Insurance against the AIB to "be utilized by the attorney general for the purpose of the investigation and prosecution of automobile insurance fraud matters referred to the attorney general by said insurance fraud bureau." The legislative enactment at issue in *Ellis* also mandated that the Office of the Attorney General "designate at least one assistant attorney general" devoted "full-time to the investigation and prosecution" of IFB-referred fraud matters. In other words, as the court put it, "the AIB not only paid for the operation of the IFB; it also provided money indirectly to the Office of the Attorney General for the prosecution of insurance fraud." The law was later broadened so assessments would also be used for automobile and workers' compensation fraud matters. "The newly-created Fraud Division," as the court observed, "was to include 'at least' thirteen assistant attorneys general: six to prosecute automobile insurance fraud, and seven to prosecute workers' compensation fraud." Since its inception, the IFB had referred more than 1,200 cases of suspected insurance fraud for criminal investigation, with 369 of those referred to the Office of the Attorney General, 28 to various district attorneys within the Commonwealth, and 11 to the state's U.S. Attorney. The Attorney General had accepted 86% of the IFB's referrals; the district attorneys, on the other hand, had accepted 79% of the referrals, with the U.S. Attorney accepting 91%.

After denying the defendant's request for an evidentiary hearing, the court in *Commonwealth v. Ellis* addressed the motion to disqualify on the merits. As the court summarized the defendant's arguments:

> In support of his motion to dismiss, the defendant argues that St. 1990, c. 338 and its progeny has created a particular relationship between the insurance industry and the Office of the Attorney General; that that relationship, based on a financial as well as an operational symbiosis, infects prosecutorial decisions of the Office of the Attorney General to the extent that such decisions are not made on an impartial and objective basis; that the biased decision to prosecute him and his co-defendants in this case for alleged acts of insurance fraud has deprived him and his co-defendants of certain constitutional and statutory protections against unfair and prejudicial enforcement of the laws of this Commonwealth; and that, for that reason, the indictments in this case should be dismissed. Specifically, the defendant has argued that, in this case, the initiation of a criminal investigation and the subsequent prosecution of charges against him and his co-defendants violate the Due Process Clause of the Fourteenth Amendment; Articles 5, 6, 7, and 12 of the Massachusetts Declaration of Rights; G.L. c. 12, § 30; and the policy of the Commonwealth proscribing discriminatory action on the part of a public prosecutor.[199]

Michigan: In Michigan, "a prosecutor must normally authorize a prosecution" and the prosecutor has "exclusive authority to decide whom to prosecute."[200] "Although the prosecutor alone is granted the discretion to determine whether to prosecute an offender," the Court of Appeals of Michigan ruled in *People v. Williams* (2001), "this is not to say that crime victims do not have rights with respect to the prosecution of their offender." In that case, the court pointed out that Michigan's constitution and the state's Crime Victim's Rights Act enumerate certain rights. "These provisions," the court emphasized, "'were intended to enable victims to be compensated fairly for their suffering at the hands of convicted offenders,'" allowing submission of victim impact statements and requiring, for instance, "notice to the victim about the processing of a criminal case and, if requested, notice of any scheduled court proceedings." "[N]owhere in the laws of this state," the court pointed out, however, "have crime victims been given authority to determine whether the code has been violated or whether the prosecution of a crime should go forward or be dismissed."[201]

The Supreme Court of Michigan has called "a prosecuting officer" a "quasi judicial officer,"[202] and observed decades ago that it was "improper" and "against the policy of our laws" for counsel "retained by private prosecutors, and at their expense, to aid in conducting the prosecution."[203] The Court of Appeals of Michigan has also noted that "[a] special duty is placed upon a prosecutor," and that the prosecutor's responsibilities are different from those of a lawyer in private practice.[204] For purposes of a malicious prosecution action in Michigan, a private person "will be treated as having initiated a prosecution where, 'by false statements, or willful concealment of facts, or improper inducement or pressure on the prosecuting officials,' the private person induced the prosecutor to initiate the prosecution."[205] In the state, private lawyers are permitted to prosecute criminal contempt cases for violation of personal protection orders.[206]

As the Court of Appeals of Michigan held in *In re Contempt of Mitan* (2002):

> [W]e do not believe that due process concerns mandate the adoption of an automatic rule barring the appointment of a party's private counsel to prosecute a contempt action. Under both the federal and state constitutions, U.S. Const, Am 14; Const 1963, art 1, § 17, due process "is flexible and satisfied as long as fundamental fairness is observed." *Genesco, Inc v Michigan Dep't of Environmental Quality,* 250 Mich. App 45, 56; 645 NW2d 319 (2002). Determining whether particular procedures are fundamentally fair, this Court considers "the private interest at stake, the risk of an erroneous deprivation of such interest through the procedures used, the probable value of additional or substitute procedures, and the state or government interest, including the function involved and the fiscal or administrative burdens imposed by substitute procedures." *Dobrzenski v. Dobrzenski,* 208 Mich. App 514, 515; 528 NW2d 827 (1995).
>
> Here, the private interest at stake is significant. In Michigan, a conviction for contempt involving a duty which is no longer within the power of a party to perform is punishable by a fine and imprisonment. MCL 600.1715(1). We find this to be a significant interest. However, we do not believe that the risk of erroneous deprivation of this interest is high. Pursuant to court rule, it is the trial judge who must decide whether a proper showing has been made to institute contempt proceedings. MCR 3.606(A). While this may not "quell concern that prosecution by an interested party may be influenced by improper motives," *Young, supra* at 807, it does provide a procedural safeguard against initiation of a contempt prosecution for reasons other than the seriousness of the accusations, which in turn minimizes the risk that defendant will be erroneously deprived of his property and liberty interest. Further, we believe the value of adopting a blanket rule prohibiting appointment of interested party's counsel is small, especially in the context of the "tremendous fiscal and administrative burdens [that] would result from" such an absolute ban. *Wilson v. Wilson,* 984 S.W.2d 898, 903 (Tenn. 1999). Further, if we were to hold that appointment of an interested party's counsel is per se a due process violation, we believe that given the heavy caseloads that already exist in the offices of Michigan prosecutors, "many citizens would be deprived of the benefits to which they already have been adjudged entitled by state courts and many state court orders would remain unenforced." *Id.* Thus, the goal of reaffirming the authority of our state judiciary

through criminal contempt proceedings would actually be undermined by such a procedure.[207]

Minnesota: The Minnesota Supreme Court has barred prosecutions by private parties. In *State ex rel. Wild v. Otis* (1977),[208] the Minnesota Supreme Court began its opinion: "These consolidated appeals raise the issue of whether a private citizen may commence and maintain private prosecutions for alleged violations of the criminal law. We hold that he may not." In that case, J. J. Wild had requested that the Hennepin and Ramsey County Attorneys—two elected county-level prosecutors covering the Twin Cities of Minneapolis and St. Paul and their surrounding suburbs—approve criminal complaints he'd prepared. After those county attorneys declined to prosecute, Wild had unsuccessfully tried to persuade grand juries to issue indictments before filing complaints himself in an attempt, as a private citizen, to prosecute the defendants. Private prosecutors, the Minnesota Supreme Court ruled, "would entail grave danger of vindictive use of the processes of the criminal law and could well lead to chaos in the administration of criminal justice." Consequently, the state's supreme court dismissed the attempted prosecutions.[209] In 1993, the Minnesota Court of Appeals confirmed that "the prosecuting authority makes the decision to commence and maintain criminal prosecutions" and that "[a] private citizen/victim does not have the unilateral right to start or stop a criminal prosecution."[210]

However, in the State of Minnesota, lawyers at private law firms have been regularly involved in conducting prosecutions. A state legislative auditor's report, looking at prosecutorial practices in 1995, took specific note of "cities using private law firms" (sometimes pursuant to "shared arrangements") to conduct non-felony prosecutions.[211] Cities in Minnesota send out requests for proposals ("RFPs") seeking prosecutorial services from lawyers at private law firms.[212] For example, one RFP sent out by the City of Virginia, Minnesota, in October 2019, included a request for the following "criminal prosecution services" to be provided pursuant to a fixed retainer fee: "Prosecution of all petty misdemeanor, misdemeanor and statutorily delegated gross misdemeanor offenses committed within the corporate limits of the City. This includes all such cases initiated by any law enforcement agency and citizen complaints including but not limited to traffic violations, DWI cases, theft and City code violations." In addition to seeking legal advice for police training and as regards criminal prosecutions, that RFP sought legal work associated with preparing criminal complaints, negotiating and entering plea bargains, and representing the city in court.[213] In the wake of George Floyd's murder in Minneapolis, the law firm of Dorsey & Whitney—Minnesota's largest law firm—ended its decades-long Minneapolis City Attorney's program, under which the law firm's lawyers provided legal services assisting in misdemeanor prosecutions in the City of Minneapolis. In announcing that program's termination, a Dorsey & Whitney statement noted: "Studies demonstrate that prosecution of misdemeanors disproportionately impact the Black community, which was an important factor in Dorsey's decision to end its involvement in Minneapolis prosecutions."[214]

Mississippi: In Mississippi, the Attorney General has the power to employ outside counsel as special assistant attorneys general[215] and special prosecutors are used, including in capital murder cases.[216] For example, in *Jordan v. State* (2005), the Supreme Court of Mississippi reviewed a criminal prosecution in which the death penalty was sought and imposed. There, the petitioner, Richard Jordan, argued in a petition for post-conviction relief that it was error for the special prosecutor to prosecute the case because that prosecutor was not "disinterested" and had "a personal vendetta against him." The state supreme court summarily rejected that argument. The court determined the claim had "already been litigated and is now procedurally barred," noting that the Fifth Circuit had ruled that where special prosecutors are appointed, district attorneys simply must retain "control of the prosecution."[217] In turning aside the petitioner's claim, the Supreme Court of Mississippi emphasized:

> In this petition as on direct appeal, Jordan fails to offer any proof that the Harrison County District Attorney's Office did not retain control over the prosecution of this case. We have already found that during most of the pre-trial hearings and at trial, the District Attorney himself or one of his assistants was always present with the special prosecutor. Likewise, Jordan fails to demonstrate the "prosecutorial vindictiveness" about which he complains. This claim has no merit.[218]

Thus, so long as the public prosecutor maintains control over the prosecution, the use of a special prosecutor in Mississippi will not result in a due process violation.[219] In a prior judicial decision, *Jordan v. State* (2001), involving Richard Jordan's case, the Supreme Court of Mississippi observed that "[w]hile Jordan presents a compelling argument about the conflicts that can arise in having an attorney who takes a personal interest in the case prosecute a criminal action, there is no limit on an Attorney General's ability to appoint" one. In that case, the state supreme court had looked to the Fifth Circuit's decision in *Faulder v. Johnson*,[220] which observed that a district attorney must only "retain control of the prosecution" when special prosecutors are appointed. In analyzing Jordan's appeal, the Supreme Court of Mississippi held that Jordan's claim failed because no proof had been offered that the public prosecutor did not retain such control. "[E]ither the District Attorney himself or one of his assistants," the court found, "were present" with the special prosecutor "during most of the pre-trial hearings and at trial." "There is absolutely nothing in the record," the court added, "on which to make an inference" that the special prosecutor's actions "were not authorized by or under the control of the District Attorney."[221]

Missouri: In Missouri, trial courts may appoint special prosecutors to handle criminal prosecutions when the regular prosecutor is disqualified.[222] As the Missouri statute reads:

> If the prosecuting attorney and assistant prosecuting attorney be interested or shall have been employed as counsel in any case where such employment is inconsistent with the duties of his or her office, or shall be related to the defendant in any criminal prosecution, either by blood or by marriage, the court having criminal jurisdiction may appoint some other attorney to prosecute or defend the cause. Such special prosecutor shall not otherwise represent a party other than the state of Missouri in any criminal case or proceeding in that circuit for the duration of that appointment and shall be considered an appointed prosecutor for purposes of section 56.360.

A prosecutor's disqualification is only called for when the prosecutor has "a personal interest of a nature which might preclude" a defendant from receiving fair treatment.[223]

Interested private prosecutions, however, are forbidden in the state as a result of the Supreme Court of Missouri's decision in *State v. Harrington* (1976).[224] In that case, the defendant was convicted of second-degree murder after a private attorney, hired by the victim's father, assisted in the defendant's prosecution. On appeal, the Supreme Court of Missouri held that "the practice of allowing private prosecutors, employed by private persons, to participate in the prosecution of criminal defendants, is fundamentally unfair."[225] "The modern day prosecutor," the *Harrington* court emphasized, "wields the power of the State's investigatory force, decides whom to indict and prosecute, decides what evidence to submit to the court, negotiates the State's position in plea bargaining and recommends punishment to the court." The court's conclusion: "The entry of a private prosecutor into a criminal prosecution exposes all of these areas to prejudicial influence. We consider such exposure intolerable."[226] In *Harrington*,[227] the state supreme court wrote: "We believe, and hold, that the practice of allowing private prosecutors, employed by private persons, to participate in the prosecution of criminal defendants, is inherently and fundamentally unfair, and that it should not be permitted on retrial of this case or in any case tried after publication of this opinion in the Southwestern Reporter."[228]

Montana: Historically, private prosecutors appeared in Montana.[229] For example, in *State v. Tighe* (1903), the Supreme Court of Montana ruled:

> For nearly 40 years the practice in the territory and state of Montana has been to permit counsel employed and paid by private persons to assist in the prosecution of criminal cases. This practice has amounted to a contemporaneous interpretation of the law, which, in view of the doubt touching the correct solu-

> tion of the question, should not be disturbed or changed by the court. The writer of this opinion, speaking for himself only, thinks the practice is in accord with the law, irrespective of the contemporaneous interpretation. The legislature may abolish the practice. As the matter stands at present, the district courts may, in their discretion, permit such counsel to appear and participate in the trial of criminal actions as assistants to county attorneys.[230]

As a note in the *Montana Law Review* observed in 1966, citing another Montana Supreme Court precedent, *State v. Moran* (1963): "Montana law permits privately compensated counsel to appear, with the court's consent, and assist the county attorney in the prosecution of criminal cases."[231] In 1985, the state's supreme court did cite with approval Canon 7 of the Model Code of Professional Responsibility, which provides that "[t]he responsibility of a public prosecutor differs from that of the usual advocate"; that the prosecutor's duty "is to seek justice, not merely to convict"; and that "the prosecutor has responsibilities different from those of a lawyer in private practice."[232]

Nebraska: The Nebraska Supreme Court has held that "a public prosecutor, acting within the general scope of his official authority in making a determination whether to file a criminal prosecution, is exercising a quasi-judicial and discretionary function."[233] That court has further held that "[a] prosecutor must be an impartial officer, and private prosecutors are not permitted under our law."[234] In 1986, the Nebraska Supreme Court cited with approval Canon 7 of the Model Code of Professional Responsibility, which—as noted—states in part that "[t]he responsibility of a public prosecutor differs from that of the usual advocate" and that "the prosecutor has responsibilities different from those of a lawyer in private practice."[235] Nebraska public prosecutors are permitted to employ private attorneys to assist in prosecutions, but they are employed by the county attorney, not interested private parties.[236] The rule prohibiting interested private prosecutors in Nebraska goes back to the early twentieth century.[237]

Nevada: The Supreme Court of Nevada has held that "the courts should not unnecessarily interfere with the performance of a prosecutor's duties." But that court has also emphasized that "a broader concern in criminal cases that cannot be overlooked" is "the defendant's right to a fair trial."[238] A prosecutor, the Nevada Supreme Court has held, "represents the state and has a duty to see that justice is done in a criminal prosecution."[239] "As representatives of the state," that court observed in *Greene v. State* (1997), "prosecutors have a special, heightened duty of fairness and responsibility, particularly in capital cases."[240]

Notably, Nevada crime victims have certain rights, including, upon request, to be informed by the prosecuting attorney, sheriff or chief of police when the defendant is released from custody at any time before or during the trial and to be told about the final disposition of the criminal case in which the victim is "directly involved."[241] "A court trying a criminal case shall provide victims and witnesses a secure waiting area which is not used by the members of the jury or the defendant and the defendant's family and friends," another provision of Nevada law reads.[242] In a domestic violence case, yet another provision reads, "a witness may designate an attendant who must by allowed to attend the preliminary hearing and the trial during the witness's testimony to provide support."[243] Another right that crime victims are afforded under Nevada law: before a sentence's imposition, "the court shall afford the victim an opportunity to: (1) Appear personally, by counsel or by personal representative; and (b) Reasonably express any views concerning the crime, the person responsible, the impact of the crime on the victim and the need for restitution." A "victim" is defined as (1) "[a] person, including a governmental entity, against whom a crime has been committed"; (2) "[a] person who has been injured or killed as a direct result of the commission of a crime"; and (3) "[a] relative of a person described in subparagraph (1) or (2)."[244]

Under a provision of Nevada's constitution, titled "Rights of victims of crime," every victim of crime in Nevada is afforded certain rights. Among them: "(a) To be treated with fairness and respect for his or her privacy and dignity, and to be free from intimidation, harassment and abuse, throughout the criminal or juvenile justice process."; "(f) To reasonably confer with the prosecuting agency, upon request, regarding the case."; "(g) To reasonable notice of all public proceedings, including delinquency proceedings, upon request, at which the defendant and the prosecutor are entitled to be present and of all parole or other postconviction release proceedings, and to be present at all such proceedings."; "(h) To be reasonably heard, upon request, at any public proceeding, including any delinquency proceeding, in any court involving release or sentencing, and at any parole proceeding."; "(j) To provide information to any public officer or employee conducting a presentence investigation concerning the impact of the offense on the victim and the victim's family and any sentencing recommendations before the sentencing of the defendant."; "(k) To be informed, upon request, of the conviction, sentence, place and time of incarceration, or other disposition of the defendant, the scheduled release date of the defendant and the release of or the escape by the defendant from custody."; and "(*l*) To full and timely restitution." "A victim has standing to assert the rights enumerated in this section in any court with jurisdiction over the case," Article 1, Section 8A of the Nevada constitution declares, adding this caveat: "This section does not alter the powers, duties or responsibilities of a prosecuting attorney. A victim does not have the status of a party in a criminal proceeding."[245]

New Hampshire: The Supreme Court of New Hampshire has held that, in that state, "prosecutions of criminal offenses that are punishable by imprisonment can only be initiated by public prosecutors." "When presented with evidence of criminal offenses punishable by imprisonment," the state supreme court ruled, "prosecutors possess the sole authority to decide whether and whom to charge, the classification of the offense charged, and whether to offer a plea bargain."[246] That court has also held: "Although a criminal contempt proceeding may be initiated and prosecuted by a private attorney, the private attorney must be disinterested. A private attorney who represents the beneficiary of a court order cannot prosecute a criminal contempt action arising from that order."[247] In *State v. Martineau* (2002), the supreme court noted that "no statute or court rule" in the state "either expressly permits, or expressly prohibits, private prosecutions by either an interested party or an interested party's attorney." That court, however, held that "[t]he common law of this State does not preclude the institution and prosecution of certain complaints by private citizens."[248]

In *Martineau*, the state supreme court noted that "[p]rior to the adoption of the New Hampshire Constitution in 1784, jurisdiction of certain criminal cases of minor importance was conferred upon justices of the peace." It then observed that New Hampshire's 1784 constitution included a provision stating: "All the laws which have heretofore been adopted, used, and approved, in the province, colony, or state of New Hampshire, and usually practiced on in the courts of law, shall remain and be in full force, until altered and repealed by the legislature; such parts thereof only excepted, as are repugnant to the rights and liberties contained in this constitution."[249] Although the court found that private prosecutions "continue to exist as a matter of New Hampshire common law," the court—after reviewing reported decisions involving private prosecutors—found that such "private criminal prosecutions" (*e.g.*, catching trout out of season, dog leash law violations) arose in classes of cases imposing penalties no more severe than a fine.[250] In holding that "the common law does not authorize private prosecutions of criminal offenses which may be punished by imprisonment," the court emphasized of private prosecutions that it was "cognizant of the dangers they pose both to the rights of criminal defendants and to the sound administration of justice."[251]

New Jersey: In New Jersey, a state rule—Rule 7:8-7(b)—permits prosecution of criminal complaints by private attorneys in municipal courts,[252] although New Jersey's courts have not permitted "private prosecutions for serious criminal charges" since "at least 1901."[253] "The court," Rule 7:8-7(b) reads, "may permit an attorney to appear as a private prosecutor to represent the State in cases involving cross-complaints."[254] "Such private prosecutions may be permitted to appear on behalf of the State," that rule continues, "only if the court has first reviewed the private prosecutor's motion to so appear and an accompanying certification submitted on a form approved by the Administrative Director of Courts."[255] If a private attorney does not comply with the certification requirements, a municipal court conviction can be voided and a new trial ordered.[256] Municipal courts, the Supreme Court of New Jersey has emphasized, must "strictly enforce Rule 7:8-7(b)" because that rule "has the beneficent purpose of ensuring that quasi-criminal actions brought in the name of the State proceed in a disinterested manner."[257]

In New Jersey, legal challenges have been brought to the use of private prosecutors for failures to comply with the provisions of Rule 7:8-7(b).[258] In *State v. Storm*, the Supreme Court of New Jersey held in 1995 that, in that state, whenever a private party's attorney applies to prosecute a complaint in the municipal court, the court should determine whether to permit the attorney to proceed.[259] That case noted that "[t]he challenge is to respect the defendant's right to a fair trial while preserving the contribution of private prosecutors to the disposition of complaints in the municipal courts," with the court noting that "municipal courts provide a safety value for society" by encouraging "the peaceful resolution of disputes." In that case, the state supreme court also observed:

> The overarching argument against private prosecutors is the risk they pose to a defendant's right to a fair trial. A private prosecutor's dual responsibilities to the complaining witness and to the State breed numerous problems.
>
> Representation of the complainant in a related civil action could invest the prosecutor with a monetary interest in the outcome of the matter. That risk is particularly high if the prosecutor has agreed to receive a contingent fee in the civil action. Even in the absence of actual conflict, the appointment as prosecutor of an attorney for an interested party creates the appearance of impropriety.
>
> Conflicting interests, moreover, can undermine a prosecutor's impartiality. The loss of impartiality can affect the prosecutor's assessment of probable cause to proceed; the disclosure of exculpatory evidence; and the willingness to plea bargain. Also implicated are the prosecutor's ethical obligation "to see that the defendant is accorded procedural justice and that guilt is decided upon the basis of sufficient evidence." In addition, private prosecutions pose the risk that the complainant will use the municipal court proceeding to harass the defendant or to obtain an advantage in a related civil action.[260]

In *State v. Storm*, the New Jersey Supreme Court determined that Rule 7:8-7(b) authorizes a municipal court to permit a private attorney to assume the role of a municipal prosecutor (and thus to represent the State in a case) only after determining on the record that certain specific conditions exist and that the attorney has submitted a proper certification.[261] "The New Jersey Supreme Court in *State v. Storm*," a New Jersey federal judge noted shortly after *Storm* was decided, "held that a private attorney wishing to prosecute a criminal action … must disclose in a written certification all facts that foreseeably may affect the fairness of the proceedings." "The relevant facts," that judge noted in summarizing the *Storm* decision, "include the identity of the complainant, indicating (1) whether the complainant is an individual, a business, or an entity with its own police department; (2) any actual conflict of interest arising from the attorney's representation of, and fee arrangement with, the complainant; (3) any civil litigation, existing or anticipated, between the complainant and the defendant; (4) whether the defendant is, or is expected to be, represented by counsel; and (5) any other facts that reasonably could affect the impartiality of the prosecutor and the fairness of the proceedings or otherwise create the appearance of impropriety."[262]

In New Jersey, public prosecutors have considerable discretion and powers.[263] It has been emphasized that "[t]he public policy behind the limitation on who may act as a 'prosecuting attorney' is well-established" and that "[b]ecause they are mandated to ensure the fairness of the process, only prosecutors, as defined in the court rules, are authorized to act in cases that may result in incarceration or other penalties of magnitude."[264] Rule 3.4(g) of the Rules of Professional Conduct states that "[a] lawyer shall not present, participate in presenting, or threaten to present criminal charges to obtain an improper advantage in a civil matter." However, the Supreme Court of New Jersey held in 2019 that "[i]t is not at all inappropriate for private counsel to make a presentation to the prosecutor's office on behalf of a victim." What the public prosecutor does with that information, though, is up to the public prosecutor. As the state supreme court ruled in that case, *In the Matter of Helmer*:

> The prosecutor represents the public and should independently assess the allegations presented. If, in the prosecution's judgment, further action is warranted, prosecutors and law enforcement officers ordinarily conduct an independent investigation. At a minimum, prosecutors have an obligation to review evidence with care and ensure early on that it satisfies the threshold requirement of probable cause.[265]

Other New Jersey judges have also addressed the issue of private prosecution. As one New Jersey superior court ruled in 1998: "[P]rivate prosecution plays an important role in the municipal court system, where, because of the large volume of cases disposed of, public prosecutors limit their involvement for the most part to complaints signed by police officers."[266] "Permitting private citizens to appear either *pro se* or through private attorneys in the municipal courts," that court held, "'facilitates access' to those courts."[267] "Without private prosecution," that court observed, "'some wrongs would not be set right.'"[268] After the New Jersey Supreme Court's decision in *State v. Storm*, a U.S. district court in New Jersey also observed that a "proper application" of New Jersey's rule "requires a court to evaluate the particular circumstances to determine if the private attorney has a conflict of interest which impinges upon a criminal defendant's due process rights so as to prevent the defendant from receiving a fair trial." "If a court finds a conflict," that court ruled, "the appropriate procedure would be to disqualify the private attorney, and if no satisfactory private prosecutor subsequently comes forward, then the court may dismiss the complaint." "This evaluation," the court emphasized, "primarily involves an inquiry into the private attorney's pecuniary or other interest in the outcome of the criminal case and whether the attorney is involved in a related civil case."[269]

New Mexico: In New Mexico, a prosecutor is viewed as "quasi-judicial officer"[270] and may be disqualified if he or she has a conflict of interest.[271] As the Supreme Court of New Mexico, in *State v. Gonzales* (2005), observed of a prosecutor's duties:

> [A] prosecutor represents the public interest, not the private interests of others or the personal interest of the prosecutor. *See generally Hill,* 88 N.M. at 219, 539 P.2d at 239 (listing two situations in which a prosecutor would have a conflict of interest that would preclude appearance before a grand jury). "'[A prosecutor] should represent public justice and stand indifferent between the accused and any private interest.'" *Chambers,* 86 N.M. at 387, 524 P.2d at 1003 (emphasis omitted) (quoting *People v. Gerold,* 265 Ill. 448, 107 N.E. 165, 177 (1914)). Further, a prosecutor must act impartially in the course of a grand jury hearing. *Hill,* 88 N.M. at 219, 539 P.2d at 239. "[H]is methods in procuring [a] conviction must accord with the fair and impartial administration of justice, and he should see that the accused receives a fair trial...." *Chambers,* 86 N.M. at 386, 524 P.2d at 1002 (quoting 2 *Thornton on Attorneys at Law,* § 712 (1914)).
>
> At one time, the ethical code for attorneys included an aspirational goal of avoiding an appearance of impropriety. *See* Flowers, *supra,* at 712–716, 766. While that aspirational goal continues to be part of the Canons of Judicial Conduct, it "was excluded from the Model Rules of Professional Conduct because it was considered to be a vague standard that was inapplicable to lawyers." *Id.* at 766; *see also id.* at 717–18. "Nevertheless, ... the concept remained ... part of the conflict-of-interest analysis...." *Romley,* 908 P.2d at 40, and "trial courts will still need to examine closely the facts of each case with an eye to the ultimate goal of maintaining confidence in the integrity of the judicial system." *Id.* at 41.
>
> Under New Mexico law, prosecutors should not be influenced by private interests. *Hill,* 88 N.M. at 219, 539 P.2d at 239; *Chambers,* 86 N.M. at 387, 524 P.2d at 1003. National standards for prosecutors also provide that a prosecutor's professional judgment should not be affected by personal interests. National District Attorneys Association, National Prosecution Standards § 7.3d (2d ed. 1991) (NDAA Standards); American Bar Association, ABA Standards for Criminal Justice: Prosecution Function and Defense Function § 3–1.3(f) (3d ed.1993). More generally, a lawyer may not allow private interests to adversely affect a client. Restatement (Third) of the Law Governing Lawyers § 125 (2000). For a prosecutor, this means at a minimum that private interests may not adversely affect his representation of the public and pursuit of a fair trial.[272]

A New Mexico statute, § 36-1-19, specifically contemplates the participation of private lawyers in certain criminal cases. As that statue reads:

> A. Except as provided in Subsections B and C of this section, no one shall represent the state or any county thereof in any matter in which the state

or county is interested except the attorney general, his legally appointed and qualified assistants or the district attorney or his legally appointed and qualified assistants and such associate counsel as may appear on order of the court, with the consent of the attorney general or district attorney.

B. Notwithstanding any other provision of law, a board of county commissioners may contract with private counsel for legal assistance to or representation of the county in any civil matter in which the county is interested. Such private counsel shall have the same powers of compromise, satisfaction or release in civil proceedings as are held by district attorneys pursuant to Section 36-1-22 NMSA 1978.

C. The private legal assistance permitted pursuant to Subsection B of this section shall not extend to the prosecution of any criminal action without the permission of the district attorney for that county, provided that such permission shall not be required for the prosecution of any violation of a county ordinance.[273]

In 2005, the Supreme Court of New Mexico noted that, "[i]n municipal court, it is contemplated that the city attorney, a municipal officer, a police officer, or a private citizen will prosecute the violation of a municipal ordinance."[274] However, the current version of Rule 8-111 of Municipal Court Procedures, titled "Non-Attorney Prosecutions," provides:

A. *Law enforcement officers.* Law enforcement officers may file criminal complaints against persons in the municipal court that has jurisdiction over the alleged offense. Criminal complaints shall be limited to charges within the jurisdiction of the court. Law enforcement officers may prosecute misdemeanor criminal complaints they have filed in municipal court, except that no law enforcement officer may prosecute any case that involves a charge of driving under the influence of intoxicating liquor or drugs.

B. *Other authorized prosecutions.* A municipal officer or employee may appear and prosecute any petty misdemeanor proceeding on behalf of the municipality if the municipality has authorized the officer or employee to institute or cause to be instituted an action on behalf of the governmental entity, except that no municipal officer or employee may prosecute through a non-attorney any case that involves a charge of driving under the influence of intoxicating liquor or drugs.

C. *Trial procedures.* In cases where law enforcement officers and non-attorney municipal employees are authorized under Paragraphs A and B of this rule to prosecute complaints they have filed, those officers and employees shall be permitted to testify and present evidence to the court. In the court's discretion, such parties may also ask questions of witnesses, either

> directly or through the court, and may make statements bringing pertinent facts and legal authorities to the court's attention.[275]

"Committee Commentary" to Rule 8-111 notes that there was once a Paragraph D and a Paragraph E to that rule but that they were withdrawn. As the Committee Commentary explains:

> Prior to December 31, 2008, this rule authorized private citizens to pursue criminal prosecutions in municipal court, either on their own or through a special prosecutor. In 2013, the Court withdrew former Paragraphs D and E in recognition of the 2008 amendment, which removed the authority for such private prosecutions. Former Paragraph D was entitled "Special prosecutor" and provided that "[n]othing in this rule shall be construed to allow a private attorney to prosecute a case for any party without first having been duly appointed as a special prosecutor by the city attorney for the municipality in which the court is located." Former Paragraph E was entitled "City attorney" and provided that "[n]othing in this rule shall be construed to prevent the city attorney of the municipality in which the complaint is filed from dismissing the case or entering an appearance and assuming prosecutorial control over the case." Paragraphs D and E are no longer necessary because they addressed the situation in which a private citizen could pursue a criminal complaint through a special prosecutor. The withdrawal of Paragraphs D and E does not preclude a municipality from appointing a special prosecutor to prosecute.[276]

Another New Mexico statute, § 36-1-23.1, allows for the appointment of "Special prosecutors" in conflict-of-interest cases. That provision reads:

> Each district attorney may, when he cannot prosecute a case for ethical reasons or other good cause, appoint a practicing member of the bar of this state to act as special assistant district attorney. Any person so appointed shall have authority to act only in the specific case or matter for which the appointment was made. An appointment and oath shall be required of special assistant district attorneys in substantially the same form as that required for assistant district attorneys in Section 36-1-2 NMSA 1978.[277]

In New Mexico, a properly appointed special prosecutor "is given all the authority and duties of the appointing district attorney to prosecute the case for which that special prosecutor was appointed, including the authority to name another special prosecutor if unable to proceed for an ethical reason or other good cause."[278] A private attorney must be authorized[279] or properly appointed by the district attorney to serve, however.[280]

New York: The State of New York used to regularly allow private prosecutions by interested parties,[281] but there is now a split of authority in the courts of the state as to their propriety. In 2008, in *Sedore v. Epstein*, the New York Supreme Court, Appellate Division, took up the question, "May a District Attorney delegate the prosecution of a criminal action to an attorney retained by the complaining witness?" Its answer: "We conclude that such a delegation is improper ...." "The private prosecution of a criminal complaint has its origins in the trial by combat that was a fixture of early English common law," the court recounted, emphasizing that American courts had "moved away ... from the concept that the criminal law is an instrument of private vengeance" and that the majority of states "have either prohibited the practice altogether or limited the private prosecutor to acting under the control of the public prosecutor."

After remarking that, in New York, "the authority to prosecute a criminal offense generally rests with the local District Attorney, as it has since 1801," the court in *Sedore* observed: "The Criminal Procedure Law defines the term 'prosecutor' as 'a district attorney or any other public servant who represents the people in a criminal action.'" "The broad authority of the District Attorney with respect to the initiation and prosecution of criminal offenses," that court pointed out, "does not mean, of course, that the District Attorney must try every case himself or herself." As the court in *Sedore*, citing various precedents, opined:

> The District Attorney may delegate prosecutorial authority to assistants, as well as to public officials outside the District Attorney's office, such as a state trooper, a deputy sheriff, or a Deputy Town Attorney. In addition, when the District Attorney is unable to appear or is disqualified from proceeding, a superior criminal court may appoint the District Attorney of another county or a private attorney to undertake the duties of the prosecutor.

In finding that "no statutory authority" existed allowed the delegation of authority to an attorney for "the complaining witness" to prosecute the alleged offense, the court in *Sedore* distinguished prior case law and held that "[a]t bottom, the prosecution of a criminal offense is a public function, not a private one."[282] The court in *Sedore*, though, held that the district attorney would not be precluded "from delegating prosecution of the complaint to an attorney outside of his office as long as that attorney has not been retained by the complaining witness."[283]

Sedore is not the only New York case to address the private prosecution issue. In 2010, in *People v. Robinson*, the New York Legal Assistance Group ("NYLAG") filed a Notice of Appearance to formally represent the complaining witness, J.R., in a domestic violence prosecution charging the defendant with first-degree rape. In its application, NYLAG sought to allow a private individual to become a party to a criminal prosecution based on her interests in it. The basis for the motion: Article 23 of the

Executive Law entitled "Fair Treatment Standards for Crime Victims." But the Supreme Court of Kings County, New York, rejected the motion, ruling that nothing in that law "provides for formal appearances by complaining witnesses or private counsel on their behalf in criminal prosecutions." "To the contrary," the court ruled, "the law of this state obligates the district attorney of each county 'to prosecute all crimes and offenses cognizable to the courts of the county for which he shall be elected . . . .'"

The *Robinson* court laid out the status of New York law as regards the handling of criminal prosecutions, which were originally private matters undertaken by the victim.[284] "The courts of this state," the *Robinson* court observed, citing a number of precedents, "have interpreted these provisions to bar private prosecutions of crimes and the delegation of this duty."[285] "In a number of jurisdictions," the *Robinson* court pointed out, "private counsel employed by a complaining witness or by other persons desirous of a conviction are allowed to appear in criminal proceedings or assist in criminal prosecutions either implicitly under common law or explicitly by statute."[286] But the court emphasized: "[T]here is no similar provision in New York Law and any common law right has been abrogated by statute. The only parties to criminal litigation in this state are the people, represented by the district attorney of the county, and the accused, represented by assigned or retained counsel. This is sound public policy and prevents much mischief."[287]

New York law has evolved when it comes to private prosecutions. For example, in *People v. Vial* (1986), the Criminal Court of the City of New York took up this question: "May a Criminal Court Judge authorize and permit the attorney for a complaining witness to act as the prosecutor against a defendant charged with a criminal violation of a petty offense?" Judge Max Sayah's answer: "In a case of apparent first impression, we hold that under the facts of this case the Court acts within its power when it authorizes the People of the State of New York to be represented by a private attorney." In that case, the defendant, James Vial, had been charged with harassment, a penal code violation. It was alleged that on April 29, 1985, at approximately 8:15 p.m. in the lobby of Carnegie Hall during a performance of the Chicago Symphony Orchestra, the complaining witness, James Jones, then "moonlighting" as an off-duty security officer for Carnegie Hall, was tasked with escorting Vial off the premises. Vail was found to be yelling loudly, shouting obscenities, and using foul and abusive language. After Vail hit Jones with his elbow and spat in his face, the altercation escalated and Vial sustained injuries to his nose. After Jones was arrested and charged with assault on the complaint of Vial, Jones requested a judge of the Criminal Court, pursuant to the procedures of the Summons All Purpose Part ("SAP"), to authorize the issuance of a Criminal Court information charging the defendant with harassment in violation of Penal Law § 240.25. Ultimately, the Court directed that James Vial stand trial and authorized Peter Blessinger, an attorney for Jones, to act "in the nature of the private prosecutor" to present the People's case against Mr. Vial. Vial thereafter moved to dismiss the charge on the ground that the court was "without power to appoint the attorney for the complainant as the acting prosecutor."

In his ruling, the presiding judge in *People v. Vial* made these observations:

We note at the outset that for several decades the Criminal Court of New York has staffed a term of the Court known as the Summons All Purpose part (SAP). Through this part pass hundreds upon hundreds of New York citizens charged with a variety of petty offenses. The offenses include traffic violations, "fare beats", sanitation violations, etc, all brought to Court by universal summonses issued by law enforcement personnel. In addition to universal summonses, Criminal Court Judges, under the authority of the New York City Criminal Court Act, Section 50, routinely authorize summonses and informations in this SAP part, based upon the sworn allegations of private citizens who seek redress for criminal acts against them. Often these New York citizens have appeared at local police precincts to register complaints as victims of a crime but are told by the police to seek remedy before the SAP court. The offenses include harassment, assaults, sexual abuse, larceny and a host of other petty crimes.

The District Attorney, either by design, policy or monetary considerations, does not staff this SAP part. Hence, there is no representative of the People to prosecute the thousands of cases before the Court. It is well established that when the District Attorney is aware of a prosecution or a term of the Court in which prosecutions are ordinarily held and he chooses not to appear therein, he is held to acquiesce to prosecution by others. Further by consenting to these Assistant-District-Attorney-unattended prosecutions, the District Attorney appears to relinquish his duty "to conduct all prosecutions for crimes and offenses cognizable by the courts of the county for which he has been elected." Where the charge brought under the SAP procedures is a petty offense and remains in the SAP part, the Court routinely takes guilty pleas, conducts hearings and trials, asks questions, permits complaining witnesses and attorneys to question those charged, and in effect, the entire proceeding, in this so called "People's Court," is generally one of private or court-conducted trial.

Where the docket which has originated in the SAP part charges a misdemeanor and cannot be resolved in this SAP part, the Court policy is to forward the proceedings to an All Purpose part (AP) for the assignment of an Assistant District Attorney. The District Attorney, for the first time, assumes his duty to conduct the prosecution under County Law Section 700. The Assistant District Attorney in the AP part investigates, moves the case to trial, or in many instances, moves the Court to dismiss when the evidence is insufficient to prove the charges beyond a reasonable doubt.

Without question, the District Attorney has the unfettered right and discretion to decide which cases and which crimes are prosecutable. This exercise of discretion may not be interfered with by the Court and remains solely within the province of the District Attorney. However, despite this unfettered right of the District Attorney, when the District Attorney is confronted with a clear conflict of interest, he may not, consistent with his duty to protect the public at large

> from any appearance of impropriety and risk of prejudice to a defendant, move to dismiss a pending case or take any action inconsistent with this intrusion into the proceeding involving his competing or disqualifying interest. It has been established that there exists in this case a conflict of interest on the part of the prosecution.

In its decision in *People v. Vial*, the Criminal Court of the City of New York observed that in *People v. Van Sickle*, where "the prosecution was conducted by the complaining witness who was the alleged victim of an assault," the majority opinion of the New York Court of Appeals "recognized that petty offenses might be prosecuted by attorneys other than the District Attorney, but limited its decision, by holding that a reversal was unwarranted simply because the District Attorney had not appeared." The opinion in the *Vial* case described the concurring opinion of Justice John Van Voorhis in *Van Sickle* as recognizing "that there are certain situations where the charges have not been preferred by public officials and where there is no one but the complaining witness to press the charge which would otherwise be dropped by default." "[A] complaining witness," it was noted in *Van Sickle*, "has prima facie the right to conduct such a prosecution if the District Attorney does not do so, but must abide by the same rules of fairness and of law which would bind a public officer if he were present." In the *Vial* opinion, the judge authoring it, citing *People v. Vlasto* (1974), further noted that "[a] well-reasoned opinion of my colleague, Honorable Alfred H. Kleinman, outlines the history of private prosecution," with the Criminal Court in *Vlasto* observing that "where a defendant is charged with a 'serious' offense, one in which the maximum sentence exceeds six months, only the District Attorney may prosecute." In *Vial*, the Criminal Court ruled as follows:

> While we agree with the reasoning of *Vlasto*, we disagree with its conclusion. We hold that once an information is docketed before the court, the court does not relinquish its jurisdiction simply because a District Attorney refuses to appear. The court has the responsibility of safeguarding both the rights of the accused and the interests of the public in the administration of criminal justice. In addition it has the obligation on its own initiative to correct real or apparent improprieties which would tend to lower the esteem for the system of justice which it is bound to uphold. Where the District Attorney has conceded the existence of a conflict of interest, the Court should constrain itself from dismissing charges brought by a sworn information, for no one has properly investigated the charges. Rather the Court should exercise its inherent power to correct any apparent impropriety.
>
> As we have indicated above, the District Attorney was invited by the Court to either select an Assistant District Attorney from another trial bureau to prosecute the instant case against Mr. Vial or to follow the procedures for the appointment of a Special District Attorney under County Law, Section 701. He declined

both invitations. Accordingly, the Court finds no bar in acting to correct the void created by the self-disqualification of the District Attorney.

We may proceed by one of two methods. This Court may forward the docket to a Supreme Court Justice who is empowered under County Law, Section 701 to order the appointment of a Special District Attorney; or in the alternative, the Court may permit private prosecution of the defendant. After due consideration of all the factors concerning the use of Section 701, we have chosen the latter procedure.

The defendant James Vial is charged with harassment, a violation which is delineated a petty offense .... Were this Court, as is contended by James Vial, obligated to act solely under the dictates of County Law, Section 701 after finding that the District Attorney was disqualified, we would procedurally refer the proceedings to a Supreme Court Justice for the appointment of a Special Prosecutor. The Supreme Court after a referral by this court for a Section 701 Special District Attorney would be duly bound to make such an appointment. It is clear that where the District Attorney, as in the case at bar, seeks to disqualify himself, the burden of proof is sustained merely by a good faith application containing the reasonable grounds for his belief that he is so disqualified. The docket would thereupon be returned for trial before a term of the Criminal Court. Considering the huge case load with which both the District Attorney and the Courts of New York County are burdened, and given the limited nature of staff and trial parts related to this case load, the appointment of a Section 701 Special District Attorney would be unwarranted. We do not believe that the Legislature of this State, in passing County Law, Section 701, sought to bring about a situation as is here presented. If it were intended that in New York County every time there was a traffic offense, a sanitation offense, a peddling offense, a harassment offense or a disorderly conduct offense, that the District Attorney was required "to wheel in his heavy artillery, then the members of the Legislature did not use common sense" and simply did not remember the aged institution of the Magistrate Courts.

As we have shown, the overwhelming weight of authority supports the proposition that the absence of representation by the District Attorney's office neither invalidates a trial nor a conviction, especially where the offense involved is a petty offense. Furthermore, this court cannot close its eyes to the practice that has developed for a century in this State in the Magistrates Courts, and currently in the SAP part, wherein thousands of cases yearly are disposed of either by plea or trial through the vehicle of court-conducted or private prosecution.

We thus hold that the attorney for the complainant James Jones may act as the private prosecutor in the trial of the defendant James Vial.

The Court is mindful that the necessity that the attorney for James Jones act as private prosecutor may itself be considered a conflict of interest, in that a private attorney, hired to pursue an individual's personal claims and interests is

> compelled by the Code of Professional Responsibility to act within the bounds of the law solely for the benefit of his client and free of compromising influences and loyalties. However, the activities of a public prosecutor are held to a different ethical standard in that the prosecutor, as a representative of the state, is mandated by his oath of office to not merely seek to obtain convictions but to seek justice.
>
> This differing standard of ethical conduct may present the private prosecutor with a conflict of competing interests as between the fiduciary duty of partisan loyalty to his client and the more abstract and metaphysical commandment that a prosecutor must pursue simple and impartial justice regardless of its result.
>
> However, no prejudice will lie if the trial court diligently monitors the proceeding with the same rules of fairness and of law which would bind the District Attorney if he were present. This Court is confident that a trial judge hearing this matter will be sensitive to the delicate balance necessary to afford all parties the fundamental fairness and substantial justice that due process requires.[288]

In yet another New York case, *People v. Garfield* (1991), the Justice Court for the Town of Clarkstown, New York, considered a case where the public prosecutor declined to prosecute a matter and the alleged victim of a hit and run became a complainant, seeking to undertake a prosecution. That court noted that two New York cases—*People v. Benoit* (1991) and *People v. Calderone* (1991)—had considered the issue of private prosecution. In *Benoit*, the Criminal Court for the City of New York, Kings County, held section 50 of the New York City Criminal Court Act to be unconstitutional because it allowed a private citizen to commence and maintain a prosecution.[289] In that case, where a landlord brought a private prosecution against a tenant after the district attorney declined to prosecute the tenant, the law allowing private prosecutions was held to violate the Fourteenth Amendment's due process and equal protection clauses and the New York Constitution's due process clause.[290] The court in *Benoit* determined: "The decision to prosecute must rest with professional assistance of duly elected prosecutors who can properly evaluate the merits of the case and who represent the interest of the People of the State of New York." Allowing individuals to use criminal cases to pursue "personal aims," that court noted, "undermines justice and the appearance of justice and it erodes the public's confidence in the criminal justice system." In *Calderone*, the Criminal Court of the City of New York, New York County, similarly held that to allow "private prosecution" by self-interested persons violates "contemporary standards of fair and impartial prosecution." The criminal case at issue there, a prosecution for fourth-degree criminal mischief, was commenced by the law firm of De Maio and Hughes on behalf of the owner of a condominium, Vincent Riso.[291] The defendant was served with the summons and arraigned on the accusatory instrument which alleged that he caused damage to the carpet, walls, and doors of the condominium building in which Riso had an interest.

De Maio and Hughes, the law firm retained by Riso, was also representing Riso in a civil lawsuit against the defendant, a condominium unit owner."[292]

The court in *Garfield* noted that *People v. Benoit* and *People v. Calderone* "detail a change in the case law relative to the issue of private prosecutions," with that court further observing that in *People v. Van Sickle* (1963)[293] the New York Court of Appeals had "upheld a defendant's conviction in a case prosecuted by a civilian complainant" even as the *Van Sickle* decision had "maintained a concern that 'private prosecutors' adhere to the same rules of fairness and law which would bind a public prosecutor."[294] The Criminal Court of the City of New York has been described as "a single, city-wide court,"[295] with summonses typically issued for alleged legal violations by authorized law enforcement agents, most commonly members of the New York City Police Department. For the time period from 2003 to 2013, the number of summonses issued on a daily basis ranged from a high of approximately 1,600 in 2006 to a low of roughly 1,200 in 2013. The New York City Police Department issued more than 97 percent of those summonses. A summons directs the recipient to go to court on a specific date to appear, in most cases, in a special courtroom called the summons part, or in some cases in a community court.[296] As of 2021, the "NYCourts.gov" website provides this information for crime victims: "in a criminal case, you can't bring criminal charges against the person that injured you. You go to the police and the police bring the criminal charges. Criminal cases are handled by a lawyer from the District Attorney's Office on behalf of the People of the State of New York."[297]

In contrast to *Calderone*, in *People v. Clymer* (2010), Judge Howard Aison of the City Court of the City of Amsterdam, New York, ruled that a defendant's accuser could properly prepare and file accusatory instrument without any prior district attorney or police involvement. In that case, the defendant—citing *Calderone* and another case—had moved to dismiss the accusatory instrument, asserting that the accuser had no right to "self charge." But Judge Aison "respectfully" disagreed "with the holding of both cases." In *Clymer*, Judge Aison—explaining his reasoning—wrote this:

> Every accusatory instrument, regardless of the person designated therein as accuser, constitutes an accusation on behalf of the state as plaintiff and must be entitled "the people of the state of New York" against a designated person, known as the defendant. A criminal action is commenced by the filing of an accusatory instrument against a defendant in a criminal court. An information or misdemeanor complaint is a written accusation by a person filed in the local criminal court. A simplified information is a written accusation by a police officer filed in the local criminal court. A prosecutor's information is a written accusation by a district attorney filed in the local criminal court. It is notable, even though the district attorney is solely responsible for prosecuting persons accused of a crime, that the legislature did not limit the filing of an information or misdemeanor complaint to a district attorney or require a district attorney's prior approval be-

fore these accusatory instruments are accepted by the court for filing. A police officer, although under no legal obligation to assist a "walk-in" accuser in preparing and filing an information or misdemeanor complaint, has no authority to prevent an accuser from filing an accusatory instrument directly with the Court as doing so would constitute an interference with the duty given solely to the prosecutor to determine who and in what manner a person should be prosecuted.

Various courts in this state have held that an accuser may prepare and file an information or misdemeanor complaint with a local criminal court without the need of any prior intervention from governmental authorities.

Requiring an accuser to have the district attorney review a complaint before a local criminal court filing would impose a burden on that office requiring the conducting of office interviews with accusers, investigations, and even preparation of the accusatory instrument if the police prior thereto decided not to assist the accuser.

In addition to a malicious prosecution cause of action the accused, charged by an accuser without prior governmental intervention, is secured due process and is protected by various provisions in the Criminal Procedure Law. When a criminal action is commenced in a criminal court a copy of the accusatory instrument shall be promptly transmitted to the appropriate district attorney. This obligation falls upon the police if the police officer is the complainant or has arrested the accused and in all other cases the clerk of the court shall transmit the papers to the district attorney. The Court, after the filing of the accusatory instrument, may issue a summons requiring the accused to appear in Court on some future date giving the district attorney time within which to review the accusatory instrument and determine whether or not it will be prosecuted. The Court, if the accusatory instrument is not sufficient on its face and if the court is satisfied on the basis of available facts or evidence that it would be impossible to draw and file an accusatory instrument that was sufficient on its face, must dismiss the accusatory instrument. Even if the accusatory instrument is sufficient on its face the Court can conduct an inquiry or an examination of witnesses in order to satisfy itself that there is reasonable cause to believe that the accused committed the offense charged. All of these sections establish procedures that contemplate an event whereby an accusatory instrument is filed by an accuser directly with the court.

This Court concludes that an accuser may prepare an accusatory instrument and thereafter file the same with the Court without prior district attorney or police involvement.[298]

North Carolina: The use of private attorneys to assist in criminal prosecutions is said to have existed in North Carolina courts "from their incipiency."[299] For example, in *State v. Moose*,[300] the North Carolina Supreme Court stated that "the law in North Carolina with respect to private prosecutors is clear: absent some evidence that the private prosecutor has in fact ignored the interests of justice in seeking a conviction, his assistance of the public prosecutor is not a per se constitutional violation."[301] That court further observed:

> [T]he defendant's concerns over the "fundamental fairness" of the use of private prosecutors in general are adequately addressed by existing safeguards. Private prosecutors, like all attorneys, are officers of the court, bound by the ethical responsibilities set forth in the Code of Professional Responsibility; guided by statutory rules and case law; and always controlled by the trial judge whose overriding concern is to insure orderly and evenhanded conduct in his courtroom.[302]

Nevertheless, when a North Carolina trial court permits a private prosecutor to be employed,[303] the district attorney must remain in control of the prosecution.[304] Even after the U.S. Supreme Court's decision in *Young*, North Carolina cases have permitted the use of private prosecutors.[305]

In *Whitfield v. Gilchrist* (1998), the Supreme Court of North Carolina—citing legal precedents in the case—specifically observed of that state's legal culture:

> It is important to recognize that there are situations in which a district attorney may obtain the assistance of private counsel. For example, an elected district attorney has the discretion to permit a private attorney to appear with him to represent the State's interest in an action, subject to the court's approval. Historically, however, private counsel functioning in this prosecutorial capacity either have been paid by private parties or have appeared *pro bono publico.* A district attorney's discretion to permit an attorney to act as a private prosecutor on behalf of the State in the prosecution of a particular case does not expressly or implicitly include the authority for the district attorney to bind the State to pay the attorney for performing the historic role of a private prosecutor.
>
> More recently, the General Assembly has expressly provided authority for the State's district attorneys to employ private attorneys to exercise a more expansive prosecutorial power than that historically exercised under our common law by private prosecutors who were empowered to act only in individual cases. N.C.G.S. § 7A-64(2) sets out the mandatory procedure for a district attorney to follow to appoint private counsel to provide temporary assistance when criminal dockets are overcrowded. N.C.G.S. § 7A-64(2) (1995). Approval by the Administrative Officer of the Courts is required before a district attorney may make any such appointment. Significantly, N.C.G.S. § 7A-64 also mandates that "[t]he length of service and compensation of such temporary appointee shall be fixed by the Administrative Officer of the Courts in each case." *Id.*, para. 2. The district attorney has no power to provide for compensation of an attorney appointed under this statute. The statute is public notice that compliance with its terms is required before such an attorney will be compensated by the State.[306]

In a prior case, *State v. Camacho* (1991), the Supreme Court of North Carolina had made this ruling:

> [T]he elected District Attorney may, in his or her discretion and where otherwise permitted by law, delegate the prosecutorial function to others. For example, where the District Attorney consents to the employment of a private prosecutor and continues in charge of the prosecution, the trial court may permit such a private prosecutor to appear for the State. The discretion to permit private prosecutors to appear when the District Attorney consents "has existed in our courts from their incipiency."
>
> More to the point here, N.C.G.S. § 114-11.6 authorizes the several elected District Attorneys of the State to permit the Special Prosecution Division of the Office of the Attorney General to prosecute individual criminal cases in their prosecutorial districts. When that statute is read *in pari materia* with article IV, section 18, of the Constitution of North Carolina, it is apparent that our Constitution and statutes give the District Attorneys of the State the exclusive discretion and authority to determine whether to request—and thus permit—the prosecution of any individual case by the Special Prosecution Division. Therefore, the trial court exceeded its authority and invaded the province of an independent constitutional officer in this case when it ordered the District Attorney to request that the Attorney General prosecute this defendant.[307]

The case of *Person v. Miller*[308] provides a notable illustration of how lower courts have analyzed the constitutionality of private prosecutors. In that case, Bobby Person, a Black citizen of North Carolina, filed a class action suit in 1984 against the Carolina Knights of the Ku Klux Klan ("CKKKK"), and, among others, its leader, Glen Miller. The suit alleged that the defendants had engaged in a series of violent and intimidating acts against Black citizens throughout North Carolina, thereby depriving them of their rights under state and federal law. After the district court certified a class consisting of "all black citizens in the State of North Carolina," the parties to the lawsuit entered into a consent decree in 1985 which, inter alia, prohibited Miller and the CKKKK from "operating a paramilitary organization and doing other acts" prohibited by North Carolina law. During the course of the litigation, Person was represented by Morris Dees, a civil rights lawyer who co-founded and served as the trial counsel for the Southern Poverty Law Center.[309]

In April 1986, Person's counsel, Dees, sought to cite Miller and the White Patriot Organization ("WPO"), the CKKKK's successor organization, for criminal contempt of court. In this respect, Person's complaint alleged that Miller and the WPO had violated the court's order by operating a paramilitary organization and engaging in conduct in violation of North Carolina law. The court initially authorized Dees to prosecute the contempt action.[310] Based upon the court's authorization, Dees actively prepared the case until June 1986. He filed several amendments to the original complaint, moved the court to add various parties as defendants, and conducted discovery.

However, in June 1986, the attorney for Miller moved to have Dees disqualified on the grounds that Dees' appointment violated the North Carolina Rules of Professional Conduct and Miller's due process right to be prosecuted by an impartial prosecutor. Ultimately, the district court ruled that the prosecution of the case must be under the "direct supervision and control" of the United States Attorney's Office, although Dees was authorized to "assist" the United States Attorney's Office "prior to and during the course of the trial."[311] At trial, Dees examined witnesses, participated in both opening and closing argument, as well as made and responded to objections and arguments.[312]

After Miller was convicted of criminal contempt, Miller appealed to the U.S. Court of Appeals for the Fourth Circuit, arguing that Dees' trial participation violated the rule established by the Supreme Court in *Young*. In particular, Miller contended that Dees functioned as "lead" or "primary" counsel, effectively controlling Miller's prosecution. In support of this contention, Miller asserted that (1) "Dees singly conducted the prosecution" until the case was referred to the United States Attorney's Office "some two weeks prior to the original trial date"; (2) "Dees took substantially more time in opening and closing arguments than did government trial counsel"; (3) "Dees examined virtually all the significant witnesses," and (4) "Dees made and responded to most of the objections and arguments at trial."[313] Accepting the accuracy of these assertions regarding the degree of Dees' participation, the Fourth Circuit held that the participation by Dees in the criminal contempt prosecution did not constitute reversible error. According to the opinion of Judge Phillips: "Dees' participation was limited in its total compass to assisting government counsel in a subordinate role."[314]

While acknowledging that the U.S. Supreme Court's decision in *Young* was relevant to the issue of Dees' trial participation, the Fourth Circuit distinguished the *Young* decision. According to the Fourth Circuit:

> *Young* flatly proscribes turning the prosecution completely over to private counsel for interested parties, but it certainly did not proscribe all participation by such counsel. Indeed, and to the contrary, the *Young* Court was at pains to point out that private counsel's greater familiarity with the case might properly "be put to use in assisting a disinterested prosecutor in pursuing the contempt action." The limits of such allowable assistance were also suggested: assistance may not extend to the point that "counsel for the private party is ... in control of the prosecution."[315]

Thus, the *Person* court read *Young* "at least implicitly to approve (or certainly not to forbid) the practice of allowing private counsel for interested parties to participate formally with government counsel in the prosecution of contempt citations" so long as three conditions were met. First, government counsel must have approved private counsel's participation. Second, that participation must consist solely of rendering assistance in a subordinate role. Finally, the participation must not rise "in practice to the level of effective control of the prosecution."[316]

North Dakota: Historically speaking, private attorneys appeared in North Dakota criminal cases in aid of the public prosecutor.[317] For example, in *State v. Kent* (1895), the state's attorney was assisted at the trial by Mr. Nye—a citizen of Minnesota and a member of the Minnesota bar. Nye had been retained by a murdered woman's brothers to assist in the prosecution. He represented to the trial judge that his clients had paid him nothing and had not talked to him about the subject of fees, but that he presumed he would be compensated for his legal services. He was neither employed by the county in which the crime was committed nor by the state's attorney of that county to assist in the prosecution. The state's attorney in open court simply declared that he desired to have Mr. Nye's assistance because he (the state's attorney) was unable, because of physical ailments, to stand the labor and strain of the case without aid. Despite defense counsel's objection, Mr. Nye was allowed to assist in the trial and played "a very active part." On appeal, defense counsel insisted that it was "prejudicial error" for Mr. Nye to participate because he was employed by private persons and not by the public.

In addressing those arguments, the Supreme Court of North Dakota in *Kent* first recounted the fact that, in England, criminal prosecutions had traditionally been "carried on by individuals interested in the punishment of the accused, and not by the public." "The private prosecutor," the court noted of the English practice, "employed his own counsel, had the indictment framed and the case laid before the grand jury, and took charge of the trial before the petit jury." "This system does not prevail in this state," the state supreme court emphasized, observing of North Dakota's practice as it made this ruling:

> Here, in each county, there is a public prosecutor, called the "state's attorney" for that county. It is his duty to prosecute all criminal offenses triable in that county. He is paid a salary for that purpose out of the public funds. He is not allowed to receive any fee or reward from or on behalf of any prosecutor or other individual for services in any prosecution or business to which it is his official duty to attend, nor be concerned as attorney or counsel for either party, other than for the state or the county, in any civil action depending on the same state of facts upon which any criminal prosecution commenced, but undetermined, shall depend. We do not think that this change in policy indicates a purpose to exclude the counsel for interested persons from all participation in the prosecution. Such counsel cannot initiate the proceedings, or conduct them. The control of criminal prosecution has been taken from private hands, and transferred to public functionaries chosen for that express purpose. But there is nothing in the statute to justify the conclusion that counsel employed by interested persons may not assist the public prosecutor, in case he and the trial judge deem this course proper. The fact that the state's attorney who controls criminal cases is not allowed to receive any compensation from private prosecutors for

> the prosecution of a criminal case does not warrant the conclusion that no counsel paid by private persons shall be permitted to assist in the trial of such a case. It is one thing to have the prosecution entirely in the hands of one who may be influenced, because of a retainer, by the strong desire of his client to secure a conviction; but it is an entirely different thing to allow such an interested counsel to aid in the prosecution one who stands affected by no other motive than that of securing the punishment of guilt, and who has absolute control over the case. The law has removed criminal prosecutions from the control of private interests, but it has not excluded such interests from all participation therein. If no error is committed on the trial, we fail to see how an accused can be prejudiced by the fact that those personally interested have employed private counsel to aid the public prosecutor. Certainly, he should not be heard to complain of the zeal of the private counsel, if such counsel has not allowed his zeal to hurry him into error.[318]

Under now-existing North Dakota law, state's attorneys regularly prosecute criminal proceedings and the state's attorney is vested with discretion to initiate those criminal prosecutions.[319] If there is a conflict of interest, though, a special prosecutor may be appointed.[320] Citing case law from other courts, including the U.S. Supreme Court's decision in *Linda R.S. v. Richard D.* (1973),[321] the Supreme Court of North Dakota has held that citizens or victims who are not parties to a criminal action do not have standing to challenge prosecutorial or judicial decisions in the action.[322]

Ohio: A provision of Ohio law, titled "Accusation by affidavit to cause arrest or prosecution," states in part that "[a] private citizen having knowledge of the facts who seeks to cause an arrest or prosecution under this section may file an affidavit charging the offense committed with a reviewing official for the purpose of review to determine if a complaint should be filed by the prosecuting attorney or attorney charged by law with the prosecution of offenses in the court or before the magistrate."[323] Under a prior version of that statute, the Court of Appeals of Ohio observed: "there were two ways that a prosecution could be initiated by a private citizen; the first method was by the filing of an affidavit with a judge or clerk of a court of record, and the second was by filing an affidavit with the prosecuting attorney who, in turn, would file a complaint." By contrast, under the statute's current version, a "peace officer" may still "cause prosecution" by filing an affidavit with a "reviewing official" (*i.e.*, a judge or a prosecutor) or the clerk of a court, but a private citizen to "cause prosecution"—as the Court of Appeals of Ohio in *State v. Jones* (2011) observed—"now must file an affidavit with a 'reviewing official' for the purpose of review to determine if a complaint should be filed by the prosecutor."[324]

Article IV, section 20 of the Ohio Constitution explicitly states: "all prosecutions shall be carried on, in the name, and by the authority, of the state of Ohio; and all indictments shall conclude, 'against the peace and dignity of the state of Ohio.'"[325] As the Court of Appeals of Ohio emphasized in *State v. Luther* (2005): "Although a person may be arrested and temporarily kept in jail on the complaint of a private individual, all criminal prosecutions are brought by the State of Ohio through its various agencies. Thus, in a criminal prosecution, the State of Ohio is the real party in interest, not the complaining witness."[326] While one Ohio statute allows a humane society to appoint attorneys to prosecute violations of law relating to "[p]revention of cruelty to animals,"[327] another Ohio statute states that, for violation of a municipal ordinance, "the magistrate or judge shall not permit prosecution of any criminal case by private attorney employed or retained by a complaining witness."[328]

Oklahoma: The Court of Criminal Appeals of Oklahoma has observed that "the decision whether to prosecute and what charge to file is within the discretion of the prosecutor."[329] In *Driskell v. State* (1983), that appellate court ruled that it was not reversible error for a private attorney to work as an assistant district attorney in a first-degree murder case that resulted in the imposition of a death sentence. In interpreting then-existing Oklahoma statutes, that court emphasized: "If the workload in a district becomes such that a district attorney or his or her assistants cannot manage it, the statutes provide that a district attorney can seek aid from other districts, or from the attorney general." As that court continued: "A district attorney may, of course, employ additional assistants if the need arises, but from the record before this Court it appears that Mr. Jones was employed for the sole purpose of assisting in the prosecution of the appellant. Although it was improper to have employed Mr. Jones as the State did, it was not reversible error. The appellant has failed to establish any prejudice resulting from Steven Jones prosecuting the case."[330]

Multiple Oklahoma cases have addressed the private prosecution issue.[331] In *Reed v. State* (1909), the Criminal Court of Appeals of Oklahoma ruled that "[t]he assistance of private counsel in the trial of criminal cases is not prohibited."[332] A current Oklahoma statute, § 215.4, however, sets out the duties and responsibilities of a district attorney, the designated public prosecutor. As that statute reads:

> The district attorney, assistant district attorneys, or special assistant district attorneys authorized by subsection C of Section 215.37M of this title, shall appear in all trial courts and prosecute all actions for crime committed in the district, whether the venue is changed or not; the district attorney or assistant district attorneys shall prosecute or defend in all courts, state and federal, in any county in this state, all civil actions or proceedings in which any county in the district is interested, or a party unless representation for the county is provided pursuant to subsection A of Section 215.37M of this title; and the district attorney or assistant district attorneys shall assist the grand jury, if required, pursuant to Section 215.13 of this title. The district attorney may at all times request the assis-

> tance of district attorneys, assistant district attorneys, district attorney investigators from other districts, or any attorney employed by the District Attorneys Council who then may appear and assist in the prosecution of actions for crime or assist in investigation of crime in like manner as assistants or investigators in the district.[333]

Oregon: The Supreme Court of Oregon has observed that, in 1864, "certain misdemeanors and lesser felonies could be prosecuted in 'Justices' Courts' rather than circuit courts, following different procedures than the circuit courts followed." "For example," the state's supreme court noted of that Civil War-era time frame in *State v. Swanson* (2011), "criminal matters were initiated in Justices' Courts by means of a private complaint, rather than an indictment, and were prosecuted by the private complainant."[334] Anyone initiating a criminal action by filing a complaint verified under oath became known as a "private prosecutor,"[335] although, in 1923, the Supreme Court of Oregon—citing precedent—accentuated that "[i]t is the duty of the attorney for the state, whether the prosecuting attorney, or private counsel employed to assist that officer, to see that the defendant has a fair and impartial trial."[336] Private parties are still permitted to initiate proceedings in limited circumstances (*e.g.*, for violation of dog control ordinances),[337] but private prosecutions fell out of favor in Oregon decades ago.[338]

Pennsylvania: Private individuals can play a role in criminal prosecutions in Pennsylvania. The prosecution of a private criminal complaint[339] is "initially subject to approval by the district attorney of the county in which the complaint is sought to be brought."[340] Rule 504 of the Pennsylvania Rules of Criminal Procedure, titled "Contents of Complaint," specifically sets forth the required contents of all complaints whether the affiant is a law enforcement or police officer or a private citizen. Rule 504 reads:

> Every complaint shall contain:
>
> (1) the name of the affiant;
> (2) the name and address of the defendant, or if unknown, a description of the defendant as nearly as may be;
> (3) a direct accusation to the best of the affiant's knowledge, or information and belief, that the defendant violated the penal laws of the Commonwealth of Pennsylvania;
> (4) the date when the offense is alleged to have been committed; provided, however:
> (a) if the specific date is unknown, or if the offense is a continuing one, it shall be sufficient to state that it was committed on or about any date within the period of limitations; and

(b) if the date or day of the week is an essential element of the offense charged, such date or day must be specifically set forth;

(5) the place where the offense is alleged to have been committed;

(6)(a) in a court case, a summary of the facts sufficient to advise the defendant of the nature of the offense charged, but neither the evidence nor the statute allegedly violated need be cited in the complaint. However, a citation of the statute allegedly violated, by itself, shall not be sufficient for compliance with this subsection; or

(b) in a summary case, a citation of the specific section and subsection of the statute or ordinance allegedly violated, together with a summary of the facts sufficient to advise the defendant of the nature of the offense charged;

(7) a statement that the acts of the defendant were against the peace and dignity of the Commonwealth of Pennsylvania or in violation of an ordinance of a political subdivision;

(8) a notation if criminal laboratory services are requested in the case;

(9) a notation that the defendant has or has not been fingerprinted;

(10) a request for the issuance of a warrant of arrest or a summons, unless an arrest has already been effected;

(11) a verification by the affiant that the facts set forth in the complaint are true and correct to the affiant's personal knowledge, or information and belief, and that any false statements therein are made subject to the penalties of the Crimes Code, 18 Pa. C.S. § 4904, relating to unsworn falsification to authorities;

(12) a certification that the complaint complies with the provisions of the *Case Records Public Access Policy of the Unified Judicial System of Pennsylvania* regarding confidential information and documents; and

(13) the signature of the affiant and the date of the execution of the complaint.

In turn, Rule 506 of the Pennsylvania Rules of Criminal Procedure, titled "Approval of Private Complaints," states that "[w]hen the affiant is not a law enforcement officer, the complaint shall be submitted to an attorney for the Commonwealth, who shall approve or disapprove it without unreasonable delay."[341]

In Pennsylvania, a criminal prosecutor, unlike a private attorney,[342] "must exercise independent judgment in prosecuting a case and 'has the responsibility of a minister of justice and not simply that of an advocate.'"[343] If the Commonwealth disapproves a private criminal complaint, the complainant can petition the Court of Common Pleas for review. Where a district attorney's denial of the private criminal complaint is based on a legal evaluation of the evidence, it has been noted, the trial court undertakes a *de novo* review of the matter. However, "[w]hen the district attorney disapproves a private criminal complaint on wholly policy considerations, or on a hybrid of legal and policy considerations, the trial court's standard of review of the district attorney's decision is abuse of discretion." As one Pennsylvania court noted of the latter standard: "This deferential standard recognizes the limitations on judicial power to interfere with the district attorney's discretion in these kinds of decisions." "The district attorney's decision not to prosecute a criminal complaint for reasons including policy matters carries a presumption of good faith and soundness," that court emphasized.[344] "The private criminal complainant has the burden to prove the district attorney abused his discretion, and that burden is a heavy one," that court stated, adding:

> In the Rule 506 petition for review, the private criminal complainant must demonstrate the district attorney's decision amounted to bad faith, fraud or unconstitutionality. The complainant must do more than merely assert the district attorney's decision is flawed in these regards. The complainant must show the facts of the case lead only to the conclusion that the district attorney's decision was patently discriminatory, arbitrary or pretextual, and therefore, not in the public interest. In the absence of such evidence, the trial court cannot presume to supervise the district attorney's exercise of prosecutorial discretion, and should leave the district attorney's decision undisturbed.[345]

Rhode Island: In 2001, the Supreme Court of Rhode Island considered whether a superior court had jurisdiction to adjudicate the private prosecution of a criminal complaint. In that case, the defendant, Dr. John Cronan, received a one-year suspended sentence and one year of probation for an assault. The victim-complainant, the doctor's estranged wife, Diane Cronan, had employed a private attorney to conduct the prosecution, during which time the Cronans were engaged in what the state's supreme court described as "a bitterly contested divorce." In affirming the conviction, Rhode Island's highest court noted that a state prosecutor from the attorney general's office had declined to prosecute the case after learning that Mrs. Cronan was prepared to proceed with her own private attorneys serving as the prosecutors for her assault complaint—one which alleged that, during a 1996 argument in their home, the defendant had "yanked her by the arm, shoved her, and kicked her." In its decision, the Supreme Court of Rhode Island pointed to a state law, Section 12-10-12, providing: "Subject to any other provisions of law relative to the filing of complaints for particular crimes, any judge of the district court or superior court may place on file any complaint in a criminal case *other than* a complaint for the commission of a felony or a complaint against a person who has been convicted of a felony *or a private complaint*." The trial court, the state supreme court ruled, "correctly construed" state law "as supportive of the conclusion that private misdemeanor prosecutors are valid in this jurisdiction." "Although an attorney from the Attorney General's office deferred to the complainant's private prosecutors when this case was reached for trial in Superior Court," the state supreme court emphasized, "this event did not cause the court's jurisdiction to lapse."

The Supreme Court of Rhode Island laid out the basis for its holding by examining the Rhode Island Constitution and specific state statutes. "In addition to § 12-10-12, other legislative enactments directly authorize prosecutions by private complaint," the Supreme Court of Rhode Island stressed, observing that while "both the Rhode Island Constitution and the General Laws exclusively confer the power and responsibility to pursue felony indictments and informations upon the Attorney General," various provisions of state law allowed misdemeanors to be prosecuted by complaint. "We are of the opinion," the state supreme court ruled, "that these statutes and constitutional provisions, construed together and in the context of a long history in this state allowing private misdemeanor prosecutions for offenses that can be charged by complaint, evidence a clear legislative authorization for the filing and prosecution of private misdemeanor complaints such as this one—especially in the absence of any contrary statutes or other legal requirements that would preclude such prosecutions." "Neither the General Assembly nor the Rhode Island Constitution has conditioned the Superior Court's subject-matter jurisdiction in misdemeanor cases such as this one upon the Attorney General's prosecution of the case," the state supreme court ruled, adding that the attorney general's office could have intervened to dismiss the case but chose not to do so.

The Supreme Court of Rhode Island thus turned aside the legal challenge to private prosecution in the appeal even as it reserved its prerogative to make a different ruling in another context. "[G]iven the historical and statutory pedigree of private prosecutions in this case, as well as the particular procedural posture of this case, we decline to exercise our supervisory powers to establish a *per se* rule prohibiting private prosecutions like this one," the court ruled. "[P]rosecutions based upon complaints filed by private individuals have a pedigree that stretches back into early English law," the court declared in rejecting the defendant's argument that the court should exercise its supervisory powers to prohibit the misdemeanor private prosecution. Notably, the Supreme Court of Rhode Island also issued this important cautionary note: "Our ruling today does not ignore the possibility that particular private prosecutions might raise legitimate constitutional, discovery, and ethical concerns. And it does not preclude the Attorney General from seeking to assert control over any criminal prosecution, even a misdemeanor charge like this one, that a private complainant has initiated." Making a narrow ruling, the state supreme court emphasized: "All we hold is that the Attorney General's failure to do so in this case did not deprive the Superior Court of jurisdiction to hear and determine the charge."[346]

South Carolina: In *In re Richland County Magistrate's Court* (2010), the Supreme Court of South Carolina held that a non-lawyer's representation of a business to prosecute a criminal misdemeanor charge in magistrate's court constitutes the unauthorized practice of law. In that case, the state's supreme court observed: "The unique nature of criminal law and the corresponding unique role of the prosecutor illustrate the danger in allowing private prosecutions. *Black's Law Dictionary* defines 'criminal law' as '[t]he body of law defining offenses *against the community at large*, regulating how suspects are investigated, charged, and tried, and establishing punishments for convicted offenders.'"[347] "Because a prosecutor is an attorney representing community, rather than private interests, the prosecutor's role is very different from that of a civil attorney," that court stated, adding: "In carrying out his duty, the prosecutor independently decides whether to prosecute, decides what evidence to submit to the court, and negotiates the State's position in plea bargaining. The South Carolina Constitution, South Carolina statutes and case law place the unfettered discretion to prosecute solely in the prosecutor's hands." As the court ruled: "If a private party is permitted to prosecute a criminal action, we can no longer be assured that the powers of the State are employed only for the interest of the community at large. In fact, we can be absolutely certain that the interests of the private party will influence the prosecution, whether the self-interest lies in encouraging payment of a corporation's debt, influencing settlement in a civil suit, or merely seeking vengeance."

In so holding, the state supreme court in *In re Richland County Magistrate's Court* decided: "We find that allowing prosecution decisions to be made by, or even influenced by, private interests would do irreparable harm to our criminal justice system. At the very least, there is 'too much opportunity for abuse and too little motivation for detachment.'" "The convenience and fiscal economy of private prosecution may be facially appealing," the majority opinion in that case observed, "but we must not embrace them at the expense of fundamental fairness and justice." The state supreme court noted that it had "previously permitted persons other than solicitors to prosecute criminal cases in magistrate's court," but it further emphasized of the non-attorneys who had been permitted to do so:

> Though this Court sanctioned the practices of allowing the arresting South Carolina Highway Patrol officer to prosecute traffic-related offenses and licensed security officers to prosecute misdemeanor cases in magistrate's court, such non-attorneys are law enforcement officers acting in the capacity of public officials and are sworn to uphold the law. Consequently, they act on behalf of the State.

Courts are accustomed to distinguishing one case from another, and that's what happened in *In re Richland County Magistrate's Court*. "As a non-lawyer representing a corporation is not a law enforcement officer," the state supreme court emphasized, "we cannot assume that he will act in the interests of the community." "Moreover," that court added, "as a non-lawyer, the representative of the corporation is not bound by professional ethical restraints. Consequently, the non-lawyer prosecutor not only acts on interests other than those of the community but is also not bound by ethical rules, yet his prosecution may result in the imprisonment of the defendant." While a dissent in *In re Richland County Magistrate's Court* contended that the decision represented "a marked departure from prior jurisprudence of this Court," the majority disagreed, saying:

> On the contrary, we rest our decision on centuries-old principles of law.... The dignity and might of the State are brought to bear in decisions to prosecute. These decisions must not be made by interested parties. We therefore find that a non-lawyer's representation of a business entity in criminal magistrate's court runs afoul of South Carolina law, is repugnant to our system of justice and constitutes the unauthorized practice of law."[348]

In a prior case, *State v. Nichols* (1997), the Supreme Court of South Carolina had considered the legality of the participation of three private attorneys hired by the victim's family to prosecute a voluntary manslaughter and criminal conspiracy case. In *Nichols*, the appellant, who had objected to the solicitor's decision to allow that participation, claimed that the participation was unconstitutional. Writing at the tail-end of the twentieth century, the Supreme Court of South Carolina observed that "[p]rivate counsel's participation in a trial to assist the solicitor" had been sanctioned in a number of prior cases, citing precedents from 1986, 1972, 1971 and 1924. The *Nichols* court, in rejecting the appellant's arguments, expressly ruled: "There is no evidence the private attorneys who acted as special assistant solicitors here stood to gain an unfair advantage in the civil matter as frowned upon in *In re Jolly* (1977). Further, the solicitor maintained control of the case. We do not find error in the use of private attorneys here."[349]

South Dakota: Historically, private prosecutors have appeared in South Dakota courts,[350] with one 1925 decision of the state's supreme court expressly allowing private counsel to aid the public prosecutor.[351] But the Supreme Court of South Dakota has also cited Ethical Consideration 7–13 of the Code of Professional Responsibility, which states, among other things, that "the prosecutor has responsibilities different from those of a lawyer in private practice."[352] As the state's supreme court emphasized in *State v. Brandenburg* (1984): "A prosecutor has an overriding obligation, shared by the court, to see that a defendant receives a fair trial. This burden weighs as heavily on prosecutors as it does on judge, jury and defense counsel. In this vein, we must be ever mindful that a prosecutor's duty is not simply to prosecute, but to obtain justice with a fair trial."[353] In *Brandenburg*, which cited Ethical Consideration 7–13, the state supreme court ordered a new trial for a defendant. In particular, it held that it exceeded harmless error to refuse to admit into evidence a secret tape recording in which a special prosecutor told a perjury defendant that defendants in a marijuana cultivation prosecution might lie to get defendant in trouble. In that case, the defendant sought to play the tape to impeach the testimony of the special prosecutor who had testified he did not recall saying that the defendants in the marijuana prosecution might lie.[354]

Tennessee: An existing Tennessee statute provides that "[e]ach district attorney general ... [s]hall prosecute in the courts of the district all violations of the state criminal statutes and perform all prosecutorial functions attendant thereto, including prosecuting cases in a municipal court where the municipality provides sufficient personnel to the district attorney general for that purpose."[355] The Court of Appeals of Tennessee has observed that, in that state, "'a private prosecutor does not control the prosecution'" and that "'[t]his is left in the hands of the District Attorney and of the Court.'"[356] In general contempt proceedings that do not require an indictment, though, "a court may appoint a private prosecutor in such proceedings to vindicate its authority."[357] As in other states, Tennessee courts distinguish between "civil contempt" and "criminal contempt," with a Tennessee judicial decision noting that, while a civil contempt "is remedial in character and is applied when a person refuses or fails to comply with a court order," a criminal contempt "is designed 'to preserve the power and vindicate the dignity and authority of the law and the court as an organ of society.'"[358]

Another Tennessee statute, § 8-7-401, expressly allows the use of privately retained counsel in criminal prosecutions. As that statute reads:

> (a) A victim of crime or the family members of a victim of crime may employ private legal counsel to act as co-counsel with the district attorney general or the district attorney general's deputies in trying cases, with the extent of participation of such privately employed counsel being at the discretion of the district attorney general. The district attorney general or a deputy shall make the final and concluding argument. The privately retained counsel shall immediately inform the district attorney general of such counsel's employment.
>
> (b)(1) No private legal counsel employed as a special prosecutor pursuant to subsection (a) is permitted to participate in any criminal hearing, trial or other proceeding unless the defendant or defendants have been notified and the court has conducted a hearing on such employment as provided in subdivision (b)(2).
>
> (2) At such hearing, the defendant or defendants have the right to be present and to raise and preserve any objections to the employment of such special prosecutor as provided by law. The court shall examine the private counsel to be employed and shall make a specific finding as to whether such person is or is not qualified under the law to serve as special prosecutor and as to whether such person has or does not have a conflict of interest as provided by law.
>
> (3) Any allegations of prosecutorial misconduct or other defects in the trial committed or caused by the special prosecutor shall be raised and disposed of at the time a motion for new trial is made by the defendant.[359]

In *State v. Bennett* (1990),[360] the Tennessee Court of Criminal Appeals held that permitting privately retained prosecutors to assist the district attorney general in a defendant's prosecution did not violate due process or equal protection of the law. In that case, the murder victim's family employed two attorneys to serve as private prosecutors,[361] but Steve Bennett—the defendant—vigorously opposed their use.[362] His objections were ultimately rejected, and a jury convicted him of second-degree murder, resulting in a sentence of 12 years of imprisonment.[363] Bennett raised multiple legal challenges to the private prosecutors, including ones grounded in the Fourteenth Amendment's Due Process and Equal Protection Clauses.[364] The Tennessee Court of Criminal Appeals, however, turned aside those challenges. Tennessee's common law had recognized the right of victims or deceased victims' families to employ private counsel to assist in criminal prosecutions, and the Tennessee General Assembly had enacted a statute in 1978—roughly a dozen years before the *Bennett* case was decided—that codified that common law rule.[365]

In the court's ruling, Judge Jones began by taking note of the history of private prosecution in Tennessee. As Judge Jones wrote: "Prior to 1978, the common law of this State recognized the right of a victim, or the family of a deceased victim, to employ private counsel to assist the district attorney general, or his assistant, in the prosecution of the person who committed the offense against the victim."[366] "In 1978," Judge Jones added, "the Tennessee General Assembly enacted a statute which recognizes the right of a victim to employ private counsel to assist in the prosecution of the accused."[367] In rejecting Bennett's arguments, the Tennessee appellate court ruled: "Contrary to the appellant's contention, the practice of permitting a privately retained prosecutor to assist a district attorney general, or his assistant, does not violate the Fourteenth Amendment to the United States Constitution or the Law of the Land provision contained in Article I, Section 8 of the Tennessee Constitution. Consequently, Tenn. Code Ann. § 8-7-401 is constitutional."[368]

In analyzing the underlying criminal proceeding, Judge Jones—writing for the Tennessee Court of Criminal Appeals—emphasized: "Our review of the record does not reveal that the application of this statute in the case *sub judice* resulted in a depravation of a constitutional right."[369] As Judge Jones further observed: "The private prosecutors did not engage in prosecutorial misconduct. Nor does the record reflect that the private prosecutors represented the family of the victim in a civil case arising out of the occurrence which gave rise to the criminal prosecution."[370] "Also," Judge Jones added, "this was not a contempt proceeding which arose out of a civil prosecution."[371] Rejecting yet another argument relating to the private prosecutor's role in making a summation to the jury,[372] Judge Jones further observed: "[t]he district attorney general maintained control over the prosecution as required by our statute."[373]

Texas: Texas law provides for the use of "special prosecutors," and many private prosecutors have appeared in state criminal prosecutions.[374] As Article 2.01 of the Texas Code of Criminal Procedure states:

> Each district attorney shall represent the State in all criminal cases in the district courts of his district and in appeals therefrom, except in cases where he has been, before his election, employed adversely. When any criminal proceeding is had before an examining court in his district or before a judge upon habeas corpus, and he is notified of the same, and is at the time within his district, he shall represent the State therein, unless prevented by other official duties. It shall be the primary duty of all prosecuting attorneys, including any special prosecutors, not to convict, but to see that justice is done. They shall not suppress facts or secrete witnesses capable of establishing the innocence of the accused.[375]

Article 2.07 of the Texas Code of Criminal Procedure provides for the appointment of either private attorneys or prosecutors from other jurisdictions within the state to take over for the recused or disqualified district or county attorney.[376] In Texas, contempt actions can also be handled by private prosecutors.[377]

Where a special prosecutor is employed, a Texas county attorney "must retain control and responsibility for the prosecution." Control of the prosecution means "control of crucial prosecutorial decisions, including, but not limited to, decisions regarding whether to prosecute, what investigative powers to utilize, and what plea bargains to strike." As the Court of Appeals of Texas stated in *Hartsfield v. State* (2006): "Control of the prosecution is not determined according to quantitative analysis or by simply looking at who was lead counsel at trial; in fact, for tactical reasons, a county attorney can give substantial portions of the conduct at trial to a particularly skilled assistant without relinquishing control." "The rationale for requiring the district or county attorney to retain control of the prosecution," that court underscored, "is to assure that the interests of society in providing justice and a fair trial are not secondary to the interests of private parties who, in some cases, pay fees to special prosecutors."[378] In another case, *Veteto v. State* (2000), the Court of Appeals had this to say where a sexual assault victim's family retained a special prosecutor to assist in the prosecution: "It is well settled that a claim of denial of due process by permitting a privately retained attorney to participate in a criminal prosecution when the district attorney consents and retains control and management of the prosecution is generally without merit." In *Veteto*, that court nonetheless emphasized that "although the use of the special prosecutor was not error in and of itself, it is the conduct of the special prosecutor that has caused the reversal of this judgment." That conduct included impermissibly commenting on the defendant's post-arrest silence.[379]

Utah: Before Utah became a state, the Supreme Court of the Territory of Utah allowed a private attorney, F. C. Goudy, to assist a district attorney in a murder prosecution. In that case, *People v. Tidwell* (1886), Goudy had assisted the district attorney at trial at the district attorney's request—and with the trial court's permission over the defense counsel's objection. Goudy was said to be "employed by the relatives or friends of the deceased." On appeal, the Supreme Court of the Territory of Utah ruled:

> While the objection is supported by high authority, we are of the opinion that the weight is to the contrary, and that the rule generally followed is to leave such permission to the discretion of the court. It often happens that two or more counsel are engaged for the defense, and justice is best promoted by a full and fair presentation of the law and the evidence. The more learning and ability brought to bear on the case, the better. The court should so control the investigations as to prevent oppression and injustice.[380]

Today, to address conflict-of-interest issues that may arise, Utah, like other states, has a statutory mechanism in place for the appointment of special prosecutors. Utah's statute provides in part: "A special prosecutor may be appointed only upon good cause shown and after the supervising judge makes a written finding that a conflict of interest exists in the Office of the Attorney General, the office of the county attorney, district attorney, or municipal attorney who would otherwise represent the state before the grand jury."[381] The statute provides: "In selecting a special prosecutor, the supervising judge shall give preference to the attorney general and assistant attorneys general, county attorneys, district attorneys, or municipal attorneys and their deputies."[382] That statute further states:

> The attorney general, county attorney, district attorney, or municipal attorney may elect to have a special prosecutor appointed by the supervising judge at the expense of the governmental entity supporting the electing prosecutor. Upon receipt of written notice from the prosecutor of that election, the supervising judge shall appoint a special prosecutor in accordance with this section. The electing prosecutor's supporting governmental entity shall reimburse the state for expenses incurred in appointment and compensation of the special prosecutor.[383]

In *Gregory v. Shurtleff* (2013), the Supreme Court of Utah addressed a question of standing to sue, with a concurring opinion observing that before the adoption of the Utah Constitution, it was "widely 'understood [that] the tort action [is] under private control and the criminal action [is] under public control'" and that (although, as factual matter, historical records show otherwise) "[e]arly American courts uniformly proscribed the private prosecution of criminal actions."[384] In so commenting, Justice Thomas Lee—the concurring opinion's author—cited Joel Bishop's *Commentaries on the Law of Criminal Procedure* (1872) that read in part: "In all the States of our

Union, and in the tribunals of the United States, criminal prosecutions are carried on by a public officer, learned in the law, and chosen for this particular purpose."[385] "Concerns about giving private parties control over claims belonging to the general public drove this proscription," Justice Lee wrote, citing a Tennessee case from 1816 for this proposition: "[c]ourts feared that 'leaving prosecutions to every attorney who will take a fee to prosecute' would frustrate '[t]he designs of the constitution' and permit 'the innocent to be oppressed or vexatiously harassed' without 'the responsibility imposed by the oath of the solicitor-general[,] by his selection for the discharge of these duties, [and] by the confidence of the public reposed in him.'"[386] "Early Utah criminal law followed this pattern and confirms that actions by individuals to prosecute public wrongs are not within the judicial power," Justice Lee emphasized, adding: "Utah courts carefully differentiated between the individual-specific harm typical to civil cases and the society-level harm involved in criminal matters. Criminal process was appropriate for the latter, but not for the former."[387]

Vermont: History shows the use of private prosecutions in Vermont, even though by the mid-nineteenth century such prosecutions were already being described as "unusual" and "not looked upon in a favorable view."[388] In 1995, the Supreme Court of Vermont made this observation: "Although, in modern times, certain public officials, particularly the state's attorney elected in each county, have been the exclusive charging authorities, we have in the past recognized the right of private persons to start criminal prosecutions. Private prosecution was rare, however, because it was 'clogged with such conditions.'"[389] The Supreme Court of Vermont, in 1967, recognized an elected prosecutor's authority to retain outside counsel to assist with prosecutorial activities. In that case, *Petition of Dusablon*, it held that a criminal defendant has no right to have the case presented solely by an elected prosecutor. That court emphasized, though, that the appointed attorney "was bound by the same standards of conduct and participation as the duly elected state's attorney whom he was assisting."[390] Rape victims in Vermont are also permitted to participate in criminal cases to determine whether the probative value of evidence outweighs its private character to protect against unwarranted public exposure of personal matters.[391]

In 2017, in an unpublished entry order of a three-justice panel, the Supreme Court of Vermont affirmed a superior court's dismissal of an inmate's declaratory judgment action seeking a declaration that the Chittenden County State's Attorney be compelled to investigate and prosecute Department of Corrections personnel whom he claimed conspired to prolong his prison sentence, thereby keeping him from his son. In 2010, the inmate had pled no contest to a charge of aggravated sexual assault and was sentenced to a term of five-to-fifteen years, which was suspended except for four years. One of the probation conditions was the inmate's completion of a treatment program for sex offenders, but after the inmate threw a wadded up piece of paper at a correctional officer in April 2013 he was terminated from the treatment program and found to have violated the probation condition. After a series of legal battles, the superior court dismissed the inmate's declaratory judgment action in part on the grounds that a state's attorney's decision whether to file criminal charges is discretionary. In affirming that dismissal, a three-justice panel observed that a statute setting forth the duties of state's attorneys "does not compel a state's attorney to prosecute a particular case anytime someone claims that a crime has been committed." "The superior court," the three justices wrote, "correctly concluded that there are no constitutional or statutory grounds for compelling the Chittenden County State's Attorney to prosecute correctional officials in this case."[392]

Virginia: In *Cantrell v. Virginia* (1985),[393] the Supreme Court of Virginia held that an attorney retained by an interested party could not prosecute the case. "A private prosecutor having a civil interest in the case," the court ruled, "so infects the prosecution with the possibility that private vengeance has been substituted for impartial application of the criminal law, that no prejudice to the defendant need be shown." In *Cantrell*, the defendant, William Cantrell, had been convicted in 1983 of first-degree murder and use of a firearm in the commission of the murder of his wife, Judy, and he'd been sentenced to life imprisonment. Cantrell, 29, had claimed at trial that three unidentified men came to his home, knocked him out, tied him up, robbed him, and then murdered his wife with a shotgun after she returned from a night class.[394] At issue on appeal: whether William Cantrell's due process rights were violated when a private attorney, Carl McAfee, employed by the victim's parents, played a dominant role in the prosecution. McAfee was paid more than $10,000.00 for his services, with McAfee saying he'd been employed to "assist the Commonwealth" even though he had not been formally appointed as a special prosecutor, was not paid by the Commonwealth, and had not taken an oath of office. William Cantrell admitted that he had affairs with other women during his nine-year marriage to Judy, although his first trial for the murder of his wife, in 1982, had ended in a hung jury.[395]

Carl McAfee—the private attorney—played dual roles in the aftermath of Judy Cantrell's murder. At William Cantrell's 1983 first-degree murder trial, McAfee acted as lead counsel, examined most of the witnesses, made and responded to motions and objections, and did the closing argument in which he told jurors, "I am speaking to you in behalf of the Commonwealth as a Special Prosecutor for the family of Judy Cantrell." McAfee had also been retained by Judy Cantrell's father in a civil case seeking a change of custody of the Cantrells' only child from the defendant, William Cantrell, to Judy's parents. In appealing his criminal conviction, Cantrell argued that McAfee's involvement in that civil matter gave McAfee a conflict of interest rendering his participation in the prosecution improper to a degree denying Cantrell due process of law. Cantrell also asserted that the murder conviction "would bar his right to inherit from his deceased wife and would set the stage for a wrongful death action against him, all to the benefit of Mr. McAfee and his civil clients." "[T]he role of privately employed prosecutors," Cantrell argued, "developed during a time when Commonwealth's Attorneys were not required to be members of the bar." "[S]ince the adoption of statutory amendments requiring bar membership for Commonwealth's Attorneys," he contended, "all justification for private prosecutors has been eliminated."

The Virginia Supreme Court in *Cantrell*—tasked with resolving the legal challenge—laid out the historical practice of private prosecutions, observing that "[t]he right of a citizen to hire a private prosecutor is rooted in the early common law of England" and that Virginia's judiciary had "approved the practice, expressly or by implication, in many of our earlier cases." Citing a 1934 precedent, *Compton v. Commonwealth*, the *Cantrell* court emphasized of the state's long tradition of private prosecution: "Only one conviction has been reversed because of the participation of a private prosecutor, but the reversal was ordered not because the private prosecutor appeared, but rather because he was in fact employed by the clerk and the sheriff, whose duty was to serve the court impartially." The *Cantrell* court, in reversing William Cantrell's murder conviction,[396] went on to make this modest, somewhat middle-of-the-road ruling: "The policy arguments advanced by the defendant for a total prohibition of privately employed prosecutors may have a sound basis in considerations of public policy, but we think it advisable to leave to the General Assembly such a basic change in the long-established common law of Virginia. Nevertheless, without disturbing the common-law rule which generally permits the appearance of private counsel to assist the prosecution, we conclude that Mr. McAfee's role, in the circumstances of this case, infringed the defendant's right to a fair and impartial trial." The *Cantrell* court emphasized that "[t]he common-law right of a crime victim, or of his family, to assist the prosecution with privately employed counsel is not absolute, but lies with the discretion and continuing control of the trial court"; that "[a] private prosecutor is subject to the same high standard of conduct in the trial of the case as is a public prosecutor" and "is absolutely prohibited from taking any position, making any argument, offering any evidence, or advocating any cause which would be forbidden to a public prosecutor"; and that the private prosecutor's role "is more limited than that of the public prosecutor."

In applying Virginia law to the specific facts of the case, and in deciding to prohibit private prosecutions in at least some cases, Virginia's highest court in *Cantrell* concluded: "A lawyer who represents the victim of a crime, or the victim's family, in a civil case arising out of the occurrence which gives rise to a criminal prosecution, for which he is hired as a special prosecutor, necessarily incurs a conflict of interest. He cannot serve two masters." As the *Cantrell* court characterized the conflict of interest: "His duty to administer the criminal law impartially, in the interest of justice, is essentially a judicial one. He also has undertaken a duty to represent the interests of his civil client with undivided fidelity and zeal. The likelihood of conflict between these two duties rises to the level of an overwhelming probability." "Even in jurisdictions in which the Commonwealth's Attorney is permitted to engage in the part-time practice of law," the court emphasized, "he may not undertake the civil representation of a victim, or the family of a victim, of a crime whose perpetrator he must prosecute." The ruling of the Supreme Court of Virginia was clear: "[T]he position of a private prosecutor having a civil interest in the case so infects the prosecution with the possibility that private vengeance has been substituted for impartial application of the criminal law, that prejudice to the defendant need not be shown. A conflict of interest on the part of the prosecution in itself constitutes a denial of a defendant's due process rights under art. I, § 11 of the Constitution of Virginia, and cannot be held harmless error."[397]

In a subsequent case, *Adkins v. Commonwealth* (1997),[398] the Court of Appeals of Virginia similarly held that the defendant's due process rights to a fair and impartial trial were violated when a participating private attorney—one retained by the victim's family and appointed as a special prosecutor to assist in the prosecution—was initially hired and paid by the victim's family to protect its interests, not those of the Commonwealth. In that case, a grand jury had indicted Kathy Myrtle Adkins for murder and use of a firearm in the commission of the murder. Prior to that indictment, the victim's family had hired David Epling, a private attorney, to assist in the case's prosecution, and Epling had worked closely with an assistant Commonwealth's attorney and participated in the decision to indict Adkins on the charges. While the criminal case was pending, Sheila Tolliver was elected to serve as the Commonwealth's Attorney, but because Tolliver had previously represented Adkins' daughter, filed a motion for leave to withdraw and for appointment of a special prosecutor. Due to Tolliver's conflict, the trial judge granted that motion and appointed Epling—the private attorney—to act as the special prosecutor. A Virginia statute allows for the appointment of an attorney to perform the duties of an attorney for the Commonwealth in the event of a conflict of interest.[399] Counsel for Adkins objected to Epling's appointment, asserting that Adkins "is entitled to a totally independent, objective prosecutor," to which Epling responded that he was no longer being compensated by the victim's family. Although the trial judge made the appointment, saying he considered Epling "a totally independent and impartial prosecutor," after Adkins was tried and convicted, the Virginia Court of Appeals reversed the convictions in light of Epling's conflict of interest.[400]

The topic of private prosecution also came up in Virginia cases after the turn of the century. In *Riner v. Commonwealth* (2003),[401] for example, the Court of Appeals of Virginia approved of the use of a private prosecutor even as it attempted to put safeguards in place. "Whether to allow a private prosecutor to participate in a particular case," the *Riner* court ruled, citing precedent, "'lies within the discretion and continuing control of the trial court.'"[402] "Factual findings related to that decision, like any factual findings made by a trial court," the *Riner* court emphasized, "are binding on appeal unless plainly wrong or without evidence to support them."[403] Still, the Court of Appeals recognized that, under its case law, legal boundaries existed. Quoting *Cantrell v. Commonwealth* (1985), the court in *Riner* explained: "'A conflict of interest on the part of the prosecution in itself constitutes a denial of a defendant's due process rights under art. I, § 11 of the Constitution of Virginia, and cannot be held harmless error.'"[404] "The Supreme Court," the *Riner* court explained of the state supreme court and its interpretation of Virginia law, "has recognized that '[a] lawyer who represents the victim of a crime, or the victim's family, in a civil case arising out of the occurrence which gives rise to a criminal prosecution, for which he is hired as a special prosecutor, necessarily incurs a conflict of interest. He cannot serve two masters.'"[405]

After laying out the governing law, the court in *Riner* then proceeded to analyze whether a conflict of interest precluded the private prosecutor's participation.[406] In that case, the appellant, Charles Riner, was charged with first-degree murder, arson, and petit larceny following the death of his wife (the victim) in 1998 in a fire in the house they shared with their three children. The appellant and the children escaped the fire, but after the fire killed Riner's wife, members of her family attempted to remove Riner as the administrator of the victim's estate and to obtain visitation with or custody of the children. In 1999, after Riner had been removed as administrator of the estate, Riner falsely told school officials he was taking the children to Pennsylvania to attend a funeral but eventually took them to Panama. While Riner was out of the country, a Virginia grand jury indicted him for arson and murder, and he was arrested in Panama and returned to Virginia, where he was later subjected to a superseding indictment for arson, robbery and capital murder.[407] Prior to Riner's trial, the Commonwealth's Attorney moved the court to allow a private prosecutor, Guy M. Harbert, III, retained by the victim's family, to participate in the appellant's prosecution. Over the appellant's objection, the trial court allowed Harbert to participate.[408]

On appeal in *Riner*, the appellant, Charles Riner, argued that private prosecutors should be outlawed. In the alternative, he contended that the specific private prosecutor in his case had conflicts of interest that should have disqualified him from serving in that role, and that the level of his participation exceeded that allowed by the *Cantrell* ruling. On the conflict of interest issue, Riner specifically asserted that Harbert had a conflict because he owed a duty of confidentiality to the Ringleys, the private citizens paying his fee, which conflicted with his duty as a prosecutor to turn over exculpatory evidence.[409] The court in *Riner* ultimately rejected Riner's arguments. "For the same reasons we are not at liberty to prevent the service of private prosecutors," the court ruled, "we must conclude that such a conflict exists neither at law nor under the specific facts of this case." "Because the common law permits the employment of private prosecutors," it determined, "the mere fact that a private citizen, most likely a member of a victim's family or someone with a similarly strong interest in the outcome of a case, pays the private prosecutor's fees does not support the conclusion that the private citizen is a client of the private prosecutor or that the private prosecutor owes any duty of confidentiality to the person who pays his fee."[410] "Here," the *Riner* court ruled, "the evidence supports the trial court's implicit finding that Harbert had no legal relationship with the Ringleys that created a duty of confidentiality or other conflict of interest."[411]

On the issue of the extent of the private prosecutor's participation, the court in *Riner* ruled: "The evidence also supports the trial court's conclusion that Harbert's participation did not exceed the bounds of *Cantrell.*"[412] In *Cantrell*, the Virginia Supreme Court had described a private prosecutor's circumscribed role in assisting the public prosecutor in this way: "His role is more limited than that of the public prosecutor. By the weight of authority, he may not initiate a prosecution or appear before the grand jury; he may appear only by leave of the trial court; he may participate only with the express consent of the public prosecutor; he may make a closing jury argument only in the court's discretion; and he may take no part in a decision to engage in plea bargaining, deciding the terms of a plea bargain, or a decision to accept a plea of guilty to a lesser crime or to enter a *nolle prosequi.*"[413] "Here," the *Riner* court stressed, "appellant makes no claim that the private prosecutor engaged in prohibited activities such as initiating the prosecution or plea bargaining." "Rather," that court summarized appellant's argument, "he contends that Harbert's 'participation dominate[d] the case' and that he impermissibly controlled the arson prosecution, the means by which the Commonwealth proved the murder charge, as well."[414] The *Riner* court found appellant's arguments unpersuasive. "Thus," the *Riner* court concluded, "we affirm both the trial court's decision to allow Harbert's participation and the level to which it permitted Harbert to participate."[415] A federal district court, in *Riner v. Edwards* (2008), also found no due process violation under the circumstances of the case.[416]

In 2020, thirty-five years after *Cantrell*, the Court of Appeals of Virginia, in *Price v. Commonwealth*, took up the subject again, considering whether a state trial court erred in allowing an attorney to serve as a private prosecutor—in that instance, at Mary Price's trial for assault and battery. In that case, the private prosecutor, attorney David Redden, simultaneously represented the victim in a civil matter against Price. Mary Price had been convicted on September 16, 2019, in a Hampton General District Court of a misdemeanor assault and battery of Veronica Drew. Price appealed to the Hampton Circuit Court and a *de novo* trial was held on November 4, 2019, with the Commonwealth's Attorney's Office for the City of Hampton electing "to permit the matter to proceed as a citizen complaint and not to enter an appearance." Redden, the attorney, appeared as a "private prosecutor" on behalf of Drew, the victim. On the day of the Circuit Court trial, Price informed the court that Redden "was representing Ms. Drew in a civil matter" against Price. Price argued that it was a due process violation for a private attorney to act as a prosecutor while "simultaneously representing one of the witnesses in the criminal case in civil litigation against the accused." On that basis, Price moved that Redden "be conflicted out of the case." There was, it was alleged, an "inherent conflict between the role of prosecutor and the role of counsel in a civil case." After Redden observed that Price had filed an initial civil suit against Drew and that Drew had filed a counterclaim against Price, Redden indicated that he wouldn't oppose being removed from the criminal case and having "the Commonwealth stepping in as prosecutor"—something the Commonwealth's Attorney had declined to do. Despite the assertion that a conflict existed that violated the defendant's due process rights, the trial court denied the motion seeking Redden's removal. After a bench trial, Price was convicted and the court sentenced Price to twelve months of incarceration. All but ten days of that sentence was suspended on the condition that Price have no contact with Drew and complete an anger management program.

In *Price v. Commonwealth*, the Court of Appeals of Virginia relied upon the decades-old *Cantrell v. Virginia* precedent as a starting point for its analysis. On appeal, Mary Price—not surprisingly—argued that the private prosecutor's appearance on behalf of the Commonwealth of Virginia violated her due process rights under the U.S. Constitution and Virginia's constitution. Price further asserted that the private prosecutor's "sole control of the prosecution" violated her due process right "to the fair-minded exercise of the Commonwealth's Attorney's discretion." In concluding that "simultaneous representation" created a conflict of interest, and in reversing Mary Price's conviction and sentence, the Virginia Court of Appeals emphasized that the prosecutor's role as "a minister of justice" carried with it "high ethical obligations and a duty of impartiality." As the Court of Appeals put it:

> A Commonwealth's attorney has duties to conduct "the impartial prosecution" of the accused and to ensure that the accused receives a fair trial. The prosecutor is "obligat[ed] to see that the defendant is accorded procedural justice and that guilt is decided upon the basis of sufficient evidence." The prosecutor is ultimately accountable not to any victim but to justice.

Quoting *Cantrell*, the Court of Appeals in *Price* observed that "'[a] conflict of interest on the part of the prosecution in itself constitutes a denial of a defendant's due process rights under art. I, § 11 of the Constitution of Virginia.'"[417] Finding reversible error and the denial of the accused's right to a fair trial, the Court of Appeals determined that the private prosecutor should have been disqualified from participation in the criminal case.[418]

In *Price*, the Virginia Court of Appeals—harkening back to *Cantrell*—observed that Virginia recognizes the "'common-law right of a crime victim, or of his family, to assist the prosecution with privately employed counsel.'" "The overarching principle governing the private prosecutor's participation," Judge William G. Petty wrote for the Court of Appeals in *Price*, "is that 'the public prosecutor must remain in continuous control of the case'" and that "[l]imits on the private prosecutor's authority ensure that the participation of a private prosecutor is only supplemental to the elected official's handling of the case." In laying out the constraints on private prosecutors, though, the Court in *Price* stressed that they may not initiate prosecutions or appear before a grand juries; "may make a closing argument to the jury only if the court, in its discretion, permits it"; and "may not participate in plea bargaining or in 'a decision to accept a plea of guilty to a lesser crime or to enter a *nolle prosequi*.'" "The prosecutor's great power carries with it great ethical obligations," the *Price* opinion declared, citing to a comment to Rule 3.8 of Virginia's Rules of Professional Conduct referencing a prosecutor's duty "to seek justice, not merely to convict." The *nolle prosequi* was a procedural device originally used by England's attorney general to terminate criminal prosecutions, and American criminal law had inherited that practice and nomenclature, with prosecutors often referring to the power to *nol pros.*[419]

The Court of Appeals in *Price*—in the opinion written by Judge Petty—highlighted the ethical obligations of a private attorney taking part in a criminal prosecution. "The prosecutor," the court stressed, "is ultimately accountable not to any victim but to justice." "When privately employed counsel assists the prosecutor," the Court of Appeals further observed, "he takes on the higher ethical obligations of the prosecutor." "Just as the public prosecutor may not entertain divided loyalties between the interests of justice and the interests of a private client," the Court of Appeals stressed, "neither may the private prosecutor attempt the same." As the ruling of the Court of Appeals put it: "All persons who hold the 'distinctive role' given to prosecutors, whether for the duration of one case or for a term of office, must maintain the impartiality befitting the system of justice. In short, if it is forbidden to the public prosecutor, it is forbidden to the private prosecutor." "Thus," the Court of Appeals concluded in *Price*, "when a private attorney steps into the shoes of a public prosecutor, he takes on the ethical obligation to maintain impartiality—an obligation that supersedes any interest of a private client that might conflict with the impartial administration of justice."[420] In noting that Price had asserted "the trial court's refusal to disqualify the private prosecutor violated her due process rights to an impartial prosecutor," the Court of Appeals cited a Virginia's attorney general's opinion from 1995 that recited that the "paramount consideration" in a criminal prosecution is that the prosecution be controlled by "an attorney who is responsible to the public."[421]

In Virginia, to this day, private citizens are allowed to initiate criminal cases. In an article in *Virginia Lawyer*, "Taking the Law into Your Own Hands: Private Criminal Complaints in Virginia," Henry Perritt, Jr. writes in the June 2020 issue: "Virginia is one of about a dozen states that permit an ordinary citizen to put the criminal justice system in motion by filing a private criminal complaint." According to § 19.2-71 of the Virginia Code: "Process for the arrest of a person charged with a criminal offense may be issued by the judge, or clerk of any circuit court, any general district court, any juvenile and domestic relations district court, or any magistrate ...." "However," that statutory section continues, "no magistrate may issue an arrest warrant for a felony offense upon the basis of a complaint by a person other than a law-enforcement officer or an animal control officer without prior authorization by the attorney for the Commonwealth or by a law-enforcement agency having jurisdiction over the alleged offense."[422] As Perritt explains: "A private citizen needs no prior authorization before going to a magistrate for misdemeanor warrants." Noting that "[a] private criminal complaint must be presented to the magistrate in writing," Perritt observes of what happens after a magistrate finds probable cause and issues a summons or warrant: "In practice, a Commonwealth's attorney's office sometimes asks for additional investigation into a case where a misdemeanor warrant was obtained from a magistrate on a private criminal complaint." In 2018, Virginia magistrates issued 110,393 felony arrest warrants and 184,476 misdemeanor arrest warrants, although statistics do not separately track the handling of private criminal complaints.[423]

Washington: Historically speaking, private lawyers employed by crime victims were allowed to assist public prosecutors in the State of Washington[424] and public prosecutors were permitted to simultaneously maintain a private law practice.[425] The Supreme Court of Washington has noted that a judge whose order is violated possesses the power to appoint a private attorney to prosecute the contempt.[426] Conflict of interest issues are of considerable concern, however. For example, the Court of Appeals of Washington has cited with approval a Pennsylvania Supreme Court case, *Commonwealth v. Eskridge* (1992), which held that there was an actual conflict of interest when a prosecuting attorney's private law firm pursued a negligence case arising out of an automobile accident in which the defendant driver had been prosecuted criminally for his role in the accident. "Clearly," the Court of Appeals of Washington emphasized in *State v. Orozco* (2008) of the facts of *Eskridge*, "a conflict of interest arose there because the prosecuting attorney, as a partner in the law firm, would benefit financially from a conviction that could be used as proof in the civil case."[427] The Court of Appeals of Washington, in *State v. Bland* (1998), further distinguished the roles of the public prosecutor and private lawyer, observing in that case that "[a] deputy prosecutor does not represent a 'client' in the traditional sense" and that "the deputy has no financial interest in the outcome of the case."[428]

West Virginia: In West Virginia, a state statute, § 7-7-8, provides: "The prosecuting attorney of each county may ... appoint practicing attorneys to assist him in the discharge of his official duties during his term of office. Any attorney so appointed shall be classified as an assistant prosecuting attorney and shall take the same oath and may perform the same duties as his principal."[429] "If, in any case," that statute further provides, "the prosecuting attorney and his assistants are unable to act, or if in the opinion of the court it would be improper for him or his assistants to act, the court shall appoint some competent practicing attorney to act in that case." "No provision of this section," the statute continues, "shall be construed to prohibit the employment by any person of a practicing attorney to assist in the prosecution of any person or corporation charged with a crime."[430]

The Supreme Court of Appeals of West Virginia has held that "[t]he right to obtain a private prosecutor in this State is not absolute and is subject to judicial control and review." That court also made clear that "[a] private prosecutor is subject to the same high standards of conduct in the trial of the case as is the public prosecutor." Emphasizing that § 7-7-8 "explicitly recognizes the practice" of private prosecution, the court—looking back at the arc of history—noted that the practice had "evolved from the common law, where under old English practice the Crown did not supply a public prosecutor to handle routine felonies," thus forcing "[t]he victim or his family ... to hire counsel to bring the guilty party into the criminal justice system." The court pointed out that § 7-7-8 "does not affirmatively authorize the system of private prosecutors," with "[t]he specific statutory language" constituting "nothing more than a proviso or exception designed to demonstrate that the Legislature did not intend to abolish the common law rule permitting the employment of a private prosecutor."[431]

Consequently, the right to use a private prosecutor is not absolute in West Virginia—the right being subject to judicial control and review.[432] In order to overturn a conviction on appeal, though, a defendant must show that the private prosecutor's misconduct in some way prejudiced the defendant.[433] A defendant is not subject to impermissible "prosecutorial overmatch" simply because a private attorney is retained by the victim's family to prosecute the case against the defendant. As the West Virginia Supreme Court of Appeals stated in *Acord v. Hedrick*: "A mere imbalance between defense counsel and prosecution does not invalidate a criminal trial. Due process of law does not require that every criminal case be prosecuted by a Thomas Dewey, defended by a Clarence Darrow, and tried before a John Marshall."[434]

The Supreme Court of Appeals of West Virginia has determined that "only law enforcement officers and prosecuting attorneys, not private citizens, can file criminal complaints."[435] Also, it's been made clear in West Virginia that an interested party's private attorney is not permitted to prosecute a criminal contempt case.[436] However, the Supreme Court of Appeals of West Virginia previously held that "in cases where a grand jury returns an indictment based on a citizen's complaint and presentation, the attestation of the prosecuting attorney to the grand jury foreperson's signature is not required and the lack of such attestation, standing alone, is insufficient grounds for dismissal of an otherwise authentic indictment."[437] Notably, the current version of Rule 7 of the West Virginia Rules of Criminal Procedure reads in part:

> The indictment or the information shall be a plain, concise and definite written statement of the essential facts constituting the offense charged. An indictment shall be signed by the foreperson of the grand jury and the attorney for the state. An information shall be signed by the attorney for the state. The indictment or the information need not contain a formal commencement, a formal conclusion, or any other matter not necessary to such statement, except that it shall conclude, against the peace and dignity of the state.[438]

Wisconsin: The State of Wisconsin, which has long required that an "impartial" public prosecutor handle criminal cases,[439] has a statute governing the use of "Special prosecutors." That statute, § 978.045, states that "[a] court on its own motion may appoint a special prosecutor ... or a district attorney may request a court to appoint a special prosecutor" under specified conditions. That statute reads in part:

> Before a court appoints a special prosecutor on its own motion or at the request of a district attorney for an appointment that exceeds 6 hours per case, the court or district attorney shall request assistance from a district attorney, deputy district attorney or assistant district attorney from other prosecutorial units or an assistant attorney general. A district attorney requesting the appointment of a special prosecutor, or a court if the court is appointing a special prosecutor on its own motion, shall notify the department of administration, on a form provided by that department, of the district attorney's or the court's inability to obtain assistance from another prosecutorial unit or from an assistant attorney general.

The Wisconsin statute further provides that "[t]he judge may appoint an attorney as a special prosecutor only if the judge or the requesting district attorney submits an affidavit to the department of administration attesting that any of the following conditions exists": (1) "There is no district attorney for the county."; (2) "The district attorney is absent from the county."; (3) "The district attorney, or a deputy or assistant district attorney for the district attorney office, is on parental leave."; (4) "The district attorney has acted as the attorney for a party accused in relation to the matter of which the accused stands charged and for which the accused is to be tried."; (5) "The district attorney is near of kin to the party to be tried on a criminal charge."; (6) "The district attorney is unable to attend to his or her duties due to a health issue or has a mental incapacity that impairs his or her ability to substantially perform his or her duties."; (7) "The district attorney is serving in the U.S. armed forces."; (8) "The district attorney stands charged with a crime and the governor has not acted ...."; or (9) "The district attorney determines that a conflict of interest exists regarding the district attorney or the district attorney staff."[440] In addition, the state statute allows for the appointment of a "special prosecutor" who is designated as a "public service special prosecutor to serve at the pleasure of the district attorney."[441]

Private citizens in Wisconsin can request the filing of criminal charges. In *State v. Unnamed Defendant* (1989), the Supreme Court of Wisconsin held that a "John Doe" criminal proceeding provision did not violate the doctrine of separation of powers and that the initiation of a criminal prosecution in the state is not exclusively an executive branch function. In that case, written by Chief Justice Nathan Heffernan, the state supreme court considered a permissive appeal of an order of the circuit court denying a motion to dismiss a criminal complaint issued after a John Doe proceeding under section 968.26 of the Wisconsin Statutes. That provision of Wisconsin law reads in part:

> (am) If a person who is not a district attorney complains to a judge that he or she has reason to believe that a crime has been committed within the

judge's jurisdiction, the judge shall refer the complaint to the district attorney or, if the complaint may relate to the conduct of the district attorney, to another prosecuting under § 978.045.

(b) If a district attorney receives a referral under par. (am), the district attorney shall, within 90 days of receiving the referral, issue charges or refuse to issue charges. If the district attorney refuses to issue charges, the district attorney shall forward to the judge in whose jurisdiction the crime has allegedly been committed all law enforcement investigative reports on the matter that are in the custody of the district attorney, his or her records and case files on the matter, and a written explanation why he or she refused to issue charges. The judge may require a law enforcement agency to provide to him or her any investigative reports that the law enforcement agency has on the matter. The judge shall convene a proceeding as described under sub. (3) if he or she determines that a proceeding is necessary to determine if a crime has been committed. When determining if a proceeding is necessary, the judge may consider the law enforcement investigative reports, the records and case files of the district attorney, and any other written records that the judge finds relevant.

(c) In a proceeding convened under par. (b), the judge shall subpoena and examine under oath the complainant and any witnesses that the judge determines to be necessary and appropriate to ascertain whether a crime has been committed and by whom committed. The judge shall consider the credibility of testimony in support of and opposed to the person's complaint.

(d) In a proceeding convened under par. (b), the judge may issue a criminal complaint if the judge finds sufficient credible evidence to warrant a prosecution of the complaint. The judge shall consider, in addition to any testimony under par. (c), the law enforcement investigative reports, the records and case files of the district attorney, and any other written reports that the judge finds relevant.[442]

In *State v. Unnamed Defendant*, the Supreme Court of Wisconsin noted of the state's law that "[f]rom the days of the Wisconsin Territory until 1945, the statutes allowed only magistrates to issue criminal complaints." The state supreme court then emphasized: "From 1945 to 1969, either a magistrate or a district attorney could charge. Only in 1969 did section 968.02(3) give district attorneys the primary power to charge criminal offenses." After observing that "[t]he provision for a John Doe criminal proceeding to commence criminal prosecution has been in the Wisconsin statutes since territorial times," the court stressed that "the John Doe proceeding has remained, substantially unchanged, in our statutes for over one hundred and fifty years." "The salient aspect of the John Doe proceeding for the purpose of this case—judicial initiation of criminal prosecution—has never appeared to be considered to be inconsistent with the doctrine of separation of powers," the court ruled.

The constitutionality of Wisconsin's statute was upheld, with the court analyzing various provisions of state law. But Chief Justice Heffernan—the former U.S. Attorney for the Western District of Wisconsin from 1962 to 1964 who served on the Wisconsin Supreme Court from 1964 to 1995—wrote a concurring opinion to the majority opinion in which he offered this perspective:

> As the author of the majority opinion, I agree with it and join it; but I cannot but feel a sense of unease over the validation of secs. 968.02(3) and 968.26, Stats., when viewed from a public policy aspect. I therefore write additionally in concurrence. The criminal law reform undertaken by the Criminal Rules Committee of the Judicial Council had as one of its purposes the elimination of the last vestiges of the pernicious practice of private prosecutions by persons who owe no allegiance to society as a whole. For a general public policy statement, see *State v. Scherr,* 9 Wis.2d 418, 426, 101 N.W.2d 77 (1960) ("It is against public policy and the impartial administration of criminal law for a court to allow attorneys for private persons to appear as prosecutors.") and *State v. Peterson,* 195 Wis. 351, 356, 218 N.W. 367 (1928) ("Our scheme contemplates that an impartial man selected by the electors of the county shall prosecute all criminal actions in the county unbiased by desires of complaining witnesses or that of the defendant.").
>
> Both of the statutes validated herein make it possible for persons to trigger the prosecutorial powers of the state *in any kind of criminal action* where "probable cause" can be established. No consistent prosecutorial policy in respect to the initiation of charges can be maintained under these circumstances. What will be charged can lie within the whim of any complainant. The *de facto* standard for prosecuting attorneys is, in the experience of this writer, but for the exceptional case, not to invoke the awesome power of the state unless the crime in all likelihood can be proved beyond a reasonable doubt. Our imprimatur upon these statutes may well give a gloss that runs counter to the legislative intent of Wisconsin's criminal law reforms. The writer is not unmindful of the predicament of a victim of a crime who is afforded no relief by a recalcitrant prosecutor. It would appear, however, that this situation might better be alleviated by legislative approval of a limited judicial review of a prosecutor's declination to prosecute. See, *State ex rel. Unnamed Petitioners v. Connors,* 136 Wis.2d 118, 134, 142, 401 N.W.2d 782 (1987).[443]

Wyoming: In Wyoming, private lawyers can participate in criminal contempt proceedings[444] and private prosecutions have been permitted even where the death penalty was sought. For example, Gerry Spence—a prominent trial lawyer—famously worked as a special prosecutor in the capital prosecution of Mark Hopkinson.[445]

Hopkinson, a former University of Arizona football player convicted on controlled substances charges in 1971, had returned to his native Wyoming after being released from federal prison. In 1975, he got embroiled in legal disputes in which Vincent Vehar, as an attorney, had played an adversarial role. In 1976, Hopkinson had asked another man about "doing a job for him" that involved "working over" Vehar, with Hopkinson agreeing to pay the man $200. Hopkinson later asked that Vehar be killed and a price of $600 was discussed. After the man had second thoughts and rejected the idea of killing Vehar, Hopkinson turned to others for ideas on how to get rid of Vehar. He ultimately settled on the idea of having a bomb tossed through a basement window of the Vehar home. Hopkinson—to be deposed by Vehar in one of the legal disputes on August 9, 1977—then managed to persuade a young man, Michael Hickey, to throw the bomb into the basement window of that home. Hopkinson had knowledge of prior criminal activity by Hickey, and Hickey later stated that Hopkinson first asked him in early 1977 if he (Hickey) would kill Vehar for $2,000 plus expenses.

With the date of his deposition approaching, a desperate Hopkinson ordered Mike Hickey to bomb the Vehar home on the night of August 6th. After drinking at Bridger Valley's Charolais Inn until 1:30 a.m., getting intoxicated on a fifth of tequila, and meeting up with a women he'd met at a local bar, Hickey acquiesced and carried out Hopkinson's demand. Driving in the middle of the night to the Vehar home, Hickey—under Hopkinson's thumb and almost-cult-like influence—then cased the Vehar home and tossed the bomb into it. The bomb exploded at approximately 3:35 a.m. on August 7th with deadly consequences, killing Vehar, his wife, and one of their children. "Mark Hopkinson was going to pay me and he just kept after and kept after me," Hickey said later, adding: "finally I just did it to get him off my back." Eventually, Hopkinson and Hickey—who were also put on trial for attempting to blow up an Arizona attorney's car,[446] for which Hopkinson (but not Hickey) was convicted and got a 10-year federal prison sentence—were implicated by another young man, Jeff Green, in the bombing of the Vehars' home. The bomb was made with 30 sticks of dynamite.[447] Tragically, the dead, badly mutilated body of Jeff Green—a 23-year-old prospective witness against Hopkinson in the grand jury investigation into the bombing deaths of the Vehar family members[448]—later turned up near an Interstate 80 off-ramp in Bridger Valley. Green's body was discovered on May 20, 1979, just two days before the scheduled opening of the grand jury's investigation into the bombing. As one journalist reported long after that torture-murder: "Authorities would later prove that Hopkinson, from a federal prison in California, orchestrated Green's murder through telephone calls. No one has ever been charged with the actual murder."[449]

In one of his books, Gerry Spence—the nationally renowned attorney—recalled his role as a private prosecutor in the Mark Hopkinson case. "I remember when, in my own state of Wyoming, I, as a special prosecutor, asked for the death penalty in a case. The defendant was guilty, all right. Killed four people, an old country lawyer, his wife, their fifteen-year-old son, and my star witness. The killer was Mark Hopkinson." As Spence described the killing of his star witness:

> Hopkinson hired some thugs to "do" our witness, as that ilk likes to say. Our witness, a tall, gangly kid named Jeff Green—looked like an adolescent Ichabod Crane—knew the whole story on Hopkinson, how he had hired another ranch kid to blow up the lawyer and his family. Used dynamite the kid's father had stored on his ranch to blow out the beaver dams that plugged up the creek. The thugs, hired by Hopkinson to "do" Green, took him to the prairie, burned out his eyes while he was still alive, burned his body with cigarettes—a "T" for traitor on his chest—burned his genitals, and then shot him and left him on the prairie for us to find him.

The prosecution of Mark Hopkinson—the man who'd left southwest Wyoming's Bridger Valley after accepting a college football scholarship only to reappear in the state after suffering a knee injury—attracted considerable press attention because of the defendant's notoriety and the grave nature of the charges. The Hopkinson murder trial began in September 1979, with one reporter describing Hopkinson as "a handsome, 29-year-old former Arizona college player."[450] Spence, who called Hopkinson a "master manipulator" who "charmed" others into carrying out his wishes,"[451] had taken on the special prosecutor role at the request of the district judge and the victims' family. "The local prosecutor had been intimidated by the defendant—his family threatened," Spence recalled, noting that the lawyer Hopkinson ordered to be killed "was Vince Vehar, one of my old friends, and his brown-eyed wife, Beverly, and their young son, John, a high school football star." As part of the prosecution team and in light of the circumstances, Spence was given special security and protection.[452] "So," Spence offered, explaining his participation in the case, "I was only doing what the state, the judge, the surviving family, and the people in Fort Bridger wanted." As for compensation, Spence said this of his work in the capital murder prosecution: "I worked pro bono, except the judge ended up giving me, as my fee, the judge's antique chair. Always admired the chair. You don't take money to do work like that, I thought. You do it because it has to be done."[453] In exchange for agreeing to testify against Hopkinson, Hickey—then 23 years old—got a 20-year prison sentence and a promise of a new name to protect himself from future harm at Hopkinson's hands.[454] As the U.S. Court of Appeals for the Tenth Circuit later put it: "Hickey testified under a grant of full immunity for the Vehar murders. In exchange for his testimony, Hickey was also assured that if he decided to plead guilty to murdering Kelly Wyckhusye, the court would accept a plea to second degree murder and sentence him to twenty to twenty-one years in prison." It was Hickey's murder of Wyckhusye, a teenage girl, that Hopkinson had knowledge of prior to the bombing of the Vehar home—knowledge that the manipulative Hopkinson used to convince Hickey to carry out that heinous act.[455]

At the trial, Gerry Spence had sought a death sentence for Hopkinson,[456] the athlete turned local businessman, with the *Billings Gazette* reporting at the trial's start: "Special Prosecutor Gerry Spence vowed … he will prove former Urie clothier Mark Hopkinson committed 'the most heinous and unbelievable series of murders that have ever been committed in this state.'"[457] In a trial that involved an alleged offer of $20,000 for perjured testimony but at which Hopkinson offered no witnesses in his defense,[458] Gerry Spence (as the *Casper Star-Tribune* later put it) "produced testimony showing Hopkinson had a grudge against Vehar—counsel for the local sewer district—for blocking Hopkinson's efforts to obtain cheap sewer hookups for a trailer park in Bridger Valley."[459] In his closing, Spence "spent 4½ hours painstakingly reconstructing the complex sequence of events[460] that led to the 1977 bombing deaths of the Vincent Vehar family followed by the tortured [d]eath of Jeffrey Green and culminating in the four-count murder trial of Mark Hopkinson." "'What once was a complex case has become a simple case of murder,' Spence pounded into the jury," a Jackson Hole newspaper reported of the trial lawyer's spell-binding closing statement. The jury deliberated 7½ hours before finding Hopkinson guilty on all four counts of first-degree murder and two counts of conspiracy to commit murder.[461] "Prosecutors quoted the Bible in urging the death penalty," one media outlet reported,[462] with Hopkinson—dressed in blue jeans and a checkered sport coat—getting three consecutive life sentences for ordering the bombing of the Vehar home and a death sentence for procuring Jeff Green's murder. Choking back tears as he addressed jurors during the trial's penalty phase, Hopkinson said: "I'm not asking for my life but I'm not going to tell you I want to die."[463]

While still maintaining his innocence after hearing his adjudicated fate, Mark Hopkinson held a 35-minute post-sentencing press conference at which he told reporters: "I think I have met the master and I don't think the man should be allowed in court, he is so good, and that's Gerry Spence."[464] "I think I'm the first man in history to be given the death penalty and never killed anybody," Hopkinson told reporters in the Teton County courtroom. "I met Vincent Vehar a total of three times in my entire life," Hopkinson said, adding, "I feel very sorry for him and his family." *The Billings Gazette* reported that Gerry Spence "was sitting on the prosecution table 10 feet away as Hopkinson spoke, and afterward Spence lambasted Hopkinson's remarks." "A man that's just been sentenced to death has the right to say anything he wants to," Spence observed, but he called Hopkinson's story a lie that—had Hopkinson taken the stand—"couldn't withstand a cross-examination on what he just said."[465] After obtaining the death sentence, Spence—citing other commitments and his faith in the abilities of the Wyoming Attorney General's office—announced a few weeks later that he would not be arguing the state's case in Hopkinson's appeal.[466]

In *The Making of a Country Lawyer* (1996), Gerry Spence wrote about the far-reaching power of prosecutors. "The power of every prosecutor is immense, a power that can destroy both the guilty and the innocent," he said. In fact, years after obtaining Hopkinson's death sentence, Spence asked Wyoming's then governor, Mike Sullivan, to commute that sentence to life imprisonment without parole. In a letter to Sullivan, Spence wrote: "My position as the special prosecutor who tried the case against Mr. Hopkinson has not changed from the date I argued to the jury for the death penalty. I was then and am now opposed to the taking of human life in the name of punishment."[467] But despite Spence's missive, reflecting his genuine after-the-fact circumspection in a criminal case that certainly did not end with the trial Spence had conducted, Wyoming's governor declined to grant a commutation.[468] Hopkinson had first been sentenced to death in 1979, but after a reversal of that sentence, he was sentenced to death again in 1982—and his continual and persistent appeals did not alter that sentence even as he called the case that Spence presented against him "manufactured bullshit."[469]

The Tenth Circuit, in *Hopkinson v. Shillinger* (1989), found that "Hopkinson's motive to kill Vehar had been demonstrated by overwhelming evidence, and his involvement in Vehar's death was established by the testimony of Hickey, the man who actually killed Vehar." "It is difficult to convey in an opinion of reasonable length," the Tenth Circuit's lengthy opinion observed, "the full strength of the prosecution's case against Hopkinson for these murders, but the proof was overwhelming."[470] Although improper statements made by Spence at trial were deemed "not prejudicial" in light of all of the evidence presented, there were still lingering questions that swirled about, and there were calls over the years to reopen Hopkinson's case. Some questions pertained to unsolved crimes, including the precise circumstances of Jeff Green's brutal murder. In 1991, the mother of a 15-year-old murder victim, Kelly Wyckhuyse, whose death prosecutors had linked to the Hopkinson murder case, specifically asked that Hopkinson's execution be delayed until authorities could be assured that the right person was arrested for Kelly's death.[471] Before the bombing of the Vehars' home, the teenage girl had gone missing. Jeff Green, the young man whose tortured body was found with more than 140 burn marks on it along with a gunshot to the neck, had implicated another young man in brutally murdering the young girl and mutilating her genitals. That young man—Mike Hickey—later confessed to the killing of Wyckhuyse, just as he ultimately confessed to bombing the Vehars' home. Hickey told Gerry Spence—as one account notes—"that Hopkinson knew about the murder and promised him an alibi if he killed Vehar."[472] In 1991, Hopkinson himself wrote an open letter to a judge suggesting in a tantalizing manner that he would "release information" to "clearly identify Jeff Green's killers." Hopkinson, facing execution at the hands of the state, called "[t]he entire scenario regarding Jeff Green's murder ... just another Gerry Spence fairy tale" and asserted that Spence "regularly makes a joke of the judicial system." According to Hopkinson's open letter written from the Wyoming State Penitentiary in Rawlins: "Spence should have never been allowed to manipulate himself into special prosecutor in the Vehar and Green cases. Spence has made it impossible for me to ever get a fair trial in Wyoming. Therefore, I will not release the above referred to information I have without certain guarantees from the governor."[473]

But such guarantees from the governor never came. After the Supreme Court of Wyoming rejected the final appeals of Hopkinson and his petition for a writ of habeas corpus fell on deaf ears,[474] the U.S. Court of Appeals for the Tenth Circuit considered—and rejected—Hopkinson's prosecutorial misconduct claims in 1989. The Tenth Circuit found that some of Hopkinson's allegations of misconduct lacked merit, but it said it was "troubled" by other statements Gerry Spence made in his closing argument. "The prosecutor," the Tenth Circuit noted, "also alluded to his own friendship with murder victim Vehar, and he incorporated personal observations of Vehar's character." Finding "improper argument" and that portions of Spence's argument "exceeded the bounds" of what was permissible, the Tenth Circuit determined that statements by Spence amounted to "testimony by the prosecutor as to matters outside the record." That was "particularly egregious" and "improper," the federal appellate court said, because Spence offered his "personal opinion on the merits of the case." "Despite this repeated, and, at times, serious prosecutorial misconduct, we will not disturb Hopkinson's convictions," the Tenth Circuit nonetheless ruled. "In the instant case," it determined, "we do not believe that the prosecutor's improper arguments, when viewed in the context of the entire trial, affected the fundamental ability of the jury to weigh the evidence fairly."[475] The U.S. Supreme Court itself refused to hear Mark Hopkinson's appeals,[476] and Hopkinson was ultimately executed by lethal injection in 1992.[477] "It was very painful for me because I hate the death penalty," Spence later said of the capital case.[478] Before being executed after a string of legal challenges and defeats, Hopkinson continually expressed his bitterness about lawyer Gerry Spence's role at his murder trial. As Hopkinson ranted: "I'm probably going to hell. You know there's a downside to that. I'm going to run into Gerry Spence there, too."[479] An Amnesty International representative, Rick Hayes, also weighed in on the private prosecution's outcome, saying that the "arbitrariness of the death penalty" in the case "is because Jackson lawyer Gerry Spence was special prosecutor."[480]

Prior to Hopkinson's execution, Wyoming's first execution in more than 25 years,[481] Spence asserted that he had only argued for the death penalty at trial on the basis of his belief in the notion of "self-defense" for society because Hopkinson "demonstrated his power to commit murder even when held in prison." "But Mr. Hopkinson has been behind bars in Wyoming these past 10 years," Spence emphasized of what led him to reconsider, asserting that "our prison authorities have been able to protect the people of Wyoming against him."[482] In appealing for clemency for Hopkinson, Spence offered: "A commutation of the death penalty in this case would speak more eloquently of justice than the executioner's straps and needle."[483] Spence made that offering even though Hopkinson, still maintaining his innocence, continually attacked Spence, saying, "I don't think you can equate my case to justice." "We all die, and if it's my time to go I'm gone," Hopkinson said dejectedly, adding bitterly: "I'll say one thing about life. To me prison is not life and that's why the thought of being executed does not bother me, but it burns my butt that I'm going to get executed for something I had nothing to do with."[484]

The Mark Hopkinson case, from beginning to end, was full of drama. On the eve of his execution, Hopkinson submitted his own petition to the Wyoming Supreme Court—a petition lacking his attorney's signature. It asked for one more chance to prove his innocence. The then 42-year-old Hopkinson named two Los Angeles area men he believed had killed Green, and he placed the blame on Spence for his impending fate. "I am trapped in the web of Gerry Spence's power," Hopkinson wrote. "If this petition is not granted, I will die in his grasp. Gerry Spence is a cult-like media personality who has long been surrounded by his hand-picked extended 'family,' those who do as he says. The control he has over those who he surrounds himself with is not unlike the control Charles Manson once seemed to exert over his 'family.'"[485] In his petition, Hopkinson stressed: "It would be a miscarriage of justice to the highest degree and display an arrogance beyond belief not to stay the execution and to verify whether the case made against Mark Hopkinson by (special prosecutor) Gerry Spence was accurate or was, instead, one of the most tragic frauds ever perpetrated upon the good people of Wyoming."[486]

Despite all the chaotic and emotionally charged last-minute appeals, Hopkinson was executed by the State of Wyoming in 1992 on a bitterly cold night in late January, his death occurring at 12:57 a.m.[487] Wyoming had long required that executions take place "before the hour of sunrise,"[488] and only 40 people braved the frigid weather to hold an execution vigil. At 1:05 a.m., shortly after Hopkinson was pronounced dead, Gov. Mike Sullivan issued a terse statement: "We have all suffered through and to this finality. Be assured one can feel only sadness that an execution has occurred." "I remained true to my personal beliefs regarding capital punishment and to my personal beliefs in this particular case and have exercised what I viewed as my responsibility as governor," the statement read, adding: "The courts have spoken, and the state has carried out the sentence. I have prayed for the victims of these heinous crimes and their families. I now pray for Mark Hopkinson and his family."[489] The high-profile execution, though, left lingering questions unsettled, as one newspaper noted in these words: "Voted the top Wyoming news story of the year by Associated Press members, the Hopkinson execution did not punish those who actually killed 23-year-old Jeffrey Green. While Green's brutal death in 1979 landed Hopkinson on death row, the unnamed murderers remain at-large."[490]

For his part, Spence was highly circumspect about Hopkinson's execution, later lamenting that the justice system "leaves the life-or-death decision of whether the death penalty will be sought in the hands of stony-souled prosecutors, and the self-righteous, ambitious politicians and book writers who decide who lives and who dies depending on what's good for them." "The justice system," he wrote, noting the lack of accountability for the death penalty because the personal responsibility for death sentences is dispersed among so many criminal justice actors, "sets up a death machine that begins with the prosecutor and ends with the governor, and no one from beginning to end bears any responsibility—not the prosecutors, not the jurors, not the judges, not the governor, not the executioner."[491] Spence, the death penalty opponent who'd nonetheless sought it at Hopkinson's trial, thus bemoaned the shell-game quality of lack of accountability for death sentences and executions, with power disbursed among attorneys, jurors, judges, and the state's governor.

The District of Columbia, U.S. Territories, and the Military

District of Columbia: The District of Columbia Court of Appeals held in *In re Taylor* (2013) that a defendant unlawfully prosecuted for criminal contempt by an interested party was not required under the plain-error standard to show that the error affected the trial's outcome. In reaching that conclusion, that court stressed the "fundamental" importance of having prosecutions conducted by "a disinterested prosecuting attorney acting as an agent of the government" in order "to fulfill the demands of due process." A complainant, the court emphasized in *In re Taylor*, is "by definition and in fact an interested party." At one time, private parties in the District of Columbia were permitted to prosecute alleged violations of orders, such as an intrafamily Civil Protection Order ("CPO"), on their initiative, with prosecutions thus becoming "private feuds." In *In re Taylor*, the District of Columbia Court of Appeals noted that, under the District of Columbia's jurisprudence, the appointment of an attorney for the beneficiary of a CPO is prohibited and that court-appointed counsel "'should be as disinterested as a public prosecutor who undertakes such a prosecution.'"[492]

In explaining its holding, the *In re Taylor* court observed that "[a] criminal prosecution conducted by a self-interested, pro se individual, rather than by a prosecutor," does not fulfill "our societal expectations for the prosecution of crime." "At the outset of a criminal case," the court pointed out, "we rely entirely on prosecutors' discretion with respect to charging decisions—a critical but largely unseen part of the criminal justice process." "Beyond determining which cases to bring to court," the court in *In re Taylor* observed, "we rely on government prosecutors to ensure that those cases are litigated fairly and justly." Prior to trial, it stressed, "prosecutors are required to provide the defense with adequate discovery, both as a matter of due process, and, pursuant to court rule, so that the defense can investigate and prepare its case." "At trial," the court further noted, "we continue to rely on prosecutors to ensure that justice is served." Not only are prosecutors prohibited from "knowingly" using false evidence, including false testimony, to obtain convictions, but prosecutors are also "precluded from making improper arguments to the fact-finder." In considering the facts of the case before it, in which a non-lawyer complainant made prosecutorial decisions, the court wrote:

> In considering the fairness of the proceedings, we also consider the absence of a public prosecutor vis-à-vis the decision to charge and prosecute this case. No neutral charging decision was ever made as to whether to bring charges or maintain them. Rather, these charges (and the ones that followed) appeared grounded in anger and vengeance.

"In short," the *In re Taylor* court concluded, "this case epitomizes why criminal contempt proceedings must not be prosecuted by private actors and must be reserved to government prosecutors acting in the court's, and ultimately the public's, interest."[493]

Guam: The Supreme Court of the Territory of Guam has written that "[p]ublic prosecutors have special duties and rights."[494] The Supreme Court of the Territory of Guam has further observed that "[p]rosecutors cannot be permitted to utilize their public office to benefit their private clients."[495]

Northern Mariana Islands: The Supreme Court of the Commonwealth of the Northern Mariana Islands has held that prosecuting attorneys are "servants of the law ... [who] must serve truth and justice first and foremost." Their job "isn't just to win, but to win fairly, staying well within the rules." "To meet that job description," that court emphasized, "prosecutors cannot prosecute cases in which they have a conflict of interest." Consistent with the U.S. Supreme Court's decision in *Young v. United States ex rel. Vuitton Et Fils S.A.* (1987), the highest court in the Northern Mariana Islands has observed, "courts generally agree that when a prosecutor's private interests and official obligations collide, the prosecutor cannot pursue both simultaneously." As that court pointed out:

> The attorney's dual representation [is] wrong because when an attorney is both a private practitioner and a prosecutor, "[h]is private interest must yield to the public one." Dual representation violates the spirit of that duty because it "necessarily tends to destroy the confidence of the public" in the administration of justice.

In *In re Matter of Woodruff* (2014), the Supreme Court of the Commonwealth of the Northern Mariana Islands specifically held:

> [T]his Court holds that a prosecuting attorney must be disinterested. This proposition is a natural corollary to the long-settled principle that the justice system must avoid even the appearance of impropriety. Allowing prosecutors to prosecute criminal or quasi-criminal cases when they have an interest in a related civil proceeding would do the exact opposite. Such representation would trigger suspicion each time a prosecutor wielded his or her extensive discretion to investigate and prosecute. That suspicion, in turn, would undermine the public's faith in the justice system. Consequently, to maximize faith in the judicial process, prosecuting attorneys must be disinterested from the start of the appointment through the close of the representation. To disqualify a prosecutor on this ground, the party seeking disqualification must show through clear and convincing evidence that the prosecuting attorney possesses any pecuniary interest

or a significant personal interest in a related civil matter that might give rise to an appearance of impropriety.[496]

Puerto Rico: The Supreme Court of Puerto Rico has, in the past, referenced the private prosecutor role.[497] For example, in *Lopez Rivera v. Matos* (1973), the Supreme Court of Puerto Rico cited a statute providing that for violations of it "the public interest shall be represented by a district attorney, his assistant, or any special prosecuting attorney designated by the Secretary of Justice, his assistant, or a private special prosecutor designated as provided by section 102 of Title 3 of the Laws of Puerto Rico Annotated."[498]

Virgin Islands: Private prosecutors have been appointed in the Virgin Islands in the past.[499] The District Court of the Virgin Islands has held that "[a]lthough the territorial judiciary *may* designate the Attorney General or the United States Attorney to prosecute criminal contempt proceedings, it is equally authorized to designate a private attorney to do so." But in exercising that power to appoint or designate private counsel, the court is required nonetheless to appoint a "*disinterested*" prosecutor. It is considered "reversible error" for an attorney to act as a special private prosecutor in a contempt proceeding if that attorney is also counsel for parties who are the beneficiaries of the court order under review.[500]

The Military: "At a time when crime control was not generally considered a responsibility of the state," an article in *The Army Lawyer* notes, "the English settlers brought the legal tradition of private prosecution with them and continued its use into the nineteenth century."[501] Decades ago, in *United States v. Smith* (1957), the Court of Military Appeals made a specific reference to "the role of a private prosecutor." "Obviously," the court observed in that case, "if a convening authority steps outside of his cloak of officiality by personally prosecuting an accused, he would bring himself within the provision of the Code which prohibits one with a personal interest in the outcome of a case from convening a court-martial to hear that particular case."[502]

Victims do have various rights in military prosecutions. "In 2013," the U.S. Air Force Court of Criminal Appeals noted in *United States v. LaSalle* (2019), "Congress enacted Article 6b, UCMJ, pursuant to the National Defense Authorization Act (NDAA) for Fiscal Year 2014," an article that incorporated additional rights of crime victims in presentencing provided in the Crime Victims' Rights Act.[503] Article 6b of the Uniform Code of Military Justice provides, in part, that a victim has the right to "reasonable, accurate, and timely notice of" public hearings concerning the continuation of confinement prior to trial of the accused, a court-martial relating to the offense, and the release or escape of the accused, unless such notice might endanger the safety of someone. Article 6b also affords victims "[t]he right to be reasonably heard" at public hearings, including sentencing hearings, and "[t]he reasonable right to confer with the counsel representing the Government at any proceedings" delineated in that provision of law.[504] In the U.S. military, the decision to refer a case to trial or withdraw it is made by the convening authority, not the trial counsel.[505] "A convening authority serves a unique role in the military justice system by possessing both judicial and prosecutorial functions that can blur together," one law review article emphasizes.[506]

7

THE ROLE OF THE PROSECUTOR

Prosecutorial Ethics, the Public Interest, and Doing Justice

The Ethical Obligations of Public Prosecutors

In the United States, public prosecutors face different ethical concerns and considerations than private lawyers.[1] In fact, they have ethical duties to defendants during every stage of the criminal process. For example, a prosecutor has an obligation to deal fairly in presenting an *ex parte* case to the grand jury. Thus, in *United States v. Hogan*,[2] an indictment was dismissed because a prosecutor's misconduct before the grand jury was fundamentally unfair.[3] Likewise, prosecutors are obligated to protect an individual's pretrial rights[4] and may not seek convictions in cases that are not supported by "probable cause."[5] The U.S. Supreme Court's 1886 decision in *Yick Wo v. Hopkins*,[6] where a Chinese individual's conviction for operating a laundry without a license was reversed, also prohibits selective prosecution that is discriminatory in nature.[7] At trial, the prosecutor is obligated not to present false evidence. As the Supreme Court has stated in numerous cases, the violation of this duty offends due process and requires the reversal of a defendant's conviction.[8] Thus, if a prosecutor becomes aware of false testimony, there is a duty to correct it by disclosing the correct information to the defendant.[9] Due process jurisprudence developed by the Supreme Court in *Brady v. Maryland*[10] specifically requires prosecutors to produce to defendants exculpatory material and evidence useful to impeach government witnesses.[11]

American law is clear that certain standards of conduct govern the prosecutorial function. "Special ethical rules are appropriate for prosecutors," one former federal prosecutor, W.J. Michael Cody, has written, "because the role of the prosecutor is significantly different from that of other attorneys." As Cody, observing that ethical prosecutors do not allow political considerations to influence prosecutorial decisions, has explained in his 1993 article, "Special Ethical Duties for Attorneys Who Hold Public Positions": "The 'formidable' power of the prosecutor includes discretion to initiate and direct investigations, to decide whether to prosecute, to designate the crimes to be charged, to effect the punishment, and to accept or reject a plea of guilt to a lesser offense. In the words of Justice Felix Frankfurter, the prosecutor 'wields the most terrible instruments of government.'" The American Bar Association—the largest membership organization for lawyers—has, in fact, adopted special ethical considerations for prosecutors, with Cody noting of the solemn duties that prosecutors have in American life: "In recognition of the distinctive roles of prosecutors, the American Bar Association and the Association of American Law Schools, in their Joint Conference Report on Professional Responsibility, concluded that a prosecutor cannot guide his conduct by 'the standards of an attorney appearing on the behalf of an individual client.'"[12] The U.S. Supreme Court has itself "long emphasized" that a prosecutor is held to "a higher standard of behavior" than defense counsel.[13]

The history of prosecutorial standards goes back a long way. In 1908, the American Bar Association promulgated the "Canons of Ethics," the first nationwide ethical code for lawyers.[14] Although phrased in somewhat vague language,[15] they proved to be popular. "Nearly every state bar association adopted the Canons," one legal scholar, Eric Fish, has noted, with Canon Five addressing the duties of prosecutors in this way: "The primary duty of a lawyer engaged in public prosecution is not to convict, but to see that justice is done. The suppression of facts or the secreting of witnesses capable of establishing the innocence of the accused is highly reprehensible."[16] Even before the Canons of Ethics were put into place, courts had spoken out about the prosecutorial role. For example, in *People v. Cahoon* (1891), the Michigan Supreme Court opined: "Zeal in a prosecuting attorney is entitled to the highest commendation, but that zeal must be exercised within proper limits." "In criminal cases," that court observed, "the prosecuting attorney is a public officer, acting in a *quasi* judicial capacity."[17] In an earlier case, *Wight v. Rindskope* (1877), the Supreme Court of Wisconsin put it this way: "A public prosecutor is a *quasi* judicial officer, retained by the public for the prosecution of persons accused of crime, in the exercise of a sound discretion to distinguish between the guilty and the innocent, between the certainly and the doubtfully guilty; never voluntarily to acquiesce in an acquittal upon certain presumption of guilt, or in conviction upon doubtful presumption of guilt."[18]

The unique role of the prosecutor,[19] which has been the subject of much commentary, was later codified in Ethical Consideration 7–13 of Canon 7 of the American Bar Association's Model Code of Professional Responsibility (1969).[20] Ethical Consideration 7–13 reads: "The responsibility of a public prosecutor differs from that of the usual advocate; his duty is to seek justice, not merely to convict." "This special duty exists," that Ethical Consideration declares, "because: (1) the prosecutor represents the sovereign and therefore should use restraint in the discretionary exercise of governmental powers, such as in the selection of cases to prosecute; (2) during the trial the prosecutor is not only an advocate but he also may make decisions normally made by an individual client, and those affecting the public interest should be fair to all; and (3) in our system of criminal justice the accused is to be given the benefit of all reasonable doubts." "With respect to evidence and witnesses," the Ethical Consideration stresses, "the prosecutor has responsibilities different from those of a lawyer in private practice: the prosecutor should make timely disclosure to the defense of available evidence, known to him, that tends to negate the guilt of the accused, mitigate the degree of the offense, or reduce the punishment." "Further," the Ethical Consideration emphasizes, "a prosecutor should not intentionally avoid pursuit of evidence merely because he believes it will damage the prosecutor's case or aid the accused."[21]

Ethical Consideration 7–13 of Canon 7 of the ABA's Model Code of Professional Responsibility was explicitly cited by the U.S. Supreme Court in 1987 as support for the prosecutor's "distinctive role." "Because of this unique responsibility," the Supreme Court observed in *Young v. United States ex rel. Vuitton et Fils S.A.* (1987), "federal prosecutors are prohibited from representing the Government in any matter in which they, their family, or their business associates have any interest."[22] Although an Ohio court noted in 1986 that "the ethical considerations of the Code of Professional Responsibility are merely 'aspirational' in character and impose no mandatory legal duty on lawyers,"[23] Ethical Consideration 7–13 has been cited in various lower-court cases for the proposition that prosecutors have various ethical responsibilities, including the duty "of pursuing the truth, regardless of what effect that effort may have on the outcome of the case";[24] the obligation "to assure a defendant a trial free from infringement of his due process rights";[25] and the responsibilities "to see that a defendant receives a fair trial,"[26] to "remain impartial in fulfilling his role as a sworn officer of the court to see that justice is done,"[27] and "to seek a just and equitable result."[28] For example, Ethical Consideration 7–13 was cited in cases to discuss the duties of prosecutors to furnish the accused with exculpatory evidence or favorable information, to refrain from suppressing such evidence, to correct the false testimony of a prosecution witness, and to refrain from using false evidence to convict an accused.[29] Ethical Consideration 7–13 was also cited in a case observing that prosecutors should not act in "an unfair, blatantly discriminatory fashion."[30]

The Model Rules of Professional Conduct, which replaced the Model Code of Professional Responsibility in most states,[31] also make the prosecutor's unique role clear: "A prosecutor has the responsibility of a minister of justice and not simply that of an advocate. This responsibility carries with it specific obligations to see that the defendant is accorded procedural justice and that guilt is decided upon the basis of sufficient evidence."[32] Rule 3.8 of the Model Rules of Professional Conduct, as written,[33] states that "[t]he prosecutor in a criminal case shall," among other things, "(a) refrain from prosecuting a charge that the prosecutor knows is not supported by probable cause"; "(b) make reasonable efforts to assure that the accused has been advised of the right to, and the procedure for obtaining, counsel and has been given reasonable opportunity to obtain counsel"; "(c) not seek to obtain from an unrepresented accused a waiver of important pretrial rights, such as the right to a preliminary hearing"; and "(d) make timely disclosure to the defense of all evidence or information known to the prosecutor that tends to negate the guilt of the accused or mitigates the offense, and, in connection with sentencing, disclose to the defense and to the tribunal all unprivileged mitigating information known to the prosecutor, except when the prosecutor is relieved of this responsibility by a protective order of the tribunal...." Rule 3.8 also states that, "except for statements that are necessary to inform the public of the nature and extent of the prosecutor's action and that serve a legitimate law enforcement purpose," a prosecutor must "refrain from making extrajudicial comments that have a substantial likelihood of heightening public condemnation of the accused and exercise reasonable care to prevent investigators, law enforcement personnel, employees or other persons assisting or associated with the prosecutor in a criminal case from making an extrajudicial statement that the prosecutor would be prohibited from making...." Rule 3.8 further states that "[w]hen a prosecutor knows of new, credible and material evidence creating a reasonable likelihood that a convicted defendant did not commit an offense of which the defendant was convicted," that prosecutor must "promptly disclose that evidence to an appropriate court or authority" and "undertake further investigation, or make reasonable efforts to cause an investigation, to determine whether the defendant was convicted of an offense that the defendant did not commit." "When a prosecutor knows of clear and convincing evidence establishing that a defendant in the prosecutor's jurisdiction was convicted of an offense that the defendant did not commit," Rule 3.8 concludes, "the prosecutor shall seek to remedy the conviction."

One comment to Rule 3.8 describes the import of that rule in this way: "A prosecutor has the responsibility of a minister of justice and not simply that of an advocate. This responsibility carries with it specific obligations to see that the defendant is accorded procedural justice, that guilt is decided upon the basis of sufficient evidence, and that special precautions are taken to prevent and to rectify the conviction of innocent persons." That comment, drafted in connection with the adoption in 1983 of the Model Rules of Professional Conduct,[34] observed that many jurisdictions had adopted the ABA's Standards of Criminal Justice Relating to the Prosecution Function, said to be "the product of prolonged and careful deliberation by lawyers experienced in both criminal prosecution and defense." The comment reflects a concern that an accused not be treated unfairly. For example, in discussing the prohibition on "extrajudicial statements that have a substantial likelihood of prejudicing an adjudicatory proceeding," the comment emphasized: "In the context of a criminal prosecution, a prosecutor's extrajudicial statement can create the additional problem of increasing public condemnation of the accused. Although the announcement of an indictment, for example, will necessarily have severe consequences for the accused, a prosecutor can, and should, avoid comments which have no legitimate law enforcement purpose and have a substantial likelihood of increasing public opprobrium of the accused."[35]

Rule 3.8 and the comment to it have been cited by various courts, including for the proposition that the prosecutor represents "the interest of society as a whole."[36] "A public prosecutor is ethically bound to charge and try only those he believes, and can prove, are guilty," the U.S. Court of Appeals for the Tenth Circuit ruled in 1986.[37] The

U.S. Supreme Court has itself recognized that the standard of disclosure imposed on prosecutors by Rule 3.8 is more demanding than that established by its decision in *Brady v. Maryland* (1963) requiring disclosures.[38] Under *Brady*, a prosecutor is obligated to provide defense counsel with exculpatory evidence on the issue of either guilt or punishment.[39] In one case citing the comment to Rule 3.8, the Ninth Circuit noted: "the government has the obligation to see that all evidence relevant to a case is presented, even if unfavorable to its position."[40] And in another case citing Rule 3.8, a state appellate court observed that the duty of disclosure "does not end" when the trial is over. "'[A]fter a conviction,'" that California appellate court emphasized, "'the prosecutor also is bound by the ethics of his office to inform the appropriate authority of after-acquired or other information that casts doubt upon the correctness of the conviction.'"[41]

In 2009, the ABA issued Formal Opinion 09–454 titled "Prosecutor's Duty to Disclose Evidence and Information Favorable to the Defense." That opinion reads in part: "Rule 3.8(d) of the Model Rules of Professional Conduct requires a prosecutor to 'make timely disclosure to the defense of all evidence or information known to the prosecutor that tends to negate the guilt of the accused or mitigates the offense, and, in connection with sentencing, [to] disclose to the defense and to the tribunal all unprivileged mitigating information known to the prosecutor.' This ethical duty is separate from disclosure obligations imposed under the Constitution, statutes, procedural rules, court rules, or court orders." That formal opinion further observes: "Rule 3.8(d) requires a prosecutor who knows of evidence and information favorable to the defense to disclose it as soon as reasonably practicable so that the defense can make meaningful use of it in making such decisions as whether to plead guilty and how to conduct its investigation." "Prosecutors are not further obligated to conduct searches or investigations for favorable evidence and information of which they are unaware," the formal opinion clarifies.[42]

There are also ABA Standards for Criminal Justice for prosecutors and the National District Attorney Association's National Prosecution Standards. The *ABA Standards for Criminal Justice: Prosecution Function and Defense Function*, the fourth edition of which were approved in 2015,[43] were "written and intended to be entirely consistent with the ABA's Model Rules of Professional Conduct" but were "not intended to modify a prosecutor's obligations under applicable rules, statutes, or the constitution." Said to be "aspirational" and to describe "best practices," the *ABA Standards for Criminal Justice* define a "prosecutor" as "any attorney, regardless of agency, title, or full or part-time assignment, who acts as an attorney to investigate or prosecute criminal cases or who provides legal advice regarding a criminal matter to government lawyers, agents, or offices participating in the investigation or prosecution of criminal cases." Those ABA standards, "intended to apply in any context in which a lawyer would reasonably understand that a criminal prosecution could result," include language from the Model Rules but address conduct or provide details beyond that governed by the Model Rules.[44]

Prosecutors have obligations to the judicial system. Standard 3–1.2 of the *ABA Standards for Criminal Justice*, titled "Functions and Duties of the Prosecutor," makes this opening declaration: "The prosecutor is an administrator of justice, a zealous advocate, and an officer of the court. The prosecutor's office should exercise sound discretion and independent judgment in the performance of the prosecution function." "The primary duty of the prosecutor," Standard 3–1.2 states, "is to seek justice within the bounds of the law, not merely to convict." As that standard further recites: "The prosecutor serves the public interest and should act with integrity and balanced judgment to increase public safety both by pursuing appropriate criminal charges of appropriate severity, and by exercising discretion to not pursue criminal charges in appropriate circumstances. The prosecutor should seek to protect the innocent and convict the guilty, consider the interests of victims and witnesses, and respect the constitutional and legal rights of all persons, including suspects and defendants." "The prosecutor," the standard continues, "is not merely a case-processor but also a problem-solver responsible for considering broad goals of the criminal justice system." The next standard, Standard 3–1.3, is titled "The Client of the Prosecutor," and emphasizes: "The prosecutor generally serves the public and not any particular government agency, law enforcement officer or unit, witness or victim."[45]

By definition, of course, the mindset of a private lawyer retained or employed by a victim of crime will be very different than that of an impartial public prosecutor. Indeed, while the Supreme Court's *Brady* ruling requires prosecutors to *disclose* information to an accused, a private client being counseled by a private lawyer will have an expectation of information remaining *confidential* by virtue of the attorney-client privilege.[46] The ABA standard stating that "[t]he prosecutor's client is the public, not particular agencies or victims," has been cited to find the attorney-client privilege inapplicable in specific situations,[47] and it has been emphasized elsewhere that "[t]he general public and public interest are the prosecutor's client, not government agencies, law enforcement bodies or personnel, or even the victims of crimes."[48] Victims themselves, in fact, may erroneously—because of their dealings with individual prosecutors—perceive that such prosecutors represent solely their interests because they may be regularly meeting to discuss pending criminal cases. As one recent law review article clarifies but notes: "Of course, prosecutors represent the state, not victims, in criminal prosecutions; however, it is likely that victims come to believe that the prosecutor is their champion, perhaps even their protector."[49] That misperception, that prosecutors are meant to serve *only* victims' interests, may be exacerbated by the fact that criminal defendants have attorneys—whether public defenders or private defense lawyers—dedicated to serving the interests of the accused. But, it must be recalled, public prosecutors' offices are structured to ensure the *independence* of prosecutors,[50] and prosecutors should maintain their integrity and independence as they make charging, plea bargaining, and other prosecutorial decisions.[51]

The *ABA Standards for Criminal Justice* lay out the prosecutor's duties in some detail, including with respect to charging decisions[52] and their relationship with victims and witnesses.[53] For instance, Standard 3–1.4, titled "The Prosecutor's Heightened Duty of Candor," notes that "the prosecutor has a heightened duty of candor to the courts and in fulfilling other professional obligations."[54] Standard 3–1.6, titled "Improper Bias Prohibited," provides in part in these hortatory terms: "The prosecutor should not manifest or exercise, by words or conduct, bias or prejudice based upon race, sex, religion, national origin, disability, age, sexual orientation, gender identity, or socioeconomic status. A prosecutor should not use other improper considerations, such as partisan or political or personal considerations, in exercising prosecutorial discretion."[55] On the topic of "Conflicts of Interest," Standard 3–1.7 gives this directive: "The prosecutor should know and abide by the ethical rules regarding conflicts of interest that apply in the jurisdiction, and be sensitive to facts that may raise conflict issues. When a conflict requiring recusal exists and is non-waivable, or informed consent has not been obtained, the prosecutor should recuse from further participation in the matter. The office should not go forward until a non-conflicted prosecutor, or an adequate waiver, is in place." That standard also provides that the prosecutor "should not participate in a matter in which the prosecutor previously participated, personally and substantially, as a non-prosecutor"; "should not be involved in the prosecution of a former client"; "should not negotiate for private employment with an accused or the target of an investigation, in a matter in which the prosecutor is participating personally and substantially, or with an attorney or agent for such accused or target"; and "should not permit the prosecutor's professional judgment or obligations to be affected by the prosecutor's personal, political, financial, professional, business, property, or other interests or relationships."[56] In one case, the Supreme Court of Colorado disqualified a district attorney's office from handling a first-degree murder case where that office had received funds from the Department of Corrections for the costs of prosecuting the defendant. Its holding: "[w]hen a district attorney's financial interest is dependent on the outcome of the trial, the district attorney can be properly disqualified."[57]

Other provisions of the *ABA Standards for Criminal Justice* emphasize that prosecutors should act "with the interests of justice and with due regard for fairness, accuracy, and rights of the defendant, victims, and witnesses," and that "[t]he prosecution function should be performed by a lawyer who is (i) a public official, (ii) authorized to practice law in the jurisdiction, and (iii) subject to the rules of attorney professional conduct and discipline." "Prosecutors whose professional obligations are devoted full-time and exclusively to the prosecution function are preferable to part-time prosecutors who have other potentially conflicted professional responsibilities," Standard 3–2.1 recites. That particular standard also observes that a prosecutor's office "should have open, effective, and well-publicized methods for communicating with, and receiving communications," with the standard making this further declaration: "If a particular matter requires the appointment of a special prosecutor from outside the office, adequate funding for this purpose should be made available. Such special prosecutors should know and are governed by applicable conflict of interest standards for prosecutors." That standard makes this hortatory observation as regards privately retained attorneys acting as prosecutors: "A private attorney who is paid by, or who has an attorney-client relationship with, an individual or entity that is a victim of the charged crime, or who has a personal or financial interest in the prosecution of particular charges, or who has demonstrated any impermissible bias relevant to the particular matter, should not be permitted to serve as prosecutor in that matter."[58] It was the latter ABA standard that the Court of Appeals of Idaho, in *State v. Johnson* (2020), invoked in holding that a defendant's right to due process "may be violated when a person who is a victim of the crime or who has a personal, financial, or attorney-client relationship with the victim of the crime prosecutes the criminal case."[59]

The third edition of the *National Prosecution Standards of the National District Attorneys Association* ("NDAA") also discuss the prosecution function and a prosecutor's duties and obligations. Like the ABA's *Standards of Criminal Justice*, the NDAA's *National Prosecution Standards* are said to be "an aspirational guide to professional conduct in the performance of the prosecutorial function." And similar to the ABA's *Standards of Criminal Justice*, the NDAA standards—which define a *prosecutor* as "any person performing the prosecution function" and a *special prosecutor* as "any person who performs the prosecution function in a jurisdiction who is not the chief prosecutor elected or appointed in the jurisdiction, or an assistant or deputy prosecutor in the jurisdiction"—are "intended to supplement rather than replace the existing rules of ethical conduct that apply in a jurisdiction." "The prosecutor is an independent administrator of justice," the NDAA's standards announce at the outset, adding: "This primary responsibility of a prosecutor is to seek justice, which can only be achieved by the representation and presentation of the truth. This responsibility includes, but is not limited to, ensuring that the guilty are held accountable, that the innocent are protected from unwarranted harm, and that the rights of all participants, particularly victims of crime, are respected." The NDAA's standards state that "[a] prosecutor should put the rights and interests of society in a paramount position in exercising prosecutorial discretion in individual cases."[60]

Like the ABA's standards, the NDAA's standards express a strong preference for public, full-time prosecutors. As NDAA Standard 1–1.3 states: "The chief prosecutor in a jurisdiction should be a full-time position. A full-time prosecutor, whether the chief prosecutor or otherwise, should neither maintain nor profit from a private legal practice." "A chief prosecutor," that standard notes, "may serve part-time in those jurisdictions that are unable or unwilling to fund a full-time prosecutor, but while serving as a part-time prosecutor may not engage in professional conduct that is inconsistent with the need for prosecutorial independence." The NDAA commentary to that standard, while noting the reality that "there are many part-time prosecutors in the United States" because of budgetary constraints on small or sparsely populated geographic jurisdictions, explains the preference for full-time public prosecutors over private or part-time prosecutors in this way: "A full-time chief prosecutor, confers many advantages on his or her jurisdiction. Among other advantages, the prosecutor is not distracted by a private law practice; is readily available for consultation with law enforcement officers; is more accountable to society for his or her decisions and performance; and, is not vulnerable to the various potential conflicts of interest that can plague a part-time prosecutor." The NDAA's standards also address "Conflicts with Private Practice" relating to those jurisdictions that "do not prohibit private practice by a prosecutor." Among other things, that conflict-of-interest standard states that "[t]he prosecutor should avoid representing to private clients or prospective clients that the status of a prosecutor could be an advantage in the private representation."[61]

Standard 17 of the NDAA standards—a standard titled "Relations with Non-Governmental Entities"—begins by stating that "[i]n all dealings with a non-governmental entity, the chief prosecutor should place the public interest above all other considerations." In a subsection of that standard addressing "Financial and Resource Assistance," one finds these items of guidance:

> a. Where permitted by law, a prosecutor's office may accept financial or resource assistance from a non-governmental source when such assistance is specifically approved by the chief prosecutor; b. When determining whether to accept assistance from a non-governmental source, the chief prosecutor should give priority consideration to the public interest over the private interests of a non-governmental source, especially when the assistance relates to a specific case or cases rather than office-wide assistance; c. The chief prosecutor should consider whether accepting assistance from a non-governmental source will create the appearance of undue influence; d. The chief prosecutor should have office procedures in place that protect the independent exercise of discretion of the office from the undue influence of a non-governmental resource that has provided assistance to the office during the investigation and prosecution of specific cases or types of cases.

The NDAA's commentary to that standard cautions: "In times of strained budgets and inadequate resources, an offer of assistance from a non-government funding source is a temptation. Such arrangements need to be carefully examined to make certain that no illegal or unethical strings are attached." "[T]he prosecutor," that commentary advises, "must be vigilant to not allow the assistance to interfere with his or her independent exercise of prosecutorial discretion."[62]

The ABA's *Standards for Criminal Justice* and the NDAA's *National Prosecution Standards* have been recognized and regularly cited by courts,[63] even though such standards are said to be "entirely nonbinding" on jurists.[64] For example, in a case decided by the Supreme Court of New Mexico, both the ABA and NDAA standards were cited for the proposition that "a prosecutor's professional judgment should not be affected by personal interests." "For a prosecutor," that court ruled, emphasizing that prosecutors should not be influenced by private interests, "this means at a minimum that private interests may not adversely affect his representation of the public and pursuit of a fair trial."[65] One scholar, Stanford Law School professor David Alan

Sklansky, has specifically taken note of the fact that the ABA's *Standards for Criminal Justice* and the NDAA's *National Prosecution Standards* are "non-binding" standards.[66] However, these standards nonetheless give a snapshot of the views of those involved in drafting them before their promulgation. Ethical lapses of public prosecutors include prosecutorial misconduct and pursuing prosecutions in spite of conflicts of interest.

In a recent case in Texas, it was revealed that Ralph Petty, an assistant prosecutor for the Midland County District Attorney's Office, "moonlighted" as a paid clerk for at least nine judges he argued criminal cases in front of, including in a capital case in which the defendant, Clinton Young, ended up on death row. In all, Petty earned $262,650 clerking for judges from 2000 to 2018, county auditor and treasurer's records revealed. "It is a breach of ethical conduct by both of them," observed Elsa Alcala, a former judge of the Texas Court of Criminal Appeals, referring to Petty and the judge who presided over Young's case. "I don't know what they were thinking," Alcala remarked of the disclosure of the conflict of interest that *USA Today* reported on in early 2021, leading Young's attorneys to seek a new trial for their client. In a court filing, Young's lawyers asserted that "the risk of a fundamentally unfair proceeding resulting from a trial judge employing a prosecutor as a judicial clerk, while that prosecutor is still representing the state in that Judge's courtroom, is so inherently violative of due process that there is scant precedent discussing it." In a thirty-page order issued on April 26, 2021, Senior Judge Sid Harle determined that Ralph Petty's actions amounted to "shocking prosecutorial misconduct that destroyed any semblance of a fair trial" in Young's case, finding that it deprived Young of due process of law. "The appearance of impropriety" was "clear," Judge Harle wrote, emphasizing that "the court's law clerk was also the prosecutor for the State" and that the DA's office "violated its statutory and constitutional obligations to protect Mr. Young's due process right to a fair trial by failing to disclose Mr. Petty's dual role to Mr. Young or his counsel during trial, and by keeping secret Mr. Petty's dual role through Mr. Young's new-trial proceeding, direct appeal, and initial postconviction proceeding."[67]

In various foreign countries, private criminal prosecutions are permitted and occur with some frequency when the public prosecutor fails to act.[68] For example, in Latin America countries, where human rights abuses by governments have a long and sordid history, private prosecution has been used to challenge corrupt public officials. One scholar, Verónica Michel-Luviano, has observed in that context that private prosecution "serves an important role as a control mechanism on the state's duty to prosecute and investigate crime." "The cases of Guatemala, Chile, and Mexico," she writes in her case study of those countries, "further show that when impunity is either the result of a state's choice or weak/inefficient institutions, private prosecutions can improve access to justice by making evident the state's failure, pushing the investigation, and giving victims a chance to access the justice system by helping the cases reach the courts."[69] In the United States, some have sought a return to a form of private prosecution, with Bennett Capers—a Fordham Law School professor—asserting that "private prosecution is in our cultural DNA" and that prosecutorial power should be restored to the people.[70] "It has sometimes been argued that the private prosecution alternative is desirable and ought to be recognized by more jurisdictions, but the generally accepted view is to the contrary," scholars Wayne LaFave, Jerold Israel, Nancy King and Orin Kerr explain in their popular criminal procedure treatise. "The 'prosecution function,'" they write, "'should be performed by a lawyer who is a public official,' as prosecution by a private party without authorization or approval of the prosecutor presents a serious 'danger of the vindictive use of the criminal law process.'"[71]

Full-time Public Prosecutors vs. Part-time or Private Prosecutors

Public prosecutors ordinarily have the power—and have long had that power—to appoint assistants and deputies, including special counsel or special prosecutors.[72] As one scholar wrote in 1976 in *The American University Law Review*: "[M]ost states provide, by statute or by case law, that the prosecuting attorney, attorney general of the state, or governor may, when the need develops, appoint special temporary prosecutors to be paid with government funds."[73] For example, in Ohio, a state statute allows a prosecuting attorney to "appoint any assistants, clerks, and stenographers who are necessary for the proper performance of the duties of his office and fix their compensation."[74] Likewise, in Indiana, a statute allows the prosecuting attorney to appoint a chief deputy prosecuting attorney and, depending on the locale's characteristics, additional deputy prosecuting attorneys. Under that statute, "[t]he various county councils shall appropriate annually for other deputy prosecuting attorneys, investigators, clerical assistance, witness fees, out-of-state travel, postage, telephone tolls and telegraph, repairs to equipment, office supplies, other operating expenses, and equipment an amount necessary for the proper discharge of the duties imposed by law upon the office of the prosecuting attorney of each judicial circuit."[75] In most cases, elected chief prosecutors—whose constituents are members of the public[76]—hire full-time prosecutors and staff to assist with the prosecution function, but part-time deputies are also a possibility.[77] A number of states also authorize courts to appoint counsel to replace the district attorney when the district attorney has an interest in the proceedings or fails to perform the duties of the office,[78] while district attorneys in some locales are specifically prohibited from engaging in the private practice of law.[79]

The highest profile examples of outside attorneys being appointed to handle criminal prosecutions in conflict-of-interest situations come from the federal "independent counsel" and "special counsel" laws and regulations. Here, a little history is in order. In 1966, Congress passed a statute vesting "[a]ll functions" of the Department of Justice, and its officers, agencies, and employees, in the Attorney General of the United States. The Attorney General, in turn, was empowered by law to delegate those functions. The statute expressly permitted the Attorney General to appoint and retain an attorney from outside of the Justice Department to act as "special assistant to the Attorney General or special attorney." Any attorney specially appointed by the Attorney General—it was provided—"may, when specifically directed by the Attorney General, conduct any kind of legal proceeding, civil or criminal, including grand jury proceedings," that U.S. attorneys are authorized by law to conduct. The U.S. Supreme Court, in *United States v. Nixon* (1974), recognized the Attorney General's authority to appoint a special counsel under those statutory provisions in the wake of the Watergate burglary. After Watergate, Congress also enacted the Ethics in Government Act of 1978—now expired—that authorized the Attorney General to refer criminal matters involving high-level government officials, including the President, to a three-judge court, which had the responsibility for the appointment of an independent investigating attorney.

The Ethics in Government Act, which created the position of "Special Prosecutor" and which was originally set to sunset after five years, was reauthorized by 1983 (though it renamed the "Special Prosecutor" as "Independent Counsel"). In 1987, Congress then established a "permanent indefinite appropriation" with the Justice Department "to pay all necessary expenses of investigations and prosecutions" by appointed independent counsel. Although the constitutionality of the independent counsel provisions of the Ethics in Government Act were upheld by the U.S. Supreme Court in *Morrison v. Olson* (1988), and the law was invoked several times to appoint special attorneys to investigate and prosecute crimes allegedly committed by members of the executive branch, the law generated intense controversy in the political realm. Congress thereafter permitted the Ethics in Government Act to sunset in 1999, leading the Justice Department shortly thereafter to issue regulations to govern the Attorney General's appointment of special counsel pursuant to the statutory scheme in existence before the Ethics in Government Act. Most recently, Special Counsel Robert Mueller was appointed pursuant to the Special Counsel Regulation, which recognizes and provides for the independence of the specially appointed lawyer. That appointment came about after then-Attorney General Jeff Sessions recused himself "from any existing or future investigations of any matters related in any way to the campaigns for President of the United States." A Justice Department regulation provides that "no employee shall participate in a criminal investigation or prosecution if he has a personal or political relationship" with any person "involved in the conduct that is the subject of the investigation or prosecution."[80]

In addition to dealing with conflicts of interest, all governmental agencies and prosecutors' offices face hiring and organizational issues. At the state and local levels, budgetary constraints can be especially challenging. Consequently, many rural counties and rural and suburban communities make use of part-time prosecutors to avoid the expense of hiring full-time prosecutors.[81] As scholar Maybell Romero observed in the *Journal of Criminal Law and Criminology* in 2017: "Cities, towns, and other small political subdivisions throughout the country frequently hire prosecutors on a part-time basis through a competitive bidding process, releasing requests for proposals (RFPs) in an effort to procure bids. This practice, however, may be observed not only in small or rural municipalities, but also in cities located near larger population centers." The drafting of the RFP is commonly followed by the publication of a legal notice announcing the solicitation of bids, with the RFP stating what legal services are requested, a schedule for the project or term of years for which the services are being requested, the qualifications needed and criteria to be evaluated, and a request for a budget (*e.g.*, salaries, supplies, any costs). Taking note of multiple RFP-issuing municipalities—Ferguson, Missouri; Kyle, Texas; Green River, Wyoming; Lakeville, Minnesota; River Falls, Wisconsin; Hortonville, Wisconsin; and Ephraim City, Utah—and observing that "contracts are generally awarded to the lowest bidder, with other factors often playing at best, a secondary role in the decision," Romero observes that outsourcing prosecution through RFPs "creates serious tensions with the professional standards that bind prosecutors." "Prosecutors hired on contract," Romero writes, are "much more vulnerable to termination from their positions than elected prosecutors, or even those assistant prosecutors who are hired by an elected prosecutorial supervisor."[82] Like part-time prosecutors who maintain private law practices, county attorneys and assistant county attorneys—by statute—are not prohibited in some locales from engaging in the private practice of law.[83]

The jurisdictions surveyed by Romero released varied RFPs for prosecution services. Some RFPs sought a two- or three-year term (with renewals to be considered and, in one case, the ability to terminate the relationship by either party with 90 days' notice), and they contemplated different compensation packages. Among the possibilities: (1) a monthly retainer and an hourly rate for services exceeding the usual monthly scope, (2) hourly or "flat fee" approaches, with costs for support staff and overhead expenses, (3) an annual salary including health insurance, and (4) an annual salary excluding health benefits. As Romero explains of the inherent vulnerability of outsourced prosecutors (which might, of course, affect their ability to truly remain independent of various pressures):

> The contractually outsourced prosecutor's job has a natural "expiration date," coupled with the additional weakness that the local government may cancel the contract, sometimes with the most minimal of notice. Elected, incumbent prosecutors, of course, have the luxury of waiting to be voted out of office (unless they have committed a rather egregious gaffe, in which case states have varying methods of removal), while even assistant prosecutors, usually hired on as at will employees, may often benefit from other protections such as collective bargaining agreements or favorable employee policies and handbooks limiting the process of termination.[84]

In the *Journal of Criminal Law and Criminology* article, Romero underscores the significant differences between public and outsourced prosecution. As Romero writes:

> Although there are widely acknowledged dangers that arise from relying on publicly elected prosecutors, such prosecutors at least wield a local govern-

> ment's power against its citizens with the understanding that if such power is abused that their elected position may be in jeopardy, while also comporting with the longstanding prosecutorial norms.... The outsourced, hired-on-contract prosecutor, however, is often much more shielded from public view. Rather than having to seek approval from the public or, in the case of an assistant prosecutor, helping one's elected supervisor secure wide public approval, the contract prosecutor only needs to perform for those who control renewal of the contract—usually a mayor, city council, county council, or city manager.

Those who provide professional services on a contract basis must, naturally, periodically renew their contracts. As one administrative law judge, in deciding whether a person providing municipal prosecution services was an employee or an independent contractor, described one such individual: "He submits a response to a Request for Proposals annually. He is appointed by the public body itself. [He] must obviously be present when court is in session, but no one... otherwise controls his comings and goings. No one formally evaluates him, or tells him how to execute his job substantively."[85] "[T]he contract prosecutor," Romero warns, "may feel a greater duty to those who make hiring decisions and to the local government itself rather than the real client to whom they owe a fiduciary duty and a duty of loyalty—the public." "A substantial conflict of interest," she writes, "is an inherent feature of a prosecutor's function when hired by way of RFP. No matter such a prosecutor's actual intentions and motivations, he or she faces competing duties to the public, to the local government, and often to their own firms." "It is in such situations," Romero explains, "that a prosecutor may decide to make choices that serve to enrich and benefit a local government rather than the citizens it would purport to serve."[86]

Part-time prosecutors thus face ethical questions that full-time public prosecutors do not. That's because part-time prosecutors are also, in some cases, attempting to take on the representation of private clients. That raises serious conflict of interest issues (*e.g.*, where a part-time prosecutor seeks to represent a private client in a tort action in which there exists an issue upon which the prosecutor has statutory prosecutorial authority),[87] with some state ethical rules—in an attempt to address concerns—specifically dealing with issues that pertain to part-time prosecutors.[88] "Lawyers who have a private practice but who also serve as part-time government lawyers," one commentator, Roy Simon Jr., notes, "face special problems that are affected not only but the Rules of Professional Conduct but also by state and local statutes and regulations."[89] "Prosecuting cases involving private clients," other scholars note, "risks disloyalty to both the private client (who may perceive that his lawyer is being disloyal by appearing against him) and the public (because of the likelihood that the prosecutor will favor the client)."[90] Conflict of interest issues can arise in any prosecutor's office, but smaller district attorney's offices in less populated counties (where at least some prosecutors may be employed on a part-time basis) may face special conflict of interest issues because of the presence of part-time prosecutors who split their time between the prosecutorial function and non-governmental employment.[91]

In their practices, lawyers must regularly deal with conflict of interest issues. In the past, lawyers have been found to have conflicts of interest requiring disqualification where, for example, a defense attorney was also a part-time assistant district attorney.[92] In one Indiana case, the Supreme Court of Indiana held that "[t]he state is entitled to a prosecutor's undivided loyalty" and that "the requirement of loyalty to a particular client prohibits a part-time prosecutor or deputy prosecutor from defending in this state persons charged with crimes."[93] In addition, part-time prosecutors have been disciplined for activities involving conflicts of interest.[94] To combat any appearance of impropriety, one Iowa ethics rule precludes a lawyer assigned to prosecute serious cases from engaging in criminal defense work, with Iowa Rule 1.11(f) providing that "[p]rosecutors for the state or county shall not engage in the defense of an accused in any criminal matter during the time they are engaged in such public responsibilities." As Gregory Sisk writes of that rule in the *Iowa Practice Series*: "Thus, if a state or county prosecutor maintains a part-time private practice, he or she may not include criminal defense work as any part of that practice. Through this rule, which preserves the longstanding standard in Iowa, the public interest in faithful prosecution is enhanced by ensuring that those prosecuting major crimes are not simultaneously seeking to defeat criminal charges against other clients (thus perhaps giving the appearance that the lawyer is riding with the cops on one day, but cheering for the robbers on another day)." As Sisk adds of the rule's implications and purpose:

> The lawyer is spared the dissonance of advocating opposing positions in different but simultaneously-pending cases, for example, in favor of suppression of evidence in one case and against suppression of evidence in another. Moreover, if a criminal defendant were to be represented by such an ambidextrous lawyer, that client might have unfounded expectations, believing that his or her defense will benefit from inside access or favored treatment because the lawyer also is part of the prosecution team in other cases.[95]

The outsourcing of traditional governmental functions has occurred in the U.S. in a number of areas, including policing and prisons. Such outsourcing and delegations to private actors raise what have been called "troubling constitutional issues"[96] and what University of Baltimore law professor Kim Wehle has called "constitutional accountability" concerns. "As government outsourcing continues," Wehle wrote in 2013, "the need to ensure proper oversight of private contractors becomes all the more salient." Taking note of the private delegation doctrine,[97] a New Deal-era doctrine developed to increase government oversight and control of private actors exercising government power,[98] she argues that "structural constraints must be in place to ensure that private interests do not trump the public good."[99] Although the use of private prosecution (which relies on private parties to act on behalf of the sovereign power) dates back centuries, the use of victim-retained private prosecutors has, in fact, become quite uncommon in modern American life. In a Kansas case, one court observed in 1993—more than twenty-five years ago—that "[t]he right to hire a private prosecutor appears to have evolved from the common law" but then took specific note of "how rare" the use of private assistant prosecutors had become.[100]

While teaching law at George Washington University, Roger Fairfax offered a pointed critique of the delegation of the criminal prosecution function to private actors. In a 2009 article, Professor Fairfax argued that "the private exercise of the tremendous discretion reserved for public prosecutors[101] represents an inappropriate delegation of sovereign prerogative." Delegating the prosecution function to private lawyers, he asserted, "presents the potential for conflicts of interest and corruption, the erosion of due process, prosecutorial underperformance, and diminished accountability." "Fundamentally," he writes, "the private exercise of the discretionary prosecutorial function—what Austin Sarat and Conor Clarke term a 'fragment of sovereignty'—challenges our settled assumptions regarding the public-private distinction and government authority." Although Fairfax acknowledges that the federal government and state and local governments have long contracted with private lawyers to represent public interests, including for the prosecution function, he contends that "the government's delegation of criminal prosecution authority to private actors is unwise or improper in most circumstances." As Fairfax observes:

> Prosecutorial decisions regarding whether and what to investigate and what tactics and tools to use in the course of an investigation can have grave consequences for those who fall under the government's scrutiny. The ability to decide whether and what to charge gives the prosecutor perhaps the most power of any single actor in the criminal justice process. Furthermore, plea bargaining, referrals for mediation, and conditional and unconditional dismissals all require the prosecutor to make significant decisions.[102]

While Professor Fairfax acknowledges the historical reality that criminal prosecutions were once privately conducted, he cites the norm of public prosecution that has emerged over time in support of his critique. "Regardless of its foggy origins in the United States," he observes, "the prosecution of crime is now firmly entrenched as a public function." "Although an ardent privatization advocate might view the lineage of the office of the modern public prosecutor as irrelevant at best," he contends, "the public nature of the prosecutorial role has been absorbed by and is intertwined with the professional identity of prosecutors." "Delegation of the prosecution function to private actors," he believes, "subverts that special professional identity now associated with the public prosecutor, along with the public confidence that the public prosecution norm engenders." Like Fairfax, others have taken notice of today's prevailing public prosecution norm. "Just as common law crimes have vanished from the scene, so has the private prosecutor," notes Professor Thomas Merrill of Columbia Law School, alluding to the rise of elected public prosecutors in American states. "As public prosecution has become the norm, and as the matter has come to be recognized to be one subject to the control and direction of the legislature," Merrill writes, "the idea that courts have inherent authority to determine who is the appropriate person to prosecute a crime has come to seem bizarre, if not unconstitutional."[103]

Of course, not all *public* prosecutors always behave in an ethical or honorable manner. Public prosecutors sometimes engage in misconduct. And lawyers at public prosecutors' office do not always act in an appropriate manner. Even those appointed to high positions of public trust abuse their authority. For example, Donald Trump's attorney general, William Barr, has been justly condemned for the manner in which he ran the U.S. Department of Justice, with one report decrying the politicization that took place during his tenure.[104] In the public context, of course, voters and periodic elections can hold public officials accountable, resulting in new political appointees or newly elected prosecutors being put in place. Delegating the prosecution function to private actors, however, carries its own problems—indeed, structural risks—that undermine confidence in the administration of justice. As Fairfax explains:

> A part-time prosecutor working under contract with a jurisdiction might feel compelled to maintain a high conviction rate to ensure the renewal of the contract. Moreover, the part-time prosecutor might be in a position to use her prosecution role to influence matters in her private practice. For example, a part-time prosecutor might hint at launching a criminal investigation against a civil litigation opponent in order to encourage settlement in the civil suit.[105]

Fairfax has also expressed concerns about other dangers and perverse incentives associated with the delegation of the prosecution function to private actors, including the financial pressures on part-time prosecutors.[106]

In his scholarship, Roger Fairfax distinguishes between "discretionary" and "ministerial" prosecutorial functions. A prosecutor's charging decision or the decision to take a position on a motion in limine, Fairfax notes, is a discretionary decision, whereas the drafting—or even arguing—of a motion in limine "might be deemed ministerial in some situations." "Likewise," he asserts, "a prosecutor's decision to seek a specific sentence following a conviction would be discretionary, whereas the drafting of the sentencing memorandum reflecting that sentencing recommendation would be largely ministerial." While Fairfax takes the position that ministerial tasks (*e.g.*, the drafting of briefs and motions) "may be appropriate for delegation to private actors" so long as the private attorneys "simply implement the discretionary blueprint set out by the government attorney," he also emphasizes that "[t]he exercise of discretion is inherent in the prosecution function and is absolutely necessary to the proper functioning of the criminal justice system." After taking note of the danger of abuse of the prosecutorial function, Fairfax—calling for greater transparency in the exercise of discretion—observes that one approach is "to cabin or guide the discretion that private actors are authorized to exercise." He makes some specific suggestions for greater accountability within the criminal justice system for private actors exercising authority delegated to them, but notes that "none is a panacea" and that "we must be vigilant to ensure that our modern commitment to public prosecution is not eschewed for whatever short-term goals such delegations are perceived to advance." Some system of prosecution must exist, so it is a question of which system is best suited to modern life and ethics. While "the danger of such abuse may be tolerable in a system of public prosecution," he observes at one point, "it becomes untenable when private actors are exercising prosecutorial discretion."[107]

The subject of what an appropriate prosecutorial system should look like has been a major subject of Professor (now Dean) Fairfax's scholarship, with Fairfax also being a nationally recognized expert on grand juries.[108] One of his articles, titled "Outsourcing Criminal Prosecution?: The Limits of Criminal Justice Privatization," was published in 2010 in the *University of Chicago Legal Forum*. The abstract of that article, laying out his position, gives this summary: "[T]he outsourcing trend in criminal justice—seen most prominently in the area of private prisons and policing—should not extend to criminal prosecution because such outsourcing is in tension with the constitutional and positive law norms regulating the public-private distinction. Furthermore, concerns about ethics, fairness, transparency, accountability, performance, and the important values advanced by the public prosecution norm all militate against the outsourcing of the criminal prosecution function to private lawyers." Fairfax notes that governments "outsource a significant amount of legal work," tapping private sector lawyers for their talents and expertise, with "a significant amount of prosecution outsourcing already ... being undertaken by smaller jurisdictions across the nation." The city of Davis, California, he observed in his 2010 article, had recently contracted with a California law firm, to be paid $180 per hour for a variety of legal services, including for the "[p]rosecution of municipal code violations." He also observed that the town of Albany, Oregon, had paid a private law firm an annual flat fee of more than $200,000 for prosecution and other legal services, and that a compensation scheme in Sequim, Washington provided that a private attorney was to be paid "a flat rate of $300 per individual case" to handle criminal appeals. Contracting with lawyers to handle civil cases is relatively common. "Governments on the local, state, and federal levels," he points out, "have contracted with private lawyers to handle all manner of government lawsuits—relating to matters from antitrust and tobacco to lead paint and handguns—often on a contingency fee basis." In Minnesota's civil lawsuit against the tobacco companies, to give but one high-profile example, the Minneapolis law firm of Robins, Kaplan, Miller & Ciresi was hired to do the legal work to recover Medicaid costs spent treating smoking-relating illnesses.[109]

In his 2010 article, Professor Fairfax returned to major themes—lack of accountability and transparency, "underperformance" by outsourced prosecutors, and ethical concerns—he had articulated before. "Prosecutors," he wrote, "wield enormous power in deciding whether and what to prosecute." "Their decisions," he pointed out, "have long-lasting consequences not only for putative criminal defendants and victims of criminal conduct, but also for law enforcement strategy, correctional resource allocation, and social policy more generally." "When private actors are contracted to perform the prosecution function," he emphasized, "they exercise this power without the democratic check that theoretically applies to public prosecutors."

His trepidation about outsourcing did not stop there. "Furthermore," Fairfax added of his detailed concerns with outsourcing the criminal prosecution function, "because private contractors perform most non-courtroom tasks in private offices away from public spaces and actors and are not subject to government information disclosure laws, there is even less transparency than we enjoy with regard to public prosecutors." "There has long been strong support among reformers for the full-time public prosecution norm because of the tremendous potential for conflicts of interest when prosecutors also represent private clients," Fairfax explains, observing that while "direct conflicts can be avoided by requiring contractor firms to recuse themselves from all criminal defense matters in the jurisdiction, the danger of conflicts of interest do not end there." "A firm," he notes, worrying about corrupting influences, "could show favoritism in a criminal case to one of its private civil clients, or might use the discretionary power of criminal investigation and prosecution as a weapon against a civil litigation adversary." "[C]orruption in the prosecutorial decision-making process, resulting in bias, favor, or prejudice," Fairfax thoughtfully asserts, observing that prosecutorial discretion, including in plea bargaining, is broad and largely unfettered, "would give rise to fairness concerns which could implicate both the Due Process and Equal Protection Clauses." "When sworn government employees rather than private lawyers litigate a criminal case," he concludes, "we may have greater confidence that the Supreme Court's admonition to 'do justice' is heeded and that the government's solemn obligation is met."[110]

In Pursuit of the "Public Interest": Public Prosecutors vs. Private Lawyers

In the American legal system, it is widely understood that private lawyers retained and paid for by private clients function as zealous advocates for those clients, though all lawyers have responsibilities to the court and to the proper functioning of the legal system as a whole. As the preamble to the American Bar Association's Model Rules of Professional Conduct state in the very first sentence: "A lawyer, as a member of the legal profession, is a representative of clients, an officer of the legal system and a public citizen having special responsibility for the quality of justice." The ABA's Model Rules of Professional Conduct, which emphasize that "a lawyer performs various functions" as a client's representative, break down each of the lawyer's unique roles and responsibilities. "As advisor," the Model Rules state, "a lawyer provides a client with an informed understanding of the client's legal rights and obligations and explains their practical implications." "As advocate," the Model Rules further assert, "a lawyer zealously asserts the client's position under the rules of the adversary system." "As a public citizen," the Model Rules continue, "a lawyer should seek improvement of the law, access to the legal system, the administration of justice and the quality of service rendered by the legal profession."

Lawyers regularly seek to avoid, and in fact have a duty to avoid,[111] conflicts of interest—a duty that is complicated by a lawyer's multiple professional roles.[112] The preamble to the Model Rules of Professional Conduct stresses of a lawyer's multiple roles and how those roles, in many cases, peacefully coexist: "A lawyer's responsibilities as a representative of clients, an officer of the legal system and a public citizen are usually harmonious. Thus, when an opposing party is well represented, a lawyer can be a zealous advocate on behalf of a client and at the same time assume that justice is being done." "In the nature of law practice, however," the Model Rules point out, "conflicting responsibilities are encountered." As the preamble to the Model Rules notes: "Virtually all difficult ethical problems arise from conflict between a lawyer's responsibilities to clients, to the legal system and to the lawyer's own interest in remaining an ethical person while earning a satisfactory living." Discerning that "many difficult issues of professional discretion can arise" within the framework of the Rules of Professional Conduct, the preamble to the Model Rules offers this observation: "Such issues must be resolved through the exercise of sensitive professional and moral judgment guided by the basic principles underlying the Rules. These principles include the lawyer's obligation zealously to protect and pursue a client's legitimate interests, within the bounds of the law, while maintaining a professional, courteous and civil attitude toward all persons involved in the legal system."[113]

In early America, long before modern-day ethical rules, chief prosecutors originally were appointed as judicial officers serving a quasi-executive function.[114] However, in American states, such prosecutors later became elected independent officeholders, with an acceleration of state and local prosecutors tied to ballot boxes in the Jacksonian Age.[115] Today, these chief prosecutors—whether appointed by the President of United States and confirmed by the U.S. Senate or elected by voters as attorneys general or district attorneys—have broad discretion to determine which cases to prosecute.[116] As the Court of Appeals of Maryland explained in 2020: "[P]rosecutors have broad prosecutorial discretion in choosing whom to prosecute, what charges to bring, and, upon conviction of a defendant, what penalties to seek from among those that the law allows." "Much of that discretion is exercised in the context of plea bargaining," the Court of Appeals of Maryland emphasized in *Brown v. State*, taking note of the relationship between legislators, prosecutors and judges in these words:

> [I]t is the Legislature that makes the general policy decisions of the criminal law—defining criminal offenses in statute, setting maximum and (in some cases) minimum penalties, creating mechanisms for defendants to earn release from custody or expungement of charges or convictions. A State's Attorney exercises prosecutorial discretion subject to the policy decisions made by the Legislature. And it is the function of the court to decide on a sentence within the range set by the Legislature as appropriate to the particular defendant.[117]

In fact, prosecutors enjoy almost unlimited discretion in deciding who and when to investigate,[118] what offense to be charged,[119] the timing of an indictment or complaint,[120] and determining the place of trial.[121] For example, the Missouri Supreme Court held in 1976: "The modern day prosecutor wields the power of the State's investigatory force, decides whom to indict and prosecute, decides what evidence to submit to the court, negotiates the State's position in plea bargaining and recommends punishment to the court." In that opinion, that court also had this to say: "The entry of a private prosecutor into a criminal prosecution exposes all of these areas to prejudicial influence. We consider such exposure intolerable."[122] Because prosecutors have such wide discretion, prosecutorial misconduct is an obvious, ever-present concern and is, in fact, a significant problem in the criminal justice system.[123] Given that misconduct does occur among public prosecutors, whose sworn duty is to serve "justice" and the "public interest," the potential for misconduct among private prosecutors, whose salaries are being paid by interested parties, is of even greater concern because of potential conflicts of interest that may arise.[124] With courts, including the U.S. Supreme Court, repeatedly pointing out that prosecutions must serve "the public interest," it is hard to see how prosecutors can do that if they are being retained and paid for by private interests.[125]

The "public interest" is a somewhat amorphous and elusive concept,[126] though it has been invoked to justify everything from infrastructure projects to various regulatory schemes.[127] Courts themselves regularly use the concept to justify awards of injunctive relief.[128] Although one commentator has noted that "it has become fashionable in some quarters to dismiss the concept of the 'public interest' as devoid of content,"[129] it is helpful to analyze in assessing the practice of private prosecution because of the directive that prosecutors serve the "public interest."[130] As the Supreme Court of Pennsylvania put it: "As an officer of the court, the prosecutor has the responsibility to serve the public interest and to 'seek justice within the bounds of the law, not merely to convict.'"[131] Likewise, the Supreme Court of Louisiana has pointed out that a prosecutor's "zealousness is not without limits, because prosecutors are public officials who must 'serve the public interest.'"[132] In Michigan, a prosecutor's failure to recognize a disqualifying conflict of interest has been expressly treated under the rubric of prosecutorial misconduct,[133] while in Kentucky, a federal district court has stressed that "the right to an impartial tribunal precludes the use of contingency fee contracts in criminal prosecutions." As the latter court explained in considering the public interest construct: "Because the prosecutor's duty to serve the public interest can be distorted by a system of remuneration that compensates him based on the outcome of cases, contingency fee 'contracts for criminal prosecutors have been recognized to be unethical and potentially unconstitutional.'"[134]

Before the concept of the "public interest" is applied in the private prosecutor context, at least three complimentary definitions should be explored. First, according to political theorist Brian Barry, the "public interest" should be defined as those interests which people have in common as members of the public.[135] This definition is consistent with the views of Jean-Jacques Rousseau, who believed that a government must serve the shared interests of the people and that "it is on the basis of this common interest alone that society must be governed."[136] The "public interest"—as one scholar notes—"clearly means different things to different people,"[137] with Cass Sunstein observing that "[t]here is a large difference between the public interest and what interests the public."[138] Second, the English philosopher Jeremy Bentham believed that the "public interest" should be defined as "the sum of the interests of the several members of the community who compose it."[139] Under that definition, if "most voters favor a certain tax limitation (i.e. the Proposition 13 in California), then its adoption coincides with the public interest."[140] Richard Flathman, describing the "public interest" as a moral concept judged by values such as "promote justice" or "maximize human freedom," provides yet another conception.[141] That view originates with Aristotle, who wrote that "the good in the sphere of politics is justice, and justice consists in what tends to promote the common interest."[142]

Under the first and third definitions of "public interest," members of the public obviously have a common interest in receiving fair treatment from the criminal justice system.[143] Indeed, because any given individual can be falsely accused of a crime, each individual in the society has a common interest in receiving "just" treatment from a prosecutor.[144] That is especially so—and very important to consider—given prosecutors' exercise of almost unbridled discretion. The purpose of the U.S. Constitution's Sixth Amendment—guaranteeing the accused the right to a speedy and public trial "[i]n all criminal prosecutions," and made applicable to the states by the Fourteenth Amendment—is to make sure "a defendant is accorded a fair trial." The Sixth Amendment, one federal district court emphasized, "is intended to eliminate the abuses that the framers of the Constitution recognized were inherent in the secret 'star chamber' proceedings formerly utilized in England." "It seeks to accomplish that purpose," that court stressed, "by enabling the public to see that the defendant receives just treatment thereby making the judge and prosecutor more keenly aware of their responsibilities, encouraging witnesses to come forward and discouraging perjury."[145]

Because of the common community interest in ensuring that prosecutors treat members of the public fairly and in a non-discriminatory fashion, the "public interest" demands the prohibition of private prosecutors so that private interests are not elevated over public ones. "It is patently unethical for a lawyer in a legal proceeding to represent an individual whose interests are adverse to another party whom the lawyer represents in other matters, even if the two representations are not related," the Supreme Court of New Jersey emphasized in 1984.[146] Indeed, under the second formulation of "public interest," while state statutes permitting the use of private prosecutors arguably express the public's interest in allowing each member of the public to hire a private prosecutor if desired, that argument is flawed for at least four reasons. First, the use of private prosecutors fails to advance community cohesion. On the contrary, the use of such prosecutors encourages vengeance-seeking and pits private citizen against private citizen.[147] Second, private prosecutions, because of the prejudice and self-interest they promote, do not further the public interest in obtaining truth or justice. On the contrary, allowing them *undermines* the pursuit of these goals, increasing the odds of improper charges and unreliable convictions and decreasing accountability and transparency. Private prosecutors have an incentive to err on the side of their private clients when deciding how to handle a case and what exculpatory material to produce, and because so much of what prosecutors do happens behind closed doors, the actions of private prosecutors have a Star Chamber-quality to them.[148] Third, only a small subset of people can afford to hire private counsel, making private prosecutions inequitable. And finally, the use of private prosecutors affects *constitutional* rights that courts must safeguard—and that must not be subject to any vote.[149] Thus, while legislative bodies ordinarily declare the contours of the public interest via statute, courts are duty-bound to invalidate statutes that disregard constitutional rights such as the right to due process and to equal protection of the laws.[150] In short, constitutional provisions, not statutory directives, must be deemed the ultimate expression of the public interest for purposes of constitutional interpretation and deciding whether a particular practice is legally permissible.[151]

In their article, "Adjudicatory Independence and the Values of Procedural Due Process," Martin Redish and Lawrence Marshall have emphasized that "the purpose of the due process clause—and indeed, of the entire Bill of Rights—is to protect the individual against the government."[152] As the U.S. Supreme Court itself stated in *In re Gault*,[153] "Due process of law is the primary and indispensable foundation of individual freedom. It is the basic and essential term in the social compact which defines the rights of the individual and delimits the powers which the state may exercise."[154] Forbidding interested private prosecutors would strengthen due process safeguards, thus fortifying the protections of the U.S. Constitution, not jeopardizing them. As Justice Felix Frankfurter emphasized: "The history of American freedom is, in no small measure, the history of procedure." In fact, the Supreme Court has said this of the value of procedural protections: "[T]he procedural rules which have been fashioned from the generality of due process are our best instruments for the distillation and evaluation of essential facts from the conflicting welter of data that life and our adversary methods present. It is these instruments of due process which enhance the possibility that truth will emerge from the confrontation of opposing versions and conflicting data."[155]

The notion that a prosecutor's obligation is to further the public interest, rather than private vengeance, is reinforced by the U.S. Supreme Court's 1976 decision in *Imbler v. Pachtman*.[156] In *Imbler*, the Supreme Court held that a public prosecutor has absolute immunity to civil rights actions brought pursuant to 42 U.S.C. § 1983.[157] In rejecting the contention that prosecutors should enjoy only qualified immunity, the Court stated as follows: "A prosecutor is duty bound to exercise his best judgment both in deciding which suits to bring and in conducting them in court. The public trust of the prosecutor's office would suffer if he were constrained in making every decision by the consequences in terms of his own potential liability in a suit for damages."[158] As the Court stated later in the *Imbler* opinion: "Qualifying a prosecutor's immunity would disserve the broader public interest. It would prevent the vigorous and fearless performance of the prosecutor's duty that is essential to the proper functioning of the criminal justice system."[159] In holding that a public prosecutor enjoys absolute immunity from § 1983 actions, the Court also reiterated what it called the "well settled" common law rule that a public prosecutor is absolutely immune from suits for malicious prosecution.[160]

While the public has a separate interest in effective law enforcement,[161] that interest cannot be advanced at the expense of an individual's constitutional rights.[162] For example, several members of the U.S. Supreme Court have observed that criminal entrapment is not "countenanced" because the "obligation" to avoid "enforcement of the law by lawless means... goes beyond the conviction of the particular defendant before the court." "Public confidence in the fair and honorable administration of justice," the Court ruled, "is the transcending value at stake."[163] Indeed, the Supreme Court has recognized that conflict of interest provisions are "designed to prohibit government officials from engaging in conduct that might be inimical to the best interests of the general public."[164] Courts, as one Texas prosecutor, Edward Wilkinson, wrote in 2002, "have almost unanimously concluded that a prosecutor cannot be sufficiently disinterested so as to satisfy constitutional concerns... when a state's attorney prosecutes a defendant in a criminal case and also represents the victim against the defendant in a civil action arising from the same offense." Although Wilkinson pointed out in his 2002 law review article that "[t]he divided *Vuitton* Court did not settle the issue of whether a prosecutor's lack of disinterestedness can constitute a per se violation of due process or whether disinterestedness is subject to harmless error," he noted of that Supreme Court decision that "courts and individual judges have applied its reasoning to other contexts where questions have been raised concerning prosecutors' personal interests or conflicts of interest."[165]

In both federal and state courts, prosecutors have regularly been referred to as "quasi-judicial" officials or as performing a "quasi-judicial" function.[166] "It is the functional comparability of their judgments to those of the judge that has resulted in both grand jurors and prosecutors being referred to as 'quasi-judicial' officers, and their immunities being termed 'quasi-judicial' as well," the U.S. Supreme Court wrote in *Imbler*.[167] "Texas courts have followed federal courts and consistently held as a matter of law that absolute immunity extends to quasi-judicial officers, including prosecutors performing such typical prosecutorial functions as initiating criminal prosecution and presenting the State's case," the Court of Appeals of Texas emphasized in line with other judicial rulings from around the country.[168] "Prosecutors act as quasi-judicial officers who 'represent[] the people and presumptively act[] with impartiality in the interest of justice,' and therefore 'must subdue courtroom zeal for the sake of fairness to the defendant," the Court of Appeals of Washington held in *State v. Thierry* (2015).[169] "[P]rosecutors are considered 'quasi-judicial officers,'" the Court of Appeals of Michigan similarly wrote in 2015,[170] with the Missouri Court of Appeals ruling: "It is clear that prosecutors, as quasi-judicial officers, have a duty to avoid even the appearance of impropriety."[171]

In yet another case, a federal district court wrote in 2018 that "when prosecuting a criminal matter," prosecutors "are acting in a quasi-judicial capacity."[172] Federal and state judges, of course, have a much different role than prosecutors, with the U.S. Supreme Court noting in *Young v. U.S. ex rel. Vuitton et Fils S.A.* (1987):

> It is true that we have indicated that the standards of neutrality for prosecutors are not necessarily as stringent as those applicable to judicial or quasi-judicial officers. This difference in treatment is relevant to *whether* a conflict is found, however, not to its gravity once identified. We may require a stronger showing for a prosecutor than a judge in order to conclude that a conflict of interest exists. Once we have drawn that conclusion, however, we have deemed the prosecutor subject to influences that undermine confidence that a prosecution can be conducted in disinterested fashion. If this is the case, we cannot have confidence in a proceeding in which this officer plays the critical role of preparing and presenting the case for the defendant's guilt.[173]

Citing various U.S. Supreme Court precedents, including *Young*, one federal district court recently put it this way:

> Prosecutors, however, are traditionally accorded wide discretion in the enforcement process, and the standards of neutrality for prosecutors are not as demanding as those applied to judicial or quasi-judicial officers. This is because unlike judges, who must always remain impartial, prosecutors are partisan advocates who are permitted to be zealous in their enforcement of the law. Accordingly, to prevail on a claim predicated upon a prosecutor's conflict or bias, a petitioner must demonstrate that her trial was rendered fundamentally unfair by such conflict or bias. The Supreme Court has said "the touchstone of due process analysis in cases of alleged prosecutorial misconduct is the fairness of the trial, not the culpability of the prosecutor."[174]

The "appearance of impropriety" standard is pertinent to situations in which prosecutors have a conflict of interest or a personal interest in the litigation. "Thus," the Court of Appeals of Michigan observed in 2021, "prosecutors may be disqualified out of fairness to the accused, or merely to avoid the appearance of impropriety even in the absence of proof of bad faith or unethical conduct."[175] Likewise, a Connecticut judicial decision from 2008 emphasized that "prosecutors and judges should always strive to avoid even the appearance of impropriety."[176] While Texas case law concerning disqualification has distinguished between an elected district attorney and prosecutors at the elected prosecutor's office, on the one hand, and "special prosecutors," on the other,[177] the Supreme Court of Wyoming—citing 18 U.S.C. § 208(a)—made this observation in 2006: "Federal prosecutors are statutorily prohibited from representing the government in any matter in which they, their family or their business associates have an interest. Although our statutes and rules do not contain a similar prohibition, it would seem advisable for prosecutors to avoid even the appearance of impropriety, by refraining from representing the state in prosecutions involving family members as victims or defendants."[178] A year earlier, in *State v. Gonzales* (2005), the Supreme Court of New Mexico had this to say: "Some commentators have argued, and some jurisdictions have concluded, that an appearance of impropriety may be the basis of disqualifying an individual prosecutor."[179] And back in 1982, the Oklahoma Court of Criminal Appeals issued this directive: "we remind all prosecutors that they must at all times avoid even the appearance of impropriety throughout all phases of a criminal proceeding."[180]

In areas of the criminal justice system outside the context of public versus private prosecutions, the Supreme Court has attempted to maximize the reliability of criminal trials and convictions.[181] For example, in *In re Winship*,[182] the Supreme Court held that due process requires the prosecution to prove every element of the crime charged "beyond a reasonable doubt."[183] "The accused during a criminal prosecution," the Court emphasized in *In re Winship*, "has at stake interests of immense importance, both because of the possibility that he may lose his liberty upon conviction and because of the certainty that he would be stigmatized by the conviction." According to the Court: "The reasonable-doubt standard plays a vital role in the American scheme of criminal procedure. It is a prime instrument for reducing the risk of convictions resting on factual error."[184] Likewise, in *Strickland v. Washington*,[185] the Supreme Court held that a defendant in a criminal case must not receive "ineffective assistance of counsel." In so holding, the Court emphasized the importance of reliable convictions: "The bench-mark for judging any claim of ineffectiveness must be whether counsel's conduct so undermined the proper functioning of the adversarial process that the trial cannot be relied on as having produced a just result."[186] Similarly, in *Taylor v. Louisiana*,[187] the Court held that a defendant's constitutional rights were violated by the exclusion of women from the jury pool because the jury venire must be composed of a "fair cross section of the community" in order to ensure the fairness of a defendant's conviction.[188] And in cases such as *Tumey v. Ohio* (1927) the Supreme Court has repeatedly held that considerations of fairness dictate that potentially biased judges not be allowed to sit in judgment.[189]

The notion that fair procedure is critical to the adversary system was specifically recognized by the U.S. Supreme Court in *In re Gault* (1967). In that case, the Supreme Court held that juveniles were constitutionally entitled to legal counsel and the privilege against self-incrimination. As the Court in *In re Gault* emphasized: "Failure to observe the fundamental requirements of due process has resulted in instances, which might have been avoided, of unfairness to individuals and inadequate or inaccurate findings of fact and unfortunately prescriptions of remedy." "Under our Constitution," the Court observed, "the condition of being a boy does not justify a kangaroo court."[190] Indeed, American jurists have emphasized procedure's importance in the real world,[191] with jurists making a distinction between *procedural due process* claims (which challenge procedures effecting a deprivation) versus *substantive due process* claims (which attack the governmental action itself).[192] As the Supreme Judicial Court of Maine explained in *Doe v. Board of Osteopathic Licensure* (2020): "The basic difference between a substantive and a procedural due process claim is that procedural due process requires that the procedures provided by the state in effecting the deprivation of liberty or property be adequate in light of the affected interest, while substantive due process imposes limits on what a state may do regardless of what procedural protection is provided."[193]

To ensure the fairness of prosecutorial decisions and the reliability of criminal convictions, the use of interested "private prosecutors" must be strictly prohibited. Interested parties should not serve as prosecutors, and it must be acknowledged that lawyers retained by private clients to prosecute criminal defendants have strong incentives—financial or otherwise—to please those private clients. Where interested parties or their representatives are involved, there is inherently bias as well as the potential for prejudicial decision-making.[194] The risk of prosecutorial misconduct is also particularly high.[195] Specifically, private prosecutors for interested parties may charge an accused vindictively or inappropriately, fail to deliver complete *Brady*/potentially exculpatory evidence, seek harsher punishments than deserved, or engage in misconduct prior to trial or at the trial itself. Because prosecutorial discretion is virtually unchecked and nearly impossible to monitor, especially for conduct that occurs outside the courtroom, the only way to ensure fairness and reliability of convictions is to prohibit the use of interested private prosecutors.[196] The legal argument that interested private prosecutors should be declared unconstitutional—one that analyzes existing U.S. Supreme Court and other case law—will be presented later in this chapter and in the book's final chapter.

Significantly, the use of interested private prosecutors undermines prosecutorial accountability.[197] Although two scholars, Harold Krent and Ethan Shenkman, have mused that private enforcement of criminal laws against murder or fraud "might be salutary," even these scholars concede that, in general, the use of public prosecutors increases prosecutorial accountability. According to their *Michigan Law Review* article: "Executive branch control over federal criminal law enforcement permits greater discretionary enforcement and greater accountability. In a world of limited resources, prosecutorial discretion allows the government to gauge the relative seriousness of particular crimes and the relative threat posed by individual criminals." "Few," they write, "would equate sound policy with the maximum enforcement authorized by law, even if sufficient funds existed." "A decision not to enforce," they explain of the allocation of resources that must be doled out in any prosecutor's office as individual prosecutors decide what kind of cases to prioritize, "may represent as significant a policy determination as one to enforce." "The potential for harassment is minimized through the process of publicly controlled prosecutions," they write, adding that "public prosecutors can temper justice with mercy."[198] Private prosecutors, on the other hand, are only concerned about the specific case they are handling—and, perhaps, in the case of the private lawyers involved, about whether they'll get another chance or referral to handle future cases. In making prosecutorial decisions, a prosecutor should only be concerned with what is just and right, not with what will help bring in the next client or additional monies.

Above all else, a prosecutor has a duty to seek and "do justice"[199] and to serve the public interest.[200] As the U.S. Supreme Court, in *Connick v. Thompson*,[201] described the unique and solemn nature of the prosecutor's role: "Prosecutors have a special 'duty to seek justice, not merely to convict.' Among prosecutors' unique ethical obligations is the duty to produce *Brady* evidence to the defense. An attorney who violates his or her ethical obligations is subject to professional discipline, including sanctions, suspension, and disbarment."[202] "The role of a prosecutor," the Court emphasized, "is to see that justice is done."[203] Prosecutors must thus seek justice impartially, and they must see to it that the defendant receives a fair and impartial trial.[204] In that regard, the Supreme Court of New Jersey has described the prosecutor's role as "uniquely challenging" because it is a "double calling—to represent vigorously the state's interest in law enforcement and at the same time help assure that the accused is treated fairly and that justice is done."[205] As Justice John Paul Stevens put it in *United States v. Agurs* (1976) of the prosecutor's dual role: "For though the attorney for the sovereign must prosecute the accused with earnestness and vigor, he must always be faithful to his client's overriding interest that 'justice shall be done.' He is the 'servant of the law, the twofold aim of which is that guilt shall not escape or innocence suffer.'"[206]

Back in 1935, the U.S. Supreme Court, in its landmark decision in *Berger v. United States*,[207] called the prosecutor—in that case, the United States Attorney—"the representative not of an ordinary party to a controversy, but of a sovereignty whose obligation to govern impartially is as compelling as its obligation to govern at all; and whose interest, therefore, in a criminal prosecution is not that it shall win a case, but that justice shall be done."[208] "As such," the Supreme Court in *Berger* wrote of the prosecutor, whose argument to the jury was described as undignified and intemperate, "he is in a peculiar and very definite sense the servant of the law, the twofold aim of which is that guilt shall not escape or innocence suffer."[209] As the Court in *Berger*—in language that was later borrowed in part in *Agurs*—went on to describe the limits of the prosecutor's discretion: "He may prosecute with earnestness and vigor—indeed, he should do so. But, while he may strike hard blows, he is not at liberty to strike foul ones. It is as much his duty to refrain from improper methods calculated to produce a wrongful conviction as it is to use every legitimate means to bring about a just one."[210] When a prosecutor delivers foul blows, the prosecutor's actions can be found to constitute prosecutorial misconduct.[211]

Since the *Burger* decision, the U.S. Supreme Court has written more about the prosecutor's unique duties. For instance, in *Kyles v. Whitley*,[212] the Supreme Court wrote: "The prosecution's affirmative duty to disclose evidence favorable to a defendant can trace its origins to early 20th-century strictures against misrepresentation and is of course most prominently associated with this Court's decision in *Brady v. Maryland*." "*Brady*," the Court in *Kyles* summarized that landmark 1963 case, "held 'that the suppression by the prosecution of evidence favorable to an accused upon request violates due process where the evidence is material either to guilt or to punishment, irrespective of the good faith or bad faith of the prosecution.'"[213] "We have never held that the Constitution demands an open file policy (however such a policy might work out in practice)," the Court noted in *Kyles*, though it also observed that the American Bar Association's Standards for Criminal Justice and the Model Rules of Professional Conduct set a higher bar for disclosure.[214] "[S]howing that the prosecution knew of an item of favorable evidence unknown to the defense," the Court in *Kyles* noted, "does not amount to a *Brady* violation, without more." "But the prosecution, which alone can know what is undisclosed," it added, "must be assigned the consequent responsibility to gauge the likely net effect of all such evidence and make disclosure when the point of 'reasonable probability' is reached."[215] Of course, given what is known about the prevalence of wrongful convictions and miscarriages of justices, prosecutors should always err on the side of disclosure, not the withholding of evidence.[216]

The disclosure of evidence, which happens through acts of prosecutorial discretion, is thus one of the prosecutor's most important obligations—although U.S. Supreme Court case law lays out the contours of prosecutors' current legal obligations. Under the U.S. Supreme Court's ruling in *United States v. Bagley*,[217] evidence withheld by the government is "material," as would require a conviction's reversal, only if there is a reasonably probability that, had the evidence been disclosed to the defense, the result of the proceeding would have been different." A "reasonable probability" is a probability sufficient to undermine confidence in the outcome."[218] But in *Kyles*, the Supreme Court spoke of the prosecutor's inexorable duty to disclose evidence favorable to the accused. As the Court stated in *Kyles*: "[W]hether the prosecutor succeeds or fails in meeting this obligation (whether, that is, a failure to disclose is in good faith or bad faith), the prosecution's responsibility for failing to disclose known, favorable evidence rising to a material level of importance is inescapable."[219] "At bottom, what the State fails to recognize," the Court stressed in *Kyles*, "is that, with or without more leeway, the prosecution cannot be subject to any disclosure obligation without at some point having the responsibility to determine when it must act."[220] "[A] prosecutor anxious about tacking too close to the wind will disclose a favorable piece of evidence," the Court in *Kyles* pointed out, quickly adding: "This is as it should be. Such disclosure will serve to justify trust in the prosecutor as 'the representative... of a sovereignty... whose interest... in a criminal prosecution is not that it shall win a case, but that justice shall be done.' And it will tend to preserve the criminal trial, as distinct from the prosecutor's private deliberations, as the chosen forum for ascertaining the truth about criminal accusations."[221]

American prosecutors, it is clear, occupy a dual role in the criminal justice system—one the requires the exercise of daily judgment calls and the exercise of tremendous power. As Charles Wolfram writes in *Modern Legal Ethics* (1986): "They are the only governmental officers responsible for obtaining convictions of the guilty in litigated criminal cases; but they also bear alone the state's considerable responsibility to see that no innocent person is prosecuted, convicted, or punished."[222] This dual role is in sharp contrast to the role of private counsel, whose primary obligation within the adversarial system is to protect a client's interests. The Model Code of Professional Responsibility explicitly states that "the duty of a lawyer . . . is to represent his client zealously within the bounds of the law."[223] The prosecutor's dual role has led Wolfram to remark that the prosecutor's job is "much nearer that of a judicial officer than that of partisan advocate."[224] "The conflict of interest inherent in criminal prosecutions conducted by privately retained attorneys is clear," another legal commentator, Matthew Nichols, has observed, noting that "[t]he prosecutor's duty is distinct from the duty a private attorney owes to an individual client."[225]

An Old Practice and the Young *Decision*

In 1987, the U.S. Supreme Court held, in the exercise of its "supervisory authority," that a district court erred in appointing counsel for an interested party to prosecute a criminal contempt action. In that case, *Young v. United States ex rel. Vuitton et Fils S.A.*,[226] the Supreme Court ruled that the appointment of counsel for an interested party created opportunities for conflicts of interest to arise and created at least an appearance of impropriety.[227] Noting irreconcilable differences in the ethical obligations of public and private advocates, the Supreme Court—refusing to apply "harmless error" analysis—reversed the contempt convictions of multiple defendants.[228] Notwithstanding the Court's pronouncement in *Young*, several American states, though not the U.S. government or the federal judiciary, which the *Young* decision plainly controls, still allow the use of privately retained prosecutors for interested parties.[229] Through the years, however, the *Young* decision has made its mark on American jurisprudence and several state-court decisions have cited it along with ethics provisions in rejecting the use of interested private prosecutors.[230]

In the *Young* case, Louis Vuitton, S.A., a French leather goods manufacturer, brought suit in 1978 against several defendants alleging that Vuitton's trademark was being infringed by the manufacture, sale, and distribution of imitation Vuitton goods. Three years later Vuitton's trademark was upheld by the Ninth Circuit, and Vuitton and the defendants then entered into a settlement agreement in 1982. Under the agreement, the defendants paid Vuitton $100,000 in damages, and they consented to the entry of a permanent injunction prohibiting them from engaging in any economic activity related to Vuitton's registered trademark.[231] The permanent injunction prohibited the defendants from, among other things, "manufacturing, producing, distributing, circulating, selling, offering for sale, advertising, promoting or displaying any product bearing any simulation, reproduction, counterfeit, copy, or colorable imitation" of Vuitton's registered trademark.[232]

In early 1983, however, a Florida investigation firm employed by Vuitton discovered possible violations of the permanent injunction in an undercover "sting" operation. Subsequently, Vuitton's attorney, J. Joseph Bainton, requested that the district court appoint him and his colleague, Robert Devlin, as special counsel to prosecute a criminal contempt action for violation of the permanent injunction. The district court granted Bainton's request, with the court finding probable cause to believe that the defendants in the earlier action were engaged in conduct violating the court's injunctive order.[233] Although Bainton informed the U.S. Attorney's Office of his appointment and impending investigation, the head of that office merely wished Bainton good luck.[234] Ultimately, despite the defendants' objections to the appointment of Bainton and Devlin as special prosecutors, the five defendants were convicted of criminal contempt for violating the injunction prohibiting the infringement of Vuitton's trademark. The defendants received sentences ranging from six months to five years.[235] Before the U.S. Court of Appeals for the Second Circuit, the defendants urged that Bainton and Devlin's appointment violated their right to be prosecuted by an impartial prosecutor. But citing its previous decision in *Musidor, B.V. v. Great American Screen*,[236] the Second Circuit rejected the defendants' arguments.[237] In particular, the Second Circuit held that the supervision of contempt prosecutions by a judge is adequate protection against the "danger that the special prosecutor will use the threat of prosecution as a bargaining chip in civil negotiations."[238] Thus, the Second Circuit affirmed the defendants' contempt convictions.

On appeal to the U.S. Supreme Court, the defendants first contended that the district court lacked the authority to appoint any private attorney to prosecute the contempt action against them. However, in rejecting the argument that only the U.S. Attorney's Office could have permissibly brought a contempt prosecution, a majority of the Supreme Court stated as follows: "It is long settled that courts possess inherent authority to initiate contempt proceedings for disobedience to their orders, authority which necessarily encompasses the ability to appoint a private attorney to prosecute the contempt."[239] According to Justice Brennan's majority opinion: "Courts cannot be at the mercy of another Branch in deciding whether such proceedings should be initiated. The ability to appoint a private attorney to prosecute a contempt action satisfies the need for an independent means of self-protection, without which courts would be 'mere boards of arbitration whose judgments and decrees would be only advisory.'"[240] As another passage of Justice Brennan's majority opinion read: "While contempt proceedings are sufficiently criminal in nature to warrant the imposition of many procedural protections, their fundamental purpose is to preserve respect for the judicial system itself. As a result, courts have long had, and must continue to have, the authority to appoint private attorneys to initiate such proceedings when the need arises."[241]

While recognizing that courts have the authority to appoint private attorneys to prosecute contempt violations, the Supreme Court specifically held in *Young* that the exercise of that authority must be restrained by the principle that "only 'the least possible power adequate to the end proposed' should be used in contempt cases."[242] In so stating, the Court held, in the exercise of its supervisory power, that the district court erred in appointing counsel for an *interested* party in connection with the contempt prosecution. Notably, multiple Supreme Court cases had previously delineated the scope of a court's "supervisory powers." In *United States v. Hasting*, for instance, the Court held in 1983 that a federal court "may, within limits, formulate procedural rules not specifically required by the Constitution or the Congress."[243] In reaching that conclusion, the Court in *Hasting* outlined the three purposes underlying the use of a court's supervisory powers: (1) "to implement a remedy for violation of recognized rights," (2) "to preserve judicial integrity by ensuring that a conviction rests on appropriate considerations validly before the jury," and (3) "as a remedy designed to deter illegal conduct."[244]

The importance of the *Young* decision is clear. According to the U.S. Supreme Court in *Young*: "Regardless of whether the appointment of private counsel in this case resulted in any prosecutorial impropriety (an issue on which we express no opinion), that appointment illustrates the potential for private interest to influence the discharge of public duty."[245] Citing numerous statutory and ethical duties related to conflicts of interest, the *Young* Court specifically emphasized that "representation of other clients may compromise the prosecutor's pursuit of the Government's interest" because a prosecutor owes an ethical duty to those other clients.[246] The Court in *Young* held: "'It is the highest claim on the most noble advocate which causes the problem—fidelity, unquestioned, continuing fidelity to the client.'"[247] That a lawyer cannot serve "two masters" is a recurring theme in Supreme Court opinions.[248] Legal scholars, too, have taken notice of that idea, with two academics—Margaret Garvin and Douglas Beloof—writing that "prosecutorial control of victims' rights provides fertile ground for ethical conflicts of interest" and that "[i]t is a mistake to define the State and victims as non-adversaries simply because both are harmed by the criminal act and both may share an interest in punishment or other disposition."[249]

With the Supreme Court in *Young* having found that the trial court erred in appointing counsel for an interested party, the Court was then compelled to address whether the government should have the opportunity to demonstrate that it was "harmless error" for the trial court to appoint such counsel.[250] Writing for four members of the Court with respect to this issue, Justice Brennan's opinion noted that "some errors 'are so fundamental and pervasive that they require reversal without regard to the facts or circumstances of the particular case.'"[251] Reiterating the general rule that an error is fundamental if it undermines confidence in the integrity of the criminal proceeding,[252] Justice Brennan concluded that "the appointment of an interested prosecutor raises such doubts."[253] According to his opinion: "Prosecution by someone with conflicting loyalties 'calls into question the objectivity of those charged with bringing a defendant to judgment.'" "It is," Brennan stressed, "a fundamental premise of our society that the state wield its formidable criminal enforcement powers in a rigorously disinterested fashion, for liberty itself may be at stake in such matters."[254]

Emphasizing that the public perception of the integrity of the criminal justice system is at stake, Justice Brennan opined that a concern for actual prejudice "misses the point."[255] "'Justice,'" it was stressed "'must satisfy the appearance of justice,' and a prosecutor with conflicting loyalties presents the appearance of precisely the opposite."[256] Accordingly, he wrote, "society's interest in disinterested prosecution . . . would not be adequately protected by harmless-error analysis, for such analysis would not be sensitive to the fundamental nature of the error committed."[257] Justice Brennan also concluded that the appointment of an interested prosecutor is "an error whose effects are pervasive," writing that "[s]uch an appointment calls into question, and therefore requires scrutiny of, the conduct of an entire prosecution, rather than simply a discrete prosecutorial decision." "Determining the effect of this appointment," Brennan observed, "thus would be extremely difficult." "A prosecution," he aptly pointed out, "contains a myriad of occasions for the exercise of discretion, each of which goes to shape the record in a case, but few of which are part of the record."[258]

In contrast to Justice Brennan's opinion, Justice Powell's opinion, joined by then-Chief Justice William Rehnquist and then-Associate Justice Sandra Day O'Connor, would have remanded the case to the Second Circuit to determine whether the error of appointing private counsel to prosecute the contempt proceeding was harmless error. Although Justice Powell's opinion asserted that, "as a general matter, courts should not appoint interested private lawyers to prosecute charges of criminal contempt," his opinion also took the position that Supreme Court precedents did not call for a "per se reversal."[259] Indeed, noting that the Second Circuit had found "no reason to believe" that the private prosecutor acted unethically before the trial court, Justice Powell's opinion intimated that the Second Circuit's findings strongly suggested that the error of appointing private counsel to prosecute the contempt proceeding was harmless. Nevertheless, Justice Powell's opinion would have remanded the case to the Second Circuit for further findings on the "harmless error" issue.[260] Neither Justice White's dissenting opinion nor Justice Scalia's concurring opinion, which argued for the reversal of the defendants' convictions on different grounds, reached the "harmless error" issue. Justice White's dissenting opinion merely stated that "there was no error, constitutional or otherwise, in the appointments made in this action and that petitioners were not denied due process of law by being tried and convicted of contempt."[261] And Justice Scalia's concurring opinion, citing Article III of the U.S. Constitution, argued that the appointment of private prosecutors was defective because the prosecution of individuals who disregard court orders is not an exercise of "the judicial power of the United States."[262] According to Justice Scalia, "The federal courts have no power to prosecute condemners for disobedience of court judgments, and no derivative power to appoint an attorney to conduct contempt prosecutions."[263]

Although the Supreme Court's decision in *Young* was based upon its "supervisory powers,"[264] Justice Harry Blackmun, in a lone concurrence, would have held that "the practice—federal or state—of appointing an interested party's counsel to prosecute for criminal contempt is a violation of due process."[265] According to Justice Blackmun's terse opinion, the concept of due process "requires a disinterested prosecutor with the unique responsibility to serve the public, rather than a private client, and to seek justice that is unfettered."[266] According to one scholar, Beth Nolan: "In its basic form, a conflict of interest arises when a person who has a duty to make decisions affecting others has some independent interest in the decision. We identify a lawyer's conflict by holding up relevant interests (of self or of others) against the lawyer's primary duties to her client." "The duties required by conflict of interest rules," Nolan explains, "are generally loyalty, confidentiality, and independent professional judgment exercised in the best interests of the client."[267] Despite the fact that Justice Blackmun identified a clear due process violation, his opinion reflected only one of nine votes—and his views did not carry the day in *Young*. In fact, post-*Young* cases allowing the use of private prosecutors for interested parties have generally ignored the *Young* decision,[268] distinguished it as merely a "supervisory authority" case,[269] or held that *Young* simply precludes private prosecutors from taking complete or effective control of criminal prosecutions.[270]

The Supreme Court's decision in *Young* has been distinguished by multiple courts, with state courts not bound by it as it was not decided on constitutional grounds.[271] State supreme courts have rejected "the rule of automatic disqualification announced in *Young*,"[272] concluding, for example, that "*Young* does not apply to state court contempt proceedings" because the *Young* ruling "was an exercise of the Court's supervisory authority and not a determination of constitutional requirements."[273] One appellate court observed that "*Young* endorsed having private lawyers assist criminal prosecutors, noting that in *Young* it was acknowledged that "counsel for the beneficiary of the court order may often be most familiar with the allegedly contumacious conduct" and "[t]hat familiarity may be put to use in *assisting* a disinterested prosecutor in pursuing the contempt action."[274] As another court emphasized shortly after the Supreme Court issued its *Young* decision: "*Young* flatly proscribes turning the prosecution completely over to private counsel for interested parties, but it certainly did not proscribe all participation by such counsel. Indeed, and to the contrary, the *Young* Court was at pains to point out that private counsel's greater familiarity with the case might properly 'be put to use in *assisting* a disinterested prosecutor in pursuing the contempt action.'"[275]

The murky and problematic nature of private prosecutions was recently in the public spotlight in the case of Steven Donziger. As an attorney, Donziger won a multi-billion-dollar judgment from an Ecuadorian court against Chevron in 2011. The lawsuit was brought on behalf of thousands of indigenous people in Ecuador's Lago Agrio region of the Amazon for exposure to toxic oil waste—exposure allegedly caused by Texaco, later owned by Chevron. But after a bench trial in New York held before U.S. District Court Judge Lewis Kaplan, that judgment was later found to be unenforceable,[276] with Chevron reportedly disposing of its Ecuadorean assets and targeting Donziger himself. Indeed, a separate civil racketeering lawsuit brought by Chevron against Donziger in the United States alleged that the Ecuadorian judgment had been obtained through bribery and fraud. In 2014, after a seven-week trial, Judge Kaplan had sided with Chevron, establishing "a constructive trust for the benefit of Chevron on all property" that Mr. Donziger either received or might receive traceable to the Ecuadorian judgment, enjoining him from "undertaking any acts to monetize or profit from" that judgment, and finding that Donziger and others had conspired to fabricate evidence—a decision upheld by the U.S. Court of Appeals for the Second Circuit in 2016.[277]

Ultimately, after the U.S. Supreme Court denied certiorari and following Mr. Donziger's refusal to produce various documents as part of post-judgment discovery proceedings, Judge Kaplan issued a supplemental judgment for costs against Donziger and others. That March 2019 order required Donziger to, *inter alia*, (1) provide a list of all his electronic devices and accounts to an appointed forensic expert; and (2) surrender those devices to the forensic expert for images. Donziger did not comply with either directive, however. In May 2019, Donziger and his law firm were found in contempt of court and Chevron was awarded millions of dollars in attorneys' fees.[278] As part of a civil contempt sanction, Donziger—in addition to facing a series of coercive fines—was also ordered to surrender his passport to the clerk of court. In addition, in the course of the dispute, Donziger lost his law license (a decision he's been fighting), though he gained the support of actor Susan Sarandon, Rogers Waters of the rock band Pink Floyd, U.S. Representative Alexandria Ocasio-Cortez, and dozens of Nobel laureates who sent a letter to Attorney General Merrick Garland demanding a halt to a criminal contempt prosecution brought against him. The Second Circuit affirmed the district court judgment awarding costs because "Donziger failed to object to the imposition of costs when he had the opportunity to do so," and the Second Circuit affirmed, with one exception, the civil contempt findings.[279]

In the criminal contempt prosecution against Donziger, a misdemeanor prosecution carrying a maximum sentence of six months, the criminal contempt trial was scheduled for—and commenced on—May 10, 2021. It was tried without a jury, and it was premised on Donziger's refusal to hand over to the court his computer, cellphone and other electronic devices. "Although no attorney without a criminal record in the federal court system has ever before been detained pretrial for a misdemeanor offense," one source reported on May 17, 2021 as the trial came to a close, "Donziger has been confined to his home for 21 months for the misdemeanor charge."[280] Nearly two years earlier, on July 31, 2019, Judge Kaplan had issued an order, pursuant to Rule 42 of the Federal Rules of Criminal Procedure,[281] directing Mr. Donziger to show cause why he should not be held in criminal contempt, in violation of 18 U.S.C. § 401(3). As Judge Loretta Preska later described that order: "The Order to Show Cause, which was made returnable before the undersigned, cited six charges for criminal contempt premised on Mr. Donziger's alleged violations of court orders contained in the RICO Judgment, the Protocol Order, and the Passport Surrender Order."[282] Although the U.S. Attorney's office for the Southern District of New York had declined to prosecute the case, the law firm of Seward & Kissel had been appointed to handle the criminal contempt prosecution. As a result of the misdemeanor prosecution, Donziger was required to stay in his New York City apartment and wear an electronic monitor on his left ankle. James Craig, a spokesperson for Chevron, denied that Chevron had anything to do with Donziger's criminal prosecution. In an email, Craig wrote: "Chevron is not a party to the criminal case, did not initiate the criminal charges, and played no role in the court's decision to charge Donziger with criminal contempt of court. The criminal charges were brought by a federal District Court."

On the eve of the criminal contempt trial, Donziger served subpoenas on the law firm of Gibson, Dunn & Crutcher LLP ("GDC")—Chevron's long-time law firm—and four of GDC's partners seeking any documents or communications involving GDC or those partners and "the Private Prosecutors." The "Private Prosecutors" were defined in the subpoenas to include "Rita Glavin, Brian P. Maloney, Sareen K. Armani, or any employee or agent of the Seward & Kissel law firm." Donziger-issued subpoenas also sought, among other things, GDC billing records pertaining to Chevron Corporation and "all electronic documents or communications" from Judge Loretta A. Preska and Judge Lewis A. Kaplan involving "anyone from Gibson Dunn." After a motion to quash the subpoenas was brought, Judge Preska granted in part and denied in part that motion, quashing the subpoenas issued to Judges Kaplan and Preska as an impermissible "fishing expedition," requiring GDC's production of "hours and dollar amounts billed to Chevron on a quarterly basis on all matters, including matters involving Mr. Donziger," and modifying the "definition of 'Private Prosecutors' to require production of responsive communications only involving employees or agents of Seward and Kissel who are involved with *this case*."[283]

In a separate order signed on May 6, 2021, Judge Preska denied Donziger's pre-trial motion to discuss the July 31, 2019 Order to Show Cause on the grounds of vindictive or selective prosecution. On December 30, 2019, Donziger had previously filed a letter seeking an order "directing the Special Prosecutors to disclose the extent to which they had been in contact with Judge Kaplan during the pendency of this criminal case." The special prosecutors had responded that "the prosecution does not work for Judge Kaplan and makes its own decisions in this case" and later clarified: "the prosecution does not seek Judge Kaplan's input with respect to our prosecution decisions or our strategy, and Judge Kaplan does not weigh in our prosecution decisions or strategy." Based on those representations, the federal district court had denied Donziger's request for disclosure. On February 27, 2020, Donziger had also sought (1) the recusal of the Court based on Judge Kaplan's transfer of the case to Judge Preska, (2) the special prosecutors' disqualification on the basis that the law firm of Seward & Kissel LLP was not disinterested, and (3) dismissal of the charges because of Judge Kaplan's "demonstrable bias" against Donziger and Judge Kaplan's assertedly improper invocation of the criminal contempt power. In response, Judge Preska expressly found that Judge Kaplan was not required to recuse himself, that the transfer to her (Judge Preska) was not "somehow inappropriate," and that disqualification of the special prosecutors was unwarranted for two reasons: first, Seward & Kissel's relationships with clients doing business with Chevron or other oil companies was too attenuated to justify relief; and second, Seward & Kissel did not have a current attorney-client relationship with Chevron and its past work for the company was limited and unrelated to the case.[284]

In her May 6, 2021 Memorandum and Order, Judge Preska wrote that "the traditional frameworks for analyzing vindictive and selective prosecution claims" did not apply in Donziger's case "because Judge Kaplan initiated the contempt charges and appointed private attorneys to prosecute the matter." "While the Court recognizes that the prosecutorial function is traditionally housed within the Executive Branch," Judge Preska wrote, "federal law spells out a separate process for criminal contempt charges" under Rule 42 of the Federal Rules of Criminal Procedure. "The Supreme Court," Judge Preska observed, citing the *Young* case, "has stressed the importance of that provision, noting that '[t]he ability to appoint a private attorney to prosecute a contempt action satisfies the need for an independent means of self-protection, without which courts would be mere boards of arbitration whose judgments and decrees would be only advisory.'" In spite of Donziger's contentions in the case that Seward & Kissel "has an attorney-client relationship to Chevron and a deep loyalty to the oil & gas sector," that "it appears [Seward & Kissel] is using this criminal case to deliver a 'payback' for an entire industry that was deeply threatened by the litigation model that Mr. Donziger openly espoused and dedicated his career to," and that Chevron and its counsel at Gibson, Dunn & Crutcher LLP effectively bankroll and control the criminal prosecution of Mr. Donziger through a "partnership" with the special prosecutors, Judge Preska rejected Donziger's allegations as being "premised solely on Mr. Donziger's conjectures and suppositions, not actual evidence." Judge Preska also rejected the argument that Rule 42 is unconstitutional as applied, with Judge Preska writing that the argument that the special prosecutors were not disinterested had already been rejected. "Mr. Donziger's assertion that 'there appears to be no case in the United States dealing with Rule 42 that is anything like this' does not alter that conclusion," Judge Preska emphasized.[285]

In the criminal contempt trial itself, the lead private prosecutor, Rita Marie Glavin, said in an opening statement: "Steven Donzigner, the defendant in this case, intentionally and repeatedly disobeyed court order after court order after court order." But before the trial began, Donziger questioned the very legitimacy of the criminal contempt prosecution. As Donziger tweeted: "As I head into my Chevron-orchestrated 'trial' today after 643 days of house arrest, please never forget what this case is really about. Chevron caused a mass industrial poisoning of the Amazon."[286] In a case that drew international attention, Judge Kaplan had turned the prosecution over to a private law firm after the U.S. attorney, Geoffrey Berman, had declined to prosecute the criminal contempt charge, with Judge Kaplan then hand-picking the judge—Judge Preska—who would oversee the case. Martin Garbus, one of Steven Donziger's attorneys, had this to say about the latter judicial decision: "He knows in choosing her, he is choosing the one judge in the Southern District, perhaps, who is going to go after

Steven in the worst possible way. And Kaplan was exactly right." Donziger and his lawyers pointed to ties between Judge Preska and Chevron, taking note of a relationship with the Federalist Society—the conservative organization that had received funding from Chevron. With the prosecution's witnesses including attorneys for Gibson, Dunn & Crutcher, who represented Chevron in litigation against Donziger and had multiple meetings with the private prosecutors, Donziger gave this assessment of the likely outcome after leaving the courtroom: "I am going to get convicted. This is not a fair proceeding." "I'm still completely fucked," Donziger said, adding: "It's not a normal public prosecution."[287]

In a subsequent letter send to Judge Preska on June 22, 2021, Martin Garbus—the lawyer for Donziger—urged the federal district court to dismiss the case. "It is clear that this criminal contempt prosecution of human rights attorney Steven Donziger by private prosecutor Rita Glavin and the Seward & Kissel firm, with the active assistance of long-time Chevron law firm Gibson Dunn & Crutcher, is illegal and a nullity per core constitutional principles." In his four-page letter, Garbus had this to say:

> The basic procedural facts of this case are deeply troubling. Ms. Glavin for months hid the fact that she worked for an oil industry law firm while pushing for the detention and imprisonment of Mr. Donziger, a human rights lawyer who had won a historic pollution judgment against Chevron, an undisclosed client of her law firm. Ms. Glavin has also vigorously advocated for the Court to continue to imprison Mr. Donziger in his home—an imprisonment now in its 23rd month even though the underlying misdemeanor charges carry a maximum jail term of six months. At trial, it was revealed that Ms. Glavin has spent an estimated $1 million in taxpayer dollars on this misdemeanor case, all the while working hand-in-glove fashion with Chevron's lead outside law firm in its civil cases against Mr. Donziger.
>
> The unconstitutionality of Ms. Glavin's appointment and lack of supervision, raised in a pre-trial motion and again at trial, lies at the foundation of all these problems. Ms. Glavin was appointed as—and has taken steps to position herself as—a free-floating "inferior officer" exercising federal executive power without any of the constraints of supervision by the President or a "superior officer" nominated by the President and confirmed by the Senate. As discussed in *Arthrex* and earlier case law, this supervision and the resulting political accountability are core "structural safeguards" guaranteed by the Appointments Clause and designed to prevent this precise type of illegal prosecution from happening.[288]

As Steven Donziger himself predicted, he was convicted of criminal contempt. U.S. District Judge Loretta Preska found that prosecutors had proven each element of criminal contempt beyond a reasonable doubt and that it was time for Donziger to "pay the piper" for refusing to obey court orders handed down in the years following Chevron's successful civil case against Donziger in 2014.[289] "At stake here is the fundamental principle that a party to a legal action must abide by court orders or risk criminal sanctions, no matter how fervently he believes in the righteousness of his cause or how much he detests his adversary," Preska wrote. Martin Garbus, one of the lawyers on Donziger's *pro bono* defense team and described as "a legendary 86-year-old litigator once hailed by *The Guardian* as one of the 'finest' trial lawyers worldwide," predicted, however, that Judge Preska's 241-page ruling of July 26, 2021,[290] would be reversed on appeal. As Garbus said: "Judge Preska admits the case, prosecution and conviction is unprecedented. Her attempt to justify the proceeding is wrong and her interpretation of the law is wrong."[291] In rejecting Mr. Donziger's assertion that the special prosecutors—private attorneys affiliated with the law firm of Seward & Kissel LLP and, later, in the case of Rita Glavin and one of her associates, the law firm of Glavin PLLC—were not "disinterested" as required by the U.S. Supreme Court's decision in *Young*, Judge Preska held that "*Young* did not hold that *the Constitution* requires the appointment of a disinterested prosecutor."[292] Judge Preska emphasized that "the Special Prosecutors are paid for their work by the federal judiciary (not Chevron), and this case was initiated by Judge Kaplan (not Chevron) based on Mr. Donziger's refusal to comply with several court orders over a period of years."[293] For his part, Donziger promptly sought a new trial after his conviction, with Ron Kuby—another of Donziger's attorneys—telling Reuters: "Simply stated, the appointment of the special prosecutors was invalid because they were not supervised by any principal officer of the United States, neither were they principal officers."[294]

Predicting the future is impossible, but the U.S. Supreme Court ultimately may declare interested private prosecutors unconstitutional in spite of their past use. In *Young*, the U.S. Supreme Court relied on its supervisory authority in issuing its ruling "to avoid the necessity of reaching any constitutional issues."[295] Obviously, this approach does not preclude—and may only foreshadow—a *constitutional* bar with respect to the use of private prosecutors, as Justice Blackmun clearly preferred. Indeed, although some lower courts, echoing the *Young* approach, have used their "supervisory powers" to prohibit private prosecutors,[296] other lower courts already have held that the practice violates due process. For example, in *Brotherhood of Locomotive Firemen & Enginemen v. United States*,[297] the appointment of an interested prosecutor was characterized as a due process violation by the Fifth Circuit. Likewise, in *Ganger v. Peyton*,[298] the Fourth Circuit ruled that a due process violation existed where a part-time prosecutor was prosecuting a man for assaulting his wife while simultaneously representing the wife in a divorce proceeding.[299]

The notion that the U.S. Supreme Court's use of its "supervisory powers" in *Young* may merely foreshadow a constitutional preclusion of interested private prosecutors is supported by several Supreme Court rulings. Thus, the Supreme Court has repeatedly exercised its supervisory authority with respect to a given issue prior to creating a due process right in connection with that issue. For example, in *United States v. Hale*,[300] the Supreme Court exercised its supervisory power to reverse a conviction based on a defendant's silence after being given *Miranda* warnings. Subsequently, in *Doyle v. Ohio*,[301] the Court adopted the right to remain silent as a due process right. Likewise, in *Offutt v. United States*,[302] the Supreme Court, pursuant to its supervisory authority, reversed a criminal contempt conviction on the grounds of judicial bias. Just a year later, in *In re Murchison*,[303] the Supreme Court held that conducting a criminal contempt trial before a personally affronted judge violates due process.[304]

The Supreme Court's pattern of using its supervisory authority with respect to a given issue before adopting a due process right with regard to that issue was recognized by the Minnesota Supreme Court in *Peterson v. Peterson*.[305] In *Peterson*, the Minnesota Supreme Court held that state courts may not impose sentences greater than six months for contempt unless a jury trial has occurred or been waived. In so holding, the *Peterson* court anticipated that the Supreme Court's "supervisory authority" decision in *Cheff v. Schnackenberg*[306] was likely to be extended to a constitutional rule and applied to the states through the Fourteenth Amendment. According to the *Peterson* court: "It is realistic to think that the United States Supreme Court's new rule, although now stated to be in the exercise of its supervisory power, may be extended to the Sixth Amendment of the Federal Constitution and made applicable to the states under the Fourteenth Amendment."[307] In fact, the *Cheff* holding, based upon the Supreme Court's supervisory authority, was later made a due process right.[308] Only time will tell what the U.S. Supreme Court decides to do the next time it is given a chance to review a case involving a private prosecutor for an interested party. But given what is at stake, a future U.S. Supreme Court decision barring the use of interested private prosecutions would be a welcome development.

8

PRIVATE PROSECUTION IN AMERICA

A Violation of Due Process and Equal Protection of the Laws

The Due Process Clauses

The Due Process Clause of the U.S. Constitution's Fifth Amendment prohibits the federal government from depriving an individual "of life, liberty, or property, without due process of law."[1] The Constitution's Fourteenth Amendment, which curtails the power of American states, similarly provides: "nor shall any State deprive any person of life, liberty, or property, without due process of law."[2] In adopting the Fifth and Sixth Amendments, which respectively guarantee the accused "due process of law" and "the right to a speedy and public trial, by an impartial jury," the framers of the U.S. Bill of Rights—as the U.S. Supreme Court has ruled—put in place two "pillars" that, as interpreted, "ensure that the government must prove to a jury every criminal charge beyond a reasonable doubt, an ancient rule that has 'extend[ed] down centuries.'"[3] The Fourteenth Amendment's Due Process Clause, ratified after the Civil War and applicable to American states, "establishes a constitutional floor, not a uniform standard," the Supreme Court has emphasized, noting that while "most cases" are "answered by common law, statute, or the professional standards of the bench and bar," the principle of due process "clearly requires a 'fair trial in a fair tribunal,' before a judge with no actual bias against the defendant or interest in the outcome of his particular case."[4]

The U.S. Supreme Court has held that due process of law "centrally concerns the fundamental fairness of government activity,"[5] and that "the fundamental requirement of due process is the opportunity to be heard at a meaningful time and in a meaningful manner."[6] "[D]ue process is flexible," the Supreme Court has stressed, observing that it "calls for such procedural protections as the particular situation demands"[7] and functions to "prevent unfair and mistaken deprivations."[8] Due process does not require a State "to adopt one procedure over another on the basis that it may produce results more favorable" to the party challenging the existing procedures.[9] But the Supreme Court has described due process of law "as a safeguard against fundamentally unfair prosecutorial conduct."[10] For instance, the guarantee of due process may be violated by prosecutorial delay that is "tactical" or "reckless"[11] or by prosecutorial "vindictiveness."[12] Due process also requires prosecutors to disclose evidence favorable to defendants,[13] and it prohibits a prosecutor "from pointing to the fact that a defendant was silent" after getting a *Miranda* warning.[14]

Due process, which protects an individual's right not to be coerced except by lawful judicial power,[15] is critical to protecting the rights of the accused. The U.S. Supreme Court has explicitly held that "[i]t is axiomatic that '[a] fair trial in a fair tribunal is a basic requirement of due process.'"[16] "The right to a fair trial, guaranteed to state criminal defendants by the Due Process Clause of the Fourteenth Amendment," the Supreme Court has opined,[17] "imposes on States certain duties consistent with their sovereign obligation to ensure "that 'justice shall be done'" in all criminal prosecutions."[18] For example, in *Estelle v. Williams* (1976),[19] the Supreme Court considered "whether an accused who is compelled to wear identifiable prison clothing at his trial by a jury is denied due process or equal protection of the laws."[20] In that case, the Court emphasized that "the State cannot, consistently with the Fourteenth Amendment, compel an accused to stand trial before a jury while dressed in identifiable prison clothes,"[21] though the Court held that the defendant in that particular case had waived any objection to being tried in prison clothes by failing to object at trial.[22]

The U.S. Constitution's Due Process Clauses[23] provides critical guarantees with respect to the administration of justice. Due process not only incorporates "the common-law rule that a judge must recuse himself when he has 'a direct, personal, substantial, pecuniary interest' in a case,"[24] but it entitles a defendant to an attorney in a criminal case.[25] Due process also provides "a safeguard against fundamentally unfair prosecutorial conduct,"[26] such as the introduction of "unduly prejudicial" evidence[27] and the prosecution's failure to disclose evidence favorable to the defense[28] or supporting a defendant's actual innocence.[29] Due process, as adjudicated through the years, thus specifically prohibits prosecutors from infecting a trial with unfairness[30] or—as noted—pointing to a defendant's silence after receiving a *Miranda* warning because an accused has the constitutional right to remain silent.[31] With the Constitution's Sixth and Seventh Amendments guaranteeing the right to a jury trial in criminal and civil cases, respectively, due process entitles a person "to an impartial and disinterested tribunal in both civil and criminal cases."[32] As the U.S. Supreme Court held in *Bracy v. Gramley*,[33] for example, "[t]he floor established by the Due Process Clause clearly requires a 'fair trial in a fair tribunal' before a judge with no actual bias against the defendant or interest in the outcome of his particular case."[34] "The 'shock the conscience' standard," it has been emphasized, "typically is employed when determining whether governmental action violates due process rights under the Fifth and Fourteenth Amendments."[35] "[I]n a due process challenge to executive action," the U.S. Supreme Court has ruled, "the threshold question is whether the behavior of the governmental officer is so egregious, so outrageous, that it may fairly be said to shock the contemporary conscience."[36] Charging decisions are traditionally seen as an executive branch function,[37] though judges—through the power of judicial review laid out in *Marbury v. Madison*—have the power to review executive branch decisions.[38] Federal and state court judges also have their own separate interest in ensuring the enforcement of judicial orders (*i.e.*, the power to punish contempt of court).[39]

The neutrality requirement—whether for judges or, to a somewhat lesser extent (as various judicial decisions have determined), for prosecutors—is critical to satisfying due process requirements.[40] In the seminal case of *Tumey v. Ohio* (1927),[41] for instance, the U.S. Supreme Court explicitly ruled almost one hundred years ago that a judge must be disqualified when there is a "direct, personal, substantial, pecuniary interest in the matter before the court."[42] That case, which ensures that judges don't have a financial incentive to rule in a particular way, has dictated the opinions of many other American jurists. As one concurrence, written by an Oklahoma Supreme Court jurist, put it: "Ever since *Tumey v. Ohio*, a tribunal's *impartiality* has been a *sine qua non* element of due process within the meaning of the Fifth and Fourteenth Amendments. Judges must be not only *neutral* but also *detached*. These prerequisites preserve both the reality and appearance of fairness."[43] Judges, the U.S. Supreme Court has held, are not allowed "to try cases" in which they have "an interest in the outcome."[44] As Chief Justice William Howard Taft wrote in *Tumey* itself: "Every procedure which would offer a possible temptation to the average man ... to forget the burden of proof required to convict the defendant, or which might lead him not to hold the balance nice, clear and true between the State and the accused, denies the latter due process of law."[45] A biased decisionmaker is, simply put, "constitutionally unacceptable,"[46] with courts stressing that "a minimal rudiment of due process is a fair and impartial decisionmaker."[47]

Due process rights are often invoked in cases involving actual bias on the part of an adjudicator, but the due process guarantee also prohibits the mere *appearance of impropriety* on the part of a decision maker. Thus, in *Offutt v. United States*,[48] the Supreme Court held that "justice must satisfy the appearance of justice."[49] That language, found repeatedly in Supreme Court[50] and other cases,[51] is often used to protect due process rights. For example, in *In re Murchison*,[52] the Supreme Court cited this language to prohibit a trial judge, who acted as a one-man grand jury, from finding two of the grand jury witnesses guilty of contempt in a subsequent proceeding. According to the Court: "A fair trial in a fair tribunal is a basic requirement of due process. Fairness of course requires an absence of actual bias in the trial of cases. But our system of law has always endeavored to prevent even the probability of unfairness ...." "To perform its high function in the best way," the Court determined, "'justice must satisfy the appearance of justice.'"[53] Although this rule, as the Court held in *Aetna Life Ins. Co. v. Lavoie* (1986),[54] "may sometimes bar trial judges who have no actual bias," it is—it has been noted—"a necessary prophylactic rule to preserve the defendant's fourteenth amendment rights because proof of actual bias may be too difficult."[55]

The law regularly seeks to avoid even the "appearance of impropriety" in various contexts. For example, one federal statute—28 U.S.C. § 455—defines the circumstances mandating the disqualification of federal judges. "Any justice, judge, or magistrate judge of the United States shall disqualify himself in any proceeding in which his impartiality might reasonably be questioned," 28 U.S.C. § 455(a) provides. "The very purpose of § 455(a)," the U.S. Supreme Court ruled in 1988, "is to promote confidence in the judiciary by avoiding even the appearance of impropriety whenever possible."[56] In that case, *Liljeberg v. Health Services Acquisition Corp.*, the Supreme Court interpreted 28 U.S.C. § 455 to require a judge's recusal if a reasonable person, knowing all the circumstances, would expect that the judge would have actual knowledge of his or her interest or bias in the litigation.[57] Federal law also requires a judge's disqualification where, among other things, the judge (1) "has a personal bias or prejudice concerning a party, or personal knowledge of disputed evidentiary facts concerning the proceeding," (2) in private practice served as a lawyer "in the matter in controversy," (3) knows that, whether "individually or as a fiduciary," the judge or the judge's "spouse or a minor child residing in the household," has "a financial interest in the subject matter in controversy... or any other interest that could be substantially affected by the outcome of the proceeding," or (4) the judge or the judge's spouse, "or a person within the third degree of relationship to either of them, or the spouse of such a person," is "known by the judge to have an interest that could be substantially affected by the outcome of the proceeding."[58] Another federal statute, 28 U.S.C. § 144, also provides: "Whenever a party to any proceeding in a district court makes and files a timely and sufficient affidavit that the judge before whom the matter is pending has a personal bias or prejudice either against him or in favor of any adverse party, such judge shall proceed no further therein, but another judge shall be assigned to hear such proceeding."[59]

The U.S. Supreme Court has decided a slew of due process cases. "An insistence on the appearance of neutrality is not some artificial attempt to mask imperfection in the judicial process, but rather an essential means of ensuring the reality of a fair adjudication," the Supreme Court emphasized in *Williams v. Pennsylvania* (2016), a case in which a former prosecutor, after becoming a judge, declined to recuse himself from a death penalty case in which he'd been involved in the decision-making as the prosecutor.[60] In the Supreme Court's decision in *Concrete Pipe and Products of California, Inc. v. Construction Laborers Pension Trust for Southern California* (1993), Justice David Souter likewise wrote: "[D]ue process requires a 'neutral and detached judge in the first instance,' and the command is no different when a legislature delegates adjudicatory functions to a private party."[61] "Before one may be deprived of a protected interest, whether in a criminal or civil setting," he observed, citing prior precedents, including *Tumey v. Ohio*, "one is entitled as a matter of due process of law to an adjudicator who is not in a situation 'which would offer a possible temptation to the average man as a judge... which might lead him not to hold the balance nice, clear and true.'" "'Justice,'" Justice Souter wrote, quoting from another U.S. Supreme Court precedent, *Marshall v. Jerrico, Inc.* (1980), "'must satisfy the appearance of justice, and this stringent rule may sometimes bar trial [even] by judges who have no actual bias and who would do their very best to weigh the scales of justice equally between contending parties.' This, too, is no less true where a private party is given statutory authority to adjudicate a dispute...."[62] In *Tumey*, the Supreme Court had emphasized "[t]hat officers acting in a judicial or quasi-judicial capacity are disqualified by their interest in the controversy to be decided is, of course, the general rule."[63]

The guarantee of due process, the concept that America's founders enshrined in the U.S. Constitution, is clearly designed to ensure impartiality and fairness in judicial proceedings.[64] Such impartiality and fairness, in fact, is critical to protecting life and liberty. In the Massachusetts Constitution of 1780, drafted by John Adams, the Massachusetts lawyer and future U.S. president, one finds this telling language: "It is essential to the preservation of the rights of every individual, his life, liberty, property, and character, that there be an impartial interpretation of the laws, and administration of justice. It is the right of every citizen to be tried by judges as free, impartial, and independent as the lot of humanity will admit."[65] In 1784, Alexander Hamilton—in a letter to "the Considerate Citizens of New York"—had this to say: "The spirit of Whiggism cherishes legal liberty, holds the rights of every individual sacred, condemns or punishes no man without regular trial and conviction of some crime declared by antecedent laws, reprobates equally the punishment of the citizen by arbitrary acts of legislature, as by the lawless combinations of unauthorized individuals...." Of the state's constitution, Hamilton added:

> The 13th article of the constitution declares, "that no member of this state shall be *disfranchised* or *defrauded of any of the rights or privileges* sacred to the subjects of this state by the constitution, unless *by the law of the land or the judgment of his peers*." If we enquire what is meant by the law of the land, the best commentators will tell us, that it means *due process of law, that is, by indictment or presentment of good and lawful men*—and trial and conviction in consequence.[66]

Elsewhere, Hamilton noted that "[t]he words '*due process*' have a precise technical import, and are only applicable to the process and proceedings of the courts of justice...."[67]

The U.S. Supreme Court is tasked with defining the contours of due process. Due process, the Supreme Court held in *Morrissey v. Brewer*,[68] "is flexible and calls for such procedural protections as the particular situation demands." Over time, the Court—as legal scholars Martin Redish and Lawrence Marshall have pointed out—has used multiple methods to determine whether a specific procedure is required in a given case.[69] Initially, the Supreme Court looked to what procedures were required by the English common law. Thus, in *Murray's Lessee v. Hoboken Land & Improvement Co.* (1855),[70] the Court analyzed the types of procedures that the framers of the Fifth Amendment would have considered "the law of the land."[71] The Due Process Clause, the Court has asserted, "has its origins in Magna Carta," with the Great Charter providing that "[n]o freeman shall be taken, or imprisoned, or be disseised of his freehold, or liberties, or free customs, or be outlawed, or exiled, or any otherwise destroyed; nor will we not pass upon him, nor condemn him, but by lawful judgment of his peers, or *by the law of the land*." When the Fifth Amendment was ratified, the words "due process of law"—as the Court has said—were understood "to convey the same meaning as the Magna Carta's words, 'by the law of the land.'"[72]

The U.S. Supreme Court, as new cases come before it, continues to wrestle with the concept of due process. And each case has been analyzed according to its own unique facts and circumstances. Due process, the U.S. Supreme Court stressed in *Rippo v. Baker* (2017),[73] may "demand recusal" even when a judge has no "actual bias" but when, objectively speaking, "the probability of actual bias on the part of the judge or decisionmaker is too high to be constitutionally tolerable."[74] In *Rippo*, a Nevada jury convicted a man, Michael Rippo, of first-degree murder and other offenses and then sentenced him to death. During his trial, Rippo received information that the judge was the target of a federal bribery probe, with Rippo surmising that the Clark County District Attorney's office, which was prosecuting him, had a role in that investigation. In moving for the judge's disqualification under the Fourteenth Amendment's Due Process Clause, Rippo contended that the judge could not impartially adjudicate the case under those circumstances. The trial judge declined to recuse himself but was later indicted on federal charges after the district attorney's office had, in fact, participated in the trial judge's investigation.[75] "In *Rippo v. Baker*, the Supreme Court vacated a Nevada Supreme Court's judgment because it applied the wrong legal standard for judicial recusal," one legal commentator emphasizes of that decision.[76] The Supreme Court of Louisiana, in applying the *Rippo* precedent, specifically held in 2018 that the appearance of bias—and the probability of actual bias—dictated a trial judge's recusal in a capital murder case where the judge had "a longtime working relationship" with the victim's widow, a court employee with whom the judge had a social media relationship. As that state supreme court ruled: "[R]ecusal may be required as a constitutional safeguard against the risk of bias and, because the defendant here faces the possibility of a death sentence, every reasonable effort must be made to ensure constitutional safeguards are met."[77]

In an earlier case, *Caperton v. A.T. Massey Coal Co.* (2009),[78] the U.S. Supreme Court reviewed the Supreme Court of Appeals of West Virginia's reversal of a trial court judgment, which had entered a jury verdict of $50 million.[79] That West Virginia case had been heard by five state supreme court justices and the vote to reverse had been extremely close: 3 to 2.[80] The question presented: whether the Fourteenth Amendment's Due Process Clause was violated when one of the justices in the majority denied a recusal motion—the basis of which was that the justice had received an extraordinary amount of campaign contributions from, and through the efforts of, the board chairman and principal officer of the corporation found liable for the $50 million in damages.[81] After noting the governing law, that "objective standards . . . require recusal when 'the probability of actual bias on the part of the judge or decisionmaker is too high to be constitutionally tolerable,'" the U.S. Supreme Court in *Caperton*, in applying its precedents, determined that "in all the circumstances of this case, due process requires recusal."[82] "Not every campaign contribution by a litigant or attorney creates a probability of bias that requires a judge's recusal," the Court observed, but it called the matter before it "an exceptional case." The Court in *Caperton* concluded that "there is a serious risk of actual bias—based on objective and reasonable perceptions—when a person with a personal stake in a particular case had a significant and disproportionate influence in placing the judge on the case by raising funds or directing the judge's election campaign when the case was pending or imminent."[83]

The neutrality requirement for judges—those tasked with presiding over the administration of justice—serves legitimate aims. It would be highly inappropriate to have a judge presiding over a case who is bought and paid for by a litigant before that judge, and requiring neutrality gives the public greater confidence that adjudications will be just and fair.[84] "This requirement of neutrality in adjudicative proceedings," the U.S. Supreme Court held in *Marshall v. Jerrico, Inc.*,[85] "safeguards the two central concerns of procedural due process, the prevention of unjustified or mistaken deprivations and the promotion of participation and dialogue by affected individuals in the decisionmaking process."[86] "The neutrality requirement," the Supreme Court observed in that case, "helps to guarantee that life, liberty, or property will not be taken on the basis of an erroneous or distorted conception of the facts or the law."[87] "At the same time," the *Marshall* Court noted, "it preserves both the appearance and reality of fairness, 'generating the feeling, so important to a popular government, that justice has been done' by ensuring that no person will be deprived of his interests in the absence of a proceeding in which he may present his case with assurance that the arbiter is not predisposed to find against him."[88] In short, due process requires a "neutral and detached judge in the first instance,"[89] with *Hamdi v. Rumsfeld* (2004), another U.S. Supreme Court case emphasizing the importance of notice and an individual's opportunity to be heard,[90] holding that "a citizen-detainee" challenging his classification as an "enemy combatant" is entitled to "notice of the factual basis for his classification, and a fair opportunity to rebut the Government's factual assertions before a neutral decision maker."[91] Without a neutral, unbiased decisionmaker, and without the opportunity to be heard in the proceeding, it is simply impossible for justice to be administered in a fair manner.

The U.S. Supreme Court's decision in *Williams v. Pennsylvania* (2016)[92] is especially notable. In that case, the Supreme Court reviewed the appeal of Terrance Williams, a man convicted and sentenced to death in Pennsylvania for first-degree murder.[93] The Supreme Court of Pennsylvania had vacated a post-conviction decision granting relief to Williams.[94] But Ronald Castille, one of the justices on the Supreme Court of Pennsylvania, had previously been the district attorney who, years earlier, had given his official approval to seek the death penalty in Williams' case.[95] "Approved to proceed on the death penalty," Castille—the elected prosecutor who served as Philadelphia's DA from 1986 to 1991—had written on a memorandum prepared by another prosecutor seeking permission from her supervisors in the district attorney's office to pursue a capital charge.[96] Castille, the state supreme court justice in question, had later denied the prisoner's recusal motion and had participated in the judicial decision to deny relief.[97] The question presented in *Williams*: "whether the justice's denial of the recusal motion and his subsequent judicial participation violated the Due Process Clause of the Fourteenth Amendment"?[98] It was specifically contended by Williams that Castille's decision as a district attorney to seek the death penalty against him barred Castille, in his role as Pennsylvania's supreme court chief justice, from later adjudicating Williams' petition to overturn his sentence.[99]

In an opinion written by Justice Anthony Kennedy, the U.S. Supreme Court in *Williams* held that "under the Due Process Clause there is an impermissible risk of actual bias when a judge earlier had significant, personal involvement as a prosecutor in a critical decision regarding the defendant's case."[100] "Due process," Justice Kennedy wrote for the Court, one in which its own members occasionally recuse themselves,[101] "guarantees 'an absence of actual bias' on the part of a judge."[102] In laying out its approach to the law, the Court emphasized: "Bias is easy to attribute to others and difficult to discern in oneself. To establish an enforceable and workable framework, the Court's precedents apply an objective standard that, in the usual case, avoids having to determine whether actual bias is present." "The Court," its opinion declared, "asks not whether a judge harbors an actual, subjective bias, but instead whether, as an objective matter, "the average judge in his position is 'likely' to be neutral, or whether there is an unconstitutional 'potential for bias.'""[103] "Of particular relevance," Justice Kennedy observed in his majority opinion, "the Court has determined that an unconstitutional potential for bias exists when the same person serves as both accuser and adjudicator in a case."[104] "The due process guarantee that 'no man can be a judge in his own case' would have little substance," Justice Kennedy concluded in wrestling with the constitutional guarantee, "if it did not disqualify a former prosecutor from sitting in judgment of a prosecution in which he or she had made a critical decision."[105]

In *Williams*, the U.S. Supreme Court paid particular attention to the former prosecutor's unique role in the capital charging decision in the case in which the very same individual, as a state supreme court justice, had later participated in reviewing the case on appeal. "No attorney," Justice Kennedy began, "is more integral to the accusatory process than a prosecutor who participates in a major adversary decision."[106] Justice Kennedy then laid out the constitutional concern: "When a judge has served as an advocate for the State in the very case the court is now asked to adjudicate, a serious question arises as to whether the judge, even with the most diligent effort, could set aside any personal interest in the outcome. There is, furthermore, a risk that the judge 'would be so psychologically wedded' to his or her previous position as a prosecutor that the judge 'would consciously or unconsciously avoid the appearance of having erred or changed position.'"[107] "[T]he constitutional principles explained in *Murchison*,"[108] Justice Kennedy wrote, citing one of the Court's precedents and finding that Williams was entitled to a new hearing,[109] "are fully applicable where a judge had a direct, personal role in the defendant's prosecution."[110] In *In re Murchison*,[111] the

Court ruled: "A fair trial in a fair tribunal is a basic requirement of due process. Fairness of course requires an absence of actual bias in the trial of cases. But our system of law has always endeavored to prevent even the probability of unfairness. . . ." "To perform its high function in the best way," the Court stressed in *In re Murchison*, "'justice must satisfy the appearance of justice.'"[112]

In numerous cases, not just in capital cases, the U.S. Supreme Court has ruled that the judicial process must be free of improper or partisan influences.[113] In one case, *Ward v. Village of Monroeville* (1972),[114] the Supreme Court—utilizing a due process analysis—invalidated a procedure in which sums produced from a mayor's court accounted for a substantial portion of municipal revenues, even though the mayor's salary was not augmented by those sums. Although the accused in *Ward* was convicted of only two minor traffic offenses and fined a total of one hundred dollars, the Supreme Court ruled that due process required the elimination of the possibility of bias. According to the Court:

> Plainly a "possible temptation" may... exist when the mayor's executive responsibilities for village finances may make him partisan to maintain the high level of contribution from the mayor's court. This, too, is a "situation in which an official perforce occupies two practically and seriously inconsistent positions, one partisan and the other judicial, and necessarily involves a lack of due process of law in the trial of defendants charged with crimes before him."[115]

In other words, the Supreme Court—utilizing due process principles—"may disqualify even decision-makers who in fact 'have no actual bias' if they might reasonably appear to be biased."[116] Avoiding the appearance of impropriety, an ethical directive and imperative, helps to ensure that the criminal justice system is not only more just and less biased, but more trusted by the public.[117] That's why, in 2013, the American Bar Association issued Formal Opinion 462, titled "Judge's Use of Electronic Social Networking Media," cautioning judges to be conscious of the way their online social media relationships will appear to others.[118] Under the Model Code of Judicial Conduct, judges are exhorted to "maintain the dignity of judicial office at all times, and avoid both impropriety and the appearance of impropriety in their professional and personal lives." Judges, the code's preamble reads, "should aspire at all times to conduct that ensures the greatest possible public confidence in their independence, impartiality, integrity, and competence."[119]

Although the U.S. Supreme Court has consistently held that judges must be free from the appearance of impropriety, the nation's highest court has also required that other actors in the criminal justice system remain bias-free. For example, in cases such as *Strauder v. West Virginia*,[120] *Batson v. Kentucky*,[121] *Taylor v. Louisiana*,[122] *Miller-El v. Dretke*,[123] and *Foster v. Chatman*,[124] the Supreme Court has emphasized that juries—the citizens who sit in judgment on the actions of the accused—must be free of racial and gender bias.[125] Other cases have likewise held that juries must be free of additional biases, misconceptions, and invidious influences.[126] For example, in *Gold v. United States*,[127] the Supreme Court reversed the conviction of an accused who was charged with violating the National Labor Relations Act by filing a false non-Communist affidavit. In that case, three members of the jury were approached by an F.B.I. agent and asked if they had received any Communist propaganda.[128] Likewise, in *Carter v. Kentucky*,[129] the Supreme Court held that "a state trial judge has the constitutional obligation, upon proper request, to minimize the danger that the jury will give evidentiary weight to the defendant's failure to testify."[130] "Judges themselves must not only avoid the appearance of impropriety but also instruct juries to do the same," one federal district court recently put it in discussing the role of jurors.[131]

In addition to judges and juries, defense counsel must also be free of influences which might adversely affect a defendant's constitutional rights. Thus, in *Glasser v. United States*,[132] the Supreme Court held that an attorney's representation of two co-defendants whose interests conflict denies a defendant his constitutional right to effective assistance of counsel.[133] "In all cases," the Court observed in *Glasser*, "the constitutional safeguards are to be jealously preserved for the benefit of the accused, but especially is this true where the scales of justice may be delicately posed between guilt and innocence."[134] Another conflict of interest case, *Holloway v. Arkansas*,[135] is also instructive. In *Holloway*, the defendant's attorney apprised the court of a conflict of interest in his having to represent three co-defendants in the same trial. Holding that an accused's right to counsel was denied where the trial court, over the defense attorney's objection, refused to provide separate counsel for the co-defendants, the Supreme Court ruled that "whenever a trial court improperly requires joint representation over timely objection reversal is automatic," and no prejudice need be shown.[136] The U.S. Constitution's Sixth Amendment affords criminal defendants the right to "the Assistance of Counsel,"[137] and that constitutional right—as the Supreme Court noted in *United States v. Cronic* (1984)—exists "not for its own sake, but because of the effect it has on the ability of the accused to receive a fair trial."[138]

In another U.S. Supreme Court case, *Cuyler v. Sullivan* (1980), two privately retained lawyers represented three criminal defendants charged with first-degree murder in Pennsylvania. In that case, the Supreme Court observed: "Defense counsel have an ethical obligation to avoid conflicting representations and to advise the court promptly when a conflict of interest arises during the course of trial." "In order to establish a violation of the Sixth Amendment," the *Cuyler* Court wrote, "a defendant who raised no objection at trial must demonstrate that an actual conflict of interest adversely affected his lawyer's performance."[139] In yet another case, *Wheat v. United States* (1988), the Supreme Court emphasized that "multiple representation of criminal defendants engenders special dangers of which a court must be aware.[140] In *Wheat*, the Court held: "Federal courts have an independent interest in ensuring that criminal trials are conducted within the ethical standards of the profession and that legal proceedings appear fair to all who observe them." "Both the American Bar Association's Model Code of Professional Responsibility and its Model Rules of Professional Conduct," the Court noted, "imposed limitations on multiple representation of clients." "Not only the interest of a criminal defendant but the institutional interest in the rendition of just verdicts in criminal cases may be jeopardized by unregulated multiple representation," the Court stressed.[141]

With constitutional law rulings already prohibiting biased or improperly influenced judges, juries, and defense attorneys, the time has come to end the anachronistic practice of allowing private prosecutions by interested parties. The U.S. Supreme Court in *Marshall* found that "the rigid requirements of *Tumey* and *Ward*, designed for officials performing judicial or quasi-judicial functions, are not applicable to those acting in a prosecutorial or plaintiff-like capacity."[142] As the Court emphasized: "Prosecutors need not be entirely 'neutral and detached.' In an adversary system, they are necessarily permitted to be zealous in their enforcement of the law." "The constitutional interests in accurate finding of facts and application of law, and in preserving a fair and open process for decision," the Court observed, "are not to the same degree implicated if it is the prosecutor, and not the judge, who is offered an incentive for securing civil penalties."[143] But prosecutors making judgments about the application of the criminal law *do* serve in a quasi-judicial capacity because of their unique duties and the ethical responsibility they have to serve the cause of justice.[144] The Court in *Marshall* itself made clear that the U.S. Constitution's Due Process Clause *does* constrain prosecutors in certain respects. "We do not suggest, and appellants do not contend, that the Due Process Clause imposes no limits on the partisanship of administrative prosecutors," the *Marshall* Court observed.[145] "Prosecutors," the Court stated, "are also public officials; they too must serve the public interest."[146] "In appropriate circumstances," it emphasized, "the Court has made clear that traditions of prosecutorial discretion do not immunize from judicial scrutiny cases in which the enforcement decisions of an administrator were motivated by improper factors or were otherwise contrary to law."[147] "A scheme injecting a personal interest, financial or otherwise, into the enforcement process," the Court in *Marshall* made clear, "may bring irrelevant or impermissible factors into the prosecutorial decision and in some contexts raise serious constitutional questions."[148] Private prosecutions by interested parties do just that; they inject improper motivations and factors into the decision-making process.

Due process principles impose limits on the "partisanship" of prosecutors,[149] who already can be disqualified—as just one example—for participating in cases in which they have a personal interest.[150] Public prosecutors have vast discretion,[151] and it is true that legislatures—out of necessity—routinely delegate power to public prosecutors to enforce the criminal law.[152] In the twenty-first century, a number of governmental functions have been delegated to *private* actors.[153] For example, state attorneys general and public agencies regularly employ experts in the private sector or lawyers in private practice to handle civil litigation matters.[154] But there are certain core governmental functions that either cannot or should not be delegated,[155] especially in the criminal law arena to those with a self-interest or a financial interest in the outcome of the governmental function in question.[156] For example, it has been argued with considerable force that the use of private, for-profit prisons impermissibly mixes profit with the core governmental function of incarceration and leads to damaging consequences for prisoners and the public alike. As Robert Craig and André Douglas Pond Cummings write in the *University of Baltimore Law Review*: "Privatization of incarceration introduces serious perverse incentives created by government and financial bias throughout the criminal justice process, and contracting a core government function to private entities undermines the legitimacy of the justice system at large."[157] Whereas private prison operators seek to fill their available prison space and then cut costs to maximize profits for their shareholders, a well-functioning prison system should have well-trained, well-resourced staff, provide educational opportunities for incarcerated individuals, and seek to rehabilitate those serving time behind bars.[158] A popular maxim of the Enlightenment was that any punishment that goes beyond necessity is "tyrannical," yet for-profit, private prison operators—because of their financial motivations—seek to encourage longer sentences, not shorter ones.[159]

In the twenty-first century, the prosecution of crime by an interested private party or that interested party's retained attorney should be seen as an impermissible delegation of power[160] because of the interested party's personal stake in the proceeding's outcome.[161] The prosecution of crime is a core governmental function,[162] and criminal prosecutions—as instances of misconduct make clear—are subject to abuse. Although victims of crime were once primarily responsible for directing them, that is simply no longer the case following the rise of public prosecutors' offices. Public prosecutors bring cases on behalf of "The State" or "The People" because the interests of the whole community are paramount.[163] It is one thing for a private party to bring a *civil* lawsuit seeking injunctive relief or money damages, but it is quite another for an interested private party to bring, control, guide or assist a *criminal* prosecution that could result in a conviction and a punishment (e.g., the death penalty's imposition, a term of imprisonment, or a criminal fine). Under existing law, not only can criminal cases deprive people of their lives or liberty, but criminal prosecutions can be stigmatizing and may have collateral consequences.[164]

The collateral consequences of criminal prosecutions should not be overlooked in assessing the practice of private prosecutions. As one scholar, Yuri Linetsky, notes: "While the criminal case may end in a dismissal or acquittal, the defendant often still suffers significant collateral consequences: legal fees, loss of liberty, loss of employment, and loss of reputation (especially in the internet age)."[165] Either a felony or a misdemeanor can have collateral consequences, so interested private prosecutions should be prohibited in both of those categories of cases.[166] Handing an interested private party the ability to cause the arrest of another person or handing an interested private party leverage over another person through the threat of a criminal prosecution is a recipe for abuse of power. Even if a court ultimately throws out the charges or later finds that there was overcharging or, perhaps, a vindictive or malicious prosecution, the damage may already have been done. In fact, there can be a wide variety of adverse consequences for anyone who faces a criminal prosecution or who ends up with a criminal record.[167] "A collateral consequence," scholar Paul Crane emphasizes, "is any sanction or disability imposed by law as a result of a criminal conviction that is in addition to the conviction's direct consequences."[168]

To evaluate due process claims, the U.S. Supreme Court—in the year of America's bicentennial—established a three-factor balancing test in *Mathews v. Eldridge* (1976).[169] "Procedural due process," the Supreme Court held in that case, "imposes constraints on governmental decisions which deprive individuals of 'liberty' or 'property' interests within the meaning of the Due Process Clause of the Fifth or Fourteenth Amendment."[170] After emphasizing that "[t]his Court consistently has held that some form of hearing is required before an individual is finally deprived of a property interest,"[171] the *Mathews* Court stressed: "[t]he fundamental requirement of due process is the opportunity to be heard 'at a meaningful time and in a meaningful manner.'"[172] "[O]ur prior decisions," the Court ruled, pointing out that due process is a flexible concept, "indicate that identification of the specific dictates of due process generally requires consideration of three distinct factors: First, the private interest that will be affected by the official action; second, the risk of an erroneous deprivation of such interest through the procedures used, and the probably value, if any, of additional or substitute procedural safeguards; and finally, the Government's interest, including the function involved and the fiscal and administrative burdens that the additional or substitute procedural requirement would entail."[173]

The three-factor *Mathews* test is applied in a variety of circumstances. In *Medina v. California* (1992),[174] though, the U.S. Supreme Court—in another opinion written by Justice Anthony Kennedy—held that "the *Mathews* balancing test does not provide the appropriate framework for assessing the validity of state procedural rules which ... are part of the criminal process."[175] "In the field of criminal law," the Court emphasized in *Medina*, it had "defined the category of infractions that violate 'fundamental fairness' very narrowly" based on the recognition that "[b]eyond the specific guarantees enumerated in the Bill of Rights, the Due Process Clause has limited operation."[176] "The Bill of Rights," the *Medina* Court stated, "speaks in explicit terms to many aspects of criminal procedure, and the expansion of those constitutional guarantees under the open-ended rubric of the Due Process Clause invites undue interference with both considered legislative judgments and the careful balance that the Constitution strikes between liberty and order."[177] "The proper analytical approach, and the one that we adopt here," the Supreme Court held in *Medina*, "is that set forth in *Patterson v. New York*, 432 U.S. 197, 97 S. Ct. 2319, 53 L.E.2d 281 (1977), which was decided one year after *Mathews*."[178] In *Patterson*, the Court ruled: "It goes without saying that preventing and dealing with crime is much more the business of the States than it is of the Federal Government, and that we should not lightly construe the Constitution so as to intrude upon the administration of justice by the individual States." "Among other things," the Court held in *Patterson*, "it is normally 'within the power of the State to regulate procedures under which its laws are carried out, including the burden of producing evidence and the burden of persuasion,' and its decision in this regard is not subject to proscription under the Due Process Clause unless 'it offends some principle of justice so rooted in the traditions and conscience of our people as to be ranked as fundamental.'"[179] The question in *Medina* was "whether the Due Process Clause permits a State to require a defendant who alleges incompetence to stand trial to bear the burden of proving so by a preponderance of the evidence."[180]

To evaluate the contours of due process, the U.S. Supreme Court once used what has been called a "frozen-in-history" approach, looking to what the English common law permitted.[181] That approach, however, ultimately gave way to a more nuanced and modern approach,[182] with the Court in *Hurtado v. California* (1884) emphasizing that "[i]t was the characteristic principle of the common law to draw its inspiration from every fountain of justice" and "we are not to assume that the sources of its supply have been exhausted."[183] Thus, in *Twining v. New Jersey*,[184] the Supreme Court stated that the meaning of the due process clause "should be gradually ascertained by the process of inclusion and exclusion in the course of decisions of cases as they arise."[185] "[T]he amount and quality of process that our precedents have recognized as 'due'" under the Fifth Amendment's Due Process Clause, the Court has acknowledged, "has changed considerably since the founding."[186] In essence, the Supreme Court abandoned the historical approach in favor of asking "whether a given procedure was essential to modern—as opposed to 17th century—notions of fairness."[187]

The modern era is characterized by practices very different than those of prior ages, some of which have medieval roots. "The 1970s brought forth what Judge Friendly characterized as a 'due process explosion,'" one legal commentator has written, noting that "the Supreme Court evolved new and broader concepts of 'property' and 'liberty' which formed the fuel for the 'due process explosion.'"[188] As yet another source, a popular criminal procedure treatise, explains of the U.S. Supreme Court's due process jurisprudence: the Court "relied upon the same 'evolving concept' of due process that had dominated due process analysis in the past," leading it "in many instances to condemn practices never thought to raise significant difficulties at common law."[189] Writing in 2013, some 145 years after the Fourteenth Amendment's ratification, the Supreme Court specifically observed that "[t]he liberty protected by the Fifth Amendment's Due Process Clause contains within it the prohibition against denying to any person the equal protection of the laws."[190] The U.S. Supreme Court in *Powell v. Alabama* (1932) interpreted the Fourteenth Amendment's Due Process Clause to require the provision of counsel for defendants in capital cases,[191] and the Fourteenth Amendment's due process and equal protection guarantees must be seen as fundamentally transforming American law.[192]

The Due Process Concerns Raised by Private Prosecutors

As shown in the book's prior chapters, private prosecutions by interested parties are not yet a thing of the past.[193] "In a few jurisdictions," one contemporary criminal procedure treatise notes of the state of American law, "private parties may institute criminal proceedings without the authorization or approval of a prosecuting attorney." "The system of private prosecution that survives in some jurisdictions has its roots in English common law," that source notes, making these observations on the past and the current state of affairs: "Over time, in both England and the United States, the use of public prosecutors increased, and the use of private prosecutors began to fall into disfavor. Today, some states prohibit altogether the use of private prosecutors on behalf of interested parties. Others allow private prosecutors to *assist* in the prosecution, but only if the public prosecutor consents and retains control over the case." In underscoring the state law variations that exist, that criminal procedure treatise makes these additional comments about American states: "Still others permit the trial court to appoint a private prosecutor when the public prosecutor has refused or neglected to perform his or her duties. Finally, other jurisdictions permit a private party to force a public prosecution only if the prosecution's failure to prosecute constitutes an abuse of discretion."[194]

In an article published in the *Alabama Law Review* in 2021, Louis Rulli—a professor at the University of Pennsylvania Law School—describes how attorneys in private practice, whether on a contractual basis or due to self-interested or financial motives, get involved in criminal cases in a variety of ways. As Rulli explains: "On occasion, law-enforcement agencies hire private lawyers to litigate on the public's behalf. State attorney-general offices sometimes engage a private law firm to temporarily expand their resources to handle a complex case, bring on special expertise, or obtain needed help during temporary periods of time." In the latter instances, Rulli writes, "private counsel are often called 'special assistants' and perform specified litigation tasks enumerated by contract." As Rulli observes of those specially employed individuals: "Special assistants are compensated on an hourly basis or for a flat amount that is set in relation to salaried members of the office. In some states, however, this traditional form of compensation has been replaced by contingency fees in which special assistants assume a personal financial stake in the outcome of the cases they handle on behalf of the public." "There is serious question as to whether private lawyers are constitutionally permitted to prosecute criminal cases, regardless of the manner of payment," Rulli stresses, taking this modern-day snapshot of the law associated with private prosecution: "Some states prohibit the practice, while others permit it as long as a district attorney retains strict control over the prosecution. In some jurisdictions, trial courts possess discretion to determine whether private attorneys may assist a district attorney when prosecuting a criminal case." The use of part-time private prosecutors, Rulli notes, brings "an increased risk of outside conflicts arising from their nongovernmental lawyering."[195]

The U.S. Supreme Court itself has taken notice of the historical use of private prosecutors on more than one occasion. For example, in *Rehberg v. Paulk*, the target of a grand jury investigation brought a section 1983 action alleging that the chief investigator for a district attorney's office violated his constitutional rights by fabricating evidence. In its 2012 ruling in the case, in which it was held that the investigator—a grand jury witness—had absolute immunity, the Supreme Court noted that "[w]hen § 1983's predecessor was enacted in 1871, it was common for criminal cases to be prosecuted by private parties, who did not enjoy absolute immunity from suit." "[P]rivate prosecutors, like private plaintiffs in civil suits, did not enjoy absolute immunity from suit," the *Rehberg* Court remarked, pointing out that "[i]nstead, 'the generally accepted rule' was that a private complainant who procured an arrest or prosecution could be held liable in an action for malicious prosecution if the complainant acted with malice and without probable cause." "In the decades after the adoption of the 1871 Civil Rights Act, however," it was emphasized of the development of American history, "the prosecutorial function was increasingly assumed by public officials, and common-law courts held that public prosecutors, unlike their private predecessors, were absolutely immune from the types of tort claims that an aggrieved or vengeful criminal defendant was most likely to assert, namely, claims for malicious prosecution or defamation." "This adaption of prosecutorial immunity accommodated the special needs of public, as opposed to private, prosecutors," the *Rehberg* Court stressed, adding of its own prior case law: "Thus, when the issue of prosecutorial immunity under § 1983 reached this Court in *Imbler*, the Court did not simply apply the scope of immunity recognized by common-law courts as of 1871 but instead placed substantial reliance on post–1871 cases extending broad immunity to public prosecutors sued for common-law torts."[196] The Supreme Court, in prior decisions, has also afforded qualified immunity—an issue that has attracted considerable public attention and debate following George Floyd's murder in Minneapolis in 2020[197]—to police officers and others performing discretionary functions.[198]

Prosecutors have long been afforded special protection through the immunity doctrine created by the U.S. Supreme Court. In *Imbler v. Patchman* (1976), the Supreme Court specifically held that a state prosecuting attorney acting within the scope of his duties in initiating and pursuing a criminal prosecution and in presenting the state's case was absolutely immune from a civil suit under 42 U.S.C. § 1983 for damages.[199] In that case, Paul Imbler had been charged with a first-degree felony murder in the shooting death at a Los Angeles market. Witnesses had identified Imbler as the gunman, but Imbler's alibi defense at trial was that he had spent the night of the shooting bar-hopping. A deputy district attorney, Richard Pachtman, had been the prosecutor at Imbler's trial—one in which Imbler was found guilty and sentenced to death. After the California Supreme Court unanimously affirmed Imbler's conviction and sentence, Patchman had written to California's governor describing newly discovered evidence, including witnesses corroborating Imbler's alibi. In that communication, Patchman further noted that leads to some of this information had been available to Imbler's counsel prior to trial but had, apparently, never been developed, although Patchman asserted that none of the new evidence was conclusive of Imbler's innocence. Patchman observed that he, as a prosecutor, "had a duty to be fair and see that all true facts whether helpful to the case or not, should be presented." Imbler's attorney lauded Pachtman's post-trial investigatory work as exemplifying a "devotion to duty" and as befitting "the highest tradition of law enforcement and justice." But Imbler's lawyer also charged that the prosecution had knowingly used false testimony and suppressed material evidence at Imbler's criminal trial. Ultimately, Imbler's death sentence was overturned. After a writ of habeas corpus was granted, the prosecution decided not to retry Imbler and he was released. Imbler then filed his section 1983 lawsuit alleging a violation of his civil rights and seeking $2.7 million in damages from each named defendant.

In its *Imbler* decision, the U.S. Supreme Court noted that the case "marks our first opportunity to address the § 1983 liability of a state prosecuting officer." After observing that some lower courts had previously addressed the issue, the Court in *Imbler* gave this historical context: "The common-law immunity of a prosecutor is based upon the same considerations that underlie the common-law immunities of judges and grand jurors acting within the scope of their duties. These include concern that harassment by unfounded litigation would cause a deflection of the prosecutor's energies from his public duties, and the possibility that he would shade his decisions instead of exercising the independence of judgment required by his public trust." After asserting that the common-law rule of prosecutorial immunity is "well settled," the Court decided that public policy considerations warranted affording absolute immunity under section 1983. "If a prosecutor had only a qualified immunity," the Court ruled, "the threat of § 1983 suits would undermine performance of his duties no less than would the threat of common-law suits for malicious prosecution." "A prosecutor," the *Imbler* Court stressed, "is duty bound to exercise his best judgment both in deciding which suits to bring and in conducting them in court." In providing the same level of immunity to prosecutors as it did for judges in *Stump v. Sparkman* (1978),[200] the Court in *Imbler* laid out the specific rationale for its decision. "The public trust of the prosecutor's office," it ruled in the mid-1970s, "would suffer if he were constrained in making every decision by the consequences in terms of his own potential liability in a suit for damages."[201]

Although the Supreme Court in *Imbler* decided to afford absolute immunity to prosecutors, it observed in dicta that prosecutorial immunity in section 1983 suits "does not leave the public powerless to deter misconduct or to punish that which occurs." As the Court wrote: "This Court has never suggested that the policy considerations which compel civil immunity for certain governmental officials also place them beyond the reach of the criminal law. Even judges, cloaked with absolute civil immunity for centuries, could be punished criminally for willful deprivations of constitutional rights on the strength of 18 U.S.C. § 242, the criminal analog of § 1983. The prosecutor would fare no better for his willful acts." The Court also noted that a prosecutor depriving someone of constitutional rights could be subject "to professional discipline by an association of his peers"—a check the Court characterized as undermining "the argument that the imposition of civil liability is the only way to insure that prosecutors are mindful of the constitutional rights of persons accused of crime."[202] As an empirical matter, though, prosecutors are only rarely disciplined by state ethics boards, diminishing the effectiveness of that check on prosecutorial abuses.[203] The absolute immunity extended to prosecutors—like the qualified immunity afforded to police officers—has come under criticism in recent years, with commentators noting that egregious prosecutorial misconduct remains a significant problem and that such misconduct can lead—and has led—to wrongful convictions. America's criminal justice system—in the words of one law professor—"lacks effective mechanisms to deter or remedy prosecutorial misconduct."[204]

The issue of the legitimacy or illegitimacy of private prosecutors has been percolating for a long time, leading to at least some writings on the subject from the nation's highest court. In *Robertson v. U.S. ex rel. Watson* (2010), the U.S. Supreme Court dismissed a writ of certiorari as "improvidently granted" in a case in which the following issue was presented for review: "Whether an action for criminal contempt in a congressionally created court may constitutionally be brought in the name and pursuant to the power of a private person, rather than in the name and pursuant to the power of the United States"? Although the writ of certiorari was ultimately dismissed in that case, Chief Justice John Roberts—joined by Justices Antonin Scalia, Anthony Kennedy and Sonia Sotomayor—wrote in a dissent that "[t]he answer to that question is no." As the dissent of Chief Justice Roberts read: "The terrifying force of the criminal justice system may only be brought to bear against an individual by society as a whole, through a prosecution brought on behalf of the government. The court below held otherwise, relying on a *dissenting* opinion in one of our cases, and on the litigating position of the United States, which the Solicitor General has properly abandoned in this Court. We should correct the lower court's error and return the case to that court to resolve the remaining questions."[205]

In his dissent in *Robertson*, Chief Justice Roberts emphasized that "[t]he protections our Bill of Rights affords those facing criminal prosecution apply to '*any* person,' '*any* criminal case,' and '*all* criminal prosecutions.'"[206] "But those protections," he wrote, adding his own emphasis, "apply only against *the government*; '[i]ndividual invasion of individual rights' is not covered." "If the safeguards of the Bill of Rights are to be available in 'all criminal prosecutions,'" he noted, "then any such prosecution must be considered to be one on behalf of the government—otherwise the constitutional limits do not apply."[207] "The court below," Chief Justice Roberts stressed of the case under consideration, "rejected this understanding, concluding that Watson's 'criminal contempt prosecution' was not 'a public action' but 'a private action,' such that it was not covered by an agreement binding the Government." As the dissent of Chief Justice Roberts continued: "But as we have explained, '[t]he purpose of a criminal court is not to provide a forum for the ascertainment of private rights. Rather it is to vindicate the public interest in the enforcement of the criminal law while at the same time safeguarding the rights of the individual defendant.'"[208] Whereas the English jurist, Sir William Blackstone, distinguished between "Private Wrongs" and "Public Wrongs,"[209] and whereas the criminal law has long been associated with public wrongs while the law of torts has dealt with private wrongs,[210] the Supreme Court of Virginia—in a pre-*Robertson* case—itself tellingly worried aloud about substituting "private vengeance" for what should be an "impartial application of the criminal law."[211]

Chief Justice Roberts and the other three dissenters in *Robertson* saw troubling implications—implications that should not be forgotten in the evaluation of the practice of private prosecutions—if the lower court ruling in the case were allowed to stand. As Chief Justice Roberts wrote:

> The holding below gives rise to a broad array of unsettling questions. Take the Due Process Clause. It guarantees particular rights in criminal prosecutions because the prosecutor is a state actor, carrying out a "duty *on the part of the Government*." *Kyles v. Whitley,* 514 U.S. 419, 433, 115 S. Ct. 1555, 131 L.Ed.2d 490 (1995) (emphasis added). But if the criminal prosecution is instead viewed as "a private action," not an exercise of sovereign power, how would those rights attach? Cf. *DeShaney v. Winnebago County Dept. of Social Servs.,* 489 U.S. 189, 195–196, 109 S. Ct. 998, 103 L.Ed.2d 249 (1989). What about *Brady v. Maryland,* 373 U.S. 83, 83 S. Ct. 1194, 10 L.Ed.2d 215 (1963)? The private prosecutor is likely to have evidence pertinent to the proceeding—particularly if, as here, the private prosecutor is also the victim of the crime. But if the prosecutor is not exercising governmental authority, what would be the constitutional basis for any *Brady* obligations? May the private prosecutor interview the defendant without *Miranda* warnings, since she is not acting on behalf of any sovereign but only in a private capacity? See *Miranda v. Arizona,* 384 U.S. 436, 86 S. Ct. 1602, 16 L.Ed.2d 694 (1966).
>
> Our entire criminal justice system is premised on the notion that a criminal prosecution pits the government against the governed, not one private citizen against another. The ruling below is a startling repudiation of that basic understanding.[212]

Though his *Commentaries on the Laws of England* was written more than 250 years ago, the "public" versus "private" distinction raised by Sir William Blackstone is still relevant and worthy of consideration today. Prosecutors—those tasked with prosecuting crime and, along with police officers, protecting public safety—have ethical responsibilities and legal obligations. "It is well established under *Brady* that prosecutors have a constitutional duty to disclose exculpatory evidence to criminal defendants," a federal district court aptly observed, setting forth the applicable rule of law established by the U.S. Supreme Court in its landmark decision in *Brady v. Maryland* (1963).[213] "Criminal convictions obtained by presentations of known false evidence or by suppression of exculpatory or impeaching evidence violate the due process guarantees of the Fourteenth Amendment and are actionable under 42 U.S.C. § 1983," that same federal district court emphasized, adding: "This is because 'deliberate deception of a court and jurors by the presentation of known false evidence is incompatible with rudimentary demands of justice.'" To establish a *Brady* violation, the following three elements must be shown: (1) the evidence at issue must be favorable to the accused either because it is exculpatory or impeaching; (2) the evidence must have been suppressed by the government, either willfully or inadvertently; and (3) prejudice must have ensued.[214] Indeed, if prosecutors engage in misconduct, criminal convictions may be reversed.[215] It has also been repeatedly held that a private citizen may not maintain an action to compel the government to bring a criminal prosecution against another person.[216]

With respect to interested private prosecutions, federal courts have taken a much different approach than several of their state counterparts, with many state court jurists, in the past, either embracing or tolerating such prosecutions. Under well-settled federal court rulings, private parties lack standing to bring criminal charges, and may not themselves prosecute crimes in federal court,[217] because private individuals—it has been determined—have no "judicially cognizable interest in the prosecution" of others.[218] "Only federal prosecutors, and not private citizens, have the authority to initiate federal criminal charges," one federal district court emphasized in making that point.[219] Similarly, in 2011, another federal district court ruled that, although a crime victim under the Crime Victims' Rights Act has "[t]he right to be reasonably heard at any public proceeding in the district court involving release, plea, sentence, or any parole proceeding," it would be "a flagrant violation" of a defendant's due process rights to permit criminal allegations to be "prosecuted by private citizens, not the government."[220] In contrast, at the state level, what is allowed by law is currently more variable, resulting in a rather *ad hoc* and unprincipled approach to private prosecutions. The bottom line: to make the law's application more principled and more protective of defendant's due process rights in the twenty-first century, interested private prosecutions—whether at the federal or state level—should be barred universally as a matter of constitutional law.[221]

Indeed, courts in California, New York, Virginia, and elsewhere have already adjudged that private prosecutions by interested parties violate an individual's due process rights,[222] although the state's mere retention of a private lawyer has not been seen as a due process violation where the outside counsel was neither hired on a contingency basis nor had a direct financial interest in the case's outcome.[223] *United States ex rel. Miller v. Myers*[224] provides a good illustration of why interested private prosecutors should be seen as violative of defendants' due process rights. In that case, a defendant charged with burglary was represented by an attorney who was simultaneously representing the owner of the allegedly burgled establishment in another matter. In reversing the defendant's conviction on the grounds that the conflict of interest violated the defendant's constitutional right to counsel, the federal district court stated that "it takes no great understanding of human nature to realize that the individuals who had been burglarized might be less than happy and might go so far as to remove the attorney from their good graces if this defendant were acquitted."[225] The judicial system should endeavor to make sure that attorneys, with all their faults and human frailties, are not placed in situations in which they have a distorting conflict of interest. Discouraging interested private prosecutions through ethical guidance is a good first step, but barring interested private prosecutions as a matter of constitutional law would draw a bright line that lawyers would then be forbidden to cross.

Existing case law is notable. In *People v. Municipal Court for the Ventura Judicial District of Ventura County* (1972), for instance, a California appellate court specifically declared that "[t]he due process clause of both United States and California Constitutions is a bar to the deprivation of liberty except by the regular administration of law and in accordance with general rules designed to protect individual rights." As that court emphasized: "Due process of law requires that criminal prosecutions be instituted through the regular processes of law. These regular processes include the requirement that the institution of any criminal proceeding be authorized and approved by the district attorney." In that case, the underlying facts were that on July 4, 1971, in a residential neighborhood of Ventura County, citizens had been shooting fireworks in the street. Douglas Bishop was driving his car down the street, honking his horn, and flashing his headlights, which offended some people watching the fireworks. A Mrs. Pellegrino and a Mr. Stromstad, concerned that Mr. Bishop was driving too fast and endangering children, ran after Mr. Bishop's car, with the court reporting that "when Bishop stopped his car at the end of the block, he was apparently assaulted by Pellegrino and Stromstad" and "[t]he police were called and reports were made." After a deputy district attorney had reviewed those reports, misdemeanor criminal complaints signed by Mr. Bishop and naming Pellegrino and Stromstad as defendants were filed with the Municipal Court of the Ventura Judicial District, with Mrs. Pellegrino contacting a private attorney, Randolph Siple, concerning the matter. On July 9, 1971, she then appeared at the office of the district attorney bearing a letter addressed to the district attorney and signed by Mr. Siple. The letter requested that Mr. Bishop be charged in a criminal complaint. Siple thereafter requested that the court "disqualify" the district attorney and appoint him (Siple) as "special prosecutor"—a request that a deputy district attorney vigorously objected to, with the deputy district attorney advising the court that, in the district attorney's opinion, there was no evidence to warrant a prosecution of Bishop.

The case arising out of the Fourth of July fireworks celebration continued to produce legal fireworks as the parties made their arguments in the judicial system. On July 23, 1971, two misdemeanor criminal complaints were filed with the court. Those complaints, each sworn to by Florence Pellegrino, alleged that Douglas Bishop had violated sections of the penal code relating to simple assault and battery and sections of the vehicle code relating to the basic speed law, exceeding 25 miles per hour in a residential district, and engaging in a speed exhibition. The record also reflected that on July 23, 1971, the municipal court—in connection with complaint No. TC 2487—ordered "Atty. Siple appointed as Special Prosecutor upon Court's Motion and finding—DDA disqualified." As to complaint No. TC 2488, the order read: "Atty. Siple appointed as Spec. Prosecutor upon Court's finding—DA office is disqualified." In holding that "the municipal court had no authority to appoint Mr. Siple as 'special prosecutor,'" the California appellate court made these observations: "Here a properly sworn complaint, approved by the district attorney, was filed against Pellegrino and Stromstad. In an apparent attempt to frustrate the prosecution, one of the defendants sought to prosecute the complaining witness. As a result, Bishop stands charged with several criminal offenses in spite of the fact that the district attorney has determined that the charges lack merit." "Equally troubling," the California appellate court stated, alluding to Pellegrino's refusal to make any statement beyond her charges due to the fact that she, herself, had been charged with criminal activity, "is the fact that the court, without authority to appoint a special prosecutor, now has before it an action filed, a charged defendant and a prosecuting witness who refuses to put forth any information except by way of a complaint in simple statutory language." "The complaints filed by Pellegrino against Bishop without the district attorney's authorization were nullities," the California appellate court concluded in *People v. Municipal Court for the Ventura Judicial District of Ventura County*.[226]

Courts are accustomed to considering conflict of interest issues,[227] and prosecutors—as with lawyers in private practice—can run into an array of conflicts of interests as they do their jobs.[228] In Virginia, that state's court of appeals explicitly held in *Price v. Commonwealth* (2020) that "[i]t constitutes a violation of the defendant's due process rights if a private prosecutor participates in the defendant's prosecution" if an "impermissible conflict of interest" exists.[229] "Virginia courts," a federal district court summarized in *Riner v. Edwards* (2008), "have held that while use of private prosecutors is permitted, the procedure may violate Article 1, § 11 of the Constitution of Virginia if the private prosecutor has a personal interest in the outcome of the case or if the public prosecutor relinquishes control of the case to the private prosecutor."[230] In *Adkins v. Commonwealth* (1997), the state's court of appeals previously held that a defendant's due process rights were violated when a private attorney who had been retained by the victim's family to assist in the process was appointed as a "special prosecutor." As the court emphasized in *Adkins*: "Having once been paid by the victim's family to protect its interest and to assist in the prosecution, Epling was prohibited for reasons of conflict of interest from becoming a special prosecutor. The conflict of interest between a special prosecutor's duty 'to seek justice' and his duty to his former client denied the defendant her right to a fair and impartial trial."[231]

In a New York case, *People v. Calderone* (1991), the legal issue was framed this way: "This case requires the court to determine whether an interested party, the victim of a criminal act or a private attorney representing such person, may prosecute a criminal action against the person alleged to have committed that act."[232] In that case, the defendant was charged with fourth-degree criminal mischief in a misdemeanor accusatory instrument. That prosecution was commenced on the application of the complainant, Vincent Riso, for a court-ordered summons pursuant to Section 50 of the New York City Criminal Court Act[233] based on the filing of the accusatory instrument in the Summons Appearance Part (SAP) of the Criminal Court. The defendant, Jack Calderone, was then served with the summons and arraigned on the accusatory instrument which alleged that he caused damage to the carpet, wall and doors of the condominium building in which Mr. Riso had an interest.[234] In *Calderone*, the Criminal Court for the City of New York described the procedure at issue and the dispute's context.[235] "Generally," the court in *Calderone* began, "the District Attorney for the County prosecutes criminal matters in the name of the People of the State of New York."[236] "However," that court continued, "pursuant to Section 50 of the New York City Criminal Court Act, private persons have, for many years, been permitted to initiate criminal actions in the Summons Appearance Part of the Criminal Court without the participation of the District Attorney."[237] "Such actions," it was noted, "are commenced by the complainant having a Clerk of the Court prepare an accusatory instrument which is docketed and the court's issuance of a summons directing that the named defendant appear before the court on a date specified for arraignment on the criminal charges."[238] As the court went on to describe the procedure: "The District Court does not appear in the Summons Appearance Part in New York County. Rather, the cases docketed in that Part are prosecuted by the complainant, who is usually the victim of the crime alleged, or by a private attorney representing the complainant."[239]

The court in *Calderone* began by observing that "[t]he question of whether there is any statutory prohibition against a person who is not specifically charged with responsibility for prosecuting criminal cases conducting the prosecution of such matters was addressed by the Court of Appeals in *People v. Van Sickle*."[240] In *Van Sickle*, the New York Court of Appeals held that the conviction should not be reversed because the victim of the crime conducted the prosecution. While the judges on the New York Court of Appeals in *Van Sickle* were divided on whether the District Attorney had a duty to be aware of such "private prosecutions," those judges were unanimous that no statutory bar existed to a private individual prosecuting a criminal case. In a concurring opinion in *Van Sickle*, Judge Van Voorhis also cited with approval attorney general opinions expressing the view that a "criminal prosecution "may be done by a private individual or a lawyer hired by the complainant."[241] The court in *Calderone* stated that, subsequent to the *Van Sickle* decision, "a number of courts have issued opinions as to whether a privately retained attorney could prosecute a criminal action."[242]

In *Calderone*, the New York court observed that "[i]t is... clear that the courts of this State have found that there is no statutory prohibition against the prosecution of a criminal case by the victim of the crime alleged or by an attorney representing such person."[243] "Those cases, however," the *Calderone* court added of such precedents, "did not address the question of whether private prosecution constitutes a per se violation of the constitutional standards of due process applicable to criminal prosecutions."[244] That, of course, is a major issue—one plainly worthy of consideration given the stakes for an accused. "Indeed," the *Calderone* court emphasized, "the majority opinion in *People v. Van Sickle*... did not address the constitutional implications of private prosecutors."[245] In distinguishing *Van Sickle* and other New York cases upholding the use of private prosecutors, the court in *Calderone* had this to say: "[R]ecent decisions of the New York Court of Appeals and the Supreme Court of the United States lead this court to conclude that private prosecutions by interested parties or their attorneys present inherent conflicts of interest which violate defendants' due process rights." "Accordingly," the court held in *Calderone*, "whether or not actual prejudice results from the inherent conflict of interest, such an interested person may not initiate a prosecution by obtaining the issuance of a summons requiring a person's appearance in the Criminal Court nor may such an interested person in any other manner prosecute the criminal charges."[246]

In *Calderone*, the Criminal Court of the City of New York, citing an earlier case, *People v. Zimmer*, in which the New York Court of Appeals reversed a conviction and dismissed an indictment obtained by a District Attorney who had a financial interest, specifically determined: "The holding in *People v. Zimmer*... that a public prosecutor's conflict of interest violates due process and requires dismissal of the accusatory instrument and conviction obtained by that prosecutor, should be applied to private prosecutions by victims of crimes or private attorneys representing such persons."[247] "While *People v. Zimmer*," the *Calderone* court stressed, "is distinguishable on its facts from *People v. Van Sickle*... in that, in *Zimmer*, the Court was applying standards concerning the duties and responsibilities of public officials charged with responsibility for investigating and prosecuting violations of the criminal statutes in the name of the people of the State, a defendant's right to due process is no different in public and private prosecutions."[248] "Clearly," the *Calderone* court continued, "the effect of criminal proceedings and the consequences of a conviction for criminal charges are no different in prosecutions by a public prosecutor than in prosecutions by a private prosecutor."[249] The *Calderone* court's conclusion: "As no viable rationale justifies a distinction between prosecutions by public officials and those by private persons with respect to the potential for prejudice that arises from inherent conflicts of interest created by the prosecutor being personally interested in the case, the reasoning of the Court in *People v. Zimmer*... requires the conclusion that a defendant's right to due process is violated when a person who is a victim of a crime or who has a personal, financial or attorney-client relationship with the victim of a crime prosecutes the criminal case."[250]

In finding a due process violation, the *Calderone* court noted that "[t]he courts of other states and federal courts which have considered this issue have divided on the question of whether private prosecutions by interested persons violate due process."[251] After the New York judge, Peter Benitez, cited case law in Kentucky allowing the practice and in Missouri and Virginia prohibiting that practice, he concluded: "Therefore, as the prosecution in this case was initiated by a person with a personal interest in the matter and is being prosecuted by a law firm which has an attorney-client relationship with the victims of the offenses alleged, such violates defendant's due process rights. Accordingly, the criminal action is dismissed without prejudice to the complainant pursuing his complaint with the District Attorney's Office."[252] Both *Calderone* and another New York case, *People v. Benoit*, detailed what a subsequent New York case, *People v. Garfield*, called "a change in the case law relative to the issue of private prosecutions." In ordering that an automobile accident victim would be disqualified from prosecuting a criminal complaint against a driver who hit him after the district attorney and the town attorney declined to prosecute, the court in *Garfield* stressed: "the failure to provide a professional evaluation of such cases by a neutral prosecutor may result in improper charges and convictions and denies a defendant the due process of law." The rationale? "Where there exists a financial interest as in this case, or other personal interest, the prospect for a fair and impartial trial diminishes to the extent that the due process of law to which all defendants are entitled may cease to exist," the *Garfield* court observed. In *Calderone*, the judge in *Garfield* wrote, "the court determined that to allow a 'private prosecution' where self-interested persons were allowed to prosecute, violates 'contemporary standards of fair and impartial prosecution.'"[253]

In *People v. Benoit*,[254] the issue—as framed by the Criminal Court of the City of New York, Kings County—was "whether a private prosecution for a crime, after the District Attorney's office declines to prosecute, constitutes a violation of the defendant's rights to due process and equal protection."[255] In that case, an altercation occurred on February 8, 1991, between the defendant, Martine Benoit, and her landlord, Marie Franck, at Ms. Franck's house where both parties lived. On that date, the police arrested Marie Franck, who was charged in a felony complaint with assaulting Ms. Benoit. After being arraigned, Franck was assigned Legal Aid counsel and then released on her own recognizance. Shortly thereafter, Franck went to the New York City Criminal Court's Summons Part at 246 Broadway in New York County[256] where a clerk prepared a misdemeanor complaint on her behalf charging Ms. Benoit with the crimes of third-degree assault, fourth-degree criminal mischief, menacing, and harassment—all of which were grounded on the same February 8th incident for which Ms. Franck herself had previously been charged. Next, Ms. Franck appeared before a judge of the Criminal Court in Kings County, swore to the truth of her allegations, and received a summons to serve on Ms. Benoit and to secure her appearance in court.[257] After the public prosecutor declined to pursue a prosecution against Benoit,[258] Benoit's counsel filed a motion to dismiss based on the applicable New York City Criminal Court Act constituting a violation of due process and equal protection.[259]

In analyzing section 50 of the New York City Criminal Court Act, the court in *Benoit* first noted that "[t]he legislative history of section 50 reveals that in 1908 the Legislature appointed a commission . . . to investigate the lower courts of criminal jurisdiction in New York City."[260] That commission's reports ultimately led "to the passage of the Inferior Criminal Courts Act, including the original version of New York City Criminal Court Act § 50.[261] The court in *Benoit* went on to observe that "the Commission found that the courts were noisy, overcrowded, and lacked any semblance of judicial procedure," with the commission recommending "reorganization of the courthouse facilities, including 'provision for the complaint clerks in a room separate from the courtroom.'"[262] After noting that "[a]ll of these measures were instituted to '*enable the defendant in all cases to have the same opportunity to be heard as the complainant*,'"[263] the *Benoit* court stressed: "Viewed in its historical context, the statute did clearly benefit the defendant at a time when, among other things, all complaints were sworn to before the court and there was no right to counsel."[264]

But the court in *Benoit* had much more to say about the law and the specific provision at issue. "New York City Criminal Court Act § 50 and the summons and complaint process it authorizes," the court explained, "was critically scrutinized in the Report of the Task Force on the Civilian-Initiated Complaint Process in the New York City Criminal Court ([Task Force], June 1989)."[265] The report of that task force, as the *Benoit* court pointed out, stated that "lack of prosecutorial involvement erodes confidence in the criminal justice system."[266] As the task force's report observed: "The decision to prosecute must rest with professional assistants of duly elected prosecutors who can properly evaluate the merits of a case and who represent the interests of the People of the State of New York. Either a case warrants prosecution or it should not be brought in Criminal Court. The alternative is to allow any individual to use a criminal case to pursue his or her own personal aims. This practice undermines justice and the appearance of justice and it erodes the public's confidence in the criminal justice system."[267] In other words, prosecutions by interested private parties were suspect because of how they affected the public's perception of the justice system.

After examining the history and modern-day critique of section 50 of the New York City Criminal Court Act, the court in *Benoit* looked at the broader history of private prosecution in New York and elsewhere. "The custom of allowing individuals to prosecute in the name of the State has its origins in English Common Law," the court began, though it explained that "in New York, since the Constitutional Convention of 1777, the Attorney-General was the chief law enforcement officer responsible for the prosecution of all persons charged with criminal offenses."[268] After the office of district attorney was created by statute in the early nineteenth century, the *Benoit* court observed, "the District Attorney has been charged with the duty to prosecute crimes and offenses."[269] Jurisdictions allowing private prosecutions based on their statutes or case law, the *Benoit* court added, shifting its focus to the practice's history elsewhere, "all have one common characteristic—the private prosecutor is always an attorney who merely assists the public prosecutor and it is the public prosecutor who actually remains in control of the case."[270] The court in *Benoit* concluded that "[p]rosecution by a disinterested prosecutor is a fundamental aspect of due process," and that the defendant would be deprived of it if the private prosecution were allowed to continue.[271]

In the past, multiple American judges determined that interested private prosecutions did not violate due process or render a criminal conviction invalid.[272] In one North Carolina case, a defendant was convicted of the first-degree murder of his father—a conviction affirmed in 1981 even though the trial court refused to permit the cross-examination of the defendant's siblings as to whether they would inherit a greater portion of their father's estate if the defendant were to be disqualified as an heir. In that case, the defendant's siblings hired a private prosecutor who assisted in the case's preparation, and that prosecutor sat with the state's prosecutor at trial.[273] The use of private attorneys in criminal cases "has existed in our courts from their incipiency" North Carolina's supreme court wrote in 1972,[274] with another North Carolina judicial decision likewise finding no due process violation. In the latter case, private attorneys were involved in both the criminal trial and as plaintiffs' attorneys in civil suits against the defendant arising out of a traffic accident that produced both the criminal charges and the civil actions. Other courts have also declined to find due process violations even while characterizing private prosecutions unfavorably. "While we think that the use of private prosecutors who are also representing plaintiffs in civil actions against the criminal defendant should be discouraged," the Fourth Circuit emphasized in 1985 in reviewing a defendant's conviction on habeas corpus, "we do not find that such use in the present case violated the constitutional rights of the appellant, and we affirm."[275] "[I]t is unseemly, to say the least," for discretion "to be exercised by a prosecutor who is not reasonably disinterested," the Sixth Circuit held in 1989, nonetheless finding no due process violation even though the lawyer who successfully prosecuted the defendant for a drunken driving offense later represented the victim of the vehicle collusion, along with her husband, in a civil case against the offender, Stanley Dick, for damages arising out of the collision. "We agree that any personal interest the prosecutor may have had was insufficient to render petitioner's conviction constitutional infirm," the Sixth Circuit ruled, rejecting Mr. Dick's habeas corpus petition.[276]

In prior decades, courts allowed private prosecutions in the face of legal challenges. For instance, in *State v. Atkins* (1979), the Supreme Court of Appeals of West Virginia ruled that it was not reversible error for a private prosecutor in a second-degree murder case to not disclose the amount of his fee.[277] That state appellate court, in 1986, specifically rejected a legal challenge to a private prosecutor's use, finding no "prosecutorial overmatch" and offering this ruling after citing a West Virginia statute: "Although the right to a private prosecutor is not absolute, the retention of a private prosecutor is perfectly just, legal, and fair in many cases."[278] In contrast, the Supreme Court of Appeals of West Virginia in *State ex rel. Koopers Co. v. International Union of Oil, Chemical and Atomic Workers* (1982) ruled that "[a] public prosecutor's fundamental duty is to do justice" and that "his or her presence should protect against overzealousness and an unrestrained pursuit of private vindication." "Participation by a private prosecutor," that decision declared, "does not obviate the need for a public prosecutor's presence, he being ultimately responsible for discretion regarding prosecution of alleged public offenders." In that decision, reviewing criminal contempt cases arising out of the violation of an injunction in a labor dispute, the Supreme Court of Appeals of West Virginia held that the defendants' due process rights were violated when they were prosecuted by the employer's lawyers.[279]

Other courts, in reviewing state law convictions in habeas corpus proceedings or in section 1983 actions, have rejected due process challenges to private prosecution or the participation of private attorneys.[280] In 1968, the U.S. Court of Appeals for the

Fifth Circuit specifically turned aside a due process challenge to the practice of private prosecution in *Powers v. Hauck*. In that habeas corpus proceeding, the petitioner, Ralph Powers, had appealed the dismissal of his petition for a writ of habeas corpus. For the highly publicized capital murder trial in Bexar County, Texas, the victim's family had hired a San Antonio-based private prosecutor, Fred Semaan, to assist with the prosecution as a "special prosecutor." Semaan participated in the trial with the district attorney's consent and—at the time—without any objection from the defendant. In addition to presenting some of the evidence against Powers, Semaan made the opening statement to jurors in which he sought the death penalty's imposition. After being convicted and sentenced to death in 1966, Powers had sought review of his conviction but it was affirmed on direct appeal. After Powers exhausted his state post-conviction remedies and the U.S. District Court for the Western District of Texas had denied his habeas corpus petition, his execution was stayed pending appeal to the Fifth Circuit. The Fifth Circuit, however, affirmed the decision of U.S. District Judge Adrian Spears, announcing that it was "in full agreement with the findings and conclusions of the district court judge."

In summarily upholding the district court's findings of fact and conclusions of law, the Fifth Circuit thus saw nothing wrong with the participation of the special prosecutor in the murder case. In his conclusions of law, Judge Spears explicitly declared: "[t]he mere participation of a special prosecutor alone is not sufficient grounds to show denial of due process, without some additional showing of a violation of the rules relating to prosecuting attorneys." As Judge Spears ruled: "There is no constitutional prohibition against the use of special prosecutors, and so long as the Criminal District Attorney retains control and management of the prosecution, the special prosecutor is not guilty of conduct prejudicial to the defendant, and the rights of the defendant are duly observed, no reason exists why such settled practice, in and of itself, should cause the reversal of a case." In his conclusions of law, Judge Spears also held that the Texas law authorizing the death penalty neither denied equal protection of the laws nor transgressed the prohibition against cruel and unusual punishments.[281] Likewise, in *Ballard v. State* (1975), the Texas Court of Criminal Appeals made this ruling: "Due process is not denied by permitting a privately retained attorney to participate in a criminal prosecution when the district attorney retains control and management of the prosecution."[282]

Other judges came to the same conclusion after considering due process challenges. In 1989, the Supreme Court of Kentucky explicitly held in *Commonwealth v. Hubbard*: "The employment of private counsel to assist the Commonwealth Attorney in the prosecution of a criminal case does not violate the due process clauses of the Fifth and Fourteenth Amendments to the United States Constitution. It has been previously held that it is permissible for the circuit court and the Commonwealth Attorney to permit a private attorney to assist the Commonwealth Attorney in prosecuting a criminal case."[283] In *Stumbo v. Seabold* (1983), decided a few years before *Hubbard*, the U.S .Court of Appeals for the Sixth Circuit made this parallel ruling in response to a habeas corpus petition challenging a first-degree murder conviction: "We do not believe that Kentucky law, which allows a privately retained prosecutor to assist the public prosecutor in criminal cases, constitutes a *per se* violation of due process." In that case, though, the Sixth Circuit emphasized that Kentucky law "requires the public prosecutor to retain control over the conduct of the trial to ensure that the state's interests are protected" and held that the habeas corpus petitioner had been deprived of a fundamentally fair trial as a result of the private prosecutor's misconduct. That misconduct included the petitioner being referred to as "Johnny Murder Boy," attempts to suggest to the jury a conspiracy to murder in spite of the absence of evidence to support that theory, and a statement to jurors that if they believed the "cock-and-bull story" murder cases would be "stacked up" in Floyd County. As the Sixth Circuit added, raising questions about the petitioner's guilt: "Had the evidence of guilt been overwhelming in this case, prosecutorial misconduct might be considered harmless error. There was little evidence, however, to support the prosecution's theory of intentional homicide and a significant amount of evidence to support the defendant's claim of accidental shooting."[284]

In a more recent case, *Erikson v. Pawnee County Board of County Commissioners* (2001), another due process challenge was rejected. In that case, the U.S. Court of Appeals for the Tenth Circuit considered Michael Erikson's 42 U.S.C. § 1983 lawsuit, which alleged that Erikson's federal due process rights were violated. In 1992, Erikson had shot and killed two men, Tony McCollum and Fred Head, on his family's ranch property, but he claimed to have done so in self-defense. Erikson was acquitted on all charges for Head's death, and although two mistrials were ultimately declared with respect to the criminal charges brought against Erikson relating to McCollum's death, a third prosecution of him for that death ended in a dismissal of the voluntary manslaughter charge. In his subsequent section 1983 lawsuit, Erikson alleged that the Oklahoma Sportsman's Association ("OSA"), OSA's president, Harland Stonecipher, and attorney Michael Turpen and his law firm had actively influenced and participated in Erikson's prosecution. In particular, Erikson alleged that OSA raised more than $25,000 from its membership and contributed that money to defendant Turpen for use in providing research assistants and investigators to assist in Erikson's prosecutions. In affirming the district court's dismissal of Erikson's section 1983 lawsuit, the Tenth Circuit found that Erikson "has failed to allege a federal constitutional violation." Citing case law from other federal circuit courts, the Tenth Circuit ruled: "the participation of a privately-retained attorney in a state criminal prosecution does not violate the defendant's right to due process under federal law unless the private attorney effectively controlled critical prosecutorial decisions." As the Tenth Circuit stated in rejecting Erikson's section 1983 lawsuit: "Plaintiff has not alleged that defendant Turpen exercised control over any critical prosecutorial decisions. Instead, plaintiff only alleges that defendant Turpen, acting on behalf of the OSA, provided research assistants and investigators...." "This," the Tenth Circuit determined, "is insufficient to state a claim for a federal due process violation."[285]

Why Interested Private Prosecutions Should Be Barred as a Violation of Due Process

Both the Fifth and Fourteenth Amendments prohibit the government from depriving an individual "of life, liberty, or property, without due process of law."[286] Those procedural safeguards, it has been emphasized, "have their historical origins in the notion that conditions of personal freedom can be preserved only when there is some institutional check on arbitrary government action."[287] Indeed, in *Marshall v. Jerrico, Inc.*,[288] the U.S. Supreme Court—as noted earlier—determined that the due process guarantee "entitles a person to an impartial and disinterested tribunal in both civil and criminal cases."[289] This neutrality requirement helps prevent "unjustified or mistaken deprivations" of liberty.[290] As the Supreme Court emphasized in *Marshall*: "The neutrality requirement helps to guarantee that life, liberty, or property will not be taken on the basis of an erroneous or distorted conception of the facts or the law." "At the same time," the *Marshall* Court observed, the neutrality requirement simultaneously "preserves both the appearance and reality of fairness, 'generating the feeling, so important to a popular government, that justice has been done,' by ensuring that no person will be deprived of his interests in the absence of a proceeding in which he may present his case with assurance that the arbiter is not predisposed to find against him.[291] Thus, an "essential safeguard" of due process is the participation of an "independent adjudicator."[292] Indeed, the independence of actors involved in the criminal justice system is critical to protecting an accused's due process rights.[293]

The American system of justice must ensure as best it can the accuracy of results, and that is especially important in criminal cases where a person's life or liberty is at stake.[294] And when prosecutors have conflicts of interest, those conflicts clearly undermine confidence in their work. "Prosecutors make discretionary decisions with significant consequences for criminal defendants and for criminal justice in general," two scholars, Bruce Green and Rebecca Roiphe, explain, adding that "[t]he law presupposes that prosecutors make these decisions disinterestedly, unaffected by their own self-interest or the interests of others." "Conflicts of interest, which are endemic to prosecutorial decision-making, threaten the legitimacy and efficacy of the criminal justice system," they emphasize. In making such discretionary decisions,[295] Green and Roiphe note, "prosecutors have a fiduciary obligation to act in the public interest, not in furtherance of private interests, including their own."[296] As prosecutors make their decisions, the appearance of fairness—so critical to maintaining public confidence in the system—is particularly vital to furthering due process principles not only because prosecutors have ethical obligations to the accused but because so much of what prosecutors do happens behind the scenes.[297] As the Supreme Court itself has repeatedly stated: "justice must satisfy the appearance of justice."[298] The appearance-of-fairness value is so indispensable to due process because—as has been said—it "generates the feeling, so important to a popular government, that justice has been done."[299]

There are instances where private actors are used to further public aims. American law, for example, recognizes the availability *qui tam* actions—civil proceedings in which private persons pursue claims on behalf of the United States and themselves to recover damages or statutory penalties.[300] *Qui tam* is the shorthand Latin phrase for "*qui tam pro domino rege quam pro si ipso in hac parte sequitur,*" or "who brings the action as well for the king as for himself."[301] Although the writ of *qui tam* was abolished in England in 1951, *qui tam* actions have long been authorized by the United States Congress, with Congress beefing up that enforcement tool in the False Claims Act ("FCA") in 1986. The FCA imposes civil liability upon persons presenting false claims for payment to or otherwise defrauding the federal treasury. "The FCA," as one North Carolina federal district court put it, "confers standing on private persons to bring a qui tam action on behalf of the United States against a person who has submitted a false or fraudulent claim for payment to the federal government."[302] In *qui tam* actions, the person who pursues the action—the "informer" or "relator"—receives a portion of any amount recovered on the government's behalf. As scholar J. Randy Beck observes of the history: "While *qui tam* statutes have been on the books since the first Congress and the FCA has contained a *qui tam* provision since the Civil War, these pre-1986 statutes generated relatively little litigation. By contrast, the generous bounty offered to informers under the 1986 legislation has resulted in an increased number of *qui tam* filings."[303] "The overwhelming weight of authority supports the view that *qui tam* suits are civil actions," another legal scholar has written of how they are viewed,[304] with courts emphasizing that the type of conflict of interest at issue in the U.S. Supreme Court's decision in *Young* is not present in *qui tam* actions, where private and public goals in obtaining civil relief are seen as congruent in remedying harm to the federal treasury.[305]

While the U.S. Constitution's guarantee of due process should prohibit interested private prosecutions, disinterested prosecutions will continue and civil actions can provide interested parties with adequate legal remedies for the harms they've suffered (but such actions must not violate another's constitutional rights). For example, if a murder has occurred, a disinterested public prosecutor will evaluate the evidence and a wrongful death claim will also provide an interested party with a forum to seek civil redress. Likewise, where someone has been assaulted, a disinterested prosecutor can bring a criminal charge and, in addition, a tort claim can be still brought by the injured party against the wrongdoer. Even though the due process guarantee should safeguard the accused from facing an interested private prosecution in a *criminal* proceeding, existing private attorneys general statutes—be they in the realm of antitrust,[306] civil rights,[307] labor law violations,[308] or RICO[309]—will allow aggrieved parties to pursue *civil* remedies.[310] The retention of private counsel to pursue civil penalties under state law has been held to be indistinguishable from a private relator's pursuit of civil penalties under the *qui tam* provisions of the False Claim Act and not to violate due process, though no civil action should ever be allowed to infringe a woman's constitutional rights under *Roe v. Wade*.[311] "The Civil False Claims Act was born in

1863 to a nation engulfed in a civil war," one federal district court has explained, observing that Congress enacted the False Claims Act at President Abraham Lincoln's urging so that suits to recover damages could be brought, with the False Claims Act amended in 1943 and 1986.[312] "[L]ower levels of prosecutorial neutrality are permissible in civil as opposed to criminal prosecutions," one court has observed.[313] Treble damages and punitive damages are sometimes available in civil suits, but civil liability and money damages do not carry the kind of stigma or dire and collateral consequences associated with criminal liability.[314]

Many American judges have already grown skeptical of interested private prosecutors, forbidding the latter from controlling prosecutions and barring their participation in civil matters arising out of the same incidents giving rise to criminal prosecutions.[315] *State v. Myerowitz*, for example, illustrates the problematic nature of private prosecutions, including the appearance of impropriety generated by them when a private party's own lawyer initiates and pursues the criminal case. In that particular matter, Howard Myerowitz—a lawyer—represented the Liberty Humane Society, a non-profit animal shelter organization. In appealing his conviction for a petty offense, Myerowitz asserted that the complainant, Donna Lerner, had filed a criminal harassment complaint against him in retaliation for a civil action that the Liberty Humane Society had previously brought against Lerner. On January 31, 2011, Myerowitz had attended a Liberty Humane Society board of directors meeting to update the board members about the status of the civil litigation against Lerner—a meeting held in a room inside the City Hall of the City of Jersey City. Although the meeting was initially open to the public, with Lerner in attendance and seeking to record the board's discussions, when it came time for Myerowitz to give his confidential litigation update, the board members asked Lerner and other members of the public to leave the room. Once the meeting room was cleared of public attendees, Myerowitz took certain personal items that those attendees had left inside the meeting room and placed them outside on the hallway floor. According to Lerner, Myerowitz also told her to stay away from the meeting room door, said he would have her escorted out of the building, and acted in a "confrontational and physically menacing" way towards her. At one point, he reportedly got "several inches away" from her face and yelled and pointed his finger at her. Although Lerner testified that Myerowitz's alleged misconduct occurred for roughly fifteen to twenty minutes, she also indicated that, in apparent defiance of the board's decision to close the meeting to the public, she had continuously walked in and out of the room. During the confrontation with Lerner, Myerowitz asked both security and Jersey City police officers for assistance to physically remove Lerner, but Lerner was allowed to stay because she was in a public building. Lerner's charge of harassment against Myerowitz was based solely on his alleged misbehavior after the board decided to close the meeting to the public.

At the start of the trial against Myerowitz on June 5, 2012, he inquired of the municipal court judge if Lerner's private attorney was, in fact, acting as the prosecutor in the case. The municipal judge's reply: "My understanding is she is. I received an application to do so." Although Myerowitz indicated he had received no such application, Lerner's attorney contended that an application had been submitted "probably four sessions ago." Myerowitz filed a motion to disqualify Lerner's attorney, but the municipal judge rejected it, finding that Lerner's private counsel "can appear in this matter." "[T]his has been on the calendar forever with today as the day to go forward," the judge said. Back on September 6, 2001, the first day of trial for harassment charges filed by Lerner against Myerowitz's wife, Diana Jeffrey, whom Myerowitz had represented as defense counsel, Lerner's private attorney had entered her appearance in that case, objected to Myerowitz serving as defense counsel for Jeffrey, and announced to the municipal court judge that she, as Lerner's lawyer, had "filed a *Storm* motion on behalf of Donna Lerner." A 1995 New Jersey Supreme Court case, *State v. Storm* requires private attorneys seeking to prosecute a case to "disclose in a written certification all facts that foreseeably may affect the fairness of the proceedings." "The relevant facts," the New Jersey Supreme Court ruled in *Storm*, "include the identity of the complainant, indicating (1) whether the complainant is an individual, a business (such as a department store), or an entity with its own police department (such as Rutgers University); (2) any actual conflict of interest arising from the attorney's representation of, and fee arrangement with, the complainant; (3) any civil litigation, existing or anticipated, between the complainant and the defendant; (4) whether the defendant is, or is expected to be, represented by counsel; and (5) any other facts that reasonably could affect the impartiality of the prosecutor and the fairness of the proceedings or otherwise create the appearance of impropriety."[316] The municipal judge in the criminal case against Diana Jeffrey had let that case go forward with Lerner's private attorney acting as the private prosecutor.

In *State v. Myerowitz*, a separate case, the Appellate Division of the Superior Court of New Jersey determined that "[t]he record corroborates" Myerowitz's claim "that Lerner's attorney did not submit a *Storm* certification requesting leave to prosecute the case against him." A letter from Lerner's attorney transmitting her own personally drafted version of the certification required by *Storm* and a New Jersey rule—a certification found not to be in compliance with the actual certification form dictated by the *Storm* decision and approved by the Administrative Director of the Courts—only referred to the case of "*State v. Diana Jeffrey*, Complaint No. S2010 009052 0906," with Lerner's attorney only previously seeking permission to serve as a private prosecutor in the criminal matter against Diana Jeffrey. Because Lerner's attorney did not comply with the requirements of New Jersey law in carrying out the private prosecution against Myerowitz, and because of the municipal court's failure to enforce the requirements of state law, the Appellate Division of the Superior Court of New Jersey found that Myerowitz's conviction for the petty disorderly offense of harassment—one that, naturally, would've resulted in a criminal record and impacted his professional reputation—was "void *ab initio*." "We remand this matter for a new trial," the Appellate Division ruled after considering the issues raised by Mr. Myerowitz's appeal.

While the private prosecution against Mr. Myerowitz involved a petty offense, private prosecutors have shown up in felony cases, too. The use of private prosecutions in capital cases, in fact, highlights the extremely consequential due process concerns associated with such prosecutions.[317] In *East v. Scott* (1995),[318] a case decided by the U.S. Court of the Appeals for the Fifth Circuit, Wayne East, a Black death row inmate/habeas corpus petitioner, had been convicted of capital murder and sentenced to die. At his trial, a private prosecutor, J. Russell "Rusty" Ormesher, had been heavily involved.[319] East had been charged in the stabbing death of Mary Eula Sears, a wealthy white philanthropist who loved to paint flowers and landscapes, with Ormesher—a seasoned prosecutor—retained by the deceased woman's nephew as part of the state's quest to obtain a death sentence. Among other things, Ormesher worked with investigators in the Taylor County District Attorney's office, interviewed witnesses, was present at counsel table throughout the trial, made objections, and actively participated by giving the State's opening and closing statements. East argued on appeal that the district court had erred in denying his habeas petition without allowing him the opportunity for discovery or an evidentiary hearing on his claim that the private prosecutor's participation violated his right to due process.[320] Prior to East's trial, the murder victim's family had retained Ormesher, a former Dallas County prosecutor, to aid Taylor County's district attorney in East's capital murder prosecution.[321] As the Fifth Circuit summarized East's claim: "East maintains that Mr. Ormesher essentially controlled all the critical trial strategy and prosecutorial decisions, and that Ormesher's role in the prosecution thus violated the Due Process Clause."[322]

In analyzing East's claim, the Fifth Circuit first discussed prior cases addressing the involvement of privately retained attorneys in criminal cases. After distinguishing the U.S. Supreme Court's "supervisory power" decision in *Young v. United States ex rel. Vuitton et Fils S.A.* (1987),[323] considering the Fifth Circuit cases of *Powers v. Hauck* (1968)[324] and *Woods v. Linahan* (1981)[325] which rejected due process claims, and adopting the Fourth Circuit's decision-making framework in *Person v. Miller* (1988)[326] for evaluating such claims, the Fifth Circuit in *East v. Scott* made this ruling: "Applying the framework developed in *Powers, Woods,* and *Person,* we conclude that these factual allegations raise the inference that Ormesher effectively controlled East's prosecution and, consequently, are facially sufficient to establish a *prima facie* due process claim."[327] The Fifth Circuit in *East* thus allowed discovery to determine whether the private prosecutor actually controlled "critical trial strategy and prosecutorial decisions." After allowing discovery on the due process claim and a *Brady* claim, a magistrate judge conducted an evidentiary hearing. Ultimately, the magistrate recommended that East's habeas petition be denied, concluding that no evidence indicated that the private prosecutor was in charge of the prosecution. Despite East's allegations pertaining to Ormesher's involvement in the prosecution, the U.S. district court adopted the magistrate judge's report and recommendation, thus dismissing East's habeas petition. In 1997, the Fifth Circuit affirmed the district court's judgment, although it vacated East's death sentence and gave the State of Texas "a reasonable time to conduct a new sentencing hearing" because of a finding that the prosecution had failed to disclose material *Brady* evidence to East at the sentencing phase.[328] Wayne East—the man sentenced to death for the 1981 murder of 77-year-old Mary Eula Sears—later entered into a plea deal in 1999, admitting that he fatally stabbed Sears and agreeing to a life sentence as part of the plea bargain.[329]

The very nature of the way in which criminal cases are conducted makes clear that interested private prosecutions should be a thing of the past. It is nearly impossible to detect the precise manner in which interested private prosecutors may shape and prejudice criminal proceedings, especially given the fact that interested private prosecutors have financial and other incentives that public prosecutors do not.[330] Prosecutors do a large part of their work behind the scenes—deciding what charges to bring, what to investigate, and what plea bargains, if any, to offer. Only a small fraction of what prosecutors do—trial work or court appearances to argue motions or appeals—takes place in the public eye, and even then, what went into their preparation and decision-making would regularly remain shrouded in secrecy. Because interested private prosecutors are not the kind of impartial actors one should expect to encounter in a quasi-judicial role, and because they create, at a minimum, an appearance of impropriety that undermines public confidence in the administration of justice, their use should be found to violate defendants' due process rights. In a world in which it is known that coerced and false confessions and wrongful convictions occur, and it which arbitrariness and racial discrimination still plague the administration of justice,[331] it is imperative that the prosecutorial function be reformed to be as fair as possible.

The offices of public prosecutors are now professionalized in a way that was certainly not the case at America's founding or in the nineteenth or early twentieth centuries. "Today," writes Rachel King of the American Civil Liberties Union, "no one can seriously doubt our system of prosecution is a public one."[332] Indeed, American public prosecutors—as historian Joan Jacoby observes—have power and discretion "vastly greater than those of any European prosecutor,"[333] with Jacoby writing that the American prosecutor "enjoys an independence and discretionary privileges unmatched in the world."[334] Eliminating the appearance of impropriety associated with interested private prosecutions will serve the public interest and—simply put—give all Americans greater confidence that justice is being done. As Justice John Marshall Harlan II stated in *Mayberry v. Pennsylvania* (1971),[335] "The appearance of evenhanded justice… is at the core of due process…."[336] Of course, public prosecutors' offices should reflect the communities that they serve. As such, those offices—often underrepresented by people of color—must redouble their efforts to diversify so that more minorities and women have seats at the table.[337] Diversity matters, and the legal profession itself must do a better job of diversifying so prosecutors' offices are populated by ethical, independent-minded prosecutors of varied backgrounds.[338]

Because fairness and the perception of fairness have always been integral aspects of due process analysis,[339] the principle of due process requires that prosecutors be fair-minded, independent adjudicators. Indeed, because interested private prosecutions are already so rare,[340] and because prosecutorial biases and prejudices can be so easily eliminated by prohibiting such prosecutions, due process requires that interested private prosecutions be outlawed. Under the U.S. Supreme Court's decision in *Mathews v. Eldridge*,[341] a court is directed to consider the value of the individual's interest, the risk of erroneous deprivation, and the government interest at stake, including the expense and administrative burden of different procedures.[342] In assessing the constitutionality of interested private prosecutors, whether under the "mechanical" balancing approach of *Mathews*[343] or the stricter *Medina* test, the conclusion is inescapable that the use of interested private prosecutors violates due process. For example, in *State v. Culbreath* (2000), where the defendants were charged with obscenity-related offenses pertaining to running sexually-oriented businesses, the Supreme Court of Tennessee determined that "the participation of a private funded prosecutor rendered the proceedings fundamentally unfair" under Tennessee's constitution. In that case, the private attorney, former Assistant U.S. Attorney Larry Parrish, received $410,931.87 from a special interest group, Citizens for Community Values, Inc. ("CCV"), creating a conflict of interest and an appearance of impropriety that violated the defendants' right to due process.[344]

In considering the factors set forth in *Mathews*, it is unquestionable that an individual has an important stake in not being prosecuted by an interested prosecutor. Prosecutors wield enormous power, and any prosecution carries significant consequences for the affected individual. As the Supreme Court stated in *Young*: "Between the private life of the citizen and the public glare of criminal accusation stands the prosecutor. That state official has the power to employ the full machinery of the state in scrutinizing any given individual." "Even if a defendant is ultimately acquitted," the Court emphasized in *Young*, "forced immersion in criminal investigation and adjudication is a wrenching disruption of everyday life." "For this reason," the Court observed in that case, "we must have assurance that those who would wield this power will be guided solely by their sense of public responsibility for the attainment of justice."[345] That an individual has an important interest in not being erroneously deprived of liberty was emphasized in *In re Winship*,[346] where the Supreme Court held that due process requires that a prosecutor prove each element of a crime "beyond a reasonable doubt." According to the Court: "The accused during a criminal prosecution has at stake interests of immense importance, both because of the possibility that he may lose his liberty upon conviction and because of the certainty that he would be stigmatized by the conviction."[347]

With respect to the second *Mathews* factor, prosecution by an interested private prosecutor greatly increases the risk of an erroneous deprivation of individual liberty. Because privately retained prosecutors are employed by—and have a desire to please and, in fact, routinely receive compensation from—interested parties, the use of such prosecutors allows influences other than "justice" or the "public interest" to enter into prosecutorial decisions.[348] Thus, the use of private prosecutors not only increases the risk that exculpatory evidence will be withheld from accused criminal defendants, but greatly increases the risk that an accused will be treated unfairly throughout or during a portion of the criminal process. As the Tennessee Supreme Court held in *Culbreath* in finding that an interested private prosecutor had an actual conflict of interest: a private prosecutor "compensated by a special interest group" owed a duty of loyalty to that group. Because the private prosecutor in that case was compensated on an hourly basis, that court emphasized, "the reality is that he acquired a direct financial interest in the duration and scope of the ongoing prosecution." That court also pointed out that the private attorney's "dual role"—with loyalties owed to both the public prosecutor's office and to the private special interest group—precluded him from exercising "his independent judgment free of 'compromising influences and loyalties.'" "Accordingly," the state supreme court observed in *Culbreath*, the private attorney's conflict of interest "tainted the entire prosecution," leading to a ruling that "the trial court did not abuse its discretion in disqualifying Parrish and the District Attorney General and his office."[349]

Finally, against the highly significant factors of the individual's interest and the risk of erroneous deprivation, the third *Mathews* factor requires that the government's interest be considered. In particular, *Mathews* asks a court to consider the expense and administrative burden of different procedures. In balancing that interest, it is clear that the elimination of interested private prosecutors would only slightly increase a state's expense in administering justice. Although interested private prosecutions were once common,[350] their use has become very infrequent in the United States, with some states having already eliminated them. In considering the critical interest an individual has in receiving fair treatment from a prosecutor, any additional expense incurred by the state due to eliminating private prosecutors must be deemed insignificant.[351] As the Tennessee Supreme Court stressed in *Culbreath* in finding that the private lawyer's participation in the prosecution rose to the level of a due process violation: "the fiscal and administrative burdens are minimal" because the public prosecutor's office was "already charged with the responsibility of investigating and prosecuting the offenses in question."[352] Thus, utilizing a *Mathews* analysis, the use of private prosecutors is unconstitutional.

If a *Mathews*-style analysis were to be employed, two U.S. Supreme Court cases decided in the early 1980s, where the Court found no due process violations, are clearly distinguishable. In the first case, *Marshall v. Jerrico, Inc.*,[353] a constitutional challenge was brought against §16(e) of the Fair Labor Standards Act after a restaurant management corporation was assessed civil penalties of $103,000 for violations of child labor laws by a regional administrator of the Employment Standards Administration ("ESA") of the Department of Labor. Section 16(e) allowed sums collected as civil penalties for the unlawful employment of child labor to be returned to the ESA in reimbursement for the costs of determining violations and assessing penalties.[354] Although this provision was alleged to create an "impermissible risk and appearance of bias" by encouraging the ESA "to make unduly numerous and large assessments of civil penalties,"[355] the Supreme Court rejected this challenge, stating that "the biasing influence… discerned in § 16(e) is… too remote and insubstantial to violate the constitutional constraints applicable to the decisions of an administrator performing prosecutorial functions."[356]

In so holding, the Supreme Court in *Marshall* noted that no official's salary was affected by the levels of the penalties and that the sums collected as child labor penalties amounted to substantially less than one percent of the ESA's annual budget.[357] Furthermore, the Supreme Court emphasized that the ESA never spent its full congressional appropriation, and that sums not spent were actually returned to the U.S. Treasury.[358] Finally, aside from noting that civil penalties were never allotted to regional offices on the basis of the total amounts of penalties collected by particular offices,[359] the Court emphasized that it was ultimately an administrative law judge, not a regional ESA administrator, who performed the function of adjudicating child labor violations.[360] The Supreme Court concluded:

> We need not say with precision what limits there may be on a financial or personal interest of one who performs a prosecutorial function, for here the influence alleged to impose bias is exceptionally remote. No government official stands to profit economically from vigorous enforcement of the child labor provisions of the Act. The salary of the assistant regional administrator is fixed by law. The pressures relied on in such cases as *Tumey v. Ohio* are entirely absent here.[361]

Thus, "'under a realistic appraisal of psychological tendencies and human weakness,'"[362] the Supreme Court held that it was "exceedingly improbable" that the assistant regional administrator's enforcement decisions would be "distorted" by improper influences or bias.[363]

In the second case, *Schweiker v. McClure*,[364] the Supreme Court also rejected a due process challenge to the system of providing federal reimbursements to insurance carriers under a Medicare provision providing medical insurance benefits. Under the challenged scheme, Congress authorized the Secretary of Health and Human Services to contract with private insurance carriers to administer the payment of qualifying claims. While the Secretary paid the carriers' costs of claims administration, the carriers, in turn, acted as the Secretary's agents. If a carrier determined that a claim met certain criteria, the carrier paid the claim out of a government trust fund. On the other hand, if a carrier denied a claim, the claimant was entitled to a "review determination," whereby the claimant could submit arguments of fact and law and written evidence. Claimants involved in a dispute greater than $100 were entitled to an oral hearing presided over by an officer, chosen by the carrier, who had not participated personally in the case prior to the hearing stage. The hearing officer's decision was not appealable.[365]

At the trial level, a federal judge in California ruled that these hearing procedures violated the constitutional guarantee to due process because of the risk of erroneous deprivation of Medicare benefits created by the carriers' hearing officers' "prior involvement and pecuniary interest."[366] The district court also held that due process required additional procedural protection, with the trial court ordering that a *de novo* hearing of record was required before an administrative law judge of the Social Security Administration. In rejecting these holdings, the U.S. Supreme Court refused to rely on the district court's "generalized assumptions of possible interest," which placed "special weight on the various connections of the hearing officers with the private insurance carriers."[367] In the words of the Supreme Court:

> The difficulty with this reasoning is that these connections would be relevant only if the carriers themselves are biased or interested. We find no basis in the record for reaching such a conclusion.... The carriers pay all... claims from federal, and not their own, funds. Similarly, the salaries of the hearing officers are paid by the Federal Government. Further, the carriers operate under contracts that require compliance with standards prescribed by the statute and the Secretary. In the absence of proof of financial interest on the part of the carriers, there is no basis for assuming a derivative bias among their hearing officers.[368]

Thus, in considering the three factors weighed by the trial court as required by *Mathews v. Eldridge*,[369] the Court in *Schweiker* found that no showing was made that the procedures prescribed by Congress and the Secretary were unfair.[370]

Unlike the situations in *Marshall* and *Schweiker*, an attorney hired by a victim or the victim's family has a fiduciary obligation arising out of the attorney-client relationship[371] and, typically, a direct financial incentive to further the client's real or perceived interests and to do exactly as the client desires. This incentive exists because the monetary success of private lawyers or law firms depends, in large part, upon the business of current clients and referrals from current and former clients.[372] Thus, if an interested private prosecutor's client does not believe that a case is being vigorously prosecuted (or, more significantly, if the private prosecutor does not "win" the case), the dissatisfied client may simply hire another attorney to prosecute the case or will not use or recommend the private prosecutor in the future. As a result, "under a realistic appraisal of psychological tendencies and human weakness"—to use the language of *Marshall*—it is not "exceedingly improbable" that significant decisions made by a private prosecutor will be "distorted" by the pressures created by his or her individual client.[373] Indeed, because an interested private prosecutor's motivation to obtain a conviction is high and anything but remote,[374] the Due Process Clauses of the U.S. Constitution's Fifth and Fourteenth Amendments should be interpreted to bar the use of such prosecutors.[375]

The contempt context is one area that warrants examination and the imposition of standards to protect the rights of those accused of contempt. In *Young*, the U.S. Supreme Court noted that "the fact that the judge makes the initial decision that a contempt prosecution should proceed is not sufficient to quell concern that prosecution by an interested party may be influenced by improper motives."[376] The Court emphasized:

> A prosecutor exercises considerable discretion in matters such as the determination of which persons should be targets of investigation, what methods of investigation should be used, what information will be sought as evidence, which persons should be charged with what offenses, which persons should be utilized as witnesses, whether to enter into plea bargains and the terms on which they will be established, and whether any individuals should be granted immunity. These decisions, critical to the conduct of the prosecution, are all made outside the supervision of the court.[377]

In light of the enormous discretionary powers that prosecutors wield, including in the context of a contempt prosecution, the prosecutorial function simply cannot be entrusted to private counsel representing the purely private interests of interested parties.

If one applies the *Medina v. California* standard, the use of interested private prosecutors must also be found to be unconstitutional as a matter of law. In *Medina,* the Supreme Court emphasized that "[i]n the field of criminal law," it had "defined the category of infractions that violate 'fundamental fairness' very narrowly." That's because, as the Court put it, "[t]he Bill of Rights speaks in explicit terms to many aspects of criminal procedure, and the expansion of those constitutional guarantees under the open-ended rubric of the Due Process Clause invites undue interference with both considered legislative judgments and the careful balance that the Constitution strikes between liberty and order."[378] "Discerning no historical basis for concluding that the allocation of the burden of proving incompetence to the defendant violates due process," the Court in *Medina* found that even though the Due Process Clause prohibits the criminal prosecution of a defendant who is not competent to stand trial, that clause permits a state to require that a defendant claiming incompetence to stand trial bear the burden of proving so by a preponderance of the evidence. "[B]ecause the States have considerable expertise in matters of criminal procedure and the criminal process is grounded in centuries of common-law tradition," the *Medina* Court determined, "it is appropriate to exercise substantial deference to legislative judgments in this area." Quoting from its decision in *Patterson v. New York*, the *Medina* Court stressed: "[W]e cannot say that the allocation of the burden of proof to a criminal defendant to prove incompetence 'offends some principle of justice so rooted in the traditions and conscience of our people as to be ranked as fundamental.'"[379]

But in spite of *Medina*'s expressed reluctance to recognize due process rights, the U.S. Supreme Court has repeatedly stressed the importance of *neutral* decisionmakers to due process analysis. In 1993, the Court specifically determined that "due process requires a 'neutral and detached judge in the first instance,' and the command is no different when a legislature delegates adjudicative functions to a private party."[380] And the Court has already characterized prosecutors as "quasi-judicial" officers,[381] with the Court making this determination almost 100 years ago in *Tumey v. Ohio* (1927): "That officers acting in a judicial or quasi-judicial capacity are disqualified by their interest in the controversy to be decided is, of course, the general rule."[382] Although prosecutors play a much different role than judges in the criminal justice system, prosecutorial decisions have considerable consequences for people's lives. Moreover, although interested private prosecutions were commonplace in colonial times and in states in America's earliest days (and thus would've been seen by eighteenth-century lawyers as consistent with constitutional principles),[383] such prosecutions were curtailed and restrained over time as public prosecution systems professionalized and jurists came to see the problematic nature of private prosecutions by interested parties.

Of considerable relevance, the ratification of the Fourteenth Amendment—a provision requiring equal protection of the laws and containing its own Due Process Clause—fundamentally changed the nature of constitutional protections and rights.[384] The Fourteenth Amendment has been referred to as America's "second constitution,"[385] and because the Fourteenth Amendment and the Supreme Court's incorporation doctrine made the states subject to provisions of the U.S. Bill of Rights, it made state practices subject to scrutiny by the nation's highest court. By virtue of the Fourteenth Amendment, equal treatment under the law became a material part of the American legal system's value system as states became constrained by the provisions of the Bill of Rights.[386] By their very nature, not only do interested private prosecutions violate an accused's due process rights, but the application of equal protection principles—as set forth in detail below—makes them highly suspect because individuals do not receive equal treatment under the law. If allowed, interested private prosecutions would arbitrarily subject just a handful of people to them while almost all other prosecutions rely on *disinterested* prosecutors to make decisions in criminal cases.

The importance of barring interested private prosecutions is, no doubt, best illustrated in the context of states that retain capital punishment. In such states, because prosecutors make the charging and plea-bargaining decisions, it is literally true that the life or death of an accused could rest in the hands of an interested private prosecutor. In light of the vengeful desires that murder victims' families often feel and express, private attorneys retained by those families experiencing grief would often be pressured not to plea bargain or to aggressively seek the death penalty. In fact, a private attorney may be expressly consulted and retained by family members *to* seek a death sentence. "Retribution is what society seeks, vengeance is what the victim wants," one source observes, adding that vengeance "is pure anger manifested by uncontrollable, prejudicial outbursts."[387] Because an attorney has an ethical obligation—indeed, a fiduciary duty—to zealously represent his or her client's interests,[388] if a murder victim's family wants the death penalty imposed, an interested private prosecutor may be incentivized or feel compelled to seek the death penalty irrespective of what justice would otherwise require.[389] Capital charges and death sentences, in fact, constitute threats of death that should be seen as an impermissible form of psychological torture that no lawyer or judge should tolerate.[390]

In the past, courts have articulated multiple reasons for retaining the right to employ a private prosecutor. For example, in *State v. Atkins*,[391] West Virginia's supreme court listed the following reasons for retaining the right to employ a private prosecutor: (1) there may be occasions when the public prosecutor is in need of assistance to carry out her duties effectively; (2) there may be occasions when the employment of a private prosecutor would satisfy the public's concern that a given case not be accorded perfunctory treatment; and (3) the victim's family may wish to satisfy itself that the case is being vigorously prosecuted.[392] Other stated rationales for retaining the use of private prosecutors include the protection of property rights,[393] reserving public prosecution for non-petty offenses,[394] and the saving of time and resources.[395] Whatever superficial appeal these reasons might have, none of them outweigh the due process concerns raised by interested private prosecutors. To begin with, the government's interest in preventing a slight increase in expenditures necessitated by a rule prohibiting interested private prosecutors pales in comparison to the defendant's interest in not being prosecuted by someone with a clear conflict of interest.[396] Indeed, because interested private prosecutions are already so infrequent, the notion that their use would save governmental financial resources is more ruse than reality. State public defenders' offices have long been more financially overburdened than public prosecutors' offices,[397] and the public, acting through its elected representatives or via referendum, is always free to devote more resources to law enforcement activities.

The argument that interested private prosecutors are necessary to assist public prosecutors likewise falls flat. Elected public prosecutors do need assistance, but that assistance should come in the form of deputies and, ideally, attorneys and support staff who are dedicated to their jobs and not to serving a private interest. Whenever private interests and monetary considerations are allowed to invade the criminal justice system, there is a risk of that system being perverted. Once again, Americans are free to devote more financial resources to law enforcement activities—and to *disinterested* prosecutors—if they so desire. Although the public interest will sometimes demand that certain anachronistic laws, like penal laws criminalizing adultery or marijuana use,[398] actually not be enforced, crimes worthy of more investigatory resources and vigorous prosecution (e.g., rape or child abuse) should be better resourced through public appropriations. Public prosecutors must make judgment calls all the time about how to spend the limited resources allocated to them. And while public prosecutors sometimes solicit and accept grants or private donations in order to fund prosecutorial priorities, there is a substantial risk to individual rights if a public prosecutor is coopted by special interests—what one source describes as "the capture of the prosecutor"—or if there is unequal access to justice.[399] If crimes worthy of more vigorous prosecution are not being appropriately handled by the local district attorney, any lax enforcement can become a campaign issue and the neglectful public prosecutor can be thrown out of office.[400]

In prohibiting interested private prosecutors, victims' rights will not be compromised. Victims or their families may already express their feelings of outrage at the sentencing stage,[401] and victims, whether of assault, robbery, or otherwise, are free to testify at trial about the facts or regarding their sense of violation at the hands of the alleged wrongdoer. Although victims' rights are of critical importance, the use of interested private prosecutors in the name of victims' rights cannot be tolerated. Such prosecutors have significant adverse effects on defendants' constitutional rights, and they are completely unnecessary to vindicate the rights of victims. Of course, during the heyday of American private prosecutions, a criminal prosecution was seen as a pitched contest between the accuser and the accused.[402] "The first half of the nineteenth century," Adam Malka writes in *The Men of Mobtown: Policing Baltimore in the Age of Slavery and Emancipation* (2018), was "the era of private prosecutions." If a fight broke out between two men, Malka explains, one of the assailants (and perhaps both) might bring charges against the other by heading to the nearest magistrate's office and securing a warrant for his opponent's arrest. The magistrate usually conducted a formal hearing with the two men representing themselves.[403]

In modern times, interested private prosecutions are increasingly rare, though many Americans—perhaps because of the country's history—continue to look on criminal prosecutions as part of the adversarial system despite the fact that most prosecutions are now pursued by public instead of private prosecutors. Eric Fish, a federal public defender in San Diego, California, writes of how modern-day prosecutors and members of the public generally perceive the criminal justice system "as an adversarial contest between two sides." As he observes of prevailing attitudes toward prosecutors and criminal trials: "The government wins this contest if the defendant is convicted and punished. The government loses if the defendant is acquitted or the conviction is later vacated. Consequently, the prosecutor is expected to advocate zealously for conviction and punishment." "This means," Fish writes of prosecutors, that "they must make strategic decisions that will maximize the likelihood of victory, just as a private lawyer would act strategically on behalf" of a client. But when a person's life or liberty is at stake, the prosecutor—in reality, a person performing a *quasi-judicial* function—must be vigilantly concerned about erroneous charges and wrongful convictions. Indeed, a prosecutor undeniably has basic obligations not just to victims but *to the accused* (*e.g.*, to disclose exculpatory evidence and to see that justice is done). Because interested private prosecutors necessarily have conflicting loyalties that may not be reconcilable, their participation should not be permitted in criminal cases as their judgment may be clouded by those conflicting loyalties.

Because public prosecutors naturally have their own views of the law and a given set of facts, and because their perspectives may diverge from those victimized or affected by crime, there will naturally be many cases in which private individuals will disagree—sometimes, strongly—with public prosecutors' decisions. Some states expressly give judges the right to approve criminal complaints filed by private parties, although most states—like the federal system—vest public prosecutors with the exclusive power to charge individuals with criminal violations.[404] Regardless of whether a private individual has the right to ask a judge to review the circumstances of a particular set of allegations, the key is to have a *disinterested* prosecutor and a *disinterested* tribunal ultimately handle the matter to ensure the fair administration of justice.[405] An ethical prosecutor should have independence and not be a tool or a mouthpiece for someone seeking vengeance or a specific result or leverage in another related dispute. Even where judges, aiming to vindicate the power of the court, appoint a private attorney to handle a contempt case, it is important that the prosecutor who is appointed be independent and not be coopted by private interests.[406] That is exactly why, at the federal level, a special counsel (formerly known as a special prosecutor or independent counsel) is appointed to investigate and handle matters in which a conflict of interest exists for the prosecutor's office normally tasked with making prosecutorial decisions.[407] For example, Robert Mueller was appointed Special Counsel for the U.S. Department of Justice by then-Acting Attorney General Rod Rosenstein after then-Attorney General Jeff Sessions recused himself.[408] Just as the American legal system does not countenance one individual taking on the role of judge, jury and executioner,[409] an interested private prosecutor should not be permitted to initiate or guide a prosecution.

The Equal Protection Clause and Private Prosecution

The U.S. Constitution's Fourteenth Amendment provides in part: "No state shall make or enforce any law which shall abridge the privileges or immunities of citizens of the United States; nor shall any state deprive any person of life, liberty, or property, without due process of law; nor deny to any person within its jurisdiction the equal protection of the laws."[410] "[T]he central purpose of the Fourteenth Amendment," the U.S. Supreme Court has ruled, "was to eliminate racial discrimination emanating from official sources in the States."[411] "In the years before and after the ratification of the Fourteenth Amendment," the Supreme Court observed in *Peña-Rodriguez v. Colorado* (2017), "it became clear that racial discrimination in the jury system posed a particular threat both to the promise of the Amendment and to the integrity of the jury trial." "It must become the heritage of our Nation to rise above racial classifications that are so inconsistent with our commitment to the equal dignity of all persons," the Court held in that case, adding: "The duty to confront racial animus in the justice system is not the legislature's alone. Time and again, this Court has been called upon to enforce the Constitution's guarantee against state-sponsored racial discrimination in the jury system." "The Nation must continue to make strides to overcome race-based discrimination," the Court stressed.[412]

As a matter of constitutional law, the Fourteenth Amendment's Equal Protection Clause must be interpreted in the context of other provisions of the U.S. Constitution, including the Fourteenth Amendment's Due Process Clause. "The Due Process Clause and the Equal Protection Clause are connected in a profound way, though they set forth independent principles," the U.S. Supreme Court emphasized in *Obergefell v. Hodges* (2015).[413] In holding that same-sex couples have the fundamental right to marry, Justice Anthony Kennedy's majority opinion found that the right was "part of the liberty promised by the Fourteenth Amendment" and "derived, too, from that Amendment's guarantee of the equal protection of the laws." As Justice Kennedy wrote for the Court of the connection between the Due Process Clause and Equal Protection Clause: "Rights implicit in liberty and rights secured by equal protection may rest on different precepts and are not always co-extensive, yet in some instances each may be instructive as to the meaning and reach of the other. In any particular case one Clause may be thought to capture the essence of the right in a more accurate and comprehensive way, even as the two Clauses may converge in the identification and definition of the right." "This interrelation of the two principles," Justice Kennedy wrote, "furthers our understanding of what freedom is and must become." "[R]ights come not from ancient sources alone," Kennedy added elsewhere in the opinion, pointing out that rights "rise, too, from a better informed understanding of how constitutional imperatives define a liberty that remains urgent in our own era."[414]

The U.S. Supreme Court's equal protection jurisprudence, not tethered to outdated eighteenth- or nineteenth-century modes of thinking, "has typically been concerned with governmental classifications that 'affect some groups of citizens differently than others.'"[415] The Fourteenth Amendment's Equal Protection Clause, the Supreme Court ruled in *City of Cleburne v. Cleburne Living Center* (1985), "is essentially a direction that all persons similarly situated should be treated alike." As the Court observed in that opinion of the Fourteenth Amendment and its equal protection jurisprudence: "Section 5 of the Amendment empowers Congress to enforce this mandate, but absent controlling congressional direction, the courts have themselves devised standards for determining the validity of state legislation or other official action that is challenged as denying equal protection." "The general rule," the Court emphasized, "is that legislation is presumed to be valid and will be sustained if the classification drawn by the statute is rationally related to a legitimate state interest." "The general rule gives way, however," the Court clarified, "when a statute classifies by race, alienage, or national origin," observing that such laws "are subjected to strict scrutiny and will be sustained only if they are suitably tailored to serve a compelling state interest." The Court noted that "[s]imilar oversight by the courts is due when state laws impinge on personal rights protected by the Constitution" and that "[l]egislative classifications based on gender also call for a heightened standard of review." Such a classification, the Court ruled in *City of Cleburne*, "fails unless it is substantially related to a sufficiently important government interest."[416]

To date, the U.S. Supreme Court has held that only "intentional discrimination" violates the Equal Protection Clause.[417] For example, in *McCleskey v. Kemp* (1987), the U.S. Supreme Court—in an infamous opinion written by Justice Lewis Powell that he came to regret in his retirement[418]—rejected an equal protection challenge to the application of Georgia's death penalty premised on compelling statistical evidence. A defendant who alleges an equal protection violation, the Court decided in its 5–4 ruling, has the burden of proving "the existence of purposeful discrimination." "[T]o prevail under the Equal Protection Clause, McCleskey must prove that the decisionmakers in *his* case acted with discriminatory purpose," the Court ruled, though the Court noted that it accepts statistics as proof of intent to discriminate "in certain limited contexts," including as regards the selection of the jury venire and under Title VII of the Civil Rights Act.[419] As two legal commentators, Mark Rosenbaum and Daniel Tokaji, wrote in the *Michigan Law Review* back in 2002 of the Court's approach to equal protection claims: "Rather than examining whether a government entity as a whole has discriminated, the Court has insisted upon an inquiry that requires equal protection plaintiffs to ferret out individual, intentional discriminators. Put another way, the Court has insisted upon a 'bad apple' paradigm instead of examining, to borrow a term from criminal procedure, whether the tree itself is poisoned."[420]

In the United States, it is clear that prosecutors exercise vast discretion in prosecuting criminal cases. It has been held, however, that a prosecutor's discretion "is subject to constitutional constraints," one of which is imposed by the Equal Protection Clause and which prevents a prosecutor from deciding whether to prosecute someone based on "an unjustifiable standard such as race, religion, or other arbitrary classification."[421] "To prevail on a selective enforcement equal protection claim," one federal district court observed in 2020, "'a plaintiff must demonstrate that enforcement had a discriminatory effect and the police were motivated by a discriminatory purpose.'" "To state a claim," that court noted, "the plaintiff must allege facts demonstrating that similarly situated individuals could have been prosecuted but were not."[422] A defendant, it has been held, may demonstrate that the law's administration is "directed so exclusively against a particular class of persons… with a mind so unequal and oppressive" that the system of prosecution amounts to "a practical denial" of the equal protection of the law.[423]

A high threshold of proof is thus required to establish an equal protection violation in the prosecution context. "Because of the presumption of regularity," the U.S. Court of Appeals for the Eleventh Circuit declared in 2021, "a defendant who seeks to establish a claim of selective prosecution in violation of the Constitution carries a 'demanding' burden."[424] As one criminal procedure treatise, in a section titled "Discriminatory prosecution," describes the existing state of the law: "Whether raised in federal court or state court, the claim is not likely to succeed; courts 'have found only a handful of equal protection violations' arising out of the charging decisions of prosecutors. This is because claimants bear a 'heavy burden' to overcome the presumption of legal regularity in enforcement of the penal law by proving the three essential elements of a discriminatory prosecution claim: (1) that other violators similarly situated are generally not prosecuted; (2) that the selection of the claimant was 'intentional or purposeful'; and (3) that the selection was pursuant to an 'arbitrary classification.'"[425]

Selective or discriminatory prosecutions are different—or at least constitute a different class or category of cases—from private prosecutions by interested parties, with selective or discriminatory prosecutions also differing in their requirements from malicious and vindictive prosecutions. The elements of malicious prosecution—a tort recognized in both English and American common law[426]—are "(1) the institution of a criminal proceedings; (2) without probable cause; (3) with malice; and (4) termination of the proceeding in favor of the accused."[427] "The elements of vindictive prosecution," by contrast, as another source puts it, "are: (1) the exercise of a protected right, (2) a prosecutorial stake in the exercise of that right, (3) unreasonableness of the prosecutor's conduct, and (4) the intent to punish a defendant for exercise of the protected right." "Vindictive prosecution," that source observes, "occurs when a prosecutor seeks to punish a defendant solely for exercising a valid legal right; such prosecution constitutes a violation of due process."[428] The use of interested private prosecutions may, of course, substantially increase the likelihood of malicious or vindictive prosecutions. As one scholar observes: "It is well acknowledged that the availability of private prosecutions in any criminal justice system risks improper and malicious prosecutions at the peril of a person's liberty."[429]

Although some scholars do not see private prosecutions as running afoul of the Fourteenth Amendment's Equal Protection Clause,[430] private prosecutions by interested parties should be seen as violative of equal protection principles.[431] First, the practice of private prosecution itself has a sordid and discriminatory past—one that should not be overlooked in assessing the practice's constitutionality. Prior to the Fourteenth Amendment's ratification, laws that forbade people of color from testifying in court precluded them from bringing criminal any prosecutions against whites.[432] As Professor Darryl Brown, of the University of Virginia School of Law, wrote in the *Minnesota Law Review* in 2018: "During the first several decades of the nineteenth century, when private citizens could prosecute crimes, many states—and not only Southern ones—either denied African Americans legal capacity as litigants or barred them from testifying under oath on the basis of race. Among other effects, those barriers barred private prosecutions by African Americans." In other words, while whites victimized by crime could freely testify in court and pursue private prosecutions against offenders as they desired, non-white persons—as a practical matter—could not access or utilize a state's private prosecution system.

After slavery was outlawed following the hard-fought Civil War through the adoption of the U.S. Constitution's Thirteenth Amendment, the passage of the Civil Rights Act of 1866 and the Enforcement Act of 1870—along with the Fourteenth Amendment's ratification—sought to give Black citizens and others equal access to the courts and to prohibit laws barring their testimony.[433] As Darryl Brown emphasizes of American history following slavery's abolition: "After 1865—an era in which rights to litigate and testify were viewed by many as more meaningful than the right to vote—those race-based legal disabilities were abolished. In the same period, private charging authority, already on the decline, was abolished in most states that still permitted it." "States that retained a formal litigation role for crime victims," he noted, "did so by allowing privately funded attorneys to assist in prosecutions filed and controlled by public prosecutors, thus ensuring that public officials are the exclusive gatekeepers of criminal law enforcement." "Between the 1840s and 1860s," Brown explains, "prosecutors had become locally elected officials in nearly all states," with Brown—taking note that "Southern whites succeeded in disenfranchising black citizens"—further observing: "Evidence for the relationship between race and the demise of private prosecution is correlative rather than causal, but it nonetheless suggests a reason for why state justice systems took a different path from other common-law jurisdictions and abolished private charging." As Brown writes: "Local white majorities had little need for a structural check on prosecutors they elected, and they likely did not want a way for African-American citizens to challenge prosecutors and independently pursue their interests in criminal courts."[434]

The nation's first federal civil rights act—the Civil Rights Act of 1866—required "like punishment" for Blacks and whites, though southern states and members of the Ku Klux Klan resisted that legal reform.[435] The Ku Klux Klan was formed shortly after Robert E. Lee's surrender at Appomattox, and it used violence and other intimation tactics to terrorize Black citizens, leading Congress to pass "The Ku Klux Klan Act" of 1871. The 1871 Act empowered the federal government to enforce the mandates of the Fourteenth and Fifteenth Amendments, the former guaranteeing "equal protection of the laws" and the latter providing that "[t]he right of citizens of the United States to vote shall not be denied or abridged by the United States or by any State on account of race, color, or previous condition of servitude."[436] Some southern states (*i.e.*, Georgia, Kentucky, Alabama, and Tennessee)—jurisdictions that sought to deny Blacks access to the courts—actually initiated systems of public prosecution after the federal Slave Trade Act of 1794, which posed a threat to slaveholders and their interests in those southern states. That federal act prohibited anyone from outfitting or preparing a ship for purposes of engaging in the slave trade with a foreign country; prohibited the taking on board of slaves obtained in the international slave trade; and provided that those convicted would forfeit their ships. The federal system had established a system of public prosecution after the U.S. Constitution's ratification, but the Slave Trade Act of 1794 provided that a portion of the fine received from a successful prosecution would be split between the United States and the person "who shall sue for and prosecute" the case. As one commentator, Jason Twede, notes: "It appears that the prosecutor referred to in the statute is not the public prosecutor" because the Act specified that any fine would be split between the United States and another.

In his Ph.D. dissertation, "Going Public: How the Government Assumed the Authority to Prosecute in the Southern United States," Jason Twede points out that, in Georgia, "slavery abolition societies' willingness and financial ability to prosecute slaveholders posed a threat to slaveholders." Although the Slave Trade Act of 1794 was a federal law, it could be enforced in the states, making it—in Twede's words—"a cause for concern for those in the South that were involved in or benefitted from the slave trade." "Public prosecution," he writes, "appears to have been initiated in Georgia—at least in part—to safeguard those slaveholder interests by taking away the ability of private parties to prosecute and vesting that authority in an appointed governmental official—the public prosecutor." "It became clear," Twede explains, "that abolition societies were willing to prosecute cases against those participating in slavery—even their own family members if necessary." "The method of appointing public prosecutors in Georgia from its inception in the late eighteenth century to the mid-nineteenth century," he writes, "appears to have been designed to create a corps of public prosecutors that were sympathetic to slaveholder interests." "If we look at the times that states in the South instituted a system of public prosecution," Twede observes, "we can see a distinct trend." As Twede reports: "Many of the states—Georgia, Kentucky, Alabama and Tennessee—initiated a system of public prosecution after the federal Slave Trade Act of 1794 was passed but before the 20 year window during which the slave trade could not be addressed." As agreed at the Constitutional Convention in Philadelphia and later ratified as part of the U.S. Constitution, Article I, section 9 of the U.S. Constitution provided that Congress could not prohibit the "importation" of slaves prior to 1808.[437]

Through the years, some American jurists have rejected equal protection challenges to private prosecutors[438] or declined the reach the constitutional dimensions of private prosecutions.[439] Such rulings were made even though the distinction between "private" and "public" prosecution was—as history reveals—tied up with issues of discrimination and racial prejudice. Yet, the dangers in allowing purely private interests to drive prosecutions has long been recognized. For example, in *People v. Acme Markets, Inc.* (1975), the Court of Appeals of New York held that "prosecution at the instance of an interest group for its private purposes constitutes discrimination violative of the equal protection clauses of the Federal and State Constitutions." In that case, the defendants were Erie County supermarkets, with complainants being business representatives of the Amalgamated Meatcutters Union, Local 34, whose territory included Erie County and western New York. "The District Attorney of Erie County," New York's Court of Appeals reported, "testified that over a seven-year period it was his policy not to prosecute actively Sunday sales law violations, but that if an arrest were made—i.e., if an information was filed—prosecution would be brought." Where the district attorney's office had last prosecuted violation of Sunday sales laws in 1964 and 1965, and where that office itself had no general enforcement plan for Sunday sales law violations but only acted upon complaints and informations filed by private citizens, the Court of Appeals of New York held that "[d]iscriminatory enforcement as a defense to a criminal action derives from the Federal and State constitutional guarantee of equal protection of the law." As that court emphasized: "The underlying concept is elemental—that persons similarly situated should be treated the same and that criminal justice should and must be evenly and equally dispensed." In dismissing the informations initiated by interested private parties, the Court of Appeals of New York made this ruling:

> Assuming the fairness of the statute on its face and ascribing the actions of the meatcutters to the District Attorney, discriminatory enforcement is established in these cases as a matter of law. As found by the courts below, the Sun-

> day sales law has fallen into a sort of desuetude by law agencies in Erie County, unenforced, save upon complaint. And then it is perhaps unenforceable in an even-handed and fair manner. Indeed, it is not an exaggeration to say that enforcement has been totally surrendered to private parties and interest groups who without constraint may manipulate the law for purely private purposes. This is an unseemly state of affairs openly inviting discrimination and harassment of one group by another.[440]

In another case, *People v. Benoit* (1991), the Criminal Court for the City of New City held that a city statute providing for prosecution by private citizens violated the Fourteenth Amendment's due process and equal protection clauses. It that case, it was contended that section 50 of the New York City Criminal Court Act was unconstitutional as applied. After the court emphasized that "[t]he custom of allowing individuals to prosecute in the name of the state" had its origins in the English common law, the court observed: "Jurisdictions which allow private prosecutions based on their case law or state statutes all have one common characteristic—the private prosecutor is always an attorney who merely assists the public prosecutor and it is the public prosecutor who actually remains in control of the case." In its opinion, the court noted that "[d]efendant's equal protection argument rests on the premise that she is entitled to prosecution by a disinterested public prosecutor, and not an interested private one." Citing *People v. Zimmer* (1980), in which the New York Court of Appeals described the public prosecutor's role as "not so much to convict as it is to achieve a just result," the court in *Benoit* concluded that *Zimmer* "dictates that a public prosecutor must be disinterested" so that the continued prosecution of a defendant by a woman "whose interest in the prosecution is beyond peradventure, would violate both the defendant's due process and equal protection guarantees."[441]

The Equal Protection Clause, as its name suggests, is designed to ensure that similarly situated individuals are treated equally.[442] The U.S. Supreme Court, for example, has observed that "like individuals should be treated alike,"[443] and that the Equal Protection Clause "keeps governmental decisionmakers from treating differently persons who are in all relevant respects alike."[444] Private prosecutions, of course, are directly contrary to that equality-of-treatment principle as those facing interested private prosecutions are treated arbitrarily and much differently than other individuals in the criminal justice system.[445] Interested private prosecutions are not justified because they treat persons facing them differently than everyone else; are arbitrary and discriminatory; and bear no rational relation to a legitimate governmental interest, let alone serve a compelling governmental interest.[446] There is not, in fact, any legitimate government interest in letting non-disinterested prosecutors conduct prosecutions. By permitting interested private prosecutions, state actors consciously and intentionally discriminate against those who ultimately face such prosecutions.[447]

Case law has already recognized that there is no constitutional right to have someone criminally prosecuted, and private citizens—as has been held—"are thus not entitled to an order requiring the arrest or prosecution of wrongdoers."[448] While private citizens, on the one hand, possess no constitutional right to have another person criminally prosecuted, a focus on the rights of the accused, on the other, should make clear the unfairness of having an interested private prosecutor involved in a criminal prosecution. The concepts of due process and equal protection of the laws are legal bulwarks against arbitrariness and unfair treatment, and in twenty-first century America, interested private prosecutions are—and must be seen as—inherently arbitrary and unjust. A typical prosecution involves decision-making by impartial or disinterested actors, but when a private interest is deliberately injected into a prosecution brought in the name of the state, it poses a clear risk of unfairness and unequal treatment.[449]

Even if it is not shown that laws permitting interested private prosecutions were enacted for discriminatory purposes, such laws should still be found to be unconstitutional in their application. The U.S. Supreme Court has ruled that "an equal protection claim can in some circumstances be sustained even if the plaintiff has not alleged class-based discrimination, but instead claims that she has been irrationally singled out as a so-called 'class of one.'"[450] To proceed on a claim of that type, a plaintiff must allege that he or she has been "intentionally treated differently from others similarly situated and that there is no rational basis for the difference in treatment."[451] "It is well settled," the Supreme Court ruled in *Engquist v. Oregon Department of Agriculture* (2008), "that the Equal Protection Clause 'protect[s] persons, not groups,' and that the Clause's protections apply to administrative as well as legislative acts."[452] One A.L.R. annotation, titled "Class-of-One Equal Protection Claims Based upon Law Enforcement Actions," summarizes the law in this area as follows: "A plaintiff not otherwise part of an identifiable group may bring a 'class-of-one' equal protection claim against government actors where there is sufficient proof that the defendant intentionally treated the plaintiff differently from other similarly situated persons or entities without a rational basis for the disparate treatment." That annotation discusses both successful and unsuccessful class-of-one claims involving prosecutorial discretion and imposition of sentences,[453] with interested private prosecutions plainly resulting in some people being treated differently than others. In two cases referenced in the A.L.R. annotation where class-of-one claims were identified as successful, the courts found that the individuals had been treated arbitrarily or more harshly than others.[454]

Although the Court in *Engquist* held that the "class-of-one theory" of equal protection does not apply in the public employment context,[455] the Court—in an earlier case, *Village of Willowbrook v. Olech* (2000)—has specifically emphasized: "[o]ur cases have recognized successful equal protection claims brought by a 'class of one,' where the plaintiff alleges that she has been intentionally treated differently from others similarly situated and that there is no rational basis for the difference in treatment." "In so doing," the Court observed, "we have explained that '[t]he purpose of the equal protection clause of the Fourteenth Amendment is to secure every person within the State's jurisdiction against intentional and arbitrary discrimination, whether occasioned by express terms of a statute or by its improper execution through duly constituted agents.'" In that case, Grace Olech and her late husband, Thaddeus, had asked the Village of Willowbrook to connect their property to the municipal water supply, and the village at first conditioned the connection on the Olechs granting a village a 33-foot easement instead of a 15-foot easement it sought from other property owners seeking access to the water supply. The Olechs asserted that the village's demand was "motivated by ill will resulting from the Olechs' previous filing of an unrelated, successful lawsuit" against the village. The Supreme Court ruled that "Olech's complaint can fairly be construed as alleging that the Village intentionally demanded a 33-foot easement as a condition of connecting her property... where the Village required only a 15-foot easement from other similarly situated property owners." "These allegations, quite apart from the Village's subjective motivation," the Court added, "are sufficient to state a claim for relief under traditional equal protection analysis."[456] If a case involving the size of an easement warranted finding an equal protection violation, then surely a case where a person's life or liberty is at stake—as is true with a criminal prosecution—should merit a similar finding in the context of an interested private prosecution.

The "class-of-one theory" of equal protection warrants special consideration in the context of interested private prosecutors. The Equal Protection Clause, the U.S. Court of Appeals for the Seventh Circuit emphasized in *Brunson v. Murray* (2016), "guards against government discrimination on the basis of race and other immutable characteristics, but it also extends to protect people from so-called 'class-of-one' discrimination in which a government arbitrarily and irrationally singles out one person for poor treatment." Such "class-of-one claims," that court observed, "are designed to prevent government actors from singling out a person for arbitrary abuse."[457] To establish an equal protection violation based on a class-of-one theory, a plaintiff must allege that the defendant: (1) intentionally (2) treated the plaintiff differently than other similarly situated individuals (3) without a rational basis.[458] As one federal district court, in considering a lawsuit brought pursuant to 42 U.S.C. § 1983, declared in 2016 of what's necessary to state a claim for an equal protection violation under a "class of one theory": "To state such a claim, the plaintiffs must allege that the officers treated them in an adverse fashion relative to other similarly-situated individuals connected with the investigation and prosecution of an alleged crime, and that the defendants' adverse treatment was arbitrary and motivated by ill-will or animus towards the plaintiffs."[459] "Closely related to a class-of-one claim," one federal court pointed out in 2015, "a claim of selective enforcement or selective prosecution arises when the government seeks to apply the law to a plaintiff differently than it would to other similarly situated individuals for constitutionally impermissible reasons such as on grounds of a plaintiff's race or malicious intent." To prevail on that claim, a plaintiff must prove: (1) that the plaintiff, compared with others similarly situated, was "selectively treated"; and (2) that "such selective treatment was based on impermissible considerations such as race, religion, intent to inhibit or punish the exercise of constitutional rights, or malicious or bad faith intent to injure a person."[460]

In an era in which disinterested public prosecutors handle almost all criminal cases, the use of interested private prosecutors should be found to be a violation of the U.S. Constitution's Equal Protection Clause. In many courts and locales, that will require reevaluating prior judicial rulings, but the time has come—and for good reason—to declare that the provisions of the U.S. Constitution and equivalent state constitutions do not allow interested private prosecutions. In 1989, in *Register v. Vasquez*, the U.S. Court of Appeals for the Ninth Circuit considered whether the constitutional rights of a California state prisoner convicted of first-degree murder were violated because he was prosecuted by a "private prosecutor." In that case, Register—who had been convicted of first-degree murder—brought a petition for writ of habeas corpus in which he alleged that "his equal protection rights were violated because he was prosecuted by a private prosecutor rather than a public prosecutor." In summarily rejecting Kash Register's petition, the Ninth Circuit—in an unpublished opinion—ruled in 1989: "In order to obtain habeas relief, a state prisoner must demonstrate that his detention violates the federal Constitution or laws. There is no support in federal law or from the facts in the record to support a claim that such procedure unlawfully discriminated against Register. Thus, the district court properly dismissed this claim."[461] Register had been convicted of first-degree murder in the Los Angeles County Superior Court in 1979 and was sentenced to life in state prison without parole.[462] His conviction was upheld in 1981, though in 1984, due to a change in California's sentencing laws, Register was resentenced to 27 years to life. "Because all of Register's claims are without merit," the Ninth Circuit declared in its 1989 ruling, "we affirm the district court's dismissal of Register's petition for writ of habeas corpus."[463]

As it turns out, Register's claims, including a claim of innocence, were meritorious. In fact, the Los Angeles City Council later paid Kash Register $16.7 million to settle his federal civil rights lawsuit after he had served thirty-four years in prison for a murder he did not commit.[464] An African-American man, Register was released from prison in 2013 after his lawyers—with the assistance of Loyola Law School students—cast doubt on the credibility of a key prosecution witness. Register had always maintained his innocence, but he nevertheless spent 34 years in custody after being convicted of the 1979 armed robbery and murder of a 78-year-old man, Jack Sasson. In 1979, prosecutors had convinced the jury that Kash Delano Register—the defendant on trial—had shot Sasson five times in the carport of his West Los Angeles home. Brenda Anderson—the prosecution's star witness—testified that Register, a young man whom she'd gone to high school with, had shot her elderly neighbor, leading to his death three weeks later. Brenda Anderson, then 19, said that she looked out the window when she heard gunfire and saw an African American man sprinting from the Sassons' carport. She specifically identified the assailant as Register in spite of an alibi offered by Register.[465]

For years, Register was denied parole. "It appears that the only reason that I have been consistently denied parole is because I have maintained my innocence," Register told the parole board at one point. But the truth eventually came out. According to a story published in the *Los Angeles Times* after Register's exoneration: "The case against Register was based on eyewitness testimony. No murder weapon was recovered and none of the fingerprints lifted at the West Los Angeles crime scene matched Register's." Although Register's girlfriend testified at trial that Register was with her at the time of the shooting, the prosecution's star witness—Brenda Anderson—told police that she heard gunshots and saw Register running away from the crime scene. More than thirty years later, however, that testimony was eviscerated. In court papers, Anderson's sisters—Sheila Vanderkam and Sharon Anderson—said that when they tried to tell a detective that their sister was not telling the truth and that the police had the wrong person, they were ignored and told to keep quiet. Register's attorneys specifically contended that police and prosecutors had suppressed exculpatory evidence.[466]

In late 2011, Vanderkam—"out of curiosity," as she later reported—had typed in Kash Register's name into a website and found, to her "horror," that Register was still in prison. Long after Register's 1979 conviction, Vanderkam told Register's attorney that Brenda Anderson's account at trial was a lie. Register's attorneys, in turn, asserted in post-conviction proceedings that Brenda Anderson only picked Register out of a photo array after police threatened to have her prosecuted for credit card forgery and theft. "According to Vanderkam," the *Los Angeles Times* reported in 2013, "at the time of the shooting, her sisters had just hidden a package of Avon products they had stolen from a neighbor" and, though "they heard gunfire," they "weren't close enough to get a good look at the shooter." Sharon Anderson had been told that her sister, Brenda, had identified Register, but Sharon had told investigators, "Well, it's not the same guy I seen." Although Vanderkam herself had worked at the same LAPD station as the detectives who investigated the shooting, Vanderkam recounted how the "[t]he detective placed his finger over this mouth (like a shush sound) and just stared at me," making it very clear to her, "without actually saying anything"—as Vanderkam put it—"that I was to stay out of it." A Los Angeles County Superior Court judge, Katherine Mader, ultimately threw out Register's conviction after Brenda Anderson recanted her original testimony ("It may or may not have been that person," she lamely offered in testimony before Judge Mader), causing Register's mother to sob with tears of joy. "Thank you Lord Jesus for giving me my child back," she cried with emotion as she thanked her son's attorneys from Loyola Law School's Project for the Innocent.[467] Just 18 at the time of the crime and only 19 when he was wrongfully convicted, Register was 53 when he was released from prison.[468] Register was released after the judge found that police and prosecutors had "repeatedly concealed relevant evidence" pointing to Register's innocence.[469]

A description of Kash Register's wrongful conviction on the website for The National Registry of Exonerations notes that "[f]ive alibi witnesses testified" at Register's trial. Alibi witnesses said that on the day of the shooting, Register was not wearing clothing consistent with the shooter's. The summary of the case from The National Registry of Exonerations gives this additional information about the miscarriage of justice that occurred:

> Sharon Anderson testified that she looked at the same photographic lineup as Brenda. She said a detective pointed to the photograph of Register and said, "Your sister, Brenda Anderson, said it's him—this one, right there." She said she told the detective that Register was not the gunman. She said that police attempted to coerce her to identify Register by threatening to arrest her for the stolen Avon products, but she still refused to identify him and, as a result, did not testify at trial.
>
> On November 7, 2013, Judge Mader vacated Register's conviction and ordered a new trial. The judge found that Brenda Anderson was an unreliable and unbelievable witness, noting that at the hearing, Brenda Anderson said that she wasn't sure the gunman was Register, that the gunman looked like someone she went to school with, that she wasn't sure who the gunman was, that she never "definitely" said the gunman was Register and that the police convinced her the gunman was Register.
>
> ....
>
> The judge found that the prosecution "repeatedly concealed relevant evidence" that would have resulted in an acquittal instead of a conviction. The evidence included Vanderkam's statement about her sister and Sharon Anderson's statement that the gunman was not Register. The prosecution also concealed the identify of another eyewitness... because she said she didn't want to get involved.

"From January to October 2013," the summary of Register's case emphasizes, "lawyers and law students from the Project for the Innocent investigated the case and discovered that the prosecution had failed to disclose that Brenda Anderson had a criminal record, including an arrest for forgery six days before the murder and convictions for petty theft and burglary prior to Register's trial."[470]

In a long article about the case titled, "A Mistake Has Been Made Here, and No One Wants to Correct It," Lara Bazelon—one of Register's lawyers—wrote in *Slate* about the failure of prosecutors to turn over exculpatory evidence. Bazelon noted that in the course of the reinvestigation of the case, a deputy district attorney had "turned over part of the prosecution's old trial file from 1979." The information that was turned over long after the fact included Brenda Anderson's rap sheet and offered a rationale for Anderson's motivation to testify against Register. As Bazelon wrote:

> The timing of her criminal record went a long way toward explaining her testimony. In addition to the threat of charges for the Avon theft, Anderson was facing a recent charge for credit-card forgery on the day she identified Register at the police station. She was in real danger of facing criminal prosecution,

> which gave her every reason to cooperate with the police. After Anderson pointed to Register's picture, the forgery charges evaporated, just like the threat of an indictment for the Avon theft. Since prosecutors had kept this information from Register's trial lawyer, the jurors had heard none of it. They also didn't learn that Anderson was on probation for two other theft-related convictions when she testified.

Just nine days before an evidentiary hearing that had been ordered by Judge Mader before Register's exoneration, the deputy district attorney had written an email to explain that he'd taken another look at the old 1979 prosecution file and found a document that he thought he should turn over because it could be "potentially" relevant. "Chillingly," Bazelon wrote in *Slate*, "the document was a memo about whether to seek the death penalty against Register." As Bazelon described the document: "It included these sentences: 'Mrs. Singleton saw the incident, but thus far has not cooperated due to the fact that her husband is afraid to have her testify,' and 'Two other witnesses, Christine Chambers and Sharon Anderson, were with Brenda Anderson and observed the incident. They cannot identify.'" In describing her reaction on getting the document, Bazelon emphasized: "Seeing this for the first time, I stared at my computer screen, reading the words 'cannot identify' over and over. In my mind, the memo confirmed everything we had argued for months. Sharon had been interviewed by the police and had not picked Register as the shooter. Neither had her mother. And Patty Singleton—blocked by her husband from coming forward—apparently hadn't made a positive identification either. Which meant that no one had." Under questioning at the hearing itself, Bazelon recounted, Brenda Anderson testified that she didn't know who the shooter was because she had "only seen a flash," adding horrifyingly, "And like everybody knows, black people all look alike."[471]

To be sure, the current state of the law makes it extremely difficult for those bringing equal protection claims in the criminal justice context. Persons alleging a "class-of-one" equal protection claim, it has been held, must show "an extremely high degree of similarity between themselves and the persons to whom they compare themselves."[472] Several class-of-one claims, in fact, have been rejected in matters involving discretionary decisionmaking,[473] including in the context of prosecutorial discretion.[474] "[A]n exercise of prosecutorial discretion, unless based on some invidious discrimination, is not typically a basis for a class-of-one challenge," the U.S. Court of Appeals for the Seventh Circuit held in *Van Dyke v. Village of Alsip* (2020).[475] As the Seventh Circuit ruled in an earlier case, *United States v. Moore* (2008): "[A] class-of-one equal protection challenge, at least where premised solely on arbitrariness/irrationality, is just as much a 'poor fit' in the prosecutorial discretion context as in the public employment context." "[T]he discretion conferred on prosecutors in choosing whom and how to prosecute is flatly inconsistent with a presumption of uniform treatment," the Seventh Circuit noted, adding that "[t]o treat like individuals differently" in the context of exercise of prosecutorial discretion—"even without a strictly rational justification"—"'is not to classify them in a way that raises equal protection concerns.'"[476] But interested private prosecutions should be seen as an equal protection violation because they are *uniformly* unfair to those subjected to them. Interested private prosecutions inject structural unfairness into the criminal justice process.

Some state courts (*e.g.*, in Indiana and Tennessee) have rejected equal protection challenges to the practice of private prosecution.[477] As noted earlier, though, in *People v. Benoit*, the Criminal Court of the City of New York found that a private prosecution violated the Fourteenth Amendment's Equal Protection Clause. In that case, the landlord had commenced the private prosecution against a tenant charging assault, criminal mischief, and menacing and harassment in connection with the same incident for which the grand jury had indicted the landlord on charges of assault and criminal possession of a weapon. The defendant's equal protection challenge was premised on the argument that she was entitled to "a disinterested public prosecutor, and not an interested private one." In analyzing the issue, the court in *Benoit* had cited a New York precedent, *People v. Zimmer* (1980), that described the public prosecutor's mission as "not so much to convict as it is to achieve a just result." The court in *Zimmer* had dismissed an indictment obtained by a district attorney against a defendant who had allegedly stolen money from a corporation of which the district attorney was both a stockholder and counsel. The *Zimmer* court ruled that it was enough of a conflict of interest such that there did not need to be a showing of actual prejudice to the defendant. The *Zimmer* court then posed these questions: "Assuming he intended to be as fair and objective as fair could be, in presenting this evidence where did his role as partisan corporate attorney end and where did that of nonpartisan District Attorney begin? At what point was he serving which of his two masters?" "To put the questions is to state the problem, a problem instinct with due process implications," the court in *Zimmer* concluded. After noting that *Zimmer* dictated that "a public prosecutor must be disinterested," the court in *Benoit* found that the defendant's continued prosecution "would violate both the defendant's due process and equal protection guarantees."[478] The *Benoit* court employed better legal reasoning than decisions rejecting equal protection challenges, and interested private prosecutions should thus be made a thing of the past not only under due process principles but equal protection principles, too.

Indeed, not only are interested private prosecutions fundamentally unfair to the accused, but their use threatens the reliability of criminal proceedings[479] and discriminates against the poor. It requires tremendous resources to commence and continue prosecutions, and the poor are the least equipped to handle such prosecutions. "Public prosecutors," scholar Darryl Brown writes, "now dominate enforcement decisions in both common law-based and civil law-based justice systems worldwide." "That is hardly surprising," he explains, "given the far-reaching regulatory scope of modern criminal law and high expectations that the state will ensure security against social disorder and innumerable harms, and will intervene in risk creation long before manifest criminal conduct or injury." Such an agenda, he emphasizes, "requires capacity, resources, and expertise that only public agencies can marshal." In his critique of private prosecutions, Brown adds: "[A] criminal enforcement regime that relied heavily on private plaintiffs would be one skewed against redress for poor victims who cannot bear litigation costs to vindicate their own interests. Without safeguards, such a regime also could be at the mercy of the varied, perhaps idiosyncratic motives and interests of private actors lodging criminal complaints."[480] "[R]equiring resources to obtain equal protection of the law is anathema to our criminal justice system," another scholar, Tania Tetlow, points out, adding: "We have already traveled too far down the road of private policing in wealthy communities, allocating the resources of law enforcement according to the ability to pay. We should not start privatizing prosecution for those who can afford it."[481]

The poor have—and should be afforded—special protection within the context of the criminal justice system. For example, in *Griffin v. Illinois*,[482] the Supreme Court utilized the equal protection and due process clauses to strike down a law requiring criminal appellants to pay for trial transcripts. As the Supreme Court stated in *Griffin*: "There can be no equal justice where the kind of trial a man gets depends on the amount of money he has. Destitute defendants must be offered as adequate appellate review as defendants who have money enough to buy transcripts."[483] Likewise, in *Gideon v. Wainwright*,[484] the Supreme Court held that every indigent criminal defendant accused of a felony is entitled to appointed counsel.[485] The guarantee of appointed counsel was subsequently broadened in *Argersinger v. Hamlin*[486] to include all prosecutions resulting in imprisonment for any term. The Supreme Court has also held that an indigent criminal defendant has a right to the assistance of a psychiatrist at state expense if the defendant's sanity will be a significant factor at trial or if the state presents psychiatric testimony during a capital sentencing proceeding.[487] As Professor Laurence Tribe has aptly observed: "Particularly noteworthy in all of these cases is the Court's willingness to mandate what amounts to state purchase of private services—legal or medical—for private citizens."[488]

In the founding era, criminal trials were frequently conducted without counsel.[489] Thankfully, in modern times, neither victims of crime nor criminal defendants have to endure that circumstance. Although some advocate for the use of interested private prosecutors, contrary to the suggestion that private prosecutors benefit law enforcement activities by providing additional resources, the use of private prosecutors only creates castes within the criminal justice system. Whereas wealthy citizens can afford to pursue questionable criminal prosecutions by hiring private prosecutors, poor individuals, who—according to Census figures—are statistically more likely to be racial minorities,[490] cannot afford access.[491] In this vein, the U.S. Supreme Court has held that rich and poor alike must be afforded "equal justice" under the Constitution. As Justice Douglas wrote for the Supreme Court in *Harper v. Virginia Board of Elections*,[492] where Virginia's poll tax was struck down: "Lines drawn on the basis of wealth or property, like those of race... are traditionally disfavored."[493] To put an end to interested private prosecutions in America, the U.S. Supreme Court should declare the practice unconstitutional and not just rely on its "supervisory power" as it did in its *Young* decision.[494]

One of the most striking features of public prosecution in the United States is that wealthy and poor individuals alike have equal access, at least theoretically, to the criminal justice system. While problems and imperfections exist, public prosecutors should treat criminal assaults on food stamp recipients just as seriously as they treat assaults on corporate executives. In contrast to this egalitarian ideal, allowing interested private prosecutors creates situations in which the criminal justice system treats wealthy individuals far better than poor individuals. There is great wealth and income inequality in the United States, and there should not be one system of justice for billionaires and millionaires and another system of justice for everyone else. Because the use of interested private prosecutors runs contrary to the concept of "equal justice,"[495] the Constitution should be read to prohibit the use of such prosecutors.[496] In short, the criminal justice system should not discriminate between rich and poor. For example, in writing for the Supreme Court in *M.L.B. v. S.L.J.* (1996) and holding that Mississippi statutes violated the Fourteenth Amendment's Equal Protection and Due Process Clauses by requiring an indigent woman to pre-pay record preparation fees estimated at $2,352.36 before she would be allowed to appeal a parental termination decree, Justice Ruth Bader Ginsburg pronounced: "We hold that, just as a State may not block an indigent petty offender's access to an appeal afforded others, so Mississippi may not deny M.L.B., because of her poverty, appellate review of the sufficiency of the evidence on which the trial court found her unfit to remain a parent."[497]

In several cases, courts have noted that private prosecutors are bound by the same standards of professional conduct as public prosecutors.[498] For example, in *Kerns v. Wolverton* (1989), the Supreme Court of Appeals of West Virginia emphasized of its ruling in a prior case, *State v. Atkins* (1979): "[T]his Court recognized that '[t]he right to obtain a private prosecutor in this State is not absolute and is subject to judicial control and review. A private prosecutor is subject to the same high standards of conduct in the trial of the case as is the public prosecutor.'"[499] According to West Virginia's supreme court, "this rule blunts, if it does not entirely dissipate, the major criticism of private prosecutors, that they will be overzealous to convict and consequently ignore the public prosecutor's fundamental obligation to do justice."[500] However, what such court rulings fail to recognize is that interested private prosecutors cannot possibly adhere to the same standards of professional conduct as public prosecutors; the conflicts of interest that arise in interested private prosecutions are simply irreconcilable. An interested private prosecutor, who is often being paid handsomely to convict someone, cannot also, without at least some subtle bias, fairly represent the interests of that person and consider the "public interest" in treating that person justly. While private law firms are still often retained by municipalities—and not the victims of crime—to handle misdemeanor and petty misdemeanor cases, even in those situations courts must ensure through rigorous disclosures that the private law firm does not have any disqualifying conflict of interest. Ideally, all prosecutions—whether in felony or misdemeanor cases—would be handled by disinterested public prosecutors with no conflict of interest potentially clouding their judgment. But if lawyers at private law firms are selected to handle criminal prosecutions, judges must evaluate the arrangement for prosecution that has been made to ensure that fee structures, financial incentives, or other factors do not themselves violate a defendant's constitutional rights.

In a normal prosecution, a public prosecutor overly anxious to secure a conviction can engage in a wide variety of prosecutorial misconduct by, among other things, pursuing impermissible lines of questioning or argument, interrupting defense counsel's examination of witnesses, or acting unfairly toward defense counsel, the accused, or defense witnesses.[501] When such misconduct occurs, courts must check it and the bar must discipline the offending prosecutor. Although abolishing interested *private* prosecutions will not mean the end of prosecutorial misconduct, their abolition will at least reduce the number of such incidents.[502] While public prosecutors may, at times, become overzealous in their desire to convict, the U.S. Supreme Court in *Young* correctly recognized that this "problem... is personal, not structural."[503] Unlike the potential personal deficiencies with public prosecutors, the problem created by interested private prosecutors is structural in nature. Unlike public prosecutors whose salaries are paid by the state, interested private prosecutors have additional structural incentives (*i.e.*, money or the desire for future referrals) to seek convictions rather than justice.[504] "In *Brady v. Maryland*," the U.S. Supreme Court reiterated in 2017, "this Court held that the government violates the Constitution's Due Process Clause 'if it withholds evidence that is favorable to the defense and *material* to the defendant's guilt or punishment.'"[505] The determination before trial of what is material and exculpatory is necessarily left to the prosecutor, and courts rely on prosecutors to exercise their broad discretion responsibly.[506] Public confidence that a prosecutor will exercise judgment responsibly is not possible when there is the presence of a private party's interest in addition to that of doing justice.[507]

Judge Friendly's opinion in *Wright v. United States*[508] supports the notion that the use of interested private prosecutors should be barred in all circumstances. In *Wright*, Judge Friendly first stated that the word "disinterested" should describe situations where a prosecutor does not have an interest which constitutes "an additional and impermissible reason in forwarding the prosecution."[509] Because of the practical difficulty or impossibility of showing that a private prosecutor for an interested party actually prejudiced a defendant,[510] Judge Friendly then concluded that the mere appearance of impropriety must be sufficient to establish a constitutional violation (in that case, a due process violation). According to his opinion in *Wright*, "the practical impossibility of establishing that a prosecutorial conflict of interest has worked to the defendant's disadvantage dictates the adoption of standards under which a reasonable potential for prejudice will suffice."[511] Because interested private prosecutors always have "an additional and impermissible reason" to forward a prosecution, namely, they *represent* private interests, the mere appearance of impropriety must be sufficient to establish a due process and equal protection violation. In the Supreme Court's own words, "justice must satisfy the appearance of justice."[512]

Even if the U.S. Supreme Court refuses to declare the use of interested private prosecutors unconstitutional in all cases, an interested prosecutor's participation at trial must invalidate any conviction obtained for any serious offense (*e.g.*, any felony conviction or one involving the imposition of imprisonment).[513] Thus, even if private prosecutors are permitted for minor offenses or petty crimes (such as those not involving any risk of imprisonment), it must be adjudicated to be a *per se* violation of a defendant's due process and equal protection rights when an interested private prosecutor participates in any proceeding which could result in jail time. In *State of New Jersey v. Kinder*,[514] a federal district court in New Jersey held that a municipal court rule allowing a defendant to be prosecuted through the use of a private attorney did not violate the defendant's due process rights, where the defendant was charged with simple assault and battery and, if convicted, would not receive a criminal record or a jail term exceeding six months.[515] But in that case, the *Kinder* court stressed: "It is important to emphasize that this is not a case involving an offense arising under federal laws subject to prosecution by federal authorities. Nor is this a prosecution for a felony or misdemeanor which can result in a criminal record, a lengthy jail term and a loss of certain privileges of citizenship." As the *Kinder* court continued, observing that state courts which had invalidated criminal prosecutions by private attorneys had often done so in cases involving serious crimes (and those involving situations where the public prosecutor had refused to prosecute): "This is not a prosecution for criminal contempt which also involves the possibility of a lengthy jail term in addition to the more concrete conflicts of interest which exist when an attorney prosecutes a person in a criminal matter while simultaneously representing that person's opponent in an underlying civil matter. This is also not a case where the public prosecutor has declined to prosecute the defendant after expressly finding that there is no probable cause for such action." "In all of those cases," the U.S. district court judge concluded in *Kinder*, "I have no doubt that a private attorney would be precluded by the United States Constitution, the federal courts' supervisory power and/or federal statutes and rules from conducting a criminal prosecution."[516]

Because of the "death is different" jurisprudence that has been developed by the U.S. Supreme Court, the use of private prosecutors is particularly inappropriate in cases involving capital crimes.[517] As Justice John Paul Stevens stated in *Barclay v. Florida*,[518] "A constant theme of our cases... has been emphasis on procedural protections that are intended to ensure that the death penalty will be imposed in a consistent, rational manner."[519] Some jurists have held that private attorneys can assist a public prosecutor and participate in death penalty cases in spite of conflict-of-interest allegations.[520] For example, *in State v. Moose* (1984), the Supreme Court of North Carolina rejected an argument that the participation of a private prosecutor employed by the family of a murder victim denied the defendant a fair trial. "[W]here it is shown that the solicitor consented to the participation of a privately employed prosecutor and retained control and management of the prosecution," the state supreme court observed, "no reason exists why such an accepted and well-settled practice, in and of itself, should cause reversal of the case."[521]

However, despite the fact that states such as Kansas and Texas have allowed the use of private prosecutors in death penalty cases,[522] there is simply too much at stake—a person's life—to allow an interested private prosecutor's involvement in a capital prosecution. As one commentator put it: "Parties that have interests in the outcomes of specific criminal proceedings provide private prosecutors to ensure that the private parties' interests are protected. Permitting interested parties to employ private attorneys to assist in the prosecution of criminal cases results in the 'overwhelming probability' that private vengeance will supplant the prosecutor's duty to ensure the rights of defendants."[523] Any interested private prosecution in a case that leads to a term of imprisonment or a death sentence should be seen not only as a due process and an equal protection violation but as a "cruel and unusual punishment" in violation of the U.S. Constitution's Eighth Amendment.[524]

CONCLUSION

American private prosecutions date back to colonial times.[1] Consequently, the history of the criminal law in early America is bound up with the then-prevailing English practice of private prosecution. Private prosecutions in the United States are, in fact, a byproduct of "our English heritage of common law," scholar Thomas Robinson once wrote, noting how a private prosecutor "could and did manage his whole prosecution just as he would manage a civil case." In the early nineteenth century, the prominent English lawyer and legal commentator, Joseph Chitty, himself emphasized in *A Practical Treatise on the Criminal Law* (1816) that, "[i]n general... every man is of common right entitled to prefer an accusation against a party whom he suspects to be guilty."[2] That common-law practice had deep roots, with a variety of locales in continental Europe having a long tradition of private prosecutions in one form or another.[3] As David Friedman explains in a book chapter titled "Private Prosecution and Enforcement in Roman Law": "Anglo-American common law developed out of a legal system, Anglo-Saxon law, in which offenses were for the most part treated as torts; a killing created a claim for compensation by the kin of the victim. The state had a claim only if and to the extent that the offense was also seen as a breach of the king's peace."[4] The laws of Anglo-Saxon monarchs—set forth in dooms, or decrees—provided for monetary or other sanctions for a variety of injuries done to another (*e.g.*, the payment of 100 shillings for killing a freeman, twelve shillings for cutting off an ear, six shillings for a front tooth).[5]

Over the centuries, Anglo-American legal customs have changed significantly, including with respect to punishments and prosecutorial norms in both England and the United States. Just as British policing work was originally carried out in a mainly *ad hoc* fashion by private citizens (*e.g.*, part-time constables, nightwatchmen, "thief-takers," and victims), private parties on both sides of the Atlantic were once expected to take on the personal responsibility—and to pick up the tab—for criminal prosecutions. Scotland, with its own distinctive legal traditions,[6] moved away from private prosecutions centuries ago by placing prosecutorial power in the hands of the Lord Advocate and procurator fiscals.[7] But England—despite its proximity to the Scottish model—retained its private prosecution system for far longer, even as that system came under increasing scrutiny.[8] "For reasons that remain obscure," Vincent Chiao writes in *Criminal Law in the Age of the Administrative State* (2019), "public prosecution in the common-law world first arose in a systematic way in North America." "Private prosecutions," he notes, "remained the norm in England until much later: the office of the Director of Public Prosecutions was not created until 1879, and another century went by before the Crown Prosecution Service was created in 1986." But the law—as it so often does—changed substantially with the times, with the societal shift from private to public prosecution occurring at different times in different places. As Chiao explains of the American experience: "[T]he practice of private prosecution persisted in the United States well after the introduction of public prosecutors, 'because some wealthy crime victims did not trust the low-paid, often inexperienced, and understaffed public prosecutors.' However, although private prosecutions remain possible today, that power is typically thoroughly circumscribed by official discretion."[9]

Private prosecutions persist around the globe,[10] including in American capital cases, despite that fact that writers like George Warvelle, in *Essays in Legal Ethics* (1902), warned as regards such cases more than a century ago that "where life or death is the issue 'it is always more honorable to defend than to prosecute.'" Counsel should "never take blood money," he contended. A practicing lawyer in Wisconsin, Warvelle wrote a number of legal treatises before becoming a law professor at the Chicago Law School and the Illinois College of Law.[11] "[W]hile an attorney may be permitted to assist in a prosecution, it is yet a privilege that he should exercise with the utmost caution and circumspection," Warvelle stressed, adding: "If he represents private interests, it has been held in some states, he cannot be retained to assist in criminal proceedings growing out of such interests ... and the rule seems to be eminently salutary and just." "There is," he observed, "something revolting to the moral sense in the spectacle of counsel selling his talents to enable an individual to satisfy his thirst for vengeance, and this, in most cases, is just what counsel does when he accepts a private retainer to assist the prosecuting officer."[12] In Islamic societies, a very different conception of "blood money"—the payment of money to avoid the death penalty's imposition for homicide or other harms—remains a familiar one.[13] In 2014, it was reported that, in just one year, the payment of "blood money" (*diya* in Arabic)[14] spared 358 Iranians from execution.[15]

In the United States, despite objections to private attorneys for interested parties conducting criminal prosecutions,[16] private prosecutions continue as a result of orders like the one is Steven Donziger's federal criminal contempt prosecution and various state statutes and judicial decisions.[17] In allowing interested private prosecutions in past decades, American courts have regularly focused on their historical roots, which—as this book has shown—date back centuries. For instance, in *State v. Atkins* (1979),[18] the Supreme Court of Appeals of West Virginia wrote of the past: "The right to hire a private prosecutor appears to have evolved from the common law, where under old English practice the Crown did not supply a public prosecutor to handle routine felonies. The victim or his family was therefore required to hire counsel to bring the guilty party into the criminal justice system."[19] In *Atkins*, the court observed that a West Virginia statute "explicitly recognizes the practice" of private prosecution,[20] adding: "The role of a private prosecutor has not received extensive treatment by this Court, although in several cases the specific conduct of the private prosecutor has been discussed."[21] "In none of these cases, however," the *Atkins* court observed, "was there a total challenge to the employment of a private prosecutor."[22] "In most jurisdictions," the opinion in *Atkins* stressed, "the courts have generally upheld the private prosecutor system against some specific claim of error without having to deal with the merits of the system as a whole."[23] Attorneys, of course, are quite accustomed to raising legal errors in criminal cases and as part of appeals, with claims of prosecutorial misconduct and various constitutional law violations raised in individual cases.[24]

The United States Constitution explicitly gave Congress the right to punish certain crimes, so long as the resulting federal laws did not impose "excessive fines" or inflict "cruel and unusual punishments."[25] Like the Articles of Confederation that preceded it, though, the U.S. Constitution did not specify the method of prosecution to be employed. Although the founders were clearly concerned about abuses of power, dividing power between different actors and branches of government,[26] because of old traditions and new approaches that arose out of experimentation in the states, both public and private prosecutions persisted on American soil after the country's founding.[27] Many American states—out of habit, if nothing else—continued utilizing private prosecutions in the generations following America's founding despite the fact that public prosecutions became normalized and the routine federal practice.[28] Private prosecutions were inherited from English law, so in the colonial era, European settlers to the New World would've expected—and been largely comfortable with—private prosecutions. For the most part, America's founders most likely simply assumed their legitimacy even as private prosecution—a practice clearly subject to abuse and glaring conflicts of interest[29]—came under increasing scrutiny in the decades and centuries to come[30] as courts imposed more restrictions on private prosecutors.[31] "Prosecution by the state was instituted to halt the system of blood vengeance and family feuds," Thomas Robinson explains of the move away from archaic Anglo-Saxon customs (*e.g.*, the payment of "blood money," or *weregild/wergild*, in medieval times in lieu of an injured clan engaging in a blood feud and exacting private revenge).[32]

America's continued use of prosecutions by interested parties allows the justice system to be corrupted and tainted by private motives.[33] "[A]llowing private persons to seek their vengeance by use of the courts," Robinson writes, recalling the long history of private prosecutions, "is a throwback to the days of personal satisfaction and vengeance."[34] It recalls the days in colonial America when, because of what's been called "the popularity of vengeance," the death penalty and draconian corporal punishments were regularly resorted to or proposed in legislation.[35] *Non-lethal* corporal punishments have been abandoned in the U.S. penal system, but the impulse for vengeance—as illustrated by the death penalty's continued use despite the now more than 250-year-old movement to abolish capital punishment—is still with us. Indeed, despite the sustained efforts to quell the base and blood-thirsty cravings of human beings to exact revenge for criminal acts that have been made for centuries, state-sanctioned executions are still being carried out. Legal historian Robert Ireland, in recounting America's history of private prosecutions, provides this telling anecdote from the mid-nineteenth century about trying to moderate vengeance-seeking in the legal profession among prospective private prosecutors: "In 1856, the eminent Philadelphia criminal lawyer, David Paul Brown, advised 'private counsel... never [to] prosecute a capital charge—*never take blood money.*' He implied that privately funded prosecutors tended to be 'butcher[s]' while public prosecutors had more of a duty to seek justice."[36]

The Due Process and Equal Protection Clauses work together to protect individual rights.[37] Because interested private prosecutors represent, or, at the very least, are logically perceived to represent, interests other than "justice" or the "public interest," the use of such prosecutors must be forbidden to ensure impartial justice and to safeguard due process rights and the equal protection of the laws. The only way to achieve *impartial prosecutions* is to require *impartial prosecutors*, and the only way to achieve *equal protection* of the laws is to treat criminal defendants *equally*, irrespective of race or other status. Because private prosecutions by interested parties risk injecting substantial unfairness into the prosecutorial function, barring interested private prosecutions will not only be a step toward achieving greater fairness but will help avoid the appearance of impropriety that is so central to building confidence in the fairness of the criminal justice system. In the words of President John F. Kennedy, "the basis of effective government is public confidence, and that confidence is endangered when ethical standards falter or appear to falter."[38]

The prevalence of private prosecutions in the past is a historical fact. They occurred in droves in England and the United States, and their use was not seriously questioned for a long period of time. But despite the general acceptance of such prosecutions in America's founding era and into the nineteenth and twentieth centuries, most prosecutions in the United States are now conducted by public prosecutors instead of private ones.[39] Private law firms are still commonly retained to handle lower-level offenses, but public prosecutor's offices now handle almost all felony charges and trials. Unlike private criminal defense lawyers and public defenders, the latter said to be "assigned the responsibility of protecting the interests and defending the rights of a client,'" American prosecutors have a solemn duty to represent "the state's or the public's interests" and not to pursue private ends.[40] As the Supreme Court of Missouri emphasized in 2019: "A prosecutor 'is not an advocate in the ordinary sense of the word, but is the people's representative....'" Pointing out that the prosecutor's "primary duty is not to convict but to see that justice is done," that court explicitly emphasized: "'The prosecutor is an officer of the state who should have no private interest in the prosecution and who is charged with seeing that the criminal laws of the state are honestly and impartially administered, unprejudiced by any motives of private gain.'" A prosecutor, that court stressed, "is under a duty to consider the public interest in the fair administration of criminal justice."[41]

In making a host of discretionary decisions—from what investigations and charges to pursue to what plea bargains[42] and immunity agreements[43] to enter into—prosecutors have been said to have "a fiduciary obligation to act in the public interest, not in furtherance of private interests, including their own."[44] An ethical prosecutor represents the people, not any private or proprietary interests, and should do so without fear or favor in the pursuit of "EQUAL JUSTICE UNDER LAW"—the motto engraved on the west pediment of the U.S. Supreme Court building in Washington, D.C.[45] When interested private prosecutors participate in criminal prosecutions, there is no way of ensuring that private interests are not infecting the integrity of such prosecutions. That's because so much of what a prosecutor does is discretionary, with prosecutors making countless judgment calls about how a case should be handled. In the twenty-first century, there should no longer be a debate about whether the justice system should ensure fairness and equal treatment; it not only *should*, it *must*. Ensuring public confidence in the criminal justice system—taking every measure possible to make sure it operates in a fair and non-discriminatory fashion—is absolutely paramount to promoting public confidence in the system. Because interested private prosecutors call into question the even-handedness and integrity of the prosecutorial system, they should no longer be permitted—period, full stop. Where elected public prosecutors or their deputies have conflicts of interest, disqualification procedures and precedents exist—and should be followed—to ensure that prosecutions are conducted fairly by individuals without disqualifying conflicts.[46] That will normally involve the appointment of another public prosecutor's office to handle the individual prosecution in question or, if necessary, the appointment of *disinterested* private attorneys to handle matters where public prosecutors are unable to do so.[47] Governments regularly contract with private firms and lawyers to provide legal services, and that is true with respect to both civil and criminal matters.[48] But when it comes to a person's life or liberty, public prosecutions should be the norm. Courts have a particularly solemn obligation to make sure that private interests are not putting at jeopardy the constitutional rights of those who appear before the bar of justice.

Victims and their families are undeniably legitimate participants in the criminal justice system, and the protection of victims' rights is incredibly important. Victims and their families have the right to observe and monitor criminal cases and to be informed about, and to consult with legal counsel about, the full panoply of their legal rights, and the victims' rights movement—especially in the past few decades—has made great strides to ensure that victims are treated with dignity and respect.[49] The voices of victims must be heard in America's criminal justice system, and victims of crime, in fact, already regularly participate in criminal proceedings in various ways—from offering eyewitness testimony to submitting victim impact statements. Those affected by crime must have access to, and be able to freely communicate with, the designated prosecutor about relevant matters. If crime victims or the family members of a murdered relative want to hire private attorneys to advise them about their legal rights, that is certainly their right to do so. After all, everyone has the right to retain counsel—and any member of the public, including any retained attorney, should be able to communicate freely with a prosecutor's office to provide whatever information is felt to be necessary for a prosecutor to make an appropriate decision, whether that involves charging, plea bargaining, sentencing, or otherwise. Indeed, only if the prosecutor is fully informed as to all the relevant facts and circumstances of a case will justice be done. But while victims and their families have many legal rights, including the ability to testify about the impact of a crime,[50] the constitutional rights of an accused must not be compromised. It is one thing for a victim or an attorney retained by a victim to pass along relevant information to a prosecutor; it is quite another for a victim or the victim's attorney to actually initiate, conduct or take an active role in coordinating a prosecution.

Criminal prosecutions can deprive individuals of their liberty—or, in capital cases, of their lives. The dire consequences of such prosecutions require that the accused receive due process and equal protection of the laws before any adverse action is taken that will affect the accused. When public prosecutors have a conflict of interest, they can voluntarily recuse themselves or be involuntarily disqualified by a judge.[51] Interested private prosecutors pose a related but different kind of problem. By infecting the criminal justice system with impermissible motives or incentives, interested private prosecutors create structural flaws in the system which, as a class, violate the U.S. Constitution's legal protections and guarantees. As one scholar, Daniel Epps, described the discomfort with private prosecutions in 2016 in the *New York University Law Review*: "[D]espite its historical pedigree, private prosecution is unlikely to be a good option for our system today. Many people would feel discomfort with the idea of giving private citizens the power to force accused wrongdoers into court to answer criminal charges. Private prosecution creates the possibility of abuse by those who might use the criminal process as a way of settling scores."[52]

As prosecutors do their work, they should not be inappropriately influenced by considerations that might inject unfairness into prosecutions. Prosecutors are advocates, but they should be advocates for justice—as concerned about the possibility of wrongful convictions as they are about securing convictions.[53] The criminal justice system does not—and should not—tolerate prosecutions tainted by either bribes or monetary payments from self-interested parties.[54] As law professors Bruce Green and Rebecca Roiphe argue in a 2020 law review article, prosecutors have a solemn duty to pursue the public interest in seeking justice. "The shift from private to public prosecutions in America," they explain, "could be seen as a shift from a private service model to a public fiduciary model." "In the Middle Ages," they observe, "crime was originally seen as a personal offense, a wrong inflicted on the victim." As they note of the law's history: "This view persisted through the nineteenth century in England and America. Private prosecution in England was justified, in part, as a restriction on the power of the Crown." But a more public-oriented view of prosecutions ultimately emerged—a development that changed the perspective of the prosecution function. In 1826, one English commentator remarked that a prosecutor "has as much a public duty to discharge as the sovereign himself, and has a public trust to exercise." And in nineteenth-century America, Green and Roiphe write, the prosecutor increasingly "came to be viewed as a fiduciary of the public at large or of the public interest in the abstract, not as an agent of an individual victim." That sentiment was echoed in many places. In 1893, the Indiana Supreme Court—in line with other judicial decisions of that era—explicitly described the prosecutor's role as a "public trust, committed by the public to an individual."[55]

The practice of privately prosecuting offenders may be an ancient one.[56] But the historical length of a practice does not, in and of itself, justify it or mean that it should continue. Indeed, if one looks back through history, one encounters all sorts of archaic ideas, barbaric institutions, and horrific punishments within the realm of law and society and the criminal law in particular. For example, one encounters slavery, the use of hooding and prolonged solitary confinement, and the infliction of an array of corporal punishments—from branding and ear cropping to lashes and the pillory.[57] In a bill Thomas Jefferson drafted in the 1770s, he hideously proposed that Virginians castrate anyone found "guilty of rape, polygamy, or sodomy" and, for any woman convicted of then-illicit sexual acts, "by cutting thro' the cartilage of her nose a hole of one half inch diameter at the least." Jefferson, utilizing a *lex talionis* approach even as he confided to his mentor, George Wythe, that "[t]he 'lex talionis' will be revolting to the humanized feelings of modern times," also proposed that anyone who "on purpose and of malice forethought shall maim another, or shall disfigure him, by cutting out or disabling the tongue, slitting or cutting off a nose, lip or ear, branding, or otherwise, shall be maimed or disfigured in like sort: or if that cannot be for want of the same part, then as nearly as may be in some other part of at least equal value and estimation in the opinion of a jury, and moreover shall forfeit one half of his lands and goods to the suffer."[58] The U.S. Constitution's Thirteenth Amendment abolished slavery and involuntary servitude, although that amendment—in a reflection of the time—contained an explicit exception for the punishment of crime. And America's penal system regrettably still makes use of extended periods of solitary confinement,[59] even though appalling bodily punishments, such as cutting off body parts, branding or whipping, or being made to sit on a gallows for hours at a time, are no longer permitted by the U.S. penal system.[60]

The U.S. Supreme Court has the weighty responsibility to interpret the U.S. Constitution and its Bill of Rights and to protect individual rights, including in criminal cases. In *Young v. United States ex rel. Vuitton et Fils S.A.*,[61] the Supreme Court issued a stern warning in deciding that private attorneys for interested parties could not prosecute criminal contempt actions. Although the *Young* Court relied on its "supervisory authority" to reach this result, the Supreme Court's decision used broad, sweeping language that could signal a future ruling with potentially constitutional dimensions. While Justice Harry Blackmun's concurrence in *Young* would have established a constitutional right to a disinterested prosecutor, the Supreme Court's decision in *Young* might foreshadow a Supreme Court ruling forbidding the use of interested private prosecutors in all criminal cases. In *Young*, the U.S. Supreme Court relied upon ethics provisions requiring lawyers to avoid conflicts of interest and to avoid the mere appearance of impropriety.[62] Courts disagree about the legal effect of a prosecutor's breach of professional ethics.[63] But the Supreme Court's decision in *Young* makes clear that professional ethics should be taken into account in analyzing a criminal defendant's rights.[64]

In recognition of the structural conflict of interest created by the use of interested private prosecutors, state legislatures should abolish the practice of allowing interested private prosecutors. While lawyers in private practice have a legitimate role to play in the criminal justice system (e.g., as defense counsel or where public prosecutors or public defenders have conflicts of interest), lawmakers should ensure that those who conduct prosecutions do not have disqualifying conflicts of interests—and that means eliminating interested private prosecutions. On the judicial front, at least until the U.S. Supreme Court addresses the constitutional implications of interested private prosecutors head-on, lower courts should endeavor to eliminate the use of such prosecutors through constitutional means[65] or, alternatively, by using their own "supervisory" authority.[66] State court judges—those tasked with interpreting state constitutions—should themselves hold that an interested private prosecution is a *per se* violation of a defendant's constitutional rights.[67] Victims and their counsel should clearly be permitted to communicate whatever information they wish to a prosecutor, but the law should forbid interested private prosecutors from overseeing criminal investigations;[68] making charging, plea bargaining or immunity decisions; or sitting with the public prosecutor at counsel's table during trial. Indeed, interested private prosecutors should not be allowed to examine witnesses, make objections or arguments in court, or engage in other courtroom activities that should be conducted by disinterested prosecutors.[69] Because structural conflicts of interest and, at a minimum, the appearance of impropriety are created by the possibility that interested private prosecutors will engage in misconduct or misuse their discretion,[70] any violation of the rule barring such prosecutors requires the automatic reversal of a defendant's conviction without a showing of prejudice.[71] With life or liberty at stake, the scales of justice should not be tipped against an accused from the outset by allowing a self-interested party to make prosecutorial decisions.

Indeed, courts should find a violation of a defendant's constitutional rights, requiring a retrial, if a private attorney for an interested party participates in anything more than *de minimis* activities outside the courtroom at the public prosecutor's request.[72] This rule recognizes that private attorneys, hired by victims or their families, have motives or incentives, financial or otherwise, to act in a vengeful or unfair manner toward a criminal defendant or to conceal exculpatory evidence uncovered during a criminal investigation. For example, if a prosecutor—who, under existing law, is cloaked with broad immunity[73]—asks a private attorney to investigate some aspect of a crime, that private attorney, because of his or her association with the retaining client, may decide not to turn over potentially exculpatory evidence or to act in a way that shows undivided loyalty to his or her client instead of to the cause of impartial justice. Private lawyers are free to advise their private clients, and it is not problematic if private lawyers communicate with public prosecutors to, for example, coordinate the logistics of testimony to be offered at trial. But because the participation of an interested party's attorney in pre-trial activity creates structural problems with the criminal process, the harmless error rule should not apply to pre-trial activity that goes beyond minor or non-substantive tasks.[74] As one state court cautioned: "The participation of a private prosecutor in the pretrial stages of litigation should be viewed with a wary eye, as it is at this point that the public prosecutor exercises 'virtually unchecked and unreviewed discretion' with respect to matters occurring outside of the courtroom."[75] The ultimate result of a prosecution should be the product of impartial justice, not impermissible or vindictive interests.

The use of private prosecutors violates the "public interest"—what Justice Felix Frankfurter once called "that vague, impalpable, but all-controlling consideration."[76] Indeed, a "quasi-judicial" label has already been attached to the work of prosecutors. In his concurrence in *Imbler v. Pactman* (1976)—one joined by Justices William Brennan and Thurgood Marshall, two members of the U.S. Supreme Court known for their fervent opposition to capital punishment[77]—Justice Byron White explicitly wrote: "[I]n deciding whether or not to prosecute, the prosecutor performs a 'quasi-judicial' function."[78] "It is the functional comparability of their judgments to those of the judge," Justice Lewis Powell observed in the Supreme Court's main opinion in *Imbler*, "that has resulted in both grand jurors and prosecutors being referred to as 'quasi-judicial' officers, and their immunities being termed 'quasi-judicial' as well."[79] In *Imbler*, the Court's main opinion emphasized: "The common-law immunity of a prosecutor is based upon the same considerations that underlie the common-law immunities of judges and grand jurors acting within the scope of their duties. These include concern that harassment by unfounded litigation would cause a deflection of the prosecutor's energies from his public duties, and the possibility that he would shade his decisions instead of exercising the independence of judgment required by his public trust."[80] While interested private prosecutions were a predominant feature of early American law in the states, and while they still stubbornly persist in some locales, the recognition that prosecutors have a quasi-judicial role should result in court rulings that forbid interested private prosecutions. If the U.S. Supreme Court takes seriously its role as the guardian of individual rights, then it will act to give true meaning and effect throughout the United States to these words found in the 1903 annual report of Philander Knox, then-Attorney General of the United States: "private prosecutions are prohibited by the fundamental law of the land."[81]

NOTES

Introduction Notes

1. Jessica M. Eaglin, *Technologically Distorted Conceptions of Punishment*, 97 Wash. U.L. Rev. 483, 492–93 (2019) ("Particularly after the 2008 economic crisis, states' budgets were pinched and a newfound attention to criminal justice reform emerged after decades of punitive policies. Public and private coalitions began endorsing the use of publicly and privately developed actuarial risk tools in the states as part of a comprehensive agenda to reduce recidivism while saving states correctional costs. By 2017, at least thirteen states required the use of actuarial risk tools at sentencing. In 2017, the American Law Institute endorsed the institutionalization of actuarial risk tools into state sentencing structures."); Rachel E. Barkow & Mark Osler, *Designed to Fail: The President's Deference to the Department of Justice in Advancing Criminal Justice Reform*, 59 Wm. & Mary L. Rev. 387, 390 (2017) ("If you follow criminal justice policy in the United States, two themes dominate the discourse of the past several years. First, large portions of society have awakened to America's record-breaking levels of mass incarceration and criminalization. One out of every three adults possesses a criminal record, and our levels of incarceration have no equal anywhere else in the world. Second, and relatedly, there has been a bipartisan call to reform this state of affairs because it is not necessary for—and often undermines—public safety and because its costs outweigh its benefits. News articles continually tout criminal justice reform as one of the few areas to bring together many Republicans and Democrats, even in Congress where common ground is hard to find.").

2 *Criminal Justice Reform*, S. Law Poverty Ctr, https://www.splcenter.org/issues/mass-incarceration (last visited Mar. 30, 2020).

3. *Bail Reform*, Am. C.L. Union, https://www.aclu.org/issues/smart-justice/bail-reform (last visited Mar. 30, 2020); *Bail Reform*, The Marshall Project, https://www.themarshallproject.org/records/1439-bail-reform (last visited Mar. 30, 2020).

4. *About the Sentencing Project*, The Sent'g Project, https://www.sentencingproject.org/about-us/ (last visited Mar. 30, 2020).

5. *Ending Mass Incarceration*, Vera Inst. of Justice, https://www.vera.org/ending-mass-incarceration (last visited Mar. 30, 2020); Lauren-Brooke Eisen, *Criminal Justice Reform at the State Level*, Brennan Ctr for Just. (Jan. 2. 2020), https://www.brennancenter.org/our-work/research-reports/criminal-justice-reform-state-level (last visited Mar. 30, 2020).

6. *An Unjust Burden: The Disparate Treatment of Black Americans in the Criminal Justice System*, Vera Inst. of Justice (May 2018), https://www.vera.org/publications/for-the-record-unjust-burden (last visited Mar. 30, 2020). Because of the country's system of federalism, there are more than fifty criminal justice systems in the U.S. John M. Scheb & John M. Scheb, II, Criminal Law and Procedure 19 (6th ed. 2008) ("Despite the differences that exist between federal and state criminal justice systems, there are certain similarities. All fifty-one criminal justice systems in the United States involve legislative bodies, law enforcement agencies, prosecutors, defense attorneys, courts of law, and corrections agencies.") (citation omitted).

7. Michelle Alexander, The New Jim Crow: Mass Incarceration in the Age of Colorblindness (10th anniversary ed. 2020).

8. John F. Pfaff, Locked In: The True Causes of Mass Incarceration and How to Achieve Real Reform (2017).

9. Brandon Garrett, End of Its Rope: How Killing the Death Penalty Can Revive Criminal Justice (2017).

10. Paul Butler, Chokehold: Policing Black Men (2017).

11. The Formerly Incarcerated Reenter Society Transformed Safely Transitioning Every Person Act, or FIRST STEP Act, which reformed the federal prison system, passed the U.S. House of Representatives on May 22, 2018 on a bipartisan vote of 360 to 59. A revised bill passed the U.S. Senate by an 87 to 12 vote on December 20, 2018, and after the House of Representatives approved that bill the same day by a vote of 358 to 36, the FIRST STEP Act was signed into law on December 21, 2018. Emily Greene, *What is the FIRST STEP Act?*, Prison Fellowship, https://www.prisonfellowship.org/2019/01/what-is-the-first-step-act/ (last visited Jan. 28, 2021).

12. Evan Hill, Ainara Tiefenthäler, Christiann Triebert, Drew Jordan, Haley Willis and Robin Stein, *8 Minutes and 46 Seconds: How George Floyd Was Killed in Police Custody*, N.Y. Times, May 31, 2020 (updated June 9, 2020), https://www.nytimes.com/2020/05/31/us/george-floyd-investigation.html; Eric Levenson, *Former Officer Knelt on George Floyd for 9 Minutes and 29 Seconds—Not the Infamous 8:46*, CNN, Mar. 30, 2021, 6:27 AM), https://www.cnn.com/2021/03/29/us/george-floyd-timing-929-846/index.html. The topic of excessive force by police is one that long predates the George Floyd case. *E.g.*, United States Commission on Civil Rights, Police Practices in the Twin Cities: A Report Prepared by the Minnesota Advisory Committee to the United States Commission on Civil Rights (1981), *available at* https://www.ncjrs.gov/pdffiles1/Digitization/83730NCJRS.pdf.

13. *E.g.*, Deborah Becker, "More Than 150 Positive COVID-19 Cases Reported Among Prisoners, Staff Inside Mass. Jails and Prisons," WBUR News, (Apr. 15, 2020), https://www.wbur.org/news/2020/04/15/jails-prisons-latest-coronavirus-cases-mtc; *see also* A State-by-State Look at Coronavirus in Prisons, The Marshall Project, https://www.themarshallproject.org/2020/05/01/a-state-by-state-look-at-coronavirus-in-prisons (noting that by March 9, 2021, "at least 388,321 people in prison had tested positive for the illness").

14. Stephanie Wykstra, *The Case Against Solitary Confinement*, Vox, Apr. 17, 2019, https://www.vox.com/future-perfect/2019/4/17/18305109/solitary-confinement-prison-criminal-justice-reform ("Thousands of people—at least 61,000 on any given day and likely many thousands more than that—are in solitary confinement across the country, spending 23 hours per day in cells not much bigger than elevators.").

15. I have written extensively about the history of the U.S. Constitution's Eighth and Fourteenth Amendments, as well as about America's use of capital punishment. These writings highlight the long history of the death penalty's use on American soil, America's anti-death penalty movement, the torturous nature of death sentences and executions, and the ongoing international efforts to abolish capital punishment. *See, e.g.*, John D. Bessler, The Baron and the Marquis: Liberty, Tyranny, and the Enlightenment Maxim that Can Remake American Criminal Justice (2019); John D. Bessler, The Death Penalty as Torture: From the Dark Ages to Abolition (2017); John D. Bessler, Cruel and Unusual: The American Death Penalty and the Founders' Eighth Amendment (2012); John D. Bessler, Death in the Dark: Midnight Executions in America (1997); John D. Bessler, "From the Founding to the Present: An Overview of Legal Thought and the Eighth Amendment's Evolution," *in* Meghan J. Ryan & William W. Berry III, eds., The Eighth Amendment and Its Future in a New Age of Punishment 11 (2020); John D. Bessler, *A Century in the Making: The Glorious Revolution, the American Revolution, and the Origins of the U.S. Constitution's Eighth Amendment*, 27 Wm. & Mary Bill of Rts. J. 989 (2019); John D. Bessler, *Taking Psychological Torture Seriously: The Torturous Nature of Credible Death Threats and the Collateral Consequences for Capital Punishment*, 11 Ne. U. L. Rev. 1 (2019); John D. Bessler, *Torture and Trauma: Why the Death Penalty Is Wrong and Should be Strictly Prohibited by American and International Law*, 58 Washburn L.J. 1 (2019); John D. Bessler, *The Abolitionist Movement Comes of Age: From Capital Punishment as a Lawful Sanction to a Peremptory, International Law Norm Barring Executions*, 79 Mont. L. Rev. 7 (2018); John D. Bessler, *The Long March Toward Abolition: From*

the Enlightenment to the United Nations and the Death Penalty's Slow Demise, 29 U. Fla. J. L & Pub. Pol'y 1 (2018); John D. Bessler, *The Concept of "Unusual Punishments" in Anglo-American Law: The Death Penalty as Arbitrary, Discriminatory, and Cruel and Unusual*, 13 Nw. J.L. & Soc. Pol'y 307 (2018); John D. Bessler, "The American Death Penalty: A Short (But Long) History," *in* Routledge Handbook on Capital Punishment (Robert M. Bohm & Gavin Lee eds, 2017); John D. Bessler, *The Inequality of America's Death Penalty: A Crossroads for Capital Punishment at the Intersection of the Eighth and Fourteenth Amendments*, 73 Wash. & Lee L. Rev. Online 487 (2016), https://scholarlycommons.law.wlu.edu/wlulr-online/vol73/iss1/22. The extensive use of private prosecutors in capital cases through the years in England and the United States will be explored throughout this book.

16. *E.g.*, Christine S. Scott-Hayward & Henry F. Fradella, Punishing Poverty: How Bail and Pretrial Detention Fuel Inequalities in the Criminal Justice System (2019) (discussing the need for bail reform); William R. Kelly, Criminal Justice at the Crossroads: Transforming Crime and Punishment (2015) (discussing the history and status of sentencing reform). America's death penalty has gotten considerable public attention in recent years not only because of the Trump Administration's resumption of federal executions but in part because liberals and conservatives alike have begun raising concerns about capital punishment. *E.g.*, Michael Tarm & Michael Kunzelman, "Trump Administration Carries Out 13th and Final Execution," Associated Press, Jan. 15, 2021, https://apnews.com/article/donald-trump-wildlife-coronavirus-pandemic-crime-terre-haute-28e44cc5c026dc16472751bbde0ead50; *2016 Democratic Party Platform*, Death Penalty Info. Ctr ("We will abolish the death penalty, which has proven to be a cruel and unusual form of punishment. It has no place in the United States of America. The application of the death penalty is arbitrary and unjust. The cost to taxpayers far exceeds those of life imprisonment. It does not deter crime. And, exonerations show a dangerous lack of reliability for what is an irreversible punishment."), *available at* https://deathpenaltyinfo.org/facts-and-research/public-opinion-polls/political-party-platforms-and-the-death-penalty; 2020 Democratic Party Platform, https://www.demconvention.com/wp-content/uploads/2020/08/2020-07-31-Democratic-Party-Platform-For-Distribution.pdf, p. 38 ("And Democrats continue to support abolishing the death penalty."); Ben Jones, *The Republican Party, Conservatives, and the Future of Capital Punishment*, 108 J. Crim. L. & Criminology 223, 233–34 (2018) ("Some leaders in the criminal justice reform movement have drawn attention to the death penalty's incompatibility with their vision for reform. For instance, one leading figure in this movement, Pat Nolan—director of the American Conservative Union Foundation's Criminal Justice Reform Project—has made clear his desire to end the death penalty and lent his assistance to state efforts toward that goal. In addition, groups like Conservatives Concerned about the Death Penalty (CCATDP) have emerged to encourage conservatives and Republicans to rethink the death penalty in light of its high costs, errors, and ineffectiveness. In short, the changing conversation on criminal justice among conservatives also has helped facilitate a new conversation on the death penalty. As a result, a number of conservative and Republican leaders are now making the case that the death penalty proves incompatible with their core values.").

17. Michael Edmund O'Neill, *Private Vengeance and the Public Good*, 12 U. Pa. J. Const. L. 659, 683 (2010) ("Although several states continue to allow private prosecutions, most jurisdictions have either disallowed privately managed prosecutions completely, or severely limited the role a private prosecutor may play."); Darryl K. Brown, *Criminal Enforcement Redundancy: Oversight of Decisions Not to Prosecute*, 103 Minn. L. Rev. 843, 869–70 (2018) ("[O]nly vestiges of *private prosecution* remain in a few states. Pennsylvania seems to have the strongest version: it permits *private prosecutions* for any offense upon the approval from a state prosecutor *or* a judge. Rhode Island authorizes *private prosecutions* only for misdemeanors. Under state common law, New Hampshire might permit the same for nonjailable offenses. Beyond that, judges in many states can issue an arrest warrant or criminal summons based on a private person's testimony, but public prosecutors control whether to go forward with the case.") (italics in original); Benjamin M. Birney, *What Can the Feds and the French Teach Us About Criminal Restitution in Maine?*, 65 Me. L. Rev. 247, 264 (2012) ("Some states still preserve the use of private prosecutors. A private prosecution grants victims procedural rights that are, in some senses, analogous to the *partie civile* system in France; the private attorney may, in most cases, perform all of the procedural tasks that a public prosecutor would perform.").

18. State v. Culbreath, 30 S.W.3d 309, 314 (Tenn. 2000) ("Under English common law, the criminal justice system required the victim of a criminal offense, or the victim's family, to initiate and pursue criminal proceedings. *See State v. Peterson*, 195 Wis. 351, 218 N.W. 367, 369 (Wis. 1928). Although the development and role of the public prosecutor in the United States over the past several centuries has largely supplanted the English common law in this regard, many jurisdictions still allow a private attorney to be retained or appointed to assist in the prosecution of a criminal case."); Allen Steinberg, *The "Lawman" in New York: William Travers Jerome and the Origins of the Modern District Attorney in Turn-of-the-Century New York*, 34 U. Tol. L. Rev. 753, 754 (2003) ("Before the invention of the modern police in American cities shortly before the Civil War, the key figures in criminal justice were the private citizen complainants and the magistrates to whom they brought their complaints. The word 'prosecutor' referred to the person we would understand to be the plaintiff. The equivalent members of what we would today call the prosecutor's office were little more than clerks. Only in very serious felony cases, like capital homicide, did the state actively prosecute a case, and even then, like private prosecutors (when they could afford it), they hired private attorneys to represent them. In the decades following the Civil War, the police replaced private citizens as the typical complainants in criminal cases, but the decisions about whether to pursue a case and to what end remained in the hands of the parties: usually the police and the people they arrested, overseen by a magistrate."); 4 Wayne R. LaFave, Jerold H. Israel, Nancy J. King & Orin S. Kerr, Crim. Proc. § 13.3(b) (4th ed. 2019) ("Some foreign jurisdictions permit private criminal prosecution when the public prosecutor fails to act, and some vestiges of this ancient practice remain in this country."); Tania Tetlow, *Granting Prosecutors Constitutional Rights to Combat Discrimination*, 14 U. Pa. J. Const. L. 1117, 1137–38 (2012) ("Most of the American colonies initially followed the English tradition of allowing victims to prosecute their own cases. States did not invest prosecutorial authority in a public prosecutor until the end of the eighteenth century, and private prosecution continued in many areas throughout the nineteenth century. Today, a number of jurisdictions allow some form of private prosecution, usually as to minor crimes."); 63C Am. Jur. 2d *Prosecuting Attorneys* § 12 (2020) ("In a number of jurisdictions, private counsel employed by the complaining witness or by other persons desirous of a conviction are permitted to assist the prosecuting attorney in the conduct of the prosecution and, as a general rule, no valid objection can be raised by the accused to allowing the prosecuting attorney to have the assistance of private members of the bar."); *see also id.* ("The common law right of a crime victim, or of the victim's family, to assist the prosecution with privately employed counsel is not absolute, but lies within the discretion and continuing control of the trial court. Moreover, the trial court, in the exercise of its discretion, must determine whether the private prosecutor has a conflict of interest."); Adam P. Karp, *Power of Private Citizen to Institute Criminal Proceedings Without Authorization or Approval by Prosecuting Attorney*, 90 A.L.R.6th 385 (2013) ("This annotation collects and discusses case having considered the propriety and procedure of privately instituting criminal prosecution."); Gerald F. Uelmen, *Fighting Fire with Fire: A Reflection on the Ethics of Clarence Darrow*, 71 Fordham L. Rev. 1543, 1556 (2003) ("The 'private' prosecutor is alive and well in our time. Many states still permit private attorneys to be retained to 'assist' the prosecution, although they generally require that the private attorney work under the direction and control of the public prosecutor."); Jason Twede, "Going Public: How the Government Assumed the Authority to Prosecute in the Southern United States," Ph.D. dissertation, University of North Dakota (May 2016), p. 15 n.6 ("Even after the establishment of public prosecutors in Georgia, charging documents would still list as 'prosecutor' the person who provided the information for the complaint. The public prosecutor would be listed by their title—'attorney general' or 'solicitor general.' The etymology is important to note, for the informant was not a prosecutor in the way the term is used today.").

19. Allen Steinberg, The Transformation of Criminal Justice, Philadelphia, 1800–1880, at 5 (1989) ("Private prosecution refers to the system by which private citizens brought criminal cases to the attention of court officials, initiated the process of prosecution, and retained considerable control over the ultimate disposition of cases—especially when compared with the two main executive authorities of criminal justice, the police and the public prosecutor."); Nadia Hajji, *After Repeal of El Salvador's Amnesty Law: Next Steps in Justice and Accountability*, 53 Tex. Int'l L.J. 77, 102 (2018) ("Private prosecution, an often-overlooked institutional feature of some criminal justice systems, allows victims or their surviving relatives to participate in the investigation and prosecution of a criminal case under the legal advice of a

lawyer who serves as the private prosecutor."); Verónica Michel & Kathryn Sikkink, *Human Rights Prosecutions and the Participation Rights of Victims in Latin America*, 47 Law & Soc'y. Rev. 873, 874 (2013) ("The right to private prosecution allows victims and their lawyers, including domestic human rights organizations, to open a criminal investigation and actively participate throughout every stage of the criminal proceedings."); *see also Private Prosecutions*, CPS, https://www.cps.gov.uk/legal-guidance/private-prosecutions ("A private prosecution is a prosecution started by a private individual, or entity who/which is not acting on behalf of the police or other prosecuting authority."); E. T. Branch, Criminal Law of Texas: Trial Briefs Arranged in Digest Form 189 (1911) ("A 'private prosecutor" is one who prefers an accusation against a party whom he suspects to be guilty (or desires to have arrested).").

20. *E.g.*, Daniel Klerman, *Settlement and the Decline of Private Prosecution in Thirteenth-Century England*, 19 Law & Hist. Rev. 1 (2001) (noting that most crimes in pre-modern societies were prosecuted privately); R. J. Walker & M. G. Walker, The English Legal System 13 (1970) ("The striking feature of ancient criminal procedure prior to the Norman Conquest was that the responsibility for bringing a person to justice lay not with the Crown but with the individual against whom the crime had been committed. Although most of the ancient procedure became obsolete under the Normans, the appeal of felony created by them perpetuated the ancient concept of private prosecution."); James A. Ballentine, A Law Dictionary of Words, Terms, Abbreviations and Phrases Which Are Peculiar to the Law and of Those Which Have a Peculiar Meaning in the Law 22 (1916) (describing "Appeal of felony" as "[a]n old English proceeding in the nature of a private prosecution wherein a relative of the injured or deceased person was usually the plaintiff or appellant"); Laurie Edelstein, *An Accusation Easily to be Made? Rape and Malicious Prosecution in Eighteenth-Century England*, 42 Am. J. Legal Hist. 351, 353–54 (1998) ("The eighteenth-century criminal justice system in England was essentially a system of private prosecution. The prosecution of almost all criminal offenses was left almost entirely in the hands of the victim. Cases were initiated, for the most part, only if a victim complained to a magistrate. Thus, if a victim wanted to bring an offender before the courts, the victim or the victim's agent was responsible for bringing the offense to the attention of the authorities. The victim also prepared for trial by assembling and interviewing witnesses, deciding upon the charges, attending the court clerks to draw the indictment, and presenting the prosecution case in open court. In some instances, the victim may have been aided by a solicitor in preparing a case for trial, although we do not know how frequently solicitors were used or what function a solicitor carried out when employed."); *see also* Danielle S. Allen, The World of Prometheus: The Politics of Punishing in Democratic Athens 3 (2000) ("Prior to the modern age, private prosecution was the norm in the ancient Greek *polis*, in the Roman Republic and Principate, in the pre-sixteenth-century French and Prussian monarchies, and in the pre-eighteenth-century English monarchy."); 1 James Fitzjames Stephen, A History of the Criminal Law of England 44–45 (1883; digital version 2014) (observing of ancient Rome: "Crimes might be prosecuted under the Empire as well as under the Republic by a private prosecutor. In such cases the procedure closely resembled that which was pursued in purely civil actions .... The accuser cited the accused before the præses to prosecute. The parties appeared before the judge. The accuser took an oath that his accusation was not calumnious, and stated the nature of his accusation."); Charles Freeman, Egypt, Greece, and Rome: Civilizations of the Ancient Mediterranean 416 (3d ed. 2014) (noting that in ancient Rome "the direct bribery of voters ... was a common subject of private prosecutions between rivals"); Ric Simmons, *Private Criminal Justice*, 42 Wake Forest L. Rev. 911, 951–52 (2007) ("Before King Henry I decreed that certain actions were 'offenses ... against the King's peace,' criminal behavior was "viewed as conflict between individuals, and an emphasis upon repairing the damage by making amends to the victim was well established.' Even after certain harms became criminalized, private prosecution was still common; as late as the seventeenth century, both the English and the colonial criminal justice systems depended upon 'a system of private prosecution, where the victim or interested individual had the right to bring and prosecute the case against a criminal offender.' John Langbein describes pre-eighteenth century criminal trials as 'lawyer-free contest[s] of amateurs' in which the victim of the crime served as the prosecutor. Although the state had some involvement in criminal cases throughout the medieval and colonial period, it was not until the eighteenth century that public prosecutors first began to appear."); Trever Homer, The Book of Origins (2007) ("In the ancient world, prisons were used for holding the accused pending trial, rather than as a

punishment. In ancient Babylonia the state did not act as the prosecuting body, but held accused persons in prison, ready for private prosecutions to be made.").

21. Tania Tetlow, *Discriminatory Acquittal*, 18 Wm. & Mary Bill Rts. J. 75, 123 n.281 (2009) ("a few American states still allow victims to retain counsel to represent their interests alongside the public prosecutor for minor crimes") (*citing* Cronan ex rel. State v. Cronan, 774 A.2d 866 (R.I. 2001) (upholding assault victim's right to initiate a private complaint and prosecute a defendant for misdemeanor assault) & John D. Bessler, *The Public Interest and the Unconstitutionality of Private Prosecutors*, 47 Ark. L. Rev. 511 (1994) (describing the use, in some American jurisdictions, of private prosecutors)). The rarity of interested private prosecutions in America goes back many decades now. 19 The New Int. Encyclopædia 272 (2d ed. 1916) ("In the United States, while prosecutions by private individuals are permissible, they are in practice rarely resorted to.").

22. Marie Manikis, *Conceptualizing the Victim within Criminal Justice Processes in Common Law Tradition, in* Darryl K. Brown, Jenia I. Turner & Bettina Weisser, eds., The Oxford Handbook of Criminal Process 249 n.12 (2019) ("In Canada, although private prosecutions are still on the books, in practice they are very rare and are generally taken over and pursued or stopped by public prosecutors."); *see also* 2 Christopher Berry Gray, ed.,. The Philosophy of Law: An Encyclopedia 698 (1999) ("[T]here are, at least in Canada, significant fetters, both practical and procedural, on the wholesale resort to the use of the power. As the seriousness of the charge in question increases, the restrictions on the ability of an individual to prosecute a case privately become more severe. Thus, while there are few, if any, restrictions on the right to prosecute a summary conviction case (that is, the most minor form of criminal charge) privately through to the conclusion of trial, matters become procedurally more complex when the charge in question is more serious and consequently must be prosecuted by indictment."); Provincial Offences Act, R.S.O. 1990, c. P.33 § 23(1) (this Ontario provision for commencing a private prosecution for a provincial offense provides: "Any person who, on reasonable and probable grounds, believes that one or more persons have committed an offence, may lay an information in the prescribed form and under oath before a justice alleging the offence."); *compare* Donald Fyson, Magistrates, Police, and People: Everyday Criminal Justice in Quebec and Lower Canada, 1764–1837, at 238 (2006) ("In England, until the nineteenth century, most cases brought before magistrates and judges, from simple assaults to murders, were prosecuted by private individuals, at their own initiative and expense, with little intervention by the state. The flip side of this prosecutorial initiative was prosecutorial discretion: if the plaintiff decided not to pursue the case, the state did not generally step in, allowing the case to drop.... In Quebec and Lower Canada, as in the American and British North American colonies, the situation was more complicated. In more serious cases the state was more directly involved in prosecution: thus, King's Bench cases were prosecuted not by victims but by the colony's law officers, to whom justices sent in the results of pre-trial hearings.... [T]he rise of public prosecution in other cases was one of ways in which the everyday criminal justice system was transformed in the nineteenth century. However, as Martin Dufresne has shown for assault cases in Quebec City in the 1830s, much as Allen Steinberg found for Philadelphia in the first half of the nineteenth century, for less serious complaints, and notably assaults, the system still retained a strong flavor of private initiative and prosecutorial discretion.").

23. Tim Hitchcock & Robert Shoemaker, Tales from the Hanging Court 39 (2006) ("In modern Britain, despite the occasional 'have-a-go hero' and private prosecution, we expect crime to be dealt with by the police and prosecution to be led by the state."); Kate Leader, *Report on England and Wales, in* Serena Quattrocolo & Stefano Ruggeri, eds., Personal Participation in Criminal Proceedings: A Comparative Study of Participatory Safeguards and *in Absentia* Trials in Europe 70–71 (2019) ("Although private prosecutions undertaken successfully by individuals are relatively rare, private prosecutions form a part of the landscape in England and Wales, most commonly being undertaken by private organisations, such as the Royal Society for Prevention of Cruelty to Animals (RSPCA) and for protection of copyright."); *id.* at 71 ("To initiate a private prosecution, an individual must provide the relevant information to a magistrate who can, if they accept the validity of the information given, then issue a summons or a warrant for arrest. If a summons is issued and the matter progresses to trial, the Crown Prosecution Service has the right to take over the prosecution and to either take it to trial or potentially discontinue it, should they decide there is insufficient evidence, or that it is not in the public interest to

proceed. It should be noted, however, that legal aid is not available to individuals instituting private prosecutions and consequently its application is arguably limited to those with the means to do it."); O'Neill, *supra* note 17, at 672 ("Although privately initiated prosecutions remain commonplace in England, what constitutes a 'private' prosecution is somewhat different from the way in which such prosecutions are understood in the United States. In England, the term 'private prosecution' has come to mean a prosecution not formally involving the police. Local governments, governmental agencies, trade and professional associations, and individuals all may bring private prosecutions."); *id.* ("Following the 1985 adoption of the Prosecution of Offenses Act, the English crown began to shoulder a greater burden of conducting criminal prosecutions. While the police may assist the private complainant in a private prosecution, oftentimes the Crown may intercede in a matter of significant public interest. If, for example, the crime is one of violence or a breach of the public order, the police will become the official complainant, and the government will handle the case. However, the Prosecution of Offenses Act did not end the practice of privately initiated prosecutions. Such prosecutions remain a cornerstone of the English criminal justice system."); *id.* ("Although the individual's right to commence and maintain a private prosecution was preserved under the Prosecution of Offenses Act, the Crown Prosecution Service (CPS) was nonetheless granted considerable authority to take over, end, or otherwise control a private prosecution."); Bambos Tsiattalou, "Private Criminal Prosecutions in the Headlines," Lawyer Monthly, July 2020, https://www.lawyer-monthly.com/2020/07/private-criminal-prosecutions-in-the-headlines/ ("Private criminal prosecutions have recently hit the headlines, with news that Boots successfully brought a private prosecution against a prolific shoplifter after the police had refused to take action. In 2019, a fraudster received an eight-year custodial sentence after a private prosecution was brought by an engineering company. Even Dominic Cummings is the subject of a private prosecution for his notorious breach of lockdown in March, during the height of the coronavirus pandemic."); *see also* TYRONE KIRCHENGAST, THE VICTIM IN CRIMINAL LAW AND JUSTICE 71 (2006) ("Private prosecution is a right expressly preserved in Australian and UK law: *Prosecution of Offences Act 1985* UK s6(1); Criminal Procedure Act 1986 NSW ss49, 174; Special Prosecutors Act 1982 Cth s6(5); Director of Public Prosecutions Act 1983 Cth s10(2). Section 6(1) of the Prosecution of Offences Act 1985 UK provides that 'nothing ... shall preclude any person from instituting any criminal proceedings or conducting any criminal proceedings to which the Director's duty to take over the conduct of proceedings does not apply.'"); Lissa Griffin, *The Correction of Wrongful Convictions: A Comparative Perspective*, 16 AM. U. INT'L L. REV. 1241, 1264 (2001) (noting of England: "With respect to the prosecution, there was no nationwide, institutional prosecutor in England until 1985, and, even now, private barristers are usually hired to represent the Crown in court."); CLIVE EMSLEY, CRIME AND SOCIETY IN ENGLAND, 1750–1900, at 223 n.56 (4th ed. 2013) ("Hay, 'Controlling the English prosecutor', pp. 178–9 lists fourteen acts, excluding the Vexatious Indictments Act, passed between 1791 and 1888 which infringed the discretion of the private prosecutor.").

24. Kelly & anor v. Ryan [2013] IEHC 321 (H. Ct.) ¶ 11 ("In *The State (Ennis) v. Farrell* [[1966] I.R. 107] the Supreme Court held that the right of private prosecution had indeed survived the enactment of the Constitution."); *id.* at ¶ 14 ("The definition of 'prosecutor' in s. 4 of the 1967 Act (as inserted by s. 8 of the 1999 Act) is one which has plainly been drafted with great care. In the case of Part IA (and s. 13) of the 1967 Act (as inserted by s. 9 of the 1999 Act)—which deals with proceedings relating to indictable offences—prosecutor is defined as meaning only the Director of Public Prosecutions. But so far as Part II and Part III of the 1967 Act is concerned, the term 'prosecutor'" is given a broader meaning by s. 4 and includes a person 'authorised by law to prosecute the offence.' There is no doubt but that at common law, a common informer was so authorised. The matter was, in any event, put beyond doubt by the Supreme Court's decision in *Ennis*."); *id.* at ¶ 15 ("This special definition of the term prosecutor—with differential definitions for different contexts—as effected by the 1999 Act gives a clear signal that the Oireachtas consciously decided not to abolish the system of private prosecution, even for indictable offences. It is true that no further practical step can be taken by a private prosecutor in relation to the prosecution of an indictable offence beyond the issuing of proceedings since it is at that point that the prosecution comes within the realm of Part 1A of the 1967 Act (as amended). It is at this point that the Director enjoys the monopoly as *dominus litis*."); *id.* at ¶ 16 ("[I]f the right of private prosecution is to be abolished one would expect to see that this had been done by clear words. As O Dálaigh C.J. observed ([1966] I.R. 107, 121) in *Ennis*, the court 'should

require clear language to abolish the valuable right of private prosecution'. Besides, the presumption against unclear changes in the law would further counsel such an approach, since it is well established that clear words are required before the courts can properly hold that well established common law rights have been displaced or even abolished: see, e.g., the judgment of Henchy J. in *Minister for Industry and Commerce v. Hales* [1967] I.R. 67b at 76–77. Indeed, in *Wedick v. Osmond & Sons* [1935] I.R. 820, 852 Hanna J. invoked this very presumption before concluding that 'clear and unmistakeable language' would be required to abolish the right of private prosecution."); *id.* at ¶ 17 ("[T]here are, in fact, many individual instances of where the right of private prosecution has been entirely excluded by statute. A notable example is provided by s. 5(2) of the Criminal Law (Amendment) Act 1990, which provides that: 'Criminal proceedings against a man in respect of the rape by him of his wife shall not be instituted except by or with the consent of the Director of Public Prosecutions.'"); *id.* at ¶ 18 ("It will be seen from this provision that proceedings for marital rape may not even be instituted, save with the consent of the Director, so that private prosecutions for marital rape are thereby necessarily excluded. The Oireachtas, could therefore, have readily employed the language appropriate to effect such an exclusion of a private prosecution but has refrained from doing so. The very fact that it has chosen not to do so is in itself telling.") (italics in original); *id.* at ¶ 19 ("Nor is the fact that the common informer cannot actually do much more other than to launch the proceedings is itself a reason for holding that the right has been abolished. Here it must be recalled that since the very earliest days of the State, the effective control of all prosecutions on indictment has remained with the law officers, first the Attorney General (via s. 9(1) of the 1924 Act) and then subsequently the DPP (following the enactment of the 1974 Act), a control underscored by Article 30.3 of the Constitution."); *id.* at ¶ 20 ("[T]he existence of a private prosecutor still acts as an external check against the risk of a rare lapse or oversight on the part of the Director. The commencement of a private prosecution is in effect an appeal from the party who claims that he or she has suffered a private injustice for the public justice envisaged by Article 30.3, so that a prosecution can be brought in the name of the People at the suit of the Attorney General or the Director of Public Prosecution beyond the point where the private prosecutor can no longer act. Even if the role of the private prosecutor is far less extensive than was the case prior to 1999, the underlying purpose of the private prosecution is still the same, namely, to draw the public prosecutor's attention to the case with the implicit request that the prosecution be taken over."); *id.* at ¶ 22 ("While it is true that the private prosecutor no longer has the right to have a preliminary examination conducted (because that system has itself been abolished), the common informer has the right to institute the prosecution, once the matter comes back before the District Court, the continuation of the prosecution is entirely contingent on whether the Director consents to summary trial or the sending forward of the accused for trial in the manner contemplated by Part IA. In the event that the Director has not so consent or direct, then the prosecutions must be struck out."); *id.* at ¶ 42.(A.) ("The right of private prosecution has not been indirectly affected by the abolition of the preliminary examination procedure by the Criminal Justice Act 1999. In the light of *The State (Ennis) v. Farrell*, clear and express statutory language would be required for this purpose. The special and varying definitions of the word 'prosecutor' now contained in s. 4 of the 1967 Act (as inserted by s. 8 of the 1999 Act) provides clear indication that the Oireachtas, so far from evincing an intention to abolish the right of private prosecution, actually intended to preserve it.").

25. John Macaulay, *Private Prosecution: The Glasgow Rape Case Revised*, The Journal, Jan. 16, 2017 (in recalling his involvement in the successful Scottish private prosecution of a rape that occurred in 1980, solicitor John Macaulay—formerly in practice in Glasgow—writes of his initial work on the case of "Carol X": "The only thing I knew about private prosecutions at the time was what I recalled from law school—that while private prosecutors were, theoretically, possible in Scotland, they were of academic interest only and that the last successful private prosecution had been the case of *J & P Coats Ltd v. Brown* in 1909."); *id.* ("Nowadays, if, as appears to be the case, private prosecution is competent and possible, it is important both for the Crown and the court to advise a socius criminis witness, as a matter of fairness, that, whenever immunity is offered by the Crown, such immunity must, of necessity, be limited and the threat of private prosecution may still hang over his or her head."); *id.* ("While the Carol X case may have been decided correctly at the time on its own particularly special circumstances, private prosecutions have their origin in the mists of legal history and, nowadays, such prosecutions sit so uncomfortably alongside a modern system of public prosecution that they simply cannot be justified."); *see also id.* ("The problem is

that private prosecutions are completely alien to a modern democracy, and certainly so to Scottish criminal procedure. Their time is up and the Scottish Government should put this ghostly relic finally, firmly and promptly to rest.").

26. Both New Zealand and South Africa, for example, allow private prosecutions. *E.g.*, Anna Prestidge, *Private Prosecutions in New Zealand—A Public Concern?*, 50 VUWLR 107 (August 26, 2019), Victoria University of Wellington Legal Research Paper, Student/Alumni Paper No. 5/2019, *available at* SSRN: https://ssrn.com/abstract=3442711 ("It is undeniable that New Zealand's criminal justice system is dramatically different from its early Anglo-Saxon roots. However, one similarity that remains is the ability of a private person to bring criminal proceedings against another. Private prosecutions are often regarded as an 'important safeguard' for New Zealand citizens. These prosecutions are rare in the modern criminal environment ...."); *id.* at 109 ("New Zealand adopted many of the key features of the British criminal justice system during the country's colonisation in the early 1840s, including the ability for private citizens to commence a prosecution."); *id.* at 110 ("Nowadays most prosecutions in New Zealand are public in nature, instigated by Crown Solicitors, the police and relevant Ministries and Crown agencies such as WorkSafe, who enforce the Health and Safety at Work Act 2015 ('HSWA'). Private prosecutions, by contrast, are rare in comparison."); National Society for the Prevention of Cruelty to Animals v Minister of Justice and Constitutional Development and Another [2016] ZACC 46, ¶ 65(3) ("It is declared that the National Society for the Prevention of Cruelty to Animals has the statutory power of private prosecution conferred upon it by section 6(2)(e) of the Societies for the Prevention of Cruelty to Animals Act 169 of 1993 read with section 8 of the Criminal Procedure Act 51 of 1977.").

27. *E.g.*, John L. Worrall, *Prosecution in America: A Historical and Comparative Account, in* John L. Worrall & M. Elaine Nugent-Borakove, eds., The Changing Role of the American Prosecutor 16–17 (2008) ("For the most part, private prosecution has given way to public prosecution across the globe, but there are exceptions. For example, public prosecutors may waive prosecution in certain cases, perhaps due to a lack of evidence, paving the way for private prosecution. Thailand permits private prosecutions, but only following an intense preliminary hearing on the matter. In other countries, when a prosecutor declines to pursue charges, victims, family members of victims, and other concerned citizens can lodge a complaint in court. Other jurisdictions maintain hybrid models of private and public prosecution. In Finland, for instance, the right to prosecute is shared by a prosecutor and the person harmed. Both individuals assume a prominent role in prosecution, quite opposite of what occurs in the United States.").

28. State of New Jersey v. Lazarchick, 314 N.J. Super. 500, 512 (1998); *see also* David Lemmings, Law and Government in England during the Long Eighteenth Century: From Consent to Command 115 (2011) ("[i]n England the common law principle of private prosecution was held dear"); David Hirschel, William Wakefield & Scott Sasse, Criminal Justice in England and the United States 169 (2d ed. 2008) ("In England, under common law, any person could commence a criminal prosecution. Thus, traditionally, the prosecution of cases was considered a private matter and it was up to the citizen to institute criminal proceedings, produce witnesses, and handle the case from the initial prosecution to the trial under the 'direction' of a magistrate.") (citation omitted). In New Jersey, individuals are allowed to sign their own complaints and hire private attorneys to prosecute them. 19 N.J. Prac., *Skills and Methods* § 2:61 (3d ed. 2019) ("Frequently, individuals sign their own complaints and then come to municipal court in order to prosecute their complaints. The municipal prosecutor may decline to take part in the prosecution of these matters. Sometimes the complaining witness hires a private attorney to prosecute his or her complaint. In such a case, it is left to the municipal court's discretion to determine whether the private attorney should be allowed to prosecute the complaint. Before the court makes its determination, the private attorney should disclose in a written certification all facts that foreseeably may affect the fairness of the proceedings.").

29. Steel Co. v. Citizens for a Better Env't, 523 U.S. 83 (1998).

30. *Id.* at 127–28 (Stevens, J., concurring). "The interest in punishing the defendant and deterring violations of the law by the defendant and others," Justice Stevens wrote, "was sufficient to support the 'standing' of the private prosecutor even if the only remedy was the sentencing of the defendant to jail or to the gallows." *Id.* at 128; *see also* Pfaff, *supra* note 8 ("Public prosecutors have existed since the colonial era—although at that time they were appointed, not elected—but they were generally not viewed with

much respect; even well after the American Revolution, victims often preferred to hire private prosecutors to try their cases, even when public prosecutors were available. Public prosecutors were generally younger, less skilled, and less well-financed than private defense counsel."); Margaret Z. Johns, *Reconsidering Absolute Prosecutorial Immunity*, 2005 B.Y.U. L. Rev. 53, 110 ("The persistence of the private prosecutor in the United States in the nineteenth century after the establishment of public prosecutors' offices has been explained by two main factors. First, because of inadequate funding of the office, public prosecutors were often incompetent. According to one delegate at the Illinois Constitutional Convention in 1847, 'The [public prosecutor's] office was generally taken by young men who desired to become acquainted with people, and get into practice; as soon as this was accomplished they gave way to others.' This view was expressed in many other jurisdictions as well. Second, public prosecutors were responsible for covering vast territories, often without any assistants, which compounded their incompetence. Traveling from county to county, the public prosecutor was often unprepared for the litigation, unfamiliar with the jury pool, and outmatched by defense counsel. As one delegate to the 1890–91 Kentucky Constitutional Convention explained, the public prosecutor was 'a rat in a strange garret.' Under these circumstances, victims and their families hired private lawyers to handle criminal prosecutions in the hope of securing convictions. Throughout the nineteenth century, private prosecution flourished in most states."). *Compare* Patrick Michel & Joëlle Huot, *Background: From the Origin of the Office of the Attorney General in England to the Creation of the Office of Director of Criminal and Penal Prosecutions in Québec (Canada)*, 53-JUL Prosecutor 22, 23 (2019) ("In 1985, the functioning of the British system became founded, in principle, on State prosecutors acting as public prosecutors. It was in that year that the Crown Prosecution Service (CPS) was established, a structured prosecution service acting under the supervision of the DPP and present throughout the territory of England and Wales to conduct the majority of criminal prosecutions."); Anna Louise Prestidge, *Private Prosecutions in New Zealand—A Public Concern?*, 50 Vict. U. Wellington L. Rev. 107, 114 (2019) ("England and Wales have the Crown Prosecution Service, an independent prosecuting authority that prosecutes cases following investigations by the police and other organisations. As part of this service, victims of crime have a special right of review for decisions not to prosecute.").

31. Mikhail v. Kahn, 991 F. Supp. 2d 596, 635–36 (E.D. Pa. 2014) ("[P]rivate criminal prosecutions once characterized the common law. In colonial America, as '[i]n England, victims prosecuted their own crimes *pro se*, without lawyers and at their own expense,' and 'American prosecutions remained private well into the nineteenth century.' 'In colonial Pennsylvania,' for instance, 'crimes were viewed as an offense against the individual victim, and private prosecutions were the most common mode by which the criminal justice system functioned.'") (citations omitted); National Crime Victim Law Institute, *Fundamentals of Victims' Rights: A Brief History of Crime Victims' Rights in the United States*, Victim L. Bull. 1 (Nov. 2011) ("At common law, it was well recognized that victims played a central role in the criminal justice process. The practice of private prosecution, whereby the crime victim initiated and controlled criminal prosecutions, dates back to the Middle Ages. Although notions of prosecuting on behalf of the Crown began in the eleventh and twelfth centuries, even at that time most crime was viewed as a wrong against the individual victim rather than against the King or society as a whole. A crime victim's right to initiate and conduct criminal proceedings remained the norm in England well into the nineteenth century."), *available at* https://law.lclark.edu/live/files/11822-fundamentals-of-victims-rights-a-brief-history-of; Steven Penrod & Daniel Linz, *Using Psychological Research on Violent Pornography to Inform Legal Change, in* Neil M. Malamuth & Edward Donnerstein, eds., Pornography and Sexual Aggression 252 (1984) ("With the growth of Victorian morality, prosecutions became more common during the nineteenth century. Private societies with the avowed purpose of suppressing vice were formed at the end of the eighteenth century and proceeded, for the next 150 years, to institute private prosecution of pornography publishers."); Jonathan Obert, The Six-Shooter State: Public and Private Violence in American Politics 5 (2018) (taking note, in late nineteenth century America and "through the turn of the century," of the prevalence of "[p]rivate forms of administering punishment, such as citizens' vigilance groups, anti-horse thief associations branches, citizen policing initiatives, and private prosecution societies"); *see also* David A. Sklansky & Stephen C. Yeazell, *Comparative Law Without Leaving Home: What Civil Procedure Can Teach Criminal Procedure, and Vice Versa*, 94 Geo. L.J. 683, 688 (2006) ("Today, of course, the civil bar and the criminal bar are largely separate, and the great majority of criminal lawyers

are employed by the government—regardless of which side they represent. In the nineteenth century, by contrast, the private bar was more unified, and it handled the bulk of litigation, both civil and criminal. Criminal prosecution, let alone criminal defense, had not yet become a government monopoly. Before the Civil War, in fact, criminal prosecution was not even a government specialty. The system relied on private prosecution, with state officials involved only in a minority of cases. So overwhelming was the caseload for such officials that citizens with an interest in seeing justice done often hired private prosecutors to marshal evidence and to prosecute the case. Understandably, such citizens were often the victims, or family members of the victims, of the crimes alleged. The real or suspected motive of vengeance provided arguments for the defendant, and, more occasionally, criticism from appellate courts. But private prosecution flourished well into the twentieth century, in large part because few public prosecutors were funded and staffed well enough to bring charges in the vast run of cases.").

32. "The Barcelona Tragedy—Cardiff Man Charged with Murder," Western Mail (Cardiff, Wales), Apr. 18, 1894, p. 6 ("Criminal proceedings in Spain differ in many respects from the English mode of procedure. Immediately [after] a crime is committed the Juge d'Instruction is summoned and takes down in writing the evidence of all persons who witnessed the deed or of others who are interested in the case. When the judge has collected all the obtainable evidence he presents it, together with a statement of the facts of the case, so far as he has been able to learn them, to the official of the Audience Chamble, called a 'Relator,' and this official makes a summary of the case in writing, which he passes on to the Fiscal or Public Prosecutor, who marks on the summary a note of the penalty which he proposes should be applied to the prisoner. The summary is then sent to the advocate of the private prosecutors, who, after a careful consideration of the facts as presented in the summary, marks on it the class of evidence that he proposes to offer and the names of the witnesses he intends to call. The summary is next delivered to the advocate of the prisoner, who deals with it in the same way and returns it to the Audience Chamber, where the magistrates consider whether the evidence proposed to be offered on either side is admissible and fix the date of the hearing of the case before a jury. To form a jury 40 men, who must be citizens, are summoned, and from these fourteen men are drawn by lot, twelve of whom are to form the jury and two are to be in reserve in case of a juryman falling ill. Either the Fiscal or the advocates of the private prosecutors and prisoner can object to any of the 40 men originally summoned without giving any reason for so doing."); "The Barcelona Tragedy—Cardiff Man Charged with Murder," Western Mail (Cardiff, Wales), Apr. 19, 1894, p. 5 ("The trial of Samuel Willie, of Cardiff, on a charge of murdering Don Jose Bofill, a merchant, of Barcelona, was resumed at the latter place on Tuesday. The public prosecution, represented by the fiscal of his Majesty, lays down the charges against Mr. Willie to be those of murder, attempted murder, and the firing of two firearm shots, which are said to have been premeditated, the tragedy having taken place on the premises of the murdered man. The prosecution asks for the first indictment the penalty of death, for the second sixteen years' penal servitude, and two years for each of the two firearm shots. There are two private accusations—one by Don Juan Bofill, who has recently renounced his action, and the other by the widow of Don Jose Maria Bofill. The latter accusation, which had up to the trial been represented by the solicitor, Don Manuel Plana y Casals, is now urged by the Procurator Don Enrique Crexans, who claims that the murder was committed with premeditation on the premises of the murdered man without the least provocation from the latter, and he, therefore, asks that a sentence of death shall be passed upon the prisoner.... Don Juan Soy y Ortega, advocate of the private prosecutor, the widow of Don Jose, is confident in the ability of the Crown Prosecutor to break down the defence ....").

33. United States v. Teodoro des Pabiladeras and Julian S. Laxaman, G.R. No. 10639, Republic of the Philippines, Supreme Court (Manila) (Dec. 6, 1915) (en banc) ("It is true that the record affirmatively discloses that counsel for the private prosecutor actively conducted the proceedings in the court below and that there is no record of any further intervention in the trial on the part of the provincial fiscal after the accused had been arraigned. But there is nothing in the rules of practice and procedure in criminal cases which denies the right of the fiscal, in the exercise of a sound discretion, to turn over the active conduct of the trial to a competent assistant or to counsel for a private prosecutor, with the understanding, of course, that he does not thereby relieve himself of responsibility for the prosecution, and that he retains the right to control the prosecution at every stage of the proceedings to the end, and to intervene at any time he sees fit. In the absence of any showing to the contrary, we assume that this is what was done in the case at bar.");

id. ("It is every day practice in this jurisdiction, as well as in the United States generally, for the prosecuting attorney to turn over the active conduct of criminal cases (especially those in which the offenses charged are of the nature of those known as private offenses under the Spanish Penal Code) to counsel employed by private prosecutors; and we see nothing objectionable in this practice, provided always that the fiscal retains control of the prosecution, and assumes full responsibility therefor."); United Sates vs. de la Santa, No. 3181, Republic of the Philippines, Supreme Court (Manila) (Oct. 10, 1907), *in* 9 David Lewis Cobb, comp., Reports of Cases Determined in the Supreme Court of the Philippine Islands from October 8, 1907, to January 23, 1908, at 22 (1908) (in a case where the complaint charged the defendant with the crime of seduction (*cstupro*) of a woman over 12 and under 23 years of age, making note of "*Rafael Palma* and *P. Salas*, for private prosecutors"); The Code of Criminal Procedure of the Philippine Islands Annotated by Guillermo B. Guevara 124 (1922) (noting that "the intervention or appearance of the so-called private prosecutors is permitted by the courts in certain cases," to wit: "those cases where the party injured by the crime is entitled to some indemnity, or civil remedy (as for example, homicide, *lesiones*, rape, robbery, etc.)"; "*Trial Conducted by Private Prosecutors.* When the prosecuting attorney is assisted by a private prosecutor, the former may turn momentarily to the latter the prosecution of the case, provided he retains full control of the same."). A search of the website for the United Nations reveals that private prosecutions are still used in various countries. *E.g., Government Support: Philippines, United Nations, Victims of Terrorism Support Portal*, https://www.un.org/victimsofterrorism/en/node/377 ("Under the Philippine legal system, the victims can be represented by private prosecutors of their choice in court, working together with the public prosecutors."); "Submission of an example of good practice in combatting violence against women for the United Nations Secretary-General's in-depth study on violence against women Feminist League, Kazakhstan," United Nations, https://www.un.org/womenwatch/daw/vaw/ngo-contribute/Feminist%20League.pdf (discussing the use of private prosecution in the Republic of Kazakhstan); User's Guide, https://www.un.org/ruleoflaw/files/MC2-3-Intro.pdf, p. 21 (a "User's Guide" that introduces the *Model Codes for Post-Conflict Criminal Justice* notes: "The extent of the involvement of victims in criminal procedures varies from state to state. In some states, victims have extensive rights such as the right to mount a 'private prosecution' against the alleged perpetrator of a criminal offense."); Handbook on Justice for Victims: On the Use and Application of the Declaration of Basic Principles of Justice for Victims of Crime and Abuse of Power, United Nations Office for Drug Control and Crime Prevention, Centre for International Crime Prevention (New York, 1999), http://www.unodc.org/pdf/crime/publications/standards_9857854.pdf, p. 39 ("[I]n a number of legal systems, the victim may prosecute for certain minor offences (so-called 'private prosecution'), where the public interest is deemed not to require public prosecution.").

34. Laura I. Appleman, *The Community Right to Counsel*, 17 Berkeley J. Crim. L. 1, 5–6 (2012); *see also id.* at 6 n.4 ("Although the (private) prosecutor was permitted to engage counsel, he usually did not. This rule held true for all felonies excluding treason, although counsel was permitted for misdemeanor trials.") (citing John H. Langbein, The Origins of Adversary Criminal Trial 11–12, 36–37 (2003)).

35. *Id.* at 6; *compare id.* at 7–8 ("The custom of barring defense counsel began to relax only slowly in England. In 1695, the Treason Act allows a defendant the use of counsel for either treason or misprision of treason. Defense counsel was permitted during the rare appeal, whether the charge was capital or not. Formally, the rule barring defense counsel stopped being enforced around 1730, although defense counsel did not play a role in English trials in any significant way until the end of the eighteenth century. The decision to allow defense representation lied in the individual judge's hands. It was not until 1836 that Parliament formally gave criminal defendants the right to be represented through counsel.") *with id.* at 9 ("The question of why a right to counsel arose in the American colonies so early and so many years before England is a mystery that has never fully been explained. In part, this is because much of the workings of the colonial criminal courts are lost to us. The common explanation—that the defendant's right to counsel arose primarily as a protest against English heavy-handedness in the American colonial criminal justice arena—can only explain why counsel rights were protected in the late eighteenth century, with revolution fomenting and the various wrongs of England foremost in colonial minds. But the right to counsel—or, at least, the defendant's ability to bring some sort of advocate to the bar—arose in the colonies before such beliefs and feelings against the England government became common.").

36. Barry Godfrey, *"Private Policing and the Workplace": The Worsted Committee and the Policing of Labor in Northern England, 1840–1880*, *in* Paul Lawrence, ed., The New Police in the Nineteenth Century 179 (2016); *see also* Wilbur R. Miller, A History of Private Policing in the United States (2020) (discussing the history of private policing); George S. Rigakos, Nightclub: Bouncers, Risk, and the Spectacle of Consumption 34 (2008) ("The Metropolitan Police of London came into being in 1830. In the Anglo-American context, this is seen as the starting point for the new public police. What must be remembered, however, is that private policing arrangements never disappeared. In fact, they re-emerged quite spectacularly in the United States less than a century later. Private policing organizations such as the Pinkerton Detective Agency ('the eye that never sleeps') played a significant and often brutal role in strike suppression and the intimidation of workers during labour unrest in the early twentieth century.") (citation omitted); *see also* Beau Riffenburgh, Pinkerton's Great Detective: The Rough-and-Tumble Career of James McParland, America's Sherlock Holmes (2013), ch. 8 n.5 ("That 'company lawyers' were allowed to join the prosecution in the Molly Maguire trials has been criticized as one of the most unethical aspects of the trials. However, this argument shows a lack of understanding of mid–nineteenth century legal practice. There was no objection at the time because private prosecution, although not as common as several decades previously, was still not infrequent and was acceptable in the eyes of the law, as it was recognized that the county district attorney would require aid to prosecute such an unusually large number of capital cases. Even Judge John P. Lavelle, whose book The Hard Coal Docket is perhaps the most notable condemnation of the fairness of the trials, acknowledged: 'It was not unusual at this time for lawyers who represented a victim's family to assist the district attorney in trying the case against the defendant.'").

37. *See generally* Mark Koyama, *Prosecution Associations in Industrial Revolution England: Provide Providers of Public Goods?*, 41 J. Legal Studies 95 (2012); *see also* Wilbur R. Miller, A History of Private Policing in the United States 51 (2019) ("In Britain before 1829, and afterward in areas that did not yet have 'New Police,' private prosecution associations pooled contributions of well-to-do-members to pay for prosecutions they themselves initiated (usually for theft). A persistent example was the Worsted Committee's Inspectorate, a specialized private police and prosecution organization in the wool-making cities of Yorkshire. This force was mainly concerned with violations within the factories, especially theft of material for workers' own use and failure to complete the contracted number of woolen goods. The committee was a prosecution society; the Inspectorate, a detective police with power of arrest."); Alison Cronin, Corporate Criminality and Liability for Fraud (2018) ("If a formal prosecution was sought, the expenses involved in both the criminal investigation and the prosecution were borne by the victim himself which meant that the availability of the criminal justice system was limited to the wealthier classes or at least those who could subscribe to a private prosecution association.") (citations omitted); "Unlawful Hunting—Redress Required," Richmond Dispatch (Richmond, VA), Oct. 13, 1869, p. 1 ("Our farmers complain of the great annoyance they suffer from persons trespassing on their ground at will on pretence of shooting game.... A movement is being made to establish a county association of farmers and fruitgrowers, one of the objects of which is the retaining a standing attorney to prosecute every case of which notice is given him; for the vexations of a private prosecutor are so many, and the loss of time so frequent and so great in securing a conviction, that most people at present will choose to endure an injury and suffer a ruffian to escape rather follow him up by a prosecution.").

38. Allyson N. May, The Bar and the Old Bailey, 1750–1850, at 20 (2003).

39. Michal R. Belknap, The Vinson Court: Justices, Rulings, and Legacy 127 (2004) ("Before 1868, the year in which the Fourteenth Amendment was added to the Constitution, the Bill of Rights placed constraints on the federal government exclusively. In 1833, Chief Justice John Marshall offered the definitive pre–Fourteenth Amendment analysis of their reach in *Barron v. Baltimore*: The Bill of Rights 'constrain[s] only the government created by the document,' the federal government."); William Davenport Mercer, Diminishing the Bill of Rights: *Barron v. Baltimore* and the Foundations of American Liberty (2017); Barron v. Baltimore, 32 U.S. (7. Pet.) 243 (1833).

40. Russell L. Christopher, *Appointed Counsel and Jury Trial: The Rights that Undermine the Other Rights*, 75 Wash. & Lee L. Rev. 703, 719–20 (2018); Gideon v. Wainwright, 372 U.S. 335 (1963). The Sixth Amendment contains additional legal protections, too. As the Sixth Amendment reads in full: "In all

criminal prosecutions, the accused shall enjoy the right to a speedy and public trial, by an impartial jury of the State and district wherein the crime shall have been committed, which district shall have been previously ascertained by law, and to be informed of the nature and cause of the accusation; to be confronted with the witnesses against him; to have compulsory process for obtaining witnesses in his favor, and to have the Assistance of Counsel for his defence." U.S. CONST., amend. VI.

41. ROBERT B. SHOEMAKER, PROSECUTION AND PUNISHMENT: PETTY CRIME AND THE LAW IN LONDON AND RURAL MIDDLESEX, c. 1660–1725, at 216 (1991) ("In identifying the prosecutors of petty crime, this discussion has so far been restricted to private individuals, in most cases the victims of the offences prosecuted. Indeed, the private prosecutor was the mainstay of the judicial system in preindustrial England, a situation markedly different from that of the present day. Nonetheless, a small but significant proportion of offences were prosecuted by public officials acting in their official capacities. As Table 8.4 demonstrates, although private prosecutors formed the vast majority of the prosecutors of recognizances and indictments, justices of the peace and parish officers (constables, night watchmen, churchwardens, and overseers of the poor) were responsible for 20% of the indictments and 12% of the recognizances."); *id.* (Table 8.4 reflects that private prosecutors were responsible for 71% of the "Recognizances" and 65% of the "Indictments").

42. Carlton F.W. Larson, *The Revolutionary American Jury: A Case Study of the 1778–1779 Philadelphia Treason Trials*, 61 SMU L. REV. 1441, 1453 (2008) ("In late eighteenth-century England, most felony cases were prosecuted by private parties, generally the victims. Treason cases, by contrast, were generally prosecuted by professional attorneys working for the crown such as the attorney general or solicitor general."); *see also* Bruce P. Smith, *The Emergence of Public Prosecution in London, 1790–1850*, 18 YALE J.L. & HUMAN. 29, 32 (2006) ("[W]hile private victims typically provided the necessary impetus for prosecuting cases of felony in the higher courts, this Article argues that public officials in London between roughly 1790 and 1850 played considerable (and considerably underappreciated) roles in prosecuting cases of misdemeanor in the city's lower criminal courts.").

43. JOHN ALLEN STEVENSON, THE REAL HISTORY OF TOM JONES 104–05 (2005) ("The starting point for understanding eighteenth-century criminal law is the institution of 'private prosecution,' and the crucial role played by the person called the 'prosecutor.' Immediately, we are forced to confront difference, because an eighteenth-century prosecutor was not a lawyer representing the state, but was, in fact, the victim; as Beattie puts it, this is 'a system of justice that puts the burden of prosecution entirely on the victim of the crime.' The law expected, indeed demanded, that victims report the crime, identify the criminal, gather witnesses, and make a case before judge and jury.... There were no police as we know them to call in England in the eighteenth century, nor indeed until the Peel Act of 1829 established the first real police force. Much law, and much legal practice, flowed from this reluctance to institute a police force—an institution that was common elsewhere in Europe (France, for instance, had both national and local police forces by the early eighteenth century), but which came very late to Britain.") (citing J. M. BEATTIE, POLICING AND PUNISHMENT IN LONDON, 1660–1750: URBAN CRIME AND THE LIMITS OF TERROR vi (2001)).

44. BEATTIE, *supra* note 43, at 375 ("[O]ne of the characteristics of trials for felonies in England had been that they were conducted essentially as direct confrontations between a private prosecutor and the accused. That remained true in the majority of cases well into the nineteenth century."); GUYORA BINDER, CRIMINAL LAW (2016) (noting that, in eighteenth-century England, "[t]he Crown offered rewards for the successful private prosecution of serious crimes, which created a profession of mercenary investigators"); *see also* WILLIAM CORNISH, STEPHEN BANKS, CHARLES MITCHELL, PAUL MITCHELL & REBECCA PROBERT, LAW AND SOCIETY IN ENGLAND 1750–1950 (2d ed. 2019) ("In a system dependent on private prosecution, some who might have prosecuted offences were, without doubt, inhibited either by their own conscience or by the knowledge that unpopular prosecutions that had capital outcomes were particularly likely to invite retribution.").

45. Powers v. Hauck, 399 F.2d 322 (5th Cir. 1968) (approving the use of a private prosecutor where the death penalty was imposed).

46. Philip Stenning, Victoria Colvin & Heather Douglas, *Introduction*, *in* VICTORIA COLVIN & PHILIP STENNING, EDS., THE EVOLVING ROLE OF THE PUBLIC PROSECUTOR: CHALLENGES AND INNOVATIONS 2 (2019) ("Modern prosecution scholars owe a considerable debt to John Langbein for explaining the origins

of the modern public prosecutor within the English common law system .... In the first place, Langbein's account is useful in dispelling what he refers to as lawyers' assumption that the modern system of lawyer-prosecutors in criminal cases 'goes back to some sort of antiquity' in English common law. He points out that in fact the public prosecutor was 'an historical latecomer' in this system, and that the confusion arises from the fact that historians have failed to distinguish between the famous State Trials that were typically prosecuted by one of the law officers of the Crown (the Attorney General or his deputy, the Solicitor General), and 'ordinary felony' cases in which lawyers did not participate on either side (prosecutor or defence) until very late in the eighteenth century, and even then by no means always.") (citations omitted); *id.* ("Perhaps more importantly, Langbein demonstrates in his very well-documented account that many of the investigative and forensic functions we associate with public prosecutors today were assumed from private complainants by the lay Justices of the Peace (nowadays usually called magistrates in the UK). This office was originally established in the fourteenth century, and the assumption of this role was not confirmed in legislation until the passage of the Marian bail and committal statutes, passed in 1554 and 1555 respectively. The role of the J.P.s did not supersede prosecution by citizens, in a tradition of 'gratuitous citizen prosecution,' but rather complemented it. It was not until the creation of 'the new police' in the early nineteenth century, and the office of the Director of Public Prosecutions in 1879, that the prosecutorial responsibility was finally entrusted entirely to state officials. A state institution of lawyer-prosecutors (the Crown Prosecution [S]ervice) was finally established in 1986 in England and Wales.") (citations omitted).

47. "The M'Farland Trial," N.Y. HERALD (New York, NY), May 10, 1870, p. 3 ("In Great Britain to this day nearly all prosecutions for the Crown are conducted by counsel employed by private prosecutors."); *accord* N.Y. TIMES, May 11, 1870, p. 2 (same); *see also* J. ANTHONY LUKAS, BIG TROUBLE: A MURDER IN A SMALL WESTERN TOWN SETS OFF A STRUGGLE FOR THE SOUL OF AMERICA 354 (1997) ("The practice of hiring private counsel to assist prosecutors was an old one in the West, where it was rare to find competent prosecuting attorneys at the county level and where the mixture of public functions and private interests was endemic. In 1884, a California court noted that the practice 'has existed and been acquiesced in almost since the organization of the state.' In two highly publicized cases pitting sheep men against cattlemen—the Diamondfield Jack case in Idaho and the Spring Creek raid case in Wyoming—sheep men made no secret of hiring and amply remunerating private attorneys to go after their sworn enemies, the cattlemen and their agents. The more remote the locale, the more visible the case, the more potent the colliding forces, and the more celebrated the defense attorney, the more often another celebrated attorney would be called in to act for the prosecution—paid sometimes by the state, sometimes by an interested corporation or association."); *id.* at 354 n.* ("In southern states, when a black man was charged with raping a white woman it was long the practice for the family of the 'victim,' bent on revenge, to provide the 'prosecutor.'")

48. An Act Providing for the Election of District Attorneys § 1 (passed May 3, 1850) ("That the qualified voters of the city and county of Philadelphia, and of each and every county in the state, shall, at the general election of the second Tuesday next, and every three years thereafter, elect one person, learned in the law, who has been two years admitted to the bar, and who shall have resided in the county for which he is elected for one year next preceding his election, who shall be called the district attorney of said county; and the officer so elected shall sign all bills of indictment, and conduct in court all criminal and other prosecutions in the name of the commonwealth, or when the state is a party, which arise in the county for which he is elected, and perform all the duties which now by law are to be performed by deputy attorney generals, and receive the same fees or emoluments of office: Provided, Said district attorney shall in no case whatever have authority to enter nolle prosequi in any criminal case, either before or after bill found, or to discharge a prisoner from custody, without first having obtained the approbation of the court, in writing."), *reprinted in* JAMES DUNLOP, COMP., THE GENERAL LAWS OF PENNSYLVANIA, FROM THE YEAR 1700, TO MAY, 1853, CHRONOLOGICALLY ARRANGED: WITH NOTES AND REFERENCES, TO ALL THE DECISIONS OF THE SUPREME COURT OF PENNSYLVANIA, GIVING CONSTRUCTION TO SAID LAWS 1111–12 (3d ed. 1853).

49. STEINBERG, *supra* note 19, at 24–69, 152–57; *see also* Robert M. Ireland, *Privately Funded Prosecution of Crime in the Nineteenth-Century United States*, 39 AM. J. LEGAL HIST. 43, 43 n.1 (1995) ("Allen Steinberg's *The Transformation of Criminal Justice: Philadelphia 1800–1880* (Chapel Hill, 1989) deals

extensively with a form of private prosecution of alleged criminality, but not that involving privately funded lawyer-prosecutors of major felonies."); *id.* ("Steinberg's private prosecutors are complaining witnesses who did not hire lawyers but usually themselves prosecuted essentially misdemeanors before minor quasi-judicial officials such as city aldermen and justices of the peace, likewise often untrained in the law. He only briefly mentions privately funded lawyer-prosecution of serious felonies."); Gerald Caplan, *Criminal Justice in the Lower Courts: A Study in Continuity*, 89 MICH. L. REV. 1694, 1694 (1991) ("*The Transformation of Criminal Justice* chronicles the administration of criminal justice in nineteenth-century Philadelphia, a period when private prosecution was the predominant method for initiating a prosecution. Historian Allen Steinberg has searched intensively through yellowed court files, prison records, and reports from long defunct Philadelphia newspapers to put together a portrait of private prosecution in the magistrates' courts. *The Transformation* is thus a great store of ordinary conflicts, injuries, and grievances; it reveals the commonplace of criminal law—neighborhood quarrels, domestic assaults, disorderly conduct, public drunkenness, destruction and theft of property. It is an unsettling account—an unpleasant reminder of the misconduct and bias which have plagued the administration of justice throughout this nation's history.") (reviewing STEINBERG, *supra* note 19).

50. Paul G. Cassell & Steven Joffee, *The Crime Victim's Expanding Role in a System of Public Prosecution: A Response to the Critics of the Crime Victims' Rights Act*, 105 NW. U. L. REV. COLLOQUY 164, 178 (2011); *see also* "The January Court," MANSFIELD ADVERTISER (Mansfield, PA), Feb. 3, 1892, p. 2 ("The following bills were ignored: Helen Shutter, assault and battery, the private prosecutor to pay the costs."); "The Second Week of Court," WELLSBORO AGITATOR (Wellsboro, PA), Dec. 9, 1891, p. 2 ("The case of the Commonwealth against Howard Petty, charged with assault and battery upon the person of Edward Payne, which was continued into the civil week, closed last Thursday with a verdict of not guilty, and that the costs be equally divided between the defendant and the private prosecutor."); "Court Proceedings," MANSFIELD ADVERTISER (Mansfield, PA), Dec. 2, 1885, p. 3 (containing the following notations: "Miles Egleston and others, assault; costs to be paid by private prosecutor, Frank Barnhart." "David Thomas, assault; costs to be paid by private prosecutor, R. H. Fleming."); "Private Iams vs. Colonel Streator," HARRISBURG STAR INDEPENDENT (Harrisburg, PA), Oct. 28, 1892, p. 2 ("PITTSBURG, Oct. 28.—The case against Colonel Alexander Hawkins, Lieutenant Colonel J. B. R. Streator and Assistant Surgeon W. S. Grim, of the Tenth regiment, for tying Private W. L. Iams by the thumbs at Homestead, was called for trial before Judge Porter yesterday.... At the opening of the case the defense moved to quash the indictment on the ground that the civil court had no jurisdiction, the alleged offense having been committed when the guard was on active duty, and if the private prosecutor had any grievance he had a tribunal to appeal to, which was created by the National Guard act of 1887, and establishing court martial."); "The Iams Case Concluded—Eight Days Consumed in Trying an Assault and Battery Case," LEBANON DAILY NEWS (Lebanon, PA), Nov. 4, 1892, p. 1 ("W. L. Iams, the private prosecutor in the case, today said that whether the jury in the present case found the defendants guilty or not he would bring suit for damages.").

51. STEINBERG, *supra* note 19, at 57.

52. Stephen C. Yeazell, *Socializing Law, Privatizing Law, Monopolizing Law, Accessing Law*, 39 LOY. L.A. L. REV. 691, 692–93 (2006).

53. AARON PALMER, A RULE OF LAW: ELITE POLITICAL AUTHORITY AND THE COMING OF THE REVOLUTION IN THE SOUTH CAROLINA LOWCOUNTRY, 1763–1776, at 74 (2014) (noting that South Carolina "drafted a revised comprehensive slave code in 1740, which included a separate system of criminal justice to deal with this huge portion of the colonial population"); 1 JOHN CODMAN HURD, THE LAW OF FREEDOM AND BONDAGE IN THE UNITED STATES 237 (1858) (reprinting and discussing the Virginia act of 1692); MARK TUSHNET, THE AMERICAN LAW OF SLAVERY, 1810–1860: CONSIDERATIONS OF HUMANITY AND INTEREST 122 (1981) ("Southern courts worked toward a separate system of law for slaves, and once that system was set off from the general system, they expressed significantly less concern for technicality"); *id.* ("Slave law used both procedure and substance to separate slave law and general law. Special courts were established for the trial of minor slave crimes, and procedural nicety was not always demanded in those courts."); Judith Kelleher Schafer, *Slaves and Crime: New Orleans, 1846–1862*, *in* CHRISTOPHER WALDREP & DONALD G. NIEMAN, EDS., LOCAL MATTERS: RACE, CRIME, AND JUSTICE IN THE NINETEENTH-CENTURY SOUTH 55–56 (2011) ("Exempting slaves from common law safeguards underscored the special nature

of slave property. The exquisite dilemma of the peculiar institution was that although slaves were property, they were also humans who could be held accountable for their misdeeds as could no horse, cow, or chicken. But to try them in the same courts under the same rules as free persons elevated them to a status that no slaveholder would or could admit. Hence the need for a separate system in which the concern was not, as with free people, procedural guarantees, but a mechanism for visiting swift, brutal, exemplary punishment on persons who had to be always reminded of their subordinate status."); Twede, *supra* note 18, at 15 ("The English courts of law still operated under [a] system of private prosecution when England began establishing colonies in America. As such, the English system of private prosecution made its way to the colonies. However, the English never sought uniformity in the way the colonial courts operated. Thus, the colonial courts were left in some regards to adapt and evolve on their own. Prosecution was one of the elements that evolved.") (citations omitted).

54. *See also* Bruce A. Green & Rebecca Roiphe, *Rethinking Prosecutors' Conflicts of Interest*, 58 B.C. L. Rev. 463, 490 n.124 (2017) ("The use of private prosecutors, typically employed by victims or their families or by individuals with potential civil lawsuits that will benefit from a criminal conviction, predates the American Revolution and has continued through the nineteenth century in many states and remains at least a theoretical possibility in some states today.").

55. Marc L. Miller & Ronald F. Wright, Criminal Procedures: Cases, Statutes, and Executive Materials 834 (2003) (noting how private prosecutions "became the exception rather than the rule as public prosecutors become more professionalized and independent of the courts, professional police departments became more common in metropolitan areas, and acquittal rates rose for privately initiated complaints").

56. *E.g.*, Joshua M. Divine, *Statutory Federalism and Criminal Law*, 106 Va. L. Rev. 127, 165 (2020); Amendments to the Bail Reform Act of 1966, Hearings before the Subcommittee on Constitutional Rights of the Committee on the Judiciary, United States Senate, Ninety-First Congress, First Session (January 21, 22, 23, 28, 29, 30, and February 4, 1969) 311 (1969).

57. Leslie B. Arffa, *Separation of Prosecutors*, 128 Yale L.J. 1078, 1088–89 (2019); *see also id.* at 1089 ("[F]rom 1800 to 1814, the Attorney General often played the role of 'an absentee cabinet member.' It was not until 1819 that the Attorney General even received a physical office."); *id.* at 1090 ("[F]or most of the nineteenth century, Congress continued to resist executive demands to centralize the law enforcement apparatus. In 1830, for example, the Senate debated but took no action on a 'bill to organize the Attorney General's department, and to erect it into an Executive office.' … [M]ost senators resisted centralization. One proclaimed that organizational innovation was 'unnecessary,' and another, Senator Daniel Webster, argued that no 'good would result from the metamorphosis of the Attorney General into the head of a bureau.' Senators expressed a fear that the Attorney General, who 'should be engaged in studying his books of law,' would instead be distracted by administrative (i.e., supervisory) duties."); *id.* ("The District Attorney position, meanwhile, enjoyed virtually unlimited independence. The attorneys lived and worked throughout the country. There was no formal chain of command within the executive branch. Furthermore, the attorneys often lacked a means of effective communication with national officials."); *id.* at 1090–91 ("Until 1854, the various Attorneys General kept up significant private practices, and many of them did not even live in Washington, D.C."); "The Macon Note Book," Atlanta Const. (Atlanta, GA), Oct. 12, 1883, p. 1 ("In the United States circuit court, to-day was taken up in making a jury in the Jamison counterfeiting case.… Counsel for Jamison moved to quash the bill of indictment on the ground that the marshal who summoned the grand jury was prosecutor. The district attorney replied that in the courts of the United States no private prosecutor is known, he being prosecutor in the name of the United States. Judge Locke promptly overruled the motion to quash.").

58. *See, e.g.*, U.S. Const. art. II, § 3 (establishing the duty of the Executive Branch to "take Care that the Laws be faithfully executed"); United States v. Armstrong, 517 U.S. 456, 467 (1996) ("[O]ne of the core powers of the Executive Branch of the Federal Government [is] the power to prosecute."); Young v. United States ex rel. Vuitton et Fils S.A., 481 U.S. 787, 816 n.2 (1987) (Scalia, J., concurring) ("At the time of the Constitution, there existed in England a longstanding custom of private prosecution. I am unaware, however, of any private prosecution of federal crimes. The Judiciary Act of 1789 provided for the appointment in each judicial district of 'a … person learned in the law to act as attorney for the United States … whose

duty it shall be to prosecute in such district all delinquents for crimes and offences, cognizable under the authority of the United States.'") (citations omitted); Note, *Permitting Private Initiation of Criminal Contempt Proceedings*, 124 HARV. L. REV. 1485, 1495 (2011) ("In federal court, from the very beginning, Congress gave to U.S. Attorneys the authority to 'prosecute in [each] district all delinquents for crimes and offences, cognizable under the authority of the United States.'"); *see also* Linda R.S. v. Richard D., 410 U.S. 614, 619 (1973) ("This Court's prior decisions consistently hold that a citizen lacks standing to contest the policies of the prosecuting authority when he himself is neither prosecuted nor threatened with prosecution. Although these cases arose in a somewhat different context, they demonstrate that, in American jurisprudence at least, a private citizens lacks a judicially cognizable interest in the prosecution or nonprosecution of another.") (citing Younger v. Harris, 401 U.S. 37, 42 (1971); Bailey v. Patterson, 369 U.S. 31, 33 (1962); Poe v. Ullman, 367 U.S. 497, 501 (1961)); Leeke v. Timmerman, 454 U.S. 83, 86–87 (1981) ("Respondents concede that the decision to prosecute is solely within the discretion of the prosecutor."); *compare id.* at 87 n.3 ("The American Bar Association Standards for Criminal Justice, The Prosecution Function 3-3.4 (2d ed. 1980), propose that where the law permits a private citizen to complain directly to a judicial officer, the complainant 'should be required to present the complaint for prior approval to the prosecutor, and the prosecutor's actions or recommendation thereon should be communicated to the judicial officer or grand jury.' Many jurisdictions contain provisions for private citizens to initiate the criminal process, and some have required or encouraged input of the prosecuting attorney before issuance of an arrest warrant.") (citing NEB. REV. STAT. § 29-404 (1979); OHIO REV. CODE ANN. § 2935.10 (1975); S.D. COMP. LAWS ANN. § 23A-2-2 (1979); WIS. STAT. § 968.02(3) (1977)).

59. GWLADYS GILLIÉRON, PUBLIC PROSECUTORS IN THE UNITED STATES AND EUROPE: A COMPARATIVE ANALYSIS WITH SPECIAL FOCUS ON SWITZERLAND, FRANCE, AND GERMANY 66 (2014) ("In 2010, the U.S. attorney's offices nationwide had a total of 6,075 full time attorneys and 5,799 support staff, the majority of them (79%) focusing on criminal prosecutions. Assistant U.S. attorneys constituted about 66% of Department attorneys with prosecution responsibilities. As of the end of the 2010 fiscal year, the U.S. attorney system consisted of 94 headquarter offices and 138 staffed branched offices."); RONALD J. BACIGAL & MARY KELLY TATE, CRIMINAL LAW AND PROCEDURE: AN OVERVIEW xxxix (4th ed. 2015) ("At the national level, the U.S. Department of Justice and U.S. Attorney's offices, distributed geographically throughout the country, initiate a prosecution for a federal offense. At the state level, the state attorney general's office may initiate certain prosecutions, but such offices normally limit their function to handling appeals of convictions.").

60. *Compare* Jane E. Kirtley & Casey Carmody, *Criminal Defamation: Still "An Instrument of Destruction" in the Age of Fake News*, 8 J. INT'L MEDIA & ENT. L. 163, 172 (2019–2020) ("Many international criminal defamation cases stem from private prosecutions, which are barred or limited in most parts of the United States.") *and* State v. Eldridge, 951 S.W.2d 775, 780 (Tenn. Ct. Crim. App. 1997) ("Being aware of the special dangers inherent in private prosecutions, some states prohibit the practice altogether.") *with* O'Neill, *supra* note 17, at 689–90 ("Alabama, Georgia, Indiana, New Jersey, New York, Ohio, Pennsylvania, Tennessee, Vermont, Virginia, West Virginia, and Wisconsin each allow private counsel to participate in a criminal prosecution in some way. Although a comprehensive examination of each of those individual state rules is beyond the scope of this Article, I will consider several other circumstances in which states, subject to various limitations, permit privately-managed prosecutions.") *and* Tyler Grove, *Are All Prosecutorial Activities "Inherently Governmental"?: Applying State Safeguards for Victim-Retained Private Prosecutions to Outsourced Prosecutions*, 40 PUB. CONT. L.J. 991, 1007 (2011) ("The states are currently split on whether victim-retained private prosecutors are permissible. Some jurisdictions prohibit the practice, while other jurisdictions allow private prosecutors as long as the district attorney retains control over the prosecution. Only a handful of states allow private prosecutions without any supervision from a public prosecutor or other safeguards.").

61. Bennett L. Gershman, *Prosecutorial Ethics and Victims' Rights: The Prosecutor's Duty of Neutrality*, 9 LEWIS & CLARK L. REV. 559, 561 (2005) ("[A] prosecutor cannot align herself exclusively with the victim. A prosecutor also owes an allegiance to constituencies that are independent of the victim—i.e., the general public and the accused. A prosecutor must attempt to reconcile this tripartite responsibility to protect the public from harm and protect the rights of the accused while at the same time protecting the rights of

the victim."); *id.* at 563 ("A prosecutor's duty of neutrality derives from several sources. First, a prosecutor does not represent a private client. A prosecutor's 'clients' are the people who live in the prosecutor's jurisdiction, including police, witnesses, crime victims, and even the accused. A prosecutor, as with all lawyers, has a fiduciary obligation to her client. But in contrast to attorneys representing private clients, a prosecutor's fiduciary duty requires the prosecutor to exercise professional judgment, as the ABA Criminal Justice Standard directs, 'solely for the benefit of the client—the people—free of any compromising influences or loyalties.'"); *id.* ("Second, as courts, commentators, and professional codes consistently declare, the role of a prosecutor is not to win a case (and achieve professional and media acclaim) but, rather, to behave in a fair and lawful manner to promote the cause of justice. This requirement to serve justice means that in order to achieve a fair and just result, a prosecutor must, again, exercise her powers in an objectively fair and disinterested manner without any implication of partiality that might tarnish her integrity."); *id.* ("Third, given a prosecutor's enormous power over people's lives, liberty, and reputations, as well as the limited checks on a prosecutor's discretion, a prosecutor has an extraordinary opportunity for her sympathies for a victim to influence the exercise of official discretion, entirely without review. The duty to remain neutral serves as an assurance to courts, individual defendants, and the public that a prosecutor's unreviewable discretionary choices presumably are unaffected by personal, political, or private interests.").

62. Adam N. Stern, *Plea Bargaining, Innocence, and the Prosecutor's Duty to "Do Justice,"* 25 Geo. J. Legal Ethics 1027 (2012).

63. Malcolm M. Feeley, Crime, Law and Society 114 (2016) ("Private prosecution was justified by the theory that crime was primarily a wrong to the victim and only secondarily an affront to the integrity of the state. This view placed considerable discretion in the hands of the victim, for if he or she did not want to prosecute, the state could not easily intervene.").

64. Mary Fan, *Adversarial Justice's Casualties: Defending Victim-Witness Protection*, 55 B.C. L. Rev. 775, 795 (2014) ("The criminal justice system was far different than the modern system, with its professional forces of public defenders, probation officers, full-time prosecutors, and trained police forces. Indeed, the State hardly had a monopoly on prosecution—with the practice of private prosecution of crimes persisting in Philadelphia, until the 19th century.").

65. Gilliéron, *supra* note 59, at 47 ("The danger in a system of private prosecution is the failure of the victim or other interested individuals to bring prosecutions. This is even truer for the poor and the powerless, particularly in view of the fact that the English justice system was intended to protect property in a society based on property. The old English system of private prosecution was a system favoring people of means. In a system of private prosecution, an individual needed to avenge himself and bear the cost of prosecution. Hence, an individual could not expect protection from the state. In addition, private prosecution produced some abuses. It was not uncommon for the accused and the accuser to meet each other in a pretrial collaboration and agree that, in exchange for payment of a percentage of the anticipated penalty by the offender to the accuser, the accuser would not prosecute the offense. As a consequence, this practice threatened the financial solvency of the courts.").

66. In the Matter of Richland County Magistrate's Courts, 699 S.E.2d 161, 162–63 (S.C. 2010); *see also id.* at 163 ("We find that allowing prosecution decisions to be made by, or even influenced by, private interests would do irreparable harm to our criminal justice system. At the very least, there is 'too much opportunity for abuse and too little motivation for detachment.'") (quoting State v. Martineau, 808 A.2d 51, 55 (N.H. 2002) (Nadeau, J., concurring)).

67. Christopher Roberts, *From the State of Emergency to the Rule of Law: The Evolution of Repressive Legality in the Nineteenth Century British Empire*, 20 Chi. J. Int'l L. 1, 30 (2019) ("While private prosecutions had been the order of the day at the start of the nineteenth century, by the century's end they had largely been replaced by public prosecutions."); Gregory M. Gilchrist, *Regulation by Prosecutor*, 56 Am. Crim. L. Rev. 315, 320 (2019) ("Prosecutors as we know them are an American contribution to common law. At the time of our founding, private prosecutions were the British norm. At common law, the criminal justice system functioned when a victim appeared before a court to make a claim. Public prosecutions are an innovation dating to colonial times. Today, American criminal justice is thoroughly public and professionalized.").

68. Pa. R. Crim. P. 506. Rule 506, entitled "Approval of Private Complaints," provides:

> (a) When the affiant is not a law enforcement officer, the complaint shall be submitted to an attorney for the Commonwealth, who shall approve or disapprove it without unreasonable delay.
>
> (b) If the attorney for the Commonwealth:
>
> (1) approves the complaint, the attorney shall indicate this decision on the complaint form and transmit it to the issuing authority;
>
> (2) disapproves the complaint, the attorney shall state the reasons on the complaint form and return it to the affiant. Thereafter, the affiant may petition the court of common pleas for review of the decision.

PA. R. CRIM. P. 506(A)-(B).

69. In re Einloth, No. 533 WDA 2020, 2020 WL 4783307, *3–4 (Pa. Super. Ct., Aug. 18, 2020); In re Obenski, No. 709 EDA 2017, 2017 WL 6546345, *3 (Pa. Super. Ct., Dec. 22, 2017); *see also* In re Colman v. SCI Albion, No. 430 WDA 2014, 2014 WL 10889769, at *2 (Pa. Super. Ct., Aug. 14, 2014) ("When a district attorney's denial of a private criminal complaint is based wholly on policy considerations, then the trial court must defer to the prosecutor's discretion absent a gross abuse of that discretion. Thereafter, the appellate court will review the trial court's decision for an abuse of discretion, in keeping with settled principles of appellate review of discretionary matters.") (*citing* In re Private Crim. Complaint of Wilson, 879 A.2d 199 (Pa. Super. Ct. 2005); Commonwealth v. Michaliga, 947 A.2d 786, 791 (Pa. Super. Ct. 2008)). "'Under Rule 506 and settled case law, the private criminal complainant has no right to an evidentiary hearing in connection with the trial court's review of the district attorney's decision to disapprove the private criminal complaint. Rule 506 merely allows the private criminal complainant the opportunity to have his complaint reviewed in the Court of Common Pleas, following the district attorney's adverse decision.'" In re Private Criminal Complaint Donald Miles, 170 Ad. 530, 536 (Pa. Super. Ct. 2017) (citation omitted).

70. DARRYL K. BROWN, FREE MARKET CRIMINAL JUSTICE: HOW DEMOCRACY AND LAISSEZ FAIRE UNDERMINE THE RULE OF LAW 232 n.96 (2016):

> Pennsylvania and Rhode Island may be the only states in which statutes still authorize a limited power of private prosecutions. In Pennsylvania, courts may approve a private prosecutor's request to take over prosecution from a district attorney who 'neglect[s] or refuse[s]' to pursue a properly grounded charge. *See* 16 PA. CONST. STAT. ANN. § 1409 (2012) (authorizing victims dissatisfied with public prosecutor to petition the court, and granting courts the power to allow victim's attorney to take over as private prosecutor). Pennsylvania courts are the rare U.S. example in which private prosecutors are recognized as part of the 'checks and balances' on public prosecutors. *See In re* Hickson, 765 A.2d 372, 377 (Pa. Super. 2000) (but denying private standing to seek judicial review of decision not to prosecute). For Rhode Island, which authorizes private misdemeanor prosecutions only, *see* R.I. GEN. LAWS §§ 12-4-1, 12-4-2, 12-4-6, 12-12-1.3 (2013); Cronan *ex rel.* State v. Cronan, 774 A.2d 866 (R.I. 2001) (approving private misdemeanor prosecution for assault under state statutes). New Hampshire might permit private prosecution of misdemeanors under state common law; *see* State v. Martineau, 148 N.H. 259, 808 A.2d 51 (2002). *See also* 63C Am. Jr. 2d Prosecuting Attorneys § 12 (2013) (citing authority in at least three states permitting private attorneys to assist public prosecutors).

71. Scott Ingram, *George Washington's Attorneys: The Political Selection of United States Attorneys at the Founding*, 39 PACE L. REV. 163, 183 (2018).

72. John C. Olson, Jr., *Discovery for Three at a Table Set for Two: An Alteration of Rule for Courts-Martial 701 to Accommodate the Practice and Philosophical Realities of the Victim as a Limited Third Party*, 2015-NOV ARMY LAW. 30, 32 (2015).

73. *E.g.*, Alan Greenblatt, "Crime Victims' Rights Added to Several States' Constitutions," GOVERNING, Nov. 6, 2018, https://www.governing.com/topics/public-justice-safety/gov-marsys-law-crime-victims-rights-ballot-measures.html.

74. O'Neill, *supra* note 17, at 695–96.

75. Charles C. Olson, *Pro Bono Publico: A History of Georgia's Prosecuting Attorneys* (1732–2012), 25 J. S. LEGAL HIST. 235, 239 (2017) ("In 1789, the General Assembly divided the state into two judicial

districts, the Eastern (based in Savannah), and the Western (based in Augusta). At the same time, the duties of the attorney general were "divided" between the attorney general and a solicitor general who were to exercise the duties of the office "jointly or severally ... and ... prosecute all delinquents for crimes and offences ...."); *see also id.* at 240 ("By 1796, the growth of the State required the creation of an additional circuit. The Judiciary Act of 1796 added a Middle Judicial Circuit made up of eight counties that had formerly been in the Eastern and Western Judicial Circuits. At the same time, the Act created another Solicitor General, thus establishing the pattern which was to be followed in the future: as the number of judicial circuits increased, so did the number of Solicitors General."); *id.* ("In 1799, the General Assembly enacted the Judiciary Act of 1799 which would govern the Georgia Judiciary and the State's prosecuting attorneys well into the twentieth century. This Act provided that there should be a solicitor general for each judicial circuit as well as an attorney general to be appointed by the General Assembly. However, in practice, the attorney general also served as the prosecuting attorney in the Eastern Judicial Circuit until 1807. In 1807, Robert Walker, the Solicitor General of the Middle Judicial Circuit which now included the State Capital, assumed the duties and title of attorney general.").

76. Peter C. Hennigan, *Property War: Prostitution, Red-Light Districts, and the Transformation of Public Nuisance Law in the Progressive Era*, 16 YALE J.L. & HUMAN. 123, 132 n.41 (2004).

77. R. KENT NEWMYER, THE TREASON TRIAL OF AARON BURR: LAW, POLITICS, AND THE CHARACTER WARS OF THE NEW NATION 40 (2012).

78. "On Trial at Nocogdoches," GALVESTON DAILY NEWS (Galveston, TX), Apr. 2, 1889, p. 3 ("NOCOGDOCHES, Tex., April 1.—The case of James P. Clevenger, charged with the murder of John J. Moore, on the 13th day of December, 1888, was called for trial on last Thursday, and there have been two special venires exhausted and only nine jurors obtained. This is one of the most interesting trials that has been tried in this county for many years. The deceased was of one of the wealthiest families in the state, while the defendant is a poor man, but has many friends, who at least are lending him their sympathies. Each side is contesting for every inch of their rights. There are several private prosecutors and one private detective assisting the state.").

79. "The Courts," PITTSBURGH DAILY POST (Pittsburgh, PA), Sept. 19, 1868, p. 4 ("The next case called was that of the Commonwealth vs. Charles Hoffman and William Schimmelfennig, indicted for aggravated assault and battery. It was charged that on the 20th of last June the two defendants above named were driving a buggy at a furious rate along Butler street, Lawrenceville, and in their reckless flight they ran over and seriously injured two little children named Catharine and William Hartz. Jacob Wiedler, the uncle and guardian of the children, appeared as private prosecutor. The case will be concluded this morning in the Common Pleas Court room."); "The August Term of Court," WELLSBORO AGITATOR (Wellsboro, PA), Sept. 3, 1889, p. 3 ("The assault and battery case against L. J. Preble was settled by consent of the Court, the private prosecutor, Will Hammond, have acknowledged satisfaction for the injury done him."); WELLSBORO AGITATOR (Wellsboro, PA), Apr. 10, 1888, p. 3 (noting that "H. L. Rockwell," a "private prosecutor," appeared consecutively in two assault and battery cases, and that, in the first, "[t]he defendant was sentenced to pay a fine of $50 and costs of prosecution" and that, in the second, "[t]he jury found the defendant not guilty, but divided the costs between the prosecutor and the defendant in equal proportions").

80. "Fined for Trespass," CAPITAL J. (Salem, OR), Nov. 12, 1894, p. 4 ("This morning Andrew Zelinskey was arraigned before Justice Johnson for trespassing. He was accused by J. F. Johnson, private prosecutor, of hunting with a gun on his premises, and the justice gave him the lowest fine of $15 and costs, being $28 all told. The prosecuting attorney conducted the case and defendant plead[ed] guilty.").

81. "November Quarter Sessions," DAILY EVENING SENTINEL (Carlisle, PA), Feb. 14, 1888, p. 1 (noting that "the defendant, Wm. L. Boswell, jr.," after pleading guilty "as to the brokerage counts," "was sentenced to pay the costs of prosecution and $800 fine, half of the fine to go to the private prosecutor, R. E. Shearer"); "Weary of Waiting—Prosecutions of Lawrence Bank Officials to Be Pushed," PITTSBURGH COMMERCIAL GAZETTE (Pittsburgh, PA), Oct. 13, 1893, p. 2 ("Some of the depositors in the defunct Lawrence bank, who lost heavily by the failure of that institution and who have grown weary of the frequent postponements of the trials of President Young and Cashier Hoerr for embezzlement, have again started a movement looking to a speedy trial of the accused. This is to be accomplished either by forcing the present criminal proceedings to an issue or by the institution of new charges. Those who have taken the matter in hand are not the

wealthy depositors who could afford to lose the cash they had entrusted to the care of that institution, but those who lost their savings of years and who have so far received back only a small percentage of the total amount originally lost. They cannot understand why Young and Hoerr should be treated with more leniency than other alleged criminals.... It now having appeared that all civil proceedings are ended and that the assignee has recovered all that is likely to be saved out of the wreck, that spirit which demands justice for a wrong done has taken possession of the many who were impoverished by criminal management of this bank and inaugurated the present move."); *id.* ("Among those who will take an active part in the renewal of the prosecutions are J. A. Welsh, of Thirty-eighth street, L. E. Williams, of Main street, Bloomfield, and William Hoffman, of 3146 Mulberry alley. There are others who do not wish their names published at present. The first named said yesterday that over fifty of the late depositors were ready to join in the movement and to subscribe to a fund to employ private counsel. These represented deposits ranging from $200 to $2,000. They had so far received about one-fourth of the original and were told that they were to be paid another small amount as soon as the assignee company realized upon the sale of certain real estate formerly owned by the bank. This might occur within a year or at the furthest two years."); *id.* ("County Detective Beltzhoover was next seen and asked why the trials mentioned had been so long delayed. He promptly replied: 'These cases have been on the list at different times and the commonwealth was ready to proceed, but each time the private counsel for the prosecutor, James E. O'Donnell, Esq., intervened and said his client was not ready to go on with the case.'"; when asked of O'Donnell, "Whom did he represent?", Detective Beltzhoover replied, "Mr. Thomas McCaffrey is the prosecutor, I believe. The cases were fixed for trial at the time the late Richard Johnston held the office of district attorney, and a day for the commencement of the same has been set on two or three occasions during Mr. Burleigh's term, but each time we were informed that the private prosecutor was not ready."; Detective Beltzhoover was then asked, "Is it is not a commonwealth case? Could not the district attorney go ahead with the trial without regard to whether the private prosecutor is ready or not?", to which the detective responded: "He could, but this might jeopardize the chances of conviction, as the private prosecutors' attorney has worked up the evidence and we would have to have his assistance to convict. The defendants were originally held in the sum of $50,000 bail, but the court grew disgusted with the frequent postponements and released both on their recognizances, as there did not appear to be any desire upon the part of the prosecution to push the case."); *id.* ("Among those who lost their all by this lamentable failure were small tradespeople, widows, orphans, laborers, mill-workers, school-teachers, dress-makers, and in fact, the blow fell upon those classes who could least afford to lose. One young lady, who taught at the Lawrence public schools, had over $1000, the result of years of saving, swallowed up in this crash.").

82. "Work in the Courts," WELLSBORO AGITATOR (Wellsboro, PA), Apr. 12, 1893, p. 3 (noting that in a criminal case taken to trial against A. J. Farr, charged with "secreting property to defraud creditors," the jury found the defendant not guilty and "directed that the private prosecutor, E. A. Smead, pay the costs").

83. "Judges and Jurors," WELLSBORO AGITATOR (Wellsboro, PA), Apr. 13, 1886, p. 3 ("The case against Valentine Nowaski, indicted for disturbing public worship, was tried, and the jury returned a verdict of not guilty, the defendant to pay one half the costs and the private prosecutor to pay the balance.").

84. "The Times Kodak," ROANOKE TIMES (Roanoke, VA), May 17, 1893, p. 2 ("The indictment found against William Woods, of this county, for stealing wood was dismissed on account of the failure of the private prosecutor to give security for costs.").

85. "Trouble in Chinatown," DAILY OREGON STATESMAN (Salem, OR), Feb. 18, 1890, p. 4 ("Hop Lee swore out a warrant yesterday before Recorder Conn against Lee Young, charging him with the unlawful destruction of property. It seems that Wing Lee was running a wash house in the building near the covered bridge and had Lee Yong employed and failed to pay him. Wing Lee was sold out under attachment and Hop Lee being the principal creditor bought him out. Lee Young finally got tired of waiting for his money went to Hop Lee and claimed that he was 'the same' as Wing Lee and demanded settlement. Upon being refused he procured a club, went into Hop Lee's wash house and proceeded to beat up his wash kettle. The case was dismissed upon motion of the private prosecutors, they agreeing to dismiss the case and pay the costs and Lee Young paying the costs of the kettle amounting to $17.").

86. Immanuel Kim, *A Voice for One, or a Voice for the People: Balancing Prosecutorial Speech Protections with Community Trust*, 86 FORDHAM L. REV. 1331, 1332 (2017) ("Prosecutors are public officials who

represent the residents of a community ('the People') and their interests in the criminal justice system.'"); Fred C. Zacharias, *The Professional Discipline of Prosecutors*, 79 N.C. L. Rev. 721, 762–63 (2001) ("In addition to the initial training of new prosecutors, many agencies maintain manuals or guidelines governing recurring prosecutorial conduct. Prosecutors tend to adhere to these regulations, not only because they provide needed guidance in resolving ethical dilemmas, but because violations may serve as a basis for internal discipline or poor performance evaluations.").

87. Brown, *supra* note 17, at 868 n.77.

88. Office of Justice Programs, Bureau of Justice Statistics: Prosecutors Offices. Access at https://www.bjs.gov/index.cfm?ty=tp&tid=27 (last visited Jan. 28, 2021).

89. National District Attorney Association, *About NDAA*, https://ndaa.org/about/aboutndaa/ (last visited Jan. 28, 2021).

90. Ron Abernethy, *The History of Public Defenders*, Napa Valley Register (June 10, 2013), https://napavalleyregister.com/the-history-of-public-defenders/article_f3c5b182-d224-11e2-bd9a-001a4bc-f887a.html ("Clara Foltz, the first female lawyer in California, had long advocated that the Constitution required the government to provide a lawyer for indigent criminal defendants. As a direct result of her advocacy and in a crowning achievement of her storied public career, the Los Angeles County Public Defender's Office was established in 1912, the first public defender's office in the nation. Other statutory public defender offices were to follow, particularly after it became clear that a statutory office was the most efficient way to provide quality indigent defense services at a reasonable cost."); *see also* Barbara Allen Babcock, *Clara Shortridge Foltz: Constitution-Maker*, 66 Ind. L.J. 849, 850 (1991) (noting that Clara Shortridge Foltz (1849–1934) became California's first female lawyer in 1878 and worked as a public defender).

91. Gideon v. Wainwright, 372 U.S. 335 (1963).

92. Steinberg, *supra* note 19, at 43.

93. *E.g.*, Thomas W. Merrill, *Is Public Nuisance a Tort?*, 4 J. Tort L. 1, 39 (2011) ("With the rise of Jacksonian democracy, the prosecution of crime increasingly was given over to elected officials. Starting with Massachusetts in 1849, states began questioning the propriety of private prosecution. Soon, a number of state supreme courts refused to affirm convictions procured by private prosecutors; other states enacted legislation outlawing private prosecutors. Today, only three states allow private prosecutions without the consent or supervision of a public prosecutor.").

94. For a comparison of private prosecution practices in just two American states, *compare* Ken Lammers, *Private Prosecutors*, Crim Law Blog, Feb. 18, 2014, http://crimlaw.blogspot.com/2014/02/private-prosecutors.html (discussing precedents in Virginia) *with* Jonathan Holbrook, "Prosecutor for Hire?", North Carolina Criminal Law: A UNC School of Government Blog, Feb. 13, 2018, https://nccriminallaw.sog.unc.edu/prosecutor-for-hire/ (discussing practices in North Carolina).

95. Vincent Chiao, Criminal Law in the Age of the Administrative State 14 (2019).

96. Laura I. Appleman, Defending the Jury: Crime, Community, and the Constitution 218 n.28 (2015) ("Connecticut was the first colony to eliminate private prosecutors, passing a statute appointing a county prosecutor to prosecute all crimes.") (citing James L. Worrall, Prosecution in America: A Historical and Comparative Account 7 (2008)); Report on Prosecution, National Commission on Law Observance and Enforcement 6–7 (1930) ("[T]he Colonies began to do away with private prosecutions and set up public prosecutors. The first statute was enacted in Connecticut in 1704, as follows: " * * * Henceforth there shall be in every countie a sober, discreet and religious person appointed by the countie courts, to be attorney for the Queen (this was in the reign of Queen Anne) to prosecute and implead in the laws all criminals and to doe all other things necessary or convenient as an attorney to suppress vice and immoralitie."); *see also id.* at 7 ("In 1711 county attorneys were commissioned in Virginia, and the example of Connecticut was soon followed in other Colonies. By the end of the century, official prosecutions by public prosecutors had become established as the American system."); Guyora Binder, Criminal Law (2016) ("Connecticut in 1704 eliminated private prosecution by statute and required appointment of an attorney for the Crown in each county. By 1711 Virginia had turned prosecution of all felonies over to attorneys general. Over the course of the eighteenth century Massachusetts developed a system of county prosecutors. By the 1820s most states had public prosecutors, and by the 1840s many of these prosecutors were popularly elected.").

97. Chiao, *supra* note 95, at 14–15 (2019); *see also id.* at 15 (discussing private prosecution associations in eighteenth-century England and observing: "These associations were designed to provide their dues-paying members with what we would now think of a public prosecutorial services. 'All associations,' Philips notes, 'offered their members at least two basic forms of assistance: in the detection and apprehension of suspected offenders, and in the prosecution of those arrested people.' However, the significance of these private prosecution clubs declined as the century wore on and professional police forces became more established and expert in investigating and prosecuting crime; over time, public law enforcement substituted for private."); *see also* Anthony Ogus, *Better Regulations—Better Enforcement, in* Stephen Weatherill, ed., Better Regulation 120 (2007) ("English law has a long tradition of the private prosecution of criminal offences but, notwithstanding a general legislative right for its continuance, there are a large number of offences in relation to which the consent of the Director of Public Prosecutions or of the Attorney-General to the prosecution is first required. In a study of this area by the Law Commission, the incidence of such consent was found to be 'haphazard' and lacking a 'unifying principle.'").

98. Mikhail v. Kahn, 991 F. Supp.2d 596, 635 (E.D. Pa. 2014).

99. Ireland, *supra* note 49, at 47–48 ("Celebrated Kentucky lawyer, John Rowan, provided one of the first in-depth denunciations of the custom of privately funded prosecutors. Appearing for the defense in 1839 in the trial of three Mississippi aristocrats for the murder of two Louisville artisans in the bar of the Galt House, Rowan devoted a major portion of his closing argument berating Ben Hardin, another famous Kentucky attorney, for appearing as a private prosecutor in the case for a fee of $1,000.00 paid by the friends of the victims. Rowan argued that the practice violated due process and the presumption of innocence. Public prosecutors, he contended, had a duty to presume that all criminal defendants were innocent; private prosecutors were paid to assume defendants were guilty. Furthermore, the practice revived the ancient and barbaric custom of trial by vengeance embodied in the private prosecutors who accepted *blood money* to secure a guilty verdict regardless of the evidence. Money, not evidence, would determine guilt or innocence. Wealthy victims or their families could always hire enough talented prosecutors to convict defendants, regardless of the evidence. Describing the practice as a violation of the commandment against murder, Rowan implored the younger lawyers of Kentucky to forsake private prosecution and urged the public to condemn it.").

100. William Marvel, Lincoln's Autocrat: The Life of Edwin Stanton 101–107 (2015).

101. 12 John D. Lawson, ed., American State Trials: A Collection of the Important and Interesting Criminal Trials Which Have Taken Place in the United States, from the Beginning of Our Government to the Present Day 640, 687, 700–705 (1919); *see also* "The Sickles Tragedy: Trial of Danial E. Sickles for the Murder of Philip Barton Key," N.Y. Times, Apr. 15, 1859, p. 1 ("Mr. Stanton wanted to know whether it was the persons engaged in the prosecution who tried to destroy this evidence. There were two prosecutors here—a public prosecutor and a private prosecutor."); "The Washington Tragedy: Trial of Daniel E. Sickles for Killing Philip Barton Key," N.Y. Daily Herald (New York, NY), Apr. 15, 1859, p. 1 ("Mr. Stanton resumed, by repeating that such law as that insisted on would conduct his client to the foot of the gallows, and that there were private prosecutors here.").

102. Walter Stahr, Stanton: Lincoln's Secretary of War (2017).

103. Louis Lusky, *United States of America, in* Constitutional Protection of Equality 43–44 (T. Koopmans, ed. 1975).

104. "Powers and Duties of United States Grand Juries," National Republican (Washington, DC), Oct. 31, 1881, p. 2 ("The following are extracts from a charge to the grand jury in the Circuit Court of the United States, delivered in 1872 by Mr. Justice Field, of the United States Supreme Court, presiding in that circuit: '... [T]here is a double duty cast upon you as grand jurors of this District; one a duty to the Government, or, more properly speaking, to society, to see that parties against whom there is just ground to charge the commission of crime shall be held to answer the charge; and on the other hand, a duty to the citizen to see that he is not subjected to prosecution upon accusations having *no better foundation than public clamor or private malice*. The Government has appointed the District-Attorney to represent its interest in the prosecution of parties charged with the commission of public offenses against the laws of the United States. He will, therefore, appear before you and present the accusations which the Government may desire to have considered by you. He will point out to you the laws which the Government deems to

have been violated, and will subpoena for your examination such witnesses as he may consider important, and also such other witnesses as you may direct.... You will not allow private prosecutors to intrude themselves into your presence and present accusations. Generally such parties are actuated by private enmity, and seek merely the gratification of their personal malice. * * * We have been led, gentlemen, to give these instructions upon the nature of your duties and the limits to the sphere of your investigations, because an impression widely prevails that the institution of the grand jury has outlived its usefulness, an impression which has been created from a disregard of those limits, and the facility with which it has, unfortunately, often been used as an instrument for the *gratification* of private malice.'") (italics in original); "King's Case Is Postponed," MEMPHIS DAILY COMMERCIAL (Memphis, TN), Nov. 25, 1890, p. 5 (noting that at 10:00 a.m. "yesterday morning" the Circuit Court of the United States "opened for business, with the Hon. E. S. Hammond presiding"; in charging the grand jury, Judge Hammond explained: "The District Attorney is the only prosecutor; there are no private prosecutors in United States courts; that their jurisdiction extended only over statutory offenses on the high seas, great lakes, rivers, navy yards, arsenals, etc."); "Among Illicit Distillers," PITTSBURGH POST (Pittsburgh, PA), Oct. 18, 1892, p. 3 ("The October term of the United States district court opened yesterday with Judge Buffington on the bench. In his charge to the grand jury Judge Buffington reminded the jurors that the United States district attorney was the prosecutor in all suits, and that there were no private prosecutors.").

105. Ireland, *supra* note 49, at 49 ("By the end of the nineteenth century, the high tribunals of Alabama, Florida, Iowa, Kansas, Kentucky, Maine, Minnesota, Mississippi, Nebraska, New Jersey, North Dakota, Texas, Utah, Vermont, and Virginia had upheld the legality of privately funded prosecutors. Most of these courts did not weigh the equities, but simply stated that the practice had been well-established and it was up to the legislature to change the law. Several, including that of Alabama and Kansas, candidly reflected upon the realities of criminal prosecution within their states, noting that public prosecutors were not infrequently young, inexperienced, and outclassed by highly paid expert defense attorneys. The Kansas Supreme Court also noted that in its state, assistance for the prosecution could only come from private sources, a condition that also prevailed in other states.").

106. Ireland, *supra* note 49, at 43, 46; *see also id.* at 47 ("Privately funded prosecution even found its way into the federal criminal justice system. In 1851, one Hanway of Pennsylvania was tried for committing treason against the United States by allegedly encouraging a band of African-Americans to assault and kill a slave owner from Maryland who had gone into Pennsylvania with a federal marshal to retrieve an escaped slave. The slave owner's family hired James Cooper, United States Senator from Pennsylvania, and R.M. Lee, a Philadelphia lawyer, to help the federal district attorney prosecute Hanway. The chief presiding judge at the trial, associate supreme court justice Robert C. Grier, found nothing illegal about the presence of privately funded prosecutors and even praised their efforts, which nonetheless were not sufficient to secure a conviction.").

107. ALBANY DAILY DEMOCRAT (Albany, OR), May 14, 1890, p. 4 ("The case of State of Oregon vs Arch McKinley, in which J W Will was private prosecutor, attracted the attention of the Justice court the fore part of last week. It seems defendant has been selling sewing machines for Mr Will and the trouble grew out of the division of the profits. The evidence went to show that the business was very lucrative and the jury evidently didn't blame Mack for trying to get more than his share of the spoils under the circumstances, for they returned a verdict of not guilty and recommended that the private prosecutor be taxed with the costs."); ALBANY DAILY DEMOCRAT (Albany, OR), Apr. 10, 1891, p. 4 (noting that the costs were "taxed against the private prosecutor" after the evidence against the defendants was found "insufficient").

108. PITTSBURGH GAZETTE (Pittsburgh, PA), July 8, 1850, p. 3 ("In Rush vs. the Commonwealth, 2nd Barr 189, it was said that as the office of the Attorney General is a public trust which involves the exercise of an almost boundless discretion by an officer, who ought to stand as impartial as a judge, it might be doubted whether even counsel employed by a private prosecutor should be heard, but that private counsel could at most be allowed to act by his permission and under his control. What impartiality is there to be expected from a private prosecutor, flushed with the excitement of victory or defeat? The officer (Attorney General) acts under the obligation of an oath, and at the peril of an impeachment—a private prosecutor under no obligation of responsibility at all, yet we are called upon, without a clear warrant, to let him wield at will the tremendous power of public prosecution.").

109. Rehberg v. Paulk, 566 U.S. 356, 364–66 (2012); *see also* Wheeler v. Nesbitt, 24 How. 544, 550, 16 L.Ed. 765 (1861) ("Undoubtedly, every person who puts the criminal law in force maliciously, and without any reasonable or probable cause, commits a wrongful act; and if the accused is thereby prejudiced, either in his person or property, the injury and loss so sustained constitute the proper foundation of an action to recover compensation"); Dinsman v. Wilkes, 12 How. 390, 402, 13 L.Ed. 1036 (1852) (no immunity "where a party had maliciously, and without probable cause, procured the plaintiff to be indicted or arrested for an offence of which he was not guilty"). A "private prosecutor" reference even worked its way into a section of the Restatement (Second) of Torts adopted in 1977. Restatement (Second) of Torts § 587 (1977); *see also* Udd v. City of Phoenix, No. CV-18-01616-PHX-DWL, 2020 WL 1536326 *24 (D. Ariz. Mar. 31, 2020) ("Under Section 587 of the Restatement (Second) of Torts, '[a] party to a private litigation or a private prosecutor or defendant in a criminal prosecution is absolutely privileged to publish defamatory matter concerning another in communications preliminary to a proposed judicial proceeding... if the matter has some relation to the proceeding.' Additionally, the comments to a different portion of the Restatement clarify that the phrase "communications preliminary to a proposed judicial proceeding" in Section 587 includes the submission of a criminal referral to a prosecutor's office.") (citing Restatement (Second) of Torts, § 598, cmt. e ("Formal or informal complaints to a prosecuting attorney or other law enforcement officer concerning violations of the criminal law are absolutely privileged under the rule stated in [section] 587.")); *compare id.* at *25 ("Nevertheless, the submission of a criminal referral doesn't automatically qualify as privileged conduct under Section 587. Comment (e) to Section 587 provides that 'the rule stated in this Section applies only when the communication has some relation to a proceeding that is contemplated in good faith and under serious consideration. The bare possibility that the proceeding might be instituted is not to be used as a cloak to provide immunity for defamation when the possibility is not seriously considered.' Here, there are disputed issues of fact as to whether Roberts actually believed the submission of the referrals would result in prosecution (which is different from whether the referrals were supported by probable cause), so Defendants are not entitled to summary judgment based upon a claim of absolute privilege.").

110. Leslie B. Arffa, *Note, Separation of Prosecutors*, 128 Yale L.J. 1078, 1095 (2019).

111. *E.g.*, Steven W. Perry & Duren Banks, "Prosecutors in State Courts, 2007—Statistical Tables," U.S. Department of Justice, Office of Justice Programs, Bureau of Justice Statistics (Dec. 2011), https://www.bjs.gov/content/pub/pdf/psc07st.pdf ("In 2007, 2,330 state prosecutors' offices served state judicial districts in the United States. The offices reported a total estimated budget of $5.8 billion in 2007 and employed nearly 78,000 attorneys, investigators, paralegals, and support staff. State prosecutors closed 2.9 million cases charged as felonies in state courts in 2007, approximately 94 cases for each prosecuting attorney on staff.").

112. Mugambi Jouet, *Reconciling the Conflicting Rights of Victims and Defendants at the International Criminal Court*, 26 St. Louis U. Pub. L. Rev. 249, 254–55 (2007) ("Unlike a civil claimant's participation, a private prosecutor's participation is not restricted to the reach of his civil claim for compensation, thereby enabling the private prosecutor to expressly seek the defendant's conviction in addition to damages. Nevertheless, government prosecutors can usually intervene and dismiss the case if they deem that prosecution is not justified. Countries have instituted different checks on the private prosecutor procedure, such as France's provision that the private prosecutor must pay for court costs and the accused's legal fees if the accused is found not guilty. Certain countries go even further, such as Spain, which allows felonies to be privately prosecuted by virtually any person, even if he is neither a victim nor a citizen, so long as the government has declined to prosecute the case.").

113. E.g., Equal Protection of the Laws in North Carolina, Report of the North Carolina Advisory Committee to the United States Commission on Civil Rights 1959–62, at 55 (1962) ("Negro attorneys in private practice sometimes appear with the solicitor in the role of private prosecutors. There are no Negroes employed by the State or counties in any of the solicitors' offices. The reason given was that none had applied.").

114. Brown, *supra* note 17, at 865–67; *see also id.* at 867 ("The standard common law model is that public prosecutors retain the power to take over privately filed charges and then either try the case

themselves, negotiate a plea bargain, or—more commonly when intervention occurs—dismiss the charges altogether.").

115. Jouet, *supra* note 112, 254–55.

116. Tyler Grove, *Are All Prosecutorial Activities "Inherently Governmental"? Applying State Safeguards for Victim-Retained Private Prosecutions to Outsourced Prosecutions*, 40 Pub. Cont. L.J. 911, 1002 (2011); *see also id.* at 1003–04 ("A number of distinctions exist between victim-retained private prosecutions and outsourced prosecutions. First, outsourced prosecutors are in privity with the state by virtue of their contract with the Government, while victim-retained private prosecutors have no such agreement with the Government. Victim-retained private prosecutors also typically bring cases that the Government has declined to prosecute itself. Outsourced prosecutors, on the other hand, only work on cases that the Government has chosen to bring (assuming that the Government has not impermissibly outsourced the initial decision of whether to prosecute). Another distinction is that victim-retained private prosecutors are "'required by the very standards of the profession to serve two masters'—the court that appointed her and the private client who pays her bills." Outsourced prosecutors, on the other hand, represent the state and not the victims of the crimes they are prosecuting.").

117. Roger A. Fairfax, Jr., *Delegation of the Criminal Prosecution Function to Private Actors*, 43 U.C. Davis L. Rev. 411, 426 (2009); *compare id.* at 436–37 ("When the government outsources the prosecution function or permits victim-retained lawyers to prosecute, the government delegates prosecutorial authority to private attorneys. These lawyers typically maintain private practices in addition to handling criminal prosecutions. In this sense, they are all part-time prosecutors. The notion that an attorney could serve simultaneously as both a prosecutor and a private practitioner has long been the subject of criticism from law reform commissions, the organized bar, and prosecutor advocacy groups. The moral hazard concerns presented when prosecutors also maintain private practices have fueled support for the full-time public prosecution norm. As such, critiques of part-time prosecutors largely have focused on ethical issues of conflicts of interest and potential corruption.").

118. Roger A. Fairfax, Jr., *Outsourcing Criminal Prosecution?: The Limits of Criminal Justice Privatization*, 2010 U. Chi. Legal F. 265, 280–81 (2010).

119. Jed Handelsman Shugerman, *Professionals, Politicos, and Crony Attorneys General: A Historical Sketch of the U.S. Attorney General as a Case for Structural Independence*, 87 Fordham L. Rev. 1965, 1986–87 (2019) ("[F]or much of English and American history, most prosecution was not an executive function at all because it was a *private* enterprise. In England, the vast majority of criminal prosecution was by private parties, as historians like John Langbein, Patrick Devlin, and many others have explained. The vast majority of American prosecutions were still private through the mid-nineteenth century, as Allen Steinberg and many other historians have demonstrated. The rough consensus is that the public prosecutor did not overtake private prosecution in America until after the Civil War, and yet private prosecution continued deep into the twentieth century. Even today, New Hampshire, New Jersey, Pennsylvania, Rhode Island, Virginia, and Texas allow private citizens to serve a role in criminal prosecutions.") (italics in original).

120. John L. Costello, Virginia Criminal Law and Procedure § 70.13 (4th ed. 2012) ("Although charges are brought by Commonwealth's attorneys, Virginia procedure allows for victim rights in the criminal process. Victims seeking retribution or punishment may hire private prosecutors to help the public prosecutor bring a case to justice. This is not an absolute right, but remains in the sound discretion of the trial court. As recently as 1997, the court reiterated this practice as a holdover from common law prosecution. At all times, however, the public prosecutor must keep 'continuous control' of the case because the private prosecutor's first duty is to be a zealous advocate for his client. The Virginia Court of Appeals made a nice distinction recently. Acknowledging the unacceptable *Cantrell* situation where the private prosecution is also counsel for the family's civil efforts to gain compensation for the defendant's misconduct, Judge Elder wrote for the Court that the mere unaccompanied fact that the victim's family was paying the private prosecutor's fees could not be counted a disqualifying conduct. Were that true, practically all private prosecutors would be barred, an intolerable result because private prosecutors have been permitted at common law and the general Assembly of Virginia has made no effort to curtail the practice."); Simon Schama, Rough Crossings: Britain, the Slaves and the American Revolution 41

(2005) (noting the use of a private prosecution for assault); AIMÉ MUYOBOKE KARIMUNDA, THE DEATH PENALTY IN AFRICA: THE PATH TOWARDS ABOLITION (2016) (in discussing Ethiopian law, observing that "[t]he *Fetha Negest* introduced capital punishment without instituting the prosecutor" and without "indicat[ing] the executioner either"; "[a]ccordingly, individuals personally initiated and prosecuted the case" and "[t]his anarchy meant that the victim's family had the latitude of determining the method of execution"; "Private prosecution of criminal cases and execution of penal sanctions undermined the policy of reconciliation. Indeed, the new law had not formally repealed compensation as a means of reconciliation. Over the years, the government felt concerned by this private justice and took measures."); *see also* Robert Allen Sedler, *The Development of Legal Systems: The Ethiopian Experience*, 53 IOWA L. REV. 562, 625 (1967) (discussing Ethiopian criminal procedure and the use of private prosecution, and noting that the Ethiopian Criminal Procedure Code "attempts to reconcile the interest of the state and the interest of the private prosecutor").

121. Rochez v. Mittleton, 839 F. Supp. 1075, 1081 (S.D.N.Y. 1993) ("Private prosecutors, while certainly not the norm, have been used in a variety of settings and jurisdictions in this country. The prosecutorial function is not, therefore, the exclusive prerogative of the state.") (citing New Jersey v. Imperiale, 773 F. Supp. 747 (D. N.J. 1991) (discussing variety of jurisdictions employing private prosecutors); Young v. United States ex rel. Vuitton et Fils, S.A., 481 U.S. 787 (1987) (holding that courts have authority to appoint private attorneys to prosecute contempt actions)).

122. *E.g.*, Douglas E. Beloof, *Weighing Crime Victims' Interests in Judicially Crafted Criminal Procedure*, 56 CATH. U. L. REV. 1135, 1138 (2007) ("In early America, private prosecutions were dominant. The system of private prosecution had been 'preferred because it avoided the tyranny of government prosecutors and the expense of providing for public prosecution.' A recent overview of the shift from private prosecution to public prosecution reveals that private prosecution survived in the United States well into the 1800s, and in petty offenses continues as a viable procedure to this day. In private prosecutions, citizens bring charges and hire counsel to prosecute crimes themselves. As Professor McDonald recounts: 'Even after identification and arrest, the victim carried the burden of prosecution. He retained an attorney and paid to have the indictment written and the offender prosecuted.' Other legal historians report that private prosecution was dominant. "Professor Nelson's history of a typical Massachusetts county between 1760 and 1810 reports that criminal trials were 'in reality a contest between subjects rather that contests between government and subjects.'" Other historians acknowledge the pre- and post-colonial prevalence of private prosecution. In sum, discretion in day-to-day litigation was ceded to private prosecutors.").

123. Allen Steinberg, *From Private Prosecution to Plea Bargaining: Criminal Prosecution, the District Attorney, and American Legal History*, 30 CRIME & DELINQ. 568, 571 (1984).

124. Carolyn B. Ramsey, *The Discretionary Power of "Public" Prosecutors in Historical Perspective*, 39 AM. CRIM. L. REV. 1309, 1322 (2002). But over time, some colonies grew skeptical of private prosecutions, the practice inherited from the mother country. *Id.* ("However, 'the colonies began to experiment with forms of publicly funded prosecution' because '[t]he system of private prosecution was criticized as elitist, inefficient, and vindictive.'") (quoting Juan Cardenas, *The Crime Victim in the Prosecutorial Process*, 9 HARV. J.L. & PUB. POL'Y 357, 369 (1986)).

125. JOHN D. BESSLER, KISS OF DEATH: AMERICA'S LOVE AFFAIR WITH THE DEATH PENALTY 16 (2003).

126. "Faulder, Joseph (Profile)," THE CANADIAN ENCYCLOPEDIA (last edited Dec. 16, 2013), https://www.thecanadianencyclopedia.ca/en/article/joseph-faulder-profile.

127. "Execution Report: Joseph Faulder," Texas Execution Information Center, http://www.txexecutions.org/reports/178-Joseph-Faulder.htm; *see also* Faulder v. State, 745 S.W.2d 327 (1987) (en banc); Mark Warren, *Bordering on Discord: The Impact of the Death Penalty on U.S.-Canada Relations*, 2006 J. INST. JUST. INT'L STUD. 79, 88 (2006) ("Canadian citizen Joseph Stanley Faulder was sentenced to death in Texas in 1977 for a murder committed during a residential burglary gone terribly wrong. After his conviction was reversed on appeal and the local authorities expressed doubt over their ability to retry the case, the victim's family hired private prosecutors to secure another death sentence."); Kelly Trainer, *The Vienna Convention on Consular Relations in the United States Courts*, 13 TRANSNAT'L LAW. 227, 249 n.141 (2000) ("This was Faulder's second conviction for the crime. The events that lead up to this conviction merit comment.

Faulder originally confessed after four days of interrogation. He signed a written statement confessing to the murder. He further admitted he had an accomplice named Linda McCann. In 1979, the Texas Court of Criminal Appeals overturned Faulder's conviction, finding that the confession was illegally obtained. The state found without the confession, there was insufficient evidence to re-prosecute Faulder. Jack Phillips, the brother of the victim, hired private prosecutors upon learning that the state was considering offering Faulder life imprisonment instead of the death penalty. Even though Linda McCann was eligible for the death penalty under Texas law, the private prosecutors offered her immunity and $15,000 in exchange for her testimony. Her husband was given $2000 to corroborate her testimony, as required by Texas law since McCann was an accomplice. In Faulder's second trial, his court-appointed attorney did not call any witnesses and failed to investigate Faulder's background. During sentencing, Faulder's attorney did not attempt to rebut the testimony of the psychiatrist who claimed that Faulder was an untreatable sociopath who would certainly kill again. In July 1981, Faulder was convicted for the second time and sentenced to death.") (citing Amnesty International, *United States of America: Adding Insult to Injury: the case of Joseph Stanley Faulder* (Nov. 1998), *available in* AI Index: AMR 51/86/98 and < http://www.amnesty.it/ailib/aipub/1998/AMR/25108698.htm>); John Cary Sims & Linda E. Carter, *Emerging Importance of the Vienna Convention on Consular Relations as a Defense Tool*, 22 CHAMPION 28, 28 (Sept./Oct. 1998) ("When Sandra Babcock graduated from law school in 1991, she became a staff attorney at the Texas Resource Center, where her practice was limited to indigent criminal defense. One of her early assignments was the case of Joseph Stanley Faulder, a Canadian citizen who had been convicted of a 1975 murder and sentenced to death.").

128. Tony Rizzo & Savanna Smith, "Despite Doubts, Judge Allows Private Prosecutors in Case of Two Slain Deputies," KANSAS CITY STAR, Jan. 9, 2019, https://www.kansascity.com/news/local/crime/article224079520.html.

129. *See, e.g.*, Maggie Kolb, *Switch Hitter: From Prosecution to Defense and Back Again, Tom Bath Is at Home on Either Side of the Courtroom*, MO. & KAN. SUPER LAWYERS MAG. (Nov. 2008), *available at* https://www.superlawyers.com/kansas/article/switch-hitter/a2586ea2-3e06-4e43-b659-980df2c59315.html ("Because of his reputation for hard work and success from either side of the courtroom, Bath has had the opportunity to assist the state as a private prosecutor through a provision of Kansas law that allows victims of crimes or families of victims to hire outside counsel to work with the prosecution. In 2004, the family of 40-year-old former Manhattan city prosecutor, lawyer and mediator Carmin Ross hired Bath as a private prosecutor after Ross was beaten and fatally stabbed in her home northwest of Lawrence on Nov. 13, 2003. Earlier that year, Ross divorced her husband of 18 years, Thomas Murray, a Kansas State University English professor, and was reportedly just weeks away from moving with their young daughter to California and marrying her new fiancé.").

130. Tony Rizzo, "Families Hire Private Lawyers to Help Prosecute Alleged Killer of Two WyCo Deputies," KANSAS CITY STAR (Kansas City, MO), Dec. 26, 2018, https://www.kansascity.com/news/local/crime/article223566290.html.

131. GEORGE H. DESSION, CRIMINAL LAW, ADMINISTRATION AND PUBLIC ORDER: SELECTED CASES, STATUTES, COMMENTARIES, AND OTHER MATERIALS ON CRIMINAL LAW, PROCEDURE AND POLICY 357 (1948).

132. CAROL HARLOW, UNDERSTANDING TORT LAW 1 (3d ed. 2005); EDWARD JENKS, A SHORT HISTORY OF ENGLISH LAW FROM THE EARLIEST TIMES TO THE END OF THE YEAR 1911, at 13 (1912); J.W. CECIL TURNER, KENNY'S OUTLINES OF CRIMINAL LAW 1 (18th ed. 1964).

133. ROSCOE LEWIS ASHLEY, MEDIEVAL CIVILIZATION: A TEXTBOOK FOR SECONDARY SCHOOLS 330 (1916) ("Among the early Germans, and to some extent in later times, there existed a law of 'fist-right,' that is, the right of personal vengeance. If one man killed another, the relatives of the latter took up the quarrel and any one of them might murder the assassin. In later times when one man accused another of crime, a duel or wager of battle was used to learn whether the accuser or the accused person was right."); MARY BONAVENTURE MROZ, DIVINE VENGEANCE: A STUDY IN THE PHILOSOPHICAL BACKGROUNDS OF THE REVENGE MOTIF AS IT APPEARS IN SHAKESPEARE'S CHRONICLE HISTORY PLAYS 71 (1971) ("Not only the right of appeal, but under certain circumstances, even private vengeance for kin was legally sanctioned, despite the progressive development of legal machinery. From the time of King Alfred English law

permitted private revenge to a husband finding his wife in adultery. A London charter of the thirteenth century sanctions revenge taken by a citizen on a man of the king or baron, who should billet himself by force in the former's house. A full century after private war had lost legal sanction in England there is acceptance of Christine de Pisan's judgment that if prisoners of war be slain without trial by King's Counsel, then 'I tell the that parents and frendes myght pursue therfore as for wronge doon.'"); *id.* ("The evidence examined points to the fact that in the Renaissance English popular opinion accepted the duty of avenging the blood of kin, by legal means, if possible—by private revenge, if convenient."); PETER ARNADE & WALTER PREVENIER, HONOR, VENGEANCE, AND SOCIAL TROUBLE: PARDON LETTERS IN THE BURGUNDIAN LOW COUNTRIES 27 (2015) ("In England blood feuds were still a legally recognized practice in the eleventh and twelfth centuries, but ceases by the reign of Edward I (1272–1307). In Scotland and Wales, however, blood feuds survived until the early sixteenth century."); CARL LUDWIG VON BAR, A HISTORY OF CONTINENTAL CRIMINAL LAW 119 (Thomas S. Bell, trans. 1916); *see also id.* at 120 ("Crime in modern penal justice is considered chiefly as an infraction of the law in its objective sense, and punishment as a means of restoring public law and order. But the sole concern in the early ages was the individual's injury; it was left to the injured party himself to procure reparation .... This authority to wreak vengeance ('Hævn') on the offender, by the aid of his kin if needed, was limited only by public opinion, founded on the natural sense of right and custom and usage. A feud, or relation of hostility, arose between the wrongdoer and the sufferer, and their respective blood-kindred; this could be settled by reconciliation alone, which frequently was attainable only after a feud ('Feide') of long duration. Such a pact was generally conditioned on the payment of a fine ('Bøde'); this was deemed to be not only reparation for the physical damage, but also satisfaction for the impeached honor."); *id.* at 120–21 ("The narratives of various events, found in the Sagas (especially from the close of the 800s to the commencement of the 1100s), which undoubtedly have a historical basis, describe almost exclusively gross acts of violence and wrong, mayhem and murder. In the latter case it behooved the kin of the slain to wreak blood vengeance (Sagas of Niala, Viga Styrs, Heidaviga, Grettis, and Vatnsdæla). While it was held to be a sacred duty not to leave unavenged the slaying of kin, and hence the acceptance of money satisfaction was deemed dishonorable, nevertheless, the circumstances were taken into consideration, especially the provocation and the mode (whether the crime was committed in the heat of passion or deliberately), and also the conduct of the wrongdoer subsequently. On this latter point the early law-texts of Sweden and Norway contain extensive provisions. Thus, under the Gotland law-text, the slayer could tender reparation for the life only after a year had elapsed; during this period he, with his nearest relatives, must at first abide in hallowed places of refuge, or sanctuaries, and thereafter in distant and unfrequented localities, in order to escape the 'Hævn', or exaction of the toll of blood for blood. Should the tender not be accepted at the expiration of that period, he must resume such a mode of life for the two following years; but the law expressly declares that the acceptance of the 'Bøde' (or, amount of penalty and satisfaction) after the lapse of the first year should not disgrace the family kin. By the Östgöta law-text the tender could be made only after three years; and similar requirements are contained in the early Gula-thing law-text. Until expiation is made (according to Andreas Suneson) the murderer must absent himself from the sight of his opponent, lest he offend him by his presence."); LESTER BERNHARDT ORFIELD, THE GROWTH OF SCANDINAVIAN LAW 280 (2002) ("From 900 to 1100 kin vengeance existed as to murder, and the acceptance of a money satisfaction was thought to be dishonorable except in certain limited situations. Private fines might be arranged for murder and other violent felonies. The introduction of Christianity resulted in limitations on private vengeance. Church mulcts might be collected under the church law of Skåne."); EMOTION, VIOLENCE, VENGEANCE AND LAW IN THE MIDDLE AGES: ESSAYS IN HONOUR OF WILLIAM IAN MILLER 221 (Kate Gilbert & Stephen D. White, eds., 2018) (noting of Scandinavia that "feuds went on ... even after King Haakon formulated a prohibition against taking kin vengeance in 1260. As sources from the fourteenth century onward make abundantly clear, local feuding cultures persisted for centuries to come."); Pragya Vohra, *Creating Kin, Extending Authority: Blood-Brotherhood and Power in Medieval Iceland, in* THE PALGRAVE HANDBOOK OF MASCULINITY AND POLITICAL CULTURE IN EUROPE 115 (Christopher Fletcher, Sean Brady, Rachel E. Moss & Lucy Riall, eds. 2018) ("[F]eud touches upon a range of interpersonal relationships that could affect an individual in medieval Iceland. Kinship obligations included the requirement for kinsmen to avenge one another. This sentiment is enshrined in Icelandic law laid down in *Grágás* which confers the right to vengeance on an injured party and his supporters. Individuals often sought the protection and support of their kin as well as their chieftains in the pursuit of vengeance."); *see also* FREDERICK O. BLUE, WHEN A STATE GOES DRY: A BRIEF STUDY IN LAW ENFORCEMENT 17 (1916) ("The lay citizen assumes that society—the state—always has prosecuted offenses against the individual and his property. Such, however, is not the fact. Even in the preserved records of European peoples punishment for injuries to the person or his property was left to the injured person or his blood kin. Vengeance was law. Criminal law began as private vengeance."); CARLO CALISSE, A HISTORY OF ITALIAN LAW 88, 90–93, 102, 173, 272, 330–31, 335, 401 (trans. Layton B. Register, 1928) (discussing "private vengeance"); G. G. COULTON, THE MEDIEVAL VILLAGE 188 (1925) ("The right of private vengeance was recognized by law far down into the Middle Ages."); VENGEANCE IN MEDIEVAL EUROPE: A READER 59, 69, 71, 73, 147, 158 (Daniel Lord Smail & Kelly Gibson, eds., 2009) (discussing killings by "next of kin," the "pay of *wergeld* for a slaying," and "*chrenecruda* (i.e., involving the kin in the payment of composition for homicide")).

134. State v. Myerowitz, 439 N.J. Super. 341, 108 A.3d 671 (2015).

135. STEINBERG, *supra* note 19, at 24–69, 152–157 (describing private prosecutions in nineteenth-century Philadelphia); Yeazell, *supra* note 52, at 692 ("Until late into the nineteenth century, most criminal prosecutions were undertaken by private parties; the participation of state prosecutors was unusual."); Ireland, *supra* note 49, at 43 ("In colonial America, because of Dutch (and perhaps French) practice and the expansion of the office of attorney general, public officials came to dominate the prosecution of crimes. By 1820, most states had established local public prosecutors known by a variety of titles, including state's attorney, county attorney, district attorney, and commonwealth's attorney. Yet, because of deficiencies in the office of public prosecutor, privately funded prosecutors constituted a significant element of the state criminal justice system throughout the nineteenth century."); O'Neill, *supra* note 17, at 673–74 ("[P]rivate criminal prosecutions in the American colonies appear to have been commonplace, but not exclusive. Scholarship tracing the origins of the prosecutorial function in colonial America demonstrates that colonial legislatures, borrowing from the Dutch, often established offices for public prosecutors. Until the late-nineteenth century, however, private prosecutions dominated the legal landscape."); D. Josev Brewer, *The Work of the United States Attorney's Offices Across the Sequential Intercept Model*, 12 LIBERTY U. L. REV. 265, 265–66 (2018) ("Jewish law recognized the role of private citizens to accomplish a criminal prosecution insofar as two private accusers were required to indict before a tribunal, called 'the Synhedrian.' Indeed, it is unequivocally America's prosecutorial heritage too, where here in the colonies and through the time of the early Republic, private prosecution was adapted from English practice and pursued, in certain municipalities, through at least the middle of the nineteenth century."); Eric S. Fish, *Prosecutorial Constitutionalism*, 90 S. CAL. L. REV. 237, 244–45 (2017) ("In the old English system, criminal prosecution was a private law matter—victims brought criminal cases against those who had harmed them. Similarly, in the United States before 1800, the main approach to criminal prosecution was for victims to pursue charges against the accused."); Olson, *supra* note 72, at 32 ("At the time when the founding fathers gathered in Philadelphia to hash out the foundation and fabric of American law, the victim was the primary player in criminal trials. Private prosecutors passed the bar to argue the guilt of the accused. At a time when crime control was not generally considered a responsibility of the state, the English settlers brought the legal tradition of private prosecution with them and continued its use into the nineteenth century. In that model, victims would often make an arrest and hire a private attorney who would then conduct the prosecution against the perpetrator; furthermore, the state's role, if any, was to help facilitate the process for a fee. Intuitively, the victim neither cared for nor adhered to the presumption of innocence much less the due process rights of the accused. Rather, the victim utilized the court system as a civilized means of retribution against an assailant whom she knew to be guilty."); Ryan W. Scott, *Standing to Appeal and Executive Non-Defense of Federal Law After the Marriage Cases*, 89 IND. L.J. 67, 79 (2014) ("For over a century, the law of many states authorized private parties to initiate criminal prosecutions in the State's name to redress injuries to the State as sovereign. Private prosecutors need not have suffered any personal injury, were not public officials, and had no formal agency relationship with the State. Yet they routinely filed court actions on behalf of the State to enforce the criminal law, as authorized by state procedures.").

136. Brown, *supra* note 17, at 868–69 ("Early public prosecutors were paid by the case or the conviction and pursued cases from private complainants. But by the mid-nineteenth century, every state had

public prosecutor offices of some sort. Increasingly, they were full-time and accompanied by public police forces. In this context, private prosecutions diminished, then vanished."); Margaret H. Lemos, *Privatizing Public Litigation*, 104 GEO. L.J. 515, 517 (2016) ("Before we had a United States Department of Justice (DOJ), it was commonplace for private lawyers to handle the federal government's work. And private prosecutions were once the norm in many jurisdictions. Over time, however, our system 'publicized' most litigation in the name of the government, shifting control from private actors to salaried public servants."); ERIC STOVER, THE WITNESSES: WAR CRIMES AND THE PROMISE OF JUSTICE IN THE HAGUE 24 (2005) ("In colonial America, victims in most colonies were considered central actors in the system and, if they succeeded in winning their claim, stood to benefit financially .... There were exceptions, however. In areas settled by the Dutch in the seventeenth century (such as New Netherland—parts of which are now Connecticut, New York, New Jersey, Pennsylvania, and Delaware), local governments eschewed private prosecutions for public ones by an official called a schout. Even when the British took New York from the Dutch in 1664, criminal prosecutions remained much as they had been under the Dutch administration."); *id.* ("By the late 1800s private prosecutions in the United States had given way to public ones."); OHIO OFFICE OF CRIMINAL JUSTICE SERVICES, STATE OF CRIME AND JUSTICE IN OHIO 13 (2004) (noting that "reliance on private prosecutions faded from practice only when law enforcement agencies began dramatically improving their investigative and evidence methods"). Practices around the world varied widely, and so, not surprisingly, immigration patterns—and the views and customs of new immigrants—influenced the way in which prosecutions were handled in individual colonies and locales. *E.g.*, 8 ERIC A. WALKER, ED., THE CAMBRIDGE HISTORY OF THE BRITISH EMPIRE 862 (1963) (noting of criminal procedure in courts of Holland: "In criminal matters it was regulated by an Ordinance of 1570. There was no right of private prosecution; the Fiscal or, in the case of country crimes, the landdrost of the district acted as public prosecutor; the system of preparatory examination was already in force; the accused was competent to give evidence and might be interrogated; testimony was not as a rule taken in open court."); DENNIS SULLIVAN, THE PUNISHMENT OF CRIME IN COLONIAL NEW YORK: THE DUTCH EXPERIENCE IN ALBANY DURING THE SEVENTEENTH CENTURY 28 (1997) ("The criminal justice ordinance of 1570 curbed these powers by limiting private prosecution as well as the right of private individuals to grant pardon or remit penalty."); "Prosecution: History of the Public Prosecutor," Encyclopedia.com, https://www.encyclopedia.com/law/legal-and-political-magazines/prosecution-history-public-prosecutor ("While public prosecution was superimposed on private prosecution in most colonies, it emerged more directly in others, especially in areas that had been settled by the Dutch in the seventeenth century. In these settlements—constituting New Netherlands and counties of parts of what are now Connecticut, New York, New Jersey, Pennsylvania, and Delaware—the Dutch brought public prosecution with them. Prosecutions were conducted by an official called a *schout*. When the British took New York from the Dutch in 1664, criminal prosecution remained much as it had been under the Dutch administration, except that the *schout* was replaced by a sheriff."); *see also* LOUIS J. PALMER, JR., THE DEATH PENALTY IN THE UNITED STATES: A COMPLETE GUIDE TO FEDERAL AND STATE LAWS 62 (2d ed. 2014) ("One aspect of the Dutch system of government that was brought with the colonists had a profound effect on Anglo-American jurisprudence. The legal system of the Dutch had an office called the 'schout.' Legal scholars rarely acknowledge the point, but it was the principles undergirding the office of schout which shaped the prosecutorial system that America would eventually adopt and utilize to this day."); *id.* ("The schout was a public prosecutor. Unlike the chaotic system of prosecution tolerated by the common law, Dutch law entrusted the task of prosecuting criminals in a single office—the office of schout. Dutch colonists did not haul their neighbors into criminal courts on real or monetarily imagined charges. If a criminal offense occurred, the office of schout prosecuted the crime."); DREWRY'S DERBY MERCURY (Derby, England), Aug. 27, 1773, p. 3 (referring to "an Officer called the Schout, who acts in every Town as a Sub-Sheriff"); "London, August 17," MARYLAND GAZETTE (Annapolis, MD), Nov. 11, 1773, p. 1 (same); "Description of the Government of the Seven United Provinces," THE TIMES (London, England), Aug 8, 1787, p. 2 ("The next office of weight and authority to that of the Burgo-masters of cities, is that of Schout, or Bailiff. He is intrusted with the direction of hospitals, lunatics, orphans and paupers. It is his province to keep order in the towns; he receives informations, takes cognizance of crimes, arrests and commits to prison, prosecutes offenders before the Sheriffs, and is charged with the execution of the sentence. He has a right of appeal to the Provincial High Court from the decision of the Sheriffs, when he thinks their sentence too favourable to the prisoner. As he is the first minister of the law, and the only officer whose duty it is to prosecute offences committed against the civil magistrate, it is of the utmost importance, that the person who fills this office should be a man of worth and integrity.").

137. William Ortman, *Probable Cause Revisited*, 60 Stan. L. Rev. 511, 548–49 n.207 (2016); *see also id.* at 549 n.207 ("By the late nineteenth century, prosecutorial offices in urban centers were staffed by full-time criminal justice professionals."); *id.* ("In the federal system, prosecutors became full-time only in the middle of the twentieth century.").

138. "Criminal Court," Pittsburgh Daily Post (Pittsburgh, PA), Jan. 15, 1868, p. 1 ("The case of the Commonwealth vs. Joseph McMullen and Thomas Hughes, indictment, felonious assault and battery, James Miller, private prosecutor, was taken up."); "Criminal Court," Pittsburgh Daily Post (Pittsburgh, PA), Jan. 21, 1868, p. 1 ("The case of the Commonwealth vs. James I. McKee, indicted for perjury was the first called up. Wm. Lock was the private prosecutor."); "The Courts," Pittsburgh Daily Post (Pittsburgh, PA), Apr. 21, 1868, p. 1 ("John Mealy was arraigned upon a charge of false pretenses. Thomas J. Campbell appeared as private prosecutor."); "The Courts," Pittsburgh Daily Post (Pittsburgh, PA), July 3, 1868, p. 1 ("Commonwealth vs. George Chess; indictment, larceny; F. Weigand, private prosecutors.").

139. Eric M. Freedman, *Habeas Corpus in Three Dimensions Dimension II: Habeas Corpus as a Legal Remedy*, 8 Ne. U. L.J. 1, 44–48 (2016) ("A truly useful history of private prosecution in America has yet to be written. Notwithstanding some initial efforts by academics, lawyers, and courts, the story of the evolving relationship between public and private prosecution on this side of the Atlantic, which varied in the past between jurisdictions and which is still in transition, has not been told in any comprehensive and well-documented way, with the result that much of the recent discussion has taken place with only a shallow grounding in primary sources. 'A lot of research remains to be done ... and the story is on the whole rather murky.'"); *see also* Jason Twede, "Going Public: How the Government Assumed the Authority to Prosecute in the Southern United States," Ph.D. dissertation, University of North Dakota (May 2016), p. 11 ("There has been no comprehensive evaluation of the history of private prosecution in the United States. Thus, we do not know exactly the practice ceased.").

140. Brown, *supra* note 17, at 867 n.75 ("By the end of the nineteenth century, state and federal justice systems were firmly committed to the principle that prosecution is an exclusive power of public officials in which private victims have no role or standing.") (citing Malley v. Lane, 115 A. 674, 676 (Conn. 1921); *cf.* Linda R.S. v. Richard D., 410 U.S. 614, 619 (1973) ("[A] citizen lacks standing to contest the policies of the prosecuting authority when he himself is neither prosecuted nor threatened with prosecution. ... [I]n American jurisprudence at least, a private citizen lacks a judicially cognizable interest in the prosecution or nonprosecution of another.")); Vt. Stat. Ann. tit. 15, § 1108(e) (2015) (codifying that the state's attorney should prosecute criminal contempt cases); Robertson v. United States *ex rel.* Watson, 560 U.S. 272, 281 (2010) (per curiam) (Roberts, C.J., dissenting) (stating that private prosecution of criminal contempt cases should be prohibited); People v. Eubanks, 927 P.2d. 310, 315 (Cal. 1996) (holding that all criminal prosecutions must be prosecuted in the name of the people of California and by their authority) (citing Cal. Gov't Code § 100(d) (West 2013)); DiSabatino v. Salicete, 671 A.2d 1344, 1353 (Del. 1996) (following *Young* and holding that an attorney for the beneficiary of an order in a civil proceeding may not represent the party in a subsequent criminal contempt prosecution); Rogers v. State, 348 S.E.2d 888, 889 (Ga. Ct. App. 1986) (holding that private parties are prohibited from acting as private prosecutors in criminal cases); Dep't of Soc. Servs. *ex rel.* Montero v. Montero, 758 P.2d 690, 693 (Haw. Ct. App. 1988) (holding that interested private prosecutors may not prosecute criminal contempt actions); State *ex rel.* LaMere v. Young, 192 N.W.2d 186, 187 (Minn. 1971) (per curiam) (holding that a petitioner's attorney may not act as a special prosecutor in a contempt action); State v. Warford, 389 N.W.2d 575, 582 (Neb. 1986) (stating that private prosecutors are not permitted); Rogowicz v. O'Connell, 786 A.2d 841, 844 (N.H. 2001) (holding that interested parties may not prosecute criminal contempt cases); State v. Valentine, 864 A.2d 433, 435–36 (N.J. Super. Ct. App. Div. 2005) (setting certification requirements for private prosecutors that disqualify interested parties from prosecuting criminal contempt); *In re* Mowery, 169 P.2d 835, 842–43 (Wash. Ct. App. 2007) (holding that Washington State law requires disinterested prosecutors); Trecost v. Trecost, 502 S.E.2d 445, 449 (W. Va. 1988) (holding that it is unconstitutional for a private, interested party to prosecute a criminal contempt case).

141. Bessler, *supra* note 21, at 512 ("[S]everal jurisdictions in the United States still allow the use of privately retain prosecutors for interested parties."); *id.* at 529 ("Although a growing number of states prohibit the use of private prosecutors, many jurisdictions adhere to the rule allowing interested parties to retain such prosecutors. These latter jurisdictions differ as to the permissible scope private prosecutors can play in such actions. While three states, Alabama, Montana, and Ohio, allow private prosecutors to participate without the consent or supervision of the district attorney, the majority of jurisdictions allow participation only with the public prosecutor's consent and retention of control over the case."); Venckus v. City of Iowa, 930 N.W.2d 792, 815 (Iowa 2019) (Appel, J., concurring in part and dissenting in part) ("In Iowa, public prosecutors have worked alongside private prosecutors since before the 1857 constitutional convention. At the constitutional convention, Mr. Harris noted that, oftentimes, private prosecutors were employed to initially present a case to a magistrate, after which they 'let the matter go to court, when the State will take charge of it. They look to the prosecuting attorney to take charge of it in the courts.'") (*quoting* 1 The Debates of the Constitutional Convention of the State of Iowa 476 (W. Blair Lord rep., 1857), www.statelibraryofiowa.org/services/collections/law-library/iaconst).... Across the country, both public and private prosecutors were subject to suit for misconduct. Private prosecutors could be sued for malicious prosecution where, for instance, they caused wrongful imprisonment or induced the seizure of property.").

142. *See, e.g.*, Rochez v. Mittleton, 839 F. Supp. 1075 (S.D.N.Y. 1993) (dismissing section 1983 action against court officers, city, and district attorney after court officer initiated private criminal prosecution of plaintiff for disorderly conduct pursuant to city policy allowing private individuals to commence criminal actions, and holding that initiation by court officer of private criminal prosecution did not constitute state action); *see also id.* at 1081 ("The private citizens prosecuting these cases are not acting jointly with the state officials, for the gravamen of Rochez's complaint is that the state officials are not acting at all. *See Lugar,* 457 U.S. at 941, 102 S.Ct. at 2755 (private party's joint participation with state officials in seizure of property sufficient to characterize private party as 'state actor' for purposes of the Fourteenth Amendment.). Under the 'symbiotic relationship' test established in *Burton v. Wilmington Parking Auth.*, 365 U.S. 715, 725, 81 S. Ct. 856, 861, 6 L.Ed.2d 45 (1961), an action will be considered that of the State if the State has 'so far insinuated itself into a position of interdependence with [the acting party] that it must be recognized as a joint participant in the challenged activity....' Again, since Rochez's complaint alleges that state officials are absent from prosecutorial decisions, Rochez's allegations can not meet the *Burton* standard. State law did not compel the Court Officers' prosecution of Rochez, *see Adickes v. S.H. Kress & Co.*, 398 U.S. 144, 170, 90 S. Ct. 1598, 1615, 26 L.Ed.2d 142 (1970), and the state's mere acquiescence in a private action does not convert that action into state action. *Flagg Bros., Inc. v. Brooks,* 436 U.S. 149, 164, 98 S. Ct. 1729, 1737, 56 L.Ed.2d 185 (1978)."); *id.* at 1081–82 ("The only involvement of the City that Rochez can allege in the present case is that private individuals are initiating prosecutions pursuant to the Municipal Policy. Rochez does not allege that the District Attorney's office has a policy of conducting unconstitutional prosecutions itself; according to her, as soon as the District Attorney's office gets involved, the unconstitutional behavior ceases. Nor does she allege that the DA's office ratifies any unconstitutional prosecutions brought by private citizens, thus adopting the unconstitutional behavior. She simply states the District Attorney is negligent in permitting a policy of allowing private citizens to bring unconstitutional prosecutions. Rochez has failed to allege the 'something more,' beyond action pursuant to the Municipal Policy, which might make the actions of private prosecutors in this case attributable to the City. Since the municipal policy can not, as a matter of law, have proximately caused Rochez's injuries and because the actions of the Court Officer Defendants are not fairly attributable to the City, Rochez's complaint must be dismissed.").

143. Rachel E. Barkow, *Criminal Justice Reform and the Courts*, 10/15/2019 U. Chi. L. Rev. Online 1 (2019) ("Prosecutors seem to be the primary target for criminal justice reformers today, and with good reason: they are key gatekeepers to whether criminal charges get brought or not, and the particular charges they bring often dictate a defendant's sentence. In a world dominated by plea bargains, prosecutors are essentially the final adjudicators in most criminal cases.").

144. Carrie Johnson, "Federal Executions Set to Resume After 17 Years with 3 Deaths Scheduled Soon," NPR, July 10, 2020, https://www.npr.org/2020/07/10/889667257/federal-executions-set-to-resume-after-17-years-with-3-deaths-scheduled-soon; Michael Tarm, "Report: Federal Execution Numbers

Top States' for 1st Time," Associated Press, Dec. 16, 2020, https://apnews.com/article/donald-trump-coronavirus-pandemic-executions-736b68c22e821be7c5faa85f1bf0b245; Michael Tarm & Michael Kunzelman, Trump Administration Carries Out 13th and Final Execution," Associated Press, Jan. 15, 2021, https://apnews.com/article/donald-trump-wildlife-conoravirus-pandemic-crime-terre-haute-28e44c-c5c026dc16472751bbde0ead50.

145. Gilliéron, *supra* note 59, at 40 ("The criminal justice system in colonial America reflected the English common law tradition. In common law, a crime was viewed as a wrong against an individual rather than against the state."); Hale v. Henkel, 201 U.S. 43, 59 (1906) ("Under the ancient English system, criminal prosecutions were instituted at the suit of private prosecutors, to which the King lent his name in the interest of the public peace and good order of society. In such cases the usual practice was to prepare the proposed indictment and lay it before the grand jury for their consideration. There was much propriety in this, as the most valuable function of the grand jury was not only to examine into the commission of crimes, but to stand between the prosecutor and the accused, and to determine whether the charge was founded upon credible testimony or was dictated by malice or personal ill will."); Ben Wilson, The Making of Victorian Values: Decency and Dissent in Britain: 1789–1837 (2007) ("In the later seventeenth and early eighteenth centuries the Society for the Reformation of Manners, a private prosecution society, had brought to account some 91,000 immoral people in thirty-three years, from prostitutes and vendors of obscene material to shopkeepers and publicans who traded on Sunday."); *compare* Human Rights Watch, Mixed Results: US Policy and International Standards on the Rights and Interests of Victims of Crime 9 (2008) ("In the 18th century, the British legal scholar William Blackstone wrote that '[i]n all cases the crime includes an injury: every public offense is also a private wrong, and somewhat more; it affects the individual, and it likewise affects the community.' This recognition that both victims and the state are harmed by crime meant that historically in Britain and the United States, victims were able to prosecutions themselves, as private prosecutors. In fact, the burden was often entirely on the victim, who had to pay to retain an attorney to have the indictment written and the offender brought to trial.") (quoting William Blackstone, Commentaries on the Laws of England, vol. 4 (1769), p. 5); Wilbur R. Miller, A History of Private Policing in the United States 51 (2019) (discussing private prosecution associations); V. A. C. Gatrell, The Hanging Tree: Execution and the English People 1770–1868, at 520 (1994) ("The high costs and inconvenience of private prosecution meant that most lawbreakers escaped the courts entirely (again, the addition to private prosecution expressed a suspicion of state prosecutions which was fueled by seventeenth-century memories)."); Bessler, *A Century in the Making*, *supra* note 15, at 989 (discussing abusive prosecutions in England before the Glorious Revolution of 1688–1689); Thomas B. Colby, *Clearing the Smoke from* Philip Morris v. Williams: *The Past, Present, and Future of Punitive Damages*, 118 Yale L.J. 392, 431–32 (2008) ("[A]s crime and tort emerged as distinct branches of the common law, the distinction between the two initially did not turn on the identity of the prosecutor; both actions were privately prosecuted by the individual victim. Nor did it turn on whose interests were being served; both actions satisfied the private interests of the victim. Rather, the distinction lay in the victim's motive for bringing the lawsuit and the remedy sought: 'The crux of the distinction between crime and tort in the early common law was the choice of vengeance or compensation.' Victims who preferred compensation could bring an action for a writ of trespass; victims who preferred vengeance could bring an appeal of felony. 'They could either put their wrongdoers to death and collect nothing [through an appeal of felony], or collect money for themselves and leave their wrongdoers alive with the rest of their wealth intact [through a writ of trespass].'").

146. Palmer, *supra* note 136, at 62 ("The chaotic private prosecutorial method that existed in England was allowed to flourish in the colonies. The inducement used to encourage colonists to prosecute criminals was the same carrot used in England. Private prosecutors reaped monetary rewards for successfully prosecuting criminals. They also reaped rewards by intimidating defendants into settling criminal charges, prior to trial, by paying them monetary sums."); Susan Howley & Carol F. Dorris, "Legal Rights for Crime Victims in the Criminal Justice System," *in* Robert C. Davis, Arthur J. Lurigio & Susan A. Herman, eds., Victims of Crime 271 (4th ed. 2013) ("During colonial times, crime victims were integral to the criminal justice process. The victim could pay the sheriff to pursue and arrest the defendant, and then the victim hired the prosecutor.").

147. Steinberg, *supra* note 19, at 56 ("Private prosecutors, despite having to negotiate a more complex legal process, still frequently took cases into the trial courts. Though they could not control the process as fully as they had during a case's primary stages, prosecutors nonetheless wielded considerable influence over the proceedings in the courts of record. Manipulation of the criminal law by the parties to cases resulted in extremes in every possible direction.").

148. *E.g.*, Ian C. Pilarczyk, "'To shudder at the bare recital of those acts'": Child Abuse, Family, and Montreal Courts in the Early Nineteenth Century," *in* G. Blaine Baker & Donald Fyson, eds., Essays in the History of Canadian Law: Quebec and the Canadas 406 n.57 (2013) ("The Montreal court of this period was a highly localized, court-driven system, in which private prosecutors initiated a considerable amount of the business heard before the courts, particularly where assaults were concerned."); *see also* Mary Anne Poutanen, Beyond Brutal Passions: Prostitution in Early Nineteenth-Century Montreal 202, 251, 257 (2015) (discussing private prosecutions).

149. Jay M. Feinman, Law 101: Everything You Need to Know About American Law 330 (4th ed. 2014).

150. *Id.*

151. *See generally* Joseph F. Lawless, Prosecutorial Misconduct: Law, Procedure, Forms (4th ed. 2019).

152. Matthew S. Nichols, *No One Can Serve Two Masters: Arguments Against Private Prosecutors*, 13 Cap. Def. J. 279 (2001).

153. State v. Culbreath, 30 S.W.3d 309, 314 (Tenn. 2000) ("Numerous courts and commentators have recognized, however, that the use of a private attorney in the prosecution of a criminal case may present ethical dilemmas, including conflicts of interest."); Sedore v. Epstein, 836 N.Y.S.2d 779, 782 (N.Y. Sup. Ct., Dutchess County, 2008) ("There is an inherent conflict and ethical dilemma for a privately retained attorney to prosecute on behalf of the District Attorney's Office based upon which this court finds it would be an abuse of discretion and in excess of lawful procedure to allow the prosecution to go forward in such manner. Accordingly, it is hereby ORDERED that the petition is granted to the extent that the respondent, Hon. Harold D. Epstein, as Town Justice of the Town of Fishkill, Dutchess County, New York, shall not proceed in the *Matter of the People v. Sedore* if prosecution is not by the District Attorney, or an Assistant District Attorney."); State v. Eldridge, 951 S.W.2d 775, 781 (Tenn. Ct. Crim. App. 1997) ("There are certain inherent conflicts that arise due to the differing roles of the government prosecutor and private prosecutor. The responsibility of a public prosecutor differs from that of the usual advocate in that it is the public prosecutor's duty to seek justice, not merely to convict.") (citing *Code of Professional Responsibility*, Tenn. S.Ct. Rule 8, EC 7-13); Paul B. Spelman, *Public Prosecutors and the Appearance of Justice: How the Court of Appeals Erred in Gatewood by Treating a State's Attorney as an Ordinary Advocate*, 65 Md. L. Rev. 1222, 1238 (2006) ("The premise that with a prosecutor's great power comes a special ethical responsibility was perhaps most clearly articulated in *Young v. United States ex rel. Vuitton et Fils S.A.*, in which the Court reversed a criminal contempt conviction because it had been prosecuted by a private prosecutor who was also representing an adverse party to the defendant in a related civil action. The Court called the use of a prosecutor with a private professional interest a fundamental error which violated the premise of the American legal system that the state 'wield its formidable criminal enforcement powers in a rigorously disinterested fashion . . . .' The Court noted that while a prosecutor may be held to a somewhat less stringent standard of neutrality than a judge, the appointment of an 'interested' prosecutor creates an appearance of impropriety that impacts the public's faith in the fairness and impartial nature of the courts. The Court went on to declare a categorical rule against appointing interested private prosecutors to preserve public confidence in the integrity of the justice system."); Andrew Sidman, Comment, *The Outmoded Concept of Private Prosecution*, 25 Am. U. L. Rev. 754, 773–80 (1976) (discussing ethical issues pertaining to private prosecution); *cf.* Note, *Permitting Private Initiation of Criminal Contempt Proceedings*, 124 Harv. L. Rev. 1485, 1493 (2011) ("A truly private prosecution could be difficult to reconcile with the requirements of constitutional due process. Separation of powers issues might arise. The ethical requirements of a prosecutor might prove incompatible with those of a private advocate.").

154. People v. Benoit, 575 N.Y.S.2d 750, 757 (N.Y. Crim. Ct. 1991) (private prosecution of tenant by landlord violated tenant's due process rights); David W. Neubauer & Henry F. Fradella, America's

Courts and the Criminal Justice System 170 (13th ed. 2019) ("Due process concerns about private prosecutions—especially potential conflicts of interest, vindictive prosecutions, corruption, accountability, and the non-delegable sovereign act of exercising prosecutorial discretion—eventually led to the overwhelming number of U.S. jurisdictions moving to the public prosecutor model .... Indeed, in *Young v. United States ex rel. Vuitton et Fils S.A.* (1987), the U.S. Supreme Court overturned a federal conviction for criminal contempt of court that was privately prosecuted by counsel appointed by a federal district court. Key to the Court's decision was that the lawyers appointed to prosecute the contempt case had a conflict of interest."); *cf.* Douglas E. Beloof, Victims' Rights: A Documentary and Reference Guide 106 (2012) ("Historically, victims had been private prosecutors. Because this was commonplace at the time of the nation's founding, it is clear that the framers of the Constitution did not intend the Constitution to exclude such private prosecutions. However, history is only one basis upon which the federal courts interpret the Constitution. There is another method of interpretation called 'evolving due process.' The reasoning behind this approach is, as civilization evolves, more civilized standards of due process evolve along with it. Thus, a procedure acceptable one hundred years ago can be scrutinized as unconstitutional now, even though the actual words of the Constitution have not changed at all.").

155. *Benoit*, 575 N.Y.S.2d at 757 (private prosecution of tenant by landlord violated tenant's equal protection rights).

156. Model Rules of Professional Conduct, Rules 1.2 & 3.8, *available at* https://www.americanbar.org/groups/professional_responsibility/publications/model_rules_of_professional_conduct/.

157. *E.g.*, Verónica Michel, Prosecutorial Accountability and Victims' Rights in Latin America 6 (2018) ("[T]he right to private prosecution is a right of the victim or their relatives to have a lawyer that represents their interests and to participate in the criminal proceedings. Whereas the public prosecutor represents the interests of the state, the private prosecutor represents the interests of the victim."); *id.* at 6–7 ("Contemporary Latin American criminal law allows for a range of different forms of prosecution. On one end of the spectrum there is 'public prosecution' (*acusación pública*), when criminal action is exercised exclusively by the state, while on the other end of the spectrum some countries also allow 'exclusive private prosecution' (*acusación privada*). Between those extremes there is a third kind of prosecution: public prosecution supported by an 'autonomous private prosecution' (*acusación particular o autónoma*). An auxiliary private prosecutor is only allowed to support the prosecution of the state and collaborate with the state throughout the investigation. Countries that allow this type of private prosecution include: Brazil, Germany, Mexico, Russia and Sweden.") (citations omitted); *id.* at 7 ("[A] autonomous private prosecutor not only has the right to collaborate throughout the criminal investigation, but also has the right to present her own indictment; this allows the victim to press for charges that are different from those introduced by the public prosecutor. This type of private prosecution can be found in countries like Chile and Guatemala, as well as in Austria, Bulgaria, Portugal, and Poland."); *id.* at 23 ("The right to private prosecution is an old right that nowadays is present in most countries in Latin America."); Lucien Karpik & Terence C. Halliday, *The Legal Complex*, 7 Ann. Rev. L. & Soc. Sci. 217, 223 (2011) (referring to "the institution of private prosecutions in Latin America"); *see also* Case of Armani Da Silva v. The United Kingdom, Application No. 5878/08, Judgment Grand Chamber, Eur. Ct. Hum. Rts. (30 Mar. 2016), ¶ 175 ("From the information available to the Court, it would appear that, leaving aside the question of private prosecutions, in at least twenty-five Contracting States the decision to prosecute is taken by a public prosecutor. That is the case in Albania, Armenia, Austria, Azerbaijan, Bulgaria, the Czech Republic, Estonia, Finland, Georgia, Hungary, Iceland, Ireland, Italy, Latvia, the Republic of Moldova, Montenegro, Poland, Portugal, Romania, Russia, Serbia, Sweden, Switzerland, Turkey and Ukraine. In a further twelve Contracting States, the prosecutorial decision is first taken by a public prosecutor before being put before a judge and/or a court. This is the position in Belgium, Cyprus, France, Germany, Lithuania, Luxembourg, the former Yugoslav Republic of Macedonia, Malta, Monaco, Slovakia, Slovenia and Spain."); In re Caceres, Case No. 1:19-mc-00405-KS-RHW, 2020 WL 2523120 *1, 7 (S.D. Miss. May 18, 2020) ("Under Honduran law, the private prosecutor is authorized to present arguments, submit evidence, and examine witnesses at pretrial hearings and during the trial of criminal matters.... In Honduras, victims of crime have the right to intervene in criminal proceedings and establish a private prosecution against the accused. Article 16 of the Honduran Code of Criminal Procedure explicitly allows a victim to 'become a private plaintiff or

complainant and intervene as such' throughout the criminal process."); *compare* Jessica G. Mecellem, *Human Rights Trials in an Era of Democratic Stagnation: The Case of Turkey*, 43 Law & Soc. Inquiry 119, 146 (referring to "[p]rivate prosecution") *with* Feridun Yenisey, Criminal Procedure Law in Turkey (May 2015), https://law.ku.edu/sites/law.ku.edu/files/docs/istanbul/criminal-procedure-istanbul-2015.pdf, p. 20 ("'The Private Criminal Prosecution' was a formal complaint filed by the victim or his legal representative against the commission of a crime. This private prosecution was only possible for the offenses listed in the Code.... The Penal Code has abolished this legal institution.").

158. Joshua D. Kadish, Stephen J. Schulhofer & Rachel E. Barkow, Criminal Law and Its Processes: Cases and Materials (10th ed. 2017) ("[I]n Great Britain and in many countries of continental Europe, a private person can initiate a criminal prosecution, become a formal party, or retain counsel to prosecute the case on her own behalf.") (*citing* Carsten Stahn, Héctor Olásolo & Kate Gibson, *Participation of Victims in Pre-Trial Proceedings of the ICC*, 4 J. Int'l Crim. Just. 219, 220 (2006)); Johanna Göhler, "Victim Rights in Civil Law Jurisdictions," *in* Darryl K. Brown, Jenia I. Turner & Bettina Weisser, eds., The Oxford Handbook of Criminal Process (2019), ch. 13 ("[I]n many though not all civil jurisdictions, the victim can appear as a private prosecutor. Hence, the victim has the right to decide whether to bring charges against a defendant and represent the prosecution during regular criminal proceedings. Private prosecution is usually limited to certain less serious offenses, such as libel and defamation."); Chantelle Feldhaus & René Koraan, Explainer: How South Africa's First Private Prosecutions Unit Will Work, The Conversation, Feb. 3, 2017, https://theconversation.com/explainer-how-south-africas-first-private-prosecutions-unit-will-work-72389 ("Private prosecutions are allowed in many countries under common law. These include Australia, Canada, Kenya, Zimbabwe, and the UK—as well as many more. The South African Criminal Procedure Act makes provision for two forms of private prosecutions. Section 7 of the act provides for private prosecution by an aggrieved individual on the basis of a certificate nolle prosequi—a declaration [of] the National Prosecuting Authority (NPA) not to prosecute. And section 8 provides for private prosecution under statutory right. This means that any person can conduct a prosecution in a court competent to try the offence."); *see also* Fidelis Munyoro, *Zimbabwe: Family Seeks Private Prosecution in Waverley Blankets Wrangle*, The Herald, Sept. 2, 2020, https://allafrica.com/stories/202009020530.html ("Under Zimbabwean practice, almost all criminal prosecutions are undertaken by the State, but there is a provision for the Prosecutor-General to allow a private prosecution."); Jamil Ddamulira Mujuzi, *Private Prosecutions in Kenya*, 11 Afr. J. Leg. Studies 33 (2018) (discussing the right to institute a private prosecution).

159. Máximo Langer & Mackenzie Eason, *The Quiet Expansion of Universal Jurisdiction*, 30 Eur. J. Int'l L. 779, 801 (2019) ("Argentina's criminal justice system includes a system of private criminal prosecution").

160. Case of Milićević v. Montenegro, Application No. 27821/16, Judgment (6 Feb. 2019), Eur. Ct. Hum. Rts, 2d Section, ¶ 57 ("[T]he Court firstly notes that the Montenegrin legal framework provides for the criminal offence of jeopardising someone's personal security. It further observes that Montenegrin criminal law distinguishes between criminal offences to be prosecuted by a State prosecutor and criminal offences to be prosecuted by means of private prosecution. It also provides for the injured party to act as a subsidiary prosecutor."); Case of Alković v. Montenegro, Application No. 66895/10, Eur. Ct. Hum. Rts., 2d Section, Judgment 5 Dec. 2017), ¶ 40 ("For crimes subject to private prosecution (*za koja se goni po privatnoj tužbi*), the authorised prosecutor would be a victim (*privatni tužilac*).").

161. Anna Louise Prestidge, *Private Prosecutions in New Zealand—A Public Concern?*, 50 Vict. U. Wellington L. Rev. 107, 107 (2019) ("It is undeniable that New Zealand's criminal justice system is dramatically different from its early Anglo-Saxon roots. However, one similarity that remains is the ability of a private person to bring criminal proceedings against another. Private prosecutions are often regarded as an 'important safeguard' for New Zealand citizens. These prosecutions are rare in the modern criminal environment and consequently, little academic attention has been paid to them. Yet, where the use of private prosecutions has been considered, concerns have been raised."); Tyrone Kirchengast, The Victim in Criminal Law and Justice 191 (2006) ("[I]n the New Zealand case of *Wallace v Abbott* (unreported), a private prosecution on indictment for murder was brought for the fatal shooting of Steven Wallace by Constable Keith Abbott. Abbott maintained that Wallace was killed in the line of duty after he

smashed the windscreen of a police car. An investigation carried out by the NZ Police Complaints Authority exonerated Abbott of any responsibility for the death. Thus, no charge was laid by the police. Exercising his right of private prosecution, Wallace's father initiated a deposition hearing in January 2002 before two justices of the peace. The justices ruled that there was not enough evidence to proceed, that Abbott acted in self-defence, and that the shooting was a matter of police policy.").

162. Case of Volodina v. Russia, Application No. 41261/17, Judgment (9 July 2019), Eur. Ct. Hum. Rts., 3d Section, ¶ 46 ("Chapter 16 of the Russian Criminal Code covers offences against the person, including murder and manslaughter (Articles 105 to 109) and three levels of assault occasioning actual bodily harm (Articles 111 to 115). 'Grievous bodily harm' (Article 111) may involve the loss of a body part or the termination of pregnancy; 'medium bodily harm' (Article 112) leads to a long-term health disorder or loss of ability to work, and 'minor bodily harm' (Article 115) covers injuries that take up to twenty-one days to heal. Causing grievous or medium bodily harm is subject to public prosecution; the offence of 'minor bodily harm' is liable to private prosecution, meaning that the institution and pursuance of criminal proceedings is left to the victim, who has to collect evidence, identify the perpetrator, secure witness testimony and bring charges before a court. Private prosecution proceedings can be terminated at any stage up until the delivery of judgment in the event that the victim has agreed to withdraw the charges."); *see also id.* at ¶ 69 ("Private prosecution cases were prohibitively onerous for a victim, who had to act as her own investigator, prosecutor and advocate. Reconciliation was considered a primary goal in such cases, leaving the victim exposed to pressure from her abuser. About 90% of private prosecution cases were discontinued, either owing to reconciliation or failure to fulfil the legal requirements. In 2015, there had been 2.37 million reports of assault, but only 26,212 cases had resulted in a criminal conviction. In 2017, out of a total of 164,000 instances of assault, only 7,000 had been subject to a criminal investigation. The applicant pointed out that once the offence of assault had been decriminalised, the authorities had failed to hold S. accountable—even under administrative law. She also emphasised that nothing remotely resembling a protection order existed in Russian law and that the Russian authorities had been unable to offer her any meaningful protection over more than two years of violence."); *id.* at ¶ 82 ("[T]he Russian law leaves the prosecution of charges of 'minor harm to health' and 'repeat battery' to the private initiative of the victim. The Court has acknowledged that the effective protection of the Convention right to physical integrity does not require public prosecution in all cases of attacks by private individuals (see *Sandra Janković v. Croatia*, no. 38478/05, § 50, 5 March 2009). Within the context of domestic violence, however, it has considered that the possibility to bring private prosecution proceedings is not sufficient, as such proceedings obviously require time and cannot serve to prevent the recurrence of similar incidents (see Bevacqua and S., cited above, § 83; see also the Council of Europe's Recommendation Rec (2002) 5, cited in paragraph 59 above). A private prosecution puts an excessive burden on the victim of domestic violence, shifting onto her the responsibility for collecting evidence capable of establishing the abuser's guilt to the criminal standard of proof. As the Government acknowledged, the collection of evidence presents inherent challenges in cases where abuse occurs in a private setting without any witnesses present, and sometimes leaves no tangible marks. The Court agrees that this is not an easy task even for trained law-enforcement officials, but the challenge becomes unsurmountable for a victim who is expected to collect evidence on her own while continuing to live under the same roof as the perpetrator, being financially dependent on him, and fearing reprisals on his part. Moreover, even if a trial results in a guilty verdict, a victim cannot be provided with the necessary protection, such as protective or restraining orders, owing to the absence of such measures under Russian legislation."); *id.* at ¶ 84 ("The authorities' failure to provide for the public prosecution of domestic-violence charges has been consistently criticised by the CEDAW [Convention on the Elimination of All Forms of Discrimination against Women] Committee. In 2015, in its concluding observations on the eighth periodic report by the Russian Federation, the Committee expressed concern regarding the high prevalence of violence against women—which was considered 'a private matter'—and recommended that the Russian State amend the relevant law to provide for the *ex officio* prosecution of domestic violence (see paragraph 64 above). In the views that it recently expressed regarding a domestic-violence complaint against Russia that was similar to the one addressed in the present case, the Committee established that placing the burden of proof on the victim of domestic violence in private prosecution cases had the effect of denying access to justice, in breach of Russia's obligations under the CEDAW Convention (see paragraph

65 above)."); *id.* at ¶ 123 ("[O]n the question whether women who are victims of domestic violence have an equal access to justice, the Court has noted above that victims have had no access to public prosecution of such offences save for a short period between July 2016 and January 2017 (see paragraph 49 above). The majority of domestic-violence cases have been classified as private prosecution offences in the Russian legal system which placed the onus of prosecution on the victim (see paragraph 82 above). The official statistics of the Judicial Department of the Supreme Court of the Russian Federation indicate that that classification has the effect of disproportionately and adversely affecting the prospects of success for victims seeking access to justice. The global number of acquittals in the Russian criminal justice system in 2013–14 amounted to less than 1% of all criminal cases considered by courts of general jurisdiction. Approximately 70% of those acquittals were pronounced in private prosecution cases (3,894 out of 5,624 cases in 2013, and 3,778 out of 5,167 cases in 2014), even though such cases made up less than 5% of all criminal cases (49,315 out of 946,747 cases in 2013, 45,427 out of 936,771 cases in 2014). Moreover, private prosecution cases were four times more likely to be discontinued on various procedural grounds in comparison to public prosecution cases (78% compared to 19% in 2013 and 76% compared to 19% in 2014). It follows that victims of domestic violence have been placed in a de facto situation of disadvantage.").

163. Case of Mučibabić v. Serbia, Application No. 34661/07, Eur. Ct. Hum. Rts., 3d Section, Judgment (12 Oct. 2016), ¶ 79 ("Most criminal offences (including those mentioned above) are subject to public prosecution, but some minor offences are only subject to private prosecution. The public prosecutor's discretion to decide whether to press charges, however, is bound by the principle of legality, which requires that he must act whenever there is a reasonable suspicion that a crime subject to public prosecution has been committed. The public prosecutor must undertake measures necessary for the preliminary investigation of crimes subject to public prosecution and the identification of the alleged perpetrators. To that end, he is vested with the power to co-ordinate the work of various law-enforcement agencies and other governmental bodies.").

164. Elisabetta Grande, *Legal Transplants and the Inoculation Effect: How American Criminal Procedure Has Affected Continental Europe*, 64 AM. J. COMP. L. 583, 598 n.62 (2016) ("In Spain, private prosecutors can ask for the case to go to trial against the prosecutor's request for dismissal.").

165. Yue Ma, *The Amended Criminal Procedure Law of China: Prosecution and Trial*, 54 No. 2 CRIM. LAW BULLETIN ART. 2 (2018) ("The crime victim may initiate private prosecution in three categories of cases."); Duan Xiaosong, *Criminal Responsibility for Arbitrators in Chinese Law: Perversion of Law in Commercial Arbitration*, 27 PACE INT'L L. REV. 1, 12 (2015) ("In the Chinese criminal justice system, one of the important aspects is the dichotomy drawn between public prosecution and private prosecution. The criminal cases are under public prosecution with exceptions of three categories of less serious crimes."); David C. Rodearmel, *Military Law in Communist China: Development, Structure and Function*, 119 MIL. L. REV. 1, 68 (1988) ("Under the Criminal Procedure Law, criminal complaints and accusations may be filed by citizens with the public security organs, the procuracy, or the courts. The procedures for servicemen to follow in bringing criminal complaints directly to the attention of military courts were outlined by the editors of *Zhongguo Fazhi Bao* (China Legal Journal) on 2 May 1986, in response to a letter from a PLA recruit in Henan province. Private prosecutions may be commenced before military courts under the provisions of the Criminal Procedure Law, with the additional requirement that the unit Party committee assist in the investigation and production of evidence. If supported by sufficient evidence, the case may be transferred to the military procuracy for initiation of public prosecution, or it may be directly investigated and heard by the military court as a private prosecution. If the evidence is insufficient to support a criminal prosecution, the case may be referred to the complainant's unit Party committee for further investigation. If sufficient evidence is developed, the unit Party committee may refer the case back to the court. Violations that do not constitute criminal offenses may be referred for possible disciplinary action. The law requires that complainants be informed of the potential legal responsibility incurred for false accusations.").

166. Mikko Vuorenpää, *Prosecutors, the Objectives of Criminal Policy and the Situation in Finland, in* LAURA ERVO, MINNA GRÄNS & ANTTI JOKELA, EDS., EUROPEANIZATION OF PROCEDURAL LAW AND THE NEW CHALLENGES TO FAIR TRIAL 212 n.51 (2009) ("In Finland, the complainant may bring a private prosecution under chapter 1, section 14 CPA [Criminal Procedure Act] if the prosecutor decides not to bring a charge."); *see also id.* at 212–13 ("Owing to the unconditional wording of chapter 1, section 16(1),

of the Finnish Criminal Procedure Act (CPA), issues of private prosecution have been beset with problems in the case law. Under that provision, the complainant forfeits his or her right to private prosecution, if he or she declares in the pre-trial investigation that he or she does not request the prosecution of the perpetrator.").

167. Taiwan: Criminal Laws, Regulations and Procedures Handbook 193 (2016) (noting that Article 319 of the criminal code provides in part: "The victim of a crime may file a private prosecution, provided that where he is without, or of limited, legal capacity, or is dead, such private prosecution may be filed by his statutory agent, lineal relative, or spouse."); Tatsuya Ota, *The Development of Victim Support and Victim Rights in Asia, in* Wing-Cheong Chan, ed., Support for Victims of Crime in Asia 133 (2008) ("In Taiwan, victims or certain persons, such as their legal representatives, lineal families or spouses (in the event of a victim's death or incompetence), may file a prosecution with a competent court against the offenders .... The Taiwanese private prosecution system is similar to that of Thailand, in that the court may dismiss the prosecution if it finds the prosecution is not well founded or if some condition for suspended-prosecution is met after a preliminary hearing.").

168. Case of Ž.B. v. Croatia, Application No. 47666/13, Eur. Ct. Hum. Rts., 2d Section, Judgment (Oct. 11, 2017), ¶ 28 ("Articles 47 to 61 regulated the rights and duties of private prosecutors and of injured parties acting as subsidiary prosecutors. A private prosecutor (*privatni tužitelj*) was an injured party who brought a private prosecution in respect of criminal offences for which such a prosecution was expressly allowed by the Criminal Code (namely, offences of a lesser degree). An injured party acting as a subsidiary prosecutor (*oštećeni kao tužitelj*) could take over criminal proceedings in respect of criminal offences subject to public prosecution where the relevant prosecuting authorities, for whatever reason, had decided not to prosecute (Article 55). When acting as a subsidiary prosecutor, the victim had the same procedural rights as the State Attorney's Office would have had as public prosecuting authority, save for those vested in the State Attorney's Office as a State body. Under Article 58, the State Attorney's Office was authorised, on a discretionary basis, to take over a prosecution from a subsidiary prosecutor at any point before the end of the trial."); Case of Škorjanec v. Croatia, Application No. 25536/14, Eur. Ct. Hum. Rts., Judgment (28 Mar. 2017), ¶ 30 ("Articles 55 to 63 regulate the rights and duties of private prosecutors and of victims acting as subsidiary prosecutors. A private prosecutor (*privatni tužitelj*) is a victim who brings a private prosecution in respect of criminal offences for which such a prosecution is expressly allowed by the Criminal Code (less serious offences). A victim acting as a subsidiary prosecutor (*oštećeni kao tužitelj*) is an individual taking over criminal proceedings in respect of criminal offences subject to public prosecution where the relevant prosecuting authorities, for whatever reason, have decided not to prosecute. When acting as a subsidiary prosecutor, the victim has all the rights in the proceedings which the State Attorney's Office would have as a public prosecuting authority, save for those vested in the State Attorney's Office as a State body. Under Article 58 § 2, the State Attorney's Office is authorised, on a discretionary basis, to take over a prosecution from a subsidiary prosecutor at any point before the end of the trial.").

169. 2 Sosteness Francis Materu, The Post-Election Violence in Kenya: Domestic and International Legal Responses 132 (2015) ("Private prosecutions are regulated under section 88 of the Kenyan Criminal Procedure Code. A private person, either personally or through an advocate, is allowed to conduct private prosecution, provided a permission *of a magistrate* is obtained.") (italics in original).

170. Shannon Vaughn Hoctor, Criminal Law in South Africa §1(V.) (2d ed. 2017) ("Private prosecutions are permitted in certain limited circumstances. A private prosecution is a very rare phenomenon in South Africa and is one in which a private individual and not the State prosecutes."). As legal treatises show, private prosecutions have a long history in places such as South Africa. *E.g.*, 4 Manfred Nathan, The Common Law of South Africa: A Treatise Based on Voet's Commentaries on the Pandects, with References to the Leading Roman-Dutch Authorities, South African Decisions, and Statutory Enactments in South Africa 2648–49 (1907) ("In all cases where the Attorney-General declines to prosecute for any alleged crime or offence, it is competent for any private party who can show some substantial and peculiar interest in the issue of the trial arising out of some injury which he individually has suffered by the commission of any such alleged crime or offence to prosecute the person alleged to have committed the same, in any competent Court. The following persons also possess this right of private prosecution: (1) a husband in respect of offences committed against his wife; (2) the

legal guardians or curators of minors or lunatics in respect of offences committed against their wards; (3) the wife or children, or, where there is no wife or child, any of the next of kin, of any deceased person, in respect of any crime or offence by which the death of such person is alleged to have been caused.") (citations omitted).

171. *Compare Private Prosecution: A Remedy for District Attorneys' Unwarranted Inaction*, 65 Yale L.J. 209, 218–19 (1955) ("Despite widespread belief that criminal actions are conducted exclusively by public officials, private prosecutors in fact play an extensive role in criminal law enforcement. In thirty jurisdictions appellate courts have decided that privately employed attorneys may assist the public prosecutor, while only three have said that they may not. Moreover, sixty-two per cent of 151 public prosecutors from forty-five states who responded to a *questionnaire* on prosecution procedures stated that they permit privately hired attorneys to assist in criminal proceedings.") *with* David W. Neubauer & Henry F. Fradella, America's Courts and the Criminal Justice System 170 (13th ed. 2019) ("Most modern prosecutors in the United States hold a public office. They are government employees in civil service."). *See also* A Proposed Constitutional Amendment to Protect Crime Victims, Hearing Before for the Committee on the Judiciary, United States Senate, 106th Cong., 1st Sess. (1999), p. 12 ("In America ... while some vestiges of private prosecutions continue to this day there was a 'meteoric rise of public prosecutions' and the office of public prosecutor grew in stature.").

172. Johanna Göhler, *Victim Rights in Civil Law Jurisdictions, in* Darryl K. Brown, Jenia I. Turner & Bettina Weisser, eds., The Oxford Handbook of Criminal Process 279 (2019) ("The existence of a right to private prosecution may astonish given the fact that the civil law tradition generally regards criminal prosecution as a state duty exercised by a public servant. Consequently, purpose and legitimacy of private prosecutions are highly controversial.").

173. Gilliéron, *supra* note 59, at 297 (noting that, in France, "the victim has the possibility to initiate proceedings and directly summon the suspect before a criminal court (*citation directe*), in case of misdemeanors and petty offenses"); *see also* Gerald L. Kock, *Criminal Proceedings in France*, 9 Am. J. Comparative L. 253, 253, 256 (1960) ("French penal law recognizes three classes of offenses (*infractions*): felonies (*crimes*), misdemeanors (*délits*) and petty offenses (*contraventions de simple police*).... There are several ways in which a case can be brought before the court. The culprit and the accuser may voluntarily appear before the court where justice will be rendered rather summarily. Another, and the most usual, way for offenses to come in is by petition of the victim or the local prosecutor (member of the ministère public attached to the local court of primary jurisdiction, the tribunal de grande instance). On receipt of this petition an order to appear (citation directe) is issued by the court and is served on the accused or at his domicile by the bailiff of the court.").

174. *E.g.*, Jamil Ddamulira Mujuzi, *Private Prosecutions in Mauritius: Clarifying Locus Standi and Making the Direction of Public Prosecutions More Accountable*, 10 African J. Leg. Studies, Iss. 1 (2017), https://doi.org/10.1163/17087384-12340016 ("Private prosecutions have been part of Mauritian law for a long period of time. In Mauritius there are two types of private prosecutions: private prosecutions by individuals; and private prosecutions by statutory bodies. Neither the Mauritian constitution nor legislation provides for the right to institute a private prosecution. Unlike legislation in some countries such as South Africa, Ethiopia, Botswana, Swaziland, Zimbabwe and Namibia, which is detailed when it comes to the manner in which private prosecutions may be conducted, the Mauritian legislation is not that detailed. The result is that Mauritian courts have had to deal with issues such as: who has *locus standi* to institute a private prosecution and the role of the Director of Public Prosecutions in private prosecutions. The Mauritian Supreme Court has held, inter alia, that a private prosecution may only be instituted by an aggrieved party (even in lower courts where this is not a statutory requirement) and that the Director of Public Prosecutions may take over and discontinue a private prosecution without giving reasons for his decision."); National Society for the Prevention of Cruelty to Animals v Minister of Justice and Constitutional Development and Another [2016] ZACC 46 (declaring that the National Society for the Prevention of Cruelty to Animals has the statutory power of private prosecution conferred upon it by section 6(2)(2) of South Africa's Societies for the Prevention of Cruelty to Animals Act 169 of 1993 read with section 8 of the Criminal Procedure Act 51 of 1977); Bothma v Els [2009] ZACC 27, ¶¶ 1, 5 (noting that, in 2007, "the applicant, Mrs Bothma, instituted a private prosecution charging that thirty-nine years before, when she

had been a thirteen year old schoolgirl, the first respondent, Ms Els, a wealthy family friend much older than herself, had taken her by car to his farm and raped her."; that the private prosecution was commenced after the Director of Public Prosecutions ("DPP") decided not to prosecute and, at the request of Mrs. Bothma, "a certificate *nolle prosequi* (refusal to prosecute)" was issued; and that Mrs. Bothma instituted the private prosecution under the terms "of section 7 of the Criminal Procedure Act (the CPA), which provides that in any case in which a DPP declines to prosecute an alleged offence, any private person who proves some substantial and peculiar interest in the issue arising out of some injury which he or she individually suffered, may institute and conduct a prosecution in respect of such offence in any court competent to try that offence").

175. *E.g.*, Viraphong Boonyobhas, *Victims of Human Trafficking in Thailand: A Study of Women and Children, in* K. Jaishankar & Natti Ronel, eds., Second International Conference of the South Asian Society of Criminology and Victimology (SASCV), 11–13, January 2013—Kanyakumari, Tamil Nadu, India 367 (2013) ("In Thailand, where the concept of a private prosecution still exists, as stipulated in the *Criminal Procedure Code*, victims of crime have the full right to bring their cases to the court themselves as joint Public Prosecutor. Although the criminal procedure laws of Thailand were modeled after civil law system, many elements of the common law were present in the laws as well as in its practices, including the concept of private prosecution.").

176. *E.g.*, Miklos Hollan, *Hungary, in* 1 Katalin Ligeti, ed., Toward a Prosecutor for the European Union (2013), ch. 8 (noting that under Hungarian criminal procedure law, "[t]he victim may act as a substitute private prosecutor, even when the offences are subject to public prosecution, if the prosecutor (the investigative authority) refuses to, or terminates the investigation or drops the charges"; "[I]n the course of a court procedure, the substitute private prosecutor shall exercise the rights of the public prosecutor, including the right to motion for a coercive measure depriving the personal freedom of the accused."); Despina Kyprianou, The Role of the Cyprus Attorney General's Office in Prosecutions: Rhetoric, Ideology and Practice 66 (2010) ("The courts have on many occasions been at pains to stress that 'there is nothing in the Constitution neutralising the position at common law as regards private prosecutions' (Ttofinis v. Theocharides 1983 2 C.L.R. 363) and 'neither the constitution nor the Criminal Procedure Law had abolished the valuable right of private prosecutions' (The Police v Athienitis 1983 C.L.R. 194). It was held that the right of a common informer to bring and conduct a prosecution for the trial of a summary offence derives from the common law and remains untouched, and indeed untrammelled, by any statutory provision. However, as the current President of the Supreme Court recognized extra-judicially, 'a private prosecution is always subject to the control of the Attorney General through his power to control, take over, continue or discontinue criminal proceedings' (Artemis 1989, p. 4032). Furthermore, it only concerns summary prosecutions as prosecutions on information can only be[] carried out by the Attorney General. Therefore, if a common informer wants to prosecute an offence tried on information, he can only do so up to the point of the preliminary inquiry. There are no official statistics about the exact number of private prosecutions that are being invoked every year, but it is common knowledge that they are very few and mainly limited to those relating to the offence of dishonoured cheques or offences regarding breaches of local administrative law.").

177. *E.g.*, Verónica Michel, Prosecutorial Accountability and Victims' Rights in Latin America 34 (2018) (noting the "pervasive presence of private prosecution in Latin America" that "became entrenched in criminal procedure in the region" as a result, among other things, of colonialism); *see also id.* at 53 ("[W]hen victims gain standing as private prosecutors they access very important remedies. They can appeal important prosecutorial decisions, including those that can end a prosecution, such as when a public prosecutor files a motion to drop charges or offers a plea bargain. In Latin America, private prosecutors can also appeal judicial decisions, including those that end a criminal prosecution, such as a dismissal with or without prejudice or a guilty or nonguilty verdict."). Historically speaking, private prosecutions in places like South America were noted in the United States long ago. "Brazil," N.Y. Herald (New York, NY), Nov. 13, 1869, p. 23 ("Another law has been published which, in some degree, removes a gross abuse. Previously, when a person tried before a jury was acquitted, and an appeal was taken by the public or private prosecutor against the acquittal, the party had to remain in custody until the appeal was decided, which involved months always and years frequently. The new act proposed by the Ministry of Justice

grants the right of bail when the penalty of the alleged crime does not exceed fourteenth years of simple imprisonment, twelve of hard labor or twenty of exile, and the term for appealing has been reduced from seven days to three.").

178. Washington v. Moore, Case No. 3-18-cv-06728-JD, 2020 WL 1082552, at *1 (N.D. Cal. Mar. 6, 2020) ("'California law does not authorize private prosecutions.'") (*quoting* People v. Eubanks, 14 Cal. 4th 580, 588 (1996)); People v. Eubanks, 14 Cal. 4th, 580, 588–89 (Cal. 1996) ("In California, all criminal prosecutions are conducted in the name of the People of the State of California and by their authority. (Gov. Code, § 100, subd. (b).) California law does not authorize private prosecutions. Instead, '[t]he prosecution of criminal offenses on behalf of the People is the sole responsibility of the public prosecutor ... [who] ordinarily has sole discretion to determine whom to charge, what charges to file and pursue, and what punishment to seek. [Citation.] No private citizen, however personally aggrieved, may institute criminal proceedings independently [citation], and the prosecutor's own discretion is not subject to judicial control at the behest of persons other than the accused.' (*Dix v. Superior Court* (1991) 53 Cal.3d 442, 451, 279 Cal. Rptr. 834, 807 P.2d 1063.)").

179. Joan E. Jacoby, *The American Prosecutor in Historical Context*, 44-DEC PROSECUTOR 38, 41 (2010) ("There are few vestiges of private prosecution in the United States today. Few states allow the use of private prosecutors, and those that do restrict their participation to limited types of cases. The opposition to private prosecution has also been clearly and consistently demonstrated by court decisions. In several states, convictions were overturned in cases where private counsel was hired to pursue a prosecution. In the opinion of the Wisconsin courts in the *State v. Peterson*, such practice was contrary to 'state policy.'") (*citing* State v. Peterson, 218 N.W. 367 (Wis. 1928)).

180. State v. Martineau, 808 A.2d 51, 54 (N.H. 2002) ("[W]hile we have never specifically defined what charges private prosecutors may bring, we have been cognizant of the dangers they pose both to the rights of criminal defendants and to the sound administration of justice. *See Waldron v. Tuttle,* 4 N.H. 149, 151 (1827) (noting that private prosecutions often originate from private quarrels, are intended to vex and harass an opponent, and often do not result in a public benefit justifying the expense); *Fletcher v. Merrimack County,* 71 N.H. 96, 102, 51 A. 271 (1901) (discussing the manner in which an interested prosecutor poses a threat to a defendant's rights). Consequently, when confronted with questions related to the governance of private criminal prosecution, we have consistently adhered to rules designed to counterbalance these concerns. *See Rogowicz v. O'Connell,* 147 N.H. 270, 274, 786 A.2d 841 (2001) (courts may not appoint the representative of an interested person to prosecute a criminal contempt action); *Rollins,* 129 N.H. at 687, 533 A.2d 331 (private prosecutors do not enjoy prosecutorial immunity); *Bokowsky v. Rudman,* 111 N.H. 57, 58–59, 274 A.2d 785 (1971) (public prosecutor may *nol pros* private prosecution over objection of private complainant); *Waldron,* 4 N.H. at 151 (private prosecutions will not be paid for from the county treasury unless they receive the sanction of the attorney general or solicitor).").

181. 481 U.S. 787 (1987).

182. *Id.* at 808. Since *Young*, that U.S. Supreme Court case has been cited numerous times. See, *e.g.*, DiSabatino v. Salicete, 671 A.2d 1344, 1352 (Del. 1996) ("Since courts possess 'inherent authority to initiate contempt proceedings for disobedience to their orders,' that authority 'necessarily encompasses the ability to appoint a private attorney to prosecute the contempt.' *Young v. United States,* 481 U.S. at 793, 107 S. Ct. at 2130. Ordinarily, however, a court 'should first request the appropriate prosecuting authority to prosecute contempt actions, and should appoint a private prosecutor only if that request is denied. Such a procedure ensures that the court will exercise its inherent power of self-protection only as a last resort,' just as it usually considers enforcing compliance with its orders through the imposition of civil contempt before it utilizes criminal contempt as a sanction. *Young v. United States,* 481 U.S. at 801–804, 107 S.Ct. at 2134–36."); *id.* at 1352–53 ("[I]n the event that a private attorney is appointed to prosecute a criminal contempt which arises from a civil proceeding, that attorney 'should be as disinterested as a public prosecutor who undertakes such a prosecution.' *Id.* Therefore, the attorney for a party that is the beneficiary of a court order in a civil proceeding 'may not be appointed as a prosecutor in a [criminal] contempt action alleging a violation of that order.' *Young v. United States,* 481 U.S. at 809, 107 S. Ct. at 2138.").

183. Aviva Abramovsky, *An Unholy Alliance: Perceptions of Influence in Insurance Fraud Prosecutions and the Need for Real Safeguards*, 98 J. CRIM. L. & CRIMINOLOGY 363, 408 (2008) ("Although the *Young*

decision rested on the Supreme Court's inherent supervisory power and considerations of prosecutorial ethics rather than constitutional due process, the Court often uses its supervisory authority to strike down an unlawful procedure as a precursor to finding that such practice amounts to a due process violation. The Tennessee courts, construing the right to prosecutorial impartiality in light of *Young*, have concluded that it 'does not preclude and probably only foreshadows a constitutional bar' with respect to the involvement of private prosecutors in criminal cases.") (citations omitted); *see also id.* at 408–09 ("In subsequent cases, other courts interpreting *Young* have held that the Due Process Clause mandates substantial restrictions on the activities of private prosecutors. The judicially imposed restrictions include requirements that private attorneys work under the direction of public prosecutors and that they not be permitted to 'effectively control critical prosecutorial decisions ... [such as] whether to prosecute, what targets of prosecution to select, what investigative powers to utilize [and] what sanctions to seek.' Other jurisdictions have held that private prosecutors with certain interests, such as representing victims who also have civil claims against the defendant, are disqualified per se from taking part in the criminal litigation.") (citations omitted).

184. *Young*, 481 U.S. at 807.

185. The Supreme Court's decision in *Young* was based on its "supervisory powers," but Justice Harry Blackmun—in a lone concurrence—would have held that "the practice—federal or state—of appointing an interested party's counsel to prosecute for criminal contempt is a violation of due process." *Young*, 481 U.S. 815–16 (Blackmun, J., concurring). According to Justice Blackmun's short opinion, due process "requires a disinterested prosecutor with the unique responsibility to serve the public, rather than a private client, and to seek justice that is unfettered." *Id.* at 816 (citing Brotherhood of Locomotive Firemen & Enginemen v. United States, 411 F.2d 312, 319 (5th Cir. 1969)).

186. Bruce A. Green & Rebecca Roiphe, *Rethinking Prosecutors' Conflicts of Interest*, 58 B.C. L. Rev. 463, 490 n.124 (2017); *see also id.* ("Had the Court decided *Vuitton* based on due process rather than judicial supervisory authority, the practice of private prosecutions would have been called into serious question, whereas after *Vuitton*, some states continued to allow private prosecutors, even if in most cases those private prosecutors were subject to the elected prosecutor's consent and supervision.").

187. Williams-Yulee v. Florida Bar, 575 U.S. 433, 453 (2015) ("Florida has reasonably determined that personal appeals for money by a judicial candidate inherently create an appearance that may cause the public to lose confidence in the integrity of the judiciary."); Caperton v. A.T. Massey Coal Co., 556 U.S. 868, 888 (2009) ("One must also take into account the judicial reforms the States have implemented to eliminate even the appearance of partiality. Almost every State—West Virginia included—has adopted the American Bar Association's objective standard: 'A judge shall avoid impropriety and the appearance of impropriety.' The ABA Model Code's test for appearance of impropriety is 'whether the conduct would create in reasonable minds a perception that the judge's ability to carry out judicial responsibilities with integrity, impartiality and competence is impaired.'") (quoting ABA Annotated Model Code of Judicial Conduct, Canon 2 (2004); Canon 2A, Commentary); Liljeberg v. Health Servs. Acquisition Corp., 486 U.S. 847, 865 (1988) ("The very purpose of § 455(a) is to promote confidence in the judiciary by avoiding even the appearance of impropriety whenever possible."); *see also* Lillian E. Kraemer, *Ethical Issues Involving Case Professionals and Other Court-Appointed Parties in Chapter 11 Proceedings*, American Law Institute—American Bar Association Continuing Legal Education, ALI-ABA Course of Study 1, 44 (Sept. 28, 1995) ("The 'appearance of impropriety' standard is derived from the American Bar Association's Model Code of Professional Responsibility, Canon 9 which states that '[a] lawyer should avoid even the appearance of professional impropriety.'") (quoting Model Code of Professional Responsibility Canon 9 (1983)); Ronald E. Mallen, 4 Legal Malpractice § 32.13 (2021) (discussing the origins of the appearance of impropriety standard); Nancy J. Moore, *Is the Appearance of Impropriety an Appropriate Standard for Disciplining Judges in the Twenty-First Century?*, 41 Loy. U. Chi. L.J. 285, 289 (2010) ("[T]he appearance of impropriety standard began to take on a life of its own in the context of lawyer disqualification. Indeed, although the term 'appearance of impropriety' disappeared altogether in the 1983 Model Rules of Professional Conduct, there are some courts that continue to disqualify a lawyer in pending litigation because of an appearance of impropriety.").

188. Like *Young*, *Robertson v. United States ex rel. Watson*, 130 S. Ct. 2184, 2185 (2010) also raised the question of whether a criminal contempt could be prosecuted by a private party. In *Robertson*, four Justices

of the Supreme Court—dissenting from a writ of certiorari as "improvidently granted"—reasoned that a criminal contempt is part of the "criminal law" and cannot be enforced by private citizens. That dissent, written by Chief Justice John Roberts, and joined by Justices Scalia, Kennedy and Sotomayor, stated: "The terrifying force of the criminal justice system may only be brought to bear against an individual by society as a whole, through a prosecution brought on behalf of the government." *Id.* at 2185 (Roberts, C.J., dissenting); *id.* at 2187–88 ("The private prosecutor is likely to have evidence pertinent to the proceeding—particularly if, as here, the private prosecutor is also the victim of the crime. But if the prosecutor is not exercising governmental authority, what would be the constitutional basis for any *Brady* obligations? May the private prosecutor interview the defendant without *Miranda* warnings, since she is not acting on behalf of any sovereign but only in a private capacity?"); *id.* at 2188 ("Our entire criminal justice system is premised on the notion that a criminal prosecution pits the government against the governed, not one private citizen against another. The ruling below is a startling repudiation of that basic understanding."); *see also id.* at 2188–89 ("To say that private parties could (and still can, in some places) exercise some control over criminal prosecutions says nothing to rebut the widely accepted principle that those private parties necessarily acted (and now act) on behalf of the sovereign. *See, e.g.*, *Cronan ex rel. State v. Cronan*, 774 A.2d 866, 877 (R.I. 2001) ('[A]ttorneys conducting private prosecutions stand in the shoes of the state'); *State v. Westbrook*, 279 N.C. 18, 36, 181 S.E.2d 572, 583 (1971) ('The prosecuting attorney, whether the solicitor or privately employed counsel, represents the State'); Andrew Sidman, *The Outmoded Concept of Private Prosecution*, 25 Am. U. L. Rev. 754, 774 (1976) ('[T]he privately retained attorney becomes, in effect, a temporary public prosecutor')[.] Indeed, many of the state court authorities Watson herself cites expressly recognize this fundamental point. *See, e.g.*, Katz v. Commonwealth, 379 Mass. 305, 312, 399 N.E.2d 1055, 1060 (1979) ('[I]t is clear with respect to the criminal aspects of the present case that the Commonwealth ... is the adverse party')").

189. Tetlow, *supra* note 18, at 1139 ("In 2010, the Supreme Court came tantalizingly close to addressing the issue of a private prosecution by a domestic violence victim in the case of *Robertson v. United States ex rel. Watson*. The Court granted certiorari in the case to consider whether the victim of domestic violence could prosecute the defendant for criminal contempt for violation of a civil restraining order. The victim proceeded over the objections of the federal prosecutor, who had previously worked out a plea bargain with the defendant to punish him for an earlier assault. Ultimately, however, a majority of the Court decided that the relevant issues were not clearly presented by the facts of the case, and the Court denied certiorari as 'improvidently granted.'"); *id.* ("Chief Justice Roberts wrote a twelve page dissent, joined by Justices Scalia, Kennedy, and Sotomayor, urging the Court to reject private prosecution because '[o]ur entire criminal justice system is premised on the notion that a criminal prosecution pits the government against the governed, not one private citizen against another. The ruling below [affirming the contempt conviction] is a startling repudiation of that basic understanding.' Chief Justice Roberts questioned whether a victim bringing criminal contempt proceedings would be subject to all of the constitutional criminal procedural requirements of a government prosecutor, including revealing exculpatory information or administering *Miranda* warnings before interviewing the defendant. Regardless of how the Court ultimately decides this issue, it is clear that our adversarial system of criminal justice does not comfortably allow for private prosecution, even in the context of contempt proceedings of a civil order.").

190. U.S. Const., amend. V. The Fifth Amendment has been described as one of the "pillars of the Bill of Rights." United States v. Haymond, 139 S. Ct. 2369, 2376 (2019). "When ratified in 1791, the Bill of Rights applied only to the Federal Government." Timbs v. Indiana, 139 S. Ct. 682, 687 (2019). *Cf.* Cohen v. Wright, 22 Cal. 293, 318 (1863) ("The terms 'due process of law' have a distinct legal signification, clearly securing to every person whether a citizen or not, without distinction of sex or race, a judicial trial, according to the established rules of law, before he can be deprived of life, liberty, or property.").

191. Bessler, Cruel and Unusual, *supra* note 15, at 204, 308.

192. Danforth v. Minnesota, 552 U.S. 264, 269–70 (2008) ("The ratification of the Fourteenth Amendment radically changed the federal courts' relationship with state courts. That Amendment, one of the post-Civil War Reconstruction Amendments ratified in 1868, is the source of this Court's power to decide whether a defendant in a state proceeding received a fair trial—*i.e.*, whether his deprivation of liberty was 'without due process of law.' U.S. Const., Amdt. 14, § 1 ('[N]or shall any State deprive any person of life,

liberty, or property, without due process of law'). In construing that Amendment, we have held that it imposes minimum standards of fairness on the States, and requires state criminal trials to provide defendants with protections 'implicit in the concept of ordered liberty.' *Palko v. Connecticut,* 302 U.S. 319, 325, 58 S.Ct. 149, 82 L.Ed. 288 (1937)."); John D. Bessler, *The Inequality of America's Death Penalty: A Crossroads for Capital Punishment at the Intersection of the Eighth and Fourteenth Amendments*, 73 WASH. & LEE L. REV. ONLINE (2016), https://scholarlycommons.law.wlu.edu/wlulr-online/vol73/iss1/22 (discussing the ratification of the Fourteenth Amendment).

193. JETHRO K. LIEBERMAN, A PRACTICAL COMPANION TO THE CONSTITUTION: HOW THE SUPREME COURT HAS RULED ON ISSUES FROM ABORTION TO ZONING xii (1999) ("Beginning in the late nineteenth century ... the Supreme Court began to apply to the state individual rights contained in the Bill of Rights, by 'incorporating' them into the Due Process Clause of the Fourteenth Amendment, which itself applies directly to the states. Through a long process of 'selective incorporation' ... the Bill of Rights today has largely been absorbed in the Fourteenth Amendment and hence is equally applicable to the states and the federal government.").

194. U.S. CONST., amend. XIV. The Fourteenth Amendment's Due Process Clause "centrally concerns the fundamental fairness of governmental activity." Quill Corp. v. North Dakota, 504 U.S. 298, 312 (1992), *overruled on other grounds*, South Dakota v. Wayfair, Inc. 138 S. Ct. 2080, 2092–93 (2018); *see also* District Attorney's Office for Third Judicial Dist. v. Osborne, 557 U.S. 52, 67 (2009) (noting that the Due Process Clause "imposes procedural limitations on a State's power to take away protected entitlements") (*citing* Jones v. Flowers, 547 U.S. 220, 226–239 (2006); Weinberger v. Wiesenfeld, 420 U.S. 636, 638 n.2, 95 S. Ct. 1225, 43 L.Ed.2d 514 (1975) ("[W]hile the Fifth Amendment contains no equal protection clause, it does forbid discrimination that is so unjustifiable as to be violative of *due process*. This Court's approach to Fifth Amendment equal protection claims has always been precisely the same as to equal protection claims under the Fourteenth Amendment." (citations and internal quotation marks omitted; alteration in original)).

195. Tetlow, *supra* note 18, at 1139.

196. Bessler, *supra* note 21. The *Arkansas Law Review* article only addressed the constitutionality of private prosecutors for interested parties. The article pointed out that the term "private prosecutor" was not to be confused with state laws that allow disinterested private attorneys to prosecute cases in the absence of a county attorney. *See, e.g.*, MINN. STAT. § 388.09, subd. 1 ("When there is no county attorney, the county board may employ any competent attorney to perform legal services for the county. The board may employ an attorney to assist the county attorney, to appear for the county or any county officer in any action in which the county or officer in an official capacity is a party, to advise the board or its members in relation to the action, or in relation to any other matter affecting the interests of the county. The county may pay the attorney out of the funds of the county."); MINN. STAT. § 388.09, subd. 2 ("Except in the counties of Ramsey and Hennepin, the county board with concurrence of the county attorney may enter into agreements with attorneys or firms of attorneys for the prosecution of gross misdemeanors, misdemeanors or petty misdemeanors, without making these attorneys or members of the firms assistant county attorneys or employees of the county where the county attorney has responsibility for the prosecution of these charges. If there is a contract between the county and any city within it which provides that the county attorney shall also prosecute municipal ordinance, municipal rule or regulation, and charter provision violations for that city, an attorney or firm engaged pursuant to this subdivision may also prosecute these violations."); Graham v. Crow Wing County Board of Commissioners, 515 N.W.2d 81, 85 (Minn. Ct. App. 1995) ("Minn. Stat. § 388.09 sets forth the circumstances under which a board may hire an attorney in place of the county attorney."); Keiver v. Koochiching County, 169 N.W. 254 (Minn. 1918) ("'When there is no county attorney, the county board may employ any competent attorney to perform legal services for the county as may be necessary.'") (quoting "section 970, Gen. St. 1913"); IDAHO CODE § 31-2603(a) ("When the prosecuting attorney for the county is absent from the court, or when he has acted as counsel or attorney for a party accused in relation to the matter of which the accused stands charged, and for which he is to be tried on a criminal charge, or when he is near of kin to the party to be tried on a criminal charge, or when he has a business connection or kinship with the complainant or defendant, or when he is unable to attend to his duties, the district court may, upon petition of the prosecuting attorney or board of

county commissioners, by an order entered in its minutes, stating the cause therefor, appoint some suitable person to perform for the time being, or for the trial of such accused person, the duties of such prosecuting attorney, and the person so appointed has all the powers of the prosecuting attorney, while so acting as such."); State v. Barber, 88 P. 418, 419 (Idaho 1907) (quoting Idaho's statute, listed as from "Session Laws of 1897, p. 74"); *see also* IDAHO CODE § 31-2603(b) ("The prosecuting attorney may petition the district judge of his county for the appointment of a special assistant attorney-general to assist in the prosecution of any criminal case pending in the county; and if it appears to the district judge to whom such petition is addressed that good cause appears for granting such petition, the district judge, may, with the approval of the attorney-general, appoint an assistant attorney-general to assist in such prosecution. The compensation of the person so appointed shall be fixed by agreement between the district judge and the attorney-general and shall be paid by the attorney-general out of appropriations made available for the conduct of his office."); State v. Corcoran, 61 P. 1034, 1035–36 (Idaho 1990):

> The third specification of error is based upon the action of the trial court in making an order designating J. H. Forney as special prosecutor and acting county attorney of Shoshone county. In determining whether the court acted correctly in this regard or not, we should keep in view the conditions that existed. In the proclamation of the governor of May 4th, which put martial law in force in Shoshone county to a limited extent, it was said, after setting forth the riot of April 29, 1899, which resulted in the death of James Cheyne, for which appellant is being prosecuted in this action, that "the perpetrators of said outrages seem to enjoy immunity from arrest and punishment through subservience of peace officers of said county of Shoshone, or through fear on the part of said officers to such bodies of lawless and armed men." In the face of this charge, either of complicity, or of disqualification through fear, the county attorney of said county, in open court, stated to the court that he was disqualified from acting as county attorney, and that he was unable to attend to the duties of said office in matters connected with or growing out of the alleged riots of April 29, 1899, in Shoshone county. It is evident to our minds that said county attorney was unable to discharge the duties of his said office, within the meaning and intent of the act of February 2, 1899. It therefore became the duty of the district court to appoint some suitable person to perform, for the time being, the duties of said office. But appellant urges that J. H. Forney was disqualified, because the record shows that he lived, not in Shoshone, but in an adjoining county, and that he was attorney for the owners of the mining property destroyed in said riot. The action of the court in this matter is to be tested solely by the provisions of the act of February 2, 1899 (Acts 1899, pp. 24, 25), the first two sections of which are as follows:
>
> > Section 1. No person shall be eligible to the office of county attorney who is not an attorney and counselor at law duly licensed to practice as such in the district courts of the state. No county attorney shall hold any other county or state office during his term of office as county attorney.
> >
> > Sec. 2. *When there is no county attorney* for the county or when he is absent from the court, or when he has acted as counsel or attorney for a party accused in relation to the matter of which the accused stands charged, and for which he is to be tried on a criminal charge, or when he is near of kin to the party to be tried on a criminal charge, or when he is unable to attend to his duties, the district court may, by an order entered in its minutes, stating the cause therefor, appoint some suitable person to perform for the time being or for the trial of such accused person, the duties of such county attorney, and the person so appointed has all the powers of the county attorney, while so acting as such.
>
> There is no showing or claim that said Forney is not a suitable person, other than the claim that he is not a resident of the county, and that he was attorney in one case for the mining company. Section 2 of the act of February 2, 1899, quoted *supra*, does not require that the appointee, who only acts temporarily, should be a resident of the county. We can readily see that contingencies might arise and had probably arisen in this case when it would be the duty of the court, in subserving the public interest, to appoint, through necessity, some lawyer living outside the county to perform, for the time being, the duties of the office of county attorney. Mr. Forney was not disqualified from acting as county attorney pro tem. by reason of his having been attorney for the

Bunkerhill & Sullivan Mining Company in a civil case. This action is between the people of the state, on one side, and the appellant, upon the other. We think that the trial court was justified in appointing Mr. Forney to act temporarily as the prosecuting officer of Shoshone county. But, even if we be mistaken in this, he acted as such, and his acts were those of an officer de facto, and entitled to recognition as such. And we do not find anything in the record before us which indicates that any substantial right of the defendant has been prejudiced by Mr. Forney's appointment, or that the result would have been different if some other suitable person had acted as prosecutor instead of Mr. Forney.

197. In England and elsewhere in the British Isles, private prosecutions were the tradition and norm for centuries. MR. MACLAURIN, COMP., ARGUMENTS AND DECISIONS IN REMARKABLE CASES, BEFORE THE HIGH COURT OF JUSTICIARY, AND OTHER SUPREME COURTS, IN SCOTLAND 253 (1774) ("From the 4th book of *Reg. Maj.* it appears, that anciently the primary right of criminal prosecution was in private parties; and it was only in case of their not exerting it that the crown could take it up. The method of private prosecution was therefore fixed."); FRANK J. GOODNOW, THE PRINCIPLES OF THE ADMINISTRATIVE LAW OF THE UNITED STATES 412 (1905) ("The English system was based upon the idea of private prosecution. The usual method of prosecution was a complaint by the individual against whom the crime had been committed to a committing magistrate who made the preliminary examination of the prisoner and sent the case up to the grand jury in case the prisoner was held."); JONATHAN SIMON, POOR DISCIPLINE: PAROLE AND THE SOCIAL CONTROL OF THE UNDERCLASS, 1890–1990, at 21 (1993) ("Prosecution in sixteenth-century Britain was almost wholly dependent on private prosecutors—usually, but not always, the victim of crime. Recognizance bonds provided a way to prevent abuse of the prosecution power in the absence of a professional bureaucracy to screen cases."); MAY, *supra* note 38, at 20 ("Victims of crime bore the chief responsibility for bringing offenders to justice: a victim's pursuit and apprehension of a suspected felon and his willingness to take that person before a local magistrate were crucial to prosecution. There were obviously disadvantages to a system of private prosecution. It did not deal adequately with public offenses, crimes in which no one had received special injury and for which no one would step forward to claim special satisfaction, and the financial burden borne by the private prosecutor must also have barred many victims of crime from seeking legal redress."); *id.* at 195 ("One of the 'great evils' in the English criminal justice system, according to an article in [the Legal Observer], was 'making the party who suffers by the crime the prosecutor in the punishment of it.' His may have been the immediate injury or loss, but 'the injury set forth in the major proposition is an injury done to society.' … 'Private prosecutors standing up and demanding exile or death against their fellow-subject,—then begging, when the trial is over, for the repayment of the expense to which they are put,—make the Old Bailey Sessions among the most painful scenes that a feeling mind can contemplate.'"); J. M. BEATTIE, THE FIRST ENGLISH DETECTIVES: THE BOW STREET RUNNERS AND THE POLICING OF LONDON, 1750–1840, at 55 (2012) ("It is impossible to learn how many private prosecutors engaged the help of the runners. Of the 18 trials at the Old Bailey in 1767 in which one or more runners gave evidence for the prosecution, six were cases in which John Fielding had paid them to investigate and apprehend the accused. In the other 12, they had been engaged by the victim.").

198. GILLIÉRON, *supra* note 59, at 46–47 ("The American public prosecutor is not part of British common law heritage. In 1976, Jack M. Kress stated that the 'district attorney is a distinctive and uniquely American contribution to common law jurisprudence. Whereas Americans typically describe their legal system as based upon the English common law, in terms of both its procedural attributes and substantive state penal codes, the public prosecutor is a figure virtually unknown to the English system, which is primarily one of private prosecution to this day.' It was only in 1879 that England established a Director of Public Prosecutions. His function was limited to making prosecution decisions in very serious cases, such as homicide. At the beginning of the eighteenth century, the colonies had already begun to introduce a system of public prosecution."); *id.* at 47–48 ("In 1704, Connecticut became the first colony to eliminate the system of private prosecution entirely, and other colonies soon followed. By the end of eighteenth century, a system of public prosecution was established in nearly every state of the union.").

199. *Id.* at 48 ("In America, the concept of public prosecution is well established. In opposition to private prosecution, where a crime is primarily a private matter between the offender and the victim, in a

system of public prosecution all criminal acts are considered against the state."). Early public prosecutors had much different professional lives than most modern-day public prosecutors. Stephanos Bibas, The Machinery of Criminal Justice 18 (2012) ("Public prosecutors were at first appointed, but by the Civil War, there was a strong trend toward electing them directly and locally. They were not necessarily full-time professionals. Most were part-time officials, hurrying to get back to their more lucrative private practices on the side. They received low salaries or fixed fees per case or conviction. Thus, they sought to dispose of their criminal cases quickly so they could earn additional money from their private clients."); Eric S. Fish, *Prosecutorial Constitutionalism*, 90 S. Cal. L. Rev. 237, 245 n.12 (2017) ("[H]istorically the distinction between public and private prosecutors has been somewhat slippery. In the nineteenth century, after public prosecution became widespread, prosecutors were still paid for each case that they brought or for each conviction that they obtained. This fee structure effectively caused public prosecutors to act as private lawyers for accusers, or as partisan advocates for conviction.").

200. The divergence of the British and American systems began before the American Revolution. Jerold H. Israel, Yale Kamisar, Wayne R. LaFave & Nancy J. King, Criminal Procedure and the Constitution 21 (2006) ("Although the British common law tradition was one of private prosecution (i.e., the complainant hired private counsel to press the prosecution), Americans had established an office of public prosecutor even before the Revolution. In most of the colonies, public prosecution was originally superimposed upon a system of private prosecution, but private prosecution was eventually seen as impracticable, too often subject to abuse, and inconsistent with the view that crimes were 'acts against the state' . . . .").

201. *Benoit*, 575 N.Y.S.2d at 752 ("Section 50 of the New York City Criminal Court Act is unconstitutional as applied to her since a private prosecution based on this statute results in a violation of the Equal Protection and Due Process clauses of the Fourteenth Amendment."). *But cf.* Cronan ex rel. State v. Cronan, 744 A.2d 866, 877 (R.I. 2001) ("The defendant complains, for example, that this private prosecution violated his due process, separation of powers, and equal protection rights under the Rhode Island and United States Constitutions. Whatever merit these contentions may have in some other case, we hold that defendant waived his right to raise these constitutional challenges to this private prosecution. By failing to raise any of these defenses or challenges to the complaint before trial, defendant could not assert them for the first time in a post-trial motion to arrest the judgment.").

202. Benjamin Franklin expressed his views on the criminal law in a letter to an Italian thinker, Gaetano Filangieri, whose book, *The Science of Legislation*, addressed criminal law issues. Benjamin Franklin to Gaetano Filangieri, Jan. 11, 1783, *Founders Online*, National Archives, https://founders.archives.gov/documents/Franklin/01-38-02-0431 ("The two first Volumes of your excellent Work, which were put into my hands by M. Pio, I perus'd with great Pleasure. They are also much esteem'd by some very judicious Persons to whom I have lent them. I should have been glad of another Copy for one of those Friends, who is very desirous of procuring it, but I suppose those you mention to have sent to M. Pio did not arrive. I was glad to learn, that you were proceeding to consider the criminal Laws. None have more need of Reformation. They are every where in so great Disorder, and so much Injustice is committed in the Execution of them, that I have been sometimes inclin'd to imagine, less would exist in the World if there were no such Laws, and the Punishment of Injuries were left to private Resentment. I am glad therefore that you have not suffered yourself to be discouraged by any Objections or Apprehensions, and that we may soon expect the Satisfaction of seeing the two Volumes on that Subject which you have now under the Press.").

203. State v. Harrington, 534 S.W.2d 44, 48–49 (Mo. 1976) (private prosecution "inherently and fundamentally unfair" despite its prior history in the state); People v. Municipal Court, 27 Cal. App. 3d 193, 206, 103 Cal. Rptr. 645, 654–55 (1972) (rejecting a trial court's authorization of a private prosecutor because due process requires that "any criminal proceeding be authorized and approved by the district attorney"); Biemel v. State, 37 N.W. 244, 247 (Wis. 1888) (describing 1887 Wisconsin statute barring private prosecutors); Meister v. People, 31 Mich. 99, 103–04 (1875) (observing that Michigan statute barring private prosecution was "designed to secure impartiality from all persons connected with criminal trials").

204. Cameron v. State, 171 P.3d 1154, 1157 n.23 (Alaska 2007); *see also* John Gilbeaut, *Indictment of a System*, 87 A.B.A. J. 34, 35–36 (2001) ("Grand juries often shielded colonists from abuses by prosecutors for the Crown, and the framers required indictment in the Fifth Amendment as a buffer between the

accused and the government."); United States v. Cook, 472 F. Supp.3d 326, 330 n.4 (N.D. Miss. 2020) ("In a now famous interview, former New York State Chief Judge Sol Wachtler stated something along the lines of 'a grand jury would 'indict a ham sandwich' if that's what [a prosecutor] wanted."); United States v. Lewis, No. 201900049, 2020 WL 3047524, at *16 n.10 (U.S. Navy-Marine Corps Ct. Crim. App. June 8, 2020) (Stephens, J., concurring) ("In January 1985, Sol Wachtler, the Chief Judge of the New York Court of Appeals told the New York Daily News, district attorneys have so much influence on grand juries that 'by and large' they could get them to 'indict a ham sandwich.' This quip was popularized in Tom Wolfe's 1987 novel 'The Bonfire of the Vanities.' Judge Wachtler was later himself indicted and convicted for extortion.").

205. In the capital cases, the U.S. Supreme has already held that the Eighth Amendment provides certain *procedural* protections, including to protect against the arbitrary and capricious imposition of death sentences. *See, e.g.*, Bosse v. Oklahoma, 137 S. Ct. 1, 2 (2016) ("A jury convicted petitioner Shaun Michael Bosse of three counts of first-degree murder for the 2010 killing of Katrina Griffin and her two children. The State of Oklahoma sought the death penalty. Over Bosse's objection, the State asked three of the victims' relatives to recommend a sentence to the jury. All three recommended death, and the jury agreed. Bosse appealed, arguing that this testimony about the appropriate sentence violated the Eighth Amendment under *Booth*. The Oklahoma Court of Criminal Appeals affirmed his sentence, concluding that there was 'no error.' We grant certiorari and the motion for leave to proceed *in forma pauperis*, and now vacate the judgment of the Oklahoma Court of Criminal Appeals."; "The Oklahoma Court of Criminal Appeals remains bound by *Booth*'s prohibition on characterizations and opinions from a victim's family members about the crime, the defendant, and the appropriate sentence unless this Court reconsiders that ban. The state court erred in concluding otherwise.") (citation omitted); Welch v. United States, 136 S. Ct. 1257, 1266 (2016) ("Decisions from this Court show that a rule that is procedural for *Teague* purposes still can be grounded in a substantive constitutional guarantee. For instance, the Court has adopted certain rules that regulate capital sentencing procedures in order to enforce the substantive guarantees of the Eighth Amendment. The consistent position has been that those rules are procedural, even though their ultimate source is substantive."); Ring v. Arizona, 536 U.S. 584, 606 (2002) ("States have constructed elaborate sentencing procedures in death cases, Arizona emphasizes, because of constraints we have said the Eighth Amendment places on capital sentencing.") (citations omitted); Sawyer v. Whitley, 505 U.S. 333, 341 (1992) ("Since our decision in *Furman v. Georgia*, 408 U.S. 238, 92 S. Ct. 2726, 33 L.Ed.2d 346 (1972), our Eighth Amendment jurisprudence has required those States imposing capital punishment to adopt procedural safeguards protecting against arbitrary and capricious impositions of the death sentence."); *see also* Beck v. Alabama, 447 U.S. 625, 637–38 (1980) ("While we have never held that a defendant is entitled to a lesser included offense instruction as a matter of due process, the nearly universal acceptance of the rule in both state and federal courts establishes the value to the defendant of this procedural safeguard. That safeguard would seem to be especially important in a case such as this. For when the evidence unquestionably establishes that the defendant is guilty of a serious, violent offense—but leaves some doubt with respect to an element that would justify conviction of a capital offense—the failure to give the jury the 'third option' of convicting on a lesser included offense would seem inevitably to enhance the risk of an unwarranted conviction. Such a risk cannot be tolerated in a case in which the defendant's life is at stake."; "To insure that the death penalty is indeed imposed on the basis of 'reason rather than caprice or emotion,' we have invalidated procedural rules that tended to diminish the reliability of the sentencing determination. The same reasoning must apply to rules that diminish the reliability of the guilt determination. Thus, if the unavailability of a lesser included offense instruction enhances the risk of an unwarranted conviction, Alabama is constitutionally prohibited from withdrawing that option from the jury in a capital case.").

206. *Benoit*, 575 N.Y.S.2d at 756 ("[T]he defendant here is deprived of even the semblance of the exercise of prosecutorial discretion, and the conflicts implicit in this private prosecution violate due process.") (citations omitted); *id.* ("Accordingly, since *Zimmer, supra*, dictates that a public prosecutor must be disinterested, continued prosecution of the defendant here by Ms. Franck, whose interest in the prosecution is beyond peradventure, would violate both the defendant's due process and equal protection guarantees.") (*citing* People v. Zimmer, 51 N.Y. 390, 434 N.Y.S.2d 206, 414 N.E.2d 705 (1980)).

Chapter 1 Notes

1. *See* 3 Encyclopedia of Crime and Justice 1286–88 (Sanford H. Kadish ed. 1983); Joan E. Jacoby, The American Prosecutor: A Search for Identity 3–39 (1980); Allen Steinberg, The Transformation of Criminal Justice: Philadelphia, 1800–1880 (1989); Juan Cardenas, *The Crime Victim in the Prosecutorial Process*, 9 Harv. J.L. & Pub. Pol'y 357, 359–71 (1986); Josephine Gittler, *Expanding the Role of the Victim in a Criminal Action*, 11 Pepperdine L. Rev. 117, 125–32 (1984); Harold J. Krent, *Executive Control Over Criminal Law Enforcement: Some Lessons from History*, 38 Am. U. L. Rev. 275, 290–96 (1989); Joan Meier, *The "Right" to a Disinterested Prosecutor of Criminal Contempt: Unpacking Public and Private Interests*, 70 Wash. U. L.Q. 85, 101–03 (1992); Thomas J. Robinson, Comment, *Private Prosecution in Criminal Cases*, 4 Wake Forest L. Rev. 300 (1968); Andrew Sidman, Comment, *The Outmoded Concept of Private Prosecution*, 25 Am. U.L. Rev. 754, 756–65 (1976); W. Scott Van Alstyne, Jr., Comment, *The District Attorney—A Historical Puzzle*, 1952 Wis. L. Rev. 125.

2. John D. Bessler, *The Public Interest and the Unconstitutionality of Private Prosecutors*, 47 Ark. L. Rev. 511, 515 n.12 (1994) (collecting citations); *see also* 1 Joel Prentiss Bishop On the Law of Pleading and Evidence and the Practice in Criminal Cases § 143 (3d ed. 1880) ("[A]t the common law, 'the king's coroner and attorney in the Court of King's Bench, usually called the master of the crown office,' may file a criminal information. He does it only on the prompting of some private prosecutor; or, as Blackstone expresses it, 'at the relation of some private person or common informer'; but the form of the information makes no mention of this, or of the prompting. In early times, this officer proceeded, says Lord Mansfield, 'upon any application, as a matter of course.' The consequence of which was, that the process was sometimes perverted to private ends; and, to remedy the evil, it was in 1692 provided by statute 4 & 5 Will. & M. c. 18, that informations should not be filed by this officer, except by leave of court, and on the prosecutor's giving security to the party proceeded against for costs. It may be doubtful how far this statute is common law in this country; but, it seems, we have no such officer, so that the law of England respecting this kind of criminal informations cannot be of practical force with us."); *id.* at § 278 ("'In general, every man is of common right entitled to prefer an accusation against a party whom he suspects to be guilty' of crime. He is termed the prosecutor. Commonly he is some person particularly aggrieved by the criminal act, but not so necessarily. In England, the greater part of criminal prosecutions are set on foot by private prosecutors, and conducted to the end by legal persons whom they employ, with only slight supervision by officers of the government.").

3. Bessler, *supra* note 2, at 515 n.13 (collecting citations); *see also* Cardenas, *supra* note 1, at 358 (noting that in the Middle Ages "vengeance and personal animosity" played a role in the justice system).

4. Sir Edward Coke, The Third Part of the Institutes of the Laws of England: Concerning High Treason, and Other Pleas of the Crown and Criminal Causes 157 (Union, NJ: The Lawbook Exchange, 2000) (reprinting London edition printed for W. Clarke and Sons in 1817). *The Third Part of the Institutes* was originally published in London in 1644. Barbara J. Shapiro, Law Reform in Early Modern England, 1500–1740: Crown, Parliament and the Press 91 n.156 (2019).

5. Sir James Stephen, A History of the Criminal Law of England 245 (1883).

6. Before the development of English law and criminal procedure, aggrieved individuals or families resorted to self-help. John Hostettler, A History of Criminal Justice in England and Wales 12 (2009) ("When Anglo-Saxon law first began to emerge in England it was primitive and harsh, reflecting contemporary life. The community was based on agriculture with the majority of people living in villages and on farms. In addition to flooding, famine and other natural disasters many lived in fear of being robbed or slain. Murder and cattle-rustling were the most common outrages and they were dealt with in turn by private vengeance and constant blood-feuds. Initially, self-help was the primary law."); *id.* at 13 ("At first, few could write or keep records and there were no courts and no public officers to pursue or inquire into crime. Injuries inflicted were punished by private vendetta on the part of those who suffered from them or their relatives, and the vengeance was savage. Gradually, however, the rulers of the four kingdoms, whose powers were increasing and who began to exercise direct personal control over their small populations, started to intervene against lawlessness and to compose laws, known as dooms. These were written in the English language derived from Wessex, instead of Latin as used on the continent.").

Private prosecutions were also used in English military tribunals. *E.g.*, OPINIONS OF ATTORNEYS GENERAL: MESSAGE FROM THE PRESIDENT OF THE UNITED STATES, TRANSMITTING OPINIONS OF ATTORNEYS GENERAL 669 (1851) ("It seems, consulting *Hough on Courts-Martial*, that the practice in England is to appoint a private prosecutor before the trial commences. And though the reasons there given for this course would by no means render it necessary that the persons selected should be the accuser, yet, from what is said of such prosecutor being sworn as a witness, it is probable that the accuser is in fact generally, perhaps uniformly, selected. The writer just referred to proceeds to declare, that it rests with the court to determine whether they will allow a private prosecutor to reply or not; and that the usual rule is to allow it, if new evidence is introduced in the defence, or if the prisoner has impugned the credit or attacked the character of the prosecutor or his witnesses."); *see also* S. V. BENÉT, A TREATISE ON MILITARY LAW AND THE PRACTICE OF COURTS-MARTIAL 141 (5th ed. 1866) ("[I]t may be added that upon military trials in this country, the prosecution is almost invariably conducted by the judge advocate, who, while pressing his proof, is at the same time bound to see that the accused has all proper assistance in bringing out his defence. In the British courts, on the other hand, the prosecutor is more frequently an officer or person acting independently as such, and who, as both accuser and prosecutor, is wholly or mainly interested in convicting the prisoner.").

7. *E.g.*, Matthew Steilen, *Bills of Attainder*, 53 HOUS. L. REV. 767, 819 & n.298 (2016) ("Christopher St. German mentions attainder in several places in *Doctor and Student*, whose two dialogues were composed between 1523 and 1530, on the cusp of the English Reformation; but the mentions are brief and clearly ancillary to other topics."; "For example, St. German's 'Student' describes for the civilian 'Doctor' the various forms of process available at common law for prosecuting a man suspected of being hired to kill another, including indictment and appeal of murder (the latter being a form of private criminal suit). The two forms treat a suspect's silence differently. If an 'appele [is] brought of the murdre [and the suspect] stand dombe & wyll not answer to the murdre,' says the Student, 'he shall be attaynted of the murdre and shall forfeyte lyfe landes and goodes'; in contrast, a suspect indicted for murder who remains silent is 'pressyd to dethe' (a form of torture designed to force the suspect to enter a plea) and forfeits only his goods."). Another source on the history of English law discusses an ancient procedure known an *actio furti*, what transformed into *appeal of larceny*. 1 SIR FREDERICK POLLOCK & FREDERIC WILLIAM MAITLAND, THE HISTORY OF ENGLISH LAW BEFORE THE TIME OF EDWARD I, at 157–58 (1898) ("When there has been a bailment and the chattel has been taken from the bailee's possession, it is natural that, so long as prosecution means speedy pursuit, the right and duty of prosecution should he his. The bailor, it may be, will never hear of the theft until it is some days old and the tell-tale hoof-marks have been effaced. When the pursuer makes his claim he will say that the thing is 'his'; but this is an assertion of possession rather than of ownership; he means that the thing was taken from him. Of any other procedure for the recovery of goods we read little or nothing in our old dooms. No doubt the bailor had some action against the bailee for the return of the goods; but whether this action was conceived as based upon ownership or as based upon contract, whether that distinction could have been clearly drawn, whether the bailee could be compelled to deliver back the very thing that had been bailed, or whether the bailor had to be content if he got its value—these are questions about which we have no certain information. In the thirteenth century this ancient procedure was not yet obsolete; but it was assuming a new form, that of the appeal of larceny. Bracton called it the *actio furti*. We should do wrong were we to reject this name as a scrap of romanizing pedantry. English law knew an action based upon theft, and, if we would speak of such an action in Latin, we can but call it *actio furti*. It still had about it many antique traits, though, as already said, it was assuming a new form, that of the appeal of larceny. We are wont to think of the appeal as of a criminal prosecution, though one that was instituted by a private prosecutor. A criminal prosecution it was, and if the appellee was convicted, he would as a general rule be sentenced to death; but still throughout the middle ages it had in it a marked recuperatory element; it was constantly spoken of as a remedy competent to the man whose goods had been stolen: it would restore those goods to him. But in Bracton's day the recuperatory element was even more visible than it was in later centuries, and we can see a close connexion between the appeal and that old procedure which we have endeavoured to describe. A little time spent over this matter will not be lost, for it is only through procedural forms that we can penetrate to substantive rights.").

8. Janelle R. Greenberg & Martin S. Greenberg, *Crime and Justice in Tudor-Stuart England and the Modern United States: The More Things Change, the More They Stay the Same*, 6 L. & Hum. Behav. 261, 263 (1982) ("If the victim decided to report the offense, he or she went to the nearest justice of the peace, who, if he believed the story, would order the arrest of the suspect. If the constable found the accused, he could arrest him and bring him before the justice of the peace, who would likely examine him along with the victim and any witnesses who were available. If the justice believed the suspect's story, he set him free. If not, he released the accused on bail if the latter were a person of wealth, or committed him to jail if he were not."); *id.* ("All witnesses and suspects were bound over until the next quarter session. At that time a grand jury, usually composed of 23 or 24 men, heard the facts of the case, with the justices questioning the victim, the accused, and the witnesses. If the grand jury found the evidence inadequate, it returned a bill of *ignoramus* ('we do not know') and the accused went free. If the grand jury found a *billa vera*, a true bill, as such juries were increasingly inclined to do in the 16th and 17th centuries, the accused stood indicted and was returned to jail or released on bail. At the next assize, presided over by the king's own justices from the great courts at Westminister, the indicted suspect would appear for trial. Here the suspect could either plead 'guilty' or 'put himself upon his country,' the latter being a plea of not guilty. A trial by jury followed.") (italics in original); *see also* Carlisle Herald (Carlisle, PA), Dec. 14, 1815, p. 3 ("It ought to be provided, that where the return of ignoramus is made by a grand jury, or where on trial a verdict of not guilty is rendered, and the prosecutor is ordered to pay the costs, the juries shall respectively determine, whether the defendant's costs, shall be paid by the prosecutor or by himself. If an indictment for a nuisance in a public road or highway is on trial not sustained, it ought for obvious reasons to be provided, that the prosecutor shall not be liable for costs, unless there be evident malice and want of probable cause.").

9. Greenberg & Greenberg, *supra* note 8, at 262; *see also id.* at 263 ("In theory, the king was the fountain of all criminal justice, and in practice this jurisdiction was primarily exercised by the Court of the King's Bench at Westminister, by the assizes, and by the quarter sessions. Assizes were special sessions supervised by the king's justices from Westminister and commissioned under the Great Seal. For administrative purposes England was divided into six circuits, in each of which, generally speaking, were held two assizes annually. The majority of criminal cases, and especially the serious offenses of murder, robbery, burglary, rape, and grand larceny, were dealt with on circuit by the king's justices."); *id.* ("In addition to the assizes, the sessions of the peace, presided over by the local justices of the peace and empowered by the commissions of the peace, also exercised criminal jurisdiction. Called 'quarter sessions' because parliamentary statute decreed that they be held four times a year, these sessions usually dealt with less serious offenses, e.g., petty larceny."); Tyrone Kirchengast, The Victim in Criminal Law and Justice 39 (2006) ("Into the latter part of the twelfth century, prosecution changed from exclusively private, to being partially controlled by the King."); 1 Sir Thomas Edlyne Tomlins, The Law-Dictionary: Explaining the Rise, Progress, and Present State of the British Law; Defining and Interpreting the Terms or Words of Art; and Comprising Also Copious Information on the Subjects of Trade and Government (3d ed. 1820) (giving the following definition of "Indictment": "Indictamentum, from the Fr. *enditer*, i. e. *indicare*, to shew. A bill or declaration of complaint drawn up in form of law, exhibited for some offence criminal or penal, and preferred to a grand jury; upon whose oath it is found to be true, before a judge or others, having power to punish or certify the offence. *Termes de Ley*. Indictment in the Scotch Law, is the form of process by which a criminal is brought to trial at the instance of the Lord Advocate. Where a private party is a principal prosecutor he brings his action in what is termed the form of criminal letters.").

10. *See generally* Thomas Jones Howell, A Complete Collection of State Trials and Proceedings for High Treason and Other Crimes and Misdemeanors from the Earliest Period to the Year 1783 (1816) (multi-volume series).

11. Criminal and Judicial Statistics, 1878–1879 - Ireland, at 48 (1879) ("In England and Wales the Coroners' inquest retains its position of importance, owing to the system of private prosecution. When the prosecution of infanticide, of other murders and of manslaughter is intrusted to private prosecutors, the Coroners' tribunal is essential to secure that crimes involving the loss of human life are not compromised or concealed."); *see also* Criminal and Judicial Statistics—1877—Ireland 57 (1878) ("The important position which the ancient Coroners' tribunal for inquiry and prosecution in cases of sudden

or suspicious death appears from these figures to occupy in England and Wales arises from the system of private prosecutions that prevails there. When the prosecution of infanticide, other murders and manslaughter is intrusted to private prosecutors, the Coroners' tribunal is essential to secure that crimes involving the loss of human life are not compromised or concealed. The cost of this machinery for checking private prosecutions, £85,667, or 38 per cent. of the whole, is however very considerable. Of the other expenditure of criminal prosecutions in England and Wales, £142,261, only £10,092 was for Government prosecutions (£1,325 in 221 Mint cases, for issuing base coins and other offences against the currency, and £8,767 for 50 other criminal cases prosecuted on indictment by the Treasury Solicitor), whilst £114,983 was for defraying certain parts of the expenses of private prosecutors in 13,598 prosecutions at the Assize Courts, Central Criminal Courts, and Quarter Sessions, and £17,186 for 17,821 proceedings under the Criminal Justice Act and Juvenile Offenders Act.").

12. John H. Langbein, *The Criminal Trial before the Lawyers*, 45 U. Chi. L. Rev. 263, 267, 282 (1978); *see also id.* at 316 ("The English system of private prosecution, with its emphasis on a nonbureaucratic pretrial procedure, kept the English trial judge from assuming sustained responsibility for investigation. The English did not develop the *Aufklärungspflicht*, the duty to clarify, which drives the Continental judge. In England the busy judges from the central courts at Westminster were loaned to the Old Bailey or to an assize court for a crowded session of at most a few days. Given the caseload that awaited him, the English trial judge had to take whatever case the private prosecutor, aided by the lay JP and the lay constable, had worked up for trial.").

13. *See* William Henry P. Phyfe, 5000 Facts and Fancies A Cyclopædia of Important, Curious, Quaint, and Unique Information in History, Literature, Science, Art, and Nature 546 (rev. ed. 1901) (including this entry for "Old Bailey": "A famous old criminal court on Old Bailey Street, London, erected in 1773, and enlarged in 1808. It is officially known as the *Central Criminal Court*, and consists of two divisions,—the *Old Court*, for the trial of serious offenses, and the *New Court*, for the trial of petty offenses. The Old Bailey adjoins Newgate Prison.") (italics in original); *see also* 1 David Sugarman, Law in History: Histories of Law and Society 296 (1996) (noting the appearance of private prosecutors at Old Bailey trials and that both criminals and their victims were often poor, although "[i]n the Old Bailey cases we often cross a class line when we move from the offender to his victim, but not a class gulf": "[t]he victim is usually more propertied than the person who victimized them, although often only slightly").

14. *See Bind Over*, The Free Dictionary, *available at* https://www.thefreedictionary.com/Bound+over.

15. John H. Langbein, *Understanding the Short History of Plea Bargaining*, 13 Law & Society Rev. 261, 262–63 (1979) (italics in original); *see also id.* at 263 ("The accused was forbidden counsel, the prosecution might be conducted by a lawyer, but in practice virtually never was. The victim or other complaining witness, sometimes aided by the lay constable and the lay justice of the peace, performed the role we now assign to the public prosecutor, gathering evidence and presenting it at trial."); *id.* ("[A]t the Old Bailey only two twelve-man jury panels were used to discharge the entire caseload of as many as a hundred felony trials in a few days. Each jury usually heard several unrelated cases before deliberating on any. Often the juries rendered verdicts in these cases of life and death 'at the bar,' that is, so rapidly that they did not even retire from the courtroom to deliberate.").

16. Jennifer T. Roberts, The Plague of War : Athens, Sparta, and the Struggle for Ancient Greece 309 (2017) (noting of the trial of Socrates: "In 399, three Athenians, Anytus, Lycon, and Meletus—all men of democratic sympathies—took Socrates to court. (It was customary in Athens for cases to be brought by private prosecutors rather than by the state.) Because of the amnesty of 403, they could not accuse him of collusion with the traitors Alcibiades and Critias, both of them men with whom he consorted regularly, so instead they accused him of not believing in the gods of the state, of introducing new gods, and of corrupting the young."); Wilfried Nippel, Ancient and Modern Democracy: Two Concepts of Liberty? (2015) (noting of Athenian democracy: "[I]n general a prosecutor who gained less than a fifth of the judges' votes—who was therefore thought to have brought a casual or abusive case—had himself to pay a fine; and if he repeated the offence he was barred from bringing any future prosecution. Trials in which everyone had a right of action, including those against office holders, were generally heard before 500 jurors; private prosecutions were heard before 200 or 400 jurors; or before 201, 401 or 501 so as to avoid a tied vote."); Joseph Roisman & J. C. Yardly, Ancient Greece form Homer to Alexander: The

Evidence 269 (2011) (noting of ancient Athenian democracy: "Private prosecutions of homicide and wounding are heard in the Areopagus, if the killing and wounding are premeditated, as are those of poisoning and arson."); Edward E. Cohen, Ancient Athenian Maritime Courts 144 (2005) (referencing "private prosecutions" in the context of ancient Athenian maritime courts).

17. Sean J. Crossan, Introductory Scots Law: Theory and Practice § 1.15 (3d ed. 2017) ("In the Ancient Rome of Julius Caesar, the criminal code was highly developed but its enforcement relied on a system of private prosecution whereby lawyers were commissioned (and petitioned) by interested parties to take on the role of prosecutors. There was no such thing as an office of State Prosecutor. In one of the most famous examples of a successful private prosecution commissioned in Ancient Rome, Marcus Tullius Cicero, the lawyer, was approached by leading members of several Sicilian communities in 70 BC who wished him to commence a prosecution against the incredibly corrupt Roman Governor of Sicily, Gaius Verres. Undoubtedly, Verres had committed terrible crimes against the people of Sicily (most Roman Governors did during their term of office), but Cicero's decision to prosecute him in the Roman law courts was not entirely altruistic. Cicero calculated that, if he won the extortion case against Gaius Verres (which he duly did in 69 BC), he would inherit Verres' patrician status and wealth, not to mention the fame and the hordes of potential clients any victory would almost certainly bring him. Cicero also had his eyes on a political career and coveted the supreme office of the Roman Republic, the Consulship or Chief Magistrate (in fact there were normally two Consuls at any one time). On such private prosecutions were the foundations of successful political careers established and Cicero became a Consul in 63 BC."); Charles Freeman, Egypt, Greece, and Rome: Civilizations of the Ancient Mediterranean 416 (3d ed. 2014) (noting that in ancient Rome "the direct bribery of voters" was "a common subject of private prosecutions between rivals"); Frederic Huidekoper, Judaism at Rome: B. C. 76 to A. D. 140, at 475–81 (1876) (discussing the Roman system of private prosecution); 4 Wilhelm Ihne, The History of Rome 133 (1882) ("The criminal procedure in Rome, as in Greece, allowed every citizen the right to act a prosecutor. The state in its earlier stages of development, after self-help by private war was abolished, left an injured party to obtain satisfaction and redress of his wrongs by prosecuting the offender by process of law."); William F. Allen & P. V. N. Myers, Ancient History for College and High Schools 246 (1896) ("The Romans had no public prosecuting officer; it was left to the interest or public spirit of individuals to bring criminals to justice, and the private prosecutors were rewarded for their services by a share of the property of their victims. Hence it became a trade, and a very lucrative one, to hunt up offences and bring them to justice. This was called *delation*, and the prosecutions *delators*.").

18. David Sacks, A Dictionary of the Ancient Greek World 130 (1995); *see also* David D. Phillips, The Law of Ancient Athens 33 (2013) ("[I]n at least some and perhaps most *dikai*, a prosecutor who failed to receive 20 percent of the votes incurred the *epôbelia*. The purpose of these penalties was to discourage sycophancy, the bringing of malicious or baseless prosecutions in the hope of harming a personal enemy and/or making money either by extorting payment for dropping charges or by securing a monetary verdict (the man who engaged in such practices was called a sycophant). To judge from the Attic orators and other contemporary sources—especially the comedies of Aristophanes—sycophancy in both public and private lawsuits was a serious problem in Classical Athens; speakers in all kinds of lawsuits accused their opponents of sycophancy as a matter of course.") (citations omitted).

19. David Brewster, comp., The Edinburgh Encyclopædia 258–59 (1830).

20. E. A. Kendall, An Argument for Construing Largely the Right of an Appellee of Murder to Insist on Trial by Battle; and Also for Abolishing Appeals 235 (3d ed. 1818); *see also id.* at 234–35 ("If the sentiments of the reader, upon the law of Appeal of Murder, are in any degree in unison with those expressed in these pages, and if his acquaintance with what has heretofore been written, and heretofore passed in Parliament concerning it, is limited, it will be with nothing short of amazement that he finds it advanced, That 'the Appeal of Murder is the *strongest barrier* our Constitution opposes to the prerogatives of the Crown;' (seeing that on a conviction by Appeal, the King has no power of pardon) that Lord Chief Justice Holt has called the Appeal of Murder 'a most noble birthright of an Englishman,' and that Mr. Moreton, Mr. Dunning (afterward Lord Ashburton) once spoke of it, in his place, in the House of Commons, as 'that great pillar of the Constitution'") (italics in original; citing "the Appendix"); Andrew Amos, Observations on the Statutes of the Reformation in the Reign of King Henry the

EIGHTH 180 (1859) ("The Reformation Parliament can scarcely be blamed for not abolishing Criminal Appeals altogether, when we find Lord Holt extolling them as 'a most noble birthright of an Englishman,' and Lord Coke upholding Trial by Battle as founded on the precedent of David and Goliath.").

21. HERBERT NEWMAN MOZLEY & GEORGE CRISPE WHITELEY, A CONCISE LAW DICTIONARY 490 (1876).

22. Yue Ma, *Exploring the Origins of Public Prosecution*, 18 INT'L CRIM. JUST. REV. 190, 191 (2008) ("In early Anglo-Saxon times, crime was a personal matter to be dealt with through private vengeance. Later in the Middle Ages, kings and tribal leaders placed restrictions on private vengeance to alleviate the disruption caused by the wild justice of vengeance. A system of *wergild*, monetary competition, was created. The law required that an injured party must first seek compensation from the offender. The aggrieved party was permitted to resort to vengeance only when the offender refused to pay legally prescribed compensation."); *id.* at 191–92 ("Although crime was predominantly a private affair, there had never been a complete lack of official interest in criminal matters. Even in Anglo-Saxon times, crime was perceived in twofold light. On one hand, it was a private matter to be resolved by the injured party. On the other hand, crime was also seen as an offense against the peace of the state. For that reason, the offender was required not only to pay *wergild* to the injured party but also a fine, known as *wite*, to the state. The king's involvement in criminal matters nonetheless was driven more by the desire to collect revenue than to help the injured party seek justice.").

23. 8 CHAMBERS'S ENCYCLOPÆDIA: A DICTIONARY OF UNIVERSAL KNOWLEDGE FOR THE PEOPLE WITH MAPS AND NUMEROUS WOOD ENGRAVINGS 243–44 (rev. ed. 1889).

24. MICHAEL MARTIN, CITY OF THE SUN: DEVELOPMENT AND POPULAR RESISTANCE IN THE PRE-MODERN WEST 167 (2017).

25. ALTINA L. WALLER, FEUD: HATFIELDS, MCCOYS, AND SOCIAL CHANGE IN APPALACHIA, 1860–1900, at 1, 10 (1988).

26. *E.g.*, PETER ARNADE & WALTER PREVENIER, HONOR, VENGEANCE, AND SOCIAL TROUBLE: PARDON LETTERS IN THE BURGUNDIAN LOW COUNTRIES 27 (2015) ("In England blood feuds were still a legally recognized practice in the eleventh and twelfth centuries, but ceased by the reign of Edward I (1272–1307). In Scotland and Wales, however, blood feuds survived until the early sixteenth century."); *id.* at 30–31 (noting the use of ducal pardon letters that resolve vendettas and conflicts, and noting that historic feuds "are a reminder that inhabitants of the Low Countries settled scores by means of private vengeance, even as city officials and ducal officers offered the means of conciliation before feuds and vendettas spun out of the[ir] control."); *see also* NICOLAI RUBINSTEIN, STUDIES IN ITALIAN HISTORY IN THE MIDDLE AGES AND THE RENAISSANCE: POLITICAL THOUGHT AND THE LANGUAGE OF POLITICS, ART AND POLITICS 180 (Giovanni Ciappelli, ed., 2004).

27. *E.g.*, Rogers v. Tennessee, 532 U.S. 451, 462–63 (2001) ("The year and a day rule is widely viewed as an outdated relic of the common law. Petitioner does not even so much as hint that good reasons exist for retaining the rule, and so we need not delve too deeply into the rule and its history here. Suffice it to say that the rule is generally believed to date back to the 13th century, when it served as a statute of limitations governing the time in which an individual might initiate a private action for murder known as an 'appeal of death'; that by the 18th century the rule had been extended to the law governing public prosecutions for murder; that the primary and most frequently cited justification for the rule is that 13th century medical science was incapable of establishing causation beyond a reasonable doubt when a great deal of time had elapsed between the injury to the victim and his death; and that, as practically every court recently to have considered the rule has noted, advances in medical and related science have so undermined the usefulness of the rule as to render it without question obsolete."); Commonwealth v. Lewis, 409 N.E.2d 771, 772 (Mass. Sup. Jud. Ct. 1980) ("Any discussion of the subject begins with the antique statute 6 Edw. 1, c. 9 (1278), which declares as to the private form of prosecution for murder called 'appeal,' that it shall not be abated so soon as it has been heretofore; but if the appellor declare the 'Deed' and the time when it was done, and with what weapon the victim was slain, the appeal shall stand and not abate 'if the Party shall sue within the Year and the Day after the Deed done.' 'Deed' was read as meaning the death, not the act of assault leading to the death, and evidently it was from the date of the death that the period was measured.").

28. *E.g.*, K.N. Chandrasekharan Pillai, Double Jeopardy Protection: A Comparative Overview 3–4 (1988) ("[P]rior to 1819, the acquittal was not always a final bar [to prosecution]. Before then, a criminal prosecution in England was conducted by a dual system, *i.e* by grand jury indictment and by private prosecution (described as 'by appeal'). The person to whom the 'suit of vengeance' was allowed could take out a writ of appeal and frame a charge thereafter against the defendant. This 'appeal' was to be brought in by the private person within a year and a day of the occurrence. An indictment could also be brought in on the same cause. Between an indictment and an appeal, the latter was to have priority. And an acquittal on appeal was a good bar to an indictment for the same offense. At first, an acquittal on indictment was also a bar to any appeal by the private party on the same cause. Thus if the defendant was arraigned on indictment and acquitted, the private party could not bring in an appeal. In order to save the suit of the private party, the practice of not trying a person indicted for murder for a year and a day was evolved by the courts. By this time, however, it was probable that witnesses had died, or they had forgotten the case. The private party was not often prompt in bringing appeals and this created an unsatisfactory situation. To remedy the situation the King enacted new legislation laying down that indictments for murder should be tried at once and that an acquittal on an indictment should be no bar to an appeal, so that if the private party wanted to bring suit after indictment and acquittal, he would still have a chance to gain punishment of the guilty. In practice, private parties began to rely primarily upon indictment, and were reluctant to proceed once indictment failed. Thus, the new legislation was eventually responsible for making the institution of appeals by private individuals obsolete and such appeals came to be abolished by legislation in 1819. At that point, an acquittal on an indictment by a court with jurisdiction was a final bar in all cases."); *see also* Kendall, *supra* note 20, at 244–45 ("When the same gentleman likened the Appeal of Murder to the Appeals of Rape and Robbery, he overlooked the important consideration, that it is only the Appeal of Murder (or rather the Appeal of Death) which can be made use of to procure a *second* criminal trial. As the law stands, if a man robs my hen-roost, I may demand a Duel with him, instead of causing him to be indicted for the offence. The two courses are equally open to me. I may indict him, if I have *evidence to produce to a Jury*, and I may fight him, if I have *none*. But I cannot do *both*. With respect to Murder, however, I may. I may cause a man or woman to be indicted—I may employ counsel against the prisoner—I may produce evidence; and if he or she is acquitted, I may afterward appeal him or her, &c. Mr. Burke allowed that Combat *was* part of the Appeal, and characterized it according to the usual common-places. He did not know, (what, in these pages, we have been so repeatedly called upon to confess) that the thing sought for by Appeal is Battle; and that the barbarism of Battle is the barbarism of Appeal. Mr. Fox, at the same time, was in error, when he described the Appeal of a Murder, as 'the only instance in our laws, in which satisfaction is allowed to the injured by the blood of another;' since the same satisfaction is allowed in regard of all capital offences.") (italics in original).

A different year-and-a-day rule developed in England, too. Thomas J. Gardner & Terry M. Anderson, Criminal Law 48 (9th ed. 2006) ("The year-and-a-day rule goes back hundreds of years in the law to 1278, when medical science was primitive. Before the American Revolutionary War, Sir William Blackstone described the rule as follows: 'In order ... to make the killing murder, it is requisite that the party die within a year and a day after the stroke (blow) received, or cause of death administered; in the computation of which the whole day upon which the hurt was done shall be reckoned the first.' Under the year-and-a-day rule, a defendant could not be convicted of murder if the victim did not die within a year and a day.").

29. James Barr Ames, Lectures on Legal History and Miscellaneous Legal Essays v, 8, 34, 39–41 (1913); 2 John Bouvier, A Law Dictionary, Adapted to the Constitution and Laws of the United States of America, and of the Several States of the American Union 219 (1885).

30. "This Day is Publish'd," Post Boy (London, England), June 6, 1719, p. 2 (noting the publication of the book); "This Day is Publish'd," Post Boy (London, England), June 9, 1719, p. 2 (same); "This Day is Publish'd," Post Boy (London, England), June 11, 1719, p. 2 (same); "Lately Published," Post Boy (London, England), June 25, 1719, p. 2. Other publications around that time also contained information on the subject of appeals. Henry Care & W. N. of the Middle Temple, comp., English Liberties, or the Free-born Subject's Inheritance 83 (5th ed. 1721) ("This Discourse of Pardons puts us in mind of another legal Pro[s]ecution, in which the Subject hath a particular Benefit, and that is by *Appeal*, of which it may be convenient to give a short account."); *id.* ("Where a Criminal deserveth to be punished with

Death for any Offence, and particularly for Murder, there are two ways to bring him to answer, one is by an Indictment, which is at the Suit of the King, and the other is by *Appeal*, which is at the Suit of the Party injured by the Murtherer; as a Widow, a Son whose Father, or a Brother whose Brother, hath been murdered."); *id.* ("Now if the Offender be found guilty upon the Indictment, a Pardon hath been sometimes obtained. But in an Appeal all agree, the King can grant no Pardon. Nay, if a Person be tried by Indictment, and acquitted, or convicted and get a Pardon, yet an Appeal may be brought, and if he be thereupon convicted, notwithstanding such his former Acquittal or Pardon, he must be hanged."); *id.* at 83–84 ("*Note*, That this Appeal must be brought within a Year and a Day after the Murder committed; for afterwards it cannot be brought at all. And anciently it was customary not to bring an Indictment for the King, till after the Year and the Day, waiting in the mean time for the Prosecution of the Party; but this was found very inconvenient, for the Party was frequently compounded with, and at the Year's end the business was forgot, and so Offenders escaped Justice."); *id.* at 84 ("And therefore the same was altered by the Statute 3 *Hen.* 7. *cap.* I. whereby it is Enacted, *That the Coroner shall do his Office, and the Offenders may be arraigned at any time within the Year, at the King's Suit, but if acquitted, yet the Party, within the Year and Day, should have liberty to bring an Appeal against such Person, either a[c]quitted or attainted, if the Benefit of the Clergy be not before thereof had. And in order thereunto, that when any Person happened to be acquitted for the Death of a Man, within the Year, the Justices before whom he is acquitted, shall not suffer him to go at large, but either to remit him again to the Prison, or else to let him to Bail, after their Discretion, till that the Day and Year be passed, that so he may be forth-coming to answer an Appeal, if it shall happen to be brought.*") (italics in original). *English Liberties, or the Free-born Subject's Inheritance* was advertised for sale in Philadelphia. "To be Sold by the Printer Hereof," PENNSYLVANIA GAZETTE (Philadelphia, PA), Nov. 14, 1734, p. 4; "To be Sold by the Printer Hereof," PENNSYLVANIA GAZETTE (Philadelphia, PA), Jan. 28, 1735, p. 4. *See also* "From the State Trials, Vol. VII. April 30, 1666," PUBLIC ADVERTISER (London, England), Mar. 14, 1765, p. 2 (noting from that historical source that a man "was hang'd upon an Appeal of Murder"); DERBY MERCURY (Derby, England), Apr. 14, 1769, p. 2 ("It is rumoured among the Lawyers, that McQuirk ought not (consistently with the Laws of this Land) to have been bailed out of Newgate; but that he ought to have remained in Goal *a Year and a Day*; because the next of Kin to the late murdered Mr. Clark might have sued out an Appeal of Murder. And it is now a Certainty, that the next of Kin to the said Mr. Clarke will, in Justice to the Public, claim and insist upon so *valuable* and transcendent a Privilege: A Privilege which the Subjects of no other Sovereign Prince in the known World can boast of, and which no English Subject, through a false Notion of Delicacy or Humanity, ought to wave; because to wave such a Privilege would be only trifling with the Law of God, in which it is said; 'Thou shalt do no Murder,' and 'Blood for Blood shall be required.'") (italics in original); BATH AND BRISTOL CHRONICLE (Bath, England), May 4, 1769, p. 4 ("An affidavit, it is said, will shortly appear from the nearest relation of Mr. Clarke, who was supposed to be killed by a blow received at Brentford, that a thousand pounds were offered if the said relation would consent to lodge an appeal for murder, against McQuirk, in order to prevent his receiving his Majesty's pardon."); "This Day Are Published," JACKSON'S OXFORD JOURNAL (Oxford, England), Dec. 8, 1770, p. 4 (referring to the publication of a book "[b]y JOHN Lord Viscount DUDLEY and WARD, and T. CUNNINGHAM, Esq." and emphasizing: "Under the Title Appeal . . . are the Proceedings in several Appeals of Murder, in the Reign of Queen Elizabeth and King James I, now first translated from the Latin Entries of Sir Edward Coke."); "This Day Are Published, by W. Griffin, in Catherine-Street, Strand," BATH CHRONICLE (Bath, England), Nov. 1, 1770, p. 4 (noting the same).

31. GILES JACOB, THE LAWS OF APPEALS AND MURDER 5 (1719) ("[I]f a Woman be slain, her next of Kin may maintain an Appeal of Murder."). The rules for "Appeal of Murder"—as established by various precedents—were summarized in numerous English treatises. *See, e.g.*, 2 A DIGESTED INDEX TO THE CROWN LAW: COMPREHENDING ALL THE POINTS RELATING TO CRIMINAL MATTERS CONTAINED IN THE REPORTS OF BLACKSTONE, BURROW, COWPER, DOUGLAS, LEACH'S CROWN LAW, LORD RAYMOND, SALKELD, STRANGE, WILSON, AND THE TERM REPORTS 75–77 (1816) (prepared by Harold Nuttall Tomlins of the Inner Temple and printed in London).

32. JACOB, *supra* note 31, at 6 ("Appeal of Death is of two Sorts; Murder and Homicide. Murder is where a Person willfully and with prepensed Malice kills another. Homicide, or Manslaughter, is the killing of a Man without any Malice, upon a sudden Provocation; and it differs from Murder in that it is done

without Malice prepensed, and from Chancemedley in that it hath a present Intent to kill. Chancemedley, or *per infortunium*, is when one is slain casually by another, without any Intent to hurt; but of this no Appeal doth lie.") (italics in original; citation omitted).

33. *Id.* at 1 (italics in original); *see also id.* at 2 ("[T]he Learned *Bracton* defines *Appeal* to be a lawful Declaration of another Man's Crime (being Felony at least) before a competent Judge, by one that sets his Name to the Declaration, and undertakes to prove it, upon the Penalty that may ensue to the contrary.") (citing Bracton Lib. 3).

34. *Id.* at 2 (italics in original).

35. David Churchill, Crime Control and Everyday Life in the Victorian City: The Police and the Public 1–2 (2017).

36. Shapiro, *supra* note 4, at 24.

37. Jacob, *supra* note 31, at 4 (italics in original; citation omitted).

38. "Appeal of Maihem," Jacob wrote, citing the English jurist Henry de Bracton, "is an Accusing of one that hath maim'd or wounded another; but this being no Felony, the Appeal thereof is but, in a manner, an Action of Trespass, because there is nothing recover'd but Damages." *Id.* at 2.

39. "Appeal of Rape," Jacob reported, "lies where a Rape is committed, (*viz.*) where a Man hath unlawful and carnal Knowledge of a Woman by Force, and against her Will, which is Felony by the Common Law ...." "By our Ancient Laws," Jacob added, "the Party ravish'd, if she gives Consent either before or after, can bring no Appeal; but if she neither before nor after give such Consent, she may appeal." *Id.* at 2. "And the Statute II *H.* 4. *c.* 13. gives Power to a Husband, or Father, or next of Blood, there being no Husband, to bring an Appeal of Rape, where a Woman is ravish'd, and afterwards gives her Consent." *Id.* at 2–3.

40. "Appeal of Robbery," per Jacob, "was a Remedy given at Common Law, where a Party was robb'd of Goods, to have the Goods restor'd to the Person from whom taken; for a Man could not have Restitution upon an Attainder, or an Indictment, because that was at the Suit of the King." "This Law being defective," Jacob editorialized, "in case of several Appeals brought against one Person; as where a Robbery is committed by one Man upon three, and they all bring Appeals against him, and he is attainted and executed at the Suit of one of the Appellants, the other two cannot be restor'd to their Goods, because the Robber being dead, cannot be attainted; the Statute 21 *H.* 8. gives Power to Justices to award Restitution of the Goods taken immediately after the Offender is found Guilty. And by this Statute Restitution is to be granted on an Indictment." *Id.* at 3 (citations omitted).

41. *Id.* at 3–4; *see, e.g.*, Henry Campbell Black, A Law Dictionary Containing Definitions of the Terms and Phrases of American and English Jurisprudence, Ancient and Modern 905–06 (2d ed. 1910) ("Pledges of prosecution. In old English law. No person could prosecute a civil action without having in the first stage of it two or more persons as pledges of prosecution; and if judgment was given against the plaintiff, or he deserted his suit, both he and his pledges were liable to amercement to the king *pro falso clamore*. In the course of time, however, these pledges were disused, and the names of fictitious persons substituted for them, two ideal persons, John Doe and Richard Rose, having become the common pledges of every suitor; and now the use of such pledges is altogether discontinued.").

42. Jacob, *supra* note 31, at 119.

43. Thomas J. Gardner & Terry M. Anderson, Criminal Law 158 (10th ed. 2009) ("In the twelfth century, a controversy arose about whether priests accused of felonies should be tried by the royal courts or the ecclesiastical courts. It was decided that the royal courts could try priests but could not put them to death for the first felony conviction. This privilege was known as the benefit of clergy, and by the end of the Middle Ages, it was extended to all laypeople who could read."); *id.* ("The test to determine who could claim the privilege of benefit of clergy was a person's ability to recite the first verse of Psalm 51: 'Have mercy upon me, O God, after Thy great goodness.' This came to be known as the *neck verse* because it saved the accused from hanging. The only punishment that could then be inflicted was imprisonment for one year and an *M* branded on the brawn of the left thumb to prevent the criminal from claiming the privilege again. For many years, only three crimes were excluded from benefit of clergy (high treason, highway robbery, and the willful burning of a house), but in 1769, Blackstone noted that 'among the variety of actions which men are daily liable to commit no less than 160 have been declared by Act of Parliament to be felonies without benefit of clergy.'").

44. Thomas J. Gardner & Terry M. Anderson, Criminal Law 120 (10th ed. 2009) (citation omitted).

45. Challenging Orthodoxies: The Social and Cultural Worlds of Early Modern Women—Essays Presented to Hilda L. Smith (Sigrun Haude & Melina S. Zook, eds., 2016) ("Benefit of clergy was obtained by reading (or memorizing) a biblical verse. This was usually Psalm 51, the 'neck verse,' because it saved one's neck. An uncompromising judge could ask for another verse, eliminating the uneducated who had memorized Psalm 51. Women did not legally receive benefit of the clergy until two statutes passed in 1623 and 1692.").

46. Henry Campbell Black, A Law Dictionary Containing Definition of the Terms and Phrases of American and English Jurisprudence, Ancient and Modern 127 (2d ed. 1910).

47. Jacob, *supra* note 31, at 4.

48. *Id.* (citation omitted); *see also id.* ("There lay an Appeal of High Treason by the Common Law, before the Statute, 1 *H.* 4. *C.* 14. And at Common Law, a Woman might have an Appeal for the Death of her Ancestor; but by Magna Charta, 'tis enacted, *Quod nullus capiatur, aut imprisonetur, propter Appellum fœminœ de morte alterius quam viri sui.*") (citation omitted); *id.* ("But the Son of a Woman may have an Appeal, (being Heir at the Death of the Ancestor) for the Son is not disabled, but the Mother only.") (citation omitted); *id.* ("The Writ of Appeal of a Woman for the Death of her Husband is annex'd to her Widowhood; so that if the Wife of the deceased marry again, her Appeal is gone, although the second Husband die within the Year; for she must, before any Appeal brought, continue *fœmina viri sui*, upon whose Death she brings her Appeal.") (citation omitted).

49. *Id.* at 6 (italics in original).

50. Joseph A. Melusky & Keith A. Pesto, Cruel and Unusual Punishment: Rights and Liberties under the Law 36–37 (2003) ("One aspect of the tradition of Anglo-Norman law almost invisible to us was that, in addition to maintaining public order, or important secondary function (and sometimes not even secondary) of the criminal law was the raising of revenue. Going all the way back to Magna Carta, one can see that King John's concessions to the barons did not include any limit on the death penalty, but included the prohibition of excessive fines near the top of the list."; "Before the establishment of the offices of professional prosecutors who acted in the name of the Crown, well into the nineteenth century, justice was still in part a private affair, and in the era of the American Revolution a criminal prosecution could be commenced by a crime victim or his or her family by filing an 'appeal,' that is, by what we would call a private criminal complaint. To return again to the Magna Carta, one of the injustices that the king promised to stop was the indignity of having a man brought to trial on the appeal of a woman."); *id.* at 37–38 ("The sovereign's assertion of the public interest in criminal actions came when the facts of the alleged crime were presented to a grand jury of twenty-three men. If indicted, the accused would stand trial before a petit jury of twelve men of equal social standing. If convicted of treason or felony after indictment, the property and lands of the criminal would be forfeited to the king. Creative interpretations of the law were often used by judges appointed by kings hungry for revenue. However, royal trial was at first really just one option available to a criminal defendant. Until it was outlawed by the Roman Catholic Church in 1215, a defendant could choose trial by ordeal. For a long while afterward, a defendant could legally choose trial by battle. Even though after the thirteenth century a jury trial was the only option in practice, because it was considered an innovation on prior settled law, a plea to stand trial 'upon my country' was considered legally necessary before the king could try a felon and forfeit his property. A man who died but did not enter a plea, even a plea of not guilty, could transmit his lands and goods to his family, whereas a person taking advantage of the king's justice might not only lose his life but also beggar his family. As a result, forcing a defendant to plead became an end in itself, as a matter not of justice but of revenue, and it was lawful to torture a defendant by a combination of starvation, thumbscrews, and *peine forte et dure*, that is, 'punishment hard and long' by loading weights on the spreadeagled defendant's chest until he should consent."; "'Pressing,' in fact, was used as late as 1692 in Massachusetts during the Salem witch trials and was not legally abolished until 1772. Other forms of torture were permitted in the colonies as investigative methods. Although the common law courts traditionally did not employ torture, it was considered lawful for the Court of Star Chamber, which existed from 1487 to 1641, to use torture.").

In medieval times, there was a split of authority over prosecution between Church and State. R. H. Helmholz, *Crime, Compurgation and the Courts of the Medieval Church*, 1 LAW & HIST. REV. 1, 2 (1983) ("The courts of the Church, which enforced the canon law of the Western Church, long played an important role in the legal life of England. For centuries they exercised jurisdiction over wide areas of human life."); *id.* at 3 ("These canon law courts have also left a considerable body of court records by which the historian may judge the extent and effectiveness of ecclesiastical jurisdiction. Among the most frequent survivals are *ex officio* Act books, which contain records of prosecutions undertaken against alleged violators of the canon law of the Church. Kept regularly by court scribes as memoranda of past actions taken and as notations of future actions to be carried out, the *ex officio* records (as opposed to 'instance' Act books) contain the records of prosecutions undertaken officially by the court against those who had publicly broken the norms laid down by ecclesiastical law."); PHILIP HAMBURGER, IS ADMINISTRATIVE LAW UNLAWFUL? 162 (2014) (discussing "private prosecutions in ecclesiastical courts"); *but cf.* In the Goods of J. M. Dillon (opinion of Hargrave, J.), *in 1* GEORGE KNOX & FREDERICK HARVIE LINKLATER, REPORTS OF CASES ARGUED AND DETERMINED IN THE SUPREME COURT OF NEW SOUTH WALES WITH TABLES OF THE CASES AND PRINCIPAL MATTERS 132, 135 (1879) ("Are we to allow private persons to make use of the prerogatives of the Crown for their own private ends? To do so would be contrary to every principle on which the Court is accustomed to act. We are now emerging from a bad system; private prosecutions have been abolished, and now barristers are not even allowed to assist the Crown in public prosecutions on behalf of private persons. It is against all constitutional principle that things which concern the public should pass into private hands.").

51. HUNT JANIN, MEDIEVAL JUSTICE: CASES AND LAWS IN FRANCE, ENGLAND AND GERMANY, 500–1500, at 17–18, 87 (2004); *see also id.* at 17 ("Not everyone was permitted to engage in trial by combat. In 1140, Pope Innocent II ordered that ecclesiastics should not take part in such a duel. Serfs could not challenge freemen. The sick, e.g., lepers, could not challenge the healthy. Bastards could not challenge those who were legitimately born. Children were not allowed to fight. Women were normally excluded from trial by combat. Very rarely, however, a wife might be allowed to fight her husband, with rigorous conditions being imposed to make the duel a fair one."); *id.* at 18 ("England even had a special category of champions known as 'approvers.' These were career criminals who had turned witness (state's evidence) in the hope of lessening their sentences. Seeking a full pardon, they had also agreed to challenge, for a relatively brief period of time, other felons to trial by battle. A contemporary case records that one Robert, son of Patrick, 'was captured at Kidderminster fleeing in company with thieves ... he confessed that he is a thief ... and he turns an approver to fight five battles.' This procedure may have been an easy way to get rid of convicted criminals: Robert himself might have been killed in combat or he might have managed to kill some or all of the other felons."); *id.* at 19 (showing an illustration depicting a trial by battle "c. 1249" between "approver" Walter Bloweberme and an accused robber, Hamo le Stare; "Blowberme, an accomplice who had turned crown witness, charged le Stare with complicity in a robbery and challenged him to trial by battle .... Le Stare was defeated. Having thus been proved guilty, he was hanged from a nearby gallows ...."); *id.* at 196 ("The court could also order trial by battle to resolve disputes for which there was no remedy at common law. Treason and homicide committed abroad are the best examples here, although such a trial might also be used to settle an unspecified 'deed or action of arms.' The legal proceedings for trial by battle began with a petition to the king in council, containing the articles of complaint. This document was then forwarded to the High Court of Chivalry, which set the date and place for the fight. The king footed the bill for preparing the field of battle, arming the combatants and even, if necessary, training them. In 1446, for example, Henry VI paid for two appellants to have lessons in fighting."). "When a case was tried by battle," USC law professor Daniel Klerman writes, "the outcome hinged on personal combat between prosecutor and defendant." Daniel Klerman, *Women Prosecutors in Thirteenth-Century England*, 14 YALE J.L. & HUMAN. 271, 290–91 (2002); *see also* Daniel Klerman, "Private Prosecution of Crime in Thirteenth Century England" (University of Chicago Law School July 1997); Daniel Klerman, *Settlement and the Decline of Private Prosecution in Thirteenth-Century England*, 19 LAW & HIST. REV. 1, 5 (2001); SUSAN N. HERMAN, THE RIGHT TO A SPEEDY AND PUBLIC TRIAL: A REFERENCE GUIDE TO THE UNITED STATES CONSTITUTION 241 (2006) ("The earliest writing on the right to speedy trial at common law is in the second volume of the encyclopedia of Henry de Bracton, *On the Laws and Customs of England:*

1240–1260, trans. Samuel Thorne (Cambridge: Harvard Univ. Press, 1968), who was considered the most reliable source on English law until Blackstone. Bracton described the procedural options open to a person accused by appeal (private prosecution) to seek release rather than be incarcerated 'for a long time.' Daniel Klerman's article, 'Settlement and Decline of Private Prosecution in Thirteenth-Century England' 19 Law & Hist. Rev. (2001): 1, 5–8, 10–11, is a useful source of information about limitations on private prosecutions during the thirteenth century, a key era in which speedy trial remedies were being developed in both private and public prosecutions.").

52. James Bradley Thayer, "The Older Modes of Trial," *in* 2 Association of American Law Schools, comp., Select Essays in Anglo-American Legal History 396–97 (1908) ("*Trial by Battle.*—This is often classified as an ordeal, 'a God's judgment,' but in dealing with our law it is convenient to discriminate it from the ordeals, for the battle has other aspects than that of an appeal to Heaven. Moreover, it survived for centuries the ordeal proper.... Although it existed among almost all the Germanic people, the Anglo-Saxons seem not to have had it; but with the Normans it came into England in full strength. In Glanvill, a century after the Conquest, we see it as one of the chief modes of trial in the king's courts: 'A debt ... is proved by the court's general mode of proof, viz., by writing or by duel.' 'They may come to the duel or other such usual proof as is ordinarily received in the courts,' etc. Of the inferior courts, also, we are told that in a lord's court, a duel may be reached between lord and man, if any of the man's peers makes himself a witness and so champion."); *id.* at 397 ("The earliest reference to the battle, I believe, in any account of a trial in England, is at the end of the case of Bishop Wulfstan *v.* Abbot Walter, in 1077. The controversy was settled, and we read: 'Thereof there are lawful witnesses ... who saw and heard this, ready to prove it by oath and battle.' This is an allusion to a common practice in the Middle Ages, that of challenging another's witness; or perhaps to one method of disposing of cases where adversary witnesses were allowed, and these contradicted each other."); *id.* at 398 ("In a great degree it was for the purpose of displacing this dangerous, costly, and discredited mode of proof that the recognitions—that is to say, juries in their first organized form—were introduced. These were regarded as a special boon to the poor man, who was oppressed in many ways by the duel. It was by enactment of Henry II. That this reform was brought about, first in his Norman dominions (in 1150–52), before reaching the English throne, and afterwards in England, sometime after he became king, in 1154."); *id.* at 400–1 ("The Year Books indicate small use of the trial by battle in later days. One sign is the particularity with which the ceremonial is described, as if it were a curiosity. Thus in 1342–3, and again in 1407, in criminal appeals, the formalities of the battle oath and subsequent matters are fully given. And in 1422 the ceremony in a battle between champions is described with curious details, down to the defaulting of the tenant on the appointed day. In 1565 Sir Thomas Smith tell us, of this mode of trial, that it was not much used, but 'I could not learn that it was ever abrogated.' This was only six years before the famous writ of right, in Lowe *v.* Paramour, which furbished up this faded learning. Dyer has a pretty full and good account of that case; but Spelman's Latin is fuller and very quaint. The trial in a writ of right, he tells us, repeating with precision the doctrine of four centuries and a half before, is by duel or the assize ... Yet, he goes on, it chanced that this last was revived in 1571, and battle was ordered .... Then comes a curious detailed account, setting forth, among other things, how Nailer, the demandant's champion, in his battle array, to the sound of fifes and trumpets, on the morning of the day fixed for the battle, *Londinum minaciter spatiatur.* It has been said that Spelman was present at Tothill Fields on that day with the thousands of spectators that assembled; he does not say so, I believe, but he writes with all the vivacity of an eye-witness. The demandant made default. Another like case occurred as late as 1638, but again there was no fight. Efforts to abolish the judicial battle were made through that century and the next, but without result. At last came the famous appeal of murder in 1819, in which the learning of the subject was fully discussed by the King's Bench, and battle was adjudged to be still 'the constitutional mode of trial' in this sort of case. As in an Irish case in 1815, so here, to the amazement of mankind, the defendant escaped by means of this rusty weapon. And now, at last, in June, 1819, came the abolition of a long-lived relic of barbarism, which had survived in England when all the rest of Christendom had abandoned it."); *id.* at 401 n.5 ("Stat. 59 Geo. III, c. 46, — reciting that 'appeals of murder, treason, felony, and other offences, and the manner of proceeding therein, have been found to be oppressive; and the trial by battle in any suit is a mode of trial unfit to be used; and it is expedient that the same should be wholly abolished.' The statute went on to enact that all such appeals 'shall cease, determine, and become void and ... utterly

abolished, [and that] in any writ of right now depending or hereafter to be brought, the tenant shall not be received to wage battle, nor shall issue be joined or trial be had by battle in any writ of right.'"); George Fisher, *The Jury's Rise as Lie Detector*, 107 YALE L.J. 575, 586 n.23 (1997) ("Before 1215, publicly initiated prosecutions, or indictments, were resolved by ordeal, while privately initiated prosecutions, or appeals, were tried by battle. One-on-one combat may have appeared to be more appropriate to private than to public prosecutions.") (citing THE TREATISE ON THE LAWS AND CUSTOMS OF THE REALM OF ENGLAND COMMONLY CALLED GLANVILL 171–73 (G.D.G. Hall ed. & trans., Nelson 1965) (c. 1188)); *id.* at 586 n.23 ("Though unused since 1492, trial by battle survived on English statute books until 1819.") (citing An Act To Abolish Appeals of Murder, Treason, Felony or Other Offences, and Wager of Battel, or Joining Issue and Trial by Battel, in Writs of Right, 1819, 59 Geo. 3, ch. 46); 1 SIR MATTHEW HALE, HISTORIA PLACITORUM CORONAE: THE HISTORY OF THE PLEAS OF THE CROWN 8 n.1 (1st Am. ed. 1847) (noting the abolition of appeals of murder and "wager of battel" in 1819 following the 1818 case of *Ashford v. Thornton*, 1 B. & Al. 405).

53. 2 D. K. SANDFORD, THOMAS THOMSON & ALLAN CUNNINGHAM, EDS., THE POPULAR ENCYCLOPEDIA; BEING A GENERAL DICTIONARY OF ARTS, SCIENCES, LITERATURE, BIOGRAPHY, HISTORY, AND POLITICAL ECONOMY 140 (1836) (entry for "CHAMPION").

54. ALFRED H. KNIGHT, THE LIFE OF THE LAW: THE PEOPLE AND CASES THAT HAVE SHAPED OUR SOCIETY, FROM KING ALFRED TO RODNEY KING 16 (1996) ("In thirteenth-century England, noblemen maintained drowning pools for disposing of people convicted in their private courts. (Bayard's castle in London had a special franchise to drown miscreants in the Thames.) Particularly egregious criminals were hanged, 'cut down while yet living,' disemboweled, castrated, and quartered.").

55. JANIN, *supra* note 51, at 13–17.

56. JAMES OLDHAM, TRIAL BY JURY: THE SEVENTH AMENDMENT AND ANGLO-AMERICAN SPECIAL JURIES 281 n.87 (2006).

57. Daniel Klerman, *Women Prosecutors in Thirteenth-Century England*, 14 YALE J.L. & HUMAN. 271, 290–91 (2002); *see also id.* at 293 ("Over half of all homicide appeals were widows prosecuting those allegedly responsible for their husbands' death. This phenomenon may stem from a norm or custom that a wife prosecute her husband's murderer. That treatises, cases, and Magna Carta explicitly allow appeals in this situation probably reflects that custom. This explanation and the previous one—women's immunity from battle—may have been related. No thirteenth-century source barred male relatives from appealing the death of a married man. The custom that widows prosecute those responsible for the deaths of their husband may have arisen because the widow, as a woman, was immune from battle."); *id.* at 307 ("The fact that lawyers were rare meant that a female prosecutor had to appear publicly and make her case. She had to come to county court to make her accusation and then, since the appellee seldom showed up until absolutely necessary, return to county court several times until he appeared or was outlawed. If she pursued the case to outlawry, as more than a quarter of women prosecutors did, she would have to appear five times at county court. If the accused appeared and remained steadfast in her determination to prosecute, as happened in about 15% of all cases, she would have to continue her prosecution in the general eyre, the most awesome manifestation of royal judicial power outside of Westminster Hall. All of these court appearances would require extensive public speaking, contrary to the norm counseling women's silence in public places."); J. Savannah Shipman, Agents of Justice: Female Plaintiffs in the King's Court in Thirteenth and Fourteenth-Century England, M.A. Thesis, History, Western Michigan University (Aug. 2016), *available at* https://scholarworks.wmich.edu/cgi/viewcontent.cgi?article=1745&context=masters_theses; *see also id.* at 2 ("[C]ourt records of the proceedings before the king and his justices reveal that medieval English women exercised legal agency during thirteenth- and fourteenth-century England. The women that litigated before the king or his justices were persistent and knowledgeable in their attempts to gain justice for alleged wrongs and had a higher degree of control over their lives than previously assumed."); *id.* at 1–2 (noting that although the Magna Carta decreed, "No one is to be arrested or imprisoned through the appeal of a woman for the death of anyone other than her husband," and although legal treatises, Glanvill's *Treatise on the Laws and Customs of the Realm of England* and Henry Bracton's *On the Laws and Customs of England*, contained statements to the effect that "English women could only prosecute men for the murder of their husbands or for bodily harm done to themselves," such statements "did not reflect reality"

as "[i]n practice hundreds of English women came to the King's Court to seek justice for crimes that included murder, assault, robbery, breaking and entering, and arson"); *id.* at 3 ("It is important to note that even among contemporary legal documents there was some confusion as to what cases women could bring to court. Glanvill's and Bracton's treatises stated that a woman could prosecute a man for the murder of her husband, if she were a witness, or for any bodily harm, most specifically rape. At the same time, the Magna Carta dictated that a woman may only seek justice for the murder of her husband but remained silent about women's other legal pleas. The sources of judicial litigation themselves, the *Curia Regis Rolls* and the *Calendar of Patent Rolls*, and contemporary legal treatises, such as *Glanvill*, Bracton, and the Magna Carta, are in conflict about the legal capacity of female plaintiffs. Documentary evidence suggests that female plaintiffs came forward in high numbers to seek justice from the royal court during the thirteenth and fourteenth centuries. In order to provide a detailed analysis of female plaintiffs in the King's Court, I have chosen to focus on court cases that took place at the beginning and end of the thirteenth century and the mid-fourteenth century. From 1198–1212, 1275–1300, 1335–1350, 404 female plaintiffs came to the king's royal court to seek justice for a number of different crimes. Over this period of time totaling just sixty-four years, 205 women appealed the crime of homicide, fifty-two women complained to the king of breaking and entering, forty-seven women appealed the crime of rape, thirty-four appealed the crime of assault, twenty-seven appealed the crime of robbery, and five the crime of arson."); *id.* at 11–12 ("For those who are unfamiliar with medieval English legal terminology, it will be useful to provide a brief paragraph defining the terms I will use throughout my thesis. Instead of using modern words like 'sue' or 'prosecute' to describe the action of bringing a complaint to court, I have chosen to use the verb 'appeal' which appears in the documents as '*appellum facere*,' and can be translated as 'to bring a case to court' or 'to make a complaint.' ... Another Anglo-Norman legal term is '*oyer* and *terminer*,' a royal order from the king to his justice 'to hear and to determine' particular open cases that had been brought to the attention of the king."). According to another source: "Before 1215, publicly initiated prosecutions, or indictments, were resolved by ordeal, while privately initiated prosecutions, or appeals, were tried by battle. One-on-one combat may have appeared to be more appropriate to private than to public prosecutions." George Fisher, *The Jury's Rise as Lie Detector*, 107 YALE L.J. 575, 586 n.23 (1997).

58. 1 STEWART RAPALJE & ROBERT L. LAWRENCE, A DICTIONARY OF AMERICAN AND ENGLISH LAW, WITH DEFINITIONS OF THE TECHNICAL TERMS OF THE CANON AND CIVIL LAWS 65 (1888) (describing *appeal of felony* as "a criminal proceeding, being an accusation by one private subject against another for some heinous crime demanding punishment, rather on account of the particular injury suffered by the individual than for the offence against the public. (4 Bl. Com. 312) Appeals were of three classes, namely, by an heir for the death (by murder or homicide) of his ancestor, by a wife for the death of her husband, and by the appellant for a wrong done to himself or herself, as robbery, rape, mayhem, &c."); ANTHONY MUSSON, MEDIEVAL LAW IN CONTEXT: THE GROWTH OF LEGAL CONSCIOUSNESS FROM MAGNA CARTA TO THE PEASANTS' REVOLT 154 (2001) ("The legal system also offered the opportunity for private individuals to seek redress before the royal justices. Actions could be initiated by obtaining a royal writ, or less formally, by providing a written bill or oral 'plaint.' The other mechanism by which private suits could be brought to court was by making an appeal of felony."); *id.* ("[W]e should not draw too much of a distinction between civil and criminal cases (suits against another individual and offences against the king) since appeals of felony could be made by private individuals with compensation in mind."); *id.* ("An appeal of felony was essentially a private prosecution which could be brought by the victim of a serious crime. If the victim was no longer alive to bring it personally, their widowed spouse, heir or relations could sue on their behalf. An appeal of felony could be initiated by making an oral complaint in the county court, duly witnessed and recorded by the coroner."); ROBERT C. PALMER, THE COUNTY COURTS OF MEDIEVAL ENGLAND, 1150–1350, at 321 (1982) ("The appeal of felony was an old and formal process initiated by plaint (or, increasingly, by writ of the king's court) by the wronged person or his next of kin against the person named (appealed) of the homicide, rape, mayhem, et cetera. When the plaint was lodged, the appellant would often be required to show his wounds or his bloodied garments to the coroners before the county court. The accused was then obliged to appear in county to defend himself."); *see also* "Crown Pleas of the Wiltshire Eyre, 1249," *in* C. A. F. MEEKINGS, ED., WILTSHIRE ARCHAEOLOGICAL AND NATURAL HISTORY SOCIETY—RECORDS BRANCH, Vol. XVI (1961), p. 69 ("The appeal of felony was an accusation made in a set

form and according to customary procedure by a plaintiff, known as the appellor, *apellator*, against one or more defendants, known as the appellees, *appellati*. In Norman times trial had been by judicial duel, save where the party's condition made this impossible, as with a woman, clerk or an aged or crippled man, when trial would be by ordeal.").

59. Philip Rawlings, Policing: A Short History 14 (2002); Mark Lunney & Ken Oliphant, Tort Law: Text and Materials 4 (5th ed. 2013).

60. Margaret H. Kerr, *Angevin Reform of the Appeal of Felony*, 13 Law & Hist. Rev. 351, 351–52 (1995); *see also id.* at 352 ("Serious crimes such as homicide, robbery, theft, rape, mayhem, or breach of the king's peace were pleas of the Crown and so were tried before the king's justices, usually when they made a visit in eyre (on circuit court) to the counties to hear criminal and land pleas. Between the Norman Conquest and the Assize of Clarendon, however, and especially during Stephen's reign (1135–53) with its civil wars, it can only be speculated whether there was a formal mechanism for the king to pursue offenders. It was the victim who prosecuted the aggressor, through the private criminal prosecution known as the appeal of felony, and it was the victim who decided whether to abandon or settle the appeal.").

61. Wayne R. LaFave, Jerold H. Israel, Nancy J. King & Orin S. Kerr, Criminal Procedure § 15.1(c) (available on Westlaw).

62. Kerr, *Angevin Reform of the Appeal of Felony*, *supra* note 60, at 352; *see also id.* ("After the abolition of the ordeal at the Fourth Lateran Council in 1215, the opinion of respectable neighbors, gathered together in a jury, was substituted for that of God in appeals that would have been tried by ordeal. Trial by battle remained available in an appeal of felony until the appeal itself was abrogated in 1819, some four centuries after it ceased to be a significant component of the criminal justice system."); Thomas P. Gallanis, *Reasonable Doubt and the History of the Criminal Trial*, 76 U. Chi. L. Rev. 941, 954–55 (2009) ("Ordeals were the most common form of *judicium Dei*, the other forms being battle and oaths. Trial by battle had been introduced into England after the Norman Conquest, but it was considered appropriate only in some instances of what was known as 'appeal of felony,' the private accusation of serious crime."). *Compare* Richard R. Cherry, Lectures on the Growth of Criminal Law in Ancient Communities 97–98 (1890) ("All through the Middle Ages, and indeed long after that period is considered to have come to a close, two systems of prosecutions for crimes continued to exist side by side. Either the party aggrieved (or his relatives in case of his death) might institute a proceeding which was called an appeal, or, if he failed to do so, the Sovereign might take up the matter and prosecute for the violation of his peace. Gradually appeals became rarer and rarer, and at least entirely obsolete; but they were not formally abolished until the year 1819. As long, however, as they continued to exist they retained all their primitive characteristics. The accused had the option of a trial by battle; and he could compound with his accuser by the payment of a pecuniary fine. When the King prosecuted, both these barbarous incidents disappeared. It was laid down by Bracton that the King did not give wager of battle; and it was obviously still more beneath his dignity to make a bargain for the life of a malefactor.").

63. Kerr, *Angevin Reform of the Appeal of Felony*, *supra* note 60, at 352; *see also* 1 Sir Frederick Pollock & Frederic William Maitland, The History of English Law before the Time of Edward I, at 540 (1898) ("If he [the king] prosecutes criminals, this is because his peace has been broken, and other lords are often proceeding against offenders who have done them 'shame and damage' by breaking their peace. In pardoning a criminal, the king only waives his rights, and he cannot waive the rights of others; he cannot prevent a private prosecutor from urging an appeal of felony.").

64. Kerr, *Angevin Reform of the Appeal of Felony*, *supra* note 60, at 382; *id.* ("Although it was used to prosecute pleas of the Crown, serious offenses over which the king had jurisdiction, it was controlled by individual appellors and not by the Crown.").

65. David J. Seipp, *The Distinction Between Crime and Tort in the Early Common Law*, 76 B.U. L. Rev. 59, 61 (1996); *see also id.* ("'Appeal' in the sense of asking a higher court to review the judgment of a lower court was a procedural term used only in the church courts. Appeals in the sense of suits by victims seeking punishment for their wrongdoers came before the king's courts when victims formally alleged that wrongdoers acted feloniously and against the king's peace.").

66. *Id.*; *see also id.* at 61–62 ("Before that time, English kings had sometimes substituted blinding and castration or amputation of a hand or foot, and some localities had customary means of execution other than hanging.").

67. In his law dictionary, Giles Jacob defined "ATTAINDER" as "[t]he *stain* or *corruption* of the blood of a criminal capitally condemned; the immediate inseparable consequence by the common law, on the pronouncing the sentence of death."; "He is then called attaint, . . . stained or blackened. He is no longer of any credit or reputation; he cannot be a witness in any court; neither is he capable of performing the functions of another man; for by an anticipation of his punishment, he is already dead in law." 1 GILES JACOB, COMP. & T. E. TOMLINS, ED., THE LAW-DICTIONARY: EXPLAINING THE RISE, PROGRESS, AND PRESENT STATE, OF THE ENGLISH LAW; DEFINING AND INTERPRETING THE TERMS OR WORDS OF ART; AND COMPRISING COPIOUS INFORMATION ON THE SUBJECTS OF LAW, TRADE, AND GOVERNMENT (2d ed. 1809) (entry for "Attainder"; italics in original).

68. "CORRUPTION OF BLOOD," the entry in Giles Jacob's law dictionary notes, is "[a]n infection growing to the state of a man, and to his issue; and is where a person is attainted of *treason* or *felony*, by means whereof his blood is said to be corrupted, and neither his children, nor any of his blood, can be heirs to him or any other ancestor; also if he is of the nobility, or a gentleman, he and all his posterity by the attainder are rendered base and ignoble; but by pardon of the King, the children born afterwards may inherit the land of their ancestor, purchased at the time of the pardon or after; but so cannot they, who were born before the pardon." *Id.* (entry for "CORRUPTION OF BLOOD"; italics in original).

69. 1 PAUL FINKELMAN, ED., ENCYCLOPEDIA OF AMERICAN CIVIL LIBERTIES 370 (2006) ("The doctrine of corruption of blood mandated that when a person committed a criminal or treasonous act, he and his entire family became outlaws. As a consequence, the offender forfeited all of his property, real and personal. In addition, the offender could no longer transfer his property, either during his lifetime or on death. The property itself fell to the crown."); *id.* ("The U.S. Constitution rejected the penalty in the Corruption of Blood Clause of Article III. It limits forfeiture for treason to the traitor's lifetime and indicates its hostility to the punishment also in the Bill of Attainder Clause.").

70. David J. Seipp, *The Distinction Between Crime and Tort in the Early Common Law*, 76 B.U. L. REV. 59, 62 (1996); *see also id.* at 62–63 ("The king received the value of any goods, chattels, and short-term interests in land possessed by a felon after the commission of the felony, or left behind by a fugitive suspected of felony. The king could also take possession, for a year and a day, of any heritable interest in land held by the felon. The king could commit 'waste' on such land, by means such as cutting down trees and pulling down houses. After the king's year and day, the land forfeited to the felon's feudal lord by way of escheat. The term 'felony' originally meant the sort of offenses for which feudal lords were entitled to end their relationships with tenants and to take back the tenants' lands."); *id.* at 63 ("The common law piled up consequences in addition to death, confiscation of goods, and forfeiture of lands. It invalidated all gifts and contracts that a felon made after committing the felony. The felon's widow and persons who held the felon's land for a term of years or for a term of life also lost their possession. Some lawyers argued that the landholding felon's widowed mother lost the land she held in dower, and that any lands a felon would have inherited from living relatives would also become forfeit at their deaths. No doubt many felons were poor folk who held no heritable land and few goods when they committed their wrongs, but for those who possessed some wealth, conviction of felony meant not only death, but also impoverishment of their surviving family members.").

71. *Id.* at 63 ("Lawyers named vengeance as the motive for bringing appeals of felony. Year Books told that in some earlier period the widow and children of a slain man personally dragged the killer to the gallows. They recorded that a victim of rape personally castrated and blinded her wrongdoer. The right and duty to avenge homicide passed like dower to a victim's widow and like inheritance to a victim's heir."); *see also id.* at 63–64 ("The Year Books thus attest to powerful feelings of vengeance on the part of these victims. The motive of vengeance was more readily understood and accepted in the Middle Ages than it is now. The church taught that vengeance was a virtue and sometimes a duty. If courts of law had not provided a means of seeking vengeance, victims would more readily have resorted to bloodfeuds, cycles of retaliation that would escalate and last for generations. The king enhanced his own authority by asserting exclusive power to put felons to death. At the same time, the king offered to exercise that power at the behest of any victim

who could prove a wrongdoer guilty of felony. Victims could appeal not only the principals who wronged them, but also any accessories who commanded, counseled, aided, or harbored the principals or assisted their escape.").

72. *Id.* at 66; *see also id.* ("Treatises directed judges to determine at the outset whether the act alleged was really a felony, or whether the plaintiff was attempting to appeal the defendant for mere bruises or scratches, theft of less than sixpence, or, in Bracton's example, 'feloniously shaking the dust off his cloak.' If the offense was not a felony, the action would go forward as a writ of trespass. In that case, the punishment could not be death or dismemberment, and the defendant could not demand trial by battle.").

73. Mikhail v. Kahn, 991 F. Supp.2d 596, 635 n.27 (E.D. Pa. 2014) ("[T]he indictment (and hence the beginning of the more intimate involvement of the Crown) was not truly born until King Henry II's Assize at Clarendon in 1166, and many years passed before the Crown instigated process resembling public criminal prosecutions in anything near the number of private 'appeals of felony,' or, in essence, private criminal prosecutions.") (citing 1 Frederick Pollock & Frederic William Maitland, *The History of English Law Before the Time of Edward I,* at 161–62 (Liberty Fund 2010) (2d ed. 1898); 2 *id.* at 672 ('[A] form of criminal procedure which had the future before it, that, namely, which is initiated by a presentment or indictment ... may have been occasionally used in England before the year 1166 when Henry II. issued his Assize of Clarendon ... [but it was] machinery that Henry II. set in motion....'); Theodore F.T. Plucknett, *A Concise History of the Common Law* bk. 2, pt. 2, ch. 1, at 424–41 (Liberty Fund 2010) (5th ed. 1956); John H. Langbein et al., *History of the Common Law* ch. 4, pt. 1 (2009)); *see also* Mikhail v. Kahn, 572 Fed. Appx. 68, 73 (3d Cir. 2019) ("as explained in detail by the District Court, section 242 of title 18 does not authorize private criminal prosecutions for alleged wrongdoings, and creates no private right of action").

74. The Constitutional History of England: A Course of Lectures Delivered by F. W. Maitland, LL.D. 128 (1908) (2001); *see also* Cynthia Nicoletti, *The American Civil War as a Trial by Battle*, 28 Law & Hist. Rev. 71, 77–78 (2010) ("While other forms of the ordeal fell into disuse after the Fourth Lateran Council of 1215, when Pope Innocent III condemned the participation of clergy in judicial ordeals, trial by battle survived, probably because it did not necessarily require the sanction of the clergy in order to take place. Over time, trial by battle faded into disuse, as jury trial became the preferred method of discerning the truthfulness of litigants and witnesses. Although its exercise became increasingly infrequent, trial by battle remained a technically valid form of proof in England until 1819, when Parliament abolished it after a defendant, who had already been acquitted by a jury, threatened to wage battle against his accuser in a subsequent appeal of felony."); Laurie C. Kadoch, *So Help Me God: Reflections on Language, Thought, and the Rules of Evidence Remembered*, 9 Rutgers J.L. & Religion 2 (2007) ("The Trial by Battle became obsolete for much the same reason as the compurgation. The church turned against it. Because it operated side by side with the more rationally based forms of adjudication that developed, it eventually appeared barbaric. It became more of a curiosity than the norm. However, there are sporadic reports of isolated cases. In England, the Trial by Battle existed until the nineteenth century as an alternative in real actions and as a means of disproving an appeal of murder. It lingered as the duel, and was in fact, a recognized judicial solution that could be and was selected by an accused until 1819."); "Imperial Parliament," Morning Chronicle (London, England), Feb. 10, 1819, p. 2 ("The Attorney-General, in moving for leave to bring in a Bill for abolishing Appeals for Murder, Felony, and Mayhem and Wager of Battle, went at some length into an historical account of the existing law on the subject."); Wex S. Malone, *The Genesis of Wrongful Death*, 17 Stan. L. Rev. 1043, 1055 (1965) ("The probable origin of the rule denying a cause of action for wrongful death was the doctrine, since discarded, that where a cause of action disclosed the commission of a felony the civil action was merged into the criminal wrong. The sources of the felony merger doctrine are lost in the obscurity of Anglo-Saxon law. The original ancient proceeding against a person who had killed his neighbor through violence was both civil and criminal in nature. Its sole purpose was to discourage the blood feud. The vengeance of the members of the deceased's clan was bought off by an award of money, the *wer* (or *capitis oestimatio*), the amount of which was fixed in terms of the status or rank of the deceased and which was distributed in definite proportions to his paternal and maternal kin. In the same proceeding there was exacted of the wrongdoer the *wite*, which was a reparation to the King or overlord for the breach of his peace or *mund*. In time, as the power of the King increased, certain of the more serious offenses came to be regarded as *unemendable*; that is to say, they could not be compensated

by the payment of *wer* to the kin of the deceased, but fell under the exclusive jurisdiction of the sovereign."); *id.* at 1055–56 ("It is probable that the desire for personal vengeance by the relatives of the deceased continued to find its appeasement through the various forms of the appeal of felony. These appeals, however, resembled the modern criminal proceeding in that no damages were awarded the offended relatives. But for many years the appeal continued to exist side by side with the criminal indictment, which developed later; and a trial and even acquittal in a modern criminal proceeding would not foreclose the possibility that the kinsman might later institute an *appeal of murdrum* against the alleged offender. Although this appeal fell into general disuse, it was not formally abolished by statute until 1819. The availability of the appeal of murdrum as a satisfaction of the personal desire for vengeance, when coupled with the fact that a civil action, if available, would probably have been of little assistance to the bereaved family (since the felon was promptly executed upon conviction and his goods confiscated by the King), would tend to induce the medieval mind to accept readily the idea that a criminal proceeding was the only appropriate remedy for a felonious killing.").

75. Harold Bloom, ed., Walt Whitman 1 (2008); April Gentry, Lisa Paddock & Carl Rollyson, Critical Companion to Herman Melville: A Literary Reference to His Life and Work 3 (2007).

76. Elizabeth L. Ihle, *Women's Admission to the University of Virginia: Tradition Transformed*, *in* Leslie Miller-Bernal & Susan L. Poulson, eds., Going Coed: Women's Experiences in Formerly Men's Colleges and Universities, 1950–2000, at 181 (2004).

77. W. P. Rogers, *Superstitions in Ancient Trials*, 8 Ohio Law Reporter 611, 613 (1911).

78. *See generally* John D. Bessler, *The Anomaly of Executions: The Cruel and Unusual Punishments Clause in the 21st Century*, 2 Brit. J. Am. Leg. Studies 297 (2013) (discussing various corporal punishments used in the past).

79. Barbara J. Shapiro, Law Reform in Early Modern England, 1500–1740: Crown, Parliament and the Press 208–9 (2019); *see also* Frank McLynn, Crime and Punishment in Eighteenth-century England xi (1989) ("The Bloody Code is the name traditionally given to the English system of criminal law during the period 1688–1815. In these years a huge number of felonies punishable by death was added to the statute book. In 1688 no more than fifty offences carried the death penalty: the crimes so punishable were treason, murder, rape, and arson. By 1765 this figure had risen to about 160; an average of one new capital offence a year was added during the thirty-three-year reign of George II. A further sixty-five capital felonies added to the Code from 1765 to 1815 brought the number of crimes that bore the death penalty to about 225 by the end of the Napoleonic wars.").

80. 2 Report of the Commissioner of Education for the Year Ended June 30, 1910, at 1055 (1911).

81. Rogers, *supra* note 77, at 611–12.

82. *Id.* at 612–13; *see also* McCoy v. Lemon, 11 Rich. 165, 172, 1856 WL 3280, at *5 (S.C. Ct. App. of Law 1856) ("In 1818, on an appeal of murder, Thornton, the appellee, threw down his glove before the Chief Justice of England, and demanded trial by battle. (1 Barn. & Ald., 405.) The case was discussed before the Judges, and it involved the question whether the right of trial by battle still existed as part of the common law of England. Upon this point Lord Ellenborough, Chief Justice, said: 'The general law of the land is in favor of the wager of battle, and it is our duty to pronounce the law as it is, and not as we may wish it to be. Whatever prejudices therefore may justly exist against this mode of trial, still, as it is the law of the land, the Court must pronounce judgment for it.'") Dean Rogers had this to say about the murky origins of *trial by battle*: "It had existed in other countries long before it crossed the borders of England, and is so hoary with age that no historian claims yet to have discovered its origin. A writer, George Neilson, says that trial by battle came into existence at a time beyond anything known in tradition concerning it, and that it had attained a vigorous manhood amongst the tribes of Northern Europe before their written history began. He further states that it reached its legal prime in the early feudal ages, and enjoyed a new era of activity under the auspices of later chivalry." As Rogers' account continued: "It assumed different forms at different periods and in different countries, but when it had come to be fixed, if not a popular proceeding in English jurisprudence, the form of trial there was as follows: He who was charged with the crime might demand the right known as wager of battle. Having done this, he was formally arraigned by the question,

'Are you guilty or not guilty?' He would make the answer, 'I am not guilty, and I am ready to defend this with my body.' He would then place one glove upon his hand and cast the other to the floor by way of challenge to his prosecutor, who was regarded as the plaintiff in the case." Once the plaintiff, or private prosecutor, took up the glove, the two parties would take their respective oaths: the plaintiff would swear the defendant to be guilty, and the defendant would attest his innocence of the crime charged. After a patch of ground sixty feet square was marked off and "arranged for the combat," which was to begin at sunrise on the day set for the trial, both parties were required to take this additional oath before fighting: "Hear this, ye justices. That I have this day neither eaten nor drunk, nor have upon me neither bone, stone, nor grass, nor any enchantment, sorcery or witchcraft whereby the law of God may be abused or the law of the devil exalted. So help me God." Rogers, *supra* note 77, at 614; *see also id.* at 616 ("There grew up many modifications and exceptions concerning the combat, giving greater discretion relating to its uses, and allowing to disputants the right of election between this method of trial and that of trial by jury."); *id.* at 616–17 ("The fact that one of the parties was physically deformed, or maimed in such manner as to be thereby less able to defend himself, came to be good ground for refusing to enter the battle. But here many refinements arose. It was determined that the loss of molar teeth was not a valid ground of excuse, but that one who had not incisors was excused, because they were excellent weapons. Women and minors were expected to fight by champions, but were not compelled to do so.").

83. "Court of King's Bench," OBSERVER (London, England), Feb. 8, 1818, p. 1.

84. Rogers, *supra* note 77, at 614–15; *see also id.* at 617 ("When we recall that all these combats, covering a period of several centuries, were conducted by legal authority and engaged in by the combatants under the belief that the right in the matter was thereby determined, the practice seems to us all the more abhorrent. If they had fought as men now fight, only in the heat of passion or in self-defense, they might be forgiven, but to thus submit affairs of vital importance, coolly and deliberately, for the sole purpose of determining by brute force what is just to the parties engaged, seems so insane that we are astounded to know that the legality of the barbarous custom so nearly touches our own generation. That one's guilt or innocence of a heinous crime, the penalty for which was death, should be settled by such a superstitious appeal to force, aided, as the combatants presumably believed, by some divine power, smacks so much of savagery that we hesitate to believe that our present civilization could so recently have developed from such crude ideas and customs."); 1 DANIEL COIT GILMAN, HARRY THURSTON PECK & FRANK MOORE COLBY, EDS., THE NEW INTERNATIONAL ENCYCLOPÆDIA 665 (1906) (noting in the entry for "APPEAL," said to denote "an accusation by a private person against another for some heinous crime, demanding punishment on ac[c]ount of the injury to the appellor, rather than for the public offense": "This method of prosecution remained in force until abolished by act of Parliament in 1819 (59 Geo. III., ch. 46), although it had been used but rarely for a century prior thereto. The last appeal of murder brought in England (which led to the enactment of the statute above referred to) was that of Ashford *vs.* Thornton, instituted in 1818, and reported in 1 Barnwell and Alderson, 405."); *see also* People ex rel. Swanson v. Fisher, 340 Ill. 250, 253, 172 N.E.2d 722, 723 (1930) ("The jury, as a temporary body, constituted for the purpose of determining disputed questions of fact, was not, even when Blackstone wrote, the exclusive mode of trial. Trial by battle, though very rarely invoked, was still a part of the law of England in his day. Practically obsolete by the end of the thirteenth century, the case of Ashford v. Thornton, 1 B. & Ald. 405, decided in 1818, showed that trial by battle persisted as 'the constitutional mode of trial' in appeals of murder. That ancient method of trial was not abolished for all purposes until 1819, by Statute 59 Geo. III, chap. 46.") (citations omitted).

85. Ashford v. Thornton, 1 B. & Ald. 405; In re Presentment by Camden County Grand Jury, 89 A.2d 416, 422 (N.J. 1952) (citations omitted), *overruled on other grounds*, In re Presentment by Camden County Grand Jury, 169 A.2d 465, 476 (N.J. 1961).

86. 4 WILLIAM BLACKSTONE, COMMENTARIES ON THE LAWS OF ENGLAND 1–2, 5 (1769) (italics in original).

87. English barristers and solicitors handled both civil and criminal matters, with the death of individuals potentially implicating both criminal and civil jurisdiction. *E.g.*, "Prosecution of Offences Act, 1879," HUDDERSFIELD DAILY CHRONICLE (Huddersfield, England), Dec. 10, 1879, p. 4 (noting that the newly authorized Director of Public Prosecutions was to be "a Barrister or Solicitor"); "Police-Court, Abergele," THE TIMES (London, England), Sept. 7, 1868, p. 9 ("At the Police-court, Abergele, on Saturday, before Mr.

T. B. Hesketh and the Rev. T. Williams, county magistrates. Mr. Edwards-Wood, solicitor, who has represented certain of the relatives of the deceased at the coroner's inquest, said he appeared on behalf of Henry Cripps (brother Charles Cripps, who was killed by the accident) for a summons against Samuel Eaton, the station-master at Lianddulas, for the manslaughter of Charles Cripps."; "Mr. Eyton, solicitor, of Rhyl, who acted as the coroner's assessor during the inquest, and who happened to be in court on other business, stated, on behalf of the coroner, that he had already bound over the police to prosecute, and that it was much better to leave the prosecution in the hands of the police, as public prosecutors, than to have the prisoners committed in one case only, on the prosecution of a private prosecutor, such as Henry Cripps was. In regard to the assertion that in the event of the death of any of the witnesses the relations of the deceased would not have the benefit of the depositions and evidence given before the jury, he would remind the magistrates that Mr. Edwards-Wood had nothing to do with the criminal part of the case. He only appeared civilly, and he did not think that the police ought to be interfered with in the prosecution of this matter by a private prosecutor. The police and their legal adviser were on the spot, and if any fresh evidence turned up they would be much more likely to discover it than Mr. Edwards-Wood and Cripps, who lived at a distance. It was undesirable that the whole proceedings should be reopened, as the result would be that if the parties went on with this second prosecution two bills of indictment would be preferred against the accused persons, entailing a double cost upon the county, and leading to no practical good.").

88. William D. Popkin, Statutes in Court: The History and Theory of Statutory Interpretation 28 (1999); *see also* Charles Arnold-Baker, The Companion to British History (Henry von Blumenthal, ed. 2015) (entry for "BLACKSTONE, Sir William (1723–80)).

89. 4 William Blackstone, Commentaries on the Laws of England 5–6 (1769) (italics in original); *compare id.* at 6–7 ("But there are crimes of an inferior nature, in which the public punishment is not so severe, but it affords room for a private compensation also: and herein the distinction of crimes from civil injuries is very apparent. For instance; in the case of battery, or beating another, the aggressor may be indicated for this at the suit of the king, for disturbing the public peace, and be punished criminally by fine and imprisonment; and the party beaten may also have his private remedy by action of trespass for the injury, which he in particular sustains, and recover a civil satisfaction in damages. So also, in case of a public nu[i]sance, as digging a ditch across a highway, this is punishable by indictment, as a common offence to the whole kingdom and all his majesty's subjects: but if any individual sustains any special damage thereby, as laming his horse, breaking his carriage, or the like, the offender may be compelled to make ample satisfaction, as well for the private injury, as for the public wrong.").

90. Rev. W. L. Clay, Our Convict Systems 7 (1862) (noting the use in England of "[t]he gallows, the pillory, the stocks, ear-cropping, flogging, branding, fining, and the like"); *see also* C. K. Blatchly, "The Man Who Comes Out of Prison," *in* The Delinquent: A Monthly Periodical, Published by the Prison Association of New York (Jan. 1918), Vol. VIII, No. 1, p. 22 ("The Colonial period was characterized by the free employment of capital punishment for offense that today would seem to warrant no such treatment. Even at the close of the eighteenth century, the English penal code still retained the death penalty for 160 offenses. The policy of England had been to superimpose upon the Colonies her own methods of punishment."); *id.* ("The gradual emancipation of the Colonies and their successors, the States, from the sanguinary and horrible tyranny of mutilation, branding, ear-cropping, flogging and the like occurred through the ultimate realization of the leaders of the political and social life of the communities that barbarous and debasing physical punishments failed to solve the problem of the reduction of crime. This realization was of slow growth.").

91. Nicholas M. McLean, *Livelihood, Ability to Pay, and the Original Meaning of the Excessive Fines Clause*, 40 Hast. Const. L. Q. 833, 857 n.89 (2013); *see also* 4 Blackstone, *supra* note 89 ("[I]t is never usual to assess a larger fine than a man is able to pay, without touching the implements of his livelihood, but to inflict corporeal punishment, or a limited imprisonment, instead of such a fine as might amount to imprisonment for life. And this is the reason why fines in the king's courts are frequently denominated ransoms, because the penalty must otherwise fall upon a man's person, unless it be redeemed or ransomed by a pecuniary fine, according to the ancient maxim, *qui non habet in crumena luat in corpore.*"); Bruce H. Mann, Republic of Debtors: Bankruptcy in the Age of American Independence 81 (2002)

("[I]mprisonment for debt was an unquestioned piece of the cultural baggage of English immigration in the seventeenth century. It could hardly have been otherwise for a practice that had existed in England for three hundred years."); Philip Girard, "Married Women's Property, Chancery Abolition, and Insolvency Law: Law Reform in Nova Scotia 1820–1867," *in* 3 PHILIP GIRARD & JIM PHILLIPS, EDS., ESSAYS IN THE HISTORY OF CANADIAN LAW 95 (1990) ("In the United States almost all of the states on the eastern seaboard had abolished debtors' prisons by 1870; in England the debtors' prisons disappeared in 1869 ...."); 2 SPENCER C. TUCKER, ED., AMERICAN REVOLUTION: THE DEFINITIVE ENCYCLOPEDIA AND DOCUMENT COLLECTION 410 (2018) ("During the colonial and early national period in the United States, the system of incarceration for debt closely resembled that of England. Debtors' prisons in each colony were privately run enterprises that operated for two primary purposes: to force debtors to pay creditors and to make a profit for those operating the prison.").

92. *E.g.*, JOHN PAUL DAVIS, A HIDDEN HISTORY OF THE TOWER OF LONDON: ENGLAND'S MOST NOTORIOUS PRISONERS 117 (2020).

93. SUSAN WILLIS FLETCHER, TWELVE MONTHS IN AN ENGLISH PRISON 254 (1884).

94. ERNEST W. PETTIFER, PUNISHMENTS OF FORMER DAYS (2017), ch. 1.

95. YALE LAW SCHOOL, LILIAN GOLDMAN LIBRARY, BLACKSTONE'S COMMENTARIES ON THE LAWS OF ENGLAND, BOOK THE FOURTH—CHAPTER THE THIRTY-SECOND: OF EXECUTION, https://avalon.law.yale.edu/18th_century/blackstone_bk4ch32.asp.

96. 4 BLACKSTONE, *supra* note 89, AT 176–77, 289–90 (italics in original). The *hue and cry* terminology became a common one associated with bringing offenders to justice. NEWCASTLE WEEKLY COURANT (Newcastle upon Tyne, England), Aug. 9, 1839, p. 3 ("If a greater number of rewards are offered in the Gazette, or Hue and Cry, for the apprehension of capital offenders, this is proved to be in consequence of Lord Normanby's anxiety that no heinous violation of the law should escape. He offered those rewards in numerous cases, such as former governments were in the habit of leaving entirely to the zeal and discretion of private prosecutors, or the local magistracy, to deal with as they pleased.").

97. W. C. HUMPHREYS, OBSERVATIONS ON THE INUTILITY OF GRAND JURIES, AND SUGGESTIONS FOR THEIR ABOLITION 5 (1842); *History of the Grand Jury*, https://www.sanmateocourt.org/court_divisions/grand_jury/history.php.

98. State v. Iosue, 19 N.W.2d 735, 739–40 (Minn. 1945):

A brief resume of the history of the grand jury system may be helpful. We find that the grand jury in English law goes back many centuries. To begin with, it not only accused, but also tried, those who had offended the criminal law. As time went on, however, it became an accusing tribunal only. No one charged with a crime amounting to felony, except in certain special cases, could be put upon trial without prior action by that body. It frequently stood as a barrier against royal persecution. The King's subjects were made more secure thereby against prosecutions by the Crown. While that reason may not have been the motivating factor in this country, the fact remains that the grand jury system was adopted here and for considerations quite similar to those of the mother country. Our adoption of the system was founded upon the theory not only of bringing wrongdoers to justice, but also of providing to one accused protection against unfounded and unreal accusations, whether these had their origin in governmental sources or were founded upon private passion or enmity. 24 Am.Jur., Grand Jury, s 3. What has been said finds support also in Hale v. Henkel, 201 U.S. 43, 59, 26 S. Ct. 370, 373, 50 L.Ed. 652, 659, where the court said: 'Under the ancient English system, criminal prosecutions were instituted at the suit of private prosecutors, to which the King lent his name in the interest of the public peace and good order of society. In such cases the usual practice was to prepare the proposed indictment and lay it before the grand jury for their consideration. There was much propriety in this, as The most valuable function of the grand jury was not only to examine into the commission of crimes, but to stand between the prosecutor and the accused, and to determine whether the charge was founded upon credible testimony or was dictated by malice or personal ill will.'

99. 4 BLACKSTONE, *supra* note 89, at 289–90; *see also id.* ("[B]y the statute of Gloucester, 6 Edw. I. c. 9. all appeals of death must be sued within a year and a day after the completion of the felony by the death of the party: which seems to be only declaratory of the old common law; for in the Gothic constitutions we find the same '*praescriptio annalis, quae currit adversus actorem, fi de homicida ei non constat intra annum*

a caede facta, nec quenquam interea arguat et accufet.'"); Donald E. Walther, *Taming a Phoenix: The Year-and-a-Day Rule in Federal Prosecutions for Murder*, 59 U. CHI. L. REV. 1337, 1338 (1992) ("The first mention of a year-and-a-day rule came in the English Statute of Gloucester in 1278: 'It is provided also, that no Appeal shall be abated so soon as they have been heretofore; but if the Appellor declare the deed was done and with that Weapon he was slain, the Appeal shall stand in effect and shall not be abated for Default of fresh Suit, if the Party shall sue within the Year and the Day after the Deed was done.' Because the statute refers to the timing of the suit (as opposed to the time of death), it makes clear that the reference to a year and a day was originally intended as a statute of limitations governing the time in which an individual might initiate a private appeal for murder."); KENDALL, *supra* note 20, at 14–16 ("The law of murder, in England, at and up to the beginning of the reign of Henry VII, exhibits only a few successive removes from that which has just been described as the law of Turkey. Murder, together with other felonies, had been early recognized as a public wrong, but it has been left with its character of private wrong also. The consequence was, that prosecutions by the Crown had been admitted, while prosecutions by individuals were still allowed. But the mischief of private prosecutions had been felt, and various limitations to their exercise had been successively established. The rational attempt to lead the people to a more sane system of jurisprudence had been pushed as far as possible; and, in the midst of the worst circumstances, the great and sacred principle of the Common Law, That no man shall be put into jeopardy of his life more than once, upon the same charge, had never been violated. Our early forefathers, barbarians as we are pleased to call them, had still the sense and the virtue to shudder at the enormity of making the same criminal charge the subject of a second trial. There were no second trials. The individuals, to whom, in cases of murder, was still conceded the right of *appealing*, were allowed *a year and a day* for its exercise. *Within that period, the Crown could not prosecute*. If, within that period, the *Appeal* was made, the accused was put on trial, either by Jury, or by other lawful mode of decision. Whatever the decision was, it was final. *The Crown was unable to prosecute after trial on Appeal*. If, on the other hand, the period of a year and day, from the date of the murder, went by, without Appeal by the wife, or heir lawfully entitled to make it, then the Crown could lawfully prosecute. In this state of the transaction, the right of Appeal had lapsed, and therefore *no Appeal could be brought after the public prosecution*. Thus, the prosecution by the Crown was equally final with the prosecution by Appeal; and the accused, in either case, was safe from a second trial.") (italics in original); Note, *The Inquisitorial Power of the Federal Grand Jury*, 6 COLUM. L. REV. 347 (1906) ("Under the English system of private prosecution the function of the grand jury was to stand between the accuser and the accused. And so it was customary to act only on a formal bill of indictment being laid before them, where acting at the instigation of a private prosecutor.").

100. YALE LAW SCHOOL, LILIAN GOLDMAN LIBRARY, BLACKSTONE'S COMMENTARIES ON THE LAWS OF ENGLAND, BOOK THE FOURTH—CHAPTER THE THIRTY-SECOND: OF EXECUTION, https://avalon.law.yale.edu/18th_century/blackstone_bk4ch23.asp, ch. 23.

101. In *A Treatise of the Pleas of the Crown*, first published in 1716, William Hawkins makes reference to both an "Appeal of Murder" and an "Appeal of Felony." WILLIAM HAWKINS, A TREATISE OF THE PLEAS OF THE CROWN (1716), Bk. I, pp. 69, 190.

102. *A Treatise of the Pleas of the Crown, or, A System of Principal Matters Relating to that Subject: Digested Under Their Proper Heads*, https://lawlibrary.wm.edu/wythepedia/index.php/Treatise_of_the_Pleas_of_the_Crown.

103. YALE LAW SCHOOL, LILIAN GOLDMAN LIBRARY, BLACKSTONE'S COMMENTARIES ON THE LAWS OF ENGLAND, BOOK THE FOURTH—CHAPTER THE THIRTY-SECOND: OF EXECUTION, https://avalon.law.yale.edu/18th_century/blackstone_bk4ch32.asp.

104. 4 WILLIAM BLACKSTONE, COMMENTARIES ON THE LAWS OF ENGLAND (1769), https://avalon.law.yale.edu/18th_century/blackstone_bk4ch23.asp, ch. 23; *see also id.* ("In the fame manner by the Irish Brehon law, in case of murder, the Brehon or judge was used to compound between the murderer, and the friends of the deceased who prosecuted him, by causing the malefactor to give unto them, or to the child or wife of him that was slain, a recompense which they called an *eriach*. And thus we find in our Saxon laws (particularly those of king Athelstan) the several *weregilds*, for homicide established in progressive order, from the death of the ceorl or peasant, up to that of the king himself. And in the laws of king Henry I, we have an account of what other offences were then redeemable by *weregild*, and what were not so. As

therefore, during the continuance of this custom, a process was certainly given, for recovering the *weregild* by the party to whom it was due; it seems that, when these offences by degrees grew no longer redeemable, the private process was still continued, in order to insure the infliction of punishment upon the offender, though the party injured was allowed no pecuniary compensation for the offence."); *Fay & Ux. v. Parker* (Dec. 1872) *in* 53 JOHN M. SHIRLEY, COMP., REPORTS OF CASES ARGUED AND DETERMINED IN THE SUPREME JUDICIAL COURT OF NEW HAMPSHIRE 342, 385 (1874) (in a case decided "March, 1873" by the Supreme Judicial Court of New Hampshire, and reported by John M. Shirley, citing the double jeopardy provisions of the U.S. Constitution and the New Hampshire Bill of Rights; indicating that those clauses set forth "maxims" that "are as old as the common law"; that "Mr. Broom mentions but one 'remarkable exception which formerly existed' to the principle stated and illustrated by these maxims"; and that "[t]his occurred in the proceedings in case of Appeal of Death (see 4 Bl. Com. 312), which might be instituted against a supposed offender after trial and acquittal, and by which punishment for some heinous crime was demanded on account of the particular injury suffered by an individual, rather than for the offence against the public; but this method of prosecution, having attracted the attention of the legislature in the celebrated case of *Ashford v. Thornton*, 1 B. & Ald. 405 (*qu. vide*), was abolished by Stat. 59, Geo. III, c. 46. Broom's Leg. Max. 258."; "Blackstone tells us that this private process for the punishment of crimes probably had its origin in those times when a private pecuniary satisfaction, called a *weregild*, was constantly paid to the party injured, or his relations, to expiate enormous crimes—a custom derived to our British ancestors, in common with other norther nations, from the ancient Germans. Tacitus Man. Ger., ch. 21. These private prosecutions by appeal, so called, and which involved not only cases of homicide, but also of treason and felony, were gradually discontinued, or abolished by statute, though, to some extent, they were still recognized as legal remedies in the days of Blackstone. But they were plainly regarded by that eminent jurist as violative of the fundamental maxims of the law; for he says,—'These appeals may be brought previous to any indictment, and if the appellee be acquitted thereon, he cannot be afterward indicted for the same offence.' And, again: 'If he hath been found guilty of manslaughter on an indictment, and hath had the benefit of clergy, and suffered the judgment of the law, he cannot afterward be appealed; for it is a maxim in law, that 'nemo bis puniture pro eodem delicto." 4 Bl. Com. 312–315.").

105. *E.g.*, MARY BILDER, MAEVA MARCUS & R. KENT NEWMYER, EDS., BLACKSTONE IN AMERICA: SELECTED ESSAYS OF KATHRYN PREYER (2014).

106. 4 WILLIAM BLACKSTONE, COMMENTARIES ON THE LAWS OF ENGLAND (1769), *available at* https://avalon.law.yale.edu/18th_century/blackstone_bk4ch23.asp, ch. 23.

107. *Id.*; *see also id.* ("And so, with us, if a man be acquitted on an indictment of murder, or found guilty, and pardoned by the king, still he may, by virtue of statute 3 Hen. VII. c. 1. be prosecuted by appeal for the same felony, not having as yet been punished for it : though, if he hath been found guilty of manslaughter on an indictment, and hath had the benefit of clergy, and suffered the judgment of the law, he cannot afterwards be appealed. For it is a maxim of law, that '*memo his punitur pro eodem delicto*.'"); *id.* ("If the appellee be found guilty, he shall suffer the same judgment, as if he had been convicted by indictment: but with this remarkable difference; that on an indictment, which is at the suit of the king, the king may pardon and remit the execution; on an appeal, which is at the suit of a private subject, to make an atonement for the private wrong, the king can no more pardon it, than he can remit the damages recovered on an action of battery. In like manner as, while the *weregild* continued to be paid as a fine for homicide, it could not be remitted by the king's authority. And the antient usage was, so late as Henry the fourth's time, that all the relations of the slain should drag the appellee to the place of execution: a custom, founded upon that savage spirit of family resentment, which prevailed universally through Europe, after the irruption of the northern nations, and is peculiarly attended to in their several codes of law ; and which prevails even now among the wild and untutored inhabitants of America : as if the finger of nature had pointed it out to mankind, in their rude and uncultivated state. However, the punishment of the offender may be remitted and discharged by the concurrence of all parties interested; and as the king by his pardon may frustrate an indictment, so the appellant by his release may discharge an appeal . . . .").

108. ALLYSON N. MAY, THE BAR AND THE OLD BAILEY, 1750–1850, at 19–20 (2003); *see also id.* at 20 ("The coroner was empowered to bind over witnesses and suspects to appear at the next assizes, to imprison anyone suspect of homicide, and to take depositions. As Langbein notes, the coroner system 'was the

closest English approximation to Continental-style public prosecution by an investigating officer.'"); *id.* at 24 ("After 1724 a new system arose whereby the Treasury paid private citizens to prosecute riot and sedition, and official views of what kind of offenses threatened the state and public order became increasingly elastic, even extending—albeit rarely—to rape, murder, and violent property offenses. The attorney general, for instance, was instructed to prosecute George Smith and three other men for the murder of Anne Bristol in 1723, and the Treasury solicitor prepared the case for trial."); *id.* ("The 'episodic' interventions of the state into criminal prosecution are intimately tied to metropolitan London, for it was a perceived increase in violent crime in that city, the seat of national government, that prompted the Whig government's actions. 'By the mid-1720s,' the undersecretaries of state 'seem to have been expecting to pay for the prosecution of at least some felonies at the Old Bailey,' including robbery and burglary. They also developed contacts with the Middlesex and Westminster benches. As Beattie indicates, the engagement of solicitors in ordinary criminal prosecutions in the first half of the eighteenth century remained the exception rather than the rule. But the government's willingness to pay costs 'perhaps established a pattern'; moreover, the utility of professional pretrial preparation had been demonstrated. When 'the central authorities wanted to strengthen a criminal prosecution, they did it by sending in the lawyers.' Their example perhaps encouraged private prosecutors to do the same."); *see also* John H. Langbein, The Origins of the Adversary Criminal Trial 4, 12 (2003) ("The English perpetuated a system of private prosecution (reinforced by amateur justices of the peace and amateur village constables) into the urban industrial age.... Private prosecution was a default system, accepted because devising an effective alternative would have required the political community to confront a nest of divisive issues about financing and controlling a public prosecutorial corps. Comparable concerns prevented the development of the uniformed police until the second quarter of the nineteenth century.").

109. *Peter Ricaut. Killing: murder. 18th February 1691*, Old Bailey records, *available at* https://www.oldbaileyonline.org/images.jsp?doc=16910218004.

110. *Lewis Hussar. Killing: murder. 14th October 1724*, Old Bailey records, *available at* https://www.oldbaileyonline.org/images.jsp?doc=172410140008.

111. *Ordinary's Account*, 7th December 1724, Old Bailey records, *available at* https://www.oldbaileyonline.org/images.jsp?doc=OA172412070001.

112. *James Cluff. Killing: murder. 9th July 1729*, Old Bailey records, *available at* https://www.oldbaileyonline.org/images.jsp?doc=172907090006.

113. *Ordinary's Account*, 25th July 1729, Old Bailey records, *available at* https://www.oldbaileyonline.org/images.jsp?doc=OA172907250001; *see also* John Hostettler, A History of Criminal Justice in England and Wales 151 (2009) ("The trial of Thomas Bambridge, on a charge of murdering Robert Castell, took place at the Old Bailey on 21 May 1729. The judges were Sir Robert Baylis, Lord Mayor of the City of London, Mr Justice Page, Mr Baron Carter, some other judges and a number of justices of the peace. The trial was very brief and the main witness was Richard Corbett, the keeper of Bambridge's sponging house. He told the court that although he told Bambridge that Castell wanted to be moved out of the house he, Corbett, had not permitted the prisoner to have contact with any smallpox victim there. On the strength of this evidence Bambridge was acquitted. Castell's widow, Mary, then decided to bring an appeal of felony (a private prosecution permitted despite the acquittal) against both Bambridge and Corbett for the murder of her husband. This was heard the following year at The Guildhall before Lord Chief Justice Raymond."). In 1735, a book was advertised and published that contained Old Bailey proceedings "for Murders, Robberies, Rapes, Sodomy, Coining, Frauds and other Offences, from the year 1720 to the present time." The book included "The Trial of James Clough, on an Appeal for Murder," and, among others, the trial of "James Cluff for the Murder of his Fellow Servant Mary Green." Old Bailey Proceedings advertisements, 16th January 1735, Old Bailey records, *available at* https://www.oldbaileyonline.org/images.jsp?doc=173501160023.

114. *E.g.*, "Swindling in England," Weekly Raleigh Register (Raleigh, NC), Nov. 28, 1855, p. 2 ("In another column we give a full report, taken from the London *Times*, of the trial of the London bankers, Paul, Strahan & Bates. Their offence was appropriating to their own use the produce of the sale of securities deposited in their hands for safe keeping. The private prosecutor was Dr. Griffith, the prebendary of Rochester who had at various times employed the defendants to invest money for him ...."); "Public Prosecutors

Bill," MORNING POST (London, England), May 5, 1870, p. 2 ("Mr. WEST said he had had much experience of the working of both systems—that of conducting prosecutions by a public prosecutor in Manchester and Leeds, and by a private prosecutor in other towns. He admitted that prosecutions were better conducted in the former case, but the prosecutors there were solicitors . . . .").

115. "Court of Queen's Bench," FREEMAN'S JOURNAL (Dublin, Ireland), Jan. 17, 1842, p. 3 (noting that "Mr. Bennett, Q.C., on the part of the private prosecutor, Mr. Whittingham, had no objection to have the prisoner admitted to bail, provided it was measured in an amount which would secure the presence of the prisoner at the next assizes"); "The Riot in College-Green on the Night of the 1st July," FREEMAN'S JOURNAL (Dublin, Ireland), Aug. 13, 1845, p. 4 ("William Tyndall, Richard Brown Harding, and James M'Math were indicted for an assault on Joseph Nugent, in the parish of St. Andrew, with intent to murder him by stabbing him in the side with a knife. There were sixteen counts in the indictment, all varying, charging Tyndall as the principal, and the other two prisoners as aiding and assisting, &c. Messrs. Armstrong, Q.C., and O'Dwyer, appeared for the crown, and Mr. Henry Grattan Curran, with Mr. Peter Casserly, as private prosecutors, for Nugent's father."); "State Prosecutions," FREEMAN'S JOURNAL (Dublin, Ireland), Feb. 8, 1849, p. 2 (referring to a "private prosecutor" applying to quash an indictment "in order that a new one should be sent up"); "Administration of Justice in Ireland," BELFAST NEWS-LETTER (Belfast, Northern Ireland), Mar. 31, 1854, p. 1 (noting that Lord Monteagle stated: "A Crown prosecutor was merely appointed to assist in the administration of justice, and did not hold a position that would enable him to prevent a private prosecutor from coming forward and proceeding with an indictment for a graver offence."); "County of Armagh," BELFAST NEWS-LETTER (Belfast, Northern Ireland), Mar. 23, 1859, p. 3 (noting under "CHARGE OF TAKING A WILL": "After some conversation, the indictment, which was not drawn up by the Crown Solicitor, but by an agent for the private prosecutor, who claimed something under the will, was quashed by his lordship, on the ground that it did not charge any fraudulent intent, which alone was an offence."); "Spring Assizes, 1859 - County of Antrim," BELFAST NEWS-LETTER (Belfast, Northern Ireland), Mar. 31, 1859, p. 4 (noting under the heading of "LARCENY": "Sir THOMAS STAPLES stated that the charge was trivial, and that, with the consent of the private prosecutor, the Crown would enter a *nolle prosequi*."); "Belfast Police Court—Yesterday," BELFAST NEWS-LETTER (Belfast, Northern Ireland), Sept. 22, 1869, p. 4 ("Mr. Seeds prosecuted on the part of the police; Mr. M'Lean appeared for Henry Crangel, the private prosecutor" on the assault charge); "Belfast Police Court—Yesterday," BELFAST NEWS-LETTER (Belfast, Northern Ireland), Oct. 7, 1869, p. 3 ("Mr HARPER said he had been instructed by the private prosecutor in the case to ask that the case should be marked 'adjourned,' not 'remanded.' He believed that the prisoner, with others, had been employed by some more wealthy person to commit the offence."); "Parliament," FREEMAN'S JOURNAL (Dublin, Ireland), June 8, 1894, p. 6 ("Mr J MORLEY—It is a fact, I believe, that summonses have been issued against four directors of the National Discount Corporation of Ireland for issuing fraudulent balance sheets, and for conspiring to defraud. Those summonses, I understand, were to be heard at the Belfast Police Court to-day, but I have not yet heard the result. The present proceedings have been instituted by a private prosecutor, and I am clearly of opinion on advice from the Irish Law officer that at the present stage the Executive could not interfere in the case."); "Police Intelligence," BELFAST NEWS-LETTER (Belfast, Northern Ireland), Feb. 16, 1880, p. 7 ("Mr. SHEALS said he had consulted with his friend Mr. Coultor, and having considered the charge on the book, they had agreed to withdraw from the present prosecution. A private prosecutor had a right to withdraw from a prosecution, and also, if he chose, to amend the charge."); "Law Intelligence," FREEMAN'S JOURNAL (Dublin, Ireland), June 16, 1876, p. 2 ("*Queen (Dower) v. Justices of Tipperary.*—"Mr. Lover appeared on behalf of the private prosecutor in the court below, to show cause against a conditional order for removing the proceedings into the superior court. The action had been for trespass on a farm at Rathbeggan, near Clonmel, and it was contended there was a question of title involved."); "Law Intelligence," FREEMAN'S JOURNAL (Dublin, Ireland), June 13, 1878, p. 3 (noting for "The Queen *v.* Mayne Brothers": "The Attorney-General had declined to prosecute, and the prosecution was conducted by the private prosecutors."); "Dungannon Quarter Sessions," BELFAST NEWS-LETTER (Belfast, Northern Ireland), Jan. 24, 1876, p. 4 ("His WORSHIP, having looked at the petty sessions book, said in this case there was an application made to the Court to direct the Clerk of the Peace to send up a bill of indictment to the Grand Jury, to be considered by them, not on the application of the Crown Solicitor, but on the application of a private prosecutor."); "Parliament," THE TIMES (London,

England), July 19, 1890, p. 8 (in response to a question about whether a pending suit by the Irish Pharmaceutical Society against chemists and druggists in Belfast could be postponed "until the sense of Parliament had been fully ascertained in reference to the Pharmacy (Ireland) Act Amendment Bill, which was passed through the House of Commons and was now before the other House of Parliament," the Attorney General for Ireland replied: "The prosecutions referred to in the question were not instituted by my directions, and appear to be at the suit of private prosecutors. I have, therefore, no power to interfere in the manner suggested in the question.").

116. "The Scotch Collieries," Glasgow Herald (Glasgow, Scotland), Sept. 8, 1866, p. 6 (noting the words of the "The Chairman" as follows: "Now, at the very outset of the statute which I have referred to, it is said that 'all proceedings for summary conviction for any offense, whether at common law or under any Act of Parliament, and all proceedings for the recovery of any penalty which may be sued for or recovered in a summary form, whether such proceedings are at the instance of a public or private prosecutor or complainer, may be instituted by way of complaint in one or other of the forms set forth in the schedule A to this Act annexed.'").

117. "Borough Magistrates' Court," Wrexham Advertiser (Wrexham, Wales), June 24, 1893, p. 6 (noting that a Mr. Wynn Evans said: "The law, which was clear, laid it down that the police could not appear as advocates except in those cases where they were in the position of private prosecutors."); "Immorality in Cardiff," Western Mail (Cardiff, Wales), June 21, 1883, p. 2 ("We hear a great deal of the immorality of the large towns of every county in England, and of every country in the world. Because the immorality of Cardiff has been brought to somewhat conspicuous notice by the deputation who waited upon the Watch Committee of the Corporation of that town yesterday it must not be imagined that Cardiff is, for its size and wealth, very much, or at all, more immoral than any other town with which it might be fairly compared. The complaint of the deputation had something more pointed in it than the proclamation which we have been accustomed to listen to at the Assizes, and which is nearly as often read at, and which, therefore, may be taken to apply quite as much to, Swansea, Brecon, Carmarthen, and Haverfordwest as Cardiff.... The deputation proposed giving private individuals the power of prosecuting, hoping thereby to supplement to a very large extent the repressive influence of the police. There are two rather weighty objections to this. In the first place, the tendency of modern ideas is to discourage, as far as possible, the proceedings of private prosecutors, who are becoming more and more identified with common informers, a set whom law and the lawyers look upon with positive disfavour. Where there is a direct violation of public morals or public peace such as gives personal offence to the party complaining, it is quite another matter, but beyond this there is always a strong disposition to prevent the private prosecutor from taking action. To give powers of the kind sought by the memorialists would be to encourage a system of espionage over the private conduct of our neighbours' affairs, and to arm the unscrupulous with a potent weapon for revenging every grudge which he wished to wipe off against an enemy. But the strongest proof of all that no such power is wanted is that, as the Head Constable pointed out, it already exists, and that it is never used."); "The House of Commons and the Tithe Riots," Wrexham Advertiser (Wrexham, Wales), July 23, 1887, p. 3 ("In the old days, every prosecutor could get a *certiorari*, but by the 5th and 6th William IV. that was altered. The vexatious power, however, was reserved to the Attorney-General because the Attorney-General was responsible to the House of Commons and the country if he abused the power. (Cheers.) After referring at length to Erskine's account of the celebrated Welsh case of the Dean of St. Asaph to show how the power of a private prosecutor's writ of *certiorari* was abused, the right hon. gentleman said he could not understand why the Attorney-General should refuse to state to the House what his reasons were for putting the court in motion. If it was because Wales was in such a condition that he could not trust a jury, that was a reason which the House was entitled to know something about. (Opposition cheers.).") (italics in original).

118. "Supreme Court," The Age (Melbourne, Australia), June 25, 1863, p. 7 ("In this colony, as in England, the word prosecutor meant exactly the same, though in special cases one might appear as a private prosecutor; whereas, in other ordinary cases, he might be a public prosecutor."); "Tasmania," Sydney Morning Herald (Sydney, Australia), Sept. 4, 1857, p. 8 (in a discussion of the conviction rate, referring to "the malice of private prosecutors"); Sydney Morning Herald (Sydney, Australia), Feb. 2, 1859, p. 8 (in a letter to the editor written by attorneys, it was stated: "The Attorney-General has invariably granted

to persons who initiated prosecutions for libel at the Police Office, in cases where a committal had taken place, liberty to employ private counsel and attorneys to conduct the prosecution, reserving to himself the right (but we have never known him to exercise it) of interfering if he thought fit. In cases where the private prosecutor has not been willing to take the duty and incur the expense of carrying on the prosecution, the Attorney-General has always declined to carry it on at the public expense."); *see also* "In re John and Solomon Nathan," THE AGE (Melbourne, Australia), Dec. 3, 1862, p. 7 ("The court could not recognize the Crown being assisted by counsel instructed by private prosecutors. The prosecution must be either public or private. If the Crown appeared at all in any case, then the prosecution was a public one. It sometimes happened, however, that the Attorney-General filed an information, and then allowed a prosecutor to carry out the prosecution at his own expense, and that was the course evidently pursued in the present case."); "Criminal Sessions. Friday, 27th October.", THE AGE (Melbourne, Australia), Oct. 28, 1865, p. 5 (noting of proceedings in *Wood v. Syme* "Before His Honor Mr Justice Williams, and a Special Jury": "Mr Wrixon said the only thing before the court was a criminal information, filed in the ordinary way. No one had applied to the Crown, under the Supreme Court Act, for leave to appear. There was no private prosecutor here. In the case of *The Queen v. O'Farrell*, it was laid down that, unless a private prosecutor applied under the Supreme Court Act, there was no recognition. His learned friends could not represent the Crown, and claim the privileges which the Crown exercised. One question that would be raised was the right of challenged. The Crown had the right, but that privilege was not conceded to a private prosecutor."); "Supreme Court Criminal Sittings," THE ARGUS (Melbourne, Australia), Oct. 28, 1865, p. 5 (noting that in *Queen v. O'Farrell*, "the Chief Justice had said that a private prosecutor had no *locus standi* unless he had previously made application, under the Supreme Court Act, for leave to file a criminal information"); PARLIAMENTARY DEBATES—SESSION 1893, at 42–43 (1894) (reporting the following remarks of Sir Bryan O'Loghlen: "Originally, in 1825, in Sydney, accused persons were tried by commissioned officers. In 1828, the Attorney-General was given power to prosecute. In 1833, petty juries were established. In 1840, there was a Crown Prosecutor appointed for Port Phillip. Under all these Acts the rights of the Attorney-General were preserved, and when this colony got autonomy the Sydney system was followed, and Crown Prosecutors were appointed subject to the direction of the Attorney-General. This question came before the House as long ago as the year 1865. Mr. Adamson was then Crown Prosecutor, and the late Chief Justice held office as Attorney-General. There were a number of cases of private libel, and, in consequence of certain observations made by Chief Justice Stawell in the case of *The Queen* v. *O'Farrell*, there was a memorandum sent to the Crown Solicitor by Mr. Higinbotham, and communicated to all the Crown Prosecutors to the effect that in cases of private libel there should be no prosecution."); "Criminal Sessions. Saturday, 28th October.", THE AGE (Melbourne, Australia), Oct. 30, 1865, p. 6 ("Mr Wrixon: The argument of my learned friend, Mr Smyth, if it has any weight, goes to the length of saying that because the Attorney-General gave a private prosecutor, rightly or wrongly—we say wrongly—leave to undertake the prosecution of his own trial, it was to continue for ever. The result would be that Mr Wood, who declined to ask the court for leave to conduct his own trial, placed himself in such a position that, failing in his proceedings against the defendant, no costs could be obtained from him. The construction put upon the Attorney-General's authority is that Mr Wood can prosecute, time after time, notwithstanding that the juries may continue to disagree, and that the defendant, by the mistempered zeal of the prosecutor, can be perpetually harassed."); "Legislative Assembly. Tuesday, 31st October." THE AGE (Melbourne, Australia) Nov. 1, 1865, p. 6 (noting the following comments of Mr. Halfey and Mr. Higinbotham relating to the *Wood v. Syme* case: "Mr HALFEY, without notice, asked the hon. the Attorney-General whether, after the result of the trial of Wood v. Syme, the Government intended to permit Mr Wood to pursue another trial under the protection of the Crown; or what course the Government intended to take." "Mr HIGINBOTHAM said that, from the report of the trial, which had appeared in the public journals, it seemed to him and to the Government that it was a subject which required them to take into serious consideration whether, in the interest of public justice, the case should be allowed to proceed to a new trial. In the course of the day he had received a communication from the defendant, expressing his desire that the Crown should not interfere, and that the case should be allowed to proceed to a second trial; and, in deference to the opinion of the judge, that the authority in the first instance was a continuing authority, he had not yet returned an answer to the request of the defendant, or reviewed the decision on the subject of the trial. He would take the opportunity of informing the House that in this instance leave had been given to a private prosecutor to conduct the case at his own expense, and by his own counsel on his own application. He found the practice had existed for some time past in the Crown law office. It appeared to him, under the particular circumstances of the case, that it was his duty not to oppose the permission; but at the same time he thought it was open to most serious objection; and now that the case had been to some extent determined, and the opportunity presented itself to alter the practice, he would publicly state that, in future, he would not grant any such permission. The hon. member might be aware that, when a person desired to put the criminal law in motion for his own satisfaction, he could do so by application to the Supreme Court for a rule for criminal trial; and if the court thought fit to grant the request, both the prosecution and the defendant would be placed in an equal position, and each party be compelled to pay costs according to the result of the trial; and when a criminal prosecution was issued to obtain private redress, it was only reasonable that these terms should be enforced. According to the practice hitherto prevailing, the prosecutor bore his own costs, but the defendant was not remunerated for the expense of conducting his case. He therefore thought it would be right to announce that, in future, the practice would be, where a private prosecutor sought redress by putting the criminal law in motion, except in the case of a public officer or some person in whom the public had an interest, he should go to the Supreme Court and ask for a rule authorising the institution of criminal proceedings.").

119. "Law Intelligence," VICTORIA DAILY TIMES (Victoria, Canada), Oct. 17, 1893, p. 5 ("Mr. Justice Drake sat in the Speedy Trials Court to hear the evidence in the case of Reg. vs. Currier, charged with the larceny of a diamond ring. W. H. Langley appeared for the crown and Lindley Crease defended. The evidence did not differ from that taken at the preliminary investigation with the exception that the defendant and his witnesses gave their testimony. Young Ramous, who laid the information against the prisoner admitted that he knew the owner of the diamond ring but did not explain why he kept it in his possession so long without notifying him. The evidence of the prisoner and of Wallace went to show that the ring was purchased from Ramous for $30. His lordship discharged the prisoner whereupon the crown prosecutor intimated that an information would be laid against Ramous for stealing the ring. The private prosecutor accordingly changed places with the prisoner and was placed under arrest by Officer Hildreth.").

120. "State Offenders and Private Prosecutors," PALL MALL GAZETTE (London, England), Nov. 15, 1866, p. 2 ("The *Herald* is of opinion that the indictment of 'Governor Eyre' by the 'Jamaica Committee' is disgraceful to our jurisprudence. Here is a public servant prosecuted by private individuals upon a charge of the highest felony for official misdeeds. Where is the Government that should arraign him if he be guilty? Where is the Government that should undertake his defence if it deems him innocent? No fault, however, can be found with the Executive, which must be ruled by the Acts of Parliament as they stand. Still, when a State wrong is done the State is insulted, and the State should vindicate its own honour. Here, however, after the Government have instituted a solemn, elaborate, and exhausting investigation Mr. Eyre is exonerated from all blame beyond that of a partial error of judgment—one of those errors, perhaps, by which nations and empires have occasionally been saved; but a little coterie, of one opinion in politics, interferes, pushes the State aside, takes possession of the law, and insists upon putting a man, lately the responsible administrator of affairs in an important British colony, in peril of his life. It is monstrous and shameful. Virtually, in this case the Jamaica committee prosecutes, nominally the Crown does so. Is there no discretion vested in the Crown, as represented by its law officers, to refuse? If not, it may be hoped that so serious a defect in the law will not long be permitted to deface and scandalize the statute book of the realm."); *see also* MORNING POST (London, England), Feb. 7, 1867, p. 4 ("Impeachment by Parliament is the remedy provided by the Constitution for abuse of the Executive power, and if the Commons of England in their discretion did not see fit to impeach Mr. EYRE and his subordinates, we do not think the duty of bring them to justice should have been undertaken by private prosecutors."); "The Legal Position of Mr. Eyre," LEEDS MERCURY (Leeds, England), Feb. 11, 1867, p. 4 ("Upon a first perusal of the Act of William III. we thought that possibly a governor of a colony could only be dealt with on the information of the Attorney-General. But obviously the method of procedure is governed by later Acts, which, read with the Act of William III., make a colonial governor amenable to the ordinary jurisdiction of the criminal courts at the suit of a private prosecutor. The only question—the question of jurisdiction being disposed of—is that raised by the Indemnity Act, which was passed by the Jamaica Legislature. Does not include Mr. Eyre?

That is for the court.—*Law Times*."); "The Market Drayton Parody on Justice," NORTH WALES CHRONICLE (Bangor, Wales), Apr. 6, 1867, p. 2 ("No one can accuse the royal commissioners of undue leniency towards Mr. Eyre, and now that he has passed through that trying ordeal it is hardly fair that he should be exposed to the ill-natured attacks of private prosecutors. It is not necessary to discuss the dreadful incidents of the Jamaica insurrection, to ascertain whether or not the repressive measures were too severe. Sitting quietly at home in a state of profound security it is easy to say that this precaution was needless, that punishment too exemplary. We must put ourselves in the position of Mr. Eyre to realize the adequacy or otherwise of his precautions : the peace and safety of a colony were committed to his care : the white population formed a mere handful among half-a-million of blacks; a massacre of whites, only equalled in barbarity by the misdeeds of the Sepeys, had already begun, and momentary success was all that was necessary to kindle revote from end to end of the island."); "The Matter of John Edward Eyre, Esq., Late Governor of Jamaica," THE TIMES (London, England), May 9, 1868, p. 11 ("This was a proceeding to compel the magistrate ... to hear and determine a charge of high crime and misdemeanor against Mr. Eyre, late Governor of Jamaica ... for declaring and executing martial law in Jamaica, on the occasion of the rebellion in that island ...."; "Mr. POWELL, Q.C., now appeared on the part of Mr. Vaughan, the magistrate (not on the part of Mr. Eyre), to submit the grounds on which he conceived he had no jurisdiction in the matter.... Mr. POWELL.— ... The policy of the Colonial Governors Acts, which relate to offenses by governors of colonies, or other high officers in the service of the Crown, was that such offences should be dealt with only in this high court, either with the approval of the Attorney-General or with the sanction of grand jury, and ought not to be brought before a common police-court at the caprice of any private prosecutor, and that it ought not to be in the power of any private parties, at their mere will and pleasure, to inflict as often as they please upon a colonial governor the ignominy and annoyance of appearance at a police-court, along with common thieves and drunkards, to answer any charge that might be preferred against him."); John Fabian Witt, *Anglo-American Empire and the Crisis of the Legal Frame (Will the Real British Empire Please Stand Up?)*, 120 HARV. L. REV. 754, 781–82 (2007) ("[T]he Jamaica Committee retained two distinguished barristers, one a Queen's Counsel, to draft an opinion on the illegality of Eyre's conduct. With the opinion in hand, the Committee pushed the government to initiate a criminal prosecution of Eyre. When the new Conservative government declined to do so (and when Disraeli went so far as to suggest that Eyre had acted appropriately under the circumstances), the Committee began two private criminal prosecutions of Eyre and a third against two military officers who had sentenced George Gordon to death: Colonel Abercrombie Nelson and Lieutenant Herbert Brand. For good measure, the Committee sponsored a private civil suit against Eyre by two Jamaicans seeking damages for injuries they had suffered during the period of martial law.").

121. Reinhold Kramer & Tom Mitchell, "'Daniel de Leon Drew up the Diagram': Winnipeg's Seditious-Conspiracy Trials of 1919–20," *in* 4 CANADIAN STATE TRIALS: SECURITY, DISSENT, AND THE LIMITS OF TOLERATION IN WAR AND PEACH, 1914–1939, at 232 (Barry Wright, Eric Tucker & Susan Binne, eds. 2015) (noting that "the 1892 Criminal Code continued to protect the right of private citizens to initiate criminal prosecutions" and that the Manitoba Court of Appeals ruled that a private prosecutor had legal standing and a right to be heard) (citing Fred Kaufman, *The Role of the Private Prosecutor: A Critical Appraisal of the Complainant's Position in Criminal Cases*, 7 MCGILL L.J. 102, 102–14 (1960) & Peter Burns, *Private Prosecutions in Canada: The Law and a Proposal for Change*, 21 MCGILL L.J. 269 (1975)); "Chamberlain Jumps Bail," WINNIPEG DAILY TRIBUNE (Winnipeg, Manitoba), Dec. 6, 1893, p. 5 (noting that a Mr. Haggart, in addressing the magistrate, said, "Well, you know, your worship, this is not a crown case and it has now been remanded several times just at the instance of a private prosecutor."); "The Fur Theft Case," MANITOBA MORNING FREE PRESS (Winnipeg, Manitoba), Jan. 4, 1894, p. 6 ("Andrew H. Smith, the tanner, who shipped a parcel of furs, the property of E. J. Rodgers, valued at $900, to Vancouver, and attempted to follow them up, was arraigned at the police court yesterday. Mr. Wade appeared for the crown and Mr. Elliott in behalf of the private prosecutor."); "Criminal Docket," WINNIPEG DAILY TRIBUNE (Winnipeg, Manitoba), Jan. 8, 1894, p. 5 ("Andrew H. Smith, the tanner who shipped a parcel of furs, the property of E. J. Rodgers, valued at $800, to Vancouver, and then went west, was charged with stealing the same. He pleaded not guilty. Mr. Wade appeared for the crow, and Mr. Elliott for Rodgers, the private prosecutor. No one appeared for the prisoner."); "A Protest from Manitou," WINNIPEG DAILY TRIBUNE (Winnipeg,

Manitoba), Apr. 17, 1894, p. 4 (a letter to the editor began: "Sir,—Two cases brought, one by the license department and one by a private prosecutor, against Mr. Shore, proprietor of the Ellis House, for allowing liquor to be consumed on his premises after hours, are to be tried here next Thursday.").

122. "Lacrosse—It Ended in Love," THE GAZETTE (Montreal, Canada), Dec. 14, 1892, p. 8 ("TORONTO, Ont., December 13.—Captain William Stuart, of the Capital Lacrosse club, is not to answer to the law for his assault upon John C. Warbrick, of the Torontos, during the match here last season. In the General Sessions to-day Crown Attorney Dewart stated that the private prosecutor, Warbrick, was not anxious to proceed. 'The matter has been settled by an exchange of compliments and bouquets,' and so, by direction of the Attorney-General, he would enter a *nolle prosequi*. Toronto lacrosse men are well satisfied with the termination of the action, and only regret cause was even given for the fighting.").

123. "Law Intelligence," MONTREAL GAZETTE (Montreal, Quebec), Mar. 17, 1857, p. 2 (containing the following notation under the heading "COURT OF QUEEN'S BENCH, (CRIMINAL TERM)": "The Court opened this morning with the case of The Queen vs. Michael Gaffey, on indictment for stealing a mare. A man named Dufresne, a farmer, resident at Longue Pointe, lost a mare; he afterwards came to the city and found the missing animal in the hands of the prisoner, whom he arrested. The only evidence on the part of the Crown was the private prosecutor, the policeman who arrested the prisoner, and a young man named Chartier, a resident of Longue Pointe."); "Court of Quarter Sessions," MONTREAL GAZETTE (Montreal, Quebec), July 6, 1857, p. 2 ("The Queen *vs.* the Harbour Commissioners of Montreal, William Dow and Joseph Warren Coleman, on conviction of a nuisance. Mr. Mack, as Counsel for the Defendants, moved that the proceedings in this case be quashed, inasmuch as the indictment did not bear the signature of any officer on the part of the Crown. It was signed by Mr. Carter on behalf of the private prosecutor. As this case was brought in the name of the Queen it should have been signed by the Counsel for the Crown. Mr. Carter opposed the motion. The motion was rejected."); "Court of General Sessions of the Peace," MONTREAL GAZETTE (Montreal, Canada), Jan. 11, 1858, p. 2 (noting the appearance of counsel "for private prosecutor"); "Assault," MONTREAL GAZETTE (Montreal, Canada), Apr. 8, 1858, p. 2 ("Mr. J. M. Loranger conducted the prosecution on behalf of the private prosecutor."); "The Canadian Extradition Case," THE TIMES (London, England), Nov. 12, 1866, p. 10 ("A Canadian paper, in explanation of the delay of a day in applying for a writ of *habeas corpus*, alleges that the practice of the court required a day's notice of the application. It is also stated, in reference to the adjournment of the case, for a day in order to allow the counsel for the private prosecutor to be head...."); "York Assizes," DAILY CITIZEN (Ottawa, Canada), Oct. 10, 1874, p. 4 ("The 11th section of the statute of last session evidently applied to cases where the Crown felt it would be to the public interest to prosecute and where the private prosecutor did not feel it necessary to act himself; where persons of distinction were concerned, such as the Governor General or Lieut.-Governor, the Crown might feel disposed to prosecute in their behalf and would then claim the privileges of the Crown."); *see also* MORNING CHRONICLE (London, England), Oct. 17, 1832, p. 2 (reprinting a story from the *Montreal Gazette*, which reported: "Messrs. CHERRINE and WALKER attempted to interfere in the case on behalf of the private prosecutors, or, more properly, persecutors : but who these were, no one could discover. Whether the former gentleman had received a fee from the faction, or whether he presumed to volunteer his interference, did not transpire. The Judges concurred in the Constitutional opinion of the Crown Counsel, and told the advocates of persecution, that they could not be allowed to offer any observations on the case, as the Crown Lawyers were the only individuals intrusted with criminal prosecutions.").

124. 3 R. MONTGOMERY MARTIN, HISTORY OF THE BRITISH COLONIES 542 (1834).

125. "Court of Queen's Bench," THE GAZETTE (Montreal, Quebec), Oct. 11, 1880, p. 3.

126. "Montreal," OTTAWA DAILY CITIZEN (Ottawa, Canada), Apr. 14, 1880, p. 1.

127. "Adjourned Till To-Morrow," VANCOUVER DAILY WORLD (Vancouver, Canada), July 28, 1891, p. 4 (noting the appearance of a "private prosecutor" at the Police Court in a case involving a broken pane of glass).

128. FREEMAN'S JOURNAL (Dublin, Ireland), June 16, 1875, p. 5 ("His lordship adverted to another matter even still more important than that of reckless driving. This was the filthy state of the streets. The subject will come before the Commission in a noteworthy form; and if the judge's remarks may be taken with a signification, it is not unlikely that this problem of street cleansing will receive a new and momentous turn. The question is at present before the Commission Court in the shape of a bill by a private prosecutor

against the Lord Mayor, aldermen, and burgesses of the city of Dublin, for a common nuisance. It is set forth in this novel indictment that the civic authorities named, having care of the streets of the city, and jurisdiction over them, and having imposed upon them the duty of keeping these streets clean and in repair, had neglected to do so, thereby causing inconvenience and loss to such of her Majesty's subjects as are occasionally obliged to use them. His lordship mentioned that the evidence to the indictment set forth that on one occasion a witness measured five feet of mud outside the pathway at Inns-quay, and that he saw a girl who was attempting to cross the road opposite the church step into it up to her ankles. No city reader will doubt the statement, for, we venture to say, there is not one among them but has been spectator or victim in some episode of the kind."); "The Commission," FREEMAN'S JOURNAL (Dublin, Ireland), June 16, 1875, p. 7 ("The Commission of Oyer and Terminer for the City and County of Dublin was opened yesterday by Mr. Justice Fitzgerald and Baron Dowse in the Courthouse, Green-street. The Right Hon. The Lord May, who was attended by the civic officers, also occupied a seat upon the bench."; "After the grand juries for the city and county had been duly sworn, Baron Dowse, addressing the city grand jury, said he was sorry to have to say that the cases before them were, many of them, of a very serious character .... The remainder of the two or three and twenty cases that were to go before them were of the ordinary character. There were cases of obtaining money under false pretences, and of larceny, and one of highway robbery. He had reserved one bill, which was a very important one, for the last. It was a bill by a private prosecutor against the Lord Mayor, aldermen, and burgesses of the city of Dublin for a common nuisance (laughter). He was quite sure that they would do their duty undismayed by the high position of the traverser and his friends (laughter). Speaking seriously, the case was in many respects the most important that was to go before them. They were not to be influenced by their private experience, however extensive, as to the condition of the streets of the city; they were to act only upon the evidence, so far as they thought they ought to act upon it. The offense charged was a nuisance at common law, for fortunately the common law was strong enough to grapple with the Lord Mayor and the aldermen and burgesses of the city of Dublin. The indictment charged that the Lord Mayor, alderman, and burgesses of the city of Dublin having care of the streets of the city and jurisdiction over them, and having imposed upon them the duty of keeping those streets clean and in repair, had neglected to repair and cleanse those streets, thereby occasioning inconvenience and loss to such of her Majesty's subjects as had been occasionally obliged to use them. The evidence was to the effect that on one occasion a witness measured five feet of mud outside the pathway at Inn's-quay, filling up the channel, and he saw a girl who was attempting to cross opposite the church, where the mud was six feet across, step into it up to her ankles; and he pointed this circumstance out to an official who was described merely by letters and figures as 150 D. If they were satisfied that the traversers had neglected their duty, for it would hardly be denied that it was their duty, of cleansing the streets, they should bring in a true bill.").

129. *E.g.*, "Alleged Embezzlement," BELFAST NEWS-LETTER (Belfast, Northern Ireland), Mar. 24, 1866, p. 3 ("Mr. LAW: My lord, I am requested on the part of the prosecutors to say that, so far as their suggestion or wishes can be considered in the matter in your lordship's estimation of the punishment, it is not their desire that the prisoner should be dealt with more heavily than your lordship would consider absolutely necessary. They brought the prosecution in the discharge of what they considered their duty."; "HIS LORDSHIP—Of course the application upon the part of the prosecutors, as well as the recommendation of the jury, alters my determination as to what I thought ought to be done. I thought it essential in the case, especially in a mercantile community like this, that when a case of this kind was so clearly established it ought to be met by exemplary punishment—not for the purpose of inflicting punishment upon the individual, but by that punishment of warning all others in a community of this kind that it is their duty and their interest to be honest and to be true."; "HIS LORDSHIP— ... [A]s the prosecutors do not press for severe punishment, I am enabled to deal with the case otherwise than I had intended. If it had not been for that, I would not have done my duty without pronouncing some sentence of penal servitude. This is no case of ordinary larceny. I have just been obliged in a case of three or four offences to impose on a prisoner—not one-half so culpable as the prisoner before me—a sentence of seven years' penal servitude. I have now to deal with a young man of better condition—of education—of family—and with all the means of religious instruction—with everything that ought to keep him right, and notwithstanding all that he has been convicted in the case. I never heard clearer evidence in a case. It did not leave open for a shade of doubt.... As the jury have recommended him to mercy—and I think this recommendation, on the first ground, is

not without foundation—regarding the loose, irregular mode the transactions were allowed to be carried on, and the want of proper surveillance—and as the prosecutors—for this is a private prosecution—one in which the public at large have not the same interest as the private prosecutors—as they do not press for punishment, it enables me to depart from the punishment I intended to impose. I can also well conceive that to the unfortunate young man now a prisoner here—that the true punishment to him is not the sentence I shall impose on him. It is the remorse which must for ever haunt him when he recollects the opportunities he has thrown away, the position he has neglected, the opportunities of acquiring wealth, the ruin he has brought upon himself and upon his family too, that is the real punishment. However, I would not be doing my duty by imposing a less sentence than that William Robinson be imprisoned and kept to hard labor for two years from the present time. The prisoner was then removed.").

130. 19 T.B. Howell, comp. A Complete Collection of State Trials and Proceedings for High Treason and Other Crimes and Misdemeanors from the Earliest Period to the Present Time, with Notes and Other Illustrations 12 n.* (1813).

131. 19 T.B. Howell, comp., A Complete Collection of State Trials and Proceedings for High Treason and Other Crimes and Misdemeanors from the Earliest Period to the Present Time 15–16 (1816); *see also id.* at 214 (noting the words of "Mr. *Brown*, for the Pannel" in the 1752 trial of James Stewart: "Gentlemen of the jury; I appear for the pannel.... [G]entlemen, if I have undertaken what I am not sufficient for, the fault lies at the door of the private prosecutor, who, before the prosecution was commenced, begun early with pre-engaging the whole counsel at the bar, who had most experience in these matters, not with an intention that they should assist in carrying on the prosecution, (for many of the gentlemen who were engaged have not appeared at the trial), but with an intention that they might not have it in their power to appear on the side of the pannel."); *id.* at 189, 205–07 (noting that James Stewart had been "active for the rebels during the 1745 Jacobite Rebellion" and that "[p]rior to the murder, James was employed by Colin Campbell of Glenure, also known as the 'Red Fox', as his assistant"; "The determination of the authorities, and power members of Clan Campbell, to prosecute and convict James Stewart, despite the deficiencies in the evidence against him, demonstrated th[e] continued tension in the area even after the Jacobite cause was soundly defeated in 1746.").

132. *Id.* at 14; Samantha Priestley, The History of Gibbeting: Britain's Most Brutal Punishment 30 (2020); Rachel E. Bennett, Capital Punishment and the Criminal Corpse in Scotland, 1740–1834, at 205–10 (2018); *see also* "The Trial of Stewart of Acharn," *in* The Journal of Jurisprudence and Scottish Law Magazine (1891), Vol. XXXV, pp. 521, 525 ("The sentence of the Court was that, on 8th November, James Stewart should be hanged on a gibbet to be erected 'on a conspicuous eminence upon the south side of and near to the said ferry' of Ballachulish, 'until he be dead, and thereafter to be hung in chains upon said gibbet.'").

133. *See also* 1 John Bouvier, Bouvier's Law Dictionary: A Concise Encyclopedia of the Law (Rawle's Revision) 708 (Francis Rawle, 3d rev. 1914) ("Court of the Lord High Steward. If the House of Lords is not sitting, cases of impeachment and temporal peers and peeresses accused of high treason, felony or misprision are tried in the Court of the Lord High Steward. He is appointed for the occasion, and is usually the Lord Chancellor. All peers who have a right to sit and vote in Parliament must be summoned. They are the sole judges of fact, and the majority, which must consist of twelve at least, decides. The Lord High Steward has a vote, and is judge of all matters of law.").

134. Thomas Edlyne Tomlins & Thomas Colpitts Granger, The Law-Dictionary, Explaining the Rise, Progress, and Present State of the British Law: Defining and Interpreting the Terms or Words of Art, and Comprising Also Copious Information on the Subjects of Trade and Government (4th ed. 1835) (entry for "BLACK-ROD").

135. "The Adventures of the Byrons: Royalists, Rebels, Roysterers, Writers—and Rectors," The Sketch, July 13, 1898, p. 492.

136. 8 Lives of Eminent and Illustrious Englishmen from Alfred the Great to the Latest Times, on an Original Plan 295 (George Godfrey Cunningham, ed. 1838).

137. "The Trial of Lawrence Earl Ferrers, for the Murder of John Johnson," *in* 19 T.B. Howell, comp., A Complete Collection of State Trials and Proceedings for High Treason and Other Crimes and Misdemeanors from the Earliest Period to the Present Time 885 (1813).

138. 19 T.B. Howell, comp., A Complete Collection of State Trials and Proceedings for High Treason and Other Crimes and Misdemeanors from the Earliest Period to the Present Time 1177–1236 (1816). The reports of the State Trials in England also contain other references to "private prosecutors." *E.g.*, 17 T.B. Howell, comp., A Complete Collection of State Trials and Proceedings for High Treason and Other Crimes and Misdemeanors from the Earliest Period to the Present Time 210–11 (1816) (noting that Robert Hales was tried at the "King's-bench bar, Westminster, by a special jury of the county of Middlesex," and that in that case, "Mr. Attorney moved for a trial at bar on an information filed by him for forgery. But it not being carried on at the expence of the crown, but of a private prosecutor, the Court held, that he must make out the usual requisites to bring it to the bar . . . ."); 20 T.B. Howell, comp., A Complete Collection of State Trials and Proceedings for High Treason and Other Crimes and Misdemeanors from the Earliest Period to the Present Time 507, 663 (1816) (quoting the following from "Mr. Wallace" in the "Trial of the Duchess of Kingston": "The prosecutor of this indictment has had the boldness to set at defiance the proceedings in the Ecclesiastical Court; and, in direct opposition to a sentence pronounced there, to prefer in a court of criminal jurisdiction a charge of felony; for although criminal prosecutions are and must be in the name of the crown, yet in both cases they are carried on by private individuals; and your lordships particularly know, in the present case, there is a private prosecutor, and one who might have applied on the score of interest to the Ecclesiastical Court, to have had that sentence reexamined."); *id.* at 663 (noting these words of Lord Mansfield: "I am most clear that the Attorney-General has a right to reply if he thinks fit, and that I cannot deprive him of it; and there is no such rule, that in no case a private prosecutor or private plaintiff shall not reply, if new matter is urged which calls for a reply; new questions of law, new observations, or any matter that makes a reply necessary. No authority at law has been quoted to the contrary."); *see also* 21 T.B. Howell, comp., A Complete Collection of State Trials and Proceedings for High Treason and Other Crimes and Misdemeanors from the Earliest Period to the Present Time 935 (1816) (making reference to "a prosecution by a private prosecutor"); 22 T.B. Howell, comp., A Complete Collection of State Trials and Proceedings for High Treason and Other Crimes and Misdemeanors from the Earliest Period to the Present Time 223 (1817) ("[T]he French minister would have taken upon himself to prosecute the defendant; but when government knew how much it affected the mind of the high and honourable person whom it concerned, it would have been a shabby part indeed, in government, to have suffered a foreign minister to come here as a private prosecutor, to protect himself against the attack of a British subject, appearing publicly at noon-day and avowing it."); 27 T.B. Howell, comp., A Complete Collection of State Trials and Proceedings for High Treason and Other Crimes and Misdemeanors from the Earliest Period to the Present Time 977 (1820) (referencing a "private prosecutor").

139. 4 Sir Spencer Walpole, A History of England from the Conclusion of the Great War in 1815, at 439 n.1 (1910).

140. Arthur Lyon Cross, A History of England and Greater Britain 903 (1914) ("In 1815 the pillory was done away with for every offense except perjury, and twenty years later it was abolished for that offense as well. The flogging of women was declared illegal in 1817. Brougham did much to simplify procedure, while Peel, who prepared the way for a better enforcement of the laws by the establishment of the metropolitan police system in 1829, greatly improved the criminal code. He abolished benefit of clergy in 1827, and, before he left office, he had reduced the capital penalties to about a dozen.").

141. "Criminal Prosecutions in Scotland," The Times (London, England), Mar. 1, 1887, p. 6 ("The Lord Advocate.—It is possible for an individual in Scotland to institute a criminal prosecution, and the fact of the person proceeded against being a police inspector makes no difference in that respect; but a private person cannot institute such a proceeding without the concurrence of the Public Prosecutor, who, however, cannot improperly or from a corrupt motive withhold his concurrence. If it can be shown that he has improperly withheld his concurrence the High Court of Justiciary will interfere to prevent injustice being done."); "Prosecution in Scotland," Glasgow Herald (Glasgow, England), Mar. 1, 1887, p. 8 (reporting the same remarks of Scotland's Lord Advocate); "High Court of Justiciary," Dundee Courier and Argus (Dundee, Scotland), Mar. 21, 1892, p. 4 ("The Court met on Saturday, Alex. Robertson ('Dundonnachie'), pleading before Lords Rutherfurd Clark, Trayner, and Wellwood, complained of having been committed under a certificate granted by Dr Charles Hay to the effect that he was insane, and he asked for

criminal letters against Dr Hay. After hearing Robertson, the Court asked if the Lord Advocate was represented. Mr Dickson, who had watched the case, said he had no instructions, because the concurrence of the Lord Advocate was not asked till after the bill was presented. Lord Trayner said that the concurrence of the Lord Advocate should have been asked. If the Lord Advocate had refused to give his concurrence, the Court could have given a warrant to the private prosecutor to proceed without his concurrence. But he thought, further, that no relevant statement whatever of any criminal charge had been made against Dr Hay upon which criminal letters could be issued. The other Judges concurred, and the application was refused."); CALEDONIAN MERCURY (Edinburgh, Scotland), Oct. 2, 1752, p. 3 (referencing the daughter of the Honourable Hugh Mackay as a "private Prosecutor"); CALEDONIAN MERCURY (Edinburgh, Scotland), Oct. 14, 1758, p. 3 (referencing a "Payment to the private Prosecutor of the Sum of 700 Merks"); CALEDONIAN MERCURY (Edinburgh, Scotland), Oct. 2, 1762, p. 3 (referencing the use of "private prosecutors" with "concourse, and also at the instance of his Majesty's Advocate, for his Majesty's interest, for the crimes of violently invading the said private prosecutors, in the month of May last, with arms, and turning them and their families out of their houses and possessions," and Lord Alemoor pronouncing sentence that "George Campbell and his sons, conjunctly and severally, to make payment to the private prosecutors, equally betwixt them, of the sum of one hundred Merks, in name of damages and expenses, and fined and amerciated each of them in the sum of three pounds Scots, to be applied for his Majesty's use; ordered George Campbell and Janet Ferguson to be incarcerate[d] within the Tolbooth of Inverary for fourteen days, and the two sons for eight days and to remain in prison after the elapse of those periods of confinement, until the sums of money above mentioned should be paid; and until each of them found bail, under the penalty of 500 Merks, that thay should live peace[a]bly and inoffensively for the space of two years, and particularly, that they should not trouble or molest the private prosecutors during that period"); "EDINBURGH," CALEDONIAN MERCURY (Edinburgh, Scotland), Sept. 18, 1771, p. 3 (referencing "the trial at the instance of Mr. Edward Maxwell, Merchant, and one of the Baillies of Dumfries, with concourse of his Majesty's Advocate, against John Bushby, Writer there, accused of insulting and attaching the private prosecutor while in the exercise of his office as a Magistrate"); CALEDONIAN MERCURY (Edinburgh, Scotland), May 21, 1777, p. 3 (making reference to "a voluntary disclamation, which had been twice read over to the private prosecutor"); "Edinburgh," CALEDONIAN MERCURY (Edinburgh, Scotland), June 23, 1777, p. 3 (making reference to "the private prosecutor" in a murder case); "Riot at Aberdeen," ABERDEEN JOURNAL, AND GENERAL ADVERTISER FOR THE NORTH OF SCOTLAND (Aberdeen, Scotland), Jan. 12, 1803, p. 2 (containing this note pertaining to "*Thursday, Jan. 6*": "This day the Court met to proceed to the trial of *Lieut. Colonel George Mackenzie*, *Captain J. B. Macdonoch*, *Ensign George Lanigan*, *Serjeant Andrew Mackay*, and *Serjeant Alexander Sutherland* ... accused at the instance of Daniel Ross, and three other private prosecutors, with concurrence of his Majesty's Advocate, of being guilty of the murder of certain persons on the 4th of June last, in the streets of the town of Aberdeen."); "High Court of Justiciary," ABERDEEN JOURNAL, AND GENERAL ADVERTISER FOR THE NORTH OF SCOTLAND (Aberdeen, Scotland), Jan. 8, 1806, p. 3 ("Friday the Court met, agreeably to adjournment, to consider the objections of the relevancy of the libel, and title of the private party to prosecute the charge of forgery against *Andrew Belch*, with the informations ordered to be given in. Their Lordships delivered their opinions at considerable length, and unanimously found, that Mr Dundas, the private prosecutor, had no sufficient title to maintain the present action before this Court upon the facts charged in the libel, the said prosecution being only with the concourse, and not at the instance of his Majesty's Advocate, and therefore dismissed the said criminal libel and the pannel from the bar."); CALEDONIAN MERCURY (Edinburgh, Scotland), Oct. 3, 1818, p. 3 (referencing a "private prosecutor"); "Opinion of the Court," CALEDONIAN MERCURY (Edinburgh, Scotland), June 17, 1833, p. 4 ("It appears that this young man, so far as he himself confessions, did, on the 6th April, enter into an inclosed field belonging to the private prosecutor, and that he was accompanied by two of his companions, and two dogs. Under these circumstances, an action was brought at the instance of the private prosecutor, with concurrence of the Procurator Fiscal (although I hold that that concurrence was not necessary, founded on the late act of his present Majesty, 17th July, 1833[)]").

142. CALEDONIAN MERCURY (Edinburgh, Scotland), July 22, 1776, p. 3.

143. *Panel*, Dictionary of the Scots Language: Scottish National Dictionary (1700-). Access at https://www.dsl.ac.uk/entry/snd/panel.

144. *Pannel*, Dictionary of the Scots Language: Scottish National Dictionary (1700-). Access at https://dictionary.thelaw.com/pannel/.

145. 2 John Hill Burton, A History of the Reign of Queen Anne 47 (1880).

146. "Riot at Aberdeen," Aberdeen Journal, and General Advertiser for the North of Scotland (Aberdeen Scotland), Jan. 12, 1803, p. 2 ("This day the Court met to proceed to the trial of *Lieut. Colonel George Mackenzie*, *Captain J. B. Macdonoch*, *Ensign George Lanigan*, *Serjeant Andrew Mackay*, and *Serjeant Alexander Sutherland*, all of the late regiment of the *Ross and Crosnarty Rangers*, accused at the instance of Daniel Ross, and three other private prosecutors, with concurrence of his Majesty's Advocate, of being guilty of the murder of certain persons on the 4th of June last, in the streets of the town of Aberdeen."); "Edinburgh, Jan. 10. Court of Justiciary," Aberdeen Journal, and General Advertiser for the North of Scotland (Aberdeen Scotland), Jan. 19, 1803, p. 2 ("Mr Clerk then addressed the Jury for the prosecution.—He said, there was nothing in the course of this long trial that gave him more pleasure than the evidence of the last witness, to the good character of the pannels. This he did not doubt—they certainly were men of an excellent character, yet this had nothing to do with the present question. A murder was committed, and the enquiry to be made was, who committed this murder? He appeared there for the private prosecutor; and although he could not explain the reasons which induced his learned friend, the Lord Advocate, to decline prosecuting, his motives were no doubt good and proper. He thanked God, however, that although the powers of Majesty's Advocate were greater than those of the public prosecutor in any county in Europe, yet a private prosecution could be carried on without him, which was fortunate for the inhabitants of this country.").

147. "Juries and Justice—A Peculiar System of Jurisprudence," Morning Call (San Francisco, CA), Oct. 29, 1893, p. 15 ("Scotch law places crime upon the proper footing of being an injury to the state, and not one confined to the individual, as is the theory in England, where the private prosecutor figures so prominently, often at his own expense. Hence in every town of any consequence, and certainly in every county, there is an official appointed during good behavior, not elected, who is called a 'Procurator Fiscal' or in popular parlance 'Fiscal.' He is virtually an attorney chosen through the crown to make a preliminary inquiry into all crimes and misdemeanors occurring within his jurisdiction and when there is a warrant to go further he 'precognosces' the witnesses thoroughly and has their 'precognitions' made available for the prosecution at the trial. Coroners and Coroners' juries are unknown in Scotland."); *see also* Caledonian Mercury (Edinburgh, Scotland), June 3, 1782, p. 3 (referring to the "Procurator-fiscal" as the "public prosecutor"); Leeds Mercury (Leeds, England), Aug. 3, 1816, p. 4 (noting that Scotland's "public prosecutor" operates "under the name of the Procurator Fiscal"); *see also* Caledonian Mercury (Edinburgh, Scotland), p. 2 ("because, being a crime against the public, none but the public prosecutor could insist in it"); Morning Chronicle (London, England), May 16, 1833, p. 2 ("Scotland enjoys inestimable advantages in its having local Judges and public prosecutors."); "House of Lords," The Observer (London, England), Mar. 30, 1834, p. 4 ("the law of Scotland recognises, which the English law does not, the office of a Public Prosecutor"); Daily News (London, England), Apr. 6, 1853, p. 2 ("There was this difference in the Scotch law and the English, that in Scotland there was a public prosecutor, who secured justice to the peasant as well as to the peer.").

148. 24 The Sessional Papers Printed by Order of the House of Lords, or Presented by Royal Command, in the Session 1847, at 355–56 (1847) (noting that "the Procurator Fiscal is appointed by the Sheriff, and is the Public Prosecutor for the County" and that that "[t]he Moment the Procurator Fiscal receives Information of an Offence, he makes an Inquiry, follows it up, if necessary, and reports to the Sheriff."; "Does the Case go to the Lord Advocate? If it is a Case of Importance it goes to the Lord Advocate; it is, as we call it, 'reported;' and then the Lord Advocate, or his Deputy, directs that it shall be tried before the High Court of Justiciary, or the Circuit Court, or before the Sheriff and a Jury, or by the Sheriff alone."; "If the Lord Advocate refuses to try a Person, do not Parties having an Interest to try him obtain the Concourse of the Lord Advocate? Yes."; "Is it not understood that the Lord Advocate is bound to give his Concourse? Yes; it is so understood."); Eighth Report of Her Majesty's Commissioners on Criminal Law 363–64 (1845) ("In Scotland, though private prosecutions are permitted by law, provided they are commenced with the concurrence of the public accuser, they are almost unknown at the present day; and criminal proceedings usually begin by an application to an officer somewhat quaintly and

erroneously denominated procurator fiscal. This officer, who is attached to every Sheriff's Court, and to most of the Royal Borough Courts, is appointed by the sheriff, or by the magistrates and counsel of the burgh to which he belongs; his office is held for life or during good behaviour; his residence is in the neighbourhood of his Court, and he is remunerated by fees, charged according to a regulated rate on the business performed. His duties in general are, to receive information of offences committed—to accuse the suspected party before the magistrate, and obtain a warrant for his apprehension and examination; to search for and arrange the proofs of his guilt, and if these be such as to create a reasonable presumption against him, to obtain his committal; and then, if the offence be one of a trifling description, to bring the accused to trial at his own instance before the inferior tribunal."); *id.* at 363 (noting that the *procurator fiscal* title, "which has been handed down from the earliest ages, evidently took its rise in those good old times when Crown prosecutions were instituted, not from any weak desire of protecting the public by the suppression of crime, but with the more tangible object of grasping the forfeitures and penalties which resulted from the conviction of offenders. In those days the *Lord High Treasurer* was the chief public accuser, the Lord Advocate being merely subsidiary to him.") (italics in original); C. S. Greaves, Esq., Q.C., *Criminal Procedure, in* THE LAW MAGAZINE AND LAW REVIEW: OR QUARTERLY JOURNAL OF JURISPRUDENCE (1866), No. XLII, p. 169 ("The procurator-fiscal received information that a crime has been committed; his duty is to make immediate inquiry; if any person is suspected, he applies to the sheriff for a warrant to apprehend him, and the party is taken before the sheriff for examination. Generally, a leading attorney in the county town is the procurator-fiscal."). *See also* Bruce P. Smith, *The Emergence of Public Prosecution in London, 1790–1850*, 18 YALE J.L. & HUM. 29, 30 (2006) (noting that, in the early years of the nineteenth century, "an official known as the 'Procurator Fiscal' essentially 'monopolized all serious criminal prosecutions'"); "Alexander Robertson v. His Majesty's Advocate, Oct. 28, 1887," *in* MIDDLETON RETTIE, JAMES PATTEN, C. C. MACONOCHIE, H. J. E. FRASER & JOHN DAVID SYM, COMP., CASES DECIDED IN THE COURT OF SESSION, COURT OF JUSTICIARY, AND HOUSE OF LORDS, FROM AUGUST 1, 1887, TO AUGUST 10, 1888, at 1–3 (1888) (statement of Lord M'Laren in the case: "With reference to the requirement of our law that the Lord Advocate should concur in private prosecutions, I venture to ask whether it would be consistent with order or with the true liberty of the subject that any citizen, however high his position, however estimable his character, however irreproachable his conduct, should be liable to be placed in the dock of a criminal Court at the suit of a private individual upon charges which might be frivolous, and the motive of which might be prejudice, ill-feeling, or spite. I say that such a state of things would be intolerable, and I am not aware that there is any civilised country in which the unlimited right of private prosecution exists. In every country of whose laws I have any experience some provision is to be found by which a check is put on the unlimited right of private prosecution. In England the Attorney-General by an entry on the record can always stop a private prosecution which, in his opinion, is frivolous or prejudicial to the public interest. In this country the check is that the preliminary consent of the Lord Advocate must be given. This is a most wholesome check, and one which I am sure this Court would be very sorry in any way to relax. Judging from past experience, the action of the office of the Lord Advocate has been so salutary that private prosecution in this country may be said to have almost ceased to exist. In every case where there was a reasonable ground for prosecution the public authorities, acting under the Lord Advocate, have been found ready to undertake it, and where the authorities were satisfied that there were no sufficient grounds for a prosecution the parties interested, with few exceptions, if any, have acquiesced in the decision. Nevertheless, the right of private prosecution does exist, and one sees that there may be cases in which the public prosecutor may not think fit to undertake the responsibility of directing a prosecution, although he may consider it his duty to give his concurrence to a private prosecution. Apparently this is not a case of that description, because the Lord Advocate has informed the Court that after full consideration he found that there was no *prima facie* case such as would justify him in giving his concurrence."); GREAT BRITAIN, PARLIAMENT, HOUSE OF COMMONS, REPORTS FROM COMMISSIONERS: CAPITAL PUNISHMENT (Session—1 February-10 August 1866) (1866), Vol. 21, p. 434 (taking note of the following questions and answers in the "Minutes of Evidence" from the Capital Punishment Commission for March 24, 1865: "But the right of private prosecution exists in Scotland at this moment?—Yes. A public prosecution was originally exceptional in Scotland, it is now the rule, and has been the rule for 100 years I suppose." "It is quite universal, is it not?—Yes, so much so that since I have been at the bar there has not, I think I may say with certainty, been a single instance of a private prosecution in the superior courts, and I know of none in any inferior court either." "I suppose that if there were ever a private prosecution the Lord Advocate would still have the power of entering what we call in England a *nolle proseuqui*, he could still stop the prosecution, could he not?—No, I do not think that he could do that. I ought to explain, however, that it is a condition of private prosecution by our law (I am speaking of a matter which is interesting rather in speculation than in practice, as you will see from the fact of the real absence of private prosecutions with us,) that the prosecutor shall have the concurrence of the Lord Advocate; that concurrence never was refused; and there are judgments to the effect that he might be compelled to give his concurrence,—application would be made to him so that he might attend to the public interest in the matter,—but the public interest is, that he offence should be prosecuted, and there is no instance I am aware of in Scotland in which the Lord Advocate has stopped a prosecution by private persons. He may always do it by prosecuting himself."); A. Edward Henderson, Henry Johnston, David Gillespie & James Paterson, The Scottish Jurist: Being Reports of Cases Decided in the Supreme Courts of Scotland and in the House of Lords on Appeal from Scotland (1873), Vol. XLV, p. 52 ("A public prosecution is raised and pursued for the sake of public justice, and for the vindication of public law, and the protection of the interests of society at large; while, in a country where there is a public prosecutor, all private prosecution in a criminal court had its origin in personal resentment. This is so stated by Baron Hume. It is because of a sense of personal wrong that private prosecution is desired, and that it is sometimes permitted. I do not estimate very highly the privilege of prosecution for personal wrong, when public law does not require it; and I have no doubt that the presumption of reason pervading all constitutional law is in favour of that prosecution which arises and is pursued for the purpose of public vindication of law, in preference to the prosecution which springs from personal resentment, and is pursued for the gratification of that feeling. It is upon that principle, and because of that presumption, that the exceptional procedure by private prosecution has, in Scotland, become so very rare."); William Chambers & Robert Chambers, comp., Chambers' Edinburgh Journal (1839), Vol. VII, p. 205 ("According to the common usage of law in Scotland, private prosecution of a criminal nature is entirely unknown, and for a very proper reason: when a person suffers an injury, as, for instance, a robbery of his property, the offence is viewed in the light of a breach of the public peace, and is investigated and punished purely on public grounds. On this account, any legal pursuit of an offender has no appearance of personal revenge, and, in point of fact, the sufferer has nothing to do with the case—he can neither prevent nor hasten the prosecution when once the cause of complaint has been lodged. The officer who stands at the head of the department of public prosecution in the Lord Advocate, who is appointed by the crown, and is assisted by a certain number of advocate-deputes.").

149. "Official Salaries Committee," Morning Chronicle (London, England), Sept. 13, 1850, p. 7 ("The Lord Advocate is so much in the character of public prosecutor in Scotland, that although private parties have the right of prosecution they very rarely exercise it; and all the prosecutions in Scotland, almost without exception, are carried on in the name of the Lord Advocate in the Court of Justiciary, where the principal prosecutions in number and importance take place, and in the name of officers for whom he is responsible even in the Sheriff's Courts."); *see also* "The Talk of London," North Wales Chronicle, and Advertiser for the Principality (Bangor, Wales), Oct. 12, 1850, p. 5 ("By the way, how much better the criminal law is *administered* in Scotland than among us. As you are aware, their *machinery* for working it out, is superior to ours. For instance they have what we want, namely, a public prosecutor.") (italics in original).

150. Caledonian Mercury (Edinburgh, Scotland), Jan. 25, 1813, p. 3 ("This day came on, before the High Court of Justiciary, the trial of Thomas Sommerville, in[n]keeper at Carstairs, accused, at the instance of private prosecutors, of perjury. As Counsel are now pleading on the relevancy of the libel, which will not be over in time for this publication, we must delay farther particulars till our next."); *see also* "Glasgow, June 10," Glasgow Herald (Glasgow, Scotland), June 10, 1822, p. 4 ("Borthwick was, on Thursday afternoon, carried off prisoner from this jail, by the senior Macer of the Justiciary Court, to Edinburgh, at the instance of the private prosecutor.").

151. "Trial for a Duel," Morning Post (London, England), Oct. 7, 1818, p. 2 ("The following curious Trial took place on the 26th ult. at Aberdeen, the action being brought upon an old statute of William III. for preventing and punishing duels. The Court proceeded to the trial of Lieutenant James Rollo, of the

59th regiment of foot, on the complaint of THOMAS RITCHIE, younger, of Cultmaluadie, private prosecutor, with concurrence of his Majesty's Advocate ….."); *accord* "Curious Trial," ABERDEEN JOURNAL, AND GENERAL ADVERTISER FOR THE NORTH OF SCOTLAND (Aberdeen, Scotland), Oct. 14, 1818, p. 4 (mentioning the "private prosecutor" in the trial of Lieutenant James Rollo); "Duelling.—Curious Trial," THE OBSERVER (London, England), Oct. 12, 1818, p. 4 (same). *See also* "Circuit Intelligence," CALEDONIAN MERCURY (Edinburgh, Scotland), Sept. 24, 1821, p. 3 (referring to a "private prosecution" for a trial involved a statute that was passed "70 years ago").

152. "The Trial of the Glasgow Bank Directors," SHEFFIELD AND ROTHERHAM INDEPENDENT (Sheffield, England), Jan. 23, 1879, p. 5 ("EDINBURGH, Wednesday. The trial of the directors and manager of the Glasgow City Bank for fraud, misrepresentation, and theft, was resumed this morning in the High Court of Justiciary, before the Lord Justice Clerk, Lord Mure, and Lord Craighill. The examination of Mr. William Morrison, formerly clerk and subsequently accountant of the City Bank, was continued by the Lord Advocate. The witness stated that the amount of deposits given in the public balance sheet for 1878 was alleged to be £8,102,000, but they were understated to the extent of £740,000. The bank notes in circulation by the bank were also incorrectly stated to the amount of £89,000. The outstanding drafts were falsely stated to the extent of £410,000. These understatements were made by the director and Mr. Stronach, the manager, and were marked on the abstract in red ink."); "The Chesterfield and North Derbyshire Bank. Proceedings against the Directors.", SHEFFIELD AND ROTHERHAM INDEPENDENT (Sheffield, England), Jan. 23, 1879, p. 5 ("At the Chesterfield Borough Police Court, yesterday morning, before the Mayor (Mr. Pearson), Mr. J. Stores Smith, and Dr. Booth, the directors of the Chesterfield and North Derbyshire Bank (David Hawkins, Josiah Elliott, Roger Wall, James Burt, and George Walker) and the manager of the same (Edward Holland) were summoned 'for circulating and publishing a written statement of account concerning the affairs of the bank, knowing the same to be false in one or more particulars, with intent to deceive or defraud the shareholders and creditors of the company.' The summonses were taken out by Mr. Henry Blandy, of Nottingham, a shareholder in the bank, and formerly a member of the committee of investigation appointed to inquire into the position of the company. The bank collapsed in September last, and when it became known that the concern was in difficulties, the great anxiety prevailed in the whole of the East Derbyshire district, where the bank had been looked upon for many years as one of the safest in the kingdom."; after a discussion of a continuance in the case, a "Mr. Barker" stated: "I must really ask that Mr. Blandy pay the costs of the day. It is an inquiry instituted by Mr. Blandy personally: He does not represent anybody but himself. He appears here as a private prosecutor, and his case has broken down because he has not taken proper legal advice. He asks for the adjournment as a matter of favour and not for any substantial reason. His case is utterly incomplete; and we are just where we were when we came into court. A great deal of trouble and expense has been incurred, and assuming my clients are innocent, as at present we are bound to assume, it is a very great hardship that we should have to come here again in a month's time. Asking for the adjournment as a favour, he is bound to pay the taxed costs of the day.").

153. "High Court of Justiciary: Case of Hare, the Accomplice," MORNING POST (London, England), Jan. 30, 1829, p. 2 ("Monday the Court being met, and the whole of the Judges … present, their Lordships proceeded to the consideration of a bill of suspension and liberation, presented on behalf of *William Hare*, present prisoner in the Tolbooth of Edinburgh, confined upon a charge of being concerned in the murder of James Wilson, more commonly known by the name of 'Daft Jamie.'"); *id.* ("Mr. Hugh Bruce appeared on behalf of Hare. The facts on which the petition was grounded, he said, were not disputed on the other side of the bar. Upon the 24th of December, an individual, William Burke, was placed at their Lordships' bar, accused of three charges of murder; one of the charges exhibited against Burke was that of the murder of James Wilson, commonly called 'Daft Jamie;' and on turning to the list of witnesses annexed to the indictment, their Lordships would find the name of the petition, W. Hare. On the 19th of Nov. last, an application was presented by the Procurator Fiscal for the county for a warrant to apprehend Hare; he was apprehended accordingly, and examined as to the murders for which Burke was afterwards indicted. Subsequently, the petitioner, Hare, was assured by the Public Prosecutor, that if he made a full disclosure of all that he knew in regard to the alleged murders, he should receive immunity in so far as he himself was concerned. He accepted of the proferred immunity, and was accordingly examined as a witness on the trial of Burke, and that without the caution or warning usually given to a witness having no promise of immunity, to avoid

stating any thing to criminate himself. Upon that trial he did make full disclosures, under the assurance of personal and individual safety."); *id.* ("It was quite notorious that disclosures were made by Hare to the Public Prosecutor, and, in particular, it was known that disclosures were made in relation to the murder of James Wilson. It is averred that, during all these proceedings, neither of the private prosecutors (Janet Wilson, alleged mother, or Janet Wilson, alleged sister of James Wilson), came forward, or pretended to come forward and caution Hare as to the evidence he was to disclose, because they intended to turn that evidence against him."); *id.* ("The question now was, whether the proceedings of the Public Prosecutor were sufficient to quash those at the instance of the Private Prosecutor. The proposition of the Learned Counsel was, that a socius being cited as a witness, acquires immunity from all proceedings against him at the instance of a Private Prosecutor, and this immunity he derives from his being enclosed and called as a witness."). The High Court of Justiciary ultimately determined that William Hare could not be prosecuted, though the relatives of James Wilson immediately thereafter commenced a civil suit against Hare. A discussion of the arguments of counsel and the resolution of the case can be found elsewhere. *See* George MacGregor, The History of Burke and Hare 191–98 (1884); "Substance of the Informations: For William Hare and Janet Wilson, Senior and Junior," Caledonian Mercury (Edinburgh, Scotland), Feb. 2, 1829, pp. 2–3; "Case of Hare," Morning Chronicle (London, England), Feb. 2, 1829, p. 4; "The Scotch Murders: The Informations for William Hare and Janet Wilson, Senior and Junior," Morning Post (London, England), Feb. 5, 1829, p. 4; "High Court of Justiciary: Opinions of the Judges in the Case of Hare," Caledonian Mercury (Edinburgh, Scotland), Feb. 9, 1829, p. 4; "High Court of Justiciary: Liberation of Hare," Aberdeen Journal, and General Advertiser for the North of Scotland (Aberdeen, Scotland), Feb. 11, 1829, p. 4; "High Court of Justiciary: Opinions of the Judges in the Case of Hare," Caledonian Mercury, Feb. 12, 1829, p. 4; "High Court of Justiciary: Opinions of the Judges in the Case of Hare," Caledonian Mercury, Feb. 14, 1829, p. 4.

154. Seán J. Crossan, Introductory Scots Law: Theory and Practice (3d ed. 2017); *see also id.* ("The most famous partially successful private prosecution in Scotland in the last 30 years was the affair that became popularly known as the Glasgow Rape Case. In 1982, a rape victim was permitted to raise a private prosecution against three of her alleged assailants. Prior to this legal action, there had been one other private prosecution in Scotland during the twentieth century and that had taken place in 1911.").

155. "West Port Murders," Caledonian Mercury (Edinburgh, Scotland), Jan. 17, 1829, p. 2; *see also* "High Court of Justiciary," Aberdeen Journal, and General Advertiser for the North of Scotland (Aberdeen, Scotland), Jan. 8, 1806, p. 3 ("Friday the Court met, agre[e]ably to adjournment, to consider the objections of the relevancy of the libel, and the title of the private party to prosecute the charge of forgery against *Andrew Belch*, with the informations ordered to be given in. Their Lordships delivered their opi[ni]ons at considerable length, and unanimously found, that Mr Dundas, the private prosecutor, had no sufficient title to maintain the present action before this Court upon the facts charged in the libel, the said prosecution being only with the concourse, and not at the instance of his Majesty's Advocate, and therefore dismissed the said criminal libel and the pannel from the bar."); Caledonian Mercury (Edinburgh, Scotland), Jan. 25, 1813, p. 3 ("This day came on, before the High Court of Justiciary, the trial of Thomas Sommerville, in[n]keeper at Carstairs, accused, at the instance of the private prosecutors, of perjury. As Counsel are now pleading on the relevancy of the libel, which will not be over in time for this publication, we must delay farther particulars till our next.").

156. Mr. Maclaurin, comp., Arguments and Decisions, in Remarkable Cases, Before the High Court of Justiciary, and Other Supreme Courts, in Scotland 172 (1774); *see also id.* at 474, 478–80 (noting that, in February 1768, at the trial of "His Majesty's Advocate, against James Archibald," indicted for murdering Peter Lawson, a "day-labourer at Duddingstown" in 1767, the King's Advocate declared that "[a] private prosecutor is in a different situation from the Advocate; because the law does not establish the same presumptions in his favour"; "Replied for the prisoner: Two capital mistakes run through the prosecutor's argument; *first*, That he has an incontroulable power over the diets of court; *2dly*, That he has a much greater power in criminal actions than a private prosecutor.... [T]he truth is, that the powers of the Advocate do not differ from those of private prosecutor; or if there is any difference, those of the latter are the most extensive. In the early periods of our law, there was no public prosecutor. It appears from our old law-books, that prosecutions anciently were brought either at the instance

of private parties having a proper title, without any public aid or concurrence, or else without any private prosecutor, upon a dittay taken up by an inquest, much in the same manner that bills are found by a grand jury in England; and a roll of these dittays was called the *Porteous roll*. Punishments, during the infancy of our law, were but few in number, and generally corporal; afterwards it became fashionable to punish by escheats, forfeitures, and fines. Hence the fisk had an interest in every trial, and its officers lent their aid to prosecutors. This practice probably crept in about the beginning of the 16th century, as before that there is no mention of the Advocate as a public prosecutor, nor indeed any mention of him at all. Long after he interfered in trials, he never proceeded without a private prosecutor, who, in our statutes, is generally denominated the *informer*.") (italics in original); ARCHIBALD ALISON, PRACTICE OF THE CRIMINAL LAW OF SCOTLAND 104 (1833) ("The true foundation of the right of a private party to prosecute, is to be found in the feelings of resentment which follow the reception of an injury, which are implanted by nature, and universally felt. As the law which prohibits private feuds cannot extinguish these feelings, it deems it safer to turn them into the regulated channel of legal proceedings. Upon this account, and because the deceased sufferer cannot himself prosecute, the near kinsmen are allowed to prosecute in cases of murder, rape, or attempt to commit these crimes. In the case of rape, a right to prosecute was sustained at the instance of the women's father, though it was objected that she was of perfect age, and did not join in the complaint; and a stepfather has been permitted to insist in his own name, and for the woman and her mother.... [I]n the case of Col. Charteris, Nov. 12, 1723, the title at the instance of the injured husband, was sustained after the Lord Advocate has withdrawn his concourse."); JOHN BURNETT, A TREATISE ON VARIOUS BRANCHES OF THE CRIMINAL LAW OF SCOTLAND 296 n.* (1811) ("The acts 1612, c. 4. and 1661, c. 26, illustrate the principle here stated, as to the nature and origin of the powers of this officer, and the preference right to prosecute, understood formally to belong to the private party. The act 1612, gives power to the woman's parents and nearest kinsmen, *or* to his Majesty's Advocate, to prosecute for the crime of *rape*, though the party injured not only consents to pass from any pursuit, but even declares that no injury was done to her. Here the forbearance of the woman to prosecute, and the risk of the crime thereby passing with impunity, is cured, by the right given to the Public Prosecutor to insist, as well as to the kindred of the injured party; while, from the words of the statute, a *priority* seems to be implied in favour of the latter. Accordingly, we find, that in interpreting the statute, the Court, in the case of Colonel Charteris, March 1723, sustained process at the instance of the woman's husband, though the King's Advocate withdrew his concurrence at the diet of compearance. The act 1661, affords a stronger illustration of this subject. By this act, the goods stolen, (which formerly, along with those of the thief himself, were, on conviction of the offender, forfeited to the King, in prejudice of the owner,) are declared to belong to the person from whom they were stolen, or their just value is to be *paid*, out of the readiest of the thief's goods, provided *the owner pursues the thief usque ad sententiam*. No mention is here made of the King's Advocate, but a boon is held out to the private party, to induce him to prosecute, namely, the restitution of his goods. At this period, the powers of the King's Advocate must have been extremely feeble, and his right to prosecute rarely exercised, when recourse was had to this sort of *stimulus*, to insure a prosecution. Accordingly, we know, that at this time, and for many years after, almost all prosecutions for crimes, touching individuals, were at the instance of the *private party*.") (italics in original).

157. "Criminal Law Notes," *in* SCOTTISH LAW JOURNAL, AND SHERIFF COURT RECORD 34–35 (Mar. 1860).

158. "EDINBURGH," CALEDONIAN MERCURY (Edinburgh, Scotland), Oct. 25, 1773, p. 2.

159. "Mr. Hope of Fentonbarns on the Game Laws," CALEDONIAN MERCURY (Edinburgh, Scotland), Oct. 10, 1865, p. 4 (noting these remarks of George Hope of Fentonbarns at the Social Science Congress: "Any person killing, selling, or buying, or having game in possession in forbidden time, forfeits £5 for each birth, and, in case of failure to pay within ten days, is liable to two months' imprisonment for each £5. These penalties admit of no modification. In one case the combined penalties against one individual amounted to £220, and the consequent imprisonment to seven years and five months; but the private prosecutor restricted his complaint to four birds, or £20 of fine. But surely this is a power too enormous for any private prosecutor to possess in the punishment of individuals."); "Hamilton.—Private Prosecution in Poaching Cases," GLASGOW HERALD (Glasgow, Scotland), Mar. 1, 1882, p. 7 ("Yesterday a couple of cases of day poaching were tried by Sheriff Birnie, and were remarkable from being at the instance of private

prosecutors. Hitherto this class of prosecutions has been conducted by the Procurator-Fiscal, but it was intimated that Mr Dykes, in view of the Summary Jurisdiction Act, declined to appear in them further.").

160. "Edinburgh, Jan. 29," Aberdeen Journal, and General Advertiser for the North of Scotland (Aberdeen Scotland), Feb. 2, 1803, p. 3 ("On Monday the 24th curt. came on at Perth, before the Magistrates and a respectable Jury, the trial of Thomas Ogilvie, dyer, and Mungo M'Pherson, occasional residenter in Perth, at the instance of Messrs Smith and Stevenson, contractors for lighting and upholding the public lamps, accusing them of having, on the morning of the 9th ult. broke no less than sixty-four of the street lamps, to the injury of the private prosecutors, and great breach of the peace. The trial last from eleven o-clock forenoon, till one the following morning, which day the Jury returned their verdict finding the pannels guilty. The Provost pronounced the sentence of the Magistrates, adjudging the panels to pay to Messrs. Smith and Stevenson 25*l.* in name of damages, and 15*l.* to the Procurator Fiscal in name of expences; to be imprisoned for two months, and to find security to keep the peach for three years.").

161. Caledonian Mercury (Edinburgh, Scotland), Dec. 1, 1777, p. 3.

162. "High Court of Justiciary," Glasgow Herald (Glasgow, Scotland), Dec. 28, 1855, p. 7.

163. Momanyi Bwonwong'a, Procedures in Criminal Law in Kenya 144 (1994) ("It is a general requirement that an intending private prosecutor has to show that he has suffered a wrong or an injury entitling him to prosecute. This injury or wrong suffered by an individual is the reason that drives him to file a private prosecution and is what is referred to as *locus standi*."); *id.* at 145 ("The requirement of locus standi is a further limitation on a private individual who wants to set in motion the machinery of the criminal law."); *id.* ("In some common law jurisdictions the issue of *locus standi* is not considered an essential element in filing private prosecutions.").

164. *Id.* at 145.

165. Burnett, *supra* note 156, at 295–96 (italics in original); *see also* Glasgow Herald (Glasgow, Scotland), Oct. 8, 1866, p. 6 ("In France the judge is charged with the duty of investigating into the truth of a charge. With us, whether there be a public prosecutor, as in Scotland, or a private prosecutor, as in England, the judge is simply a moderator between the two parties to a litigation and has no duty of inquiry beyond putting questions at the trial as to points which happen to be left obscure by one party or the other. He has nothing to do with the preliminary examination either of witnesses or of the prisoner, except in Scotland, when he may happen to have taken the prisoner's declaration."); "French Criminal Trials," Worthington Advance (Worthington, MN), Dec. 7, 1882, p. 1 ("At the close of the evidence the public prosecutor leads off with a simple statement of the facts on which he expects a verdict of guilty, if they are private prosecutors who wish to get pecuniary damages out of a prisoner, besides seeing him punished, then these advocates follow. For French law allows the court not only to sentence a murderer to death, but to make him pay a heavy fine to the relatives of the victim.").

166. Cases Decided in the Court of Session and Also in the Court of Justiciary and House of Lords, from July 20, 1913, to July 22, 1914, at 78 (J. S. Leadbetter, ed. 1914) ("It is certainly a remarkable circumstance that a prosecution for the crime of compounding a felony has never, so far as we know, taken place in Scotland; and there are excellent reasons why, in a country where the conduct of the prosecution of crimes is entrusted to a public prosecutor, in should not be necessary to create a more or less artificial crime, one purpose of which in England seems to be to stimulate the activities of private prosecutors.").

167. 1 John Bouvier, Bouvier's Law Dictionary: A Concise Encyclopedia of the Law (Rawle's Revision) 574 (Francis Rawle, ed., 3d rev. 1914); *see also id.* ("The compounding of misdemeanors, as it is also a perversion or defeating of public justice, is in like manner an indictable offence at common law.").

168. Rachel E. Bennett, Capital Punishment and the Criminal Corpse in Scotland, 1740–1834, at 31 (2018) ("In Scotland, since the sixteenth century the responsibility for prosecuting offenders was vested in the legal profession, from the Lord Advocate in Edinburgh to the procurator fiscals who would gather evidence, or precognitions, in their local areas and build up the case. In more serious cases the fiscals would send the precognitions to the Crown Office where the Lord Advocate, or in most cases one of his deputes, would decide whether to prosecute in the High Court or its circuit courts. This system

of public prosecution was perhaps more comparable to other Continental European practices than elements of the English system with its heavy reliance upon private prosecution.").

169. BURNETT, *supra* note 156, at 296–97 (citations omitted; italics in original). In Scotland, there were different evidentiary practices for private prosecutions versus those involving the public prosecutor. *Id.* at 429–30 ("[N]o precise rule has been followed by our Courts, at least in criminal prosecutions, farther than that the nearest relations of husband and wife, father, son, and brother, do not appear to have been held as competent witnesses for the prosecutor, in trials where the prosecution was solely at the instance of the private party. But it is deducible more from the general spirit of our law, and the silence of the records as to any question upon the competency of such witnesses, even at a period too when private prosecutions were more frequent, than from any direct authorities upon the subject."); *id.* at 430 ("This, however, seems to be held, that where the prosecution is at the instance solely of the private party, and is mainly directed to pecuniary reparation, the near kindred of the prosecutor and *inhabile* witnesses. A father, son, or brother, at least, is not to be received, unless in extraordinary cases, and where there is a penury of witnesses; and the same ought to hold when the prosecution is only for the punishment of the offender, and without any pecuniary view, though at the instance solely of the private party; more especially as it is now considered to be the peculiar duty of the public prosecutor, in all cases of atrocious injury, (and it is the general practice) to insist in his own name, or give his *instance* along with the private party; where this does not happen, it is generally owing, either to the case not being clear upon its merits, or to some impropriety in the conduct of the private party; in either of which cases, it is proper that the evidence of those who are nearly related to the private party ought not to be received.") (italic in original); *id.* ("In prosecutions, however, at the *joint* instance of the public prosecutor and the private party, the usage seems to have been to receive the evidence of the nearest relations of the latter in behalf of the prosecution; and this even in cases where the private party insists also for pecuniary reparation, it being held unreasonable that, in cases where the interposition of the public accuser is deemed necessary, the near relations of the private party should be excluded, merely because one consequence of the *conviction* may be to give reparation to him; and when, perhaps, the case is of that kind that calls loudly both for *punishment* and *reparation*.") (italics in original).

170. JOHN LOUTHIAN, THE FORM OF PROCESS, BEFORE THE COURT OF JUSTICIARY IN SCOTLAND 120 (2d ed. 1752) ("If the private Party intends to prosecute the Complaint, then a *Memorandum* for drawing a Bill of Criminal Letters, is made out by his Majesty's Advocate, or his Deputes. ——And the Bill being framed in terms of the *Memorandum*, his Majesty's Advocate grants his Concurrence thereto, and signs the same, or the Person who is appointed by him for that Purpose, writes on the Bill thus: ——*Edinburgh, the —— Day of ——, Concurrence granted for his Majesty's Advocate*; ——and signs the same.").

171. BURNETT, *supra* note 156, at 297–98.

172. *See generally* JOHN D. BESSLER, THE BARON AND THE MARQUIS: LIBERTY, TYRANNY, AND THE ENLIGHTENMENT MAXIM THAT CAN REMAKE AMERICAN CRIMINAL JUSTICE (2019).

173. BURNETT, *supra* note 156, at 298–300, 302 (italics in original).

174. The oath of calumny itself sometimes begat legal disputes. For example, in one case from 1888, two music sellers in Aberdeen, Scotland, were charged with fraudulently pawning harmoniums. In an Aberdeen newspaper that reported the charges, it was noted that the complainer was a private prosecutor. The solicitor tasked with defending against the charges insisted the complainer take the oath. As that Aberdeen newspaper reported: "Mr. J. M. I. Scott, solicitor, who appeared for the accused, said that as the complainer had adopted a rather unusual and somewhat antiquated mode of procedure, he, on behalf of the defenders, would do the same, and ask his Lordship to adopt one of the old forms. Where a charge was made by a private prosecutor it was competent that before the case is proceeded with he take the oath of calumn[y], and Mr Scott moved that it be done in the present instance." "Of course," a Mr. Wilson, the solicitor for the complainer, replied, "if it were necessary to administer the oath of calumn[y] he would ask for an adjournment of the case." A robust argument between the sheriff, Mr. Wilson and Mr. Scott followed as to whether the oath of calumny was necessary or unnecessary in that particular instance. "Alleged Fraudulent Pawning of Harmoniums," ABERDEEN WEEKLY JOURNAL AND GENERAL ADVERTISER FOR THE NORTH OF SCOTLAND (Aberdeen, Scotland), June 9, 1888, p. 5.

175. *See, e.g.*, David Martin Jones, Conscience and Allegiance in Seventeenth Century England: The Political Significance of Oaths and Engagements (1999).

176. *Oath*, Dictionary of the Scots Language: Scottish National Dictionary (1700-). Access at https://www.dsl.ac.uk/entry/snd/oath; *see also* John Finlay, Legal Practice in Eighteenth-Century Scotland 163 (2015) ("According to an Act of Parliament in 1430, the oath *de calumnia* was originally sworn by counsel and by the parties, if present, at the commencement of an action. In substance it was an oath that the swearer believed in the justness of the cause he pursued and the truth of the facts he asserted. In eighteenth-century practice, the oath was only ever given by a party when demanded by his opponent or the judge, and it was never demanded of counsel."); *id.* ("There are examples in the sixteenth century of the oath being sworn at both the request of a party and by order of the lords of session. According to Bell's *Dictionary*, the oath of calumny was little used after 1715."). Robert Bell's *Dictionary of the Law of Scotland* also references private prosecutions. 1 Robert Bell, Dictionary of the Law of Scotland Intended for the Use of the Public at Large, as Well as of the Profession 182 (2d ed. 1815) ("Concourse of Actions. This is the authorising of several actions on the same ground of action, which was admitted in the Roman law; but with us no concourse of civil actions is allows. It is in criminal actions, where a person may be tried civilly or criminally on the same act; there the private prosecutor may proceed to the effect of recovering his debt or damages, whether the prosecution at the instance of the public prosecutor proceeds or not."); 2 Robert Bell, Dictionary of the Law of Scotland Intended for the Use of the Public at Large, as Well as of the Profession 712 (2d ed. 1815) ("The sheriff's criminal jurisdiction extends to the trial of murder, though the frequent and regular circuits of Justiciary have removed the necessity of the sheriff's taking cognizance of this plea of the Crown. He may take cognisance of theft, either at the instance of the private prosecutor, or by indictment . . . .").

177. 6 The Encyclopædia Britannica 29 (7th ed. 1842).

178. Angus Stevenson, ed., Oxford Dictionary of English 250 (3d ed. 2010) (defining *calumny*).

179. Max Radin, The Jews Among the Greeks and Romans 333 (1915). The "Oath of Calumny" has been described as "an oath which both parties in a cause were obliged to take: the plaintiff that he did not bring his charge, and the defendant that he did not deny it, with a design to abuse each other, but because they believed their cause was just and good; that they would not deny the truth, nor create unnecessary delays, nor offer the judge or evidence any gifts or bribes." 6 The Encyclopædia Britannica 29 (7th ed. 1842).

180. Burnett, *supra* note 156, at 302, 304–6 (citations omitted; italics in original); *id.* at 306–7 ("Certain it is, that the right which his Majesty, and in his name his Advocate, has, to be informed of, and to watch over all prosecutions *ad vindictam publicam*, and more particularly that *interest* which his Majesty has in the fines and forfeitures, which arise upon convictions for crimes, if they did not originate, did mainly contribute to the concourse being held as a necessary and essential form in all private prosecutions. Being now considered as such, (indeed without it the private party who comes into the criminal Court cannot be heard,) it is understood, that his Majesty's Advocate cannot refuse his *concourse*, and may be compelled to give it, in all cases where the complaint of the private party is founded on a known and relevant *point of dittay*, and as to which he has, *prima facie*, a *title* to insist. On the other hand, such *concourse* his Majesty's Advocate may refuse, in cases that are clearly of an opposite description; a power, which seems to result from the nature of his office, and from what seems to have been in part the principle on which such concourse was originally deemed necessary.") (italics in original).

181. Archibald Alison, Practice of the Criminal Law of Scotland 111 (1833); *see also id.* at 217 ("The privilege of appearing by indictment belongs to the Lord Advocate alone; any inferior functionary, as a procurator-fiscal, must pursue in the form of criminal letters. But if the indictment is raised in the name and at the *instance* of the Lord Advocate, the injured party, if his prosecutes jointly with him, may sign after his lordship or his deputes. But if the prosecution is at the instance of the private party, with *concourse* only of his lordship, which is generally the case with private prosecutions, the libel must be in the form of criminal letters; and that is the form universally adopted now in such cases."). "Criminal letters," a Scotch procedure, has been described as "[a] prosecution similar to one upon an information." James A. Ballentine, A Law Dictionary of Words, Terms, Abbreviations and Phrases Which Are Peculiar to the Law and of Those Which Have a Peculiar Meaning in the Law 100 (1923);

see also WALTER A. SHUMAKER & GEORGE FOSTER LONGSDORF, THE CYCLOPEDIC LAW DICTIONARY COMPRISING THE TERMS AND PHRASES OF AMERICAN JURISPRUDENCE, INCLUDING ANCIENT AND MODERN COMMON LAW, INTERNATIONAL LAW, AND NUMEROUS SELECT TITLES FROM THE CIVIL LAW, THE FRENCH AND THE SPANISH LAW, ETC. ETC. 257 (James C. Cahill, ed., 2d ed. 1922) ("CRIMINAL LETTERS. In Scotch law. A summons issued by the lord advocate or his deputies as the means of commencing a criminal process. It differs from an indictment, and is like a criminal information at common law.").

182. ABERDEEN JOURNAL, AND GENERAL ADVERTISER FOR THE NORTH OF SCOTLAND (Aberdeen, Scotland), Jan. 19, 1803, p. 2 ("Mr Clerk then addressed the Jury for the prosecution.—He said, there was nothing in the course of this long trial that gave him more pleasure than the evidence of the last witness, to the good character of the pannels. This he did not doubt—they certainly were men of an excellent character, yet this had nothing to do with the present question. A murder was committed, and the enquiry to be made was, who committed this murder? He appeared there for the private prosecutor; and although he could not explain the reasons which induced his learned friend, the Lord Advocate, to decline prosecuting, his motives were no doubt good and proper. He thanked God, however, that although the powers of his Majesty's Advocate were greater than those of the public prosecutor in any country in Europe, yet a private prosecution could be carried on without him, which was fortunate for the inhabitants of this country.").

183. "Court of Session," CALEDONIAN MERCURY (Edinburgh, Scotland), Jan. 26, 1807, p. 3 ("An action was brought against one of the gentlemen prosecuted by a member of the Association for the preservation of Game in the county of Mid-Lothian, and the Procurator Fiscal of the county, for the penalty of 100l. Scots, imposed by the act of Parliament 1621, for having killed game without the qualification of a ploughgate of land; also, upon the statute 13 of Geo. III. for having game in his possession;—and likewise, for a treaspass for having encroached on the property of the gentlemen of the Association, in which the Sheriff decerned for payment of the statutory penalties, enacted by both statutes; and prohibited the defender from trespassing on the property of the private prosecutor in future."); GLASGOW HERALD (Glasgow, Scotland), July 8, 1822, p. 1 ("On the 4th of May, not many days after the Glasgow Circuit terminated, Mr. Alexander intimated to the Crown Agent his intention to prosecute Borthwick at his own instance, as private prosecutor. From that time, the prosecution against Borthwick was at the instance of the private party alone, and was no longer under the control, direction, or management of the Public Prosecutor.").

184. CALEDONIAN MERCURY (Edinburgh, Scotland), Dec. 27, 1828, p. 2 (taking note of "the Aberdeen riots," and observing: "[T]he parties were brought to trial at the instance of a private prosecutor. His Lordship was of counsel for the pannels, and they were acquitted. Not satisfied with this, however, the private prosecutor reared up a new indictment upon new grounds. And he could never forget the feeling which was excited, by this attempt to bring the parties acquitted to a second trial, in the Court, the Bar, and the country at large; there was one general cry of indignation against a proceeding so shameless and oppressive; the consequence of which was, that the private prosecutor became alarmed, and the attempt was quashed."); CALEDONIAN MERCURY (Edinburgh, Scotland), Jan. 29, 1829, p. 4 (noting that a man was "apprehended by the Private Prosecutors for Wilson's murder: he was examined without the presence of an agent—and was committed for farther examination, and to close confinement").

185. In 1848, a Scottish solicitor wrote of Scotland: "We have no private prosecutor in criminal causes, the crown, in all cases, by the lord-advocate or procurator-fi[s]cal, being prosecutor." "Copies of Indictments and Lists of Juries in Political Trials," DAILY NEWS (London, England), Oct. 17, 1848, p. 3; *see also* "Notes of the Month," *in* JOHN INDERMAUR & CHARLES THWAITES, EDS., THE LAW STUDENTS' JOURNAL 224 (Oct. 1, 1901) ("The system of public prosecution in Scotland is so complete and efficient that criminal prosecutions at the instance of private persons are of very rare occurrence. In Scotland, as in England, a person injured by a criminal offence is entitled to prosecute the offender, but, in striking contrast with the English practice, the right is very seldom exercised. In summary complaints for the contravention of statutes, private individuals sometimes come forward as prosecutors, but, in so far as indictable offences are concerned, private prosecutions in Scotland are entirely obsolete."); ROGER DAVIDSON & GAYLE DAVIS, THE SEXUAL STATE: SEXUALITY AND SCOTTISH GOVERNANCE, 1950–80, at 275 (2012) ("In contrast to developments in England, there were no private prosecutions in Scotland after *McBain v. Crichton* in 1961,

when the High Court refused a petition to prosecute a bookseller who had sold a copy of *Lady Chatterly's Lover* . . . .").

186. MORNING CHRONICLE (London, England), June 26, 1822, p. 1 ("The Lord Advocate was the public prosecutor in almost all instances in Scotland. Upon his own authority he instituted a prosecution. There was not, it was to be recollected, in Scotland the intervention of a Grand Jury. In the institution of all prosecutions the Learned Lord therefore exercised judicial functions; on his own authority he could proceed, and without his concurrence no private prosecutor had power to originate a criminal prosecution. In 1701, a restraint was imposed by Statute on the powers of the Lord Advocate. But even under that Statute, if the prosecutor deserted the diet, *pro loco et tempore*, the imprisonment of the accused might be prolonged, from sixty to one hundred and forty days. A private prosecutor was bound to give security for the payment of the expences; he must subscribe to an oath . . .; he must be personally present during the prosecution. No claim from illness or emergent business had any effect. In addition to all these obstacles to a private prosecution, he must shew that he had sustained a personal and individual injury. Even in the case of murder he cannot prosecute, unless within a degree of propinquity; and in the case of a nuisance in his neighborhood, the individual cannot interfere without the concurrence of the Lord Advocate. Those powers, in the administration of the Criminal Law of Scotland, were administered by the Lord Advocate, the Solicitor General, and the Advocate Depute, who were the miniature representatives of the Learned Lord; and it was rarely that the individual prosecutors appeared."); *see also* GLASGOW HERALD (Glasgow, Scotland), June 28, 1822, p. 2 ("The Noble and Learned Lord was nearly the sole prosecutor in Scotland, and the greatest difficulties were thrown in the way of the private prosecutor. There was no Grand Jury to limit the authority of the Noble Lord. The act of 1701 had imposed some restraints, one of which was a compulsion to bring the criminal to trial in the space of sixty days. But the Learned Lord, in deserting the diet, might keep the criminal in person 140 days. He then adverted to the difficulties thrown in the way of the private prosecutor. He was obliged, if required, to take a previous oath of calumny; he was obliged to prove that he had received a personal injury, and if he failed in the prosecution he had to pay the whole expences. He was also obliged to appear personally at the Bar of the Court; and the consequence of all these difficulties was that there were but few private prosecutions."). But in an 1829 editorial titled "The Public Prosecutor and His Apologists," published in Edinburgh's *Caledonian Mercury*, the writer defended the use of private prosecutors, putting it this way of the requirements for conducting a private prosecution: "To entitle a private party to prosecute, he must have an *interest*, not remote or feeble, but immediate and powerful in the cause; the wrongs alleged must be wrongs done to the *person*, and 'of a high and aggravated king, such as may naturally excite strong feelings of anguish and resentment in the minds of the *kindred* of the sufferer;" an oath of calumny must be taken by the prosecutor, if required by the party accused; caution must found to insist in the prosecution; and the law also subjects the private prosecutor in expenses, and even in penalties, if he insist in a groundless or malicious accusation." "The Public Prosecutor and His Apologists," CALEDONIAN MERCURY (Edinburgh, Scotland), Jan. 8, 1829, p. 3 (italics in original).

187. "Under Secretary of State (Scotland)," THE STANDARD (London, England), June 16, 1858, p. 2.

188. "The Fortnightly Review, No. VI. London: Chapman and Hall.", CALEDONIAN MERCURY (Edinburgh, Scotland), Aug. 12, 1865, p. 6 ("Among the other articles there is a very good one by Mr Herbert Graham on 'Public and Private Prosecutors,' explaining and comparing the practice of England and Scotland in this respect, and expressing, on several grounds shown, a decided preference for that of the latter."). In *The Fortnightly Review*, Herbert Graham observed that "[i]t has been frequently proposed to introduce into the criminal jurisprudence of England a system of public prosecution." Graham lamented that although "[t]he attention of Parliament has more than once been directed to the subject," and although "[c]ommissions of inquiry have been appointed, and evidence taken before them," "the old system still remains, and with as little appearance of change as ever." As Graham described private prosecutions: "Criminal prosecutions are generally carried on at the instance of the person injured by the crime, or his relatives; but they may, as I have said, be instituted by any one who feels inclined to do so. The prosecutor selects his own law agent and counsel to act for him. The whole procedure thus merges into something like a private litigation—the prosecutor being the plaintiff, and the accused the defendant. The conviction and consequent punishment of the accused is the sole object of the prosecutor, and in this he endeavours to succeed by every means in his power, because he has no doubt that the accused is guilty of the crime with

which he is charged. The guilt or innocence of the accused becomes a private instead of a public question; and the protection of the public interest by the prosecution of criminals is left almost entirely in the hands of private individuals." "In general," Graham added, "prosecutors are entitled to be reimbursed their expenses, but the fees allowed by Government are so very small that they frequently fall short of the expenses actually incurred." In extensively laying out his objections to private prosecutions, Graham added: "The public interest is not protected as it ought to be by leaving the prosecution of criminals in the hands of private individuals. Many criminals go unpunished, because the person injured has no wish to incur trouble and expense, and other people have no desire to mix themselves up in a matter with which they have no personal connection, and for their trouble in regard to which they would receive no adequate remuneration, but, on the contrary, run the risk of being involved in subsequent litigation, and, it may be, compelled to pay heavy damages. Many prosecutions, too, are compromised—as when, for instance, in the case of robberies, a portion of the property stolen is returned on a withdrawal of the prosecution, the prosecutor deeming it more for his own interest to get back part of his property without punishing the thief, than to have the bare satisfaction of punishing the thief without succeeding in recovering any of his property. Evidence to this effect has more than once been given before Parliamentary Commissioners, by men who were in a position to speak from experience of the working of the system of prosecutions at the instance of private individuals." As Graham stressed: "The public interest is thus injured in two ways—by failure to prosecute, and compromise after the prosecution has been commenced. This ought not to be." Herbert Graham, "Public and Private Prosecutions," *in* 1 GEORGE HENRY LEWES, ED., THE FORTNIGHTLY REVIEW 675–77 (1865).

189. J. Y. WONG, DEADLY DREAMS: OPIUM AND THE ARROW WAR (1856–1860) IN CHINA 30 n.193 (1998); JOSEPH FOSTER, MEMBERS OF PARLIAMENT, SCOTLAND, INCLUDING THE MINOR BARONS, THE COMMISSIONERS FOR THE SHIRES AND THE COMMISSIONERS FOR THE BURGHS, 1357–1882, ON THE BASIS OF THE PARLIAMENTARY RETURN, 1880, WITH GENEALOGICAL AND BIOGRAPHICAL NOTICES 254 (1882).

190. "Social Science Congress. Second Day. Tuesday, September 25. The Lord-Advocate's Address," GLASGOW DAILY HERALD, Sept. 26, 1860, p. 2; *see also* "National Association for the Promotion of Social Science," CALEDONIAN MERCURY (Edinburgh, Scotland), Sept. 26, 1860, p. 3 (reporting that the Lord Advocate said this as part of his address: "As regards the question of a public prosecutor, I can only say that every year's experience has convinced me that it tends most admirably to the protection of the innocent and the punishment of the guilty. No doubt a public prosecutor in an arbitrary state would be dangerous to the liberty of the people; but in a country like this, where the public prosecutor is under the influence of public opinion and Parliamentary control, I consider that no system could be more advantageous. Crime is a public wrong, and its punishment should not be left to a private prosecutor; and it would be most desirable if such a change was made in the English system.").

191. David Hall to Benjamin Franklin (June 23, 1763); Benjamin Franklin to Richard Jackson (Feb. 11, 1764); Benjamin Franklin to William Franklin (Apr. 16, 1768); Benjamin Franklin to Joseph Galloway (May 14, 1768). Access at https://founders.archives.gov.

192. *Wilkes, John*, Encyclopedia.com, https://www.encyclopedia.com/people/history/british-and-irish-history-biographies/john-wilkes (last accessed Feb. 21, 2021) ("John Wilkes was a London radical who favored revolutionary changes in England's political structure. His newspaper articles irritated King George III and British lawmakers (Parliament) so much that he was several times expelled from his seat in Parliament. The public was outraged over this treatment, and the important question was raised—whether Parliament could ignore the will of voters. Wilkes became known as a champion of the common people and a crusader for freedom of the press and the reform of Parliament. American colonists made a hero out of him because of his support for the American Revolution (1775–83).").

193. Committee of the Boston Sons of Liberty to John Wilkes (June 6, 1768), National Archives. Access at https://founders.archives.gov.

194. *1715 Riot Act*, SPARTACUS EDUCATIONAL (Sept. 1997), https://spartacus-educational.com/Lriot.htm.

195. Benjamin Franklin to Joseph Galloway (May 14, 1768). Access at https://founders.archives.gov.

196. ANTHONY BABINGTON, MILITARY INTERVENTION IN BRITAIN: FROM THE GORDON RIOTS TO THE GIBRALTAR INCIDENT 20 (1990).

197. "An Essay on Petitioning the King," NORTH BRITON, No. 132, p. 209 (1769); ANTHONY BABINGTON, MILITARY INTERVENTION IN BRITAIN: FROM THE GORDON RIOTS TO THE GIBRALTAR INCIDENT 20 (2016); "A Summary of the Trial of Donald Maclane, for the Murder of Mr. William Allen the Younger," *in* 1 THE OXFORD MAGAZINE: OR, UNIVERSITY MUSEUM 72–75 (1768); *see also* "A short Account of the Trial of Donald Maclane at Guildford for the wilful murder of young Mr. Allen, on the 10th of May 1768," *in* 3 THE POLITICAL REGISTER, AND IMPARTIAL REVIEW OF NEW BOOKS FOR MDCCLXVIII 179–86 (1768) (containing an account of the trial of Donald Maclane).

198. THE MONUMENTAL INSCRIPTIONS IN THE OLD CHURCHYARD OF ST. MARY, NEWINGTON, SURREY 8 (1880) (privately printed in London).

199. *Old Bailey Proceedings, 6th July 1768*, https://www.oldbaileyonline.org/print.jsp?div=17680706.

200. Stephan Landsman, *The Rise of the Contentious Spirit: Adversary Procedure in Eighteenth Century England*, 75 CORNELL L. REV. 497, 583–86 (1990); DAVID J. COX, CRIME IN ENGLAND, 1688–1815, at 21–25 (2014); 1 ROBERT BISSETT, THIS HISTORY OF THE REIGN OF GEORGE III, at 282 (new ed. 1822); 16 THE PARLIAMENTARY HISTORY OF ENGLAND, FROM THE EARLIEST PERIOD TO THE YEAR 1803, at 428 (1813); THE ANNUAL REGISTER, OR A VIEW OF THE HISTORY, POLITICKS, AND LITERATURE FOR THE YEAR 1768, at 137, 227–34 (1768); 2 NOTES AND QUERIES: A MEDIUM OF INTER-COMMUNICATION FOR LITERARY MEN, ARTISTS, ANTIQUARIES, GENEALOGISTS, ETC. 333 (1851); THE GUILDHALL MISCELLANY 12 (1952); GEORGE RUDÉ, PARIS AND LONDON IN THE EIGHTEENTH CENTURY 241 (1973); "*A cursory Sketch of the Trial of* Samuel Gillam, *Esq; for Murder*," *in* THE LONDON MAGAZINE, OR, GENTLEMAN'S MONTHLY INTELLIGENCER 362–64 (1768); Samuel Gillam, *Killing: murder. 6th July 1768*, Old Bailey records, *available at* https://www.oldbaileyonline.org/images.jsp?doc=176807060052; "Today in London Riotous History, 1768: The "Massacre of St. George's Fields," PAST TENSE (May 10, 2019), https://pasttenseblog.wordpress.com/2019/05/10/today-in-london-riotous-history-1768-the-massacre-of-st-georges-fields/.

201. 1 SIR HENRY CAVENDISH'S DEBATES OF THE HOUSE OF COMMONS, DURING THE THIRTEENTH PARLIAMENT OF GREAT BRITAIN, COMMONLY CALLED THE UNREPORTED PARLIAMENT 321 (1841) ("drawn up from the original manuscripts, by J. Wright, editor of the Parliamentary History of England, &c."); *see also id.* at 321 n.1 ("Mr. Gillam, charged with the murder of William Redburn, he having, on the 10th of May, given the order to the soldiers to fire, had been tried at the Old Bailey, on the 11th of ... July. The judges were Mr. Justice Gould, Lord Chief Baron Parker, and Mr. Justice Aston. The counsel for the prosecution were Mr. Serjeant Glynn and Mr. Lucas; for Mr. Gillam, Sir Fletcher Norton and the attorney and solicitor general."); WALTER HARRISON, NEW AND UNIVERSAL HISTORY, DESCRIPTION AND SURVEY OF THE CITIES OF LONDON AND WESTMINSTER, THE BOROUGH OF SOUTHWARK, AND THEIR ADJACENT PARTS 654 (1776) ("On the 7th of July a bill of indictment for murder was found by the grand jury of the county of Middlesex, against Samuel Gillam, Esq. the justice of the peace who ordered the guards to fire on the 10th of May in St. George's Fields. In consequence of which he was tried at the Old Bailey for the murder of William Redburn, but was acquitted without entering upon his defence, and a copy of his indictment was granted him by the court."); "The Trial of Samuel Gillam, Esq; at the Old Bailey, for the willful murder of William Redburn, who was killed in St. George's Fields on the 10th of May, 1768," *in* 3 THE POLITICAL REGISTER, AND IMPARTIAL REVIEW OF NEW BOOKS FOR MDCCLXVIII 171–79 (1768).

202. 6 THE POLITICAL REGISTER, AND IMPARTIAL REVIEW 297 (1770).

203. "Court of King's Bench, Nov. 21," MORNING CHRONICLE (London, England), Nov. 23, 1807, p. 3 ("The ATTORNEY GENERAL moved for a Rule to shew cause why a criminal information should not be filed against Mr. Ralph Dod, a gentleman who, after having seet on foot for a scheme for making a turnpike road under the River Thames, had now become the founder of two institutions publickly advertised in the papers; the one for constituting a Public Distillery, the other for the manufacture of paper. These institutions were contrary to an Act of Parliament.... The ATTORNEY GENERAL stated, that this was moved at the instance of a private Prosecutor....").

204. MORNING CHRONICLE (London, England), Dec. 10, 1819, p. 3 (noting that the Lord Chancellor stated: "In Crown cases, where there was what was called a private prosecutor, the defendant, through entitled to carry down the record if the prosecutor did not proceed, yet he must tender himself for trial and abide by the consequences."); "LAW INTELLIGENCE: COURT OF KING'S BENCH," FREEMAN'S JOURNAL (Dublin, Ireland), Jan. 18, 1837, p. 3 (noting of the case of *The King v. Connolly*: "Mr. Macdonagh applied in this

case to have the defendant admitted to bail. The crown would, he understood, offer no opposition. The charge against his client in the informations and the committal was for a conspiracy to do an offence. There was of course a private prosecution in the case."). On June 1, 1837, in testimony before a select committee on metropolis police offices, E. G. Wakefield, Esq., had this to say on the subject of prosecution: "[W]ould it not also be desirable that some means should be adopted for the prosecution of criminals, and that it should no longer be left to individuals; that is to say, would it not be desirable to establish an officer to be the public prosecutor?" In making the case for a public prosecutor, Wakefield emphasized: "[A]nother great evil arising from the want of a public prosecutor is not so much that the private prosecutor is liable to be tampered with, as that he is engaged about his own occupations, in which he has incurred a loss, and he is quite unwilling to incur another in giving up a great deal of his time and some of his money in the pursuit of the ends of justice; he has suffered; the object of the law in punishing the individual who has injured him is not to revenge his wrong, it is to benefit the public, and yet the public leaves the person injured to be the only prosecutor of the criminal. It is therefore only in human nature, that unless the prosecutor be a man of a vindictive turn of mind, unless he be actuated by some angry feeling, he will never be a diligent prosecutor; in a great number of cases he would not prosecute at all; he will do just enough to avoid forfeiting his recognizance, and the prisoner will escape; I consider the want of a public prosecutor, even if detection were well secured, which it is not, would vitiate any system of police." REPORT FROM THE SELECT COMMITTEE ON METROPOLIS POLICE OFFICES; WITH THE MINUTES OF EVIDENCE, APPENDIX AND INDEX 126 (1837).

205. "Coroner's Court," MORNING POST (London, England), Aug. 22, 1821, p. 3 ("I have also understood that the duties of a Coroner's Court, *super visum corporis*, was merely that of inquiry from the vicinage—that they have no authority to hear either accusation or defence against or by any one—that if the ATTORNEY GENERAL or any private prosecutor, *has* occasion to become an accuser, his recourse ought to be to a Grand Jury—if he has been injured or has ground for complaint (on suspicion) that his appeal should be to a Magistrate, by his warrant to put the constitutional officer, known by the name of the Constable, into motion.") (italics in original); *see also* MORNING CHRONICLE (London, England), Jan. 14, 1825, p.2 ("The Law of England, as has been well said, 'divides the consideration of the grounds against a prosecutor among very different parties; the private Prosecutor, the Magistrate committing, and the Grand Jury. Equitable as this system appears in theory, it leads in practice to a division of the responsibility, which operates most grievously against the prisoner.'"); LEEDS MERCURY (Leeds, England), Dec. 12, 1891, p. 6 ("A curious instance, writes a legal correspondent, recently came to light before Mr. Justice Grantham on circuit of the injustice, at times unintentionally, wrought by the law. A statute of the present reign, passed soon after the Queen came to the throne, provided that 'in any case of an indictment or information by a private prosecutor for the publication of any defamatory libel, if judgment shall be given for the defendant, he shall be entitled to recover from the prosecutor the costs sustained by the said defendant by reason of such indictment or information,' and this, which appears on the face of it an extremely fair and reasonable provision, has undoubtedly had a good effect in restraining the unnecessary multiplication of this class of cases. But in a case which came before Mr. Justice Grantham at Nottingham, the Grand Jury, acting under the direction of the Judge, found no true bill in a prosecution for a defamatory libel, and the defendant was unable to recover costs from the prosecutor because judgment had not been given for him. The result is that where there is *primâ facie* evidence to go to a jury, and the defendant succeeds, he may get his costs from the prosecutor; but where the charge ought never to have been brought, since in the opinion of the Grand Jury there is not even a *primâ facie* case against the defendant, the unfortunate man has no remedy as to the expenses he has incurred. Mr. Justice Grantham expressed his regret that he could not help the defendant, but in the present state of the law he was unable to do so."); "Legal Competition," DERBY MERCURY (Derby, England), Feb. 1, 1882, p. 5 ("The Watch Committee of the Derby Corporation and the Borough Justices have been in correspondence with the Home Secretary on the question of the distribution of briefs in the case of prosecutions at Assizes and Quarter Sessions. The result of that correspondence is summed up in the following letter, which appears in the report of the committee to be presented to the Town Council at their quarterly meeting to-day:—Whitehall. 21st January, 1862.–Sir—I am directed by Secretary Sir William Vernon Harcourt to acknowledge the receipt of your letter of the 12th inst., respecting the distribution of copies of depositions in cases of prisoners committed for trial at the Derby Borough

Sessions and Assizes. In reply, I am to acquaint you that the rule to be observed appears to the Secretary of State to be quite clear; but, in giving the following opinion, I am to say that he has only done so because it has been expressly asked for. It is for the justices to determine whom they shall bind over to prosecute, and for the prosecutor to select his solicitor. Hence (1) in all cases in which the police are bound to prosecute, whether the charge is originated by them or not, they are the prosecutors, and the selection of a solicitor should be left to the Watch Committee. (2) In cases in which either a Government Department prosecutes, or a private prosecutor is willing to undertake at his personal liability the proper conduct of the case, the selection of a solicitor should be left to the Department or to such private prosecutor.—I am, Sir, your obedient servant, A. F. O. LIDDELL. The Clerk to the Justices for the Borough of Derby.").

206. "Bandon Sessions," MORNING CHRONICLE (London, England), Oct. 31, 1843, p. 3.

207. SYDNEY MORNING HERALD (Sydney, Australia), Oct. 17, 1843, p. 2.

208. SYDNEY MORNING HERALD (Sydney, Australia), Aug. 2, 1844, p. 2 ("The COLONIAL SECRETARY supported the view taken by the Attorney-General, that it was absolutely necessary that there should be a Crown Prosecutor in the Courts of Quarter Sessions, in order to secure the due administration of justice, and that unless a properly qualified officer were appointed, the interests of the public would be severely injured. The honorable member who had last spoken entertained some apprehension of there not being a sufficient revenue to meet the expense; he entertained no such fear whatever. He believed that in most instances at home, prosecutions were conducted by private prosecutors."); *id.* ("Mr. WINDEYER observed that it was not the fact that private prosecutors were engaged in the majority of the cases. He had carefully observed the proceedings in the Central Criminal Court in London for several years and there private prosecutors were rarely employed; cases in which they were employed, formed rather the exception than the rule."); *id.* ("The ATTORNEY-GENERAL said, that the honorable member for Durham, in the course of the observations which he addressed to the Committee, had stated, that he was shocked on his arrival in this colony at the mode of conducting criminal prosecutions. The honorable and learned member laid some stress of his opportunity of observation in England. He, the Attorney-General, had recently been in England, and he had endeavoured to profit something by visiting courts of all descriptions, inferior as well as superior, and he could not discover that the prosecutions here were carried on at all differently from similar prosecutions in England. It was no doubt the case that there was no one Crown Prosecutor, as there had been, and it was proposed to continue here, but in ten cases to one there were private prosecutors, whose costs were allowed by the Courts, and paid by the counties. The private prosecutors in England and in Ireland exhibited the same zeal, the same rigour in their prosecutions as the honorable and learned member had been shocked with here; and it was rather a measure of economy to appoint a single Crown Prosecutor, than to pursue the system of allowing costs to be paid by the public, which was pursued at home.").

209. "Alleged Bribery at the Late Ipswich Borough Election," IPSWICH JOURNAL (Ipswich, England), Apr. 20, 1880, p. 3 (in the prosecution against a tailor and a shoemaker for bribery at a borough election, defense lawyer, Mr. Moseley, "addressed the Bench on behalf of the accused," saying in part: "This is a prosecution—and I say it at the outset, and I believe I shall be backed in my opinion by a very large majority of the inhabitants of this town—that ought never to have been brought here at all. It has been instituted by a private prosecution, as sanctioned by the Act; it is not a public prosecution on behalf of a man who really has the welfare of the town at his heart. It is impossible to shut one's eyes to the fact that this prosecution has been instituted for the purposes of private interests, with an ulterior object."). Private prosecutors were, on occasion, accused of having ulterior political motives. *See, e.g.*, "Court of Queen's Bench, Westminster, May 5," THE TIMES (London, England), May 7, 1860, p. 27 ("Mr. V. WILLIAMS showed cause against the rule, and contended that the Court ought not to interfere, particularly on the application of private prosecutors, who, he said, were actuated by political motives. The proper party to prosecute, if any proceeding were necessary, was the Attorney-General.").

210. "The *Town Talk* Libel Case," HUDDERSFIELD DAILY CHRONICLE (Huddersfield, England), Oct. 27, 1879, p. 4 ("Mr. Watkin Williams, Q.C., M.P., on behalf of Mr. Cornwallis West, said that, as this was a prosecution by private prosecutors, it was no part of their duty or wish to pursue anybody to vengeance, or to indulge personal vindictiveness. As to the interest of the public and public justice, it appeared to them that the defendant Rosenberg, in the first place, having pleaded guilty to the publication of a false and

defamatory libel and having been already convicted of the publication of a false and defamatory paper, knowing it to be false and defamatory, the public interest would be satisfied if we are content with a verdict of guilty against him on this indictment, and not to offer any evidence on the more aggravated count of the indictment charging the defendant with a knowledge that it was false. With regard to the printer, their position was quite different. Printers, publishers, and writers should know that they cannot print such things, and thus help in their dissemination, with impunity."); *accord* "Central Criminal Court, Oct. 25," THE TIMES (London, England), Oct. 27, 1879, p. 4.

211. The Attorney General in England only rarely got involved in criminal cases, usually when the case was of particular concern to the Crown. *E.g.*, "To the Editor of the Morning Chronicle," MORNING CHRONICLE (London, England), Sept. 28, 1818, p. 3 ("It is true that the ATTORNEY GENERAL is called the public prosecutor, but he never interferes unless the King or the State is more immediately concerned. A real active prosecutor on behalf of the Crown, on all ordinary occasions, is required by justice and a well regulated police, for the hardship of subjecting individuals to such proceedings is at once impolitic and intolerably oppressive.").

212. The idea of *pursuer-generals* to oversee private prosecutors and to perform the function of private prosecutors in case of their unavailability was one proposed by Jeremy Bentham in 1790. *See* DRAUGHT OF A CODE FOR THE ORGANISATION OF THE JUDICIAL ESTABLISHMENT (1790). Jeremy Bentham specifically described the contemplated role of *pursuer-generals* in "penal matters." Their function, he said, is (1) "To superintend the proceedings of every private prosecutor; to assist him, in case of oversight or unskil[l]-fulness; and to watch over him, and prevent collusion with the defendant"; (2) "To reclaim the execution of all penal laws, by performing the functions of prosecutor where no private prosecutor has first presented himself, and in the cases, if any, where individuals are not admitted to prosecute." *Id.*, ch. VI; *see also* 4 THE WORKS OF JEREMY BENTHAM, Vol. 4 (John Bowring, ed. 1843) ("Title XI: Of Pursuer-Generals"); Jason Twede, "Going Public: How the Government Assumed the Authority to Prosecute in the Southern United States," Ph.D. dissertation, University of North Dakota (May 2016), pp. 40–41 ("To understand Bentham's proposed prosecution legislation, it is important to understand what the existing system of prosecution was in England at the time he wrote it. Bentham wrote two separate pieces of proposed legislation at separate times. The first was written in 1790, and the second was published in 1843. At both times, the criminal justice system operated under a system of pure private prosecution; it was not until 1879 when the Prosecution of Offenses Act (Summary Jurisdiction Acts, 1887) was passed that this system of pure private prosecution was abrogated. In both pieces of proposed legislation, Bentham advocated a prosecution system that utilized both private and public prosecutors. Where private prosecution was the norm at the time of his writing, he was advocating a shift of control in the system of prosecution from private parties to the government."). In 1829, in a collection of essays, another prominent Englishman, James Mill, embraced Bentham's idea, writing: "Besides the judge and his deputy, there are two adjuncts to every tribunal, which are of the utmost importance: indispensable, indeed, to the due administration of justice. These are, a *pursuer-general*, and a *defender-general*." As Mill explained their contemplated joint and respective functions: "The business of both pursuer-general, and defender-general is to reclaim the execution of all laws in the execution of which the nation has a peculiar interest, though individuals may not." As Mill wrote: "The peculiar business of the pursuer-general is, to act on behalf of the administrative authority, in its character of plaintiff, and on behalf of every plaintiff who is without the means of engaging another advocate; to obviate any prejudice he sees likely to arise to justice from the conduct of plaintiffs, whether in civil matters or penal; and to perform, in the case of all offences, where no private prosecutor appears, the office of prosecutor. The peculiar duty of the defender-general is, to act on behalf of the administrative authority in its capacity of defendant, and on behalf of every defendant who has not the means of engaging another advocate, and to obviate any prejudice he sees likely to result to justice from want of skill or other causes on the part of a defendant who pleads his own cause, or on the part of the advocate who pleads it for him." JAMES MILL, ESSAYS ON GOVERNMENT, JURISPRUDENCE, LIBERTY OF THE PRESS, AND LAW OF NATIONS 41 (1829); *see also* ALEXANDER BAIN, JAMES MILL: A BIOGRAPHY 235–36 (1882) (noting the embrace by James Mill of Jeremy Bentham's idea of a pursuer-general and a defender-general, and that "[n]either has yet found his way into the English courts"); 5 THE FOREIGN REVIEW, AND CONTINENTAL MISCELLANY 165–66 (1830) (calling for "two officers, named a prosecutor-general, and defender-general," who

would be "on precisely the same footing as the judges," and emphasizing: "With regard to the prosecution of crimes, there are four different ways by which criminals may be brought to justice. First, by admitting all voluntary prosecutors; secondly, offering rewards to prosecutors; thirdly, appointing public prosecutors; fourthly, combining these three methods. Mr. Bentham proves, in the most convincing manner, that neither of the three first methods, taken *singly*, will fulfil the ends of justice. The different motives in individuals to forego the labour, expense, and anxiety of a public prosecution, and the consequent advantages to offenders, are enumerated with great ability.") (italics in original). In his writings, Jeremy Bentham had taken notice of the practice of private prosecution and focused, among other things, on penal reform and what he saw as the proper organization of the criminal justice system. 6 The Works of Jeremy Bentham (John Bowring, ed. 1843) ("1. Under the Roman system, the conduct of the business, from beginning to end, in the case of those crimes of high degree, which, affording no individual prompted by peculiar interest to take upon himself the vexation and expense attached to the station of private prosecutor, are left to be prosecuted for, as well as decided upon, by the judge. 2. Under the English system, the preparatory inquiry conducted by a justice of the peace, in the case of a crime of the rank of felony. 3. Under the same English system, the inquiries conducted by tribunals organized on special occasions, for special purposes—whether by the authority of either house of parliament, under the name of a committee—or under the authority of the whole legislature, under the name of a commission of inquiry."); 2 The Works of Jeremy Bentham 213–14 (John Bowring, ed. 1843) ("In this country, where, properly speaking, there is no public prosecutor, many offences, which no individual has any peculiar interest in prosecuting, are liable to remain unpunished. In the way of remedy, the law offers from £10 to £20, to be levied upon the goods of the offender, to whoever will successfully undertake this function: sometimes it is added, that the expenses will be repaid in case of conviction: sometimes this is not promised. These expenses may amount to thirty, fifty, and even one hundred pounds; it is seldom they are so little as twenty pounds. After this, can we be surprised that the laws are imperfectly obeyed? It may be added, that it is considered dishonourable to attend to this summons of the laws. An individual who in this manner endeavours to serve his country, is called an informer; and lest public opinion should not be sufficient to brand him with infamy, the servants of the law, and even the laws themselves, have on some occasions endeavoured to fix the stain. The number of private prosecutors would be much more numerous, if, instead of the insidious offer of a reward, an indemnification were substituted. The dishonourable offer being suppressed, the dishonour itself would cease. And who can say, when by such an arrangement the circumstance which offends it is removed, whether honour itself may not be pressed into the service of the laws?").

213. Jeff Wallenfeldt, ed., The United Kingdom: England 273 (2014); "Narrative of the Manchester Massacre," *in* The Chronicle of the Kings of England, from William the Norman to the Death of George III, at 5, 9 15, 34–36 (1821); Eric J. Evans, Britain Before the Reform Act: Politics and Society 1815–1832, at 17 (2d ed. 2014); Guide to the Henry Hunt Papers MS 563 1760–1838, University of Chicago Library (access at https://www.lib.uchicago.edu/e/scrc/findingaids/view.php?eadid=ICU.SPCL.MS563HHUNT); Robert Reid, The Peterloo Massacre (2018); "The Trial of Henry Hunt, Esq.," The Annual Register, or a View of the History, Politics, and Literature, of the Year 1820, at 849 (1822) (noting that "the trial of Mr. Hunt and the other defendants, indicted for conspiracy on the 16th of August last, at Manchester, commenced at York").

214. "Criminal Information Against the Manchester Magistrates," Morning Chronicle (London, England), Nov. 9, 1819, p. 3; *accord* "Court of King's Bench, London, November 8, Criminal Information against the Manchester Magistrates," The Irishman (Belfast), Nov. 19, 1819 (reporting the same incident). Members of the Bar were allowed to appear in court as private prosecutors. "Law Intelligence: Court of Queen's Bench," Freeman's Journal (Dublin, Ireland), Jan. 28, 1841, p. 3 ("There was, however, one mistake committed by counsel for the defendants, in supposing that the Attorney-General was ex-officio counsel for the prosecution, which was far from being the case, as he only exercised the privilege of any member of the bar in appearing as a private prosecutor.").

215. 41 T. C. Hansard, comp., The Parliamentary Debates from the Year 1803 to the Present Time 373 (1820).

216. "The Peterloo Massacre," Law and Lawyers (Aug. 15, 2019), http://obiterj.blogspot.com/2019/08/the-peterloo-massacre-bicentenary.html.

217. *E.g.*, "Public Prosecutors," CHAMPION AND WEEKLY HERALD (London, England), Nov. 4, 1838, p. 4 (discussing the proposal to have a "public prosecutor," that is, "an officer, whose business it shall be to take up and conduct prosecutions, instead of the same thing being done as at present, by the party who may have suffered from the act of the criminal, or by some one whom a magistrate may appoint to prosecute"; "[t]he Whig press, too, have for some time back been complaining of the barbarian defect of our law in this particular, and pointing to the superiority of criminal proceedings in *Scotland*, in which country they have public prosecutors"); NEWCASTLE COURANT (Newcastle upon Tyne), Oct. 2, 1840, p. 2 ("The appointment of a public prosecutor in criminal cases, whose duty it is to put the law in force against offenders, instead of leaving prosecutions to the frequently capricious and possibly revengeful feelings of individuals, is a part of the system of criminal jurisprudence which is found among our French neighbours, which, under certain modifications, might, we think, be introduced with advantage into this country."); "The Execution of William Ross," HUDERSFIELD CHRONICLE AND WEST YORKSHIRE ADVERTISER (Huddersfield, England), Aug, 24, 1850, p. 6 ("The want of a public prosecutor in England has often been severely commented upon, but generally with a view to the obstacles it throws in the way of convicting the guilty. The want of such a public functionary is, perhaps, still more to be regretted on account of the facilities it may at times afford to the condemnation of the innocent."); "Want of a Public Prosecutor," LLOYD'S WEEKLY NEWSPAPER (London, England), Aug. 25, 1850, p. 5 (raising the same concerns after the execution of William Ross, and noting that "[p]enal prosecutions are the concerns of the public, not of individuals" but that England lacks a public prosecutor and that "[t]he task of prosecuting is either devolved upon the injured parties, or is left to a subordinate set of functionaries, the police, of whose regular duties it is scarcely considered a part, and whose discharge of it is therefore remissly and leniently watched"; "A public prosecutor would not have been liable either to the suspicion of personal enmity, or to doubts as to his capacity for the discharge of his duty. No doubts could have arisen, had a public prosecutor conducted the case, that sufficient grounds existed for a prosecution, and that every allowance was made to which the accused was entitled. In such circumstances even those who deny the right of society to take life in any case would not have been haunted by the additional painful reflection that the sufferer may have been innocent."); "An Attorney-General for Everybody," HUDERSFIELD CHRONICLE AND WEST YORKSHIRE ADVERTISER (Huddersfield, England), Nov. 9, 1850, p. 3 ("It has often been said, that, to secure the ends of justice, we want a Public Prosecutor in this country. The truth of that assertion was never so manifest as it is now, when everybody feels how much such an officer is wanted, to in order to prosecute the Public's right of way through Glen Tilt."); "Evasions of Justice," THE EXAMINER (London, England), Dec. 21, 1850, p. 1 ("It is hardly possible to take up a report of proceedings in Criminal Courts without finding some example of the necessity for a public prosecutor."); "A Public Prosecutor," MORNING POST (London, England), Mar. 31, 1851, p. 2 ("However widely opinions may differ as to the policy of appointing a public prosecutor, it seems to be a question beyond dispute, that some greater regularity is required in our criminal proceedings, and that the time has arrived for adopting some system by which certainty may be secured in the prosecution of offenders.").

218. MORNING CHRONICLE (London, England), Sept. 29, 1825, p. 2; *see also id.* (*The Edinburgh Review* further noted of private prosecution: "In the one case, he undergoes all the expence of a prosecution, with the risk of at least not being allowed his expences (and lately a Judge refused to order this allowance, because one of the witnesses for the prosecution offended him by his demeanor). In the other case, he may, if he pleases, avoid the law expences, but he is subject to the trouble and personal expence of attending to give evidence; and in both cases it depends on his good will and pleasure whether he ever appears to prosecute or give evidence or not. If the prosecution is voluntary, he may drop it; if he is bound over, he may forfeit the small sum in the recognizance, and he hears no more about it; nor does the prisoner—for he is acquitted for want of prosecution, & can never be tried again."); *id.* ("Substantially then, there is nothing like a public prosecutor in England; a person charged with putting the criminal law in motion, and giving the public some security that offences shall not escape unpunished, from private fear, favour, or corruption.").

219. Douglas Hay, *Controlling the English Prosecutor*, 21 OSGOODE HALL L.J. 165, 167 (1983); *see also id.* ("A handful of cases were prosecuted by the Treasury Solicitor, acting for the government in coining cases and thus in some sense as a state prosecutor."); *id.* at 167–68 ("[A] very small number of cases, fewer

than one percent of the total, were prosecuted at the direction of the Attorney-General or his agents. Almost all of these were state trials, usually for treason or seditious libel. The latter, which were more numerous, were usually prosecuted in the eighteenth and nineteenth centuries by the Attorney-General, exercising his unique privilege of prosecuting grave misdemeanours by an *ex officio* information in the King's Bench. This procedure eliminated the grand jury, could allow the careful packing of a special jury, and saddled the defendant with heavy costs even if the Crown lost."); *id.* at 168 ("[T]he typical prosecution in England was on indictment at the initiative of a private citizen who was the victim of crime and who conducted the prosecution in almost all cases. Blackstone's only mention of this obvious fact of eighteenth-century English criminal law was the remark that 'indictments ... are preferred ... in the name of the King, but at the suit of any private prosecutor....'"); *id.* at 168–69 (noting that "ninety-four percent" of private prosecutors were men, and that they "enjoyed discretion at many crucial points" and that "[e]ven the indictment, the only formal written record of the charge, could be drawn by his own lawyer on his instructions, rather than by the Clerk of the Court," with "[t]he effective result" that often the prosecutor "could choose among a variety of likely penalties" and "had much influence in deciding what witnesses to take before the magistrate for the preliminary hearing ... and before the grand jury"); *id.* at 169 ("If, for whatever reasons, the prosecutor decided to drop the charge, the could do so without resulting official inquiry."); *id.* at 169–70 ("The private prosecutor also strongly influenced the outcome of the trial through the fact that he chose his own solicitor, who instructed counsel (if a barrister was retained) to conduct the case in the manner most likely to yield the outcome he wished. In these circumstances, it was not unknown for the prosecuting lawyer to be unhappy with the result. In one case in 1787 the barrister petitioned for a pardon for a prisoner whom he had just successfully prosecuted, declaring that he: 'was so unfortunate as to be Counsel against the prisoner at his trial, that His prosecutors discovered the most rancorous malice and revenge upon the Occasion, and that there were not wanting circumstances on his trial which rendered him an Object of great Compassion.' Finally, after a conviction, the Government and the King would pay great attention to the wishes of the prosecutor in deciding whether or not to grant a free or conditional pardon, particularly in cases in which the death sentence had resulted."); *id.* at 170 ("Small wonder, then, given the range of prosecutorial discretion, that one frequently finds eighteenth-century private prosecutors reflecting gravely on their power. As one observed in 1796 in a theft case: '[I]f I succeed I shall most certainly hang the culprit. It is certainly more honourable to detect felons than it is to committ Felonys. However I wish to hold the scales of justice even and never suffer one's power to border upon Tyranny.' ... When the prosecutor was determined to proceed in the face of sharp public criticism, he would commonly defend his actions in the press, as in this appeal published after an execution in 1802: 'Edward Allen, one of the unfortunate Men who suffered on Washwood Heath on Monday last for a Forgery on the Bank of England, having persisted in his Innocence to the last, and accused me of being his Murderer, I think it a Justice due to myself to state to the Public, through the Medium of your paper, the Circumstances which led to his detection and Conviction....'"); *id.* ("The danger of anonymous malice damage to property, particularly in rural parishes, undoubtedly subjected some prosecutors to strong pressure to drop charges, to reduce the charge between the preliminary inquiry and the grand jury hearing, or not to begin at all. Within the community itself this greatly accentuated the pressure to reach accommodations outside the courts."); *id.* at 171 ("Legislation enacted in the eighteenth and, especially, the nineteenth centuries gradually increased the costs granted to prosecutors, in an effort to spur them on to greater action.").

220. "Operation of the New Law of Evidence Act," Belfast News-Letter (Belfast, Northern Ireland), Nov. 19, 1851, p. 1 ("Hitherto punishment of witnesses for perjury has, in great measure, been left to the discretion of private prosecutors, who have often used this power rather as a means of extorting terms from an adversary than of furthering the ends of public justice.").

221. *E.g.*, Morning Post (London, England), Jan. 28, 1851, p. 2.

222. "Court of Queen's Bench.—June 2," Daily News (London, England), June 3, 1856, p. 6. Indeed, all the way across the Atlantic, the *New York Daily Herald*—aware of the oftentimes collusive reputation of the English justice system—made this report in 1857: "In England, indictments are prosecuted by private complaints at their own expense and by private counsel. The practice has excited attention from its abuses, such as private compoundings of felonies, private settlement of crime and withdrawals of charges or

witnesses, and the subject of our own system of public attorneys has been up before the British Parliament." "Court of General Sessions. Before Judge Russell," N.Y. DAILY HERALD (New York, NY), Nov. 18, 1857.

223. LEEDS MERCURY (Leeds, England), Oct. 2, 1866, p. 4 ("The accusation he made was against CAPTAIN JERVIS, who had held the post of his housekeeper or steward, and was to the effect that this officer had appropriated stores belonging to the Commander-in-Chief to his own use. He, therefore, appeared not only as public prosecutor, but as private prosecutor—a confusion of offices which, though necessary, was not conducive to justice."); *see also* "The Great Indian Pickle Case," LIVERPOOL MERCURY (Liverpool, England), Oct. 25, 1866, p. 6 ("It was Sir William Mansfield's own wrongful acts that betrayed Captain Jervis into the only offences of which the court convicted him. Considering, too, that Sir William Mansfield combined in his own person the ill-assorted characters of private prosecution and judge, he might excusably have distrusted his own impartiality, and permitted the recommendation of an unbiassed tribunal to temper the rigour of military law. Not so, however, thinks Sir William Mansfield. He unhesitatingly confirms the legal sentence of the court, and rejects with something like indignation the lenient suggestion that accompanied it. More than this, and infinitely than this, he actually re-asserts the truth of the very charges on which the prisoner had been acquitted.").

224. MARTYN WHITTOCK, A BRIEF HISTORY OF LIFE IN THE MIDDLE AGES: A SOCIAL HISTORY OF MEDIEVAL ENGLAND (2009), ch. 7 ("A key feature of the administration of local justice was a system known as *Frankpledge*. With its roots in Late Anglo-Saxon times it made all freemen (except for clergy and knights) join a *tithing* of ten men, who were responsible for the behavior of each other. In the event of one of them being accused of a crime, the other members of the tithing had the task of bringing the accused to face justice, or compensating the injured party. In practice the checking that everyone was a member of a tithing—called the *View of Frankpledge*—was the task of the manorial *Court Leet*. Any man not in a tithing as fined and the money went to the lord of the manor."); Phillipp R. Schofield, "The Late Medieval View of Frankpledge and the Tithing System: An Essex Case Study," *in* MEDIEVAL SOCIETY AND THE MANOR COURT 408 (Zvi Razi & Richard Smith, eds. 1996) ("The main function of the frankpledge system was to provide mutual surety: the good behaviour of an individual member of the community was the responsibility of that individual's kin and neighbours. All males, both free and servile, over the age of 12 were expected to be members of frankpledge. Wealthy freemen were exempt, their status surety in itself for their good conduct; women and clergy were also exempt. Each frankpledge unit was based, in theory, upon a vill or township, and each unit was divided into a number of tithings, or *decennae*, which, was their name implies, were intended to contain ten men. Each tithing was presided over by one, or sometimes two, chief pledges. The chief pledges were responsible for the behaviour of those in their tithing and for the allocation of tithing of strangers and those reaching the age of 12. Chief pledges represented their tithings at annual or biannual views of frankpledge and it was at such views that a tithing penny was collected from all those in tithing. The frankpledge system thus offered annual remuneration for those administering it, a fact which in part explains why, although intended as a national system to be run from the hundred courts by royal officials, it frequently fell into the hands of local lords.").

225. CAROLYN BOYES-WATSON WITH SUSAN T. KRUMHOLZ, CRIME AND JUSTICE: LEARNING THROUGH CASES 207 (3d ed. 2018) ("In England, a community system known as the *frankpledge* required that every male above the age of twelve join the *tything*, a group of ten able-bodied men sworn to deliver to court any neighbor or who committed a crime. Ten tythings were under the supervision of a constable appointed by the local nobleman. A hundred of these were grouped into shires under the leadership of a 'shire reeve' or sheriff who was appointed by the local landowner representing the king.") (italics added); *see also* ERIC H. MONKKONEN, POLICE IN URBAN AMERICA, 1860–1920, at 33 (1981) ("[I]f we step back to the era prior to the Statute of Winchester, before the codification of community law enforcement, we discover that from the time of the Norman conquest until the thirteenth century the Anglo-Saxon inhabitants of Britain, ruled by the Normans, had been under the compulsory social control system of *frankpledge*. Frankpledge, described by its historian as a '"system of compulsory collective bail fixed for individuals, not after their arrest for a crime, but as a safeguard in anticipation of it,"' forced the community to accept responsibility for the behavior of its individual members, to produce offenders for trial, or, if unable to discover the offender, to pay the fines. Thus, frankpledge demanded that the conquered Anglo-Saxons preserve Norman-defined law and order within the community."); *compare* BRADLEY CHAPIN, CRIMINAL JUSTICE IN

Colonial America, 1606–1660, at 68–69 (2010) ("Scattered all over England in 1600 were hundreds, perhaps thousands, of local courts. These courts baron and courts leet were incidences of a franchise and were held either by the lord of a manor or a borough corporation. The franchise had been created either by prescriptive custom or royal grant. The court baron dealt with obligations related to copyhold tenure and was not a court of record. The court leet was a royal court of record. The leet had a broad criminal jurisdiction. In it justice was done in the king's name, though the fees and fines belonged to the holder of the franchise. The lawyers saw court baron and court leet as two distinct tribunals."); *id.* ("The jurisdiction of each leet was set out in its articles of view, and though these articles varied, they had much in common, including view of frankpledge, which by this time meant assurance that all had taken the oath of allegiance; matters that could be inquired into and presented but not punished, primarily the common law felonies; matters that could be determined in the leet, among them 'common annoyances,' damage to the environment, certain assaults, 'evil persons,' breaches of the assize of ale and bread, and duties imposed by statutes regulating, among many other matters, hunting, apparel, conspiracy to raise wages, highway repair, and drunks.").

226. Giles Jacob, A New Law-Dictionary: Containing the Interpretation and Definition of Words and Terms Used in the Law; and Also the Whole Law, and the Practice Thereof, Under All the Heads and Titles of the Same (5th ed. 1744; The Lawbook Exchange, 2004) (observing that "Frank-pledge" is "a *Pledge* or Surety for the Behaviour of *Freeman*; it being the antient Custom of this Kingdom, borrowed from the *Lombards*, that for the Preservation of the publick Peace, every Free-born man at the Age of Fourteen (Religious Persons, Clerks, &c. excepted) should give Security for his Truth towards the King and his Subjects, or be committed to Prison; whereupon a certain Number of Neighbours, usually became bound one for another, too see each Man of their Pledge forth-coming at all Times, or to answer the Transgression done by any gone away ....").

227. John H. Langbein, *The Origins of Public Prosecution at Common Law*, 17 Am. J. Legal Hist. 313, 317 (1973).

228. Ric Simmons, *Private Criminal Justice*, 42 Wake Forest L. Rev. 911, 923 & n.49 (2007).

229. Charles J. Rzepka & Lee Horsley, eds., A Companion to Crime Fiction 391 (2020) ("The first Sherlock Holmes short story, 'A Scandal in Bohemia,' appeared in the monthly *Strand Magazine* in July 1891.").

230. Gary Mason, The Official History of the Metropolitan Police (2004); *see also* David A. Campion, "'Policing the Peelers': Parliament, the Public, and the Metropolitan Police, 1829–33," *in* London Politics, 1760–1914, at 41 (Matthew Cragoe & Antony Taylor, eds. 2005) ("In 1829, the 'Bill for Further Improving the Police of the Metropolis' abolished the parish system and replaced it with one department, the Metropolitan Police. The jurisdiction of the Metropolitan Police extended in a 12-mile radius from Charing Cross and was composed of 19 'divisions,' each designated by a letter of the alphabet. These corresponded not to traditional parish boundaries but rather to geographic areas measured in square miles. The Police Act also completely overhauled the system by which policing had been previously financed. Where the parishes had once controlled their own budgets and determined rates among local residents for the operational costs of their constabularies, the government introduced a new universal rate paying system throughout London in which funds were allocated to the various divisions at the discretion of the central police administration. Additionally, it mandated uniform standards of recruitment, training and attire among its men. Most importantly, the Police Act placed administrative control of the 'New' Police under the Secretary of State for the Home Office."); Jelle Janssens, State-Building in Kosovo: A Plural Policing Perspective 19 (2015) ("In England, the first 'modern' police force was established when Robert Peel, then Home Secretary, introduced the Metropolitan Police Bill, which created the London Metropolitan Police in 1829, which was a community-based decentralised policing model.") (citation omitted).

231. The Standard (London, England), Jan. 29, 1829, p. 4.

232. Sydney Morning Herald (Sydney, Australia), June 8, 1840, p. 7 ("The usual Prosecutor, in England where there is substantially no private Prosecutor, is the Clerk of the Peace."); *see also* Sydney Morning Herald (Sydney, Australia), June 8, 1840, p. 6 ("I have reason to fear that at present the

punishment of offenders could not, with safety, be left as in the Mother Country, to the zeal of private Prosecutors").

233. THE STANDARD (London, England), Nov. 17, 1829, p. 2.

234. "Northern Circuit. Durham, Friday, March 5," THE TIMES (London, England), Mar. 8, 1847, p. 8.

235. "A Friend at Court," BUFFALO ENQUIRER (Buffalo, NY), Jan. 14, 1893, p. 2.

236. "Central Criminal Court, Dec. 19," THE TIMES (London, England), Dec. 13, 1892, p. 7; "Central Criminal Court," DAILY NEWS (London, England), Dec. 13, 1892, p. 2. The grand jury system had been in use in England for centuries, and was at times subject to abuses. *E.g.*, 2 WILLIAM BLACKSTONE, COMMENTARIES ON THE LAWS OF ENGLAND 302–3 (1753) ("In the time of king Richard the First (according to Hoveden) the process of electing the grand jury ordained by that prince was as follows: four knights were to be taken from the county at large, who chose two more out of every hundred; which two associated to themselves ten other principal freemen, and those twelve were to answer concerning all particulars relating to their own district. This number was probably found too large and inconvenient; but the traces of this institution still remain in that some of the jury must be summoned out of every hundred. This grand jury are previously instructed in the articles of their inquiry by a charge from the judge who presides upon the bench. They then withdraw, to sit and receive indictments, which are preferred to them in the name of the king, but at the suit of any private prosecutor; and they are only to hear evidence on behalf of the prosecution: for the finding of an indictment is only in the nature of an inquiry or accusation, which is afterwards to be tried and determined; and the grand jury are only to inquire upon their oaths whether there be sufficient cause to call upon the party to answer it. A grand jury, however, ought to be thoroughly persuaded of the truth of an indictment so far as their evidence goes, and not to rest satisfied merely with remote probabilities; a doctrine that might be applied to very oppressive purposes."); DAILY JOURNAL (Montpelier, VT), Nov. 18, 1859, p. 4 ("The institution of the Grand Jury was not created by a republican form of government. It first came into existence in England long before the liberties of the people of that kingdom had assumed the inviolable character which they now possess; at a time when every prosecuting officer throughout the realm held office at the pleasure of the crown. These officers were the instruments of the king, not responsible in any sense to the people, but to him alone, for all their actions. They could institute prosecutions for political as well as other offences, when the power that created them required them to do so, and put a stop to such prosecutions at pleasure. The favorites of the government, however great their crimes, always escaped punishment, while its enemies were continually subjected to groundless accusations. The Grand Jury was among the first concessions made by the English crown to the imperative demands of the people, and its main purpose was the security of the subject, and the bringing to justice those whom government favoritism had theretofore protected. Its first duty was to hear complaints preferred by any *private* prosecutor, and it was only bound to present an indictment when its members were thoroughly persuaded of its truth.") (italics in original). *Compare* THE STANDARD (London, England), Nov. 28, 1833, p. 1 ("As to the ordinary class of criminal informations which are not filed *ex officio*, but for which the permission of the court must be obtained, they were the favourite mode of process in the notorious Court of Star Chamber, the members of which judged of the law, the fact, and the penalty, dispensing with both grand and petty juries, as only clogs and impediments to the simple and rapid energy of their despotic proceedings. When that court was abolished by the 16th Car. I., cap. 10, the process by criminal information developed on the Court of King's Bench, where the Master of the Crown Office could, of his own authority, file such informations at the instance of any private prosecutor, by which great oppression was occasioned to the subject, and malice and revenge worked its private ends, to the scandal and degradation of the first court of criminal judicature in the realm. At length the vexation exercise of this power become so intolerable, that a remedy was obliged to be applied at the Revolution, or soon after. That remedy was a partial one, for instead of abolishing criminal informations altogether—as, by dispensing with a grand jury, they were at variance with the principles of the British constitution—they were only regulated so that they could no longer be filed at the arbitrary discretion of the Master of the Crown Office, on the application of a private prosecutor.").

237. There is clear evidence of English solicitors assisting private prosecutors in preparing criminal cases for trial back in the eighteenth century. JOHN H. LANGBEIN, THE ORIGINS OF THE ADVERSARY CRIMINAL TRIAL 109 (2003) ("Across the eighteenth century, solicitors came to play an ever increasing role in

the work of investigating criminal cases, shaping criminal charges, and preparing evidence for trial, a role whose essentials survive in modern English practice. I emphasize in this chapter the work of solicitors for what I call institutional prosecutors (the Mint, the Bank of England, the Treasury, and the Post Office), as well as the growing use of solicitors by private prosecutors. Further, I point to the reinforcement for private prosecution that resulted from the development of associations for the prosecution of felons, voluntary societies that were intimately aligned with the solicitor's profession. The use of prosecution solicitors was associated with a perceptible increase in the use of counsel to prosecute felony cases at trial, further exaggerating the imbalance between the unaided accused and a lawyer-conducted prosecution."); *id.* at 124 ("The most valuable window that I have found on the activity of solicitors working for private prosecutors in the early decades of the eighteenth century is an anonymous tract published in London in 1728, titled *Directions for Prosecuting Thieves without the Help of Those False Guides, the Newgate Sollicitors [sic]* .... Although the author tells his readers that his 'profession is not directly the Law,' he was close enough to the London legal scene to dedicate the pamphlet to the influential recorder of London, Sir William Thompson; and he was knowledgeable enough about criminal practice to devote the back half of the pamphlet to an exposition of the rudiments of criminal practice derived from Hawkins' *Pleas of the Crown*. A main theme of *Directions* is the superiority of counsel as an advisor in a criminal matter by comparison with a solicitor. Even though the tract is hostile to solicitors, it underscores the contemporary perception that solicitors were becoming increasingly important in organizing and preparing prosecution cases at the Old Bailey and in the lesser London criminal courts.").

238. Donald W. Shriver & Peggy L. Shriver, *Law, Religion, and Restorative Justice in New Zealand*, 28 J. Law & Religion 143 (2013).

239. *See, e.g.*, Douglas Hay, *Controlling the English Prosecutor*, 21 Osgoode Hall L.J. 165, 171 (1983) (taking note of the "Association for the Prosecution of Felons," and further observing: "There were hundreds of such groups throughout the country—probably about a thousand by the mid-nineteenth century. Their growth is discernable from the middle of the eighteenth century, although some appear as early as the late 1600s."); *see also id.* at 172 ("In a typical case the members entered into articles of association and agreed to share costs, pool any rewards obtained on convictions, offer rewards to witnesses, and elect a committee to decide which cases to prosecute. Sometimes associations also organized foot and horse patrols, paid retainers to keepers of turnpike gates to watch for stolen horses, and agreed at least to consider undertaking cases on behalf of poorer victims of crime who could not afford to go to law themselves."); *id.* ("These private bodies undoubtedly affected the administration of the criminal law to a considerable extent. Although their members probably constituted fewer than ten percent of the adult male population, they accounted for as much as a quarter or more of prosecutions."); *id.* ("One Midlands association in the 1770s provided that if any members should 'screen, forgive, or otherwise overlook any Felony or Felonies' they should pay a healthy fine. Others promised to prosecute their members for compounding offences. Still others provided for expulsion from the association.").

240. F. W. M. (Fred) McElrea, *Restorative Justice as a Procedural Revolution: Some Lessons from the Adversary System*, *in* David J. Cornwell, John Blad & Martin Wright, eds., Civilising Criminal Justice: An International Restorative Agenda for Penal Reform 87–88 & n.22 (2013).

241. David Sunderland, Social Capital, Trust and the Industrial Revolution, 1780–1880, at 130 (2007).

242. "From the London Morning Journal, of 12th September," The Democrat (Huntsville, Alabama), Nov. 20, 1829, p. 2; *cf.* Morning Post (London, England), Mar. 3, 1830, p. 2 ("Perhaps it never happened before that a Lord Chancellor was a private prosecutor for a libel; he hoped there never might be occasion for his being so again; but was that any reason why, if he were malignantly libeled, he should not bring the offender to justice according to the laws of the land?"); *see also* Caledonian Mercury (Edinburgh, Scotland), Mar. 6, 1830, p. 2 (noting the remarks of the Attorney General as follows: "I shall discuss the topics introduced by my Honourable and Learned Friend in the order in which he has given them. In the first place, he makes a charge that the Lord Chancellor had commenced proceedings in the Court of King's Bench upon a private prosecution for the libel against Fisher and Alexander, and that when the Court had granted a rule upon the application first made in those proceedings the nature of the prosecution was altered, and the Attorney-General though fit to file an ex-officio information.").

243. 2 John Marius Wilson, A Memoir of Field Marshal The Duke of Wellington: With Interspersed Notices of His Principal Assistants in Council, and Companions and Opponents in Arms 505 (1853).

244. Morning Chronicle (London, England), Mar. 27, 1841, p. 3.

245. "Melbourne, Tuesday, 8th August, 1893," The Age (Melbourne, Australia), Aug. 8, 1893, p. 4.

246. Even wealthy individuals in the British Isles sometimes balked at the costs associated with private prosecutions. *See, e.g.*, Michael Moss, The Duel Between Sir Alexander Boswell and James Stuart: Scottish Squibs and Pistols at Dawn 146 (2019) ("Robert Alexander was furious that he had been denied the opportunity to set the record straight: 'Posterity will see the whole affair in its proper colours'. Lady Boswell hankered after a private prosecution, but was advised by her husband's friend, the now retired Viscount Sidmouth, that 'the Expense would be enormous.'").

247. "The Recovery of Stolen Goods," Pall Mall Gazette (London, England), Mar. 4, 1875, p. 3 ("[T]he Crown never, or very rarely, prosecutes in cases of larceny or robbery, and the bare expenses allows to private prosecutors are very inadequate, added to which conviction is not restitution.").

248. The parish constable and justices of the peace, neither of which were intended to supplant private prosecution, had been around for a long time in English life. Yue Ma, *Exploring the Origins of Public Prosecution*, 18 Int'l Crim. Just. Rev. 190, 193–94 (2008) ("In the 13th century, the parish constable was the chief law enforcement officer. He had the duty to maintain law and order in the local community. The constable had the power to make an arrest when an offender was caught red-handed. Operating on his own, however, he could hardly have done much in way of investigation. The burden of investigating crimes thus fell on the shoulders of justice of the peace. Justices of the peace first appeared in the 14th century, were residents of the community appointed by the king to serve as keepers of the peace. They were given the power to inquire into crimes committed in the local community and present the accused before the grand jury. The power assigned to the constable and justices of the peace was not designed to replace private prosecution. The constable and justices of the peace stepped in only when private individuals were not interested in pursuing the matter.") (citations omitted).

249. "Parliamentary Intelligence," The Times (London, England), Aug. 7, 1857, p. 6 (making this note for the "House of Lords, Thursday, August 6": "Lord Campbell ... expressed an earnest wish that in other branches of the law the sanction of some public officer might be necessary before criminal prosecutions were instituted. He had frequently observed that the most frightful abuses arose from the facilities which were given to private prosecutors, without any notice whatever to the parties accused, to prefer bills of indictment and immediately obtain warrants thereon. That was the case particularly with regard to charges of perjury and conspiracy. Those indictments were frequently preferred for the sake of extortion. If some public functionary were responsible for the institution of those proceedings it would be a great improvement in our criminal jurisprudence. He had a good deal of conversation with the late Attorney-General, Sir A. Cockburn, on the subject, and his learned friend had made up his mind to propose a Bill to remedy the evil. He hoped that a Bill of that nature would ere long receive the sanction of the Legislature. For the present he thought it was highly desirable that no person should be liable to any prosecution for breach of trust without the previous sanction of a public functionary."); *see also* "Imperial Parliament," Morning Post (London, England), Feb. 16, 1860, p. 2 (noting that "Mr. Collier" said this in the House of Commons on February 15th: "As to public prosecutors being appointed for the offence of bribery, the present machinery was defective. The house did not always at present fix and get hold of the principal offenders. It was impossible for the Attorney-General to afford the time necessary for this branch of the administration of justice. The house had affirmed the principle of a public prosecutor being appointed, and it received the assent and support of the present Chief Justice of England. In these matters, however, it was most of all desirable that a public prosecutor should be appointed, for the offence tended to sap our public institutions; and secondly, bribery was that sort of offence which private prosecutors could be least entrusted with. The omission to prosecute a man who stole a sheep was condemned by public opinion, but the man who would prosecute bribery was said to be looked upon as spiteful and vindictive."); The Isle of Man Weekly Times (Douglas, England), Sept. 26, 1874, p. 4 ("Our readers will remember the untiring efforts we some two years ago put forth to induce the Insular Legislature to appoint a public prosecutor for this Island, and they will as readily call to mind the reception which the proposition met with at the hands

of the House of Keyes. The argument as to the necessity of such an official, or officials, being appointed was altogether on the side of the supporters of the change in our existing method of criminal procedure. Case after case arose in this Island in which justice was either delayed or defeated in consequence of the defective machinery we possessed for impartiality and vigorously administering our criminal law. It was clearly demonstrated that the amount of cost and trouble entailed upon an individual who, on account of injury received, desired to set the law in motion was so great, that, perhaps, in three cases out of five, prosecutions were either never instituted, or, if instituted were abandoned in one or other of their earlier stages.... The fifth and final report of the English Judicature Commission was published a few days ago, and in it the appointment of public prosecutors for England meets with the unanimous recommendation and approval of the Commissioners.... They have had before them, as we have had in the Island, undeniable instances where the punishment of crime has become a matter of chance and uncertainty—cases where unprincipled persons have compromised serious offences; and the records of our Courts disclose how often unscrupulous people have dared to put the criminal law in motion for the express purpose of extorting money from the accused. With reference to the first class of cases, the report of the Commission states that 'there are cases in which, after a private prosecutor has employed an attorney, and the case has been proceeded with for some time, the prosecution is dropped, under such circumstances as to give reason to suspect that the accused or his friends have made terms with the prosecutor, and that the case, although one which ought to be prosecuted, is compromised.' The rich criminal with his gold can thus purchase immunity from punishment; the wretch whom, perhaps, poverty has driven into crime, must suffer the full penalty of the law, because he has nothing wherewith to bribe his accuser."); "THE ATTORNEY-GENERAL," SYDNEY MORNING HERALD (Sydney, Australia), June 20, 1836, p. 3 ("A letter appeared in Friday's *Australian*, which more than insinuated that the present Attorney-General, while acting as Crown Prosecutor, received fees from private prosecutors. This, certainly, was a startling announcement, inasmuch as, if the accusation were true, no man can question the justice and propriety of our contemporary's remark, that it was in principle tantamount to bribing a Grand Jury. Upon the assembling of the Supreme Court, however, on the same day, the Attorney-General rose and called the attention of the Judges to the publication, which, he stated, was altogether erroneous throughout. The learned gentleman said, that previous to his nomination to the office of Attorney-General, he had been retained as counsel by the Association for the Suppression of Cattle Stealing; but that immediately on being appointed to the office he now holds, he returned all his briefs. Their Honors were of opinion that the learned Gentleman's explanation was perfectly satisfactory."); "House of Commons," *in* GARDENERS' CHRONICLE 388 (1841) (in speaking about the need to pursue a bribery case, a Mr. Wynn in the House of Commons stated to this effect: "I had also been said that these [types of] cases were open to private prosecutors. True; but prosecutions in these cases, he considered, were too often collusive to be safely left in private hands."); THE STANDARD (London, England), Mar. 3, 1859, p. 8 ("That prosecutions are followed up or dropped, according as interested motives may happen to influence private prosecutors, has long been surmised. It is, however, satisfactory to perceive that the subject has at last attracted judicial notice. In a recent case, 'The Queen v. Skeene and another,' the Lord Chief Baron observed—'And now the prosecutors do not appear.' Mr. Giffard, Q.C.—'They have obtained their money.' The Court—'And having got that, they do not care how the criminal law may be defeated.'—Report of 'Crown cases reserved,' January 24, 1859.").

250. Over the years, another problem identified by public officials was that private prosecutors were not always incentivized to come forward to prosecute cases. *E.g.*, "Unseaworthy Ships," THE TIMES (London, England), Feb. 16, 1874, p. 11 (at the annual meeting of the Liverpool Chamber of Commerce, Mr. W. Rathbone, an M.P., made comments along these lines: "In England it was presumed that there was always some private individual whose interest and duty it was to prosecute every offence; but for many of those offences which injured society most there was no such voluntary private prosecutor. For various reasons, which he would not trouble them by repeating, in cases of sending unseaworthy ships to sea, and in cases of great commercial frauds, no such private prosecutor appeared; and what they wanted was a public prosecutor; and Mr. Walpole and Mr. Russell Gurney joined Mr. Eykyn and himself in introducing a Bill to provide such an officer.").

251. THE TIMES (London, England), Aug. 7, 1850, p. 5. "Such a check," *The Times* offered, "would not exclude private co-operation, or lay our whole administration of justice at the feet of any official."

Straddling both sides of the public prosecutor-private prosecutor divide, *The Times* concluded: "Public duty and private zeal might be made mutually to aid each other, and economy, justice, and morality would all thrive by such an arrangement." *Id.*

252. Philip B. Kurland & D. W. M. Waters, *Public Prosecutions in England, 1854–79: An Essay in English Legislative History*, 1959 DUKE L.J. 493, 499.

253. "House of Commons, Tuesday, Feb. 14," THE TIMES (London, England), Feb. 15, 1854, p. 9. Phillimore "proposed that the Crown should distribute the different circuits into a certain number of divisions, and appoint to each division a public prosecutor, who should hold office upon the tenure of good behavior." "In addition, he proposed the appointment of district agents to collect and examine evidence, to transmit all cases to the public prosecutor for his opinion, and also to conduct the proceedings before the magistrates." "[H]e thought there should be a change in the administration of the law; and that means should be taken to put the law itself upon a sounder, more liberal, and more enlightened footing, so that it should be enabled to correspond better with the exigencies of the age. (Hear, hear.). They should not be content with making the Sovereign the nominal prosecutor, but they should recollect that a criminal offence was an offence against society, and that society was bound to interfere in administering justice to the offenders." *Id.*; *see also* "The Appointment of Public Prosecutors," THE MORNING CHRONICLE (London, England), Feb. 15, 1854, p. 6 ("Mr. PHILLIMORE moved for leave to bring in a bill to provide for the appointment of public prosecutors in criminal cases. The honourable member stated that he was anxious, by means of the provisions of his bill, to simplify and improve one part of the public justice of the country which had hitherto remained in a scandalous and discreditable state."); "In the House of Commons," DAILY NEWS (London, England), Feb. 15, 1854, p. 5 ("On the motion of Mr. J. G. PHILLIMORE, leave was given to bring in a bill for the appointment of public prosecutors, to whom should be entrusted the conduct of actions before the criminal tribunals. The present system, as the hon. member contended, fostered private animosity, enhanced expense, and led very often to the defeat of justice."); MORNING CHRONICLE (London, England), Feb. 16, 1854, p. 4 ("Mr. JOHN PHILLIMORE has just obtained leave to bring in a Bill to remedy this glaring inconsistency between the profession and practice of the law. He proposes to establish public prosecutors. We have said that the law of England already recognises the theory of a public prosecutor; and sanguine reformers have not been wanting who think that all legal proceedings ought to be conducted—whether they relate to the public peace and morality, or to private wrongs—by a public officer, and at the common expense of the State. We must wait, however, for this consummation until the settlement of the kingdom of Utopia and the establishment of the new Atlantis."); "Public Prosecutors," LIVERPOOL MERCURY AND LANCASHIRE, CHESHIRE, AND GENERAL ADVERTISER (Liverpool, England), Feb. 21, 1854, p. 6 ("In reforming our laws we have too often omitted to consider the defects visible in their administration. In this particular there is much to be done, but one want especially craves notice. The prosecution of public offenders is the business of society, and should not be left to the animosity and revenge which may animate private individuals. Mr. Phillimore has obtained leave to bring in a bill on this subject, and he proposed to divide the circuits into districts, to appoint a public prosecutor for each district, with district agents to examine the evidence and conduct the proceedings before the magistrates...."); "Appointment of a Public Prosecutor," BELFAST NEWS-LETTER (Belfast, Northern Ireland), Feb. 17, 1854, p. 1 ("Mr. Napier expressed his approval of the principle of appointing a public prosecutor, and stated that it was already in adoption in Ireland, where Crown solicitors were appointed upon every circuit.... He considered that a prosecution ought not to be left to the caprice or malice of a private prosecutor, who would not have the same responsibility and interest in arriving at the truth as a public prosecutor, but who would be frequently actuated by indirect motives."); "Imperial Parliament," YORK HERALD (York, England), May 6, 1854, p. 3 ("The Public Prosecution Bill, which stood for second reading, was withdrawn by Mr. Phinn, the Attorney-General having undertaken to bring in a measure on the subject."); "The Work of the Session," LIVERPOOL MERCURY (Liverpool, England), May 12, 1854, p. 12 ("Of the bills introduced by members unconnected with the Government, Mr. Phillimore's proposition for appointing Public Prosecutors will be revised and re-introduced when the Attorney-General is at leisure"); "A Public Prosecutor," MORNING CHRONICLE (London, England), May 31, 1854, p. 2 ("Lord BROUGHAM, availing himself of a pause in the business before the house, said he once more begged to entreat the attention of their lordships to that most important subject—the establishment of a public prosecutor; and he ventured to say that even at this period of the

session it would not be found too late to make a beginning towards achieving that most important and absolutely necessary improvement of the criminal law."); "Public Prosecutor," MORNING POST (London, England), June 20, 1854, p. 3 ("Mr. J. G. Phillimore asked the Attorney-General when the promised bill on the subject of public prosecutors would be laid upon the table—(laughter);—but the Attorney-General not being in his place the question remained unanswered."); "Hull Borough Sessions," HULL PACKET AND EAST RIDING TIMES (Hull, England), July 7, 1854, p. 8 ("The present Attorney-General, on the presenting of a bill, which was brought forward by a friend of mine in the House of Commons (Mr. Phillimore), for the establishing of a public prosecutor, procured the withdrawal of that bill, by an assurance that the government would take up such a measure. The Attorney-General then stated that such were the difficulties which he also found environing this subject, that he could not hold out a hope of introducing a comprehensive measure relating to it during the present session, but he pledged himself to look into the case in all directions, and come prepared, if possible, with such a bill during the next session.").

254. JAMES FITZJAMES STEPHEN, A GENERAL VIEW OF THE CRIMINAL LAW OF ENGLAND 30, 154–55, 169, 171–73 (1863); *see also id.* at 171 ("Our system not only cripples the efficiency of prosecutions and favours the escape of criminals, but it inflicts cruel hardship on innocent persons who have the misfortune to be accused. A day-labourer or mechanic is accused of an offence, and committed to trial at the assizes. If he is unable to procure bail, or the magistrates are unwilling to take it, he must remain in prison for several months, during which he has no means of supporting his family. In order to raise a few pounds for legal assistance he has to sell his furniture, and even if he is acquitted he leaves prison a beggar."). In a second edition of his treatise, published in 1890, Stephen emphasized that "the most characteristic principle of the law of England" is that "everyone, without exception, has the right to use the Queen's name for the purpose of prosecuting any person for any crime." "This," he wrote, "is subject only to the condition that the Attorney-General has power on his own authority to stop any prosecution by entering a *nolle prosequi*." SIR JAMES FITZJAMES STEPHEN, A GENERAL VIEW OF THE CRIMINAL LAW OF ENGLAND 156 (2d ed. 1890). "It was not until the thirteenth century that a split occurred in the way prosecutions were handled in Europe," one scholar explains. As that scholar, Jason Twede, writes in his dissertation: "Until then, England and the rest of Europe had handled prosecution in much the same way, via a system [of] private prosecution. It was during the thirteenth century that continental Europe generally switched to an inquisitorial system of prosecution that utilized government officials in the accusation process. England held to a system that used laymen in the accusation process. In other words, England maintained a system of private prosecution while continental Europe switched to a system of public prosecution." Jason Twede, "Going Public: How the Government Assumed the Authority to Prosecute in the Southern United States," Ph.D. dissertation, University of North Dakota (May 2016), pp. 14–15.

255. *E.g.*, NORTH-EASTERN DAILY GAZETTE (Middlesbrough, England), Oct. 2, 1874, p. 2 ("[T]he task of the prosecutor was one of no ordinary difficulty. It was a duty which ought never to be placed in the hands of an independent and irresponsible individual—a blunder in getting up the evidence—personal friendship, a dislike to the task, the expense, and a great many other circumstances might induce a private prosecutor to give up an important case like this, and thus allow the guilty to escape. Public prosecutors ought to be appointed who know the law, and are accustomed to unearth the mysteries of a complicated case, and thus take the unpleasant responsibility off private individuals.").

256. GEORGE ROBB, WHITE-COLLAR CRIME IN MODERN ENGLAND: FINANCIAL FRAUD AND BUSINESS MORALITY 1845–1929, at 71 (1992).

257. "Overend and Gurney Directors, in Relation to Working Men," LLOYD'S WEEKLY NEWSPAPER (London, England), Feb. 7, 1869, p. 12. This same letter to the editor also ran in *Reynolds's Newspaper* in London a week later. "Overend and Gurney Directors in Relation to Working Men," REYNOLDS'S NEWSPAPER (London, England), Feb. 14, 1869, p. 7.

258. THE TIMES (London, England), July 1, 1869, p. 8.

259. "Private Prosecutors," PALL MALL GAZETTE (London, England), Apr. 17, 1869, p. 3 ("The *Economist* has seen few stronger illustrations of the necessity of a public prosecutor than the advertisement of Mr. Thom, the private prosecutor of Overend and Gurney's directors, that he will conduct his own case at the trial. Whatever may be the motive of Mr. Thom, whether want of means or excessive confidence in his own powers, or something that cannot be guessed at, it is most unfortunate that a prosecution so

imperatively demanded in the public interest, if there is room for it at all, should be played with in this manner. No case ever required more laborious and skil[l]ful guidance, or a longer purse; think only of the array of zealous counsel opposed, and the intricate matters of accounting that witnesses must be examined and cross-examined on; and yet whether it shall be adequately conducted or not is left to the judgment of a mere private individual, who may by accident by right, but is far more likely to be wrong, and who may not command such resources as to be altogether a free agent. Till now the evil of private prosecutions has been the risk of arrangements between the prosecutor and the accused; but Mr. Thom has revealed a new peril. The *Economist* trusts it is not yet too late to avert the scandal which the breakdown of such a prosecution through deficient management would cause—in other words, that Mr. Thom, who deserves no little credit for his public spirit, will at the last moment be better advised."); *accord* "Private Prosecutors," SHEFFIELD AND ROTHERHAM INDEPENDENT (Sheffield, England), Apr. 20, 1869, p. 3 (reprinting the same piece). *See also* "Public Prosecutors," PALL MALL GAZETTE (London, England), July 3, 1869, p. 3 ("There is not an income-tax payer in England who is not the poorer for the conduct of the directors of Overend, Gurney, and Co., and an inquiry whether that conduct was legal or not is, if for that reason alone, within the legitimate business of the Government."; "The *Economist* holds that the better it is proved that the Overend and Gurney case is not of the class which the Treasury prosecutor takes up, the more clearly it is shown that we should have a different organization of our system of criminal prosecutions. Here is an important case which was manifestly going to be wrecked and mismanaged in private hands, and for which it could not be hoped that private prosecutors would be adequate on the mere ground of the great expense involved; yet by our law it must be left to the chance efforts of volunteers, like almost all other cases."; "The imperfection of our law is just this, that it imposes on the sufferers by a crime the duty of prosecuting—that is to say, provides that they shall suffer more; and this is not only sheer barbarity in all cases, but in many cases will not work. The arrangement presupposes a spirit of resentment among the victims against the criminal, and trusts to it to secure his punishment, but it is barbarous to stimulate this feeling—the civilized principles in dealing with crime being the defence of the community and the reformation of the criminal. And the arrangement fails, because in a civilized community resentment is weak and the notion is ineradicable that the hunting of criminals is the business of the community and not of individuals."); "The Overend, Gurney, and Co. Case," LEEDS MERCURY (Leeds, England), July 5, 1869, p. 3 (reprinting the *Economist* editorial calling for public prosecutions and noting: "Mr. Adam Thom, the prosecutor in Overend and Gurney's case, writes that he is quite willing to forego the right of advocating his own cause providing the public will supply him with sufficient funds to engage Counsel worthy of the occasion.").

260. CAROLE RAWCLIFFE & RICHARD WILSON, EDS., NORWICH SINCE 1550, at 372 (2004); 2 SIR JOHN CLAPHAM, THE BANK OF ENGLAND: A HISTORY 263 (1966) ("It was on Thursday, 10 May 1866, that Overend, Gurney & Co. Ltd. Failed for over five millions; and Friday, 11 May, was the City's Black Friday.").

261. THE TIMES (London, England), July 1, 1869, p. 8 ("There now seems little, if any, doubt that, unless the LORD CHIEF JUSTICE comes to the rescue at the last moment, the OVERAND and GURNEY case must break down, and a miscarriage of justice ensue such as would be possible in no other civilized country in the world. But, whether the case break down or not, the mere possibility, or rather the imminent probability, of so grave a scandal has done good service by bringing forcibly and clearly home to the comprehension of the general public a strange defect in our criminal jurisprudence which has long been felt by law reformers. Thirty-five years ago Lord BROUGHAM declared that the appointment of a Public Prosecutor was then contemplated by Government, and ever since the measure has been from time to time taken up, to be for a brief period strenuously advocated by this or that distinguished lawyer, and then quietly dropped. It might, indeed, possibly have continued this spasmodic and checkered career of activity and repose for another five-and-thirty years but for the interest felt in the extraordinary miscarriage of justice which the want of a Public Prosecutor now threatens to occasion."); *see also* "Imperial Parliament," MORNING POST (London, England), May 31, 1854, p. 2 ("Lord BROUGHAM remarked that he considered the appointment of a public prosecutor by the Government was most desirable. Even at this advanced period of the season he thought it was not too late to make a beginning towards that important measure."); *id.* ("Lord CAMPBELL believed that great improvement in the administration of justice would follow if a public prosecutor were appointed. He had had many opportunities of seeing how advantageous such an officer was in Scotland, and he had no doubt similar advantages might follow in England, though the case was attended with

a great deal of difficulty. He had no doubt such an office would be a great saving in the long run, though, in the first instance, there would be a good deal of expenses in salaries; and though he should rejoice exceedingly to see such a measure adopted, he feared it would tend to injure the prospects of young aspirants at the bar.").

262. "House of Commons.—Yesterday," WESTERN MAIL (Cardiff, Wales), July 2, 1869, p. 2; "House of Commons, Yesterday," LEEDS MERCURY (Leeds, England), July 2, 1869, p. 3.

263. THE GUARDIAN (London, England), Nov. 8, 1869, p. 2 ("Dr. Thom's application to the Court of Chancery suggests that the prosecution of the Directors of OVEREND, GURNEY, & CO., Limited, is again, for financial reasons, in a critical condition, and that there is still some chance of a collapse. Such a result would on many grounds be extremely unfortunate. Whatever view may be taken of the probabilities of the case, on one side or the other, it is impossible to deny that if the prosecution, after having been carried so far, were now allowed to drop, there would be a failure of justice. Either the gentlemen arranged committed the offences imputed to them, or they have been most grossly and cruelly calumniated. In the former event, they ought, of course, to be punished in the manner prescribed by law; in the latter, the least that is due to men who have been so deeply wronged is a public vindication of their honour such as can be obtained only by a solemn judicial decision, based upon a complete and searching investigation of the whole facts of the case."); *id.* ("In an ordinary case the expense are small, the prosecutor seldom gives them a thought and they are paid out of a public fund as a matter of course. But in a great case where the outlay is reckoned by thousands of pounds, a private prosecutor is naturally more timid. At best, it is certain that his expenses will be much beyond the taxed costs allowed, and the authorities will be more scrupulous as to repaying him just in proportion to the amount and the peculiar character of the proceedings.").

264. "Overend-Gurney Case," SYDNEY MORNING HERALD (Sydney, Australia), Sept. 2, 1869, p. 3; *see also* "The Prosecution of the Directors of Overend, Gurney, and Co.," MORNING POST (London, England), Dec. 23, 1869, p. 2 ("This was the ninth and last day of the trial of the late directors of Overend, Gurney, and Co. (Limited), for conspiracy to defraud Adam Thom and other shareholders in that company.").

265. GEORGE ROBB, WHITE-COLLAR CRIME IN MODERN ENGLAND: FINANCIAL FRAUD AND BUSINESS MORALITY 1845–1929, at 71 (1992) ("The trial of the Overend and Gurney directors centered on allegations that they had concealed from shareholders the true state of the company's affairs. After the 1866 crash, it was revealed that the old, private bill-brokering firm Overend and Gurney had fallen on hard times during the 1850s due to a series of bad loans. In an attempt to stave off ruin, the business was floated as a public, limited company in 1865. Due to the firm's celebrated reputation, the floatation was fully subscribed, bringing in millions in new capital. The prospectus, however, had not disclosed the insolvency of the old firm. This sin of omission led shareholders to resist paying claims of almost £5 million against the now bankrupt company on the grounds that they had become members due to false information. The courts eventually rejected the shareholders' plea, and, to add insult to injury, the directors were acquitted of fraud. The shareholders only had moral force on their side, the directors the inadequate provisions of company law which failed to specify the content of prospectuses. Overend's shareholders consequently lost millions of pounds, and the company's debts were not fully discharged until 1893."). The private prosecution of Adam Thom was followed in the press not just by English subjects, but by American citizens, too. "Our Credit Abroad," PHILADELPHIA INQUIRER (Philadelphia, PA), June 29, 1870, p. 3 ("[W]e have not forgotten the astonishing revelations in the case of the Overend-Gurney concern—nor the technical difficulties which the English Judiciary interposed between Dr. Thom, the private prosecutor in that affair, and the ends of justice. If Dr. Thom had been favored with a fair chance instead of being systematically snubbed and thwarted by the Bench, the result of that trial might have been very different.").

266. "Public Prosecutors," PALL MALL GAZETTE (London, England), Mar. 9, 1870, p. 3 ("AFTER the experience of the last few years and the very strong observations of the Chief Justice in the course of the Overend, Gurney trial, it is by no means creditable to the Government that they should have thrown the responsibility of legislating on the subject of public prosecutors upon the shoulders of a private member. Fortunately, Mr. Eykyn has not been daunted by the refusal of the Home Secretary to do his duty in the matter, and has brought forward a very simple and practical proposal which, if it does not give us all we might perhaps desire in the shape of an active prosecution of criminals by and on behalf of the public, does at least go far to systematize and bring into regular working order the loose, capricious, and often

scandalously defective arrangements by which this branch of the administration of justice is at present supposed to be provided for.").

267. "Moving Forward," BRADFORD OBSERVER (Bradford, England), May 7, 1870, p. 3; *see also* "Public Prosecution," BRADFORD OBSERVER (Bradford, England), Apr. 29, 1871, pp. 1–2 ("England is the only civilized country in the world which is without a public prosecutor. Ireland and Scotland have each their systems of public prosecution. In Ireland there are thirty-three public prosecutors, or one for each county, acting under the supervision of the legal authorities of Dublin Castle. The expense of the system is not above £7000 a year. In Scotland, wherever there is a sheriff there is a prosecutor-fiscal to inquire into and take charge of all criminal cases. The prosecutor-fiscal's first duty is to inquire and to report to the Lord Advocate, with whom rests the ultimate decision as to whether or not there are sufficient grounds and evidence for laying any indictment. In Scotland this system of public prosecution is old. It works well and cheaply.... Both in Ireland and Scotland the public prosecutors are leading solicitors or attorneys in their districts.... The Public Prosecutor's Bill, which the House of Commons sanctioned in principle the other night, proposes to make the Attorney-General, assisted by three consulting counsel, the commander-in-chief of an army of local public prosecutors, appointed by the Secretary of State on the recommendation of the magistrates of the several districts.... The scheme of the bill is that there should be about 700 public prosecutors appointed as above, who, throughout England and Wales, would vindicate the rights of society against people charged with crimes and offences. The private prosecutor will not be superseded and suppressed by the scheme. The object is to supplement rather than to extinguish the present system.... At present the haphazard system of prosecution gives every criminal so many chances that philosophic criminals can calculate with certainty upon many chances of escape to one of conviction. The Recorder of London is very well acquainted with the administration of criminal jurisdiction, and he declares that according to his experience the present mode of conducting prosecutions is neither conducive to the protection of innocence nor to the detection and punishment of guilt. Thousands escape because the private prosecutors are irresponsible and fail to appear, or because they are ignorant and mismanage the evidence. Then policemen are in reality assuming to a large and dangerous extent the double character of prosecutors and witnesses. Until there are public prosecutors this evil is inseparable from the duties thrown on the police.").

The complexity and expense of banking and securities cases were major obstacles to private prosecutions. *E.g.*, "Trade and Finance," DAILY NEWS (London, England), Aug. 3, 1875, p. 4 ("All securities, as we have shown, being liable to be manipulated for purposes of fraud by the creation of an artificial market, the proper cure is to so amend the law that the fraudulent manipulation, and any fraudulent misrepresentation accompanying it, can be made a punishable offence. There is now a difficulty in bringing home offences like these, because there is no direct connection between the rogue and his victims. The fraudulent manœuvres and misrepresentations are addressed to nobody in particular, and the fraudulent sales and purchases through the agency of dealers and brokers take place between people who do not see each other.... To complete the improvement, there ought also to be a public prosecutor able to pounce upon the offenders when not expected, and under an obligation to prosecute without fear or favour. The frauds in these cases are often too complicated for private prosecution, and a private prosecutor, we fear, is only too frequently tempted to rest content when the threat of putting the criminal law in motion has sufficed to procure the redress of his private wrong.").

268. In Ireland, if the Crown stepped in, it could override the wishes of the private prosecutor. "THE DERRYMACASH AFFRAY," FREEMAN'S JOURNAL (Dublin, Ireland), Jan. 8, 1862, p. 4 ("Mr. M'Mechan, on behalf of the private prosecutors, was proceeding to object to the application, and to state his reasons why some of the cases at least ought to be tried at the quarter sessions, when [t]he Chairman interrupted him, saying he would be happy to hear him in support of the application made on behalf of the crown, but that as the crown, who were the proper parties, had taken the conduct of the case into their own hands, he did not consider the private prosecutor at all entitled to object to the application made on behalf of the crown, which, in his opinion, and in that of the entire bench, was a most reasonable and proper one, and should, therefore, be granted; and he directed an order to be made accordingly, and that the parties and the several witnesses should be rebound to take their trial at the ensuing assizes."); *see also* "Court of Queen's Bench," FREEMAN'S JOURNAL (Dublin, Ireland), Apr. 29, 1875, p. 2 (noting that "Mr. Justice Barry sat to dispose of

motions" and that "Mr. Maybury called his lordship's attention to an old rule of the court which rendered the present motion necessary, as the grand jury could not be summoned at the instance of a private prosecutor without the special leave of the court."; "His Lordship directed the grand jury to be summoned upon such day as would be most convenient to the sheriff."). There was clearly concerns among the Irish judiciary with the potential for abuse by private prosecutors. "Assize Intelligence. County of Armagh," BELFAST NEWS-LETTER (Belfast, Northern Ireland), Mar. 7, 1862, p. 4 ("[T]he fact of setting aside jurors by a private prosecutor—the effect of that practice is to enable him to pack a jury. A private prosecutor has an unlimited right to direct jurors to stand by when they come to be sworn. That right can only be exercised by the Attorney-General subject to public responsibility—to Parliamentary responsibility; but when it is exercised by a private prosecutor there is no such responsibility; and I quite concur with the observation made that it is a most objectionable power, and liable to great abuse."); "The Prosecution of the Rev. Mr. Quinn," FREEMAN'S JOURNAL (Dublin, Ireland), Mar. 8, 1862, p. 4 (noting the remarks of "Mr. Justice Fitzgerald" as follows: "[T]he prosecutor ... expresses ... confidence, that the effect of setting aside jurors, if carried out to an abuse, does enable a prosecutor to do what is called 'pack a jury.' He has an unlimited right of directing jurors to stand aside as they come to be sworn, without assigning any cause of challenge. The Attorney-General or his nominee exercises this right, subject to public responsibility—responsibility to parliament, and official responsibility to the public; but when it is exercised by a private prosecutor, there is no such responsibility, and I agree in the observation that it is a power, the exercise of which in the hands of a private prosecutor is most objectionable and liable to great abuse."); "Assize Intelligence. County of Armagh.", BELFAST NEWS-LETTER, Mar. 7, 1862, p. 4 (noting the following remarks of "HIS LORDSHIP" in a charge to the jury: "I have to remind you that we are now upon our respective oaths disposing of a criminal prosecution. What has occurred in the course of this case has induced me to think that the Scotch course is a wise one—that there should be no such thing as a private prosecutor, and every case entrusted to the public prosecutor."); "The Prosecution of the Rev. Mr. Quinn," FREEMAN'S JOURNAL (Dublin, Ireland), Mar. 8, 1862, p. 4 ("I have to remind you that we—you and I—are now upon our respective oaths disposing of a criminal prosecution. A matter that has occurred in the course of this case induced me to think that the Scotch principle would be the wise one, that there should be no such thing as private prosecutions, and that every prosecution should be entrusted to a responsible public prosecutor ....").

269. "Criminal Law in England," N.Y. DAILY HERALD (New York, NY), Feb. 23, 1875, p. 4; *accord* "Criminal Law in England," ST. JOSEPH GAZETTE (St. Joseph, MO), Feb. 27, 1875, p. 3 (reprinting the same article). *See also* "Police Intelligence," MORNING POST (London, England), Oct. 19, 1877, p. 7 ("Sir R. Carden said that the case down to the present time had been conducted in the most able and zealous manner by Mr. Grain, but the inquiry was clearly one of vast magnitude and importance, and would press too heavily upon the resources of any private prosecutor to carry it out in a satisfactory manner. He was very glad, therefore, to find that the inquiry had been taken up by the Treasury, and he felt that it was only reasonable that the application made by Mr. Pollard should be granted.").

270. IRELAND, CRIMINAL AND JUDICIAL STATISTICS, 1878–1879, at 27 (1879).

271. *E.g.*, "The British Association," IRISH TIMES (Dublin, Ireland), Aug. 20, 1877, p. 6 ("Dr. Hancock read a paper 'On the cost of adopting a complete system of prosecution in England, as illustrated by the results of the Scotch and Irish system of public prosecution.' He showed that the extension to England of the system of public prosecution which had long existed in Scotland and Ireland was apparently only a question of time. In 1872, Mr. Walpole had said, 'it was really a disgrace, and he used the word advisedly, that England was the only country in the world where prosecutions for crime were left at the mercy of private individuals, who might or might not procced with them as they thought fit.' That the delay in adopting so essential a reform is connected with fears of the cost, appears from the observation of the Home Secretary, who, while announcing that a bill was prepared, said a 'public prosecutor was an expensive luxury.' The Scotch system of a local Crown Solicitor, called Procurator-Fiscal, in 60 districts in Scotland, taking charge under the direction of the Lord Advocate (who corresponds to the English and Irish Attorney General) of all prosecutions from the very commencement to the final stage, costs only £27,960 a year .... The effect of this public local officer taking charge of prosecutions arising out of sudden deaths was to dispense altogether with coroners' inquests, the inquiry by the Crown Solicitor into every sudden death that might possibly have resulted from crime being accepted as a complete substitute for coroners'

inquests, which do not exist in Scotland.... The Irish system does not meet one class of cases as to which there is a strong demand for a public prosecutor intervening—frauds connected with private companies, and embezzlement on private people; these are left to the private prosecutor."); "The Chambers of Commerce and the Administration of the Laws," SHEFFIELD AND ROTHERHAM INDEPENDENT (Sheffield, England), Oct. 1, 1877, p. 2 ("Another reform in the administration of the law which the Associated Chambers of Commerce call for, is the appointment of public prosecutors throughout the country, whose official duty it would be to examine into cases of suspected crime on the earliest information of their occurrence, and to undertake the task of bringing the offenders to justice. The Chambers, or at least the majority of them, appear to hold a very strong and decided opinion on the public necessity of appointing such officials, and have expressed the opinion several times during the last few years. The question however is one with respect to which the country may be said to be in a halting mood. It has undergone considerable discussion from time to time, yet no very enthusiastic feeling has yet arisen upon the subject. Law reform indeed has never been a subject upon which the majority of Englishmen have manifested a very deep interest; whilst the lawyers themselves, being as a class perhaps the most conservative section of the community, for the most part look upon this indifference with satisfaction and complacency. The question of appointing public prosecutors has had the attention not only of the present but of the late Government, and towards the close of last session the present Home Secretary intimated that 'he was prepared, whenever an opportunity offered, to bring in a bill on the subject.' At the same time he added a warning that public prosecutors may be a very expensive luxury."); *id.* ("Instances constantly occur of neglect or indifference on the part of the private prosecutor leading to a failure of justice, and this neglect or indifference cannot in every case be characterised as culpable, when we consider the legal expenses and the trouble and loss of time which a prosecution often involves."); *cf.* "Social Science Congress - Aberdeen Meeting," THE ABERDEEN JOURNAL, AND GENERAL ADVERTISER FOR THE NORTH OF SCOTLAND (Aberdeen, Scotland), Sept. 24, 1877, p. 6 ("The proceedings were opened by the address of the Lord-Advocate, as President of the Repression of Crime section.... He preferred the public prosecutor of Scotland to the private prosecutor of England; and thought their English friends should seriously consider the advantages of the Scotch mode, though it would also be necessary to consider the complaint brought against the Scotch system—that it proceeds on the results of a secret enquiry, in which the accused is allowed no opportunity of cross-examining witnesses or of showing that the charge brought against him is not sufficiently well founded to warrant his being committed for trial."); *accord* "Social Science Congress," GLASGOW HERALD (Glasgow, Scotland), Sept. 24, 1877, p. 4 (taking note of the Lord Advocate's address discussing public vs. private prosecutions and comparing the Scotch and English systems). On occasion, reformers cited other legal systems as well, such as the public prosecution system in Prussia. "Department of Jurisprudence," FREEMAN'S JOURNAL (Dublin, Ireland), Aug. 17, 1861, p. 3 ("Baron Holtzendorf read a paper 'On Public Prosecutions in Prussia.' Previous to 1818 no provision existed in Germany for public prosecution by special officers; but when the revolution swept over the Rhine one of the changes introduced was the appointment of a 'Judge of Instruction.' Within one year the whole system of criminal prosecution was remodeled, and the right of prosecuting vested in public prosecutors or state attorneys. On the whole this system was found to work satisfactory both in securing the detection and punishment of crime, and also preventing prosecutions from being unnecessarily and improperly brought against individuals. No charge could be brought in public court against any individual unless the evidence was first examined by the responsible officer of the crown, who had the power of refusing to allow the prosecution to proceed if he thought the evidence did not warrant the probability of a conviction. The defect of the system as now carried out in Prussia was that the aggrieved party had no power, in cases where the officer refused to take up the prosecution, of obtaining redress against the individual, if guilty. Cases had occurred in which from private or improper motives the public prosecutor refused to proceed. This would be remedied by allowing the private prosecutor to prosecute the case himself if the public prosecutor declined proceeding. The subject would soon be under discussion in Berlin, and he hoped that some such provision would be the result."); *see also* "Social Science Congress," LLOYD'S WEEKLY NEWSPAPER (London, England), Aug. 25, 1861, p. 7 (at the Social Science Congress held in Dublin under the presidency of Lord Brougham, Lord Brougham said: "Though there might be defects in the Prussian system, the institution of public prosecutors was of a very great benefit: and he thought it very desirable to have a responsible minister of justice for this country. The want of such a system was a very great defect in England. He could take no blame to himself in this matter, for one of the last efforts he made before quitting office was to introduce a system of public prosecutors: but it was thought too large a step to take at once to involve the whole country in a system of public prosecutors. In Scotland the private prosecutor was technically required to obtain the 'concurrence' of the lord advocate, but that concurrence was never withheld unless in extraordinary cases in which there was obvious cause for so doing.").

272. Thomas D. Lynch & Todd J. Dicker, eds., Handbook of Organizational Theory and Management: The Philosophical Approach 116 (1998); 4 Alexander Taylor Milne, ed., The Collected Works of Jeremy Bentham: The Correspondence of Jeremy Bentham xxiv (2017); Michael S. Pike, The Principles of Policing 6, 7, 135, 195 n.15 (1985); Steven M. Cox, David Massey, Connie M. Koski & Brian D. Fitch, Introduction to Policing 20 (4th ed. 2020); K. G. Simpson, ed., Henry Fielding, Justice Observed 17 (1985); Kurland & Waters, *supra* note 252, at 497.

273. May, *supra* note 108, at 194; *see also id.* ("Previous customs and formed habits, however, mitigated against the innovation, for the English were wont to equate public prosecution with political tyranny."); *id.* at 194–95 ("In the 1830s public prosecution was not in the forefront of the reformers' minds, and only a few references to it can be found either in the parliamentary records or the legal professional press. The *Law Magazine*'s review of Wontner's *Old Bailey Experience* remarked in passing, '[T]he criminal business of the metropolis can never be conducted in a satisfactory manner, until a public prosecutor shall have been appointed.' ... The *Legal Observer* raised the issue in the course of its discussion of prisoners' counsel. One of the 'great evils' in the English criminal justice system, according to an article in that journal, was 'making the party who suffers by the crime the prosecutor in the punishment of it.' His may have been the immediate injury or loss, but 'the injury set forth in the major proposition is an injury done to society.' Vengeance 'thus belongs to the public, and should be demanded in the name of the public.' 'Private prosecutors standing up and demanding exile or death against their fellow-subject,—then begging, when the trial is over, for the repayment of the expense to which they are put,—make the Old Bailey Sessions among the most painful scenes that a feeling mind can contemplate.' Lushington too had suggested to the criminal law commissioners 'the great importance of considering whether there ought not to be some public prosecutor,' someone who would not only oversee the prosecution in court but look earlier to the evidence and see that the prosecution was properly brought."). In the late eighteenth century and early nineteenth century, prominent British reformers, including Jeremy Bentham and Sir Robert Peel, argued that the system of private prosecutions was breeding unacceptable evils. Among those evils was the initiation of prosecutions for revenge and personal animosity and arrangements between attorneys and police to secure prosecutions. Cardenas, *supra* note 1, at 362; *see also* Kurland & Waters, *supra* note 252, at 497–99 (detailing proposals to implement a public prosecution system in England, including those of the Select Committee of 1798, those suggested, among others, by Jeremy Bentham, Henry Fielding, Sir Samuel Romilly, Sir Robert Peel, Lord John Russell when he was Home Secretary, Lord Chief Justice Denman, and Lord Brougham); 5 The Foreign Review, and Continental Miscellany 166 n.† (1830) ("It seems to us that the system of private prosecutions has been chiefly founded on the belief, that *revenge*, not the *prevention of crime*, is the proper end of punishment.") (italics in original); 5 Sir Joseph Arnould, Lives of the Chief Justices of England 90–93 (1881) (noting that in 1819 Lord Denman, as penal reformer and a member of Parliament, "spoke in favor of the Attorney-General, Sir Samuel Shepherd's, Bill for abolishing the antiquated abuses of appeals of murder, and wager of battle on writs of right").

274. *See generally* Works of Henry Lord Brougham (1873).

275. The Times (London, England), Apr. 13, 1855, p. 6 ("The resolutions on the criminal law recently moved by Lord Brougham in the House of Lords are deserving of respect and consideration, not only on account of the high authority from which they emanate, but of the numerous and important questions which they suggest. In 18 resolutions the whole career of a criminal, from his apprehension to his trial, conviction, and imprisonment, is sketched out .... [B]ut it will not be denied that the most disputable as well as the most important of these recommendations is that for the establishment of a Public Prosecutor, which runs as follows:—'That the prosecution of offenders should be intrusted to an officer appointed by the Government, with such number of subordinate officers as may be required for conducting prosecutions in the counties and larger towns.' We confess that at the present moment we are more struck with the

difficulties than with the advantages of this scheme, and, as the matter is involved with some obscurity of thought and ambiguity of words, we will offer a few observations on the several meanings which may be attached to the term 'Public Prosecutor.'"). Lord Brougham was very active in issues pertaining to the court system and the judicial system. "Department of Jurisprudence," FREEMAN'S JOURNAL (Dublin, Ireland), Aug. 17, 1861, p. 3 ("The President of the Association, the Right Hon. Lord Brougham, was in present in this department, and occupied the chair for a considerable time during the proceedings, and took an active part in the discussions of the department."); "County Court Returns," THE TIMES (London, England), Mar. 19, 1858, p. 6 ("His proposition was that the defendant in a criminal suit should have the right if he chose of being examined upon oath, subject to the cross-examination of the prosecution. It was absurd to say that the Crown was the prosecutor. In 99 cases out of every 100 there was a private prosecutor, who could be examined upon oath, and cross-examined, while the mouth of the accused was stopped.").

276. THE TIMES (London, England), Apr. 13, 1855, p. 6. Jeremy Bentham, the newspaper wrote, "dwelt much on the hardship of making a man pay for bringing to justice another who had wronged him, and no doubt he was right; but this abuse has been long remedied, and every prosecutor is now indemnified at the public expense, unless for some flagrant misconduct the Court see fit to disallow his expenses, a discretion to which no reasonable man can object." "So long as the plan of circuits is retained," *The Times* editorialized, "something must be found for our young barristers to do, and we know no better training than that of conducting criminal cases." *Id.*; *see also* "Imperial Parliament," MORNING CHRONICLE (London, England), July 13, 1855, p. 2 ("Mr. M'MAHON moved the following new clause . . . :—'Whereas by law every nuisance of a public nature is abateable by indictment, but the expense attending the prosecution thereof has deterred parties suffering thereby from seeking the remedy given by law, and great inconv[en]ience has arisen, and a great degree of injury has been and is now sustained by her Majesty's subjects in various parts of the United Kingdom in consequence of this state of the law, be it enacted, that in case of any indictment or information by a private prosecutor for any nuisance whatsoever, if judgment shall be given for the defendant, he shall be entitled to recover from the prosecutor the costs sustained by the said defendant by reason of such indictment or information, and in the abatement of the nuisance pursuant to the judgment of the Court, such costs so to be recovered by the defendant or prosecutor respectively to be taxed by the proper officer of the Court before which the said indictment or information is tried.' The ATTORNEY-GENERAL opposed the insertion of the clause as at variance with the general spirit of the bill. The clause was negatived."); DAILY NEWS (London, England), July 13, 1855, p. 2 ("Mr. M'MAHON proposed a clause that 'in case of an indictment or information by a private prosecutor, for a nuisance, costs to abide the event.' The ATTORNEY-GENERAL objected to the clause. It would introduce a principle that was somewhat novel, and totally without the scope of the bill. The clause was negatived without a division.").

277. LORD BROUGHAM'S SPEECH ON CRIMINAL LAW PROCEDURE, HOUSE OF LORDS, 23RD MARCH, 1855, at 17 (1855). As Lord Brougham further stated of private prosecution in his 1855 speech: "It is the relic of days when the great body of the people were held in property as slaves by a few landowners; when one class of the community was privileged from capital punishment because capable of reading; when men were tried, not by the evidence of witnesses, but by the belief of their adherents, ignorant of the whole matter, or by their own skill and courage in single combat; nay, when trial by jury had not yet superseded the ordeal of fire and water. In those dismal times, all crimes could be compounded by the payment of a sum of money, or a number of beasts while money was not yet known; every man's head being valued at a certain price,—his Weregeld, as the Saxon called it, his Eric, as the Celt had it,—from the Sovereign down to the peasant." *Id.*

278. "Public Prosecutors. Recommendations of the Select Committee," THE GUARDIAN (London, England), May 29, 1856, p. 4. This proposal met with some opposition, with one editorial in *The Standard* arguing that private prosecutors should be awarded more costs and that a public prosecution system would be flawed. THE STANDARD (London, England), Jan. 9, 1857, p. 2 ("[N]ow there is a scheme proposed which we cannot contemplate without apprehension. We allude to the plan for the establishment of public prosecutors. The present law, regulating prosecutions, is in one respect defective. The costs which the private prosecutor incurs in the discharge of his duty to the public are very seldom covered by the costs which the Court allows him. This is unjust, and the rate of allowance should be made more liberal than it is; but his remedy has not met with half the official favour that the idea of establishing public prosecutors has met

with. Yet, we believe, that anyone considering the subject, and having before his eyes the late disclosures concerning official mismanagement, would willingly experience in his own person the average degree of trouble and expense incurred in instituting a prosecution rather than see the detection of crime and the protection of life and property handed over to placeholders. As the criminal law stands now it is difficult indeed for a guilty man to escape. The business of prosecution is confided in London to men of proved ability, indeed, but by no means in a secure position, while on circuit it is confided to men whose position is yet to make. A flaw in the indictment, or a blunder in cross-examination, would shake the reputation of a senior, and might fatally damage that of a junior. The result of this is, that none but men of talent get prosecutions to conduct, and that those who do get them conduct them with great care; but we have no security that either of these facts will exist when the choice of a prosecutor is entrusted to men whose living does not depend, like that of an attorney, on the skill with which the object of their choice performs his duty, and when the public prosecutor himself knows that his salary is independent of his abilities or his industry. An attorney dare not habitually employ a stupid or idle barrister, because he is a relation or a friend, but a minister may easily appoint an incompetent public prosecutor to oblige an ally or secure a vote. A rising barrister will work hard, because if he blunders in one case he will not easily get another, but a place-holder draws his salary every quarter whether he does his work well or ill.").

279. "Obituary," THE LAW JOURNAL (June 11, 1881), pp. 258–59.

280. The Jurist: Containing Articles on Legal Subjects, All Important Statutes, the Rules and Orders of the Various Courts, the Gazettes, Cause Lists, and Miscellaneous Legal Information for the Year 1856 (1857), Vol. II, Part II, pp. 296–98. For centuries, English private prosecutions and public prosecutions for "breach of the king's peace" coexisted. RICHARD R. CHERRY, LECTURES ON THE GROWTH OF CRIMINAL LAW IN ANCIENT COMMUNITIES 97 (1890) ("The gradual change from a system of private revenge or pecuniary compensation to a true system of Criminal Law was… materially assisted by the growth of the royal power.… [O]nce the Sovereign became strong enough to preserve the peace, the reasons in favour of a system of fines for the sake of preserving order and putting an end to blood feuds ceased to exist…."); *id.* at 97–98 ("Royal prosecutions did not at once supersede prosecutions by the parties themselves. This was only a gradual process. All through the Middle Ages, and indeed long after that period is considered to have come to a close, two systems of prosecutions for crimes continued to exist side by side. Either the party aggrieved (or his relatives in case of his death) might institute a proceeding which was called an appeal, or, if he failed to do so, the Sovereign might take up the matter and prosecute for the violation of his peace. Gradually appeals became rarer and rarer, and at last entirely obsolete; but they were not formally abolished until the year 1819.").

Chapter 2 Notes

1. ANTHONY CHADWICK, AN EMERALD GUIDE TO THE ENGLISH LEGAL SYSTEM: A COMPREHENSIVE GUIDE TO ALL ASPECTS OF THE ENGLISH LEGAL SYSTEM 64–65 (2011); *see also* F. W. MAITLAND, THE CONSTITUTIONAL HISTORY OF ENGLAND: A COURSE OF LECTURES DELIVERED BY F. W. MAITLAND 481 (H. A. L. Fisher, ed. 1974) ("The king's Attorney-General has power to stop any criminal prosecution without pardon. All criminal proceedings (now that appeals are abolished) are in law at the suit of the king—*Rex v. A. B.* If the king's Attorney-General states that he will not prosecute (enters a *nolle prosequi*) then proceedings are at an end, though other proceedings may be begun. This power is sparingly exercised to stop prosecutions which are obviously vexatious. The safeguard consists in this, that the Attorney-General is expected to be a member of the House of Commons, and according to usage a member of the Ministry, though not of the Cabinet. Any use he may make of this power might thus be called in question: he could not use it for political purposes without the approval of the House of Commons."); *id.* ("The king has had officers, 'law officers,' Attorney-General and Solicitor-General, charged with the duty of bringing the greatest offenders to justice, but it is in the power of any man to begin a criminal prosecution by presenting a bill of indictment to a grand jury, and as a matter of fact, until very lately, it has generally been left to those who have suffered by crime to bring an ordinary criminal to justice. This work is now falling more and more into the hands of a Director of Public Prosecutions….").

2. "A Public Prosecutor," LEEDS MERCURY (Leeds, England), Feb. 22, 1879, p. 11 ("Among the Government measures which will be welcomed by the majority of the community and by which medico-legal work generally is likely to be facilitated is Bill 68, to provide for the appointment of a solicitor for public prosecutions, paid by salary, and armed with authority and power, though in no way interfering with the rights and privileges of private prosecutors. It is much to be desired that this measure, amended as may hereafter appear expedient, should find its way to the statute book."); "The Prosecution of Offences Bill," MORNING POST (London, England), Mar. 15, 1879, p. 3 (containing debate in Parliament over the bill to provide for the appointment of persons to institute prosecutions); "Local and District News," HAMPSHIRE ADVERTISER (Southampton, England), Oct 15, 1879, p. 3 ("The measure providing a public prosecutor was an excellent and much desired one. It created a public prosecutor, with a central office, whose duty it would be to advise and assist private prosecutors and the police, who were, in some sense, private prosecutors; whilst in cases of difficulty and expense he would be himself the prosecutor, and thus obviate that failure of justice which often occurred, especially in cases of ingenious fraud. What was everybody's business was too often no one's, and people who had been swindled out of their money preferred often with strong language to pocket the first loss rather than prosecute and throw good money after bad in further legal proceedings."). As Parliament debated the bill to create a Director of Public Prosecutions, it was well known that the vast majority of criminal cases in England were brought by private prosecutors. THE STANDARD (London, England), Dec. 19, 1878, p. 5 ("In theory, of course, the QUEEN is the prosecutor in all criminal cases, and is so in fact whenever the prosecution passes into the hands of the Treasury or the police. But the great majority of cases, and the most important, especially from a commercial point of view, are as a rule in the hands of private prosecutors, who, being *domini litis*, are able at any moment to effect a questionable compromise. In the interests of public justice, a criminal charge once preferred ought to be persistently carried through. Were this the rule, not only should we avoid the scandal of seeing our police-courts converted into a mechanism for the prompt recovery of doubtful debts, but we should also be spared the graver disgrace of knowing that actual offenders had bought themselves off by prompt and full payment. Were a Public Prosecutor appointed for each district, and were it not possible to take criminal proceedings, even in their most initial stages, without his *fiat*, abuses of the kind to which we have alluded would become extinct."); SYDNEY MORNING HERALD (Sydney, Australia), Nov. 29, 1875, p. 3 ("There could be no doubt that in England a majority of the prosecutions were conducted at the expense of a private prosecutor, the Attorney-General not interfering unless in some case of public importance."); *see also* GERHARD FALK, THE AMERICAN CRIMINAL JUSTICE SYSTEM: HOW IT WORKS, HOW IT DOESN'T, AND HOW TO FIX IT 23–24 (2012) ("it has been estimated that the English prosecutors handled only about 8 percent of all complaints").

3. Thomas J. Robinson, *Private Prosecution in Criminal Cases*, 4 WAKE FOREST INTRAMURAL L. REV. 300, 306 (1968); *see also* Prosecution of Offenses Act of 1908, 8 Edw. 7, ch. 3, § 2 ("Nothing in the Prosecution of Offenses act, 1879, and 1884, or in this Act, shall preclude any person from instituting or carrying on any criminal proceedings, but the Director of Public Prosecutions may undertake at any stage, the conduct or those proceedings if he thinks fit.").

4. "Prosecution of Offences Act, 1879," HUDDERSFIELD DAILY CHRONICLE (Huddersfield, England), Dec. 10, 1879, p. 4; *see also* THE DAILY NEWS (London, England), Dec. 20, 1879, p. 5 ("It will be interesting to know what steps the Government is about to take in the case of the important Act of Parliament which comes into operation on New Year's Day. The appointment of a Public Prosecutor has been so much canvassed, and so generally approved that there should be no delay in giving complete efficiency to the provisions of the Act. Much will depend on the adequacy of the selected official. The salary is 2,000*l.*; and this ought to secure a thoroughly efficient man, nor should the appointment of the minor officials be delayed. The Act is but a step in the reconstruction of our whole system of criminal jurisprudence. But then it is the first step. There can be no doubt that it will be supplemented by subsequent legislation. In the meantime the first start should be made with purpose and vigour. It is easy to cite cases where the original appointment of unwilling or incapable officials has made important statutes utterly nugatory. The Act which becomes law next month is worded in the very spirit of compromise. It reserves all private prosecutors the power to institute, undertake, or carry our any criminal proceedings. It gives to the ATTORNEY-GENERAL the right to make, rescind, vary, and add to the regulations for carrying its own provisions into effect. This

it is at once ancillary to the old system and but tentative in the very theory of its own operation. It becomes the more imperative that it should be fairly launched in its career by the nomination of an efficient man."); *see also* "The Shooting Case at St. John's-Wood," THE TIMES (London, England), Jan. 12, 1881, p. 10 ("Mr. W. Lane O'Neill, solicitor for the prosecution in this case, writes to us that, during the proceedings before the magistrate on Friday, he used the following words:—'The Act appointing Public Prosecutors does without prejudice to private prosecutors.' Mr. O'Neill explains that by section 7 of the Public Prosecutors Act, 1879, 42 and 43 Vic., cap. 22, it is expressly provided that nothing in that Act shall interfere with the rights of any person to institute, undertake, or carry on any criminal proceedings. Mr. O'Neill cannot conceive that any person can have a higher or more sacred right to institute such proceedings than the father, mother, brothers, and sisters of the deceased who he represents."); "The St. John's Wood Shooting Case," DAILY NEWS (London, England), Jan. 15, 1881, p. 6 ("On the prisoner being placed in the dock, Mr. O'Neill, who, at the second hearing of the case, had prosecuted for the relatives of the deceased, again drew attention to the fact that the Public Prosecutor had intervened and taken the case out of his hands. He contended that the Public Prosecutor could not oust a private prosecutor."); FALK, *supra* note 2, at 24 ("The history of British public prosecution did not really begin until 1879, when Parliament passed the Prosecution of Offences Act—this, despite early criticism of the private prosecution of crimes. In fact, Henry VIII proposed in 1534 that the penal statutes of England be prosecuted by public prosecutors throughout the kingdom .... His suggested was rejected by Parliament.").

5. SARAH OWEN & JAMIE MACKENZIE, THE COMPLETE GUIDE TO INVESTIGATIONS AND ENFORCEMENT (2010) (noting the appointment of Sir John Maule as the Director of Public Prosecutions); JOSHUA ROZENBERG, THE CASE FOR THE CROWN: THE INSIDE STORY OF THE DIRECTOR OF PUBLIC PROSECUTIONS 19 (1987) (same); JAMES TAYLOR, BOARDROOM SCANDAL: THE CRIMINALIZATION OF COMPANY FRAUD IN NINETEENTH-CENTURY BRITAIN 191 (2013) (same).

6. "The Judicature Commission and the Appointment of a Public Prosecutors," ECONOMIST (Sept. 5, 1874), p. 1076 ("The 'Fifth and Final Report' of the Judicature Commission relates mainly to the subject of a 'public prosecutor,' and is not doubt somewhat disappointing. The Commissioners, though commending the institution of the office as likely to 'add materially to the efficiency of the administration of criminal justice in the country,' have not agreed among themselves as to the best method of constituting the office."); *see also id.* ("There are two ways in which the present system of private prosecution is visibly defective. The *first* is that the private prosecutor who has suffered by the crime of the accused has often no interest, more than that of any other private individual, to prosecute. The law trusts to a feeling of private vindictiveness which frequently does not exist, and which will perhaps continue to diminish as the subject is looked at more and more from the point of view of enlightened self-interest. Especially as regards petty crimes, the expense and trouble of a prosecution to an individual are quite out of proportion to any possible gratification of his vindictive feelings which is his supposed inducement to prosecute, while frequently there can be no real vindictive feeling at all, the prosecution being recognised as useful for the protection of society but nothing more. To impose upon individuals among whom such opinions prevail the duty of prosecuting is to make sure that the duty will be neglected, and the wonder perhaps is that the loss to the community by the neglect is not greater than it is. It is sometimes urged, indeed, that the private prosecutor should be animated by some public spirit, but unfortunately for this view he is the person who has suffered most previously by the particular crime in question, and is consequently the last person who should be called on by the community to undertake any troublesome and expensive duty, which necessarily means an additional loss, in connection with it. The *second* way in which private prosecution is mischievous is the disposition which seems to have been growing up of late to use the criminal law as a means of recovering damages, or for some similar motive. The private prosecutor, having the right of initiative, holds up the criminal law *in terrorem* over the accused, and makes the abandonment of the prosecution conditional on the success of his personal object.") (italics in original).

7. The Lord Advocate has long played a prominent role in Scotland. Robinson, *supra* note 3, at 309 ("Scotland, in 1587, gave a public prosecutor the unquestioned right to prosecute all crimes. The status of the public prosecutor in Scotland is very well summarized in the case of *King's Advocate v. Lord Douglas*: 'The King's Advocate was authorized to act as public prosecutor in the time of James VI. This is implied in (The Act of) 1579, c.78, and still more by (The Act of) 1587, c.77, which authorized the ... Advocate to

pursue, although the private party did not. He may have had power previously from the Sovereign to prosecute in the pleas of the Crown; but in that large class of crimes, then prosecuted at the instance of the private party, his power was confirmed and finally recognized by these statutes; so that, since the date of the latter Act his right to prosecute all crimes has been unquestioned.' The Act of 1587 referred to did not withdraw from the party injured his right to prosecute, but allowed the Lord Advocate to gradually assume complete control over the administration of criminal law.").

8. THE TIMES (London, England), Dec. 24, 1879, p. 9; *see also id.* ("In France, and almost everywhere but in England, the business of punishing crime is deemed to be too high and perilous a prerogative to be placed in private hands, and is made peculiarly the duty of the Government. The Act which comes into force on the 1st of January does not incorporate this principle, and will not assimilate our law in this respect to that of other countries. It will leave untouched the rights of private person to prefer bills for criminal offences or to apply for summonses against any one they think fit to assail. The strange and, if it be well considered, somewhat barbarous idea that a crime is an offence against the injury party for which he ought to have vengeance in the form of a prosecution will continue. The Government has often been recommended, and sometimes by authorities of great weight, to put an end to this anomaly in our legal system. The LORD CHIEF JUSTICE, for instance, at a time when the Judicature Commission was engaged in its labours, strongly urged the establishment of a Public Prosecutor, who should institute personally, or by his representatives, all prosecutions. Theoretically, this is probably the best and only proper system But it would necessitate the appointment of a large number of officials. Thousands of prosecutions are annually conducted at Assizes or Quarter Sessions. In thousands of instances investigation must be made to see whether there is ground for taking criminal proceedings. This work is parceled out among a vast number of persons, and if it were to be taken out of their hands and to devolve on any one department, the staff must be immense; and the cost of carrying out those multifarious duties would be such as to deter most Governments from submitting to the House of Commons a scheme of the necessary dimensions. All rounded and complete measures for the establishment of Public Prosecutors have been hitherto wrecked on the question of expense, and the Act of last Session was adopted only because it was tentative and fragmentary. It was well understood that it would have no appreciable effect on the run of trials at Assizes and Quarter Sessions, and it became law when a more ambitious scheme would have been doomed."). The Judicature Commission did an extensive study of the private versus public prosecution issue. *See* REPORTS FROM COMMISSIONERS, Vol. (1874) ("First Appendix" containing papers on public prosecutors with minutes of evidence from the Judicature Commission and "The Memorandum of the Lord Chief Justice of England on the Advisability of Appointing a Public Prosecutor").

9. THE TIMES (London, England), Dec. 24, 1879, p. 9; *see also id.* ("In the case of many crimes against society there is no one especially injured, and therefore no one who has any direct interest to call for the enforcement of the law. And if a private prosecutor is found, what security is there that he will do his duty? He is exposed to solicitations of all sorts; and if he be weak or corrupt, or too compassionate, a crime which ought to have been laid bare in all its ramifications and punished with due solemnity will be covered by some secret compromise. He may be tempted to abuse his position and strange powers in order to gain a personal end; and too often a prosecution is from first to last an unworthy attempt to procure circuitously an advantage which is not to be got by any civil remedy, or to indulge a base passion which could not be avowed in a court of justice. The public little know the degree to which the criminal law is perverted into an instrument of petty extortion. It is only occasionally and accidentally that this iniquity, this tampering with justice at its springs, crops up. Of course a practical people could not allow the state of things which we have described to remain without seeking a remedy, and various palliatives have been applied. A rude system of public prosecutions exists. If an important crime is brought to the attention of the Home Secretary, this Solicitor to the Treasury sooner or later intervenes, and the Attorney-General prosecutes. Sometimes a public department or a municipality, having more or less remote connexion with a crime, takes up the prosecution of it. Sometimes, too—and this is the more common case—pure accident determines who is bound over to prosecute. It must be owned that crimes which excite wide interest are pretty sure to be investigated by the Law Officers.... But there are obscure crimes which never come to the notice of the Solicitor to the Treasury, and the perpetrators of which go unpunished. Suspicious events, with, in all probability, a core of crime in them, are allowed to pass without examination.... The new Act which Mr.

Maule has to carry out may help a little to diminish these scandals. He will be able, at all events, to attend to details which the Law Officers of the Crown cannot follow. But a Director of Public Prosecutions cannot root up abuses which must, it is to be feared, accompany every system of private prosecution. The Act is, perhaps, most valuable as an earnest and promise of what may exist if ever Parliament should see fit to deny the inborn right of every Englishman to set the criminal law in motion whenever it seems good to him in his wisdom or folly.").

10. Newcastle Weekly Courant (Newcastle upon Tyne), Dec. 23, 1879, p. 4 ("An important step has just been taken towards the reform of our criminal law, by the appointment of Mr Maule, Recorder of Leeds, to the post of Director of Public Prosecutions, under the Prosecution of Offences Act of last Session. Great hardship has been inflicted by the onus of prosecution in many extensive banking frauds at first being thrown upon individuals, although the expenses and responsibility are ultimately borne by the Treasury. Three classes of cases are expected to be dealt with by the new official: very important cases in which nobody cares to prosecute; others in which private prosecutors find the work too expensive or difficult; and a third class, which do not properly lie outside the ordinary routine, but to which for certain reasons the special attention of the Director may be called, just as in some severe sentences the Home Secretary is memorialised for a reversal. The details of this arrangement are to be worked out by the Attorney-General, subject to the revision of the Lord Chancellor and the approval of Parliament; and although not obtaining the ample powers possessed by a French Procureur Royal, the Director will be doubtless furnished with powers to supply the long-felt want of a public prosecutor, which has allowed many criminals to escape punishment."); The Standard (London, England), Dec. 24, 1879, p. 5 ("The Government have at length taken the first step towards the practical realisation of the Reforms in the Criminal Law promised by the Prosecution of Offences Act of last Session. The appointment of Mr. Maule, Q.C., to the post of Director of Public Prosecutions, which was created by that Act, will be welcomed not only by the Profession to which he belongs, but by the public who entertain, perhaps, somewhat extravagant hopes respecting the benefits to be conferred upon them under his superintendence. Some little curiosity has been felt in the Profession, ever since the Act became law, as to the manner in which the post it created was to be filled up, and more than one name has been mentioned in connection with the appointment, but no one can doubt the propriety of the choice which has at length been made. Mr. Maule is a Bencher of the Inner Temple, having been called in the year 1847, and having received the honour of a silk gown in 1866. He is also Recorder of Leeds, where he is, we believe, presiding today at the Borough Sessions; and, though not a prominent advocate, he has always been regarded as a skilled and experienced lawyer, having for some time represented the Inner Temple on the Incorporated Council of Law Reporting, and also on the Council of Legal Education. In addition to these positions, Mr. Maule is well known as having acted for the Government on several important inquiries, particularly that which related to the Jamaica disturbances in 1865, and the Commission which more recently investigated the administration of Dr. Barnardo's schools for destitute boys. In August 1868, Mr. Maule was appointed to inquire into the pay and organisation of the Metropolitan Police, and he may be presumed to have acquired, in the course of this experience, much valuable information with respect to the department over which he is now called upon to preside. In short, there can be no doubt that the new Director of Public Prosecutions will be thoroughly qualified by training and actual experience for the discharge of the novel and important duties which will devolve upon him."); *id.* ("It is an obvious remark, which in no way diminishes the sincerity of this expression of belief, that no one as yet knows clearly what those duties are. In moving the second reading of the Bill in the House of Lords, last May, Lord Cairns stated that the object with which it had been introduced was to meet exceptional cases, such as large commercial frauds, in which private persons could not be expected to undertake the expense of prosecutions. Every one knows that such cases as these, and many others of like magnitude, are already undertaken by the Treasury, and had the Bill aimed at no more than this it would have been little more in effect than an act for regulating the position and amending the title of the Treasury Solicitor. As a matter of fact, it professes, on the face of it, to do a good deal more. The Second Section declares that it shall be the duty of the Director of Public Prosecutions, under the superintendence of the Attorney General, to institute, undertake, or carry on such criminal proceedings, and to give such advice and assistance to chief officers of police, clerks to justices, and other persons, whether officers or not, concerned in any criminal proceeding, respecting the conduct of that proceeding, as may

for the time being be prescribed by certain regulations to be made under the Act, or may be directed in special instances by the ATTORNEY GENERAL. It is plain that the real duties thrown upon the Director of Public Prosecutions will depend almost entirely upon the interpretation of this Section, and the nature of the rules made under it. It can hardly be supposed that the Director will be regarded as a consulting criminal Barrister, to whose chambers private prosecutors may resort from all parts of the country to get indictments drawn and opinions on evidence written without the necessity of paying a fee. Not one, nor twenty Directors, would be sufficient to get through the mass of work which would be showered upon so accommodating and convenient an officer. On the other hand, it is clear that the Director's functions will not be confined to those cases, such as charges of murder or commercial fraud, with which the Solicitor to the Treasury is at present called upon to deal. A comparison of the Second and Seventh Sections of the Act will show that while the Director is expected to undertake certain prosecutions, and conduct them in his own name on behalf of the Government, very much as the Treasury Solicitor does now, there is clearly another class of cases contemplated which are to remain in the hands of private prosecutors, subject to official superintendence and advice. The conclusion would appear to be that there are to be three classes of criminal cases instituted, to one of which every case that is brought under the notice of the department will be assigned, at the discretion of the Director. The first class comprises all those cases which Government will conduct, either because of their special importance or because nobody else can be found to undertake them, though they are too serious to be allowed to drop. The second class will be made up of those cases of less magnitude where there is a private prosecutor, but one whom the difficulties or importance of the case entitle to official assistance and advice, though not to absolute relief. The third class will include all those cases which are of so trivial or common-place a character as to be left to the ordinary administration of justice, in which it may be presumed that the Director will refuse to interfere, unless his attention is drawn to the fact that something is going wrong. Anything like a compounding of a felony, for example, such as the Fifth Section appears to contemplate, would be a miscarriage of justice which even in a trivial case would demand correction and rebuke.").

11. "Cheshire Quarter Sessions," CHESHIRE OBSERVER (Chester, England), Oct. 18, 1879, p. 7; *see also* "City Quarter Sessions," BERROW'S WORCESTER JOURNAL (Worcester, England), Oct. 18, 1879, p. 7 (in a grand jury charge to the Michaelmas Quarter Sessions of the Peace before "Mr. F. A. Bosanquet, Recorder," the "learned RECORDER," in laying out the law, said the following in his charge: "Another Act of great importance provided for a want which had been generally felt. There had not hitherto been a public prosecutor. The new Act provided for the establishment of a director of public prosecutions, whose duty it would be to give advice and assistance to chief officers of police, justices' clerks, and other persons concerned in criminal proceedings in cases of difficulty and extraordinary importance, and also in cases which might be prescribed by rules made under the Act. The Act provided that the director of public prosecutions should have returned to him all proceedings and documents in any cases which he might require, so that he might have an opportunity of properly conducting prosecutions, and also that he should have returned to him any cases where a private prosecutor withdrew from a prosecution or refused to failed to proceed with it, the object being to prevent private persons withdrawing from prosecutions which it was the public interest should be proceeded with. The Act did not take away the right of any private prosecutor to conduct a prosecution himself."); "Hull Chamber of Commerce and Shipping," LEEDS MERCURY (Leeds, England), Oct. 31, 1879, p. 3 (at the annual meeting of the Hull Chamber of Commerce and Shipping held at Bowlalley-lane, the following remarks were made about the new law passed by the members of Parliament: "They had got the appointment of public prosecutor. The Home Secretary had the power to appoint a gentleman—a barrister, of course, of a certain number of years' standing—as a director of prosecutions, and he could appoint six assistants. That was an important measure, because there was no doubt that in past years grave frauds had been allowed to escape the proper consequences of their conduct, from the mismanagement or indifference of private prosecutors. Now there was power for the Government to step in, and they could take prosecutions into their own hands. (Hear, hear.)"); *accord* "Hull Chamber of Commerce. Mr. Norwood, M.P., on the Work of the Past Session.", YORK HERALD (York, England), Oct. 31, 1878, p. 6.

12. THE TIMES (London, England), Apr. 12, 1883, p. 9; *see also id.* ("It is not necessary, and it would be quite unjust, to throw the blame of the shortcomings upon the present eminent occupier of the office. His

powers are limited. His means of acting with efficiency are not at all what they should be. The so-called Director of Public Prosecutions has singularly little power either to direct or to prosecute. Mr. Justice Hawkins made, last December, at the Old Bailey, very strong remarks upon the fact that prosecutions of the most important character were left to shift for themselves; and the Lord Chief Justice expressed on Monday, in the case of 'The Queen v. Taylor,' his surprise that an inquiry so pre-eminently suitable for the intervention of the Director of Public Prosecutions should have been left to private enterprise. In the House of Commons, too, there have been not a few complaints as to the timidity or inactivity of that functionary. Probably all these criticisms have been coloured more or less by the erroneous assumption that Sir John Maule is Public Prosecutor, when, in truth, he is nothing of the sort. He is armed with no powers worth speaking of which do not belong to any member of the public. He is little more than an appendage to the Solicitor to the Treasury, with a fine-sounding name added thereto; and the title of Public Prosecutor might with less inaccuracy be reserved for the Attorney-General, who directs the Director, and who has, in fact, certain substantial privileges. It is the duty of the Director to institute, undertake, or carry on criminal proceedings under the superintendence of the Attorney-General, and to give advice and assistance to the chief officers of police, clerks to justices, and other persons concerned in any criminal proceedings. But any private person has as good a right as he to set the criminal law in motion. That free trade in prosecutions which has so long been the characteristic of our criminal law is retained.... Limited though the conception of his office was, it is in fact much less than was intended. Parliament contemplated the appointment of no fewer than six assistants to the Director; and it is a partial and very important explanation of the poverty of the results, too apt to be forgotten, that up to this date only one has been appointed."); *id.* ("The Official Judicial Statistics of the country—by the way, probably the most defective documents of the kind published by any civilized State—throw no light on the amount or nature of the business transacted by the new department. Indeed, its name does not once occur therein. It appears to be the deliberate opinion of those who frame these statistics that the new office is not worth mentioning. They have some excuse. We should be much surprised if a review of the facts of the case since 1880 did not show that there has been no sensible improvement in the conduct of public prosecutions since the Prosecution of Offences Act came into operation. The Act which established the new office was, as may now be seen, one of those showy pieces of legislation which are in the main intended more to silence a troublesome cry than to meet a clear want of the time. People talked much about the propriety of having a Public Prosecutor, and a sort of toy was given them instead of the reality. The very real evils which led to the demand for a Public Prosecutor still exist, it is to be feared, with little diminution.").

13. *E.g.*, The Times (London, England), Aug. 3, 1883, p. 7 (containing Parliamentary debate on the subject).

14. *See also* Morning Post (London, England), Aug. 6, 1883, p. 4 ("The vote for the salaries and expenses incident to the office of Director of Public Prosecutions, which was taken at the close of last week, merited a far more exhaustive discussion than was accorded to it.").

15. *Id.*; *see also id.* ("In the case of misdemeanours private prosecutors have always been considered entitled to abandon the prosecution at pleasure, and hence the frequent recurrence of those unedifying scenes in public courts, when after, with much parade, a formidable case has been opened against a defendant, those conducting the prosecution have at a subsequent adjournment declared that on reconsideration it was felt that the case could not be sustained, and would, therefore, not be proceeded with, the real explanation being that the application of the screw supplied by the Criminal Law had compelled the defendant to disgorge and removed the only motive which induced the complainant to take action. In this, and in many similar cases, the question constantly arose, why is there not a Public Prosecutor; what cannot the State undertake the duty of vindicating its outraged laws and afform protection to its citizens by the punishment of offenders? At length Parliament gave the reply that was desired, and with a very great flourish of trumpets a Director of Public Prosecutions was called into existence.").

16. Sir Thomas Edlyne Tomlins, The Law-Dictionary, Explaining the Rise, Progress, and Present State of the British Law: Defining and Interpreting the Terms or Words of Art, and Comprising Also Copious Information on the Subjects of Trade and Government (4th ed. 1835) (entry for "Compounding Felony"); *see also* "Borough Sessions," Liverpool Mercury and Lancashire, Cheshire, and General Advertiser (Liverpool, England), Jan. 16, 1880, p. 6 ("The law against

compounding a felony, although perhaps not very often acted upon, was nevertheless a very beneficial one for many reasons. It was for the public good that felons should be prosecuted, and it would be a monstrous thing if private individuals should be allowed, for the purpose of getting money—even the money of which they had been robbed—to make a prosecution the subject matter of a bargain. The object of a prosecution was not to enable persons to get back their property, but to vindicate the law, and after steps had been taken at the public expense to bring offenders to justice, it would be a monstrous thing that, even for the purpose of getting back his money, a private prosecutor should be allowed to let off the person who was charged. But the real reason why bargains of that kind should be prohibited, was that they would give an opening to very serious extortion.").

17. Sir William Blackstone, Commentaries on the Laws of England: In Four Books; with an Analysis of the Work 95 (1832) (from the eighteenth London edition with a life of the author, and notes, by "Christian, Chitty, Lee, Hovenden, and Ryland").

18. Herbert Newman Mozley & George Crispe Whiteley, A Concise Law Dictionary 79–80 (1876) (italics in original).

19. Morning Post (London, England), Aug. 6, 1883, p. 4; *see also id.* ("The office was created to supply a want; but not only was the want not supplied, but a condition of things was created far worse than that which it was intended to remedy. Public complaints became frequent and loud; though, being unable to penetrate behind the scenes, the critics were by no means sure to whom the blame of a transparent failure ought to be attributed. Some were inclined to think that it was the fault of the individual who filled the office of Director of Public Prosecutions, and that all that was necessary was to replace him by one more competent to discharge his duties; others, on the contrary, went deeper in search of the root of the evil, and declared that the legislative restrictions imposed by Parliament were of a nature to paralyse the action of any official, however able or zealous."); *id.* ("The fact that the Government have practically recognised the failure of the scheme so recently sanctioned by the Legislature by the appointment of a committee to inquire into its shortcomings, renders it the less necessary to dwell now on its defects.... We are bound to conclude that it has been simply due to our inexperience in such matters that the late experiment has proved a failure. In Scotland a Public Prosecutor is one of the established institutions of the country, and in Ireland there are Crown Prosecutors in the various counties. In the Continental States the intervention of private individuals in setting the Criminal Law in motion is absolutely forbidden, all prosecutions being conducted by officials appointed for that purpose. To the French and other European systems there are, however, objections which would prove insuperable to our national prejudices, and all we can hope to attain is the creation of a department which will, at all events by its intervention, prevent those miscarriages of justice which are now of daily occurrence, owing to the poverty or the indifference of the victims of fraud and crime. What is required is an official who, when satisfied by the facts submitted to him that a criminal prosecution is necessary in the interests of society, will undertake it at the expense of the State. Hitherto we have been so accustomed to leave this duty to private individuals, save in what were rightly described in the House the other evening as 'sensational cases,' that it is difficult to reconcile ourselves to a burden heretofore so deftly avoided. But if the English Public Prosecutor is to be a reality instead of a sham, he must be put on a different footing and entrusted with very much larger discretionary power than at present. This, as we have already remarked, is acknowledged by the Government, and we can only hope that our next efforts in legislation in this direction will be more successful than the last. If we are to have a Public Prosecutor at all it is imperative that he should possess ample powers and be willing to use them.").

20. "The Harrogate Shooting Case," Blackburn Standard and Weekly Express (Blackburn, England), Dec. 10, 1892, p. 3.

21. "The Case of Colonel Valentine Baker," Pall Mall Gazette (London, England), July 29, 1875, p. 8.

22. "A Public Prosecutor," The Times (London, England), Feb. 15, 1888, p. 6 (reporting the Lord Ellenborough's words as follows: "In London a man was tried for murder said to be brought about by arson, when the jury brought in a verdict of not guilty. The prisoner was subsequently tried for arson, found guilty, and received an adequate punishment. The case, at Birmingham was that of a man and a woman tried for the murder of Colonel Fendall. The grand jury brought in a true bill for murder. A robbery clearly was committed with violence. The clothes of the murdered man were found with the parents of the man who was

tried for murder. He was found guilty of manslaughter, and received a trifling punishment only, not being subsequently tried for robbery with violence, though it resulted in death. He submitted that in the two cases quoted there was a great inequality before the law."). Lord Ellenborough was not the only one who believed that England lacked a public prosecutor. "Mr. John Morley and Mr. Thorburn, M.P.," THE TIMES (London, England), Nov. 2, 1887, p. 10 (in a letter to the editor of *The Times*, Walter Thorburn wrote: "In that part of Great Britain called England there is no public prosecutor on whose responsibility the criminal law is set in motion. Criminal charges are left to private prosecutors, with the result that criminal prosecution is not infrequently a mere weapon of private revenge, and is conducted on much the same terms as private litigation. It is not strange, therefore, that the criminal system in England is encumbered by many pedantries and inefficiencies which find no place in Scotland, where the whole criminal machinery is under the charge of a high officer of State, the Lord Advocate, his deputies, and the procurators fiscal.").

23. "A Public Prosecutor," THE TIMES (London, England), Feb. 15, 1888, p. 6 (the Lord Chancellor also stated: "Not knowing what cases would be cited by the noble lord, he had not acquainted himself with the details of the two that had been mentioned. But from the circumstances that had been stated he did not see how the action of a Public Prosecution could have averted the failures of justice which had been suggested."); *see also* "The Office of Public Prosecutor," THE STANDARD (London, England), Feb. 15, 1888, p. 2 (noting the comments of the Lord Chancellor in response to Lord Ellenborough, with the Lord Chancellor's remarks including these: "He believed Sir Augustus Stephenson performed his duty with skill and diligence, and he had heard no complaint. It was not the present intention of the Government to appoint an officer to look after all prosecutions.").

24. REYNOLDS'S NEWSPAPER (London, England), Jan. 3, 1892, p. 5.

25. "London Correspondence," BIRMINGHAM DAILY POST (Birmingham, England), Apr. 11, 1893, p. 4 ("A somewhat curious instruction to Committee is to be moved by the Under-Secretary for the Home Department (Mr. Herbert Gladstone) at the time for private business to-morrow as to the Salford Improvement Bill, empowering the repeal of a section of a local Act of fifteen years ago, which confers, or is alleged to confer, on the clerk for borough business the right to conduct, to the exclusion of the Director of Public Prosecutions and of private prosecutors, all prosecutions at assizes and quarter sessions for offences committed in Salford. This solicitude for the Public Prosecutor on the part of the Home Office is the more remarkable because that official takes no particular pains to keep himself in evidence, his refusal to proceed in the Howard de Walden case and his lukewarmness in regard to the Liberator frauds having sufficiently shown his little is attempted to be done by his department.").

26. "Oscar Wilde Angry," BUFFALO ENQUIRER (Buffalo, NY), Mar. 2, 1895, p. 1; "Oscar Wilde Begins a Libel Suit," WILMINGTON DAILY COMMERCIAL (Wilmington, DE), Mar. 2, 1895, p. 3.

27. Gordon Turriff, *The Importance of Being Earnestly Independent*, 2012 MICH. ST. L. REV. 281, 282–84:

> On Friday, March 1, 1895, Oscar Wilde visited a solicitor, C.O. Humphreys, in Humphreys's offices in Giltspur Chambers, Holborn Viaduct, London. Humphreys was "a most experienced criminal lawyer." Wilde was forty. "Two of his plays were running in the West End of London, both of them huge successes." A few years earlier, Wilde had taken up with Lord Alfred Douglas, a son of the eighth Marquis of Queensberry. Douglas, who was known as Bosie, was twenty-four in early 1895. Queensberry, who had developed the rules of boxing, was livid about his son's association with Wilde. Wilde and Douglas—Bosie particularly so—were bothered by Queensberry's opposition and resisted it. As events later proved, they didn't take Queensberry seriously enough.
>
> Ten days before Wilde saw Humphreys, Queensberry had left a card for Wilde with a porter at the Albemarle Club, off Picadilly. The porter, whose name was Wright, had read the card. Later he claimed not to have understood its meaning. On the card, although part of the message is very hard to decipher, Queensberry had written: "For Oscar Wilde posing as Somdomite." "Somdomite" was Queensberry's slip. Wright had placed the card in an envelope, probably without having shown it to anyone. On February 28th, Wright had given Wilde the envelope. Wilde was upset by Queensberry's imputation. He described Queensberry's words as "hideous." Douglas encouraged Wilde to prosecute Queensberry for criminal libel. Wilde didn't know what to do. Late that night, he consulted his friend, Robert Ross. Ross was twenty-five. Probably against

Ross's advice, Wilde went the next morning with Ross and Douglas to Humphreys's chambers. After some discussion, Humphreys recommended the proposed prosecution. That course proved to be disastrous for Wilde. Responsibility for the disaster is not uniformly placed on the same shoulders by Wilde biographers. Half a century later, Humphreys's son justified his father's endorsement of the prosecution as "natural and proper" "with the knowledge of the parties which [his father] then possessed."

It is said that before Humphreys gave Wilde his advice he had "asked Wilde point-blank on his solemn oath whether there was any truth in the libel [and that] Wilde solemnly assured him that he was absolutely innocent." Wilde's solemn assurance was a lie. His prosecution of Queensberry quickly collapsed under the weight of expected evidence of rent boys, turned up by Queensberry, apparently with help from an actor, Charles Brookfield, who is thought to have been "jealous of Wilde's success." On the Queensberry evidence, Wilde was himself successfully prosecuted for conduct that is no longer criminal, although it took two trials to convict him. He was sentenced to and served two years imprisonment with hard labor. After his release, he produced only one further work of art—*The Ballad of Reading Gaol*—although a long letter to Douglas, now known as De Profundis, which he brought with him out of prison, is very interesting. Wilde died an outcast in 1900, just forty-six. He was witty to the end. He had once declined an invitation "owing to a subsequent engagement." In his last weeks, spent very uncomfortably in bed at the Hotel d'Alsace in Paris, he quipped that either he or the wallpaper in his room had to go and that he was dying beyond his means.

In *The Ballard of Reading Gaol*, Oscar Wilde summed up his experience with the legal system in this way: I know not whether Laws be right, Or whether Laws be wrong; / All that we know who lie in goal Is that the wall is strong. / And that each day is like a year, A year whose days are long. Marilyn Aitken Robert, *Legal Lore: Sir Edward Carson Cross-Examines Oscar Wilde*, 30 LITIGATION 51, 67 (Spring 2004).

28. "Our London Letter," BELFAST NEWS-LETTER (Belfast, Northern Ireland), Feb . 11, 1892, p. 5; *see also* "London's Stage," ST. LOUIS POST-DISPATCH (St. Louis, MO), Feb. 20, 1892, p. 1 ("The event of the week in the theatrical world will be the production to-night at the St. James Theater of Mr. Oscar Wilde's play, 'Lady Windermere's Fan.' This is the first one of his plays to be produced in England, and there is much interest manifested in theatrical circles as to the reception of Mr. Wilde's first venture."); "Oscar Wilde's Play—'Lady Windermere's Fan' Successfully Presented in London," ST. LOUIS POST-DISPATCH (St. Louis, MO), Feb. 21, 1892, p. 3 ("Oscar Wilde's new play 'Lady Windermere's Fan' at the St. James Theater to-night, was a success. There were recalls after each act, and the author was demanded at the fall of the curtain.").

29. "The London Boards," DAILY PICAYUNE (New Orleans, LA), Nov. 13, 1892, p. 2; "Oscar Wilde's Play," WESTERN MAIL (Cardiff, Wales), Apr. 8, 1893, p. 4; "Haymarket Theatre," MORNING POST (London, England), Apr. 20, 1893, p. 5.

30. *George Bernard Shaw on An Ideal Husband - 1895, in* OSCAR WILDE: THE CRITICAL HERITAGE (Karl Beckson, ed. 2005); Marilyn Aitken Robert, *Legal Lore: Sir Edward Carson Cross-Examines Oscar Wilde*, 30 LITIGATION 51, 51 (Spring 2004).

31. PATRICIA FLANAGAN BEHRENDT, OSCAR WILDE: EROS AND AESTHETICS 158–59 (1991).

32. Joseph Bristow, *Homosexual Blackmail in the 1890s: The Fitzroy Street Raid, the Oscar Wilde Trials, and the Case of Cotsford Dick*, 22 AUSTRALASIAN J. VICTORIAN STUDIES 1, 11 (2018).

33. BUFFALO EXPRESS (Buffalo, NY), Feb. 28, 1895, p. 5.

34. ROY MORRIS, JR., DECLARING HIS GENIUS: OSCAR WILDE IN NORTH AMERICA (2013); Anne B. Goldstein, *Reasoning about Homosexuality: A Commentary on Janet Halley's "Reasoning about Sodomy: Act and Identity in and after* Bowers v. Hardwick," 79 VA. L. REV. 1781, 1786 (1993); Marilyn Aitken Robert, *Legal Lore: Sir Edward Carson Cross-Examines Oscar Wilde*, 30 LITIGATION 51, 52 (Spring 2004).

35. "The Charge against Lord Queensberry," MORNING POST (London, England), Apr. 4, 1895, p. 6.

36. Richard Davenport-Hines, "The Marquess of Queensberry: Wilde's Nemesis by Linda Stratmann," THE GUARDIAN, Apr. 17, 2013, https://www.google.com/amp/s/amp.theguardian.com/books/2013/apr/17/marquess-queensberry-linda-stratmann-review.

37. "General News," DAILY EXAMINER (San Francisco, CA), Nov. 20, 1882, p. 3.

38. Linda Stratmann, The Marquess of Queensberry: Wilde's Nemesis (2013); C. W. Oldborn, "Before the Public—Latest Bid for Notoriety by Two Queer Englishmen," Davenport Sunday Democrat (Davenport, IA), Mar. 24, 1895, p. 8.

39. 2A William Morris & Norman Kelvin, The Collected Letters of William Morris, 1881–1884, at 137 n.2 (1987).

40. The Gazette (Montreal, Canada), Mar. 23, 1895, p. 11; Marilyn Aitken Robert, *Legal Lore: Sir Edward Carson Cross-Examines Oscar Wilde*, 30 Litigation 51, 53 (Spring 2004).

41. "The Latest Oscar Wildeisms," Akron Daily Democrat (Akron, OH), Mar. 9, 1895, p. 3; The Fort Wayne News (Fort Wayne, IN), Mar. 12, 1895, p. 3; "The Latest Oscar Wildeisms," The Gazette (York, PA), Mar. 11, 1895, p. 5.

42. "The Trial of Lord Queensberry," The Standard (London, England), Apr. 4, 1895, p. 6.

43. Franny Moyle, Constance: The Tragic and Scandalous Life of Mrs. Oscar Wilde (2012); Eleanor Fitzsimons, Wilde's Women: How Oscar Wilde Was Shaped by the Women He Knew (2015).

44. "Oscar Wilde Sues for Libel," Scranton Times (Scranton, PA), Mar. 2, 1895, p. 1.

45. C. W. Oldborn, "Before the Public—Latest Bid for Notoriety by Two Queer Englishmen," Davenport Sunday Democrat (Davenport, IA), Mar. 24, 1895, p. 8; Medical Aspects of Boxing 5–6 (Barry D. Jordan, ed. 1992) (laying out "The Queensberry Rules").

46. 2 E. H. Mikhail, ed., Oscar Wilde: Interviews and Recollections 262 (1979).

47. Matthew Hofer & Gary Scharnhorst, eds., Oscar Wilde in America: The Interviews 2–4 (2010).

48. "Mr. Oscar Wilde and the Marquis of Queensberry," Trewman's Exeter Flying Post (Exeter, England), Mar. 2, 1895, p. 8.

49. "The Queensberry Libel Case," The Standard (London, England), Mar. 11, 1895, p. 2.

50. "Marquis of Queensbury Arraigned in Court for Defaming Oscar Wilde," Victoria Times (Victoria, British Columbia), Mar. 2, 1895, p. 1; "Wilde Was Wild," St. Paul Sunday Globe (St. Paul, MN), Mar. 3, 1895, p. 1.

51. "A Society Libel Case," Sydney Morning Herald (Mar. 11, 1895), p. 5.

52. Freya Drohan, "'Queensberry Curse' Blamed for Oscar Wilde's Downfall Claims Another Victim: Lady Beth Douglas (18)," Irish Central, Nov. 12, 2018, https://www.irishcentral.com/culture/lady-beth-douglas-queensberry-curse-oscar-wilde.

53. Neil McKenna, The Secret Life of Oscar Wilde: An Intimate Biography (2005); Ashley H. Robins, Oscar Wilde: The Great Drama of His Life—How His Tragedy Reflected His Personality 176 (2012).

54. Richard Ellmann, Oscar Wilde 384–86, 391–92 (1987).

55. Oscar Wilde, The Picture of Dorian Gray 15–16 (2015) ("In mid-1891 Lionel Johnson introduced Wilde to Lord Alfred Douglas, an undergraduate at Oxford at the time. Known to his family and friends as 'Bosie', he was a handsome and spoilt young man. An intimate friendship sprang up between Wilde and Douglas and by 1893 Wilde was infatuated with Douglas and they consorted together regularly in a tempestuous affair. If Wilde was relatively indiscreet, even flamboyant, in the way he acted, Douglas was reckless in public. Wilde, who was earning up to £100 a week from his plays (his salary at The Woman's World had been £6), indulged Douglas's every whim: material, artistic or sexual."); *id.* at 16 ("Douglas soon dragged Wilde into the Victorian underground of gay prostitution and Wilde was introduced to a series of young, working class, male prostitutes from 1892 onwards by Alfred Taylor. These infrequent rendezvous usually took the same form: Wilde would meet the boy, offer him gifts, dine him privately and then take him to a hotel room."); *see also* Neil McKenna, The Secret Life of Oscar Wilde: An Intimate Biography (2005), foreword ("There is a surprising wealth of material about Oscar's sexual and emotional life. Some of it is new and exciting, like the recently discovered witness statements made by the boys Oscar had sex with, and to which I was fortunate enough to be granted exclusive access. The boys' statements bring Oscar's sexual behaviour vividly to life. Taken in conjunction with the publication, earlier this year, of the full and unexpurgated transcript of the trial of the Marquis of Queensberry for criminally libelling Oscar,

these statements made it possible for me to reconstruct Oscar's immensely rich and complicated sexual life between 1892 and 1895, the years of his love affair with Bosie.").

56. "The Queensberry rules," BRITANNICA, https://www.britannica.com/sports/boxing/The-Queensberry-rules.

57. JOHN BARTLETT, FAMILIAR QUOTATIONS: A COLLECTION OF PASSAGES, PHRASES, AND PROVERBS TRACED TO THEIR SOURCES IN ANCIENT AND MODERN LITERATURE 566 (16th ed. 1992).

58. "Oscar Wilde Charges Libel," BROOKLYN DAILY EAGLE (Brooklyn, NY), Mar. 2, 1895, p. 1; "Marquis of Queensbury," BIRMINGHAM NEWS (Birmingham, AL), Mar. 3, 1895, p. 1.

59. "The Action Against the Marquis of Queensberry," DUNDEE COURIER AND ARGUS (Dundee, Scotland), Mar. 9, 1895, p. 3; "Charge of Libel Against the Marquis of Queensberry," MORNING POST (London, England), Mar. 4, 1895, p. 7.

60. "A Green Carnation," INDIANAPOLIS JOURNAL (Indianapolis, IN), Mar. 25, 1895, p. 3 (reprinting item from the *New York Recorder*).

61. "The Oscar Wilde Libel Case—Why Sir George Lewis Retired," LEEDS MERCURY (Leeds, England), Mar. 12, 1895, p. 3 ("As considerable misapprehension seems to have arisen by the retirement of Sir George Lewis from the defence in the proceedings take by Mr. Oscar Wilde against the Marquis of Queensberry, we are authorised to state that Sir George Lewis did not retire in consequence of any opinion that he had formed upon the case, but upon purely personal grounds. The advice of Sir George Lewis had at various times been sought in other matters by both Lord Queensberry and Mr. Oscar Wilde, and in these circumstances he decided not to act for either party."); MICHAEL S. FOLDY, THE TRIALS OF OSCAR WILDE: DEVIANCE, MORALITY, AND LATE-VICTORIAN SOCIETY 156 (1997) (discussing Sir George Lewis); Marilyn Aitken Robert, *Legal Lore: Sir Edward Carson Cross-Examines Oscar Wilde*, 30 LITIGATION 51, 52 (Spring 2004) ("Queensberry ... retained Wilde's previous solicitor and friend, Sir George Lewis, who later commented that knowing of blackmail attempts against Alfred Douglas, he would have advised Wilde to tear up the card and take no action.").

62. "Mr. Oscar Wilde and Lord Queensberry," LEEDS MERCURY (Leeds, England), Mar. 11, 1895, p. 8; Marilyn Aitken Robert, *Legal Lore: Sir Edward Carson Cross-Examines Oscar Wilde*, 30 LITIGATION 51, 52 (Spring 2004).

63. "Mr. Oscar Wilde and Lord Queensberry," THE STAR (Guernsey, England), Apr. 4, 1895, p. 2; *John Douglas, 9th Marquess of Queensberry*, https://en.wikipedia.org/wiki/John_Douglas,_9th_Marquess_of_Queensberry.

64. *Albemarle Club*, https://en.wikipedia.org/wiki/Albemarle_Club.

65. MERLIN HOLLAND, THE FIRST COMPLETE RECORD: THE REAL TRIAL OF OSCAR WILDE 4 (2004); "Wilde the Chief Witness," BROOKLYN DAILY EAGLE (Brooklyn, NY), Apr. 3, 1895, p. 1; "Police," THE TIMES (London, England), Mar. 4, 1895, p. 3.

66. Steven Lubet, *The Importance of Being Honest*, 8 GREEN BAG 2d 163, 164–65 (2005).

67. HOLLAND, *supra* note 65, at 5; Marilyn Aitken Robert, *Legal Lore: Sir Edward Carson Cross-Examines Oscar Wilde*, 30 LITIGATION 51, 51 (Spring 2004).

68. LINDA STRATMANN, THE MARQUESS OF QUEENSBERRY: WILDE'S NEMESIS 216 (2013); "Mr. Oscar Wilde and the Marquis of Queensberry," NOTTINGHAMSHIRE GUARDIAN (Nottingham, England), Mar. 9, 1895, p. 5.

69. LINDA STRATMANN, THE MARQUESS OF QUEENSBERRY: WILDE'S NEMESIS 218 (2013); HOLLAND, *supra* note 65, at 3–5; "Charge of Libel Against the Marquis of Queensberry," MORNING POST, Mar. 4, 1895, p. 7.

70. LINDA STRATMANN, THE MARQUESS OF QUEENSBERRY: WILDE'S NEMESIS 218 (2013); "Telegraphic News Notes," MARION BAPTIST (Marion, Kansas), Mar. 1895; "Queensberry Arrested: The Marquis Charged with Libeling Oscar Wilde," STANDARD UNION (Brooklyn, NY), Mar. 2, 1895, p. 1.

71. "The Wilde-Queensberry Libel Case," THE TIMES-PICAYUNE (New Orleans, LA), Mar. 10, 1895, p. 12; "Pretty Oscar Wilde," DAILY CLARION-LEDGER (Jackson, MS), Mar. 9, 1895, p. 1; "Stands By It: Called Oscar Wilde a Hard Name and Won't Apologize," HELENA INDEPENDENT (Helena, MT), Mar. 10, 1895, p. 1; *see also* "Gleanings," BIRMINGHAM DAILY POST (Birmingham, England), Mar. 9, 1895, p. 7 ("Sir Edward

Clarke, Q.C., M.P., and Mr. Charles Mathews have been retained for the prosecution in the charge against the Marquis of Queensberry of publishing a defamatory libel of and concerning Mr. Oscar Wilde.").

72. "Society Scandal," WESTERN MAIL (Cardiff, Wales), Mar. 11, 1895, p. 5.

73. "A Marquis Sued," BROOKLYN CITIZEN (Brooklyn, NY), Mar. 9, 1895, p. 1.

74. OSCAR WILDE, DE PROFUNDIS AND OTHER PRISON WRITINGS (2013) ("Notes"); THE SPEEDICUT PAPERS: ROYAL SCANDALS—1884–1895 (Christopher Joll, ed. 2016).

75. HOLLAND, *supra* note 65, at 9–10, 13.

76. *Id.* at 13.

77. Peter Solomon, *Abolition of Secrecy in the Preferment of Indictments*, 17 MODERN L. REV. 336, 840 (1954).

78. "Pretty Oscar Wilde," DAILY CLARION-LEDGER (Jackson, MS), Mar. 9, 1895, p. 1; Marilyn Aitken Robert, *Legal Lore: Sir Edward Carson Cross-Examines Oscar Wilde*, 30 LITIGATION 51, 51 (Spring 2004).

79. MERLIN HOLLAND, THE REAL TRIAL OF OSCAR WILDE 13 (2004); "Mr. Oscar Wilde's Charge Against Lord Queensberry," THE OBSERVER (London, England), Mar. 10, 1895, p. 5. "Mr. Carson," *The Observer* of London reported, "said he was aware that the magistrate had nothing to do with the truth of the libel, but surely he was entitled to raise the question that Lord Queensberry had the privilege of giving advice to his own son." *Id.*

80. "Committed for Trial: Preliminary Hearing of the Wilde vs. Marquis of Queensberry Case," FORT WAYNE NEWS (Fort Wayne, IN), Mar. 8, 1895, p. 5; "Oscar Wilde, Author," BOSTON DAILY GLOBE (Boston, MA), Mar. 9, 1895, p. 4.

81. HOLLAND, *supra* note 65, at 21–22; "Charge of Libel Against the Marquis of Queensberry," MORNING POST (London, England), Mar. 4, 1895, p. 7.

82. "Charge of Libelling Oscar Wilde," LLOYD'S WEEKLY NEWSPAPER (London, England), Mar. 17, 1895, p. 5.

83. HOLLAND, *supra* note 65, at 17–18.

84. *Id.* at 13.

85. *Id.* at 13–14; THOMAS WRIGHT, BUILT OF BOOKS: HOW READING DEFINED THE LIFE OF OSCAR WILDE 229 (2008).

86. N.Y. TIMES, Mar. 10, 1895, p. 1.

87. Steven Lubet, *The Importance of Being Honest*, 8 GREEN BAG 2d 163, 163 (2005).

88. ASHLEY H. ROBINS, OSCAR WILDE—THE GREAT DRAMA OF HIS LIFE: HOW HIS TRAGEDY REFLECTED HIS PERSONALITY 10–11 (2012).

89. RICHARD E. MILLER, ON THE END OF PRIVACY: DISSOLVING BOUNDARIES IN A SCREEN-CENTRIC WORLD (2019) (describing the marriage to Ethel Weeden and the circumstances of the annulment of that marriage); *The Douglas Archives*, http://www.douglashistory.co.uk/history/john9thmarquessofqueensberry.htm (describing the marriage to Sibyl Montgomery in 1866 and the divorce in 1887).

90. The Marquess of Queensberry's eldest son, Francis, had died in 1894. PAUL FISHER, HOUSE OF WITS: AN INTIMATE PORTRAIT OF THE JAMES FAMILY 409 (2008) ("In October 1894, the young Francis Viscount Drumlanrig died in a 'shooting accident' that was widely understood to be a suicide. This handsome young Scottish lord evidently feared blackmail or the politically damaging exposure of his sexual relation with Lord Rosebery, at that point the foreign secretary."); *see also id.* ("Drumlanrig was the eldest son of the homophobic and pugilistic Marquess of Queensberry and the brother of Lord Alfred Douglas, the lover of Oscar Wilde.").

91. FOLDY, *supra* note 61, at 22 ("It has ... been surmised that the pressure on the Crown to convict Wilde at all costs came from Queensberry. Both of Wilde's major biographers, H. Montgomery Hyde and Richard Ellmann, intimate that Queensberry possessed some sort of evidence implicating persons high in the government, and in particular, Lord Rosebery, the Prime Minister. The evidence itself, of unknown form and content, was suspected of containing information confirming a 'homosexual' link between Rosebery and Queensberry's eldest son, Francis Archibald Douglas, Viscount Drumlanrig. Drumlanrig, who had served as private secretary to Lord Rosebery, then Foreign Minister, was killed in a mysterious shooting accident on October 18, 1894. Although the death was officially listed as 'accident,' suicide was suspected. It was believed by persons in a position to know that Drumlanrig had been threatened with exposure

over his alleged affair with Rosebery and had elected instead to take his own life in order to avoid implicating him. Ellmann reports that Queensberry had long been suspicious of Rosebery's influence on his favorite and most successful son (also his heir), and was furious with him because of it.").

92. "The Wilde Suit—Strong Support by Marquis of Queensbury's Sons," DEMOCRAT AND CHRONICLE (Rochester, NY), Mar. 10, 1895, p. 1; ANGELA KINGSTON, OSCAR WILDE AS A CHARACTER IN VICTORIAN FICTION 274 n.1 (2007); ASHLEY H. ROBINS, OSCAR WILDE—THE GREAT DRAMA OF HIS LIFE: HOW HIS TRAGEDY REFLECTED HIS PERSONALITY 10 (2012); A.N. WILSON, THE VICTORIANS 562 (2003) (discussing the death of Lord Drumlanrig and noting, "The death of this unfortunate young man removed a very considerable occasion of scandal from the public scene. Quite what Drumlanrig and Rosebery ever did when they were alone together we shall probably never know, but they were widely believed to have been lovers, and the belief is far from implausible.... Six months before the shooting, in March 1894, Gladstone had resigned as prime minister and Lord Rosebery had succeeded him. Even in today's relaxed and tolerate climate there would surely be misgivings about a prime minister who had promoted his apparently talentless and very young secretary to a peerage.")

93. Steven Lubet, *The Importance of Being Honest*, 8 GREEN BAG 2d 163, 165–66 (2005).

94. "Queensberry Held for Libel," EXAMINER (San Francisco, CA), Mar. 10, 1895, p. 1; "Queensberry Held for Trial," ST. LOUIS POST-DISPATCH (St. Louis, MO), Mar. 10, 1895, p. 9; ST. JOHN G. ERVINE, SIR EDWARD CARSON AND THE ULSTER MOVEMENT 51 (1916) (noting that Carson was "Solicitor-General for Ireland in 1892 and Solicitor-General for England from 1900 until 1906").

95. "Queensberry's Boys Side with Oscar Wilde and Say Their Father Is a Madman," THE SUN (New York, NY), Mar. 10, 1895, p. 1.

96. "Interesting Items," VISALIA DAILY TIMES (Visalia, CA), Mar. 11, 1895, p. 3.

97. "Oscar Wilde to Duel," TOPEKA STATE JOURNAL (Topeka, KS), Mar. 15, 1895, p. 1; *see also* "Will Oscar Fight the Marquis?", DAILY MINERS' JOURNAL (Pottsville, PA), Mar. 15, 1895, p. 2 ("MONTE CARLO, March 14.—Oscar Wilde and the Marquis of Queensberry have arrived here. It is rumored that Mr. Wilde and the marquis have visited this place to settle their personal differences in a duel."); ALEXANDRIA GAZETTE (Alexandria, VA), Mar. 16, 1895, p. 2 ("MAY FIGHT A DUEL.–A duel between Oscar Wilde and the Marquis of Queensberry is imminent. Both the æsthete and the Marquis, who Oscar charges with gross libel, are at Monte Carlo, that scene of many contests on the field of honor. Mr. Wilde is accompanied by Lord Alfred Douglas, son of the Marquis, who has taken sides against his own father in the sensational imbroglio, which has been the talk of London clubs for a fortnight. The Marquis is out of jail under heavy bonds for appearance later for trial. There is no question that he has gone to Monte Carlo to get satisfaction, if possible, with pistol or rapier. The trouble between the two men started, so far as the public knows, in the Marquis sending to a London club a postal addressed to Mr. Wilde, calling him every kind of vile thing."); "The Society Scandal—Mr. Wilde and Lord Alfred Douglas Leave London," WESTERN MAIL (Cardiff, Wales), Mar. 15, 1895, p. 4 ("The London correspondent of a French paper states that Mr. Oscar Wilde's departure from London with Lord Alfred Douglas was so sudden that many of his friends are ignorant of his destination, though it is supposed he has gone to Paras, whither he was preceded by an intimate friend last week. Mr. Wilde, according to the same authority, took with him a considerable quantity of luggage. Justification having been pleaded, the case of Mr. Oscar Wilde against the Marquis of Queensberry will not be ready for trial at the next Old Bailey Sessions, but will probably stand over to the following sessions.").

98. "Not by Queensbery Rules," BOSTON DAILY GLOBE (Boston, MA), Mar. 15, 1895, p. 1.

99. THE TIMES (Richmond, VA), Mar. 17, 1895, p. 18 ("The report that the Marquis of Queensberry and Oscar Wilde had arrived at Cannes was erroneous. It was true in regard to Oscar Wilde, but instead of the Marquis of Queensberry, the other arrival at the Riviera resort was Lord Arthur Douglas, a relative of the Marquis. The latter is in London."); *see also* "Oscar Wilde Returns to London," UNION WEEKLY LEADER (Wilkes-Barre, PA), Mar. 22, 1895, p. 5 ("A paper announces the return to London of Oscar Wilde and Lord Alfred Douglas, son of the Marquis of Queensberry, who had been making a short visit to Monte Carlo.").

100. "Queensberry Indicted," STANDARD UNION (Brooklyn, NY), Mar. 25, 1895, p. 1; *see also* "Queensberry Libel Case," PALL MALL GAZETTE (London, England), Mar. 25, 1895, p. 7 ("At the opening of the March session at the Central Criminal Court to-day the Recorder, in charging the grand jury, referred to

the charge of libel brought by Mr. Oscar Wilde against the Marquis of Queensberry. He said he would not go into the case, but would merely explain that if the Marquis of Queensberry wrote the words upon the card produced, whether he was justified or not, it constituted a libel. Moreover, the defendant intended to plead justification. It was therefore their duty to return a true bill.").

101. "Apologized to Oscar Wilde," DAILY PRESS (Asbury Park, NJ), Apr. 1, 1895, p. 2 ("The Observer has apologized to Oscar Wilde and Lord Alfred Douglas for the statement published by that paper on March 25 to the effect that after staying a day at a hotel at Monte Carlo the proprietor, at the request of the other English guests, informed Wilde and Lord Alfred that their rooms had been engaged by others.").

102. *Id.*; *see also* "Denial of a Story Concerning Oscar Wilde and Lord Douglas," CINCINNATI ENQUIRER (Cincinnati, OH), Apr. 1, 1895, p. 1 ("Both Wilde and Lord Alfred assure the editor of the paper that there was not the slightest foundation for the statement. The Observer continues: 'We take the earliest opportunity of expressing our sincere regret and apologies for the pain and annoyance the statement has caused them.'"); SAN FRANCISCO CHRONICLE (San Francisco, CA), Apr. 2, 1895, p. 6 ("It was very malicious for the London *Observer* to print a dispatch from Nice declaring flatly that Oscar Wilde and Lord Alfred Douglas had been forced to leave one of the hotels because of the protests of the other English guests. The inference conveyed by the dispatch was that the playwright and his companion were socially ostracized, which is seems is not the case, for the newspaper has made a sweeping apology.").

103. "The Queensberry Libel Case," BUFFALO COMMERCIAL (Buffalo, NY), Mar. 25, 1895, p. 15; "Indicted for Libel," BUFFALO EXPRESS (Buffalo, NY), Mar. 26, 1895, p. 2.

104. "The Queensberry Libel Case," PALL MALL GAZETTE (London, England), Mar. 26, 1895, p. 7.

105. "News from England," KANSAS SEMI-WEEKLY CAPITAL (Topeka, KS), Apr. 2, 1895, p. 2.

106. "Wilde Goes Suddenly," OAKLAND TRIBUNE (Oakland, CA), Apr. 2, 1895, p. 1.

107. Bristow, *supra* note 32, at 13, 16.

108. "To What Depths," TOPEKA STATE JOURNAL (Topeka, KS), Apr. 3, 1895, p. 1.

109. THE INTERNATIONAL WHO'S WHO: WHO'S WHO IN THE WORLD—A BIOGRAPHICAL DICTIONARY OF THE WORLD'S NOTABLE LIVING MEN AND WOMEN 300 (H. L. Motter, ed. 1912).

110. HOLLAND, *supra* note 65, at 25. *See also* Douglas O. Linder, *Famous Trials*, University of Missouri-Kansas City Law School, https://famous-trials.com (listing various nineteenth-century trials).

111. "Wilde the Chief Witness," BROOKLYN DAILY EAGLE (Brooklyn, NY), Apr. 3, 1895, p. 1.

112. "Mr. Oscar Wilde and Lord Queensberry," THE STAR (Guernsey, England), Apr. 4, 1895, p. 2.

113. "Oscar Wilde Libel Case," PALL MALL GAZETTE (London, England), Apr. 3, 1895, p. 7.

114. "As a Witness," ST. LOUIS POST-DISPATCH (St. Louis, MO), Apr. 3, 1895, p. 2.

115. "The Charge Against Lord Queensberry," LEEDS MERCURY (Leeds, England), Apr. 4, 1895, p. 7.

116. "Wilde the Chief Witness," BROOKLYN DAILY EAGLE (Brooklyn, NY), Apr. 3, 1895, p. 1; "The Wilde-Queensberry Libel Case," YORKSHIRE HERALD AND YORK HERALD (York, England), Apr. 4, 1895, p. 5.

117. "Oscar Wilde's Queer Ways," THE WORLD (New York, NY), Apr. 3, 1895, p. 1 (Evening Edition).

118. "Oscar Wilde Libel Case," PALL MALL GAZETTE (London, England), Apr. 3, 1895, p. 7.

119. HOLLAND, *supra* note 65, at 26; "Passion Poet," BOSTON DAILY GLOBE (Boston, MA), Apr. 3, 1895, p. 1; "A Nasty Mess," EVENING EXPRESS (Los Angeles, CA), Apr. 3, 1895, p. 1.

120. ROBERT ALDRICH & GARRY WOTHERSPOON, EDS., WHO'S WHO IN GAY AND LESBIAN HISTORY: FROM ANTIQUITY TO WORLD WAR II 252 (2001); ROBERT ALDRICH & GARRY WOTHERSPOON, EDS., WHO'S WHO IN GAY & LESBIAN HISTORY 299 (2020); Offences Against the Person Act 1861, c. 100, §§ 61–62, https://www.legislation.gov.uk/ukpga/Vict/24-25/100/section/61/enacted & https://www.legislation.gov.uk/ukpga/Vict/24-25/100/section/62/enacted; NORENA SHOPLAND, A PRACTICAL GUIDE TO SEARCHING LGBTQIA HISTORICAL RECORDS (2021); *see also* Mary Ann Case, *Of "This" and "That" in* Lawrence v. Texas, 55 SUP. CT. REV. 75, 123 (2003) ("At the beginning of the nineteenth century in Britain, sodomy was a capital offense for which a record number of more than fifty men were executed in the first third of the century. After several decades without executions, the 1861 Offenses Against the Person Act replaced the death penalty for buggery with sentences of from ten years to life."); Nancy J. Knauer, *The Politics of Eradication and the Future of LGBT Rights*, 21 GEO. J. GENDER & L. 615, 624 n.59 (2020) (citations omitted):

In England, sodomy was first criminalized during the reign of Henry VIII. The penalty for "the detestable and abominable vice of buggery committed with mankind or beast" was death. Eskridge reports that "the English crime of buggery was generally applicable in the American colonies, either as a matter of common law or statutory decree." Under English law, the death penalty for sodomy was not removed until the Offences Against the Person Act of 1861. Both Edward Coke and William Blackstone believed that the very nature of the act was unmentionable and described sodomy as "the infamous crime against nature." The Labouchere Amendment to the Criminal Law Amendments Act of 1885 criminalized oral sex between men with the creation of a separate criminal offense of "gross indecency with another male person." Eskridge reports that in the United States, a number of states later amended their sodomy laws to include oral sex.

121. *See, e.g.*, Yi Wei, *Towards the Full Promise of Liberty: A Comparative Approach to the Decriminalization of Male Homosexual Sex in Singapore*, 20 ASIAN-PAC. L. & POL'Y J. 50, 55 (2018) (discussing the Labouchere Amendment); William N. Eskridge, Jr., *Law and the Construction of the Closet: American Regulation of Same-Sex Intimacy, 1880–1946*, 82 IOWA L. REV. 1007, 1026–27 (1997) ("Literally an appendage to a major prostitution law reform bill, the Labouchere Amendment is conceptually significant in its insistence that illegal sexual acts between men must not be limited to anal sex (sodomy and buggery, as understood by Anglo-American lawyers). Coming at a time when subcultures of male inverts had formed at the fringes of society, Labouchere's Amendment was an important regulatory expansion that permitted English authorities to regulate those subcultures through arrests for oral sex (which was understood to be the chief object of 'gross indecency'). Indeed, this is the law that snared Oscar Wilde in 1895. His trials for gross indecency were publicized in the United States as well as England ...."). Indeed, it wasn't long before Oscar Wilde found himself as the defendant in a criminal case faces charges under the Labouchere Amendment. *See, e.g.*, Marco Wan, *From the Rack to the Press: Representation of the Oscar Wilde Trials in the French Newspaper* Le Temps, 18 LAW & LITERATURE, 47, 47–48 (2006) ("The narrative of the three Wilde trials in England is well known: furious over Wilde's relationship with his son, the Marquis of Queensberry left a card at the Albemarle Club accusing Wilde of 'posing as a somdomite [*sic*].' The playwright instituted a libel trial against the Marquis, with Edward Clarke acting as the prosecution lawyer, and Edward Carson acting as the defense lawyer. The case was subsequently dropped. Shortly afterward, Wilde was brought back to court for allegedly committing acts of gross indecency under the Labouchère amendment of the Criminal Law (Amendment) Act of 1885. The roles were now reversed, with Wilde standing in the dock as the accused. The jury's inability to reach a verdict necessitated a third trial, in which Wilde was prosecuted by the Solicitor-General himself. He was found guilty and sentenced to hard labor for two years.").

122. HOLLAND, *supra* note 65, at 26–27.

123. Roy Robert Ray, *Truth: A Defense to Libel*, 16 MINN. L. REV. 43, 55 (1931).

124. HOLLAND, *supra* note 65, at 29.

125. Bristow, *supra* note 32, at 9–10.

126. HOLLAND, *supra* note 65, at 30–31.

127. "The Wilde Prosecution," YORKSHIRE HERALD, AND THE YORK HERALD (York, England), May 23, 1895, p. 5.

128. "Oscar Wilde Libel Case," PALL MALL GAZETTE (London, England), Apr. 3, 1895, p. 7.

129. "A Disgusting Libel Suit on Tap in London," HUTCHINSON NEWS (Hutchinson, KS), Apr. 3, 1895, p. 1.

130. HOLLAND, *supra* note 65, at 30–31.

131. MAX BEERBOHM, COMP., HERBERT BEERBOHM TREE: SOME MEMORIES OF HIM AND OF HIS ART (2d ed. 1969).

132. "Wilde the Chief Witness," BROOKLYN DAILY EAGLE (Brooklyn, NY), Apr. 3, 1895, p. 1.

133. "Trial of Lord Queensberry," THE STANDARD (London, England), Apr. 4, 1895, p. 6; "Mr. Oscar Wilde's Action for Libel," DAILY NEWS (London, England), Apr. 4, 1895, p. 2; THE CAMBRIDGE COMPANION TO OSCAR WILDE 150 (Peter Raby, ed. 1997); *see also* OSCAR WILDE: THE IMPORTANCE OF BEING EARNEST AND OTHER PLAYS xv (Peter Raby, ed. 1995) (noting of *A Woman of No Importance*: "The distinguished actor manager Herbert Beerbohm Tree, impressed by *Lady Windermere's Fan*, had asked Wilde for a play.").

134. "Oscar Wilde Libel Case," PALL MALL GAZETTE (London, England), Apr. 3, 1895, p. 7.

135. THE LETTERS OF OSCAR WILDE 326 (Rupert Hart-Davis, ed. 1962); "Trial of the Marquis of Queensberry," LIVERPOOL MERCURY (Liverpool, England), Apr. 4, 1895, p. 5.

136. "Wilde the Chief Witness," BROOKLYN DAILY EAGLE (Brooklyn, NY), Apr. 3, 1895, p. 1.

137. "Trial of Lord Queensberry," THE STANDARD (London, England), Apr. 4, 1895, p. 6; https://www.sothebys.com/en/auctions/ecatalogue/lot.174.html/2010/rimbaud-verlaine-mallarm-and-their-friends-books-manuscripts-and-photographs-from-the-poetical-collection-of-eric-and-marie-hlne-b-pf1040.

138. NORBERT KOHL, OSCAR WILDE: THE WORKS OF A CONFORMIST REBEL 178 (David Henry Wilson, trans. 1989).

139. Xavier Giudicelli, "Butterflies, Orchids and Wasps—Polyglossia and Aesthetic Lives: Foreign Languages in *The Spirit Lamp* (1892–1893)," AESTHETICISM AND DECADENTISM, Vol. 78 (2013), https://journals.openedition.org/cve/930. Oscar Wilde published several items in *The Spirit Lamp*.

140. HOLLAND, *supra* note 65, at 33–34.

141. *Id.* "[N]or indeed," Clark said, "need I mention any incident until one comes to the early part of 1894 when Lord Alfred Douglas who had been to Cairo and had returned to this country in, I think, February 1894, again lunched at the Café Royal in the public room of the Café and they again met Lord Queensberry." At that lunch, Clarke made clear, the Marquis of Queensberry had shaken hands with both Oscar Wilde and his son and "a conversation of a most friendly character" had taken place. *Id.*

142. *Id.* at 34–35.

143. *Id.* at 37–38.

144. *Id.* at 38–40.

145. "On Trial—Oscar Wilde's Libel Suit Against Lord Queensberry," STANDARD UNION (Brooklyn, NY), Apr. 3, 1895, p. 1.

146. "Wilde the Chief Witness," BROOKLYN DAILY EAGLE (Brooklyn, NY), Apr. 3, 1895, p. 1.

147. "Oscar Wilde Libel Case," PALL MALL GAZETTE (London, England), Apr. 3, 1895, p. 7

148. "Wilde the Chief Witness," BROOKLYN DAILY EAGLE (Brooklyn, NY), Apr. 3, 1895, p. 1.

149. "Trial of Lord Queensberry," THE STANDARD (London, England), Apr. 4, 1895, p. 6; ANDRÉ GIDE, OSCAR WILDE: A STUDY 3–4 (1905).

150. LINDA STRATMANN, THE MARQUESS OF QUEENSBERRY: WILDE'S NEMESIS (2013).

151. "A Disgusting Libel Suit on Tap in London," HUTCHINSON NEWS (Hutchinson, KS), Apr. 3, 1895, p. 1.

152. "Wilde and Queensbery," DAYTON EVENING HERALD (Dayton, OH), Apr. 3, 1895, p. 1.

153. "Central Criminal Court, April 3," THE TIMES (London, England), Apr. 4, 1895, p. 10.

154. "Wilde the Chief Witness," BROOKLYN DAILY EAGLE (Brooklyn, NY), Apr. 3, 1895, p. 1.

155. "Oscar Wilde Libel Case," PALL MALL GAZETTE (London, England), Apr. 3, 1895, p. 7; "Trial of Lord Queensberry," THE STANDARD (London, England), Apr. 4, 1895, p. 6. At one point, Wilde testified: "I rarely write what I believe is true." "Wilde and Queensbery," DAYTON EVENING HERALD (Dayton, OH), Apr. 3, 1895, p. 1.

156. "Trial of Lord Queensberry," THE STANDARD (London, England), Apr. 4, 1895, p. 6.

157. "Oscar Wilde's Tastes," SPOKESMAN-REVIEW (Spokane, WA), Apr. 4, 1895, p. 2 ("Carson then drew out Wilde's opinion regarding literature in general, to which line of cross-examination plaintiff made many responses in the same line as in his plays. 'The interpretation of my works does not concern me,' said Wilde. 'I do not care tuppence for what the Philistines think of me.'").

158. *The Picture of Dorian Gray*, https://en.wikipedia.org/wiki/The_Picture_of_Dorian_Gray.

159. "Trial of Lord Queensberry," THE STANDARD (London, England), Apr. 4, 1895, p. 6.

160. *Id.*; Marilyn Aitken Robert, *Legal Lore: Sir Edward Carson Cross-Examines Oscar Wilde*, 30 LITIGATION 51, 52–53 (Spring 2004).

161. "Trial of Lord Queensberry," THE STANDARD (London, England), Apr. 4, 1895, p. 6; Marilyn Aitken Robert, *Legal Lore: Sir Edward Carson Cross-Examines Oscar Wilde*, 30 LITIGATION 51, 52–53 (Spring 2004).

162. "Trial of Lord Queensberry," THE STANDARD (London, England), Apr. 4, 1895, p. 6.

163. "Wilde the Chief Witness," BROOKLYN DAILY EAGLE (Brooklyn, NY), Apr. 3, 1895, p. 1.

164. "Oscar Wilde's Libel Suit," EVENING GAZETTE (Cedar Rapids, IA), Apr. 3, 1895, p. 2; "A Society Libel Case," WESTERN MAIL (Cardiff, Wales), Apr. 4, 1895, p. 6; Marilyn Aitken Robert, *Legal Lore: Sir Edward Carson Cross-Examines Oscar Wilde*, 30 LITIGATION 51, 63–64 (Spring 2004).

165. Marilyn Aitken Robert, *Legal Lore: Sir Edward Carson Cross-Examines Oscar Wilde*, 30 LITIGATION 51, 63–66 (Spring 2004).

166. "It Was True—What Queensberry Said of Oscar Wilde," BOSTON GLOBE (Boston, MA), Apr. 5, 1895, p. 1.

167. "Wilde the Chief Witness," BROOKLYN DAILY EAGLE (Brooklyn, NY), Apr. 3, 1895, p. 1; "Trial of Lord Queensberry," THE STANDARD (London, England), Apr. 4, 1895, p. 6.

168. "Day of Trial Fixed," ELMIRA GAZETTE AND FREE PRESS (Elmira, NY), Mar. 28, 1895, p. 1 ("London, March 27.—In the Criminal Court, Old Bailey, to-day counsel on behalf of the Marquis of Queensberry and Oscar Wilde represented their clients as both being anxious to have the case of Wilde against Queensberry tried at the earliest possible moment. Justice Collins fixed April 3 as the day for the trial.").

169. "Terrible Ordeal for Oscar Wilde—The Aesthetic Poet's Relations with Lord Alfred Douglass Aired in Court," PHILADELPHIA INQUIRER (Philadelphia, PA), Apr. 4, 1895, p. 2.

170. "Oscar Wilde Is Pitilessly Scored," CHICAGO DAILY TRIBUNE (Chicago, IL), Apr. 5, 1895, p. 3.

171. *Id.*

172. Bristow, *supra* note 32, at 6–7 ("A well-educated man who attended Marlborough College and had at one time held a commission in the Royal Fusiliers. Taylor was not known as a blackmailer, and he appears not to have been involved in receiving money through selling his body. He was the bankrupted heir to a cocoa manufacturing fortune of £45,000, which—for reasons that he never properly expounded—had been squandered rapidly. His name and identity attracted immense publicity when he was successfully tried alongside Oscar Wilde, in April and May 1895, for committing acts of gross indecency .... As the lengthy criminal proceedings against Wilde revealed, Taylor was known for hosting parties in his rooms at 13 Little College Street, Westminster, and he did the same for his gay friends in his next set of lodgings at 3 Chapel Street. By September 1892, when Taylor met Wilde for the first time, the thirty-year-old had for some years been living on a small allowance from his family, which he presumably supplemented with additional sums made from procuring young men for wealthy clients.").

173. *Alfred Taylor*, https://spartacus-educational.com/FWWtaylorAT.htm; NEIL BARTLETT, WHO WAS THAT MAN? A PRESENT FOR MR OSCAR WILDE 85 (1988); GARY SCHMIDGALL, THE STRANGER WILDE: INTERPRETING OSCAR 218 (1994); PETER FARRER, MEN IN PETTICOATS: A SELECTION OF LETTERS FROM VICTORIAN NEWSPAPERS 20 (1987).

174. "Oscar Wilde's Case Closed," THE TIMES (Philadelphia, PA), Apr. 5, 1895, p. 1.

175. "The Oscar Wilde Libel Action," SHEFFIELD AND ROTHERHAM INDEPENDENT (Sheffield, England), Apr. 5, 1895, p. 6.

176. Bristow, *supra* note 32, at 1–2 & n.1 (noting that twenty men were arrested just before midnight on August 12, 1894, at a raid at 46 Fitzroy Street in central London, and that those arrested included Alfred Taylor and Charles Parker, with two men—John Severs and Arthur Marling—charged under the Vagrancy Act 1824 "with being idle and disorderly persons").

177. "The Oscar Wilde Libel Action," SHEFFIELD AND ROTHERHAM INDEPENDENT (Sheffield, England), Apr. 5, 1895, p. 6; "The Society Libel Case—Mr. Oscar Wilde Again in the Witness-Box," WESTERN MAIL (Cardiff, Wales), Apr. 5, 1895, p. 6.

178. "Oscar Wilde Libel Case," PALL MALL GAZETTE (London, England), Apr. 5, 1895, p. 7.

179. "Arrest of Oscar Wilde," WESTERN MAIL (Cardiff, Wales), Apr. 6, 1895, p. 5; "Wilde Is Arrested," PIERRE WEEKLY FREE PRESS (Pierre, SD), Apr. 11, 1895, p. 2.

180. *Id.*; "Branded Before All the World—An Indelible Mark of Shame Set Upon Oscar Wilde," ST. LOUIS POST-DISPATCH (St. Louis, MO), Apr. 5, 1895, p. 1.

181. "Oscar Wilde Disgraced," KANSAS CITY STAR (Kansas City, MO), Apr. 5, 1895, p. 1.

182. "Oscar Wilde and the Marquis of Queensberry," YORKSHIRE HERALD (York, England), Apr. 6, 1895, p. 5; "Wilde Is Arrested," PIERRE WEEKLY FREE PRESS (Pierre, SD), Apr. 11, 1895, p. 2.

183. GLASGOW HERALD (Glasgow, Scotland), Apr. 6, 1895, p. 4; "Wilde History," THE INDEPENDENT (London, England), Apr. 3, 2017, sec. 2.

184. "The Queensberry Libel Case," The Standard (London, England), Apr. 6, 1895, p. 4.

185. *Alfred Taylor*, https://spartacus-educational.com/FWWtaylorAT.htm.

186. Merlin Holland, The First Complete Record: The Real Trial of Oscar Wilde 10 (2004); "Arrest of Oscar Wilde," Western Mail (Cardiff, Wales), Apr. 6, 1895, p. 5; "Branded Before All the World—An Indelible Mark of Shame Set Upon Oscar Wilde," St. Louis Post-Dispatch (St. Louis, MO), Apr. 5, 1895, p. 1.

187. Steven Lubet, *The Importance of Being Honest*, 8 Green Bag 2d 163, 166–67 (2005).

188. "The Affairs of Oscar Wilde," North-Eastern Daily Gazette (Middlesbrough, England), Aug. 23, 1895, p. 3 ("At the London Bankruptcy Court yesterday th[e] accounts were issued under the failure of Oscar Wilde, now of Her Majesty's Prison, Wandsworth. The liabilities are expected to rank at £3,591, and no available assets are shown. Debtor states his income, which he estimates at £2,000 a year, has been derived chiefly from royalties received on plays and literary works written by him. He attributes his insolvency to the failure of legal proceedings taken by him against the petitioning creditor the Marquis of Queensberry, and to his conviction in the recent trial of Regina v. Wilde. The Official Receiver observes, however, 'that it would appear debtor has been insolvent for at least two years, and that his household and personal expenditure has been considerably in excess of his income.'").

189. "Trial of Lord Queensberry," The Standard (London, England), Apr. 5, 1895, p. 6.

190. "The Wilde Case," Western Mail (Cardiff, Wales), Apr. 8, 1895, p. 5.

191. "The Wilde Case," Northern Echo (Dalington, England), Apr. 9, 1895, p. 3.

192. "The Oscar Wilde Trial," Manchester Weekly Times (Manchester, England), May 3, 1895, p. 3.

193. "Wilde–Taylor," Reynolds's Newspaper (London, England), Apr. 28, 1895, p. 1.

194. "Wilde Fully Committed," Brooklyn Daily Times (Brooklyn, NY), Apr. 19, 1895, p. 1. At their prior arraignment, one newspaper gave this description: "Oscar Wilde and his friend, Alfred Taylor, were arraigned in the Bow street police court at noon to-day for further examination. Wilde looked greatly fatigued and really ill. His hair was ruffled, and his general appearance indicated carelessness." At that preliminary hearing, Charles Parker had been called to the stand and testified that "Taylor upon one occasion told him" that he (Taylor) had "gone through" a marriage ceremony with a young man in which Taylor wore women's clothes. A detective also testified that he had "searched the rooms occupied by Taylor in Chapel street," where he found checks payable to that young man, and "telegrams from Wilde to Taylor arranging and cancelling meetings." "Trial of Wilde and Taylor," Berrow's Worchester Journal (Worcester, England), Apr. 27, 1895, p. 5.

195. "Wilde–Taylor," Reynolds's Newspaper (London, England), Apr. 28, 1895, p. 1.

196. *Id.*

197. "Wilde–Taylor," Reynolds's Newspaper (London, England), Apr. 28, 1895, p. 1.

198. "The Oscar Wilde Scandal," Glasgow Herald (Glasgow, Scotland), May 1, 1895, p. 9.

199. Foldy, *supra* note 61, at 31–39.

200. Liverpool Mercury and Lancashire, Cheshire, and General Advertiser (Liverpool, England), May 2, 1895, p. 5.

201. "The Charge Against Oscar Wilde," North-Eastern Daily Gazette (Middlesbrough, England), Apr. 24, 1895, p. 3.

202. "The Oscar Wilde Case—Prisoners To Be Tried Separately," The Bury and Norwich Post, and Suffolk Standard (Bury, England), May 21, 1895, p. 5.

203. "Wilde Scandal," Western Mail (Cardiff, Wales), May 22, 1895, p. 6.

204. "The Trial of Taylor," The Star (Guernsey, England), May 23, 1895, p. 1.

205. "Alfred Taylor Convicted," Wilmington Messenger (Wilmington, NC), May 22, 1895, p. 1; *see also* "Wilde's Friend Taylor Convicted," The Gazette (York, PA), May 22, 1895, p. 1 (London, May 21.—Alfred Taylor, who was indicted with Oscar Wilde, but whose trials were ordered separate, was found guilty today on several counts of the indictment. Court deferred sentence.").

206. "Found Guilty," Standard Union (Brooklyn, NY), May 21, 1895, p. 1.

207. "Taylor Convicted," Record-Union (Sacramento, CA), May 22, 1895, p. 1 ("The Marquis of Queensberry and his younger son, Lord Alfred Douglas, had an exciting quarrel in Piccadilly this afternoon. Both were arrested, charged with breaking the peace and released on bail. Lord Alfred Douglas

received severe chastisement from his father. The latter's high hat was somewhat battered. The crowd outside the police station loudly cheered the Marquis of Queensberry.").

208. "Peers at Fisticuffs," THE AGE (Melbourne, Australia), May 23, 1895, p. 5; "The Wilde Scandal," THE AGE (Melbourne, Australia), May 23, 1895, p. 5.

209. LINDA STRATMANN, THE MARQUESS OF QUEENSBERRY: WILDE'S NEMESIS (2013).

210. *See also* "The Queensberry Case—Fight Between Father and Son," THE ILLUSTRATED POLICE NEWS: LAW COURTS AND WEEKLY RECORD (London, England), June 1, 1895, p. 3 ("Shortly after the termination of the trial of Taylor at the Old Bailey on Tuesday last week an exciting fracas occurred in Piccadilly Circus, the principal persons concerned being the Marquis of Queensberry and his son, Lord Douglas. The affray appears to have been short and determined, and but for the intervention of the police might have had more serious results. What preceded the altercation it is not possible to explain at present, but considerable violence must have been used by both father and son. The Marquis of Queensberry appears to have met his son quite accidentally in Piccadilly, near Bond Street. A considerable crowd had surrounded the principals of this exceptional episode in a fashionable highway, when Police-constable 6 C R, assisted by another officer, escorted the marquis and his son to Vine Street police station, which is a short distance from the scene of disorder.").

211. "Hopes for Oscar Wilde—The Chances for His Conviction Are Thought to Be Slight," SAN FRANCISCO CHRONICLE, May 21, 1895, p. 1.

212. THE PROVINCE (Victoria, British Columbia), June 1, 1895, p. 4.

213. "The Trial of Oscar Wilde," BELFAST NEWS-LETTER (Belfast, Northern Ireland), May 27, 1895, p. 6.

214. Foldy, *supra* note 61, at 39–47.

215. "The Trial of Oscar Wilde—Accused Found Guilty and Sentenced to Two Years' Hard Labour," YORKSHIRE HERALD (York, England), May 27, 1895, p. 5.

216. "Wilde-Taylor Trial—Both Prisoners Found Guilty," DUNDEE COURIER AND ARGUS (Dundee, Scotland), May 27, 1895, p. 3.

217. "The Trial of Oscar Wilde," BELFAST NEWS-LETTER (Belfast, Northern Ireland), May 27, 1895, p. 6.

218. FOLDY, *supra* note 61, at 46–47; "Summary of News," THE INDEPENDENT (Sheffield, England), May 27, 1895, p. 4 ("At the Old Bailey, on Saturday evening, the Wilde case was concluded, a verdict of guilty on all the counts submitted to them being found by the jury. Mr. Justice Wills sentenced the prisoner to two years' hard labour. The accused man, Taylor, who was found guilty of similar practices earlier in the week, was brought into court and sentenced also to two years' hard labour."); *see also* ILLUSTRATED POLICE NEWS: LAW COURTS AND WEEKLY RECORD (London, England), June 1, 1895, p. 3 (discussing the sentence imposed on Oscar Wilde).

219. LEEDS MERCURY (Leeds, England), May 27, 1895, p. 4; "The Trial of Oscar Wilde—Accused Found Guilty and Sentenced to Two Years' Hard Labour," YORKSHIRE HERALD (York, England), May 27, 1895, p. 5.

220. "The Oscar Wilde Case," FREEMAN'S JOURNAL (Dublin, Ireland), May 27, 1895, p. 6.

221. "What Wilde Will Do Now," WESTERN MAIL (Cardiff, Wales), May 28, 1895, p. 3.

222. "Oscar Wilde in Gaol," IPSWICH JOURNAL (Ipswich, England), June 1, 1895, p. 5. *But cf.* "Oscar Wilde's Health—Recent Rumours Contradicted," NORTH-EASTERN DAILY GAZETTE (Middlesbrough, England), June 7, 1895, p. 3 (saying that rumors about Oscar Wilde's health and treatment in the Pentonville Prison are "absolutely without foundation").

223. NICHOLAS FRANKEL, OSCAR WILDE: THE UNREPENTANT YEARS 1, 5 (2017).

224. Jennifer Latson, "When Oscar Wilde's Wit Couldn't Save Him," *TIME*, May 25, 2015, https://time.com/3890539/oscar-wilde-trial-history/.

225. "Oscar Wilde in Court—His Bankruptcy Affairs," REYNOLD'S NEWSPAPER (London, England), Nov. 17, 1895, p. 3.

226. FRANKEL, *supra* note 223, at 1–2, 5–8; OSCAR WILDE AND MODERN CULTURE: THE MAKING OF A LEGEND 235 (Joseph Bristow, ed. 2008); *Oscar Wilde*, https://en.wikipedia.org/wiki/Oscar_Wilde; *The Importance of Being Earnest*, https://en.wikipedia.org/wiki/The_Importance_of_Being_Earnest.

227. Oscar Wilde, De Profundis, The Ballad of Reading Gaol and Other Writings 89 (2002); Oscar Wilde, The Soul of Man and Prison Writings 131 (Isobel Murray, ed. 1990); Frankel, *supra* note 223, at 8.

228. A. Lawrence Lowell, The Government of England 135 (1914).

229. Shortly prior to this development in English law, an article published in 1984 laid out the long history of efforts to move away from private prosecutions. Steve Uglow, Comment, *Independent Prosecutions*, 11 J. L. & Society 233, 233 (1984) ("There will be the novel sight of public prosecutors operating throughout England and Wales if the recommendations of a recent White Paper are carried through. This particular reform of the criminal justice system has been sought for 150 years without success, despite the support that has been voiced from time to time by the legal profession and the judiciary."); *id.* at 234 ("The pressure to develop a national system for prosecuting dates from at least 1845 when the Eighth Report of the Royal Commission on the Criminal Law was published. This evidence on the need for public prosecutors was echoed in two other major studies—a Select Committee of the House of Commons in 1855 and the Judicature Commission in 1875. The complaints were that the system was ineffective in allowing too many criminals to go unprosecuted, that it placed too great a burden on the citizen in terms of cost and inconvenience and that it encouraged corruption especially among the police and justices' clerks who 'consorted with low attornies' to divide up the prosecutions and share the fees and costs and accrued.").

230. Gary Slapper, Organisational Prosecutions (2018) (section on "The Private Prosecution").

231. Jacqueline Martin, The English Legal System § 16.13.3 (8th ed. 2016).

232. Prosecution of Offences Act 1985, § 2. *See also* Falk, *supra* note 2, at 24 ("[I]n 1978 the Royal Commission on Criminal Procedure was appointed. In 1981, the commission published a report that sought to reform the process by making several recommendations, including the recommendation to Parliament that an independent prosecuting authority be initiated. This led to the passage of the amended Prosecution of Offences Act of 1985, which further expanded the powers and duties of the Public Prosecution Service . . . .").

233. *About CPS - The Crown Prosecution Service*, https://www.cps.gov.uk/about-cps; *The Director of Public Prosecutions*, In Brief, https://www.inbrief.co.uk/legal-system/director-of-public-prosecutions/.

234. John D. Bessler, *The Public Interest and the Unconstitutionality of Private Prosecutors*, 47 Ark. L. Rev. 511, 515–16 & nm.14–15 (1994) (collecting citations). *See generally* Sam Tate & Charlotte Thompson, "English Private Prosecutions Are Now Too Important to Ignore," The FCPA Blog, June 18, 2019, https://fcpablog.com/2019/06/18/english-private-prosecutions-are-now-too-important-to-ignore/ (noting that "private prosecutions became front page news around the world when proceedings," ultimately "thrown out by the High Court," "were brought against Boris Johnson, the likely next British prime minister, over claims that he lied during the 2016 Brexit referendum"; that "[p]rivate prosecutions begin when a magistrate issues a summons or warrant, following the 'laying on information' by the private prosecutor (a summary of the case)"; that "[p]rivate prosecutions (as opposed to public prosecutions) are those started by private individuals or entities not acting on behalf of the police or any other enforcement or prosecuting authority," with "[t]he right to bring ... long-established and contained in 6(1) of the Prosecution of Offences Act (POA) 1985"; that "[a]s regards scope, private prosecutions can be used for any offense, including fraud, and Proceeds of Crime Act 2002 offenses"; that "private prosecutors are subject to obligations to act as ministers of justice" and "English solicitors conducting private prosecutions must maintain high standards of integrity"; and that "[t]he Director of Public Prosecutions (DPP) can take over proceedings at any stage, and decide to discontinue the prosecution . . . ."); Julia Faure Walker & Hannah Thomas, "Who Is the Private Prosecutor?" 2 Hare Court, Sept. 14, 2018, https://www.2harecourt.com/training-and-knowledge/who-is-the-private-prosecutor/ ("By section 6 of the Prosecution of Offences Act 1985, Parliament reaffirmed, albeit in qualified terms, the right of '*any person*' to bring a prosecution. Part 7 of the Criminal Procedure Rules 2015, providing for the commencement of a prosecution, refers to '*a prosecutor*' laying an information."; "[A] prosecution can be commenced by a body corporate and the courts have generally been unwilling to allow informations to fail on such technicalities where the prosecutor is easily identifiable. However, it is 'preferable' that a prosecution is commenced by a named individual. The prosecutor must have legal personality and the authority to bring the prosecution.") (italic in original); Paul Cassell, "Is the Private Prosecution of the Hillsborough Disaster a Model for the U.S.?", Wash. Post, Apr.

15, 2014, https://www.washingtonpost.com/news/volokh-conspiracy/wp/2014/04/15/is-the-private-prosecution-of-the-hillsborough-disaster-a-model-for-the-u-s/ ("[C]rime victims in England have the clear opportunity to bring their own criminal cases by initiating a 'private prosecution.' Such an opportunity is not unfettered. As I understand English criminal procedure, public prosecutors are free to intervene in such a private prosecution for the purpose of dismissing charges that are not well-founded."). For more information about the process by which private prosecutions are commenced in England, as well as about how they can be discontinued, see the Crown Prosecution Service's website, which contains information on those subjects. Private Prosecutions, Crown Prosecution Service, https://www.cps.gov.uk/legal-guidance/private-prosecutions (updated October 2019).

235. State v. Storm, 661 A.2d 790, 793 (N.J. 1995); *see also id.* ("Private prosecution derives from the practice of trial by combat, which evolved into the prosecution of criminal charges by private parties. By the early nineteenth century, Britain's system of private prosecution was in retreat. In 1879, Parliament created the Office of Public Prosecutions, which prosecuted serious crimes. Twenty-nine years later, Parliament enacted the Prosecution of Offenses Act, which allows the Director of Public Prosecutions to supersede a private prosecution.") (citations omitted); *id.* ("English justice became the dominant influence in the development of New Jersey's criminal justice system. By the eighteenth century, New Jersey had established an extensive system of public prosecution. Even so, in the last century, the former New Jersey Supreme Court described private prosecution as 'the settled practice in this State....' Notwithstanding the reforms of the judicial and criminal justice systems in the 1947 Constitution, the practice of private prosecution has survived.") (citation omitted; quoting Gardner v. State, 55 N.J.L. 17, 33, 26 A. 30 (1892)).

236. *See* Elizabeth Gilchrist, *Attitudes Towards Victims of Crime: A Double-Edged Sword? in* Jane Wood & Theresa Gannon, eds., Public Opinion and Criminal Justice 146 (2009) ("In England and Wales, although there is now a public prosecution service, historically criminal proceedings were private matters. Even the police prosecuted as private bodies on behalf of the victims. Also, while the right is not always exercised and it is possible for the Crown Prosecution Service to 'take over' a private prosecution case and discontinue it, it is still possible in England and Wales for a victim to pursue a private prosecution through the criminal courts. In this system, particularly in sexual offences and offences from within a domestic setting, the victim as a more central role. However, although it is common to hear that victims have 'dropped the charges', charges can only be dropped with the consent of the Crown Prosecution Service. If the CPS does not consent then the prosecution goes ahead.").

237. Gary Slapper & David Kelly, The English Legal System: 2015–2016, at 19 (16th ed. 2015) ("It should not be forgotten that although prosecution of criminal offences is usually the prerogative of the State, it remains open to the private individual to initiate a private prosecution in relation to a criminal offence. It has to be remembered, however, that even in the private prosecution, the test of the burden of proof remains the criminal one requiring the facts to be proved beyond reasonable doubt. An example of the problems inherent in such private actions can be seen in the case of Stephen Lawrence, the young black man who was gratuitously stabbed to death by a gang of white racists whilst standing at a bus stop in London. Although there was strong suspicion, and indeed evidence, against particular individuals, the CPS [Crown Prosecution Service] declined to press charges against them on the basis of insufficiency of evidence. When the lawyers of the Lawrence family mounted a private prosecution against the suspects, the action failed for want of sufficient evidence to convict. As a consequence of the failure of the private prosecution, the rule against double jeopardy meant that the accused could not be retried for the same offence at any time in the future, even if the police subsequently acquired sufficient new evidence to support a conviction."); *see also id.* (noting that "a Law Commission report recommended the removal of the double jeopardy rule and provision to remove it, under particular circumstances and subject to strict regulation, was contained in ss 77–79 of the Criminal Justice Act 2003"; that in September 2010, two men, Gary Dobson and David Norris, were arrested for Stephen Lawrence's murder, even though Dobson had been one of the people originally charged in the private prosecution; and that both Dobson and Norris were prosecuted in 2011 and convicted of Lawrence's murder in 2012 after the Court of Appeals held that there was sufficient new scientific evidence justify a retrial under the Criminal Justice Act 2003).

238. "A Guide to Private Prosecution Procedure in England and Wales," McCue Law, http://www.mccue-law.com/wp-content/uploads/2011/09/UK-guide-to-private-prosecution1.pdf.

239. David D. Friedman, *Making Sense of English Law Enforcement in the Eighteenth Century*, 2 U. CHI. L. SCH. ROUNDTABLE 475, 476 (1995); *see also id.* ("Under English law, any Englishman could prosecute any crime. In practice, the prosecutor was usually the victim. It was up to him to file charges with the local magistrate, present evidence to the grand jury, and, if the grand jury found a true bill, provide evidence for the trial."); *id.* at 477–78 ("Dissatisfaction with the perceived problems of private prosecution, and concerns with what was perceived as a high and rising crime rate, eventually led to the introduction of full-scale paid police forces, first in London in 1829 and later elsewhere in England. The police took over from the private prosecutors much of the responsibility for identifying and apprehending criminals. As the century passed, the police also took over much of the job of prosecuting criminals. By the end of the century, prosecution was still for the most part nominally private, but the private prosecutor was usually a police officer."); Dietrich Oberwittler, *Crime and Authority in Eighteenth Century England: Law Enforcement on the Local Level*, 15 HISTORICAL SOCIAL RESEARCH 3, 16 (1990) ("[I]n the eighteenth century there were no police to carry out investigations and no public prosecutor to bring a suspected criminal to trial; instead, the burden of criminal prosecution was entirely left to the victim."); *id.* at 17 ("Many victims preferred the compounding of a property crime to a criminal prosecution, if the stolen goods could be recovered in this way. In the capital, advertisements in the newspapers were a frequently used medium for communication between the victim and the thief. Another reason not to deliver the criminal to the courts was public disapproval of a criminal law which inflicted capital punishment or transportation for the mere theft of the proverbial silk handkerchief.").

240. JOHN HOSTETTLER, A HISTORY OF CRIMINAL JUSTICE IN ENGLAND AND WALES 119 (2009) ("Three factors are generally put forward to explain the entry of defence lawyers in criminal trials and their introduction of adversary trial. The first is the creation of a rewards culture for bounty hunters. By a series of statutes at the end of the seventeenth century, and into the first half of the nineteenth century, prosecutors and their witnesses could receive substantial sums of money from the state for informing that led to a conviction. Hundreds of thousands of pounds were paid out in this way and not unnaturally this led to a good deal of perjury and accusations against innocent people."); *see also* MIA MAHMUDUR RAHIM, LEGAL REGULATION OF CORPORATE SOCIAL RESPONSIBILITY: A META-REGULATION APPROACH OF LAW FOR RAISING CSR IN A WEAK ECONOMY 158 (2013) ("Facilitating the function of bounty hunters within the domain of regulation is an old idea that can be traced back to the qui tam writs in the English state during the fourteenth and fifteenth centuries. 'A writ of *qui tam* is a writ whereby a private individual who assists a prosecution can receive all or part of any penalty imposed.'").

241. CHRISTOPHER BLAKE, BARRIE SHELDON & PETER WILLIAMS, POLICING AND CRIMINAL JUSTICE (2010). The conduct of thief-takers was the subject of considerable controversy and public debate. THE REGULATOR: OR, A DISCOVERY OF THE THIEVES, THIEF-TAKERS, AND LOCKS, ALIAS RECEIVERS OF STOLEN GOODS IN AND ABOUT THE CITY OF LONDON (1718) ("By a Prisoner in NEWGATE"); *see also* JOHN FIELDING, A PLAN FOR PREVENTING ROBBERIES WITHIN TWENTY MILES OF LONDON, WITH AN ACCOUNT OF THE RISE AND ESTABLISHMENT OF THE REAL THIEFTAKERS (1755); *see also* RACHEL WEIL, A PLAGUE OF INFORMERS: CONSPIRACY AND POLITICAL TRUST IN WILLIAM III'S ENGLAND (2013) ("Thief-takers straddled the border between crime and law enforcement. They helped victims to make a 'composition' with a thief (that is, to buy their stolen goods back at a price that was less than their value but high enough to make the effort of stealing them worthwhile for the thief). The thief-takers were able to negotiate such settlements, of course, because they had connections among criminals, often heading up the gangs of thieves that committed the robbery in the first place. Yet they were tolerated and sometime protected by magistrates. Such tolerance was justifiable as the least of all possible evils: thief-takers 'helped' the victim, and because they were sometimes willing to act as informants and witnesses they helped control crime. But it made the magistrate into the thief's accomplice, subjecting him (fairly or unfairly) to charges of corruption."); DAVID LEMMINGS, LAW AND GOVERNMENT IN ENGLAND DURING THE LONG EIGHTEENTH CENTURY (2011) ("[T]he enduring existence of large incentives to catch thieves helped to accelerate the tendency towards professional policing as substitute constables and 'thief-takers' made a lucrative trade out of prosecuting criminals, sometimes earning the princely sum of £140 per head. It is true that 'policing' of this private enterprise kind tended to corruption, for criminal entrepreneurs like Jonathan Wild combined prosecuting for profit with organizing theft and returning stolen goods for gratuities. Also there were

several major reward scandals, whereby prosecutions which had led to execution were found to have been fabricated by thief-takers."). The term "blood money" was the slang used to describe "[t]he reward given by the legislature on the conviction of highwaymen, burglars, &c." CAPTAIN GROSE, COMP., LEXICON BALATRONICUM: A DICTIONARY OF BUCKISH SLANG, UNIVERSITY WIT, AND PICKPOCKET ELOQUENCE (1811) (entry for blood money); "Police of the Metropolis," *in* 33 T. C. HANSARD, ED., THE PARLIAMENTARY DEBATES FROM THE YEAR 1803 TO THE PRESENT TIME: FORMING A CONTINUATION OF THE WORK ENTITLED "THE PARLIAMENTARY HISTORY OF ENGLAND FROM THE EARLIEST PERIOD TO THE YEAR 1803" 888–89 (1816) ("Mr. *Bennet* rose to move for a committee to inquire into the state of the Police of the Metropolis. The question, he said, had been often before considered—in 1772, in 1791, and again in 1812; in consequence of the atrocious acts (the murder of the Marrs and Williamsons) which had struck the metropolis with horror and alarm.... He should first state, that he considered the system of giving 40*l.* on convictions for offences of magnitude a very bad one: the money was technically called *blood money*; and the consequence was, that offenders were allowed to escape, till by the process of crime; they increased in value. The giving of sums of money in the way of rewards had also been found very pernicious on the same principle."); FRANCIS GROSE, A CLASSICAL DICTIONARY OF THE VULGAR TONGUE (2d ed. 1788) (defining "THIEF TAKERS" as follows: "Fellows who associate with all kinds of villains, in order to betray them, when they have committed any of those crimes which entitle the persons taking them to a handsome reward, called blood money. It is the business of these thief takers to furnish subjects for a handsome execution, at the end of every sessions."). For a discussion of how private prosecutors worked with magistrates and "runners" and got assistance with investigations in eighteenth-century England, *see* J. M. BEATTIE, THE FIRST ENGLISH DETECTIVES: THE BOW STREET RUNNERS AND THE POLICING OF LONDON, 1750–1840, at 3, 52, 55, 95, 109, 205 (2012).

242. The Code for Crown Prosecutors (Oct. 26, 2018), General Principle 2.1, *available at* https://www.cps.gov.uk/publication/code-crown-prosecutors.

243. Ward v. State, 427 A.2d 1008, 1012 (Md. 1981) ("Apparently the first reported case discussing the entry of a nolle prosequi in a criminal prosecution was *Stretton and Taylors Case,* 1 Leon. 119, 74 Eng. Rep. 111 (K.B. 1588), where the Attorney General entered a '*non vult prosequi* ' for purpose of preventing a private prosecution. Since that time, the nolle prosequi has been a means whereby the government exercises control over pending criminal cases. Thus ... a '*Nolle prosequi* in criminal practice (for it pertains also to civil), is a declaration of record from the legal representative for the government, that he will no further prosecute the particular indictment or some designated part thereof.' It is 'an abandonment of the prosecution,' or a 'discontinuance of a prosecution by the authorized attorney' for the state."); *see also* Hoskins v. Maricle, 150 S.W.3d 1, 30 n.27 (Ky. 2004) (concurring in part and dissenting in part) (discussing the history of the *nolle prosequi* practice).

244. The High Court in England, in 2019, blocked a private prosecution of Tory leader Boris Johnson. Jane Croft, "High Court Blocks Private Prosecution of Boris Johnson," *Financial Times*, June 7, 2019, https://www.ft.com/content/d3be7ec8-890c-11e9-a028-86cea8523dc2; *see also Ball v Johnson*, https://en.wikipedia.org/wiki/Ball_v_Johnson ("*Ball v Johnson* was an attempted private prosecution application by Marcus Ball and his company Brexit Justice Limited, on 29 May 2019, against Boris Johnson for three counts of alleged misconduct in public office. The applicants alleged that Johnson 'in his position as a Member of Parliament and Mayor of London, abused the public's trust during the 2016 Brexit referendum by lying about the United Kingdom's spending on European Union membership.'").

245. The Code for Crown Prosecutors (Oct. 26, 2018), General Principles 2.7 & 2.8, *available at* https://www.cps.gov.uk/publication/code-crown-prosecutors.

246. 19 THE NEW INTERNATIONAL ENCYCLOPÆDIA 272 (2d ed. 1916); *see also* THE EXAMINER (London, England), Feb. 16, 1867, p. 4 ("The framers of the Act of 1854 seem to have known well what they were about in placing bribery in the category of indictable offences triable at the assizes, and in order to guard against the risk of innocent persons being harassed by prosecutions for bribery, they, in a spirit of exceptional legislation, have in sections 12 and 13 made the following provisions: 'In case of any indictment or information by a private prosecutor for any offence against the provisions of this Act, if judgment be given for the defendant, *i.e.*, he shall be entitled to recover from the prosecutor the costs sustained by the

defendant by reason of such indictment or information, such costs to be taxed by the proper officer of the Court in which such judgment shall be given.'").

247. "Justice for Sale," THE INDEPENDENT (London, England), Aug. 16, 2014, p. 2 (editorial). A century and a half earlier, English private prosecutions had come under attack on multiple fronts even though it would take decades for a Director of Public Prosecutions to be appointed (and many more decades for English private prosecutions to precipitously decline). WENDIE ELLEN SCHNEIDER, ENGINES OF TRUTH: PRODUCING VERACITY IN THE VICTORIAN COURTROOM 35 (2015) ("Legislation establishing the office of a Public Prosecutor was not passed until 1879...."); *id.* at 35–36 ("The limitations of private prosecution led both to overenforcement of dubious cases and to underenforcement of possibly meritorious cases. As one barrister described the situation in 1855, private prosecution was responsible for a litany of evils: 'escape of criminals for want of prosecution; deliberate mismanagement of prosecutions; improper compromise and abandonment of prosecutions; the securing of prosecutions by 'low attorneys';... the high cost of private prosecutions; and the failure properly to instruct grand juries.' Perjury prosecutions motivated by revenge or the desire to inconvenience an opponent could be added to that list. Perjury prosecutions, in particular, were also singled out by the Attorney General as too frequently settled by the parties in exchange for compensation, rather than proceeding to adjudication."); David G. T. Williams, "Prosecution, Discretion and the Accountability of the Policy," *in* ROGER HOOD, ED., CRIME, CRIMINOLOGY AND PUBLIC POLICY: ESSAYS IN HONOUR OF SIR LEON RADZINOWICZ 166 (1975) ("Nowadays the number of private prosecutions each year is extremely small, partly because of a growing acceptance of the role of the police as prosecutors and partly because of the prohibitive cost of instituting and conducting the proceedings."). For more information on the development of English public prosecutions, the duly appointed public prosecutors, and the creation of the Crown Prosecution Service, *see* JOSHUA ROZENBERG, THE CASE FOR THE CROWN: THE INSIDE STORY OF THE DIRECTOR OF PUBLIC PROSECUTIONS (1987).

Chapter 3 Notes

1. DAVID W. NEUBAUER & HENRY F. FRADELLA, AMERICA'S COURTS AND THE CRIMINAL JUSTICE SYSTEM 170 (13th ed. 2019) ("In 1704, Connecticut enacted the first statutory scheme for public prosecutions. And in 1711, 'Virginia established a formal system of county prosecuting attorneys.'") (citation omitted); Jason Twede, Going Public: How the Government Assumed the Authority to Prosecute in the Southern United States, Ph.D. thesis, University of North Dakota (May 2016), p. 21 ("Connecticut's statute of 1704 reads: 'Henceforth there shall be in every county a sober, discreet and religious person appointed by the county courts, to be attorney for the Queen to prosecute and implead in the law all criminals and to do all other things necessary or convenient as an attorney to suppress vice and immorality.'"); OLIVER PERRY CHITWOOD, JUSTICE IN COLONIAL VIRGINIA 120–21 (1905) ("In 1711, it was found necessary to appoint prosecuting attorneys for the counties. At that time breaches of the penal laws were prosecuted in the counties by those persons who had reported them to the courts, and informers were given one-half of all the fines imposed for offenses reported by them. It sometimes happened that the informer would compound with the accused for half of the fines and would then stop the prosecution. This would cause the case to be thrown out of court, and, so the crown would fail to receive its half of the fine. There was need, therefore, of a better method of prosecuting offenders in the counties, and Governor Spottswood, following a recommendation of the attorney-general, issued a proclamation appointing prosecuting attorneys for the counties. These new officers came to stay, and from this time on we find them performing their duties in the county courts.").

2. State v. Gerry, 38 A. 272, 273 (N.H. 1896) ("By the common law of the colony no one could be subjected to a trial for any criminal offense beyond the jurisdiction of a justice of the peace, except upon an indictment returned by a grand jury in cases of felony, or in the case of misdemeanors, on such indictment, or upon an information filed by the attorney general. The English common law respecting appeals of murder and other crimes (4 Bl. Comm. 312–316), and its rule that one found guilty of a felony by the verdict of a jury in a civil cause might, without other accusation, be put on trial for the crime (1 Chit. Cr. Law, 164, 165; Bac. Abr. 'Indictment,' B.), were never adopted here."); *see also* Barnet v. Ihrie, 17 Serg. &

Rawle 174, 214, 1828 WL 2411, at *32 (Pa. 1828) (Huston, J., dissenting) ("The original settlers of this country, and their successors for more than a century, had no doubt on this subject. No one thought of going to the times of Edward and Richard for correct views of the rights or remedies necessary for more enlightened times. Trial by battel, and attaints, and assize were equally unknown. We must now decide whether they are to remain so, or are to be dug from the rubbish in which they had been forgotten, and introduced to our courts, and forced on our citizens, till again experience sends them back to obscurity. The only difficulty, or at least, the greatest which meets us, is the fact, that in 1809, there was an assize of nuisance tried in this county, and about the same time, the judges, as is supposed, reported that several acts of parliament prescribing the forms, &c., of assize, were in force. As to the trial, let those who choose read it, and those who wish for such another say so. As to the report of the judges, it is not so explicit as could have been wished. Their notes to several statutes, 'to be incorporated,' and 'this statute, or certain sections of it, are in force,' leaves an uncertainty as to what is really meant in each case. I shall show that the words 'to be incorporated,' did not mean, as they do not purport to mean, that the statute has ever been in use in this country. I think no one will say, that an appeal of murder or felony was ever in use in Pennsylvania, or that it can be, since the present constitution; yet four statutes (the last in 1300) are mentioned, and have the note 'to be incorporated,' added to them; and if incorporated, we may see a trial by battel, for it is as much a part of the law as the appeal."); *see also* "Brief for Petitioner," Robertson v. United States ex rel. Watson, 2010 WL 360209, at *22–25 (U.S.) (Appellate Brief):

> The appeal, a vestigial remnant of the "primitive conditions of society," Riddell, *supra* n.10 at 1, was in virtual disuse in England by the late eighteenth century. While Stephen explained that "the only appeals which can be said to have ... formed a substantial part of the criminal procedure of [England] were appeals of murder," 1 Stephen, *History of the Criminal Law* at 248, he noted that even the appeal of murder virtually had ended in England by the late eighteenth century. *See id.* at 248–49. Blackstone felt constrained to describe appeals, but only while simultaneously noting that the practice was already then in virtual disuse: "As this method of prosecutions is still in force, I cannot omit to mention it: but as it is very little in use ... I shall treat of it very briefly." 4 *Commentaries* *308.
>
> Perhaps more important than its declining status in England at the time of the framing, the practice never took hold in the Colonies. *See generally Burns v. Reed*, 500 U.S. 478, 493 (1991) ("[I]t is American common law that is determinative."). Early jurisprudence in the States recognized the appeal of felony as an oddity of the English common law, never practiced after independence on this side of the ocean. *See Boston & W.R. Corp. v. Dana*, 67 Mass. (1 Gray) 83, 97–98 (1854) ("No one has ever heard of an appeal of felony ... in our courts. So far therefore as we know the origin of the rule and the reasons on which it was founded, it would seem very clear that it was never adopted here as part of our common law."); *State v. Gerry*, 38 A. 272, 273 (N.H. 1896) ("The English common law respecting appeals of murder and other crimes and its rule that one found guilty of a felony by the verdict of a jury in a civil cause might, without other accusation, be put on trial for the crime were never adopted here.") (citations omitted); *In re Presentment by Camden County Grand Jury*, 89 A.2d 416, 423–24 (N.J. 1952) (noting "no record of its use has been located" in New Jersey); *Barnet v. Ihrie*, 17 Serg. & Rawle 174, 214 (Pa. 1828) (Huston, J., dissenting) ("I think no one will say, that an appeal of murder or felony was ever in use in Pennsylvania, or that it can be, since the present constitution."); *Allison v. Farmers' Bank of Va.*, 27 Va. (6 Rand.) 204, 225 (1828) ("In all these respects, the policy and spirit of our Laws are the reverse of those of the English Laws. We have no appeal, in which the right to a civil action can merge.").
>
> The colorful words of a Pennsylvania court reflect American distaste for the private criminal suit:
>
>> The old common-law right of prosecuting the higher felonies by appeal, which had sprung from a barbarous state of society, was left by our ancestors in the lumber garrets of the law at home.... These are not the days to encourage individuals, or the masses, to snatch the reins from the constituted organs of the government.... Astounding results proceed from small beginnings; and we have already beheld appalling scenes enacted in our commercial emporium with impunity, and almost without resistance, by men who took the law into their own hands in the name of the people.

Commonwealth v. Burrell, 7 Pa. 34, 39 (1847).

This Court previously identified only a single instance of the appeal used here, a 1765 case in the Maryland province, *Soaper v. Negro Tom*, 1 H. & McH. 227 (Md. 1765), where under English law a private appeal of murder resulted in the hanging of a slave. *See Hurtado v. California*, 110 U.S. 516, 526 (1884). Notably, the private cause of action was subsequently deemed inconsistent with the Maryland Constitution. *See* William Kilty, *A Report of English Statutes* 141, 143, 158 (1811); *see generally Dashiell v. Attorney General*, 5 H. & J. 392 (Md. 1822) (relying on *A Report of English Statutes* to determine which English statutes were applicable in Maryland). In *Louisville, Evansville, & St. Louis R.R. Co. v. Clarke*, 152 U.S. 230 (1894), this Court described the English practice of the appeal, but recognized that "we do not in this country depend upon the injured party, or his representative, to institute criminal prosecutions." 152 U.S. at 235–36.

3. John W. Stickels, *Victim Impact Evidence: The Victims' Right that Influences Criminal Trials*, 32 Tex. Tech L. Rev. 231, 234 (2001) ("The English who settled the North American colonial frontier during the seventeenth century brought the English common law with them. The colonists also imported the English tradition of private prosecutions. As in England, the victim had the obligation to initiate and prosecute a criminal case against a perpetrator."); *see also* Roger A. Fairfax, Jr., *Delegation of the Criminal Prosecution Function to Private Actors*, 42 U.C. Davis L. Rev. 411, 421 (2009) ("Although prosecutorial power in the early colonies initially often was concentrated in a representative of the Crown, the English tradition of private prosecution dominated the early American experience before the Revolution."); Sue Anna Moss Cellini, *The Proposed Victims' Rights Amendment to the Constitution of the United States: Opening the Door of the Criminal Justice System to the Victim*, 14 Ariz. J. Int'l & Comp. L. 839, 844 (1997) ("In the American colonies, building on European legal concepts, the first statutes establishing the office of public prosecutor merely authorized public prosecution, but did not withdraw from the private individual the right to instigate a criminal prosecution if the public official did not."); Paul G. Cassell & Steven Joffee, *The Crime Victim's Expanding Role in a System of Public Prosecution: A Response to the Critics of the Crime Victims' Rights Act*, 105 Nw. U. L. Rev. Colloquy 164, 178 (2011) ("[L]egal scholars report that private prosecutions were the dominant form of prosecution during the colonial period."); *id.* at 180 ("Although private prosecution was firmly entrenched in the history of the colonies and the states, it does not appear to have been extensively used in the federal system."); Douglas E. Beloof & Paul G. Cassell, *The Crime Victim's Right to Attend the Trial: The Reascendant National Consensus*, 9 Lewis & Clark L. Rev. 481, 485 (2005) ("[H]istories of colonial and post-constitutional criminal justice generally acknowledge the prevalence of private prosecution.") (citing Richard Gaskins, *Changes in the Criminal Law in Eighteenth-Century Connecticut*, 25 Am. J. Legal Hist. 309 (1981); Michael S. Hindus, *The Contours of Crime and Justice in Massachusetts and South Carolina, 1767–1878*, 21 Am. J. Legal. Hist. 212 (1977); William H. Loyd, Jr., *The Courts of Pennsylvania in the Eighteenth Century Prior to the Revolution*, 56 U. Pa. L. Rev. 28, 46 (1908); Erwin C. Surrency, *The Evolution of an Urban Judicial System: The Philadelphia Story, 1683–1968*, 18 Am. J. Legal Hist. 95 (1974)); Alexis de Tocqueville, Democracy in America, 96 (Anchor Books ed., 1969) ("the officers of the public prosecutor's office are few, and the initiative in prosecutions is not always theirs"); "Colonial Legislation," Morning Post (London, England), Dec. 30, 1819, p. 4 ("That English Colonies should be governed as much as possible in the spirit and genius of the English law, is a rule as old as our Colonial establishments. It is the common style of the records in the Council books on all proceedings like the present, to set forth the power granted to the Colonial Legislatures to make laws, which are to be 'as near as conveniently may be agreeable to the laws and statutes of this kingdom.' The same provision appears in all the Colonial charters extant, particularly in those of Maryland, 1681; Hudson's Bay, 1670; Pennsylvania, 1682; and Massachusett's Bay, 1691. The reason of the rule was obviously to keep up such an identity of feeling and sentiment between the colonies and the mother country, as would ensure the attachment of the former to the latter.").

4. George C. Thomas III, *Colonial Criminal Law and Procedure: The Royal Colony of New Jersey 1749–57*, 1 NYU J. L. & Liberty 671, 671–73, 679 (2005), https://www.law.nyu.edu/sites/default/files/ECM_PRO_060913.pdf; *see also id.* at 710 ("The colonial historian Anton-Hermann Chroust wrote that after New Jersey became a royal colony in 1702, it 'probably followed more closely the common law of England and English precedents than any other American colony.'").

5. Josephine Gittler, *Expanding the Role of the Victim in a Criminal Action: An Overview of Issues and Problems*, 11 PEPP. L. REV. 117, 125–26 (1984).

6. FRANCIS WHARTON, A TREATISE ON THE CRIMINAL LAW OF THE UNITED STATES: COMPRISING A GENERAL VIEW OF THE CRIMINAL JURISPRUDENCE OF THE COMMON AND CIVIL LAW, AND A DIGEST OF THE PENAL STATUTES OF THE GENERAL GOVERNMENT, AND OF MASSACHUSETTS, NEW YORK, PENNSYLVANIA, VIRGINIA AND OHIO; WITH THE DECISIONS ON CASES ARISING UPON THOSE STATUTES 268 (4th & rev. ed. 1857) ("The institution of grand juries presents questions of a political as well as a legal character, which have been the subject of a conflict of opinion in this country in recent times, as great as that which existed with regard to the same agency in England before the revolution. The point of discussion, however, is not the same. In the time of James II., when Lord Somers' famous tract was written, a barrier was needed against frivolous state prosecutions, and this barrier grand juries presented. In our own times a restraint is required upon the malice of private prosecutors, and the violence of popular excitement; and it is to the adequacy of grand juries for that purpose, that public attention has been turned. Assuming, therefore, as now settled definitely, that on all prosecutions instituted either by government or individuals, the grand jury has an absolute veto at the outset, the fundamental question still remains, have grand juries anything more than the power of veto, or in other words, can they originate prosecutions, and if so, with what qualifications?"); Harold J. Krent, *Executive Control Over Criminal Law Enforcement: Some Lessons from History*, 38 AM. U. L. REV. 275, 292 (1989) ("Although Congress never vested victims with a general right to prosecute defendants under federal criminal provisions, citizens in the first years under the Constitution evidently presented evidence of crimes directly to the grand jury. More commonly, individuals continued as at common law to bring evidence of crimes before magistrates and then, upon the magistrate's approval, to obtain a bench warrant for the defendant's arrest.").

7. Carolyn B. Ramsey, *The Discretionary Power of 'Public' Prosecutors in Historical Perspective*, 39 AM. CRIM. L. REV. 1309, 1325–26 (2002); *see also id.* at 1326 ("Indeed, private citizens continued to initiate and litigate criminal prosecutions in New York until the 1840s or 1850s, and even as late as 1891, relatives of a murder victim might urge the District Attorney to charge an individual whom they suspected. Before mid-century, activities like searching for evidence, drafting legal documents, and empanelling a jury corresponded to a fee schedule; the complaining witness paid the District Attorney for services rendered. Moreover, in the early 1800s, private lawyers (rather than the District Attorney) commonly presented criminal cases in New York courts—sometimes representing the victim in one matter and the defendant in another.").

8. CAROLYN BOYES-WATSON WITH SUSAN T. KRUMHOLZ, CRIME AND JUSTICE: LEARNING THROUGH CASES 207 (3d ed. 2018); *see also* THEODORE FERDINAND, BOSTON'S LOWER CRIMINAL COURTS, 1814–1850, at 97 (1992) ("In the beginning the American colonies assumed a system of private prosecution based on an age-old practice followed in England. An attorney general, appointed by the royal governor, pursued cases of special political importance, as in England, but routine criminal cases were prosecuted by private individuals, usually the victim.") (citation omitted); RANDALL G. SHELDEN & PAVEL V. VASILIEV, CONTROLLING THE DANGEROUS CLASSES: A HISTORY OF CRIMINAL JUSTICE IN AMERICA 106 (3d ed. 2018) ("In colonial America, the victim hired a private prosecutor (usually a privately retained lawyer) for the case.... The grand jury was originally tied to private prosecution."); Marty C. Marran, *"Ubi Jus, Ibi Remedium"—Sed Non Hodie:* Bandoni v. State of Rhode Island, *a Ten Year Retrospective*, 13 ROGER WILLIAMS U. L. REV. 594, 599 n.22 (2008) ("private prosecution, no doubt, flourished in colonial times"); 1 CLAIRE M. RENZETTI & JEFFREY L. EDLESON, EDS., ENCYCLOPEDIA OF INTERPERSONAL VIOLENCE 408 (2008) ("As early as 1641, the Massachusetts Bay Colony legislated against wife-beating in its *Body of Liberties*. However, absent organized police and public prosecutors, there was no criminal justice system as we recognize it today. If law was to be enforced, it was through private prosecution, with either the victim or her representatives arguing her case before a magistrate."); Charles C. Olson, *"Pro Bono Publico": A History of Georgia's Prosecuting Attorneys (1732–2012)*, 25 J. S. LEGAL HIST. 235, 236 (2017) ("[T]he colony's founder, General James Oglethorpe, proudly declared in 1739 that 'no lawyers (were) allowed to plead for hire, nor no attorneys to take money, but (as in old times in England) every man pleads his own cause.' However, that did not mean that there was no court system or that crimes were not prosecuted—the Charter specifically empowered the Trustees to erect courts. During the Trustee period, cases were heard

in the Town Court of Savannah, with '[o]ne of the first cases,... a murder case,' tried on July 17, 1739. It meant rather that from 1733 until 1754, criminal prosecutions were brought either by the victim of the crime or by the constables before lay judges who had no legal training."); *see also* Stephanie Cole, "Keeping the Peace: Domestic Assault and Private Prosecution in Antebellum Baltimore," *in* CHRISTINE DANIELS & MICHAEL V. KENNEDY, EDS., OVER THE THRESHOLD: INTIMATE VIOLENCE IN EARLY AMERICA 148, 149 (1999) ("The procedures for prosecuting criminal assault in antebellum Maryland contributed to dependents' abilities to use the legal system to negotiate patriarchy; consequently, understanding judicial procedures is crucial to interpreting records of domestic assault. In early nineteenth-century Maryland, for example, victims generally had to institute and pursue criminal prosecutions."). In Native American communities, a practice known as peacemaking was often used to resolve disputes. Ghazi Hashimi, *Helping Afghanistan's Informal Dispute Resolution Systems Follow Afghan Law in Criminal Matters: What Afghanistan Can Learn from Native American Peacemaking Program,* 25 MICH. ST. INT'L L. REV. 77, 109 (2017) ("With the evolution of tribal government, criminal law and procedure has changed. Even though the U.S. federal government gave authority to the Navajo and other Indian tribes to run their own courts approximately a century ago, the Navajo Nation maintains traditional values of dispute resolution to a greater extent than other tribal courts in many other American Indian communities. Many Native American courts have different programs in their prosecutor's office that include community justice and formal dispute resolution. Peacemaking is one good way to recommend appropriate disciplinary actions to the criminal or defendant and to address victims' rights. Parties to the conflict; victims and its relatives; and defendant and its relatives, settle and agree on the terms of sentence and ask a Peacemaker to deliver it for them."); *id.* at 104–05 ("Although Indian tribes were given the authority to run their own court systems a century ago, some of them preferred to maintain traditional values of dispute resolution to a greater extent over formal courts. Thus, tribal courts have been using traditional law in different areas of law. The method of using traditional law varies from tribe to tribe; however, they all share a similar purpose reflective of native customs and traditions. The Navajo Nation has a 'horizontal' traditional model of justice that is to show equality among people and, according to which, no person is above another. In this system, victims, defendants, and others who are effected by the committed crime, get together to discuss the situation, find the causes of crime, express their emotions, and agree on compensation that would restore the lost harmony to all concerned. In addition, the horizontal model of dispute resolution shares the same principles related to the healing of parties. The traditional indigenous and restorative justice movement trends deal with very concrete processes to settle disputes, especially adult criminal and juvenile wrongdoing cases."); Jessica Metoui, Comment, *Returning to the Circle: The Reemergence of Traditional Dispute Resolution in Native American Communities,* 2007 J. DISP. RESOL. 517, 519–20 ("The creation of adversarial justice systems by agents of American jurisprudence illuminated many of the conflicts between Western and Native American ideologies about the nature of law. The United States imposed its ideology because of the pervading view that a Western legal system represented the correct way to administer justice, despite any conflicts with native culture that the imposition of such a system might cause. This divergence remained largely unexamined at the end of the nineteenth and early twentieth centuries, when Indian court systems were being formed."); *id.* at 520–21 ("The imposition of Western style courts alienated tribal societies from the laws which governed them. Recent institutionalization of dispute resolution methods that utilize traditional concepts of justice, such as peacemaking circles, represents a move within Native American communities to replace the adversarial systems imposed by the United States' colonization efforts with culturally relevant systems of justice."); Mary Ellen Reimund, *Is Restorative Justice on a Collision Course with the Constitution?,* 3 APPALACHIAN J.L. 1, 12 (2004) ("Sentencing circles find their origins in Native Canadian and Native American community peacemaking processes. People participating sit in a circle while a 'talking piece' is passed from person to person as each speaks about their feelings regarding the crime and expresses their support for the victim and offender. The most extensive use of circles is in Saskatchewan, Manitoba, and the Yukon, although their usage is growing in the United States, especially in Minnesota.").

9. ANDREW KARMEN, CRIME VICTIMS: AN INTRODUCTION TO VICTIMOLOGY 420 (9th ed. 2016) ("In colonial America before the Revolution, criminal acts were handled as private conflicts between individuals. Police departments and public prosecutors did not exist yet. A victim in a city could call upon night watchmen for help, but they might not be on duty, or the offender might flee beyond their jurisdiction. If

the injured party sought the aid of a sheriff, he had to pay a fee. If the sheriff located the alleged perpetrator, he would charge extra to serve a warrant against the defendant. When the suspect was taken into custody, the complainant had to hire a lawyer to draw up an indictment. Then the complainant either prosecuted the case personally or hired an attorney for an additional fee to handle the private prosecution. If the accused was found guilty, the person he harmed could gain substantial benefits. Convicted thieves were required to repay their victims three times as much as they had stolen. Thieves who could not hand over such large amounts were compelled to be servants until their debts were paid off. If the victims wished, they could sell these indentured servants for a hefty price, and they had one month in which to find a buyer. After that, victims were responsible for the costs of maintaining the offenders behind bars. If they didn't pay the fees, the convicts were released.") (citations omitted); *see also* Angela J. Davis, *The American Prosecutor: Independence, Power, and the Threat of Tyranny*, 86 Iowa L. Rev. 393, 449–50 (2001) ("Criminal prosecutions in colonial America mirrored the early English experience. Before the American Revolution, the crime victim maintained sole responsibility for apprehending and prosecuting the criminal suspect. The victim conducted the investigation and acted as prosecutor if the case went to trial. Alternatively, the victim hired a detective and a private lawyer to perform these functions. If convicted, the court frequently ordered the subject to pay restitution to the victim. Poor criminal defendants paid for their crimes by working for the victim as a servant or having their services sold for the financial benefit of the victim. If the victim did not want these services or was unable to sell them, the law mandated that the victim pay the jailer for maintaining custody of the prisoner."); William F. McDonald, *The Role of the Victim in America*, *in* Assessing the Criminal: Restitution, Retribution and the Legal Process 295 (Randy E. Barnett & John Hagel III eds., 1977) (discussing the practice of private prosecution in colonial America); Rachelle K. Hong, *Nothing to Fear: Establishing an Equality of Rights for Crime Victims Through the Victims' Rights Amendment*, 16 Notre Dame J.L. Ethics & Pub. Pol'y 207, 209 (2002) ("Colonists brought the principles of English common law, including private criminal prosecutions, with them to the New World. Private prosecutions provided victims of felonies the active role of not only initiating, but also prosecuting their offenders on their own, without a public prosecutor. This practice was 'widespread' in colonial America....").

10. Susan E. Gegan & Nicholas Ernesto Rodriguez, *Victims' Roles in the Criminal Justice System: A Fallacy of Victim Empowerment?*, 8 J. Civ. Rights & Econ. Development 225, 225 n.3 (1992). *See also* Michael Edmund O'Neill, *Private Vengeance and the Public Good*, 12 U. Pa. J. Const. L. 659, 673–74 (2010) ("Mirroring the English view of considering crime to be a private concern, private criminal prosecutions in the American colonies appear to have been commonplace, but not exclusive. Scholarship tracing the origins of the prosecutorial function in colonial America demonstrates the colonial legislatures, borrowing from the Dutch, often established offices for public prosecutors. Until the late-nineteenth century, however, private prosecutions dominated the legal landscape."); Michael Clemente, *A Reassessment of Common Law Protections for "Idiots"*, 124 Yale L.J. 2746, 2773 (2015) ("First, as a baseline matter, we know relatively little about criminal justice in the colonies. As Lawrence Friedman said, 'The colonial world is not easy to capture in a few short pages, and its criminal justice system is no less elusive. The further we go back in time, the dimmer the world gets, and the stranger.' In their casebook, Langbein, Lerner, and Smith likewise acknowledge that 'little is known about the conduct of criminal prosecutions in colonial America....' Second, the colonies were not homogenous; they varied across geographical regions."); Note, Sierra Elizabeth, *The Newest Spectator Sport: Why Extending Victims' Rights to the Spectators' Gallery Erodes the Presumption of Innocence*, 58 Duke L.J. 275, 285 (2008) ("In colonial America, individual victims of crime were the ones in charge of 'law enforcement and the administration of justice.' In the early eighteenth century, however, as the broader criminal-justice goals of deterrence and retribution started to garner support, once-private criminal prosecutions become public, and individual victims of crime had to yield their control to government prosecutors.").

11. Mikhail v. Kahn, 991 F. Supp.2d 596, 636 (E.D. Pa. 2014).

12. In re Hickson, 821 A.2d 1238, 1244 (Pa. 2003) (quoting Note, *The Constitutional Validity of Pennsylvania Rule of Criminal Procedure 133(B)(2) and the Traditional Role of the Pennsylvania Courts in the Prosecutorial Function*, 52 U. Pitt. L. Rev. 269, 274 (1990)); *see also In re Hickson*, 821 A.2d at 1244 ("This was consonant with the English common law principle that 'the Crown did not supply a public prosecutor

to handle routine felonies. The victim or his family was therefore required to hire counsel to bring the guilty party into the criminal justice system.'") (quoting State v. Atkins, 163 W. Va. 502, 261 S.E.2d 55, 57 (1979)).

13. Clare A. Lyons, *Mapping an Atlantic Sexual Culture: Homoeroticism in Eighteenth-Century Philadelphia*, *in* LONG BEFORE STONEWALL: HISTORIES OF SAME-SEX SEXUALITY IN EARLY AMERICA 177 (Thomas A. Foster, ed. 2007).

14. The 1768 "Report of Advocate, Attorney, and Solicitor General to Secretary Hillsborough," the latter individual "one of His Majesty's Principal Secretaries of State," read in part as follows: "[W]e are humbly of opinion, that his Ma'ty may, if he shall so please, signify to the Deputy Governor of Pen[n]Sylvania, that the evidence transmitted to England not appearing to be sufficient to convict either of the Persons of the Murder for which they are committed, His Ma'ty does not think fit to cause the said Persons to be sent over to England for the purpose of their being brought to a Trial for the same; And that it is His Ma'tys Pleasure, if no private Prosecutor should appear therein, that all further Prosecution thereof should cease, and that the said Prisoners should be discharged from their Imprisonment, as far as His Ma'ty is concerned therein, in such manner as shall be most agreeable to the Laws and Forms of Proceeding established in the said Colony." The report, dated July 24, 1768, was signed by James Marriott, Wm. De Grey and J. Dunning. 4 SAMUEL HAZARD, COMP., PENNSYLVANIA ARCHIVES: SELECTED AND ARRANGED FROM ORIGINAL DOCUMENTS IN THE OFFICE OF THE SECRETARY OF THE COMMONWEALTH, CONFORMABLY TO ACTS OF THE GENERAL ASSEMBLY, FEBRUARY 15, 1851, & MARCH 1, 1852, at 304 (1853).

15. Beloof & Cassell, *supra* note 3, at 485.

16. William Livingston, "Have You Been Drinking Tonight Ms. Prynne?" *Ohio's Scarlett Letter for OVI/DUI Offenders: A Violation of First Amendment Protection Against Compelled Speech*, 59 CLEV. ST. L. REV. 745, 762 (2011); *see also* Elizabeth Pleck, *Criminal Approaches to Family Violence, 1640–1980*, 11 CRIME & JUST. 19, 22–28 (1989) (discussing Puritan-inspired laws in New England). The concept of vengeance and punishment has, throughout time, been counterbalanced by notions of forgiveness, including those rooted in religious texts. MARTHA MINOW, WHEN SHOULD LAW FORGIVE? 24–25 (2019) ("Arguments for lessening legal sanctions have ancient roots. The famous retributive punishment notion of matching the loss of an eye by taking the eye of the offender was in fact an effort to confine punishment that otherwise could escalate into a blood feud. Punishment can never make a victim whole, so the desire for ever more punishment can spiral without limit. Hence the notion of proportionality captured in 'an eye for an eye' has a forgiving theme against the alternative of escalating responses.").

17. John E. Witte, Jr. & Thomas C. Arthur, *The Three Uses of the Law: A Protestant Source of the Purposes of Criminal Punishment?*, 10 J.L. & RELIGION 433, 436–37, 450 (1994); *see also id.* at 452 ("From these premises, the English and American jurists argued that the criminal law serves three uses or purposes in the lives of the criminal and the community. These they variously called: (1) deterrence or prevention; (2) retribution or restitution; and (3) rehabilitation or reformation—the classic purposes of criminal law and punishment that every law student learns still today."); *id.* at 451 n. 58 ("It was common, particularly in colonial America, to draw criminal law provisions directly from the Bible, and to classify criminal laws in accordance with the commandments in the Decalogue.") (citations omitted); Cotton Mather, *The Call of the Gospel Applied Unto all Men in General, and Unto a Condemned Malefactor in Particular* 58 (2d ed., Richard Pierce, 1687).

18. *E.g.*, FRANCIS WHARTON, PRECEDENTS OF INDICTMENTS AND PLEAS ADAPTED TO THE USE BOTH OF THE COURTS OF THE UNITED STATES AND THOSE OF ALL THE SEVERAL STATES: TOGETHER WITH NOTES ON CRIMINAL PLEADING AND PRACTICE, EMBRACING THE ENGLISH AND AMERICAN AUTHORITIES GENERALLY 33, 69, 82, 86–89, 91, 102, 104–05, 107, 111, 144, 146–47, 151, 388–89, 391, 403, 416, 422, 780 (2d rev. ed. 1857) (taking note of the "by the instigation of the devil" language in multiple criminal charges); 6 NATHAN DANE, A GENERAL ABRIDGMENT AND DIGEST OF AMERICAN LAW, WITH OCCASIONAL NOTES AND COMMENTS 657 (1824) (same); THE TRYALS, CONVICTIONS & SENTENCE OF TITUS OTES, UPON TWO INDICTMENTS FOR WILLFUL, MALICIOUS, AND CORRUPT PERJURY: AT THE KINGS-BENCH-BARR AT WESTMINSTER, BEFORE THE RIGHT HONOURABLE GEORGE LORD JEFFREYS 2–3, 5 (1685) (taking note of the same language); GEORGE NEILSON, TRIAL BY COMBAT 329 (2007) (in a book originally published in 1890, noting the "by the instigation of the Devil" language appeared in the 1817 case of *Ashford v. Thornton*).

19. John D. Bessler, The Death Penalty as Torture: From the Dark Ages to Abolition 4–5 (2017). *See also* Lawrence M. Friedman, A History of American Law 294 (2d ed. 1985) ("If crime was sin ... before the Revolution, it gradually shifted to concern for protection of private property.... [There was a] rapid decline of prosecutions for victimless crime.... By 1800, more than forty percent of all prosecutions ... studied were for theft, only seven percent for offenses against morality.") (citing William E. Nelson, *Emerging Notions of Modern Criminal Law in the Revolutionary Era: An Historical Perspective*, 42 N.Y.U. L. Rev. 450, 452–59 (1967)). In his article in the *New York University Law Review*, William Nelson described criminal law and punishment practices at the close of the colonial period from 1760 to 1774.

20. Bennett Capers, *Against Prosecutors*, 105 Cornell L. Rev. 1561, 1575 & n.83 (2020) (quotation from Joan E. Jacoby, The American Prosecutor: A Search for Identity 13 (1980)).

21. Lawrence M. Friedman, *Notes Toward a History of American Justice, in* Lawrence M. Friedman & Harry N. Scheiber, eds., American Law and the Constitutional Order: Historical Perspectives 16 (enlarged ed. 1988); William E. Nelson, *Emerging Notions of Modern Criminal Law in the Revolutionary Era: An Historical Perspective, in* Friedman & Scheiber, *supra*, at 165–72 (enlarged ed. 1988) (reprinting William E. Nelson, *Emerging Notions of Modern Criminal Law in the Revolutionary Era: An Historical Perspective*, 42 N.Y.U. L. Rev. 450 (1967)); Allen Steinberg, The Transformation of Criminal Justice, Philadelphia, 1800–1800, at 7 (1989).

22. Scott Ingram, *George Washington's Attorneys: The Political Selection of United States Attorneys at the Founding*, 39 Pace L. Rev. 163, 182 (2018).

23. The Judiciary Act of 1789 (Sept. 24, 1789), https://avalon.law.yale.edu/18th_century/judiciary_act.asp. Section 35 of the Judiciary Act of 1789 further provided that "in all courts of the United States, the parties may plead and manage their own causes personally or by assistance of such counsel or attorneys at law as by the rules of the said courts respectively shall be permitted to manage and conduct causes therein." *Id.*

24. Ingram, *supra* note 22, at 181 n.113.

25. *Id.* at 182 (citing George Washington to Edmund Randolph (Sept. 28, 1789), *available at* https://founders.archives.gov)).

26. Linda Myrsiades, Medical Culture in Revolutionary America: Feuds, Duels, and a Court-Martial 152–54 (2009) (discussing a private prosecution in early American in which John Morgan acted as the "prosecutor"; noting that "Morgan arrived at the compounded position of plaintiff-prosecutor as the result of two congressional resolves, November 16 and December 24, 1779, which presumably responded to letters he had sent to Congress"; emphasizing that "[i]n the mantle of private prosecutor, Morgan argued the essential unfairness of his having to assume the responsibility not only to provide evidence that proved the charges but to do so 'opposed to a man holding in his hands the means to bribe and seduce witnesses'; and further observing: "Private prosecution relied upon an older model of the law in which victims gathered evidence and pursued their complaints in their own time and at their own expense."); *see also* Justin McHenry, *John Morgan vs. William Shippen: The Battle that Defined the Continental Medical Department*, J. of Am. Revolution (Jan. 28, 2020), https://allthingsliberty.com/2020/01/john-morgan-vs-william-shippen-the-battle-that-defined-the-medical-department/.

27. Ingram, *supra* note 22, at 183–85, 187; *see also* Scott Ingram, *Representing the United States Government: Reconceiving the Federal Prosecutor's Role through a Historical Lens*, 31 Notre Dame J.L. Ethics & Pub. Pol'y 293 (2017).

28. Note, Stephanie A.J. Dangel, *Is Prosecution a Core Executive Function?* Morrison v. Olson *and the Framers' Intent*, 99 Yale L.J. 1069, 1071 (1990); *see also id.* at 1072 ("While American colonial statutes appear to have vested public 'prosecutors' with more prosecutorial responsibility than their English ancestors, recent studies focusing on prosecutorial practice show the persistence of a primarily private system of colonial prosecution. Many of the crimes today viewed as related to property (e.g., cases involving theft of goods in trade or destruction of land improvements or crops) were civil actions, and thus prosecuted privately. Even in the smaller category of colonial criminal cases, justices of the peace or aldermen summarily handled their caseload of privately initiated prosecutions with informal procedures. Private parties retained ultimate control, often settling even after grand juries returned indictments.").

29. *Id.* at 1072 & 1074 & n. 33 (citing, *inter alia*, Commonwealth v. Williams, 56 Mass. (2 Cush.) & People v. Wabash, St. L. & Pac. Ry., 12 Ill. App. 263 (1883)); *see also id.* at 1073 ("The work of colonial public 'prosecutors' resembled that of their English counterparts in four respects. First, colonial attorneys general and district attorneys performed non-prosecutorial tasks: Attorneys general provided opinions and advice to governors, councils, legislatures, and courts, while local public prosecutors handled land transfers and patent applications. Second, while colonial public prosecutors conducted most cases that directly infringed the state's interests, private individuals at times prosecuted even 'great public wrongs.' Third, public prosecutors performed the administrative tasks of a quasi-judicial official or adjunct to the court. Finally, the only discretionary prosecutorial task exercised by public officials in common criminal cases was the decision to end, rather than to initiate or conduct, prosecutions. Yet colonial prosecutors confined even this power to cases of malicious prosecution and misdemeanors where the parties consented.").

30. Mitchell v. Warden, No. TSRCV124009415, 2015 WL 8487896, at *3 (Conn. Super. Ct. Nov. 17, 2015).

31. Watson v. Walker, 854 N.E.2d 1247, 1248 (Mass. Super. Jud. Ct. 2006); *see also* Commonwealth v. Kardas, 106 N.E.3d 1129, 1134 (Mass App. Ct. 2018) ("'[T]he decision to nol pros a criminal case is within the discretion of the executive branch of government, free from judicial intervention.'") (citation omitted).

32. Diaz v. Perez, Civil Action No. 16-11860-RGS, 2016 WL 6871233, at *5 (D. Mass. Nov. 21, 2016); *see also* United States v. Saena Tech Corp., 140 F. Supp.3d 11, 28 (D. D.C. 2015):

> [T]he decision to prosecute is "particularly ill-suited to judicial review." *Wayte*, 470 U.S. at 607, 105 S. Ct. 1524. Thus, " '[t]he presumption of regularity supports' ... prosecutorial decisions and, 'in the absence of clear evidence to the contrary, courts presume that they have properly discharged their official duties.' " *United States v. Armstrong*, 517 U.S. 456, 464, 116 S. Ct. 1480, 134 L.Ed.2d 687 (1996) (quoting *United States v. Chem. Found., Inc.*, 272 U.S. 1, 14–15, 47 S. Ct. 1, 71 L.Ed. 131 (1926)); *see also Nader*, 497 F.2d at 679 n. 18 ("The federal courts have customarily refused to order prosecution ...").
>
> Not only is the Judicial Branch ill-suited to review prosecutorial decisions—given the complex factors involved—but judicial intervention would also undermine the Executive Branch's ability to "take Care that the Laws be faithfully executed." U.S. Const. art. II, § 3. As the Supreme Court elaborated:
>
>> Judicial supervision in this area, moreover, entails systemic costs of particular concern. Examining the basis of a prosecution delays the criminal proceeding, threatens to chill law enforcement by subjecting the prosecutor's motives and decision-making to outside inquiry, and may undermine prosecutorial effectiveness by revealing the Government's enforcement policy. All these are substantial concerns that make the courts properly hesitant to examine the decision whether to prosecute.
>
> *Wayte*, 470 U.S. at 607–08, 105 S. Ct. 1524.
>
> Furthermore, "a district judge must be careful not to exceed his or her constitutional role." *United States v. Microsoft Corp.*, 56 F.3d 1448, 1462 (D.C. Cir. 1995). The judiciary is separated from the prosecutorial function, "keep[ing] the courts as neutral arbiters in the criminal law generally." *Nader*, 497 F.2d at 679 n. 18. "When a judge assumes the power to prosecute, the number [of branches] shrinks to two." *In re United States*, 345 F.3d 450, 454 (7th Cir. 2003); *see also United States v. Cox*, 342 F.2d 167, 171 (5th Cir. 1965) ("It follows, as an incident of the constitutional separation of powers, that the courts are not to interfere with the free exercise of the discretionary powers of the attorneys of the United States in their control over criminal prosecutions."). These institutional concerns must shape any analysis of the Court's role in reviewing the government's decision to offer a defendant a deferred-prosecution agreement.

33. State v. Matthews, 933 N.W.2d 152, 156 (Wis. Ct. App. 2019) (citations omitted).

34. Brosky v. Miller, Civil Action No. 14-89, 2015 WL 8533689 *5 (W.D. Pa. 2015) (quoting Wayte v. United States, 470 U.S. 598, 607 (1985)); *see also* Klein v. Met Ed, Civil No. 3:19-CV-725, 2020 WL 94077, at *5 (M.D. Pa. Jan. 8, 2020) ("It is well established that decisions regarding the filing of criminal charges are the prerogative of the executive branch of government, are consigned to the sound discretion of prosecutors, and under the separation of powers doctrine are not subject to judicial fiat. Indeed, it has long

been recognized that the exercise of prosecutorial discretion is a matter, 'particularly ill-suited to judicial review.'") (quoting Wayte v. United States, 470 U.S. 598, 607 (1985)).

35. 1 WAYNE R. LAFAVE, JEROLD H. ISRAEL, NANCY J. KING & ORIN S. KERR, CRIMINAL PROCEDURE § 1.6(b) (4th ed. 2019) (discussing the colonial period); *see also id.* ("The county prosecutor then bore the responsibility of presenting the case at trial and also had the power to terminate the prosecution by entering a *nolle prosequi* (as was frequently done). Private prosecutions were still permitted, (and were quite significant in some of the colonies), but in other colonies, the public prosecutor gradually came to assume responsibility for proceeding on most serious offenses. Thus, the official of colonial prosecutor laid the groundwork for the eventual monopolization of all criminal prosecutions by public officials in this country."); *id.* ("[W]here the charge was bound over for trial and there was no confession, in many colonial communities, there remained a very good chance that the accused would never reach the trial stage. A substantial portion of the prosecutions, ranging as high as fifty percent, were dismissed on the prosecutor's filing of a *nolle prosequi* motion or on the failure of witnesses, the defendant, or sometimes even the prosecutor, to appear. In some instances, the dismissal probably was the result of the accused and the victim having reached a mutually agreeable settlement, but many dismissals were a product of the inefficiency of constables or the reluctance of complainants to undertake the necessary travel and expense."); *compare id.* at n.85 ("Various explanations have been offered as to why some colonies placed primary responsibility for the prosecution in the hands of a public official. Those explanations include: a desire to curb abuses, such as malicious proceedings and compounding, associated with private prosecutions; a democratic urge to eliminate the class distinctions associated with private prosecution; colonial conditions that rendered private prosecution impracticable, including the scarcity of persons learned in the law; and a view of the law as based on important moral principles and therefore too important to allow its enforcement to depend on 'the whims, and the pocketbooks, of individual victims.'"); Twede, *supra* note 1, at 15 ("The English courts of law still operated under this system of private prosecution when England began establishing colonies in America. As such, the English system of private prosecution made its way to the colonies. However, the English never sought uniformity in the way the colonial courts operated. Thus, the colonial courts were left in some regards to adapt and evolve on their own. Prosecution was one of the elements that evolved.").

36. "Judge Dillon's Charge to the Grand Jury," DAILY IOWA STATE DEMOCRAT (Davenport, Iowa), Jan. 26, 1859, p. 1 (noting this language in the charge to the grand jury: "If there is a private prosecutor, the foreman will endorse his name on the indictment."); "His First Charge," EVENING DEMOCRAT-GAZETTE (Davenport, IA), Sept. 15, 1887, p. 1 (noting that Judge Waterman, in charging the grand jury of Clinton County, observed: "No indictment can be found without the concurrence of at least five of your number; when found it should be indorsed 'a true bill' and this indorsement signed by your foreman. If the indictment is found at the instance of a private prosecutor, the indorsement should so state and the name of such prosecutor be given, and in every case the names of all witnesses on whose testimony it is found must appear on the back of the indictment."); "Right," MUSCATINE EVENING JOURNAL (Muscatine, IA), Dec. 6, 1872, p. 4 ("In his instructions to the Grand Jury in Clinton county, on Monday, Judge Brannan charged that where it was apparent the prosecuting witness was governed by a vengeful spirit that his name be returned as private prosecutor, to the end that if the prosecution should fail, the county might be relieved of the burden of the cost."). *See also* "Judge Dillon's Sentiments Concerning the System," MORNING DEMOCRAT (Davenport, IA), May 18, 1872, p. 4 (noting that the grand jury system "is liable to great abuse because it is open to private prosecutions, and conducts its investigations secretly and without notice to the party accused"); *accord* "Judge Dillon on Grand Juries," LEAVENWORTH DAILY COMMERCIAL (Leavenworth, KS), May 21, 1872, p. 2; *see also* "Traction Conspiracy," THE TIMES (Philadelphia, PA), Feb. 7, 1890, p. 2 ("George P. Rich, counsel for the Moncayos, asked that the name of the prosecutor be put on the bill before the jury was empaneled so that it would be known that the Traction Company was back of the case. This was opposed by District Attorney Graham, as the matter was one affecting the administration of public justice, and it would be improper to name any private prosecutor.").

37. United States v. Marion, 404 U.S. 307, 329 (1971) (Douglas, J., concurring) (*citing* G. DESSION, CRIMINAL LAW, ADMINISTRATION AND PUBLIC ORDER 356 (1948)).

38. 2 THE WORKS OF JAMES WILSON: ASSOCIATE JUSTICE OF THE SUPREME COURT OF THE UNITED STATES, AND PROFESSOR OF LAW IN THE COLLEGE OF PHILADELPHIA 445–47 (James DeWitt Andrews, ed. 1896).

39. *Id.* at 449–50. In his lecture on the criminal law, Wilson added of *appeals*: "On this subject there is, in our law books, an immense profusion of professional learning. As the appeal is now but little used, I decline any minute inquiry concerning it: as it is still in force, it would have been improper wholly to have omitted it." *Id.* at 450; *see also id.* at 471 (in the context of discussing peremptory challenges, Wilson also wrote: "True it is, that, at the common law, the king might challenge peremptorily, as well as the prisoner. The distinction between a public and a private prosecutor was not sufficiently regarded.").

40. "An Act for punishing Treasons and Felonies, and for the better regulating the Proceedings in Cases of Felony" (passed Feb. 21, 1788), *in* 2 THOMAS GREENLEAF, COMP., LAWS OF THE STATE OF NEW-YORK, COMPRISING THE CONSTITUTION AND THE ACTS OF THE LEGISLATURE, SINCE THE REVOLUTION, FROM THE FIRST TO THE FIFTEENTH SESSION, INCLUSIVE 73, 76 (1792) (section VIII of the statute reads in part: "That such party to whom appeal of murder is or shall be given by the law, may commence, take and sue appeal of murder in the same county where the party feloniously stricken or poisoned, shall die, as well against the principal and principals, as against every accessary to the same offences, in whatsoever county or place the accessary or accessaries shall be guilty to the same; and the justices before whom any such appeal shall be commenced, sued and taken, within the year and day after such murder and manslaughter committed and done, shall proceed against all and every such principal and principals, accessary and accessaries, in the same county where such appeal shall be so taken, in like manner and form as if the same offence or offences had been committed and done in the same county where such appeal shall be so taken...."); *see also id.* at 54, 58 (another New York law, passed on February 20, 1788, states in part: "That this act, or any thing therein contained, shall not extend to any writ, declaration or suit of appeal of felony or murder, nor to any indictment or presentment of felony, murder, treason, or other matter, nor to any process upon any of them....").

41. Chapman & Nelson v. Sloan, 2 N.H. 464, 1822 WL 425 (N.H. Super. Ct. Judicature 1822) ("[T]hat statute allows any pleas whatever, except in penal actions and in appeals of felony."); In re Presentment by Camden County Grand Jury, 89 A.2d 416, 424 (N.J. 1952) ("The appeal [of felony], which dated back to the Norman Conquest, was gradually superseded by presentments, indictments and informations on the criminal side and by trespass civilly, although an appeal of murder was heard in England as late as 1818") (*citing* Ashford v Thornton, 1 B. & Ald. 405); United States v. Guiteau, 1 Mackey 498, 524, 1882 WL 19929, at *19 (D.C. Sup. Ct. 1882) ("[I]n England there was a proceeding very common, that of appeal of murder, in which the wife, or near relative of the deceased party, could recover both compensation for the loss sustained, and at the same time a judgment as severe as if the offender had been indicted. That proceeding, involving both the vindication of private right and public justice, could be instituted in the county where the mortal blow was struck, although death ensued in another county."); State v. Baker, 24 Mo. 437, 442, 1857 WL 5428, at *3 (Mo. 1857) ("[E]very English authority, for one hundred years, admits that on a charge of high treason, or an appeal of murder, the deposition of the witness is not legal evidence, but he must meet the accused face to face."); *see also* Martin's Executrix v. Martin, 25 Ala. 201, 204, 1854 WL 263, *2 (Ala. 1854) (noting that W. Garrott, counsel for the appellant, argued: "Appeals of felony never have existed, and never can exist, in this country, until our constitution is altered or abolished; because no man can be put on his trial for an indictable offence, except on presentment of a grand jury.--Const. Ala., art. 1, § 10. Even in England appeals of felonies have been abolished by stat. 59 Geo. III, c. 46.--1 Bac. Abr. 291."

42. HENRY CAMPBELL BLACK, A LAW DICTIONARY CONTAINING DEFINITIONS OF THE TERMS AND PHRASES OF AMERICAN AND ENGLISH JURISPRUDENCE, ANCIENT AND MODERN (2d ed. 1910).

43. Lynne N. Henderson, *The Wrongs of Victim's Rights*, *in* TOWARDS A CRITICAL VICTIMOLOGY 144 n.21 (Ezzat A. Fattah, ed. 1992) ("Goebel and Naughton's history of the development of a criminal justice system in colonial New York notes the system was a mixed one of public and private prosecutions, depending on the location of the prosecution. Officials frequently brought formal accusations, however, and the office of the attorney general conducted many criminal prosecutions in the name of the Crown by the 1700s.") (citing JULIUS GOEBEL, JR. & T. RAYMOND NAUGHTON, LAW ENFORCEMENT IN COLONIAL NEW YORK 329 n.14, 330–31, 337, 619–21 (1944) and further observing: "in Easthampton, offences were

prosecuted on complaints of injured persons or informers; in New York City, the sheriff filled role of law enforcement official and prosecutor; the Attorney General's power increased throughout 1700s as direct representative of the Crown's interests")).

44. *See, e.g.*, FRANK MONAGHAN & MARVIN LOWENTHAL, THIS WAS NEW YORK: THE NATION'S CAPITAL IN 1789, at 221 (1945) ("So great was the business of the Court of General Sessions that by January 1797 Mayor Varick and his colleagues urged that a session of one week be held the first Tuesday of every other month, beginning in April. In writing to Governor Jay, Mayor Varick added that—none of the Magistrates have for some time past appeared willing to sit & try any Man at a Justices or Bridewell Court. And I [have] expressly declared that I will much rather Resign my Office than again sit in a Court where myself & my Brethren may stand accused before the Assembly of this State by the Perjury of any Rascal in the Community or be the object of private prosecution thro the contemptible & officious Zeal of even an Alexander Hamilton himself."); MIKE MCCONVILLE & CHESTER L. MIRSKY, JURY TRIALS AND PLEA BARGAINING: A TRUE HISTORY 28 (2005) ("At the outset of the nineteenth century, the prosecutorial system leading to trials in General Sessions was at once private-entrepreneurial and publicly administered. The importance of the citizen in crime control functions in New York is traceable to the moral reformation project of mid-eighteenth century England in which reformers contended that the solution to the 'crime panic' was that citizens should take responsibility for apprehending offenders and co-operating with magistrates in the suppression of vice and in the execution of the laws against public offending. In New York City, a private citizen who was aware that a felony had been committed had the responsibility to file a complaint at the Police Office. Thus, the mainspring of the criminal justice system in the first half of nineteenth century New York was the private prosecutor. It was the private prosecutor—the victim or someone acting on his or her behalf—who initiated the overwhelming majority of complaints and in whose name complaints were launched."); *id.* ("Private prosecutors came from all walks of life many of whom were members of the underclass of labourers, servants and free blacks. Without the moving force of the private prosecutor, many prosecutions would never have been brought or, if brought, would have failed through lack of evidence. As in England, there was statutory recognition of this in providing compensation for time and expenses to the citizen prosecutor and witnesses. In addition, the administrative structure which supported the private prosecutor was itself based upon market principles: the marshals, constables, magistrates and part-time District Attorneys were compensated according to a schedule of fees for acts undertaken on behalf of the citizen."); *id.* at 29 (discussing the way in which private prosecutions were conducted in practice and before the Court of General Sessions); Bennett Capers, *Against Prosecutors*, 105 CORNELL L. REV. 1561, 1580 (2020) ("The legal historian Nicholas Parrillo... not[es] that throughout much of the nineteenth century, 'American public prosecutors made their income from fees, usually based on the number of cases they brought or the number of convictions they won.' Stephanos Bibas is specific: 'Until the mid-nineteenth century, New York prosecutors searched for evidence, drafted legal documents, and empaneled juries upon victims' paying them set fees.'"); SELECT CASES OF THE MAYOR'S COURT OF NEW YORK CITY, 1674–1784, at 57–59, 302–27 (R. Morris ed. 1935) (noting that in the 1780s, in *Rutgers v. Waddington*, "victim used private prosecution for trespass to vindicate anti-Tory state policy in derogation of Sixth Article of the Treaty of Peace"); *accord* Michael Edmund O'Neill, *Private Vengeance and the Public Good*, 12 J. CONST. L. 659, 677 n.103 (2010) (discussing *Rutgers v. Waddington*). *See also* MIKE MCCONVILLE & CHESTER L. MIRSKY, JURY TRIALS AND PLEA BARGAINING: A TRUE HISTORY 38 (2005) ("In the eighteenth century, the Mayor's Court attracted lawyers of ability and distinction. Originally a small group of these lawyers provided the entirety of legal representation but this was subsequently expanded to include all lawyers admitted to practice in the state Supreme Court. By the end of the eighteenth century, prominent lawyers continued to dominate and included such notables as Alexander Hamilton, Aaron Burr, Edward Livingston and the 'American Erskine', Josiah Ogden Hoffman."); *id.* at 253 ("[A]fter 1850 private lawyers no longer represented the interests of the private prosecutor. Whilst the District Attorney may have hired private lawyers to act as Assistant District Attorneys when necessary, for the most part private lawyers became identified with defence work...."); *id.* at 248 ("After 1850, responsibility for the management of prosecutions in the court decisively shifted away from the private citizen to state actors."); *id.* at 28 ("[A]t the outset of the nineteenth century, the prosecutorial system leading to trials in General Sessions was at once private-entrepreneurial and publicly administered."); *id.* at 35 ("when the District Attorney did not

attend the prosecution, the court had the authority to appoint one of the private lawyers in the court who would then prosecute and could be compensated for services").

45. Darryl K. Brown, Free Market Criminal Justice: How Democracy and Laissez Faire Undermine the Rule of Law 42 (2016); *see also* id. ("In accord with English tradition, American jurisdictions in the first half of the nineteenth century widely authorized private individuals to prosecute crimes, and they often relied heavily on them. In some places during this era, private prosecutions made up the majority of criminal cases. In Philadelphia, private citizens routinely charged fellow residents with crimes if magistrates confirmed a sufficient evidentiary basis.").

46. Hurtado v. People of State of California, 110 U.S. 516, 526 (1884) (italics in original; citations omitted); *see also* David S. Rudstein, *A Brief History of the Fifth Amendment Guarantee Against Double Jeopardy*, 14 Wm. & Mary Bill Rts. J. 193, 218 (2005) ("Modern double jeopardy law began to emerge in England in the last half of the seventeenth century. By that time, prosecutions by the King had begun replacing private prosecutions by appeal as the preferred method of prosecution, thereby fulfilling the 'prerequisite to a true double jeopardy situation.'"); 6 Sir John Baker, The Oxford History of the Laws of England (1483–1558), at 514 (2003) ("In later periods, the principal use of the appeal was to initiate a prosecution where a grand jury would not approve an indictment; but in the early Tudor period it was common for an appeal to be accompanied by a parallel prosecution on indictment. This had the advantage to the prosecutor that it ousted battle, and also served to demonstrate that the appeal was not malicious. The appeal took priority, and the judges decided in 1482 that arraignment on an indictment for homicide should in all cases be delayed for a year and a day 'so that the party's suit may be saved'. This rule was reversed by statute in 1487, on the grounds that 'the party is oftentimes slow, and also agreed with, and by the end of the year all is forgotten, which is another occasion of murder'. Nevertheless, if an appeal had been commenced it was still given priority, and in practice arraignment 'at the king's suit' often followed the formal discontinuance of an appeal by nonsuit. In such cases the defendant was arraigned at the king's suit upon the declaration in the appeal rather than upon the indictment. The statute of 1487 may have diminished the bargaining power of the widow or heir, though an acquittal on indictment did not free the defendant from the possibility of conviction upon a subsequent appeal. The principal deterrent to potential appellors was no doubt the risk of having to pay heavy damages on acquittal if the appeal was found to have been malicious.").

47. Securing "pledges of prosecution" had a long history. Henry Campbell Black, A Law Dictionary Containing Definitions of the Terms and Phrases of American and English Jurisprudence, Ancient and Modern 905 (2d ed. 1910) (noting of "Pledges of prosecution": "In old English law. No person could prosecute a civil action without having in the first stage of it two or more persons as pledges of prosecution; and if judgment was given against the plaintiff, or he deserted his suit, both he and his pledges were liable to amercement to the king *pro falso clamore*.").

48. South Atlantic Q. (1968), Vol. 67, p. 536; (noting that the stabbing of Thomas Soaper occurred on November 6, 1764; that "Negro Tom" was enslaved by "Samuel Sweringen" and "acquitted on indictment, Nov. 1764"; and that after the death warrant was issued on October 30, 1765, "Negro Tom" was hanged on November 2, 1765).

49. *Id.* at 530–32, 535.

50. *See also* State v. Rogers, 992 S.W.2d 393, 395–96 (Tenn. 1999) (taking note of "the common law year-and-a-day rule" and observing: "The year-and-a-day rule is deeply rooted in the common law. Its lineage is generally traced to the thirteenth century where the rule was originally utilized as a statute of limitations governing the time in which an individual might initiate a private action for murder known as 'appeal of death.' The 'appeal of death' was a private and vindictive action instituted by an interested party and derived from the Germanic custom of 'weregild,' or compensation for death. 'Appeal of death' actions became obsolete and were abolished in 1819. By the eighteenth century, however, the year-and-a-day rule had been extended to the law governing public prosecutions so that a homicide prosecution could not be brought unless the victim died within a year and one day of the injury. Though the rule began in England, its applicability to criminal prosecutions in this country was acknowledged by the United States Supreme Court in 1894 as follows: 'In cases of murder the rule at common law undoubtedly was that no person should be adjudged "by any act whatever to kill another who does not die by it within a year and a day

thereafter. . . ." And such is the rule in this country in prosecutions for murder, except in jurisdictions where it may be otherwise prescribed by statute.'") (citations omitted).

51. Soaper v. Negro Tom, 1 Har. & McH. 227 (Md. 1765). The 1765 decision would later be included in a collection of "the most important law cases" from Maryland's provincial judiciary. Thomas Harris, Jr. & John M'Henry, comp., Maryland Reports Being a Series of the Most Important Law Cases, Argued and Determined in the Provincial Court and Court of Appeals of the Then Province of Maryland, from the Year 1700 Down to the American Revolution 227 (1809).

52. Two Centuries' Growth of American Law 1701–1901, at 85 (1902) (written by members of the faculty of the Yale Law School).

53. Stuart Banner, The Death Penalty: An American History 73 (2002); John D. Bessler, Cruel and Unusual: The American Death Penalty and the Founders' Eighth Amendment 270 (2012); Ben Cohen, Calvin Johnson & William P. Quigley, *An Analysis of the Economic Cost of Maintaining a Capital Punishment System in the Pelican State*, 21 Loy. J. Pub. Int. L. 1, 9–10 (2019); Andrew Drilling, *Capital Punishment: The Global Trend Toward Abolition and Its Implications for the United States*, 40 Ohio N.U. L. Rev. 847, 849 (2014); Margaret Vandiver & Michel Coconis, *"Sentenced to the Punishment of Death": Pre-*Furman *Capital Crimes and Executions in Shelby County, Tennessee*, 31 U. Mem. L. Rev. 861, 885–86 (2001).

54. Kevin M. Barry, *The Death Penalty and the Fundamental Right to Life*, 60 B.C. L. Rev. 1545, 1569 (2019); *see also* Seth Kotch & Robert P. Mosteller, *The Racial Justice Act and the Long Struggle with Race and the Death Penalty in North Carolina*, 88 N.C. L. Rev. 2031, 2044 n.46 (2010).

55. Bessler, *supra* note 53, at 217. Whipping was used as a punishment in some American locales well into the twentieth century. Casey Adams, *Banishing the Ghost of Red Hannah: Proportionality, Originalism, and the Living Constitution in Delaware*, 27 Widener L. Rev. 23, 24 & n.11 (2021) (noting that between 1900 and 1942, Delaware "conducted 1,604 whippings and the punishment was used on 22% of all convicted prisoners"; that the constitutionality of whipping as a punishment was upheld in 1963; and that only on July 6, 1972, did Delaware's governor, Russell W. Peterson, sign into law a revised criminal code that finally removed the whipping post—known as Red Hannah—from the state's law books).

56. Drew D. Gray, Crime, Policing and Punishment in England, 1660–1914, at 14 (2016).

57. 1 Legal Papers of John Adams 8 (L. Kinvin Wroth & Hiller B. Zobel, eds. 1965).

58. Chaim M. Rosenberg, The Loyalist Conscience: Principled Opposition to the American Revolution 42 (2018).

59. 1 Legal Papers of John Adams 8 (L. Kinvin Wroth & Hiller B. Zobel, eds. 1965).

60. 9 Nelson's Encyclopædia: Everybody's Book of Reference 152 (Frank Moore Colby & George Sandeman, eds. 1907).

61. Gary B. Nash, The Unknown American Revolution: The Unruly Birth of Democracy and the Struggle to Create America 97 (2005); Alfred F. Young, "Ebenezer Mackintosh: Boston's Captain General of the Liberty Tree," *in* Revolutionary Founders: Rebels, Radicals, and Reformers in the Making of the Nation 28 (Alfred F. Young, Gary B. Nash & Ray Raphael, eds. 2012).

62. 1 Legal Papers of John Adams 8 (L. Kinvin Wroth & Hiller B. Zobel, eds. 1965).

63. Jeff Wallenfeldt, "Boston Massacre," https://www.britannica.com/event/Boston-Massacre#ref1224191; *see also* Robert Treat Paine Papers, Vol. 2, http://www.masshist.org/publications/rtpp/index.php/view/RTP2d470 (an editorial note reads: "The trial of Richardson began on Apr. 20, 1770. Josiah Quincy acted for the defense, and Samuel Quincy and RTP [Robert Treat Paine] for the prosecution. Richardson was found guilty of murder on Apr. 21, 1770 and was kept in jail until Mar. 10, 1772, when his pardon by the King was announced.").

64. William Molineux to Robert Treat Paine, Robert Treat Paine Papers, Vol. 2, http://www.masshist.org/publications/rtpp/index.php/view/RTP2d470; see also "Editorial Note," Legal Papers of John Adams, vol. 3, p. 11, http://www.masshist.org/publications/adams-papers/index.php/view/LJA03p34 ("The Town, too, had been active in collecting prospective evidence. At the meeting of 12 March, James Bowdoin, Joseph Warren, and Samuel Pemberton were voted a committee to obtain 'a particular Account of all proceedings relative to the Massacre in King Street on Monday Night last, that a full and Just representation may be made thereof.'").

65. Dan Abrams & David Fisher, John Adams Under Fire: The Founding Father's Fight for Justice in the Boston Massacre Murder Trial (2020), ch. 2; Colin Nicolson & Owen Dudley Edwards, Imaginary Friendship in the American Revolution: John Adams and Jonathan Sewall n. 69 (2019) (noting that on March 14, 1770 "the town appointed a special prosecutor, Robert Treat Paine, to assist the King's attorney").

66. John D. Bessler, *The Italian Enlightenment and the American Revolution: Cesare Beccaria's Forgotten Influence on American Law*, 37 Mitchell Hamline L.J. Pub. Pol'y & Prac. 1, 33 (2016), http://digitalcommons.hamline.edu/jplp/vol37/iss1/1; *see also* John Ferling, John Adams: A Life 67 (1992) ("After what must have seemed an attorney to the frightened soldiers, [John] Adams agreed to head their defense. He was to be assisted principally by Josiah Quincy, the brother of both the prosecutor and of John's first love, Hannah....").

67. Randolph G. Adams, New Light on the Boston Massacre 259, 339 (1937), *available at* https://www.americanantiquarian.org/proceedings/44806960.pdf; *Boston Massacre*, History.com (updated Feb. 21, 2020), https://www.history.com/topics/american-revolution/boston-massacre.

68. "London," Public Advertiser (London, England), May 28, 1770, p. 2 ("No Person has been tried in this Kingdom on an Appeal for Murder since the Month of May, 1726, when a French Barber was tried at the Old Bailey for murdering his Wife, whose Brother brought an Appeal, upon which he was a second Time tried, convicted, sentenced, and hanged."; Public Advertiser (London, England), June 1, 1770, p. 2 ("A Correspondent informs us, that notwithstanding the Waiter at the Green Lettice is mentioned in the Papers as the last tried on Appeal was indicted for the Murder of his Sweet-heart and acquitted, but on a second Trial was found guilty and executed, denying the Fact to the last Moment; and as he was a young Fellow of good Character, and only circumstantial Evidence appeared against him, he was greatly pitied, and believed to be innocent, is not however the last Person tried in Appeal of Murder. One Nickolls was tried at Hertford in 1729 for the Murder of a Farmer near Bishops-Stortford by cutting his Throat after having robbed him. The Farmer lived some Time, saw Nickolls, was positive of his being the Man, and would have made Oath of it, but before a Justice of Peace could be procured he died. Nickolls was tried at Hertford, and upon strong circumstantial Evidence proved to be on the Spot, he was found guilty, but reprieved from Time to Time before he was discharged. The Widow lodged an Appeal, upon which Nickolls was removed to Town, and tried at the King's Bench Bar by a Hertfordshire Jury, and acquitted."). Later, other reports were made in the English press about the appeal of murder procedure. Jackson's Oxford Journal (Oxford, England), Mar. 15, 1783, p. 1 ("A Report is in Circulation that Dr. Magennis, during the ensuring Term, will be re-tried for the Murder of Mr. Hardy, on an Appeal at the Suit of the Widow of the Deceased, and that in case a second Verdict be given against him, he must suffer Death; as the Royal Mercy cannot interpose. It is true the King cannot interpose in case of a Conviction on an Appeal for Murder, because the Prosecution is not at the Suit of the Crown; but the Royal Power operates almost to the same Effect as a Pardon; for the Sovereign can respite *sine Die*.") (italics in original).

69. Dan Abrams & David Fisher, John Adams Under Fire: The Founding Father's Fight for Justice in the Boston Massacre Murder Trial (2020), ch. 5 ("The law in America was still developing its unique character, responding to the needs of a new and growing country, while still retaining both the majesty and quirks of centuries of developed British law. Among those remnants was the medieval right known as an appeal of felony, which did not require a review of the trial, but allowed a close relation of a murder victim to bring a quasi-personal action against the accused killer. In response, the defendant had the option of insisting on trial by battle, literally a fight to surrender or death. As Blackstone explained it, it was based on the belief that 'God would always interpose miraculously, to vindicate the guiltless.' Some patriots in Boston urged close kin of the victims to bring this appeal against Preston. But, among other things, the specter of fighting a well-trained British officer proved daunting. When that effort failed, it was suggested those wounded that night bring civil actions against Preston for damages. To escape this nuisance, Preston relocated back to the safety of the military fortress at Castle William."); *see also* "London, *(Monday)* April 30," Drewry's Derby Mercury (Derby, England), May 4, 1770, p. 3 ("Saturday Night, after the passing Sentence on the Prisoners, the Widow of Bigby, the Watchman, presented an Appeal of Murder, against Patrick and Matthew Kennedy; on which Patrick was ordered to be detained in Newgate till next Session, in order to be tried thereon. Matthew, was last Week delivered to be Transported for his

Life."); JACKSON'S OXFORD JOURNAL (Oxford, England), May 5, 1770, p. 3 ("It is said, that when the Court was moved at the Old Bailey to charge Patrick Kennedy with the Appeal for Murder, and also to have a Warrant from that Bench for bringing back Matthew Kennedy, who was on board a Transport Ship at Gravesend, a Law Officer told the Counsel who made the Motion, that he had no Power to stop him, nor even to hold him if he had been present, unless a Bill had been found in consequence of the Appeal: To which the Lord Mayor told him, that he would take it upon himself; he would sign the Warrant (which he did) and dispatch it immediately; his Lordship ordered Mr. Akerman to detain Patrick Kennedy also; and that he himself would be answerable for every bad Consequence which might arise from the supposed illegal Method of bringing Kennedy from the Ship, to take his Trial at the next Quarter Sessions."); "London," PENNSYLVANIA GAZETTE (Philadelphia, PA), July 12, 1770, p. 5 (reporting the same story); "London," PUBLIC ADVERTISER (London, England), May 28, 1770, p. 2 ("A Correspondent informs us, that on Friday the two Sheriffs of the City of London were fined 500*l.* each in the Court of King's Bench, for not making a Return on the Writ of Habeas Corpus issued out of that Court, commanding them to produce the Body of Matthew Kennedy (who was sentenced to Death the last Sessions at the Old Bailey for the Murder of the Watchman on Westminster-Bridge last Christmas, but had received his Majesty's Pardon) in order to be tried a second Time for the same, pursuant to the Appeal brought by his Wife."); *id.* ("The Public have been grossly and cruelly misled by a Paragraph extolling the Widow for refusing to take Money to release her Appeal; for the Acceptance of a Recompence for that Purpose is so far from being in the Nature of a corrupt Bribe, that it is a well-known legal Proceeding, authorized by every Law-Book that treats on the Subject, and founded on Principles of Christian Mercy; none but the Ignorant can support the contrary Doctrine, and none but the Blood-Thirsty can wish to carry it into Execution. The Law of Appeal was invented by the Founders of our Constitution for no other Purpose than that of giving a Compensation to the nearest Relation for the Death of the Person slain: A more rational Proceeding was afterwards adopted, namely, that by Indictment; for when Barbarity abated, the true Principle of Punishment became known, and Example was consider'd as the only End for which Punishments were inflicted. According to this Rule surely the Sufferings of these poor Boys have been sufficient to deter others from rendering themselves liable to the fatal Consequences that may follow from immoderate Intoxication.—The periodical Carnage at Tyburn is not able to impress the Mind with Horror equal to that of three Preparations for Death, and the cruel Disappointment of being brought back from the Seas after full Assurances of Safety; But notwithstanding the Humanity which is generally called the Characteristic of Englishmen, there are Men even in this Country to be found so destitute of Compassion and Patriotism as rather to procure an illegal Warrant for the Apprehension of this poor Lad, than permit him to attone for his Crimes by perpetual Banishment.").

70. PETER C. HOLLORAN, HISTORICAL DICTIONARY OF NEW ENGLAND 215 (2d ed. 2017); DIANE SMOLINSKI, IMPORTANT PEOPLE OF THE REVOLUTIONARY WAR 8 (2001).

71. THE STATE GAZETTE OF NORTH-CAROLINA (New Bern, NC), June 29, 1792, pp. 1, 4; 2 GRIFFITH J. MCREE, LIFE AND CORRESPONDENCE OF JAMES IREDELL, ONE OF THE ASSOCIATE JUSTICES OF THE SUPREME COURT OF THE UNITED STATES 353–53 (1858) (reprinting the same grand jury charge); *see also* "A charge delivered to the grand jury for South Carolina district, in the circuit court of the United States for the said district, held in Columbia, the 14th day of May last, by James Iredell, one of the associate judges of the Supreme Court of the United States," AMERICAN MUSEUM, OR, UNIVERSAL MAGAZINE (1792), p. 39.

72. Donna J. Spindel, *The Administration of Criminal Justice in North Carolina, 1720–1740*, 25 AM. J. LEG. HIST. 141, 146, 162 (1981).

73. Charles A. Boston, "Appeals of Death," *in* LAW NOTES (Dec. 1897), p. 128 ("[I]t may interest you to know that in Maryland, at least, appeal of death was actually invoked in one reported case, to wit, the case of 'Sarah Soaper v. Negro Tom' in the September Term 1765, in the Provincial Court of the Province of Maryland, reported 1 Harris & McHenry 227, and that in that case the defendant was sentenced to be hanged."); *see also* SOUTH ATLANTIC Q., Vol. 67 (1968), p. 530 (discussing Sarah Soaper's legal action).

74. *See, e.g.*, A CATALOGUE OF LIBRARY OF THE STATE OF VIRGINIA, ARRANGED ALPHABETICALLY UNDER DIFFERENT HEADS, WITH THE NUMBER AND SIZE OF THE VOLUMES OF EACH WORK SPECIFIED 46 (1856) (noting the library contained John Hansard's 1685 "A Book of Entries: of Declarations and other Pleadings in King's Bench; also a Collection of Special Writs &c. To which are added Appeals of Murder

and Mayheme with Pleadings therein."); 9 ESEK COWEN, COMP., REPORTS OF CASES ARGUED AND DETERMINED IN THE SUPREME COURT; AND IN THE COURT FOR THE TRIAL OF IMPEACHMENTS AND THE CORRECTION OF ERRORS IN THE STATE OF NEW YORK 655, 656 (3d ed. 1859) (noting the following argument by H. B. Davis, for the prisoners, in the New York case of *The People v. Peter Van Santvoord and Gilbert Oakley* (1821): "And Ld. Ellenborough, C. J. who delivered the opinion of the court, supposes, that, in an appeal of murder, it is necessary, where the stroke is laid on one day, and the death on another, to lay the latter day as within a year and a day of that on which the stroke is charged to have been given; otherwise the crime is not made out."). In *Hoffman v. Carow* (1839), decided by the Court for the Correction of Errors of New York, the plaintiff, Mr. Carow, had brought an action of trover in the superior court of the City of New York against Hoffman & Co., Baltimore auctioneers, for merchandise stolen from the plaintiff in New York and then forwarded by the thief to the Hoffman & Co. to be sold at auction. The thief was indicted and convicted of the felony in May of 1833, prior to which the goods had been sold and the proceeds paid over to thief without notice of the commission of the felony. Carow's lawsuit against Hoffman & Co. was thereafter brought in October 1834, whereupon Hoffman & Co. moved for a nonsuit on the basis that the proceeds of the auctioned goods were paid over to the thief before his arrest and before Hoffman & Co. had notice of the robbery. After the superior court judge refused a nonsuit and directed the jury to bring in a verdict for the plaintiff, which it did, Hoffman & Co. appealed the judgment, which was affirmed by the supreme court and, then, by New York's Court for the Correction of Errors. The Chancellor's written opinion in the case, which finally resolved the matter, noted that "the courts in England will not sustain a suit in favor of the owner of the stolen property, either against the thief or against a purchaser from him, until he has proceeded criminally against the thief for the felony." "This practice," the Chancellor emphasized, "undoubtedly proceeds upon the ancient common law principle that the civil injury is merged in the felony; but as the revised statutes of 1801, which abolished appeals of felony in this state, also declared that the civil remedy should not be merged in the felony, or in any manner affected thereby, this English rule does not apply to suits commenced here." "In the present case," the Chancellor ruled in affirming the judgment for the plaintiff, "the plaintiff had convicted the thief before the commencement of his suit" and "was therefore entitled to recover according to the English practice." Hoffman v. Carow, 22 Wend. 285, 285–86, 293–94 (N.Y. Ct. Corr. Errs. 1839).

The Chancellor's opinion also noted of English practice:

> It is known to the professional members of the court, that in the market towns of England there are periodical fairs, where property is bought and sold, called market days; and that by the custom of the city of London, every day except Sunday, is a market day, and every trademan's shop is a market overt for those things in which he usually deals at that place; and that by the common law, a sale in a market overt actually changes the title to the property in favor of a *bona-fide* purchaser thereof, even though it has been stolen from the rightful owner. 5 *Coke's R.* 83, *a.* The only remedy of the owner of stolen property to recover it again, under such circumstances, at the common law, was to pursue his *appeal* against the felon to conviction then he was entitled to restitution of his goods, although they had been sold in a market overt. *Coke's 2d Inst.* 714. So, also, if goods were stolen, and the thief abandoned or waived them in his flight, they were forfeited to the crown, or the lord of the manor, unless the owner proceeded upon his *appeal* to attaint the thief. *Foxley's case,* 5 *Coke,* 109, *a.* But as this proceeding to convict the felon by a private suit was very inconvenient and expensive to the owner of stolen property, the statute 21 *Hen.* VIII. *ch.* 11, was enacted, by which the stolen goods were directed to be restored to the owner upon his procuring a conviction of the thief, upon an *indictment* in the ordinary way, without the necessity of an appeal. *Staunf. P. C. ed. of* 1583, *p.* 167. Under this statute, it is the settled law in England, that upon the conviction of the offender, the owner is entitled to be restored to his property, notwithstandi[n]g it may have been sold to a *bona fide* purchaser in a *market overt. Burgess v. Koney, Trem. P. C.* 315. *Coke's* 2d *Inst.* 714. *J. Kelyng's R.* 48." *Hoffman*, 22 Wend. at 290–91.

See also FRANK A. ERWIN, CASES ON SALES OF PERSONAL PROPERTY 253 n.1 (2d ed. 1909).

In *Carow*, Senator Verplanck's opinion also had this to say:

The statute, 21 *Hen.* VIII, gave the party robbed a right to immediate restitution after conviction. Several decisions upon the act gave it a construction in conformity with the old law of appeal. It

> was strictly held that the civil action was merged in the felony. After conviction of the felon, the stolen goods could be reclaimed even if sold in *market overt,* and whoever sold them after that date was deemed a tortious converter. But it has been expressly decided that the owner who had prosecuted the thief to conviction, cannot recover the value of his goods from one who bought them from the thief, and sold them again before conviction, even with notice. 2 *T. R.* 750. In the words of Chief Justice Best, in another case, *Simpson v. Woodhert,* 2 *Carr. & Payne,* 41, 'The law is this: you must do your duty to the public before you seek a benefit to yourself; and then there is no necessity for a civil action. The decisions, says he, go not only to the case of an action against the felon, but also against persons who derive title under him. If such actions could be maintained, there would be no criminal prosecutions.' The authority of these and similar decisions has been much shaken, and certainly much narrowed in their application, by the case of *Peer v. Humphrey,* 2 *Ald, & Ellis,* 195, decided in 1835. There the court of king's bench held, that in trover for oxen feloniously sold by a servant, their value might be recovered from the *bona fide* purchaser who had sold them again before conviction.

Hoffman, 22 Wend. at 320–21 (opinion of Senator Verplanck); *see also id.* at 321–22 (opinion of Senator Verplanck) ("[I]n my opinion, we are not called upon to reconcile these cases, or to decide between them, for whatever may be the law of England, it is quite clear that these peculiar exceptions to the general principle of the law, obtaining on special grounds of policy, have no application within this state. Not only has the foundation of the doctrine been removed by the abolition of *appeals of felony* and of the former statutory provision of restitution, but a contrary doctrine has been expressly substituted. The English law established the universal rule that the felony excluded or suspended the civil suit until after conviction. Our revised statutes enact thus, *part* 3, *ch.* 4 *tit.* 1: 'The right of any person injured by felony, shall not in any case be merged in such felony or be in any manner affected thereby.' The first part of the section may, perhaps, by a strict construction, be confined to the action against the felon himself, which was formerly held to be merged in the felony; but the concluding words have no force or effect unless they extend to cases like the present. Chief Justice Best, as just cited, says: 'The decisions go not only to the case of an action against the felon, but also against persons claiming under him.' As the action against the felon is restored by the first part of the section, so that against persons claiming under him must be comprehended under the final words: 'the rights of any person injured by any felony, shall not be in any manner affected thereby.' The abrogation of the whole policy of the English law on this head, removes the only exception before known to the general right of the real owner to follow his property and recover its value in any hands whatever. But we need not rest merely on the general terms of this enactment. The whole policy of the statute of restitution upon which the English decisions stand, has been altered in our statute. Instead of requiring a conviction before stolen goods are restored, lest (as Hale and Blackstone says) 'felonies should be made up and healed,' our revised statutes direct that 'upon receiving satisfactory proof of the title of any owner, the magistrate who shall take the examination of an accused person, may order the same to be delivered to such owner.' And again: 'If stolen property shall come into the custody of any magistrate, upon satisfactory proof of the title of any owner thereof, it shall be delivered to him.' Finally, the English statute is in substance re-enacted, with this remarkable addition: 'if the property shall not before have been delivered to the owner.' These several provisions, taken in connection with the abolition of appeals of felony and of the merger of the civil remedy in the criminal prosecution, shew, I think, conclusively, that the English doctrine on this head, even in the more limited sense as laid down by Chief Justice Denman, has no application in this state.").

75. Aurora General Advertiser (Philadelphia, PA), Mar. 13, 1795, p. 3. That same New York bill for the more effectual prevention of crimes, said to be "now before the legislature of this state," also contemplated the death penalty's abolition for capital punishment, except in cases of treason and murder. *Id.* "It must give pleasure to every humane and benevolent heart," the *Aurora General Advertiser* reported, "that under the administration of our free and republican governments in the United States, penalties and punishments for crimes are assuming a less oppressive and sanguinary aspect." "Pennsylvania," that paper observed, "has the honour to take the lead in this reformation, and we rejoice to see her sister states every where adopting similar principles." *Id.*; *see also* "New-York, March 13," Pennsylvania Gazette (Philadelphia, PA), Mar. 18, 1795, p. 3 (reporting the same news story).

76. Rutland Herald (Rutland, VT), July 18, 1796, p. 2.

77. Laws of the State of New Jersey 244, 263 (1821) (reprinting the 1796 New Jersey law).

78. 319 N.W.2d 400 (Minn. 1982).

79. *Id.* at 402.

80. *Id.*

81. *Id.*

82. *Id.* at 403 (citations omitted); *see also id.* ("Whatever its origin, it is apparent that trespass retained a strong quasi-criminal character. In the earlier trespass cases, compensatory damages in the modern sense were almost unknown; the defendant usually would be required to pay an amount fixed by law rather than compensation for the plaintiff's actual injuries. *See* 2 F. Pollock & F. Maitland, *supra*, at 522–23. The nature of the trespass actions remained essentially punitive even as courts began to award actual damages, and the rule prohibiting the survival of such causes of action was retained. *See* Winfield, *Death as Affecting Liability in Tort*, 29 Colum. L. Rev. 239, 242 (1929). It was modified by statute during the reign of Edward III to permit causes of action for the loss, damage or conversion of personal property to survive the death of the plaintiff. *See* 4 Edw. 3 ch. 7 (1330); 25 Edw. 3, st. 5, ch. 5 (1351).").

83. Mark Lunney & Ken Oliphant, Tort Law: Text and Materials 4 (5th ed. 2013).

84. Paul R. Hyams, Rancor and Reconciliation in Medieval England 233 (2003); *see also id.* ("Ordinary people were sometimes unable to secure the sheriff's ear, still less able to spur him into action. They needed royal assistance to compel him to attach the defendant by sureties. At first, the provision of writs hardly changed the ways that the courts understood these procedures and the rights that underlay them. Only very gradually did the constraints of an increasingly professional system begin to sharpen the choices available to litigants. The boundary between the two main procedures that became trespass and appeal of felony remained extremely porous, and the cases long remained compatible with an analysis that simply saw two forms of the same set of remedies for traditional wrong."); Patrick Lynn Rivers, Governing Hate and Race in the United States and South Africa 48 (2008) ("[T]ort emerged in the English common law appeal of felony. Wrongs in common law were originally treated as criminal, not civil, offenses. If a defendant was judged to be wrong, then that defendant was not only incarcerated but the defendant's property was ceded to the Crown. The appeal of felony was eventually replaced by a writ of trespass. As action, writs of trespass allowed the wronged to pursue criminal charges and seek restitution against the individual doing wrong, all in one legal proceeding. Here, civil and criminal actions, while still intricately connected, were being differentiated in order to, eventually, be broken into civil and criminal actions that would relieve the wrong and sanction the individual doing the wrong."); David Friedman, *Beyond the Tort/Crime Distinction*, 76 B.U. L. Rev. 103, 106 (1996) ("To the extent that the hope of gain motivated private prosecutions, whether payment for compounding an appeal of felony or damages awarded in a writ of trespass, victims had a stronger incentive to prosecute rich criminals than poor ones. There may well have been situations in which a rich felon would be convicted and fined and a poor one would be convicted and executed. There were surely also situations, however, in which it was worth prosecuting a rich felon but not a poor one.") *id.* at 109 ("Consider the English legal system of the Middle Ages as described by Professor Seipp. Precisely the same offense can be prosecuted in four different ways. An appeal of felony (Column C on Table 1) is private prosecution with punishment, an indictment of felony is public prosecution with punishment (Column D on Table 1), a writ of trespass is private prosecution with wealth transfer (Column E on Table 1), and an indictment of trespass is public prosecution with wealth transfer (Column F on Table 1). Thus a single wrong, with, one presumes, a single moral status, can result in legal actions corresponding to all possible combinations of the choices shown by the first two rows of the table."); John C.P. Goldberg, *The Constitutional Status of Tort Law: Due Process and the Right to a Law for the Redress of Wrongs*, 115 Yale L.J. 524, 548 n.126 (2005) ("Blackstone placed his discussion of the appeal of felony in Book IV rather than Book III. As noted above, the appeal was a private prosecution that, like actions for trespass and case, was not terminable by officials, but that, in principle, would result in punishment of the offender rather than payment of damages. (I say 'in principle' because 'appealed' defendants seem often to have reached monetary settlements with their accusers.) There were at least two considerations at work here. First, the appeal was already a relic by the mid-eighteenth century. Second, the appeal's availability hinged on the commission of a felony, and therefore arguably was best presented in the

Book devoted to specifying the content of that category of wrongs.") (citations omitted); G. William Rice, *Of Cold Steel and Blueprints: Musings of an Old Country Lawyer on Crime, Jurisprudence, and the Tribal Attorney's Role in Developing Tribal Sovereignty*, 7 KAN. J.L. & PUB. POL'Y 31, 41–42 (1997) ("The slow but steady amalgamation of the old with the new resulted in four different, yet related, forms of action designed to remedy wrongs done: the appeal of felony, the writ of trespass, the indictment of felony, and the indictment of trespass. The appeal of felony, still extant in Blackstone's day, was not an appeal to a higher court but rather an original action through which a private citizen obtained redress upon the wrongdoer by a private prosecution for a felony. As in the writ of trespass, in which the victim requested damages, an appeal of felony could neither be dismissed nor pardoned by the King, but only by the victim or the victim's heir entitled to bring the appeal. Further, an appeal of felony could be brought after a defendant had been acquitted, or found guilty and pardoned (not punished), at the suit of the King upon indictment, but no indictment could be brought by the King after an acquittal upon an appeal of felony. The private victim-prosecutor ran some risk in that the defendant could demand trial by battle, and the victim-prosecutor could be killed. Further, if the action were lost, the prosecutor would be fined in a small amount by the king. They were attractive, however, in that so long as such actions could be settled out of court, the defendant and his relatives literally bet the defendant's life on the jury verdict if they refused to compensate the victim.").

85. FED. R. CRIM. P. 6(a)(1) ("When the public interest so requires, the court must order that one or more grand juries be summoned. A grand jury must have 16 to 23 members, and the court must order that enough legally qualified persons be summoned to meet this requirement."); *accord* METHODOLOGICAL ISSUES IN APPLIED SOCIAL PSYCHOLOGY 223 (Fred B. Bryant, et al., eds., 1992).

86. LAWRENCE M. FRIEDMAN, CRIME AND PUNISHMENT IN AMERICAN HISTORY 21 (1993).

87. THE PRACTICAL STATUTES OF THE SESSION 1854; (17 & 18 VICT.) WITH INTRODUCTION, NOTES, AND INDEX 185 (W. Paterson, ed. 1854) ("In case of any indictment or information by a private prosecutor for any offence against the provisions of this act, if judgment shall be given for the defendant, he shall be entitled to recover from the prosecutor the costs sustained by the defendant by reason of such indictment or information, such costs to be taxed by the proper officer of the court in which such judgment shall be given."); *id.* at 185–86 ("It shall not be lawful for any court to order payment of the costs of a prosecution for any offence against the provisions of this act, unless the prosecutor shall, before or upon the finding of the indictment or the granting of the information, enter into a recognizance, with two sufficient sureties, in the sum of two hundred pounds (to be acknowledged in like manner as is now required in cases of writs of *certiorari* awarded at the instance of a defendant in an indictment), with the conditions following; that is to say, that the prosecutor shall conduct the prosecution with effect, and shall pay to the defendant or defendants, in case he or they shall be acquitted, his or their costs."); 25 THE DISTRICT REPORTS OF CASES DECIDED IN ALL THE JUDICIAL DISTRICTS OF THE STATE OF PENNSYLVANIA DURING THE YEAR 1916, at 882 (1916) (reprinting *Commonwealth v. Crone* in which the Court of Quarter Sessions decided it would not set aside a finding of a grand jury imposing costs on a private prosecutor, with the court stating that P. L. Fortenbaugh, the prosecutor in the case, "was not a duly elected or legally appointed constable, policeman, sheriff or other peace officer whose duty it was to arrest offenders on view of a breach of the peace" and that "[t]he prosecutor made this information against several parties with whom he got into an altercation himself, which resulted in a street fight between him and them," thus making "[t]he affair... a personal and not an official matter"); *see also* 21 GEORGE ROSS ESHLEMAN, THE LANCASTER LAW REVIEW, CONTAINING THE DECISIONS OF THE SEVERAL COURTS OF LANCASTER COUNTY, LEGAL MISCELLANY, ETC. 397 (1904) (taking note of *Commonwealth v. Koffroth*, a decision of the Court of Quarter Sessions of Lancaster County, which held that constable "who arrests a horse thief on a complaint made by a private prosecutor is not entitled to the reward of $20 provided by the Act of March 15, 1821, P.L., 90").

88. *E.g.*, Joan E. Jacoby, *The American Prosecutor in Historical Context, available at* https://cdn.ymaws.com/mcaa-mn.org/resource/resmgr/Files/About_Us/AmericanProsecutorHistorical.pdf:

> The Dutch colonies of New York and New Jersey were familiar with Dutch law and the duties of the Dutch judicial officer, the *schout*. The first courts in New Amsterdam (1653) and Bergen (1661) consisted of a director general, three magistrates and a presiding officer, the *schout*, whose duties in the court were to present criminal charges against alleged criminals. The schout was a

combination constable and court officer with limited discretion in charging. He presented the case against the defendant and notified all accused of the charges being leveled against them. He had some powers of arrest and was involved in the collection of evidence, but he served more as a central figure that controlled access to the court than as an officer who initiated prosecutions.

Early records of the New Amsterdam court show that the first *schout,* Cornelius Van Tienhoven, appeared as plaintiff in a criminal trial for the first time on February 17, 1653, and consistently thereafter in most criminal matters until his replacement in 1665. *Schouts* remained in office for the next 20 years and even weathered the change of flags over the colony. In 1664, the English captured the settlement in the name of the crown and the Duke of York. Under the interim code of law known as the "Duke's Law" the schout remained as an officer of the court.

In 1674 English common law was established in New York, New Jersey and in other former Dutch settlements in Delaware and Pennsylvania. Although the title of *schout* disappeared, his function as police-prosecutor was carried on through the office of the sheriff. When the propriety of this was questioned for lack of precedent in the English courts, "the Governor's council issued a plainly-worded reply which stated that the sheriff was to put the law into execution, apprehend and prosecute violators."

The separation of the police-prosecutor functions was not clearly distinguished in the early days. Records exist of an ordinance established by the English governor of Newcastle, Delaware, in 1676 directing the sheriff to act as principal officer in the execution of the laws. Subsequent records show him acting as the prosecutor in a notorious murder case in the Newcastle courts. In 1686 the Quaker communities of Burlington, New Jersey, and in 1687, the county of Philadelphia, both established the position of county prosecutor. Both towns were in close geographic proximity to former Dutch settlements in whose courts *schouts* had conducted prosecutions only 10 years earlier.

89. FRIEDMAN, *supra* note 86, at 23–24, 27–28.

90. *Id.* at 31, 57–58 (italics in original).

91. MARTIN ALAN GREENBERG, CITIZENS DEFENDING AMERICA: FROM COLONIAL TIMES TO THE AGE OF THE TERRORISM 28 (2005).

92. JOAN E. JACOBY, THE AMERICAN PROSECUTOR: A SEARCH FOR IDENTITY xvii (1980) ("After early settlement, the responsibility for bringing criminal actions in each of the thirteen colonies was lodged in a centralized figure—the King's Attorney or Attorney General."); *see also* LOUIS J. PALMER, JR., THE DEATH PENALTY IN THE UNITED STATES: A COMPLETE GUIDE TO FEDERAL AND STATE LAWS 61 (2d ed. 2014) ("The Crown appointed attorney generals in all of the colonies. The first appointment was made in Virginia in 1643. The primary task of colonial attorney generals was to promote and protect the financial interests of the Crown. This meant that the bulk of the legal work performed by the colonial attorney generals was civil in nature."); *id.* ("The attitude of colonial attorney generals was the same as their brethren in England, i.e., if the Crown did not obtain a substantial benefit from criminal prosecutions, there would be no prosecution by the sovereign authority whose duty it was to prosecute all crimes. Colonial judges did not challenge the discretion exercised by colonial attorney generals.").

93. PALMER, *supra* note 92, at 61. *Compare* HOMER CUMMINGS, FEDERAL JUSTICE: CHAPTERS IN THE HISTORY OF JUSTICE AND THE FEDERAL EXECUTIVE 12–13 (1937) ("The English attorney general possessed full power to conduct criminal trials in behalf of the King, but in practice only those of great state importance received his attention. The colonial attorneys general, on the other hand, not only possessed the power but early began to exercise it in both the important and the unimportant cases. To explain how this came about is to explain the origin of a fundamental distinction between the administration of criminal justice in England and America—a distinction which exists in a considerable degree to this day. In England private citizens were expected and encouraged to prosecute those suspected of crime. But private prosecution, though certainly legal in the colonies, was not suited to survive in pioneer society. It entailed both effort and expense to the private prosecutor, who was obliged to employ a lawyer to conduct the preliminary stages of the prosecution and even the trial itself. Furthermore, criminal business as compared with civil litigation was not extensive. Few lawyers could hope to make a living from criminal cases.

Indeed, not until the abolition of the rule denying counsel to felons, near the time of the Revolution, was there occasion for the 'criminal lawyer' to appear.").

94. Cynthia Nicoletti, *The American Civil War as a Trial by Battle*, 28 LAW & HIST. REV. 71, 78 n.14 (2010) (citations omitted); *see also* Laurie C. Kadoch, *So Help Me God: Reflections on Language, Thought, and the Rules of Evidence Remembered*, 9 RUTGERS J. L. & RELIGION 2 n.147 (2007) (noting that Theodore F.T. Plucknett, in *A Concise History of the Common Law* (5th ed. 1956), "relates a curious incident with the trial by battle that pitted the American colonies against England"; "In 1774 because of various events occurring in Boston, the British governor decided to improve the methods of justice by abolishing the battle on appeals for murder. This proposal aroused furor in England from those who regarded the trial by battle to be 'a great pillar of the constitution.' The mode remained a viable choice. The last attempt to bring an appeal of murder by trial by battle was frustrated by the act abolishing trial by battle in both real actions and appeal of murder.").

95. Wex S. Malone, *The Genesis of Wrongful Death*, 17 STAN. L. REV. 1043, 1056 n.65 (1965) ("In 1774 the ministerial majority in Parliament attempted to abolish the appeal for the Province of Massachusetts, but the opposition defended the ancient institution in the strongest terms as a "'great pillar of the constitution,'" and the measure was defeated.") (*citing* MORRIS, STUDIES IN THE HISTORY OF AMERICAN LAW 248 (1930)); *see also* "Editorial Note," *Founders Online*, National Archives, https://founders.archives.gov/documents/Adams/05-03-02-0001-0001. [Original source: *The Adams Papers*, Legal Papers of John Adams, vol. 3, *Cases 63 and 64: The Boston Massacre Trials*, ed. L. Kinvin Wroth and Hiller B. Zobel. Cambridge, MA: Harvard University Press, 1965, pp. 1–43.] (noting of Captain Thomas Preston, one of the men indicted after the Boston Massacre in 1770, and of the aftermath of that historical event: "Though he was a free man, Preston's troubles had not ended. 'They have endeavourd to lodge an Appeal against me, in behalf of one of the relations of the deceasd, but it won't lie, as there are not any near enough of kin now surviving.' The word 'appeal' here connotes not a review of the trial, but an ancient procedure whereby the near kin of a murder victim could prosecute a quasi-personal action against the purported offender. This mode of vengeance had almost died out by 1770; the last case of appeal of felony arose in England in 1819, quickly to be followed by an act of Parliament abolishing it. It is worth realizing (as apparently whoever suggested prosecuting an appeal against Preston did not) that the accused in an appeal of felony could insist on trial by battle. This feature precipitated the demise of the procedure in 1819. Curiously, for some unexplained reason, at the time of the Intolerable Acts, passed in 1774 as a consequence of the Boston Tea Party, the English government decided 'to improve the administration of justice in Massachusetts by means of a bill which *inter alia* abolished battle on appeals of murder. This proposal roused opposition in England from those who affected to regard trial by battle as a great pillar of the constitution, and in the end it was withdrawn on the more liberal grounds that parliament ought not to restrain the liberties of the colonies.' Preston also found himself threatened with 'endless lawsuits' for damages alleged to have resulted from the various woundings.").

96. Twede, *supra* note 1, at ix ("The findings of this research indicate that slavery abolition societies' willingness and financial ability to prosecute slaveholders posed a threat to slaveholders that a system of private prosecution was not adequate to protect against. Public prosecution appears to have been initiated in Georgia—at least in part—to safeguard those slaveholder interests by taking away the ability of private parties to prosecute and vesting that authority in an appointed government official—the public prosecutor."); *see also id.* at 23–24 n.12 ("In addition to Connecticut, the following states had ambiguously worded statutes regarding the extent of control public prosecutors were to have over prosecutions: Arkansas—*Laws of Arkansas Territory* (1835); Colorado—*Revised Statutes of Colorado* (1868); Florida—*Manual or Digest of the Statute Law of the State of Florida* (1848); Illinois—*Revised Code of Laws of Illinois* (1827); Kansas—*Statutes of the Territory of Kansas* (1855); Kentucky—*Collection of all the Public and Permanent Acts of the General Assembly of Kentucky* (1802); Maine—*Laws of the State of Maine* (1830); Massachusetts—*Compendium and Digest of the Laws of Massachusetts* (1809); Michigan—*Laws of the Territory of Michigan* (1827); Minnesota—*Revised Statutes of the Territory of Minnesota* (1851); Missouri—*Digest of the Laws of Missouri Territory* (1818); Nevada—*Compiled Laws of the State of Nevada* (1873); New Hampshire—*Laws of the State of New Hampshire* (1830); North Carolina—*Revised Statutes of the State of North Carolina* (1837); North Dakota—*Revised Codes of the Territory of Dakota* (1877); Ohio—*Statutes of Ohio*

and of the Northwestern Territory (1834); Oklahoma—*Statutes of Oklahoma* (1891a); Pennsylvania—*Digest of the Laws of Pennsylvania* (1852); South Dakota—*Revised Codes, State of South Dakota* (1903); Tennessee—*Statute Laws of the State of Tennessee* (1831); Virginia—*Code of Virginia* (1849); Wisconsin—*Statutes of the Territory of Wisconsin* (1839); Wyoming—*Compiled Laws of Wyoming* (1876). In the majority of these cases, the ambiguity hinges on the use of one of two pieces of phraseology. First, many statutes state it is the public prosecutor's duty to prosecute all cases in which the state is interested. What this meant is unclear.... While some state courts provided some guidance on how to interpret those statutes, most did not. As such, pinpointing when that control was wrested from private individuals becomes difficult."); *id.* at 24–25 ("Even if the statutes were crystal clear in their intent, the difficulty of the task of tracking the transition from private prosecution to public prosecution is further compounded by the fact that practice did not always follow law. There is indication that private prosecution continued in courts in New York, Massachusetts and Philadelphia well beyond the time it would have been barred by law.") (citations omitted).

97. *See generally* BARBARA JEANNE FIELDS, SLAVERY AND FREEDOM ON THE MIDDLE GROUND: MARYLAND DURING THE NINETEENTH CENTURY (1985).

98. "Prince George's County," The Maryland State Archives Presents - Beneath the Underground: The Flight to Freedom and Communities in Antebellum Maryland, http://slavery.msa.maryland.gov/html/antebellum/pg.html ("There were large clusters of African Americans, mainly enslaved, [w]ith Prince George's County. The holding of thirteen slaves per capita by 1850 only partially reveals the clustering of the black population. Of the 879 slave holders in the county by that year, 177 (20%) held at least twenty enslaved blacks, thirty-two (4%) held at least fifty slaves, and nine (1%) enslaved seventy-five or more. There was also a concentration of these holders in and around the county seat, Upper Marlborough. It was little more than a hamlet, but in 1850 tobacco planters kept 2,793 black slaves there.").

99. "Third Dispatch," WASH. SENTINEL (Washington, DC), Oct. 13, 1853, p. 3 (noting that in a case in Baltimore, Maryland, involving "Deputy Marshals Jenkins and Crossier, who were arrested last week on a charge of assault and battery on Bill Thomas, a fugitive slave, and arrested by them at Wilkesbarre," Judge Grier said he "would not allow the lawyers Brown employed by abolitionists to come as private prosecutors into court and interfere with the officers of the government in the execution of their duties"); *accord* "The Wilkesbarre Fugitive Slave Case," N.Y. TIMES, Oct. 13, 1853, p. 1 ("Judge GRIER said he would not allow Lawyer BROWN, employed by the Abolitionists, to come as a private prosecutor into Court, and interfere with the officers of Government in the execution of their duties."); "An Independent Judge," VICKSBURG WHIG (Vicksburg, MS), Nov. 2, 1853, p. 1 ("Two of the U.S. Deputy Marshals, by virtue of a warrant of a commissioner, arrested a negro slave named Bill Thomas, at Wilkesbarre, Penn. An attempt was made to rescue the prisoner, and as he was a little unruly himself, the officers used sufficient force to bring him to subjection to their authority. An abolitionist named Gilchrist, made affidavit, on behalf of the negro, and had a warrant issued from a justice of the Peace, on which the U.S. Officers were arrested for assault and battery. Judge Grier, of the U.S. Supreme Court, presiding in that circuit, granted a habeas corpus to bring these officers before him, out of the hands of the State officers, and the proof of the commissioner being given, that he had issued the warrant, and that the marshals were performing their duty, Judge Grier declared that he would permit no petty Justice, instigated by the abolitionist, or hear no lawyer employed by the abolitionists as a private prosecutor to interfere, with the U.S. officers, and therefore discharged them."). One scholar has observed that "private prosecution was the standard in fugitive cases, and it was not uncommon for private prosecutors to assist public prosecutions." Linda Myrsiades, *Legal Practice and Pragmatics in the Law: The 1821 Trials of John Reed, "Fugitive Slave"*, 138 PA. MAG. HIST. & BIOGRAPHY 305, 320 (2014).

100. James Wilson, of Pennsylvania, discussed private prosecutions in the context of a discussion of peremptory challenges. 2 COLLECTED WORKS OF JAMES WILSON 1197 (Mark David Hall & Kermit L. Hall, ed. 2007) ("When a prosecution, as well as the defence of it, was viewed as the cause of an individual, it might be reasonable enough that, in this view, the power of challenging jurors should, on both sides, be equal. But when a prosecution is considered as the cause of the community, by a part of which community this very cause is to be tried; matters now assume a very different appearance. This important difference was fully explained in the account which I gave of the radical principles, as I may call them, of the trial by

jury. The accused stands alone on one side: on the other side stand the whole community: the jury are indeed a *selected* part; but still they are a *part* of the whole community: the power of challenging, therefore, ought not, on both sides, to be equal. True it is, that, at the common law, the king might challenge peremptorily, as well as the prisoner. The distinction between a publick and a private prosecutor was not sufficiently regarded.").

101. Nathaniel Chipman, Sketches of the Principles of Government 166–67 (1793). Malicious prosecution claims were frequently brought against unsuccessful private prosecutors. Eric M. Freedman, Making Habeas Work: A Legal History 58 (2018) ("One common fact pattern arose when someone who had been the defendant in a criminal action initiated by a private prosecutor was acquitted and sued the prosecutor for malicious prosecution. For instance, in a 1762 New Hampshire case, Oliver Farwell launched a private criminal prosecution against Daniel Stearns and others for trespassing on his property, assaulting him, and destroying his crops. Stearns was acquitted in a jury trial and sued Farwell. After losing below, Stearns prevailed on appeal and was awarded damages of £40 plus £34.8s in costs."); *id.* ("Similarly, in a 1768 case from Virginia, John Knox initiated a felony prosecution in the King's name against one Peter Daniel, who was promptly acquitted. Daniel thereupon brought a malicious prosecution action against Knox. In that action the jury found that Knox in bringing the criminal charges had acted 'maliciously, and unjustly to vex, injure and oppress' Daniel, and had caused him to be bound over for trial 'without any just or reasonable cause.' The jury accordingly awarded £75 in damages plus costs, and the court subsequently denied a motion to arrest that judgment."); Martin L. Newell, A Treatise on the Law of Malicious Prosecution, False Imprisonment, and the Abuse of Legal Process, as Administered in the Courts of the United States of America, Including a Discussion of the Law of Malice and Want of Probable Cause, Advice of Counsel, End of the Prosecution, Etc. 355 (1892) (discussing private prosecutors and malicious prosecution); 1 Joel Prentiss Bishop On the Law of Pleading and Evidence and the Practice in Criminal Cases § 690 (3d ed. 1880) ("We have seen that, in England, indictments are generally found at the instigation of a private prosecutor, and sometimes they are here."); *id.* at § 691 ("Such prosecutor is, at the common law, under some liabilities; as, for instance, if the prosecution was both malicious and without probable cause, the prisoner, on being acquitted, may maintain against him a civil action for damages."); *id.* ("Under statutes existing to some extent in both countries, the prosecutor is in certain circumstances, not in all, liable to pay the costs of the proceeding when it is frivolous or malicious, or even when it simply fails. And, on the other hand, in England, he is sometimes compensated or reimbursed from the public treasury for a successful prosecution, or occasionally for proper steps taken short of a conviction, or the defendant is required to pay costs to him."); *cf.* George Buchan, An Accurate and Authentic Narrative of the Origin and Progress of the Dissentions at the Presidency of Madras: Founded on the Original Papers and Correspondence 157 (1810) ("A private prosecutor, of a malicious prosecution, is liable to an action on the case, for a malicious prosecution in preferring such an indictment before a grand jury. Yet, if the same person, serving on the grand jury, were maliciously to present, or to find such an indictment, no action would lie. Thus, it is clear, that the same act done by the same person, and proceeding from the same evil motive, is or is not actionable, according to his acting in a private, or a public capacity.").

102. Chipman, *supra* note 101, at 44 ("In the first rude stages of society, men have no idea of general rules, or public punishments, for the prevention of private injuries. They are unable to connect private injuries with the common concerns of the nation. The redress and prevention of these, are left to the care of each individual. In a situation like this, hatred and revenge are the only possible external checks. These passions go to the nature of each individual. Hatred is a rooted aversion of one man to another, on account of a real, or supposed, fixed and intentional opposition to his interest, or happiness. Revenge, is a desire in one person, to inflict an evil on another, for a real, or supposed injury received. Hatred dictates the avoidance of its object, as disagreeable or noxious. Revenge pursues its object, and is gratified, only with retaliating the injury.").

103. *Id.* at 167–68 n.*; *see also id.* at 168 ("The practice of admitting common informers, who are to receive a share of the penalty, as a reward for prosecuting, is still less to be justified. This practice can never be necessary, in any state of manners.... It often serves the purpose of private malice; always to cultivate a spirit of revenge, and to disseminate jealousies, and private animosities among the citizens.").

104. *See generally* JOANNE B. FREEMAN, AFFAIRS OF HONOR: NATIONAL POLITICS IN THE NEW REPUBLIC (2001); *see also* JOHN COCKBURN, THE HISTORY OF DUELS (1720) (discussing the history of duels); STEPHEN BANKS, DUELS AND DUELLING (2012) (same); Alfred I. Phillips, "Trial by Battle," *in* 26 PROCEEDINGS OF THE NUMISMATIC AND ANTIQUARIAN SOCIETY OF PHILADELPHIA FOR THE YEARS 1910, 1911, 1912, at 160–61 (1913) ("The private prosecution was called an 'Appeal,' which did not mean an application to a higher court to review the proceedings in a lower one, but the word was used to indicate a call or demand in an original private suit to answer a complaint. The accused then had the right to defend himself in a duel. If the defendant was found guilty in such private prosecution the same punishment was inflicted as if conviction had resulted upon indictment by the crown. In murder cases the right of suit accrued to the heir and under a revision of the law upon the subject in the time of Henry VII it became the duty of the crown to prosecute first and in the event of an acquittal by a jury the heir of the murdered person could begin a private prosecution to test the question of guilt a second time. These private appeals are said to have been established with the view of assisting in the collection of *weregilds* which represented pecuniary payments for the private settlement of criminal offences. Our ancestors seem to have arranged *weregilds* with much nicety and established a scale of prices to be paid for the commission of various crimes. Appeals appear to have been popular and several efforts to abolish them failed."); ROGER W. SHUY, THE LANGUAGE OF DEFAMATION CASES 16–17 (2010) ("Today, the standard remedy for the offending party in a defamation case is monetary compensation. But it wasn't always that way. In more barbaric times, people who were insulted, defamed, or otherwise offended by others simply whacked them on the head or even killed them. In medieval Europe, this barbaric violence continued for years, even after such physical retribution morphed into a newer version of ritualized civil justice, called judicial trial by combat, had begun to find its place in society. As the number of these ritualized battles grew, it became commonplace for knights in armor to challenge other knights according to a gradually evolving code of honor. Solving disputes by personal combat in this way seemed to appeal to aristocrats in particular. . . . [P]rivate duels of honor continued in one form or another into the nineteenth century, with elaborate rules by which honorable parties were expected to abide.") (citation omitted); *compare* ANN GOLDBERG, HONOR, POLITICS, AND THE LAW IN IMPERIAL GERMANY, 1871–1914, at 209 (2010) ("In the nineteenth century the upper bourgeoisie, mirroring the values of their social superiors and empowered by changes in the legal codes, adopted the *Privatklage* as an extension of the aristocratic dueling concept of 'private prosecutions.'") *with* "Prevalence of Duels in America," *in* 11 THE LITERARY PANORAMA, BEING A COMPENDIUM OF NATIONAL PAPERS AND PARLIAMENTARY REPORTS, ILLUSTRATIVE OF THE HISTORY, STATISTICS, AND COMMERCE OF THE EMPIRE 293 (1812) (discussing duels in America) *and* THOMAS GAMBLE, SAVANNAH DUELS AND DUELLISTS 1733–1877 (1923) (discussing duels in that locale).

105. *See* "Survival of the Duel," BURLINGTON DAILY NEWS (Burlington, VT), June 21, 1918, p. 4 (reprinting this commentary from the *New York Commercial*: "In some countries libel suits have taken the place of duels. In England a man in public life is often forced by public opinion to bring a libel suit. When he is accused of committing a punishable offence or an act that should exclude him from decent society he prosecutes a criminal libel case to vindicate his reputation. Such cases are often brought for the sole purpose of enabling the plaintiff or private prosecutor to tell his side of the story under oath and submit himself to cross-examination.").

106. 1 R. S. ROSE, KENTUCKY CRIMINAL LAW PROCEDURE AND FORMS 393 (1918) ("Dueling is a misdemeanor at common law, and to either challenge another to fight a duel, or to be the bearer of such a challenge, or to provoke another to send a challenge are each and all misdemeanors."); *see also id.* ("In the history of the United States and of Kentucky, dueling is very prevalent. A great many controversies were settled by the dueling code; a great many prominent and useful citizens of this commonwealth have fallen in dueling.... Soon after the Hamilton-Burr duel, the constitutional conventions and state legislatures denounced dueling by attaching heavy penalties, such as disqualifying every person who challenged another to fight a duel or aiding or assisting or in any way promoting dueling, and under such constitutions and statutes as were enacted in Kentucky...."); WILLIAM L. CLARK & WILLIAM L. MARSHALL, A TREATISE ON THE LAW OF CRIMES 635–36 (Herschel Bouton Lazell, ed., 2d ed. 1905) (noting of dueling: "In some countries it is not unlawful, but it is a misdemeanor at common law in England and in this country. It is also a misdemeanor at common law to give a challenge to fight a duel, either by words or by letter, or to

knowingly be the bearer of such a challenge, or to designedly provide such a challenge."); 1 THE PHILOSOPHY OF LAW: AN ENCYCLOPEDIA 231 (Christopher Berry Gray, ed., 2012) ("Dueling was not considered a specific offense in English common law. Duelists who fought in public were charged with aggravated affray. Survivors of deadly combat faced murder charges."); *id.* ("In 1803, the Statutes of George III made dueling a specific offense, but apparently with little deterrent effect. In 1844, Prime Minister Peel revised the army pension statute to deny a benefice to the widows of duelists. The English duel went into decline thereafter, but proving a causal connection is not easy.").

107. LARRY MAY & ZACHARY HOSKINS, EDS., INTERNATIONAL CRIMINAL LAW AND PHILOSOPHY 77 (2010); Thomas J. Carmody, *The Anti-Dueling Movement, in* A NEW HISTORY OF THE SERMON: THE NINETEENTH CENTURY 341–42 (Robert H. Ellison, ed. 2010); C.A. Harwell Wells, *The End of the Affair? Anti-Dueling Laws and Social Norms in Antebellum America*, 54 VANDERBILT L. REV. 1805, 1805–1814 (2001); *see also id.* at 1814 ("When the English began to settle North America, they brought with them the common law and its prohibitions against dueling. Especially considering how popular dueling became in the nineteenth-century, it is surprising to realize that only a handful of duels took place in English America between 1620 and 1760, and that in these rare instances duelists were usually punished."); *see also* LAWRENCE M. FRIEDMAN, A HISTORY OF AMERICAN LAW 76 (3d ed. 2005) ("In Pennsylvania (1838) any person who fought a duel, or sent a challenge, or aided or abetted in fighting a duel, was 'deprived of the right of holding any office of honor or profit in this State.'").

108. Bennett Capers, *Against Prosecutors*, 105 CORNELL L. REV. 1561, 1578 (2020).

109. WEX S. MALONE, ESSAYS ON TORTS 78 (1986).

110. NATHANIEL CHIPMAN, SKETCHES OF THE PRINCIPLES OF GOVERNMENT 165, 168–69 (1793).

111. "Important to Lumberman.—Bridges on the Ottawa," OTTAWA DAILY CITIZEN (Ottawa, Canada), Dec. 4, 1860, p. 2 (noting the appearance of "Mr. E. Carter, for the private prosecutors"); "The Shooting Case," REGINA LEADER (Regina, Canada), Oct. 25, 1883, p. 4 (noting that "D. L. Scott represented private prosecutor" in a case where the charge was for "unlawfully and maliciously shooting at one Thomson from a pistol loaded with powder and ball with intent to do him grievous bodily harm"); "Fred Pryce Discharged," CALGARY DAILY HERALD (Calgary, Canada), Aug. 11, 1891, p. 4 (reporting that G. E. Jacques said under examination: "I am the private prosecutor in the case. I lost a large quantity of jewelry in January last, consisting of watches, chains, rings, etc., valued at between three and four thousand dollars. I lost it from the safe, the safe was broken into and the jewelry stolen."); "On Trial for Embezzlement," VANCOUVER DAILY WORLD (Vancouver, Canada), July 18, 1891, p. 5 (noting the appearance of "private prosecutors" in an embezzlement case); "The Embezzlement Case," VANCOUVER DAILY WORLD (Vancouver, Canada), Aug. 5, 1891, p. 5 ("When the case of Reg. *vs* Isen came up in the Police Court this morning, Mr. Jordan who appeared for the private prosecutor stated that he had been instructed by his client that a settlement of the case had been made and he wished to withdraw the charge."); "Police Court," VANCOUVER DAILY WORLD (Vancouver, Canada), Nov. 18, 1891, p. 4 ("John Donaldson, charged with having stolen a coat, the property of Gabriel Thomas, pleaded not guilty. Evidence was given by the private prosecutor, when the Bench sentenced him to three months with hard labor."); "Formally Acquitted," SACRAMENTO DAILY RECORD-UNION (Sacramento, CA), Mar. 31, 1880, p. 2 ("MONTREAL, March 30th. — Sir Francis Hincks and the other Directors of the Consolidated Bank, against whom true bills were found at the last assizes for making false returns, were formally acquitted at the Court of Queen's Bench to-day, the Private Prosecutor having withdrawn the accusation and the Crown having no evidence to offer."); "Montreal's Broken Bank," THE SUN (New York, NY), June 27, 1880, p. 5 ("MONTREAL, June 25.—At the last meeting of the shareholders of the insolvent Consolidated Bank, held here, a resolution was passed, by an overwhelming majority, to enter civil actions against the directors to recover the losses which have been sustained through their maladministration of the affairs of the bank. The Chairman of the meeting, John Rankin, had to acknowledge, in reply to a shareholder, that John Monk, the private prosecutor of Sir Francis Hincks and the other directors, was paid $20,000 in cash to drop the prosecutions. This caused a great sensation, and it is sure to stimulate the unfortunate shareholders in pursuit of their claims."); "Montreal," OTTAWA DAILY CITIZEN (Ottawa, Canada), Mar. 1, 1875, p. 4 ("Mr. John O'Farrell, advocate of Quebec, has been suspended from practice for three months, for voluntarily acting as constable in a case in which he was employed as private prosecutor."); *see also* "From New Brunswick," THE GAZETTE (Montreal, Quebec), July 16, 1879, p. 3 ("The

Government has decided not to prosecute Annie Parker, who became well known through the Osborne case, and unless she is prosecuted privately, she will be discharged. A few months ago she was arrested at the instance of the Osborne family on a charge of perjury, she having given evidence against them on their trial for the murder of Timothy McCarthy. They thought the Government would bear the expense of the trial, but the Attorney-General has decided otherwise.").

112. BRADLEY CHAPIN, CRIMINAL JUSTICE IN COLONIAL AMERICA, 1606–1660, at 33–34 (2010) (discussing the methods of prosecution in England and noting that "[t]he colonies used all of the English modes of prosecution, though often in somewhat variant form"); DOUGLAS E. BELOOF, VICTIMS' RIGHTS: A DOCUMENTARY AND REFERENCE GUIDE 15 (2012) ("In Colonial America where the English common law was the law of the land, the system of private prosecutions was widely used...."); *see also* Lynne N. Henderson, "The Wrongs of Victim's Rights," *in* TOWARDS A CRITICAL VICTIMOLOGY 144 n.21 (Ezzat A. Fattah, ed. 1992) ("Goebel and Naughton's history of the development of a criminal justice system in colonial New York notes the system was a mixed one of public and private prosecutions, depending on the location of the prosecution. Officials frequently brought formal accusations, however, and the office of the attorney general conducted many criminal prosecutions in the name of the Crown by the 1700s.") (citing JULIUS GOEBEL, JR. & T. RAYMOND NAUGHTON, LAW ENFORCEMENT IN COLONIAL NEW YORK 329 n.14, 330–31, 337, 619–21 (1944) and noting that "in Easthampton, offences were prosecuted on complaints of injured persons or informers; in New York City, the sheriff filled role of law enforcement official ad prosecutor; the Attorney General's power increased through 1700s as direct representative of the Crown's interests").

113. The Articles of Confederation (1781) emphasized in Article II that "[e]ach state retains its sovereignty, freedom, and independence, and every power, jurisdiction, and right, which is not by this Confederation expressly delegated to the United States, in Congress assembled." It further provided in Article III: "The said States hereby severally enter into a firm league of friendship with each other, for their common defense, the security of their liberties, and their mutual and general welfare, binding themselves to assist each other, against all force offered to, or attacks made upon them, or any of them, on account of religion, sovereignty, trade, or any other pretense whatever." Although the individual states retained their sovereignty, Article IV of the Articles of Confederation did contain this clause: "If any person guilty of, or charged with, treason, felony, or other high misdemeanor in any State, shall flee from justice, and be found in any of the United States, he shall, upon demand of the Governor or executive power of the State from which he fled, be delivered up and removed to the State having jurisdiction of his offense." Decisions to prosecute were made at the state level. Kelsy Deye, *Can Corporations Be Held Liable Under the Alien Tort Claims Act?*, 94 KY. L.J. 649, 651 (2005) ("Marbois, the French Consul General, was assaulted by another Frenchman, DeLongchamps, while walking on a Philadelphia street. Although Marbois complained to the Continental Congress at the time, there was little they could do under the Articles of Confederation. It was left to the state of Pennsylvania to prosecute the action in the criminal sense."); Jeffrey G. Miller & Brooke S. Dorner, *The Constitutionality of Citizen Suit Provisions in Federal Environmental Statutes*, 27 J. ENVTL. L. & LITIG. 401, 424 (2012) ("The complete lack of connection between prosecution and executive power in the wording and history of the Constitution suggests the framers of the Constitution had no intent to place prosecution in the executive power. It most strongly suggests the framers simply were not thinking of prosecution when they framed the Constitution and wrote The Federalist because they did not envision prosecution as a major federal function, executive or otherwise. There could be several reasons for this. First, they envisioned prosecution of traditional common law crimes as a state rather than a federal function. Second, they conceived of state and private parties performing many of the functions of federal prosecution. Third, they viewed prosecution of federal criminal statutes as of limited importance, as they did not establish punishments for common law crimes within federal jurisdiction until its second session. Finally, there had been no prosecutorial function under the Articles of Confederation."). *But cf.* J. Andrew Kent, *Congress's Under-Appreciated Power to Define and Punish Offenses Against the Law of Nations*, 85 TEX. L. REV. 843, 900 (2007) ("An individual conception of the Piracies and Felonies Clause—seeing it as power to constitute tribunals, appoint prosecutors, define individual crimes, or affix punishments—is very plausible in light of the history of attempts to reform the Articles of Confederation. The Articles gave the

Continental Congress the power of 'appointing courts for the trial of piracies and felonies committed on the high seas.'").

114. Harold J. Krent, *A Symposium on* Morrison v. Olson: *Addressing the Constitutionality of the Independent Counsel Statute: Executive Control Over Criminal Law Enforcement: Some Lessons from History*, 38 Am. U.L. Rev. 275, 291–92 (1989) ("In the United States, because the Articles of Confederation did not provide for general federal criminal law enforcement, private citizens were primarily responsible for criminal law enforcement in the period prior to the ratification of the Constitution.").

115. *Id.* at 292–93.

116. Jeffrey G. Miller & Brooke S. Dorner, *The Constitutionality of Citizen Suit Provisions in Federal Environmental Statutes*, 27 J. Envtl. L. & Litig. 401, 426 (2012).

117. William Bradford was the Pennsylvania lawyer who succeeded George Washington's first Attorney General Edmund Randolph to become the second Attorney General of the United States.

118. Krent, *supra* note 114, at 293–96 (italics in original):

> After ratification of the Constitution, victims did not directly participate in criminal prosecutions in federal court, as they had in the colonies and continued to a certain extent to do in the states. When Congress under the 1789 Judiciary Act established the office of district attorney, it implicitly vested the district attorneys with exclusive authority to prosecute *all* federal crimes within their jurisdiction.
>
> Nonetheless, private citizens helped initiate prosecutions by contacting the grand jury and attempting to persuade it to issue presentments against suspects. More commonly, judges on their own volition exhorted grand juries to investigate certain conduct or to issue presentments against particular individuals. Members of the grand jury could share with other members any evidence of crime that came to their attention. Although individuals or judges were also free to present evidence of wrongdoing to the district attorneys, they retained the discretion to bypass the executive branch at this early stage of the criminal process and contact the grand jury directly.
>
> An early opinion by Attorney General Bradford indicates that the colonial practice of privately-initiated prosecutions continued at least for a brief period under the Constitution. Bradford responded to a request made by the Secretary of State on behalf of the British consul stationed in Norfolk, Virginia. Apparently, a crowd had gathered outside the consul's residence in early 1794, insulting him and demanding that he deliver individuals within the residence to the crowd, presumably because the crowd believed that the individuals had committed various criminal violations. The district attorney declined to prosecute members of the crowd on the ground that violence perpetrated upon a consul did not constitute a federal crime.
>
> The Attorney General thus plainly believed that private citizens could, in effect, lobby the grand jury, even if the Executive had already determined not to press charges.
>
> Instead of contacting the grand jury directly, private citizens could appear before a federal or state judicial official and swear out a complaint against a suspected criminal. The magistrate was empowered to order the defendant incarcerated pending further proceedings before a grand jury. Since there was no federal police force and there were so few district attorneys, this direct involvement of private citizens was important to effective law enforcement.
>
> The proceedings in *United States v. Skinner* are illustrative. Upon application of a private citizen, Justice Livingston issued warrants against three suspects for violation of the Neutrality Act. This Act proscribed, in part, outfitting ships with the intent of employing those ships against foreign nations with whom the United States was at peace. The Act set criminal penalties and included a qui tam provision providing that, upon conviction, the ships would be forfeited.
>
> Counsel for the defendants moved in part that their clients be released on the ground that the prosecution had been commenced without direction from the government. Private counsel for the informer argued that the involvement of the district attorney was not needed, and the court agreed in emphatic terms:
>
> [N]o instructions were necessary on the part of the president, or any other officer of government, to justify the issuing a warrant for the violation of this or any other law.... Nor was it necessary that the application for a warrant should be made by the district attorney, as any

individual might complain of the infraction of a law, and he considered it his duty to award a warrant whenever complaint was made to him on oath of a crime's being committed, whether such warrant were applied for by the district attorney or any other person.

Prosecutions were thus launched by private initiative, and private citizens could participate in the legal process even after the arrest.

Despite the involvement of private citizens at the initial phase of criminal prosecutions, district attorneys apparently retained the discretion not to act on presentments brought by grand juries. Public prosecutors on numerous occasions dropped prosecutions for any number of reasons, whether for reasons of strategy, legal judgment, or politics. As Chief Justice John Marshall noted, 'the usage in this country has been, to pass over, unnoticed, presentments on which the district attorney does not think it proper to institute proceedings.' The case in *Hill* itself arose out of the district attorney's issuance of a series of *nolle prosequis*. Thus, while individuals played a role in starting the prosecution process, they did not control the prosecutions once begun.

Despite agreeing with the district attorney that federal prosecution was not warranted, the Attorney General apprised the Secretary of State that an avenue of redress was still available to the consul. Attorney General Bradford stated that:

> [I]f the party injured is advised or believes that the federal courts are competent to sustain the prosecution, I conceive he ought not to be concluded by my opinion or that of the district attorney. If he desires it, he ought to have access to the grand jury with his witnesses; and if the grand jury will take it upon themselves to *present* the offense in that court, it will be the duty of the district attorney to reduce the presentment into form, and the point in controversy will thus be put in a train for *judicial* determination.

Bradford's name also shows up as part of a description of a case, captioned "Respublica *versus* Griffiths," heard in the June 1790 term of the Supreme Court of Pennsylvania. 2 A. J. Dallas, Reports of Cases Ruled and Adjudged in the Several Courts of the United States and Pennsylvania, Held at the Seat of the Federal Government 105, 112 (1790). That description reads as follows:

> Leave having been granted, on the motion of *Sergeant*, to file an information against the defendant, one of the justices of the peace for Chester county, it became a question, whether the information should be drawn, filed and prosecuted by the attorney general, or by the party at whose instance it was awarded.
>
> The attorney general (*Bradford*) objected, that it is not the duty of the attorney general to draw and file this information. It must, indeed, be in the name of the commonwealth, and the prosecutor may make use of the name of the officer, who prosecutes for the state. But there is in England a known and established distinction, between informations filed by the attorney general, and those filed by him at the relation of a private person, in the name of the master of the crown office. The former are always filed *ex officio;* and the court will not, upon motion of the attorney general, give him leave to file an information against any person, 3 Burr. 1812. They cannot be quashed on motion of the prosecutor, (Dougl. 227) nor is the prosecutor liable for costs. But informations, at the relation of private persons, are in a great measure private suits. They are moved for, and conducted, not by the officers of the crown, but by counsel employed by the prosecutor. The prosecutor is, in many cases, liable to costs, 3 Burr. 1270, 1305. The court will not grant it where the prosecutor appears unworthy, Burr. 548, 869. And on a motion for an information for a libel, oath must be made of the falsity of the charges contained in the libel, a circumstance quite immaterial, where the prosecution is wholly on the part of the public. The prosecutor, therefore, ought to be at the expense and employ his own counsel, in this proceeding, in which he is really interested. If it be the duty of the attorney general to file this information, it is his duty to prosecute it also. Dall. 2.
>
> No informations (except those *qui tam*) have hitherto been filed in Pennsylvania; and it is of consequence to settle this point. No fees are provided for the duty, in the bill of fees, and the attorney general ought not, on this occasion, to be considered as the mere drawer of an information, for which he is not to be paid, and with the future prosecution of which he has nothing to do.

> *By the Court.—The objection is reasonable and just. But, *pro forma*, the attorney general must allow his name to be used by the prosecutor.
>
> *Id.* at 112–13.

That source also gives a description of a 1762 case from the Supreme Court of Pennsylvania captioned "The King *v.* John Lukens." That description reads as follows:

> The Act of 1705, requiring the prosecutor's name to be inserted on an indictment, applies only where there is an actual prosecutor; and proof of the person prosecuting cannot be made by the defendant.
>
> Indictment for a nuisance.—*Mr. Dickenson,* for the defendant, moved that a prosecutor should be indorsed on the indictment, agreeably to the act of assembly, before the defendant should be put to plead—*Mr. Chew,* Attorney General, urged that such a construction ought to be put on the act as that public justice may not be eluded; and that there should be no necessity to indorse a prosecutor, unless it be proved that there is some person active in carrying on a prosecution; because, if it took its rise from the grand jury, or a justice of the peace, no person could be indorsed; and offenders of the highest nature would escape being brought to justice.
>
> By the Court. It often happens that all the witnesses necessary to support a public prosecution are brought unwillingly to give evidence; and the act could never intend there should be a prosecutor indorsed, unless there was really a prosecutor existing, for the words in the act are, *the prosecutor*. And as no person in the present case is proved to be active in carrying on the prosecution, the defendant must plead to the indictment without any indorsement.
>
> It was then moved, that the defendant himself might be sworn to prove the person prosecuting but denied by the court, who said it must be proved by indifferent witnesses.

1 A. J. Dallas, Reports of Cases Ruled and Adjudged in the Courts of Pennsylvania, Before and Since the Revolution 5–6 (1790) (italics in original; citing 4 Ann. c. 37, see 1 State Laws, 49, Dall. 1).

119. "The Federal Courts—Judge Buffington Makes His First Jury Charge," Scranton Republican (Scranton, PA), Mar. 8, 1892, p. 5 (noting Judge Buffington's grand jury charge and emphasizing that "[t]he March term of the United States District and Circuit Courts opened in this city at 10 o'clock yesterday morning, with Judges Acheson and Buffington presiding."); "Uncle Sam's Court," Scranton Republican (Scranton, PA), Mar. 7, 1893, p. 5 (also noting that, in another grand jury change, Judge Buffington pointed out that no private prosecutor are permitted in the United States District Courts).

120. *E.g.*, Robert M. Ireland, *The Register of the Kentucky Historical Society*, Vol. 88, No. 1 (Winter 1990), pp. 1–23 (discussing the 1845 private prosecution and execution of Dr. Abner Baker for the murder of Daniel Bates in the Commonwealth of Kentucky, and observing: "The prosecution numbered four: Commonwealth's Attorney William B. Moore and three private lawyers hired by the Bates's executors. Relatives and friends of murder victims in Kentucky and most other states hired private counsel to assist in the prosecution of their allegedly murdered loved ones. Although none of the three private prosecutors lived in Clay County, each had established a prestigious career in adjoining counties.").

121. James M. Farrell, *Pretrial Publicity in 1830 Salem: Daniel Webster, New England News, and the Knapp-White Trial*, 44 Journalism Hist. 232, 232 (Winter 2019) ("More than five hundred newspaper stories appeared in New England newspapers between April 8, 1830, and Sept. 1, 1830, concerning the murder of Captain White, and the trial of Frank Knapp. New England newspapers had published, on average, more than three stories per day for the 116 days between the murder and the beginning of the first Knapp trial. Even accounting for the republication of some stories, the White murder in Salem was a news event that generated unprecedent journalistic interest.").

122. Over the course of his career, Daniel Webster argued more than 200 cases before the U.S. Supreme Court. Mark Stein, How the States Got Their Shapes Too: The Behind the Border-Lines 142 (2011).

123. Robert V. Remini, Daniel Webster: The Man and His Time 337 (1997); "Webster Enters the Case," American Heritage (June 1960), Vol. 11, Iss. 4, https://www.americanheritage.com/webster-enters-case. Initially, it was rumored that Daniel Webster might make an appearance as a defense lawyer in the case—rumors the *Salem Gazette* later dispelled. Charleston Courier (Charleston, SC), July 2, 1830,

p. 2 ("We observe that it is repeated in many papers that the Hon. Daniel Webster and Jeremiah Mason, are employed to defend the persons in our jail; as to Mr. Webster it has been positively denied.... We understand that the Hon. Lemuel Shaw is employed as Counsel for Col. Selman, and Franklin Dexter, Esq. for the two Knapps.").

124. "Trial of John Francis Knapp for the Murder of Capt. Joseph White," DUNDAFF REPUBLICAN, AND CANAL & RAIL ROAD INTELLIGENCER, Sept. 1, 1830, p. 1.

125. Marilynne K. Roach, THE SALEM WITCH TRIALS: A DAY-BY-DAY CHRONICLE OF A COMMUNITY UNDER SIEGE (2002); BRYAN F. LE BEAU, THE STORY OF THE SALEM WITCH TRIALS (2d ed. 2016).

126. "The Trial of John Francis Knapp for the Murder of Joseph White, Salem, Massachusetts, 1830," *in* 7 JOHN D. LAWSON, ED., AMERICAN STATE TRIALS: A COLLECTION OF THE IMPORTANT AND INTERESTING CRIMINAL TRIALS WHICH HAVE TAKEN PLACE IN THE UNITED STATES, FROM THE BEGINNING OF OUR GOVERNMENT TO THE PRESENT DAY 395 (1917).

127. NATIONAL GAZETTE (Philadelphia, PA), May 31, 1830, p. 2 (noting a report of the *Boston Patriot*); "The Salem Murder," CHARLESTON COURIER (Charleston, SC), June 7, 1830, p. 2 (same).

128. R. KENT NEWMYER, SUPREME COURT JUSTICE JOSEPH STORY: STATESMAN OF THE OLD REPUBLIC 167 (2004).

129. Rita Sheridan Pollard, "Against the Law and Beyond the Evidence," ABA J. (Feb. 1977), Vol. 63, p. 205; 6 THE WORKS OF DANIEL WEBSTER 41–42 (17th ed. 1877); "The Murder of Captain Joseph White by the Knapp Brothers, 1830," Historical Crime Detective, http://www.historicalcrimedetective.com/ccca/murder-of-captain-joseph-white-1830/; E.J. Wagner, "A Murder in Salem," SMITHSONIAN MAG. (Nov. 2010), https://www.smithsonianmag.com/history/a-murder-in-salem-64885035/.

130. "The Murder," RICHMOND ENQUIRER (Richmond, VA), June 8, 1830, p. 4.

131. "The Salem Murder," FARMER'S HERALD (St. Johnsbury, VT), June 23, 1830, p. 2.

132. CHRISTOPHER JON LUKE DOWGIN SUB ROSA: MORE TALES OF THE TUNNELS IN SALEM, PLANNED ECONOMIC CYCLES, THE HISTORY OF THE BIRTH OF THE FEDERAL RESERVE, AND THE ASSASSINATION OF TWO PRESIDENTS BEFORE THE CIVIL WAR, AND OTHER WAYS SALEM SHAPED YOUR LIVES AND AMERICAN HISTORY 130 (2017).

133. 6 THE WORKS OF DANIEL WEBSTER 42–43 (17th ed. 1877).

134. Walker Lewis, "The Murder of Captain Joseph White: Salem, Massachusetts, 1830," ABA J. (May 1968), pp. 460–61.

135. 1 JOHN W. JOHNSON, ED., HISTORIC U.S. COURT CASES: AN ENCYCLOPEDIA 376–77 (2d ed. 2001); Sturges v. Crowninshield, 17 U.S. (4 Wheat.) 122 (1819).

136. RALPH D. PAINE, THE SHIPS AND SAILORS OF OLD SALEM: THE RECORD OF A BRILLIANT ERA OF AMERICAN ACHIEVEMENT 232 (1909).

137. ROBERT BOOTH, DEATH OF AN EMPIRE: THE RISE AND MURDEROUS FALL OF SALEM, AMERICA'S RICHEST CITY 27–29 (2011).

138. BROOK THOMAS, EXAMINATION OF LAW AND LITERATURE: COOPER, HAWTHORNE, STOWE, AND MELVILLE 58 (1990).

139. E.J. Wagner, "A Murder in Salem," SMITHSONIAN MAG. (Nov. 2010), https://www.smithsonianmag.com/history/a-murder-in-salem-64885035/.

140. EVENING POST (New York, NY), June 3, 1830, p. 2.

141. NATIONAL GAZETTE (Philadelphia, PA), May 31, 1830, p. 2.

142. Walker Lewis, "The Murder of Captain Joseph White: Salem, Massachusetts, 1830," ABA J. (May 1968), pp. 460–62.

143. "The Murder of Mr. White explained," NATIONAL GAZETTE (Philadelphia, PA), June 2, 1830, p. 2.

144. Walker Lewis, "The Murder of Captain Joseph White: Salem, Massachusetts, 1830," ABA J. (May 1968), pp. 460–63; E.J. Wagner, "A Murder in Salem," SMITHSONIAN MAG. (Nov. 2010), https://www.smithsonianmag.com/history/a-murder-in-salem-64885035/.

145. Daniel Webster was not involved in the Crowninshield prosecution. LANCASTER JOURNAL (Lancaster, PA), Nov. 19, 1830, p. 2 ("Mr. Saltonstall has taken the place of Mr. Webster as assistant to the Solicitor general, on the trial of Crowninshield.").

146. Walker Lewis, "The Murder of Captain Joseph White: Salem, Massachusetts, 1830," ABA J. (May 1968), p. 463; E.J. Wagner, "A Murder in Salem," SMITHSONIAN MAG. (Nov. 2010), https://www.smithsonianmag.com/history/a-murder-in-salem-64885035/.

147. "Webster Enters the Case," AMERICAN HERITAGE (June 1960), Vol. 11, Iss. 4, https://www.americanheritage.com/webster-enters-case.

148. "Wild," CINCINNATI ENQUIRER (Cincinnati, OH), Oct. 14, 1900, p. 9 ("The private prosecutor of the murderers was Stephen White, a connection of Judge Story by marriage, and this Stephen White was the employer of Daniel Webster. So the counsel for the defense had objected to Webster's appearance on the law ground that the public prosecutors should not receive any fee. Webster replied that he had no pecuniary inducement. But he had received a fee from Stephen White for assisting to convict Francis Knapp, the other brother, three months previously. This is admitted by Mr. Webster's biographer, George Tighnor Curtis, who wrote 39 years afterwards.").

149. Walker Lewis, "The Murder of Captain Joseph White: Salem, Massachusetts, 1830," ABA J. (May 1968), pp. 463–64.

150. Daniel Feller, "The Bank War," *in* THE AMERICAN CONGRESS: THE BUILDING OF DEMOCRACY 166 (Julian E. Zelizer, ed. 2004) (biographical sketch of Daniel Webster).

151. *See* Farrell, *supra* note 121, at 235 ("Webster came late to the case. The murder of Captain White occurred on the night of April 6, 1830, and was discovered the next morning. At the time of the murder, Webster was in Washington, attending to his Senate business. Although he had received correspondence regarding the case from Joseph Story, and had likely read some accounts of it in the newspapers, he remained in Washington throughout the spring. The Knapp and Crowninshield brothers were not arrested until May 26, 1830. Richard Crowninshield, the principal murderer, took his own life in prison on June 15. It was only then that the peculiar legal challenge in the case arose. Webster arrived home in Boston on June 28. The trial of Frank Knapp had been scheduled to begin on July 27, but even then, Webster, apparently, had not yet been engaged by the prosecution to assist in the case. Judge Isaac Parker died on the night of July 25–26, forcing a postponement in the trial until Aug. 3. By then, Webster *had* joined the prosecution's team.") (italics in original).

152. Walker Lewis, "The Murder of Captain Joseph White: Salem, Massachusetts, 1830," ABA J. (May 1968), p. 464.

153. 7 LAWSON, *supra* note 126, at 472; *see also id.* (noting that Mr. Dexter argued to jurors: "While the official prosecutors are competent to discharge the duties of their office, why are they surrounded and replaced by this extraordinary assistance? Is there anything in this cause that threatens to turn aside public justice from its proper victim?").

154. "Trial at Salem," EVENING POST (New York, NY), Aug. 7, 1830, p. 2.

155. "Salem Murder," HURON REFLECTOR (Norwalk, OH), Aug. 31, 1830, p. 2.

156. 11 THE WRITINGS AND SPEECHES OF DANIEL WEBSTER—LEGAL ARGUMENTS AND DIPLOMATIC PAPERS 56 (national ed. 1903); *see also* 7 LAWSON, *supra* note 126, at 513–18; *id.* at xiv ("The White tragedy closes with the acquittal of *George Crowninshield* (p. 640), the brother of Richard, the actual perpetrator, and who certainly was cognizant of some, at least, of the details of the conspiracy. Was it to Mr. Webster's absence from the trial that he owed his life, or was it that the jury thought that in the two brothers Knapp the State had taken enough victims and the crime had been sufficiently avenged."); E.J. Wagner, "A Murder in Salem," SMITHSONIAN MAG. (Nov. 2010), https://www.smithsonianmag.com/history/a-murder-in-salem-64885035/ ("George Crowninshield, the remaining conspirators, had spent the night of the murder with two ladies of the evening, who provided him with an alibi. After two trials he was acquitted by a now-exhausted court.").

157. "Knapp's Trial," KENTUCKY REPORTER (Lexington, KY), Sept. 15, 1830, p. 1.

158. 7 LAWSON, *supra* note 126, at 519, 521, 572.

159. "Salem Murder," HURON REFLECTOR (Norwalk, OH), Aug. 31, 1830, p. 2 ("The Boston Courier of Saturday says:—At eleven o'clock yesterday morning the jury came into Court, stating that they could not agree on a verdict, some difficulty having arisen in the minds of some of the jurors respecting the presence of Knapp in Brown street at the time of the murder, agreeably to a previous arrangement, performing his part in aiding and abetting, he would be implicated, and be liable under the indictment, as much

as if he had been the chamber of Captain White. If he were there only from curiosity, or for the purpose of receiving information when the deed was done, he was not present.").

160. "The Salem Trials," NATIONAL GAZETTE (Philadelphia, PA), Aug. 18, 1830, p. 2 (noting that "[t]he prosecution is continued by the Solicitor General and Mr. Webster"; that "[t]hree or four reports of the first trial of J. F. Knapp, were published in Boston on Saturday, and many thousand copies of them sold during the day"; and that "[t]he Court, on Saturday morning, proceeded with the trial of John F. Knapp" and that "[t]he same witnesses were examined as on the former trial, and the testimony as far as it was given, was substantially the same"); *see also* "The Salem Murder," NATIONAL GAZETTE (Philadelphia, PA), Aug. 20, 1830, p. 1 (reporting on the trial of John Francis Knapp for the murder of Captain Joseph White).

161. "Salem Murder," EVENING POST (New York, NY), Aug. 16, 1830, p. 2 ("The case was committed to the Jury on Thursday, and they were called into Court at 7 P.M. of that day; and on Friday at 9, 10 and 11 A.M. they said they were not agreed. On Friday at 2, P.M. the Jury reported that they *could not* agree. The papers were then taken from them, and they forever discharged from the consideration of the case of the Commonwealth vs. J. Francis Knapp. The interest of the public increases as the uncertainty of guilt is developed."). Despite the hung jury, the *Salem Gazette* reported of Daniel Webster's performance: "Mr. Webster has sustained the prosecution in a manner that all would expect; he is the only great man we ever knew that does not at any time fall short of the expectations of the public." *Id.*; *see also* "Salem Trials," BELLOWS FALLS INTELLIGENCER (Bellows Falls, VT), Aug. 23, 1830, p. 3 ("On the trial of John Francis Knapp, the jury to whom the case was submitted, after 24 hours deliberation, could not agree, and were discharged by the Court.").

162. "Salem Trials," WORKING MEN'S BULLETIN (Buffalo, NY), Aug. 28, 1830, p. 3 ("The second jury impannelled to try John Francis Knapp, for the murder of Capt. Joseph White, have r[e]turned a verdict of GUILTY, and he has been sentenced to be hung; but the time of his execution is to be determined by the executive council.").

163. Book Review, 50 N. AM. REV. 539, 541–42 (1864) (reviewing THE WORKS OF NATHANIEL HAWTHORNE (Boston: Ticknor and Fields)); *see also* Klaus P. Stich, *"Cap'n Hathorn": Hawthorne's Reconnection to Ancient Deeds during Bowdoin's Fiftieth Anniversary Celebration of Its First Graduating Class*, 34 NATHANIEL HAWTHORNE REV. 103 (2008).

164. Walker Lewis, "The Murder of Captain Joseph White: Salem, Massachusetts, 1830," ABA J. (May 1968), p. 464; E.J. Wagner, "A Murder in Salem," SMITHSONIAN MAG. (Nov. 2010), https://www.smithsonianmag.com/history/a-murder-in-salem-64885035/; "The Trial of John Francis Knapp for the Murder of Joseph White, Salem, Massachusetts, 1830," *in* 7 LAWSON, *supra* note 126, at 395–593 (italics in original); Rita Sheridan Pollard, "Against the Law and Beyond the Evidence," ABA J. (Feb. 1977), Vol. 63, p. 205.

165. "Trial of Knapp," VERMONT GAZETTE (Bennington, VT), Aug. 31, 1830, p. 3.

166. Walker Lewis, "The Murder of Captain Joseph White: Salem, Massachusetts, 1830," ABA J. (May 1968), p. 465.

167. VERMONT AURORA (Vergennes, VT), Oct. 7, 1830, p. 3; "Execution of John Francis Knapp," THE REPERTORY (St. Albans, VT), Oct. 7, 1830, p. 3 (reporting the same information).

168. "Execution of J. F. Knapp," VERMONT GAZETTE (Bennington, VT), Oct. 5, 1830, p. 3. Before the execution of Frank Knapp, one newspaper reported: "A new party is breaking out in the lower end of Massachusetts, called the Frank Knapp and anti-Knapp party—one in favour of his pardon, and the other of his hanging." In the same edition of that newspaper, it was noted that "Daniel Webster is spoken of by the Clay party as a candidate for the Presidency." "A Diary," WESTERN CAROLINIAN (Salisbury, NC), Oct. 5, 1830, p. 3.

169. "Execution of John Francis Knapp," ANTI-MASONIC REPUBLICAN (Middlebury, VT), Oct. 20, 1830, p. 3.

170. Walker Lewis, "The Murder of Captain Joseph White: Salem, Massachusetts, 1830," ABA J. (May 1968), p. 465.

171. "Trial of Joseph J. Knapp," NATIONAL GAZETTE (Philadelphia, PA), Nov. 15, 1830, p. 2.

172. *See also* "Salem Trials," NATIONAL GAZETTE (Philadelphia, PA), Nov. 13, 1830, p. 2 ("The counsel for the prisoner objected to the appearance of Mr. Webster as assistant counsel on the part of the Government, on the ground that such appearance would be contrary to the statute, which implies that no person

shall appear in behalf of the Government, except the officers appointed for that purpose."); "John Jenkins Knapp," AMERICAN WHIG, VERMONT LUMINARY & EQUAL RIGHTS (Woodstock, VT), Nov. 17, 1830, p. 2 ("After a jury was empannelled, the Attorney General was proceeding to open the cause when the counsel for the prisoner enquired who was to conduct the cause for the prosecution, saying that he understood that the distinguished gentleman who conducted the former trials for this murder was not under the retainer of the Commonwealth, but of a private individual, and asserting that his appearance was contrary to the statute which implies that no person shall appear in behalf of the government, except the officers appointed for that purpose.").

173. Walker Lewis, "The Murder of Captain Joseph White: Salem, Massachusetts, 1830," ABA J. (May 1968), p. 464 n.15.

174. "The Trial of Joseph Jenkins Knapp, Jr., as an Accessory in the Murder of Joseph White, Salem, Massachusetts, 1830," *in* 7 LAWSON, *supra* note 126, at 597.

175. "Salem Trials," UNITED STATES GAZETTE (Philadelphia, PA), Nov. 16, 1830, p. 4.

176. *See also* Commonwealth v. Knapp, 10 Pick. 477, 27 Mass. 477, 490–91, 1830 WL 2680, *4–5 (Mass. Supreme Jud. Ct. Nov. 1830) (Putnam, J.):

> The counsel in behalf of the prisoner object, and contend that the statute of 1807, *c.* 18, (revived by *St.* 1811, *c.* 10,) respecting the offices and duties of the attorney-general, solicitor-general and county-attorney, makes it their duty exclusively to conduct the prosecutions on the part of the Commonwealth.
>
> We have examined that statute and are of opinion that it was not intended to prohibit the appointment of the counsellors of this Court in aid of the law officers, whenever the circumstances of the case should require the Court, in the exercise of a sound discretion, to make such appointments. It is one of the incidental powers of the Court, and has heretofore been exercised in cases within our own recollection.
>
> In cases where civil rights are in controversy and the form of proceeding is by indictment or information, the Court do not perceive any objection against permitting the party in interest to employ counsel in aid of the law officers. The same reasons would not apply to cases involving public considerations only. In such cases the statute supposes that the prosecution will be conducted by the law officers, for their salaries, and without any other compensation whatever.
>
> In the present case Mr. *Webster* avows that he is induced to aid the attorney-general merely at his request, and without any other consideration; so that this case presents the question, whether a counsellor may, at the request of the attorney-general, be admitted to aid him in the prosecution, without any pecuniary consideration being paid to him, or any other consideration which may be supposed to influence him, excepting a disinterested regard for the public good. And we all think that under these circumstances the application should be granted.
>
> It is to be recollected, that at the trial of John Francis Knapp, Mr. *Webster* was, at the request of the law officers, appointed to aid them, and that there was no objection then made by the prisoner or his counsel. And although that appointment strictly was for the then pending trial, yet if the other trials had followed immediately, the counsel for the government would have had reason to suppose that they were to receive his assistance in those trials, unless good objections should have been made. It is said by the law officers, that the preparations for this trial have been made under a similar expectation on their part, and no objection was made to this measure until the jury were empannelled.
>
> It is to be understood that the solicitor-general concurs in this application on the part of the attorney-general, and that two gentlemen only are to address the jury in the case, in behalf of the Commonwealth. It is further to be understood, that the "direction and control of the prosecution is to be with the attorney-general"; who acts under oath and upon his official responsibility.
>
> We give no opinion upon any application of this nature under any other circumstances than such as are found in the case now before us.

177. HOWARD A. BRADLEY & JAMES A. WINANS, DANIEL WEBSTER AND THE SALEM MURDER 19 (2007) (originally published in 1956); Letter of Daniel Webster to Justice Story (Aug. 11, 1830), *in* THE PRIVATE CORRESPONDENCE OF DANIEL WEBSTER 506 (Fletcher Webster, ed., 1857).

178. ROBERT V. REMINI, DANIEL WEBSTER: THE MAN AND HIS TIME 337 (1997).

179. *Id.* at 338 (noting that Webster "did not mention the fact that on August 14 he had already received a fee of one thousand dollars from Stephen White in payment for his efforts in the first trial").

180. MAURICE G. BAXTER, ONE AND INSEPARABLE: DANIEL WEBSTER AND THE UNION 544 n.18 (1984).

181. *Id.* at 161.

182. HOWARD A. BRADLEY & JAMES A. WINANS, DANIEL WEBSTER AND THE SALEM MURDER 68 (2007) (originally published in 1956).

183. 7 LAWSON, *supra* note 126, at 611–17.

184. *Id.* at 617–19.

185. *Id.* at 625.

186. "Salem Murder," VERMONT AURORA (Vergennes, VT), Nov. 18, 1830, p. 2.

187. "Sentence of J. J. Knapp, Jr.," NEW-YORK EVENING POST (New York, NY), Nov. 19, 1830, p. 2.

188. ELLEN COHN, CRIMINAL JUSTICE IN MASSACHUSETTS 84 (2004).

189. "Salem, Dec. 31, 1830," VERMONT REPUBLICAN & JOURNAL (Windsor, VT), Jan. 8, 1831, p. 3; Walker Lewis, "The Murder of Captain Joseph White: Salem, Massachusetts, 1830," ABA J. (May 1968), p. 465; "The Trial of Joseph Jenkins Knapp, Jr., as an Accessory in the Murder of Joseph White, Salem, Massachusetts, 1830," *in* 7 LAWSON, *supra* note 126, at 594.

190. "Execution of Knapp," NATIONAL GAZETTE (Philadelphia, PA), Jan. 3, 1831, p. 2.

191. FALL RIVER MONITOR (Fall River, MA), Nov. 27, 1830, p. 2.

Chapter 4 Notes

1. BRUCE DORSEY, REFORMING MEN AND WOMEN: GENDER IN THE ANTEBELLUM CITY 107 (2002) (noting that "Philadelphia's first penny-press paper, the *Public Ledger*, began publishing accounts of the daily docket of the mayor's court in the mid-1830s," with that local court becoming a place "where working-class men and women could settle disputes through private prosecution"); *see also* MICHAEL MERANZE, LABORATORIES OF VIRTUE: PUNISHMENT, REVOLUTION, AND AUTHORITY IN PHILADELPHIA, 1760–1835, at 244 (1996) ("The system of private prosecution that underlay the cases for assault and battery was a vibrant form of popular conflict resolution that the city's poor employed to help police their own affairs and neighborhoods. That many of these prosecutions were trifling and indeed vindictive, and that the aldermen colluded in the practice to secure fees, are true.").

2. "Court of Quarter Sessions: Trial of E. Sprogel, Williams, and Boon, for Highway Robbery," PUBLIC LEDGER (Philadelphia, PA), July 4, 1836, p. 2.

3. Stephanie Hoover, "Pennsylvania's Court of Quarter Sessions," PennsylvaniaResearch.com, http://www.pennsylvaniaresearch.com/pennsylvania-quarter-sessions-court.html.

4. "Correspondence of the National Gazette," NATIONAL GAZETTE (Philadelphia, PA), Aug. 22, 1839, p. 2; *see also* STATE CAPITOL GAZETTE (Harrisburg, PA), Sept. 4, 1839, p. 2 (referring to "John Adams Fisher, Esq." as "counsel of the private prosecutors"); "Commonwealth vs. Edwin W. Hutter & John J. C. Cantine," GETTYSBURG COMPILER (Gettysburg, PA), Feb. 9, 1841, p. 3 (noting that Thaddeus Stevens appeared as "the private prosecutor").

5. "Speech of Mr. Buchanan, of Pennsylvania," THE KEYSTONE (Harrisburg, PA), June 15, 1842, p. 1.

6. Douglas E. Beloof & Paul G. Cassell, *The Crime Victim's Right to Attend the Trial: The Reascendant National Consensus*, 9 LEWIS & CLARK L. REV. 481, 486 (2005).

7. *Id.* ("Steinberg cites numerous examples of private prosecutors handling cases in the daily Philadelphia criminal docket. Thus, in Philadelphia (the only city for which a comprehensive nineteenth century history has been compiled) private prosecution continued for decades after the American Revolution.").

8. ALLEN STEINBERG, THE TRANSFORMATION OF CRIMINAL JUSTICE, PHILADELPHIA 1800–1880, at 82 (1989).

9. "Citizens of Luzerne County," CARBONDALE JOURNAL (Carbondale, PA), Sept. 5, 1839, p. 2.

10. SHAE IRVING, ED., NOLO'S PLAIN-ENGLISH LAW DICTIONARY 286 (2009).

11. STEINBERG, *supra* note 8, at 1–2, 5, 8, 17, 25, 28.

12. WILBUR R. MILLER, ED., THE SOCIAL HISTORY OF CRIME AND PUNISHMENT IN AMERICA: AN ENCYCLOPEDIA 1347 (2012).

13. In addition, private prosecutions were used in cases involving gambling and riots, larceny and other property crimes, and by parents of young women for seduction.

14. STEINBERG, *supra* note 8, at 29, 38, 42, 44, 46, 48–53, 56–57, 66–67, 69, 71–72, 80–81, 84–85, 138; *see also* MONONGAHELA VALLEY REPUBLICAN (Monongahela, PA), Feb. 18, 1897, p. 3 (noting the appearance of a "private prosecutor" in an "aggravated assault and battery" case); "A Seduction Case," OREGON WEEKLY STATESMAN (Salem, OR), July 17, 1896, p. 5 ("Maud M. Wagnon, the daughter of Dan Wagnon, of Highland addition to Salem, is private prosecutor in a seduction case instituted in City Recorder Edes' court against Arthur Townsend, the bicyclist. The criminal information on file with that official bears date of July 13th and reads as follows: 'Comes now Maud M. Wagnon who, being first duly sworn, says that Arthur Townsend is guilty of the crime of seduction committed as follows: The said Arthur Townsend, on the 16th day of June, 1896, in the county of Marion, did then and there unlawfully, wrongfully and feloniously, and under a pretense of marriage, seduce and have illicit connection with one Maud M. Wagnon, an unmarried female of previous chaste character, contrary to the statutes,' etc."). It was also suggested in Pennsylvania, in a letter to the editor written by one "G. R." in 1885, that private prosecutors provide $1,000 to $5,000 bonds in cases having to do with criminal cases involving gambling or lotteries. "'Playing with Justice,'" THE TIMES (Philadelphia, PA), May 14, 1885, p. 3. In other American states, it was also common for private prosecutors to strike deals before trial with those against whom they had initiated private prosecutions. *See, e.g.*, "Municipal Affairs," EL PASO TIMES (El Paso, TX), Nov. 26, 1889, p. 7 ("In police court yesterday morning when the cases of the state of Texas vs. Taylor, Look and Morehouse were called, Judge Nugent, who appeared for the state, moved to dismiss the cases at the request of the private prosecutors who had instigated the suit, on the ground that a compromise had been effected between the prosecutor and prosecuted, on the basis that defendants would cease to violate the law if all prosecutions for past offenses was withdrawn.").

15. *See* "The Duties of District Attorney," CARLISLE WEEKLY HERALD (Carlisle, PA), Jan. 15, 1880, p. 2 ("When a District Attorney publicly declared that every criminal prosecution must be begun by a private prosecutor before a justice of the peace, he was simply in error. Such is not the law. On the contrary, a District Attorney, whenever in possession of facts sufficient to warrant a conviction for a violation of the criminal law, is bound to lay such facts before the grand jury, and can do so without previous binding over before a justice of the peace, and so acting in his public capacity is not liable for costs, because not a 'private' prosecutor within the meaning of our statute. The statute of 1850, relating to District Attorneys, is merely supplementary. Prior to its passage, there were no District Attorneys in this State, the duties of the office being discharged by Deputy Attorneys-General. The statute referred to concludes by devolving upon the District Attorney 'all the duties now performed by the Deputy Attorney-General.'"); *id.* ("Bishop on Criminal Procedure states the matter in a nut-shell: 'The efficacy of every indictment comes from the finding of a grand jury. In the United States, where there are Prosecuting Attorneys, the party who received the injury is usually, *though not necessarily or always*, the person who puts the machinery of the law in motion, and is known as the 'private prosecutor.'") (italics in original); *id.* ("The 29th section of the act of 1860, clearly implies the doctrine that indictments may be found by the grand jury without any private prosecutor, when it provides that no person shall be required to answer any indictment, 'unless the prosecutor's name, *if any there be*, is endorsed thereon.'") (italics in original); *see also* REVISED STATUTES OF THE TERRITORY OF IOWA 108 (1911) (reprinting an 1843 act pertaining to grand juries, section 29 of which provided: "The foreman shall endorse upon the indictment the names of the witnesses upon whose testimony the same was found, as well as the name of the private prosecutor, (when there has been one) who shall be liable for the costs in case the defendant is acquitted on the trial."). In the United States, the district attorney's role in relation to private prosecutors became a subject of considerable interest. *See, e.g.*, "That's the Way the Money Goes," SANTA CRUZ WEEKLY SENTINEL (Santa Cruz, CA), Dec. 7, 1878, p. 2 ("In reference to an article in our local columns touching some Court matters, we beg to make a suggestion. A party feels aggrieved and goes to the District Attorney, who finds that there is no ground for an accusation and refuses to appear in the matter. The informer, however, from some private cause, desiring a prosecution, employs some person who

may or may not be an attorney and an affidavit is sworn to before a Justice, warrants are issued, witnesses are summoned, a jury is empaneled and before long a bill is presented to the Supervisors for from ten to twenty-five dollars. While the District Attorney is unwilling to spend the county's money uselessly the private prosecutor squanders it, and the taxpayer is the only sufferer. We believe it is the contemplation of the law that the District Attorney shall prosecute all criminal causes, and if on being notified he refuses to act, the presumption is that there is no legal cause for a prosecution.").

16. Steinberg, *supra* note 8, at 183, 185, 199 & 271 n.8; John Binns, Binns's Justice, or Magistrate's Daily Companion: A Treatise on the Office and Duties of Aldermen and Justices of the Peace, in the Commonwealth of Pennsylvania, Including All the Required Forms of Process and Docket-Entries 343 (Frederick C. Brightly, ed., 9th ed. 1886); *see also* The City Government of Philadelphia: A Study in Municipal Administration 259 (1893) ("Prior to 1850 the district attorney existed as the deputy attorney-general of the State, and prosecuted violations of the criminal law in the county for which he was appointed; but in 1850 the department of district attorney was constituted."); "Correspondence," Bedford County Press and Everett Press (Everett, PA), June 9, 1869, p. 2 ("The District Attorney holds his office for three years. His fees are fixed by law and are governed in amount by the grade of crimes. They are paid by the county but are taxed with the costs in the case, and are afterwards collected from the party sentenced to pay the costs, by which means the county is reimbursed. The highest fee which this officer can receive in any case is twelve dollars. The office is worth about six hundred dollars a year. The power of the District Attorney to control the prosecution of a case against a prisoner, formerly was so exclusive as, if he chose to do so, to deprive private counsel, retained by the informer or private prosecutor to assist him, from throwing the weight of his skill into the case, even if the private prosecutor so desired. It thus sometimes happened, that, when the District Attorney had prejudices in favor of a party charged with and brought to trial for an offence, he prevented the private counsel retained to assist him, from taking part in some stages of the suit. And the instance which gave occasion for the change of this law occurred in this county, when John Palmer, being the commonwealth's attorney and P. F. Smith and John Cessna were private counsel retained to assist him, in the case against Reed for the killing of Crouse, refused to permit Mr. Cessna to close the argument to the jury. Mr. Cessna then prepared a bill, which was passed by the legislature and which in certain cases gives the entire management of the case to the private counsel for the prosecution."). In Pennsylvania, grand jurors frequently put costs upon the private prosecutor when proposed criminal charges were ignored. "Judge and Jurors," Wellsboro Agitator (Wellsboro, PA), Feb. 5, 1896, p. 3 ("The grand jury ignored seven bills, and in almost every case put the costs upon the private prosecutor.").

17. "Jury Out All Night," Rochester Democrat and Chronicle (Rochester, NY), June 6, 1891, p. 10 (Judge Rumsey, in giving the charge to the "Gentlemen of the Jury," said: "It is not necessary in this state, it never was necessary in this state since it ceased to be colony of England that there should be a private prosecutor in a criminal case. The state through its district attorney and by its grand jury assumes the prosecution of criminal actions, and when the state sees fit by the district attorney and through the grand jury to present to a trial jury a man for trial upon a charge of any crime, it is not necessary nor is it proper for a trial jury to look any farther than to the great personality which stands at the head and front of the proceedings. Private prosecutors are unknown in this state and the only prosecutor that there can be, the only prosecutor that there needs to be, is the great body of people of the state of New York who see fit to present and who deem it proper to present for your final judgment persons whom they see fit to accuse of a crime."); "Court of General Sessions. Before Judge Russell," N.Y. Daily Herald (New York, NY), Nov. 18, 1857 ("When the City Judge took his seat upon the bench this morning, he rendered the following decision in reference to the Lippincott & Roberts indictment, for an alleged issue of fraudulent stock:—*The People vs. Lippincott & Roberts.*—A motion was made before the Court in behalf of a private prosecutor to have an attorney deputed to prosecute an indictment for issuing fraudulent coal stock, on an allegation that the District Attorney showed himself indifferent to the case. The motion cannot be entertained in practice, even were the grounds of the motion founded in fact. The public prosecutor has a discretion to bring on for trial, or not, any indictment, subject only to the impeachment provided for by statute.... The Attorney General and District Attorney have very large discretion in prosecutions. They are supposed to know their own business best, and are at liberty to decide whether indictments ought to be tried, and the order in

which they should be tried. There are often reasons not advisable to let the public know, which control their course—the same as with Judges—so that Judges and prosecuting attorneys are often compelled to bear in silence ill natured public criticism, which is not founded in fact. Although the District Attorney expressed himself very willing to allow his successor elect, Mr. Sweeny, to act as District Attorney, I see no reason to take the indictment from his hands or from those of his associate, Mr. Sedgwick, in both of whom I have the highest confidence in their integrity and ability to discharge their public duty. On the contrary, I am of opinion that the District Attorney acted wisely in not trying the case whilst underhanded private litigation was going on. Whilst at the bar I have had frequent occasion to resist prosecutions of a private nature instituted in criminal courts. District Attorneys are often deceived by these specious prosecutions. But this is the first case that has come to my judicial notice, and I should do great injustice to the community if I did not act promptly in this matter.... Negotiations for a private settlement are renewed from the complainant, and the counsel for the accused—highly eminent counsel, too—Messrs. Cram and Fowler—promptly inform the District Attorney, and demand a trial. The District Attorney refuses to bring on the case because the calendar of the Court is crowded with more important felonies, such as murder, robbery, &c. The complainant commits himself in writing to some kind of an intimation that he has the witnesses for the people under his control, and offers settlement again. Without tendering any opinion as to whether the acts constitute an offence, I shall send the papers before the Grand Jury, that they may there be examined."); *see also* "Not Seeking the Truth—The Prosecution in the Gould-Field Interest," N.Y. Times, Nov. 19, 1885, p. 8 (in a dispute involving the Manhattan Railway Company and the *Wall Street Daily News*, when the judge announced that all was ready to proceed, a "Mr. Strahan for Mr. Keep" arose and said: "I am not prepared to go on at the moment, and shall not be until a representative from the District Attorney's office is here. I have to-day made an official complaint to him as to the manner in which his alleged representatives here have been conducting this case, and he has promised to send here his assistant, Mr. Ambrose H. Purdy."; after a "Mr. Goodwin" renewed his motion to proceed, Mr. Strahan objected to him speaking, with Mr. Goodwin "excitedly" replying: "I don't care if you do. The District Attorney designated my firm as his representative. I have a right to speak and proposed to exercise that that right, so just sit down." "Sit down, do you say?" Mr. Strahan shouted in response, adding, "It will take a good deal more than you to make me sit down."; Mr. Strahan then addressed the court as follows: "I object to Mr. Goodwin appearing here, and I want the objection made matter of record. Your Honor has held that there was no private prosecutor in the matter. You have sustained Mr. Goodwin in concealing the identity of the person or persons or corporation who is the father and prosecutor of this proceeding. That is your act. You have ruled over and over again that the people was the prosecution in the present case. Now, your Honor, I assert that the gentleman who appears here is the private counsel of Mr. Cyrus W. Field and Mr. Jay Gould, or one or both of them, and that he is not here as representing the public, and is not authorized to represent the public."). *See also* "Philadelphia Affairs," Baltimore Sun (Baltimore, MD), June 7, 1890, p. 1 ("District Attorney Graham has made up his mind that it is his duty as public prosecutor to take up the cases of the men who wrecked the Bank of America and the American Life Insurance Company without waiting for private prosecutors to appear. He has accordingly asked the depositors to appoint an expert to examine the books for his information and guidance. As he has no fund with which to pay for such work, he advises the depositors to provide a fund for the purpose. As the affairs of the two corporations are almost inextricably mixed the district attorney wants only one expert to go over both, and will give him all needed legal advice and backing."); "The Fitzporter Case," St. Louis Post-Dispatch, Nov. 25, 1884, p. 2 ("The Court of Appeals this morning affirmed the judgment of the Court of Criminal Correction in the case of the State against Dr. John L. Fitzporter. Dr. Fitzporter was tried and convicted of an attempted to commit an abortion on one Annie Fanger and was fined $500. He appealed the case to the Court of Appeals, and sought a reversal of the judgment of the lower court on the ground that he could prove by newly discovered evidence that no abortion had ever been committed, as Annie Fanger had admitted to one Harriet Jones that she was still enc[ei]nte after the alleged abortion had been performed. The Court this morning in it opinion disposes of this point by saying that Dr. Fitzporter had been convicted not of committing an abortion, but of an attempt to commit an abortion, and even granting that this evidence could be produced on a new trial it would not alter the verdict or judgment. With regard to the stipulation filed in the case by Mr. Robert Goode, acting as special prosecutor in the case, Mr. James M. Loring, the defendant's counsel, the

Court thus delivers itself: 'A stipulation has been filed between a member of the bar professing to represent the State as associated with the Prosecuting Attorney of the Court of Criminal Correction and the defendant[']s counsel, to the effect that this Court enter judgment reversing the judgment of the Court of Criminal Correction, and remanding the cause of that Court, because of alleged newly-discovered evidence. If this evidence were true, it would have no tendency to controvert the facts charged in the indictment which the jury, by their verdict, have found to be true. But aside from this we decline to enter judgment in conformity with the stipulation, because the stipulation is not signed by the proper officer of the State. Nor do we say that we should accede to if it were so signed, but because it is not so signed we shall not consider it at all, holding as we do that counsel retained by private prosecutors have no power to give the consent of the State to the reversal of a judgment which the State has obtained in a criminal prosecution. The judgment is accordingly affirmed. All the judges concur.'"); "Quarter Sessions Reforms. The District Court the Proper Officer to Prosecute All Criminal Cases," THE TIMES (Philadelphia, PA), May 16, 1877, p. 4:

> When the Hart creek sewer assault case was called for trial before Judge Elcock a day before it was tried a continuance was asked on account of the absence of Mr. White, who represented the prosecutor. Judge Elcock allowed the case to go over until the next day, but condemned the employment of private counsel to prosecute the Commonwealth's case. He said the District Attorney was the proper officer for that purpose, and that all persons should be willing to entrust their cases in his hands. Judge Biddle yesterday, upon being informed that the prosecution of a public case was to be conducted by private counsel, said that he would not hear any case wherein the Commonwealth was not represented by its proper officer. He further said: "In the criminal courts the only offenses tried are those against the Commonwealth, and they are not to be prosecuted to suit the vindictiveness of private suitors, but the demands of public justice. The officers of the Commonwealth are under the obligation of an oath to see that the prosecution is conducted with that view alone, and they are responsible to the law for its proper performance. A prisoner in our State is entitled to impartiality from the prosecuting officer as well as from the Judge and jury. When the District Attorney desires to associate private counsel with himself in the prosecution, for public reasons, permission can always be obtained from the court. This is no new doctrine, although it may have been lost sight of. Chief Justice Gibson said thirty years ago, in the case of Rush v. Cavenaugh: 'As the office of Attorney General is a public trust which involves, in the discharge of it, an almost boundless discretion by one officer who stands as impartial as a judge, it might be doubted whether counsel retained by a private prosecutor can be allowed to perform any part of his duty. Certainly no, unless in subservience to his will and instructions.' "This," continued his Honor, "is sound law, and I propose to adhere to it."

18. "Court of Quarter Sessions," EVENING TELEGRAPH (Philadelphia, PA), Oct. 15, 1868, p. 8 ("Judge Ludlow.—William H. Ruddiman, Prosecuting Attorney.—The court met this morning and resumed the trial of prison cases. In the midst of the squal'd, abandoned looking occupants of the prison dock sat a fair, blue-eyed lad of eleven or twelve summers, whose open, manly countenance in that strange place attracted the attention of many persons. Mr. P. F. Ransford, a member of the Bar, on entering Court, was at once enlisted by the child's appearance into his interest, and in a gentle manner asked what offense he had committed? The little prisoner frankly confessed that he had, under the persuasion of an older boy, stolen two watches, but protested warmly that he did not appreciate the wrong he was doing. Mr. Ransford at once appealed to the good nature of the private prosecutor, who generously consented to abandon the prosecution; to which charitable proposition Mr. Ruddiman kindly gave his assent.").

19. *E.g.*, "County Court Notes," DAILY REPUBLICAN (Monongahela, PA), May 2, 1905, p. 4 ("Joe Alexis was up and pleaded guilty to carrying concealed weapons in Monongahela. Leo Logan was the private prosecutor."); BRADFORD STAR (Towanda, PA), Feb. 2, 1899, p. 2 ("It seems that the views of men depend very largely upon how they are situated personally. When Senator Quay was several years ago the private prosecutor of a minor libel case in Beaver county he had the District Attorney set aside every Democrat, presumably in his own interest. Now Senator Quay is on the other side of the criminal table, and wishes the power he once exercised to be set aside entirely."); *see also* "Judge and Jury," MANSFIELD ADVERTISER (Mansfield, PA), Feb. 13, 1895, p. 3 (noting a bill was "ignored" in a case involving a "private prosecutor").

20. Filarsky v. Delia, 566 U.S. 377, 380, 384–85 (2012) (citing Commonwealth v. Gibbs, 70 Mass. 146 (1855); White v. Polk County, 17 Iowa 413 (1864)).

21. "Reddy's Masterly Appeal," SPOKANE DAILY CHRONICLE (Spokane, WA), Sept. 27, 1892, p. 1 (reporting in a "Second Edition—4:00 P.M." that in Coeur d'Alene, Idaho, "Mr. Reddy, the great San Francisco lawyer, commenced the closing argument for the defense in the conspiracy cases against the miners"; "'I join with Attorney Wood in congratulating the jury,' said he, 'who will soon go home to meet bright eyes and warm hearts and hope that you will accord the same to the defendants who toil for a living the same as you.' He then paid his compliments to Attorney Wood: 'Why did the able district attorney leave his post of honor to give it to paid private prosecutors, and who prosecute these unfortunate defendants, not because they are guilty, but because the power of wealth, influence and the press has been brought against them. The jury stands as a barrier against these oppressors and for the liberty and privileges of the defendants.'"); *accord* "In the Jury's Hands—Arguments Finished in the Case Against the Coeur d'Alene Miners," ANACONDA STANDARD (Anaconda, MT), Sept. 28, 1892, p. 1 (reporting that Mr. Reddy referred to Fremont Wood and remarked: "Why did the able district attorney leave his post of honor to give it to a paid private prosecutor?").

22. "Sprawozdanie Angielskie," DZIENNIK CHICAGOSKI (Chicago, IL), July 21, 1899, p. 1 (noting the appearance of "Mr. Geeting as private prosecutor" for a "prosecuting witness").

23. "Nic Newcomb Indicted," ROCK ISLAND ARGUS (Rock Island, IL), Sept. 26, 1898, p. 5 ("The Scott county grand jury has returned an indictment against Nic Newcomb, the Davenport saloonkeeper, on the charge of larceny by embezzlement, in the case of Daniel Drost vs. Nic Newcomb. The witnesses examined by the grand jury were Daniel Drost, John Looney, Frank H. Kelly, William Keys and A. B. Truesdale. The indictment was found at the instance of Daniel Drost, private prosecutor. The grand jury based the indictment on private prosecution, because it did not desire to take any responsibility for the outcome of the trial. It is the first time for 15 years in Davenport that the responsibility for a trial has been thus placed by a grand jury."); "The State Rests," DAVENPORT DAILY TIMES (Davenport, IA), Oct. 5, 1898, p. 2 ("Drost gave bond covering the expenses of the trial and naming him as the private prosecutor. The county attorney hesitated before entering upon the trial of the case and A. P. McGuirk was therefore retained.").

24. "Local Items," ALMA NEWS (Alma, KS), Mar. 30, 1871, p. 3 ("State of Kansas vs. J. M. Matheny, aiding and abetting assault and battery, was dismissed at request of private prosecutor."); "The Walkup Case," ST. LOUIS GLOBE-DEMOCRAT, Oct. 27, 1885, p. 1 (EMPORIA, KAN., October 26.—The Walkup case opened with a full house.... If your Honor please, and you, gentlemen of the jury. Nor words from me are necessary to impress upon your minds the grave importance of the issue to be decided by you, wherein the great State of Kansas, of which we are all proud to be citizens, on one side represented by its County Attorney and by paid private prosecutors, is the plaintiff; and this young lady, not yet 17 years of age, is the defendant."); *accord "From Tuesday's Daily,"* EMPORIA WEEKLY REPUBLICAN (Emporia, KS), Oct. 29, 1885, p. 1.

25. "In the Jury's Hands," OWENSBORO DAILY MESSENGER (Owensboro, KY), Sept. 9, 1893, p. 1 ("Hon. W. T. Ellis for the defense followed Mr. Noe. He said he would not prolong the torture of the jury by an elaborate speech. He regretted that Mr. Noe had appeared as a private prosecutor in the case. He (Noe) had argued the same old way with all old prosecutors, their consciences became hardened, and wanted conviction whether guilty or not."); NEW ENGLAND FARMER (Boston, MA), Feb. 22, 1896, p. 4 ("Randall Litsey of Harrodsburg, Kentucky, at one time an extensive Jersey breeder has been tried for forgery..., the private prosecutors being the American Jersey cattle club.").

26. "The Conviction of Myers," RICHMOND ENQUIRER (Richmond, VA), Dec. 6, 1859, p. 4 (an article reprinted from the *Maryland Union*, which noted that "[t]he prosecution was conducted for private prosecutors by Judge Watts and A. B. Sharpe, read as follows: "Emanuel Myers, who was kidnapped from Maryland, in June last, has been tried and convicted in the Court of Quarter Sessions, of Cumberland County, at Carlisle, Pennsylvania, for arresting certain runaway negroes of Warfield and Hoffman, of this State, when duly authorized to do so."); "The Christiana Treason Trials," BALTIMORE SUN (Baltimore, MD), Dec. 3, 1851, p. 4 (noting these remarks of defense counsel Theodore C. Cuyler: "The State of Maryland is here to-day, in the person of her Attorney-General, and his coadjutors,—a private prosecutor in a criminal cause—Far be it from me to say, that she thirsts for the blood of this man; and yet I have seen events occur upon the trial of this case which might almost justify this remark. It has ever been the merciful doctrine of

the law, that the sworn officer of the law, its public prosecutor, was not justified in exhibiting the particular zeal of private counsel in pressing for a conviction. This duty was to aid the court in doing justice, to seek the disclosure of the whole truth . . . .").

27. "Sayings and Doings," Detroit Free Press, Oct. 16, 1878, p. 1 ("The complaint against Reuben Russell for alleged assault with intent to kill Theodore Negro, was dismissed by Police Justice Miner yesterday on motion of Col. Larned, private prosecutor for Negro, and with the consent of the Assistant Prosecuting Attorney Miller. Negro declared that he knew Russell did not intend to kill him; that he (Negro) was the aggressor, and that he objected to going on with the case. Mr. Chipman said the complaint was made by a police officer, but neither he nor any person else had any right under the law to swear to a complaint in any matter in which he has not seen the offense committed. Justice Miner said that was an open question.").

28. Michael P. Mills, *Josephine (A Slave) v. The State of Mississippi*, 88 Miss. L.J. 273, 280 (2017) ("Under antebellum Mississippi law, a slave owner could receive from the state treasury up to one-half the value of a slave who was convicted and hanged for a capital offense, but only if the sentence were imposed by a court of competent jurisdiction within the state. Thus, slave owners had an economic incentive to allow due process of the law to obtain in capital cases involving their slaves. The law also required the owner to pay for counsel to represent the slave defendants, and further allowed private counsel to be hired to prosecute criminal cases.").

29. "Case of William Rushworth," N.Y. Daily Tribune (New York, NY), Oct. 23, 1843, p. 2 ("In the case of this individual indicted for being concerned as an accomplice in robbing the porter of the Long Island Bank of some $25,000, Mr. Warner, of counsel, moved that the accused be discharged from his recognizance, for the reason that a long period had elapsed and the case not brought to trial, because, as he stated, the District Attorney and the private counsel for prosecution had not been ready to try the issue. The Court denied the motion for the present, receiving the papers, and saying that unless the defendant should be brought to trial the next term, the motion would be entertained."); "Non-Enforcement of the Laws," Buffalo Morning Express and Illustrated Buffalo Express (Buffalo, NY), Dec. 18, 1855, p. 2 ("The *N. Y. Tribune* of Saturday, contains a well digested article under the above caption, much of which applies to this city as well as to that. Of all the numerous objections so pertinaciously urged against laws prohibiting the sale of intoxicating drinks, the one which has the most weight—we might almost say, the one which alone has any weight—with persons really friendly to the object of such laws, is the oft-repeated assertion that they cannot be enforced.... So exceedingly imperfect, so utterly inadequate is our present system of criminal justice, and so little trustworthy the persons to whom its administration is committed, that the only offenses which at present run any considerable risk of punishment are those which, by making some sudden and notable attack upon person and property, stir up for their enforcement, in addition to all the machinery of the police, the anger and spirit of retaliation of some persevering private prosecutor.").

30. "The City," The Observer (Raleigh, NC), Mar. 22, 1877, p. 3 ("The defendants were all present, and represented by their Attorney, J. C. Logan Harris, Esq. Mr. W. J. Edwards, the private prosecutor, was not represented by counsel."); "Glover Was Persecuted—North Carolina Judge Threw Out Charges Against a Boston Man and Said Prosecutors Should Pay Costs," Boston Globe (Boston, MA), Aug. 24, 1893, p. 2 ("The Asheville Daily Citizen states that Judge Armfield declared from the bench that the district attorney and lawyers of the prosecutors had evidently been misled in the Glover cases by their clients, and that he did not think that the county should pay the costs of prosecution, but that they should be borne by the private prosecutors."); "More Pardons by Russell," Charlotte Daily Observer (Charlotte, NC), Dec. 22, 1897, p. 8 ("Governor Russell pardoned Robert Dougherty, convicted of manslaughter at June term, 1891, of Buncombe Criminal Court, and sentenced to twenty years in the penitentiary. He gives the following reasons: 'This pardon is recommended by E. D. Carter, who prosecuted the case and whose letter gives reasons sufficient and satisfactory for granting it. It is also advised by V. S. Lusk, the private prosecutor, and by the widow of the deceased and by all the jury who tried the case; by many members of the bar of Buncombe and by a number of responsible citizens. It appears that his homicide was without malice or premeditation or actual intent to kill and was not without some provocation. Dougherty has been in the penitentiary about six years and has suffered enough.'"); "No Pardon for Robertson," Morning Post (Raleigh, NC), Jan. 22, 1898, p. 4 ("Governor Russell has refused to pardon Thos. Robertson, the young man

from this county, who is serving a five year's sentence on the county roads for seduction of Miss Julia Hester. Application was made to the Governor, upon a written agreement that the prisoner pay the private prosecutor $1,000 and the county all the costs in the same. The costs amount to about $150."); ASHEVILLE DAILY CITIZEN (Asheville, NC), Apr. 30, 1895, p. 1 ("Mr. Webb moved that Dr. A. M. Ballard be marked a private prosecutor and his Honor directed the clerk to enter the motion.").

31. "Assaulted," DAILY OREGON STATESMAN (Salem, OR), Dec. 12, 1894, p. 1 ("M. Holbert is the private prosecutor in the case of the state vs. Leonard Brown, charged with the crime of assault and battery on Saturday last. The claim of Mr. Holbert is that he was attacked by Brown in North Salem. The defendant will have a hearing before Justice H. A. Johnson at 10 o'clock tomorrow morning."); "Hillsboro Notes," DAILY EUGENE GUARD (Eugene, OR), Aug. 8, 1893, p. 1 ("HILLSBORO, Aug. 7.—James Lee was examined before Justice Knight Saturday on a charge of rape alleged to have been committed on his 15-year-old sister-in-law, Caroline Ziegler. It appearing that it was only a family row, Lee was dismissed and the costs assessed against the private prosecutor, William D. Zeigler."); "Arrested Without Cause," CORVALLIS GAZETTE (Corvallis, OR), June 15, 1894, p. 1 (explaining that "[i]t often happens that an innocent person is arrested for an imaginary offense," and pointing to a very recent occurrence in which "a party by the name of Thomas Martin arrived here from Lane county, with a band of horses, which he placed in a pasture near town"; after "a cayuse pony, worth, probably, $30, followed his band of horses along the road, and "Martin was arrested on a warrant from Lane County, issued on the complaint of the owner of the pony, and taken to Junction yesterday morning for a preliminary examination, where he will no doubt explain the matter to the entire satisfaction of the court, and be discharged"; "In such an event, it is to be hoped that the costs will be taxed to the private prosecutor for owning a horse that would run away, and for causing the arrest of a man, who, upon investigation, he would have found innocent of the charge."); "Arrested," DAILY EUGENE GUARD (Eugene, OR), Feb. 16, 1894, p. 4 ("On a complaint charging Rev. F. S. Beck with the crime of larceny, Deputy Sheriff Croner arrested the reverend father this morning. The complaint alleges that the said F. S. Beck did, on or about Feb. 5th, 1894, take, steal and carry away from St. Mary's Catholic church, in Eugene, the following described property, to wit: One statute [sic] of the 'Blessed Virgin,' of the probable value of $60; four set[s] of church vestments, $125; one monstrance, $60; two altar cloths, $5, contrary to the peace and dignity of the state of Oregon, in such cases made and provided. Louis Aya is the private prosecutor. The examination will take place before Justice Kinsey some time tomorrow afternoon. Mr. Beck was released on his own recognizance."); "Justification," DAILY EUGENE GUARD, Mar. 16, 1894, p. 1 ("EDITOR GUARD: In No. 57 you brought the news: Father Beck arrested for larceny. Louis Aya is the private prosecutor. In next number you announced the case dismissed on motion of the prosecuting witness. The matter is herewith not settled. I always waited for a certificate of revocation and satisfaction from the part of said complaint. But without any result. Hence I publicly declare said Louis Aya a liar, calumniator and detractor of first rate, so long as he does not give full satisfaction or prove his bold accusation. REV. F. S. BECK."); "An Officer Arrested," DAILY OREGON STATESMAN, Oct. 2, 1892, p. 4 ("Yesterday evening Marshal Minto placed Constable T. P. Welch under arrest on a warrant sworn out before Recorder Goodell by Peter Brown, private prosecutor. Welch is charged with 'compounding a crime for a reward.' This arrest grows out of the constable's endeavor to close up a crap game Thursday night when he arrested the proprietor of the game and afterwards released him upon the crap man paying $30 to the complainant. Constable Welch will have a hearing Monday morning, having given bonds in sum of $250 for his appearance. His sureties were J. C. Smith and Chas. Smith."); *see also* "The Gervais Examination," OREGON DAILY STATESMAN (Salem, OR), Oct. 28, 1885, p. 3 ("The little town is considerably shaken up with the robbery, and if the true burglars are caught, there will be plenty of private prosecutors to see them to the penitentiary.").

32. "'Blind Tiger' Cases in Crockett," GALVESTON DAILY NEWS (Galveston, TX), Sept. 2, 1877, p. 2 (noting "Mr. Leaverton being private prosecutor").

33. "The Virginian Duelist," N.Y. TIMES, Aug. 23, 1882, p. 5 ("LUNENBERG COURT-HOUSE, Va., Aug. 22—The court convened for the Garland trial at 9:30 o'clock this morning, at which hour the prisoner was brought from the jail to the court-room, looking sallow, and apparently more concerned about his trial than on any previous day.... After the reading of the instructions there was a lengthy argument between counsel for the Commonwealth and the defense as to who should open and close the argument in the case, counsel for defendant claiming that Mr. George C. Orgain, the Commonwealth's attorney, should open and

close the argument, not the counsel employed by the private prosecutors. Mr. Orgain, replying to counsel for the defense, said that he did not intend that defendant's counsel should dictate to him how he should conduct this prosecution. The court said he never knew a case where such a question was raised, and instructed the Commonwealth's attorney to exercise his own discretion in the conduct of the trial. Subsequently, by mutual agreement of counsel on both sides, it was agreed that Mr. Orgain should open the case for the Commonwealth and that Mr. H. A. Taylor, of Baltimore, and Judge Drury A. Hinton, of Petersburg, should close for the prosecution."); *see also* "The Virginia Duel Trial," The Times (Philadelphia, PA), Aug. 23, 1882, p. 1 ("The Prosecution Close. Mr. Orgain was followed by A. H. Taylor, of Baltimore, representing the prosecution, who said it was a pleasure to him to appear before the jury if for nothing else but to clear away the misrepresentations that had been made by counsel for the defense. We had been spoken of as private prosecutors, and the unjust aspersion of private malice was cast upon Addison's family. Mr. Taylor said he was a life-long friend of the Addison family; he came here to assist this court in the prosecution of the murderer of Joseph Addison."); "The Virginia Duel Trial," The Times (Philadelphia, PA), Aug. 24, 1882, p. 1 ("The trial of Duelist Garland still attracts the deepest interest. The only men who do not seem particularly concerned are the jurors. One of them, Bruce by name, has borrowed Garland's fiddle to play for the amusement of his fellow-jurymen after the adjournment of the court every day. After the court had been called to order to-day, Charles F. Finch, of Mecklenburg county, opened for the defense. He began by saying that Mr. Taylor and Judge Hinton had been employed by the Addison family as prosecutors. The speaker wanted to know, as this case might possibly go to the Supreme Court of Appeals, what right Judge Hinton had to come here to prosecute this prisoner for the gold of the Addison family—for blood-money. In this connection Mr. Finch said that Judge Hinton and Mr. Taylor had the right to put their legal talents up to the highest bidder for blood-money, but this was the first time in the history of Virginia that a member of the Court of Appeals of the State had ever been found trailing its white ermine for blood-money. His (Finch's) talents could not be bought for blood-money.").

34. Wheeling Daily Register (Wheeling, WV), Mar. 27, 1876, p. 4 ("The case of the State of West Virginia vs. Hamilton, of the Wild Gazelle, in which the Brown Brothers, owners of the Luella and Humming Bird, are private prosecutors, began in the County Court of Point Pleasant, West Virginia, Friday, on appeal from the Magistrate on a peace bond for $4,000. Some forty witnesses are in attendance."); "Charleston Liquor Cases," Wheeling Daily Intelligencer (Wheeling, WV), Apr. 26, 1898, p. 7 ("The statutes of this state have clearly provided for the allowance of costs in all civil proceedings to the party substantially prevailing, but in criminal proceedings they only allow costs to be recovered against the accused in case of some conviction, and in some cases in his favor on acquittal against a private prosecutor, but never against the public, the state or its authorized representative.").

35. "A Just Judge," Racine Daily Journal (Racine, WI), Dec. 7, 1882, p. 2 ("Janesville, Wis., Dec. 6. The trial of Hartley Clifford for the murder of Capt. W. R. Pugh opened here yesterday.... At the opening of the case, an objection was raised by the defense to the appearance of Mr. Fish, Mr. Cooper's assistant in the case. The objection was overruled and great confusion was the result of Mr. Ebbets' attempt to show that Mr. Fish appeared in the case as a private prosecutor to be paid with the money of the relatives of the deceased. Mr. Fish opened the case to the jury with great clearness, and ably anticipated all the issues which are likely to be developed in the trial. In the parallel he drew between the slayer and his victim which consisted of inferences from the facts of the homicide to be proven, his words were a fitting tribute to the memory of generous and wholesouled Capt. Pugh, and a judicious and in no way inappropriate condemnation of his cowardly assassin."); "Trial of Clifford," Racine Daily Journal (Racine, WI), Dec. 6, 1882, p. 3 ("The trial of Hartley Clifford on the charge of the murder of Capt. Wm. R. Pugh, began in the Rock County Circuit Court yesterday, on change of venue from Racine County. The trial attracts considerable attention here and the court room at the opening was filled with spectators. John T. Fish and District Attorney Cooper appeared for the state...."); "Hartley Clifford's Case Disposed of by the Supreme Court," State Gazette (Green Bay, WI), June 9, 1883, p. 2 ("The motion filed by the attorneys of Hartl[e]y Clifford, the Milwaukee gambler who killed Capt. Pugh at Racine, asking for a stay of the execution of sentence, was sharply argued before the Supreme Court to-day by W. H. Ebbets for petitioner and the assistant Attorney General and John T. Fish, of Racine, for the State."). John T. Fish—a private practice lawyer—was also involved in a successful lawsuit for malicious prosecution and represented the Traders' Insurance

Company in a trial in which two sisters—Mary Melendy and Sarah E. Westcott—were charged with arson. "Victory for Racine Lawyers," RACINE DAILY JOURNAL, Oct. 10, 1885, p. 3 ("John T. Fish and J. V. Quarles who have been at Sparta, Wis., conducting a case against Geo. Hiles, malicious prosecution, obtained a verdict yesterday against the gentleman for $9,000 damages. The case is one of more than usual interest for the reason that Hiles is a wealthy lumberman of Dexterville and is reputed to be worth a million. The suit was brought against him by a Mrs. Spear, who with George Haney, and husband John Spear, was arrested for arson. Some buildings belonging to Hiles were burned. The suit was conducted by District Attorney Williams, and arrests were made upon his advice. Hiles was the complainant. The defendants waived an examination and asked to be sent to the Grand Rapids jail. They were sent there and remained between five and six weeks, finally being bailed out by parties living at Grand Rapids. They had their trial there and were acquitted, hence their suit for false imprisonment."); "The Melendy Trial," CHICAGO DAILY TRIBUNE, Nov. 8, 1885, p. 14 (describing John T. Fisk's role in the arson case); *see also* "Racine, Wis.," CHICAGO DAILY TRIBUNE, Nov. 1, 1885, p. 11 ("It is quite generally admitted that John T. Fish of Racine has been offered the First Assistant Solicitorship of the St. Paul Railroad, in place of David S. Wegg, who resigned last spring. Mr. Fish has refused the offer and will move to Milwaukee to be one of the firm of Jenkins, Winker & Smith.").

36. *Filarsky*, 566 U.S. at 384; *id.* at 384–85:

> As one commentator has observed, there was at that time "no very clear conception of a professional office, that is, an office the incumbent of which devotes his entire time to the discharge of public functions, who has no other occupation, and who receives a sufficiently large compensation to enable him to live without resorting to other means." F. Goodnow, Principles of the Administrative Law of the United States 227 (1905). Instead, to a significant extent, government was "administered by members of society who temporarily or occasionally discharge[d] public functions." *Id.*, at 228. Whether government relied primarily upon professionals or occasional workers obviously varied across the country and across different government functions. But even at the turn of the 20th century, a public servant was often one who "does not devote his entire time to his public duties, but is, at the same time that he is holding public office, permitted to carry on some other regular business, and as a matter of fact finds his main means of support in such business or in his private means since he receives from his office a compensation insufficient to support him." *Id.*, at 227.

37. "An Awful Crime and Speedy Punishment," SPRINGFIELD DAILY REGISTER, May 14, 1853; *see also* 2 EARL SCHENCK MIERS, ED., LINCOLN DAY BY DAY: A CHRONOLOGY 1809–1865, at 98 (1960) (noting that, on May 9, 1853, "[w]ith important rape case coming for trial, court orders Lincoln to act as prosecutor for remainder of term" and Lincoln "writes indictment of Thomas Delany Watlen, signing 'Lincoln atty Pro tem."; and noting with respect to May 10, 1853: "Lincoln is prosecutor in People *v.* Watlen. Defendant is accused of raping seven-year-old girl. Jury brings in verdict of guilty and court sentences accused to penitentiary for 18 years."); *see also* id. at 156 (noting in entry for October 29, 1855: "Eleven of Lincoln & Lamon's cases are called.... Lincoln writes indictment in People *v.* Griffith, altering agreement, for Lamon as prosecuting attorney, who signs.").

38. *Lincoln Legal Career Timeline*, Abraham Lincoln Online, http://www.abrahamlincolnonline.org/lincoln/education/lawhighlights.htm.

39. "Circuit Court," DEWITT COURIER (Clinton, IL), Nov. 2, 1855, p. 2; "The Trial of Wyant," THE WEEKLY PANTAGRAPH (Bloomington, IL), Apr. 8, 1857, p. 3; "That Celebrated Case," THE PANTAGRAPH (Bloomington, IL), Jan. 14, 1882, p. 4.

40. ALLEN D. SPIEGEL, A. LINCOLN, ESQUIRE: A SHREWD, SOPHISTICATED LAWYER IN HIS TIME 38, 193, 219 (2002); "Obscure History Story Had Error," THE PANTAGRAPH (Bloomington, IL), June 29, 2000, p. A2; "Joseph W. Fifer Begins Eighty-Second Year Today," THE DAILY PANTAGRAPH (Bloomington, IL), Oct. 28, 1921, p. 5; *see also* "Lincoln v. Chloroform Insanity," Anesthesiology Reflections, http://watermark.silverchair.com ("During a dispute over a property boundary in June of 1855, Isaac Wyant was shot by a gun-wielding man named Anson Rusk. According to one witness, after surgical amputation of his arm, Wyant emerged from his chloroform anesthetic 'ever after morbidly fearful that Rusk would kill him... and complained greatly about his head and exhibited many signs of being unsettled in his intellect.'").

Additional information on *People v. Wyant* can be found online. The Law Practice of Abraham Lincoln (Second Edition), http://www.lawpracticeofabrahamlincoln.org/Details.aspx?case=136798 (last accessed Mar. 20, 2021).

41. "That Celebrated Case," THE PANTAGRAPH (Bloomington, IL), Jan. 14, 1882, p. 4.

42. "Police Court," BOSTON POST (Boston, MA), Sept. 2, 1836, p. 2 ("The discussion of this question was opened yesterday, in the case of the Commonwealth *vs.* Samuel H. Moore and William Moore, who were charged with keeping a gambling house, the inmates of which were routed on Saturday night last. Mr *William Joseph Snelling* was the complainant, and of course private prosecutor, and a witness."); "Municipal Court," BOSTON PORT (Boston, MA), July 16, 1840, p. 2 ("MR VOSE yesterday retracted his plea of 'not guilty,' on the indictment for assaulting two Canadian females, and entered a plea that he would not contend with the Commonwealth. He has made pecuniary reparations to the private prosecutors to the extent of his limited means, and the sentence on the indictment has been suspended till the August term, to allow him to procure the needful to meet the judgment and liquidate the heavy bill of costs, which have accrued in the course of the prosecution."); BOSTON PORT (Boston, MA), Oct. 4, 1841, p. 2 ("*The Grand Jury*, for the Municipal Court, will come together at 9 o'clock this morning. Witnesses and private prosecutors will take due notice, and govern themselves accordingly."); "*Municipal Court*," BOSTON PORT (Boston, MA), Jan. 3, 1842, p. 2 (referring to "the private prosecutor" in "the last cases of Doe and Alker"); *see also* "Municipal Court," BOSTON PORT (Boston, MA), May 22, 1837, p. 2 ("As a general rule, the Police Court does not entertain criminal suits, when there are adverse civil actions pending upon the subject matter of the complaint. Why the Court in this case departed from this judicious practice, does not appear very obvious, for it was quite a manifest, that Low had a good ground of action, under the usury law, as that he had mistaken his legal remedy, in trusteeing Delano, and arresting the notes in his possession. If every person, who attaches property upon an erroneous process, should be prosecuted as a thief, the monthly catalogue of indictments would be exceedingly increased. There is a distinction between civil and criminal suits, that jurors and the public should never lose sight of: —it is this—in the criminal suit, the private prosecutor's mouth in *open* in court, but the defendant's is *shut*.") (italics in original). Private prosecutions were also used in the military. EVENING POST (New York, NY), Nov. 30, 1829, p. 2 ("It is laid down by Hough, in his treatise on Court Martials, that 'Whether the prosecution shall be conducted by the Judge Advocate, or by a private prosecutor, must be determined by the Commanding General.'").

43. "Conclusion of the Trial of Edwin Kelly for the Alleged Murder of Thomas J. Sharpe—The Recorder's Charge—Verdict of Not Guilty," N.Y. DAILY HERALD (New York, NY), May 1, 1868, p. 5.

44. *Filarsky*, 566 U.S. at 385.

45. "Brief Mention," DALLES DAILY CHRONICLE (The Dalles, OR), Nov. 21, 1895, p. 3 ("The Rothermel trial is on its third day and bids fair to last out the week. The case is one of importance, but is proving very wearisome because of the slowness of its progress. The private prosecutor, August Morsbach, was upon the stand all day yesterday and as he is not familiar with the English language, the court appointed Mr. E. Jacobsen interpreter. The reading of letters in German and necessitating translation took up a great portion of the time.").

46. *See, e.g.*, "What They Found—Result of the Grand Jury's Investigation," READING TIMES (Reading, PA), June 19, 1890, p. 1 (noting that "[a]fter the private prosecutor was satisfied and the costs paid in the Quarter Sessions office, two hundred and seventy-five dollars was deposited at the Keystone Bank in an envelope").

47. "Judges and Jurors," WELLSBORO AGITATOR (Wellsboro, PA), Sept. 1, 1885, p. 3 ("John Quillott, indicted for carrying concealed weapons, was found not guilty, and the costs were imposed on Fred. Costley, the private prosecutors. Quillott has appeared in Court a number of times within the last year and half actively engaged in prosecuting certain parties in Knoxville and vicinity for illegally selling liquor. At the last term he was indicted as a common barrator, but the case was never tried. By his constantly causing the arrest of liquor men and the subpoenaing of many witnesses to bring them here to Court he excited the indignation of a large number of people in the neighborhood of Knoxville, who threatened and armed himself with revolvers and signified his intention of using the same if molested. The jury by their finding vindicated his action.").

48. "June Jottings," DALLES DAILY CHRONICLE (The Dalles, OR), June 21, 1893, p. 3 ("In Justice Davis' court yesterday in the case of the state of Oregon vs. Chas. Casson, the defendant was discharged and costs taxed to I. C. Matney private prosecutor. This case was about that Mill creek road again. It appears to be the custom out there to fence up the county road whenever it suits an individual's convenience to do so. Mr. Matney had Mr. Casson arrested for tearing down a fence which it suited his convenience to place across said road.").

49. "Letter from Bradford," VERMONT UNION (Lyndon, VT), Apr. 8, 1870, p. 2; *compare* "A State Police," ST. ALBANS WEEKLY MESSENGER (Saint Albans, VT), Oct. 28, 1870, p. 4 ("Our present law offers as attractive pecuniary inducements to private prosecutors as the bill in question and it lays equally exacting obligations upon the authorities. We are firmly persuaded that this, with the moral influence of the press, the family and the church, is the hope of the temperance cause.").

50. "J. H. Wilson's Answer," GALVESTON DAILY NEWS (Galveston, TX), Dec. 14, 1890, p. 28 ("Colonel S. N. Wood, a member of the bar of the supreme court of the United States, and during the republic of Texas a practicing lawyer in this state, was engaged by Mrs. Cross, the widow of one of the murdered men, as well as by Mr. Wilcox, whose brother was murdered, and by Herbert Tonney as private prosecutor to aid the United States attorney in prosecuting those cases."); "The Wolf Homicide," PITTSBURGH POST-GAZETTE (Pittsburgh, PA), Nov. 19, 1885, p. 3 (noting that in Washington, Pennsylvania, "District Attorney Taylor" appeared "for the Commonwealth" and that "Mrs. Jane Mason, sister of the deceased, is the private prosecutor, and has no counsel"); "Homicides," DAILY REPUBLICAN (Monongahela, PA), Jan. 6, 1899, p. 4 ("Of those charged with the foregoing, the coroner's jury in the case of Wm. Phennicle exonerated him, as he had done it in self defense. An information having been made by a private prosecutor when the deed was committed. The case went to court and was ignored by the grand jury."); "Dorsey Murder Trial," DAILY REPUBLICAN (Monongahela, PA), May 23, 1896, p. 1 ("Beside the district attorney for the commonwealth, the private prosecutor has retained McCracken & McGiffins, Braden & Campbell and A. M. Templeton, Esqrs."); "A Horrible Crime," STATE RIGHTS DEMOCRAT (Albany, OR), Dec. 11, 1896, p. 1 ("The preliminary examination of Willard Birchard, who resides two miles east of Stayton on the charge of rape, alleged to have been committed on this daughter Minnie Birchard, June 1, 1896, H. N. Huntley private prosecutor, was held before Justice Johnson at Salem yesterday. Two married daughters, Mrs. H. N. and Mrs. J. O. Huntley swore that their father had committed the same crime with them from the time they were 11 and 12 until they were married, that they were afraid of their father and never told, as he threatened them.").

51. "Work of the Court," WELLSBORO AGITATOR (Wellsboro, PA), Dec. 6, 1893, p. 3 (noting that "[t]he private prosecutor, Mr. Ross, charged his co-partner with the fraudulent appropriation of $925.36 of the firm's money on the 27th day of February last"); "Hazlett Guilty as Indicted," PITTSBURGH PRESS (Pittsburgh, PA), Nov. 25, 1899, p. 7 (noting that "counsel for the private prosecutor... presented the arguments for the commonwealth" in a case involving a banker, Samuel Hazlett, charged with embezzlement for "receiving funds after he knew himself to be insolvent"); "Hazlett on Trial," PITTSBURGH PRESS (Pittsburgh, PA), Nov. 28, 1898, p. 7 (noting that ex-banker, Samuel Hazlett, "would try to repay to W. D. Roberts, the private prosecutor, but Judge Taylor, from the bench this morning, stated that the case must be settled in open court"); "Trembling Stockholders," LANCASTER INTELLIGENCER (Lancaster, PA), Sept. 28, 1877, p. 2 ("Mr. John S. Morton has put on an appearance of great candor ever since the discovery of his fraud, and appeared to desire to tell everything while in reality concealing much. No doubt he has been more full in his confession to his fellow-stockholders, else they surely would not be disposed to handle with gloves the man who has done them the largest injury and has secured the largest profit. Yesterday Mr. Morton appeared before the committing magistrate as a witness against his co-conspirators, Huhn and Nagle. He declared that the over-issue of stock amounted altogether to eleven thousand shares, of which Nagle & Co. got twenty-five hundred shares, upon which they borrowed a hundred dollars a share. He failed to account, and in fact does not appear to have been asked by Wm. B. Mann, the counsel of Huhn and Nagle, to account, for the small balance of eighty-five hundred shares; and the only conclusion we are left to draw is that they were applied by Morton to his own use. Yet Huhn and Nagle were held in $50,000 bail each, while Morton was required by the accommodating magistrate to furnish but $10,000. Clearly his action was inspired by the private prosecutors; and just as clearly they must have had some strong reason for making so invidious and apparently unjustifiable a distinction between the prisoners.").

52. "Work of the Court," WELLSBORO AGITATOR (Wellsboro, PA), Dec. 6, 1893, p. 3 (noting that "[t]he following bills were ignored by the grand jury": "Marion Willard, assault and battery," "Jerry Hurley, assault and battery," "John Clark, assault and battery," "George Silverman, selling liquors without a license," and "John Wilson, Garry Smith, Levi Woodward, Samuel Woodward and John Henry, riot and assault, etc.," and Charles Stodard, forcible entry and detainer," with the respective private prosecutors in those cases to "pay costs"); "Judge and Jurors," WELLSBORO AGITATOR (Wellsboro, PA), Oct. 3, 1894, p. 3 (noting several "bills" for "assault and battery" that were ignored, with the private prosecutors "to pay costs"); WELLSBORO AGITATOR (Wellsboro, PA), Nov. 29, 1899, p. 1 ("The bill against Michael Ryan, for assault and battery, was ignored and the costs placed upon the private prosecutor, John Blunt."); "Case Continued," DAILY OREGON STATESMAN (Salem, OR), Feb. 8, 1896, p. 5 (noting the appearance of a "private prosecutor" in an assault and battery case); "Dismissed," OREGON WEEKLY STATESMAN (Salem, OR), July 16, 1897, p. 5 ("The assault and battery charges against H. J. Bigger, E. Nordyke, F. Baker and J. Young, entered in Justice Johnson's court Monday by Isham B. Small as the result of a row which occurred in the court house hall during the forenoon, were dismissed yesterday at the request of the private prosecutor.").

53. "'Billy' Egan in Trouble," OREGON DAILY STATESMAN (Salem, OR), July 23, 1896, p. 5.

54. "A Gypsy Girl Arrested," OREGON STATESMAN (Salem, OR), May 13, 1898, p. 5 ("Pearl Boyd first became known in police court circles last October. She was, with her people, encamped in North Salem, and first appeared in City Recorder Edes' court in the role of private prosecutor in that she swore out a warrant for the arrest of her alleged brother, Geo. Buttler, whom she accused of threatening to take her life. Buttler was tried and acquitted on October 28, 1897, and on the following day was examined for insanity, but was discharged.").

55. "Trespass Case," DAILY EUGENE GUARD (Eugene, OR), Sept 13, 1898, p. 4 ("An exciting trespass case was tried yesterday before Justice C K Hale, of Cheshire precinct, and a jury wherein L P Taliman was private prosecutor...."); *see also* "By Justice Johnson," OREGON WEEKLY STATESMAN (Salem, OR), Oct. 29, 1897, p. 3 (noting a trespass case had been dismissed on motion of the district attorney, with a "private prosecutor" being mentioned by name).

56. "Court Proceedings," DAILY REPUBLICAN (Monongahela, PA), Aug. 19, 1896, p. 1 ("The case of James Smith charged with perjury occupied the greater part of the day. A verdict is expected today. The defendant is charged by Thomas S. Briggs with having cultivated two lots belonging to the private prosecutor and in judicial proceedings growing out of said action to have sworn that the title to the lots was vested in himself. The parties are all from Stockdale, on the Monongahela. Messrs. Baird and Bible represented the private prosecutor and James I. Brownson, Jr., the defendant.").

57. "The New Law of Libel," SUNDAY NEWS-DEALER (Wilkes-Barre, PA), Dec. 27, 1885, p. 2 ("The trial of Alex. McClure in the Criminal Court of this county a few days since has by reason of some of its features attracted considerable attention.... The private prosecutor, J. C. Coon, is the editor of this paper. The defendant, McClure, is the editor of the Philadelphia *Times*, whose influence is, perhaps, not exceeded by any other journal published in Pennsylvania. Whilst in every criminal prosecution there must be a private accuser, it must not be lost sight of that the charge always made is that, in some special manner, the defendant has violated the public law of the State, and imperilled the peace and order of society. It was the Commonwealth, and not Mr. Coon, who caused Mr. McClure to be indicted, arraigned and tried. The Grand Inquest declared that from the testimony, submitted to them, the defendant had committed an offense against the public law, that, in their judgment, he had published a libelous attack upon Mr. Coon, and should, for this alleged public crime, be put upon trial. The indictment charged that the defendant, on the 21st day of May, 1885, published in the Philadelphia *Times* a special dispatch from Washington, which stated that J. C. Coon and another gentleman from Wilkes-Barre and come to Washington to deal out Luzerne county offices, and it went on to falsely accuse Mr. Coon of several heinous crimes.").

58. "The Saloon and the Speak-Easy," WILKES-BARRE RECORD (Wilkes-Barre, PA), Mar. 11, 1896, p. 4 ("In this State the enforcement of the criminal law as to offenses ranking only as misdemeanors is made to depend too much on the zeal, intelligence and pertinacity of some private prosecutors. The Law and Order Society has been the chief prosecutor of violators of the laws relating to liquor selling, but it concerns itself chiefly with those selling liquors on Sunday. Those selling without a license on week-days only are apt to escape the attention of the Law and Order Society."); "The Courts," PITTSBURGH DAILY POST (Pittsburgh,

PA), Dec. 22, 1868, p. 1 ("Commonwealth vs. Henry Thompson, indictment, selling liquor to minors; William Pittman, private prosecutor. The defendant is a tavern keeper at Tarentum, and is charged with selling liquor to a step-son of Pittman. On trial."); "A Costly Liquor Case," MONONGAHELA VALLEY REPUBLICAN (Monongahela, PA), Aug. 28, 1884, p. 3 ("WASHINGTON, PA., August 22.—The jury in the case of John Boyle, of Coal Centre, for violation of the liquor laws, returned a verdict this morning of not guilty. Mr. Boyle who keeps a wholesale store in connection with his distillery, was charged with furnishing whisky to men of known intemperate habits. The suit was bought by Constable Freeman, the private prosecutors being, it is stated, members of the Woman's Christian Temperance Union. The county pays the cost, amounting probably to $2,000."); "Selling Cider," DAILY REPUBLICAN (Monongahela, PA), Feb. 18, 1888, p. 4 ("On Friday, at Court, Jacob Kurtzsock of Midway, was charged with violation of the liquor law, Officer McBurney being the prosecutor. The defendant keeps a store in Midway, where he sold soft drinks. It was said that he sold a drink called cider, which would make persons drinking it intoxicated. The defendant claimed that he sold nothing but sweet cider. The jury returned a verdict of not guilty, and the private prosecutors, David and John Wright, pay half of the costs and the defendant the other half."); "A Rum Rebellion," LEAVENWORTH WEEKLY TIMES (Leavenworth, KS), Sept. 9, 1886, p. 4 ("The murder of Rev. George C. Haddock at Sioux City, Ia., was the outcome of an attempt to enforce the prohibitory law by private prosecutors. Sioux City has long been notorious for its open defiance of the liquor law. The saloons have elected the mayor and the city council and the mayor, as is the case at Leavenworth, licenses the saloons and gambling-houses in defiance of the law, collecting 'license fees,' which are really black-mail for police protection, every month. All the other officers of the law acquiesced in the action of the mayor. It was the duty of the sheriff and district attorney to prosecute violations of the liquor law, and the duty of the judges to remove these officers if they did not prosecute, but nobody lifted a hand and free rum throve... A law and order league was formed to fight the evil, but the 'saloon party' threatened to shoot any man who signed an information for their arrest. Then two women signed the informations and the ministers in the law and order league undertook to carry the prosecutions forward. It was in this work that Haddock was shot. The president of the league, another minister, has his house guarded every night to prevent a similar fate."); *see also* "Rebellion," LEAVENWORTH TIMES (Leavenworth, KS), Sept. 14, 1886, p. 1 (discussing the killing of Rev. Haddock in Sioux City, Iowa, and noting in part: "The saloon keepers of Sioux City seemed to have everything their own way. They elected the mayor, they controlled the election of the sheriff. They quieted the district attorney and they soothed the judges. There was only one thing left now to fear. That was the private prosecutors. The officers of the law they controlled, they must guard against private prosecution. So, in order to guard against this danger surely and successfully, they declared against private prosecutions. Their declaration was very loud. It was very definite. IT WAS DEATH! Death to the man who signed a petition to enjoin a saloon. That seemed to settle matters.... The saloon held absolute sway and wielding its unmerciful scepter with merciless power. Upon this scene of treason, of shame, of wickedness, of degr[a]dation there came two mothers. God bless Mrs. F. O. Brown. God bless Mrs. A. R. Comstock. The saloon keepers should silence men, but they could not silence these mothers. . . . The clergy of Sioux City stepped to the side of these brave mothers. George C. Haddock was at their head. He held no office.... Upon him the threatened death penalty was executed. Like cowards they struck him in the dark."); "The Defense—W. W. Erwin Makes the Last Address to the Jury for the Defense," SIOUX CITY JOURNAL (Sioux City, IA), Dec. 9, 1887, p. 2 (in his closing, defense lawyer W. W. Erwin argued that "private prosecutors took control of the coroner's inquest, and there suppressed evidence"); "The Haddock Murder," WORTHINGTON ADVANCE (Worthington, MN), Dec. 15, 1887, p. 3 (noting that W. W. Erwin spoke of "the inalienable right of Americans to drink what they please, and then "proceeded to attack... the 'private prosecutors,' as he sneeringly terms the gentlemen at the state's table, and the press as 'conspirators.'"). *Compare* "Orange County Supreme Court," UNITED OPINION (Bradford, VT), Mar. 18, 1870, p. 3 ("Badger vs. Woodward et. al.—This was an action for false imprisonment brought by the plf. against the justice, constable and private prosecutor for arresting and detaining him on a charge of drunkenness in August, 1868. The defendants pleaded the facts of the intoxication legal complaint, warrant and arrest, in justification. Plaintiff replied to the plea that the justice was not duly elected, that a private prosecutor has no right to enter complaints under the Liquor Law, and that the recognizance on the warrant was informal. To this replication the defendants demurred, and a hearing was had before the Co. court, and judgment rendered for the defendants sustaining the demurrer. To this decision the plaintiff took exceptions. Judgment for defendants affirmed and execution issued in favor of defendants."); *accord* "Orange County Supreme Court," VERMONT JOURNAL (Windsor, VT), Mar. 26, 1870, p. 1.

59. "Local Affairs," DAILY POST (Pittsburgh, PA), Apr. 6, 1869, p. 4 ("The case of the Commonwealth vs. James Thackeray indicted for malicious mischief, was next taken up. M. W. Canning, Manager of the Opera House, and W. C. Smythe, Manager of the American Theatre, were the private prosecutors. It was alleged that the defendant did wilfully and maliciously tear down and deface the bills and posters of the places of amusement managed by the prosecutors. There were two indictments, and the defendant was found guilty upon both.").

60. "Police Court," DAILY OREGON STATESMAN (Salem, OR), Feb. 8, 1896, p. 5 ("When the case against Bradley for indecent exposure was called the private prosecutor failed to show up, so there was a dismissal at his cost. The matter had been amicably fixed up outside of court so as to relieve all parties of embarrassing publicity."); "Butler in Jail—He Is Held as the Prosecuting Witness in the Burrus Case," OREGON WEEKLY STATESMAN (Salem, OR), May 21, 1897, p. 3 ("B. Butler is in jail. He is the fellow who played the part of private prosecutor in the criminal information against Mary Burrus, charging her with polygamy, an account of her arrest being published in the Sunday Statesman. Butler called upon Justice H. A. Johnson yesterday and offered to pay the costs in the case against the Burrus woman, providing the complaint would be dismissed. Justice Johnson permitted Butler to talk as much as he desired to and when he finished his story the justice consulted District Attorney Hayden and as a result of the conference Butler was held under $100 bonds as the prosecuting witness against Mrs. Burrus. This was a great surprise to Butler; he couldn't see how it was possible for such action to be taken against him and he fears that he will yet be landed in the penitentiary. Not putting up the necessary bonds he was ordered to jail."); "Justice Court," DAILY CAPITAL JOURNAL (Salem, OR), Dec. 11, 1896, p. 4 ("A Chinaman, known as George, was arrested Thursday afternoon charged with larceny from the dwelling of R. A. Smiley, who resides north of Salem, of several tools, valued at about $10. Mr. Smiley, who is a woodchopper by occupation, is private prosecutor and the complaint alleges the tools were stolen on the 8th inst."); "Stirrup Lodged in the Jail," OREGON WEEKLY STATESMAN (Salem, OR), Dec. 11, 1896, p. 12 (noting that a German man, Felix Stirrup, was charged with larceny for stealing jewelry and clothes, and that "Stirrup admitted that he took the jewelry and clothes but thought the private prosecutor had placed too great a value upon the former when he heard the charge read, $20 being the sum"); DALLES DAILY CHRONICLE (The Dalles, OR), July 3, 1895, p. 3 (taking note of a "private prosecutor" in a larceny case involving a horse and saddle); "Over a Gun," DAILY OREGON STATESMAN (Salem, OR), Dec. 8, 1894, p. 1 ("The case of the state vs. M. P. Baker, charged with larceny by bailee of a gun belonging to S. G. Dorris, was heard by Justice H. A. Johnson yesterday afternoon. The affair ended by the defendant being discharged and the costs taxed to the private prosecutor."); "That Gun," STATE RIGHTS DEMOCRAT (Albany, OR), Dec. 14, 1894, p. 1 ("The case of the state vs. Mrs. M P Baker, charged with larceny by bailee of a gun belonging to S G Dorris, of Albany, was heard by Justice H A Johnson, of Salem yesterday afternoon. The affair ended by the defendant being discharged and the costs taxed to the private prosecutor, which means that Sid will have to rustle for the costs or be in hot water. It seems that Mr Dorris was coming down from Crook county at the same time Mrs Baker was crossing the mountains. He borrowed $5 of her, gave the gun as security, to be kept as such a certain length of time. About a month after the time was up Mrs Baker sold the gun for $5.25 and sent Dorris the 25 cents. As the gun was worth about $40 he wanted it and tendered the money; but it was too late. Then he had her arrested....").

61. WELLSBORO AGITATOR (Wellsboro, PA), Feb. 2, 1866, p. 3 ("The first case was from Morris township. The private prosecutor was a carpenter by the name of Harry Keissler who charged Ernest Watkins with stealing from his room his trunk, watch, some old clothes and a pair of boots. It appeared in evidence that Kiessler, who boarded with Carlos Watkins the father of the defendant, was owing something over $17 on his board bill and was secretly to remove his things from his room one night about twelve o'clock and 'jump' his board, when he was discovered by the defendant, who seized his goods and held them till he should secure his board bill.... A verdict of not guilty was taken, and the defendant was discharged.").

62. "Baker vs. Baker," OREGON WEEKLY STATESMAN (Salem, OR), Jan. 28, 1898, p. 2 ("David Hammond, a baker, was arrested by Deputy Sheriff A. T. Wain yesterday afternoon and taken before Justice H.

A. Johnson to answer the charge of larceny of a Columbia bicycle valued at $15. George A. Bach, of the Home bakery, is the private prosecutor, and alleges that Hammond committed the theft on December 24th last. Hammond was arraigned and, pleading not guilty, his preliminary examination was set for 1 p.m. tomorrow.").

63. "An Indian Stole Cider," OREGON DAILY STATESMAN (Salem, OR), Dec. 16, 1897, p. 4 ("Wm. Tooley, an Indian at Chemawa, was arrested yesterday by Deputy Sheriff E. E. Cooper on a warrant charging him with the larceny of a barrel of the value of $4 and eight gallons of cider of the value of $2, the private prosecutor being C. Baltimore, who resides near that village. Mr. Baltimore alleges that the theft was committed on the 10th inst. On being taken before Justice H. A. Johnson, Tooley entered a plea of guilty and he was committed to the county jail for thirty days.").

64. "The Benwood Murder Case," WHEELING DAILY INTELLIGENCER (Wheeling, WV), Oct. 15, 1878, p. 1. For instance, under the headline, "The Benwood Murder Case," *The Wheeling Daily Intelligencer* of West Virginia, made this report on October 15, 1878: "The prosecution is being conducted by James E. Hooton, Esq., Prosecuting Attorney, assisted by E. G. Cracraft, Esq., of Wheeling, who is employed by the friends of the deceased, as a private prosecutor."

65. "Taken to a Higher Court," CEDAR RAPIDS EVENING GAZETTE (Cedar Rapids, IA), Apr. 30, 1891, p. 2.

66. *E.g.*, "A Desperate Scoundrel," COURIER-JOURNAL (Louisville, KY), Apr. 6, 1866, p. 1 (noting the "[t]he Portland (Oregon) Oregonian, in referring to the escape of Jarvine J. Bush, as murder," had related, among other things, the following: "As soon as the sheriff of Clark county had a favorable opportunity he took Bush into custody. The trial was set, but before it came to the day, the private prosecutor was 'made way with' by Bush's friends, or frightened into leaving the country, as he was not to be found, and has not been heard of to this day. Bush was soon again at his dead-fall, retailing poison to his followers, where remained up to the time the circumstances happened which resulted in the death of Sheriff Sullivan and J. P. Dennison, for which he was detained here at the time of his escape.").

67. "The Sequel," DALLES DAILY CHRONICLE (The Dalles, OR), Apr. 14, 1894, p. 3 ("Dr. Morrison, the deceiver of Mrs. Rose Brown, was released before Justice Schutz' court this morning, the private prosecutor failing to appear and he could no longer be held."); *compare* "Over the River," OREGON DAILY STATESMAN (Salem, OR), Aug. 5, 1885, p. 3 ("The parties to the defense, Mr. and Mrs. Brower, appeared before the Eola tribunal yesterday, and the private prosecutor and injured person, alleged, not appeared he dismissed the case."); "The Polk County War," OREGON DAILY STATESMAN (Salem, OR), Aug. 6, 1885, p. 3 ("The Brower-Teller war, in Polk county, still goes on, with no promise of a truce or cessation of hostilities. Yesterday morning this paper informed its readers that the case before Squire Pearce, of Eola, had been dismissed. Mr. and Mrs. Brower were arrested on a charge of assault on Miss Belle Teller, but the private prosecutor not appearing they were dismissed. There was no authority to do this in the absence of the injured party, and Mr. and Mrs. Brower were re-arrested yesterday and the trial commenced yesterday afternoon before T. Pearce, justice of the peace, of Eola precinct.").

68. "Murder Case Nolle Prosequied," DALLAS HERALD, Dec. 13, 1881, p. 5 ("County-Attorney Seay entered a nolle prosequi yesterday in the District Court in the case of the State vs. Colonel A. T. Obenchain, charged with killing Dr. J. W. Calder on the 4th day of September, 1878. The following are his reasons for thus disposing of the case:... 2d. — The private prosecutor in the cause has abandoned the prosecution of the cause as have the relatives of the deceased J. W. Calder, and by this the prosecution is greatly crippled."); *see also* "Judge Dick—Mr. Gudger's Letter," THE OBSERVER (Raleigh, NC), Nov. 15, 1877, p. 2 (a letter signed by H. A. Gudger contains the following statement: "When the case of State vs. Ray and Rice, for the killing of one Jervis, was tried by Judge Dick, he expressly held that he could not hear an affidavit in the cause made by the father of the deceased, unless the father would allow himself to be marked a private prosecutor, and thereby become responsible for the costs. The father refusing to do so, the counsel for the State were forced to offer a *nol. pros.* To this the attorneys for the defence objected and the court ordered a verdict of *not guilty* to be entered, though there was, in fact, no trial had. The father of the deceased and many of his friends and neighbors were accused of being Ku Klux, and the District Attorney, with the approval of the Judge, threatened wholesale prosecutions of these parties unless they would abandon the prosecution of Ray and Rice. These parties were almost, if not entirely driven from the prosecution by said

threats as will appear more clearly when it is remembered that when the father decided to go home and take no further steps in the matter, an order was issued for those who were charged with being Ku Klux in the neighborhood where the homicide was committed, to go home and that no more arrests be made.").

69. "The Commonwealth's Criminal Suits Break Down for Want of Witnesses," The Times (Philadelphia, PA), May 30, 1882, p. 3.

70. "Gambling House Bills Submitted," Philadelphia Inquirer (Philadelphia, PA), Apr. 29, 1884, p. 3.

71. John Anthon, The Law Student, or Guides to the Study of Law in Its Principles 166–67 (1850); "Trial of Joseph Jenkins Knapp, Jr.," American Whig (Woodstock, VT), Nov. 24, 1830, p. 2 ("Messr. Dexter and Gardiner made some remarks respecting the employment of Mr. Webster on the retainer of a private prosecutor.—But on Mr. W. repeating what he had before stated, that he was engaged to aid the prosecution by the Attorney General himself, and that his motive in consenting to act as counsel for the Government, was a desire to promote public justice, &c. the subject was dropped."); *see also* Arkansas Gazette (Arkansas Post, AR), Dec. 29, 1830, p. 1 ("This trial commenced at Salem, on the morning of the 9th Nov.... The former counsel in the case of J. F. Knapp, appeared on behalf of the prisoner, and the Attorney General and Mr. Webster for the commonwealth.... The prisoner's counsel then objected to the employment of counsel in aid of the regular prosecuting officers of the government—urging that the prisoner's case ought not to be prejudiced by the extraordinary array of counsel against him; and that the law did not recognize the right of carrying on a public prosecution at the expense of private prosecutor. This point was also argued. Mr. Webster rose merely to state that he attended at the request of the Attorney General, and that no other consideration would have brought him there. The Court reserved their decision on the question for the present, directing the trial to proceed."); "Proceedings of Court," Saturday Evening Express (Lancaster, PA), Dec. 3, 1853, p. 2 ("In the case of *Wm. Hazard*, the prosecutor not having appeared at this term or the last, District Attorney Thompson, by leave of Court, entered a *nol pros.* and defendant was discharged.").

72. "Circuit Court of the United States: United States vs. John Henderson," Daily Delta (New Orleans, LA), Jan. 4, 1851, p. 2.

73. Edward Harold Mott, Between the Ocean and the Lakes: The Story of Erie 488–91 (1899).

74. W. A. Swanberg, Jim Fisk: The Career of an Improbable Rascal 272–73 (1959); Laura Fleischmann, "A Murder on Broadway: Josie Mansfield and the Grand Central Hotel," Off the Grid: Village Preservation Blog, Apr. 9, 2019, https://www.villagepreservation.org/2019/04/09/a-murder-on-broadway-josie-mansfield-and-the-grand-central-hotel/.

75. Seymour's Reminiscences: An Interesting Condensed History of Jay Gould and James Fisk, Jr.'s Mismanagement of the Erie Road in Contrast with the Management of Commodore Vanderbilt, with Other Interesting Reading 29 (1893).

76. Charles Sutton, The New York Tombs; Its Secrets and Its Mysteries: Being a History of Noted Criminals, with Narratives of Their Crimes 563 (James B. Mix & Samuel A. MacKeever, 1874); "The Fisk Inquest," N.Y. Herald (New York, NY), Jan. 9, 1872, p. 3.

77. The Murder of Jim Fisk for the Love of Josie Mansfield, ch. 21, *available at* https://erenow.net/biographies/the-murder-of-jim-fisk-for-the-love-of-josie-mansfield/21.php.

78. "The Fisk Murder," N.Y. Times, July 4, 1872, p. 2.

79. *John R. Fellows*, https://en.wikipedia.org/wiki/John_R._Fellows.

80. *E.g.*, "Judge Fullerton Appears as Counsel for Mrs. Burke," N.Y. Herald (New York, NY), May 31, 1870, p. 10; *see also* "Tweed Paying His Counsel," Minneapolis Daily Trib. (Minneapolis, MN), Nov. 27, 1873, p. 1 (noting that William M. Tweed 'is indebted" to "ex-Judge William Fullerton, one of his counsel," and transferred to him "a large block of real estate" valued at $80,000).

81. "The Trial of Stokes," New England Farmer (Boston, MA), Dec. 28, 1872, p. 2; "Second Trial of Stokes," Boston Daily Globe (Boston, MA), Dec. 19, 1872, p. 5.

82. "The Press on the Verdict," Vermont Record and Farmer (Brattleboro, VT), Jan. 10, 1873, p. 4.

83. H. W. Brands, The Murder of Jim Fisk for the Love of Josie Mansfield: A Tragedy of the Gilded Age 110–11, 186–87 (2011); "How Stokes Killed Fisk and Why," Cincinnati Enquirer (Aug. 24, 1913), p. 5; "Fisk—Mansfield—Stocks," Chicago Tribune (Chicago, IL), Jan. 11, 1872, p. 6.

84. "Stokes Death Sentence," Vermont Record and Farmer (Brattleboro, VT), Jan. 10, 1873, p. 4.

85. *Id.*; John D. Bessler, Death in the Dark: Midnight Executions in America 47–48 (1997).

86. "Stokes Death Sentence," Vermont Record and Farmer (Brattleboro, VT), Jan. 10, 1873, p. 4.

87. J. North Conway, King of Heists: The Sensational Bank Robbery of 1878 that Shocked America 131 (2009).

88. Norm Cohen, Long Steel Rail: The Railroad in American Folksong 91–92 (2d ed. 2000); Edward J. Renehan, Jr., Dark Genius of Wall Street: The Misunderstood Life of Jay Gould, King of the Robber Barons (2005), ch. 21; J. North Conway, The Big Policeman: The Rise and Fall of Thomas Byrnes, America's First, Most Ruthless, and Greatest Detective 85–101 (2010); "The Jim Fisk Murder," The News (Newport, PA), Dec. 5, 1895, p. 4; *compare* Denis Tilden Lynch, The Story of a Grim Generation: "Boss" Tweed 388 (2017) ("In a jealous rage, Fisk published an unsupported affidavit of Miss Mansfield's discharged butler. This manifestly false testimony, accusing Stokes and Miss Mansfield of conspiring to blackmail Fisk, was the flimsy pretext of an indictment against Stokes. The spurned lover then published the servant's statement. Immediately Miss Mansfield had Fisk arrested for criminal libel. This case was pending when Stokes, temporarily insane from the persecutions of Fisk, shot him.").

89. "Court of General Sessions," N.Y. Daily Herald (New York, NY), Jan. 3, 1869, p. 3.

90. Sutton, *supra* note 76, at 649–56; "Stokes' Appeal," N.Y. Herald (New York, NY), Feb. 17, 1876, p. 7; "Tammany Nominations," Buffalo Express (Buffalo, NY), Oct. 15, 1872, p. 1.

91. "The Probate Judgeship," LaFayette Sun (LaFayette, AL), Feb. 2, 1898, p. 2 (noting of a judgeship: "The duties of this office are many and of great responsibility.... As a court in the trial of cases, especially criminal charges, the Judge should, without prejudice—determine the questions presented promptly, firmly, and in a spirit of fairness tempered with charity and mercy, taking no delight in the punishment of even the most inexcusably guilty, but enforcing the laws—and all of the laws with impartiality as a means of protecting society, and for the reformation of the offender and not to wreak vengeance, or gratify the malice of private prosecutors."); "Beamish Case—Continued," Daily Record of the Times (Wilkes-Barre, PA), Sept. 24, 1875, p. 3 ("The case was then opened for the defense by John Lynch, Esq., who began clearly and distinctly to state what the defense expected to prove. He pointed to the Commonwealth's table and called the attention of the jury to the absence of the District Attorney, who was elected and paid to prosecute the pleas of the Commonwealth, but in his stead there sat four private counsel, paid for by private prosecutors, who composed the Taxpayers' Association of the city of Scranton. The President of this association was himself charged with stealing ten thousand dollars from the city, and some of its members—Royce, Lynde and others—were indicted in the Scranton courts for embezzlement. His client, Mr. Beamish, was a young man of Scranton who was striving to gain an honest livelihood—the same as he (Mr. Lynch) and the members of the jury were—and whom Black, Royce and Lynde were endeavoring to crush.").

92. "Quarter Sessions," Intelligencer Journal (Lancaster, PA), Aug. 19, 1878, p. 2 (in speaking to a grand jury, Judge Livingston said: "In case you find that the prosecutor is a constable or other public officer who prosecutes solely in the discharge of his public duty and in his public capacity, as in cases of disturbances at elections, neglect of duty on the part of supervisors, or wherever the law makes it his special duty to report to the court, you cannot compel him to pay costs; he is protected in the discharge of such public duty. But where a constable or public officer turns private prosecutor for the purposes of making money and accumulating costs, he, like any other private individual, should be made to pay costs, and the grand jury should direct that he do so."); *see also* "Court and Jury," The Weekly New Era (Lancaster, PA), Aug. 24, 1878, p. 5 ("Judge Livingston delivered a clear and concise charge to the Grand Inquest, containing the usual instructions, and animadverted severely upon the conduct of the officer in the case of Kemple, where a number of suits were brought by the officer himself, who turned private prosecutor for the purpose of making fees.").

93. "Another Bawdy House Case," Pittsburgh Weekly Gazette, Aug. 25, 1868, p. 8 ("The crusade against houses of ill repute is still kept alive, but whether with a view to a reformation in the morals in this city of wickedness, or for the less laudable purpose of levying black mail, we do not pretend to say. There are doubtless cases in which the welfare of the public prompts the prosecution, or, if not for the public weal, the peace and comfort of the private prosecutor, who is a part of the public, and hence entitled to protection from annoyances resulting from the maintaining of a house of ill fame in any community, at the hands of the law. On the other hand, there is no doubt whatever that in many instances the prosecutions are made for the purpose of blackmailing not only the keepers of the house, but all those who are willing to pay rather than have their names used in connection with such affairs. The greatest evidence of this latter fact is the character of many of the prosecutors, who in some instances are themselves engaged in the same business. The latest case is that of Mary Brown, who makes information before Alderman Strain, charging Sallie White, 'Gib' Miller and others with maintaining a bawdy house on Liberty street in the Ninth ward. The accused were arrested and held for a hearing.").

94. "Powers and Duties of Grand Juries in the Courts of the United States—Charge to the Grand Jury—Circuit Court, District of California—August 22, 1872," *in* 2 L. S. B. Sawyer, comp., Reports of Cases Decided in the Circuit and District Courts of the United States for the Ninth Circuit 667, 673–74 (1875); *see also id.* at 674 (noting the following additional language in Justice Field's grand jury charge: "There has hardly been a session of the grand jury of this court for years, at which instances have not occurred of personal solicitation to some of its members to obtain or prevent the presentment or indictment of parties. And communications to that end have frequently been ad[d]ressed to the grand jury filled with malignant and scandalous imputations upon the conduct and acts of those against whom the writers entertained hostility, and against the conduct and acts of former and present officers of this court, and of previous grand juries of this district.").

95. "Our Grand Jury System," Camden Daily Courier (Camden, NJ), Mar. 21, 1887, p. 2 ("The grand jury, as we have it in New Jersey, is objected to because it is not a professional body. The fact that it is body of men drawn from the people gives to it the appearance of being a tribunal that is impartial in its dealings. If it were only to find out according to the evidence whether a prima facie case of crime is made out, it would be well, but when it acts contrary to the evidence and dismisses a culprit out of fear or regard for party affiliation it becomes worse than useless.... It is the boast of politicians that they can pack any grand jury in the state, and they frequently made good their boast. The work of selecting a jury is not always left to the sheriff. It is done for him by those who have the axes to grind. He is simply the official that summons the jurymen together. It is not unusual for one jury to refuse to indict and another to find the true bill. A remarkable feature about jury-packing is that it can be so adroitly done that detection is impossible. There can only be one remedy, and that is the total abolition of the grand jury system, which no longer stands as a barrier to the citizen against malicious and tyrannical action of private prosecutors, but screens and shields public offenders from being tried by a jury of their countrymen."); "Grand Jury," Neosho County Republican (Osage Mission, KS), Mar. 1, 1883, p. 3 ("Much is being said pro and con in reference to the calling of a grand jury by the county commissioners for the next term of the district court of this county. The greatest objection seems to be the expense that will be incurred by the county, and that no material good will result from the labors of a grand jury. Now the violators of the law can only be reached by indictment or information. There are very few individuals who are willing to take upon themselves the responsibility of filing an information against the violator of a law, although they are cognizant of the fact, for the reason that the public does not look with favor on private prosecutions, and in nine cases out of ten the private prosecutor is subjected to the most bitter calumny. And again private prosecutions are often malicious, and innocent parties are dragged into court and compelled to defend a 'made up' case in order to vindicate their good name. With a grand jury it is different. Here fifteen sworn and unprejudiced men listen to the testimony of witnesses and find indictments only when twelve of the jurymen concur. While a grand jury may be some expense to the county, we think it is the most effectual, speedy and fair way of reaching the violators of the law.").

96. "The Grand Jury," Chicago Tribune, Aug. 3, 1878, p. 8 ("There was published in The Tribune yesterday a decision of Judge Rogers, sitting in the Criminal Court, to the effect that all complaints which persons desired to make to the Grand Jury should first be submitted to the State's Attorney, and could be

heard by the Grand Jury only with his approval. The decision was, in brief, that the State's Attorney held the keys of the Grand-Jury room except in jail cases and others where persons had been bound over to appear before the Grand Jury. There was yesterday morning in several quarters strong expressions of disapproval with this decision, which, it was stated, took diametrically opposed ground from the one which Judge Moore made while he was sitting in the Court last month. It was claimed that to give this power to the State's Attorney would be to divest the Grand Jury of its legitimate functions.... Inquiry of Assistant State's-Attorney Weber as to the law on the question shows that the rule adopted was based on the opinion of Judge Field, of the United States Supreme Court, in California in 1873, where the same point was raised. The Judge held that: First, the Judge of the Court could send matters to the jury; second, the District Attorney; third, the jurors themselves where they had a personal knowledge of the matter at issue; and, fourth, all committing Magistrates. Judge Field held that there were no other ways than these to reach the jury, and especially did he deprecate the allowing of private prosecutors to intrude upon the jury, on the ground that such persons were usually actuated by malice and a spirit of vindictiveness. His ideas have become the law, and are observed by all of the Federal Courts, and by most of the Courts in the States."); "The Charge delivered by the Hon. Robert P. Dick, U.S. Judge for the Western District of North Carolina at the opening of the District Court, at Ashville, N. C., on Tuesday the 4th day of November, A. D., 1873," West-Carolina Record (Rutherfordton, NC), Nov. 29, 1873, p. 1 (in addressing "Mr. Foreman, and Gentlemen of the Jury," the Hon. Robert P. Dick stated in part in his charge to the grand jury: "I desire now, Gentlemen of the Grand Jury, to give you some instructions as to the nature of your duties in making enquiries of violations of law, and as to the extent of your investigation. In doing so, I will use a part of a charge given to a Grand Jury in California, by Mr. Justice Field, of the Supreme [C]ourt of the United States. I approve of his sentiments, and will employ the language in which he so forcibly expresses them. 'We, therefore, instruct you that your investigations must be limited.... You will not allow private prosecutors to intrude themselves into your presence, and present accusations by private enmity, and seek merely the gratification of their personal malice. If they possess any information, justifying the accusation of the person against whom they complain, they should impart it to the District Attorney, who will seldom fail to act in a proper case. But if the District Attorney should refuse to act, they can make their complaint committing to a Magistrate, before whom the matter can be investigated. A preliminary examination of the accused before a Magistrate, when he can, meet his prosecutor face to face, and cross examine him, and the witnesses, produced by him, and have the benefit of counsel, is the "usual mode of instituting proceedings in criminal cases, and is the one which presents to the citizen the greatest security against false accusation."'"); "Judge Roberts' Charge to the Grand Jury," The Sun (Baltimore, MD), May 10, 1898, p. 9 (noting the Chief Judge Roberts, in Westminster, Maryland, gave a grand jury charge to this effect at the May term of the Circuit Court for Carroll County: "He also impressed upon the jury 'that they should not allow private prosecutors to intrude themselves in their presence and present accusations, as generally such parties are actuated by private enmity and malice.'"); *see also* "The Grand Jury. Impaneling of the Indictment-Finders for the January Term.", Chicago Tribune, Jan. 17, 1882, p. 7 (noting that Judge Barnum "called attention to the law on the subject of disclosing what took place during the sessions of the body, and cautioned them not to allow 'private prosecutors' to intrude themselves into their presence and present accusations."; Judge Barnum said that "Complaints should come through the State's-Attorney or a committing magistrate."); "Charge to the Grand Jury," Yellowstone Journal (Miles City, MT), Apr. 21, 1883, p. 1 (noting that Judge Wade, in a charge to the grand jury, observed: "One more word of caution before proceeding more definitely to point out the work before you. You will permit no private prosecutor to intrude before you. You will investigate no matters except such as are given you in charge by the court, or such as the prosecuting attorney may lay before you; or such, as from their notoriety, you may know of your own knowledge. Keeping within these bounds you will escape becoming the tools of private malignity, hatred, or ill-will."); "United States Courts," Salt Lake Herald (Salt Lake City, UT), Nov. 10, 1896, p. 5 (noting the Judge Marshall's grand jury charge included the following directive: "That you may not be made the instrument of ill will rather than of justice, you will not permit private prosecutors to appear before you."). *Cf.* Marc L. Miller & Ronald F. Wright, Criminal Procedures: Prosecution and Adjudication 205 (2005) ("Although private prosecutors appeared before grand juries in the nineteenth century, at the turn of the century courts began to exclude them from the grand jury proceedings.") (citing

Hartgraves v. State, 114 P. 343 (Okla. 1911)). In *Hartgraves v. State*, R.P. Phillips, a member of the bar who was not the duly elected county attorney or deputy county attorney of Custer County but who was employed by the prosecuting witness in the case, was present before—and presented to—the grand jury and conducted the examination of grand jury witnesses. In that case, the Oklahoma Court of Criminal Appeals held that "no one should be permitted to be present during the sessions of the grand jury except the witnesses and the officers duly authorized by law to so appear." "Here," that appellate court ruled, "the record shows that, while the prosecution was nominally being conducted in the name of the state, as a matter of fact it was in the hands of a private attorney employed by the prosecuting witness." "We think that such conduct is a direct violation of the Constitution of this state," the court ruled, adding: "If a county attorney can turn a defendant over to the paid counsel of private parties, or if private parties can usurp the powers of a county attorney before a grand jury where the defendant cannot be heard and has no one to represent him, no man is safe from persecution in Oklahoma, and the abuses of the grand jury system will be perpetuated among us. This is the evil that the people have tried to destroy. The law therefore prohibits all persons from being in the grand jury room except the officers authorized by law to examine witnesses and the witness to be examined, and the presence of any other person in the grand jury room at any stage of the proceedings when a witness is being examined, or when the grand jury are considering the advisability of finding an indictment vitiates the entire proceedings. There is no exception to this rule. The sessions of the grand jury being secret, it is impossible for a defendant to protect himself against danger from this source. Therefore the law protects him by rigidly excluding from the grand jury room all persons except those expressly authorized by law to be present." Hartgraves v. State, 5 Okla. Crim. 266, 267–71 (1911); *see also* id. at 272–73 ("In the case at bar the attorney who appeared before the grand jury was not the deputy county attorney and he had no appointment from the district judge to act in place of the county attorney on account of the disqualification of that officer. He was merely requested by the county attorney to go before the grand jury. While we are satisfied that neither the county attorney nor the attorney who appeared for him before the grand jury were actuated by improper motives in this case, yet this cannot cause us to sanction a proceeding which is unauthorized by law, is contrary to public policy, and which, if allowed to stand, would establish a precedent repugnant to reason and pregnant with danger to justice and innocence. A county attorney has no right to turn a defendant over to his enemies, after having first armed them with the entire power of the state to be used as they see fit in his prosecution. If such prosecutions were permitted, they would soon become a great scandal and absolutely odious to a fair-minded and justice-loving people. Honest men against whom naught could be truthfully alleged have been greatly mortified and have had their good names called in question by just such proceedings as this, prompted alone by the malice and cowardice of their enemies, when if they had been faced by their accusers, and given the right of cross-examination, those who sought to destroy them through the secret inquisitorial proceedings of a grand jury would have been covered with defeat and infamy. In 1876, when the writer of this opinion was practicing law in Texas, a preacher who had some bitter enemies was indicted for stealing hogs. Upon the final trial it was conclusively shown that the parties who had caused his indictment were themselves the thieves. While the preacher was acquitted, yet he carried to his grave the stain upon his name of having been indicted for hog stealing. We are pleased to be able to say that these remarks do not apply to the county attorney of Custer county or to the attorney who appeared for the private prosecution before the grand jury in this case. We call attention to these matters to illustrate the consequences which might grow out of this precedent if we allowed it to stand. The extreme illustration is always the test of a rule. Fairness and justice demand that a criminal prosecution should at all times be under the direction of a regularly constituted public officer, who is charged by law with the performance of this duty."); WATONGA HERALD (Watonga, OK), Apr. 13, 1911, p. 9 ("There is no provision of law authorizing a private prosecutor to have any voice in the selection of a trial judge. The county attorney does not represent the private prosecutor, but he represents the entire people of the state and it is his duty as it is also the duty of the judge to be entirely impartial in the discharge of their duties and not to consult any private parties or persons interested in the trial of a criminal case. Our constitution by express provision protects the citizens of this state against private prosecutions. For a full discussion of this question see, Hartgraves vs. State, decided at this term."). An interesting and notable collection of American grand jury charges before 1801 was recently compiled and published. *See* GENTLEMEN OF THE GRAND JURY: THE SURVIVING GRAND JURY CHARGES FROM COLONIAL, STATE, AND LOWER FEDERAL COURTS BEFORE 1801 (Stanton D. Krauss, ed. 2012).

97. "United States District Court—Tuesday, June 3rd, 1873," RALEIGH NEWS (Raleigh, NC), June 4, 1873, p. 1 (noting that Judge Brooks gave the following charge to the "GENTLEMEN OF THE GRAND JURY": "I therefore instruct you, that your investigations are to be limited.... You should not allow private prosecutors to intrude themselves upon you—and present accusations, for generally, such parties are actuated by private enmity, and seek merely the gratification of their personal malice. If such prosecutors possess any information justifying the accusation of the person against whom they complain, they should impart it to the District Attorney, who will seldom fail to act in a proper case. But if the District Attorney should refuse to act, they can make their complaint to the Court, or to any committing Magistrate, before whom the matter can be investigated, and if sufficient evidence be produced of the commission of a public offence by the accused he can be held to bail to answer to the action of the Grand Jury. When the court does not deem the matter of sufficient importance to call your attention to it, and the District Attorney does not think it expedient to... submit it for your consideration, and the private prosecutor neglects to proceed before a committing Magistrate, I think it may be safely inferred that public interests will not suffer if the matter is not considered by you."); "Judge Person's High Motives in Calling Grand Jury," DETROIT FREE PRESS, Nov. 17, 1899, p. 1 (noting the following words from Judge Person's grand jury charge: "When the court does not deem a matter of sufficient importance to call your attention to it, and the prosecuting attorney does not think it expedient to submit the matter to your consideration and the private prosecutor neglects to proceed before the committing magistrate, I think it may be safely inferred that public justice will not suffer if the matter is not considered by you."); "Chittenden County Court," BURLINGTON FREE PRESS & TIMES, Sept. 16, 1885, p. 4 (noting that the following words were spoken by Judge Taft in a grand jury charge at the regular September term of the Chittenden County Court in Burlington, Vermont: "You should not allow private prosecutors to intrude themselves into your room to present accusations."); "Judge Shinn's Charge to the Grand Jury," GREENWOOD COUNTY REPUBLICAN (Eureka, KS), Sept. 7, 1888, p. 1 (recording that, in his charge to the grand jury in Greenwood County, Kansas, Judge Shinn said: "The Grand Jury serves as a barrier against unjust, friv[o]lous or malicious prosecutions, and a protection against the vicious and depraved. Thus it serves as a protection to the individual and to society. It may, and should on the one hand shield the good name and fair reputation of the citizen against the malice of the private prosecutors, while it brings to the bar of justice those whose disregard for the rights of others has been fairly shown upon competent testimony."); "U.S. Court—The Empaneling of the Grand Jury Completed and S. K. McGinnis Appointed Foreman," BISMARCK DAILY TRIBUNE (Bismarck, ND), Apr. 16, 1890, p. 3 (noting that Judge Thomas delivered a grand jury charge that "warned them against allowing private prosecutors to introduce themselves into the grand jury room to present accusations"; part of the charge was as follows: "It is of the utmost importance that grand juries be secured against outside influence and improper interference. If allowed it will introduce a flood of evils disastrous to the purity of the administration of criminal justice and subversive of all public confidence in the actions of these bodies.").

98. "District Court," BILLINGS HERALD (Billings, MT), Oct. 13, 1883, p. 3 ("The first district court held in this county, opened to-day at 2:30 p.m., Chief Justice Wade presiding.... The Judge then delivered an able and exhaustive charge to the Grand Jury on the duties of their office and the proper mode of its performance. This was the first grand Jury of Yellowstone County, and the manner in which they performed their duties would form a precedent for their successors in office.... Their duty was to present any person whom they knew to be guilty of an offence, but not to act at the instigation of any private prosecutor as, if this were allowed, grand juries might be made instruments of oppression and the tools of malice."); *see also* "Grand Jury Report," DAILY HERALD (Billings, MT), Oct. 12, 1883, p. 2 ("The able and lengthy report filed yesterday by the Grand Jury, at the conclusion of their labors, contains many matters of deep interest to everyone in this county. Yellowstone County was fortunate in numbering among its first Grand Jury so many gentlemen of intelligence and public spirit, and the example set by the jury, in earnestly inquiring into existing public abuses, irrespective of the parties concerned, is one that may well be followed by its successors.... They draw attention to the practice of compounding felonies, a matter which has grown almost to be a custom, where the defendant or his friends can raise the money necessary to satisfy the private prosecutors['] demands.").

99. "Judge Garrison's Charge," CAMDEN DAILY COURIER (Camden, NJ), May 6, 1890, p. 1; *see also* "May Term," MORNING POST (Camden, NJ), May 6, 1890, p. 1 (noting that Judge Garrison's grand jury charge "was one of the best charges that has ever been delivered to a Grand Jury in the Camden Court House"; "[T]he learned Judge made reference to the matters to be considered by the Grand Jury. He said that some private prosecutors seemed to think they had a right to prosecute by coming secretly before the Grand Jury. He said there were two bodies who could bring matters before the Grand Jury—the State's Prosecutor and the Court—unless it was other matters of which members of the Grand Jury have personal knowledge.").

100. "Ready for Work," DAILY PICAYUNE (New Orleans, LA), Dec. 6, 1892, p. 3; *see also* "New Grand Jury," TIMES-DEMOCRAT (New Orleans, LA), June 6, 1893, p. 3 (summarizing Judge Moise's grand jury charge as follows: "Special attention was called to section 883 of the Revised Statutes. The grand jury was told to be careful and circumspect in considering accusations made by private prosecutors. Such persons were said to be generally actuated by private enmity. They merely sought the gratification of their personal malice."); "Criminal District Court," DAILY PICAYUNE (New Orleans, LA), June 5, 1894, p. 1 (noting that Judge J. C. Moise gave a grand jury charge in which he told the grand jurors: "[Y]ou should present no man from envy, hatred or malice. Be careful and circumspect in considering accusations made by private prosecutors. Such parties are frequently actuated by private enmity and seek the gratification of their personal malice. If they possess any information implicating certain persons in the commission of crime they should impart it to the district attorney or his assistant, who will not fail to act in a proper case.").

101. *See, e.g.*, "Quarter Sessions Court," LANCASTER EXAMINER (Lancaster, PA), Apr. 19, 1899, p. 8 (noting that Judge Landis delivered the following grand jury charge: "Gentlemen of the Grand Inquest.... Your office is a most responsible one. It has been handed down to us from former generations that when liberty has been threatened by excess of authority the grand jury, springing from the people, has proved an important safe-guard to liberty. Standing as it does between the Commonwealth and its citizens, it has proved a barrier against the malice of private prosecutors and the violence of popular excitement...."); "Court Opened To-Day," WILKES-BARRE TIMES (Wilkes-Barre, PA), Sept. 2, 1895, p. 2 (noting that Judge Bennett charged the grand jury as follows: "[A]nother branch of your oath is that you will present no one through envy, hatred, malice or ill will; and herein as also from your just sense of the natural principles of right and your own conceptions as law abiding citizens, consists a proper protection to the accused from the persecution and annoyance which private malice or personal animosity might subject him to were the private prosecutor thus influenced, allowed to bring his accusation directly before the petit jury and subject the accused to trial without your sanction.").

102. "Judge Edmunds Tells the Jury to Beware of Private Prosecutors Whom He Severely Scores," ST. LOUIS POST-DISPATCH, Mar. 6, 1893, p. 1. A year earlier, another judge in St. Louis, Judge Castleman, told jurors: "You are specially cautioned against lending audience to the 'private prosecutor,' he who seeks in the first instance your body to secure the institution of prosecution in which he has a personal concern." "Not Master," ST. LOUIS POST-DISPATCH, Oct. 10, 1892, p. 4.

103. "Pattison's Culpability," HARRISBURG TELEGRAPH (Harrisburg, PA), Sept. 30, 1882, p. 4.

104. "Grand Juries," CARBONDALE LEADER (Carbondale, PA), Sept. 12, 1892, p. 2; *see also* id. (further noting of grand juries in discussing their history: "They heard evidence on behalf of the prosecution only, for the finding of an indictment is in the nature of an inquiry or accusation, the trial taking place before another jury. But the Grand Jury was also required to make due presentment of all such matters as had otherwise come to the knowledge of its members, and, no doubt, in early days the body found useful employment in calling the attention of the court and authorities to offences within the knowledge of the jurors, with a view to indictment, and also to public evils that the courts might remedy. In our days these presentments frequently cover a very wide field. They sometimes relate not only to the business brought before the jury, but to matters of legislation or administration about which a single juryman desires to express his opinion; and, to do so persuades his fellow-jurymen to endorse his views in the presentment.").

105. HENRY CAMPBELL BLACK, A LAW DICTIONARY CONTAINING DEFINITIONS OF THE TERMS AND PHRASES OF AMERICAN AND ENGLISH JURISPRUDENCE, ANCIENT AND MODERN 583 (2d ed. 1910); "The Shinn Case," ALEXANDRIA GAZETTE (Alexandria, VA), Jan. 11, 1878, p. 3 ("Mr. Edmund Burke, counsel for defendant, then moved to quash the indictment and began his argument. He reviewed the institution

and organization of grand juries at common law, and claimed that that they were instituted for the protection of the citizen against frivolous State prosecutions, and, latterly, they were a necessity as a bar to the malice of the private prosecutor. No citizen could be put upon trial for a felony without an indictment first had by a competent grand jury."). Judges became highly suspicious of the power of private prosecutors. In giving a charge to a New York grand jury in 1856, Judge Capron of the Court of General Sessions instructed the jurors: "It is the shield of defense which the fundamental law of the State had interposed for the protection of the citizen against the malice of private prosecutors, and the violence of popular prejudice and excitement. You will, therefore, make all your official action subservient to this cardinal object." "Important Charge to the Grand Jury," N.Y. TIMES, Feb. 5, 1856, p. 1; *accord* "Court of General Sessions," N.Y. DAILY HERALD (New York, NY), Feb. 5, 1856, p. 8 (reporting the same grand jury charge).

106. "Private information conveyed to a Grand Jury," those Commissioners determined, "has led to numberless prosecutions prompted by private interest, and to speculations upon the fears of the unfortunate, which would have been defeated by a public scrutiny or by an opportunity afforded to the accused of explaining or defending himself against the charge."

107. "Good Advice to the Grand Jury," THE SUN (New York, NY), Apr. 12, 1891, p. 6; *see also id.* ("The existing Code of Criminal Procedure, in section 259, provides that if a member of the Grand Jury knows or has reason to believe that a crime has been committed which is triable in the county, he must declare the same to his fellow jurors, who must thereupon investigate the matter. This provision, substantially in its present form, was recommended to the Legislature for enactment by the Commissioners we have mentioned, in 1850, but did not become a part of the express law of the State until 1881. It is not intended to make a private prosecutor of any member of the Grand Jury, but is declarative merely of the obligation of a grand juror to cause proper inquiry to be instituted with reference to any offences of which he has personal information. In the rural portions of the State the grand jurors usually represent all parts of the county, and it may well happen that some of them have heard of crimes concerning which the District Attorney or the community at large knows little or nothing. The intention of the law is to require a frank disclosure of any such information by one member of the Grand Jury to his associates.").

108. "The Trial of Judge Wilkinson, Dr. Wilkinson and John Murdaugh for the Murder of John Rothwell and Alexander H. Meeks, Kentucky, 1839," *in* 1 AMERICAN STATE TRIALS: A COLLECTION OF IMPORTANT AND INTERESTING CRIMINAL TRIALS WHICH HAVE TAKEN PLACE IN THE UNITED STATES, FROM THE BEGINNING OF OUR GOVERNMENT TO THE PRESENT DAY xviii-xix, 132–34 (John D. Lawson, ed. 1914).

109. JOHN E. KLEBER, ED., THE KENTUCKY ENCYCLOPEDIA 403 (1992).

110. "The Trial of Judge Wilkinson, Dr. Wilkinson and John Murdaugh for the Murder of John Rothwell and Alexander H. Meeks, Kentucky, 1839," *in* 1 AMERICAN STATE TRIALS, *supra* note 108, at xviii-xix, 132–37, 282, 290; Roger A. Fairfax, Jr., *Delegation of the Criminal Prosecution Function to Private Actors*, 43 U.C. DAV. L. REV. 411, 423 n.34 (2009); *see also* THE KENTUCKY ENCYCLOPEDIA 403 (John E. Kieber, ed., 2015) ("In the trial of the Wilkinsons and Murdaugh in Harrodsburg in March 1839 for the alleged murder of two Louisville artisans, friends of the victims paid Hardin a fee of $1,000 to act as special private prosecutor. Defense attorney John Rowan's blistering attack on the tradition of private criminal prosecutors, plus the weight of the evidence, caused Hardin to lose the case despite a brilliant summation to the jury. Hardin's persuasive powers, however, usually enabled him to win such trials, no matter which side of the case he represented. Until Hardin entered the prosecution of one Spencer in 1842 for the murder of his stepson, all, including the commonwealth's attorney, believed Spencer to be innocent. Hardin secured a conviction and heard the condemned confirm the accuracy of the judgment in a confession on the gallows."); "Should a Lawyer Appear against a Prisoner in a Capital Case?" LEISURE HOUR (Oxford, NC), Oct. 18, 1859, p. 1 ("Some years ago, Judge Wilkinson and others were indicted in the Kentucky courts for murder. On account of the high position of the parties, and the peculiar circumstances attending the killing, the trial excited public attention to an unusual degree. Several of the ablest lawyers were engaged in the defence, among whom were Judge Rowan, and several other distinguished lawyers from Kentucky and S. S. PRENTISS, of Mississippi. Mr. Hardin assisted the State's Solicitor in the prosecution. Judge Rowan, in his argument in the defense, made a violent and scathing attack on Mr. Hardin, for appearing for the prosecution, and in which he denounced in no measured terms the habit of lawyers appearing against a prisoner in a capital case.").

111. "The Trial of Judge Wilkinson, Dr. Wilkinson and John Murdaugh for the Murder of John Rothwell and Alexander H. Meeks, Kentucky, 1839," *in* 1 AMERICAN STATE TRIALS, *supra* note 108, at 173–75, 182–84.

112. *See generally* THE LAW OF HOMICIDE TOGETHER WITH THE TRIAL FOR MURDER OF JUDGE WILKINSON, DR. WILKINSON AND MR. MURDAUGH: INCLUDING THE INDICTMENTS, EVIDENCE AND SPEECHES OF HON. S. S. PRENTISS, HON. BENJAMIN HARDIN, E. J. BULLOCK, ESQ., JUDGE ROWAN, COL. ROBERTSON, AND JOHN B. THOMPSON, ESQ., OF COUNSEL IN FULL (1882).

113. "The Trial of Judge Wilkinson, Dr. Wilkinson and John Murdaugh for the Murder of John Rothwell and Alexander H. Meeks, Kentucky, 1839," *in* 1 AMERICAN STATE TRIALS, *supra* note 108, at 186, 189–91, 193, 202–03, 226–27.

114. *Id.* at 283–85 (italics in original).

115. *Id.* at 285–86.

116. REV. JOHN PLATTS, A DICTIONARY OF ENGLISH SYNONYMES: COMPREHENDING THE DERIVATIONS AND MEANINGS OF THE WORDS; AND THE DISTINCTIONS BETWEEN THE SYNONYMES ILLUSTRATED BY EXAMPLES 221 (1825).

117. "The Trial of Judge Wilkinson, Dr. Wilkinson and John Murdaugh for the Murder of John Rothwell and Alexander H. Meeks, Kentucky, 1839," *in* 1 AMERICAN STATE TRIALS, *supra* note 108, at 286–88.

118. *Id.* at 288–89.

119. WILLIAM C. SNEED, A REPORT ON THE HISTORY AND MODE OF MANAGEMENT OF THE KENTUCKY PENITENTIARY, FROM ITS ORIGIN, IN 1798, TO MARCH 1, 1860, at 215 (1860); "Latest News," THE REPORTER (Lexington, KY), Nov. 27, 1826, p. 3; NATIONAL BANNER AND NASHVILLE WHIG (Nashville, TN), June 27, 1828, p. 3.

120. SOUTHERN BANNER (Holly Springs, MS), Feb. 15, 1839, p. 3 (letter to editor signed by John Rowan); *see also* "Mechanics and Pedagogues," SOUTHERN SUN (Jackson, MS), Nov. 12, 1839, p. 3 ("The Hon. John Rowan, of Kentucky, who is a native of Pennsylvania, and the Hon. S. S. Prentiss, now of Mississippi, but originally from New England, were both engaged in behalf of Judge Wilkinson, his brother Dr. Wilkinson, and Mr. Murdough, all of Mississippi, who it will be recollected, were indicted for murder committed in the Galt House of Louisiana.").

121. "The Trial of Judge Wilkinson, Dr. Wilkinson and John Murdaugh for the Murder of John Rothwell and Alexander H. Meeks, Kentucky, 1839," *in* 1 AMERICAN STATE TRIALS, *supra* note 108, at 289–90.

122. *Id.* at 290–91.

123. *Id.* at 291–94; Robert M. Ireland, *Privately Funded Prosecution of Crime in the Nineteenth-Century United States*, 39 AM. J. LEGAL HIST. 43, 47–48 (1995) ("Celebrated Kentucky lawyer, John Rowan, provided one of the first in-depth denunciations of the custom of privately funded prosecutors. Appearing for the defense in 1839 in the trial of three Mississippi aristocrats for the murder of two Louisville artisans in the bar of the Galt House, Rowan devoted a major portion of his closing argument berating Ben Hardin, another famous Kentucky attorney, for appearing as a private prosecutor in the case for a fee of $1,000.00 paid by the friends of the victims. Rowan argued that the practice violated due process and the presumption of innocence. Public prosecutors, he contended, had a duty to presume that all criminal defendants were innocent; private prosecutors were paid to assume defendants were guilty. Furthermore, the practice revived the ancient and barbaric custom of trial by vengeance embodied in the private prosecutors who accepted blood money to secure a guilty verdict regardless of the evidence. Money, not evidence, would determine guilt or innocence. Wealthy victims or their families could always hire enough talented prosecutors to convict defendants, regardless of the evidence. Describing the practice as a violation of the commandment against murder, Rowan implored the younger lawyers of Kentucky to forsake private prosecution and urged the public to condemn it.").

124. In 1898, defense counsel in one murder case in Washington State made this argument: "The prosecuting attorney of Snohomish county is the only attorney who has the right to represent the state in this case and any other counsel here stands before you in the light of a private prosecutor. The Hon. J. T. Ronald, the ablest prosecutor in this state, has been brought here to influence this jury by his eloquence. Either this case has ceased to be a criminal prosecution and has become a persecution or the state's case is

so weak that outside counsel must be obtained to bolster it up." SEATTLE POST-INTELLIGENCER (Seattle, WA), Dec. 25, 1898, pp. 1–2.

125. "The Fight Is On. Mr. Shire Objects to 'Private Prosecutors' in the Trial of Mr. Duggan.", BUFFALO ENQUIRER (Buffalo, NY), Feb. 6, 1893, p. 1.

126. "Murder," IOWA DAILY STATE REGISTER (Des Moines, IA), Nov. 29, 1873, p. 4.

127. "The Death Shot," IOWA DAILY STATE REGISTER (Des Moines, IA), Dec. 3, 1873, p. 4.

128. "Murder," IOWA DAILY STATE REGISTER (Des Moines, IA), Nov. 29, 1873, p. 4; *see also id.* ("Judge Jones was sworn and stated that he appeared, as he understood it at the request of the District Attorney. Mr. Jones, as coming from the District Attorney, asked me to assist Gen. Given. He said he was not able to pay me for my services, but would see if the father of the widow could pay me. Messrs Jones and Sturman called on me and said the widow had property and would pay. I refused to deal with her, but said I would take the case if they would be responsible, which they agreed to do and I consequently appear."; "Gen. Given sworn—Before the filing of preliminary information, J. C. Jones called on me and I urged him to employ Judge Phillips to help me, but he declined to do so. I asked Judge Phillips and he refused on the ground that the State wouldn't pay. He declined."); "Yard Released," IOWA DAILY STATE REGISTER (Des Moines, IA), July 19, 1873, p. 4; "The Jones Murder," IOWA DAILY STATE REGISTER (Des Moines, IA), Nov. 18, 1873, p. 4.

129. "The Murder Trial," IOWA DAILY STATE REGISTER (Des Moines, IA), Nov. 30, 1873, p. 4; *see also id.* ("The discussion by the attorneys that followed the introduction of this paper was heated and earnest, and the decision of the Judge was not wanting in spice. It concluded by stating that the trial of the cause should proceed, General Given for the State and Judge Phillips for the Governor, but he did not think the Governor had any right to make such appointment. Thereupon Judge Phillips appeared and formally withdrew from the case, and the District Attorney excepted to the rulings of the Court that the Court had no right to appoint an Assistant District Attorney, and to the employment by private parties.").

130. "Lawyer Hogate's Trial," THE POST (Camden, NJ), Feb. 10, 1891, p. 1.

131. "Private Counsel Ruled Out," CAMDEN DAILY COURIER (Camden, NJ), Feb. 9, 1891, p. 1.

132. "Hogate's Bail, $10,000," THE POST (Camden, NJ), Oct. 21, 1891, p. 1.

133. "Hogate," THE POST (Camden, NJ), Oct. 22, 1891, p. 1.

134. Meister v. People, 31 Mich. 99, 107 (1875).

135. "The Nicely Brothers," Murder by Gaslight, http://murderbygaslight.com/2015/03/the-nicely-brothers.html?m=1.

136. Appeal of Nicely, 18 A. 737, 130 Pa. 261, 269–70 (1889).

137. "Escaped from Jail—The Nicely Brothers Make a Break for Liberty, but Are Soon Captured," JEFFERSONIAN DEMOCRAT (Brookville, PA), Sept. 18, 1889, p. 1; "Sawed Out of Jail—The Nicely Brothers Escape Once More from the Somerset Authorities," PITTSBURG DISPATCH, Nov. 30, 1890, p. 1; "Joe Nicely's Story," THE TIMES (Altoona, PA), Dec. 4, 1890, p. 1; "The Nicelys Hanged!" SOMERSET HERALD (Somerset, PA), Apr. 2, 1891, p. 1.

138. Appeal of Nicely, 130 Pa. 261, 268, 18 A. 737, 737–38 (1889); "Doomed to Death—Joe and Dave Nicely Must Hang," SOMERSET HERALD (Somerset, PA), Nov. 13, 1889, p. 3; "A Mother's Devotion," HARRISBURG DAILY INDEPENDENT (Harrisburg, PA), Mar. 4, 1891, p. 1.

139. Rush v. Cavenaugh, 2 Pa. 187, 189–90, 1845 WL 5210 *2 (1845); *see also id.* at 190 ("But the professional assistant, like the regular deputy, exercises not his own discretion, but that of the attorney-general whose locum tenens at sufferance he is; and he consequently does so under the obligation of the official oath.").

140. "Justice Asserting Her Majesty," THE TIMES (Philadelphia, PA), May 16, 1877, p. 2.

141. Biemel v. State, 37 N.W. 244, 245–47 (Wis. 1888); *see also id.* at 245–46 ("Section 752, Rev. St., says: 'It shall be the duty of the district attorney to prosecute all criminal actions in the circuit courts of his county, etc., and all criminal actions, except common assault and battery, and actions for breaches of the peace by the use of abusive or threatening words, before any magistrate, when requested by the magistrate before whom the action is pending, and upon like request to attend all criminal examinations before any magistrate; and at the request of a grand jury to appear before them and examine witnesses, to give advice, to draw all bills of indictment and informations, and issue subpœnas and other processes for the

attendance of witnesses.' Section 754 reads as follows: 'No district attorney shall receive any fee or reward for or on behalf of any prosecutor, or other individual, for services in any prosecution, to which it shall be his official duty to attend; nor be concerned as attorney or counsel for either party, other than for the state or county, in any civil action depending upon the same state of facts upon which any criminal prosecution commenced but not determined shall depend;' 'nor shall any district attorney while in office be eligible to or hold any judicial office whatever.' Section 750 provides for the appointment of a person in the place of the district attorney when the office is vacant, or when the district attorney is absent from the court unable to attend to his duties, or when he shall have acted as attorney for or be near of kin to the accused, and 'when the person shall be so appointed by the court he shall for the time being perform all the duties and have all the powers of the district attorney.' Section 4649 directs that all informations for crimes shall be signed by the district attorney and filed by him. In addition to these provisions, the legislature, recognizing the propriety of giving the district attorney the aid of other counsel in the prosecution of important or intricate cases, by chapter 354, Laws 1887, have provided 'that the circuit judges, within their respective circuits, are authorized in their discretion to appoint counsel to assist the district attorney in the prosecution of persons charged with crime in all cases when the crime charged is punishable by imprisonment in the state prison. Such additional counsel shall be paid in the same manner as now provided by law for the payment of counsel for indigent criminals.' This last act was undoubtedly passed, recognizing the fact that in some criminal cases there was great propriety if not the necessity for furnishing the district attorney aid in their prosecutions. The propriety of such aid had been recognized by this court in the cases cited below; and it may be reasonably inferred that this act was passed to sanction the custom of the courts which had grown up in the state of allowing the district attorney the aid of assistant counsel in difficult cases, and at the same time to regulate and limit it to the appointment of counsel who are not paid by private parties, but from the public funds, thereby placing the assistant attorney in the same impartial and unprejudiced position as the prosecuting attorney. It cannot be claimed that either before or since the passage of the act of 1887 private parties could thrust their hired attorneys into the courts to take charge of or assist the district attorney in the prosecution of any criminal case, without the consent of the court and the district attorney."). As the Wisconsin Supreme Court explained the history in that state: "Whenever attorneys other than the district attorney have been heretofore permitted to appear in a criminal case, they have come in by the consent of both the court and the district attorney, and not upon any claim of right to be there by the employment of private individuals. Heretofore no case has come before this court where the trial judge has permitted any one to appear as the assistant of the district attorney when it was shown that he was employed by private parties, and came into court at their request." *Id.* at 245–46.

142. *See* Meister v. People, 31 Mich. 99, 101 (1875) ("Under the English practice, prosecution by private parties has been the rule rather than the exception, and there is no public prosecutor who has general charge of criminal business. The necessity of such an officer has been urged repeatedly by many of the ablest jurists; and the chief reason suggested has been the abuse of criminal proceedings for private ends, and the subordination of public justice to private control."); *id.* at 102 ("In this country we have usually had in every state some officer, or class of officers, appointed for the express purpose of managing criminal business; but the extent and nature of their powers and duties have not been uniform. Sometimes the officers have been permanent, and sometimes counsel have been appointed by the courts to act for the term; and the duties have often been left under vague regulations. Under our territorial statutes, and until the Revised Statutes of 1838, the legislation was not very specific. But by the Revised Statutes of 1838 a regulation was introduced, that was borrowed from the laws of Massachusetts, and that has been preserved ever since. The prosecuting attorney of each county is required to prosecute all criminal cases in the courts of his county, and may be required also to appear for the same purpose before any magistrate, except in certain municipal courts. And he is expressly debarred from receiving any fee or reward from any private person for any services within his official business, and from being retained, except for the public, in any civil action depending on the same state of facts on which a criminal prosecution shall depend."); *id.* at 103 ("It has been quite common in this state for prosecuting attorneys to be aided by counsel, and probably in some cases they have had the help of those retained by private prosecutors. As no objections have been taken in these cases, and no attention has been called to the statute, it cannot be said there has been any practical construction of the statute; and we are obliged to consider the case as one requiring the law to be

enforced according to its fair meaning."); *id.* at 103–04 ("It is impossible to account for the change in our statutes requiring the exclusive control of criminal procedure to be in the hands of public officers who are forbidden to receive pay or in anyway become enlisted in the interests of private parties, unless we assume the law to have been designed to secure impartiality from all persons connected with criminal trials. The law never has prevented, and does not now prevent, private complaints before magistrates, who have a discretion in regard to calling in the prosecuting attorney. In the ordinary course of things the case for the prosecution is brought out on that examination, and justice requires that it should be, where a defendant does not waive examination. But when the charge is presented on which the respondent is to be tried at the circuit (where he must be tried for all statutory and common-law felonies, except petit larceny), the law requires the public prosecutor to assume and retain exclusive charge of the cause, until the case is ended by acquittal or conviction. The chief dangers which the statute intends to guard against must be those attendant on the trial, inasmuch as the preliminary proceedings usually determine the nature and extent of the accusation, and those may be under the charge of private parties. And we must conclude that the legislature do not consider it proper to allow the course of the prosecuting officer during the trial to be exposed to the influence of the interests or passions of private prosecutors."). Although the Michigan Supreme Court flirted with a retreat from its prohibition in an 1889 case, the ban on private prosecutors was reaffirmed only a year later. *Compare* People v. Schick, 42 N.W. 1008 (Mich. 1889) (although the record failed to establish that an assistant prosecutor had been retained by private parties, the court stated that even if such facts were established, the questioning of one witness and the argument of one motion would not require reversal) *with* People v. Hillhouse, 45 N.W. 484, 485–86 (Mich. 1890) (regardless of a private prosecutor's fairness toward a criminal defendant, the private prosecutor's participation constituted error).

143. *Compare* Commonwealth v. Williams, 56 Mass. (2 Cush.) 582 (1849) (although a private attorney was permitted to assist the prosecutor at trial, there was no evidence that the private attorney received any pecuniary compensation for his services) *with* Commonwealth v. Gibbs, 70 Mass. (4 Gray) 146 (1855) (the syllabus of the case notes: "A counsellor, appointed by the court to perform the duties of prosecuting officer in the absence of the district attorney, cannot act as such in a criminal case depending upon the same state of facts as a civil action in which he had been previously employed; and if he is allowed to conduct such prosecution, against the objection of the defendant, it is ground of exception."); *see also* Meister v. People, 31 Mich. 99, 104–05 (1875) ("The courts of Massachusetts have passed upon their statute several times. It was first brought to their attention in the case of *Commonwealth v. Knapp,* 10 Pick. R., 477, where it appeared that Mr. Webster had aided without objection in the trial of the principal felon whose accessories were on trial, and that reliance had been had on his aid in the case at bar, and that he was acting without any pecuniary inducement. The court, under these circumstances, holding it had a right to allow the prosecuting officer to obtain help in a proper case, considered it admissible in that instance, but reserved their opinion as to any different circumstances, and laid stress upon the absence of any interest in Mr. Webster beyond "a disinterested regard for the public good." In *Commonwealth v. Williams,* 2 Cush., 582, a similar course was sustained, but the court said it could only be allowed for stringent reasons, and referred again to the absence of any pecuniary compensation from any private individual. They said that such counsel is not under ordinary circumstances to be permitted, yet, when sanctioned by the court under the limitations suggested, it would not furnish sufficient ground for setting aside the verdict. In *Commonwealth v. Gibbs,* 4 Gray, 146, a conviction was set aside because the court had, in the absence of the district attorney, appointed counsel to act in his place, who had been retained by private parties in civil litigation of the same matter. In *Commonwealth v. King,* 8 Gray, 501, a gentleman was allowed to act as counsel who had acted in aid of the prosecution on the preliminary examination, and had also sat upon a commission of inquest concerning the fire which was the occasion of the prosecution. The court held this peculiar familiarity with the facts would make his help valuable; and no suggestion was made by anyone that he was not disinterested, as no interested person, it must be supposed, would have been allowed to sit on the commission.").

144. Biemel v. State, 37 N.W. 244, 245–47 (Wis. 1888).

145. "Private Counsel Ruled Out," CAMDEN DAILY COURIER (Camden, NJ), Feb. 9, 1891, p. 1.

146. Commonwealth v. Williams, 56 Mass. 582, 2 Cush. 582 (1849).

147. *Biemel,* 37 N.W. at 248–49 (Wis. 1888).

148. "Thompson vs. Fath," THE POST (Camden, NJ), Oct. 4, 1894, p. 1.

149. "Private Counsel Ruled Out," CAMDEN DAILY COURIER (Camden, NJ), Feb. 9, 1891, p. 1.

150. *E.g.*, "Public or Private Prosecutors," N.Y. TIMES, Dec. 15, 1872, p. 4 ("Offenses against the State it is proper that the State should take care of, and, generally speaking, every crime is heinous primarily as an offense against the State, against society, and only secondarily as an offense against the individual, inasmuch as the whole is greater than the part. When a man is murdered, for example, he suffers an extreme injury; but society, if it fail to avenge him, suffers a greater injury by multiplying the possibilities of murder. And if these offenses against the State were left to the chances of private prosecution, how often would they be punished? How often would want of money, want of time, want of energy, want of courage, deter the plaintiff from pushing his own case through the aid of private prosecution? How often would the criminal go unwhipt of justice, without the presence of an officer specially detached on behalf of the State to avenge the injury done to the State?"); *id.* ("Nor is it anything but the shallowest sophistry to say that because in England, under the system of private prosecution, criminals are punished, while in New-York, with a public prosecution, criminals escape, therefore the former system is the best. On the contrary, if in England criminals are punished, it is in spite of the absence of a public prosecutor; in spite of his presence that in New-York they go free.").

151. SOMERSET HERALD (Somerset, PA), June 4, 1879, p. 2 ("Now that the riot investigating committee at Harrisburg has reported that certain members and others have been guilty of violations of the Constitution and laws of the State, the next step in order is to see that the violators are properly and promptly punished. It is not to be expected that private prosecutors will volunteer to perform this service to the State."); *see also* "'The Best Workers,'" WEEKLY NEW ERA (Lancaster, PA), Nov. 22, 1879, p. 2 (in the context of an election fraud dispute, the newspaper observed: "There is a great danger in delaying the prosecution of this most important public matter, and if the District Attorney is so busy that he cannot find time to attend to his business, a private prosecutor should be appointed to look after it for him.").

152. "Howard's Letter," BOSTON GLOBE (Boston, MA), May 6, 1894, p. 24 ("NEW YORK, May 5—... You know how we feel when we find a privately paid lawyer assisting the district attorney in the prosecution of a man accused of crime. We resent the interference. I can conceive of nothing more hazardous before a jury than a private prosecutor, and whenever such have appeared disaster has attended the people of the state. Private counsel aided in the prosecution of Ned Stokes, private counsel assisted in the prosecution of MacFarlane, and neither man was convicted.").

153. "To Prevent Cruelty," HELENA INDEPENDENT (Helena, MT), May 26, 1890, p. 5 (at a meeting of the newly organized Society for the Prevention of Cruelty to Animals, the president of the association said "[a] private prosecutor is considered a public persecutor"); "Sergt. Clark Discharged," DETROIT FREE PRESS, Aug. 2, 1887, p. 8 (it was noted by Col. Sylvester Larned that "there was nothing illegal as provided by statute in private prosecutor assisting the officials, but he said that it too often occurred that private prosecutors are private persecutors, that they were apt to be prejudiced against the person they were endeavoring to punish"); *see also* PITTSBURGH POST (Pittsburgh, PA), Feb. 5, 1893, p. 4 ("A BILL is before the legislature, advised by Governor PATTISON, abolishing the right of the commonwealth to set aside jurors, and giving it only the same number of challenges that the defense has. It should pass. If the power was only used for public purposes, there might not be so much against its exercise; but the wrong comes in when it is perverted to accomplish the ends of private prosecutions, in cases of misdemeanor or felony. The conviction of DEMPSEY and BEATTY would have carried much greater weight had they been allowed the same privilege in making up the jury that the commonwealth, or private counsel acting for the commonwealth, exercised. The appeal is made to workingmen on their behalf that the jury was packed against them, and the fact cited that under the commonwealth's power of setting aside no workingmen were permitted on the jury. In those cases the defense had only four challenges, but in the capital case, now on trial, the defense had twenty, and, the panel being exhausted, the prosecution was compelled to accept some of the jurors it had stood aside. It is not in capital cases where the wrong and injustice of the 'king's jury' is so manifest as in a lower grade of offenses, where the venom of private persecution often enters in. For this reason the law should be modified as advised by the governor.").

154. *E.g.*, "List of Acts passed by the Legislature of Iowa at the present Session," DEMOCRATIC BANNER (Davenport, IA), Feb. 4, 1853, p. 2 (taking note of the passage of "An act to make private prosecutors liable

for cost in certain cases); "Crime's Consequences," NEW ERA (Lancaster, PA), Aug. 17, 1885, p. 4 (noting that Judge Patterson ordered aldermen and constables to be "investigated" in a charge to the grand jury; per the newspaper report, Judge Patterson conveyed the following to grand jurors: "The Grand Inquest should inquire if the aldermen and constables had persuaded the parties to bring suit. If the Grand Inquest should find from an examination that the aldermen or constables had incited any one to a prosecution, they should put the costs on them, as they were the real prosecutors, and could not shield themselves behind their office, standing in the same capacity as private prosecutors.").

155. *E.g.*, "Iowa Legislature," QUAD-CITY TIMES (Davenport, IA), Jan. 19, 1866, p. 4 ("Senator Powers introduced a bill for an act to award costs against private prosecutors in criminal cases the same as in private cases. Read a second time and referred to the Judiciary Committee."); "Legislative Summary," WEEKLY OTTUMWA COURIER (Ottumwa, IA), Feb. 8, 1866, p. 1 (noting the passage of a bill "for taxing cost to private prosecutors"); QUAD-CITY TIMES (Davenport, IA), June 8, 1868, p. 2 (reprinting "AN ACT to Provide for the Payment of Witness Fees and Jurors' Fees in State Cases," with section 1 reading in part "that nothing in this act shall be construed as preventing courts from taxing costs against private prosecutors").

156. "Criminal Trials Last Week," WELLSBORO AGITATOR (Wellsboro, PA), Feb. 1, 1893, p. 5.

157. Jerry L. Anderson, *The Origins and Efficacy of Private Enforcement of Animal Cruelty in Britain*, 17 DRAKE J. AGRICULTURAL L. 263, 265–66 (2012) (discussing the Royal Society for the Prevention of Cruelty to Animals ("RSPCA"), reportedly "the largest non-governmental law enforcement agency in England and Wales," and observing: "In the United States, private prosecution of animal abuse began in New York City in 1866, after the American Society for the Prevention of Cruelty to Animals (ASPCA) was organized by Henry Bergh, using the RSPCA as his model. In some ways, the ASPCA enjoyed even greater powers than its British counterpart. For example, the New York legislature gave the society a right to issue its own arrest warrants in certain cases, a 'truly extraordinary' delegation of criminal enforcement authority."); "To Prevent Cruelty," HELENA INDEPENDENT (Helena, MT), May 26, 1890, p. 5 (at a meeting of the newly organized Society for the Prevention of Cruelty to Animals, the president of the association addressed it as follows: "Ladies and Gentlemen: ... I can also outline what I consider to be the power, and what should be the policy of the association. Perhaps I can best state that policy, by remarking that no law can be enforced which does not meet with public approbation. As proof of that I will call your attention to the fact that, although the law preventing cruelty to animals was enacted in 1881, there have been comparatively no prosecutions for violations of the law. This would not have been the case, had public opinion demanded the enforcement of the law. This association is the first utterance of public opinion that this law must be obeyed. The best policy of the association, in my opinion, demands that its acts should be but the voice of public opinion at the time of the act.... I am opposed to having any special officer of the association. Special officers do not meet with especial favor; there is a public feeling which I have frequently met, which prevents jurors from giving to the testimony of such officers the same weight as is given to the evidence of the regular officers of the law. Perhaps that feeling may best be described as a fear that the special officer may act so as to appear to be earning his salary. I think that we can rely upon the county and city officials. I believe that their neglect to act in the past is due to the fact that they did not know of this law of the land, and I feel that all that should be done will be done when we have called their attention to the law. When they refuse to act, we can act, and by acting wisely we can increase the number of those who act with us, and I can assure you that so acting, we will have the officers of the law with us, even though it should be against their will. That, however, is a fear which we need not entertain, for I firmly believe that all the officers will act heartily with us. For similar reasons, I would depend solely upon the county attorney as a prosecuting officer. You cannot overcome the prejudice which does exist against the retaining of private counsel for the prosecution of criminal cases. A private prosecutor is considered a public persecutor. The present county attorney is able, and, I believe, he is willing to prosecute for the violation of that law which we seek to have enforced."); "Cruelty to Animals," CAPITAL JOURNAL (Salem, OR), Dec. 11, 1895, p. 4 ("The case of the State v. Chas. R. McCarty and Thos. Pickeus, with H. W. Downing the private prosecutor, was on trial before Justice Johnson this afternoon. The defendants were charged with cruelty to animals...."). Private prosecutions relating to animal cruelty continue to be brought in certain locales. *E.g.*, JUSTIN MARCEAU, BEYOND CAGES: ANIMAL LAW AND CRIMINAL PUNISHMENT 93 (2019) ("The only way to ensure that prosecutors remain steadfast in their commitment to prosecute animal cruelty is to pay a prosecutor

to bring such cases. To most students of the American legal system, this would seem an impossibility. After all, a hallmark of the American justice system is that *only* the government can bring criminal charges against an individual. As a testament to their creativity and tenacity, animal protection groups have nonetheless achieved notable success in this effort as well.") (italics in original); *id.* ("In Ohio, county humane societies are authorized to appoint persons to aid in the prosecution of individuals charged with animal cruelty. At least one attorney has served as a private attorney general prosecuting animal cruelty under this statute. The attorney became well known in the state for his ambitious and aggressive animal cruelty prosecutions, and he was paid his usual rate from private practice by the Ohio Humane Societies. He made just as much money prosecuting cruelty cases as he did billing private clients and had no qualms about noting that he preferred prosecution to his normal civil docket. By all accounts, this arrangement has been advantageous to the funders because the attorney 'has been remarkable successful in getting convictions.'"); *see also id.* at 93–94 ("Moving beyond special prosecutors, however, the Animal Legal Defense Fund has set the gold standard for 'bankrolling' prosecutions. The organization has created, funded, and apparently selected a full-time prosecutor in Oregon whose only job is to prosecute animal related crimes. The prosecutor, Jake Kamins, is a fully-sworn member of the district attorney's office, but his salary is funded entirely by ALDF, and he prosecutes only animal cruelty or neglect cases. The terms of his funding, as revealed in the contract between him and ALDF, make clear that the continued funding of the position is tied, at least informally, to the success he has in obtaining more and longer terms of incarceration. ALDF expects some returns on their investment, and presumably a prosecutor who was dismissing charges, suggesting treatment instead of incarceration, or otherwise offering lenient plea bargains would not expect their funding to continue.").

158. ALTOONA TRIBUNE (Altoona, PA), Mar. 1, 1888, p. 4 (quoting from the *Philadelphia Press*); *see also* ALTOONA TRIBUNE (Altoona, PA), Mar. 1, 1888, p. 4 (of the perspective of the *Philadelphia Press, The Altoona Tribune* offered this viewpoint: "These are true words and they are commended to the consideration of those otherwise good citizens who refuse to assist in the organization of a Law and Order league on the ground that it is the duty of our officials to enforce the laws, and that private citizens should not be asked to undertake so vexatious and unpopular a task. The fact is that if the laws are to be well enforced and criminals promptly punished, private citizens must engage actively in the work. In many cities and towns the leading people realize the truth just stated and have gone to work on behalf of good government.").

159. Nathan Cree, "The Metropolitan Police Question," WYANDOTT HERALD (Kansas City, KS), Aug. 30, 1888, p. 2 (italics in original).

160. *Posse comitatus*, Legal Information Institute, https://www.law.cornell.edu/wex/posse_comitatus; C. J. Williams, *An Argument for Putting the Posse Comitatus Act to Rest*, 85 MISS. L.J. 99, 164 (2016).

161. "Justices Must Hedge," MEDFORD MAIL (Medford, OR), July 31, 1896, p. 4 (noting that Douglas County justices of the peace were admonished: "All justices of the peace of Douglas county, Oregon, are hereby cautioned against issuing warrants for the arrest of persons charged with petty offenses, unless the justice should be satisfied that the evidence is sufficient to convict, or that the accused is attempting to leave the county or state, and when warrant is issued to notify the district attorney or his deputy, and in all cases where practicable, such as where defendant is not attempting to leave the county or state, to submit a full statement of the case to the district attorney or his deputy before issuing a warrant. Special attention of all justices of the peace is called to the following section of the code: 'Section 2172—The justice may, in his discretion, require the private prosecutor in a criminal action to give security for costs and disbursements, before filing or receiving the complaint therein, in the amount authorized in civil action, and not otherwise.'").

162. OREGON DAILY STATESMAN (Salem, OR), Apr. 9, 1897, p. 5 ("The commissioners court made an order yesterday as follows: 'In the matter of the fees of prosecuting witnesses in state cases: It appearing to the county court that criminal complaints are made by irresponsible persons in the various justices courts in the county, and it being apparent that in some instances such complaints are made by private prosecutors for the purpose of venting personal spites, and in some cases for the purpose of individual gain, and in several instances it having happened that it was necessary for the justice of the peace to dismiss such complaints for the failure of the prosecuting witness to attend upon the trial, and in many other cases after complaints have been made the prosecuting witness has refused to appear and testify as a witness unless

being first subpoenaed, which has caused additional and unwarranted expense to the county and to the taxpayers of the county; for the purpose of correcting such abuses and to protect the taxpayers of the county, who are innocent sufferers by reason of such wrongful practices, this court desires to suggest to the various justices of the peace in Marion county, that hereafter when a criminal complaint or information is filed in any such justice's court, that unless the prosecuting witness is a person of sufficient property interest to enable the county to collect a judgment against the prosecuting witness for costs should such prosecuting witness fail or neglect to attend the examination or trial and for such reason the case be dismissed, that the justice require such prosecuting witness to give an undertaking before the issuance of any warrant of arrest, with sufficient sureties, to the effect that he will appear and testify as a witness in such proceeding against the defendant in such court with like effect as though a subpoena had been served upon him requiring such attendance, and that if such prosecution should be found to be malicious, that he will pay such judgment as may be rendered against him by the court. It is further ordered that the district attorney be requested to use his best endeavors to correct such abuses of the criminal processes of the justice's courts and that he use his best efforts to see that the foregoing directions are enforced. That a copy of this order be mailed to each justice of the peace in Marion county and one to the district attorney of the third judicial district.'").

163. "Special Counsel in Libel Cases," THE EXAMINER (San Francisco, CA), Jan. 21, 1898, p. 6.

164. "Shooting at Big Elk," CORVALLIS GAZETTE (Corvallis, OR), June 6, 1890, p. 4.

165. "A Desperate Fight," STATE RIGHTS DEMOCRAT (Albany, OR), Sept. 5, 1890, p. 3 ("A warrant was sworn out in Justice Turney's court last Saturday evening by Thomas Reed as private prosecutor against Mrs Nancy Slator. The officers arrested and brought the accused before his honor yesterday morning, who on being arraigned plead not guilty. We will not undertake to recite any of the facts that led to the fight, but suffice it to say that Mrs Slator is a tenant on Reed's ranch and that controversies and bad blood had existed between them for some months. Last Saturday they met in battle array. Clubs were used very freely, and while Mrs Slator was badly bruised about the fact and arms, Mr Reed got an arm and a finger broken and otherwise badly used up. Both called physicians to their assistance and their wounds have been partially patched up, but the law will undertake to sift out the whys and wherefores on Monday.... Tom Reed is well known in Albany. He has probably had more quarrels and trouble than any man in Oregon."); *see also* ALBANY DAILY DEMOCRAT (Albany, OR), Sept. 17, 1890, p. 5 (noting that Tom Reed, aged 79, "is not a successful litigator" and that "he has been involved in civil and criminal suits" throughout his life and "has never yet been successful in one," and that yesterday he was ordered to pay "a fine and costs" of $61 and taxed for his role as a "private prosecutor" in the case of "State versus Nancy Slator").

166. "Justice's Court," OREGON DAILY STATESMAN (Salem, OR), Oct. 22, 1885, p. 4 ("Before Justice Coffey yesterday the private prosecutor in the case of the State against Mrs. Sheridan filed satisfaction, paid the costs of the action, and the charge was dismissed.").

167. "Discouraging Litigation," MORNING ASTORIAN (Astoria, OR), Jan. 14, 1883, p. 1. Section 1 of the bill read: "The name of every person who voluntarily appears before any justice of the peace or grand jury to prosecute any person in a criminal action, either for a misdemeanor or felony shall be endorsed upon the complaint, information or indictment as private prosecutor; and if it shall be found by any justice or court trying said action or hearing said proceedings that the prosecution is malicious or without probable cause, said fact shall be entered upon record in said action or proceedings by said justice or court." "Upon making the entry prescribed in section 1 of this act," section 2 of the bill read, "the justice or court must immediately render judgment against the private prosecutor for the cost and disbursements of the action or proceeding, which may be enforced by execution, in the same manner as a judgment in the civil action." *Id.*; *see also* "Oregon Legislature," CORVALLIS GAZETTE-TIMES (Corvallis, OR), Sept. 29, 1882, p. 3 ("S. B. 27—Providing for taxing costs and disbursements of criminal actions against private prosecutors when found to be malicious or without probable cause. Referred to judiciary committee."); "What Was Done—The Legislature's Work," MORNING ASTORIA (Astoria, OR), Oct. 31, 1882, p. 1 ("S. B. 27—An act providing for taxing private prosecutors with costs and disbursements of criminal actions where found to be malicious, etc. Approved Oct. 20."). In Seattle, Washington, a municipal ordinance was also proposed—and quickly passed in 1884—to allow Justices of the Peace to make judicial inquiries of private complainants and to require private prosecutors to give security for costs. Signed into law by Mayor John

Leary in December 1884, that ordinance—Ordinance No. 628—provided in section 1: "That when any complaint shall be made by a person other than an officer of the city of Seattle in the course of his official duty, before any Justice of the Peace for a criminal violation of an Ordinance of the city, it shall be the duty of such Justice of the Peace, before issuing a warrant for the arrest of the accused, to investigate the charge and to examine the complainant on oath as to the facts and circumstances of the case and the number of witnesses cognizant thereof, and the names and whereabouts of such witnesses; and such Justice of the Peace may, in his discretion, after such investigation, require any complainant, except an officer of the city when acting in the course of his official duty, to furnish sufficient security, by a bond with sureties, or cash deposit, for all costs of the case in the event of an acquittal of the person or persons accused, upon the trial." Section 2 of the Ordinance, spelling out the consequences of the failure to provide such security, then read: "That when any Justice of the Peace shall require security for costs in any case, as provided by this Ordinance, if the complainant shall fail to give such security to the satisfaction of such Justice of the Peace, such case shall be dismissed without further proceedings therein." The bonds required by the Ordinance were to be in favor of the City of Seattle and conditioned "for the payment of all costs taxable" in the cases for which such bonds were filed, to cover "fees of juries, in case a jury trial shall be demanded, and the expense, if any, of boarding and maintaining the accused while in custody, if the accused shall be acquitted upon the trial of such case." "Ordinance No. 628," SEATTLE DAILY POST-INTELLIGENCER (Seattle, WA), Dec. 30, 1884, p. 2; *see also* "Notice of Special Meeting," SEATTLE DAILY POST-INTELLIGENCER (Seattle, WA), Dec. 25, 1884, p. 1 ("A special meeting of the Common Council is hereby called for Friday, December 26, 1884, at 7 o'clock p.m., for the purpose of considering and acting upon the following matters, to wit:... An Ordinance to require private prosecutors to give security for costs.").

168. "New Law Denounced," LEBANON DAILY NEWS (Lebanon, PA), June 17, 1897, p. 2 ("Judge Yerker, of the Montgomery county court, is an able, fearless expounder of the law and has acquired a wide reputation as such. In charging the grand jury on Monday he scathingly commented on an act of assembly passed May 25, 1897. It provides that in all prosecutions for larceny where the value of the goods is less than $10, if the bill be returned 'ignored' the grand jury shall decide whether the county or the prosecutor shall pay the costs. It is further provided that in the event of an acquittal in cases where the value of the goods is less than $10 the petit jury trying the case shall determine whether the costs shall be born[e] by the county or the prosecutor. Heretofore juries were permitted to and frequently did impose the costs on the accused."; "The judge said in part: 'The thief may now invade the humble abode of the laboring man or the poor woman and steal their belongings, precious to them, but of little money value, or upon the lone highway may attempt to outrage a beloved child, and if afterwards it appears that the prosecutors were mistaken in the identity of the felon or property, and had the temerity to arrest a cowardly sneak thief or prowling tramp, who it was believed perpetrated the deed, they may incur the risk of taking the place of the criminal in the cell because of non-payment of costs. But if the rich man, who owns more valuable property, is robbed of more than $10 in value, and makes a mistake in prosecuting a thief, he stands in no peril of the vengeance of the law. The effect of this act is to discourage prosecutions for felonies. This hesitancy on the part of the citizens to perform a most important duty is due largely to unwise legislation in the past, which has impressed the community that it is the duty of public officers to institute prosecutions. This act in effect says to the private prosecutor, there can be in law two kinds of thieves—the protected, privileged thief and the $10 class. A man is not a felon because he steals, but because he steals in quantity. Again, it becomes a temptation to the public officer, constable and every prosecutor to exaggerate the value of stolen property or the character of an assault to escape the possible penalty for costs.").

169. CORVALLIS TIMES (Corvallis, OR), Jan. 28, 1895, p. 4 ("Senator Alley is much interested in his bill amending the criminal code so as to require private prosecutors to give security for costs and disbursements. It is designed, of course, to prevent the abuses which have crept into criminal practice by reason of irresponsible prosecutions. He has a bill of expenses from a Lane county justice court and other data, showing what it has cost the county for frivolous prosecutions, instigated from spite."); *see also* STATE RIGHTS DEMOCRAT (Albany, OR), Feb. 1, 1895, p. 2 ("A justice of the peace hereafter, or as soon as the new law is approved by the governor, shall require the private prosecutor in a criminal action to give security for costs and disbursements before filing or receiving the complaint therein, in the amount authorized in civil actions, and not otherwise. This law is to be enacted owing to the fact that many irresponsible parties

are repeatedly instituting actions on frivolous pretexts, resulting in needless expense to taxpayers."); "Should Give Bonds," OREGON MIST (St. Helens, OR), June 21, 1895, p. 2 ("A great deal is said nowadays as to whether or not a justice of the peace has authority to require a private prosecutor or complaining witness to give security for the cost in a criminal action, for the purpose of securing the county in case of no conviction, and especially in cases of malicious prosecution. Below we quote a few of the many sections of Hill's code bearing upon this question.... It will be seen by the foregoing sections that the justice has the right, always, to require the complainant to give security for the cost. The justice not only has the right but it is a duty he owes taxpayers of the county to require security given for the costs in all cases. Then would a case of malicious prosecution be unheard of, and then and not until then, will the county be protected against the many petty spite-work cases that are continually occupying the time of the justice courts while the county foots the bill. This method would not deprive any man of justice, since if he has a good case it will be an easy matter to furnish the required bonds, and if he has not a good case the sooner it is disposed of the better for all concerned.").

170. "From Brownsville," GALVESTON DAILY NEWS (Galveston, TX), Dec. 24, 1874, p. 1 ("The trial of Burko and others commenced to-day. Messrs. Powers and Maxan are for the defendants, District Attorney Scat for the State, and Judge Russell is private prosecutor. Maxan made a point requiring him to disclose by whom he had been employed. Half an hour was allowed him to consult with his employers. The time expired and no report was made.... It is reported that $800 have been raised, here and in Matamoros, to pay the private prosecutor, etc."); *cf.* "Abe Rothschild. No Progress Made Thus Far—His Lawyers Fighting Hard—The Court's Ruling Generally Unfavorable to Him," CINCINNATI ENQUIRER, Dec. 20, 1877, p. 1 ("JEFFERSON, TEXAS, December 19.—The entire day has been consumed by counsel in arguing a motion offered by Rothschild's counsel, that the State's Attorney be ordered to disclose to the Court if there by any private prosecutor in the case. The State's counsel resisted this as being premature, as this inquiry could be made at the proper time, which would be after the announcement by the defendant that he was ready for trial. Counsel for defendant introduced, accompanying their motion to disclose the private prosecutors, a list, purporting to be a subscription-list, signed by sundry parties, donating money to employ attorneys to prosecute Rothschild, and desired the Court to permit the defendant to institute an inquiry, under oath, by placing the signers of the paper upon the stand, stating that their object was to ascertain who were the private prosecutors and those connected with them, that they could object to them when selecting the jury, and that this was a proper subject of inquiry before announcing their readiness for trial. The Court overruled the motion, to which ruling the defendant took a bill of exceptions."); "The Rothschild Trial," TRI-WEEKLY HERALD (Marshall, TX), Dec. 20, 1877, p. 2 ("Counsel for the defense offered a motion to the effect that private prosecutors had enlisted against the defendant, and that their names should be all known and placed on the record. The defence presented in the motion a subscription, dated in February last of money subscribed by citizens to employ counsel, in which there were thirty-seven names. The entire morning hour was consumed in discussing this motion. The Messrs. Todd filed a reply stating that the contract had never been completed, and was wholly repudiated by them; that they appeared as voluntary counsel for the State, to promote the ends of justice, and for which they had never received a dollar.... Mr. C. S. Todd made the opening speech after dinner, and presented very clearly and forcibly the relations of counsel to the State in the prosecution of his case, contending that there were no private prosecutors employed, and that there never had been. He was followed by Col. Culberson in one of his happiest efforts, in which he maintained that every man who had signed the subscription paper was, in fact and in law, a private prosecutor and neither he nor any one related to him, within the third degree of consanguinity or affinity, could properly act as a juror in this trial. It was certainly a very nice point, and ably argued on both sides."); *id.* ("The whole of yesterday was consumed in the discussion. At its termination the Judge overruled the motion of the defence. He said the signers to the subscription were not private prosecutors within the meaning of the act. The defense filed a bill of exceptions to this ruling."); "Abe Rothschild on Trial," GALVESTON NEWS (Galveston, TX), Dec. 22, 1877, p. 1 ("Count convened this morning at the usual hour. Defendant's counsel presented a written motion to quash the bill of indictment, because it is uncertain and duplicitous in this, that the time and place where the fatal shot was made are not alleged, and because it is not clear whether defendant is charged with the killing of one or three white women, to wit: Bessie Moore, Diamond Bessie or Bessie Rothschild. The discussion on this motion lasted until the hour

of adjournment for dinner. When the court reassembled the judge overruled the motion."); *id.* ("Counsel for the defense offered another motion, to the effect that money had been paid on the subscription to employ counsel. One lawyer, it was alleged, had received thirty-five dollars; and the defense were prepared to prove that present counsel for the State had called for money on the subscription to buy books, and to pay other expenses of the trial. If this was deemed insufficient to constitute them private prosecutors, defense were further prepared to prove that there were, outside of that paper, private prosecutors. The judge held that a subscription to simply employ counsel, and money paid on it, did not constitute a private prosecutor; but if there were, as stated, private prosecutors, the defendant had a right to know the fact. After some parleying, P. H. Rowell and P. M. Allen were put on the stand. Their testimony elected nothing beyond the subscription to pay lawyers to subserve the ends of justice."); "The Trial of John W. Wilson, in the District Court of Shawnee County, for the Shooting of J. Clarke Swayze," WEEKLY COMMONWEALTH (Topeka, KS), May 31, 1877, p. 2 (recounting that the defense counsel, W. C. Webb, told the jury: "The prosecution is in the name of the state, and the state is the people—you and I, and the citizens sitting here listening. Do you think that in a case of this kind the sole object is to convict and punish? has not the state as much interest in acquitting an innocent man as in convicting a guilty one? The state is represented by the county attorney in this case—chosen by the people, and it is his duty to prosecute this case, and it is hoped he will perform his duty and nothing more. There is one novel feature in this case; every wrong is of a two-fold nature, the public and the individual are both wronged. Some man assails your character and you go into court as a private prosecutor. If a man's father or brother is slain, the survivor is apt to become the prosecutor, and sits by to assist the counsel for the state in the calling and examining witnesses. So too, if your horse is stolen, you make complaint, and become the private prosecutor. In this case learned and able counsel come in and sit beside the public prosecutor and assist him; but who has been sitting and advising with the law officer of the county in this case. In all former experience there has been some person assisting; there is no pretense that counsel had volunteered in this case; honorable counsel do not do that; but who was the private prosecutor that had employed these learned gentlemen? It was the duty of the public prosecutor when the coroner's verdict was returned, to file an information, and summon to court *all persons* who might be supposed to know anything of the cause of Swayze's death. It was a singular fact that counsel came in here, and so far as could be seen, representing nobody, should actively assist the public prosecutor, who is amply competent to conduct the case. The fact is disclosed in the testimony that three of the witnesses called as to the particular facts in relation to Swayze's death. Were also witnesses before the coroner's jury. Why were not Blue and Miller, who were both present and active in their duty as officers, called to testify by the state, if the whole truth in the case was desired.") (italics in original); *see also* "Court of Appeals—Synopsis of Opinions of the Court of Appeals, Tyler Term, 1882," DALLAS DAILY HERALD (Dallas, TX), Nov. 23, 1882, p. 2 ("Heacock vs. the State; from Van Zandt county. The mere fact that a person has paid or promised to pay money to aid in the prosecution of a person charged with crime, is not sufficient to constitute such person a private prosecutor under the statute.").

171. *E.g.*, "The Factory Conspirators—The Rights of Labor—The Uses of Wealth," DAILY MORNING POST (Pittsburgh, PA), Feb. 15, 1849, p. 2 (noting that little girls who worked in a factory were prosecuted for rioting after throwing rotten eggs and mud, with *The Daily Morning Post* emphasizing: "These are the prominent facts of the case, as we have learned them. And for *this* the little girls were prosecuted by the factory proprietors;—none but *private counsel* appearing and pleading before court and jury, on the part of the prosecution. If it was a 'bold, palpable and aggravated riot,' where was the Commonwealth's counsel? Why was his voice not heard? The Mayor and the Police of Allegheny City, the public officers of the law, were present at the scene; why did they not institute the prosecution, if it was a 'bold, palpable and aggravated riot?'") (italics in original).

172. "A Strange Way," LANCASTER INTELLIGENCER (Lancaster, PA), July 27, 1892, p. 2; *see also* "Critchlow Not Guilty," BOSTON DAILY GLOBE (Boston, MA), Nov. 24, 1892, p. 10 (taking note of the acquittal of "Sylvester Pritchlow, the Homestead steel worker, accused of slaying T. J. Connor, a Pinkerton detective, in the battle at Fort Frick on July 6 last"; "The finding of the jury was not a surprise, as the alibi established by the defence was so strong that the united efforts of Carnegie's six private prosecutors and the district attorney of Alleghany county could not shake it, their oratorical bombshells falling, like blank cartridges in a sham battle, short of their mark.").

173. Paul Kahan, The Homestead Strike: Labor, Violence, and American Industry 97 (2014); Sean Dennis Cashman, America in the Gilded Age: From the Death of Lincoln to the Rise of Theodore Roosevelt 127 (3d ed. 1993); *see also* James Howard Bridge, The Inside History of the Carnegie Steel Company 243 (1903) ("On September 21st true bills were found against one hundred and sixty-seven participants in the Homestead battle—three for murder and the rest for aggravated riot and conspiracy. The next day Mr. Lovejoy, secretary of the Carnegie Company, was arrested at the behest of the Amalgamated Association on a charge of aggravated riot and assault and battery; and Mr. Frick and a dozen other officials of the company were included in the indictment."); *id.* ("With the exemption of three ringleaders of the rioters, who were held on a murder charge, all of these persons were admitted to bail. The murder charges duly came to trial. In two cases the accused had no difficulty in proving an alibi; and the third, that of O'Donnell, resulted in an acquittal. Nine months later the cases against the Carnegie officials were dropped; and the same day an order of court was issued releasing from bail the strikers who were under indictment.").

174. "Shocking Tragedy at Lexington, Virginia," Wash. Sentinel (Washington, DC), Jan. 21, 1854, p. 4.

175. *See* Daniel S. Morrow, Murder in Lexington: VMI, Honor and Justice in Antebellum Virginia (2013).

176. Ollinger Crenshaw, *The School of Law, 1849–1949: A Century Revisited*, 6 Wash. & Lee L. Rev. 12, 12 (1949); W. Hamilton Bryson, *The History of Legal Education in Virginia*, 14 U. Rich. L. Rev. 155, 183 (1979).

177. "Trial for Murder," Richmond Dispatch (Richmond, VA), Apr. 28, 1854, p. 1.

178. *See* Morrow, *supra* note 175.

Chapter 5 Notes

1. State v. Mansy, 262 A.2d 817, 818 (Conn. Cir. Ct. 1969).

2. Andrew Sidman, Comment, *The Outmoded Concept of Private Prosecution*, 25 Am. U.L. Rev. 754, 762 (1976).

3. *Id.* at 763; Thomas J. Robinson, Comment, *Private Prosecution in Criminal Cases*, 4 Wake Forest L. Rev. 300, 308 (1968); *see also* Gerard "Chuck" Rainville, 40-Dec. Prosecutor 32, 35 (2006) ("In 1704, Connecticut became the first colony to discontinue the practice of private prosecution by naming public prosecutors adjuncts to all county courts. Though these local prosecutors remained the counsel for the Queen (of England) they were entrusted to prosecute criminals and suppress vice—functions that were not of particular concern to the monarchy.").

4. Jack M. Kress, *Progress and Prosecution*, 423 Annals Am. Acad. Pol. & Soc. Sci. 99, 103 (1976).

5. *Mansy*, 262 A.2d at 818.

6. Sidman, *supra* note 2, at 763; Robinson, *supra* note 3, at 309.

7. Joan E. Jacoby, *The American Prosecutor in Historical Context*, 44 Prosecutor 38, 45 (Dec. 2010); Juan Cardenas, *The Crime Victim in the Prosecutorial Process*, 9 Harv. J.L. & Pub. Pol'y 357, 370 (1986). Private prosecutions became even less common in 1751, when the Virginia courts forced all crime victims to consult with the deputy attorney general before filing criminal complaints. Those deputies assumed complete control over all prosecutions within their respective counties in 1789. *Id.*

8. Sidman, *supra* note 2, at 763.

9. Cardenas, *supra* note 7, at 369.

10. *Id.* at 370. "When the English took over Dutch settlements in the Seventeenth Century, the English governor revoked all Dutch law and government—except for the schout, who eventually took control of prosecutorial power." *Id.* (citing Robinson, *supra* note 3, at 308). For experiences of other colonies with respect to the growth of the public prosecutor, *see* Josephine Gittler, *Expanding the Role of the Victim in a Criminal Action*, 11 Pepperdine L. Rev. 126 n.31 (1984) (listing citations for the colonies of New York, New Hampshire, Maryland, and Rhode Island).

11. Robinson, *supra* note 3, at 308.

12. Stephanie A.J. Dangel, *Is Prosecution a Core Executive Function?* Morrison v. Olson *and the Framers' Intent*, 99 YALE L.J. 1069, 1073–74 (1990).

13. Michael J. Ellis, *The Origins of the Elected Prosecutor*, 121 YALE L.J. 1528, 1537 (2012).

14. *Id.* at 1530, 1540–69.

15. Tyler Grove, *Are All Prosecutorial Activities "Inherently Governmental"?: Applying State Safeguards for Victim-Retained Private Prosecutions to Outsourced Prosecutions*, 40 PUB. CONT. L.J. 991, 1007 (2011); *see also* "Prosecuting Attornies," BUCYRUS JOURNAL (Bucyrus, OH), Mar. 18, 1870, p. 2 ("We are glad to note that a bill is pending before the Legislature, to increase the salaries of Prosecuting Attornies."); *id.* ("The public prosecutor, or Prosecuting Attorney, is, ex-officio, the guardian of the personal rights and property of community, and the prosecutor of all crimes against them. As such he is the conservator of the peace and order of society, and the protector of our property."); *id.* ("Such an officer should be one of the best paid in the county, and should rank in official dignity and importance only inferior to the Common Pleas Judge.").

16. Yue Ma, *Exploring the Origins of Public Prosecution*, 18 INT'L CRIM. JUST. REV. 190, 206 (2008) ("The American judiciary has taken an extremely deferential approach toward prosecutorial decision making. The origin of the deferential approach can be traced back to the second half of the 19th century when public prosecutors first rose to prominence. The prosecutor's authority to not bring charges or to drop already-filed charges came from English attorney general's power to enter the writ of *nolle prosequi*. The prosecutor's power to exercise this authority was upheld by the courts in the early days of the nation's existence. In *Commonwealth v. Wheeler* (1806), a Massachusetts court stated that 'the power of entering a *nolle prosequi* is to be exercised at the discretion of the attorney who prosecutes for the government, and for its exercise he alone is responsible.'"); *id.* at 206–07 ("The support to prosecutors did not come only from the state courts. It came from the U.S. Supreme Court as well. The Supreme Court echoed the state courts in upholding prosecutors' power to enter the writ of *nolle prosequi*. In the Confiscation Cases (1868), the U.S. Supreme Court held that 'public prosecutions, until they come before the court . . . are within the exclusive direction of the district attorney, and even after they are entered in court, they are so far under his control that he may enter a *nolle prosequi* at any time before the jury is empanelled for the trial of the case.'") (citing Confiscation Cases, 74 U.S. 454, 454–55 (1868)); *cf.* The Role of Victims of Crime in the Criminal Trial Process: History, Concepts and Theory, Victorian Law Reform Commission, Information Paper 1, at 7–8 (May 2015), http://www.antoniocasella.eu/restorative/Victorian_law_Reform_may2015.pdf ("From the 1200s, the role of the King's Attorney as the Crown's representative in court included the power to place people on trial. In 1461 the Attorney became a member of the House of Lords and assumed the title of Attorney-General. From this time, the role of the Attorney-General developed progressively, so that by the 1700s the Attorney-General possessed the common law power to commence and discontinue a prosecution. This prosecutorial role was focused on the most serious crimes which threated the security of the monarch or the realm (for example treason, counterfeiting, riots), rather than on criminal offences against individual victims.").

17. Ma, *supra* note 16, at 203.

18. Michael J. Ellis, *The Origins of the Elected Prosecutor*, 121 YALE L.J. 1528, 1569 (2012). The importance of the office of public prosecutor in the United States was only further reinforced by its shift in the nineteenth century from an appointive office to an elective office. "After Andrew Jackson was elected in 1828," historian Joan Jacoby writes, "the expansion of democracy in the form of elected positions swept the country." "Hanging on the coattails of the movement to elect local judges was the prosecutor," Jacoby explains, taking note of how Mississippi, in 1832, "became the first state to include in its constitution a provision for the popular election of local district attorneys." "By 1859," Jacoby observed, "the trend was clear and irreversible—the prosecutor was a locally elected position." JOAN E. JACOBY, THE AMERICAN PROSECUTOR: A SEARCH FOR IDENTITY 37–38 (1980).

19. *Criminal Discovery Under* Brady v. Maryland: *Current Developments*, THE CALIFORNIA PROSECUTOR, 2013 WL 5910804 (Sept. 18, 2013); *see also* Ma, *supra* note 16, at 203 ("In many states, the change to the elective system of prosecutorial selection came as a result of amendment to the state constitution. In these states, prosecutors simultaneously acquired constitutional status. In 1912, of the 48 states in the union, 38 of them provided for a prosecuting attorney in the state constitution. In the remaining states,

although the constitution did not provide for the office directly, it contained provisions mandating the legislature to establish the office of the prosecuting attorney.") (citation omitted).

20. Ma, *supra* note 16, at 202.

21. Charles C. Olson, *"Pro Bono Publico": A History of Georgia's Prosecuting Attorneys (1732–2012)*, 25 J. S. Legal Hist. 235, 242–43 (2017).

22. *See* People v. Powell, 25 P. 481 (Cal. 1891); State v. Rue, 75 N.W. 235 (Minn. 1893); Gardner v. State, 26 A. 30 (N.J. 1892); State v. Kent, 62 N.W. 631 (N.D. 1895); People v. Tidwell, 12 P. 61 (Utah 1886), *reh'g denied*, 12 P. 638 (Utah 1887); Jackson v. Commonwealth, 30 S.E.2d 452 (Va. 1898).

23. *See* Allen Steinberg, The Transformation of Criminal Justice: Philadelphia, 1800–1880 (1989) (detailing private prosecutions in Philadelphia); *see also id.* at 1–2 ("Private prosecution—one citizen taking another to court without the intervention of the police—was the basis of law enforcement in Philadelphia and an anchor of its legal culture, and this had been so since colonial times."); *id.* at 25 ("Early in the century, private cases were overwhelmingly dominant, but as the decades passed state prosecution became ever more prominent."). Notably, Allen Steinberg defines "private prosecution" as "the system by which private citizens brought criminal cases to the attention of court officials, initiated the process of prosecution, and retained considerable control over the ultimate disposition of cases—especially when compared with the two main executive authorities of criminal justice, the police and the public prosecutor." *Id.* at 5.

24. Domestic disputes short of assault also came before the court. Thus, "parents of young women prosecuted men for seduction; husbands prosecuted their wives' paramours for adultery; wives prosecuted their husbands for desertion." According to an 1863 article published by the Philadelphia Society for Alleviating the Miseries of Public Prisons, honest private prosecutors were quite rare: "Most of the complaints that come before our aldermen are brought by those who seek to gratify personal animosity and a sudden desire of vengeance rather than any wish to punish the wrong-doer for the sake of right." *Id.* at 44, 48, 50, 199. Some private prosecutions in Philadelphia bordered on the bizarre. For example, "Henry Blake's wife prosecuted him for refusing to come to bed and making too much noise, preventing her from sleeping. He was bound over to come to bed when called." *Id.*; *see also id.* at 57 (defining "bound over" as "bound over for trial"). Likewise, a Southwark man "charged a fortune teller with conspiracy for beguiling his wife into believing that for a fee information could be provided about his infidelities." *Id.* (footnote omitted). In effect, private prosecutions "gave citizens the power, in practice, to define crime. Because the minor judiciary let them do so, almost anything that annoyed or irritated a person could be treated as a crime, for whatever motives a prosecutor might have." *Id.* at 77. To discourage abuses of the private prosecution system, Philadelphia did—for decades—tax court costs against unsuccessful private prosecutors. *Id.* at 183; *see also* "August Grand Jury Convenes at Washington," Daily Republican (Monongahela, PA), Aug. 22, 1933, p. 3 ("After delivering the usual charge Judge Hughes directed the Grand Jury's attention to a recent law passed by the last Legislature in which the costs may be placed on the prosecutor when a bill is ignored in a larceny case in which the value of the stolen articles is $100 or under. Heretofore the Grand Jury only had the power to place the costs on the private prosecutor in a larceny case in which the value of the stolen goods was $10 or under. This is optional with the Grand Jury and not mandatory."). Under Philadelphia's system of private prosecution, many defendants sought to control the criminal process by becoming prosecutors themselves and initiating "cross-bills." Steinberg, *supra* note 23, at 46. According to one account: "Lewis Conrad's squirrel was attacked by Benjamin Morris's dog. Conrad kicked the dog, Morris kicked Conrad, and 'a regular scraping took place.' Morris accused Conrad before Alderman Binns, and Conrad brought Morris before Alderman Mitchell. 'The dog and squirrel came off without harm, and have thus far avoided lawsuits,' added the reporter." *Id.* Occasionally such "cross-prosecutions" resulted in dual convictions. *Id.* at 67.

25. *See* Commonwealth v. Williams, 56 Mass. (2 Cush.) 582 (1849) (although a private attorney was permitted to assist the prosecutor at trial, there was no evidence that the private attorney received any pecuniary compensation for his services).

26. Commonwealth v. Gibbs, 70 Mass. (4 Gray) 146 (1855).

27. Commonwealth v. Herman, 149 N.E. 198 (Mass. 1925).

28. *See* Meister v. People, 31 Mich. 99 (1875).

29. People v. Schick, 42 N.W. 1008 (Mich. 1889) (although the record failed to establish that an assistant prosecutor had been retained by private parties, the court stated that even if such facts were established, the questioning of one witness and the argument of one motion would not require reversal).

30. People v. Hillhouse, 45 N.W. 484, 485–86 (Mich. 1890) (regardless of a private prosecutor's fairness toward a criminal defendant, the private prosecutor's participation constituted error).

31. 37 N.W. 244, 245–48 (Wis. 1888).

32. *Id.* at 245.

33. *Id.* at 245–48. In *State v. Peterson*, 218 N.W. 367 (Wis. 1928), a case decided forty years after *Biemel*, the Wisconsin Supreme Court reiterated its disdain for private prosecutors. According to the *Peterson* court:

> In an early day in England private parties prosecuted criminal wrongs which they suffered. They obtained an indictment from a grand jury, and it became the duty and the privilege of the person injured to provide a prosecutor at his own expense to prosecute the indicted person. Our scheme of government has changed all this. It is now deemed the better public policy to provide for the public prosecution of public wrongs without any interference on the part of private parties, although they may have been injured in a private capacity different from the general public injury that accrues to society when a crime is committed. So under our system we have private prosecution for private wrongs and public prosecution for public wrongs.

Id. at 369.

34. Scheldberger v. State, 235 N.W. 419 (Wis. 1931) (a private attorney was permitted to take witnesses' statements and do investigatory work).

35. *See* State v. Scherr, 101 N.W.2d 77 (Wis. 1960); State v. Peterson, 218 N.W. 367 (Wis. 1928); Rock v. Ekern, 156 N.W. 197 (Wis. 1916).

36. *See, e.g.*, Margaret Z. Johns, *Unsupportable and Unjustified: A Critique of Absolute Prosecutorial Immunity*, 80 Fordham L. Rev. 509, 522 (2011) ("The common law as of 1871 did not confer absolute immunity for prosecutorial misconduct. Indeed, no court adopted absolute prosecutorial immunity until 1896—twenty-five years after the adoption of § 1983. In fact, in 1871, although the office of the public prosecutor existed, the private prosecution of crimes was widespread, and both public and private prosecutors were liable or malicious prosecution. Indeed, as one court observed, it was especially appropriate and necessary to hold prosecutors liable for malicious prosecutions given their power and the need to hold them accountable for the abuse of that power."); State v. Rand, 112 P.2d 1034, 1035 (Or. 1941) ("These two sections of the code last mentioned were enacted in 1882 (Laws 1882, page 13), under the following title: 'An act providing for taxing private prosecutors with cost and disbursements of criminal actions when found to be malicious or without probable cause.' It is apparent, both from the title and the body of the 1882 act, that the purpose of enacting that law was to deter the institution of prosecutions malicious or without probable cause, by imposing the costs and disbursements thereof as a penalty."); Darryl K. Brown, *Judicial Power to Regulate Plea Bargaining*, 57 Wm. & Mary L. Rev. 1225, 1246 (2016) ("[P]rivate prosecutors who lost might be ordered to pay the defendant's costs or face liability for malicious prosecution."); "Rawlings Replies in 'Graft' Action—Woodbury County Denies Editor's Activity Invalidated Indictments," Muscatine Journal and News-Tribune (Muscatine, IA), Mar. 20, 1936, p. 1 ("[Woodbury County Attorney M. E.] Rawlings said the section of the Iowa code which requires endorsement by a private prosecutor serves only to make 'such private prosecutor liable for the costs if it is found the prosecution was malicious or without probable cause.'").

37. Rehberg v. Paulk, 566 U.S. 356, 364 (2012) (citations omitted); *compare id.* at 365 ("In the decades after the adoption of the 1871 Civil Rights Act, however, the prosecutorial function was increasingly assumed by public officials, and common-law courts held that public prosecutors, unlike their private predecessors, were absolutely immune from the types of tort claims that an aggrieved or vengeful criminal defendant was most likely to assert, namely, claims for malicious prosecution or defamation.") (citations omitted); *id.* at 365–66 ("This adaptation of prosecutorial immunity accommodated the special needs of public, as opposed to private, prosecutors. Because the daily function of a public prosecutor is to bring criminal charges, tort claims against public prosecutors 'could be expected with some frequency, for a defendant often will transform his resentment at being prosecuted into the ascription of improper and

malicious actions to the State's advocate.' Such 'harassment by unfounded litigation would cause a deflection of the prosecutor's energies from his public duties,' and would result in a severe interference with the administration of an important public office. Constant vulnerability to vexatious litigation would give rise to the 'possibility that [the prosecutor] would shade his decisions instead of exercising the independence of judgment required by his public trust.'") (citations omitted).

38. Vt. St. Ann. § 7259 (provision of Vermont law, titled "Private prosecutors—Liability for and right to costs," reads: "When a person other than an informing officer, becomes a prosecutor, he or she shall enter his or her name and place of residence at the foot of the complaint, information or indictment, and shall be liable to pay costs on such prosecution, and, on conviction, may receive costs."); *see also* Stewart v. Sonneborn, 98 U.S. 187, 198 (1878) (Bradley, J., dissenting) ("[E]very man in the community, if he has probable cause for prosecuting another, has a perfect right, by law, to institute such prosecution, subject only, in the case of private prosecutions, to the penalty of paying the costs if he fails in his suit.").

39. Michael Edmund O'Neill, *Private Vengeance and the Public Good*, 12 U. Pa. J. Const. L. 659, 683 (2010) ("Iowa and North Dakota... have laws prohibiting a private attorney from accepting a fee for prosecuting a criminal case.").

40. William H. Danne, Jr., John A. Gebauer, Thomas Muskus & Alan Weinstein, 27 C.J.S. *District and Prosecuting Attorneys* § 85 (2020) ("By the great weight of authority the court may, in its discretion, permit the prosecuting attorney to have the assistance of counsel employed by the prosecuting witness or other persons interested in securing a conviction; but such appointment, it has been held, can be made only on the request or consent of the prosecuting attorney, which, however, may be presumed from the fact of participation and assistance without objection.").

41. State v. Martineau, 808 A.2d 51, 52 (N.H. 2002) (noting that certain states "allow private prosecutors to *assist* in the prosecution, but only if the public prosecutor consents and retains control over the cases") (citing *Erikson v. Pawnee County Bd. of County Com'rs*, 263 F.3d 1151, 1154 (10th Cir. 2001), *cert. denied*, 535 U.S. 971 (2002); *Com. v. Hubbard*, 777 S.W.2d 882, 883 (Ky. 1989); *State v. Moose*, 310 N.C. 482, 313 S.E.2d 507, 512 (1984); *State v. ex. rel. Koppers v. Intern. Union of Oil, Chemical and Atomic Workers*, 171 W.Va. 290, 298 S.E.2d 827, 829–30 (1982); *Ates v. State*, 141 Fla. 502, 194 So. 286, 286–87 (1939); *Brown v. State*, 242 Ga. 536, 250 S.E.2d 438, 439 (1978); *State v. Addis*, 257 S.C. 482, 186 S.E.2d 415, 417 (1972); *People v. Farnsley*, 53 Ill.2d 537, 293 N.E.2d 600, 605 (1973); *State v. Basham*, 84 S.D. 250, 170 N.W.2d 238, 241 (1969); *Veteto v. State*, 8 S.W.3d 805, 817–18 (Tex. App. 2000)); State v. Eldridge, 951 S.W.2d 775, 780 (Tenn. Ct. Crim. App. 1997) ("The majority of jurisdictions that allow the use of private prosecutors, by statute or case law, require the public prosecutor's consent and retention of control over the case.").

42. *Eldridge*, 951 S.W.2d at 780 (citations omitted); *see also* Fred C. Zacharias, *The Professional Discipline of Prosecutors*, 79 N.C. L. Rev. 721, 724 n.7 (2001) (containing a collection of cases in which part-time prosecutors have been disciplined for participating in both criminal and civil actions).

43. Bennett L. Gershman, *Prosecutorial Ethics and Victims' Rights: The Prosecutor's Duty of Neutrality*, 9 Lewis & Clark L. Rev. 559, 567 (2005) ("A good example of a constitutional violation by a private prosecutor is *Hughes v. Bowers*. In that case, a federal district court vacated the defendant's manslaughter conviction based on the misconduct of a private attorney hired by the victim's family as a 'special prosecutor' to assist the district attorney. Despite a request from the defense for evidence of the existence of insurance policies on the life of the deceased that would have impeached the testimony of relatives of the deceased, the special prosecutor, apparently with the district attorney's knowledge and acquiescence, misled the defense and the court by falsely denying the existence of such policies and then eliciting testimony that no policies existed. The federal court concluded that the presence of a special prosecutor is not constitutionally improper per se, and that a defendant must establish either that the district attorney failed to retain control and management of the case or that the special prosecutor engaged in specific misconduct that prejudiced the defendant's right to a fair trial. The court found that the special prosecutor had a personal financial stake in securing the defendant's conviction, and that his nondisclosure of the existence of the insurance policies constituted prejudicial misconduct.") (citing Hughes v. Bowers, 711 F. Supp. 1574 (N.D. Ga. 1989)).

44. State v. Martineau, 808 A.2d 51, 52 (N.H. 2002) ("Because we conclude that New Hampshire common law prevents a private complainant from prosecuting a class A misdemeanor, which is the charge at

issue in this case, we do not reach the broader constitutional question of whether private prosecutions by an interested party violate a criminal defendant's due process rights."); *id.* at 53 ("Because the legislature has never limited the initiation of the criminal process to public prosecutors, private prosecutions continue to exist as a matter of New Hampshire common law, so long as they are not 'repugnant to the rights and liberties' contained in the constitution."); *id.* at 53–54 ("Although we have never before defined the class of cases private prosecutors may bring, all of the reported decisions that the parties have cited, and that we have been able to find, involving convictions after private criminal prosecutions arose in cases imposing penalties no more severe than a fine.") (citing *State v. Wilson,* 7 N.H. 543 (1835) (military mustering violation); *State v. Tufts,* 56 N.H. 137 (1875) (violation of liquor laws); *State v. Roberts,* 59 N.H. 484 (1879) (catching trout out of season); *State v. Gratta,* 101 N.H. 87, 133 A.2d 482 (1957) (assault); *State v. Merski,* 115 N.H. 48, 49, 333 A.2d 159 (1975) (dog leash law violation)); *id.* at 54 ("We conclude from a review of our case law that the common law does not authorize private prosecutions of criminal offenses which may be punished by imprisonment. Because the complaint in this case charges the defendant with a class A misdemeanor, which carries a potential prison term of up to a year, we hold that Premo is barred from prosecuting the complaint.").

45. Agacoili v. Gonzo, Civil Action No. 09-CV-2147 (DMC), 2010 WL 606697 (D. N.J. Feb. 18, 2010), at *3 n.3 ("'Our courts have not recognized private prosecutions for serious criminal charges since at least 1901.' 'In the modern era, it has been the responsibility of the public prosecutor to investigate and prosecute serious crimes, and it has been the role of the victim or concerned citizen to report knowledge of criminal activities to the proper law enforcement authorities.'") (citations omitted); In re Grand Jury Appearance Request by Loigman, 870 A.2d 249, 253 (N.J. 2005) ("Our courts have not recognized private prosecutions for serious criminal charges since at least 1901. In the modern era, it has been the responsibility of the public prosecutor to investigate and prosecute serious crimes, and it has been the role of the victim or concerned citizen to report knowledge of criminal activities to the proper law enforcement authorities.") (citations omitted).

46. State v. Myerowitz, 108 A.3d 671, 673 (N.J. Super. Ct. 2015) ("conviction for harassment is procedurally defective and cannot stand as matter of law"); *id.* at 673–74 ("The record of the municipal court proceedings presented for de novo review to the Law Division shows that the Secaucus Municipal Court permitted the private attorney retained by the complaining witness to assume the authority ordinarily reserved to duly appointed municipal prosecutors without adhering to the procedural requirements of *Rule* 7:8-7(b)."); *id.* at 674 ("Specifically, the private attorney retained by the complaining witness prosecuted the case against defendant without submitting the certification required by *Rule* 7:8-7(b). The municipal court erred in permitted this private attorney to exercise prosecutorial authority without adhering strictly to the rules governing such practices. Failure to follow the procedures established in *Storm* violated defendant's due process rights and did not 'preserve the integrity of municipal courts, protect the rights of defendants, and [] make the system work.'") (quoting State v. Storm, 661 A.2d 790 (N.J. 1995)); *id.* at 679 ("Our review of the record leads us to conclude that the private attorney who prosecuted this case against defendant did not submit the certification required by *Rule* 7:8-7(b), and was thus not vested with the authority to represent the State at the time she prosecuted defendant. In permitting this attorney to assume the role of prosecutor in this case, the municipal court judge mistakenly relied on a certification this same attorney submitted in support of an application to prosecute a case against defendant's wife, Diana Jeffrey. The Law Division erred in upholding the municipal court judge's decision under these circumstances."); *id.* at 679–80 ("We further hold that the failure of the municipal court to enforce the requirements of *Rule* 7:8-7(b) renders defendant's conviction void *ab initio.* As we stated in *State v. Valentine,* 374 N.J. Super. 292, 297–98, 864 A.2d 433 (App. Div. 2005), judicial oversight in this context and adherence to the requirements of the rule are necessary to prevent a 'structural rift in the framework of the entire judicial process[.]'"); *id.* at 681 ("*Rule* 7:8-7(b) authorizes the municipal court to permit a private attorney to assume the role of municipal prosecutor and represent the State in a particular case, only after determining on the record that certain specific conditions exist, and that the attorney has submitted a certification, in the form approved by the Administrative Director of the Courts, addressing all of the questions contained therein."); *id.* ("In the absence of actual cross-complaints that create an insurmountable conflict of interest for the prosecutor, there are no legal grounds for the municipal court to permit a private attorney to represent the

State. Because public policy favors that prosecutions be conducted by duly appointed independent prosecutors, the municipal court judge should obtain a statement from the municipal prosecutor, on the record, confirming the existence of this conflict of interest, requiring his or her recusal in the case."); *id.* at 682 ("Use of the form approved by the Administrative Director of the Courts is not discretionary. The questions contained in the form, including the precise phraseology used, constitutes the expressed method adopted by the Supreme Court to accommodate the public policy concerns expressed in *Storm, supra*, 141 *N.J.* at 254, 661 *A.*2d 790."); *id.* ("The certification form attached here as Exhibit B was approved by the Administrative Director of the Courts in 1999 to comply with the mandate of *Rule* 7:8–7(b). The certification is electronically available to all of the municipal courts of this State. Municipal Courts have an obligation to provide this certification form to any private attorney seeking leave to assume the role of prosecutor in a given case."); *id.* at 683 ("The municipal court's failure to enforce the requirements of *Rule* 7:8–7(b) rendered defendant's conviction for the petty disorderly offense of harassment void *ab initio*. Thus, we need not reach the remaining issues raised by defendant in this appeal. We remand this matter for a new trial.").

47. Gittler, *supra* note 10, at 127.

48. *See* Jacoby, *supra* note 18, at 3; Sidman, *supra* note 2, at 763; *see also* Ma, *supra* note 16, at 197 ("Official prosecution made its appearance on the continent in the 12th century, but its development was not completed in all detail until the 17th and 18th centuries. Take the development in France, for example. In France, prior to the 12th century, pursuit of crime was a private affair. The law strictly limited the right to bring criminal accusation to the injured party. It was unlawful for any one to bring an accusation except for himself or for his kindred. In murder or homicide cases, the accuser would not be heard if he was not connected with the deceased by blood relationship or if she was not the deceased's wedded wife. The only exception to the rule was that if there were no family members or relatives left to avenge the deceased, the king had the authority to bring the accusation on behalf of the deceased.") (citations omitted).

49. *See* Jacoby, *supra* note 18, at 3; Gittler, *supra* note 10, at 127–129 & n.34; *see also* Ma, *supra* note 16, at 197 ("The French king employed the *procureur du roi* (the king's prosecutor) to protect his own interests. The king's prosecutor would not intervene in criminal matters unless the crime implicated an interest relevant to the king. It was only in rare instances that the public authority would intervene in an efficacious manner."); *id.* at 198 ("Although by the 16th century public prosecution had become an established institution on the European continent, the modern day prosecutorial system was developed in the mid-19th century in the wake of the French Revolution. The basic structure of the French public prosecution was created by the Code of Criminal Procedure of 1808. The influence of the public prosecution service established in the Napoleon era was not confined within the French borders. The French system of public prosecution, like the French Civil Code, was brought to other countries by Napoleon's military expansion."); Cardenas, *supra* note 7, at 370 ("The Dutch civil law employed a public official known as a *schout* to conduct criminal prosecutions. Wherever the Dutch migrated, they were known to take their laws and customs with them; therefore, Dutch settlements in America (Connecticut, New York, New Jersey, Pennsylvania and Delaware) had the services of a *schout*, who was much like a sheriff and public prosecutor."); *id.* ("Scottish influence was extensive in some areas of southern colonial America, with large settlements of colonists of Scottish origin."); *id.* at 371 ("The concept of public prosecution was also well-established in France at the time of America's colonization. The French system of a public prosecutor's office prosecuting all crimes in the king's name can be traced back to the Fifteenth Century. The French did, however, retain private prosecution as a check upon the system of public prosecution; in the event of neglect, inertia or corruption of the public authorities, a crime victim could pursue a private prosecution.").

50. Jacoby, *supra* note 18, at 3.

51. Comment, *Private Prosecution: A Remedy for District Attorneys' Unwarranted Inaction*, 65 Yale L.J. 209, 224 (1955) [hereinafter, "Comment, *Private Prosecution*"].

52. United States v. Stevens, 239 F. Supp.3d 417, 419 (D. Conn. 2017); *see also* Darryl K. Brown, Free Market Criminal Justice: How Democracy and Laissez Faire Undermine the Rule of Law 41 (2016) ("In all modern criminal justice systems today, public officials initiate and control the overwhelming majority of criminal prosecutions. But in all U.S. jurisdictions the public prosecutor's monopoly power seems to be more absolute than in many other advanced democracies.").

53. Carolyn B. Ramsey, *The Discretionary Power of "Public" Prosecutors in Historical Perspective*, 39 Am. Crim. L. Rev. 1309, 1324–25 (2002) ("W. Scott Van Alstyne, Jr. pioneered the influential thesis that the District Attorney had Dutch (rather than English) origins and that New York led the way to state control over prosecution. An official called the *schout*, who doubled as a constable and fiscal agent for the Dutch West India Company, brought criminal charges against defendants as early as 1653 in New Netherland, the colony that later became New York, New Jersey, Connecticut, Delaware, and Pennsylvania. Even after the English seized control of the colony and imposed their laws in 1665, the *schout* continued to bring cases. He now bore the designation of sheriff, and his efforts to exercise prosecutorial power engendered some concern; however, according to Van Alstyne, the English made no serious effort to halt the *schout*'s activities.").

54. Louis J. Palmer, Jr., The Death Penalty: An American Citizen's Guide to Understanding Federal and State Laws 48–49 (1998).

55. Jacoby, *supra* note 18, at 14; "New York's First Charter," Brooklyn Daily Eagle (Brooklyn, NY), Nov. 24, 1901, p. 17 ("In 1650, in a 'provisional order' of the directors of the West India Company, clause 17 states: 'And within the City of New Amsterdam shall be erected a burgher government consisting of a schout, two burgomasters and five schepens.'"); "The Surrogate's Court," The Sun (New York, NY), Mar. 27, 1911, p. 6 ("When the Dutch settled New Amsterdam all judicial power was vested in a council composed of the Director-General, the vice-director and the schout fiscal."); "Lee's History Says Bergen County Was Created in 1675," Evening Record and Bergen County Herald (Hackensack, NJ), Jan. 25, 1917, p. 1 ("'The municipal government of Bergen had been organized upon the 5th of September, 1661, and a schout, an officer holding in part the position of sheriff, judge and district attorney, had been selected by the Dutch authorities at New Amsterdam.'"); "Prosecutor of the Pleas: Story of a 300-Year-Old Office Under Flags of Three Nations," Bergen Evening Record (Hackensack, NJ), Marc. 29, 1937, p. 5 ("Fragmentary and fading documents give a rather hazy picture of the colonial prosecutors in office here from about 1650 to the Revolutionary War. Not until the present century do the records really begin to reveal much about the men charged with prosecuting all the serious and minor criminal offenses which take place each year."); *id.* ("One of the first prosecutors to follow the Dutch Schepens when England whipped the Netherlands for control of the prized New York area was tall, lean, hard Cortlandt Skinner, Crown Prosecutor of Bergen County in 1775 and aristocratic Royal attorney general for King George's thriving colony here."); *id.* ("From 1652 to 1661 the court of Burgomasters and Schepens had jurisdiction over Bergen County for the royal Netherlands government. Dutch prosecutors and judges had to swear to 'maintain the Reformed Religion and no other.' Members of that first ancient court were Tielman Van Vleck, Michael Jansen, Herman Smeeman and Casper Stainmets. An early trial recorded in the minutes of Nov. 11, 1673, resulted in a fine of 250 Dutch guilders against Captain John Berry for taking hogs from Major Kingsland at what is now Lyndhurst. In 1676 the same Captain Berry was commissioned schout or presiding judge of the very court which had convicted him three years before."); *id.* ("In those far off days one-half of all fines went to the prosecutor for his services, one-third of the remaining one-half went to the Dutch church, the second one-third to the poor and the last one-third to the judge.").

56. Jacoby, *supra* note 18, at 14.

57. W. Scott Van Alstyne, Jr., *The District Attorney—A Historical Puzzle*, 1952 Wis. L. Rev. 125, 128–33, 135, 138.

58. Craig B. Little & Christopher P. Sheffield, *Frontiers and Criminal Justice: English Private Prosecution Societies and American Vigilantism in the Eighteenth and Nineteenth Centuries*, 48 Am. Sociological Rev. 796, 804 (1983).

59. Ann-Marie Szymanski, *Stop, Thief! Private Protective Societies in Nineteenth-Century New England*, 78 New England Q. 407, 407–12, 417, 419–24, 434 (2005); *see also id.* at 435–38 (appendix listing all of the protective societies that were formed in New England in Connecticut, Maine, Massachusetts, New Hampshire, Rhode Island and Vermont); *compare id.* at 429 ("After the Civil War, antitheft societies, along with other regional associations, declined more in the urban Northeast than in other, more rural, parts of the country. In New England, most protective societies were either moribund or purely social by the 1880s, and by 1905, most of the remaining ones existed solely as social organizations that held (and in some cases continue to hold) an annual dinner."); *id.* at 430 ("The most likely explanation for this decline is that as

municipal police forces arose in the region's smaller cities and towns, such societies were no longer needed."); PROCEEDINGS OF THE TENTH NATIONAL TEMPERANCE CONVENTION HELD AT SARATOGA SPRINGS, N.Y., JULY 15 AND 16, 1891, at 172 (1891) ("On the 22d day of February, 1883, delegates from eight States, representing more than one hundred law and order leagues, met in Tremont Temple, Boston, and formed 'The Citizens' Law and Order League of the United States.' This association has met annually since that time, inviting all law and order leagues and other societies having kindred objects to send delegates."); 6 EDWARD E. HALE, LEND A HAND: A RECORD OF PROGRESS 6 (1891) ("There are now about twelve hundred law and order leagues in the Unites States and Canada. While our people have been accustomed for many years to associate themselves together for the purpose of influencing legislation, the combination of people for the purpose of influencing executive officers and endeavoring to secure a better administration of the laws is of recent date. It is not easy to learn just when the first of these organizations was formed, nor what particular law was the subject of the first efforts in this direction. The law and order leagues came into being for the especially purpose of securing a better administration of the laws placing restrictions upon the liquor traffic.").

60. Ma, *supra* note 16, at 198–203 (citations omitted).

61. "Complete Text of Supreme Court Opinion Upholding Margiotti's Right to Name Self as Prosecutor," MORNING HERALD (Uniontown, PA), Dec. 12, 1936, p. 3 ("The English common law furnished the basis of American jurisprudence.").

62. "Judge Charges Jury in Trial of Cy Broome," TUCSON CITIZEN (Tucson, AZ), June 22, 1918, p. 3 (noting that former Judge J. H. Campbell was the lead defense lawyer, and reporting a charge that "it is evident that behind the private prosecutors, assisting the county attorney, there is an unseen hand and some money at work" and that "Judge Campbell referred to this 'sinister conspiracy'").

63. "Mr. Williams Explains," L.A. TIMES, Feb. 26, 1907, p. 18 ("All day Tuesday I was about town in my ordinary business. Wednesday while the McKinley case was on trial, I was in Justice Pierce's court while the case was being heard, and saw Attorney Davis, the private prosecutor in the case, and if he looked up he saw me as I passed by him."); "A Strange Set of Affairs at the Bay," SANTA ANA DAILY REGISTER (Santa Ana, CA), Mar. 30, 1907, p. 1 (noting that the mayor and thirteen of the fifteen members of the board of supervisors for San Francisco were under indictment and that "[i]n the place of government by Boss Ruef there is now virtually government by grand jury and a few private citizens who, in the role of private prosecutors and reformers, are holding a big stick over the heads of the indicted supervisors"); "Ruef Squirms Under Guard," L.A. TIMES, Mar. 31, 1907, p. 5 ("For the first time since his capture a month ago at the Trocadero, Abraham Ruef, the indicted political boss of San Francisco, today turned on his prosecutors and unsparingly denounced the 'conspiracy," which he declared responsible for his present plight. Ruef made the following statement to the Associated Press: ... [Ruef] is being prosecuted—not by the regularly elected and duly authorized District Attorney—but by a private lawyer, especially appointed a deputy for the purpose, and a former Secret Service officer who is not even a citizen of this State, both of whom were privately retained and are being privately paid out of a private fund raised and guaranteed by a private citizen—to wit, Rudolph Spreckels."); "Abe Ruef Takes Refuge in Charge of Conspiracy," SUNDAY ADVERTISER (Honolulu, HI), Mar. 31, 1907, p. 1 ("Abe Ruef, in an interview, denounces his prosecutors and declares that he is kept in a private prison, in violation of precedent and legality, is in the care of a private jailor, and is hounded by private prosecutors privately paid; yet he is charged with public offenses."); "Administering Justice as a Private and Personally Conducted Enterprise," OAKLAND TRIBUNE (Oakland, CA), Oct. 7, 1907, p. 6 ("An example of justice as a private and personally conducted enterprise was furnished when the trial of Tirey L. Ford was abruptly halted while the private prosecutor went before the grand jury and had indicted two contract witnesses who had testified contrary to the wishes of the court manager."); "Name of Heney in Bartnett's Letters to Brown Gives Shock," OAKLAND TRIBUNE (Oakland, CA), June 17, 1908, p. 9 ("The spectators in the court room, at the sound of the private prosecutor's name, laughed audibly, and an expression of wonderment could be distinguished upon the faces of many."); "Heney and Ach Again Clash—Private Prosecutor Is Taken to Task for Abusing Witness Not Present to Defend Himself," OAKLAND TRIBUNE, Aug. 7, 1908, p. 11 ("The verbal war which has been going on between Special Prosecutor Francis J. Heney and Attorney Ach, representing Abraham Ruef, in the Burns contempt proceedings before Judge Lawlor, was resumed this morning...."); "Calhoun's Counsel Allege

Heney Has No Right to Act as Prosecutor and that Court Is Biased," OAKLAND TRIBUNE, June 21, 1909, p. 2 ("Heney a Private Prosecutor—'Another reason why we think neither your honor nor Mr. Heney should participate in these trials is because he was appointed at the request of a private prosecutor. The evidence shows that Rudolph Spreckels raised a fund a prosecute these cases, among others.'").

64. "Leftwich Breaks Silence at Last," FORT COLLINS EXPRESS (Fort Collins, CO), June 17, 1909, p. 8 ("The case was conducted on the part of the state by a private prosecutor. It resulted in a hung jury.").

65. "Williams' Case Is Expected to Go to Jury Friday: Final Pleas of Counsel Were Heard During Morning Sitting of the Court," CHARLOTTE NEWS AND EVENING CHRONICLE (Charlotte, NC), Apr. 8, 1921, pp. 1–2 (reporting that in Covington, Georgia, a former congressman, Mr. Howard, was "the paid attorney of 'private prosecutors'" in a murder case against John S. Williams, described as a "county planter," for the murder of an African-American man); "Jury Will Get the Williams Case Today," GASTONIA DAILY GAZETTE (Gastonia, NC), Apr. 8, 1921, p. 1 (reporting the same remarks); "Georgia Murder Case at Climax," CHATTANOOGA NEWS (Chattanooga, TN), Apr. 8, 1921, p. 1 (same); "Williams' Fate May Go the Jury This Eve," SELMA TIMES-JOURNAL (Selma, AL), Apr. 8, 1921, p. 1 (same).

66. "Nurse Will Employ Private Prosecutor—Friends of Polo Player Try to Discredit Charge," EL PASO HERALD-POST (El Paso, TX), Aug. 22, 1933, p. 7.

67. "Russell C. Brown Acquitted," INDIANAPOLIS JOURNAL (Indianapolis, IN), Mar. 21, 1903, p. 7 (noting the employment of a "private prosecutor"); "Demurrer Is Sustained," INDIANAPOLIS NEWS (Indianapolis, IN), Apr. 16, 1918, p. 3 (noting that Judge B. S. Alkman, a circuit court judge, "held it was legal for an individual or group of citizens to hire special prosecutors to return an indictment against and to prosecute 'certain classes of individuals, such as robbers, etc.'").

68. "Mayor Answers Questions," SIOUX CITY JOURNAL (Sioux City, IA), Jan. 7, 1904, p. 6 (taking note of the "Anti-Saloon league" and "private prosecutors"); "Sheriff Finds More Evidence in Kuehl Case—J. B. Simon Identifies Part of Stolen Grapes and May Prosecute," DAILY TIMES (Davenport, IA), Aug. 31, 1921, p. 8 (noting that an allegation of the theft of grapes from a farm would be prosecuted through "a private prosecutor" as there was dissatisfaction "with the work of the county officials in prosecuting the case"); "Private Prosecutors To Be Hired by City Tonight; Grill Spies," DAVENPORT DEMOCRAT AND LEADER (Davenport, IA), Dec. 14, 1921, p. 1 (noting that the law firm of Betty & Betty was to be retained as private prosecutors to push investigation of the misuse of municipal funds); *see also* "Mulct Law in Question," WATERLOO DAILY COURIER (Waterloo, IA), Jan. 20, 1904, p. 1 (noting a challenge to the constitutionality of the Iowa mulct law, and emphasizing that "[t]he petition declares that 'the statutes named are unlawful, unconstitutional and void because under their provisions private prosecutors who are irresponsible, and without the necessity of giving security for costs or of furnishing any bond whatever, without any protection or guard for the rights of citizenship, but merely for the purpose of personal and private gain and for the gratification of personal malice, may be permitted to prosecute and force the defendants or those whom they may allege have violated the provisions of the statutes to incur expense and costs, loss of time and deprive them of their property without due process of law.'").

69. "The Redemption of Shawnee County," TOPEKA DAILY CAPITAL (Topeka, KS), Oct. 31, 1906, p. 4 ("If elected county attorney and sheriff, Frank Foster and John M. Wilkerson will make these offices a positive and active force for the detection, punishment and suppression of crime. They will neither sit idly in their offices waiting for private prosecutors to notify them that crime is being perpetrated under their noses, nor will they discriminate between criminals, being active in the pursuit of some and indifferent to others.").

70. *See* "Scrub Bull to Go on Trial in Lincoln Parish," MONROE NEWS-STAR (Monroe, LA), Nov. 10, 1927, p. 1 ("While it is though[t] that District Attorney Hammons will lead in the prosecution, it is planned to employ strong private prosecutors.").

71. "Police Liable for Costs—Counsel for Board Gives Opinion on Judge Dobler's Decision," THE SUN (Baltimore, MD), Dec. 5, 1902, p. 12 (noting that Mr. Miles' opinion to the Board of Police Commissioners stated in part: "[I]n my judgment, Section 340 of the Baltimore City Charter refers only to private prosecutors at whose instance prosecution may be commenced against an alleged offender, and not to the officers of the law who are charged with making arrests for offenses committed in their presence" and that "the

law ... is meant solely to apply to private prosecutors who, out of malice or without any probable cause, swear out a warrant or commence prosecution against an innocent person.").

72. "Woman's Love Turns to Hate—Suit in Mississippi Follows Attempt at Assassination," St. Louis Post-Dispatch (St. Louis, MO), Feb. 17, 1901, p. 6 (noting that in a Mississippi case, "the state's attorney is assisted by a private prosecutor").

73. "Judgeship Was Burney's Dream," St. Joseph Union-Observer (St. Joseph, MO), Feb. 10, 1033, p. 1 (noting in an obituary for Judge Clarence A. Burney that "he first gained the recognition of the Democratic leaders and lawyers by his vigorous prosecution of fraudulent registration cases in which he had been employed as private prosecutor").

74. "Stories of Witnesses—Good Progress in Tighe Murder Trial," Anaconda Standard (Anaconda, MT), May 23, 1902, p. 7 (noting that the court allowed the participation of a private prosecutor in a murder trial); "Precedent Is Established," Billings Daily Gazette (Billings, MT), Jan. 6, 1903, p. 3 (noting an argument by the counsel about "the case of State vs. Tighe" in which it was emphasized: "One of the errors alleged was that the trial court had permitted private counsel to assist in the prosecution. The supreme court sustained the lower court in this. In his dissent Justice Milburn said that a private prosecutor had been employed by a stranger and represented vengeance, and that the county prosecutor represented law and justice and was a regular officer of the court."); *id.* ("This morning after Clerk Williams had read yesterday's proceedings of the district court Mr. Johnston, attorney for L. M. Hayden, arose and said that he wished to enter an objection to the appearance of O. F. Goddard as associate counsel for the prosecution for the reason that he had not been retained by the county, but appeared as the representative of private parties.... The objection was overruled and Mr. Goddard continues as counsel.").

75. "Recommend Radical Change—Bar Association Makes Points for Legislative Thought," Nebraska State Journal (Lincoln, NE), Nov. 24, 1908, p. 5 ("In districts having populous cities like Lincoln and Omaha, suitable provisions should be made for the requisite number of deputies or assistants. In many districts of the state private prosecutors are required to assist county attorneys. In such districts the expense of the employment of such private prosecutors is greater than the salary of a district attorney.").

76. "Court Proceedings," Asheville Citizen (Asheville, NC), Feb. 14, 1902, p. 1 ("The case of State against Sam Branch and others, charged with a forcible trespass, was resumed today, the trial having been begun yesterday. G. W. Davis is the private prosecutor. The state is assisted in the case by Frank Carter who represents the private prosecution."); "The Argument Is Half Over," News and Observer (Raleigh, NC), Oct. 11, 1903, p. 3 ("It was cruel, declared Mr. Holding. If the State had indicted him for manslaughter, Mr. Haywood would have been saved the trouble and expense of preparing a defense against the charge of murder. The treasury of the State could be drawn on in behalf of private prosecutors, but the defendant had no such treasury to draw upon."); "Ernest Haywood Acquitted. Jury Out Just 15 Minutes," Morning Post (Raleigh, NC), Oct. 15, 1903, p. 1 ("Col. Argo criticized the course of the prosecution showing that the state's duty was not to conceal evidence but to bring out all the facts. The attorneys represented not the state but private prosecutors."); "Not Guilty, the Jury's Verdict," News and Observer (Raleigh, NC), Oct. 15, 1903, p. 4 (noting of Colonel Argo's assertion that there had been a "failure of the State in its duty to the defendant, to the law and to the jury," with these spoken words reported: "The prosecuting attorneys had been bold enough to say they had no apologies to make for appearing on that side, and that they considered it their duty to engage in this prosecution. Duty to whom? They are not sworn officers of the law. They are simple lawyers. To say that out of the forty lawyers in Raleigh only two could be found to prosecute this case was an imputation upon the lawyers of Raleigh, Or else it must be that they exercised their right of discriminating in favor of innocence. What was that duty to come here to Wake county to administer justice? Their duty was merely to their private retainers, the private prosecutors who had employed them."); "Authorities Still in the Air," Greensboro Daily News and Telegram (Greensboro, NC), Sept. 17, 1911, p. 1 (reporting out of Hendersonville, North Carolina: "The Hawkins family today employed the firm of Staten and Rector as private prosecutors to aid in the case."); *accord* "To Fix Night of Death Screams," Durham Recorder (Durham, NC), Sept. 19, 1911, p. 1 (reporting on the retention of the Staten and Rector firm by the Hawkins family).

77. "Steenrod Is Declared 'Not Guilty'—Verdict Was Reached in 45 Minutes," El Reno Daily (El Reno, OK), Sept. 19, 1909, p. 1 (referring to a "private prosecutor hired by the father of the deceased");

"District Court Proceedings," PAULS VALLEY DEMOCRAT (Pauls Valley, OK), Jan. 26, 1911, p. 1 (noting the appearance of a "private prosecutor," R. T. Jones); "Libel Charge Is Quashed by Hoel," PAYNE COUNTY NEWS (Stillwater, OK), July 10, 1931, p. 1 ("[J. M.] Springer was paid for his services by contributions from private citizens, making him a private prosecutor, the defense pointed out.").

78. "Driving on Path—Two Men Charged with Injuring Bicycle Roadway," OREGON STATESMAN (Salem, OR), Jan. 24, 1900, p. 4 (taking note of the use of "private prosecutor" in a case charging two "cattle-buyers" with "injuring a bicycle path in the Lake Labish vicinity, by driving a horse thereupon"); "Was Bound Over," OREGON STATESMAN (Salem, OR), Mar. 8, 1900, p. 2 (noting in a larceny case: "Geo. S. Downing, the private prosecutor, appeared for the state, while John A. Carson conducted the defense"); "Mill City Whiskey," DAILY JOURNAL (Salem, OR), Apr. 6, 1900, p. 3 ("[A] charge was entered against McCarty for selling liquor to a minor, and against Curtis for selling liquor without a license. Curtis took the alarm and skipped out, which seems to be satisfactory to the private prosecutor."); "Additional Local," OREGON MIST (St. Helens, OR), May 4, 1900, p. 3 (noting the settlement of a controversy over property rights where Tony Barber was the "private prosecutor"); *see also* "Win Out Again—The State and Private Prosecutors Get Verdict in Cooper Case," DAILY OREGON STATESMAN (Salem, OR), July 21, 1904, p. 1.

79. PITTSBURG PRESS (Pittsburgh, PA), Jan. 19, 1900, p. 7 (referencing a "private prosecutor" in a case involving an individual hit several times with a blunt instrument); "Fred Bell's Case," DAILY REPUBLICAN (Monongahela, PA), Feb. 22, 1900, p. 1 (noting that Frederick Bell is "[t]he private prosecutor" in a case charging Samuel Senderusky "with aggravated assault and battery, simple assault and battery and malicious mischief," but that "District Attorney Templeton is conducting the prosecution"); "The Grand Jury Makes Its Report," ROGUE RIVER COURIER (Grant's Pass, OR), Oct. 5, 1906, p. 1 (giving the following report of "the grand jury for the County of Josephine, State of Oregon, drawn for the September, 1906, term of the circuit court": "we have examined into many complaints brought by private prosecutors, and returned true bills where justifiable, and dismissed the others"); *accord* "Austin Dam Case Goes Over Again—Private Prosecutor Asks Delay Fearing Trial Now Will Injure His Case," EVENING REPUBLICAN (Meadville, PA), Sept. 23, 1913, p. 1.

80. "Another Chapter Opened in Watertown Robbery Case," SIOUX CITY JOURNAL (Sioux City, IA), Jan. 15, 1904, p. 3 (noting of a charge of perjury that grew out of a criminal prosecution for the robbery of $600 of jewelry in Watertown, South Dakota: "The case has attracted wide attention and is unique. The state's attorney has refused to prosecute, and Dennis O'Connell has hired a private prosecutor.").

81. "Renders a Decision—Governor Russell Honors Requisition for Shemwell," MORNING POST (Raleigh, NC), Apr. 14, 1900, p. 6 ("The question is, shall the Governor refuse to surrender the prisoner if he is satisfied that the prosecution is instituted by private parties in the hope that they will by means of criminal proceedings procure from the defendant the settlement of their claim. The bank of Knoxville, Tenn., from which the money was obtained, is the prosecutor. It seems that the State's attorney in Tennessee required them to become responsible for the costs of the prosecution and that the Governor of Tennessee required the prosecutor to indemnify the State against the expense of the extradition. It is well known that generally in such cases the prosecutor is after his money, and when the defendant offers that, the prosecutor ceases to prosecute and urges the State's attorney to proceed no further.").

82. "Two Noted Cases Now Up in Dallas Courts," EL PASO HERALD (El Paso, TX), July 30, 1901, p. 1 ("The relatives of the deceased policeman have employed a private prosecutor to assist the state."); "Burton Acquitted—Conviction Not Probable, So Attorneys Agreed to It," GALVESTON DAILY NEWS (Galveston, TX), May 31, 1905, p. 4 (noting that in Dallas, Texas news report that two private prosecutors appeared in a case of attempted criminal assault); "Woman To Face Ordeal," FORT WORTH RECORD AND REGISTER (Fort Worth, TX), Sept. 30, 1912, p. 7 (noting that Cullen F. Thomas "will assist the prosecution as private prosecutor" in a woman's trial in Dallas, Texas, for killing her husband); "57 Felony Cases Docketed for Trial in 67th District Court, Beginning Monday," FORT WORTH RECORD (Fort Worth, TX), Sept. 3, 1913, p. 5 ("on account of the 'large array of private prosecutors,' his friends prevailed upon him to retain attorneys for his defense"); "Prosecutors Seek Change of Venue in Weatherford Case," FORT WORTH RECORD (Fort Worth Record), Sept. 9, 1913, p. 2 (noting the appearance of private prosecutors in the case); *accord* "Arson Trials Halted Till May Next Year; Couple Fined $1,000—Private Prosecutors Granted Further Delay in Baptist Church Cases by Judge McKensey at Weatherford," FORT WORTH RECORD (Fort Worth,

TX), Nov. 4, 1913, p. 1; "Klan Members Are Excused from Jury in McKenzie Trial," HOUSTON POST-DISPATCH (Houston, TX), Dec. 16, 1924, p. 5.

83. "Question Is, Will Vacos Escape Rope?", SALT LAKE TRIBUNE (Salt Lake City, UT), Sept. 15, 1909, p. 13 ("Instead of sentencing the prisoner, Judge Howell, after hearing arguments for the state and for the defense, refused absolutely to accept the recommendations of District Attorney Nathan J. Harris and District Attorney Fred Loofbourow of Salt Lake who had been retained by the family of John Contos, the slain man, as a private prosecutor.").

84. "Private Prosecutor Leaves Case Because of Solicitor—D. H. Parsons Withdraws as Private Prosecutor Because, He Charges, Jarrell Refused to Let Him Present Evidence," HIGH POINT ENTERPRISE (High Point, NC), Oct. 15, 1941, p. 5.

85. "Grand Jury Is Probing the Lorena Tragedy—Forty-Six Witnesses Are Summoned Before the Grand Jury in the Lorena Tragedy in Which Louis Crow Was Killed and Sheriff Bob Buchanan and Others Were Wounded," BRYAN DAILY EAGLE (Bryan, TX), Oct. 13, 1921, p. 1 ("'The county attorneys department will handle the investigation before the grand jury without aid from any outside sources,' said County Attorney Frank B. Tirey in connection with the offer of C. S. Farmer's services made by Lorena citizens and of the governor's tender of the 'civil and military forces of the state.' Atto[r]ney Tirey said he would permit no private prosecutor to enter the sanctum off the grand jury while the investigation was in progress."). There was a continual concern with private prosecutors manipulating grand jurors. *E.g.*, "Urges Acquittal of Police Indicted in Whitman Probe," BROOKLYN DAILY EAGLE (Brooklyn, NY), Nov. 25, 1921, p. 3 ("Ex-Judge Leonard Snitkin today before Judge Alfred J. Talley in General Sessions, denounced the Grand Jury system making special reference to the so-called Whitman Grand Jury, and said that those bodies 'were absolute and in the hands of a private prosecutor became dangerous weapons.'").

86. "Help for Solicitors," GREENSBORO PATRIOT (Greensboro, NC), Jan. 30, 1919, p. 4 (after taking note of an attorney's article in the *News and Observer* advocating a plan to employ lawyers to assist solicitors in important cases, *The Greensboro Patriot* wrote: "In our Federal courts no privately employed attorney can appear for the government, and there are many who think we ought to have such a state law. Sometimes strong lawyers are employed by private prosecutors to assist the solicitor—not so much as a matter to see that justice shall be done in the case, but sometimes personal enmity against the defendant is the moving element for private counsel to assist the solicitor."); "Two Murder Cases to Come Up Next Week," ASHEVILLE CITIZEN (Asheville, NC), Nov. 5, 1920, p. 9 (noting that a "Mark W. Brown will appear as private prosecutor" in a case); *cf.* EVENING TELEGRAM (Rocky Mount, NC), Apr. 20, 1939, p. 2 ("In its decision this week, the Supreme court held that five continuances of a criminal prosecution, procured at the instance of the private prosecutor, and extending over 22 months are not evidence of abuse of process where the case originally got into the court on the defendant's appeal from a conviction and there was nothing to show that he objected to the continuances.").

87. "Young Men Will Defy the Gang—Agree to Support W. D. Grimes, Who Announces Candidacy for District Attorneyship," PITTSBURGH DAILY POST (Pittsburgh, PA), Mar. 26, 1906, pp. 1, 5 (noting that Assistant District Attorney William D. Grimes, in announcing his candidacy for District Attorney, said this: "The office of district attorney is one of the most powerful that belongs to our system of government. Its influence upon the conditions of a community, political, social and moral, is of the utmost importance. In addition to the conduct of criminal cases to the number of 5,000 and upward in this community every year, which are instituted by private prosecutors, it is important to understand what appears to be not generally known, even to the profession: that the district attorney has a vast reserve power in instituting proceedings and investigations in behalf of the public interest on occasions of great public concern."; "The reluctance of private prosecutors to commence criminal prosecutions is as strong now as ever for various reasons. A district attorney with an adequate conception of his powers and a full sense of his responsibility in this behalf, is a prime necessity in the present aroused state of the public conscience."); "Grimes Puts His Case Up to Voters—He Announces His Candidacy for the Office of District Attorney," GAZETTE TIMES (Pittsburgh, PA), Mar. 31, 1913, p. 8 ("In addition to the routine cases which are instituted by private prosecutors, there is a vast reserve power in the district attorney in instituting proceedings and investigations in behalf of the public interest, and which on proper occasions can be exercised to the advantage of the community."); *compare* "Grimes Resigns Job to Probe Frauds," PITTSBURGH POST (Pittsburgh, PA),

Sept. 19, 1906, p. 3 (noting that William D. Grimes, a candidate for District Attorney, alleged "many frauds being unearthed in the returns of the recent Republican primary election," and that Mr. Grimes' letter of resignation read in part: "As it is almost impossible for a private prosecutor to successfully carry such cases through the criminal courts, and as I have a sufficient number of cases to make the matter one of great public importance, my attorneys advise the placing of them in the hands of the district attorney."); *see also* "Fuller Comments on Sacco-Vanzetti," WILKES-BARRE TIMES LEADER (Wilkes-Barre, PA), Aug. 22, 1927, p. 2 (a judge observed in a grand jury charge: "You are one of the links in the legal chain between the preparation of crime and its punishment, viz:... Information of complaint, often by public officer, but commonly by private prosecutor accompanied by a warrant of arrest.").

88. "Railey Trial On," HOUSTON POST (Houston, TX), Oct. 22, 1907, p. 5; "Earl McFarlane Hearing," HOUSTON POST (Houston, TX), Apr. 13, 1910, p. 11; "Clay County District Court Proceedings," WICHITA DAILY TIMES (Wichita Falls, TX), May 4, 1914, p. 4.

89. Comment, *Private Prosecution*, *supra* note 51, at 210–11.

90. "Personal Shorts," PHILADELPHIA INQUIRER (Philadelphia, PA), July 25, 1905, p. 8; *compare* "Personal Shorts," PHILADELPHIA INQUIRER (Philadelphia, PA), Dec. 8, 1909, p. 14 ("'J. K.'—A person wrongfully arrested and subsequently acquitted has a right of action against the private prosecutor. If there are certain elements in the case; but the State of Pennsylvania is not required to pay out damages under any such facts.").

91. "'Peculiar Conception of Duty,'" WYOMING DEMOCRAT (Tunknannock, PA), Sept. 7, 1906, p. 3 ("All criminal cases have to have a prosecutor; either an officer or private citizen, and many persons to their sorrow have found after furnishing evidence through officers that the jury returned a verdict that they were the real prosecutors and placed the costs on them. A cursory examination of the indictments found in this county will show that more than half, probably three-fourths, are brought by private prosecutors.").

92. "Doings of the Court," DAILY TIMES (Mauch Chuck, PA), Apr. 12, 1924, p. 1; "One Held for Green County Man's Killing," DAILY NOTES (Canonsburg, PA), Nov. 11, 1936, p. 6; "Grindstone Pair Wins Acquittal in Murder Case," MORNING HERALD (Uniontown, PA) Mar. 4, 1943, p. 2.

93. "The Retreat of the Mayor," PHILADELPHIA INQUIRER (Philadelphia, PA), Apr. 12, 1906, p. 8.

94. "Nearing the Close—Epting Trial, as Side Line to the Boyce-Sneed Case, About Over," TUSLA WEEKLY DEMOCRAT (Tulsa, OK), Jan. 23, 1913, p. 1; *see also* "State Will Be Ready—Selection of Veniremen in Sneed Case to Begin Today," WACO MORNING NEWS (Waco, TX), Feb. 11, 1913, p. 5 ("Private prosecutors had asked for time to ascertain whether certain important witnesses would be present. [District Attorney] Spencer disagreed with the private prosecutors this afternoon and determined to act. He said that the state desires no unnecessary delay.").

95. Byron Ford, "Argument Heard in Epstein Case," NEWS AND OBSERVER (Raleigh, NC), Dec. 9, 1916, p. 3.

96. "Judge Will Not Hear Evidence," YORK GAZETTE (York, PA), Apr. 9, 1918, p. 6 ("The district attorney is the proper officer before whom to lay the facts, when no private prosecutor desires to assume the responsibility of bringing an information. If the facts are sufficient to warrant the prosecution, it will then be ordered and conducted by the district attorney officially.").

97. "The Position of District Attorney Bell," PHILADELPHIA INQUIRER, July 21, 1906, p. 8; *see also id.* ("This power, which is really in contravention of the principles of the Constitution, guaranteeing a preliminary hearing to everyone accused of crime, is rarely exercised. George S. Graham has declared publicly that he never filed such a District Attorney's bill in the eighteen years of his service. Yet, this was the extraordinary procedure which it was first demanded by Mayor Weaver and Mr. Gordon that Mr. Bell should take. This he declined to do."); "Bell Not to Act in City Trust," PHILADELPHIA INQUIRER, Sept. 22, 1906, p. 16 (noting that a letter of John C. Bell, the District Attorney, who declined to take criminal action against the treasurer of the City Trust who swore to the financial health of a company before its failure, read as follows: "I do not, of course, wish or intend this decision by me to be construed as precluding the bringing of any criminal action by any private prosecutor....").

98. "The Position of District Attorney Bell," PHILADELPHIA INQUIRER, July 21, 1906, p. 8; *see also* "Needed Legislation," PITTSBURGH POST, Sept. 2, 1906, p. 8 ("Although the press was full of charges of dishonesty against the contractors for the Philadelphia filtration plant, the district attorney of that city held

that it was not his duty to institute proceedings against the accused men, but that some private prosecutor must undertake the task."). In a very different forum, at a Law Enforcement League gathering in Mississippi, the inherent limitations of private prosecutions were described this way, however: "For crimes of certain kinds there is always some interested private prosecutor, as in the case of a murder, when the victim's relatives are interested, or that of a man whose person or property is injured. But other offenses do not produce a prosecutor because all who know it are interested to conceal it, resorting to perjury if necessary." The Law Enforcement League," JACKSON DAILY NEWS (Jackson, Mississippi), Feb. 20, 1909, p. 5.

99. Comment, *Private Prosecution, supra* note 51, at 218–19.

100. *Id.* at 219 n. 51 (citing Commonwealth v. Williams, 56 Mass. 582 (1849) (dictum); Meister v. People, 31 Mich. 99 (1875); Biemel v. State, 71 Wis. 444, 37 N.W. 244 (1888) & Commonwealth v. Herman, 253 Mass. 516, 149 N.E. 198 (1925) (no reversible error if a private attorney occupies the district attorney's trial table to confer with the prosecutor); Commonwealth v Knapp, 27 Mass. (10 Pick.) 477 (1830) (conviction approved since the private assistant, Daniel Webster, was a volunteer and received no compensation from any interested party); People v. Schick, 75 Mich. 592, 42 N.W. 1008 (1889) (privately hired attorney permitted to ask a few questions and argue a motion to quash the indictment); People v. Bemis, 51 Mich. 422, 16 N.W. 794 (1883) (Board of County Commissioners permitted to hire a private prosecutor); Scheldberger v. State, 204 Wis. 235, 235 N.W. 419 (1931) (investigation and taking statements from witnesses by a private attorney are proper)).

101. Comment, *Private Prosecution, supra* note 51, at 221; *see also id.* at 221–22 ("*Questionnaire* responses disclosed that in at least twenty-eight states, it is a common practice for private attorneys to prosecute criminal actions in the lesser courts. Since these courts customarily have jurisdiction over all misdemeanors, private citizens may initiate criminal actions which result in jail terms up to one year. In many states the latitude of private prosecutors is extended by the fact that the public prosecutor need not attend such courts unless the presiding official requests his appearance. If the district attorney chooses, he can control the proceedings in these courts; in his absence, a private attorney is in complete charge of the prosecution. Some states fortify private prosecution in these courts by statutes which prohibit exclusion by a public prosecutor of assisting private attorneys.").

102. *Id.* at 219; *see also id.* ("A few states have enacted statutes that give private parties the right to hire assistant prosecutors."); *id.* at 219 n.55 ("Under KAN. GEN. STAT. § 19-717 (1949), counsel hired by the prosecuting witness on any type of action will be recognized as the associate prosecutor. Minnesota and New Jersey statutes authorize any private citizen to hire an attorney to assist the public prosecutor in enforcing election laws. MINN. STAT. ANN. § 211.33 (West 1947); N.J. STAT. ANN. § 19:34-63 (1940). W. VA. CODE ANN. § 404 (1955) implies that a private citizen has a right to hire an assistant prosecutor.").

103. *Id.* at 219–20; *see also id.* at 220–21 ("Through his role as assistant prosecutor, the private attorney frequently controls the criminal action. Many states permit privately hired counsel to conduct criminal prosecutions alone with the permission of the public prosecutor and the trial court. While most jurisdictions require that the public prosecutor be present to supervise, no limitation has been imposed on the scope or extent of the private prosecutor's activities. In response to the *questionnaire*, many prosecutors stated that they permit private attorneys to control criminal prosecutions. Unless the privately hired attorney violates the defendant's right to a fair trial by using unfair tactics, appellate courts will not ordinarily reverse a successful private prosecution. However, some courts will reverse a conviction if the relationship between the accused and private prosecutor or hiring citizen might have produced unfairness.").

104. "Mr. Hoffman's Valedictory," THE CHARLESTON COURIER (Charleston, SC), May 26, 1835, p. 2 ("From the N.Y. Com. Adv., May 18); CHARLES WARREN, A HISTORY OF THE AMERICAN BAR 369 n.1 (1911).

105. "Great Tribute from the Bar to Samuel P. Rotan," PHILADELPHIA INQUIRER, Oct. 1, 1909, pp. 1, 6.

106. PHILADELPHIA INQUIRER, Oct. 26, 1909, p. 2.

107. "Assault and Battery—A Horse Trainer and a Doctor Come to Blows," DAILY OREGON STATESMAN (Salem, OR), Apr. 26, 1901, p. 3; "Justice Trial," DAILY JOURNAL (Salem, OR), Aug. 26, 1901, p. 4; "In the Minor Courts—Sam Castro Tried for Assault and Battery," DAILY OREGON STATESMAN (Salem, OR), Aug. 27, 1901, p. 3; "Was Found Guilty—Edward Gregory Convicted of Assault and Battery," DAILY OREGON STATESMAN (Salem, OR), Dec. 27, 1901, p. 3; "His Own Juryman," ALBANY DEMOCRAT (Albany, OR),

Feb. 16, 1906, p. 4; "Homicide Case Is Still Unfinished," Daily Republican (Monongahela, PA), Feb. 17, 1906, p. 1; "Local Negro Found Guilty of Serious Crime and Sentenced This Afternoon—Deputy Gibson Acquitted—Stonerod Case Still On," Monongahela Valley Republican (Monongahela, PA), Nov. 21, 1906, p. 1; "Woman Must Serve Time for Beating Teacher—Fine of $5 and 10 Days in Jail Meted Out to Washington Mother," Pittsburgh Sunday Post (Pittsburgh, PA), Jan. 13, 1907, p. 1; "True Bill Returned by Grand Jury," Daily Republican (Monongahela, PA), May 10, 1907, p. 1; "Three Years in Penitentiary," Daily Notes (Canonsburg, PA), May 15, 1907, p. 1; "Four Months for Webster—Young Colored Man Pleads Guilty to Charge Against Him," Daily Notes (Canonsburg, PA), June 5, 1907, p. 1; "Grand Jury Grinds Out True Bills," Daily Notes (Canonsburg, PA), Aug. 11, 1909, p. 1; "Grand Jury Work," Daily Republican (Monongahela, PA), Aug. 12, 1909, p. 1; "Ritson's Bail Is Fixed at $1,000," Daily Notes (Canonsburg, PA), Sept. 10, 1909, p. 1; "The Grand Jury Indicts Anderson," Daily Notes (Canonsburg, PA), May 5, 1910, p. 1; "Several Local Cases Heard," Daily Republican (Monongahela, PA), May 14, 1910, p. 1; "Third Offense Is Costly to Miller," Daily Notes (Canonsburg, PA), Feb. 13, 1914, p. 1; "Criminal Court List Completed Yesterday," Daily Republican (Monongahela, PA), May 14, 1921, p. 1; "Two Defendants Take Appeal," Huntsville Times (Huntsville, AL), June 15, 1927, p. 8; "Brown Released, Battery Charges—Claims Johnson Hit First in Beer Parlor Row; Circus Man Held," Oregon Statesman (Salem, OR), Aug. 18, 1936, p. 7.

108. "Gibson Held to Answer," Daily Oregon Statesman (Salem, OR), July 31, 1902, p. 6; "Verdicts Returned Today," Daily Notes (Canonsburg, PA), Sept. 2, 1905, p. 1; "Would Be Murderer Bound Over to Grand Jury," Coos Bay Times (Marshfield, OR), July 4, 1907, p. 1; "Three Local Cases Were Heard," Daily Republican (Monongahela, PA), July 11, 1907, p. 4; Daily Notes (Canonsburg, PA), Nov. 12, 1908, p. 1. The wife was described as the private prosecutor in various instances. *E.g.*, Daily Notes (Canonsburg, PA), Feb. 12, 1908, p. 5; "City News," Daily Capital Journal (Salem, OR), Sept. 8, 1909, p. 8.

109. "Two Pleaders Sentenced," Daily Republican (Monongahela, PA), Nov. 30, 1909, p. 1.

110. Crimes victims or those who sought to prosecute offenders became known as "private prosecutors." *Cf.* "Criminal Court Began Trial of Cases Today," Daily Notes (Canonsburg, PA), Feb. 13, 1905, p. 1 ("There are not many cases of much importance at this term and consequently there will not be many attorneys figure in court. The private prosecutors in almost every case will be represented by the commonwealth's representative, District Attorney Owen C. Underwood."). In Pennsylvania, they were required to sign the bill of indictment; in Oregon, the private prosecutor was named in the indictment. "District Attorney Tells Law Academy of the Various Modes of Instituting Criminal Proceedings," Philadelphia Inquirer (Philadelphia, PA), May 28, 1904, p. 6 (noting of District Attorney John C. Bell's address to eminent jurists and members of the bar in Horticultural Hall at the annual meeting of the Law Academy: "Allusion is not infrequently made to the District Attorney as the public prosecutor. The term is in a sense misleading, and somewhat anomalous in a jurisdiction where—in all cases save the few exceptional ones already noted—it is the right by express legislative enactment of the person accused to refuse to plead until the name of the private prosecutor is indorsed on the bill of indictment—so zealously indeed are the rights of the accused citizen protected, for it is the policy of the law that there shall be a responsible prosecutor."); "Poaching Charged," Daily East Oregonian (Pendleton, OR), Apr. 6, 1906, p. 8 ("In the indictments, O. F. Turner is named as private prosecutor...."); "Deer Slayers Are Heavily Fined," Evening Statesman (Walla Walla, WA), Apr. 9, 1906, p. 3 ("O. F. Turner, recently appointed deputy game warden, was principally instrumental in bringing the men to justice, and his name appeared as private prosecutor in the indictment."). *See also* Daily Oregon Statesman (Salem, OR), June 10, 1904, p. 1 ("'The men upon whom warrants were served, appeared in court yesterday afternoon at 1:30 o'clock and demanded that the private prosecutor appear in court before they would enter their pleas.").

111. "Up for Assault," Daily Oregon Statesman (Salem, OR), Mar. 16, 1904, p. 1.

112. "Sentences Imposed on Pleas of Guilty," Daily Notes (Canonsburg, PA), Feb. 7, 1905, p. 1. *See also* "Criminal Cases Being Disposed of Rapidly," Daily Notes (Canonsburg, PA), Feb. 17, 1905, p. 1 ("Henry Swickey is being tried before Judge Taylor on a charge of assault and battery. The private prosecutor is A. C. Campbell. The trouble occurred in a barber shop in the river town, Swickey alleging that Campbell struck him on the head with a black jack which was offered in evidence in court.").

113. "Weston," Spokesman-Review (Spokane, WA), Jan. 2, 1906, p. 9; "Arrested as He Left Prison," Daily Notes (Canonsburg, PA), Mar. 10, 1905, p. 1; "Goes Up for Four Years," Daily Notes (Canonsburg, PA), May 2, 1905, p. 1; "True Bill Found Against James Love," Daily Republican (Monongahela, PA), May 4, 1905, p. 1; "Basil Brown Is Placed o[n] Trial," Daily Notes (Canonsburg, PA), May 11, 1905, p. 1; "Monongahela Cases at Court," Daily Republican (Monongahela, PA), Aug. 15, 1905, p. 4; "Wilbur Sharp Trial Begins," Daily Notes (Canonsburg, PA), Nov. 17, 1905, p. 1; "Reforms in Morrow County," Daily East Oregonian (Pendleton, OR), Nov. 28, 1905, p. 8; "Supreme Court Opens Its Term," Pittsburgh Post (Pittsburgh, PA), Oct. 10, 1906, p. 3; "Murder Trial Began Today," Daily Notes (Canonsburg, PA), Feb. 18, 1907, p. 1; "Coal Bluff Murder Case on Trial," Daily Republican (Monongahela, PA), Feb. 19, 1907, p. 1; "Fourteen Charges Will Be Brought Against Former Cashier of Defunct Bank," Daily Notes (Canonsburg, PA), May 10, 1907, p. 6; "Case Is Called, Paxton Absent," Daily Notes (Canonsburg, PA), Aug. 20, 1908, p. 1; "Local News Notes," Daily Republican (Monongahela, PA), Nov. 12, 1908, p. 1; "Underwood Failed to Put in Appearance," Daily Republican (Monongahela, PA), Feb. 10, 1909, p. 1; Daily Republican (Monongahela, PA), Feb. 16, 1909, p. 1; "Court Instructed Jury to Return Verdict of Not Guilty for Underwood," Daily Republican (Monongahela, PA), May 11, 1909, p. 1; "Criminal Court Is Still Busy," Daily Republican (Monongahela, PA), May 14, 1909, p. 1; "Italians Not Guilty," Daily Notes (Canonsburg, PA), May 15, 1909, p. 1; "Kises Not Guilty," Daily Republican (Monongahela, PA), Aug. 20, 1909, p. 4; "Many Cases Were Heard on Friday," Daily Republican (Monongahela, PA), Nov. 11, 1911, p. 1; Daily Republican (Monongahela, PA), Aug. 14, 1912, p. 4; "Raleigh Sharp Is Arrested Here," Semi-Weekly Democrat (Albany, OR), Feb. 21, 1913, p. 3; "Local Hotel Men Indicted Yesterday," Daily Republican (Monongahela, PA), Nov. 8, 1921, p. 1.

114. "Many True Bills Being Returned," Daily Notes (Canonsburg, PA), Aug. 16, 1905, p. 1; "Finds True Bill vs. Clara Fields," Monongahela Valley Republican (Monongahela, PA), Aug. 17, 1905, p. 3; *see also* "Important Cases Come Up Next Week," Daily Republican (Monongahela, PA), Nov. 13, 1905, p. 1 ("Chief Logan is the private prosecutor. On Tuesday of next week but one case is listed, that of Joe Delmarsio, charged by County Detective McCleary with the murder of Chas. Dalfi. On Wednesday the case of Clara Fields is scheduled. She is charged with murder and concealing a bastard child."); *see also* "Constable Fee Case," Wilkes-Barre Semi-Weekly Record (Wilkes-Barre, PA), Mar. 20, 1906, p. 6.

115. "Young Girl Being Tried for Murder," Daily Notes (Canonsburg, PA), Nov. 22, 1905, p. 1.

116. "Three Local Cases Were Heard," Daily Republican (Monongahela, PA), July 11, 1907, p. 4.

117. "Newsy Notes," Daily Republican (Monongahela, PA), Nov. 18, 1905, p. 4.

118. "Grand Jury Found Many True Bills," Daily Republican (Monongahela, PA), Nov. 10, 1911, p. 1; *see also* "Rosemovicz Faces Jury for Murder," Evening News (Wilkes-Barre, PA), Apr. 22, 1912, p. 1 (referring to Chief of Police Killeen as "the private prosecutor in the case" of "a bad gang of criminals who infest a couple of the West Side towns").

119. "To Workhouse One Year," Daily Republican (Monongahela, PA), May 10, 1912, p. 1.

120. "Condemn Police as Prosecutors," Pottsville Republican (Pottsville, PA), Jan. 7, 1922, p. 1.

121. "Court Will Hear Licenses on Tuesday," Evening Herald (Shenandoah, PA), Jan. 7, 1922, p. 3.

122. *E.g.*, "Jury Fails to Agree in Trial of Edith Grebe," Oregon Statesman (Salem, OR), Nov. 5, 1921, p. 4 ("Barney Goldstein of Portland appeared as private prosecutor in the case, collaborating with District Attorney Carson."). The views of district attorneys and private prosecutors could diverge, of course. *Cf.* "Jetton Found Not Guilty of Murder," Charlotte Daily Observer (Charlotte, NC), Feb. 22, 1914, p. 7 ("Mr. Cansler declared that while he did not know what the mouthpiece of the State of North Carolina was going to ask, he did know that not one of the private prosecutors had had the nerve to stand up and ask the jury to return a verdict of murder in the first degree. The most they had done was to beg that he be not allowed to go free, but should be convicted of some crime.").

123. "Coal Bluff Murder Case on Trial," Monongahela Valley Republican (Monongahela, PA), Feb. 21, 1907, p. 4. Sometimes, however, the constables were the criminal defendants in cases brought by private prosecutors. *E.g.*, "Constable Acquitted of Assault," Daily Notes (Canonsburg, PA), Aug. 23, 1913, p. 1.

124. "Court Concludes with Guilty Plea," Jeffersonian Democrat (Brookville, PA), Sept. 23, 1954, p. 1.

125. Gazette Times (Pittsburgh, PA), Sept. 4, 1906, p. 3.

126. "Case Closed on Testimony," Daily Notes (Canonsburg, PA), Nov. 16, 1906, p. 1; "Revoked Application," Daily Republican (Monongahela, PA), Nov. 13, 1907, p. 1; "Attacks the Law," Houston Post (Houston, TX), June 28, 1908, p. 1; "Lenhart Case Being Heard in Criminal Court," Daily Notes (Canonsburg, PA), Aug. 25, 1908, p. 1; "Remanded to Jail—Henry Becker Must Stand Trial for Attempted Arson," Lebanon Daily News (Lebanon, PA), Nov. 24, 1909, p. 1.

127. "Clutter Case Taken Up," Daily Notes (Canonsburg, PA), Feb. 20, 1907, p. 1; "Washington Constable Convicted," Daily Republican (Monongahela, PA), Feb. 22, 1907, p. 1.

128. "City Urged to Hire Private Prosecutor in Reservoir Cases," Fort Worth Record (Fort Worth, TX), Aug. 5, 1913, p. 5; *see also* "Gillespie Will Be Retained, Says Milam—Former Congressman to Prosecute Dam Cases for City," Fort Worth Star-Telegram (Fort Worth, TX), Aug. 6, 1913, p. 7 ("Mayor Milam said Wednesday the retaining of O. W. Gillespie as private prosecutor in the reservoir cases is certain, although the city commission has not formally approved the mayor's arrangement with the former congressman.").

129. *E.g.*, "Is No Verdict—Jury Disagreed in Trial of Harvey Walker for Assault and Battery," Daily Oregon Statesman (Salem, OR), Apr. 20, 1904, p. 1; "County Court Miscellany," Monongahela Valley Republican (Monongahela, PA), May 11, 1905, p. 3; "Assault and Battery," Daily Republican (Monongahela, PA), Mar. 24, 1906, p. 1; "Assault and Battery," Monongahela Valley Republican (Monongahela, PA), Mar. 29, 1906, p. 3; "Had Beginning in Dance Hall," Scranton Times (Scranton, PA), Feb. 8, 1907, p. 5; "Jas. King Fined $1 and the Costs," Daily Notes (Canonsburg, PA), Feb. 12, 1907, p. 1; "Polish Girl Held for Court Action," Daily Notes (Canonsburg, PA), Aug. 19, 1931, p. 3.

130. "Local Cases Heard Yesterday," Daily Republican (Monongahela, PA), Aug. 28, 1911, p. 1; "Local Case Being Heard," Daily Republican (Monongahela, PA), Aug. 30, 1911, p. 1.

131. *E.g.*, "Salem Justice Court," Daily Journal (Salem, OR), Sept. 23, 1901, p. 4; "Court Sentences," Canonsburg Notes (Canonsburg, PA), Aug. 27, 1902, p. 1; "Haberly Placed under Arrest," Oregon Daily Journal (Portland, OR), May 30, 19030, p. 15; "Are Arrested for Larceny," Daily Oregon Statesman (Salem, OR), May 30, 1903, p. 3; "Ryan Found Guilty," Daily Capital Journal (Salem, OR), Jan. 5, 1905, p. 5; "Colored Boy Is Convicted," Daily Notes (Canonsburg, PA), May 12, 1905, p. 1; "Local Cases in Criminal Court," Daily Notes (Canonsburg, PA), Feb. 15, 1907, p. 1; "Hopkins Is Sent to Dixmont," Daily Republican (Monongahela, PA), May 16, 1907, p. 1; "Bradley Is Given Eight-Month Term," Daily Notes (Canonsburg, PA), Feb. 4, 1908, p. 1; "Sent to Huntington," Daily Republican (Monongahela, PA), Apr. 13, 1909, p. 1; "Not Guilty, Wilquit Plea," Capital Journal (Salem, OR), Nov. 23, 1922, p. 1; "Accuse Ben Jory of Theft of Mule," La Grande Evening Observer (La Grande, OR), June 13, 1932, p. 1; "Case Dismissed," Oregon Statesman (Salem, OR), Oct. 21, 1932, p. 5.

132. "Murder Cases for Next Week," Daily Notes (Canonsburg, PA), Feb. 16, 1907, p. 1.

133. "'You're a Liar by the Clock,' Yells Plaintiff and Case Is Continued," Daily Notes (Canonsburg, PA), Nov. 16, 1925, p. 3.

134. "Threat Charge Case Continued—Marcenkus Offers to Make Apology but Prosecutor Wants Case Tried," Oregon Statesman (Salem, OR), p. 5 ("Insistence of Josephine Yankauskas, private prosecutor, that the case be tried led to postponement yesterday of disposition of the state's charge against Charlie Marcenkus of pointing a firearm at her. After seeking unsuccessfully to get the matter settled, Judge L. H. McMahan continued the case for jury trial. Marcenkus offered to make amends by apology or some other manner.").

135. "Graft Postponement Stirs Luzerne Co.—Private Prosecutor Disgusted Because of Latest Halt in Proceedings and Alleges Insincerity," Philadelphia Inquirer, June 22, 1911, p. 1; *see also* "Clancy Is Visitor of Valentine—Tells District Attorney He Is Now Ready to Fight Cases," Evening News (Wilkes-Barre, PA), Sept. 12, 1911, p. 1 ("'We have lost in our attempt to get different counsel in the court house cases, and will now go on and do the best we can' was the statement of Thomas B. Clancy, of New York, the private prosecutor who yesterday tried to get rid of District Attorney W. Alfred Valentine, whom he said he did not believe should be given charge of the cases.").

136. "Several Cases of Interest," Daily Republican (Monongahela, PA), Nov. 5, 1909, p. 1.

137. "Harris Murder Case" HOUSTON POST (Houston, TX), Feb. 23, 1904, p. 8 (noting the involvement of a "private prosecutor"); Trial Finished," HOUSTON POST, July 9, 1922, p. 28 (same); "Jury in the Carlile Case Is in Deadlock," MARSHALL MORNING NEWS (Marshall, TX), Nov. 26, 1925, p. 1; "Sneed Prosecutor Pleads to Jury for Death Verdict," FORT WORTH STAR-TELEGRAM (Fort Worth, TX), Nov. 29, 1912, p. 1 ("Sitting directly behind County Attorney Baskin and the private prosecutors was Mrs. Al G. Boyce Sr., widow of the man Beal Sneed killed, and Miss Mary Hamilton and James Burrows, her cousins."); "James Callan Murder Case Given to Jury," FORT WORTH STAR-TELEGRAM, May 16, 1920, p. 1 ("The conclusion of a two hours' speech by Attorney Blanton, private prosecutor, the James Callan murder case went to the jury Saturday afternoon."); *see also* "Soon to Fix Date for M'Mahon Trial," CAMDEN POST-TELEGRAM (Camden, NJ), Sept. 6, 1911, p. 10; "No Verdict in Hefner Case," MORNING STAR (Wilmington, NC), Aug. 2, 1912, p. 6; *cf.* "Girl, 16, on Trial for Killing Father," EVENING PUBLIC LEDGER (Philadelphia, PA), Jan. 12, 1922, p. 1 (noting that "there is a hint that a private prosecutor will appear" and might try the case).

138. "Austin Cases All Quashed," ELMIRA STAR-GAZETTE (Elmira, NY), Dec. 9, 1913, p. 2 (noting of a Pennsylvania case: "Private prosecutors presented petitions requesting the step on the ground that they believed that there could be no conviction of the defendants for involuntary manslaughter under the facts in the case. Settlements of the civil actions for damages against the company opened the way for securing the consent of the private prosecutors to drop the criminal cases."); "Brooklyn Man Held in Highway Wreck," EVENING TELEGRAM (Rocky Mount, NC), Jan. 13, 1937, p. 3 (taking note of a private prosecutor in Edgecombe County superior court in a manslaughter case arising out of a highway accident); "Judge Sets Aside Part of Verdict—Directs County, Instead of Prosecutor, To Share Costs in Manslaughter Trial of Two Men," GAZETTE AND BULLETIN (Williamsport, PA), Nov. 30, 1937, p. 2 (noting a private prosecutor, County Detective Roy Wilcox, in the context of a manslaughter case); "Joe Small Gets Prison Sentence," EVENING TELEGRAM (Rocky Mount, NC), Mar. 15, 1939, p. 9 (noting a guilty plea in a manslaughter case, with it noted that an attorney assisted the solicitor as "private prosecutor").

139. "Harris to Appeal to Supreme Court—Attorneys Seek to Have Death Sentence Commuted for Condemned Man," BIRMINGHAM NEWS (Birmingham, AL), Nov. 24, 1920, p. 28; "More on Norris," READING TIMES (Reading, PA), Jan. 25, 1927, p. 16; "Rehearing in Death Case Reversals Sought," VERNON DAILY RECORD (Vernon, TX), Dec. 23, 1929, p. 1.

140. "His Own Blood Is Against Him in Murder Case—George Briggs Goes to Trial Next Week at West Union on Capital Charge," EVENING GAZETTE (Cedar Rapids, IA), Nov. 10, 1919, p. 1.

141. "Ray Houghton Left No Will; Open Estate," DAILY TIMES (Davenport, IA), Mar. 8, 1921, p. 15.

142. "Sensational Suits in Justice Court," DAILY JOURNAL (Salem, OR), May 24, 1901, p. 4; "Moser Bound Over—Silverton Man Accused of Shocking Crime Must Answer to Circuit Court," DAILY OREGON STATESMAN (Salem, OR), June 1, 1905, p. 1; "Rev. P. B. Urban Put on Trial," DAILY NOTES (Canonsburg, PA), Aug. 20, 1906, p. 1; "Soup Caused the Trouble," DAILY NOTES (Canonsburg, PA), May 9, 1903, p. 1; *see also* "Petition for Pardon," DAILY JOURNAL (Salem, OR), Aug. 9, 1901, p. 4 (noting with regard to a petition for the pardon of Nick Jenkins, sentenced for rape in 1899: "An unusual feature of the petition is that the father, mother[,] brother and other relatives of the private prosecutor head the petition list with their names."); "Judge Brownson Meets Out Severe Sentence," THE DAILY REPUBLICAN (Monongahela, PA), Aug. 30, 1923, p. 1 ("Sandy Gore, a Washington Italian, was convicted of a statutory offense before Judge Brownson yesterday afternoon and sentenced to pay costs, a fine of $1, to serve from eighteen months to three years in the Western penitentiary and to pay the private prosecutor, Lulu May Byrd, $2.50 a week for five years for the support of her child, born June 23 this year. The private prosecutor is an orphan colored girl, 14 years of age, who was employed at the Washington hospital where the defendant was also employed."); "News of the County Courts," WELLSBORO AGITATOR (Wellsboro, PA), Dec. 7, 1927, p. 3 (noting that Arthur DeLong was the "private prosecutor" in a trial of a man, William K. Dibble, indicted on a charge of statutory rape).

143. "Gets Rehearing," DAILY OREGON STATESMAN (Salem, OR), Mar. 14, 1905, p. 4; "Barn Burner to Stand Trial," DAILY NOTES (Canonsburg, PA), Aug. 11, 1908, p. 1.

144. "Riot Case Was Again Delayed," PITTSBURG PRESS (Pittsburgh, PA), May 26, 1904, p. 4; "Trial of Tucker on Riot Charge," ENTERPRISE NEWS-RECORD (Enterprise, OR), Nov. 10, 1909, p. 1.

145. "Serious Charge—Roy Orey Arrested in Woodburn on Charge of Enticing Girl from Home," Daily Oregon Statesman (Jan. 13, 1904), p. 4.

146. "Pason Charged with Perjury," Weekly Herald (Albany, OR), Mar. 27, 1908, p. 4.

147. "Political Comment," Evening News (Wilkes-Barre, PA), Apr. 20, 1910, p. 6.

148. "Sarver Case Is Now Being Heard," Daily Republican (Monongahela, PA), Feb. 16, 1912, p. 1; "Highwayman Was on Trial Yesterday," Daily Republican (Monongahela, PA), May 17, 1913, p. 1.

149. "Supervisors Acquitted," Daily Notes (Canonsburg, PA), Feb. 14, 1907, p. 1.

150. "Criminal Court Begins Trial of Cases This Afternoon," Daily Notes (Canonsburg, PA), Nov. 12, 1906, p. 1; "Bunola Men Face Charge of Conspiracy," Daily Republican (Monongahela, PA), Oct. 23, 1907, p. 1; "Interesting Case of Drum and Ward to Close in Court Today," Daily Republican (Monongahela, PA), Sept. 1, 1909, p. 1.

151. "George Hunt, Canonsburg, Will Spend 60 Days in Jail for Jumping Board Bill," Daily Notes (Canonsburg, PA), May 7, 1907, p. 1.

152. "M'Callister in Toils Again," Daily Notes (Canonsburg, PA), Oct. 31, 1907, p. 5; "Committed to Jail," Daily Republican (Monongahela, PA), Dec. 4, 1907, p. 1; "Sent to Jail," Daily Republican (Monongahela, PA), July 8, 1908, p. 1.

153. "Will Bring Him Back," Weekly Oregon Statesman (Salem, OR), June 12, 1903, p. 5.

154. "Scales of Justice," Wellsboro Agitator (Wellsboro, PA), Oct. 2, 1901, p. 1; "Case Went to Jury Today," Daily Republican (Monongahela, PA), Feb. 17, 1908, p. 1.

155. "Chief Snow Is Now on Trial," Daily Notes (Canonsburg, PA), Aug. 25, 1905, p. 1

156. "Defendants Are Acquitted," Daily Notes (Canonsburg, PA), Aug. 31, 1905, p. 1.

157. "The Court Disposes of Many Cases," Daily Notes (Canonsburg, PA), Aug. 23, 1905, p. 8; "Odette Is Also Discharged," Detroit Free Press (Detroit, MI), Dec. 14, 1905, p. 12; "Stonerod Placed on Trial Today," Daily Notes (Canonsburg, PA), Aug. 28, 1906, p. 1; "Supervisors Found Guilty," Daily Notes (Canonsburg, PA), Nov. 14, 1906, p. 1; Daily Republican (Monongahela, PA), Nov. 19, 1908, p. 1; "Man Who Swindled Foreigners Sent to the Workhouse," Daily Notes (Canonsburg, PA), May 8, 1925, p. 5.

158. "Trespass Is Charged—Two Farmers, Near Neighbors, Take Their Troubles into the Justice Court," Daily Oregon Statesman (Salem, OR), July 1, 1902, p. 4; "A Plain Case," Daily Oregon Statesman (Salem, OR), Aug. 16, 1903; p. 7; Morning Register (Eugene, OR), Apr. 18, 1909, p. 8. Like accused criminals, private prosecutors were sometimes required to post a bond as part of the process. "Could Not Give Bonds—Charles Hammond Will Have to Answer to the Circuit Court," Daily Oregon Statesman (Salem, OR), Aug. 18, 1903, p. 6 (noting that the accused, Charles "Red" Hammond "was bound over to the circuit court under $200 bonds" which he was unable to pay, resulting in his transfer to the Marion county jail, and that "W. E. Lynch, the private prosecutor, was also placed under bonds in the sum of $100 by Recorder Judah, to insure his appearance when the case is called in the circuit court. Lynch furnished the required bond yesterday afternoon.").

159. "Was Released from Charge—Frank Robinson Found Not Guilty of Disorderly Conduct and Costs Placed on Private Prosecutor," Monongahela Valley Republican (Monongahela, PA), Sept. 29, 1904, p. 3; "Rosenburg on Trial," Daily Notes (Canonsburg, PA), May 16, 1906, p. 1; "Fine and Costs Are $23.54," Daily Notes (Canonsburg, PA), Mar. 23, 1908, p. 1; "Court Upholds Justice's Finding," Daily Notes (Canonsburg, PA), May 18, 1905, p. 1.

160. "Arguments Being Made in Epting Case," Bryan Daily Eagle and Pilot (Bryan, TX), Jan. 22, 1913, p. 1.

161. "Old Election Cases Dropped," Philadelphia Inquirer, Nov. 15, 1911, p. 2; "4 Election Law Violators Fined," Robesonian (Lumberton, NC), Aug. 22, 1938, p. 4.

162. "Hazlett Cases All Settled—Washington County Banker Enters Nollo Contendere Plea," Pittsburg Press, May 16, 1901, p. 1 ("There are nearly 40 indictments against Mr. Hazlett, and there are 25 attorneys concerned for the private prosecutors."); "Contractor Lucas Discharged—Part of the Money Belonged to Him," Daily Journal (Salem, OR), Jan. 31, 1902, p. 4 (noting a private prosecutor brought an embezzlement case); "Bumgartner Got Six Months," Daily Republican (Monongahela, PA), May 14, 1904, p. 1 (noting that W. A. James was the private prosecutor in an embezzlement case); "Court Notes," Allentown Morning Call (Allentown, PA), Dec. 21, 1906, p. 1 (noting that "Mr. Gernerd" appeared

"for the private prosecutor"); "Embezzlement Case Before the Court," DAILY NOTES (Canonsburg, PA), Aug. 21, 1908, p. 1 (noting the appearance of a private prosecutor); *accord* "Four Sentenced on Their Pleas—Pinkerton Brothers, Arrested in Canonsburg on Embezzlement Charges, Get Off Light," DAILY NOTES (Canonsburg, PA), Mar. 30, 1909, p. 1; "Realty Dealer Jailed—Gets Eighteen Months for Embezzling as Agent," PHILADELPHIA INQUIRER (Philadelphia, PA), Oct 9, 1919, p. 8.

163. "With Grand Jury," DAILY NOTES (Canonsburg, PA), Feb. 7, 1906, p. 4; "Bank 'Snatchers' To Be Tried Soon," EUGENE REGISTER-GUARD (Eugene, OR), Mar. 24, 1933, p. 10; DAILY NEWS (Canonsburg, PA), Feb. 18, 1911, p. 1 (noting the appearance of a "private prosecutor" in a case where a man charged with wife "with unfaithfulness").

164. "Prominent Doctor Is Under Arrest," DAILY NOTES (Canonsburg, PA), Mar. 16, 1908, p. 1; "Rockpile Charge Against Finley—Complaint Alleges that He Has Failed to Support His Wife," DAILY OREGON STATESMAN (Salem, OR), Mar. 13, 1909, p. 2; "Arrested for Non-Support," DAILY CAPITAL JOURNAL (Salem, OR), Dec. 24, 1909, p. 1.

165. "News of the County Court," WELLSBORO AGITATOR (Wellsboro, PA), May 28, 1930, p. 1.

166. "Another Brown Gets Out," DAILY NOTES (Canonsburg, PA), July 11, 1907, p. 1 ("Before Judge Taylor yesterday, Charles Brown, of the Brown family which has been in some trouble lately, entered a plea of guilty to the charge of fornication. He had been living, it was alleged, with Mrs. Annie Brown, at Midland No. 1, representing that she was his housekeeper. The husband of Mrs. Brown was the private prosecutor. Brown was sentenced to pay the costs and a fine of 6¹/4 cents.").

167. "Gilmore Acquitted," DAILY REPUBLICAN (Monongahela, PA), Aug. 27, 1907, p. 1.

168. "Bright Gets Ten Months at Works," DAILY REPUBLICAN (Monongahela, PA), May 18, 1906, p. 1.

169. "Criminal Court Adjourns for Week," DAILY NOTES (Canonsburg, PA), Nov. 18, 1916, p. 1; "Case Dismissed," OREGON STATESMAN (Salem, OR), Oct. 23, 1926, p. 5; "O'Hare Charge Changed," OREGON STATESMAN (Salem, OR), Feb. 18, 1934, p. 5.

170. "Was Convicted," DAILY REPUBLICAN (Monongahela, PA), Feb. 22, 1912, p. 1; "Mrs. Wiggins Acquitted," DAILY REPUBLICAN (Monongahela, PA), Aug. 25, 1913, p. 1.

171. "Arsenic Found in Cup of Tea," WEEKLY HERALD (Albany, OR), Oct. 25, 1906, p. 1.

172. "Must Keep the Peace—W. W. Slaughter of Woodburn Placed Under $500 Bonds by Justice Turner," DAILY OREGON STATESMAN (Salem, OR), May 19, 1906, p. 2.

173. "Many Verdicts Are Returned in Court," DAILY NOTES (Canonsburg, PA), May 13, 1910, p. 1.

174. "The Court Was Lenient with Foreigners," DAILY REPUBLICAN (Monongahela, PA), Aug. 20, 1909, p. 1; "Rush Wood Convicted of Felonious Assault and Battery," DAILY REPUBLICAN (Monongahela, PA), Sept. 1, 1923, p. 1.

175. "Badly Injured," DAILY OREGON STATESMAN (Salem, OR), Sept. 12, 1905, p. 5; "Mrs. Kimsay Will Fight for Children," DAILY CAPITAL JOURNAL (Salem, OR), Aug. 30, 1910, p. 8; "Moore Acquitted by Jury," DAILY REPUBLICAN (Monongahela, PA), Nov. 21, 1923, p. 1.

176. "Court Dealing Out Justice to Law Breakers," DAILY NOTES (Canonsburg, PA), Aug. 21, 1903, p. 1; "Many Cases Being Heard in Court Today," DAILY NOTES (Canonsburg, PA), Nov. 17, 1904, p. 1; "Sentenced on Guilty Pleas," DAILY NOTES (Canonsburg, PA), Aug. 15, 1905, p. 4; "Court News," DAILY REPUBLICAN (Monongahela, PA), Aug. 23, 1905, p. 4; "Other Cases Before the Criminal Court," DAILY NOTES (Canonsburg, PA), Nov. 17, 1906, p. 1; "Lock No. 4 Man Gets Four Years," DAILY REPUBLICAN (Monongahela, PA), Feb. 14, 1907, p. 1.

177. "Gun Case Appealed," DAILY REPUBLICAN (Monongahela, PA), Aug. 29, 1911, p. 4.

178. "In Trouble Again—Clayton Bradley Persists in Pointing Guns at Mr. Southwick," DAILY OREGON STATESMAN (Salem, OR), Nov. 5, 1902, p. 6.

179. "Expensive Mischief," DAILY REPUBLICAN (Monongahela, PA), Aug. 28, 1912, p. 1.

180. "John Francis Placed on Trial," SCRANTON TIMES (Scranton, PA), Oct. 10, 1902, p. 3.

181. "Grocer Charged with Giving Short Weight," DAILY NOTES (Canonsburg, PA), Jan. 18, 1922, p. 1.

182. "True Bills Against the Robinsons," DAILY REPUBLICAN (Monongahela, PA), Feb. 7, 1907, p. 1; "Stokes Is Guilty - Entered the Above Plea to Bigamy Charges—Sentenced to Pay Costs Fine of $1 and Serve Three Months in Jail," DAILY REPUBLICAN (Monongahela, PA), Jan. 25, 1910, p. 1.

183. "Criminal Court Opened Monday with Interesting Cases," DAILY REPUBLICAN (Monongahela, PA), Aug. 18, 1908, p. 1.

184. "Two Pleaders Are Sentenced by the Court," DAILY REPUBLICAN (Monongahela, PA), July 20, 1909, p. 1.

185. "In Criminal Court," DAILY REPUBLICAN (Monongahela, PA), Aug. 19, 1908, p. 1.

186. "Canonsburg Man Sent Up," DAILY NOTES (Canonsburg, PA), Aug. 26, 1905, p. 1 ("Joseph Palmer of Canonsburg pleaded guilty to a charge of sodomy and buggery, and Judge Taylor sentenced him to the insane asylum at Dixmont. Joseph B. Wilson of Canonsburg was the private prosecutor."); "Last Case on in Criminal Court," DAILY NOTES (Canonsburg, PA), Sept. 12, 1906, p. 1 (noting that "J. M. Patterson" is "the private prosecutor" in a case involving allegations of "sodomy and buggery, indecent exposure and indecent assault and battery").

187. *E.g.*, "Cameron Will Push Bank Cases—Judge Pipes Will Be Retained by Incoming District Attorney to Continue Prosecution of Officials of Wrecked Institution," OREGON DAILY JOURNAL (Portland, OR), June 12, 1906, p. 1 ("District Attorney-Elect Cameron will retain Martin L. Pipes as the private prosecutor in the remaining cases against the indicted officials of the Title Guarantee & Trust company, and will cooperate with him in the trial of the cases.").

188. "Dick Keene Pleads Guilty," WEEKLY HERALD (Albany, OR), Aug. 2 1906, p. 2.

189. "Will Deport C. Yashito," DAILY OREGON STATESMAN (Salem, OR), Dec. 13, 1908, p. 1.

190. "Teacher on Trial for Whipping Pupil—Charles Heimer Accused of Having Unlawfully Punished Boy at McClelland School," DAILY NOTES (Canonsburg, PA), Feb. 16, 1917, p. 1.

191. "Wasn't a Fight But a Tea Party," ANACONDA STANDARD (Anaconda, MT), Sept. 7, 1906, pp. 1, 3; "Sporting Writer Placed on Stand," BUTTE INTER MOUNTAIN (Butte, MT), Sept. 7, 1906, p. 1.

192. "Horse Whip a Minister—Irate Women of Salem Assault Preacher After Meeting and Are Placed Under Arrest," COOS BAY TIMES (Marshfield, OR), Apr. 9, 1908, p. 1; "Youths Arraigned," OREGON STATESMAN (Salem, OR), Feb. 27, 1925, p. 3.

193. DAILY NOTES (Canonsburg, PA), Nov. 9, 1909, p. 1.

194. "Hammock Dismissed—Was Arrested for Killing China Pheasants Out of Season," WEEKLY OREGON STATESMAN (Salem, OR), Oct. 7, 1902, p. 5; "Case Was Dismissed," DAILY JOURNAL (Salem, OR), Oct. 7, 1902, p. 2.

195. "Recorder Postpones Trial of Ridgeway," DAILY OREGON STATESMAN (Salem, OR), Apr. 16, 1907, p. 6 (noting "Mr. Leo Stanwood" was "the private prosecutor" in a case involving an allegation of unlawfully practicing optometry); "Veterinary Arrested—Dr. Long Is Charged with Practicing Without License but Later Produces Certificate," WEEKLY OREGON STATESMAN (Salem, OR), Mar. 31, 1905, p. 3 (noting that "Dr. Long prescribed medicine for a sick horse belonging to the private prosecutor on February 2, 1905, for which the latter paid the veterinary a fee of one dollar.").

196. "Kelly Says Ordinance Interferes with Rights," OREGON STATESMAN (Salem, OR), Oct. 3, 1919, p. 6.

197. "Defective Brakes Charged," OREGON STATESMAN (Salem, OR), Oct. 7, 1924, p. 5.

198. "Many Cases Disposed of During Week," DAILY REPUBLICAN (Monongahela, PA), Nov. 13, 1920, p. 1.

199. "Missing Girl from Brooks Is Located; Two Men Are Held," OREGON DAILY JOURNAL (Portland, OR), Feb. 28, 1921, p. 3; "Nine Arrested on Vice Count," OREGON STATESMAN (Salem, OR), Apr. 7, 1925, p. 1.

200. "Goes Up for Four Years," DAILY NOTES (Canonsburg, PA), May 2, 1905, p. 1; "Bobinski Not Guilty," DAILY REPUBLICAN (Monongahela, PA), Aug. 24, 1908, p. 4.

201. "Arden Man Sent Up," DAILY NOTES (Canonsburg, PA), Feb. 15, 1911, p. 1; "Arrested for Selling Liquor Without License," DAILY REPUBLICAN (Monongahela, PA), Aug. 19, 1920, p. 1.

202. "Charged with Selling Liquor to Minor," DAILY OREGON STATESMAN (Salem, OR), July 7, 1908, p. 1.

203. BUTLER CITIZEN (Butler, PA), June 21, 1915, p. 1.

204. "Thirty Days," DAILY NOTES (Canonsburg, PA), Aug. 26, 1907, p. 1.

205. "Houston Couple Are Sentenced," DAILY NOTES (Canonsburg, PA), June 19, 1907, p. 1; "Gets Salty Sentence," DAILY REPUBLICAN (Monongahela, PA), June 19, 1907, p. 1.

206. "Witnesses Swear Inquisitors Visited Store of Accused Cocaine Seller," PITTSBURGH SUNDAY POST, May 12, 1907, p. 4.

207. "News from the County Court House," DAILY NOTES (Canonsburg, PA), Aug. 19, 1903, p. 1 ("Before Judge Taylor on Tuesday afternoon was heard the case of the commonwealth against Samuel Rosenberg, for peddling shoes without a license in the village of Westland. J. B. Ritson, constable, is the private prosecutor.").

208. "Local News," ROSEBURG REVIEW (Roseburg, OR), Oct. 24, 1908, p. 4; *accord* "Talley Acquitted," EVENING NEWS (Roseburg, OR), Apr. 8, 1913, p. 2 (noting in the context of a charge of "violating the fish laws," that "[i]n dismissing the case, Justice Marsters warned the several game wardens against the institution of future actions through malice or personal motives").

209. "Hunts Without a License," OREGON STATESMAN (Salem, OR), Sept. 28, 1940, p. 10.

210. "Municipal Judge of Philadelphia Must Face Trial," WILMINGTON MORNING NEWS (Wilmington, DE), Dec. 17, 1918, p. 7 (reporting on Philadelphia: "John M. Nobre, former city surveyor, was indicted on a charge of libel, in which Senator Vare is the private prosecutor."); "Expect Crowds at News Trial," DAILY TIMES (Davenport, IA), Jan 24, 1919, p. 13 ("Attorneys involved in the H. M. Hamilton criminal libel case which is to be tried during the later days of next week, stated today that undoubtedly the trial would be one of the most important in the local court for some time.... The state's case may be conducted against Hamilton by a private prosecutor as is the custom in criminal libel cases. W. M. Chamberlin represents the complaining witnesses."); "True Bills Against Dr. Delk," EVENING SENTINEL (Carlisle, PA), Apr. 8, 1919, p. 6 (noting that the indictment of a man by the grand jury on four bills charging criminal libel, and taking note of a "private prosecutor," Lieutenant David Craig, in the case).

211. "Grand Jury Finds Many True Bills—Agents of Foreign Insurance Company Indicted," DAILY NOTES (Canonsburg, PA), Aug. 14, 1908, p. 1; *accord* "Labor Leader on Trial—James Cronin Charged with Conspiracy to Defraud," PHILADELPHIA INQUIRER, Apr. 10, 1919, p. 17.

212. "Cases Heard in Criminal Court Today," DAILY NOTES (Canonsburg, PA), Aug. 18, 1908, p. 1.

213. "Personal Mention," DAILY OREGON STATESMAN (Salem, OR), June 22, 1906, p. 4; *see also* "Tallow in the Lard," DAILY CAPITAL JOURNAL (Salem, OR), July 10, 1906, p. 3 (noting that the "private prosecutor" was "Dairy and Food Commissioner J. W. Bailey" and that "[t]he specific charge was that the butcher was mixing tallow with his lard which he had contracted to furnish the penitentiary"); "Four Criminal Courts To Be at Work Next Week," PITTSBURGH PRESS, Nov. 19, 1909, p. 9 (noting that "Charles L. Shoop is the private prosecutor" in "[a]bout a dozen pure food cases"); "Court News of Past Week," WELLSBORO AGITATOR (Wellsboro, PA), Dec. 15, 1926, p. 1 (noting that Frank Bolger, of the Pure Food Commission, "appeared as the private prosecutor").

214. EVENING NEWS (Roseburg, OR), Feb. 11, 1914, p. 5 (noting that "Deputy Food Commissioners Shrock and Duncan were the private prosecutors").

215. "4 Held for Fraud; Involved in Theft of 500 Autos Here—Arrests Follow Demands by Mayor and Insurance Companies," PHILADELPHIA INQUIRER, Dec. 14, 1918, p. 1 (noting that "[f]our of the prisoners arrested yesterday" were held by the magistrate "on the advice of David J. Smyth, former Director of Public Safety, who is acting as private prosecutor for the insurance companies").

216. "Charged with Cutting Wires," DAILY NOTES (Canonsburg, PA), Aug. 30, 1905, p. 1; "Admitted His Guilt," DAILY REPUBLICAN (Monongahela, PA), June 20, 1911, p. 1.

217. "Martin Daughtery Acquitted," DAILY REPUBLICAN (Monongahela, PA), Aug. 23, 1913, p. 1.

218. "Echo of the Vandegrift Case Heard," DAILY REPUBLICAN (Monongahela, PA), May 13, 1909, p. 1.

219. "Goes Up for Four Years," DAILY NOTES (Canonsburg, PA), May 2, 1905, p. 1; "Basil Brown Is Placed o[n] Trial," DAILY NOTES (Canonsburg, PA), May 11, 1905, p. 1; DAILY REPUBLICAN (Monongahela, PA), May 11, 1905, p. 4; "Midland Parties on Trial for Keeping a Disorderly House," DAILY NOTES (Canonsburg, PA), Sept. 1, 1905, p. 1; "Jury Finds Chas. Taylor Innocent," DAILY REPUBLICAN (Monongahela, PA), Sept. 1, 1905, p. 1; "Blanche Thompson Held—Must Answer to Court for Running Disorderly House," DAILY NOTES (Canonsburg, PA), Apr. 4, 1908, p. 1; "Local Cases Heard in Court at Washington Monday

and Today," DAILY REPUBLICAN (Monongahela, PA), Mar. 7, 1911, p. 1. Prosecutions for "disorderly houses" were also brought in the founding era. Thomas Boylston Adams to Abigail Adams, Jan. 22, 1794, *Founders Online,* National Archives, https://founders.archives.gov/documents/Adams/04-10-02-0022 ("It is true I commenced my career at the Bar, as the Prosecutor of a Female—The cause was of such a nature, that there was no necessity for personal or general remarks in the manner you allude to; I took occasion to remark to the Jury on the evil tendency of Disorderly houses—that they were a common nuisance in the Neighborhood where they existed, & a general evil, by the effects of them upon the Manners & Morals of the Citizens. That the Evil was rapidly increasing, and the frequency of complaints upon this subject was the best evidence that they called for suppression—The testimony was insufficient to convince the Jury that the person Indicted really did keep a house of the above description and therefore they found a verdict of Not Guilty.").

220. "Can Now Play Ball," DAILY EUGENE GUARD (Eugene, OR), May 7, 1903, p. 1; "Verdicts in Three Cases," DAILY NOTES (Canonsburg, PA), Aug. 29, 1905, p. 1; "Pearson Fined $75 in Police Court—Founded Guilty of Selling Whiskey on Sunday," ASHEVILLE CITIZEN (Asheville, NC), Nov. 29, 1905, p. 5; "Another Effort Made to Bribe Law and Order Men," POTTSVILLE REPUBLICAN (Pottsville, PA), Apr. 25, 1906, p. 1; "Spicy Testimony in Liquor Cases," MINERS JOURNAL (Pottsville, PA), Apr. 25, 1906, p. 5; ROSEBURG REVIEW (Roseburg, OR), July 27, 1908, p. 4; "Local News," ROSEBURG REVIEW (Roseburg, OR), Aug. 3, 1908, p. 4; "Man and Wife Arrested - McGovern Couple Charged with Illegal Liquor Selling," DAILY NOTES (Canonsburg, PA), Aug. 4, 1908, p. 1; "Westland Liquor Case," DAILY NOTES (Canonsburg, PA), Aug. 19, 1908, p. 5; "Found Indicted on Conspiracy Charge," DAILY NOTES (Canonsburg, PA), Nov. 2, 1909, p. 1. *Compare* "Not to Enforce Blue Laws—Philadelphia Police Chief Says Latitude Should Be Allowed," THE SUN (Baltimore, MD), July 23, 1914, p. 1 (noting that "Superintendent of Police Robinson, according to a statement made by him... said that judgment should be used in making arrests" for offenses under "the Sunday blue laws of 1794" and that "there would not be any action taken under the blue laws in these cases unless some private prosecutors stepped in and caused arrests"); "'Blue Law' Fading," ADAMS COUNTY FREE PRESS (Corning, IA), June 16, 1917, p. 4 (noting that the local county attorney issued this statement: "Until further directions from the Attorney General no further prosecutions will be initiated by the county attorney nor will peace officers be required to investigate infractions of the Sunday law nor to sign informations charging the offense. Private prosecutors may, upon furnishing to the county attorney evidence which would probably warrant an arrest and conviction, file information charging violations of the Sunday law in this county.").

221. "Alleged Common Scold on Trial," DAILY NOTES (Canonsburg, PA), Feb. 14, 1911, p. 1 ("Mrs. Lizzie Baxley of Finleyville, a negress, is on trial charged with being a common scold. Mrs. Randolph, the private prosecutor, alleges that Mrs. Baxley circulated false reports as to the prosecutrix's character. The colored population of Finleyville is well represented. The case is rather amusing."); *see also* "$216.40 Cost of a Law Suit," DAILY REPUBLICAN (Monongahela, PA), Feb. 16, 1911, p. 4 ("It is very expensive to settle little differences in court. This Mrs. Ida B. Randolph, a private prosecutor, and Mrs. Lizzie Baxley, a defendant, both colored, of the Finleyville section, have found this out. In the case in which Mrs. Baxley was charged with being a common scold, the jury found the defendant not guilty, but put one-half the costs on her and one-half on the private prosecutor. It cost each of the negresses just $108.20 to have the jury pass upon their troubles, in addition to the time they spent in court, paid out for lodging, railroad fare, etc. They gave bond for the payment of the sums within ten days. Otherwise they would have to go to jail.").

222. "Springer Was Bound Over—Will Answer Serious Criminal Charge in the Circuit Court," DAILY OREGON STATESMAN (Salem, OR), Aug. 5, 1903, p. 1; *see also* "More Trouble for Springer—Will Be Arrested Charged with Letting Down Fences Belonging to J. W. La Follett," DAILY OREGON STATESMAN (Salem, OR), Feb. 11, 1904, p. 1; "Is Not Guilty—Mathias Springer Cleared of Charge of Throwing Down Fence," DAILY OREGON STATESMAN (Salem, OR), Feb. 20, 1904, p. 1.

223. "Democracy Protects Its Rascals," SEATTLE POST-INTELLIGENCER (Seattle, WA), July 9, 1900, p. 4.

224. "Lenhart on Stand in His Own Behalf," DAILY NOTES (Canonsburg, PA), Feb. 18, 1909, p. 1.

225. "No Poison Charge Made; O'Malley's Wife Out on Bail," THE TIMES (Philadelphia, PA), July 11, 1902, p. 3 ("[D]espite the intervention of the Western officials, the stepping in of the Philadelphia District Attorney and his detectives, and all the efforts made by the private prosecutors to find proof of her guilt,

there remains not a single bit of strength to the unspoken charge that the young bride tried to kill her husband by secretly giving him deadly drugs."); "Ernest Haywood Asks that Trial by Postponed," NEWS AND OBSERVER (Raleigh, NC), Mar. 25, 1903, p. 3 ("I am informed that at least one man has been employed by the private prosecutors in this case to make something of a canvass of the South-western portion of Wake county ostensibly looking up witnesses, but that this man devotes a great deal of his time to creating a public sentiment against me.").

226. "Sent Back to the Army—Former Street Car Conductor Pleaded Guilty to Taking Day's Receipts," PHILADELPHIA INQUIRER, Nov. 21, 1902, p. 16 ("George Leib, who was formerly employed as a sub-contractor on the Twelfth and Sixteenth streets division of the Philadelphia Rapid Transit Company, was arraigned before Judge Wiltbank, in the Criminal Court, yesterday and pleaded guilty to an indictment charging him with larceny. Attorney Samuel A. Boyle appeared as private prosecutor for the railway company, in conjunction with Assistant Attorney Gray.").

227. *E.g.*, CAMERON HERALD (Cameron, TX), Apr. 17, 1902, p. 8 (noting of a murder case: "The state was not only represented by the strong prosecutors of Bell county, but by three private prosecutors two of whom were from Washington county and are considered the ablest and strongest prosecutors in that part of the state.").

228. "Wanted Shoes Badly," DAILY JOURNAL (Salem, OR), Jan. 13, 1902, p. 3; "Burglary Is the Charge," DAILY OREGON STATESMAN (Salem, OR), June 24, 1902, p. 4; "Court Settles Down to Monotonous Grind," DAILY NOTES (Canonsburg, PA), Nov. 15, 1904, p. 1; "Jury Is Out in Chadwick Case," DAILY NOTES (Canonsburg, PA), Nov. 15, 1905, p. 1; "Boys on Trial for 'Swiping' Two Pigeons," SCRANTON TIMES (Scranton, PA), Apr. 2, 1907, p. 11; "Costs Placed on Prosecutor," DAILY NOTES (Canonsburg, PA), May 18, 1907, p. 1; "Goldstein Not Guilty," DAILY REPUBLICAN (Monongahela, PA), July 23, 1907, p. 1; "Not Guilty," DAILY REPUBLICAN (Monongahela, PA), July 26, 1907, p. 1; "Squire Elwood's First Case," DAILY REPUBLICAN (Monongahela, PA), Apr. 7, 1908, p. 1; "Criminal Cases Being Heard by Judge and Jury," DAILY NOTES (Canonsburg, PA), Nov. 9, 1908, p. 1; "Several Cases of Interest Tried in Criminal Court," DAILY REPUBLICAN (Monongahela, PA), Nov. 13, 1908, p. 1; "November Term of Criminal Court at End," DAILY NOTES (Canonsburg, PA), Nov. 20, 1908, p. 1; "Several Pleas Were Entered," DAILY REPUBLICAN (Monongahela, PA), Apr. 20, 1909, p. 4; "Three Men Plead Guilty," DAILY REPUBLICAN (Monongahela, PA), Oct. 12, 1909, p. 1; "August Term of Court Is Ended," DAILY NOTES (Canonsburg, PA), Sept. 2, 1910, p. 1; "Boy's Tongue Tied; Defendant Acquitted," DAILY NOTES (Canonsburg, PA), Feb. 23, 1911, p. 1; "Cleaver Bone of Contention," DAILY REPUBLICAN (Monongahela, PA), May 13, 1916, p. 2; "Criminal Court Convened Today," DAILY NOTES (Canonsburg, PA), Nov. 13, 1916, p. 6; "Miner Exonerated," DAILY NOTES (Canonsburg, PA), Oct. 4, 1930, p. 1.

229. "A Small Boy Before Court," DAILY OREGON STATESMAN (Salem, OR), Aug. 2, 1903, p. 1.

230. "County Court Notes," DAILY REPUBLICAN (Monongahela, PA), May 2, 1905, p. 4; "Defendants Are Acquitted," DAILY NOTES (Canonsburg, PA), Aug. 31, 1905, p. 1; "Culprits Are Facing Court Law," DAILY REPUBLICAN (Monongahela, PA), Aug. 17, 1910, p. 1.

231. "He Sold Oleo for Real Thing," DAILY NOTES (Canonsburg, PA), May 9, 1907, p. 1.

232. "It Must Have Hurt," WEEKLY OREGON STATESMAN (Salem, OR), June 12, 1903, p. 8.

233. "Declares Prosecutor's Office Has Been Prostituted," L.A. HERALD, May 18, 1907, p. 1; "Synopsis," L.A. TIMES, May 18, 1907, p. 1; "Calhoun Emphatically Denies that He Ever Bribed the Supervisors," EVENING TELEGRAM (Salt Lake City, UT), May 18, 1907, p. 2; "'It's All a Spreckels Plot' Says Calhoun," OAKLAND EXAMINER, May 18, 1907, p. 1.

234. "Judge Jones Raps Compromises in Goose Creek Case," HOUSTON POST, Aug. 1, 1923, p. 2 ("This thing of having a private prosecutor go behind closed doors and try to coerce men to plead guilty and then by the consent of the criminal district judge dismiss perjury cases in order to get men to plead guilty and take a $100 fine in my opinion is a travesty on justice, and is something that should never be permitted in Harris county."); *id.* ("I will not permit any man to plead guilty in this case if he says he is not guilty. I understand that men who pleaded guilty in the criminal court were not guilty, and I understand that some of the men whose cases were dismissed were supposed to have been guilty and were turned loose, and that the private prosecutor received a fee of $10,000 in order to get these men to plead guilty; a blood-sucking conviction, I call it. The district attorney, as I understand it, has not been permitted to go into the grand

jury room in these cases, and by a stroke of the pen men have been indicted without any evidence against them by permission of the criminal district judge."); READING TIMES (Reading, PA), Jan. 22, 1926, p. 6 (taking note of discriminatory treatment in the context of the trial for the killing of Jonathan Klopp and stating: "When these three negroes were tried, a private prosecutor sat by the elbow of the district attorney and he said he came to see that all three of them paid for the life of Klopp.").

235. "To Rule in Libel Case," CHICAGO DAILY TRIBUNE, Feb. 3, 1900, p. 8 ("The doubts of the court were shared by Attorney Wing, leading counsel for the defense, and in arguing against the motion he scored severely the private counsel for the prosecuting witness, John Barton Payne, ridiculing the proposition to deprive a defendant in a criminal procedure of his right to trial by jury. 'This motion must have emanated from the misguided zeal of the private prosecutor,' said Attorney Wing. 'I cannot believe that it is authorized by the State's Attorney. It is something new under the sun for a jury to be asked to find a verdict for the people in a criminal case.'"); *accord* "Libel Suit Ending," DAILY INTER OCEAN (Chicago, IL), Feb. 3, 1900, p. 3 ("Mr. Wing.—I never expected that I would live long enough to argue a question of that sort in a case, and I do not believe that any such motion has ever been presented in Illinois by any prosecutor who was elected by the people to represent people. It could only emanate from the misguided zeal of a private prosecutor."); "Court House Graft Cases Finally Brought to Trial—Attorney Lenahan Scores the Private Counsel for Prosecution and Calls Them 'Bandits' and 'Buccaneers' in the First Clash," EVENING NEWS (Wilkes-Barre, PA), Sept. 18, 1911, p. 1 ("Attorney Lenahan then took the floor and with his old time vigor attached the private prosecutor and his private counsel. He called the prosecutors the 'Bowery gang,' and said that they were capable of anything...."); "Two Attorneys in Hicks Case Still Wear War Paint," OREGON DAILY JOURNAL (Portland, OR), Mar. 20, 1912, p. 15 (noting that in the first-degree murder trial of Burt Hicks, charged with murdering machinist union picket W. A. Wortman in 1911, Dan Malarkey—counsel for the defense—criticized "Special Prosecutor" Davis' "attempts to 'badger, bulldoze and intimidate the state's own witnesses because they didn't have to testify as the private prosecutor would have them testify'" and criticized the "zeal," "malice," and "spleen" of the "private prosecutor," saying that "it is an outrage for the power of the state of Oregon to be in the hands of a private prosecutor"); "Unionism Caused Murder," L.A. TIMES, Apr. 7, 1912, pt. IV, p. 8 ("The unions are trying to have him hanged for protecting his own life, and have employed private prosecutors to secure his conviction.").

236. "Rule Lawyer Out Duling Murder Case—Court Holds Murder Victim's Widow Has No Right to Employ Private Prosecutor," THE BEE (Danville, VA), Feb. 15, 1937, p. 8 ("Judge J. L. Almond, Jr., of Hustings Court, Roanoke, sitting at the request of Judge A. H. Hopkins, of Franklin county circuit court, this morning denied J. B. Allman the right to sit as counsel for Mrs. T. J. Richards when Paul and Hubbard Duling face trial here tomorrow charged with killing Mrs. Richards' husband, a deputy sheriff, several years ago. Judge Almond held that no lawyer has a right to enter such a case for the prosecution without the consent of the commonwealth's attorney."); *accord* "Carter Lee Wins Case in Franklin—Court Holds His Consent Needed Before Private Prosecutor Can Act," BRISTOL HERALD COURIER (Bristol, VA-TN), Feb. 16, 1937, p. 10 (reporting the same story).

237. *E.g.*, "Stories of Witnesses—Good Progress in Tighe Murder Trial," ANACONDA STANDARD (Anaconda, MT), May 23, 1902, p. 7 ("The Tighe murder trial made good progress here today.... The objection to the appearance of Purcell, who is acting as assistant to County Attorney Goodman, was based on allegations that Mr. Purcell had not been employed by the county commissioners to assist in the prosecution of the case; that he had been employed by private persons, the money being paid to him coming from private sources; that the county attorney was not in any way incapacitated from representing the interests of the state in the prosecution and had not solicited the aid of the attorney general of the state, and for the reason that Mr. Purcell appeared in the case as a private prosecutor at the instance of private persons, receiving his compensation exclusively from private sources. The objections were overruled."); *see also* "Testing a Technicality—Right of Private Prosecutor Under Plumbers' Ordinance Questioned," PITTSBURG PRESS (Pittsburgh, PA), Aug. 15, 1905, p. 4; "Dr. Messner's New Scheme to Get Free—Claims the Grand Jury Hadn't Any Right to Indict Him," SPOKANE DAILY CHRONICLE (Spokane, WA), Sept. 14, 1905, p. 1 ("If said indictment was found at the instance of a private prosecutor, or upon a complaint sworn to before an officer authorized to administer oaths, and presented by the prosecuting attorney, then, it is claimed, the indictment is irregular and void and not in conformity to the provisions of the state."); "Much Legal Lore

Is Hurled at Judge Poindexter in an Effort to Show That the Late Inquisitorial Body Was Not Properly Organized Nor Conducted," SPOKANE PRESS (Spokane, WA), Sept. 15, 1905, p. 1 ("[E]ndorsed on the indictment did not appear the name of 'Mr. Blank,' a private citizen who should have instituted the proceedings before the grand jury and should have had his name endorsed on the indictment as the 'private prosecutor.'"); "Attorney M. C. Chapman Mercilessly Flays Man Who as Private Prosecutor Runs District Attorney Langdon's Office," OAKLAND TRIBUNE (Oakland, CA), May 19, 1908, p. 1 (assailing "private prosecutor"); "Question of Information," DAILY OKLAHOMAN (Oklahoma City, OK), Sept. 26, 1908, p. 9 ("Evans set up the claim that the information against him was sworn to by a private prosecutor, and not a legalized prosecutor."); "Christian Science vs. The Doctors," SANDUSKY REGISTER (Sandusky, OH), Apr. 23, 1911, p. 7 (noting that, in an appeal to the court, members of the Church of Christ, Scientist, it was stated: "private prosecutors are likely to become unconscious fanatics and persecutors").

238. "Order Venue Change in Beamon Trial," CORSICANA DAILY SUN (Corsicana, TX), Mar. 30, 1963, pp. 1, 14 (noting that "[a] motion submitted by the defendant through his court-appointed attorneys . . . asking the court to quash and abate the indictment" included the argument that "participation on the part of Mr. A. P. Mays, a purely private prosecutor hired by persons interested in revenge, was highly improper and in complete derogation of the rights of this defendant guaranteed him by the Constitution of the State of Texas, United States, and the laws and statutes of the State of Texas").

239. "Iden's Attorney Makes Formal Demand for Certain Papers—Calls Complaining Witness the 'Private Prosecutor' and Refers to District Attorney as ex-Officio Attorney to Said Private Prosecutor," VISALIA DAILY TIMES (Visalia, CA), Sept. 1, 1913, p. 1; "Judge Allen Orders $3000 Increase in Bonds of Iden—Attorneys Clash when Clack Refers to Power as Private Prosecutor; Latter Resents Insinuation and Court Is Compelled to Restore Order," VISALIA DAILY TIMES (Visalia, CA), Sept. 29, 1913, p. 1; "Says He Did Not Admit Defects in Walker Complaint," MEDFORD MAIL TRIBUNE (Medford, OR), July 14, 1923, p. 6; "Argument of Prosecutor Is Basis for New Trial," GALVESTON DAILY NEWS (Galveston, TX), Nov. 2, 1925, p. 5; *see also* "Convicted Man May Get Retrial," THE ROBESONIAN (Lumberton, NC), Sept. 3, 1953, p. 5 ("The attorney general's office conceded to the Supreme Court yesterday that it could offer no arguments in support of statements made to the trial jury by the private prosecutor."); "Supreme Court Grants New Trial to Sheriff's Slayer," THE LANDMARK (Statesville, NC), Sept. 24, 1953, p. 1 ("The high court ordered the new trial on grounds that Judge Allen H. Gwyn allowed a private prosecutor to make prejudicial statements to the jury in his plea for a guilty verdict."); "Church of God Bishop Skips Sheet for Shirttail in Court Appearance," THE INDEX-JOURNAL (Greenwood, SC), Nov. 9, 1953, p. 1 (noting of a North Carolina case: "Dockery was convicted last April 18, and sentenced to die in the gas chamber. The Supreme Court granted him a new trial, holding arguments made to the jury by a private prosecutor were improper.").

240. "Attack Made on Marshall, H. M. Havner—Editor Accused of Being Private Prosecutor," CARROLL DAILY HERALD (Carroll, IA), Mar. 16, 1936, p. 1; *see also* "Insulting Court Talk Has Certain Limits in Old North State," DOTHAN EAGLE (Dothan, AL), Nov. 3, 1949, p. 19 (noting of a Supreme Court of North Carolina decision: "'A severe reprimand by the court would have been justified,' the seven justices said, when a private prosecutor in the case of the State vs. Correll characterized the defendant on trial for murder as 'a small-time racketeering gangster.'"); "Request to Drop Hibbins Case Slated Tuesday," DAILY PANTAGRAPH (Bloomington-Normal, IL), Sept. 27, 1954, p. 3 ("Defense attorneys have charged that the indictment should be rejected as the work of 'a volunteer, private prosecutor.' They contend Lyons was motivated by 'private enmity' against Chief Hibbens.").

241. "Liquor Law in N. Dakota," ST. PAUL GLOBE (St. Paul, MN), Feb. 18, 1901, p. 4 ("There has been a good deal of criticism through the state recently of the methods of the State Enforcement league in bringing actions for the prosecutions of the liquor law.... Senator LaMoure, of Pembina county, unfolded some of the practices of the league in the state senate when his bill to shut out Bosard & Bosard and other private prosecutors came up for passage. The bill provides that the state's attorney of each county shall be, with the attorney general, the only public prosecutor in that county and that he can only be relieved of his duties upon a showing before the district court. It also provides that where private counsel is appointed to prosecute it must be appointed from the county where the actions are pending. This bill will effectively shut out the firm of Bosard & Bosard and other private prosecutors....").

242. *E.g.*, "Iowa Opinions and Notes," EVENING TIMES-REPUBLICAN (Marshalltown, IA), Dec. 2, 1907, p. 4 ("Further enforcement has depended on private prosecution, which is seriously objectionable."); *see also* SAN FRANCISCO CHRONICLE, Oct. 22, 1909, p. 6 ("San Francisco has no use for private prosecutors, least of all for the kind whose hands are dirty."). Sometimes, lawyers in general were the target. "Hard After the Lawyers," ABILENE DAILY REPORTER (Abilene, TX), June 26, 1907, p. 4 ("The Farmer makes some pretty strong points and has arguments that are hard to answer. It might be added that district attorneys and private prosecutors as a class are just as ready to convict an innocent man as the lawyers for the defense are to acquit a red handed murderer or an offending corporation that habitually breaks every statute of the state.").

243. *Cf.* "Editorials of People," DAILY OREGON STATESMAN (Salem, OR), Nov. 29, 1902, p. 6 (satirically questioning, in response to another published article, whether officers of the law who witnessed crimes would have to wait for a private prosecutor to arrive to make an arrest).

244. "Ninth Judicial Convention," GREENSBORO PATRIOT (Greensboro, NC), Sept. 10, 1902, p. 3 (noting that the Hon. A. L. Brooks, the Democratic nominee for solicitor of the Ninth Judicial District of North Carolina, said this in accepting the nomination: "I am persuaded that we have a more difficult task and a higher duty to perform to the public and the law. And that is to vigilantly guard our dockets so that the criminal law is not used for the mere purpose of collecting civil debts out of insolvent debtors; and that the state docket is not made the vehicle of envy and spleen whereby private prosecutors in the name of the public good so frequently seek to reek their vengeance upon a weak and helpless defendant whom they have clandestinely gotten upon the docket."); "Loyalty to Country Laws," DAILY OREGON STATESMAN (Salem, OR), Oct. 23, 1902, p. 3 (noting that an address of Judge Stephen A. Lowell, of Pendleton, included these remarks: "The statutes of the states which protect the Sabbath, prohibit gambling and the social evil, and impose a penalty upon bribery, are impressive monuments to the purity of the past, but are recognized today only in short spasms of public virtue or the vengeance of some political boss or private prosecutor."). In England, the system of private prosecution also continued to be scrutinized. THE TIMES (London, England), Apr. 30, 1906, p. 9 ("The lot of a private prosecutor is at present unpleasant. 'What would it become if, in addition to his having to attend before the magistrates and the assizes where the prisoner was convicted, he were to be compelled to follow the case to the Court of Appeal at his own expense?'"); *see also* "Calhoun Styles Heney 'Hireling of a Private Prosecutor,'" THE CALL (San Francisco, CA), May 28, 1907, p. 2. Meanwhile, in some locales outside the United States, private prosecutions were eliminated. "Crown to Appear in Police Cases—New Procedure Means the Elimination of Private Prosecutors," OTTAWA JOURNAL (Ottawa, Canada), Nov. 21, 1935, p. 4. *Compare* "May Appeal," LETHBRIDGE HERALD (Lethbridge, Alberta), Feb. 10, 1938, p. 4 ("When informed of the premier's statement, George H. Steer, K.C. counsel in the private prosecution which led to conviction of the two men, said: 'If they do not surrender tomorrow, I intend to take whatever action is appropriate and necessary, acting in my capacity as counsel for the private prosecutor.'"); "Prosecution Asks 30 Year Sentence for Young Dancer," STREATOR DAILY TIMES (Streator, IL), July 24, 1947, p. 1 (noting that, in Havana, Cuba, two prosecutors—one, Gustave Reno, a private prosecutor—recommended that 21-year-old Patricia Schmidt, accused of shooting John Lester Mee, receive a 30-year sentence); "Lover Murderer's Trial Due Today," LA GRANDE EVENING OBSERVER (La Grande, OR), Sept. 17, 1947, p. 2 ("The private prosecutor is Dr. Gustavo Reno. He was hired by Dr. Lester Mee, father of the victim and a socially prominent Chicago physician, to see that Miss Schmidt gets all that is coming to her. That would be a maximum of 30 years in prison, if she is found guilty by a five-judge court for murdering her lover in cold blood."); "Satira Trial Nears Ends," INDIANA EVENING GAZETTE (Indiana, PA), Dec. 18, 1947, p. 9 (noting that, although the public prosecutor sought a manslaughter conviction, "Felipe Sarrian, private prosecutor retained by Mee's family, asked that Patricia be convicted of murder and given the maximum sentence of 30 years....").

245. "Court Term Gets Along—The Work of Judge Parson's Justice Mill Last Week," HAWAII HERALD (Hilo, HI), July 26, 1906, p. 1.

246. "Judge Andrade Hits Back Hard at Lawyer M'Bride," HAWAIIAN STAR (Honolulu, HI), Oct. 15, 1910, p. 1.

247. *E.g.*, "Woman Convicted in Death Husband Awarded New Trial—Statements of Sheriff and Prosecutor Give Woman Chance," CORSICANA DAILY SUN (Corsicana, TX), Mar. 30, 1932, p. 1 ("the court held

that argument of a private prosecutor and certain testimony of the Kleburg county sheriff were prejudicial to the defendant").

248. CHICAGO SUNDAY TRIBUNE, Apr. 5, 1914, p. 20 (including this statement from United States District Attorney James H. Wilkerson in an advertisement to "Vote Against the Revision of the Municipal Court Act": "A situation which permits the institution of prosecution for felony upon complaint of private prosecutors made on information and belief would be intolerable. This is probably one of the worst sections ever incorporated in any statute anywhere on earth."); "Those Wood Endorsements," HOT SPRINGS NEW ERA (Hot Springs, AR), May 20, 1918, p. 3 ("I will not permit my grand jury to be turned over to private prosecutors, or to be used as an instrument of oppression to any class or profession."); "A. V. Dinwiddie—Republican Candidate for County Attorney," OKLAHOMA STATE REGISTER (Guthrie, OK), June 30, 1932, p. 8 (stating in campaign ad, "When a heinous crime is committed why be compelled to employ a private prosecutor when one is maintained by the county?"); "Ray Alexander—Democratic Candidate for District Attorney (Solicitor) June 4th Runoff Primary," HIGH POINT ENTERPRISE (High Point, NC), June 1, 1974, p. 5 (noting in political advertisement that the candidate had "practiced in both criminal and civil cases" and had worked "both as a defense attorney and public and private prosecutor").

249. "Attorney Opposed to 'Third Degree' Plan," OREGON DAILY JOURNAL (Portland, OR), Apr. 2, 1912, p. 3 (noting that Walter H. Evans, a candidate for district attorney, declared that "the successful candidate for the district attorney's office should not favor any one"; "He should not listen to the ranting and threats of selfish or unthinking people. The speaker touched upon the question of the county hiring private prosecutors. He said none would be hired if he is elected."; "'The district attorney is paid $4000 a year,' said Evans, 'and I consider that a pretty good salary. A man on this salary should be able to deliver the goods.'").

250. "Taxpayers Pay $750.00 for Private Prosecutor in Case of State vs. Bryant," CORVALLIS GAZETTE-TIMES (Corvallis, OR), May 13, 1930, p. 6. In 1951, Maurice Epstein, a Republican candidate for district attorney, touted the fact that he had, "[i]n the past 3½ years," assisted the Bradford County District Attorney "as private prosecutor in cases" and that convictions were obtained in such cases. EVENING TIMES (Sayre & Athens, PA), July 23, 1951, p. 12.

251. "Reelect Michael A. Hanna District Attorney," DAILY REPUBLICAN (Monongahela, PA), May 15, 1963, p. 8.

252. "F. W. Bolowicz Files Papers—Larksville Attorney to Seek Office of District Attorney," WILKES-BARRE RECORD (Wilkes-Barre, PA), Aug. 11, 1931, p. 4.

253. "To the Voters," KERRVILLE MOUNTAIN SUN (Kerrville, TX), Oct. 13, 1932, p. 10.

254. "The Private Prosecutor," CARTER'S WEEKLY (North Wilkesboro, NC), Nov. 19, 1920, p. 4; *see also* NEWS AND OBSERVER (Raleigh, NC), Jan. 3, 1922, p. 4 ("In a New Year's suggestion just received Judge Frank Winston says:... 'Stop private prosecutors from appearing in courts.'").

255. THE GRAPHIC (Nashville, NC), Jan. 31, 1924, p. 8.

256. "We're Curious That Way," THE LANDMARK (Statesville, NC), Sept. 4, 1930, p. 12.

257. *E.g.*, "The Public Conscience Versus the Governor's Malice," THE ISSUE: A MAGAZINE INTERPRETING THE SOUTH (Jackson, MS), May 14, 1914, p. 9 ("The governor's attitude... towards this prosecution... would seem to indicate that the executive does not want what the public conscience wants; he does not desire a fair trial, but a conviction; and does not seem to care by what means it may be procured.... He has come into court, openly, as the prosecutor; not as public prosecutor, not as the district attorney would come, to urge the conviction of the accused in the name of law and of justice, but as a private prosecutor, seeking revenge upon a personal and political enemy, whose conviction must be accomplished, at any cost, that his malice, and not the ends of justice may be satisfied."); "Kidnap Trial Is Near Close," DE KALB DAILY CHRONICLE (De Kalb, IL), Jan. 22, 1934, p. 1 ("'This whole case,' McCormick told the jury, 'smacks of private persecution by private prosecutors.'"); *accord* "Scheme of Saloon Men—Effort to Show that O'-Mara and Piety Were 'Private Prosecutors,'" INDIANAPOLIS NEWS, Mar. 5, 1918, p. 3.

258. "Bondmen Request They Be Relieved," PITTSBURGH POST, Aug. 2, 1913, p. 2.

259. "Attorneys Seek to Justify Both Sides in Sneed Argument," FORT WORTH STAR-TELEGRAM (Fort Worth, TX), Feb. 22, 1913, p. 1.

260. "Best Shots Ever Fired in Texas Were Those Which Killed Al Boyce, Said Walter Scott in Speech," WACO MORNING NEWS (Waco, TX), Feb. 25, 1913, p. 2.

261. "Dumas Incent Case Goes to the Jury," FORT WORTH RECORD (Fort Worth, TX), Feb. 3, 1914, p. 4.

262. "Harris to Pay Supreme Price for His Crime—Governor Declines to Commute Sentence to Life Imprisonment," CHARLOTTE SUNDAY OBSERVER (Charlotte, NC), Sept. 25, 1921, p. 1.

263. *See, e.g.*, "A Report from District Attorney Kenneth E. Fox Jr.," NEW CASTLE NEWS (New Castle, PA), May 3, 1965, p. 3 (noting that "the charges in the cases involving 132 persons were withdrawn by the private prosecutors who had caused them to be instituted").

264. *E.g.*, "Anderson Set at Liberty—Portland Authorities Will Not Prosecute Him - The Man Arrested in Salem Charged with the Larceny of Harness from a Barn Freed upon Request of the Prosecution," DAILY OREGON STATESMAN (Salem, OR), Apr. 12, 1902, p. 4; "Assault Charges Dropped," PHILADELPHIA INQUIRER, May 21, 1920, p. 7; *see also* "Case 'Reopened and Dismissed,'" KNOXVILLE NEWS-SENTINEL (Knoxville, TN), Jan. 17, 1960, p. 2 ("City Court Clerk Ed Ware says he doesn't remember the case but he says that 'usually' such a dismissal occurs when the 'private prosecutors' or prosecution witnesses—let it be known they're willing to drop the case.").

265. "News in a Nutshell," HAWAIIAN STAR (Honolulu, HI), Feb. 20, 1911, p. 8.

266. "Pardons Granted," NEWS AND OBSERVER (Raleigh, NC), June 14, 1908, p. 13 (taking note of the case of R. A. Bradley); "Pardons Granted," DAILY INDUSTRIAL NEWS (Greensboro, NC), Dec. 6, 1908, p. 2; "Governor Grants Xmas Pardons," FORT WORTH TELEGRAM (Fort Worth, TX), Dec. 11, 1908, p. 1; "One Pardon and Few Paroles Are Granted," TWIN CITY SENTINEL (Winston-Salem, NC), Dec. 16, 1921, p. 2.

267. *E.g.*, "Granted Full Pardon," DAILY OREGON STATESMAN (Salem, OR), Apr. 18, 1903, p. 7; NEW BERN WEEKLY JOURNAL (New Bern, NC), Jan. 19, 1906, p. 1; "Pardon Day for the Governor," TIMES DISPATCH (Richmond, VA), Jan. 19, 1906, p. 5; "Leo Hamilton Gets Pardon from Prison—Private Prosecutor's Name on List of Those Asking for Executive Clemency," NEWS AND OBSERVER (Raleigh, NC), Mar. 20, 1917, p. 5.

268. "Piper Sentenced to Penitentiary," GAZETTE TIMES (Pittsburgh, PA), Feb. 23, 1909, p. 8.

269. "Whitehead Commutation—Reasons Why Governor Changed the Sentence," NEWS AND OBSERVER (Raleigh, NC), Apr. 9, 1910, p. 5.

270. "Asked Help for Negro—Attorney in Bennett Case Wrote to Governor," HOUSTON POST, Jan. 2, 1914, p. 9.

271. Sometimes, the very identity of private prosecutors remained hidden, at least temporarily, or were attempted to be concealed or obscured by counsel. "Exciting Scenes—In the Court Room at the Pitt Murder Trial," EL PASO DAILY HERALD (El Paso, TX), Nov. 20, 1900, p. 4 (noting that when Judge Edwards asked if there were any private prosecutors in the case of *State of Texas vs. Sidney Pitt* for the murder of Hinks Hill in Ward County, Judge Hammond of Colorado City—who had been employed to assist the district attorney—stepped forward and said, "I am assisting the district attorney," but then declined to say who he was representing, at which point the defense filed a motion to have the name of the person who had employed any private prosecutor disclosed); "Examining of Witnesses," PALESTINE DAILY HERALD (Palestine, TX), Sept. 21, 1904, p. 1 ("The defense also called upon the state to know who were the private prosecutors in the case. This consumed several minutes."); "Dumas's Daughter on Witness Stand," FORT WORTH RECORD (Fort Worth, TX), Jan. 30, 1914, p. 5 ("Attorneys for Dumas asked the private prosecutor who employed him and he 'declined to answer,' and Thursday morning they had him summoned as a witness."); "Metz Is Confused in Some of His Replies in Trial on Friday," NEWS-HERALD (Franklin and Oil City, PA), Nov. 20, 1926, p. 2 ("G. G. Martin, of defense counsel, said of the prosecution, 'Was it begun in good faith by state officers or is there a private prosecutor who does not appear?' 'Do you know who provided private counsel in this case?' Mr. Martin asked and objection to the question was sustained."); *see also* "Ferguson's Name Figures in Watson Case," CAMERON HERALD (Cameron, TX), Nov. 2, 1916, p. 1 (noting in the context of a capital murder trial: "Just after the first venireman had been examined counsel for the defense insisted that the private prosecutors in the case tell whom they represented. No objection was offered, and Lud T. Williams of Waco said he was in the case at the solicitation of Governor Ferguson,

who had employed him, as governor. Cullen F. Thomas of Dallas said he was employed by Mrs. Patterson, widow of the decedent, and her brother, Arthur Carnes of Moody.").

272. "Private Lawyers Are Not in Favor—Surprising Order Made in Criminal Court Against a Practice That Is Regarded Now as an Abuse," PITTSBURG PRESS (Pittsburgh, PA), Nov. 2, 1900, p. 7. In the early twentieth century, the district attorney would sometimes await the receipt of evidence from private prosecutors before considering bringing criminal charges. "Bell and Gordon Split on Filtration Suits," PHILADELPHIA INQUIRER, July 12, 1905, p. 1 ("The District Attorney specifically pointed out that he had no evidence on which such prosecutions could be begun, but offered to co-operate the instant the private prosecutors would furnish the evidence and take the initiative.").

273. "Gambling Cases Net Constable Good Sum—Receives One-Half Penalty Imposed in Justice Court and Also Other Fees," COOS BAY TIMES (Coos Bay, OR), Mar. 15, 1921, p. 6 ("Under the state law, the private prosecutor gets one-half of the fines imposed.").

274. "Court News," MONONGAHELA VALLEY REPUBLICAN (Monongahela, PA), May 17, 1900, p. 3 (noting of the grand jury for the May term: "Of all the cases before the jury, but seven bills were ignored, the costs on four of these being placed on the county and the remainder on the private prosecutors."); "A Full Court Week," WELLSBORO AGITATOR (Wellsboro, PA), Oct. 3, 1900, p. 1 ("The jury found the defendant not guilty, but placed two-thirds of the costs upon him and the remaining one-third of the costs upon the private prosecutor, Mike Rose."); "A Eugene Boy," DAILY EUGENE GUARD (Eugene, OR), Sept. 23, 1901, p. 1 ("Justice Robinett decided that Blair was not guilty of a misdemeanor and taxed the cost of the case to the private prosecutor."); "January Court," MANSFIELD ADVERTISER (Mansfield, PA), Feb. 4, 1903, p. 3 ("Charles Dorrance, assault and battery, was acquitted but sentenced to pay two-thirds of the costs, the private prosecutor the other third."); "The County Court," WELLSBORO AGITATOR (Wellsboro, PA), Oct. 1, 1902, p. 1 (noting that private prosecutors were ordered to pay costs in two cases).

275. "Urban-Tyszka Case Ruling," DAILY NOTES (Canonsburg, PA), Apr. 24, 1907, p. 1; "Last Cases in Criminal Court," DAILY NOTES (Canonsburg, PA), Sept. 2, 1907, p. 1 (noting that after a not guilty verdict, the cost were placed on two of the private prosecutors).

276. "Sentenced for Costs," DAILY REPUBLICAN (Monongahela, PA), May 5, 1904, p. 1. Some private prosecutions were ignored by grand juries for lack of evidence. *E.g.*, "Grand Jury Is Discharged," DAILY REPUBLICAN (Monongahela, PA), Aug. 18, 1913, p. 1 (noting that the grand jury "ignored" a case "of the commonwealth against Ida Glamm, of Bentleyville, charged with arson and felonious breaking and entry and larceny" where "Samuel Dudra was the private prosecutor" and "[m]ost of the evidence" against Glamm "was circumstantial").

277. "Dividing Costs in the Many Trivial Cases," DAILY REPUBLICAN (Monongahela, PA), May 15, 1913, p. 1.

278. "Mrs. Pizzica Is Found Not Guilty," DAILY REPUBLICAN (Monongahela PA), Aug. 24, 1906, p. 1; "Found Not Guilty," DAILY REPUBLICAN (Monongahela, PA), May 18, 1907, p. 1.

279. "Dividing Costs in the Many Trivial Cases," DAILY REPUBLICAN (Monongahela, PA), May 15, 1913, p. 1; *see also id.* ("The parties came from Catsburg, and it was simply a fight. Ban alleged that during the fracas the defendant had severely cut him, and the defendant claimed that Ban was the aggressor in the trouble. The defendant paid his part of the costs, amounting to $9.20. The private prosecutor could not raise the amount he had to pay and went to jail.").

280. "Costs were Divided," DAILY REPUBLICAN (Monongahela, PA), Nov. 16, 1904, p. 1.

281. "In County Court," DAILY REPUBLICAN (Monongahela, PA), May 12, 1905, p. 1.

282. "Local Man Cleared of Embezzlement Charges," DAILY NOTES (Canonsburg, PA), Nov. 16, 1922, p. 1.

283. "Mills of Justice Grinding Slowly," DAILY NOTES (Canonsburg, PA), Nov. 16, 1905, p. 1.

284. "Alleged Bank Swindler Put on Trial in Criminal Court," DAILY NOTES (Canonsburg, PA), Nov. 15, 1906, p. 1; *see also* "Verdicts Given in Criminal Court," DAILY NOTES (Canonsburg, PA), Aug. 22, 1908, p. 1 ("The jury returned a verdict of not guilty, but placed one-fourth of the costs on the defendant. The remainder of the costs were placed on the private prosecutor."); "Mrs. Mitchell Not Guilty," DAILY REPUBLICAN (Monongahela, PA), Feb. 13, 1909, p. 4 ("Not guilty, and placing three-fourths of the costs on the private prosecutor, William R. Scott, and one fourth on the defendant, Mrs. Mary Mitchell, of Eldora, was

the verdict returned yesterday in the prosecution of Mrs. Mitchell on the charge of larceny. Private prosecutor and defendant were sentenced to pay costs or give security for the payment of the same in ten days.").

285. "Local Youth Freed of Assault Charge," DAILY REPUBLICAN (Monongahela, PA), Nov. 14, 1930, p. 1.

286. "Homicide Case Called in Court," DAILY NOTES (Canonsburg, PA), May 19, 1913, p. 1.

287. Sometimes, the private prosecutors held the cards in their hands when it came to costs. "Made Restitution to Bank," WILLINGTON MESSENGER (Willington, NC), Nov. 22, 1905, p. 1 ("The defendants, J. C. Haigh and G. G. Myrover came into court accompanied by their counsel and plead[ed] guilty to the bill of indictment pending against them, and it appearing to the court that restitution has been made, upon the recommendation of the Bank of Fayetteville, the private prosecutor and by the consent of the solicitor, it is ordered that judgment be, and the same hereby is, suspended upon the payment of the costs of this action, to be taxed by the clerk of this court.").

288. "Judge and Jury," MANSFIELD ADVERTISER (Mansfield, PA), Dec. 11, 1901, p. 3 (noting that "[t] he costs were divided between defendants and V. K. Jones the private prosecutor"); *see also* "Canonsburg Woman on Trial," DAILY NOTES (Canonsburg, PA), Aug. 16, 1904, p. 1 ("In the case of the commonwealth against Hannah Crumpton on the charge of larceny, tried this morning, the jury found the defendant guilt[y] but divided the cost. The defendant is from Canonsburg as is the private prosecutor, Joseph Simons."); "Grand Jury's Work Finished," DAILY NOTES (Canonsburg, PA), Aug. 19, 1908, p. 1 ("The jurors evidently thought one was as much to blame as the other, as they found the defendant not guilty, but divided the costs between him and the private prosecutor."); "Happenings in the County Courts," DAILY REPUBLICAN (Monongahela, PA), Nov. 15, 1910, p. 1 ("Charles Verdikel, a miner of Hackett, was found not guilty of malicious mischief and assault and battery, but was assessed one-half the costs. The other half was placed on the private prosecutor, a fellow countryman. The two men had trouble over some beer.").

289. "Leib Case in Hands of Jury Today," EVENING PUBLIC LEDGER (Philadelphia, PA), Dec. 5, 1919, p. 2; *see also* "Prosecutors Fined—Two Given Penalties for Bringing of Unwarranted Charges," PHILADELPHIA INQUIRER, Mar. 24, 1920, p. 10 ("Two private prosecutors who were responsible for unwarranted prosecutions were fined yesterday by a jury before Judge McCullen, in Quarter Sessions Court. The jurors in each case acquitted the defendants accused and imposed the costs of the prosecution on the private prosecutors.").

290. "Beaver County Judge to Assist Next Week," DAILY NOTES (Canonsburg, PA), May 17, 1913, p. 1 ("The private prosecutor having stated to the district attorney that he had received full satisfaction of the injury done him, the case of the commonwealth against Frank Labor, Sam Ladula and Fortunata Ladula of Cokeburg, charged with felonious assault, has been settled. The private prosecutor alleged he was attacked by these men and cut."); LANCASTER EXAMINER (Lancaster, PA), May 31, 1913, p. 4 ("When the trial of three former police officers and two organization workers, charged with election crime, was called in court yesterday, the Committee of Seventy and George Wharton Pepper, private prosecutors, astounded spectators by announcing an agreement to drop prosecution."); "Bass Charges Withdrawn—Colored Sculptor Takes Back Larceny Accusation," PHILADELPHIA INQUIRER, Dec. 5, 1913, p. 3 (noting that "[b]y agreement of counsel for the private prosecutor and the District Attorney's office," that indictments "were submitted for verdicts of not guilty").

291. "John Shinko Released From Jail," DAILY REPUBLICAN (Monongahela, PA), Oct. 3, 1907, p. 1.

292. "Robert Bell Must Serve Five Years," DAILY REPUBLICAN (Monongahela, PA), Nov. 16, 1906, p. 1; "In the Superior Court—Several Important Cases Settled Last Week," CAROLINA WATCHMAN (Salisbury, NC), Feb. 20, 1907, p. 7; "Items of Interest from Washington Co. Courts," DAILY NOTES (Canonsburg, PA), Feb. 22, 1928, p. 4.

293. "Scales of Justice," WELLSBORO AGITATOR (Wellsboro, PA), Dec. 4, 1901, p. 1.

294. "For Stealing a Bike," DAILY OREGON STATESMAN (Salem, OR), July 19, 1902, p. 4.

295. "The Cash Settlements in Court," THE LANDMARK (Statesville, NC), Aug. 4, 1930, p. 4; *see also id.* ("Because private prosecutors may be satisfied with reparations and express a desire that the defendant be allowed to go without a day, does not settle the bill to society, which has a very great interest in such matters. Laws are passed for the protection of all the people, and their violation is not a matter for agreement on the part of individuals."). In some instances, private prosecutors—sometimes threatening to withdraw

from representation—got into attorneys' fee disputes with the lawyers they retained. *E.g.*, "A Temporary Jury in the Hyde Case," ARIZONA REPUBLIC (Phoenix, AZ), Apr. 15, 1910, p. 1 (noting in the context of "the Hyde murder trial" in Kansas City that there was a dispute "over the size of the attorney's fees" between "Mrs. L. O. Swope and special counsel she has employed to assist the state in the prosecution of her son-in-law, Dr. Hyde"; that Mrs. Swope "objected to the amount of the fee and suggested a smaller one"; and that "[o]ther members of the Swope family refusing to aid in defraying expenses attached to the employment of lawyers, the burden of payment fell upon Mrs. Swope"). The employment of attorneys for private prosecutions was expensive, and sometimes those victimized by offenders could not afford to hire attorneys to pursue criminal cases, especially against wealthy, white-collar offenders. "The Big Criminals," BOSTON GLOBE (Boston, MA), June 30, 1910, p. 10 ("Why do big criminals go free? innocently asks a contemporary. This query can be answered in several ways. If the offender represents trust interests there are always funds enough in the safe or bank to prolong a lawsuit almost indefinitely, as President Taft has pointed out, and a private prosecutor soon retires from the field."). Sometimes, citizens simply chose not to pursue criminal cases as private prosecutors even though they wished that public authorities would pursue criminal charges. "Drunken Driving Grows; Fines Called Too Light—Courts, Police Blame Public for Failing to Carry Prosecution Under State Law," KNOXVILLE NEWS-SENTINEL (Knoxville, TN), July 31, 1949, p. A-12 (quoting City Judge Charles G. Kelly as follows: "Citizens as individuals just won't take an interest in the cases in which they are privately involved. Private prosecutors won't come to court to push charges against the defendant, although they have demanded that the officer bring the charges."); "4 Freed of Charges in Drunken Driving," KNOXVILLE NEWS-SENTINEL (Knoxville, TN), Nov. 29, 1950, p. 19 ("Three men were freed of city and state charges of drunken driving today in City Court when private prosecutors failed to appear to push charges against them.").

296. "In Justice Court," DAILY JOURNAL (Salem, OR), Oct. 4, 1990, p. 4 (noting "the private prosecutor had failed to appear"); "Court Proceedings," MANSFIELD ADVERTISER (Mansfield, PA), Sept. 24, 1902, p. 3 ("The private prosecutor not appearing, Herbert Gardner and E. G. Kelts under indictment for burglary and larceny, were declared not guilty and were discharged."); "Court Hears Surety Cases," DAILY NOTES (Canonsburg, PA), May 8, 1907, p. 1 ("Only one bill was ignored during the day, and it was where the private prosecutor was absent . . . ."); "Frey Acquitted," PHILADELPHIA INQUIRER, June 30, 1908, p. 6 (noting that "the private prosecutor had failed to appear in court to press the charges" and that "Judge Magill directed that the bills of indictment be submitted for verdicts of not guilty"); "Acquitted of Liquor Selling, Costs on the Prosecutor," DAILY NOTES (Canonsburg, PA), Sept. 6, 1911, p. 1 ("The case of the commonwealth was somewhat weakened by the non-appearance of the private prosecutor, the court declaring that when one man charged another with breaking the law he should not be afraid to face him in court."); "Prosecutor Failed to Appear," DAILY REPUBLICAN (Monongahela, PA), May 14, 1915, p. 1 (noting that the private prosecutor failed to appear and that the court directed a non-guilty verdict and that costs be placed on the prosecutor); *see also* "Former City Auditor Freed in Driving Case," KNOXVILLE NEWS-SENTINEL (Knoxville, TN), Feb. 12, 1949, p. 1 (noting that a charge of drunken driving was dropped "because of absence of a private prosecutor who didn't appear at hearing yesterday in City Court"); "Lack of Licenses Ignored in Drunk Driving Cases," KNOXVILLE NEWS-SENTINEL, Mar. 10, 1950, p. 1 (noting that "private prosecutors . . . sometimes don't like to prosecute a case all the way"); "Driver Freed in Accident Which Killed Woman," KNOXVILLE NEWS-SENTINEL, Apr. 5, 1950, p. 21 (noting that a drunken driving charge was dismissed "when a private prosecutor, S. T. Hunley, Powell, failed to appear").

297. "Coerper Drops Bolte Charge," HAWAIIAN STAR (Honolulu, HI), Oct. 23, 1909, p. 1 (noting the withdrawal of a charge of adultery by a private prosecutor).

298. "Defendant Says He Meant No Harm—Alleged Statutory Case Involving Lebanon Young Man Dismissed—Private Prosecutor Backs Down," WEEKLY HERALD (Albany, OR), Jan. 2, 1908, p. 2.

299. "Crime Has Increased," LEBANON DAILY NEWS (Lebanon, PA), Dec. 8, 1902, p. 1 ("The assault and battery charge against William Gregg, of this city, was withdrawn by the private prosecutor, Timothy Hartnett."); Case Compromised," RALEIGH TIMES (Raleigh, NC), Nov. 27, 1905, p. 3 ("Mrs. Wiggins has withdrawn as private prosecutor in the criminal proceeding against Mr. Featherston, who was charged with kicking the Army worker from his liquor shop several weeks ago.").

300. 15A Jeanne M. Naffky, C.J.S. *Compounding Offenses* § 4 (June 2021 Update) ("At common law, the compounding of a misdemeanor was, at least in a restricted sense, an indictable offense, as well as the compounding of a felony. Apart from statutes expressly making the compounding of a misdemeanor an indictable offense, it is to be noted that some statutes refer to the offense compounded in general terms, such as 'crime' or 'violation of statute,' but under other statutes, the compounding of offenses is limited to felonies."); Wight v. Rindskopf, 43 Wis. 344, 361 (1877) ("[i]t is supposed by some that compounding an offense was anciently an offense of equal grade with the offense compounded. However that may be, compounding a felony has been so long a crime as to have come down to us with his Saxon name of *theft-bote*, and compounding a misdemeanor of an essentially public nature has almost as long been an indictable *obstruction of the course of public justice*") (emphasis added). *Compare* David D. Friedman, *Making Sense of English Law Enforcement in the Eighteenth Century*, 2 U. Chi. Sch. Roundtable 475, 486 (1995) ("One way of resolving a civil suit is through out-of-court settlement. The equivalent in a system of private enforcement of criminal law is for the prosecutor to compound the offense—to agree, in exchange for some sort of compensation, not to press charges. Compounding a misdemeanor was legal in eighteenth-century England. Indeed, magistrates seem to have felt that part of their job was to encourage private settlements between the offender and the injured party, thus keeping disputes out of the courts."); *with id.* at 487 ("Compounding a felony was illegal; once a prosecutor had filed felony charges, he was supposed to carry the case through to trial. It appears to have also been common. One of the criticisms of the system of private prosecution, especially during the nineteenth-century attempts to establish a system of public prosecutors, was that many cases were dropped because of agreements between the prosecutor and the defendant.").

301. C. C. Daniels, "Suggestions to Magistrates: Information of Value Not Only to Magistrates and Mayors But to All Citizens," News and Observer (Raleigh, NC), Mar. 11, 1906, p. 1.

302. Friedman, *supra* note 300, at 487; *see also* Laurie Edelstein, *An Accusation Easily to Be Made? Rape and Malicious Prosecution in Eighteenth-Century England*, 42 Am. J. Legal Hist. 351, 380 n.110 (1998) ("Making private arrangements and settling out of court, or 'compounding' a *felony*, was technically illegal, although it is believed that it was widely practiced and hardly ever punished. Compounding a misdemeanor, in contrast, was legal and often encouraged by magistrates who wished the parties, particularly in trespass and assault cases, to settle privately and out of court.") (citations omitted).

303. "Judge Jones's Charge," Montgomery Advertiser (Montgomery, AL), Nov. 5, 1901, p. 5 (noting that Judge Jones gave the following charge to the grand jury: "The law wisely excludes any private prosecutor from appearing before you, or directing your attention to matters which you should investigate. If this were permitted you would often become the medium of unjust and oppressive accusation."); "Judge Jones Charges Jury," Montgomery Advertiser (Montgomery, AL), May 25, 1910, p. 7 ("Different from the State court, a private prosecutor cannot appear. The only persons who are authorized to go before you are the District Attorney, the Assistant District Attorney, and in some cases which will be brought to your attention, at this term, special assistants to the Attorney General, who have been appointed by him in pursuance of law for the investigation of certain matters.").

304. "Grand Jury Drawn," Fresno Morning Republican (Fresno, CA), Oct. 23, 1900, p. 7 (noting that Judge Risley read the following charge to grand jurors: "You will not allow private prosecutors to intrude themselves into your presence and present accusations. Generally such parties are actuated by private enmity and seek merely the gratification of their personal malice. If they possess any information justifying the accusation of the person against whom they complain, they should impart it to the district attorney, who will seldom fail to act in a proper case; but if the district attorney should refuse to act, they can make their complaint to a committing magistrate before whom the matter can be investigated, and if sufficient evidence be produced of the commission of a public offense by the accused, he can be held to answer to the charge.").

305. "Judge Estee's Charge to the Grand Jury," Pacific Commercial Advertiser (Honolulu, HI), Apr. 10, 1901, p. 9 (noting that at the first federal grand jury for the territory, the grand jury charge by Judge Estee included the following remarks: "I particularly instruct you not to allow private prosecutors or private defenders to intrude themselves upon your attention."); *see also* "The Grand Jury Given Its Work," Evening Bulletin (Honolulu, HI), Sept. 19, 1901, p. 1 ("They should not allow any private prosecutor to

appear before them."); "County Attorney on Grand Jury and the Tribune," HAWAII HERALD (Hilo, HI), Dec. 3, 1908, p. 1 (noting that the judge's grand jury charge included the following language: "It is not your duty to act upon vague rumors or reports, nor to listen to tales told you outside the jury room, nor to admit private prosecutors to attend your sessions."); "Charge to the Grand Jury," HAWAII HERALD, Dec. 2, 1909, p. 2 ("nor shall you permit any private prosecutor to appear before you for the purpose of making charges, instituting proceedings, or of invoking your assistance for any purpose").

306. "Grand Jury Quit—Three Days Work Gets No Results So They Adjourn," CANEY NEWS (Caney, KS), Jan. 28, 1921, p. 1 (noting of Judge Holdren's instruction to the grand jury convened in Independence, Kansas: "He also told them to look to the county attorney for legal advice. No other person than the county attorney is permitted to enter the grand jury room. No private prosecutors are allowed to enter the jury room. Such private prosecutors, the judge told the jury, can present their evidence to the county attorney or if not satisfied with his actions, may present it to any magistrate of the county who in turn can communicate it to the district court.").

307. "Throng at Opening of Superior Court," BANGOR DAILY NEWS (Bangor, ME), Sept. 3, 1919, p. 3 (noting that Justice Bertram L. Smith's grand jury charge in Penobscot county's superior court included the following language: "You should be very cautious in finding indictments based upon complaints of private prosecutors of a friv[o]lous character and should especially scrutinize testimony in cases which sometimes arise, where the purpose sought is not the vindication of the laws and the protection of the public, but a design to subserve some private interest—as for instance the collection of a debt.").

308. "April Grand Jury Warned Against Partisan Actions—Judge Franklin Ferriss Carefully Outlines Scope of That Body's Work," ST. LOUIS REPUBLIC (St. Louis, MO), Apr. 2, 1901, p. 2 ("Judge Ferriss warned the body against allowing private prosecutors to prevent accusations for the gratification of personal malice."); "Hard Words of the Court," KANSAS CITY STAR (Kansas City, MO) pp. 1–2 (noting that Judge Hazell gave the following grand jury charge: "You will not allow, under any circumstances, private prosecutors to intrude themselves into your presence and present accusations. Such parties are generally actuated by private malice, and seek gratification of personal malice."); "New Grand Jury Told to Carry Vote Inquiry On," ST. LOUIS POST-DISPATCH, Dec. 6, 1920, pp. 1–2 (noting that Judge Landwehr "cautioned the grand jurors to be especially guarded in entertaining accusations made by private prosecutors, and said all anonymous communications should be disregarded").

309. "Grand Jury Begins Work of Inquiry," LINCOLN DAILY EVENING NEWS (Lincoln, NE), Apr. 29, 1907, p. 1 (noting that Judge Lincoln Frost gave the following grand jury charge: "You should not allow private prosecutors to intrude themselves into your presence and present accusations, as such parties are usually actuated by private enmity, and seek merely gratification of their personal malice."); *accord* "Grand Jury Is Starting Work," LINCOLN DAILY STAR (Lincoln, NE), Apr. 29, 1907, p. 4 (reporting the same charge).

310. "September Term of Monmouth Court Opens—Justice Bodine Delivers Unusual Charge to Grand Jury," MONMOUTH DEMOCRAT (Freehold, NJ), Sept. 29, 1932, p. 1 (noting that Justice Joseph Bodine's grand jury charge included the following instruction: "You will not allow private prosecutors to intrude themselves into your presence and present accusations. The reason is obvious. The grand jury is an impartial body earnestly seeking to determine whether there have been infractions of the criminal law.")

311. "Grand Jury Informed of Protected Vice," N.Y. TIMES, Dec. 4, 1900, p. 3 (noting that Judge Warren W. Foster, in charging the grand jury, gave this instruction: "But, gentlemen, beware of the private prosecutor. Let him not intrude into your room, and through malice or hatred, influence your action against his enemy.").

312. "State Election To Be Probed by U.S. Grand Jury," SHAWNEE DAILY HERALD (Shawnee, OK), Jan. 10, 1911, p. 1 (noting that a federal judge, Judge Cotteral, "cautioned" the grand jury "against private prosecutors, and against giving attention to anonymous letters").

313. "The January Term," WELLSBORO AGITATOR (Wellsboro, PA), Jan. 30, 1901, p. 1 (noting that Judge Jerome B. Niles "took up the subject of costs" in his grand jury charge and "explained under what circumstance the costs might be put upon the private prosecutor: that the private prosecutor named in the indictment might be only a 'stool-pigeon' and that in that event the grand jury could seek out the real prosecutor and place the costs upon him in proper cases, but that the costs ought never to be placed upon

such a prosecutor unless he be a witness before them or brought before them and given an opportunity to explain his actions").

314. "First Jury of Kind Called in County," LA CROSSE TRIBUNE (La Crosse, WI), Jan. 8, 1912, p. 6 (noting that Judge Higbee's charge to a La Crosse County grand jury included the following language: "You will not allow private prosecutors to intrude themselves into your presence, and present accusations. Generally such parties are actuated by private enmity, and seek merely the gratifications of their personal malice.").

315. *See also* EDWARDSVILLE INTELLIGENCER (Edwardsville, IL), Dec. 22, 1917, p. 3 ("The courts have previously held that 'private prosecutors are not allowed to intrude themselves to the grand jury since generally such parties are actuated by private enmity and seek merely the gratification of their personal malice.'").

316. "Judge Parsons Opens the February Term," HILO TRIBUNE (Hilo, HI), Feb. 21, 1905, p. 6; "Grand Jury Charged by Judge Parsons," HAWAII HERALD (Hilo, HI), Mar. 1, 1906, p. 1.

317. "Private Prosecutors," ST. LOUIS POST-DISPATCH, Apr. 2, 1900, p. 2.

318. "Love to Head Grand Jury," SAN MATEO TIMES (San Mateo, CA), Mar. 11, 1953, p. 2 ("The jurist warned the jury not to allow private prosecutors to intrude themselves into its presence and present accusations.").

319. "Bankers Decide to Fight," PITTSBURG PRESS (Pittsburgh, PA), Nov. 1, 1905, p. 1.

320. "Epting Trial Arguments—Special Prosecutor Delivers Speech Before Jury," AUSTIN STATESMAN (Austin, TX), Jan. 23, 1913, p. 3.

321. "Life Sentenced Reversed—Joe M'Kay of Antelope Gets New Trial," SUNDAY STATE JOURNAL (Lincoln, NE), Oct. 8, 1911, p. 10; "Supreme Court Syllabi," LINCOLN DAILY STAR (Lincoln, NE), Oct. 10, 1911, p. 7.

322. HENRY P. STODDART, ED., REPORTS OF CASES IN THE SUPREME COURT OF NEBRASKA (1912), Vol. 90, pp. 63, 69–71, 73–75.

323. "Private Prosecutors," READING TIMES (Reading, PA), Dec. 15, 1928, p. 8; *see also id.* ("When these private prosecutor cases are not brought for vengeance then they are brought to coerce and force under the duress of the fear of jail the payment of damage claims. This is not blackmail simply and solely because the law makes it legal."); *id.* ("In so far as the private prosecutor's action is used to force settlement of claims, it is as iniquitous as our aldermanic system, the motive being the collection of fees and not justice."). The *Reading Times* expressed its disapproval of private prosecution, using a biblical reference to make its points. "When we do this, then like Pontius Pilate, having found no wrong in the man ourselves," the paper wrote, "we wash our hands and turn him over as a sacrifice to those who far from a desire to see justice done, hunger only for revenge and reprisal." *Id.*

324. "Improving the Legal System," READING TIMES (Reading, PA), June 26, 1929, p. 6; *see also* "Using the Jail for Private Gain," READING TIMES (Reading, PA), Dec. 12, 1929, p. 8 ("Confronted as we are by the cruel and clownish injustices inherent in the twin evils of the private prosecutor and the aldermanic system, we are prone to grow callous. We have been taught to gloss over and wink at the perversion and downright degeneracy of the law and our court procedure into instruments of cold blooded legalistic blackmail. Here every day in Berks we see the criminal statutes used in the high name of the People of the Commonwealth to hound victims into settling civil suits."); *id.* ("Jail was meant for the punishment of criminals and for the detention of those accused of crime. It was not meant for men and women charged with no crime. It is not to punish or harass men and women at the whim of a lawyer. It is high time the state and our courts prevented the use of the jail by private citizens and their lawyers for private gain and private purposes.").

In 1930, in an editorial titled "Justice—A Tragic Joke," the *Reading Times* lamented that "[c]ountless pieces of wicked prosecution have been started and countless thousands of dollars have gone to greedy aldermen and avaricious lawyers" under the private prosecution system. As the newspaper pointedly observed: "At every term of our court the dignity of the Commonwealth of Pennsylvania is being dragged in the dirt and made a mockery of from motives combined of spite and of greed. The spite is on the part of those who fancy they are aggrieved but have no case at law. The greed is on the part of the aldermen and constables and lawyers who are lining their pockets with fees mulcted from angry plaintiffs and bewildered and unfortunate defendants." In its 1930 editorial, the *Reading Times* put it this way: "What is this private prosecution system? It is a system whereby any lawyer representing a private individual, whose case in most instances is so weak and poor that the public prosecutor will not touch it, becomes, for the mere asking, virtually a deputy district attorney, clothed with the full power of that mighty office and privileged to use and misuse it almost as he pleases." "Justice—A Tragic Joke," READING TIMES (Reading, PA), Sept. 19, 1930, p. 6. The private prosecution system, the *Reading Times* observed, "can be done away with in a single day, in the twinkling of an eye," if Paul Schaeffer, the president judge of the Berks County Courts, would only condemn it. To put "an effectual check on the private prosecutor," the paper advised, President Judge Schaeffer "has only to put upon it the official condemnation it deserves and bring the truly tremendous force and prestige of his high office against it." "He," it concluded, "has merely to announce from the bench that henceforth the court will sign no 'nolle prosse' orders without full explanation made in open court and that it will roundly and publicly rebuke every lawyer every time when, in the opinion of the court, he has either used our criminal law for a civil purpose or appeared as private prosecutor in a case where the testimony shows a wealth of spite and venom and a sad lack of sound evidence." *Id.* In describing how the private prosecution system worked (and was put to use by private lawyers for their clients), the *Reading Times* further observed: "The district attorney asks the indictment of the chosen victim as a matter of routine. That indictment returned, this lawyer is free to take the time of our courts to prosecute if he pleases or he can, and very often does, blackjack the defendant into a money settlement and then at his request the district attorney and the court 'nolle prosse' or kill the case." "It is a system," the *Reading Times* stressed, "which invites abuse and encourages wicked, if not illegal, collusions and alignments between lawyers and their clients and aldermen." "It is a system," the newspaper added, "which consistently robs the poor and the ignorant and breeds hatred and contempt of law in this community.

325. READING TIMES (Reading, PA), Sept. 22, 1931, p. 4; *see also* "Mr. Wanner's Program," READING TIMES (Reading, PA), Nov. 7, 1931, p. 4 ("[T]his is an excellent opportunity to point out that this is an excellent time for our judges to abolish the private prosecutor whose abuses are as great as those of avaricious aldermen. Here no state law is required. Just a change in the rules of the court so that, as in some other counties, every criminal case must be prosecuted by the public prosecutor and on his responsibility. As it is now, any vengeful person can, and does hire a lawyer who from that time takes over the whole power of the district attorney's office, harrowing and hounding men and women the district attorney would never dream of proceeding against. Just a change in court rules and instead of this, the private prosecutor would have to sit dumb in court making certain prosecution is not persecution."); *id.* ("Alone Mr. Wanner can accomplish a great deal. With the help of the judges, the lawyers and the decent aldermen he can come close to wiping out this abuse. And the judges can wipe out the private prosecutor abuse, with a stroke of the pen. Let us wish every success to the new district attorney and let us hope he is given the support he should have."); "Private Persecutors," READING TIMES (Reading, PA), Apr. 15, 1932, p. 10 ("Lawyers are hired as private prosecutors for one of two purposes only: either to obtain private vengeance or to use the criminal law to collect private debts. They are in short, private persecutors, hired and paid by private persons yet operating in the name of the commonwealth. We elect and we pay a district attorney and his staff to represent the commonwealth and there is no legitimate reason why any criminal case should be tried except by these elected officials. The debts the private prosecutor uses the criminal law to blackjack and often blackmail defendants into paying, should be collected by civil suit. Many states have abolished the private prosecutor and more progressive Pennsylvania counties have banished him almost altogether by rule of the court."). *Compare* "Are Not Bosses, Lawyer Tells Minor Judiciary," READING TIMES (Reading, PA), Apr. 27, 1939, p. 24 ("Members of Berks county's minor judiciary—aldermen in the city and justices of the peace in boroughs and township—last night were told by Bertram J. Murphy, attorney and former assistant district attorney, that they 'are their own bosses' and should arrive at their decisions independent of public or private prosecutors, counsel or other interested parties."; "A practice has grown up," Murphy said, "where various magistrates seem to take orders from the district attorney's office, private prosecutors, and other officers in many criminal cases."); "Wants Aldermen Paid by Salary," WILKES-BARRE TIMES LEADER (Wilkes-Barre, Pa), Sept. 7, 1940, p. 14 ("Sharp criticism of aldermen who surround themselves with constables and professional private prosecutors and who are permitted county-wide jurisdiction became a matter of court record yesterday.... Attorney Mattes declared that under the

law alderman are placed in the position of having to depend upon fees derived from the volume of business, which should be rectified by substitution of the present system by the placing of a qualified minor judiciary of limited numbers and on a salary basis.").

326. "Limit Private Prosecution," THE LANDMARK (Statesville, NC), Feb. 4, 1929, p. 4.

327. "Legal Practice in Prosecuting Case Is Changed—Private or Special Prosecutors Are Eliminated by Order," MORNING HERALD (Uniontown, PA), Feb. 29, 1944, pp. 1–2. The district attorney was frequently referred to as a "quasi-judicial officer." *E.g.*, "Blasted Hopes," PHILADELPHIA INQUIRER, Dec. 15, 1885, p. 3 ("The defense objected to this proposition on the ground that in a former case Judge Biddle had declined to permit private counsel to prosecute because the District Attorney, being a quasi judicial officer, stood between a prisoner and the Commonwealth, and that private counsel, in his zeal for his client, might go further and do things which the District Attorney would not do."); "Powers of the Court and Rights of District Attorney," THE NEW ERA (Lancaster, PA), June 2, 1894, p. 4 ("In the exercise of his office certain things are entrusted to his judgment, which, in the sphere of his duties, may be and often is superior to that of the Judge. He is a constitutional officer; he is a 'quasi judicial officer.'").

328. "Davis Trial Is Nearing Close," DECATUR DAILY (Decatur, AL), Oct. 25, 1950, p. 1 (noting that "Bennett Eslick, a private prosecutor," was assisting the attorney general and his assistant); "Attorneys Begin Jury Arguments," DAILY TIMES-NEWS (Burlington, NC), June 17, 1960, p. 17 (noting that in a murder trial, for the killing of Charles Alfred Johnson, the private prosecutor was W. R. Dalton); "Foust Gets 10–20 Years for Murder," DAILY TIMES-NEWS (Burlington, NC), Mar. 9, 1962, pp. 1B, 7B (noting that 16-year-old was sentenced on a second-degree murder charge in which a private prosecutor, Louis Allen Jr. of Burlington, participated).

329. "Thurman Jury Not Complete," LUBBOCK EVENING JOURNAL (Lubbock, TX), Oct. 24, 1950, p. 1 (noting that "a private prosecutor, Billy Hall of Littlefield," would be assisting in the prosecution).

330. "News of the County Court," WELLSBORO AGITATOR (Wellsboro, PA), Nov. 29, 1950, p. 4.

331. "Moses Wilson Released on $1,000 Bond," OREGON STATESMAN (Salem, OR), Feb. 27, 1951, p. 12.

332. "Larceny Charged," KNOXVILLE JOURNAL (Knoxville, TN), June 27, 1961, p. 7.

333. "Rape Attempt Charged," KNOXVILLE NEWS-SENTINEL (Knoxville, TN), Apr. 12, 1960, p. 9.

334. *E.g.*, "Jury Is Selected," DAILY INDEPENDENT (Kannapolis, NC), Apr. 3, 1956, p. 2 ("A private prosecutor, retained by the family of the slain man, said the crime was a 'mad dog slaying'").

335. "Portsmouth Father Pleads Guilty to Beating Infant Son," PORTSMOUTH HERALD (Portsmouth, NH), Aug. 31, 1951, p. 1 (noting that "ATTY. Wyman P. Boyton, representing Mrs. Walsh as a private prosecutor," appeared in a case in which a father, John Walsh, was charged with beating his year-old son, causing severe injuries).

336. "Newton Hanes Case Put in Jury's Hands," HIGH POINT ENTERPRISE (High Point, NC), Jan. 11, 1952, p. 1 (reporting from New Bern on the second-degree murder trial of Newton Hanes: "Private prosecutor Jack Grantham, in his final argument, said this was 'the most brutal and cold-blooded murder in this county since I've been practicing law.'"); "Jury to Get Murder Case," STATESVILLE DAILY RECORD (Statesville, NC), Mar. 21, 1952, p. 14 (noting the private prosecutor's role in the murder case of a Burlington bulldozer operator); "Regan Acquitted in Trial of Drunken Driving Charge," THE ROBESONIAN (Lumberton, NC), Jan. 27, 1955, p. 4 (noting that a private prosecutor, William Smith of Wilmington, was assisting Solicitor Leon D. Smith); "Klan Trial Opens to Crowded Court," THE ROBESONIAN (Lumberton, NC), Mar. 11, 1958, p. 1 (noting that "Luther J. Britt... was employed as private prosecutor by Frank S. White of Pembroke"); "Judge," DAILY TIMES-NEWS (Burlington, NC), Aug. 21, 1958, p. 3 ("Presenting the first argument for the state was Bonner D. Sawyer of Hillsboro, private prosecutor for the Dorrity family."); "No Assistance Offered Dominy—Woman Scared When She Shot Mate," GASTONIA GAZETTE (Gastonia, NC), Mar. 1, 1972, p. B1 (noting the involving of a "private prosecutor" in a first-degree murder charge); "Testimony Comes Out in Reverse," GASTONIA GAZETTE (Gastonia, NC), Oct. 16, 1972, p. B1 ("A Gastonia lawyer, employed as a private prosecutor, was red-faced in District Court Monday when he called a witness for the state who testified for the defense instead."); "In Gaines Murder Trial: Under Heavy Guard, Jury Picking Continues," GASTONIA GAZETTE (Gastonia, NC), Apr. 17, 1973, p. 11 ("A private prosecutor for the Gaines family is assisting Childs in presenting the case for the state."); "State Seeks First Degree in

Shotgun Murder Trial," DAILY TIMES-NEWS (Burlington, NC), Dec. 5, 1973, p. B1 (noting that "a private prosecutor hired by Mrs. Langley" was participating in the capital murder trial).

337. "Gene Rehberg Admits Second City Burglary," OREGON STATESMAN (Salem, OR), Jan. 25, 1952, p. 5.

338. "Poison Case To be Argued in Court," BRISTOL COURIER (Bristol, PA), June 30, 1952, pp. 1, 5 (noting that "Attorney S. Hare, a resident of the Quakertown area, is the private prosecutor on one of the cases"); "Judge Continues Mt. Pleasant Case," DAILY NOTES (Canonsburg, PA), Aug. 27, 1952, p. 1 (noting the involvement of "private prosecutors").

339. "Prosecutors Must Attend City Court," KNOXVILLE JOURNAL (Knoxville, TN), Jan. 18, 1952, p. 13 ("Private prosecutors in City Court cases must appear in court from now on, either voluntarily or by subp[o]ena, under a new city policy outlined by Trial Attorney Len Broughton Jr."); "23 Witnesses Subp[o]enaed for Trials of Drunk Driving Cases," KNOXVILLE NEWS-SENTINEL (Knoxville, TN), Mar. 4, 1952, p. 1 ("Court subp[o]enas have been issued for 24 private prosecutors to appear at tomorrow's City Court traffic session in which 33 defendants have been scheduled for hearings on charges of drunken driving, City Trial Atty. Len Broughton Jr., said today."); "Warrant Served After Two Years, Charge Dropped," KNOXVILLE JOURNAL (Knoxville, TN), Jan. 4, 1953, p. 20 ("A larceny warrant sworn out here two years ago was served yesterday, but the private prosecutor had a change of heart and dropped the charge."); "Theft Suspect Bound to Grand Jury," KNOXVILLE JOURNAL (Knoxville, TN), Feb. 28, 1953, p. 8 (noting that private prosecutors represented six businesses that were burglarized).

340. "Operation Stalls Trial for Murder—Defendant Has Appendectomy Night Before," GILMER MIRROR (Gilmer, TX), June 10, 1954, pp. 1, 8 (noting that "Leslie Florence, employed by the Robinson family as a private prosecutor for the state," appeared in addition to County Attorney F. L. Garrison); *see also* MARSHALL NEWS MESSENGER (Marshall, TX), July 21, 1954, p. 3 (a letter to the editor from "SAM FORD AND FAMILY" in Marshall, Texas: "It has been called to our attention that misrepresentations are being made by a few people concerning our employment of private prosecutors. We employed the law firm of Felid and Woodall, have paid them a reasonable fee and for no purpose at all except to see that justice is done. This was without solicitation from anyone."); "Odessa Trial Set for Duval Clerk," ABILENE REPORTER-NEWS (Abilene, TX), Jan. 8, 1958, p. 10-B (noting that Sidney Chandler, a former assistant attorney general, "now is a private prosecutor in some of the Duval County cases").

341. "Hodges Trial Set Friday in Cross Slaying Case," THE BEE (Danville, VA), Oct. 19, 1976, p. 9 (noting that in a murder case in the circuit court of Pittsylvania County, Virginia, the family of Mary Cross—the murder victim—had "retained John D. Epperly of the Martinsville firm of Broaddus, Epperly and Broaddus in the case," with Epperly to assist the commonwealth's attorney, George A. Jones Jr., in the prosecution).

342. "Castalia Citizens Take Action to Round Up Reckless Driver," EVENING TELEGRAM (Rocky Mount, NC), July 9, 1963, p. 8; "Driver Faces Second Charge," KNOXVILLE JOURNAL (Knoxville, TN), Aug. 13, 1963, p. 2.

343. "Court Issues Bench Warrants," GETTYSBURG TIMES (Gettysburg, PA), Oct. 9, 1980, p. 5.

344. Wally Avett, "Bradshaw Murder Trial Winding Up in Superior Court - Lawyers Complete Arguments in Nash," EVENING TELEGRAM (Rocky Mount, NC), Jan. 11, 1963, p. 5; Celestine Sibley, "Prosecutors Agree Little Trial Should Move," ATLANTA CONSTITUTION, Apr. 15, 1975, p. 11; *see also* "Joan Little Case: First of Defense Motions Wrapped Up at Hearing," THE BEE (Danville, VA), Apr. 18, 1975, p. 10 ("In response to a question, 'Do you think Joan Little killed Clarence Alligood in self defense?', 58 per cent of the whites said they did not believe it was self defense, while only one per cent of the blacks responded that way.").

345. "Judge Opposes Trial Delay," DAILY TIMES-NEWS (Burlington, NC), July 9, 1975, p. 1A; Cathy Steele Roche, "Jury Selection in Little Case Is Expected to Take Two Weeks," INDEX-JOURNAL (Greenwood, SC), July 11, 1975, p. 6; *see also* Cathy Steele Roche, "Bomb Threat Fails to Halt Little Trial Jury Selection," GREELY DAILY TRIBUNE (Greeley, CO), July 15, 1975, p. 15 ("Hobgood planned to rule today on a defense motion to remove private prosecutor John Wilkinson from the case. Wilkinson was hired by the slain jailer's family to aid Beaufort County Dist. Atty. William Griffin. The defense charged that Wilkinson's role in the prosecution was a conflict of interest, because he represented Miss Little in two previous shoplifting

cases. She was acquitted in each."); "Joan Little's Attorneys File a Surprise Motion," INDEX-JOURNAL (Greenwood, SC), July 18, 1975, p. 5 ("Judge Hamilton Hobgood had still not ruled Thursday on the participation of Beaufort County attorney John Wilkinson as a private prosecutor in the case. The ethics of committee of the North Carolina State Bar was reportedly still studying the question of a possible conflict of interest in Wilkinson's role."); "On Little Jury—Black Housewife Seated," HIGH POINT ENTERPRISE (High Point, NC), July 22, 1975, p. 2 ("Hobgood made the decision to allow Wilkinson to continue as a private prosecutor after the State Bar ethics committee ruled that his previous role as a defense attorney for Miss Little was not a conflict of interest."); "Charges Reduced in Joan Little Case; Defense Seeks a Dismissal," INDEX-JOURNAL (Greenwood, SC), Aug. 7, 1975, p. 13 (noting Wilkinson's role as private prosecutor in the case). Sometimes, murder victim's family hired more than one attorney to serve as a private prosecutor. George Stein, "Abner Murder Case Is Heading Back to Court," DAILY TIMES-NEWS (Burlington, NC), Aug. 24, 1975, p. A1 ("A three-man team of private prosecutors hired by the Abner family hammered at the Barbour defense, disputing his claim that he was acting as a police officer when he killed Abner.").

346. "White Gets 30 Years in Case," DAILY TIMES-NEWS (Burlington, NC), Apr. 9, 1975, p. 3A.

347. "'Private' Prosecutors Cut into Trial Jam—Traffic Cases Speeded by Civic Action," SALT LAKE TRIBUNE (Salt Lake City, UT), Dec. 18, 1962, p. 17. The "special prosecutors" served without pay as they took on the 320-case jury trial backlog of cases. Richard Dibblee, the Salt Lake County Bar Association president, specifically urged the City Commission to hire as many extra full-time prosecutors as were needed to keep the jury trial backlog "within reasonable bounds." *Id.*

348. "Fresno State Disturbances—Extra Prosecutors Are Hired to Handle College Case Load," SANTA CRUZ SENTINEL (Santa Cruz, CA), June 3, 1970, p. 16.

349. U.S. Department of Justice, Bureau of Justice Statistics, Report to the Nation on Crime and Justice (2d ed. 1988), p. 74. As that *Report to the Nation on Crime and Justice* added, private defenders provided pursuant to contract systems "serve as an overflow for public defender offices and also represent codefendants in cases of conflict of interest." *Id.*

350. DAVID W. NEUBAUER & HENRY F. FRADELLA, AMERICA'S COURTS AND THE CRIMINAL JUSTICE SYSTEM 154 (12th ed. 2017) ("Due to the small size or budgetary restrictions (both of which are typically applicable in rural areas), some U.S. jurisdictions have adopted one of two models of quasi-public prosecution. Under the *prosecution outsourcing model*, the jurisdiction might contract with a nongovernmental lawyer in private practice or a law firm to prosecute cases on behalf of the state either on a fixed time basis (e.g., for a year) or on an *ad hoc* basis when the need arises. Under the *part-time prosecutor model* that is used in approximately 25 percent of the states, lawyers are hired or elected to serve as part-time government prosecutors, but they are simultaneously permitted to maintain a private law practice."). In some instances, attorneys in private practice are tapped by public officials to handle specific criminal cases. *E.g.*, David Thomas, *Hogan Lovells' Katyal, Others to Prosecute Officers Charged in Floyd Death*, Law.com (July 14, 2020, 12:07 PM), https://www.law.com/americanlawyer/2020/07/14/hogan-lovells-katyal-others-to-prosecute-officers-charged-in-floyd-death/ (noting that three law firm partners and one corporate counsel, including a former U.S. solicitor general at Hogan Lovells, "are temporarily joining the Minnesota Attorney General's Office for the prosecution of the police officers who killed George Floyd" on "a pro bono basis").

351. "Pittsburgh's Red Leaders Are Held," WARREN TIMES-MIRROR (Warren, PA), Sept. 6, 1950, p. 1.

352. "Judges Hike Nelson's Bond to $100,000," DAILY REPUBLICAN (Monongahela, PA), Sept. 7, 1950, p. 1.

353. "Quash Conviction of Steve Nelson," KANE REPUBLICAN (Kane and Mt. Jewett, PA), Jan. 25, 1954, p. 6; *see also* "Musmanno Files Appeal, Attacks Freeing of Nelson," MORNING HERALD (Uniontown, PA), Jan. 30, 1954, p. 7 ("A Pennsylvania Supreme Court justice told his colleagues today they were wrong in setting aside the sedition conviction of Communist Steve Nelson. And he told them if they don't void the decision, he's going to ask the U.S. Supreme Court to do so. Justice Michael A. Musmanno, who was private prosecutor of Nelson before being elevated to the Supreme Court, filed an appeal with his own court, declaring that the court's opinion freeing Nelson 'contains serious errors in law and fact.'"); *id.* ("Musmanno, a judge at the German war crime trials, led a raid on Pittsburgh Communists headquarters that resulted in the arrest of Nelson, former Western Pennsylvania Communist party chairman."); "Musmanno Says Blast in Communist Case Is Not Bid for Governor," KANE REPUBLICAN (Kane and Mt. Jewett, PA), Feb. 1,

1954, p. 6 ("Musmanno petitioned the Supreme Court for a re-hearing of the case in his role as private prosecutor, but was refused. He also has offered to aid Atty. Gen. Frank Truscott in an appeal. The attorney general announced plans to appeal Saturday."); "Smith Backs Musmanno's View of Act," RICHMOND TIMES-DISPATCH (Richmond, VA), Feb. 16, 1954, p. 10 (reporting from Washington, D.C.: "Musmanno is opposing a recent Pennsylvania Supreme Court ruling that set aside a conviction of Steve Nelson, Pittsburgh Communist. Musmanno acted as private prosecutor of Nelson, later was elected to the court, but disqualified himself from participating in the ruling. The jurist said he was in Washington as a 'private citizen' to gather information for Frank Truscott, Pennsylvania attorney-general, who has petitioned the Pennsylvania Supreme Court to reconsider its decision, and to prepare for a possible appeal to the Supreme Court of the United States.").

A little more than a decade later, in 1961, in Charlotte, North Carolina, the murder trial of real estate tycoon George King Cutter—a millionaire charged with beating to death a divorcee, his long-time companion—got underway, with the press reporting that two private prosecutors, retained by the victim's family, were involved in the case. "Jury Selected, Cutter Trial Gets Underway—Charged in Woman's Death," THE BEE (Danville, VA), Sept. 13, 1961, p. 6-B; *see also* "Cutter Denies Killing But Admits Moving Body, Burning Dress," INDEX-JOURNAL (Greenwood, SC), Sept. 16, 1961, p. 1 ("The millionaire realtor returned to the witness stand for cross-examination today by private prosecutor Allen A. Bailey."); "Cutter Insists He's Innocent in Death Case," FLORENCE MORNING NEWS (Florence, SC), Sept. 17, 1961, p. 9-B ("Cutter underwent a slashing, relentless three-hour cross-examination by private prosecutor Allen A. Bailey Saturday."). It was a capital murder trial in which Cutter was ultimately acquitted, with the disappointed private prosecutors going on to file civil suits for hundreds of thousands of dollars on behalf of the relatives of the deceased woman. Charles L. West, "Cutter Case Due to Reach Jury Today," EVENING TELEGRAM (Rocky Mount, NC), Sept. 22, 1961, p. 1 (noting it was a capital case); "Damage Judgments Are Sought Against Charlotte Millionaire," FLORENCE MORNING NEWS (Florence, SC), Oct. 6, 1961, p. 3-B (noting that two civil suits sought damages from millionaire George King Cutler, who was acquitted by a jury two weeks earlier of first-degree murder, second-degree murder and manslaughter charges; "Mrs. Sarah Emory, aunt of Mrs. Nycum and executrix of her estate, filed one suit for $300,000 and Mrs. Nycum's two children, Ricky, 15, and Sandra, 16—filed the other for $300,000."; "Attorneys Charles E. Knox and Allen A. Bailey, who served as private prosecutors in the trial, brought the civil action in Mecklenburg Superior Court in behalf of Mrs. Emory and the children.").

354. "Food for Thought," GAZETTE AND DAILY (York, PA), Dec. 7, 1954, p. 20.

355. *E.g.*, "Stabbing Case Goes to Knox Grand Jury," KNOXVILLE JOURNAL (Knoxville, TN), Mar. 4, 1951, p. 12; $50 Fine Given on Hit-Run Charge," KNOXVILLE NEWS-SENTINEL (Knoxville, TN), Mar. 6, 1951, p. 2; *see also* "Stiffer Prosecution of Drivers Planned," KNOXVILLE NEWS-SENTINEL (Knoxville, TN), Jan. 26, 1958, p. 10 ("Mr. Garrison emphasized that most drunk driving cases which the city has lost have been those in which private prosecutors failed to show up.").

356. *E.g.*, "His Alcohol Was in Car, Driver Assures Judge," KNOXVILLE JOURNAL (Knoxville, TN), Mar. 16, 1951, p. 24; "Six Are Charged as Drunk Drivers," KNOXVILLE NEWS-SENTINEL (Knoxville, TN), Dec. 10, 1960, p. 8; *see also* "Citizen Makes Fourth Trip to Win Conviction," KNOXVILLE JOURNAL (Knoxville, TN), Apr. 25, 1953, p. 14 ("A private prosecutor showed in City Court for the fourth time yesterday and was finally able to dispose of a drunken driving case he was pushing because the defendant was 'endangering lives by driving recklessly.'"); "Private Prosecutors May Get Weary at Having to Make Many Court Trips," KNOXVILLE JOURNAL (Knoxville, TN), Apr. 27, 1953, p. 4 (discussing the case of Inskip resident who had to make four trips to City Court for purposes of prosecuting a drunken driving case).

357. Marvin Eury, "A 'Girl Friday': Mrs. Dorothy Barbee Is Veteran of Cabarrus County Court," DAILY INDEPENDENT MAGAZINE (Kannapolis, NC), Dec. 17, 1967, pp. 1-C, 2-C (in a profile of Mrs. Dorothy C. Barbee, assistant clerk of Superior Court assigned to Recorder's Court, reporting: "Mrs. Barbee said another thing that is not tolerated is a person failing to appear as a prosecuting witness. She said there are fewer instances now but it used to be a regular practice to swear out a warrant in the heat of an argument and then fail to appear in court to press the charge. Persons failing to appear as prosecuting witnesses now are arrested on capiases and may be fined for malicious prosecution.").

358. "New Law Lends Itself to Graft, Knox Officials Say," KNOXVILLE NEWS-SENTINEL (Knoxville, TN), Mar. 30, 1955, p. 17.

359. *E.g.*, "Grand Jury Returns Three Indictments," WELLSBORO AGITATOR (Wellsboro, PA), Apr. 21, 1955, p. 1; "Fees Question Raised in Case," EVENING TELEGRAM (Rocky Mount, NC), June 15, 1955, p. 11; "Probable Cause in Assault Case," EVENING TELEGRAM (Rocky Mount, NC), Jan. 4, 1956, p. 9; "Tenth DWD Conviction Draws 'Book,'" KNOXVILLE JOURNAL (Knoxville, TN), Jan. 10, 1956, p. 11; "Fine $25 on Selling Pictures," KNOXVILLE JOURNAL (Knoxville, TN), Mar. 17, 1956, p. 1; "Charged with Assault," KNOXVILLE NEWS-SENTINEL (Knoxville, TN), June 20, 1959, p. 3; "In Alleged Assault Councilman Faces $30,000 Lawsuit," THE ROBESONIAN (Lumberton, NC), Aug. 3, 1967, p. 1; "Greene Jury Indicts Five," EVENING STANDARD (Uniontown, PA), Nov. 3, 1970, p. 6.

360. *E.g.*, "Court Cleared in Kidnapping, Murder Case," THE REGISTER (Danville, VA), July 16, 1970, p. 5-D.

361. "3 Sent to Prison Over Involvement in Theft Cases," LEADER-TIMES (Kittanning, PA), Feb. 27, 1976, p. 2.

362. "Imes Is Found Guilty of Assault by Threat," STATESVILLE RECORD & LANDMARK (Statesville, NC), May 4, 1964, p. 3 ("Attorney Jack R. Harris was private prosecutor in the case. He has been employed by the Statesville Merchants Association to prosecute persons charged with shoplifting. Harris said the total value of merchandise stolen in Statesville annually is $100,000. He said that persons thinking of stealing should know that this is one town where such offenses will not be considered lightly.").

363. Alex Kingsbury, "How the Red Scare Destroyed a Small-Town Teacher," BOSTON GLOBE, Feb. 4, 2016, https://www.bostonglobe.com/magazine/2016/02/04/how-red-scare-destroyed-small-town-teacher/OyzaMTrsxMsx54liP1YX9I/story.html.

364. ALAN AXELROD, THE REAL HISTORY OF THE COLD WAR: A NEW LOOK AT THE PAST 290 (2009).

365. "Civil Liberty," GAZETTE AND DAILY (York, PA), Dec. 2, 1954, p. 20.

366. Connor Jones, "Man Gets 30 Years for Dynamiting," DAILY TIMES-NEWS (Burlington, NC), May 10, 1962, p. B1.

367. Myron A. Kautsch, "Bartel Presses Efforts To Be 'Private Prosecutor,'" IOWA CITY PRESS-CITIZEN (Iowa City, IA), Apr. 6, 1971, pp. 1A-2A; *compare id.* at 2A ("No cases in Iowa appear to answer these or a host of other questions. Only one scholarly work directly on the question appears to exist—a 1952 student article in the Drake Law Review. The article, citing history and various written authorities, contends that Iowa law should not be interpreted to eliminate private prosecutors.").

368. Bill Noblitt, "This Afternoon in North Carolina—Rising Crime Trend, Overpopulated Prisons, Death Row Show Best Efforts Have Failed," THE ROBESONIAN (Lumberton, NC), Jan. 8, 1976, p. 6.

369. "To Aid in Prosecuting Rape Charge—Pierce Rejects Paul's Legal Services," DAILY TIMES-NEWS (Burlington, NC), Mar. 19, 1976, p. 11.

370. "Kunstler Offers His Services," GAFFNEY LEDGER (Gaffney, SC), Dec. 5, 1979, p. 3. The high-profile lawyer who had represented defendant such as Little and the "Chicago Seven," William Kunstler had been approached by members of New York's Communist party to serve as a private prosecutor in the pending trials of 15 men charged with murder and conspiracy in the deaths of five people at an anti-Ku Klux Klan rally. Although Kunstler told a Greensboro newspaper, "I'd be delighted to do it," District Attorney Schlosser announced that he would prosecute the cases because they occurred within Guilford County. *Id.*

371. THE TRIAL OF THE CHICAGO 7: THE OFFICIAL TRANSCRIPT (Mark L. Levine, George C. McNamee & Daniel L. Greenberg, eds. 2020).

372. "To Aid in Prosecuting Rape Charge—Pierce Rejects Paul's Legal Services," DAILY TIMES-NEWS (Burlington, NC), Mar. 19, 1976, p. 11.

373. "Re-elect Herbert F. (Herb) Pierce—Democrat as District Solicitor (District Attorney," DAILY TIMES-NEWS (Burlington, NC), May 6, 1974, p. 16.

374. "Mebane's Parents Very Upset," DAILY TIMES-NEWS (Burlington, NC), Jan. 29, 1977, p. 15. Dissatisfaction with plea bargains led *The Anderson Herald* in Indiana to write an editorial that the use of private prosecutors should at least be considered. "Private Prosecutors," ANDERSON HERALD (Anderson, IN), July 9, 1977, p. 4 ("A New York consumer advocate, David B. Saxbe, has raised an interesting proposal for

checking the misuse of plea bargaining in criminal cases. Noting that public opinion, expressed through polls, takes a dim view of plea bargaining, Saxbe suggests that private prosecution be allowed. This would allow a court to permit the victim of a crime to hire a private prosecutor who would prosecute the case in place of the inactive prosecuting attorney."); *id.* ("Under a system of private prosecution, the injured party would be allowed to hire his own attorney to prosecute the accused to the full extent of the law.... Private prosecution would still require the prosecuting attorney to be primarily responsible for criminal prosecutions but a judge would be empowered to hear testimony from any interested party regarding the propriety of the plea bargain or inaction in a particular case. If the judge found the plea bargain to be unwarranted, the victim would have the opportunity to retain a lawyer to prosecute the felon.").

375. "Harrington to Get New Trial," DAILY STANDARD (Sikeston, MO), June 12, 1975, p. 1.

376. "Court Overturns Murder Convictions," MEXICO LEDGER (Mexico, MO), Mar. 8, 1976, pp. 1, 5.

377. "State Court May Review Rules for Minor Judiciary," DELAWARE COUNTY DAILY TIMES (Chester, PA), Jan. 19, 1974, p. 10.

378. "Told of New Law," EVENING HERALD (Shenandoah, PA), Dec. 29, 1973, p. 1; *see also* "Changes Ordered for Crime Code," MEYERSDALE REPUBLIC (Meyersdale, PA), Jan. 10, 1974, p. 6 (summarizing the changes as follows: "[P]ersons who have no police powers in the future will be required to file criminal complaints as a private prosecutor. Before an individual can file such a complaint, he must submit his complaint to the district attorney, who then either approves or disapproves. If the DA approves, the individual then files charges with a magistrate. If he disapproves, the individual may petition the court for consideration, and the court may either approve or disapprove. There is one exception to this new ruling—if the offense involves a clear or present danger to any person or community, then the magistrate can issue a complaint. Magistrate Robert Philson of Meyersdale explained the changes which are now effective.").

379. "State Court May Review Rules for Minor Judiciary," DELAWARE COUNTY DAILY TIMES (Chester, PA), Jan. 19, 1974, p. 10.

380. "State's Attorney Relates Influence of His Office," FREEPORT JOURNAL-STANDARD (Freeport, IL), Feb. 26, 1974, p. 4.

381. Cardenas, *supra* note 7, at 372–73.

382. WILLIAM WRIGHT, THE VON BÜLOW AFFAIR: THE OBJECTIVE BEHIND-THE-SCENES ACCOUNT OF THE SHOCKING ATTEMPTING MURDER CASE (2014), ch. 18; "Defense Offers Its Own Villain," JOURNAL GAZETTE (Mattoon, IL), Jan. 23, 1982, p. 2; *see also* ALAN M. DERSHOWITZ, REVERSAL OF FORTUNE, INSIDE THE VON BÜLOW CASE (2013); Sam Roberts, "Herald Price Fahringer, a Defender of Free Speech, Dies at 87," N.Y. TIMES, Feb. 19, 2015, https://www.nytimes.com/2015/02/19/nyregion/herald-price-fahringer-a-defender-of-free-speech-dies-at-87.html.

383. State v. von Bülow, 474 A.2d 995, 1003 (1984); *see also id.* ("Consequently, we also recognize that rulings of admission or exclusion of evidence insofar as they relate solely to the claim of private prosecution would be non-prejudicial in their effect."); Cardenas, *supra* note 7, at 372–73.

384. Letter from U.S. Senators Edward J. Markey and Sheldon Whitehouse to Hon. Roslynn R. Mauskopf, Director, Administrative Office of the U.S. Courts, July 29, 2021, *available at* https://www.markey.senate.gov/imo/media/doc/markey-whitehouse_letter_to_judge_mauskopf1.pdf.

385. Sofia Andrade, "This Attorney Took on Chevron. Then Chevron-Linked Judges and Private Prosecutors Had Him Locked Up." Slate, Aug. 12, 2021, https://slate.com/news-and-politics/2021/08/chevron-judge-loretta-preska-steven-donziger.html.

386. The Texas law, known as Senate Bill 8, deputized private citizens to sue doctors or anyone who "aids or abets" an abortion performed after roughly six weeks of a woman's pregnancy, with the law purporting to allow $10,000 in "statutory damages" and attorney's fees for prevailing plaintiffs. The U.S. Department of Justice, led by Attorney General Merrick Garland, quickly declared that S.B. 8 was passed "in open defiance of the Constitution" and long-standing U.S. Supreme Court case law, including *Roe v. Wade*. Ruth Graham, Adam Liptak & J. David Goodman, "Lawsuits Filed Against Texas Doctor Could Be Best Tests of Abortion Law," N.Y. TIMES, Sept. 21, 2021; Alan Feuer, "The Texas Abortion Law Creates a Kind of Bounty Hunter. Here's How It Works." N.Y. TIMES, Sept. 10, 2021 (updated Sept. 20, 2021).

387. Adam Liptak, J. David Goodman & Sabrina Tavernise, "Supreme Court, Breaking Silence, Won't Block Texas Abortion Law," N.Y. Times, Sept. 1, 2021 (updated Sept. 19, 2021); Devin Dwyer, "2 Disbarred Attorneys Outside Texas Sue Abortion Doctor under SB8," ABC News, Sept. 21, 2021, https://abcnews.go.com/Politics/disbarred-attorneys-texas-sue-abortion-doctor-sb8/story?id=80147133; Press Release (Sept. 13, 2021), "In Win for Abortion Providers, Texas State Court Enters Temporary Injunction Against Texas Right to Life," Planned Parenthood, https://www.plannedparenthood.org/about-us/newsroom/press-releases/breaking-in-win-for-abortion-providers-texas-state-court-enters-temporary-injunction-against-texas-right-to-life.

Chapter 6 Notes

1. National Commission on Law Observance and Enforcement, Report on Prosecution 6–7 (Apr. 22, 1931). After taking note of England's private prosecution system, the report pointed out that "in the first years of the eighteenth century, the Colonies began to do away with private prosecutions and set up public prosecutors." "This public prosecutor, given sole charge of all criminal causes," the report stressed, "was quite unknown to English law." *Id.*

2. The countries of continental Europe moved toward public prosecution much earlier than England. Joan E. Jacoby, The American Prosecutor: A Search for Identity 10 (1980) ("The French had operated under a ... system [of private prosecution] beginning in the twelfth century but had begun, in progressive stages, to adopt public prosecution within the following 300 years. They eventually abandoned the private system of prosecution, retaining private complaint only as a method of correcting a neglectful prosecutor. The Dutch and the Germans similarly adopted related forms of public prosecution. Only the British persisted with this medieval institution at the time of the colonization of the North American continent.").

3. 12 Stat. at Large, 285, § 1.

4. National Commission on Law Observance and Enforcement, Report on Prosecution 7–12 (Apr. 22, 1931); *see also id.* at 18–19 ("[I]n the English common law prosecutions were ordinarily private. Hence a necessary check existed in the power of the Attorney General, as representing the Crown, to inform the court that the Crown was unwilling to prosecute and so bring the private prosecution to an end. This could be done at any stage of the proceeding down to the final judgment of conviction. In America the power passed to the prosecuting attorney as a local attorney general. At common law exercise of this power is beyond control of courts, and American courts have in general adopted the common law in this respect. As one court puts it, the power is 'absolute.' The prosecutor 'is not even required to give a reason for his dismissal.' In some States by statute reasons are required to be put on file and in some by statute or long judicial practice leave of court must be had. But in practice, with the crowded dockets of the modern city, these checks have been applied perfunctorily and are achieving little or nothing. In origin a public check on private prosecutions, when private prosecutions came to an end and all prosecutions became public or official it ceased to be a check and became an additional mitigating or dispensing device."); Gerald V. Bradley, *Law Enforcement and the Separation of Powers*· 30 Ariz. L. Rev. 801, 841 (1988) ("It was the Judiciary Act of 1789 which established the monopoly on federal prosecutions by United States Attorneys that continues to the present ...."); *id.* at 803 ("A widely-noted passage in *United States v. Nixon* said that the 'Executive Branch has exclusive authority and absolute discretion to decide whether to prosecute a case.'") (quoting United States v. Nixon, 418 U.S. 683, 693 (1974)). On the other hand, the report observed that state systems of prosecution vary considerably "from State to State," with the report taking note of the powers of state attorneys general and local prosecutors operating under titles such as county attorney, district attorney, solicitor general, and county solicitors.

5. Lewis Coe, The Telegraph: A History of Morse's Invention and Its Predecessors in the United States (1993); *see also* 1 Encyclopedic Dictionary: Analytical Historical Reference 57 (1906) ("Colonies and States had their Attorneys-General before 1789. The Judiciary Act of that year, organizing the Federal judiciary under the new Constitution, provided for an Attorney-General of the United States, to act as government counsel, with a salary of $1,500. At first he had little to do, and could

practice for himself; but he was always a member of the Cabinet. In 1858 he was provided with an assistant. In 1861 he was given charge of U.S. district attorneys and marshals. In 1870 the office was organized as the Department of Justice.").

6. *Private Prosecution: A Remedy for District Attorneys' Unwarranted Inaction*, 65 YALE L.J. 209, 210 n.8, 218–21 & nn.60–61 (1955); *see also* Callahan v. Johns, 93 P.2d 326, 331–32 (Wash. 1939) ("[A]ppellants cite the opinion of the supreme court of New Mexico, in the case of *Baca v. Padilla*, 26 N.M. 223, 190 P. 730, 11 A.L.R. 1188, in which it was held that a contract for legal services entered into between an attorney and a private party, under the terms of which the attorney, for a contingent fee, was to act as private prosecutor in a criminal case, was void as against the policy of the law, the court, however, holding, in an action by the attorney, that the contract was neither malum in se nor malum prohibitum, and that a recovery should be allowed on the basis of a quantum meruit. It does not appear that any statute similar to § 4138 was in force in New Mexico, and the attorney who was allowed to recover was not holding a state or county office.").

7. State ex rel. Koppers Co., Inc. v. International Union of Oil, Chemical and Atomic Workers, 298 S.E.2d 827, 829–30 (W. Va. Sup. Ct. App., 1982) ("Participation by a private prosecutor does not obviate the need for a public prosecutor's presence, he being ultimately responsible for discretion regarding prosecution of alleged public law offenders. If the government's prosecutor fails to perform his duties, he is answerable under W.Va. Const. art. IX, § 4 and art. IV, § 6.") (citations omitted); *id.* at 830 ("Although a private prosecutor is held to the same high standards as a public one, the apparent conflict of interest and pressure of 'wearing two hats' militates against permitting a party's private counsel to prosecute a criminal contempt charge stemming from a civil suit; and it makes no difference whether he acts as private lawyer or by appointment as special prosecutor.") (citing Code of Professional Responsibility, W.Va. Code, App., EC-7-13, EC-5-1, EC-5-11, EC-5-14, EC-5-23; ABA Standards for Criminal Justice (2d Ed. 1980), Standard 3-2.1 and comments, p. 3.13); *id.* at 831 ("Justice is better served by avoiding appearances of impropriety and of inherent conflicts of interest, presented when a private party's counsel in a civil suit is permitted to prosecute a criminal contempt against an opposing party."); *id.* at 832 ("Cheek and Rhodes were denied due process of law when their criminal contempts were prosecuted by Koppers' lawyers.").

8. Thomas J. Robinson, *Private Prosecution in Criminal Cases*, 4 WAKE FOREST INTRAMURAL L. REV. 300, 312–13, 316 (1968).

9. Andrew Sidman, *The Outmoded Concept of Private Prosecution*, 25 AM. U. L. REV. 754, 765–67, 770–72 (1976).

10. *E.g.*, John D. Bessler, *The Public Interest and the Unconstitutionality of Private Prosecutors*, 47 ARK. L. REV. 511 (1994).

11. State v. Smith, No. 2018-0416, 2020 WL 1071066, at *3 (N.H. Mar. 6, 2020) ("Prosecutors are important gatekeepers of our criminal justice process. Indeed, we have held that, in New Hampshire, prosecutions of criminal offenses that are punishable by imprisonment can only be initiated by public prosecutors.") (citing State (Premo Complainant) v. Martineau, 808 A.2d 51 (N.H. 2002)); Frese v. MacDonald, 425 F. Supp.3d 64, 77 (D. N.H. 2019) ("Under New Hampshire law, individuals can initiate private prosecutions for criminal offenses that does not carry a possible penalty of imprisonment."); *see also id.* ("Since as early as 1827, New Hampshire courts have recognized the potential 'dangers to both the public interest and to the sound administration of justice' that private prosecutions pose.") (citing Richard B. McNamara, New Hampshire Practice, Criminal Practice and Procedure § 15.04[1] (6th ed. 2017) (quoting Waldron v. Tuttle, 4 N.H. 149, 151 (1827)).

12. Cooper v. District Court, 133 P.3d 692, 696–711 (Alaska Ct. App. 2006). Private prosecutions were once permitted in Alaska. *See* Rollins v. State *ex rel.* Municipality of Anchorage, 748 P.2d 767, 769, 771 (Alaska Ct. App. 1988) (upholding criminal contempt prosecution by interested party); *see also* Note, *Permitting Private Initiation of Criminal Contempt Proceedings*, 124 HARV. L. REV. 1485, 1504 (2011) ("Although no state offers a perfect example, many suggest that the concept of a 'private prosecutor' may be erroneous. Rather than providing for true prosecutions, these states allow beneficiaries of court orders to file ex parte motions requesting that the court issue an order to show cause why the alleged contemnor should not be punished. In Alaska, upon 'a proper showing on ex parte motion supported by affidavits,' a court must issue either an order to show cause or a bench warrant for the arrest of the accused party. Such

a motion can be made 'by the aggrieved party whose right or remedy in an action has been defeated or prejudiced or who has suffered a loss or injury by the act constituting a contempt.' Then, when the alleged contemnor appears, 'the court or judicial officer shall proceed to investigate the charge by examining the defendant and witnesses for or against the defendant.' As the rules describe it, this proceeding is almost inquisitorial: it is not clear that there is any prosecutor at all.").

13. People v. Dehle, 166 Cal. App.4th 1380, 1386–90 (Cal. Ct. App., 3d Dist. 2008).

14. Ga. Uniform Super. Ct. R. 42.1 ("Private special prosecutors retained by the family or relatives of one named as a victim in an indictment or accusation may not participate in the prosecution of a criminal case. Special assistant district attorneys appointed by the district attorney including attorneys from personnel of public agencies may prosecute criminal cases."); *see also* Gay v. Gay, 485 S.E.2d 187, 188 (Ga. 1997) (allowing a wife, a physician, to prosecute her former husband in a contempt case, but noting: "[W]here, as here, the trial court orders a party incarcerated for more than 20 days, the contempt order should contain sufficient facts to support the court's finding of more than one contemptuous act. Because the trial court failed to specify more than one contemptuous violation of its order, we find that any sentence in excess of 20 days imprisonment was unauthorized under OCGA § 15-6-8(5). Accordingly, we remand the case so that the trial court may reconsider the issue of contempt consistent with this opinion.").

15. State v. Johnson, 470 P.3d 1263, 1264, 1268–69 (Idaho Ct. App. 2020).

16. Michael T. McCormack, *The Need for Private Prosecutors: An Analysis of Massachusetts and New Hampshire Law*, 37 Suffolk U. L. Rev. 497, 498 (2004) ("For nearly 150 years, Massachusetts citizens have been prohibited from hiring a private attorney to prosecute a criminal offense.").

17. In *State ex rel. Wild v. Otis*, the Minnesota Supreme Court held that, absent legislative authority, a system of private prosecution would not be permitted. 257 N.W.2d 361 (Minn. 1977), *cert. denied*, 434 U.S. 1003 (1978). Noting that it could find no such authority, the court stated, "this lack of authority is not surprising because to permit such prosecutions would entail grave danger of vindictive use of the processes of the criminal law and could well lead to chaos in the administration of criminal justice." *Id.* at 365.

18. The State of Massachusetts doesn't allow, or confer standing upon, private parties to seek criminal complaints in non-misdemeanor cases. Commonwealth v. Orbin O., 89 N.E.3d 1151, 1158 (Mass. Sup. Jud. Ct., Berkshire, 2018) ("We have noted that '[t]he right of a citizen to obtain a criminal complaint is itself something of an anomaly, because in modern times[,] the formal initiation and prosecution of criminal offenses is usually the domain of public officials. Accordingly, even where the Legislature has given a private party the opportunity to seek a criminal complaint, we have uniformly held that the denial of a complaint creates no judicially cognizable wrong.' Bradford, 427 Mass. at 751, 695 N.E.2d 1068. *See* Victory Distribs., Inc., 435 Mass. at 142, 755 N.E.2d 273 ('a private party suffers no judicially cognizable wrong when its application for a criminal complaint is denied'); Taylor v. Newton Div. of the Dist. Court Dep't, 416 Mass. 1006, 1006, 622 N.E.2d 261 (1993) ('it is settled beyond cavil that a private citizen has no judicially cognizable interest in the prosecution of another'). Because a private party has no right to the issuance of a criminal complaint where there is probable cause, and because the issuance of such a complaint is within the sound discretion of the clerk-magistrate following a show cause hearing, a judge deciding a motion to dismiss a civilian complaint issued pursuant to § 35A may consider whether the clerk-magistrate abused his or her discretion in issuing the complaint, and, in doing so, may consider whether dismissal of the complaint is in the best interests of the child and in the interests of justice."); Victory Distributors, Inc. v. Ayer Div. of Dist. Ct. Dept., 755 N.E.2d 273, 278 (Mass. Sup. Jud. Ct. 2001) ("Victory concedes, as it must, that a private citizen has no right to the issuance of a criminal complaint. Our prior decisions have held consistently that, if a judge or clerk-magistrate denies an application for a criminal complaint, a private party has no constitution or statutory right to challenge that decision.") (citations omitted); *id.* ("A private party's rights with respect to the criminal complaint process are limited to the filing of an application and court action on that application. Once a private party alerts the court of the alleged criminal activity through the filing of an application and the court responds to that application, the private party's rights have been satisfied."); *id.* ("We recognize that our holding in this and prior decisions, that a private party suffers no judicially cognizable wrong when its application for a criminal complaint is denied, encompasses cases where an application is refused on the basis of an erroneous interpretation of the law, as was the situation in the Marlborough court. That possibility is implicit in the system of citizen complaints, and is

consistent with the notion that the right to pursue a criminal prosecution belongs not to a private party but to the Commonwealth."); Commonwealth v. DiBennadetto, 764 N.E.2d 338, 340 (Mass. Sup. Jud. Ct., Suffolk, 2002) ("The Commonwealth, acting through its respective district attorneys, has a substantial interest in prosecuting the commission of crimes. Indeed, 'the Commonwealth may well be the only party that has standing to challenge the [court's] actions in the case before us.' *Commonwealth v. Clerk of the Boston Div. of the Juvenile Court Dep't,* 432 Mass. 693, 698, 738 N.E.2d 1124 (2000). '[T]he right[ ] to pursue criminal prosecution '[is] not private but [is] in fact lodged in the Commonwealth as it may proceed to enforce its laws." *Bradford v. Knights,* 427 Mass. 748, 751, 695 N.E.2d 1068 (1998), quoting *Whitley v. Commonwealth,* 369 Mass. 961, 962, 339 N.E.2d 890 (1975). No statute provides the Commonwealth a right of appeal from an adverse determination of probable cause by a judge in the BMC or District Court Department."); Whitley v. Commonwealth, 339 N.E.2d 890, 890 (Mass. Sup. Jud. Ct., Suffolk, 1975) ("The rights asserted by the petitioners are not private but are in fact lodged in the Commonwealth as it may proceed to enforce its laws. Pugach v. Klein, 193 F.Supp. 630, 635 (S.D.N.Y. 1961). '(I)n American jurisprudence ... a private citizen lacks a judicially cognizable interest in the prosecution or nonprosecution of another.' S. v. D., 410 U.S. 614, 619, 93 S. Ct. 1146, 1149, 35 L.Ed.2d 536 (1973).").

19. Koch v. Grimminger, 223 N.W.2d 833, 837 (Neb. 1974).

20. People v. Robinson, 27 Misc.3d 635 (Sup. Ct., Kings County, N.Y. 2010).

21. In re Richland County Magistrate's Court, 699 S.E.2d 161, 162–63 (S.C. 2010).

22. Wayne A. Logan, *A Proposed Check on the Charging Discretion of Wisconsin Prosecutors,* 1990 Wis. L. Rev. 1695, 1705 ("From a relatively early date, Wisconsin took steps to ensure that its public prosecutors upheld their obligation to impartially administer the criminal laws. In 1888, the Wisconsin Supreme Court decided *Biemel v. State,* holding that the use of prosecuting attorneys compensated by private person in criminal actions was against public policy.").

23. Trial Handbook for Massachusetts Lawyers § 1:21 (3d ed. 2019) ("The trial court, in its discretion, may permit a privately-employed attorney to assist the district attorney in the prosecution of a criminal case where the interests of public justice so require. Com. v. Herman, 253 Mass. 516, 149 N.E. 198 (1925); Commonwealth v. Lane, 254 Mass. 46, 149 N.E. 663 (1925). The statute prohibiting a prosecuting officer from receiving any private reward for the performance of official duties, M.G.L. c. 12, § 30, is not applicable to this situation, because the district attorney has complete control and conduct of the case and is simply taking advantage of an obvious source of information. Com. v. Herman, 253 Mass. 516, 149 N.E. 198 (1925)."); Bradford v. Knights, 695 N.E.2d 1068, 1071 (Mass. Sup. Jud. Ct., Suffolk, 1998) ("the Legislature has allowed private parties to seek criminal complaints in the case of misdemeanors"); Katz v. Commonwealth, 399 N.E.2d 1055, 1060 (Mass. 1979) ("The power of the Housing Court to punish for contempt is confirmed by statute. G.L. c. 185C, s 3. 'In numerous contempt cases a sentence has been imposed partly remedial and partly punitive, partaking both of civil and criminal features.' Root v. MacDonald, 260 Mass. 344, 363, 157 N.E. 684, 691 (1927). Private parties to civil litigation have the right 'to press both the civil and criminal aspects of the case.' *Id.* at 365, 157 N.E. at 691. *See* Stow v. Marinelli, 352 Mass. 738, 745, 227 N.E.2d 708 (1967). Contrary to the landlord's contention, a private citizen may prosecute a purely criminal complaint in the Housing Court, as in a District Court. G.L. c. 185C, § 19. Commonwealth v. Haddad, 364 Mass. 795, 798, 308 N.E.2d 899 (1974)."); Bradford v. Knights, 695 N.E.2d 1068, 1070–71 (Mass. Sup. Jud. Ct., Suffolk, 1998) ("[E]ven where the Legislature has given a private party the opportunity to seek a criminal complaint, we have uniformly held that the denial of a complaint creates no judicially cognizable wrong. See *Whitley v. Commonwealth,* 369 Mass. 961, 962, 339 N.E.2d 890 (1975) (the rights to pursue criminal prosecution 'are not private but are in fact lodged in the Commonwealth as it may proceed to enforce its laws'). *See also Tarabolski v. Williams,* 419 Mass. 1001, 642 N.E.2d 574 (1994); *Taylor v. Newton Div. of the Dist. Court Dep't,* 416 Mass. 1006, 1006, 622 N.E.2d 261 (1993) ('it is settled beyond cavil that a private citizen has no judicially cognizable interest in the prosecution of another'). Nonetheless the Legislature has allowed private parties to seek criminal complaints in the case of misdemeanors. G.L. c. 218, § 35A."); *see also* Mass. Stat., ch. 218, § 35A ("If a complaint is received by a district court, or by a justice, associate justice or special justice thereof, or by a clerk, assistant clerk, temporary clerk or temporary assistant clerk thereof under section 32, 33 or 35, as the case may be, the person against whom such complaint is made, if not under arrest for the offense for which the complaint is made, shall, in the case of

a complaint for a misdemeanor or a complaint for a felony received from a law enforcement officer who so requests, and may, in the discretion of any said officers in the case of a complaint for a felony which is not received from a law enforcement officer, be given an opportunity to be heard personally or by counsel in opposition to the issuance of any process based on such complaint unless there is an imminent threat of bodily injury, of the commission of a crime, or of flight from the commonwealth by the person against whom such complaint is made.").

24. DeGeorge v. Warheit, 741 N.W.2d 384, 392 (Mich. Ct. App. 2007).

25. Pearl v. Mickelson-Dera, No. CV136022964S, 2014 WL 2854021, at *9 (Conn. Super. Ct., Jud. Dist. of New Britain, May 16, 2014) (citations omitted); State v. Leingang, 763 N.W.2d 769, 774 (N.D. 2009).

26. Rhode Island has also allowed private prosecutions in misdemeanor cases. Cronan ex rel. State v. Cronan, 774 A.2d 866, 870–77 & n.3 (R.I. 2001). Notably, in some locales through history, even some misdemeanors were considered too serious to allow prosecutions by private parties. *E.g.*, People v. Vlasto, 355 N.Y.S.2d 983, 990–91 (Crim. Ct. City N.Y., N.Y. County, 1974) ("The right of persons other than the District Attorney to prosecute criminal actions has never been extended beyond 'petty crimes and offenses'.... To permit a complaining witness or his attorney to represent the People before a jury would negate the rules of fairness required of a prosecutor.... Accordingly, I hold, the defendant having been charged with a crime where the maximum authorized penalty exceeds six months, it is a 'serious' crime which only the District Attorney may prosecute."); *see also* People on Complaint of Allen v. Citadel Management Co., 355 N.Y.2d 976, 982 (Crim. Ct. City N.Y., N.Y. County, 1974) (holding that in the "Summons Parts, where complaints are commonly instituted by private persons and prosecutions conducted by them or their personal counsel," the District Attorney need not be physically present as that "would work a great injustice to the spirit of the law, on persons who feel themselves aggrieved but might otherwise have no other recourse, and would revolutionize a procedure with the sanction of a long tradition and which today has the force of law.").

27. *E.g.*, Ala. Code § 28-4-314 (1990) ("Any district attorney in the county whose duty it is to prosecute criminal cases on behalf of the state shall not be prohibited from commencing prosecution on his own affidavit against any party violating any provision of any law of the State of Alabama for the suppression of the evils of intemperance, and every such district attorney, upon receiving information giving him probable cause to believe that there has been a violation of any statute upon the subject named, shall proceed to lay the matter before the grand jury or to institute a criminal prosecution against said party by affidavit before a court or judge of competent jurisdiction, if he is willing and able to make such affidavit for the institution of a criminal prosecution. If he is not, he must superintend the preparation of the papers and the institution of the prosecution if any citizen is willing to make an affidavit for the institution of a criminal prosecution against any party for such violation; provided, that the district attorney is of opinion from the facts at hand that there is reasonable ground to believe that the offense has been committed."); Kan. Stat. Ann. § 19-717 (1988) (allowing the employment of a private prosecutor to assist the county attorney in any criminal matter); N.J. Stat. Ann. § 19-34-63 (allowing any citizen to "employ an attorney to assist the prosecutor," and requiring that such attorney be recognized by the prosecutor and the court as "associate counsel"); Or. Rev. Stat. § 135.165 (1990) (allowing a complainant to "employ counsel to appear against the defendant in every stage of the preliminary hearing"); Or. Rev. Stat. § 131.025 (1990) (the prosecuting party in a criminal case is the State of Oregon "[e]xcept for offenses based on municipal or county ordinances"); Tenn. Code Ann. § 8-7-401 (1993) ("A victim of crime or the family members of a victim of crime may employ private legal counsel to act as co-counsel with the district attorney general or the district attorney general's deputies in trying cases, with the extent of participation of such privately employed counsel being at the discretion of the district attorney general. The district attorney general or a deputy shall make the final and concluding argument. The privately retained counsel shall immediately inform the district attorney general of such counsel's employment."); *cf.* W. Va. Code § 7-7-8 (1993) ("No provision of this section shall be construed to prohibit the employment of any person of a practicing attorney to assist in the prosecution of any person or corporation charged with a crime.").

28. Private Criminal Complaints—Private Criminal Complaint Process, Wayne County, PA, https://waynecountypa.gov/794/Private-Criminal-Complaints ("Pennsylvania law allows for private citizens to file Private Criminal Complaints through its court system with certain restrictions which are detailed in

Title 234 Pennsylvania Rules of Criminal Procedure (Pa. R. Crim. P) Rule 420 (Summary Violations), Rules 504 (Contents of Complaint) and Rule 506 (Approval for Private Complaints)."); *cf. id*:

> *A Private Criminal Complaint should never be used to address a monetary or other dispute which is properly the subject of a civil action.* You must understand that filing criminal charges against another individual is a serious matter which requires that a crime has been committed and that the person(s) accused has committed this crime. There are other legal requirements that will also be addressed by the District Attorney's Office such as the statute of limitations, proper jurisdiction, etc.
>
> Before you file a Private Criminal Complaint, you must understand there are numerous laws in the Pennsylvania Crimes Code that address False Swearing (18 Pa. CS §4903), Unsworn Falsification (18 Pa. CS §4904) and False Reports to Law Enforcement (18 Pa. CS §4906).
>
> In order to avoid being in violation of these and possibly other sections of the Crimes Code, you must be complete, detailed, honest and accurate when describing the facts in the affidavit and in all conversations with detectives. Anyone violating these laws is subject to criminal prosecution. Prior to writing your criminal complaint we recommend you review the Pennsylvania Crimes Code Title 18, Crimes and Offenses to determine which section(s) you believe address the actions you are accusing the defendant of committing.

29. Margaret H. Lemos, *Privatizing Public Litigation*, 104 Geo. L.J. 515, 561 nn.243–44 (2016) (citing an article "describing state laws and judicial decisions permitting private attorneys to assist in prosecutions" and noting that "[m]ost courts to consider the question have held that private prosecutions are constitutionally permissible as long as public officials retain formal control over the litigation").

30. *Ex parte* Landry, 117 So. 3d 714, 717 (Ala. Civ. App. 2013) (per curiam) (a mother could independently pursue a motion for criminal contempt against the defendant-father); Hall v. State, 411 So.2d 831, 839 (Ala. Crim. App. 1981) (permitting special prosecutor to assist government prosecution).

31. Olmstead v. Olmstead, 284 S.W.3d 27, 28 (Ark. 2008) ("On April 10, 2008, Olmstead filed a petition for writ of certiorari with this court seeking to stay his trial, contending, inter alia, that he was being prosecuted by an unauthorized private prosecutor in violation of *Young v. United States ex rel. Vuitton et Fils S.A.*, 481 U.S. 787, 107 S. Ct. 2124, 95 L.Ed.2d 740 (1987). This court denied the writ without prejudice on April 10, 2008.").

32. Eichhorn v. Kelley, 111 P.3d 544, 548 (Colo. App. 2004) (declining to adopt a rule prohibiting a beneficiary of an order from prosecuting for contempt); Davis v. People, 238 P. 25 (Colo. 1925) ("There are authorities which support the position that a special prosecutor, privately employed, may not appear over defendant's objection, and in some states the practice is prohibited by statute. But the great weight of authority, and we think of reason, is to the contrary. It has been decided that the public prosecutor must retain control of the case for the people and be held accountable for its conduct; that privately employed counsel may assist him on his request or by his consent; that such request or consent is presumed in the absence of a showing to the contrary; that such assistance, so requested or consented to, as well as the number of assistants, rests in the sound discretion of the trial court; that objection thereto must be made in proper time and manner and be supported by the necessary showing; that in exercising its discretion the trial court should be guided only by the requirements of justice, the enforcement of the law, and the preservation of its guarantees. We so hold.").

33. State v. Wilson, 545 A.2d 1178, 1180–81 (Del. 1988) (noting that, in 1987, the mother of an 11-year-old alleged victim appeared before a Justice of the Peace to file a complaint against a 12-year-old body for assault, but that the Family Court held that new Family Court Criminal Rules, in effect, removed from the Attorney General "the option or discretion to permit private prosecution of delinquency proceedings, even before masters"; observing that on appeal, "the Attorney General disputes the power of the Family Court, through its rule-making authority, to require public prosecution of delinquency petitions to the exclusion of private petitioner and in derogation of the Attorney General's constitutional prerogatives"; and holding, "We agree with the State's contention that Family Court Criminal Rule 7 cannot be construed to require the Attorney General to prosecute all delinquency petitions before masters nor can the Rule be applied to preclude private petitioners from initiating and presenting delinquency petitions before masters in the Family Court."). Under the facts of *State v. Wilson*, the Supreme Court of Delaware—in a case in which the

Attorney General "initiated the prosecution through the filing of a formal petition signed by a deputy attorney general"—did note: "A court may, through its inherent authority to regulate the status of those who appear before it in a representative capacity, preclude the privatization of prosecutions initiated by a public prosecutor. This result is simply a corollary of the principle that the courts possess the exclusive right to govern the practice of law." *Id.* at 1183.

34. Marcisz v. Marcisz, 357 N.E.2d 477, 480 (Ill. 1976) (allowing counsel to prosecute criminal contempt for the beneficiary's order); People v. Ford, 168 N.E.2d 33, 37 (Ill. 1960) ("At the trial, Peyton Berbling, an attorney and resident of a neighboring county, appeared with the Pulaski County State's Attorney in prosecution of this case and was compensated partially by Unger's widow and partially by the State's Attorney. We see no error in this regard inasmuch as we have consistently held that a trial court, in its discretion, may permit a privately employed attorney to assist the State's Attorney in the prosecution of a criminal case so long as the defendant is adequately represented, and have held the statute prohibiting a State's Attorney from receiving any private reward for performing official duties (Ill.Rev.Stat.1951, chap. 14, par. 7) is not applicable to this situation. Hayner v. People, 213 Ill. 142, 72 N.E. 792; People v. O'Farrell, 247 Ill. 44, 93 N.E. 136; People v. Strosnider, 264 Ill. 434 106 N.E. 229; People v. Kingsbury, 353 Ill. 11, 186 N.E. 470; People v. Stark, 324 Ill. 289, 155 N.E. 271; People v. Donaldson, 255 Ill. 19, 99 N.E. 62; People v. Hartenbower, 283 Ill. 591, 119 N.E. 605; People v. Miller, 13 Ill.2d 84, 148 N.E.2d 455. From the record it appears that defendant was represented by an experienced and able attorney of his choice and was not prejudiced by the presence of privately employed counsel. Although defense counsel initially objected to the appearance of Berbling, it appears that the objection was for the purpose of determining if any of the jurors had contributed towards his employment and was not directed against his participation in the case as special prosecutor.").

35. State v. Sandstrom, 595 P.2d 324, 329 (Kan. 1979) ("It has long been the rule of law in this state that the family of the deceased in a murder prosecution is entitled to retain special counsel to assist the local prosecutor in the preparation of the case.").

36. Commonwealth v. Hubbard, 777 S.W.2d 882, 883 (Ky. 1991) ("The employment of private counsel to assist the Commonwealth Attorney in the prosecution of a criminal case does not violate the due process clauses of the Fifth and Fourteenth Amendments to the United States Constitution. It has been previously held that it is permissible for the circuit court and the Commonwealth Attorney to permit a private attorney to assist the Commonwealth Attorney in prosecuting a criminal case. *Goehring v. Commonwealth,* Ky., 370 S.W.2d 822 (1963); *Earl v. Commonwealth,* Ky. App., 569 S.W.2d 686 (1978). The Sixth Circuit Court of Appeals in *Stumbo v. Seabold,* 704 F.2d 910 (6th Cir.1983) held that the employment of private counsel to assist an elected prosecutor is not *per se* unconstitutional. *See also, Jones v. Richards,* 776 F.2d 1244 (4th Cir.1985), cited in 63A Am.Jur.2d *Prosecuting Attorneys* § 13 (1988 pocket pt. p. 48). *Also see* 27 C.J.S., *District and Prosecuting Attorneys* § 28(2a), pp. 710–712, 1988 pocket pt. p. 196.").

37. Long v. Hutchins, 926 So. 2d 556, 567 (La. Ct. App. 2006) (en banc) (Brown, C.J., concurring) ("The fact that private parties traditionally and naturally prosecute contempt proceedings is the fundamental difference between criminal cases and contempt proceedings. The Fourteenth Amendment's Due Process Clause does not impose upon states the requirement that charges be initiated by an independent state prosecutor.").

38. State v. Rollins, 533 A.2d 331, 331 (N.H. 1987) (stating that, in New Hampshire, "[t]he common law ... does not preclude the institution and prosecution of certain criminal complaints by private citizens"); State v. Fleury, 364 A.2d 625, 626 (N.H. 1976) (in prosecution for resisting arrest, trial court did not abuse its discretion in allowing a private attorney who represented a police office in a pending civil rights arising out of the events relating to the arrest to sit with the county attorney during trial and to participate in the prosecution; "The case was in the control of the county attorney, who was at all times present and who conducted the prosecution. What occurred was within the discretion of the trial court, and we find no violation of any rights of the defendant."); *see also* State v. Martineau, 808 A.2d 51, 52–53 (N.H. 2002) ("In New Hampshire, no statute or court rule either expressly permits, or expressly prohibits, private prosecutions by either an interested party or an interested party's attorney.... However, we have held that '[t]he common law of this State does not preclude the institution and prosecution of certain criminal complaints by private citizens.'") (citing State v. Rollins, 553 A.2d 331 (N.H. 1987)); Rogowicz v. O'Connell,

786 A.2d 841, 843–44 (2001) ("The authority to appoint a private prosecutor, however, should be exercised with restraint in accord with the notion that "only the least possible power adequate to the end proposed should be used in contempt cases." *Id.* at 801, 107 S. Ct. 2124 (brackets and quotation omitted). We agree with the Court in *Young* that criminal contempt should, in the first instance, be referred to the executive branch for prosecution. *See id.* We are confident that in most cases the executive branch will act to preserve respect for judicial authority. In the unusual case in which a court believes that prosecution is necessary, even after the executive branch has declined to act, a court may appoint a private prosecutor.").

39. *E.g.*, State of New Jersey v. Bazin, 912 F. Supp. 106, 111 (D. N.J. 1995); N.J. R. Mun. Ct. R. 7:8-7(b) ("The municipal prosecutor, municipal attorney, Attorney General, county prosecutor, or county counsel, as the case may be, may appear in any municipal court in any action on behalf of the State and conduct the prosecution either on the court's request or on the request of the respective public official. The court may also, in its discretion and in the interest of justice, direct the municipal prosecutor to represent the State. The court may permit an attorney to appear as a private prosecutor to represent the State in cases involving cross-complaints. Such private prosecutors may be permitted to appear on behalf of the State only if the court has first reviewed the private prosecutor's motion to so appear and an accompanying certification submitted on a form approved by the Administrative Director of the Courts. The court may grant the private prosecutor's application to appear if it is satisfied that a potential for conflict exists for the municipal prosecutor due to the nature of the charges set forth in the cross-complaints. The court shall place such a finding on the record."); State v. Ciepoch, Docket No. A-3596-18T1, 2020 WL 3459076, at *1–2 (N.J. Super. Ct., June 25, 2020) (noting the appearance of a private prosecutor in a municipal court case for simple assault); N.J. Directive 13-08 (titled "Certification Application for Appointment of a Private Prosecutor" and dated October 8, 2008); N.J. R. Mun. Ct. R. 7:7-7(a) ("If the government is represented by the municipal prosecutor or a private prosecutor in a cross complaint case, discovery shall be available to the parties only as provided by this rule, unless the court otherwise orders. All discovery requests by defendant shall be served on the municipal prosecutor, who shall be responsible for making government discovery available to the defendant. If the matter is, however, not being prosecuted by the municipal prosecutor, the municipal prosecutor shall transmit defendant's discovery requests to the private prosecutor in a cross complaint case, pursuant to R. 7:8-7(b)."); 17A Robert Ramsey, N.J. Prac., *Municipal Court Practice* § 43.7 (3d ed. 2019) ("A private attorney who wishes to appear as a prosecutor must make a good cause showing on the record to the court that his or her appearance as prosecutor would be in the interests of justice. The attorney must also file a motion seeking to be admitted as private prosecutor, complete with a detailed certification on a form prescribed by the Administrative Director of the Courts."); 17 Robert Ramsey, N.J. Prac., *Municipal Court Practice* § 12.7 (3d ed. 2019) ("The Legislature permits municipal prosecutors, with the approval of the municipal court, to authorize private attorneys to prosecute citizen complaints that are filed in municipal court. This grant of authority is somewhat different from that contained in the Rules of Court. Specifically, Rule 7:8-7(b) indicates that the court may make a determination in its own discretion and in the interests of justice to permit a private prosecutor to represent the government."); In re Grand Jury Appearance Request by Loigman, 870 A.2d 249, 253 n.1 (N.J. 2005) ("Private prosecutions in municipal court are a permissible, *R.* 7:8–7(b), but not favored, practice.") (citing *State v. Storm,* 141 *N.J.* 245, 252–54, 661 *A.*2d 790 (1995); *State v. Ward,* 303 *N.J.Super.* 47, 52, 696 *A.*2d 48 (App.Div.1997)).

40. Whitfield v. Gilchrist, 497 S.E.2d 412, 415 (N.C. 2008) ("[T]here are situations in which a district attorney may obtain the assistance of private counsel. For example, an elected district attorney has the discretion to permit a private attorney to appear with him to represent the State's interest in an action, subject to the court's approval. *State v. Camacho,* 329 N.C. 589, 593, 406 S.E.2d 868, 871 (1991). Historically, however, private counsel functioning in this prosecutorial capacity either have been paid by private parties or have appeared *pro bono publico. See State v. Best,* 280 N.C. 413, 186 S.E.2d 1 (1972). A district attorney's discretion to permit an attorney to act as a private prosecutor on behalf of the State in the prosecution of a particular case does not expressly or implicitly include the authority for the district attorney to bind the State to pay the attorney for performing the historic role of a private prosecutor."); State v. Camacho, 406 S.E.2d 868, 871 (N.C. 1991) ("[T]he elected District Attorney may, in his or her discretion and where otherwise permitted by law, delegate the prosecutorial function to others. For example, where the District Attorney consents to the employment of a private prosecutor and continues in charge of the

prosecution, the trial court may permit such a private prosecutor to appear for the State. The discretion to permit private prosecutors to appear when the District Attorney consents "has existed in our courts from their incipiency.") (citing *State v. Best*, 280 N.C. 413, 416–17, 186 S.E.2d 1, 3–4 (1972)); *see also State v. Misenheimer*, 304 N.C. 108 (1981) ("Several of defendant's brothers and sisters, including four who testified for the state at trial, hired a private prosecutor to represent the family. He aided in preparation and sat with the state's prosecutor at trial, but did not examine or cross-examine witnesses."); WILLIAM FRANK MCDONALD, CRIMINAL JUSTICE AND THE VICTIM 35 (1976) ("Projections about the impact of the use of private prosecutor laws can be extrapolated on an unscientific basis from some observations on how the system works in North Carolina—one of the few states where it continues to be used regularly. It is believed by some that the existence of the private prosecution system is one of the reasons for the comparatively large number of convicts on death row. However, David Kendall, an attorney directly familiar with 34 North Carolina death row cases, reports that private prosecutors were involved in only about 10 cases ....").

41. State v. Ray, 143 N.E.2d 484, 485 (Ohio Ct. App., 4th Dist. 1956) (allowing private prosecutions; "[w]e know of no statutory or constitutional reason for prohibiting" the practice of private prosecution "and, in our opinion, it is well and wise that the policy of the law permits the appearance of private counsel, especially in courts with limited jurisdiction"); Bechtel v. City of Eastlake, Ohio, Case No. 1:19CV1159, 2020 WL 137075, at *1, 5 (N.D. Ohio Jan. 13, 2020) (where a plaintiff filed a complaint asserting a violation of her rights under the U.S. Constitution's First, Fourth and Fourteenth Amendments, with the plaintiff alleging that defendants unlawfully delegated prosecutorial duties to private attorneys employed by the Lake Humane Society, the court dismissed that complaint and held that "the prosecution by counsel employed by a humane society of a criminal action relating to cruelty to animals does not violate the constitutional requirement that prosecutions be carried on in the name of and by the authority of the state" and that the individuals who prosecuted the animal cruelty case "were employed by Lake Humane Society in the exercise of its independent authority pursuant to R.C. 2931.18").

42. OR. REV. STAT. § 157.030 ("The appeal is taken in the same manner and within the same time as in the case of an appeal from a judgment in a civil action, except that: (1) The noticed thereof shall be served upon the district attorney for the county, or the deputy of the district attorney, or upon the private prosecutor in the action ....").

43. 16 PA. STAT. § 7710 (statute titled "When private counsel allowed to prosecute" reads: "If any district attorney, within this commonwealth, shall neglect or refuse to prosecute, in due form of law, any criminal charge, regularly returned to him, or to the court of the proper county; or if, at any stage of the proceedings, the district attorney of the proper county, and the private counsel, employed by the prosecutor, should differ as to the manner of conducting the trial, it shall be lawful for the prosecutor to present his or her petition to the court of the proper county, setting forth the character of the complaint, and verify the same by affidavit; whereupon, if the court shall be of the opinion that it is a proper case for a criminal proceeding or prosecution, it shall be lawful for it to direct any private counsel, employed by such prosecutor, to conduct the entire proceeding, and where an indictment is necessary, to verify the same, by his own signature, as fully as the same could be done by the district attorney; and this act shall apply to all criminal proceedings heretofore commenced, and still pending, as well as to those which shall be instituted hereafter."); 16 PA. STAT. § 1409 (statute titled "When private counsel may prosecute" reads: "If any district attorney shall neglect or refuse to prosecute in due form of law any criminal charge regularly returned to the district attorney or to the court, or if at any stage of the proceedings the district attorney and the private counsel employed by the prosecutor shall differ as to the manner of conducting the trial, the prosecutor may present a petition to the court, setting forth the character of the complaint, and verify the same by affidavit. If the court shall be of the opinion that it is a proper case for a criminal proceeding or prosecution, it may direct any private counsel employed by such prosecutor to conduct the entire proceeding, and where an indictment is necessary, to verify the same by the private counsel's own signature, as fully as the same could be done by the district attorney."); 234 PA. R. CRIM. P. 506(B) (2018) ("If the attorney for the Commonwealth ... (2) disapproves the complaint, the attorney shall state the reasons on the complaint form and return it to the affiant. Thereafter, the affiant may petition the court of common pleas for review of the decision."); PA. R. NORTHUMBERLAND CTY. R. CRIM. P. Rule NCR-313(b) ("A motion for nolle prosequi not resulting from a plea agreement shall include a certification that the prosecuting officer

or private prosecutor received notice of the hearing."); PA. R. BERKS CTY. J. ADMIN. Rule 1901.03(a) (rule, titled "Termination of Inactive Criminal and Summary Cases Before District Justices," makes reference to "private prosecuting attorney").

44. Cronan *ex rel.* State v. Cronan, 774 A.2d 866, 871 (R.I. 2001) ("[P]rivate misdemeanor prosecutions are valid in this jurisdiction."); Darryl K. Brown, *Criminal Enforcement Redundancy: Oversight of Decisions Not to Prosecute*, 103 MINN. L. REV. 843, 870 (2018) ("Rhode Island authorizes private prosecutions only for misdemeanors.").

45. TENN. CODE. ANN. § 8-7-401(a) ("A victim of crime or the family members of a victim of crime may employ private legal counsel to act as co-counsel with the district attorney general or the district attorney general's deputies in trying cases, with the extent of participation of such privately employed counsel being at the discretion of the district attorney general. The district attorney general or a deputy shall make the final and concluding argument. The privately retained counsel shall immediately inform the district attorney general of such counsel's employment."); Wilson v. Wilson, 984 S.W.2d 898, 903–04 (Tenn. 1998):

> A defendant found guilty of general contempt in Tennessee may be punished by fine or by imprisonment, or both. However, any fine imposed may not exceed fifty dollars and any term of imprisonment may not exceed ten days. Tenn. Code Ann. § 29-9-103 (Supp.1998). The risk that a defendant's liberty interest will be erroneously deprived by the current practice which allows a litigant's private attorney to prosecute contempt is slight because it is the trial judge, not the private attorney, who actually decides whether a contempt action may proceed. *See* Tenn. R. Crim. P. 42(b). Since the risk of erroneous deprivation is minimal, there is no real benefit or value in adopting a rule which would preclude a litigant's private attorney from prosecuting a contempt. Finally, tremendous fiscal and administrative burdens would result from a substitute procedural requirement. Contempt proceedings often arise in domestic relations cases in state courts. However, unlike the federal system, there is no fund in Tennessee from which to compensate private counsel appointed to prosecute criminal contempt actions. It is unrealistic to expect district attorneys to prosecute contempt actions arising from alleged violations of civil court orders. District attorneys already have a heavy case load prosecuting violations of the general criminal laws. *See State ex rel O'Brien v. Moreland,* 778 S.W.2d 400, 406 (Mo.App.1989) (discussing similar practical problems surrounding the rule of automatic disqualification). Were we to hold that due process precludes a litigant's private attorney from prosecuting contempt proceedings, many citizens would be deprived of the benefits to which they already have been adjudged entitled by state courts and many state court orders would remain unenforced. The minimal risk that a defendant will be erroneously deprived of his or her liberty interest if a litigant's private attorney prosecutes a contempt proceeding is far outweighed by the very real fiscal and administrative burdens certain to accompany the adoption of a substitute procedure. We hold that Due Process does not mandate adoption of a rule which automatically disqualifies a litigant's private counsel from prosecuting a contempt action.

46. Hott v. Yarbrough, 245 S.W. 676, 678–79 (Tex. 1922) ("Equally clear is the right of any one who may consider himself aggrieved by the actual or supposed commission of a crime to call the matter to the attention of the grand jury for investigation and action. The law does not restrict the method by which this may be done.").

47. Cantrell v. Commonwealth, 329 S.E.2d 22, 26 (Va. 1985) (stating that, in Virginia, the common law "generally permits the appearance of private counsel to assist the prosecution"). *But cf.* Riner v. Edwards, Civil Action No. 7:07-cv-00455, 2008 WL 4388788, at *13 (W.D. Va. 2008) ("Virginia courts have held that while use of private prosecutors is permitted, the procedure may violate Article I, § 11 of the Constitution of Virginia if the private prosecutor has a personal interest in the outcome of the case or if the public prosecutor relinquishes control of the case to the private prosecutor. *Cantrell v. Commonwealth,* 229 Va. 387, 329 S.E.2d 22, 26–27 (Va.1985).").

48. State v. Crouch, 445 S.E.2d 213, 218–19 (W. Va. 1994) (private prosecution held to be allowed to permit a victim's family to pursue a case).

49. Michael Edmund O'Neill, *Private Vengeance the Public Good*, 12 U. Pa. J. Const. L. 659, 689 (2010) ("Alabama, Georgia, Indiana, New Jersey, New York, Ohio, Pennsylvania, Tennessee, Vermont, Virginia, West Virginia, and Wisconsin each allow private counsel to participate in a criminal prosecution in some way."). The District of Columbia also has a provision for the appointment of a private prosecutor for a criminal contempt case. D.C. Dom. Violence Rule 14(b)(2)(C) (Superior Ct. Rules of the Family Division) ("A motion for criminal contempt will be referred to the Office of the Attorney General for the District of Columbia and the United States Attorney's Office for review. If both public prosecutors decline to prosecute, the court may appoint a private prosecutor to independently review the motion."); D.C. Dom. Violence Rule 14(b)(2)(D) (Superior Ct. Rules of the Family Division) ("If a public or private prosecutor decides to proceed, the prosecutor must file an information or complaint in accordance with Criminal Rule 7. After an information or complaint is filed, all proceedings are governed by the Superior Court Rules of Criminal Procedure."); Ryan W. Scott, *Standing to Appeal and Executive Non-Defense of Federal Law after the Marriage Cases*, 89 Ind. L.J. 67, 81 n.103 (2014) ("The Circuit Court for the District of Columbia ... routinely exercised jurisdiction over private criminal prosecutions brought in the name of the United States. That court was organized under Article I, see Act of Feb. 27, 1801, ch. 15, § 3, 2 Stat. 103, 105–06 ....") (citing United States v. Birch, 24 F. Cas. 1147 (C.C.D.C. 1809) (No. 14,595); United States v. Dulany, 25 F. Cas. 923 (C.C.D.C. 1809) (No. 15,000); United States v. Lyles, 26 F. Cas. 1024 (C.C.D.C. 1806) (No. 15,645); United States v. Sandford, 27 F. Cas. 952 (C.C.D.C. 1806) (No. 16,221); Virginia v. Dulany, 28 F. Cas. 1223 (C.C.D.C. 1802) (No. 16,958)); *see also* In re Peak, 759 A.2d 612, 617 (D.C. Ct. App. 2000) ("It is well settled that criminal contempt proceedings may be prosecuted by private attorneys appointed by the court for that purpose."); Seth Davis, *Standing Doctrine's State Action Problem*, 91 Notre Dame L. Rev. 585, 611–12 (2015) ("History also shows, however, that the legislature could authorize private litigants to stand for the government even if the common law did not. Private litigants could prosecute crimes in the District of Columbia and the territories, suggesting, at a minimum, that Article I, Article II, and the Due Process Clause were not perceived to prohibit private enforcement of the United States' interest in enforcing the laws. The practice of qui tam litigation, in turn, suggests that Article III courts could entertain government suits brought by formally private plaintiffs. When the legislature specially provided for it, a private relator could sue on behalf of the government to enforce the law, with the relator retaining part of the recovery as a bounty. During the Founding era Congress enacted several *qui tam* statutes, a practice that has continued into the modern day. Federal courts have long recognized standing under these statutes.").

50. Lopez v. State, 437 S.W.2d 268, 269 (Tex. Ct. Crim. App. 1968) (trial court did not abuse its discretion in permitting attorney employed by family of deceased to assist in homicide prosecution); Ex parte Powers, 487 S.W.2d 101, 104 (Tex. Ct. Crim. App. 1972) (rejecting contention that "the petitioner was 'denied a fair and impartial trial by virtue of the Special Prosecutor who was not sworn or duly elected, nor appointed to represent the State of Texas, but was only hired by the family of the deceased to avenge the personal feelings and emotions of the family of the deceased and such a procedure is unconstitutional in violation of the Sixth and Fourteenth Amendments of the Constitution of the United States'").

51. N.J. Stat. Ann. § 19:34-63 (L. 1930, c. 187, ¶ 495, p. 909).

52. In re Ringwood Fact Finding Committee, 324 A.2d 1, 2 (N.J. 1974).

53. Ruvoldt v. Tumulty, 107 N.J. Super. 545, 555 (1969).

54. Minn. Stat. Ann. § 211A.08 (Laws 1988, c. 578, art. 2, § 8, eff. July 1, 1988, *repealed by* Laws 2004, c. 277, § 13); Minn. Stat. Ann. § 211B.16 (Laws 1988, c. 578, art. 3, § 16, eff. July 1, 1988, *repealed by* Laws 2004, c. 277, § 13).

55. Donald J. Hall, *The Role of the Victim in the Prosecution and Disposition of a Criminal Case*, 28 Vand. L. Rev. 931, 976 (1975). The practice of requiring public prosecutors to control a criminal prosecution is at odds with some nineteenth-century practices, such as those of Philadelphia. Allen Steinberg, The Transformation of Criminal Justice: Philadelphia, 1800–1880, at 82 (1989) ("The discretion of the private parties in criminal cases was not checked by the public prosecutor. Instead, the public prosecutor in most cases adopted a stance of passive neutrality. He was essentially a clerk, organizing the court calendar and presenting cases to grand and petit juries. Most of the time, he was either superseded by a private attorney or simply let the private prosecutor and his witnesses take the stand and state their case.").

56. State v. Page, 206 S.E.2d 771, 772 (N.C. Ct. App. 1974).

57. State v. Riser, 294 S.E.2d 461, 465 (W.V. 1982).

58. *See Alabama*, Hall v. State, 411 So. 2d 831, 838 (Ala. Crim. App. 1981) ("The appearance by a qualified attorney for a private person ... does not require an appointment by any court, the District Attorney, or any of his assistants."); *Montana*, State v. Cockrell, 309 P.2d 316, 319 (Mont. 1957) ("The record does not show whether any appointment was made under the authority of this statute [authorizing the board of county commissioners 'to employ, or authorize the county attorney to employ, special counsel to assist in the prosecution of any criminal case pending in such county']. However the general rule is, that on a collateral attack such as this, the court will indulge the presumption that the appointment was regularly made in the absence of a showing to the contrary."); *Ohio*, State v. Ray, 143 N.E.2d 484 (Ohio App. 1956) (private prosecutor was permissible despite fact that private counsel admitted that he was not affiliated with the city solicitor's office in any manner). However, in these states, the trial court has the discretion to preclude private prosecutors. *See, e.g., Hall*, 411 So.2d at 838–39 (trial court can, for good cause, preclude the participation of a private prosecutor).

59. *E.g.*, State v. Dressler, 738 P.2d 830, 838 (Kan. 1987) ("[A]n attorney hired by the prosecuting witness to assist the prosecutor must participate in discovery pursuant to K.S.A. 22–3212 by disclosing requested evidence which is in the attorney's possession, custody, or control.").

60. *E.g., California*, People v. Powell, 25 P. 481 (Cal. 1891); *Colorado*, Davis v. People, 238 P. 25 (Colo. 1925); *Florida*, Ates v. State, 194 So. 286 (Fla. 1940); *Georgia*, Allen v. State, 257 S.E.2d 5 (Ga. App. 1979); Brown v. State, 250 S.E.2d 438 (Ga. 1978); *Illinois*, People v. Farnsley, 293 N.E.2d 600, 605 (Ill. 1973); Hayner v. People, 72 N.E. 792 (Ill. 1904); *Kansas*, State v. Baker, 819 P.2d 1173 (Kan. 1991); State v. Berg, 694 P.2d 427, 431 (Kan. 1985); State v. Sandstrom, 595 P.2d 324 (Kan. 1979); *Kentucky*, Stumbo v. Seabold, 704 F.2d 910 (6th Cir. 1983) (applying Kentucky law); Commonwealth v. Hubbard, 777 S.W.2d 882 (Ky. 1989); Earl v. Commonwealth, 569 S.W.2d 686 (Ky. App. 1978); *Louisiana*, State v. Hopper, 203 So. 2d 222, 229 (La. 1967) ("The jurisprudence has been legion that private counsel may be employed to assist the Attorney General or the district attorney in the trial of a criminal cause."); Hon. Leander H. Perez, Jr., District Attorney, Pointe-A-La-Hache, LA, 1978–79 La. Op. Atty. Gen. 65, La. Atty. Gen. Op. No. 79-49, 1979 WL 38543 (Jan. 19, 1979) ("[I]t appears settled the district attorney can retain private counsel for proceedings conducted by his office."); *Maine*, State v. Bartlett, 74 A. 18, 19 (Me. 1909); *New Jersey*, State v. Wouters, 177 A.2d 299 (N.J. Super. 1962); *New Mexico*, State v. Baca, 688 P.2d 34, 35 (N.M. 1984) (noting that a New Mexico statute, § 36-1-19, "authorizes an associate counsel to prosecute for the district attorney and 'on ruling of the court,'" thus requiring "an explicit order of the court"; "We hold that where the record does not demonstrate such explicit approval, the proper authority is not vested in the private counsel to prosecute."); *North Carolina*, State v. Moose, 313 S.E.2d 507 (N.C. 1984); *North Dakota*, State v. Kent, 62 N.W. 631 (N.D. 1895); *Oklahoma*, Ryals v. State, 434 P.2d 488 (Okla. Crim. App. 1967); *Pennsylvania*, Commonwealth v. Musto, 35 A.2d 307 (Pa. 1944); *South Carolina*, State v. Addis, 186 S.E.2d 415, 417 (S.C. 1972) ("'By the great weight of authority the court may, in its discretion, permit the prosecuting attorney to have the assistance of counsel employed by the prosecuting witness or other persons interested in securing a conviction; but such appointment, it has been held, can be made only on the request or consent of the prosecuting attorney, which, however, may be presumed from the fact of participation and assistance without objection.'") (quoting 29 C.J.S. District and Prosecuting Attorneys § 29(1) (1959)); *South Dakota*, State v. Basham, 170 N.W.2d 238, 241 (S.D. 1969) (noting that a statute did not prohibit "prohibit employment of an attorney, who is not interested in a civil suit involving the same facts as are involved in the criminal action, by private parties to assist in prosecution if agreeable to the state's attorney and the latter retains control of the prosecution"); *Tennessee*, State v. Bennett, 798 S.W.2d 783 (Tenn. App. 1990); *Texas*, Urdiales v. Canales, 475 F. Supp. 622, 628 (S.D. Tex. 1979) ("notwithstanding the required 'control and management' by the public prosecutor, the Texas Court of Criminal Appeals has routinely approved very active participation in criminal trials by special prosecutors"); Ballard v. State, 519 S.W.2d 426 (Tex. Crim. App. 1975); Lopez v. State, 437 S.W.2d 268 (Tex. Crim. App. 1969); *Utah*, People v. Tidwell, 12 P. 61 (Utah 1886) (allowing the use of special prosecutor in a murder trial); *Vermont*, State v. Dunbar, 566 A.2d 970, 977 (Vt. 1989) (complaining witness' attorney did not exceed permissible limits established for private prosecutor in *State v. Gonyaw*, 507 A.2d 944, 947 (Vt. 1985), in sexual assault prosecution, though attorney was heard on issues of joinder and severance, dismissal for lack of prima facie case, seating arrangements,

appointment of substitute counsel, and continuance, and where he strongly urged incarceration of defendant at sentencing); *Virginia*, Cantrell v. Commonwealth, 329 S.E.2d 22 (Va. 1985); *Virgin Islands*, Tonkin v. Michael, 349 F. Supp. 78, 81 (V.I. 1972) ("A private citizen, in my opinion, is still authorized to file a complaint if the prosecutor refuses or neglects to do so. However, as stated above, and for policy reasons, I believe that the public prosecutor must supervise the actual conduct of the case."; "[T]he Court may, pursuant to Rule 132, appoint private prosecutors. It would be advisable, for the purposes of the rule, that the prospective private prosecutor seek the permission of the Attorney General to prosecute before attempting to obtain leave of Court."); *West Virginia*, State ex rel. Koppers Co. v. International Union of Oil, Chemical & Atomic Workers, 298 S.E.2d 827, 829 (W. Va. 1982) ("Participation by a private prosecutor does not obviate the need for a public prosecutor's presence, he being ultimately responsible for discretion regarding prosecution of alleged public law offenders."); State v. Riser, 294 S.E.2d 461, 465 (W. Va. 1982) ("In *State v. Atkins*, W.Va., 261 S.E.2d 55 (1979), *cert. denied*, 445 U.S. 904, 100 S. Ct. 1081, 63 L.Ed.2d 320 (1980) ... this Court declined to abolish the common law private prosecutor system, recognizing there were sound policy reasons for its retention.").

A handful of states allow only minimal participation by private prosecutors. *E.g.*, State v. Newman, 568 S.W.2d 276, 282–83 (Mo. App. 1978) (prosecution witness has right to have private attorney appear, but witness' counsel had no right to otherwise participate in process of examination). Other jurisdictions have yet to articulate the permissible level of assistance that private prosecutors can provide in specific contexts. *E.g.*, Smith v. State, 426 N.E.2d 364 (Ind. 1981) (private attorney introduced as "assistant" sat with public prosecutor at trial but did not participate); Sedelbauer v. State, 455 N.E.2d 1159, 1164 (Ind. App. 1983) (private prosecutor may assist in criminal trial); State v. von Bulow, 475 A.2d 995, 1003 (R.I. 1984) (stating merely that claim of private prosecution is "utterly without merit").

61. State v. Best, 186 S.E.2d 1, 3–4 (N.C. 1972) ("[t]he discretion vested in the trial judge to permit private counsel to appear with the solicitor has existed in our courts from their incipiency"; "'[i]t is within the discretion of the trial judge to allow special counsel to aid the prosecution of a case, and such discretion will be interfered with only on a showing of abuse thereof'"; "the appearance of private counsel for the prosecution was a matter under the control and in the sound discretion of the presiding judge"); State v. Woodruff, 392 S.E.2d 434, 436 (N.C. App. 1990) (noting that the trial judge has the discretion "'to determine whether a private attorney may assist the District Attorney in the prosecution of a case'"), *aff'd*, 399 S.E.2d 114 (N.C. 1991) (per curiam). In such jurisdictions, it is often held that the trial judge's discretion in such matters will only be interfered with upon a showing of abuse of discretion. State v. Boykin, 259 S.E.2d 883, 891 (N.C. 1979) ("The employment of private prosecution is a discretionary practice which has long been approved in North Carolina. The trial court's discretion in allowing or disallowing private prosecution will be interfered with only upon a showing of abuse.") (citations omitted); *accord Woodruff*, 392 S.E.2d at 436.

62. Hall v. State, 411 So.2d 831, 839 (Ala. Ct. Crim. App. 1981).

63. State v. Atkins, 261 S.E.2d 55, 58 (W.V. 1979).

64. In a few states, statutes prohibiting adultery—though rarely put to use in the modern era—only permit the affected spouse to commence a criminal prosecution. *See, e.g.*, Susan L. Thomas, *Proof of Adultery as Grounds for Dissolution of Marriage*, 49 Am. Jur. Proof of Facts 3d 277, at § 21 (1998; updated Apr. 2021) ("Although prosecutions for adultery have become rare in modern times, many states continue to have statutory provisions that prohibit adultery."); Ariz. Rev. Stat. Ann. § 13-1408(B) ("No prosecution for adultery shall be commenced except upon complaint of the husband or wife."); Mich. Comp. Laws § 750.31 ("No prosecution for adultery, under the preceding section, shall be commenced, but on the complaint of the husband or wife; and no such prosecution shall be commenced after 1 year from the time of committing the offense."); Minn. Stat. Ann. § 609.36, subd. 2 ("No prosecution shall be commenced under this section [prohibiting adultery] except on complaint of the husband or the wife, except when such husband or wife lacks the mental capacity, nor after one year from the commission of the offense."); N.D. Cent. Code § 12.1-20-09, subd. 2 ("No prosecution shall be instituted under this section [prohibiting adultery] except on the complaint of the spouse of the alleged offender, and the prosecution shall not be commenced later than one year from commission of the offense."); Okla. Stat. Ann. § 871 ("Prosecution for adultery can be commenced and carried on against either of the parties to the crime only by his or her

own husband or wife as the case may be, or by the husband or wife of the other party to the crime: Provided, that any person may make complaint when persons are living together in open and notorious adultery."); State v. Lynch, 562 P.2d 1386, 1391 (Ariz. Ct. App. 1977) (holding that "the legislature has decided that, as a matter of public policy," acts of "adultery" or "adulterous conduct" are "to be prosecuted as a crime only under certain circumstances" and that a prosecution cannot be initiated "except on a complaint of the husband or wife"); *see also* Lee v. State, 231 P. 324, 325 (Okla. Crim. App. 1924) (adultery is a "private wrong" that must be initiated by the injured person); Dale v. State, 449 P.2d 921, 925 (Okla. Crim. App. 1969) (statutory provision that adultery prosecution can be commenced and carried on only by husband or wife of either party should be construed to harmonize with general provisions of criminal procedure, and "commenced" implied that injured party may start the proceedings by signing a complaint but that after prosecution has been so commenced it must be carried on largely by county attorney); State v. La Bounty, 116 P. 1073 (Wash. 1911) (the crime of adultery can only be prosecuted by a spouse); 1 GILLESPIE MICH. CRIM. L. & PROC. § 9:3 (2d ed. 2020) ("The fact that a criminal proceeding for adultery must be commenced by the husband or wife of one of the guilty parties does not make the complainant a party to the case, and the people and the defendant are the only parties. If one of the parties is unmarried, the complaint may be made by the husband or wife of the opposite party."). *Compare* Elizabeth F. Emens, *Monogamy's Law: Compulsory Monogamy and Polyamorous Existence*, 29 N.Y.U. REV. L. & SOC. CHANGE 277, 365 n.446 (2004) (noting the "four state statutes that condition" a prosecution for adultery "on a complaint by the other spouse") *with* Gregory A. Mccarthy, *Reforming Chapter 14 of Arizona's Criminal Code: Bringing Consistency, Clarity, Contemporaneity, and Constitutionality to Sexual Offenses in Arizona*, 33 ARIZ. ST. L.J. 229, 257–58 (2001) (discussing Arizona's adultery statute, Ariz. Rev. Stat. § 13-1408, and observing: "This statute is objectionable because its subsection (B) places the decision whether to prosecute in the hands of the aggrieved spouse. Ordinarily, the decision to prosecute belongs to a prosecutorial agency and not to a private person. Entrusting this critical decision to the discretion of a private citizen ensures that the statute will be enforced in an arbitrary fashion. The implicit assumption that the harm is specific to the spouse and does not more generally and substantially affect society militates against criminalizing adultery in the first place.") *and Right of Injured Spouse to Discontinue Prosecution for Adultery*, 61 A.L.R. 973 (1929) ("The rule that, while statutory provision to the effect that no prosecution for adultery 'shall be commenced' except on complaint of the husband or the wife of offending party is mandatory, a prosecution, where once commenced by such husband or wife, is no longer within the control of complainant, but within the control of the court, and that complainant therefore has no right to have the prosecution discontinued or dismissed, is supposed by the following cases .... The theory behind the cases supporting this rule is that, while adultery is an offense against the injured party, and primarily a private concern, after the complaint is filed it is no longer a matter of private concern, but partakes of all the attributes of a public offense, relieving the injured spouse of further right to control the proceedings by repenting and demanding a dismissal.").

65. *See* Patricia Moran, Note, *Private Prosecutors in Criminal Contempt Actions Under Rule 42(b) of the Federal Rules of Criminal Procedure*, 54 FORDHAM L. REV. 1141, 1154 n.54 (1986) (citing cases). A 1983 Alabama case, one scholar notes, "is the only 20th century case holding unequivocally that a private prosecutor who also represents plaintiffs in a civil action arising out of the same proceeding presents no inherent due process or ethical problems." *Id.* at 1155 n.57 (citing Hopkins v. State, 429 So. 2d 1146, 1154 (Ala. Crim. App. 1983)). For a discussion of case law with respect to prosecutors' conflicts of interest, see Moran, *supra*, at 1155–62; Richard H. Underwood, *Part-Time Prosecutors and Conflicts of Interest: A Survey and Some Proposals*, 81 KY. L.J. 1 (1992–93).

66. Ahuruonye v. United States Department of Interior, 312 F. Supp.3d 1, 12 (D. D.C. 2018) ("As to the criminal claims asserted by the plaintiff against the defendants, see generally Compl.; see also Pl.'s Opp›n at 53–56 (discussing the various criminal violations purportedly committed by the defendants), the defendants argue that these claims should be dismissed due to the Court's lack of subject-matter jurisdiction because "private citizens lack Article III standing to bring claims under criminal statutes," Defs.' Mot. at 19. The Court agrees."); *id.* ("It is well-settled that 'a citizen lacks standing to contest the policies of the prosecuting authority when he himself is neither prosecuted nor threatened with prosecution,' and 'a private citizen lacks a judicially cognizable interest in the prosecution or nonprosecution of another.' Linda R.S. v.

Richard D., 410 U.S. 614, 619, 93 S. Ct. 1146, 35 L.Ed.2d 536 (1973). And contrary to the plaintiff's contention, see Pl.'s Opp'n at 53 (asserting that the 'prosecution of the defendants for their criminal actions [is] at the discretion of the [C]ourt,' and that he 'is entitled to the requisite economic and financial damage as a victim of [their] criminal conduct'), '[t]he power to decide when to investigate, and when to prosecute, lies at the core of the Executive's duty to see to the faithful execution of the laws,' Cmty. for Creative Non–Violence v. Pierce, 786 F.2d 1199, 1201 (D.C. Cir. 1986). Accordingly, the plaintiff cannot pursue criminal claims against the defendants, and the Court must therefore grant this aspect of the defendants' motion and dismiss these claims for lack of subject-matter jurisdiction."); Chagolla v. Cluff, No. CV-19-00243-PHX-SPL, 2019 WL 1777268, at *1 (D. Ariz. Apr. 23, 2019) ("[T]o the extent the Complaint appears to assert any criminal charges, the Court notes that 'a private citizen lacks a judicially cognizable interest in the prosecution or nonprosecution of another.'") (quoting Linda R.S. v. Richard D., 410 U.S. 614, 619 (1973)); Kastis v. Alvarado, Case No. 1:18-cv-01325-DAD-BAM, at *9 (E.D. Cal. July 11, 2019) ("Plaintiff is advised ... that he may not pursue criminal charges or a criminal prosecution against defendants by way of a federal civil rights action."); Engelbrecht v. Kern Cty. Tax Assessor, No. 2:17-cv-01229 KJM AC PS, 2017 WL 2618492, at *2 (E.D. Cal. June 16, 2017) (there is no right of private prosecution in federal court; a private individual cannot criminally prosecute, or cause the government to criminally prosecute, another private individual); Owens v. Doe of Store Vintage Wine and Spirits, No. 18-CV-10278 (CM), 2019 WL 2743204 *2 (S.D.N.Y. July 1, 2019) ("A private individual cannot prosecute a criminal action in federal court."); *see also* Douglas E. Beloof & Paul G. Cassell, *The Crime Victim's Right to Attend the Trial: The Reascendant National Consensus*, 9 Lewis & Clark L. Rev. 481, 487–88 (2005) ("While private prosecution is firmly entrenched in the history of the colonies and the states, it was not extensively used in the federal system. One important reason is that the early federal criminal code established 'crimes against the Federal Government qua Federal Government and thus, public officials prosecuted these public crimes.' Moreover, from the very inception of the federal system, starting with the Judiciary Act of 1789, public prosecutors—the Attorney General along with U.S. Attorneys—were available to prosecute federal cases. Private citizens, however, still had some limited involved in federal criminal prosecutions. They could initiate prosecutions, by obtaining 'bench warrants from magistrates for the arrest of defendants' and by presenting 'evidence of crimes directly to grand juries.' In addition, they could pursue a private qui tam action for some offenses (a vestige of private prosecution that remains viable to this day).").

67. Allen v. City of New York, No. 1:20-CV-3868 (LLS), 2020 WL 3546883, at *2 (S.D.N.Y. June 29, 2020); *see also* Panetta v. Cassel, 7:20-CV-2255 (PMH), 2020 WL 2521533, at *2 (S.D.N.Y. May 18, 2020) (same); Johnson El ex rel. v. DeProspo, 1:19-CV-8426 (CM), 2019 WL 6311882, at *3 (S.D.N.Y. Nov. 22, 2019) (same).

68. Article III of the U.S. Constitution, which created the U.S. Supreme Court and authorized Congress to set up "such inferior courts as the Congress may from time to time ordain and establish," is the part of the Constitution that deals with the "judicial power." From the start, Article III courts did not look favorably upon private prosecutions. *E.g.*, Ann Woolhandler & Caleb Nelson, *Does History Defeat Standing Doctrine?*, 102 Mich. L. Rev. 689, 699–700 (2004) ("Although private prosecutions occasionally occurred in territorial courts and in the courts of the District of Columbia, Article III courts were different: they did not recognize private citizens as the proper people to prosecute public offenses. As the U.S. Supreme Court put it in 1842, 'from the very nature of an indictment and the sentence thereon, the government alone has the right to control the whole proceedings and execution of the sentence.' At least when it came to criminal prosecutions, then, private individuals were not understood to be able to go to federal court to vindicate public rights, whether on their own behalf or in the name of the American people at large.").

69. *See also* Ryan W. Scott, *Standing to Appeal and Executive Non-Defense of Federal Law after the Marriage Cases*, 89 Ind. L.J. 67, 79 n.102 (2014) ("The lack of private prosecutions in Article III courts did not stem from standing requirements, but from choices made by Congress. One was a requirement of public prosecution for all federal crimes. *See* Judiciary Act of 1789, ch. 20, § 35, 1 Stat. 73, 92–93; United States v. Murphy, 41 U.S. 203, 209 (1842); Ann Woolhandler & Caleb Nelson, *Does History Defeat Standing Doctrine?*, 102 Mich. L. Rev. 689, 697 (2004) .... Another was the Supreme Court's asymmetrical appellate jurisdiction in federal-question cases, see Judiciary Act of 1789 § 25, which made it impossible for States to appeal from state-court decisions erroneously accepting a federal-law defense."); *see also* Johnson v.

United States Department of Justice, Civil No. 3:12-CV-1842, 2013 WL 1909566, at *1 (M.D. Pa. May 3, 2013) ("Before the court is the report and recommendation, (Doc. No. 5), of Judge Martin C. Carlson recommending that plaintiff's complaint, (Doc. No. 1), be dismissed without leave to amend. In particular, Judge Carlson finds that plaintiff's claims are categorically barred by various principles of immunity and prohibitions against private criminal prosecutions in federal court. (Doc. No. 5.) After reviewing the record *de novo,* the court will adopt the report and recommendation and dismiss plaintiff's complaint with prejudice.").

70. Mikhail v. Kahn, 991 F. Supp. 2d 596, 634 (E.D. Pa. 2014) (*quoting* Linda R.S. v. Richard D. 410 U.S. 614, 619 (1973) (emphasis added by court in *Mikhail*).

71. Mikhail v. Kahn, 991 F. Supp. 2d 596, 634–35 (E.D. Pa. 2014) ("Lower federal courts, including the Third Circuit Court of Appeals, have consistently enforced this rule by dismissing private attempts to prosecute.") (*citing* Johnson v. U.S. DOJ, 541 Fed. Appx. 160, 161 (3d Cir. 2013) (per curiam) ("Nor could Johnson bring a private criminal complaint against the judges or prosecutors, as 'a private citizen lacks a judicially cognizable interest in the prosecution ... of another.'") (quoting *Linda R.S.*, 410 U.S. at 619)); United States ex rel. Nagy v. Patton, Misc. Action No. 11-267, 2012 WL 1858983, at *1 (E.D. Pa. May 22, 2012) ("[T]he Court is aware of no provision under which the plaintiff could bring an action as a 'relator' or 'private attorney general' to enforce the criminal laws of the United States of America. Federal law provides for occasional situations in which a private party may sue as relator on the Government's behalf for the recovery of money owed to the Government. *See, e.g.*, 31 U.S.C. §§ 3729 *et seq.* (False Claims Act); *Vt. Agency of Natural Res. v. United States ex rel. Stevens,* 529 U.S. 765, 774–77, 120 S. Ct. 1858, 146 L.Ed.2d 836 (2000) (discussing history of *qui tam* actions). But the plaintiff's complaint here does not invoke any such provisions; the plaintiff seeks, instead, to charge and prosecute the defendants with criminal offenses."); *see also id.* at *2 ("The prosecution of violations of federal criminal law in federal court is a function of the federal government, not private parties. 'Under the authority of Art. II, § 2 [of the U.S. Constitution], Congress has vested in the Attorney General the power to conduct the criminal litigation of the United States Government.' *United States v. Nixon,* 418 U.S. 683, 694, 94 S. Ct. 3090, 41 L.Ed.2d 1039 (citing 28 U.S.C. § 516); *see also Keenan v. McGrath,* 328 F.2d 610, 611 (1st Cir. 1964) (per curiam) ('[W]e are unaware of any authority for permitting a private individual to initiate a criminal prosecution in his own name in a United States District Court ....'); *Smith v. Krieger,* 389 F. App'x 789, 798–99 (10th Cir. 2010) ('Congress has by statute conferred the power to prosecute crimes in the name of the United States on the United States Attorney General and his delegates. The long-standing view of the Supreme Court is that such power is exclusive.' (internal citation omitted)); *United States ex rel. Savage v. Arnold,* 403 F. Supp. 172, 174 (E.D. Pa. 1975) ('[T]he essential role of the government (i.e. the U.S. Attorney) in the prosecution of criminal violations must of necessity preclude complaints by private citizens.')."); *id.* at *3 ("The plaintiff's complaint, construed as an effort to initiate a private prosecution of federal criminal law, will be dismissed.").

72. Mikhail v. Kahn, 991 F. Supp. 2d 596, 635 (E.D. Pa. 2014) ("[A] private individual cannot sue—at least in federal court—to compel the state or federal government to investigate or prosecute an alleged crime.") (*citing* Williams ex rel. Faison v. U.S. Penitentiary Lewisburg, 377 Fed. Appx. 255, 256 (3d Cir. 2010) (per curiam) ("Because Williams requested only criminal prosecution of those allegedly responsible for her brother's death, her claims are not cognizable."); United States v. Nixon, 418 U.S. 683, 693 (1974) ("[T]he Executive Branch has exclusive authority and absolute discretion to decide whether to prosecute a case.")); *see also* United States ex rel. Nagy v. Patton, Misc. Action No. 11-267, 2012 WL 1858983, at *2 n.3 (E.D. Pa. May 22, 2012) ("The old system of private criminal prosecutions is largely but not entirely absent from modern federal practice. *See, e.g., United States v. Dixon,* 509 U.S. 688, 692–93, 113 S. Ct. 2849, 125 L.Ed.2d 556 (1993) (private prosecution of criminal contempt); *New Jersey v. Kinder,* 701 F. Supp. 486, 487 & n.1, 491–93 (D. N.J.1988) (private prosecution of state disorderly persons offense heard in federal court in removal jurisdiction).").

A few cases can be found where private prosecutors made their way into federal court. "The old system of private criminal prosecution is largely but not entirely absent from modern federal practice," the U.S. District Court for the Eastern District of Pennsylvania wrote in 2012 in *United States ex rel. Nagy v. Patton.* In that case, the district court judge stated that "the Court is aware of no provision under which the plaintiff could bring an action as a 'relator' or 'private attorney general' to enforce the criminal laws of the United States of America." "Federal law," that court observed, making reference to the False Claims Act and the history of *qui tam* actions, "provides for occasional situations in which a private party may sue as relator on the Government's behalf for the recovery of money owed to the Government." But in that case, the district court judge noted that the plaintiff had impermissibly sought "to charge and prosecute the defendants with criminal offenses" despite the fact that "[t]he prosecution of violations of federal criminal law is a function of the federal government, not private parties." United States ex rel. Nagy v. Patton, Misc. Action No. 11-267, 2012 WL 1858983, at *1–2 (E.D. Pa. May 22, 2012); *id.* at *2 ("'Under the authority of Art. II, § 2 [of the U.S. Constitution], Congress has vested in the Attorney General the power to conduct the criminal litigation of the United States Government.' *United States v. Nixon*, 418 U.S. 683, 694, 94 S. Ct. 3090, 41 L.Ed.2d 1039 (citing 28 U.S.C. § 516); *see also Keenan v. McGrath*, 328 F.2d 610, 611 (1st Cir. 1964) (per curiam) ('[W]e are unaware of any authority for permitting a private individual to initiate a criminal prosecution in his own name in a United States District Court ....'); *Smith v. Krieger*, 389 F. App'x 789, 798–99 (10th Cir. 2010) ('Congress has by statute conferred the power to prosecute crimes in the name of the United States on the United States Attorney General and his delegates. The long-standing view of the Supreme Court is that such power is exclusive.' (internal citation omitted)); *United States ex rel. Savage v. Arnold*, 403 F. Supp. 172, 174 (E.D. Pa. 1975) ('[T]he essential role of the government (i.e. the U.S. Attorney) in the prosecution of criminal violations must of necessity preclude complaints by private citizens.').").

The court in *United States ex rel. Nagy v. Patton* pointed to two cases in which private prosecutors were allowed to appear in federal court. First, in *United States v. Dixon*, the U.S. Supreme Court examined whether the U.S. Constitution's Double Jeopardy Clause barred criminal prosecutions for conduct that had previously been the subject of trials for criminal contempt of court for violating court orders that prohibited them from engaging in that conduct. The Supreme Court, in a decision written by Justice Antonin Scalia, held that double jeopardy protections apply to non-summary criminal contempt prosecutions, with Justice Scalia emphasizing that "[a]t common law, the criminal contempt power was confined to sanctions for conduct that interfered with the orderly administration of judicial proceedings." United States v. Dixon, 509 U.S. 688, 691, 694 (1993) (citing 4 W. Blackstone, Commentaries *280-*285). "That limitation," Justice Scalia concluded in Part II of his opinion, "was closely followed in American courts." *Id.* at 694 (citing United States v. Hudson, 7 Cranch 32, 34, 3 L.Ed. 259 (1812); R. Goldfarb, The Contempt Power 12–20 (1963)); *see also id.* at 694 ("Federal courts had power to 'inforce the observance of order,' but those 'implied powers' could not support common-law jurisdiction over criminal acts. *Hudson, supra,* at 34. In 1831, Congress amended the Judiciary Act of 1789, allowing federal courts the summary contempt power to punish generally 'disobedience or resistance' to court orders. § 1, Act of March 2, 1831, 4 Stat. 487–488. See *Bloom v. Illinois,* 391 U.S. 194, 202–204, 88 S.Ct. 1477, 20 L.Ed.2d 522 (1968) (discussing evolution of federal courts' statutory contempt power)."); *id.* at 695 ("English and earlier American cases do report instances in which prosecution for criminal contempt of court—as originally understood—did not bar a subsequent prosecution for a criminal offense based on the same conduct. *See, e.g., King v. Lord Ossulston,* 2 Str. 1107, 93 Eng. Rep. 1063 (K.B. 1739); *State v. Yancy,* 4 N.C. 133 (1814). But those contempt prosecutions were for disruption of judicial process, in which the disruptive conduct happened also to be criminal."). *Compare Civil Rights Removal After* Rachel *and* Peacock: *A Limited Federal Remedy*, 121 U. Pa. L. Rev. 351, 351 ("Congressional protection of civil rights has taken both substantive and procedural form. One major procedural guarantee, first enacted in the post Civil War period, permits removal of state criminal prosecutions to the federal courts under certain circumstances. Early Supreme Court decisions restricted the applicability of this civil rights removal provision to the situation where a facially unconstitutional state statute is involved."), *with* Wisconsin v. Walker, No. 10–C–335, 2010 WL 1805380, at *2 (E.D. Wis. May 5, 2010) ("The removal statute was meant to protect federal agents in the performance of their official duties from interference by states unfriendly to their ends."); Donald H. Zeigler, *Twins Separated at Birth: A Comparative History of the Civil and Criminal Arising Under Jurisdiction of the Federal Courts and Some Proposals for Change*, 19 Vt. L. Rev. 673, 730–31 (1995) ("As Reconstruction continued, Congress enacted additional legislation to protect the newly-freed slaves, Union Army officers, and northern government officials supervising Reconstruction. These enforcement acts followed a similar pattern. They created new substantive rights, imposed criminal sanctions and provided private civil remedies for violation of the rights, and gave the federal courts original or removal jurisdiction or both over cases arising under the acts.").

73. 481 U.S. 787 (1987).

74. Some state laws specifically prohibit the use of private prosecutors. For example, in Georgia, Superior Court Rule 42.1 provides that "private special prosecutors retained by the family or relatives of one named as a victim in an indictment or accusation may not participate in the prosecution of a criminal case." *But see* Sustakovitch v. State, 290 S.E.2d 77 (Ga. 1982) (the victim's attorney, who was allowed to sit at counsel table, was not a special prosecutor); Rutledge v. State, 267 S.E.2d 199, 200 (Ga. 1980) (participation of special prosecutor hired by the victim's family did not violate the defendant's due process rights in a murder prosecution where the special prosecutor (1) was subject to the control and direction of the district attorney and (2) was not paid or reimbursed for his expenses by the district attorney's office).

75. *Young*, 481 U.S. at 804.

76. Price v. Commonwealth, 849 S.E.2d 140, 145 (Va. Ct. App. 2020) (citing *Young*); In re Wilson, 2014 WL 12684935, at *4 (V.I. Super. Ct., Div. St. Croix, Apr. 11, 2014) (same); State v. Eldridge, 951 S.W.2d 775, 781–82 (Tenn. Ct. Crim. App. 1997) (same); *see also* Woodside v. Woodside, No. 01-A-01-9503-PB00121, 1995 WL 623077, at *5 (Tenn. Ct. App. 1995) (declining to follow *Young*).

77. Venckus v. City of Iowa City, 930 N.W.2d 792, 824 (Iowa 2019) (Appel, J., concurring in part and dissenting in part) ("One incident of prosecutorial misconduct is one too many. One study found that, since 1970, prosecutorial misconduct led to dismissal of charges, reversal of conviction, or reduction of sentence in more than 2000 cases. Steve Weinburg, *Harmful Error: Breaking the Rules*, Ctr. for Pub. Integrity, (updated May 19, 2014), https://publicintegrity.org/accountability/breaking-the-rules/ [https://perma.cc/AX5L-AW7F]. As one jurist put it, 'There is an epidemic of *Brady* violations abroad in the land. Only judges can put a stop to it.' *United States v. Olsen*, 737 F.3d 625, 626 (9th Cir. 2013) (Kozinski, J., dissenting from order denying petition for rehearing en banc); *see also* John C. Jeffries, Jr., *The Liability Rule for Constitutional Torts*, 99 Va. L. Rev. 207, 227 & n.68 (2013) [hereinafter Jeffries] (collecting evidence on 'widespread noncompliance' with *Brady*)."); Peter A. Joy, *The Relationship Between Prosecutorial Misconduct and Wrongful Convictions: Shaping Remedies for a Broken System*, 2006 Wis. L. Rev. 399, 400 (2006) ("[P]rosecutorial misconduct is largely the result of three institutional conditions: vague ethics rules that provide ambiguous guidance to prosecutors; vast discretionary authority with little or no transparency; and inadequate remedies for prosecutorial misconduct, which create perverse incentives for prosecutors to engage in, rather than refrain from, prosecutorial misconduct. These three conditions converge to create uncertain norms and a general lack of accountability for how prosecutors view and carry out their ethical and institutional obligations."); *Venckus*, 930 N.W.2d at 824 (Appel, J., concurring in part and dissenting in part) ("Without civil liability, deterrents to prosecutorial misconduct are insufficient. As Justice White wrote for himself and two other Justices, '[O]rdinarily, liability in damages for unconstitutional or otherwise illegal conduct has the very desirable effect of deterring such conduct. Indeed, this was precisely the proposition upon which § 1983 was enacted.' *Imbler*, 424 U.S. at 442, 96 S. Ct. at 1000 (White, J., concurring in the judgment).").

78. Moore v. LaSalle Corrections, Inc., Civil Action No. 3:16-CV-01007, 2020 WL 6389182, at *10 (W.D. La. Oct. 30, 2020) ("I think it highly unlikely that we would deny prosecutorial immunity to those private attorneys increasingly employed by various jurisdictions in this country to conduct high-visibility criminal prosecutions."); *Venckus*, 930 N.W.2d at 817 (Appel, J., concurring in part and dissenting in part):

> At the turn of the twentieth century, there were also decisions holding prosecutors absolutely immune from suit for malicious prosecution. The first case anywhere was in Indiana. *See Griffith v. Slinkard*, 146 Ind. 117, 44 N.E. 1001, 1002 (1896); *see* Johns, *Reconsidering Absolute*, 2005 BYU L. Rev. at 114. The *Griffith* court held that a public prosecutor is a judicial officer, not in the sense of a judge but insofar as he performs judicial duties requiring exercise of judgment, and is therefore entitled to absolute immunity. 44 N.E. at 1002. In *Smith v. Parman*, 101 Kan. 115, 165 P. 663, 663 (1917), the Kansas Supreme Court recognized that much of a public prosecutor's work is advocacy. However, because "the important matter of determining what prosecutions shall be instituted is committed in a considerable degree to his sound judgment," the court held that "the reason for granting immunity to judges and grand jurors applies with practically equal force to a

> public prosecutor in his relations to actions to punish infractions of the law." *Id.* The court reasoned that absolute immunity would not foster abuse of power because of "the risk of being called to account criminally for official misconduct." *Id.* at 663–64. In *Kittler v. Kelsch*, 56 N.D. 227, 216 N.W. 898, 898 (1927), a public prosecutor was sued after he made out a criminal complaint and brought criminal charges based on false information. The court held that the prosecutor's action was state action and constituted a judicial mistake to which absolute immunity applied. *Id.* at 904. This immunity, the court said, was "for the protection of the public, and to insure the active and independent action of the officers charged with the prosecution of crime, for the protection of life and property." *Id.* at 905. In a dissent, Justice Burr argued that a prosecutor should be immune from "passing upon complaints' but not from 'making the complaint himself." *Id.* (Burr, J., dissenting).
>
> In *Watts v. Gerking*, 111 Or. 641, 228 P. 135, 141 (1924), a majority of the Oregon Supreme Court sustained a demurrer of a complaint for malicious prosecution against a public prosecutor. The majority said, "Because of their tendency to obstruct the administration of justice, it is the policy of the law to discourage actions for malicious prosecution." *Id.* Noting that a public prosecutor is subject to criminal sanctions, the majority further stated, "The public policy of the state affords ample protection to the innocent, and a prosecutor's endeavors should not be weakened by backfires in the nature of malicious prosecution." *Id.* Two Justices dissented. Justices Burnett and Rand emphasized that a prosecutor should not be immune from civil suit when he prosecuted a person the prosecutor knew to be innocent of the charges. *Id.* at 142 (Burnett, J., dissenting); *id.* at 143–44 (Rand, J., dissenting).

Venckus, 930 N.W.2d at 818 (Appel, J., concurring in part and dissenting in part) ("Jurisdictions across our country remain divided on whether prosecutors are entitled to absolute immunity. To be sure, the greater weight of modern precedent affords absolute immunity to prosecutorial functions. *See Knapper v. Connick*, 681 So. 2d 944, 946 n.8 (La. 1996) (collecting authorities); George A. Weiss, *Prosecutorial Accountability After* Connick v. Thompson, 60 Drake L. Rev. 199, 231 & n.231 (2011) (same); *see also* Restatement (Second) of Torts § 656, at 414 (Am. Law Inst. 1977) ('A public prosecutor acting in his official capacity is absolutely privileged to initiate, institute, or continue criminal proceedings.')."); *Venckus*, 930 N.W.2d at 818–19 (Appel, J., concurring in part and dissenting in part) ("The United States Supreme Court has held prosecutors absolutely immune to common law torts and § 1983 actions. In *Yaselli v. Goff*, 275 U.S. 503, 48 S. Ct. 155, 72 L.Ed. 395 (1927) (per curiam), in a one-sentence opinion, the Supreme Court of the United States affirmed a lower court decision holding public prosecutors absolutely immune from a civil action for malicious prosecution. The *Yaselli* Court cited its decisions upholding absolute immunity of judges. *Id.*; *see Alzua v. Johnson*, 231 U.S. 106, 111, 34 S. Ct. 27, 29, 58 L.Ed. 142 (1913); *Bradley v. Fisher*, 80 U.S. 335, 347, 13 Wall. 335, 20 L.Ed. 646 (1871). The Court's decisions on absolute prosecutorial immunity in § 1983 actions began in 1976. *See Imbler v. Pachtman*, 424 U.S. 409, 431, 96 S. Ct. 984, 995, 47 L.Ed.2d 128 (1976). In short, the Court has determined that a prosecutor is entitled to absolute immunity when functioning as an advocate and qualified immunity when functioning as an administrator or investigator. *Id.* at 430–31, 96 S. Ct. at 995; *see Van de Kamp v. Goldstein*, 555 U.S. 335, 338–39, 129 S. Ct. 855, 858–59, 172 L.Ed.2d 706 (2009); *Kalina*, 522 U.S. at 129–31, 118 S. Ct. at 509–10 (majority opinion); *Buckley v. Fitzsimmons*, 509 U.S. 259, 261, 275–76, 113 S. Ct. 2606, 2609, 2617, 125 L.Ed.2d 209 (1993); *Burns v. Reed*, 500 U.S. 478, 494–96, 111 S. Ct. 1934, 1943–44, 114 L.Ed.2d 547 (1991)."); *Venckus*, 930 N.W.2d at 819–20 (Appel, J., concurring in part and dissenting in part) ("Some states have departed from the majority and limit or deny absolute prosecutorial immunity. In *Cashen v. Spann*, 66 N.J. 541, 334 A.2d 8, 10, 12 (1975), the New Jersey Supreme Court distinguished prosecutorial immunity from judicial immunity and held the former was not absolute. The *Cashen* court reviewed a lower state court decision finding '[n]o rationalization could possibly shield evil acts of such magnitude' as the subornation of perjury involved in the reviewed case. *Id.* at 13 (quoting *DeGroot v. Muccio*, 115 N.J.Super. 15, 277 A.2d 899, 907 (N.J. Super. Ct. Law Div. 1971)). The *Cashen* court concluded that 'there are indeed circumstances in which a prosecutor will incur civil liability for his official conduct' and '[t]he public interest is best served by recognizing that prosecutors enjoy only a limited form of immunity.' *Id.* The *Cashen* court did not consider the contours of prosecutorial immunity because it found the record 'd[id] not support any inference that the prosecutor in this case acted out of personal motive, with malicious intent, or in excess of his jurisdiction.' *Id.*at 14. In a subsequent case, the New Jersey Supreme Court explained that 'reasonable grounds for the belief formed at the time and in light of all the circumstances, coupled with good-faith belief, … affords a basis for qualified immunity of executive officers for acts performed in the course of official conduct.' *Burke v. Deiner*, 97 N.J. 465, 479 A.2d 393, 397 (1984) (quoting *Scheuer v. Rhodes*, 416 U.S. 232, 247–48, 94 S. Ct. 1683, 1692, 40 L.Ed.2d 90 (1974), *abrogated on other grounds by Davis v. Scherer*, 468 U.S. 183, 191, 104 S. Ct. 3012, 3017, 82 L.Ed.2d 139 (1984)). *Cashen* remains the law in New Jersey. *See, e.g., Pitman v. Ottehberg*, No. 10-2538, 2015 WL 179392, at *9 (D.N.J. Jan. 14, 2015) (recognizing continuing vitality of *Cashen*); *Newsome v. City of Newark*, No. 13-CV-06234, 2014 WL 4798783, at *4 (D.N.J. Sept. 25, 2014) (same)."); *Venckus*, 930 N.W.2d at 820 (Appel, J., concurring in part and dissenting in part) ("Public prosecutors acting in a prosecutorial function are also subject to suit in Nebraska. In *Koch v. Grimminger*, 192 Neb. 706, 223 N.W.2d 833, 836 (1974), the Nebraska Supreme Court relied on the common law notion of quasi-judicial immunity. The *Koch* court said that, in determining whether to file a complaint, the prosecutor must ascertain the law, apply the law to the facts, and weigh the reliability of evidence, all of which constitute quasi-judicial and discretionary functions. *Id.* at 836–37. In conclusion, the *Koch* court said, 'We hold that a public prosecutor, acting within the general scope of his official authority in making a determination whether to file a criminal prosecution, is exercising a quasi-judicial and discretionary function and that where he acts in good faith he is immune from suit for an erroneous or negligent determination. This rule would not protect a prosecutor who, knowing that a particular charge is groundless in law or in fact, nonetheless intentionally files a charge and thus acts through a corrupt motive. In such a case he would not be acting within the scope of his authority.' *Id.* at 837. *Koch* remains the law in Nebraska. *See, e.g., Anderson v. Nebraska*, No. 4:17-CV-3073, 2018 WL 4354952, at *8 (D. Neb. Sept. 12, 2018) (recognizing continued vitality of *Koch*); *Gallion v. Woytassek*, 244 Neb. 15, 504 N.W.2d 76, 83 (1993) (same)."); *Venckus*, 930 N.W.2d at 820 (Appel, J., concurring in part and dissenting in part) ("Public prosecutors may also be sued in Hawaii. '[A]bsolute immunity is not a defense under Hawai'i law in an action for malicious prosecution.' *Wong v. Cayetano*, 111 Hawai'i 462, 143 P.3d 1, 18 (2006). '[T]he prosecuting attorney is an officer of the executive branch of appellant, and thus subject to liability for his tortious conduct.' *Orso v. City of Honolulu*, 56 Haw. 241, 534 P.2d 489, 493 (1975) (footnote omitted), *overruled on other grounds by Kahale v. City of Honolulu*, 104 Hawai'i 341, 90 P.3d 233, 239 (2004)."); *Venckus*, 930 N.W.2d at 821–22 (Appel, J., concurring in part and dissenting in part) ("In a conclusory fashion, the majority flatly declares, 'The same public-interest considerations that justify the judicial process immunity apply whether the legal claims arise under common law or the state constitution.' Of course, there was no such absolute at the time of the adoption of the Iowa Constitution of 1857, but the majority declines to engage in originalist reasoning. In any event, I strongly disagree with the notion that constitutional torts are simply garden variety torts.").

79. *E.g.*, CAL. GOV'T CODE § 821.6 (stating that "[a] public employee is not liable for injury caused by his instituting or prosecuting any judicial or administrative proceeding within the scope of his employment, even if he acts maliciously and without probable cause"); *id.* § 820.2 ("Except as otherwise provided by statute, a public employee is not liable for an injury resulting from his act or omission where the act or omission was the result of the exercise of the discretion vested in him, whether or not such discretion be abused."); COLO. REV. STAT. ANN. § 20-1-106.1(2) ("In the absence of the bad faith performance of the duties specified in this section, the district attorneys of the state of Colorado shall be immune from liability for the performance of said duties; except that such immunity shall not apply to charges of perjury in the first degree, perjury in the second degree, or false swearing brought pursuant to section 18-8-502, 18-8-503, or 18-8-504, C.R.S., respectively."); GA. CONST. art. 6, § 8, ¶ 1(e) ("District attorneys shall enjoy immunity from private suit for actions arising from the performance of their duties."); 42 PA. CONS. STAT. ANN. § 8546 (titled "Defense of official immunity"); TENN. CODE ANN. § 40-3-208 ("The district attorney general and assistant district attorneys general, district attorney general's investigators, district attorney general's secretaries and any other employee of the district attorney general shall not be civilly or criminally liable for acts performed pursuant to this part or in furtherance of the purposes of this part except as those acts relate to expenditure of an accounting of moneys collected under this part.").

80. *See Venckus*, 930 N.W.2d at 816-17 (Appel, J., concurring in part and dissenting in part) ("Public prosecutors remained subject to suit in many states well into the twentieth century. In *Arnold v. Hubble*, 38 S.W. 1041, 1041 (Ky. 1897), the court suggested that a public prosecutor could be liable for malicious prosecution if acting with malicious or corrupt motives. In *Carpenter v. Sibley*, 153 Cal. 215, 94 P. 879, 879–80 (1908), the California Supreme Court held that a public prosecutor and a sheriff were subject to suit for malicious prosecution for the use of false testimony. In *Buhner v. Reusse*, 144 Minn. 450, 175 N.W. 1005, 1006 (1920), the Minnesota Supreme Court explained that an action for malicious prosecution against a public prosecutor required plaintiff to prove both malice and want of probable cause. In *Leong Yau v. Carden*, 23 Haw. 362, 368 (1916), the Hawaii court held that public prosecutors are immune from suits based on actions 'done in good faith though with erroneous judgment, but private individuals are entitled to the protection of the law against any conduct of such officers which is at once reckless, malicious and damaging.' The *Leong Yau* court specifically rejected the notion that public prosecutors act in a judicial function, explaining, 'Public prosecuting officers are, properly speaking, executive officers. Though, like all enrolled attorneys, they are officers of the courts, they are not part of the courts. In discharging their duties executive officers are at times required to perform acts of a judicial nature, but even then they act no more than quasi-judicially.' *Id.* at 367. Finally, in *Schneider v. Shepherd*, 192 Mich. 82, 158 N.W. 182, 184 (1916), the Michigan Supreme Court held that a public prosecutor's instigation of arrest did not even warrant the immunity of a quasi-judicial officer. The court noted that the prosecutor prosecuted criminal charges based on vague investigative reports, without further inquiry, that did not connect the criminal defendant with the alleged crime. *Id.*").

81. Coello v. Dileo, Civil Action No. 20-1682 (SDW) (LDW), 2020 WL 6156695, at *1 (D. N.J. Oct. 21, 2020) ("On January 17, 2007, non-party Shirley Messina ('Messina') filed a citizen's complaint in Linden Municipal Court against Coello, alleging that Coello had harassed her. At the time, Coello was dating David Figueroa ('Figueroa'), Messina's ex-boyfriend. The charge was initially dismissed, but later reinstated, although neither the reason for the dismissal nor the reinstatement are included in the record. On February 26, 2007, Kathleen Estabrooks, Esq. ('Estabrooks'), who was 'simultaneously representing Messina in other civil actions against Figueroa ... in Superior Court of Union County, Family Court,' sought appointment to serve as the acting prosecutor of Messina's complaint. Prior to being appointed, Estabrooks was required to submit an affidavit disclosing any conflicts of interest, indicating whether the municipal prosecutor, Nicholas P. Scutari ('Scutari') had elected not to prosecute the matter, and averring that there were 'no other facts that could reasonably affect the impartiality of the private prosecutor and the fairness of the proceedings or otherwise create an appearance of impropriety.' Estabrooks' affidavit did not disclose that she was representing Messina in Family Court and did not certify that Scutari had declined to prosecute Coello's case.") (citations omitted); *id.* at *5 ("Generally, prosecutors are responsible for initiating criminal proceedings, but '[d]ecisions have recognized that a § 1983 malicious prosecution claim might be maintained against one who furnished false information to, or concealed information from, prosecuting authorities.' *Gallo v. City of Phila.*, 161 F.3d 217, 220 n.2 (3d Cir. 1998). Here, Plaintiff has pled that Estabrooks 'investigated, initiated, maintained, pursued and/or pressed criminal proceedings against' her. In support of that claim, Plaintiff alleges that Estabrooks actively sought appointment to prosecute Coello by means of a deficient affidavit, and subsequently initiated the post-trial hearing which led to Coello's incarceration. These allegations are sufficient at this stage to permit Plaintiff's claim to proceed.") (citations omitted); *id.* at *5 ("Plaintiff has pled that the citizen's complaint lacked probable cause, and that the facts surrounding the initial dismissal and later reinstatement of that case were motivated by a desire to improve Messina's position in family court, rather than to hold Plaintiff accountable for actionable harassment. Taking Plaintiff's allegations as true, as is required on a motion to dismiss, Plaintiff has sufficiently pled that the charges against her lacked probable cause.") (citations omitted); *id.* ("Here, having determined that the pleadings sufficiently allege an absence of probable cause, this Court may infer malice. In addition, Plaintiff pleads that Estabrooks 'had malicious motive to investigate, initiate, maintain, pursue, and/or press criminal charges including but not limited to utilizing gains she realized in the criminal prosecution for the benefit of her client Messina in separate legal matters involving ... Figueroa,' suggesting that she was motivated, at least in part, by animus, rather than belief in the propriety of the prosecution. Because Plaintiff has sufficiently pled the five elements of a malicious prosecution claim, the motion to dismiss Counts Nine and Ten will be denied.") (citation omitted); *see*

also Hogan v. Rose, Case No. 7:16-CV-1325 (LEK/ATB), 2020 WL 6118573, at *1, 6 (N.D. N.Y. Oct. 16, 2020) (in an action in which the plaintiffs sued both their neighbors and various local officials under 42 U.S.C. § 1983 and New York law in a property-related dispute, the court held: "Normally, a citizen who reports a crime to law enforcement authorities cannot be held liable for malicious prosecution under § 1983. Indeed, in § 1983 actions in general, state actors generally can be held liable, while private citizens generally cannot be."; "In the context of malicious prosecution claims in particular, the existence of the institution of the public prosecutor generally precludes liability for private citizens who report crimes, because it is typically not within the private citizen's power to determine whether charges are brought, but rather within the absolute power of the public prosecutor."); Betts v. Shearman, 751 F.3d 78, 84–86 (2d Cir. 2014) (noting that "[u]nder 42 U.S.C. § 1983, constitutional torts are only actionable against state actors or private parties acting 'under the color of' state law," and that a private citizen is only so regarded when acting "in concert with the state actor to commit an unconstitutional act.") (internal quotation marks omitted); White v. Frank, 855 F.2d 956, 962 (2d Cir. 1988) ("Unlike the private prosecutor, the public prosecutor is absolutely immune from suit for malicious prosecution. The exercise of independent judgment by the public prosecutor and his active role in initiating criminal prosecutions may decrease the likelihood that a complaining witness will be considered to have 'caused' or 'procured' the prosecution, thus defeating grounds for liability under this initial prong of the common law standard.") (internal quotation marks and citations omitted).

82. Rogowicz v. O'Connell, 786 A.2d 841, 843–44 (N.H. 2001).

83. In re Jackson, 51 A.3d 529, 540–41 (D.C. Ct. App. 2012).

84. State v. Ward, 696 A.2d 48, 55 (N.J. Super. Ct., App. Div. 1997).

85. Brown v. State, 250 S.E.2d 438, 439 (Ga. 1978) ("A special prosecutor, who is subject to the direction and control of the district attorney, may be employed by the family of the deceased to assist the district attorney in prosecuting the case. The fact that the special prosecutor represents the deceased's family in civil litigation arising from his death is no ground for disqualification.") (citations omitted); Rutledge v. State, 267 S.E.2d 199 (Ga. 1980) (allowing the participation of a special prosecutor hired by the victim's family in a murder prosecution; "[t]he participation of the special prosecutor did not violate Code Ann. § 24-2914."); State v. Trice, 258 S.E.2d 270, 271 (Ga. Ct. App. 1979) ("A special prosecutor may take part in the prosecution of a case on behalf of the state . . . .").

86. Robert M. Ireland, *Privately Funded Prosecution of Crime in the Nineteenth-Century United States*, 39 Am. J. Legal Hist. 43, 57 n.25 (1995); Charles C. Olson, *"Pro Bono Publico": A History of Georgia's Prosecuting Attorneys (1732–2012)*, 25 J. S. Legal Hist. 235, 245 n.133 (2017).

87. Ga. Uniform Superior Court R. 42.1; *compare* Rogers v. State, 348 S.E.2d 888 (Ga. App. 1986) (there was no violation of rule prohibiting private special prosecutors retained by victim's family or relatives from participating in prosecution of criminal case, when private attorney, who was representing parents of victim in pending civil suit against defendant, helped to arrange for appearance of expert witness for State in defendant's prosecution, where parents' attorney did not sit at counsel table and took no part in actual trial of case, attorney did not assist in preparation of State's case and was not present when expert witness had been interviewed, and expert was paid by State); Ga. Code Ann. § 15-18-5(a)-(b) (providing that "[w]hen a district attorney's office is disqualified from interest or relationship to engage in a prosecution, the district attorney shall notify the Attorney General of the disqualification" and "the Attorney General shall . . . [a]ppoint a competent attorney to act as district attorney pro tempore in place of the district attorney"; "A private attorney acting as district attorney pro tempore pursuant to paragraph (3) of subsection (a) of this Code section is subject to all laws and regulations established pursuant to Code Section 15-18-19 governing district attorneys. Such private attorney shall receive the same compensation from state funds appropriated for the operations of the district attorneys at the same rate as the district attorney during the term of such appointment and shall incur the same penalties in the discharge of the duties of said office."); Ga. Code Ann. § 15-18-5(d) ("The appointment of the district attorney pro tempore shall specify in writing the court or courts to which the appointment applies, the county or counties where located, the time period covered, and the name of the case or cases to which such appointment shall apply. A copy of the appointment shall be filed with the clerk of court and copies shall be provided to the presiding judge and the Prosecuting Attorneys' Council of the State of Georgia and opposing counsel in any action affected by such order. An order appointing a private attorney pursuant to this Code section

shall also specify whether such attorney will serve on a full-time or part-time basis and any restrictions which may apply to such attorney's private practice of law during the term of such appointment. Private attorneys who serve on a part-time basis shall be compensated at an hourly rate determined by the Prosecuting Attorneys' Council of the State of Georgia based on the annual salary of district attorneys paid from state funds. The Prosecuting Attorneys' Council of the State of Georgia shall establish such procedures or guidelines as may be necessary to ensure proper accountability of any funds paid to a private attorney pursuant to this Code section.").

88. Ga. Code Ann. § 15-18-5(a)-(b).

89. Rogers v. State, 348 S.E.2d 888, 889 (Ga. Ct. App. 1986).

90. 777 S.W.2d 882 (Ky. 1989).

91. 369 S.E.2d 706, 718–19 (W. Va. 1988), *cert. denied*, 488 U.S. 895 (1988).

92. As one commentator has noted:

> Because the allegiance owed by a private prosecutor to a possibly vengeful client must coexist with the impartiality demanded in the role of solicitor, a fair termination of any plea bargaining based on the equities of the situation is highly unlikely. The public solicitor who is in control of the plea bargain is less likely to be fair if he is assisted and counseled by a private advocate. If the private prosecutor is given control of the plea bargaining, the interest of his client might override those of the public in determining whether a plea to a lesser crime should be accepted.

John A.J. Ward, Note, *Private Prosecution—The Entrenched Anomaly*, 50 N.C. L. Rev. 1171, 1175–76 (1972) (footnote omitted).

93. Park v. State, 170 S.E.2d 687 (Ga. 1969), *vacated in part*, 408 U.S. 935 (1972) (attorney allowed to assist prosecutor in murder case despite representation of widow in wrongful death action); State v. Addis, 186 S.E.2d 415 (S.C. 1972) (attorney representing family of deceased in wrongful death action allowed to participate in involuntary manslaughter prosecution).

94. 648 F.2d 973 (5th Cir. 1981).

95. The new district attorney made the opening statement, examined witnesses, and made the closing statement.

96. *Woods*, 648 F.2d at 977.

97. *Id.* In light of the Supreme Court's holding in *Young* that harmless error analysis is inappropriate, the *Woods* case is superseded by *Young* in that "prejudice" to the defendant is no longer the appropriate focus when considering whether a due process violation has occurred. Indeed, because the focus in *Young* was on the appearance of justice, the notion in *Woods* that prejudice is important is no longer relevant. *See* In re Davidson, 908 F.2d 1249, 1251 (5th Cir. 1990) (adopting as its own rule the position put forth by a plurality of the *Young* Court that "where, as here, there is a *Young* violation, 'harmless error analysis is inappropriate' "); In re Reed, 161 F.3d 1311, 1314 (11th Cir. 1998) ("*Young* further held that a district court's appointment of counsel for an interested party as a contempt prosecutor is not subject to a harmless error analysis."); Matter of Hipp, Inc., 895 F.2d 1503, 1509 (5th Cir. 1990) ("Here, by contrast, the private party's counsel actively prosecuted the entire contempt trial, securing and presenting the evidence and arguing the case. To distinguish the present case from *Young* on the basis of the degree of participation by the prosecutor 'prosecutor' would render *Young* essentially meaningless.... [W]here, as here, there is a *Young* violation, 'harmless error analysis is inappropriate.'"); In re Grand Jury Proceedings, 875 F.2d 927, 933 n.7 (1st Cir. 1989) (discussing *Young* and observing: "Four justices would have ruled that harmless-error analysis could not be applied to the appointment of an interested party's attorney to prosecute a charge of criminal contempt. A fifth, Justice Scalia, would have ruled that courts never may appoint private prosecutors, citing concerns about the separation of the executive branch's power to enforce laws and the judicial branch's limited power to issue orders only in cases brought before the courts."); Rebecca A. Pinto, Note, *The Public Interest and Private Financing of Criminal Prosecutions*, 77 Wash. U. L.Q. 1343, 1362 n.106 (1999) (citing *Young* and arguing that "appellate review of a privately financed conviction focusing only on a defendant's rights would seem to provide insufficient protection if the court applied harmless error analysis."). *But see* Webber v. Scott, 390 F.3d 1169, 1175–76 (10th Cir. 2004) (participation of a privately-retained attorney in a state criminal prosecution held not to violate the defendant's right to due process under federal law unless the private attorney effectively controlled critical prosecutorial decisions, and

distinguishing *Young*, in which a plurality of the Supreme Court concluded that the appointment of a private prosecutor is structural error not subject to harmless error analysis).

98. Powers v. Hauck, 399 F.2d 322 (5th Cir. 1968) (murder); Brooks v. State, 228 So. 2d 24 (Ala. Crim. App. 1969) (murder); Lopez v. State, 437 S.W.2d 268 (Tex. App. 1968) (murder); *see also* Comment, *Private Prosecution: A Remedy for District Attorneys' Unwarranted Inaction*, 65 Yale L.J. 209, 220 & n.57 (1955) (citing cases where private prosecutors have been used to prosecute, among other crimes, murder, manslaughter, burglary, larceny, criminal libel, adultery, and rape). Pre-*Young* cases from other jurisdictions also have upheld the constitutionality of private prosecutors. For example, in *Jones v. Richards*, 776 F.2d 1244 (4th Cir. 1985), the defendant claimed that his constitutional right to an impartial prosecutor was violated by the simultaneous involvement of private attorneys (retained by the victim's family) in filing civil actions and assisting in North Carolina's prosecution of his criminal case. *But see* Ganger v. Peyton, 379 F.2d 709, 713 (4th Cir. 1967) (where a prosecutor was representing the defendant's wife in a divorce action at the same time that he was prosecuting the defendant, the defendant's prosecutor "was not in a position to exercise fair-minded judgment with respect to (1) whether to decline to prosecute, (2) whether to reduce the charge to a lesser degree of assault, or (3) whether to recommend a suspended sentence or other clemency"). Although the Fourth Circuit, applying North Carolina law, noted that the private attorneys had a financial interest in the outcome of the civil actions, the Fourth Circuit held that no evidence demonstrated the private attorneys attempted to use their position as prosecuting attorneys "to exact a more generous settlement of the civil actions." *Jones*, 776 F.2d at 1246; *see also* North Carolina State Bar Ethics Opinion 595 ("It is ethical for an attorney who has represented the private prosecution in a criminal action growing out of an automobile collision to later represent the same party in a civil action for damages growing out of the same collision."). The *Jones* case quoted Ethics Opinion 595 of the North Carolina State Bar. *Jones*, 776 F.2d at 1247.

99. City of Caldwell, Idaho—Request for Qualifications for Prosecution Services, Licensed Idaho Attorneys, https://www.cityofcaldwell.org/home/showdocument?id=9435; "Nampa City Council to Discuss Misdemeanor Prosecution, NDC," Idaho Press, Feb. 15, 2014, https://www.idahopress.com/news/local/nampa-city-council-to-discuss-misdemeanor-prosecution-ndc/article_745829f6-96c9-11e3-be88-0019bb2963f4.html; Request for Proposals, Prosecution Services for the City of Indianola, Iowa, http://www.indianolaiowa.gov/DocumentCenter/View/7169/REQUEST-FOR-PROPOSALS-City-Prosecutor?bidId=; Request for Proposal—Prosecution Services City of Clawson, https://www.cityofclawson.com/RFP-LEGALSERVJHKrev2.pdf; Request for Qualifications and Proposals to Provide Prosecution Legal Services to the Cities of Buffalo, Annandale, and Howard Lake, City of Buffalo, County of Wright, State of Minnesota (Feb. 2020), https://www.ci.buffalo.mn.us/wp-content/uploads/2020/02/request-for-proposal-prosecution-services-2020.pdf; Request for Proposal, Town of Plaistow, Plaistow Police Department, Full-Time Prosecution Services (Jan. 14, 2019), https://www.plaistow.com/sites/g/files/vyhlif1071/f/uploads/rfp_prosecution_services.pdf; Request for Proposals and Qualifications for Prosecuting Attorney Services (City of Minot, North Dakota), https://www.minotnd.org/DocumentCenter/View/5734/Request-for-Proposals-and-Qualifications-for-Prosecuting-Attorney-Services_Final?bidId=; City of Kyle, Texas, Request for Proposals (RFP), RFP No. 2016-03-PM, Prosecution Services for Municipal Court, https://www.cityofkyle.com/sites/default/files/fileattachments/finance/page/371/rfp_-_court_prosecution_services_2016.pdf; City of Duvall, Request for Qualification and Proposal Prosecution Services, http://www.duvallwa.gov/DocumentCenter/View/3788/Prosecutor-RFP-2017?bidId=; Request for Qualifications and Proposal—Prosecution Services, City of Lakewood, Washington, https://www.tpcba.com/wp-content/uploads/2015/05/RFP-RFQ-Contract-Prosecutor.pdf; City of Mukilteo, Request for Proposals for Prosecution Services, https://mukilteowa.gov/wp-content/uploads/Prosecutor-RFP-FINAL.pdf; City of Edmonds, Request for Proposal, http://mrsc.org/getmedia/9ed7192e-a827-44a9-a29c-5d94d352de54/e3prosecutorRFP.pdf.aspx; City of Tukwila, Request for Qualifications and Proposals for Prosecution Services, http://records.tukwilawa.gov/WebLink/1/edoc/307057/2018-09-06%20-%20Request%20for%20Qualifications%20-%20Prosecution%20Services.pdf.

100. Farmington City—Request for Proposal for Prosecutorial Services, http://www.farmington.utah.gov/img/File/Request%20for%20Proposal%20for%20Prosecutorial%20Services.pdf.

101. Handley v. State, 106 So. 692, 694 (Ala. 1925).

102. *Id.* at 694–95.

103. Oliver v. State, 175 So. 305, 306–08 (Ala. 1937); *see also* Langley v. State, 383 So.2d 868, 872 (Ala. Ct. Crim. App. 1980) ("The law in Alabama is clear that a special prosecutor may appear as an assistant to the prosecution with the consent of the court."); Hall v. State, 411 So.2d 831, 838–39 (Ala. Ct. Crim. App. 1981) ("In our opinion, the appearance by a qualified attorney, which Mr. McDonald is and was, does not require an appointment by any court, the District Attorney, or any of his assistants. Of course, the trial court would have the right, for good cause, to refuse to permit an attorney to appear as a special prosecutor in any case, but no effort was made to show any cause why Mr. McDonald, a former assistant district attorney, employed by Mr. Berdaux who had been shot by one of the robbers, should not appear and actively engage in the trial, which he did.").

104. McCrory v. State, 505 So.2d 1272, 1279–80 (Ala. Ct. Crim. App. 1986).

105. McCain v. City of Montgomery, 92 So.2d 678, 680 (Ala. Ct. App. 1956) (citation omitted), *cert. denied*, 92 So.2d 682 (1956).

106. Johnson v. State, 69 So. 396, 397 (Ala. Ct. App. 1915), *cert. denied*, Ex parte State, 69 So. 1020 (1915) (citation omitted).

107. *E.g.*, Hall v. State, 411 So.2d 831, 838–39 (Ala. Ct. Crim. App. 1981) ("In our opinion, the appearance by a qualified attorney, which Mr. McDonald is and was, does not require an appointment by any court, the District Attorney, or any of his assistants. Of course, the trial court would have the right, for good cause, to refuse to permit an attorney to appear as a special prosecutor in any case, but no effort was made to show any cause why Mr. McDonald, a former assistant district attorney, employed by Mr. Berdaux who had been shot by one of the robbers, should not appear and actively engage in the trial, which he did."); *id.* at 839 ("The action of the trial court in not sustaining defendant's objection to the appearance of Mr. McDonald as special prosecutor was free of error."); Langley v. State, 383 So.2d 868, 872–73 (Ala. Ct. Crim. App. 1980) ("The law in Alabama is clear that a special prosecutor may appear as an assistant to the prosecution with the consent of the court. Moreover, such special prosecutor need not show the authority under which he is employed or acting. In the case at bar, Mr. Gilmore, at the request of defense counsel and out of the hearing of the jury venire, nevertheless told defense counsel who his employer was, and the trial court determined that Mr. Gilmore was appearing with the consent of the State and approved his appearance as such special prosecutor. We are of the opinion that the trial court properly permitted Mr. Gilmore to appear in this cause and no error is shown by this record. This Court judicially knows that Mr. Gilmore was the district attorney for the circuit in which he appeared for a number of years."); Howard v. State, 678 So.2d 302, 304–05 (Ala. Ct. Crim. App. 1996) (rejecting motion to disqualify special prosecutor based on an alleged conflict of interest).

108. Cooper v. District Court, 133 P.3d 692, 696–711 (Alaska 2006); *see also id.* at 699 ("The government prosecutor might not view the facts in the same way as the victim, and thus the prosecutor might conclude that no crime had been committed. Or the prosecutor might agree that a crime had probably been committed, but nevertheless conclude that the case could not be proved in court. Or the prosecutor might disagree with the victim concerning the proper charges to file against the defendant. Or, after charges were filed and the case brought to court, the prosecutor might disagree with the victim concerning how the case should be litigated, or whether (and on what terms) the case should be settled, or what punishment should be sought in the event of the defendant's conviction."); Richard Allen, Note, *Is the Office Closed? The Role of the Office of Victims' Rights After* Cooper v. District Court, 24 ALASKA L. REV. 263, 277 (2007) ("The Alaska Code was annotated after *Cooper* to clarify that the Office of Victims' Rights does not have 'an independent right to file lawsuits that the victims themselves could not file.'"). In Alaska, "if a private person makes an accusation of criminal misconduct about another to an official, the person must believe that the accusation or information is true." Greywolf v. Carroll, 151 P.3d 1234, 1242 (Alaska 2007). The following elements are required to maintain a cause of action for the tort of malicious prosecution: "(1) a criminal proceeding instituted or continued by the defendant against the plaintiff; (2) termination of the proceeding in favor of the plaintiff; (3) absence of probable cause for the proceeding; and (4) 'malice' or a primary purpose other than that of bringing an offender to justice." *Id.* at 1241. Prior to the *Cooper* decision, the Court of Appeals of Alaska had raised a question about the propriety of permitting a

contempt action to be prosecuted by the attorney who represented an interested party. *See* Carter v. Brodrick, 750 P.2d 843, 845–46 (Alaska Ct. App. 1988):

> Carter has also argued that the trial court erred in permitting the contempt action to be prosecuted by the attorney who represented his former wife. Carter relies on the United States Supreme Court's recent ruling in *Young v. United States ex rel. Vuitton Et Fils S.A.*, 481 U.S. 787, 107 S.Ct. 2124, 95 L.Ed.2d 740 (1987).
>
> In *Rollins v. State of Alaska ex rel. Municipality of Anchorage*, 748 P.2d 767 (Alaska App.1988), this court, in light of *Young*, expressed concern about the wisdom of routinely appointing, as prosecutor in a criminal contempt action, counsel for the aggrieved party in the underlying civil litigation. We nevertheless declined to apply *Young* to the circumstances in *Rollins*, because the party appointed to prosecute that case was not a private party, but, rather, was the Municipality of Anchorage, a governmental body that was duly authorized to and, in fact, regularly did perform the functions of a public prosecutor.
>
> This case, in contrast, presents a far more difficult issue, because it involves a prosecution by a private party. However, Carter did not object below to the superior court's order appointing his former wife's counsel to prosecute the case, and the superior court did not have the opportunity to consider its appointment in light of the Supreme Court's decision in *Young*. Because Carter's conviction must be reversed on other grounds, we believe it preferable to allow the superior court an opportunity to consider in the first instance the conflict issue raised by *Young*. In the event of a retrial, the superior court should give due consideration to *Young* and *Rollins* in resolving the question of appointing a prosecutor for this case.

109. Matter of Martinez, 462 P.3d 36, 41 (Ariz. 2020).

110. Pool v. Superior Court in and for Pima County, 677 P.2d 261 (Ariz. 1984) (quoting Berger v. United States, 295 U.S. 78, 88 (1935)).

111. Johnson v. Vederman in and for the County of La Paz, Nos. 1-CA-SA 17-0105, 1 CA-SA 17-0111, 1 CA-SA 17-0112, 2017 WL 2438059 (Ariz. Ct. App., Div. 1, June 6, 2017) (citations omitted).

112. *Id.* at *1; *see also id.* ("In response to the motions to disqualify, the State (represented by Schilder) informed the superior court that Schilder 'is not controlled by, nor answers to, the County Attorney as a 'deputy.' As Schilder declared at oral argument in the superior court, he has 'independent power without the day-to-day oversight' of the County Attorney. Moreover, in response to questioning by the superior court, Schilder agreed that the County Attorney has ceded to him all authority over the cases to which he has been appointed. Further, Schilder told the superior court that although he 'consult[s]' with the County Attorney, he is not required to do so.").

113. *Id.* at *2–3 (citations omitted).

114. State v. Carter, No. 1 CA-CR 18-0278, 2019 WL 1130353, at *1 n.1 (Ariz. Ct. App., Div. 1 Mar. 12, 2019) ("This was the La Paz County Attorney's third appointment of a special prosecutor in the case. Carter moved to disqualify the first and objected to the second, both of whom were private practitioners. The motion to disqualify was denied, which resulted in a special action to this court. We vacated the denial and directed the superior court to hold an evidentiary hearing and reconsider the motion. *Johnson v. Vederman*, 1 CA-SA 17-0105, 2017 WL 2438059, at *3, ¶ 12 (Ariz. App. June 6, 2017). On remand, the La Paz County Attorney appointed a different special prosecutor before appointing the Chief Deputy Attorney of Mohave County. No evidentiary hearing was held because the parties agreed the motion to disqualify was moot.").

115. Olmstead v. Olmstead, 284 S.W.3d 27, 28 (Ark. 2008); *see also* Weems v. Anderson, 516 S.W.2d 895, 898 (Ark. 1974) ("Section 24–108, Arkansas Statutes, provides that it is the duty of the Court to appoint an attorney to 'conduct the prosecution' when there is an indictment of the prosecuting attorney, but this statute makes no provision for the appointment of an attorney to assist the grand jury in the investigation of the alleged crime or in the drafting of an indictment. Section 24–117, Arkansas Statutes, provides that if a prosecuting attorney shall neglect or fail to attend to the courts of the circuit and to prosecute as required by law, it is the duty of the court to appoint an attorney to 'prosecute for the state during the term.' A literal reading of the statutory provision expresses an intent that a special prosecutor shall be appointed only when the prosecuting attorney both fails to attend court and to prosecute as required by law."); *id.*

("The absence of specific statutory authority for the appointment of a special prosecuting attorney under the circumstances of this case does not mean that the court is without authority to do what justice, reason and common sense dictate must be done. In other jurisdictions where there was the same lack of statutory authority for the appointment of a special prosecuting attorney under circumstances such as those here presented, the courts have held that there is an inherent power in the courts to make such an appointment. We hold that the Arkansas Circuit Courts also have such inherent power.").

116. Mili Patel, *Guarding Their Sanctuary on the Offense: Criminal Contempt Actions by Domestic Violence Victims in Private Capacity*, 18 CARDOZO J.L. & GENDER 141, 160 & n.148 (2011); Standridge v. State, 423 S.W.3d 677, 682 (Ark. Ct. App. 2012); *see also id.*:

> Appellant notes that prosecutors are quasi-judicial officers, who are supposed to serve in the distinctive role of disinterested and impartial public advocates. He cites several cases from other jurisdictions regarding broad policy arguments regarding the need for prosecutors to act impartially in prosecutorial actions and circumstances requiring disqualification. *See State v. Robinson*, 143 N.M. 646, 179 P.3d 1254 (N.M. Ct. App.2008); *State v. King*, 956 So.2d 562 (La. 2007); *State v. Gonzales*, 138 N.M. 271, 119 P.3d 151 (2005); *State v. Cope*, 30 Kan.App.2d 893, 50 P.3d 513 (2002); *State v. Hill*, 88 N.M. 216, 539 P.2d 236 (N.M. Ct. App. 1975); *State v. Chambers*, 524 P.2d 999 (N.M. Ct. App. 1974); *State v. Cox*, 246 La. 748, 167 So.2d 352 (1964); and *State v. Tate*, 185 La. 1006, 171 So. 108 (1936).
>
> Appellant submits that courts recognize two primary policy considerations underlying the disqualification of prosecuting attorneys for a conflict of interest. The first policy served by the rule is fairness to the accused. The second policy served by disqualification of a prosecuting attorney for conflict of interest is the preservation of public confidence in the impartiality and integrity of the criminal justice system. Appellant points out that no finding of intentional misconduct on the prosecutor's part is necessary to establish a conflict of interest. *Young v. States ex rel. Vuitton et Fils S.A*, 481 U.S. 787, 107 S. Ct. 2124, 95 L.Ed.2d 740 (1987).
>
> Appellant's argument and citations to several other jurisdictions as authority to support broad policy arguments regarding the need for prosecutors to act impartially were not made below; therefore, they are not preserved for appeal. *Flowers v. State*, 92 Ark.App. 337, 213 S.W.3d 648 (2005).

117. People v. Turcott, 3 P. 461, 461 (Cal. 1884).

118. People v. Blackwell, 27 Cal. 65, 67–68 (1864) (citation omitted); *id.*:

> On the cross-examination of the prosecutrix, defendant's counsel asked the witness if she had employed Budd & Carr and Heslep & Jenkins to assist the district attorney in the prosecution. The district attorney objected to the question, on the ground that the proof was incompetent. The objection was sustained and the defendant excepted.
>
> We cannot determine, nor is it either necessary or proper for us to inquire, what, if any, effect an affirmative answer to the question would have had on the minds of the jury. The defendant had a right to ask the question. If a witness retain counsel in a case to which he is not a party, and in the result of which he has no interest, it is a fact going to the credibility of the witness. The witness may have thus interposed on considerations of humanity, or of public justice, or he may have been influenced by private grudge; but the party against whom the witness is produced is always entitled to inquire of the witness as to the fact, and, if admitted, it goes to the jury for whatever it is worth; and such explanation of motives as the witness may give for his action goes with it. (1 Greenl. Ev., Secs. 449, 450; *Baker v. Joseph*, 16 Cal. 173).
>
> Judgment reversed and cause remanded for further proceedings.

119. HENRY CAMPBELL BLACK, A LAW DICTIONARY CONTAINING DEFINITIONS OF THE TERMS AND PHRASES OF AMERICAN AND ENGLISH JURISPRUDENCE, ANCIENT AND MODERN 959 (2d ed. 1910); Allen v. State, 700 S.W.2d 924, 933–34 (Tex. Ct. Crim. App. 1985) (Teague, J., concurring):

> Members of this Court have for many, many years referred to the victim of a sexual assault as "the prosecutrix", if such person was the complainant in a criminal prosecution. And such usage has always been understandable by most rational persons because in point of semantical fact, it is not erroneous to call the female victim of a sexual assault "the prosecutrix" in a criminal proceeding

if she has, indeed, appeared as the chief witness for the State. That is precisely what the word "prosecutrix" means according to all of the authorities. In *Arnold v. State,* 148 Tex. Cr. R. 310, 186 S.W.2d 995, 997 (Tex.Cr.App.1945), this Court defined "a private prosecutor" as "one who prefers an accusation against a party whom he suspects to be guilty." Also see *Williams v. State,* 321 S.W.2d 72 (Tex. Cr. App. 1958).

"Prosecutrix" is an agent noun, which is a noun denoting the performer of an action, as confirmed by the etymological notes that appear both in *Webster's New International Dictionary of the English Language* and the *Oxford English Dictionary.* The word "prosecutrix" is derived through Middle English, from a feminine ending in Latin for agent nouns, where the current masculine or generic ending is "-or"; "-tress" is the feminine ending usually associated with the masculine or generic ending "-er", taken in this instance from Old English, which evidently received it from Greek through late Latin.

Thus, but as easily observed, the word "prosecutrix" nicely fits into the meaning of an agent noun, just as the word "prosecutor" does. Further, because the word "prosecutrix" is formed by appending a gender-specific suffix to the verb "prosecute," the resulting construction is necessarily feminine. Likewise, "prosecutor" is masculine, although not necessarily so, since it also serves a generic function; the context will determine in which sense the word is to be understood.

Until recent times, the terms "prosecutor" and "prosecutrix" were universally understood to be roughly synonymous with "complaining witness" or "complainant", which words are derived from a participle of the verb "complaint", not from the addition of an agent noun suffix to it, and so do not exist in separate masculine and feminine forms. Although such usage may sound slightly odd to those citizens who reside in Dallas County, I find that Webster's does not yet report that the word "prosecutrix" is either archaic or regional, let alone rare or obsolete. It is therefore patently false to maintain that the word "prosecutrix" does not have the above meaning, even if it has others as well.

120. People v. Dehle, 166 Cal. App.4th 1380, 1386–90 (Cal. Ct. App., 3d Dist. 2008):

"In California, all criminal prosecutions are conducted in the name of the People of the State of California and by their authority. (Gov. Code, § 100, subd. (b).) California law does not authorize private prosecutions. Instead, '[t]he prosecution of criminal offenses on behalf of the People is the sole responsibility of the public prosecutor .... [¶][who] ordinarily has sole discretion to determine whom to charge, what charges to file and pursue, and what punishment to seek. [Citation.] No private citizen, however personally aggrieved, may institute criminal proceedings independently [citation], and the prosecutor's own discretion is not subject to judicial control at the behest of persons other than the accused.' (*Dix v. Superior Court* (1991) 53 Cal.3d 442, 451, 279 Cal. Rptr. 834, 807 P.2d 1063.)

"The district attorney of each county is the public prosecutor, vested with the power to conduct on behalf of the People all prosecutions for public offenses within the county. (Gov. Code, § 26500; *Hicks v. Board of Supervisors* (1977) 69 Cal.App.3d 228, 240, 138 Cal. Rptr. 101.) Subject to supervision by the Attorney General (Cal. Const., art. V, § 13; Gov. Code, § 12550), therefore, the district attorney of each county independently exercises all the executive branch's discretionary powers in the initiation and conduct of criminal proceedings. (*People ex rel. Younger v. Superior Court* (1978) 86 Cal.App.3d 180, 203, 150 Cal. Rptr. 156; *People v. Municipal Court (Pellegrino)* (1972) 27 Cal.App.3d 193, 199–204, 103 Cal. Rptr. 645.) The district attorney's discretionary functions extend from the investigation and gathering of evidence relating to criminal offenses (*Hicks v. Board of Supervisors, supra,* 69 Cal.App.3d at p. 241, 138 Cal. Rptr. 101), through the crucial decisions of whom to charge and what charges to bring, to the numerous choices the prosecutor makes at trial regarding 'whether to seek, oppose, accept, or challenge judicial actions and rulings.' (*Dix v. Superior Court, supra,* 53 Cal.3d at p. 452, 279 Cal. Rptr. 834, 807 P.2d 1063; see also *People v. Superior Court (Greer)* (1977) 19 Cal.3d 255, 267, 137 Cal. Rptr. 476, 561 P.2d 1164 [giving as examples the manner of conducting voir dire examinations, the granting of immunity, the use of particular witnesses, the choice of arguments, and the negotiation of plea bargains].)

"The importance, to the public as well as to individuals suspected or accused of crimes, that these discretionary functions be exercised 'with the highest degree of integrity and impartiality, and with the appearance thereof' (*People v. Superior Court (Greer), supra,* 19 Cal.3d at p. 267, 137 Cal. Rptr. 476, 561 P.2d 1164) cannot easily be overstated. The public prosecutor ' "is the representative not of any ordinary party to a controversy, but of a sovereignty whose obligation to govern impartially is as compelling as its obligation to govern at all; and whose interest, therefore, in a criminal prosecution is not that it shall win a case, but that justice shall be done. As such, he is in a peculiar and very definite sense the servant of the law, the twofold aim of which is that guilt shall not escape or innocence suffer." ' (*Id.* at p. 266, 137 Cal. Rptr. 476, 561 P.2d 1164, quoting *Berger v. United States* (1935) 295 U.S. 78, 88, 55 S. Ct. 629, 633, 79 L.Ed. 1314, 1321.)

"The nature of the impartiality required of the public prosecutor follows from the prosecutor's role as representative of the People as a body, rather than as individuals. 'The prosecutor speaks not solely for the victim, or the police, or those who support them, but for all the People. That body of "The People" includes the defendant and his family and those who care about him. It also includes the vast majority of citizens who know nothing about a particular case, but who give over to the prosecutor the authority to seek a just result in their name.' (Corrigan, *On Prosecutorial Ethics* (1986) 13 Hastings Const. L.Q. 537, 538–539.) Thus the district attorney is expected to exercise his or her discretionary functions in the interests of the People at large, and not under the influence or control of an interested individual. (*People v. Superior Court (Greer), supra,* 19 Cal.3d at p. 267, 137 Cal. Rptr. 476, 561 P.2d 1164.)

"While the district attorney does have a duty of zealous advocacy, 'both the accused and the public have a legitimate expectation that his zeal ... will be born of objective and impartial consideration of each individual case.' (*People v. Superior Court (Greer), supra,* 19 Cal.3d at p. 267, 137 Cal. Rptr. 476, 561 P.2d 1164.) 'Of course, a prosecutor need not be disinterested on the issue whether a prospective defendant has committed the crime with which he is charged. If honestly convinced of the defendant's guilt, the prosecutor is free, indeed obliged to be deeply interested in urging that view by any fair means. [Citation.] True disinterest on the issue of such a defendant's guilt is the domain of the judge and the jury—not the prosecutor. It is a bit easier to say what a disinterested prosecutor is not than what he is. He is not disinterested if he has, or is under the influence of others who have, an axe to grind against the defendant, as distinguished from the appropriate interest that members of society have in bringing a defendant to justice with respect to the crime with which he is charged.' (*Wright v. United States* (2d Cir.1984) 732 F.2d 1048, 1056.)" (*People v. Eubanks* (1996) 14 Cal.4th 580, 588–590, 59 Cal.Rptr.2d 200, 927 P.2d 310)

As our long quote from *Eubanks* makes clear, the People have an interest in being heard throughout the course of a criminal prosecution and it is the duty of the district attorney to advocate on the People's behalf in an effort to achieve a fair and just result.

In this matter, both the defendant and Debra Bodine had a voice at the restitution hearing; the People did not. The district attorney, having left the proceedings, did not allow the People to be heard on several issues that may have affected a fair and just result on the question of victim restitution. While we express no opinion on the resolution of these issues, they include, among others, the following: given the fact that it appears that the decedent was not wearing a seatbelt at the time of the accident, whether the decedent's own negligence contributed to his death and whether the defendant should be required to make restitution for economic harm caused in part by the victim himself; whether it was just to deny Debra Bodine restitution for her attorney fees in the underlying action against the insurance carrier because her attorney refused to produce his billing records; whether the proper measure of Debra Bodine's economic loss was the loss of John Bodine's gross income to age 67, adjusted as it was by Debra Bodine's expert witness, or something less than that, such as John Bodine's taxable income; whether it was appropriate to reduce John Bodine's gross income by 30 percent per year based on an estimate of his personal consumption; and whether the victim restitution statutes allow for or require compensation for the loss of a decedent's services around the home and, if so, the proper measure of that compensation.

We recognize that many of the questions that arose during the restitution hearing are the subject of developed law in a civil action for wrongful death. But the focus of a restitution hearing in a criminal matter—economic compensation to the victim, rehabilitation of the offender, and the deterrence of the offender and others from similar conduct—is different from the focus of a civil wrongful death action even though the former raises many of the same issues as the latter. The goals of a restitution hearing are matters that the People expect will be achieved in a just and fair manner which can only be accomplished with the participation of the district attorney acting in accordance with his responsibilities to the criminal justice system.

We also recognize that, in September 2006, approximately four months prior to the restitution hearing, the district attorney submitted a letter to the court requesting restitution to Debra Bodine in the amount of $985,324. The letter does not explain the process by which the district attorney arrived at that number. While that letter is some indication of the district attorney's point of view regarding restitution in September 2006, we cannot say it was a figure informed by the evidence and issues presented four months later at the restitution hearing. The district attorney's obligation to the People to seek a just and fair result can only be accomplished by his presence at the hearing and his consideration of the evidence and issues presented as they bear on the ultimate goals of victim restitution in a criminal case.

Finally, we note that it has long been the law in California that the trial court may permit private counsel to assist the district attorney in a given prosecution. Thus, in *People v. Blackwell* (1864) 27 Cal. 65, 1864 WL 715, our high court said: "It appears from the record that the court, by the request of the district attorney, permitted other counsel to assist him at trial. Before trial commenced, however, the counsel of the appellant moved the court to vacate the order. The motion was overruled and the defendant excepted.

"It appears that the district attorney had the active superintendence and management of the case during the progress of the trial. Whether the State, through him, should be allowed to avail itself of additional professional aid, was a matter addressed to the discretion of the court, and there is nothing in the record showing that the court abused its discretion in granting the request of the attorney. [Citation.]" (*Id.* at p. 67.)

In *People v. Turcott* (1884) 65 Cal. 126, 3 P. 461, the same issue arose. In *Turcott,* the trial court allowed private counsel to assist the district attorney in the prosecution of the case. The defendant claimed error. In resolving the issue, the *Turcott* court wrote: "The practice allowing district attorneys to have the assistance of other counsel in the prosecution of criminal cases has existed and been acquiesced in almost since the organization of the State, and this practice seems to have been sanctioned by legislative action. In prescribing the course of the trial the legislature has provided by the second subdivision of section 1093 of the Penal Code, that the district attorney or other counsel for the people must open the cause and offer the evidence in support of the charge, and by section 1095—that if the indictment or information be for an offense punishable with death—two counsel on each side may argue the cause to the jury. We think the point not well taken." (*Turcott, supra,* 65 Cal. 126 at pp. 126–127, 3 P. 461.)

Section 1093, still in effect and not amended as pertinent to our discussion, now provides in subdivision (b): "The district attorney or *other counsel for the people,* may make an opening statement in support of the charge." (§ 1093, subd. (b); emphasis added.)

In this matter however, Debra Bodine's attorney was not appearing on behalf of the district attorney or the People, he was appearing solely on behalf of Debra Bodine. We have not been cited to a case, and we are aware of none, where the district attorney in a criminal proceeding has been permitted to simply walk away from an important part of the criminal proceedings, leaving conduct of the restitution hearing to a private attorney who has a duty only to his client and no duty to the People.

The trial court abused its discretion when it allowed the restitution hearing to go forward without the presence of the People and there must be a new restitution hearing.

121. 246 Cal. App. 4th Supp. 1, 8, 201 Cal. Rptr. 3d 443 (Cal. App. Div., Sup. Ct., Orange County, 2016) ("'In California, all criminal prosecutions are conducted in the name of the People of the State of

California and by their authority. (Gov.Code § 100, subd. (b).) California law does not authorize private prosecutions. Instead, '[t]he prosecution of criminal offenses on behalf of the People is the sole responsibility of the public prosecutor.... [¶] [who] ordinarily has sole discretion to determine whom to charge, what charges to file and pursue, and what punishment to seek. [Citation.] No private citizen, however personally aggrieved, may institute criminal proceedings independently [citation], and the prosecutor's own discretion is not subject to judicial control at the behest of persons other than the accused." [Citation.]'"); *id.* ("'The district attorney of each county is the public prosecutor, vested with the power to conduct on behalf of the People all prosecutions for public offenses within the county. [Citations.]... [¶] ... [¶] ... "The prosecutor speaks not solely for the victim, or the police, or those who support them, but for all the People. That body of 'The People' includes the defendant and his family and those who care about him. It also includes the vast majority of citizens who know nothing about a particular case, but who give over to the prosecutor the authority to seek a just result in their name." [Citation.] Thus the district attorney is expected to exercise his or her discretionary functions in the interests of the People at large, and not under the influence or control of an interested individual. [Citation.]'") (citing *Dehle,* 166 Cal.App.4th at 1387–1388, 83 Cal.Rptr.3d 461.).

122. 166 Cal. App. 4th 1380, 1387, 83 Cal. Rptr. 3d 461, 465 (Cal. Ct. App., 3d Dist. 2008) ("'In California, all criminal prosecutions are conducted in the name of the People of the State of California and by their authority. (Gov. Code, § 100, subd. (b).) California law does not authorize private prosecutions. Instead, '[t]he prosecution of criminal offenses on behalf of the People is the sole responsibility of the public prosecutor .... [¶][who] ordinarily has sole discretion to determine whom to charge, what charges to file and pursue, and what punishment to seek. [Citation.] No private citizen, however personally aggrieved, may institute criminal proceedings independently [citation], and the prosecutor's own discretion is not subject to judicial control at the behest of persons other than the accused.' (*Dix v. Superior Court* (1991) 53 Cal.3d 442, 451, 279 Cal.Rptr. 834, 807 P.2d 1063.)").

123. 86 Cal. App. 4th 781, 796–98, 104 Cal. Rptr.2d 31, 42–43 (Cal. Ct. App., 3d Dist. 2001) ("A district attorney must be independent of private influences because our law does not authorize private prosecutions. (*Eubanks, supra,* 14 Cal.4th at p. 588, 59 Cal.Rptr.2d 200, 927 P.2d 310; see Gov.Code, § 100, subd. (b).) "One of the reasons often cited for the institution of public prosecutions is that 'Americans believed that an officer in a position of public trust could make decisions more impartially than could the victims of crimes or other private complainants,' persons who often brought prosecutions under the older English system of criminal justice. [Citations.] This advantage of public prosecution is lost if those exercising the discretionary duties of the district attorney are subject to conflicting personal interests which might tend to compromise their impartiality. In short, the prosecuting attorney "'is the representative of the public in whom is lodged a discretion which is not to be controlled by the courts, or *by an interested individual. ...*"' (Italics added.) [Citation.]" (*People v. Superior Court (Greer), supra,* 19 Cal.3d at p. 267, 137 Cal.Rptr. 476, 561 P.2d 1164.)"; "The 'disinterest' demanded of a prosecutor is not the type of true disinterest that is the domain of the judge and jury. (*Eubanks, supra,* 14 Cal.4th at p. 590, 59 Cal.Rptr.2d 200, 927 P.2d 310.) A prosecutor has a duty of zealous advocacy and need not be disinterested on the issue of whether the prospective defendant has committed a crime. (*Ibid.*) If convinced of the defendant's guilt, the prosecutor is free, and indeed obligated, to be deeply interested in urging that view by any fair means. (*Ibid.*) In this respect, however, the prosecutor's interest should coincide with the interest of the public in bringing a criminal to justice and should not be under the influence of third parties who have a particular axe to grind against the defendant. (*Ibid.*) In this light, it can be seen that the interest to be served by a motion to disqualify a prosecutor is the defendant's interest in fair treatment. A defendant has the right to be treated the same as any other person in the same circumstances and thus has the right to expect the prosecutor to be free of the influence of private parties who may have a particular reason for wanting to see the defendant prosecuted and convicted. But a defendant does not have a right or expectation of falling through the cracks for want of resources or lack of prosecutorial zeal. (*Eubanks, supra,* 14 Cal.4th at pp. 590, 599, 59 Cal.Rptr.2d 200, 927 P.2d 310.)"; "The prosecutorial function is an executive branch function, and the prosecutor's independence is founded in part on the principle of separation of powers. (*People v. Birks, supra,*19 Cal.4th at p. 134, 77 Cal.Rptr.2d 848, 960 P.2d 1073.) A prosecutor is not required to be wholly independent of executive branch influences. (See *Sundance v. Municipal Court* (1986) 42 Cal.3d 1101,

1132, 1134, 232 Cal. Rptr. 814, 729 P.2d 80.) While the Constitution requires each county to have a district attorney who serves as public prosecutor (Cal. Const., art. XI, §§ 1, subd. (b); 4, sub. (c); Gov. Code, § 26500), the district attorney is a county officer (Gov. Code, § 24000, subd. (a)) subject to the authority of the county board of supervisors. (Cal. Const., art. XI, §§ 1, subd. (b), 4, subd. (f); Gov. Code, § 25300.) The district attorney's office is funded with county funds pursuant to the county budget established by the board of supervisors and, except as otherwise provided by law, is limited in the making of expenditures or the incurring of liabilities to the amount of appropriations allowed by the budget. (Gov. Code, § 29120.)").

124. The Supreme Court of California, however, has observed that "[n]either this court nor the United States Supreme Court has delineated the limitations due process places on prosecutorial conflicts of interest." People v. Vasquez, 45 Cal. Rptr.3d 372, 380 (Cal. 2006); *id.* at 381 ("Defendants' reliance on *Vuitton* for the proposition that participation of an interested prosecutor universally or generally infringes due process suffers from a fatal flaw: *Vuitton* was decided not on constitutional grounds but under the United States Supreme Court's supervisory powers over the lower federal courts. (*Vuitton, supra,* 481 U.S. at pp. 790, 809, 107 S. Ct. 2124.) Only Justice Blackmun, in a concurring opinion, wrote that 'the practice—federal or state—of appointing an interested party's counsel to prosecute for criminal contempt is a violation of due process.' (*Id.* at pp. 814–815, 107 S. Ct. 2124 (conc. opn. of Blackmun, J.).) *Vuitton* stands as an example of how external influences might affect discretionary prosecutorial decisionmaking, but does not establish a due process test for prosecutorial conflicts."); *id.* at 381–82 ("Several lower federal courts and courts of our sister states have squarely addressed prosecutorial conflicts as a due process problem. The most influential decision has been *Ganger v. Peyton* (4th Cir.1967) 379 F.2d 709 (*Ganger*), which like *Vuitton* involved a prosecutor's simultaneous representation of a private party with an interest in the criminal case. The *Ganger* court found Ganger's Virginia assault conviction constitutionally invalid because the prosecuting attorney had simultaneously 'represented Ganger's wife in the prosecution of a divorce action ... based upon the same alleged assault on Mrs. Ganger. Ganger testified that the prosecuting attorney offered to drop the assault charge if Ganger would make a favorable property settlement in the divorce action.' The prosecutor's self-interest ('including the possibility that the size of his fee would be determined by what could be exacted from defendant') thus made it impossible for him to exercise 'fairminded judgment' with regard to whether and how to prosecute Ganger criminally. 'We think the conduct of this prosecuting attorney in attempting at once to serve two masters, the people of the Commonwealth and the wife of Ganger, violates the requirement of fundamental fairness assured by the Due Process Clause of the Fourteenth Amendment.'") (citations omitted); *id.* at 382 ("More recently, the court in *State v. Eldridge* (Tenn. Crim. App. 1997) 951 S.W.2d 775, 782, also found a due process violation in the participation of 'special prosecutors who represent the victim in a civil matter arising from the same incident giving rise to the criminal prosecution.' The potential for influence on the prosecution by a private interest is simply too great in situations involving such simultaneous representation: "Just as a special prosecutor may be tempted to bring a tenuously supported prosecution if such a reward promises financial or legal rewards for the private client, a special prosecutor may also be tempted to suggest the abandonment of a meritorious prosecution if a settlement providing benefits to the private client is conditioned on a recommendation against criminal charges." (*Id.* at p. 781.)").

125. Victims' Bill of Rights Act of 2008, Cal. Const. art. I § 28; Cal. Penal Code §§ 3041.5, 3043. Article 1, section 28 of the California Constitution provides:

> Sec. 28. (a) The People of the State of California find and declare all of the following:
>
> (1) Criminal activity has a serious impact on the citizens of California. The rights of victims of crime and their families in criminal prosecutions are a subject of grave statewide concern.
>
> (2) Victims of crime are entitled to have the criminal justice system view criminal acts as serious threats to the safety and welfare of the people of California. The enactment of comprehensive provisions and laws ensuring a bill of rights for victims of crime, including safeguards in the criminal justice system fully protecting those rights and ensuring that crime victims are treated with respect and dignity, is a matter of high public importance. California's victims of crime are largely dependent upon the proper functioning of government, upon the criminal justice system and upon the expeditious enforcement of the rights of victims of crime described herein, in order

to protect the public safety and to secure justice when the public safety has been compromised by criminal activity.

(3) The rights of victims pervade the criminal justice system. These rights include personally held and enforceable rights described in paragraphs (1) through (17) of subdivision (b).

(4) The rights of victims also include broader shared collective rights that are held in common with all of the People of the State of California and that are enforceable through the enactment of laws and through good-faith efforts and actions of California's elected, appointed, and publicly employed officials. These rights encompass the expectation shared with all of the people of California that persons who commit felonious acts causing injury to innocent victims will be appropriately and thoroughly investigated, appropriately detained in custody, brought before the courts of California even if arrested outside the State, tried by the courts in a timely manner, sentenced, and sufficiently punished so that the public safety is protected and encouraged as a goal of highest importance.

(5) Victims of crime have a collectively shared right to expect that persons convicted of committing criminal acts are sufficiently punished in both the manner and the length of the sentences imposed by the courts of the State of California. This right includes the right to expect that the punitive and deterrent effect of custodial sentences imposed by the courts will not be undercut or diminished by the granting of rights and privileges to prisoners that are not required by any provision of the United States Constitution or by the laws of this State to be granted to any person incarcerated in a penal or other custodial facility in this State as a punishment or correction for the commission of a crime.

(6) Victims of crime are entitled to finality in their criminal cases. Lengthy appeals and other post-judgment proceedings that challenge criminal convictions, frequent and difficult parole hearings that threaten to release criminal offenders, and the ongoing threat that the sentences of criminal wrongdoers will be reduced, prolong the suffering of crime victims for many years after the crimes themselves have been perpetrated. This prolonged suffering of crime victims and their families must come to an end.

(7) Finally, the People find and declare that the right to public safety extends to public and private primary, elementary, junior high, and senior high school, and community college, California State University, University of California, and private college and university campuses, where students and staff have the right to be safe and secure in their persons.

(8) To accomplish the goals it is necessary that the laws of California relating to the criminal justice process be amended in order to protect the legitimate rights of victims of crime.

(b) In order to preserve and protect a victim's rights to justice and due process, a victim shall be entitled to the following rights:

(1) To be treated with fairness and respect for his or her privacy and dignity, and to be free from intimidation, harassment, and abuse, throughout the criminal or juvenile justice process.

(2) To be reasonably protected from the defendant and persons acting on behalf of the defendant.

(3) To have the safety of the victim and the victim's family considered in fixing the amount of bail and release conditions for the defendant.

(4) To prevent the disclosure of confidential information or records to the defendant, the defendant's attorney, or any other person acting on behalf of the defendant, which could be used to locate or harass the victim or the victim's family or which disclose confidential communications made in the course of medical or counseling treatment, or which are otherwise privileged or confidential by law.

(5) To refuse an interview, deposition, or discovery request by the defendant, the defendant's attorney, or any other person acting on behalf of the defendant, and to set reasonable conditions on the conduct of any such interview to which the victim consents.

(6) To reasonable notice of and to reasonably confer with the prosecuting agency, upon request, regarding, the arrest of the defendant if known by the prosecutor, the charges filed, the

determination whether to extradite the defendant, and, upon request, to be notified of and informed before any pretrial disposition of the case.

(7) To reasonable notice of all public proceedings, including delinquency proceedings, upon request, at which the defendant and the prosecutor are entitled to be present and of all parole or other post-conviction release proceedings, and to be present at all such proceedings.

(8) To be heard, upon request, at any proceeding, including any delinquency proceeding, involving a post-arrest release decision, plea, sentencing, post-conviction release decision, or any proceeding in which a right of the victim is at issue.

(9) To a speedy trial and a prompt and final conclusion of the case and any related post-judgment proceedings.

(10) To provide information to a probation department official conducting a pre-sentence investigation concerning the impact of the offense on the victim and the victim's family and any sentencing recommendations before the sentencing of the defendant.

(11) To receive, upon request, the pre-sentence report when available to the defendant, except for those portions made confidential by law.

(12) To be informed, upon request, of the conviction, sentence, place and time of incarceration, or other disposition of the defendant, the scheduled release date of the defendant, and the release of or the escape by the defendant from custody.

(13) To restitution.

(A) It is the unequivocal intention of the People of the State of California that all persons who suffer losses as a result of criminal activity shall have the right to seek and secure restitution from the persons convicted of the crimes causing the losses they suffer.

(B) Restitution shall be ordered from the convicted wrongdoer in every case, regardless of the sentence or disposition imposed, in which a crime victim suffers a loss.

(C) All monetary payments, monies, and property collected from any person who has been ordered to make restitution shall be first applied to pay the amounts ordered as restitution to the victim.

(14) To the prompt return of property when no longer needed as evidence.

(15) To be informed of all parole procedures, to participate in the parole process, to provide information to the parole authority to be considered before the parole of the offender, and to be notified, upon request, of the parole or other release of the offender.

(16) To have the safety of the victim, the victim's family, and the general public considered before any parole or other post-judgment release decision is made.

(17) To be informed of the rights enumerated in paragraphs (1) through (16).

(c)(1) A victim, the retained attorney of a victim, a lawful representative of the victim, or the prosecuting attorney upon request of the victim, may enforce the rights enumerated in subdivision (b) in any trial or appellate court with jurisdiction over the case as a matter of right. The court shall act promptly on such a request.

(2) This section does not create any cause of action for compensation or damages against the State, any political subdivision of the State, any officer, employee, or agent of the State or of any of its political subdivisions, or any officer or employee of the court.

(d) The granting of these rights to victims shall not be construed to deny or disparage other rights possessed by victims. The court in its discretion may extend the right to be heard at sentencing to any person harmed by the defendant. The parole authority shall extend the right to be heard at a parole hearing to any person harmed by the offender.

(e) As used in this section, a "victim" is a person who suffers direct or threatened physical, psychological, or financial harm as a result of the commission or attempted commission of a crime or delinquent act. The term "victim" also includes the person's spouse, parents, children, siblings, or guardian, and includes a lawful representative of a crime victim who is deceased, a minor, or physically or psychologically incapacitated. The term "victim" does not include a person in custody for an offense, the accused, or a person whom the court finds would not act in the best interests of a minor victim.

(f) In addition to the enumerated rights provided in subdivision (b) that are personally enforceable by victims as provided in subdivision (c), victims of crime have additional rights that are shared with all of the People of the State of California. These collectively held rights include, but are not limited to, the following:

(1) Right to Safe Schools. All students and staff of public primary, elementary, junior high, and senior high schools, and community colleges, colleges, and universities have the inalienable right to attend campuses which are safe, secure and peaceful.

(2) Right to Truth-in-Evidence. Except as provided by statute hereafter enacted by a two-thirds vote of the membership in each house of the Legislature, relevant evidence shall not be excluded in any criminal proceeding, including pretrial and post conviction motions and hearings, or in any trial or hearing of a juvenile for a criminal offense, whether heard in juvenile or adult court. Nothing in this section shall affect any existing statutory rule of evidence relating to privilege or hearsay, or Evidence Code Sections 352, 782 or 1103. Nothing in this section shall affect any existing statutory or constitutional right of the press.

(3) Public Safety Bail. A person may be released on bail by sufficient sureties, except for capital crimes when the facts are evident or the presumption great. Excessive bail may not be required. In setting, reducing or denying bail, the judge or magistrate shall take into consideration the protection of the public, the safety of the victim, the seriousness of the offense charged, the previous criminal record of the defendant, and the probability of his or her appearing at the trial or hearing of the case. Public safety and the safety of the victim shall be the primary considerations.

A person may be released on his or her own recognizance in the court's discretion, subject to the same factors considered in setting bail.

Before any person arrested for a serious felony may be released on bail, a hearing may be held before the magistrate or judge, and the prosecuting attorney and the victim shall be given notice and reasonable opportunity to be heard on the matter.

When a judge or magistrate grants or denies bail or release on a person's own recognizance, the reasons for that decision shall be stated in the record and included in the court's minutes.

(4) Use of Prior Convictions. Any prior felony conviction of any person in any criminal proceeding, whether adult or juvenile, shall subsequently be used without limitation for purposes of impeachment or enhancement of sentence in any criminal proceeding. When a prior felony conviction is an element of any felony offense, it shall be proven to the trier of fact in open court.

(5) Truth in Sentencing. Sentences that are individually imposed upon convicted criminal wrongdoers based upon the facts and circumstances surrounding their cases shall be carried out in compliance with the courts' sentencing orders, and shall not be substantially diminished by early release policies intended to alleviate overcrowding in custodial facilities. The legislative branch shall ensure sufficient funding to adequately house inmates for the full terms of their sentences, except for statutorily authorized credits which reduce those sentences.

(6) Reform of the parole process. The current process for parole hearings is excessive, especially in cases in which the defendant has been convicted of murder. The parole hearing process must be reformed for the benefit of crime victims.

(g) As used in this article, the term "serious felony" is any crime defined in subdivision (c) of Section 1192.7 of the Penal Code, or any successor statute.

126. Cal. Penal Code § 290.46.

127. Cal. Const. art. I, § 28(c)(1).

128. People v. Eubanks, 927 P.2d 310, 315 (Cal. 1996); *see also* County of Santa Clara v. Superior Court, 235 P.3d 21, 31 (Cal. 2010) ("[A]lthough there are virtually no cases considering the propriety of compensation of public prosecutors pursuant to a contingent-fee arrangement, it would appear that under most, if not all, circumstances, such a method of compensation would be categorically barred. This is so because giving a public prosecutor a direct pecuniary interest in the outcome of a case that he or she is prosecuting 'would render it unlikely that the defendant would receive a fair trial.'").

129. Washington v. Moore, Case No. 3:18-cv-06728-JD, 2020 WL 1082552, at *1 (N.D. Cal. Mar. 6, 2020) (citing People v. Eubanks, 14 Cal. 4th 580, 588 (1996)).

130. Critchfield v. People, 13 P.2d 270, 272 (Colo. 1932) ("Error is assigned in granting permission for the appearance of special counsel for the people. The motion, order, and objection thereto are hereinbefore set forth. We do not approve of the action of the district attorney or the trial court in this respect, and suggest that counsel should be given ample notice of all counsel to appear in the trial of a cause, so that the opportunity of interrogating prospective jurors may be full and complete. If, after accepting the jury, defendant's counsel had desired further opportunity of examining them, with reference to their relations and acquaintance with newly entered counsel, and such request had been denied by the trial court, an entirely different situation would have presented itself for our determination; however, herein, there is no indication that the substantial rights of the defendant were prejudiced, and, in the absence thereof, we cannot say that error was committed.").

131. Kailey v. Chambers, 261 P.3d 792, 794 (Colo. Ct. App. 2011) (citation omitted); *see also* People v. Jiminez, 528 P.2d 913, 915 (Colo. 1974) ("The final ground for reversal relates to the improper interest of the district attorney in the outcome of the case. It was shown, without dispute, at the hearing on appellant's motion for a new trial that the district attorney, prior to filing criminal charges against appellant, had been employed as counsel in his private capacity to represent one of the injured passengers and the family of the deceased passenger in their respective claims for damages against appellant and his liability insurance carrier. Although the appellant knew, prior to the commencement of trial, of the district attorney's private interest in the case, he made no objection to the prosecution of the case by the district attorney, nor did he move for the district attorney's recusation. The trial court was not aware of this conflict of interest until it was raised by appellant in his motion for a new trial. After a full hearing, the court found that the appellant, having full knowledge of the private interest of the district attorney in the civil litigation arising out of the transaction involved, had waived his right to have the district attorney disqualified from prosecuting the criminal action against him. The court denied appellant's motion for a new trial predicated upon this ground. We do not disagree with the court's ruling under the circumstances of this case."); *id.* at 916 ("Under the circumstances of the dual representation in the present case, upon motion the district attorney would have been disqualified and a special prosecutor appointed. The matter, however, was not brought to the court's attention, even though counsel for appellant knew about it. The court, as heretofore noted, found that appellant had waived his right to have the district attorney disqualified. A defendant will not be permitted, as a matter of trial strategy, to conceal error during trial and gamble on a favorable verdict, and upon an adverse result assert as grounds for reversal the error he should have revealed to the court.").

132. Colo. Rev. Stat. Ann. § 16-5-209; *see also* Kailey v. Chambers, 261 P.3d 792, 795 (Colo. Ct. App. 2011) ("We review de novo the district court's application of the statutory abuse of discretion standard (i.e., 'arbitrary or capricious and without reasonable excuse') to the district attorney's decision.").

133. Pearl v. Mickelson-Dera, No. CV136022964S, 2014 WL 2854021, at *9 (Conn. Super. Ct., Jud. Dist. of New Britain, May 16, 2014) (citations omitted); *see also* Lewis v. Mashantucket Pequot Gaming Commission, 2 Mash. 242, 243, 1997 WL 34641752, at *2 (Mash. Pequot Tribal Ct. Dec. 10, 1997) ("Alleged violations of Connecticut criminal statutes may not be prosecuted by a private party; only the State of Connecticut or the Mashantucket Pequot Tribe, when it is enforcing state law as tribal law, possesses that authority."); Chapnick v. Dilauro, NNHCV186086166S, 2019 WL 3249891, at *2 (Conn. Super. Ct., Jud. Dist. of New Haven, June 17, 2019) ("Our Supreme Court has stated: 'The policy of encouraging private citizens to assist in law enforcement is vindicated, in the law of malicious prosecution, by providing a limited immunity in the form of the first element that the plaintiff must prove to maintain his cause of action. A private person can be said to have initiated a criminal proceeding if he has insisted that the plaintiff should be prosecuted, that is, if he has brought pressure of any kind to bear upon the public officer's decision to commence the prosecution ... But a private person has not initiated a criminal proceeding if he has undertaken no more than to provide potentially incriminating information to a public officer. In such a case, if the defendant has made a full and truthful disclosure and has left the decision to prosecute entirely in the hands of the public officer, he cannot be held liable for malicious prosecution.'") (citations omitted).

134. *E.g.*, Anderson v. Kubish, No. CV010084133, 2001 WL 1178521, at *1 (Conn. Super. Ct. 2001).

135. DiSabatino v. Salicete, 671 A.2d 1344, 1352 (Del. 1996) (citations omitted).

136. Seth v. State, 592 A.2d 436, 438–42 (Del. 1991); *see also id.* at 442–43 ("We recognize that there is a potential for financial and other conflicts to develop when a private attorney becomes a prosecutor, even for a brief period of time. *See generally* R. Underwood & W. Fortune, *Trial Ethics* § 14.3.4, Prosecutor's Conflicts (Supp.1990); C. Wolfram, *Modern Legal Ethics* § 8.9 (1986); Supreme Court Advisory Committee, *A Comparative Study of the ABA Standards for Criminal Justice with Present Delaware Law*, the Prosecution Function Std. 1.2 comment at 288 (1976) (improper for a member of the Attorney General's office to practice with a firm that handles any legal matters involving the State of Delaware). However, we find no bar to the Lend–A–Prosecutor program on ethical grounds where no actual conflict between the public and private interest is presented. *See, e.g.*, ABA Committee on Ethics and Professional Responsibility, Informal Op. C–772 (1964) (State Prosecuting Attorney may engage in private practice where permitted by law and no conflict of interest involved); ABA Committee on Ethics and Professional Responsibility, Formal Op. 278 (1948)."); *Seth*, 592 A.2d at 443 ("Absent the existence of a conflict, we further will not bar the Lend–A–Prosecutor program based on an unarticulated concern for the "appearance of impropriety." *See* Rule 1.10 comment, Lawyers moving between firms. *See also* Wolfram, *Modern Legal Ethics* § 7.1.4 (criticizing appearances test as imprecise and leading to ad hoc results). The Rules may not be used for tactical purposes to disqualify prosecutors where no realistic likelihood of conflict appears. *See Infotechnology*, 582 A.2d at 220–221. We therefore find no merit to defendant's claim that the program violates the Rules.").

137. Gordon v. State, 960 So.2d 31, 37–39 (Fla. D.C. App., 4th Dist. 2007).

138. *Id.* at 39.

139. Plank v. State, 190 So.3d 594, 606 (Fla. 2016).

140. Roberts v. State, 634 S.E.2d 790, 792 (Ga. Ct. App. 2006) (citations omitted).

141. Ga. Uniform Superior Court R. 42.1; *see also* Rogers v. State, 348 S.E.2d 888 (Ga. App. 1986) (there was no violation of rule prohibiting private special prosecutors retained by victim's family or relatives from participating in prosecution of criminal case, when private attorney, who was representing parents of victim in pending civil suit against defendant, helped to arrange for appearance of expert witness for State in defendant's prosecution, where parents' attorney did not sit at counsel table and took no part in actual trial of case, attorney did not assist in preparation of State's case and was not present when expert witness had been interviewed, and expert was paid by State); Ga. Code Ann. § 15-18-5(a)-(b) (providing that "[w]hen a district attorney's office is disqualified from interest or relationship to engage in a prosecution, the district attorney shall notify the Attorney General of the disqualification" and "the Attorney General shall ... [a]ppoint a competent attorney to act as district attorney pro tempore in place of the district attorney"; A private attorney acting as district attorney pro tempore pursuant to paragraph (3) of subsection (a) of this Code section is subject to all laws and regulations established pursuant to Code Section 15-18-19 governing district attorneys. Such private attorney shall receive the same compensation from state funds appropriated for the operations of the district attorneys at the same rate as the district attorney during the term of such appointment and shall incur the same penalties in the discharge of the duties of said office."); Ga. Code Ann. § 15-18-5(d) ("The appointment of the district attorney pro tempore shall specify in writing the court or courts to which the appointment applies, the county or counties where located, the time period covered, and the name of the case or cases to which such appointment shall apply. A copy of the appointment shall be filed with the clerk of court and copies shall be provided to the presiding judge and the Prosecuting Attorneys' Council of the State of Georgia and opposing counsel in any action affected by such order. An order appointing a private attorney pursuant to this Code section shall also specify whether such attorney will serve on a full-time or part-time basis and any restrictions which may apply to such attorney's private practice of law during the term of such appointment. Private attorneys who serve on a part-time basis shall be compensated at an hourly rate determined by the Prosecuting Attorneys' Council of the State of Georgia based on the annual salary of district attorneys paid from state funds. The Prosecuting Attorneys' Council of the State of Georgia shall establish such procedures or guidelines as may be necessary to ensure proper accountability of any funds paid to a private attorney pursuant to this Code section.").

142. Rogers v. State, 348 S.E.2d 888 (Ga. Ct. App. 1986).

143. Susan W. Brenner & James Geoffrey Durham, *Towards Resolving Prosecutor Conflicts of Interest*, 6 Geo. J. Legal Ethics 415, 420 (1993); *see also id.* ("no state statute indicates whether Hawaiian prosecutors in general are part-time or full-time").

144. Revised Charter of the City & County of Honolulu 1973 (2017 Edition), June 30, 2017, *available at* http://www.honolulu.gov/rep/site/cor/rch/Online_Charter_-_07.01.2020.pdf.

145. Okuda v. Ching, 785 P.2d 943 (Haw. 1990).

146. *Id.* at 946.

147. People v. Biles, 6 P. 120, 120–21 (Idaho 1885) (citing People v. Turcott, 3 P. 461 (Cal. 1884) (holding that the district attorney, in prosecuting a criminal case, may be permitted by the court to have the assistance of private counsel).

148. Derting v. Walker, 739 P.2d 354, 357 (Idaho 1987); *see also id.* ("In sum, our Constitution, while making clear that a county prosecutor is to receive only 'compensation for services as may be fixed by law,' such services do not include the prosecution of city misdemeanors. I.C. § 31–2604. Any compensation received for prosecution of city misdemeanors is outside the scope of either Id. Const. art. 5 § 18 or art. 18 § 7."). *But see id.* at 358 (Bistline, J., dissenting) ("It is bewildering that three members of this Court, constituting a majority and thus speaking for the Court, rationalize that a person who is elected (or appointed in case of vacancy) to the office of prosecutor, can all at the same time while prosecuting criminals and advising county officials with authority to, as prosecutor, make contracts with cities, then, as an individual, reap and retain for himself personally monies earned under that contract. By virtue of the office, he is receiving the salary which is set by the legislature. It is all the compensation which he, as an individual, can be paid for that office. He cannot enjoy the benefits of a private legal practice. He owes to the county complete fealty—which means any legal work he does will be attributable to his duties and functions as a prosecutor.").

149. State v. Johnson, 470 P.3d 1263, 1264, 1268–69 (Idaho Ct. App. 2020) (citing People v. Calderone, 573 N.Y.S.2d 1005, 1009 (N.Y. Crim. Ct. 1991); quoting ABA Standard 3–2.1(c)).

150. People v. Hartenbower, 283 Ill. 591, 600–01 (1918) (citations omitted).

151. People v. Wiggins, 231 Ill. App. 467, 474 (Ill. App. Ct. 1923).

152. People v. Husband, 123 N.E.2d 315, 316 (1954); *see also* People v. Miller, 148 N.E.2d 455, 469 (Ill. 1958) (upholding the use of private prosecutor in a prosecution for murder and observing: "The record discloses the court entered an order appointing a private counsel to assist the State's Attorney, and defendant now insists that it was without jurisdiction to do so inasmuch as the statutory prerequisites for the appointment of a special prosecutor were not met. The statute relied upon relates to the procedure to be followed when a State's Attorney is sick, absent or unable to attend, or the office is vacant, and has no application to this case. On the other hand, this court has repeatedly held the trial court is vested with discretion in permitting private counsel to assist a State's Attorney, and that it may do so as fairness and justice require and without oppression of a defendant. We find nothing in the present case, which was twice-tried, complex and exhaustively defended by cocounsel for defendant, which shows an abuse of discretion in this respect.") (citations omitted).

153. People v. Farnsley, 293 N.E.2d 600, 605 (Ill. 1973); *see also id.* (noting that in an earlier Illinois case, *Hayner v. People*, it was held that "a duty was imposed upon the trial court to prevent oppression of the accused and to insure that such appointment is 'not being used to gratify malice or personal ends.'").

154. In re Estate of Wernick, 530 N.E.2d 1127, 1130 (Ill. App. Ct., 1st Dist. 1988).

155. Del Dotto v. Olsen, 628 N.E.2d 1156, 1158 (Ill. App. Ct., 1st Dist. 1993).

156. State ex rel. Johnson v. White Circuit Court, 77 N.E.2d 298, 301 (Ind. 1948) ("Nor may private individuals institute criminal prosecution. 'Criminal prosecutions cannot be instituted by private individuals.'"); *see also* King v. State, 397 N.E.2d 1260, 1267–68 (Ind. Ct. App. 1979) ("King correctly asserts in his brief that criminal prosecutions cannot be instituted by private individuals. However, this case was not instituted by a private individual. Rather it was initiated by a special prosecutor who, at minimum, was a de facto public official.") (citing *Johnson v. White Circuit Court* (1948)).

157. 455 N.E.2d 1159 (Ind. Ct. App. 1983).

158. *Id.* at 1164; *see also* Bebout v. State, 714 N.E.2d 1152, 1153 (Ind. Ct. App. 1999) ("A prosecutor may enlist the assistance of other attorneys without petitioning to have the attorneys appointed as special

prosecutors. *See, e.g.*, Sedelbauer v. State, 455 N.E.2d 1159, 1164 (Ind. Ct. App. 1983). There, we found no error where a member of an anti-pornography group was admitted *pro hac vice* to assist the prosecutor in an obscenity trial but was not named a special prosecutor. We recognized the 'long-standing principle in Indiana that courts exercising criminal jurisdiction have the inherent power and duty to appoint attorneys to *assist* in the trial of criminal cases.' We noted that the co-counsel appeared with, and not in place of, the deputy prosecutor, and that there was no indication the co-counsel 'represented the State's interest outside of legal boundaries or inconsistent with the State's interest.'") (citations omitted).

159. Ind. Code 33-39-10-2.

160. State of Indiana ex rel. Kirtz v. Delaware Circuit Court No. 5, 916 N.E.2d 658, 659–61 (Ind. 2009).

161. Jones v. State, 901 N.E.2d 655, 658 (Ind. Ct. App. 2009).

162. State v. Young, 863 N.W.2d 249, 258 (Iowa 2015).

163. State v. Tolson, 82 N.W.2d 105, 106 (Iowa 1957) ("[A prosecutor] owes a second duty, of no less importance, to see that the accused has a fair trial."); *accord* State v. Coleman, 907 N.W.2d 124, 153 (Iowa 2018) (Appel, J., concurring in part and dissenting in part).

164. State v. Plain, 898 N.W.2d 801, 818 (Iowa 2017) (citations omitted).

165. State v. Ronek, 176 N.W.2d 153, 154–155 (Iowa 1970) ("Defendant was charged by preliminary information signed by one Otto R. Donath filed in Municipal Court of Dubuque with having committed adultery with Ellen Donath, wife of informant. Subsequently appellant was indicted by the Dubuque county grand jury and pleaded not guilty. He then filed motion to dismiss based on grounds section 702.1, Code, 1966, is unconstitutional for: (1) said statute is an unlawful delegation by the legislature of exclusive authority to institute the criminal charge of adultery, (2) it is an unlawful delegation of power to an individual permitting the individual to choose whom to punish for a crime, (3) it is violative of Amendment 14 of the United States Constitution and Article 1, § 6, of the Iowa Constitution by granting to the offended husband or wife the right exclusive to institute prosecution against either party to an adulterous relationship, (4) it deprives a defendant of his right to equal protection in violation of the last cited constitutional provisions, and (5) it deprives the defendant of due process of law. The motion to dismiss was overruled, defendant withdrew his plea of not guilty, pleaded guilty and was sentenced to a term in jail and assessed a fine, and in its order and judgment the court directed entry of judgment for costs against defendant, including fees paid to defendant's court-appointed counsel. In his motion in arrest of judgment appellant reiterated all of the constitutional questions raised in the motion to dismiss and in addition claimed appellant had been deprived of effective assistance of counsel because of threats of violence to appellant by the prosecuting witness, the husband of defendant's associate in the claimed adultery. The motion in arrest of judgment was overruled. We affirm the trial court."); *see also id.* at 155–56:

> The constitutional issues presented in appellant's first assignment of error and which were raised in the motion to dismiss filed in advance of the appellant's withdrawal of his plea of not guilty and the entry of his guilty plea and were later raised in the motion in arrest of judgment subsequent to sentence, are all directed at the last sentence of section 702.1, which provides no prosecution for the crime of adultery can be commenced except on the complaint of the husband or wife. The complaint here was made by Otto R. Donath, the husband of Ellen Donath, with whom the defendant pleaded guilty to having committed adultery. Succinctly stated, the appellant's contentions are that the criticized sentence of section 702.1 is violative of the concept of separation or distribution of powers provided for in both the federal and Iowa state constitutions; in other words, is an undue delegation of powers over criminal law to a private individual. He further contends it is violative of the equal protection clause of both the federal and state constitutions and of the due process as well as the privileges and immunities clauses. Appellant's principal contention appears to be that because the statute gives sole power to the injured or offended spouse to complain, hence, to commence prosecution for adultery, that the legislature has placed judicial powers over criminal law in the hands of a private person in derogation of the separation of powers concept. We do not believe the separation of powers concept has been violated by the legislature in enacting section 702.1, Code. The separation of powers concept, as we understand it, has to do with the distribution of governmental functions as among the executive, legislative and judicial branches of the government, and recognizes the constitutional prohibition against

one department's exercising another's powers, since all departments of government derive their authority from the same source, they in equal degree represent the sovereignty, and each within its own sphere is supreme and independent, and the several departments are not merely equal but are also exclusive. Therefore it necessarily follows the enactment of section 702.1 was a proper legislative function. The legislature has the power to proscribe certain acts as crimes and to provide penalties for the violation of the same. Appellant does not seem to question the right of the legislature to define adultery as a public offense, and to fix punishment therefor. Adultery is an offense against the husband or wife of the guilty party, but it is nonetheless an offense against the public for that reason. All offenses against persons or property are in some sense offenses against an injured individual but they are also offenses against the public. The provision in section 702.1 that 'no prosecution for adultery shall be commenced but on the complaint of the husband or wife' does not fix the character of the offense. State v. Corliss, 85 Iowa 18, 20, 51 N.W. 1154. The provision is grounded in the regard which the law has for the marital relation and the rights of the husband and wife to condone the wrongs of either toward the other. That the offender cannot be prosecuted except at the instance of the injured husband or wife does not render his crime any the less an offense against the public. State v. Corliss, supra. In determining the question as to whether or not the criticized portion of section 702.1 is an unconstitutional delegation of judicial authority to a private individual, we should consider whether or not it is the result of a constitutional policy determination by the legislature balancing policy considerations with the concept of crimes being injuries to the public. The Minnesota case of State v. Allison, 175 Minn. 218, 220 N.W. 563, was the subject of a comment in 28 Columbia Law Review 1102, 1103. The Minnesota court held the offended spouse could not terminate a prosecution for adultery once she or he had begun it, and the writer of the law review article noted two alternate policy considerations involved in the Minnesota statute which incidentally is virtually indistinguishable from the Iowa statute: (1) the phrase in the statute on commencement of prosecution indicates the state considers the offense primarily an offense against the unoffending spouse rather than against society and will not prosecute except at the request or upon the complaint of the injured spouse, and (2) conceding the offense to be one against society, as Iowa does, State v. Corliss, supra; State v. Clemenson, 123 Iowa 524, 525, 99 N.W. 139, the state is reluctant to prosecute except on the complaint of the offended spouse because of the incidental injury that could result to the innocent spouse and children. Under either policy consideration, the statute makes allowances for a possibility of reconciliation which would not be the case if a prosecuting attorney were to institute prosecution on his own and against the wishes of the offended spouse. These policy factors of course do not apply after a complaint is made and prosecution is commenced. Hence the Iowa rule that prosecution may continue even though the injured spouse recants and wishes to secure a dismissal of the prosecution. State v. Athey, 133 Iowa 382, 384, 385, 108 N.W. 224.

166. *Id.* at 155 (quoting Section 702.1, Code, 1966).

167. Venckus v. City of Iowa City, 930 N.W.2d 792, 815 (Iowa 2019) (Appel, J., concurring in part and dissenting in part) (citing 1 *The Debates of the Constitutional Convention of the State of Iowa* 475–77 (W. Blair Lord rep., 1857), www.statelibraryofiowa.org/services/collections/law-library/iaconst); *see also id.* ("Across the country, both public and private prosecutors were subject to suit for misconduct. Private prosecutors could be sued for malicious prosecution where, for instance, they caused wrongful imprisonment or induced the seizure of property. This court said, for example, that '[t]he prosecution of an innocent person without using reasonable care to ascertain the facts is certainly not justifiable.' Public prosecutors were also subject to suit for malicious prosecution.") (citations omitted); *id.* at 823 ("When the Iowa Constitutions were adopted in 1846 and 1857, neither public nor private prosecutors enjoyed absolute immunity from lawsuits concerning their litigation misconduct. Indeed, at the time, 'there was *not a single decision* affording prosecutors *any kind* of immunity defense from liability for malicious prosecution.'") (citations omitted).

168. "Legislative Enactments," SEMI-WEEKLY INDEPENDENT-NEW ERA (Coffeyville, KS), Apr. 26, 1901, p. 7; "Some New Laws," THE MARSHALL COUNTY NEWS (Marysville, KS), Mar. 22, 1901, p. 4.

169. Kan. Stat. Ann. § 19-717; *see also* Kan. Stat. Ann. § 19-705 ("No county attorney shall receive any fee or reward from or on behalf of any prosecutor or other individuals, except such as are allowed by law for services in any prosecution or business to which it shall be his official duty to attend, nor be concerned as attorney or counsel for either party other than the state or county, in any civil action depending upon the same state of facts upon which any criminal prosecution, commenced but undetermined, shall depend; nor shall any county attorney while in office be eligible to or hold any judicial or other county office whatsoever.").

170. Thomas Dever, "Read the Law," Junction City Sentinel (Junction City, KS), Mar. 29, 1901; *see also id.* (in comparing the 1885 statute and the 1901 statute, the newspaper noted: "It will be seen that the former of these sections gave to any citizen the power to employ etc., while the latter gives such power only to the prosecuting witness. However, the latter law has no more application to the prohibitory law than to any other law of the state, while the former has application to none other than the prohibitory law.").

171. 819 P.2d 1173 (Kan. 1991).

172. Section 19-717 of the Kansas Statutes provided as follows: "That the prosecuting witness in any criminal action or proceeding may, at his own expense, employ an attorney or attorneys to assist the county attorney to perform his duties in any criminal action or proceeding under any of the laws of the state of Kansas, and such attorney or attorneys shall be recognized by the county attorney and court as associate counsel in such action or proceeding, and no prosecution shall be dismissed over the objection of such associate counsel until the reason of the county attorney for such dismissal, together with the objections thereto of such associate counsel, shall have been filed in writing, argued by counsel, and fully considered by the court." Kan. Stat. Ann. § 19-717 (1988).

173. Section 19-717 of the Kansas Statutes governs the use of assistant prosecutors, while section 22-2202(17) of the Kansas Statutes defines a "prosecuting attorney" as "any attorney who is authorized by law to appear for and on behalf of the state of Kansas in a criminal case, and includes the attorney general, an assistant attorney general, the county or district attorney, an assistant county or district attorney, and any special prosecutor whose appearance is approved by the court." The Kansas Supreme Court has discussed the difference between a special prosecutor and an assistant prosecutor. State v. Berg, 694 P.2d 427, 431 (Kan. 1985) ("An attorney hired by the complaining witness to assist the prosecutor pursuant to 19-717 is not a 'special prosecutor' within the meaning of 22-2202(19). Although we find no Kansas cases which define 'special prosecutor,' we are of the opinion that ... it refers to one who is temporarily appointed by the court to replace the absent county attorney pursuant to K.S.A. 19-711 or 19-715. The 19-717 attorney does not take over the role of the prosecutor. The controlling word in 19-717 is 'assist.' The attorney is to assist the prosecutor who will maintain ultimate control of the case.").

174. *Baker*, 819 P.2d at 1184. In *Berg*, the Kansas Supreme Court held that an assistant prosecutor retained by the complaining witness did not have the right to take appeal from an order dismissing the criminal complaint. *Berg*, 694 P.2d at 429–31; *see also* State v. Glant, 13 Wash. App.2d 356, 371 (Wash. Ct. App. 2020) ("*State v. Berg* addressed a Kansas statute that allowed for a complaining witness to hire private counsel as associate counsel to the prosecutor to assist in the criminal proceeding. Jerry Berg, a complaining witness in a case against his ex-wife, hired private counsel to assist in the prosecution. But, after further investigation, the prosecutor moved to dismiss the charges. Over the objections of private counsel, the trial court dismissed the case. The court held that private counsel could not overrule the prosecutor's decision to dismiss the charges, stating that a prosecutor must be independent.") (citations omitted); State ex rel. Rome v. Fountain, 678 P.2d 146, 153 (Kan. 1984) (a complaining witness has no right to challenge a decision by the prosecutor to dismiss).

175. *Baker*, 819 P.2d at 1183.

176. *Id.* at 1176, 1190. The Kansas Supreme Court has recognized that "an attorney who is hired by a complaining witness must act in the interest of his client which may not be in the interest of the general public." *Berg*, 694 P.2d at 432. *But cf.* Rome, 678 P.2d at 152 (a person representing the State must be a "law-trained, independent public prosecutor rather than a vengeful prosecutor").

177. Pabst v. State, 192 P.3d 630, 633–34 (Kan. 2008).

178. *Id.* at 634.

179. *Id.*

180. *Id.* at 635.

181. *Id.* at 635–36.

182. *Id.* at 636–37 (citations omitted).

183. *Id.* at 640; *see also* id. at 638 ("Granted, we have pointed out that there is an inherent difference between the attorney occupying the public office of prosecutor and an attorney hired by the prosecuting witness to assist the public prosecutor. The public prosecutor is expected to be conflict-free, whereas we have acknowledged that the victim-retained 'assistant' comes to the table with built-in divided loyalties. Nevertheless, we need not exacerbate the inherent conflict by absolving the retained attorney of all of the prosecutorial constraints of K.S.A. 19–705. Therefore, we find the K.S.A. 19–717 attorney is subject to the statutory conflict rule of K.S.A. 19–705, *i.e.*, the victim-retained attorney is precluded from representing a party in a civil action that depends on the same state of facts as the ongoing criminal prosecution in which the attorney is assisting the public prosecutor."); *id.* at 639 ("Pabst does not identify a substantial right that has been unequivocally violated. He cites to a portion of the *Young* opinion that says the harm in having an interested party bring a contempt prosecution is that it creates '*opportunities* for conflicts to arise' and creates 'at least the *appearance* of impropriety.' 481 U.S. at 806, 107 S. Ct. 2124. However, we are directed by K.S.A. 60–261 to 'disregard any error or defect in the proceeding which does not affect the substantial rights of the parties.' The mere potential for having an effect on substantial rights is not excepted from the harmless error rule.").

184. Pabst v. McKune, 438 Fed. Appx. 674, 676 (10th Cir. 2011) ("Defendant's first contention is that Irigonegaray's conflicted role in his murder trial violated constitutional due process. On this issue we need not rely on AEDPA deference to the state court. We held in *Erikson v. Pawnee County Board of County Commissioners*, 263 F.3d 1151 (10th Cir.2001), that 'the participation of a privately-retained attorney in a state criminal prosecution does not violate the defendant's right to due process under federal law unless the private attorney effectively controlled critical prosecutorial decisions,' *id.* at 1154. Here, both the state trial court and the federal district court found that Irigonegaray did not have such control. Accordingly, this contention fails."). In 2021, after a local Kansas prosecutor declined to bring rape charges, a 22-year-old woman who alleged that what began as consensual sex in a college dorm room became a rape invoked a Kansas law to summon a grand jury. Peter Kendall, "Kansas Prosecutor Says No to a Rape Charge, So a College Student Calls Her Own Grand Jury," Star Tribune (Minneapolis, MN), May 19, 2021, https://www.startribune.com/kansas-prosecutor-says-no-to-a-rape-charge-so-a-college-student-calls-her-own-grand-jury/600059053/ ("Madison Smith will be just a few months out of college when her story is heard this fall by a most unusual Kansas grand jury—one she convened. For three years, the local prosecutor has resolutely refused to make her case: that what began as consensual sex in a college dorm room became a rape, and that she was unable to say 'stop' because her classmate was strangling her."); *id.* ("Smith invoked a vestige of frontier justice that allows citizens in Kansas to summon a grand jury when they think prosecutors are neglecting to bring charges in a crime. The law, dating to the 1800s, was originally used to go after saloonkeepers when authorities ignored violations of statewide prohibition. The 22-year-old graduate is believed to be the first to convene a citizen grand jury after a prosecutor declined to pursue a sex-crime charge."); *id.* ("Only five other states, all in the Great Plains or the West, have similar laws still on the books. The Kansas statute requires an individual to gather a certain number of signatures of support ...."); *id.* ("The 1887 Kansas law allow[s] citizens to go around reluctant prosecutors to seek an indictment on their own. A state appeals court looking into its origins cited contemporary newspaper reports saying it was intended to aid citizens frustrated with prosecutors who refused to enforce temperance laws. It was quickly successful, according to an 1889 story in the Topeka Capital-Commonwealth: 'As soon as the first grand jury met, every whisky joint, about seventy-five in the county, and every drug store selling without a license had disappeared. The long-dormant statute had been dusted off in this century by activists aiming to prosecute abortion providers and operators of adult bookstores. 'Kansas has the lowest threshold for bringing one of these petitions, so it makes it easy for someone who has an agenda to bring one,' said Marissa Hotujac, a Kansas attorney who as a law student published a legal journal article on citizen grand juries."). For more information on citizen grand juries, see Richard D. Younger, The People's Panel: The Grand Jury in the United States, 1634–1941, at 27–28 (1963) (discussing the influence of citizen grand juries); Marissa Hotujac, *The Jury Is Still Out: Should Kansas Continue to Allow Its Citizens to Initiate Grand*

Juries?, 29 KAN. J.L. & PUB. POL'Y 72, 73 (2019) ("Kansas is one of only six states to allow citizens to initiate a grand jury. Kansas's citizen-initiated grand jury law allows individuals to submit a petition to the court, and the court may then summon a grand jury to investigate the petitioner's allegations of suspected criminal wrongdoing. The petition must meet the substantive requirements listed in the Kansas grand jury statute, and it must be accompanied by signatures from electors in the county. In Kansas, a petition for a grand jury must include signatures from 100 voters in the county where the court sits, plus two percent of the total number of votes cast in the county's last gubernatorial election. After the legitimacy of the signatures on the petition is verified, the judge, or judges, of the district court will determine if the petition complies with the statutory requirements. If the court determines that the petition is in proper form and bears the requisite number of signatures, the court will summon a grand jury."). *See also* Roger Roots, *The Originalist Case for the Fourth Amendment Exclusionary Rule*, 45 GONZ. L. REV. 1, 11–12 (2010):

> Criminal procedure in the United States has literally been transformed over the course of American history. During the late eighteenth century, when the Constitution was debated and ratified, there were no professional police officers to enforce criminal laws. Criminal law enforcement was mostly the province of private citizens, who conducted investigations, made arrests and initiated complaints in criminal court. Constables and sheriffs were not salaried but instead paid by user fees. When a crime was alleged, a sheriff or constable might be given a warrant to arrest a suspect and draw upon other citizens in a posse comitatus to assist him.
>
> At the time of the American Revolution, many criminal cases were privately prosecuted without government attorneys general. The distinction between civil and criminal cases was still emerging, and most criminal accusations were simply controversies between private parties. Citizen grand juries investigated and indicted suspected criminals without the assistance—or even the approval—of government prosecutors. Searches and seizures by state officials were rare because the domain of the state was substantially smaller than it is today. Usually, a private person would complain to a justice of the peace or a grand jury and occasionally accompany constables on the search if a warrant was issued. When no constable was available, a justice or magistrate would deputize a private citizen to perform executive duties such as searches and arrests. Occasionally, private citizens served and executed their own search warrants after magistrates signed them.

185. Earl v. Commonwealth, 569 S.W.2d 686 (Ken. Ct. App. 1978) (citing Catron v. Commonwealth, 130 S.W. 951 (Ky. 1910); Tackett v. Commonwealth, 12 S.W.2d 289 (Ky. 1928); Fields v. Commonwealth, 9 S.W.2d 990 (Ky. 1928); Price v. Caperton, 62 Ky. 207 (1864)).

186. Commonwealth v. Hubbard, 777 S.W.2d 882, 883–84 (Ky. 1989).

187. State v. Boasberg, 50 So. 162, 165 (La. 1909).

188. LA. CODE CRIM. P., Art. 63.

189. State v. Petrich, 47 So. 438, 439 (La. 1908).

190. State ex rel. Stewart v. Reid, 37 So. 866, 867–68 (La. 1905) (citations omitted).

191. State v. Young, 476 A.2d 188, 187 (Me. 1984). *Compare* State v. McBreairty, 137 A.3d 1012, 1018 (Me. 2016) ("That a party has offered the court an accord and satisfaction signed by the injured party agreeing to dismiss the charges does not in itself, however, mandate dismissal of the charges. A court may reject a proffered accord and satisfaction and refuse to dismiss criminal charges; when the court does so, its decision is reviewed for an abuse of discretion.") (citing *State v. Young*); *id.* ("In this case, the accord and satisfaction offered by McBreairty was presented on the first day of trial. The court acted well within its discretion in deferring action on the motion until after the jury's verdict. By that time, the parties disputed the validity of the accord and satisfaction. The State offered a letter written by the executive director of North Maine Woods, who had signed the original accord and satisfaction, explaining that he had been misled as to the nature of the charges against McBreairty. The letter stated that if he had known the nature of the charges, he would not have signed the accord and satisfaction. Due to the lack of clarity regarding the validity of the accord and satisfaction offered, the court did not abuse its discretion in allowing the convictions on Counts 10 and 12 (theft of services) to stand.").

192. ME. REV. STAT. ANN. 15 § 1256.

193. Petition of Thomas, 434 A.2d 503, 508 (Me. 1981).

194. Md. R. Crim. R. 4-211(b)(1) ("*Before Any Arrest.* Except as otherwise provided by statute, a judicial officer may file a statement of charges in the District Court against a defendant who has not been arrested for that offense upon written application containing an affidavit showing probable cause that the defendant committed the offense charged. If not executed by a peace officer, the affidavit shall be made and signed before a judicial officer."); Md. R. Crim. R. 4-211(b)(2) ("*After Arrest.* When a defendant has been arrested without a warrant, unless an information is filed in the District Court, the officer who has custody of the defendant shall (A) forthwith cause a statement of charges to be filed against the defendant in the District Court and (B) at the same time or as soon thereafter as is practicable file an affidavit containing facts showing probable cause that the defendant committed the offense charged."); *see also* Md. Crim. Proc. § 11-105 ("On a finding of probable cause and before the issuance of an arrest warrant or a summons, a judicial officer shall provide to an individual filing an application for a statement of charges under Maryland Rule 4-211(b) an opportunity to request reasonable protections for the safety of an alleged victim or the victim's family.").

195. Applicant for Statement of Charges, District Court of Maryland, https://mdcourts.gov/sites/default/files/import/district/commissioners/forms/dccr001.pdf.

196. Brandy R. Cannon & Lauren M. Taylor, "Advocating within the Criminal Justice System," Maryland State Bar Association, Domestic Violence Cases: Handling Them Effectively in Maryland District and Circuit Courts (2017).

197. Victory Distribs., Inc. v. Ayer Div. of Dist. Ct. Dept., 755 N.E.2d 273 (Mass. Sup. Jud. Ct. 2001); *see also* Whitley v. Commonwealth, 369 Mass. 961, 962, 339 N.E.2d 890 (1975) (rights to pursue criminal prosecution "are not private but are in fact lodged in the Commonwealth as it may proceed to enforce its laws"); Commonwealth v. DiBennadetto, 764 N.E.2d 338, 340 (Mass. Sup. Jud. Ct., Suffolk, 2002) ("'[T]he right[ ] to pursue criminal prosecution '[is] not private but [is] in fact lodged in the Commonwealth as it may proceed to enforce its laws.'"") (citing Bradford v. Knights, 427 Mass. 748, 751, 695 N.E.2d 1068 (1998), quoting Whitley v. Commonwealth, 369 Mass. 961, 962, 339 N.E.2d 890 (1975)); Commonwealth v. Clerk of the Boston Division of the Juvenile Court Department, 738 N.E.2d 1124, 1128 (Mass. Sup. Jud. Ct., Suffolk, 2000) (same); Commonwealth v. Orbin O., 89 N.E.3d 1151, 1158 (Mass. Sup. Jud. Ct., Berkshire, 2018):

> We have noted that "[t]he right of a citizen to obtain a criminal complaint is itself something of an anomaly, because in modern times[,] the formal initiation and prosecution of criminal offenses is usually the domain of public officials. Accordingly, even where the Legislature has given a private party the opportunity to seek a criminal complaint, we have uniformly held that the denial of a complaint creates no judicially cognizable wrong." Bradford, 427 Mass. at 751, 695 N.E.2d 1068. See Victory Distribs., Inc., 435 Mass. at 142, 755 N.E.2d 273 ("a private party suffers no judicially cognizable wrong when its application for a criminal complaint is denied"); Taylor v. Newton Div. of the Dist. Court Dep't, 416 Mass. 1006, 1006, 622 N.E.2d 261 (1993) ("it is settled beyond cavil that a private citizen has no judicially cognizable interest in the prosecution of another").

See also Commonwealth v. Tuck, 37 Mass. 356, 364–65 (Mass. Sup. Jud. Ct. 1838) ("The authority of the attorney general, when present, to conduct and manage all criminal prosecutions, is unquestionable .... It is his exclusive duty to do so; and although he may seek assistance from his brethren of the bar, yet a private prosecutor has no right to employ counsel to aid him. *Commonwealth v. Knapp*, 10 Pick. 481. The law, in the district attorneys, has provided the proper assistance. In England, the practice is entirely different. There, in ordinary cases, criminal trials are conducted by counsel employed by the private prosecutor. It is true that in many respects the duties and powers of the attorney general in England and in this Commonwealth are similar, but in others they are dissimilar and diverse. And upon the question now before us, we derive little light from English books.").

198. Bradford v. Knights, 695 N.E.2d 1068, 1070–71 (Mass. Sup. Jud. Ct., Suffolk, 1998) (citing Whitley v. Commonwealth, 339 N.E.2d 890 (Mass. 1975) (the rights to pursue criminal prosecution "are not private but are in fact lodged in the Commonwealth as it may proceed to enforce its laws"); Taylor v. Newton Div. of the Dist. Court Dep't, 622 N.E. 261 (Mass. 1993) ("it is settled beyond cavil that a private citizen has no judicially cognizable interest in the prosecution of another"). As to misdemeanors, the Massachusetts

court ruled: "Perhaps this encourages a sense of public participation in the enforcement of the criminal law, and also these often more minor matters may include the frictions and altercations of daily life, which may not attract the attention of the police or the public prosecutor but yet may rankle enough that resolution is required if peace is to be maintained. It appears that clerks and magistrates often use the hearings which the statute requires as an occasion to effect an informal settlement of grievances, and if that happens regularly it is reason enough for the procedure." *See also* Katz v. Commonwealth, 399 N.E.2d 1055, 1060 (Mass. Sup. Jud. Ct. 1979) ("The power of the Housing Court to punish for contempt is confirmed by statute. G.L. c. 185C, s 3. "In numerous contempt cases a sentence has been imposed partly remedial and partly punitive, partaking both of civil and criminal features." Root v. MacDonald, 260 Mass. 344, 363, 157 N.E. 684, 691 (1927). Private parties to civil litigation have the right "to press both the civil and criminal aspects of the case." Id. at 365, 157 N.E. at 691. See Stow v. Marinelli, 352 Mass. 738, 745, 227 N.E.2d 708 (1967). Contrary to the landlord's contention, a private citizen may prosecute a purely criminal complaint in the Housing Court, as in a District Court. G.L. c. 185C, s 19. Commonwealth v. Haddad, 364 Mass. 795, 798, 308 N.E.2d 899 (1974).").

199. Commonwealth v. Ellis, 8 Mass. L. Rptr. 678 (Mass. Super. Ct. July 31, 1998).

200. People v. Williams, 625 N.W.2d 132, 134 (Mich. Ct. App. 2001); *see also id.* at 135 ("The authority to prosecute for violation of those offenses is vested solely and exclusively with the prosecuting attorney. Const. 1963, art. 7, § 4; MCL 49.153; MSA 5.751. A prosecutor, as the chief law enforcement officer of a county, is granted the broad discretion to decide whether to prosecute or what charges to file. *People v. Jackson,* 192 Mich. App. 10, 15, 480 N.W.2d 283 (1991); *Williams, supra* at 609, 465 N.W.2d 376. The prosecution is not for the benefit of the injured party, but for the public good. See *Morrow, supra* at 163, 542 N.W.2d 324. Crimes not only injure the victim, but society in general, and the conviction of a crime results not only in a sentence enumerating the punishment in quantitative amounts, but also carries with it society's formal moral condemnation.").

201. *Williams,* 625 N.W.2d at 135 (citations omitted).

202. Schneider v. Shepherd, 158 N.W. 182, 184 (Mich. 1916).

203. People v. Welch, 45 N.W. 482, 484 (Mich. 1890); *see also* People v. Hurst, 1 N.W. 1027, 1031–32 (Mich. 1879) ("We discover no error except in the allowance of assistance in the prosecution by the counsel of private prosecutors. We are not at liberty to overlook such an error from any impression that the conviction would have been had without him. The rejection of such prosecutors is in the public interest, and the rule is one which should be enforced."); People v. Meister, 31 Mich. 99, 101–07 (1875):

> At the opening of the trial an objection was made that counsel had been retained by private prosecutors, and at their expense, to aid in conducting the prosecution. Defendants offered to show this fact, and asked to have one of the assisting counsel sworn, who declined to be sworn, and the court refused to require him; and the prosecuting attorney stating the gentlemen referred to were acting at his request, the court permitted them to assist, and overruled the objection. This question has never been presented to the court before. Under the English practice, prosecution by private parties has been the rule rather than the exception, and there is no public prosecutor who has general charge of criminal business. The necessity of such an officer has been urged repeatedly by many of the ablest jurists; and the chief reason suggested has been the abuse of criminal proceedings for private ends, and the subordination of public justice to private control.
>
> In this country we have usually had in every state some officer, or class of officers, appointed for the express purpose of managing criminal business; but the extent and nature of their powers and duties have not been uniform. Sometimes the officers have been permanent, and sometimes counsel have been appointed by the courts to act for the term; and the duties have often been left under vague regulations. Under our territorial statutes, and until the Revised Statutes of 1838, the legislation was not very specific. But by the Revised Statutes of 1838 a regulation was introduced, that was borrowed from the laws of Massachusetts, and that has been preserved ever since. The prosecuting attorney of each county is required to prosecute all criminal cases in the courts of his county, and may be required also to appear for the same purpose before any magistrate, except in certain municipal courts. And he is expressly debarred from receiving any fee or reward from any private person for any services within his official business, and from being retained, except for

the public, in any civil action depending on the same state of facts on which a criminal prosecution shall depend.—*C. L., §§ 529, 530, 534.*

The courts may appoint counsel to act in his place when he is absent or unable to perform his duties, or where the office is vacant; but no other power of appointment is given. Any recognition of other counsel, if valid, can only be by the request of the prosecuting attorney. He cannot abdicate his duties, and the court cannot divide or relieve them, or give to other counsel any authority whatever, independent of his responsibility.—*U. S. v. Morris,* 1 Paine, 209; *Hite v. State,* 9 Yerg., 198; *Com. v. Knapp,* 10 Pick., 477; *Com. v. Williams,* 2 Cush. R., 582.

The question, therefore, seems to narrow itself to the inquiry whether or not the persons allowed to act at the request or by the assent of the prosecuting attorney are subject to any restrictions applicable to him, or whether they may act without reference to their relations to private parties.

It has been quite common in this state for prosecuting attorneys to be aided by counsel, and probably in some cases they have had the help of those retained by private prosecutors. As no objections have been taken in these cases, and no attention has been called to the statute, it cannot be said there has been any practical construction of the statute; and we are obliged to consider the case as one requiring the law to be enforced according to its fair meaning.

The mere appointment of public prosecutors is not inconsistent with private prosecutions, either separately or under official supervision. When the crown officers intervene at common law, they must, as we suppose, have control of the proceedings. The proposals in England to establish a new system do not aim at entirely destroying the right of private prosecution.--See *Edinburgh Review, No. 220, Art. 2, on Criminal Procedure in England and Scotland.* But so long as the present system exists, it appears to make it not only the right, but the duty, of individuals to complain of felonious crimes; and the disability against bringing private actions before prosecuting for felonies was imposed to encourage such complaints, and to ensure private diligence in bringing offenders to justice. The premiums offered to informers stand on a similar footing.

The policy of allowing *qui tam* actions has not been encouraged in this state, and criminal penalties have been devoted to public purposes. Neither is the felonious character of an injury held to prevent an action before, any more than after a criminal prosecution. And one of the reasons given for this is the establishment of public prosecutors.—*Hyatt v. Adams,* 16 Mich., 180.

It is impossible to account for the change in our statutes requiring the exclusive control of criminal procedure to be in the hands of public officers who are forbidden to receive pay or in anyway become enlisted in the interests of private parties, unless we assume the law to have been designed to secure impartiality from all persons connected with criminal trials. The law never has prevented, and does not now prevent, private complaints before magistrates, who have a discretion in regard to calling in the prosecuting attorney. In the ordinary course of things the case for the prosecution is brought out on that examination, and justice requires that it should be, where a defendant does not waive examination. But when the charge is presented on which the respondent is to be tried at the circuit (where he must be tried for all statutory and common-law felonies, except petit larceny), the law requires the public prosecutor to assume and retain exclusive charge of the cause, until the case is ended by acquittal or conviction. The chief dangers which the statute intends to guard against must be those attendant on the trial, inasmuch as the preliminary proceedings usually determine the nature and extent of the accusation, and those may be under the charge of private parties. And we must conclude that the legislature do not consider it proper to allow the course of the prosecuting officer during the trial to be exposed to the influence of the interests or passions of private prosecutors. His position is one involving a duty of impartiality not altogether unlike that of the judge himself. We have had occasion heretofore to refer to this duty in these officers of justice. Their position is a trying one, but the duty nevertheless exists, and the law has done much to remove hindrances to its performance, and in no case more plainly than by the prohibition in question here, and that against allowing a circuit judge to act as counsel in his own court, before another judge, as was done in *Bashford v. People,* 24 Mich., 245. See for illustrations *Wellar v. People,* 30 Mich., 16; *Wagner v. People,* 30 Mich., 384; *Hurd v. People,* 25 Mich., 416.

The courts of Massachusetts have passed upon their statute several times. It was first brought to their attention in the case of *Commonwealth v. Knapp,* 10 Pick. R., 477, where it appeared that Mr. Webster had aided without objection in the trial of the principal felon whose accessories were on trial, and that reliance had been had on his aid in the case at bar, and that he was acting without any pecuniary inducement. The court, under these circumstances, holding it had a right to allow the prosecuting officer to obtain help in a proper case, considered it admissible in that instance, but reserved their opinion as to any different circumstances, and laid stress upon the absence of any interest in Mr. Webster beyond "a disinterested regard for the public good." In *Commonwealth v. Williams,* 2 Cush., 582, a similar course was sustained, but the court said it could only be allowed for stringent reasons, and referred again to the absence of any pecuniary compensation from any private individual. They said that such counsel is not under ordinary circumstances to be permitted, yet, when sanctioned by the court under the limitations suggested, it would not furnish sufficient ground for setting aside the verdict. In *Commonwealth v. Gibbs,* 4 Gray, 146, a conviction was set aside because the court had, in the absence of the district attorney, appointed counsel to act in his place, who had been retained by private parties in civil litigation of the same matter. In *Commonwealth v. King,* 8 Gray, 501, a gentleman was allowed to act as counsel who had acted in aid of the prosecution on the preliminary examination, and had also sat upon a commission of inquest concerning the fire which was the occasion of the prosecution. The court held this peculiar familiarity with the facts would make his help valuable; and no suggestion was made by anyone that he was not disinterested, as no interested person, it must be supposed, would have been allowed to sit on the commission.

The supreme court of Maine, in *State v. Bartlett,* 55 Maine, 200, allowed Gen. Shepley to act with the prosecuting attorney, though under retainer from the insurance company at whose instance the case was prosecuted; and disposed of the Massachusetts cases by saying that in the only one where the conviction was set aside, the counsel complained of was in effect acting district attorney, and so within the words of the statute, which they held should only apply to that officer.

The Massachusetts court, in both of the earlier cases, made the absence of compensation a prominent feature; and in all the cases, spoke of the employment of associates as exceptional, and not generally allowable. They do not bear out the Maine decision in their reasoning. And that can only stand on its own reasoning, upon the assumption that the control of the prosecuting attorney will destroy any influence or mischief which might result from the private interests of his colleagues.

But a theory which holds them as any thing but his deputies, or assistants in office, would render it difficult to reconcile their appearance with the law, which compels him to conduct the prosecution. Such counsel, in the courts of the United States, are required to take the oath of office, and are made expressly public officers.—*16 L. U. S., 165.* The experience of trials shows that any other position is fallacious. When counsel are introduced into a cause, and aid in the trial or argument, it is little short of absurd to suppose they can be prevented from having their own way. It would be unseemly and unprofitable for one counsel, during a trial, to interfere with his associate's questions or argument; and competent auxiliaries would not be engaged on terms which would subject them to open slights. We must look at things as they exist; and every one knows that if a prosecuting attorney allows the counsel of private parties to intervene, it must usually be for the reason that they will save him labor, and assume the burden of the prosecution. The mischief which the law aims to avoid is, prosecution by interested parties; and if such is the policy of the law, it ought to be carried out. It does not assume that there is anything dishonorable in such employment, but it does assume that it is not proper to entrust the administration of criminal justice to any one who will be tempted to use it for private ends, and it assumes that a retainer from private parties tends to this.

The great scandals which have occurred from the abuse of criminal process to further purposes of gain or vindictiveness, have often demanded notice; and no better remedy has been suggested than the policy of our statute. It does not prevent any one from hunting up proofs, or furnishing every facility to the officers of the law. But it will be very inefficient, if it is possible to allow those who have a direct pecuniary interest in convicting a prisoner, to take an active part in his trial. Until the legislature see fit to restore the common-law rule, and leave cases to private prosecution, it must be assumed that they regard it as unsafe, and opposed to even-handed justice.

204. Bay County Prosecutor v. Bay County District Judge, 311 N.W.2d 399, 402 (Mich. Ct. App. 1981).

205. Betzoldt v. Travis, Docket No. 280942, 2008 WL 4762363, at *1 (Mich. Ct. App. Oct. 30, 2008) (citations omitted); *see also* Walsh v. Taylor, 689 N.W.2d 506, 516–17 (Mich. Ct. App. 2004) ("In maintaining a claim of malicious prosecution, a plaintiff bears the burden of proving that (1) the defendant has initiated a criminal prosecution against him, (2) the criminal proceedings terminated in his favor, (3) the private person who instituted or maintained the prosecution lacked probable cause for his actions, and (4) the action was undertaken with malice or a purpose in instituting the criminal claim other than bringing the offender to justice."); Matthews v. Blue Cross and Blue Shield of Michigan, 572 N.W.2d 603, 612–13 (Mich. 1998) ("The plaintiff failed to show that defendant's agents instituted the proceeding or maintained it. The prosecutor authorized the warrant, and Detective Waldron was the complainant. The warrant request was based on Waldron's independent investigation, not on the information the defendant's agent submitted. As the chief law enforcement officer of the county, a prosecutor has independent authority to initiate criminal prosecutions. M.C.L. § 764.1; M.S.A. § 28.860. A warrant may not be issued without the prosecutor's written authorization unless security for costs is given. *Bloss v. Williams,* 15 Mich.App. 228, 233, 166 N.W.2d 520 (1968). Thus, in Michigan, the prosecutor's exercise of his independent discretion in initiating and maintaining a prosecution is a complete defense to an action for malicious prosecution. *Christy v. Rice,* 152 Mich. 563, 565, 116 N.W. 200 (1908).").

206. Rastelli v. Rastelli, Docket No. 317547, 2014 WL 7157415, at *4 (Mich. Ct. App. Dec. 16, 2014) ("Respondent next argues that the court violated his constitutional rights when it allowed petitioner's lawyer to prosecute him for criminal contempt. Under Michigan law, the party who procured a PPO may hire a lawyer to prosecute a criminal contempt arising from the violation of the PPO. MCL 764.15b(7); MCR 3.708(G). And this Court has already rejected a challenge to the constitutionality of these provisions under federal law. See *DeGeorge v. Warheit,* 276 Mich.App 587, 392–393; 741 NW2d 384 (2007). The trial court did not err by permitting petitioner's lawyer to prosecute the contempt.").

207. In re Contempt of Mitan, Nos. 222230 & 222231, 2002 WL 31082190, at *10 (Mich. Ct. App. Sept. 17, 2002).

208. 257 N.W.2d 361, 364–65 (Minn. 1977) ("In arguing that a private citizen has a right to commence and maintain a criminal prosecution, plaintiff makes many of the arguments that are made in the leading law review article on the subject. What plaintiff neglects to mention is that the authors of the comment concluded that legislative authority was needed for a system of permitting private prosecution. Comment, 65 Yale L.J. 209, 233."; "Plaintiff has not cited and we have not found any authority justifying the instant actions. This is not surprising because to permit such prosecutions would entail grave danger of vindictive use of the processes of the criminal law and could well lead to chaos in the administration of criminal justice."), *cert. denied* 434 U.S. 1003 (1978).

209. *Wild,* 257 N.W.2d at 365; *see also* Peterson v. Peterson, 153 N.W.2d 825, 830 (Minn. 1967) ("We also believe that constructive criminal contempts should not be prosecuted by attorneys other than those representing the state.").

210. State v. Johnson, Nos. C4-92-2517 & C6-92-2518, 1993 WL 205242, at *2 (Minn. Ct. App. June 15, 1993); *see also* Miller v. Minneapolis Underwriters Ass'n, 33 N.W.2d 48, 52 (Minn. 1948) ("Whether a private citizen may be authorized to conduct a criminal action need not be determined.").

211. "Non-Felony Prosecution: A Best Practices Review," https://www.auditor.leg.state.mn.us/ped/pedrep/9707-sum.pdf; *see also* "Non-Felony Prosecution—A Best Practice Review," Office of the Legislative Auditor, State of Minnesota, Report #97-07, Apr. 1997, https://www.leg.mn.gov/docs/pre2003/other/970245.pdf.

212. *E.g.*, Request for Qualifications and Proposals to Provide Prosecution Legal Services to the Cities of Buffalo, Annandale, and Howard Lake, City of Buffalo, County of Wright, State of Minnesota (Feb. 2020), https://www.ci.buffalo.mn.us/wp-content/uploads/2020/02/request-for-proposal-prosecution-services-2020.pdf; Request for Proposals for Attorney Services, City of Northfield, June 2009, https://icma.org/sites/default/files/302066_approve-rfp-for-city-attorney-services-motion-attachment.pdf.

213. City of Virginia, Minnesota Request for Proposals for Legal Services (Oct. 9, 2019), http://www.virginiamn.us/docs/RFP%20Atty%20Services%202019.pdf.

214. Press release, "Dorsey & Whitney Ends Misdemeanor Prosecutions Program," Dorsey & Whitney, June 2, 2020, https://www.dorsey.com/newsresources/news/press-releases/2020/06/dorsey-ends-misdemeanor-prosecutions-program; see also Final Report, "Low Level Offenses in Minneapolis: An Analysis of Arrests and Their Outcomes," Council of Crime and Justice (Nov. 2004), p. 3 (a study done by Julie Atella, Becky Ericson, Laura Schauben, Ebony Ruhland and Tom Johnson found that Black citizens "were 15 times more likely" to be arrested than whites" and "7 times more likely" than whites to be convicted).

215. Miss. Code Ann. 7-5-5(b):

> The Attorney General may employ outside counsel as special assistant attorneys general on a fee or contract basis; the Attorney General shall be the sole judge of the compensation in such cases except as otherwise provided in Section 7-5-8.
>
> (i) Any contract for services of outside counsel shall require current and complete written time and expense records that describe in detail the time, in increments of no greater than one tenth (1/10) of an hour, and money spent each day in performance of the contract.
>
> (ii) On conclusion of the matter for which the outside legal services were obtained, outside counsel shall provide a complete written statement of all fees and expenses, and the final complete time and expense records.

216. Goldsby v. State, 123 So.2d 429, 437 (Miss. 1960):

> This Court takes judicial notice of the fact that it has been the custom in this State from time immemorial for individuals interested in the punishment of an accused, such as the husband of the deceased, to employ a special prosecutor in whom they have particular confidence to assist the State's attorney in the prosecution. This practice has been uniformly permissible in this State. Edwards v. State, 1873, 47 Miss. 581, 587; Carlisle v. State, 1895, 73 Miss. 387, 394–395, 19 So. 207. It represents a common law practice, and that of a large majority of the states of the Union.
>
> The rule, with citations of numerous authorities supporting it, is summarized in 42 Am. Jur., Prosecuting Attorneys, Sec. 10: 'At common law, criminal prosecutions were generally carried on by individuals interested in the punishment of the accused, and not by the public.
>
> The private prosecutor employed his own counsel, had the indictment found and the case laid before the grand jury, and took charge of the trial before the petit jury. While under the present practice officers are appointed or elected for the express purpose of managing criminal business, the old practice survives in most jurisdictions to the extent that counsel employed by the complaining witness or by other persons desirous of a conviction are permitted to assist the prosecuting attorney in the conduct of the prosecution, and as a general rule no valid objection can be raised by the accused to allowing the prosecuting attorney to have the assistance of private members of the bar.'
>
> Moreover, the employment of a special prosecutor by the husband of the deceased and his participation in the trial of the case, in addition to the several official legal representatives of the state, was not a violation of Code Sec. 2521. The restriction there is that only two counsel for the state 'shall be heard', which quoted phrase is confined to arguments of counsel for the state after the evidence has been presented to the jury. The trial court limited the argument of counsel to two counsel for the State and two for the defendant. Moreover, Sec. 2521 places the ultimate decision in the discretion of the trial court, and there is no evidence which indicates any abuse of that discretion.

217. Jordan v. State, 912 So.2d 800, 810, 821–22 (Miss. 2005) (quoting Faulder v. Johnson, 81 F.3d 515, 517 (5th Cir. 1996)).

218. *Id.* at 822 (citation omitted).

219. Hollingsworth v. State, 852 So.2d 612, 617 (Miss. Ct. App. 2003):

> Hollingsworth asserts that his due process rights were violated when Martin Kilpatrick was appointed special prosecutor because, at that time, the State lost control over the prosecution of Hollingsworth. He cites *Jordan v. State*, 786 So.2d 987, 1011 (¶ 75) (Miss. 2001) as support for his contention that control of the prosecution must remain under the control of the district attorney.

> Hollingsworth contends that the district attorney's loss of control is evidenced by Kilpatrick's motion to revoke bond after the district attorney's office had agreed not to revoke bond, by requesting that Hollingsworth's guilty plea be rejected after the State had agreed to the plea agreement, and by Kilpatrick's request to the trial judge that the maximum sentence be given, in violation of the plea agreement that the State would remain silent on the matter of sentencing.
>
> The State contends that Hollingsworth's due process rights were not violated because the special prosecutor, Martin Kilpatrick, did not control crucial prosecutorial decisions such as the targets of the prosecution, decisions whether to prosecute, what investigative powers to use, sanctions to seek, plea bargains to strike, or immunities to grant. The State agrees with Hollingsworth that a district attorney must retain control of the prosecution when a special prosecutor is appointed, but, as might be expected, differs with Hollingsworth's assessment as to who remained in control. We have reviewed the record and find that the State did maintain control of this case. The district attorney decided to allow Hollingsworth to plead guilty to a lesser charge of manslaughter in spite of the special prosecutor's opposition. The State did not renege on the plea agreement, and notwithstanding Hollingsworth's assertions to the contrary, the record does not support his emphatic contention that the State agreed not to pursue an increase or revocation of his bond. The record reflects that at best some confusion or misunderstanding occurred between the district attorney's office, the court, and Hollingsworth's counsel concerning the State's intention regarding Hollingsworth's bond. Nevertheless, we are at a loss to understand the point Hollingsworth seeks to make regarding the bond issue since the trial judge neither increased nor revoked Hollingsworth's bond.

220. 81 F.3d 515, 517 (5th Cir. 1996). In *Jordan*, the Supreme Court of Mississippi had this to say about the *Faulder* decision:

> The Fifth Circuit has ruled that, where special prosecutors are appointed, district attorneys must "retain control of the prosecution." *Faulder v. Johnson*, 81 F.3d 515, 517 (5th Cir.1996). In *Faulder*, Hill, a special prosecutor, had participated in the defendant's first trial as an assistant district attorney.
>
> The other special prosecutor, Burleson, was a former prosecutor and a well known criminal defense attorney. When the resulting conviction was overturned due to the erroneous admission of the defendant's confession, Burleson was hired by the victim's family to determine whether a second prosecution was possible without the use of the confession. The district attorney assigned an assistant with two years of experience to help Hill and Burleson during the trial. The defendant complained that the use of special prosecutors violated his constitutional rights. The Fifth Circuit held that, because of "Hill's prior relationship with the district attorney's office, the frequent communication between counsel and clear understanding of the district attorney's final decision-making authority," the district attorney controlled the defendant's prosecution.

Jordan, 786 So.2d at 1011.

221. *Jordan*, 786 So.2d at 1011.

222. State v. Swartz, 517 S.W.3d 40, 53–54 (Mo. 2017); State v. Kroenung, 188 S.W.3d 89, 92–93 (Mo. Ct. App. 2006); *see also* State ex rel. Bennett v. Ravens, 258 S.W.3d 929, 931 (Mo. Ct. App. 2008) (finding that a judge "inappropriately interfered" with plea agreement discussions and "abused his discretion in appointing a special prosecutor from the attorney general's office").

223. State v. Stewart, 869 S.W.2d 86, 90 (Mo. Ct. App. 1993); *see also id.* ("Stewart's motion to dismiss, in which he requested the appointment of a special prosecutor on those grounds, was necessarily directed to the trial court's sound discretion. The only evidence Stewart adduced in support of his request for a special prosecutor was contained in an affidavit supporting his motion, in which Stewart stated that shortly before being stopped for speeding, he had voted in the Democratic primary for David Raithel, who was running against then Boone County Prosecutor Joe Moseley. The trial court did not abuse its discretion in refusing to disqualify Moseley on the basis of this evidence, which is conclusory at best and wholly insufficient to justify disqualification.") (citing Mo. Stat. § 56.110 (1986); State v. Choate, 722 S.W.2d 643, 647 (Mo. App. 1986); State v. Harris, 477 S.W.2d 42, 45 (Mo. 1972)).

224. 534 S.W.2d 44 (Mo. 1976) (en banc).

225. *Id.* at 48.

226. *Id.* at 50. Thus, the court held that the use of a private prosecutor should not be permitted on retrial of the case or "in any case tried after publication of this opinion in the Southwestern Reporter." *Id.* at 48. A dissenting opinion in *Harrington* would have upheld the use of private prosecutors. "My dissent," Judge Holman wrote, "is based on the point which rules that privately employed attorneys may no longer assist prosecuting attorneys in this state." *Id.* at 50 (Holman, J., dissenting). According to that dissenting opinion: "The practice of employing private counsel is rarely used in this state. I see no necessity for this court, however, to decree that the practice is absolutely outlawed." *Id.* at 52. Since the *Harrington* decision, the Missouri Court of Appeals for the Western District has reaffirmed that, in *Harrington*, "our Supreme Court has recognized that to allow private prosecutors, employed by private citizens, to participate in the prosecution of a defendant 'is inherently and fundamentally unfair.'" Damon v. City of Kansas City, 419 S.W.3d 162 (Mo. Ct. App. 2013) (citing State v. Harrington, 534 S.W.2d 44, 48 (Mo. 1976)); *see also* Crow v. Crawford & Co., 259 S.W.3d 104, 117, (Mo. Ct. App. 2008) ("Green did not participate at the criminal trial of Mr. Crow.... Even if true [that Green transported witnesses to the criminal prosecution], these same witnesses were his clients, whom he had represented in their depositions, and transportation hardly amounts to acting as a private prosecutor in the manner forbidden by the Missouri Supreme Court in *State v. Harrington*, 534 S.W.2d 44 (Mo. Banc 1976). Point denied."); State *ex rel.* O'Brien v. Moreland, 778 S.W.2d 400, 406–07 (Mo. Ct. App. 1989) (upholding a private prosecution for criminal contempt).

227. 534 S.W.2d 44 (Mo. 1976) (en banc).

228. *Id.* at 48; *see also id.* at 49 ("This Court has recognized the inherent vice and potential prejudice arising from the participation of privately retained prosecutors in the prosecution of criminal defendants, but, nevertheless, has yet to strike down a conviction because of a private prosecutor's participation. The decisions have cast the burden on the defendant to allege and prove prejudice. We have come to believe that, by reason of the public policy enunciated by the Legislature, such a burden is unwarranted."); Crow v. Crawford & Co., 259 S.W.3d 104, 117 (Mo. Ct. App., Eastern Dist. 2008):

> Appellants also contend that Green acted as a private prosecutor. The record reflects that this contention is not supported by summary judgment facts. Green was present at several depositions that Assistant AG did not attend. However, Green was not representing the State of Missouri, but rather was present representing the deponents, who had a right to counsel. While it is true that the court reporter erroneously noted that Green was representing the State, Assistant AG stated in his deposition that this was a mistake, and that he had contacted Green and the court reporter to correct that error. Assistant AG's deposition also states that while Green was erroneously listed as representing the State in several depositions, the record of those same depositions also indicated that Green was there on behalf of the deponent and on behalf of Cassens. Green did not participate at the criminal trial of Mr. Crow. Appellants also argue in their brief that Green transported several witnesses to the criminal prosecution of Mr. Crow. Even if true, these same witnesses were his clients, whom he had represented in their depositions, and transportation hardly amounts to acting as a private prosecutor in the manner forbidden by the Missouri Supreme Court in *State v. Harrington*, 534 S.W.2d 44 (Mo. banc 1976). Point denied.

229. State v. Trueman, 85 P. 1024, 1026 (Mont. 1906).

> Thomas D. Long, an attorney, was employed by Mrs. McCabe, relict of James McCabe, the deceased, to assist in the prosecution, and from the record it appears that he assumed the role of leading counsel for the state and did most of the work of interrogating witnesses at the trial. During the course of the trial Mr. Long's conduct became the subject of many protests from counsel for the defendant, and it is urged that the district court abused its discretion in permitting him to continue in the case, and that his conduct was such as to prevent the defendant from having a fair trial. There may be some question as to whether these matters are properly presented in the record. This we do not determine. The matters are discussed as though properly before us, except that the attorney general contends that the objection to privately employed counsel appearing for the state should have been made before or at the time the trial commenced.

230. State v. Tighe, 71 P. 3, 6 (Mont. 1903), *overruled on other grounds*, State v. Sherman, 90 P. 981, 982 (Mont. 1907); *see also Tighe*, 71 P.3d at 5–6:

> At the beginning of the trial the defendant objected to the appearance in behalf of the state of R. R. Purcell, Esq., whose name had, on motion of the county attorney, been entered as an assistant to that officer, on the ground that Mr. Purcell had been employed by private prosecutors, by whom, and by whom alone, he was to be compensated. In support of the objection the defendant offered to prove the truth of the averments, but the court refused to permit this to be done, and overruled the objection. Much might be said in favor of the action of the court, and much against it. Many courts declare that counsel employed and compensated by private persons may, with the court's consent, assist in the prosecution of criminal cases. State v. Wilson, 24 Kan. 189, 36 Am. Rep. 257; U. S. v. Hanway, 2 Wall. Jr. 139, 26 Fed. Cas. 105, 129 (No. 15,-299); Polin v. State, 14 Neb. 540, 16 N. W. 898; Bradshaw v. State, 17 Neb. 147, 22 N. W. 361, 5 Am. Cr. Rep. 499; State v. Bartlett, 55 Me. 200, 220; Hopper v. Com., 6 Grat. 684; Siebert v. State, 95 Ind. 471, 476. And see 1 Bish. Cr. Proc. § 251, and People v. Blackwell, 27 Cal. 66. Other courts have interpreted statutory provisions prohibiting the state's attorney from receiving any compensation from or in behalf of any prosecutor for his services in a criminal case as preventing the appearance for the state of counsel employed by or in behalf of private persons. Biemel v. State, 71 Wis. 444, 37 N. W. 244; Meister v. People, 31 Mich. 99; People v. Hurst, 41 Mich. 328, 1 N. W. 1027; Com. v. Knapp, 10 Pick. 477, 20 Am. Dec. 534; and Com. v. Williams, 2 Cush. 582.

Accord State v. Whitworth, 66 P. 748, 750–51 (Mont. 1901):

> It appears from the record that the county attorney of Broadwater county appeared in open court and asked that the county attorney of Meagher county and Max Waterman, Esq., be appointed to assist him in the trial of the cause, at the same time filing his affidavit setting forth that he (the county attorney of Broadwater county) was then and there physically unable to assume the entire burden of the prosecution; and the court, finding that the attorney general was absent from the county of Broadwater, and that the cause was then ready for trial, granted the motion of the said county attorney of Broadwater county, and said county attorney of Meagher county and the said Max Waterman, Esq., were then appointed by the court to assist in the prosecution of the cause, and the objection of the defendant to the appearance of said parties as assistants to the county attorney of Broadwater county was then and there overruled. At the time of the making of the defendant's objection, his counsel made and filed the affidavit of said counsel to the effect that the county attorney of Broadwater county was not sufficiently ill to prevent him from giving the necessary attention to the case. It appears also that the said Waterman had been, before the defendant's preliminary examination in Meagher county, employed by the chairman of the board of county commissioners of Meagher county as special counsel to assist in prosecuting the charge, and had appeared for the state at said examination. It does not appear that any one of the three attorneys appearing for the state had received or been promised any compensation by any one whomsoever, except possibly such compensation as may be inferred as promised because of the employment of Mr. Waterman by the chairman of the board of county commissioners of Meagher county. Defendant's counsel, in his argument, inquires: First, "What county attorney prosecutes in Broadwater county?" and, second, "May the court permit a private attorney to represent the state in prosecuting a criminal charge?" In the light of the provisions of the Penal Code pertinent to the matter, it is apparent what answer must be given to the first question; that is to say, the county attorney of the county to which the cause is removed must prosecute, in the same manner as if the action had been begun in that county. Counsel cites a large number of authorities tending to show that the court may not, over the objection of the defendant in a criminal action, permit a "private attorney" to represent the state in the prosecution. Examination of these authorities not only shows that they are not relevant to the question raised in the record at the time of the objection of the defendant to the appearance of the assistant attorneys, but at least one of them (Com. v. Knapp, 10 Pick. 477, 20 Am. Dec. 534) even fails to support the proposition advocated by counsel for defendant,—that the statute which declares who shall prosecute excludes the appointment of other attorneys by the court over the objection of the defendant; the case referred to being one wherein Mr. Webster was allowed to appear as counsel for the prosecution, over the objection of the defendant, upon the request of the prosecution. It is not necessary to pass in this

> opinion upon the question asked by the counsel, for it does not appear that the county attorney of Meagher county or Mr. Waterman, in any wise, in this case, was a "private attorney." A private attorney, as in the view of the courts whose opinions are cited by counsel, is an attorney employed by, and in the interest of, private persons, and not paid out of public funds. He is one who has a special interest in the securing of a conviction, being employed by private persons to prosecute. He is not one who, like a public prosecutor, is presumed to do his duty in an earnest and faithful manner, impartially, and with the sole purpose of presenting the whole truth to the court and jury, both as to law and facts. We do not find anything in the record to show that either of the two assistant counsel appointed by the court was employed in the interest of any private person. It is contended by counsel in the argument that the county may have assistance only as provided in sections 4318 and 4319 of the Political Code, except that the attorney general may appear, and that the court, when it finds itself "without a prosecuting officer," may "supply one temporarily." The two sections of the Political Code do not apply, as they are intended to provide for as many deputies in the office of any county officer, except a county commissioner and a justice of the peace, "as may be necessary for the faithful and prompt discharge of the duties of his office." It is obvious that these provisions do not pertain to the appointment by the court of such assistant counsel as it may think necessary in the prosecution of any particular criminal case, when, in the opinion of the court, owing to the physical weakness of the county attorney, assistance is needed. We think the great weight of authority is in support of our opinion that the court may legally, in its discretion, appoint counsel from the members of its bar to assist the prosecution, over the objection of the defendant, and that no error was made by the court in the present case in the matter. In support of our position that the statute declaring who shall be charged with the duty of prosecuting persons charged with crime does not exclude the power of the court to appoint assistant counsel, we refer to the numerous citations in Tull v. State, 99 Ind. 238, wherein the court says that: "The people do not surrender the right to employ just means of prosecuting criminals by choosing an officer and charging him with the special duty of prosecuting the pleas of the state. *** The community does not avow that it will not employ counsel to assist him when the occasion demands." Numerous other authorities might be cited.

231. Shelton C. Williams, Note, *Discretion Exercised by Montana County Attorneys in Criminal Prosecutions*, 28 MONT. L. REV. 41, 49 n.31 (1966) (citing State v. Moran, 384 P.2d 777, 788 (Mont. 1963) ("The fact that counsel appearing to assist a county attorney upon the trial of an action receives compensation from independent sources does not make him a party in interest so it could be charged that he has a financial interest in the prosecution.")).

232. State v. Warnick, 699 P.2d 1049, 1052 (Mont. 1985); *see also* Portland Cattle Loan Co. v. Featherly, 241 P. 322, 328 (Mont. 1925):

> The authorities quite generally agree that a contract which tends to suppress the investigation of a criminal offense is illegal, even though it does not amount to compounding a crime, and this for the reason that such a contract is contrary to good morals and public policy. 13 C. J. 449; 17 A. L. R. 326. The rule is stated concisely in 2 Page on the Law of Contracts, § 919, as follows:
>
> "Criminal prosecutions should be instituted, conducted or dismissed, as the case may be, solely for the good of organized society and not for the private gain of prosecuting witnesses, prosecuting attorneys, or third persons. Accordingly, a contract by which A agrees to pay B. a thing of value, in consideration that B. will refrain from instituting a criminal proceeding or will dismiss a criminal proceeding which has already been instituted, and which is entered into for the private gain of the promisee, is illegal. Such a contract is invalid although the accused is not under arrest. The fact that the accused is not guilty of the crime does not render such contract valid."

233. Koch v. Grimminger, 223 N.W.2d 833, 837 (Neb. 1974) ("We hold that a public prosecutor, acting within the general scope of his official authority in making a determination whether to file a criminal prosecution, is exercising a quasi-judicial and discretionary function and that where he acts in good faith he is immune from suit for an erroneous or negligent determination. This rule would not protect a prosecutor who, knowing that a particular charge is groundless in law or in fact, nonetheless intentionally files

a charge and thus acts through a corrupt motive. In such a case he would not be acting within the scope of his authority.").

234. State v. Warford, 389 N.W.2d 575, 582 (Neb. 1986) (citing McKay v. State, 132 N.W. 741 (Neb. 1911); Rogers v. State, 149 N.W. 318 (Neb. 1914)); *see also* Snide v. Smith, 167 N.W. 573, 573 (Neb. 1918):

> While Snide was cultivating a field of corn, Smith was likewise engaged in a contiguous cabbage patch. Under a lease Smith claimed a share of the corn as rental for the land, and asserted the right to participate in its cultivation. Snide had undertaken to raise the corn on the shares, and disputed Smith's right to cultivate it under existing conditions. After a controversy between the two, a warrant for Snide's arrest was issued on a complaint filed by Smith. In a few days each party, with his counsel, appeared before the justice of the peace who had issued the warrant. Snide objected to being prosecuted by private counsel. The county attorney had not been consulted about the filing of the complaint, had not personally investigated the facts, declined on behalf of the county to incur liability for costs under the circumstances, and refused to prosecute Snide under Smith's complaint. The justice of the peace excluded private counsel for the prosecution, and the proceeding was consequently dismissed, without a trial or a finding on the merits of the case. The present suit by Snide against Smith for malicious prosecution followed.

See also Flege v. State, 142 N.W. 276, 277–78 (Neb. 1913):

> It appears from the record, and as shown by our former opinion, that the principal witness on the part of the state, one Albert Eichtencamp, who testified to having seen defendant kill his sister (Louise Flege), had testified to a different state of facts at the coroner's inquest, the effect of which was the complete exoneration of defendant. While the witness was never arrested nor charged in any legal proceeding with the commission of the crime, there appears to have arisen a known suspicion on the part of some that he might be the guilty party. He and his relatives employed an attorney to assist in the prosecution of defendant at the preliminary trial, and upon the former trial in the district court, evidently under the belief that the conviction of defendant would remove all suspicion from Eichtencamp. The attorney appeared and took an active part in the prosecution at the two trials, and was paid for his services by Eichtencamp and his relatives. After the cause was removed to Thurston county, the state was represented by the county attorney of Dixon county and the county attorney of Thurston county, when application was made to the court for the appointment of Eichtencamp's former attorney to assist the two county attorneys in the prosecution of the case in the approaching trial. The application was resisted upon the ground that the attorney's former employment as a private prosecutor, employed by Eichtencamp, rendered him an improper person to have charge or any part in the prosecution, the purpose of which was for the protection of Eichtencamp. The attorney was called to the stand and candidly stated his relations with Eichtencamp, which continued up to the close of the former trial, which resulted in the conviction of defendant. The objection of defendant was overruled, the appointment made, and the attorney entered upon and took an active part throughout the trial, making, to say the least, a vigorous argument to the jury, which in some respects we cannot approve. While we intend no personal reflections upon the attorney, yet we do not hesitate to say that the appointment should not have been made and that it was prejudicial error to make it. It is impossible to conceive of an attorney, after having served Eichtencamp as he had and for the purpose for which he had been employed, to enter upon the trial with the single purpose of impartially seeking to know the truth, protecting the rights of defendant, and seeing that they were maintained, if need be, at all hazards. Not only this court, but all courts, have so clearly stated the judicial duties of a public prosecutor as to leave no room for doubt as to the entire impartial attitude of a prosecutor so as to leave no room for question upon this point. In Liniger v. State, 85 Neb. 98, 122 N. W. 705, we said: "Public prosecutors and peace officers owe no greater obligation to the public than to a defendant charged with crime, and they should as zealously protect the one as the other." This being true and maintained by all courts, it must appear to the mind at once that the appointment of a partisan special prosecutor was not in the interest of the fair and impartial trial guaranteed by the Constitution. The obligation of an attorney to his client, when once employed in a particular case or matter, can never be shaken off. It is a perpetual obligation, which abides to the end

of life, unless, in a proper case, waived by the client. With this obligation resting upon the memory of a conscientious lawyer, as the appointee no doubt was and is, it would be impossible for him to forget his sworn duty to his former client, and there would be a constant inclination to ask of himself: "What effect will this evidence or argument have upon the rights of my first client to whom I am still bound by every principle of law and honor? I should be faithful to my trust and protect Eichtencamp in every way possible. If defendant is convicted, Eichtencamp is forever cleared of the suspicion resting against him." We are forced to the conclusion that no honest and conscientious attorney could be able, nor should he, if he could, withstand such an appeal.

McMartin v. State, 145 N.W. 695, 701 (Neb. 1914) (Hamer, J., dissenting):

It is well to remember that it is a serious thing to go to the penitentiary even just one year. Mr. Harrington went into the case of McKay v. State, 90 Neb. 63, 132 N. W. 741, 39 L. R. A. (N. S.) 714, Ann. Cas. 1913B, 1034, at the "request" of the county attorney, at least the county attorney was not unwilling, and by "the order of the court * * * is permitted to assist the county attorney in the prosecution of this case." Now the substantial objection to Mr. Harrington was the *private interest* he had in the case, being employed and "paid by the brothers and sisters of the deceased." This same objection to private counsel is further emphasized in Flege v. State, 93 Neb. 610, 142 N. W. 276, where it is held that "no attorney should be appointed who is known to be a partisan as against the accused, and who has theretofore been employed and paid by another suspected person." If the doctrine applied to the McKay and Flege Cases, and which seems mainly responsible for their reversal, should be applied to the instant case, it is difficult to see how McMartin had a fair trial, because Mr. Patrick had a *private interest* to sustain by securing McMartin's conviction, not a private interest existing because of fees which had been paid him in some other proceeding, but Mr. Patrick was not the county attorney of Sarpy county, and he was in the case as Mr. Harrington was in the McKay Case, and as private counsel was in the Flege Case, by request of other counsel, and by permission of the court, and he had a *personal interest* in the enforcement of the amendment of which he was the author.

235. State v. Borchardt, 395 N.W.2d 551, 558 (Neb. 1986), *overruled on other grounds*, State v. Baue, 607 N.W.2d 191, 195 (Neb. 2000).

236. Barr v. State, 211 N.W. 188, 188–89 (Neb. 1926):

The errors assigned and relied on are: Error of the court in permitting M. F. Harrington, an attorney, to assist the county attorney in the prosecution of the defendant; error in refusing the defendant's request that said Harrington be not permitted to make the closing argument to the jury; error in permitting the said Harrington to give his opinion as to the guilt of the defendant in his argument to the jury and in making inflammatory and prejudicial statements to the jury in the course of his argument; error in the exclusion of certain proffered evidence; and, finally, that the verdict is not sustained by sufficient evidence.

It is argued that Mr. Harrington was a private prosecutor employed by or at the instance of Mr. Kain, whose hogs had been stolen, and that he was not a fair and impartial person and was, therefore, not a proper person to assist the county attorney in the prosecution of the case. An examination of the evidence upon this point fails to show that Mr. Harrington was ever in the employ of Mr. Kain, or had ever acted as his attorney. It does show that Mr. Kain approached the county attorney, asking to have some one assist him in the prosecution, and that the county attorney evinced his willingness to have such assistance; that Mr. Kain, with the purpose of employing him, called on Mr. Harrington, but the latter informed Mr. Kain that he could not accept a retainer from him; nor could he act as a prosecutor or assistant prosecutor except that he be appointed by the court and employed and paid by the county. Thereafter, 30 or 40 citizens called upon the county board and petitioned for the appointment of Mr. Harrington to assist in the prosecution of the case. The county board passed a resolution to employ Mr. Harrington and fixed the compensation that the county should pay therefor. Mr. Harrington appeared in the county court, pursuant to this resolution, and assisted at the preliminary hearing. In the district court objections were made to his appointment, and the facts above related developed. Thereupon, the court, on its own motion, called Mr. Harrington to the witness stand and fully and thoroughly interrogated him as to his relations to the prosecuting witness and to the defendant, from which it appears that there was no occasion for any feeling of hostility on the part of Mr. Harrington towards the defendant, and that there was no reason why he could not, and would not, be fair and impartial in the prosecution of the case as an assistant to the county attorney. Thereupon, the court made the appointment upon the application of the county attorney.

Section 4916, Comp. St. 1922, provides that the county attorney of any county may, under the direction of the district court, procure such assistance in the trial of any person, charged with a felony, as may be necessary for the trial thereof, and such assistant, or assistants, shall be allowed such compensation for his services as the county board shall determine. The application of the county attorney for the appointment of Mr. Harrington to assist in the prosecution presented a question addressed to the sound discretion of the trial court.

In Baker v. State, 112 Neb. 654, 200 N. W. 876, it is held:

"Where a county attorney requests and the court appoints counsel to assist in the prosecution of a felony case, a verdict will not be vacated for that reason in the absence of a showing which discloses that the defendant has been thereby prejudiced in his substantial rights."

And in Gragg v. State, 112 Neb. 732, 201 N. W. 338, it is held:

"When, under section 4916, Comp. St. 1922, a county attorney, under the court's direction, procures counsel to assist in the prosecution of a person charged with a felony, it is not error for the court to overrule defendant's objection to such appointment, unless it is shown that the appointment was made under a mistake of fact or under such circumstances as would reasonably tend to preclude the accused from having a fair and impartial trial and thereby prejudicially affect his substantial rights."

In the instant case it is not made to appear that the appointment was made under a mistake of fact or under such circumstances as would preclude the accused from having a fair and impartial trial. No abuse of discretion on the part of the court in making the appointment is shown. The assignment of error is not well taken.

With respect to the assignment that the court erred in permitting Mr. Harrington to make the closing argument to the jury, it may be observed that the record fails to show that Mr. Harrington made any argument to the jury. Error will not be presumed, but, to be available, it must be made to appear from the record.

As to the assignment that Mr. Harrington, in his argument to the jury, made inflammatory statements and stated his opinion of defendant's guilt, it is sufficient to say that the record fails to disclose that any such inflammatory statements were made, or that the opinion of Mr. Harrington was ever stated to the jury. The assignment is without merit.

Compare Goldsberry v. State, 137 N.W. 1116, 1118 (Neb. 1912):

The abstract in this case shows that counsel for the defendant in the motions and objections made in the trial of the case recited that Mr. Robinson was a nonresident and was unsworn, but these recitals do not establish the fact, and the abstract does not show, that section 3 above quoted was not complied with by the court. The presumption is that the court performed its duty in that regard. It is further insisted that Mr. Robinson had been retained by private individuals to prosecute this case, and that he had been by them paid at least in part for his services. The abstract shows that Mr. Robinson renounced any employment by private individuals, and returned all fees that they had paid him for his services in this case. Whether an attorney who had been procured by the county attorney, under the direction of the court, to assist in the prosecution, for compensation to be paid by the county, would be disqualified by receiving additional compensation from private individuals was not considered or determined in McKay v. State, supra, and it is not necessary to determine that question in this case for the reason above stated. It is the duty of the trial court to see that proper selection is made in the interest of the state, and for the promotion of justice in determining the guilt or innocence of the accused, and the presumption is that the trial court has properly exercised its discretion in that regard.

237. McKay v. State, 135 N.W. 1024, 1025 (Neb. 1912):

> Our opinion in relation to the employment of private counsel, as embodied in paragraphs 4, 5, and 6 of the syllabus, is next assailed. We deem it unnecessary to again discuss that question. We are satisfied with our former opinion upon that point and adhere thereto. This case presents a good illustration of the sufficiency of the reasons which prompted the Legislature to amend the statute in relation to the employment of private counsel in felony cases, and of the soundness of our former holding. Here we have private counsel, employed by relatives of the deceased, not only dominating the trial of a felony case in the court below, but obtruding himself into this court, after the Attorney General and the county attorney had accepted the opinion and obtained the issuance of a mandate, and attempting to further serve his private clients by a persistent contention at variance with the orderly course then being pursued by the able prosecuting officers of the state.

See also McKay v. State, 132 N.W. 741, 744–46 (Neb. 1911):

> Section 16, c. 7, Comp. St. 1911, makes it the duty of the county attorney to appear in the several courts of their respective counties and prosecute and defend on behalf of the state and county all actions, civil or criminal. Section 20 provides: "The county attorney may appoint one or more deputies, who shall act without any compensation from the county, to assist him in the discharge of his duties: Provided, that the county attorney of any county may, under the direction of the district court, procure such assistance, in the trial of any person charged with the crime of felony, as he may deem necessary for the trial thereof, and such assistant or assistants shall be allowed such compensation as the county board shall determine for his services, to be paid by order on the county treasurer, upon presenting to said board the certificate of the district judge before whom said cause was tried, certifying to services rendered by such assistant or assistants." The stipulation of Mr. Harrington, which we have given above, does not state that the county attorney had, under the direction of the district court, procured his assistance, but, on the contrary, states that he had been employed and was being paid by the brothers and sisters of the deceased; that he had not been appointed by the court to prosecute the case "but has been permitted by the court to prosecute the same." When placed upon the witness stand and examined by counsel for defendant, Mr. Harrington testified as follows: "Q. Now, have you ever been appointed under the statutes of this state, the method of which you understand well, to assist the county attorney in the prosecution of this case? A. No; not at public expense. Q. You have simply been permitted to appear? A. I don't know; I have been employed by relatives of the deceased, his brothers and sisters. Q. These relatives live in Beemer county, Iowa? A. I don't know what county. Q. Live near Gritole, in Iowa? A. Some of them, I think. Q. Any of them residents of this section? A. Not that I know of. Q. They employed you and are paying you? A. Yes, sir. Q. And you are appearing here in the capacity of private prosecutor? A. Yes, sir."
>
> The question of the right of private counsel to appear in the prosecution of a criminal action has been before this court a number of times. The first reported case is Polin v. State, 14 Neb. 540, 16 N. W. 898. That case was decided in 1883. We there held, under the statute as it then existed, that the district attorney in a criminal trial may have the assistance of counsel employed on private account. The next case is Bradshaw v. State, 17 Neb. 147, 151, 22 N. W. 361, 363, where the rule in Polin v. State was reannounced. In that case, however, it appears from the opinion, that "the record shows that before any evidence was introduced the district attorney stated to the court that he desired the assistance of Mr. Ashby in the trial of the cause on account of the magnitude of the case; that he had before that time requested his aid," etc. It will be observed that the facts in that case are very different from those in the case at bar. The next case was Gandy v. State, 27 Neb. 707, 723, 43 N. W. 747, 752, where the rule in Polin v. State was again announced. In that case it was insisted by counsel that Polin v. State and Bradshaw v. State, supra, arose under the statute existing prior to the passage of the act of March 10, 1885 (Laws 1885, c. 40). The opinion then sets out the sections of the statute referred to, which are substantially the same as those now in force. In commenting thereon, Cobb, J., said: "But it by no means appears that Martin and Falloon were deputies of the district attorney appointed under the provisions of the twentieth section, but were his assistants, procured by him under the direction of the district court, in accordance with the

proviso of said section, and were not required to take an official oath, other than that as attorneys of the court." It appears from this statement in the opinion that the appearance of Messrs. Martin and Falloon in that case was strictly in accordance with the requirements of statute. The next case is Blair v. State, 72 Neb. 501, 515, 101 N. W. 17, 22. In that case the syllabus holds: "(10) An objection to the appearance of private counsel to assist the county attorney in conducting a criminal prosecution, to be available, should be made at a suitable time and in the proper manner, and must be supported by at least some showing that the county attorney did not request or require any assistance, and the court had not appointed such counsel for that purpose. (11) Held, that a general objection to the appearance of such counsel, made during the trial in connection with the examination of a witness, and without any showing to support it, was properly overruled." In the opinion, Barnes, J., said: "No statement was made, or evidence offered, showing, or tending to show, that the prosecution had not requested the assistance of counsel, or that the court had not properly appointed them to render such assistance." Under those facts the decision in that case was clearly right. It is urged by the state that the question of employment of private counsel in the prosecution of a criminal case has been very recently discussed by this court in Burnett v. State, 88 Neb. 638, 130 N. W. 263. In that case the question was not raised at any time during the trial. Moreover, it could not have been raised under the statute above quoted for the reason that that case was a misdemeanor simply, and not a felony. To such a case the statute has no application. The only other authority cited by the state upon this point is the note to State v. Bartlett, 24 L. R. A. (N. S.) 564 (105 Me. 212, 74 Atl. 18, 134 Am. St. Rep. 542). There the principal case was simply a misdemeanor. An examination of the copious notes will show that there is a conflict in the holdings of the different states upon this point. In his brief the Attorney General says: "I cannot see that the statute of 1893, quoted by counsel, provides for any change of this general rule." In Biemel v. State, 71 Wis. 444, 37 N. W. 244, and Bird v. State, 77 Wis. 276, 45 N. W. 1126, it is held that a statute very similar to ours does change the rule, and that under it an unofficial member of the bar may not assist in the prosecution for a fee to be paid by private persons.

In support of his contention, defendant cites Biemel v. State, 71 Wis. 444, 37 N. W. 244; Meister v. People, 31 Mich. 99; People v. Bussey, 82 Mich. 49, 46 N. W. 97, and other cases. We are impressed with and prefer to follow the rule announced by the Supreme Court of Wisconsin and the other states that are in harmony therewith. We are not unmindful of the fact that in many cases, particularly in sparsely settled counties, young lawyers of little experience are ofttimes, from necessity, elected to the office of county attorney, and, if the prosecution of felony cases were left to such a county attorney alone, crime might go unpunished. In such cases it is to the interest of the state that such a county attorney should have the assistance of outside counsel; and, if there were nothing in the statute providing therefor, as was the case when Polin v. State, supra, was decided, we would adhere to the rule there announced; but our Legislature, by the statute under consideration, has wisely provided for just such emergencies. In doing so, however, it has not left it to outside parties to select the assistant counsel. It has imposed that duty upon the county attorney and district court, and has provided that the county attorney may, under the direction of the district court, procure such assistance. Counsel thus procured will not be actuated by sordid motives. He will enter upon the discharge of his duties in the same spirit that any honorable county attorney would enter upon the same, viz., with the desire simply to see that justice is done. It is just as much the duty of a county attorney to see that an innocent man is not convicted as to see that the guilty receive their just deserts. As said by Mr. Chief Justice Christiancy, in Hurd v. People, 25 Mich. 405, 416: "The only legitimate object of the prosecution is 'to show the whole transaction, as it was, whether its tendency be to establish guilt or innocence.' The prosecuting officer represents the public interest, which can never be promoted by the conviction of the innocent. His object, like that of the court, should be simply justice; and he has no right to sacrifice this to any pride of professional success." Counsel called to assist in the prosecution should govern his actions in like manner, and when procured in the manner and for the compensation contemplated by the statute quoted would doubtless do so; while counsel employed by outside parties, and, in the case of a homicide, by relatives of the deceased, would not feel bound by any

> such rule of conduct. He appears as private counsel simply, to represent the wishes, prejudice, and animosities of his clients; to secure a conviction at all hazards. Such is not the policy of the law as indicated by the Legislature, and we must decline to give it our sanction. In the case at bar there is nothing to show that the county attorney, who is a lawyer of known ability, requested the assistance of Mr. Harrington, nor that he had been in any manner previously consulted in reference thereto. The mere fact that the court permitted Mr. Harrington to assist in the prosecution cannot be held to be a compliance with the statute, which provides that private counsel may be procured by the county attorney, under the direction of the court. This provision of the statute calls for affirmative action by the county attorney and the court. Mere acquiescence in or assent to the appearance of private counsel does not constitute the affirmative action required by the statute, and is not sufficient. If, in the further prosecution of this case, the court and county attorney deem it necessary to have the assistance of outside counsel, it is their duty to follow the plain provisions of the statute in procuring the same.

238. State v. Eighth Jud. Dist. Ct. (Zogheib), 321 P.3d 882, 886 (Nev. 2014).

239. Jimenez v. State, 918 P.2d 687, 692 (Nev. 1996); *see also* State v. Huebler, 275 P.3d 91, 98 (Nev. 2012) (citing authorities).

240. Greene v. State, 931 P.2d 54, 62 (Nev. 1997) (citations omitted).

241. Nev. Rev. Stat. Ann. § 178.5698(1)(a) & (c); *see also* Nev. Rev. Stat. Ann. § 200.601(1) ("The prosecuting attorney in any trial brought against a person on a charge of harassment, stalking or aggravated stalking shall inform the alleged victim of the final disposition of the case."); Nev. Rev. Stat. Ann. § 205.980(3) ("The prosecutor shall notify the victim concerning the disposition of the criminal charges against the defendant within 30 days after the disposition. The notice must be sent to the last known address of the victim.").

242. Nev. Rev. Stat. Ann. § 178.5696(1).

243. Nev. Rev. Stat. Ann. § 178.571(1).

244. Nev. Rev. Stat. Ann. § 176.015(3), (5).

245. Nev. Const. art. 1, §8A.

246. State v. Smith, 238 A.3d 1014, 1017 (2020) (citing State (Premo Complainant) v. Martineau, 808 A.2d 51 (N.H. 2002)).

247. Mortgage Specialists, Inc. v. Davey, 904 A.2d 652, 673 (N.H. 2006).

248. State v. Martineau, 808 A.2d 51, 52–53 (N.H. 2002); State (Haas Complainant) v. Rollins, 533 A.2d 331 (N.H. 1987).

249. State v. Martineau, 808 A.2d 51, 53 (N.H. 2002) (citing N.H. Const., pt. II, art. 90).

250. *Id.* at 53–54.

251. *Id.* at 54.

252. N.J. Mun. Ct. R. 7:8-7(b). This rule was adopted October 6, 1997, to be effective February 1, 1998, and was amended June 15, 2007, to be effective September 1, 2007. The rule was originally adopted to comply with—and supplement and codify—the requirements laid down by the Supreme Court of New Jersey in *State v. Storm*, 661 A.2d 790 (N.J. 1995). State v. Myerowitz, 108 A.3d 671, 673 (N.J. Super. Ct. 2015).

253. Agacoili v. Gonzo, Civil Action No. 09-CV-2147 (DMC), 2010 WL 606697, at *3 n.3. (D. N.J. Feb. 18, 2010).

254. N.J. Mun. Ct. R. 7:8-7(b).

255. *Id.* That rule further states: "The court may grant the private prosecutor's application to appear if it is satisfied that a potential for conflict exists for the municipal prosecutor due to the nature of the charges set forth in the cross-complaints. The court shall place such a finding on the record." *Id.*; *see also* John H. Klock, 2A N.J. Prac., Court Rules Annotated R. 7:8-7(b) (2019) ("The court may permit an attorney to appear as a private prosecutor to represent the State in cases involving cross-complaints. Such private prosecutors may be permitted to appear on behalf of the State only if the court has first reviewed the private prosecutor's motion to so appear and an accompanying certification submitted on a form approved by the Administrative Director of the Courts. The court may grant the private prosecutor's application to appear

if it is satisfied that a potential for conflict exists for the municipal prosecutor due to the nature of the charges set forth in the cross-complaints. The court shall place such a finding on the record.").

256. State v. Guzman, Docket No. A-5271-17T4, 2020 WL 3055649, at *2 (N.J. Super. Ct. June 9, 2020); State v. Myerowitz, 108 A.3d 671, 673–80 (N.J. Super. Ct., App. Div. 2015); *see also* State v. Jenkins, 2012 WL 2474923, at *3 (N.J. Super. Ct., App. Div., June 29, 2012) (per curiam) ("On appeal, Jenkins, through newly-retained appellate counsel, argues that the failure to comply with the provisions of *Rule* 7:8–7(b) with respect to the use of private prosecutors is fatal to the claims against him under the precedent established by *State v. Storm,* 141 *N.J.* 245 (1995), recognizing the potential for conflicts of interest that may undermine the impartiality of the proceedings in private prosecutions, *id.* at 253–55, and *State v. Valentine,* 374 *N.J. Super.* 292, 297–98 (App. Div. 2005), declaring that, in the absence of compliance with *Rule* 7:8–7, a conviction resulting from a private prosecution cannot stand. Significantly, the State, which is the only other party to appear on appeal, concedes that point.").

257. State v. Burkert, 174 A.3d 987, 990 n.2 (N.J. 2017).

258. State v. Jenkins, 2012 WL 2474923 (N.J. Sup. Ct. June 29, 2012) (per curiam).

259. State v. Storm, 661 A.2d 790, 792 (N.J. 1995).

260. *Storm*, 661 A.2d at 790.

261. State v. Myerowitz, 108 A.2d 671, 681 (N.J. 2015) (discussing the holding in *State v. Storm*); *see also id.*:

> Distilled into manageable subparts, the first step under *Rule* 7:8–7(b) requires the municipal court judge to determine whether the parties have filed cross-complaints against each other. In such a scenario, the municipal prosecutor is placed in an untenable situation because each party is a defendant in one case and a complaining witness in the other. Here, the record shows defendant did not have a cross-complaint against Lerner. Although defendant represented the Liberty Humane Society in a pending civil action against Lerner, there is no evidence that defendant had a pending personal complaint against Lerner before the municipal court.
>
> In the absence of actual cross-complaints that create an insurmountable conflict of interest for the prosecutor, there are no legal grounds for the municipal court to permit a private attorney to represent the State. Because public policy favors that prosecutions be conducted by duly appointed independent prosecutors, the municipal court judge should obtain a statement from the municipal prosecutor, on the record, confirming the existence of this conflict of interest, requiring his or her recusal in the case. However, "[i]f the municipal prosecutor insists on proceeding with the prosecution, the prosecutor's decision should be final." *Storm, supra,* 141 *N.J.*at 255, 661 *A.*2d 790.
>
> The second step under *Rule* 7:8–7(b) requires the municipal court to review the private attorney's motion to assume the role of prosecutor. This motion must be accompanied by a "*certification submitted on a form approved by the Administrative Director of the Courts.*" *R.* 7:8–7(b) (emphasis added). Here, the Law Division's finding that the municipal court judge consolidated defendant's case with Jeffrey's case is not supported by the record. Lerner's attorney did not file a formal motion seeking leave to prosecute the case against defendant or submit the certification required by *Rule* 7:8–7(b).

See also State v. Farzan, 2007 WL 461295, at *1 (N.J. Super. Ct., App. Div. 2007) (per curiam) ("A municipal court, on good cause shown, 'may permit a private prosecutor to represent the government.' *R.* 7:8-7(b). 'The propriety of appointing a private prosecutor will vary from case-to-case, depending on the facts of each case.'") (quoting *State v. Storm*).

262. State of New Jersey v. Bazin, 912 F. Supp. 106, 111 (D. N.J. 1995).

263. State v. Vitiello, 873 A.2d 591, 593 (N.J. Super. Ct., App. Div. 2005) ("The State, and only the State, can appeal a dismissal, particularly where the matter is being handled by a public prosecutor, and a citizen, including the complainant, who has not been designated 'private prosecutor,' does not have standing.").

264. State v. Bradley, 19 A.3d 479, 481–82 (N.J. Super. Ct., App. Div. 2011).

265. In the Matter of Helmer, 202 A.3d 1261, 1265, 1270 (N.J. 2019).

266. State v. Lazarchick, 715 A.2d 365, 371 (N.J. Superior Ct., 1998) (citation omitted).

267. *Id.* (citation omitted).

268. *Id.*

269. State v. New Jersey v. Bazin, 912 F. Supp 101, 111 (D. N.J. 1995); *see also id.* at 112 ("[T]he mere fact that a private attorney is getting paid does not create a conflict of interest that is so severe as to intrude upon a defendant's constitutional rights. There is no evidence that Ms. Utley-Williams has any other pending or imminent action against Defendant Bazin. Neither Mr. Lewis nor Stark & Stark have represented Ms. Utley-Williams or the union before. There is no indication that Mr. Lewis' fee is contingent. The circumstances do not appear to present an intolerable conflict of interest that would rise to a violation of Defendant's due process rights. The defendant's motion to dismiss on this ground shall be denied.").

270. State v. Gonzales, 119 P.3d 151, 160 (N.M. 2005).

271. *E.g.*, State v. Barnett, 965 P.2d 323, 329–30 (N.M. 1998):

> Given the tremendous discretion possessed by a prosecutor in the plea bargaining process, a defendant could be seriously prejudiced by the prosecutor's knowledge regarding the defendant's character and conduct acquired in prior representation. For example, the prosecutor could refuse to bargain with a defendant whose danger to society would be apparent from confidential communications during the prior representation. In the present case, we consider it significant that Prosecutor conducted the plea negotiations on the State's behalf after she had been closely involved in counseling Defendant's plea in a prior criminal matter. This situation creates a significant risk that information relating to the prior representation which concerns Defendant's personality, credibility, and negotiating style will be used to his disadvantage in assessing the State's ability to obtain a favorable plea agreement, avoid trial, or otherwise exploit the trust that was developed as a result of the prior representation. *Cf. Lepe*, 211 Cal. Rptr. at 434 (criminal defendant's "personality traits, lifestyle, associations, thought patterns, attitudes—all are eventually known to thoughtful and prepared counsel."). Such prior knowledge of a former client's credibility or personality also may be used to his or her disadvantage in the prosecuting attorney's assessment of whether or under what terms the former client should be released from detention.
>
> Thus, the specific circumstances of this case suggest a substantial relationship between the matters at issue. Prosecutor admitted that she counseled Defendant's plea of guilty to burglary and conspiracy charges in 1993, continued to represent him on DWI charges in 1995, and later negotiated with Defendant on the State's behalf to obtain his guilty plea on another set of burglary and conspiracy charges in 1996. It is also undisputed that Prosecutor used the prior convictions obtained while she represented Defendant in 1993 to add a habitual offender sentence to the convictions she obtained on the State's behalf in 1996. At the plea hearing, Prosecutor admitted that if the case went to trial, it would involve conflicting testimony between Defendant and another witness, thus making Defendant's credibility as a potential witness a key issue in the case. Finally, at the close of the plea hearing when Defendant requested to be released from detention for a few days to put his affairs in order, Prosecutor commented on his prior history in an attempt to persuade the trial court that Defendant was a flight risk and should not be released.
>
> Under these circumstances, we determine that the trial court erred in concluding that "a conflict was not present in this case." The fact that this case involves a plea agreement, and the exchange of concessions and advantages necessary to such an agreement, does not eliminate or diminish the likelihood or appearance of a conflict of interest, especially when the prosecuting attorney who negotiates the plea agreement previously sat on the opposite side of the table and counseled the defendant's plea in another case concerning similar charges. Had Defendant raised the issue prior to his conviction, the conflict of interest would have provided a basis for disqualifying Prosecutor from participating in the plea negotiations.

272. *Gonzales*, 119 P.3d at 160–61.

273. N.M. Stat. Ann. § 36-1-19.

274. State v. Rodriguez, 116 P.3d 92, 103 (N.M. 2005).

275. N.M. R. Mun. Ct. P. Rule 8-111.

276. *Id.*, committee commentary.

277. N.M. Stat. Ann. § 36-1-23.1.

278. State v. Surratt, 363 P.3d 1204, 1205 (N.M. 2015).

279. State v. Baca, 688 P.2d 34, 35–36 (N.M. Ct. App. 1984):

The state is the plaintiff in any criminal proceeding in the metropolitan court. NMSA 1978, Metro. R. 40(a) (Repl. Pamp. 1981). Although NMSA 1978, Section 36–1–18 A (Rep. Pamp. 1984) does not require the district attorney to appear in a non-record court such as metro court, Section 36–1–19 prohibits anyone other than the attorney general's office and district attorney's office from representing the state in a criminal proceeding, except on order of the court and with the consent of those offices. *State v. Lucero,* 20 N.M. 55, 146 P. 407 (1915). The question of the lawful authority of Salaz's attorney to prosecute, and thus the jurisdiction of metro court, involves the granting of permission by the district attorney's office *and* an order of the metro court.

The state makes various arguments by which it attempts to show that the district attorney's office consented to the private prosecution of the matter. These arguments do not fully address the issue. Section 36–1–19, which authorizes an associate counsel to prosecute for the district attorney with the consent of the district attorney *and* "on ruling of the court", requires an explicit order of the court. The state infers the existence of an order of the court. A party may not infer the existence of an order because the case proceeded to trial before the court. What the state seeks is judicial surgery on Section 36–1–19 when what would be appropriate is legislative therapy. *City of Albuquerque v. Sanchez,* 81 N.M. 272, 466 P.2d 118 (Ct.App.1970). We note that in *State v. Lucero* the record demonstrated that an order of the court was sought and obtained, and that there was no question of proper court approval in that situation.

We hold that where the record does not demonstrate such explicit approval, the proper authority is not vested in the private counsel to prosecute. Without this authority, the metro court lacked criminal jurisdiction to proceed. *State v. Reese.* Therefore, the district court lacked criminal jurisdiction to hear the case, and render a judgment and sentence. *See State v. Lynch.*

280. State v. Rivera, 268 P.3d 40, 44 (N.M. 2012) ("Defendant maintains that lack of prejudice is immaterial because an unauthorized prosecution deprives the trial court of jurisdiction. Defendant relies on *State v. Hollenbeck,* 112 N.M. 275, 814 P.2d 143 (Ct.App.1991) and *State v. Baca,* 101 N.M. 716, 688 P.2d 34 (Ct.App.1984) for this proposition. In both *Hollenbeck* and *Baca,* the accused was prosecuted by a *private* attorney who the district attorney had failed to properly appoint or otherwise authorize to conduct the prosecution. *Hollenbeck,* 112 N.M. at 276, 814 P.2d at 144; *Baca,* 101 N.M. at 717, 688 P.2d at 35. Once it was established that the private attorney lacked authority to prosecute, our Court of Appeals concluded in each case that the trial court lacked subject matter jurisdiction, thereby reversing the convictions. *Hollenbeck,*112 N.M. at 277–78, 814 P.2d at 145–46; *Baca,* 101 N.M. at 718, 688 P.2d at 36."). *Cf.* State v. Cherryholmes, 930 P.2d 1139, 1141 (N.M. 1996) ("Section 36–1–23.1 requires only that the appointment and oath of a special prosecutor be in 'substantially the same form' as the appointment and oath of an assistant district attorney. We do not believe that Section 36–1–23.1 requires strict compliance to further the goal of the legislature.").

281. *See, e.g.,* Gary Muldoon, Handling a Criminal Case in New York § 1:16 (2019) ("A private person may seek to prosecute a criminal charge. For example, a 'cross-complaint' might be filed by one defendant against the original complainant. A private prosecutor is held to the same standards of fairness that a district attorney would uphold. Such a prosecution must be conducted with the knowledge and consent of the district attorney."); People v. Soddano, 655 N.E.2d 161, 161–62 (N.Y. Ct. App. 1995) ("County Law § 700(1) provides that '[i]t shall be the duty of every district attorney to conduct all prosecutions for crimes and offenses cognizable by the courts of the county for which he or she shall have been elected or appointed.' It is well settled, however, that this statute does not require the District Attorney's personal presence at every criminal hearing in a county, and the prosecution of petty crimes or offenses may be delegated to subordinates and other public or administrative officers and even to private attorneys (*see, People v. DeLeyden,* 10 N.Y.2d 293, 294, 220 N.Y.S.2d 961, 177 N.E.2d 924 [prosecution by Deputy Sheriff who made the speeding charge]; *People v. Czajka,* 11 N.Y.2d 253, 254, 228 N.Y.S.2d 809, 183 N.E.2d 216 [prosecution of traffic offense by Deputy Town Attorney]). District Attorneys, of course, retain the ultimate, nondelegable responsibility for prosecuting all crimes and offenses, but they may allow appearances by public officers or private attorneys so long as they are kept aware of all the criminal prosecutions in the county (*see, People v. Van Sickle,* 13 N.Y.2d 61, 62–63, 242 N.Y.S.2d 34, 192 N.E.2d 9).").

282. Sedore v. Epstein, 864 N.Y.S.2d 543, 544–47 (N.Y. Sup. Ct., App. Division, 2d Dept. 2008) (citations omitted); *see also id.* at 547 n.1 ("No issue is presented here as to the extent New York City Criminal Court Act § 50 may provide authority for private prosecutions (*see People v. Vial,* 132 Misc.2d 5, 502 N.Y.S.2d 930). However, courts have questioned the prudence of doing the same (*see People v. Benoit,* 152 Misc.2d 115, 120, 575 N.Y.S.2d 750; *People v. Calderone,* 151 Misc.2d 530, 535–536, 573 N.Y.S.2d 1005)."); *see also id.* at 547–49:

> The District Attorney asserts, however, that the Court of Appeals has endorsed such delegations in *People v. Van Sickle,* 13 N.Y.2d 61, 242 N.Y.S.2d 34, 192 N.E.2d 9. There is a facial appeal to the District Attorney's argument in this regard. Nevertheless, upon closer analysis, the holding in *Van Sickle* is not as broad as the District Attorney would have us read it. As we see it, moreover, to the extent that *Van Sickle* can be read as supporting the conclusion the District Attorney would have us reach, its authority has been compromised by the more recent holdings of the Court of Appeals with respect to the proper role of the prosecutor in a criminal case.
>
> The issue in *Van Sickle* was narrowly defined by Chief Judge Desmond, writing for the majority, as "must a criminal conviction be reversed solely because the lay complaining witness was allowed to conduct the prosecution" (*id.* at 62, 242 N.Y.S.2d 34, 192 N.E.2d 9). In holding that reversal was not required, the Court of Appeals wrote, as Judge Van Voorhis noted in concurring, against a common-law background in New York that recognized the right of a complainant to prosecute minor offenses personally (*id.* at 64, 242 N.Y.S.2d 34, 192 N.E.2d 9; *see People v. Citadel Mgt. Co.,* 78 Misc.2d 626, 355 N.Y.S.2d 976; *Matter of Santacrose v. Bean,* 52 Misc.2d 167, 275 N.Y.S.2d 418). Unlike the concurring judges, however, the majority did not rely on that authority to reach its conclusion. The majority determined only that it was sufficient to sustain the conviction that the prosecution before it did not violate the District Attorney's statutory responsibility to prosecute. To the extent that the Court impliedly approved the delegation of prosecutorial authority to a private individual, provided that the District Attorney had "set up a system" for monitoring those prosecutions, it did so expressly in dictum.
>
> The reluctance of the *Van Sickle* majority to embrace the broader holding urged by the concurring judges evidences the Court's concern about the evolving role of the public prosecutor in our criminal justice system. "The [prosecutor] is the representative not of an ordinary party to a controversy, but of a sovereignty whose obligation to govern impartially is as compelling as its obligation to govern at all; and whose interest, therefore, in a criminal prosecution is not that it shall win a case, but that justice shall be done" (*Berger v. United States,* 295 U.S. 78, 88, 55 S. Ct. 629, 79 L.Ed. 1314). The duty of the District Attorney, therefore, is not merely to obtain convictions, but to see that justice is done (*see People v. Santorelli,* 95 N.Y.2d 412, 420–421, 718 N.Y.S.2d 696, 741 N.E.2d 493, *cert. denied* 532 U.S. 1008, 121 S. Ct. 1736, 149 L.Ed.2d 660; *People v. Steadman,* 82 N.Y.2d 1, 6, 603 N.Y.S.2d 382, 623 N.E.2d 509; *People v. Bailey,* 58 N.Y.2d 272, 277, 460 N.Y.S.2d 912, 447 N.E.2d 1273; ABA Standards for Criminal Justice, Prosecution Function and Defense Function, Standard 3–1.2[c] [3d ed. 1993]). The practical obligations that flow from the prosecutor's duty to do justice have given heightened recognition to the singular nature of that role (*see Brady v. Maryland,* 373 U.S. 83, 87, 83 S. Ct. 1194, 10 L.Ed.2d 215; *People v. Rosario,* 9 N.Y.2d 286, 213 N.Y.S.2d 448, 173 N.E.2d 881, *cert. denied* 368 U.S. 866, 82 S. Ct. 117, 7 L.Ed.2d 64).
>
> The duty of a prosecutor is thus somewhat different from that of an attorney retained by a party, as the canons of professional ethics recognize (*see* Code of Professional Responsibility EC 7–13). The attorney's obligation is to exercise professional judgment "solely for the benefit of the client and free of compromising influences and loyalties" (Code of Professional Responsibility EC 5–1), to represent the client zealously within the bounds of the law (*see* Code of Professional Responsibility Canon 7), and "to seek the lawful objectives of the client through reasonably available means permitted by law and the Disciplinary Rules" (Code of Professional Responsibility DR 7–101 [A] [1] [22 NYCRR 1200.32(A)(1)]). In the case of the prosecutor, all of these obligations flow not to the complainant, but to the public, which is the client (*see People v. Harris,* 154 Misc.2d 554, 558, 585 N.Y.S.2d 684; *see also Berger v. United States,* 295 U.S. at 88, 55 S. Ct. 629; *People v. Zimmer,* 51 N.Y.2d at 393, 434 N.Y.S.2d 206, 414 N.E.2d 705; ABA Standards for Criminal Justice,

Prosecution Function and Defense Function, Commentary, Standard 3–1.3 [3d ed. 1993]). In light of this, the conflict inherent in permitting the prosecutor to be paid by the complainant is readily apparent (*see People v. Garfield,* 152 Misc.2d 51, 574 N.Y.S.2d 501; *People v. Benoit,* 152 Misc.2d 115, 575 N.Y.S.2d 750; *People v. Calderone,* 151 Misc.2d 530, 573 N.Y.S.2d 1005).

While it is true that the Code of Professional Responsibility permits an attorney, with the client's consent, to accept payment from a third party (*see* DR 5–107 [22 NYCRR 1200.26]), that provision simply does not contemplate the unique role of the public prosecutor. "The prosecutor is appointed solely to pursue the public interest ... A private attorney appointed to prosecute a criminal [offense] therefore certainly should be as disinterested as a public prosecutor who undertakes such a prosecution" (*Young v. United States ex rel. Vuitton et Fils S.A.,* 481 U.S. 787, 804, 107 S. Ct. 2124, 95 L.Ed.2d 740). "The administration of justice must not only be above reproach, it must also be beyond the suspicion of reproach" (*People v. Savvides,* 1 N.Y.2d 554, 556, 154 N.Y.S.2d 885, 136 N.E.2d 853). Thus, even assuming that the District Attorney, as the public official charged with prosecutorial responsibility, could consent on behalf of the public to such an arrangement, the conflict is not resolved.

Moreover, even the statutory authority of the District Attorney to prosecute must yield when a conflict of interest potentially impairs the prosecutor's obligation to do justice (*see People v. Shinkle,* 51 N.Y.2d 417, 434 N.Y.S.2d 918, 415 N.E.2d 909; *People v. Zimmer,* 51 N.Y.2d 390, 434 N.Y.S.2d 206, 414 N.E.2d 705). In *Zimmer,* the District Attorney was also the general counsel of, and a shareholder in, the corporation that was allegedly the victim of the crime. Recognizing the unique role of the public prosecutor, and the inherent conflict between the District Attorney's public and private roles, the Court of Appeals held that the defendant's motion to dismiss the indictment should have been granted even without any proof that the District Attorney had acted improperly or prejudiced the defendant. The delegation of prosecutorial authority to an attorney retained by the complaining witness would, essentially, place the attorney in the same position as the disqualified District Attorney in *Zimmer.*

At bottom, the prosecution of a criminal offense is a public function, not a private one. "Every accusatory instrument, regardless of the person designated therein as accuser, constitutes an accusation on behalf of the state as plaintiff and must be entitled 'the people of the State of New York' against a designated person, known as the defendant" (CPL 1.20[1]). "The idea that the criminal law, unlike other branches of the law such as contracts and property, is designed to vindicate public rather than private interests is now firmly established. The participation of a responsible public officer in the decision to prosecute and in the prosecution of the charge gives greater assurance that the rights of the accused will be respected ... The absence of a trained prosecution official risks abuse or casual and unauthorized administrative practices and dispositions that are not consonant with our traditions of justice" (ABA Standards for Criminal Justice, Prosecution Function and Defense Function, Commentary, Standard 3–2.1 [3d ed. 1993]). Prosecution of a criminal complaint by an attorney retained by the complaining witness is simply inconsistent with these principles.

For these reasons, we conclude that the District Attorney may not delegate the authority to prosecute a criminal offense to an attorney retained by the complaining witness.

283. Sedore v. Epstein, 56 A.D.3d 60, 61–63 (N.Y. App. Div., 2d Dept. 2008).

284. People v. Cortes, 3 Misc.3d 1106(A), 2004 WL 1190995, at *7 n.5 (N.Y. Sup. Ct., Bronx County, May 26, 2004).

285. People v. Robinson, 27 Misc.3d 635, 636 (N.Y. Sup. Ct., Kings County 2010) (citing People v. DiFalco, 44 N.Y.2d 482, 406 N.Y.S.2d 279, 377 N.E.2d 732; Sedore v. Epstein, 56 A.D.3d 60, 864 N.Y.S.2d 543; Kinberg v. Kinberg, 48 A.D.3d 387, 853 N.Y.S.2d 27; People v. Memminger, 121 Misc.2d 953, 469 N.Y.S.2d 323; People v. Rodgers, 205 Misc. 1106, 131 N.Y.S.2d 622).

286. People v. Robinson, 27 Misc.3d 635, 636 (N.Y. Sup. Ct., Kings County 2010) (citing Goldsby v. State, 240 Miss. 647, 123 So.2d 429; State v. Mattoon, 287 S.C. 493, 339 S.E.2d 867; Cantrell v. Commonwealth, 229 Va. 387, 329 S.E.2d 22; Cronan ex rel. State v. Cronan, 774 A.2d 866; Kan. Stat. Ann. § 19–717).

287. People v. Robinson, 27 Misc.3d 635, 636–37 (N.Y. Sup. Ct., Kings County 2010) (citing Sedore v. Epstein, 56 A.D.3d at 65; 864 N.Y.S.2d 543).

288. People v. Vial, 502 N.Y.S.2d 930, 132 Misc. 2d 5 (N.Y. Crim. Ct. 1986) (citations omitted).

289. Section 50 of the City Criminal Court Act reads:

> Provision shall be made at all times in each part of the court in which a judge is sitting as a magistrate whereby the clerk, the clerk's assistants or other employees whose duty it is to prepare complaints shall have proper accommodations and the necessary room or rooms separate from but convenient to the room in which the court is held, and therein shall be at all times conspicuously posted a notice legibly printed in English, Spanish, Italian and Yiddish, respectively, and such other language as a rule or order of court shall prescribe, to the effect that any person to whom permission is refused to make and verify a complaint and who is thereby aggrieved will be heard upon application to the judge in person before the closing of the pending session of the court. It shall be the duty of each such judge before opening and again before closing a session to cause to be intelligibly announced to all persons in and about his courtroom that the court will then and there hear all complaints which have not been taken by the complaint clerk.

N.Y. Consol. Laws, City Crim. Ct. Act § 50, *available at* https://www.nysenate.gov/legislation/laws/CRC/50.

290. People v. Benoit, 575 N.Y.S.2d 750 (N.Y. Crim. Ct. 1991).

291. 573 N.Y.S.2d 1005 (N.Y. Crim. Ct. 1991); *see also* Kampfer v. Vonderheide, 216 F. Supp.2d 4, 8 (N.D.N.Y. 2002) (citing *Calderone* and stating that "Kampfer would not personally be able to commence a New York State criminal action against the person(s) who vandalized his home").

292. *Calderone*, 573 N.Y.S.2d at 1005. Under the facts of *Calderone*, a New York court granted the defendant's motion to disqualify the law firm of De Maio and Hughes. In so holding, the court concluded that private prosecutions by interested parties or their attorneys present inherent conflicts of interest which violate a defendant's due process rights. Id. at 1007. According to the court:

> Compelling support for this conclusion is found in the opinions of Justices Brennan and Blackmun in *Young v. United States*. The Supreme Court of Wisconsin, one hundred years ago in *Biemel v. State*, 37 N.W. 244, 244–45 (Wis. 1888), stated, "We think public policy, and the fair, just, and impartial administration of the criminal law of the state, make it the duty of the courts to exclude the paid attorneys of private persons from appearing as prosecutors." This court agrees and goes further, holding that due process requires that the individual who prosecutes a criminal case not have any personal or financial interest in the prosecution nor an attorney-client relationship with any of the parties.

Id. at 1009 (citing Young v. United States ex rel. Vuitton et Fils S.A., 481 U.S. 787, 810, 814–15 (1987) (Justice Brennan's and Justice Blackmun's opinions)). Significantly, several other New York cases have discussed the propriety of private prosecutors. *Compare* People v. Garfield, 574 N.Y.S.2d 501, 502 (N.Y. Just. Ct. 1991) ("In the opinion of this Court ... the failure to provide a professional evaluation of such cases by a neutral prosecutor may result in improper charges and convictions and denies a defendant the due process of law."); People v. Benoit, 575 N.Y.S.2d 750, 757 (N.Y. Crim. Ct. 1991) (private prosecution of tenant by landlord violates the tenant's due process and equal protection rights); People v. Zimmer, 434 N.Y.S.2d 206 (N.Y. 1980) (conviction of a corporation manager reversed where the district attorney had a financial interest in the corporation); People v. Franklin, 369 N.Y.S.2d 531 (A.D.2d 1975) (permitting attorney representing one of complaining witnesses who was under indictment on unrelated charge to sit at counsel table and to object to questions put to witness on cross-examination was error that required new trial); People v. Vlasto, 355 N.Y.S.2d 983 (N.Y. Crim. Ct. 1974) (private prosecution of a Class A misdemeanor not authorized) *with* Read v. Sacco, 375 N.Y.S.2d 371 (N.Y.A.D. 2d Dept. 1975) (private prosecution of a Class A misdemeanor authorized); People v. Cuozzo, 412 N.Y.S.2d 748, 752 (City Ct. White Plains 1978) (court denied private attorney leave to prosecute a police officer involved in a traffic accident with his client-defendant because it was "virtually impossible to ask the defense attorney, or any defense attorney so situated, to act with objectivity and complete impartiality as a prosecutor in a criminal proceeding against a police officer who is responsible for the charge against his client"); People v. Vial, 502 N.Y.S.2d 930 (N.Y. Crim. Ct. 1986) (attorney for defendant prosecuted by district attorney permitted to act as prosecutor in cross-complaint against his accuser); Peter L. Davis, *The Crime Victim's "Right" to a Criminal Prosecution: A Proposed Model Statute for the Governance of Private Criminal Prosecutions*, 38 DEPAUL L. REV. 329 (1989) (detailing New York case law regarding the use of private prosecutors); *see also* Rochez v. Mittleton, 1993 WL 530947 (S.D.N.Y. Dec. 20, 1993) (dismissal of a 42 U.S.C. § 1983 action against the City of New York, the Bronx District Attorney, and others alleging a deprivation of constitutional rights because of a municipal policy allowing private prosecutions to be commenced by any "complaining witness," including interested parties).

293. People v. Van Sickle, 242 N.Y.S.2d 34 (N.Y. Ct. App. 1963). The substantive opinion in *Van Sickle* was short and read in its entirety:

> I join in the court's negative answer to the only question presented to us on this appeal, that is: must a criminal conviction be reversed solely because the lay complaining witness was allowed to conduct the prosecution? If there was before us for decision the must broader question as to the District Attorney's rights and duties I would say that the courts as well as the District Attorney himself must obey the plain, clear mandate of subdivision 1 of section 700 of the County Law, Consol. Laws, c. 11. That statute does not necessarily mean that the District Attorney or his deputy must be physically present at every criminal hearing in the county. However, it means at least that the District Attorney, as the elected representative of the people and charged with this responsibility, must carry the responsibility and must set up a system whereby he knows of all the criminal prosecutions in his county and either appears therein in person or by assistant or consents to appearance on his behalf by other public officers or private attorneys.

A concurring opinion in *Van Sickle*, made by Judge Van Voorhis, made this observation:

> It is an ancient right of the individual litigant to appear in propria persona written into some statutes (Civil Practice Act, s 236; Justice Court Act, s 32), which is, of course, primarily applicable to civil actions inasmuch as criminal causes are prosecuted in the name of the People of the State. The withdrawal of this right by statute in certain criminal prosecutions indicates, however, that it is not considered to be confined to civil action, but extends to criminal proceedings of a minor nature (e.g., former N. Y. City Criminal Courts Act, § 37). The decision on appeal in the case of a trial in a Court of Special Sessions, where the individual has prosecuted without the assistance of counsel or a public officer, as in any other case, should turn on whether the defendant's rights have been prejudiced by the course of the trial or the conduct of the Justice or Judge, instead of a categorical rule of thumb query whether an attorney or public officer 'prosecuted'. In these courts there are certain to be situations, like the present, where the charges have not been preferred through public officials and where there would be no one but the complaining witness to press the charge which would otherwise be dropped by default. It would be impractical, nor do we consider that the statute requires that a lawyer be employed in every instance to act ad hoc under and with the consent of the District Attorney if the District Attorney or his office cannot be present. A threshold problem would almost always arise in such instances: who would compensate the lawyer?
>
> We consider that a complaining witness has prima facie the right to conduct such a prosecution if the District Attorney does not do so, but must abide by the same rules of fairness and of law which would bind a public law officer if he were present.
>
> We disagree with the statement in the opinion by Chief Judge DESMOND that the District Attorney must know of all the criminal prosecutions in the Justices' Courts in his county, and must either appear therein in person or by assistant or that all such prosecutions must be conducted by some public officer or private attorney with the consent of the District Attorney.
>
> The order of the County Court should be reversed and the matter remitted to the County Court to rule on the facts in its appellate capacity pursuant to section 543-b of the Code of Criminal Procedure.

Van Sickle, 242 N.Y.S.2d at 37 (Van Voorhis, J., concurring).

294. People v. Garfield, 574 N.Y.S.2d 501, 502–503 (N.Y. Just. Ct. 1991) (citing People v. Benoit, 575 N.Y.S.2d 750 (N.Y. Crim. Ct. City, Kings Cnty. 1991); People v. Calderone, 573 N.Y.S.2d 1005 (N.Y. Crim. Ct. City, N.Y. Cnty. 1991)); *see also Garfield*, 574 N.Y.S.2d at 503:

> While no court has held that it is unconstitutional in every case to permit a civilian to personally prosecute under facts as in the case at bar, this Court is mindful of the duty of a prosecutor to do justice, and to provide a fair and impartial atmosphere within which a guilty defendant is held accountable, and the innocent exonerated. Where there exists a financial interest as in this case, or other personal interest, the prospect for a fair and impartial trial diminishes to the extent that the due process of law to which all defendants are entitled may cease to exist.
>
> Therefore, unless and until the District Attorney and Town Attorney determine which office has the responsibility to prosecute this case, and one office or the other undertakes the prosecution of this case, the prosecution herein shall not be permitted, and the complainant Marvin Koplic is hereby disqualified from acting as a prosecutor in view of the appearance of a conflict of interest.
>
> The parties are directed to appear on the date set for trial, September 3, 1991 at 3 P.M. at which time the District Attorney shall advise the Court whether it elects to undertake the prosecution of this case or in the alternative designate the Town Attorney to do so. The failure of either the District Attorney to make a designation pursuant to County Law Section 701 or undertake the prosecution himself, would result in a dismissal of the charges pending against the defendant. The matter should be considered carefully by the People to ensure that justice is done to all parties.

See also Brief for Respondent, *The People of the State of New York, Respondent, against Terrence Carter and Solomon Witherspoon, Defendants-Appellants*, Court of Appeals, State of New York, Sept. 5, 1990, pp. 41–42 ("New York courts have upheld criminal convictions in a variety of proceedings in which the prosecutor was not a lawyer. In fact, the practice of non-lawyer prosecutions has been institutionalized in one form or another in virtually all parts of the state."); *id.* at 42 ("In New York City, prosecutions by non-attorneys are routinely conducted in the Summons All Purpose Part, located at 346 Broadway in Manhattan. Prior to 1975, each borough had its own summons party. Cases in the SAP part may be prosecuted by law enforcement personnel who are not attorneys. Victims of crime may also prosecute their own cases, or can even employ their own private counsel to do so.") (citations omitted); *id.* at 43 ("The validity of private prosecutions in the SAP Part has been repeatedly upheld, in spite of the absence of any statutory authorization for such proceedings in the Criminal Procedural Law and the language of County Law § 927, which purports to vest authority for the prosecution of 'all crimes and offenses cognizable by the courts' in the district attorneys of the five boroughs. Courts have found authority for the SAP part proceedings both in historical precedent and in Section 50 of the New York City Criminal Court Act, which recognizes the right of individuals to file criminal complaints.").

295. N.Y.C. Crim. Ct. Act § 20; Barry Kamins, Criminal Law Handbook of New York, including Penal Law, Criminal Procedural Law, Correction Law, N.Y.C. Criminal Court Act, Uniform Rules for Courts Exercising Criminal Jurisdiction, Related Statutes, Offenses and Classifications for the Penal Law (2020).

296. Preeti Chauhan, Megan Welsh, Adam G. Fera & Ervin Balazon, The Summons Report: Trends in the Issuance and Disposition of Summonses in New York City, 2003–2013: A Report of the Misdemeanor Justice Project at John Jay College of Criminal Justice (Apr. 27, 2015), https://www.jjay.cuny.edu/sites/default/files/news/Summons_Report_DRAFT_4_24_2015_v8.pdf.

297. *Crime Victims*, http://www.nycourts.gov/courthelp/Criminal/crimeVictims.shtml (last accessed Jan. 17, 2021).

298. People v. Clymer, 902 N.Y.S.2d 922, 923–24 (City Ct., City of Amsterdam, 2010).

299. State v. Best, 186 S.E.2d 1, 3 (N.C. 1972). In North Carolina, the use of private prosecutors has been upheld in numerous cases. State v. Westbrook, 181 S.E.2d 572 (N.C. 1971), *vacated in part*, 408 U.S. 939 (1972); State v. Carden, 183 S.E. 898 (N.C. 1936), *cert. denied*, 298 U.S. 682 (1936); *see also* State v. Branch, 220 S.E.2d 495, 517 (N.C. 1975), *cert. denied*, 433 U.S. 909 (1977) (use of a private prosecutor did not create an atmosphere in which it was impossible for the defendant to receive a trial consistent with the requirements of due process). Nevertheless, the permissibility of private prosecutors in North Carolina rests within the discretion of the trial judge. *Branch*, 220 S.E.2d at 577; State v. Lippard, 25 S.E.2d 594, 599 (N.C. 1943), *cert. denied*, 320 U.S. 749 (1943).

300. 313 S.E.2d 507 (N.C. 1984).

301. *Id.* at 512 (citations omitted).

302. *Id.* at 513.

303. In North Carolina, trial courts have the discretion to allow the use of private prosecutors. State v. Boykin, 259 S.E.2d 883, 891 (N.C. 1979), *cert. denied*, 446 U.S. 911 (1980). The trial court's discretion in this regard is only interfered with upon a showing of abuse of discretion. *Id.*; State v. Carden, 183 S.E. 898 (N.C. 1936), *cert. denied*, 298 U.S. 682 (1936); *see also* CATHY PICKENS, TRUE CRIME STORIES OF EASTERN NORTH CAROLINA 105 (2020) (noting that, in a murder case, "[l]ocal attorney Elsie Webb, later one of the cofounders of the North Carolina (later Rockingham) Motor Speedway, was hired by the Hines family as a private prosecutor"). In some instances, the use of private prosecutors to assist the public prosecution has been denied. *E.g.*, SPOMA JOVANOVIC, DEMOCRACY, DIALOGUE, AND COMMUNITY ACTION: TRUTH AND RECONCILIATION IN GREENSBORO 11 (2012) ("The survivors, who had wanted but were denied a private prosecutor to assist with the case, expressed concerns that the Greensboro district attorney's office in charge of the prosecution had made legal strategy decisions that public comments that belittled the position of the survivors."); SINGE WALLER, LOVE AND REVOLUTION: A POLITICAL MEMOIR—PEOPLE'S HISTORY OF THE GREENSBORO MASSACRE, ITS SETTING AND AFTERMATH 282 (2002) ("In February, Judge James Long denied without a hearing our motion that the court appoint a private prosecutor to assist the prosecution. William Kunstler had agreed to serve in this role.").

304. State v. Moose, 313 S.E.2d 507, 513 (N.C. 1984) ("The record before us discloses that the district attorney was at all times in control of the prosecution; that he adequately supervised the participation of the private prosecutor; and that the two attorneys worked as a team sharing the workload evenly."); State v. Page, 206 S.E.2d 771, 772 (N.C. Ct. App. 1974), *cert. denied*, 209 S.E.2d 287 (N.C. 1974).

305. State v. Camacho, 406 S.E.2d 868 (N.C. 1991); State v. Woodruff, 392 S.E.2d 434 (N.C. Ct. App. 1990), *aff'd*, 399 S.E.2d 114 (N.C. 1991) (per curiam).

306. Whitfield v. Gilchrist, 497 S.E.2d 412, 415 (N.C. 1998) (State v. Camacho, 406 S.E.2d 868, 871 (N.C. 1991); State v. Best, 186 S.E.2d 1 (N.C. 1972)).

307. State v. Camacho, 406 S.E.2d 868, 871 (N.C. 1991) (citations omitted).

308. 854 F.2d 656 (4th Cir. 1988).

309. *See* MORRIS DEES, A SEASON FOR JUSTICE (1991).

310. *Person*, 854 F.2d at 659.

311. *Id.*

312. *Id.* at 663.

313. *Id.*

314. *Id.*

315. *Person*, 854 F.2d at 663 (*quoting Young*, 481 U.S. at 806 n.17). According to the *Person* court:

> The more appropriate analytic focus is on the evil at which the *Young* rule forbidding total abdication to private counsel for interested parties was aimed. That evil was the possibility that the criminal contempt sanction would be invoked and prosecuted by private counsel, operating in the adversarial mode, solely to secure advantage to his client and hence without regard for any interests of the defendant and the public in fairness of the criminal process. That evil is sufficiently guarded against—both in appearance and reality—by the presence of disinterested government counsel effectively in a position and manifestly prepared to exercise control over the critical prosecutorial decisions—most critically, whether to prosecute, what targets of prosecution to select, what investigative powers to utilize, what sanctions to seek, plea bargains to strike, or immunities to grant. It is control over these critical prosecutorial decisions which determine the fairness of particular prosecutions that is the important consideration; operational conduct of the trial is actually of subordinate concern, except as it may actually impact upon the more fundamental prosecutorial decisions.

Id. at 663–64 (citations omitted).

316. *Id.* In this final respect, the *Person* court stated as follows: "We can conceive of situations in which without ever relinquishing effective control of the prosecution government counsel might for tactical reasons give over even more substantial portions of the actual conduct of trial to particularly skilled or knowledgeable private counsel." *Id.*

317. State v. Stepp, 178 N.W. 951, 953 (N.D. 1920); *see also* Ex parte Corliss, 114 N.W. 962, 962–63 (N.D. 1907) ("Petitioner admits that prior to such official appointments and employment he had been employed by private individuals to prosecute certain criminal cases against one Edward G. Patterson for alleged violation of the law of this state prohibiting the manufacture and sale of intoxicating liquors, and that said official appointments and official employment were made for the purpose of investing him with legal authority in said criminal prosecutions, and to authorize him to attend before said grand jury in the interest of such private employers. Petitioner concedes that his appointment as assistant state's attorney was and is void for the reason that he is a nonresident of Burleigh county. His employment by the board of county commissioners was concededly for a nominal consideration. It was not a good-faith employment for the purpose of assisting the state's attorney in the discharge of his public duties, but was, as conceded by him, as above stated, for the purpose of gaining admission to the sessions of the grand jury for the purpose of discharging his duties under such private employment. Even if a good-faith employment by the county commissioners would legally qualify him to visit the grand jury session, which we seriously question, we are clear that he had no such right under the employment in question, as he concedes, as before stated, that it was merely to enable him to fulfill a contract of employment entered into with private individuals. Under such facts, it was manifestly improper for him to appear before such grand jury, and the district judge properly excluded him therefrom.").

318. State v. Kent, 62 N.W. 631, 633–34 (N.D. 1895). In its opinion, the Supreme Court of North Dakota added:

> The best mode of reaching the truth is by the strenuous contentions of opposing counsel, each animated by the conviction that the cause he has espoused is just. The public have some interests at stake in a criminal prosecution. May all the zeal be displayed on one side, and none be tolerated on the other? The public interests demand that a prosecution should be conducted with energy and skill. While the prosecuting officer should see that no unfair advantage is taken of the accused, yet he is not a judicial officer. Those who are required to exercise judicial functions in the case are the judge and the jury. The public prosecutor is necessarily a partisan in the case. If he were compelled to proceed with the same circumspection as the judge and the jury, there would be an end to the conviction of criminals. Zeal in the prosecution of criminal cases is therefore to be commended, and not condemned. It is the zeal of counsel in the court room, alone, of which the accused can complain. No decision can be found which questions the right of the prosecuting officer to consult with, and receive all manner of aid, even during the trial, from counsel for private parties, outside of the court room. And if such zeal in the court room, on the trial, does not result in error, what conceivable difference can it make whether such assistant was employed by the public, or by private persons? May not cross-examination of witnesses be conducted, and arguments to court and jury be made, by one who is as much convinced of the guilt of the accused as his counsel is persuaded of his innocence? The manner of conducting the case in the court room cannot work legal prejudice to the accused, without resulting in error for which the conviction will be set aside. It is therefore of no legal importance what inspires the zeal of the attorney who assists in the trial. Whatever is done to the injury of the prisoner by private counsel, for which he can have no redress, is done out of court; for instance, by concealing or fabricating evidence. At just this point, where the zeal of counsel employed by private parties may be deadly to the accused, no kind of safeguard is or can be thrown around him. The prosecuting officer may consult with, and be entirely governed by the advice of, such private counsel; and yet the accused has no remedy, if the private counsel does not participate in the trial. If he does so participate, his zeal works no more prejudice to the accused than the zeal of any other equally able counsel who may be employed by the public. The cases all agree that an assistant hired by the public may engage in the trial without giving the prisoner any legal cause for complaint. Of course, the latter may think he is prejudiced because of being compelled to confront an exceptionally able and experienced prosecutor, but this furnishes no legal ground for overthrowing the conviction. The question can be placed in a clear light by the following statement of it: Can a defendant in a criminal case, who is obliged to submit to the zeal of an assistant prosecutor employed by the public, insist that the zeal of an assistant counsel employed by interested parties shall not be

displayed against him, although it results in no error on the part of the prosecution in the management of the case? We think there is only one answer to this question, and that is against the right of the accused to complain in either case, so long as no error has been committed by the assistant on the trial. The rule is different, however, in Michigan and Massachusetts, under statutes very similar to ours. Meister v. People, 31 Mich. 99; Sneed v. People, 38 Mich. 251;People v. Hurst, 41 Mich. 328, 1 N. W. 1027; People v. Bemis (Mich.) 16 N. W. 794; Com. v. Gibbs, 4 Gray, 146. The reasoning of Judge Campbell in Meister v. People, while very plausible, does not convince us that there should be interpolated into the statute an implied prohibition against counsel employed by interested parties assisting in the prosecution. We are unable to discover in the statute any other policy than that of transferring the control of criminal prosecutions from private to public hands. We think that the control of the public prosecutor over the proceedings is a sufficient guaranty that the accused will not be made the innocent victim of overzealous prosecution by private persons. While aware that Judge Campbell has made out a strong case in support of his view, we cannot discover in the legislation of this state the evidence of a policy hostile to the quite general practice of allowing the prosecuting officer to be assisted by counsel retained by those having a personal interest in the prosecution distinct from that of the general public. In support of our ruling on this point, we cite the following cases: State v. Helm, (Iowa) 61 N. W. 246; Keyes v. State (Ind. Sup.) 23 N. E. 1097; Polin v. State (Neb.) 16 N. W. 899; State v. Bartlett, 55 Me. 220; State v. Fitzgerald, 49 Iowa, 260; State v. Wilson, 24 Kan. 189; Burkhard v. State, 18 Tex. App. 599–618; Gardner v. State, 55 N. J. Law, 17, 26 Atl. 30; Benningfield v. Com. (Ky.) 17 S. W. 271; People v. Tidwell (Utah) 12 Pac. 61; 1 Bish. Cr. Proc. § 281; Whart. Cr. Pl. & Prac. § 555. See, also, People v. Powell (Cal.) 25 Pac. 481; Jackson v. State (Wis.) 51 N. W. 89; U. S. v. Hanway, 2 Wall. Jr. 139, Fed. Cas. No. 15,299. See, particularly, the reasoning of Judge Elliott in Keyes v. State (Ind. Sup.) 23 N. E. 1097, and Judge Brewer in State v. Wilson, 24 Kan. 189. The decision of the Wisconsin supreme court in Biemel v. State, 37 N. W. 249, sustaining the Michigan and Massachusetts doctrine, appears to be based upon legislation in that state authorizing the trial judge to appoint an assistant whenever he thinks the public interests require it, and providing that such assistant shall be paid out of the public funds. See pages 248 and 249. The case of Lawrence v. State (Wis.) 7 N. W. 343, is distinguished in the Biemel Case on the ground that it was decided before the new statute was passed, giving the trial judge power to appoint an assistant to be paid out of the public treasury. The Lawrence Case is more in harmony with, than opposed to, our views. We hold that it was not error to permit Mr. Nye to assist in the prosecution, at the request of the state's attorney, because of his having been employed by the brothers of the murdered woman.

State v. Kent, 62 N.W. 631, 634–35 (N.D. 1895).

319. Saefke v. Stenehjem, 673 N.W.2d 41, 47 (N.D. 2003).

320. State v. Flohr, 301 N.W.2d 367, 369 (N.D. 1980).

321. 410 U.S. 614 (1973).

322. State v. Leingang, 763 N.W.2d 769, 774 (N.D. 2009) (citing various cases); *see also* Wishnatsky v. Bergquist, 550 N.W.2d 394, 399 (N.D. 1996) ("[W]here a private citizen merely summons the police for assistance or to report an offense, and does not specifically request that the person be arrested nor supply false information, no liability for false arrest arises. *See Harrison,* 544 S.W.2d at 693; Landis, 98 A.L.R.3d at § 2; 32 Am.Jur.2d *False Imprisonment* § 41 (1995). And there is no liability where a private citizen merely provides information to the police and leaves the decision whether to arrest to the officer's judgment and discretion. *E.g., Johnson,* 300 N.W.2d at 13; 3 Lee & Lindahl, at § 41.02; Prosser & Keeton, Torts § 11 (5th ed.1984); Restatement (Second) of Torts, at § 45A cmt. c; *see also Larson v. Baer,* 418 N.W.2d 282, 287 (N.D. 1988) (there is no liability for malicious prosecution if a private citizen merely gives authorities information he believes to be true and leaves the decision to prosecute to the officer's discretion).").

323. Ohio Stat. § 2935.09; *see also* State v. Bergandine, No. 19 CAC 10 0054, 2020 WL 2462560, at *5 (Ohio Ct. App., 5th Dist., Delaware County May 12, 2020) ("[A] private citizen, to 'cause prosecution,' now must file an affidavit with a 'reviewing official' for the purpose of review to determine if a complaint should be filed by the prosecutor.") (citations omitted); Mango v. City of Columbus, Case Nos. 2:19-cv-31202:19-cv-5282, 2020 WL 5247939, at *1 (S.D. Ohio Sept. 3, 2020) ("Ohio law permits a private citizen to initiate

criminal proceedings using the following procedure: 'A private citizen having knowledge of the facts who seeks to cause an arrest or prosecution under this section may file an affidavit charging the offense committed with a reviewing official for the purpose of review to determine if a complaint should be filed by the prosecuting attorney or attorney charged by law with the prosecution of offenses in the court or before the magistrate. A private citizen may file an affidavit charging the offense committed with the clerk of a court of record before or after the normal business hours of the reviewing officials if the clerk's office is open at those times. A clerk who receives an affidavit before or after the normal business hours of the reviewing officials shall forward it to a reviewing official when the reviewing official's normal business hours resume.'") (citing OHIO REV. CODE ANN. § 2935.09(D) (West 2020)); *id.* at *20 ("It is difficult to find instances of private citizens so deeply involved in the initiation of a criminal prosecution as Ms. Mango alleges was the case here. Indeed, this country abolished the use of private prosecutors some time ago. Given this history, there can be no doubt that a private citizen who initiates a prosecution is a state actor under the public function test. To declare otherwise would allow a government to farm out its prosecutorial power with impunity.") (citations omitted); *id.* at *21 ("Ohio Rev. Code § 2935.09(D) requires all Complaints to be filed by a prosecutor even if they are initiated by a private citizen"; "the filing of a Complaint by a private citizen is significant involvement in the State's criminal process, one normally reserved for a prosecutor (i.e., the government)"); Mills v. Westlake, 70 N.E.3d 1189, 1195–96 (Ohio Ct. App., 8th Dist., Cuyahoga County 2016) ("[T]he Ohio Supreme Court has recognized that a malicious prosecution action may be brought against an individual who is not a government employee. A 'private person who initiates or procures the institution of criminal proceedings against another is not subject to liability unless the person against whom the criminal proceedings were initiated proves all * * * of the above-listed elements' of malicious prosecution.") (citing Ash v. Ash, 651 N.E.2d 945 (Ohio 1995)).

324. State v. Jones, 2011 WL 4553117, at *5 (Ohio Ct. App. 11th Dist., Portage County Sept. 30, 2011) (citations omitted).

325. OHIO CONST., art. IV, § 20.

326. State v. Luther, No. 2003-A-0130, 2005 WL 517473, at *2 (Ohio Ct. App. Mar. 4, 2005). *Compare* State v. Berry, 1983 WL 4870, at *1 (Ohio Ct. App., 2nd Dist., Clark County Mar. 24, 1983) ("Historically Ohio has never restricted the right of attorneys to engage in a general practice of law while representing one of its subdivisions as prosecutor. The reasons are discussed by the trial judge in his opinion and are immaterial here. Small counties still do not need or cannot afford to maintain an exclusive staff with essential facilities for the variety of legal services they require. The debate over complete separation of public and private services of prosecutors surfaces periodically and continues across the nation. *Ethical Considerations in Prosecution*, National College of District Attorneys (1977)."); State v. Broady, 321 N.E.2d 890 (Ohio Ct. App. 1974) (citing EC 7-13 of the Code of Professional Responsibility providing in part: "The responsibility of a public prosecutor differs from that of the usual advocate; his duty is to seek justice, not merely to convict.").

327. OHIO STAT. § 2931.18(A).

328. OHIO STAT. § 2938.13.

329. Carpenter v. State, 929 P.2d 988, 995 (Okla. Ct. App. 1996); *see also id.*:

> At Proposition IV Petitioner claims the district attorney acted as a special prosecutor in seeking the death penalty by allowing his decision to seek the death penalty to be controlled by the wishes of the victim's family. There is no dispute that the district attorney here consulted the victim's family during plea negotiations with Petitioner. However, his consultation with the family concerning their feelings is hardly proof that the district attorney, as claimed by Petitioner, allowed the victim's family to completely control all decisions concerning plea negotiations. The record reflects that the district attorney consulted with the victim's family and conveyed to Petitioner that the family considered a plea arrangement of life to be unacceptable. However, the district attorney also testified that he never seriously considered offering Petitioner a life sentence as he felt it was not appropriate in this case.
>
> Regardless, Petitioner's characterization of the district attorney as a "special" or "private" prosecutor is inapposite here. The record reflects that the State's counsel was, at all times, in control of the case before us. The fact that he consulted the victim's family and kept them informed, at all

times, of the case's progress, is not *prima facie* evidence he abdicated his role as prosecutor and assumed the role of avenger. It is well established that the State is under no obligation to plea bargain with a defendant. *State ex rel. Stout v. Craytor,* 753 P.2d 1365, 1368 (Okl.Cr.1988). Likewise, the decision whether to prosecute and what charge to file is within the discretion of the prosecutor. *Id.*

Nothing in Petitioner's argument persuades this Court that the decision to pursue the death penalty in this case was either improper and/or unsupported by the law and facts. Moreover, even if Petitioner could quantify and document the extent to which the victim's family participated in any decision concerning the charging and prosecution of this case, he alleges nothing which shows that the course of action pursued by the State would have been any different had the family been absent during the entire process. Additionally, Petitioner has cited no supporting authorities to bolster his position that it is improper to advise a victim's family of case developments, or to consider their feelings regarding the case.

We agree that had the State appointed a special prosecutor, abdicated its duty by formally delegating its authority to another to prosecute the case, or allowed the family to hire private counsel to represent them, then Petitioner's cited authorities as to the impropriety of engaging the services of a special prosecutor would have been relevant. There was no special prosecutor and the victim's family did not hire their own counsel to represent them. Likewise, the citation to *Robison v. Maynard,* 829 F.2d 1501 (10th Cir.1987) is inapplicable here. That case dealt with the exclusion of testimony from the victim's family members as to whether the death penalty was the appropriate punishment. That is not the case before this Court, and it does not support the argument advanced by Petitioner. We find no error here.

330. Driskell v. State, 659 P.2d 343, 346–47 (Okla. Ct. Crim. App. 1993).

331. *E.g.*, Evans v. Willis, 97 P. 1047, 1051 (Okla. 1908) ("[S]ince the adoption of our state Constitution, no person can be prosecuted criminally in any court of record in this state for felony or misdemeanor other than by presentment of an indictment by a grand jury, or by information exhibited by the county attorney or other officer authorized by law. The information filed in this case by the private prosecutor, who was neither the county attorney nor any officer authorized by law, was void."); Roberts v. State, 115 P.2d 270, 272–73 (Okla. Crim. Ct. App. 1941) ("The Code of Criminal Procedure directs that all informations shall be signed by the county attorney. This is required as a guaranty of good faith and to protect a defendant against prosecution by private parties without authority of law; but where a defendant pleads to an information which is not signed by the county attorney, and without objection goes to trial thereon, he waives all right to afterwards object to the information upon this ground, and cannot be heard upon appeal to complain that the information was not signed by the county attorney as directed by law."); Lee v. State, 231 P. 324, 325 (Okla. Crim. Ct. App. 1924) ("Under our statutes a private individual cannot become a public prosecutor, nor can a county attorney act purely as a private prosecutor. Section 5741, Comp. Stat. 1921, provides that it shall be the duty of the county attorney to appear and prosecute and defend, on behalf of the state or county, all actions or proceedings, civil or criminal, in which the state or county is interested or a party.").

332. Reed v. State, 103 P. 1042, 1052 (Okla. Ct. Crim. App. 1909); *see also* id. ("The laws of this state only prohibit persons other than the county attorney, or his deputies, from performing such acts in the prosecution of crimes as are strictly official, such as appearing before and advising the grand jury, verifying informations, approving complaints, etc. The assistance of private counsel in the trial of criminal cases is not prohibited. This is a matter entirely in the discretion of the county attorney, who has complete control in conducting public prosecutions, subject only to the supervision of the court upon the trial. Regardless of the ability and the zeal of county attorneys, the proper administration of the criminal law often requires such assistance. County attorneys are prohibited from accepting private compensation. As wealth, influence, and eminent ability are often arrayed on the side of the defense, it is well and wise that the policy of the law permits such assistance to the prosecution.").

333. Okla. Stat. Ann. § 215.4. *See also* Haney v. State, 850 P.2d 1087, 1092 (Okla. 1993):

District attorneys have a statutory duty to prosecute or defend any action in which a county in their district is interested or is a party. They are prohibited from engaging in the private practice of law. Further, a district attorney cannot act as a purely private prosecutor. These statements merely recognize a district attorney represents the public interest, not the interests of private individuals. If the intent of the Legislature was to recognize or establish an attorney-client relationship between a district attorney and a custodial parent in a situation under the statutory scheme at issue here, a situation would exist which would foster or raise the potential for serious conflicts of interest within that relationship. For example, a district attorney would be compelled to prosecute his "client" should the individual violate criminal statutes. Further, if custody of the child is transferred to another, the district attorney could be compelled to enforce support payments against his former "client", which inherently would pose confidentiality problems. We simply do not believe the Legislature intended such potential results, but instead at all times recognized district attorneys were deemed to represent the interests of the State, rather than the custodial parent.

334. State v. Swanson, 266 P.3d 45, 48 n.5 (Or. 2011).

335. State v. Rand, 112 P.2d 1034, 1035 (Or. 1941):

This complaint meets the requirement of § 28–602, O.C.L.A., which provides that in a justice's court, likewise in a municipal court (§ 95–204, O.C.L.A.), a criminal action is commenced by the filing of a complaint therein, verified by the oath of the person commencing the action, who is thereafter known as the private prosecutor.

Section 26–1217, O.C.L.A., is relied upon by the defendant in his contention that the complaint was "fatally defective". That section provides that the name of every person who voluntarily appears before any justice of the peace to prosecute any person in a criminal action shall be endorsed upon the complaint "as private prosecutor" and if it be found by the justice or court trying the action or hearing the proceeding that the prosecution is malicious or without probable cause, that fact "shall be entered upon record in said action or proceeding by said justice or court." The following section, § 26–1218, O.C.L.A., provides that upon making the entry prescribed in the preceding section the justice or court must immediately render judgment "against the private prosecutor for the costs and disbursements of the action or proceeding, which may be enforced by execution, in the same manner as judgment in a civil action".

These two sections of the code last mentioned were enacted in 1882 (Laws 1882, page 13), under the following title: "An act providing for taxing private prosecutors with cost and disbursements of criminal actions when found to be malicious or without probable cause." It is apparent, both from the title and the body of the 1882 act, that the purpose of enacting that law was to deter the institution of prosecutions malicious or without probable cause, by imposing the costs and disbursements thereof as a penalty.

336. State v. Pointer, 213 P. 621, 626 (Or. 1923).

337. Hood River County v. Stevenson, 33 P.3d 325, 329 (Or. 2001) ("the county ordinance permits a private party to initiate a proceeding of the dog control ordinances").

338. State v. Rogers, 836 P.2d 1308, 1317 (Or. 1992) (en banc):

In determining what the term "complainant" means in the context of ORS 136.220, we look to the legislation itself. The term "complainant," which was added to the statute in a 1961 amendment to ORS 136.220, Or. Laws 1961, ch 444, § 1, 5 is not defined in ORS chapter 136. The 1961 amendment to ORS 136.220 substituted the term "complainant" for the phrase "the person indorsed thereon as the prosecutor" in both subsections (1) and (2) of ORS 136.220. The amendment also reworded and divided former subsection (2) into subsections (2)(a) to (c) and (3) and added the word "or information" after indictment in referring to the charging instrument. It appears that the legislature intended no major substantive changes by the 1961 amendment. In the minutes of the Senate Judiciary Committee, the bill was referred to as a "housekeeping" amendment that would "delete 'prosecutor' because the private prosecutor no longer exists in the law." Minutes, Senate Judiciary Committee (HB 1171), April 13, 1961.

339. Private prosecutions were common in colonial Pennsylvania and early America. In re Hickson, 821 A.2d 1238, 1244–45 (Pa. 2003):

> In colonial Pennsylvania, crimes were viewed "as an offense against the individual victim[,]" and private prosecutions were the most common mode by which the criminal justice system functioned in the colonial era. Note, *The Constitutional Validity of Pennsylvania Rule of Criminal Procedure 133(B)(2) and the Traditional Role of the Pennsylvania Courts in the Prosecutorial Function,* 52 U. Pitt. L. Rev. 269, 274 (1990) (hereinafter "*Pennsylvania Courts in the Prosecutorial Function* "). This was consonant with the English common law principle that "the Crown did not supply a public prosecutor to handle routine felonies. The victim or his family was therefore required to hire counsel to bring the guilty party into the criminal justice system." *State v. Atkins,* 163 W. Va. 502, 261 S.E.2d 55, 57 (1979). In fact, the victim served a multi-function role, in which he apprehended, prosecuted, and sometimes even jailed the accused. *Pennsylvania Courts in the Prosecutorial Function, supra,* at 274.
>
> In the post-Revolutionary era, the state, as the representative for society as a whole, began to be seen as the injured party in criminal matters, and the role of the government in prosecuting criminal matters began to grow; ultimately, the Pennsylvania Legislature established the office of district attorney in 1850. *See id.* at 275. Yet, with this shift in how crimes were generally prosecuted, a citizen's right to pursue his victimizer in criminal courts via a private criminal complaint was never abolished in this Commonwealth. Rather, the Legislature enshrined it in statutory enactments, *id.,* and later, this court provided an avenue via the predecessor to Rule 106.
>
> Based on this history, we find that provisions authorizing private criminal complaints, such as Rule 106, have their roots in a time when crimes were viewed as an offense against individuals rather than the state, visiting upon directly involved parties a harm greater than that experienced by the population as a whole. Thus, in contrast to the prosecutions initiated by the Commonwealth, it is the recognition that a crime has caused an individual a substantial, direct, and immediate injury that is a personal one that animates Rule 106 prosecutions. This is the interest—the interest of seeking justice for harm arising from a crime that directly impacted on oneself—that must be established to show that a party may seek judicial review of the disapproval of a private criminal complaint brought pursuant to Rule 106.

Rule 106, which is renumbered and is now titled "Continuances in Summary and Court Cases," was referenced in previous cases. *E.g.,* In re Hickson, 765 A.2d 372, 378 (Pa. Super. 2000):

> In Pennsylvania then, the right of private individuals to compel the district attorney, via the courts, to file charges is found in statute (Section 1409) and in rule (106). Rule 106 differs in some respects from the right under Section 1409. In the former, the conduct and competence of the district attorney to handle the matter is not questioned, although court intervention is necessary to trigger the prosecution. In the latter it is the district attorney's conduct and, perhaps, her lack of objectivity or competence, that prompts court intervention and results in her replacement. Still, Section 1409 and Rule 106 both address the rights and remedies accorded a private individual who is at odds with a district attorney over the handling of a particular case.
>
> To determine the necessity and definition of standing in bringing private criminal complaints, we trace the history. Historically, both Section 1409 and Rule 106 have developed as mechanisms designed to maintain victims' rights. Prior to the introduction of the public prosecutor's office in the late 1700s, victims personally dealt with individuals who committed crimes against them. *See* Note, *The Constitutional Validity of Pennsylvania Rule of Criminal Procedure 133(B)(2) and the Traditional Role of the Pennsylvania Courts in the Prosecutorial Function,* 52 U. Pitt. L. Rev. 269, 275 (1990). "Prior to the Revolutionary War, private citizens were the driving force behind criminal prosecutions.... [T]he victim searched for the criminal, arrested him ..., drew up indictments, prosecuted the criminal personally ..., and sometimes even served as the criminal's jailer...." *Id.*
>
> Although the public character of the office of the prosecutor has been firmly entrenched in our justice system, concern that the victim's voice not be lost remains. The victim has been characterized as an essential party to the criminal process and permitting the victim's participation in a criminal proceeding, even in the face of opposition by the publicly elected prosecutor, is considered by many as vital to a successful system of justice. *See generally* Benson, *The Lost Victim*

and Other Failures of the Public Law Experiment, 9 Harv. J.L. & Pub. Pol'y 399 (1986); Cardenas, *The Crime Victim in the Prosecutorial Process,* 9 Harv. J.L. & Pub. Pol'y 357 (1986); Note, *Private Prosecution: A Remedy for District Attorneys' Unwarranted Inaction,* 65 Yale L.J. 209 (1955).

See also Michaels v. Barrasse, 681 A.2d 1362, 1365 (Pa. Super. 1996):

> We note that the law does not give a private complainant a right to an evidentiary hearing. *See Commonwealth v. Eisemann,* 276 Pa. Super. 543, 544 n. 4, 419 A.2d 591, 592 n. 4 (1980) (the court is not required to grant a hearing pursuant to Rule 106; the rule merely gives the private prosecutor the opportunity to have his complaint reviewed following an adverse decision by a district attorney). Thus, it was well within the trial judge's discretion to conduct a conference to review the private criminal complaints.
>
> While the trial court was not required to conduct a hearing on the record, it is necessary for this court, as a reviewing court, to examine the trial court's reason(s) for its denial of the private criminal complaint. As stated earlier, our review is limited to determining whether the trial court abused its discretion or committed an error of law; we are limited to ascertaining the propriety of the trial court's actions. *Brown, supra; McGinley, supra.* Thus, we are required to review the trial court's *de novo* review of the complaint and its determination of whether a *prima facie* case was established. *Brown, supra; McGinley, supra.* Here, the trial court's order did not contain sufficient information for an appropriate review by this court; it simply affirmed the district attorney's disapproval without explanation. We, therefore, must remand this matter to the trial court for the preparation of an opinion in support of its order. Such a measure will enable this court to review the propriety of the trial court's actions.

340. Landmesser v. Office of Luzerne County Dist. Attorney, No. 310 C.D. 2019, 2019 WL 3814876, at *2 (Pa. Commonwealth Ct. Aug. 14, 2019).

341. Pa. R. Crim. P. 506.

342. A private attorney may conduct a prosecution in Pennsylvania. 16 Pa. Stat. § 1409 ("If any district attorney shall neglect or refuse to prosecute in due form of law any criminal charge regularly returned to the district attorney or to the court, or if at any stage of the proceedings the district attorney and the private counsel employed by the prosecutor shall differ as to the manner of conducting the trial, the prosecutor may present a petition to the court, setting forth the character of the complaint, and verify the same by affidavit. If the court shall be of the opinion that it is a proper case for a criminal proceeding or prosecution, it may direct any private counsel employed by such prosecutor to conduct the entire proceeding, and where an indictment is necessary, to verify the same by the private counsel's own signature, as fully as the same could be done by the district attorney.").

343. Commonwealth v. Briggs, 12 A.3d 291, 331 (Pa. 2011).

344. In re Private Criminal Complaints of Rafferty, 969 A.2d 578, 581 (Pa. Super. 2009).

345. Id. at 581–82 (citing Commonwealth v. Michaliga, 947 A.2d 786, 791–92 (Pa. Super. 2008). *See also* Commonwealth v. Sennett, No. 1275 WDA 2018, 2019 WL 2121356, at *2 (Pa. Super Ct. May 14, 2019):

> In addressing a district attorney's refusal to prosecute a private criminal complaint, our Court has consistently held that a determination that a private criminal complaint "lacks prosecutorial merit" is a policy determination. *In re Private Complaint of Adams,* 764 A.2d 577, 581 (Pa. Super. 2000). When a district attorney's denial of a private criminal complaint is based wholly on policy considerations, the trial court must defer to the prosecutor's discretion absent a gross abuse of that discretion. *In re Wilson,* 879 A.2d 199, 215 (Pa. Super. 2005). An appellate court will review the trial court's decision for an abuse of discretion, in keeping with settled principles of appellate review of discretionary matters. *Commonwealth v. Michaliga,* 947 A.2d 786, 791–792 (Pa. Super. 2008).

In re Hamelly, 200 A.3d 97, 101 (Pa. Super. Ct. 2018):

> "A private criminal complaint must at the outset set forth a *prima facie* case of criminal conduct." *In re Ullman,* 995 A.2d at 1213. Nevertheless, "a well-crafted private criminal complaint cannot be the end of the inquiry for the prosecutor." *Id.* (quoting *In re Private Criminal Complaint of Adams,* 764 A.2d 577, 580 (Pa. Super. 2000)). The district attorney must investigate the

allegations of a properly drafted complaint to permit a proper decision on whether to approve or disapprove the complaint. *In re Ullman*, 995 A.2d at 1213. "[S]uch investigation is not necessary where the allegations of criminal conduct in the complaint are unsupported by factual averments." *Id.* (quoting *Commonwealth v. Muroski*, 352 Pa.Super. 15, 506 A.2d 1312, 1317 (1986) (*en banc*)). Both the district attorney and the trial court have a responsibility to prevent the misuse of judicial and prosecutorial resources in the pursuit of futile prosecutions. *In re Ullman*, 995 A.2d at 1213.

Armolt v. Kerestes, No. 2013 MDA 2015, 2016 WL 32223423, at *3 (Pa. Super. Ct. June 10, 2016):

In addressing a District Attorney's refusal to prosecute a private criminal complaint, our Court has consistently held that a determination that a private criminal complaint "lacks prosecutorial merit" is a policy determination. *In re Private Complaint of Adams*, 764 A.2d 577, 581 (Pa. Super. 2000). When a District Attorney's denial of a private criminal complaint is based wholly on policy considerations, then the trial court must defer to the prosecutor's discretion absent a gross abuse of that discretion. *In re Wilson*, 879 A.2d 199, 215 (Pa. Super. 2005). An appellate court will review the trial court's decision for an abuse of discretion, in keeping with settled principles of appellate review of discretionary matters. *Commonwealth v. Michaliga*, 947 A.2d 786, 791–92 (Pa. Super.2008).

A District Attorney's decision not to prosecute a criminal complaint for policy reasons carries a presumption of good faith and soundness. *Id.* at 792. To challenge that decision before the trial court, a complainant must show that the District Attorney's decision amounted to bad faith, fraud, or unconstitutionality. *In re Private Criminal Complaint of Rafferty*, 969 A.2d 578, 581–82 (Pa. Super.2009). Specifically, he must show that the facts of the case lead only to the conclusion that the District Attorney's decision was patently discriminatory, arbitrary or pretextual, and therefore, not in the public interest. *Michaliga*, 947 A.2d at 792.

346. Cronan ex rel. State v. Cronan, 774 A.2d 866, 870–77 & n.3 (R.I. 2001). The *Cronan* case was later cited by a dissent in *Robertson v. U.S. ex rel. Watson*, 560 U.S. 272, 279–80 (2010) (Roberts, C.J., dissenting):

To say that private parties could (and still can, in some places) exercise some control over criminal prosecutions says nothing to rebut the widely accepted principle that those private parties necessarily acted (and now act) on behalf of the sovereign. See, *e.g.*, *Cronan ex rel. State v. Cronan*, 774 A.2d 866, 877 (R.I.2001) ("[A]ttorneys conducting private prosecutions stand in the shoes of the state"); *State v. Westbrook*, 279 N.C. 18, 36, 181 S.E.2d 572, 583 (1971) ("The prosecuting attorney, whether the solicitor or privately employed counsel, represents the State"); Sidman, The Outmoded Concept of Private Prosecution, 25 Am. U.L. Rev. 754, 774 (1976) ("[T]he privately retained attorney becomes, in effect, a temporary public prosecutor"). Indeed, many of the state court authorities Watson herself cites expressly recognize this fundamental point. See, *e.g.*, *Katz v. Commonwealth*, 379 Mass. 305, 312, 399 N.E.2d 1055, 1060 (1979) ("[I]t is clear with respect to the criminal aspects of the present case that the Commonwealth ... is the adverse party").

347. In re Richland County Magistrate's Court, 699 S.E.2d 161, 162–63 (S.C. 2010) (quoting Black's Law Dictionary 403 (8th ed. 2004) (italics in original).

348. *Id.* at 162–65; *see also* Gibson v. State, 514 S.E.2d 320, 325 (S.C. 1999) ("The overriding theme of the *Brady* cases is the emphasis the Supreme Court has placed on the prosecutor›s responsibility for fair play. In close cases, 'the prudent prosecutor will resolve doubtful questions in favor of disclosure. This is as it should be. Such disclosures will serve to justify trust in the prosecutor as the representative ... of a sovereignty ... whose interest ... in a criminal prosecution is not that it shall win a case, but that justice shall be done.'").

349. State v. Nichols, 481 S.E.2d 118, 122–23 (S.C. 1997) (citing In re Jolly, 239 S.E.2d 490 (S.C. 1977)); *see also* State v. Mattoon, 339 S.E.2d 867, 868–69 (S.C. 1986):

Private counsel may participate in the trial of a case to assist the solicitor. *State v. Addis*, 257 S.C. 482, 186 S.E.2d 415 (1972); *State v. Lee*, 255 S.C. 309, 178 S.E.2d 652 (1971); *State v. Gregory, et al.*, 172 S.C. 329, 174 S.E. 10 (1924). Appellant asserts Gonzales' participation went beyond permissible limits since he served as chief prosecutor and had full control of the case.

In 1984, the general assembly enacted S.C. Code Ann. Section 1-7-405 (Supp.1984), which grants solicitors authority to appoint assistant solicitors and to vest them with "such responsibility as he directs." The statute does not permit a solicitor to relinquish prosecutorial control to a private attorney, but it removes any limitations upon his actual trial participation arguably imposed by our prior decisions. It was not error to allow Gonzales to try the case without the solicitor being present.

Appellant next argues Gonzales should have been disqualified from prosecuting the case because of a conflict of interest. She asserts Gonzales was not disinterested because he was prosecuting appellant at the same time he was representing the City which initiated the charges against her.

We have recognized that a special assistant solicitor is not automatically disqualified because of his simultaneous representation of an interested person. *State v. Addis, supra.* Disqualification occurs when a special assistant solicitor attempts to use his authority in the criminal action to the advantage of his civil client, or otherwise compromises his neutrality in the criminal proceeding. *Jones v. Richards,* 776 F.2d 1244 (4th Cir.1985). Nothing in this record suggests any improper motives or action on Gonzales' part.

Although we find no error in this case, we express our disapproval of the practice of appointing private counsel to prosecute criminal cases. Because of the increased possibility of a conflict when private counsel is involved, we believe the practice should be discouraged.

350. State v. Ferguson, 204 N.W. 652, 660 (S.D. 1925).

351. State v. Magnuson, 202 N.W. 638 (S.D. 1925) (adopting "the reasoning and conclusions reached by the North Dakota court, in so far as such reasoning applies to the right of members of the bar of this state employed by private persons to assist the state's attorney, upon his request or with his assent") (citing State v. Kent, 62 N.W. 631 (N.D. 1895)).

352. In the Matter of the Discipline of Russell, 797 N.W.2d 77, 87 n.9 (S.D. 2011) (citing State v. Brandenburg, 344 N.W.2d 702, 706 (S.D. 1984)).

353. State v. Brandenburg, 344 N.W.2d 702, 705 (S.D. 1984).

354. *Id.* at 706.

355. Tenn. Code Ann. § 8-7-103.

356. Bovat v. Nissan North America, 2013 WL 6021458 (Tenn. Ct. App. Nov. 8, 2013) (quoting Pera v. Kroger Co., 674 S.W. 715, 722 (Tenn. 1984)).

357. Baker v. State, 417 S.W.3d 428, 437 (Tenn. 2013).

358. *Id.* at 436; *see also id.* at 436–37:

Civil contempt is remedial in character and is applied when a person refuses or fails to comply with a court order. *Beeler,* 387 S.W.3d at 520. A civil contempt action is brought to force compliance with the order and thereby secure private rights established by the order. *Overnite Transp. Co. v. Teamsters Local Union No. 480,* 172 S.W.3d 507, 510 (Tenn. 2005) (citing *Robinson v. Air Draulics Eng'g Co.,* 214 Tenn. 30, 377 S.W.2d 908, 912 (1964)). When a trial court orders imprisonment after finding civil contempt, the confinement is remedial and coercive in nature, designed to compel the contemnor to comply with the court's order. Consequently, compliance with the order will result in the contemnor's immediate release from confinement. *Id.* at 511. It has long been said that in a civil contempt case, the contemnor "carries the keys to his prison in his own pocket." *State ex rel. Anderson v. Daugherty,* 137 Tenn. 125, 191 S.W. 974, 974 (1917).

Criminal contempt, by contrast, is designed "to preserve the power and vindicate the dignity and authority of the law and the court as an organ of society." *Beeler,* 387 S.W.3d at 520 (quoting *Black v. Blount,* 938 S.W.2d 394, 398 (Tenn. 1996)); *Daugherty,*191 S.W. at 974. Sanctions for criminal contempt are generally both punitive and unconditional in nature, designed to punish past behavior, not to coerce directly compliance with a court order or influence future behavior. *See Beeler,* 387 S.W.3d at 520; *Black,* 938 S.W.2d at 398. Therefore, when a court imposes a definite term of confinement for conduct constituting criminal contempt, the contemnor cannot shorten the term by agreeing not to continue in the behavior that resulted in his confinement. *Gompers,*

> 221 U.S. at 442, 31 S. Ct. 492. "Such imprisonment operates not as a remedy coercive in its nature, but solely as punishment for the completed act of disobedience." *Id.* at 442–43, 31 S. Ct. 492.
>
> Criminal contempt is often regarded as a "crime" because certain substantial rights and constitutional privileges afforded criminal defendants are also afforded criminal contemnors. For example, indirect criminal contempt may only be punished after the accused contemnor has been given notice and an opportunity to respond to the allegations at a hearing. Tenn. R. Crim. P. 42(b); *Cooke v. United States,* 267 U.S. 517, 537, 45 S. Ct. 390, 69 L.Ed. 767 (1925); *State v. Maddux,* 571 S.W.2d 819, 821 (Tenn.1978). In addition to the notice requirements, the United States Supreme Court and this Court have long recognized that an alleged criminal contemnor, like a person charged with a criminal offense, is presumed to be innocent, must be proven guilty beyond a reasonable doubt, and cannot be compelled to testify against himself. *Gompers,* 221 U.S. at 444, 31 S. Ct. 492; *Daugherty,* 191 S.W. at 974. An alleged contemnor is also entitled to an attorney and may have an attorney appointed to represent him at no cost if he is not able to afford one. *See Cooke,* 267 U.S. at 536–37, 45 S. Ct. 390; *Cottingham v. Cottingham,* 193 S.W.3d 531, 536 (Tenn. 2006); *see also* Tenn. Sup. Ct. R. 13, § 1(d)(1)(B).
>
> Not all rights afforded criminal defendants are available to alleged criminal contemnors, however. Contemnors are not entitled to a jury trial if the criminal contempt is not "serious" enough to require the protection of the constitutional right to a jury trial. *Bloom v. Illinois,* 391 U.S. 194, 198, 88 S. Ct. 1477, 20 L.Ed.2d 522 (1968). Although the Supreme Court has not expressly defined what constitutes a "serious contempt," the Court has repeatedly held that a jury trial is not required if the contempt is punished by confinement of six months or less. *See Taylor v. Hayes,* 418 U.S. 488, 496, 94 S. Ct. 2697, 41 L.Ed.2d 897 (1974); *Cheff v. Schnackenberg,* 384 U.S. 373, 379–80, 86 S. Ct. 1523, 16 L.Ed.2d 629 (1966); *cf. Bloom,* 391 U.S. at 211, 88 S. Ct. 1477 (concluding that a contempt punished by a two-year term of imprisonment is a "serious offense" to which the right to trial by jury applies); *Int'l Union, United Mine Workers of Am. v. Bagwell,* 512 U.S. 821, 837–38, 114 S. Ct. 2552, 129 L.Ed.2d 642 (1994) (holding that a fifty-two million dollar fine could not be imposed as a sanction for criminal contempt except through a jury trial). Similarly, in this State "[t]he general rule is that a constitutional guaranty of jury trial does not apply to proceedings to punish for contempt of court whether in a court of law, a court of equity, a court having criminal jurisdiction, or other court." *Pass v. State,* 181 Tenn. 613, 184 S.W.2d 1, 3 (1944) (internal quotation marks omitted); *see also Ahern v. Ahern,* 15 S.W.3d 73, 82 (Tenn.2000).

See also Baker v. Baker, No. M2010-01806-COA-R3-CV, 2012 WL 764918, at *7 (Tenn. Ct. App. Mar. 9, 2012):

> In *Wilson v. Wilson,* our Supreme Court held unequivocally that "no constitutional principle nor ethical standard automatically disqualifies a private attorney representing the beneficiary of a court order from simultaneously prosecuting a contempt action which alleges a violation of the order." *Wilson,* 984 S.W.2d 898, 905 (Tenn.1998). The court further noted that it was "unrealistic" to expect district attorneys to prosecute contempt actions arising from alleged violations of civil court orders. *Id.* at 903.

359. Tenn. Code Ann. § 8-7-401; *see also* State v. Parks, No. E2010-02557-CCA-R3-CD, 2012 WL 525500, at *7-8 (Tenn. Ct. Crim. App. Feb. 17, 2012):

> In Tennessee, victims have the right to hire a special prosecutor. T.C.A. § 8–7–401 (2002). Our Supreme Court has held that special prosecutors are not automatically disqualified because of due process concerns. *See Wilson v. Wilson,* 984 S.W.2d 898, 903–04 (Tenn. 1998) (holding that if "due process precludes a litigant's private attorney from prosecuting contempt proceedings, many citizens would be deprived of the benefits to which they already have been adjudged entitled by state courts and many state court orders would remain unenforced"). Further, as stated in *Wilson,* the Tennessee Supreme Court has found "no ethical standard which mandates adoption of an automatic rule of disqualification." *Id.* at 904.
>
> In *State v. Bennett,* this Court has analyzed whether a deprivation of a constitutional right was related to the participation of a private prosecutor, describing four circumstances when the involvement of a private prosecutor could cause a constitutional violation: (1) when the private

prosecutor engages in prosecutorial misconduct; (2) if the private prosecutor represents the victim or the family of the victim in a civil case arising out of the same criminal action(s); (3) it is a contempt proceeding arising out of a civil prosecution; and (4) the district attorney general does not maintain control of the case as required by statute. 798 S.W.2d 783, 786 (Tenn. Crim. App. 1990).

Three of the four the situations that would amount to constitutional violations, as described in *Bennett,* do not apply to this case: the Defendant did not claim prosecutorial misconduct, this matter is not a contempt proceeding, and the Assistant District Attorney maintained control of the case by participating in bench conferences and delivering the final rebuttal, which satisfies the statutory requirements discussed above. *See id.;* T.C.A. § 8–7–401 (2002). The trial court held a pretrial hearing to determine the qualifications of Special Prosecutor Petty, and the trial court found him fit to proceed with the criminal case. Therefore, the single remaining issue is whether a civil case arose from the same occurrence as the criminal case, causing a violation of the Defendant's due process rights.

In this case, Syiek paid Special Prosecutor Petty a flat fee retainer to send the Defendant a letter to remind him to comply with a previous agreement made with the trial court, whereby his charges would be dismissed if he paid restitution to Syiek for the damage the Defendant caused to Syiek's property. Special Prosecutor Petty's letter reminded the Defendant that he would be subject to re-indictment on the theft charge if he did not comply with the agreement. Special Prosecutor Petty stated in the letter that he will "proceed directly to the District Attorney's Office and see what can be done to enforce the payment of this restitution and follow through with the orders of the Court." The trial court found that, despite the special prosecutor's authorship of the letter, Special Prosecutor Petty did not file a civil suit on behalf of Syiek against the Defendant. As a result, no civil suit existed, and the trial court held that the special prosecutor's involvement "is not a violation of the due process rights of the [D]efendant." Therefore, considering the record and applicable law, we agree with the conclusion of the trial court. The Defendant is not entitled to relief on this issue.

Compare State v. Crump, No. M2006-02244-CCA-R3-CD, 2009 WL 723524, at *33 (Tenn. Ct. Crim. App. 2009):

On appeal, the defendant argues that under *State v. Culbreath,* 30 S.W.3d 309 (Tenn. 2000), the trial court should have dismissed the indictment or stricken the State's notice of intent to seek the death penalty based upon prosecutorial misconduct. In *Culbreath,* a private prosecutor operated on behalf of the district attorney's office to prosecute crimes involving adult-oriented businesses. The private prosecutor was appointed a special assistant district attorney general. The private prosecutor's fees and some of his expenses were paid by Citizens for Community Values, Inc. The defendants were charged with crimes related to their operation of sexually-oriented businesses and sought disqualification of the district attorney's office and the private prosecutor. The supreme court held that the private prosecutor had a conflict of interest by virtue of his compensation by the special interest group and his role as a prosecutor with the district attorney's office, because he owed a duty of loyalty to both. The court noted that in rare instances, prosecutorial misconduct may rise to the level of violating a defendant's due process rights and mandate dismissal of the indictment. The court concluded that the involvement of the private prosecutor had so infected the proceedings, from before the indictment was returned and continuing throughout the entire proceedings, that the trial court properly disqualified the private prosecutor and the district attorney's office and correctly dismissed the indictment. *Id.*

360. 798 S.W.2d 783 (Tenn. Ct. Crim. App. 1990).

361. *Id.* at 785 ("One of the attorneys was active in the Blount County Democratic Party. The other attorney was active in the Blount County Republican Party. Both had served as county chairman for their respective parties. The attorneys actively participated in all phases of the prosecution against the appellant.").

362. *Id.* ("The appellant vigorously opposed the right of the private prosecutors to participate in the trial on the merits. He filed a pretrial motion challenging their right to participate in the prosecution on

constitutional grounds. The trial judge denied the motion. He subsequently appealed by permission to this Court pursuant to Rule 9, Tenn. R. App. P. The appellant's application was denied. Thereafter, the appellant sought permission to appeal the issue to the Tennessee Supreme Court pursuant to Rule 10, Tenn. R. App. P. The Supreme Court denied the appellant's application on the ground that the issue had become moot.").

363. *Id.* at 785. Since the appellant, Steve Bennett, used a firearm in the commission of the offense, the trial judge imposed an additional sentence of five years. The sentences were to be served consecutively, so the effective sentence imposed by the trial judge was 17 years in the Department of Corrections. *Id.* In its initial charge, the State of Tennessee had sought the death penalty against Bennett, though the jury ultimately rejected the first-degree murder charge. *Id.* at 786–87 ("The state gave notice to the appellant that it intended to seek the death penalty. The aggravating circumstance alleged in the notice contended that the appellant 'knowingly created a great risk of death to two or more persons other than the victim.' The appellant moved to strike this aggravating circumstance on the ground it was not warranted by the facts or the law. The appellant also sought the entry of an order requiring the district attorney general to declare the standards or criteria he used in determining whether he should seek the death penalty in his case. The trial judge denied both motions. These issues are moot. As previously indicated, the jury found the appellant guilty of murder in the second degree. The jury's verdict means that the appellant was acquitted of murder in the first degree.").

364. *Id.* at 785–86 ("In this Court the appellant contends that the statute permitting the utilization of private prosecutors violates the Due Process and Equal Protection Clauses of the Fourteenth Amendment to the United States Constitution and the Law of the Land Clause contained in Article I, Section 8 of the Tennessee Constitution. He further contends that the statute is unconstitutional in the manner in which it was applied in this case.").

365. *Id.* at 786 (citing TENN. CODE ANN. § 8-7-401 (1988)).

366. *Id.* at 786.

367. *Id.*

368. *Id.*

369. *Id.*

370. *Id.*

371. *Id.*

372. *Id.* ("The appellant's complaint that a private prosecutor was permitted to argue during summation to the jury is likewise without merit. The statute does not prohibit a private prosecutor from making the opening argument to the jury. Only the rebuttal, or last argument, must be made by the district attorney general or his assistant. This issue is without merit.").

373. *Id.*

374. Brent E. Newton, *A Case Study in Systemic Unfairness: The Texas Death Penalty, 1973–1994*, 1 TEX. F. C.L. & C.R. 1, 18 n.112 (1994) ("[I]n numerous Texas death penalty cases, the murder victims' families utilized a Texas law that permitted them to retain private trial prosecutors. In each case, the local elected district attorneys opted not to try the case, so affluent family members of the victims hired private prosecutors, paying them handsome fees of as much as $275/hour (in 1981 dollars).") (citing Petition for Writ of Habeas Corpus, *Faulder v. Collins*, No. 6:92-CV-755 (N.D. Tex., pending)).

375. TEX. CODE. CRIM. P., art. 2.01; *see also* Powell v. State, 898 S.W.2d 821, 831 n.3 (Tex. Ct. Crim. App. 1994) (Clinton, J., concurring):

> A long line of authorities is to same effect, again without the Court distinguishing public prosecuting attorneys from private counsel. See, e.g., *Ballard v. State*, 519 S.W.2d 426, at 428 (Tex. Cr. App. 1975) (not violative of due process for private "special prosecutor" to assist district attorney where case is tried and also district attorney where offense committed) reversed on rehearing for other ground; *Lopez v. State*, 437 S.W.2d 268 (Tex. Cr. App. 1968) (no abuse of discretion to permit same attorney in *Ex Parte Powers*, supra, to participate as "special prosecutor" with consent of same district attorney; need not take constitutional oath of office as prerequisite to appearing in case); *Figueroa v. State*, 375 S.W.2d 907 (Tex. Cr. App. 1964) (no abuse of discretion in overruling *objection* to private counsel assisting as "special prosecutor" on ground that he also represented injured party in criminal case arising out of same transaction); *Bingham v. State*, 163

Tex. Cr. R. 352, 290 S.W.2d 915, at 918–919 (1956) (under general rule stated *ante,* no abuse of discretion to overrule *motion* to preclude district attorney of another judicial district from assisting in prosecution at request of local district attorney); *Phillips v. State,* 159 Tex. Cr. R. 286, 263 S.W.2d 159, 160 (1953) (allowing over *objection* "special prosecutor" to participate in trial not error under general rule, citing 15 Tex. Jur. 288, § 5); *Davis v. State,* 148 Tex. Cr. R. 499, 188 S.W.2d 397, at 399–400 (1945) (no statutory inhibition against any lawyer, with consent of district attorney or assistant, from participating in prosecution); *Emerson v. State,* 54 Tex. Cr. R. 628, 114 S.W. 834, at 835–836 (1908) (attorney assisting county attorney on account of absence of assistant county attorney not "disqualified" by prior brief casual discussion with accused about fee to represent him). See also *Fitzgerald v. State,* 722 S.W.2d 817, at 820 (Tex. App.—Tyler 1987), *affirmed on other grounds* 782 S.W.2d 876 (Tex. Cr. App. 1990) (not error for assistant district attorney of Walker County to assist district attorney of Anderson Count at trial).

There is yet another category of putative prosecutors: "volunteer counsel." That is, one who is not employed or paid a fee for his services, but volunteers his services as counsel to assist the State in the prosecution of a particular case. After cautionary comments the Court ultimately left the matter to the discretion of the trial court. *Loshe v. State,* 160 Tex. Cr. R. 561, 272 S.W.2d 517, at 519, 520 (1954); see also *Nacol v. State,* 590 S.W.2d 481, at 483–484 (Tex.Cr.App.1979).

The Court makes no meaningful distinction between "special prosecutors" and "volunteer counsel" in terms of functions performed in assisting the incumbent prosecutor on behalf of the State. See 31 Tex.Jur.3d §§ 56 and 58, at 641–644, 645–646 (1994); *Nacol v. State,* supra; see also Exhibit in *Powers v. Hauck,* supra, at 324 (Findings of Fact II) and at 325 (Conclusions of Law (1), (2) and (3)).

376. State ex rel. Wice v. Fifth Judicial Dist. Ct. App., 581 S.W.3d 189, 192 (Tex. Ct. Crim. App. Nov. 21, 2018).

377. Luttrell v. El Paso County, 555 S.W.3d 812, 823 n.9 (Tex. Ct. App. 2018):

> [B]ecause contempt proceedings are triggered by actions which defy the state's authority and entail possible penal sanctions, Texas courts have characterized such proceedings as being quasi-criminal proceedings that should conform as nearly as practicable to those in criminal cases. *See Ex parte Johnson,* 654 S.W.2d 415, 420 (Tex. 1983) (citing *Deramus v. Thornton,* 160 Tex. 494, 333 S.W.2d 824, 829 (1960); *Ex parte Scott,* 133 Tex. 1, 123 S.W.2d 306, 311 (1939)). In most instances, this will require a trial court to appoint either a public or private prosecutor to present evidence and testimony to support the contempt charges. *See generally Ex parte Daniels,* 722 S.W.2d 707, 709 (Tex. Crim. App. 1987) (recognizing that it is necessary to require testimony or the production of evidence—put forth by either a public or private prosecutor—to establish that a contempt occurred); *see also United States v. Time,* 21 F.3d 635, 638–39 (5th Cir. 1994) (in a criminal contempt action conducted pursuant to Federal Rule of Criminal Procedure 42(b), the judge may not prosecute the contempt and at the same time act as judge) (citing *American Airlines, Inc. v. Allied Pilots Ass'n,* 968 F.2d 523 (5th Cir. 1992)).

El Paso Elec. Co. v. Texas Dept. of Ins., 937 S.W.2d 432, 439 (Tex. 1996):

> Regardless of how the representational authority is allocated between the Attorney General, District Attorney, and County Attorney, we have held that the Legislature may not divest these officials of their collective constitutional authority by shifting representation to some other attorney employed by the State or under contract to the State. *See Hill County v. Sheppard,* 142 Tex. 358, 178 S.W.2d 261, 264 (1944); *Maud v. Terrell,* 109 Tex. 97, 200 S.W. 375, 376 (1918). We made clear in *Maud,* however, that the Legislature may authorize an agency to retain private counsel to prosecute actions, as long as such counsel's authority is subordinate to that of the Attorney General, County Attorney, or District Attorney.

378. Hartsfield v. State, 200 S.W.3d 813, 817 (Tex. Ct. App. 2006); *see also* In re Cox, 481 S.W.3d 289, 293–94 (Tex. Ct. App. 2015):

> A "special prosecutor," though enlisted by a district attorney to help in a particular case, is not part of the district attorney's staff. *Coleman v. State,* 246 S.W.3d 76, 82 (Tex. Crim. App. 2008). Unlike the district attorney and the attorneys employed in the district attorney's office, a special

prosecutor is not required to sign the oath of office. *Id.* Commissioning a special prosecutor does not require court approval. *Id.* Additionally, unlike a prosecutor, who is statutorily prohibited from appearing adversely to the State, a private attorney asked to serve as a special prosecutor is under no such prohibition. *See* Tex. Code Crim. Proc. Ann. art. 2.08(a). Unlike a prosecutor in the district attorney's office whose position is constitutionally mandated and protected, the position of a special prosecutor enjoys no such constitutional underpinnings. *Cf. Landers*, 256 S.W.3d at 303. If one private attorney appointed as a special prosecutor is disqualified in a particular case, a district attorney may appoint a different private attorney to serve as a special prosecutor. In short, the policy reasons articulated by the court of criminal appeals to support disqualification of an entire district attorney's office on the basis of a conflict of interest simply do not apply to an attorney in private practice appointed as a special prosecutor in a single case. *Accord id.* at 304. A private attorney appointed as a special prosecutor nonetheless remains a private attorney and is disqualifiable on conflict-of-interest grounds that need not rise to the level of a due-process violation.

379. Veteto v. State, 8 S.W.3d 805, 808, 817 (Tex. Ct. App. 2000), *abrogated on other grounds*, State v. Crook, 248 S.W.3d 172 (Tex. Ct. App. 2008); *see also* Stephens v. State, 978 S.W.2d 728, 730–31 (Tex. Ct. App. 1998):

> Appellant argues that the elected district attorney of the 51st Judicial District had the duty and obligation to represent the State in all criminal cases within the district but did not do so in the instant case. *See* Tex. Const. art. V, § 21; Tex. Code Crim. Proc. Ann. art. 2.01(West Supp.1998); Tex. Gov't Code Ann. § 43.130 (West 1988). Appellant acknowledges that there is a procedure for the appointment of an attorney pro tem, but contends that the basis or grounds for replacing the district attorney as required by article 2.07 were not met. Tex. Code Crim. Proc. Ann. art. 2.07 (West 1997 & Supp.1998). Appellant asserts that Lisa Tanner, an assistant attorney general, and the purported attorney pro tem, represented the State in the instant case without legal authority to do so. He claims that he was deprived of the right to deal with the prosecutor elected by the people.
>
> Appellant argues that Tanner was without authority to prosecute the case because an attorney pro tem can be appointed under article 2.07(a) only when the attorney for the State is disqualified to act, is absent from the county or district, is otherwise unable to perform the duties of his office, or in any instance where there is no attorney for the State. Appellant contends that none of these requirements were met with regard to the elected district attorney. The district attorney's motion for the appointment of a "special prosecutor" was based on the assertion that the victim and her family had requested the appointment of a "special prosecutor" and that the district attorney did not oppose the request. The trial court granted the motion finding that the reasons set forth were sufficient.
>
> Article 2.07(b–1) provides that an attorney for the State who is not disqualified to act may request the trial court to permit him to recuse himself in a case for good cause and upon approval by the court is disqualified. This is the procedure that was followed in the instant case. The district attorney was removed from the case and his disqualification met the requirement in article 2.07(a). Lisa Tanner took the oath as attorney pro tem and was in control and management of the case.
>
> Moreover, appellant's trial counsel was aware of the trial court's action and the appointment of a "special prosecutor." At no time during the trial did appellant object to the authority of the attorney pro tem to conduct the prosecution. The failure to object waived any error. *See* Tex. R. App. P. 33.1 (former Rule 52(a)); *Stanley v. State*, 880 S.W.2d 219, 220 (Tex.App.—Fort Worth 1994, no pet.); *see also Ethington v. State*, 819 S.W.2d 854, 859–60 (Tex. Crim. App. 1991). Further, in the absence of a showing to the contrary, the presumption obtains that the person who acted and was recognized by the trial court in prosecuting the case was duly authorized and qualified. *See Eppes v. State*, 10 Tex. 474, 475 (1853); *see also Cook v. State*, 146 Tex. Crim. 523, 176 S.W.2d 941, 943 (1944) (where prosecutor was at least an "officer de facto," no collateral attack on his authority was permitted).

. . .

Because the terms "special prosecutor" and "attorney pro tem" were used interchangeably in the instant record, we call attention to the distinction between the terms. A "special prosecutor," with the consent of the district attorney, assists the district attorney in the investigation and prosecution of a particular case, but the district attorney is responsible for the prosecution, control and management of the case. *See State v. Rosenbaum,* 852 S.W.2d 525, 529 (Tex. Crim. App. 1993) (Clinton, J., concurring); *Rogers v. State,* 956 S.W.2d 624, 625 n. 1 (Tex. App.—Texarkana 1997, pet. ref'd). The "special prosecutor" need not be appointed by the trial court and is not required to take the constitutional oath of office where he acts with the permission of the district attorney. *See Rosenbaum,* 852 S.W.2d at 529 n.2 (Clinton, J., concurring); *Lopez v. State,* 628 S.W.2d 77, 80 (Tex. Crim. App. 1982); *Reed v. State,* 503 S.W.2d 775, 776 (Tex. Crim. App. 1974); *Lopez v. State,* 437 S.W.2d 268, 269 (Tex. Crim. App. 1968). The utilization of a special prosecutor is not predicated upon the absence or disqualification of the elected district attorney. *See Davis v. State,* 840 S.W.2d 480, 487 (Tex. App.—Tyler 1992, pet. ref'd).

An "attorney pro tem" is appointed by the district court in accordance with statutory provisions. *See* Tex. Code Crim. Proc. Ann. art. 2.07 (West 1997 & Supp.1998). After taking the required constitutional oath of office, the appointee assumes the duties of the elected district attorney and in effect replaces the latter in performing germane functions of the office for purposes contemplated by the appointment. *See Rosenbaum,* 852 S.W.2d at 529 (Clinton, J., concurring); *Rogers,* 956 S.W.2d at 625 n.1.

The term "special prosecutor" is commonly used in an expansive and often improper manner by the bench and bar when reference should be to "attorney pro tem" as contemplated by article 2.07. This confusion of terms is reflected in appellate opinions. *See, e.g., Rosenbaum,* 852 S.W.2d at 526 n. 1; *Ballard v. State,* 519 S.W.2d 426, 428 (Tex. Crim. App. 1975); *State v. Broaddus,* 952 S.W.2d 598, 599 (Tex. App.—Houston [14th Dist.] 1997, pet. granted); *see also Busby v. State,* No. 1284–97, slip op. 1–3, —S.W.2d —, ———(Tex. Crim. App. Sept. 16, 1998) (Mansfield, J., dissenting).

In the instant case, the terms were used interchangeably, but it is clear that the trial court appointed an attorney pro tem under article 2.07. We do not understand appellant to contend otherwise. In such cases, the motion for the appointment of an attorney pro tem, the order appointing such officer, and the constitutional oath should be carefully worded to distinguish between an "attorney pro tem" and a "special prosecutor." The first point of error is overruled.

380. People v. Tidwell, 12 P. 61, 64 (Utah 1886).

381. Utah Code Ann. § 77-10a-12(2).

382. *Id.*, § 77-10a-12(3).

383. *Id.*, § 77-10a-12(5).

384. Gregory v. Shurtleff, 299 P.3d 1098, 1122–23 (Utah 2013) (Lee, J., concurring in part and dissenting in part) (quoting Ann Woolhandler & Caleb Nelson, *Does History Defeat Standing Doctrine?*, 102 Mich. L. Rev. 689, 696 (Utah 2004)).

385. *Id.* at 1123 n.10 (*quoting* 1 Joel Prentiss Bishop, Commentaries on the Law of Criminal Procedure § 26, at 15 (2d ed. 1872)).

386. *Id.* at 1123 (quoting Foute v. State, 4 Tenn. 98, 98–100 (1816)).

387. *Id.* (citing Snow v. Snow, 43 P. 620, 622 (Utah 1896) (though a private party may benefit from a criminal contempt charge, it is imposed "to vindicate the authority and dignity of the people, as represented in and by their judicial tribunals").

388. State Treasurer v. Rice, 11 Vt. 339, 343 (1839) ("There is a striking and important difference in prosecutions for criminal offences here and in England. In this state, prosecutions for offences before the county court, which has original and exclusive jurisdiction of most offences, are conducted by a public officer appointed for that purpose, and responsible for the manner in which he discharges his duty. In England they are usually instituted and conducted by private prosecutors, and, frequently, are only for the purpose of obtaining redress of a private injury. In many cases the civil action is suspended until the prosecution for the offence is terminated. Although private prosecutions are here recognized in some

cases, yet they are unusual, and are not looked upon in a favorable view, and it is rare that the attention of the court has been called to proceedings under the sections of the statute before mentioned, or to the authority of magistrates in such prosecutions."); *accord* In re Barker, 56 Vt. 14 (1884) (same); *see also* State v. Freeman, 10 A. 752, 753 (Vt. 1887) ("This was a complaint by a private prosecutrix for breach of the peace."); Bowen v. Buck, 28 Vt. 308, 315 (1856) ("I question, very seriously, whether, in this state, a private person has any right to use any public or private prosecution for crime of any grade, for the purpose of inducing a settlement, security or payment of a private claim for private loss or injury. At all events it must be considered as well settled everywhere, that no such use can be made of a prosecution for a crime of the character here indicated.").

389. In re D.L., 669 A.2d 1172, 1178 n.6 (Vt. 1995) (quoting Henry Harman, The Vermont Justice and Public Officer: A Manual of Vermont Law Relating to Civil and Criminal Business Before Justices of the Peace, and to the Duties of Sheriffs, Notaries Public, Town Clerks, Selectmen, Overseers of Poor, and Various Other Public Officers § 585, at 476 (1905)).

390. Petition of Dusablon, 230 A.2d 797, 799 (Vt. 1967) ("The prosecution was instituted by an information filed by the state's attorney of Chittenden County. According to the findings, the attorney general of Vermont requested the Govern[o]r to appoint Richard E. Davis, Esq., as a 'special assistant attorney general or prosecutor.' The request cited the heavy case load on the criminal docket and the need of assistance for the state's attorney's office to expedite the disposition of criminal causes in Chittendon County. The request was granted and the appointment was recorded in the executive office. By virtue of this authority, Mr. Davis became engaged in the prosecution of the complaint presented against the petitioner."); *id.* ("Since the early days of our government it has been the practice in this state to engage the services of special counsel to aid state's attorneys in the prosecution of serious criminal offenses.") (citations omitted); *id.* at 800 ("The predominant interest of the State and the public at large in the administration of criminal justice in its most populous county clearly justified the executive appointment of special counsel to expedite disposition of an overcrow[d]ed criminal docket. Whether the attorney called upon to serve the State in this capacity was designated special assistant attorney general or special prosecutor is of no legal significance in the disposition of the present petition. The attorney appointed was bound by the same standards of conduct and participation as the duly elected state's attorney whom he was assisting. And there is no suggestion that the case against the petitioner was unfairly or improperly presented, either before the plea of guilty was entered or in the matter of sentence.").

391. State v. Gonyaw, 507 A.2d 944, 947 (Vt. 1985); *see also* State v. Dunbar, 566 A.2d 970 (Vt. 1989) (complaining witness' attorney did not exceed permissible limits established for private prosecutor, in sexual assault prosecution, though attorney was heard on issues of joinder and severance, dismissal for lack of prima facie case, seating arrangements, appointment of substitute counsel, and continuance, and he strongly urged incarceration of defendant at sentencing, in that none of attorney's activities tended to unfairly slant criminal proceeding against defendant or usurp prosecutorial role).

392. Cavett v. Donovan, Docket No. 2017–167, 2017 WL 5010798, at *1-2 (Vt. Oct. 27, 2017) (citing State's Attorney v. Attorney General, 138 Vt. 10, 13 (1979); Linda R.S. v. Richard D., 410 U.S. 614, 619 (1973)).

393. 329 S.E.2d 22 (Va. 1985), *cert. denied*, 496 U.S. 911 (1990).

394. "Cantrell Gets Life Term," News Leader (Staunton, VA), July 14, 1983, p. 15.

395. "Man Sentenced After 2 Other Trials, 1 Conviction," Daily Press (Hampton Roads, VA), June 29, 1986, p. 18.

396. "Court: 2nd Conviction Not Double Jeopardy," Daily Press (Hampton Roads, VA), Apr. 2, 1989, p. 41.

397. *Cantrell*, 329 S.E.2d. at 24- 27.

398. Adkins v. Commonwealth, 492 S.E.2d 833 (Va. Ct. App. 1997).

399. Va. Code Ann. § 19.2-155.

400. In its ruling, the *Adkins* court had this to say:

> Virginia adheres to "the common-law rule which generally permits the appearance of private counsel *to assist* the prosecution." *Cantrell v. Commonwealth*, 229 Va. 387, 392, 329 S.E.2d 22, 26 (1985) (emphasis added). "At common law, a prosecuting attorney 'is the representative of the

public in whom is lodged a discretion ..., which is not to be controlled by the courts or *by an interested individual.*'" *Ganger v. Peyton,* 379 F.2d 709, 713 (4th Cir. 1967) (citation omitted). "'[T]he breadth of discretion that our country's legal system vests in prosecuting attorneys carries with it the potential for individual and institutional abuse.'" *Lux v. Commonwealth,* 24 Va. App. 561, 568, 484 S.E.2d 145, 148 (1997) (quoting *Bordenkircher v. Hayes,* 434 U.S. 357, 365, 98 S. Ct. 663, 669, 54 L.Ed.2d 604 (1978)). Thus, we require impartiality in the exercise of discretion on the part of the prosecutor. *See Berger v. United States,* 295 U.S. 78, 88, 55 S. Ct. 629, 633, 79 L.Ed. 1314 (1935).

This case is governed by the principles the Supreme Court of Virginia set forth in *Cantrell.* There, an attorney was hired by a murder victim's family "to help get ... Cantrell convicted." 229 Va. at 391, 329 S.E.2d at 25. Although the Commonwealth's attorney was present at the trial and took an active role, the private prosecutor examined most of the witnesses, generally acted as lead counsel, and made the closing argument to the jury. The private prosecutor was also retained by the family in a civil suit to seek a change in custody of Cantrell's child from Cantrell to the victim's parents. *See id.*

Cantrell argued that the private prosecutor's employment by the victim's family created a conflict of interest which rendered the private prosecutor's participation in the criminal prosecution improper to a degree that denied Cantrell due process of law. He also argued that the private prosecutor had an incentive other than the impartial administration of justice to seek a conviction.

In discussing the limitations on the role of a private prosecutor, the Supreme Court stated that when a private prosecutor has been engaged to assist in a criminal proceeding, "the public prosecutor must remain in continuous control of the case." *Id.* at 393, 329 S.E.2d at 26. Noting the different roles of a private and a public prosecutor, the Court stated that the duty of a private prosecutor is to zealously represent his client's interests while a public prosecutor's duty is "'to seek justice, not merely to convict.'" *Id.* Thus, the Supreme Court ruled that the private prosecutor's dual role as prosecutor and civil attorney created a conflict of interest which interfered with the fair administration of justice. The Court held that, under the circumstances, the private prosecutor's role infringed on the defendant's right to a fair and impartial trial.

The Commonwealth contends that in *Cantrell* the private prosecutor had not been formally appointed as a special prosecutor, was not being paid by the Commonwealth, and had not taken an oath of office. The Commonwealth argues that Epling was formally appointed as special prosecutor and that, although Epling was initially hired by the victim's family to help in the prosecution of Adkins, he never represented them in any civil matter. Also, Epling terminated his representation of the family upon his appointment and was no longer being compensated by them.

While the facts in this case differ from those in *Cantrell,* the rationale of *Cantrell* still applies. A public prosecutor is vested with a duty not merely to convict but to see that the accused receives a fair and impartial trial. A special prosecutor appointed by the trial judge steps into the role of public prosecutor and necessarily accepts that duty of impartiality. However, where a special prosecutor has a "personal interest in the outcome of the prosecution," *Lux,* 24 Va. App. at 569, 484 S.E.2d at 149, "his objectivity and impartiality are called into question," *id.,* and a defendant's right to a fair and impartial trial is violated. A special prosecutor who was formerly employed by the victim's family in connection with the same proceeding is incapable of exercising the fair-minded prosecutorial discretion to which the defendant is entitled, *see id.,* due to his pre-existing interest in securing the conviction of the defendant. Once the private prosecutor who has been paid by the victim's family to obtain a conviction becomes the special prosecutor with full discretionary authority, obviously, the opportunity to give full reign to the partiality that initially existed is unchecked.

Epling was initially hired and paid by the victim's family to protect its interest, not the interest of the Commonwealth. When Epling was appointed special prosecutor, he was no longer merely assisting in the prosecution; he was given ultimate control of the case. In view of Epling's earlier receipt of payment by the victim's family to represent them in the prosecution of Adkins, he owed his allegiance to those clients and had a duty not to act adversely to their interest. We cannot say that when the trial judge appointed Epling as special prosecutor, with sole authority to make prosecutorial decisions, Epling was then able to act with fair-minded discretion and impartially or unprejudiced by motives related to his earlier private gain. "The likelihood of conflict between those two duties rises to the level of an overwhelming probability." *Cantrell,* 229 Va. at 393, 329 S.E.2d at 26.

Having once been paid by the victim's family to protect its interest and to assist in the prosecution, Epling was prohibited for reasons of conflict of interest from becoming a special prosecutor. The conflict of interest between a special prosecutor's duty "to seek justice" and his duty to his former client denied the defendant her right to a fair and impartial trial. *See id.* at 394, 329 S.E.2d at 26–27. Accordingly, we reverse the convictions and remand for further proceedings.

Adkins, 492 S.E.2d at 834–36 (italics in original).

401. 579 S.E.2d 671 (Va. Ct. App. 2003).

402. *Id.* at 686 (citing Cantrell v. Commonwealth, 329 S.E.2d 22 (Va. 1985)).

403. *Id.* (citing *Martin v. Commonwealth,* 4 Va. App. 438, 443, 358 S.E.2d 415, 418 (1987)).

404. *Id.* (quoting *Cantrell,* 229 Va. at 394, 329 S.E.2d at 26–27).

405. *Id.* (citing *Cantrell,* 229 Va. at 393, 329 S.E.2d at 26).

406. *Id.* at 687 ("We acknowledge appellant's argument that a conflict appears to exist based on the fact that a private citizen rather than the government pays a private prosecutor's fees. Nevertheless, this conflict is one not considered a disabling conflict at common law, as indicated by the very practice of allowing private prosecutors. Whatever wisdom we might see in discontinuing the practice, *id.* at 392, 329 S.E.2d at 25 (recognizing '[t]he policy arguments advanced by the defendant for a total prohibition of privately employed prosecutors may have a sound basis in considerations of public policy'), it still exists at common law, and as the Supreme Court recognized in *Cantrell,* any decision to further limit or abrogate the practice must be made by the General Assembly rather than the courts. Thus, we are left to consider whether any cognizable conflicts of interest existed that prevented appellant from having a fair trial and whether the level of Harbert's participation exceeded the bounds of *Cantrell.*") (citations omitted).

407. *Id.* at 676–77.

408. *Id.* at 686.

409. *Id.* at 687.

410. *Id.*; *see also id.* ("The Supreme Court recognized implicitly in *Cantrell* that no attorney-client relationship arises between a private prosecutor and the person who pays the fees incurred for that purpose. Only if the private prosecutor directly represents the person paying his fee in some other capacity does such a conflict arise.").

411. *Id.*; *see also id.* ("The trial court accepted Harbert's statement that his retention letter indicated his 'agreement with [the Ringleys] ... to represent *the Commonwealth*' in return for the Ringleys' 'paying [Harbert's] fee.'"; "Harbert stated his belief that he did not represent the Ringleys, that 'there has been nothing the Ringleys have told me that I am holding in confidence' and 'that everything that constituted [*Brady*] material has been turned over to the defense in this case.' Harbert, an insurance defense lawyer, testified the relationship was much like the one that exists when an insurance company pays him to represent an insured involved in an auto accident. The trial court found these representations credible, and they support the conclusion that Harbert's relationship with the Ringleys was not a disqualifying conflict of interest."); *id.* ("Harbert's representations also support the trial court's implicit conclusion that neither Harbert nor his law firm had a contemporary, or even recent, attorney-client relationship with CIGNA, parent of LINA, the company liable on the victim's life insurance policy. In light of Harbert's representations that he had performed a conflict-of-interest check and that his firm had last represented CIGNA ten years previously, the court was entitled to credit his representations over a Martindale-Hubbell entry that listed CIGNA as one of the firm's representative clients.").

412. *Id.*

413. *Cantrell,* 329 S.E.2d at 26 (citations omitted). As long as "the public prosecutor ... remain[s] in continuous control of the case," the Virginia Supreme Court held in *Cantrell,* "there is no arbitrary limitation as to the *proportion* of work which may be done by a private prosecutor." *Id.* (emphasis added).

414. *Riner*, 579 S.E.2d 688; *see also id.* ("The Commonwealth represents Harbert conducted direct examination of just over 20% of the Commonwealth's witnesses in its case-in-chief and cross-examined 20% of appellant's witnesses during appellant's case-in-chief and surrebuttal. In the Commonwealth's rebuttal, Harbert did not examine any of the Commonwealth's five witnesses. Appellant does not expressly challenge the Commonwealth's calculations. In light of these calculations, we hold the Commonwealth's utilizing Harbert's admitted arson expertise by focusing his participation predominantly on the examination of witnesses related to the fire did not violate *Cantrell.* Permitting private prosecutors to handle only innocuous witnesses and evidentiary matters would effectively abrogate the common-law principle that still permits their appointment. As set out above, abrogation is a task for the General Assembly rather than the courts. In the absence of such abrogation, we hold Harbert's participation in appellant's prosecution did not violate the principles in *Cantrell.*").

415. *Id.*

416. Riner v. Edwards, Civil Action No. 7:07-cv-00455, 2008 WL 4388788, at *15 (W.D. Va. Sept. 26, 2008):

> Pursuant to § 2254(e)(1), this court will presume correct the state court's finding that the Commonwealth's Attorney remained in continuous control of the criminal case against Riner. *Riner*, 601 S.E.2d at 569. Furthermore, the court concludes that this finding is fully supported by the record and is dispositive of the federal due process issue. Riner presents no evidence that Harbert played any role whatsoever in the critical prosecutorial actions in Riner's case, including the indictment process, plea discussions, and the decision about what penalties to seek. It is undisputed that the Commonwealth's Attorney continuously retained all of these functions. Moreover, Riner presents no evidence that Harbert's participation in presenting evidence, examining witnesses, and making argument to the jury interfered with the Commonwealth's Attorney's independence in making the critical prosecutorial decisions in Riner's case. Indeed, the facts of Riner's case are far less indicative of potentially prejudicial conflicts on the part of the private prosecutor than were the facts of the *Jones* case, in which the Fourth Circuit found no due process violation. 776 F.2d at 1245–46. Cheryl Ringley, one of the victim's sisters, and her husband, Greg Ringley, paid Harbert a set fee for his assistance to the prosecutor. The Ringleys and others of Denise's family were involved in litigation after the fire, seeking visitation with and then custody of the Riner children, challenging Riner's insurance claims, and suing him for monetary damages in relation to Denise's death. The record does not indicate, however, that Harbert served as the legal representative of any of Denise's family members in any of these other legal matters. The record also does not indicate any likelihood that Harbert would receive greater compensation if Riner was convicted than if he was acquitted. Thus, the court finds no evidence of conflicts in interest of the type that the Fourth Circuit found objectionable in the *Ganger* case. The court will, therefore, deny relief on the federal due process claim.

417. Price v. Commonwealth, 849 S.E.2d 140 (Va. Ct. App. Nov. 4, 2020).

418. The Court of Appeals in *Price* stated:

> A pecuniary or other tangible interest in the outcome of a prosecution—one which corresponds to a factually-related civil case—certainly warrants a private prosecutor's disqualification. But the absence of such an interest does not eliminate the greater ethical conflict that arises whenever an attorney attempts to "serve two masters." The private attorney owes his loyalty to the client; the prosecutor owes his loyalty to the impartial administration of justice. Any conflict between these loyalties, direct or implied, violates the defendant's due process rights guaranteed under the United States Constitution and the Constitution of Virginia. This is why a trial court can disqualify a prosecutor if that prosecutor "has an interest pertinent to a defendant's case that *may*"—not "will"—conflict with the prosecutor's duties.
>
> The Commonwealth argues, however, that even if the trial court erred in failing to disqualify Redden, such error was harmless. We disagree. Harmless-error analysis is inappropriate when evaluating the effect of an interested prosecutor in a criminal case, because "such analysis would not be sensitive to the fundamental nature of the error committed." As opposed to the review of "discrete exercises of judgment by lower courts," the rule governing disqualification of an

> interested prosecutor "requires no subtle calculations of judgment" by a reviewing court. Because a prosecutor's many decisions are often not contained in the record, the precise moments of misconduct arising from such a situation cannot be easily identified and evaluated. Such error has "fundamental and pervasive effects" that infect the entire proceeding with prejudice.
>
> A concern for actual prejudice in such circumstances misses the point, for what is at stake is the public perception of the integrity of our criminal justice system. "[J]ustice must satisfy the appearance of justice," and a prosecutor with conflicting loyalties presents the appearance of precisely the opposite. Society's interest in disinterested prosecution therefore would not be adequately protected by harmless-error analysis, for such analysis would not be sensitive to the fundamental nature of the error committed. Therefore, we heed the guidance of the United States Supreme Court and of our own Supreme Court, and we decline to apply a harmless-error analysis.

Price, 849 S.E.2d at 147–48 (citations omitted).

419. Rebecca Krauss, *The Theory of Prosecutorial Discretion in Federal Law: Origins and Development*, 6 SETON HALL CIRCUIT REV. 1 (2009).

420. In applying Virginia law to the facts of *Price*, the Court of Appeals of Virginia ruled:

> Here, an impermissible conflict of interest existed because of Redden's concurrent representation of the victim in a civil case against Price, and the trial court should have disqualified Redden from participating in Price's prosecution. As the victim's private attorney, Redden owed duties of loyalty and confidentiality to his client, Va. R. of Prof. Conduct 1.6–1.7, and he was encouraged to act with "zeal in advocacy" on her behalf, Va. R. of Prof. Conduct 1.3 cmt. 1. As a prosecutor, Redden was expected to rid himself of all partialities, disclose exculpatory evidence, and pledge his efforts to nothing but the independent administration of justice. "The likelihood of conflict between these two duties rises to the level of an overwhelming probability." *Cantrell*, 229 Va. at 393, 329 S.E.2d 22. Redden's representation of the victim in a civil case created a conflict of interest which warranted his disqualification in Price's prosecution. His participation in the case despite this conflict of interest violated Price's due process rights.

Price, 849 S.E. at 488–89.

421. *Price*, 849 S.E.2d at 146–47 & nn.4–5.

422. VA. CODE ANN. § 19.2-71.

423. Henry H. Perritt, Jr., *Taking the Law into Your Own Hands: Private Criminal Complaints in Virginia*, 69 VIRGINIA LAWYER 30–31, 54 (June 2020).

424. State v. Hoshor, 67 P. 386, 388 (Wash. 1901) ("It is insisted that the court committed error in denying defendant's motion to exclude counsel employed by the prosecuting witness from assisting the prosecuting attorney. In support of this motion affidavits were filed charging that such counsel was employed upon a contingent fee, and other charges not necessary to enumerate here. These charges are denied by affidavits filed in the cause, and the court, after hearing these affidavits, overruled the motion. This court in State v. Elswood, 15 Wash. 453, 46 Pac. 727, held that it was within the discretion of the trial court to allow special counsel to aid the prosecuting attorney in the prosecution of a case, and that such discretion would be interfered with only upon a showing of abuse thereof. After a careful reading of the affidavits, we are satisfied that the court did not abuse its discretion in this regard.").

425. State ex rel. Becker v. Wiley, 133 P.2d 507, 513 (Wash. 1943) ("If recognition of a course of conduct is to be considered in the interpretation of a statute, then certainly it can be argued that it has for so long been the practice of prosecuting attorneys to carry on, in the office provided by the county for their offic[i]al business, what private practice they may have, and such practice is so well known, that it is reasonable to assume that the legislature must have known of such practice, and if it had been the desire or intent of the legislature to prohibit such practice, it would have specifically so provided."); *id.* ("it was not the intent of the legislature to prohibit prosecuting attorneys from engaging in certain types of private practice"); *id.* at 514 ("[I]n view of the fact that the above section has been in effect for so many years, it is impossible to escape the conclusion that the legislature has approved of a prosecuting attorney engaging in private practice, so long as such practice does not conflict with the duties imposed upon him as prosecuting attorney."); *id.* ("As a practical proposition, it is generally recognized that in the smaller counties at least, because of the law salaries paid, it would be practically impossible to procure a prosecutor, if he were not permitted

to supplement his office salary by private practice."); *id.* ("Our conclusion in regard to prosecutors engaging in private practice, and our conclusion as to the practical reasons for allowing them to engage in such practice, are borne out, we think, by certain acts passed by the 1941 legislature."); *id.* ("Conceding ... that a prosecuting attorney may engage in private practice, and that the commissioners have the implied power to expend county funds for the maintenance of an office for the prosecutor outside the county seat, we are of the opinion that it logically follows, and that it is desirable, that the prosecutor conduct such private practice as he may have, in the office provided by the county for his official business."); *id.* ("[W]e are of the opinion it is fair to assume the legislature has recognized that such private practice would be conducted in the office provided for his official duties, and that such private practice does not make illegal the expenditure of county funds for the maintenance of the prosecutor's office."); *id.* ("We may add that it undoubtedly has been recognized that it is a distinct advantage to the county to have the prosecuting attorney spend all of his time in the office provided for his official business, rather than have him spend part of his time in another office, where he would be compelled to go in order to conduct his private practice.").

426. In re Dependency of A.K., 174 P.3d 11, 21 n.6 (Wash. 2007).

427. State v. Orozco, 186 P.3d 1078, 1080 (Wash. Ct. App. 2008); *see also id.* at 1079 ("Christina Orozco appeals her conviction for stalking. She argues that the trial court erred by refusing to disqualify the Snohomish County Prosecutor's Office (Prosecutor's Office) because one of its attorneys assisted her victim in obtaining a civil antiharassment order. She fails to properly raise any relevant Washington rule, statute, or case to support her claim that a prosecutor's office cannot assist a county employee in obtaining a civil antiharassment order against another county employee and then later prosecute the offending employee criminally without creating an impermissible conflict of interest. We affirm.").

428. State v. Bland, 953 P.2d 126, 128 n.4 (Wash. Ct. App. 1998); *see also* State v. Galvin, No. 37350-5-II, 2009 WL 2849639, at *2 (Wash. Ct. App. Sept. 3, 2009) ("the relationship between a crime victim and a prosecutor does not constitute an attorney-client relationship"). In the State of Washington, Rule 2.1 of the Criminal Rules for Courts of Limited Jurisdiction ("CrRLJ") states: "Except as otherwise provided in this rule, all criminal proceedings shall be initiated by a complaint." WASH. REV. CODE, CRIM. RULES FOR COURTS OF LIMITED JURISDICTION, Rule 2.1(a)(1). One subsection of that rule, titled "Citizen Complaints," provides: "Any person wishing to institute a criminal action alleging a misdemeanor or gross misdemeanor shall appear before a judge empowered to commit person charged with offenses against the State, other than a judge pro tem. The judge may require the appearance to be made on the record, and under oath. The judge may consider any allegations on the basis of an affidavit sworn to before the judge. The court may also grant an opportunity at said hearing for evidence to be given by the county prosecuting attorney or deputy, the potential defendant or attorney of record, law enforcement or other potential witnesses. The court may also require the presence of other potential witnesses." *Id.*, Rule 2.1(c). "In addition to probable cause," the subsection states, "the court may consider: (1) Whether an unsuccessful prosecution will subject the State to costs or damages claims under RCW 9A.16.110, or other civil proceedings; (2) Whether the complainant has adequate recourse under laws governing small claims suits, anti-harassment petitions or other civil actions; (3) Whether a criminal investigation is pending; (4) Whether other criminal charges could be disrupted by allowing the citizen complaint to be filed; (5) The availability of witnesses at trial; (6) The criminal record of the complainant, potential defendant and potential witnesses, and whether any have been convicted of crimes of dishonesty as defined by ER 609; and (7) Prosecution standards under RCW 9.94A.440." *Id.* That subsection of the rule then reads: "If the judge is satisfied that probable cause exists, and factors (1) through (7) justify filing charges, and that the complaining witness is aware of the gravity of initiating a criminal complaint, of the necessity of a court appearance or appearances for himself or herself and witnesses, of the possible liability for false arrest and of the consequences of perjury, the judge may authorize the citizen to sign and file a complaint in the form prescribed in CrRLJ 2.1(a) The affidavit may be in substantially the following form ...." *Id.* The prescribed affidavit reads in part: "I, the undersigned complainant, understand that I have the choice of complaining to a prosecuting authority rather than signing this affidavit. I elect to use this method to start criminal proceedings. I understand that the following are some but not all of the consequences of my signing a criminal complaint: (1) the defendant may be arrested and placed in custody; (2) the arrest if proved false may result in a lawsuit against me; (3) if I have sworn falsely I may be prosecuted for perjury; (4) this charge will be prosecuted even though I

might later change my mind; (5) witnesses and complainant will be required to appear in court on the trial date regardless of inconvenience, school, job, etc." *Id.*

This rule has been called the "citizen complaint rule." *See* Stout v. Felix, No. 98613-4, 2021 WL 3778382, at * 1 (Wash. Aug. 26, 2021) ("Under the citizen complaint rule, '[a]ny person' may initiate criminal proceedings. CrRLJ 2.1(c). To begin the process, the person must appear before a judge to present their allegations. They may also file an affidavit, and the judge may provide the potential defendant, the prosecuting attorney, and other potential witnesses an opportunity to be heard. Then, the judge considers the evidence, makes a probable cause determination, and weighs a number of factors before authorizing the citizen to sign and file the criminal complaint."); *id.* at *2 ("The parties dispute whether a citizen's affidavit initiates criminal proceedings under the citizen complaint rule. The parties also dispute the constitutionality of the citizen complaint rule. We will not reach a constitutional issue 'unless absolutely necessary to the determination of the case.' Therefore, we first address the statute of limitations issue.") (citation omitted); *id.* (noting that "the citizen complaint rule... has been used seemingly rarely"); *id.* at *3 ("a citizen's affidavit cannot initiate criminal proceedings because it does not provide any notice to the potential defendant, who has a due process right to notice of the accusations against them"); *id.* at *4 ("It is incumbent on any citizen who seeks to file such a complaint to ensure that they come before a judge to move their case forward before any statute of limitations passes. If, as in this case, the complaining citizen fails to timely act to prosecute their matter and the statute of limitations passes, the citizen complaint fails."); *id.* (Yu, J., dissenting in part and concurring in part) ("I cannot join the majority because it assumes that Thomas Stout's private prosecution of Geene Felix could have proceeded without violating the separation of powers doctrine if only it were timely filed. The majority never questions this assumption, citing our general practice of declining to reach constitutional issues. This form of constitutional avoidance is the best and wisest course of action in the vast majority of cases. But in this case, to avoid the constitutional question is to avoid the heart of the matter.") (citation omitted); *id.* at *5 (Yu, J., dissenting in part and concurring in part) ("The citizen complaint rule is not merely bad policy. It also derogates our constitutional vision of separation of powers among three branches of government. Within this constitutional framework, a judicial officer cannot determine in the first instance whether criminal charges should be filed against an individual without usurping the authority of the executive branch. But that is precisely what the plain language of the citizen complaint rule requires judges to do. Therefore, on its face, the citizen complaint rule violates the separations of powers doctrine, " 'one of the cardinal and fundamental principles of the American constitutional system' " that 'forms the basis of our state government.' In failing to acknowledge this constitutional violation, the majority signals its view that a citizen complaint is an appropriate means of seeking public redress through criminal prosecution for a private grievance. I do not share this view.") (citations omitted); *id.* (Yu, J., dissenting in part and concurring in part) ("I would hold that reaching the constitutional question in this case is necessary and that the answer to that question is clear. The citizen complaint rule is unconstitutional on its face. Therefore, the only appropriate outcome in this and every citizen complaint case is summary dismissal with prejudice. I thus respectfully concur only in the result."); *id.* at *7 (Yu, J., dissenting in part and concurring in part) ("[I]t should be clear that the citizen complaint rule blatantly violates the separation of powers doctrine by requiring a judicial officer to exercise the charging authority that is supposed to be vested in the executive branch. This throws off the careful balance that the coordinate branches of government are supposed to provide in every criminal case...."); *id.* at *13 (Yu, J., dissenting in part and concurring in part) ("In addition to the damage caused by all such cases, every attempted private prosecution causes harms unique to the case. Just one example from this case is Stout's mistitling his appeal to superior court as 'State v. Felix' to make it appear as though this were an actual criminal case, instead of the unsuccessful citizen complaint case that it is. This was an intentional act of dishonesty rather than a simple mistake; Stout did the same thing in district court, and the judge explicitly admonished him that the case title 'is and it should be[,] on our documents [and] also on our computer system[,] In Regards to the Citizen's Complaint, Petitioner Thomas Stout.' ") (citations omitted); *id.* at *14 (Yu, J., dissenting in part and concurring in part) ("It is long past time for the wasteful pretense of citizen complaints to end. I would affirm the district court's order of dismissal on the alternative basis that this and every citizen complaint case must be summarily dismissed with prejudice because CrRLJ 2.1(c) is unconstitutional on its face. I therefore respectfully concur only in the result.").

429. W. Va. Code § 7-7-8.

430. *Id.*

431. State v. Atkins, 261 S.E.2d 55, 58 (W. Va. 1979).

432. Acord v. Hedrick, 342 S.E.2d 120, 126 (W. Va. 1986); State v. Atkins, 261 S.E.2d 55, 58 (W. Va. 1979), *cert. denied*, 445 U.S. 904 (1980).

433. *Acord*, 342 S.E.2d at 126; State v. Riser, 294 S.E.2d 461, 466 (W. Va. 1982); *see also Atkins*, 261 S.E.2d. at 59 (it was not reversible error for private prosecutor not to disclose the amount of his fee).

434. *Acord*, 342 S.E.2d at 123 (citing Macklin Fleming, The Price of Perfect Justice 5 (1974)); *see also* State v. Moose, 313 S.E.2d 507, 513 (N.C. 1984) ("Nor do we find persuasive the argument that assistance of a private prosecutor results in a 'mismatching' of legal talent and experience to a defendant's disadvantage. We know of no law that requires counsel to be equal to or better or greater in number than counsel for the opposition.").

435. Amos v. Courtney, No. 13–1064, 2014 WL 1672930, at *4 (W. Va. Sup. Ct. App. Apr. 25, 2014).

436. In re Frieda Q., 742 S.E.2d 68, 85 n.20 (W. Va. Sup. Ct. App. 2013) ("In a footnote in *State ex rel. Koppers v. International Union of Oil, Chemical and Atomic Workers,* 171 W.Va. 290, 293 n. 2, 298 S.E.2d 827, 829 n. 2 (1982), this Court overruled *Arnold* insofar as *Arnold* had held that 'a criminal contempt proceeding is not an actual criminal trial.' The sole issue in *Koppers* was whether a jury trial in a criminal contempt case could be prosecuted by private counsel rather than the county prosecutor; we held that it could not."); Trecost v. Trecost, 502 S.E.2d 445, 449 (W. Va. Sup. Ct. App. 1998) ("In this case, the hearing before the circuit court below was an indirect criminal contempt proceeding in which the Appellee's private attorney was permitted to prosecute the Appellant. The state's attorney was not involved in the prosecution in any respect. By allowing the Appellee's lawyer to conduct the prosecution, the circuit court clearly violated the rules articulated in *Koppers, supra.* We have previously stated that '[t]he failure to follow proper contempt procedure is reversible error.' *P.G. & H. Coal Co. v. International Union, United Mine Workers of America,* 182 W.Va. 569, 390 S.E.2d 551 (1988). Therefore, we conclude that the circuit court committed reversible error in allowing the Appellee's private lawyer to prosecute the criminal contempt.").

437. State ex rel. R.L. v. Bedell, 452 S.E.2d 893, 897 (W. Va. Sup. Ct. App. 1994).

438. W. Va. R. Crim. P. 7.

439. State v. Peterson, 218 N.W. 367, 369 (Wis. 1928) ("In an early day in England private parties prosecuted criminal wrongs which they suffered. They obtained an indictment from a grand jury, and it became the duty and the privilege of the person injured to provide a prosecutor at his own expense to prosecute the indicted person. Our scheme of government has changed all this. It is now deemed the better public policy to provide for the public prosecution of public wrongs without any interference on the part of private parties, although they may have been injured in a private capacity different from the general public injury that accrues to society when a crime is committed. So under our system we have private prosecution for private wrongs and public prosecution for public wrongs. Our scheme contemplates that an impartial man selected by the electors of the county shall prosecute all criminal actions in the county unbiased by desires of complaining witnesses or that of the defendant.") (citing Biemel v. State, 37 N.W. 244 (Wis. 1888)).

440. Wis. Stat. Ann. § 978.045.

441. *Id.*, subd. (3)(a)-(c):

> (3)(a) If an attorney is available and willing to serve as a special prosecutor without state compensation, the district attorney may appoint the attorney as a public service special prosecutor to serve at the pleasure of the district attorney. The public service special prosecutor may perform the duties and has the powers of the district attorney while acting under such an appointment, but is not subject to the appointment procedure under subs. (1g) and (1r) or to the compensation under sub. (2). A full-time public service special prosecutor may not engage in a private practice of law while serving under this paragraph. A part-time public service special prosecutor may engage in a private practice of law while serving under this paragraph.
>
> (b) A law firm or other employer employing an attorney who is appointed as a public service special prosecutor may continue to pay, for a period of not more than 4 months, the salary and fringe benefits of the attorney while he or she serves under par. (a). If the public service special

prosecutor receives any such payments, the prosecutor's law firm and the prosecutor are subject to the following restrictions:

1. The law firm may not participate in any of the cases in which the public service special prosecutor participates.

2. The public service special prosecutor may not consult with any attorney in or employee of the law firm about any criminal case in which the public service special prosecutor participates except as necessary to ensure compliance with this subsection.

(c) An attorney serving as a public service special prosecutor under par. (a) is considered to be a public employee for purposes of s. 895.46. A law firm or employer described under par. (b) is not liable for any acts or omissions of a public service special prosecutor while acting in his or her official capacity or performing duties or exercising powers under par. (a).

In a concurring opinion in *State ex rel. Two Unnamed Petitioners v. Peterson*, 866 N.W.2d 165, 213, 222 (Wis. 2015), Judge David Prosser noted that Wis. Stat. § 978.045 "dates back to 1989" and enables "[t]he *court*" to appoint special prosecutors. *Id.* at 223 (italics in original); *see also id.* at 224 (italics in original):

> ¶ 209 There are several reasons why one of the nine conditions *must* exist in order for the court to make an appointment. First, the Department of Administration is required to pay for a special prosecutor who is properly appointed under these subsections. Wis. Stat. § 978.045(2)(b) ("The department of administration *shall* pay the compensation ordered by the court from the appropriation under s. 20.475(1)(d).") (emphasis added). The department does not appear to have authority to reject payment for a properly appointed special prosecutor. However, the legislature did establish conditions for these appointments before requiring the department of administration to pay.
>
> ¶ 210 Second, if the conditions in subsection (1r) did not have to be followed, courts could grant requests from district attorneys for an unlimited number of special prosecutors to supplement district attorney staffs. In other words, individual judges could effectively disregard the number of positions for assistant district attorneys set out in statute. *Cf.* Wis. Stat. § 16.505. District attorneys in the state's largest counties already may appoint "temporary counsel" *as authorized by the department of administration.* Wis. Stat. § 978.03(3). Section 978.045 does not permit an alliance between a district attorney and a judge to override statutory limitations on prosecutor appointments.
>
> ¶ 211 Third, if the conditions in subsection (1r) did not have to be followed, courts could appoint special prosecutors on their own motion for "investigations" of interest to an individual judge without any involvement by the local district attorney. This would present a significant separation of powers issue.
>
> ¶ 212 Fourth, courts could appoint special prosecutors with "all the powers of the district attorney," without the accountability of any checks on the special prosecutor's conduct, except from the appointing court. A special prosecutor appointed on the court's own motion would not necessarily be overseen by a district attorney. The special prosecutor could not be recalled or defeated for reelection, never having been elected to the special prosecutor position. The special prosecutor could be appointed by a reserve judge who would never again face the electorate.

442. Wis. Stat. Ann. 968.26.

443. State v. Unnamed Defendant, 441 N.W.2d 696, 702 (Wis. 1989) (Heffernan, C.J., concurring).

444. Private lawyers in Wyoming are permitted to participate in "Indirect (Constructive) Contempt Proceedings." Wyo. R. Crim. P. 42(c)(4) ("The judge may conduct a hearing without assistance of counsel or may be assisted by the attorney for the state or by an attorney appointed by the court for that purpose.").

445. Judge R.A. (Jim Randall), *The Death Penalty*, 14 Hamline J. Pub. L. & Pol'y 154 n.1 (1993) (noting in a book review: "The defendant, Mark Hopkinson, had been duly convicted by a rural Wyoming jury of his peers of putting out a contract that led to the dynamite bombing death of an attorney, his wife, and a son. It came out during the trial that Hopkinson had also ordered the killing of his own accomplice to silence him. Wyoming is a state where private prosecutors can be hired to bring charges. The deceased was a long time friend of Gerry Spence who had known his family, and after much soul searching, Spence agreed to take the case for the prosecution.").

446. "Judge Balks in Bomb Charge Case," NAPA REGISTER AND THE NAPA J. (Napa, CA), Dec. 28, 1978, p. 6 ("The presiding judge in the case of two men charged in an alleged plot to blow up an Arizona lawyer's car says he will block any evidence during a trial linking them to two unsolved Wyoming murders."); *see also* Karen Scherting, "Man Who Killed 4 People Lives Quietly in Wyoming's Bridger Valley," BILLINGS GAZETTE, May 1, 2011 (updated May 4, 2015), https://billingsgazette.com/news/state-and-regional/wyoming/man-who-killed-4-people-lives-quietly-in-wyomings-bridger-valley/article_077eb6c9-d476-57f9-ae67-30b675780630.html.

447. "Hopkinson Case Review: 12 Years of Wyoming Controversy," CASPER STAR-TRIBUNE (Casper, WY), Jan. 21, 1992, p. 1.

448. "Hopkinson Case Review: 12 Years of Wyoming Controversy," CASPER STAR-TRIBUNE (Casper, WY), Jan. 21, 1992, pp. A1, A10.

449. Hopkinson v. State, 632 P.2d 79, 94–99 (Wyo. 1981); Karen Scherting, "Man Who Killed 4 People Lives Quietly in Wyoming's Bridger Valley," BILLINGS GAZETTE, May 1, 2011 (updated May 4, 2015), https://billingsgazette.com/news/state-and-regional/wyoming/man-who-killed-4-people-lives-quietly-in-wyomings-bridger-valley/article_077eb6c9-d476-57f9-ae67-30b675780630.html.

450. "Jury Selection Begins in Hopkinson Murder Trial," BILLINGS GAZETTE (Billings, MT), Sept. 5, 1979, p. 13.

451. David Ansley, "Prosecutor Calls Hopkinson 'Master Manipulator,'" CASPER STAR-TRIBUNE (Casper, WY), Sept. 8, 1979, p. 15.

452. "Prosecutors Given Special Protection in Murder Case," RAPID CITY JOURNAL (Rapid City, SD), Aug. 3, 1979, p. 21.

453. David Ansley, "Sentencing Hearing Is Months Away," CASPER STAR-TRIBUNE (Casper, WY), July 3, 1981, p. 1 (noting that Gerry Spence "served without pay as special prosecutor during the investigation and trial"). The 3½-week trial itself was quite costly, with Gerry Spence noting that witness fees and expense alone amounted to approximately $10,000. "Hopkinson Trial Cost Teton County about $44,000," BILLINGS GAZETTE (Billings, MT), Oct. 5, 1979, p. 5-B.

454. Karen Scherting, "Man Who Killed 4 People Lives Quietly in Wyoming's Bridger Valley," BILLINGS GAZETTE, May 1, 2011 (updated May 4, 2015), https://billingsgazette.com/news/state-and-regional/wyoming/man-who-killed-4-people-lives-quietly-in-wyomings-bridger-valley/article_077eb6c9-d476-57f9-ae67-30b675780630.html.

455. Hopkinson v. Shillinger, 866 F.2d 1185, 1194 n.3 (10th Cir. 1989).

456. GERRY SPENCE, O.J.: THE LAST WORD 69–71 (1997).

457. "Prosecutor Vows to Prove Hopkinson Guilty of Murder," BILLINGS GAZETTE (Sept. 8, 1979), p. 1.

458. "Perjury Offer Claimed," SALT LAKE TRIBUNE (Salt Lake City, UT), Sept. 21, 1979, p. 20; "Hopkinson Has No Witnesses in Defense," BILLINGS GAZETTE (Billings, MT), Sept. 22, 1979, p. 5.

459. Katharine Collins, "Hopkinson Appeal Denied," CASPAR STAR-TRIBUNE (Casper, WY), Dec. 19, 1991, p. 1; *see also* Hopkinson v. Shillinger, 866 F.2d 1185, 1193–94 (10th Cir. 1989):

> In December 1975, Hopkinson requested the Fort Bridger, Wyoming, Sewer and Water Board to annex a trailer court owned by his family, then under construction, to the Fort Bridger Sewer District and to hook the entire trailer court onto the district's sewer lines for the usual $100 hookup fee. VIII–D R. 96. Vincent Vehar, the board's attorney, advised the board that $100 was inadequate payment for connecting the entire trailer court onto the sewer. *Id.* at 97, 100–01. Before the board took any official action on the request, a petition which Vehar drafted, *id.* at 234–35, and which ninety-five percent of the district's membership signed, was presented to the board, requesting it to increase Hopkinson's connection fee. *Id.* at 235, 257–58. After conducting several public hearings, the board entered into a contract with Hopkinson providing for the annexation of his property to the district and requiring the payment of $300 for each trailer connected, for a total of $12,300. *Id.* at 106. Pursuant to the contract Hopkinson agreed to pay the connection fee in installments, *id.* at 115, and to pay a monthly service fee of $120, *id.* at 238.
>
> Hopkinson connected the trailer court to the sewer but then refused to pay amounts owing under the contract. *Id.* at 199–200; VIII–E R. at 339–41. The board, represented by Vehar,

> decided to sue him. This lawsuit, filed on January 28, 1977, sought the $12,300 fee, plus additional monies for legal and engineering costs incurred in connecting the trailer park to the system. VIII–D R. at 115–17. The suit also sought $1,000 actual damages and $50,000 punitive damages for threats Hopkinson allegedly made against the board members to convince them to disavow the contract. *Id.* at 129. Once the suit was filed, Vehar withdrew from the case because he anticipated being called as a witness. *Id.* at 105. His associate, John Troughton, replaced him. *Id.*
>
> On August 1, 1977, the board met to discuss the lawsuit and to assist Troughton in preparing for Hopkinson's deposition. VIII–E R. 280–81. Hopkinson attended part of this meeting and repeatedly asked the board to fire Vehar and to submit the dispute to arbitration. *Id.* at 286–87, 301–02. The board decided, however, to maintain the lawsuit. On August 3, Troughton sent notice to Hopkinson's attorney that he would depose Hopkinson on August 9 in connection with the sewer board's lawsuit. VIII–D R. 118–21.
>
> At approximately 3:35 a.m. on August 7, an explosion destroyed Vehar's home and killed Vehar, his wife, and his younger son. Another son, Tony, was injured in the blast but survived. An investigation by the federal Bureau of Alcohol, Tobacco and Firearms revealed that a dynamite bomb caused the explosion. VIII–H R. 1326. A few days later, Hopkinson told a sewer board member, "I'm glad the old son-of-a-bitch [Vehar] is dead. If somebody wouldn't have done it, I would have done it myself." VIII–E R. 367.

The Tenth Circuit's decision in *Hopkinson v. Shillinger*, 866 F.2d 1185 (10th Cir. 1989) contains an extensive recitation of events pertaining to the conviction of Mark Hopkinson.

460. Teri Gomes, Local Arrested for '79 Murder," Park Record (Park City, UT), Aug. 6, 1987, p. 1 ("The month-long trial saw flamboyant Jackson attorney, Gerry Spence, appointed as special prosecutor. A major portion of his 1982 best-selling 'Gunning for Justice' book is devoted to the sensational case involving varied elements, from sewer connections to drug deals.").

461. Mark Rohde, "It Became a Question of Who the Jury Believed," Jackson Hole Guide (Jackson Hole, WY), Sept. 27, 1979, p. A3; Mark Rohde, "Jury Convicts on All Six Counts: Hopkinson Guilty of First Degree Murder," Jackson Hole Guide (Jackson Hole, WY), Sept. 27, 1979, p. A1. It was a complex series of events leading up to Hopkinson's murder trial and Gerry Spence's appearance as a special prosecutor in the case. *E.g.*, Joan Barron, "He Came Not to Rap Spence But to Praise Him," Sunday Star-Tribune (Casper, WY), Mar. 12, 1989, p. 10.

462. "Hopkinson Still Awaiting Jury's Decision on Fate," Rapid City Journal (Rapid City, SD), Sept. 27, 1979, p. 13.

463. Mark Rohde, "Hopkinson Sentenced to Gas Chamber," Jackson Hole Guide (Jackson, WY), Oct. 4, 1979, p. 1.

464. "Hopkinson Gets Death for Contract Slaying," Salt Lake Tribune (Salt Lake City, UT), Sept. 28, 1979, p. 28.

465. "Hopkinson and Spence Trade Jibes after Trial," Billings Gazette (Billings, MT), Sept. 30, 1979, p. 69. Years later, Mark Hopkinson said that Gerry Spence was "powerful in Wyoming," adding, "There is no person in this state who could control Spence. If I was going to book it like a bookie, I would bet Spence could convince a jury in Wyoming that the Pope isn't Catholic." "Death-row Inmate Hopkinson Hopes for Conviction Reversals," Billings Gazette (Billings, MT), Nov. 17, 1985, p. 4-B.

466. "Spence Will Not Appear in Hopkinson Appeal," Billings Gazette (Billings, MT), Apr. 10, 1980, p. 2B. In 1983, Hopkinson moved again for a new trial. "Convicted Killer Files Again for New Trial," Billings Gazette (Billings, MT), Nov. 17, 1983, p. 7-B; "Hopkinson Again Seeks Relief from Death Sentence," Jackson Hole News (Jackson, WY), July 25, 1984, p. ("Hopkinson was sentenced to die for ordering Green's death. Hopkinson also is seeking to prevent Jackson attorney Gerry Spence, who acted as special prosecutor in the trial, and his partners from interfering with investigations by the Wyoming Public Defender's Office on the case.").

467. Dan Whipple, "Spence Opposes Hopkinson Execution," Casper Star-Tribune (Casper, WY), Sept. 18, 1990, p. 1.

468. Gerry Spence, The Making of a Country Lawyer: An Autobiography 330 (1996).

469. "Hopkinson Case Review: 12 Years of Wyoming Controversy," CASPER STAR-TRIBUNE (Casper, WY), Jan. 21, 1992, p. 1.

470. Hopkinson v. Shillinger, 866 F.2d 1185, 1202–03, 1210 (10th Cir. 1989).

471. Katharine Collins, "Asks Sullivan to Delay Hopkinson's Execution," CASPER STAR-TRIBUNE (Casper, WY), May 16, 1991, p. B1.

472. William Browning, "Of Murder and Moving On: Man who Killed Four People Lives Quietly in Bridger Valley," CASPER STAR-TRIBUNE, May 1, 2011, https://trib.com/news/local/of-murder-and-moving-on/article_3bd18d7f-7c64-5fc6-8f76-fb395b3a942b.html; Karen Scherting, "Man Who Killed 4 People Lives Quietly in Wyoming's Bridger Valley," BILLINGS GAZETTE, May 1, 2011 (updated May 4, 2015), https://billingsgazette.com/news/state-and-regional/wyoming/man-who-killed-4-people-lives-quietly-in-wyomings-bridger-valley/article_077eb6c9-d476-57f9-ae67-30b675780630.html; *see also* Hopkinson v. Shillinger, 866 F.2d 1185, 1194 (10th Cir. 1989):

> [I]n 1979, Michael Hickey confessed to bombing the Vehars' home. Testifying at trial under a grant of immunity, Hickey stated that Hopkinson first asked him in early 1977 whether he would kill Vehar for $2,000 plus expenses. VIII–G R. at 916. Hopkinson knew at that time that Hickey had killed a local fifteen-year-old girl, Kelly Wyckhuyse. *Id.* at 913–15. Over a period of several months, the two discussed various methods of accomplishing Vehar's murder. *Id.* at 917–29. As the deposition in the sewer board case neared, Hickey testified that Hopkinson became "desperate," *id.* at 930, and decided that a dynamite explosion of Vehar's house would be the best way to kill Vehar, *id.* at 930–33, 971–72. Hickey agreed to bomb the house for the offered sum plus Hopkinson's help should Hickey be charged for Wyckhuyse's murder. *Id.* at 932. Hopkinson told Hickey that he did not care if the bomb killed everyone in the house, *id.* at 932, 971, 987, or if it killed half of Evanston, Wyoming, VIII–H R. 1231, so long as it killed Vehar.

473. "Is Kip Croft Interested in Who Killed Jeff Green?", CASPER STAR-TRIBUNE (Casper, WY), July 21, 1991, pp. 10–11.

474. Hopkinson v. State, 798 P.2d 1186 (Wyo. 1990).

475. Hopkinson v. Shillinger, 866 F.2d 1185, 1205–11 (10th Cir. 1989); Katharine Collins, "Court Chastises Spence's Conduct During Stint as Special Prosecutor," CASPER STAR-TRIBUNE (Casper, WY), Feb. 13, 1989, p. 1; *see also* "Trial Set for Suspect in '79 Slaying," BILLINGS GAZETTE (Billings, MT), Apr. 13, 1990, p. 8 ("Hopkinson, in letters from death row at the Wyoming State Penitentiary, has maintained that the case against him was manufactured by special prosecutor Gerry Spence. Hopkinson claims the state refuses to pursue any investigation that does not conform to Spence's case.").

476. "Supreme Court Refused to Hear Hopkinson Appeal," JACKSON HOLE NEWS (Jackson, WY), Oct. 9, 1985, p. 24.

477. Angela Pelkey & Katharine Collins, "Execution Set for 12:30 a.m. Wednesday," CASPER STAR-TRIBUNE (Casper, WY), Jan. 18, 1992, p. 1; Katharine Collins, "Hopkinson Maintains Innocence," CASPER STAR-TRIBUNE (Casper, WY), Jan. 18, 1992, p. 1.

478. "A 'Real People' Lawyer's Hardest Case," CHICAGO TRIBUNE, June 11, 1992, https://www.chicagotribune.com/news/ct-xpm-1992-06-11-9202220012-story.html.

479. "1990 Marked by Lively Remarks," CASPER STAR-TRIBUNE (Casper, WY), Jan. 1, 1991, p. 3.

480. Katharine Collins, "Groups Seek Clemency for Death-row Inmate," CASPER STAR-TRIBUNE (Casper, WY), Jan. 8, 1992, p. B1.

481. "Anatomy of Murder Unsolved—Hopkinson Execution Would Leave Intriguing Questions Unanswered," BILLINGS GAZETTE (Billings, MT), Sept. 23, 1990, p. 1C.

482. Joy Ufford, "Spence: No Responsibility for Hopkinson Sentence," JACKSON HOLE GUIDE (Jackson, WY), Sept. 19, 1990, p. 1.

483. Angus M. Thuermer Jr., "Spence Opposes Death of Killer Hopkinson - Spence Delivers Eloquent Plea for Killer's Life," JACKSON HOLE NEWS (Jackson, WY), Sept. 19, 1990, pp. 1, 8.

484. Angela Pelkey & Katharine Collins, "Execution Set for 12:30 a.m. Wednesday," CASPER STAR-TRIBUNE (Casper, WY), Jan. 18, 1992, pp. 1, 10; *see also* "Hopkinson Execution Won't Kill Killers," TIME-NEWS (Twin Falls, ID), p. A-11 ("Ironically, Gerry Spence, the famed Jackson lawyer and special prosecutor who

convinced jurors to sentence Hopkinson to death, has urged Gov. Mike Sullivan to spare the 42-year-old Hopkinson. All the while Hopkinson, like most death row inmates, has maintained his innocence.").

485. "Hopkinson Files Own Appeal to Justices," BILLINGS GAZETTE (Billings, MT), Jan. 21, 1992, p. B1.

486. "No Stay in Hopkinson Execution," BILLINGS GAZETTE (Billings, MT), Jan. 21, 1992, p. 1. Jim Fitzgerald, Michael Hickey's defense attorney, would later compare *Hopkinson* to Charles Manson. Fitzgerald described Hopkinson as a "(Charles) Manson in pinstripes," someone who conned and "pulled" people like Hickey and Jeff Green "under his influence." Karen Scherting, "Man Who Killed 4 People Lives Quietly in Wyoming's Bridger Valley," BILLINGS GAZETTE, May 1, 2011 (updated May 4, 2015), https://billingsgazette.com/news/state-and-regional/wyoming/man-who-killed-4-people-lives-quietly-in-wyomings-bridger-valley/article_077eb6c9-d476-57f9-ae67-30b675780630.html.

487. Julie Prodis & Angela Pelkey, "Hopkinson Maintains Innocence to the End—State Declares Death at 12:57 a.m.," CASPER STAR-TRIBUNE (Casper, WY), Jan. 23, 1992, p. 1.

488. JOHN D. BESSLER, DEATH IN THE DARK: MIDNIGHT EXECUTIONS IN AMERICA 4, 89, 91–92 (1997).

489. Julie Prodis & Angela Pelkey, "Hopkinson Maintains Innocence to the End—State Declares Death at 12:57 a.m.," CASPER STAR-TRIBUNE (Casper, WY), Jan. 23, 1992, p. 1.

490. Kurt J. Repanshek, "Execution Top Story of '92," RAPID CITY JOURNAL (Rapid City, SD), Dec. 28, 1992, p. B2.

491. GERRY SPENCE, O.J.: THE LAST WORD 71 (1997).

492. *In re Taylor*, 73 A.3d 85, 89, 98–103 (D.C. 2013); *see also* Crockett v. District of Columbia, 95 A.3d 601, 605 n.3 (D.C. Ct. App. 2014) (describing the holding of *In re Taylor*); *see also* In re Peak, 759 A.2d 612, 617 (D.C. Ct. App. 2000):

> It is well settled that criminal contempt proceedings may be prosecuted by private attorneys appointed by the court for that purpose. *Young v. U.S. ex rel. Vuitton et Fils, S.A.*, 481 U.S. 787, 793, 800–01, 107 S. Ct. 2124, 95 L.Ed.2d 740 (1987). "Private attorneys appointed to prosecute a criminal contempt action represent the United States, not the party that is the beneficiary of the court order allegedly violated." *Young*, 481 U.S. at 804, 107 S. Ct. 2124. Criminal contempt proceedings which arise out of civil litigation are between the defendant and the public, rather than a part of the original action. *Id.* (citing *Gompers v. Bucks Stove & Range Co.*, 221 U.S. 418, 445, 31 S. Ct. 492, 55 L.Ed. 797 (1911)). When a private attorney is appointed solely for contempt prosecution, that attorney "is appointed to pursue the public interest in vindication of the court's authority." *Id.* Thus, for purposes of the contempt proceeding, the attorney so appointed represents the sovereign. *Id.*
>
> Having been appointed to represent the government for purposes of the contempt proceeding, such attorney necessarily must have the authority to execute, on behalf of the sovereign, a conditional plea agreement under Super. Ct. Crim. R. 11(a)(2). To preclude the private prosecutor from functioning within the rules pertaining to the proceeding would severely restrict the court's inherent authority over contempt proceedings, including its ability to prosecute through a private attorney. *See id.* at 793, 107 S. Ct. 2124. Therefore, we hold that a private attorney appointed to prosecute contempt actions, consistent with the provisions of Super. Ct. Crim. R. 11(a)(2), may consent to a conditional plea agreement entered by the contemnor.

493. *In re Taylor*, 73 A.3d at 100–02, 105.

494. Attorney General of Guam v. Gutierrez, No. CVA09-024, 2011 WL 6937265, at *9 (Guam Terr. June 28, 2011).

495. Guerrero v. Moylan, No. CVA01-020, 2002 WL 31119472, at *13 (Guam Terr. Sept. 26, 2002).

496. In re Matter of Woodruff, Sup. Ct. No. 2013-SCC-0030-CIV, 2014 WL 10486959, at *1–3 (Mariana Islands Aug. 26, 2014).

497. Santos v. Tribunal Superior, 102 D.P.R. 171, 1974 WL 36890 (P.R. 1974).

498. Lopez Rivera v. Matos, 101 D.P.R. 740, 1973 WL 35606 (P.R. 1973).

499. Tonkin v. Michael, 349 F. Supp. 78, 79 (V.I. 1972).

500. Government of the Virgin Islands v. Santiago, 937 F. Supp. 1157, 1161 (D.C. V.I., St. Croix Div., App. Div. 1996) (italics in original).

501. John C. Olson, Jr., *Discovery for Three at a Table Set for Two: An Alteration of Rule for Courts-Martial 701 to Accommodate the Practice and Philosophical Realities of the Victim as a Limited Third Party*, ARMY LAWYER, pp. 30, 32 (Nov. 2015).

502. United States v. Smith, 23 C.M.R. 402, 406, 8 U.S.C.M.A. 178, 182 (Ct. Mil. App. 1957).

503. United States v. LaSalle, 2019 WL 3991102, at *2 (U.S. Air Force Ct. Crim. App., Aug. 21, 2019).

504. 10 U.S.C.A. § 806b. The *Military Law Review* once pointed out that private prosecutions have been used in the Chinese military. *See* Captain Daivd C. Rodearmel, *Military Law in Communist China: Development, Structure and Function*, 119 MIL. L. REV. 1, 68 (1988):

> Under the Criminal Procedure Law, criminal complaints and accusations may be filed by citizens with the public security organs, the procuracy, or the courts. The procedures for servicemen to follow in bringing criminal complaints directly to the attention of military courts were outlined by the editors of *Zhongguo Fazhi Bao* (China Legal Journal) on 2 May 1986, in response to a letter from a PLA recruit in Henan province. Private prosecutions may be commenced before military courts under the provisions of the Criminal Procedure Law, with the additional requirement that the unit Party committee assist in the investigation and production of evidence. If supported by sufficient evidence, the case may be transferred to the military procuracy for initiation of public prosecution, or it may be directly investigated and heard by the military court as a private prosecution. If the evidence is insufficient to support a criminal prosecution, the case may be referred to the complainant's unit Party committee for further investigation. If sufficient evidence is developed, the unit Party committee may refer the case back to the court. Violations that do not constitute criminal offenses may be referred for possible disciplinary action. The law requires that complainants be informed of the potential legal responsibility incurred for false accusations.

505. *Military Legal Ethics: Perjury and the Prosecutor*, ARMY LAWYER (Nov. 1975), p. 6 (reporting the remarks of Colonel Donald W. Hansen to the FBA Ethics Seminar in Atlanta, Georgia, on September 10, 1975).

506. Taylor S. West, *The Convening Authority and Ex Parte Communications: A Threat to the Legitimacy of Military Justice?*, 30 GEO. J. LEGAL ETHICS 1115, 1115 (2017). *But cf.* Leo Shane III, *Plan to Remove Handling of Military Sexual Misconduct from Chain of Command Sees New Momentum*, MILITARY TIMES, Feb. 24, 2021, https://www.militarytimes.com/news/pentagon-congress/2021/02/24/plan-to-remove-handling-of-military-sexual-misconduct-from-chain-of-command-sees-new-momentum/ ("The chairman of the Senate Armed Services Committee said he is considering plans to establish an independent prosecutor to handle all sex crimes in the military, a potentially major change to the Uniform Code of Military Justice stemming from years of frustration over the Defense Department's handling of the issue.").

Chapter 7 Notes

1. *E.g.*, Strickler v. Greene, 527 U.S. 263, 281 (1999) (taking note of "the special role played by the American prosecutor in the search for truth in criminal trials"); State ex rel. Hamstead v. Dostert, 313 S.E.2d 409, 414 (W. Va. Sup. Ct. App. 1984) (noting "the public prosecutor's unique role in the criminal justice system"); In the Matter of Murray, Case No. 14-O-00412, 2016 WL 6651388, at *11 n.9 (Review Dept. of State Bar Ct. of Cal., Nov. 10, 2016) ("Our recognition of a higher standard of conduct for prosecutors is not only derived from case law. As a result of a prosecutor's unique position in the administration of justice, we note that the American Bar Association adopted a rule of professional conduct detailing the "Special Responsibilities of a Prosecutor." (See ABA Model Rules Prof. Conduct, rule 3.8.).").

2. 712 F.2d 757 (2d Cir. 1983).

3. *Id.* at 759–62; *see also* United States v. Serubo, 604 F.2d 807 (3d Cir. 1979); United States v. Chanen, 549 F.2d 1306 (9th Cir. 1977), *cert. denied*, 434 U.S. 825 (1977).

4. Under the Model Rules of Professional Conduct, a prosecutor "shall ... make reasonable efforts to assure that the accused has been advised of the right to, and the procedure for obtaining, counsel and has

been given reasonable opportunity to obtain counsel...." Model Rules of Professional Conduct Rule 3.8(b) (1984).

5. Model Code of Professional Responsibility DR 7-103(A) (1982); Model Rules of Professional Conduct Rule 3.8(a) (1984); Calif. R. 7-102; Prosecution Function Standards § 3-3.9 (approved 1979); *see also* Minnesota Rules of Professional Conduct Rule 3.8(a) (1988); United States v. Lovasco, 431 U.S. 783 (1977) (it is "unprofessional conduct for a prosecutor to recommend an indictment on less than probable cause"); Commonwealth v. Hawkins, 469 A.2d 252, 255 (Pa. Super. 1983) (action should not go forward absent probable cause); In re Gonyo, 245 N.W.2d 893 (Wis. 1976) (prosecutor disciplined for breach of obligation to prosecute only on probable cause). Notably, some scholars have argued that prosecutors should be required to be personally convinced that the accused is guilty beyond a reasonable doubt before commencing a prosecution. Monroe Freedman, Lawyers' Ethics in an Adversary System 85–88 (1975).

6. 118 U.S. 356 (1886).

7. In *Yick Wo*, the record demonstrated that almost all Chinese individuals who applied for a license were refused, while nearly all non-Chinese applicants received licenses. Under those facts, the U.S. Supreme Court in *Yick Wo* held that discriminatorily selective enforcement is a complete bar to prosecution; it was irrelevant that the accused was guilty of the underlying criminal offense.

8. Miller v. Pate, 386 U.S. 1 (1967); Alcorta v. Texas, 355 U.S. 28 (1957); Mooney v. Holohan, 294 U.S. 103 (1935); *see also* United States v. Kelly, 543 F. Supp. 1303, 1309–10 (D. Mass. 1982) (a prosecutor may not present evidence that "he actually knows, or should know, to be false"); Mooney v. Holohan, 294 U.S. 103, 110, 112 (1935) (noting that the due process requirement, "in safeguarding the liberty of the citizen against deprivation through the action of the State, embodies the fundamental conceptions of justice which lie at the base of our civil and political institutions," in the context of a case containing these allegations: "Petitioner charges that the State holds him in confinement without due process of law in violation of the Fourteenth Amendment of the Constitution of the United States. The grounds of his charge are, in substance, that the sole basis of his conviction was perjured testimony, which was knowingly used by the prosecuting authorities in order to obtain that conviction, and also that these authorities deliberately suppressed evidence which would have impeached and refuted the testimony thus given against him.").

9. United States v. Agurs, 427 U.S. 97, 103–04 (1976); Giglio v. United States, 405 U.S. 150 (1972); Napue v. Illinois, 360 U.S. 264 (1959); Mooney v. Holohan, 294 U.S. 103 (1935).

10. 373 U.S. 83 (1963). The Supreme Court in *Brady* held that "suppression by the prosecution of evidence favorable to an accused upon request violates due process where the evidence is material either to guilt or punishment." *Id.* at 87.

11. *Id.* at 87; United States v. Bagley, 473 U.S 667, 676 (1985); Giglio v. United States, 405 U.S. 150, 154 (1972). In *Bagley*, the Supreme Court held that the prosecution must disclose evidence "if there is some reasonable probability that, had the evidence been disclosed to the defense, the result of the proceeding would have been different." A "reasonable probability" is one that is "sufficient to undermine confidence in the outcome." *Bagley*, 473 U.S. at 682. For a discussion of this issue, see Terrence Galligan, *The Prosecutor's Duty to Disclose Exculpatory Evidence After* United States v. Bagley, 1 Geo. J. L. Ethics 213 (1987).

12. W.J. Michael Cody, *Special Ethical Duties for Attorneys Who Hold Public Positions*, 23 Memphis State U. L. Rev. 453, 456, 458–59 (1993).

13. United States v. Young, 470 U.S. 1, 25 (1985) (Brennan, J., concurring in part and dissenting in part).

14. The Alabama State Bar Association adopted a code of ethics for the legal profession in 1887. Allison Marston, *Guiding the Profession: The 1887 Code of Ethics of the Alabama State Bar Association*, 49 Ala. L. Rev. 471 (1998); *see also id.* at 472, 496 (noting that George Sharswood, a University of Pennsylvania Law School professor who delivered lectures on ethics summarized and published in his 1854 *Essay on Professional Ethics*, "drew the line at an attorney's acting as a private prosecutor against a man he believed to be innocent"); *see also* Walter Burgwyn Jones, *Canons of Professional Ethics, Their Genesis and History*, 7 Notre Dame L. Rev. 483, 494 (1932) ("'While Sharswood's *Essay on Professional Ethics* was doubtless the inspiration for the Alabama Code, the profession is nevertheless indebted for that Code's existence to the initiative of Col. Thomas Goode Jones, afterwards Governor of Alabama, and now United States Judge

for the Middle District of Alabama, who in 1881 suggested the adoption of a Code of Professional Ethics by the State Bar Association and afterwards compiled it.'").

15. Peter A. Joy, *The Relationship Between Prosecutorial Misconduct and Wrongful Convictions: Shaping Remedies for a Broken System*, 2006 WIS L. REV. 399, 411 ("The lack of clarity or specificity in the 1908 Canons concerning the prosecutor's ethical obligations was perhaps as much a reflection of the overall structure of the 1908 Canons as an inability to define concrete steps that a prosecutor could take 'to see that justice is done.' Many of the other 1908 Canons were similarly general and vague, and one commentator described them as 'vaporous platitudes... which have somewhat less usefulness as guides to lawyers in the predicaments of the real world than do valentine cards as guides to heart surgeons in the operating room.' Analyzing the 1908 Canons in the context of ethical issues specific to prosecutors and defense lawyers, another commentator concluded that 'the Canons of Ethics are so vague, so ambiguous, and so contradictory that they are little or no help in resolving these problems [of ethical conduct of prosecutors and defense counsel], and that almost any position, on a given issue, can reasonably be defended with support from the [C]anons.'"); *see also* Fred C. Zacharias, *The Humanization of Lawyers*, 2002 PROF. LAW. 9, 17 n.34 (2002) ("The 1908 CANONS OF ETHICS did little more than propose generalized standards to govern the role of lawyers. The 1969 CODE OF PROFESSIONAL RESPONSIBILITY moved towards the inclusion of enforceable rules, but still relied heavily on broad "ethical considerations" that sought solely to provide guidance.").

16. Eric S. Fish, *Against Adversary Prosecution*, 103 IOWA L. REV. 1419, 1438 (2018); *see also* Michael Ariens, *Brougham's Ghost*, 35 N. ILL. U. L. REV. 263, 293 (2015) ("The American Bar Association began work on its Canons of Ethics in 1905, which it adopted in 1908. Roscoe Pound, then an obscure academic, gave a famous speech at the 1906 Annual Meeting of the ABA attacking the view that a lawsuit was akin to a game, which 'leads counsel to forget that they are officers of the court and to deal with the rules of law and procedure exactly as the professional foot ball coach with the rules of the sport.'"); David Keenan, Deborah Jane Cooper, David Lebowitz & Tamar Lerer, *The Myth of Prosecutorial Accountability After* Connick v. Thompson: *Why Existing Professional Responsibility Measures Cannot Protect Against Prosecutorial Misconduct*, 121 YALE L.J. ONLINE 203, 222 n.93 (2011) ("The ABA promulgated its first ethics code, the Canon of Ethics, in 1908. By 1914, the Canons had been adopted by thirty-one bar associations.") (citing James M. Altman, *Considering the A.B.A.'s 1908 Canons of Ethics*, 71 FORDHAM L. REV. 2395, 2395–96 (2003)).

17. People v. Cahoon, 50 N.W. 384, 385 (Mich. 1891).

18. Wight v. Rindskopf, 43 Wis. 344, 354 (1877); *see also* People v. Fielding, 158 N.Y. 542, 547 (N.Y. Ct. App. 1899) ("Language which might be permitted to counsel in summing up a civil action cannot with propriety be used by a public prosecutor, who is a quasi judicial officer, representing the people of the state, and presumed to act impartially in the interest only of justice. If he lays aside the impartiality that should characterize his official action, to become a heated partisan, and by vituperation of the prisoner and appeals to prejudice seeks to procure a conviction at all hazards, he ceases to properly represent the public interest, which demands no victim, and asks no conviction through the aid of passion, sympathy, or resentment."); In re Moegenberg, 120 N.W. 1132, 1133 (Neb. 1909) ("The county attorney is the public prosecutor, and his office is quasi judicial. In the discharge of the functions of that office he is called upon to exercise a sound discretion to distinguish between the guilty and the innocent, and to refrain from prosecuting those persons whose guilt is so doubtful that in his judgment justice will not be subserved by prosecutions, and there should not be anything in the way of private interest to possibly sway that judgment or to tempt him to depart from a disinterested and conscientious discharge of his duty.") (citing *Wight*, 43 Wis. at 354); Ex parte Bentine, 196 N.W. 213, 216–17 (Wis. 1923) ("'A public prosecutor is a quasi judicial officer, retained by the public for the prosecution of persons accused of crime, in the exercise of a sound discretion to distinguish between the guilty and the innocent, between the certainly and the doubtfully guilty.' The office of district attorney is a constitutional office. It is held as a public trust, and the incumbent is charged with the grave responsibilities calling for the exercise of learning in the law and sound judgment. The duties of the office should be discharged vigorously, and without fear or favor. At the same time they should be discharged fairly; so discharged that persons accused of crime will not be deprived of their constitutional rights. Before filing the information it is the duty of the district attorney to make full

examination of all the facts and circumstances connected with the case, and it is not to be presumed that his decision will be influenced by any personal bias or excessive zeal.") (quoting *Wight*, 43 Wis. at 354 and citing Rock v. Ekern, 156 N.W. 197, 198 (Wis. 1916)).

19. *E.g.*, State v. Johnson, 470 P.3d 1263, 1268 (Idaho Ct. App. 2020) ("Allowing a non-party to intervene in a defendant's criminal proceeding would bring complicated consequences, including the potential to undermine the critical and distinct role of the prosecutor. Unlike private counsel, a prosecutor has the unique role as 'a minister of justice and not simply that of an advocate.' Idaho Rules of Professional Conduct, 3.8 cmt.1. While a prosecutor has a duty to communicate with the crime victim, *see* IDAHO CONST. art. I, § 22, '[t]he prosecutor generally serves the public and not any particular government agency, law enforcement officer or unit, witness or victim.' ABA Standard 3-1.3.").

20. ABA Model Code of Professional Responsibility, https://njdc.info/wp-content/uploads/2014/05/ABA-Model-Code-of-Professional-Responsibility.pdf.

21. Model Code of Professional Responsibility EC 7-13 (1982); Hearings before a Subcommittee of the Committee on Government Operations, House of Representatives, Ninety-Fifth Congress, First Session, June 9, 21; July 21 and 27, 1977, at 104–05 (1977) (noting that the House of Delegates of the American Bar Association adopted Ethical Consideration 7–13 in 1969); *see also* ABA Standards for Criminal Justice, Standard 3-1.1(c) (1979) ("The duty of the prosecutor is to seek justice, not merely to convict."); Vandenades v. United States, 523 F.2d 1220, 1225 n.12 (5th Cir. 1975) ("Ethical Consideration 7–13 . . . urges prosecutors to 'seek justice, not merely to convict.'"); Commonwealth v. Diana, 314 A.2d 262, 263 n.* (Pa. 1974) ("It should not be necessary to state that counsel for the prosecution in a criminal case, no less than counsel for the defense, have an obligation to their clients and to the court to 'represent a client zealously within the bounds of the law.' Canon 7 of the Code of Professional Responsibility. The Code, of course, is a rule of this Court. See Rule 205, 12 P.S. Appendix and Rule 17–3. The public prosecutor's responsibility under this Canon is delineated in ethical consideration EC 7–13 in the Code. The obligation to assist the court to a correct and just result which rests upon appellant's counsel in a criminal case (see section 3.2, Counsel on appeal, and comment f. thereto (the lawyer's duty to assist the court) of the American Bar Association's Standards Relating to Criminal Appeals (Tentative Draft, March, 1969)), lies equally upon counsel for the state."); ABA Standards for Criminal Justice, Standard 3-1.1 cmt. (1979) ("It is fundamental that the prosecutor's obligation is to protect the innocent as well as convict the guilty, to guard the rights of the accused as well as to enforce the rights of the public."); *see also* Polo Fashions, Inc. v. Stock Buyers Int'l, Inc., 760 F.2d 698, 704–05 (6th Cir. 1985); *cf.* Donnelly v. DeChristoforo, 416 U.S. 637, 648–49 (1974) ("The function of the prosecutor under the Federal Constitution is not to tack as many skins of victims as possible to the wall. His function is to vindicate the right of people as expressed in the laws and give those accused of crime a fair trial.").

22. Young v. United States ex rel. Vuitton et Fils S.A., 481 U.S. 787, 803–04 (1987) (citing 18 U.S.C. § 208(a)). State laws have similar ethics provisions for prosecutors. *E.g.*, Minnesota Rules of Professional Conduct Rule 3.8 (1988); *see also* State v. Marshall, 586 A.2d 85 (N.J. 1991) (court can disqualify prosecutor for personal interest or financial stake in outcome of criminal prosecution). Significantly, many states have enacted laws which prohibit prosecutors from accepting fees from private parties and from participating in civil actions whose facts form the basis of a criminal case. Andrew Sidman, Comment, *The Outmoded Concept of Private Prosecution*, 25 AM. U.L. REV. 754, 778 & n.132 (1976) (citing statutes). For a recent annotation addressing the issue of when a prosecuting attorney must be disqualified based upon a relationship with the alleged victim or the victim's family, see Christopher Vaeth, *Disqualification or Recusal of Prosecuting Attorney Because of Relationship with Alleged Victim or Victim's Family*, 12 A.L.R. 5th 909 (1993) (citing cases); *see also id.* at § 2[a] ("A trial court has the power to disqualify a prosecuting attorney from proceeding with a particular criminal prosecution if the prosecuting attorney suffers from a conflict of interest which might prejudice him against the accused, such as where he has a personal interest in convicting the accused, or where he has a pecuniary interest in the outcome."). All attorneys are subject to professional discipline, a court's contempt power, and a court's "supervisory authority." CHARLES W. WOLFRAM, MODERN LEGAL ETHICS, § 13.10.2, at 760–61 (1986) (citations omitted); *see also* State v. Wilson, 545 A.2d 1178, 1183 (Del. 1988) ("a court may, through its inherent authority to regulate the status of

those who appear before it in a representative capacity, preclude the privatization of prosecutions initiated by a public prosecutor").

23. State of Ohio v. Jones, No. 1266, 1986 WL 5234 *4 (Ohio Ct. App. 1986); *see also* State v. Johnson, 702 S.W.2d 65, 69 (Mo. 1985) (en banc) ("Ethical Consideration 7–13 points out that 'the responsibility of a public prosecutor differs from that of the usual advocate; his duty is to seek justice, not merely to convict.' This ethical consideration, though admittedly only aspirational in nature, is given greater weight and meaning by the substance of Disciplinary Rule 7–103(A) and (B), which in combination prohibit a prosecuting attorney from instituting criminal charges without probable cause and require him to disclose to a criminal defendant any evidence that tends to negate guilt, mitigate the degree of the offense or serves to reduce the punishment. Thus, it becomes apparent that the 'partisan' interest normally attributed to the private practitioner who serves as trial advocate differs in a fundamental way when the trial advocate is a prosecuting attorney.").

24. United States v. Kelly, 543 F. Supp. 1303, 1310 (D. Mass. 1982).

25. People v. Bonilla, 420 N.Y.S.2d 665, 669 (N.Y. Sup. Ct. 1979).

26. State v. Brandenburg, 344 N.W.2d 702, 705 (S.D. 1984).

27. Shuttleworth v. State, 469 N.E.2d 1210, 1216 (1984); *see also id.* at 1217 ("[A] prosecutor must 'represent public justice and stand indifferent as between the accused and any private interest.' In other words, an attorney's private employment must not influence his prosecutorial decision whether or not to bring criminal charges based upon the same set of facts available in the civil case.") (citations omitted).

28. North Fulton Community Hospital, Inc. v. State Health Planning & Development Agency, 310 S.E.2d 764, 770 (Ga. Ct. App. 1983).

29. *E.g.*, State v. Spurlock, 874 S.W.2d 602, 611–12 (Tenn. Ct. App. 1993).

30. People v. Harrison, 205 N.W.2d 900, 907 (Mich. Ct. App. 1973).

31. Roger LeRoy Miller & Mary Meinzinger, Paralegal Today: The Essentials 88 (7th ed. 2017) ("Today's state ethical codes are based, for the most part, on later revisions of the ABA canons: the *Model Code of Professional Responsibility* (published in 1969) and the *Model Rules of Professional Conduct* (first published in 1983 to replace the *Model Code* and revised many times since then). Although most states have adopted laws based on the *Model Rules*, the *Model Code* is still in effect in some states. New York still uses the *Model Code*, for example, while California and Maine have developed their own rules.").

32. Model Rules of Professional Conduct Rule 3.8 cmt. (1984).

33. Stern v. United States District Court for the District of Massachusetts, 214 F.3d 4, 8 (1st Cir. 2000) ("In 1990, the American Bar Association (the ABA) amended Rule 3.8 of the Model Rules of Professional Conduct by adding a new paragraph (f)...."); Commission for Lawyer Discipline v. Hanna, 513 S.W.3d 175, 181 (Tex. Ct. App. 2016) ("The American Bar Association amended Model Rule 3.8 in 2008 to include two new subsections that explicitly impose on prosecutors a duty to disclose evidence learned post-conviction and to attempt to rectify an improper conviction....").

34. Bruce A. Green, *Prosecutorial Ethics as Usual*, 2003 U. Ill. L. Rev. 1573, 1576 (2003).

35. "Rule 3.8 Special Responsibilities of a Prosecutor—Comment," American Bar Association, https://www.americanbar.org/groups/professional_responsibility/publications/model_rules_of_professional_conduct/rule_3_8_special_responsibilities_of_a_prosecutor/comment_on_rule_3_8/.

36. United States v. Miller, 953 F.3d 1095, 1104 (9th Cir. 2020).

37. Bowen v. Maynard, 799 F.2d 593, 604 n.5 (10th Cir. 1986).

38. United States v. Klein, No. 16-cr-442 (JMA), 2017 WL 1316999, at *15 (E.D.N.Y. Feb. 10, 2017) (citing Kyles v. Whitley, 514 U.S. 419, 437 (1995)); *see also id.* ("Unlike the duties set out under *Brady* and its progeny, however, Rule 3.8 does not constitute a constitutional guarantee, and district courts enforcing the rules of professional conduct do so at their own discretion."); United States v. Starusko, 729 F.2d 256, 264 (3d Cir. 1984) ("It is clear that 'a prosecutor who intentionally fails to make disclosure to the defense, at the earliest feasible opportunity, of the existence of evidence which tends to negate the guilt of the accused as to the offense charged,' violates certain standards of professional conduct, Standards for Criminal Justice § 3-3.11 (1980). *See also* Model Rules of Professional Conduct Rule 3.8 (1983).").

39. 373 U.S. 83 (1963).

40. United States v. Chu, 5 F.3d 1244, 1249 (9th Cir. 1993).

41. People v. Garcia, 17 Cal.App.4th 1169, 1179 (Cal. Ct. App., 4th Dist. 1993).

42. In re: Petition to Stay the Effectiveness of Formal Ethics Opinion 2017-F-163, 582 S.W.3d 200, 206–07 (Tenn. 2019).

43. ABA Standards for Criminal Justice: Prosecution Function and Defense Function (4th ed. 2015), https://lalegalethics.org/wp-content/uploads/107d.pdf.

44. *Id.*, Standard 3–1.1(a)-(b).

45. *Id.*, Standard 3–1.2 & 3–1.3.

46. Rebecca Gray Klotzle, "Attorney-Client Privilege," *in* 2 ROBIN L. CAUTIN & SCOTT O LILIENFELD, EDS., THE ENCYCLOPEDIA OF PSYCHOLOGY 235 (2015) ("A *privilege* is the legal right to prevent disclosure of certain information, usually information that was originally communicated in a professional relationship. The attorney-client privilege is one of the oldest recognized privileges, dating back to sixteenth-century England, and protects against the disclosure of confidential communications made between an attorney and his or her client for purposes of legal advice or assistance.").

47. Nice v. City of Akron, Case No. 18-cv-1565, 2019 WL 6771156, at *4 n.2 (N.D. Ohio Dec. 12, 2019).

48. Mildred Scott, *Prosecutorial Misconduct: Shouldn't the Punishment Fit the Crime?*, 60 S. TEX. L. REV. 325, 329 (2019).

49. Jason Kreag, *Disclosing Prosecutorial Misconduct*, 72 VAND. L. REV. 297, 334 (2019).

50. Daniel J. Bussel, *Ethics for Examiners*, 84 FORDHAM L. REV. 2073, 2077 n.34 (2016):

> Conventionally, American prosecutors are said to represent the "State," the "Government," or, most generically, the "People," but prosecutors' offices are typically structured to act independently of other government officials. Unlike lawyers with "real" clients, and very much like bankruptcy examiners, "the only mind the prosecutor must make up is his own." John S. Edwards, *Professional Responsibilities of the Federal Prosecutor*, 17 U. Rich. L. REV. 511, 513 (1983). Prosecutors often do identify with several constituencies: crime victims, law enforcement agencies and personnel with whom they work closely, and other officials. A prosecutor may even in some senses "represent" these constituents in the criminal process, but certainly as a formal and an ethical matter they are not his clients, and they can neither direct nor discharge him. *See* ABA STANDARDS FOR CRIMINAL JUSTICE: PROSECUTORIAL INVESTIGATIONS std. 26-1.2(a) (2014) (reaffirming the prosecutor's role as a "member of an independent institution the primary duty of which is to seek justice," but noting the prosecutor's client is "the public, not particular government agencies or victims").

51. *E.g.*, Katrina Lynne Baker, Note, *Don't Forget the Family: A Proposal for Expanding Immediate Protection to Families of Human Trafficking Survivors*, 30 FORDHAM INT'L L.J. 836, 853–54 (2007):

> In the current U.S. prosecutorial scheme, the victim no longer has a role in initiating criminal proceedings. Instead, because U.S. jurisdictions employ public and independent prosecution, a prosecutor's clients are the individuals who live in her jurisdiction. These people include law enforcement officials, victims, witnesses, and can include the defendant.
>
> Like other attorneys, the prosecutor has a fiduciary obligation to her clients. But, hers is a greater obligation to remain independent. She must be independent from police, victims, and families of victims. This duty of neutrality assures everyone within the judicial system that the unreviewable discretion a prosecutor has will not be affected by her own interests or any other party's interests.
>
> Furthermore, the prosecutor is not to be a counselor to victims of crimes because her client is the people. Prosecutors often discuss cases with victims, but should not defer to them, as the prosecutor is the ultimate decision-maker. But if the case goes to trial, the prosecutor often will need the victim to testify in order to secure a conviction. This necessity creates a tension—the prosecutor must maintain trust between herself and the victim, but only until she is finished using the victim in the trial, at that point she no longer needs to sustain the relationship. If a victim decides not to testify, a prosecutor has tools to motivate a witness, including contempt citations or arrest. The decision to use these tools could also implicate a prosecutor's duty of neutrality to the extent that she employs coercive tactics to get an unwilling victim to testify.

> Neutrality is not unattainable—it does not mean that the prosecutor should not be concerned for the victim's safety or injury. The prosecutor must merely avoid using her position to further personal motivations against the defendant or motivations to favor the victim, if that favoritism is at odds with the prosecutor's duty of neutrality. Prosecutorial ethics scholars argue that prosecutors must reconcile the need to remain neutral and protect the public with ensuring the rights of the accused and the victim.

52. ABA Standards for Criminal Justice: Prosecution Function and Defense Function (4th ed. 2015), https://lalegalethics.org/wp-content/uploads/107d.pdf., Standard 3-4.2(a) ("While the decision to arrest is often the responsibility of law enforcement personnel, the decision to institute formal criminal proceedings is the responsibility of the prosecutor. Where the law permits a law enforcement officer or other person to initiate proceedings by complaining directly to a judicial officer or the grand jury, the complainant should be required to present the complaint for prior review by the prosecutor, and the prosecutor's recommendation regarding the complaint should be communicated to the judicial officer or grand jury."); *id.*, Standard 3-4.4(b) ("In exercising discretion to file and maintain charges, the prosecutor should not consider: (i) partisan or other improper political or personal considerations; (ii) hostility or personal animus towards a potential subject, or any other improper motive of the prosecutor;....").

53. *Id.*, Standard 3-3.4; *see also id.*, Standard 3-3.4(i) ("Consistent with any specific laws or rules governing victims, the prosecutor should provide victims of serious crimes, or their representatives, an opportunity to consult with and to provide information to the prosecutor, prior to making significant decisions such as whether or not to prosecute, to pursue a disposition by plea, or to dismiss charges.").

54. *Id.*, Standard 3-1.4(a).

55. *Id.*, Standard 3-1.6(a).

56. *Id.*, Standard 3-1.7(a).

57. People v. Perez, 238 P.3d 665, 671 (Colo. 2010).

58. ABA Standards for Criminal Justice: Prosecution Function and Defense Function (4th ed. 2015), https://lalegalethics.org/wp-content/uploads/107d.pdf, Standard 3-1.9(a) & Standard 3-2.1(a)-(c); *compare id.*, Standard 3-2.1(d) ("Unless impractical or unlawful, the prosecutor's office should implement a system for allowing qualified law students, cross-designated prosecutors from other offices, and private attorneys temporarily assigned to the prosecutor's office, to learn about and assist with the prosecution function.").

59. State v. Johnson, 470 P.3d 1263, 1268-69 (Idaho 2020).

60. National District Attorneys Association, National Prosecution Standards (3d ed. with Revised Commentary), https://ndaa.org/wp-content/uploads/NDAA-NPS-3rd-Ed.-w-Revised-Commentary.pdf, "Definitions" and Standard 1-1.1 & 1-1.2.

61. *Id.*, Standard 1-1.3, Standard 1 commentary, and Standard 1-3.2.

62. Standard 2-17.1, Standard 2-17.2, and Standard 17 Commentary.

63. *E.g.*, State v. Jumpp, H15NCR180698275T, H15NCR1906321308S, H15NCR180264758T, 2020 WL 927702, at *2 (Conn. Super. Ct. Jan. 22, 2020); Evans v. State, 212 A.3d 308, 319 n.58 (Del. Super. Ct. 2019); State v. White, 2000 WL 73143, No. CR 1199106088, at *3 (Conn. Super. Ct. Jan. 10, 2000); *see also* State v. Surratt, 363 P.3d 1204, 1208-09 (N.M. 2015) ("[T]he State suggests that Section 36-1-23.1 is not invoked when an elected district attorney requests, for a specific case, that another elected district attorney prosecute the case instead. Applying well established rules of statutory construction, we disagree. An ordinary reading of the statute's plain language suggests the Legislature intended the statute to apply to the appointment of both private counsel and other public prosecutors. While the terms 'special prosecutor' and 'special assistant district attorney' are not specifically defined within the statute, its text is inclusive of both private counsel and other public prosecutors in its generic reference to 'a practicing member of the [New Mexico] bar.' This plain-language reading is consistent with the definition of special prosecutor adopted by the National District Attorney's Association as 'any person who performs the prosecution function in a jurisdiction who is not the chief prosecutor elected or appointed in the jurisdiction, or an assistant or deputy prosecutor in the jurisdiction.' National District Attorney's Association, *National Prosecution Standards* 2 (3d ed.2009), *available at* http://www.ndaa.org/pdf/NDAA NPS 3rd Ed. w Revised Commentary.pdf (last visited Dec. 7, 2015).").

64. Eric S. Fish, *Prosecutorial Constitutionalism*, 90 So. Cal. L. Rev. 237, 280–81 (2017); *see also* R. Michael Cassidy, 13 Geo. J. Legal Ethics 361, 383 (2000) (describing the NDAA's National Prosecution Standards as a "non-binding" code).

65. State v. Gonzales, 119 P.3d 151, 161 (N.M. 2005).

66. David Alan Sklansky, *The Nature and Function of Prosecutorial Power*, 106 J. Crim. L. & Criminology 473, 501 n.161 (2016).

67. Jessica Priest, "Moonlighting Prosecutor Sent Texas Man to Death Row; 17 Years Later, He Could Get a New Trial," USA Today, Feb. 4, 2021, https://www.usatoday.com/in-depth/news/investigations/2021/02/04/texas-death-row-inmate-could-get-new-trial/4255647001; "Trial Court Recommends New Trial for Death-Row Prisoner Whose Prosecutor Secretly Also Served as the Court's Law Clerk," Death Penalty Info. Ctr., May 4, 2021, https://deathpenaltyinfo.org/news/trial-court-recommends-new-trial-for-death-row-prisoner-whose-prosecutor-secretly-also-served-as-the-courts-law-clerk.

68. Verónica Michel-Luviano, Access to Justice, Victims' Rights, and Private Prosecution in Latin America: The Cases of Chile, Guatemala, and Mexico, Ph.D. thesis, University of Minnesota, Aug. 2012, https://conservancy.umn.edu/bitstream/handle/11299/138850/MichelLuviano_umn_0130E_13062.pdf?sequence=1&isAllowed=y, pp. 2–3 ("The right to private prosecution empowers victims of crime in ways that the US criminal system cannot conceive. As private prosecutor, the victim's lawyer has standing to intervene during the hearings and trial, and can even contradict the public prosecutor. The private prosecutor even has certain controls over the state in terms of how to conduct an investigation (e.g. sometimes by forcing the public prosecutor to follow a certain line of investigation) and when to end a prosecution (e.g., by requesting to a judge to keep the criminal investigation open or to take the case to trial)."); *id.* at pp. 3–4 ("Although in most Latin American criminal procedure codes (CPCs) this right can only be claimed by the victim or the victim's family, some countries allow other state agencies and even NGOs to litigate as private prosecutors in favor of an individual victim or the collective interest."); Verónica Michel & Kathryn Sikkink, *Human Rights Prosecutions and the Participation Rights of Victims in Latin America*, 47 Law & Soc'y Rev. 873, 874–75 (2013) ("The right to private prosecution allows victims and their lawyers, including domestic human rights organizations, to open a criminal investigation and actively participate throughout every stage of the criminal proceedings. In this article, we make two main claims: (1) private prosecution works as the vehicle through which societal actors engage in legal mobilization, bring human rights claims to the courts, and use and introduce international human rights law; and (2) that legal fights take place within a political and institutional context in which, at the very least, private prosecution opens doors for accountability by offering legal resources for societal actors to push for justice. Private prosecution also helps overcome barriers that state prosecutors face in holding other state officials accountable. Since human rights violations usually involve crimes committed by state officials, we might say that the state has a conflict of interest when it comes to human rights prosecutions. Even where the state is efficient in prosecuting ordinary crime, it may not be good at prosecuting itself. Private prosecutors thus assist in initiating and in keeping open human rights cases that would not have prospered without their involvement."); Jessica G. Mecellem, *Human Rights Trials in an Era of Democratic Stagnation: The Case of Turkey*, 43 Law & Soc. Inquiry 119, 129 (2016) ("Private prosecution occurs in countries that provide victims and NGOs the ability to advocate for victims' rights actively throughout court proceedings—mirroring public prosecutor advocacy of the state. This right was a major driving force in Latin American human rights trials of military officials, especially in Chile and Argentina, which have experienced a comparatively high number of prosecutions for human rights crimes (Michel and Sikkink 2013). Michel and Sikkink demonstrate that this right was a key causal mechanism for two reasons: it has been used to introduce new arguments regarding international and regional human rights law, which were eventually relied on in Supreme Court decisions (2013, 898); and second, private prosecution allowed victims, and NGOs representing them, to keep court cases open, even in the absence of political will to examine accusations against state actors (889). The authors argue that private prosecution is fundamental because it provides a mechanism through which civil society actors can use the law to advocate for victims' rights."); *see also* James G. Stewart, *The Turn to Corporate Criminal Liability for International Crimes: Transcending the Alien Tort Statute*, 47 N.Y.U. J. Int'l L. & Pol. 121, 184–85 (2014) ("In terms of case-specific opportunities to affect prosecutorial discretion, a range of legal mechanisms allow victims and others

to either force subtly the issue or, more powerfully, to stand in for reluctant state prosecutors. For example, many civil law countries entertain concepts like partie civile; Germany and other countries have compulsory prosecution principles (called Legalitätsprinzip); and the notion of private prosecutions remains in various common law systems.").

69. Access to Justice, Victims' Rights, and Private Prosecution in Latin America: The Cases of Chile, Guatemala, and Mexico, Ph.D. thesis, University of Minnesota, Aug. 2012, https://conservancy.umn.edu/bitstream/handle/11299/138850/MichelLuviano_umn_0130E_13062.pdf?sequence=1&isAllowed=y, pp. 296, 298.

70. Bennett Capers, *Against Prosecutors*, 105 CORNELL L. REV. 1561, 1564, 1573, 1581, 1609 (2020).

71. Wayne R. LaFave, Jerold H. Israel, Nancy J. King & Orin S. Kerr, 4 Crim. Proc. § 13.3(b) (4th ed.); *compare id.* ("But while there may be good reasons for not permitting a private person through his own counsel to actually pursue a criminal prosecution, it does not inevitably follow that a private citizen should be barred from seeking approval from another public authority after he has not received satisfaction from the prosecutor. Even under this system, of course, there is some danger that this opportunity could work against rather than in favor of uniformity in law enforcement. The better view, therefore, is that the private person should be able to force a public prosecution only upon a showing of an 'abuse of discretion' by the prosecutor. And in those jurisdictions holding to the view that a private citizen may file an application for a criminal complaint, this may require that a judicial officer act on the application, but it does not necessarily follow that a private citizen has any right to issuance of the complaint even when probable cause supporting it is shown."); *see also* Herbert B. Chermside Jr., *Power of Private Citizen to Institute Criminal Proceedings Without Authorization or Approval by Prosecuting Attorney*, 66 A.L.R.3d 732, § 1[a] ("This annotation collects the cases which deal with the power of a private citizen to institute criminal proceedings without the authorization or approval of the prosecuting attorney. In jurisdictions wherein the applicable statutes or rules permit a private citizen to institute criminal proceedings by complaining directly to a judicial officer or to the grand jury, the right of a private citizen to institute such proceedings independently of the prosecuting attorney is clear."); Peter L. Davis, *The Crime Victim's "Right" to a Criminal Prosecution: A Proposed Model Statute for the Governance of Private Criminal Prosecutions*, 38 DEPAUL L. REV. 329, 330 (1989) ("The thesis of this Article is that the public prosecution should not have a monopoly on criminal prosecutions; some supplementary system of private criminal prosecution should be available. Two such systems, or models, currently exist in New York. The first model, available statewide, theoretically allows a complainant to initiate a non-felony criminal prosecution without any screening by a prosecutor or judge. This system is unwise, unworkable, and illusory because it obscures the exercise of judicial discretion and focuses the court's attention on the wrong issues, usually precluding the crime victim's complaint. The second model, limited by statute to New York City, allows an aggrieved person to apply to a judge for the issuance of a criminal complaint. This model, though far preferable to the first model, is in need of substantial refinement. The exercise of judicial discretion should be guided and circumscribed by explicit statutory guidelines. This Article suggests such guidelines in the form of a model statute to govern the initiation and litigation of private criminal prosecutions.").

72. Lonnie E. Griffith, 7A C.J.S. *Attorney General* § 6 (2020) ("A state attorney general ordinarily has the power to appoint necessary deputies and assistants including special counsel or assistant attorneys general for particular actions or proceedings, special prosecutors, an attorney appointed for an investigation, or an assistant to handle a matter as to which the attorney general may have an actual conflict of interest.").

73. Sidman, *supra* note 22, at 764.

74. Ohio R.C. § 309.06.

75. IND. CODE § 33-39-6-2.

76. Newton v. Rumery, 480 U.S. 386, 395 n.5 (1987).

77. *E.g.*, ARK. CODE ANN. § 16-21-158.

78. Sidman, *supra* note 22, at 764–65.

79. Haney v. State, 850 P.2d 1087, 1092 (Okla. 1993) ("District attorneys have a statutory duty to prosecute or defend any action in which a county in their district is interested or is a party. They are prohibited from engaging in the private practice of law. Further, a district attorney cannot act as a purely private

prosecutor. These statements merely recognize a district attorney represents the public interest, not the interests of private individuals.").

80. United States v. Stone, 394 F. Supp.3d 1, 17–18 (D. D.C. 2019) (citations omitted); In re Grand Jury Investigation, 916 F.3d 1047, 1050 (D.C. Cir. 2019); United States v. Nixon, 418 U.S. 683 (1974); Morrison v Olson, 487 U.S. 654 (1988); 28 C.F.R. § 45.2; *see also* United States v. Manafort, 312 F. Supp.3d 60, 67 (D. D.C. 2018):

> In accordance with Department of Justice regulations, Deputy Attorney General Rod Rosenstein serves as the Acting Attorney General in cases in which the Attorney General is recused. *See* 28 C.F.R. § 600.1. In that capacity, he issued an order on May 17, 2017, appointing Robert Mueller to serve as Special Counsel for the U.S. Department of Justice. Appt. Order. The Acting Attorney General stated that he issued the order "[b]y virtue of the authority vested in me as Acting Attorney General, including 28 U.S.C. §§ 509, 510, and 515, in order to discharge my responsibility to provide supervision and management of the Department of Justice, and to ensure a full and thorough investigation of the Russian government's efforts to interfere in the 2016 presidential election." *Id.*

81. Patrick Emery Longan, *Legal Ethics*, 69 MERCER L. REV. 157, 201 (2017); *see also id.* at 181–82 ("The most recent (and possibly only widely available) national survey of prosecutors in smaller jurisdictions was undertaken by the Department of Justice's Bureau of Justice Statistics (BJS), which released its findings on state and local prosecutors' offices in January 2003. While most popular media such as television or movies depict prosecutors in large and gritty cities, about 23% of the nation's prosecutors' offices have a chief prosecutor who was hired on a part-time basis, running counter to the usual public perception of the job. The median budget for offices with part-time prosecutors was only $95,000. Nearly 9 in 10 of the nation's prosecutors practice in an office servicing populations of less than 250,000: This figure represents almost 40% of the nation's population. The prosecutors' offices in these smaller districts overwhelmingly have had difficulties hiring new attorneys given their scant budgets and inability to offer competitive salaries to new attorneys. Although this data is interesting and hints at the challenges posed to prosecutors in small districts, including those where a city, county, or other governmental subdivision is unable or unwilling to find a full-time prosecutor, the BJS survey unfortunately only covered, 'all chief prosecutors that tried felony cases in State courts of general jurisdiction.'").

82. Maybell Romero, *Profit-Driven Prosecution and the Competitive Bidding Process*, 107 J. CRIM. L. & CRIMINOLOGY 161, 162, 166 (2007); *see also id.* at 169–70 ("American criminal prosecutors were also not originally full-time government employees, given that criminal prosecutions had originally been victim-funded, but usually took such positions to supplement income from private practices or other business ventures. As such, attorneys employed as public prosecutors were often 'young, inexperienced attorneys or older, generally incompetent ones.' Prosecutorial budgets in the early republic were often anemic, resulting in complaints of overwork for too little pay. Talented, experienced criminal law attorneys, therefore, were disincentivized from considering such work, choosing to work as either defense counsel or private prosecutors hired by victims."); *id.* at 172–73 ("A multitude of other states addressed the further question of whether attorneys engaged in private practice should be allowed to handle criminal actions on behalf of certain jurisdictions, and many of these cases were heard by state supreme courts throughout the 1800s. For example, the Michigan Supreme Court held that that appointment of an additional prosecutor during the pendency of a forgery case was permissible given that this attorney 'was not employed by any private party, that he had no interest in the matter, that he was associated in business with the prosecuting officer, and had attended the prosecution on behalf of the people in the justice's court.' Such cases present the early formation of a normative standard that prosecutors are expected to meet—that they should somehow be shielded from external or private interests and should only concern themselves with the public good and with the fair administration of justice rather than deal with the external pressures that come from running separate legal practices.").

83. KY. REV. STAT. §15.765(4); KY. REV. STAT. §15.770(3).

84. Romero, *supra* note 82, at 198; *see also id.* at 198–99 ("Financial pressures faced by contracted prosecutors may cause perverse incentives to, on the one hand, over-perform, and on the other, underperform. Just as any other private service provider, prosecutors hired on contract will be 'motivated to maximize

profit.' The attorney who has advanced an hourly pay arrangement may have a greater tendency, conscious or not, to spend more time 'padding' their hours on a prosecution job—in essence making every task take as long as possible. Conversely, attorneys working on flat fee per case or monthly retainer bases may become more lax in fulfilling their duties, doing as little as possible while getting paid as much as possible under the contract. Since government employees are not usually rewarded for cost-saving, some praise competitive bidding as a way to control costs by awarding contracts to those who would purportedly provide services more cheaply. Contracted prosecutors who are chosen because of their cost-saving measures, in reality, 'might be even more motivated than government actors to provide low-quality service.'").

85. Lanza v. Board of Trustees, Public Employees' Retirement System, Docket No. A-2685-16T2, 2019 WL 1040670, at *5 (N.J. Super. Ct. Mar. 5, 2019).

86. Romero, *supra* note 82, at 200–01; *see also id.* at 203 ("The hiring of prosecutors through a public bidding process also allows local governments an undue ability to shield themselves from accountability for a prosecutor's actions, and disincentivizes them from seeking to provide good service.").

87. *E.g.*, James R. Fisher, Debra H. Miller & Thomas B. Merritt, 23 Ind. Prac., Personal Injury Law & Practice § 1:9 (2020) ("A conflict of interest can exist between a proposed private employment and an existing or previous government service. A part-time prosecutor may not represent a private client in a tort action in which there exists an issue upon which the prosecutor has statutory prosecutorial authority or responsibilities. A lawyer generally may not represent a private client in connection with a matter in which the lawyer participated personally and substantially as a public officer or employee."); Richard A. Revell, Diana L. Skaggs & Michelle Eisenmenger Mapes, Kentucky Divorce (2020) ("If an attorney is a part-time public employee and also engaged in private practice, the attorney must be exceedingly cautious in accepting private employment in matters in which the attorney has participated personally and substantially as a public officer or employee. There is a great potential for a conflict of interest if an attorney, acting as a Commonwealth Attorney or County Attorney, is prosecuting a defendant on a criminal charge and simultaneously is handling a private case involving a claim against the same individual, as the prosecutor may attempt to use the promise of probation or some other concession as an undo leverage to obtain a settlement with the defendant in the civil case which is favorable to the attorney's client in the private case. For example, a Commonwealth Attorney or County Attorney handling a criminal charge against the defendant, while representing the defendant's spouse in a dissolution action, could make unfair concessions in the criminal matter in order to entice the defendant to sign a property settlement agreement in the dissolution action which is unduly favorable to the attorney's private client.").

88. *E.g.*, Patrick Emery Longan, *Legal Ethics*, 69 Mercer L. Rev. 157, 201–02 (2017) ("The Georgia Supreme Court approved three significant amendments to the Georgia Rules of Professional Conduct during the survey period. Rule 1.7 was amended to deal with the problem of part-time prosecutors. Many rural counties use part-time prosecutors to avoid the expense of a full-time prosecutor. Under the prior version of Rule 1.7, the part-time prosecutor arguably had a conflict of interest that would prevent the prosecutor from representing criminal defendants, even in another part of the state. For example, if you assume that the prosecutor's client is the State of Georgia, then the prosecutor is in an attorney-client relationship with the State, and the lawyer could not represent a defendant being prosecuted by the State, without consent, because the lawyer would be representing a client (the defendant) against a current client (the State). Rural counties likely would have a hard time recruiting part-time prosecutors if that job disqualified the lawyer (and all associated lawyers) from criminal defense cases. Rule 1.7(d) was added to Rule 1.7: '(d) Though otherwise subject to the provisions of this Rule, a part-time prosecutor who engages in the private practice of law may represent a private client adverse to the state or other political subdivision that the lawyer represents as a part-time prosecutor, except with regard to matters for which the part-time prosecutor had or has prosecutorial authority or responsibility.' Comment 4 was amended to eliminate the 'automatic' conflict that kept a part-time prosecutor from representing criminal defense clients....").

89. Roy D. Simon Jr., Simon's NY Rules of Prof. Conduct § 1.7:25 (2019).

90. Bruce A. Green & Rebecca Roiphe, *Rethinking Prosecutors' Conflicts of Interest*, 58 B.C. L. Rev. 463, 486 & n.104 (2017).

91. *See, e.g.*, Roy D. Simon Jr., Simons NY Rules of Prof. Conduct § 1.11:41 (2019) ("What happens if every attorney in a District Attorney's office is disqualified under Rule 1.11(d)? This would not happen in

a large urban office where dozens of prosecutors work, but it might be the case in a small community, especially in a small D.A.'s office where a number of the prosecutors are part time, splitting their time between private practice (or other nongovernmental employment) and public prosecution. The solution, rarely invoked, is found in N.Y. County Law § 701(1)(a), which provides for appointment of a special prosecutor when an entire District Attorney's office is disqualified.").

92. State v. White, 114 S.W.3d 469, 478 (Tenn. 2003) ("[E]thical duties and principles demonstrate that the Court of Criminal Appeals properly concluded that McDaniel's dual roles as assistant district attorney general and defense counsel in the same county were inherently antagonistic and thus, created an actual conflict of interest. The ethical obligations of these dual roles required McDaniel to represent the interests of two adverse parties simultaneously and forced him to attempt to reconcile his duty to vigorously prosecute criminal offenses on behalf of the State with his duty to zealously defend the criminal defendant. In his capacity as an assistant district attorney, for example, his ethical duties required him to advocate for the public and to seek justice. In his capacity as defense counsel, however, his ethical duties required him to be a zealous advocate of White and an adversary to his fellow assistant district attorneys in Shelby County.").

Courts looking into conflict of issues have reached differing conclusions in those cases. For a discussion of the range of conflict of issues that can occur in criminal cases, see Wayne R. LaFave, Jerold H. Israel, Nancy J. King & Orin S. Kerr, 3 Crim. Proc. § 11.9(a) (4th ed. 2019) (section of treatise titled "The range of possible conflicts of interest"); *see also* John M. Burkoff, Criminal Defense Ethics § 6:11 (2d ed. 2020) ("Courts addressing the question whether or not it is an unconstitutional conflict of interest for counsel to simultaneously represent a criminal defendant and also be employed full- or part-time to prosecute crimes in the same or a neighboring jurisdiction have reached differing conclusions."). *Compare id.* ("The Fifth Circuit Court of Appeals, for example, has concluded that there was no Sixth Amendment violation of a defendant's right to conflict-free counsel where his defense attorney also worked as a part-time city traffic court prosecutor. As the Fifth Circuit concluded, '[a]lthough it may be that the representation of a defendant in a state court criminal trial by a city court prosecutor creates the 'appearance of professional impropriety,' it is not the province of this court to police the officers of local courts, unless their actions violate federal statutory or constitutional standards.'") *with id.* ("Other courts are less sanguine about such conflicts. The Illinois Supreme Court, for example, has reversed a defendant's conviction on ineffective assistance of counsel grounds where two witnesses called to establish probable cause were police officers in the city where defense counsel also served as prosecutor. As the Illinois Supreme Court recognized, '[t]he attorney was obliged to cross-examine and attempt to discredit one of the officers whose veracity and credibility he vouched for when acting as a prosecutor for his municipality. Certainly the possibility was raised that the attorney's duty of undivided loyalty to the accused was affected by contradicting obligations.'") *and id.* ("Still other courts have reversed convictions on this ground without pointing to specific instances of potential conflict. The Oklahoma Court of Criminal Appeals, for example, has reversed a conviction obtained against an indigent defendant who was represented by a part-time district attorney, holding that such appointments should never be made by trial courts on both ethical and constitutional grounds: 'A district attorney represents the State of Oklahoma to enforce its criminal laws. His first and foremost duty is to represent the State in criminal proceedings, and, he cannot represent a defendant where the State of Oklahoma is the opposing party. One cannot adequately serve two masters; these positions are inherently antagonistic and irreconcilable.' The Fourth Circuit Court of Appeals has likewise concluded that: 'Since conflicts of interest are so likely... and since in most cases in which they are not apparent on the surface, one cannot know with assurance that there were no subliminal or concealed conflicts which may have affected the outcome of the trial, we think it may well be that the only workable rule of the future will be a per se one, in which it would be presumed that one involuntarily represented by a public prosecutor in a criminal trial has not had the fair trial to which he is constitutionally entitled.' For similar reasons, the New Jersey Supreme Court has ruled—prospectively—that municipal prosecutors may not simultaneously serve as defense counsel in the same county.").

93. In re Cole, 738 N.E.2d 1035, 1037 (2000); *see also* People v. Cooper, 593 N.Y.S.2d 733, 736 (County Ct., Erie County, N.Y. 1992) ("I find, therefore, that Adrian's representation of defendant at the same time as he was a part-time prosecutor for the Town of West Seneca constituted an obvious and actual conflict of interest."); *see also* Beaver v. Thompson, 93 F.3d 1186 (4th Cir. 1996) (no conflict of interest existed in

state trial counsel's representation of defendant even though counsel was part-time assistant prosecutor in neighboring county); People v. Herr, 86 N.Y.2d 638, 639 (N.Y. Ct. App. 1995) (that defense counsel in prosecution by district attorney's office for various sex offenses was part-time village prosecutor did not create opportunity for abuse of confidences or create appearance of impropriety sufficient to violate defendant's right to counsel, where defense counsel could not prosecute crimes with which defendant was charged, did not try cases in his prosecutorial capacity in court in which defendant's trial was held, did not work with law enforcement personnel who investigated case, and was not supervised or even in communication with district attorney's office that conducted prosecution).

94. Bruce A. Green & Rebecca Roiphe, *Rethinking Prosecutors' Conflicts of Interest*, 58 B.C. L. Rev. 463, 485–86 & n.104 (2017) (noting that "[p]rosecutors have occasionally been sanctioned for obvious conflicts arising out of their duties to current or former private clients (or, in the case of part-time prosecutors, duties to current clients)," and citing *In re* Ridgely, 106 A.2d 527, 528–30 (Del. 1954) (disciplining lawyer for prosecuting case while representing the victim in related civil litigation); *In re* Cole, 738 N.E.2d 1035, 1037–38 (Ind. 2000) (disciplining part-time prosecutor for appearing as a prosecutor in cases involving private clients); In re Toups, 773 So.2d 709, 711–12, 715 (La. 2000) (sanctioning part-time district attorney for appearing as prosecutor against ex-spouse of his private divorce client); Va. State Bar v. Gunter, 11 Va. Cir. 349 (1969) (reprimanding part-time prosecutor who filed bigamy charge while representing the defendant's wife in a divorce action)). It has been emphasized elsewhere that a number of disciplinary actions "have been against part-time prosecutors for conflicts between their public responsibilities and their private practices." Bruce A. Green & Samuel J. Levine, *Disciplinary Regulation of Prosecutors as a Remedy for Abuses of Prosecutorial Discretion: A Descriptive and Normative Analysis*, 14 Ohio St. J. Crim. L. 143, 154 n.72 (2016) (citing In re Holste, 358 P.3d 850 (Kan. 2015) (part-time prosecutor suspended for threatening criminal action to gain an advantage for a civil client); Ky. Bar Ass'n v. Ballard, 349 S.W.3d 922 (Ky. 2011) (disciplining part-time prosecutor for negotiating plea agreement with creditor client's manager); In re Cole, 738 N.E.2d 1035 (Ind. 2000) (disciplining part-time prosecutor for appearing as a prosecutor in cases involving private clients); In re Toups, 773 So.2d 709 (La. 2000) (sanctioning part-time prosecutor for appearing as prosecutor against spouses of private divorce clients); In re Jones, PR 08-0216, slip op. at 1–2 (Mont. June 24, 2009); In re Thrush, 448 N.E.2d 1088 (Ind. 1983) (disciplining part-time prosecutor who failed to recuse himself in criminal case filed against a divorce client); Va. State Bar v. Gunter, 11 Va. Cir. 349 (Va. Cir. Ct. 1969) (reprimanding part-time prosecutor who filed bigamy charge against a man while representing the man's wife in a divorce action)).

95. Gregory C. Sisk, 16 Ia. Prac., Lawyer and Judicial Ethics § 5:11(d)(2); *see also* Peter A. Joy, *Lawyers Serving as Judges, Prosecutors, and Defense Lawyers at the Same Time: Legal Ethics and Municipal Courts*, 2017 Prof. Law. 65, 89–90 (2017) ("[M]ore than fifteen years ago the New Jersey Supreme Court enacted a court rule that expressly prohibits a lawyer from simultaneously serving as a prosecutor and defense counsel in the same county. In 2000, the New Jersey Supreme Court ruled on a claim of ineffective assistance of counsel lodged against a defense lawyer who had represented a defendant in the superior Court for Middlesex County, while he was a part-time municipal prosecutor in New Brunswick, also located in Middlesex County. The defendant argued that he did not know of the lawyer's employment as a prosecutor and that his lawyer's role as a prosecutor created a conflict that deprived the defendant of effective assistance of counsel. The court determined that because there was no rule or law prohibiting the defendant's lawyer from simultaneously serving as a municipal prosecutor and representing the defendant in the Superior Court of the same county there was no actual conflict or prejudice to the defendant. The case, though, prompted the court to consider the issue, and it determined that a court rule that prohibited a municipal prosecutor from representing a defendant in the municipal court in which the lawyer was a prosecutor should be amended "to preclude a municipal prosecutor from simultaneously serving as a defense counsel in the same county in which he or she serves as municipal prosecutor." The court then proceeded to amend New Jersey Court Rule 1:15-3(b) to state, in pertinent part: 'A municipal prosecutor shall not represent a defendant in any other municipal court in that county or in a criminal proceeding in the Superior Court in that county but may represent a defendant in a municipal court or in a criminal proceeding in the Superior Court in a county other than the one in which he or she serves as a municipal prosecutor.'").

96. City of Houston v. Houston Firefighters' Relief and Retirement Fund, 502 S.W.3d 469, 474 (Tex. Ct. App. 2016) ("Delegations to private entities raise more troubling constitutional issues than delegations to public entities because private delegates are not elected by the people, appointed by a public official or entity, or employed by the government and such delegations may allow one with a personal or pecuniary interest to adversely affect the public interest. Nevertheless, private delegations are frequently necessary and desirable but are subject to more stringent requirements and less judicial deference than public delegations, and courts apply an eight-factor test to analyze constitutionality.") (citations omitted); *see also* American Horse Protection Ass'n, Inc. v. Veneman, Civil Action No. 01-00028 (HHK), 2002 WL 34471909, at *4 (D. D.C. July 9, 2002) ("delegations to a private party are particularly suspect when the private actor's objectivity may be questioned due to a conflict of interest"); Texas Boll Weevil Eradication Found., Inc. v. Lewellen, 952 S.W.2d 454, 469 (Tex. 1997) ("[W]e believe it axiomatic that courts should subject private delegations to a more searching scrutiny than their public counterparts.").

97. Kim Wehle, formerly Kim Brown, has discussed the private delegation doctrine extensively in her scholarship. Kimberly N. Brown, *Outsourcing, Data Insourcing, and the Irrelevant Constitution*, 49 Ga. L. Rev. 607, 656–57 (2015) ("The private delegation doctrine offers another approach to limiting the government's ability to partner with the private sector for purposes of engaging in government functions, including surveillance. In theory, it insists that the powers vested by the Constitution in Congress must be exercised by that branch of government and cannot be transferred elsewhere. Such a claim featured prominently in post-New Deal litigation around the propriety of the burgeoning administrative state. In *Panama Refining Co. v. Ryan*, the Court struck down a provision of the National Industrial Recovery Act (NIRA) that empowered the President to manage a prohibition on interstate shipment of petroleum on the grounds that Congress had set 'no criterion to govern the President's course.' The Supreme Court has since declined to apply the doctrine on the theory that Congress has broad delegation authority so long as its enabling legislation includes an 'intelligible principle' to guide the exercise of discretion. The Court's landmark decision in *Chevron U.S.A., Inc. v. Natural Resources Defense Council, Inc.*—which requires courts to defer to agency constructions of ambiguous statutory text—effectively shores up Congress's authority to hand off legislative power with vague directives to agencies charged with administering a statute.").

98. Andrea Nishi, *Privatizing Sentencing: A Delegation Framework for Recidivism Risk Assessment*, 119 Colum. L. Rev. 1671, 1673 (2019); *see also* Gillian E. Metzger, *Privatization as Delegation*, 103 Colum. L. Rev. 1367, 1370 (2003) ("To the extent private delegations are considered, it is under the rubric of private delegation doctrine, which assesses whether the Constitution's separation of powers and due process requirements prohibit the [G]overnment from delegating certain types of powers to private hands. But constitutional law makes no attempt to link the constitutionality of a private delegation to the risk that it will place government power outside of constitutional controls. Private delegations of government power are upheld without examining whether private actions taken pursuant to such delegations will come within the Constitution's purview.").

99. Kimberly N. Brown, *"We the People," Constitutional Accountability, and Outsourcing Government*, 88 Ind. L.J. 1347, 1360, 1379 (2013).

100. Uhlrig v. Harder, No. 93-1009-PKF, 1993 WL 246006, at *1 n.2 (D. Kan. June 3, 1993). In that case, the private assistant prosecutor was hired by Mr. Uhlrig to assist in the criminal prosecution of his wife's murderer. *Id.* at *2. In Kansas, it has been held that a private attorney for a complaining witness has no standing—and does not have the right—to bring an appeal from a district court's dismissal of a criminal complaint. "The complaining witness has no right to challenge a decision by the prosecutor to dismiss," the Kansas Supreme Court ruled in 1985. State v. Berg, 694 P.2d 427, 429, 432 (Kan. 1985); *see also* State ex rel. Rome v. Fountain, 678 P.2d 146, 148 (Kan. 1984) (where district court dismisses criminal complaint, complaining witness does not have right to appeal from order of dismissal to appellate court; right to appeal is vested in public prosecutor).

101. American prosecutors have vast discretion. *E.g.*, Bordenkircher v. Hayes, 434 U.S. 357, 364 (1978) ("In our system, so long as the prosecutor has probable cause to believe that the accused committed an offense defined by statute, the decision whether or not to prosecute, and what charge to file or bring before a grand jury, generally rests entirely in his discretion.").

102. Roger A. Fairfax, Jr., *Delegation of the Criminal Prosecution Function to Private Actors*, 43 U.C. Davis L. Rev. 411, 413–15, 427–28 (2009); *see also id.* at 419 ("Today, nearly one out of every four state prosecutors is a so-called 'part-time' prosecutor—a publicly-paid government lawyer permitted to maintain a full-fledged private law practice. In other words, these lawyers are employed as prosecutors but permitted to 'moonlight' or engage in private practice. Under the jurisdiction's laws, regardless of whether these private lawyers assume the job of public prosecutor through direct election, political appointment, or civil service hiring and, therefore, are bona fide government officials, they are permitted to maintain a private practice."); *id.* at 419 n.24 ("Estimates of the number of part-time prosecutors hover between one-quarter and one-third of all state prosecutors."); *id.* at 420 n.28 ("This Article's definition of 'part-time prosecutor' does not include those prosecutors who, for family or other personal reasons, choose to work a part-time schedule. For instance, in Montgomery County, Maryland, the State's Attorneys Office employs a number of prosecutors who work a modified or 'flex-time' partial work schedule of fewer than 40 hours per week."); *id.* at 419–20 ("For example, some publicly elected prosecutors are permitted, by statute, to maintain a private practice despite their service as chief public prosecutor. In addition, in a handful of jurisdictions, government officials such as the mayor, town council, or the county executive appoint the prosecutor. In some of these jurisdictions, the lawyer, who is appointed to prosecute criminal offenses, may maintain a private practice. Whether elected or appointed, these chief prosecutors typically hire assistant prosecutors if there is sufficient budgetary authority to staff such positions."); *id.* at 427 ("Prosecution outsourcing and part-time prosecution are confined largely to sparsely populated rural or suburban jurisdictions and sometimes are limited to less serious criminal offenses.").

103. Thomas W. Merrill, *Is Public Nuisance a Tort?*, 4 J. Tort L. 1, 39 (2011).

104. George Croner, "Ethics Groups Say Barr's Use of DOJ Shredding Its Essential Independence," Just Security, Oct. 26, 2020, https://www.justsecurity.org/73014/ethics-groups-say-barrs-use-of-doj-is-shredding-its-essential-independence/.

105. Roger A. Fairfax, Jr., *Delegation of the Criminal Prosecution Function to Private Actors*, 43 U.C. Davis L. Rev. 411, 413–15, 439–40 (2009).

106. *Id.* at 441–42 ("Another danger of delegating prosecution authority to private or part-time prosecutors is the possibility that they will not devote the requisite time and attention to their public duties. A part-time, outsourced, or victim-retained prosecutor faces not only conflicting loyalties regulated by ethical rules, but competing demands on her time and attention. The private practice of law is as demanding as any professional vocation. The development, servicing, and maintenance of clients; the managing of an office, junior lawyers, and support staff; and other duties make it difficult to strike a proper work-life balance, much less allow for the focus required of a prosecutor."); *id.* at 442 ("[T]he financial pressures of the part-time prosecutor's full-time job (law practice or otherwise) will be brought to bear. The desire to turn his attention to more lucrative private client work might prompt a part-time prosecutor to give short shrift to the criminal cases. Given the economic realities of part-time prosecutorial pay, there exist 'incentives for part-time prosecutors . . . to avoid time-consuming proceedings.' As a result, there is the chance that the prosecution of crime by private practitioners could be marked by suboptimal performance, allocation of time, and attention.").

107. *Id.* at 435, 448–56; *see also id.* at 452–53 ("Other possibilities for mitigating the perceived harm of having private actors wield prosecutorial authority relate to transparency in the decision-making process. If private actors are permitted to exercise prosecutorial discretion and are not limited to mere ministerial tasks, at least such decisions can be better exposed to public scrutiny. Proposed reforms to the public prosecution function have aspired to increase transparency in prosecutorial decision making for some time, and the transparency rationale applies with perhaps greater force to the prosecution outsourcing context."); *id.* at 453 ("One mechanism for greater transparency in the exercise of discretion by private actors might be a public reporting requirement, whereby contracted prosecutors are required to prepare a report on all the cases that they have considered, including matters that they have declined to prosecute, as well as dispositions and outcomes in matters that they have prosecuted. Community review boards provide another potential mechanism for enhancing the transparency of private exercises of prosecutorial discretion. Such review boards could be made up of members of the bar, laypersons, or some combination of the two. Such boards could review a cross section of matters handled by the private prosecutor to

determine adherence to prosecutorial guidelines or the compatibility of prosecution, declination, and plea bargaining decisions with community values and preferences. The findings of such boards could then be made public via written report or public hearing, and would serve as a vehicle for assessment of the private actor's performance of the public function by the citizenry and government officials.").

108. Roger A. Fairfax, Jr., ed., Grand Jury 2.0: Modern Perspectives on the Grand Jury (2011); Roger A. Fairfax, Jr., *Grand Jury Discretion and Constitutional Design*, 93 Cornell L. Rev. 703 (2008).

109. "Law Firm From Tobacco Case to Help Government," Tampa Bay Times, Sept. 29, 2005, https://www.tampabay.com/archive/1999/04/07/law-firm-from-tobacco-case-to-help-government/?outputType=amp.

110. Roger A. Fairfax, Jr., *Outsourcing Criminal Prosecution?: The Limits of Criminal Justice Privatization*, 2010 U. Chi. Legal Forum 265, 278–88, 295.

111. American Bar Association, Model Rules of Professional Conduct, Rule 1.7 ("Conflict of Interest: Current Clients"); *id.*, Rule 1.8 ("Current Clients: Specific Rules"); *id.*, Rule 1.11 ("Special Conflicts of Interest for Former & Current Government Officers & Employees").

112. There is a clear need to avoid conflicts of interest to protect a criminal defendant's rights. Elizabeth M. Bosek, et al., Carmody-Wait 2d § 184:205 (2020) ("The representation of a defendant by an attorney who is simultaneously employed as a part-time town prosecutor creates a conflict of interest that denies the defendant the right to conflict-free, effective counsel. Thus, a conflict of interest question arises when a town attorney seeks to practice on the defense side.").

113. American Bar Association, Model Rules of Professional Conduct, preamble, https://www.americanbar.org/groups/professional_responsibility/publications/model_rules_of_professional_conduct/model_rules_of_professional_conduct_preamble_scope/. A lawyer has various professional duties, as the Model Rules make clear: "In all professional functions a lawyer should be competent, prompt and diligent. A lawyer should maintain communication with a client concerning the representation. A lawyer should keep in confidence information relating to representation of a client except so far as disclosure is required or permitted by the Rules of Professional Conduct or other law." *Id.* Likewise, the Model Rules state: "A lawyer's conduct should conform to the requirements of the law, both in professional service to clients and in the lawyer's business and personal affairs. A lawyer should use the law's procedures only for legitimate purposes and not to harass or intimidate others. A lawyer should demonstrate respect for the legal system and for those who serve it, including judges, other lawyers and public officials. While it is a lawyer's duty, when necessary, to challenge the rectitude of official action, it is also a lawyer's duty to uphold legal process." *Id.*

114. Joan E. Jacoby, The American Prosecutor: A Search for Identity 13 (1980) ("In 1643, an officer was appointed to the courts of the Virginia colonies as a representative of the King."); *id.* at 23 ("At the beginning of the nineteenth century in America, the district attorney was viewed as a minor figure in the court, an adjunct to the judge. His position was primarily judicial, and perhaps only quasi-executive.").

115. *Id.* at 25 ("After Andrew Jackson was elected in 1828, the trend toward more electable offices, toward wider franchise so long restrained, swept the United States and changes were made in almost every state. In the next 20 years, seven of the thirteen founding states altered their constitutions to accommodate this new spirit. Lower court judges and justices of the peace were elected in Rhode Island (1842), and New York (1846), and justices of the peace only, in Pennsylvania and Delaware. The Attorney General become an elected position in Rhode Island and New York. In Georgia, the state that had first provided for elected jurists, an amendment to the constitution in 1839 provided for Prosecuting Attorneys in each county elected by the General Assembly."); *id.* ("In 1832 Mississippi became the first state to include in its constitution a provision for the popular election of local district attorneys. It also allowed for the election of all judges on the circuit and appellate levels. Similarly Iowa decided to hold popular election for its judges and county attorneys in 1846. Massachusetts had created the office District and County Attorney in a statute of 1817. The law, however, had placed this under the nominal supervision of the Attorney General. By 1843, the position had become so independent that the Attorney General's office was abolished as being unnecessary. In New York the prosecuting attorney became a constitutional office in 1846. The District Attorney was established by the Pennsylvania legislature on May 3, 1850, a move that was motivated by 'a wave of home rule sentiment in the country.'"); *id.* at 37–38 ("After Andrew Jackson was elected in 1828, the expansion of

democracy in the form of elected positions swept the country. Hanging on the coattails of the movement to elect local judges was the prosecutor. In 1832, Mississippi became the first state to include in its constitution a provision for the popular election of local district attorneys. By 1859 the trend was clear and irreversible—the prosecutor was a locally elected position.").

116. Garrett v. United States, 471 U.S. 773 (1985); Wayte v. United States, 470 U.S. 598 (1985); *see also* Kenneth J. Melilli, *Prosecutorial Discretion in an Adversary System*, 1992 B.Y.U. L. Rev. 669, 672 (1992) (footnotes and citations omitted) ("In exercising the charging function, the prosecutor enjoys broad, indeed virtually unlimited, discretion. Indeed, the prosecutor has been fairly described 'as the single most powerful figure in the administration of criminal justice.'").

117. Brown v. State, 236 A.3d 488, 506–507 (Md. 2020).

118. United States v. Martinez, 785 F.2d 663 (9th Cir. 1986).

119. Ball v. United States, 470 U.S. 856 (1985).

120. United States v. Lovasco, 431 U.S. 783 (1977).

121. United States v. Bagnell, 679 F.2d 826 (11th Cir. 1982), *cert. denied*, 460 U.S. 1047 (1983). In addition, prosecutors have the discretion to arrest, plea bargain, grant immunity, and make bail and sentencing recommendations. Katherine Lowe, Project, *Twenty-Second Annual Review of Criminal Procedure: United States Supreme Court and Courts of Appeal 1991–1992*, 81 Geo. L.J. 853, 1029–32 (1993). Because most of these decisions are made outside the courtroom, very little of the prosecutor's discretionary authority is subject to judicial supervision. Indeed, it is well-settled that judicial deference "to a prosecutor's broad discretion to initiate and conduct criminal prosecutions" is generally guided by "the recognition that the decision to prosecute is particularly ill-suited to judicial review." *Id.* at 1029 (citing Wayte v. United States, 470 U.S. 598, 607 (1985) and Town of Newton v. Rumery, 480 U.S. 386, 396 (1987)).

122. State v. Harrington, 534 S.W.2d 44, 50 (Mo. 1976); *see also* Mo. Stat. § 56.360 ("It shall be unlawful for any prosecuting attorney or circuit attorney, or any assistant prosecuting attorney or any assistant circuit attorney, during the term of office for which he shall have been elected or appointed, to accept employment by any party other than the state of Missouri in any criminal case or proceeding; provided, that nothing in this section shall be deemed to preclude the officers specified in this section from engaging in the civil practice of law. Any violation of the provisions of this section shall be deemed a misdemeanor.").

123. *See* Michael T. Fisher, Note, *Harmless Error, Prosecutorial Misconduct, and Due Process: There's More to Due Process Than the Bottom Line*, 88 Colum. L. Rev. 1298, 1322 (1988) (citations omitted) ("Courts and commentators have expressed frustration and concern over the frequent occurrence of prosecutorial misconduct."); *see also* Albert W. Alschuler, *Courtroom Misconduct by Prosecutors and Trial Judges*, 50 Tex. L. Rev. 629 (1972).

124. One historian has argued for a return to a system of private prosecution based upon the principle of "self-government." Allen Steinberg, The Transformation of Criminal Justice: Philadelphia, 1800–1880, at 114, 223 (1989); *see also id.* at 230 ("The world of private prosecution... was relatively democratic, flexible, expandable, and familiar."). However, that same historian details the corruption, misconduct, and abuses inherent in such a system. *See* Gerald Caplan, *Criminal Justice in the Lower Courts: A Study in Continuity*, 89 Mich. L. Rev. 1694, 1703 (1991) (footnote omitted) (Steinberg's "examples evidence garden variety judicial misconduct—impulsive, arbitrary, biased, and no cause for nostalgia or romantic reminiscences about revitalizing democracy in twentieth-century America. Even to an ardent populist, to one highly suspicious of lawyers, the power of citizen prosecutors to 'define crime' would be unacceptable.") (reviewing Steinberg's book; citing Steinberg, *supra*, at 1, 26, 56, 61, 77, 106, 230); *see also* Caplan, *supra*, at 1694 (Steinberg's study of private prosecution in nineteenth-century Philadelphia provides "an unsettling account—an unpleasant reminder of the misconduct and bias which have plagued the administration of justice throughout this nation's history."); Steinberg, *supra*, at 47 (some private prosecutions were "manipulative"); *id.* at 230 (stating that the system of private prosecution was "corrupt, easily manipulated, harsh, and sometimes even cruel").

125. Marshall v. Jerrico, Inc., 446 U.S. 238, 249 (1980); McNeil v. Community Probation Services, LLC, No. 1:18-cv-00033, 2021 WL 365844, at *13 (M.D. Tenn. Feb. 3, 2021) (noting that prosecutors "must serve the public interest"); Brucker v. City of Doraville, 391 F. Supp.3d 1207, 1217 (N.D. Ga. 2019); Condon v. Wolfe, Case No. 1:03cv897, 2006 WL 8437981, at *13 (S.D. Ohio May 25, 2006); *see also* State v.

Gonzales, 119 P.3d 151, 160 (N.M. 2005) ("a prosecutor represents the public interest, not the private interests of others or the personal interest of the prosecutor").

126. Steven K. Berenson, *Public Lawyers, Private Values: Can, Should, and Will Government Lawyers Serve the Public Interest?*, 41 B.C. L. REV. 789, 802–03 (2000) ("Numerous commentators have argued that the concept of the public interest is too ill-defined to be particularly useful in establishing appropriate professional roles for government lawyers. Fred Zacharias advances this thesis in an important article regarding the ethics of prosecutorial trial practice. Zacharias, who refers to prosecutors' duty to serve the public interest as the 'do justice standard,' contends that the standard "establishes no identifiable norm." He contends that the standard's 'vagueness leaves prosecutors with only their individual sense of morality to determine just conduct.' This ambiguity, he concludes, makes the likelihood that prosecutors will in fact advance the public interest completely unreliable."); Fred C. Zacharias, *Structuring the Ethics of Prosecutorial Trial Practice: Can Prosecutors Do Justice?*, 44 VAND. L. REV. 45, 48 (1991) ("The codes' failure to define prosecutors' ethical obligations at trial has significant costs. As 'professionals,' prosecutors probably are capable of exercising discretionary judgment in a manner consistent with general norms of behavior. The 'do justice' standard, however, establishes no identifiable norm. Its vagueness leaves prosecutors with only their individual sense of morality to determine just conduct. Some will decide that justice lies in conviction at all cost; others will bend over backwards to vindicate defendants' rights—in the process underestimating their obligation to the community to assure that criminals are convicted. The result is inconsistent trial practice, both within a single prosecutor's case load and among lawyers in the prosecution corps."); *id.* at 103–04 ("The generality of any rule based on justice heightens the importance of enforcement and better definition through disciplinary proceedings. The notion of professionalism may include some expectation that every lawyer will exercise good judgment to implement standards of conduct in the public interest. But the vaguer a norm—the more it is allowed to become subject to varying interpretations—the less valuable it becomes. Prosecutors who lack a lodestar for behavior will bow to the instinct to minimize their responsibilities. Once the pattern of prosecutorial behavior settles at a low ethical level, institutional and peer pressure to obey a higher standard of conduct naturally will disappear. External pressures, such as occasional media comment, will not influence behavior because prosecutors and their superiors can rationalize particular conduct and claim disagreement over the extent of the ethical requirements.").

127. AMY KLOBUCHAR, UNCOVERING THE DOME xviii (1982); Asaf Wiener, *How to Evaluate the Constitutional Legitimacy of Regulating Speech Intermediaries: Lessons from a Century-Long Experience of Media Regulation*, 29 FORDHAM INTELL. PROP. MEDIA & ENT. L.J. 803, 811 (2019); Alaska Structures, Inc. v. Hedlund, 323 P.3d 1082, 1085 (Wash. Ct. App. 2014). ("California courts have defined 'public interest' as 'any issue in which the public is interested.'").

128. *See generally* 11 WRIGHT & MILLER, FEDERAL PRACTICE AND PROCEDURE, § 2948, at 430–31 (1973) (listing the "public interest" as one of four factors for a court to consider in determining the propriety of granting a preliminary injunction). Thus, "it frequently has been emphasized that whether the public interest either might be furthered or might be injured by an injunction should be given considerable weight." *Id.* at 457 (footnote omitted) (citing Yakus v. United States, 321 U.S. 414 (1944); Hecht Co. v. Bowles, 321 U.S. 321 (1944); Inland Steel Co. v. United States, 306 U.S. 153 (1939)).

129. BRIAN BARRY, POLITICAL ARGUMENT 207 (1965).

130. Marshall v. Jerrico, Inc., 446 U.S. 238, 249 (1980) (prosecutors "must serve the public interest"); *Young*, 481 U.S. at 804 ("The prosecutor is appointed solely to pursue the public interest in the vindication of the court's authority."); Town of Newton v. Rumery, 480 U.S. 386, 395 n.5 (1987) ("The constituency of an elected prosecutor is the public, and such a prosecutor is likely to be influenced primarily by the general public interest."); *see also* Haney v. State, 850 P.2d 1087, 1092 (Okla. 1993) ("A district attorney represents the public interest, not the interests of private individuals."); Cantrell v. Commonwealth, 329 S.E.2d 22, 26 (Va. 1985), *cert. denied*, 496 U.S. 911 (1990) ("It is as much the duty of a Commonwealth's Attorney to protect his fellow citizens from unjustified prosecutions as it is to prosecute the guilty. His duty is 'to seek justice, not merely to convict.' "); *cf.* Model Code of Professional Responsibility EC 8-4 (1981) (when "the lawyer purports to act on behalf of the public, he should espouse only those changes which he conscientiously believes are in the public interest"). A comment to Standard 3-2.1 of the ABA Standards for Criminal Justice states as follows: "The idea that the criminal law, unlike other branches of

the law such as contracts and property, is designed to vindicate public rather than private interests is now firmly established. The participation of a responsible public officer in the decision to prosecute and in the prosecution of the charge gives greater assurance that the rights of the accused will be respected." ABA Standards for Criminal Justice, Standard 3-2.1 cmt. (1979). A former United States Attorney, Kenneth Melilli, has reiterated the notion that a prosecutor's role is to serve the public interest. "Prosecutors do not have individual, identifiable clients. They are lawyers for the state. As such, prosecutors represent the public interest. Prosecutors represent the interests of society as a whole, including the interests of defendants as members of that society." Kenneth J. Melilli, *Prosecutorial Discretion in an Adversary System*, 1992 B.Y.U. L. REV. 669, 698 (1992) (footnotes omitted); *see also* W.J. Michael Cody, *Special Ethical Duties for Attorneys Who Hold Public Positions*, 23 MEM. ST. U. L. REV. 453, 456 (1993) (footnote omitted) ("A prosecutor's duty... is not to seek convictions, but to seek justice."); Carol Corrigan, *On Prosecutorial Ethics*, 13 HASTINGS CONST. L.Q. 537, 537–38 (1986) ("The prosecutor represents society as a whole. His goal is truth and the achievement of a just result."). For an article discussing the concept of the "public interest" as it relates to government lawyers, see Beth Nolan, *Removing Conflicts from the Administration of Justice: Conflicts of Interest and Independent Counsels Under the Ethics in Government Act*, 79 GEO. L.J. 1, 36–43 (1990); *cf. id.* at 42 ("The government lawyer has obligations to the public interest as well as to the mission of her agency. The fact that the government lawyer takes instruction from those invested with policy making powers does not mean that she does so in the service of the agency without regard to the agency's obligations to the public.").

131. Officer of Disciplinary Counsel v. Fina, 225 A.3d 568, 570 (Pa. 2020); *see also* State v. Owen, 207 A.3d 17, 24–25 (Conn. 2019) (noting that "[i]t is highly significant that a prosecutor is an officer of the court" and citing the ABA standard stating that the prosecutor "serves the public interest").

132. State v. Griffin, 180 So.3d 1262, 1272 (La. 2015).

133. People v. Vannortrick, No. 350799, 2021 WL 1589763, at *3 (Mich. Ct. App. Apr. 22, 2021).

134. Merck Sharp & Dohme Corp. v. Conway, 861 F. Supp.2d 802, 812 (E.D. Ky. 2012) (citations omitted).

135. BRIAN BARRY, POLITICAL ARGUMENT 190 (1965). In this regard, Barry makes a distinction between the "public interest" and the "common interest." In recapping Barry's work, one scholar has articulated the distinction as follows:

> The common interest is simply an interest shared between individuals. Legal academics have a common interest in a good pay settlement for university teachers, even though we may each gain different amounts. The public interest is used to describe where the net interests which people have qua member of the public or the community. It is this idea of public interest as an interest in our role as members of the community which is perhaps the key to seeing public interest as a subspecies of arguments about the collective welfare. In this way, "the public interest is simply the class of human interests of any group of human beings where the unity of the group is determined by its organization under a common public authority."

John Bell, *Public Interest: Policy or Principle?*, *in* LAW AND THE PUBLIC INTEREST 30 (Proceedings of the 1992 ALSP Conference) (Roger Brownsword ed.) (1993). Thus, "public interest emerges as a set of fundamental values in society." *Id.*

136. JEAN JACQUES ROUSSEAU, SOCIAL CONTRACT, Book II, at 23 (1947); *see also* Brady v. Maryland, 373 U.S. 83, 87 (1963) ("society wins not only when the guilty are convicted but when criminal trials are fair").

137. Matthew Keller, *"Damn the Torpedoes! Full Speed Ahead": The FCC's Decision to Deregulate Media Ownership and the Threat to Viewpoint Diversity*, 12 J.L. & POL'Y 891, 933 (2004).

138. Cass R. Sunstein, *Television and the Public Interest*, 88 CALIF. L. REV. 499, 501 (1999).

139. JEREMY BENTHAM, AN INTRODUCTION TO THE PRINCIPLES OF MORALS AND LEGISLATION 3 (1948).

140. AMY KLOBUCHAR, UNCOVERING THE DOME xviii (1982).

141. RICHARD E. FLATHMAN, THE PUBLIC INTEREST: AN ESSAY CONCERNING THE NORMATIVE DISCOURSE OF POLITICS 67 (1966).

142. ARISTOTLE, THE POLITICS OF ARISTOTLE 1282b (1962).

143. The Supreme Court has specifically recognized "the public interest in the accuracy and justice of criminal results." Standefer v. United States, 447 U.S. 10, 25 (1980) (quoting United States v. Standefer, 610 F.2d 1076, 1093 (3d Cir. 1979)). In fact, the Supreme Court has held that the Fourth Amendment's prohibition of unreasonable searches and seizures was designed to protect the "common interest" of the community against unlawful invasion of the home. Miller v. United States, 357 U.S. 301, 313 (1958); *see also* Gannett Co., Inc. v. DePasquale, 443 U.S. 368, 383 (1979) (noting "public interest" in seeing that justice is "fairly administered," and noting the "great public interest" in having a criminal case heard by a jury); Arizona v. Washington, 434 U.S. 497, 510 & n.27 (1978) (recognizing the "public interest" in "fair judgments" and "just judgments").

144. According to the U.S. Supreme Court:

> The use of the reasonable-doubt standard is indispensable to command the respect and confidence of the community in applications of the criminal law. It is critical that the moral force of the criminal law not be diluted by a standard of proof that leaves people in doubt whether innocent men are being condemned. It is also important in our free society that every individual going about his ordinary affairs have confidence that his government cannot adjudge him guilty of a criminal offense without convincing a proper factfinder of his guilt with utmost certainty.

In re Winship, 397 U.S. 358, 364 (1970); *see also* Strunk v. United States, 412 U.S. 434, 439 n.2 (1973) ("the public interest in a broad sense, as well as the constitutional guarantee, command prompt disposition of criminal charges."); Mooney v. Holohan, 294 U.S. 103, 112 (1935) (the due process requirement "in safeguarding the liberty of the citizen against deprivation through the action of the State, embodies the fundamental conceptions of justice which lie at the base of our civil and political institutions").

145. Fayerweather v. Moran, 749 F. Supp. 43, 44–45 (D. R.I. 1990).

146. Matter of Garber, 472 A.2d 566, 572 (N.J. 1984); *see also id.* at 576 ("The case involves a matter that implicates the most important public interest in the justice system—the prosecution of crime. For all members of the profession, the administration of justice invokes a high moral sensitivity and impells [sic] a strict adherence to ethical standards.").

147. The U.S. Supreme Court has stated that "the purpose of a criminal court is not to provide a forum for the ascertainment of private rights." "Rather," the Supreme Court stated, "it is to vindicate the public interest in the enforcement of the criminal law while at the same time safeguarding the rights of the individual defendant." Standefer v. United States, 447 U.S. 10, 25 (1980) (quoting United States v. Standefer, 610 F.2d 1076, 1093 (3d Cir. 1979)).

148. The "public interest" is greatly disserved if the wrong person is convicted. According to Justice William Brennan, "a miscarriage of justice that imprisons an innocent accused also leaves a guilty party at large, a continuing threat to society." Richmond Newspapers, Inc. v. Virginia, 448 U.S. 555, 596 (1980) (Brennan, J. concurring).

149. *See* Bivens v. Six Unknown Named Agents of Fed. Bureau of Narcotics, 403 U.S. 388, 398, 407 (1971) (Harlan, J., concurring) ("The Bill of Rights is particularly intended to vindicate the interests of the individual in the face of the popular will as express in legislative majorities . . . ."). As Justice Harlan stated in another case:

> Legislatures are, as this Court has often acknowledged, the "main guardian" of the public interest, and, within their constitutional competence, their understanding of that interest must be accepted as "well-nigh" conclusive. This principle does not, however, reach all the questions essential to the resolution of this case. The legislative judgments at issue here embrace assessments of the necessity and wisdom of procedural guarantees; these are questions which the Constitution has entrusted at least in part to courts, and upon which courts have been understood to possess particular competence.

In re Gault, 387 U.S. 1, 70 (1967) (Harlan, J., concurring in part and dissenting in part) (citation omitted).

150. Under the positivist view of procedural due process, courts have no role to play in defining what procedures are necessary to satisfy the Constitution. "Rather, the term 'due process' dictates that individuals be afforded whatever procedures the legislature has mandated—no more and no less." Martin H. Redish & Lawrence C. Marshall, *Adjudicatory Independence and the Values of Procedural Due Process*, 95 YALE L.J.

455, 457 (1986). Although the first Supreme Court case construing the Due Process Clause rejected this view, the positivist approach has been advocated by some members of the Court, including former Chief Justice William Rehnquist. *Compare* Murray's Lessee v. Hoboken Land and Improvement Co., 59 U.S. (18 How.) 272, 276 (1855) ("It is manifest that it was not left to the legislative power to enact any process which might be devised. The article is a restraint on the legislative as well as on the executive and judicial powers of the government, and cannot be so construed as to leave congress free to make any process 'due process of law' by its mere will.") *with* Cleveland Bd. of Educ. v. Loudermill, 470 U.S. 532, 561 (1985) (Rehnquist, J., dissenting) (the Court "ought to recognize the totality of the State's definition of the property right"). However, the positivist approach—which would effectively "rubber stamp" all legislative enactments—has been thoroughly discredited. Martin H. Redish & Lawrence C. Marshall, *Adjudicatory Independence and the Values of Procedural Due Process*, 95 YALE L.J. 455, 456 (1986) ("The historical evidence upon which the positivists rely offers no real support for any particular conception of the clause, even if one accepts the controversial principle that modern constitutional interpretation is rigidly controlled by the intent of the framers."); *see also id.* at 457–68 (outlining the flaws in the positivist approach and demonstrating, both historically and analytically, why courts must determine how much "due process" is constitutionally required).

151. For example, in *Llewelyn v. Oakland County Prosecutor's Office*, a federal district court granted a movie exhibitor's motion for a preliminary injunction against a county attorney who had been seizing copies of a film and making arrests on the basis of a zoning ordinance that prohibited the exhibition of obscene films within 1,000 feet of a residence. 402 F. Supp. 1379 (E.D. Mich. 1975). In so ruling, the court stated that the First Amendment precluded the court from finding that the "public interest" would be harmed by the showing of a film yet to be found obscene because "it may be assumed that the Constitution is the ultimate expression of the public interest." *Id.* at 1393.

152. Martin H. Redish & Lawrence C. Marshall, *Adjudicatory Independence and the Values of Procedural Due Process*, 95 YALE L.J. 455, 493 (1986).

153. 387 U.S. 1 (1967). In *Gault*, the Court held that Arizona's juvenile delinquency process denied a juvenile due process of law.

154. *Id.* at 20 (footnote omitted); *see also Loudermill*, 470 U.S. at 541 ("The right to due process 'is conferred, not by legislative grace, but by constitutional guarantee....' ") (quoting Arnett v. Kennedy, 416 U.S. 134, 167 (1974) (Powell, J., concurring in part and concurring in result in part)).

155. *In re Gault*, 387 U.S. at 21.

156. 424 U.S. 409 (1976).

157. Title 42 U.S.C., section 1983, originally enacted as § 1 of the Civil Rights Act of 1871, 17 Stat. 13, reads as follows:

> Every person who, under color of any statute, ordinance, regulation, custom, or usage, of any State or Territory, subjects, or causes to be subjected, any citizen of the United States or other person within the jurisdiction thereof to the deprivation of any rights, privileges, or immunities secured by the Constitution and laws, shall be liable to the party injured in an action at law, suit in equity, or other proper proceeding for redress.

Significantly, federal prosecutors are also absolutely immune from civil suit for constitutional violations. Butz v. Economou, 438 U.S. 478 (1978). *But see* Burns v. Reed, 111 S. Ct. 1934 (1991) (prosecutors have only qualified immunity when sued for constitutional violations arising out of legal advice given to police). Judges have immunity under *Pierson v. Ray*, 386 U.S. 547 (1967).

158. *Imbler*, 424 U.S. at 424–25. As the Court further stated: "The affording of only a qualified immunity to the prosecutor also could have an adverse effect upon the functioning of the criminal justice system. Attaining the system's goal of accurately determining guilt or innocence requires that both the prosecution and the defense have wide discretion in the conduct of the trial and the presentation of evidence." *Id.* at 426 (footnote omitted).

159. *Id.* at 427–28 (footnote omitted)

160. *Id.* at 424; *see also* Yaselli v. Goff, 275 U.S. 503 (1927) (per curiam) (affirming a decision of the U.S. Court of Appeals for the Second Circuit that a special assistant to the Attorney General of the United States is absolutely immune from a civil action for malicious prosecution). According to the Court:

> The common-law immunity of a prosecutor is based upon the same considerations that underlie the common-law immunities of judges and grand jurors acting within the scope of their duties. These include concern that harassment by unfounded litigation would cause a deflection of the prosecutor's energies from his public duties, and the possibility that he would shade his decisions instead of exercising the independence of judgment required by his public trust.

Imbler, 424 U.S. at 422–23 (footnote omitted); *see also* Gannett Co., Inc. v. DePasquale, 443 U.S. 368, 384 n.12 (1979) ("The responsibility of the prosecutor as a representative of the public surely encompasses a duty to protect the societal interest in an open trial. But this responsibility also requires him to be sensitive to the due process rights of a defendant to a fair trial.").

161. United States v. Ross, 456 U.S. 798, 804 (1982) (noting the "public interest in effective law enforcement").

162. *See* Gibson v. Florida Legislative Investigation Comm., 372 U.S. 539, 566 (1963) (Douglas, J., concurring) ("'The public interest in the suppression of crime, for example, cannot be weighed against a constitutional provision that accused persons may not be denied the right to counsel.'") (quoting Laurent Frantz, *The First Amendment in the Balance*, 71 YALE L.J. 1424, 1441 (1962)).

163. Richmond Newspapers, Inc. v. Virginia, 448 U.S. 555, 594 n.19 (1980) (Brennan, J., concurring) (citing Sherman v. United States, 356 U.S. 369, 380 (1958) (Frankfurter, J., concurring in result)).

164. United States v. Mississippi Valley Generating Co., 364 U.S. 520, 548 (1961). Because public prosecutors, unlike private prosecutors, have absolute immunity from suit and are therefore free to advance the positions that they believe are in the public interest, prohibiting interested private prosecutors will undoubtedly further the public interest. *Cf.* Butz v. Economou, 438 U.S. 478 (1978); Imbler v. Pachtman, 424 U.S. 409 (1976).

165. Edward L. Wilkinson, *Conflicts of Interest in Texas Criminal Cases*, 54 BAYLOR L. REV. 171, 187 (2002).

166. Mitchell v. Forsyth, 472 U.S. 511, 520 (1985); Butz v. Economou, 438 U.S. 478, 511–12 (1978); *see also* Quadri v. Rivera-Mercado, 303 So.3d 250, 254 (Fla. Dist. Ct. App. 2020) ("It is well settled that the various officers of the State Attorney's Office are quasi-judicial officers, as established by article V, section 17 of the Florida Constitution."); Mobley v. O'Donnell, No. 19AP-440, 2020 WL 703690, at *5 (Ohio Ct. App. Feb. 11, 2020) ("Courts consider prosecutors 'quasi-judicial officers' entitled to the absolute immunity granted to judges...."); State v. Carter, No. 77068-3-I, 2019 WL 1255732, at *2 (Wash. Ct. App. Mar. 18, 2019) ("As quasi-judicial officers, prosecutors have a duty to act impartially in the interest of justice."); State v. Bellah, No. 74213-2-I, 2017 WL 571075, at *4 (Wash. Ct. App. Feb. 13, 2017) ("[U]nlike criminal defense attorneys, prosecutors are quasi-judicial officers and are presumed to act impartially; thus, their opinion has the danger of carrying particular weight with the jury."). On the legislative front, a Colorado statute explicitly refers to the "quasi-judicial capacity" of district attorneys. COLO. REV. STAT. ANN. § 20-1-106.1(1) ("The district attorneys of the several judicial districts in the state of Colorado shall: (a) Rending, in their quasi-judicial capacity, legal advice to peace officers, upon the request of such officers or of the court, pertaining to the preparation and review of affidavits and warrants for arrests, searches, seizures, nontestimonial identification items, and court orders for the production of records....").

167. Imbler v. Pachtman, 424 U.S. 409, 423 n.20 (1976); *accord* Rehberg v. Paulk, 566 U.S. 356, 372 n.3 (2012) (quoting that language from *Imbler v. Pachtman*).

168. Brown v. Lubbock County Comm. Court, 185 S.W.3d 499, 505 (2005).

169. State v. Thierry, 360 P.3d 940, 945 (Wash. Ct. App. 2015).

170. West Michigan Film LLC v. Metz, Docket No. 319119, 2015 WL 404933, at *4 (Mich. Ct. App. Jan. 29, 2015).

171. State v. Harris, 939 S.W.2d 915, 919 (Mo. Ct. App. 1996); *see also* Roberta K. Flowers, *What You See Is What You Get: Applying the Appearance of Impropriety Standard to Prosecutors*, 63 MO. L. REV. 699 (1998).

172. Hasan v. Onondaga County, 5:18-CV-806 (GLS/ATB), 2018 WL 4055296, at *9 (N.D.N.Y. Aug. 2, 2018); *see also* State v Hollingworth, No. 71614-0-I, 2015 WL 4530263, at *3 (Wash. Ct. App. July 27, 2015) ("A prosecutor represents the people in a quasi-judicial capacity and must temper courtroom zeal in

fairness to the defendant."); *cf.* Pitman v. Ottehberg, Civil No. 10–2538, 2015 WL 179392, at *10 (D. N.J. Jan. 14, 2015):

> Mere employment by the prosecutor's office, however, is not a sufficient basis to invoke prosecutorial immunity. *See Drisco v. City of Elizabeth,* No. Civ. A. 03–397, 2010 WL 1253890, at *8 n. 18 (D.N.J. Mar. 23, 2010) ("New Jersey law, like federal law, determines the level of immunity afforded prosecutors based on whether prosecutors are operating in a quasi-judicial capacity. Under section 3–3, immunity is qualified where a prosecutor is involved in the conduct of an investigation."); *cf. Hayes,* 217 N.J. Super. at 622, 526 A.2d 737 (investigator is entitled to a specific qualified immunity). Rather, to the extent Defendant Woshnak was conducting only investigatory duties, he would be entitled to qualified immunity rather than the near-absolute immunity afforded to prosecutors.

173. Young v. U.S. ex rel. Vuitton et Fils S.A., 481 U.S. 787, 810–11 (1987).

174. Conklin v. Hill, Case No. 16-cv-02860-JSW, 2018 WL 11225865, at *16 (N.D. Cal. Nov. 6, 2018) (citations omitted); *accord* Grey v. McEwen, No. CV 11-7510 CJC(JC), 2014 WL 7149442, at *8 (C.D. Cal., Dec. 15, 2014).

175. People v. Mienkwic, No. 347863, 2021 WL 299292, at *3 & n.6 (Mich. Ct. App. Jan. 28, 2021); *see also* State v. Harris, 939 S.W.3d 915, 919 (Mo. Ct. App. 1996) ("It is clear that prosecutors, as quasi-judicial officers, have a duty to avoid even the appearance of impropriety.") (citing State v. Boyd, 560 S.W.2d 296, 297 (Mo. Ct. App. 1977)). *But see* State v. Washington, 189 A3d 43, 65 (R.I. 2018) ("It is insufficient for the defendant to merely allege that there was an appearance of impropriety because one of the prosecutors in the defendant's case had a working relationship with the trial justice's daughter, without asserting any supporting evidence that would demonstrate judicial bias. Thus, the defendant has failed to meet the "substantial burden" required to prevail on a recusal motion."); People v. Perez, 201 P.3d 1220, 1232 (Colo. 2009) (en banc) ("[O]ur precedent establishes that the current version of the disqualification statute, by listing only three grounds for the disqualification of prosecutors, eliminates the previous 'appearance of impropriety' standard. To the extent that the trial court based its disqualification ruling on any 'appearance of impropriety' it perceived from the possible use of Edwards' legal work in this case, the court considered an improper ground for disqualification.") (citations omitted); Adkins v. State, 169 S.W.3d 916, 921 (Mo. Ct. App. 2005) ("Here, the motion is to set aside a conviction on grounds that trial counsel was ineffective, and the *Strickland* test applies. Therefore, Mr. Adkins must show prejudice. This misapplication of conflict of interest cases also appears to underlie Mr. Adkins's incorrect assertion that prosecutors must avoid the 'appearance of impropriety.'").

176. Iannazzi v. Warden, No. CV054000419, 2008 WL 853557, at *4 (Conn. Super. Ct. Mar. 13, 2008).

177. *See* In re Cox, 481 S.W.3d 289, 293–94 (Tex. Ct. App. 2015):

> The standard for disqualification of an elected district attorney and her entire office is different from the standard for disqualification of a special prosecutor. A trial court may not disqualify a district attorney on the basis of a conflict of interest unless that conflict rises to the level of a due-process violation. *Landers v. State,* 256 S.W.3d 295, 304 (Tex. Crim. App. 2008) (citing *State ex rel. Hill v. Pirtle,* 887 S.W.2d 921, 927 (Tex. Crim. App. 1994) (orig. proceeding)). A due-process violation occurs only when the defendant can establish "actual prejudice," not just the threat of possible prejudice to her rights. *Id.* Actual prejudice would occur, for example, if the prosecuting attorney had previously represented the defendant in the same matter or in a substantially-related matter and in that representation had obtained confidential information and used it to the defendant's disadvantage. *Id.* at 304–05. A trial court's authority to disqualify a prosecutor comes from the court's duty to protect the accused's constitutional due-process rights, *see, e.g., Ex parte Morgan,* 616 S.W.2d 625, 626 (Tex. Crim. App. 1981) (orig. proceeding), and the statute barring a prosecutor from representing the State in the same matter on which he or she has been previously employed adversely, *see* Tex. Code Crim. Proc. Ann. art. 2.01 (West 2005).
>
> The heightened burden for disqualification of a district attorney is policy driven; unlike a private attorney, a district attorney is an elected official whose office is constitutionally mandated and protected. *Landers,* 256 S.W.3d at 303; *State ex rel. Eidson v. Edwards,*793 S.W.2d 1, 6 (Tex. Crim. App.1990) (orig. proceeding) (plurality op. on reh'g). District attorneys and their

prosecutors are subject to the rules of disciplinary conduct, "but they must police themselves at the trial court level because of their status as independent members of the judicial branch of government." *Eidson,* 793 S.W.2d at 6. And because the district attorney is an elected official, "[s] hould h[er] conduct [and the conduct of the prosecutors in her office] create too much appearance of impropriety and public suspicion, [s]he will ultimately answer to the voters." *Id.*

....

A "special prosecutor," though enlisted by a district attorney to help in a particular case, is not part of the district attorney's staff. *Coleman v. State,* 246 S.W.3d 76, 82 (Tex. Crim. App. 2008). Unlike the district attorney and the attorneys employed in the district attorney's office, a special prosecutor is not required to sign the oath of office. *Id.* Commissioning a special prosecutor does not require court approval. *Id.* Additionally, unlike a prosecutor, who is statutorily prohibited from appearing adversely to the State, a private attorney asked to serve as a special prosecutor is under no such prohibition. *See* Tex. Code Crim. Proc. Ann. art. 2.08(a). Unlike a prosecutor in the district attorney's office whose position is constitutionally mandated and protected, the position of a special prosecutor enjoys no such constitutional underpinnings. *Cf. Landers,* 256 S.W.3d at 303. If one private attorney appointed as a special prosecutor is disqualified in a particular case, a district attorney may appoint a different private attorney to serve as a special prosecutor. In short, the policy reasons articulated by the court of criminal appeals to support disqualification of an entire district attorney's office on the basis of a conflict of interest simply do not apply to an attorney in private practice appointed as a special prosecutor in a single case. *Accord id.* at 304. A private attorney appointed as a special prosecutor nonetheless remains a private attorney and is disqualifiable on conflict-of-interest grounds that need not rise to the level of a due-process violation.

178. Reichert v. State, 134 P.3d 268, 277 n.3 (Wyo. 2006).

179. State v. Gonzales, 119 P.3d 151, 160 (N.M. 2005) (citations omitted).

180. Wacoche v. State, 644 P.2d 568, 574 (Okla. Ct. Crim. App. 1982).

181. Discovering truth is the primary function of the adversary system. United States v. Havens, 446 U.S. 620 (1980).

182. 397 U.S. 358 (1970).

183. *Id.* at 364.

184. *Id.* at 363.

185. 466 U.S. 668 (1984). To prove an "ineffective assistance of counsel" claim, the Supreme Court has held that a defendant must show that counsel's performance was deficient and that the deficient performance prejudiced the defense. *Id.* at 687; *see also* Hill v. Lockhart, 474 U.S. 52 (1985) (same). Significantly, the requirement that prejudice be shown to establish an "ineffective assistance" claim does not lead to the conclusion that prejudice also has to be shown to reverse a conviction obtained by a private prosecutor. First, whereas prejudice is required with respect to ineffective assistance claims because the government has no control over defense counsel's errors, *Strickland,* 466 U.S. at 693, it is prosecutorial conduct that is at stake in the private prosecutor context. Second, while ineffective assistance claims do not involve conflict of interest issues, the use of private prosecutors directly implicates such concerns. Indeed, under *Cuyler v. Sullivan,* 446 U.S. 335 (1980), prejudice to a defendant is presumed if it is demonstrated that defense counsel "actively represented conflicting interests" and that "an actual conflict of interest adversely affected" the lawyer's performance. *Id.* at 348, 350; *see also* Burger v. Kemp, 483 U.S. 776, 783 (1987) (same); *Strickland,* 466 U.S. at 692 (conflicts of interest affecting counsel's performance are presumptively prejudicial). Because prosecutors, in representing the public interest, have an affirmative obligation to represent the interests of a defendant as a member of the general public, private prosecutors are presumptively prejudicial to defendant's rights under *Cuyler* because they actively represent conflicting interests. Finally, unlike ineffective assistance claims, where the Supreme Court is concerned with whether defense counsel's performance was actually deficient, the mere appearance of impropriety is the critical concern in evaluating the propriety of private prosecutors.

186. *Strickland*, 466 U.S. at 686. The *Strickland* Court stated that "the purpose of the Sixth Amendment guarantee of counsel is to ensure that a defendant has the assistance necessary to justify reliance on the outcome of the proceeding." *Id.* at 691–92.

187. 419 U.S. 522 (1975).

188. The right of a defendant to challenge prospective jurors for cause to ensure an impartial jury is also well established. Lewis v. United States, 146 U.S. 370 (1892).

189. *Tumey*, 273 U.S. at 532.

190. 387 U.S. 1, 20–21, 28, 34–50 (1967). *But cf.* Allen v. Illinois, 478 U.S. 364, 372 (1986) (citing case law distinguishing *In re Gault*).

191. Amary v. JP Morgan Chase Bank, N.A., Civil Action No. 12-10777-NMG, 2013 WL 6979525, at *2 (D. Mass. Jan. 13, 2013).

192. Pereira v. Fu, No. 2:15-cv-00503-KJM-AC, 2015 WL 5436767, at *8 (E.D. Cal. Sept. 15, 2015); *see also* Tristan Montaque, *Policing the Police: Analzying the Legal Implications of the Sequestration of Cellphone Video Footage*, 22 J. Tech. L. & Pol'y 1, 17 (2018) (taking note of the "the fundamental difference between a substantive due process claim and a procedural due process claim" and observing that whereas "a substantive due process claim requires an illegitimate deprivation of rights or property" a "procedural due process claim" involves a deprivation of "fair and adequate procedure"); 16C C.J.S. *Constitutional Law* § 1863 n.9 ("Substantive due process implicates the essence of state action rather than its modalities; procedural due process differs from substantive due process by focusing not on what a person has been deprived of but rather on how the deprivation was accomplished.").

193. Doe v. Board of Osteopathic Licensure, 242 A.3d 182, 189 n.8 (Maine Sup. Jud. Ct. 2020).

194. Black's Law Dictionary 171, 1218 (8th ed. 2004) (defining bias as "[i]nclination; prejudice; predilection," and defining prejudice as "[a] preconceived judgment formed without a factual basis; a strong bias"); Compton v. Henrie, 364 S.W.2d 179, 182 ("Bias, in its usual meaning, is an inclination toward one side of an issue rather than to the other, but to disqualify, it must appear that the state of mind of the juror leads to the natural inference that he will not or did not act with impartiality. Prejudice is more easily defined, for it means prejudgment, and consequently embraces bias; the converse is not true."); 22 Tracy Bateman, et al., Ohio Jur.3d Courts and Judges § 128—*Bias or prejudice of judge—Bias or prejudice defined* (June 2021 Update) ("The term 'bias or prejudice' in the canon requiring a judge to perform judicial duties without bias or prejudice implies a hostile feeling or spirit of ill will or undue friendship or favoritism toward one of the litigants or his or her attorney, with the formation of a fixed anticipatory judgment on the part of the judge, as contra-distinguished from an open state of mind which will be governed by the law and the facts."); 46 Glenda K. Harnad, et al., Am. Jur.2d Judges § 124 (May 2021 Update)—*Definitions of "bias" and "prejudice" with reference to disqualification of judge* ("'Prejudice' involves a prejudgment or forming of an opinion without sufficient knowledge or examination. 'Bias' is a leaning of the mind or an inclination toward one person or another. In construing the words 'bias or prejudice,' it has been said that such conditions must exist which reflect prejudgment of the case by the judge or a leaning of his or her mind in favor of one party to the extent that his or her decision in the matter is based on grounds other than the evidence placed before him or her.").

195. John D. Bessler, *The Public Interest and the Unconstitutionality of Private Prosecutors*, 47 Ark. L. Rev. 511, 569 (1994); *cf.* State v. Culbreath, 30 S.W.3d 309, 318 (2000) ("The defendants' liberty interests are obviously significant, as they have been charged with multiple felony offenses. We also believe, for the reasons already described, that the risk of erroneous deprivation of these interests, i.e., prejudice to the defendants, stemming from the participation of a private attorney compensated by a special interest group, is also substantial. In short, the participation of a privately funded prosecutor rendered the proceedings fundamentally unfair. Finally, unlike *Wilson*, the fiscal and administrative burdens are minimal because the District Attorney General and his staff are already charged with the responsibility of investigating and prosecuting the offenses in question. Indeed, two assistant district attorneys were directly involved in the investigation of these cases along with Parrish. Given these factors, we agree with the lower courts that the defendants were denied their right to due process."); State v. Crump, No. M2006-02244-CCA-R3-CD, 2009 WL 723524, at *33 (Mar. 18. 2009) ("In *Culbreath*, a private prosecutor operated on behalf of the district attorney's office to prosecute crimes involving adult-oriented businesses. The private prosecutor was

appointed a special assistant district attorney general. The private prosecutor's fees and some of his expenses were paid by Citizens for Community Values, Inc. The defendants were charged with crimes related to their operation of sexually-oriented businesses and sought disqualification of the district attorney's office and the private prosecutor. The supreme court held that the private prosecutor had a conflict of interest by virtue of his compensation by the special interest group and his role as a prosecutor with the district attorney's office, because he owed a duty of loyalty to both. The court noted that in rare instances, prosecutorial misconduct may rise to the level of violating a defendant's due process rights and mandate dismissal of the indictment. The court concluded that the involvement of the private prosecutor had so infected the proceedings, from before the indictment was returned and continuing throughout the entire proceedings, that the trial court properly disqualified the private prosecutor and the district attorney's office and correctly dismissed the indictment.").

196. *See* Fuentes v. Shevin, 407 U.S. 67, 97 (1972) (due process is required to minimize "substantially unfair or mistaken deprivations"); LAURENCE H. TRIBE, AMERICAN CONSTITUTIONAL LAW TRIBE § 10-7, at 667 (1988) (same).

197. The concept of prosecutorial accountability strongly militates against the use of private prosecutors. In fact, if a private prosecution is botched, the doctrine of double jeopardy greatly reduces prosecutorial accountability because the government cannot re-prosecute an individual after an acquittal is obtained. Harold J. Krent & Ethan G. Shenkman, *Of Citizen Suits and Citizen Sunstein*, 91 MICH. L. REV. 1793, 1804 n.40 (1993). Thus, while public prosecutors are directly accountable to the electorate when a prosecution goes awry, elected prosecutors are only indirectly accountable—to the extent they did not appropriately supervise a prosecution—for the conduct of private prosecutors.

198. *Id.* at 1803; *see also id.* ("Moreover, accountability concerns suggest that the individual making such determinations be subject to the political process. Accountability benefits not only the public as a whole, but the criminally accused whose very liberty is at stake."); *id.* ("The shortcomings of exclusive private enforcement—which have always existed—have . . . become more glaring with the growth of the country and of federal criminal law. For instance, there is little reason to entrust private citizens with the prosecution of victimless crimes like drug use or gambling. Even for crimes with identified victims such as murder or theft, centralized enforcement may well generate benefits. The potential for harassment is minimized through the process of publicly controlled prosecutions. Furthermore, public prosecutors can temper justice with mercy, and only a centralized executive can modulate enforcement of the laws as social conditions change. If the President devotes too few resources to combatting drug use or insider trading, he or she is responsible at election time for decisions to enforce as well as not to enforce."); *id.* at 1803 n.37 ("Because only the sovereign can deprive a citizen of liberty, the need for accountability in criminal prosecution is probably greater than in the civil context. The concern for accountability might explain in part the evolution toward public prosecution."); *see also* Evan Caminker, Comment, *The Constitutionality of Qui Tam Actions*, 99 YALE L.J. 341, 368 (1989) ("Because prosecutors within the executive branch are accountable to the President and, through her, ultimately to the people, they are presumably less likely to enforce the law oppressively or overzealously."). A recent U.S. Supreme Court decision ruled that the unreviewable authority wielded by Administrative Patent Judges is incompatible, under the Appointments Clause, with tier appointment by the Secretary of Commerce to an inferior office. United States v. Arthrex, Inc., Nos. 19-1434, 19-1452 & 19-1458, 2021 WL 2519433, at *13 (U.S. June 21, 2021) ("Today, we reaffirm and apply the rule from *Edmond* that the exercise of executive power by inferior officers must at some level be subject to the direction and supervision of an officer nominated by the President and confirmed by the Senate. The Constitution therefore forbids the enforcement of statutory restrictions on the Director that insulate the decisions of APJs from his direction and supervision. To be clear, the Director need not review every decision of the PTAB. What matters is that the Director have the discretion to review decisions rendered by APJs. In this way, the President remains responsible for the exercise of executive power—and through him, the exercise of executive power remains accountable to the people.").

199. State ex rel. Koppers Co., Inc. v. International Union of Oil, Chemical and Atomic Workers, 298 S.E.2d 827, 829 (W. Va. Sup. Ct. App., 1982) ("A public prosecutor's fundamental duty is to do justice; his or her presence should protect against overzealousness and an unrestrained pursuit of private vindication.") (citing Code of Professional Responsibility, EC-7-13, West Virginia Code, Appendix; ABA Standards

of Criminal Justice (2d Ed. 1980), Standard 3-1.1(c); 44 A.B.A.J. 1159, 1218 (1958); ABA Opinion 150 (1936)); *see also* ABA Comm. on Professional Ethics and Grievances, Formal Op. 150 (1936) ("The prosecuting attorney is the attorney for the state, and it is his primary duty not to convict but to see that justice is done.").

200. Bruce A. Green & Rebecca Roiphe, *Rethinking Prosecutors' Conflicts of Interest*, 58 B.C. L. Rev. 463, 469–70 (2017) ("The concept of a conflict of interest is necessarily different and more complex for prosecutors than for private lawyers because prosecutors do not have traditional clients. In a private representation, the lawyer ordinarily has an identifiable client who defines the objectives of the representation. The lawyer can judge whether, at least in theory, a personal interest may compromise her ability to achieve the client's objectives. For prosecutors, however, there is room for debate about how to identify the client. Some suggest that prosecutors represent the victim or the police in some literal sense. In that case, close alliances with the victim or law enforcement might not create a conflict but, to the contrary, might be said to strengthen the prosecutor's loyalty. Nevertheless, the contemporary understanding is that prosecutors do not represent the victim or the police. Instead, they represent the government, state or locality, or the public in an abstract sense. Prosecutors therefore serve the public interest.").

201. 563 U.S. 51 (2011).

202. *Id.* at 65–66 (citing LSBA, Articles of Incorporation, Art. 15, §§ 5, 6 & Art. 16, EC 7–13 & DR 1–102 (1971); ABA Standards for Criminal Justice 3–1.1(c) (2d ed.1980); ABA Model Rule of Prof. Conduct 3.8(d) & 8.4 (1984)).

203. Connick v. Thompson, 563 U.S. 51, 71 (2011) (citing Berger v. United States, 295 U.S. 78, 88 (1935)).

204. Norton v. State, No. W2018-01420-CCA-R3-PC, 2019 WL 4594273, at *6 (Tenn. Ct. Crim. App. Sept. 20, 2019); People v. Brown, No. 340069, 2019 WL 3312509, at *3 (Mich. Ct. App. July 23, 2019); *see also* State v. Ponder, No. M2018-00998-CCA-R3-CD, 2019 WL 3944008, at *12 (Tenn. Ct. Crim. App. Aug. 21, 2019) ("Our supreme court has emphasized 'that prosecutors must balance zealous advocacy with their obligations to seek justice and ensure that defendants receive fair trials' and 'urge[d] prosecutors to err on the side of restraint and temperance when presenting closing arguments.'") (citation omitted).

205. State v. McNeil-Thomas, 209 A.3d 845, 855 (N.J. 2019).

206. United States v. Agurs, 427 U.S. 97, 110–11 (1976).

207. 295 U.S. 78 (1935).

208. *Id.* at 88.

209. *Id.*

210. *Id.* This duty of fairness has been held to apply even where the prosecutor strongly believes that the accused is guilty. State v. Sha, 193 N.W.2d 829 (Minn. 1972).

211. *E.g.*, Wend v. People, 235 P.3d 1089, 1096–99 (Colo. 2010); *see also* Seth Apfel, *Prosecutorial Misconduct: Comparing American and Foreign Approaches to a Pervasive Problem and Devising Possible Solutions*, 31 Ariz. J. Int'l & Comp. L. 835, 837 (2014) ("The high import of the issue of prosecutorial misconduct has been repeatedly and eloquently recognized by the U.S. Supreme Court. Many of the seminal cases addressing the issue have engaged sweeping philosophical pronouncements intended as profound statements implicating notions of fairness and justice. Perhaps the most renowned and oft cited epithet was penned by Justice Sutherland in *Berger v. United States:* '[W]hile [the prosecutor] may strike hard blows, he is not at liberty to strike foul ones.' While condemning misconduct committed by a U.S. Attorney, Sutherland describes the ideal function of a prosecutor as having an interest not to win, but to do justice, and as a 'servant of the law, the twofold aim of which is that guilt shall not escape or innocence suffer.' More recently Justice Ginsburg, recognizing the importance of full prosecutorial disclosure of evidence, the absence of which may result in wrongful conviction, opined that 'it is unconscionable not to impose reasonable controls impelling prosecutors to bring the information to light.'"); Jacob A. Stein, Closing Arguments § 1:16 (2020–2021 ed.) ("A criminal prosecutor is but an appendage of the people of the jurisdiction, a 'servant of the law.' Nonetheless, the prosecutor must be careful not to suggest to the jury that he or she represents the 'citizens' of the community. He or she is duty bound to prosecute in a fair and impartial manner. Thus, it is as much a prosecutor's duty to refrain from improper methods calculated to produce a wrongful conviction as it is to use every legitimate means to bring about a just one.").

212. 514 U.S. 419 (1995).

213. *Id.* at 432 (citing Brady v. Maryland, 373 U.S. 83, 86 (1963)).

214. *Id.* at 437 ("We have never held that the Constitution demands an open file policy (however such a policy might work out in practice), and the rule in *Bagley* (and, hence, in *Brady*) requires less of the prosecution than the ABA Standards for Criminal Justice, which call generally for prosecutorial disclosures of any evidence tending to exculpate or mitigate.") (*citing* ABA Standards for Criminal Justice, Prosecution Function and Defense Function 3–3.11(a) (3d ed. 1993) ("A prosecutor should not intentionally fail to make timely disclosure to the defense, at the earliest feasible opportunity, of the existence of all evidence or information which tends to negate the guilt of the accused or mitigate the offense charged or which would tend to reduce the punishment of the accused"); ABA Model Rule of Professional Conduct 3.8(d) (1984) ("The prosecutor in a criminal case shall... make timely disclosure to the defense of all evidence or information known to the prosecutor that tends to negate the guilt of the accused or mitigates the offense, and, in connection with sentencing, disclose to the defense and to the tribunal all unprivileged mitigating information known to the prosecutor...."); *see also* In the Matter of Attorney C, 47 P.3d 1167, 1171 (Colo. 2002) (en banc) (citing ABA Standard 3–3.11(a) and noting that "we read Rule 3.8(d) as containing a requirement that a prosecutor disclose exculpatory, outcome-determinative evidence that tends to negate the guilt or mitigate the punishment of the accused").

215. *Kyles*, 514 U.S. at 437–38 (*citing Brady*, 373 U.S. at 87); *see also id.* at 437 ("This in turn means that the individual prosecutor has a duty to learn of any favorable evidence known to the others acting on the government's behalf in the case, including the police.").

216. More information about wrongful convictions can be found at the websites for the Innocence Project and the National Registry of Exonerations. Innocence Project, https://innocenceproject.org; The National Registry of Exonerations, https://www.law.umich.edu/special/exoneration/Pages/about.aspx.

217. 473 U.S. 667 (1985).

218. *Id.* at 682.

219. *Kyles*, 514 U.S. at 437–38 (*citing Brady*, 373 U.S. at 87).

220. *Id.* at 439; *see also id.* ("Indeed, even if due process were thought to be violated by every failure to disclose an item of exculpatory or impeachment evidence (leaving harmless error as the government's only fallback), the prosecutor would still be forced to make judgment calls about what would count as favorable evidence, owing to the very fact that the character of a piece of evidence as favorable will often turn on the context of the existing or potential evidentiary record. Since the prosecutor would have to exercise some judgment even if the State were subject to this most stringent disclosure obligation, it is hard to find merit in the State's complaint over the responsibility for judgment under the existing system, which does not tax the prosecutor with error for any failure to disclose, absent a further showing of materiality. Unless, indeed, the adversary system of prosecution is to descend to a gladiatorial level unmitigated by any prosecutorial obligation for the sake of truth, the government simply cannot avoid responsibility for knowing when the suppression of evidence has come to portend such an effect on a trial's outcome as to destroy confidence in its result.").

221. *Kyles*, 514 US. at 439–40 (quoting Berger v. United States, 295 U.S. 78, 88 (1935); citing Rose v. Clark, 478 U.S. 570, 577–78 (1986); Estes v. Texas, 381 U.S. 532, 540 (1965); United States v. Leon, 468 U.S. 897, 900–01 (1984)).

222. Wolfram, *supra* note 22, at § 13.10.1, at 759.

223. Model Code of Professional Responsibility EC 7-1 (1984).

224. Wolfram, *supra* note 22, at § 13.10.1, at 759 (footnote omitted); *see also* Fred Zacharias, *Structuring the Ethics of Prosecutorial Trial Practice: Can Prosecutors Do Justice?*, 44 Vand. L. Rev. 45 (1991) (outlining the ethical duty of prosecutors to "do justice").

225. Matthew S. Nichols, *No One Can Serve Two Masters: Arguments Against Private Prosecutors*, 13 Cap. Def. J. 279, 281, 289 (2001).

226. 481 U.S. 787 (1987).

227. *Id.* at 807.

228. *Id.* at 813. For an analysis of the *Young* decision, see Terri L. Braswell, Comment, *Criminal Procedure—*Young v. United States ex rel. Vuitton et Fils S.A.: *The Right to a Disinterested Prosecutor in a*

Federal Criminal Contempt Proceeding Arising from the Underlying Civil Litigation, 18 MEM. ST. U. L. REV. 143 (1987).

229. *See* Chapter 5.

230. *E.g.*, *Young*, 481 U.S. at 803–06 & nn.14–16; State v. Harrington, 534 S.W.2d 44, 50 (Mo. 1976); *see also* ABA Standards for Criminal Justice, Standard 3-2.1 (1979) (emphasis added) ("The prosecution function should be performed by a public prosecutor who is a lawyer subject to the standards of professional conduct and discipline.").

231. *Young*, 481 U.S. at 790–92.

232. *Id.*

233. *Id.* at 792–93.

234. *Id.* at 793.

235. *Id.* at 790–91 n.1, 793.

236. 658 F.2d 60 (2d Cir. 1981), *cert. denied*, 455 U.S. 944 (1982). In *Musidor*, the Second Circuit held that neither due process nor Rule 42 of the Federal Rules of Criminal Procedure requires a court to select counsel from the staff of the United States Attorney's Office to prosecute a criminal contempt. *Id.* at 64.

237. United States ex rel. Vuitton et Fils S.A. v. Klayminc, 780 F.2d 179 (2d Cir. 1985).

238. *Id.* at 184.

239. *Young*, 481 U.S. at 794.

240. *Id.* at 797 (*citing* Gompers v. Bucks Stove & Range Co., 221 U.S. 418, 450 (1911)).

241. *Young*, 481 U.S. at 801–02.

242. *Id.* at 802 (quoting United States v. Wilson, 421 U.S. 309, 319 (1975) and Anderson v. Dunn, 6 Wheat. 204, 231 (1821)). "This principle of restraint in contempt counsels caution in the exercise of the power to appoint a private prosecutor." *Young*, 481 U.S. at 802.

243. United States v. Hasting, 461 U.S. 496, 505 (1983). *But cf.* Thomas v. Arn, 474 U.S. 140, 148 (1985) ("Even a sensible and efficient use of the supervisory power... is invalid if it conflicts with constitutional or statutory provisions."). In so holding, the *Hasting* Court ruled that a court could not, by an assertion of its supervisory power, avoid the rule that a prosecutorial comment on the failure of an accused to testify is not per se error requiring automatic reversal of a conviction if the whole record indicates that the error was harmless beyond a reasonable doubt.

244. *Hasting*, 461 U.S. at 505. In a subsequent case, *Bank of Nova Scotia v. United States*, the Supreme Court also held that a court's supervisory power may not be invoked "to circumvent the harmless error inquiry prescribed by Federal Rule of Criminal Procedure 52(a)." 487 U.S. 250, 254 (1988) (citing Fed. R. Crim. P. 52(a)). As Justice Anthony Kennedy wrote in that case: "Rule 52 is, in every pertinent respect, as binding as any statute duly enacted by Congress, and federal courts have no more discretion to disregard the Rule's mandate than they do to disregard constitutional or statutory provisions. The balance struck by the Rule between societal costs and the rights of the accused may not casually be overlooked 'because a court has elected to analyze the question under the supervisory power.'" *Bank of Nova Scotia*, 487 U.S. at 255 (quoting United States v. Payner, 447 U.S. 727, 736 (1980)). In *Bank of Nova Scotia*, for an error not to be harmless, the Court held that the prosecutorial misconduct involved in that case must have "substantially influenced" the grand jury's decision to indict, thereby creating a "grave doubt" that the indictment was free from substantial influence. *Bank of Nova Scotia*, 487 U.S. at 256.

245. *Young*, 481 U.S. at 806; *id.* at 807 (footnote omitted) ("The appointment of counsel for an interested party to bring the contempt prosecution in this case at a minimum created opportunities for conflicts to arise, and created at least the appearance of impropriety."). According to the Court: "The prosecutor is appointed solely to pursue the public interest in vindication of the court's authority. A private attorney appointed to prosecute a criminal contempt therefore certainly should be as disinterested as a public prosecutor who undertakes such a prosecution." *Id.* at 805 (footnote omitted).

246. *Id.* at 804–05.

247. *Id.* at 805 (quoting Brotherhood of Locomotive Firemen & Enginemen v. United States, 411 F.2d 312, 319 (5th Cir. 1969)). In a footnote, Justice Brennan asserted that the potential for misconduct that arises through the appointment of an interested prosecutor is not outweighed by the fact that an attorney for the beneficiary of the court order may often be the most familiar with the underlying facts of the

dispute. In so stating, Justice Brennan suggested in dicta that "that familiarity may be put to use in assisting a disinterested prosecutor in pursuing the contempt action, but cannot justify permitting counsel for the private party to be in control of the prosecution." *Young*, 481 U.S. at 807 n.17.

248. *E.g.*, United States v. Mississippi Valley Generating Co., 364 U.S. 520, 549 (1961) (statute prohibiting financial conflict-of-interest "has its foundation in the Biblical admonition that no man may serve two masters"); Glasser v. United States, 315 U.S. 60, 75 (1942) (representation of multiple codefendants created impermissible "struggle to serve two masters").

249. Margaret Garvin & Douglas E. Beloof, *Crime Victim Agency: Independent Lawyers for Sexual Assault Victims*, 13 OHIO ST. J. CRIM. L. 67, 86 (2015).

250. The harmless error rule provides that "any error, defect, irregularity or variance which does not affect substantial rights shall be disregarded." Fed. R. Crim. P. 52(a). A constitutional error at trial requires the reversal of a conviction unless the government can establish that the error was harmless beyond a reasonable doubt. Chapman v. California, 386 U.S. 18 (1967).

251. *Young*, 481 U.S. at 810–11 (quoting Delaware v. Van Arsdall, 475 U.S. 673, 681 (1986)). Only four members of the Supreme Court joined Part III B of the *Young* opinion, which holds, among other things: "We establish a categorical rule against the appointment of an interested prosecutor, adherence to which requires no subtle calculations of judgment. Given the fundamental and pervasive effects of such an appointment, we therefore hold that harmless-error analysis is inappropriate in reviewing the appointment of an interested prosecutor in a case such as *Young*." *Id.* at 814. Notably, in *New Jersey v. Imperiale*, the State of New Jersey argued that criminal defendants in private prosecutor cases only suffer due process violations if their actual trial was fundamentally unfair. 773 F. Supp. 747 (D. N.J. 1991). The court in *Imperiale* noted: "This is the 'harmless error' approach, which stands bruised but intact given that Part III B of the *Young* opinion only carried four votes." *Imperiale*, 773 F. Supp. at 753 (footnote omitted). *But see* In re Davidson, 908 F.2d 1249, 1251 (5th Cir. 1990) (noting that the Fifth Circuit has adopted as its own rule the position put forth by a plurality of the *Young* Court that "where as here, there is a *Young* violation, 'harmless error analysis is inappropriate'") (citing Matter of Hipp, Inc., 895 F.2d 1503, 1509 (5th Cir. 1990)); *see also* Ganger v. Peyton, 379 F.2d 709, 714 (4th Cir. 1967) (harmless error analysis inappropriate where constitutional deficiency of conviction arises from conflicting roles of private attorney and prosecutor).

252. *Young*, 481 U.S. at 811 (citing Rose v. Clark, 478 U.S. 570, 577–78 (1986); Van Arsdall, 475 U.S. at 681–82; Vasquez v. Hillery, 474 U.S. 254, 263–64 (1986)).

253. *Young*, 481 U.S. at 811.

254. *Id.* at 811.

255. *Id.* at 813.

256. *Id.* at 812–83 (quoting Offutt, 348 U.S. at 14).

257. *Young*, 481 U.S. at 813.

258. *Id.* at 813–14 (citing Holloway v. Arkansas, 435 U.S. 475 (1978) (rejecting application of the harmless-error rule to a defense attorney's conflict in representing three codefendants)). In *Holloway*, the Supreme Court stated as follows: "In a case of joint representation of conflicting interests the evil—it bears repeating—is in what the advocate finds himself compelled to refrain from doing, not only at trial but also as to possible pretrial negotiations and in the sentencing process." *Holloway*, 435 U.S. at 490–91.

259. *Young*, 481 U.S. at 827 (Powell, J., concurring in part and dissenting in part).

260. *Id.*

261. *Young*, 481 U.S. at 828 (White, J., dissenting).

262. *Young*, 481 U.S. at 816 (Scalia, J., concurring) (citing U.S. Const., Art. III, §§ 1, 2).

263. *Id.* at 826.

264. Justice Brennan's opinion in *Young* noted that the Court was relying on its supervisory authority "to avoid the necessity of reaching any constitutional issues." *Young*, 481 U.S. at 810 n.21.

265. *Young*, 481 U.S. at 815–16 (Blackmun, J., concurring).

266. *Id.* at 816 (citing Brotherhood of Locomotive Firemen & Enginemen v. United States, 411 F.2d 312, 319 (5th Cir. 1969)).

267. Beth Nolan, *Removing Conflicts from the Administration of Justice: Conflicts of Interest and Independent Counsels Under the Ethics in Government Act*, 79 GEO. L.J. 1, 33–35 (1990) (footnotes omitted).

268. *See* State v. Camacho, 406 S.E.2d 868, 871 (N.C. 1991) (no citation to *Young*); State v. Woodruff, 392 S.E.2d 434 (N.C. App. 1990), *aff'd*, 399 S.E.2d 114 (N.C. 1991) (per curiam) (same); State v. Bennett, 798 S.W.2d 783, 785–86 (Tenn. Crim. App. 1990) (same); State v. Dunbar, 566 A.2d 970 (Vt. 1989) (same); *cf.* Dick v. Scroggy, 882 F.2d 192 (6th Cir. 1989) (no citation to *Young* in the majority opinion); Hughes v. Bowers, 711 F. Supp. 1574, 1583 (N.D. Ga. 1989), *aff'd*, 896 F.2d 558 (11th Cir. 1990) (without citing *Young*, the court held that "the presence of a special prosecutor hired by the family of the victim is not constitutionally improper per se"); Kerns v. Wolverton, 381 S.E.2d 258, 262 (W. Va. 1989) (without citing *Young*, the West Virginia Supreme Court stated in dicta that "this Court has countenanced the participation of a private prosecutor at trial").

269. Dick v. Scroggy, 882 F.2d 192, 198 n.2 (6th Cir. 1989) (Celebrezze, J., concurring); New Jersey v. Imperiale, 773 F. Supp. 747, 752 (D. N.J. 1991); New Jersey v. Kinder, 701 F. Supp. 486, 490 & n.6 (D. N.J. 1988); Commonwealth v. Hubbard, 777 S.W.2d 882, 883 (Ky. 1989). *See* Sassower v. Sheriff of Westchester County, 824 F.2d 184, 191 (2d Cir. 1987) (*Young* distinguished on the ground that no pretrial investigation or other prosecutorial conduct was required in order to make a criminal contempt determination; a private party's motion for criminal contempt "simply concerns the routine New York State practice of bringing contempts to the attention of the court by motion," and the criminal contempt conviction was enforceable "because the court already had before it all the facts needed to establish Sassower's commission of the multiple contempts" i.e., failure to make a required appearance); *see also* Ex parte Williams, 799 S.W.2d 304, 307 n.10 (Tex. Crim. App. 1990) (noting that *Young* was decided pursuant to the Supreme Court's "supervisory powers," the court stated that "we have found nothing in our rules of procedure or prior case law which requires that prosecution of criminal contempt arising out of Texas civil suits be deemed a separate proceeding from that suit, or be brought on behalf of the State"). It is well-established that U.S. Supreme Court decisions based on the Court's supervisory authority over federal courts are not binding on the states. Smith v. Phillips, 455 U.S. 209, 221 (1982).

270. Person v. Miller, 854 F.2d 656, 663 (4th Cir. 1988). For example, in 1989, the Kentucky Supreme Court held in *Commonwealth v. Hubbard*: "It is our opinion that *Young* does not require a reversal of Hubbard's conviction. Unlike *Young, supra,* the Commonwealth Attorney's office maintained control over the prosecution of the case. It should be noted that the ethical conduct of any private counsel should be measured by the same standard as applied to the Commonwealth Attorney. Private counsel who undertake the duties of prosecution may not become involved in any civil matter related to the criminal prosecution. DR 9–101(B)."

271. *E.g.*, Commonwealth v. Hubbard, 777 S.W.2d 882, 883 (Ky. 1989) ("The Court of Appeals for the Second Circuit has determined in *Sassower v. Sheriff of Westchester County*, 824 F.2d 184, 191 (2nd Cir.1987), that *Young v. United States, ex rel Vuitton et Fils S.A.*, 481 U.S. 787, 107 S. Ct. 2124, 95 L.Ed.2d 740 (1987), the case relied on by our Court of Appeals panel in deciding this issue, is not applicable to state criminal contempt proceedings because it was decided under the U.S. Supreme Court's supervisory authority over federal courts, and not as a federal constitutional ruling. Decisions of the U.S. Supreme Court based on its supervisory authority over federal courts are not binding on the states. *Smith v. Phillips*, 455 U.S. 209, 221, 102 S. Ct. 940, 948, 71 L.Ed.2d 78 (1982). A majority of the U.S. Supreme Court in *Young, supra,* declined to adopt the concurring opinion of Justice Blackmun which found a due process clause violation, but rather, the Court held that, 'We rely today on that (supervisory) authority to hold that counsel for a party that is the beneficiary of a court order may not be appointed as prosecutor in a contempt action alleging a violation of that order.' *Young*, at 481 U.S. at 808, 107 S. Ct. at 2137, 95 L.Ed.2d 759.").

272. Wilson v. Wilson, 984 S.W.2d 898, 902 (Tenn. 1998).

273. Eichhorn v. Kelley, 111 P.3d 544, 547 (Colo. Ct. App. 2004); *see also* Cronan ex rel. State v. Cronan, 774 A.2d 866, 876 (R.I. 2001) ("[W]e note that *Young* relied upon the United States Supreme Court's supervisory powers over lower federal courts. Because that decision was not based upon the United States Constitution, it does not bind us here.").

274. Priceline.com Inc. v. City of Anaheim, 103 Cal. Rptr.3d 521, 535 (Cal. Ct. App., 4th Dist. 2010) (citing *Young*, 481 U.S. at 806 n.17); *see also* East v. Scott, 55 F.3d 996, 1000 n.2 (5th Cir. 1995) ("*Young* was decided under the Court's supervisory power over federal courts, not as a matter of federal constitutional law"). *Cf.* United States v. Arpaio, 887 F.3d 979, 982 (9th Cir. 2018) ("The long-standing practice of the

United States Supreme Court is to use its inherent authority to appoint disinterested counsel to represent the position taken by the United States below when the United States refused to defend its prior position.").

275. Person v. Miller, 854 F.2d 656, 663 (4th Cir. 1988) (quoting *Young*, 107 S. Ct. at 2137 n.17).

276. Chevron v. Donziger, 974 F. Supp.2d 362, 384 (S.D.N.Y. 2014) ("Upon consideration of all of the evidence, including the credibility of the witnesses—though several of the most important declined to testify—the Court finds that Donziger began his involvement in this controversy with a desire to improve conditions in the area in which his Ecuadorian clients live. To be sure, he sought also to do well for himself while doing good for others, but there was nothing wrong with that. In the end, however, he and the Ecuadorian lawyers he led corrupted the Lago Agrio case. They submitted fraudulent evidence. They coerced one judge, first to use a court-appointed, supposedly impartial, "global expert" to make an overall damages assessment and, then, to appoint to that important role a man whom Donziger hand-picked and paid to 'totally play ball' with the LAPs. They then paid a Colorado consulting firm secretly to write all or most of the global expert's report, falsely presented the report as the work of the court-appointed and supposedly impartial expert, and told half-truths or worse to U.S. courts in attempts to prevent exposure of that and other wrongdoing. Ultimately, the LAP team wrote the Lago Agrio court's Judgment themselves and promised $500,000 to the Ecuadorian judge to rule in their favor and sign their judgment. If ever there were a case warranting equitable relief with respect to a judgment procured by fraud, this is it.").

277. Chevron Corp. v. Donziger, 833 F.3d 74, 151 (2d Cir. 2016) ("We have considered all of the arguments of Donziger and the LAP Representatives on this appeal and have found in them no basis for dismissal or reversal. The judgment of the district court is affirmed.").

278. 3 Richard W. Blackburn & Jeffrey J. Binder, Successful Partnering Between Inside and Outside Counsel § 47:27 n.35 (April 2021 Update); *see also* Chevron Corp. v. Donziger, Nos. 18-855-cv (L), 18-2191-cv, 19-1584-cv, RICO Bus. Disp. Guide ¶ 13,477 (2d Cir. Mar. 4, 2021) ("We conclude that the district court did not err in awarding costs to Chevron under Federal Rule of Civil Procedure 54(d). We also affirm the district court's finding that Donziger violated the Injunction in several respects and its judgment of civil contempt relating to those violations. However, we hold that the Injunction, previously affirmed by this Court and clear and far-reaching on its own terms, was insufficiently clear and unambiguous, when read alongside the district court's explanation of that Injunction in a subsequent opinion, in prohibiting Donziger from raising funds by selling interests in the Ecuadorian Judgment. Thus, we conclude that the district court erred in finding Donziger in contempt for engaging in that conduct.").

279. Chevron Corp. v. Donziger, 990 F.3d 191, 196 (2d Cir. 2021).

280. Sharon Lerner, "Steven Donziger Describes Contempt Case as a 'Charade' as Trial Comes to a Close," The Intercept, May 17, 2021, https://theintercept.com/2021/05/17/chevron-steven-donziger-trial/.

281. *Compare* United States v. Arpaio, 887 F.3d 979, 981 (9th Cir. 2018) ("[W]e conclude that we have the authority to appoint counsel under Federal Rule of Criminal Procedure 42, which prescribes procedures for dealing with criminal contempt.... In Rule 42(a)(2)'s most common application, the district court appoints a special prosecutor to investigate and try a criminal contempt when the government declines to perform that function. But the operation of Rule 42(a)(2) is not confined to investigations and trials in the district court. A private attorney appointed under the rule has the authority to act as a special prosecutor not only in the district court but also in the court of appeals. Our attention has not been directed to, nor have we found, a case in which a special prosecutor was appointed by a court of appeals after the government declined to oppose the contemnor's arguments on appeal. However, we see no reason why such appointment should not take place under Rule 42(a)(2).") (citing various authorities, including Hollingsworth v. Perry, 570 U.S. 693, 725 (2013) (Kennedy, J., dissenting) ("Federal Rule of Criminal Procedure 42(a)(2) allows a court to appoint a private attorney to investigate and prosecute potential instances of criminal contempt.")) *and Arpaio*, 887 F.2d at 982 ("The long-standing practice of the United States Supreme Court is to use its inherent authority to appoint disinterested counsel to represent the position taken by the United States below when the United States refuses to defend its prior position. The Supreme Court has relied on its inherent judicial power to appoint appellate counsel specifically in the context of contempt. In *United States v. Providence Journal Co.*, 485 U.S. 693, 108 S. Ct. 1502, 99 L.Ed.2d 785 (1988), the Court held that a special prosecutor appointed under Rule 42 needs the permission of the Solicitor General to litigate a contempt case in the Supreme Court. The Court noted that the

independence of the judiciary 'might appear to be threatened' by this holding, especially in cases in which the contemnor was convicted by the district court, the Court of Appeals affirmed, and the Solicitor General refused to either defend the judgment below or authorize the special prosecutor to do so. However, the Supreme Court explained that '[t]his threat… is inconsequential' because of the Court's inherent authority to appoint an amicus to appear before the Court to defend the judgment below: '[I]t is well within this Court's authority to appoint an *amicus curiae* to file briefs and present oral argument in support of that judgment.'") (citations omitted) *and* James A. Cohen, *Self-Love and the Judicial Power to Appoint a Special Prosecutor*, 16 HOFSTRA L. REV. 23, 23 (1987) ("Judicial appointment of private attorneys as special prosecutors has occurred and is permitted to occur in a variety of contexts other than when the executive branch is faced with a potential or actual conflict of interest. Until recently, the Second Circuit Court of Appeals and, of course, district courts within the Second Circuit, have interpreted Rule 42(b) of the Federal Rules of Criminal Procedure to permit judicial appointment of a private attorney to prosecute conduct allegedly violative of a court order as criminal contempt.") *with id.* at 24–25 ("Although there is no federal statute or rule authorizing judicial appointment of private attorneys as criminal prosecutors, the court [in *Young v. U.S. ex rel. Vuitton et Fils*] held that 'courts possess inherent authority to initiate contempt proceedings for disobedience to their orders, authority which necessarily encompasses the ability to appoint a private attorney to prosecute the contempt.' Relying on notions of 'inherent authority' and 'necessity,' eight justices agreed that courts have the power to appoint a private attorney to prosecute conduct constituting a violation of a court order as criminal contempt. The Court reversed petitioners' convictions because the particular attorney appointed to investigate and prosecute the contempt was *interested*, that is, he was also the attorney for the party on whose behalf the court order was secured.") (italics in original) *and* David E. Rigney, Participation of private counsel for beneficiary of court order allegedly violated by defendant, in prosecution of federal criminal contempt proceeding, 96 A.L.R. Fed. 519 § 1 (1990) ("The court in *Polo Fashions, Inc. v Stock Buyers International, Inc.* (1985, CA6 Ohio) 760 F2d 698, 226 USPQ 117, cert den 482 US 905, 96 L Ed 2d 373, 107 S Ct 2480, held that it was an abuse of discretion for a court to appoint an attorney for the beneficiary of an injunction granted in the underlying litigation, concerning trademark infringement, to conduct criminal contempt proceedings as sole or primary counsel, although it stated that these attorneys could assist either a United States Attorney or disinterested court-appointed counsel in such a prosecution. Upon motion of the interested party, the District Court had entered an order, pursuant to Rule 42(b) of the Federal Rules of Criminal Procedure, appointing counsel to prosecute a criminal contempt charge. All appointed counsel had been attorneys for the beneficiary of the underlying injunction, while no one from the office of the United States Attorney appeared in the contempt proceedings. While the court observed that the Second Circuit had consistently approved the appointment of opposing counsel to prosecute criminal contempt actions, it stated that Rule 42(b) did not explicitly permit prosecution of a criminal contempt by the attorney for a party in the underlying proceedings, since by its terms the Rule merely permitted the court to give notice to a defendant by an order to show cause or an order of arrest on application of an attorney appointed by the court for that purpose. The practicality of having an attorney familiar with the facts of the underlying litigation involved in a criminal contempt prosecution was obvious, said the court, but our system of justice recognizes higher values than speed and efficiency.")

282. United States v. Donziger, No. 19-CR-561 (LAP), No. 11-CV-691 (LAK), 2021 WL 1845104, at *1-2 (S.D.N.Y. May 7, 2021).

283. United States v. Donziger, No. 19-CR-561 (LAP), No. 11-CV-691 (LAK), 2021 WL 1865376, at *1-10 (S.D.N.Y. May 10, 2021).

284. United States v. Donziger, No. 19-CR-561 (LAP), No. 11-CV-691 (LAK), 2021 WL 1820190, at *1-2 (S.D.N.Y. May 6, 2021).

285. United States v. Donziger, No. 19-CR-561 (LAP), No. 11-CV-691 (LAK), 2021 WL 1820190, at *5-8 (S.D.N.Y. May 6, 2021) (quoting *Young*, 481 U.S. at 796 (emphasis added)); *see also id.* at *9 ("In his notice of motion, Mr. Donziger, for a third time, requests that the Court recuse itself. (*See* dkt. no. 258.) Mr. Donziger does not elaborate much on that argument in his memorandum of law, however, offering only that the Judge Kaplan 'hand-picked private prosecutors . . . who also appear to have personal ties to the presiding judge, having served on a law school alumni committee together.' (Dkt. no. 259 at 7.) The

Court understands Mr. Donziger to be referring to the undersigned's and Ms. Glavin's membership on the Board of Directors of the Fordham Law School Alumni Association ('FLAA'), an organization with more than 100 members. Canon 4 of the Code of Conduct of United States Judges expressly authorizes a judge to 'engage in extrajudicial activities, including law-related pursuits and civic, charitable, educational, religious, social, financial, fiduciary, and governmental activities.' The undersigned's involvement with the FLAA provides no basis for recusal.").

286. Bob Van Voris, "Chevron Gadfly Donziger Faces Criminal Charges in N.Y. Trial," Bloomberg, May 10, 2021, https://www.bloomberg.com/news/articles/2021-05-10/after-8-6-billion-ruling-lawyer-who-sued-chevron-goes-on-trial; Sharon Lerner, "Law Students Denounce Chevron's Law Firm over Steven Donziger Case," The Intercept, Apr. 7, 2021, https://theintercept.com/2021/04/07/chevron-steven-donziger-law-gibson-dunn-boycott/.

287. Sharon Lerner, "Steven Donziger Describes Contempt Case as a 'Charade' as Trial Comes to a Close," The Intercept, May 17, 2021, https://theintercept.com/2021/05/17/chevron-steven-donziger-trial/.

288. Letter dated June 22, 2021 from Martin Garbus, Esq. to Hon. Loretta Preska, pp. 1–2. In a submission to the Court dated June 8, 2021, Martin Garbus—counsel for the defendant in the criminal contempt case—submitted proposed "Findings and Conclusions and Offer of Proof." In that document, Garbus wrote that "[f]or the first time in the history of the United States, a private law firm with substantial ties to the oil and gas industry has been granted the powers of the United States to prosecute an adverse party and human rights attorney." "Even more disturbing," Garbus wrote, "is that this appears to be the nation's first corporate prosecution given that the oil company (Chevron) against whom Mr. Donziger won a large pollution judgement in Ecuador is a client of the very law firm (Seward & Kissel) now prosecuting him after the charges were declined by the U.S. attorney." The proposed findings stated, among other things, that "the appointment of the private law firm Seward & Kissel to prosecute Mr. Donziger violates the principles set forth in *United States ex rel Vuitton et Fils S.A.*, 481 U.S. 787 (1987), which requires a disinterested prosecution"; that "the lead private prosecutor, Rita Glavin, did not disclose her law firm's flagrant conflict of interest until pressed, eventually revealing that her firm had Chevron has a client as recently as 2018 and that the client relationship still exists"; that "the private prosecutors submit to no supervisory authority in the Department of Justice, or anywhere else, creating what appears to be for the first time a private prosecutor floating out in middle of nowhere billing hundreds of thousands of dollars to U.S. taxpayers"; that "the private prosecutor has refused to disclose evidence of her unethical, secret, *ex parte* communications with the charging judge (Kaplan), saying only that they did not discuss prosecution strategy"; and that "Mr. Donziger is the only lawyer in U.S. history to be prosecuted for criminal contempt after inviting the court to impose a civil contempt so he could have a direct appeal of the discovery order (which covers counts I through III of Judge Kaplan's charging document)." Findings and Conclusions and Offer of Proof, United States v. Steven Donziger, 11 Cr. 0691 (LAP), S.D.N.Y., https://static1.squarespace.com/static/5ac2615b8f5130fda4340fcb/t/60c0f3966b33d51521819c4c/1623258008452/2021-06-08-defense-proposed-findings-counts-i-iii.pdf, pp. 1–3; *see also id.* at 3–4 ("Underscoring the many questions surrounding this Chevron-funded attack, Mr. Donziger's case is the *first* criminal prosecution by a private prosecutor in the 232-year history of the Southern District of New York, which was founded in 1789 as our nation's first court. Apart from a single case in the Eastern District in 1994 involving well-known defense lawyer Bruce Cutler, in which a private prosecutor was appointed as a *protection* for Cutler's due process rights given the famously antagonistic relationship between him and the federal prosecutor, there has been no other such case.") (italics in original); *id.* at 7–8 ("There are thousands of practicing criminal law attorneys in the New York Metropolitan area, many of whom have significant federal prosecution experience. Judge Kaplan, acting alone, made the decision of who to appoint as private prosecutor for this case. Judge Kaplan again has refused to explain the basis of his decision-making. He selected an attorney and law firm that had an attorney-client relationship with Chevron. The law firm, Seward & Kissel, has a substantial oil and gas industry practice and, if Chevron views their performance in this lawsuit favorably, is poised to receive significant business in the future. Judge Kaplan also selected an individual attorney from that firm, Rita Glavin, to lead the private prosecution. Glavin is known for playing a key role in one of the most notorious prosecutorial misconduct cases in recent decades. She also serves on the board of a Fordham Law School alumni committee with none other than Judge Preska ....") (citations omitted).

289. Debra Cassens Weiss, "'It's time to pay the piper': Ex-lawyer found guilty of criminal contempt in long-running Chevron battle," ABA J., July 26, 2021, https://www.abajournal.com/news/article/judge-finds-disbarred-lawyer-guilty-of-criminal-contempt-in-long-running-chevron-battle.

290. "Findings of Fact & Conclusions of Law," United States v. Donziger, July 26, 2021, *available at* https://www.abajournal.com/files/PreskaDonziger.pdf. The opinion of U.S. District Judge Loretta A. Preska is also available on Westlaw. United States v. Donziger, No. 19-CR-561 (LAP), No. 11-CV-691 (LAK), 2021 WL 3141893 (S.D.N.Y., July 26, 2021).

291. Jason Grant, "Donziger Is Convicted of Criminal Contempt of court," N.Y. L.J., July 21, 2021, https://www.law.com/newyorklawjournal/2021/07/26/donziger-is-convicted-of-criminal-contempt-of-court/?slreturn=20210809122438.

292. "Findings of Fact & Conclusions of Law," July 26, 2021, p. 123 (italics in original), *available at* https://www.abajournal.com/files/PreskaDonziger.pdf.

293. *Id.* at 128.

294. Sebastien Malo, "After Contempt Conviction, Attorney Donziger Asks for New Trial," Reuters, Aug. 4, 2021, https://www.reuters.com/legal/government/after-contempt-conviction-attorney-donziger-asks-new-trial-2021-08-04/.

295. *Young*, 481 U.S. at 809 n.21.

296. Polo Fashion, Inc. v. Stock Buyers Int'l, Inc., 760 F.2d 698 (6th Cir. 1985), *cert. denied*, 482 U.S. 905 (1987).

297. 411 F.2d 312, 319 (5th Cir. 1969) (*cited in Young*, 481 U.S. at 808 n.19).

298. 379 F.2d 709 (4th Cir. 1967).

299. *Id.* at 714–15; *see also* Cantrell v. Commonwealth, 329 S.E.2d 22, 26 (Va. 1985), *cert. denied*, 496 U.S. 911 (1990) (*citing Ganger*) (a private prosecutor having a civil interest in the case so infects the prosecution with the possibility that "private vengeance has been substituted for impartial application of the criminal law, that prejudice to the defendant need not be shown"); *id.* at 27 (harmless error analysis inapplicable).

300. 422 U.S. 13 (1975).

301. 426 U.S. 610 (1976).

302. 348 U.S. 11 (1954).

303. 349 U.S. 133 (1955).

304. *Accord Kent v. United States*, 383 U.S. 541 (1966) (the Court stated that certain minimum due process protections apply to juveniles tried under the Juvenile Court Act, without explicitly adopting them as due process rights); In re Gault, 387 U.S. 1 (1967) (due process clause applies to juvenile delinquency hearings).

305. 153 N.W.2d 825, 828 n.3 (Minn. 1967).

306. 384 U.S. 373 (1966).

307. *Peterson*, 153 N.W.2d at 828.

308. *Compare* Cheff v. Schnackenberg, 384 U.S. 373 (1966) (establishing a right to a jury trial for nonpetty contempts under the Court's supervisory authority) *with* Bloom v. Illinois, 391 U.S. 194 (1968) (the right to a jury trial was adopted as a due process right).

Chapter 8 Notes

1. U.S. Const., amend. V.

2. U.S. Const., amend. XIV, § 1. It is firmly established that prosecutors' actions "may constitute state action within the purview of the Fourteenth Amendment." Mooney v. Holohan, 294 U.S. 103 (1935); *see also* Andrew Sidman, Comment, *The Outmoded Concept of Private Prosecution*, 25 Am. U.L. Rev. 754, 787–88 (1976) (same).

3. United States v. Haymond, 139 S. Ct. 2369, 2376 (2019); *see also* Hurst v. Florida, 577 U.S. 92, 97 (2016) ("The Sixth Amendment provides: 'In all criminal prosecutions, the accused shall enjoy the right to a speedy and public trial, by an impartial jury....' This right, in conjunction with the Due Process

Clause, requires that each element of a crime be proved to a jury beyond a reasonable doubt.") (citations omitted); Alleyne v. United States, 570 U.S. 99, 104 (2013) ("The Sixth Amendment provides that those 'accused' of a 'crime' have a right to a trial 'by an impartial jury.' This right, in conjunction with the Due Process Clause, requires that each element of a crime be proved to the jury beyond a reasonable doubt."); *see also* Alafair S. Burke, *Prosecutorial Agnosticism*, 8 Ohio St. J. Crim. L. 79, 79 (2010) ("Most legal ethicists maintain that an ethical prosecutor should pursue criminal charges against a defendant only if the prosecutor personally believes that the defendant is guilty."); Bruce A. Green, *Why Should Prosecutors "Seek Justice"?*, 26 Fordham Urb. L.J. 607, 640–41 (1999) ("Prosecutors have the power, freedom and responsibility to make decisions for the sovereign in the criminal context.... They must satisfy themselves of an individual's guilt as a precondition to determining that the conviction of an individual is an end to be sought on behalf of the state or the federal government."); Bennett L. Gershman, *A Moral Standard for the Prosecutor's Exercise of the Charging Decision*, 20 Fordham Urb. L.J. 513, 522 (1993) ("[B]efore making the ultimate decision to charge, the prosecutor should then assure herself that she is morally certain that the defendant is both factually and legally guilty.... [T]he prosecutor who acknowledges moral uncertainty about a defendant's guilty but decides nonetheless to bring charges, violates the prosecutor's special obligation to seek justice, and tacitly invites the system to miscarry.").

4. Bracy v. Gramley, 520 U.S. 899, 904–05 (1997) (citations omitted).

5. North Carolina Dep't of Revenue v. The Kimberly Rice Kaestner 1992 Family Trust, 139 S. Ct. 2213, 2219 (2019).

6. Mathews v. Eldridge, 424 U.S. 319, 333 (1976) (citation omitted). The Supreme Court "consistently has held that some form of hearing is required before an individual is finally deprived of a property interest." *Id.*; *accord* Wolff v. McDonnell, 418 U.S. 539, 557–58 (1974).

7. Jennings v. Rodriguez, 138 U.S. 830, 852 (2018); Morrisey v. Brewer, 408 U.S. 471, 481 (1972); *see also* Cafeteria & Restaurant Workers Union v. McElroy, 367 U.S. 886, 895 (1961) ("[C]onsideration of what procedures due process may require under any given set of circumstances must begin with a determination of the precise nature of the government function involved as well as of the private interest that has been affected by governmental action.").

8. Fuentes v. Shevin, 407 U.S. 67, 97 (1972).

9. Medina v. California, 505 U.S. 437, 451 (1992) (citations omitted).

10. Betterman v. Montana, 136 S. Ct. 1609, 1613 (2016) (citing United States v. Lovasco, 431 U.S. 783, 789 (1977)).

11. *Id.*

12. Alabama v. Smith, 490 U.S. 794, 800 n.3 (1989) ("We adopted a similar prophylactic rule to guard against vindictiveness by the prosecutor at the postconviction stage in *Blackledge v. Perry*, 417 U.S. 21, 94 S. Ct. 2098, 40 L.Ed.2d 628 (1974). There the prosecutor charged the defendant with a felony when the latter availed himself of *de novo* review of his initial conviction of a misdemeanor for the same conduct. He received a sentence of five to seven years for the felony compared to the 6-month sentence he had received for the misdemeanor. On these facts, we concluded that a presumption of vindictiveness arose analogous to that in *Pearce* because the 'prosecutor clearly has a considerable stake in discouraging convicted misdemeanants from appealing.'"); *see also* U.S. v. Hollywood Motor Car Co., 458 U.S. 263, 267–68 (1982):

> *Blackledge v. Perry*, 417 U.S. 21, 94 S. Ct. 2098, 40 L.Ed.2d 628 (1974), on which respondents base the merits of their claim of vindictive prosecution, was an application of the principles announced in *North Carolina v. Pearce*, 395 U.S. 711, 89 S. Ct. 2072, 23 L.Ed.2d 656 (1969), to conduct on the part of a prosecutor. In *Perry* the defendant had been convicted in a state court of limited jurisdiction, and had exercised his statutory right to a *de novo* appeal to the state court of general jurisdiction. Prior to the commencement of the latter trial, the prosecutor obtained an indictment charging the defendant with crimes more severe than those for which he was initially convicted. Because the facts suggested "a realistic likelihood of 'vindictiveness,'" 417 U.S., at 27, 94 S. Ct., at 2102, we deemed it necessary to apply the "prophylactic rule of *Pearce*," *id.*, at 26, 94 S. Ct., at 2102, in order to discourage retaliation by the State for the defendant's exercise of his procedural right.

See also United States v. Goodwin, 457 U.S. 368, 380–84 (1982):

There is good reason to be cautious before adopting an inflexible presumption of prosecutorial vindictiveness in a pretrial setting. In the course of preparing a case for trial, the prosecutor may uncover additional information that suggests a basis for further prosecution or he simply may come to realize that information possessed by the State has a broader significance. At this stage of the proceedings, the prosecutor's assessment of the proper extent of prosecution may not have crystallized. In contrast, once a trial begins—and certainly by the time a conviction has been obtained—it is much more likely that the State has discovered and assessed all of the information against an accused and has made a determination, on the basis of that information, of the extent to which he should be prosecuted. Thus, a change in the charging decision made after an initial trial is completed is much more likely to be improperly motivated than is a pretrial decision.

In addition, a defendant before trial is expected to invoke procedural rights that inevitably impose some "burden" on the prosecutor. Defense counsel routinely file pretrial motions to suppress evidence; to challenge the sufficiency and form of an indictment; to plead an affirmative defense; to request psychiatric services; to obtain access to government files; to be tried by jury. It is unrealistic to assume that a prosecutor's probable response to such motions is to seek to penalize and to deter. The invocation of procedural rights is an integral part of the adversary process in which our criminal justice system operates.

Thus, the timing of the prosecutor's action in this case suggests that a presumption of vindictiveness is not warranted. A prosecutor should remain free before trial to exercise the broad discretion entrusted to him to determine the extent of the societal interest in prosecution. An initial decision should not freeze future conduct. As we made clear in *Bordenkircher*, the initial charges filed by a prosecutor may not reflect the extent to which an individual is legitimately subject to prosecution.

The nature of the right asserted by the respondent confirms that a presumption of vindictiveness is not warranted in this case. After initially expressing an interest in plea negotiation, respondent decided not to plead guilty and requested a trial by jury in District Court. In doing so, he forced the Government to bear the burdens and uncertainty of a trial. This Court in *Bordenkircher* made clear that the mere fact that a defendant refuses to plead guilty and forces the government to prove its case is insufficient to warrant a presumption that subsequent changes in the charging decision are unjustified. Respondent argues that such a presumption is warranted in this case, however, because he not only requested a trial—he requested a trial by jury.

We cannot agree. The distinction between a bench trial and a jury trial does not compel a special presumption of prosecutorial vindictiveness whenever additional charges are brought after a jury is demanded. To be sure, a jury trial is more burdensome than a bench trial. The defendant may challenge the selection of the venire; the jury itself must be impaneled; witnesses and arguments must be prepared more carefully to avoid the danger of a mistrial. These matters are much less significant, however, than the facts that before either a jury or a judge the State must present its full case against the accused and the defendant is entitled to offer a full defense. As compared to the complete trial *de novo* at issue in *Blackledge*, a jury trial—as opposed to a bench trial—does not require duplicative expenditures of prosecutorial resources before a final judgment may be obtained. Moreover, unlike the trial judge in *Pearce*, no party is asked "to do over what it thought it had already done correctly." A prosecutor has no "personal stake" in a bench trial and thus no reason to engage in "self-vindication" upon a defendant's request for a jury trial. Perhaps most importantly, the institutional bias against the retrial of a decided question that supported the decisions in *Pearce* and *Blackledge* simply has no counterpart in this case.

There is an opportunity for vindictiveness, as there was in *Colten* and *Chaffin*. Those cases demonstrate, however, that a mere opportunity for vindictiveness is insufficient to justify the imposition of a prophylactic rule. As *Blackledge* makes clear, "the Due Process Clause is not offended by all possibilities of increased punishment... but only by those that pose a realistic likelihood of 'vindictiveness.'" 417 U.S., at 27, 94 S. Ct., at 2102. The possibility that a prosecutor would respond to a defendant's pretrial demand for a jury trial by bringing charges not in the public interest that could be explained only as a penalty imposed on the defendant is so *unlikely* that a presumption of vindictiveness certainly is not warranted.

13. Kyles v. Whitley, 514 U.S. 419, 432–34 (1995):

The prosecution's affirmative duty to disclose evidence favorable to a defendant can trace its origins to early 20th-century strictures against misrepresentation and is of course most prominently associated with this Court's decision in *Brady v. Maryland,* 373 U.S. 83, 83 S. Ct. 1194, 10 L.Ed.2d 215 (1963). See *id.,* at 86, 83 S. Ct., at 1196 (relying on *Mooney v. Holohan,* 294 U.S. 103, 112, 55 S. Ct. 340, 341–342, 79 L.Ed. 791 (1935), and *Pyle v. Kansas,* 317 U.S. 213, 215–216, 63 S. Ct. 177, 178–179, 87 L.Ed. 214 (1942)). *Brady* held "that the suppression by the prosecution of evidence favorable to an accused upon request violates due process where the evidence is material either to guilt or to punishment, irrespective of the good faith or bad faith of the prosecution." 373 U.S., at 87, 83 S. Ct., at 1196–1197; see *Moore v. Illinois,* 408 U.S. 786, 794–795, 92 S. Ct. 2562, 2567–2568, 33 L.Ed.2d 706 1972). In *United States v. Agurs,* 427 U.S. 97, 96 S. Ct. 2392, 49 L.Ed.2d 342 (1976), however, it became clear that a defendant's failure to request favorable evidence did not leave the Government free of all obligation. There, the Court distinguished three situations in which a *Brady* claim might arise: first, where previously undisclosed evidence revealed that the prosecution introduced trial testimony that it knew or should have known was perjured, 427 U.S., at 103–104, 96 S. Ct., at 2397–2398; second, where the Government failed to accede to a defense request for disclosure of some specific kind of exculpatory evidence, *id.,* at 104–107, 96 S. Ct., at 2398–2399; and third, where the Government failed to volunteer exculpatory evidence never requested, or requested only in a general way. The Court found a duty on the part of the Government even in this last situation, though only when suppression of the evidence would be "of sufficient significance to result in the denial of the defendant's right to a fair trial." *Id.,* at 108, 96 S. Ct., at 2400.

In the third prominent case on the way to current *Brady* law, *United States v. Bagley,* 473 U.S. 667, 105 S. Ct. 3375, 87 L.Ed.2d 481 (1985), the Court disavowed any difference between exculpatory and impeachment evidence for *Brady* purposes, and it abandoned the distinction between the second and third *Agurs* circumstances, *i.e.,* the "specific-request" and "general- or no-request" situations. *Bagley* held that regardless of request, favorable evidence is material, and constitutional error results from its suppression by the government, "if there is a reasonable probability that, had the evidence been disclosed to the defense, the result of the proceeding would have been different." 473 U.S., at 682, 105 S. Ct., at 3383 (opinion of Blackmun, J.); *id.,* at 685, 105 S. Ct., at 3385 (White, J., concurring in part and concurring in judgment).

14. Salinas v. Texas, 570 U.S. 178, 188 n.3 (2013) (discussing the holding of *Doyle v. Ohio,* 426 U.S. 610, 617–18 (1976) but noting "that rule does not apply where a suspect has not received the warnings' implicit promise that any silence will not be used against him"). In *Darden v. Wainwright* (1986), the Supreme Court observed that a prosecutor's improper comments will be held to violate the U.S. Constitution only if they "'so infect the trial with unfairness as to make the resulting conviction a denial of due process.'" Darden v. Wainwright, 477 U.S. 168, 181 (1986) (quoting Donnelly v. DeChristoforo, 416 U.S. 637, 643 (1974)); *accord* Parker v. Matthews, 567 U.S. 37, 45 (2012).

15. J. McIntyre Machinery, Ltd. v. NiCastro, 564 U.S. 873, 877 (2011).

16. Caperton v. A.T. Massey Coal Co., Inc., 556 U.S. 868, 876 (2009) (quoting Murchison, 349 U.S. 133, 136 (1955)); *see also id.* at 876–77 ("The *Tumey* Court concluded that the Due Process Clause incorporated the common-law rule that a judge must recuse himself when he has 'a direct, personal, substantial, pecuniary interest' in a case. *Ibid.* This rule reflects the maxim that '[n]o man is allowed to be a judge in his own cause; because his interest would certainly bias his judgment, and, not improbably, corrupt his integrity.' The Federalist No. 10, p. 59 (J. Cooke ed.1961) (J. Madison); see Frank, Disqualification of Judges, 56 Yale L.J. 605, 611–612 (1947). Under this rule, 'disqualification for bias or prejudice was not permitted'; those matters were left to statutes and judicial codes. *Lavoie, supra,* at 820, 106 S. Ct. 1580; see also Part IV, *infra* (discussing judicial codes). Personal bias or prejudice 'alone would not be sufficient basis for imposing a constitutional requirement under the Due Process Clause.' *Lavoie, supra,* at 820, 106 S. Ct. 1580."); *id.* at 877 ("As new problems have emerged that were not discussed at common law, however, the Court has

identified additional instances which, as an objective matter, require recusal. These are circumstances 'in which experience teaches that the probability of actual bias on the part of the judge or decisionmaker is too high to be constitutionally tolerable.' *Withrow,* 421 U.S., at 47, 95 S. Ct. 1456."); Withrow v. Larkin, 421 U.S. 35, 47 (1975) ("Not only is a biased decisionmaker constitutionally unacceptable but 'our system of law has always endeavored to prevent even the probability of unfairness.' In pursuit of this end, various situations have been identified in which experience teaches that the probability of actual bias on the part of the judge or decisionmaker is too high to be constitutionally tolerable. Among these cases are those in which the adjudicator has a pecuniary interest in the outcome and in which he has been the target of personal abuse or criticism from the party before him.") (citations omitted).

17. Cone v. Bell, 556 U.S. 449 (2009).

18. *Id.* at 451 (citing *United States v. Agurs,* 427 U.S. 97, 111, 96 S. Ct. 2392, 49 L.Ed.2d 342 (1976) (quoting *Berger v. United States,* 295 U.S. 78, 88, 55 S. Ct. 629, 79 L.Ed. 1314 (1935)); *see also* Rivera v. Illinois, 556 U.S. 148, 158 (2009) ("The Due Process Clause, our decisions instruct, safeguards not the meticulous observance of state procedural prescriptions, but 'the fundamental elements of fairness in a criminal trial.'") (quoting *Spencer v. Texas,* 385 U.S. 554, 563–564, 87 S. Ct. 648, 17 L.Ed.2d 606 (1967)).

19. 425 U.S. 501 (1976).

20. *Id.* at 502.

21. *Id.* at 512.

22. *Id.* at 512–13.

23. *See supra* text (quoting the language of the U.S. Constitution's Due Process Clauses). *See also* Bracy v. Gramley, 520 U.S. 899, 904 (1997) ("[T]he Due Process Clause of the Fourteenth Amendment establishes a constitutional floor, not a uniform standard. Instead, these questions are, in most cases, answered by common law, statute, or the professional standards of the bench and bar.") (citing Aetna Life Ins. Co. v. Lavoie, 475 U.S. 813, 828 (1986); Tumey v. Ohio, 273 U.S. 510, 523 (1927); 28 U.S.C. §§ 144, 455; ABA Code of Judicial Conduct, Canon 3C(1)(a) (1980)).

24. Caperton v. A.T. Massey Coal Co., Inc., 556 U.S. 868, 876 (2009).

25. Sanchez-Llamas v. Oregon, 548 U.S. 331, 350 (2006) ("A foreign national detained on suspicion of crime, like anyone else in our country, enjoys under our system the protections of the Due Process Clause. Among other things, he is entitled to an attorney, and is protected against compelled self-incrimination."); *compare* United States v. Gonzalez-Lopez, 548 U.S. 140, 146 (2006) ("'The Constitution guarantees a fair trial through the Due Process Clauses, but it defines the basic elements of a fair trial largely through the several provisions of the Sixth Amendment, including the Counsel Clause.'") (quoting Strickland v. Washington, 466 U.S. 668, 684–85 (1984)).

26. Betterman v. Montana, 136 S. Ct. 1609, 1613 (2016) (citing United States v. Lovasco, 431 U.S. 783, 789, 795 n.17 (1977)). In *United States v. Lovasco,* the case cited in *Betterman,* the Supreme Court discussed the Due Process Clause in the context of deciding that a prosecutor did not violate due process in filing charges after a lapse of time. *Lovasco,* 431 U.S. at 790 ("[T]he Due Process Clause does not permit courts to abort criminal prosecutions simply because they disagree with a prosecutor's judgment as to when to seek an indictment. Judges are not free, in defining 'due process,' to impose on law enforcement officials our 'personal and private notions' of fairness and to 'disregard the limits that bind judges in their judicial function.' Rochin v. California, 342 U.S. 165, 170, 72 S. Ct. 205, 209, 96 L.Ed. 183 (1952). Our task is more circumscribed. We are to determine only whether the action complained of here, compelling respondent to stand trial after the Government delayed indictment to investigate further violates those 'fundamental conceptions of justice which lie at the base of our civil and political institutions,' Mooney v. Holohan, 294 U.S. 103, 112, 55 S. Ct. 340, 342, 79 L.Ed. 791 (1935), and which define 'the community's sense of fair play and decency,' Rochin v. California, supra, 342 U.S., at 173, 72 S. Ct. at 210. See also Ham v. South Carolina, 409 U.S. 524, 526, 93 S. Ct. 848, 850, 35 L.Ed.2d 46 (1973); Lisenba v. California, 314 U.S. 219, 236, 62 S. Ct. 280, 289, 86 L.Ed. 166 (1941); Hebert v. Louisiana, 272 U.S. 312, 316, 47 S. Ct. 103, 104, 71 L.Ed. 270 (1926); Hurtado v. California, 110 U.S. 516, 535, 4 S. Ct. 111, 120, 28 L.Ed. 232 (1884)."); *Lovasco,* 431 U.S. at 790–92 ("It requires no extended argument to establish that prosecutors do not deviate from 'fundamental conceptions of justice' when they defer seeking indictments until they have probable cause to believe an accused is guilty; indeed it is unprofessional conduct for a prosecutor to recommend an indictment on

less than probable cause. It should be equally obvious that prosecutors are under no duty to file charges as soon as probable cause exists but before they are satisfied they will be able to establish the suspect's guilt beyond a reasonable doubt. To impose such a duty 'would have a deleterious effect both upon the rights of the accused and upon the ability of society to protect itself,' United States v. Ewell, supra, 383 U.S., at 120, 86 S. Ct., at 776. From the perspective of potential defendants, requiring prosecutions to commence when probable cause is established is undesirable because it would increase the likelihood of unwarranted charges being filed, and would add to the time during which defendants stand accused but untried.... Thus, no one's interests would be well served by compelling prosecutors to initiate prosecutions as soon as they are legally entitled to do so."); *id.* at 795–96 ("investigative delay is fundamentally unlike delay undertaken by the Government solely 'to gain tactical advantage over the accused,' United States v. Marion, 404 U.S., at 324, 92 S. Ct., at 465, precisely because investigative delay is not so one-sided. Rather than deviating from elementary standards of 'fair play and decency,' a prosecutor abides by them if he refuses to seek indictments until he is completely satisfied that he should prosecute and will be able promptly to establish guilt beyond a reasonable doubt. Penalizing prosecutors who defer action for these reasons would subordinate the goal of 'orderly expedition' to that of 'mere speed,' Smith v. United States, 360 U.S. 1, 10, 79 S. Ct. 991, 997, 3 L.Ed.2d 1041 (1959). This the Due Process Clause does not require. We therefore hold that to prosecute a defendant following investigative delay does not deprive him of due process, even if his defense might have been somewhat prejudiced by the lapse of time."); *id.* at 795 n.17 ("In *Marion* we noted with approval that the Government conceded that a 'tactical' delay would violate the Due Process Clause. The Government renews that concession here, Brief for United States 32, and expands it somewhat by stating: 'A due process violation might also be made out upon a showing of prosecutorial delay incurred in reckless disregard of circumstances, known to the prosecution, suggesting that there existed an appreciable risk that delay would impair the ability to mount an effective defense,' id., at 32–33, n. 25. As the Government notes, however, there is no evidence of recklessness here.").

27. Kansas v. Carr, 136 S. Ct. 633, 644 (2016) ("[I]t is the Due Process Clause that wards off the introduction of 'unduly prejudicial' evidence that would 'rende[r] the trial fundamentally unfair.' *Payne v. Tennessee,* 501 U.S. 808, 825, 111 S. Ct. 2597, 115 L.Ed.2d 720 (1991); see also *Brown v. Sanders,* 546 U.S. 212, 220–221, 126 S. Ct. 884, 163 L.Ed.2d 723 (2006).").

28. Smith v. Cain, 565 U.S. 73, 75 (2012) ("Under *Brady,* the State violates a defendant's right to due process if it withholds evidence that is favorable to the defense and material to the defendant's guilt or punishment.") (citing *Brady,* 373 U.S. at 87); Cone v. Bell, 556 U.S. 449, 451 (2009) ("In *Brady v. Maryland,* 373 U.S. 83, 83 S. Ct. 1194, 10 L.Ed.2d 215 (1963), we held that when a State suppresses evidence favorable to an accused that is material to guilt or to punishment, the State violates the defendant's right to due process, 'irrespective of the good faith or bad faith of the prosecution.' *Id.,* at 87, 83 S. Ct. 1194."); Brady v. Maryland, 373 U.S. 83, 87 (1963) ("We now hold that the suppression by the prosecution of evidence favorable to an accused upon request violates due process where the evidence is material either to guilt or to punishment, irrespective of the good faith or bad faith of the prosecution.").

29. Wearry v. Cain, 136 S. Ct. 1002, 1002 (2016) (per curiam) ("Michael Wearry is on Louisiana's death row. Urging that the prosecution failed to disclose evidence supporting his innocence and that his counsel provided ineffective assistance at trial, Wearry unsuccessfully sought postconviction relief in state court. Contrary to the state postconviction court, we conclude that the prosecution's failure to disclose material evidence violated Wearry's due process rights."); *id.* at 1006 ("'[T]he suppression by the prosecution of evidence favorable to an accused upon request violates due process where the evidence is material either to guilt or to punishment, irrespective of the good faith or bad faith of the prosecution.' *Brady, supra,* at 87, 83 S. Ct. 1194. See also *Giglio v. United States,* 405 U.S. 150, 153–154, 92 S. Ct. 763, 31 L.Ed.2d 104 (1972) (clarifying that the rule stated in *Brady* applies to evidence undermining witness credibility). Evidence qualifies as material when there is "'any reasonable likelihood'" it could have "'affected the judgment of the jury.'" *Giglio, supra,* at 154, 92 S. Ct. 763 (quoting *Napue v. Illinois,* 360 U.S. 264, 271, 79 S. Ct. 1173, 3 L.Ed.2d 1217 (1959)). To prevail on his *Brady* claim, Wearry need not show that he 'more likely than not' would have been acquitted had the new evidence been admitted. *Smith v. Cain,* 565 U.S. 73, --------, 132 S. Ct. 627, 629–631, 181 L.Ed.2d 571 (2012) (internal quotation marks and brackets omitted). He must show only that the new evidence is sufficient to 'undermine confidence' in the verdict. *Ibid.*").

30. Parker v. Matthews, 567 U.S. 37, 45 (2012) (noting that, under the U.S. Supreme Court's decision in *Darden v. Wainwright*, 477 U.S. 168 (1986), a prosecutor's improper comments will be held to violate the Constitution only if they "'so infected the trial with unfairness as to make the resulting conviction a denial of due process'").

31. Salinas v. Texas, 570 U.S. 178, 188 n.3 (2013) (citing Doyle v. Ohio, 426 U.S. 610, 617–18 (1976)); *see also* Albert W. Alschuler, *A Peculiar Privilege in Historical Perspective: The Right to Remain Silent*, 94 MICH. L. REV. 2625, 2638 ("The history of the modern privilege against self-incrimination can be divided roughly into three stages, each of them captured by its own distinctive formulation of the doctrine. At the earliest stage, the privilege against self-incrimination was expressed in maxims like *Nemo tenetur seipsum accusare* ('No one shall be required to accuse himself') and *Nemo tenetur prodere seipsum* ('No one shall be required to produce himself" or "No one shall be required to betray himself'). At the second stage, the formulation was that of the United States Constitution: No person 'shall be compelled in any criminal case to be a witness against himself.' At the third stage (the modern stage), the warnings mandated by *Miranda v. Arizona* express the general although not universal understanding of the privilege: 'You have a right to remain silent.'"); Gerardo Schiano, Note, *"You Have the Right to Remain Selectively Silent": The Impractical Effect of Selective Invocation of the Right to Remain Silent,"* 38 NEW ENG. J. ON CRIM. & CIV. CONFINEMENT 177, 177 (2012) ("The right of criminal defendants to remain silent has been established both as a matter of procedure at trial and after a suspect has been arrested and taken into custody. This right's origin stems from the privilege against self-incrimination explicit in the language of the Fifth Amendment, yet the interpretation of the right has been the subject of countless constitutional challenges as criminal defendants attempt to invoke that right in order to suppress evidence at trial.").

32. Marshall v. Jerrico, Inc., 446 U.S. 238, 242 (1980).

33. 520 U.S. 899 (1997).

34. *Id.* at 904–05 (quoting Withrow v. Larkin, 421 U.S. 35, 46 (1975)). In *Bracy v. Gramley*, a man who was sentenced to death alleged that the judge in his case had taken bribes in criminal cases and that his due process rights were violated. *Id.* at 900–01 ("Petitioner William Bracy was tried, convicted, and sentenced to death before then-Judge Thomas J. Maloney for his role in an execution-style triple murder. Maloney was later convicted of taking bribes from defendants in criminal cases. Although he was not bribed in this case, he 'fixed' other murder cases during and around the time of petitioner's trial. Petitioner contends that Maloney therefore had an interest in a conviction here to deflect suspicion that he was taking bribes in other cases, and that this interest violated the fair-trial guarantee of the Fourteenth Amendment's Due Process Clause. We hold that petitioner has made a sufficient factual showing to establish 'good cause,' as required by Habeas Corpus Rule 6(a), for discovery on his claim of actual judicial bias in his case."); *id.* at 905 ("A judge who accepts bribes from a criminal defendant to fix that defendant's case is 'biased' in the most basic sense of that word, but his bias is directed against the State, not the defendant. Petitioner contends, however, that Maloney's taking of bribes from some criminal defendants not only rendered him biased against the *State* in those cases, but also induced a sort of compensatory bias against *defendants* who did *not* bribe Maloney. Maloney was biased in this latter, compensatory sense, petitioner argues, to avoid being seen as uniformly and suspiciously 'soft' on criminal defendants. The Court of Appeals, in its opinion, pointed out that this theory is quite speculative; after all, it might be equally likely that a judge who was 'on the take' in *some* criminal cases would be careful to at least appear to favor *all* criminal defendants, so as to avoid apparently wild and unexplainable swings in decisions and judicial philosophy. 81 F.3d, at 689–690. In any event, difficulties of proof aside, there is no question that, if it could be proved, such compensatory, camouflaging bias on Maloney's part in petitioner's own case would violate the Due Process Clause of the Fourteenth Amendment.").

35. Rosales-Mireles v. United States, 138 S. Ct. 1897, 1906 (2018) (citing County of Sacramento v. Lewis, 523 U.S. 833, 847 n.8 (1998) ("[I]n a due process challenge to executive action, the threshold question is whether the behavior of the governmental officer is so egregious, so outrageous, that it may fairly be said to shock the contemporary conscience."); *id.* ("This Court has said that the 'shock the conscience' standard is satisfied where the conduct was 'intended to injure in some way unjustifiable by any government interest,' or in some circumstances if it resulted from deliberate indifference.") (citation omitted); *id.* at 1908 ("In broad strokes, the public legitimacy of our justice system relied on procedures that are 'neutral,

accurate, consistent, trustworthy, and fair,' and that 'provide opportunities for error correction.'") (citation omitted).

36. County of Sacramento v. Lewis, 523 U.S. 833, 847 n.8 (1998).

37. *Compare* In re Flynn, 961 F.3d 1215, 1224 (D.C. Cir. 2020) ("Our precedents emphatically leave prosecutorial charging decisions to the Executive Branch and hold that a court may scrutinize a motion to dismiss only on the extraordinary showing of harassment of the defendant or malfeasance such as bribery....") *and id.* at 1227 ("When the court scrutinizes a selective prosecution claim, it exercises the core Article III power by protecting individuals from improper and unconstitutional prosecutions. Yet unwarranted judicial scrutiny of a prosecutor's motion to dismiss places the court in an entirely different position. Rather than allow the Executive Branch to dismiss a problematic prosecution, the court assumes the role of inquisitor, prolonging a prosecution deemed illegitimate by the Executive. Judges assume that role in some countries, but Article III gives no prosecutorial or inquisitorial power to federal judges.") (citing Young v. United States ex rel. Vuitton et Fils S.A., 481 U.S. 787, 816 (1987) (Scalia, J., concurring in the judgment) ("The judicial power... includes the power to serve as a neutral adjudicator in a criminal case."), *with In re Flynn*, 961 F.3d at 1232–33 (Wilkins, J., dissenting in part) ("It is an unremarkable proposition that, pursuant to his constitutional duty to 'take Care that the Laws be faithfully executed,' U.S. Const. art II, § 3, the Executive has 'broad discretion' over prosecutorial matters, and that a 'presumption of regularity' attaches to the exercise of that discretion. It is (or should be) equally uncontroversial that such discretion is not absolute and that the presumption of regularity does not shield such discretion for review. Indeed, the Supreme Court said as much in *Rinaldi*, where the Court '[did] not presume[] bad faith on the part of the Government at the time it sought leave to dismiss the indictment,' yet nonetheless conducted an 'independent evaluation' of the record to determine whether the unopposed Rule 48(a) motion should have been granted. The same principle holds true in the selective-prosecution context, where the district court may dismiss an indictment if it finds 'the decision to prosecute [was] 'deliberately based upon an unjustifiable standard such as race, religion, or other arbitrary classification." While the Supreme Court has iterated some separation-of-powers concerns around the conduct of discovery pursuant to such a motion, it has never cited the separation of powers as prohibiting the district court from holding a hearing on such a motion. To the contrary, courts have allowed not just plain hearings (or oral arguments) on such motions to dismiss, but *evidentiary* hearings where the prosecutor is subject to questioning under oath. In other words, it is not inconsistent with the separation of powers for a district court to conduct regular proceedings and afford consideration to a motion, even if the eventual grant or denial of the motion might intrude on the Executive's exercise of his prosecutorial discretion.") (citations omitted; italics in original).

38. Bartlett v. Bowen, 816 F.2d 695, 710 (D.C. Cir. 1987) ("Judicial review has been with us since *Marbury v. Madison*...."); *see also* Robert J. Reinstein & Mark C. Rahdert, *Reconstructing* Marbury, 57 Ark. L. Rev. 729, 771 (2005) ("In asserting a power of constitutional judicial review, Marshall's opinion in *Marbury v. Madison* confirmed a view of judicial power that had been widely accepted in the ratification debates of 1788, and that had surprisingly deep roots in English common law.").

39. Ex parte Robinson, 86 U.S. 505, 510 (1873) ("The power to punish for contempts is inherent in all courts; its existence is essential to the preservation of order in judicial proceedings, and to the enforcement of the judgments, orders, and writs of the courts, and consequently to the due administration of justice. The moment the courts of the United States were called into existence and invested with jurisdiction over any subject, they became possessed of this power."). Rule 42 of the Federal Rules of Criminal Procedure, addressing the subject of "Criminal Contempt," expressly allows the court to request that a contempt be prosecuted by an attorney for the government. Fed. R. Crim. P. 42(a)(2). "If the government declines the request," Rule 42 reads, "the court must appoint another attorney to prosecute the contempt." *Id.*

40. Bruce A. Green & Rebecca Roiphe, *Rethinking Prosecutors' Conflicts of Interest*, 58 B.C. L. Rev. 463, 471 (2017) ("Prosecutors are said to have a duty to 'do justice,' which requires, among other things, impartiality, neutrality, and, especially, disinterestedness."); *see also* McNeil v. Community Probation Servs., LLC, No. 1:18-cv-00033, 2021 WL 365844, at *13 (M.D. Tenn. Feb. 3, 2021) ("The due process neutrality requirement has also been applied to officials who perform prosecutorial/enforcement functions, based on language from the Supreme Court's opinion in *Marshall v. Jerrico, Inc.*, 446 U.S. 238, 100 S. Ct. 1610, 64 L.Ed. 2d 182 (1980)."); Guzman v. State, 552 S.W.3d 936, 943–44 (Tex. Ct. App. 2018):

> Although due process guarantees an "impartial and disinterested tribunal in both civil and criminal cases," the standards of neutrality that apply to judges are not so stringently required of prosecutors. *Marshall v. Jerrico, Inc.*, 446 U.S. 238, 242, 248, 100 S. Ct. 1610, 64 L.Ed.2d 182 (1980). "Prosecutors need not be entirely neutral and detached[.] In an adversary system, they are necessarily permitted to be zealous in their enforcement of the law." *Id.* at 248, 100 S. Ct. 1610 (internal quotation and citation omitted). The Supreme Court recognized, however, that the Due Process Clause nevertheless places limits on the "partisanship of . . . prosecutors." *Id.* at 249, 100 S. Ct. 1610. "A scheme injecting a personal interest, financial or otherwise, into the enforcement process may bring irrelevant or impermissible factors into the prosecutorial decision and in some contexts raise serious constitutional questions." *Id.* at 249–50, 100 S. Ct. 1610. Although the court declined to specify when a prosecutor's personal interest necessitates recusal or disqualification, it left open the possibility that "different considerations might be held to apply if the alleged biasing influence contributed to prosecutions against particular persons, rather than to a general zealousness in the enforcement process." *Id.* at 250 & n.12, 100 S. Ct. 1610.

Merck Sharp & Dohme Corp. v. Conway, 861 F. Supp.2d 802, 811–12 (E.D. Ky. 2012):

> The requirement of neutrality is much narrower in the case of prosecuting attorneys. "The constitutional interests in accurate finding of facts and application of law, and in preserving a fair and open process for decision, are not to the same degree implicated if it is the prosecutor, and not the judge, who is offered an incentive for securing civil penalties." *Marshall v. Jerrico, Inc.*, 446 U.S. 238, 248–49, 100 S. Ct. 1610, 64 L.Ed.2d 182 (1980). In other words, "[p]rosecutors need not be entirely neutral and detached." *Id.* at 248, 100 S. Ct. 1610 (internal quotation marks omitted). As a result, a "financial interest that would disqualify a judge . . . may be 'too remote and insubstantial to violate the constitutional constraints applicable to the decisions of [one] performing prosecutorial functions.'" *Dick v. Scroggy*, 882 F.2d 192, 197 (6th Cir. 1989) (quoting *Marshall*, 446 U.S. at 243–44, 100 S. Ct. 1610).

41. 273 U.S. 510, 523 (1927).

42. As Justice William Brennan observed, due process may require a judge's recusal when his or her participation may affect nonpecuniary interests. *See* Aetna Life Ins. Co. v. Lavoie, 475 U.S. 813, 829–30 (1986) (Brennan, J., concurring). Indeed, the mere participation of a judge in a decision may violate due process even if the judge's participation would not necessarily affect the outcome of the proceeding. *See* id. at 831 (Blackmun, J., concurring) (a judge's "mere participation in the shared enterprise of appellate decision making—whether or not he ultimately wrote, or even joined, the Alabama Supreme Court's opinion—posed an unacceptable danger of subtly distorting the decision making process"). According to another passage from Justice Brennan's opinion:

> While the influence of any single participant in this process can never be measured with precision, experience teaches us that each member's involvement plays a part in shaping the court's ultimate disposition. The participation of a judge who has a substantial interest in the outcome of a case of which he knows at the time he participates necessarily imports a bias into the deliberative process. This deprives litigants of the assurance of impartiality that is the fundamental requirement of due process.

Id. at 831 (Brennan, J., concurring).

43. Fent v. Oklahoma Capitol Improvement Authority, 984 P.2d 200, 216 (Okla. 2009) (Opala, J., concurring) (italics in original).

44. In re Murchison, 349 U.S. 133, 136 (1955). Under *Murchison*, it is not necessary to establish that the judge's interest actually altered his or her decision. On the contrary, the relevant inquiry focuses on the "possible temptation" which might lead the judge "not to hold the balance nice, clear and true between the State and the accused." Ward v. Village of Monroeville, 409 U.S. 57, 60 (1972); *see also* Aetna Life Ins. Co. v. Lavoie, 475 U.S. 813, 825 (1986).

45. *Tumey*, 273 U.S. at 532 (emphasis added); *see also* Peter David Blanck, et al., Note, *The Appearance of Justice: Judges' Verbal and Nonverbal Behavior in Criminal Jury Trials*, 38 Stan. L. Rev. 89 (1985) (footnotes omitted) (citing supporting case law).

> The trial judge's "appearance," or conduct and behavior, in a criminal jury trial must never indicate to the jury that the judge believes the accused to be guilty. The appearance of bias alone is grounds for reversal even if the trial judge is, in fact, completely impartial. Due process violations have been found when a trial judge's behavior created just the appearance of partiality, and courts have held such behavior sufficient to reverse criminal convictions.

Id. at 89–90.

46. Withrow v. Larkin, 421 U.S. 35, 47 (1975).

47. Guthrie v. Wisconsin Employment Relations Commission, 331 N.W.2d 331, 335 (Wis. 1983); *see also* Goldberg v. Kelly, 397 U.S. 254, 271 (1970) ("an impartial decision maker is essential"); In re Spivey, 480 S.E.2d 693, 700 (N.C. 1997) ("Due process requires a neutral decision-maker."). *Cf.* Richard J. Pierce, Jr., *How Should the U.S. Public Law System React to President Trump?*, 4 ALR ACCORD 41, 56 (2018) ("Courts have long distinguished between biased decisionmakers and biased prosecutors. A decision in an adjudication by a decisionmaker who is biased against the individual or firm that loses the case is a violation of due process. However, a decision against an individual or firm in a case in which the prosecutor is biased against the firm or individual is not a violation of due process. As long as the decisionmaker is unbiased, the potential effects of prosecutor's bias are too remote to invalidate the decision on constitutional grounds.") (citing Tumey v. Ohio, 273 U.S. 510, 532 (1927) (a system of adjudication in which the adjudicator benefitted from a decision against a defendant found to be unconstitutional) and Marshall v. Jerrico, 446 U.S. 238, 250–52 (1980) (a provision of the Fair Labor Standards Act assessing civil penalties for child labor violations and allowing the agency to collect the penalties on behalf of the agency found not to violate due process)).

48. 348 U.S. 11 (1954).

49. *Id.* at 14.

50. *E.g.*, Aetna Life Ins. Co. v. Lavoie, 475 U.S. 813, 822 (1986) (quoting *In re Murchinson*); Richmond Newspapers, Inc. v. Commonwealth of Virginia, 448 U.S. 555, 594 (1980) (Brennan, J., concurring) (quoting *Offutt*); Levine v. United States, 362 U.S. 610, 616 (1960) (quoting *Offutt*).

51. State ex rel. Koopers Co. v. International Union of Oil, Chemical and Atomic Workers, 298 S.E.2d 827, 830–31 (1982) ("Although a private prosecutor is held to the same high standards as a public one, the apparent conflict of interest and pressure of 'wearing two hats' militates against permitting a party's private counsel to prosecute a criminal contempt charge stemming from a civil suit; and it makes no difference whether he acts as private lawyer or by appointment as special prosecutor.... Justice is better served by avoiding appearances of impropriety and of inherent conflicts of interest, presented when a private party's counsel in a civil suit is permitted to prosecute a criminal contempt against an opposing party.").

52. 349 U.S. 133 (1955).

53. *Id.* at 136 (quoting *Offutt*).

54. Aetna Life Ins. Co. v. Lavoie, 475 U.S. 813, 825 (1986).

55. Jon Bancone, Note, *Article III and Due Process Limitations on the FSLIC's Adjudicatory Role During Its Receiverships*, 76 GEO. L.J. 1845, 1861 (1988) (quoting Taylor v. Hayes, 418 U.S. 488, 501 (1974)).

56. Liljeberg v. Health Servs. Acquisition Corp., 486 U.S. 847, 865 (1988); *see also id.* at 864 ("We conclude that in determining whether a judgment should be vacated for a violation of § 455(a), it is appropriate to consider the risk of injustice to the parties in the particular case, the risk that the denial of relief will produce injustice in other cases, and the risk of undermining the public's confidence in the judicial process. We must continuously bear in mind that 'to perform its high function in the best way 'justice must satisfy the appearance of justice.''") (quoting In re Murchison, 349 U.S. 133, 136 (1955) (citation omitted)).

57. *Liljeberg*, 468 U.S. at 865.

58. 28 U.S.C. § 455(b)(1), (b)(4), (b)(5)(iii). A "financial interest" is statutorily defined as the "ownership of a legal or equitable interest, however small, or a relationship as director, advisor, or other active participant in the affairs of a party." *Id.* at § 455(d)(4). For an article discussing this federal disqualification statute, see Susan B. Hoekema, Comment, *Questioning the Impartiality of Judges: Disqualifying Federal District Court Judges under 28 U.S.C. § 455(a)*, 60 TEMP. L.Q. 697 (1987). Although federal law provides for the disqualification of judges under particular circumstances, 28 U.S.C. § 455, the Constitution itself may mandate disqualification depending on the circumstances. *See Lavoie*, 475 U.S. at 828 ("The Due Process

Clause demarks only the outer boundaries of judicial disqualifications. Congress and the states, of course, remain free to impose more rigorous standards for judicial disqualification ....").

59. 28 U.S.C. § 144; *see also* Nevada Com'n on Ethics v. Carrigan, 564 U.S. 117, 123–24 (2011):

> Federal conflict-of-interest rules applicable to judges also date back to the founding. In 1792, Congress passed a law requiring district court judges to recuse themselves if they had a personal interest in a suit or had been counsel to a party appearing before them. Act of May 8, 1792, ch. 36, § 11, 1 Stat. 278–279. In 1821, Congress expanded these bases for recusal to include situations in which "the judge ... is so related to, or connected with, either party, as to render it improper for him, in his opinion, to sit on the trial of such suit." Act of Mar. 3, 1821, ch. 51, 3 Stat. 643. The statute was again expanded in 1911, to make any "personal bias or prejudice" a basis for recusal. Act of Mar. 3, 1911, § 21, 36 Stat. 1090. The current version, which retains much of the 1911 version's language, is codified at 28 U.S.C. § 144. See generally *Liteky v. United States*, 510 U.S. 540, 544, 114 S. Ct. 1147, 127 L.Ed.2d 474 (1994); Frank, *Disqualificaiton of Judges*, 56 Yale L.J. 605, 626–630 (1947) (hereinafter Frank). There are of course differences between a legislator's vote and a judge's, and thus between legislative and judicial recusal rules; nevertheless, there do not appear to have been any serious challenges to judicial recusal statutes as having unconstitutionally restricted judges' First Amendment rights.

60. Williams v. Pennsylvania, 136 U.S. 1899, 1909 (2016); *see also id.* ("A multimember court must not have its guarantee of neutrality undermined, for the appearance of bias demeans the reputation and integrity not just of one jurist, but of the larger institution of which he or she is a part."); *id.* at 1909–10 ("Both the appearance and reality of impartial justice are necessary to the public legitimacy of judicial pronouncements and thus to the rule of law itself. When the objective risk of actual bias on the part of a judge rises to an unconstitutional level, the failure to recuse cannot be deemed harmless.").

61. Concrete Pipe and Prods. of Cal., Inc. v. Construction Laborers Pension Trust for S. Cal., 124 L.E.2d 539, 560–61 (1993) (quoting Ward v. Village of Monroeville, 409 U.S. 57, 61–62 (1972); citing Schweiker v. McClure, 456 U.S. 188, 195 (1982)).

62. *Concrete Pipe and Prods. of Cal., Inc.*, 124 L.E.2d at 561.

63. Tumey v. Ohio, 273 U.S. 510 (1927).

64. Much has been written about "due process of law," America's founders' conception of it, and the concept's use in the modern legal system. *See, e.g.*, Timothy M. Tymkovich, Joshua Dos Santos & Joshua J. Craddock, *A Workable Substantive Due Process*, 95 Notre Dame L. Rev. 1961, 1965–67 (2020):

> Skipping to the American Founding, all agree the Fifth Amendment's Due Process Clause was supposed to incorporate this Magna Carta guarantee of compliance with the law of the land. But, perhaps unsurprisingly, what Americans in 1789 thought of as "due process of law" may not have been the same as what their cousins across the pond thought. Much ink has thus been dedicated to refining just what "due process of law" meant to the Founders.
>
> Coke is a key figure here. His ideas formed "a chief source of early American constitutionalism." Since it seems plausible to attribute Coke's views to those of our Constitution's Framers, there is debate about what Coke's precise formulation of "due process of law" was. In particular, did Coke think of the "law of the land" as including some kind of higher, "fundamental law"—law that even Parliament could not transgress? If so, this would make Coke's conception of due process a kind of substantive limit on law *as well as* a guarantee of compliance with law. Some have read Coke's commentary and decisions to say exactly that. Others disagree.
>
> While the bulk of scholarship concludes Coke did not incorporate higher law into his definition of due process of law, there is strong evidence the Framers understood due process to include substantive limits on laws passed by the legislature. In part, the Framers did hold the commonsense interpretation. As due process of law was commonly understood before the Founding, neither king nor Parliament could deprive someone of life, liberty, or property except through a common-law court so deciding by *applying settled law*. That is, the deprivation could only be authorized by valid law already existing at the time of the deprivation. By itself, this is a minimal substantive requirement, of course.

But Nathan Chapman and Michael McConnell have persuasively argued the Framers of the original Constitution also understood due process to impose a stronger, and substantive, limitation on legislatures: legislatures could not, consistent with due process, authorize other branches of government to deprive others of property without adjudication by a common-law court, nor could they deprive specific individuals of rights or property—the latter being a violation of the separation of powers.

This is not to say the Founders had anything like a modern notion of "substantive due process"—which places a number of *nonprocedural* rights beyond the legislature's power to regulate. But the Founders did believe due process required more than executive compliance with the law on the books. Rather, Americans tended to think legislatures had to comply with the "law of the land," and to them, the "law of the land" included common-law procedural protections. Indeed, some of the American Revolutionaries' principal objections to Parliament's legislation came wrapped in this theory of due process. Parliament, they thought, could not abrogate common-law protections, as those were the (unalterable) law of the land, the basic Rights of Englishmen. And various state court cases held legislative acts incompatible with the law of the land because they either (1) allowed the executive to deprive persons of property without adjudication by a common law court, or (2) directly deprived specific individuals of property. To Americans, the latter was legislative usurpation of the judicial power. And that violated the separation of powers, a rule that they thought indispensable for any scheme to bear the name "due process of law."

65. Mass. Const., pt. 1, art. XXIX.

66. A Letter from Phocion to the Considerate Citizens of New York (1–27 Jan. 1784), *Founders Online*, National Archives, https://founders.archives.gov/documents/Hamilton/01-03-02-0314. (citing Coke upon Magna Charta, Chap. 29, Page 50) [Original source: *The Papers of Alexander Hamilton*, vol. 3, *1782–1786*, ed. Harold C. Syrett. New York: Columbia University Press, 1962, pp. 483–497.]

67. New York Assembly. Remarks on an Act for Regulating Elections, [6 Feb. 1787], *Founders Online*, National Archives, https://founders.archives.gov/documents/Hamilton/01-04-02-0017 ("We had in a former debate, travelled largely over the ground of the constitution, as applied to legislative disqualifications; He [Alexander Hamilton] would not repeat what he had said, but he hoped to be indulged by the house in explaining a sentence in the constitution, which seems not well understood by some gentlemen. In one article of it, it is said no man shall be disfranchised or deprived of any right he enjoys under the constitution, but by the *law of the land*, or the judgment of his peers. Some gentlemen hold that the law of the land will include an act of the legislature. But Lord Coke, that great luminary of the law, in his comment upon a similar clause, in Magna Charta, interprets the law of the land to mean presentment and indictment, and process of outlawry, as contradistinguished from trial by jury. But if there were any doubt upon the constitution, the bill of rights enacted in this very session removes it. It is there declared that, no man shall be disfranchised or deprived of any right, but by *due process of law*, or the judgment of his peers. The words '*due process*' have a precise technical import, and are only applicable to the process and proceedings of the courts of justice; they can never be referred to an act of legislature."). Original source: *The Papers of Alexander Hamilton*, vol. 4, *January 1787–May 1788*, ed. Harold C. Syrett. New York: Columbia University Press, 1962, pp. 34–37.

68. 408 U.S. 471 (1972).

69. *See generally* Martin H. Redish & Lawrence C. Marshall, *Adjudicatory Independence and the Values of Procedural Due Process*, 95 Yale L.J. 455, 468–72 (1986); *see also* Laurence H. Tribe, American Constitutional Law § 10-13, at 714–15 (1988) (outlining the Supreme Court's shifting methods of determining what process is due).

70. 59 U.S. (18 How.) 272 (1855).

71. *Id.* at 277.

72. Kerry v. Din, 576 U.S. 86, 91 (2015). Unlike the Fourteenth Amendment, the Fifth Amendment does not contain an equal protection provision. However, the U.S. Supreme Court has determined that the equal protection concept is still relevant in deciding Fifth Amendment issues. *See* Weinberger v. Wiesenfeld, 420 U.S. 636, 638 n.2 (1975) ("[W]hile the Fifth Amendment contains no equal protection clause, it does forbid discrimination that is so unjustifiable as to be violative of due process. The Court's approach

to Fifth Amendment equal protection claims has always been precisely the same as to equal protection claims under the Fourteenth Amendment."); *accord* Sessions v. Morales-Santana, 137 S. Ct. 1678, 1686 n.1 (2017) (same); United States v. Windsor, 570 U.S. 744, 774 (2013) ("The liberty protected by the Fifth Amendment's Due Process Clause contains within it the prohibition against denying to any person the equal protection of the laws. While the Fifth Amendment itself withdraws from Government the power to degrade or demean in the way this law does, the equal protection guarantee of the Fourteenth Amendment makes that Fifth Amendment right all the more specific and all the better understood and preserved.").

73. 137 S. Ct. 905 (2017).

74. *Id.* at 907 (*quoting* Aetna Life Ins. Co. Lavoie, 475 U.S. 813, 825 (1986) & Withrow v. Larkin, 421 U.S. 35, 47 (1975)); *see also* Williams v. Pennsylvania, 136 S. Ct. 1899, 1903 (2016) ("This Court's precedents set forth an objective standard that requires recusal when the likelihood of bias on the part of the judge "'is too high to be constitutionally tolerable.'" *Caperton v. A.T. Massey Coal Co.*, 556 U.S. 868, 872, 129 S. Ct. 2252, 173 L.Ed.2d 1208 (2009) (quoting *Withrow v. Larkin*, 421 U.S. 35, 47, 95 S. Ct. 1456, 43 L.Ed.2d 712 (1975)). Applying this standard, the Court concludes that due process compelled the justice's recusal."); *Williams*, 136 S. Ct. at 1905 ("The Court asks not whether a judge harbors an actual, subjective bias, but instead whether, as an objective matter, the average judge in his position is likely to be neutral, or whether there is an unconstitutional potential for bias.").

75. Rippo v. Baker, 137 S. Ct. 905, 906 (2017).

76. Barbara E. Bergman & John D. Cline, Everytrial Criminal Defense Resource Book § 72:1 (2020).

77. State v. Daigle, 241 So.3d 999, 1000 (La. 2018).

78. 556 U.S. 868 (2009).

79. *Id.* at 872.

80. *Id.*

81. *Id.*; *see also id.* at 873 ("Don Blankenship is Massey's chairman, chief executive officer, and president. After the verdict but before the appeal, West Virginia held its 2004 judicial elections. Knowing the Supreme Court of Appeals of West Virginia would consider the appeal in the case, Blankenship decided to support an attorney who sought to replace Justice McGraw. Justice McGraw was a candidate for reelection to that court. The attorney who sought to replace him was Brent Benjamin."); *id.* ("In addition to contributing the $1,000 statutory maximum to Benjamin's campaign committee, Blankenship donated almost $2.5 million to 'And For The Sake Of The Kids,' a political organization formed under 26 U.S.C. § 527. The § 527 organization opposed McGraw and supported Benjamin. 223 W.Va. 624, 700, 679 S.E.2d 223, 299 (2008) (Benjamin, Acting C.J. concurring). Blankenship's donations accounted for more than two-thirds of the total funds it raised. App. at 150a. This was not all. Blankenship spent, in addition, just over $500,000 on independent expenditures—for direct mailings and letters soliciting donations as well as television and newspaper advertisements—"'to support… Brent Benjamin.'" *Id.*, at 184a, 186a, 200a (quoting Blankenship's state campaign financial disclosure filings; bold typeface omitted)."); ("Benjamin won. He received 382,036 votes (53.3%), and McGraw received 334,301 votes (46.7%). 223 W.Va., at 702, 679 S.E.2d., at 301 (Benjamin, Acting C.J., concurring)."); *id.* at 873–74 ("In October 2005, before Massey filed its petition for appeal in West Virginia's highest court, Caperton moved to disqualify now-Justice Benjamin under the Due Process Clause and the West Virginia Code of Judicial Conduct, based on the conflict caused by Blankenship's campaign involvement. Justice Benjamin denied the motion in April 2006. He indicated that he 'carefully considered the bases and accompanying exhibits proffered by the movants.' But he found 'no objective information… to show that this Justice has a bias for or against any litigant, that this Justice has prejudged the matters which comprise this litigation, or that this Justice will be anything but fair and impartial.' App. 336a–337a.").

82. *Id.* at 872.

83. *Id.* at 884; *see also id.* ("The inquiry centers on the contribution's relative size in comparison to the total amount of money contributed to the campaign, the total amount spent in the election, and the apparent effect such contribution had on the outcome of the election."); *id.* ("Applying this principle, we conclude that Blankenship's campaign efforts had a significant and disproportionate influence in placing Justice Benjamin on the case. Blankenship contributed some $3 million to unseat the incumbent and replace

him with Benjamin. His contributions eclipsed the total amount spent by all other Benjamin supporters and exceeded by 300% the amount spent by Benjamin's campaign committee. App. 288a. Caperton claims Blankenship spent $1 million more than the total amount spent by the campaign committees of both candidates combined. Brief for Petitioners 28."); *id.* at 885 ("Due process requires an objective inquiry into whether the contributor's influence on the election under all the circumstances 'would offer a possible temptation to the average ... judge to ... lead him not to hold the balance nice, clear and true.' *Tumey, supra,* at 532, 47 S. Ct. 437. In an election decided by fewer than 50,000 votes (382,036 to 334,301), see 223 W.Va., at 702, 679 S.E.2d, at 301, 2008 WL 918444, Blankenship's campaign contributions—in comparison to the total amount contributed to the campaign, as well as the total amount spent in the election—had a significant and disproportionate influence on the electoral outcome. And the risk that Blankenship's influence engendered actual bias is sufficiently substantial that it 'must be forbidden if the guarantee of due process is to be adequately implemented.' *Withrow, supra,* at 47, 95 S. Ct. 1456."); *id.* at 886 ("The temporal relationship between the campaign contributions, the justice's election, and the pendency of the case is also critical. It was reasonably foreseeable, when the campaign contributions were made, that the pending case would be before the newly elected justice. The $50 million adverse jury verdict had been entered before the election, and the Supreme Court of Appeals was the next step once the state trial court dealt with post-trial motions. So it became at once apparent that, absent recusal, Justice Benjamin would review a judgment that cost his biggest donor's company $50 million. Although there is no allegation of a *quid pro quo* agreement, the fact remains that Blankenship's extraordinary contributions were made at a time when he had a vested stake in the outcome. Just as no man is allowed to be a judge in his own cause, similar fears of bias can arise when—without the consent of the other parties—a man chooses the judge in his own cause. And applying this principle to the judicial election process, there was here a serious, objective risk of actual bias that required Justice Benjamin's recusal."); *id.* at 886–87 ("Due process 'may sometimes bar trial by judges who have no actual bias and who would do their very best to weigh the scales of justice equally between contending parties.' *Murchison,* 349 U.S., at 136, 75 S. Ct. 623. The failure to consider objective standards requiring recusal is not consistent with the imperatives of due process. We find that Blankenship's significant and disproportionate influence—coupled with the temporal relationship between the election and the pending case—"''offer[s] a possible temptation to the average ... judge to ... lead him not to hold the balance nice, clear and true."'" *Lavoie,* 475 U.S., at 825, 106 S. Ct. 1580 (quoting *Monroeville,* 409 U.S., at 60, 93 S. Ct. 80, in turn quoting *Tumey,* 273 U.S., at 532, 47 S. Ct. 437). On these extreme facts the probability of actual bias rises to an unconstitutional level.").

84. 6 Wayne R. LaFave, Jerold H. Israel, Nancy J. King & Orin S. Kerr, Crim. Proc. § 22.4(a)—*Right to impartial judge* (4th ed. 2020) ("Just as the defendant has a constitutional right to 'impartial' jury, he also has a constitutional right to an impartial judge. Judicial conduct codes that use more exacting standards will resolve most disqualification disputes, the Court has noted, so that 'application of the constitutional standard ... will thus be confined to rare instances.' The Court in *Caperton,* noted four examples of those rare instances where recusal would be required in order to satisfy due process: a direct, personal, substantial pecuniary interest of the judge in the case; an indirect financial interest in the case's outcome; certain contempt scenarios; and, the extreme case before it where one of the parties had donated $3 million to the judge's election campaign."); People v. Hawkins, 690 N.E.2d 999 (Ill. 1998) (defendants denied due process in their murder trial by judge's willingness to accept bribe for acquittal, even though judge ultimately returned bribe money and convicted defendants; judge was motivated to return verdict that would not spark suspicions of authorities); Penny J. White, *The Other Costs of Judicial Elections,* 67 DePaul L. Rev. 369, 384 (2018) ("judges who take bribes violate due process because implicit in the concept of due process is the notion that a fair tribunal is presided over by a fair arbiter").

85. 446 U.S. 238 (1980).

86. *Id.* at 242.

87. *Id.* (citing Matthews v. Eldridge, 424 U.S. 319, 344 (1976)); *see also Marshall,* 446 U.S. at 242–43 ("The requirement of neutrality has been jealously guarded by this Court. In *Tumey v. Ohio, supra,* the Court reversed convictions rendered by the mayor of a town when the mayor's salary was paid in part by fees and costs levied by him acting in a judicial capacity. The Court stated that the Due Process Clause would not permit any 'procedure which would offer a possible temptation to the average man as a judge to

forget the burden of proof required to convict the defendant, or which might lead him not to hold the balance nice, clear and true between the state and the accused.' 273 U.S., at 532, 47 S. Ct., at 444. *Tumey* was applied in *Ward v. Village of Monroeville, supra,* to invalidate a procedure by which sums produced from a mayor's court accounted for a substantial portion of municipal revenues, even though the mayor's salary was not augmented by those sums. The forbidden 'possible temptation,' we concluded, is also present 'when the mayor's executive responsibilities for village finances may make him partisan to maintain the high level of contribution from the mayor's court.' 409 U.S., at 60, 93 S. Ct., at 83. We have employed the same principle in a variety of settings, demonstrating the powerful and independent constitutional interest in fair adjudicative procedure. Indeed, 'justice must satisfy the appearance of justice,' *Offutt v. United States,* 348 U.S. 11, 14, 75 S. Ct. 11, 13, 99 L.Ed. 11 (1954), and this 'stringent rule may sometimes bar trial by judges who have no actual bias and who would do their very best to weigh the scales of justice equally between contending parties,' *In re Murchison,* 349 U.S. 133, 136, 75 S. Ct. 623, 625, 99 L.Ed. 942 (1955). See also *Taylor v. Hayes,* 418 U.S. 488, 94 S. Ct. 2697, 41 L.Ed.2d 897 (1974).").

88. *Marshall,* 446 U.S. at 242; Joint Anti-Fascist Committee v. McGrath, 341 U.S. 123, 172 (1951) (Frankfurter, J., concurring); *see also* Turner v. United States, 137 S. Ct. 1885, 1888 (2017) ("In *Brady v. Maryland,* 373 U.S. 83, 83 S. Ct. 1194, 10 L.Ed.2d 215 (1963), this Court held that the government violates the Constitution's Due Process Clause 'if it withholds evidence that is favorable to the defense and *material* to the defendant's guilt or punishment.'") (quoting Smith v. Cain, 565 U.S. 73, 75 (2012); italics in original).

89. Concrete Pipe & Products of Cal., Inc. v. Constr. Laborers Pension Trust for Southern Cal., 508 U.S. 602, 617 (1993).

90. *E.g.,* Dusenbery v. United States, 534 U.S. 161, 167 (2002) ("The Due Process Clause of the Fifth Amendment prohibits the United States, as the Due Process Clause of the Fourteenth Amendment prohibits the States, from depriving any person of property without 'due process of law.' From these 'cryptic and abstract words,' we have determined that individuals whose property interests are at stake are entitled to "notice and an opportunity to be heard.") (citations omitted); LaChance v. Erickson, 522 U.S. 262, 266 (1998) ("The core of due process is the right to notice and a meaningful opportunity to be heard.").

91. Hamdi v. Rumsfeld, 542 U.S. 507, 533 (2004).

92. 136 S. Ct. 1899 (2016).

93. *Id.* at 1903.

94. *Id.*

95. *Id.*

96. *Id.*

97. *Id.*; *see also id.* at 1905 ("Two weeks after the Pennsylvania Supreme Court decided Williams's case, Chief Justice Castille retired from the bench.").

98. *Id.* at 1903.

99. *Id.* at 1905; *see also id.* ("Chief Justice Castille, Williams argues, violated the Due Process Clause of the Fourteenth Amendment by acting as both accuser and judge in his case.").

100. *Id.*; *see also id.* at 1908–09 ("Chief Justice Castille's significant, personal involvement in a critical decision in Williams's case gave rise to an unacceptable risk of actual bias. This risk so endangered the appearance of neutrality that his participation in the case 'must be forbidden if the guarantee of due process is to be adequately implemented.'") (*quoting Withrow,* 421 U.S., at 47, 95 S. Ct. 1456).

101. Anthony J. Scirica, *Judicial Governance and Judicial Independence,* 90 N.Y.U. L. Rev. 779, 800 (2015) ("[T]he Justices do recuse themselves with some degree of regularity; from October Terms 2008 to 2012, Justices recused themselves fifty-five times, with the majority of those recusals coming from Justice Elena Kagan as a result of her work as Solicitor General. What is clear is that the Supreme Court Justices carefully consider the decision to recuse by consulting the Code of Conduct, legal precedent, and scholarly works, as well as advice from colleagues, the Court's legal office, and the Judicial Conference Committee on the Codes of Conduct.").

102. *Williams,* 136 S. Ct. at 1905 (quoting In re Murchison, 349 U.S. 133, 136 (1955)).

103. *Id.* (quoting *Caperton,* 556 U.S. at 881). *Caperton* held that a judge was required to recuse himself "when a person with a personal stake in a particular case had a significant and disproportionate influence

in placing the judge on the case by raising funds or directing the judge's election campaign when the case was pending or imminent." Caperton v. A.T. Massey Coal Co., 556 U.S. 868, 884 (2009). The recusal remedy was based on a litigant's due process right to a fair trial before an unbiased judge. *See* Withrow v. Larkin, 421 U.S. 35, 46 (1975).

104. *Williams*, 136 S. Ct. at 1905 (*citing Murchison*, 349 U.S. at 136–37); *see also id.* at 1905–06 ("This objective risk of bias is reflected in the due process maxim that 'no man can be a judge in his own case and no man is permitted to try cases where he has an interest in the outcome.'") (*citing Murchison*, 349 U.S. at 136).

105. *Id.* at 1906; *see also id.* ("This conclusion follows from the Court's analysis in *In re Murchison.* That case involved a 'one-man judge-grand jury' proceeding, conducted pursuant to state law, in which the judge called witnesses to testify about suspected crimes. *Id.*, at 134. During the course of the examinations, the judge became convinced that two witnesses were obstructing the proceeding. He charged one witness with perjury and then, a few weeks later, tried and convicted him in open court. The judge charged the other witness with contempt and, a few days later, tried and convicted him as well. This Court overturned the convictions on the ground that the judge's dual position as accuser and decisionmaker in the contempt trials violated due process: 'Having been a part of [the accusatory] process a judge cannot be, in the very nature of things, wholly disinterested in the conviction or acquittal of those accused.' *Id.*, at 137."); *id.* ("The facts of *Murchison,* it should be acknowledged, differ in many respects from a case like this one. In *Murchison,* over the course of several weeks, a single official (the so-called judge-grand jury) conducted an investigation into suspected crimes; made the decision to charge witnesses for obstruction of that investigation; heard evidence on the charges he had lodged; issued judgments of conviction; and imposed sentence.").

106. *Id.*

107. *Id.* (*quoting Withrow*, 421 U.S. at 57); *see also id.* ("In addition, the judge's 'own personal knowledge and impression' of the case, acquired through his or her role in the prosecution, may carry far more weight with the judge than the parties' arguments to the court.") (citing *Murchison*, 349 U.S. at 138; *Caperton*, 556 U.S. at 881).

108. Gerard J. Clark, Caperton*'s New Right to Independence in Judges*, 58 Drake L. Rev. 661, 667 (2010) ("In *In re Murchison*, a state court judge held a hearing to determine whether criminal charges should be brought. Two witnesses were called. One answered questions, but the judge found him untruthful and charged him with perjury. The second declined to answer on the ground that he did not have counsel with him, as state law seemed to permit. The judge charged the witness with contempt and proceeded to try and convict the witness. The Supreme Court set aside the convictions because the judge had a conflict of interest at the trial stage based on his earlier participation in charging the witnesses. Thus, the Due Process Clause required disqualification. The Court recited the general rule that 'no man can be a judge in his own case,' adding that 'no man is permitted to try cases where he has an interest in the outcome.'").

109. *Williams*, 136 S. Ct. at 1910 ("Allowing an appellate panel to reconsider a case without the participation of the interested member will permit judges to probe lines of analysis or engage in discussions they may have felt constrained to avoid in their first deliberations."); *id.* ("Chief Justice Castille's participation in Williams's case was an error that affected the State Supreme Court's whole adjudicatory framework below. Williams must be granted an opportunity to present his claims to a court unburdened by any 'possible temptation... not to hold the balance nice, clear and true between the State and the accused.'") (quoting *Tumey v. Ohio,* 273 U.S. 510, 532, 47 S. Ct. 437, 71 L.Ed. 749 (1927)); *id.* ("Due process entitles Terrance Williams to 'a proceeding in which he may present his case with assurance' that no member of the court is 'predisposed to find against him.'") (quoting *Marshall v. Jerrico, Inc.*, 446 U.S. 238, 242, 100 S. Ct. 1610, 64 L.Ed.2d 182 (1980)).

110. *Williams*, 136 S. Ct. at 1906. As the Court in *Williams* concluded: "The involvement of other actors and the passage of time are consequences of a complex criminal justice system, in which a single case may be litigated through multiple proceedings taking place over a period of years. This context only heightens the need for objective rules preventing the operation of bias that otherwise might be obscured." *Id.* at 1906–07. The Court in *Williams* determined that Chief Justice Castille's prior decision to seek

authorization of the death penalty against Williams constituted "significant, personal involvement" and that, "as a result, Chief Justice Castille's failure to recuse from Williams's case presented an unconstitutional risk of bias." *Id.* at 1907. On the issue of recusal, the Court in *Williams* stressed: "Due process 'demarks only the outer boundaries of judicial disqualifications.' Most questions of recusal are addressed by more stringent and detailed ethical rules, which in many jurisdictions already require disqualification under the circumstances of this case.") (quoting Aetna Life Ins. Co. v. Lavoie, 475 U.S. 813, 828 (1986); citing Brief for American Bar Association as *Amicus Curiae* 5, 11–14); *see also* ABA Model Code of Judicial Conduct Rules 2.11(A)(1), (A)(6)(b) (2011) (no judge may participate "in any proceeding in which the judge's impartiality might reasonably be questioned," including where the judge "served in governmental employment, and in such capacity participated personally and substantially as a lawyer or public official concerning the proceeding"); 28 U.S.C. § 455(b)(3) (recusal required where judge "has served in governmental employment and in such capacity participated as counsel, adviser or material witness concerning the proceeding"); *see also Williams*, 136 S. Ct. at 1907 ("Within a large, impersonal system, an individual prosecutor might still have an influence that, while not so visible as the one-man grand jury in *Murchison*, is nevertheless significant. A prosecutor may bear responsibility for any number of critical decisions, including what charges to bring, whether to extend a plea bargain, and which witnesses to call. Even if decades intervene before the former prosecutor revisits the matter as a jurist, the case may implicate the effects and continuing force of his or her original decision. In these circumstances, there remains a serious risk that a judge would be influenced by an improper, if inadvertent, motive to validate and preserve the result obtained through the adversary process. The involvement of multiple actors and the passage of time do not relieve the former prosecutor of the duty to withdraw in order to ensure the neutrality of the judicial process in determining the consequences that his or her own earlier, critical decision may have set in motion."); *id.* at 1909 ("The Court has little trouble concluding that a due process violation arising from the participation of an interested judge is a defect 'not amenable' to harmless-error review, regardless of whether the judge's vote was dispositive. The deliberations of an appellate panel, as a general rule, are confidential. As a result, it is neither possible nor productive to inquire whether the jurist in question might have influenced the views of his or her colleagues during the decisionmaking process. Indeed, one purpose of judicial confidentiality is to assure jurists that they can reexamine old ideas and suggest new ones, while both seeking to persuade and being open to persuasion by their colleagues.") (quoting Puckett v. United States, 556 U.S. 129, 141 (2009)); *id.* ("[I]t does not matter whether the disqualified judge's vote was necessary to the disposition of the case. The fact that the interested judge's vote was not dispositive may mean only that the judge was successful in persuading most members of the court to accept his or her position. That outcome does not lessen the unfairness to the affected party.").

111. 349 U.S. 133 (1955).

112. *Id.* at 136 (quoting *Offutt*).

113. Cuyler v. Sullivan, 446 U.S. 335 (1980) (defense counsel cannot have an actual conflict of interest); Connally v. Georgia, 429 U.S. 245 (1977) (per curiam) (system invalidated in which justices of the peace were paid for issuance but not for nonissuance of search warrants); Taylor v. Hayes, 418 U.S. 488 (1974) (prohibiting the trial of a defendant before a judge who had previously held the defendant in contempt); Gibson v. Berryhill, 411 U.S. 564 (1973) (prohibiting an administrative board consisting of optometrists in private practice from hearing charges filed against optometrists competing with board members); Morrissey v. Brewer, 408 U.S. 471 (1972) (prohibiting parole officers from making parole revocation decisions); Tumey v. Ohio, 273 U.S. 510 (1927) (judges must be free from bias); *cf.* Marshall v. Jerrico, Inc., 446 U.S. 238 (1980) (articulating standard for administrative prosecutors).

114. 409 U.S. 57 (1972).

115. *Id.* at 60 (quoting *Tumey*, 273 U.S. at 534).

116. Tribe, *supra* note 69, at 745 (citing Morrissey v. Brewer, 408 U.S. 471, 485–86 (1972); Goldberg v. Kelly, 397 U.S. 254, 271 (1970)); *see also* Aetna Life Ins. Co. v. Lavoie, 475 U.S. 813, 825 (1986) ("The Due Process Clause 'may sometimes bar trial judges who have no actual bias and who would do their best to weigh the scales of justice equally between contending parties.'") (quoting *Murchison*, 349 U.S. at 136); Marshall v. Jerrico, Inc., 446 U.S. 238, 243 (1980) (quoting Offutt v. United States, 348 U.S. 11 (1954) & In re Murchison, 349 U.S. 133 (1955)) ("'Justice must satisfy the appearance of justice,'" and this 'stringent

rule may sometimes bar trial by judges who have no actual bias and who would do their very best to weigh the scales of justice equally between contending parties.'").

117. David Barnhizer, *"On the Make": Campaign Funding and the Corrupting of the American Judiciary*, 50 CATH. U. L. REV. 361, 368 (2001) ("The legal profession generally—and judges specifically—are governed by ethical mandates requiring them to avoid even the appearance of impropriety.").

118. Daniel D. Dubnicki, *Disqualification or Recusal of Judge Based upon Use or Attributed Use of Social Media*, 33 A.L.R.7th, Art. 9, § 2 (2017) ("So powerful was the rise of social media among lawyers and judges that, in 2013, the American Bar Association issued Formal Opinion 462 entitled 'Judge's Use of Electronic Social Networking Media' to address several concerns with social media usage among the judiciary. While the ABA recognizes the utility of social media for judges, it does caution judges to exercise 'judicial discretion' in the way they use social media and interact with others online so as not to create the impression of bias or impropriety, which would necessitate the recusal or disqualification of the judge.").

119. Agnieszka McPeak, *The Internet Made Me Do It: Reconciling Social Media and Professional Norms for Lawyers, Judges, and Law Professors*, 55 IDAHO L. REV. 205, 230 n.204 (2019).

120. 100 U.S. 303 (1880).

121. 476 U.S. 79 (1986) (race-based peremptory challenges are unconstitutional); *see also* Edmonson v. Leesville Concrete Co., 500 U.S. 614 (1991) (banning race-based strikes by either party in civil litigation); Powers v. Ohio, 111 S. Ct. 1364 (1991) (peremptory challenges cannot be used to exclude jurors not of the same race as the defendant). The Supreme Court has also ruled that gender-based peremptory challenges are unconstitutional. J.E.B. v. Alabama ex rel. T.B., 511 U.S. 127 (1994).

122. 419 U.S. 522 (1975).

123. 545 U.S. 231 (2005).

124. 136 S. Ct. 1737 (2016).

125. *See also* TED A. DONNER, JURY SELECTION STRATEGY AND SCIENCE § 32:1—*Significance of questions concerning racial bias* ("The predispositions of jurors to racial or gender bias should have no place in how any case is decided in the United States.").

126. *See* Remmer v. United States, 350 U.S. 377 (1956).

127. 352 U.S. 985 (1957) (per curiam).

128. "In a criminal case, any private communication, contact, or tampering, directly or indirectly, with a juror during a trial about the matter pending before the jury is deemed presumptively prejudicial, if not made in pursuance of known rules of the court and with full knowledge of the parties." CHESTER ANTIEAU, MODERN CONSTITUTIONAL LAW: THE INDIVIDUAL AND THE GOVERNMENT § 5:62, at 348 (1969) (citing Remmer v. United States, 347 U.S. 227 (1954)). As the Supreme Court has firmly stated: "Due process requires a fair trial by an impartial jury free from outside influences." Sheppard v. Maxwell, 384 U.S. 333 (1966).

129. 450 U.S. 288 (1981).

130. *Id.* at 305.

131. Audio MPEG, Inc. v. Dell, Inc., 219 F. Supp.3d 563, 576 (E.D. Va. 2016); Towler v. State, 372 S.E.2d 242, 244 (Ga. Ct. App. 1998) ("There is nothing more threatening to the integrity of our legal system than the possibility that the person or persons—whether judge or jury—charged with the responsibility for finding a defendant guilty or not guilty may be corrupted by the intrusion of interested outsiders into the sanctity of the factfinder's deliberations. It matters not whether the incentive be money, influence, or some other tangible or intangible entity. Jurors, like Caesar's wife, must avoid the very appearance of impropriety."); State v. Shipp. 116 P.3d 317, 320 (Utah 2005) ("In *Pike*, the defendant, after being convicted in a jury trial, requested a new trial on the basis that he was unfairly prejudiced when three jurors had a brief conversation with a key State witness during a recess in the trial. We held that '[a]nything more than the most incidental contact during the trial between witnesses and jurors casts doubt upon the impartiality of the jury and at best gives the appearance of the absence of impartiality.' We reiterated our rule that such contact 'raises a rebuttable presumption of prejudice,' which places the burden upon 'the prosecution to prove that the unauthorized contact did not influence the juror.'"); United States v. Kyles, 40 F.3d 519, 524 (6th Cir. 1994) ("Quite apart from the Sixth Amendment's requirements, the Supreme Court, in its supervisory capacity over the federal judiciary, has stated that a federal trial judge should usually grant a criminal

defendant's request to inquire into racial bias, in order to dispel any appearance of injustice."); Smith v. Phillips, 455 U.S. 209, 215 (1982) ("This Court has long held that the remedy for allegations of juror partiality is a hearing in which the defendant has the opportunity to prove actual bias."); *id.* at 217 ("Due process means a jury capable and willing to decide the case solely on the evidence before it, and a trial judge ever watchful to prevent prejudicial occurrences and to determine the effect of such occurrences when they happen."); *cf.* David P. Goldstein, *The Appearance of Impropriety and Jurors on Social Networking Sites: Rebooting the Way Courts Deal with Juror Misconduct*, 24 GEO. J. LEGAL ETHICS 589, 603–04 (2011):

> In order to protect public confidence in the judicial system, instances of juror misconduct via social networking sites and the use of sanctions to address such behavior must be evaluated under the appearance of impropriety standard. Currently, juror misconduct is viewed through the lens of prejudice. If the misconduct is not prejudicial against the defendant, a judge will generally not punish it. This standard is designed to protect the defendant's Sixth Amendment right to a fair trial. However, the prejudice standard does not account for potential damage to the judicial system's public image, something the *Model Code for Judicial Conduct* Rule 1.2 is designed to protect. News stories involving jurors Tweeting about evidence or posting Facebook messages describing deliberations reflect negatively on the judiciary as a whole, regardless of the prejudicial effect of that behavior. Allowing judges to apply the appearance of impropriety standard empowers them to punish misconduct that "create[s] in reasonable minds a perception" that jurors were engaged in "conduct that reflects adversely" on their "honesty, impartiality, temperament, or fitness to serve." This new ability would permit judges to assure the public of the "independence, impartiality, and integrity" of the judiciary, which in turn promotes public confidence in the judicial system. Public confidence is a prerequisite for an effective judicial system.

See also State v. Montgomery, 432 So.2d 340, 344–45 (La. Ct. App. 1983) ("The purpose of sequestering jurors is to protect them from outside influences and from basing their verdict upon anything other than evidence developed at trial.").

132. 315 U.S. 60 (1942).

133. In *Glasser*, the record indicated that the attorney failed to cross-examine a government witness whose testimony linked Glasser with the conspiracy and failed to object to the admission of arguably inadmissible evidence. *Id.* at 73–75. This failure was viewed by the Supreme Court as a result of the defense attorney's "struggle to serve two masters." *Id.* at 75.

134. *Id.* at 67.

135. 435 U.S. 475 (1978).

136. *Id.* at 488–91; *see also* Wood v. Georgia, 450 U.S. 261, 271 (1981) (observing that there is a constitutional right to counsel and "a correlative right to representation that is free from conflicts of interest").

> To determine the precise degree of prejudice sustained by Glasser as a result of the district court's appointment of Stewart as counsel for the co-defendant is at once difficult and unnecessary. The right to have the assistance of counsel is too fundamental and absolute to allow courts to indulge in nice calculations as to the amount of prejudice arising from its denial.

Glasser, 315 U.S. at 75–76.

137. Mickens v. Taylor, 535 U.S. 162, 166 (2002).

138. United States v. Cronic, 466 U.S. 648, 658 (1984).

139. Cuyler v. Sullivan, 446 U.S. 335, 346, 348 (1980); *cf.* Burger v. Kemp, 483 U.S. 776 (1987) ("We have never held that the possibility of prejudice that 'inheres in almost every instance of multiple representation' justifies the adoption of an inflexible rule that would presume prejudice in all such cases. Instead, we presume prejudice 'only if the defendant demonstrates that counsel 'actively represented conflicting interests' and that 'an actual conflict of interest adversely affected his lawyer's performance.'") (citations omitted).

140. Wheat v. United States, 486 U.S. 153, 159 (1988).

141. *Id.* at 160 (citations omitted).

142. *Marshall*, 446 U.S. at 248; *see also id.* ("The constitutional interests in accurate finding of facts and application of law, and in preserving a fair and open process for decision, are not to the same degree implicated if it is the prosecutor, and not the judge, who is offered an incentive for securing civil penalties.").

"Our legal system," the Court emphasized in *Marshall*, "has traditionally accorded wide discretion to criminal prosecutors in the enforcement process, and similar considerations have been found applicable to administrative prosecutors as well." *Marshall*, 446 U.S. at 248 (*citing* Linda R. S. v. Richard D., 410 U.S. 614 (1973) & Moog Industries, Inc. v. FTC, 355 U.S. 411, 414 (1958)); *see also Marshall*, 446 U.S. at 250 ("[W]e need not say with precision what limits there may be on a financial or personal interest of one who performs a prosecutorial function, for here the influence alleged to impose bias is exceptionally remote. No governmental official stands to profit economically from vigorous enforcement of the child labor provisions of the Act. The salary of the assistant regional administrator is fixed by law."); *id.* at 250–51 ("Nor is there a realistic possibility that the assistant regional administrator's judgment will be distorted by the prospect of institutional gain as a result of zealous enforcement efforts. As we have noted, the civil penalties collected under § 16(e) represent substantially less that 1% of the budget of the ESA. In each of the relevant years, the amount of the ESA's budget that was returned to the Treasury was substantially greater than the amount collected as civil penalties. Unlike in *Ward* and *Tumey*, it is plain that the enforcing agent is in no sense financially dependent on the maintenance of a high level of penalties. Furthermore, since it is the national office of the ESA, and not any assistant regional administrator, that decides how to allocate civil penalties, such administrators have no assurance that the penalties they assess will be returned to their offices at all."); *id.* at 251–53 ("The District Court's conclusion that the reimbursement provision violated the Due Process Clause was evidently premised on its perception that an assistant regional administrator might be tempted to devote an unusually large quantity of resources to enforcement efforts in the hope that he would ultimately obtain a higher total allocation of federal funds to his office. This increase in enforcement effort, the court suggested, might incline the assistant regional administrator to assess an unjustified number of penalties, and to make those penalties unduly high. But in light of the factors discussed above, it is clear that this possibility is too remote to violate the constraints applicable to the financial or personal interest of officials charged with prosecutorial or plaintiff-like functions.").

143. *Marshall*, 446 U.S. at 248–49 (*quoting* Ward v. Village of Monroeville, Ohio, 409 U.S. 57, 62 (1972)); *see also id.* at 249 ("The distinction between judicial and nonjudicial officers was explicitly made in *Tumey*, 273 U.S., at 535, 47 S. Ct., at 445, where the Court noted that a state legislature 'may, and often ought to, stimulate prosecutions for crime by offering to those who shall initiate and carry on such prosecutions rewards for thus acting in the interest of the state and the people.'").

144. Wright v. Fischer, No. 99-3901, 2000 WL 517788, at *3 (7th Cir. Apr. 26, 2000) ("Prosecutors cannot be sued for initiating a prosecution and presenting a case. Absolute immunity protects prosecutors performing quasi-judicial functions, such as evaluating evidence or preparing a case for trial or indictment.") (citing Buckley v. Fitzsimmons, 509 U.S. 259, 273 (1993)); DeCamp v. Douglas County Franklin Grand Jury, 978 F.2d 1047, 1052 (8th Cir. 1992) (noting that "[p]rosecutors enjoy their absolute immunity for quasi-judicial acts they undertake when *prosecuting* individuals") (italics in original); Murray v. Clower, No. 88-5178, 1988 WL 102517, at *2 (6th Cir. Oct. 5, 1988) ("The issuance of arrest warrants is a quasi-judicial function, and prosecutors have absolute immunity from claims arising out of the performance of that function."); Land v. Del Papa, No. 93-16489, 1994 WL 68245, at *1 (9th Cir. Mar. 3, 1994) ("[P]rosecutors are entitled to absolute immunity for 'quasi-judicial activities taken within the scope of their authority.' Because filing an opposition to a petition for habeas corpus clearly falls within the prosecutor's role as a judicial officer, the district court properly dismissed the complaint as to these two defendants."); *see also* Burton v. Infinity Capital Management, 862 F.3d 740, 748 (9th Cir. 2017):

> Absolute immunity has been extended to attorneys for performing the duties of a prosecutor. *Butz v. Economou*, 438 U.S. 478, 517, 98 S. Ct. 2894, 57 L.Ed.2d 895 (1978); *Imbler v. Pachtman*, 424 U.S. 409, 431, 96 S. Ct. 984, 47 L.Ed.2d 128 (1976); *Stapley v. Pestalozzi*, 733 F.3d 804, 811–12 (9th Cir. 2013). Prosecutors enjoy immunity when they take "action that only a legal representative of the government could take." *Stapley*, 733 F.3d at 812. However, the Supreme Court has not extended the immunity beyond the prosecutorial function. *Id.* at 811–12. Even court-appointed defense attorneys do not enjoy immunity because, despite being "officers" of the court, "attorneys [are not] in the same category as marshals, bailiffs, court clerks or judges." *Ferri v. Ackerman*, 444 U.S. 193, 202 n.19, 100 S. Ct. 402, 62 L.Ed.2d 355 (1979). In *Ferri*, the Supreme Court declined to extend immunity to defense attorneys because "the primary office performed by appointed

counsel parallels the office of privately retained counsel" where an attorney owes a duty to his client, not the public. *Id.* at 204, 100 S. Ct. 402. This implied disinclination to grant immunity to private counsel was solidified after the Supreme Court concluded that "private actors are not entitled to the absolute immunity granted to some government officials, such as prosecutors and judges." *Kimes v. Stone*, 84 F.3d 1121, 1128 (9th Cir. 1996) (citing *Wyatt v. Cole*, 504 U.S. 158, 164–65, 112 S. Ct. 1827, 118 L.Ed.2d 504 (1992)).

145. *Marshall*, 446 U.S. at 249.

146. *Id.*

147. *Id.*

148. *Id.* at 250 (*citing* Bordenkircher v. Hayes, 434 U.S. 357, 365 (1978); *cf.* 28 U.S.C. § 528 (1976 ed., Supp. III) (disqualifying federal prosecutor from participating in litigation in which he has a personal interest)); *compare id.* at 250 ("But the strict requirements of neutrality cannot be the same for administrative prosecutors as for judges, whose duty it is to make the final decision and whose impartiality serves as the ultimate guarantee of a fair and meaningful proceeding in our constitutional regime."), *with* Aetna Life Ins. Co. v. Lavoie, 475 U.S. 813 (1986) (a state supreme court's affirmance of a damage award was vacated where a justice on the state's highest court with a similar suit pending in a lower state court had cast an apparently decisive vote).

149. *See* Schweiker v. McClure, 456 U.S. 188, 195 (1982) (citations omitted) ("due process demands impartiality on the part of those who function in judicial or quasi-judicial capacities").

150. Bordenkircher v. Hayes, 434 U.S. 357 (1978) (federal prosecutor disqualified from participating in litigation in which he has a personal interest). In some cases, attorneys acquainted with victims have been permitted to appear in cases and sit at counsel table. *E.g.*, Smith v. State, 426 N.E.2d 364, 365 (Ind. 1981):

> The record shows that attorney Marcia Burgdorf requested permission of the trial judge to enter an appearance with the prosecutor for the State of Indiana for the trial of defendant. The deputy prosecuting the case, John D. Krisor, Jr., indicated to the court that attorney Burgdorf was acquainted with the victim, that she was licensed to practice law in the State of Indiana, and that she had been sworn in as a special deputy prosecutor for the trial of this case only. The trial court indicated that since Mrs. Burgdorf was a licensed attorney he would allow her to participate as an assistant or in a passive role. Appellant's objection seemed to be that Mrs. Burgdorf appeared as the victim's private attorney and that her presence was prejudicial to the defendant in that it lent credence to the victim's testimony by implication.
>
> Nowhere in the record does it appear that Mrs. Burgdorf was, in fact, the victim's private counsel nor was she introduced to the jury as such. The introduction to the jury indicated only that Mrs. Burgdorf was going to be assisting the prosecutor and the record does not show that she did anything whatsoever in the trial. Although she sat with the prosecuting attorney at the counsel table, she did not participate in the trial. The defendant, therefore, has not shown that the presence of Mrs. Burgdorf created any prejudice or harm to the defendant other than the speculative statement that it could have influenced the jury's verdict. Also, since the prosecuting attorney indicated to the court that Mrs. Burgdorf had been sworn as a deputy prosecuting attorney, she had a perfect right to appear for the State in a criminal case and it was not incumbent on the trial judge to refuse her appearance particularly since no sound reason was given for doing so. We find no error on this issue.

151. *E.g.*, Timothy Fry, Comment, *Prosecutorial Training Wheels: Ginsburg's* Connick v. Thompson *Dissent and the Training Imperative*, 102 J. CRIM. L. & CRIMINOLOGY 1275, 1278–79 (2012) ("Prosecutors have enormous, wide-ranging discretion to choose what crimes to investigate, whether to entertain plea bargains, when to grant immunity to a potential witness, how to organize the state's case, which charges to prosecute, and even in which jurisdiction to bring a case. Prosecutors are powerful actors, controlling the criminal justice system with an outsized impact on the wider political system. Prosecutors' day-to-day decisions happen behind closed doors and are virtually unreviewable. Prosecutors are answerable only to other prosecutors, who rarely prosecute such misconduct."); Venckus v. City of Iowa City, 930 N.W.2d 792, 828–29 (Iowa 2019) (Appel, J., concurring in part and dissenting in part) ("Our system of criminal justice

gives prosecutors remarkable power and wide discretion. Rachel E. Barkow, *Institutional Design and the Policing of Prosecutors: Lessons from Administrative Law*, 61 STAN. L. REV. 869, 874, 884 (2009) (characterizing prosecutors as 'leviathans' with 'unchecked power'). At the same time, we expect a prosecutor's interest to be 'not that [he] shall win a case, but that justice shall be done.' *Berger v. United States*, 295 U.S. 78, 88, 55 S. Ct. 629, 633, 79 L.Ed. 1314 (1935). '[W]hile he may strike hard blows, he is not at liberty to strike foul ones. It is as much his duty to refrain from improper methods calculated to produce a wrongful conviction as it is to use every legitimate means to bring about a just one.' Id.").

152. Jason Iuliano & Keith E. Whittington, *The Nondelegation Doctrine: Alive and Well*, 93 NOTRE DAME L. REV. 619, 643 (2017) ("[I]n 1924, a California court upheld a state law that gave prosecutors the ability to determine whether a criminal's second conviction for the unlawful possession of narcotics should be upgraded from a misdemeanor to a felony offense. In 1975, an Illinois state court ruled that a prosecutor can constitutionally be delegated the authority to decide whether to charge an individual with a felony or misdemeanor.").

153. *See, e.g.*, GOVERNMENT PRIVATIZATION: HISTORY, EXAMPLES, AND ISSUES, COMMISSION ON GOVERNMENT FORECASTING AND ACCOUNTABILITY (Oct. 2006); *see also* Behm v. City of Cedar Rapids, 922 N.W.2d 524, 571–72 (Iowa 2019) ("The *Texas Boll Weevil* court developed an eight-factor test to determine the validity of delegations of public authority to private agencies: 1. Are the private delegate[e]'s actions subject to meaningful review by a state agency or other branch of state government? 2. Are the persons affected by the private delegate[e]'s actions adequately represented in the decisionmaking process? 3. Is the private delegate[e]'s power limited to making rules, or does the delegate[e] also apply the law to particular individuals? 4. Does the private delegate[e] have a pecuniary or other personal interest that may conflict with his or her public functions? 5. Is the private delegate[e] empowered to define criminal acts or impose criminal sanctions? 6. Is the delegation narrow in duration, extent, and subject matter? 7. Does the private delegate[e] possess special qualifications or training for the task delegated to it? 8. Has the Legislature provided sufficient standards to guide the private delegate[e] in its work? *Id.* at 472.").

154. Tyler Grove, Note, *Are All Prosecutorial Activities "Inherently Governmental"?: Applying State Safeguards for Victim-Retained Private Prosecutions to Outsource Prosecutions*, 40 PUB. CONT. L.J. 991, 994 (2011).

155. Angela E. Addae, *Challenging the Constitutionality of Private Prisons: Insights from Israel*, 25 WM. & MARY J. RACE, GENDER & SOC. JUST. 527, 536 (2019) ("The Supreme Court of the United States has also acknowledged that there are certain governmental functions that cannot be delegated to private parties, a concept known as the nondelegation doctrine.") (citing Carter v. Carter Coal Co., 298 U.S. 238, 310 (1936)); *see also id.* at 537–38 ("Deprivation of liberty may be one function that is inherently governmental and should not be delegated to private parties. Though the U.S. Supreme Court has never adjudicated this particular issue, strong arguments exist that 1) liberty deprivation should be classified as a solely state function, and 2) the delegation of incarceration to private corporations violates the nondelegation doctrine. The primary challenge to a nondelegation argument is that the U.S. Supreme Court considers the doctrine moribund. The use of the doctrine has dissipated over time, among the likes of substantive due process and the restrictive commerce clause doctrines of the New Deal Era. The cases that presented successful claims against delegations to private parties under the nondelegation doctrine all occurred during this period. Still, the New Deal era cases primarily dealt with property interests, not liberty interests. Since then, the Court has hinted at the revival of the nondelegation doctrine and has insinuated that delegations interfering with liberty interests may warrant a higher standard.").

156. *See, e.g.*, Harold J. Krent, *The Private Performing the Public: Delimiting Delegations to Private Parties*, 65 U. MIAMI L. REV. 507, 525 (2011) ("Scholars across a wide spectrum of ideologies agree that the Constitution does not empower governmental officials to offload governmental powers to private entities that could in turn exercise those powers outside the constraints faced by public actors. Indeed, in the criminal law context, Chief Justice Roberts recently commented that delegations to private parties should be prohibited because '[a] basic step in organizing a civilized society is to take that sword out of private hands and turn it over to an organized government, acting on behalf of all the people.' The constitutional framework does not countenance delegation of at least some type of governmental authority to private individuals and groups.") (quoting Robertson v. United States ex rel. Watson, 130 S. Ct. 2184, 2190 (2010)

(Roberts, J., dissenting)); Seth Davis, *Standing Doctrine's State Action Problem*, 91 NOTRE DAME L. REV. 585, 610–11 (2015) ("Due process also limits private delegations, but leaves legislatures with substantial discretion to privatize government functions. *Carter v. Carter Coal Co.*, the foundational private nondelegation case, held that Congress violated the Due Process Clause of the Fifth Amendment by delegating to coal producers and miners the power to make wage and hour laws. When Congress later reenacted the statute, this time tasking an agency with adopting the standards, the Court held the delegation was constitutional because Congress had not 'delegated its legislative authority to the industry.' Thus, the Court set an outer limit on 'clearly arbitrary' delegations of lawmaking authority to private parties."); *see also* Roger A. Fairfax, Jr., *Delegation of the Criminal Prosecution Function to Private Actors*, 43 U.C. DAVIS L. REV. 411, 413–14 (2009) ("This Article argues that the private exercise of the tremendous discretion reserved for public prosecutors represents an inappropriate delegation of sovereign prerogative. The Article asserts that delegating the prosecution function to private lawyers presents the potential for conflicts of interest and corruption, the erosion of due process, prosecutorial underperformance, and diminished accountability. Also, examining the important values associated with the modern public prosecution norm, the Article seeks to unravel the knotty issues inherent in the state's delegation of discretionary prosecutorial functions to private actors. Fundamentally, the private exercise of the discretionary prosecutorial function—what Austin Sarat and Conor Clarke term a 'fragment of sovereignty'—challenges our settled assumptions regarding the public-private distinction and government authority. Moreover, it calls into question the role and professional identity of the prosecutor in the modern system of criminal justice and, perhaps, the essential nature of the system itself.").

157. Robert Craig & André Douglas Pond Cummings, *Abolish Private Prisons: A Constitutional and Moral Imperative*, 49 U. BALT. L. REV. 261, 266–67 (2020); *see also id.* at 282–83 ("Private incarceration represents 'delegation in its most obnoxious form; for it is not even delegation to an official or an official body, presumptively disinterested, but to private persons whose interests may be and often are adverse to the interests of' the incarcerated. The 'intelligible principles' test may have rendered the public nondelegation doctrine toothless; '[n]ot so, however, in the case of private entities to whom the Constitution commits no executive power.' Although courts have not explicitly delineated the structural underpinnings of the private nondelegation doctrine, two main themes drive their decisions: first, core governmental functions cannot be delegated to private parties; and second, executive branches cannot grant legal enforcement power to entities outside the government over whom the executive does not exercise control. Each of these themes point toward the result that private incarceration violates the United States Constitution.").

158. Rachel Christine Bailie Antonuccio, *Prisons for Profit: Do the Social and Political Problems Have a Legal Solution?*, 33 J. CORP. L. 577, 590 (2008) ("[G]iven the nature of the business at issue, the goal of making money often puts prison corporations' interests in diametric opposition to general societal goals. Private prison corporations do not have a financial interest in promoting a society focused on preventing crime, imprisoning only individuals who pose an active threat, and rehabilitating and/or educating incarcerated individuals so that they may avoid future imprisonment. If these goals are realized, private prisons lose the primary source of their profits—the prisoners. Instead, it is in private prisons' interest to encourage longer sentences, incarceration as a punishment for more crimes, and reduced reliance on parole or probation. None of these options benefit either the prisoners or society as a whole.").

159. For a history of the origins and development of the Enlightenment maxim, see JOHN D. BESSLER, THE BARON AND THE MARQUIS: LIBERTY, TYRANNY, AND THE ENLIGHTENMENT MAXIM THAT CAN REMAKE AMERICAN CRIMINAL JUSTICE (2019).

160. *E.g.*, Behm v. City of Cedar Rapids, 922 N.W.2d 524, 572 (Iowa 2019) ("[T]he cases also recognize that some types of government functions are simply not delegable. For example, the Secretary of Defense cannot delegate war-making authority to the Rand Corporation, and the Attorney General cannot delegate the decision whether to prosecute to a private attorney. *See* Paul R. Verkuil, *Public Law Limitations on Privatization of Government Functions*, 84 N.C. L. REV. 397, 425 (2006). In federal procurement, the Office of Management and Budget's Circular A-76 prohibits contracting of "inherently governmental" activities, including activities that involve '[d]etermining, protecting, and advancing economic... interests by... contract management' and activities '[s]ignificantly affecting the life, liberty, or property of private persons.' *Id.* at 438."). Courts have analyzed the role and responsibility of private parties in relation to public

actors in various contexts. *See, e.g.*, Herman v. Lackey, 309 Fed. Appx. 778, 782 (4th Cir. 2009) ("joint participation of public and private actors may turn private conduct into state conduct for purposes of a § 1983 claim"); Andrews v. Federal Home Loan Bank of Atlanta, 998 F.2d 214, 217 (4th Cir. 1993) ("A private party can be deemed a state actor in four contexts: (1) when the state has coerced the private actor to commit an act that would be unconstitutional if done by the state; (2) when the state has sought to evade a clear constitutional duty through delegation to a private actor; (3) when the state has delegated a traditionally and exclusively public function to a private actor; or (4) when the state has committed an unconstitutional act in the course of enforcing a right of a private citizen. If the conduct does not fall into one of these four categories, then the private conduct is not an action of the state.").

161. Coercive private power is especially problematic when *interested* private actors are handling or involved in criminal prosecutions. Adrian Vermeule, *Optimal Abuse of Power*, 109 Nw. U. L. Rev. 673, 675–76 (2015) ("The architects of the modern administrative state were not only worried about abuse of power by governmental officials; they were equally worried about 'private' abuses—abuses effected through the self-interested behavior of economic actors wielding delegated state power under the rules of the common law of property, tort, and contract, and under corporate law. The administrative state thus trades off governmental and 'private' abuse; it accepts increased risks of official abuse and distorted decisionmaking to give governmental officials more power to suppress 'private' abuses, to increase the activity level of the government as a whole, and to give administrators sufficient information to combat the evils that arise in complex sectors of the economy."); *cf.* Association of American Railroads v. United States Dep't of Transportation, 821 F.3d 19, 31 (D.C. Cir. 2016) (noting that "[c]urbing the misuse of public power was the aim of the Magna Carta, and the Supreme Court has consistently concluded the delegation of coercive power to private parties can raise ... due process concerns") (citing Eubank v. City of Richmond, 226 U.S. 137 (1912); City of Eastlake v. Forest City Enters., Inc., 426 U.S. 668, 677–78 (1976); Silverman v. Barry, 727 F.2d 1121, 1126 (D.C. Cir. 1984)).

162. *E.g.*, Ridings v. Lane County, Or., 862 F.2d 231, 235 (9th Cir. 1988) ("The prosecution of crimes is no less a traditional governmental function than is the operation of a police force. Law enforcement includes both the investigation of crimes and the prosecution of criminal proceedings."); Spencer v. Lee, 864 F.2d 1376, 1380 (7th Cir. 1989) ("That Socrates was prosecuted by a private denouncer does not place the prosecution of crime in Illinois today outside the core of governmental functions. Every function performed by government has an analogue that was performed privately when government was rudimentary, or before there *was* government—for social order is older than government. The tradition that establishes a core of exclusive governmental functions does not reach back so far."). *But see id.* ("There have been citizen arrests for as long as there have been public police—indeed much longer. In ancient Greece and Rome, and in England until the nineteenth century, most arrests and prosecutions were by private individuals. (Some crimes, e.g., shoplifting, are still privately prosecuted in England.) Arrest has never been an exclusively governmental function. Not all state-authorized coercion is government action."). One regulation, published at 32 C.F.R. § 169.3, notes that "[g]overnmental functions normally fall into two categories," one of which involves "[t]he discretionary exercise of Governmental authority." "Examples," that regulation reads, "include criminal investigations, prosecutions, and other judicial functions; management of Government programs requiring value judgments....").

163. Paul Gewirtz, *Victims and Voyeurs at the Criminal Trial*, 90 Nw. U. L. Rev. 863, 865 (1996):

> The existence of a victim, of course, is what prompts the criminal trial. The earliest court proceedings in England denominated "criminal" were, in fact, private prosecutions brought by the victim directly. But as the criminal process evolved, prosecution became a government function. The victim became a trigger and a witness for the prosecution, rather than the prosecution's director. Put another way, the victim was no longer the guiding narrator of the proceedings but became instead just one of many storytellers at trial. Today, criminal litigation against the alleged wrongdoer is controlled by a government prosecutor, not by the victim, and it is the government, not the victim, that decides which witnesses to present, guides the stories they tell, and shapes opening and closing statements to the jury. Thus, the modern prosecution is not really a battle between the victim and the accused. A criminal prosecution claiming that Smith was robbed by defendant Jones is not captioned Smith v. Jones but is called The State v. Jones or The People v.

Jones. The abstraction of the "state" calls the wrongdoer to account, displacing the victim because the wrong is seen as one against the community as much as any particular victim.

164. Even when someone contemplates a civil lawsuit in the context of a criminal case, that information is relevant to a prosecuting witness' credibility. Martin v. State, 775 A.2d 385, 391 (Md. 2001) ("The question posed by defense counsel here was whether the witness had hired an attorney to file a civil lawsuit against petitioner, arising from the same set of circumstances as the criminal prosecution in which the witness was testifying. We hold that the trial court erred in refusing to permit defense counsel to attempt to impeach the credibility of the prosecuting witness by eliciting testimony regarding a contemplated lawsuit."); *id.* ("The jury had to decide whether to accept petitioner's version of the events or Guevera's version. Thus, credibility was a central issue in the case. Since Guevera's retaining a lawyer to bring a civil lawsuit was relevant to his credibility, it was error to preclude defense counsel from cross-examining him about it. Guevera testified that petitioner simply took $300 from the Guevera's pocket, placed it in his own pocket, and left. Petitioner's version of events, however, is that Guevera taunted him verbally and waved the money in his face, that he then took the money from Guevera's hand in anger, and that he forgot momentarily that he had the money when he responded to a call to duty. These versions of the incident differ significantly, and the jury's assessment of who was telling the truth was critical. Petitioner was denied the opportunity to establish the bias or pecuniary interest of the witness. Thus, the complete denial to petitioner of an opportunity to impeach the witness's credibility was not harmless error.").

165. Yuri R. Linetsky, *A Rule 11 for Prosecutors*, 87 Tenn. L. Rev. 1, 4 (2019).

166. *Cf.* Roger A. Fairfax, Jr., *Delegation of the Criminal Prosecution Function to Private Actors*, 43 U.C. Davis L. Rev. 411, 432 (2009) ("Sarat and others present criminal prosecution as an inherently public function, with profound impact on life and liberty, unsuitable for delegation to private hands. As such, they provide a compelling rationale for withholding such discretion from private actors.").

167. Jamie Connolly, Note, *Prosecutorial Discretion and Collateral Consequences: Rethinking the Alabama Rules of Professional Conduct*, 43 J. Legal Prof. 269, 270 (2019) ("Collateral consequences include a variety of legal and regulatory restrictions from revoking a business license to withholding the right to vote. These consequences pose unique harms that can be impossible to escape. The mere fact of a criminal record can bar an individual from fundamental rights such as housing and education. In Alabama, a felony or misdemeanor conviction carries up to 307 potential consequences aside from traditional prison and probation sentences, and an additional 455 consequences accompany convictions for other offenses such as child-support offenses, recreational license offenses, and motor vehicle offenses.").

168. Paul T. Crane, *Charging on the Margin*, 57 Wm. & Mary L. Rev. 775, 785 (2016).

169. 424 U.S. 319 (1976).

170. *Id.* at 332.

171. *Id.* at 333 (citations omitted).

172. *Id.* (quoting Armstrong v. Manzo, 380 U.S. 545, 552 (1965)).

173. *Id.* at 334–35 (citations omitted). *Compare* Swarthout v. Cooke, 562 U.S. 216, 219 (2011) ("As for the Due Process Clause, standard analysis under that provision proceeds in two steps: We first ask whether there exists a liberty or property interest of which a person has been deprived, and if so we ask whether the procedures followed by the State were constitutionally sufficient.") (citing *Kentucky Dept. of Corrections v. Thompson*, 490 U.S. 454, 460, 109 S. Ct. 1904, 104 L.Ed.2d 506 (1989)).

174. 505 U.S. 437 (1992). *Compare* Nelson v. Colorado, 137 S. Ct. 1249 (2017) (the procedural due process inspection instructed by *Mathews v. Eldridge*, 424 U.S. 319 (1976), requiring a court to evaluate the private interest affected, the risk of erroneous deprivation of that interest through the procedures used, and the governmental interest at stake, governed the determination of whether Colorado's statutory scheme requiring exonerated defendants to prove their innocence by clear and convincing evidence to obtain the refund of costs, fees, and restitution paid pursuant to an invalid conviction violated due process, rather than the standard from *Medina v. California*, 505 U.S. 437 (1992), requiring a court to ask whether defendants were exposed to a procedure offensive to a fundamental principle of justice, since the scheme addressed the continuing deprivation of property after a conviction had been reversed or vacated, with no prospect of reprosecution), *with Nelson*, 137 S. Ct. at 1258–59 (Alito, J., concurring in the judgment):

The proper framework for analyzing these cases is provided by *Medina v. California*, 505 U.S. 437, 112 S. Ct. 2572, 120 L.Ed.2d 353 (1992). *Medina* applies when we are called upon to "asses[s] the validity of state procedural rules which... are part of the criminal process," *id.*, at 443, 112 S. Ct. 2572 and that is precisely the situation here. These cases concern Colorado's rules for determining whether a defendant can obtain a refund of money that he or she was required to pay pursuant to a judgment of conviction that is later reversed. In holding that these payments must be refunded, the Court relies on a feature of the criminal law, the presumption of innocence. And since the Court demands that refunds occur either automatically or at least without imposing anything more than "minimal" procedures, see *ante*, at 1257, it appears that they must generally occur as part of the criminal case. For these reasons, the refund obligation is surely "part of the criminal process" and thus falls squarely within the scope of *Medina*. The only authority cited by the Court in support of its contrary conclusion is a footnote in a dissent. See *ante*, at 1255 (citing *Kaley v. United States*, 571 U.S. —, —, n.4, 134 S. Ct. 1090, 1110 n.4, 188 L.Ed.2d 46 (2014) (opinion of Roberts, C.J.)). Under *Medina*, a state rule of criminal procedure not governed by a specific rule set out in the Bill of Rights violates the Due Process Clause of the Fourteenth Amendment only if it offends a fundamental and deeply rooted principle of justice. 505 U.S., at 445, 112 S. Ct. 2572. And "[h]istorical practice is probative of whether a procedural rule can be characterized as fundamental." Id., at 446, 112 S. Ct. 2572. Indeed, petitioners invite us to measure the Colorado scheme against traditional practice, reminding us that our "'first due process cases'" recognized that "'traditional practice provides a touchstone for constitutional analysis,'" Brief for Petitioners 26 (quoting *Honda Motor Co. v. Oberg*, 512 U.S. 415, 430, 114 S. Ct. 2331, 129 L.Ed.2d 336 (1994)). Petitioners then go on to argue at some length that "[t]he traditional rule has always been that when a judgment is reversed, a person who paid money pursuant to that judgment is entitled to receive the money back." Brief for Petitioners 26; see *id.*, at 26–30. See also Brief for National Association of Criminal Defense Lawyers as *Amicus Curiae* 4–14 (discussing traditional practice).

The Court, by contrast, turns its back on historical practice, preferring to balance the competing interests according to its own lights. The Court applies the balancing test set out in *Mathews v. Eldridge*, 424 U.S. 319, 96 S. Ct. 893, 47 L.Ed.2d 18 (1976), a modern invention "first conceived" to decide what procedures the government must observe before depriving persons of novel forms of property such as welfare or Social Security disability benefits. Dusenbery v. United States, 534 U.S. 161, 167, 122 S. Ct. 694, 151 L.Ed.2d 597 (2002). Because these interests had not previously been regarded as "property," the Court could not draw on historical practice for guidance. *Mathews* has subsequently been used more widely in civil cases, but we should pause before applying its balancing test in matters of state criminal procedure. "[T]he States have considerable expertise in matters of criminal procedure and the criminal process is grounded in centuries of common-law tradition." *Medina, supra*, at 445–446, 112 S. Ct. 2572. Applying the *Mathews* balancing test to established rules of criminal practice and procedure may result in "undue interference with both considered legislative judgments and the careful balance that the Constitution strikes between liberty and order." *Medina, supra*, at 443, 112 S. Ct. 2572. Where long practice has struck a particular balance between the competing interests of the State and those charged with crimes, we should not lightly disturb that determination. For these reasons, *Medina*'s historical inquiry, not *Mathews*, provides the proper framework for use in these cases.

175. *Medina*, 505 U.S. at 443. The Court in *Medina* stressed: "*Mathews* itself involved a due process challenge to the adequacy of administrative procedures established for the purpose of terminating Social Security disability benefits, and the *Mathews* balancing test was first conceived to address due process claims arising in the context of administrative law. Although we have since characterized the *Mathews* balancing test as 'a general approach for testing challenged state procedures under a due process claim,' *Parham v. J.R.*, 442 U.S. 584, 599, 99 S. Ct. 2493, 2502, 61 L.Ed.2d 101 (1979), and applied it in a variety of contexts, *e.g., Santosky v. Kramer*, 455 U.S. 745, 102 S. Ct. 1388, 71 L.Ed.2d 599 (1982) (standard of proof for termination of parental rights over objection); *Addington v. Texas*, 441 U.S. 418, 99 S. Ct. 1804, 60 L.Ed.2d 323 (1979) (standard of proof for involuntary civil commitment to mental hospital for indefinite

period), we have invoked *Mathews* in resolving due process claims in criminal law cases on only two occasions." *Medina*, 505 U.S. at 444; *see also id.* ("In *United States v. Raddatz*, 447 U.S. 667, 100 S. Ct. 2406, 65 L.Ed.2d 424 (1980), we cited to the *Mathews* balancing test in rejecting a due process challenge to a provision of the Federal Magistrates Act which authorized magistrates to make findings and recommendations on motions to suppress evidence. In *Ake v. Oklahoma*, 470 U.S. 68, 105 S. Ct. 1087, 84 L.Ed.2d 53 (1985), we relied upon *Mathews* in holding that, when an indigent capital defendant has made a preliminary showing that his sanity at the time of the offense is likely to be a significant factor at trial, due process requires that the defendant be provided access to the assistance of a psychiatrist. Without disturbing the holdings of *Raddatz* and *Ake*, it is not at all clear that *Mathews* was essential to the results reached in those cases."); *see also* Nelson v. Colorado, 137 S. Ct. 1249, 1255 (2017) ("*Medina* 'provide[s] the appropriate framework for assessing the validity of state procedural rules' that 'are part of the criminal process.'").

176. *Medina*, 505 U.S. at 443 (citing Dowling v. United States, 493 U.S. 341, 352 (1990) & United States v. Lovasco, 431 U.S. 783, 790 (1977)).

177. *Id.*; *see also id.* at 443–444 ('As we said in *Spencer v. Texas*, 385 U.S. 554, 564, 87 S. Ct. 648, 653, 17 L.Ed.2d 606 (1967), 'it has never been thought that [decisions under the Due Process Clause] establish this Court as a rule-making organ for the promulgation of state rules of criminal procedure.'").

178. *Id.* at 445; *id.* ("In *Patterson*, we rejected a due process challenge to a New York law which placed on a criminal defendant the burden of proving the affirmative defense of extreme emotional disturbance. Rather than relying upon the *Mathews* balancing test, however, we reasoned that a narrower inquiry was more appropriate....").

179. *Id.* (citations omitted); *see also id.* at 445–46 ("As *Patterson* suggests, because the States have considerable expertise in matters of criminal procedure and the criminal process is grounded in centuries of common-law tradition, it is appropriate to exercise substantial deference to legislative judgments in this area. The analytical approach endorsed in *Patterson* is thus far less intrusive than that approved in *Mathews*."). "Historical practice," the Court noted in *Medina*, "is probative of whether a procedural rule can be characterized as fundamental." *Id.* at 446. The Court in *Medina* further observed that "[c]ontemporary practice" is "of limited relevance to the due process inquiry." *Id.* at 447.

180. *Medina*, 505 U.S. at 439. *See also* White v. State, 837 S.E.2d 838, 844 n.5 (Ga. 2020) ("The Court noted in *Medina* that the *Mathews* balancing test was first conceived to address procedural due process claims arising in the context of administrative law, that the Court had invoked *Mathews* to resolve due process claims in criminal law cases on only two occasions, and that it was not at all clear that *Mathews* was essential to the results reached in those cases."); Kaley v. United States, 571 U.S. 320, 334 (2014) (declining got address arguments about, or to define the respective reach of, *Mathews* and *Medina*).

181. 1 WAYNE R. LAFAVE, JEROLD H. ISRAEL, NANCY J. KING & ORIN S. KERR, CRIM. PROC. § 2.7(c)—*Due process methodology* (Dec. 2020 update):

> In the Supreme Court's first major ruling on the procedural content of due process, *Murray's Lessee v. Hoboken Land and Improvement Co.*, the Court asked the question: "To what principles * * * are we to resort to ascertain whether * * * [a] process, enacted by Congress, is due process?" Its answer was "to look to those settled usages and modes of proceeding existing in the common law and statute law of England, before the immigration of our ancestors, and which are shown not to have been unsuited to their civil and political condition by having been acted on by them after settlement of this country." The procedure at issue in *Murray's Lessee*, a summary distress warrant process, was upheld as consistent with that standard. Since that procedure was fully in accord with English common law and with "the laws of many of the States at the time of the adoption of * * * [the Fifth] Amendment," it could not "be denied to be due process."
>
> The reasoning of *Murray's Lessee* suggested a due process clause that was "frozen-in-history." If the challenged procedure had been accepted at the common law as it existed at the time of the adoption of the Constitution, it was per se consistent with the mandate of due process. If the challenged procedure had been rejected at common law (either by a direct ruling or by being in conflict with what was required at common law), it was a per se violation of due process. Where the practice was not known at common law, and was not inconsistent with the procedure

employed at common law, it presumably was constitutionally acceptable under this reading of *Murray's Lessee* because it did not contradict the "law of the land" mandated by due process.

182. Redish & Marshall, *supra* note 69, at 469.

183. *See, e.g.*, Daniel S. McConkie, *Structuring Pre-Plea Criminal Discovery*, 107 J. CRIM. L. & CRIMINOLOGY 1, 39–40 (2017):

> Although the core purpose of due process has always been to make fair and accurate adjudicatory decisions, the Supreme Court has used different tests over time for determining whether a particular feature of criminal procedure comported with due process. An important early case is *Murray's Lessee* (1855), involving the federal government's use of a nonjudicial warrant to recover embezzled funds. The Supreme Court decided what constituted due process in that case by reference to the common law and accepted practices at the time of the Fifth Amendment's passage. In other words, the Court took history for its guide.
>
> A later case, *Hurtado v. California* (1884), took a markedly different approach in assessing a state's procedural innovation. The Supreme Court held that California had not violated the Fourteenth Amendment's Due Process Clause by allowing prosecutors in felony cases to dispense with the grand jury indictment and to proceed instead by way of a judicial probable cause determination. The *Hurtado* Court took a different view of the common law than *Murray's Lessee*: "[I]t was the characteristic principle of the common law to draw its inspiration from every fountain of justice, [and] we are not to assume that the sources of its supply have been exhausted." Even if California's procedure did not comport with the common law, as long as the procedure was consistent with "fundamental principles of liberty and justice," due process was satisfied. The new procedure must be non-arbitrary and substantially equivalent to the common law procedure in its protections afforded to defendants.

184. 211 U.S. 78 (1908).

185. *Id.* at 100 (emphasis added).

186. Kerry v. Din, 576 U.S. 86, 90 (2015).

187. Redish & Marshall, *supra* note 69, at 468 (citing *Twining*, 211 U.S. at 101); *see also* Adamson v. California, 332 U.S. 46, 61 (1947) (Frankfurter, J., concurring) (asking whether procedures are necessary for the "protection of ultimate decency in a civilized society"); Snyder v. Massachusetts, 291 U.S. 97, 116 (1934) ("due process of law," according to Justice Cardozo, "requires that the proceedings shall be fair"). For a source containing essays regarding the "original intent" debate, see INTERPRETING THE CONSTITUTION: THE DEBATE OVER ORIGINAL INTENT (Jack Rakove ed. 1990).

188. 1 CHARLES H. KOCH, JR., ADMIN. L. & PRAC. § 2:20 (3d ed. Feb. 2021 update).

189. 1 WAYNE R. LAFAVE, JEROLD H. ISRAEL, NANCY J. KING & ORIN S. KERR, CRIM. PROC. § 2.7(c)—*Due process methodology* (4th ed. Dec. 2020 update); *see also* 1 WAYNE R. LAFAVE, JEROLD H. ISRAEL, NANCY J. KING & ORIN S. KERR, CRIM. PROC. § 2.9(d)—*The original understanding* (4th ed. Dec. 2020 update):

> Historically accepted practices have also been rejected on the ground that the practice conflicts with a more fully developed subsequent understanding of the general principles underlying a particular guarantee. Thus, the practice of not providing court appointed counsel for indigent felony defendants was held to violate the Sixth Amendment in light of experience establishing the "obvious truth that the average defendant does not have the professional legal skill" to ensure that he receives a fair trial. So too, the right to jury trial was held to extend to criminal contempt proceedings, notwithstanding a well established common law practice of allowing judges to try contempt cases without juries, because "experience teaches that convictions for criminal contempts * * * are indistinguishable from those obtained under ordinary criminal laws" and safeguards developed over the years to minimize "the malfunctioning of the jury system" ensured that jury participation would not undermine the judicial interest in vindicating its authority through contempt sanctions. The analysis applied in such cases is reconciled with originalism on the assumption that the Framers would not have wanted a constitutional framework designed for the future as well as the present to lock-in their specific, immediate expectations on the application of a guarantee without regard to what might be learned through subsequent experience in

applying that guarantee to a variety of different settings. When such experience reveals that a practice originally thought to be consistent with the guarantee's core purpose is, in fact, in conflict with that purpose, requiring a choice between the Framers' specific expectation and their overall objective, they presumably would have expected coherence in effectuating that overall objective to prevail.

The concepts of changed circumstances, guarantees that absorb the "evolving gloss of civilized standards," and re-examination in light of the deeper, experienced-based understanding of a guarantee's core purpose, provide ample leeway for holding unconstitutional any historically sanctioned practice viewed by today's Court as inconsistent with the general thrust of its current interpretation of a particular guarantee. Whether that will occur depends in large part on that point within the spectrum of judicially recognized approaches to constitutional interpretation at which a Court majority can be formed. Over the years, individual justices have varied considerably in their basic positions on originalism, and their willingness to override historical sanction on any or all of the above guards resulting in sometimes substantial and sometimes subtle shift's as the composition of the Court changes.

190. United States v. Windsor, 570 U.S. 744, 774 (2013).

191. Powell v. Alabama, 287 U.S. 45 (1932); *see also* State Farm Mut. Auto. Ins. Co. v. Campbell, 538 U.S. 408, 416 (2003) ("The Due Process Clause of the Fourteenth Amendment prohibits the imposition of grossly excessive or arbitrary punishments on a tortfeasor.").

192. Joel K. Goldstein, *Teaching the Transformative Fourteenth Amendment*, 62 St. Louis U. L.J. 581, 582 (2018) ("The Fourteenth Amendment has made the Constitution much more rights-focused and rights-protective, restructured the relationship between national and state government, and changed the role and work of branches of the national government, among other things. And it gave equality and fairness a more exalted and prominent place in American constitutional ideals, thereby recognizing and celebrating American pluralism as among the Constitution's strengths and intrinsic and enduring commitments. The transformation occurred largely through the process of incorporation of rights as against the states and through the development of the Equal Protection and Due Process Clauses over time, and these three Fourteenth Amendment streams together have made the theory and practice of American constitutional government quite different from what previously existed.").

193. *See also* Tyler Grove, *Are All Prosecutorial Activities "Inherently Governmental"?: Applying State Safeguards for Victim-Retained Private Prosecutions to Outsourced Prosecutions*, 40 Pub. Cont. L.J. 991, 1003 (2011) ("Though it receives relatively little commentary or attention, the United States has a long history that continues to this day of allowing victim-retained private attorneys to initiate and prosecute crimes. The role private prosecutors play in a trial can range from providing minor ministerial assistance to the public prosecutor to a much more significant role of lead attorney. Victim-retained private prosecutors at trial often perform the same tasks as their public counterparts: examining witnesses, making objections, and conducting opening and closing arguments.").

194. Barbara E. Bergman, Theresa M. Duncan & Marlo Cadeddu, 1 Wharton's Criminal Procedure § 1.1—*Who Makes the Decision* (updated Jan. 2021).

195. Louis S. Rulli, *Prosecuting Civil Asset Forfeiture on Contingency Fees: Looking for Profit in All the Wrong Places*, 72 Ala. L. Rev. 531, 556–57 (2021).

196. Rehberg v. Paulk, 566 U.S. 356, 364–66 (2012); *see also id.* at 361 ("Section 1983, which derives from § 1 of the Civil Rights Act of 1871, 17 Stat. 13, creates a private right of action to vindicate violations of 'rights, privileges, or immunities secured by the Constitution and laws' of the United States. Under the terms of the statute, "'[e]very person' who acts under color of state law to deprive another of a constitutional right [is] answerable to that person in a suit for damages." ") (quoting *Imbler v. Pachtman*, 424 U.S. 409, 417, 96 S. Ct. 984, 47 L.Ed.2d 128 (1976) (citing 42 U.S.C. § 1983)").

197. Madeleine Carlisle, "The Debate Over Qualified Immunity Is at the Heart of Police Reform. Here's What to Know," Time, June 3, 2021, https://time.com/6061624/what-is-qualified-immunity/.

198. *E.g.*, Stacey Haws Felkner, *Proof of Qualified Immunity Defense in 42 U.S.C.A. § 1983 or Bivens Actions Against Law Enforcement Officers*, 59 Am. Jr. Proof of Facts 3d 291, at § 1 (2000; updated Apr. 2021) ("Qualified immunity is a judicially created affirmative defense which protects state or local officials

sued in their individual capacity under 42 U.S.C.A. § 1983, or federal officials sued in their individual capacity under *Bivens v. Six Unknown Fed. Narcotics Agents*."); *id.* ("The doctrine of qualified immunity is a judicially created affirmative defense protecting public officials sued for violations of constitutional rights. Recognizing that constitutional law is constantly evolving, and that public officials cannot be 'expected to predict the future course of constitutional law,' the Supreme Court has decided that government officials performing discretionary functions should be shielded from liability for civil damages insofar as their conduct does not violate clearly established statutory or constitutional rights of which a reasonable person would have known. The qualified immunity defense is intended to provide 'protection to all but the plainly incompetent or those who knowingly violate the law.'"); *see also* Correctional Services Corp. v. Malesko, 534 U.S. 61 (2001) (there was no implied private right of actions, pursuant to *Bivens*, for damages against private entities that engaged in alleged constitutional deprivations while acting under color of federal law); Minneci v. Pollard, 565 U.S. 118, 120, 131 (2011) (prisoner could not assert an Eighth Amendment *Bivens* claim for damages against private prison employees; "[b]ecause we believe that in the circumstances present here state tort law authorizes adequate alternative damages actions—actions that provide both significant deterrence and compensation—we cannot do so, with the Supreme Court citing *Bivens v. Six Unknown Fed. Narcotics Agents*, 403 U.S. 388, 389 (1971) and another case, *Wilkie v. Robbins*, 551 U.S. 537, 550 (2007) for the proposition that there can be "no *Bivens* action where 'alternative, existing' processes provide adequate protection"; "[W]here, as here, a federal prisoner seeks damages from privately employed personnel working at a privately operated federal prison, where the conduct allegedly amounts to a violation of the Eighth Amendment, and where that conduct is of a kind that typically falls within the scope of traditional state tort law (such as the conduct involving improper medical care at issue here), the prisoner must seek a remedy under state tort law. We cannot imply a *Bivens* remedy in such a case."). *Compare* Cooper v. Parrish, 203 F.3d 937, 952–53 (6th Cir. 2000) (private attorney working alongside a prosecutor may not assert qualified immunity), *with* Cullinan v. Abramson, 128 F.3d 301, 310–11 (6th Cir. 1997) (private attorneys serving as outside counsel to a city may assert qualified immunity).

199. By contrast, in *Richardson v. McKnight*, 521 U.S. 399 (1997), an inmate brought a section 1983 action against two prison guards who were employees of a private, for-profit corporation which had a contract with the state to manage a correctional facility. The inmate alleged that the restraints used on him by the guards caused him serious injury requiring his hospitalization. In an opinion written by Justice Stephen Breyer, the U.S. Supreme Court held, in a 5 to 4 decision, that the prison guards were not entitled to qualified immunity from suit. *Id.* at 401. In reaching that conclusion, the Court emphasized that "[h]istory does *not* reveal a 'firmly rooted' tradition of immunity applicable to privately employed prison guards." *Id.* at 404. "*Government*-employed prison guards may have enjoyed a kind of immunity defense arising out of their status as public employees at common law," the Court ruled. *Id.* at 405 (citing Procunier v. Navarette, 434 U.S. 555, 561–62 (1978) (extending qualified immunity to state prison guards)), "[b]ut correctional functions"—as the Court emphasized—"have never been exclusively public." *Id.* As the Court observed, citing the work of historians: "Private individuals operated local jails in the 18th century, and private contractors were heavily involved in prison management during the 19th century." *Id.*; *see also id.* (as regards the nineteenth century, the Supreme Court noted: "During that time, some States, including southern States like Tennessee, leased their entire prison systems to private individuals or companies which frequently took complete control over prison management, including inmate labor and discipline."); *id.* at 405–06 ("Private prison lease agreements (like inmate suits) seem to have been more prevalent after § 1983's enactment, see generally M. Mancini, One Dies, Get Another (1996), but we have found evidence that the common law provided mistreated prisoners in prison leasing States with remedies against mistreatment by those private lessors. *See, e.g., Dade Coal Co. v. Haslett*, 83 Ga. 549, 550–551, 10 S.E. 435, 435–436 (1889) (convict can recover from contractor for injuries sustained while on lease to private company); *Boswell v. Barnhart*, 96 Ga. 521, 522–523, 23 S.E. 414, 415 (1895) (wife can recover from contractor for chain-gang-related death of husband); *Dalheim v. Lemon*, 45 F. 225, 228–230 (1891) (contractor liable for convict injuries); *Tillar v. Reynolds*, 96 Ark. 358, 360–361, 365–366, 131 S.W. 969, 970, 971–972 (1910) (work farm owner liable for inmate beating death); *Weigel v. Brown*, 194 F. 652 (C.A.8 1912) (prison contractor liable for unlawful whipping); see also *Edwards v. Pocahontas*, 47 F. 268 (CC Va. 1891) (inmate can recover from municipal corporation for injuries caused by poor jail conditions); *Hall v. O'Neil Turpentine*

Co., 56 Fla. 324, 47 So. 609 (1908) (private prison contractor and subcontractor liable to municipality for escaped prisoner under lease agreement); see generally Mancini, *supra* (discussing abuses of 19th-century private lease system). Yet, we have found no evidence that the law gave purely private companies or their employees any special immunity from such suits. Cf. *Almango v. Board of Supervisors of Albany County*, 32 N.Y.Sup.Ct. 551 (1881) (no cause of action against private contractor where contractor designated state instrumentality by statute)."); *id.* at 407 ("Our research, including the sources that the parties have cited, reveals that in the 19th century (and earlier) sometimes private contractors and sometimes government itself carried on prison management activities. And we have found no conclusive evidence of a historical tradition of immunity for private parties carrying out these functions. History therefore does not provide significant support for the immunity claim."); *id.* at 412 ("Our examination of history and purpose thus reveals nothing special enough about the job or about its organizational structure that would warrant providing these private prison guards with a governmental immunity. The job is one that private industry might, or might not, perform; and which history shows private firms did sometimes perform without relevant immunities. The organizational structure is one subject to the ordinary competitive pressures that normally help private firms adjust their behavior in response to the incentives that tort suits provide—pressures not necessarily present in government departments. Since there are no special reasons significantly favoring an extension of governmental immunity, and since *Wyatt* makes clear that private actors are not *automatically* immune (*i.e.*, § 1983 immunity does not automatically follow § 1983 liability), we must conclude that private prison guards, unlike those who work directly for the government, do not enjoy immunity from suit in a § 1983 case.").

It is sometimes litigated as to whether an individual is acting in an individual capacity, rather than in official capacity as a prosecutor. *See, e.g.*, Champluvier v. Couch, 557 F. Supp.2d 748, 753–54 (N.D. Miss. 2008):

> Deborah Champluvier alleges in her complaint that defendant Couch cannot enjoy prosecutorial immunity because he acted in his individual capacity, rather than his official capacity as prosecutor. All of Couch's actions of which the plaintiff complains, however, were taken within the course and scope of his duties as a prosecutor. Indeed, the plaintiff's sole allegation regarding Couch is that he improperly interpreted Mississippi's embezzlement statute and used that improper interpretation to prosecute Champluvier for the State of Mississippi.... As all of Couch's actions relevant to this case were taken during the course and scope of Couch's prosecution of Champluvier, the court finds that he was acting in his official capacity as a prosecutor.

200. Stump v. Sparkman, 435 U.S. 349, 359, 363–64 (1978) ("A judge is absolutely immune from liability for his judicial acts even if his exercise of authority is flawed by the commission of grave procedural errors."; "Despite the unfairness to litigants that sometimes results, the doctrine of judicial immunity is thought to be in the best interests of 'the proper administration of justice... [, for it allows] a judicial officer, in exercising the authority vested in him [to] be free to act upon his own convictions, without apprehension of personal consequences to himself.' The fact that the issue before the judge is a controversial one is all the more reason that he should be able to act without fear of suit.") (citation omitted); 2 Ivan E. Bodensteiner & Rosalie Berger Levinson, State and Local Government Civil Rights Liability § 2:5—*Absolute immunity—Prosecutorial functions* (June 2021 Update) ("The Supreme Court held in *Imbler v. Pachtman* that 'in initiating and in presenting the [government's] case,' prosecutors act 'quasi-judicially' and therefore enjoy the same absolute immunity as judges. This immunity also extends to prosecutors who initiate certain civil proceedings. In general, the Court has stressed that the prosecutor's role is integral to the judicial process and requires both the exercise of broad discretion as well as the courageous exercise of that discretion."); Beck v. Texas State Bd. of Dental Examiners, 204 F.3d 629, 634 (5th Cir. 2000) ("It is well settled that judges and prosecutors are entitled to absolute immunity.") (citing Stump v. Sparkman, 435 U.S. 349, 355 (1978) (judicial immunity) & Imbler v. Pachtman, 424 U.S. 409, 430–31 (1976)); *see also* McConnell v. Lassen County, Ca., No. CIV. S-05-0909 FCD DAD, 2005 WL 8176687, at *2 (E.D. Cal. Sept. 21, 2005) ("'It is well settled that judges and prosecutors are entitled to absolute immunity.'") (citations omitted); Margaret Z. Johns, *Reconsidering Absolute Prosecutorial Immunity*, 2005 B.Y.U. L. Rev. 53, 117 (2005) ("Instead of denying absolute prosecutorial immunity based on the common law of 1871, the *Imbler* Court misread the 1871 common law and erroneously concluded that prosecutors enjoyed

absolute immunity. As discussed above, the *Imbler* Court found that at common law, prosecutors enjoyed absolute immunity for the same policy reasons that judges and legislators were shielded by immunity. Indeed, the Court concluded that this immunity was 'well settled.' But the Court cited no precedent recognizing prosecutorial immunity before 1871. And as the following discussion will show, the Court's initial conclusions about the 1871 common law were unfounded since none of the 1871 common-law immunities afforded prosecutors absolute immunity.").

201. "Such suits," the U.S. Supreme Court observed, "could be expected with some frequency, for a defendant often will transform his resentment at being prosecuted into the ascription of improper and malicious actions to the State's advocate." "[I]f the prosecutor could be made to answer in court each time such a person charged him with wrongdoing, his energy and attention would be diverted from the pressing duty of enforcing the criminal law." Suits surviving the pleadings "would pose substantial danger of liability even to the honest prosecutor," the Court stressed, adding: "The prosecutor's possible knowledge of a witness' falsehoods, the materiality of evidence not revealed to the defense, the propriety of a closing argument, and ultimately in every case the likelihood that prosecutorial misconduct so infected a trial as to deny due process, are typical of issues with which judges struggle in actions for post-trial relief, sometimes to differing conclusions. The presentation of such issues in a § 1983 action often would require a virtual retrial of the criminal offense in a new forum, and the resolution of some technical issues by the lay jury." "[A] prosecutor inevitably makes many decisions that could engender colorable claims of constitutional deprivation," the Court pointed out, concluding: "Defending these decisions, often years after they were made, could impose unique and intolerable burdens upon a prosecutor responsible annually for hundreds of indictments and trials." The Court acknowledged that affording "absolute immunity" under section 1983 "does leave the genuinely wronged defendant without civil redress against a prosecutor whose malicious or dishonest action deprives him of liberty." "But the alternative of qualifying a prosecutor's immunity would disserve the broader public interest," the Court decided, noting that it "would prevent the vigorous and fearless performance of the prosecutor's duty that is essential to the proper functioning of the criminal justice system." Notably, the debate over immunity, including qualified immunity for police offices, has divided lawmakers in their talks on police reform legislation. Matthew Brown, "Qualified Immunity Divides Lawmakers in Police Reform Talks. What Is that Legal Defense", USA TODAY, June 13, 2021 (updated June 14, 2021), https://www.usatoday.com/in-depth/news/politics/2021/06/13/qualified-immunity-explained-behind-legal-shield-police/7614386002/.

202. Imbler v. Pachtman, 424 U.S. 409, 410–31 (1976).

203. Venckus v. City of Iowa City, 930 N.W.2d 792, 826 (Iowa 2019) (Appel, J. concurring in part and dissenting in part); *see also* Adam M. Gershowitz, *The Race to the Top to Reduce Prosecutorial Misconduct*, 89 FORDHAM L. REV. 1179, 1179 (2021) ("Prosecutorial misconduct is a serious problem in the United States. Unfortunately, the two main mechanisms to deal with the problem—lawyer disciplinary boards and adjudicatory remedies—have not been up to the task. State ethics boards rarely discipline prosecutors and courts rarely reverse convictions for prosecutorial misconduct."). There are, at least occasionally, cases in which prosecutors are disciplined or disbarred for misconduct. *E.g.*, Fred C. Zachariasa, *The Professional Discipline of Prosecutors*, 79 N.C. L. REV. 721, 744–45 (2001) ("The study, though not all-encompassing, revealed over 100 cases in which prosecutors have been disciplined. This result dispels at least one myth: that prosecutors are never disciplined. Nevertheless, many of the cases are old, making the number of reported cases far from staggering in light of the many prosecutors and criminal cases that exist. Still, the body of cases is not entirely negligible. The research suggests at least that, in appropriate cases, courts and disciplinary organizations sometimes have been willing to address prosecutorial misconduct."); Derek Hawkins, "Dallas Prosecutor Disbarred for Withholding Evidence that Could Have Cleared Men of Murder Charges," SEATTLE TIMES, May 15, 2021, https://www.seattletimes.com/nation-world/dallas-prosecutor-disbarred-for-withholding-evidence-that-could-have-cleared-men-of-murder-charges/ ("When former Dallas County prosecutor Richard Jackson put two homeless Black men on trial in 2000 for the murder of a local pastor, he allegedly withheld a heap of evidence that could have cleared them."); *id.* ("Jackson surrendered his law license last month after the State Bar of Texas said that he had withheld exculpatory evidence in the trials of Allen and Mozee. State appellate judges had previously reached the same conclusion. The disbarment was first reported by *The Dallas Morning News*.").

204. Margaret Z. Johns, *Unsupportable and Unjustified: A Critique of Absolute Prosecutorial Immunity*, 80 Fordham L. Rev. 509, 510 (2011); *see also* Kate Cohn, *When the Home Team Calls Their Own Balls and Strikes: The Problem of* Brady *Violations, Accountability, and Making the Case for a Washington State Commission on Prosecutorial Conduct*, 19 Seattle J. for Soc. Just. 161, 163 (2020) ("Most prosecutors who commit *Brady* violations are shielded from accountability due to the absolute immunity afforded to them and the gaps left by current corrective structures."); Timothy Fry, Comment, *Prosecutorial Training Wheels: Ginsburg's* Connick v. Thompson *Dissent and the Training Imperative*, 102 J. Crim. L. & Criminology 1275, 1281–83 (2012) ("The first American case to extend immunity to a prosecutor was an 1896 Indiana Supreme Court decision affirming dismissal of a complaint for malicious prosecution. This decision became the majority rule in the United States. By 1927, the Supreme Court endorsed this rule by affirming per curiam the Second Circuit's holding that a prosecutor 'is immune from ... malicious prosecution based on an indictment and prosecution....' The Second Circuit grounded this rule in public policy considerations. In 1976, the Supreme Court extended this common law rule of immunity to § 1983 civil rights claims. This holding was limited to the 'judicial phase of the criminal process.' In subsequent cases, the Supreme Court further extended prosecutorial immunity. In *Van de Kamp v. Goldstein*, the Court extended absolute immunity to administrative tasks, such as training, supervision, and management of information systems. The Court's rationale for this expansion was that these administrative tasks relied on the prosecutor's 'legal knowledge and the exercise of related discretion.' In other circumstances, the Court has granted qualified immunity to provide a 'defense of good faith' for prosecutors performing certain official duties. These official duties include: (1) advising the police; (2) interacting with the media; and (3) testifying as a complaining witness. Qualified immunity will protect a prosecutor unless he or she knowingly violates clear constitutional standards.").

205. Robertson v. U.S. ex rel., 560 U.S. 272, 273 (2010) (Roberts, C.J., dissenting).

206. *Id.* (citing U.S. Const., amdts. 5, 6 (emphasis added by Chief Justice Roberts)).

207. *Id.* at 276–77 (citing *Civil Rights Cases*, 109 U.S. 3, 11, 3 S. Ct. 18, 27 L.Ed 835 (1883)).

208. *Id.* at 277 (quoting *Standefer v. United States*, 447 U.S. 10, 25, 100 S. Ct. 1999, 64 L.Ed.2d 689 (1980) (internal quotation marks omitted)); *see also* Kenneth J. Melilli, *Prosecutorial Discretion in an Adversary System*, 1992 BYU L. Rev. 669, 669 (1992) ("I viewed myself as having a very different role [than a lawyer in private practice], a view shared by many of my prosecutor colleagues. My understanding was that my obligation as a prosecutor was to the public interest, an obligation fundamentally different than that of lawyers to their private clients.").

209. Michael O. Eshleman, *A History of the Digests*, 110 L. Libr. J. 235, 241 (2018); *see also* Kevin C. Walsh, *In the Beginning There Was None: Supreme Court Review of State Criminal Prosecutions*, 90 Notre Dame L. Rev. 1867, 1877–78 (2015) ("Blackstone divided his two books on 'wrongs' between 'private wrongs' (Book III) and 'public wrongs' (Book IV). Book III is largely devoted to the 'redress of private wrongs, by suit or action in the courts.' Book IV, by contrast, studies the criminal law, or what Blackstone called the 'pleas of the crown' because the king 'is supposed by the law to be the person injured by every infraction of the public rights belonging to [the] community, and is, therefore, in all cases, the proper prosecutor for every public offense.'"); George P. Fletcher, *Domination in Wrongdoing*, 76 B.U. L. Rev. 347, 347 (1996) ("Blackstone had a point in identifying crimes as public wrongs and torts as private wrongs. Both crimes and torts claim victims, however, the victims' responses vary according to context. In criminal cases, the victim responds by hoping that the government will apprehend and successfully prosecute the offender. In tort disputes, the victim responds by demanding compensation.").

210. Ambrose Y. K. Lee, *Public Wrongs and the Criminal Law*, 9 Crim. L. & Phil. 155, 157 (2015); *see also* James Lindgren, *Why the Ancients May Not Have Needed a System of Criminal Law*, 76 B.U. L. Rev. 29, 39 (1996) ("[T]he Romans distinguished between torts and crimes according to whether the action was private or public, not according to whether it involved moral blameworthiness."); Richard W. Wright, *The Grounds and Extent of Legal Responsibility*, 40 San Diego L. Rev. 1425, 1430 (2003) ("Tort law and contract law deal with 'private wrongs,' unjust discrete injuries to the persons or property of specific individuals. Criminal law deals with 'public wrongs,' unjust nondiscrete injuries to the dignity and security of each member of society that result from (or are constituted by) criminals' acting in disregard of the society's norms of public peace and order, thereby declaring themselves to be outside the law ('outlaws').").

211. Cantrell v. Commonwealth, 329 S.E.2d 22, 26 (Va. 1985).

212. *Robertson*, 560 U.S. at 277–78.

213. Brady v. Maryland, 373 U.S. 83 (1963).

214. Powell v. Miller, 104 F. Supp.3d 1298, 1306–07, 1309 (W.D. Okla. 2015).

215. *See* Eric Hatfield, Case Comment, *Six Wrongs Take Away a Right: The Odyssey of Curtis Flowers and the Prosecutorial Misconduct that Caused It*, 47 S.U. L. REV. 347, 349 (2020) ("Remedies for prosecutorial misconduct include sanctions against the violating prosecutor, discipline by the state bar against the prosecutor, and the reversal of convictions. These remedies have limitations. Even when a conviction is reversed, the accused often remain incarcerated awaiting a decision regarding future action (e.g., retrial or dismissal) in the criminal proceeding. Further, conviction reversals often result in no practical consequences for a prosecutor in violation.").

216. Drew v. United States, No. 3:18-cv-01070, 2018 WL 3336484, at *1 (D. Conn. July 6, 2018); *see also* Jonathan Remy Nash, *Nontraditional Criminal Prosecutions in Federal Court*, 53 ARIZ. ST. L.J. 143, 159 (2021) ("On the federal side of the ledger, private parties do not have the general power to pursue criminal prosecutions. However, there is some historical evidence that private parties in the early Republic may have had the chance to play some role in starting federal criminal proceedings, 'including directly appealing to grand juries.'"); *id.* at 145 ("In a typical federal criminal prosecution, the local U.S. Attorney's Office, acting on behalf of the United States Department of Justice ('DOJ'), prosecutes a criminal defendant under a provision of the federal criminal code. Such a prosecution proceeds under the auspices of the U.S. Attorney for the district, who, in the ordinary course, is appointed by the President with the advice and consent of the Senate. The typical prosecution takes place in a federal district court and is governed procedurally by the Federal Rules of Criminal Procedure. If there is a conviction, sentencing is accomplished with reference to the (now-advisory) United States Sentencing Guidelines, and any prison sentence is administered by the DOJ's Bureau of Prisons. Appeal lies to the appropriate regional federal court of appeals, with certiorari review thereafter available by the U.S. Supreme Court."); *id.* at 190–91:

> [F]ederal law has long allowed the removal of certain state criminal prosecutions to federal court. First, with antecedents dating back to 1815, the current federal-officer removal statute allows for removal to federal district court of prosecutions brought in state court against federal officers for "any act under color" of their office. Second, the civil rights removal statute—which dates back to Reconstruction-era statutes—today provides for removal to federal district court of state court prosecutions "[a]gainst any person who is denied or cannot enforce in the [state] courts . . . a right under any law providing for the equal civil rights of citizens of the United States, or of all persons within the jurisdiction thereof." Last, a provision today allows members of the armed services facing state court prosecution to remove those cases to federal district court. While the very thing that allowed the initial removal of a state court prosecution to federal district court often results in quick dismissal of the prosecution on immunity grounds, still the prosecution must have representation in federal court.

Id. at 195:

> Lower federal courts handling removed private prosecutions have applied the *Erie* analysis to uphold the effectiveness of such provisions: They are at least somewhat substantive in nature, and they do not conflict with any federal procedural rule. Indeed, the federal courts have hosted a few removed private state prosecutions, and appellate courts have accepted appeals by private prosecutors. The one limitation they have placed on state-authorized private prosecutors is that, pursuant to the Supreme Court's *Young* opinion (or perhaps a more general Due Process Clause concern), the private prosecutor can pursue only low-level criminal penalties and introduce no intolerable conflict of interest.

217. Glassey v. Amano Corp., No. C-05-01604 RMW, 2006 WL 889519, at *3 (N.D. Cal. Mar. 31, 2006) ("Private parties generally lack standing to enforce federal criminal statutes."), *aff'd*, 285 Fed. Appx. 426 (9th Cir. 2008); *cf.* Brotherhood of Locomotive Firemen and Enginemen v. Bangor & Aroostook R.R. Co., 380 F.2d 570, 580 (D.C. Cir. 1967) ("Appellants' arguments regarding lack of standing beg the question of whether this is a criminal contempt action (wherein private parties would unarguably lack standing to initiate such proceedings), FED. R. CRIM. P. 42(b), a question we have disposed of above.").

218. Dietrich v. Schaaf Excavating Contractors, Inc., 2:18-cv-01697-RJC, 2021 WL 807712, at *7 (W.D. Pa. Mar. 3, 2021).

219. Cox v. Vieyra, Civil Action No. 3:20-cv-178-DJH, 2021 WL 796152, at *4 (W.D. Ky. Mar. 2, 2021); *see also* Ezekwo v. Neri, 20-CV-9505 (LLS), 2021 WL 603268, at *3 (S.D.N.Y. Feb. 12, 2021) ("Plaintiff cannot initiate the arrest and prosecution of an individual in this Court because "the decision to prosecute is solely within the discretion of the prosecutor." *Leeke v. Timmerman*, 454 U.S. 83, 87 (1981). Nor can Plaintiff direct prosecuting attorneys to initiate a criminal proceeding against Defendants, because prosecutors possess discretionary authority to bring criminal actions, and they are "immune from control or interference by citizen or court." *Conn. Action Now, Inc. v. Roberts Plating Co.*, 457 F.2d 81, 87 (2d Cir. 1972).").

220. United States v. McMahan, Case No.: SACR 07-00249-CJC, 2011 WL 13208839, at *2 (C.D. Cal. Nov. 16, 2011) (citing 18 U.S.C. § 3771).

221. *See generally* Mary M. Cheh, *Constitutional Limits on Using Civil Remedies to Achieve Criminal Law Objectives: Understanding and Transcending the Criminal-Civil Law Distinction*, 42 Hastings L.J. 1325, 1410 (1991) ("[C]ourts and commentators have concluded—though by no means uniformly—that, despite the historical practice of private prosecution by victims, prosecution by an interested prosecutor violates due process of law.") (citation omitted).

222. Some judicial opinions declined to reach the due process issues raised. *E.g.*, State v. Martineau, 808 A.2d 51, 52 (N.H. 2002) ("Because we conclude that New Hampshire common law prevents a private complainant from prosecuting a class A misdemeanor, which is the charge at issue in this case, we do not reach the broader constitutional question of whether private prosecutions by an interested party violate a criminal defendant's due process rights.").

223. City of Norco v. Mugar, 59 Cal. App.5th 786, 793–97 (Cal. Ct. App., 4th Dist., Div. 2, 2020); *see also* City of Monrovia v. White, Case No. B282713, 2019 WL 366469, at *6 (Cal. Ct. App., 2d Dist., Div. 2, Jan. 30, 2019) ("The City was not precluded from retaining private counsel to prosecute its public nuisance action against White. Contrary to White's assertion, *People ex rel. Clancy v. Superior Court* (1985) 39 Cal.3d 740 (*Clancy*) does not prohibit the City from doing so. In that case, the California Supreme Court held that the City of Corona could not retain outside counsel, on a contingency fee basis, to prosecute a public nuisance action against an adult bookstore. (*Id.* at pp. 747–748.) The high court reasoned that the city's contingent fee arrangement with a private attorney was inappropriate because it gave the attorney a financial interest in the outcome of the case and was "antithetical to the standard of neutrality that an attorney representing the government must meet when prosecuting a public nuisance abatement action." (*Id.* at p. 750.) The City's attorneys in this case were not retained on a contingency fee basis, as is evident from the billing statements and declaration in support of the City's motion for attorney fees. *Clancy* accordingly is inapposite.").

224. 253 F. Supp. 55 (E.D. Pa. 1966).

225. *Id.* at 57.

226. People v. Municipal Court for the Ventura Judicial Dist. of Ventura County, 103 Cal. Rptr. 645, 647–55 (Cal. Ct. App. 1972). *But cf.* Steen v. Appellate Div., Super. Ct., 331 P.3d 136, 138 (Cal. 2014) ("[T]he prosecutor may validate a complaint filed by someone else by approving, authorizing or concurring in it. Here, the relevant prosecutorial agency has, through an established practice, implicitly approved in advance the clerk's routine issuance of complaints for the offense of failure to appear, including the complaint against petitioner. Accordingly, the complaint was valid and the prosecution timely commenced.").

227. *E.g.*, State v. Nickels, 434 P.3d 535, 537–38 (Wash. Ct. App. 2019) ("When an attorney transitions from representing individual clients to the position of elected prosecutor, conflicts of interest can arise, restricting not only the attorney's ability to work on a given case, but also necessitating recusal of the entire prosecutor's office. The standard set by the Washington Supreme Court is that when an elected prosecutor has previously represented a criminally accused person in a case that is the same, or substantially the same, as the one currently pending prosecution, the entire prosecutor's office should ordinarily be disqualified from further participation."); *id.* at 494–95 ("The parties agree the elected prosecutor, Garth Dano, has a disqualifying conflict of interest and must be recused from Mr. Nickels's case. The only issue to be decided is whether Mr. Dano's entire office must be recused as well. Our review is de novo."); *id.* at 495 ("Where the

prosecuting attorney (as distinguished from a deputy prosecuting attorney) has previously personally represented the accused in the same case or in a matter so closely interwoven therewith as to be in effect a part thereof, the entire office of which the prosecuting attorney is administrative head should ordinarily also be disqualified from prosecuting the case and a special deputy prosecuting attorney appointed. This is not to say, however, that anytime a prosecuting attorney is disqualified in a case for any reason that the entire prosecuting attorney's office is also disqualified. Where the previous case is not the same case (or one closely interwoven therewith) that is being prosecuted, and where, for some other ethical reason the prosecuting attorney may be totally disqualified from the case, if that prosecuting attorney separates himself of herself from all connection with the case and delegates full authority and control over the case to a deputy prosecuting attorney, we perceive no persuasive reason why such a complete delegation of authority and control and screening should not be honored if scrupulously maintained."); *id.* at 499 ("Generally, an attorney's representation of a client will involve acquisition of privileged information through confidential communications. Thus, an elected prosecutor and his or her office will typically need to be recused from prosecuting a case in which the elected prosecutor previously served as defense counsel. But in unusual circumstances, the elected prosecutor's prior representation may have been so brief, or so attenuated, that no confidential communications were shared. Such circumstances would be extraordinary and might not necessitate recusal of the entire prosecutor's office."); *id.* at 500 ("Given the significant commitment of resources necessary for a death penalty prosecution, it is difficult to imagine that an elected prosecutor, tasked with prioritizing a county's prosecution resources, can ever be fully walled off from a death penalty prosecution. It is perhaps for this reason that in 1997 the WSBA's RPC Committee issued an advisory opinion, stating that, in death penalty cases, recusal of an elected prosecutor based on prior representation in the same criminal case must result in recusal of the prosecutor's office as a whole. WSBA Advisory Op. 1773. But in less significant prosecutions, there is a greater chance that an elected prosecutor could be effectively walled off from a case brought by his or her office."); *id.* at 502 ("Because Mr. Nickels has been charged with a serious offense, the same offense about which the Grant County prosecuting attorney has acquired privileged information through work product and attorney-client communications during his time as a private attorney, the entire Grant County Prosecuting Attorney's Office must be recused from Mr. Nickels's first degree murder prosecution. The trial court's ruling to the contrary is reversed.").

228. Susan W. Brenner & James Geoffrey Durham, *Towards Resolving Prosecutor Conflicts of Interest*, 6 GEO. J. LEGAL ETHICS 415, 417 (1993) ("The organized bar has done a poor job of providing ethical guidance to criminal prosecutors. This article examines and analyzes the conflict of interest rules that apply to prosecutors, an area of legal ethics in which the organized bar has left prosecutors with little guidance except by extrapolation from rules primarily drafted to deal with conflicts of interest for lawyers in private practice. Like private practice lawyers, prosecutors can have 'generic conflicts,' conflicts of interest arising from prior representations or personal interests. In addition, prosecutors are faced with 'system conflicts,' conflicts of interest inherent in their distinct responsibilities: the political reality of having to please the electorate; the necessity of being an advocate; and the ethical requirement of being an 'administrator of justice.' Finally, many jurisdictions allow 'part-time prosecutors' to also engage in private law practice, resulting in 'role conflicts,' which are conflicts arising because part-time prosecutors serve both the state and private clients.").

229. Price v. Commonwealth, 849 S.E.2d 140, 145–48 (Va. Ct. App. 2020).

230. Riner v. Edwards, Civil Action No. 7:07-cv-00455, 2008 WL 4388788, at *13 (W.D. Va. Sept. 26, 2008).

231. Adkins v. Commonwealth, 492 S.E.2d 833, 835–36 (Va. Ct. App. 1997).

232. People v. Calderone, 573 N.Y.S.2d 1005 (Crim. Ct., City of New York, New York County, Part SAP II, 1991); *see also* Kampfer v. Vonderheide, 216 F. Supp.2d 4, 8 (N.D.N.Y. 2002) ("Kampfer would not personally be able to commence a New York State criminal action against the person(s) who vandalized his home.") (citing *Calderone*, 573 N.Y.S.2d at 1007 (holding that "decisions of the New York Court of Appeals and Supreme Court of the United States lead this court to conclude that private prosecutions by interested parties or their attorneys present inherent conflicts of interest which violate defendants' due process rights")).

233. Section 50 of the New York City Criminal Court Act reads as follows: "Provision shall be made at all times in each part of the court in which a judge is sitting as a magistrate whereby the clerk, the clerk's assistants or other employees whose duty it is to prepare complaints shall have proper accommodations and the necessary room or rooms separate from but convenient to the room in which the court is held, and therein shall be at all times conspicuously posted a notice legibly printed in English, Spanish, Italian and Yiddish, respectively, and such other language as a rule or order of court shall prescribe, to the effect that any person to whom permission is refused to make and verify a complaint and who is thereby aggrieved will be heard upon application to the judge in person before the closing of the pending session of the court. It shall be the duty of each such judge before opening and again before closing a session to cause to be intelligibly announced to all persons in and about his courtroom that the court will then and there hear all complaints which have not been taken by the complaint clerk." N.Y. CTY. CR. CT. ACT § 50.

234. *Calderone*, 573 N.Y.S.2d at 1005; *see also id.* at 1005–06 ("Mr. Riso is a sponsor of the condominium and an officer of its Board of Directors. Mr. Riso commenced this action on behalf of the Board and certain unit owners of the condominium. The criminal action is being prosecuted by the law firm De Maio and Hughes, which represents complainant Mr. Riso and the condominium Board in this action. That firm also represents Mr. Riso, the condominium Board and a number of unit owners in civil litigation that they have brought against defendant, who is also a unit owner, and other unit owners. Additionally, a member of the law firm is also a member of the condominium Board.").

235. *Id.* at 1006 ("Defendant moves to disqualify the firm of De Maio and Hughes from prosecuting this action alleging that its role as prosecutor is not authorized under the County Law, constitutes a conflict of interest, violates defendant's rights to due process, and violates the Canons of Professional Responsibility. Complainant argues that the law firm has no financial interest in the civil or criminal actions apart from its attorney-client relationship with the condominium board and various unit owners and further argues that this action is not being prosecuted under the Criminal Procedure Law, but rather, under the Criminal Court Act.").

236. *Id.*

237. *Id.*

238. *Id.*

239. *Id.*

240. *Id.* (citing People v. Van Sickle, 13 N.Y.2d 61, 242 N.Y.S.2d 34, 192 N.E.2d 9 (1963)).

241. *Calderone*, 573 N.Y.S.2d at 1006 (*citing Van Sickle*, 13 N.Y.2d at 64).

242. *Id.* at 1007 (citing *People v. Vlasto,* 78 Misc.2d 419, 355 N.Y.S.2d 983 (Crim.Ct., NY Co.1974), [private prosecution not authorized in class A misdemeanor prosecution]; *People v. Citadel Mgt. Co.*, 78 Misc.2d 626, 355 N.Y.S.2d 976 (Crim.Ct. NY Co.1974), [private prosecution of violation authorized]; *People v. Cuozzo,* 97 Misc.2d 871, 412 N.Y.S.2d 748 (City Ct. White Plains 1978); *People v. Vial,* 132 Misc.2d 5, 502 N.Y.S.2d 930 (Crim.Ct. NY Co.1986), [attorney for defendant prosecuted by District Attorney permitted to act as prosecutor in cross-complaint against his accuser]; and *Read v. Sacco,* 49 A.D.2d 471, 375 N.Y.S.2d 371 (2nd Dept.1975), [private prosecution of class A misdemeanor authorized].). "In each of those cases except *People v. Vlasto*," the *Calderone* court emphasized, "the court, relying primarily on *People v Van Sickle*... held that a privately retained attorney could appear as a prosecutor in a criminal action." *Id.* at 1007.

243. *Id.* at 1007.

244. *Id.*

245. *Id.*; *see also id.* ("Rather, in the cases cited above where private prosecutions were upheld, the courts expressed the view that due process could be insured in private prosecutions through the court's monitoring of the prosecution for actual prejudice resulting from the clear conflicts of interest presented by the complainant or his or her attorney acting as the prosecutor.").

246. *Id.* In particular, the *Calderone* court cited the decisions of the New York Court of Appeals in *People v. Zimmer*, 51 N.Y.2d 390, 434 N.Y.S.2d 206, 414 N.E.2d 705 (1980) and the U.S. Supreme Court's decision in *Young v. United States ex rel. Vuitton Et Fils SA*, 481 U.S. 787 (1987). *See Calderone*, 573 N.Y.S.2d at 1008 ("In *People v. Zimmer,* 51 N.Y.2d 390, 434 N.Y.S.2d 206, 414 N.E.2d 705 (1980), the Court reversed a conviction and dismissed an indictment obtained by a District Attorney who had a financial interest in

the corporation in the course of whose management the defendant is alleged to have committed the offenses for which he was prosecuted. The Court held that where the District Attorney has a financial interest in and is the 'legal spokesman' for the corporation which is alleged to be directly affected by the defendant's alleged actions, that District Attorney has a conflict of interest which prohibits him from conducting the prosecutions of the case."); *Calderone*, 573 N.Y.S.2d at 1008 ("[I]n *People v. Zimmer* the Court found that, 'due process implications' were presented when there existed any potential for prejudice to a defendant due to a prosecutor's conflict of interest. Stating, at p. 394, 434 N.Y.S.2d 206, 414 N.E.2d 705, that it was 'simplistic... to think of the impact of a prosecutor's conflict of interest merely in terms of explicit instances of abuse,' the Court concluded that the avoidance of possible prejudice was not achieved by judicial scrutiny of the prosecutor's actions to determine if the prosecutor's conflict of interest actually prejudiced the defendant. Rather, the Court held that the existence of any 'reasonable potential for prejudice will suffice [to require that the prosecutor be recused].' See, *People v. Zimmer,* supra, at 395, 434 N.Y.S.2d 206, 414 N.E.2d 705. The Court found that the District Attorney's financial and attorney-client relationship with the corporation which was alleged to have been affected by the defendant's actions was a conflict of interest which clearly presented a potential for prejudice to the defendant."); *Calderone*, 573 N.Y.S.2d at 1008 ("In *Young v. United States ex rel. Vuitton Et Fils SA,* 481 U.S. 787, 107 S. Ct. 2124, 95 L.Ed.2d 740 (1987), the Court held that the District Court's appointment of one of the attorneys in a civil case to prosecute an opposing party in the case on a charge of criminal contempt arising out of the violation of the court's injunction was improper. Six Justices found it unnecessary to determine whether this error violated the defendants' due process rights, relying instead on the Court's supervisory power to hold that the same conflicts which, under federal statutes and contemporary standards of fair and impartial prosecution, prohibit prosecution by an interested government prosecutor also prohibit prosecution by an interested private prosecutor. Justice Blackmun concurred with those six Justices and further stated that such conflicts also violate due process.").

247. *Calderone*, 573 N.Y.S.2d at 1009.

248. *Id.*

249. *Id.*; *see also id.* ("Additionally, the standards of professional conduct applicable to public prosecutors are not required because such individuals are public officials, but rather, are required because of the functions they perform and the authority and discretion that they possess in our system of criminal justice. A defendant in a criminal case is entitled to no less justice when prosecuted by a private citizen or by an attorney representing such person than when prosecuted by a public prosecutor.").

250. *Id.*; *see also id.* ("Compelling support for this conclusion is found in the opinions of Justices Brennan and Blackmun in *Young v. United States,* supra. The Supreme Court of Wisconsin, one hundred years ago in *Biemel v. State,* 71 Wis. 444–445, 37 N.W. 244–245 (1888), stated, 'We think public policy, and the fair, just, and impartial administration of the criminal law of the state, make it the duty of the courts to exclude the paid attorneys of private persons from appearing as prosecutors.' This court agrees and goes further, holding that due process requires that the individual who prosecutes a criminal case not have any personal or financial interest in the prosecution nor an attorney-client relationship with any of the parties. The holding of *People v. Van Sickle,* supra, reached more than twenty-five years ago, can no longer be viewed as controlling authority for permitting such private prosecutions in light of the Court's more recent due process analysis set forth in *People v. Zimmer,* supra."); *id.* at 1009–10 ("[A]s the prosecution in this case was initiated by a person with a personal interest in the matter and is being prosecuted by a law firm which has an attorney-client relationship with the victims of the offenses alleged, such violates defendant's due process rights. Accordingly, the criminal action is dismissed without prejudice to the complainant pursuing his complaint with the District Attorney's Office.").

251. *Calderone,* 573 N.Y.S.2d at 1007 n.3 (citing *Commonwealth v. Hubbard,* 777 S.W.2d 882 (Ky. 1989) (permitting attorney for decedent's family to prosecute); *State v. Harrington,* 534 S.W.2d 44 (Mo. Sup. Ct. App. 1976) (en banc) (prohibiting prosecution by attorney retained by interested party); *Cantrell v. Va.,* 329 S.E.2d 22 (Va. 1985) (prohibiting prosecution by attorney retained by interested party); *Brotherhood of Locomotive Firemen v. United States,* 411 F.2d 312, 319 (5th Cir. 1969) (prohibiting private prosecution) & *State v. Atkins,* 261 S.E.2d 55 (W. Va. 1979) (citing decisions of other states' courts concerning the question)).

252. *Calderone*, 573 N.Y.S.2d at 1009–10.

253. People v. Garfield, 574 N.Y.S.2d 501, 502–03 (Just. Ct., Town of Clarkstown, Rockland County, 1991).

254. 575 N.Y.S.2d 750 (N.Y. Crim. Ct. 1991).

255. *Id.* at 751.

256. *Id.* at 751 n.1 ("In 1988, over 36,000 prosecutions were initiated by civilian complaints in the Criminal Courts of the City of New York. Over 20,000 of these cases were diverted to alternative dispute resolution (which are various forms of conciliation, mediation and arbitration, often referred to as 'ADR'). The other 16,000 cases remained in Criminal Court.") (citing Report of Task Force on Civilian-Initiated Complaint Process in N Y City Crim Ct [June 1989])).

257. *See also id.* at 751 ("The Judge who issued the summons for the defendant was unaware that Ms. Franck had already been arrested for the very same conduct of which she accused Ms. Benoit. In fact, the summons clerk's intake sheet merely indicates that Ms. Franck was referred to the Summons Part by her attorney and that she refused mediation."); *id.* ("As a result of being served with the summons, the defendant appeared in this court with her attorney and was arraigned. Ms. Franck and her attorney were present at the defendant's arraignment. At arraignment, the court was advised that Ms. Franck had been indicted by a Kings County Grand Jury for assault in the second degree and criminal possession of a weapon in the fourth degree for allegedly assaulting the defendant on February 8, 1991. Since this was the first time the District Attorney's office had an opportunity to review the summons-initiated case in light of the pending indictment, the court inquired if the People were going to assume prosecution of the defendant. Counsel for Ms. Franck submitted a motion and affirmation requesting that the District Attorney's office not be permitted to dismiss this prosecution and for an adjournment to allow her to move in Supreme Court for the appointment of a Special Prosecutor.").

258. *Id.* at 751 ("The People consented to an adjournment and filed a written response to Ms. Franck's motion. The response reads, in pertinent part: 'The People's position concerning *People v. Benoit*, 91K008301, is that the People have not assumed prosecution of this matter. Furthermore, the People will not assume prosecution of this matter in the future. The People have no position concerning the appointment of a special prosecutor.'").

259. *Id.* at 752 ("[D]efendant's counsel filed a written motion to dismiss pursuant to CPL 170.30 (f). Specifically, defendant argues that if Ms. Franck is allowed to prosecute, the defendant will be deprived of the many constitutional safeguards to a fair trial that other defendants who are prosecuted by the District Attorney enjoy. In essence, defendant asserts that New York City Criminal Court Act § 50 is unconstitutional as applied to her since a private prosecution based on this statute results in a violation of the Equal Protection and Due Process Clauses of the Fourteenth Amendment. Counsel for Marie Franck acknowledged it would be improper for her to assume the prosecutor's role by responding to defendant's motion to dismiss. Since the defendant challenged the constitutionality of New York City Criminal Court Act § 50, this court notified the Attorney-General's office to allow it an opportunity to intervene. *(See,* Executive Law § 71; CPLR 1012 [b].) The Attorney-General's office has declined, in writing, to intervene at this stage of the proceedings and this court has therefore addressed the merits of the defendant's motion.").

260. *Id.* at 752.

261. *Id.* at 753 (citing L 1910, ch 659, art. IV, § 58; L 1933 ch 746, § 8).

262. *Id.*

263. *Id.* (citing Commn's Final Report, at 85 (emphasis added)).

264. *Id.* (citing People v. Minuto, 71 Misc.2d 800).

265. *Id.*; *see also id.* ("Describing section 50 as an 'antiquated provision,' the Task Force report recommended its repeal. The report found the existing system to be deficient in almost every respect.") (citing Task Force report, at 30 n.15).

266. *Id.*

267. *Id.* (quoting Task Force report at 31). In *Calderone*, the Criminal Court of the City of New York also favorably cited the 1989 report written by the Task Force on the Civilian-Initiated Complaint Process in the New York City Criminal Court. *Calderone*, 573 N.Y.S.2d at 1007 n.2 ("In 1989, after reviewing the practices relating to private prosecutions in the Criminal Court of the City of New York, the Task Force on

the Civilian–Initiated Complaints Process expressed the opinion that private prosecutions allow individuals 'to use a criminal case to pursue their own personal aims' in direct contrast to prosecutions by public officials which pursue the interests of the people of the State as a whole. Task Force Report, p. 31. The Task Force stated that 'this practice undermines justice and the appearance of justice and it erodes the public's confidence in the criminal justice system.' Task Force Report, at p. 31. Accordingly, the Task Force recommended that 'the Criminal Court should no longer entertain civilian initiated complaints and should only adjudicate cases drawn and prosecuted by the duly-elected District Attorneys. Section 50 of the Criminal Court Act... should be repealed.' Task Force Report, at p. 11. Section 50 has not been repealed.").

268. *People v. Benoit*, 575 N.Y.S.2d 750, 753–54 (N.Y. Crim. Ct. 1991). The common law's recognition of private prosecutions has been noted by U.S. Supreme Court justices. *See, e.g.*, United States v. Marion, 404 U.S. 307, 329 (1971) (Douglas, J., concurring; joined by Justices Brennan and Marshall) ("[M]ore basically, the 18th century criminal prosecution at the common law was, in general, commenced in a completely different way from that with which we are familiar today. By the common law of England which was brought to the American colonies, the ordinary criminal prosecution was conducted by a private prosecutor, in the name of the King. In case the victim of the crime or someone interested came forward to prosecute, he retained his own counsel and had charge of the case as in the usual civil proceeding. Procedurally, the criminal prosecution was commenced by the filing of a lawsuit, and thereafter the filing of an application for criminal prosecution or rule nisi or similar procedure calling for the defendant to show cause why he should not be imprisoned. The English common law, with which the Framers were familiar, conceived of a criminal prosecution as being commenced prior to indictment. Thus, in that setting, the individual charged as the defendant in a criminal proceeding could and would be an 'accused' prior to formal indictment.") (citing G. Dession, Criminal Law, Administration and Public Order 356 (1948)).

269. *Benoit*, 575 N.Y.S.2d at 753–54 (citations omitted).

270. *Id.* at 755 (citations omitted); *see also* Faulder v. Johnson, 81 F.3d 515, 517 (5th Cir. 1996) ("[T]he use of special prosecutors raises concerns that the prosecutor's loyalty to the person who pays the special prosecutor may override the interests of society in justice and a fair trial of the accused. We require, therefore, that the district attorney retain control of the prosecution, the special prosecutor not be guilty of conduct prejudicial to the defendant, and the rights of the defendant be duly observed."); *id.* ("Control of the prosecution means control of crucial prosecutorial decisions, such as whether to prosecute, what targets of prosecution to select, what investigative powers to utilize, what sanctions to seek, plea bargains to strike or immunities to grant."). It was alleged in Joseph Faulder's case that private prosecutors violated Faulder's due process rights. *See* Third Amended Application for Writ of Habeas Corpus, *Ex parte Joseph Stanley Faulder* (filed Nov. 23, 1992), p. 3 ("Before Mr. Faulder's 1981 trial, Jack Phillips, the victim's son, discovered that the state was considering offering Mr. Faulder a plea bargain. At that point, he called Mr. Burleson, a prominent defense attorney with offices in Dallas, Texas. Phillips asked Burleson to intervene in the case and to encourage the Gregg County District Attorney's office to prosecute Mr. Faulder for capital murder. Burleson agreed, in exchange for a retainer and payment at his usual hourly rate, which in 1981 was in the vicinity of $150 to $200 per hour."); *id.* ("The state handed over its files on Mr. Faulder to Burleson, who reviewed them at Phillips' behest. After Burleson reviewed the Gregg County district attorney's files, he recommended that the state try Mr. Faulder for capital murder. Relying on Burleson's assessment of the case, the state agreed to seek the death penalty for Mr. Faulder."); Brief in Support of Petitioner's Proposed Conclusions of Law, *Joseph Stanley Faulder v. James A. Collins*, No. 6:92-CV-755 (U.S. Dist. Ct., Tex., Lufkin Div., Jan. 7, 1994) (signed by Sandra Babcock, Texas Resource Center), p. 4 ("[T]he private prosecutorial team in Mr. Faulder's case marshalled tremendous resources to ensure Mr. Faulder's conviction. The victim's son, Jack Phillips, retained two private prosecutors, Odis Hill and Phil Burleson. He paid Mr. Burleson approximately $72,000 for his work on the case. Mr. Hill received close to $17,000. Mr. Phillips further retained a private investigator, Bob Stephens, at a cost of approximately $12,000."); *id.* at 5 ("Before the victim's son, Jack Phillips, retained private counsel in Mr. Faulder's case, the Gregg County District Attorney's office had publicly stated that there were serious evidentiary problems with Mr. Faulder's case. District Attorney Odis Hill, before resigning from office in January 1981, was debating whether to try Mr. Faulder for capital murder, murder, or conspiracy to commit burglary. Mr. Hill resigned on January 9, 1981. The

recommendation to move forward with a capital murder prosecution came from Phil Burleson, whom Mr. Phillips retained in January, 1981—just as the newly appointed district attorney assumed office.").

271. *Benoit*, 575 N.Y.S.2d at 757; *see also id.* ("Section 50, as applied here, is also violative of the Due Process Clause of the State Constitution (NY Constitution, Art. I, Sec. 6).").

272. State v. Ray, 142 N.E.2d 484, 485 (Ohio Ct. App. 1956) ("if such counsel is not guilty of conduct which prevents the litigants from having a fair trial, the defendant would have no right to complain"; "[t]he defendant in the instant case makes no complaint as to the conduct of the attorney appearing on behalf of the complaining witness, and, even if we held such appearance by private counsel to be improper, unless the defendant was prevented from having a fair trial, the error would not be prejudicial"); State v. Addis, 186 S.E.2d. 415, 417 (S.C. 1972) ("We cannot say that the participation of private counsel violates the constitution or any statutory or common law principle."); State v. Bennett, 798 S.W.2d 783, 785–86 (Tenn. Cr. App. 1990) ("In this Court the appellant contends that the statute permitting the utilization of private prosecutors violates the Due Process and Equal Protection Clauses of the Fourteenth Amendment to the United States Constitution and the Law of the Land Clause contained in Article I, Section 8 of the Tennessee Constitution. He further contends that the statute is unconstitutional in the manner in which it was applied.... Contrary to the appellant's contention, the practice of permitting a privately retained prosecutor to assist a district attorney general, or his assistant, does not violate the Fourteenth Amendment to the United States Constitution or the Law of the Land provision contained in Article I, Section 8 of the Tennessee Constitution."); Hepburn v. Eagleton, Civil Action No. 6:11-cv-2016-RMG, 2012 WL 4051126, at *4 (D. S.C. Sept. 13, 2012) ("The PCR judge did not incorrectly apply federal law in finding the use of a private prosecutor is not a violation of due process. The judge found that the county solicitor was present and involved at the trial, and that he did not turn over all control of the case. There was no evidence that the private prosecutor was simultaneously involved in a civil case against the Petitioner. In these circumstances, the PCR judge did not unreasonably apply federal law in holding Petitioner's right to due process was not violated.") (citations omitted); State v. Reed, No. 1 CA-CR 17-0620, 2020 WL 8678504, at *5 (Ariz. Ct. App. Oct. 20, 2020) ("Reed's counsel suggests that the victim's attorney 'acted as a private prosecutor' and that '[i]t violates due process to allow a private attorney, who represents the victim in a criminal case, to help prosecute the criminal case.'... The State (not the victim's attorney) prosecuted the case against Reed, while the victim's attorney represented the victim and her rights. This representation properly included offering evidence and argument at the restitution hearing, given '[t]he state does not represent persons who have suffered economic loss at the [restitution] hearing but may present evidence or information relevant to the issue of restitution.' A.R.S. § 13-804(G). Because Reed's counsel has not shown the victim's attorney improperly participated in the prosecution of the case in a way that violated Reed's due process rights, this argument fails.").

273. State v. Misenheimer, 282 S.E.2d 790, 797 (N.C. 1981).

274. State v. Best, 186 S.E.2d 1, 3 (1972).

275. Jones v. Richards, 776 F.2d 1244, 1246–47 (4th Cir. 1985); *see also* 6 Wayne R. LaFave, Jerold H. Israel, Nancy J. King & Orin S. Kerr, Crim. Proc. § 22.5(a) (4th ed. 2019) ("Just as due process is violated where the judge has a personal interest in the exercise of his authority, it is also violated where the prosecutor's exercise of discretion may be motivated by interests 'other than the impartial administration of justice.' Thus, the Fourth Circuit has held that a conviction must be reversed where obtained by a private prosecutor against a defendant from whom the attorney was seeking a civil judgment on a claim arising from the same incident. In such a case, the court noted, it could not be assumed that the prosecutor, who was obviously 'serving two masters,' had been 'free to exercise the fair discretion which he owed to all persons charged with crime.'") (*quoting* Cantrell v. Commonwealth, 329 S.E.2d 22, 25 (Va. 1985) & Ganger v. Peyton, 379 F.2d 709, 714 (4th Cir. 1967)).

276. Dick v. Scroggy, 882 F.2d 192, 193, 195 (6th Cir. 1989).

277. State v. Atkins, 261 S.E.2d 55, 59 (W. Va. Sup. Ct. App. 1979).

278. Acord v. Hedrick, 342 S.E.2d 120, 123, 125 (W. Va. 1986); *see also id.* at 126 ("At the appellate level, a complaint against a private prosecutor must be bottomed on an instance of the private prosecutor's misconduct that in some way prejudiced the defendant. Mr. Acord has failed to establish any prejudice resulting from Mr. Thornhill's prosecuting the case that would rise to a constitutional level.") (citing State

v. Riser, 294 S.E.2d 461, 466 (W. Va. 1982). In the course of its ruling, the court in *Acord* stressed: "A mere imbalance between defense counsel and prosecution does not invalidate a criminal trial. Due process of law does not require that every criminal case be prosecuted by a Thomas Dewey, defended by a Clarence Darrow, and tried before a John Marshall." *Acord*, 342 S.E.2d at 123. In another case, the Supreme Court of Appeals of West Virginia emphasized that "a private prosecutor is bound by the same standards of professional conduct as a public prosecutor" but found that where a private prosecutor "did no more than to relay the wish of deceased's family that the case be vigorously prosecuted" (thus resulting in the public prosecutor's withdrawal of a plea offer), there was no prosecutorial misconduct on the part of the private prosecutor. State v. Worley, 369 S.E.2d 706, 718–19 (W. Va. Sup. Ct. App. 1988). *Compare* State ex rel. Moran v. Ziegler, 244 S.E.2d 550 (W. Va. Sup. Ct. App. 1978) (observing that "public prosecutors" must "observe the highest standards of conduct" and "we see no reason why private prosecutors should not be held to the same high standards," and finding that, even though an attorney was never retained by a criminal defendant, where that defendant had initially contacted that attorney to represent him in the criminal matter there was an appearance of a conflict of interest that required the attorney's disqualification when the attorney appeared as the private prosecuting attorney in the defendant's prosecution).

279. *State ex rel. Koopers Co. v. International Union of Oil, Chemical and Atomic Workers*, 298 S.E.2d 827, 829–30, 832 (1982).

280. Sedelbauer v. State, 455 N.E.2d 1159, 1164 (Ind. Ct. App. 1983); Hopkins v. Sellers, No. 1:09-cv-304, 2011 WL 2173859, *4–5 (E.D. Tenn. June 2, 2011) ("Plaintiff asserts the due process clause of the Fourteenth Amendment protects him from being criminally prosecuted by a private attorney, acting on behalf of the state, who has some personal interest in the prosecution. According to Plaintiff, this is precisely what Sellers' participation in the arraignment hearing subjected him to. Plaintiff also at times appears to argue that Sellers violated his Fourteenth Amendment due process rights by prosecuting him without probable cause. Additionally, Plaintiff argues that even if the Fourteenth Amendment does not directly confer the right not to be prosecuted by an interested private attorney, the due process clause of the Fourteenth Amendment protects a state law-created liberty interest in not being prosecuted by a private attorney who has not first been approved as qualified and free of conflicts in a court hearing.... Following *Young* and *Polo Fashions,* this Court is unwilling to find in the due process clause of the Fourteenth Amendment a hitherto unrecognized right not to be prosecuted by an interested private attorney."); Phipps v. Vaugh, No. CV 06-100-MO, 2006 WL 1050631, at *1 (D. Ore. Apr. 18, 2006) ("Plaintiff alleges that a prosecutor and two private attorneys involved in his criminal case and resulting civil case used false and misleading evidence against him, and withheld evidence from the trial courts in violation of his rights to due process and equal protection.... According to plaintiff, defendants Burris and Jonasson are private attorneys. Accordingly, they are not state actors for purposes of § 1983.").

281. Powers v. Hauck, 399 F.2d 322, 322–25 (5th Cir. 1968).

282. Ballard v. State, 519 S.W.2d 426, 428 (Tex. Cr. App. 1975); *see also* Powers v. Hauck, 399 F.2d 322, 325 (5th Cir. 1968) ("The mere participation of a special prosecutor alone is not sufficient grounds to show a denial of due process, without some additional showing of a violation of the rules relating to prosecuting attorneys."); Urdiales v. Canales, 475 F. Supp. 622, 628 (S.D. Tex. 1979) ("[T]he Texas Court of Criminal Appeals has routinely approved very active participation in criminal trials by special prosecutors. Apparently, the only requirement is that the public prosecutor or a member of his staff remain present during the trial and accept ultimate responsibility for the various decisions made during the trial.").

283. Commonwealth v. Hubbard, 777 S.W.2d 882, 883 (Ky. 1989) (citing Goehring v. Commonwealth, 370 S.W.2d 822 (Ky. 1963); Earl v. Commonwealth, 569 S.W.2d 686 (Ky. App. 1978)). The Supreme Court of Kentucky in *Hubbard* further noted that "[t]he Sixth Circuit Court of Appeals in *Stumbo v. Seabold*, 704 F.2d 910 (6th Cir. 1983) held that the employment of private counsel to assist an elected prosecutor is not *per se* unconstitutional." *Hubbard*, 777 S.W.2d at 883.

284. Stumbo v. Seabold, 704 F.2d 910, 911–12 (6th Cir. 1983). Other state court decisions have found that a conflict of interest on the part of the prosecution (e.g., where the private prosecutor has a civil interest in the criminal case that infects the prosecution) constitutes a denial of a defendant's due process rights and cannot be harmless error. *E.g.*, Cantrell v. Commonwealth, 329 S.E.2d 22, 26–27 (Va. 1985).

285. Erikson v. Pawnee County Board of County Commissioners, 263 F.3d 1151, 1154 (10th Cir. 2001) (citing East v. Scott, 55 F.3d 996, 1000–01 (5th Cir. 1995); Person v. Miller, 854 F.2d 656, 663–64 (4th Cir. 1998)).

286. U.S. Const. amend. V; U.S. Const. amend XIV, § 1.

287. Tribe, *supra* note 69, at § 10-7, at 664.

288. 446 U.S. 238 (1980).

289. *Id.* at 242.

290. *Id.* (citing Carey v. Piphus, 435 U.S. 247, 259–62, 266–67 (1978)).

291. *Id.* (citations omitted) (quoting Joint Anti-Fascist Committee v. McGrath, 341 U.S. 123, 172 (1951) (Frankfurter, J., concurring)).

292. Redish & Marshall, *supra* note 69, at 475 ("It is our position that the participation of an independent adjudicator is such an essential safeguard, and may be the only one."); *id.* at 477 ("the use of an 'independent' adjudicator is a sine qua non of procedural due process"). According to Redish and Marshall:

> Review of historical evidence demonstrates that the right to an independent adjudicator was considered a crucial element of procedural justice by the common law, by those that established the law of the colonies, and, perhaps most important, by the Framers of the United States Constitution. This historically fundamental role adds significant weight to the conclusion that the right to an independent adjudicator constitutes the floor of due process.

Id. at 479. The purpose of due process is to ensure the most accurate decision possible, with protections like notice, hearing, right to counsel, and cross-examination all contributing to that worthy goal. *Id.* at 476.

293. *Id.* at 475 ("If a given value cannot be protected absent the use of specific procedure, then that procedure must be deemed essential to the achievement of due process in all cases. It is our position that the participation of an independent adjudicator is such an essential safeguard, and may be the only one."); *id.* at 483 ("Of all the values informing the due process guarantee, the perception-of-fairness value most clearly dictates use of a truly independent adjudicator. Whether or not it can be proven that a particular decisionmaker allows her personal interests to sway her resolution of a dispute, the perception-of-fairness value demands that she be enjoined from deciding the case if she has some identifiable *potential* bias.") (italics in original).

294. *See* In re Winship, 397 U.S. 358 (1970) (due process requires that the prosecution prove the guilt of the defendant "beyond a reasonable doubt").

295. Prosecutors make a whole host of discretionary decisions—from charging and plea bargaining to those at trial—as they do their work. Norman Abrams, "Prosecutorial Discretion," *in* 3 Sanford H. Kadish, ed., Encyclopedia of Crime and Justice 1272–86 (1983).

296. Bruce A. Green & Rebecca Roiphe, *Rethinking Prosecutors' Conflicts of Interest*, 58 B.C. L. Rev. 463, 466, 471, 535 (2017).

297. Powell v. Amguard Ins. Co., C.A. No. K17C-11-003 JJC, 2020 WL 996734, at *8 (Del. Mar. 2, 2020) ("Criminal prosecutors have a dual role: to present the State's case earnestly *and* to advance justice by providing the defendant a fair and adequate trial.") (italics in original). According to Beth Nolan:

> Justice requires the appearance of justice for the same reason that conflict-free representation requires the appearance of conflict-free representation: in both cases, those outside the process must believe that the process is fair. It is a question of confidence in government. The appearance standard accepts that seeing is believing: if the public sees the process as unjust, or unfair, it cannot be expected to believe otherwise.

Beth Nolan, *Removing Conflicts from the Administration of Justice: Conflicts of Interest and Independent Counsels Under the Ethics in Government Act*, 79 Geo. L.J. 1, 55–56 (1990) (footnote omitted); *see also* David Harris, *The Appearance of Justice: Court TV, Conventional Television, and Public Understanding of the Criminal Justice System*, 35 Ariz. L. Rev. 785, 790 (1993) (footnote omitted) ("The appearance of justice will affect public perception of the system's legitimacy. A system consistently seen as unjust will eventually lose the allegiance of its citizens. If people perceive the courts as less than fair decision makers, the moral force courts depend on to ensure compliance with decisions they make diminishes.").

298. *E.g.*, In re Murchison, 349 U.S. 133, 136 (1955); Offutt v. United States, 348 U.S. 11, 14 (1954).

299. Joint Anti-Fascist Refugee Committee v. McGrath, 341 U.S. 123, 171–72 (1951) (Frankfurter, J., concurring).

> Of all the values informing the due process guarantee, the perception-of-fairness value most clearly dictates use of a truly independent adjudicator. Whether or not it can be proven that a particular decision maker allows her personal interests to sway her resolution of a dispute, the perception-of-fairness value demands that she be enjoined from deciding the case if she has some identifiable potential bias. Few situations more severely threaten trust in the judicial process than the perception that a litigant never had a chance because the decision maker may have owed the other side special favors.

Martin H. Redish & Lawrence C. Marshall, *Adjudicatory Independence and the Values of Procedural Due Process*, 95 YALE L.J. 455, 483 (1986).

300. Jason S. Rathod, *Emerging Markets, Vanishing Accountability: How Populations in Poor Countries Can Use Aggregate Litigation to Vindicate Their Rights*, 24 TRANSNAT'L L. & CONTEMP. PROBS. 69, 87–88 (2014) ("Some jurisdictions, such as California and Washington D.C., have 'private attorneys general' statutes in which citizens are given the same power to bring suit and seek recovery on behalf of the general public. Qui Tam actions are in a similar vein, authorizing a private individual to sue on behalf of the government to redress an injury suffered by the government as the preserver of the public treasury and share in the damages and financial penalties recovered for the government."); United States of America ex rel. Givler v. Smith, 775 F. Supp. 172 n.4 (E.D. Pa. 1991) ("The law authorizes *qui tam* plaintiffs to sue in the name of the United States. In contrast, private attorneys general statutes merely permit citizen plaintiffs to sue on their behalf.").

301. BLACK'S LAW DICTIONARY 1251 (6th ed. 1991); Evan Caminker, Comment, *The Constitutionality of Qui Tam Actions*, 99 YALE L.J. 341, 341 & n.1 (1989).

302. United States ex rel. Howard v. Caddell Constr. Co., No. 7:11-CV-270-H-KS, 2018 WL 2291300, at *2 (E.D. N.C. Feb. 23, 2018); *see also* United States ex rel. Sanders v. Allison Engine Co., 364 F. Supp.2d 716, 718 (S.D. Ohio 2005) ("Where the Government declines to intervene, the relator is empowered as a private prosecutor."); United States ex rel. Lamers v. City of Green Bay, Wis., 924 F. Supp. 96, 98 (E.D. Wis. 1996) ("The False Claims Act empowers the qui tam relator to act as a private prosecutor but does not empower it to replace the government."); Bagley v. United States, 963 F. Supp.2d 982, 991 (C.D. Cal. 2013):

> The FCA establishes liability for "[a]ny person" who "knowingly presents, or causes to be presented, to an officer or employee of the United States Government . . . a false or fraudulent claim for payment or approval." *Vermont ANR v. United States ex rel. Stevens,* 529 U.S. 765, 120 S. Ct. 1858, 146 L.Ed.2d 836 (2000) (quoting 31 U.S.C. § 3729(a)). The defendant is liable for up to treble damages and a civil penalty of up to $10,000 per claim. 31 U.S.C. § 3729(a). The Act authorizes both the Attorney General and private persons to bring civil actions to enforce the Act. 31 U.S.C. § 3730. An action brought by a private person under Section 3730(b) of the FCA is termed a "qui tam" suit, and the person who brings such an action is referred to as a "relator" or "informer." *Kelly,* 9 F.3d at 761. Various other terms have also been used by courts to describe the role of the relator: "a private prosecutor," or a "private attorney general." *See Kelly,* 9 F.3d. at 760; *see also United States ex rel. Milam v. Univ. of Texas,* 961 F.2d 46, 49 (4th Cir.1992) ("A *qui tam* relator is essentially a self-appointed private attorney general, and his recovery is analogous to a lawyer's contingent fee.").

303. Caminker, *supra* note 301, at 342–43; J. Randy Beck, *The False Claims Act and the English Eradication of* Qui Tam *Legislation*, 78 N.C. L. REV. 539, 541–42 (2000).

304. Robert W. Fischer, Jr., Comment, Qui Tam *Actions: The Role of the Private Citizen in Law Enforcement*, 20 UCLA L. REV. 778, 786 (1973) (citing cases); *see also* Donald J. Hall, *The Role of the Victim in the Prosecution and Disposition of a Criminal Case*, 28 VANDERBILT L. REV. 931, 974 & n.234 (1975) ("Closely related to private prosecution is the qui tam action. Created by statute, this action allows a private citizen to receive part of a fine or penalty for successfully suing persons involved in a wide variety of crimes. The plaintiff need not prove special damages, and both the government and plaintiff share in the penalty (a 50–50 division is common). The plaintiff in a qui tam action is usually described as an informer who 'himself [has] no interest whatever in the controversy other than that given by statute . . . .' The action does

not force criminal prosecution of the accused; rather, it is characterized as a 'remedial' proceeding that imposed only a civil sanction. Therefore, the qui tam action is not an appropriate legal avenue for the victim seeking to force criminal prosecution.") (citations omitted). Potential constitutional issues have been flagged in the past about qui tam suits. *See, e.g.*, Ammex, Inc. v. Wenk, 936 F.3d 355, 365 (6th Cir. 2019) (Bush, J., concurring in the judgment):

> Members of the Supreme Court have noted that substantial constitutional issues arise from certain arguable delegations of federal executive power to non-Article II actors. *See Friends of the Earth, Inc. v. Laidlaw Envtl. Servs. (TOC), Inc.*, 528 U.S. 167, 197, 120 S. Ct. 693, 145 L.Ed.2d 610 (2000) (Kennedy, J., concurring) ("Difficult and fundamental questions are raised when we ask whether exactions of public fines by private litigants, and the delegation of Executive power which might be inferable from the authorization, are permissible in view of the responsibilities committed to the Executive by Article II of the Constitution of the United States."); *see also id.* at 209–10, 120 S. Ct. 693 (Scalia, J., dissenting) (observing the same). Not only have several justices highlighted constitutional concerns posed by certain arguable delegations of federal executive power to private parties, but a majority of justices have, in the context of *qui tam* suits, explicitly reserved judgment on the issue until the appropriate time. *See Vt. Agency of Nat. Res. v. United States ex rel. Stevens*, 529 U.S. 765, 778 n.8, 120 S. Ct. 1858, 146 L.Ed.2d 836 (2000) ("[W]e express no view on the question whether *qui tam* suits violate Article II, in particular the Appointments Clause of § 2 and the 'take Care' Clause of § 3.").

See also Sierra Club v. Khanjee Holding (US) Inc., 655 F.3d 699, 705 n.3 (6th Cir. 2011):

> Justice Kennedy's concurrence in *Laidlaw* merely stated that neither the litigants nor the court of appeals had considered whether "exactions of public fines by private litigants, and the delegation of Executive power which might be inferable from the authorization, are permissible in view of the responsibilities committed to the Executive by Article II of the Constitution of the United States." *Id.* As a result, Justice Kennedy believed that "these matters [were] best reserved for a later case." *Id.*

In the *Laidlaw* case, the Supreme Court—in an opinion written by Justice Ruth Bader Ginsburg—held that environment groups had standing to bring a citizen suit pursuant to the Clean Water Act seeking both injunctive relief and *civil* penalties. Friends of the Earth, Inc. v. Laidlaw Environmental Services (TOC), Inc., 528 U.S. 167 (2000).

305. Fallon v. Accudyne Corp., 921 F. Supp. 611, 623–24 (W.D. Wis. 1995); United States ex rel. Kelly v. Boeing Co., 9 F.3d 743, 760 (9th Cir. 1993).

306. Shearson/American Express, Inc. v. McMahon, 482 U.S. 220, 241 (1987) ("Antitrust violations generally have a widespread impact on national markets as a whole, and the antitrust treble-damages provision gives private parties an incentive to bring civil suits that serve to advance the national interest in a competitive economy."); Edward Cavanagh, *Antitrust Remedies Revisited*, 84 Or. L. Rev. 147, 152–53 (2005) ("The antitrust laws also create a private right of action for individuals or entities harmed by anticompetitive acts. Congress created the private right of action to supplement public enforcement because it was aware that the government would not have the necessary resources to uncover, investigate, and prosecute all violations of the antitrust laws. To encourage private enforcement, Congress built in powerful incentives: mandatory treble damages; attorneys' fees for prevailing plaintiffs (although not for prevailing defendants); and in cases where a civil action follows a successful criminal prosecution, the factual findings in the criminal action are given prima facie effect in the civil action and, if applicable, issue preclusive effect. Private parties may also seek injunctive relief in appropriate cases."); Peter J. Hammer & William M. Sage, *Antitrust, Health Care Quality, and the Courts*, 102 Colum. L. Rev. 545, 565 (2002) ("Federal antitrust law provides several enforcement avenues: criminal and civil enforcement by the Department of Justice (DOJ), civil administrative enforcement by the Federal Trade Commission (FTC), civil enforcement by state attorneys general, and civil actions by private parties with the prospect of treble damages (as well as defensive antitrust pleadings by private parties in civil litigation).").

307. Whitfield v. Riley, Civil Action No. 09-1877, 2009 WL 1269243, at *1 n.1 (E.D. La. May 6, 2009) ("In this case, the civil cause of action is lodged in private persons, who act as 'private attorneys general' for purposes of enforcing fundamental constitutional rights under Section 1983.").

308. Fleming v. Matco Tools Corp., 384 F. Supp.3d 1124, 1132 (N.D. Cal. 2019) ("PAGA [Private Attorney General Act] 'authorizes an employee to bring an action for civil penalties on behalf of the state against his or her employer for Labor Code violations committed against the employee and fellow employees, with most of the proceeds of that litigation going to the state.' It was enacted to (i) provide civil penalties for violations of parts of the labor code that had previously only carried criminal penalties, and (ii) to make up for the shortage of government enforcement resources to combat violations of the labor code. To compensate for the shortage of resources, PAGA permitted aggrieved employees to act as private attorneys general to collect civil penalties for labor code violations, with seventy five percent of recovered penalties distributed to the California Labor and Workforce Development Agency.").

309. Roop v. Southern Pharmaceutical Corp., Cause No. 1:09CV222-M-D, 2010 WL 11643323, at *3 (N.D. Miss. June 30, 2010) ("The object of the civil RICO statute is to 'bring to bear the pressure of "private attorneys general" on a serious national problem for which public prosecutorial resources are deemed inadequate.'"); Innovative Metal Design, Inc. v. U.S. Bank Nat'l Ass'n, Case No. 3:15-cv-00560-SB, 2015 WL 9434779, at *6 (D. Or. Sept. 18, 2015) ("'The object of civil RICO is... to turn [victims] into prosecutors, 'private attorneys general,' dedicated to eliminating racketeering activity.' Wearing a prosecutor's hat confers upon civil RICO plaintiffs an important responsibility, and one that plaintiffs and their counsel must not take lightly.") (citations omitted). In civil RICO cases, successful plaintiffs can recover treble damages and attorney's fees. McSweeney v. Kahn, Civil Action File No. 4:05-CV-0132-HLM, 2006 WL 8439260, at *16 (N.D. Ga. Jan. 20, 2006) ("The object of civil RICO is not merely to compensate victims, but to turn them into prosecutors, 'private attorneys general,' dedicated to eliminating racketeering activity. A person injured by a violation of RICO's criminal provisions may recover treble damages and attorney's fees in a civil RICO action."); *see also* Indiana ex rel. Carter v. Pastrick, 384 F. Supp.2d 1261, 1265–66 (N.D. Ind. 2005) ("RICO provides for a dual system of enforcement—criminal and civil. The private enforcement component of RICO was designed 'not merely to compensate victims but to turn them into prosecutors, "private attorneys general, dedicated to eliminating racketeering activity."'") (quoting Rotella v. Wood, 528 U.S. 549, 557–58 (2000)); Chevron v. Donziger, 296 F.R.D. 168, 206 (S.D.N.Y. 2013) ("The United States has an interest also in ensuring that its laws are enforced. And, '[a]lthough the interest of the United States in criminal and civil enforcement suits is normally stronger than its interest in private disputes,' this distinction is less significant where, as here, claims are brought under RICO, which has the effect 'intended by Congress... of enforcing the law by means of "private attorney generals."' The Supreme Court has recognized that RICO 'bring[s] to bear the pressure of "private attorneys general" on a serious national problem for which public prosecutorial resources are deemed inadequate.'"); Julie R. Lewis, *An Offer He Couldn't Refuse:* Firestone v. Galbreath *Finds that the Racketeer Influenced and Corrupt Organizations Act (RICO) Is Unconstitutionally Vague*, 23 U. Tol. L. Rev. 619, 624 (1992) ("Private attorneys general is the term used for private plaintiffs who use civil suits to punish criminal defendants for the harm that was personally inflicted on them by the crime."); John D. Corrigan, *Restricting RICO under FSIA*, 84 St. John's L. Rev. 1477, 1487–88 (2010) ("[A]s organized crime infected legitimate businesses, Congress shifted focus away from a pure prosecutorial approach to include regulatory reforms. Notably, civil litigation was seen as a potential weapon against organized crime, turning citizens into 'private attorneys general.' Thus, Congress enacted RICO and created a civil private right of action whereby victims of statutorily proscribed criminal activity could sue in federal court for treble damages."); Michael A. DiMedio, *A Deterrence Theory Analysis of Corporate RICO Liability for "Fraud in the Sale of Securities,"* 1 Geo. Mason U. L. Rev. 135, 155 (1994) ("RICO's legislative history reveals that the treble damage provisions were intended to encourage citizens to supplement federal enforcement measures with private suits. This is the so-called 'private Attorney General' role of civil RICO plaintiffs. The same legislative history reveals that Congress' original targets were organized criminals such as the Mafia and La Cosa Nostra families. The statute involved legitimate businesses only to the extent that it provided them with a remedy against organized criminals who infiltrated their businesses."); Thomas J. Miles, *Dupes and Losers in Mail Fraud*, 77 U. Chi. L. Rev. 1111, 1127–28 (2010) ("The RICO statute has many unusual features. It is primarily a criminal statute, but unlike most criminal prohibitions, it has a complex-compound structure. It also permits private civil enforcement and even encourages private attorneys general by providing for treble damage awards.").

310. *Compare* United States v. Ferranti, 928 F. Supp. 206, 218 (E.D.N.Y. 1996) ("Post-medieval parallel and almost simultaneous growth of private tort law and public criminal law separated the individual interest in compensation from the social interest in punishment and deterrence. There were overlaps, of course. Tort law served a public purpose of deterrence and, like the criminal law, provided a sense of justice mollifying the urge for self help and revenge. Criminal law does sometimes deter and compensate the state through fines for some of the costs of prosecution and harm to the state. *See, e.g.* 26 U.S.C. §§ 7201 (tax evasion), 7203 (costs of prosecution); *see also United States v. Terrell,* 390 F. Supp. 371 (1975) (defendant received substantial income upon which substantial taxes were due, and his failure to file returns was deliberate). Private attorney general prosecutions through class actions, whistle blower suits, qui tam actions, fines and compensations by administrative agencies and other quasi-private and quasi-public procedures are developing. They have begun to blur our sharp civil-criminal-administrative law distinctions.").

311. American Bankers Management Co. v. Heryford, 885 F.3d 629, 631 (9th Cir. 2018).

312. United States ex rel. Newsham v. Lockheed Missiles & Space Co., 722 F. Supp. 607, 609 (N.D. Cal. 1989).

313. National Paint & Coatings Association, Inc. v. State of California, 58 Cal. App. 4th 753, 765 (Cal. Ct. App. 1997).

314. Paul H. Robinson, *The Criminal-Civil Distinction and the Utility of Desert,* 76 B.U. L. Rev. 201, 206 (1996) ("Criminal liability signals moral condemnation of the offender, while civil liability does not."); Caminker, *supra* note 301, at 371 (footnotes omitted) ("Our legal system generally considers criminal behavior to be more opprobrious than civil misconduct and criminal sanctions to be both quantitatively and qualitatively more severe than civil sanctions. The structural check against oppressive prosecution in the form of frivolous suits or excessive punishments that is created by executive oversight and discretion ought to be much more stringent in the criminal than the civil context, just as due process safeguards are more stringent against erroneous conviction than erroneous civil liability.") (citing Wayne LaFave & Austin Scott, Criminal Law 12–16 (2d ed. 1986) (listing distinctions between civil and criminal sanctions) and Hart, *The Aims of the Criminal Law,* 23 Law & Contemp. Probs. 401, 402–06 (1958) (same)); *see also* Richard Epstein, *Crime and Tort: Old Wine in Old Bottles, in* Assessing the Criminal 231 (R. Barnett & J. Hagel eds. 1977) (distinguishing between civil and criminal law). Unlike private prosecutions, *qui tam* actions are statutorily created and allow a private citizen to receive part of a fine or penalty for successfully suing a wrongdoer. A *qui tam* action is not a criminal prosecution; rather, it is a "remedial" proceeding that imposes only civil sanctions. United States ex rel. Marcus v. Hess, 317 U.S. 537, 549 (1943); *see also* Caminker, *supra* note 301, at 370 ("qui tam lawsuits seek only civil remedies and bring only private enforcement machinery to bear"); *cf.* Robert W. Fischer, Comment, *Qui Tam Actions: The Role of the Private Citizen in Law Enforcement,* 20 UCLA L. Rev. 778, 786 (1973) (footnote omitted) ("The overwhelming weight of authority supports the view that qui tam actions are civil actions."). To the extent any *qui tam* statutes permit the pursuit of *criminal* responsibility by interested private parties, such statutes must be declared unconstitutional. *Cf.* United States ex rel. Kelly v. Boeing Co., No. 92-36660 (9th Cir. Sept. 7, 1993), 62 U.S.L.W. 2165 (rejecting a due process challenge to a *qui tam* provision of the False Claims Act, but noting that a criminal prosecution might require a higher level of prosecutorial disinterest than would be necessary in a civil enforcement action under the False Claims Act).

315. State v. Eldridge, 951 S.W.2d 775, 780 (Tenn. Ct. App. 1997) ("The majority of jurisdictions that allow the use of private prosecutors, by statute or case law, require the public prosecutor's consent and retention of control over the case. Another restriction that is placed upon the use of private prosecutors in most states is the prohibition of their participation in related civil matters. We are aware of only one twentieth century case holding unequivocally that a private prosecutor who also represents plaintiffs in a civil action arising out of the same proceeding presents no inherent due process or ethical problems.") (citations omitted); *id.* at 782 ("Numerous cases have either found express due process violations or due process implications relating to the participation of an interested prosecutor.") (citations omitted); *id.* ("We have no hesitation in concluding that the participation by special prosecutors who represent the victim in a civil matter arising from the same incident giving rise to the criminal prosecution is a violation of the

defendant's rights under the Due Process Clause of the Fourteenth Amendment to the United States Constitution as well as the Law of the Land provision in Article I, § 8 of the Tennessee Constitution.").

316. State v. Storm, 661 A.2d 790, 795 (N.J. 1995).

317. *Compare* Brief of Petitioner-Appellant, *Wayne East v. Wayne Scott*, No. 94-10730 (Dec. 23, 1994, 5th Cir.) (brief signed by Sandra L. Babcock, Texas Resource Center, counsel for Mr. East.), pp. 9–10 ("In the months following the victim's death, the Sears family retained J. Russell 'Rusty' Ormesher, a seasoned prosecutor who had spent several years in the office of the Dallas County District Attorney, to prosecute Mr. East. Ormesher had successfully prosecuted several death penalty cases in Dallas County. He was an expert in trial preparation, and had trained prosecutors across the state. The Sears family retained him with the hope that his skills would ensure a death sentence for Mr. East.") (citations omitted); *id.* at 10 ("Ormesher reported case developments to his client, Tim Eyssen, the nephew of the deceased. Eyssen, who was himself a prosecutor in Wichita Falls, at times worked hand in hand with Ormesher in developing and preparing the state's case for trial. At a critical juncture in Mr. East's prosecution, Ormesher made the decision to strike a deal with Deedee Martin, and thereby obtained the testimony of the state's star witness."); *id.* ("At trial, Ormesher examined the state's two most important witnesses...."); *id.* at 11 ("He gave the State's opening statement, and gave closing arguments at both phases. He made objections throughout the trial, and examined half the prospective jurors. Ormesher was present at counsel table throughout trial."); *id.* ("Mr. Ormesher retained a separate set of prosecution files which, absent a court order, he refused to turn over to postconviction counsel for Mr. East."), *with* Brief of Respondent-Appellee, *Wayne East v. Wayne Scott*, No. 94-10730 (Jan. 14, 1995, 5th Cir.) (brief signed by William C. Zapalac, Assistant Attorney General), p. 9 ("East states in his brief that 'Ormesher's aim was to procure a death sentence for East in accordance with the wishes of his paying client.' This statement is not supported by reference to anything in the record or by any extra-record citation."); *id.* at 9 n.3 ("In addition to receiving some payment from the victim's family, Ormesher was paid in part by the Texas Prosecutor Council, 'a centralized agency of the judicial department of government capable of delivering technical assistance, educational services, and professional development training to the prosecutors of Texas and their assistants and to improve the administration of criminal justice through professionalization of the prosecuting attorney's office.'"); *id.* at 11 ("Here, it is plain that Patricia Elliott, the District Attorney of Taylor County, was in complete charge of the case."); *id.* at 11 n.6 ("Nothing in the record indicates that the decision to charge East with a capital crime was made by anyone other than the district attorney, and East offered nothing save his unsupported speculation that the decision was made by anyone other than the district attorney.").

318. 55 F.3d 996 (5th Cir. 1995). *East v. Scott*, 55 F.3d 996 (5th Cir. 1995) has been described as "a significant case in that it uses an 'evolving due process' interpretation to determine whether a defendant's due process rights were violated when a private prosecutor, hiring by the victim's family, controlled the case." DOUGLAS E. BELOOF, VICTIMS' RIGHTS: A DOCUMENTARY AND REFERENCE GUIDE 106 (2012).

319. *East*, 55 F.3d at 998–99.

320. *Id.* at 999; Michael Hall, *Who Killed Mary Eula Sears?*, TEXAS MONTHLY (Nov. 2011), https://www.texasmonthly.com/articles/who-killed-mary-eula-sears/.

321. *East*, 55 F.3d at 999–1000.

322. *Id.* at 1000; Brief of Petitioner-Appellant, *East v. Scott* (5th Cir.), No. 94-10730, at p. 5, 9–11, 15 (Dec. 23, 1994). East made the following allegations regarding Mr. Ormesher's role: (1) "Ormesher controlled all the significant trial strategy decisions for the prosecution, including the decision to offer a plea bargain to Dee Dee Martin, the prosecution's key witness linking East to Sear's murder"; (2) "Ormesher conducted an independent pre-trial investigation and maintained a separate case file"; (3) "Ormesher interviewed all the state's key witnesses independent of the supervision or control of the Taylor County district attorney"; (4) "Ormesher played a key role during the trial," with Ormesher delivering opening and closing arguments and participating in the direct examination of important prosecution witnesses; and (5) "Ormesher was a 'seasoned' veteran of capital murder prosecutions, while the district attorney prosecuting the case had little experience." *East*, 55 F.3d at 1001.

323. 481 U.S. 787 (1987); *East*, 55 F.3d at 1000 n.2 ("East argues that the Supreme Court's decision in *Young v. United States ex rel. Vuitton et Fils S.A.*, 481 U.S. 787, 107 S. Ct. 2124, 95 L.Ed.2d 740 (1987) creates a strict blanket prohibition against the participation of private prosecutors and, therefore, impliedly

overrules *Woods* and *Powers*. We disagree that *Young* alters the analysis set out in *Woods* and *Powers*. *Young* merely held that the counsel for a party in the position to gain from a criminal contempt proceeding cannot be appointed by the court to prosecute the party charged with contempt. In contrast to *Woods* and *Powers*, the private prosecutor in *Young* acted as the government's sole representative throughout the trial. Moreover, *Young* was decided under the Court's supervisory power over federal courts, not as a matter of federal constitutional law.").

324. 399 F.2d 322, 325 (5th Cir. 1968); *see also East*, 55 F.3d at 1000 ("*Powers v. Hauck* was the first decision by this court to expressly address whether the participation of a private prosecutor in a criminal prosecution violates the Due Process Clause.").

325. 648 F.2d 973, 976 (5th Cir. 1981); *see also East*, 55 F.3d at 1000 ("In *Woods v. Linahan*, 648 F.2d 973, 976 (5th Cir.1981), the court similarly held that the participation of a privately-retained attorney in a murder prosecution did not offend due process even though the attorney exercised independent control over the prosecution during its pre-trial stages. The private prosecutor in *Woods* conducted the pre-trial investigation, interviewed witnesses, filed and argued pre-trial motions, and made pre-trial strategy decisions without the supervision or control of the district attorney. According to the court, the private prosecutor's pretrial activity 'border[ed] on a constitutional violation' because 'these activities were not carried out under the direction, control, or knowledge of the district attorney.' However, the court concluded that there was no due process violation in *Woods* because the district attorney assumed control of the prosecution once the trial started. After the trial started, the district attorney assumed control over trial strategy decisions, gave the state's opening and closing arguments, and examined all the witnesses. While the private prosecutor assisted the district attorney during the trial, he never acted without the district attorney's consent or supervision. Thus, as in *Powers*, the *Woods* court held that the private prosecutor's actions did not offend due process because he did not control important phases of the prosecution.") (citation omitted).

326. 854 F.2d 656 (4th Cir. 1988), *cert. denied*, 489 U.S. 1011 (1989); *see also East*, 55 F.3d at 1000–01 ("In *Person v. Miller*... the Fourth Circuit followed similar reasoning in concluding that a private prosecutor must effectively control a prosecution to violate the accused's due process rights. The court reasoned that, for purposes of due process, it is important to determine whether a private prosecutor controlled crucial prosecutorial decisions, such as 'whether to prosecute, what targets of prosecution to select, what investigative powers to utilize, what sanctions to seek, plea bargains to strike, or immunities to grant.' According to the court, 'It is control over these critical prosecutorial decisions which determine the fairness of particular prosecutions that is the important consideration; operational conduct of the trial is actually of subordinate concern, except as it may actually impact upon the more fundamental prosecutorial decisions.' The court reasoned that, while the quantitative division of trial work has some relevance to determining control, the ultimate question must be whether the private prosecutor controlled these crucial prosecutorial decisions.") (citations omitted); *East*, 55 F.3d at 1001 ("We agree with the Fourth Circuit's characterization of the proper framework for resolving East's claim. We therefore turn to East's pleadings to determine whether he alleges specific facts suggesting that Mr. Ormesher effectively controlled critical prosecutorial decisions throughout East's prosecution.").

327. *East*, 55 F.3d at 1001. In *Woods*, the Fifth Circuit held in 1981 that the participation of a privately retained attorney in a murder prosecution did not offend due process even though the attorney exercised independent control over the pre-trial stages of the prosecution, including the pre-trial investigation, interviewing witnesses, filing and arguing pre-trial motions, and made pre-trial strategy decisions without the supervision or control of the district attorney. The court in *Woods*, however, ultimately found no due process violation because the district attorney "assumed control of the prosecution once the trial started." East v. Scott, 55 F.3d 996, 1000 (5th Cir. 1995) (discussing *Woods v. Linahan*, 648 F.2d 973, 976 (5th Cir. 1981)).

328. East v. Johnson, 123 F.3d 235, 236–37, 241 (5th Cir. 1997).

329. "Convicted Killer Agrees to Life in Prison," THE MONITOR (McAllen, TX), Sept. 11, 1999, p. 16; "An Update to the Mary Eula Sears Case," TEXAS MONTHLY (Nov. 2011), https://www.texasmonthly.com/articles/an-update-to-the-mary-eula-sears-case/.

330. John A. J. Ward, *Private Prosecution—The Entrenched Anomaly*, 50 N.C. L. REV. 1171, 1177 (1972) ("To determine if a defendant has been deprived of due process by a particular practice, the crucial

question is whether the practice inherently is so prejudicial as to infringe the defendant's fundamental right to a fair trial."); *id.* at 1178 ("[T]he difficulty in determining whether in specific cases the private prosecutor has actually prejudiced the defendant militates towards a ruling that private prosecutors should be banned in all cases, especially since the countervailing state interest in continuing the practice is miniscule. Arguably, any process which subjects the accused to the abuses inherent in the questioned method of trial deprives him of the fundamental fairness required by the due process clause.").

331. *See, e.g.*, Flowers v. Mississippi, 139 S. Ct. 2228, 2242 (2019) ("Equal justice under law requires a criminal trial free of racial discrimination in the jury selection process."); Davis v. Ayala, 135 S. Ct. 2187, 2208 (2015) ("The pattern of peremptory challenges in this case was sufficient to raise suspicions about the prosecution's motives and to call for the prosecution to explain its strikes. As we have held, the Fourteenth Amendment prohibits a prosecutor from striking potential jurors based on race. Discrimination in the jury selection process undermines our criminal justice system and poisons public confidence in the even-handed administration of justice.").

332. Rachel King, *Why a Victims' Rights Constitutional Amendment Is a Bad Idea: Practical Experiences from Crime Victims*, 68 U. Cin. L. Rev. 357, 367 (2000).

333. Joan E. Jacoby, The American Prosecutor: A Search for Identity 3 (1980).

334. Id.

335. 400 U.S. 455 (1971).

336. *Id.* at 469 (Harlan, J., concurring).

337. Melba V. Pearson, *Data as a Tool for Racial Justice*, 36 Crim. Just. 4, 5 (2021) ("Another challenge is diversity within prosecutors' offices. People of color are often absent in senior leadership. Offices find it difficult to hire and retain prosecutors of color. There are many reasons that can drive this, including the notorious low pay of prosecutors' offices, feelings of isolation once in the office, and not seeing a pathway into promotion. Again, elected prosecutors need to take the lead by meaningfully engaging with their staff to ascertain what is needed. Prosecutors' offices need to recruit from a wider area than their backyards—and can do so by forming partnerships with the National Black Law Students Association (https://www.nblsa.org/) and National Hispanic Bar Association (https://hnba.com/) as well as the National Black Prosecutors Association (http://blackprosecutors.org/), to name a few. Organizations such as these have job fairs that can bring diverse talent together with elected prosecutors who center diversity as part of their mission."); Donald R. Caster & Brian C. Howe, *Taking a Mulligan: The Special Challenges of Narrative Creation in the Post-Conviction Context*, 76 Md. L. Rev. 770, 771 (2017) ("[O]nly eight percent of Assistant United States Attorneys are black. The lack of diversity among America's prosecutors can hardly be surprising: as of the most recent Census in 2010, whites accounted for eighty-eight percent of attorneys across the country. The significance of racial disparities in prosecutors' offices becomes even larger in light of recent scholarship that emphasizes the role individual prosecutors play in creating or addressing systemic problems."); Olivia Dana & Sherene Crawford, *Restorative Prosecution? Rethinking Responses to Violence*, 64 N.Y.L. Sch. L. Rev. 53, 55 n.7 (2019/2020) ("'Ninety-five percent of elected prosecutors in the U.S. are white and that more than 60 percent of the nation's 50 states have exactly zero black prosecutors in office. The study found that, of the 2,437 elected prosecutors serving around the country, which includes officials at the state and local levels, just 61 are black—and of those, more than half are concentrated in Virginia and Mississippi. In 14 states, all elected prosecutors are white.'") (quoting Leon Neyfakh, *Why Aren't There More Black Prosecutors*?, Slate (July 8, 2015), https://slate.com/news-and-politics/2015/07/prosecutors-and-race-why-arent-there-more-black-prosecutors.html).

338. *E.g.*, Shaun Ossei-Owusu, *Criminal Legal Education*, 58 Am. Crim. L. Rev. 413, 427 (2021) ("Legal education is an underexplored site for criminal justice reform. The few empirical studies on race and gender in prosecutorial offices indicate that both categories matter, yet these issues, along with poverty, amongst other categories, occupy undersized space in criminalization. It is no secret that diversity in the legal profession is an issue, but there is a related and arguably deeper issue of how future criminal justice practitioners—irrespective of their race and gender—are socialized into understanding the relevance of those categories to their lawyering. The legal system tasks a relatively unrepresentative set of attorneys with prosecuting and representing criminal defendants in a world where race, gender, and poverty influence assumptions about crime as well its regulation.").

339. *See* John Nowak, Ronald Rotunda & J. Nelson Young, Constitutional Law 557 (2d ed. 1983) (stating the essential guarantee of due process is fairness).

340. Stumbo v. Seabold, 704 F.2d 910, 911 (6th Cir. 1983) (noting that many states have private prosecutor statutes but that they are "rarely used"); *see also* Charles W. Wolfram, Modern Legal Ethics §13.10.1, at 759 (1986) (noting that a few jurisdictions continue to allow the "barbaric" practice of private prosecutions).

341. 424 U.S. 319 (1976).

342. *Id.* at 335. While the *Mathews* test is usually applied in civil cases, it has also been used to test the sufficiency of criminal procedures. Ake v. Oklahoma, 470 U.S. 68, 77–82 (1985) (applying *Mathews* test and holding that an indigent defendant is entitled to access to a psychiatrist if the defendant's sanity is a significant factor); *see also* United States v. Raddatz, 447 U.S. 667, 677–81 (1980) (applying test to right to de novo hearing of suppression motion); *see also* Wofford v. Wainwright, 748 F.2d 1505, 1507–08 (11th Cir. 1984); Shepard v. United States Bd. of Parole, 541 F.2d 322, 326–29 (2d Cir. 1976).

343. In *Mathews v. Eldridge*, 424 U.S. 319 (1976), articulated an approach to due process that involves a "mechanical" balancing of interests, articulating three areas of critical importance for a court to consider in determining what process is due: First, the private interest that will be affected by the official action; second, the risk of an erroneous deprivation of such interest through the procedures used, and the probable value, if any, of additional or substitute procedural safeguards; and finally, the Government's interest, including the function involved and the fiscal and administrative burdens that the additional or substitute procedural requirement would entail. *Mathews*, 424 U.S. at 335; *see also* Connecticut v. Doehr, 501 U.S. 1 (1991). Notably, "the word 'fairness' did not appear in the balancing test. Redish & Marshall, *supra* note 69, at 472. In spite of that, the Supreme Court has reiterated that "procedural due process" remains "a guarantee of fair procedure." Zinermon v. Burch, 494 U.S. 113, 125 (1990) (emphasis added).

344. State v. Culbreath, 30 S.W.3d 309, 310–12, 318 (Tenn. 2000).

345. *Young*, 481 U.S. at 814.

346. 397 U.S. 358 (1970).

347. *Id.* at 363. As the Supreme Court stated in *Ake*: "The private interest in the accuracy of a criminal proceeding that places an individual's life or liberty at risk is almost uniquely compelling. Indeed, the host of safeguards fashioned by this Court over the years to diminish the risk of erroneous conviction stands as a testament to that concern." *Ake*, 470 U.S. at 78.

348. The Court of Criminal Appeals of Tennessee made just such a finding. State v. Culbreath, No. 02C01-9805-CR-00145, 1999 WL 134685, at *5 (Mar. 9, 1999) ("[T]he use of an interested prosecutor allows influences other than 'justice' or the 'public interest' to weigh upon prosecutorial decisions.") (citing John D. Bessler, *The Public Interest and the Unconstitutionality of Private Prosecutors*, 47 Ark. L. Rev. 511, 576 (1994)). Permission to appeal the decision by the Court of Criminal Appeals of Tennessee was granted on September 13, 1999, ultimately resulting in the Supreme Court of Tennessee's decision in *State v. Culbreath* on October 20, 2000. State v. Culbreath, 30 S.W.3d 309 (Tenn. 2000).

349. *Culbreath*, 30 S.W.3d at 316–17.

350. *See* Chapter 1.

351. "The Court has had occasion to recall even recently that 'procedural due process is not intended to promote efficiency' and that a procedural safeguard must be afforded 'if that may be done without prohibitive cost.'" Tribe, *supra* note 69, at § 10-13, at 717 (quoting Fuentes v. Shevin, 407 U.S. 67, 90 n.22 (1972) and Goss v. Lopez, 419 U.S. 565, 580 (1975) (emphasis added)). In *Ake*, the Supreme Court held that indigent criminal defendants must be provided access to a psychiatrist if insanity is likely to be a significant issue at trial or if the state presents psychiatric testimony of the defendant's future dangerousness at a capital sentencing proceeding. In so holding, the Supreme Court rejected the argument that providing such assistance would result in a "staggering burden" to the State of Oklahoma. *Ake*, 470 U.S. at 78. According to the Court: "In such a circumstance, where the potential accuracy of the jury's determination is so dramatically enhanced, and where the interests of the individual and the state in an accurate proceeding are substantial, the State's interest in its fisc must yield." *Id.* at 83.

352. *Culbreath*, 30 S.W.3d at 318.

353. 446 U.S. 238 (1980).

354. *Id.* at 239.

355. *Id.* at 241.

356. *Id.* at 243–44.

357. *Id.* at 245 & n.6.

358. *Id.* at 246. The amounts returned to the U.S. Treasury substantially exceeded the sums collected under § 16(e) in all relevant years. *Id.* at 246 (footnote omitted).

359. *Id.*

360. *Id.* at 248. Administrative law judges perform de novo review of ESA assessments, and administrative law judges were not entitled to reimbursement in conjunction with § 16(e). *Id.* at 245, 248 n.10.

361. *Id.* at 250 (footnote and citations omitted). According to the Supreme Court: "We need not say whether different considerations might be held to apply if the alleged biasing influence contributed to prosecutions against particular persons, rather than to a general zealousness in the enforcement process." *Id.* at 250 n.12.

362. *Id.* at 252 (quoting Withrow v. Larkin, 421 U.S. 35, 47 (1975)).

363. *Id.*

364. 456 U.S. 188 (1982).

365. *Id.* at 190.

366. *Id.* at 192.

367. *Id.* at 196 (footnote omitted).

368. *Id.* at 196–97 (citations and footnote omitted).

369. 424 U.S. 319 (1976).

370. *Schweiker*, 456 U.S. at 200.

371. *See, e.g.*, Casey W. Baker, *Attorney-Client Sexual Relationships in the #MeToo Era: Understanding Current State Approaches and Working Towards a Better Rule*, 49 Sw. L. Rev. 243, 248 (2020) ("The attorney-client relationship is a fiduciary relationship. As a fiduciary, the attorney owes the client the duty of care, consistent with a certain minimum level of skill or expertise as well as diligence, and the duty of loyalty and fidelity, including the duties of confidentiality, candor, and disclosure. It is fundamental to the attorney-client relationship that the attorney faithfully, honestly, and consistently represent the interests and protect the rights of the client—and the attorney must fulfill these duties to the client with the highest degree of fidelity and in utmost good faith."); Charles S. Hale, II, *Market Impact in the Information Age: Protecting Hotel Owners from Hotel Management Companies*, 108 W. Va. L. Rev. 573, 577–78 (2005) ("A fiduciary relationship arises when one party, the fiduciary, is under a duty to act for the benefit of another party, the beneficiary. A fiduciary duty is 'a duty of utmost good faith, trust, confidence, and candor... a duty to act with the highest degree of honesty and loyalty toward another person and in the best interests of the other person.' Some examples of fiduciary relationships are trustee-beneficiary, guardian-ward, principal-agent, and attorney-client, and these relationships require 'an unusually high degree of care.' The Restatement of Agency states that 'an agent is a fiduciary with respect to matters within the scope of his agency,' meaning the principal is the beneficiary of the relationship. Among the specific duties of an agent to the principal are the duties to act 'solely for the benefit of the principal in all matters connected with the agency [and to] not act secretly in the same transaction on the agent's own account or act for an adverse party without the principal's consent.'")

372. Sally J. Schmidt, Selling Your Lawyers On Client Surveys, The American Lawyer Management Serv. (1990–2000 ed.), vol. 1, at 10.17 (research shows that a firm's current clients can be responsible for up to 80% of its business through on-going work or referrals); Stuart A. Forsyth, *Good Client Relations = The Key to Success*, 34 Ariz. Att'y 20, 23 (May 1998) ("As much as 80 percent of your future clients will come from word-of-mouth referrals by your current and former clients.").

373. Private clients often have great influence over their attorneys. For example, courts have recognized that payment of fees by a client can affect a lawyer's loyalties. *See* Wood v. Georgia, 450 U.S. 261, 268–69 (1981) ("Courts and commentators have recognized the inherent dangers that arise when a criminal defendant is represented by a lawyer hired and paid by a third party, particularly when the third party is the operator of the alleged criminal enterprise."); *see also* Beth Nolan, *Removing Conflicts from the Administration of Justice: Conflicts of Interest and Independent Counsels Under the Ethics in Government Act*,

79 Geo. L.J. 1, 52 (1990) ("The human-nature rationale for regulation of potential conflicts of interest accepts that the ability of individuals to rise above their conflicting loyalties (even when it is theoretically possible to do so) is limited."). In *Wood*, an attorney, paid by the employer, represented two employees in a criminal prosecution for distributing obscene material. Under those facts, the Court held that the record was unclear "whether counsel was influenced in his basic strategic decisions by the interests of the employer who hired him," although the record did demonstrate at least the "possibility of a conflict of interest." *Wood*, 450 U.S. at 272. Consequently, the Court remanded for a determination, pursuant to the due process guarantee, as to whether the employees' convictions were tainted by an attorney's conflict of interest. *Id.* at 273–74.

374. The Supreme Court has stated that some interests are so "minute, remote, trifling or insignificant" that they do not create due process violations. *See Tumey*, 273 U.S. at 532; *see also* Aetna Life Ins. Co. v. Lavoie, 475 U.S. 813 (1986) (noting that a judge's interest that was "highly speculative and contingent" would not violate due process). Although the Supreme Court stated in dicta in *Commonwealth Coatings v. Continental Casualty Co.* that *Tumey* required a decision to be set aside where "the slightest pecuniary interest" existed, the Supreme Court has since declined to read *Tumey* "as constitutionalizing any rule that a decision rendered by a judge with 'the slightest pecuniary interest' constitutes a violation of the Due Process Clause." Commonwealth Coatings v. Continental Casualty Co., 393 U.S. 145, 148 (1968); *Lavoie*, 475 U.S. at 825 n.3. Because of the strong financial incentives that interested private prosecutors have to obtain convictions, such prosecutors do not implicate merely "minute" or "remote" interests. As the Supreme Court stated in *Tumey*:

> The mayor received for his fees and costs in the present case $12, and from such costs under the prohibition act for seven months he made about $100 a month, in addition to his salary. We can not regard the prospect of receipt or loss of such an emolument in each case as a minute, remote, trifling or insignificant interest. It is certainly not fair to each defendant brought before the mayor for the careful and judicial consideration of his guilt or innocence that the prospect of such a prospective loss by the mayor should weigh against his acquittal.

Id. at 531–32.

375. *See* Blackledge v. Perry, 417 U.S. 21, 28–29 (1974) (due process requires that the "potential for vindictiveness" not enter into prosecutorial decisions). Under Article III of the Constitution, "the Judges, both of the supreme and inferior courts, shall hold their offices during good behavior, and shall, at stated Times, receive for their Services a Compensation, which shall not be diminished during their Continuance in Office." U.S. Const. art. III, § 1. The salary provisions of Article III, designed to protect the judiciary's independence, were based on the conclusion that "in the general course of human nature, a power over a man's subsistence amounts to a power over his will." The Federalist No. 79, at 583 (A. Hamilton) (E. Earle ed. 1937); *see also* Northern Pipeline Constr. Co. v. Marathon Pipe Line Co., 458 U.S. 50 (1982).

376. *Young*, 481 U.S. at 807.

377. *Id.*

378. *Medina*, 505 U.S. at 443.

379. *Id.* at 446.

380. Concrete Pipe & Products of Cal., Inc. v. Construction Laborers Pension Trust for Southern Cal., 508 U.S. 602, 617 (1993) (quoting Ward v. Village of Monroeville, 409 U.S. 57, 61–62 (1972); citing Schweiker v. McClure, 456 U.S. 188, 195 (1982)); *see also* Isom v. Arkansas, 140 S. Ct. 342, 344 (2019) (Sotomayor, J., statement respecting denial of cert.) ("I write ... to encourage vigilance about the risk of bias that may arise when trial judges peculiarly familiar with a party sit in judgment of themselves. The Due Process Clause's guarantee of a neutral decisionmaker will mean little if this form of partiality is overlooked or underestimated.").

381. Mitchell v. Forsyth, 472 U.S. 511, 520 (1985) (including prosecutors among those performing "quasi-judicial" functions); Imbler v Pachtman, 424 U.S. 409, 423 n.20 (1976) ("It is the functional comparability of their judgments to those of the judge that has resulted in both grand jurors and prosecutors being referred to as 'quasi-judicial' officers, and their immunities being termed 'quasi-judicial' as well.") (citations omitted).

382. Tumey v. Ohio, 273 U.S. 510, 522 (1927); *see also Concrete Pipe & Products of Cal.*, 508 U.S. at 617 ("Before one may be deprived of a protected interest, whether in a criminal or civil setting, one is entitled as a matter of due process of law to an adjudicator who is not in a situation "'which would offer a possible temptation to the average man as a judge... which might lead him not to hold the balance nice, clear and true....'"") (citations omitted).

383. *See* Danielle Levine, *Public Wrongs and Private Rights: Limiting the Victim's Role in a System of Public Prosecution*, 104 Nw. U. L. Rev. 335, 337–38 (2010) ("During colonial America and early American independence, private prosecutions played a role in the criminal process. Despite the debate over the extent of private prosecutions during early American history, the victim was often responsible for many, if not all, aspects of the criminal prosecution. He was responsible for arresting the offender, investigating the crime, filing charges, and prosecuting the alleged criminal. For example, if a shopkeeper caught a thief in his store, the shopkeeper had to use his money and resources to bring the offender to justice. This was often an expensive undertaking; consequently, prosecuting an offender depended on the victim's financial means."); *see also id.* at 338 ("Although private prosecutions played a role in early American history, the role of a public prosecutor appeared earlier in America than in England, 'due to the greater egalitarianism of American society.' The United States developed public prosecutors for both philosophical and practical reasons. Philosophically, the Enlightenment shifted the focus of criminal prosecutions from serving the private interests of victims to the greater societal interests of deterrence, rehabilitation, and retribution. Practically, as the police forces, prisons, and penal codes expanded, a professional government-run prosecutorial force emerged and began to displace the private prosecution system.").

384. Peña-Rodriguez v. Colorado, 137 S. Ct. 855, 867 (2017) ("'[T]he central purpose of the Fourteenth Amendment was to eliminate racial discrimination emanating from official sources in the States.'") (quoting McLaughlin v. Florida, 379 U.S. 184, 192 (1964)).

385. Earl H. Fry, *Sovereignty and Federalism: U.S. and Canadian Perspectives Challenges to Sovereignty and Governance*, 20 Can.-U.S. L.J. 303, 315 n.47 (1994); *see also* David Ray Papke, *A Democracy for the Pursuit of Happiness*, 35 Ind. L. Rev. 1005, 1008–09 (2002) ("After the Civil War, the victorious North changed the Constitution by adding the Thirteenth, Fourteenth, and Fifteenth Amendments. These are the heart of the 'second' Constitution. The Thirteenth Amendment eliminates slavery and other forms of involuntary servitude. The Fourteenth Amendment makes anyone born or naturalized in the United States a citizen of both the nation and a state and warns that the individual states may not deny the fundamental national rights of citizens. The Fifteenth Amendment says citizens' right to vote should not be denied because of race, color or earlier enslavement. 'The people who drafted those amendments believed they were necessary because the Civil War had shown the southern states unwilling to protect the fundamental rights of free men, black or white.'") (reviewing John Denvir, Democracy's Constitution: Claiming the Privileges of American Citizenship (2001)).

386. John M. West, *Expert Services and the Indigent Criminal Defendant: The Constitutional Mandate of* Ake v. Oklahoma, 84 Mich. L. Rev. 1326, 1334–35 (1986) (discussing the importance of due process and equal protection jurisprudence following the Fourteenth Amendment's ratification).

387. William Hauptman, *Lethal Reflection: New York's New Death Penalty and Victim Impact Statements*, 13 N.Y.L. Sch. J. Hum. Rts. 439, 478–79 (1997).

388. *See* Model Rules of Professional Conduct (1983) (preamble) ("As advocate, a lawyer zealously asserts the client's position under the rules of the adversary system."); *see also* Model Rules of Professional Conduct Rule 1.7 cmt. (1983) ("Loyalty is an essential element in the lawyer's relationship to a client."); Model Rules of Professional Conduct Rule 1.2(a) (1983) ("A lawyer shall abide by a client's decisions concerning the objectives of representation...."); Olson v. Fraase, 421 N.W.2d 820 (N.D. 1988) (an attorney must follow the client's specific instructions); Foothills Dev. Co. v. Clark County Bd., 730 P.2d 1369 (Wash. App. 1986) (an attorney must follow the client's specific instructions). *But cf.* Model Rules of Professional Conduct Rule 1.2 cmt. (1983) ("At the same time, a lawyer is not required to pursue objectives or employ means simply because a client may wish that the lawyer do so.").

389. In states that allow private prosecutors, it is often recited that private prosecutors are bound by the same standards of conduct as public prosecutors, presumably requiring private prosecutors to disregard the wishes of their clients when "justice" or the "public interest" so requires. Aside from the ethical

tension that standard creates (and regardless of whether private prosecutors, as a practical matter, can actually refuse to honor their clients' wishes), incentives will always exist in close cases to err on the side of a private client, rather than with the accused. This situation is especially true given the subjective nature of "justice" and the "public interest." Attorneys in private practice are accustomed to regularly advising and conferring with their clients and to acting in a manner consistent with the interests of those clients. Attorney Grievance Commission of Maryland v. Powers, 164 A.3d 138, 150–51 (Md. 2017) ("Rule 1.2(a) provides that a lawyer 'shall abide by a client's decisions concerning the objectives of the representation and, when appropriate, shall consult with the client as to the means by which they are to be pursued.' Further, '[a] lawyer may take such action on behalf of the client as is impliedly authorized to carry out the representation.' An attorney's failure to inform a client of the status of his or her case, which denies the client the ability to make informed decisions may be a violation of Rule 1.2(a). Additionally, an attorney may violate Rule 1.2(a) if he or she fails to follow the client's instructions.") (citation omitted); United States v. McTizic, 377 Fed. Appx. 391, 394 (5th Cir. 2010) ("In general, attorneys are obliged to follow the explicit instructions of their clients."); Wolf v. Ramirez, No. 08-19-00147-CV, 2020 WL 5110635, at *13 (Tex. Ct. App. Aug. 31, 2020) ("Attorneys in particular owe their clients the duty to act with integrity and fidelity, which includes a number of additional duties beyond those owed by other types of fiduciaries. Among those additional duties, and implicated in the instant case by the facts alleged in Appellant's complaint, are the duty to act with absolute candor and honesty, and without any concealment or deception; the duty to inform the client of all matters material to the representation; and the duty to follow the client's instructions.") (citation omitted); In re Mirabile, 975 S.W.2d 936, 939 (Mo. 1998) (en banc) ("Attorneys generally must follow their clients' instructions, but only within the limits of the law." 'The client has ultimate authority to determine the purposes to be served by legal representation, within the limits imposed by law and the lawyer's professional obligations.'") (citations omitted); Olfe v. Gordon, 286 N.W.2d 573, 577–78 (Wis. 1980) ("The attorney-client relationship in such contexts is one of agent to principal, and as an agent the attorney 'must act in conformity with his authority and instructions and is responsible to his principal if he violates this duty.' While actions for disregard of instructions can be based upon fiduciary and contractual principles, the principal's cause of action for an agent's breach of duty may also lie in tort.") (citation omitted); People v. Betillo, 279 N.Y.S.2d 444, 452 (N.Y. Sup. Ct., N.Y. Cty, Trial Term, Part XXX, 1967) ("An attorney is a mere agent of his client and is supposed to follow his instructions and carry out the agreement of his principal lower. A delicate and confidential relationship exists between attorney and client. It is a rule of first importance governing the conduct of a lawyer that his relationship to his client should be personal; that his responsibility should be direct. Without specific authority from his principal, an agent has no power to delegate his trust.") (citations omitted); Nave v. Baird, 12 Ind. 318, 319, 1859 WL 4663, at *1 (1859) ("[I]t is the duty of the attorney to advise his client to the best of his judgment; and it is generally the wiser course for the client to act upon the advice so given; but if he is unwilling to do so, it is safer for the attorney to follow the instructions of his client, so far as the rules of law may permit. But if he does not do so, and the client sues for damages, it will devolve upon him to show, presumptively, that he was injured by the course pursued by the attorney, in order to recover more, at least, than nominal damages.").

390. John D. Bessler, *Torture and Trauma: Why the Death Penalty Is Wrong and Should Be Strictly Prohibited by American and International Law*, 58 Washburn L.J. 1 (2019); John D. Bessler, *Taking Psychological Torture Seriously: The Torturous Nature of Credible Death Threats and the Collateral Consequences for Capital Punishment*, 11 Ne. U. L. Rev. 1 (2019).

391. 261 S.E.2d 55 (W. Va. 1979), *cert. denied*, 445 U.S. 904 (1980).

392. *Id.*

393. Handley v. State, 106 So.2d 692, 695 (Ala. 1925).

394. People ex rel. Allen v. Citadel Management Co., 355 N.Y.S.2d 976 (N.Y. Crim. Ct. 1974); *see also* People v. Black, 282 N.Y.S. 197, 201 (Ostego County Ct. 1935) (minor infractions do not necessitate "heavy artillery" of district attorney or Attorney General).

395. *See* United States v. Crawford Enter., Inc., 643 F. Supp. 370, 380 (S.D. Tex. 1986), *order aff'd and appeal dismissed*, 826 F.2d 392 (1987) ("To require a government prosecutor to present facts supporting criminal contempt and a private attorney to present facts supporting civil contempt would be an injudicious use of the court's, government's and the private attorney's time and resources."). Because the

American system of justice recognizes "higher values than speed and efficiency," the use of private prosecutors, even in the contempt context where such individuals may possess a greater understanding of the underlying facts, is inappropriate. Stanley v. Illinois, 405 U.S. 645, 656 (1972).

396. The fact that prohibiting private prosecutors may produce more intangible benefits while allowing private prosecutors may produce real cost savings, however small those may be, does not preclude a rule barring private prosecutors. According to two scholars:

> By their very nature, procedural safeguards impose administrative costs and burdens on the government that would not otherwise exist. At the same time, the benefits of such safeguards are not always immediately recognizable. Often it is not clear that the ultimate outcome in a particular case will be more just or efficient when specific procedures are employed than when they are not. In an important sense, then, the benefits of procedural due process—at least when measured from a purely efficiency standpoint—are prophylactic in nature.

Redish & Marshall, *supra* note 69, at 473. Significantly, even the use of private prosecutors involves public costs. Thus, in states that allow private prosecutors, public prosecutors are still required to supervise and control the activities of private prosecutors.

397. Dziubak v. Mott, 503 N.W.2d 771, 775 (Minn. 1993) ("Public Defender offices are grossly under-funded."). According to one law review article, a politician "at best, has little to gain by advocating large expenditure for the defender office, and at worst, much to lose." Suzanne E. Mounts, *Public Defender Programs, Professional Responsibility, and Competent Representation*, 1982 Wis. L. Rev. 473, 482. To ensure the proper administration of justice, there needs to be equity in terms of staffing and resources as between prosecutors' offices and public defenders' offices.

398. *See, e.g.*, Sabrina Margret Bierer, *Bettering Prosecutorial Engagement to Reduce Crime, Prosecutions, and the Criminal Justice Footprint*, 32 Fed. Sent. R. 221, 214–15 (2020) ("Taking advantage of new data emerging in states that have legalized or decriminalized marijuana possession, and to have a better understanding of the consequences of ending marijuana prosecutions entirely, in 2018 the Manhattan DA's Office conducted interviews and gathered data from prosecutors, regulators, and law enforcement representatives from jurisdictions that have legalized or decriminalized marijuana. The resulting report confirmed what many prosecutors already knew from experience: marijuana prosecutions consume an inordinate amount of prosecutorial resources for little public safety, rehabilitative, or deterrent impact, and they have disparate results for communities of color. On August 1, 2018, DA Vance announced a new policy to summarily decline to prosecute marijuana possession and smoking cases. The next month, DA Vance dismissed 3,042 marijuana smoking and possession cases, eliminating the collateral consequences associated with having an open marijuana case and giving New Yorkers the freedom to interact with law enforcement without fearing arrest or collateral consequences, such as deportation, from such prosecutions. In 2019, the New York State Legislature decriminalized, although it did not legalize, possession of small amounts of marijuana. In the absence of such legislative change in other states, prosecutors can still implement policies to improve the fairness of the justice system and to increase the prosecutorial resources available to pursue more serious cases.").

399. Jordan C. Harris, *Justice for Sale: The Cost of Private Financing of Prosecution, When Is It Worth It?*, 31 Geo. J. Legal Ethics 635, 654 (2018).

400. Notably, even if a local district attorney refuses to prosecute a worthy case, some state laws already provide the victim or the victim's family with alternate remedies. *See generally* Sidman, *supra* note 2, at 764–65, 790 (describing statutes, which exist in a majority of states, that permit the appointment of special temporary prosecutors to be paid with government funds or that authorize courts to appoint counsel to replace the district attorney when he or she fails to perform his or her duties or has an interest in the proceedings); *cf.* ABA Standards for Criminal Justice, Standard 3-2.1 cmt. (1979) ("Private prosecution ... should be distinguished from the process available in some jurisdictions whereby a private citizen may file a complaint if the prosecutor refuses to act."); ABA Standards for Criminal Justice, Standard 3-2.10(a) (1979) ("Procedures should be established by appropriate legislation to the end that the governor or other elected state official is empowered by law to suspend and supersede a local prosecutor upon making a public finding, after reasonable notice and hearing, that the prosecutor is incapable of fulfilling the duties of office."); ABA Standards for Criminal Justice, Standard 3-2.10(b) (1979) ("The governor or other elected

official should be empowered by law to substitute special counsel in the place of the local prosecutor in a particular case, or category of cases, upon making a public finding that this is required for the protection of the public interest."). For example, in *State ex rel. Wild v. Otis*, when the elected officials refused to prosecute a case, the Minnesota Supreme Court noted that an aggrieved citizen might (1) petition the district court to appoint a special prosecutor, (2) appeal to the governor, who then might order the Attorney General to commence prosecution, or (3) seek mandamus. 257 N.W.2d 361, 364–65 (Minn. 1977), *cert. denied*, 434 U.S. 1003 (1978); *see also* Kentucky v. Hubbard, 777 S.W.2d 882, 885 (Ky. 1989) (Leibson, J., dissenting) (if county attorney is incapable, unable, or unwilling to prosecute, the aggrieved citizen can apply for relief to the "prosecutors advisory council" created by Ky. Rev. Stat. § 15.705 (Michie/Bobbs-Merrill 1988)). Under federal law, the Attorney General of the United States can appoint qualified private attorneys to assist United States attorneys in the prosecution of cases. 28 U.S.C. § 543(a) (1988) ("The Attorney General may appoint attorneys to assist United States attorneys when the public interest so requires, including the appointment of qualified tribal prosecutors and other qualified attorneys to assist in prosecuting Federal offenses committed in Indian country.").

401. Payne v. Tennessee, 501 U.S. 808 (1991) (admission of testimony of murder victim's mother during the sentencing phase of a capital case did not violate the defendant's due process rights); *see also* Williams v. New York, 337 U.S. 241, 246 (1949) (sentencer has wide discretion in types of information used to determine sentence).

402. Eric S. Fish, *Against Adversary Prosecution*, 103 Iowa L. Rev. 1419 (2018).

403. Adam Malka, The Men of Mobtown: Policing Baltimore in the Age of Slavery and Emancipation 33 (2018).

404. Darryl Brown, *The Judicial Role in Criminal Charging and Plea Bargaining*, 46 Hofstra L. Rev. 63, 73–74 (2017) ("Many states give judges the authority to approve criminal complaints (as well as warrant requests) filed by private citizens. Given that judicial approval of charges is not required to commence a prosecution in most jurisdictions, this process represents a modest version of judicial power to initiate a criminal case independently of the prosecutor's office. This is surely a remnant of procedures, common in the nineteenth century in some states, in which judges approved private prosecutions handled by victims' private attorneys. In most states, it is solely up to the prosecutor's office whether to file charges or otherwise allow private criminal complaints to proceed. If they choose not to, prosecutors can request or dictate their dismissal."); *id.* at 74 ("In a few states, however, legislatures have granted judges review over prosecutors' decisions to press charges. Colorado, Michigan, Nebraska, and Pennsylvania all have similar statutes that authorize judges to review public prosecutors' decisions not to charge based on private criminal complaints. Each state requires prosecutors to provide reasons for declining to prosecute in certain kinds of cases. State law empowers trial judges to assess prosecutors' discretionary declination decisions, and those explanations provide a basis for judicial review of prosecutorial decision-making. If judges find the decision unmerited, they can *order* that the prosecution proceed, either by compelling the public prosecutor to litigate it or by appointing a special prosecutor.") (italics in original); *id.* at 75 ("In one sense, this procedure looks familiar. It is a classic structure of checks and balances on the government's decision about a criminal charge—a decision in which alleged victims have a direct, substantial interest, in addition to the generic public interest in criminal law enforcement. On the other hand, this scheme is radical, because U.S. judges and legislatures normally grant extreme deference to prosecutors. And judging from appellate reports, it seems that courts may have continued that tradition under these statutes. There is little published evidence of courts using this statutory power to overrule prosecutors. It may be that they are presented with few plausible challenges to prosecutors' declination decisions. But it is also the case that, as they do in the context of dismissals in the interest of courts, appellate courts direct trial judges to give great deference to prosecutors when exercising this power to second-guess non-charging decisions."); Stuart P. Green, *Private Challenges to Prosecutorial Inaction: A Model Declaratory Judgment Statute*, 97 Yale L.J. 488 (1988) ("Given a statute upon which to base a claim, private persons can successfully challenge the decisions of prosecutors not to prosecute. Although federal law lacks such a statute, at least nine states have, or recently had, statutory schemes that potentially enable private persons to challenge prosecutorial inaction.").

405. *See* Sidman, *supra* note 2, at 793 ("The better reasoned view appears to be that the presence of a private prosecutor creates a situation of inherent bias or prejudice sufficient to enable a defendant to

invoke the guarantees of the due process clause."); *id.* at 793–94 ("The presence of an attorney who is being paid to secure a conviction seems calculated to unfairly tip the scales of justice against the defendant.").

406. United States v. Schwartz, 692 F. Supp. 331, 342 (D. Del. 1988) ("In applying separation of powers analysis, the Supreme Court has sometimes focused on the necessity for any action by one branch that infringes upon another branch. *See Young v. United States ex rel. Vuitton et Fils S.A.*, 481 U.S. 787, 107 S. Ct. 2124, 2134, 95 L.Ed.2d 740 (1987) (court's authority to appoint private prosecutor in contempt proceedings based upon necessity); *Schor,* 106 S. Ct. at 3260 (exercise of Article III jurisdiction limited to that which is necessary to enable non-Article III tribunal to fulfill its function). And in *Morrison,* the Court found limitation of the removal power necessary to fulfill Congress's intent to create independence for the special prosecutor. 108 S. Ct. at 2618–21."). Separation-of-powers considerations have been raised in the context of the initiation of prosecutions and in the private prosecution context. *E.g.*, Joshua D. Kadish, Stephen J. Schulhofer & Rachel E. Barkow, Criminal Law and Its Processes: Cases and Materials (10th ed. 2017) ("American courts have uniformly held that separation-of-powers requirements prohibit judges from compelling an unwilling prosecutor to file charges. A Wisconsin statute, for example, provided that if a judge finds probable cause to believe that an individual has committed an offense and the district attorney nonetheless refuses to file a complaint, the judge can direct the commencement of a prosecution. The statute was tested in *State ex rel. Unnamed Petitioners v. Connors*, 401 N.W.2d 782 (Wis. 1987), where a female dancer alleged that she had been assaulted by two professional football players in her dressing room at a Milwaukee night club. When the prosecutor acknowledged the existence of probable cause but refused to proceed, because he had doubts about his ability to win convictions at trial, a circuit judge invoked the statute and ordered the prosecution to go forward. The Wisconsin Supreme Court reversed, holding that the statute violated the separation-of-powers requirements of the state constitution. A recent decision from the California Supreme Court raised similar separation-of-powers concerns about a state law that could have been read to allow a judicial employee to issue misdemeanor complaints for failure to appear in court; the court read the law narrowly to require prosecutorial approval in order to avoid the constitutional question. Steen v. Appellate Div., Superior Court, 331 P.3d 136 (Cal. 2014)."); Abby L. Dennis, *Reining in the Minister of Justice: Prosecutorial Oversight and the Superseder Power*, 57 Duke L.J. 131, 151 (2007) ("[T]he statutory authority for courts to remove prosecutors and appoint special prosecutors may need to be 'narrowly drawn' to avoid violating the constitutional doctrine of separation of powers. Specifically, a broad interpretation of these statutes would enable trial courts to appoint special prosecutors over the objections of prosecuting attorneys, stripping the executive branch of its power to prosecute and transferring that power to the judiciary. Thus, not surprisingly, the doctrine of separation of powers has invalidated private challenge statutes in at least one state and formed the basis of criticisms of the jurisdictions that continue to allow victims to petition trial courts for private prosecutors."); Joshua D. Kadish, Stephen J. Schulhofer & Rachel E. Barkow, Criminal Law and Its Processes: Cases and Materials (10th ed. 2017) ("Private prosecution, like judge-initiated prosecution, likewise violates American separation-of-powers principles. People v. Municipal Court, 103 Cal. Rptr. 645 (Ct. App. 1972). The Supreme Court of South Carolina in *In re Richland County Magistrate's Court*, 389 S.C. 408, 412 (2010), offers additional functional arguments against the practice: 'If a private party is permitted to prosecute a criminal action, we can no longer be assured that the powers of the State are employed only for the interest of the community at large. In fact, we can be absolutely certain that the interests of the private party will influence the prosecution, whether the self-interest lies in encouraging payment of a . . . debt, influencing settlement in a civil suit, or merely seeking vengeance.'").

407. Eric R. Glitzenstein & Alan B. Morrison, *The Supreme Court's Decision in* Morrison v. Olson: *A Common Sense Application of the Constitution to a Practical Problem*, 38 Am. U.L. Rev. 359, 382 (1989) ("The independent counsel provisions of the Ethics in Government Act, which have now been upheld by the Supreme Court, are not only permitted by the Constitution but are essential to safeguard our constitutional system."); *id.* at 379 ("The Supreme Court's decision last year in *Young v. United States*, confirms the importance of the interests served by the Ethics Act. The Court reaffirmed that federal courts may appoint private attorneys to prosecute criminal contempt actions, reasoning that '[i]f the Judiciary were completely dependent on the Executive Branch to redress direct affronts to its authority, it would be powerless to protect itself if that branch declined prosecution.' The rationale for the appointment of independent

counsels is at least as powerful; Congress determined that the nation cannot be entirely dependent on high executive officials to investigate and prosecute crimes where there is an actual or potential conflict of interest."); *see also* Earl C. Dudley, Jr., Morrison v. Olson: *A Modest Assessment*, 38 Am. U.L. Rev. 255 (1989) (discussing the *Morrison v. Olson* decision); Morrison v. Olson, 487 U.S. 654 (1988) (finding that the independent counsel provisions of the Ethics in Government Act of 1978 did not violate the U.S. Constitution or the principle of separation of power).

408. Bruce Ledewitz, *What Is the Best Model for Investigating Presidential Wrongdoing, Today?*, 57 Duq. L. Rev. 225, 231 (2019).

409. Cruz v. Ferre, 571 F. Supp. 125, 133 (S.D. Fla. 1983) ("The indecency ordinance permits the City Manager to initiate complaints against the licensee, assess the validity of the complaint, preside over the hearing on the complaint, admit evidence at the hearing, make a determination, and issue sanctions, all in an area of moral judgment that might well try the neutrality and impartiality of Solomon. The risk of arbitrary or capricious governmental action under these circumstances is intolerably high. The Court consequently finds that these procedures, by concentrating the functions of complainant, jury, judge and 'executioner' in one person, do not comport with the fundamental notion of fairness implicit in due process.").

410. U.S. Const., art. XIV.

411. McLaughlin v. Florida, 379 U.S. 184, 192 (1964).

412. Peña-Rodriguez v. Colorado, 137 S. Ct. 855, 867, 871 (2017).

413. Obergefell v. Hodges, 576 U.S. 644, 672 (2015); *see also id.* ("Rights implicit in liberty and rights secured by equal protection may rest on different precepts and are not always co-extensive, yet in some instances each may be instructive as to the meaning and reach of the other. In any particular case one Clause may be thought to capture the essence of the right in a more accurate and comprehensive way, even as the two Clauses may converge in the identification and definition of the right.").

414. *Id.* at 671–72; *see also* Truax v. Corrigan, 257 U.S. 312, 331–32 (1921) ("This brings us to consider the effect in this case of that provision of the Fourteenth Amendment which forbids any state to deny to any person the equal protection of the laws. The clause is associated in the amendment with the due process clause and it is customary to consider them together. It may be that they overlap, that a violation of one may involve at times the violation of the other, but the spheres of the protection they offer are not coterminous. The due process clause brought down from Magna Charta was found in the early state constitutions and later in the Fifth Amendment to the federal Constitution as a limitation upon the executive, legislative and judicial powers of the federal government, while the equality clause does not appear in the Fifth Amendment and so does not apply to congressional legislation. The due process clause requires that every man shall have the protection of his day in court, and the benefit of the general law, a law which hears before it condemns, which proceeds not arbitrarily or capriciously, but upon inquiry, and renders judgment only after trial, so that every citizen shall hold his life, liberty, property and immunities under the protection of the general rules which govern society. Hurtado v. California, 110 U.S. 516, 535, 4 Sup. Ct. 111, 28 L. Ed. 232. It, of course, tends to secure equality of law in the sense that it makes a required minimum of protection for every one's right of life, liberty, and property, which the Congress or the Legislature may not withhold. Our whole system of law is predicated on the general fundamental principle of equality of application of the law. 'All men are equal before the law,' 'This is a government of laws and not of men,' 'No man is above the law,' are all maxims showing the spirit in which Legislatures, executives and courts are expected to make, execute and apply laws. But the framers and adopters of this amendment were not content to depend on a mere minimum secured by the due process clause, or upon the spirit of equality which might not be insisted on by local public opinion. They therefore embodied that spirit in a specific guaranty.").

415. Engquist v. Or. Dep't of Agric., 553 U.S. 591, 601 (2008) (quoting McGowan v. Maryland, 366 U.S. 420, 425 (1961)); Ross v. Moffitt, 417 U.S. 600, 609 (1974) ("'Equal protection' ... emphasizes disparity in treatment by a State between classes of individuals whose situations are arguably indistinguishable"); San Antonio Independent School Dist. v. Rodriguez, 411 U.S. 1, 60 (1973) (Stewart, J., concurring) ("[T]he basic concern of the Equal Protection Clause is with state legislation whose purpose or effect is to create discrete and objectively identifiable classes").

416. City of Cleburne, Tex. v. Cleburne Living Center, 473 U.S. 432, 439–441 (1985). In an recent immigration reform bill, it was sagely proposed to remove the dehumanizing term "alien" from U.S. immigration laws and replace it with the word "noncitizen." Nicole Acevedo, "Biden Seeks to Replace 'Alien" with Less 'Dehumanizing Term" in Immigration Laws," NBC News, Jan. 22, 2021, https://www.nbcnews.com/news/latino/biden-seeks-replace-alien-less-dehumanizing-term-immigration-laws-n1255350.

417. Hinterberger, 49–50 LLC v. City of Indianapolis, No. 1:16-cv-01341-SEB-MJD, 2019 WL 1439159, at *10 (S.D. Ind. Mar. 30, 2019) (citing Washington v. Davis, 426 U.S. 229, 242 (1976)).

418. "Justice Powell's New Wisdom," N.Y. Times, June 11, 1994, https://www.nytimes.com/1994/06/11/opinion/justice-powell-s-new-wisdom.html ("Too late for Warren McCleskey and numerous other executed prisoners, retired Justice Lewis Powell now concedes that he was wrong to cast the deciding fifth Supreme Court vote to uphold Mr. McCleskey's death sentence in a major case.").

419. McCleskey v. Kemp, 481 U.S. 279, 292–93 (1987).

420. Mark D. Rosenbaum and Daniel P. Tokaji, Book Review, 98 Mich. L. Rev. 1941, 1949 (2000) (reviewing David Cole, No Equal Justice: Race and Class in the American Criminal Justice System (1999)).

421. United States v. Armstrong, 517 U.S. 456, 464 (1996); Bolling v. Sharpe, 347 U.S. 497, 500 (1954); Oyler v. Boles, 368 U.S. 448, 456 (1962); United States v. Padilla-Caban, 995 F. Supp.2d 19, 20 (D. Puerto Rico 2014); *see also* United States v. Temple, 261 F. Supp.3d 971, 982 (E.D. Mo. 2017) ("[P]rosecutorial discretion has limits; it violates the Due Process Clause for a prosecutor to engage in vindictive prosecution—to punish a defendant for exercising her statutory or constitutional rights.") (citing United States v. Goodwin, 457 U.S. 386, 372 (1982)).

422. Hansen v. Schaefer, Case No.: 2-19-cv-02234-APG-BNW, 2020 WL 5534622, at *4 (D. Nev. Sept. 14, 2020).

423. United States v. Davis, No. 4:16CR495 CDP/NCC, 2017 WL 2703863, at *3 (E.D. Mo. May 24, 2017) (citing Yick Wo v. Hopkins, 118 U.S. 356, 373 (1886)).

424. United States v. Cannon, 987 F.3d 924, 937 (11th Cir. 2021).

425. 4 Wayne R. LaFave, Jerold H. Israel, Nancy J. King & Orin S. Kerr, Crim. Proc. § 13.4(a)—*Discriminatory prosecution* (4th ed. 2020); *accord* United States v. McKinley, 48 M.J. 280, 282 (U.S. Ct. App. for the Armed Forces, 1998). "[I]t is well settled that defendants subjected to or threatened with discriminatory prosecution have standing to bring an equal protection claim." Parkhurst v. Tabor, 569 F.3d 861, 865 (8th Cir. 2009).

426. Margaret Z. Johns, *Reconsidering Absolute Prosecutorial Immunity*, 2005 B.Y.U. L. Rev. 53, 111:

> While the office of public prosecutor was not well established in the late nineteenth century, the tort of malicious prosecution was clearly recognized in both the English and American common law. The elements of the action were: (1) that the prosecution terminated in favor of the plaintiff; (2) that there was no probable cause; and (3) that the defendant acted with malice. Although there was no prosecutorial immunity defense at the time, the elements of a cause of action for malicious prosecution essentially allowed for the same result as qualified immunity, since the plaintiff was required to prove malice and lack of probable cause. As explained in Blackstone's Commentaries, these requirements were necessary, "[f]or it would be a very great discouragement to the public justice of the kingdom if prosecutors, who had a tolerable ground of suspicion, were liable to be sued at law whenever their indictments miscarried."

See also McDonough v. Smith, 139 S. Ct. 2149, 2156 (2019) ("Common-law malicious prosecution requires showing, in part, that a defendant instigated a criminal proceeding with improper purpose and without probable cause.") (citations omitted); Beaman v. Freesmeyer, 131 N.E.3d 488, 496–97 (Ill. 2019) ("It is useful to examine the history of the common-law tort of malicious prosecution. In the 1800s, 'it was common for criminal cases to be prosecuted by private parties.' *Rehberg v. Paulk*, 566 U.S. 356, 364, 132 S. Ct. 1497, 182 L.Ed.2d 593 (2012). Those private parties did not enjoy immunity from suit; rather, 'a private complainant who procured an arrest or prosecution could be held liable in an action for malicious prosecution if the complainant acted with malice and without probable cause.' *Rehberg*, 566 U.S. at 364, 132 S. Ct. 1497. 'Both English and American courts routinely permitted plaintiffs to bring actions alleging that the defendant had made a false and malicious accusation of a felony to a magistrate or other judicial officer.'

Briscoe v. LaHue, 460 U.S. 325, 351, 103 S. Ct. 1108, 75 L.Ed.2d 96 (1983) (Marshall, J., dissenting, joined by Blackmun, J.). After 1871, criminal cases were increasingly prosecuted by public officials who, unlike private prosecutors, were absolutely immune from tort claims for malicious prosecution. *Rehberg*, 566 U.S. at 365, 132 S. Ct. 1497. However, courts have continued to recognize claims for malicious prosecution against private individuals whose conduct led to the plaintiff's criminal prosecution.").

427. Martin A. Schwartz, Sec. 1983 Litig. Claims & Defenses § 3.18—*Malicious Prosecution; Abuse of Civil Process* (4th ed. 2020-2 Supplement); *see also* McDonough v. Smith, 139 S. Ct. 2149, 2156 (2019) ("Common-law malicious prosecution requires showing, in part, that a defendant instigated a criminal proceeding with improper purpose and without probable cause."); 1 Fed. Proc. Forms § 1A:235 *Complaint—Malicious prosecution* ("The elements of the common-law tort of malicious prosecution include: (1) a criminal prosecution instituted or continued by the present defendant; (2) with malice and without probable cause; (3) that terminated in the plaintiff accused's favor; and (4) caused damage to the plaintiff accused.") (citing Black v. Wigington, 811 F.3d 1259 (11th Cir. 2016)).

428. Anne E. Melley, et al., 11 Cyc. of Federal Proc. § 39.12—*Defense of vindictive prosecution* (3d ed. Apr. 2021).

429. Anna Louise Prestidge, *Private Prosecutions in New Zealand—A Public Concern?*, 50 Vict. U. Wellington L. Rev. 107, 118 (2019).

430. *See, e.g.*, Michael Edmund O'Neill, *Private Vengeance and the Public Good*, 12 U. Pa. J. Const. L. 659, 719–20 (2010):

> The Supreme Court has established varying tests to determine whether an equal protection violation has occurred: generally, it depends on the type of classification the state has made and its effect on fundamental rights. Traditionally, the Court finds a state classification constitutional if it has a rational basis "related to a legitimate state interest." The Supreme Court, however, will strictly scrutinize a distinction when it involves a "suspect distinction." Here, the argument might be that the poor are discriminated against in a system that relies on private prosecution because they are unable to avail themselves of prosecutors. "In order for a classification to be subject to strict scrutiny, however, it must be shown that the state law or its administration is intended to discriminate" and that there would be no legitimate state purpose. It would be difficult, if not impossible, to prove whether a state that permitted private prosecutions intended to discriminate against anyone. Moreover, the Court has never found economic status to be a "suspect class" in the same way as race or national origin. The Court also applies a strict scrutiny test if the classification interferes with a fundamental right—such as a First Amendment right or the right to vote. The Court, however, has never found an affirmative "right to prosecution." Thus, it is difficult to see how the Court would countenance an equal protection challenge to a private prosecution on the ground of economic inequality. And while the wealthy presumably would have better access to more talented attorneys, it is unclear that the poor would be disadvantaged in a system that permitted private prosecutions as an adjunct to the general, and more common and equally available, system of public prosecutions. One could argue that, as a practical matter, if those who could afford private criminal prosecutions (like wealthy individuals or corporations) shouldered the financial burden for crimes committed against them, then more resources might be available for the government to pursue crimes committed against persons less fortunate and therefore less able to afford to hire private counsel—in turn, making "equal protection" more likely, not less.
>
> An alternative equal protection argument might be that a particular defendant was "selectively prosecuted" and that a public prosecutor might not have brought the case. Essentially, this criticism demands that equal protection requires all individuals to be prosecuted by a public prosecutor and, that if some individuals were to be prosecuted by a private prosecution, as opposed to a public one, the Equal Protection Clause would be violated. While this sort of argument is invoked in several contexts, it would be difficult to show that the "system" of private prosecutions violated the Equal Protection Clause. After all, the system would function similarly to the public one in which one prosecutor in the District Attorney's Office might be more inclined to recommend prosecution than another.

> More likely, in situations such as these a claim would be based on an "as applied" challenge levied against a particular prosecutor and would not invalidate a system using privately managed prosecutions. Even with respect to an "as applied" challenge to an individual prosecutor, however, the claimant would have to demonstrate that similarly situated individuals were not being prosecuted. Aside from the practical difficulties of making such a showing, it is unclear a prosecution could be sustained absent a showing to the court of sufficient evidence consistent with guilt. If grand jury indictment were required prior to commencing a private prosecution, presumably no case undeserving of prosecution would go forward. Moreover, such concerns would also be alleviated to the extent that appointment of the private prosecutor was certified by the public prosecutor or the trial court. In any event, an Equal Protection challenge to private prosecutions, especially a facial challenge to a statute or rule allowing such prosecutions, would likely be of little merit.

See also id. at 749–50 ("Although many scholars have argued that criminal defendants have a constitutional right to an 'impartial' (i.e., public) prosecutor, the Supreme Court has never so held. Nor is it clear that defendants ought to possess such a right on due process or equal protection grounds. The Framers of both the Constitution and Bill of Rights, doubtless aware of the existence of private criminal prosecutions, recognized the need to protect defendants' interests, and therefore established important procedural protections to ensure that criminal trials would be fair. While the Framers explicitly provided rights to counsel, grand juries, impartial judges, public trials, and petite juries, private prosecutions were never forbidden.").

431. Ahmed A. White, *Victims' Rights, Rule of Law, and the Threat to Liberal Jurisprudence*, 87 KY. L.J. 357, 378 n.55 (1999) ("Private prosecutions violate the Due Process and Equal Protection Clauses.") (citations omitted).

432. Alfred Avins, *The Right to Be a Witness and the Fourteenth Amendment*, 30 MO. L. REV. 471, 481–82 (1966) ("The denial of protection in criminal cases was equally clear. The Supreme Court of Alabama held that a mulatto assaulted by a white man could not testify to the assault in a criminal prosecution against the latter. The United States Circuit Court for the District of Columbia likewise held that, if colored victims were the only witnesses to a crime, the defendants could not be prosecuted. Thus, in one case defendants were convicted of a cheat in passing off a paper having the appearance of a bank note upon a free Negro. The only witnesses were free Negros and mulattoes, and the court held that the conviction would have to be reversed and the prosecution dropped. It was even held that a Negro might not testify as to his freedom against a white defendant charged with kidnapping him."); *see also id.* at 471 ("Although the right to give evidence has been all but obliterated from current legal thinking, to confer this right was a major factor in the insertion of the Equal Protection Clause into the Fourteenth Amendment of the United States Constitution. Indeed, it is this type of right which the framers conceived of as conferring 'protection' equally to all persons within the jurisdiction of the state. Because the right to testify so largely shaped the original conception of the Equal Protection Clause, it is still worthy of attention.").

433. John D. Bessler, *The Inequality of America's Death Penalty: A Crossroads for Capital Punishment at the Intersection of the Eighth and Fourteenth Amendments*, 73 WASH. & LEE L. REV. ONLINE 487, 515–16 (2016) (reprinting the language of the Civil Rights Act of 1866); Alfred Avins, *The Right to Be a Witness and the Fourteenth Amendment*, 30 MO. L. REV. 471, 483 (1966) ("The first congressional attack on the exclusionary rule came from Senator Henry Wilson, the Radical Republican from Massachusetts. Wilson observed that the 1717 Maryland statute, which made Negroes and mulattoes incompetent as witnesses where white persons were parties, was still in force in the District of Columbia in 1862."); *id.* at 484 ("The next Senate attack came from Wilson's colleague, Senator Charles Sumner, the equalitarian Radical. On February 29, 1864, he made a lengthy report for the Committee on Slavery and the Treatment of Freedmen, proposing to abolish the exclusionary rule in all federal courts. Sumner commenced by pointing out that there was no direct federal statute excluding colored witnesses, but that it had been the uniform practice of federal courts to follow rules of evidence of state courts in the state in which they sat. After discussing in detail the various statutes and case on exclusion, Sumner concluded that even though in theory Negroes were protected by the criminal law, in actuality it left them, whether slave or free, without remedy for crimes committed against them by white persons when no other white person was present."); *id.* at 498 ("Representative Bingham of Ohio, the framer of the second sentence of the first section of the Fourteenth

Amendment, had once denounced southern statutes which did not allow Negroes to testify."); *id.* at 499 ("In reporting the Fourteenth Amendment to the House of Representatives from the Joint Committee on Reconstruction, Representative Thaddeus Stevens of Pennsylvania, leader of the House Radical Republicans and committee chairman on the part of the House, explained the Equal Protection Clause as follows: 'Whatever law protects the white man shall afford 'equal' protection to the black man. Whatever means of redress is afforded to one shall be afforded to all. Whatever law allows the white man to testify in court shall allow the man of color to do the same.... Now color disqualifies a man from testifying in courts.... I need not enumerate these partial and oppressive laws. Unless the Constitution should restrain them those States will all, I fear, keep up this discrimination, and crush to death the hated freedman.'"); *id.* at 501 ("The Enforcement Act of 1870, the first law passed to enforce the Fourteenth Amendment,... extended the right to testify to all persons and was not limited to citizens as the 1866 statute was. The section making this extension was designed for the benefit and protection of the west coast Chinese, and was referred to as the 'Chinese bill.'"); *id.* at 504 ("The history of the abolition of the rule against permitting Negroes to testify in case where white persons were parties throws a strong and clear light on the meaning of the word 'protection' in the Equal Protection Clause of the Fourteenth Amendment."); *id.* ("The rule against allowing Negroes to testify was a practical denial of such protection. Hence, it was the motivation and need for the Fourteenth Amendment. Here was the evil to be remedied and the words used to remedy this evil.").

434. Darryl K. Brown, *Criminal Enforcement Redundancy: Oversight of Decisions Not to Prosecute*, 103 MINN. L. REV. 843, 872–73 (2018).

435. Bessler, *The Inequality of America's Death* Penalty, *supra* note 433, at 515.

436. Catherine E. Smith, *(Un)Masking Race-Based Intracorporate Conspiracies under the Ku Klux Klan Act*, 11 VA. J. SOC. POL'Y & L. 129, 135–38 (2004); U.S. CONST., amends. XIV & XV.

437. Jason Twede, "Going Public: How the Government Assumed the Authority to Prosecute in the Southern United States," Ph.D. dissertation, University of North Dakota (May 2016), pp. ix-x, 113–20 (citing *Public Statutes at Large of the United States, Vol. 1*, 1848), *available at* https://commons.und.edu/cgi/viewcontent.cgi?article=2976&context=theses; *see also id.* at 121 ("Instituting a system of public prosecution was indirectly reactionary to the threat posed by prosecutions from abolition societies. It was not that the Slave Trade Act of 1794 itself posed a threat to Southern slave holder interests. Rather, the willingness of abolition societies to prosecute those involved with slavery—both at the federal and state level—posed the problem."); *id.* at 124 ("[T]he public prosecutors for Georgia were appointed by the legislature of the state (Georgia Constitution, 1798). In order to qualify for the appointment, a person would have to be able to post a bond.... It only permitted the rich to be public prosecutors. Where wealth in the South during this time in large part corresponded with slave ownership, the bond would seem to permit only slave owners—or at least those wealthy enough to purchase slaves—to be public prosecutors. Thus, it would appear that the bond requirement served to assure that only those with interests in slavery would be able to assume the office of public prosecutor."); *id.* at 127–28 ("Slave ownership for the time period in question (1795–1855) can be determined from federal census records and Georgia tax records. Slave ownership information for 106 Georgia public prosecutors was obtained. Of those 106 public prosecutors, 87 (82%) owned at least one slave."); *id.* at 172 ("The picture we get of public prosecution in antebellum Georgia is one in which public prosecution protected the interests of slaveholders. While the protection of slaveholder interests may not have been the sole reason that public prosecution was initiated in Georgia, it certainly appears to be one of the primary reasons.").

438. State v. Bennett, 798 S.W.2d 783, 785–86 (Tenn. Ct. Crim. App. 1990):

> In this Court the appellant contends that the statute permitting the utilization of private prosecutors violates the Due Process and Equal Protection Clauses of the Fourteenth Amendment to the United States Constitution and the Law of the Land Clause contained in Article I, Section 8 of the Tennessee Constitution. He further contends that the statute is unconstitutional in the manner in which it was applied in this case.
>
> Prior to 1978, the common law of this State recognized the right of a victim, or the family of a deceased victim, to employ private counsel to assist the district attorney general, or his assistant, in the prosecution of the person who committed the offense against the victim. In 1978 the

Tennessee General Assembly enacted a statute which recognizes the right of a victim to employ private counsel to assist in the prosecution of the accused. This statute provides:

> A victim of crime or the family members of a victim of crime may employ private legal counsel to act as co-counsel with the district attorney general or his deputies in trying cases, with the extent of participation of such privately employed counsel being at the discretion of the district attorney general. The district attorney general or his deputys [sic] shall make the final and concluding argument.

Contrary to the appellant's contention, the practice of permitting a privately retained prosecutor to assist a district attorney general, or his assistant, does not violate the Fourteenth Amendment to the United States Constitution or the Law of the Land provision contained in Article I, Section 8 of the Tennessee Constitution. Consequently, Tenn. Code Ann. § 8–7–401 is constitutional.

Our review of the record does not reveal that the application of this statute in the case *sub judice* resulted in a depravation of a constitutional right. The private prosecutors did not engage in prosecutorial misconduct. Nor does the record reflect that the private prosecutors represented the family of the victim in a civil case arising out of the occurrence which gave rise to the criminal prosecution. Also, this was not a contempt proceeding which arose out of a civil prosecution.

The district attorney general maintained control over the prosecution as required by our statute.

See also Register v. Vasquez, 874 F.2d 816, 1989 WL 46718, at *1 (9th Cir. May 1, 1989):

> Register alleges that his equal protection rights were violated because he was prosecuted by a private prosecutor rather than a public prosecutor. In order to obtain habeas relief, a state prisoner must demonstrate that his detention violates the federal Constitution or laws. 28 U.S.C. § 2241(c)(3); *Pulley v. Harris*, 465 U.S. 37, 41 (1984); Gutierrez v. Griggs, 695 F.2d 1195, 1197 (9th Cir. 1983). There is no support in federal law or from the facts in the record to support a claim that such a procedure unlawfully discriminated against Register. Thus, the district court properly dismissed this claim.

439. Cronan ex rel. State v. Cronan, 774 A.2d 866, 877 (R.I. 2001) ("The defendant complains, for example, that this private prosecution violated his due process, separation of powers, and equal protection rights under the Rhode Island and United States Constitutions. Whatever merit these contentions may have in some other case, we hold that defendant waived his right to raise these constitutional challenges to this private prosecution. By failing to raise any of these defenses or challenges to the complaint before trial, defendant could not assert them for the first time in a post-trial motion to arrest the judgment."); *cf.* Commonwealth v. Cooper, 710 A.2d 76, 81 (Pa. Super. Ct. 1998):

> [A]ppellant contends that allowing the district attorney's refusal to prosecute his complaint denies him due process and equal protection of the laws as afforded by the United States and Pennsylvania constitutions. Appellant does not allege that the trial court departed in any respect from Pa. R. Crim. P. 106 (establishing the procedure for handling private civil complaints). We have held that "the provision in the Rule allowing an appeal of the district attorney's disapproval of such charges to the court constitutes sufficient checks and balances upon the district attorney's actions to comply with constitutional due process requirements." *See Commonwealth v. Eisemann*, 308 Pa.Super. 16, 20, 453 A.2d 1045, 1047 (1982). Thus, appellant's due process claims lack merit.
>
> Appellant's equal protection claim is based upon his status as a prisoner. Appellant contends that the district attorney showed deliberate indifference to the crime committed against him because of that status. This court, however, only reviews issues first presented to the lower court. *See* Pa. R. A. P. 302; *Petition of Piscanio*, 235 Pa.Super. 490, 494–96, 344 A.2d 658, 661 (1975) (finding that constitutional challenges to a denial of a private criminal complaint were waived by the affiant's failure to raise the constitutional issues in the lower court); *see also Commonwealth v. Widmer*, 547 Pa. 137, 689 A.2d 211 (1997) (explaining that, although post-sentence motions are no longer required to preserve issues in criminal matters, issues must still be raised initially in the lower court). Appellant did not allege discrimination in the petition for review he filed with the lower court. In fact, the sole allusion to any constitutional violation appellant presented to the

> court below is the single sentence, "I feel an investigation should have been done and at least an attempt to recover the vehicle and that not to do so is in violation of my constitutional rights." (Petition for Review of Decision of District Attorney 3/17/97, at 4.) This language pertains to only the procedure followed below (*i.e.*, appellant is claiming that the district attorney should have conducted further investigation before denying the petition). It does not in any manner suggest that appellant believes he was the victim of discrimination. Because the issue of whether the district attorney discriminated against appellant was not raised below, appellant's equal protection claims are waived.

440. People v. Acme Markets, Inc., 372 N.Y.S.2d 590, 591–94 (1975). *But see* S. S. Kresge Co. v. State, 546 S.W.2d 928, 930–31 (Tex. Ct. Civ. App., 1977):

> Appellants cite People v. Acme Markets Inc., 37 N.Y.2d 326, 372 N.Y.S.2d 590, 334 N.E.2d 555 (1975) and contend that it should be controlling in this jurisdiction. In that case, the evidence showed that prosecutions for violation of the State Sunday sales law was limited to cases in which complaints were filed by the officials of a local labor union. The majority of that court reasoned that enforcement of the law had been totally surrendered to private parties and interest groups with the ability to manipulate the law for purely private purposes. Consequently, the court held that the constitutional rights of the food supermarkets were violated because there was open discrimination and harassment of one group by another. Because the power and prestige of the district attorney was given to the union's campaign, the court held that the union's actions became those of the State and resulted in a violation of the equal protection guaranty of the federal constitution.
>
> We are more persuaded by the dissenting opinion in that case which took the view that the motivation of a private party in filing a complaint is not necessarily imputed to the district attorney when he enforces the statute by prosecution. Although the private party may be motivated by selfish interest, this in itself is not a denial of equal protection under the Constitution. To establish a denial of equal protection, it must be shown that the State itself was enforcing the statute not only for the purpose of executing legislative intent, but also for the purpose of discrimination. We agree with this rationale and decline to follow the holding of the Acme Markets case.
>
> Also, Tex. Rev. Civ. Stat. Ann. art. 9001, § 4 (Vernon Supp.1976), is distinguishable from the New York Penal Statute. This statute permits any person to obtain injunctive relief in addition to its penal provisions. Whereas, the New York Statute provides only that a violation is punishable as a misdemeanor. The Texas Statute does not give the district attorney the specific responsibility for enforcing the statute by securing injunctions. The Retail Merchants Association could have filed for injunctive relief itself although it chose not to do so. The record does not reveal the motivation of the association in filing the complaint. Whatever its motivation might have been, we do not agree that it is automatically imputed to the State. The assistant district attorney testified that a shortage of man power required him to rely upon complaints from private parties as a source of prosecution. No evidence was presented showing that the district attorney had any other motivation to enforce the statute than that of attempting to carry out the intent of the legislature. He testified that he would prosecute all complaints filed including those of the appellant. Thus, the record does not reveal purposeful discrimination on the part of the State which is required to sustain an allegation of a denial of equal protection under our constitutions. Accordingly, we hold that the trial court was correct in instructing a verdict and granting a permanent injunction since the appellants failed to establish a defense of purposeful discrimination.

441. State v. Benoit, 575 N.Y.S.2d 750, 751–56 (N.Y. Crim. Ct., City of N.Y., Kings County, Part AP 9, 1991).

442. City of Cleburne, Tex. v. Cleburne Living Center, 473 U.S. 432, 439–40 (1985) ("The Equal Protection Clause of the Fourteenth Amendment commands that no State shall 'deny to any person within its jurisdiction the equal protection of the laws,' which is essentially a direction that all persons similarly situated should be treated alike. Section 5 of the Amendment empowers Congress to enforce this mandate, but absent controlling congressional direction, the courts have themselves devised standards for determining the validity of state legislation or other official action that is challenged as denying equal protection. The

general rule is that legislation is presumed to be valid and will be sustained if the classification drawn by the statute is rationally related to a legitimate state interest.") (citations omitted); Club Retro, L.L.C. v. Hilton, 568 F.3d 181, 212–13 (5th Cir. 2009) ("The Fourteenth Amendment prohibits a state from 'deny[ing] to any person within its jurisdiction the equal protection of the laws.' This "Equal Protection Clause 'is essentially a direction that all persons similarly situated should be treated alike.'" To maintain an equal protection claim, a plaintiff typically alleges that he 'received treatment different from that received by similarly situated individuals and that the unequal treatment stemmed from a discriminatory intent.'") (citations omitted); *see also* Donald J. Trump for President, Inc. v. Secretary of Pennsylvania, 830 Fed. Appx. 377, 388 (3d Cir. 2020) ("A violation of the Equal Protection Clause requires more than variation from county to county. It requires unequal treatment of similarly situated parties.").

443. Engquist v. Oregon Dept. of Agr., 553 U.S. 591, 605 (2008); *cf.* State of La. ex rel. Francis v. Resweber, 329 U.S. 459, 465 (1947) ("So long as the law applies to all alike, the requirements of equal protection are met."); Southern Railway Co. v. Greene, 216 U.S. 400, 412 (1910) ("The equal protection of the laws means subjection to equal laws, applying alike to all in the same situation. If the plaintiff is a person within the jurisdiction of the state of Alabama within the meaning of the 14th Amendment, it is entitled to stand before the law upon equal terms, to enjoy the same rights as belong to, and to bear the same burdens as are imposed upon, other persons in a like situation."); Walston v. Nevin, 128 U.S. 578, 582 (1888) ("[W]henever the law operates alike on all persons and property, similarly situated, equal protection cannot be said to be denied.").

444. Nordlinger v. Hahn, 505 U.S. 1, 10 (1992).

445. *See* Smith v. Severn, 129 F.3d 419, 429 (7th Cir. 1997) ("An equal protection violation occurs only when different legal standards are arbitrarily applied to similarly situated individuals."). *But cf.* James v. City of Costa Mesa, 700 F.3d 394, 405 (9th Cir. 2012) ("There is no unequal treatment, and thus no equal protection violation.").

446. *E.g.*, Reed v. Reed, 404 U.S. 71, 75–76 (1971) ("The Equal Protection Clause of th[e] [Fourteenth] [A]mendment does . . . deny to States the power to legislate that different treatment be accorded to persons placed by a statute into different classes on the basis of criteria wholly unrelated to the objective of that statute. A classification 'must be reasonable, not arbitrary, and must rest upon some ground of difference having a fair and substantial relation to the object of the legislation, so that all persons similarly circumstanced shall be treated alike.'"); *id.* at 77 ("By providing dissimilar treatment for men and women who are thus similarly situated, the challenged section violates the Equal Protection Clause.").

447. Mejia v. Sessions, 723 Fed. Appx. 266, 267 (5th Cir. 2018) ("To bring a successful equal protection claim, Mejia must show that similarly situated persons were treated differently, and the unequal treatment resulted from discriminatory intent."); *cf.* Williams v. Lane, 851 F.2d 867, 881 (7th Cir. 1988) ("Prisoners do not surrender their rights to equal protection at the prison gate. Unequal treatment among inmates, however, is justified if it bears a rational relation to legitimate penal interest.") (citations omitted). *See also* Truax v. Corrigan, 257 U.S. 312, 332–33 (1921) (noting that the equal protection guarantee "was aimed at undue favor and individual or class privilege, on the one hand, and at hostile discrimination or the oppression of inequality, on the other"; that it "sought an equality of treatment of all persons, even though all enjoyed the protection of due process"; and that it "was intended to secure equality of protection not only for all but against all similarly situated"); F.S. Royster Guano Co. v. Commonwealth of Va., 253 U.S. 412, 415 (1920) ("It is unnecessary to say that the 'equal protection of the laws' required by the Fourteenth Amendment does not prevent the states from resorting to classification for the purposes of legislation. Numerous and familiar decisions of this court establish that they have a wide range of discretion in that regard. But the classification must be reasonable, not arbitrary, and must rest upon some ground of difference having a fair and substantial relation to the object of the legislation, so that all persons similarly circumstanced shall be treated alike.").

448. Hamilton v. McCune, Civil Action No. H-19-1901, 2019 WL 2869220, at *2 (S.D. Tex. July 3, 2019); Sattler v. Johnson, 857 F.2d 224, 227 (4th Cir. 1988) (rejecting an equal protection claim under § 1983 because neither a member of the public nor the victim has a right to have another criminally prosecuted); *see also* Brunson v. City of Sumter, C/A No. 3:11-2662-JFA-PJG, 2011 WL 6122624, at *3 (D. S.C. Oct 24, 2011) ("In the absence of allegations that protective services such as criminal investigations and

charges are being withheld solely for an illegally discriminatory reason, a private citizen may not recover damages under § 1983 based on the failure of law enforcement or prosecuting authorities to charge or prosecute certain other private citizens criminally."); Hudson v. Spears, C/A No. 4:11-2210-HFF-TER, 2011 WL 5403317, at *2 (D. S.C. Aug. 30, 2011) ("[S]everal federal courts have held that, in absence of allegations that protective services such as criminal investigations and charges are being withheld *solely* for an illegally discriminatory reason, a private citizen, such as the Plaintiff, may not recover damages under 42 U.S.C. § 1983 based on the failure of law enforcement or prosecuting authorities to charge or prosecute certain other private citizens criminally.") (italics in original); Karagi v. South Carolina, C/A No. 3:09-1316-JFA-JRM, 2009 WL 1834384 *3 (D. S.C. June 26, 2009) (same).

449. *Compare* 36 David B. Brooks, Tex. Prac., County and Special District Law § 21.19 (Oct. 2020 update) ("The attorney general has opined that a statutory denial of private practice by a county attorney does not deny equal protection of the laws. The attorney general concluded that the legislature could discriminate regarding private practice by prosecutors in an effort to provide for a more 'efficient and effective administration of justice' pursuant to the constitutional authority to create courts."), *with* Brown, *supra* note 434, at 871–72 ("Private prosecutions *should* be rare in well-functioning public prosecution systems, because public agencies pursue most provable cases and because private actors must bear considerable costs to press charges themselves. Moreover, other rules and institutions—including other safeguards on prosecutorial charging—endure despite few indications of their utility. There has never been a successful claim that a criminal charge violated the Equal Protection prohibition on racially biased charging, but few argue the doctrine lacks at least normative value. Grand juries rarely reject prosecutors' charging requests for indictments, but courts continue to tout them as a structural check on prosecutors. Like private prosecution, these safeguards may work by deterring biased or ill-conceived prosecutorial decisions; their efficacy is probably impossible to measure.") (italics in original).

450. Engquist v. Or. Dep't of Agric., 553 U.S. 591, 601 (2008).

451. *Id.* (quoting Vill. Of Willowbrook v. Olech, 528 U.S. 562, 564 (2000)); Zahl v. New Jersey Dep't of Law and Public Safety Div. of Consumer Affairs, 428 Fed. Appx. 205, 209 (3d Cir. 2011); Straser v. City of Athens, No. 3:18-cv-187, 2019 WL 2505036, at *4 (E. D. Tenn. June 17, 2019); *see also* Tenser v. Ryan, Case No. CV 19-05496 VBF (RAO), 2020 WL 4760192, at *11 (C.D. Cal. May 26, 2020):

> To succeed on a "class of one" claim, Plaintiff must demonstrate that Defendants intentionally treated Plaintiff differently than other similarly situated individuals without a rational basis. *Gerhart v. Lake Cty., Mont.*, 637 F.3d 1013, 1022 (9th Cir. 2011). "The class-of-one doctrine does not apply to forms of state action that 'by their nature involve discretionary decisionmaking based on a vast array of subjective, individualized assessments.'" *Towery v. Brewer*, 672 F.3d 650, 660 (9th Cir. 2012) (quoting *Engquist v. Oregon Dep't of Agric.*, 553 U.S. 591, 603 (2008)).

Washington. v. White, Case No. 18-cv-00333-WHO, 2018 WL 2287676, at *7 (N.D. Cal. May 18, 2018):

> "In order to claim a violation of equal protection in a class of one case, the plaintiff must establish that the [government] intentionally, and without rational basis, treated the plaintiff differently from others similarly situated." *N. Pacifica LLC v. City of Pacifica*, 526 F.3d 478, 486 (9th Cir. 2008) (citation omitted). The plaintiff bears the burden of pleading that others are similarly situated with him and how they are similarly situated. *Scocca v. Smith*, No. 11-cv-1318-EMC, 2012 WL 2375203, at *5 (N.D. Cal. June 22, 2012). "A class of one plaintiff must show that the discriminatory treatment was intentionally directed just at him, as opposed to being an accident or a random act." *N. Pacifica*, 526 F.3d at 486 (ellipses and quotation marks omitted). Showing that the treatment was "intentional" does not require showing subjective ill will. *Gerhart v. Lake Cnty., Mont.*, 637 F.3d 1013, 1022 (9th Cir. 2011).

452. Engquist v. Oregon Dept. of Agr., 553 U.S. 591, 597 (2008) (citing Adarand Constructors, Inc. v. Peña, 515 U.S. 200, 227 (1995); Raymond v. Chicago Union Traction Co., 207 U.S. 20, 35–36 (1907)).

453. Darian B. Taylor, *Class-of-One Equal Protection Claims Based upon Law Enforcement Actions*, 86 A.L.R.6th 173, at §§ 11–12 (2013); *see also, e.g.*, In re Complaint as to the Conduct of Daniel J. Gatti, 8 P.3d 966, 977 (Or. 2000) (en banc) ("The accused has shown only that the Bar believed that it did not have evidence to press charges against certain government lawyers in response to his complaint in 1992. The accused has not demonstrated that the Bar has a policy of prosecuting lawyers in private practice but not

prosecuting government lawyers who are accused of violating the Code of Professional Responsibility. On the facts of this case, we reject the accused's claim that the Bar violated Article I, section 20, or the Equal Protection Clause, in bringing this proceeding.").

454. Goldhaber v. Higgins, 576 F. Supp.2d 694, 722 (W.D. Pa. 2007) ("The Fourteenth Amendment forbids a State to 'deny to any *person* within its jurisdiction the equal protection of the laws.' U.S. CONST. amend. XIV (emphasis added). The word 'person' appears in the singular form, indicating that arbitrary or irrational discrimination against a single person runs afoul of the constitutional prohibition. Contrary to the Defendants' contentions, Goldhaber need not allege that he was a member of a broader class in order to allege a violation of the Equal Protection Clause. (Document No. 29, p. 16). Discrimination against a particular individual (i.e., discrimination against a 'class of one') violates the Equal Protection Clause when it bears no rational relationship to any legitimate governmental interest."); Cooey v. Kasich, 801 F. Supp.2d 623, 653 (S.D. Ohio 2011) ("Plaintiff has produced sufficient evidence to persuade this Court that he has a strong likelihood of prevailing on his class of one claim. Plaintiff has demonstrated that the only rationale for core deviations that eliminate safeguards and introduce greater uncertainty into the execution process is to simply complete the executions at all or nearly all costs. Mere pursuit of administrative convenience that risks flawed executions is not a legitimate state interest.").

455. *But cf.* Garcia v. City and County of Honolulu, Civ. No. 18-00100 ACK-KSC, 2018 WL 6028691, at *13 (D. Haw. Nov. 16, 2018):

> [T]he Court notes that the class-of-one theory does not apply to government action that "involve[s] discretionary decisionmaking based on a vast array of subjective, individualized assessments." Engquist v. Oregon Dep't of Agric., 553 U.S. 591, 603 (2008). Although the holding in *Engquist* was limited to barring class-of-one claims in the public employment context, id. at 605, the circuit courts are divided as to whether the class-of-one claim is a viable equal protection theory in the context of other discretionary forms of government action, such as law enforcement. Several circuits have held that such claims are impermissible. See, e.g., Flowers v. Minneapolis, 558 F.3d 794, 799–800 (8th Cir. 2009) (holding that a police officer's investigative decisions may not be attacked in a class-of-one equal protection claim); United States v. Moore, 543 F.3d 891, 901 (7th Cir. 2008) (holding that the exercise of prosecutorial discretion may not be challenged in a class-of-one equal protection claim). On the other hand, the Seventh Circuit has permitted such claims in other law enforcement situations. See Hanes v. Zurick, 578 F.3d 491, 492 (7th Cir. 2009) (holding that a class-of-one claim was permitted where officers repeatedly arrested plaintiff for reasons of personal animus).

456. Vill. Of Willowbrook v. Olech, 528 U.S. 1073, 1074–75 (2000).

457. Brunson v. Murray, 843 F.3d 698, 705 (7th Cir. 2016).

458. Garcia v. City and County of Honolulu, Civ. No. 18-00100 ACK-KSC, 2018 WL 6028691, at *13 (D. Haw. Nov. 16, 2018); *see also* Noel v. Coltri, No. 10 C 8188, 2017 WL 4620868, at *5 (N.D. Ill. Oct. 13, 2017):

> To succeed on a class-of-one equal protection claim, a plaintiff must show that a state actor discriminated against her with no rational basis. *Miller v. City of Monona*, 784 F.3d 1113, 1120 (7th Cir. 2015). While a common way to establish such discrimination is through the use of a comparator who was treated differently than the plaintiff, this is not required. *Id.* If the plaintiff can show that the state actor discriminated against her out of malice, a comparator is unnecessary. *Miller*, 784 F.3d at 1120.

459. Flinchum v. City of Beattyville, 224 F. Supp.3d 536, 542 (E.D. Ky. 2016); *see also* Goodfellas, Inc. v. Dunkel, Civil Action No. 3:15-CV-1633, 2016 WL 6599977, at *10 n.4 (M.D. Pa. Nov. 8, 2016):

> Although the line between the two claims has become blurred, a selective enforcement claim and a class-of-one equal protection claim are traditionally distinct causes of action. *See Dombrosky v. Stewart*, 2012 WL 3686779, at *7 (M.D. Pa. Aug. 27, 2012). A class-of-one equal protection claim "typically focuses on the sheer irrationality in the manner in which the plaintiff was treated," and is based on the premise that there was no rational basis for the government's action. *Casciani v. Nesbitt*, 659 F. Supp. 2d 427, 435 (W.D.N.Y. 2009); *see Dombrosky*, 2012 WL 3686779, at *7 (explaining that "differential treatment without a rational basis states a 'class of one' claim, while

> differential treatment motivated by an intent to discriminate on an impermissible basis is a selective enforcement claim").

460. Gray v. Town of Easton, No. 3:12-cv-00166 (JAM), 2015 WL 4458805, at *5 (D. Conn. July 20, 2015); *see also* United States v. Channon, Cr. No. 13-966 JCH, 2014 WL 12788057, at *18 (Sept. 22, 2014):

> The standard for proving selective prosecution is "'demanding.'" *Deberry*, 430 F.3d at 1299 (quoting *Armstrong*, 517 U.S. at 463, 116 S. Ct. 1480). "Caution is required when evaluating selective-prosecution claims" because the defendant "is asking the judiciary to exercise power over a 'special province' of the executive branch, a province in which, for good reason, the executive possesses broad discretion." *Id.* at 1299; *see Armstrong*, 517 U.S. at 464, 116 S. Ct. 1480. Provided there is probable cause to believe a person committed an offense, the decision to prosecute "generally rests entirely in [the prosecutor's] discretion." *Armstrong*, 517 U.S. at 464, 116 S. Ct. 1480 (internal quotation marks omitted). Thus courts are "'properly hesitant to examine the decision whether to prosecute.'" *Id.* (quoting *Wayte*, 470 U.S. at 608, 105 S. Ct. 1524). "'Examining the basis of a prosecution delays the criminal proceeding, threatens to chill law enforcement by subjecting the prosecutor's motives and decisionmaking to outside inquiry, and may undermine prosecutorial effectiveness by revealing the Government's enforcement policy.'" *Id.* (quoting *Wayte*, 470 U.S. at 607, 105 S. Ct. 1524).

461. Register v. Vasquez, No. 88-5692, 1989 WL 46718, at *1 (9th Cir. May 1, 1989).

462. Register v. Rackley, No. 2:13-cv-1372-JAM-EFB P, 2013 WL 5554767, at *2 (E.D. Cal. Oct. 8, 2013); Register v. Salinas, No. 2:10-cv-0889 KJM DAD P, 2012 WL 4711969, at *1 (E.D. Cal. Oct. 3, 2012).

463. Register v. Vasquez, No. 88-5692, 1989 WL 46718, at *2 (9th Cir. May 1, 1989); *Kash Register*, The National Registry of Exonerations, https://www.law.umich.edu/special/exoneration/Pages/casedetail.aspx?caseid=4324. The California judge who reviewed the evidence pertaining to Kash Register's wrongful conviction recently published a book. KATHERINE MADER, INSIDE THE ROBE: A JUDGE'S CANDID TALE OF CRIMINAL JUSTICE IN AMERICA (2020).

464. "Los Angeles to Pay $24.3M to 2 Wrongly Convicted Men," THE HERALD (Bradenton, FL), Jan. 20, 2016, p. A5; Emily Alpert Reyes & Matt Lait, "L.A. to Pay $24 Million for Wrongful Convictions," L.A. TIMES, Jan. 20, 2016, pp. A1, A11; Tim Walker, "$17m Cash Payout for American Wrongly Jailed for 34 Years (Called Kash Register)," THE INDEPENDENT (London, England), Jan. 21, 2016, p. 24; *see also* Patrick McGreevy, "$3 Million in Payouts Advance," L.A. TIMES, July 3, 2017, p. B3 (reporting on an additional payment of $1.7 million to Kash Register approved by the state senate).

465. Ashley Powers, "34-Year Wait for Justice is Over," L.A. TIMES, Nov. 8, 2013, pp. AA1, AA4; "Judge Throws Out L.A. Man's Murder Conviction," SACRAMENTO BEE (Sacramento, CA), Nov. 9, 2013, p. A.4.

466. Kate Linthicum, "Savoring His New Freedom," L.A. TIMES, Nov. 11, 2013, p. AA1.

467. Lara Bazelon, *Ending Innocence Denying*, 47 HOFSTRA L. REV. 393, 426 n.295 (2018) (citing Emily Alpert Reyes & Matt Lait, *L.A. to Pay $24 Million to Two Men Imprisoned for Decades After Wrongful Murder Convictions*, L.A. TIMES (Jan. 19, 2016, 7:43 PM), http://www.latimes.com/local/lanow/la-me-ln-wrongful-convictions-20160119-story.html).

468. "At 53, Freed Man Ponders His Lost Years," L.A. TIMES, Nov. 11, 2013, p. A1; Associated Press, "No Retrial for Los Angeles Prisoner Freed After 34 Years," TIMES-DELTA / ADVANCE-REGISTER (Visalia, CA), Dec. 14–15, 2013, p. 7B.

469. Laurie Levenson & Barry Scheck, "Evidence of Unfairness," L.A. TIMES, Dec. 16, 2014, p. A15 (op-ed).

470. *Kash Register*, The National Registry of Exonerations, https://www.law.umich.edu/special/exoneration/Pages/casedetail.aspx?caseid=4324; *see also* Laurie L. Levenson, Finding Justice: Remarks for Constitution Day University of Akron School of Law, 8 ConLawNow 91, 97–98 (2016–2017):

> In 1979, an elderly white man was robbed and shot at close range. The physical evidence at the scene did not establish Mr. Register as the suspect. Nonetheless, he spent 34 years in prison for the crime. The reason was revealed years later when LPI discovered that the prosecutors used witnesses who were obviously lying.
>
> There were two so-called eyewitnesses in Mr. Register's case. The first, Brenda Anderson, lived in an apartment on the same street as the shooting. On the day of the shooting, she was out

stealing Avon products left on people's doorsteps. In exchange for her testimony, she was not charged with that crime—a key piece of information prosecutors failed to share with Mr. Register's defense counsel. The police also did not tell the prosecutor, so the prosecutor did not tell defense counsel, that Brenda had told her older sister, Sheila Vanderkam, that she had only seen the back of the shooter's head. When Vanderkam, who worked as a detective's assistant at the police station, told the investigating detective that her sister could not make the identification and was also completely unreliable, he responded by placing his finger over his lips and saying, "ssshhh."

The second witness was Elliott Singleton. He claimed that he had been painting the house across the street from the victim's house when he saw the shooting. At trial, he testified that he left the apartment and chased after the armed suspect for blocks. After about six blocks, the man stopped and pointed the gun at him. According to Singleton, that is when he got a good look at the robber, said, "I'm cool," and then walked away. Later, when interviewed LPI, Singleton denied ever seeing the murder. Rather, he said the police had knocked on his door in an effort to get his pregnant wife to testify. She, however, was never called as a witness and an internal District Attorney memorandum showed that the prosecutors did not have confidence in either witness.

471. Lara Bazelon, "'A Mistake Has Been Made Here, and No One Wants to Correct It,'" SLATE, Dec. 17, 2013, https://slate.com/news-and-politics/2013/12/the-exoneration-of-kash-register-and-the-problem-of-false-eyewitness-testimony.html.

472. Schrock v. Kirkpatrick, No. 16-CV-6364 CJS, 2019 WL 8807887, at *10 (W.D. N.Y. Mar. 27, 2019); *see also* Every v. Town of Littleton, New Hampshire, Case No. 18-cv-43-SM, 2018 WL 4344998, at *8 (D. N.H. Sept. 11, 2018):

> In Village of Willowbrook v. Olech, 528 U.S. 562, 564 (2000), the Supreme Court recognized that arbitrary exercises of power can deprive a "class of one" of equal protection. To bring a "class of one" equal protection claim, a plaintiff must allege that he was "intentionally treated ... differently from others similarly situated and there was no rational basis for this disparate treatment." Najas Realty, LLC v. Seekonk Water Dist., 821 F.3d 134, 144 (1st Cir. 2016) (citations omitted). "[P]laintiffs claiming an equal protection violation must first identify and relate specific instances where persons situated similarly in all relevant aspects were treated differently". Cordi-Allen v. Conlon, 494 F.3d 245, 250–51 (1st Cir. 2007) (quoting Buchanan v. Maine, 469 F.3d 158, 178 (1st Cir. 2006)) (emphasis in original).
>
> Specific comparators and their similarities must be alleged with "reasonable particularity" at the Rule 12(b)(6) stage, as "[a]n equal protection claimant 'may not prevail [against a Rule 12(b)(6) motion] simply by asserting an inequity and tacking on the self-serving conclusion that the defendant was motivated by a discriminatory animus.'" Barrington Cove, LP v. R.I. Housing and Mortg. Fin. Corp., 246 F.3d 1, 8, 10 (quoting Coyne v. Somerville 972 F.2d 440, 444 (1st Cir. 1992)). Ultimately, "[a]n individual is 'similarly situated' to others for equal protection purposes when 'a prudent person, looking objectively at the incidents, would think them roughly equivalent and the protagonists similarly situated.'" Davis v. Coakley, 802 F.3d 128, 133 (1st Cir. 2015) (quoting Barrington Cove, 246 F.3d at 8). In claims such as Every's, the plaintiff must ordinarily plead facts that show that the defendants' "differential treatment of the plaintiff was motivated by 'bad faith or malicious intent to injure.'" Snyder v. Gaudet, 756 F.3d 30, 34 (1st Cir. 2014) (quoting Rubinovitz v. Rogato, 60 F.3d 906, 911 (1st Cir. 1995)).

Heyliger v. City of Binghamton, 3:11-CV-1293 (NAM/DEP), 2016 WL 1048999, at *16 (N.D.N.Y. Mar. 11, 2016):

> A plaintiff may also pursue a "class of one" equal protection claim, that is, a claim that he "has been intentionally treated differently from others similarly situated and that there is no rational basis for the difference in treatment." *Analytical Diagnostic Labs, Inc. v. Kusel*, 626 F.3d 135, 140 (2d Cir. 2010) (internal quotation marks omitted). The plaintiff must identify at least one comparator with whom he shares "an extremely high degree of similarity" sufficient to "provide an inference that the plaintiff was intentionally singled out for reasons that so lack any reasonable nexus with a legitimate governmental policy that an improper purpose—whether personal or

otherwise—is all but certain." *Clubside, Inc. v. Valentin*, 468 F.3d 144, 159 (2d Cir. 2006) (internal quotation marks omitted).

Flanders v. Dzugan, Civil Action No. 12-1481, 2015 WL 5022734, at *3 n.2 (W.D. Pa. Aug. 24, 2015) ("An equal protection claim under a 'class of one' theory requires a plaintiff to show that he was treated differently from others who are similarly situated."); *Bernett v. Redevelopment Auth. of the Cnty. of Washington*, Civ. No. 13–1409, 2013 U.S. Dist. LEXIS 181510, *6–7, 2013 WL 6881960, at *2 (W.D. Pa. 2013) ("While a claim under the Equal Protection Clause usually involves the disparate treatment of a class of individuals, such a claim can be brought by a 'class' of a single individual, where the plaintiff alleges that he has been intentionally treated differently from others similarly situated and that there is no rational basis for the difference in treatment.") (citations omitted).

473. Towery v. Brewer, 672 F.3d 650, 660 (9th Cir. 2012) ("The class-of-one doctrine does not apply to forms of state action that by their nature involve discretionary decisionmaking based on a vast array of subjective, individualized assessments.") (internal quotation marks omitted); Strohmeyer v. Belanger, 3:14-CV-00661-RCJ-WGC, 2018 WL 3581141, at *7 (D. Nev. Mar. 27, 2018) ("[I]nvestigative or prosecutorial decisions cannot be attacked via a 'class of one'-type claim.") (citing Flowers v. City of Minneapolis, 558 F.3d 794, 799–800 (8th Cir. 2009); United States v. Moore, 543 F.3d 891, 901 (7th Cir. 2008)); Katz-Crank v. Haskett, 843 F.3d 641, 649 (7th Cir. 2016) ("[A] class-of-one claim cannot be used to challenge *discretionary* governmental action, like the decision to initiate prosecution.") (italics in original); Wade v. Collier, 783 F.3d 1081, 1089 (7th Cir. 2015) ("Nor is an equal protection claim well-suited to a case involving prosecutorial discretion...."); Avila v. Pappas, 591 F.3d 552, 554 (7th Cir. 2010) ("[C]lass-of-one claims cannot rest on governmental activity that is discretionary by design, a good description of prosecutorial selectivity in criminal law."); Artec Construction and Development Corp. v. City of New York, 15 Civ. 9494 (KPF), 2017 WL 5891817, at *10 (S.D.N.Y. Nov. 28, 2017):

> While the Second Circuit clarified in *Kusel* that "*Engquist* does not bar all class-of-one claims involving discretionary state action," 626 F.3d at 142, it could not have been that Court's intention to hold that door ajar for a claim like Plaintiff's, which would grant a constitutional "class of one" claim to every target of a criminal investigation and every defendant in a criminal prosecution. The day-to-day work of a prosecutor necessarily involves the selection of certain individuals to investigate and charge—this is the very type of government discretion that the Supreme Court removed from equal protection review in *Engquist*. Accordingly, the Court holds that Plaintiff's claim that Defendant placed it in a "class of one" through participation in criminal investigations of it is barred under *Engquist*, and the Court will not consider the merits of this claim.

But see Fey v. Washington, Civil Action No. 16-cv-03103-WJM-MEH, 2017 WL 1344451, at *9 n.15 (D. Colo. Apr. 12, 2017):

> The Court recognizes that, following the Supreme Court's opinion in *Engquist v. Or. Dep't of Agric.*, 553 U.S. 591 (2008), some circuits held that a "class of one" equal protection claim is inapplicable in the prosecutorial-discretion context. *See United States v. Moore*, 543 F.3d 891, 898–99 (7th Cir. 2008). However, the Tenth Circuit has specifically declined to adopt this broad of an interpretation of *Engquist Kan. Penn Gaming, LLC v. Collins*, 656 F.3d 1210, 1217 n.1 (10th Cir. 2011).

474. *E.g.*, Hansen v. Schaefer, Case No.: 2-19-cv-02234-APG-BNW, 2020 WL 5534622, at *4–5 (D. Nev. Sept. 14, 2020) (citations omitted):

> I read Hansen's complaint to allege two separate Fourteenth Amendment claims. First, Hansen alleges a "class of one" claim by alleging he was arrested and prosecuted when other similarly situated street performers were not. Hansen also alleges that street performers who exercise their First Amendment rights are an identifiable protected class and that the defendants prosecute them for obstructing sidewalks on the Strip but do not prosecute tourists for blocking the sidewalks when they stop to take pictures or watch free performances, such as the water fountains at Bellagio.
>
> Hansen fails to plausibly allege a selective enforcement "class of one" claim. He alleges that "there were many other Street Performers that were not arrested." This conclusory allegation provides no details on who these other street performers are, what conduct they were engaged

in, and whether they also received prior warnings. However, Hansen may be able to assert facts demonstrating selective enforcement. I thus dismiss this claim without prejudice and allow Hansen to file an amended complaint if he has sufficient facts to support it.

475. Van Dyke v. Village of Alsip, 891 Fed. Appx. 431, 432 (7th Cir. 2020); *see also* Donahoe v. Arpaio, 869 F. Supp.2d 1020, 1074 (D. Ariz. 2012) ("Plaintiffs' equal protection claims arise mainly from allegedly unlawful decisions by Defendants in the investigation and prosecution of criminal charges and institution of civil proceedings against Plaintiffs. Because these decisions are all discretionary ones, no class of one equal protection claim can be stated."); Paddock v. Otter, Case No.: 1:16-CV-00222-EJL-REB, 2017 WL 4077025, at *4 (D. Idaho Feb. 17, 2017) ("Discretionary decisions by a sheriff and prosecutor during the investigation and prosecution of criminal charges cannot be the basis for class-of-one equal protection claim.").

476. United States v. Moore, 543 F.3d 891, 901 (7th Cir. 2008) (quoting *Engquist*, 128 S. Ct. at 2155); *see also* Browne v. Waldo, Cause No.: 2-20-CV-196-JVB-APR, 2021 WL 325871, at *6 (N.D. Ind. Feb. 1, 2021) (observing that "'discretionary decisionmaking,' based on the facts of a particular case, does not sustain a class of one claim" and noting that *United States v. Moore* rejected "class of one claims in the context of prosecutorial discretion"). Notably, the appointment of interested private prosecutors is unlike the ordinary exercise of prosecutorial discretion. Whereas public prosecutions must make many discretionary decisions in the course of a prosecution, the appointment of—or the consent to—an interested private prosecutor injects an element of structural unfairness into the criminal justice process because an interested private party (or that person's agent) has incentives to convict that may not align with the imperative to do justice.

477. Sedelbauer v. State, 455 N.E.2d 1159, 1164 (Ind. Ct. App. 1983) (trial court did not err in allowing Bruce Taylor, a member of an anti-obscenity group, Citizens for Decency through Law, to serve as "co-counsel" for the prosecution; "Sedelbauer contends that allowing someone so opposed to pornographic materials to aid in prosecution is highly prejudicial and amounts to a deprivation of due process and equal protection of law. He fails to cite authority in support of this contention, nor does he demonstrate any actual prejudice in this regard. There is no indication that Mr. Taylor represented the State's interest outside of legal boundaries or inconsistent with the State's interest. Therefore, his argument on this issue must fail."); State v. Bennett, 798 S.W.2d 783, 785–86 (Tenn. Cr. App. 1990) ("In this Court the appellant contends that the statute permitting the utilization of private prosecutors violates the Due Process and Equal Protection Clauses of the Fourteenth Amendment to the United States Constitution and the Law of the Land Clause contained in Article I, Section 8 of the Tennessee Constitution. He further contends that the statute is unconstitutional in the manner in which it was applied.... Contrary to the appellant's contention, the practice of permitting a privately retained prosecutor to assist a district attorney general, or his assistant, does not violate the Fourteenth Amendment to the United States Constitution or the Law of the Land provision contained in Article I, Section 8 of the Tennessee Constitution.").

478. *Benoit*, 575 N.Y.S.2d at 757; *see also id.* ("This court is well aware of the strong presumption that legislative enactments are constitutional. Nonetheless, the foregoing analysis clearly establishes that NYCCCA § 50, as applied here, is unconstitutional and violative of the Due Process and Equal Protection Clauses of the U.S. Constitution.").

479. The importance of the reliability of criminal law adjudications is obvious. *See, e.g.*, Loper v. Beto, 405 U.S. 473, 483–84 (1972) (plurality opinion) ("use of convictions constitutionally invalid under *Gideon v. Wainwright* to impeach a defendant's credibility deprives him of due process of law" because the prior convictions "lac[k] reliability").

480. Brown, *supra* note 434, at 864–65.

481. Tania Tetlow, *Granting Prosecutors Constitutional Rights to Combat Discrimination*, 14 U. Pa. J. Const. L. 1117, 1140 (2012).

482. 351 U.S. 12 (1956).

483. *Id.* at 19; *see also* Evitts v. Lucey, 469 U.S. 387 (1985) (entitling defendants to effective assistance of counsel on first appeal of right); Little v. Streater, 452 U.S. 1 (1981) (state must pay for blood test of indigent defendant in paternity action); Boddie v. Connecticut, 401 U.S. 371 (1971) (requiring indigent to

pay court costs to obtain divorce violates due process); Douglas v. California, 372 U.S. 353 (1963) (indigent convicted criminal defendants are entitled to counsel on first appeal of right).

484. 372 U.S. 335 (1963). In *Gideon*, the Court held that the "noble ideal" of "fair trials before impartial tribunals" cannot be realized "if the poor man charged with crime has to face his accusers without a lawyer to assist him." *Id.* at 344.

485. *Compare* Turner v. Rogers, 564 U.S. 431, 441 (2011) ("We must decide whether the Due Process Clause grants an indigent defendant, such as Turner, a right to state-appointed counsel at a civil contempt proceeding, which may lead to his incarceration. This Court's precedents provide no definitive answer to that question. This Court has long held that the Sixth Amendment grants an indigent defendant the right to state-appointed counsel in a *criminal* case. *Gideon v. Wainwright,* 372 U.S. 335, 83 S. Ct. 792, 9 L.Ed.2d 799 (1963). And we have held that this same rule applies to *criminal contempt* proceedings (other than summary proceedings). *United States v. Dixon,* 509 U.S. 688, 696, 113 S. Ct. 2849, 125 L.Ed.2d 556 (1993); *Cooke v. United States,* 267 U.S. 517, 537, 45 S. Ct. 390, 69 L.Ed. 767 (1925)."); *id.* at 444–45 ("We here consider an indigent's right to paid counsel at such a contempt proceeding. It is a civil proceeding. And we consequently determine the 'specific dictates of due process' by examining the 'distinct factors' that this Court has previously found useful in deciding what specific safeguards the Constitution's Due Process Clause requires in order to make a civil proceeding fundamentally fair. *Mathews v. Eldridge,* 424 U.S. 319, 335, 96 S.Ct. 893, 47 L.Ed.2d 18 (1976) (considering fairness of an administrative proceeding). As relevant here those factors include (1) the nature of 'the private interest that will be affected,' (2) the comparative 'risk' of an 'erroneous deprivation" of that interest with and without 'additional or substitute procedural safeguards,' and (3) the nature and magnitude of any countervailing interest in not providing 'additional or substitute procedural requirement[s].' *Ibid.*"); *id.* at 448 ("We consequently hold that the Due Process Clause does not *automatically* require the provision of counsel at civil contempt proceedings to an indigent individual who is subject to a child support order, even if that individual faces incarceration (for up to a year). In particular, that Clause does not require the provision of counsel where the opposing parent or other custodian (to whom support funds are owed) is not represented by counsel and the State provides alternative procedural safeguards equivalent to those we have mentioned (adequate notice of the importance of ability to pay, fair opportunity to present, and to dispute, relevant information, and court findings).").

486. 407 U.S. 25 (1972); *see also* Gerald Caplan, *Criminal Justice in the Lower Courts: A Study in Continuity*, 89 MICH. L. REV. 1694, 1707 (1991) ("[T]he Supreme Court's decision in *Argersinger v. Hamlin,* conferring a right to counsel in misdemeanor cases where there was a possibility of incarceration, worked significant changes. The wholesale introduction of defense counsel into every stage of a criminal proceeding, combined with more frequent and searching appellate oversight, made due process more evident in the lower courts.").

487. Ake v. Oklahoma, 470 U.S. 68 (1985). The *Ake* Court viewed its holding as consistent with "the belief that justice cannot be equal where, simply as a result of his poverty, a defendant is denied the opportunity to participate meaningfully in a judicial proceeding in which his liberty is at stake." *Id.* at 76.

488. TRIBE, *supra* note 69, at § 16-40, at 1635.

489. *See, e.g.,* Portuondo v. Agard, 529 U.S. 61, 65–66 (2000) ("The process by which criminal defendants were brought to justice in 1791 largely obviated the need for comments of the type the prosecutor made here. Defendants routinely were asked (and agreed) to provide a pretrial statement to a justice of the peace detailing the events in dispute. See Moglen, The Privilege in British North America: The Colonial Period to the Fifth Amendment, in The Privilege Against Self-Incrimination 109, 112, 114 (R. Helmholz et al. eds.1997). If their story at trial—where they typically spoke and conducted their defense personally, without counsel, see J. Goebel & T. Naughton, Law Enforcement in Colonial New York: A Study in Criminal Procedure (1664–1776), p. 574 (1944); A. Scott, Criminal Law in Colonial Virginia 79 (1930)—differed from their pretrial statement, the contradiction could be noted. See Levy, Origins of the Fifth Amendment and Its Critics, 19 Cardozo L. Rev. 821, 843 (1997). Moreover, what they said at trial was not considered to be evidence, since they were disqualified from testifying under oath. See 2 J. Wigmore, Evidence § 579 (3d ed.1940). The pretrial statement did not begin to fall into disuse until the 1830's....").

490. John Creamer, "Poverty Rates for Blacks and Hispanics Reached Historic Lows in 2019: Inequalities Persist Despite Decline in Poverty for All Major Race and Hispanic Origin Groups," United States Census Bureau, Sept. 15, 2020, https://www.census.gov/library/stories/2020/09/poverty-rates-for-blacks-and-hispanics-reached-historic-lows-in-2019.html; *see also* THE WORLD ALMANAC AND BOOK OF FACTS 395 (1993).

491. According to one source:

> Under a system of private prosecution, the prosecution of criminal offenses depends upon the ability and willingness of the victim or other interested individuals to bring prosecutions, which the poor and powerless are less able and willing to do. Accordingly, one of the reasons for establishing the office of public prosecutor might have been to ensure that poor victims as well as rich victims would be able to obtain redress for crimes committed against them or their property.

Josephine Gittler, *Expanding the Role of the Victim in a Criminal Action*, 11 PEPPERDINE L. REV. 117, 130 (1984) (footnote omitted). Notably, one historian has argued that private prosecution, at least in nineteenth-century Philadelphia, "represented the dignity and citizenship of Philadelphia's poor and working classes at least as much as it represented their oppression." ALLEN STEINBERG, THE TRANSFORMATION OF CRIMINAL JUSTICE: PHILADELPHIA, 1800–1880, at 114 (1989). According to Steinberg:

> Private prosecution was, for the citizen litigants of Philadelphia, a democratic form of law enforcement and criminal justice, involving in great numbers citizens of all social and economic groups with state officials who responded directly and personally (if not always satisfactory) to their requests.... Through private prosecution, even the poor, many of them disenfranchised, had a stake in the legal and political process, received something palpable from it, and asserted that democracy in America was something special.

Id. at 231.

However, Steinberg's thesis, especially as applied in modern times, has several flaws. First, because modern-day public prosecutors are elected, every citizen—whether rich or poor—already has a responsive official with whom to lodge complaints. Second, because courts are unlikely to allow non-lawyers to assist in bringing criminal prosecutions, the high cost of legal services in modern society precludes the poor, as a practical matter, from hiring private prosecutors. Finally, a system of private prosecution favors the rich, not the poor. Indeed, Steinberg himself acknowledges that the poor, even in nineteenth-century Philadelphia, were sometimes oppressed by the private prosecution system. *Id.* at 86 ("Bouvier a Philadelphia court recorder explicitly accused the poor of being responsible for petty litigation and implied that, if they had not been poor, they would have been like other Americans who brought civil actions against one another. Instead they initiated criminal cases involving themselves, the only objects of value they possessed."); *id.* at 26 (footnote omitted) ("A newspaper court reporter marveling in 1848 at how 'the miserable outcasts of society' race to the alderman's office over their petty quarrels, 'each endeavoring to ... have their opponents arrested before they were taken into custody themselves' and, in so doing, 'expend ... the greatest portion of the money that falls by accident within their grasp.'").

492. 383 U.S. 663 (1966).

493. *Id.* at 668; *see also* Edwards v. California, 314 U.S. 160 (1941) (a California law making it a misdemeanor to knowingly bring a non-resident indigent into the state was struck down).

494. Sanchez-Llamas v. Oregon, 548 U.S. 331, 345 (2006) ("To the extent Sanchez–Llamas argues that we should invoke our supervisory authority, the law is clear: 'It is beyond dispute that we do not hold a supervisory power over the courts of the several States.'") (quoting *Dickerson v. United States*, 530 U.S. 428, 438 (2000)); *see also Smith v. Phillips*, 455 U.S. 209, 221 (1982) ("Federal courts hold no supervisory authority over state judicial proceedings and may intervene only to correct wrongs of constitutional dimension").

495. The U.S. Constitution's Fourteenth Amendment provides that "no state shall... deny to any person within its jurisdiction the equal protection of the laws." Although the federal government is not governed by the Fourteenth Amendment, an equal protection requirement is also imposed under the Fifth Amendment's due process clause because "it would be unthinkable that the same Constitution would impose a lesser duty on the Federal Government." Bolling v. Sharp, 347 U.S. 497, 500 (1954) (footnote omitted).

496. Tate v. Short, 401 U.S. 395 (1971) (equal protection is violated where punishment is limited to a fine for those able to pay it but is converted to imprisonment for those unable to pay it); Williams v. Illinois, 399 U.S. 235, 244 (1970) (equal protection guarantee requires that maximum term of imprisonment be the same for all defendants regardless of economic status); *see also* CHRISTOPHER SMITH, COURTS AND THE POOR 12–40, 73–143 (1991) (detailing the lack of access the poor have to the criminal justice system and summarizing Supreme Court precedent in that area).

497. M.L.B. v. S.L.J., 519 U.S. 102, 107 (1996).

498. *E.g.*, New Jersey v. Imperiale, 773 F. Supp. 747, 751 n.7 (D. N.J. 1991); Kentucky v. Hubbard, 777 S.W.2d 882, 883–84 (Ky. 1989); Cantrell v. Commonwealth, 329 S.E.2d 22, 25 (Va. 1985), *cert. denied*, 496 U.S. 911 (1990); Kerns v. Wolverton, 381 S.E.2d 258, 261 (W. Va. 1989); State v. Worley, 369 S.E.2d 706, 718 (W. Va. 1988); Kennedy v. State, 342 S.E.2d 251, 258 (W. Va. 1986); State v. Riser, 294 S.E.2d 461, 465 (W.Va. 1982); State v. Atkins, 261 S.E.2d 55, 58 (W. Va. 1979), *cert. denied*, 445 U.S. 904 (1980); State ex rel. Moran v. Ziegler, 244 S.E.2d 550 (W. Va. 1978).

499. Kerns v. Wolverton, 381 S.E.2d 258, 261 (W. Va. Sup. Ct. App. 1989) (quoting State v. Atkins, 261 S.E.2d 55 (W. Va. 1979), *cert. denied*, 445 U.S. 904 (1980)).

500. State v. Atkins, 261 S.E.2d 55, 58 (W. Va. 1980), *cert. denied*, 445 U.S. 904 (1980) (footnote omitted).

501. CHARLES F. WOLFRAM, MODERN LEGAL ETHICS § 13.10.4, at 766 (1986) (citations omitted).

502. That private prosecutors engage in misconduct is demonstrated by the case of *Hughes v. Bowers*, 711 F. Supp. 1574 (N.D. Ga. 1989), *aff'd*, 896 F.2d 558 (11th Cir. 1990). In *Hughes*, the defendant was convicted of voluntary manslaughter after a private prosecutor represented to defense counsel that no policies of insurance existed which might serve to impeach one of the state's key witnesses. However, when defense counsel later discovered the existence of an impeaching insurance policy, the defendant's petition for habeas corpus was granted, with the court holding that the participation of a private prosecutor, hired by the victim's family, rendered the defendant's trial fundamentally unfair. In so holding, the court emphasized that the private prosecutor, in addition to participating in the criminal prosecution, also represented a member of the victim's family on a claim brought pursuant to the concealed policy of insurance. The court stated as follows: "An actual conflict of interest arose when the defense moved for production of insurance policies. The special prosecutor had a duty to disclose the policy but had a conflicting interest to conceal it. He chose to conceal it. By any standard, this deliberate, affirmative concealment from the court and the defense of important evidence constitutes a serious act of misbehavior which disregarded the rights of the defendant. The special prosecutor abdicated his duty to seek justice rather than conviction, and Hughes's trial was rendered fundamentally unfair." *Id.* at 1584.

Likewise, in *Stumbo v. Seabold*, 704 F.2d 910, 912 (6th Cir. 1983) (applying Kentucky law), the Sixth Circuit held that a defendant's trial was rendered fundamentally unfair by a private prosecutor's misconduct in accusing the defendant of a conspiracy that was unsupported by the evidence and in referring to the defendant as "Johnny Murder Boy." Even courts that have approved of the use of private prosecutors have warned of the dangers of overzealous private prosecutors. *E.g.*, State v. Addis, 186 S.E.2d 415, 417 (S.C. 1972) ("We are not unaware of the fact that sometimes private counsel, assisting the solicitor, has a tendency to become eager in the prosecution. It therefore becomes the duty of the trial judge, as well as the solicitor, to be solicitous of defendant's rights, working to the end that defendant's rights be fully protected."); *cf.* State of New Jersey v. Imperiale, 773 F. Supp. 747, 748 (D. N.J. 1991) ("Individuals can and do utilize such criminal proceedings to bolster a related civil proceeding or merely for vindictive or harassing purposes."); New Jersey v. Kinder, 701 F. Supp. 492 (D. N.J. 1988) ("While there is the possibility of frivolous suits and vindictive behavior by some complaints, abuses are checked and deterred by the Court's discretion and by the various other remedies available for malicious prosecution.").

503. *Young*, 481 U.S. at 809 n.18; *see also* Polo Fashions, Inc. v. Stock Buyers Int'l, Inc., 760 F.2d 698, 705 (1985), *cert. denied*, 482 U.S. 905 (1987) (In disapproving the use of an interested contempt prosecutor, the court stated that overzealousness "does not have its roots in a conflict of interest. When it manifests itself the courts deal with it on a case-by-case basis as an aberration. This is quite different from approving a practice which would permit the appointment of prosecutors whose undivided loyalty is pledged to a party interested only in a conviction."). The fact that private prosecutors create structural defects in the criminal justice system makes prosecutorial misconduct cases, which require a showing of prejudice,

irrelevant. Thus, cases such as *Darden v. Wainwright* and *Donnelly v. DeChristoforo*, where the relevant inquiry is "whether the prosecutors' comments so infected the trial with unfairness as to make the resulting conviction a denial of due process," address only situations involving personal misconduct. Darden v. Wainwright, 477 U.S. 168, 181 (1986); Donnelly v. DeChristoforo, 416 U.S. 637, 643 (1974).

504. According to one court:

> The question of what constitutes an "impartial" prosecutor demands clarification. A prosecutor is not "partial" simply because she zealously seeks conviction. Rather, "partiality" in this context is similar to a conflict of interest in the sense that the prosecutor has a personal interest or stake in the outcome of the criminal prosecution. Thus, "partiality" refers not to "personal" zeal but to "structural" problems where personal interests (including non-pecuniary interests) generate a structural conflict of interest.

New Jersey v. Imperiale, 773 F. Supp. 747, 750 (D. N.J. 1991).

505. Turner v. United States, 137 S. Ct. 1885, 1888 (2017) (italics in original; quoting Smith v. Cain, 565 U.S. 73, 75 (2012)).

506. *Cf.* United States v. Valenzuela-Bernal, 458 U.S. 858 (1982) (prosecutor has discretion to determine whether illegal aliens may be deported or must be kept in United States to testify at trial).

507. For example, in *Hughes v. Bowers*, a private prosecutor failed to disclose *Brady* material, and his prosecutorial misconduct resulted in the defendant's habeas corpus petition being granted. 711 F. Supp. 1574 (N.D. Ga. 1989), *aff'd*, 896 F.2d 558 (11th Cir. 1990).

508. 732 F.2d 1048 (2d Cir. 1984), *cert. denied*, 469 U.S. 1106 (1985).

509. *Id.* at 1056 n.7.

510. Several courts have held that a defendant's conviction will not be overturned absent a showing that the conduct of a private prosecutor actually "prejudiced" the defendant's trial. *See, e.g.*, Powers v. Hauck, 399 F.2d 322, 325 (5th Cir. 1968) (the use of a special prosecutor is not improper where "the special prosecutor is not guilty of conduct prejudicial to the defendant, and the rights of the defendant are duly observed"); Hughes v. Bowers, 711 F. Supp. 1574 (N.D. Ga. 1989), *aff'd*, 896 F.2d 558 (11th Cir. 1990) ("To demonstrate a denial of due process, the petitioner... must show evidence of specific misbehavior on the part of the prosecutor which prejudiced the defendant."); State v. Cockrell, 309 P.2d 316, 320 (Mont. 1957); State v. Ray, 143 N.E.2d 484, 485 (Ohio Ct. App. 1956).

511. *Wright*, 732 F.2d at 1056.

512. *Murchison*, 349 U.S. at 136; *see also* Richmond Newspapers, Inc. v. Virginia, 448 U.S. 555, 571–72 (1980) (quoting Offutt v. United States, 348 U.S. 11, 14 (1954)) ("To work effectively, it is important that society's criminal process 'satisfy the appearance of justice'....").

513. It is a well-settled principle of constitutional law that due process rights increase as the consequences of the governmental action to the individual become more severe. *See* Argersinger v. Hamlin, 407 U.S. 25 (1972) (defendant entitled to legal representation when defendant faces imprisonment); Baldwin v. New York, 399 U.S. 66 (1970) (serious offenses require a trial by jury); Bloom v. Illinois, 391 U.S. 194 (1968) (criminal contempt defendants have the right to a jury trial if the contempt charged is serious); *see also* 18 U.S.C. § 3172(2) (1985) (statutory right to speedy trial under Speedy Trial Act applies only to serious offenses). A criminal contempt is considered serious if the sentence is for more than six months. Cheff v. Schnackenberg, 384 U.S. 373, 380 (1966).

514. 701 F. Supp. 486 (D. N.J. 1988).

515. *See id.* at 490 (distinguishing *Young* on the ground that the defendants in that case were given sentences ranging up to five years); *see also id.* at 491 ("The United States Supreme Court has itself recognized that the full panoply of procedural protections is not required where lesser charges are involved and minimal punishment is authorized.") (citing Duncan v. Louisiana, 391 U.S. 145 (1968) (right to jury trial does not apply to crimes with possible punishments of six months or less)).

516. *Kinder*, 701 F. Supp. at 491–92 (citation omitted) (emphasis added); *compare* State of New Jersey v. Imperiale, 773 F. Supp. 747, 755 (D. N.J. 1991) ("Although defendant agrees that private prosecutors are not *per se* unconstitutional, it is the existence of the conflict or private interests which implicates defendant's due process rights, and thus, the analysis should turn on the nature and magnitude of the conflict, not the penalty.").

517. "Because sentences of death are 'qualitatively different' from prison sentences, this Court has gone to extraordinary measures to ensure that the prisoner sentenced to be executed is afforded process that will guarantee, as much as is humanly possible that the sentence was not imposed out of whim, passion, prejudice, or mistake." Eddings v. Oklahoma, 455 U.S. 104, 117–18 (1982) (O'Connor, J., concurring); *see also* Saffle v. Parks, 494 U.S. 484, 492–93 (1990); Whitmore v. Arkansas, 495 U.S. 149, 167 (1990) (Marshall, J., dissenting) ("It is by now axiomatic... that the unique, irrevocable nature of the death penalty necessitates safeguards not required for other punishments."); Caldwell v. Mississippi, 472 U.S. 320, 329 (1985); California v. Ramos, 463 U.S. 992, 998–99 (1983) ("The qualitative difference of death from all other punishments requires a correspondingly greater degree of scrutiny of the capital sentencing determination."). Even in the nineteenth century, the propriety of a private attorney prosecuting a capital crime was questioned:

> Prominent attorney David Paul Brown's memoirs often refer to criminal cases that were conducted by private counsel. A major concern of his was to advise lawyers to abandon prosecutions if they discovered that they were dishonest and, as a rule, not to prosecute a capital charge—"never take blood money." Brown implied that capital offenses and other "great public wrongs" should be conducted by the public prosecutor....

See also George W. Warvelle, Essays in Legal Ethics (1902):

> It not infrequently happens that private counsel are employed to assist the state. This is now generally regarded as an allowable practice, but for many years an attorney accepting such a retainer, particularly when his fee was paid by private parties, was considered as having violated an ethical canon of the profession. This was always the case when the charge involved a capital crime. "Never take blood money," say the old writers, and if we are to credit the biographies of the ancient worthies they never did. In fact, the old Ciceronian idea seems at one time to have thoroughly pervaded the bar, and numerous admonitions have come down to us that where life or death is the issue, "it is always more honorable to defend than to prosecute." *Id.* at 142 (citing Brown's Forum , Vol. 2, p. 40); *id.* at 143 ("There is something revolting to the moral sense in the spectacle of counsel selling his talents to enable an individual to satisfy his thirst for vengeance, and this, in most cases, is just what counsel does when he accepts a private retainer to assist the prosecuting officer.").

518. 463 U.S. 939 (1983).

519. *Id.* at 960 (Stevens, J., concurring); *see also* Godfrey v. Georgia, 446 U.S. 420, 427 (1980) (plurality opinion) ("The penalty of death may not be imposed under sentencing procedures that create a substantial risk that the punishment will be inflicted in an arbitrary and capricious manner.").

520. *E.g.*, State v. Spade, Appellate Case No. 2014-000448, 2016 WL 3670561, at *4 (S.C. Ct. App. July 6, 2016). *Cf.* Jordan v. Epps, 740 F. Supp.2d 802, 820 (S.D. Miss. 2010) ("It was the Mississippi Supreme Court that authorized the prosecution to seek the death penalty during the fourth trial. Finally, Owen was not a 'private prosecutor,' in the sense that he was hired and paid by an interested party. Instead, he was appointed by the Mississippi Attorney General, pursuant to statutes that give him unlimited power to do so. Miss. Code Ann. §§7-5-5 and -7 (1972). For all of these reasons, Jordan has not established a claim of prosecutorial vindictiveness that is cognizable on habeas review, and he is not entitled to relief on this issue.").

521. State v. Moose, 313 S.E.2d 507, 512–13 (1984). *But cf.* State v. White, 211 S.E.2d 445, 449–50 (N.C. 1975) ("This Court has consistently held that, in a capital case, any argument made by the solicitor, or by private prosecution appearing for the State, which suggests to the jury that they can depend upon either judicial or executive review to correct any errors in their verdict, and to share their responsibility for it, is an abuse of privilege and prejudicial to the defendant.").

522. Brent E. Newton, *A Case Study in Systemic Unfairness: The Texas Death Penalty, 1973–1994*, 1 Tex. F. on C.L. & C.R. 1, 18 n.112 (1994) ("in numerous Texas death penalty cases, the murder victims' families utilized a Texas law that permitted them to retain private trial prosecutors. In each case, the local elected district attorneys opted not to try the case, so affluent family members of the victims hired private prosecutors, paying them handsome fees of as much as $275/hour (in 1981 dollars).").

523. Matthew S. Nichols, *No One Can Serve Two Masters: Arguments Against Private Prosecutors*, 13 Cap. Def. J. 279, 305 (2001).

524. *E.g.*, Godfrey v. Georgia, 446 U.S. 420, 427 (1980) ("[T]he penalty of death may not be imposed under sentencing procedures that create a substantial risk that the punishment will be inflicted in an arbitrary and capricious manner."); Patrick Mulvaney & Katherine Chamblee, *Innocence and Override*, 126 Yale L.J. Forum 118, 118 n.5 (2016) ("The Eighth Amendment... bars sentencing procedures that create a 'substantial risk' that a punishment will be carried out in an 'arbitrary and capricious' manner.") (citations omitted).

Conclusion Notes

1. Juan Cardenas, *The Crime Victim in the Prosecutorial Process*, 9 Harv. J.L. & Pub. Pol'y 357, 366 (1986) ("Colonial America was heavily influenced by English common law and procedure. Most of the colonists were of English origin; therefore, an English-style approach dominated the law enforcement machinery. The colonies maintained the philosophical attitude that crime was primarily an offense against the individual victim, not an attack against the society, and that, therefore, it was not the government's duty to play an active role in apprehending and prosecuting criminals."); *id.* ("Law enforcement was the general responsibility of the private citizen. Thus, during the Seventeenth Century, the crime victim was largely on his own if he desired to arrest and prosecute."). During the Enlightenment and the eighteenth century in particular, history reveals, many intellectuals advocated for reforms in the administration of criminal justice. *Id.* at 369 ("[G]overnment officials were aware that a movement towards public prosecution had begun in continental Europe. Enlightenment thinkers, most notably Cesare Beccaria, advanced the notion that crime was not a private concern between the aggressor and the victim, but a societal concern. It was argued, therefore, that the criminal justice system should serve the interests of society, not the individual victim. Thus, the process of allowing the victim to control the decisions concerning prosecution was criticized."); *id.* ("Crime victims acting as private prosecutors were viewed as inherently partisan, using the powerful spurs of the criminal process to exact unfair financial benefits. The system of private prosecutions was criticized as elitist, inefficient, and vindictive.").

2. Thomas J. Robinson, *Private Prosecution in Criminal Cases*, 4 Wake Forest Intramural L. Rev. 300, 300–02 (1968); 1 Joseph Chitty, A Practical Treatise on the Criminal Law; Comprising the Practice, Pleadings, and Evidence Which Occur in the Course of Criminal Prosecutions, Whether by Indictment or Information: With a Copious Collection of Precedents of Indictments, Informations, Presentments, and Every Description of Practical Forms, with Comprehensive Notes as to Each Particular Offence, the Process, Indictment, Plea, Defence, Evidence, Trial, Verdict, Judgment, and Punishment 1–2 (1816); *see also id.* at 9 ("[T]he costs of prosecutions for misdemeanours must in general be borne by the prosecutor, yet the Court are empowered, wherever there appears reasonable ground for the investigation, either after a conviction or an acquittal, in case of felony, to award to the prosecutor his reasonable expenses, and, if he be poor, a compensation for his loss of time, on his petition."); *id.* at 9–10 ("The law always ensures to the prosecutor all due protection in the discharge of his duty. And as it would be a great discouragement to public justice, if he were liable to an action, when he was mistaken in the object of his suspicions, it is settled that he cannot be sued for indicting a party, unless his proceedings were both actuated by malice and destitute of any probable foundation.") (citations omitted).

3. Danielle S. Allen, The World of Prometheus: The Politics of Punishing in Democratic Athens 3 (2000) ("Prior to the modern age, private prosecution was the norm in the ancient Greek *polis*, in the Roman Republic and Principate, in the pre-sixteenth-century French and Prussian monarchies, and in the pre-eighteenth-century English monarchy.").

4. David Friedman, *Private Prosecution and Enforcement in Roman Law, in* Roman Law and Economics: Exchange, Ownership, and Disputes 327 (Giuseppe Dari-Mattiacci & Dennis P. Kehoe, eds. 2020); *see also id.* at 344 ("Roman law probably originated in the context of a decentralized system of self-help, a feud system where enforcement was private and the court system provided a mechanism for providing an authoritative verdict on private disputes. In the earliest form of which we have a good account, the private role both in bringing the defendant to court and in enforcing the verdict made Roman

civil law more private than modern tort law. As the system developed, under first the Republic and then the Empire, the state took an increasingly active role. But even in its final form as codified by Justinian, prosecution of both civil and criminal offenses was primarily the responsibility of private citizens.").

5. Theodore Sedgwick, A Treatise on the Measure of Damages, or an Inquiry into the Principles Which Govern the Amount of Compensation Recovered in Suits at Law 9–12 (1847); Charles E. Tucker J., *Anglo-Saxon Law: Its Development and Impact on the English Legal System*, 2 USAFA J. Leg. Stud. 127, 151–52 (1991); *see also id.* at 144 ("Aethelbert's dooms defined existing legal custom and provided a fairly inflexible list of tariffs of compensation to be paid for violent attacks against people or property."); *id.* at 145 ("[B]reaching the king's peace resulted in a heavy fine, or *mulct*, being paid to the king with the amount of the *mulct* being based upon the degree of the breach; the greater the interest that was breached, the greater the compensation that was due the king."); *id.* at 146 ("[T]he concept of the king's peace was protected not only with heavy compensation to the victim (or his family), but also with a heavy fine payable to the king."); *id.* at 146–47 ("[I]t is clear that Aethelbert's dooms also addressed the ancient Anglo-Saxon custom of the 'blood feud.' As we have seen, the early Anglo-Saxons were organized on a traditional tribal basis with heavy reliance paid to kindred affiliation. In fact, it is believed by some historians that within these tribal units, Anglo-Saxon kindred encompassed all blood relations within the sixth degree (i.e., to fourth cousins) and served as the primary institution though which the law functioned. The mechanism by which blood relationships created the basic tenets of Anglo-Saxon customary law was the concept that Anglo-Saxon kindred had the right to protect members of their extended families. This 'protection' was effectuated through the wide-spread use of private warfare, technically called the *faehcle*, or feud, and was considered to be the inalienable right/obligation of every Anglo-Saxon freeman."); *id.* at 147 ("[B]y providing for the payment of cash to help alleviate the need for the blood feud, Aethelbert's codes helped foster the transition of Anglo-Saxon society from a society based upon family loyalty (i.e., tribalism), to one based upon governmental authority."); *id.* at 148 ("The customary practice encoded in Aethelbert's doom of assigning a fixed value to be paid for the death of a particular victim based upon that victim's social status (i.e., based upon that person's *wergild*) was known as 'composition,' and every member of Anglo-Saxon society had his or her *wergild* established and fixed by the doom. Therefore, the death of a member of the nobility, for example, would require the payment of a *wergild* which was three times higher than the *wergild* to be paid in the case of a death of a peasant. Additionally, injuries less than death required a partial payment of the victim's *wergild* and were also dependent on the victim's social status.").

6. *See, e.g.*, Ethan J. Leib, *A Comparison of Criminal Jury Decision Rules in Democratic Countries*, 5 Ohio St. J. Crim. L. 629, 637 (2008) ("Scotland uses fifteen member randomly-selected juries serving for single criminal cases, though trial by jury is not especially common. A vote by eight jurors to convict is sufficient for a verdict of guilty; any fewer votes to convict results in an acquittal. Acquittals come in two forms: verdicts of 'not guilty' and verdicts of 'not proven.'").

7. "By 1800," one legal scholar notes, "countries on the European Continent had long come to rely on public officials to investigate and conduct criminal cases." Bruce P. Smith, *The Emergence of Public Prosecution in London, 1790–1850*, 18 Yale J.L. & Human. 29, 30 (2006). "In Scotland, since the sixteenth century," one legal historian, Rachel Bennett, emphasizes, "the responsibility for prosecuting offenders was vested in the legal profession, from the Lord Advocate in Edinburgh to the procurator fiscals who would gather evidence, or precognitions, in their local areas and build up the case." Rachel E. Bennett, Capital Punishment and the Criminal Corpse in Scotland, 1740–1834, at 31 (2018); *see also* The Journal of Jurisprudence (1877), Vol. XXI, p. 376 ("Why private prosecution has fallen in desuetude in Scotland, although still competent (*Macintosh of Holm* v. *The Lord Advocate*, Feb. 22, 1872, 2 Couper 250), is not difficult to discover, in the pecuniary interest which Procurators-Fiscal and Crown Counsel had for long in its discouragement. While it may be that in England private prosecution has been, in the relief of counties and Exchequer, pushed to an extreme, it might (but not with the same good effect, since Fiscals have been put on salaries) be very beneficially resuscitated in Scotland."). As Rachel Bennett writes: "In more serious cases the fiscals would send the precognitions to the Crown Office where the Lord Advocate, or in most cases one of his deputes, would decide whether to prosecute in the High Court or its circuit courts. This system of public prosecution was perhaps more comparable to other

Continental European practices than elements of the English system with its heavy reliance upon private prosecution." BENNETT, *supra*, at 31.

8. THE NEW CABINET CYCLOPÆDIA AND TREASURY OF KNOWLEDGE (1900), Vol. VII, pp. 69–70.

9. VINCENT CHIAO, CRIMINAL LAW IN THE AGE OF THE ADMINISTRATIVE STATE 13–15 (2019).

10. DARRYL K. BROWN, FREE MARKET CRIMINAL JUSTICE: HOW DEMOCRACY AND LAISSEZ FAIRE UNDERMINE THE RULE OF LAW 43 (2016) ("England and other Commonwealth countries still permit private prosecutions, where they now constitute a small but meaningful portion of cases. Procedural codes of many civil law countries also authorize private citizens to initiate criminal prosecutions independently of public prosecutors. Germany's code specifies several relatively minor crimes that *only* private parties can initiate, including trespass, bodily injury, property damage, invasion of privacy and defamation, as well as a range of commercial offenses such as copyright infringement. German prosecutors are barred from charging these offenses without a private citizen's complaint.").

11. GEORGE WILLIAM WARVELLE, ESSAYS IN LEGAL ETHICS 8–12 (Daniel Warvelle Harbaugh, ed. 2013).

12. Richard H. Underwood, *Part-Time Prosecutors and Conflicts of Interest: A Survey and Some Proposals*, 81 KY. L.J. 1, 8 n.20 (1992).

13. Haider Ala Hamoudi, *Resurrecting Islam or Cementing Social Hierarchy?: Reexamining the Codification of "Islamic" Personal Status Law*, 33 ARIZ. J. INT'L & COMP. L. 329, 365 (2016) ("Blood money is due to a decedent if someone intentionally or accidentally kills or injures the decedent. Across the various Islamic schools and sects, the amount that is due varies depending on the intent associated with the killing or injury, and the gender, religion, and status of the victim."); Daniel Pascoe, *Is Diya a Form of Clemency?*, 34 B.U. INT'L L.J. 149, 150 (2016) ("*Diya* is the payment of 'blood money' to a victim or a victim's family in order to compensate for death or injury caused by a serious offense against the person and also to provide the perpetrator relief from retaliation in kind under Islamic Sharia law. The question of whether *diya* in a murder case constitutes a form of clemency or pardon—that is, a final non-judicial relief against a death sentence, commonly granted by the executive—is an important issue that has not been sufficiently addressed by scholars of Islamic Law or by scholars of capital punishment."); Mary Carter Duncan, *Playing by Their Rules: The Death Penalty and Foreigners in Saudi Arabia*, 27 GA. J. INT'L & COMP. L. 231, 239 (1998) ("A murderer will be executed only if all of the victim's heirs demand it. If one heir refuses to ask for the death penalty, then the execution does not occur. The family may also choose to forgive the murderer, and instead receive blood money from the murderer. The family may also elect to forego both the death penalty and blood money. In the event that the victim's family does not choose the death penalty, the murderer will receive a jail sentence, usually of five years or less."); Elizabeth Peiffer, *The Death Penalty in Traditional Islamic Law and as Interpreted in Saudi Arabia and Nigeria*, 11 WM. & MARY J. WOMEN & L. 507, 525 (2005) ("Qisas crimes are also subject to fixed punishments; for example, the punishment for murder is public beheading. The murderer will only be executed, however, if all of the victim's heirs demand it, and the family has the option to collect blood money from the defendant rather than demanding the death penalty."); Jane McAdam, *Australian Complementary Protection: A Step-by-Step Approach*, 33 SYDNEY L. REV. 687, 696 (2011) ("[S]ome states have a long-standing moratorium on the death penalty, some leave open the possibility of late pardons while others permit the payment of 'blood money' to have a death sentence commuted."); *see also* Hossein Esmaeili & Jeremy Gans, *Islamic Law Across Cultural Borders: The Involvement of Western Nationals in Saudi Murder Trials*, 28 DENV. J. INT'L L. & POL'Y 145, 165 (2000) ("[A] defendant may be convicted of murder under conditions that fail to satisfy the requirements for capital punishment. For example, the murder may not have been intentional or not committed with a deadly weapon, or it may have been proved by eyewitnesses who nonetheless could not give sufficiently detailed accounts of the murder. Under such circumstances, the victim's heirs' rights under Qisas are limited to two options: to forgive the defendant completely or to receive a fixed amount of monetary compensation, termed Diyya (blood money.) Diyya has a dual role in Islamic law: as a punishment in some criminal matters and as a compensation device in civil matters."); Mehmet Celik, *Reforming Criminal Justice in the Ottoman Empire: Police, Courts and Prisons in Rusçuk, 1839–1864*, 60 AM. J. LEGAL HIST. 109, 122 (2020) ("Article 171 of the Penal Code of 1858 clarifies that 'the effect of the law cannot defeat the personal rights', referring to the blood money under Islamic law. In fact, two of four murder cases at the Sharia Court in

Rusçuk were settled with a payment of the blood money (*diyet*), while the other two were referred to the government, most likely to be investigated first at the *meclis-i kebir* and then tried at the higher courts in Istanbul. The Penal Code of 1858 retained the Islamic legal practice of settling cases with the payment of blood money, but still required imprisonment. A victim's relatives could choose to accept the blood money under Islamic law, but the *meclis* could reopen the case and impose imprisonment or even the death penalty."); *Exclusive Customary Laws*, 80 IUS GENTIUM 399, 413 (2020) ("In contrast to Mongol customs, Kazakh customary law is less lenient and human, with more capital punishment for grave crimes such as revolt, high treason, manslaughter and adultery. Blood feud was common but in case of manslaughter, the loss could be compensated by blood money called *khūn* (a Persian word for blood also in use among Pashtuns). Compensation paid for crimes other than manslaughter, that is, various forms of injuries were called *ayb* (from the Arabic word for mistake, fault) the sum of which was less than that of a *khun*. Blood money for women, the half paid for men. For killing a man, 100 horses had to be given on average, for a woman only 50.").

14. Katharine M. E. Adams, *A Permanent Framework for Condolence Payments in Armed Conflict: A Vital Commander's Tool*, 224 MIL. L. REV. 314, 340 (2016); Elizabeth Peiffer, *The Death Penalty in Traditional Islamic Law and as Interpreted in Saudi Arabia and Nigeria*, 11 WM. & MARY J. WOMEN & L. 507, 533 (2005) ("Although death is the penalty for intentional homicide, the penalty can be replaced by the payment of blood money, or diya, if the next of kin request it.").

15. "Iran: 'Blood Money' Saved 358 from Death Penalty," Contro La Pena di Morte Nel Mondo, http://www.handsoffcain.info/archivio_news/201404.php?iddocumento=18303913&mover=0; *cf.* Amnesty International, Suliamon Olufemi: Forgotten on Death Row in Saudi Arabia 5 (2020), *available at* https://www.amnesty.org/download/Documents/ACT5017772020ENGLISH.PDF ("According to Shari'a law in Saudi Arabia, if a crime is punished under the rule of *qisas* (retribution), as in Suliamon Olufemi's case, relatives of the murder victim have the right to decide if the offender should be executed or pardoned, in which case the death penalty is dropped, sometimes in return for *diya* (compensation or 'blood money'). Pardons by victims' relatives must be certified by courts of law. However, this does not automatically mean that a convicted person is spared from execution since judges have the power to invoke *hadd* (divinely prescribed fixed offences and punishments) and consider the murder as harmful to public order in addition to it being a crime against the victim and his family.").

16. People ex rel. Luceno v. Cuozzo, 412 N.Y.S.2d 748, 749 (City Ct. of White Plains, 1978) ("One of the objections to a private lawyer conducting a criminal proceeding is that he will not act with the objectivity and fairness of a District Attorney, who is [a] quasi-public officer."); *id.* at 752 ("[I]t is virtually impossible to ask Luceno's defense attorney, or any defense attorney so situated, to act with objectivity and complete impartiality as a prosecutor in a criminal proceeding against a police officer who is responsible for the charge against his client.").

17. MARC L. MILLER, RONALD F. WRIGHT, JENIA I. TURNER & KAY L. LEVINE, CRIMINAL PROCEDURES: PROSECUTIONS AND ADJUDICATION—CASES, STATUTES, AND EXECUTIVE MATERIALS 174 (6th ed. 2019) ("Traces of the older private prosecution system remain visible today, and are gaining renewed attention as a method of empowering the victims of crime. More than half the states still have statutes or constitutional provisions that allow private counsel, retained by a crime victim, to participate in criminal proceedings.").

18. 261 S.E.2d 55 (W. Va. Sup. Ct. App. 1979).

19. *Id.* at 57 (citing 1 J. Bishop, New Criminal Procedure (2d ed. 1913), p. 245; 63 Am.Jur.2d Prosecuting Attorneys § 9; Note, *Private Prosecution: The Entrenched Anomaly*, 50 N.C. L. REV. 1171 (1972)); *see also* State v. Crouch, 445 S.E.2d 213, 218 (W. Va. Sup. Ct. App. 1994) ("Mr. Crouch contends that the circuit court abused its discretion in allowing the participation of a private prosecutor, Warren R. McGraw, in the hearing on the motion for a new trial. Although Mr. McGraw was hired by the victim's family before Mr. Crouch's murder trial and appeared at all stages of the proceeding, Mr. Crouch concedes that the public prosecutor retained control of the case and the presentation of the evidence at the trial level. At the hearing on the motion for new trial, however, Mr. Crouch argues that Mr. McGraw exceeded normal bounds allowable for a private prosecutor by virtually handling the entire case. We disagree."); *id.* ("Under *W. Va. Code* 7-7-8 [1993], the employment of a practicing lawyer to assist the State in a criminal prosecution, although

not affirmatively authorized, is not prohibited."); *id.* ("Although we held in *State v. Atkins,* 163 W.Va. 502, 506, 261 S.E.2d 55, 59 (1979), *cert. denied,* 445 U.S. 904, 100 S. Ct. 1081, 63 L.Ed.2d 320 (1980) that '[t]he specific statutory language [of *W. Va. Code* 7-7-8 [1993]] is nothing more than a proviso or exception designed to demonstrate that the Legislature did not intend to abolish the common law rule permitting the employment of a private prosecutor,' we declined to delineate the exact degree of participation allowable for a private prosecutor."); *id.* at 219 ("Mr. McGraw was hired by the victim's family to serve as a private prosecutor in order to ensure that the case would be prosecuted vigorously. As the lower court recognized, because Mr. McGraw was involved in the case from its inception, it was proper to continue the hearing with his participation. Moreover, because the public prosecutor could not attend the hearing on the motion for new trial, it was also proper that Mr. McGraw, who was better acquainted with the case than the assistant prosecutor present, handle the hearing. For these reasons, we find the lower court did not abuse its discretion in allowing Mr. McGraw to participate in the hearing on the motion for new trial.").

20. *Atkins,* 261 S.E.2d at 57. Citing West Virginia Code § 7-7-8, the court in *Atkins* emphasized that "[t]his statute makes a clear distinction between a special prosecutor, who is appointed by the court because of a disqualification or inability to act on the part of a public prosecutor, and the private prosecutor." *Id.*; *see also id.* at 58 ("We observe initially that W. Va. Code, 7-7-8, does not affirmatively authorize the system of private prosecutors. The specific statutory language is nothing more than a proviso or exception designed to demonstrate that the Legislature did not intend to abolish the common law rule permitting the employment of a private prosecutor.").

21. *Id.* at 57–58 (citing State ex rel. Moran v. Ziegler, W.Va., 244 S.E.2d 550 (1978); State v. Lohm, 97 W.Va. 652, 125 S.E. 758 (1924); State v. Stafford, 89 W.Va. 301, 109 S.E. 326 (1921)).

22. *Id.* at 58.

23. *Id.* (citing Powers v. Hauck, 399 F.2d 322 (5th Cir. Tex.1968); Brooks v. State, 45 Ala. App. 196, 228 So.2d 24 (1969); Thomas v. State, 59 So.2d 517 (Fla.1952); Territory v. Chong Chak Lai, 19 Haw. 437 (1909); State v. Bartlett, 105 Me. 212, 74 A. 18 (1909); Commonwealth v. Knapp, 27 Mass. (10 Pick.) 477, 20 Am. Dec. 534 (1830); Goldsby v. State, 240 Miss. 647, 123 So.2d 429, 124 So.2d 297, 129 So.2d 127 (1960); Baca v. Padilla, 26 N.M. 223, 190 P. 730 (1920); State v. Best, 280 N.C. 413, 186 S.E.2d 1 (1972); State v. Kent, 4 N.D. 577, 62 N.W. 631 (1895); Lopez v. State, 437 S.W.2d 268 (Tex.Cr.App.1968); Contra, State v. Harrington, 534 S.W.2d 44 (Mo.1976)).

24. Christopher M. Champagne, *Prosecutorial Misconduct in Connecticut: A Review,* 78 Conn. B.J. 196, 197 (2004) ("The Connecticut Supreme Court first tackled the issue of prosecutorial misconduct more than a century ago."); Jeffrey W. Bower, *Clarity and Balance: Appellate Review of Harmless Error, Fundamental Error, and Prosecutorial Misconduct After* State v. Perry, 48 Idaho L. Rev. 85, 88 (2011) ("Generally speaking, prosecutorial misconduct occurs when a prosecutor improperly or illegally avoids a required disclosure or persuades the jury to wrongfully convict a defendant or to assess a defendant with an unjustified punishment. In Idaho, the doctrine of prosecutorial misconduct was introduced just after the turn of the century.").

25. U.S. Const., amend. VIII.

26. Daniel Epps, *Checks and Balances in the Criminal Law,* 74 Vand. L. Rev. 1, 12 (2021) ("The precise relationship between the separation of powers and criminal punishment in the Framers' thinking is not fully clear; they rarely seem to have specifically referenced criminal punishment when discussing the benefits of separate powers in constitutional design generally. The Founding generation was, however, unquestionably familiar with the English tradition... as well as with Montesquieu's and Beccaria's insights. And certainly they thought that dividing up authority among institutions would help prevent serious abuses of the state's power over citizens' life and liberty.").

27. Crime Victims' Rights Amendment: Report together with Additional and Minority Views, Committee on the Judiciary, U.S. Senate (Nov. 7, 2003), pp. 68–69 ("The clear trend during the colonial period and immediately after the Revolution was for the expansion of public prosecutions and, with it, the decline of private prosecutions. These developments, as well as the social, economic, and intellectual factors that led to these developments, were clear at the time of the framing and would have been appreciated by the Framers of the Constitution and Bill of Rights. In Virginia—home of some of the foremost architects of these documents—a deputy attorney general was appointed to each in the early 1700s and 'had complete

control over all prosecutions within his county' by 1789. North Carolina established prosecuting attorneys for each county in 1738, 'to carry on all Proceedings in the [County] Courts for the Punishing of crimes.' Connecticut adopted a system of county prosecutors in 1704—over 80 years before the Constitution was written. In other colonies, particularly in areas settled by the Dutch in the 17th century, public prosecution emerged earlier and more directly.").

28. Gerhard Falk, The American Criminal Justice System: How It Works, How It Doesn't and How to Fix It 23 (2010) ("The U.S. Constitution does not provide for a public prosecutor. Instead, the office developed gradually from the common law based on the colonial experience. The outcome of this evolution is an office that has, according to Supreme Court Justice Robert H. Jackson, 'more control over life, liberty, and reputation than any other person in America.'").

29. Gwladys Gilliéron, Public Prosecutors in the United States and Europe: A Comparative Analysis with Special Focus on Switzerland, France, and Germany 47 (2014) ("The old English system of private prosecution was a system favoring people of means. In a system of private prosecution, an individual needed to avenge himself and bear the cost of prosecution. Hence, an individual could not expect protection from the state. In addition, private prosecution produced some abuses. It was not uncommon for the accused and the accuser to meet each other in a pretrial collaboration and agree that, in exchange for payment of a percentage of the anticipated penalty by the offender to the accuser, the accuser would not prosecute the offense."); *cf.* Daniel Epps, *Adversarial Asymmetry in the Criminal Process*, 91 N.Y.U. L. Rev. 762, 840–41 (2016) ("[A] wide range of crimes today are often 'victimless,' and in those cases there would be no relevant private party to handle the litigation. Such crimes often require extensive investigative work to detect and prove, and private litigants are likely not the best parties to lead such efforts. For these and other reasons, private prosecution fell by the wayside in this country, and there are good arguments against turning back the clock.").

30. *E.g.*, New Zealand: Parliamentary Debates: Second Session of the Fifth Parliament—Legislative Council and House of Representatives Comprising the Period from the Sixteenth Day of July to the Twenty-Ninth Day of August, 1872 (1872), Vol. 12, p. 418 ("The present system of private prosecution did not prevail in any civilized country excepting England or colonies where the laws of England were in force. Generally, throughout the Continent of Europe, and in a part of the British Empire, the system of public prosecution existed, and it was found to work remarkably well. It had been well observed that the system of private prosecution was a remnant of barbarism, a remnant of that old time when every man had to protect himself by his own right hand, and the law was found to be powerless to give the necessary security to either life or property. If they were to continue a system not adapted to the exigencies of modern life, they had better revert to the practice of having disputes settled by wager of battle, and guilt determined by making the accused person walk over red-hot ploughshares."). *Compare* Cardenas, *supra* note 1, at 374 ("Professor Moley, writing in 1929, found that the amount of private prosecution in the United States was 'great and apparently enlarging.'") *and id.* ("Another commentator, writing in 1955, also found that 'private prosecutors in fact play an extensive role in criminal law enforcement.' That commentor wrote: 'Private prosecution is especially common before magistrates, municipal courts and justices of the peace.... [I]t is a common practice for private attorneys to prosecute criminal actions in the lesser courts. Since these courts customarily have jurisdiction over all misdemeanors, private citizens may initiate criminal actions which result in jail terms up to one year.'"), *with id.* ("Today, the role of private prosecution is much more limited than it was in earlier common law history. Nowhere today does the aggrieved crime victim hire his own counsel to prosecute his private interest before the grand jury or before the petit jury. The development of a state prosecutor has severely restricted the crime victim's rights to prosecute or to complain directly to a grand jury. Courts generally grant the public prosecutor the exclusive power to initiate criminal proceedings."); *id.* at 378 ("Despite the fact that the general rule is that private attorneys may participate in prosecution proceedings only if the district attorney controls and manages the prosecution, it is not uncommon for private prosecutors to dominate the proceedings. Many cases, particularly older ones, show that privately hired counsel have even conducted criminal prosecutions alone so long as permission to do so from the trial court and public prosecutor was granted. Older cases have held that if the public prosecutor is present the privately hired counsel can have exclusive control over the conduct of the trial. While it is doubtful that most modern courts would

permit such complete delegation of prosecutorial authority to a private counsel, the question of just how much control a privately hired attorney can exercise over the prosecution has not yet been clearly articulated in any reported case."); People ex rel. Luceno v. Cuozzo, 412 N.Y.S.2d 748, 751 (1978) ("Private [prosecutors] must show fairness and objectivity of the same caliber as the District Attorney. This factor militates against their conduct of a criminal proceeding. On the other hand, there may be matters which private persons should be allowed to prosecute because the District Attorney for one or more reasons will not or cannot act. Cases which present important public issues, rank unfairness or injustice should not be kept from judicial scrutiny. The court is in a better position to control the unusual case by the exercise of discretion than in fashioning an absolute role that in all cases or in no cases can such private attorney proceed.").

31. In locales permitting private prosecutions, American jurists put certain restraints upon such prosecutions. In *Atkins*, the West Virginia court observed that "[t]here are several positive reasons for retaining the right to employ a private prosecutor." *Atkins*, 261 S.E.2d at 58. In that case, three specific reasons were given for wanting to retain private prosecution. *Id.* ("First, we recognize that there may be occasions when the public prosecutor is in need of assistance in order to carry out his duties effectively. Second, there may be those occasions when the employment of a private prosecutor would satisfy the public's concern that a given case not be accorded perfunctory treatment. Finally, it is not inappropriate to consider that in certain cases, the victim's family may wish to satisfy itself that the case is being vigorously prosecuted."). But while the court in *Atkins* opined that "there are legitimate reasons for retaining private prosecutors," it specifically emphasized that "the right is not absolute." *Id.* "The ultimate responsibility for permitting the participation of a private prosecutor," the *Atkins* court observed, "rests with the trial judge." *Id.* at 58–59. As the *Atkins* court continued: "A competent public prosecutor should ordinarily not be forced to accept a private prosecutor as an associate. It should also be stressed that our recognition of the role of a private prosecutor does not imply that he should be favored for selection as special prosecutor where the regular prosecutor is disqualified under W. Va. Code, 7-7-8." *Id.* at 59. Despite the fact that it used that qualifying language, the court in *Atkins* ultimately rejected the errors raised by the defendant. *Id.* ("In regard to the specific errors raised by the defendant, we do not find error in the fact that the private prosecutor did not disclose the amount of his fee. As required by *State v. Lohm*, 97 W. Va. 652, 125 S.E. 758 (1924), he disclosed who had employed him. He also stated that the amount of his fee would be based upon the time spent in connection with the case, an indication that it was to be calculated on a Quantum meruit basis, and thus could not be determined until the trial had been completed. We are not aware of, nor have we been cited, any case where the failure to disclose the amount of the private prosecutor's fee was held to be reversible error."); *id.* ("The defendant also asserts that the private prosecutor dominated the prosecution of the trial and that where the public prosecutor plays only a limited role at trial, error should arise from this fact alone. We decline to adopt such a rule. In *State v. Stafford*, 89 W. Va. 301, 109 S.E. 326 (1921), a similar argument was advanced and rejected. There, as here, the record revealed that the public prosecutor was present at the trial and assisted in the case, although in *Stafford* the public prosecutor left the trial when his wife became seriously ill. Here, the public prosecutor was present throughout the trial. It does appear, however, that he did not participate in the examination of witnesses to the same extent as the private prosecutor."); *id.* ("We do not believe it is possible or desirable to establish an arbitrary line as to the degree of participation of the public prosecutor in the trial. The fundamental question is not the extent of the private prosecutor's participation, but whether his actions result in prejudicial error to the defendant. As previously stated, the private prosecutor is bound to follow the same high standards of conduct in the trial of the case as the public prosecutor, and this should afford the defendant adequate protection.").

32. Volker Krey, About Death Penalty Reflections on Legal History: From the Code of Hammurabi and Sumerian Precursors up to Germanic Law, the Roman Empire and the Middle Ages (2019); *see also* Sigrid Undset, Gunnar's Daughter xvii (Arthur G. Chater, trans. & Sherrill Harbison, ed. 1998) ("As it could be considered shameful to accept blood money for one's kin, settlements by *weregild* did not always end a dispute, and if no peaceful agreement could be reached by mediation, blood vengeance was the recognized recourse."); Nancy Amoury Combs, *From Prosecutorial to Reparatory: A Valuable Post-Conflict Change of Focus*, 36 Mich. J. Int'l L. 219, 274 (2015) ("[B]efore the thirteenth century, in both England and on the Continent, criminal acts did not give rise to criminal sanctions; they

instead gave rise to civil compensatory obligations. That is, before the thirteenth century, a murderer was not sentenced to prison or the gallows but rather was required to make a compensation payment-a *wergild*-to the victims' family. These compensation payments were designed to eliminate the need for blood feuds that otherwise would have erupted between the families and tribes of victims and the families and tribes of perpetrators. Although compensation payments were clear improvements over blood feuds, they were by no means an optimal response to criminal activity. But at that point in history, 'the kings were too weak to centralize the control of judicial functions in their own hands' and as such, they also were too weak to gain custody over offenders and impose criminal sanctions thereon. Later, when King Henry II gained control over the government from the feudal lords and concomitantly gained control over the administration of justice, there followed 'a strong shift away from Anglo-Saxon feud and *wergild* to Angevin public prosecution' and from 'predominantly private prosecution through monetary compensation to predominantly capital punishment at the hands of the crown.'").

33. Private prosecutors have long been motivated by self-interest or revenge. Epps, *supra* note 29, at 786–87 ("Private prosecutors were highly adversarial in their drive to punish alleged wrongdoers. Given that prosecutors either were themselves, or were lawyers paid by, the victims (or family members of the victim) of the alleged crimes, the desire for vengeance played a significant role in their motives. Yet in addition to that, the legal system itself gave private prosecutors 'various financial inducements' to obtain convictions. Victims could obtain restitution of stolen goods as well as punitive damages. If the defendant could not afford to pay, he was required to serve the victim as an indentured servant; the victim could also sell the defendant's labor to a third party. In some circumstances, private prosecutors could reach financial settlements with defendants, which may also have encouraged aggressive prosecution.").

34. Robinson, *supra* note 2, at 326–27.

35. Meagan E. Costello, *Smashing the Tragic Illusion of Justice: The Reprehensibility of the Death Penalty in Virginia*, 41 CATH. LAW 255, 257–58 (2002); Jonathan Simon, *Why Do You Think They Call It Capital Punishment? Reading the Killing State*, 36 LAW & SOC'Y REV. 783, 805–06 (2002) (reviewing AUSTIN SARAT, WHEN THE STATE KILLS: CAPITAL PUNISHMENT AND THE AMERICAN CONDITION (2001)); *see also* John D. Bessler, *The Anomaly of Executions: The Cruel and Unusual Punishments Clause in the 21st Century*, 2 BRIT. J. AM. LEGAL STUD. 297 (2013) (describing the use and subsequent abandonment of various corporal punishments); Emily Cock, *Proportionate Maiming: The Origins of Thomas Jefferson's Provisions for Facial Disfigurement in Bill 64*, TRANSACTIONS OF THE ROYAL HISTORICAL SOCIETY 29 (2019), pp. 127–151.

36. Robert M. Ireland, *Privately Funded Prosecution of Crime in the Nineteenth-Century United States*, 39 AM. J. LEGAL HIST. 43, 48 n.9 (1995) (citing Brown, 2 *The Forum; or Forty Years Full Practice at the Philadelphia Bar*, 40, 2 vols., (Philadelphia: Robert H. Small, 1856)).

37. *See, e.g.*, Obergefell v. Hodges, 135 S. Ct. 2584, 2602–03 (2015) ("The right of same-sex couples to marry that is part of the liberty promised by the Fourteenth Amendment is derived, too, from that Amendment's guarantee of the equal protection of the laws. The Due Process Clause and the Equal Protection Clause are connected in a profound way, though they set forth independent principles. Rights implicit in liberty and rights secured by equal protection may rest on different precepts and are not always co-extensive, yet in some instances each may be instructive as to the meaning and reach of the other. In any particular case one Clause may be thought to capture the essence of the right in a more accurate and comprehensive way, even as the two Clauses may converge in the identification and definition of the right. See *M.L.B.*,519 U.S., at 120–121, 117 S. Ct. 555; *id.*, at 128–129, 117 S. Ct. 555 (KENNEDY, J., concurring in judgment); *Bearden v. Georgia*, 461 U.S. 660, 665, 103 S. Ct. 2064, 76 L.Ed.2d 221 (1983). This interrelation of the two principles furthers our understanding of what freedom is and must become."); *id.* at 2603 ("[I]n interpreting the Equal Protection Clause, the Court has recognized that new insights and societal understandings can reveal unjustified inequality within our most fundamental institutions that once passed unnoticed and unchallenged."); *id.* at 2604–05 ("[T]he right to marry is a fundamental right inherent in the liberty of the person, and under the Due Process and Equal Protection Clauses of the Fourteenth Amendment couples of the same-sex may not be deprived of that right and that liberty. The Court now holds that same-sex couples may exercise the fundamental right to marry. No longer may this liberty be denied to them."); *see also* United States v. Windsor, 570 U.S. 744, 769–70 (2013) ("DOMA seeks to injure the very class New York seeks to protect. By doing so it violates basic due process and equal protection principles applicable to the

Federal Government. See U.S. Const., Amdt. 5; *Bolling v. Sharpe*, 347 U.S. 497, 74 S. Ct. 693, 98 L.Ed. 884 (1954). The Constitution's guarantee of equality 'must at the very least mean that a bare congressional desire to harm a politically unpopular group cannot' justify disparate treatment of that group. *Department of Agriculture v. Moreno*, 413 U.S. 528, 534–535, 93 S.Ct. 2821, 37 L.Ed.2d 782 (1973). In determining whether a law is motived by an improper animus or purpose, "'[d]iscriminations of an unusual character'" especially require careful consideration. *Supra*, at 2692 (quoting *Romer, supra*, at 633, 116 S. Ct. 1620). DOMA cannot survive under these principles. The responsibility of the States for the regulation of domestic relations is an important indicator of the substantial societal impact the State's classifications have in the daily lives and customs of its people. DOMA's unusual deviation from the usual tradition of recognizing and accepting state definitions of marriage here operates to deprive same-sex couples of the benefits and responsibilities that come with the federal recognition of their marriages. This is strong evidence of a law having the purpose and effect of disapproval of that class. The avowed purpose and practical effect of the law here in question are to impose a disadvantage, a separate status, and so a stigma upon all who enter into same-sex marriages made lawful by the unquestioned authority of the States.").

38. Special Message to Congress on Conflict-of-Interest Legislation and on Problems of Ethics in Government, 152 Pub. Papers 326 (Apr. 27, 1961).

39. The American Bar Association explicitly encourages public prosecutions. 4 Wayne R. LaFave, Jerold H. Israel, Nancy J. King & Orin S. Kerr, Crim. Proc. § 13.3(b) (4th ed. 2019) ("The 'prosecution function should be performed by a lawyer who is a public official,' as prosecution by a private party without authorization or approval of the prosecutor present a serious 'danger of the vindictive use of the criminal law process.'") (citing ABA Standards for Criminal Justice, Prosecution Function § 3-2.1 (4th ed. 2015)).

40. Shaffer v. Fayette County of Pennsylvania, 163 F. Supp.3d 280, 297 (W.D. Pa. 2016).

41. In re Schuessler, 578 S.W.3d 762, 773 (Mo. 2019) (en banc).

42. Plea bargaining is regularly conducted outside the courtroom, and thus outside the ability of judges to oversee. Bruce P. Smith, *Plea Bargaining and the Eclipse of the Jury*, 1 Ann. Rev. L. & Soc. Sci. 131, 131–32 (2005) ("But while radiant in constitutional principle, criminal jury trial has long been eclipsed in actual practice. By 1860, less than three generations after the framers' era, most felony cases in New York City—America's largest and most influential jurisdiction—were resolved by guilty pleas rather than by jury verdicts (Moley 1928). By the late 1920s, guilty pleas accounted for over 80% of felony convictions not only in New York, but in cities such as Chicago, Cleveland, and Los Angeles as well (Moley 1928). Recent data reveal that the eclipse of criminal jury trial in America is, by now, virtually complete: Of the roughly 1.05 million adults convicted of felony offenses in American state courts in 2002, 95% pleaded guilty (US Dep. Justice 2004), and the 75,000 or so convicted in federal courts in that year pleaded guilty at even higher rates (Admin. Office US Courts 2004).").

43. Wayne R. LaFave, Jerold H. Israel, Nancy J. King & Orin S. Kerr, Criminal Procedure § 8.11(e) (4th ed. 2020) ("Where the witness is willing to testify under a grant of immunity, the prosecutor may prefer to provide immunity through an agreement whereby the witness agrees to testify in exchange for a promise of non-prosecution or non-use."); *id.* ("Most courts view informal immunity agreements as within the exercise of the prosecutor's traditional discretion over the decision to prosecute.").

44. Bruce A. Green & Rebecca Roiphe, *Rethinking Prosecutors' Conflicts of Interest*, 58 B.C. L. Rev. 463, 471 (2017); *see also* Bruce A. Green & Rebecca Roiphe, *A Fiduciary Theory of Prosecution*, 69 Am. U. L. Rev. 805, 809 (2020) ("Courts and scholars of prosecution in the United States agree that prosecutors have a duty to seek justice. Fiduciary theory helps make that obligation less amorphous. Prosecutors, this Article argues, are fiduciaries who represent the public but are appointed or elected to pursue a particular abstract public interest, the interest in justice.").

45. Helen J. Knowles, Bruce E. Altschuler & Jaclyn Schildkraut, Lights, Camera, Execution! Cinematic Portrayals of Capital Punishment 24 (2019).

46. *E.g.*, Abby L. Dennis, *Reining in the Minister of Justice: Prosecutorial Oversight and the Superseder* Power, 57 Duke L.J. 131, 147 (2007):

> [M]ost recusal statutes provide little guidance as to when a prosecutor should request a special prosecutor. North Carolina's statute, for example, is silent on the matter. Other states' recusal

> statutes do somewhat better, focusing on when prosecutors have a "personal interest in the cause." Commentators, however, have noted the difficulty in defining prosecutorial conflicts of interest. Such difficulty arises from the nature of the prosecutorial function itself: rather than advocating for one client, the prosecutor represents a number of constituencies—including the community, the victim, the defendant, and the state. As such, professional disciplinary boards and courts have only imposed sanctions for conflicts of interest when the prosecutor has "an axe to grind" or a direct personal interest in the litigation.

1B Gillespie Mich. Crim. L. &. Proc. § 20.177—*Disqualification of prosecuting attorneys* (2d ed. 2020):

> A prosecuting attorney with a conflict of interest must be disqualified to insure that the public's interest in having a prosecutor who will obtain justice and not merely convict and in maintaining the impartiality and integrity of the criminal justice system will be served. The appearance of impropriety is sufficient to justify disqualification of a prosecuting attorney on the basis of a conflict of interest. A defendant is not required to prove actual bad faith or unethical conduct on the part of the prosecutor and his or her staff.
>
> A conflict of interest involving the elected county prosecutor requires recusal of the prosecutor and the entire staff. A conflict of interest involving an assistant prosecuting attorney requires recusal of the entire staff only where the assistant prosecutor in question has supervisory authority over other attorneys in the office or has policy-making authority.
>
> A trial court's determination regarding the disqualification of the prosecuting attorney and the appointment of a special prosecutor pursuant to a statute that permits disqualification on the basis of a conflict of interest or an inability by the prosecuting attorney at attend to his or her duties involves a question of fact and will not be reversed on appeal unless it is found to be clearly erroneous.

See also Eli Wald, *Disqualifying a District Attorney When a Government Witness Was Once the District Attorney's Client: The Law Between the Courts and the State*, 85 Denv. U. L. Rev. 369 (2007); Bruce A. Green & Fred C. Zacharias, *Prosecutorial Neutrality*, 2004 Wis. L. Rev. 837 (2004).

47. *Compare* Roger A. Fairfax, Jr., *Delegation of the Criminal Prosecution Function to Private Actors*, 43 U.C. Davis L. Rev. 411 (2009) (exploring whether it is appropriate to delegate criminal prosecutorial authority to private actors) *with* Richard H. Underwood, *Part-time Prosecutors and Conflicts of Interest: A Survey and Some Proposals*, 81 Ky. L.J. 1 (1992–93) (attempting to provide guidelines for the private attorney navigating conflicts of interest when acting as a prosecutor).

48. *E.g.*, Maybell Romero, *Profit-Driven Prosecution and the Competitive Bidding Process*, 107 J. Crim. L. & Criminology 161 (2017) (discussing cities, counties, and other political governmental subdivisions relying on "contracting out" prosecutorial services through a competitive bidding process); Lauren-Brooke Eisen, Inside Private Prisons: An American Dilemma in the Age of Mass Incarceration (2018) ("Some cities even contract out the role of the prosecutor. Officials in Albany, Oregon, recently paid a private law firm an annual fee of more than $200,000 for prosecution and other legal services."); Patrick McFadden, *The First Thing We Do, Let's Outsource All the Lawyers: An Essay*, 33 Pub. Cont. L.J. 443, 448 (2004) ("The Federal Deposit Insurance Corporation's (FDIC) practice of contracting out for legal services provides an example of mechanisms put in place to ensure that private attorneys provide legal services in an ethical fashion that maintains the public interest as the ultimate goal of government lawyering. Professor Luneburg's analysis of government contracting for legal services examines the FDIC's practice in detail. One interesting approach the FDIC took to minimize the possibility of unnecessary billing for duplicative research projects was to create a 'brief bank' of previously conducted major research projects. The FDIC also provided outside counsel with detailed instructions for representing the agency.").

49. 1 Wayne R. LaFave, Jerold H. Israel, Nancy J. King & Orin S. Kerr, Crim. Proc. § 1.5(k) (4th ed. 2020) ("Over the last few decades, there has been a widespread reevaluation of the appropriate legal status of the victim. Although hardly restored to the central position he once occupied, the victim is now recognized to be not simply a source of evidence, but an interested third party whose concerns must be considered (though not necessarily vindicated) by police, prosecutor, and judge. This development is

largely the product of what came to be known as the 'victims' rights' movement. That movement was initiated in the 1960s, gathered momentum in the 1970s and early 1980s, and has continued ever since as one of the most significant and successful forces for reshaping the criminal justice process."); 6 Wayne R. LaFave, Jerold H. Israel, Nancy J. King & Orin S. Kerr, Crim. Proc. § 24.7(b) n.42 (4th ed. 2020) ("The federal Crime Victims Rights Act provides that victims in federal criminal cases must be informed that they may seek the assistance of counsel, but the Act does not specify what that attorney's role at trial might be.") (citing 18 U.S.C. § 3771).

50. *Compare* Booth v. Maryland, 482 U.S. 496 (1987) (invalidating a state law providing for victim impact statements at sentencing trials in capital proceedings) *with* Payne v. Tennessee, 111 S. Ct. 2597 (1991) (overruling *Booth* and holding that a state has a legitimate interest in presenting relevant victim impact evidence in a capital sentencing proceeding).

51. Bruce A. Green & Rebecca Roiphe, *Rethinking Prosecutors' Conflicts of Interest*, 58 B.C. L. Rev. 463, 491–98 (2017) (discussing voluntary recusal and judicial disqualification).

52. Epps, *supra* note 29, at 840–41.

53. ABA Standards for Criminal Justice, Standard 3-1.1 cmt. (1979) ("The prosecutor has sometimes been described as a 'minister of justice' or as occupying a quasi-judicial position.").

54. *E.g.*, In re Wilson, 258 P.2d 433, 436–37 (Ariz. 1953) (per curiam) (county attorney disbarred for accepting money not to prosecute a case); In re Cowdery, 10 P. 47, 65–66 (Cal. 1886) (en banc) (city attorney suspended for accepting bribe); In re Norris, 57 P. 528, 531 (Kan. 1899) (prosecutor disbarred for accepting bribes for commencing or dismissing prosecutions); Commonwealth ex rel. Pike County Bar Ass'n v. Stump, 57 S.W.2d 524, 527–28 (Ky. 1933) (accepting bribe to discontinue investigation of a theft resulted in disbarring of prosecutor); In re Robinson, 420 N.Y.S.2d 430, 432 (App. Div. 1979) (per curiam) (assistant U.S. attorney disbarred for providing confidential information to members of organized crime); In re Crum, 215 N.W. 682, 687–89 (N.D. 1927) (prosecutor suspended for accepting campaign contributions from persons under investigation); In re Simpson, 192 P. 1097, 1098–99 (Okla. 1920) (county attorney disbarred for accepting bribes to decline to pursue prosecutions); In re McMahon, 513 P.2d 796, 798 (Or. 1973) (en banc, per curiam) (attorney suspended from practice for accepting money and gifts from a bail bondsman); State v. Hays, 61 S.E. 355, 357–58 (W. Va. 1908) (county attorney disbarred for receipt to monies from the owner of a "speak-easy" to avoid prosecution).

55. Bruce A. Green & Rebecca Roiphe, *A Fiduciary Theory of Prosecution*, 69 Am. U. L. Rev. 805, 811, 814–15 (2020) (citing State ex rel. Gibson v. Friedley, 34 N.E. 872, 875 (Ind. 1893)); *see also* State ex rel. Black v. Taylor, 106 S.W. 1023, 1027 (Mo. 1907) (refusing to allow the Attorney General to "farm out" obligations to private parties because a prosecution is a "public trust"); People ex rel. Peabody v. Attorney General, 13 How. Pr. 179, 183 (N.Y. Sup. Ct. 1856) (rejecting a writ of mandamus seeking to force the prosecutor to bring an action on the application of a private party and stating: "Our legislature have seen fit to invest the attorney general with this discretion. His office is a public trust. It is a legal presumption that he will do his duty—that he will act with strict impartiality. In this confidence he has been endowed with a large discretion, not only in cases like this, but in other matters of public concern. The exercise of such discretion is, in its nature, a judicial act, from which there is no appeal, and over which courts have no control"); Commonwealth v. Burrell, 7 Pa. 34, 39 (Sup. Ct. 1847) ("the office of the attorney-general is a public trust").

56. Daniel Klerman, Settlement and the Decline of Private Prosecution in Thirteenth-Century England, Independent Institute Working Paper #19 (Jan. 2000), p. 2 ("Although modern societies generally entrust enforcement of the criminal law to public prosecutors, most crimes in pre-modern societies were prosecuted privately. In classical Athens, ninth-century Germany, and England before the nineteenth century, there were no public prosecutors for most crimes. Instead, the victim or a relative initiated and litigated the cases."), *available at* https://pdfs.semanticscholar.org/26c7/ec28f280897a2964e6e95b5eb-5391fac47be.pdf.

57. John D. Bessler, *The Anomaly of Executions: The Cruel and Unusual Punishments Clause in the 21st Century*, 2 Brit. J. Am. Legal Stud. 297 (2013); "'Punishment, Penitence, and Reform': Eastern State Penitentiary and the Controversy Over Solitary Confinement," Pa. Heritage (Winter 1999), http://paheri tage.wpengine.com/article/punishment-penitence-reform-eastern-state-penitentiary-controversy

-solitary-confinement/ ("[Z]ealous Quaker reformers convinced Commonwealth officials to impose solitary confinement so that inmates had the opportunity to meditate about their past sins and resolve to live better lives. Every effort was made to isolate prisoners from human contact. When first brought in or transferred within the facility, prisoners wore hoods to prevent their becoming aware of other prisoners or planning escape routes.").

58. Cock, *supra* note 35, at 128; *see also id.* at 147 ("Jefferson observed that some of Bill 64's punishments had precedent in the treatment of slaves. From testimonies, runaway advertisements and other sources, we see slaves marked in a wide variety of ways. Ear-cropping is a recurring one, as is the branding of the master's initials or the letter 'R' for 'runaway' on the face and/or body. A Virginia law of 1699 stipulated that a slave convicted of hog-stealing once would be whipped, and twice would have both ears torn at the pillory."); Erin E. Braatz, *The Eighth Amendment's Milieu: Penal Reform in the Late Eighteenth Century*, 106 J. CRIM. L. & CRIMINOLOGY 405, 429 (2016) (discussing Jefferson's proposal); John D. Bessler, *The Italian Enlightenment and the American Revolution: Cesare Beccaria's Forgotten Influence on American Law*, 37 MITCHELL HAMLINE L.J. PUB. POL'Y & PRAC. 1, 149 (2016) (discussing Jefferson's correspondence with George Wythe in 1778).

59. "United States: Prolonged Solitary Confinement Amounts to Psychological Torture, Says UN Expert," United Nations Human Rights, Office of the High Commissioner, Feb. 28, 2020, https://www.ohchr.org/EN/NewsEvents/Pages/DisplayNews.aspx?NewsID=25633 ("The Mandela Rules, updated in 2015, are a revised minimum standard of UN rules that defines solitary confinement as 'the confinement of prisoners for 22 hours or more a day without meaningful human contact.' Solitary confinement may only be imposed in exceptional circumstances, and 'prolonged' solitary confinement of more than 15 consecutive days is regarded as a form of torture.").

60. *E.g.*, John D. Bessler, *Taking Psychological Torture Seriously: The Torturous Nature of Credible Death Threats and the Collateral Consequences for Capital Punishment*, 11 NE U. L. REV. 1, 35–36 (2019) ("[I]n colonial Massachusetts, in an effort to curtail stealing, a 1736 law subjected thieves to increasing penalties—and escalating threats of death—for each offense. A first-time offender was to be fined or whipped; a second offense required the thief to pay tremble damages, sit upon the gallows platform for an hour with a rope around his neck, and then to receive up to thirty stripes at the whipping post; and, finally, to be hanged for a third offense. 'The colonists' rationale,' one historian notes, 'was clear: anyone impervious to the fine and the whip, who did not mend his ways after an hour with a noose about him, was uncontrollable and therefore had to be executed.' The punishment of sitting on the gallows continued to exist in Massachusetts after the Revolutionary War, though it eventually passed from the scene along with the corporal punishments of branding, whipping, ear cropping, and standing in the pillory.").

61. 481 U.S. 787 (1987).

62. *Young*, 481 U.S. at 805 & nn.14–15; *accord* ABA Standards for Criminal Justice, Standard 3-1.2 (1979) ("A prosecutor should avoid the appearance or reality of a conflict of interest with respect to official duties."); ABA Standards for Criminal Justice, Standard 3-1.2 cmt. (1979) ("It is of utmost importance that the prosecutor avoid participation in a case in circumstances where any implication of partiality may cast a shadow over the integrity of the office."); Model Code of Professional Responsibility Canon 9 (1983) ("A lawyer should avoid even the appearance of professional impropriety."). Although the Model Rules of Professional Conduct do not contain the "appearance of impropriety" language, largely because the drafters of the Model Rules felt the standard was too vague, the principle of Canon 9 is very much alive. First Am. Carriers, Inc. v. Kroger Co., 787 S.W.2d 669, 671–72 (Ark. 1990) ("The fact that Canon 9 is not in the Model Rules does not mean that lawyers no longer have to avoid the appearance of impropriety .... The principle of Canon 9 still applies because its meaning pervades the Rules and embodies their spirit."); *see also* Andrew Kaufman, Problems in Professional Responsibility 54 (2d ed. 1984) (*appearance of impropriety* "evokes the potential erosion of confidence in the profession that may occur if its members are seen in situations that carry the potential for improper conduct even if in particular cases there is no actual misconduct").

63. *Compare* Universal Athletic Sales Co. v. American Gym, Recreational & Athletic Sales Equip. Corp., 546 F.2d 530, 539 (3d Cir. 1976), *cert. denied*, 430 U.S. 984 (1977) (holding that ethical rules regulate attorney conduct but do not "delineate the rules of evidence") *with* United States v. Hammad, 858 F.2d

834, 840 (2d Cir. 1988) (holding that suppression or exclusion of evidence may be a proper remedy for a prosecutor's ethical breach); United States v. Killian, 639 F.2d 206, 210 (5th Cir.), *cert. denied*, 451 U.S. 1021 (1981) (same); United States v. Springer, 460 F.2d 1344, 1353–54 (7th Cir. 1972)_(same); United States v. Lopez, 765 F. Supp. 1433 (N.D. Cal. 1991) (same).

64. *Accord* Wheat v. United States, 486 U.S. 153, 160 (1988) ("Federal courts have an independent interest in ensuring that criminal trials are conducted within the ethical standards of the profession and that legal proceedings appear fair to all who observe them.").

65. *See* Terri L. Braswell, Comment, *Criminal Procedure*—Young v. United States ex rel. Vuittion et Fils S.A.: *The Right to a Disinterested Prosecutor in a Federal Criminal Contempt Proceeding Arising from the Underlying Civil Litigation*, 18 Mem. St. U. L. Rev. 143, 163 (1987) ("A state court might conclude that the appointment of the private, interested attorney does violate fourteenth amendment due process. Arguments for this result are found in the 'harmless error' analysis advanced by the Court in *Young*. Even though the Court's reversal was in reliance upon its supervisory authority to avoid the necessity of reaching the constitutional issues, the Court applied a constitutional standard in deciding that this error could not be considered harmless.") (footnote omitted); *see also id.* at 162 ("A recent trend in state constitutional law is that state courts are frequently interpreting their respective constitutions to 'guarantee rights that the Supreme Court has held that the federal Constitution does not secure.'") (quoting Barbara Kritchevsy, *Justiciability in Tennessee, Part One: Principles and Limits*, 15 Mem. St. U. L. Rev. 1, 1–2 nn.1–2 (1984)).

66. *Young*, 481 U.S. at 808 n.18 (court can exercise its inherent supervisory power to disqualify certain individuals from acting as prosecutors); State v. Marshall, 586 A.2d 85 (N.J. 1991) (court can disqualify prosecutor for "nefarious" interest); *see also* Commonwealth v. Hubbard, 777 S.W.2d 882, 885 (Ky. 1989) (Leibson, J., dissenting) ("we should decide whether the proper performance of the supervisory authority entrusted to us by the Kentucky Constitution" requires the elimination of the use of interested private prosecutors). In addition, courts should use their authority to control who appears before them to prohibit the use of private prosecutors. Chambers v. Nasco, 501 U.S. 32 (1991) (courts have inherent authority "to manage their own affairs so as to achieve the orderly and expeditious disposition of cases," including the authority to control who may appear before the court) (citing Link v. Wabash R. Co., 370 U.S. 626, 630–31 (1962)); *see also* State of New Jersey v. Imperiale, 773 F. Supp. 747, 756 (D. N.J. 1991) (court has inherent authority to control who appears before it); Bartone v. United States, 375 U.S. 52, 54 (1963) (per curiam) (Supreme Court and Courts of Appeals have broad powers of supervision over federal proceedings).

67. As the U.S. Supreme Court has previously acknowledged, certain errors may involve "rights so basic to a fair trial that their infraction can never be treated as harmless error." Gideon v. Wainwright, 372 U.S. 335 (1963) (right to counsel); Tumey v. Ohio, 273 U.S. 510 (1927) (impartial judge).

68. With respect to pre-trial activity, courts should also prohibit private attorneys for interested parties from interfering in the criminal process. For example, as the Supreme Court of Appeals of West Virginia held in *Kerns v. Wolverton*, a private attorney for an interested party should not be allowed to appear before or participate in a grand jury proceeding. The *Kerns* court stated that "the presence of a private prosecutor in a grand jury room is inconsistent with the traditional view that the grand jury should be impartial and independent, and thus free of even the possibility that outside pressure or influence will infiltrate the process." Kerns v. Wolverton, 381 S.E.2d 258, 262 (W. Va. 1989); *see also* id. (footnote omitted) ("Obviously, the presence of a private prosecutor before a grand jury could only serve to enhance the public perception that a grand jury is an instrument controlled by the desires of the prosecution."). As one prominent legal encyclopedia observed way back in 1968: "The presence and participation in general jury proceedings of a person assuming the role of a private prosecutor, retained by outside interests for the purpose of obtaining an indictment against particular individuals, is generally considered highly improper." 38 Am. Jur.2d *Grand Jury* § 35 (1968) (quoted in *Kerns*, 381 S.E.2d at 261); *see also* Nichols v. State, 87 S.E. 817 (Ga. App. 1916) (same); Flege v. State, 142 N.W. 276 (Neb. 1913) (same); Cantrell v. Commonwealth, 329 S.E.2d 22, 25 (Va. 1985) (same); In re Grand Jury Appearance Request by Loigman, 870 A.2d 249, 256 (N.J. 2005) ("Unlike private citizens, prosecutors are guided and governed by the Rules of Professional Conduct and our case law to ensure fairness in the process. For example, prosecutors are forbidden from 'prosecuting a charge that the prosecutor knows is not supported by probable cause.' *RPC* 3.8(a). They must present exculpatory evidence and may not mislead the grand jury by allowing the telling of a "'half-truth'"

or "a distorted version of the facts." *Hogan, supra,* 144 *N.J.* at 236, 676 *A.*2d 533. The prosecutor's 'primary duty' is 'to see that justice is done....' *State v. Frost,* 158 *N.J.* 76, 83, 727 *A.*2d 1 (1999) (quotations omitted). A prosecutor is enjoined from using 'improper methods calculated to produce a wrongful conviction....' *Ibid.* (quotations omitted). Those principles of fairness are particularly important in a grand jury setting in which the prosecutor questions witnesses, introduces evidence, and explains the law to the jurors without a judge or defense attorney in attendance.").

69. In *Young,* the U.S. Supreme Court stated in dicta that a private party's attorney's "familiarity" with the underlying facts "may be put to use in assisting a disinterested prosecutor in pursuing the contempt action, but cannot justify permitting counsel for the private party to be in control of the prosecution." *Young,* 481 U.S. at 807 n.17. This language should not be construed to allow an interested party's attorney to participate in a criminal proceeding or prosecute a criminal case, with the only requirement being that the attorney play a subordinate role to that of the public prosecutor. Instead, the "assist" language should be read narrowly, allowing an interested party's attorney only to familiarize the public prosecutor with his or her version of the facts consistent with the party's First Amendment rights. A private attorney should not be allowed to "assist" the public prosecutor with any aspect of the criminal process because of the discretionary and unreviewable nature of prosecutors' work.

70. Obviously, prosecutorial misconduct or the misuse of prosecutorial discretion hinders the discovery of truth, which is the primary function of the court and the fundamental purpose of the adversary system. *E.g.,* United States v. Havens, 446 U.S. 620 (1980).

71. Some constitutional errors create "structural defects in the constitution of the trial mechanism, which defy analysis by 'harmless-error' standards." Arizona v. Fulminante, 499 U.S. 279, 319 (1991). "The existence of such defects—deprivation of the right to counsel, for example—requires automatic reversal of the conviction because they infect the entire trial process." Brecht v. Abrahamsom, 507 U.S. 619, 629–30 (1993).

72. *See* Kerns v. Wolverton, 381 S.E.2d 258, 262 (W. Va. 1989). *But cf.* Scheldberger v. State, 235 N.W. 419 (Wis. 1931) (although private prosecutors are not permitted under Wisconsin law, a private attorney was allowed to take witnesses' statements and do investigatory work). Significantly, the Fourth Amendment freedom from unreasonable searches and seizures by the State does not apply to actions by private individuals. Mapp v. Ohio, 367 U.S. 643 (1961); *see also* United States v. Jacobsen, 466 U.S. 109, 113 (1984); Coolidge v. New Hampshire, 403 U.S. 443 (1971); Burdeau v. McDowell, 256 U.S. 465, 467 (1921); United States v. Andrews, 618 F.2d 646, 648–52 (10th Cir. 1980); United States v. Winbush, 428 F.2d 357, 359 (6th Cir. 1970); People v. Randazzo, 34 Cal. Rptr. 65, 69–71 (Cal. App. 1963); People v. Moreno, 135 Cal. Rptr. 340, 342 (Sup. Ct. 1976); State v. Clark, 454 So. 2d 232, 234–37 (La. App. 1984); District Attorney for Plymouth District, 434 N.E.2d 1276, 1279 (Mass. 1982); Waters v. State, 575 A.2d 1244, 1246 (Md. 1990); State v. Jenkins, 259 N.W.2d 109, 111–12 (Wis. 1977). Accordingly, "when a private individual obtains incriminating matter from an accused, no matter how improperly, and such matter comes into the possession of the government without a violation of the accused's rights by government authority, the exclusionary rule does not prohibit its use at trial." *Waters,* 575 A.2d at 1246; State v. Von Bulow, 475 A.2d 995, 1012 (R.I. 1984); *see also* Colorado v. Connelly, 479 U.S. 157, 166 (1986) ("The most outrageous behavior by a private party seeking to secure evidence against a defendant does not make that evidence inadmissible under the Due Process Clause."); State v. Clark, 743 P.2d 822, 826 (Wash. App. 1987). A private search or seizure only triggers Fourth Amendment protections if the private individual whose actions are in question, "in light of all the circumstances of the case, must be regarded as having acted as an 'instrument' or agent of the state." *Coolidge,* 403 U.S. at 487. To be an instrument or agent of the state, a private party must be involved directly as a participant in the search or indirectly as an "encourager" or instigator of the private citizen's actions. United States v. Walther, 652 F.2d 788, 791 (9th Cir. 1981); *Clark,* 743 P.2d at 826. A government may not exceed the scope of a private search unless it has the right to make an independent search. Walter v. United States, 447 U.S. 649, 657 (1980); *Von Bulow,* 475 A.2d at 1018.

73. Under existing law, prosecutors enjoy absolute immunity from section 1983 lawsuits, so it is particularly hard to hold prosecutors accountable for misconduct. Van de Kamp v. Goldstein, 555 U.S. 335, 340–41 (2009) ("Over a half century ago Chief Judge Learned Hand explained that a prosecutor's absolute immunity reflects 'a balance" of "evils.' *Gregoire v. Biddle,* 177 F.2d 579, 581 (C.A.2 1949). '[I]t has been

thought in the end better,' he said, 'to leave unredressed the wrongs done by dishonest officers than to subject those who try to do their duty to the constant dread of retaliation.' *Ibid.* In *Imbler, supra,* this Court considered prosecutorial actions that are 'intimately associated with the judicial phase of the criminal process.' *Id.*, at 430, 96 S. Ct. 984. And, referring to Chief Judge Hand's views, it held that prosecutors are absolutely immune from liability in § 1983 lawsuits brought under such circumstances. *Id.*, at 428, 96 S. Ct. 984."). *But see* Van de Kamp v. Goldstein, 555 U.S. 335, 342 (2009) ("The Court made clear that absolute immunity may not apply when a prosecutor is not acting as 'an officer of the court,' but is instead engaged in other tasks, say, investigative or administrative tasks.") (citation omitted); *id.* at 343 ("In the years since *Imbler,* we have held that absolute immunity applies when a prosecutor prepares to initiate a judicial proceeding, *Burns, supra,* at 492, 111 S. Ct. 1934, or appears in court to present evidence in support of a search warrant application, *Kalina, supra,* at 126, 118 S. Ct. 502. We have held that absolute immunity does not apply when a prosecutor gives advice to police during a criminal investigation, see *Burns, supra,* at 496, 111 S. Ct. 1934, when the prosecutor makes statements to the press, *Buckley v. Fitzsimmons,* 509 U.S. 259, 277, 113 S. Ct. 2606, 125 L.Ed.2d 209 (1993), or when a prosecutor acts as a complaining witness in support of a warrant application, *Kalina, supra,* at 132, 118 S. Ct. 502 (Scalia, J., concurring). This case, unlike these earlier cases, requires us to consider how immunity applies where a prosecutor is engaged in certain administrative activities."); *Van de Kamp*, 555 U.S. at 346 ("Once we determine that supervisory prosecutors are immune in a suit directly attacking their actions related to an individual trial, we must find they are similarly immune in the case before us."); *id.* at 348 ("We recognize, as Chief Judge Hand pointed out, that sometimes such immunity deprives a plaintiff of compensation that he undoubtedly merits; but the impediments to the fair, efficient functioning of a prosecutorial office that liability could create lead us to find that *Imbler* must apply here.").

74. A criminal defendant's constitutional rights are not affected by the pre-trial activity of a private attorney who is not acting at the request of a public prosecutor. This rule recognizes that a public prosecutor has no control over private attorneys or private investigators. However, evidence obtained through private means must remain subject to the usual constitutional rules once it is turned over to the prosecutor's office. *See Von Bulow*, 475 A.2d at 1012 (when the government significantly expands a prior private search without first procuring a search warrant and no recognized exception to the warrant requirement exists to justify such expansion, the independent governmental search is subject to the proscriptions of the Fourth Amendment).

75. *See* Kerns v. Wolverton, 381 S.E.2d 258, 262 (W. Va. 1989).

76. Felix Frankfurter, Felix Frankfurter Reminisces 72 (1960).

77. *See generally* Michael Mello, Against the Death Penalty: The Relentless Dissents of Justices Brennan and Marshall (1996).

78. Imbler v. Pachtman, 424 U.S. 409, 438 (1976) (White, J., concurring) (citations omitted).

79. *Id.* at 423 n.20 (citations omitted).

80. *Id.* at 422–23. Comparing judges and prosecutors, the U.S. Supreme Court in another case, *Butz v. Economou* (1978), had this to say on the subject of immunity: "Judges have absolute immunity not because of their particular location within the Government but because of the special nature of their responsibilities. This point is underlined by the fact that prosecutors—themselves members of the Executive Branch—are also absolutely immune." Butz v. Economou, 438 U.S. 478, 511–12 (1978). *Compare* Marshall v. Jerrico, 446 U.S. 238, 248–52 (1980):

> The rigid requirements of *Tumey* and *Ward,* designed for officials performing judicial or quasi-judicial functions, are not applicable to those acting in a prosecutorial or plaintiff-like capacity. Our legal system has traditionally accorded wide discretion to criminal prosecutors in the enforcement process, see *Linda R. S. v. Richard D.,* 410 U.S. 614, 93 S. Ct. 1146, 35 L.Ed.2d 793 (1973), and similar considerations have been found applicable to administrative prosecutors as well, see *Moog Industries, Inc. v. FTC,* 355 U.S. 411, 414, 78 S. Ct. 377, 380, 2 L.Ed.2d 370 (1958); *Vaca v. Sipes,* 386 U.S. 171, 182, 87 S. Ct. 903, 912, 17 L.Ed.2d 842, (1967). Prosecutors need not be entirely "neutral and detached," cf. *Ward v. Village of Monroeville,* 409 U.S., at 62, 93 S.Ct., at 84. In an adversary system, they are necessarily permitted to be zealous in their enforcement of the law. The constitutional interests in accurate finding of facts and application of law, and in preserving

a fair and open process for decision, are not to the same degree implicated if it is the prosecutor, and not the judge, who is offered an incentive for securing civil penalties. The distinction between judicial and nonjudicial officers was explicitly made in *Tumey,* 273 U.S., at 535, 47 S.Ct., at 445, where the Court noted that a state legislature "may, and often ought to, stimulate prosecutions for crime by offering to those who shall initiate and carry on such prosecutions rewards for thus acting in the interest of the state and the people." See also *Hortonville School Dist. v. Hortonville Ed. Assn.,* 426 U.S. 482, 495, 96 S.Ct. 2308, 2315, 49 L.Ed.2d 1 (1976)

We do not suggest, and appellants do not contend, that the Due Process Clause imposes no limits on the partisanship of administrative prosecutors. Prosecutors are also public officials; they too must serve the public interest. *Berger v. United States,* 295 U.S. 78, 88, 55 S.Ct. 629, 633, 79 L.Ed. 1314 (1935). In appropriate circumstances the Court has made clear that traditions of prosecutorial discretion do not immunize from judicial scrutiny cases in which the enforcement decisions of an administrator were motivated by improper factors or were otherwise contrary to law. See *Dunlop v. Bachowski,* 421 U.S. 560, 567, n. 7, 568–574, 95 S. Ct. 1851, 1858, n. 7, 1858–1861, 44 L.Ed.2d 377 (1975); *Rochester Telephone Corp. v. United States,* 307 U.S. 125, 59 S. Ct. 754, 83 L.Ed. 1147 (1939). Moreover, the decision to enforce—or not to enforce—may itself result in significant burdens on a defendant or a statutory beneficiary, even if he is ultimately vindicated in an adjudication. Cf. 2 K. Davis Administrative Law Treatise 215–256 (2d ed. 1979). A scheme injecting a personal interest, financial or otherwise, into the enforcement process may bring irrelevant or impermissible factors into the prosecutorial decision and in some contexts raise serious constitutional questions. See *Bordenkircher v. Hayes,* 434 U.S. 357, 365, 98 S. Ct. 663, 669, 54 L.Ed.2d 604 (1978); cf. 28 U.S.C. § 528 (1976 ed., Supp. III) (disqualifying federal prosecutor from participating in litigation in which he has a personal interest). But the strict requirements of neutrality cannot be the same for administrative prosecutors as for judges, whose duty it is to make the final decision and whose impartiality serves as the ultimate guarantee of a fair and meaningful proceeding in our constitutional regime.

In this case, we need not say with precision what limits there may be on a financial or personal interest of one who performs a prosecutorial function, for here the influence alleged to impose bias is exceptionally remote. No governmental official stands to profit economically from vigorous enforcement of the child labor provisions of the Act. The salary of the assistant regional administrator is fixed by law. 5 U.S.C. § 5332 (1976 ed. and Supp. III). The pressures relied on in such cases as *Tumey v. Ohio, supra; Gibson v. Berryhill,* 411 U.S. 564, 579, 93 S.Ct. 1689, 1698, 36 L.Ed.2d 488 (1973); and *Connally v. Georgia,* 429 U.S. 245, 250, 97 S.Ct. 546, 548, 50 L.Ed.2d 444 (1977) (*per curiam*), are entirely absent here.

Nor is there a realistic possibility that the assistant regional administrator's judgment will be distorted by the prospect of institutional gain as a result of zealous enforcement efforts. As we have noted, the civil penalties collected under § 16(e) represent substantially less that 1% of the budget of the ESA. In each of the relevant years, the amount of the ESA's budget that was returned to the Treasury was substantially greater than the amount collected as civil penalties. Unlike in *Ward* and *Tumey,* it is plain that the enforcing agent is in no sense financially dependent on the maintenance of a high level of penalties. Furthermore, since it is the national office of the ESA, and not any assistant regional administrator, that decides how to allocate civil penalties, such administrators have no assurance that the penalties they assess will be returned to their offices at all. See *Dugan v. Ohio,* 277 U.S. 61, 48 S. Ct. 439, 72 L.Ed. 784 (1928).

Moreover, the ESA's administration of the Act has minimized any potential for bias. In the only year in which the ESA elected to allocate part of the civil penalties to the regional offices, it did so in proportion to the expenses incurred in investigating and prosecuting child labor violations, not on the basis of the amounts of penalties collected. Thus, even if an assistant regional administrator were to act on the assumption that civil penalties would be returned to his office in any given year, his decision to assess an unjustifiable large penalty in a particular case would be of no benefit to his office, since that decision would not produce an increase in the level of expenses.

The District Court's conclusion that the reimbursement provision violated the Due Process Clause was evidently premised on its perception that an assistant regional administrator might be tempted to devote an unusually large quantity of resources to enforcement efforts in the hope that he would ultimately obtain a higher total allocation of federal funds to his office. This increase in enforcement effort, the court suggested, might incline the assistant regional administrator to assess an unjustified number of penalties, and to make those penalties unduly high. But in light of the factors discussed above, it is clear that this possibility is too remote to violate the constraints applicable to the financial or personal interest of officials charged with prosecutorial or plaintiff-like functions. In order to produce the predicted result, the ESA would be required to decide to allocate civil penalties to regional offices; the sums allocated to the particular regional office would have to exceed any amount of that office's budget returned to the Treasury at the end of the fiscal year; the assistant regional administrator would have to receive authorization from his superiors to expend additional funds to increase his enforcement expenditures to the desired level; the increased expenditures would have to result in an increase in penalties; and the administrative law judge and reviewing courts would have to accept or ratify the assistant regional administrator's assessments. "[U]nder a realistic appraisal of psychological tendencies and human weakness," *Withrow v. Larkin*, 421 U.S. 35, 47, 95 S.Ct. 1456, 1464, 43 L.Ed.2d 712 (1975), it is exceedingly improbable that the assistant regional administrator's enforcement decisions would be distorted by some expectation that all of these contingencies would simultaneously come to fruition. We are thus unable to accept appellee's contention that, on this record and as presently administered, the reimbursement provision violates standards of procedural fairness embodied in the Due Process Clause.

The judgment of the District Court is reversed, and the case is remanded to that court for further proceedings consistent with this opinion.

81. Annual Report of the Attorney-General of the United States for the Year 1903, at 386 (1903). In America, judicial review of applications by private parties alleging criminal conduct still takes place in some locales. *See, e.g.*, In re Rega, Private Criminal Complaint, No. 657 WDA 2020, 2021 WL 2774963, at *3 (Pa. Super. Ct. July 1, 2021) ("We are constrained to reject the characterization of the District Attorney's disapproval as a policy determination. Here, the private criminal complaint clearly states that it was disapproved because it 'lacks evidence.' Private Criminal Complaint. The District Attorney did not elaborate on its decision with any type of policy reasoning. Therefore, on its face the phrase describes a solely legal conclusion based on an evaluation of the evidence. The record contains no grounds to perceive the phrase as anything other than a legal determination. That conclusion is subject to *de novo* review."); *id.* ("Accordingly, we remand to the trial court for it to determine, based on a de novo review, whether the District Attorney reached a proper legal conclusion when it disapproved Rega's private criminal complaint because it lacked evidence."). However, in today's world, it is, by and large, *disinterested* public prosecutors who are expected to evaluate the facts and the law and to make the decisions as to who, if anyone, will be prosecuted for conduct or behavior and on what charges. *E.g.*, Robert Leider, *The Modern Common Law of Crime*, 111 J. Crim. L. & Criminology 407, 457 (2021) ("[P]ublic prosecutors likely maintain their monopoly over criminal prosecutions because we expect them not to prosecute trivial or blameless cases. In early America, private prosecutors brought most criminal complaints. One familiar quasi-criminal mode of prosecution was the *qui tam* suit, in which a private informer split the penalty with the government. But private prosecutions produced undesirably high levels of enforcement, and they have been largely abandoned.") (italics in original).

Interested private prosecutions that may result in death, imprisonment or the stigma of a criminal charge or conviction are especially problematic in America's justice system not only because of what is at stake (life, liberty, or other adverse consequences), but because governmental power—in particular, prosecutorial power—should be exercised by *impartial*, not *interested*, actors. That is especially true in the twenty-first century now that America's public prosecution system is so well established and interested private prosecutions are relatively rare. *Cf.* Jonathan Remy Nash, *Nontraditional Criminal Prosecutions in Federal Court*, 53 Ariz. St. L.J. 143, 159 (2021) ("The eighteenth and nineteenth centuries witnessed a significant volume of state criminal private prosecutions. A few states today retain the possibility of private prosecutions for low-level crimes. On the federal side of the ledger, private parties do not have the general power to pursue criminal prosecution. However, there is some historical evidence that private parties in the early Republic may have had the chance to play some role in starting federal criminal proceedings, 'including directly appealing to grand juries.'"); *id.* at 168 ("[T]he power of federal courts to appoint private attorneys to prosecute contempt of court passes muster. It is critical to bear in mind, however, that such private prosecutions are sui generis: They arise in this narrow context out of the inherent power of the federal courts to protect their authority and legitimacy."); *id.* at 196 ("[P]otentially problematic for private criminal plaintiffs' standing is an argument advanced by Chief Justice Roberts in an opinion—joined by three other Justices—dissenting from the Supreme Court's 2010 dismissal of certiorari as improvidently granted. *Robertson v. United States ex rel. Watson* involved a private criminal contempt prosecution under local D.C. law by a woman against her ex-boyfriend John Robertson for violation of a civil protective order she had obtained against him. Robertson argued that the private prosecution violated a plea agreement into which he had entered with the U.S. Attorney's Office, the entity responsible for local prosecutions in the District of Columbia. He pleaded guilty to an aggravated assault charge, and in return the U.S. Attorney's Office agreed to dismiss other charges and not to bring other charges arising out of the same incident. When the local D.C. courts upheld Robertson's conviction under the private prosecution, Robertson sought review by the United States Supreme Court. The Court initially granted review on the question of whether, in pursuing her private criminal prosecution, Watson acted in her own personal interest or instead on behalf of the government but subsequently dismissed the writ of certiorari as improvidently granted."); *id.* at 196–97 ("Writing in dissent from the dismissal of the writ of certiorari, Chief Justice Roberts argued that, whoever the prosecutor, criminal prosecutions only can be undertaken on behalf of, and as an exercise of the power of, the government. Chief Justice Roberts conceded the historical practice of so-called private prosecutions but found their existence not inconsistent with the notion that they, like typical publicly administered prosecutions, are brought on the government's behalf.").

Ultimately, the delegation of prosecutorial power to interested private parties corrupts the criminal justice process. *E.g.*, Johnson v. Vederman, Nos. 1 CA-SA 17-0105, 1 CA-SA 17-0111 & 1 CA-SA-17-0112 (Consolidated), 2017 WL 2438059, at *2 (Ariz. Ct. App. June 6, 2017) ("In the usual case, discretionary decision-making inherent in the power to prosecute may not be delegated to unelected private counsel. To the contrary, important due-process rights are implicated when an elected prosecutor cedes all control over a prosecution to a private lawyer.") (citations omitted); *id.* at *3 ("[W]hen all responsibility for the prosecution of a criminal matter is ceded to an unelected special prosecutor, the resulting lack of accountability infringes the due-process rights of the accused, regardless of whether the special prosecutor is working for free. In such a case, the accused is deprived of his or her due-process right to prosecution … of an elected officer who owes 'a special and enduring duty to 'seek justice.''") (citation omitted); People v. Smakaj, No. 03867-2008, 28 Misc.3d 1201(A), 2010 WL 2574051 (N.Y, Sup. Ct., Bronx County, June 14, 2010) (where the New York Legal Assistance Group (NYLAG) brought a motion to file a notice of appearance on behalf of the complaining witness, Mimoza Smakaj, in a criminal case being handled by the Bronx County District Attorney in which the defendant was charged with second-degree attempted murder and other related charges pertaining to the stabbing of Smakaj, the court denied that motion; in that case, the public prosecutor contended that "[t]he job and discretion of a prosecutor can't be delegated to private citizens" and, after Judge Miriam R. Best observed in the case that the NYLAG had "made a similar application before the Honorable Matthew J. D'Emic, in the case of *People v. Robinson*, 898 N.Y.S.2 438, 2010 WL 1254666, 2010 N.Y. Slip Op 29112 (Sup Ct Kings County 2010), which was also opposed by the People and by defendant," the court in *People v. Smakaj* determined that "Judge D'Emic … cogently stated in *Robinson*": "To allow the entry of a private interest, even the interest of an honest and aggrieved victim into this process [involving investigation, prosecution, negotiation of plea bargains, recommendations as to punishment, and decisions whether to seek, oppose, accept, appeal or challenge judicial rulings and actions] could expose all of those areas to intolerable prejudicial influence, where the participant in the prosecution is the servant of his or her interests and not exclusively 'the servant of the law, the twofold aim of which is that guilt shall not escape or innocence suffer.'") (quoting Berger v. United States, 295 U.S. 78 (1935)); *see also* People v. Robinson, 898 N.Y.S.2 438, 439-40, 2010 WL 1254666, 2010 N.Y. Slip Op 29112 (Sup. Ct. Kings County 2010) (noting in the context of a first-degree rape prosecution where the NYLAG moved to file a notice of appearance to formally represent the complaining witness, J.R.: "In this application, NYLAG seeks to allow a private individual to become a party to a criminal prosecution and, in effect, allow her to assert rights and impose obligations on the People, the defendant and the court, based upon her interests in this criminal prosecution.... [T]he law of this state obligates the district attorney of each county 'to prosecute all crimes and offenses cognizable to the courts of the county for which he shall be elected...' The courts of this state have interpreted these provisions to bar private prosecutions of crimes and the delegation of this duty.... The only parties to criminal ligation in this state are the people, represented by the district attorney of the county, and the accused, represented by assigned or retained counsel. This is sound public policy and prevents much mischief.") (citations omitted).

Much has been written—and in a variety of ways and from a variety of perspectives—about the delegation of governmental powers, including prosecutorial power, to private entities or individuals. *Compare* Harold J. Krent, *The Private Performing the Public: Delimiting Delegations to Private Parties*, 65 U. Miami L. Rev. 507, 524–25 (2011) ("Delegation to private entities masks that chain of command. Indeed, the very notion of private exercise of governmental power contradicts our supposition of what is meant by 'government': 'One can have a government... that benefits from expertise without being ruled by experts.' Scholars across a wide spectrum of ideologies agree that the Constitution does not empower governmental officials to offload governmental powers to private entities that could in turn exercise those powers outside the constraints faced by public actors. Indeed, in the criminal law context, Chief Justice Roberts recently commented that delegations to private parties should be prohibited because '[a] basic step in organizing a civilized society is to take that sword out of private hands and turn it over to an organized government, acting on behalf of all the people.' The constitutional framework does not countenance delegation of at least some type of governmental authority to private individuals and groups.") *and* Aaron Gordon, *Nondelegation*, 12 N.Y.U. J. L. & Liberty 718, 817–18 (2019) ("One proposal is to revive the robust form of the Nondelegation Doctrine only in the criminal context. Justice Gorsuch has spoken favorably about such an approach, remarking that it is 'easy enough to see why a stricter [nondelegation] rule would apply in the criminal arena. The criminal conviction and sentence represent the ultimate intrusions on personal liberty and carry with them the stigma of the community's collective condemnation—something quite different than holding someone liable for a money judgment because he turns out to be the lowest cost avoider.' This proposal is not without historical support. Madison's 1799 committee report on the Alien Act seemed especially concerned about delegations of the power to issue rules backed by criminal penalties: 'the powers referred to [the executive] department[] may be so general and undefined, as to be of a legislative, not of an executive or judicial nature; and may for that reason be unconstitutional. Details, to a certain degree, are essential to the nature and character of a law; and, *on criminal subjects*, it is proper, that details should leave as little as possible to the discretion of those who are to apply and to execute the law.' The Supreme Court has explicitly left open the question of whether Congress has less latitude to delegate powers in the criminal context. And at least two states' judiciaries hold that their state constitutions impose greater restrictions on delegations of power to define crimes."), *with* Alexander "Sasha" Volokh, *The Shadow Debate Over Private Nondelegation in* Dot v. Association of American Railroads, 2015 Cato Sup. Ct. Rev. 359, 371–72 ("[A] delegation of governmental power to religious groups can violate the Establishment Clause. An excessively vague delegation of power to courts and juries to determine what acts are criminal violates the Fifth and Sixth Amendments. A delegation of 'private attorney general' power to a *qui tam* plaintiff might violate the Appointments Clause. And a delegation of regulatory power to self-interested private parties could also violate the Due Process Clause."); Roger A. Fairfax, Jr., *Delegation of the Criminal Prosecution Function to Private Parties*, 43 U.C. Davis L. Rev. 411, 413 (2009) (arguing that "delegating the prosecution function to private lawyers presents the potential for conflicts of interest and corruption" and "the erosion of due process"); *and* Civ. Qui Tam Actions 7366224 (C.C.H.), 2020 WL 7366224, § 4.11 *Constitutionality of the Relator's Role* ("*Qui tam* provisions also have been challenged on the basis that they violate the Due Process Clause of the Constitution.... The primary due process concern raised by *qui tam* litigation revolves around the bounty provisions of the FCA [False Claims Act]. Those who represent the government in litigation must seek a just and fair result, an obligation not imposed on private litigators whose primary ethical obligation is to zealously pursue their client's interests. The *qui tam* percentage shares of recoveries give a relator a financial *incentive* to maximize the reward that will unavoidably conflict with the pursuit of evenhanded justice. While many of the judicial precedents disapproving interested government prosecutors involve criminal or quasi-criminal actions, their holdings may be relevant to the FCA. A body of case law holds that the Act is penal rather than remedial, and it is the penal nature of a statute, rather than its superficial classification as criminal or civil, that triggers heightened due process protections.").

Just as private parties—as a matter of constitutional law—must not be allowed to obstruct or impede women's constitutional rights under *Roe v. Wade*, enter into or judicially enforce unconstitutional and highly offensive racially restrictive covenants, or even veto a bar's liquor license application, interested private parties should not be handed prosecutorial power to wield as they see fit in violation of defendants' due process and equal protection rights. *See, e.g.*, Jacyln Diaz, *The Justice Department Wants a Federal Judge to Block Texas' New Abortion Ban, NPR, Sept. 15, 2021*, https://www.npr.org/2021/09/15/1037224086/the-justice-department-wants-a-federal-judge-to-block-texas-new-abortion-ban ("In court documents, attorneys for the Justice Department said Texas' law, also called SB 8, is unconstitutional and cannot stand."); Laurence H. Tribe, *Opinion: What the Justice Department Should Do to Stop the Texas Abortion Law*, WASH. POST, Sept. 5, 2021, https://www.washingtonpost.com/opinions/2021/09/05/justice-department-stop-texas-abortion-law-laurence-tribe/ ("The Texas legislature and five Supreme Court justices have joined forces to eviscerate women's abortion rights—the legislature by creating and the justices by leaving in place a system of private bounties designed to intimidate all who would help women exercise the right to choose. But the federal government has—and should use—its own powers, including criminal prosecution, to prevent the law from being enforced and to reduce its chilling effects."); Erwin Chemerinsky, "*Roe v. Wade* Hasn't Been Overturned. The Rule of Law Might Have Been." WASH. POST, Sept. 2, 2021, https://www.washingtonpost.com/outlook/2021/09/02/roe-overturn-texas-constitution/ ("The Texas law at issue now, in clear violation of Roe, prohibits abortions after a fetal heartbeat can be detected, at around the sixth week of pregnancy, a time before many women even know that they are pregnant and many weeks earlier than science has found that a fetus would be viable.... Beyond that, to thwart the Constitution—the highest law in the land—the Texas law enlists private citizens (even those with no connection to a woman seeking an abortion) to enforce its unconstitutional ban by giving them the right to sue anyone who performs an abortion after about six weeks of pregnancy, with an award of at least $10,000 for successful suits. In effect, in Texas, there is now a bounty on many of those exercising their constitutional right to choose to have an abortion, but the court's majority said nothing in defense of the Constitution, or its own role in enforcing it.... The appropriate action in the current case, *Whole Woman's Health v. Jackson*, would have been for the court's justices to enjoin the Texas law from going into effect...."); Whole Woman's Health v. Jackson, 2021 WL 3910722, at *1 (U.S. Sept. 1, 2021) (Roberts, C.J., dissenting) ("The statutory scheme before the Court is not only unusual, but unprecedented. The legislature has imposed a prohibition on abortions after roughly six weeks, and then essentially delegated enforcement of that prohibition to the populace at large. The desired consequence appears to be to insulate the State from responsibility for implementing and enforcing the regulatory regime."); *id.* at *2 (Breyer, J., dissenting) ("I agree with THE CHIEF JUSTICE, Justice SOTOMAYOR, and Justice KAGAN. Texas's law delegates to private individuals the power to prevent a woman from obtaining an abortion during the first stage of pregnancy. But a woman has a federal constitutional right to obtain an abortion during that first stage. *Planned Parenthood of Southeastern Pa. v. Casey*, 505 U.S. 833, 846, 112 S. Ct. 2791, 120 L.Ed.2d 674 (1992); *Roe v. Wade*, 410 U.S. 113, 164, 93 S. Ct. 705, 35 L.Ed.2d 147 (1973). And a 'State cannot delegate... a veto power [over the right to obtain an abortion] which the state itself is absolutely and totally prohibited from exercising during the first trimester of pregnancy.' *Planned Parenthood of Central Mo. v. Danforth*, 428 U.S. 52, 69, 96 S. Ct. 2831, 49 L.Ed.2d 788 (1976) (internal quotation marks omitted). Indeed, we have made clear that 'since the State cannot regulate or proscribe abortion during the first stage... the State cannot delegate authority to any particular person... to prevent abortion during the same period.' *Ibid.* The applicants persuasively argue that Texas's law does precisely that."); Shelley v. Kraemer, 334 U.S. 1, 20 (1948) ("We hold that in granting judicial enforcement of the restrictive agreements in these cases, the States have denied petitioners the equal protection of the laws and that, therefore, the action of the state courts cannot stand. We have noted that freedom from discrimination by the States in the enjoyment of property rights was among the basic objectives sought to be effectuated by the framers of the Fourteenth Amendment. That such discrimination has occurred in these cases is clear. Because of the race or color of these petitioners they have been denied rights of ownership or occupancy enjoyed as a matter of course by other citizens of different race or color."); Larkin v. Grendel's Den, Inc., 459 U.S. 116, 122 (1982) ("As the Massachusetts Supreme Judicial Court concluded, § 16C [of Chapter 138 of the Massachusetts General Laws vesting in the bodies of schools and churches the power to prevent issuance of liquor licenses for premises within a 500-foot radius of the school or church by objection] delegates to private, nongovernmental entities power to veto certain liquor license applications. This is a power ordinarily vested in agencies of government."); *id.* at 125 ("The churches' power under the statute is standardless, calling for no reasons, findings, or reasoned conclusions. That power may therefore be used by churches to promote goals beyond insulating the church from undesirable neighbors; it could be employed for explicitly religious goals, for example, favoring liquor licenses for members of that congregation or adherents of that faith."); *id.* at 127 ("The Framers did not set up a system of government in which important, discretionary governmental powers would be delegated to or shared with religious institutions."); *id.* ("Section 16C substitutes the unilateral and absolute power of a church for the reasoned decisionmaking of a public legislative body acting on evidence and guided by standards, on issues with significant economic and political implications. The challenged statute thus enmeshes churches in the processes of government, and creates the danger of '[p]olitical fragmentation and divisiveness on religious lines.' Ordinary human experience and a long line of cases teach that few entanglements could be more offensive to the spirit of the Constitution."); Brian Hutler, *Religious Arbitration and the Establishment Clause*, 33 Ohio St. J. On Disp. Resol. 337, 340 (2018) ("The origin of the nondelegation doctrine is *Larkin v. Grendel's Den*, in which the Supreme Court struck down a state law granting churches the power to veto liquor licenses on the grounds that the law was an impermissible delegation of the government's authority to religious institutions."). It is one thing for a legislative body to authorize a civil litigant to enforce, say, the provisions of a consumer protection statute or a law forbidding anticompetitive conduct, but private parties should never be permitted to infringe upon another person's constitutional rights (such as the right to obtain an abortion under the authority of *Roe v. Wade*).

In the context of the criminal law, the U.S. Supreme Court should recognize a constitutional right to a *disinterested* prosecutor and outlaw interested private prosecutions at the next available opportunity. *Compare* Madgett v. United States, Case No. 19-CV-630-NJR, 2021 WL 1263903, at *7 (S.D. Ill. Apr. 6, 2021) ("In *Young v. U.S. ex rel. Vuitton et Fils S.A.*, 481 U.S. 787 (1987), the Supreme Court explained the 'requirement of a disinterested prosecutor,' and in its discussion relied on case law applying federal constitutional principles. However, the majority did not establish any constitutional standards—but relied on its supervisory authority over the lower federal courts because the matter concerned review of the federal district court's appointment of an attorney to prosecute criminal contempt.") (citations omitted); United States v. Quiros, Case No. 5:19-cr-76, 2020 WL 519807, at *11 (D. Vt. Jan. 28, 2020) ("[D]ue process does require a 'disinterested' prosecutor, but the requirements for prosecutors are different than the requirements for judges and juries."); Crowe v. Smith, 151 F.3d 217, 227–28 (5th Cir. 1998) (rights of insurance company and counsel were violated when district court failed to appoint disinterested prosecutor in disciplinary proceeding but instead appointed attorney who represented plaintiffs in RICO action; "where criminal contempt is involved, there must actually be an independent prosecutor of some kind, because the district court is not constitutionally competent to fulfill that role on its own") (italics in original); *and* United States v. Siegelman, Case No. 2:05-CR-119 (CDL), 2014 WL 12839185, at *4 (Dec. 18, 2014) ("It is indisputable that a defendant in a criminal prosecution is entitled to an impartial, disinterested prosecutor who does not have a personal financial interest in the prosecution.") (citing *Young*, 481 U.S. at 803-04, 809-10), *with Madgett*, 2021 WL 1263903, at *7 n. 4 (noting that "[o]ther courts have recognized a due process right to a disinterested prosecutor"); State v. Villanueva, 488 P.3d 680, 690 (N.M. Ct. App. 2021) ("The purpose of the Supreme Court's requirement for appointment of the district attorney to prosecute criminal contempt is part of the Court's effort to ensure that due process is provided. Prosecution by an independent, disinterested prosecutor protects the defendant's right to a fair trial."); In re Taylor, 73 A.3d 85, 89 (D.C. Ct. App. 2013) ("To satisfy due process guarantees, any court-appointed counsel must be 'disinterested,' just as a government prosecutor in a CPO contempt case would be."); In re Jackson, 51 A.3d 529, 531 (D.C. Ct. App. 2012) ("We further hold that trial judges must be scrupulously aware of due process considerations in these types of criminal contempt cases and afford a defendant due process and other protections, including a disinterested prosecutor, an impartial decision maker, an attorney, and confrontation of witnesses."); Conant v. Credit Suisse Group Securities (USA) LLC, 831 Fed. App. 793, 794 (9th Cir. 2020) ("Those individuals on whom criminal sanctions are imposed are 'entitled to the right to be advised of the charges, the right to a disinterested prosecutor, the right to assistance of counsel, a presumption of innocence, proof beyond a reasonable doubt,' and other due process protections applicable in the criminal context.") (citing F.J. Hanshaw Enters., Inc. v. Emerald River Dev., Inc., 244 F.3d 1128, 1139 (9th Cir. 2001)); *and* State of New Jersey v. Imperiale, 773 F. Supp. 747, 750 (D. N.J. 1991) ("The question of what constitutes an "impartial" prosecutor demands clarification. A prosecutor is not 'partial' simply because she zealously seeks conviction. Rather, 'partiality' in this context is similar to a conflict of interest in the sense that the prosecutor has a personal interest or stake in the outcome of the criminal prosecution. Thus, 'partiality' refers not to 'personal' zeal but to 'structural' problems where personal interests (including non-pecuniary interests) generate a structural conflict of interest."); People v. Benoit, 575 N.Y.S.2d 750, 756-57 (N.Y. Crim. Ct., Kings County, 1991) (observing that "a public prosecutor must be disinterested"; that "[p]rosecution by a disinterested prosecutor is a fundamental aspect of due process that this defendant would be deprived of if this private prosecution is allowed to continued"; and that an interested private prosecution "would violate both the defendant's due process and equal protection guarantees"). As Justice Harry Blackmun emphasized in his concurrence in *Young* of the due process concept: "This constitutional concept, in my view, requires a disinterested prosecutor with the unique responsibility to serve the public, rather than a private client, and to seek justice that is unfettered." *Young*, 481 U.S. at 815 (Blackmun, J., concurring).

Interested private prosecutions are inherently problematic because of the clear conflict of interest associated with private parties (or lawyers retained by them) making decisions that are supposed to be rooted in the "public interest." Over the centuries, many high-profile private prosecutions have taken place. These include the 1830 prosecutions of the Knapp brothers in Salem, Massachusetts, conducted by U.S. Senator Daniel Webster, leading to their execution; the 1850 capital prosecution of Dr. John Webster for the murder of George Parkman, a Boston Brahmin, a trial in which a privately retained lawyer, George Bemis, actively participated, ultimately resulting in the hanging of Dr. Webster, a lecturer at Harvard Medical College; and the 1871 capital murder trial of Laura Fair for fatally shooting her lover, California lawyer Alexander Crittenden, a prosecution in San Francisco conducted by the district attorney with the assistance of Crittenden's own former law partner. *See e.g.*, "Former Murder Trials," Boston Sunday Globe, Dec. 25, 1910, p. 38 (noting that "about the only time Daniel Webster ever appeared in the character of the law's prosecutor" was at the trial of Knapp brothers and that George Bemis "appeared for the prosecution" at John Webster's trial); Barbara Allen Babcock, *Women Defenders in the West*, 1 Nev. L.J. 1, 7 (2001) ("Laura Fair was tried for shooting Alexander Crittenden, her married lover. Her defense was temporary insanity, brought on, she claimed, because he had 'ruined' her—and her daughter as well. Crittenden was a well-known lawyer, and his law partner joined the prosecution as special counsel."); Holly Cole, *The Laura Fair Affair: Women & the Death Penalty in Victorian San Francisco*, CSCHS Newsletter (Spring/Summer 2006), p. 7, *available at* https://www.cschs.org/wp-content/uploads/2014/08/2006-Newsletter-Spring-Laura-Fair-Affair.pdf (noting that the prosecuting district attorney, Henry H. Byrne, "was assisted by Crittenden's law partner, Alexander Campbell, a former municipal judge who practiced primarily criminal law"); "Is It Murder! Waiting for the Verdict," San Francisco Chronicle, Apr. 23, 1871, p. 1 (noting that Laura Fair's trial started on March 27, 1871, with Alexander Campbell, Jr. assisting District Attorney Henry H. Byrne for the prosecution; that Campbell "[o]pened for the prosecution" and "closed at the night session, after speaking almost seven hours"; and that Campbell had a reputation as "one of the ablest criminal lawyers practicing in the Courts of California"); "Trial of Mrs. Fair—Four Jurors Sworn Thus Far," Daily Examiner (San Francisco, CA), Mar. 27, 1871, p. 3 ("Judge Alexander Campbell appeared for the prosecution, in connection with the District Attorney.").

Such high-profile private prosecutions, like the one of Laura Fair, attracted so much attention because of the high stakes of them (in her case, life versus death) and the potential for prejudice and personal vendettas. *E.g.*, Benedetta Faedi Duramy, Book Review, 33 Law & Hist. Rev. 248, 248 (2015) ("On November 3, 1870, the four-time married, twice divorced, and twice widowed Laura Fair embarked on a San Francisco ferry, anxiously searching for her married and much older lover Alexander Parker Crittenden. Doubting, after much promise, the intention of Crittenden to divorce his current wife Clara and finally introduce Laura respectably to society as his future spouse, Laura decided to witness her paramour greeting Clara and their three children as they debarked from the train and then take the ferry together. When running through the decks, Laura finally found Crittenden comfortably seated on a bench with his family showing affection to his wife. Laura pulled a gun out of her cloak and fatally shot him. After declaring 'I did it and I don't deny it. He ruined me and my daughter,' she was immediately arrested.") (reviewing CAROL HABER, THE TRIALS OF LAURA FAIR: SEX, MURDER, AND INSANITY IN THE VICTORIAN WEST (2013)); *id.* ("In *The Trials of Laura Fair: Sex, Murder, and Insanity in the Victorian West,* Tulane University history professor Carole Haber recounts what became one of the most sensational nineteenth century criminal proceedings. Tried for murder a few months later, Laura pleaded not guilty on the grounds of temporary insanity caused by dysmenorrhea, a medical condition of painful menstrual cycles. Despite the efforts of the defense to prove Laura's lack of memory of and control over her actions and the events that occurred on the ferry, the first jury decided to disregard her testimony. The court chose to focus on the prosecutors' portrayal of Laura Fair as a dishonorable woman, who, in the words of Haber, embodied 'the horrors of free love, wanton sexuality, and radical thinking'. Meanwhile, women's rights activists such as Elizabeth Cady Stanton viewed Fair as a victim of the much older, deceitful, and powerful Crittenden."); *id.* ("After an appellate court overturned the original verdict and during her second trial, Laura Fair refused to testify, and increasingly embraced the role of an innocent woman plagued by her mental and physical disturbance."); *id.* at 249 ("During Fair's second trial, her counsel portrayed her as an innocent single mother who had been failed multiple times by the men of her life, and was finally deceived by her devious lover. Doctors testified that her biological condition impaired her capacity to control her behavior and emotions, whereas prosecutors, on the other hand, described her as a mischievous and unscrupulous woman whose 'heart was evil, [and] her hands smeared with the blood of revenge'. Convinced by an effective defense supported by distinguished medical opinions on the connection between insanity and women's biological cycles, the jury returned a not guilty verdict to the astonishment of the entire country."); Jerry Thompson, Book Review, 50 AM. J. LEGAL HIST. 460, 460 (2010) ("In 1870, Laura Fair was charged with the murder of Alexander P. Crittenden, a San Francisco lawyer who was also her lover. Fair admitted to the killing, but claimed that she suffered maniacal spells due to delayed menstruation. She also claimed that when she and Crittenden first met, he lied about being married and relentlessly pursued her romantically. Once she found out he was married, Chittenden promised to divorce his wife, but, alas, his duplicity eventually made her so insane that she had no memory of killing him. In contrast, the prosecution argued that the killing was deliberate and that Fair was an 'unchaste' woman who defied Victorian values.") (reviewing GORDON MORRIS BAKKEN & BRENDA FARRINGTON, WOMEN WHO KILL MEN: CALIFORNIA COURTS, GENDER, AND THE PRESS (2009)); *id.* ("Many prominent women's suffragists attended Fair's trial to highlight that women themselves could not serve on juries even when a woman was the one being judged. After a lengthy and highly publicized trial, jurors returned a verdict of guilty. But the California Supreme Court overturned the verdict on two grounds: first, that evidence of Fair's chastity was irrelevant and second, that the defense, not the prosecution should close last. On retrial, the jurors returned a verdict of not guilty by reason of insanity and Fair was free.").

Questions about the integrity of interested private prosecutions—some dating back centuries—abound. *Compare* Michael S. Ariens, *American Legal Ethics in an Age of Anxiety*, 40 ST. MARY'S L.J. 343, 380-82 (2008) ("In late March 1850, Dr. John Webster, a professor at the Harvard Medical School, was tried and convicted of the murder of George Parkman, a Boston Brahmin, and sentenced to die. The case may have been the most notorious murder case in nineteenth century America. Shortly before he disappeared on November 23, 1849, Parkman visited Webster at the medical school to demand payment of a large outstanding debt Webster owed Parkman. The wealthy Parkman family offered a large reward for information concerning his disappearance. The police learned of Parkman's visit to Webster and arrested Webster after they found dismembered parts of a body in Webster's laboratory. The Commonwealth's star witness at the trial was the Harvard Medical School janitor, Ephraim Littlefield. Littlefield told of an argument between Webster and Parkman on November 23, and also told of his belief that Webster had murdered Parkman as soon as Parkman's disappearance was publicized. After Parkman's disappearance, Littlefield began digging through a wall separating his apartment at the medical school from Webster's laboratory. He led police to a partially dismembered body found there, later identified by experts at trial as that of George Parkman.

Littlefield was poorly paid by Harvard Medical School and supplemented his income as a body snatcher (called a 'resurrectionist' in Boston). Thus, one possible motive for Littlefield's actions was the reward offered by Parkman's family, which Littlefield later disclaimed on the witness stand. On cross-examination, Webster's lawyers failed miserably in attacking Littlefield's credibility and wholly avoided, contrary to their client's request, Littlefield's resurrectionist work. The prosecution, led by special counsel George Bemis, offered a host of expert witnesses, including the first dental expert and an early handwriting expert, whose testimony was fraught with holes, but whose credibility again remained unsullied after cross-examination. The case was tried, as a matter of law, by the entire Massachusetts Supreme Judicial Court, including its chief justice, Lemuel Shaw, whose prejudice against Webster was roundly criticized by other lawyers.") *and* Robert Kirsch, "1849 Murder at Harvard Probed," L.A. TIMES, Aug. 10, 1971, p. 46 ("At dawn Aug. 30, 1850, Harvard Prof. Dr. John White Webster was hanged for the murder of another Harvard man, Dr. George Parkman, one of the richest men in Boston, an alumnus who had endowed a chair of anatomy in the medical school.... But the execution did not provide a neat end to the matter.... There are those... who saw the conviction of Dr. Webster as a miscarriage of justice, and the most recent of these is another Harvard graduate, Judge Robert Sullivan, whose research into the cause celebre has produced THE DISAPPEARANCE OF DR. PARKMAN (Little, Brown: $6.95; illustrated.... Working from newly available documents including Dr. Webster's notes of instruction to his defense attorney, the papers and journals of the prosecutor and a large number of letters by those involved in the case and its aftermath, Judge Sullivan raises a number of disquieting points.") *with* Peter Levine, "When Justice Triumphed: Boston's Famous Parkman Mystery—Just 90 Years Ago," ATLANTA CONSTITUTION, Nov. 26, 1939, p. 46 ("Dr. Webster did not take the stand. The jury took the case at 8 p.m., March 30, and three hours later returned a verdict of guilty. Dr. Webster, who had appeared composed and confident through the trial, reacted as though some one had stabbed him and twisted the knife in his vitals. Several weeks later, having been sentenced to be hanged, he made what was described as a full confession to a clergyman. In this he admitted the killing but asserted that he had struck Dr. Parkman in a burst of rage in the course of a bitter quarrel.... This confession failed of its purpose, for Dr. Webster was hanged the following August 30.").

Where private interests are allowed to corrupt the integrity of criminal prosecutions and the reliability of convictions, the constitutional rights of defendants are jeopardized and violated, diminishing public confidence in the criminal justice itself. *E.g.*, "Murder Case Defense Assails Use of 'Private Prosecutors,'" ST. LOUIS POST-DISPATCH, June 12, 1966, p. 42 (reporting from Maryville, Tennessee, about a man facing the death penalty in the shooting death of Lance Russell, a high school student shot on Halloween, and observing: "Attorneys for a man charged with murder have asked the Tennessee Supreme Court to prevent the victim's family from hiring high-powered 'private prosecutors.'"); *id.* ("Russell's family has hired two attorneys, Jerry Cunningham and Kelly Thomas, to assist the district attorney's office in prosecuting the case. Defense attorneys asked the state Supreme Court to review the use of private prosecutors in the case after the state's Court of Appeals upheld their use. In the appeal to the Supreme Court, one defense attorney, Charles Fels, contends that it is unfair for Bennett, a truck driver with an eighth-grade education, to be prosecuted by prestigious lawyers with political connections. Fels said the attorneys hired as private prosecutors 'represent both major political parties' in Blount County, where the case is being heard."); *see also* Robert M. Ireland, *Privately Funded Prosecution of Crime in the Nineteenth-Century United States*, 39 AM. J. LEGAL HIST. 43, 46 (1995) ("There is evidence that some of the prosecutors of Frank James, on trial in 1883 in Gallitan, Missouri for murder and train robbery, were hired by railroad companies which had allegedly been robbed by the James brothers and their gang."); Camelia Foster, "Loesch Commits Suicide," WACO CITIZEN (Waco, TX), Oct. 29, 1982, p. 2 ("New Mexico attorney James Kreimeyer was hired as special prosecutor by the victim's family."); "Murder Trial Jury Sworn In," NASHVILLE TENNESSEAN, Jan. 11, 1961, p. 2 (noting that "[a] jury was sworn" in Manchester, Tennessee, "to hear the case against a mild-mannered highly respected Tullahoma, Tenn., insurance salesman accused of the sadistic slaying of a 17-year-old Tullahoma beauty"; that "[t]he defendant Roger Ivey, 33, has maintained since his arrest that the death of Anna Kelnhofer was an accident, that he struck her with his car as she was walking toward Duck River to go fishing and then hid her body out of fright"; and that the state's prosecutor, Gerald Ewell, was "being assisted by Winchester attorney Walter M. (Pete) Haynes, a former Tennessee lieutenant governor hired as special prosecutor by neighbors of the victim's family").

In criminal cases, there is simply too much at stake—and the risk of wrongful charges or wrongful convictions is too high—for the judicial system in the twenty-first century to tolerate interested private prosecutions (which are already rare). *E.g.*, Michael Martinez, "Plea Bargain? Not so fast," KANSAS CITY TIMES (Kansas City, MO), Feb. 10, 1990, pp. 1, 15 (noting that when prosecutors were proposing a plea bargain with one of the individuals charged in a murder case, the murder victims' families invoked a Kansas law from 1901 and hired an "associate counsel" who "functions as a special prosecutor with limited powers"; that "[s]ince the families hired the special prosecutor last month, they haven't heard any more talk from prosecutors about plea bargains"; that "there can be strained relations between the district attorney and the special prosecutor, or between the prosecutor and the victims' families"; and quoting Attorney General Bob Stephan as saying of the Kansas law, "It's used very infrequently," "there are drawbacks, the biggest one being money," and "[h]iring an associate counsel can be expensive"); "'Hired-gun' Prosecutors Still Legal in Tennessee," THE TENNESSEAN (Nashville, TN), July 22, 1991, p. 2 ("Although used infrequently, 'hired-gun' prosecutors are still legal in Tennessee. These are lawyers hired by a crime victim's family or relatives to help state prosecutors. Steven Bennett, tried and convicted in Blount County, Tenn., in 1988 on murder charges, felt he was facing three prosecutors: one for the state, two for the victim's family."). As Charles Fels, a lawyer in Knoxville, Tennessee, put it: "I think we shouldn't let someone use the power of public prosecutors to seek private revenge." "Private Lawyers Stepping in as 'Hired Gun' Prosecutors," SOUTHERN ILLINOISAN (Carbondale, IL), July 22, 1991, p. 5; *see also id.* (noting that "private prosecutors," though "used rarely," have "proved controversial," with Charles Fel—the lawyer who'd asked the nation's highest court to reverse a client's conviction because of the participation of two private prosecutors—arguing, "It shouldn't have been a capital punishment case but that's the way it was prosecuted. This was a matter of a victim's wealthy family trying to buy its own brand of justice through the hired-gun law.").

* * *

As *Private Prosecution in America* was going to press, U.S. District Court Judge Robert Pitman issued a preliminary injunction on October 6, 2021, prohibiting Texas, its state court judges and clerks, and private individuals from enforcing the anti-abortion law known as Senate Bill 8 ("S.B. 8"). Finding S.B. 8 unconstitutional and determining that the United States has "standing to file suit" to protect citizens' constitutional rights and the chilling of those rights, Judge Pitman ruled: "principles of equity allow the United States to seek an injunction to protect its sovereign rights, and the fundamental rights of its citizens under the circumstances present here." In his 113-page ruling, Judge Pitman wrote that "S.B. 8 prevents individuals from exercising their right to obtain abortions in Texas, and an injunction will restore that right." United States Attorney General Merrick Garland aptly called Judge Pitman's decision "a victory for women in Texas and for the rule of law." Ryan Lucas, "A U.S. Judge Blocks Enforcement of Texas' Controversial New Abortion Law," NPR, Oct. 6, 2021, https://www.npr.org/2021/10/06/1040221171/a-u-s-judge-blocks-enforcement-of-texas-controversial-new-abortion-law; Order of U.S. District Court Judge Robert Pitman, *United States of America v. Texas*, Case No. 1:21-CV-796-RP (W.D. Tex. Oct. 6, 2021), pp. 28–39, 63, 67, 105; *see also id.* at 56-57 ("[T]he United States seeks to enjoin three categories of obligors: (1) the State, (2) state actors, and (3) private individuals. Based on the analysis below, the Court concludes it has the authority to enjoin the State, its officials, and private individuals."); *id.* at 59–60 ("[T]he State has its prints all over the statute. The operation and enforcement of S.B. 8 requires the State and its employees to act, whether those acts are the maintenance of a lawsuit or carrying out a court order regarding the enforceability of S.B. 8. The State enacted S.B. 8 when Governor Abbott signed it into law; the law represents the State's pre-viability abortion policy; the State chose to partially delegate its enforcement authority to private individuals; and the State's judiciary accepts and hears S.B. lawsuits.... Employing a private cause of action neither relieves the State of its obligations to enforce and maintain its own law nor exempts the State from this federal court's authority to impose an injunction.") (citations omitted); *id.* at 60 ("The Supreme Court recognized that states cannot avoid the preservation of constitutional rights through a scheme of deflection in *Cooper v. Aaron*, 358 U.S. 1 (1958)."); *id.* at 60–61 ("[T]he State's scheme to disguise its enforcement role and disclaim accountability collapses upon cursory inspection. The State enacted S.B. 8 and created a private enforcement scheme that clothes private individuals with the State's enforcement power. That delegation alone would have been sufficient to show state action. The practical operation of an S.B. 8 lawsuit in Texas courts deepens the State's enforcement. As set out above, the State plays a role at every step of a S.B. 8's lifecycle in Texas courts. A private cause of action enforcement scheme is meaningless without state action. Yet, the State endeavors to use it as a sword (to effectuate its regulation of abortion) and a shield (to insulate those regulations from federal review). That State cannot pin the enforcement of S.B. 8 solely on the backs of private individuals and avoid federal judicial review or injunctive relief. An injunction properly runs against the State.") (citation omitted); *id.* at 63 ("Given that it is the threat of S.B. lawsuits that deters providers from offering abortion care services, an injunction must halt existing S.B. lawsuits and prevent new suits from being maintained by the state judiciary. Even though private individuals filed S.B. 8 lawsuits, the state judiciary plays a role in the lawsuits through several official actions including docketing, maintaining, hearing, and rendering relief in an S.B. 8 lawsuit.") (citation omitted); *id.* at 67-68 ("[P]rivate individuals enforcing S.B. 8 are properly regarded as state actors.... Courts have characterized private parties as state actors where a state allows or is involved with conduct that would be unconstitutional should the state itself engage in that conduct. Apt is *Shelley*, a 1948 case brought by Kraemers, a white couple, against the Shelleys, a Black couple, to stop the Shelleys from moving into the house they had just purchased in a St. Louis neighborhood. The Kraemers sought to enforce the terms of a restrictive covenant that specifically excluded Blacks from occupying the property. Before the Supreme Court, the Shelleys, who were unaware of the restrictive covenant when they purchased their home, argued that they had been denied equal protection of the laws. Confident that racial restrictive covenants violate the Fourteenth Amendment when they involve 'action by state legislature or city councils,' the Court considered whether 'agreements among private individuals' to discriminate removed the state action necessary to invoke the Fourteenth Amendment.... The Supreme Court imputed the unconstitutional acts of the private individuals to the state because the state 'grant[ed] judicial enforcement' of the unconstitutional act. Likewise here, the State has granted judicial enforcement of private causes of action brought under S.B. 8 and has done more. In addition to allowing its judiciary to enforce a likely unconstitutional S.B. 8, the State designed S.B. 8's private cause of action enforcement mechanism and authorized private individuals to bring suit on its behalf, and the private individuals who bring an S.B. suit 'make extensive use' of the state judicial system. The fact that the enforcement of S.B. 8 begins with a private individual does not immunize the State.") (citations omitted). "Tonight's ruling is an important step forward toward restoring the constitutional rights of woman across the state of Texas," Jen Psaki, the White House press secretary, emphasized in the wake of Judge Pitman's ruling. Sarah N. Lynch, "U.S. Judge Blocks Enforcement of Near-Total Abortion Ban in Texas," Reuters, Oct. 7, 2021, https://www.reuters.com/world/us/us-judge-blocks-enforcement-near-total-abortion-ban-texas-2021-10-07/.

Shortly after Judge Pitman issued a preliminary injunction, the U.S. Court of Appeals for the Fifth Circuit reinstated Texas's anti-abortion law. "U.S. Appeals Court Temporarily Reinstates Enforcement of Texas' Restrictive Abortion Law," NBC News, Oct. 8, 2021 (updated Oct. 9, 2021), https://www.nbcnews.com/politics/politics-news/texas-asks-appeals-court-allow-enforcement-nation-s-toughest-abortion-n1281153 ("A one-page order by the 5th U.S. Circuit Court of Appeals reinstated the nation's strictest abortion law, which bans abortions once cardiac activity is detected, usually around six weeks. It makes no exceptions in cases of rape or incest.... [B]arely 48 hours passed before the appeals court accepted Texas' request to set aside Pitman's ruling—at least for now—pending further arguments. It gave the Biden administration, which had brought the lawsuit, until Tuesday to respond."). "If Texas's scheme is permissible, no constitutional right is safe from state-sanctioned sabotage of this kind," the U.S. Department of Justice argued to the Fifth Circuit in the wake of the appellate court's order. "Justice Department Again Presses to Halt Texas Abortion Law," NBC News, Oct. 12, 2021, https://www.nbcnews.com/politics/justice-department/justice-department-again-presses-halt-texas-abortion-law-n1281305. The U.S. Supreme Court, which heard oral argument on the law on November 1, 2021, will ultimately determine the fate of S.B. 8. *See, e.g.*, Joanna L. Grossman, "Shame on Texas: Playing Ping-Pong with the Lives of Pregnant People," Justia, Oct. 12, 2021, https://verdict.justia.com/2021/10/12/shame-on-texas-playing-ping-pong-with-the-lives-of-pregnant-people ("The federal government will now again seek relief from the U.S. Supreme Court, which has already revealed itself to be uninterested in enforcement of existing constitutional precedents.... There are also several lawsuits working their way through state courts that raise independent challenges to SB 8.").

INDEX

J

K

N

O

Q

W